The American Promise

A HISTORY OF THE UNITED STATES

Third Edition

BASEBALL TEAM OF McINTIRE CHILDREN'S HOME (ZANESVILLE, OHIO), c. 1874–1900
Photographer unknown. Reproduced by permission of the Ohio Historical Society.

The American Promise

A HISTORY OF THE UNITED STATES

Third Edition

James L. Roark
Emory University

Michael P. Johnson
Johns Hopkins University

Patricia Cline Cohen
University of California, Santa Barbara

Sarah Stage
Arizona State University West

Alan Lawson
Boston College

Susan M. Hartmann
The Ohio State University

BEDFORD/ST. MARTIN'S
Boston ◆ New York

FOR BEDFORD/ST. MARTIN'S

Executive Editor for History: Mary Dougherty
Director of Development for History: Jane Knetzger
Senior Developmental Editor: Heidi L. Hood
Senior Production Editor: Karen S. Baart
Senior Production Supervisor: Joe Ford
Senior Marketing Manager: Jenna Bookin Barry
Editorial Assistant: Elizabeth Harrison
Production Assistants: Amy Derjue, Anne E. True
Copyeditor: Patricia Herbst
Text Design and Page Layout: Wanda Kossak Design
Photo Research: Pembroke Herbert/Sandi Rygiel, Picture Research Consultants & Archives, Inc.
Indexer: Maro Riofrancos
Cover Design: Donna Lee Dennison
Cartography: Mapping Specialists Ltd.
Composition: TechBooks
Printing and Binding: R.R. Donnelley & Sons Ltd.

President: Joan E. Feinberg
Editorial Director: Denise B. Wydra
Director of Marketing: Karen Melton Soeltz
Director of Editing, Design, and Production: Marcia Cohen
Managing Editor: Elizabeth M. Schaaf

Library of Congress Control Number: 2004102163

Manufactured in the United States of America.

9 8 7 6 5 4
f e d c b a

For information, write: Bedford/St. Martin's, 75 Arlington Street, Boston, MA 02116 (617-399-4000)

ISBN: 0–312–40687–8 (combined edition)   EAN: 978–0–312–40687–5
ISBN: 0–312–40688–6 (Vol. I)   EAN: 978–0–312–40688–2
ISBN: 0–312–40689–4 (Vol. II)   EAN: 978–0–312–40689–9

Cover Art: *Baseball Team of McIntire Children's Home (Zanesville, Ohio), c. 1874–1900.* Photographer unknown. Reproduced by permission of the Ohio Historical Society.

BRIEF CONTENTS

CONTENTS

CHAPTER 1

Ancient America: Before 1492   3

CHAPTER 6
The British Empire and the Colonial Crisis, 1754–1775　173

CHAPTER 7
The War for America, 1775–1783　211

CHAPTER 8
Building a Republic, 1775–1789 249

CHAPTER 9
The New Nation Takes Form, 1789–1800 285

CHAPTER 18
The West in the Gilded Age, 1870–1900 635

CHAPTER 19
The City and Its Workers, 1870–1900 669

CHAPTER 12
The New West and Free North, 1840–1860   395

CHAPTER 13
The Slave South, 1820–1860   437

CHAPTER 20

Dissent, Depression, and War, 1890–1900 709

CHAPTER 21

Progressivism from the Grass Roots to the White House, 1890–1916 747

CHAPTER 30
America Moves to the Right, 1969–1989 1103

CHAPTER 31
The End of the Cold War and the Challenges of Globalization: Since 1989 1141

MAPS, FIGURES, AND TABLES

Maps

HISTORICAL QUESTION

THE PROMISE OF TECHNOLOGY

THIS NEW EDITION OF *The American Promise* is a cause for celebration, for it proudly announces the successful reception of earlier editions. Preparing this edition, however, allowed us the opportunity to revisit our original premises, evaluate our earlier efforts, take stock of what worked, and decide how to build on those successes. The result of our careful reexamination is a major revision of *The American Promise*. While the third edition rests securely on our original goals and draws on our continuing engagement with American history as classroom teachers, we have also benefited from the invaluable suggestions of many of our adopters. As our textbook established its place among introductory surveys of American history, an ever-growing community of book users informed our efforts to make this good text even better. We are grateful for their suggestions and are confident the result is a text that will be even more useful to students and instructors.

From the beginning, *The American Promise* has been shaped by our firsthand knowledge that the survey course is the most difficult to teach and the most difficult to take. Collectively, we have logged more than a century in introductory American history classrooms in institutions that range from small community colleges to large research institutions. Drawing on our practical experience, we set an ambitious goal, one that we continue to focus on in the third edition: to produce the most teachable and readable introductory American history textbook available.

Our experience as teachers informs every aspect of our text, beginning with its framework. Many survey texts emphasize either a social or a political approach to history, and by focusing on one, they inevitably slight the other. In our classrooms, we have found that students need **both** the structure a political narrative provides **and** the insights gained from examining social and cultural experience. To write a comprehensive,

balanced account of American history, we focused on the public arena—the place where politics intersects social and cultural developments—to show how Americans confronted the major issues of their day and created far-reaching historical change.

We also thought hard about the concerns most frequently voiced by instructors: that students often find history boring, unfocused, and difficult and their textbooks lifeless and overwhelming. Getting students to open the book is one of the biggest hurdles instructors face. We asked ourselves how our text could address these concerns and engage students in ways that would help them understand and remember the main developments in American history. To make the political, social, economic, and cultural changes vivid and memorable and to portray fully the diversity of the American experience, we stitched into our narrative the voices of hundreds of contemporaries—from presidents to pipefitters, sharecroppers to suffragists—whose ideas and actions shaped their times and whose efforts still affect our lives. By incorporating a rich selection of authentic American voices, we seek to capture history as it happened and to create a compelling narrative that captures students' interests and sparks their historical imagination.

Our title, *The American Promise*, reflects our emphasis on human agency and our conviction that American history is an unfinished story. For millions, the nation has held out the promise of a better life, unfettered worship, representative government, democratic politics, and other freedoms seldom found elsewhere. But none of these promises has come with guarantees. And promises fulfilled for some have meant promises denied to others. As we see it, much of American history is a continuing struggle over the definition and realization of the nation's promise. Abraham Lincoln, in the midst of what he termed the "fiery trial" of the Civil War, pronounced the

> We set an ambitious goal to produce the most teachable and readable introductory American history textbook available.

nation "the last best hope of Earth." Kept alive by countless sacrifices, that hope has been marred by compromises, disappointments, and denials, but it lives still. We believe that *The American Promise*, Third Edition, with its increased attention to making history come alive, will help students become aware of the legacy of hope bequeathed to them by previous generations of Americans stretching back nearly four centuries, a legacy that is theirs to preserve and build on.

Features

From the beginning, readers have proclaimed this textbook a visual feast, richly illustrated in ways that extend and reinforce the narrative. The third edition furthers this benefit by nearly doubling the number of **illustrations** to more than 750. Many in full color and large enough to study in detail, these illustrations are contemporaneous with the period of the chapter in which they appear. In our effort to make history tangible and memorable, we expanded and enriched the art program's acclaimed use of **artifacts** and added **all-new embedded artifacts**—100 small images of material culture—from boots and political buttons to guns and sewing machines—folded into the lines of the narrative. These, combined with full-page **chapter-opening artifacts** and other captioned artifacts throughout, emphasize the importance of material culture in the study of the past and enrich the historical account. Similarly, within our **new illustrated chapter chronologies** we placed thumbnail-size images from the chapter to reinforce the narrative and stimulate students' power of recall. A striking **new design** highlights the illustration program and makes the most of our **comprehensive captions** while enticing students to delve deeper into the text itself.

Our highly regarded **map program** offers more maps than any other U.S. survey text—over 170 maps in all (20 more than in the previous edition). Each chapter offers, on average, four **full-size maps** showing major developments in a wide range of areas, from environmental and technological issues to political, social, cultural, and diplomatic matters. New maps reflect our increased attention to Native American peoples and to the West in particular, and they cover such varied topics as zones of empire in eighteenth-century North America; Indian war in the West, 1777–1781; western mining, 1848–1890; urban riots, 1965–1968; and the election of 2000. In addition, each chapter includes two to three **spot maps,** small, single-concept maps embedded in the narrative to strengthen students' grasp of crucial issues. Unique to *The American Promise,* new spot maps in the third edition highlight such topics as Spanish missions in California, frontier land opened by Indian removal in the 1830s, the Mexican cession, the Battle of Glorieta Pass, the Samoan Islands, selected Indian relocations from 1950 to 1970, the Cuban missile crisis, contemporary Liberia, contemporary Israel, and the recent conflict in Afghanistan. Another unique feature is our brief **Atlas of the Territorial Growth of the United States,** a series of full-color maps at the end of each volume that reveal the changing cartography of the nation.

Imaginative and effective pedagogy remains a hallmark of our text. All chapters are constructed to preview, reinforce, and review the narrative in the most memorable and engaging means possible. To prepare students for the reading to come, each chapter begins with a **new chapter outline** to accompany the vivid **opening vignette** that invites students into the narrative with lively accounts of individuals or groups who embody the central themes of the chapter. Each vignette ends with a **narrative overview** of all of the chapter's main topics. New vignettes in this edition include, among others, Roger Williams being banished from Puritan Massachusetts, runaway slave William Gould enlisting in the Union navy, Native American boarding school students celebrating Indian Citizenship Day, Henry Ford putting

Spanish Missions in California

America on wheels, Colonel Paul Tibbets dropping the bomb on Hiroshima, Phyllis Schlafly promoting conservatism, and Colin Powell adjusting to the post–cold war world. To further prepare students as they read, major sections within each chapter have **introductory paragraphs** that preview the subsections that follow. Throughout each chapter, **two-tiered running heads** with dates and topical headings remind students where the sections they are reading fall chronologically, and **call-outs** reinforce key points. In addition, **new thematic chronologies** reinforce and extend points in the narrative, and a **new Glossary of Historical Vocabulary** makes history even more accessible. To help students understand the role of geography in American history and to teach them how to read maps and how map content relates to chapter content, we include twice as many of our popular **map exercises** as in the last edition—now two per chapter.

MAP 7.2 Loyalist Strength and Rebel Support
The exact number of loyalists can never be known. No one could have made an accurate count at the time; in addition, political allegiance often shifted with the winds. This map shows the regions of loyalist strength on which the British relied—most significantly the lower Hudson valley and the Carolina Piedmont.

READING THE MAP: Which forces were stronger, those loyal to Britain or those rebelling? (Consider size of areas, centers of population, and vital port locations.) What areas were contested? If the contested areas ultimately sided with the British, how would the balance of power change?

CONNECTIONS: Who was more likely to be a loyalist, and why? How many loyalists left the United States? Where did they go?

FOR MORE HELP ANALYZING THIS MAP, see the map activity for this chapter in the Online Study Guide at bedfordstmartins.com/roark.

At the end of each chapter, an annotated and **illustrated chapter chronology** reviews important events, and a **conclusion** critically reexamines central ideas and provides a bridge to the next chapter.

An enriched array of special features reinforces the narrative and offers teachers more points of departure for assignments and discussion. By providing two entirely new types of features (on 41 topics) in this edition, we supply a widened variety of choices to spark students' interest while helping them understand that history is both a body of knowledge and an ongoing process of investigation. The two new types of boxed features we added are designed to expand and deepen students' understanding

of the American story and make it come alive for them. The **new American Places** feature brings history home to students through a brief essay in each chapter on an American locale related to the discussion at hand—such as Jamestown, the California Mission Trail, Lowell National Historic Park, Antietam National Battlefield, the Lower East Side Tenement Museum, and Alcatraz Island—that students can visit today in person and on the Web. Too often, written history seems to float detached from the landscape in which events occurred, untouched by the powerful influences of place. By discussing the history of specific historical sites and describing what visitors today will find there, we hope to illustrate that history is rooted in both time *and* place and provide students with a tangible, and thus memorable, bridge to the past. This feature concludes with a cross-reference to our **new PlaceLinks** feature on the book's companion Web site (at bedfordstmartins.com/roark) for virtual visits to each described site and to other sites throughout the United States.

AMERICAN PLACES

Antietam National Battlefield, Sharpsburg, Maryland

Bloody Lane
Antietam National Battlefield.

Fresh from their victory at Second Manassas, General Robert E. Lee's troops reached Sharpsburg, Maryland, on September 15 and took up positions on the low ridge that runs along the western side of Antietam Creek. General George McClellan's army arrived on and firing with demoniacal fury and shouting and laughing hysterically." So intense was the firing, Hooker remembered, that quickly "every stalk of corn in the . . . field was cut as closely as could have been done with a knife." Rival soldiers surged back and forth. Ac-

Because we understand that students need help making connections with historical geographies outside the United States as well, we complement attention to international topics in the narrative with twelve essays in our **new Beyond America's Borders** feature. Essays as varied as "American Tobacco and European Consumers," "Back to Africa: The United States and Liberia," "Transnational Feminisms," and "Jobs in a Globalizing Era" challenge students to consider the effects of transnational connections. These essays seek to widen students' perspectives, to help them see that this country did not develop in isolation. This broader notion of American history will help students understand more fully

BEYOND AMERICA'S BORDERS

Transnational Feminisms

When large numbers of American women began to protest sex discrimination in the 1960s, most were unaware that they belonged to a movement stretching more than one hundred years back in history and across oceans. In 1850, Ernestine Rose, who had been born in Poland and lived in Berlin, Paris, and London, told a women's rights convention in Massachusetts, "We are not contending here for the rights of the women of New England, or of old England,

assumption of superiority or of patronage on the part of Europe or America . . . will alienate . . . the womanhood of Asia and Africa." White, Christian women from the United States and Europe dominated the organization and all too readily assumed that they could speak for all women. But oppression and discrimination looked quite different to women in other parts of the world. For example, in **colonized** countries such as India and Egypt, feminism arose alongside movements for inde-

jected sex discri pressed hard for including Eleano delegate to the U the commission declaration; Har and women's rig India; and Miner the Dominican R

These and commitments to went far beyond teed to women b legal system or t nations, thereby and raising expe for example, asse to equal pay in 1 before the U.S. C

the complex development of their nation's history and help prepare them to live in the world.

Fresh topics in our three enduring special features further enrich this edition. Each **Documenting the American Promise** feature juxtaposes three or four primary documents to dramatize the human dimension of major events and show varying perspectives on a topic or issue. Feature introductions and document headnotes contextualize the sources, and Questions for Analysis and Debate promote critical thinking about primary sources. New topics in this edition include "Missionaries Report on California Missions," "Families Divide over the Revolution," "Young Women Homesteaders and the Promise of the West," and "Voices of Protest." Illustrated **Historical Questions** essays pose and interpret specific questions of continuing interest so as to demonstrate the depth and variety of possible answers, thereby countering the belief of many beginning students that historians simply gather facts and string them together into a chronological narrative. New questions in this edition include "How Long Did the Seven Years' War Last in Indian Country?" and "Social Darwinism: Did Wealthy Industrialists Practice What They Preached?" The **Promise of Technology** essays examine the ramifications—positive and negative—of technological developments in American society and culture. New topics in this edition include "Stoves Transform Cooking," "C.S.S. *H. L. Hunley:* The First Successful Submarine," "Artificial Limbs: Filling the 'Empty Sleeve,'" and "Solar Energy."

nings of American history means fresh material throughout the text and a new post–Civil War chapter, "The West in the Gilded Age." We also give more coverage to the environment, Native Americans, Mexicans, Latinos, Chinese workers, and other topics often related to the history of the West. We enriched the discussion of pre-Columbian America in chapter 1 (the prologue in the second edition) with more discussion of Native Americans on the eve of European contact, to complement the chapter's introduction to the process—and limits—of historical investigation.

To strengthen coverage and increase clarity and accessibility, we reorganized certain chapters. In particular, reorganization in the chapters on antebellum America and the Gilded Age provides clearer themes with smoother transitions and better places the West in the national narrative. We also provide stronger post-1945 chapters, reorganized to make themes more compelling and chronology clearer. These post-1945 chapters also include a fresh array of voices, pay greater attention to the West and related topics, and, of course, provide up-to-date coverage of the George W. Bush administration, the Middle East, and the war on terrorism.

Staying abreast of current scholarship is of perennial concern to us, and this edition reflects that keen interest. We incorporated a wealth of new scholarship into the third edition in myriad ways to benefit students. Readers will note that we made good use of the latest works on a number of topics, such as Spanish borderlands, Native Americans in the Seven Years' War, the role of political wives in the early Republic, the social history of the gold rush, the active participation of blacks in their own liberation during the Civil War, mining and commercial farming in the Gilded Age West, race and Americanization, Mexican migration into the American Southwest and how this compares to black migration into the North, the story of the atomic bomb, the black civil rights struggle in global context, and the rise of contemporary conservatism.

Textual Changes

In our ongoing effort to offer a comprehensive text that braids all Americans into the national narrative, we give particular attention to diversity and the influence of class, religion, race, ethnicity, gender, and region. For example, increased coverage of the West and its peoples from the begin-

Supplements

Developed with our guidance and thoroughly revised to reflect the changes in the third edition, the comprehensive collection of print and electronic resources accompanying the textbook provide a host of practical learning and teaching aids. Again, we learned much from the book's community of adopters, and we broadened the scope of the supplements to create a learning package that responds to the real needs of instructors and students. Cross-references in the textbook to the groundbreaking Online Study Guide and to the primary source reader signal the tight integration of the core text with the supplements.

For Students

Reading the American Past: Selected Historical Documents, **Third Edition.** Edited by Michael P. Johnson (Johns Hopkins University), one of the authors of *The American Promise,* and designed to complement the textbook, *Reading the American Past* provides a broad selection of over 150 primary source documents, as well as editorial apparatus to help students understand the sources. Emphasizing the important social, political, and economic themes of U.S. history courses, 31 new documents (one per chapter) were added to provide a multiplicity of perspectives on environmental, western, ethnic, and gender history and to bring a global dimension to the anthology.

Online Study Guide at bedfordstmartins.com/ roark**.** The popular Online Study Guide for *The American Promise* is a free and uniquely personalized learning tool to help students master themes and information presented in the textbook and improve their historical skills. Assessment quizzes let students evaluate their comprehension and pro-

vide them with customized plans for further study through a variety of activities. Instructors can monitor students' progress through the online Quiz Gradebook or receive e-mail updates.

NEW *Maps in Context: A Workbook for American History.* Written by historical cartography expert Gerald A. Danzer (University of Illinois, Chicago), this skill-building workbook helps students comprehend essential connections between geographic literacy and historical understanding. Organized to correspond to the typical U.S. history survey course, *Maps in Context* presents a wealth of map-centered projects and convenient pop quizzes that give students hands-on experience working with maps.

NEW *History Matters: A Student Guide to U.S. History Online.* This new resource, written by Alan Gevinson, Kelly Schrum, and Roy Rosenzweig (all of George Mason University), provides an illustrated and annotated guide to 250 of the most useful Web sites for student research in U.S. history as well as advice on evaluating and using Internet sources. This essential guide is based on the acclaimed "History Matters" Web site developed by the American History Social Project and the Center for History and New Media.

Telecourse Guide for *Shaping America: U.S. History to 1877.* This guide by Kenneth G. Alfers (Dallas County Community College District) is designed for students using *The American Promise* in conjunction with the Dallas TeleLearning telecourse *Shaping America* (see p. xxxvii). Lesson overviews, assignments, objectives, and focus points provide structure for distance learners, while enrichment ideas, suggested readings, and brief primary sources extend the unit lessons. Practice tests help students evaluate their mastery of the material. *Note:* The telecourse and guide for *Transforming America: U.S. History since 1877* will be available in fall 2005.

Bedford Series in History and Culture. Over 70 titles in this highly praised series combine first-rate scholarship, historical narrative, and important primary documents for undergraduate courses. Each book is brief, inexpensive, and focused on a specific topic or period. Package discounts are available.

Historians at Work Series. Brief enough for a single assignment yet meaty enough to provoke thoughtful discussion, each volume in this series examines a single historical question by combining unabridged selections by distinguished historians, each with a different perspective on the issue, with helpful learning aids. Package discounts are available.

PlaceLinks at bedfordstmartins.com/roark. Extending the goals of the "American Places" textbook feature, PlaceLinks provides access to over 100 Web sites about locations in all fifty states, such as specific monuments, parks, and museums, that connect students to the places where history happened.

DocLinks at bedfordstmartins.com/doclinks. This Web site provides over 750 annotated Web links to online primary documents, including links to speeches, legislation, treaties, social commentary, Supreme Court decisions, essays, travelers' accounts, personal narratives and testimony, newspaper articles, visual artifacts, songs, and poems. Students and teachers alike can search documents by topic, date, or specific chapter of *The American Promise*. Links can be selected and stored for later use or published to a unique Web address.

HistoryLinks at bedfordstmartins.com/history links. Recently updated, HistoryLinks directs instructors and students to over 500 carefully selected and annotated links to history-related Web sites, including those containing image galleries, maps, and audio and video clips for supplementing lectures or assignments. Users can browse these Internet starting points by date, subject, medium, keyword, or specific chapter in *The American Promise*. Instructors can assign these links as the basis for homework assignments or research projects, or students can use them in their own history research. Links can be selected and stored for later use or published to a unique Web address.

A Student's Online Guide to History Reference Sources at bedfordstmartins.com/benjamin. This Web site provides links to history-related databases, indexes, and journals, plus contact information for state, provincial, local, and professional history organizations.

Research and Documentation Online at bedfordstmartins.com/resdoc. This Web site provides clear advice on how to integrate primary and secondary sources into research papers, how to cite sources correctly, and how to format in MLA, APA, *Chicago,* or CBE style.

The St. Martin's Tutorial on Avoiding Plagiarism at bedfordstmartins.com/plagiarismtutorial. This online tutorial reviews the consequences of plagiarism and explains what sources to acknowledge, how to keep good notes, how to organize research, and how to integrate sources appropriately. The tutorial includes exercises to help students practice integrating sources and recognize acceptable summaries.

Critical Thinking Modules at bedfordstmartins .com/historymodules. This Web site offers over two dozen online modules for interpreting maps, audio, visual, and textual sources, centered on events covered in the U.S. history survey. An online guide correlates modules to textbook chapters and to books in the Bedford Series in History and Culture.

For Instructors

Instructor's Resource Manual. This popular manual by Sarah E. Gardner (Mercer University) offers both experienced and first-time instructors tools for presenting textbook material in exciting and engaging ways—annotated chapter outlines, lecture strategies, discussion starters, and film and video recommendations. The new edition includes in-class activities on analyzing visual sources and primary documents from the textbook, as well as a chapter-by-chapter guide to all of the supplements available with *The American Promise.* An extensive guide for first-time teaching assistants and sample syllabi are also included.

Transparencies. This set of over 160 full-color acetate transparencies includes all full-size maps and many other images from the textbook to help instructors present lectures and teach students important map-reading skills.

Book Companion Site at bedfordstmartins.com/ roark. The companion Web site gathers all the electronic resources for *The American Promise*, including the Online Study Guide and related Quiz Gradebook, at a single Web address, providing convenient links to lecture, assignment, and research materials such as PowerPoint chapter outlines, DocLinks, HistoryLinks, and Map Central.

Computerized Test Bank. This test bank by Bradford Wood (Eastern Kentucky University) and Peter Lau (University of Rhode Island) provides easy-to-use software to create tests. Over 80 exercises are provided per chapter, including multiple-choice, fill-in-the-blank, map analysis, short essay, and full-length essay questions. Instructors can customize quizzes, add or edit both questions and answers, as well as export questions and answers to a variety of formats, including WebCT and Blackboard. The disc includes correct answers and essay outlines.

Instructor's Resource CD-ROM. This disc provides instructors with ready-made and customizable PowerPoint multimedia presentations built around chapter outlines, maps, figures, and selected images from the textbook. The disc also includes images in jpeg format, an electronic version of the *Instructor's Resource Manual,* outline maps in pdf format for quizzing or handouts, and quick start guides to the Online Study Guide.

Map Central at bedfordstmartins.com/mapcentral**.** Map Central is a searchable database of over 750 maps from Bedford/St. Martin's history texts for classroom presentation and over 50 basic political and physical outline maps for quizzing or handouts.

Using the Bedford Series in History and Culture in the U.S. History Survey at bedfordstmartins.com/usingseries**.** This online guide helps instructors integrate volumes from the highly regarded Bedford Series in History and Culture into their U.S. history survey course. The guide not only correlates themes from each series book with the survey course but also provides ideas for classroom discussions.

Blackboard Course Cartridge and **WebCT e-Pack.** Blackboard and WebCT content are available for this book.

Videos and Multimedia. A wide assortment of videos and multimedia CD-ROMs on various topics in American history is available to qualified adopters. Also available are segments from the telecourse *Shaping America.*

The American Promise **via Telecourse.** We are pleased to announce that *The American Promise* has been selected as the textbook for the award-winning U.S. history telecourse *Shaping America* and the forthcoming *Transforming America* telecourse by Dallas TeleLearning, the LeCroy Center, Dallas County Community College District. Guides for students and instructors fully integrate the narrative of *The American Promise* into each telecourse. The telecourse package for *Shaping America: U.S. History to 1877,* updated for *The American Promise,* Third Edition, will be available for examination in fall 2004. The telecourse package for *Transforming America: U.S. History since 1877* will premiere in fall 2005. For more information on these distance-learning opportunities, visit the Dallas TeleLearning Web site at http://telelearning.dcccd.edu, e-mail tlearn@dcccd.edu, or call 972-669-6650.

Acknowledgments

We gratefully acknowledge all of the helpful suggestions from those who have read and taught from the previous editions of *The American Promise,* and we hope that our many classroom collaborators will be pleased to see their influence in the third edition. In particular, we wish to thank the talented scholars and teachers who gave generously of their time and knowledge to review this book; their critiques and suggestions contributed greatly to the published work: Eric Arnesen, *University of Illinois, Chicago;* Carl H. Boening, *Shelton State Community College;* Tommy L. Bynum, *Georgia Perimeter College;* Lawrence Cebula, *Missouri Southern State College;* Michael Connolly, *Tidewater Community College;* Gary Darden, *Rutgers University;* David Engerman, *Brandeis University;* Maurine W. Greenwald, *University of Pittsburgh;* David Igler, *University of Utah;* Peter F. Lau, *University of Rhode Island;* Charles H. Martin, *University of Texas, El Paso;* April Masten, *State University of New York, Stony Brook;* Jim R. McClellan, *Northern Virginia Community College;* Constance McGovern, *Frostburg State University;* Karen Merrill, *Williams College;* Peggy Renner, *Glendale Community College;* Steven Reschly, *Truman State University;* Leo Ribuffo, *The George Washington University;* Christine Sears, *University of Delaware;* Michael Sherry, *Northwestern University;* Steven Stoll, *Yale University;* Diana Turk, *New York University;* Elliott West, *University of Arkansas;* Jon A. Whitfield, *Central Texas College, Fort Knox;* Thomas Winn, *Austin Peay State University;* and Thomas Zeiler, *University of Colorado at Boulder.*

A project as complex as this requires the talents of many individuals. First, we would like to acknowledge our families for their support, forbearance, and toleration of our textbook responsibilities. Pembroke Herbert and Sandi Rygiel of Picture Research Consultants, Inc., contributed their unparalleled knowledge, soaring imagination, and diligent research to make possible the extraordinary illustration program. Susan Dawson at the Ohio State University provided helpful research assistance.

We would also like to thank the many people at Bedford/St. Martin's who have been crucial to this project. No one contributed more than senior editor Heidi L. Hood, who managed the entire revision and oversaw the development of each chapter. The results of her dedication to excellence and commitment to creating the best textbook imaginable are evident on every page. We thank as well executive editor Elizabeth Welch, senior editor Louise Townsend, and freelance editor Ellen Kuhl for their help with the manuscript. Thanks also go to editorial assistant Elizabeth Harrison, who provided unflagging assistance and who coordinated the supplements. We are also grateful to Jane Knetzger, director of development for history, and Mary Dougherty, executive editor, for their support and guidance. For their imaginative and tireless efforts to promote the book, we want to thank Jenna Bookin Barry, marketing manager, and Amanda Byrnes, marketing associate. With great skill and professionalism, Karen Baart, senior production editor, pulled together the many pieces related to copyediting, design, and typesetting, with the able assistance of Amy Derjue and Anne True and the guidance of managing editor Elizabeth Schaaf and assistant managing editor John Amburg. Senior production supervisor Joe Ford oversaw the manufacturing of the book. Designer and page makeup artist Wanda Kossak, copyeditor Patricia Herbst, and proofreaders Janet Cocker and Mary Lou Wilshaw-Watts attended to the myriad details that help make the book shine. Maro Riofrancos provided an outstanding index. Associate new media editor Bryce Sady and new media production coordinator Coleen O'Hanley made sure that *The American Promise* remains at the forefront of technological support for students and instructors. Editorial director Denise Wydra provided helpful advice throughout the course of the project. Finally, Joan E. Feinberg, president, and Charles H. Christensen, former president, took a personal interest in *The American Promise* from the start and guided all editions through every stage of development.

James L. Roark

Born in Eunice, Louisiana, and raised in the West, James L. Roark received his B.A. from the University of California, Davis, in 1963 and his Ph.D. from Stanford University in 1973. His dissertation won the Allan Nevins Prize. He has taught at the University of Nigeria, Nsukka; the University of Nairobi, Kenya; the University of Missouri, St. Louis; and, since 1983, Emory University, where he is Samuel Candler Dobbs Professor of American History. In 1993, he received the Emory Williams Distinguished Teaching Award, and in 2001–2002 he was Pitt Professor of American Institutions at Cambridge University. He has written *Masters without Slaves: Southern Planters in the Civil War and Reconstruction* (1977). With Michael P. Johnson, he is author of *Black Masters: A Free Family of Color in the Old South* (1984) and editor of *No Chariot Let Down: Charleston's Free People of Color on the Eve of the Civil War* (1984). He has received research assistance from the American Philosophical Society, the National Endowment for the Humanities, and the Gilder Lehrman Institute of American History. Active in the Organization of American Historians and the Southern Historical Association, he is also a fellow of the Society of American Historians.

Michael P. Johnson

Born and raised in Ponca City, Oklahoma, Michael P. Johnson studied at Knox College in Galesburg, Illinois, where he received a B.A. in 1963, and at Stanford University in Palo Alto, California, earning a Ph.D. in 1973. He is currently professor of history at Johns Hopkins University in Baltimore, having previously taught at the University of California, Irvine, San Jose State University, and LeMoyne (now LeMoyne-Owen) College in Memphis. His publications include *Toward a Patriarchal Republic: The Secession of Georgia* (1977); with James L. Roark, *Black Masters: A Free Family of Color in the Old South* (1984)

and *No Chariot Let Down: Charleston's Free People of Color on the Eve of the Civil War* (1984); *Abraham Lincoln, Slavery, and the Civil War: Selected Speeches and Writings* (2001); *Reading the American Past: Selected Historical Documents*, the documents reader for *The American Promise*; and articles that have appeared in the *William and Mary Quarterly*, the *Journal of Southern History, Labor History*, the *New York Review of Books*, the *New Republic*, the *Nation*, and other journals. Johnson has been awarded research fellowships by the American Council of Learned Societies, the National Endowment for the Humanities, and the Center for Advanced Study in the Behavioral Sciences and Stanford University, and the Times Mirror Foundation Distinguished Research Fellowship at the Huntington Library. He has directed a National Endowment for the Humanities Summer Seminar for College Teachers and has been honored with the University of California, Irvine, Academic Senate Distinguished Teaching Award and the University of California, Irvine, Alumni Association Outstanding Teaching Award. He won the *William and Mary Quarterly* award for best article in 2002 and the Organization of American Historians ABC-CLIO *America: History and Life* Award for best American history article in 2002. He is an active member of the American Historical Association, the Organization of American Historians, and the Southern Historical Association.

Patricia Cline Cohen

Born in Ann Arbor, Michigan, and raised in Palo Alto, California, Patricia Cline Cohen earned a B.A. at the University of Chicago in 1968 and a Ph.D. at the University of California, Berkeley in 1977. In 1976, she joined the history faculty at the University of California, Santa Barbara. Cohen has written *A Calculating People: The Spread of Numeracy in Early America* (1982; reissued 1999) and *The Murder of Helen Jewett: The Life and Death of a Prostitute in Nineteenth-Century New York* (1998). She has also published articles on quantitative literacy, mathematics education, prostitution, and murder in journals including the *Journal of Women's History, Radical History Review,* the *William and Mary Quarterly,* and the *NWSA Journal.* Her scholarly work has received support from the National Endowment for the Humanities, the National Humanities Center, the University of California President's Fellowship in the Humanities, the Mellon Foundation, the American Antiquarian Society, the Schlesinger Library, and the Newberry Library. She is an active associate of the Omohundro Institute of Early American History and Culture, sits on the advisory council of the Society for the History of the Early American Republic, and is president of the Western Association of Women Historians. She has served as chair of the Women's Studies Program and as acting dean of the humanities and fine arts at the University of California at Santa Barbara. In 2001–2002 she was the Distinguished Senior Mellon Fellow at the American Antiquarian Society. Currently she is chair of the history department at Santa Barbara and is working on a book about women's health advocate Mary Gove Nichols.

SARAH STAGE

Sarah Stage was born in Davenport, Iowa, and received a B.A. from the University of Iowa in 1966 and a Ph.D. in American studies from Yale University in 1975. She has taught U.S. history for more than twenty-five years at Williams College and the University of California, Riverside. Currently she is professor of Women's Studies at Arizona State University West, in Phoenix. Her books include *Female Complaints: Lydia Pinkham and the Business of Women's Medicine* (1979) and *Rethinking Home Economics: Women and the History of a Profession* (1997), which has been translated for a Japanese edition. Among the fellowships she has received are the Rockefeller Foundation Humanities Fellowship, the American Association of University Women dissertation fellowship, a fellowship from the Charles Warren Center for the Study of History at Harvard University, and the University of California President's Fellowship in the Humanities. She is at work on a book entitled *Women and the Progressive Impulse in American Politics, 1890–1914.*

ALAN LAWSON

Born in Providence, Rhode Island, Alan Lawson received his B.A. from Brown University in 1955 and his M.A. from the University of Wisconsin in 1956. After Army service and experience as a high school teacher, he earned his Ph.D. from the University of Michigan in 1967. Since winning the Allan Nevins Prize for his dissertation, Lawson has served on the faculties of the University of California, Irvine, Smith College, and, currently, Boston College. He has written *The Failure of Independent Liberalism* (1971) and coedited *From Revolution to Republic* (1976). While completing the forthcoming *Ideas in Crisis: The New Deal and the Mobilization of Progressive Experience,* he has published book chapters and essays on political economy, the cultural legacy of the New Deal, multiculturalism, and the arts in public life. He has served as editor of the *Review of Education* and the *Intellectual History Newsletter* and contributed articles to those journals as well as to the *History of Education Quarterly.* He has been active in the field of American studies as director of the Boston College American studies program and as a contributor to the *American Quarterly.* Under the auspices of the United States Information Agency, Lawson has been coordinator and lecturer for programs to instruct faculty from foreign nations in the state of American historical scholarship and teaching.

SUSAN M. HARTMANN

Professor of history at Ohio State University, Susan M. Hartmann received her B.A. from Washington University and her Ph.D. from the University of Missouri. After specializing in the political economy of the post–World War II period and publishing *Truman and the 80th Congress* (1971), she expanded her interests to the field of women's history, publishing many articles and three books: *The Home Front and Beyond: American Women in the 1940s* (1982); *From Margin to Mainstream: American Women and Politics since 1960* (1989); and *The Other Feminists: Activists in the Liberal Establishment* (1998). Her work has been supported by the Truman Library Institute, the Rockefeller Foundation, the National Endowment for the Humanities, and the American Council of Learned Societies. At Ohio State she has served as director of women's studies, and in 1995 she won the Exemplary Faculty Award in the College of Humanities. Hartmann has taught at the University of Missouri, St. Louis, and Boston University, and she has lectured on American history in Australia, Austria, France, Germany, Greece, Japan, Nepal, and New Zealand. She is a fellow of the Society of American Historians, has served on award committees of the American Historical Association, the Organization of American Historians, the American Studies Association, and the National Women's Studies Association, and currently is on the Board of Directors at the Truman Library Institute. Her current research is on gender and the transformation of politics since 1945.

The American Promise

A HISTORY OF THE UNITED STATES

Third Edition

ANASAZI EFFIGY

Ancient North Americans crafted human likenesses in stone, clay, and wood, as well as depicting human forms on canyon walls, pottery, and elsewhere. An Anasazi Indian in the Southwest carved this artifact from stone sometime around AD 1200. The unmistakably human features of the object tempt us to believe that it might be an ancient American self-portrait. Certainly the carver took care to give the object a recognizably human face, neck, arms, hands, legs, and feet. The brightly colored pigments suggest clothing or body decorations. The Anasazi who painted the object had a clear idea of what should be painted orange, turquoise, and red. Red belonged on wrists, not on lips. This color code that made perfect sense to the Anasazi remains obscure to us, a hint that the carver may have intended to depict a deity or supernatural being who had some human features. For example, the artifact lacks ears and sexual organs. The polished tip of the nose contrasts with the rough surface of the torso and legs, suggesting that Anasazi often rubbed the nose. Experts refer to this artifact and others like it as effigies, that is, objects that presumably had ritualistic or spiritual significance. Instead of showing us what the Anasazi considered a self-portrait, this effigy probably depicts one of their many gods. Yet, since the Anasazi—like other human beings—probably created gods in their own image, the effigy may somewhat resemble Anasazi people.

Jerry Jacka Photography.

Ancient America

Before 1492

GEORGE MCJUNKIN, the manager of the Crowfoot Ranch near Folsom, New Mexico, rode out to mend fences and to look for missing cattle after a violent rainstorm in August 1908. An American of African descent, McJunkin had been born a slave in Texas and had been riding horses since he was a boy. After he became free at the end of the Civil War in 1865, McJunkin worked as a cowboy in Colorado and New Mexico before becoming the Crowfoot manager in 1891. Now, as he rode across the ranch land he knew so well to survey damage caused by the recent storm, McJunkin noticed that floodwater had washed away the bank of a gulch called Wild Horse Arroyo and exposed a deposit of stark white bones. Curious, he dismounted and chipped away at the deposit until he uncovered an entire fossilized bone. The bone was much larger than the parched skeletons of range cattle and buffalo that McJunkin often saw, so he strapped it to his saddle and saved it, hoping someday to identify it.

Four years later, in 1912, McJunkin met Carl Schwachheim, a white man in Raton, New Mexico. Schwachheim, a blacksmith, shared McJunkin's curiosity about fossils, and the two men became friends. McJunkin told Schwachheim about the fossil deposit he had discovered, but Schwachheim could not get out to the ranch to take a look for himself. Ten years later, a few months after McJunkin's death, Schwachheim finally drove out to Wild Horse Arroyo, dug out several bones, and brought them back to Raton. But, like McJunkin, he could not identify an animal that had such big bones.

In 1926, Schwachheim delivered cattle to the stockyards in Denver, and he took some of the old bones to the Denver Museum of Natural History and showed them to J. D. Figgins, a paleontologist who was an expert on fossils of ancient animals. Figgins immediately recognized the significance of the fossils and a few months later began an excavation of the Folsom site that revolutionized knowledge about the first Americans.

When Figgins began his dig at Folsom, archaeologists (individuals who examine **artifacts** left by long-vanished peoples as part of the study of **archaeology**) believed that Native Americans had arrived relatively recently in the Western Hemisphere, probably no more than three or four thousand years earlier when, experts assumed, they had paddled small boats across the icy waters of the Bering Strait from what is now Siberia. At Folsom, Figgins learned that the bones McJunkin had first spotted belonged to twenty-three giant bison, a species known to have been extinct for at least 10,000 years. Far more startling, Figgins found among the bones nineteen flint spear points

George McJunkin

This photo shows McJunkin a few years after he discovered the Folsom site but about fifteen years before anyone understood the significance of his find. He appears here in his work clothes on horseback, as he probably was when he made the discovery. The fossilized bones he discovered belonged to an extinct bison species that was much larger than modern bison; the horns of the ancient animal often spanned six feet, wide enough for McJunkin's horse to have stood sideways between the horns.

Eastern New Mexico University, Blackwater Draw Site, Portales, New Mexico 88130.

years before that moment in 1492 when a few of them stood on the beach of a small island in the Caribbean and watched Christopher Columbus and his men row ashore.

Archaeology and History

Archaeologists and historians share the desire to learn about people who lived in the past, but they usually employ different methods to obtain information. Both archaeologists and historians study artifacts as clues to the activities and ideas of the humans who created them. They concentrate, however, on different kinds of artifacts. Archaeologists tend to focus on physical objects such as bones, stones, pots, baskets, jewelry, textiles, clothing, graves, and buildings. Historians direct their attention mostly to writings, which encompass personal and private jottings such as diary entries and love letters, official and public pronouncements such as laws and speeches, as well as an enormous variety of other documents such as court decisions, censuses, business ledgers, newspapers, books, and even shopping lists. Although historians are interested in other artifacts and archaeologists do not neglect written sources if they exist, the characteristic concentration of historians on writings and archaeologists on other physical objects denotes a rough cultural and chronological boundary between the human beings studied by the two groups of scholars, a boundary marked by the use of writing.

Writing is defined as a system of symbols that record spoken language. Writing originated among ancient peoples in China, Egypt, and Central America about 8,000 years ago, within the most recent 2 percent of the 400 millennia that modern human beings (*Homo sapiens*) have existed. Writing came into use even later in most other places in the world. The ancient Americans who inhabited North America in 1492, for example, possessed many forms of symbolic representation, but not writing.

The people who lived during the millennia before writing were biologically nearly identical to us. Their DNA was the template for ours. But they differed from us in many other ways. Unlike us, they did not use writing to communicate across space and time. They had a long history, both individual and collective. They moved across the face of the globe; they invented hundreds of spoken languages; they learned to sur-

(Folsom points, they have since been called), proof that human beings had been alive at the same time as the giant bison. One spear point remained stuck between two ribs of a giant bison, just where a Stone Age hunter had plunged it more than 10,000 years earlier. No longer could anyone doubt that human beings had inhabited North America for at least ten millennia.

The Folsom discovery sparked other major finds of ancient artifacts that continue to this day. Since the 1930s, archaeologists have tried to reconstruct the history of ancient Americans, to understand not only the hunters who killed giant bison with flint-tipped spears, but also their ancestors who first arrived in North America, their descendants who built southwestern pueblos and eastern burial mounds, and *their* descendants who encountered the Europeans who arrived in 1492. Although the story scholars have assembled is incomplete and controversial, they have learned enough to bring into focus the identity of ancient Americans, where they came from, and some basic features of their complex cultures and histories during the thousands of vive and even to thrive in almost every natural environment; they chose and honored leaders; they traded, warred, and worshipped; and, above all, they learned from and taught each other. Much of what we would like to know about their experiences remains unknown because it took place before writing existed. The absence of writing forever muffled their words and thus their history.

Archaeologists specialize in learning about people who did not document their history in writing. They study the millions of artifacts created by these people, trying to decipher what the objects tell us about their lives. By also scrutinizing soil, geological strata, pollen, climate, and other environmental features, they attempt to reconstruct the outlines of the history of ancient peoples. Still, much of their history remains unknowable. No documents chronicle their births and deaths, comings and goings, pleasures and pains, victories and defeats. Despite these silences, archaeologists have learned to make ancient artifacts tell a great deal about the people who made them.

Anasazi Pictograph

This unusual pictograph was painted about AD 1300 on the wall of an Anasazi dwelling in what is now Canyonlands National Park in Utah. The colorful design presumably had a specific meaning for the Anasazi who created it, but that meaning remains indecipherable to experts today.

J. Q. Jacobs.

Since ancient America was the long first phase of the history of the United States, this chapter relies on the work of archaeologists to sketch a brief overview of this important era. Our desire to understand the origins and development of our own society in the last five centuries requires beginning that story when humans first arrived in the Western Hemisphere. These ancient Americans and their descendants did not consider their history a prelude to a future that included us. They resided in North America for thousands of years before Europeans arrived. They created societies and cultures of amazing diversity and complexity. But because they did not use written records, their history cannot be reconstructed with the detail and certainty made possible by writing. Yet their remarkable longevity and creativity make it far preferable to abbreviate and oversimplify their history than to ignore it.

The First Americans

The first human beings to arrive in the Western Hemisphere immigrated from Asia. They brought with them hunting skills, weapon- and tool-making techniques, and a full range of other forms of human knowledge and expertise developed during previous millennia in Africa, Europe, and Asia. These first Americans specialized in hunting mammoths, giant elephant-like creatures they had learned in Europe and Asia to kill, butcher, and process for food, clothing, building materials, and many other purposes. Most likely, these first Americans wandered into the Western Hemisphere more or less accidentally, hungry and in pursuit of their prey.

African and Asian Origins

Human beings lived elsewhere in the world for hundreds of thousands of years before they reached the Western Hemisphere. In effect, humans lacked an effective means of transportation to it because, millions of years before humans evolved anywhere on the globe, North and South America became detached from the gigantic common landmass scientists now call Pangaea. About 240 million years ago, powerful forces deep within the earth began to fracture Pangaea and slowly to push the continents apart to approximately their present positions (Map 1.1). This process of continental drift encircled the

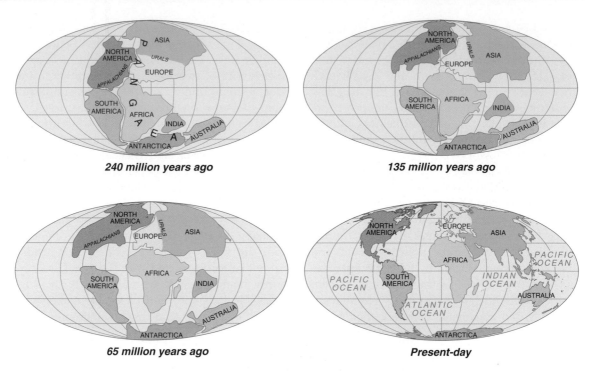

240 million years ago

135 million years ago

65 million years ago

Present-day

MAP 1.1   Continental Drift
Massive geological forces separated North and South America from other continents eons before human beings evolved in Africa in the last 1.5 million years.

READING THE MAP: Which continents separated from Pangaea earliest? Which ones separated from each other last? Which are still closely connected to each other?

CONNECTIONS: How does continental drift explain why human life developed elsewhere on the planet for hundreds of thousands of years before the first person entered the Western Hemisphere during the last 15,000 years?

FOR MORE HELP ANALYZING THIS MAP, see the map activity for this chapter in the Online Study Guide at bedfordstmartins.com/roark.

land of the Western Hemisphere with large oceans that isolated it from the other continents, long before early human beings (*Homo erectus*) first appeared in Africa about 2 million years ago. (Hereafter in this chapter, the abbreviation *BP*—archaeologists' notation for "years before the present"—is used to indicate dates earlier than 2,000 years ago. Dates more recent than 2,000 years ago are indicated with the common and familiar notation *AD*—for example, AD 1492.)

More than a million and a half years after *Homo erectus* appeared, or about 400,000 BP, modern humans (*Homo sapiens*) evolved in Africa. All human beings throughout the world today are literally descendants of these ancient Africans. Slowly, over many millennia, *Homo sapiens* migrated out of Africa and into Europe and Asia. Unlike North and South America, Europe and Asia retained land connections to Africa, making migration possible for *Homo sapi-*

ens, who traveled principally on foot and occasionally in small boats that could navigate rivers and lakes but could not survive the rigors of transoceanic travel. The vast oceans encircling North and South America kept human beings away for roughly 97 percent of the time *Homo sapiens* have been on earth.

Two major developments made it possible for human beings to migrate to the Western Hemisphere. First, humans successfully adapted to the frigid environment near the Arctic Circle. Second, changes in the earth's climate reconnected North America to Asia.

By about 25,000 BP, *Homo sapiens* had spread from Africa throughout Europe and Asia. People, presumably women, had learned to use bone needles to sew animal skins into warm clothing that permitted them to become permanent residents of extremely cold regions like northeastern Siberia. Ancient Siberians made the trip to North America on land that now lies sub-

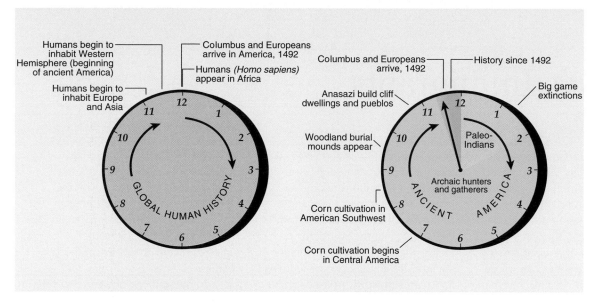

FIGURE 1.1   Human Habitation of the World and the Western Hemisphere
These clock faces illustrate the long global history of modern humans (left) and of human history in the Western Hemisphere since the arrival of the first ancient Americans (right). If the total period of human life on earth is considered, American history since the arrival of Columbus in 1492 comprises less than one minute (or 1/10 of 1 percent) of modern human existence. And if the total period of human life in the New World is converted from millennia to a 12 hour clock, then ancient American history makes up the first 11½ hours and all history since the arrival of the Europeans in 1492 occupies only the last half hour.

merged beneath sixty miles of water that separates easternmost Siberia from westernmost Alaska. But during the last great global cold spell—the Wisconsin glaciation, which endured from about 80,000 BP to about 10,000 BP—snow piled up in glaciers that did not melt, causing the sea level to drop as much as 350 feet below its current level. This natural transformation of seawater into glacial ice exposed the sea floor currently submerged beneath the waters of the Bering Strait and turned it into dry land that formed what experts refer to as a land bridge between Asian Siberia and American Alaska. This land bridge, which scientists call Beringia, opened a pathway about a thousand miles wide between the Eastern and Western Hemispheres.

Siberian hunters presumably roamed into Beringia for centuries in search of game animals. (See "Beyond America's Borders," page 8.) Grasses and small shrubs that covered Beringia supported herds of mammoth, bison, and numerous smaller animals. As the hunters ventured farther and farther east, they had no idea that they walked where humans had never before set foot. They had no awareness that their pursuit of prey made them pioneers of human life in the Western Hemisphere. Their migrations probably had very little influence on their own lives, which continued more or less in the traditional ways they had learned from their Siberian ancestors. Unbeknownst to them, however, their migrations revolutionized the history of the world, both for their descendants in the Western Hemisphere and for the descendants of their ancestors back in Asia, Europe, and Africa.

Archaeologists speculate that these Siberian hunters traveled in small bands of no more than twenty-five people. How many such bands arrived in North

Beringia

> The transformation of seawater into glacial ice exposed the sea floor beneath the waters of the Bering Strait and turned it into a land bridge between Asian Siberia and American Alaska.

Nature's Immigrants

Like the first human beings who came to the New World, most of the large animals in ancient America were descendants of migrants from elsewhere on the globe. Mammoths, the signature prey of the Clovis hunters of ancient America, illustrate the persistent immigration of animals from Asia to North America. The ancestors of the mammoths that Clovis hunters stalked about 12,000 years ago had immigrated from Asia about 1.7 million years earlier. The first mammoth migrants from Asia followed in the tracks of hundreds of other animal species that had made their way across Beringia to North America for more than 60 million years. These immigrants and their descendants populated the natural environment of America that ancient Americans first encountered. Clearly, America was a land of immigrants long before the first humans arrived.

An extraterrestrial event created the basic precondition for these animal migrations. Scientists have discovered convincing evidence that about 65 million years ago a meteorite about six miles in diameter slammed into the Yucatán peninsula in Mexico. Experts estimate that the meteorite sped toward Yucatán at about 54,000 miles an hour and cratered into the earth with an explosion equivalent to trillions of atomic bombs. Coming in at a low angle to the curvature of the earth from the direction of the Southern Hemisphere, the meteorite incinerated almost all the exposed animals and plants in North America with a blast of heat a thousand times hotter than that reaching the earth from the sun. The plume of dust and smoke propelled into the atmosphere by the impact of the meteorite darkened skies, reduced or eliminated photosynthesis, and showered the earth with sulfuric acid. These catastrophic changes in the global environment caused the extinction of many animals worldwide, including dinosaurs who had ruled the earth for more than 100 million years. But outside the fiery blast zone that extended thousands of miles north from ground zero in Yucatán, many animals survived the mass extinction and became the ancestors of animals that eventually migrated to North America.

Among the animals that survived the great extinction were small ratlike creatures, the ancestors of mammals that began to multiply and remultiply, ultimately filling many of the environmental niches previously occupied by dinosaurs and other extinct species. For example, a tiny hoofed mammal now called *Procerberus* made the trek across Beringia from Asia to North America and within about 4 million years spawned dozens of new species of hoofed mammals in the New World, the largest the size of a small pony. *Procerberus* became the ancient ancestor of both horses and camels, species that evolved first in North America.

In the millions of years that followed ancestor species' initial migration from Asia, distinctive North American descendants evolved, just as horses and camels did. The ancestor of North American cats migrated from Asia about 17 million years ago, but within a few million years, North America had evolved distinctive cat species, including lions roughly twice as large as the largest male African lions today. Similarly, nature's migrants from Asia developed into distinctive North American elephants (including mammoths), rhinoceroses, and pigs, as well as many smaller creatures such as beavers, skunks, and weasels. Although the migration of ancient birds is less well known because of the scarcity of fossil remains, the ancestor of today's common raven made the colossal journey to North America over millions of years by flying through Asia from its starting point in Australia.

Some animals that evolved in North America eventually migrated back to Asia and beyond. Horses and camels illustrate this two-way traffic on the Beringian land bridge. Horses evolved in North America for about 20 million years before they first wandered across the land bridge to Asia. They didn't stop there. Modern-day zebras on the plains of Africa are the descendants of those

Meteor Impact in North America, 65 Million Years Ago

North America

ATLANTIC OCEAN

PACIFIC OCEAN

South America

Saber-Toothed Cat Skeleton

Saber-toothed cats ranged throughout North America when the first Americans arrived. This fossilized skeleton came from the La Brea tar pits in present-day Los Angeles, California. For millennia before the arrival of human beings in the New World, these cats and 660 other animal species became bogged down in the tar pits, which ultimately served to preserve their remains. Hundreds of thousands of saber-toothed cat bones have been recovered from the tar pit deposits. The cats probably used their huge incisors to tear open the throats or abdomens of their prey. Unlike the swift-footed big cats of today, saber-toothed cats did not chase down their prey. Since they weighed about twice as much as modern lions, they crouched in ambush and leaped on unsuspecting victims nearby. This mode of attack probably accounts for the many fossils in the tar pits. Cats who attacked prey mired in the sticky tar probably became trapped themselves sometimes. Like many other big mammals that inhabited North America during the Paleo-Indian era, the saber-toothed cat became extinct about 11,000 BP.

George C. Page Museum.

On the eve of the arrival of ancient Americans in the New World, the large mammals they would prey upon—and in some cases compete with for prey—were the descendants of migrants who had preceded the first Americans millions of years earlier. The giant bison who roamed the plains—and whose fossilized remains George McJunkin excavated early in the twentieth century—descended from Asian migrants. So did the giant sloths that measured eighteen feet from nose to tail and weighed three tons. So did the massive short-faced bear that ran down its prey despite weighing the better part of a ton. So did the saber-toothed cat that, fossil deposits prove, feasted on young mammoths. And so did the mammoths themselves. The human beings who first set foot in the New World were pioneers of human migration to North America, but they were only the latest of latecomers among the thousands of nature's migrants from Asia that had been pioneering in North America for more than 60 million years.

BIBLIOGRAPHY

Jordi Agusti and Mauricio Anton, *Mammoths, Sabertooths, and Hominids* (2002).

Miles Barton et al., *Prehistoric America: A Journey through the Ice Age and Beyond* (2002).

Claudine Cohen, *The Fate of the Mammoth: Fossils, Myth, and History* (2002).

Tim Flannery, *The Eternal Frontier: An Ecological History of North America and Its Peoples* (2001).

Richard Fortey, *Life: A Natural History of the First Four Billion Years of Life on Earth* (1997).

Ian Lange, *Ice Age Mammals of North America* (2002).

ancient American migrant horses. Camels were much more recent outmigrants, wending their way from North America to Asia only about 4 million years ago. Dogs, evidently one of the few native North American mammals, also migrated to Asia, along with other distinctive species. But the dominant stream of nature's migrants was in the other direction, from Asia to North America. The greater variety of well-established species in the larger Asian landmass made it difficult for many North American species to get a foothold there. Conversely, migrants from Asia more readily carved out an environmental niche for themselves in the New World.

Mammoth Cave Painting

Like Clovis people in ancient America, human beings elsewhere in the world hunted mammoths. An ancient artist painted this portrait of mammoths on the wall of a cave in southern France about 16,000 BP. The painting conveys the artist's close observation of mammoths. It is easy to understand why the artist and hunters throughout the world paid respectful attention to mammoths. North American mammoths hunted by Clovis Paleo-Indians stood about fourteen feet tall at the shoulder and weighed eight to ten tons. Their tusks stretched to sixteen feet in length. Each of their four teeth was about the size of a shoebox. Although mammoths were vegetarians, they presumably knew how to throw their weight around against puny humans. Hunters armed with stone-tipped wooden spears needed to study such formidable prey to identify their vulnerabilities.

Musée de l'Homme.

America before Beringia once again disappeared beneath the sea will never be known. When they came is hotly debated by experts. The first migrants probably arrived sometime after 15,000 BP. Scattered and inconclusive evidence suggests that they may have arrived a few thousand years earlier. Certainly humans inhabited the Western Hemisphere by 13,000 BP.

Archaeologists refer to these first migrants and their descendants for the next few millennia as Paleo-Indians. While the date of their arrival is somewhat uncertain, they certainly originated in Asia. Some archaeologists have speculated that the Paleo-Indians may have sailed across the South Pacific from Polynesia or across the North Atlantic from Europe, but no evidence conclusively supports such views. Instead, detailed analyses of Native American languages, blood proteins, and DNA patterns, along with extensive archaeological discoveries, provide conclusive evidence of the first Americans' Asian origins.

Paleo-Indian Hunters

When humans first arrived in the Western Hemisphere, massive glaciers covered most of present-day Canada. A narrow corridor not entirely obstructed by ice ran along the eastern side of the Canadian Rockies, and most archaeologists believe that Paleo-Indians migrated through the ice-free passageway in pursuit of game. They may also have traveled along the coast in small boats, hopscotching from one desirable landing spot to another. At the southern edge of the glaciers, Paleo-Indians entered a hunters' paradise. North, Central, and South America teemed with wildlife that had never before confronted wily two-legged predators armed with razor-sharp spears. The abundance of game presumably made hunting relatively easy. Ample food permitted the Paleo-Indian population to grow. Within a thousand years or so, Paleo-Indians had migrated to the southern tip of South America and virtually everywhere else in the Western Hemisphere.

Paleo-Indians used a distinctively shaped spearhead known now as a Clovis point, named for the place in New Mexico where it was first excavated. Archaeologists' discovery of Clovis points throughout North and Central America in sites occupied between 11,500 BP and 11,000 BP is powerful evidence that these nomadic hunters shared a common ancestry and way of life. The Paleo-Indians probably hunted smaller animals, but most of the artifacts that have survived from this era indicate that the first Americans specialized in hunting mammoths. One mammoth kill supplied meat for weeks or, if dried, for months. Mammoth hide and bones provided clothing, shelter, tools, and much more.

About 11,000 BP, Paleo-Indians confronted a major crisis. The mammoths and other big-game

Clovis Spear Straightener

Clovis hunters used this bone spear straightener about 11,000 BP at a campsite in Arizona where archaeologists discovered it lying among the butchered remains of two mammoth carcasses and thirteen ancient bison. Similar objects often appear in ancient sites in Eurasia, but this is the only bone artifact yet discovered in a Clovis-era site in North America. Presumably Clovis hunters stuck their spear shafts through the opening and then grasped the handle of the straightener and moved it back and forth along the length of the shaft to remove imperfections and make the spear a more effective weapon.

Arizona State Museum, University of Arizona.

animals they hunted became extinct. Scientists are not completely certain why the extinction occurred, although the changing environment probably contributed to it. About this time the Wisconsin glacial period came to an end, glaciers melted, and sea levels rose. Some large mammals probably had difficulty adapting to the warmer climate. Many archaeologists also believe, however, that Paleo-Indians contributed to the New World extinctions by killing these animals more rapidly than they could reproduce. Within just a few thousand years of their arrival in the Western Hemisphere, Paleo-Indian hunters helped bring about a radical change in the natural environment—namely the extinction of large mammals that had existed for millions of years and whose presence had initially drawn hunters west across Beringia.

Paleo-Indians adapted to the drastic environmental change of the big-game extinctions by making at least two important changes in their way of life. First, hunters began to prey more intensively on smaller animals. Second, Paleo-Indians devoted more energy to foraging, that is, to collecting wild plant foods such as roots, seeds, nuts, berries, and fruits. When Paleo-Indians made these changes, they replaced the apparent uniformity of the big-game-oriented Clovis culture* with great cultural diversity. This diversity arose because ancient Americans adapted to the many natural environments throughout the hemisphere, ranging from icy tundra to steamy jungles.

Post-Clovis adaptations to local environments resulted in the astounding variety of Native American cultures that existed when Europeans arrived in AD 1492. By then, more than three hundred major tribes and hundreds of lesser groups inhabited North America alone. Hundreds more lived in Central and South America. These peoples spoke different languages, practiced different religions, lived in different dwellings, followed different subsistence strategies, and observed different rules of kinship and inheritance. Hundreds of other ancient American cultures had disappeared or transformed themselves as their people constantly adapted to environmental and other changes. A full account of those changes and the cultural diversity they created is beyond the scope of this textbook. But we cannot ignore the most important changes and adaptations made by ancient Americans during the last eleven millennia.

> About 11,000 BP, Paleo-Indians confronted a major crisis. The mammoths and other big-game animals they hunted became extinct.

Archaic Hunters and Gatherers

Archaeologists use the term **Archaic** to describe both the many different hunting and gathering cultures that descended from Paleo-Indians and the long period of time when those cultures dominated the history of ancient America, roughly from 10,000 BP to somewhere between 3000 BP and 4000 BP. Although the cultural and the chronological boundaries of the Archaic era are not sharply defined, the term usefully describes the important era in the history of ancient America that followed the Paleo-Indian big-game hunters and preceded the development of agriculture. It also denotes a hunter-gatherer way of life that persisted throughout most of North America well into the era of European colonization.

Like their Paleo-Indian ancestors, Archaic Indians hunted with spears; but they also took smaller game with traps, nets, and hooks. Unlike their Paleo-Indian predecessors, most Archaic peoples used a variety of stone tools to prepare food from wild plants. A characteristic Archaic artifact is a grinding stone used to pulverize seeds into edible form. Most Archaic Indians migrated from place to place to harvest plants and hunt animals. They usually did not establish permanent villages, although they often returned to the same river valley or fertile meadow from year to year to take advantage of abundant food resources. In certain regions with especially rich resources—such as present-day California and the Pacific Northwest—they developed permanent settlements. Many groups became highly proficient basket makers in order to collect and

---

* The word *culture* is used here to connote what is commonly called "way of life." It refers not only to how a group of people supplied themselves with food and shelter but also to their family relationships, social groupings, religious ideas, and other features of their lives. For most prehistoric cultures—as for the Clovis people—more is known about food and shelter because of the artifacts that have survived. Ancient American's ideas, assumptions, hopes, dreams, and fantasies were undoubtedly important, but we know very little about them.

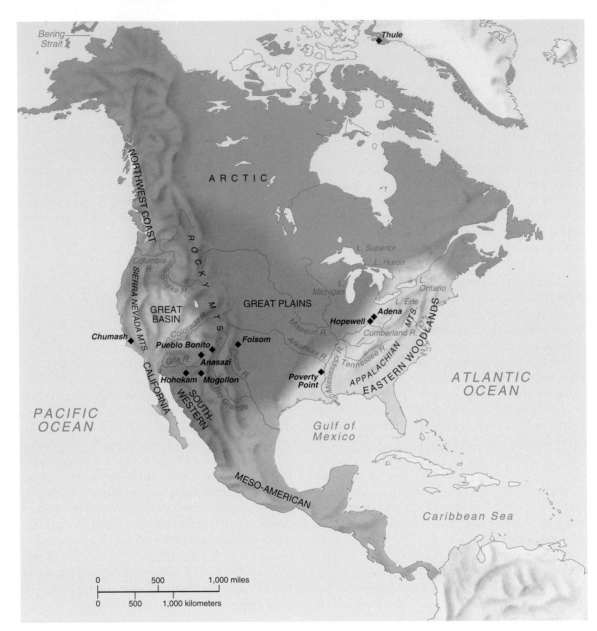

MAP 1.2   Native North American Cultures
Environmental conditions defined the boundaries of the broad zones of cultural similarity among ancient North Americans.

READING THE MAP: What crucial environmental features set the boundaries of each cultural region? (The topography indicated on Map 1.3, "Native North Americans about 1500," may be helpful.)

CONNECTIONS: How did environmental factors and variations affect the development of different groups of Native American cultures? Why do you think historians and archaeologists group cultures together by their regional positions?

FOR MORE HELP ANALYZING THIS MAP, see the map activity for this chapter in the Online Study Guide at
bedfordstmartins.com/roark.

store plant food. Above all, Archaic folk did not depend on agriculture for food. Instead, they gathered wild plants and hunted wild animals. Archaic peoples expressed these general traits in distinctive ways in the major environmental regions of North America (Map 1.2).

Great Plains Bison Hunters

After the extinction of large game such as mammoths, some hunters began to concentrate on huge herds of bison that grazed the grassy, arid plains stretching for hundreds of miles east of the Rocky Mountains. For almost a thousand years after the big-game extinctions, Archaic Indians hunted bison with Folsom points like those found at the site discovered by George McJunkin.

Like their nomadic predecessors, Folsom hunters moved constantly to maintain contact with their prey. Often two or three hunters from a band of several families would single out a few bison from a herd and creep up close enough to spear them. Great Plains hunters also developed trapping techniques that made it easier to kill large numbers of animals. At the original Folsom site, careful study of the bones McJunkin found suggests that early one winter hunters drove bison into the arroyo and speared twenty-three of them. At many other sites, hunters stampeded large numbers of bison over cliffs, killing some and injuring others, which Indians then readily slaughtered.

Bows and arrows reached Great Plains hunters from the north about AD 500. They largely replaced spears, which had been the hunters' weapon of choice for millennia. Bows permitted hunters to wound an animal from farther away, and arrows made it easy to shoot repeatedly. These new weapons did not otherwise alter the age-old techniques of bison hunting that ancient Americans had practiced since the Folsom era.

Great Basin Cultures

Archaic peoples in the Great Basin between the Rocky Mountains and the Sierra Nevada inhabited a region of great environmental diversity. Some Great Basin Indians lived along the shores of large marshes and lakes that formed during rainy periods. They ate fish of every available size and type, catching them with bone hooks and nets. Other cultures survived in the foothills of mountains between the blistering heat on the desert floor and the cold, treeless mountain heights. Hunters killed deer, antelope, and sometimes bison, as well as smaller game like rabbits, rodents, and snakes. These broadly defined zones of habitation changed constantly, depending largely on the amount of rainfall.

Despite the variety and occasional abundance of animals, Great Basin peoples relied on plants as the most important source of food. Unlike meat and fish, plant food could be collected in large quantities and stored in baskets for long periods to protect against shortages caused by the fickle rainfall. Many Great Basin peoples depended on ample supplies of piñon nuts as a dietary staple. By diversifying their food sources and migrating to favorable locations to collect and store them, Great Basin peoples adapted to the severe environmental challenges of the region and maintained their Archaic hunter-gatherer way of life for centuries after AD 1492.

Pacific Coast Cultures

The richness of the natural environment made present-day California the most densely settled area in all of ancient North America. The abundant resources of both land and ocean offered

Folsom Point at Wild Horse Arroyo

In 1927, paleontologist J. D. Figgins found this spear point (subsequently named a Folsom point) at the site discovered by George McJunkin. Embedded between the fossilized ribs of a bison that had been extinct for 10,000 years, this point proved that ancient Americans had inhabited the hemisphere at least that long. The importance of this find led one paleontologist to hold up several Folsom points and proclaim, "In my hand I hold the answer to the antiquity of man in America." Although he exaggerated (Folsom was only part of the answer), this discovery in Wild Horse Arroyo stimulated archaeologists to rethink the history of ancient Americans and to uncover fresh evidence of their many cultures.

such ample food that California peoples remained hunters and gatherers for hundreds of years after AD 1492. The diversity of California's environment encouraged corresponding diversity among native peoples. The mosaic of Archaic settlements in California included about five hundred separate tribes speaking some ninety languages, each with local dialects. No other region of comparable size in North America exhibited such cultural variety.

The Chumash, one of the many California cultures, emerged in the region surrounding what is now Santa Barbara about 5000 BP. Comparatively plentiful food resources—especially acorns—permitted Chumash people to establish relatively permanent villages. Conflict frequently broke out among the villages, documented by the notable proportion of skeletons in Chumash burial grounds that display signs of violent deaths. Archaeologists believe that these conflicts arose in part from efforts by Chumash villagers to restrict access to their valuable acorn-gathering territory. Although few other California cultures achieved the population density and village settlements of the Chumash, all shared the hunter-gatherer way of life and reliance on acorns as a major food source.

Another rich natural environment lay along the Pacific Northwest coast. Like the Chumash, Northwest peoples built more or less permanent villages. Abundant fish and marine life permitted ancient Americans in this region to devote substantial time and energy to activities other than hunting and gathering. After about 5500 BP, they concentrated on catching large quantities of salmon, halibut, and other fish, which they dried to last throughout the year and to trade with people who lived hundreds of miles from the coast. Fishing freed Northwest peoples to develop sophisticated woodworking skills. They fashioned elaborate wood carvings that denoted wealth and status as well as huge canoes, some big enough to hold fifty people, for fishing,

> Fishing freed Northwest peoples to develop sophisticated woodworking skills.

Ancient California

hunting, and conducting warfare against neighboring tribes. Much of the warfare among Archaic northwesterners grew out of attempts to defend or gain access to prime fishing sites. Northwestern peoples also carved distinctive totem poles to adorn their houses with images of animals, ancestors, and supernatural beings.

Eastern Woodland Cultures

East of the Mississippi River, Archaic peoples adapted to a forest environment that included many local variants, such as the major river valleys of the Mississippi, Ohio, Tennessee, and Cumberland; the Great Lakes region; and the Atlantic coast (see Map 1.2). Throughout these

Chumash Necklace
Long before the arrival of Europeans, ancient Chumash people in southern California made this elegant necklace of abalone shell. The carefully formed, polished, and assembled pieces of shell illustrate the artistry of the Chumash and their access to the rich and diverse marine life of the Pacific coast. Since living abalone cling stubbornly to submerged rocks along the coast, Chumash divers presumably pried abalone from their rocky perches to obtain their delicious flesh; then one or more Chumash artisans recycled the inedible shell to make this necklace. Its iridescent splendor demonstrates that Chumash people wore beautiful as well as useful adornments.
Natural History Museum of Los Angeles County.

Ozette Whale Effigy
This carving of a whale fin decorated with hundreds of sea otter teeth was discovered along with thousands of other artifacts of daily life at Ozette, an ancient village on the tip of the Olympic Peninsula in present-day Washington that was inundated by a catastrophic mud slide about five hundred years ago. The fin illustrates the importance of whale hunting to the residents of Ozette, who set out in canoes carrying eight men armed with harpoons to catch and kill animals weighing twenty to thirty tons.
Richard Alexander Cooke III.

diverse locales, Archaic peoples followed similar survival strategies.

Woodland hunters stalked deer as their most important prey. Deer supplied Woodland people with food as well as with hides and bones that they crafted into clothing, weapons, needles, and many other tools. Like Archaic peoples elsewhere, Woodland Indians gathered edible plants, seeds, and especially nuts. Most commonly, they gathered hickory nuts, but they also collected pecans, walnuts, acorns, and hazelnuts. About 6000 BP, some Woodland groups established more or less permanent settlements of 25 to 150 people, usually near a river or lake that offered a wide variety of plant and animal resources. The existence of such settlements has permitted archaeologists to locate numerous Archaic burial sites that suggest Woodland people had a life expectancy of about eighteen years.

Around 4000 BP, Woodland cultures added two important new features to their basic hunter-gatherer lifestyles: agriculture and pottery. Gourds and pumpkins that originated thousands of years earlier in Mexico spread to North America through trade and migration, and Woodland peoples began to grow them in parts of Missouri and Kentucky. After the introduction of these Mexican crops, Woodland peoples also began to cultivate local species such as sunflowers. They probably also grew small quantities of tobacco, another import from South America, since stone pipes for smoking appeared by about 3500 BP. Corn, the most important plant food in Mexico, became a significant Woodland food crop more than a thousand years later. These cultivated crops added to the quantity, variety, and predictability of Woodland food sources, but they did not fundamentally alter Woodland peoples' dependence on gathering wild plants, seeds, and nuts.

Techniques for making ceramic pots probably also originated in Mexico. Traders and migrants probably brought them into North America along with Central and South American seeds. Pots were more durable than baskets for cooking and storage of water and food, but they were also much heavier. Nomadic people elsewhere in North America relied on baskets since pots were too heavy to move readily. The permanent settlements of Woodland peoples made the heavy weight of pots much less important than their advantages compared to leaky and fragile baskets.

> Around 4,000 years ago, the Woodland cultures added two important features to their hunter-gatherer lifestyles: agriculture and pottery.

Woodland Hairpins
Ancient Americans in present-day Florida crafted these hairpins from bone between roughly 4500 BP and AD 800. The intricate designs incised on the pins demonstrate the artists' interest and skill in decoration. The differences in design hint at the diversity of cultural styles among the Woodland people who produced them.
Courtesy of Barbara A. Purdy; photo by Roy Craven.

While pottery and agriculture introduced changes in Woodland cultures, ancient Woodland Americans retained the other basic features of their Archaic hunter-gatherer lifestyle, which persisted in most areas to 1492 and beyond.

> All southwestern peoples confronted the challenge of a dry climate and unpredictable fluctuations in rainfall that made the supply of wild plant food very unreliable. These ancient Americans probably adopted agriculture in response to this basic environmental condition.

Agricultural Settlements and Chiefdoms

Among Eastern Woodland peoples and other Archaic cultures, agriculture supplemented rather than replaced hunter-gatherer subsistence strategies. Reliance on wild animals and plants required most Archaic groups to remain small and mobile. But beginning about 4000 BP, distinctive southwestern cultures slowly came to depend on agriculture and to build permanent settlements. Later, around 2500 BP, Woodland peoples in the vast Mississippi valley began to construct burial mounds and other earthworks that suggest the existence of social and political hierarchies that archaeologists term chiefdoms. Although the hunter-gatherer lifestyle never entirely disappeared, the development of agricultural settlements and chiefdoms represented important innovations to the Archaic way of life.

Southwestern Cultures

Ancient Americans in what is now Arizona, New Mexico, and southern portions of Utah and Colorado developed cultures characterized by agriculture and eventually by multiunit dwellings called pueblos. All southwestern peoples confronted the challenge of a dry climate and unpredictable fluctuations in rainfall that made the supply of wild plant food very unreliable. These ancient Americans probably adopted agriculture in response to this basic environmental condition.

Until about 5000 BP, few people lived in the Southwest. As the population slowly grew during the next 1,500 years, southwestern hunters and gatherers began to cultivate their signature food crop, corn, which had been grown in Central and South America since about 7000 BP. During the next 3,000 years, corn became the most important cultivated crop for ancient Americans throughout North America. In the Southwest, the demands of corn cultivation encouraged hunter-gatherers to restrict their migratory habits in order to tend the crop. A vital consideration was access to water. Southwestern Indians became irrigation experts, conserving water from streams, springs, and rainfall and distributing it to thirsty crops.

Ancient Agriculture
Dropping seeds into holes punched in cleared ground by a pointed stick, known as a "dibble," this ancient American farmer sows a new crop while previously planted seeds—including the corn and beans immediately opposite him—bear fruit for harvest. Created by a sixteenth-century European artist, the drawing misrepresents who did the agricultural work in many ancient American cultures—namely women rather than men. However, the three-foot dibble would have been used as shown here.
The Pierpont Morgan Library/Art Resource, NY; Jerry Jacka Photography.

About AD 200, small farming settlements began to appear throughout southern New Mexico, marking the emergence of the Mogollon culture. Typically, a Mogollon settlement included a dozen pit houses, made by digging out a rounded pit about fifteen feet in diameter and a foot or two deep and then erecting poles to support a roof of branches or dirt. Larger villages usually had one or two bigger pit houses that may have been the predecessors of the circular *kivas*, the ceremonial rooms that became a characteristic of nearly all southwestern settlements. About AD 1000, Mogollon culture began to decline, for reasons that remain obscure. Its descendants included the Mimbres peoples in southwestern New Mexico, who produced spectacular pottery often adorned with human and animal designs. By about AD 1250, the Mimbres culture also disappeared.

Around AD 500, while the Mogollon culture prevailed in New Mexico, other ancient people migrated from Mexico to southern Arizona and established the distinctive Hohokam culture. Hohokam settlements used sophisticated grids of irrigation canals to take advantage of the abundant sunshine that permitted them to plant and harvest twice a year. Irrigation produced comparatively high crop yields, permitting the Hohokam population to grow and seek out more land to settle. Hohokam culture reflected the continuing influence of its origins in Mexico. The people built sizable platform mounds and ball courts characteristic of many Mexican cultures to the south. Hohokam culture declined about AD 1400, for reasons that remain a mystery.

North of the Hohokam and Mogollon cultures, in a region that encompassed southern Utah and Colorado and northern Arizona and New Mexico, the Anasazi culture began to flourish about AD 100. The early Anasazi built pit houses on mesa tops and used irrigation much like their neighbors to the south. Beginning around AD 1000 (again, it is not known why), Anasazi began to move to large, multistory cliff dwellings whose spectacular ruins still exist at Mesa Verde, Colorado, and

Southwestern Cultures

Canyon de Chelly, Arizona. Other Anasazi communities—like the one whose impressive ruins can be visited at Chaco Canyon, New Mexico (see "American Places," page 20)—erected huge, stone-walled pueblos with enough rooms to house everyone in the settlement. Pueblo Bonito at Chaco Canyon, for example, contained more than eight hundred rooms. Anasazi pueblos and cliff dwellings typically contained one or more kivas used for secret ceremonies, restricted to men, that sought to communicate with the supernatural world.

Drought began to plague the region about AD 1130, and it lasted for more than half a century, triggering the disappearance of Anasazi culture. By AD 1200, the large Anasazi pueblos had been abandoned. The prolonged drought probably intensified conflict among pueblos and made it impossible to depend on the techniques of irrigated agriculture that worked for centuries. Some Anasazi migrated toward regions with more reliable rainfall and settled in Hopi, Zuñi, and Acoma pueblos that their descendants in Arizona and New Mexico have occupied ever since.

Hohokam "Cigarettes"
Ancient Hohokam smokers in present-day Arizona stuffed these reeds (which probably grew near their irrigation canals) with shredded tobacco. They wrapped cotton thread around each reed to protect their fingers from heat while they inhaled the smoke of the burning tobacco. When hunting or tending their crops, Hohokam smokers probably found these "cigarettes" more convenient than their heavier and more cumbersome stone or ceramic pipes, which were better suited for sedentary occasions.
Jerry Jacka Photography.

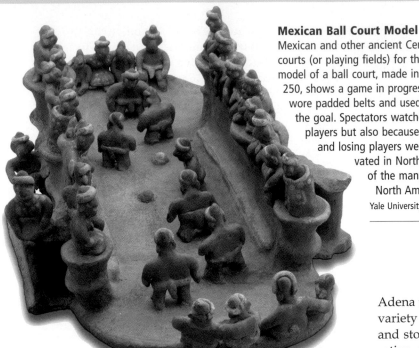

Mexican Ball Court Model
Mexican and other ancient Central American cultures commonly built special courts (or playing fields) for their intensely competitive ball games. This rare model of a ball court, made in Mexico sometime between 2200 BP and AD 250, shows a game in progress, complete with players and spectators. Players wore padded belts and used their hips to hit the hard rubber ball through the goal. Spectators watched intently, not only to admire the skills of the players but also because a lot was at stake. Spectators bet on the game, and losing players were often killed. A few ball courts have been excavated in North America, providing compelling evidence of one of the many connections between ancient Mexicans and North Americans.

Yale University Art Gallery. Stephen Carlton Clark, B.A. 1903, Fund.

Woodland Burial Mounds and Chiefdoms

No other ancient Americans created dwellings similar to pueblos, but around 2500 BP, Woodland cultures throughout the vast drainage of the Mississippi River began to build burial mounds. The size of the mounds, the labor and organization required to erect them, and the differences in the artifacts buried with certain individuals suggest the existence of a social and political hierarchy that archaeologists term a chiefdom. Experts do not know the name of a single chief, nor do they know the organizational structure a chief headed. But the only way archaeologists can account for the complex and labor-intensive burial mounds and artifacts found in them is to assume that one person—whom scholars term a chief—had the ability to command the labor and obedience of very large numbers of other people, who comprised the chief's chiefdom.

Between 2500 BP and 2100 BP, Adena people built hundreds of burial mounds radiating from central Ohio. In the mounds, the

Major Mississippian Mounds, AD 800–1500

Adena usually accompanied burials with a wide variety of grave goods, including spear points and stone pipes as well as decorative and ritualistic items such as thin sheets of mica (a glasslike mineral) crafted into shapes of birds, beasts, and human hands. Over the body and grave goods Adena people piled basketful after basketful of dirt until a mound formed. Sometimes burial mounds were constructed all at once, but often they were built up slowly over many years.

About 2100 BP, Adena culture evolved into the more elaborate Hopewell culture, which lasted about 500 years. While centered in Ohio, Hopewell culture extended throughout the vast drainage of the Ohio and Mississippi rivers. Hopewell people built larger mounds and filled them with more magnificent grave goods than had their Adena predecessors.

Burial was probably reserved for the most important members of Hopewell groups. Most people were cremated. Burial rituals appear to have brought many people together to honor the dead person and to help build the mound. Hopewell mounds were often 100 feet in diameter and 30 feet high. Careful analysis of skeletons in one Hopewell mound suggests the high status of hunters. Elbows of men in the more important graves showed signs of arthritis associated with stress to the elbow joint caused by repetitive spear-throwing. Grave goods at Hopewell sites testify to the high quality of Hopewell crafts and to the existence of a thriving trade network that ranged from Wyoming to Florida. Archaeologists believe that Hopewell chiefs probably played an important role in this sprawling interregional trade.

lasted until about AD 1500. Major Mississippian sites included huge mounds with platforms on top for ceremonies and for the residences of great chiefs. The largest Mississippian site was Cahokia, located in present-day Illinois near the confluence of the Mississippi and Missouri rivers at St. Louis, Missouri.

At Cahokia, more than one hundred mounds of different sizes and shapes were grouped around large open plazas. Monk's Mound, the largest, covered sixteen acres at its base and was one hundred feet tall. Dwellings at one time covered five square miles and may have housed as many as thirty thousand inhabitants, easily qualifying Cahokia as the largest settlement in ancient North America. At Cahokia and other Mississippian sites, people evidently worshipped a sun god; the mounds probably were supposed to elevate elites nearer to the divine power of the sun. One Cahokia burial mound suggests the authority a great chief exercised. One man—presumably the chief—was buried with the bodies of more than sixty people who had been killed at the time of burial, including fifty young women who had been strangled. Such a mass sacrifice shows the coercive power a Cahokia chief wielded and the obedience he commanded.

Cahokia and other Mississippian cultures had dwindled by AD 1500. When Europeans arrived, most of the descendants of Mississippian cultures, like those of the Hopewell culture, lived in small dispersed villages supported by hunting and gathering supplemented by agriculture.

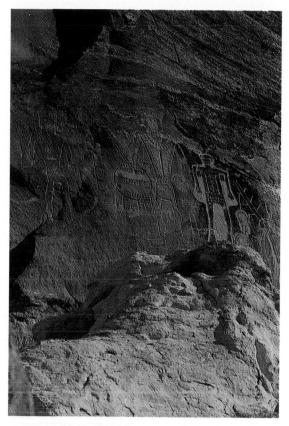

Ashley Creek Petroglyph
Ancient Americans incised this large petroglyph on a rock wall in present-day Utah. The elaborate shield and regalia (the headdress, breastplate, belt, and skirt) suggest that the larger figure depicts a chief or a warrior (who may also have been a chief). Experts do not know the meaning of these and other petroglyphs, although the care with which they were rendered proves that they were significant to the ancient Southwestern artists who made them.
J. Q. Jacobs.

FOR MORE HELP ANALYZING THIS IMAGE, see the visual activity for this chapter in the Online Study Guide at bedfordstmartins.com/roark.

Hopewell culture declined about AD 400 for reasons that are obscure. Archaeologists speculate that bows and arrows, along with increasing reliance on agriculture, made small settlements more self-sufficient and, therefore, less dependent on the central authority of the Hopewell chiefs who were responsible for the burial mounds.

Four hundred years later, another mound-building culture flourished. The Mississippian culture emerged in the floodplains of the major southeastern river systems about AD 800 and

Woodland Eagle Carving
This eagle effigy topped a post in a charnel house where Woodland Indians deposited the remains of their dead ancestors sometime between 1,500 and 1,000 years ago at a site in present-day Florida. The significance of the eagle is unknown; it may have represented the clan of the deceased in the charnel house.
The Detroit Institute of Arts.

Chaco Culture National Historical Park, Nageezi, New Mexico

Visitors to Chaco Culture National Historical Park can literally walk in the footsteps of ancient Americans. You can roam around plazas of Anasazi pueblos where hundreds of people lived; stroll through rooms where they cooked, conversed, and slept; enter kivas where they worshipped and performed secret rituals; climb up stairs they carved in steep cliffs; and hike for miles along straight roadways they built that seemingly lead to nowhere. Located in northwestern New Mexico about 200 miles west of George McJunkin's discovery at Folsom, Chaco is one of the most spectacular ancient sites in North America. About AD 1000, the massive residential and ceremonial buildings you can visit today stood at the center of Chacoan culture that extended over more than 20,000 square miles into the present-day Four Corners region at the intersection of Utah, Colorado, Arizona, and New Mexico.

The Chaco people were expert builders, constructing hundreds of masonry structures of awe-inspiring size and complexity. Like other Southwestern peoples, the Anasazi at Chaco hunted game and used irrigation to grow corn and other crops. But the scale and magnificence of their buildings strongly suggests that they were engaged in far more than simple subsistence. Large quantities of turquoise have been found in Chaco sites, providing evidence that Anasazi brought this valuable stone to Chaco Canyon for gifts, offerings, or trade. The numerous large kivas suggest that many people may have come to Chaco to participate in ceremonies and rituals. Major buildings appear to have been aligned to mark important astronomical events, such as the spring and winter solstices and the phases of the lunar cycle.

These solar and lunar alignments provide striking evidence that Chaco people were keenly attuned to heavenly events. They hint that the ceremonies held at Chaco may have symbolized the site's potent connection between earth and sky, between humans and the omnipotent celestial ruler. Even the carefully constructed roads that radiated for miles from major Chaco buildings seem to have been used for ceremony rather than transportation. Researchers continue to study the multitude of Chacoan artifacts to attempt to unravel the many mysteries of Anasazi history. Few visitors to Chaco will fail to be amazed by the stunning achievements of Anasazi minds and hands. And few will fail to be awed by the silent majesty of this premier ancient American place.

For Web links related to this site and other American Places, see "PlaceLinks" at bedfordstmartins.com/roark.

Pueblo Bonito, Chaco Canyon, New Mexico
Richard Alexander Cooke III.

Native Americans in the 1490s

About thirteen millennia after Paleo-Indians first migrated to the Western Hemisphere, a new migration—this time from Europe—began in 1492 with the journey of Columbus. In the decades before the arrival of Columbus, Native Americans continued to employ their ancestors' time-tested survival strategies of hunting, gathering, and agriculture. Those strategies succeeded in both populating and shaping the new world Europeans encountered.

By the 1490s, Native Americans lived throughout North America, but their total population is a subject of heated debate among scholars. Some experts claim Native Americans numbered 18 million to 20 million, while others place the population at no more than a million. A prudent estimate is about 4 million. On the eve of European colonization, the small island nation of England had about the same number of people as all of North America. This comparison highlights the low population density in North America. In England, every hundred square miles of land had a population of about 8,000. In North America, the same area had only about sixty people. Compared to England and elsewhere in Europe, Native Americans were spread thin across the land, an outgrowth of their survival strategies of hunting, gathering, and agriculture.

FIGURE 1.2 Native American Population in North America, about 1492 (Estimated)
On the eve of the arrival of Europeans, about a fifth of all native North Americans lived along the Pacific coast—in California and the Northwest—where rich marine resources supported hunter-gatherers in much higher population densities than elsewhere in North America. About a quarter of native North Americans resided in the Southwest, where they depended on agriculture, unlike the Pacific coast peoples. Since sparse rainfall made the southwestern environment less bountiful than that of the Pacific coast, the population density in the Southwest was roughly half that on the West Coast. Woodland peoples east of the Mississippi River—in the Northeast and Southeast—comprised almost a third of native North Americans. Woodland deer and plants supplemented by agriculture supported a lower population density than in the Southwest or the West Coast. The population density on the enormous expanses of the Great Plains, Great Basin, and Arctic regions was very low, although in total about a quarter of all native North Americans resided in these areas. Overall, the population density in North America was less than 1 percent of the population density of England, which helps explain why European colonists tended to view North America as a comparatively empty wilderness.

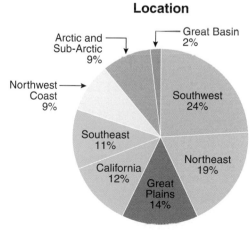

Regions in North America with abundant resources had relatively high population densities. In food-rich California and the Northwest Coast, the population density was, respectively, six times greater and four times greater than the average for the whole continent. In the food-scarce Great Plains and Great Basin, the population density was, respectively, half and one-third as much as the continental average. But even in the most densely inhabited region of North America, California, the population density was still just one-twentieth of England's.

By the 1490s, about a third of Native Americans lived in the Eastern Woodland region, which stretched west from the Atlantic coast nearly to the Mississippi, and from the Great Lakes south to the Gulf of Mexico. Eastern Woodland peoples clustered into three broad linguistic and cultural groups: Algonquian, Iroquoian, and Muskogean.

Algonquian tribes inhabited the Atlantic seaboard, the Great Lakes region, and much of the upper Midwest (Map 1.3). The relatively mild climate along the Atlantic permitted the coastal Algonquians to grow corn and other crops as well as to hunt and fish. Around the Great Lakes and in northern New England, however, cool summers and severe winters made agriculture impractical. Instead, the Abenaki, Penobscot, Chippewa, and other tribes concentrated on hunting and fishing, using canoes both for transportation and for gathering wild rice.

MAP 1.3 Native North Americans about 1500
Distinctive Native American peoples resided throughout the area that, centuries later, would become the United States. This map indicates the approximate location of some of the larger tribes about 1500. In the interest of legibility, many other peoples who inhabited North America at the time are omitted from the map.

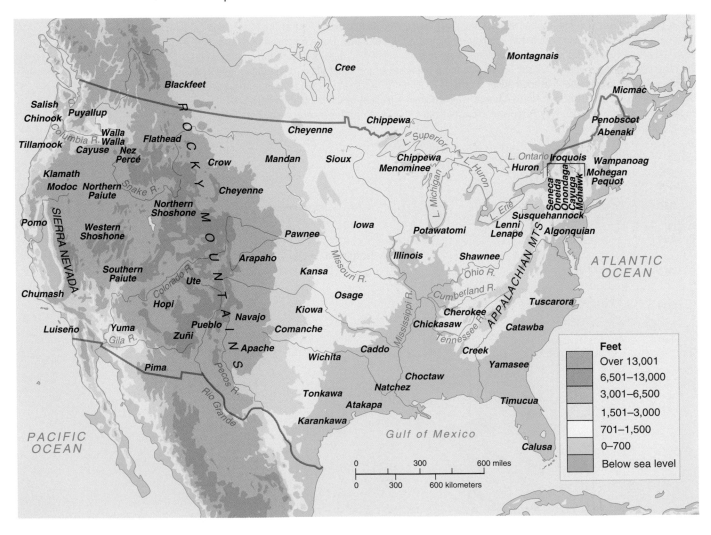

Inland from the Algonquian region, Iroquoian tribes occupied territories centered in Pennsylvania and upstate New York, as well as the hilly upland regions of the Carolinas and Georgia. Several features distinguished Iroquoian tribes from their neighbors. First, their success in cultivating corn and other crops allowed them to build permanent settlements, usually consisting of several bark-covered longhouses up to one hundred feet long and housing five to ten families. Second, Iroquoian societies adhered to matrilineal rules of descent. Property of all sorts, including land, children, and inheritance, belonged to women. Women headed family clans and even selected the chiefs (normally men) who governed tribes. Third, for purposes of war and diplomacy, an Iroquoian confederation—including the Seneca, Onondaga, Mohawk, Oneida, and Cayuga tribes—formed the League of Five Nations, which remained powerful well into the eighteenth century.

Muskogean peoples spread throughout the Southeast, south of the Ohio River and east of the Mississippi. Including Creek, Choctaw, Chickasaw, and Natchez tribes, Muskogeans inhabited a bountiful natural environment that provided abundant food from hunting, gathering, and agriculture. Remnants of the earlier Mississippian culture still existed in the religious rites common among the Muskogean. They practiced a form of sun worship, and the Natchez even built temple mounds modeled after those of their Mississippian ancestors.

Great Plains peoples accounted for about one out of seven Native Americans. Inhabiting the huge region west of the Eastern Woodland people and east of the Rocky Mountains, many tribes had migrated to the Great Plains within the last century or two, forced westward by Iroquoian and Algonquian tribes. Some Great Plains tribes—especially the Mandan and Pawnee—farmed successfully, growing both corn and sunflowers. But the Teton Sioux, Blackfeet, Comanche, Cheyenne, and Crow on the northern plains and the Apache and other nomadic tribes on the southern plains depended on buffalo for subsistence.

Southwestern cultures included about a quarter of all native North Americans. These descendants of the Mogollon, Hohokam, and Anasazi cultures lived in settled agricultural communities, many of them pueblos. They continued to grow corn, beans, and squash with methods they had refined for centuries. However, their communities came under attack by a large number of warlike Athapascan tribes who invaded the Southwest beginning around AD 1300. The Athapascans—principally Apache and Navajo—were skillful warriors who preyed on the sedentary pueblo Indians, reaping the fruits of agriculture without the work of farming.

About a fifth of all native North Americans resided along the Pacific coast. In California, abundant acorns and nutritious marine life supported high population densities but retarded the development of agriculture. Similar dependence on hunting and gathering persisted along the Northwest coast, where fishing reigned supreme. Salmon was so abundant that at the Dalles site on the Columbia River, Northwest peoples caught millions of pounds of salmon every summer and traded it as far away as California and the Great Plains. Although important trading centers existed throughout North America, particularly in the Southwest, it is likely that the Dalles site was the largest Native American trading center on the continent.

While trading was common—especially for such luxury items as highly nutritious dried salmon, or much prized stones, shells, and feathers—all native North Americans in the 1490s still depended on hunting and gathering for a major portion of their food. Most of them also practiced agriculture. Some used agriculture to supplement hunting and gathering; for others, the balance was reversed. People throughout North America used bows, arrows, and other weapons for hunting and warfare. None of them employed writing, expressing themselves instead in many other ways. They made drawings on stones, wood, and animal skins. They wove patterns in baskets and textiles. (See "The Promise of Technology," page 24.) They painted designs on pottery and crafted beadwork, pipes, and other decorative items. They danced, sang, and played music. They performed elaborate burial ceremonies and other religious rites.

These rich and varied cultural resources of Native Americans did not include features of life common in Europe during the 1490s. Native Americans did not use wheels; sailing ships were unknown to them; they had no large domesticated animals such as horses, cows, or

> Iroquoian societies adhered to matrilineal rules of descent. Property of all sorts, including land, children, and inheritance, belonged to women.

Ancient American Weaving

Weaving—like other ancient American activities such as cooking, hunting, and worship—required transmission of knowledge from person to person. The workbasket of a master weaver shown here illustrates the technology of ancient American textile production. Found in the Andes in a woman's grave dating from 1,000 years ago, the workbasket contains tools for every stage of textile production.

Most likely, the ancient American woman who owned this workbasket taught her skills to her daughters and other kinswomen. Novices learned by watching, by copying, and by listening to advice about what they did wrong. Since ancient Americans had no instruction manuals for weaving or anything else, all technological knowledge had to be remembered and passed from one person to another. Over time, details of knowledge accumulated into sophisticated technologies that produced marvels of human artistry such as the weaving shown here.

Mastery of the technology of weaving took many years of training and experience. Imagine that you were handed this workbasket and asked to make the weaving pictured here. First of all, you would need to know how to use the various tools in the workbasket. You would need to take fiber from cotton plants or animal wool (such as llama or alpaca) and spin it into thread. To make colored threads, you would dye the fibers before spinning, using different vegetable and mineral concoctions. The pointed sticks wrapped with thread (left center) are spindles for transforming the colored fibers into thread. You would use the small ceramic cup to hold one end of the spindle while you twisted the fiber through your fingers to create strong, thin thread. The two pieces of chalk (to the right of the ceramic cup) served to make a powder that lubricated your fingers to allow the thread to wind smoothly onto the spindle. Skeins of finished thread removed from their spindles are just to the left of the ceramic cup. This small workbasket contained more than 150 spindles for the many varieties of thread required. The beadlike objects at the center are whorls for placing on spindles to anchor the thread and provide decoration. On the right, above the ceramic cup, are bobbins used to pass the thread through the weaving, a bone pick to press down on the threads to tighten the weave, and a long spine needle with a tiny hole, to use for sewing and embroidery.

This simple example demonstrates that technology involves more than just physical objects—tools. Human beings must learn how to use the tools. The tools themselves embody the results of human learning that took place over many centuries. Presumably, a woman once discovered that it was easier to twist thread by holding the end of the spindle in a small cup. She probably taught the technique to friends. Eventually, this piece of knowledge became common

An Ancient American Weaver's Workbasket
Gift of Charles H. White. Courtesy of Museum of Fine Arts, Boston.

knowledge among weaving women, and they acquired a cup like the one in this workbasket.

Chances are, however, even if trained to use the tools in the weaver's workbasket, you could never weave fabrics like the one shown here. Weavers had to learn how to combine color, texture, and shape into a specific design or pattern. Designs were learned and passed from one person to another. Patterns such as those depicted on the weaving shown here required the weaver to learn, express, and transmit knowledge about much more than textile production. To weave an appropriate pattern, the weaver needed to know, for example, how to represent gods, omens, powerful leaders, or sacred places. She had to be familiar with the culture of the people she lived among—their religion, politics, economy, and social organization. Even in the unlikely event that you could *copy* this weaving, you could not possibly design other fabrics like an ancient American weaver without knowing and understanding her culture as she did. While weavers possessed specialized training and skill, their technological knowledge had to be used within the specific cultural contours of the people they lived among. A design for a commoner was not fit for a chief, nor was a woman's outfit suitable for a warrior.

The technologies of weaving, pottery-making, cooking, hunting, agriculture, and much more fit into distinctive cultural patterns among the thousands of diverse ancient American societies. Archaeologists use these cultural patterns to distinguish one group of ancient Americans from another. The enormous diversity of these patterns over the millennia of human occupation of the Western Hemisphere and throughout the vast geography of

Ancient Weaving

This tunic for Peruvian royalty illustrates the artistry a master weaver could achieve. Woven with wool and cotton sometime between AD 250 and AD 550, the tunic incorporates complex images denoting religious and political authority. In order to know what images to use and how to portray them, the weaver had to be as familiar with Peruvian culture as with the techniques of weaving.

Art Institute of Chicago.

North, Central, and South America reflects a basic fact about ancient American technology. Technological developments—such as weaving—occurred when and where they did partly because of subsistence needs and challenges posed by the natural environment. But the technology of weaving, like other technologies, depended above all on human knowledge that passed from one person to another in cycle after cycle of teaching and learning.

Over time, technological knowledge accumulated and achievements—like this weaving—could reach masterful levels of artistry. But the cycle of teaching and learning was fragile. A weaver's knowledge could die with her if it had not been taught to somebody else. Wars, famines, droughts, epidemics, and other disasters could—and did—extinguish technological knowledge along with its possessors. The fragility of the transmission of human knowledge helps explain the tremendous diversity among ancient American cultures. When the cycle of teaching and learning was broken, technologies and cultures died. Fresh and often distinctive technological knowledge had to be created anew, accumulated, and passed on. The technology of weaving practiced by the owner of this workbasket was developed by the women she learned from and passed on to the women she taught.

oxen; their use of metals was restricted to copper; and metallurgy did not exist in North America. However, the absence of these European conveniences was profoundly irrelevant to native North Americans. Their cultures had developed as adaptations to the natural environment local to each tribe and to the social environment among neighboring peoples. That great similarity—adaptation to natural and social environments—underlay all the cultural diversity among native North Americans.

> The absence of European conveniences was profoundly irrelevant to native North Americans.

It would be a mistake, however, to conclude that native North Americans lived in blissful harmony with nature and each other. Archaeological sites provide ample evidence of violent conflict among Native Americans. Skeletons bear the marks of wounds as well as of ritualistic human sacrifice and even cannibalism. Other forms of conflict—such as religious, economic, and familial—must have existed, but they left few archaeological traces and therefore remain in obscurity. In general, fear and anxiety must have been at least as common among Native Americans as feelings of peace and security.

Native Americans not only adapted to the natural environment; they also changed it in many ways. They built thousands of structures, from small dwellings to massive pueblos and enormous mounds, permanently altering the landscape. Their gathering techniques selected productive and nutritious varieties of plants, thereby shifting the balance of local plants toward useful varieties. The first stages of North American agriculture, for example, probably resulted from Native Americans gathering wild seeds and then sowing them in a meadow for later harvest. It is almost certain that fertile and hardy varieties of corn were developed in just this way, first in Mexico and later in North America.

Native Americans also altered the natural environment by fires. In addition to cooking, Indians used fires to provide food, communicate, and make war. Fires set for hunting probably left the largest imprint on the landscape. Great Plains hunters often set fires to hunt buffalo. Sometimes they circled a herd with a ring of fire that concentrated the animals and made them easy to slaughter. At other times hunters left an outlet in the ring of fire and killed buffalo as they passed through the opening. They also set widely separated parallel lines of fire and drove frightened buffalo between the fires toward a cliff over which they plunged to their destruction.

Eastern Woodland, Southwest, and Pacific coast Indians also used fire to hunt deer and other valuable prey. Frequently, hunters waited downwind from a brushy area while their companions set a fire upwind; the hunters then killed the animals that fled toward them from the burning underbrush. Over thousands of square miles throughout North America, Indians set fires along the edges of woods to burn off shrubby undergrowth and encroaching tree seedlings. These burns encouraged the growth of tender young plants that attracted deer and other game animals, bringing them within convenient range of hunters' weapons. Such burns also encouraged the growth of numerous plants Indians relished, such as blackberries, strawberries, and raspberries.

Because fires usually burned until they ran out of fuel or were extinguished by rain or wind, enormous regions of North America were burned over. In some places, fires were set once or twice a year; in other areas, decades passed between fires. In the long run, fires created and maintained light-dappled meadows for hunting and agriculture, cleared entangling underbrush from forests, and promoted a diverse and productive natural environment. Fires, like other activities of Native Americans, shaped the landscape of North America long before Europeans arrived in 1492.

The Mexica: A Meso-American Culture

The indigenous population of the New World numbered roughly 80 million in the 1490s, about the same as the population of Europe. Almost all these people lived in Central and South America. Like their much less numerous North American counterparts, they too lived in a natural environment of tremendous diversity. They too developed hundreds of cultures, far too numerous to catalog here. But among all the Central and South American cultures, the Mexica stood out. (Europeans often called these people Aztecs, a name the Mexica did not use.) Their empire stretched from coast to coast across central Mexico, encompassing as many as 25 million people. We know more about the Mexica than about any other Native American society of the time, principally because of their massive monuments and their Spanish conquerors' well-documented interest in subduing them. Their significance in the history of the New World after 1492 dictates a brief consideration of their culture and society.

The Mexica began their rise to prominence about 1325 when small bands settled on a marshy island in Lake Texcoco, the site of the future city of Tenochtitlán, the capital of the Mexican empire. Resourceful, courageous, and cold-blooded warriors, the Mexica often hired out as mercenaries for richer, more settled tribes. By 1430, the Mexica succeeded in asserting their dominance over their former allies and leading their own military campaigns in an ever-widening arc of empire building. Despite pockets of resistance, by the 1490s the Mexica ruled an empire that covered more land than Spain and Portugal combined and contained almost three times as many people.

The empire exemplified the central values of Mexican society. The Mexica worshipped the war god Huitzilopochtli. Warriors held the most exalted positions in the Mexican social hierarchy, even above the priests who performed the sacred ceremonies that won Huitzilopochtli's favor. In the almost constant battles necessary to defend and extend the empire, young Mexican men exhibited the courage and daring that would allow them to rise in the carefully graduated ranks of warriors. The Mexica considered capturing prisoners the ultimate act of bravery. Warriors usually turned over the captives to Mexican priests, who sacrificed them to Huitzilopochtli by cutting out their hearts. (See "Historical Question," page 28.)

The empire contributed far more to Mexican society than victims for sacrifice. At the most basic level, the empire functioned as a military and political system that collected tribute from subject peoples. The Mexica forced conquered tribes to pay tribute in goods, not money. Tribute redistributed to the Mexica as much as one-third of the goods produced by conquered tribes. It included everything from candidates for human sacrifice to textiles and basic food products such as corn and beans as well as exotic luxury items such as gold, turquoise, and rare bird feathers.

Tribute reflected the fundamental relations of power and wealth that pervaded the Mexican empire. The relatively small nobility of Mexican warriors, supported by a still smaller priesthood, possessed the military and religious power to command the obedience of thousands of non-noble Mexicans and of millions of other non-Mexicans in subjugated provinces. The Mexican elite exercised their power to obtain tribute and thereby to redistribute wealth from the conquered to the conquerors, from the commoners to the nobility, from the poor to the rich. This redistribution of wealth made possible the achievements of Mexican society that eventually amazed Spaniards: the huge cities, fabulous temples, teeming markets, and luxuriant gardens, not to mention the storehouses stuffed with gold and other treasures.

On the whole, the Mexica did not interfere much with the internal government of conquered regions.

> Despite pockets of resistance, by the 1490s the Mexica ruled an empire that covered more land than Spain and Portugal combined and contained almost three times as many people.

Salado Ritual Figure
About AD 1350—more than a century before Columbus arrived in the Western Hemisphere—this figure was carefully wrapped in a reed mat with other items and stored in a cave in a mountainous region of New Mexico by people of the Salado culture, descendants of the Mimbres, who had flourished three centuries earlier. The face of this figure is as close to a self-portrait of ancient Americans on the eve of their encounter with Europeans as we are ever likely to have. Adorned with vivid pigments, cotton string, bright feathers, and stones, the effigy testifies to the human complexity of all ancient Americans, a complexity visible in artifacts that have survived the millennia before the arrival of Europeans.
© 2000 The Art Institute of Chicago.

Why Did the Mexica Practice Human Sacrifice?

The Mexica practiced human sacrifice on a scale unequaled in human history. That does not mean that they intentionally killed more people than any other society. Plenty of other societies, both before and since, have systematically killed other human beings. Only a partial accounting from the years 1930 to 1945, for example, would include millions of Jews and others murdered by German Nazis and their European sympathizers, millions of Russians killed by the Soviet leader Joseph Stalin, hundreds of thousands of Chinese slaughtered by the Japanese, and hundreds of thousands of Japanese annihilated by atomic bombs the United States dropped on Hiroshima and Nagasaki. Warfare of any kind involves intentional sacrifice of human life. However, the human sacrifice practiced by the Mexica was different. For them, human sacrifice was an act of worship—in fact, the ultimate act of worship.

Looking back from our vantage point five hundred years later, we may find it difficult to understand why the Mexica accepted human sacrifice as a normal and reasonable activity. Yet it is perfectly clear that they did. Although the precise number of victims is unknown, experts estimate that about 20,000 people were sacrificed each year throughout the Mexican empire. Celebration of an important victory or the appointment of a new emperor often involved the sacrifice of hundreds, sometimes thousands.

Most of the victims were prisoners captured in battle or rendered in tribute. However, ordinary Mexican citizens—especially young men, women, and children—were often sacrificed in religious rituals. Every eighteen months, for example, a greatly honored young man was sacrificed to Tezcatlipoca, the god of human fate. From time to time, all Mexica practiced sacrificial bloodletting, piercing themselves with stingray spines or cactus thorns to demonstrate their religious devotion. Both as symbol and in reality, human sacrifice was an integral part of daily life in Mexican communities.

Mexica employed several different techniques of sacrifice, all supervised and carried out by priests. By far the most common sacrifice was performed at an altar on the top of a temple, where a priest cut out the still-beating heart of a victim and offered it to the gods. The victim's

Mexican Human Sacrifice
This graphic portrait of human sacrifice was drawn by a Mexican artist in the sixteenth century, after Spanish conquest. It shows the typical routine of human sacrifice practiced by the Mexica for centuries before Europeans arrived. The victim climbed the temple steps, then was stretched out over a stone pillar (notice the priest's helper holding the victim's legs) to make it easier for the priest to plunge a stone knife into the victim's chest, cut out the still-beating heart, and offer it to the bloodthirsty gods. The body of the previous victim has already been pushed down from the temple heights and is about to be dragged away. The Mexica's blood-caked priests and temples repulsed Spanish conquerors, who considered human sacrifice barbaric. The intent watchfulness among the people portrayed at the base of the temple suggests their keen interest in the gory spectacle as a way of obtaining favors from supernatural powers.
Scala / Art Resource, NY; Biblioteca Nazionale, Florence, Italy.

Mexican Sacrificial Knife
This flint knife—embellished and personalized with eyes and teeth made of shell, turquoise, and obsidian—was a symbol of human sacrifice. The knife, as well as two additional knives, human skulls, and other objects, was excavated from a temple where ancient Mexica placed them as offerings to Huitzilopochtli, the powerful god of war. Since this specific knife was an offering, it probably was not used to cut out the hearts of sacrifice victims. But knives just like it, made of flint and seven or eight inches long, were used by Mexican priests to sacrifice tens of thousands of people.

Photo by Michel Zabe / Banco Mexicano de Imagenes (BMI).

head and limbs were then severed, and the torso was fed to wild animals kept in cages in and near the temple. Heads were displayed on large racks at the base of the temple; limbs were cooked and eaten in sacred rituals. It is likely that participation in this ritualistic cannibalism was restricted to a minority of Mexica, principally warriors, priests, and wealthier merchants. However, every Mexica participated in symbolic cannibalism by eating small cakes made of flour mixed with blood and shaped into human forms.

To us, these rituals may seem ghoulish and disgusting, as they certainly did to sixteenth-century Europeans who eventually witnessed them. Yet the Mexica devoted so much time, energy, and resources to such rituals that it is impossible to doubt their importance to them. But why was human sacrifice so important?

In recent times, some scholars have argued that the Mexica practiced human sacrifice and cannibalism to remedy protein deficiencies in their diet. However, the Mexican diet contained many sources of protein, including turkeys, chickens, fish, turtles, and eggs as well as corn and beans. For most Mexica, dietary protein was adequate or better.

Mexican religious beliefs offer a far more persuasive explanation for human sacrifice. Scholars know a good deal about Mexican religion because, in the years immediately following European conquest, Catholic priests studied Mexican religion in order to convert the people more readily to Christianity. These sources make clear that the Mexica inhabited a world suffused with the power of supernatural beings. A special deity oversaw nearly every important activity. Mexica believed that their gods communicated with human beings through omens, signs that the gods were either happy or displeased. In turn, the people communicated their own reverence for the gods by observing appropriate rituals. Bad omens such as an unexplained fire or a lightning bolt striking a temple meant that a god was angry and needed to be appeased with the proper rituals. Since almost every occurrence could be interpreted as an omen that revealed the will of a god, the routine events of daily life had a profound, supernatural dimension.

The Mexica's most powerful gods were Huitzilopochtli, the war god, and Quetzalcoatl, the god who gave sustenance to human beings. Mexica believed that these two gods had created the world, the sun, the moon, the first human beings, the whole array of lesser deities, and everything else in the universe. Since the moment of creation, the earth had passed through four different epochs, which Mexica called the Four Suns, each of which had ended in catastrophe. It fell to Quetzalcoatl and other potent deities to begin the Fifth Sun by re-creating human beings and all the other features of the universe. After years of work, Quetzalcoatl and the other gods had accomplished everything except the creation of the sun. Finally, two gods agreed to sacrifice themselves by jumping into a fire. Thereby they became the sun and the moon, and other gods quickly followed them into the fire to keep the sun burning. But the sacrifice of the gods was sufficient only to ignite the sun. To maintain the light of the sun and keep it moving across the sky every day required human beings to follow the example of the gods and to feed the sun with human blood. Without the sacrificial blood, the world would go dark and time would stop. Mexica considered the Fifth Sun the final stage of the universe, which would end when cataclysmic earthquakes destroyed the earth and supernatural monsters ravaged human life. By feeding the sun with human sacrifices, Mexica believed they could delay that horrible final reckoning.

For the Mexica, human sacrifice was absolutely necessary for the maintenance of life on earth. Victims of sacrifice fulfilled the most sacred of duties. Through the sacrifice of their lives, they fed the sun and permitted others to live. The living demonstrated their respect and reverence for victims of sacrifice by eating their flesh. As one sixteenth-century Catholic priest explained, "The flesh of all those who died in sacrifice was held truly to be consecrated and blessed. It was eaten with reverence, ritual, and fastidiousness—as if it were something from heaven." From the Mexica's perspective, it was not wrong to engage in human sacrifice; it was wrong not to.

Instead, they usually permitted the traditional ruling elite to stay in power—so long as they paid tribute. For their efforts, the conquered provinces received very little from the Mexica, except immunity from punitive raids by the dreaded Mexican warriors. Subjugated communities felt exploited by the constant payment of tribute to the Mexica. By depending on military conquest and constant collection of tribute, the Mexica failed to create among their subjects a belief that Mexican domination was, at some level, legitimate and equitable. The high level of discontent among subject peoples constituted the soft, vulnerable underbelly of the Mexican empire. Instead of making friends for the Mexica, the empire created many bitter and resentful opponents, a fact Spanish intruders exploited after AD 1492 to conquer the Mexica.

Conclusion: The World of Ancient Americans

Ancient Americans shaped the history of human beings in the New World for more than twelve thousand years. They established continuous human habitation in the Western Hemisphere from the time the first big-game hunters crossed Beringia until 1492 and beyond. Much of their history remains irretrievably lost because they relied on oral rather than written communication. But much can be pieced together from artifacts they left behind, like the Folsom points among the bones discovered by George McJunkin. Ancient Americans achieved their success through resourceful adaptation to the hemisphere's many and ever-changing natural environments. They also adapted to social and cultural changes caused by human beings— such as marriages, deaths, political struggles, and warfare—but the sparse evidence that has survived renders those adaptations almost entirely unknowable. Their creativity and artistry are unmistakably documented in the artifacts they left behind at kill sites, camps, and burial mounds. Those artifacts sketch the only likenesses of ancient Americans we will ever have— blurred, shadowy images that are indisputably human but forever silent.

In the five centuries after 1492—just 4 percent of the time human beings have inhabited the Western Hemisphere—Europeans and their descendants began to shape and eventually to dominate American history. Native American peoples continued to influence major developments of American history for centuries after 1492. But the new wave of strangers that at first trickled and then flooded into the New World from Europe and Africa forever transformed the peoples and places of ancient America.

FOR ADDITIONAL FIRSTHAND ACCOUNTS OF THIS PERIOD, see Chapter 1 in Michael Johnson, ed., *Reading the American Past,* Third Edition.

TO ASSESS YOUR MASTERY OF THE MATERIAL IN THIS CHAPTER, see the Online Study Guide at bedfordstmartins.com/ roark.

FOR WEB LINKS RELATED TO TOPICS IN THIS CHAPTER, see "HistoryLinks," "DocLinks," and "PlaceLinks" at bedfordstmartins.com/roark.

CHRONOLOGY

("BP" is an abbreviation used by archaeologists for "years before the present.")

c. 80,000–10,000 BP

- Wisconsin glaciation exposes Beringia, land bridge between Siberia and Alaska.

c. 13,000 BP

- First humans arrive in North America.

c. 11,500–11,000 BP

- Paleo-Indians in North and Central Americas use Clovis points to hunt big game.

c. 11,000 BP

- Mammoths and many other big-game prey of Paleo-Indians become extinct.

c. 10,000–3,000 BP

- Archaic hunter-gatherer cultures dominate ancient America.

c. 7000 BP

- Corn cultivation begins in Central and South Americas.

c. 4000 BP

- Some Eastern Woodland peoples grow gourds and pumpkins and begin making pottery.

c. 3500 BP

- Southwestern cultures begin corn cultivation.
- Stone pipes for tobacco smoking appear in Eastern Woodland regions.

c. 2500 BP

- Eastern Woodland cultures start to build burial mounds.

c. 2500–2100 BP

- Adena culture develops in Ohio.

c. 2300 BP

- Some Eastern Woodland peoples begin to cultivate corn.

c. 2100 BP–AD 400

- Hopewell culture emerges in Ohio and Mississippi valleys.

c. AD 200–AD 900

- Mogollon culture emerges in New Mexico.

c. AD 500

- Bows and arrows appear in North America south of Arctic.
- Pacific Northwest cultures denote wealth and status with elaborate wood carvings.

c. AD 500–AD 1400

- Hohokam culture develops in Arizona.

c. AD 800–AD 1500

- Mississippian culture flourishes in Southeast.

c. AD 1000–AD 1100

- Anasazi peoples build cliff dwellings at Mesa Verde, Colorado, and pueblos at Chaco Canyon, New Mexico.

c. AD 1325–AD 1500

- Mexica conquer neighboring peoples and establish Mexican empire.

AD 1492

- Christopher Columbus arrives, beginning European colonization of New World.

BIBLIOGRAPHY

General Works

Robson Bonnichsen and Karen L. Turnmire, *Ice Age Peoples of North America* (1999).

Thomas M. Bonniksen, *America's Ancient Forests: From the Ice Age to Discovery* (2000).

Karen Olsen Bruhns, *Ancient South America* (1994).

Karen Olsen Bruhns and Karen E. Stothert, *Women in Ancient America* (1999).

Michael D. Coe and Rex Koontz, *Mexico: From the Olmecs to the Aztecs* (5th ed., 2002).

Michael Coe, Dean Snow, and Elizabeth Benson, *Atlas of Ancient America* (1986).

Thomas D. Dillehay, *The Settlement of the Americas: A New Prehistory* (2000).

E. James Dixon, *Quest for the Origins of the First Americans* (1993).

Roger Downey, *Riddle of the Bones: Politics, Science, Race, and the Story of Kennewick Man* (2000).

Penelope Ballard Drooker and Laurie D. Webster, *Beyond Cloth and Cordage: Archaeological Textile Research in the Americas* (2000).

Brian M. Fagan, *The Journey from Eden: The Peopling of Our World* (1990).

Brian M. Fagan, *Ancient North America: The Archaeology of a Continent* (1991).

Brian M. Fagan, *Kingdoms of Gold, Kingdoms of Jade: The Americas before Columbus* (1991).

Stuart J. Fiedel, *Prehistory of the Americas* (2nd ed., 1992).

Virginia M. Fields and Victor Zamudio-Taylor, *The Road to Aztlan: Art from a Mythic Homeland* (2002).

Robert L. Hall, *An Archaeology of the Soul: North American Indian Belief and Ritual* (1997).

David Henige, *Numbers from Nowhere: The American Indian Contact Population Debate* (1998).

Francis Jennings, *The Founders of America: How Indians Discovered the Land . . .* (1993).

Jesse D. Jennings, *Prehistory of North America* (1974).

Jesse D. Jennings, ed., *Ancient North Americans* (1983).

Alvin M. Josephy Jr., *America in 1492: The World of the Indian Peoples before the Arrival of Columbus* (1992).

Jake Page, *In the Hands of the Great Spirit: The Twenty-Thousand-Year History of American Indians* (2003).

David Hurst Thomas, *Skull Wars: Kennewick Man, Archaeology, and the Battle for Native American Identity* (2000).

Richard Townsend, ed., *The Ancient Americas: Art from Sacred Landscapes* (1992).

Frederick Hadleigh West, ed., *American Beginnings: The Prehistory and Paleoecology of Beringia* (1996).

North American Cultures

Mary J. Adair, *Prehistoric Agriculture in the Central Plains* (1988).

Kenneth M. Ames and Herbert D. G. Maschner, *Peoples of the Northwest Coast: Their Archaeology and Prehistory* (1999).

David G. Anderson, *The Savannah River Chiefdoms: Political Change in the Late Prehistoric Southeast* (1994).

Alex W. Barker and Timothy R. Pauketat, eds., *Lords of the Southwest: Social Inequality and the Native Elites of Southeastern North America* (1992).

Timothy G. Baugh and Jonathon E. Ericson, eds., *Prehistoric Exchange Systems in North America* (1994).

John Howard Blitz, *Ancient Chiefdoms of the Tombigbee* (1993).

Sally A. Kitt Chappell, *Cahokia: Mirror of the Cosmos* (2002).

Linda S. Cordell, *Prehistory of the Southwest* (1984).

Linda S. Cordell and George R. Gumerman, eds., *Dynamics of Southwest Prehistory* (1989).

Richard J. Dent Jr., *Chesapeake Prehistory: Old Traditions, New Directions* (1995).

E. James Dixon, *Bones, Boats, and Bison: Archeology and the First Colonization of Western North America* (1999).

Don Dumond, *Eskimos and Aleuts* (2nd ed., 1987).

Thomas E. Emerson and R. Barry Lewis, eds., *Cahokia and the Hinterlands: Middle Mississippian Cultures of the Midwest* (1991).

Thomas E. Emerson et al., eds., *Late Woodland Societies: Tradition and Transformation across the Midcontinent* (2000).

Brian M. Fagan, *The Great Journey: The Peopling of Ancient America* (1987).

William Fitzhugh, ed., *Crossroads of Continents: Cultures of Siberia and Alaska* (1988).

William W. Fitzhugh and Valerie Chaussonnet, eds., *Anthropology of the North Pacific Rim* (1994).

Franklin Folsom, *Black Cowboy: The Life and Legend of George McJunkin* (1992).

Nelson Foster and Linda S. Cordell, eds., *Chilies to Chocolate: Food the Americas Gave to the World* (1992).

Julie E. Francis, *Ancient Visions: Petroglyphs and Pictographs From . . . Wyoming and Montana* (2002).

Kendrick Frazier, *People of Chaco: A Canyon and Its Cultures* (1986).

George C. Frison, *Prehistoric Hunters of the High Plains* (2nd ed., 1991).

George Gumerman, *A View from Black Mesa* (1984).

George Gumerman, ed., *Themes in Southwest Prehistory* (1994).

Robert F. Heizer, ed., *Handbook of North American Indians*, vol. 8, *California* (1978).

R. Douglas Hurt, *Indian Agriculture in America: Prehistory to the Present* (1987).

Barry L. Isaac, ed., *Prehistoric Economies of the Pacific Northwest Coast* (1988).

Sissel Johannessen and Christine A. Hastorf, eds., *Corn and Culture in the Prehistoric New World* (1994).

Roger G. Kennedy, *Hidden Cities: The Discovery and Loss of Ancient North American Civilization* (1994).

Sarah A. Kerr, *Beyond Chaco: Great Kiva Communities on the Mogollon Rim Frontier* (2001).

J. C. H. King, *First People, First Contacts: Native Peoples of North America* (1999).

Ruth Kirk, *Hunters of the Whale* (1975).

Theodora Kroeber, *Ishi in Two Worlds* (1965).

Steven A. LeBlanc, *The Mimbres People: Ancient Pueblo Potters of the American Southwest* (1983).

Steven A. LeBlanc, *Prehistoric Warfare in the American Southwest* (1999).

Stephen H. Lekson, *The Chaco Meridian: Centers of Political Power in the Ancient Southwest* (1999).

Edward J. Lenik, *Picture Rocks: American Indian Rock Art in the Northeast Woodlands* (2002).

Mary Ann Levine et al., eds., *The Archaeological Northeast* (1999).

R. G. Matson, *The Origins of Southwestern Agriculture* (1991).

William E. McGoun, *Prehistoric Peoples of South Florida* (1993).

Jonathan Merli, *Shadow House: Interpretations of Northwest Coast Art* (2001).

Jerald T. Milanich, *Archaeology of Precolumbian Florida* (1994).

Claudia G. Mink, *Cahokia: City of the Sun: Prehistoric Urban Center in the American Bottom* (1992).

Michael J. Moratto, *California Archaeology* (1984).

William N. Morgan, *Precolumbian Architecture in Eastern North America* (1999).

Jon Muller, *Archaeology of the Lower Ohio Valley* (1986).

Alfonso Ortiz, ed., *Handbook of North American Indians,* vol. 9, *Southwest* (1979).

Alfonso Ortiz, ed., *Handbook of North American Indians,* vol. 10, *Southwest* (1983).

Timothy R. Pauketat, *The Ascent of Chiefs: Cahokia and Mississippian Politics in Native North America* (1994).

Timothy R. Pauketat and Thomas E. Emerson, eds., *Cahokia: Domination and Ideology in the Mississippian World* (2000).

Jefferson Reid and Stephanie Whittlesley, *The Archaeology of Ancient Arizona* (1997).

Karl H. Schlesier, *Plains Indians, A.D. 500–1500: The Archaeological Past of Historic Groups* (1994).

Lynne Sebastian, *The Chaco Anasazi: Sociopolitical Evolution in the Prehistoric Southwest* (1992).

Lynda Shaffer, *Native Americans before 1492: The Moundbuilding Centers of the Eastern Woodlands* (1992).

Dennis Slifer, *Signs of Life: Rock Art of the Upper Rio Grande* (1998).

Bruce D. Smith, ed., *The Mississippian Emergence* (1990).

Marvin T. Smith, *Coosa: The Rise and Fall of a Southeastern Mississippian Chiefdom* (2000).

Dean Snow, *The Archaeology of New England* (1980).

Katherine A. Spielmann, *Interdependence in the Prehistoric Southwest: An Ecological Analysis of Plain-Pueblo Interaction* (1991).

David E. Stuart, *Anasazi America* (2000).

Kenneth B. Tankersley and Barry L. Isaac, eds., *Early Paleoindian Economies of Eastern North America* (1990).

Bruce G. Trigger, *The Children of Aataentsic: A History of the Huron People to 1660* (1972).

Bruce G. Trigger, *Natives and Newcomers* (1985).

Bruce G. Trigger, ed., *Handbook of North American Indians,* vol. 15, *Northeast* (1978).

J. A. Tuck, *Onondaga Iroquois Prehistory* (1971).

Christy G. Turner II and Jacqueline A. Turner, *Cannibalism and Violence in the Prehistoric American Southwest* (1999).

R. Gwinnn Vivian and Bruce Hilpert, *The Chaco Handbook* (2002).

William Snyder Webb, *The Adena People* (1974).

Randolph J. Widmer, *The Evolution of the Calusa: A Nonagricultural Chiefdom on the Southwest Florida Coast* (1988).

Joseph C. Winter, *Tobacco Use by Native North Americans: Sacred Smoke and Silent Killer* (2000).

Biloine Whiting Young and Melvin L. Fowler, *Cahokia: The Great Native American Metropolis* (1999).

The Mexica

Philip P. Arnold, *Eating Landscape: Aztec and European Occupation of Tlalocan* (1999).

Elizabeth Hill Boone, *Stories in Red and Black: Pictorial Histories of the Aztecs and Mixtecs* (2000).

David Carrasco, *Quetzalcoatl and the Irony of Empire: Myths and Prophecies in the Aztec Tradition* (1992).

David Carrasco, *City of Sacrifice: The Aztec Empire and the Role of Violence in Civilization* (1999).

David Carrasco et al., eds., *Mesoamerica's Classic Heritage: From Teotihuacan to the Aztecs* (2000).

Inga Clendinnen, *Aztecs: An Interpretation* (1991).

Marty W. Eubanks, *Corn in Clay: Maize Paleoethnobotany in Pre-Columbian Art* (1999).

Ross Hassig, *War and Society in Ancient Mesoamerica* (1992).

Ross Hassig, *Time, History, and Belief in Aztec and Colonial Mexico* (2001).

Alan Knight, *Mexico: From the Beginning to the Spanish Conquest* (2002).

Mary Ellen Miller, *The Art of Meso-America: From Olmec to Aztec* (2001).

Eduardo Matos Moctezuma and Felipe Solis Olguin, *Aztecs* (2002).

Felipe Solis and Ted Leyenaar, *Art Treasures of Ancient Mexico* (2002).

Richard F. Townsend, *The Aztecs* (1992).

E. Michael Whittington, *The Sport of Life and Death: The Mesoamerican Ballgame* (2002).

TAINO ZEMI BASKET
This basket is an example of the effigies Tainos made to represent *zemis*, their deities. The effigy illustrates the artistry of the basket maker, almost certainly a Taino woman. Crafted sometime between 1492 and about 1520, the effigy demonstrates that Tainos readily incorporated goods obtained through contacts with Europeans into their own traditional beliefs and practices. The basket maker used African ivory and European mirrors as well as Native American fibers, dyes, and designs.

Archìvio Fotogràfico del Museo Preistòrico Etnografico L. Pigorini, Roma.

Europeans Encounter the New World

1492–1600

A HALF HOUR BEFORE SUNRISE on August 3, 1492, Christopher Columbus commanded three ships to catch the tide out of a harbor in southern Spain and sail west. Just over two months later, in the predawn moonlight of October 12, 1492, Columbus glimpsed an island on the western horizon. At last, he believed, he had found what he had been looking for—the western end of a route across the Atlantic Ocean to Japan, China, and India. At daybreak, Columbus could see people on the shore who had spotted his ships. He rowed ashore and, as the curious islanders crowded around, he claimed possession of the land for Ferdinand and Isabella, king and queen of Spain, who had sponsored his voyage. He named the island San Salvador, in honor of the Savior, Jesus Christ.

A day or two afterward, Columbus described that first encounter with the inhabitants of San Salvador in an extensive diary he kept during his voyage. He called these people Indians, assuming that their island lay somewhere in the East Indies near Japan or China. The Indians were not dressed in the finery Columbus expected. "All of them go around as naked as their mothers bore them; and the women also," he observed. Their skin color was "neither black nor white." They were not familiar with the Spaniards' weapons. "I showed them swords," Columbus wrote, "and they took them by the edge and through ignorance cut themselves." This first encounter led Columbus to conclude, "They should be good and intelligent servants, for I see that they say very quickly everything that is said to them; and I believe that they would become Christians very easily, for it seemed to me that they had no religion."

The people Columbus called Indians called themselves Tainos, which to them meant "good" or "noble." They inhabited most of the Caribbean islands Columbus visited on his first voyage, as had their ancestors for more than two centuries. The Tainos were an agricultural people who grew cassava, a nutritious root, as well as sweet potatoes, corn, cotton, tobacco, and other crops. To fish and to travel from island to island, they built canoes from hollowed-out logs. The Tainos worshiped gods they called *zemis*, the spirits of ancestors and of natural objects like trees and stones. They made effigies of zemis and performed rituals to honor them. "It seemed to me that they were a people very poor in everything," Columbus wrote. But the Tainos mined gold in small quantities, enough to catch the eye of Columbus and his men.

What the Tainos thought about Spaniards we can only surmise, since they left no written documents. At first, Columbus believed that the Tainos thought he and his men came from heaven. After six weeks of contact, Columbus

Cacique's Canoe
This sixteenth-century drawing of a large canoe carrying a cacique, or chief, and powered by twenty oarsmen probably resembles the canoes used by Tainos and the other Native Americans who paddled out to visit the ships of Columbus and other European explorers. The influence of such European contacts may be reflected in the flags flying from the corners of the leafy awning that shades the enthroned cacique and rowers.
The Pierpont Morgan Library / Art Resource, NY.

concluded that in fact he did not understand Tainos. Late in November 1492, he wrote that "the people of these lands do not understand me nor do I, nor anyone else that I have with me, them. And many times I understand one thing said by these Indians . . . for another, its contrary."

The confused communication between Europeans and Tainos suggests how different, how strange, each group seemed to the other. Columbus's perceptions of Tainos were shaped by European ideas, attitudes, and expectations, just as Tainos's perceptions of Europeans must have been colored by their own culture. Yet the word that Columbus coined for the Tainos— *Indians*, a word that originated in a colossal misunderstanding—hinted at the direction of the future. To Europeans, *Indians* came to mean all native inhabitants of the New World, the name they gave to the lands in the Western Hemisphere. After 1492, the perceptions, the cultures, and even the diseases of Europeans began to exert a transforming influence on the New World and its peoples.

Long before 1492, certain Europeans restlessly expanded the limits of the world known to them. Their efforts made possible Columbus's encounter with the Tainos. In turn, Columbus's landfall in the Caribbean changed the history not only of the Tainos, but also of Europe and

the rest of the world. Beginning in 1492, the promise of the New World lured more and more Europeans to venture their lives and fortunes on the western shores of the Atlantic, a promise realized largely at the expense of New World peoples like Tainos.

Europe in the Age of Exploration

Historically, the East—not the West—attracted Europeans. Around the year 1000, Norsemen ventured west across the North Atlantic and founded a small fishing village as L'Anse aux Meadows on the tip of Newfoundland. After a decade or so, the Norse left and did not return because the world's climate cooled, choking the North Atlantic with ice. Viking sagas memorialized the Norse "discovery," but it had virtually no other impact in the New World or in Europe. Instead, wealthy Europeans developed a taste for luxury goods from Asia and Africa, and merchants competed to satisfy that taste. As Europeans traded with the East and with one another, they acquired new information about the world they inhabited. Some learned that the world they knew was not all there was to know. A few people—sailors, merchants, and aristocrats—took the risks of exploring beyond the limits of the world known to Europeans. Those risks were genuine and could be deadly. But sometimes they paid off in new information, new opportunities, and eventually in the discovery of a world entirely new to Europeans.

Mediterranean Trade and European Expansion

From the twelfth through the fifteenth centuries, spices, silk, carpets, ivory, gold, and other exotic goods traveled overland from Persia, Asia Minor, India, and Africa and then were funneled into continental Europe through Mediterranean trade routes (Map 2.1). Dominated primarily by the Italian cities of Venice, Genoa, and Pisa, this lucrative trade enriched Italian merchants

and bankers, who fiercely defended their near-**monopoly** of access to eastern goods. Instead of trying to displace the Italians, merchants in other European countries chose the safer alternative of trading with them. The vitality of the Mediterranean trade offered few incentives to look for alternatives. New routes to the East and the discovery of new lands were the stuff of fantasy.

Preconditions for turning fantasy into reality developed in fifteenth-century Europe. In the mid-fourteenth century, Europeans suffered a catastrophic epidemic of bubonic plague. The Black Death, as it was called, killed about a third of the European population. This devastating pestilence had

> The risks of exploring were genuine and could be deadly. But sometimes they paid off in new information, new opportunities, and eventually in the discovery of a world entirely new to Europeans.

MAP 2.1 European Trade Routes and Portuguese Exploration in the Fifteenth Century
The strategic geographic position of Italian cities as a conduit for overland trade from Asia was slowly undermined during the fifteenth century by Portuguese explorers who hopscotched along the coast of Africa and eventually found a sea route that opened the rich trade of the East to Portuguese merchants.

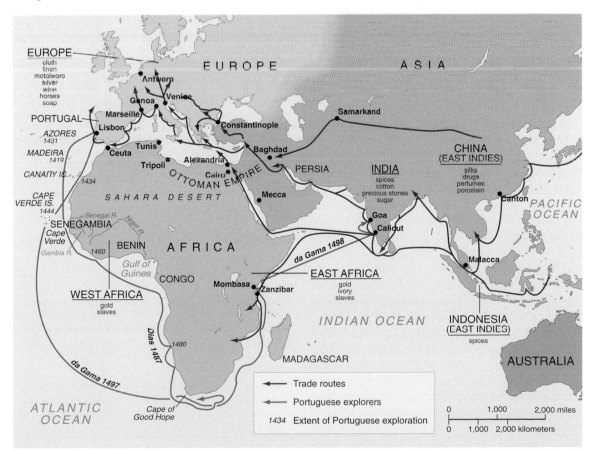

major long-term consequences. It significantly reduced the pressure of Europe's now-reduced population on food resources. Many who survived inherited property from plague victims, giving new chances for advancement. The turmoil caused by the plague also prompted peasants to move away from their homes and seek opportunities elsewhere.

Understandably, most Europeans perceived the world as a place of alarming risks where the delicate balance of health, harvests, and peace could quickly be tipped toward disaster by epidemics, famine, and violence. Most people protected themselves from the constant threat of calamity by worshipping the supernatural, by living amid kinfolk and friends, and by maintaining good relations with the rich and powerful. Curiously, the insecurity and uncertainty of fifteenth-century European life encouraged a few people to take greater chances, such as embarking on a dangerous sea voyage through uncharted waters to points unknown.

Monarchs who hoped to enlarge their realms and enrich their dynasties also had reasons to sponsor journeys of exploration. More territory meant more subjects who could pay more taxes, provide more soldiers, and participate in more commerce, magnifying monarchs' power and prestige. Voyages of exploration also could stabilize monarch's regimes by diverting the military energies of unruly noblemen toward distant lands. Sometimes monarchs sponsored expeditions by young sons of aristocratic families that had fallen on hard times. Other explorers, like Columbus, were not of noble birth and hoped to be elevated to the aristocracy as a reward for their daring achievements. Exploration promised fame and fortune in European societies to those who succeeded, whether they were commoners or kings.

Scientific and technological advances also helped set the stage for exploration. The invention of movable type made printing easier and cheaper, stimulating diffusion of information, including news of discoveries, among literate Europeans. By 1400, crucial navigational aids employed by maritime explorers like Columbus were already available: compasses; hourglasses, which allowed calculation of elapsed time, useful in estimating speed; and the astrolabe and the quadrant, devices for determining latitude. Detailed sailing maps called *portulanos* illustrated shoreline topography and noted compass headings for sailing from one port to another. Many people throughout fifteenth-century

Ivory Saltcellar

This exquisitely carved sixteenth-century ivory saltcellar combines African materials, craftsmanship, and imagery in an artifact for Portuguese tables. Designed to hold table salt in the central globe, the saltcellar portrays a victim about to be beheaded by the armed man who has already beheaded five others. To Portuguese eyes, the saltcellar dramatized African brutality and quietly suggested the superiority of Portuguese virtues and their beneficial influence in Africa.

Archivio Fotogràfico del Museo Preistòrico Etnografico L. Pigorini, Roma.

Europe knew about these and other technological advances. The Portuguese were the first to use them in a campaign to sail beyond the limits of the world known to Europeans.

A Century of Portuguese Exploration

In many ways, Portugal was an unlikely candidate to take the lead in exploration. With less than 2 percent of the population of Christian Europe, the country devoted far more energy and wealth to the geographical exploration of the world between 1415 and 1460 than all the other countries of Europe combined.

Facing the Atlantic on the Iberian Peninsula, the Portuguese lived on the fringes of the thriving Mediterranean trade. As a Christian kingdom, Portugal cooperated with Spain in the Reconquest, the centuries-long drive to expel Muslims from the Iberian Peninsula. The religious zeal that propelled the Reconquest also justified expansion into what the Portuguese considered heathen lands. The key victory came in 1415 when Portuguese forces conquered Ceuta, the Muslim bastion at the mouth of the Strait of Gibraltar that had blocked Portugal's access to the Atlantic coast of Africa.

The most influential advocate of Portuguese exploration was Prince Henry the Navigator, son of the Portuguese king. From 1415 until his death in 1460, Henry collected the latest information about sailing techniques and geography, supported new crusades against the Muslims, encouraged fresh sources of trade to fatten Portuguese pocketbooks, and pushed explorers to go farther still. Both the Portuguese king and the Christian pope supported Henry's efforts to extend the Reconquest down the African coast. African expeditions also promised to wrest wheat fields from their Moroccan owners and to obtain gold, the currency of European trade. Gold was scarce in Europe because the quickening pace of commerce increased the need for currency while purchases in the East drained gold away from European markets.

Neither the Portuguese nor anybody else in Europe knew the immensity of Africa or the length or shape of its coastline, which, in reality, fronted the Atlantic for more than 7,000 miles— about five times the considerable distance from Genoa, Columbus's hometown, to Lisbon, the Portuguese capital. At first, Portuguese mariners cautiously hugged the west coast of Africa, seldom venturing beyond sight of land. By 1434, they had reached the northern edge of the

Sahara Desert, where strong westerly currents swept them out to sea. They soon learned to ride those currents far away from the coast before catching favorable winds that turned them back toward land, a technique that allowed them to reach Cape Verde by 1444 (see Map 2.1). To stow the supplies necessary for long periods at sea and to withstand the battering of waves in the open ocean, the Portuguese developed the caravel, a sturdy ship that became explorers' vessel of choice. In caravels, Portuguese mariners sailed into and around the Gulf of Guinea and as far south as the Congo by 1480.

Fierce African resistance confined Portuguese expeditions to coastal trading posts, where they bartered successfully for gold, slaves, and ivory. Portuguese merchants learned that relatively peaceful trading posts on the coast were far more profitable than attempts at violent conquest and **colonization** of inland regions. In the 1460s, the Portuguese used African slaves to develop sugar plantations on the Cape Verde Islands, inaugurating an association between enslaved Africans and plantation labor that would be transplanted to the New World in the centuries to come.

About 1480, Portuguese explorers began a conscious search for a sea route to Asia. In 1488, Bartolomeu Dias sailed around the Cape of Good Hope at the southern tip of Africa and hurried back to Lisbon with the exciting news that it appeared to be possible to sail on to India and China. In 1498, after ten years of careful preparation, Vasco da Gama commanded the first Portuguese fleet to sail to India. Portugal quickly capitalized on the commercial potential of da Gama's new sea route. By the early sixteenth century, the Portuguese controlled a far-flung commercial empire in India, Indonesia,

Benin Queen Mother
Early in the sixteenth century, as the Portuguese began their forays along the African coast, the Oba (king) of Benin, in present-day Nigeria, introduced the notion of a queen mother who possessed the ability to communicate with supernatural deities. Brass castings of Benin queen mothers like the one shown here appeared on altars in royal palaces. The distinctive headdress apparently signified the queen mother's semidivine status.
The National Museums, Liverpool.

and China (collectively referred to as the East Indies). Their new sea route to the East eliminated overland travel and the numerous intermediate merchants and markups of the old Mediterranean trade routes controlled by the Italians. The new route allowed Portuguese merchants to charge much lower prices for the eastern goods they imported, and still make handsome profits.

Portugal's African explorations during the fifteenth century broke the monopoly of the old Mediterranean trade with the East, dramatically expanded the world known to Europeans, established a network of Portuguese outposts in Africa and Asia, and developed methods of sailing the high seas that Columbus employed on his revolutionary voyage west.

A Surprising New World in the Western Atlantic

In retrospect, the Portuguese seemed ideally qualified to venture across the Atlantic. They had pioneered the **frontiers** of seafaring, exploration, and geography for almost a century. However, the knowledge and experience they gained while navigating around Africa made them cautious about the risks of trying to sail west across the Atlantic. Portuguese and most other European experts believed doing so was literally impossible. The European discovery of America required someone bold enough to believe that the experts were wrong and the risks were surmountable. That person was Christopher Columbus. His explorations inaugurated a geographical revolution that forever altered Europeans' understanding of the world and its peoples, including themselves. Columbus's landfall in the Caribbean originated a thriving exchange between the people, ideas, cultures, and institutions of the Old and New Worlds that continues to this day.

The Explorations of Columbus

Born in 1451 into the family of an obscure master weaver in Genoa, Italy, Columbus went to sea when he was about fourteen. Sometime around 1476, he arrived in Lisbon

and within a few years married Felipa Moniz. Felipa's father had been raised in the household of Prince Henry the Navigator, and her family retained close ties to the prince. Through Felipa, Columbus gained access to explorers' maps and papers crammed with information about the tricky currents and winds encountered in sailing the Atlantic. Columbus himself ventured into the Atlantic frequently and at least twice sailed all the way to the central coast of Africa.

Like other educated Europeans, Columbus believed that the earth was a sphere and that theoretically it was possible to reach the East Indies by sailing west. Most Europeans believed, however, that the earth was simply too big for anyone to sail west from Europe to Asia. Sailors would die of thirst and starvation long before they reached Asia.

Columbus rejected this conventional wisdom. With flawed calculations, he estimated that Asia was only about 2,500 miles from the westernmost boundary of the known world, a shorter distance than Portuguese ships routinely sailed between Lisbon and the Congo. In fact, the shortest distance to Japan from Europe's jumping-off point was nearly 11,000 miles. Convinced by his erroneous calculations, Columbus became obsessed with a scheme to prove he was right.

First, Columbus tried to convince the Portuguese king to sponsor an expedition to the west. But Columbus's peculiar notions about geography did not divert the Portuguese monarchy from its lucrative African voyages. After years of unsuccessful lobbying in Spain, England, and France, Columbus finally won financing for his journey from Spain's King Ferdinand and Queen Isabella in 1492. The Spanish monarchs saw Columbus's venture as an inexpensive gamble: The potential loss was small while the potential gain was huge. The Spanish monarchs gave Columbus a letter of introduction to China's Grand Khan of the Mongols, the ruler they hoped he would meet on the other side of the Atlantic.

After scarcely three months of hurried preparation, Columbus and his small fleet—the *Niña* and *Pinta*, both caravels, and the *Santa María*, a larger merchant vessel—headed west. Six weeks after leaving the Canary

Columbus's First Voyage to the New World, 1492–1493

12 Oct. 1492
First landing on San Salvador I.

Gulf of Mexico

Cuba

ATLANTIC OCEAN

Santiago (Jamaica)

Hispaniola

Santo Domingo

Caribbean Sea

0   200   400 miles
0   400 kilometers

Islands, where he stopped for supplies, Columbus landed on a tiny Caribbean island about three hundred miles north of the eastern tip of Cuba.

Columbus and his men understood that they had made a momentous discovery. Yet they found it frustrating. Although the Tainos proved friendly, they did not have the riches Columbus expected to find in the East. For three months Columbus cruised from island to island, looking for the king of Japan and the Grand Khan of China. In mid-January 1493, he started back to Spain, taking seven Tainos with him. When he reached Isabella and Ferdinand, they were overjoyed by his news. With a voyage that had lasted barely eight months, Columbus appeared to have catapulted Spain from a secondary position in the race for a sea route to Asia into that of a serious challenger to Portugal, whose explorers had not yet sailed to India or China. Columbus and his Taino companions became the toast of the royal court. The Spanish monarchs elevated Columbus to the nobility and awarded him the title "Admiral of the Ocean Sea." The seven Tainos were baptized as Christians, and King Ferdinand became their godfather.

Soon after Columbus arrived in Spain, the Spanish monarchs rushed to obtain the pope's support for their claim to the new lands in the west. When the pope, a Spaniard, complied, the Portuguese feared their own claims to recently discovered territory were in jeopardy. To protect their claims, the Portuguese and Spanish monarchs negotiated the Treaty of Tordesillas in 1494. The treaty drew an imaginary line eleven hundred miles west of the Canary Islands (Map 2.2). Land discovered west of the line belonged to Spain; Portugal claimed land to the east.

Ferdinand and Isabella moved quickly to realize the promise of their new claims. In the fall of 1493 they dispatched Columbus once again, this time with a fleet of seventeen ships and more than a thousand men who planned to locate the Asian mainland, find gold, and get rich. When Columbus returned to the island of Hispaniola, where a shipwreck near the end of his first voyage had forced him to leave behind thirty-nine of his sailors, he received disturbing news. In Columbus's absence, his sailors had terrorized the Tainos, kidnapping their women and confining them to harems. In retaliation, Taino chiefs had killed all the Spaniards. This small episode prefigured much of what was to happen in encounters between Native Americans and Europeans in the years ahead.

Before Columbus died in 1506, he returned to the New World two more times without relinquishing his belief that the East Indies were there, someplace. Other explorers continued to search for a passage to the East or some other source of profit. Before long, however, prospects of beating the Portuguese to Asia began to dim along with the hope of finding vast hoards of gold. Nonetheless, Columbus's discoveries forced sixteenth-century Europeans to think about the world in new ways. He proved that it was possible to sail from Europe to the western rim of the Atlantic and return to Europe. Most important, Columbus made clear that beyond the western shores of the Atlantic lay lands entirely unknown to Europeans.

> Columbus made clear that beyond the western shores of the Atlantic lay lands entirely unknown to Europeans.

The Geographic Revolution and the Columbian Exchange

Within thirty years of Columbus's initial discovery, Europeans' understanding of world geography underwent a revolution. An elite of perhaps twenty thousand people with access to Europe's royal courts and trading centers learned the exciting news about global geography. But it took a generation of additional exploration before they could comprehend the larger contours of Columbus's discoveries.

European monarchs hurried to stake their claims to the newly discovered lands. In 1497, King Henry VII of England, who had spurned Columbus a decade earlier, sent John Cabot to look for a "Northwest Passage" to the Indies across the North Atlantic (see Map 2.2). Cabot reached the tip of Newfoundland, which he believed was part of Asia, and hurried back to England, where he assembled a small fleet and sailed west again in 1498. But he was never heard from again. Three thousand miles to the south, a Spanish expedition landed on the northern coast of South America in 1499 accompanied by Amerigo Vespucci, an Italian businessman. In 1500, Pedro Álvars Cabral commanded a Portuguese fleet bound for the Indian Ocean that accidentally made landfall on the coast of Brazil as it looped westward into the Atlantic.

By 1500, European experts knew that several large chunks of land cluttered the western Atlantic. A few cartographers speculated that these chunks were connected to one another in a landmass that was not Asia. In 1507, Martin Waldseemüller, a German cartographer, published the first map that showed the New World separate from Asia; he named the land America, in honor of Amerigo Vespucci.

Two additional discoveries confirmed Waldseemüller's speculation. In 1513, Vasco Núñez de Balboa crossed the isthmus of Panama and reached the Pacific Ocean. Clearly, more water lay between the New World and Asia.

MAP 2.2   European Exploration in Sixteenth-Century America
This map illustrates the approximate routes of early European explorations of the New World.

READING THE MAP: Which countries were most actively exploring the New World? Which countries were exploring later than others?

CONNECTIONS: What were the motivations behind the explorations? What were the motivations for colonization?

FOR MORE HELP ANALYZING THIS MAP, see the map activity for this chapter in the Online Study Guide at **bedfordstmartins.com/roark**.

Columbian Exchange

The arrival of Columbus in the New World initiated an ongoing transatlantic exchange of goods, people, and ideas. Spaniards brought domesticated animals from the Old World, including horses, cattle, goats, chickens, cats, and sheep (left). The novelty of such animals is demonstrated by the Nahua words the Mexican people initially used to refer to these strange new beasts: for horses, they used the Nahua word for deer; a cow was "one with horns"; a goat was a "bearded one with horns"; a chicken was a "Spanish turkey hen"; a cat was a "little cougar"; a sheep was referred to with the word for cotton, linking the animal with its fibrous woolen coat. Spaniards brought many other alien items such as cannon, which the Mexica at first termed "fat fire trumpets," and guitars, which the Mexica called "rope drums." Spaniards also carried Old World microorganisms that caused devastating epidemics of smallpox, measles, and other diseases (center). Ancient American people, goods, and ideas made the return trip across the Atlantic. Columbus's sailors quickly learned to use Indian hammocks and became infected with syphilis in sexual encounters with Indian women; then they carried both hammocks and syphilis back to Europe. Smoking tobacco, like the cigar puffed by the ancient Mayan lord (right), became such a fashion in Europe that some came to believe, as a print of two men relaxing with their pipes was captioned, "Life Is Smoke." The strangeness of New World peoples and cultures also reinforced Europeans' notions of their own superiority. Although the Columbian exchange went in both directions, it was not a relationship of equality. Europeans seized and retained the upper hand.

University of California at Berkeley, The Bancroft Library; Arxiu Mas; Collection of Dr. Francis Robicsek.

How much water Ferdinand Magellan discovered when he led an expedition to circumnavigate the globe in 1519. Sponsored by King Charles I of Spain, Magellan's voyage took him first to the New World, around the southern tip of South America, and into the Pacific late in November 1520. Crossing the Pacific took almost four months. By the time he reached the Philippines, his crew had been decimated by extreme hunger and thirst. Magellan himself was killed by Philippine tribesmen. A remnant of his expedition continued on to the Indian Ocean and managed to transport a cargo of spices back to Spain in 1522.

In most ways Magellan's voyage was a disaster. One ship and 18 men crawled back from an expedition that had begun with five ships and more than 250 men. But the geographic information it provided left no doubt that America was a continent separated from Asia by the enormous Pacific Ocean. The voyage made clear that Columbus was dead wrong about the identity of what he had discovered. It was possible to sail west to reach the East Indies, but that was a

> After Magellan, most Europeans who sailed west had their sights set on the New World, not on Asia.

terrible way to go. After Magellan, most Europeans who sailed west set their sights on the New World, not on Asia.

Columbus's arrival in the Caribbean anchored the western end of what might be imagined as a sea bridge that spanned the Atlantic, connecting the Western Hemisphere to Europe. That sea bridge ended the age-old separation of the hemispheres and initiated the **Columbian exchange**, a transatlantic exchange of goods, people, and ideas that has continued ever since.

Spaniards brought novelties to the New World that were commonplace in Europe, including Christianity, iron technology, sailing ships, firearms, wheeled vehicles, horses and other domesticated animals, and much else. (See "The Promise of Technology," page 46.) Unknowingly, they also smuggled along many Old World microorganisms that caused epidemics of smallpox, measles, and other diseases that would kill the vast majority of Indian peoples during the sixteenth century and continue to decimate survivors in later centuries. European diseases made the Columbian exchange catastrophic for Native Americans. In the long term, these diseases were decisive in transforming the dominant peoples of the New World from descendants of Asians, who had inhabited the hemisphere for millennia, to descendants of Europeans and Africans, recent arrivals from the Old World by way of the newly formed sea bridge.

Ancient American goods, people, and ideas made the return trip across the Atlantic. Europeans were introduced to New World foods such as corn and potatoes as well as exotic fruits like pineapples, named for their resemblance to pinecones. Columbus's sailors became infected with syphilis in sexual encounters with New World women and then unwittingly carried the deadly parasite back to Europe, where it may already have had a foothold. New World tobacco created a European fashion for smoking that ignited quickly and has yet to be extinguished. But for almost a generation after 1492, this Columbian exchange did not reward Spaniards with the riches they yearned to find.

> Hernán Cortés, who became the richest and most famous conquistador, arrived in the New World in 1504, an obscure nineteen-year-old Spaniard seeking adventure and the chance to make a name for himself.

Spanish Exploration and Conquest

During the sixteenth century, the New World helped Spain become the most powerful monarchy in both Europe and the Americas. Initially, Spanish expeditions reconnoitered the Caribbean, scouted stretches of the Atlantic coast, and established settlements on the large islands of Hispaniola, Puerto Rico, Jamaica, and Cuba. Spaniards enslaved Caribbean tribes and put them to work growing crops and mining gold. But the profits from these early ventures barely covered the costs of maintaining the settlers. After almost thirty years of exploration, the promise of Columbus's discovery seemed illusory.

Soon after 1519, however, that promise was fulfilled, spectacularly. The mainland phase of exploration began in 1519 with Hernán Cortés's march into Mexico. By about 1545, Spanish conquests extended from northern Mexico to southern Chile, and New World riches filled Spanish treasure chests. Cortés's expedition served as the model for Spaniards' and other Europeans' expectations that the New World could yield bonanza profits for its conquerors.

The Conquest of Mexico

Hernán Cortés, who became the richest and most famous conquistador (conqueror), arrived in the New World in 1504, an obscure nineteen-year-old Spaniard seeking adventure and the chance to make a name for himself. He fought in the conquest of Cuba and elsewhere in the Caribbean. In 1519, the governor of Cuba authorized Cortés to organize an expedition to investigate rumors of a fabulously wealthy kingdom somewhere in the interior of the mainland. A charming, charismatic leader, Cortés quickly assembled a force of about six hundred men, loaded his ragtag army aboard eleven ships, and set out.

Cortés's confidence that he could talk his way out of most situations and fight his way out of the rest fortified the small band of Spaniards. But Cortés could not speak any Native American language. Landing first on the Yucatán peninsula, he had the good fortune to receive a gift from a chief of the Tobasco people. Among about twenty other women given to Cortés was a fourteen-year-old girl named Malinali who spoke several native languages, including Mayan and Nahuatl, the language of Mexica, the most powerful people in what is now Mexico and Central America (see chapter 1). Malinali had acquired her linguistic fluency painfully. Born into a family of the Mexican nobility, she learned Nahuatl as a young child. After her father died and her mother remarried and had a son, Malinali's stepfather sold her as a slave to Mayan-speaking Indians who subsequently gave the slave girl to the Tobascans. Malinali, whom the Spaniards called Marina, soon learned Spanish and became Cortés's interpreter. She also became one of Cortés's several mistresses and bore him a son. (Several years later, after Cortés's wife arrived in New Spain, Cortés cast Marina aside, and she married one of his soldiers.) Although no word uttered by Marina survives in historical documents, her words were the Spaniards' essential conduit of communication with the Indians. "Without her help," wrote one of the Spaniards who accompanied Cortés, "we would not have understood the language of New Spain and Mexico." With her help, Cortés talked and fought with Indians along the Gulf coast of Mexico, trying to discover the location of the fabled kingdom. By the time Marina died at age twenty-four, the people she had grown up among—the people who had taught her languages, enslaved her, and given her to Cortés—had been conquered by the Spaniards with her help.

In the capital of the Mexican empire, Tenochtitlán, the emperor Montezuma heard rumors about some strange creatures sighted along the coast. (Montezuma and his people are often called Aztecs, but they called themselves Mexica.) He feared that the strangers were led by the god Quetzalcoatl, returning to Tenochtitlán as predicted by Mexican religion. Montezuma sent representatives to meet with the strangers and bring them gifts fit for gods. Marina had told Cortés about Quetzalcoatl, and when Montezuma's messengers arrived, Cortés donned the regalia they had brought, almost certain proof to the Mexica that he was indeed the god they feared. The Spaniards astounded the messengers by blasting their cannon and displaying their swords.

The messengers hurried back to Montezuma with their amazing news. The emperor arranged for large quantities of food to be sent to the coast to welcome the strangers and perhaps to postpone Quetzalcoatl's dreaded arrival in the capital. Before the food was served to the Spaniards, the Mexica sacrificed several hostages and

Cortés Arrives in Tenochtitlán

This portrayal of the arrival of Cortés and his army in the Mexican capital illustrates the importance of Malinali, who stands at the front of the Spaniards' procession, serving as their translator and intermediary with Montezuma (not pictured), who has come out to greet the invaders. Painted by a Mexican artist after the conquest, the work contrasts Cortés—dressed as a Spanish gentleman, respectfully doffing his hat to Montezuma and accompanied by his horse and African groom—with his soldiers, who are armed and ready for battle. The painting displays the choices confronted by the Mexica: accepting the pacific overtures of Cortés or facing the lances, swords, and battle axes of the Spanish soldiers. Also notable is the importance of Indian porters who carried the Spaniards' food and other supplies. What do you think was the significance of the winged image on the flag? Bibliothèque Nationale, Paris.

soaked the food in their blood. This fare disgusted the Spaniards and might have been enough to turn them back to Cuba. But along with the food, the Mexica also brought the Spaniards another gift, a "disk in the shape of a sun, as big as a cartwheel and made of very fine gold," as one of the Mexica recalled. Here was conclusive evidence that the rumors of fabulous riches heard by Cortés had some basis in fact.

In August 1519, Cortés marched inland to find Montezuma. Leading about 350 men armed with swords, lances, and muskets and supported by ten cannon, four smaller guns, and sixteen horses, Cortés had to live

Cortés's Invasion of Tenochtitlán, 1519–1521

Gulf of Mexico

Zautla
Otumba
Jalapa
Texcoco
Tenochtitlán   Tlaxcala   Veracruz
Cholula

→ Cortés' original route, 1519
→ Cortés' retreat, 1520
→ Cortés' return route, 1520–1521

Horses: A New Native American Technology

An Indian on horseback: few images better evoke the American West. Yet Native Americans had no knowledge of horses before Columbus and other Spaniards arrived in the New World. Only after Spanish conquest did Native Americans learn to ride horses. Horses illustrate the widespread transfer of European technology to America in the wake of conquest and its transformation in the new context of the American West.

Horses existed throughout the hemisphere (and the world) when the first humans arrived in North America about 13,000 years ago. Like mammoths and other large mammals, however, ancient horses became extinct in America about 11,000 years ago. Paleo-Indians almost certainly contributed to their extinction by killing them for food. They reappeared in the New World less than two years after the arrival of Europeans. In January 1494, Columbus brought 24 stallions and 10 mares from Spain to the island of Hispaniola. Spaniards brought hundreds more horses on later voyages and began to breed and raise horses in New Spain.

The reappearance of horses in the New World epitomized the connections that already interlaced the globe by 1494. Columbus, an Italian mariner born in Genoa, a center of the old Mediterranean trade, had married a woman from Portugal, a monarchy that had pioneered voyages of exploration along the African coast that eventually undermined the Mediterranean trade. Now Columbus, who commanded a Spanish fleet seeking a western route to the East to compete with both the Portuguese trade around Africa and the old Mediterranean trade, brought back to the New World the descendants of horses that had originally evolved there millions of years earlier, after *their* ancestors had migrated to North America from Asia millions of years earlier still.

Horses had survived for millennia outside North America for two basic reasons. First, horses can convert the energy stored in tough, sparse grasses into strong bones and muscles. Horses achieve this energy conversion with a specialized intestine that allows them to digest large quantities of poor-quality grass that cannot sustain cattle.

Second, horses survived because they proved to be very useful to human beings. For hundreds of thousands of years, ancient humans probably saw horses mainly as a source of meat, just as Paleo-Indians did. But about 6,000 years ago in the Ukraine, a young nomad got close enough to a horse to leap on its back and hold on for dear life, initiating a revolution in human transportation. The domestication of horses, probably launched by a wild ride on the Ukrainian plains, spread throughout Eurasia.

From China to England, people learned to harness the great strength and energy of horses to carry burdens and pull loads. Horse users invented numerous technological devices and tinkered with them endlessly: saddles for carrying riders and packs; harnesses for control and to connect with carts or plows; spurs and whips to goad and punish; stirrups for a rider's comfort and to provide leverage for driving a lance through an opponent's chest; and much else, from magnificent armor to lowly horseshoes.

Columbus and other Spaniards made room for horses on their ships partly because the prevailing technology of horses made them useful for hauling loads and tilling fields. But above all, horses were on board Spanish ships because they carried conquistadors. Horses were as much a part of conquistadors' military equipment as swords and cannon. For a glimpse of the superiority of a

off the land, establishing peaceful relations with indigenous tribes when he could and killing them when he thought necessary. On November 8, 1519, Cortés reached Tenochtitlán. Montezuma came out to welcome the Spaniards. After presenting Cortés with gifts, Montezuma welcomed the Spaniards to the royal palace and showered them with lavish hospitality. Quickly, Cortés took Montezuma hostage and held him under house arrest, hoping to make him a puppet through which the Spaniards could rule the Mexican empire. This uneasy peace existed for several months until, after a brutal massacre of many Mexican nobles by one of Cortés's suborconquistador on horseback compared to a plebeian on foot, imagine a mounted soldier swinging a long, razor-sharp sword at everyone within reach. The deadly combination of mobility, speed, and height that horses gave conquistadors created an aura of power and authority around any Spaniard on horseback. The military technology of horses helped Spaniards exercise the political authority of conquest.

The Mexica who first saw Cortés's horses thought they were strange supernatural deer. Before long, however, the Mexica and other Native Americans learned that horses were neither deer nor supernatural. Native Americans soon grasped that technology that was good for the conquerors could also be good for the conquered.

Despite Spaniards' best efforts, some of their horses were stolen by Indians or ran away and thrived in the wild by grazing marginal lands, as their ancestors had done for millennia. The horses that ultimately made their way to North America were wild descendants of the domesticated horses brought to the New World in the holds of Spanish ships. By the early seventeenth century, Spanish merchants in the Southwest and elsewhere also traded horses to Native Americans along with guns and many other goods.

Native Americans adapted horses to their own cultures. They collected horses by taming wild animals, breeding, and raiding the herds of Spaniards and nearby tribes. Tasks that had previously been assigned to domesticated dogs, such as pulling loads or carrying packs, were now given to horses that readily hauled four times more weight. With their ability to move heavy loads while they searched for grazing and hunting lands, nomadic Indians accumulated all kinds of goods, including ceremonial items that reinforced tribal political and religious hierarchies. Horses also made age-old methods of buffalo hunting faster and more efficient, freeing young men to undertake other activities, particularly raids and reprisals against their enemies.

Horses probably intensified and certainly modified warfare among Native Americans in the West. Tactics shifted from massed groups of warriors engaged in pitched battles to small numbers of highly mobile horsemen springing surprise attacks. Bows and spears became shorter and shields smaller and lighter. The goals of warriors often included capturing their enemies' horses, which increased the warriors' military might while correspondingly diminishing that of their enemies. In these and many other ways, Indians in the American West adopted and transformed the technology of horses initiated by ancient Ukrainians and imported by fifteenth- and sixteenth-century Spaniards.

Teton Sioux Hide Painting
This hide painting illustrates the significance of horses in Indian warfare on the Great Plains. Painted by a Teton Sioux artist in the late nineteenth century, the images document the prowess of Indian warrriors in combining their deadly weapons with the strength and speed of horses. Unhorsed individuals had little chance against their mounted adversaries, the painting shows. Horses are the dominant figures in the painting and are rendered as distinctive individual animals, suggesting the artist's understanding of their importance to the warriors astride them. Horses had become so deeply integrated into Teton Sioux culture that a warrior and a horse were considered a single fighting unit. These assumptions and military tactics developed in the centuries after the arrival of Columbus, when Spaniards reintroduced horses to the New World.
Thaw Collection, Fenimore Art Museum, Cooperstown, NY. John Bigelow Taylor, NYC.

dinates, the population of Tenochtitlán revolted, murdered Montezuma, and mounted a ferocious assault on the Spaniards. On June 30, 1520, Cortés and about a hundred other Spaniards fought their way out of Tenochtitlán and retreated toward the coast about one hundred miles to Tlaxcala, a stronghold of bitter enemies of the Mexica. The friendly Tlaxcalans—who had long resented Mexican power—allowed Cortés to regroup, obtain reinforcements, and plan a strategy to conquer Tenochtitlán.

In the spring of 1521, Cortés mounted a complex campaign against the Mexican capital. The Spaniards and tens of thousands of Indian allies laid siege to the city. With a relentless, scorched-earth strategy, Cortés finally defeated the last Mexican defenders on August 13, 1521. (See "Historical Question," page 46.) The great capital of the Mexican empire "looked as if it had been ploughed up," one of Cortés's soldiers remembered. A few years later, one of the Mexica described the utter despair of the defeated:

> Broken spears lie in the roads;
> we have torn our hair in grief.
> The houses are roofless now, and their walls
> are red with blood. . . .
> We have pounded our hands in despair
> against the adobe walls,
> for our inheritance, our city, is lost and dead.

The Search for Other Mexicos

Lured by their insatiable appetite for gold, conquistadors quickly fanned out from Tenochtitlán in search of other sources of treasure like Mexico. The most spectacular prize fell to Francisco Pizarro, who conquered the Incan empire in Peru. The Incas controlled a vast, complex region that contained more than nine million people and stretched along the western coast of South America for more than two thousand miles. In 1532, Pizarro and his army of fewer than two hundred men captured the Incan emperor Atahualpa and held him hostage. As ransom, the Incas gave Pizarro the largest treasure yet produced by the conquests: gold and silver equiva-

Artifacts of Spanish Conquest

Spaniards reveled in their victories over the Mexica and other native peoples in the New World. About 1522, Cortés sent this Mexican shield as a trophy of conquest to a bishop in Spain. Made by a Mexican featherworker and probably looted from its Mexican owner by Cortés's soldiers, the shield was constructed of reeds, reenforced by sticks and rawhide, and decorated with feathers of exotic Central American birds. The animal outlined in strips of gold on the shield probably depicts the coyote effigy of Mexican warriors. The shield displayed to Spaniards the artistry of the Mexica as well as their weakness: Feathers, reeds, and coyotes were no match for Spaniards' steel, gunpowder, and Christianity. Contrast the vulnerability of the featherwork shield to Spaniards' razor-sharp swords and the comparative invulnerability of the Spanish war helmet to the Mexica's wooden spears and stone points. Like the shield, the helmet was a sign of Spaniards' technological superiority, which made conquest possible and justified it: People of feathers and reeds would—and should—be conquered by people of steel, the trophies suggested to Spaniards. The gold ingot was another trophy of conquest. Shortly after Cortés and his army entered Tenochtitlán, they found the treasure-house of Montezuma filled with golden artifacts. The Spaniards confiscated the treasure and melted the golden artworks into ingots slightly bent to allow them to be strapped in belts around soldiers' waists. In 1521, when the Mexica revolted against the Spaniards and temporarily drove them out of Tenochtitlán, many of Cortés's soldiers were forced to drop their heavy waistbands of gold in order to escape. This gold ingot, excavated in Mexico City in 1982, is probably one dropped by the retreating Spaniards. The ingot hints of the looting and destruction that accompanied conquest.

Museum of Volkerkunde, Vienna; Wallace Collection, London, UK / Bridgeman Art Library; Museo Nacional de Antropologia, CONACULTA-INAH, 10-220012.

lent to half a century's worth of precious-metal production in Europe. With the ransom safely in their hands, the Spaniards executed Atahualpa. The Incan treasure proved that at least one other Mexico did indeed exist, and spurred the search for others.

Juan Ponce de León had sailed along the Florida coast in 1513. Encouraged by Cortés's success, he went back to Florida in 1521 to find riches, only to be killed in battle with Calusa Indians. A few years later, Lucas Vázquez de Ayllón explored the Atlantic coast north of Florida to present-day South Carolina. In 1526 he established a small settlement on the Georgia coast that he named San Miguel de Gualdape, the first Spanish attempt to establish a foothold in what is now the United States. Within a few months, however, Ayllón and most of the other settlers sickened and died, and the few survivors retreated to Spanish settlements in the Caribbean.

Pánfilo de Narváez surveyed the Gulf coast from Florida to Texas in 1528. The Narváez expedition ended disastrously with a shipwreck on the Texas coast near present-day Galveston. Indians enslaved the few survivors of the Narváez expedition. After several years in Indian captivity, four of the survivors managed to escape and were rescued by Spanish slave hunters in northern Mexico.

In 1539, Hernando de Soto, a seasoned conquistador who had taken part in the conquest of Peru, set out with nine ships and more than six hundred men to find another Peru in North America. Landing in Florida, de Soto literally slashed his way through much of southeastern North America for three years, searching for the rich, majestic civilizations he thought were there. After many brutal battles and much hardship, de Soto became sick and died in 1542. His men buried him in the Mississippi River before turning back to Mexico, disappointed.

Tales of the fabulous wealth of the mythical Seven Cities of Cíbola also lured Francisco Vásquez de Coronado to search the Southwest and Great Plains of North America. In 1540, Coronado left northern Mexico with more than three hundred Spaniards, a thousand Indians, fifteen hundred horses, and a priest who claimed to know the way to what he called "the greatest and best of the discoveries." Cíbola turned out to be a small Zuñi pueblo of about a hundred families. When the Zuñi shot arrows at the Spaniards, Coronado attacked the pueblo and routed the defenders after a hard battle. Convinced that the

Zuñi Defend Pueblo against Coronado
This sixteenth-century drawing by a Mexican artist shows Zuñi bowmen fighting back against the arrows of Coronado's men and the entreaties of Christian missionaries. Intended to document the support some Mexican Indians gave to Spanish efforts to extend the conquest into North America, the drawing depicts the Zuñi defender at the bottom of the pueblo aiming his arrow at a Mexican missionary armed only with religious weaponry: a crucifix, a rosary, and a book—presumably the Bible.
Hunterian Museum Library, University of Glasgow. Glasgow University Library, Department of Special Collections.

rich cities must lie somewhere over the horizon, Coronado kept moving all the way to central Kansas before deciding in 1542 that the rumors he had pursued were just that, nothing more.

Juan Rodríguez Cabrillo led an expedition in 1542 that sailed along the coast of California. Cabrillo died on Santa Catalina Island, offshore from present-day Los Angeles, but his men sailed on to the border of Oregon, where a ferocious storm forced them to turn back toward Mexico.

These probes into North America by de Soto, Coronado, and Cabrillo persuaded Spaniards that enormous territories stretched northward but their inhabitants had little to loot or exploit. After a generation of vigorous exploration, Spaniards concluded that there was only one Mexico and one Peru.

Why Did Cortés Win?

By conquering Mexico, Hernán Cortés demonstrated that Columbus had in fact discovered a New World of enormous value to the Old. But how did a few hundred Spaniards so far away from home defeat millions of Indians fighting on their home turf?

First, several military factors favored the Spaniards. They possessed superior military technology, which partially offset the Mexica's numerical superiority. They fought with weapons of iron and steel against the Mexica's stone, wood, and copper. They charged on horseback against Mexican warriors on foot. They ignited gunpowder to fire cannon and muskets toward attacking Mexica, whose only source of power was human muscle. But the Mexica's immense numerical superiority could overpower the Spaniards' weaponry.

Spaniards also possessed superior military organization, although they were far from a highly disciplined, professional fighting force. Cortés's army was composed of soldiers of fortune, young men who hoped to fight for God and king and get rich. The unsteady discipline among the Spaniards is suggested by Cortés's decision to beach and dismantle the ships that had brought his small army to the Mexican mainland. After that, his men had no choice but to go forward.

The Spaniards were a well-oiled military machine compared with the Mexica, who tended to attack from ambush or in waves of frontal assaults, showing great courage but little organization or discipline.

The Mexica seldom sustained attacks, even when they had the Spaniards on the run. In the siege of Tenochtitlán, for example, the Mexica often paused to sacrifice Spanish soldiers they had captured, taking time to skin "their faces," one Spaniard recalled, "which they afterward prepared like leather gloves, with their beards on." Spanish tactics, in contrast, concentrated their soldiers to magnify the effect of their firepower and to maintain communication during the thick of battle.

But perhaps the Spaniards' most fundamental military advantage was their concept of war. The Mexican concept was shaped by the nature of the empire. The Mexica fought to impose their tribute system on others and to take captives for sacrifices. They believed that war would make their adversaries realize the high cost of continuing to fight and would give them a big incentive to surrender and pay tribute. To the Spaniards, war meant destroying the enemy's ability to fight. In short, the Spaniards sought total victory; the Mexica sought surrender. All these military factors weakened the Mexica's resistance but were insufficient to explain Cortés's victory.

Disease played a major part in the Mexica's defeat. When the Mexica confronted Cortés, they were not at full strength. An epidemic of smallpox and measles had struck the Caribbean in 1519, arrived in Mexico with Cortés and his men, and lasted through 1522. Thousands of Indians died, and many others became too sick to fight. When the Spaniards

were regrouping in Tlaxcala after their disastrous evacuation of Tenochtitlán, a great plague broke out in the Mexican capital. As one Mexica explained to a Spaniard shortly after the conquest, the plague lasted for seventy days, "striking everywhere in the city and killing a vast number of our people. Sores erupted on our faces, our breasts, our bellies. . . . The illness was so dreadful that no one could walk or move. . . . They could not get up to search for food, and everybody else was too sick to care for them, so they starved to death in their beds."

The sickness was not confined to Tenochtitlán. It also killed and weakened people in the areas surrounding the city, spreading back along the network of trade and tribute that fed the city, reducing its food supply and further weakening the survivors. While the Mexica were decimated by their first exposure to smallpox and measles, the Spaniards were for all practical purposes immune, having previously been exposed to the diseases. European viruses probably played at least as large a role in the conquest as weapons and military tactics.

Religion also contributed to the Mexica's defeat. Mexican religious doctrine led Montezuma to be hesitant and uncertain in confronting the Spaniards during the months when they were most vulnerable. While Cortés marched toward Tenochtitlán, the Indians thought that the Spaniards and their horses were immortal deities. Cortés worked hard to maintain the illusion, hiding Spaniards who died. But by the time Cortés retreated from Tenochtitlán, the Mexica knew that the Spaniards could be killed, and their resistance stiffened accordingly.

While the Mexica's religion reduced their initial resistance to the

Mexican Warrior

Warriors held the most exalted status in Mexican society. This sixteenth-century Mexican painting of a warrior in full battle regalia illustrates the Mexica's careful attention to their magnificent, awe-inspiring costumes. The elaborate clothing and decorative adornments (notice the ornamental stone plug in the warrior's lower lip) expressed warriors' high status; they also were intended to intimidate enemies who dared oppose the fearsome Mexica. Spanish soldiers developed healthy respect for the military skills of the Mexica but were not intimidated by the costumes of Mexican warriors. They did not understand the meaning the costumes had for the Mexica—for example, the costumes' evocation of supernatural support. In addition, although Mexican wooden swords lined with sharp stones could inflict deadly wounds, they proved no match for Spanish body armor, steel swords, horses, and guns.

Bibliothèque Nationale, Paris.

conquistadors, Christianity strengthened the Spaniards. The Spaniards' Christianity was a confident and militant faith that commanded its followers to destroy idolatry, root out heresy, slay infidels, and subjugate nonbelievers. Their religious zeal had been honed for centuries in the battles of the Reconquest. Christianity was as much a part of the conquistadors' armory as swords and gunpowder.

Mexican military commanders often turned to their priests for military guidance. Spaniards routinely celebrated mass and prayed before battles, but Cortés and his subordinates—tough, wily, practical men—made the military and diplomatic decisions. When the Spaniards suffered defeats, they did not worry that God had abandoned them. However, when the Mexica lost battles advised by their priests, they confronted the distressing fear that their gods no longer seemed to listen to them. The deadly sickness sweeping through the countryside also seemed to show that their gods had abandoned them. "Cut us loose," one Mexica pleaded, "because the gods have died."

Finally, political factors proved decisive in the Mexica's defeat. Cortés shrewdly exploited the tensions between the Mexica and the people they ruled in their empire. Cortés's small army was reinforced by thousands of Indians who were eager to seek revenge against the Mexica. With skillful diplomacy, Cortés obtained cooperation from thousands of Indian porters and food suppliers. Besides fighting alongside Cortés, the Spaniards' Indian allies provided the invaders with a fairly secure base from which to maneuver against the Mexican stronghold. Hundreds of thousands of Indians helped the Spaniards by not contributing to the Mexica's defense. These passive allies of the Spaniards prevented the Mexica from fully capitalizing on their overwhelming numerical superiority. In the end, although many factors contributed to the conquest, Cortés won because the Mexican empire was the source not only of the Mexica's impressive wealth and power but also of their crippling weakness.

Spaniards created the distinctive colonial society of New Spain that gave other Europeans a striking illustration of how the New World could be made to serve the purposes of the Old.

New Spain in the Sixteenth Century

For all practical purposes, Spain was the dominant European power in the Western Hemisphere during the sixteenth century (Map 2.3). Portugal claimed the giant territory of Brazil under the Tordesillas treaty but was far more concerned with exploiting its hard-won trade with the East Indies than in colonizing the New World. England and France were absorbed by domestic and diplomatic concerns in Europe and largely lost interest in America until late in the century. In the decades after 1519, Spaniards created the distinctive colonial society of New Spain that gave other Europeans a striking illustration of how the New World could be made to serve the purposes of the Old.

The Spanish monarchy claimed ownership of most of the land in the Western Hemisphere and gave the conquistadors permission to explore and plunder. (See "Documenting the American Promise," page 54.) The crown took one-fifth, called the "royal fifth," of any loot confiscated and allowed the conquerors to divide the rest. In the end, most conquistadors received very little after the plunder was divided among Cortés and his favorite officers. After the conquest of Tenochtitlán, Cortés decided to compensate

MAP 2.3   New Spain in the Sixteenth Century

Spanish control spread throughout Central and South America during the sixteenth century, with the important exception of Portuguese Brazil. North America, though claimed by Spain under the Treaty of Tordesillas, remained peripheral to Spain's New World empire.

READING THE MAP: Track Spain's efforts at colonization by date. How did political holdings, the physical layout of the land, and natural resources influence where the Spanish directed their energies?

CONNECTIONS: What was the purpose of the Treaty of Tordesillas? How might the location of silver and gold mines have affected Spain's desire to assert its claims over regions still held by Portugal after 1494, and Spain's interest in California, New Mexico, and Florida?

FOR MORE HELP ANALYZING THIS MAP, see the map activity for this chapter in the Online Study Guide at bedfordstmartins.com/roark.

Testerian Catechism

After conquest, Catholic missionaries tried to teach the Mexica the basic doctrines of Christianity by using pictures (pictographs) that resembled the symbols in preconquest Mexican codices (books composed of pictographs). Missionaries hoped to appeal to the Mexica's respect for the authority of the ancient texts. These Testerian catechisms demonstrate the missionaries' awareness that the Mexica often retained their faith in their preconquest gods. The catechism shown here incorporates symbols of both Christian and Mexican belief. Try to puzzle out the identity of the various figures and the meanings Catholic missionaries intended them to convey to the Mexica.

his disappointed, battle-hardened men by giving them towns the Spaniards had subdued.

The distribution of conquered towns institutionalized the system of *encomienda*, which empowered conquistadors to rule the Indians and the lands in and around their towns. The concept of encomienda was familiar to the Spaniards, who had used it to govern regions recaptured from the Muslims during the Reconquest. In New Spain, encomienda transferred to the Spanish *encomendero* (the man who "owned" the town) the tribute that the town had previously paid to the Mexican empire.

In theory, encomienda involved a reciprocal relationship between the encomendero and

"his" Indians. In return for the tribute and labor of the Indians, the encomendero was supposed to encourage the Indians to convert to Christianity, to be responsible for their material well-being, and to guarantee order and justice in the town. Catholic missionaries labored earnestly to convert Indians to Christianity. Missionaries fervently believed that God expected them to save Indians' souls by convincing them to abandon their old, sinful beliefs and to embrace the one true Christian faith. After baptizing tens of thousands of Indians, the missionaries learned that many Indians continued to worship their own gods along with the Christian God. Most friars came to believe that the Indians

Justifying Conquest

The immense riches Spain reaped from its New World empire came largely at the expense of Indians. A few individual Spaniards raised their voices against the brutal exploitation of Indians. Their criticisms prompted the Spanish monarchy to formulate an official justification of conquest that, in effect, blamed Indians for resisting Spanish dominion.

DOCUMENT 1
Montecino's 1511 Sermon

In 1511, a Dominican friar named Antón Montecino delivered a blistering sermon that astonished the Spaniards gathered in the church in Santo Domingo, headquarters of the Spanish Caribbean.

Your greed for gold is blind. Your pride, your lust, your anger, your envy, your sloth, all blind. . . . You are in mortal sin. And you are heading for damnation. . . . For you are destroying an innocent people. For they are God's people, these innocents, whom you destroyed. By what right do you make them die? Mining gold for you in your mines or working for you in your fields, by what right do you unleash enslaving wars upon them? They have lived in peace in this land before you came, in peace in their own homes. They did nothing to harm you to cause you to slaughter them wholesale. . . . Are you not under God's command to love them as you love yourselves? Are you out of your souls, out of your minds? Yes. And that will bring you to damnation.

SOURCE: Zvi Dor-Ner, *Columbus and the Age of Discovery* (New York: Morrow, 1991), 220–21.

DOCUMENT 2
The Requerimiento

Montecino returned to Spain to bring the Indians' plight to the king's attention. In 1512 and 1513, King Ferdinand met with philosophers, theologians, and other advisers and concluded that the holy duty to spread the Christian faith justified conquest. To buttress this claim, the king had his advisers prepare the Requerimiento. According to the Requerimiento, Indians who failed to welcome Spanish conquest and all its blessings deserved to die. Conquistadors were commanded to read the Requerimiento to Indians before any act of conquest. Beginning in 1514, they routinely did so, speaking in Spanish while other Spaniards brandishing unsheathed swords stood nearby.

On the part of the King . . . [and] queen of [Spain], subduers of the barbarous nations, we their servants notify and make known to you, as best we can, that the Lord our God, living and eternal, created the heaven and the earth, and one man and one woman, of whom you and we, and all the men of the world, were and are descendants. . . .

God our lord gave charge to one man called St. Peter, that he should be lord and superior to all the men in the world, that all should obey him, and that he should be the head of the whole human race, wherever men should live . . . and he gave him the world for his kingdom and jurisdiction.

And he commanded him to place his seat in Rome, as the spot most fitting to rule the world from. . . . This man was called Pope, as if to say, Admirable Great Father and Governor of men. The men who lived in that time obeyed that St. Peter and took him for lord, king, and superior of the universe. So also they have regarded the others who after him have been elected to the pontificate, and so has it been continued even till now, and will continue till the end of the world.

One of these pontiffs, who succeeded that St. Peter as lord of the world . . . made donation of these islands and mainland to the aforesaid king and queen [of Spain] and to their successors. . . .

were lesser beings inherently incapable of fully understanding the Christian faith.

In practice, encomenderos were far more interested in what the Indians could do for them than in what they or missionaries could do for the Indians. Encomenderos subjected Indians to chronic overwork, mistreatment, and abuse. As one Spaniard remarked, "Everything [the Indians] do is slowly done and by compulsion. They are malicious, lying, [and] thievish." Economically, however, encomienda recognized a fundamental reality of New Spain: The most important treasure the Spaniards could plunder from the New World was not gold but uncompensated Indian labor. To exploit that labor, New Spain's richest natural resource, encomienda

So their highnesses are kings and lords of these islands and mainland by virtue of this donation; and . . . almost all those to whom this has been notified, have received and served their highnesses, as lords and kings, in the way that subjects ought to do, with good will, without any resistance, immediately, without delay, when they were informed of the aforesaid facts. And also they received and obeyed the priests whom their highnesses sent to preach to them and to teach them our holy faith; and all these, of their own free will, without any reward or condition have become Christians, and are so, and the highnesses have joyfully and graciously received them, and they have also commanded them to be treated as their subjects and vassals; and you too are held and obliged to do the same. Wherefore, as best we can, we ask and require that you consider what we have said to you, and that you take the time that shall be necessary to understand and deliberate upon it, and that you acknowledge the Church as the ruler and superior of the whole world, and the high priest called Pope, and in his name the king and queen [of Spain] our lords, in his place, as superiors and lords and kings of these islands and this mainland by virtue of the said donation, and that you consent and permit that these religious fathers declare and preach to you. . . .

If you do so . . . we . . . shall receive you in all love and charity, and shall leave you your wives and your children and your lands free without servitude, that you may do with them and with yourselves freely what you like and think best, and they shall not compel you to turn to Christians unless you yourselves, when informed of the truth, should wish to be converted to our holy Catholic faith. . . . And besides this, their highnesses award you many privileges and exemptions and will grant you many benefits.

But if you do not do this or if you maliciously delay in doing it, I certify to you that with the help of God we shall forcefully enter into your country and shall make war against you in all ways and manners that we can, and shall subject you to the yoke and obedience of the Church and of their highnesses; we shall take you and your wives and your children and shall make slaves of them, and as such shall sell and dispose of them as their highnesses may command; and we shall take away your goods and shall do to you all the harm and damage that we can, as to vassals who do not obey and refuse to receive their lord and resist and contradict him; and we protest that the deaths and losses which shall accrue from this are your fault, and not that of their highnesses, or ours, or of these soldiers who come with us.

Indians who heard the Requerimiento could not understand Spanish, of course.

No native documents survive to record the Indians' thoughts upon hearing the Spaniards' official justification for conquest, even when it was translated in a language they recognized. But one conquistador reported that when the Requerimiento was translated for two chiefs in Colombia, they responded that if the pope gave the king so much territory that belonged to other people, "the Pope must have been drunk."

SOURCE: Adapted from A. Helps and M. Oppenheim, eds., *The Spanish Conquest in America and Its Relation to the History of Slavery and to the Government of the Colonies*, 4 vols. (London and New York, 1900–1904), 1:264–67.

QUESTIONS FOR ANALYSIS AND DEBATE

1. How did the Requerimiento answer the criticisms of Montecino? According to the Requerimiento, why was conquest justified? What was the source of Indians' resistance to conquest?

2. What arguments might a critic like Montecino have used to respond to the Requerimiento's justification of conquest? What arguments might the Mexican leader Montezuma have made against those of the Requerimiento?

3. Was the Requerimiento a faithful expression or a cynical violation of Spaniards' Christian faith?

gave encomenderos the right to force Indians to work when, where, and how the Spaniards pleased.

Encomienda engendered two groups of influential critics. A few of the missionaries were horrified at the brutal mistreatment of the Indians. The cruelty of the encomenderos made it difficult for priests to persuade Indians of the tender mercies of the Spaniards' God. "What will [the Indians] think about the God of the Christians," Fray Bartolomé de Las Casas asked, when they see their friends "with their heads split, their hands amputated, their intestines torn open? . . . Would they want to come to Christ's sheepfold after their homes had been destroyed, their children imprisoned, their wives

Catholic Feather Mosaic

In sixteenth-century Europe, Catholic churches conveyed religious messages in paintings, sculptures, and stained glass. The visual images both dramatized Christian stories and made religious doctrines accessible to the majority of Europeans who could not read. This feather mosaic produced by Mexican craftsmen in 1539 had a similar purpose. It follows European Christians' example of portraying a major event in Christian faith—Christ's resurrection after his death on the cross—in the distinctively Mexican medium of a mosaic of feathers collected from New World birds. Can you detect any other hints that the mosaic was designed to be understood by the Mexica?

The Mass of St. Gregory, 1539, feather mosaic, Auch, Musée des Jacobins, France (Gers).

chy moved to abolish encomienda in an effort to replace swashbuckling old conquistadors with royal bureaucrats as the rulers of New Spain.

One of the most important blows to encomienda was the imposition in 1549 of a reform called the *repartimiento*, which limited the labor an encomendero could command from his Indians to forty-five days per year from each adult male. The repartimiento, however, did not challenge the principle of forced labor, nor did it prevent encomenderos from continuing to cheat, mistreat, and overwork their Indians. Slowly, as the old encomenderos died, repartimiento replaced encomienda as the basic system of exploiting Indian labor.

The practice of coerced labor in New Spain grew directly out of the Spaniards' assumption that they were superior to the Indians. As one missionary put it, the Indians "are incapable of learning. . . . The Indians are more stupid than asses and refuse to improve in anything." Therefore, most Spaniards assumed, Indians' labor should be organized by and for their conquerors. Indians who resisted Spaniards' labor demands did so at great peril. Spaniards seldom hesitated to use violence to punish and intimidate recalcitrant Indians.

From the viewpoint of Spain, the single most important economic activity in New Spain after 1540 was silver mining. Spain imported more New World gold than silver in the early decades of the century, but that changed with the discovery of major silver deposits at Potosí, Bolivia, in 1545 and Zacatecas, Mexico, in 1546. As the mines swung into large-scale production, an ever-growing stream of silver flowed from New Spain to Spain (Figure 2.1). Overall, exports of precious metals from New Spain during the sixteenth century were worth about twenty-five times more than hides, the next most important export. The mines required large capital investments and many miners. Typically, a few Spaniards supervised large groups of Indian miners, who were supplemented by African slaves later in the sixteenth century. The mines and their products were valuable principally for their contribution to the wealth of Spain, not to that of the colony.

For Spaniards, life in New Spain was relatively easy. Only a few thousand Spaniards actually fought during the conquests. Although the riches they won fell far short of their expectations, the benefits of encomienda gave them a comfortable, leisurely life that was the envy of many Spaniards back in Europe. As one colonist

raped, their cities devastated, their maidens deflowered, and their provinces laid waste?" Las Casas and other outspoken missionaries softened few hearts among the encomenderos, but they did win some sympathy for the Indians from the Spanish monarchy and royal bureaucracy. Royal officials interpreted encomenderos' brutal treatment of the Indians as part of the larger general problem of the troublesome autonomy of encomenderos. The Spanish monarwrote to his brother in Spain, "Don't hesitate [to come]. . . . This land [New Spain] is as good as ours [in Spain], for God has given us more here than there, and we shall be better off."

During the century after 1492, about 225,000 Spaniards settled in the colonies. Virtually all of them were poor young men of common (non-noble) lineage who came directly from Spain. Laborers and **artisans** made up the largest proportion, but soldiers and sailors were also numerous. Throughout the sixteenth century, men vastly outnumbered women, although the proportion of women grew from about one in twenty before 1519 to nearly one in three by the 1580s. The gender and number of Spanish settlers shaped two fundamental features of the society of New Spain. First, despite the thousands of immigrants, Europeans never made up more than 1 or 2 percent of the total population. Although Spaniards ruled New Spain, the population was almost wholly Indian. Second, the shortage of Spanish women meant that Spanish men frequently married Indian women or used them as concubines.

The tiny number of Spaniards, the masses of Indians, and the frequency of intermarriage created a steep social hierarchy defined by perceptions of national origin and race. Natives of Spain—*peninsulares* (people born on the Iberian Peninsula)—enjoyed highest social status in New Spain. Below them but still within the white elite were creoles, the children born in the New World to Spanish men and women. Together, peninsulares and creoles made up barely 1 or 2 percent of the population. Below them on the social pyramid was a larger group of mestizos, the offspring of Spanish men and Indian women, who comprised 4 or 5 percent of the population. So many of the mestizos were illegitimate that the term *mestizo* (after the Spanish word for "mixed") became almost synonymous with *bastard* in the sixteenth century. Some mestizos worked as artisans and labor overseers and lived well, and a few rose into the ranks of the elite, especially if their Indian ancestry was not obvious from their skin color. Most mestizos, however, were lumped with Indians, the enormous bottom mass of the population.

The society of New Spain established the precedent for what would become a pronounced pattern in the European colonies of the New World: a society stratified sharply by social origin and race. All Europeans of whatever social origin considered themselves superior to Native Americans; in New Spain, they were a dominant minority in both power and status.

> New Spain established the precedent for what would become a pronounced pattern in the European colonies of the New World: a society stratified sharply by social origin and race.

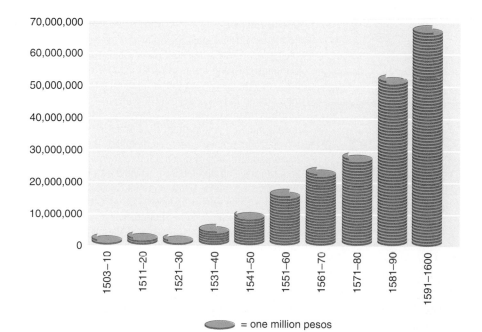

70,000,000
60,000,000
50,000,000
40,000,000
30,000,000
20,000,000
10,000,000
0

1503–10 1511–20 1521–30 1531–40 1541–50 1551–60 1561–70 1571–80 1581–90 1591–1600

⬭ = one million pesos

FIGURE 2.1 New World Gold and Silver Imported into Spain during the Sixteenth Century, in Pesos
Spain imported more gold than silver during the first three decades of the sixteenth century, but the total value of this treasure was quickly eclipsed during the 1530s and 1540s when rich silver mines were developed. Silver accounted for most of the enormous growth in Spain's precious-metal imports from the New World.

The Toll of Spanish Conquest and Colonization

By 1560, the major centers of Indian civilization had been conquered, their leaders overthrown, their religion held in contempt, and their people forced to work for the Spaniards. Profound demoralization pervaded Indian society. As a Mexican poet wrote:

> Nothing but flowers and songs of sorrow
> are left in Mexico . . .
> where once we saw warriors and wise men. . . .
> We are crushed to the ground;
> we lie in ruins.
> There is nothing but grief and suffering
> in Mexico.

Adding to the culture shock of conquest and colonization was the deadly toll of European diseases. As conquest spread, Indians succumbed to virulent epidemics of measles, smallpox, and respiratory illnesses. Indians had built up no immunity to these diseases because they had not been exposed to them before the arrival of Europeans. By 1570, only a half-century after Cortés entered Tenochtitlán, the Indian population of New Spain had fallen about 90 percent from what it had been when Columbus arrived. The destruction of the Indian population was a

Mixed Races
Residents of New Spain maintained a lively interest in each person's racial lineage. These eighteenth-century paintings illustrate forms of racial mixture common in the sixteenth century. In the first painting, a Spanish man and an Indian woman have a mestizo son; in the fourth, a Spanish man and a woman of African descent have a mulatto son; in the fifth, a Spanish woman and a mulatto man have a *morisco* daughter. The many racial permutations of parents led residents of New Spain to develop an elaborate vocabulary of ancestry. The child of a morisco and a Spaniard was a *chino*; the child of a chino and an Indian was a *salta abas*; the child of a salta abas and a mulatto was a *lobo*; and so on. Can you detect hints of some of the meanings of racial categories in the clothing depicted in these paintings?
Bob Schalkwijk/INAH.

FOR MORE HELP ANALYZING THIS IMAGE, see the visual activity for this chapter in the Online Study Guide at bedfordstmartins.com/roark.

A Sign of Conquest

This skull of an Indian man in his fifties was recently excavated from the site of a Native American village in southwestern Georgia visited by de Soto's expedition in 1540. The skull shows that the man suffered a fatal sword wound above his right eye. Combined with slashed and severed arm and leg bones from the same site, the skull demonstrates the brutality de Soto employed against indigenous peoples on his voyage through the Southeast. No native weapons could have inflicted the wounds indelibly left on this skull and the other bones.

Robert L. Blakely.

African Slaves Mining Gold *(below)*

This sixteenth-century illustration depicts African slaves mining gold in New Spain. Spaniards imported African slaves in substantial numbers after the Native American population had been decimated by conquest and disease. Here, the two slaves on the right dig ore, from which the gold is separated by the slave in the center and then washed in hot water over the fire, before the clean nuggets are given to the Spaniard, who carefully weighs and saves them. How did the artist emphasize the differences between the Spaniard and the slaves? Is it possible to detect the artist's point of view about who was more "civilized"?

The Pierpont Morgan Library, New York. MA 3900, f.100.

catastrophe unequaled in human history. A Mayan Indian recalled that when sickness struck his village, "Great was the stench of the dead. . . . The dogs and vultures devoured the bodies. The mortality was terrible. . . . So it was that we became orphans. . . . We were born to die!" For most Indians, New Spain was a rapidly growing graveyard.

For Spaniards, Indian deaths meant that the most valuable resource of New Spain—Indian labor—dwindled rapidly. By the last quarter of the sixteenth century, Spanish colonists felt the pinch of a labor shortage. To help redress the need for laborers, the colonists began to import African slaves. Some Africans had come to Mexico with the conquistadors; one Mexica recalled that among Cortés's men were "some black-skinned one with kink hair." In the years before 1550 while Indian labor was still adequate, only 15,000 slaves were imported from Africa. Even after Indian labor began to decline, the relatively high cost of African slaves kept imports low, approximately 36,000 from 1550 to the end of the century. During the sixteenth century, New Spain continued to rely primarily on a diminishing number of Indians.

Spanish Outposts in Florida and New Mexico

After the explorations of de Soto, Coronado, and Cabrillo, officials in New Spain lost interest in North America. The monarchy claimed that Spain owned North America and insisted that a few North American settlements be established to give some tangible reality to its claims. Settlements in Florida would have the additional benefit of protecting Spanish ships from pirates and privateers who lurked along the southeastern coast, waiting for the Spanish treasure fleet sailing toward Spain.

In 1565, the Spanish king sent Pedro Menéndez de Avilés to create settlements along the Atlantic coast of North America. In early September, Menéndez founded St. Augustine in Florida, the first permanent European settlement within what became the United States. By 1600, St. Augustine had a population of about five hundred, the remaining Spanish beachhead on the vast Atlantic shoreline of North America (see "American Places," page 61).

More than sixteen hundred miles west of St. Augustine, the Spaniards founded another outpost in 1598. Juan de Oñate led an expedition of about five hundred people to settle northern Mexico, now called New Mexico, and claim the booty rumored to exist there. Oñate had impeccable credentials for both conquest and mining. His father had helped to discover the bonanza silver mines of Zacatecas, and his wife was Isabel Tolosa Cortés Montezuma—the granddaughter of Cortés, the conqueror of Mexico and the great-granddaughter of Montezuma, the emperor of Mexico before conquest.

After a two-month journey from Mexico, Oñate and his companions reached pueblos near present-day Albuquerque and Santa Fe. He solemnly convened the pueblos' leaders and received their oath of loyalty to the Spanish king and to the Christian God. Oñate sent out scouting parties to find the legendary treasures of the region and to locate the ocean, which he believed must be nearby. Meanwhile, many of his soldiers planned to mutiny, and relations with the Indians deteriorated. When Indians in the Acoma pueblo revolted against the Spaniards, Oñate ruthlessly suppressed the uprising, killing 800 men, women, and children. Although Oñate reconfirmed the Spaniards' military superiority, he did not bring peace or stability to the region. Another pueblo revolt occurred in 1599, and many of Oñate's settlers returned to Mexico, dis-illusioned. New Mexico lingered as small, dusty assertions of Spanish claims to the North American Southwest.

The New World and Sixteenth-Century Europe

The riches of New Spain helped make the sixteenth century the Golden Age of Spain. After the deaths of Queen Isabella and King Ferdinand, their sixteen-year-old grandson became King Charles I of Spain in 1516. Three years later, just as Cortés ventured into Mexico, Charles I used judicious bribes to secure his selection as Holy Roman Emperor Charles V. His empire encompassed more than that of any other European monarch. Charles V used the wealth of New Spain to protect his sprawling empire and promote his interests in the fierce dynastic battles of sixteenth-century Europe. He also sought to defend orthodox Christianity from the insurgent heresy of the **Protestant Reformation**. The power of the Spanish monarchy spread throughout sixteenth-century Europe the clear message that a New World empire could bankroll Old World ambitions.

The Protestant Reformation and the European Order

In 1517, Martin Luther, an obscure Catholic priest in central Germany, initiated the Protestant Reformation by publicizing his criticisms of the Catholic Church. Luther's ideas, though shared by many other Catholics, were considered extremely dangerous by church officials and by Charles V and many other monarchs who believed with total conviction that, just as the church spoke for God, they ruled for God.

Luther preached a doctrine known as *justification by faith*: Individual Christians could obtain salvation and life everlasting only by having faith that God would save them. Giving offerings to the church, following the orders of priests, or participating in church rituals would not put believers one step closer to heaven. Also, the only true source of information about God's will was the Bible, not the church. By reading the Bible, any Christian could learn as much about God's commandments as any priest. Indeed, Luther called for a "priesthood of all believers."

AMERICAN PLACES

St. Augustine, Florida

St. Augustine, Florida, occupies the site of the oldest continuous settlement of Europeans in the United States. Founded in 1565 by the Spanish explorer Don Pedro Menéndez de Avilés on lands of a Timucuan Indian village, St. Augustine represented a projection of the power of the Spanish monarchy into the unknown lands of North America. Spaniards intended the settlement to defend Spanish ships that cruised along the Florida coast on their return to Spain and to assert Spain's claims against those of European and Native American rivals. A priest arrived with the first settlers and soon began missionary work among the Timucuan Indians.

The Mission of Nombre de Dios stands on the site of the first church and can be visited today.

Shortly after the Spaniards arrived, they mounted an attack on a nearby settlement of French Protestants (called Huguenots). More than 100 of the French settlers were killed when they refused to renounce their faith. At the site of the massacre, the Spaniards erected temporary fortifications and, much later, Fort Matanzas, which can still be visited. Other Spanish fortifications in St. Augustine were replaced in the late seventeenth century by what became Castillo de San Marcos, which is now the oldest fort built by Europeans in the United States.

Spaniards took care to fortify Castillo de San Marcos against attacks from sea and land. The drawbridge shown in the photograph allowed access to the only doorway entering the fort. In case of attack, the drawbridge would be raised; attackers who tried to cross the flooded moat would be vulnerable to weapons fired from the notched openings along the top of the fort. The design and size of Castillo de San Marcos demonstrate the military significance of St. Augustine in Spain's New World empire.

Visitors to St. Augustine today can have a taste of the daily life of settlers in colonial Spanish Florida by exploring Spanish Quarter Village, a vivid reminder of the long history of Spanish influence in North America.

FOR WEB LINKS RELATED TO THIS SITE AND OTHER AMERICAN PLACES, see "PlaceLinks" at bedfordstmartins.com/roark.

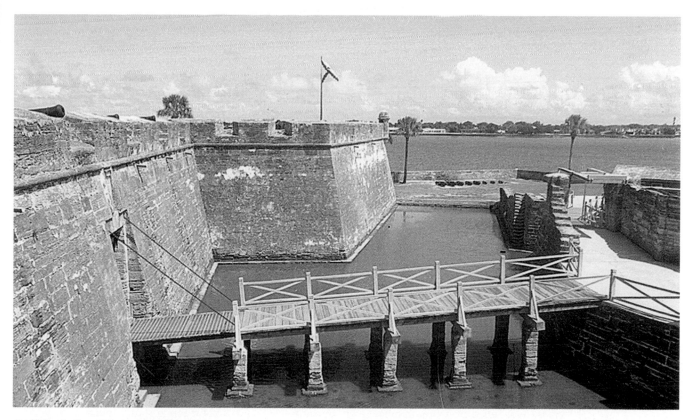

Castillo de San Marcos Fortification
Casa de San Marcos; photo by Linda Chandler.

In effect, Luther charged that the Catholic Church was in many respects fraudulent. Despite the church's claims to the contrary, Luther insisted that priests were unnecessary for salvation, and that they encouraged Christians to violate God's will by promoting religious practices not specifically commanded by the Bible. The church, Luther declared, had neglected its true purpose of helping individual Christians understand the spiritual realm revealed in the Bible and had wasted its resources in worldly conflicts of politics and wars. Luther hoped his ideas would reform the Catholic Church, but instead they ruptured forever the unity of Christianity in western Europe.

> Luther hoped his ideas would reform the Catholic Church, but instead they ruptured forever the unity of Christianity in western Europe.

Charles V pledged to exterminate Luther's **Protestant** heresies. The wealth pouring into Spain from the New World fueled his efforts to defend orthodox Catholic faith against Protestants, as well as against Muslims in eastern Europe and against any nation bold or foolhardy enough to contest Spain's supremacy. As the wealthiest and most powerful monarch in Europe, Charles V, followed by his son and successor, Philip II, assumed responsibility for upholding the existing order of sixteenth-century Europe.

New World Treasure and Spanish Ambitions

Both Charles V and Philip II fought wars throughout the world during the sixteenth century. Mexican silver funneled through the royal treasury into the hands of military suppliers, soldiers, and sailors wherever in the world Spain's forces fought. New World treasure was dissipated in military adventures that served the goals of the monarchy but did little to benefit most Spaniards.

In a sense, American wealth made the Spanish monarchy too rich and too powerful among the states of Europe. The ambitions of Charles V and Philip II were so great that the expenses of constant warfare far outstripped the revenues arriving from New Spain. To help meet military expenditures, both kings raised taxes in Spain more than fivefold during the sixteenth century. Since the nobility, by far the wealthiest class, was exempt from taxation, the burdensome new taxes fell mostly on poor peasants. The ambitions of the monarchy impoverished the vast majority of Spain's population and brought the nation to the brink of bankruptcy. When taxes failed to produce enough revenue to fight its wars, the monarchy borrowed heavily from European bankers. By the end of the sixteenth century, interest payments on royal debts swallowed two-thirds of the crown's annual revenues. In retrospect, the riches from New Spain proved a short-term blessing but a long-term curse.

But sixteenth-century Spaniards did not see it that way. As they looked at their accomplishments in the New World, they saw unmistakable signs of progress. They had added enormously to their knowledge and wealth. They had built mines, cities, Catholic churches, and even universities on the other side of the Atlantic. Their military, religious, and economic achievements gave them great pride and confidence.

Europe and the Spanish Example

The lessons of sixteenth-century Spain were not lost on Spain's European rivals. Spain proudly displayed the fruits of its New World conquests. In 1520, for example, Charles V exhibited some of the gifts Montezuma had given to Cortés. The objects astonished the German artist Albrecht Dürer, who wrote in his diary about "the things which were brought to the King from the New Golden Land: a sun entirely of gold, a whole fathom [six feet] broad; likewise a moon, entirely of silver, just as big. . . . I have never seen in all my days what so rejoiced my heart. . . . For I saw among them amazing objects, and I marveled over the subtle ingenuity of the men in these distant lands." Dürer's reaction illustrates the excitement the New World generated among some Europeans. But the most exciting news about "the men in these distant lands" was that they could serve the interests of Europeans as Spain had shown. With a few notable exceptions, Europeans saw the New World as a place for the expansion of European influence, a place where, as one Spaniard wrote, Europeans could "give to those strange lands the form of our own."

France and England tried to follow Spain's example. Both nations warred with Spain in Europe, preyed on Spanish treasure fleets, and ventured to the New World, where they too hoped to find an undiscovered passageway to the East Indies or another Mexico or Peru.

In 1524, France sent Giovanni da Verrazano to scout the Atlantic coast of North America from North Carolina to Canada, looking for a

Algonquian Ceremonial Dance
When the English artist John White visited the coast of present-day North Carolina in 1585 as part of Raleigh's expedition, he painted this watercolor portrait of an Algonquian ceremonial dance. This and White's other portraits are the only surviving likenesses of sixteenth-century North American Indians that were drawn from direct observation in the New World. White's portrait captures the individuality of these Indians' appearances and gestures while depicting a ceremony that must have appeared bizarre and alien to a sixteenth-century Englishman. The significance of this ceremonial dance is still a mystery, although the portrait's obvious signs of order, organization, and collective understanding show that the dancing Indians knew what it meant.
Copyright © The British Museum.

Northwest Passage (see Map 2.2). Eleven years later, France probed farther north with Jacques Cartier's voyage up the St. Lawrence River. Encouraged, Cartier returned to the region with a group of settlers in 1541, but the colony they established—like the search for a Northwest Passage—came to nothing.

English attempts to follow Spain's lead were slower but equally ill fated. Not until 1576, almost eighty years after John Cabot's voyages, did the English try again to find a Northwest Passage. This time Martin Frobisher sailed into the frigid waters of northern Canada. His spon-

sor was the Cathay Company, which hoped to open trade with China (see Map 2.2). Like many other explorers who preceded and followed him, Frobisher was mesmerized by the Spanish example and was sure he had found gold. But the tons of "ore" he hauled back to England proved worthless, the Cathay Company collapsed, and English interests shifted southward.

English explorers' attempts to establish North American settlements were no more fruitful than their search for a northern route to China. Sir Humphrey Gilbert led expeditions in 1578 and 1583 that made feeble efforts to found colonies in Newfoundland until Gilbert vanished at sea. Sir Walter Raleigh organized an expedition in 1585 to settle Roanoke Island off the coast of present-day North Carolina. The first group of explorers left no colonists on the island, but two years later Raleigh sent a contingent of more than one hundred settlers to Roanoke under John White's leadership. White returned to England for supplies, and when he came back to Roanoke in 1590, the colonists had disappeared, leaving only the word *Croatoan* (whose meaning is unknown) carved on a tree. The Roanoke colonists most likely died from a combination of natural causes and unfriendly Indians. By the end of the century, England had failed to secure a New World beachhead.

Roanoke Settlement, 1585–1590

Conclusion: The Promise of the New World for Europeans

The sixteenth century in the New World belonged to the Spaniards, who employed Columbus, and to the Indians, who greeted him as he stepped ashore. Spaniards initiated the Columbian exchange between the New World and the Old that continues to this day. The exchange subjected Native Americans to the ravages of European diseases and Spanish conquest. Spanish explorers, conquistadors, and colonists forced Indians to serve the interests of Spanish settlers and the Spanish monarchy. The exchange illustrated one of the most important lessons of the sixteenth century: After millions of years, the Atlantic no longer was an impermeable barrier separating the Eastern and Western Hemispheres. After the voyages of Columbus, European sailing ships regularly bridged the Atlantic and carried people, products, diseases, and ideas from one shore to the other.

No European monarch could forget the seductive lesson taught by Spain's example: The New World could vastly enrich the Old. Spain remained a New World power for almost four centuries, and its language, religion, culture, and institutions left a permanent imprint. By the end of the sixteenth century, however, other European monarchies had begun to contest Spain's dominion in Europe and to make forays into the northern fringes of Spain's New World preserve. To reap some of the benefits the Spaniards enjoyed from their New World domain, the others had to learn a difficult lesson: how to deviate from Spain's example. That discovery lay ahead.

FOR ADDITIONAL FIRSTHAND ACCOUNTS OF THIS PERIOD, see Chapter 2 in Michael Johnson, ed., *Reading the American Past*, Third Edition.

TO ASSESS YOUR MASTERY OF THE MATERIAL IN THIS CHAPTER, see the Online Study Guide at bedfordstmartins.com/roark.

FOR WEB LINKS RELATED TO TOPICS IN THIS CHAPTER, see "HistoryLinks," "DocLinks," and "PlaceLinks" at bedfordstmartins.com/roark.

CHRONOLOGY

1415 • Portugal conquers Ceuta at Strait of Gibraltar, gaining access to western coast of Africa.

1444 • Portuguese explorers reach Cape Verde.

1451 • Christopher Columbus born in Genoa, Italy.

1480 • Portuguese ships reach Congo.

1488 • Bartolomeu Dias rounds Cape of Good Hope.

1492 • Columbus lands on Caribbean island that he names San Salvador, initiating contact between Europe and the New World.

1493 • Columbus makes second voyage to the New World. In retaliation for mistreatment, Tainos kill many of Columbus's sailors.

1494 • Portugal and Spain negotiate Treaty of Tordesillas to establish their claims to newly discovered lands.

1497 • John Cabot searches for Northwest Passage.

1498 • Columbus makes third voyage to the New World and lands in Venezuela. Vasco da Gama sails to India.

1500 • Pedro Álvars Cabral makes landfall in Brazil.

1502 • Columbus makes fourth voyage to New World.

1507 • German mapmaker Martin Waldseemüller names the New World "America."

1513 • Vasco Núñez de Balboa crosses isthmus of Panama and learns that the Pacific Ocean separates America from Asia.

1517 • Protestant Reformation begins in Germany, intensifying religious and political turmoil in Europe.

1519 • Hernán Cortés leads expedition to find and conquer Mexico.

• Malinali (Doña Marina) becomes Cortés's translator and mistress.

• Ferdinand Magellan sets out to sail around the world.

• Charles I of Spain becomes Holy Roman Emperor Charles V.

1520 • Mexica in Tenochtitlán revolt against Spaniards.

1521 • Cortés, with the help of his Indian allies, conquers the Mexica at Tenochtitlán.

• Juan Ponce de León lands in Florida.

1526 • Lucas Vázquez de Ayllón establishes San Miguel de Gualdape on Georgia coast.

1528 • Pánfilo de Narváez leads expedition to survey Gulf coast from Florida to Texas.

1532 • Francisco Pizarro begins conquest of Peru.

1535 • Jacques Cartier explores St. Lawrence River.

1539 • Hernando de Soto launches exploration of southeastern North America.

1540 • Francisco Vásquez de Coronado starts to explore the Southwest and Great Plains of North America.

1542 • Juan Rodriguez Cabrillo explores California coast.

1549 • Repartimiento reforms begin to replace encomienda.

1565 • Pedro Menéndez de Avilés establishes St. Augustine, Florida.

1576 • Martin Frobisher sails into northern Canadian waters.

1578 • Sir Humphrey Gilbert attempts to found colonies in Newfoundland.

1587 • English colonists under Sir Walter Raleigh settle Roanoke Island.

1598 • Juan de Oñate leads expedition into New Mexico.

1599 • Pueblos revolt against Oñate.

BIBLIOGRAPHY

General Works

Richard Boyer and Geoffrey Spurling, eds., *Colonial Lives: Documents on Latin American History, 1550–1850* (2000).

Alfred W. Crosby Jr., *The Columbian Exchange: Biological and Cultural Consequences of 1492* (1972).

Barry W. Cunliffe, *Facing the Ocean: The Atlantic and Its Peoples, 8000 BC–AD 1500* (2001).

Zvi Dor-Ner, *Columbus and the Age of Discovery* (1991).

J. H. Elliott, *The Old World and the New, 1462–1650* (1970).

Felipe Fernández-Armesto, *Before Columbus: Exploration and Colonization from the Mediterranean to the Atlantic, 1229–1492* (1987).

Jonathan Locke Hart, *Representing the New World: The English and French Uses of the Example of Spain* (2001).

Jonathan Locke Hart, *Columbus, Shakespeare, and the Interpretation of the New World* (2003).

John L. Kessell, *Spain in the Southwest: A Narrative History of Colonial New Mexico, Arizona, Texas, and California* (2002).

D. W. Meinig, *The Shaping of America* (1986).

William D. Phillips and Carla Rahn Phillips, *The Worlds of Christopher Columbus* (1992).

David B. Quinn, *North America from Earliest Discovery to First Settlements* (1977).

A. J. R. Russell-Wood, *The Portuguese Empire, 1415–1808: A World on the Move* (1998).

Jayme A. Sokolow, *The Great Encounter: Native Peoples and European Settlers in the Americas, 1492–1800* (2003).

Stanley J. Stein and Barbara H. Stein, *Silver, Trade, and War: Spain and America in the Making of Early Modern Europe* (2000).

Hugh Thomas, *Conquest: Montezuma, Cortés, and the Fall of Old Mexico* (1993).

John Thornton, *Africa and Africans in the Making of the Atlantic World, 1400–1680* (1992).

David J. Weber, *The Spanish Frontier in North America* (1992).

Explorers and Empires

Jan De Vries, *The Economy of Europe in an Age of Crisis, 1600–1750* (1976).

William Eccles, *Canadian Frontier, 1534–1760* (1969).

Mary E. Giles, *Women in the Inquisition: Spain and the New World* (1999).

Henry Arthur Francis Kamen, *Spain's Road to Empire: The Making of a World Power, 1492–1763* (2002).

Karen Ordahl Kupperman, *Roanoke: The Abandoned Colony* (1984).

Peggy K. Liss, *Isabel the Queen: Life and Times* (1992).

John Lynch, *Spain, 1516–1598: From Nation State to World Empire* (1992).

Harry A. Miskimin, *The Economy of Later Renaissance Europe, 1460–1600* (1977).

David B. Quinn, *England and the Discovery of America, 1481–1620* (1974).

David B. Quinn, *Set Fair for Roanoke* (1985).

Francesc Relaño, *The Shaping of Africa: Cosmographic Discourse and Cartographic Science in Late Medieval and Early Modern Europe* (2002).

A. C. de C. M. Saunders, *A Social History of Black Slaves and Freedmen in Portugal, 1441–1555* (1982).

Roger C. Smith, *Vanguard of Empire: Ships of Exploration in the Age of Columbus* (1993).

Robert S. Weddle, *The Gulf of Mexico in North American Discovery, 1500–1685* (1985).

Europeans Encounter the New World

James Axtell, *Natives and Newcomers: The Cultural Origins of North America* (2002).

Robert F. Berkhofer Jr., *The White Man's Indian: Images of the American Indian from Columbus to the Present* (1978).

Philip P. Boucher, *Cannibal Encounters: Europeans and Island Caribs, 1492–1763* (1992).

Nicholas Canny and Anthony Pagden, *Colonial Identity in the Atlantic World, 1500–1800* (1987).

Rebecca Catz, *Christopher Columbus and the Portuguese, 1476–1498* (1993).

Alfred W. Crosby, *Ecological Imperialism: The Biological Expansion of Europe, 900–1900* (1986).

James Robert Enterline, *Erikson, Eskimos, and Columbus: Medieval European Knowledge of America* (2002).

William W. Fitzhugh, ed., *Cultures in Contact: The Impact of European Contacts on Native American Cultural Institutions, 1000–1800* (1985).

Valerie J. Flint, *The Imaginative Landscape of Christopher Columbus* (1992).

Anthony Grafton, *New Worlds, Ancient Texts: The Power of Tradition and the Shock of Discovery* (1992).

Peter Hulme, *Colonial Encounters: Europe and the Native Caribbean, 1492–1797* (1986).

William F. Keegan, *The People Who Discovered Columbus: An Introduction to the Prehistory of the Bahamas* (1992).

Anthony Pagden, *The Fall of Natural Man: The American Indian and the Origins of Comparative Ethnology* (1981).

Anthony Pagden, *European Encounters with the New World: From Renaissance to Romanticism* (1993).

Anthony Pagden, *Lords of All the World: Ideologies of Empire in Spain, Britain, and France, 1500–1800* (1995).

Irving Rouse, *The Tainos: Rise and Decline of the People Who Greeted Columbus* (1992).

Samuel M. Wilson, *Hispaniola: Caribbean Chiefdoms in the Age of Columbus* (1990).

Conquest and New Spain

Ida Altman, *Emigrants and Society: Extremadura and Spanish America in the Sixteenth Century* (1989).

Ida Altman, *Transatlantic Ties in the Spanish Empire: Brihuega, Spain, and Puebla, Mexico, 1560–1620* (2000).

Gary Clayton Anderson, *The Indian Southwest, 1580–1830: Ethnogenesis and Reinvention* (1999).

Kenneth J. Andrien, *Andean Worlds: Indigenous History, Culture, and Consciousness under Spanish Rule, 1532–1825* (2001).

Santa Arias, ed., *Mapping Colonial Spanish America: Places and Commonplaces of Identity, Culture, and Experience* (2002).

Elinore M. Barrett, *Conquest and Catastrophe: Changing Rio Grande Settlement Patterns in the Sixteenth and Seventeenth Centuries* (2001).

Herman L. Bennett, *Africans in Colonial Mexico: Absolutism, Christianity, and Afro-Creole Consciousness, 1570–1640* (2003).

Peter J. Blackwell, *Silver Mining and Society in Colonial Mexico: Zacatecas, 1546–1700* (1971).

Peter J. Blackwell, *Miners of the Red Mountain: Indian Labor in Potosí, 1545–1650* (1984).

Virginia Marie Bouvier, *Women and the Conquest of California, 1548–1840* (2001).

Frederick P. Bowser, *The African Slave in Colonial Peru, 1524–1650* (1974).

Gordon Brotherston, *Image of the New World: The American Continent Portrayed in Native Texts* (1979).

Louise M. Burkhart, *The Slippery Earth: Nahua-Christian Moral Dialogue in Sixteenth-Century Mexico* (1989).

Magali Marie Carrera, *Imagining Identity in New Spain: Race, Lineage and the Colonial Body in Portraiture and Casta Paintings* (2003).

Inga Clendinnen, *Aztecs: An Interpretation* (1991).

Noble David Cook, *Born to Die: Disease and New World Conquest, 1492–1650* (1998).

Noble David Cook, ed., *Secret Judgments of God: Old World Disease in Colonial Spanish America* (2001).

Kathleen A. Deegan, ed., *America's Ancient City: Spanish St. Augustine, 1565–1763* (1991).

David Ewing Duncan, *Hernando de Soto: A Savage Quest in the Americas* (1995).

Richard Flint and Shirley Cushing Flint, *The Coronado Expedition* (2003).

Patricia Galloway, *The Hernando de Soto Expedition: History . . . and "Discovery" in the Southeast* (1997).

Charles Gibson, *Spain in America* (1966).

Serge Gruzinski, *The Conquest of Mexico: The Incorporation of Indian Societies into the Western World, Sixteenth–Eighteenth Centuries* (1993).

Ramón A. Gutiérrez, *When Jesus Came, the Corn Mothers Went Away: Marriage, Sexuality, and Power in New Mexico, 1500–1846* (1991).

Robert T. Himmerich, *The Encomenderos of New Spain, 1521–1555* (1991).

Paul E. Hoffman, *A New Andalucía and a Way to the Orient: The American Southeast during the Sixteenth Century* (1990).

Robert H. Jackson, *Race, Caste, and Status: Indians in Colonial Spanish America* (1999).

Robert H. Jackson, ed., *Indians, Franciscans, and Spanish Colonization: The Impact of the Mission System on California Indians* (1995).

Richard L. Kagan, *Urban Images of the Hispanic World, 1493–1793* (2000).

Robert L. Kapitzke, *Religion and Politics in Colonial St. Augustine* (2001).

Kenneth F. Kiple and Stephen V. Beck, eds., *Biological Consequences of European Expansion, 1450–1800* (1997).

Andrew L. Knaut, *The Pueblo Revolt of 1680: Conquest and Resistance in Seventeenth-Century New Mexico* (1995).

James Lang, *Conquest and Commerce: Spain and England in the Americas* (1975).

Clark Spencer Larsen and George R. Milner, eds., *In the Wake of Contact: Biological Responses to Conquest* (1994).

James Lockhart, *The Nahuas after Conquest: A Social and Cultural History of the Indians of Central Mexico, Sixteenth through Eighteenth Centuries* (1992).

James Lockhart, ed., *We People Here: Nahuatl Accounts of the Conquest of Mexico* (1993).

Lyle N. McAlister, *Spain and Portugal in the New World, 1492–1700* (1984).

Sabine McCormack, *Religion in the Andes: Vision and Imagination in Early Colonial Peru* (1991).

Bonnie G. McEwan, *The Spanish Missions of La Florida* (1993).

Jerald T. Milanich, *Florida Indians and the Invasion from Europe* (1995).

Jerald T. Milanich, *Laboring in the Fields of the Lord: Spanish Missions and Southwestern Indians* (1999).

Jerald T. Milanich and Charles Hudson, *Hernando De Soto and the Indians of Florida* (1993).

Shannon Miller, *Invested with Meaning: The Raleigh Circle in the New World* (1998).

Barbara E. Mundy, *The Mapping of New Spain: Indigenous Cartography and the Maps of the Relaciones Geográficas* (2000).

Colin A. Palmer, *Slaves of the White God: Blacks in Mexico, 1570–1650* (1976).

José Rabasa, *Writing Violence on the Northern Frontier: The Historiography of Sixteenth Century New Mexico and Florida and the Legacy of Conquest* (2000).

Carroll L. Riley, *Rio del Norte: People of the Upper Rio Grande from Earliest Times to the Pueblo Revolt* (1995).

Carroll L. Riley, *The Kachina and the Cross: Indians and Spaniards in the Early Southwest* (1999).

Susan Schroeder, *Native Resistance and the Pax Colonial in New Spain* (1998).

Stuart B. Schwartz, ed., *Victors and Vanquished: Spanish and Nahua Views of the Conquest of Mexico* (2000).

Robert Silverberg, *The Pueblo Revolt* (1994).

Steve J. Stern, *Peru's Indian Peoples and the Challenge of Spanish Conquest: Huamanga to 1640* (1982).

David Hurst Thomas, ed., *Ethnology of the Indians of Spanish Florida* (1991).

David Hurst Thomas, ed., *The Missions of Spanish Florida* (1991).

Richard F. Townsend, *The Aztecs* (2000).

Charles A. Truxillo, *By the Sword and the Cross: The Historical Evolution of the Catholic World Monarchy in Spain and the New World, 1492–1825* (2001).

Thomas M. Whitmore and Billie Lee Turner II, *Cultivated Landscapes of Middle America on the Eve of Conquest* (2001).

Stephanie Gail Wood, *Transcending Conquest: Nahua Views of Spanish Colonial Mexico* (2003).

ALGONQUIAN POUCH

This pouch belonged to an important Algonquian Indian, possibly even the chief Powhatan, whose people inhabited the region first settled by the Virginia colonists. One or more Algonquian women probably made the pouch. Dangling from each end are two arrow-shaped pendants decorated with nearly 6,000 beads made from shells collected from Virginia's beaches. Algonquians—again, probably women—cut beads from the shells and perforated each bead with a tiny hole through which they threaded sinew interwoven with strips of deer hide to make the elaborate beaded design. Only a powerful Algonquian dignitary could command the labor and materials necessary to produce such a pouch. In turn, the pouch signaled the dignitary's importance when he wore it. The wearer draped the pouch over a belt that passed through the fold at the top. The opening to the pouch is on the inside of the fold and not visible here. The wearer probably used the pouch to carry tobacco and ritualistic objects that symbolized his authority. Most likely, however, the main function of the pouch was to dazzle ordinary Algonquians with the wearer's magnificence.

Ashmolean Museum, Oxford, England.

3

The Southern Colonies in the Seventeenth Century

1601–1700

I N December 1607, barely six months after arriving at Jamestown with the first English colonists, Captain John Smith was captured by warriors of Powhatan, the supreme chief of about fourteen thousand Algonquian people who inhabited the coastal plain of present-day Virginia, near the Chesapeake Bay. According to Smith, Powhatan "feasted him after their best barbarous manner." Then, after the chief consulted with his men, "two great stones were brought before Powhatan: then as many [Indians] as could layd hands on [Smith], dragged him to [the stones], and thereon laid his head, and being ready with their clubs, to beate out his braines." At that moment, Pocahontas, Powhatan's eleven-year-old daughter, rushed forward and "got [Smith's] head in her armes, and laid her owne upon his to save him from death." Pocahontas, Smith wrote, "hazarded the beating out of her owne braines to save mine, and . . . so prevailed with her father, that I was safely conducted [back] to James towne."

This romantic story of an Indian maiden rescuing a white soldier and saving not only his life but also Jamestown and ultimately English **colonization** of North America has been enshrined in the writing of American history since 1624 when Smith published his *Generall Historie of Virginia* and was even dramatized in a Disney movie. Historians believe that this episode actually happened more or less as Smith described it. But Smith did not understand why Pocahontas acted as she did. Many commentators have claimed that her love for Smith caused her to rebel against her father's authority. Pocahontas herself left no document that explains her motives; most likely, she could not write. Everything known about her comes from the pens of Smith or other Englishmen. When their writings are considered in the context of what is known about the Algonquian society Pocahontas was born into, her actions appear in an entirely different light.

When Pocahontas intervened to save Smith, she almost certainly was a knowing participant in an Algonquian ceremony that expressed Powhatan's supremacy and his ritualistic adoption of a subordinate chief, or *werowance*. Most likely, what Smith interpreted as Pocahontas's saving him from certain death was instead a ceremonial enactment of Powhatan's willingness to incorporate Smith and the white strangers at Jamestown into Powhatan's empire. The ceremony displayed Powhatan's power of life or death over a subordinate chief—Smith—and Powhatan's willingness to give protection to those who acknowledged his supremacy—in this case, the interlopers at Jamestown. By appearing to save Smith, Pocahontas was probably acting out Smith's new status as an adopted member of Powhatan's extended family. Rather than a rebellious, lovestruck girl, Pocahontas was almost certainly a dutiful daughter playing the part prescribed for her by her father and her culture.

Smith went back to England about two years after the adoption ritual. In the meantime, Pocahontas frequently visited the English settlement and often brought gifts of food to the colonists from her father. Powhatan routinely at-

tached his sons and daughters to subordinate tribes as an expression of his protection and his dominance. It appears that Pocahontas's attachment to the English colonists grew out of Powhatan's attempt to treat the tribe of white strangers at Jamestown as he did other tribes in his empire, an attempt that failed.

In 1613, after relations between Powhatan and the English colonists had deteriorated into bloody raids by both parties, the colonists captured Pocahontas and held her hostage at Jamestown. Within a year she converted to Christianity and married one of the colonists, a widower named John Rolfe. After giving birth to a son, Thomas, Pocahontas, her husband, and the new baby sailed for England in the spring of 1616. There, promoters of the Virginia colony dressed her as a proper Englishwoman and arranged for her to meet dignitaries. She even went to a ball attended by the English king and queen.

When John Smith heard that Pocahontas was in London, he went to see her. According to Smith, Pocahontas said, "You did promise Powhatan what was yours should bee his, and he the like to you; you called him father, being in his land a stranger, and by the same reason so must I doe you." It seems likely that Pocahontas understood what was happening to her in England as a counterpart to the adoption ritual Powhatan had staged for John Smith in Virginia back in 1607.

Pocahontas died in England in 1617. Her son, Thomas, ultimately returned to Virginia, and by the time of the American Revolution his descendants numbered in the hundreds. But the world Thomas Rolfe and his descendants inhabited was shaped by a reversal of the power ritualized when his mother "saved" John Smith. By the end of the seventeenth century, Native Americans were far from vanquished, but—unlike Powhatan—they no longer dominated the newcomers who arrived in the Chesapeake with John Smith.

During the seventeenth century, English colonists learned how to deviate from the example of New Spain (see chapter 2) by growing tobacco, a crop Native Americans had cultivated in small quantities for centuries. The new settlers, however, grew enormous quantities of tobacco, far more than they could smoke, chew, or sniff themselves, and they exported most of it to England. Instead of incorporating Powhatan's people into their new society, the settlers encroached on lands surrounding the Chesapeake

Pocahontas in England

Shortly after Pocahontas and her husband John Rolfe arrived in England in 1616, an engraver made this portrait of her dressed in English clothing suitable for a princess. The portrait captures the dual novelty of England for Pocahontas and of Pocahontas for the English. Ornate, courtly clothing probably signified to English observers that Pocahontas was royalty and to Pocahontas that the English were accepting her as befitted the "Emperor" Powhatan's daughter. The mutability of Pocahontas's identity is displayed in the engraving's identification of her as "Matoaka" or "Rebecca."

Library of Congress.

Bay that had supported ancient Americans for millennia, and they built new societies on the foundation of tobacco agriculture and transatlantic trade.

To produce large crop surpluses for export required hard labor and people who were willing—or could be forced—to do it. For the most part, Native Americans refused to be conscripted into the colonists' fields. Instead, the settlers depended on the labor of family members, **indentured servants**, and, by the last third of the seventeenth century, African slaves. By the end of the century, the southern colonies had become sharply different both from the world dominated by Powhatan when the Jamestown settlers first arrived and from contemporary English society. In ways unimaginable to Powhatan, Pocahontas, or John Smith, the colonists paid homage to the international market and the English monarch by working mightily to make a good living growing crops for sale to the Old World.

An English Colony on the Chesapeake

When James I became king of England after the death of Queen Elizabeth I in 1603, he eyed North America as a possible location for colonies. Spain claimed all of North America under the 1494 Treaty of Tordesillas (see chapter 2), but Spain's claim meant little if it could not be defended. King James had reason to believe England could encroach on the outskirts of Spain's New World empire. In 1588, England had defeated the Spanish Armada, a large fleet of warships sent to invade England and bring it under Spanish rule. England's success in defending itself from this Spanish attack suggested that England might now succeed in defending new colonies in North America. And English colonies might well become enormously profitable, just as Spain's New World empire had proved for more than a century to be profitable for Spain.

In 1606, a number of "knightes, gentlemen, merchauntes, and other adventurers of our cittie of London" organized the Virginia Company, a joint stock company. English merchants had used joint stock companies for many years to pool capital and share risks in trading voyages to Europe, Asia, and Africa. The Virginia Company

Secotan Village
This engraving, published in 1612, was copied from an original drawing John White made in 1585 when he visited the village of Secotan on the coast of North Carolina. The drawing provides a schematic view of daily life in the village, which may have resembled one of Powhatan's settlements. White noted on the original that the fire burning behind the line of crouching men was "the place of solemne prayer." The large building in the lower left was a tomb where the bodies of important leaders were kept. Dwellings similar to those illustrated on John Smith's map of Virginia lined a central space, where men and women ate. Corn is growing in the fields along the right side of the village. The engraver included hunters shooting deer at the upper left. Hunting was probably never so convenient—no such hunters or deer appear in White's original drawing. This drawing conveys the message that Secotan was orderly, settled, religious, harmonious, and peaceful (notice the absence of fortifications), and very different from English villages.
Princeton University Libraries, Department of Rare Books and Special Collections.

FOR MORE HELP ANALYZING THIS IMAGE, see the visual activity for this chapter in the Online Study Guide at bedfordstmartins.com/roark.

had ambitions larger than trade. The company petitioned King James for permission to establish a colony in North America. The king complied, giving the company over six million acres extending inland from the Atlantic coast. In effect, the king's **land grant** to the Virginia Company was a royal license to poach on both Spanish claims and Powhatan's chiefdom.

The investors in the Virginia Company hoped to found an empire that would strengthen England both overseas and at home. Richard Hakluyt, a strong proponent of colonization, claimed that a colony would provide work for swarms of poor "valiant youths rusting and hurtfull by lack of employment" in England. Jobless Englishmen could find work in the colony, producing goods that England now had to import from other nations. They could also provide a ready colonial market for English manufactured goods. More trade and more jobs would benefit many people in England, but the main reason the Virginia Company investors were willing to risk their capital in Virginia was their fervent hope for quick profits.

Investors did not know exactly how they could make money in Virginia. Enthusiastic reports from the Roanoke voyages twenty years earlier (see chapter 2) declared that in Virginia "the earth bringeth foorth all things in aboundance, as in the first creation, without toile or labour." Even if these reports exaggerated, investors reasoned, maybe some valuable exotic crop could be grown profitably in this Eden. Maybe the apparently limitless forests could be tapped to produce pitch and tar, essentials for watertight ships. Or maybe rich lodes of gold and silver awaited discovery, as they had in New Spain. Gold and silver that did not need to be discovered nestled in the holds of Spanish ships that cruised up the Atlantic coast to catch the trade winds that would take them home. Virginia Company investors dreamed about the quick and easy profits they could reap from an occasional raid on these Spanish treasure ships. One way or another, the new colony promised to reward the company's investors. Or so they thought. They failed to appreciate the difficulties of adapting European desires and expectations to the New World environment, especially the Native Americans who already inhabited the region. Within two decades, the struggling Jamestown settlement managed to survive in unexpected ways, and royal government replaced the private Virginia Company, which never earned a penny for its investors.

The Fragile Jamestown Settlement

In December 1606, the ships *Susan Constant*, *Discovery*, and *Godspeed* carried 144 Englishmen toward Virginia. They arrived at the mouth of the Chesapeake Bay on April 26, 1607. That night while the colonists rested on shore, one of them later recalled, a band of Indians "creeping upon all foure, from the Hills like Beares, with their Bowes in their mouthes," attacked and dangerously wounded two men. The attack gave the colonists an early warning that the North American wilderness was not quite the paradise described by the Virginia Company's publications in England. On May 14, they went ashore on a small peninsula in the midst of Powhatan's chiefdom. With the memory of their first night in America fresh in their minds, they quickly built a fort, the first building in the settlement they named Jamestown. (See "American Places," page 73.)

The Jamestown fort showed the colonists' awareness that they needed to protect themselves from Indians and Spaniards. Spain employed spies to stay informed about the new English colony. Spain planned to wipe out Jamestown when the time was ripe, but that time never came. Powhatan's people defended Virginia as their own. During May and June 1607, the settlers and Powhatan's warriors skirmished repeatedly. English muskets and cannon repelled Indian attacks on Jamestown, but the Indians' superior numbers and knowledge of the Virginia wilderness made it risky for the settlers to venture far beyond the peninsula. Late in June, Powhatan sensed a stalemate and made peace overtures.

The settlers soon confronted dangerous, invisible threats: disease and starvation. During the summer, many of the Englishmen lay "night and day groaning in every corner of the Fort most pittiful to heare," wrote George Percy, one of the settlers. By September, 50 of the colonists had died. "Our men were destroyed with cruel diseases [such] as Swellings, Fluxes, [and] Burning Fevers," Percy recalled. The colonists increased their misery by bickering among themselves, leaving crops unplanted and food supplies shrinking. "For the most part [the settlers] died of meere famine," Percy wrote; "there were never Englishmen left in a forreigne Countrey in such miserie as wee were in this new discovered Virginia."

Powhatan's people came to the rescue of the weakened and demoralized Englishmen. Early

AMERICAN PLACES

Jamestown, Virginia

The first colonists chose the site for Jamestown in 1607 because it seemed defensible. Located about thirty miles up the James River from the open waters of the Chesapeake Bay, the site offered protection against surprise attack by marauders from Spain. A small island separated from the mainland promised protection against Indian attacks and a convenient escape route down the James River, should escape become necessary. Quickly, the colonists built a triangular fort and mounted artillery at the corners in order, George Percy wrote, to make "our selves sufficiently strong for these Savages." Although colonists ventured outside the fort to explore, trade with Indians, plant crops, and eventually to live, the fort remained a well-entrenched safe haven for Jamestown's early inhabitants.

At first, the Jamestown settlers held religious services under an old ship's sail stretched between several trees. Inside their fort they soon erected a wooden church, "a homely thing like a barn," John Smith observed. When that church burned in 1608, the colonists put up another wooden structure, where Pocahontas and John Rolfe solemnized their marriage. Between 1617 and 1619, Jamestown residents built a larger wooden church on a foundation of big cobblestones still visible in the floor of the church shown here. Twenty years later, prosperous planters funded the replacement of the wooden structure with a new brick church, which included the tower visible at the right end of the church in the photo. In September 1676, during Bacon's Rebellion, the rebels burned down the brick church, but the tower survived. It stood for the next two centuries until it was incorporated into the present-day church. Today, the church tower is the only seventeenth-century building at Jamestown.

Fire and decay eventually eliminated every visible sign of the original fort. Since 1994, careful archaeological excavations have uncovered the outlines of the fort and many other structures. Under the surface of the soil, archaeologists found unmistakable evidence of the wooden posts that made up the walls of the fort. And jumbled together in and around the fort were numerous **artifacts** the early settlers lost or tossed away.

Today, visitors to Jamestown can see the site of the original fort and watch the continuing archaeological investigations. Exhibits display examples of armor and weapons used by the colonists, pipes they smoked, coins they spent, and dishes that held their food. At least as revealing as the many fascinating archaeological finds is the swampy, heavily wooded natural environment that surrounds Jamestown. On a stroll, bicycle ride, or drive through the wilderness around Jamestown, visitors can imagine what this strange new land must have looked like to the early colonists.

For Web links related to this site and other American Places, see "PlaceLinks" at bedfordstmartins.com/roark.

Jamestown Church
The Association for the Preservation of Virginia Antiquities

John Smith's Map of Virginia

In 1612, John Smith published a detailed map that showed not only geographic features of early Virginia but also the limits of exploration (indicated by small crosses), the locations of the houses of the Indian "kings" (indicated by dwellings that look like Quonset huts), and "ordinary houses" of indigenous people (indicated by dots). The map shows the early settlers' intense interest in knowing where the Indians were—and were not. Notice the location of Jamestown (upriver from Point Comfort) and of Powhatan's residence at the falls (just to the right of the large *P* outside the hut in the upper left corner). The drawing of Powhatan surrounded by some of his many wives (upper left corner) was almost certainly made by an English artist who had never been to Virginia or seen Powhatan but tried to imagine the scene as described by John Smith.

Princeton University Libraries, Department of Rare Books and Special Collections.

in September 1607, they began to bring corn to the colony for barter. When that was insufficient to keep the colonists fed, the settlers sent Captain John Smith to trade (and plunder) for corn with Indians upriver from Jamestown. His efforts managed to keep 38 of the original settlers alive until a fresh supply of food and 120 more colonists arrived from England in January 1608.

It is difficult to exaggerate the fragility of the early Jamestown settlement. Although the Virginia Company sent hundreds of new settlers to Jamestown each year, few survived. During the "starving time" winter of 1609–10, food became so short that one or two famished settlers resorted to eating their recently deceased neighbors. When a new group of colonists arrived in 1610, they found only about 60 of the 500 previous settlers still alive. When told they might be taken back to England, the survivors responded with "a general acclamation, and shoutte of joy," an observer wrote. The Virginia Company continued to pour people into the colony, promising in a 1609 pamphlet that "the place will make them rich." But most settlers went instead to an early grave.

Cooperation and Conflict between Natives and Newcomers

Powhatan's people stayed in contact with the English settlers but maintained their distance. The Virginia Company boasted that the settlers bought from the Indians "the pearles of earth [corn] and [sold] to them the pearles of heaven [Christianity]." In fact, few Indians converted to Christianity, and the English devoted scant effort to proselytizing. Marriage between Indian women and English men was also rare, despite the acute shortage of English women in Virginia in the early years. Few settlers other than John Smith troubled to learn the Indians' language. His notes on the Indians' vocabulary show that settlers quickly adopted the Virginia Algonquian words *tomahawk* and *moccasin*. It is safe to speculate that few English words entered Powhatan's vocabulary, given the distance the Indians maintained.

Powhatan's people regarded the English with suspicion, for good reasons. While the settlers often made friendly overtures to the Indians, they did not hesitate to use their guns and swords to enforce English notions of proper Indian behavior. More than once the Indians refused to trade their corn to the settlers, evidently hoping to starve them out. Each time the English broke the boycott by attacking the uncooperative Indians, pillaging their villages, and confiscating their corn.

Powhatan's people retaliated against English violence, but for fifteen years they did not organize an all-out assault on the European intruders, probably for several reasons. Although Christianity held few attractions for the Indians, the power of the settlers' God impressed them. One chief told John Smith that "he did believe that our [English] God as much exceeded theirs as our guns did their bows and arrows." Powhatan probably concluded that these powerful strangers would make better allies than enemies. As allies, the English strengthened Powhatan's dominance over the tribes in the region. They also traded with his people, usually exchanging European goods for corn. Native Virginians had some copper weapons and tools before the English arrived, but they quickly recognized the superiority of the intruders' iron and steel knives, axes, and pots and traded eagerly to obtain them.

The trade that supplied Indians with European conveniences provided English settlers with a necessity: food. But why did the settlers prove unable to feed themselves for more than a decade? First, as the staggering death rate suggests, many settlers were too sick to be productive members of the colony. Second, very few farmers came to Virginia in the early years. Instead, most of the newcomers were gentlemen and their servants, men who, in John Smith's words, "never did know what a day's work was." The proportion of gentlemen in Virginia in the early years was six times greater than in England, a reflection of the Virginia Company's urgent need for investors and settlers. In a 1610 pamphlet, the company declared that nobody should think that Virginia "excludeth Gentlemen . . . for though they cannot digge, use the square, nor practise the axe and chizell, yet [they know] . . . how to employ the force of knowledge, the exercise of counsel, the operation and power of their best breeding and qualities." In Virginia breeding and quality proved worthless for growing corn, catching fish, or even hunting deer. John Smith declared repeatedly that in Virginia "there is no country to pillage [as in New Spain] . . . all you can expect from [Virginia] must be by labor." For years, however, colonists clung to English notions that gentlemen should not work with their hands and tradesmen should work only in trades for which they had been trained,

John Smith's Dictionary of Powhatan's Language

In 1612, John Smith published this list of the English equivalents of words used by Powhatan's people, almost the only record of the coastal Algonquian language that exists. Smith probably compiled this list by pointing and listening carefully. Can you find any of Powhatan's words that made their way into common English usage? What do the words in the list suggest about Smith's encounters with Powhatan's people? What interested Smith? What compelled the interest of his informants?

Princeton University Libraries, Department of Rare Books and Special Collections.

Becaufe many doe defire to know the manner of their Language, I haue inferted thefe few words.

KA katorawincs yowo. What call you this.
Nemarough, a man.
Crenepo, a woman.
Marowancheffo, a boy.
Yehawkans, Houfes.
Matchcores, Skins, or garments.
Mockafins, Shooes.
Tuffan, Beds. Pokatawer, Fire.
Attawp, A bow. Attonce, Arrowes.
Monacookes, Swords.
Aumoubhowgh, A Target.
Pawcuffacks, Gunnes.
Tomahacks, Axes.
Tockahacks, Pickaxes.
Pamefacks, Kniues.
Accowprets, Sheares.
Pawpecones, Pipes. Mattaffin, Copper
Vffawaffin, Iron, Braffe, Silver, or any white mettall. Muffes, Woods.
Attaffkuff, Leaues, weeds, or graffe.
Chepfin, Land. Shacquohocan. A ftone.
Wepenter, A cookold.
Suckahanna, Water. Noughmaff, Fifh.
Copotone, Sturgeon.
Weghfhaughes, Flefh.
Sawwehone, Bloud.
Netoppew, Friends.
Marrapough, Enemies.
Maskapow, the worft of the enemies.
Mawchick chammay, The beft of friends
Cafacunnakack, peya quagh acquintan vttafantafough, In how many daies will there come hither any more Englifh Ships.
　Their Numbers.
Necut, 1. Ningh, 2. Nuff, 3. Yowgh, 4.
Paranske, 5. Comotinch, 6. Toppawoff, 7
Nuffwafh, 8. Kekatawgh, 9. Kaskeke 10
They count no more but by tennes as followeth.
Cafe, how many.
Ninghfapooeksku, 20.
Nuffapooeksku, 30.

Yowghapooeksku, 40.
Parankeftaffapooekfku, 50.
Comatincktaffapooekfku, 60.
Nuffwafhtaffapooekfku, 70.
Kekataughtaffapooekfku, 90.
Necuttoughtyfinough, 100.
Necuttwevnquaough, 1000.
Rawcofowghs, Dayes.
Kefkowghes, Sunnes:
Toppquough. Nights.
Nepawwefhowghs, Moones.
Pawpaxfoughes, Yeares.
Pummahumps, Starres.
Ofies, Heavens.
Okees, Gods.
Quiyougheofoughs, Pettie Gods, and their affinities.
Righcomoughes, Deaths.
Kekughes, Liues.
Mowchick woyawgh tawgh noeragh kaquere mecher, I am very hungry? what fhall I eate?
Tawnor nehiegh Powhatan, Where dwels Powhatan.
Mache, nehiegh yourowgh, Orapaks. Now he dwelsa great way hence at Orapaks.
Vittapitchewayne anpechitchs nehawper Werowacomoco, You lie, he ftaid ever at Werowacomoco.
Kator nehiegh mattagh neer vttapitchewayne, Truely he is there I doe not lie.
Spaughtynere keragh werowance mawmarinough kekatē wawgh peyaquaugh. Run you then to the King Mawmarynough and bid him come hither.
Vtteke, e peya weyack wighwhip, Get you gone, & come againe quickly.
Kekaten Pokahontas patiaquagh ningh tanks manotyens neer mowchick rawrenock audowgh, Bid Pokahontas bring hither two little Baskets, and I will giue her white Beads to make her a Chaine. *FINIS.*

Trade Goods

These objects excavated from the site of early Jamestown illustrate the trade between the settlers and Powhatan's people. Colonists desperately needed the Indians' corn to survive. To trade for corn, settlers had to have a surplus of something the Algonquians desired. The Indians wanted firearms, but the struggling colonists could ill afford to increase the Indians' military strength. Instead, the colonists tried to appeal to the Indians' interest in items for decoration and display. Jamestown residents often traded cheap glass beads like the one shown here (top left). Made in Venice, Italy, this colorful bead incorporated sophisticated techniques of glassmaking unknown to Indians; they readily used such glass beads as substitutes for the shell beads they had made so laboriously for centuries. Algonquians used copper before the arrival of Europeans, but their supplies were limited and difficult to obtain, as Jamestown settlers quickly learned. Colonists cut their own sheets of copper into shapes desired by the Indians for jewelry, like the triangular copper ornament at bottom left, pierced for easy attachment. As colonists learned more about Indians' fashions, they began to craft items like the bone pendant shown here (bottom, center). To our eyes, it looks as if it were made by Indians, but iron file marks along the edges are strong evidence that English settlers made the pendant, using materials and designs familiar to the Indians. In modern language, the pendant reflects the results of Jamestown settlers' market research about what Algonquians would accept in exchange for corn. The pottery shards are from an Indian clay pot that probably contained corn English settlers received for their trade goods.

The Association for the Preservation of Virginia Antiquities.

ideas about labor that made more sense in labor-rich England than in labor-poor Virginia. In the meantime, the colonists depended on the Indians' corn for food. (See "The Promise of Technology," page 78.)

The persistence of the Virginia colony, precarious as it was, created difficulties for Powhatan's chiefdom. Steady contact between natives and newcomers spread European viruses among the Indians, who suffered deadly epidemics in 1608 and between 1617 and 1619. The settlers' insatiable appetite for corn introduced other tensions within Powhatan's villages. Producing enough corn for both survival and trade with the English made agriculture, which was women's work, more important for Indians. But from the Indians' viewpoint, the most important fact about the Virginia colony was that it was surviving, barely.

Powhatan died in 1618, and his brother Opechancanough replaced him as supreme

Wolf Head Pendant

A Susquehanna man probably wore this pendant suspended from the deer hide necklace (dyed red) extending from the back of the wolf head. The Native American who made the pendant in the mid-seventeenth century took the jawbone and teeth of a wolf and skillfully stitched them into a head shaped from deer hide stuffed with deer hair, taking care to display the wolf's menacing teeth. Inside the wolf's jaws, the maker sewed a realistic tongue (not visible in the picture) made of blue cloth obtained in trade with European colonists. Whether a wolf's tongue crafted from a European textile conveyed Susquehanna interpretation of words spoken by Europeans is unknown.

Courtesy, Skokloster Castle, Uppland, Sweden.

chief. In 1622, Opechancanough organized an all-out assault on the English settlers. Striking on March 22, the Indians killed 347 settlers, nearly a third of the English population. But the attack failed to dislodge the colonists. In the aftermath, the settlers unleashed a murderous campaign of Indian extermination that in a few years pushed Indians beyond the small circumference of white settlement. Before 1622, the settlers knew that the Indians, though dangerous, were necessary to keep the colony alive. After 1622, most colonists considered Indians their perpetual enemies.

From Private Company to Royal Government

The 1622 uprising came close to achieving Opechancanough's goal of pushing the colonists back into the Atlantic—so close that it prompted a royal investigation of affairs in Virginia. The investigators discovered that the appalling mortality among the colonists was caused more by disease and mismanagement than by Indian raids. In 1624, King James revoked the charter of the Virginia Company and made Virginia a royal colony, subject to the direction of the royal government rather than to the company's private investors, an arrangement that lasted until 1776.

The king now appointed the governor of Virginia and his council, but most other features of local government established under the Virginia Company remained intact. In 1619, for example, the company had inaugurated the House of Burgesses, an assembly of representatives (called burgesses) elected by the colony's inhabitants. (Historians do not know exactly which settlers were considered inhabitants and were thus qualified to vote.) Under the new royal government, laws passed by the burgesses had to be approved by the king's bureaucrats in England rather than by the company. Otherwise,

Advertisement for Jamestown Settlers
While Virginia imported thousands of indentured servants to labor in tobacco fields, the colony advertised in 1631 for settlers like those pictured here. The notice features men and women equally, although men heavily outnumbered women among actual newcomers to the Chesapeake. How would the English experiences of the individuals portrayed in the advertisement be useful in Virginia? Why would such individuals want to leave England and go to Virginia? If indentured servants were pictured, how might they differ in appearance from these people?
Harvard Map Collection, Pusey Library, Harvard University.

Corn, the "Life-Giver"

Europeans first learned about corn from Columbus. As soon as he returned to Spain in 1493, he told the royal court about amazing things he had seen on his voyage to the other side of the Atlantic, including a plant he called maize, his version of *mahiz*, the Taino word for corn, which meant "life-giver." Ancient Americans had been growing corn for about seven thousand years. From its origin in central Mexico, corn had spread throughout the Western Hemisphere by the time Columbus arrived. Although the rest of the world had never seen or heard of corn, within a generation after 1493 travelers carried seeds throughout the Old World. By the early sixteenth century, corn seeds had sprouted in Europe, the Middle East, Africa, India, and China.

Accustomed to growing wheat and eating foods derived from it, Europeans at first did not like corn. A few years before the settlers arrived in Jamestown, an English botanist expressed the common European view that "the barbarous Indians which know no better, are constrained to make a vertue of necessitie, and think [corn is] a good food; whereas we may easily judge that it nourisheth but little, and is of hard and evill digestion, a more convenient foode for swine than for man."

Early in the seventeenth century, English settlers in North America discovered that hunger quickly made a virtue of necessity. John Smith wrote that during the spring of 1609 Jamestown residents became so hungry that "they would have sould their soules" for a half-basket of Powhatan's corn. Before settlers could reliably subsist in the Chesapeake region, they had to learn the technology of corn.

From the perspective of the twenty-first century, it may seem odd to speak of the technology of

Ancient Corn Popper
Long before movies and microwaves, ancient Americans munched popcorn. This corn popper comes from the Mochica culture, which thrived on the northern coast of Peru for about 600 years after the birth of Christ. The Mochica presumably nestled the popper on a bed of coals with the opening facing up, placed corn inside, and covered the opening with a lid (not shown) while the kernels popped. The Mochica and other ancient Americans did not pop most of the corn they grew. Instead, they ground it into cornmeal, which they used in a wide variety of dishes, probably including ancient counterparts of modern tortillas.
The Field Museum #A112961c, Chicago. Photographer: Diane Alexander Whites.

corn. Today, we tend to think that the word *technology* refers only to machinery such as engines, computer chips, or airplanes. But it also refers to a much broader range of human experience involving the use of knowledge for practical purposes. Nowadays, technological knowledge has found countless practical uses for corn as food, sweetener, and oil, as well as in such products as medicines, tires, batteries, and lipstick. The roots of these modern-day uses of corn stretch back to ancient Americans who first developed the technology of growing, processing, and consuming corn, a technology English settlers of North America sought to learn for the practical purpose of eating.

Corn needs help to grow. If you bury an ear of corn in the soil, the seeds that sprout will strangle each other in an overcrowded quest for light. But if you strip the husk from a ripe ear of corn, rub the seeds out of the cob, and plant the separated seeds on a spring day in a spot with sufficient heat, light, and water, then during the summer each seed will be capable of producing a stalk with two or more ears, each bearing hundreds of edible corn seeds. An awestruck English visitor described corn's "marveillous great increase; of a thousand, fifteene hundred and some two thousand fold."

To obtain this impressive yield, early-seventeenth-century European settlers throughout North America watched Native Americans cultivate corn. "In place of ploughs" commonly used in England, one observer reported, "they use an instrument of hard wood, shaped like a spade" to break up the soil and prepare it for planting, work usually done by men. Then women used a stick to "make a hole [in the soil] wherein they put out four grains . . . And cover them." Another colonist acknowledged that Native Americans were "our first instructors for the planting of their Indian corne, by teaching us to cull out the finest seede, to observe the fittest season, to keepe distance for holes, and fit measure for hills, to worme it, and weede it; to prune it, and dresse it as occasion shall require." Jamestown's early settlers did not depend on chance observations of this planting technology. John Smith boasted that two hostages the colonists captured from Powhatan "taught us how to order and plant our fields" while they were held as "fettered prisoners."

Along with corn, Indians usually planted beans. "When they [beans] grow up they interlace with the corn. . . . And they keep the ground very free from weeds," one newcomer noticed. Ancient Americans' association of beans with corn had a sound biochemical basis. Beans fixed nitrogen in the soil, a function corn roots cannot perform. Corn plants then absorbed the nitrogen to produce higher yields. Beans also made corn more nutritious. Beans contain niacin, an essential nutrient lacking in corn. Together, corn and beans provided the basic ingredients for a healthy diet.

As every popcorn eater knows, corn kernels are hard enough to crack a tooth. European settlers had no difficulty eating green or sweet corn, the immature form of ripening corn commonly consumed today as corn on the cob. But to obtain the nutritious interior of mature corn

Corn God Figurine
This Mayan figurine signals the importance of corn among ancient Americans who lived in present-day Guatemala. Made sometime between 1400 BP and 1100 BP, the figurine shows the corn god dancing in honor of the source of human sustenance, corn.

Museo Nacional de Arqueologia y Etnologia, Guatemala City. Photograph © Justin Kerr.

kernels without cracking their teeth they had to learn ancient American technology. For millennia Native Americans had soaked or boiled corn kernels with wood ash or other alkaline material. The alkali softened and loosened the tough hull protecting the corn's nutrients. Treated in this way, corn kernels that otherwise were rock-hard could be separated from their hulls and readily mashed into dough for tortillas or mixed with beans or other foods in tasty stews. Early colonists copied this process to make the softened corn

foods they called samp, or hominy, or grits.

Since settlers were accustomed to wheat ground into a fine flour, they preferred cornmeal obtained by the much more laborious process of pulverizing corn kernels with a mortar and pestle or grinding them between stones, both processes familiar to Native Americans. From cornmeal dough cooked on an iron griddle or baked in the coals of a cookfire, Europeans made corn bread, corn pone, hoecake, and johnnycake— English names for ancient American food.

Unlike wheat, many varieties of corn pop open when heated, an astonishing trait Columbus duly reported to his Spanish sponsors. **Archaeologists** speculate that ancient Americans first thought to cultivate corn when a few grains accidentally landed in a campfire and out popped a morsel of readily edible food. For millennia, ancient Americans enjoyed popcorn, not least because it so easily avoided the need to soak, boil, or grind hard corn kernels. They also ground popped corn into a nutritious and portable powder that could be mixed with water and other foods for a satisfying meal. The New England minister Roger Williams wrote that he "made a good dinner and supper" with "a spoonfull of this meale and a spoonfull of water from the brooke." Other colonists, too, learned the ancient technology of popcorn. Today, at the cineplex and on the couch, every American consumes about 50 quarts of popped corn each year, participating— usually unwittingly—in a technology that reaches back in unbroken continuity to a campfire in central Mexico about 7,000 years ago.

the House of Burgesses continued as before, acquiring distinction as the oldest representative legislative assembly in the British colonies. Under the new royal government, all free adult men in Virginia could vote for the House of Burgesses, giving it a far broader and more representative constituency than the English House of Commons.

The demise of the Virginia Company marked the end of the first phase of colonization of the Chesapeake region. From the first 105 adventurers in 1607, the population had grown to about 1,200 by 1624. Despite mortality rates higher than the worst epidemics in London, new settlers still came. Their arrival and King James's willingness to take over the struggling colony reflected a fundamental change in Virginia. After years of fruitless experimentation, it was becoming clear that English settlers could make a fortune in Virginia by growing tobacco.

All free adult men in Virginia could vote for the House of Burgesses, giving it a far broader and more representative constituency than the English House of Commons.

Tobacco Wrapper
This wrapper labeled a container of "Virginia Planters Best Tobacco." It shows a colonial planter supervising slaves who hold the hoes they use to chop weeds that rob the leafy tobacco plants of nutrients and moisture. The planter enjoys a pipe in the shade of an umbrella held by a slave. After the tobacco was harvested and dried, it was pressed tightly into barrels, like those shown here, for shipment overseas. How does this illustration indicate the differences between the planter and the slaves?
Colonial Williamsburg Foundation.

A Tobacco Society

Tobacco grew wild in the New World, and Native Americans used it for thousands of years before Europeans arrived. *Tobacco* was a Caribbean Indian word that referred to a leaf of the tobacco plant rolled into a cigar-like shape. Indians lit the rolled leaf and inhaled the smoke, a practice Columbus observed in Cuba on his first journey of discovery. Many sixteenth-century European explorers commented on the Indians' odd habit of "drinking smoke." During the sixteenth century, Spanish colonists in the New World sent tobacco to Europe, where it was an expensive luxury used sparingly by a few. During the next century, English colonists in North America sent so much tobacco to European markets that it became an affordable indulgence used often by many people. (See "Beyond America's Borders," page 82.)

Tobacco never featured in the initial plans of the Virginia Company. "As for tobacco," John Smith wrote, "we never then dreamt of it." John Rolfe—Pocahontas's husband-to-be—planted West Indian tobacco seeds in 1612 and learned that they flourished in Virginia. By 1617, the colonists had grown enough tobacco to send the first commercial shipment to England, where it

sold for a high price. After that, the same Virginia colonists who had difficulty growing enough corn to feed themselves learned quickly to grow as much tobacco as possible. Virginia pivoted from a colony of rather aimless adventurers into a society of dedicated tobacco **planters**.

Dedicated they were. In 1620, with fewer than a thousand colonists, Virginia shipped 60,000 pounds of tobacco to England. By 1700, nearly 100,000 colonists lived in the Chesapeake region (encompassing Virginia, Maryland, and northern North Carolina), and they exported over 35 million pounds of tobacco. Per capita tobacco exports grew fivefold during the century, demonstrating that Chesapeake colonists had mastered the demands of tobacco agriculture. To a large degree, the "Stinkinge Weede" (a seventeenth-century Marylander's term for tobacco) also mastered the colonists. Settlers lived by the rhythms of tobacco agriculture, and their endless need for labor attracted droves of English indentured servants to work in Chesapeake tobacco fields (Map 3.1).

Tobacco Agriculture

A demanding crop, tobacco required close attention and a great deal of hand labor year-round. Colonists sowed the tiny seeds in the spring, transplanted the sprouts, and hoed around the growing plants all summer while carefully grooming the plants to produce marketable leaves. Early in the fall when the leaves began to yellow, colonists cut down the plants and strung them up in a shed to dry and cure. The next spring when the dried leaves became pliable in the moist climate, workers stripped the tobacco leaves from the stalks and packed them tightly into hogsheads (large barrels) for shipment to market. By the time last year's crop was being packed, this year's crop already had to be in the ground.

Primitive tools and methods made this intensive cycle of labor taxing. Like the Indians, colonists "cleared" fields by cutting a ring of bark from trees (a procedure known as *girdling*), thereby killing them. Girdling brought sunlight to clearings but left fields studded with tree stumps, making the use of plows impractical. Instead, colonists tilled their tobacco fields with heavy hoes, one hoe-chop at a time. To plant, a visitor observed, colonists "just make holes [with a stick] into which they drop the seeds," much as the Indians did. Because colonists also

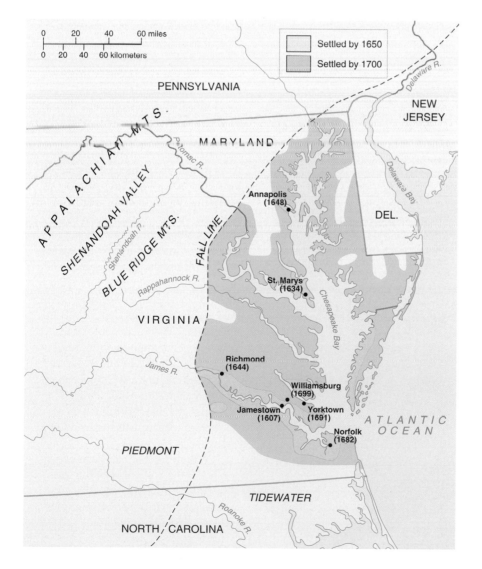

MAP 3.1   The Chesapeake Colonies in the Seventeenth Century

The intimate association between land and water in the settlement of the Chesapeake in the seventeenth century is illustrated by this map. The fall line indicates the limit of navigable water, where rapids and falls prevented further upstream travel. Although Delaware had excellent access to navigable water, it was claimed and defended by the Dutch colony at New Amsterdam (discussed in chapter 4) rather than by the English settlements in Virginia and Maryland shown on this map.

READING THE MAP: Using the notations on the map, create a chronology of the establishment of towns and settlements. What physical features correspond to the earliest habitation by English settlers?

CONNECTIONS: Why was access to navigable water so important? Given the settlers' need for defense against native tribes, what explains the distance between settlements?

FOR MORE HELP ANALYZING THIS MAP, see the map activity for this chapter in the Online Study Guide at bedfordstmartins.com/roark.

American Tobacco and European Consumers

English colonies in the Chesapeake were "wholly built upon smoke," King Charles I remarked. The king's shrewd comment highlighted the fundamental reason why the seventeenth-century Chesapeake colonies prospered by growing ever-increasing crops of tobacco: because people on the eastern side of the Atlantic were willing to buy ever-increasing quantities of tobacco to smoke—and to sniff, chew, and drink, and even to use for enemas. Europeans' desire for tobacco was the only reason it had commercial value. If Europeans had considered tobacco undesirable, the history of both the British North American colonies and the rest of the world would have been very different.

Some Europeans did hate tobacco, England's King James I foremost among them. In *A Counterblaste to Tobacco*, a pamphlet published in 1611, James declared that smoking was "A custome lothsome to the eye, hatefull to the Nose, harmefull to the braine, dangerous to the Lungs, and in the blacke stinking fume thereof, neerest resembling the horrible . . . smoke of the pit that is bottomelesse." James pulled out all the stops in attacking smoking. "What honour or policie can moove us to imitate the barbarous and beastly manners of the wilde, godlesse, and slavish *Indians*, especially in so vile and stinking a custome?" he asked. "Why doe we not as well imitate them in walking naked as they doe? in preferring glasses, feathers, and such toyes, to golde and precious stones, as they do? yea why do we not denie God and adore the Devill, as they doe?" James reviled the "filthy smoke," the "stinking Suffumigation," the "spitting," the "lust," the "shameful imbecilitie," and the "sin" of tobacco. James's fulminations acknowledged that "the

Tobacco Cutter

Tobacconists in Europe used this machine to chop tobacco leaves into small pieces. Then they often flavored the chopped tobacco with oils, herbs, and spices much as coffeehouse baristas today add hazelnut, mocha, or vanilla flavors to lattes and cappucinos. The picture on the side of the cutter refers to the Native American origins of the tobacco processed by the cutter's screws, clamps, and blades.

Niemeyer Nederlands Tabacologisch Museum.

generall use of Tobacco" was "daily practiced . . . by all sorts and complexions of people." He noted, "The publike use [of tobacco], at all times, and in all places, hath now so farre prevailed that a man cannot heartily welcome his friend now, but straight they must bee in hand with *Tobacco*. . . . It is become . . . a point of good fellowship, and he that will refuse to take a pipe of *Tobacco* among his fellows . . . is accounted peevish and no good company." Clearly, James championed a lost cause.

When Spaniards first brought tobacco to Europe during the sixteenth century, physicians praised it as a wonder drug. One proclaimed that "to seek to tell the virtues and greatness of this holy herb, the ailments which can be cured by it, and have been, the evils from which it has saved thousands would be to go on to infinity . . . this precious herb is so general a human need [that it is] not only for the sick but for the healthy." Such strong recommendations from learned men were reinforced by everyday experiences of commoners. Sailors returning from the New World "suck in as much smoke as they can," one Spaniard observed, "[and] in this way they say that their hunger and thirst are allayed, their strength is restored and their spirits are refreshed; [and] . . . their brains are lulled by a joyous intoxication." That joyous intoxication—"a bewitching quality" King James called it—made tobacco irresistible to most Europeans. And, as we know all too well today, the bewitching intoxication of tobacco was highly addictive.

Feeding that habit was expensive at the beginning of the seventeenth century because tobacco was scarce. In 1603, for example, England imported only about 25,000

Smoking Club

In Europe, tobacco smokers congregated in clubs to enjoy the intoxicating weed. This seventeenth-century print satirizes smokers' promiscuous gatherings of fashionable men, women, and children who indulged their taste for tobacco. Emblems of the tobacco trade adorn the wall; pipes, spittoons, and other smoking implements are close at hand; and the dog cleans up after those who cannot hold their smoke.

Koninklijke Bibliotheek, The Hague.

pounds of tobacco, all from New Spain. By 1700, England imported nearly 40 million pounds of tobacco, almost all from the Chesapeake colonies. The huge increase in tobacco supply caused prices to plummet. A quantity of tobacco that sold for a dollar in 1600 cost less than two and a half cents by 1700.

The low prices made possible by bumper crops harvested by planters in the Chesapeake transformed tobacco consumption in England and elsewhere in Europe. Per capita tobacco use in England grew over 200-fold during the seventeenth century, from less than a fifth of an ounce in the 1620s to 2.3 pounds by 1700. American tobacco became the first colonial product of mass consumption by Europeans, blazing a trail fol-lowed by New World sugar, coffee, and chocolate.

Tobacco altered European culture. It spawned new industries, new habits, and new forms of social life. Smoking was the most common form of tobacco consumption in the seventeenth century, and smokers needed far more than tobacco to light up. They needed pipes, and hundreds of pipe makers supplied them with millions of ceramic pipes. They needed boxes or tins to hold their tobacco and a container to hold the embers they used to light the tobacco, or a flint and steel to strike sparks; they needed pipe cleaners; they needed spittoons if they were smoking in a respectable place that disapproved of spitting on the floor. European merchants and manufac-turers supplied all these needs, along with tobacco itself, which had to be graded, chopped, flavored, pack-aged, stored, advertised, and sold. Men and women smoked in taverns, in smoking clubs, around dinner ta-bles, and in bed. A visitor to London noted that tobacco was not only in "frequent use . . . at every hour of the day but even at night [smokers] keep the pipe and steel at their pil-lows and gratify their longings."

The somewhat cumbersome paraphernalia of smoking caused many tobacco users to shift to snuff, which became common in the eigh-teenth century. Snuff use eliminated smoke, fire, and spitting with the more refined arts of taking a pinch of powdered, flavored tobacco from a snuffbox and sniffing it into one or both nostrils, which produced a fash-ionable sneeze followed by a genteel wipe with a dainty handkerchief. Sneezing induced by snuff was con-sidered not only fashionable but healthful. One snuff taker explained that "by its gently pricking and stim-ulating the membranes, [snuff] causes Sneezing or Contractions, whereby the Glands like so many squeezed Sponges, dismiss their Seriosities and Filth."

Whether consumed by smoking, by sniffing, or in other ways, tobacco profoundly changed European habits, economies, and societies. It is no exaggeration to conclude that planters, servants, and eventually slaves in the Chesapeake made it possible for Europeans to become hooked on tobacco.

BIBLIOGRAPHY

Jordan Goodman, *Tobacco in History: The Cultures of Dependence* (1993).

Jason Hughes, *Learning to Smoke: Tobacco Use in the West* (2003).

Joseph C. Winter, *Tobacco Use by Native North Americans: Sacred Smoke and Silent Killer* (2000).

had to grow food crops in the midst of the tobacco production cycle, there was little time for idleness. But in spare moments, they enjoyed the fruits of their labor. One traveler reported that "Everyone smokes while working or idling . . . men, women, girls, and boys, from the age of seven years."

English settlers worked hard because their labor promised greater rewards in the Chesapeake region than in England. One colonist proclaimed that "the dirt of this Province affords as great a profit to the general Inhabitant, as the Gold of Peru doth to . . . the Spaniard." Although he exaggerated, it was true that a hired man could expect to earn two or three times more in Virginia tobacco fields than in England. Better still, in Virginia land was so abundant that it was extremely cheap, compared to land in England. By the mid-seventeenth century, common laborers could buy a hundred acres for less than their annual wages—an impossibility in England. New settlers who paid their own transportation to the Chesapeake received a grant of fifty acres of free land (termed a *headright*). The Virginia Company initiated the headright policy to encourage settlement, and the royal government continued it for the same reason.

A Servant Labor System

Headrights, cheap land, and high wages gave poor English folk powerful incentives to immigrate to the New World. Yet many potential immigrants could not scrape together the fare to cross the Atlantic. Their poverty and the colonists' crying need for labor formed the basic context for the creation of a servant labor system.

Today, people think of the colonial South as a slave society. The seventeenth-century Chesapeake region, however, was fundamentally a servant society. Twenty Africans arrived in Virginia in 1619, and they probably were enslaved, although scanty records make it impossible to be certain. For the next fifty years, however, only a small number of slaves labored in Chesapeake tobacco fields. (Large numbers of slaves came in the eighteenth century, as chapter 5 explains.) About 80 percent of the immigrants to the Chesapeake during the seventeenth century were indentured servants. Along with tobacco, servants profoundly influenced nearly every feature of Chesapeake society.

> The seventeenth-century Chesapeake region was fundamentally a servant society.

To buy passage aboard a ship bound for the Chesapeake, an English immigrant had to come up with about £5, roughly a year's wages for an English servant or laborer. Saving a year's wages was no easier then than it is now. The purchasing power of wages was declining because England's population was growing faster than its food supply, causing prices to rise. Earning wages at all was difficult since job opportunities were shrinking. Many country gentlemen needed fewer farmhands because they fenced fields they had formerly planted with crops and began to pasture sheep in the enclosures. Unemployed people drifted into seaports like Bristol, Liverpool, and London, where they learned about the plentiful jobs in North America.

Unable to pay for their trip across the Atlantic, poor immigrants agreed to a contract called an *indenture*. In effect, an indenture functioned as a form of credit. By signing an indenture, an immigrant borrowed the cost of transportation to the Chesapeake from a merchant or ship captain in England. To repay this loan, the indentured person agreed to work as a servant for four to seven years in North America. Once the indentured person arrived in the colonies, the merchant or ship captain sold his right to the immigrant's labor to a local tobacco planter. To obtain the servant's labor, the planter paid about twice the cost of transportation and agreed to provide the servant with food and shelter during the term of the indenture. When the indenture expired, the planter owed the former servant "freedom dues," usually a few barrels of corn and a suit of clothes.

Ideally, indentures allowed poor immigrants to trade their most valuable assets—their freedom and their ability to work—for a trip to the New World and four to seven years of servitude followed by freedom in a land of opportunity. Planters reaped more immediate benefits. Servants meant more hands to grow more tobacco. As one Virginian declared, "our principall wealth . . . consisteth in servants." For every newly purchased servant, planters also received a headright of fifty acres of land from the colonial government. Since a planter expected a servant to grow enough tobacco in one year to cover the price the planter paid for the indenture, the next three to six years of the indenture promised a handsome profit for the planter. But roughly half of all servants became sick and died before serving out their indentures, reducing planters' gains.

About three out of four servants were men, the great majority between the ages of fifteen and twenty-five when they arrived in the Chesapeake. Typically they shared the desperation of sixteen-year-old Francis Haires, who indentured himself for seven years because "his father and mother and All friends [are] dead and he [is] a miserable wandering boy." Like Francis, most servants had no special training or skills, although the majority had some experience with agricultural work. "Hunger and fear of prisons bring to us only such servants as have been brought up to no Art or Trade," one Virginia planter complained. A skilled craftsman could obtain a shorter indenture, but few risked coming to the colonies since their prospects were better at home.

Women were almost as rare as skilled craftsmen in the Chesapeake and more ardently desired. In the early days of the tobacco boom, the Virginia Company shipped young single women servants to the colony as prospective wives for male settlers willing to pay "120 weight [pounds] of the best leaf tobacco for each of them," in effect getting both a wife and a servant. The company reasoned that, as one official wrote in 1622, "the plantation can never flourish till families be planted, and the respect of wives and children fix the people on the soil." The company's efforts as a marriage broker proved no more successful than its other ventures. Women remained a small minority of the Chesapeake population until late in the seventeenth century. The servant labor system perpetuated the gender imbalance. Although female servants cost about the same as males and generally served for the same length of time, only about one indentured servant in four was a woman. Planters preferred male servants for fieldwork, although many servant women hoed and harvested tobacco fields. Most women servants also did household chores such as cooking, washing, cleaning, gardening, and milking.

Servant life was harsh by the standards of seventeenth-century England and even by the **frontier** standards of the Chesapeake. Unlike servants in England, Chesapeake servants had no control over who purchased their labor—and thus them—for the period of their indenture. Many servants were bought and sold several times before their indenture expired. A Virginia servant protested in 1623 that his master "hath sold me for £150 sterling like a damnd slave." A ship captain reported in 1625 that "servants were sold here [in Virginia] upp and downe like

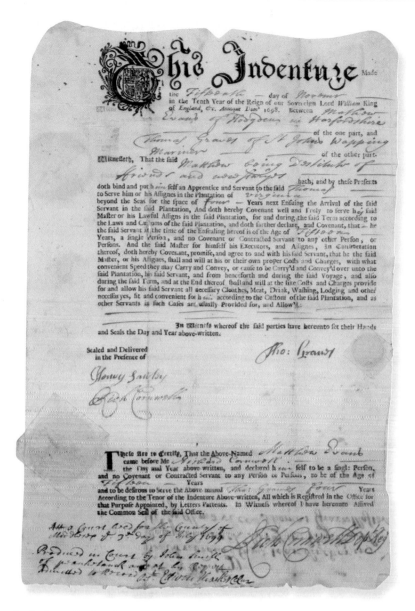

Indenture Contract
Indenture contracts were so common that forms were printed with blank spaces for details to be written in. In mid-November 1698, fifteen-year-old Matthew Evans, a friendless boy from Harfordshire, agreed to serve mariner Thomas Graves, or anybody to whom Graves sold his rights, for four years in Virginia. The contract specifies that Graves will carry Evans to Virginia and provide during the term of the indenture "all necessary Cloathes, Meat, Drink, Washing, Lodging and other necessaryes, fit and convenient for him according to the Custom of the said Plantation, as other Servants in such Cases are usually Provided for. . . ."
The Library of Virginia.

horses." But tobacco planters' need for labor muffled such qualms about treating servants as property.

Some former servants argued that indentured servitude had advantages, despite its rigors. But most found otherwise. James Revel, an

Tobacco Plantation
This print illustrates the processing of tobacco on a seventeenth-century plantation. Workers cut the mature plants and put the leaves in piles to wilt (left foreground and center background). After the leaves dry somewhat, they are suspended from poles in a drying barn (right foreground), where they are seasoned before being packed in casks for shipping. Sometimes, tobacco leaves are left to dry in the fields (center background). The print suggests the labor demands of tobacco by showing twenty-two individuals, all but two of them actively at work with the crop. The one woman, hand in hand with a man in the left foreground, may be on her way to work, on the harvested leaves, but it is more likely that she and the man are overseeing the labor of their servants or employees.
From "About Tobacco," Lehman Brothers.

eighteen-year-old thief who was punished by being indentured to a Virginia tobacco planter, described experiences common to most servants. In verse, Revel chronicled what happened when he arrived at his new master's plantation:

My Europian clothes were took from me,
Which never after I again could see.
A canvas shirt and trowsers then they gave,
With a hop-sack frock in which I was to slave:
No shoes nor stockings had I for to wear,
Nor hat, nor cap, both head and feet were bare.
Thus dress'd into the Field I next must go,
Amongst tobacco plants all day to hoe,
At day break in the morn our work began,
And so held to the setting of the Sun.

Severe laws aimed to keep servants in their place. Punishments for petty crimes stretched servitude far beyond the original terms of indenture. Christopher Adams, for example, had to serve three extra years for running away for six months. Richard Higby received six extra years of servitude for killing three hogs. After midcentury, the Virginia legislature added three or more years to the indentures of most servants by requiring them to serve until they were twenty-four years old.

Women servants were subject to special restrictions and risks. They were prohibited from marrying until their servitude had expired. A servant woman, the law assumed, could not serve two masters at the same time: one who owned her indentured labor and another who was her husband. However, the predominance of men in the Chesapeake population inevitably pressured women to engage in sexual relations. The pressure was strong enough that about a third of immigrant women were pregnant when they got married. Pregnancy and childbirth sapped a woman's strength, and a new child diverted her attention, reducing her usefulness to her master. As a rule, if a woman servant gave birth to a child, she had to serve two extra years and pay a fine. However, for some servant women, premarital pregnancy was a path out of servitude: The father of an unborn child sometimes purchased the indenture of the servant mother-to-be, freed, and married her.

Such punishments reflected four fundamental realities of the servant labor system. First, planters' hunger for labor caused them to demand as much labor as they could get from their servants, including devising legal ways to extend the period of servitude. Second, servants hoped to survive their servitude and use their freedom to obtain land and start a family. Third, servants' hopes frequently conflicted with planters' demands. Since servants saw themselves as free people in a temporary status of servitude, they often made grudging, half-hearted workers. Finally, both servants and planters put up with this contentious arrangement because the alternatives were less desirable.

Planters could not easily hire free men and women because land was readily available and free people preferred to work on their own land, for themselves. Nor could planters depend on much labor from family members. The preponderance of men in the population meant that families were few, were started late, and thus had few children. And, until the 1680s and 1690s, slaves were expensive and hard to come by. Before then, masters who wanted to expand their labor force and grow more tobacco had few alternatives to buying indentured servants.

Cultivating Land and Faith

Villages and small towns dotted the rural landscape of seventeenth-century England, but in the Chesapeake acres of wilderness were interrupted here and there by tobacco farms. Tobacco was such a labor-intensive crop that one field-worker could tend only about two acres of the plants in a year (an acre is slightly smaller than a football field), plus a few more acres for food crops. A successful farmer needed a great deal more land, however, because tobacco quickly exhausted the fertility of the soil. Since each farmer cultivated only 5 or 10 percent of his land at any one time, a "settled" area comprised swatches of cultivated land surrounded by forest. Arrangements for marketing tobacco also contributed to the dispersion of settlements. Tobacco planters sought land that fronted a navigable river in order to minimize the work of transporting the heavy hogsheads of tobacco onto ships. A settled region thus resembled a lacework of farms stitched around waterways.

Settlement Patterns along the James River

Most Chesapeake colonists were nominally **Protestants**. Attendance at Sunday services and conformity to the doctrines of the Church of England were required of all English men and women. Few clergymen migrated to the Chesapeake, however, and too few of those who did come were models of righteousness and piety. Certainly some colonists took their religion seriously. Church courts punished fornicators, censured blasphemers, and served notice on parishioners who spent Sundays "goeing a fishing." But on the whole, religion did not awaken the zeal of Chesapeake settlers, certainly not as it did the New England settlers in these same years (see chapter 4). What quickened the pulse of most Chesapeake folk was a close horse race, a bloody cockfight, or—most of all—an exceptionally fine tobacco crop. The religion of the Chesapeake colonists was Anglican, but their faith lay in the turbulent, competitive, high-stakes gamble of survival as tobacco planters.

The situation was similar in the Catholic colony of Maryland. In 1632, England's King Charles I granted his Catholic friend Lord Baltimore about six and a half million acres in the northern Chesapeake region. In return, the king specified that Lord Baltimore pay him the token rent of "two Indian arrowheads" a year. Lord Baltimore intended to create a refuge for Catholics, who suffered severe discrimination in England. He fitted out two ships, the *Ark* and the *Dove*, gathered about 150 settlers, and sent them to the new colony, where they arrived on March 25, 1634. However, Maryland failed to live up to Baltimore's hopes. The colony's population grew very slowly for twenty years, and most settlers were Protestants rather than Catholics. The religious turmoil of the **Puritan** Revolution in England (discussed in chapter 5) spilled across the Atlantic, creating conflict between Maryland's few Catholics—most of them wealthy and prominent—and the Protestant majority, most of them neither wealthy nor prominent. During the 1660s, Maryland began to attract settlers as readily as Virginia, mostly Protestants. Although Catholics and the Catholic faith continued to exert influence in Maryland, the colony's society, economy, politics, and culture became nearly indistinguishable from Virginia's. Both colonies shared a devotion to tobacco, the true faith of the Chesapeake.

> The religion of the Chesapeake colonists was Anglican, but their faith lay in the turbulent, competitive, high-stakes gamble of survival as tobacco planters.

The Evolution of Chesapeake Society

The system of indentured servitude sharpened inequality in Chesapeake society by the mid-seventeenth century, propelling social and political polarization that culminated in 1676 with Bacon's Rebellion. The rebellion prompted reforms that stabilized relations between elite planters and their lesser neighbors and paved the way for a social hierarchy based less overtly on land and wealth than on race. (See "Historical Question," page 90.) Amid this social and political evolution, one thing did not change: the dedication of Chesapeake colonists to growing tobacco.

Social and Economic Polarization

The first half of the seventeenth century in the Chesapeake was the era of the **yeoman**—a farmer who owned a small plot of land sufficient to support a family and tilled largely by servants and a few family members. A small number of elite planters had larger estates and commanded ten or more servants. But for the first several decades, few men lived long enough to accumulate a fortune sufficient to set them much apart from their neighbors. Until midcentury, the principal division in Chesapeake society was less between rich and poor planters than between free farmers and unfree servants. While these two groups contrasted sharply in their legal and economic status, their daily lives had many similarities. Servants looked forward to the time when their indentures would expire and they would become free and eventually own land. On the whole, a rough, frontier equality characterized free families in the Chesapeake until about 1650.

Three major developments splintered that equality during the third quarter of the century. First, as planters grew more and more tobacco, the ample supply depressed tobacco prices in European markets. Cheap tobacco reduced planters' profits and made it more difficult for freed servants to save enough to become landowners. Second, because the mortality rate in the Chesapeake colonies declined, more and more servants survived their indentures, and landless freemen became more numerous and grew more discontented. Third, declining mortality also encouraged the formation of a planter elite. By living longer, the most successful planters compounded their success. The wealthiest planters also began to serve as merchants, marketing crops for their less successful neighbors, importing English goods for sale, and giving credit to hard-pressed customers.

By the 1670s, the society of the Chesapeake had become polarized. Landowners—the planter elite and the more numerous yeoman planters—clustered around one pole. Landless colonists, mainly freed servants, gathered at the other. Each group eyed the other with suspicion and mistrust. For the most part, planters saw land-less freemen as a dangerous rabble rather than as fellow colonists with legitimate grievances. Governor William Berkeley feared the political threat to the governing elite posed by "six parts in seven [of Virginia colonists who] . . . are poor, indebted, discontented, and armed."

Government Policies and Political Conflict

In general, government and politics amplified the distinctions in Chesapeake society. The most vital distinction separated servants and masters, and the colonial government enforced it with an iron fist. Poor men like William Tyler complained that "nether the Governor nor Counsell could or would doe any poore men right, but that they would shew favor to great men and wronge the poore." Most Chesapeake colonists, like most Europeans, assumed that "great men" should bear the responsibilities of government. Until 1670, all freemen could vote, and they rou-

Governor William Berkeley

This portrait illustrates the distance that separated Governor Berkeley and the other Chesapeake grandees from poor planters, landless freemen, servants, and slaves. Berkeley's clothing suited the genteel interiors of Jamestown, not the rustic dwellings of lesser Virginians. His haughty, satisfied demeanor suggests his lack of sympathy for poor Virginians, who, he was certain, deserved their lot.
Courtesy of Berkeley Castle Charitable Trust, Gloucestershire.

tinely elected prosperous planters to the legislature. No former servant served in either the governor's council or the House of Burgesses after 1640. Yet Tyler and other poor Virginians believed that the "great men" used their government offices to promote their selfish personal interests, rather than governing impartially.

As discontent mounted among the poor during the 1660s and 1670s, colonial officials tried to keep political power in safe hands. Beginning in 1661, for example, Governor Berkeley did not call an election for the House of Burgesses for fifteen years. In 1670, the House of Burgesses outlawed voting by poor men, permitting only men who headed a household and were landowners to vote.

In 1660, the king also began to tighten the royal government's control of trade and to collect substantial revenue from the Chesapeake. The 1660 Navigation Act required all tobacco and other colonial products to be sent only to English ports. The act supplemented laws of 1650 and 1651 that specified that colonial goods had to be transported in English ships with predominantly English crews. A 1663 law stipulated that all goods sent to the colonies must pass through English ports and be carried in English ships by English sailors. Together, these navigation acts were designed to funnel the colonial import trade exclusively into the hands of English merchants and shippers. The navigation acts reflected the English government's **mercantilist** assumptions about the colonies: What was good for England should determine colonial policy.

These mercantilist assumptions also underlay the import duty on tobacco inaugurated by the 1660 Navigation Act. The law assessed an import tax of two pence on every pound of colonial tobacco brought into England, about the price a Chesapeake tobacco farmer received. The tax gave the king a major financial interest in the size of the tobacco crop. During the 1660s, these tobacco import taxes yielded about a quarter of all English customs revenues.

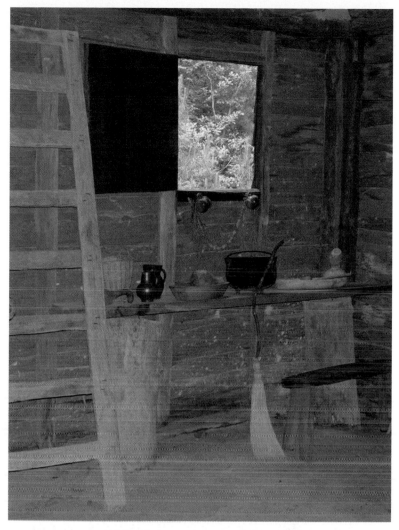

Inside a Poor Planter's House
The houses of seventeenth-century Chesapeake settlers were typically "earthfast": The structural timbers that framed the house were simply placed in holes in the ground, and the floor was packed dirt. No seventeenth-century house was substantial enough to survive until today. This photo shows a carefully documented historical reconstruction of the interior of a poor planter's house at St. Mary's City, Maryland. The wall of this one-room dwelling with a loft features a window with a shutter but no glass; when the shutter was closed, the only source of light was a candle or a fire. Notice the rustic, unfinished bench, table, and walls. These meager furnishings were usually accompanied by a storage chest and some bedding but not a bed. If and when planters became more prosperous, a bed was likely to be their first acquisition, suggesting that the lack of a good night's sleep was one of their major discomforts.
Image courtesy of Historic St. Mary's City.

Bacon's Rebellion

Colonists, like residents of European monarchies, accepted social hierarchy and inequality as long as they believed government officials ruled for the general good. When rulers violated that precept, ordinary people felt justified in rebelling. In 1676, Bacon's Rebellion erupted as a dispute over Virginia's Indian policy. Before it was over, the rebellion convulsed Chesapeake politics and society, leaving in its wake death, destruction, and a legacy of hostility between the great planters and their poorer neighbors.

Opechancanough, the Algonquian chief who had led the Indian uprising of 1622 in Virginia, mounted another surprise attack in 1644

Why Did English Colonists Consider Themselves Superior to Indians and Africans?

Were seeds of the racial prejudice that has been such a powerful force in American history planted in the seventeenth-century Chesapeake? To answer that question, historians have paid close attention to the language colonists used to describe Indians, Africans, and themselves.

In the mid-1500s, the English adopted the words *Indian* and *Negro* from Spanish, where they had come to mean, respectively, an aboriginal inhabitant of the New World and a black person of African ancestry. Both terms were generic, homogenizing an enormous diversity of tribal affiliations, languages, and cultures. Neither term originated with the people to whom it referred. The New England minister Roger Williams, who published a book on Indian languages in 1643, reported, "They have often asked mee, why we call them Indians," a poignant question that reveals the European origins of the term.

After *Indians*, the word the settlers used most frequently to describe Native Americans was *savages*. The Indians were savages in the colonists' eyes because they lacked the traits of English civilization. As one Englishman put it in 1625, the natives of Virginia were "so bad a people, having little of humanitie but

shape, ignorant of Civilitie, of Arts, of Religion; more brutish than the beasts they hunt, more wild and unmanly than that unmanned wild countrey, which they range rather than inhabite; captivated also to Satans tyranny in foolish pieties, mad impieties, wicked idlenesse, busie and bloudy wickednesse." Some English colonists counterbalanced this harsh indictment with admiration for certain features of Indian behavior. They praised Indians' calm dignity and poise, their tender love and care for family members, and their simple, independent way of life in apparent harmony with nature.

Color was not a feature of the Indians' savagery. During the seventeenth century, colonists never referred to Indians as "red." Instead, they saw Indians' skin color as tawny or tanned, the "Sun's livery," as one settler wrote. Many settlers held the view that Indians were innately white like the English but in other ways woefully un-English.

Despite their savagery in English eyes, Indians controlled two things colonists desperately wanted: land and peace. Early in the seventeenth century, when English settlements were small and weak, peace with Indians was a higher priority than land. In this period, English

comments on Indian savagery noted the obvious differences between settlers and Indians, but the colonists' need for peace kept them attuned to ways to coexist with Indians. By the middle of the seventeenth century, as colonial settlements grew and the desire for land increased, violent conflict with Indians erupted repeatedly. The violence convinced settlers that the only way to achieve both land and peace was to eliminate Indians, either by killing them or pushing them far away from colonial settlements. Colonists' convictions about Indians' savagery became the justification for chronic violence against Indians. English assumptions of their superiority to savage Indians gave a gloss of respectability to colonists' relentless grab of Indian lands.

The colonists identified Africans quite differently. Only a few Africans lived in the Chesapeake early in the seventeenth century. The first recorded arrival of Africans occurred in 1619, when a Dutch man-of-war brought to Virginia "20. and odd Negroes," as John Rolfe wrote. Rolfe's usage illustrates the colonists' most common term for Africans: *Negroes*. But the other word the colonists frequently used to refer to Africans was not *savage* or *heathen* but *black*. What struck English colonists most forcefully about Africans was not their un-English ways but their un-English skin color.

Black was not a neutral color to the colonists. According to the *Oxford English Dictionary* (which catalogs the changing meaning of words), *black* meant to the English people who settled the Chesapeake "deeply stained with dirt; soiled, dirty, foul . . . having dark or deadly purposes, malignant; pertaining to or involving death, deadly; baneful, disastrous, sinister . . . foul, iniqui-

Katarina, "Moorish Woman"

Albrecht Dürer, one of the foremost artists of the Renaissance, drew this portrait of Katarina early in the sixteenth century. It is among the first portraits of Africans made in Renaissance Europe. Katarina was the servant of a Portuguese merchant whom Dürer visited in the Netherlands in the spring of 1521. The portrait was completed before the Atlantic slave trade had begun to boom, but well after Portuguese merchants had brought thousands of African slaves to Europe. Dürer's meticulous portrait betrays no trace of racial prejudice. Katarina wears European clothing and is depicted with the same respect and dignity Dürer accorded Europeans whose likenesses he drew. In what ways might this portrait have been different if it had been executed by an artist in the southern colonies of North America in the late seventeenth century?

Foto Marburg / Art Resource, NY.

A Young Virginian

In 1645, the Dutch artist Wenceslaus Hollar drew this portrait of a twenty-three-year-old Indian man from Virginia. The young man had evidently been brought to London, where he posed for this likeness. Hollar portrayed the exotic adornment of the man—the animal claw headband, shell earrings and necklace, facial markings, Mohawk haircut, and bare-chested torso. Yet these distinctly non-European features did not cause Hollar to compromise his humane, dignified depiction of this man, whose gaze seems to be fixed steadily and without shame on the observer. If this young Virginian had been back in the Chesapeake rather than in London, he would probably have been engaged in the deadly warfare triggered by Opechancanough's 1644 uprising. How might this portrait have been different if it had been drawn by a Virginia colonist in 1645?

© Copyright The British Museum.

---

tous, atrocious, horrible, wicked." Black was the opposite of white, which connoted purity, beauty, and goodness—attributes the colonists identified with themselves. By the middle of the seventeenth century, the colonists referred to themselves not only as English but also as free, implying that people who were not English were not free. After about 1680, colonists often stated that implication in racial terms by referring to themselves as white. By the end of the seventeenth century, blacks were triply cursed in English eyes: un-English, un-white, and un-free.

A few Englishmen dissented from such views. Thomas Phillips, a slave ship captain, declared in 1694

(continued)

that he could not "imagine why they [blacks] should be despis'd for their colour, being what they cannot help, and the effect of the climate it has pleas'd God to appoint them. I can't think there is any intrinsick value in one colour more than another, nor that white is better than black, only we think it so because we are so, and are prone to judge favourably in our own case, as well as the blacks, who in odium of the colour, say, the devil is white, and so paint him." But these observations did not prevent Phillips or other colonists from enslaving Africans for their labor.

Virginians did not legally define slavery as permanent, lifelong, inherited bondage until 1660. The sparse surviving evidence demonstrates, however, that colonists practiced slavery long before that. Although there is no way to be certain, it is likely that the "20. and odd Negroes" who arrived in 1619 were slaves. And the

punishments handed out to blacks who broke the law usually took for granted that their servitude could not be extended, presumably because they were already in bondage for life, not—like servants—for a limited number of years.

The debasements of slavery strengthened colonists' prejudice toward blacks, while racial prejudices buttressed slavery. A Virginia law of 1662, for instance, provided that "if any christian shall committt Fornication with a negro man or woman, hee or shee soe offending" had to pay a double fine. The law also demonstrates that, despite racial prejudices, sexual relations between white and black settlers were prevalent enough to attract the attention of the legislature.

For most of the seventeenth century, possession of a black skin did not automatically and necessarily condemn a person to the status of

slave in the eyes of whites. Some Africans in the Chesapeake served for limited periods of time like white servants, became free like white servants, and even acquired land, reared families, and participated in local affairs like former white servants. In fact, white colonists' prejudice against blacks echoed wealthy colonists' attitudes toward servants and other poor white people. Masters often considered white servants, like blacks, "the vile and brutish part of mankind."

Colonists' attitudes toward Indians and Africans exaggerated and hardened English notions about social hierarchy, about superiority and inferiority. Colonists' convictions of their own superiority to Indians and Africans justified, they believed, their exploitation of Indians' land and Africans' labor. Those justifications planted the seeds of pernicious racial prejudices that flourished in America for centuries.

and killed about 500 Virginia colonists in two days. During the next two years of bitter fighting, the colonists eventually gained the upper hand, capturing and murdering the old chief. The treaty that concluded the war established policies toward the Indians that the government tried to maintain for the next thirty years. The Indians relinquished all claims to land already settled by the English. Wilderness land beyond the fringe of English settlement was supposed to be reserved exclusively for Indian use. The colonial government hoped to minimize contact between settlers and Indians and thereby maintain the peace.

Had the Chesapeake population remained constant, the policy might have worked. But the number of land-hungry colonists, especially poor, recently freed servants, continued to multiply. In their quest for land, they pushed beyond the treaty limits of English settlement and encroached steadily on Indian land. During the

1660s and 1670s, violence between colonists and Indians repeatedly flared along the advancing frontier. The government, headquartered in the tidewater region near the coast, far from the danger of Indian raids, took steps to calm the disputes and reestablish the peace. Frontier settlers thirsted for revenge against what their leader, Nathaniel Bacon, termed "the protected and Darling Indians." Bacon minced no words about his intention: "Our Design [is] not only to ruine and extirpate all Indians in Generall but all Manner of Trade and Commerce with them." Indians were not the only enemies Bacon and his men singled out. Bacon also urged colonists to "see what spounges have suckt up the Publique Treasure." He charged that "Grandees," or elite planters, operated the government for their private gain, a charge that made sense to many colonists. Bacon crystallized the grievances of the small planters and poor farmers against both the Indians and the colonial rulers in Jamestown.

Hoping to maintain the fragile peace on the frontier in 1676, Governor Berkeley pronounced Bacon a rebel, threatened to punish him for treason, and called for new elections of burgesses who, Berkeley believed, would endorse his get-tough policy. To Berkeley's surprise, the elections backfired. Almost all the old burgesses were voted out of office, their places taken by local leaders, including Bacon. The legislature was now in the hands of minor grandees who, like Bacon, chafed at the rule of the elite planters.

In June 1676, the new legislature passed a series of reform measures known as Bacon's Laws. Among other changes, the laws gave local settlers a voice in setting tax levies, forbade office-holders from demanding bribes or other extra fees for carrying out their duties, placed limits on holding multiple offices, and restored the vote to all freemen. Under pressure, Berkeley pardoned Bacon and authorized his campaign of Indian warfare. But elite planters soon convinced Berkeley that Bacon and his men were a greater threat than Indians.

When Bacon learned that Berkeley had once again branded him a traitor, he declared war against Berkeley and the other grandees. For three months, Bacon's forces fought the Indians, sacked the grandees' plantations, and attacked Jamestown. Berkeley's loyalists retaliated by plundering the homes of Bacon's supporters. The fighting continued until late October, when Bacon unexpectedly died, most likely from dysentery, and several English ships arrived to bolster Berkeley's strength. With the rebellion crushed, Berkeley hanged several of Bacon's allies and destroyed farms that belonged to Bacon's supporters.

The rebellion did not dislodge the grandees from their positions of power. If anything, it strengthened their position. When the king learned of the turmoil in the Chesapeake and its devastating effect on tobacco exports and customs duties, he ordered an investigation. Royal officials replaced Berkeley with a governor more attentive to the king's interests, nullified Bacon's Laws, and instituted an export tax on every hogshead of tobacco as a way of paying the expenses of government without having to obtain the consent of the tightfisted House of Burgesses.

In the aftermath of Bacon's Rebellion, tensions between great planters and small farmers gradually lessened. Bacon's Rebellion showed, a governor of Virginia said, that it was necessary "to steer between . . . either an Indian or a civil war." The ruling elite concluded that it was safer for colonists to fight Indians rather than each other, and the government made little effort to restrict settlers' encroachment on Indian lands. Tax cuts were another policy welcomed by all freemen. The export duty on tobacco imposed by the king allowed the colonial government to reduce taxes by 75 percent between 1660 and 1700. In the long run, however, the most important contribution to political stability was the declining importance of the servant labor system. During the 1680s and 1690s, fewer servants arrived in the Chesapeake, partly because of improving economic conditions in England. Accordingly, the number of poor, newly freed servants also declined, reducing the size of the lowest stratum of free society. In 1700, as many as one-third of the free colonists still worked as tenants on land owned by others, but the social and political distance between them and the great planters, enormous as it was, did not seem as profound as it had been in 1660. The main reason was that by 1700 the Chesapeake was in the midst of transition to a slave labor system that minimized the differences between poor farmers and rich planters and magnified the differences between whites and blacks.

> Bacon crystallized the grievances of the small planters and poor farmers against both the Indians and the colonial rulers in Jamestown.

Religion and Revolt in the Spanish Borderland

While English colonies in the Chesapeake grew and prospered with the tobacco trade, the northern outposts of the Spanish empire in New Mexico and Florida stagnated. Instead of attracting settlers and growing crops for export, New Mexico and Florida appealed to Spanish missionaries seeking to harvest Indian souls. The missionaries baptized thousands of Indians in Spanish North America during the seventeenth century, but they also planted the seeds of Indian uprisings against Spanish rule.

Few Spaniards came to New Spain's northern borderland during the seventeenth century. Only about 1,500 Spaniards lived in Florida and roughly twice as many inhabited New Mexico. One royal governor complained that "no [Spaniard] comes . . . to plow and sow [crops], but only to eat and loaf." In both colonies, Indians outnumbered Spaniards ten or twenty to one.

Royal officials seriously considered eliminating both colonies because their costs greatly exceeded their benefits. Every three years, oxen pulled a caravan of wagons out of Mexico City crammed with things Spaniards in New Mexico considered necessities, including nails, raisins, oysters, and communion wine. Florida required even larger subsidies because, unlike New Mexico, it housed a garrison of soldiers to menace European interlopers who sought to prey on Spanish ships. The soldiers also protected the missionaries and their faith; Christian crosses even adorned the stirrups on their saddles. Catholic missionaries persuaded the Spanish government that, instead of being losing propositions, the colonies represented golden opportunities to convert heathen Indians to Christianity. Royal officials reasoned that the missionaries' efforts would pacify Indians and be a relatively cheap way to preserve Spanish footholds in North America.

Dozens of missionaries came to Florida and New Mexico, as one announced, to free Indians "from the miserable slavery of the demon and from the obscure darkness of their idolatry." Pueblo Indians in New Mexico and southeastern tribespeople in Florida had to be taught, missionaries believed, that their religious beliefs and rituals were idolatrous devil worship and that their way of life was barbaric. Missionaries followed royal instructions that Indians should be taught "to live in a civilized manner, clothed and wearing shoes . . . [and] given the use of bread and wine and oil and many other essentials of life—bread, linen, horses, cattle, tools, and weapons, and all the rest that Spain has had." In effect, missionaries sought to convert Indians not just into Christians but also into surrogate Spaniards.

Missionaries supervised the building of scores of Catholic churches across Florida and New Mexico. Typically, they conscripted Indian women and men to do the construction labor. Adopting practices common elsewhere in New Spain, missionaries forced Indians both to work and to pay tribute in the form of food, blankets, and other goods. Supported by Indians' coerced labor, missionaries taught Christian doctrines, performed Christian rituals, and celebrated Christian—that is, Spanish—civilization. While missionaries congratulated themselves on the many Indians they converted, their coercive methods subverted their goals. A missionary reported that an Indian in New Mexico asked him, "if we [missionaries] who are Christians caused so much harm and violence [to Indians], why should they [i.e., Indians] become Christians?"

Indians retaliated repeatedly against Spanish exploitation, but Spaniards suppressed the violent uprisings by taking advantage of the disunity among Indians much as Cortés did in the conquest of Mexico (see chapter 2). In 1680, however, Pueblo Indians organized a unified revolt under the leadership of Popé, who ordered his followers, as one recounted, to "break up and burn the images of the holy Christ, the Virgin Mary, and the other saints, the crosses, and everything pertaining to Christianity." During the Pueblo Revolt, Indians desecrated churches, killed two-thirds of Spanish missionaries, and drove Spaniards out of New Mexico to present-day El Paso, Texas. Spaniards managed to return to New Mexico by the end of the seventeenth century, but only by curtailing missionaries and reducing labor exploitation. Florida Indians never mounted a unified attack on Spanish rule, but they too organized sporadic uprisings and resisted conversion, causing a Spanish official to report by the end of the seventeenth century that "the law of God and the preaching of the Holy Gospel have now ceased."

Toward a Slave Labor System

Spaniards had few qualms about exploiting Indian labor, but European diseases continued to wreak havoc among vulnerable Native Americans. During the sixteenth century, Spaniards and Portuguese supplemented Indian laborers in the New World with enslaved Africans. On this foundation, European colonizers built African slavery into the most important form of coerced labor in the New World. During the seventeenth century, British colonies in the West Indies followed the Spanish and Portuguese examples and developed sugar plantations with slave labor. In the British North American colonies, however, a slave labor system did not emerge until the last quarter of the seventeenth century. During the 1670s, settlers from Barbados brought slavery to the new English mainland colony of Carolina, where the imprint of the West Indies remained strong for decades. In Chesapeake tobacco fields at about the same time, slave labor began to replace servant labor, marking the transition toward a society of freedom for whites and slavery for Africans.

Sugar Mill

This seventeenth-century drawing of a Brazilian sugar mill highlights the heavy equipment needed to extract the juice from sugarcane. A vertical waterwheel turns a large horizontal gear that exerts force on the jaws of the press that squeezes the cane. Workers remove crushed cane from the press and replace it with freshly harvested cane as it is unloaded from an oxcart. Except for the overseer (just to the right of the waterwheel), all of the workers are black, presumably slaves from Africa, as suggested by their clothing. All of the mill workers appear to be men, a hint of the predominance of men among newly imported African slaves.

Musées Royaux des Beaux-Arts de Belgique.

The West Indies: Sugar and Slavery

The most profitable part of the British New World empire in the seventeenth century lay in the Caribbean (Map 3.2). The tiny island of Barbados, colonized in the 1630s, was the jewel of the British West Indies. During the 1640s, Barbadian planters began to grow sugarcane with such success that a colonial official proclaimed Barbados "the most flourishing Island in all those American parts, and I verily beleive in all the world for the production of sugar." Sugar commanded high prices in England, and planters rushed to grow as much as they could. By midcentury, annual sugar exports from the British Caribbean totaled about 150,000 pounds; by 1700, exports reached nearly 50 million pounds.

Sugar transformed Barbados and other West Indian islands. Poor farmers could not afford the expensive machinery that extracted and refined the sugarcane juice. Planters who had the necessary capital to grow sugar got rich. By 1680, the wealthiest Barbadian sugar planters were, on average, four times richer than tobacco grandees in the Chesapeake. The sugar grandees differed from their Chesapeake counterparts in another crucial way: The average sugar baron in Barbados in 1680 owned 115 slaves.

African slaves planted, cultivated, and harvested the sugarcane that made West Indian planters wealthy. Beginning in the 1640s, Barbadian planters purchased thousands of slaves to work their plantations, and the African population on the island mushroomed. During the 1650s, when blacks made up only 3 percent of the Chesapeake population, they had already become the majority on Barbados. By 1700, slaves constituted more than three-fourths of the island's population.

> By 1700, slaves constituted more than three-fourths of the population of Barbados.

For slaves, work on a sugar plantation was a life sentence to brutal, unremitting labor. Slaves had short life expectancies and high death rates. Since slave men outnumbered slave women two to one, few slaves could form families and have children. These grim realities meant that in Barbados and elsewhere in the West Indies, the slave population did not grow by natural reproduction. Instead, planters continually purchased enslaved Africans. Although sugar plantations did not gain a foothold in North America in the seventeenth century, the West Indies nonetheless exerted a powerful influence on the development of slavery in the mainland colonies.

Carolina: A West Indian Frontier

The early settlers of what became South Carolina were immigrants from Barbados. In 1663, a Barbadian planter named John Colleton and a group of seven other men obtained a charter from England's King Charles II to establish a colony south of the Chesapeake and north of the Spanish territories in Florida. The men, known as "proprietors," hoped to siphon settlers from Barbados and other colonies and encourage them to develop a profitable export crop comparable to West Indian sugar and Chesapeake tobacco. Following the Chesapeake example, the proprietors offered headrights of up to 150 acres of land for each settler. In 1670, they established the first permanent English settlement in the colony, on the west bank of the Ashley River just across from the peninsula where the king's namesake city, Charles Towne (later spelled Charleston), was founded (see Map 3.2).

As the proprietors had planned, most of the early settlers were from Barbados. In fact, Carolina was the only seventeenth-century English colony to be settled principally by colonists from other colonies rather than from England. The Barbadian immigrants brought their slaves with them. More than a fourth of the early settlers were slaves, and as the colony continued to attract settlers from Barbados, the black population multiplied. By 1700, slaves made up about

MAP 3.2   The West Indies and Carolina in the Seventeenth Century
Although Carolina was geographically close to the Chesapeake colonies, it was culturally closer to the West Indies in the seventeenth century because its early settlers—both blacks and whites—came from Barbados. South Carolina retained strong ties to the West Indies for more than a century, long after the arrival of many of its subsequent settlers from England, Ireland, France, and elsewhere.

READING THE MAP: Locate English colonies in America and English holdings in the Caribbean. Which European country controlled most of the mainland bordering the Caribbean? Where was the closest mainland English territory?
CONNECTIONS: Why were colonists in Carolina so interested in Barbados? What goods did they export? Describe the relationship between Carolina and Barbados in 1700.

FOR MORE HELP ANALYZING THIS MAP, see the map activity for this chapter in the Online Study Guide at bedfordstmartins.com/roark.

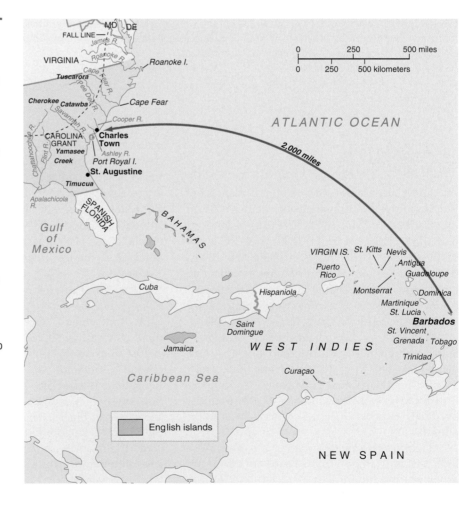

half the population of Carolina. The new colony's close association with Barbados caused English officials to refer routinely to "Carolina in ye West Indies."

The Carolinians experimented unsuccessfully to match their semitropical climate with profitable export crops of tobacco, cotton, indigo, and olives. In the mid-1690s, colonists identified a hardy strain of rice and took advantage of the knowledge of rice cultivation among their many African slaves to build rice plantations. During the first generation of settlement, however, Carolina remained an economic colony of Barbados. Settlers sold livestock and timber to the West Indies. They also exploited another "natural resource": They captured and enslaved several thousand local Indians and sold them to Caribbean planters. Both economically and socially, seventeenth-century Carolina was a frontier outpost of the West Indian sugar economy.

Slave Labor Emerges in the Chesapeake

By 1700, more than eight out of ten people in the southern colonies of British North America lived in the Chesapeake. Until the 1670s, almost all Chesapeake colonists were white people from England. In 1700, however, one out of eight people in the region was a black person from Africa. Although a few blacks had lived in the Chesapeake since the 1620s, the black population increased fivefold between 1670 and 1700 as hundreds of tobacco planters made the transition from servant to slave labor, purchasing slaves rather than servants to work in their tobacco fields. For planters, slaves had several obvious advantages over servants. Although slaves cost three to five times more than servants, slaves never became free. Since the mortality rate had declined by the 1680s, planters could reasonably expect slaves to live longer than a servant's period of indenture. Slaves also promised to be a perpetual labor force, since children of slave mothers inherited the status of slavery.

For planters, slaves had another important advantage over servants. They could be controlled politically. Bacon's Rebellion had demonstrated how disruptive former servants could be when their expectations were not met. A slave labor system promised to avoid the political problems caused by the servant labor system. Slavery kept discontented laborers in permanent servitude, and their color was a badge of their bondage.

Bell of Slave Ship
The English slave ship *Henrietta Marie* sailed from England to the west African coast in 1699, loaded a cargo of slaves, made the **Middle Passage** to the West Indies, where the slaves were sold, then started back to England, but sank with all aboard off the Florida Keys. Centuries later, this bronze bell was recovered from the wreckage.
© 1991 Mel Fisher Maritime Heritage Society, Key West, FL. Photo: Dylan Kibler.

The slave labor system polarized Chesapeake society along lines of race and status: All slaves were black, and nearly all blacks were slaves; almost all free people were white, and all whites were free or only temporarily bound in indentured servitude. Unlike Barbados, however, the Chesapeake retained a vast white majority. Among whites, huge differences of wealth and status still existed. In fact, the emerging slave labor system sharpened the economic differences among whites because only prosperous planters could afford to buy slaves. By 1700, more than three-quarters of white families had neither servants nor slaves. Nonetheless, poor white farmers enjoyed the privileges of free status. They could own property; they could marry, have families, and bequeath their property and their freedom to their descendants; they could move when and where they wanted; they could associate freely with other people; they could serve on juries, vote, and hold political office; and they could work, loaf, and sleep as they chose. Such distinctions between free people and slaves made lesser white folk feel they had a genuine stake in the existence of slavery, even if they did not own a single slave. By emphasizing the privileges of freedom shared by all white people, the slave labor system reduced the tensions between poor folk and grandees that had plagued the Chesapeake region in the 1670s.

In contrast to Barbados, most slaves in the seventeenth-century Chesapeake colonies had frequent and close contact with white people.

> Both economically and socially, seventeenth-century Carolina was a frontier outpost of the West Indian sugar economy.

Slaves and white servants performed the same tasks on tobacco plantations, often working side by side in the fields. For slaves, work on a tobacco plantation was less onerous than on a sugar plantation. But slaves' constant exposure to white surveillance made Chesapeake slavery especially confining. Slaves took advantage of every opportunity to slip away from white supervision and seek out the company of other slaves, "going abroad" to visit slaves on neighboring plantations. Planters often feared that slaves would turn such seemingly innocent social pleasures to political ends, either to run away or to conspire to strike against their masters. Slaves often ran away, but they usually were captured or returned after a brief absence. Despite planters' nightmares, slave insurrections did not occur.

While slavery resolved the political unrest caused by the servant labor system, it created new political problems. By 1700, the bedrock political issue in the Chesapeake was keeping slaves in their place, at the business end of a hoe in a tobacco field. The Chesapeake was developing a slave labor system that stood midway, both geographically and socially, between the sugar plantations and black majority of Barbados to the south and the small farms and homogeneous villages that developed in seventeenth-century New England to the north (see chapter 4).

Conclusion: The Growth of English Colonies Based on Export Crops and Slave Labor

By 1700, the colonies of Virginia, Maryland, and Carolina were firmly established. The staple crops they grew for export provided a livelihood for many, a fortune for a few, and valuable revenues for shippers, merchants, and the English monarchy. Their societies differed markedly from English society in most respects, yet the colonists considered themselves English people who happened to live in North America. They claimed the same rights and privileges as English men and women while they denied those rights and privileges to Native Americans and African slaves.

The English colonies also differed from the example of New Spain. Settlers and servants flocked to English colonies, in contrast to Spaniards who trickled into New Spain. Few English missionaries sought to convert Indians to Protestant Christianity, unlike the numerous Catholic missionaries in New Mexico and Florida. Large quantities of gold and silver never materialized in British North America. English colonists never adopted the system of encomienda (see chapter 2) because Indians were too few and too hostile and their communities too small and decentralized compared with those of the Mexica. Yet forms of coerced labor and racial distinction that developed in New Spain had North American counterparts, as English colonists employed servants and slaves and defined themselves as superior to Indians and Africans.

By 1700, the remnants of Powhatan's people still survived. As English settlement pushed north, west, and south of the Chesapeake Bay, Indians faced the new colonial world that Powhatan and Pocahontas had encountered when John Smith and the first colonists arrived at Jamestown. By 1700, the many descendants of Pocahontas's son, Thomas, as well as other colonists and Native Americans, understood that the English had come to stay.

For additional firsthand accounts of this period, see Chapter 3 in Michael Johnson, ed., *Reading the American Past*, Third Edition.

To assess your mastery of the material in this chapter, see the Online Study Guide at bedfordstmartins.com/roark.

For Web links related to the topics in this chapter, see "HistoryLinks," "DocLinks," and "PlaceLinks" at bedfordstmartins.com/roark.

CHRONOLOGY

1588 • England defeats Spanish Armada.

1606 • Virginia Company of London receives royal charter to establish colony in North America.

1607 • English colonists found Jamestown settlement; Pocahontas "rescues" John Smith.

1609 • Starvation plagues Jamestown.

1612 • John Rolfe begins to plant tobacco in Virginia.

1617 • First commercial tobacco shipment leaves Virginia for England.
• Pocahontas dies in England.

1618 • Powhatan dies, and Opechancanough becomes supreme chief of the Algonquians.

1619 • First Africans arrive in Virginia.
• House of Burgesses begins to meet in Virginia.

1622 • Opechancanough leads Indian uprising against Virginia colonists.

1624 • Virginia becomes royal colony.

1632 • King Charles I grants Lord Baltimore land for colony of Maryland.

1634 • Colonists begin to arrive in Maryland.

1640s • Barbados colonists begin to grow sugarcane with labor of African slaves.

1644 • Opechancanough leads Indian uprising against Virginia colonists.

1660 • Navigation Act requires colonial tobacco to be shipped to English ports and to be assessed customs tax.

1663 • Carolina proprietors receive charter from King Charles II for Carolina colony.

1670 • Charles Towne, South Carolina, founded.

1670–1700 • Slave labor system emerges first in Carolina and more gradually in Chesapeake colonies.

1676 • Bacon's Rebellion convulses Virginia, leading eventually to the decline of indentured servitude and the rise of slavery.

1680 • Pueblo Revolt erupts in New Mexico, temporarily pushing Spanish officials out of pueblos.

BIBLIOGRAPHY

Please consult the bibliographies of chapters 2 and 4 for more readings on related topics.

General Works

Kenneth R. Andrews, *Trade, Plunder, and Settlement: Maritime Enterprise and the Genesis of the British Empire* (1984).

David Armitage and Michael Braddick, eds., *The British Atlantic World, 1500–1800* (2002).

James Axtell, *Natives and Newcomers: The Cultural Origins of North America* (2001).

Bernard Bailyn and Philip D. Morgan, eds., *Strangers within the Realm: Cultural Margins of the First British Empire* (1991).

Robert M. Bliss, *Revolution and Empire: English Politics and the American Colonies in the Seventeenth Century* (1990).

Ruth H. Bloch, *Gender and Morality in Anglo-American Culture, 1650–1800* (2003).

Joyce E. Chaplin, *Subject Matter: Technology, the Body, and Science on the Anglo-American Frontier, 1500–1676* (2001).

Linda Colley, *Captives* (2002).

Seymour Drescher and Stanley L. Engerman, eds., *A Historical Guide to World Slavery* (1998).

Betty Fussell, *The Story of Corn* (1992).

Alison Games, *Migration and the Origins of the English Atlantic World* (1999).

Iain Gately, *Tobacco: The Story of How Tobacco Seduced the World* (2001).

Richard Godbeer, *Sexual Revolution in Early America* (2002).

Jack P. Greene and J. R. Pole, eds., *Colonial British America: Essays in the New History of the Early Modern Era* (1984).

Eric Hinderaker and Peter C. Mancall, *At the Edge of Empire: The Backcountry in British North America* (2003).

Winthrop D. Jordan, *White over Black: American Attitudes towards the Negro, 1550–1812* (1968).

Karen Ordahl Kupperman, *Indians and English: Facing Off in Early America* (2000).

John J. McCusker and Russell R. Menard, *The Economy of British America, 1607–1789* (1985).

Edmund S. Morgan, *American Slavery, American Freedom: The Ordeal of Colonial Virginia* (1975).

Mary Beth Norton, *Founding Mothers and Fathers: Gendered Power and the Forming of American Society* (1996).

David Ormrod, *The Rise of Commercial Empires: England and the Netherlands in the Age of Mercantilism, 1650–1770* (2003).

James Walvin, *Fruits of Empire: Exotic Produce and British Trade, 1660–1800* (1997).

Indians

James Axtell, *The Indians' New South: Cultural Change in the Colonial Southeast* (1997).

Philip L. Barbour, *Pocahontas and Her World* (1970).

Kathryn E. Holland Braund, *Deerskins and Duffels: The Creek Indian Trade with Anglo-America, 1685–1815* (1993).

James F. Brooks, *Confounding the Color Line: The Indian-Black Experience in North America* (2002).

Wesley Frank Craven, *White, Red, and Black: The Seventeenth-Century Virginian* (1971).

Robbie Etheridge and Charles Hudson, eds., *The Transformation of the Southeastern Indians, 1540–1760* (2002).

Alan Gallay, *The Indian Slave Trade: The Rise of the English Empire in the American South, 1670–1717* (2002).

Frederic W. Gleach, *Powhatan's World and Colonial Virginia: A Conflict of Cultures* (1997).

Charles Hudson and Carmen Chaves Tesser, eds., *The Forgotten Centuries: Indians and Europeans in the American South, 1521–1704* (1994).

J. A. Leo Lemay, *Did Pocahontas Save Captain John Smith?* (1992).

James H. Merrell, *The Indians' New World: Catawbas and Their Neighbors from European Contact through the Era of Removal* (1989).

Michael Leroy Oberg, *Dominion and Civility: English Imperialism and Native America, 1585–1685* (1999).

Daniel K. Richter, *Facing East from Indian Country: A Native History of Early America* (2001).

Helen C. Rountree, *Pocahontas's People: The Powhatan Indians of Virginia through Four Centuries* (1990).

Helen C. Rountree and E. Randolph Turner III, *Before and after Jamestown: Virginia's Powhatans and Their Predecessors* (2002).

Bernard W. Sheehan, *Savagism and Civility: Indians and Englishmen in Colonial Virginia* (1980).

Timothy Silver, *A New Face on the Countryside: Indians, Colonists, and Slaves in South Atlantic Forests, 1500–1800* (1990).

Jayme A. Sokolow, *The Great Encounter: Native Peoples and European Settlers in the Americas, 1492–1800* (2003).

Peter H. Wood et al., eds., *Powhatan's Mantle: Indians in the Colonial Southeast* (1989).

Chesapeake Society

Stephen Adams, *The Best and Worst Country in the World: Perspectives on the Early Virginia Landscape* (2001).

Edward L. Bond, *Damned Souls in a Tobacco Colony: Religion in Seventeenth-Century Virginia* (2000).

Carl Bridenbaugh, *Jamestown, 1544–1699* (1980).

Kathleen Brown, *Good Wives, Nasty Wenches, and Anxious Patriarchs: Gender, Race, and Power in Colonial Virginia* (1996).

Lois Green Carr et al., *Robert Cole's World: Agriculture and Society in Early Maryland* (1991).

Lois Green Carr et al., eds., *Colonial Chesapeake Society* (1988).

James Deetz, *Flowerdew Hundred: The Archaeology of a Virginia Plantation, 1619–1864* (1993).

James Horn, *Adapting to a New World: English Society in the Seventeenth-Century Chesapeake* (1994).

Ivor Noël Hume, *The Archaeology of Martin's Hundred* (2001).

David W. Jordan, *Foundations of Representative Government in Maryland, 1632–1715* (1987).

Jon Kukla, *Political Institutions in Virginia, 1619–1660* (1989).

Aubrey C. Land et al., eds., *Law, Society, and Politics in Early Maryland* (1977).

Kenneth A. Lockridge, *The Diary, and Life, of William Byrd II of Virginia, 1674–1744* (1987).

Gloria Lund Main, *Tobacco Colony: Life in Early Maryland, 1650–1720* (1982).

Debra Meyers, *Common Whores, Vertuos Women, and Loveing Wives: Free Will Christian Women in Colonial Maryland* (2003).

John Ruston Pagan, *Anne Orthwood's Bastard: Sex and Law in Early Virginia* (2003).

James Perry, *The Formation of a Society on Virginia's Eastern Shore, 1615–1655* (1990).

Jacob M. Price, *Perry of London: A Family and a Firm on the Seaborne Frontier, 1615–1753* (1992).

Darrett B. Rutman and Anita H. Rutman, *A Place in Time: Middlesex County, Virginia, 1650–1750*, 2 vols. (1984).

Terri L. Snyder, *Brabbling Women: Disorderly Speech and the Law in Early Virginia* (2003).

Linda L. Sturtz, *Within Her Power: Propertied Women in Colonial Virginia* (2002).

Thad W. Tate and David L. Ammerman, eds., *The Chesapeake in the Seventeenth Century: Essays on Anglo-American Society* (1979).

Margaret Holmes Williamson, *Powhatan Lords of Life and Death: Command and Consent in Seventeenth-Century Virginia* (2003).

Servants and Slaves

Ira Berlin, *Many Thousands Gone: The First Two Centuries of Slavery in North America* (1998).

Robin Blackburn, *The Making of New World Slavery: From the Baroque to the Modern, 1492–1800* (1997).

David Eltis, *The Rise of African Slavery in the Americas* (2001).

Leland G. Ferguson, *Uncommon Ground: Archaeology and Early African America, 1650–1800* (1992).

David W. Galenson, *White Servitude in Colonial America: An Economic Analysis* (1981).

David W. Galenson, *Traders, Planters, and Slaves: Market Behavior in Early English America* (1986).

Paul E. Lovejoy, ed., *Africans in Bondage: Studies in Slavery and the Slave Trade* (1986).

Russell R. Menard, *Migrants, Servants and Slaves: Unfree Labor in Colonial British America* (2001).

Hugh Thomas, *The Slave Trade* (1997).

Spanish Borderlands

Gary Clayton Anderson, *The Indian Southwest, 1580–1830: Ethnogenesis and Reinvention* (1999).

James F. Brooks, *Captives and Cousins: Slavery, Kinship, and Community in the Southwest Borderlands* (2002).

Ramón A. Gutiérrez, *When Jesus Came, the Corn Mothers Went Away: Marriage, Sexuality, and Power in New Mexico, 1500–1846* (1991).

John L. Kessell, *Spain in the Southwest: A Narrative History of Colonial New Mexico, Arizona, Texas, and California* (2002).

Jane Landers, *Black Society in Spanish Florida* (1999).

Jerald T. Milanich, *Laboring in the Fields of the Lord: Spanish Missions and Southeastern Indians* (1999).

Robert W. Preucel, *Archaeologies of the Pueblo Revolt: Identity, Meaning, and Renewal in the Pueblo World* (2002).

Carroll L. Riley, *The Kachina and the Cross: Indians and Spaniards in the Early Southwest* (1999).

David J. Weber, *The Spanish Frontier in North America* (1992).

Carolina Society

Cara Anzilotti, *In the Affairs of the World: Women, Patriarchy, and Power in Colonial South Carolina* (2002).

Alan Vance Briceland, *Westward from Virginia: The Exploration of the Virginia-Carolina Frontier, 1650–1710* (1987).

Kirsten Fischer, *Suspect Relations: Sex, Race, and Resistance in Colonial North Carolina* (2002).

Lorri Glover, *All Our Relations: Blood Ties and Emotional Bonds among the Early South Carolina Gentry* (2000).

Thomas M. Hatley, *The Dividing Paths: Cherokees and South Carolinians through the Era of the American Revolution* (1993).

Daniel C. Littlefield, *Race and Slaves: Ethnicity and the Slave Trade in Colonial South Carolina* (1981).

Aaron M. Shatzmann, *Servants into Planters: The Origin of an American Image: Land Acquisition and Status Mobility in Seventeenth-Century South Carolina* (1989).

Richard Waterhouse, *A New World Gentry: The Making of a Merchant and Planter Class in South Carolina, 1670–1770* (1989).

Robert M. Weir, *Colonial South Carolina: A History* (1983).

Peter H. Wood, *Black Majority: Negroes in Colonial South Carolina from 1670 through the Stono Rebellion* (1974).

The West Indies

Carl Bridenbaugh and Roberta Bridenbaugh, *No Peace beyond the Line: The English in the Caribbean, 1624–1690* (1972).

Richard S. Dunn, *Sugar and Slaves: The Rise of the Planter Class in the English West Indies, 1624–1713* (1972).

Jerome S. Handler and Frederick W. Lange, *Plantation Slavery in Barbados* (1978).

Kenneth F. Kiple, *The Caribbean Slave: A Biological History* (1984).

Herbert S. Klein, *African Slavery in Latin America and the Caribbean* (1986).

Sidney W. Mintz, *Sweetness and Power: The Place of Sugar in Modern History* (1985).

Richard B. Sheridan, *Sugar and Slavery: An Economic History of the British West Indies, 1623–1775* (1974).

Eric Williams, *From Columbus to Castro: The History of the Caribbean, 1492–1969* (1970).

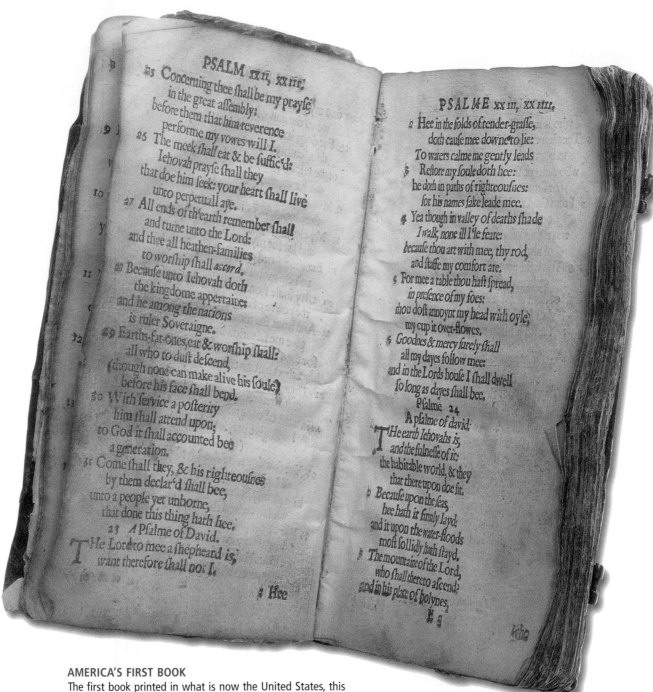

AMERICA'S FIRST BOOK

The first book printed in what is now the United States, this well-thumbed copy of *The Whole Booke of Psalmes Faithfully Translated into English Metre* was published in Cambridge, Massachusetts, in 1640. Puritan services banned musical instruments and other diversions from God's holy word. Worshippers used this book and others to sing psalms, celebrating with a chorus of voices the wonders of God's Truth. The famous Twenty-third Psalm begins near the bottom of the left-hand page and concludes on the facing page. Read the psalm aloud to re-create the experience of seventeenth-century New England Puritan congregations.

The Northern Colonies in the Seventeenth Century

1601–1700

ROGER WILLIAMS AND HIS WIFE MARY arrived in Massachusetts in February 1631. Fresh from a superb education at Cambridge University and a stint as a private chaplain for a wealthy family, the twenty-eight-year-old Williams was "a godly [Puritan] minister," noted John Winthrop, governor of the new colony. The Boston church honored Williams with an invitation to become its minister. Williams refused because the church had not openly declared its utter rejection of the corrupt Church of England. The leading church of Puritan New England was not pure enough for Williams.

Williams and his wife moved to Plymouth colony for two years; while there, he assisted another minister and spent a great deal of time among the Narragansett Indians. "My soul's desire was to do the natives good," he said By doing good he meant trying to learn about their language, their religion, and their culture, not trying to covert them to Christianity. Although Williams believed Indians were pagans, he insisted that their religion and other beliefs should be respected since all human beings should live according to their consciences as revealed to them by God. Williams avowed that "Nature knows no difference between Europeans and Americans in blood, birth, [or] bodies . . . God having made of one blood all mankind." His respect for Indians led him to condemn English colonists for their "sin of unjust usurpation" of Indian lands. The colonists' land claims were legally, morally, and spiritually invalid, Williams proclaimed.

Massachusetts officials defended colonists' settlement on Indian land. If land "lies common, and hath never been replenished or subdued, [it] is free to any that possess or improve it," Governor Winthrop explained. Besides, he said, "if we leave [the Indians] sufficient [land] for their use, we may lawfully take the rest, there being more than enough for them and us." Although Winthrop's arguments prevailed, Williams refused to knuckle under. "God Land," he said, "[is] as great a God with us English as God Gold was with the Spaniards." While New Englanders claimed to worship God in heaven, Williams observed, "the truth is the great Gods of this world are God-belly, God-peace, God-wealth, God-honour, [and] God-pleasure."

William Bradford, the governor of Plymouth, praised Williams as "a man godly and zealous, having many precious parts" but also "some strange opinions." Most New England leaders were less generous. One minister censured

Williams for his "self-conceited, and unquiet, and unlamblike frame of . . . Spirit." Rather than submitting lamblike to the colony's rulers, Williams continued to espouse his strange opinions, which ultimately caused him to be banished from the colony.

Williams accepted an invitation to become the minister at Salem, Massachusetts, in 1633. Like other New England Puritans, the members of the Salem church had solemnly agreed to "**Covenant** with the Lord and one with another; and doe bynd our selves in the presence of God, to walke together in all his waies, according as he is pleased to reveale himself unto us in his Blessed word of truth [the Bible]." Most New England Puritans believed that since the Bible clearly defined God's way, churches and governments should enforce both godly belief and behavior. Like other Puritans, Williams believed that the Bible revealed the word of God. But unlike New England's leaders who claimed that "the Word of God is so clear," Williams believed the Bible shrouded the word of God in "mist and fog." Williams pointed out that devout and pious Christians could and did differ about what the Bible said and what God expected. That observation led him to denounce the emerging New England order as impure, ungodly, and tyrannical.

New England's government required everyone to attend church service, whether or not they were church members. Williams argued that forcing people who were not Christians to attend church was wrong in four major ways. First, Williams preached, it was akin to requiring "a dead child to suck the breast, or a dead man [to] feast." The only way for any person to become a true Christian was by God's gift of faith revealed to the person's conscience. Second, churches should be reserved exclusively for those already converted. Churches, Williams declared, must separate "holy from unholy, penitent from impenitent, [and] godly from ungodly." He characterized requiring godly and ungodly to attend church as "False Worshipping" that would create "spiritual drunkenness and whoredom, a soul sleep and a soul sickness." Third, the government—any government—had no business ruling on spiritual matters. Williams termed New England's regulation of religious behavior and belief "spiritual rape" that inevitably would lead governments to use coercion and even violence to enforce the government's misguided way, not God's true way. Finally and most fundamentally, Williams believed that governments

should tolerate all religious beliefs, whether Christian or not. He argued that because only God knows the truth, all people of all religions have to struggle to decipher God's inscrutable will; no person and no religion can understand God with absolute certainty. "I commend that man," Williams wrote, "whether Jew, or Turk, or Papist, or whoever, that steers no otherwise than his conscience dares." In Williams's view, toleration of religious belief and liberty of conscience were the only paths to religious purity and political harmony.

New England's leaders denounced Williams's arguments. One minister wrote that Williams sought "liberty to enfranchise all false Religions," which was "the greatest impiety in the World." Genuine **liberty**, he said, was "to contend earnestly for the Truth; to preserve unity of Spirit, Faith, ordinances, to be all like minded, of one accord." Like-minded New Englanders banished Williams for his "extreme and dangerous" opinions. He escaped from an attempt to ship him back to England and in January 1636, "exposed to the mercy of an howling Wilderness in Frost and Snow," spent fourteen weeks walking south to Narragansett Bay. There he founded the colony of Rhode Island, which enshrined "Liberty of Conscience" as a fundamental ideal and became a refuge for other dissenters from Puritan like-mindedness.

Although New England's leaders expelled Williams from their holy commonwealth, his dissenting ideas arose from orthodox Puritan doctrines. By urging believers to search for evidence of God's grace, **Puritanism** encouraged the faithful to listen for God's whisper of truth and faith. Puritanism combined rigid insistence on conformity to God's law and aching uncertainty about how to identify and act upon it. Despite the best efforts of New England's leaders to render God's instructions in no uncertain terms, Puritanism inspired believers like Roger Williams to draw their own conclusions and stick to them.

During the seventeenth century, New England's Puritan zeal—exemplified by Roger Williams and his persecutors—cooled. The goal of founding a holy New England faded. Late in the century, new "middle" colonies—New York, New Jersey, and Pennsylvania—featuring greater religious and ethnic diversity than New England were founded. Religion remained important throughout all the colonies, but it competed with a growing faith that the promise of a better life required less of the Puritans' intense focus on salvation and more attention to the mundane affairs of family, work, and trade.

As settler populations increased throughout the British mainland colonies—northern and southern—settlements encroached on Indian lands, causing violent conflict to flare up repeatedly. Political conflict also arose among colonists, particularly in response to major political upheavals in England. By the end of the seventeenth century, the English monarchy exerted greater control over its far-flung North American empire. The lifeblood of the empire remained, however, the continual flow of products, people, and ideas that pulsed between England and the colonies, energizing both.

Puritan Origins: The English Reformation

The religious roots of the Puritans who founded New England reached back to the Protestant Reformation, which arose in Germany in 1517 (see chapter 3). The **Reformation** spread quickly to other countries, but the English church initially remained within the Catholic fold and continued its allegiance to the pope in Rome. King Henry VIII, who reigned from 1509 to 1547, understood that the Reformation offered him an opportunity to break with Rome and take control of the church in England. In 1534, Henry formally initiated the English Reformation. At his insistence, Parliament passed the Act of Supremacy, which outlawed the Catholic Church and proclaimed the king "the only supreme head on earth of the Church of England." Henry seized the vast properties of the Catholic Church in England as well as the privilege of appointing bishops and other members of the church hierarchy.

In the short run, the English Reformation allowed Henry VIII to achieve his political goal of controlling the church. In the long run, however, the Reformation brought to England the political and religious turmoil that Henry had hoped to avoid. Henry himself sought no more than a halfway Reformation. Protestant doctrines held no attraction for Henry; in almost all matters of religious belief and practice he remained an orthodox Catholic. Many English Catholics wanted to revoke the English Reformation; they

English Monarchy and the Protestant Reformation

1509–1547	Henry VIII	Leads the English Reformation, outlawing the Catholic Church in England and establishing the English monarch as supreme head of the Church of England.
1547–1553	Edward VI	Moves religious reform in a Protestant direction.
1553–1558	Mary I	Outlaws Protestantism and strives to reestablish the Catholic Church in England.
1558–1603	Elizabeth I	Reaffirms the English Reformation and tries to position the Church of England between extremes of Catholicism and Protestantism.
1603–1625	James I	Authorizes a new, Protestant, translation of the Bible, but is unsympathetic to Puritan reformers.
1625–1649	Charles I	Continues James I's move away from the ideas of Puritan reformers. Puritan-dominated Parliament orders his beheading during the Puritan Revolution.
1642		Puritan Revolution (English Civil War) begins.
1644–1660	Oliver Cromwell	Leads Puritan side to victory in the English Civil War. Parliament proclaims England a Puritan republic (1649) and declares Cromwell the nation's "Lord Protector" (1653).
1660–1685	Charles II	Is restored to the monarchy by Parliament and attempts to enforce religious toleration of Catholics and Protestant dissenters from Church of England.
1685–1688	James II	Mounts aggressive campaign to appoint Catholics to government posts, then flees to France when English Protestants in Parliament offer the throne to his Dutch son-in-law, William. The peaceful accession of William and his wife (the daughter of James II) as corulers is called a "Glorious Revolution" (1688).
1689–1694	William III and Mary II	Reassert Protestant influence in England and its empire.

> Many English Catholics wanted to revoke the English Reformation. But many other English people insisted on a genuine, thoroughgoing Reformation; these people came to be called Puritans.

hoped to return the Church of England to the pope and to restore Catholic doctrines and ceremonies. But many other English people insisted on a genuine, thoroughgoing Reformation; these people came to be called Puritans.

During the sixteenth century, Puritanism was less an organized movement than a set of ideas and religious principles that appealed strongly to many dissenting members of the Church of England. They sought to purify the Church of England by eliminating what they considered the offensive features of Catholicism. For example, they demanded that the church hierarchy be abolished and that ordinary Christians be given greater control over religious life. They wanted to do away with the rituals of Catholic worship and instead emphasize an individual's relationship with God developed through Bible study, prayer, and introspection. Although there were many varieties and degrees of Puritanism, all Puritans shared a desire to make the English church thoroughly Protestant.

The fate of **Protestantism** waxed and waned under the monarchs who succeeded Henry VIII. When he died in 1547, the advisers of the new king, Edward VI—the nine-year-old son of Henry and his third wife, Jane Seymour—initiated religious reforms that moved in a Protestant direction. The tide of reform reversed in 1553 when Edward died and was succeeded by Mary I, the daughter of Henry and Catherine of Aragon, his first wife. Mary was a steadfast Catholic, and shortly after becoming queen, she married Philip II of Spain, Europe's most powerful guardian of Catholicism. Mary attempted to restore the pre-Reformation Catholic Church. She outlawed Protestantism in England and persecuted those who refused to conform, sentencing almost three hundred to burn at the stake.

The tide turned again in 1558 when Mary died and was succeeded by Elizabeth I, the daughter of Henry and his second wife, Anne Boleyn. During her long reign, Elizabeth reaffirmed the English Reformation and tried to position the English church between the extremes of Catholicism and Puritanism. Like her father, she asserted her control over the Church of England. Elizabeth was less concerned with theology than with politics. Above all, she desired a church that would strengthen the monarchy and the nation. By the time Elizabeth died in 1603, many people in England looked on Protestantism as a defining feature of national identity.

When her successor, James I, came to the throne, English Puritans petitioned for further reform of the Church of England. The king authorized a new translation of the Bible, known ever since as the King James version. However, neither James I nor his son Charles I, who became king in 1625, was receptive to the ideas of Puritan reformers. James and Charles moved the Church of England away from Puritanism. They enforced conformity to the Church of England and punished dissenters, both ordinary Christians and ministers. In 1629, Charles I dissolved Parliament—where Puritans were well represented—and initiated aggressive anti-Puritan policies. Many Puritans despaired about continuing to defend their faith in England and began to make plans to emigrate. Some left for Europe, others for the West Indies. The largest number set out for America.

Persecution of English Protestants

This sixteenth-century drawing shows Protestant prisoners being marched to London to be tried for heresy during the reign of Queen Mary I, a staunch Catholic. The artist emphasizes the severity of the Catholic persecutors by depicting the use of four well-armed guards, two on horseback, to escort some fifteen prisoners, including at least five women who are roped together but not because they appear menacing or likely to run away. The guards seem to be necessary less to maintain order among the prisoners than to discourage sympathetic citizens from rushing forward and freeing the prisoners. The artist seems to assume that most citizens opposed the queen's persecution of Protestants. The Bible verse from the book of Matthew underscores the Protestants' fealty to Christ rather than to mere "Princes and rulers" like Queen Mary.

Folger Shakespeare Library.

You shall be led before Princes and rulers for my names sake. *Math.* 10.

Puritans and the Settlement of New England

Puritans who emigrated aspired to escape the turmoil and persecution of England and to build a new, orderly, Puritan version of England. Their faith shaped the colonies they established in almost every way. Although many New England colonists were not Puritans, Puritanism remained a paramount influence in New England's religion, politics, and community life during the seventeenth century.

The Pilgrims and Plymouth Colony

One of the first Protestant groups to emigrate, later known as Pilgrims, espoused a heresy known as separatism: These Separatists sought to withdraw—separate—from the Church of England, which they considered hopelessly corrupt. In 1608, they moved to Holland; by 1620, they realized that they could not live and worship there as they had hoped. William Bradford, a leading member of the group, recalled that "many of their children, by . . . the great licentiousness of youth in [Holland], and the manifold temptations of the place, were drawn away by evil examples." Believing that America was a place where they might protect their children's piety and preserve their community, the Separatists obtained permission to settle in the extensive lands granted to the Virginia Company (see chapter 3). To finance their journey, they formed a joint stock company with London investors. The investors provided the capital; the Separatists, their labor, lives, and a share in all profits for seven years. In August 1620, following months of delay in Holland and England, 102 settlers, mostly families, finally boarded the *Mayflower*. After eleven weeks at sea, all but one of them arrived at the outermost tip of Cape Cod, in present-day Massachusetts.

The Pilgrims realized immediately that they had landed far north of the Virginia grant and had no legal authority from the king to settle in the area. To provide order and security as well as a claim to legitimacy, they drew up the Mayflower Compact on the day they arrived. In signing the document, they agreed to "covenant and combine ourselves together into a civil Body Politick, for our better Ordering and Preservation"; the signers (all men) agreed to enact and obey necessary and just laws.

The Pilgrims settled at Plymouth and elected William Bradford their governor. That first winter "was most sad and lamentable," Bradford wrote later. "In two or three months' time half of [our] company died . . . being the depth of winter, and wanting houses and other comforts [and] being infected with scurvy and other diseases."

In the spring, Indians rescued the floundering Plymouth settlement. First Samoset, then Squanto—both of whom had learned English from previous contacts with sailors and fishermen—befriended the settlers. Samoset arranged for the Pilgrims to meet and establish good relations with Massasoit, the chief of the Wampanoags, whose territory included Plymouth. Squanto, Bradford recalled, "was a special instrument sent of God for their [the Pilgrims'] good. . . . He directed them how to set their corn, where to take fish, and to procure other commodities, and was also their pilot to bring them to unknown places." With Squanto's help and their own hard labor, the Pilgrims managed to store enough food to guarantee their survival through the coming winter, an occasion they celebrated in the fall of 1621 with a feast of thanksgiving attended by Massasoit and many of his warriors.

Still, the colony struggled to survive. Only seven dwellings were erected that first year; half the original colonists died; and a new group of thirty-six threadbare, sickly settlers arrived in November 1621, requiring the colony to adopt stringent food rationing. The colonists quarreled with their London investors, who became frustrated when the colony failed to produce the expected profits.

Although the colony's status remained precarious, the Pilgrims lived quietly and simply, coexisting in relative peace with the Indians. They paid Massasoit when settlers gradually encroached on Wampanoag lands. By 1630, Plymouth had become a permanent settlement, but it failed to attract many other English Puritans. (See "American Places," page 109.)

The Founding of Massachusetts Bay Colony

In 1629, shortly before Charles I dissolved Parliament, a group of Puritan merchants and country gentlemen obtained a royal charter for the Massachusetts Bay Company. The charter provided the usual privileges granted to joint stock companies. It granted land for **colonization** in an area spanning present-day Massachusetts, New Hampshire, Vermont, Maine, and upstate New York. In addition, the charter contained a unique provision: The government of the Massachusetts Bay Company could be located in the colony rather than in England. Thus, with royal permission, Puritans could exchange their position as a harassed minority in England for self-government in Massachusetts.

To lead the emigrants, the stockholders of the Massachusetts Bay Company elected John Winthrop, a prosperous lawyer and landowner, to serve as governor. In March 1630, eleven ships crammed with seven hundred passengers sailed for Massachusetts; six more ships and another five hundred emigrants followed a few months later. Winthrop's fleet arrived in Massachusetts Bay in early June. Unlike the Separatists, Winthrop's Puritans aspired to reform the corrupt Church of England (rather than separate from it) by setting an example of godliness in the New World. Winthrop and a small group chose to settle on the peninsula that became Boston, and other settlers clustered at promising locations nearby (Map 4.1).

In a sermon to his companions aboard the *Arbella* while they were still at sea—probably the most famous sermon in American history— Winthrop explained the cosmic significance of their journey. The Puritans had "entered into a covenant" with God to "work out our salvation under the power and purity of his holy ordinances," Winthrop proclaimed. This sanctified agreement with God meant that "the Lord will [not] bear with such failings at our hands as he doth from those among whom we have lived" in England. The Puritans had to make "extraordinary" efforts to "bring into familiar and constant practice" religious principles that most people in England merely preached. The Puritans had to subordinate their individual interests to the common good. "We must be knit together in this work as one man," Winthrop declared. "We must delight in each other, make others' conditions our own, rejoice together, mourn together, labor and suffer together, always having before our eyes . . . our community as members of the same body." The stakes could not be higher, Winthrop told his listeners: "We must consider that we shall be as a city upon a hill. The eyes of all people are upon us."

That belief shaped seventeenth-century New England as profoundly as tobacco shaped the Chesapeake. Winthrop's vision of a city on a hill fired the Puritans' fierce determination to keep their covenant and live according to God's laws, unlike the backsliders and compromisers who accommodated to the Church of England. Their determination to adhere strictly to God's plan charged nearly every feature of life in seventeenth-century New England with a distinctive, high-voltage piety.

> The vision of a city on a hill fired the Puritans' fierce determination to keep their covenant and live according to God's laws.

Seal of Massachusetts Bay Colony

In 1629, the Massachusetts Bay Company designed this seal depicting an Indian man inviting English settlers to "Come Over And Help Us." Of course, such an invitation was never issued. The seal was an attempt to lend an aura of altruism to the Massachusetts Bay Company's colonization efforts. In English eyes, the Indian man obviously needed help. The only signs that he was more civilized than the pine trees flanking him were his girdle of leaves, his bow and arrow, and his miraculous use of English. In reality, colonists in Massachusetts and elsewhere were far less interested in helping Indians than in helping themselves. For the most part, that suited the Indians, who wanted no "help" from the colonists. Courtesy of Massachusetts Archives.

FOR MORE HELP ANALYZING THIS IMAGE, see the visual activity for this chapter in the Online Study Guide at bedfordstmartins.com/roark.

AMERICAN PLACES

Plimoth Plantation, Plymouth, Massachusetts

Plymouth Fort and Meetinghouse
Courtesy of Plimoth Plantation, Inc., Plymouth, MA.

Wᴵᴸᴸᴵᴬᴹ Bradford, the governor of Plymouth colony, expressed the aspirations of the Plymouth settlers and many other seventeenth-century New Englanders when he wrote, "As one small candle may light a thousand, so the light here kindled hath shone unto many, yea in some sort to our whole nation." A recent authoritative poll by the Pew Forum on Religion in Public Life found evidence that Bradford's small candle, among other sources, succeeded in kindling religious illumination among Americans. The March 2002 poll reported that two-thirds of all Americans believe that the United States is a Christian nation; nearly 60 percent believe that the strength of America

derives from the religious faith of its people, and despite the Islamist terrorist attacks of September 11, 2001, almost half believe that the United States has enjoyed special protection from God for most of its history.

While most Americans today—like Bradford and other colonists at Plymouth and elsewhere in New England—affirm the significance of religious faith, few people today would find the Plymouth colonists' routines of daily life familiar or particularly desirable. When Bradford strolled through the woods shortly after arriving at Plymouth, he noticed a sapling bent over some acorns scattered on the ground. When he went over to look at the bent sapling, "it gave a sudden jerk

up, and he was immediately caught by the leg" in a deer trap, one of his companions wrote. Visitors who walk through Plimoth Plantation today do not risk getting snared by a deer trap, but they can experience the flavor of daily life in Plymouth and elsewhere in seventeenth-century New England.

Reproductions of seventeenth-century buildings, based on scrupulous archaeological excavations and historical research, permit visitors to stroll through a colonial village populated by well-informed interpreters who go about daily chores that would be familiar to Bradford and his fellow colonists. Plimoth Plantation includes a careful reproduction of the *Mayflower*, a Wampanoag house, and many other features of Native American and colonial activity. Visitors can watch interpreters act as if they were seventeenth-century colonists cultivating gardens, harvesting crops, cooking meals, sewing clothes, chopping wood, and going about the colonists' myriad other tasks. The arduous work demonstrates that the colonists had much more than religion on their minds. Visitors are encouraged to question the interpreters, who are trained to answer as if they were voicing the thoughts of the original colonists. In the bustle of all this unfamiliar activity, however, it is easy for a visitor to lose sight of the light of faith kindled by the small candle so important to Bradford and other New Englanders.

Fᴏʀ Wᴇʙ ʟɪɴᴋs ʀᴇʟᴀᴛᴇᴅ ᴛᴏ ᴛʜɪs sɪᴛᴇ ᴀɴᴅ ᴏᴛʜᴇʀ Aᴍᴇʀɪᴄᴀɴ Pʟᴀᴄᴇs, see "PlaceLinks" at bedfordstmartins.com/roark.

The new colonists, as Winthrop's son John wrote later, had "all things to do, as in the beginning of the world." Unlike the early Chesapeake settlers, the first Massachusetts Bay colonists encountered few Indians because the local population had been almost entirely exterminated by an epidemic more than a decade earlier. Still, as in the Chesapeake, the colonists fell victim to

MAP 4.1   New England Colonies in the Seventeenth Century

New Englanders spread across the landscape town by town during the seventeenth century. (For the sake of legibility, only a few of the more important towns are shown on the map.)

READING THE MAP: Using the notations on the map, create a chronology of the establishment of towns in New England. What physical features correspond to the earliest habitation by English settlers?

CONNECTIONS: Why were towns so much more a feature of seventeenth-century New England than of the Chesapeake (see also chapter 3)? How did Puritan dissent influence the settlement of New England colonies?

FOR MORE HELP ANALYZING THIS MAP, see the map activity for this chapter in the Online Study Guide at bedfordstmartins.com/roark.

deadly ailments. More than 200 settlers died during the first year, including one of Winthrop's sons and eleven of his servants. About the same number decided by the spring of 1631 that having "all things to do, as in the beginning of the world," was more than they had bargained for, and they returned to England on the first outbound ship. But Winthrop maintained a confidence that proved infectious. "I like so well to be heer," he wrote his wife, "as I do not repent my comminge. . . . I would not have altered my course, though I had forseene all these Afflictions." And each year from 1630 to 1640, ship after ship followed in the wake of Winthrop's fleet. In all, more than 20,000 new settlers came, their eyes fixed on the Puritans' city on a hill.

Often, when the Church of England cracked down on a Puritan minister in England, he and many of his followers uprooted and moved together to New England. By 1640, New England had one of the highest ratios of preachers to population in all of Christendom. But the ratio was still not high enough to provide a trained minister for every band of settlers who hungered for religious instruction; one colonist complained that ordinary "fellowes which keepe hogges all weeke preach on the Saboth." A few ministers sought to carry the message of Christianity to Indians, accompanied by instructions about proper civilized (that is, English) behavior to re-

place what missionary John Eliot termed Indians' "unfixed, confused, and ungoverned . . . life, uncivilized and unsubdued to labor and order." (See "Documenting the American Promise," page 116.) For the most part, however, the colonists focused on saving Indians' souls less than on saving their own.

The occupations of New England immigrants reflected the social origins of English Puritans. On the whole, the immigrants came from the middle ranks of English society. Few representatives of the nobility or the landed gentry came to Massachusetts; Winthrop was an exception. The vast majority of immigrants were either farmers or tradesmen, including carpenters, tailors, and textile workers. Servants, whose numbers dominated the Chesapeake settlers, accounted for only about a fifth of those headed for New England. Most New England immigrants paid their way to Massachusetts, even though the journey often took their life savings. To such people, reports like the one Winthrop sent his son must have been encouraging: "Here is as good land as I have seen there [in England]. . . . Here can be no want of anything to those who bring means to raise out of the earth and sea."

In contrast to the Chesapeake, where immigrant women and children were nearly as rare as atheists in Boston, New England immigrants usually arrived as families. In fact, more Puritans came with family members than did any other group of immigrants in all of American history. A ship that left Weymouth, England, in 1635 carried 106 passengers, 98 of whom belonged to one of the 14 families aboard—typically a husband, wife, and children, sometimes accompanied by a servant or two. In this group, women and children made up a solid majority.

As Winthrop reminded the first settlers in his *Arbella* sermon, each family was a "little commonwealth" that mirrored the hierarchy among all God's creatures. Just as humankind was sub-

ordinate to God, so young people were subordinate to their elders, children to their parents, and wives to their husbands. The immigrants' family ties reinforced their religious beliefs with universally understood notions of hierarchy and mutual dependence. While immigrants to the Chesapeake were disciplined mostly by the coercions of servitude and the caprices of the tobacco market, immigrants to New England entered a social order defined by the interlocking institutions of family, church, and community.

New England Great Chair
This thronelike chair belonged to Michael Metcalf, a teacher in seventeenth-century Dedham, Massachusetts. The oldest known piece of New England furniture inscribed with a date, 1652, the chair was made in Dedham specifically for Metcalf (notice the initials flanking the date), who turned sixty-six in that year. Metcalf stored books, presumably including a Bible, in the enclosed compartment under the seat. No overstuffed recliner, the chair is suited less for a relaxing snooze than for alert concentration. The panels under the arms served to block chilly drafts. Otherwise, the chair shows few concessions to comfort or ease. The carved chair back—rigidly upright—displays motifs often found on Puritan tombstones. The grand austerity of the chair hints at the importance of serious Bible study and unflinching introspection in Puritan New England.
Dedham Historical Society / photo by Forrest Frazier.

European Throne Chair
In contrast to the New England great chair, this late-sixteenth-century European throne chair is embellished on every surface with elaborate carvings proclaiming the worldly magnificence of the chair's owner. This chair illustrates the ostentatious display of luxury and refinement that disgusted Puritans considered signs of the vanity and false pride that distracted people from seeking and following God's Truth.
Courtesy of Huntington Antiques Ltd., Gloucestershire, England.

The Evolution of New England Society

The New England colonists, unlike their counterparts in the Chesapeake, settled in small towns, usually located on the coast or by a river (see Map 4.1). Massachusetts Bay colonists founded 133 towns during the seventeenth century, each with one or more churches. Church members' fervent piety, buttressed by the institutions of local government, enforced remarkable religious and social conformity in the small New England settlements. During the century, tensions within the Puritan faith and changes in New England communities splintered religious orthodoxy and weakened Puritan zeal. By 1700, however, Puritanism still maintained a distinctive influence in New England.

Church, Covenant, and Conformity

Puritans believed that the church consisted of men and women who had entered a solemn covenant with one another and with God. Winthrop and three other men signed the original covenant of the first Boston church in 1630, agreeing to "Promisse, and bind our selves, to walke in all our wayes according to the Rule of the Gospell, and in all sincere Conformity to His holy Ordinaunces, and in mutuall love, and respect to each other, so neere as God shall give us grace." Each new member of the covenant had to persuade existing members that she or he had fully experienced conversion. Fervent Puritans among the early colonists, whose faith had been tempered by persecution in England and by the journey to Massachusetts, had little difficulty meeting the test of covenant membership. By 1635, the Boston church had added more than 250 names to the four original subscribers to the covenant.

Puritan views on religion and church membership derived from **Calvinism**, the doctrines of John Calvin, a sixteenth-century Swiss Protestant theologian who insisted that Christians strictly discipline their behavior to conform to certain religious ideas. As followers of Calvin's ideas, the Puritans believed in **predestination**—the idea that all-powerful God, before the creation of the world, decided which few human souls would receive eternal life, and that nothing a person did in his or her lifetime could alter God's inscrutable choice. According to Calvinist doctrine, only God knows the identity of these fortunate, predestined individuals—the "elect" or "saints." And no person can know for certain whether she or he is predestined for salvation in heaven with the elected few or for damnation in hell with the doomed multitude.

Despite this looming uncertainty, Puritans believed that if a person lived a rigorously godly life—constantly winning the daily battle against sinful temptations—his or her behavior was likely to be a hint, a visible sign, that he or she was one of the elect. Puritans thought that "sainthood" would become visible in individuals' behavior, especially if they were privileged to know God's Word as revealed in the Bible.

The connection between sainthood and saintly behavior, however, was far from certain. Some members of the elect, Puritans believed, had not heard God's word as revealed in the Bible, and therefore their behavior did not necessarily signal their sainthood. One reason Puritans required all town residents to attend church services was to enlighten anyone who was ignorant of God's Truth. The slippery relationship between saintly behavior—observable by anybody—and God's predestined election—invisible and unknowable to anyone—caused Puritans to worry constantly that individuals who acted like saints were fooling themselves and others. Nevertheless, Puritans thought that "visible saints"—persons who passed their demanding tests of conversion and church membership—probably, though not certainly, were among God's elect.

Members of Puritan churches ardently hoped that God had chosen them to receive eternal life and tried to demonstrate saintly behavior. Their covenant bound them to help each other attain salvation and to discipline the entire community by saintly standards. Church members kept an eye on the behavior of everybody in town. Infractions of morality, order, or propriety were reported to Puritan elders, who summoned the wayward to a church inquiry. The watchfulness that set the tone of life in Puritan communities is suggested by one minister's note that "the church was satisfied with Mrs. Carlton as to the weight of her butter." By overseeing every aspect of life, including Mrs. Carlton's butter, the visible saints enforced a remarkable degree of righteous conformity in Puritan communities. Total conformity, however, was never achieved, and Puritan doctrine even spelled out the fiery punishment for failure to conform: A servant in Roxbury declared that "if hell were ten times

THE
World turn'd upside down:
OR,
A briefe defcription of the ridiculous Fafhions
of thefe diftracted Times.

By T.J. a well-willer to King, Parliament and Kingdom.

London : Printed for John Smith. 1647.

The Puritan Challenge to the Status Quo

This title page of "The World Turn'd Upside Down" satirizes the Puritan notion that the contemporary world was deeply flawed. Printed in London in 1647, the pamphlet refers to the "distracted Times" of the Puritan Revolution in England. The drawing ridicules criticisms of English society that were also common among New England Puritans. The drawing shows at least a dozen examples of the conventional world of seventeenth-century England turned upside down. Can you identify them? Puritans, of course, would claim that the artist had it wrong—that the conventional world turned God's order upside down. How might the drawing have been different if a devout Puritan had drawn it?

By permission of The British Library.

hotter, [I] had rather be there than [I] would serve [my] master."

Despite the central importance of religion, churches played no direct role in the civil government of New England communities. Puritans did not want to emulate the Church of England, which they considered a puppet of the king rather than an independent body that served the Lord. They were determined to insulate New England churches from the contaminating influence of the civil state and its merely human laws. Although ministers were the most highly respected figures in New England towns, they were prohibited from holding government office.

Puritans had no qualms, however, about their religious beliefs influencing New England governments. As much as possible, the Puritans tried to bring public life into conformity with their view of God's law. Most Puritans agreed that the Sabbath began at sunset on Saturday evening, and enforcement of proper Sabbath behavior was taken seriously. On the Sabbath, townsfolk could not work, play, or travel. Fines were issued for Sabbath-breaking activities such as playing a flute, smoking a pipe, and visiting neighbors.

Puritans mandated other purifications of what they considered corrupt English practices. They refused to celebrate Christmas or Easter because the Bible did not mention either one. They outlawed religious wedding ceremonies; couples were married by a magistrate in a civil ceremony (the first wedding in Massachusetts to be performed by a minister did not occur until 1686). Puritans prohibited elaborate, colorful clothing, censuring finery such as lace trim and frowning on short sleeves—"whereby the nakedness of the arm may be discovered." Cards, dice, shuffleboard, and other games of chance were banned, as were music and dancing. The distinguished minister Increase Mather insisted that "Mixt or Promiscuous Dancing . . . of Men and Women" could not be tolerated since "the unchaste Touches and Gesticulations used by Dancers have a palpable tendency to that which is evil." On special occasions, Puritans proclaimed days of fasting and humiliation, which, as one preacher boasted, amounted to "so many Sabbaths more."

> As much as possible, the Puritans tried to bring public life into conformity with their view of God's law.

Government by Puritans for Puritanism

It is only a slight exaggeration to say that seventeenth-century New England was governed by Puritans for Puritanism. The charter of the Massachusetts Bay Company empowered the company's stockholders, or freemen, to meet as a body known as the General Court and make the laws needed to govern the company's affairs. The colonists transformed this arrangement for running a joint stock company into a structure for governing the colony. Hoping to ensure that godly men would decide government policies,

Sabbath Breakers

These seventeenth-century prints show some of the punishments to which Sabbath breakers could be subjected by man and God. In the upper illustration, a person who gathered sticks on the Sabbath is stoned to death as Puritans believed the Bible commanded. In the lower print, three women who broke the Sabbath by preparing flax to be spun and woven into linen suffer God's retribution when they are burned to death. New Englanders differed about exactly when the Sabbath began. Some thought it started at sunset on Saturday evening, but John Winthrop believed the Sabbath began about three o'clock Saturday afternoon. Given the extreme punishments inflicted on Sabbath breakers, New Englanders needed to be careful about what they did between Saturday afternoon and Monday morning.

Divine Examples of God's Severe Judgements upon Sabbath-Breakers (London, 1671).

the General Court ruled in 1631 that freemen had to be male church members. Only freemen had the right to vote for governor, deputy governor, and other colonial officials. As new settlers were recognized as freemen, the size of the General Court grew until it became too large to meet conveniently. So in 1634, the freemen in each town agreed to send two deputies to the General Court to act as the colony's legislative assembly. All other men were classified as "inhabitants," and they had the right to vote, hold office, and participate fully in town government.

A "town meeting," composed of a town's inhabitants and freemen, chose the selectmen and other officials who administered local affairs. New England town meetings routinely practiced a level of popular participation in political life that was unprecedented elsewhere during the seventeenth century. Almost every adult man could speak out in town meetings and fortify his voice with a vote. However, all women—even church members—were prohibited from voting, and towns did not permit "contrary-minded" men to become or remain inhabitants. Although town meeting participants wrangled from time to time, widespread political participation tended to reinforce conformity to Puritan ideals.

One of the most important functions of New England government was land distribution. Settlers who desired to establish a new town entered a covenant and petitioned the General Court for a grant of land. The court granted town sites to suitably pious petitioners but did not allow settlement until the Indians who inhabited a grant agreed to relinquish their claim to the land, usually in exchange for manufactured goods. For instance, William Pynchon purchased the site of Springfield, Massachusetts, from the Agawam Indians for "eighteen fathams [arms' lengths] of Wampam, eighteen coates, 18 hatchets, 18 hoes, [and] 18 knives."

Having obtained their grant, town founders apportioned land among themselves and any newcomers they permitted to join them. Normally, each family received a house lot large enough for an adjacent garden as well as one or more strips of agricultural land on the perimeter of the town. Although there was a considerable difference between the largest and smallest family plots, most clustered in the middle range—roughly fifty to one hundred acres—resulting in a more nearly equal distribution of land in New England than in the Chesapeake. Towns reserved some common land, which all inhabitants could use for grazing livestock and cutting wood, and

Joseph Capen House

This substantial house was built in 1683 for Joseph Capen, a Harvard graduate who had recently arrived in Topsfield, Massachusetts, to serve as the local minister. The town granted Capen twelve acres for a homesite, and he probably paid for the house with the dowry of his new wife, Priscilla Appleton, the daughter of a wealthy colonist in nearby Ipswich, Massachusetts. The plain but imposing house suggests the sturdy ties between preachers and their congregations and, more generally, between families, faith, and communities. Capen lived in the house and preached to the Topsfield church for more than forty years until his death in 1725. Now, more than three centuries after Capen built the house, it still stands, a monument to New England colonists' convictions that they were building a society to endure for the ages.

Picture Research Consultants & Archives.

saved the rest for new settlers and the descendants of the founders.

The physical layout of New England towns encouraged settlers to look inward toward their neighbors, multiplying the opportunities for godly vigilance. Most people considered the forest that lay just beyond every settler's house an alien environment that was interrupted here and there by those oases of civilization, the towns. Footpaths connecting one town to another were so rudimentary that even John Winthrop once got lost within half a mile of his house and spent a sleepless night in the forest, circling the light of his small campfire and singing psalms.

The Splintering of Puritanism

Almost from the beginning, John Winthrop and other leaders had difficulty enforcing their views of Puritan orthodoxy. In England, persecution as a dissenting minority had unified Puritan voices in opposition to the Church of England. In New England, the promise of a godly society and the Puritans' emphasis on individual Bible study led New Englanders toward different visions of godliness. Puritan leaders, however, interpreted dissent as an error caused either by a misguided believer or by the malevolent power of Satan. Whatever the cause, errors could not be tolerated. As one Puritan minister proclaimed, "God doth no where in his word tolerate Christian States, to give Tolerations to . . . adversaries of his Truth, if they have power in their hands to suppress them. The Scripture saith . . . there is no Truth but one."

Shortly after banishing Roger Williams, Winthrop confronted another dissenter, this time—as one New Englander observed—a "Woman that Preaches better Gospell then any of your black-coates that have been at the Ninneversity." The woman was Anne Hutchinson, a devout Puritan steeped in Scripture and absorbed by religious questions. Hutchinson had received an excellent education from her father in England. The mother of fourteen children, she served her neighbors as a skilled midwife. After she settled into her new

> Almost from the beginning, John Winthrop and other leaders had difficulty enforcing their views of Puritan orthodoxy.

King Philip Considers Christianity

Beginning in 1646, the Puritan minister John Eliot served as a missionary to New England's Indians, trying to teach the doctrines of Christianity and proper English behavior. During his half-century tenure as leader of the Puritan congregation in Roxbury, Massachusetts, Eliot studied the languages, customs, and beliefs of Native Americans, hoping to help them along the path to Christian piety and to strengthen them against colonists' unscrupulous encroachment on their lands. The efforts of Eliot and other missionaries convinced some Indians to leave their own communities and settle in "praying towns" populated by Native Americans who had agreed to live in conformity with English ways. Most Indians, however, did not move into praying towns or adopt the faith or manners of the colonists.

In Indian Dialogues, *a book published in 1671, Eliot illustrated the challenge he and other missionaries confronted as they tried to convince Native Americans of the errors of their ways. Based on his decades of missionary experience, Eliot created imaginary conversations between converted Indians and those who resisted Christianity. Eliot's invented conversations echoed arguments he and other missionaries had encountered repeatedly. The following selection from an imaginary dialogue between two praying Indians, Anthony and William, and King Philip (or*

Metacomet), the chief (or sachem) of the powerful Wampanoags, documents Eliot's perception of the attractions of Christianity and one Indian leader's doubts about it, doubts that ultimately prevailed when King Philip led the Wampanoags in an all-out attack against the settlers in 1675.

Anthony: Sachem, we salute you in the Lord, and we declare unto you, that we are sent by the church, in the name of our Lord Jesus Christ, to call you, and beseech you to turn from your vain conversation unto God, to pray unto God, and to believe in Jesus Christ for the pardon of your sins, and for the salvation of your soul. . . . So we are come this day unto you, in the name of Jesus Christ, to call you to come unto the Lord, and serve him. . . . We hear that many of your people do desire to pray to God, only they depend on you. We pray you to consider that your love to your people should oblige you to do them all the good you can. . . . You will not only yourself turn from sin unto God . . . , but all your people will turn to God with you, so that you may say unto the Lord, oh Lord Jesus, behold here am I, and all the people which thou hast given me. We all come unto thy service, and promise to pray unto God so long as we live. . . . Oh how happy will all your people be. . . . It

will be a joy to all the English magistrates, and ministers, and churches, and good people of the land, to hear that Philip and all his people are turned to God, and become praying Indians. . . .

Philip: Often have I heard of this great matter of praying unto God, and hitherto I have refused. . . . Mr. Eliot himself did come unto me. He was in this town, and did persuade me. But we were then in our sports, wherein I have much delighted, and in that temptation, I confess, I did neglect and despise the offer, and lost that opportunity. Since that time God hath afflicted and chastised me, and my heart doth begin to break. And I have some serious thoughts of accepting the offer, and turning to God, to become a praying Indian, I myself and all my people. But I have some great objections, which I cannot tell how to get over, which are still like great rocks in my way, over which I cannot climb. And if I should, I fear I shall fall down the precipice on the further side, and be spoiled and undone. By venturing to climb, I shall catch a deadly fall to me and my posterity.

The first objection that I have is this, because you praying Indians do reject your sachems, and refuse to pay them tribute, in so much that if any of my people turn to pray unto God, I do reckon that I have lost him. He will no longer own me for his sachem, nor pay me any tribute. And hence it will come to pass, that if I should pray to God, and all my people with me, I must become as a common man among them, and so

home in Boston in 1634, women gathered there to hear her weekly lectures on recent sermons, a proper female activity since, according to one minister, it "water[ed] the seeds publikely sowen." As the months passed, Hutchinson began to lecture twice a week, and crowds of sixty to eighty women and men gathered to listen to her.

Hutchinson expounded on the sermons of John Cotton, her favorite minister. Cotton stressed what he termed the "covenant of lose all my power and authority over them. This is such a temptation as . . . I, nor any of the other great sachems, can tell how to get over. Were this temptation removed, the way would be more easy and open for me to turn praying Indian. I begin to have some good likance of the way, but I am loth to buy it at so dear a rate.

William: . . . I say, if any of the praying Indians should be disobedient (in lawful things) and refuse to pay tribute unto their sachems, it is not their religion and praying to God that teaches them so to do, but their corruptions. . . . I am sure the word of God commandeth all to be subject to the higher powers, and pay them tribute. . . . And therefore, beloved sachem, let not your heart fear that praying to God will alienate your people from you . . . for the more beneficent you are unto them, the more obligation you lay upon them. And what greater beneficence can you do unto them than to further them in religion, whereby they may be converted, pardoned, sanctified, and saved? . . .

Philip: I have another objection stronger than this, and that is, if I pray to God, then all my men that are willing to pray to God will (as you say) stick to me, and be true to me. But all such as love not and care not to pray to God, especially such as hate praying to God, all these will forsake me, yea will go and adjoin themselves unto other sachems that pray not to God. And so it will come to pass, that if I be a praying sachem, I shall be a poor and weak one, and

easily trod upon by others, who are like to be more potent and numerous. And by this means my tribute will be small, and my people few, and I shall be a great loser by praying to God. In the way I am now, I am full and potent, but if I change my way and pray to God, I shall be empty and weak. . . .

William: . . . Suppose all your subjects that hate praying to God should leave you. What shall you lose by it? You are rid of such as by their sins vitiate others, and multiply transgression, and provoke the wrath of God against you and yours. But consider what you shall gain by praying to God. . . . All the praying Indians will rejoice at it, and be your friends, and they are not a few. . . . [And] you shall gain a more intimate love of the Governor, and Magistrates. . . . They will more honor, respect, and love you, than ever they did. . . . The Governor and Magistrates of the Massachusetts will own you, and be fatherly and friendly to you. . . . Yea more, the King of England, and the great peers who . . . yearly send over means to encourage and promote our praying to God, they will take notice of you.

Philip: I perceive that in your praying to God, and in your churches, all are brought to an equality. Sachems and people they are all fellow brethren in your churches. Poor and rich are equally privileged. The vote of the lowest of the people hath as much weight as the vote of the sachem. Now I doubt [worry] that this way will lift up the heart of the poor to

too much boldness, and debase the rulers to[o] low. This bringing all to an equality will bring all to a confusion. . . . [T]here is yet another thing that I am much afraid of, and that is your church admonitions and excommunications. I hear that your sachems are under that yoke. I am a sinful man as well as others, but if I must be admonished by the church, who are my subjects, I know not how I shall like that. I doubt [worry] it will be a bitter pill, too hard for me to get down and swallow. . . . I feel your words sink into my heart and stick there. You speak arrows. . . . I desire to ponder and consider of these things. . . . I am willing they should still lie soaking in my heart and mind.

SOURCE: John Eliot, *Indian Dialogues* (Cambridge, 1671) in Henry W. Bowden and James P. Ronda, eds., *John Eliot's Indian Dialogues: A Study in Cultural Interaction* (Westport, Conn.: Greenwood Press, 1980), 120–31.

QUESTIONS FOR ANALYSIS AND DEBATE

1. To what degree is Eliot's dialogue a reliable guide to Philip's doubts about the wisdom of becoming a praying Indian?
2. According to Eliot, was Philip's religion a stumbling block to his acceptance of Christianity? What made Philip fear that he would "fall down the precipice"?
3. If Philip had written a dialogue proposing that Eliot convert to the Wampanoag way of life, what arguments might he have made?

grace"—the idea that individuals could be saved only by God's grace in choosing them to be members of the elect. Cotton contrasted this familiar Puritan doctrine with the "covenant of works," the erroneous belief that a person's behavior—

one's works—could win God's favor and ultimately earn a person salvation. Belief in the covenant of works and in the possibility of salvation for all was known as Arminianism. Cotton's sermons strongly hinted that many Puritans, including ministers, embraced Arminianism, which claimed—falsely, Cotton declared—that human beings could influence God's will. Anne Hutchinson agreed with Cotton. Her lectures emphasized her opinion that many of the colony's leaders affirmed the Arminian covenant of works. Like Cotton, she preached that only God's covenant of grace led to salvation.

The meetings at Hutchinson's house alarmed her nearest neighbor, John Winthrop, who believed that she was subverting the good order of the colony. In 1637, Winthrop had formal charges brought against Hutchinson and confronted her in court as her chief accuser. He denounced Hutchinson's lectures as "not tolerable nor comely in the sight of God nor fitting for your sex." He told her, "You have stept out of your place, you have rather bine a Husband than a Wife and a preacher than a Hearer; and a Magistrate than a Subject."

As Winthrop and Hutchinson confronted each other in court, he proved no match for her learning, wit, and insight. Hutchinson pointed to passages in the Bible that instructed women to meet and teach one another. When Winthrop claimed that those scriptures did not apply to her, she asked him, "Must I shew my name written therein?" Besides, she said, if it was "not lawful for me to teach women . . . why do you call me to teach the court?" Outsmarted and off-balance, Winthrop pressed forward with the investigation, fishing for a heresy he could pin on Hutchinson.

Winthrop and other Puritan elders referred to Hutchinson and her followers as **antinomians**, people who oppose the law. Hutchinson's opponents charged that she believed that Christians could be saved by faith alone and did not need to act in accordance with God's law as set forth in the Bible and as interpreted by Winthrop and the colony's other leaders. Hutchinson nimbly defended herself against the accusation of antinomianism. Yes, she acknowledged, she believed that men and women were saved by faith alone; but no, she did not deny the need to obey God's law. "The Lord hath let me see which was the clear ministry and which the wrong," she said. Finally, her interrogators cornered her. How could she tell which ministry was which? "By an immediate revelation," she replied, "by the voice of [God's] own spirit to my soul." Winthrop spotted in this statement the heresy of prophecy, the view that God revealed his will directly to a believer instead of exclusively through the Bible, as every right-minded Puritan knew.

In 1638, the Boston church formally excommunicated Hutchinson. The minister decreed, "I doe cast you out and . . . deliver you up to Satan that you may learne no more to blaspheme to seduce and to lye. . . . I command you . . . as a Leper to withdraw your selfe out of the Congregation." Banished, Hutchinson and her family moved first to Roger Williams's Rhode Island and then to present-day New York, where she and most of her family were killed by Indians.

The strains within Puritanism exemplified by Anne Hutchinson and Roger Williams caused it to splinter repeatedly during the seventeenth century. Thomas Hooker, a prominent minister, clashed with Winthrop and other leaders over the composition of the church. Hooker argued that men and women who lived godly lives should be admitted to church membership even if they had not experienced conversion. This issue, like most others in New England, had both religious and political dimensions, for only church members could vote in Massachusetts. In 1636, Hooker led an exodus of more than 800 colonists from Massachusetts to the Connecticut River valley, where they founded Hartford and neighboring towns. In 1639, the towns adopted the Fundamental Orders of Connecticut, a quasi-constitution that could be altered by the vote of freemen, who did not have to be church members, though nearly all of them were.

Other Puritan churches divided and subdivided throughout the seventeenth century as acrimony developed over doctrine and church government. Sometimes churches split over the appointment of a controversial minister. Sometimes families who had a long walk to the meetinghouse simply decided to form their own church nearer their houses. These schisms arose from ambiguities and tensions within Puritan belief. As the colonies matured, other tensions developed as well.

Religious Controversies and Economic Changes

A revolutionary transformation in the fortunes of Puritans in England had profound consequences in New England. Disputes between King Charles I and Parliament, dominated by Puritans, escalated in 1642 to civil war in England, a conflict known as the Puritan Revolution. Parliamentary forces led by the staunch Puritan Oliver Cromwell were victorious, executing Charles I in 1649 and proclaiming England a Puritan republic. From 1649 to 1660, England's rulers—principally Oliver Cromwell—were not monarchs who suppressed Puritanism but believers who championed it. In a half century, English Puritans had risen from being a harassed group of religious dissenters to become a dominant power in English government.

When the Puritan Revolution began, the stream of immigrants to New England dwindled to a trickle, creating hard times for the colonists. They could no longer consider themselves a city on a hill setting a godly example for humankind. English society was being reformed by Puritans in England, not New England. Furthermore, when immigrant ships became rare, the colonists faced sky-high prices for scarce English goods and few customers for their own colonial products. As they searched to find new products and markets, they established the enduring patterns of New England's economy.

New England's rocky soil and short growing season ruled out cultivating the southern colonies' crops of tobacco and rice that found a ready market in Atlantic ports. Exports that New Englanders could not get from the soil they took instead from the forest and the sea. During the first decade of settlement, colonists traded with Indians for animal pelts, which were in demand in Europe. By the 1640s, fur-bearing animals had become scarce unless traders ventured far beyond the **frontiers** of English settlement. Trees from the seemingly limitless forests of New England proved a longer-lasting resource. Masts for ships and staves for barrels of Spanish wine and West Indian sugar were crafted from New England timber.

But the most important New England export was fish. During the religious and political turmoil of the 1640s, English ships withdrew from the rich North Atlantic fishing grounds, and New England fishermen quickly took their place. Dried, salted codfish found markets in southern Europe and the West Indies. The fish trade also stimulated colonial shipbuilding and trained generations of fishermen, sailors, and merchants, creating a commercial network that endured for more than a century. But the export economy remained peripheral to most New England colonists. Their lives revolved around their farms, their churches, and their families.

Although immigration came to a standstill in the 1640s, the population continued to boom, doubling every twenty years. In New England, almost everyone married and women often had eight or nine children. Long, cold winters prevented the warm-weather ailments of the south-

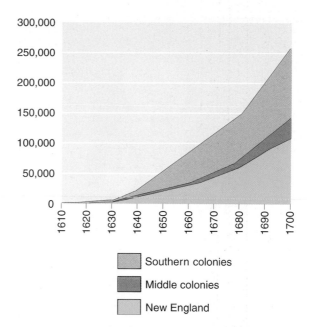

FIGURE 4.1 Population of the British North American Colonies in the Seventeenth Century
The colonial population grew at a steadily accelerating rate during the seventeenth century. New England and the southern colonies each comprised about half the total colonial population until after 1680, when growth in Pennsylvania and New York contributed to a surge in the population of the middle colonies.

ern colonies and reduced New England mortality. The descendants of the immigrants of the 1630s multiplied and remultiplied, boosting the New England population to roughly equal that of the southern colonies (Figure 4.1).

During the last half of the seventeenth century, under the pressures of steady population growth and integration into the Atlantic economy, the white-hot piety of the founders cooled. After 1640, the population grew faster than church membership. All residents attended sermons on pain of fines and punishment, but many could not find seats in the meetinghouses. Boston's two churches in 1650 could house only about a third of the city's population. By the 1680s, women were the majority of full church members throughout New England. In some towns, only 15 percent of the adult men were members. A growing fraction of New Englanders, especially men, embraced what one historian has termed "horse-shed Christianity": They attended sermons but loitered outside near the horse shed, gossiping about the weather, fishing, their crops, or the scandalous behavior of neighbors.

David, Joanna, and Abigail Mason

This 1670 painting depicts the children of Joanna and Anthony Mason, a wealthy Boston baker. The artist lavished attention on the children's elaborate clothing. Fashionable slashed sleeves, fancy laces, silver-studded shoes, six-year-old Joanna's and four-year-old Abigail's necklaces, and nine-year-old David's silver-headed cane suggest not only the Masons' wealth but also their desire to display and memorialize their possessions and adornments. The painting hints that the children themselves were adornments, young sprouts of the Mason lineage, which could afford such finery. The portrait is unified not by signs of warm affection, innocent smiles, or familial solidarity but by trappings of wealth and sober self-importance. The painting expresses the growing respect for wealth and its worldly rewards in seventeenth-century New England.

Fine Arts Museums of San Francisco. Gift of Mr. and Mrs. John D. Rockefeller III.

This slackening of piety led Puritan minister Michael Wigglesworth to ask, in verse,

> How is it that I find
>   In stead of holiness Carnality,
> In stead of heavenly frames an Earthly mind,
>   For burning zeal luke-warm Indifferency,
> For flaming love, key-cold Dead-heartedness,
>   For temperance (in meat, and drinke, and cloaths) excess?
> Whence cometh it, that Pride, and Luxurie
>   Debate, Deceit, Contention, and Strife,
> False-dealing, Covetousness, Hypocrisie
>   (With such Crimes) amongst them are so rife,
> That one of them doth over-reach another?
>   And that an honest man can hardly trust his Brother?

Most alarming to Puritan leaders, many of the children of the visible saints of Winthrop's gen-

eration failed to experience conversion and attain full church membership. Puritans tended to assume that sainthood was inherited—that the children of visible saints were probably also among the elect. Acting on this premise, churches permitted saints to baptize their infant sons and daughters, symbolically cleansing them of their contamination with original sin. As these children grew up during the 1640s and 1650s, however, they seldom experienced the inward transformation that signaled conversion and qualification for church membership. The problem of declining church membership and the watering-down of Puritan orthodoxy became urgent during the 1650s when the children of saints, who had grown to adulthood in New England but had not experienced conversion, began to have children themselves. Their sons and daughters—the grandchildren of the founders of the colony—could not receive the protection that baptism afforded against the terrors of death because their parents had not experienced conversion.

Puritan churches debated what to do. To allow anyone, even the child of a saint, to become a church member without conversion was an unthinkable retreat from fundamental Puritan doctrine. In 1662, a synod of Massachusetts ministers reached a compromise known as the **Halfway Covenant**. Unconverted children of saints would be permitted to become "halfway" church members. Like regular church members, they could baptize their infants. But unlike full church members, they could not participate in communion or have the voting privileges of church membership. The Halfway Covenant generated a controversy that sputtered through Puritan churches for the remainder of the century. With the Halfway Covenant, Puritan churches came to terms with the "luke-warm Indifferency" that had replaced the founders' burning zeal.

Nonetheless, New England communities continued to enforce piety with holy rigor. Beginning in 1656, small bands of Quakers—or members of the Society of Friends, as they called themselves—began to arrive in Massachusetts. Many of their beliefs were at odds with orthodox Puritanism. Quakers believed that God spoke directly to each individual through an "inner light," and that individuals needed neither a preacher nor the Bible in order to discover God's Word. Maintaining that all human beings were equal in God's eyes, Quakers refused to conform to mere temporal powers such as laws and governments unless God requested otherwise. Quakers affronted Puritan doctrines of faith and social order. For example, they refused to observe the Sabbath because they insisted that God had not set aside any special day for worship but instead expected the faithful to worship every day.

New England communities treated Quakers with ruthless severity. Some Quakers were branded on the face "with a red-hot iron with [an] H. for heresie." Several Quaker women were stripped to the waist, tied to the back of a cart, and whipped as they were paraded through towns. When Quakers refused to leave Massachusetts, Boston officials sentenced two men and a woman to be hanged in 1659. The three Quakers walked to the gallows "Hand in Hand, all three of them, as to a Weding-day, with great cheerfulness of Heart," one colonist observed.

New Englanders' only partial success in realizing the promise of a godly society ultimately undermined the intense appeal of Puritanism. In the pious Puritan communities of New England, leaders tried to eliminate sin. In the process, they diminished the sense of utter human depravity that was the wellspring of Puritanism. By 1700, New Englanders did not doubt that human beings sinned, but they were more concerned with the sins of others than with their own.

Witch trials held in Salem, Massachusetts, were signs of the erosion of religious confidence and assurance. In 1692, the frenzied Salem proceedings accused more than 100 people of witchcraft, a capital crime. (See "Historical Question," page 122.) Most of the accused were middle-aged women who, according to their accusers, were in thrall to Satan, who had tortured and bedeviled the accusers. The Salem court executed 19 accused witches, signaling enduring belief in the supernatural origins of evil and gnawing doubt about the strength of Puritan New Englanders' faith.

The Founding of the Middle Colonies

South of New England and north of the Chesapeake, a group of middle colonies were founded in the last third of the seventeenth century. Before the 1670s, few Europeans settled in the region. For the first two-thirds of the seventeenth century, the most important European outpost in the area was the relatively small Dutch colony of New Netherland. By 1700, however, the English monarchy had seized New Netherland, renamed it New York, and encouraged the creation of a Quaker colony led by William Penn. Unlike the New England colonies, the middle colonies of New York, New Jersey, and Pennsylvania originated as **land grants** by the English monarch to one or more proprietors, who then possessed both the land and the extensive, almost monarchical, powers of government (Map 4.2). These middle colonies attracted settlers of more diverse European origins and religious faiths than were found in New England.

From New Netherland to New York

In 1609, the Dutch East India Company dispatched Henry Hudson to search for a Northwest Passage to the Orient. Hudson sailed

Valuables Chest

This sturdy chest used to hold jewelry and valuable papers commemorated the wedding of Joseph and Bathsheba Pope in 1679. Quakers, the Popes lived in Salem, Massachusetts. Thirteen years after acquiring this chest, the Popes became participants in the 1692 Salem witch trials. They both accused neighbors of being witches. Bathsheba succumbed to fits that she attributed to the witchcraft of Martha Corey. Joseph testified that John Proctor claimed to have powers to exorcise Satan. Both Corey and Proctor were convicted of witchcraft and hanged.
Peabody Essex Museum, Salem, MA.

Why Were Some New Englanders Accused of Being Witches?

Almost everybody in seventeenth-century North America—whether Native Americans, slaves, or colonists—believed that supernatural spirits could cause harm and misfortune. Outside New England, however, few colonists were legally accused of being witches—that is, persons who had become possessed by Satan. More than 95 percent of all legal accusations of witchcraft in the North American colonies occurred in New England, a hint of Puritans' enduring preoccupation with sin and evil. In 1691 and 1692, an epidemic of witchcraft accusations broke out in Salem, Massachusetts, but long before that many New Englanders had whispered privately that particular individuals were witches. To accuse a person of witchcraft was a serious matter. A 1641 Massachusetts law stated, "If any man or woman be a witch . . . they shall be put to death." The other New England colonies had identical laws. During the seventeenth century, courts carried out the letter of the law: Thirty-four accused witches were legally executed, nineteen of them during the Salem outbreak.

To understand the peculiar New England obsession with witchcraft, historians have gathered a great deal of information about accused witches and the dark deeds their accusers attributed to them. Almost anyone could be accused of being a witch, but 80 percent of the accusations were leveled against women. About two-thirds of the accused women were over forty years old, past the normal age of childbearing. About half of the men who were accused as witches were relatives of accused women. Usually, one family member did not accuse another. Nor did accusers single out a stranger as a witch. Instead, accusers pointed to a neighbor they knew well.

Almost always the accused person denied the charge. Occasionally, the accused confessed to having made a pact with the devil. A confession could sometimes win sympathy and a reduced punishment from officials. During the Salem witch-hunt, those who confessed usually saved their own skins by naming other people as witches. The testimony of a confessed witch was then used to accuse others.

Accusers of all descriptions stepped forward to testify against alleged witches. Witchcraft investigations often stretched over weeks, months, or even years as courts accumulated evidence against (and sometimes in favor of) the accused. About 90 percent of accusers were adults, about six out of ten of them men. Young women between the ages of sixteen and twenty-five made up almost all of the remaining 10 percent of accusers; typically, they claimed to be tortured by the accused.

At Salem, for example, afflicted young girls shrieked in pain, their limbs twisted into strange, involuntary contortions as they pointed out the witches who tortured them. At the trial of Bridget Bishop in Salem, the court record noted that if Bishop "but cast her eyes on them [the afflicted], they were presently struck down. . . . But upon the touch of her hand upon them, when they lay in their swoons, they would immediately revive." The bewitched girls testified that "the shape of the prisoner did oftentimes very grievously pinch them, choke them, bite them, and afflict them; urging them to write their names in a book"—the devil's book.

Such sensational evidence of torture by a witch was relatively rare in witch-hunts and trials. Usually, accusers attributed some inexplicable misfortune they had suffered to the evil influence of an accused witch. One woman testified against a woman who, she insisted, had bewitched her cow, causing it to give discolored milk. Another woman accused a witch whom she feared would "smite my chickens," and "quickly after [the suspected witch went away] one chicken died." A man was accused as a witch because

along the Atlantic coast and ventured up the large river that now bears his name until it dwindled to a stream that obviously did not lead to China. A decade later, the Dutch government granted the West India Company—a group of Dutch merchants and shippers—exclusive rights to trade with the Western Hemisphere. In 1626, Peter Minuit, the resident director of the company, purchased Manhattan Island from the Manhate Indians for trade goods worth the

Witches Show Their Love for Satan

Mocking pious Christians' humble obeisance to God, witches willingly debased themselves by standing in line to kneel and kiss Satan's buttocks—or so it was popularly believed. This seventeenth-century print portrays Satan with clawlike hands and feet, the tail of a rodent, the wings of a bat, and the head of a lustful ram attached to the torso of a man. Notice that women predominate among the witches eager to express their devotion to Satan and to do his bidding.

UCSF Library/Center for Knowledge Management.

his "spirit bewitched the pudding," which was inexplicably "cut lengthwise . . . as smooth as any knife could cut it." Mary Parsons testified that she suspected her husband, Hugh, of being a witch "because almost all that he sells to anybody does not prosper."

From our present-day perspective, the accusers seem to have been victims not of witchcraft but of simple accidents, of overheated imaginations, or—in the case of the possessed young women—of emotional distress. But why did seventeenth-century New Englanders find the testimony of accusers persuasive?

Seventeenth-century New Englanders believed that almost nothing happened by chance. Supernatural power, whether God's or Satan's, suffused the world and influenced the smallest event, even the color of a cow's milk. When something bad happened, an unhappy God may have caused it to show his displeasure with the victim, who had perhaps sinned in some way. But maybe the victim was not in fact responsible for the misfortune. Maybe Satan, acting through a witch, had caused it. If misfortunes could be pinned on a witch in thrall to Satan, the accuser was absolved from responsibility. The accuser became a helpless victim rather than a guilty party. Witches were an explanation for the disorder that continually crept into New England communities, an explanation that attributed the disorder not to chance or to the faults of individuals but to the witches' evil deeds, commanded by Satan.

Accusers usually targeted a vulnerable neighbor, such as an older, often poor woman. Historians have noted that accusers often complained that the accused individuals were quarrelsome, grumbled about being mistreated, muttered vague threats about getting even, and seemed to be dissatisfied with their lives. Researchers have pointed out that many New Englanders had such feelings after about 1650, but most people did not express them openly or, if they did, felt guilty about doing so. Accused witches often expressed and acted on feelings that other people shared but considered inappropriate, shameful, or sinful in their zeal to lead the saintly lives prescribed by their Puritan religion. Witches made it somewhat easier for New Englanders to consider themselves saints rather than sinners.

equivalent of a dozen beaver pelts. New Amsterdam, the small settlement established at the southern tip of Manhattan Island, became the principal trading center in New Netherland and the colony's headquarters.

Unlike the English colonies, New Netherland did not attract many European immigrants. Like New England and the Chesapeake colonies, New Netherland never realized the profits of its sponsors' dreams. The company tried to stimulate immigration by granting patroonships—allotments of eighteen miles of land along the Hudson River—to wealthy stockholders who would bring fifty families to the colony and settle them as serflike tenants on their huge domains. Only one patroonship succeeded; the others failed to attract settlers, and much of the land was sold back to the company.

Although few in number, the New Netherlanders were remarkably diverse, especially compared with the homogeneous English settlers to the north and south. Religious dissenters and immigrants from Holland, Sweden, France, Germany, and elsewhere made their way to the colony. A minister

> Although few in number, the New Netherlanders were remarkably diverse. Religious dissenters and immigrants from Holland, Sweden, France, Germany, and elsewhere made their way to the colony.

of the Dutch Reformed Church complained to his superiors in Holland that several groups of Jews had recently arrived, adding to the religious mixture of "Papists, Mennonites and Lutherans among the Dutch [and] many Puritans . . . and many other atheists . . . who conceal themselves under the name of Christians."

The West India Company struggled to govern the motley colonists. Peter Stuyvesant, governor from 1647 to 1664, tried to enforce conformity to the Dutch Reformed Church, but the company declared that "the consciences of men should be free and unshackled," making a virtue of New Netherland necessity. The company never permitted the colony's settlers to form a representative government. Instead, the company appointed government officials who set policies, including taxes, which many colonists deeply resented.

In 1664, New Netherland became New York. Charles II, who became king of England in 1660 when Parliament restored the monarchy, gave his brother James, the Duke of York, an enormous grant of land that included New Netherland. Of course, the Dutch colony did not belong to the king of England. But that legal technicality did not impede the king or his brother. The duke quickly organized a small fleet of warships, which appeared off Manhattan Island in late summer 1664, and demanded that Stuyvesant surrender. With little choice, he did.

As the new proprietor of the colony, the Duke of York exercised almost the same unlimited authority over the colony as had the West India Company. The duke never set foot in New York, but his governors struggled to impose order on the unruly colonists. Like the Dutch, the duke permitted "all persons of what Religion soever, quietly to inhabit . . . provided they give no disturbance to the publique peace, nor doe molest or disquiet others in the free exercise of their religion." This policy of religious toleration was less an affirmation of liberty of conscience and more a recognition of the reality of the most heterogeneous colony in seventeenth-century North America.

New Jersey and Pennsylvania

The creation of New York led indirectly to the founding of two other middle colonies, New Jersey and Pennsylvania (see Map 4.2). In 1664, the Duke of York subdivided his grant and gave the portion between the Hudson and Delaware

New Amsterdam

In the background of this 1673 Dutch portrait of New Amsterdam appears the settlement on Manhattan Island—complete with a windmill. Wharves connect Manhattan residents to the seaborne commerce of the Atlantic world. In the foreground, the Dutch artist placed native inhabitants of the mainland, drawing them in such a way that they resemble Africans rather than Lenni Lenape (Delaware) Indians. Dutch merchants carried tens of thousands of African slaves to New World ports, New Amsterdam among them. Probably, the artist had never seen Indians, had never been to New Amsterdam, and depended on well-known artistic conventions about the appearance of Africans to create his Native Americans. The portrait contrasts orderly, efficient, businesslike New Amsterdam with the exotic natural environment of America, to which the native woman clings as if she is refusing to succumb to the culture represented by those neat rows of rectangular houses across the river.

© Collection of the New-York Historical Society.

N. AMSTERDAM, ou N. IORK in Amerig.

MAP 4.2   Middle Colonies in the Seventeenth Century
For the most part, the middle colonies in the seventeenth century were inhabited by settlers who clustered along the Hudson or Delaware rivers. The vast geographic extent of the colonies shown in this map reflects land grants authorized in England. Most of this area was inhabited by Native Americans rather than settled by colonists.

The Quakers' concept of an open, generous God who made his love equally available to all people manifested itself in unusually egalitarian worship services and in social behavior that continually brought Quakers into conflict with the English government. Quaker leaders were ordinary men and women, not specially trained preachers. More than any other seventeenth-century sect, Quakers allowed women to assume positions of religious leadership. "In souls there is no sex," they said. Since all people were equal in the spiritual realm, Quakers considered social hierarchy false and evil. They called everyone "friend" and shook hands instead of curtsying or removing their hats—even when meeting the king. These customs enraged many non-Quakers and provoked innumerable beatings and worse.

William Penn
This portrait was drawn about a decade after the founding of Pennsylvania. At a time when extravagant clothing and fancy wigs proclaimed that their wearer was an important person, Penn is portrayed informally, lacking even a coat, his natural hair neat but undressed—all a reflection of his Quaker faith. Penn's full face and double chin show that his faith did not make him a stranger to the pleasures of the table. No hollow-cheeked ascetic or wild-eyed enthusiast, Penn appears sober and observant, as if sizing up the viewer and reserving judgment. The portrait captures the calm determination—anchored in faith—that inspired Penn's hopes for his new colony.
Historical Society of Pennsylvania.

rivers to two of his friends. The proprietors of this new colony, New Jersey, soon discovered that Puritan and Dutch settlers already in the region stubbornly resisted the new government. The continuing strife persuaded one of the proprietors to sell his share to two Quakers. When the Quaker proprietors began to quarrel, they called in a prominent English Quaker, William Penn, to arbitrate their dispute. Penn eventually worked out a settlement that continued New Jersey's proprietary government but did little to end the conflict with the settlers. In the process, Penn became intensely interested in what he termed a "holy experiment" of establishing a genuinely Quaker colony in America.

Unlike most Quakers, William Penn came from an eminent family. His father had served both Cromwell and Charles II and had been knighted. Born in 1644, the younger Penn trained for a military career, but the ideas of dissenters from the reestablished Church of England appealed to him, and he became a devout Quaker. By 1680, he had published fifty books and pamphlets and spoken at countless public meetings, although he had not won official toleration for Quakers in England.

Penn was jailed four times for such offenses, once for nine months.

Despite his many run-ins with the government, Penn remained on good terms with Charles II, who granted him land to found a Quaker colony in America. Partly to rid England of the troublesome Quakers, in 1681 Charles made Penn the proprietor of 45,000 square miles for his new colony, called Pennsylvania.

Toleration and Diversity in Pennsylvania

When Penn announced the creation of his colony, Quakers flocked to English ports in numbers exceeded only by the great Puritan migration to New England fifty years earlier. Between 1682 and 1685, nearly 8,000 immigrants arrived in Pennsylvania, most of them Quakers from England, Ireland, and Wales. They represented a cross section of the **artisans**, farmers, and laborers who predominated among English Quakers. Quaker missionaries also encouraged immigrants from the European continent, and many came, giving Pennsylvania greater ethnic diversity than any other English colony except New York. Pennsylvania prospered, and the capital city, Philadelphia, soon rivaled New York—though not yet Boston—as a center of commerce. By 1700, the city's 5,000 inhabitants participated in a thriving trade exporting flour and other food products to the West Indies and importing textiles and manufactured goods.

> Despite its toleration and diversity, Pennsylvania was as much a Quaker colony as New England was a stronghold of Puritanism.

Penn was determined to live in peace with the Indians who inhabited the region. His Indian policy expressed his Quaker ideals and contrasted sharply with the hostile policies of the other English colonies. As he explained to the chief of the Lenni Lenape (Delaware) Indians, "God has written his law in our hearts, by which we are taught and commanded to love and help and do good to one another . . . [and] this great God has been pleased to make me concerned in your parts of the world, and the king of the country where I live has given unto me a great province therein, but I desire to enjoy it with your love and consent." Penn instructed his agents to obtain the Indians' consent by purchasing their land, respecting their claims, and dealing with them fairly.

Penn declared that the first principle of government was that every settler would "enjoy the free possession of his or her faith and exercise of worship towards God." Accordingly, Pennsylvania tolerated Protestant sects of all kinds as well as Roman Catholics. All voters and officeholders had to be Christians, but the government did not compel settlers to attend religious services, as in Massachusetts, or to pay taxes to maintain a state-supported church, as in Virginia.

Despite its toleration and diversity, Pennsylvania was as much a Quaker colony as New England was a stronghold of Puritanism. Penn had no hesitation about using civil government to enforce religious morality. One of the colony's first laws provided severe punishment for "all such offenses against God, as swearing, cursing, lying, profane talking, drunkenness, drinking of healths, obscene words . . . all prizes, stage plays, cards, dice, May games, gamesters, masques, revels, bull-baitings, cock-fightings, bear-baitings, and the like, which excite the people to rudeness, cruelty, looseness, and irreligion." The ethnic and religious diversity of Pennsylvania prevented strict enforcement of pious behavior, but Quaker expectations of godly order and sobriety set the tone of Pennsylvania society.

As proprietor, Penn had extensive powers, subject only to review by the king. He appointed a governor who maintained the proprietor's power to veto any laws passed by the colonial council, which was elected by property owners who possessed at least one hundred acres of land or who paid taxes. The council had the power to originate laws and administer all the affairs of government. A popularly elected assembly served as a check on the council; its members had the authority to reject or approve laws framed by the council.

Penn stressed that the exact form of government mattered less than the men who served in it. In Penn's eyes, "good men" staffed Pennsylvania's government because Quakers dominated elective and appointive offices. Quakers, of course, differed among themselves. Members of the assembly struggled to win the right to debate and amend laws, especially tax laws. They finally won the battle in 1701 when a new Charter of Privileges gave the proprietor the power to appoint the council and in turn stripped the council of all its former powers and gave them to the assembly, which became the only unicameral legislature in all the British colonies.

The Colonies and the British Empire

From the king's point of view, proprietary grants of faraway lands to which he had tenuous claims were a cheap way to reward friends. As the colonies grew, however, the grants became more valuable. After 1660, the king took initiatives to channel colonial trade through English hands and to consolidate royal authority over colonial governments. These initiatives defined the basic relationship between the colonies and England that endured until the American Revolution (Map 4.3).

Royal Regulation of Colonial Trade

English economic policies toward the colonies were designed to yield customs revenues for the monarchy and profitable business for English merchants and shippers. In addition, the policies were intended to divert the colonies' trade from England's enemies, especially the Dutch and the French.

The Navigation Acts of 1650, 1651, and 1660 set forth two fundamental regulations governing colonial trade. First, all colonial goods imported into England had to be transported in English ships using primarily English crews. Second, the Navigation Acts listed ("enumerated," in the language of the time) specific colonial products

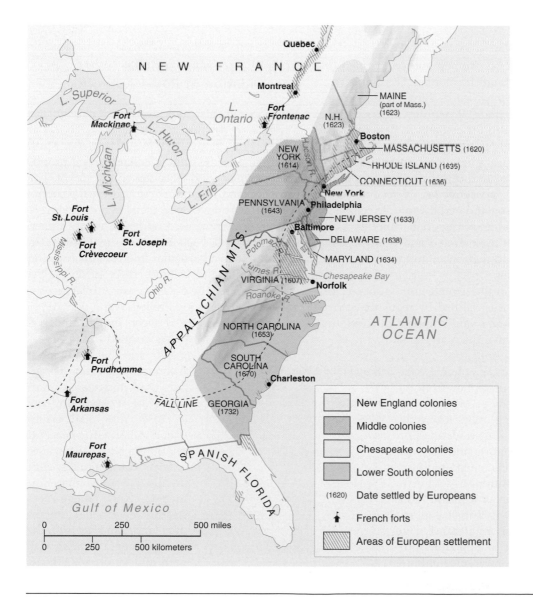

MAP 4.3 American Colonies at the End of the Seventeenth Century
By the end of the seventeenth century, settlers inhabited a narrow band of land that stretched more or less continuously from Boston to Norfolk, with pockets of settlement farther south. The colonies' claims to enormous tracts of land to the west were contested by Native Americans as well as by France and Spain.

READING THE MAP: What geographic feature acted as the western boundary for colonial territorial claims? Which colonies were the most settled and which the least?

CONNECTIONS: The map divides the colonies into four regions. Can you think of an alternative organization? On what criteria would it be based?

FOR MORE HELP ANALYZING THIS MAP, see the map activity for this chapter in the Online Study Guide at bedfordstmartins.com/roark.

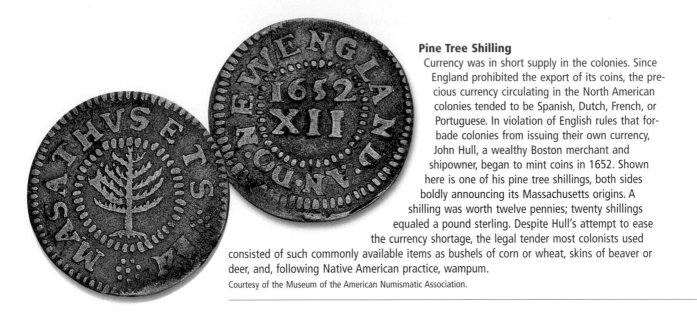

Pine Tree Shilling
Currency was in short supply in the colonies. Since England prohibited the export of its coins, the precious currency circulating in the North American colonies tended to be Spanish, Dutch, French, or Portuguese. In violation of English rules that forbade colonies from issuing their own currency, John Hull, a wealthy Boston merchant and shipowner, began to mint coins in 1652. Shown here is one of his pine tree shillings, both sides boldly announcing its Massachusetts origins. A shilling was worth twelve pennies; twenty shillings equaled a pound sterling. Despite Hull's attempt to ease the currency shortage, the legal tender most colonists used consisted of such commonly available items as bushels of corn or wheat, skins of beaver or deer, and, following Native American practice, wampum.
Courtesy of the Museum of the American Numismatic Association.

that could be shipped only to England or to other English colonies. The Staple Act of 1663 imposed a third regulation on colonial trade. It required all goods imported into the colonies to pass through England (see chapter 3). While these regulations prevented Chesapeake **planters** from shipping their tobacco directly to the European continent, they interfered less with the commerce of New England and the middle colonies, whose principal exports—fish, lumber, and flour—were not enumerated and could legally be sent directly to their most important markets in the West Indies.

By the end of the seventeenth century, colonial commerce was defined by regulations that subjected merchants and shippers to royal supervision and gave them access to markets throughout the British empire. In addition, colonial commerce received protection from the British navy. By 1700, colonial goods (including those from the West Indies) accounted for one-fifth of all British imports and for two-thirds of all goods reexported from England to the European continent. In turn, the colonies absorbed more than one-tenth of British exports. The commercial regulations gave economic value to England's proprietorship of American colonies.

King Philip's War and the Consolidation of Royal Authority

The monarchy also took steps to exercise greater control over colonial governments. Virginia had been a royal colony since 1624; Maryland, South Carolina, and the middle colonies were proprietary colonies with close ties to the crown. The New England colonies possessed royal charters, but they had developed their own distinctively Puritan governments. Charles II, whose father, Charles I, had been executed by Puritans in England, took a particular interest in harnessing the New England colonies more firmly to the British Empire. The occasion was a royal investigation following King Philip's War.

In 1675, warfare between Indians and colonists erupted in the Chesapeake and New England. Although Massachusetts settlers had massacred hundreds of Pequot Indians in 1637, they had established relatively peaceful relations with the more potent Wampanoags. But in the decades that followed, New Englanders steadily encroached on Indian lands, and, in 1675, the Wampanoags struck back with attacks on settlements

King Philip's War, 1675

King Philip (Metacomet)
No portrait of Metacomet, or King Philip, was made during his lifetime. The artist of this likeness imagines him as a proud warrior wrapped in a shawl and armed with a musket, which indicates both his adoption of this European weapon and his willingness to use it against English colonists.
Library of Congress.

dozen. By the spring of 1676, Indian warriors ranged freely within seventeen miles of Boston. The colonists finally defeated the Indians, principally with a scorched-earth policy of burning their food supplies. King Philip's War left the New England colonists with an enduring hatred of Indians, a large war debt, and a devastated frontier. And in 1676, an agent of the king arrived to investigate whether New England was abiding by English laws.

Not surprisingly, the king's agent found all sorts of deviations from English rules, and the English government decided to govern New England more directly. In 1684, an English court revoked the Massachusetts charter, the foundation of the distinctive Puritan government. Two years later, royal officials incorporated Massachusetts and the other colonies north of Maryland into the Dominion of New England. To govern the dominion, the English sent Sir Edmund Andros to Boston. Some New England merchants cooperated with Andros, but most colonists were offended by his flagrant disregard of such Puritan traditions as keeping the Sabbath. Worst of all, the Dominion of New England invalidated all land titles, confronting every

> King Philip's War left the New England colonists with an enduring hatred of Indians, a large war debt, and a devastated frontier.

in western Massachusetts. Metacomet—whom the colonists called King Philip—was the chief of the Wampanoags and the son of Massasoit, who had befriended William Bradford and his original band of Separatists. Metacomet probably neither planned the attacks nor masterminded a conspiracy with the Nipmucks and the Narragansetts, as the colonists feared. But when militias from Massachusetts and other New England colonies counterattacked all three tribes, a deadly sequence of battles killed over a thousand colonists and thousands more Indians. The Indians utterly destroyed thirteen English settlements and partially burned another half

King Philip's Sash
This woolen sash belonged to Wampanoag chief Metacomet, or King Philip. Small white glass beads, obtained through trade with Europeans, are stitched into the sash in the shape of a serpent.
Peabody Museum of Archaeology and Ethnology, Harvard University.

landowner in New England with the horrifying prospect of losing his or her land.

Events in England, however, permitted Massachusetts colonists to overthrow Andros and retain title to their property. When Charles II died in 1685, he was succeeded by his brother James II, a zealous Catholic. James's aggressive campaign to appoint Catholics to government posts engendered such unrest that in 1688 a group of Protestant noblemen in Parliament invited the Dutch ruler William of Orange, James's son-in-law, to claim the English throne. When William landed in England at the head of a large army, James fled to France and William and his wife Mary (James's daughter) became corulers in a bloodless "Glorious Revolution," which reasserted Protestant influence in England and its empire. Rumors of the revolution raced across the Atlantic and emboldened colonial uprisings against royal authority in Massachusetts, New York, and Maryland.

In Boston, rebels seized Andros and other English officials and tossed them in jail. Then the rebellious colonists destroyed the Dominion of New England and reestablished the former charter government. New Yorkers followed the Massachusetts example. Under the leadership of Jacob Leisler, rebels seized the royal governor and ruled the colony for more than a year. But when King William's governor of New York arrived in 1691, he executed Leisler for treason. In Maryland, the Protestant Association, led by John Coode, overthrew the colony's pro-Catholic government in 1689, fearing it would not recognize the new Protestant king. Coode's men ruled until the new royal governor arrived in 1692 and ended both Coode's rebellion and Lord Baltimore's proprietary government.

Much as they chafed under increasing royal control, the colonists still valued English protection from hostile neighbors. While the northern colonies were distracted by the Glorious Revolution, French forces from the fur-trading regions along the Great Lakes and in Canada attacked villages in New England and New York. Known as King William's War, the conflict with the French was a colonial outgrowth of William's war against France in Europe. The war dragged on until 1697 and ended inconclusively in both Europe and the colonies. But it made clear to many colonists that along with English royal government came a welcome measure of military security.

In Massachusetts, John Winthrop's city on a hill became another royal colony in 1691, when a new charter was issued. The charter said that the governor of the colony would be appointed by the king rather than elected by the colonists' representatives. But perhaps the most unsettling change was the new qualification for voting. Possession of property replaced church membership as a prerequisite for voting in colony-wide elections. Wealth replaced God's grace as the defining characteristic of Massachusetts citizenship.

Conclusion: An English Model of Colonization in North America

By 1700, the diverse English colonies in North America had developed along lines quite different from the example New Spain had set in 1600. In the North American colonies, English immigrants and their descendants created societies of settlers unlike the largely Indian societies in New Spain ruled by a tiny group of Spaniards. Although many settlers came to North America from other parts of Europe and a growing number of Africans arrived in bondage, English laws, habits, ideas, and language dominated all the colonies.

Economically, the English colonies thrived on agriculture and trade instead of mining silver and exploiting Indian labor as in New Spain. Southern colonies grew huge crops of tobacco and rice with the labor of indentured servants and slaves, while farmers in the middle colonies planted wheat and New England fishermen harvested the sea. Although servants and slaves could be found throughout the North American colonies, many settlers depended principally on the labor of family members. Relations between settlers and Native Americans often exploded in bloody warfare, but Indians seldom served as an important source of labor for settlers, as they did in New Spain.

Protestantism prevailed in the North American settlements, relaxed in some colonies and straitlaced in others. The convictions of Puritanism that motivated John Winthrop and others to build a new England in the colonies became muted as the New England colonies matured and dissenters like Roger Williams multiplied. Catholics, Quakers, Anglicans (members of the Church of England), Jews, and others settled in the middle and southern colonies, creating considerable religious toleration, especially in Pennsylvania and New York.

Politics and government differed from colony to colony, although the imprint of English institutions and practices existed everywhere. And everywhere, local settlers who were free adult white men had an extraordinary degree of political influence, far beyond that of colonists in New Spain or ordinary citizens in England. A new world of settlers that Columbus could not have imagined, that Powhatan only glimpsed, had been firmly established in English North America by 1700. During the next half century,

that English colonial world would undergo surprising new developments built on the achievements of the seventeenth century.

For additional firsthand accounts of this period, see Chapter 4 in Michael Johnson, ed., *Reading the American Past,* Third Edition.

To assess your mastery of the material in this chapter, see the Online Study Guide at bedfordstmartins.com/roark.

For Web links related to the topics in this chapter, see "HistoryLinks," "DocLinks," and "PlaceLinks" at bedfordstmartins.com/roark.

CHRONOLOGY

1534 • King Henry VIII breaks with Roman Catholic Church and initiates English Reformation.

1609 • Henry Hudson searches for Northwest Passage for Dutch East India Company.

1620 • English Pilgrims found Plymouth colony and elect William Bradford governor.

1626 • Peter Minuit purchases Manhattan Island for Dutch West India Company and founds New Amsterdam.

1629 • Massachusetts Bay Company receives royal charter for colony.

1630 • John Winthrop leads Puritan settlers to Massachusetts Bay, founding the largest New England colony.

1636 • Roger Williams, banished from Massachusetts, establishes Rhode Island colony as a haven for religious dissenters.
• Thomas Hooker leaves Massachusetts and helps found Connecticut colony.

1638 • Anne Hutchinson, accused of antinomianism, is excommunicated from Boston church.

1642 • Puritan Revolution inflames England, pitting Puritans against royalists in civil war and sharply reducing immigration to New England.

1649 • English Puritans win civil war, execute King Charles I, and declare England a Puritan republic.

1656 • Quakers arrive in Massachusetts and are persecuted there.

1660 • Monarchy restored in England; Charles II becomes king.
• Navigation Act requires colonial goods to be shipped in English ships through English ports.

1662 • Many Puritan congregations adopt Halfway Covenant, relaxing standards for baptism and church membership.

1663 • Staple Act requires all colonial imports to come from England.

1664 • English seize New Netherland colony from Dutch, rename it New York.
• Duke of York subdivides colony, creating colony of New Jersey.

1675 • Indians and colonists clash in King Philip's War, leaving a legacy of hostility toward Indians and prompting English monarchy to attempt to govern New England more directly.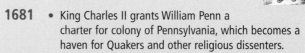

1681 • King Charles II grants William Penn a charter for colony of Pennsylvania, which becomes a haven for Quakers and other religious dissenters.

1686 • Royal officials create Dominion of New England.

1688 • King James II ousted in a "Glorious Revolution"; William III and Mary II become corulers of England.

1691 • Massachusetts becomes royal colony.

1692 • Witch trials flourish at Salem, Massachusetts.

BIBLIOGRAPHY

Please consult the bibliographies of chapters 2 and 3 for more readings on related topics.

General Works

Patricia U. Bonomi, *Under the Cope of Heaven: Religion, Society, and Politics in Colonial America* (1986).

Jon Butler, *Awash in a Sea of Faith: Christianizing the American People* (1990).

Colin G. Calloway, *New Worlds for All: Indians, Europeans, and the Remaking of Early America* (1998).

Patrick Collinson, *The Birthpangs of Protestant England: Religious and Cultural Change in the Sixteenth and Seventeenth Centuries* (1988).

David Hackett Fischer, *Albion's Seed: Four British Folkways in America* (1989).

Stephen Foster, *The Long Argument: English Puritanism and the Shaping of New England Culture, 1570–1700* (1991).

Alison Games, *Migration and the Origins of the English Atlantic World* (1999).

Jack P. Greene, *Pursuits of Happiness: The Social Development of Early Modern British Colonies and the Formation of American Culture* (1988).

David D. Hall, *Worlds of Wonder, Days of Judgment: Popular Religious Belief in Early New England* (1989).

Stephen Innes, *Creating the Commonwealth: The Economic Culture of Puritan New England* (1995).

David Jaffee, *People of the Wachusett: Greater New England in History and Memory, 1630–1860* (1999).

David S. Lovejoy, *Religious Enthusiasm in the New World: Heresy to Revolution* (1985).

Perry Miller, *The New England Mind: From Colony to Province* (1953).

Carla Pestana and Sharon V. Salinger, *Inequality in Early America* (1999).

Robert Blair St. George, *Possible Pasts: Becoming Colonial in Early America* (2000).

Martha Saxton, *Being Good: Women's Moral Values in Early America* (2002).

Alan Taylor, *American Colonies* (2001).

Helena M. Wall, *Fierce Communalism: Family and Community in the American Colonies in the Seventeenth Century* (1990).

Native Americans

Russell Bourne, *Gods of War, Gods of Peace: How the Meeting of Native and Colonial Religions Shaped Early America* (2002).

Colin G. Calloway, *The Western Abenaki of Vermont, 1600–1800: War, Migration, and the Survival of an Indian People* (1990).

Richard W. Cogley, *John Eliot's Mission to the Indians before King Philip's War* (1999).

William Cronon, *Changes in the Land: Indians, Colonists, and the Ecology of New England* (1983).

Matthew Dennis, *Cultivating a Landscape of Peace: Iroquois-European Encounters in Seventeenth-Century America* (1993).

Carol Devens, *Countering Colonization: Native American Women and Great Lakes Missions, 1630–1900* (1992).

James David Drake, *King Philip's War: Civil War in New England, 1675–1676* (2000).

Nicholas Griffiths and Fernando Cervantes, eds., *Spiritual Encounters: Interactions between Christianity and Native Religions in Colonial America* (1999).

Francis Jennings, *The Ambiguous Iroquois Empire: The Covenant Chain Confederation of Indian Tribes with English Colonies from Its Beginnings to the Lancaster Treaty of 1744* (1983).

Yasughide Kawashima, *Puritan Justice and the Indian: White Man's Law in Massachusetts, 1630–1763* (1986).

Jill Lepore, *The Name of War: King Philip's War and the Origins of American Identity* (1998).

James W. Mavor, *Manitou: The Sacred Landscape of New England's Native Civilization* (1989).

Michael Leroy Oberg, *Dominion and Civility: English Imperialism and Native America, 1585–1685* (1999).

Jean M. O'Brien, *Dispossession by Degrees: Indian Land and Identity in Natick, Massachusetts, 1650–1790* (1997).

Ann Marie Plane, *Colonial Intimacies: Indian Marriages in Early New England* (2000).

Daniel K. Richter, *The Ordeal of the Longhouse: The Peoples of the Iroquois League in the Era of European Colonization* (1992).

Daniel K. Richter and James H. Merrell, *Beyond the Covenant Chain: The Iroquois and Their Neighbors in Indian North America, 1600–1800* (1987).

Neal Salisbury, *Manitou and Providence: Indians, Europeans, and the Making of New England, 1500–1643* (1982).

Alden T. Vaughan, ed., *New England Encounters: Indians and Euroamericans, ca. 1600–1850* (2000).

Richard White, *The Middle Ground: Indians, Empires, and Republics in the Great Lakes Region, 1650–1815* (1991).

New England

David Grayson Allen, *In English Ways: The Movement of Societies and the Transferal of English Local Law and Custom to Massachusetts Bay in the Seventeenth Century* (1981).

Douglas Anderson, *William Bradford's Book of Plimmoth Plantation and the Printed Word* (2003).

Virginia Dejohn Anderson, *New England's Generation: The Great Migration and the Formation of Society and Culture in the Seventeenth Century* (1991).

Paul Boyer and Stephen Nissenbaum, *Salem Possessed: The Social Origins of Witchcraft* (1974).

Theodore Dwight Bozeman, *To Live Ancient Lives: The Primitivist Dimension in Puritanism* (1988).

Louise A. Breen, *Transgressing the Bounds: Subversive Enterprises among the Puritan Elite in Massachusetts, 1630–1692* (2001).

Francis J. Bremer, *Shaping New Englands: Puritan Clergymen in Seventeenth-Century England and New England* (1994).

Francis J. Bremer, *John Winthrop: America's Forgotten Founding Father* (2003).

Jonathan M. Chu, *Neighbors, Friends, or Madmen: The Puritan Adjustment to Quakerism in Seventeenth-Century Massachusetts Bay* (1985).

Charles Lloyd Cohen, *God's Caress: The Psychology of Puritan Religious Experience* (1986).

James F. Cooper Jr., *Tenacious of Their Liberties: The Congregationalists in Colonial Massachusetts* (1999).

David Cressy, *Coming Over: Migration and Communication between England and New England in the Seventeenth Century* (1987).

Bruce C. Daniels, *The Connecticut Town: Growth and Development, 1635–1790* (1979).

Bruce Colin Daniels, *Puritans at Play: Leisure and Recreation in Colonial New England* (1995).

Cornelia Hughes Dayton, *Women before the Bar: Gender, Law, and Society in Connecticut, 1639–1789* (1995).

John Demos, *A Little Commonwealth: Family Life in Plymouth Colony* (1970).

John Putnam Demos, *Entertaining Satan: Witchcraft and the Culture of Early New England* (1982).

Stephen Foster, *The Long Argument: English Puritanism and the Shaping of New England Culture, 1570–1700* (1991).

Edwin S. Gaustad, *Liberty of Conscience: Roger Williams in America* (1999).

Richard P. Gildrie, *The Profane, the Civil, and the Godly: The Reformation of Manners in Orthodox New England, 1679–1749* (1994).

Richard Godbeer, *The Devil's Dominion: Magic and Religion in Early New England* (1992).

Lisa M. Gordis, *Opening Scriptures: Bible Reading and Interpretive Authority in Puritan New England* (2003).

Judith S. Graham, *Puritan Family Life: The Diary of Samuel Sewall* (2000).

Philip Gura, *A Glimpse of Sion's Glory: Puritan Radicalism in Seventeenth-Century New England, 1620–1660* (1984).

Michael G. Hall, *The Last American Puritan: The Life of Increase Mather, 1639–1723* (1988).

Stephen Innes, *Labor in a New Land: Economy and Society in Seventeenth-Century Springfield* (1983).

Sydney V. James, *The Colonial Metamorphoses in Rhode Island: A Study of Institutions in Change* (2000).

Jane Kamensky, *Governing the Tongue: The Politics of Speech in Early New England* (1997).

Carol F. Karlsen, *The Devil in the Shape of a Woman: Witchcraft in Colonial New England* (1987).

Karen Ordahl Kupperman, *Providence Island, 1630–1641: The Other Puritan Colony* (1993).

Mary Lou Lustig, *The Imperial Executive in America: Sir Edmund Andros, 1637–1714* (2002).

Gloria L. Main, *Peoples of a Spacious Land: Families and Cultures in Colonial New England* (2001).

Bruce H. Mann, *Neighbors and Strangers: Law and Community in Early Connecticut* (1987).

Carolyn Merchant, *Ecological Revolutions: Nature, Gender, and Science in New England* (1989).

Edmund S. Morgan, *The Puritan Dilemma: The Story of John Winthrop* (1958).

Edmund S. Morgan, *Visible Saints: The History of a Puritan Idea* (1963).

Edmund S. Morgan, *Roger Williams: The Church and the State* (1967).

Margaret Ellen Newell, *From Dependency to Independence: Economic Revolution in Colonial New England* (1999).

Mary Beth Norton, *In the Devil's Snare: The Salem Witchcraft Crisis of 1692* (2002).

Carla Gardina Pestana, *Quakers and Baptists in Colonial Massachusetts* (1991).

Mark A. Peterson, *The Price of Redemption: The Spiritual Economy of Puritan New England* (1998).

Amanda Porterfield, *Female Piety in Puritan New England: The Emergence of Religious Humanism* (1992).

Michael J. Puglisi, *Puritans Besieged: The Legacies of King Philip's War in the Massachusetts Bay Colony* (1991).

Elizabeth Reis, *Damned Women: Sinners and Witches in Puritan New England* (1997).

Phillip H. Round, *By Nature and by Custom Cursed: Transatlantic Civil Discourse and New England Cultural Production, 1620–1660* (1999).

Robert Blair St. George, *Conversing by Signs: Poetics of Implication in Colonial New England Culture* (1998).

Timothy J. Sehr, *Colony and Commonwealth: Massachusetts Bay, 1649–1660* (1989).

Kenneth Silverman, *The Life and Times of Cotton Mather* (1984).

Richard C. Simmons, *Studies in the Massachusetts Franchise, 1631–1691* (1989).

Darren Staloff, *The Making of an American Thinking Class: Intellectuals and Intelligentsia in Puritan Massachusetts* (1997).

Harry S. Stout, *The New England Soul: Preaching and Religious Culture in Colonial New England* (1986).

Rebecca J. Tannenbaum, *The Healer's Calling: Women and Medicine in Early New England* (2002).

Roger Thompson, *Divided We Stand: Watertown, Massachusetts, 1630–1680* (2001).

Lawrence William Towner, *A Good Master Well Served: Masters and Servants in Colonial Massachusetts, 1620–1750* (1998).

Laurel Thatcher Ulrich, *Good Wives: Image and Reality in the Lives of Women in Northern New England, 1650–1750* (1982).

Lisa Wilson, *Ye Heart of a Man: The Domestic Life of Men in Colonial New England* (1999).

Michael P. Winship, *Seers of God: Puritan Providentialism in the Restoration and Early Enlightenment* (1996).

Michael P. Winship, *Making Heretics: Militant Protestantism and Free Grace in Massachusetts, 1636–1641* (2002).

Avihu Zakai, *Exile and Kingdom: History and Apocalypse in the Puritan Migration to America* (1992).

Middle Colonies

Thomas J. Archdeacon, *New York City, 1664–1710: Conquest and Change* (1976).

Patricia U. Bonomi, *A Factious People: Politics and Society in Colonial New York* (1971).

Richard S. Dunn and Mary Maples Dunn, eds., *The World of William Penn* (1986).

Sung Bok Kim, *Landlord and Tenant in Colonial New York: Manorial Society, 1664–1775* (1978).

Cathy Matson, *Merchants and Empire: Trading in Colonial New York* (1998).

Donna Merwick, *Possessing Albany, 1630–1710: The Dutch and English Experiences* (1990).

Donna Merwick, *Death of a Notary: Conquest and Change in Colonial New York* (1999).

David E. Narrett, *Inheritance and Family Life in Colonial New York City* (1992).

Gary B. Nash, *Quakers and Politics: Pennsylvania, 1681–1726* (1968).

John E. Pomfret, *Colonial New Jersey: A History* (1973).

Oliver A. Rink, *Holland on the Hudson: An Economic and Social History of Dutch New York* (1986).

Robert C. Ritchie, *The Duke's Province: A Study of New York Politics and Society, 1664–1691* (1977).

Allen Tully, *Forming American Politics: Ideals, Interests, and Institutions in Colonial New York and Pennsylvania* (1994).

Stephanie Grauman Wolf, *Urban Village: Population, Community, and Family Structure in Germantown, Pennsylvania, 1683–1800* (1976).

Karin A. Wulf, *Not All Wives: Women of Colonial Philadelphia* (2000).

COLONIAL SLAVE DRUM

An African in Virginia made this drum sometime around the beginning of the eighteenth century. The maker of the drum was probably a man who had been enslaved in Africa, transported across the Atlantic in the hold of a slave ship, and sold to a tobacco planter in the Chesapeake. The drum combines deerskin and cedar wood from North America with African skills and designs the maker had mastered before enslavement. The drum signifies the millions of enslaved African men, women, and children who were among the many goods bought and sold in the booming transatlantic trade of the eighteenth century. At a time when Benjamin Franklin and other whites—both native-born and immigrants from Europe—were finding opportunities to better their lives in America, tens of thousands of Africans were arriving in the British North American colonies in hereditary, lifetime bondage. The drum embodies slaves' use of African cultural resources in the alien and oppressive environment of New World slavery. During moments of respite from work, slaves played drums to accompany dances learned in Africa. They also drummed out messages from plantation to plantation. Whites knew slaves used drums for communication, but they could not decipher the meanings of the rhythms and sounds. Fearful that drums signaled rebellious up-risings, whites outlawed drumming but could not eliminate it. Most likely, the messages expressed by the hands that struck this drumhead included lamentations about a life of bondage in America.

Colonial America in the Eighteenth Century

1701–1770

EARLY ON A SUNDAY MORNING in October 1723, young Benjamin Franklin stepped from a wharf along the Delaware River onto the streets of Philadelphia. As he recalled in his autobiography, "I was dirty from my Journey; my Pockets were stuff'd out with Shirts and Stockings; I knew no Soul, nor where to look for Lodging. I was fatigu'd with Travelling, Rowing and Want of Rest. I was very hungry."

Born in 1706, Benjamin Franklin grew up in Boston, where his father, Josiah, worked making soap and candles. The father of seventeen children, Josiah apprenticed each of his sons to learn a trade. At the age of twelve, Benjamin signed a contract to serve for nine years as an apprentice to his brother James, a printer. In James's shop, Benjamin learned the printer's trade and had access to the latest books and pamphlets, which he read avidly. In 1721, James inaugurated the *New England Courant*, avowing to "expose the Vice and Follies of Persons of all Ranks and Degrees" with articles written "so that the meanest ploughman . . . may understand them."

Benjamin's responsibilities in the print shop grew quickly, but he chafed under his brother's supervision. "My Brother was passionate and had often beaten me," he remembered. Benjamin resolved to escape from his apprenticeship "to assert my Freedom" and to run away to New York, nearly three hundred miles from anyone he knew. When he could not find work, he wandered to the Delaware River and then talked his way aboard a small boat heading toward Philadelphia. After rowing half the night, Franklin arrived in the city and went straight to a bakery where he purchased "three great Puffy Rolls." Then he set off for the wharf, "with a Roll under each Arm," to wash down the bread with "a Draught of the River Water." After quenching his thirst, Franklin followed "many clean dress'd People . . . to the great Meeting House of the Quakers. . . . I sat down among them, and . . . I fell fast asleep, and continu'd so till the Meeting broke up."

Franklin's account of his life in Boston and his arrival in Philadelphia is probably the most well-known portrait of life in eighteenth-century America. It illustrates everyday experiences that Franklin shared with many other colonists: a large family; long hours of labor subject to the authority of a parent, relative, or employer; and a restless quest for escape from the ties that bound, for freedom. Franklin's account hints at other, less tangible trends: ambition to make something of oneself in this world rather than worry too much about the hereafter; eagerness to subvert orthodox opinion by publishing dissenting views expressed in simple, clear language understandable by

Mrs. Charles Willing

This portrait of Mrs. Charles Willing of Philadelphia illustrates the prosperity achieved by numerous women and men in the eighteenth-century colonies. Painted by the Philadelphia artist Robert Feke in 1746, the portrait depicts the close connections between Europe and the North American colonies made possible by thriving transatlantic commerce. Scholars have discovered that Anna Maria Garthwaite, an established textile designer in Spitalfields—a silk-weaving center near London—designed the silk used to make Mrs. Willing's dress in 1743. A Spitalfields weaver, Simeon Julins, then wove the fabric in the months between the fall of 1743 and the spring of 1744 and sold it to a merchant who exported it to Philadelphia in 1744. Mrs. Willing must have spotted the silk in a shop much like the one Benjamin Franklin eventually ran with his wife Deborah after he had become more established in Philadelphia. Mrs. Willing would have purchased enough to have this fashionable gown sewn and fitted for her portrait, only three years after Anna Garthwaite first sketched the design in Spitalfields. The portrait demonstrates that, like other prosperous colonists, Mrs. Willing kept abreast of the latest London fashions available in the shops of colonial merchants.

Courtesy, Winterthur Museum, gift of Mrs. George P. Bissell Jr.

"the meanest ploughman"; confidence that, with a valued skill and a few coins, a young man could make his way in the world, confidence few young women could dare assert; and a slackening of religious fervor displayed, for example, in Franklin's quiet snooze—rather than rapt attention—during the Quaker meeting he wandered into on his first day in Philadelphia.

Franklin's story introduces some of the major changes that affected all the British colonies in eighteenth-century North America. Social and economic changes tended to reinforce the differences among New England, the middle colonies, and the southern colonies, while important cultural and political developments tugged in the opposite direction, creating common experiences, aspirations, and identities. In 1776, when *E Pluribus Unum* (Latin meaning "From Many, One") was adopted as the motto for the Great Seal of the United States, the changes in eighteenth-century America that strengthened *Pluribus* also planted the seeds of *Unum*.

In contrast to the British colonies, which experienced vigorous economic growth and political maturation, the Spanish and French colonies in North America remained thinly populated outposts of European empires interested principally in maintaining a toehold in the vast North American territories they claimed. The social, cultural, and religious developments that tended to unify the British North American colonies were unique to what would soon become the United States of America.

A Growing Population and Expanding Economy in British North America

The most important fact about eighteenth-century British America is its phenomenal population growth: In 1700, colonists numbered about 250,000; by 1770, they tallied well over 2 million. An index of the emerging significance of colonial America is that in 1700 there were 19 people in England for every American colonist, but by 1770 there were only 3. The eightfold growth of the colonial population signaled the maturation of a distinctive colonial society. That society was by no means homogeneous. Colonists of different ethnic groups, races, and religions lived in varied environments under thirteen different colonial governments, all of them part of the British Empire.

In general, the growth and diversity of the eighteenth-century colonial population derived from two sources: immigration and natural increase (growth through reproduction). Natural increase contributed about three-fourths of the population growth, immigration about one-fourth. Immigration shifted the ethnic and racial balance among the colonists, making them by 1770 less English and less white than ever before. Fewer than 10 percent of eighteenth-century immigrants came from England; about 36 percent were Scots-Irish, mostly from northern Ireland; 33 percent arrived from Africa, almost all of them slaves; nearly 15 percent had left the many German-language principalities (the nation of Germany did not exist until 1871); and almost 10 percent came from Scotland. In 1670, more than 9 out of 10 colonists were of English ancestry, and only 1 out of 25 was of African ancestry. By 1770, only about half the colonists were of English descent, while more than 20 percent descended from Africans. By 1770, the people of the colonies had a distinctive colonial—rather than English—profile (Map 5.1).

The booming population of the colonies hints at a second major feature of eighteenth-century colonial society: an expanding economy. Today, societies with rapidly growing populations often have more people than they can adequately feed; or, put another way, they have a high ratio of people to land. In the eighteenth-century colonies, very different conditions prevailed.

In 1700, after almost a century of settlement, nearly all the colonists lived within fifty miles of the Atlantic coast, on the edge of a vast wilderness peopled by native Indians and a few trappers and traders. The almost limitless wilderness gave the colonies an extremely low ratio of people to land. Consequently, land was cheap. Land in the colonies commonly sold for a fraction of its price in the Old World, often for only a shilling an acre, at a time when a carpenter could earn three shillings a day. Along the **frontiers** of settlement, many newcomers who lacked the money to buy land lived as squatters on unoccupied land, hoping it might eventually become theirs.

Without labor, land was almost worthless for agriculture. The abundance of land in the colonies made labor precious, and the colonists

> The most important fact about eighteenth-century colonial America is its phenomenal population growth.

"Dummy Board" of Phyllis, a New England Slave

This life-size portrait of a slave woman named Phyllis, a mulatto who worked as a domestic servant for her owner, Elizabeth Hunt Wendell, was painted sometime before 1753. Known as a "dummy board," it was propped against a wall or placed in a doorway or window to suggest that the residence was occupied and to discourage thieves, a hint of the strangers from throughout the Atlantic world who strolled by prosperous homes in colonial cities. Phyllis is portrayed as a demure, well-groomed woman whose dress and demeanor suggest that she was capable, orderly, and efficient. Unlike Mrs. Willing, Phyllis did not appear in the latest fashions of silk and lace. Instead, she wore the clothing of a servant woman, like thousands of other slave women who labored in the homes of prosperous white families. Phyllis illustrates the integration of the mundane tasks of housekeeping with the shifting currents of transatlantic commerce. Although tens of thousands of slaves were brought from Africa to the British North American colonies during the eighteenth century (like the maker of the drum shown at the beginning of this chapter), Phyllis was probably not one of them. Instead, she was most likely born in the colonies of mixed black and white parentage.

Courtesy of the Society for the Preservation of New England Antiquities / photo by David Bohl.

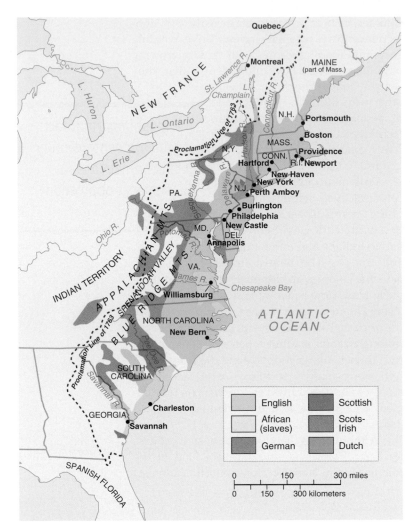

MAP 5.1   Europeans and Africans in the Eighteenth Century
This map illustrates regions where Africans and certain immigrant groups clustered. It is important to avoid misreading the map. Predominantly English and German regions, for example, also contained colonists from other places. Likewise, regions where African slaves resided in large numbers also included many whites, slave masters among them. The map suggests the polyglot diversity of eighteenth-century colonial society.

New England: From Puritan Settlers to Yankee Traders

The New England population grew sixfold during the eighteenth century but lagged behind the growth in the other colonies. Why did New England fail to keep pace? Most immigrants chose other destinations because of New England's relatively densely settled land and because Puritan orthodoxy made these colonies comparatively inhospitable to religious dissenters and those indifferent to religion. As the population grew, many settlers in search of farmland dispersed from towns, and Puritan communities lost much of their cohesion. Nonetheless, networks of economic exchange laced New Englanders to their neighbors, to Boston merchants, and to the broad currents of Atlantic commerce. In many ways, trade became a faith that competed strongly with the traditions of **Puritanism**.

Natural Increase and Land Distribution

The New England population grew mostly by natural increase, much as it had during the seventeenth century. Nearly every adult woman married. Most married women had children—often many children, thanks to the relatively low mortality rate in New England. The perils of childbirth gave wives a shorter life expectancy than husbands, but wives often lived to have six, seven, or eight babies. When a wife died, her husband usually remarried quickly. A wife's labor and companionship were too vital for a family to do without. Benjamin Franklin's father had seven children with his first wife and ten (including Benjamin) with his second.

The burgeoning New England population pressed against a limited amount of land. The interior of New England was smaller than that of colonies farther south (see Map 5.1). Moreover, as the northernmost group of colonies, New England had a contested northern and western frontier. Powerful Indian tribes, especially the Iroquois and Mahicans, jealously guarded their territories. When provoked by colonial or European disputes, the French (and Catholic) colony of Quebec also menaced the English (and **Protestant**) colonies of New England.

During the seventeenth century, New England towns parceled out land to individual families. In most cases, the original settlers prac-

always needed more. The colonists' insatiable demand for labor was the fundamental economic environment that sustained the mushrooming population. Economic historians estimate that the standard of living of free colonists (those who were not **indentured servants** or slaves) improved during the eighteenth century. By 1770, most free colonists had a higher standard of living than the majority of people elsewhere in the Atlantic world. The unique achievement of the eighteenth-century colonial economy was not the wealth of the most successful colonists but the modest economic welfare of the vast bulk of the free population.

ticed partible inheritance (they subdivided land more or less equally among sons). By the eighteenth century, the original land allotments had to be further subdivided to accommodate grandsons and great-grandsons, and many plots of land became too small for subsistence. Sons who could not hope to inherit sufficient land to farm had to move away from the town where they were born.

During the eighteenth century, colonial governments in New England abandoned the seventeenth-century policy of granting land to towns. Needing revenue, the governments of both Connecticut and Massachusetts sold land directly to individuals, including speculators. Now money, rather than membership in a community bound by a church **covenant**, determined whether a person could obtain land. The new land policy eroded the seventeenth-century pattern of settlement. As colonists moved into western Massachusetts and Connecticut and north into present-day New Hampshire and Maine, they tended to settle on individual farms rather than in the towns and villages that characterized the seventeenth century. New Englanders still depended on their relatives and neighbors for help in clearing land, raising a house, worshipping God, and having a good time. But far more than in the seventeenth century, they regulated their behavior in newly settled areas by their own individual dictates.

Farms, Fish, and Trade

A New England farm was a place to get by, not to get rich. New England farmers grew food for their families, but their fields did not produce a huge marketable surplus. Instead of one big crop, farmers grew many small ones. If they had extra, they sold to or traded with neighbors. Poor roads made travel difficult, time-consuming, and expensive, especially with bulky and heavy agricultural goods. The one major agricultural product the New England colonies exported—livestock—walked to market on its own legs. By 1770, New Englanders had only one-fourth as much wealth as free colonists in the southern colonies.

As consumers, New England farmers were the foundation of a diversified commercial economy that linked remote farms to markets throughout the world. Merchants large and small stocked imported goods—English textiles, ceramics, and metal goods; Chinese tea; West Indian sugar; and Chesapeake tobacco. Farmers'

needs for sturdy shoes, a warm coat, a sound cart, and a solid building supported local shoemakers, tailors, wheelwrights, and carpenters. Larger towns and especially Boston, housed skilled tradesmen such as cabinetmakers and silversmiths, along with printers like Benjamin Franklin's brother. Shipbuilders clustered in Boston and other ports, and they tended to do better than other **artisans** because they served the most dynamic sector of the New England economy.

Many New Englanders made their fortunes at sea, as they had since the seventeenth century. Fish accounted for more than a third of New England's eighteenth-century exports; livestock and timber made up another third. The West Indies absorbed two-thirds of all New England's exports. Slaves on Caribbean sugar plantations ate dried, salted codfish caught by New England fishermen, filled barrels crafted from New England timber with molasses and refined sugar, and loaded those barrels aboard ships bound ultimately for Europeans with a sweet tooth (Map 5.2). Almost all the rest of New England's exports went to England and continental Europe. This Atlantic commerce benefited the entire New England economy, providing jobs for laborers and tradesmen as well as for ship captains, clerks, and merchants.

Merchants dominated the commercial economy of New England and stood at the hub of trade between local folk and the international market. The largest and most successful merchants lived in Boston, where they not only bought and sold imported goods but also owned and insured the ships that carried the merchandise. When John Adams, a Massachusetts lawyer who became a leader during the American Revolution and ultimately the second president of the United States, was invited to a wealthy Boston merchant's home, he was stunned by its magnificence. It was a house "for a noble Man, a Prince," he wrote: "The Turkey Carpets, the painted Hangings, the Marble Tables, the rich Beds with crimson Damask Curtains and Counterpins, the beautiful Chimney Clock, the Spacious Garden, are the most magnificent of any Thing I have ever seen." The contrast Adams noted between the luxurious home of this merchant prince and the lives of other New Englanders indicates the polarization

> New Englanders still depended on relatives and neighbors, but far more than in the seventeenth century, they regulated their behavior in newly settled areas by their own individual dictates.

MAP 5.2   Atlantic Trade in the Eighteenth Century
This map illustrates the economic outlook of the colonies in the eighteenth century—east toward the Atlantic world rather than west toward the interior of North America. The long distances involved in the Atlantic trade and the uncertainties of seaborne travel suggest the difficulties Britain experienced governing the colonies and regulating colonial commerce.

READING THE MAP: What were the major markets for trade coming out of Europe? What goods did the English colonies import and export?
CONNECTIONS: In what ways did the flow of raw materials from the colonies affect English industry? How did English colonial trade policies influence the Atlantic trade?

FOR MORE HELP ANALYZING THIS MAP, see the map activity for this chapter in the Online Study Guide at bedfordstmartins.com/roark.

of wealth that occurred in Boston and other seaports during the eighteenth century. By 1770, the richest 5 percent of Bostonians owned about half the city's wealth; the poorest two-thirds of the population owned less than one-tenth.

Although the rich got richer and everybody else had a smaller share of the total wealth, the incidence of genuine poverty did not change much. Roughly 5 percent of the New England population qualified for poor relief throughout the eighteenth century. The colonies' growing population increased the sheer numbers of unemployed or sick, but compared with the poor in England, the colonists were better off. A Connecticut traveler wrote from England in 1764, "We in New England know nothing of poverty and want, we have no idea of the thing, how much better do our poor people live than 7/8 of the people on this much famed island."

The contrast with English poverty had meaning because the overwhelming majority of New Englanders traced their ancestry to England; New England was more homogeneous than any other region. People of African ancestry (almost all of them slaves) remained few. New Englanders had no hesitation about acquiring slaves, and many Puritan ministers owned one or two. In the Narragansett region of Rhode Island, numerous slaves were imported by the colony's prominent slave traders to raise livestock. But New England's family farms were unsuited for slave labor. Instead, slaves concentrated in towns, especially Boston, where most of them worked as domestic servants and laborers. Although the black population of New England grew to over 15,000 by 1770, it barely diluted the region's 97 percent white majority.

By 1770, the population, wealth, and commercial activity of New England differed from what they had been in 1700. Ministers still enjoyed high status, but Yankee traders had replaced Puritan saints as the symbolic New Englanders.

The Middle Colonies: Immigrants, Wheat, and Work

In 1700, almost twice as many people lived in New England as in the middle colonies of Pennsylvania, New York, New Jersey, and Delaware. But by 1770, the population of the middle colonies had multiplied tenfold—mainly from an influx of German, Irish, Scottish, and other immigrants—and nearly equaled the population of New England. Immigrants made the middle colonies a uniquely diverse society. By 1800, barely one-third of Pennsylvanians and less than half the total population of the middle colonies traced their ancestry to England.

German and Scots-Irish Immigrants

Germans made up the largest contingent of migrants from the European continent to the middle colonies. By 1770, about 85,000 Germans had arrived in the colonies. Their fellow colonists often referred to them as "Pennsylvania Dutch," an English corruption of *Deutsch*, the word the immigrants used to describe themselves.

Most German immigrants came from what is now southwestern Germany, although some hailed from German-speaking parts of Switzerland, Austria, and the Netherlands. Throughout Europe, peasants suffered from exploitation by landowners and governments and had few opportunities to improve their lives. Many German peasants, one observer noted, were "not as well off as cattle elsewhere." Devastating French invasions of Germany during Queen Anne's War (1702–1713) made ordinarily bad conditions even worse and triggered the first large-scale migration. German immigrants included numerous artisans and a few merchants, but the great majority were farmers and laborers. Economically, they represented "middling" folk, neither the poorest (who could not afford the trip) nor the better off (who did not want to leave).

By the 1720s, Germans who had established themselves in the colonies wrote back to their friends and relatives, as one reported, "of the civil and religious liberties [and] privileges, and

German Hymnal

This manuscript hymnal contains words and music created by Johann Conrad Beissel, the founder of the Seventh-Day Baptists and among the earliest musical composers in the colonies. A German sect that migrated to Pennsylvania in 1732, the Seventh-Day Baptists, like many other German immigrants, continued to worship in their native German long after arriving in the British colonies. Once owned by Benjamin Franklin, this book expresses on its title page the hymns' evocation of the Seventh-Day Baptists' vision of this world and the next: "The Bitter good, or the song of the turtledove, the Christian church here on earth, in the valley of sadness, where it bemoans its 'widowhood'; and at the same time sings of another future reunion [with God]." Roger Foley/Library of Congress.

of all the goodness I have heard and seen." Such letters prompted still more Germans to pull up stakes and embark for America, to exchange the miserable certainties of their lives in Germany for the uncertain attractions of life in the colonies.

Similar motives propelled the Scots-Irish, who considerably outnumbered German immigrants. The term *Scots-Irish* was another misleading label coined in the colonies. Immigrants labeled "Scots-Irish" actually hailed from the north of Ireland, Scotland, and northern England. Some of the Scots-Irish were Irish natives who had no personal or ancestral connection whatever with Scotland.

Like the Germans, the Scots-Irish were Protestants, but with a difference. Most German immigrants worshiped in Lutheran or German Reformed churches; many others belonged to dissenting sects such as the Mennonites, Moravians, and Amish, whose adherents sought relief from persecution they had suffered in Europe for their refusal to bear arms and to swear oaths, practices they shared with Quakers. In contrast, the Scots-Irish tended to be militant Presbyterians who seldom hesitated to bear arms or swear oaths. Like German settlers, however, Scots-Irish immigrants were clannish, residing when they could among relatives or neighbors from the old country.

In the eighteenth century, wave after wave of Scots-Irish immigrants arrived, beginning in 1717, cresting every twelve or fifteen years thereafter, and culminating in a flood of immigration in the years just before the American Revolution. Deteriorating economic conditions in northern Ireland, Scotland, and England pushed many toward America. Most of the immigrants were farm laborers or tenant farmers fleeing droughts, crop failures, high food prices, or rising rents. By 1773, British officials became so concerned about the drain of people to the colonies that they began to quiz prospective settlers about why they were leaving. The answers Scots-Irish gave echoed the motives of their predecessors: "out of work"; "poverty"; "tyranny of landlords"; and the desire to "do better in America."

Both Scots-Irish and Germans probably heard the common saying that "Pennsylvania is heaven for farmers [and] paradise for artisans," but they almost certainly did not fully understand the risks of their decision to leave their native lands. Gottfried Mittelberger, a musician who traveled from Germany to Philadelphia in 1750, described the grueling passage to America commonly experienced by eighteenth-century emigrants. Mittelberger's trip from his home village in the interior to the port of Rotterdam took seven weeks and cost four times more than the trip from Rotterdam to Philadelphia. Nearly two-thirds of all German emigrants arrived at their port of departure with no money to stock up on extra provisions for the trip or even to buy a ticket. Likewise, they could not afford to go back home. Ship captains, aware of the hunger for labor in the colonies, eagerly signed up the penniless emigrants as "redemptioners," a variant of indentured servants. A captain would agree to provide transportation to Philadelphia, where redemptioners would obtain the money to pay for their passage by borrowing it from a friend or relative who was already in the colonies or, as most did, by selling themselves as servants. Impoverished Scots-Irish emigrants, especially the majority who traveled alone rather than with families, typically paid for their passage by contracting before they sailed to become indentured servants.

Mittelberger enjoyed the amenities reserved for passengers who paid their way to Pennsylvania, but he witnessed the distress among the four hundred other Germans aboard his ship, most of them redemptioners. They were packed "as closely as herring" in bunks two feet by six feet. Seasickness compounded by exhaustion, poverty, poor food, bad water, inadequate sanitation, and tight quarters encouraged the spread of disease. The dismal conditions on Mittelberger's ship were not unusual. One historian has noted that on the sixteen immigrant ships arriving in Philadelphia in 1738, over half of all passengers died en route.

When his ship finally approached land, Mittelberger wrote, "everyone crawls from below to the deck . . . and people cry for joy, pray, and sing praises and thanks to God." Unfortunately, their troubles were far from over. Once the ship docked, passengers who had paid their fare could go ashore. Redemptioners and indentured servants—the majority of the passengers—had to stay on board until somebody came to purchase their labor. Unlike indentured servants, redemptioners negotiated independently with their purchasers about their period of servitude.

> Both Scots-Irish and Germans heard the saying that "Pennsylvania is heaven for farmers [and] paradise for artisans," but they almost certainly did not fully understand the risks of leaving their native lands.

Typically, a healthy adult redemptioner agreed to four years of labor. Indentured servants commonly served five, six, or seven years, as did weaker, younger, and less skilled redemptioners. Children ten years old or younger usually had to become indentured servants until they were twenty-one.

Pennsylvania: "The Best Poor [White] Man's Country"

New settlers, whether free or in servitude, poured into the middle colonies because they perceived unparalleled opportunities, particularly in Pennsylvania, "the best poor Man's Country in the World," as indentured servant William Moraley wrote in 1743. Although Moraley reported that "the Condition of bought Servants is very hard" and masters often failed to live up to their promise to provide decent food and clothing, opportunity abounded because there was more work to be done than workers to do it.

Most servants toiled in Philadelphia, New York City, or one of the smaller towns or villages. Artisans, small manufacturers, and shopkeepers prized the labor of male servants. Female servants

> New settlers, whether free or in servitude, poured into the middle colonies because they perceived unparalleled opportunities.

New York City Street

This painting depicts John Street, a residential neighborhood of New York City, in 1768, as recalled by the artist Joseph B. Smith early in the nineteenth century. The painting highlights the urbane pleasures of casual encounters and friendly conversations on the street. Unlike many urban streets today, John Street was quiet. People could talk casually while a horseman rode past. The street appears safe and secure. Men, women, and children show no sign of caution about theft or assault. People sit on their porches, doors ajar. Modest dwellings adjoin more elaborate homes, suggesting a mix of wealth and taste among John Street residents. Notice that fences separate house yards from the street, rather than houses from one another, hinting of friendly relations among neighbors.
Old John Street United Methodist Church.

Wampum Belt and Game Table

Delaware Indians presented this wampum belt to William Penn in the late seventeenth century to attest to peaceful land transfer and continuing friendship between the Indians and the Pennsylvania colonists. Delawares and other Indians valued wampum as currency, but the land they alienated to Penn and other colonists in the middle colonies became the foundation of prosperous farms that undermined and ultimately eliminated wampum as a form of wealth. By the eighteenth century, the hands joined on this wampum belt might have been reinterpreted by Delawares less as a symbol of friendship than of grasping colonists snatching land from reluctant Indians.

Wealth accumulated by prosperous eighteenth-century colonists supported urban artisans, such as the cabinetmaker in New York who built this elegant Chippendale table for sociable games of backgammon and cards. The table symbolizes the shift from hands joined in amity and friendship (on the wampum belt) to hands in competition with one another in games of chance that rewarded luck, shrewdness, and self-interest.

Belt: Historical Society of Pennsylvania; table: The Metropolitan Museum of Art, Rogers Fund, 1937. (37.122) Photograph by Richard Cheek. Photograph © 1984 The Metropoliton Museum of Art.

---

made valuable additions to households, where nearly all of them cleaned, washed, cooked, or minded children. From the masters' viewpoint, servants were a bargain. A master could purchase five or six years of a servant's labor for approximately the wages a common laborer would earn in four months. Wage workers could walk away from their jobs when they pleased, and they did so often enough to be troublesome to employers. Servants, however, were legally bound to work for their masters until their terms expired.

A few black slaves worked in shops and homes in Philadelphia and New York City. After Benjamin Franklin became prosperous, he purchased five slaves. Since a slave cost at least three times as much as a servant, only affluent colonists could afford the long-term investment in slave labor. While the population of African ancestry (almost all slaves) in the middle colonies grew to over 30,000 in 1770, it represented only about 7 percent of the total population, and in most of the region much less. The reason more slaves were not brought to the middle colonies was that farmers, the vast majority of the population, had little use for them. Most farms operated with family labor. Wheat, the most widely grown crop, did not require more

labor than farmers could typically muster from relatives, neighbors, and a hired hand or two.

During the eighteenth century, most slaves came to the middle colonies and New England from the West Indies. Enough arrived to prompt colonial assemblies to pass slave codes that punished slaves much more severely than servants for the same transgressions. "For the least trespass," servant Moraley reported, slaves "undergo the severest Punishment." In practice, both servants and slaves were governed more by their masters than by the laws. But in cases of abuse, servants could and did charge masters with violating the terms of their indenture contracts. The terms of a slave's bondage were set forth in a master's commands, not in a written contract.

Small numbers of slaves managed to obtain their freedom, but free African Americans did not escape whites' firm convictions about black inferiority and white supremacy. Whites' racism and blacks' lowly social status made African Americans scapegoats for European Americans' suspicions and anxieties. In 1741, when arson and several unexplained thefts plagued New York City, officials suspected a murderous slave conspiracy. On the basis of little more than evidence of slaves' "insolence" (refusal to conform fully to whites' expectations of servile behavior), city authorities had thirteen slaves burned at the stake and eighteen others hanged. Although slaves were certifiably poor (they usually had no property whatever), they were not included among the poor for whom the middle colonies were reputed to be the best country in the world.

Immigrants swarmed to the middle colonies because of the availability of land. The Penn family encouraged immigration to bring in potential buyers for their enormous tracts of land in Pennsylvania. From the beginning, Pennsylvania followed a policy of negotiating with Indian tribes to purchase additional land. This policy greatly reduced the violent frontier clashes evident elsewhere in the colonies. Yet the Penn family did not shrink from pushing its agreements with Indian tribes to the limit and beyond. In a dispute with tribes on the northern Delaware River in 1737, the Penn family pulled out a document showing that in 1686 local tribes had granted the Penns land that stretched as far as a man could walk in a day and a half. Under the terms of this infamous "Walking Purchase," the Penns sent out three runners, two of whom collapsed before the thirty-six hours expired. The third runner managed to cover sixty miles of wilderness, approximately doubling the size of the Penns' claim.

Few colonists drifted beyond the northern boundaries of Pennsylvania. Owners of the huge estates in New York's Hudson valley preferred to rent rather than sell their land, and thus they attracted fewer immigrants. The Iroquois dominated the lucrative fur trade of the St. Lawrence valley and eastern Great Lakes, and they had the political and military strength to defend their territory from colonial encroachment. Few settlers wanted to risk having their scalps lifted by Iroquois warriors in northern New York when they could choose to settle instead in the comparatively safe environs of Pennsylvania.

The price of farmland depended on soil quality, access to water, distance from a market town, and the extent of improvements. One hundred acres of improved land that had been cleared, plowed, fenced, and ditched, and per-

Patterns of Settlement, 1700–1770

haps had a house and barn built on it, cost three or four times more than the same acreage of uncleared, unimproved land. Since the cheapest land always lay at the margin of settlement, would-be farmers tended to migrate to promising areas just beyond already improved farms. From Philadelphia, settlers moved north along the Delaware River and west along the Schuylkill and Susquehanna rivers. By midcentury, settlement had reached the eastern slopes of the Appalachian Mountains, and newcomers spilled south down the fertile valley of the Shenandoah River into western Virginia and the Carolinas. Thousands of settlers migrated from the middle colonies through this back door to the South.

Farmers made the middle colonies the breadbasket of North America. They planted a wide variety of crops to feed their families, but they grew wheat in abundance. Flour milling was the number-one industry and flour the number-one export, constituting nearly three-fourths of all exports from the middle colonies. Pennsylvania flour fed residents in other colonies, in southern Europe, and, above all, in the West Indies (see Map 5.2). For farmers, the world grain market proved risky but profitable. Grain prices rose steadily after 1720; by 1770, a bushel of wheat was worth twice (in real terms, that is, adjusted for inflation) what it had been fifty years earlier.

The standard of living in rural Pennsylvania was probably higher than in any other agricultural region of the eighteenth-century world. The comparatively widespread prosperity of all the middle colonies permitted residents to indulge in a half-century shopping spree for English imports. The middle colonies' per capita consumption of imported goods from England more than doubled between 1720 and 1770, far outstripping the per capita consumption of English goods in New England and the southern colonies.

At the crossroads of trade in wheat exports and English imports stood Philadelphia. By 1776, Philadelphia had a larger population than any other city in the entire British Empire except London. Merchants occupied the top stratum of Philadelphia society. In a city where only 2 percent of the residents owned enough property to qualify to vote, merchants built grand homes and dominated local government. Many of Philadelphia's wealthiest merchants were Quakers. Quaker traits of industry, thrift, honesty, and sobriety encouraged the accumulation of wealth. A colonist complained that a Quaker "prays for his neighbor on First Days [the Sabbath] and then preys on him the other six."

The ranks of merchants reached downward to aspiring tradesmen like Benjamin Franklin. After he started to publish the *Pennsylvania Gazette* in 1728, Franklin opened a shop, run mostly by his wife, Deborah, that sold a little bit of everything: cheese, codfish, coffee, goose feathers, sealing wax, soap, and now and then a slave. In 1733, Franklin began to publish *Poor*

Bethlehem, Pennsylvania

This view of the small community of Bethlehem, Pennsylvania, in 1757 dramatizes the profound transformation of the natural landscape wrought in the eighteenth century by highly motivated human labor. Founded by Moravian immigrants in 1740, Bethlehem must have appeared at first like the dense woods on the upper left horizon. In fewer than twenty years, precisely laid-out orchards and fields replaced forests and glades. By carefully penning their livestock (lower center right) and fencing their fields (lower left) farmers safeguarded their livelihoods from the risks and disorders of untamed nature. Individual farmsteads (lower center) and impressive multistory brick town buildings (upper center) integrated the bounty of the land with the delights of community life. Few eighteenth-century communities were as orderly as Bethlehem, but many effected a comparable transformation of the environment.

Print Collection, Miriam and Ira D. Walsh Division of Art, Prints and Photographs, The New York Public Library. Astor, Lenox, and Tilden.

FOR MORE HELP ANALYZING THIS IMAGE, see the visual activity for this chapter in the Online Study Guide at bedfordstmartins.com/roark.

ARCH STREET FERRY, PHILADELPHIA.

Philadelphia Wharf

This early-nineteenth-century drawing of the Arch Street wharf in Philadelphia approximates the world Benjamin Franklin entered when he stepped ashore in 1723. The wharf was a center of industrious activity; almost everyone depicted appears to be working. The pulse of Atlantic commerce propels casks of products from the deck of the small local sailboat (right) toward the hold of large ocean-going ships (center) bound for England and Europe, ships that had unloaded European products in Philadelphia, such as the silk brocade for Mrs. Willing's dress (page 136). The small rowboat carrying four people (just to the right of the large ships) is probably similar to the boat Franklin rowed to the city. Coordinating the complicated comings and goings of people and goods that moved through the wharf required individuals who combined intelligence, energy, and discipline with efficiency, reliability, and trustworthiness—traits Franklin and other eighteenth-century colonists sought to cultivate.

Rare Book Department, The Free Library of Philadelphia.

Richard's Almanack, a calendar of weather predictions, astrological alignments, and pithy epigrams. Poor Richard preached the likelihood of long-term rewards for tireless labor. The *Almanack* sold thousands of copies, quickly becoming Franklin's most profitable product.

The popularity of *Poor Richard's Almanack* suggests that many Pennsylvanians thought less about the pearly gates than about their pocketbooks. Where were the mysteries of divine providence in what might be considered Poor Richard's motto for the middle colonies, "God gives all Things to Industry"? The promise of a worldly payoff made work a secular faith in the middle colonies. Poor Richard advised, "Work as if you were to live 100 years, Pray as if you were to die Tomorrow."

William Penn's Quaker utopia became a center of worldly affluence whose most famous citizen, Franklin, was neither a Quaker nor a utopian. Quakers remained influential, but Franklin spoke for most colonists with his aphorisms of work, discipline, and thrift that echoed Quaker rules for outward behavior. Franklin's maxims did not look to the Quakers' divine inner light for guidance. They depended instead on the spark of ambition and the glow of gain.

The Southern Colonies: Land of Slavery

Between 1700 and 1770, the population of the southern colonies of Virginia, Maryland, North Carolina, South Carolina, and Georgia grew almost ninefold. By 1770, about twice as many people lived in the South as in either the middle colonies or New England. As elsewhere, natural increase and immigration accounted for the rapid population growth. Many Scots-Irish and German immigrants funneled from the middle colonies into the southern backcountry. Other immigrants were indentured servants (mostly English and Scots-Irish) who followed their seventeenth-century predecessors. But slaves made the most striking contribution to the booming southern colonies, transforming the racial composition of the population. Slavery became the defining characteristic of the southern colonies during the eighteenth century, shaping the region's economy, society, and politics.

The Atlantic Slave Trade and the Growth of Slavery

The number of southerners of African ancestry (nearly all of them slaves) rocketed from just over 20,000 in 1700 to well over 400,000 in 1770. The black population increased nearly three times faster than the South's briskly growing white population. Consequently, the proportion of southerners who were black grew from 20 percent in 1700 to 40 percent in 1770.

Southern colonists clustered into two distinct geographic and agricultural zones. The colonies in the upper South, surrounding the Chesapeake Bay, specialized in growing tobacco, as they had since the early seventeenth century. Throughout the eighteenth century, nine out of ten southern whites and eight out of ten southern blacks lived in the Chesapeake region. The upper South retained a white majority during the eighteenth century.

In the lower South, a much smaller cluster of colonists inhabited the coastal region and spe-cialized in the production of rice and indigo (a plant used to make blue dye). Lower South colonists made up only 5 percent of the total population of the southern colonies in 1700 but inched upward to 15 percent by 1770. South Carolina was the sole British colony along the southern Atlantic coast until 1732, when Georgia was founded. (North Carolina, founded in 1711, was largely an extension of the Chesapeake region.) Blacks in South Carolina, in contrast to every other British mainland colony, outnum-bered whites almost two to one; in some low-country districts, the ratio of blacks to whites exceeded ten to one.

The enormous growth in the South's slave population occurred through natural increase

---

MAP 5.3   The Atlantic Slave Trade

Although the Atlantic slave trade lasted from about 1450 to 1870, its peak occurred during the eigh-teenth century, when more than six million African slaves were imported to the New World. Only a small fraction of the African slaves imported to the Western Hemisphere were taken to British North America; most went to sugar plantations in Brazil and the Caribbean.

READING THE MAP: From where in Africa did most slaves originate? Approximately how far was the trip from the busiest ports of origin to the two most common New World destinations?

CONNECTIONS: Why were so many more African slaves sent to the West Indies and Brazil than to British North America?

FOR MORE HELP ANALYZING THIS MAP, see the map activity for this chapter in the Online Study Guide at bedfordstmartins.com/roark.

TABLE 5.1	SLAVE IMPORTS, 1451–1870

Estimated Slave Imports to the Western Hemisphere

1451–1600	275,000
1601–1700	1,341,000
1701–1810	6,100,000
1811–1870	1,900,000

and the flourishing Atlantic slave trade (Map 5.3 and Table 5.1). Slave ships brought almost 300,000 Africans to British North America between 1619 and 1780. Of these Africans, 95 percent arrived in the South and 96 percent arrived during the eighteenth century. Unlike indentured servants or redemptioners, these Africans did not choose to come to the colonies. Most of them had been born into free families in villages located within a few hundred miles of the West African coast. Although they shared African origins, they came from many different African cultures, including Akan, Angolan, Asante, Bambara, Gambian, Igbo, Mandinga, and others. They spoke different languages, worshipped different deities, followed different rules of kinship, grew different crops, and recognized different rulers. The most important experience they had in common was enslavement. Captured in war, kidnapped, or sold into slavery by other Africans, they were brought to the coast, sold to African traders who assembled slaves for resale, and sold again to European or colonial slave traders or ship captains, who bought them for shipment to the New World. Packed below decks in the holds of a slave ship, two to three hundred or more slaves were subjected to the infamous **Middle Passage** crossing of the Atlantic and then sold yet again by the ship captain to a colonial slave merchant or to a southern **planter**.

The voices of Africans caught up in the slave trade have been enveloped in a deafening historical silence, with one major exception. In 1789, Olaudah Equiano published *The Interesting Narrative*, an account of his own enslavement that hints at the stories that might have been told by the thousands of silenced Africans. Equiano was born in 1745 in the interior of what is now Nigeria. "I had never heard of white men or Europeans, nor of the sea," he recalled. One day when Equiano was eleven years old, two men and a woman, all Africans, broke into his home, seized him and his sister, and carried them off. The kidnappers soon separated Equiano from his sister, leaving him "in a state of distraction not to be described. I cried and grieved continually, and for several days did not eat anything but what they forced into my mouth."

During the next six or seven months, Equiano was sold to several different African masters, each of whom moved him closer to the coast. When he arrived at the coast, a slave ship waited offshore. Equiano feared that he had "gotten into a world of bad spirits," that he was going to be killed and "eaten by those white men with horrible looks, red faces, and loose hair."

Olaudah Equiano

This portrait was painted by an unknown English artist about 1780, when Equiano was in his mid-thirties, more than a decade after he had bought his freedom. The portrait evokes Equiano's successful acculturation to the customs of eighteenth-century England. His clothing and hairstyle reflect the fashions of respectable young Englishmen. In his *Interesting Narrative*, Equiano explained that he had learned to speak and understand English while he was a slave. He wrote that he "looked upon [the English] . . . as men superior to us [Africans], and therefore I had the stronger desire to resemble them, to imbibe their spirit and imitate their manners; I therefore embraced every occasion of improvement, and every new thing that I observed I treasured up in my memory." Equiano's embrace of English culture did not cause him to forsake his African roots. He honored his dual identity by campaigning against slavery. His *Narrative* was one of the most important and powerful antislavery documents of the time.

Royal Albert Memorial Museum, Exeter, Devon, UK / Bridgeman Art Library.

Once the ship set sail, many slaves died from sickness, crowded together in suffocating heat fouled by filth of all descriptions. "The shrieks of the women and the groans of the dying rendered the whole a scene of horror almost inconceivable," Equiano recalled. Most of the slaves on the ship were sold in Barbados, but Equiano and other leftovers were shipped off to Virginia, where Equiano "saw few or none of our native Africans and not one soul who could talk to me." Equiano felt isolated and "exceedingly miserable" because he "had no person to speak to that I could understand." He finally was sold to a white man, the captain of a tobacco ship bound for England. Equiano remained a slave for ten years, traveling frequently from England to the West Indies and North America until he bought his freedom in 1766.

Only about 15 percent of the slaves brought into the southern colonies came as Equiano did, aboard ships from the West Indies. Merchants in the North American colonies often specialized in this trade; Equiano himself was owned for several years by a Quaker merchant from Philadelphia who traded extensively with the West Indies. All the other slaves brought into the southern colonies came directly from Africa, and almost all the ships that brought them (roughly 90 percent) belonged to British merchants. Most slaves on board were young adults, men usually outnumbering women two to one. Children under the age of fourteen, like Equiano, were typically no more than 10 or 15 percent of a cargo.

Mortality during the Middle Passage varied considerably from ship to ship. On average, about 15 percent of the slaves died, but sometimes half or more perished. The average mortality among the white crew of slave ships was often nearly as bad. In general, the longer the voyage lasted, the larger was the number of deaths. Recent studies suggest that many slaves succumbed not only to virulent epidemic diseases such as smallpox and dysentery but also to acute dehydration caused by fluid loss from heavy perspiration, vomiting, and diarrhea combined with a severe shortage of drinking water.

Normally an individual planter purchased at any one time a relatively small number of newly arrived Africans, or "new Negroes," as they were called. Planters preferred to purchase small groups of slaves to permit the newcomers to be trained by the planters' other slaves. Like Equiano, newly arrived Africans were often profoundly depressed, demoralized, and disoriented. Planters counted on their other slaves—either those born into slavery in the colonies (often called "country-born" or "creole" slaves) or Africans who had arrived earlier—to help new Negroes become accustomed to their strange new surroundings.

Planters' preferences for slaves from specific regions of Africa aided slaves' acculturation (or "seasoning," as it was called) to the routines of bondage in the southern colonies. Chesapeake planters preferred slaves from Senegambia, the Gold Coast, or—like Equiano—the Bight of Biafra, the origin of 40 percent of all Africans imported to the Chesapeake. South Carolina planters favored slaves from the central African Congo and Angola regions, the origin of about 40 percent of the African slaves they imported (see Map 5.3). Although slaves within each of these regions spoke many different languages, enough linguistic and cultural similarities existed that they could usually communicate with other Africans from the same region.

Seasoning acclimated new Africans to the physical as well as the cultural environment of the southern colonies. Slaves who had just endured the Middle Passage were poorly nourished, weak, and sick. In this vulnerable state they encountered the alien diseases of North America without having developed a biological arsenal of acquired immunities. As many as 10 or 15 percent of newly arrived Africans, sometimes more, died during their first year in the southern colonies.

While newly enslaved Africans poured into the southern colonies, slave women made an especially significant contribution to the growth of the black population by giving birth to slave babies, causing the slave population in the South to mushroom. Slave owners encouraged these births. Thomas Jefferson explained, "I consider the labor of a breeding [slave] woman as no object, that a [slave] child raised every 2 years is of more profit than the crop of the best laboring [slave] man." The growing number of slave babies set the southern colonies apart from other New World slave societies, which experienced a natural decrease of the slave population (slave deaths exceeded births). The high rate of natural increase in the southern colonies meant that by the 1740s the majority of southern slaves were country-born. The large numbers of newly enslaved Africans made the influence of African culture in the eighteenth-century South stronger than ever before—or since.

The African Slave Trade

The African slave trade existed to satisfy the New World's demand for labor and Europe's voracious appetite for such New World products as sugar, tobacco, and rice. African men, women, and children, like those pictured in this early eighteenth-century engraving of a family residence in Sierra Leone, were kidnapped or captured in wars—typically by other Africans—and enslaved. Uprooted from their homes and kin, they were usually taken to coastal enclaves where African traders and European ship captains negotiated prices, made deals, and often branded the newly enslaved people. The collaboration between Europeans and their African trading partners is evident in the seventeenth-century Benin bronze box in the shape of a royal palace in Nigeria guarded by massive predatory birds and two Portuguese soldiers. Jammed into the holds of slave ships, enslaved Africans made the dreaded Middle Passage to the New World. The model of a slave ship shown here was used in parliamentary debates by antislavery leaders in Britain to demonstrate the inhumanity of shipping people as if they were just so much tightly packed cargo. The model does not show another typical feature of slave ships: weapons. Slaves vastly outnumbered the crews aboard the ships, and crew members justifiably feared slave uprisings.

Staatliche Museen Zu Berlin, Preussischer Kulturbesitz; Courtesy, Earl Gregg Swen Library, College of William and Mary, Williamsburg, Virginia; Wilberforce House, Hull City Museums and Art Galleries, UK / Bridgeman Art Library.

Slave Labor and African American Culture

Southern planters expected slaves to work from sunup to sundown and beyond. George Washington wrote that his slaves should "be at their work as soon as it is light, work til it is dark, and be diligent while they are at it." The conflict between the masters' desire for maximum labor and the slaves' reluctance to do more than necessary made the threat of physical punishment a constant for eighteenth-century slaves. Masters preferred black slaves to white indentured servants, not just because slaves served for life but also because colonial laws did not limit the force masters could use against slaves. As a traveler observed in 1740, "A new negro . . . will require more discipline than a young spaniel. . . . let a hundred men show him how to hoe, or drive a wheelbarrow; he'll still take the one by the bottom and the other by the wheel and . . . often die before [he] can be conquered." Slaves, the traveler noted, were not stupid or simply obstinate; despite the inevitable punishment, they resisted their masters' demands because of their "greatness of soul," their stubborn unwillingness to conform to their masters' definition of them as merely slaves.

Some slaves escalated their acts of resistance to direct physical confrontation with the master, mistress, or an overseer. But a hoe raised in anger, a punch in the face, or a desperate swipe with a knife led to swift and predictable retaliation by whites. Throughout the southern colonies, the balance of physical power rested securely in the hands of whites.

Rebellion occurred, however, at Stono, South Carolina, in 1739. Before dawn on a September Sunday, a group of about twenty slaves attacked a country store, killed the two storekeepers, confiscated the store's guns, ammunition, and powder, and set out toward Spanish Florida after pausing to set the severed heads of their victims on the store's front steps. Enticing other rebel slaves to join the march south, the group plundered and burned more than a half dozen plantations and killed more than twenty white men, women, and children. A mounted force of whites quickly suppressed the rebellion. They placed rebels' heads atop mileposts along the road, grim reminders of the consequences of rebellion. The Stono rebellion illustrated that eighteenth-century slaves had no chance of overturning slavery and very little chance of defending themselves in any bold strike for freedom. After the rebellion, South Carolina legislators enacted repressive laws designed to guarantee that whites would always have the upper hand. No other similar uprising occurred during the colonial period.

Slaves maneuvered constantly to protect themselves and to gain a measure of autonomy within the boundaries of slavery. In Chesapeake tobacco fields, most slaves were subject to close supervision by whites. In the lower South, the task system gave slaves some control over the pace of their work and some discretion in the use of the rest of their time. A "task" was typically defined as a certain area of ground to be planted, cultivated, and harvested or a specific job to be completed. A slave who completed the assigned task might use the remainder of the day to work in a garden, fish, hunt, spin, weave, sew, or cook. When masters sought to boost productivity by increasing tasks, slaves did what they could to defend customary practices.

Eighteenth-century slaves also planted the roots of African American lineages that branch out to the present. Historians are only beginning to explore the kin networks slaves built; much remains unknown. But it is clear that slaves valued family ties and that, as in West African societies, kinship structured slaves' relations with one another. Slave parents often gave a child the name of a grandparent, aunt, or uncle. In West Africa, kinship not only identified a person's place among living relatives; it also linked the person to ancestors among the dead and to descendants in the future. Newly imported African slaves usually arrived alone, like Equiano, without kin. Often slaves who had traversed the Middle Passage on the same ship adopted one another as "brothers" and "sisters." Likewise, as new Negroes were seasoned and incorporated into existing slave communities, established families often adopted them as "fictive" kin.

When possible, slaves expressed many other features of their West African origins in their lives on New World plantations. They gave their children traditional dolls and African names such as Cudjo or Quash, Minda or Fuladi. They grew food crops familiar to those in Africa, such as yams and okra. They constructed huts with mud walls and thatched roofs similar to African residences. They fashioned banjos, drums, and other musical instruments, held dances, and observed funeral rites that echoed African practices. In these and many

Eliza Lucas Pinckney's Gown

When Eliza Lucas was sixteen years old in 1738, she took over day-to-day management of her father's rice plantations when he was called to duty in the British army. Highly educated, independent, and energetic, Lucas relished her duties and introduced numerous innovations on the plantations, including the cultivation of indigo— which became a major export crop in South Carolina— and silk worms. She married Charles Pinckney, a wealthy rice planter, in 1744 and continued her interest in agricultural innovation while raising four children. The gown shown here was made for Eliza Lucas Pinckney out of silk she grew on her plantation and sent to England to be dyed and woven.

Smithsonian Institution, Washington, D.C.

other ways, slaves drew upon their African heritages to endow their personal lives with relationships and meanings that they controlled, as much as the oppressive circumstances of slavery permitted.

Tobacco, Rice, and Prosperity

Slaves' labor bestowed prosperity on their masters, British merchants, and the monarchy. The southern colonies supplied 90 percent of all North American exports to England. Rice exports from the lower South exploded from less than half a million pounds in 1700 to eighty million pounds in 1770, nearly all of it grown by slaves. Exports of indigo also boomed. Together, rice and indigo made up three-fourths of lower South exports, nearly two-thirds of them going to England and most of the rest to the West Indies, where sugar-growing slaves ate slave-grown rice. Tobacco was by far the most important export from British North America; by 1770, it represented almost one-third of all colonial exports and three-fourths of all Chesapeake exports. And under the provisions of the Navigation Acts (see chapter 4), nearly all of it went to England, where the monarchy collected a lucrative tax on each pound. British merchants then reexported more than 80 percent of the tobacco to the European continent, pocketing a nice markup for their troubles.

These products of slave labor made the southern colonies by far the richest in North America. The per capita wealth of free whites in the South was four times greater than that in New England and three times that in the middle colonies. At the top of the wealth pyramid stood the rice grandees of the lower South and the tobacco gentry of the Chesapeake. These elite families commonly resided on large estates in handsome mansions adorned by luxurious gardens, maintained and supported by slaves. The extravagant lifestyle of one gentry family astonished a young tutor from New Jersey, who noted that during the winter months the family kept twenty-eight large fires roaring, requiring six oxen to haul in a heavy cartload of slave-cut wood four times a day. By contrast, **yeoman** families—who supported themselves on small plots of land without slaves and cut their own wood—normally warmed themselves around one fire.

The vast differences in wealth among white southerners engendered envy and occasional tension between rich and poor, but remarkably

Westover Plantation House
William Byrd II, a leading Virginia planter and large slaveholder, built this house about 1730 and
named it Westover, after a relative of a previous Virginia governor. Facing the James River and visible from every ship that sailed past, the house embodies the devotion of Byrd and other prominent Virginians to principles of order, symmetry, and balance commonly found among fine English
homes of the era. The house evokes the Virginia gentry's widely shared sense of confidence, stability, and permanence.
Picture Research Consultants & Archives.

little open hostility. In private, the planter elite
spoke disparagingly of humble whites but in
public acknowledged their lesser neighbors as
equals, at least in belonging to the superior—in
their minds—white race. Looking upward,
white yeomen and tenants (who owned neither
land nor slaves) sensed the gentry's condescen-
sion and veiled contempt. But they also appreciated the gentry for granting favors, upholding
white supremacy, and keeping slaves in their
place. While racial slavery made a few whites
much richer than others, it also gave those who
did not get rich a powerful reason to feel similar
(in race) to those who were so different (in
wealth).

The slaveholding gentry dominated the politics and economy of the southern colonies. In
Virginia, only adult white men who owned at
least one hundred acres of unimproved land or
twenty-five acres of land with a house could
vote. This property-holding requirement prevented about 40 percent of white men in Virginia
from voting for representatives to the House of
Burgesses. In South Carolina, only fifty acres of
land were required to vote, and most adult white
men qualified. But in both colonies, voters
elected members of the gentry to serve in the
colonial legislature. The gentry passed elected
political offices from generation to generation,
almost as if they were hereditary. Politically, the
gentry built a self-perpetuating oligarchy—rule
by the elite few—with the votes of their many
humble neighbors.

The gentry also set the cultural standard in
the southern colonies. They entertained lavishly,
gambled regularly, and attended Anglican
(Church of England) services more for social
than for religious reasons. Above all, they culti-

vated the leisurely pursuit of happiness. They did not condone idleness, however. Their many pleasures and responsibilities as plantation owners kept them busy. Thomas Jefferson, a phenomenally productive member of the gentry, recalled that his earliest childhood memory was of being carried on a pillow by a family slave— a powerful image of the slave hands supporting the gentry's leisure and achievement.

Unifying Experiences

While the societies of New England, the middle colonies, and the southern colonies became more sharply differentiated during the eighteenth century, colonists throughout British North America shared certain unifying experiences that eluded settlers in Spanish and French colonies. The first was economic. The economies of all three British regions had their roots in agriculture. But the tempo of commerce quickened during the eighteenth century. Colonists sold their distinctive products in markets that, in turn, offered to consumers throughout British North America a more or less uniform array of goods. A second unifying experience was a decline in the importance of religion. Some settlers called for a revival of religious intensity, but for most people religion mattered less, the affairs of the world more, than they had in the seventeenth century. Third, white inhabitants throughout British North America became aware that they shared a distinctive identity as *British* colonists. Thirteen different governments presided over these North American colonies, but all of them answered to the British monarchy. Royal officials who expected loyalty from the colonists often had difficulty obtaining obedience. The British colonists asserted their prerogatives as British subjects to defend their special colonial interests.

Commerce and Consumption

Eighteenth-century commerce whetted the appetite to consume. Colonial products spurred the development of mass markets throughout the Atlantic world (Figure 5.1). Huge increases in the supply of colonial tobacco and sugar brought the price of these small luxuries within reach of most free whites. Colonial goods brought into focus an important lesson of eighteenth-century commerce: Ordinary people, not just the wealthy elite, would buy the things that they desired in addition to what they absolutely needed. Even

news, formerly restricted mostly to a few people through face-to-face conversations or private letters, became an object of public consumption through the innovation of newspapers. (See "The Promise of Technology," page 156.) With the appropriate stimulus, market demand seemed unlimited.

The Atlantic commerce that took colonial goods to markets in England brought objects of consumer desire back to the colonies. English merchants and manufacturers recognized that colonists made excellent customers, and the Navigation Acts (see chapter 4) gave English exporters privileged access to the colonial market. By midcentury, export-oriented industries in England were growing ten times faster than firms attuned to the home market. Most English exports went to the vast European market, where potential customers outnumbered those in the colonies by more than one hundred to one. But as European competition stiffened, colonial markets became increasingly important. English exports to North America multiplied eightfold between 1700 and 1770, outpacing the rate of population growth after midcentury (Figure 5.1). When the colonists' eagerness to consume exceeded their ability to pay, English exporters willingly extended credit, and colonial debts soared.

Imported mirrors, silver plate, spices, bed and table linens, clocks, tea services, wigs, books, and more infiltrated parlors, kitchens, and bedrooms throughout the colonies. Despite the many differences among the colonists, the consumption of English exports built a certain material uniformity across region, religion, class, and status. Consumption of English exports did not simply tie the colonists to the British economy. It also made the colonists look and feel more British even though they lived at the edge of a wilderness an ocean away from England.

The rising tide of colonial consumption had other less visible but no less important consequences. Consumption presented women and men with a novel array of choices. In many respects, the choices might appear trivial: whether to buy knives and forks, teacups, or a clock. But such small choices confronted eighteenth-century consumers with a big question: "What do

> Colonial goods brought into focus an important lesson of eighteenth-century commerce: Ordinary people, not just the wealthy elite, would buy the things that they desired in addition to what they absolutely needed.

The Printing Press: "The Spring of Knowledge"

James Franklin's Printing Press
Newport Historical Society.

In the eighteenth century, colonial printers began to publish newspapers. Since the 1630s, colonial printers had used presses to churn out books, pamphlets, broadsides, government announcements, legal forms, invitations, and even promissory notes. The innovation of compiling newsworthy information and publishing it on a regular schedule began in 1704 with the appearance of the *Boston News-Letter*, which was usually printed on both sides of a single sheet of paper smaller than conventional typing paper. Each week the *News-Letter* contained reprints of articles that had appeared in English newspapers, along with a few tidbits of local news such as deaths, fires, storms, and ship arrivals.

For years, the audience for such information remained small; the editor complained in 1719 that he could not sell three hundred copies of each issue. Nonetheless, a competing newspaper, the *Boston Gazette*, began publication in that year. It was printed by James Franklin on his press, which he had brought from England. Both the *Gazette* and the *News-Letter* submitted their copy to the governor for official approval before the newspapers were printed. Frustrated by this official scrutiny, Franklin started a new paper, the

New England Courant, which set out to thumb its nose at officialdom, both governmental and religious. The *Courant* pledged "to entertain the Town with the most comical and diverting Incidents of Humane Life" and to "expose the Vice and Follies of Persons of all Ranks and Degrees." Franklin's press—operated faithfully by his apprentice brother, Benjamin— broadcast to the reading public dissenting opinions previously confined to private conversations.

By 1740, more than a dozen newspapers were being published in the colonies, and their numbers continued to increase. Relatively high rates of literacy gave them a large audience. In the northern colonies, readers included well over half of adult men and nearly half of adult women. In the southern colonies, literacy rates among whites were slightly lower but still considerably above those in Europe. Since whites tried to prevent slaves from learning to read, literacy rates remained low among southern blacks.

The information that newspapers printed spread far beyond readers. Newspapers were often read aloud, not just at home but in workshops, taverns, and courthouses. In these public places, people who could not read listened to the controversial ideas, partisan accusations, and salacious rumors that printers relished. An eighteenth-century poem illustrates the many connections between news and audiences cultivated by colonial newspapers:

News'papers are the spring of
   knowledge,
The gen'ral source throughout the
   nation.
Of ev'ry modern conversation.
What would this mighty people do,
If there, alas! were nothing new?

A News-paper is like a feast,
Some dish there is for ev'ry guest;
Some large, some small, some strong,
   some tender,
For ev'ry stomach, stout or slender;
Those who roast beef and ale delight
   in,
Are pleas'd with trumpets, drums, and
   fighting;
For those who are more puny made,
Are arts and sciences, and trade;
For fanciful and am'rous blood,
We have a soft poetic food;
For witty and satyric folks,
High-season'd, acid, BITTER JOKES;
And when we strive to please the mob,
A jest, a quarrel, or a job.

If any gentleman wants a wife,
(A partner, as 'tis termed, for life)
An advertisement does the thing,
And quickly brings the pretty thing.

If you want health, consult our pages,
You shall be well, and live for ages. . . .

Our services you can't express,
The good we do you hardly guess;
There's not a want of human kind,
But we a remedy can find.

When newspapers employed the technology of printing to publish everything from political news to advertisements for a spouse, all kinds of information and ideas began to diffuse more readily beyond official channels and to help form public opinion. Combining the old technology of printing with the new currents of commerce, dissent, and enlightenment, eighteenth-century newspapers created a novel awareness of the problems and possibilities of public life.

John Peter Zenger's Newspaper

This issue of John Peter Zenger's *New-York Weekly Journal* contained on the third of its four pages an article criticizing New York's governor. For this and other critical articles, the governor had Zenger tried for seditious libel in 1735. The jury sided with Zenger and acquitted him, although the law favored the governor. Like Zenger, printers throughout the colonies continued to be harassed by public officials who tried to censor irreverent and independent publishers. But colonial governments were too weak to suppress dissenting opinions for very long. Vigorous political commentary like that featured on the page shown here found an avid audience among colonial readers.

Courtesy, American Antiquarian Society.

FIGURE 5.1

Colonial Exports, 1768–1772

These pie charts provide an overview of the colonial export economy in the 1760s. The first two show that almost two-thirds of colonial exports came from the South and that the majority of the colonies' exports went to Great Britain. The remaining charts illustrate the distinctive patterns of exports in each colonial region. Fish, livestock, and wood products were New England's most important exports; they were sent primarily to the West Indies, only a small fraction going to Great Britain. From the colonial breadbasket in the middle colonies, grain products made up three-fourths of all exports, most of which went to the West Indies or to southern Europe. The Chesapeake also exported some grain, but tobacco accounted for three-fourths of the region's export trade, nearly all of it bound for Great Britain as mandated by the Navigation Acts. Rice and indigo comprised three-fourths of the exports from the lower South, the bulk of which was sent to Great Britain. Taken together, these charts reveal Britain's economic interest in the exports of the North American colonies.

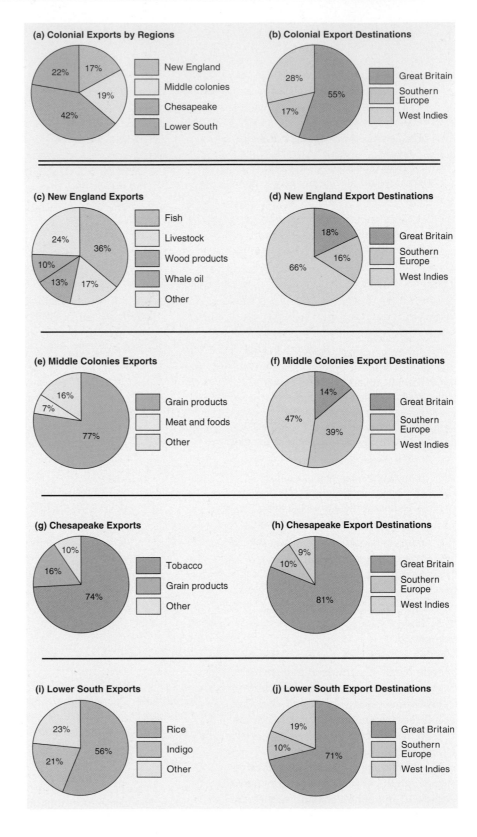

you want?" As colonial consumers defined and expressed their desires with greater frequency during the eighteenth century, they became accustomed to thinking of themselves as individuals who had the power to make decisions that influenced the quality of their lives—attitudes of significance in the hierarchical world of eighteenth-century British North America.

Religion, Enlightenment, and Revival

Eighteenth-century colonists could choose from almost as many religions as consumer goods. Virtually all of the bewildering variety of religious denominations represented some form of Christianity, almost all of them Protestant. Slaves made up the largest group of non-Christians. A few slaves converted to Christianity in Africa or after they arrived in North America, but most continued to embrace elements of indigenous African religions. Roman Catholics concentrated in Maryland as they had since the seventeenth century, but even there they were outnumbered by Protestants.

The varieties of Protestant faith and practice ranged across an extremely broad spectrum. The thousands of immigrants in the middle colonies and the southern backcountry included militant Baptists and Presbyterians. Huguenots who had fled persecution in Catholic France peopled congregations in several cities. In New England, old-style Puritanism splintered into strands of Congregationalism that differed over fine points of theological doctrine. The Congregational Church was the official established church in New England, and all residents paid taxes for its support. Throughout the plantation South and in urban centers like Charleston, New York, and Philadelphia, prominent colonists belonged to the Anglican Church. The Anglican Church in the South, like the Congregational Church in New England, received support in the form of tax monies. But in both regions, dissenting faiths grew, and in most colonies adherents of other faiths won the right to worship publicly, although the established churches retained official sanction.

Many educated colonists became deists, looking for God's plan in nature more than in the Bible. Deists shared the ideas of eighteenth-century European **Enlightenment** thinkers. Participating in a multifaceted intellectual movement that challenged many conventional ideas, Enlightenment thinkers tended to agree that science and reason could disclose God's laws in the natural order. In the colonies as well as in Europe, Enlightenment ideas encouraged people to study the world around them, to think for themselves, and to ask whether the disorderly appearance of things masked the principles of a deeper, more profound natural order. From New England towns to southern drawing rooms, individuals met to discuss such matters. Philadelphia was the center of these conversations, especially after the formation of the American Philosophical Society in 1769, an outgrowth of an earlier discussion group organized by Benjamin Franklin, who was a deist. The American Philosophical Society fostered communication among leading colonial thinkers; Benjamin Franklin was its first president, Thomas Jefferson its third. Among the purposes of these discussions was to find ways to improve society. Franklin's interest in electricity, stoves, and eyeglasses exemplified the shift of focus among many eighteenth-century colonists from heaven to the here and now.

Most eighteenth-century colonists went to church seldom or not at all, although they probably considered themselves Christians. A minister in Charleston observed that on the Sabbath "the Taverns have more Visitants than the Churches." In the leading colonial cities, church members were a small minority of eligible adults, no more than 10 to 15 percent. Anglican parishes in the South rarely claimed more than one-fifth of eligible adults as members. In some regions of rural New England and the middle colonies, church membership embraced two-thirds of eligible adults, while in other areas only one-quarter of the residents belonged to a church. The dominant faith overall was religious indifference. As a late-eighteenth-century traveler observed, "Religious indifference is imperceptibly disseminated from one end of the continent to the other."

The spread of religious indifference, of deism, of denominational rivalry, and of comfortable backsliding profoundly concerned many Christians. A few despaired that, as one wrote, "religion . . . lay a-dying and ready to expire its last breath of life." To combat what one preacher called the "dead formality" of church services, some ministers set out to convert nonbelievers and to revive the piety of the faithful with a new style of preaching that appealed more to the heart than to the head. Historians have termed this wave of revivals the **Great Awakening**. In Massachusetts during the mid-1730s, the fiery Puritan minister Jonathan Edwards reaped a harvest of souls by reemphasizing traditional Puritan doctrines of humanity's utter depravity and God's vengeful omnipotence. The title of Edwards's most famous sermon, "Sinners in the

> To combat what one preacher called the "dead formality" of church services, some ministers set out to convert nonbelievers and to revive the faithful with preaching that appealed more to the heart than to the head.

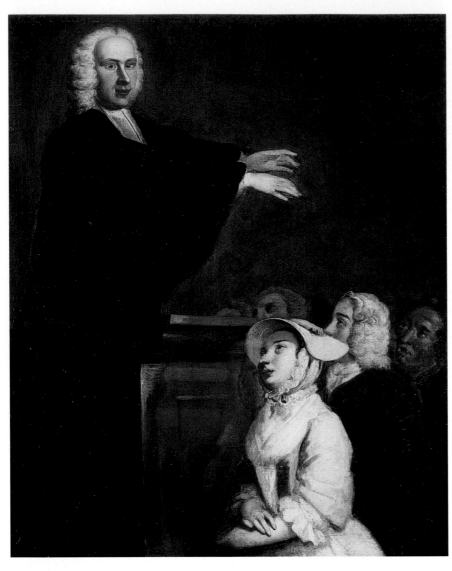

George Whitefield

An anonymous artist portrayed George Whitefield preaching, emphasizing the power of his sermons to transport his audience to a revived awareness of divine spirituality. Light from above gleams off Whitefield's forehead. His crossed eyes and faraway gaze suggest that he spoke in a semihypnotic trance. Notice the absence of a Bible at the pulpit. Rather than elaborating on God's word as revealed in Scripture, Whitefield speaks from his own inner awareness. The young woman bathed in light below his hands appears transfixed, her focus not on Whitefield but on some inner realm illuminated by his words. Her eyes and Whitefield's do not meet, yet the artist's use of light suggests that she and Whitefield see the same core of holy Truth. The other people in Whitefield's audience appear not to have achieved this state. They remain intent on Whitefield's words, failing so far to be ignited by the divine spark. National Portrait Gallery, London.

The most famous revivalist in the eighteenth-century Atlantic world was George Whitefield. An Anglican, Whitefield preached well-worn messages of sin and salvation to large audiences in England using his spellbinding, unforgettable voice. Whitefield visited the North American colonies seven times, staying for more than three years during the mid-1740s and attracting tens of thousands to his sermons, including Benjamin Franklin. Whitefield's preaching transported many in his audience to emotion-choked states of religious ecstasy. About one revival, he wrote, "the bitter cries and groans were enough to pierce the hardest heart. Some of the people were as pale as death; others were wringing their hands; others lying on the ground; others sinking into the arms of their friends; and most lifting their eyes to heaven, and crying to God for mercy. They seemed like persons . . . coming out of their graves to judgment."

Whitefield's successful revivals spawned many lesser imitations. Itinerant preachers, many of them poorly educated, toured the colonial backcountry after midcentury, echoing Whitefield's medium and message as best they could. Educated and established ministers often regarded them with disgust. Bathsheba Kingsley, a member of Jonathan Edwards's flock, preached the revival message informally—as did an unprecedented number of other awakened women throughout the colonies—causing her congregation to brand her a "brawling woman" who had "gone quite out of her place." The revivals awakened and refreshed the spiritual energies of thousands of colonists struggling with the uncertainties and anxieties of eighteenth-century America. The conversions at revivals did not substantially boost the total number of church members, however. After the revivalists moved on, the routines and pressures of everyday existence reasserted their primacy in the lives of many converts. But revivals imparted an important message to colonists, both converted and unconverted. They communicated that every soul mattered, that men and women could choose to be saved, that individuals had the power to make a

Hands of an Angry God," conveys the flavor of his message. In Pennsylvania and New Jersey, Presbyterian William Tennent led revivals dramatizing conventional appeals for spiritual rebirth with accounts of God's miraculous powers—such as raising his son, William Tennent Jr., from the dead.

decision for everlasting life or death. Colonial revivals expressed in religious terms many of the same democratic and egalitarian values expressed in economic terms by colonists' patterns of consumption. One colonist noted the analogy by referring to itinerant revivalists as "Pedlars in divinity." Like consumption, revivals contributed to a set of common experiences that bridged colonial divides of faith, region, class, and status.

Bonds of the British Empire

The plurality of peoples, faiths, and communities that characterized the North American colonies arose from the somewhat haphazard policies of the eighteenth-century British empire. Since the Puritan Revolution of the mid-seventeenth century, British monarchs had valued the colonies' contributions to trade and encouraged their growth and development. Unlike Spain and France whose policies of excluding Protestants and foreigners kept the population of their North American colonial territories tiny—Britain kept the door to its colonies open to anyone, and tens of thousands of non-British immigrants settled in the North American colonies and raised families. The open door did not extend to trade, however, as the seventeenth-century Navigation Acts restricted colonial trade to British ships and traders. These policies evolved because they served the interests of the monarchy and of influential groups in England and the colonies. The policies also gave the colonists a common framework of political expectations and experiences.

At a minimum, British power defended the colonists from foreign enemies. Each colony organized a militia, and privateers sailed from every port to prey on foreign ships. But the British navy and army bore responsibility for colonial defense. Royal officials warily eyed the small North American settlements of New France and New Spain for signs of threats to the colonies. Alone, neither New France (in present-day Canada, from the St. Lawrence River, around the Great Lakes, and down the Mississippi valley to present-day Louisiana) nor New Spain (in present-day Florida, Alabama, Texas, New Mexico, Arizona, and California) jeopardized British North America, but with Indian allies they could become a potent force that kept colonists on their guard.

Defending the Borderlands of Empire: Indians and French and Spanish Outposts

All along the ragged edge of settlement, colonists encountered Indians. Native Americans' impulse to defend their territory from colonial incursions warred with their desire for trade, which tugged them toward the settlers. As a colonial official observed in 1761, "A modern Indian cannot subsist without Europeans . . . [the European goods that were] only conveniency at first [are] now become necessity." To obtain such necessities as guns, ammunition, clothing, sewing utensils, and much more that was manufactured largely by the British, Indians trapped beaver, deer, and other fur-bearing animals throughout the interior.

Colonial traders and their respective empires competed to control the fur trade (Map 5.4). British, French, Spanish, and Dutch officials monitored the trade to prevent their competitors from deflecting the flow of furs toward their own markets. Indians took advantage of this competition to improve their own prospects, playing one trader and empire off against another. The Iroquois, for example, promised the French exclusive access to the furs and territory of the Great Lakes region and at the same time made the same pledge of exclusive rights to the English. Indian tribes and confederacies also competed among themselves for favored trading rights with one colony or another, a competition colonists encouraged.

British, French, Spanish, and Dutch traders competed to control the fur trade. Indians took advantage of this competition to improve their own prospects.

The shifting alliances and complex dynamics of the fur trade struck a fragile balance along the frontier. The threat of violence from all sides was ever present, and the threat became reality often enough for all parties to be prepared for the worst. In the Yamasee War of 1715, Yamasee and Creek Indians—with French encouragement—mounted a coordinated attack against colonial settlements in South Carolina and inflicted heavy casualties. The Cherokees, traditional enemies of the Creeks, refused to join the attack. Instead, they protected their access to British trade goods by allying with the colonists and turning the tide of battle, thus triggering a murderous rampage of revenge by the colonists against the Creeks and Yamasees.

Relations between Indians and the colonists differed from colony to colony and from year to

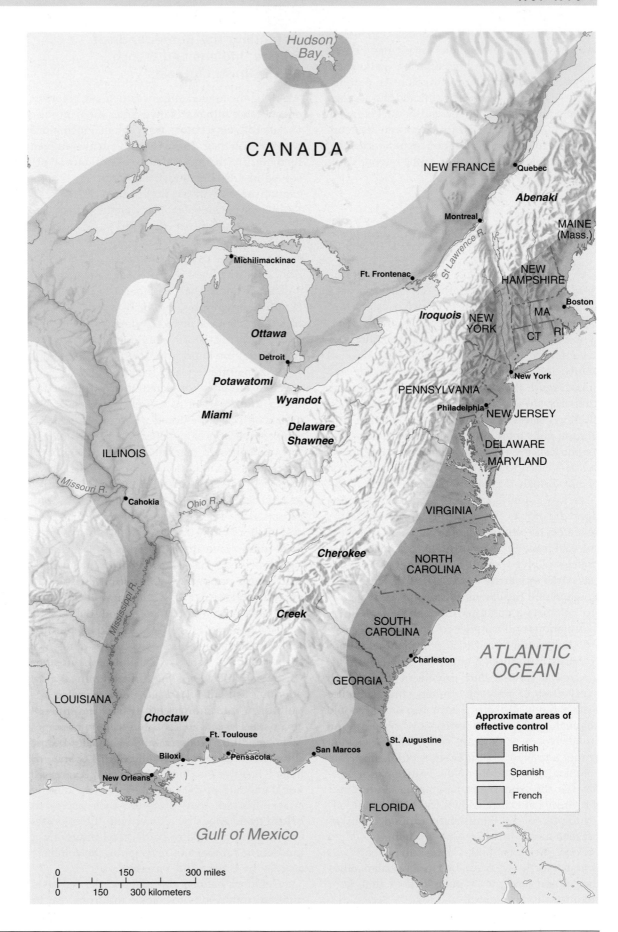

Hudson Bay

CANADA

NEW FRANCE   • Quebec

Abenaki

Montreal •   MAINE (Mass.)

St. Lawrence R.

• Michilimackinac   Ft. Frontenac •   NEW HAMPSHIRE

Iroquois   NEW YORK   • Boston

Ottawa   MA

Detroit •   CT   RI

Potawatomi   • New York

Wyandot   PENNSYLVANIA

Miami   Philadelphia •   NEW JERSEY

Delaware
Shawnee   DELAWARE

ILLINOIS   MARYLAND

Missouri R.   VIRGINIA

• Cahokia   Ohio R.

Cherokee   NORTH
CAROLINA

Mississippi R.

Creek   SOUTH
CAROLINA

• Charleston

GEORGIA   ATLANTIC
OCEAN

LOUISIANA   **Approximate areas of
effective control**

Choctaw   • St. Augustine   British

Ft. Toulouse •   Spanish

• Biloxi   • Pensacola   • San Marcos   French

• New Orleans

FLORIDA

Gulf of Mexico

0   150   300 miles

0   150   300 kilometers

Monterey Presidio

This eighteenth-century portrait of the Monterey Presidio illustrates the military significance of the Spanish outposts in California. The walled enclosure and proximity to the bay (in the background) served defensive purposes, principally against Russian expansion but also against British and French interlopers. The Indian men and women working in the fields and hanging out laundry served to support the soldiers in the presidio. Notice that no Spaniard is pictured at work. Contrast this languid scene with the picture of the Arch Street wharf in Philadelphia (see page 147), where the hustle and bustle of commerce prevailed. At Monterey and elsewhere in Spanish California, the presidios and missions focused on maintaining outposts of empire rather than on developing booming settlements or producing goods for export.

University of California at Berkeley, Bancroft Library.

year. But the colonists' nagging perceptions of menace on the frontier kept them continually hoping for help from the British in keeping the Indians at bay and in maintaining the essential flow of trade. In 1754, the colonists' endemic competition with the French flared into the Seven Years' War (also known as the French and Indian War), which would inflame the frontier for years (see chapter 6). Before the 1760s, neither the colonists nor the British developed a coherent policy toward Indians. But both agreed that Indians made deadly enemies, profitable trading partners, and powerful allies. As a result, the British and the colonists kept an eye on the Spanish Empire to the west and relations with the Indians there.

Indians' potential as allies prompted officials in New Spain to mount a campaign to block Russian access to present-day California by building forts (called *presidios*) and missions. Russian hunters in search of seals and sea otters ventured along the California coast and threatened to become a permanent presence on New Spain's northern frontier.

◀ **MAP 5.4   Zones of Empire in Eastern North America**

British colonies extending westward from the Atlantic coast were much more densely settled than the zones under French, Spanish, or Indian control. The comparatively large number of settlers made British colonists more secure than the relatively few colonists in the vast regions claimed by France and Spain or settlers among the many Indian peoples in the huge area between the Mississippi River and the Appalachian Mountains. Yet British colonists were not powerful enough to dominate the French, Spanish, or Indians. Instead, British colonists had to guard against powerful Indian groups who allied with either the French or the Spanish, since such alliances threatened settlers in the region under British control.

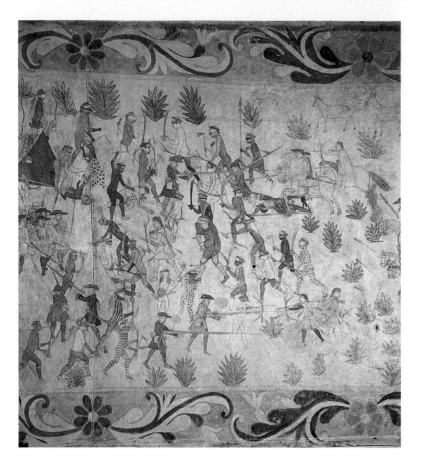

Ambush of Spanish Expedition
This detail from a remarkable hide painting depicts an ambush of a Spanish expedition by French soldiers and their Pawnee and Oto allies in August 1720. Two and a half months earlier, the governor of New Mexico had sent forty-three Spanish soldiers along with sixty Pueblo Indian allies to expel French intruders from the northern borderlands of New Spain. When the expedition reached the confluence of the Platte and Loup rivers in present-day Nebraska, they were surprised by an attack by French, Pawnees, and Otos, who killed thirty-three Spaniards and twelve Pueblos and drove the expedition back to New Mexico. Shortly afterward, an artist—whether Indian or Spanish is unknown—recorded the disastrous ambush of the Spaniards in this painting. The priest in the center of the detail shown here was Father Juan Minguez, the first priest assigned to Albuquerque; he was killed in the ambush. The Indian directly in front of the priest was Joseph Naranjo, who was also killed; he came from the Santa Clara Pueblo. He was the leader of the Spaniards' Pueblo allies and was the son of Domingo Naranjo, a leader of the Pueblo Revolt against the Spaniards in 1680.
Museum of New Mexico.

In 1769, an expedition headed by a military man, Gaspar de Portolá, and a Catholic priest, Junípero Serra, traveled north from Mexico to present-day San Diego, where they founded the first California mission, San Diego de Alcalá. They soon journeyed all the way to Monterey, which became the capital of Spanish California. There Portolá established a presidio in 1770 "to defend us from attacks by the Russians," he wrote. The same year Father Serra founded Mission San Carlos Borroméo de Carmelo in Monterey to convert Indians and to recruit them to work to support the soldiers and other officials in the presidio. By 1772, Serra had established other missions (see "American Places," page 165) on the northward path from San Diego to Monterey.

For Indians, the Spaniards' California missions had horrendous consequences, as they had elsewhere in the Spanish borderlands. European diseases decimated Indian populations, Spanish soldiers raped Indian women, and missionaries beat Indians and subjected them to near slavery. Indian uprisings against the Spaniards occurred repeatedly (see "Documenting the American Promise," page 166), but the presidios and missions endured as feeble projections of the Spanish Empire along the Pacific coast.

Colonial Politics in the British Empire

British attempts to exercise political power in their colonial governments met with success so long as British officials were on or very near the sea. Colonists acknowledged—although they did not always readily comply with—British authority to collect customs duties, inspect cargoes, and enforce trade regulations. But when royal officials tried to wield their authority on land, in the internal affairs of colonies, they invariably encountered colonial resistance. A governor appointed by the king in each of the nine royal colonies (Rhode Island and Connecticut selected their own governors) or by the proprietors in

Spanish Missions in California

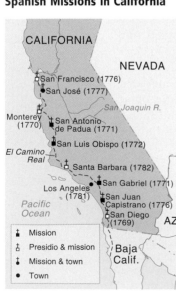

AMERICAN PLACES

California Mission Trail

Between 1769 and 1823, Spanish authorities built twenty-one missions in California. The missions usually included a church, a presidio (fort), a school, housing for missionaries, Indians, and soldiers, and various outbuildings. The missions extend from the first one, in San Diego, northward more than 500 miles, beyond the Spanish capital of California at Monterey, where the magnificent Mission San Carlos Borroméo de Carmelo is still an active church, all the way to Sonoma, north of present-day San Francisco.

Visitors today can travel from one mission to another, following in the footsteps of Spanish missionaries, soldiers, and government officials as well as Indians who converted to Christianity and those who resisted. Mission La Purisíma Concepcíon, located north of Santa Barbara near Lompoc, has been restored to its late-eighteenth-century condition. Unlike most of the other missions, which today are in urban settings or are only partially preserved, La Purisíma stands in a rural area that is much like the setting of all the missions in the eighteenth century. Visitors to La Purisíma can tour the chapel, barracks, and other restored buildings and try to imagine how the quiet, bucolic scene of today would have been different in the eighteenth century.

In effect, the California missions established by Junípero Serra and other Franciscans were small islands of Spanish culture surrounded not by villages of Spaniards—as in Spain—but by numerous settlements of California hunter-gatherers who did not worship the Spaniards'

god, speak the Spaniards' language, wear the Spaniards' clothing, or build their houses or places of worship in the Spaniards' style. The missions signified Spaniards' determination to force native Californians to conform to Spanish culture.

The elegant buildings that survive at Mission San Diego and some of the other missions tend to obscure the coercion and brutality that were common features of mission life for Indians. One Spanish soldier praised the work of the missionar-

Mission San Diego de Alcalá
Courtesy of the Mission San Diego de Alcalá.

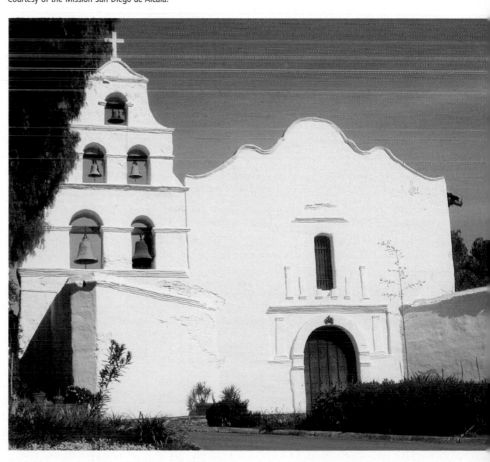

ies, writing in 1792 that "With flattery and presents [missionaries] attract the savage Indians and persuade them to adhere to life in society and to receive instruction for a knowledge of the Catholic faith, the cultivation of the land, and the arts necessary for making the instruments most needed for farming." Whippings and near enslavement were among the forms of persuasion that missionaries frequently used to bring Indians to the missions and keep them there. It is easy for visitors traveling today from one beautiful mission to another on the California Mission Trail to forget this silent and invisible—but very real—history.

FOR WEB LINKS RELATED TO THIS SITE AND OTHER AMERICAN PLACES, see "PlaceLinks" at bedfordstmartins.com/roark.

Missionaries Report on California Missions

Catholic missionaries sent regular reports to their superiors in Mexico City, New Spain's capital city. The reports described what the missionaries considered their successes in converting pagan Indians—whom they called gentiles—as well as the difficulties caused by the behavior of both Spaniards and Indians.

DOCUMENT 1
Father Luis Jayme
Describes Conditions
at Mission San Diego
de Alcalá, 1772

Father Luis Jayme, a Franciscan missionary, reported on the deplorable behavior of some of the Spanish soldiers at Mission San Diego, who frequently raped Indian women, causing many Indians to resist the efforts of the missionaries.

With reference to the Indians, I wish to say that great progress [in converting Indians] would be made if there was anything to eat and the soldiers would set a good example. We cannot give them anything to eat because what Don Pedro [the governor] has given is not enough to last half a year for the Indians from the Californias who are here. Thus little progress will be made under present conditions. As for the example set by the soldiers, no doubt some of them are good exemplars and deserve to be treated accordingly, but very many of them deserve to be hanged on account of the continuous outrages which they are committing in seizing and raping the women. There is not a single mission where all the gentiles have not been scandalized, and even on the roads, so I have been told. Surely, as the gentiles themselves state, they [the soldiers] are committing a thousand evils, particularly of a sexual nature. . . .

At one of these Indian villages near this mission of San Diego, which said village is very large, and which is on the road to Monterey, the gentiles therein many times have been on the point of coming here to kill us all, and the reason for this is that some soldiers went there and raped their women, and other soldiers who were carrying the mail to Monterey turned their animals into their fields and they ate up their crops. Three other Indian villages . . . [near] here have reported the same thing to me several times. For this reason on several occasions when . . . I have gone to see these Indian villages, as soon as they saw us they fled from their villages and fled to the woods or other remote places. . . . They do this so that the soldiers will not rape their women as they have already done so many times in the past.

No wonder the Indians here were bad when the mission was first founded. To begin with, they did not know why [the Spaniards] had come, unless they wanted to take their lands away from them. Now they all want to be Christians because they know that there is a God who created the heavens and earth and all things, that there is a Hell and Glory, that they have souls, etc., but when the mission was first founded . . . they thought they were like animals, and . . . they were very loath to pray, and they did not want to be Christians at all. . . . [Now] they all know the natural law, which, so I am informed, they have observed as well or better than many Christians elsewhere. They do not have idols; they do not go on drinking sprees; they do not marry relatives; and they have but one wife. The married men sleep with their wives only. . . . Some of the first adults whom we baptized, when we pointed out to them that it was wrong to have sexual intercourse with a woman to whom they were not married, told me that they already knew that, and that among them it was considered to be very bad, and so they do not do so at all. "The soldiers," they told me, "are Christians and, although they know that God will punish them in Hell, do so, having sexual intercourse with

---

Maryland and Pennsylvania headed the government of each colony. The British envisioned colonial governors as mini-monarchs able to exert influence in the colonies much as the king did in England. But colonial governors were not kings, and the colonies were not England.

Eighty percent of colonial governors had been born in England, not in the colonies. Some governors stayed in England, close to the source of royal patronage, and delegated the grubby details of colonial affairs to subordinates. Even the best-intentioned colonial governors had diffiour wives." "We," they said, "although we did not know that God would punish us for that in Hell, considered it to be very bad, and we did not do it, and even less now that we know that God will punish us if we do so." When I heard this, I burst into tears to see how these gentiles were setting an example for us Christians.

DOCUMENT 2
Father Junípero Serra Describes the Indian Revolt at Mission San Diego de Alcalá, 1775

Father Junípero Serra, the founder of many of the California missions, reported to his superiors in Mexico City that an Indian uprising had destroyed Mission San Diego. He recommended rebuilding and urged officials to provide additional soldiers to defend the missions, but not to punish the rebellious Indians.

As we are in the vale of tears, not all the news I have to relate can be pleasant. And so I make no excuses for announcing . . . the tragic news that I have just received of the total destruction of the San Diego Mission, and of the death of the senior of its two religious ministers, called Father Luis Jayme, at the hand of the rebellious gentiles and of the Christian neophytes [Indians who lived in the mission]. All this happened, November 5th, about one or two o'clock at night. The gentiles came together from forty rancherías,

according to information given me, and set fire to the church, after sacking it. They then went to the storehouse, the house where the Fathers lived, the soldiers' barracks, and all the rest of the buildings. They killed a carpenter . . . and a blacksmith. . . . They wounded with their arrows the four soldiers, who alone were on guard at the . . . mission. . . .

And now, after the Father has been killed, the Mission burned, its many and valuable furnishings destroyed, together with the sacred vessels, its paintings, its baptismal, marriage, and funeral records, and all the furnishings for the sacristy, the house, and the farm implements—now the forces [of soldiers] of both presidios [nearby] come together to set things right. . . . What happened was that before they set about reestablishing the Mission, they wanted to . . . lay hands on the guilty ones who were responsible for the burning of the Mission, and the death of the Fathers, and chastise them. The harassed Indians rebelled anew and became more enraged. . . . And so the soldiers there are gathered together in their presidios, and the Indians in their state of heathenism. . . .

While the missionary is alive, let the soldiers guard him, and watch over him, like the pupils of God's very eyes. That is as it should be. . . . But after the missionary has been killed, what can be gained by campaigns [against the rebellious Indians]? Some will say to frighten them and prevent them from killing

others. What I say is that, in order to prevent them from killing others, keep better guard over them than they did over the one who has been killed; and, as to the murderer, let him live, in order that he should be saved—which is the very purpose of our coming here, and the reason which justifies it.

SOURCES: Maynard Geiger, trans. and ed., *Letter of Luís Jayme, O.F.M.: San Diego, October 17, 1772* (Los Angeles, 1970), 38–42.

Antonine Tibesar, O.F.M., ed., *The Writings of Junípero Serra* (Washington, D.C.: 1956), 2:401–07.

QUESTIONS FOR ANALYSIS AND DEBATE

1. In what ways did Jayme and Serra agree about the motivations of Indians in and around Mission San Diego? In what ways did they disagree? How would Serra's recommendations for rebuilding the mission address the problems identified by Jayme that caused the revolt?

2. How did the goals and activities of the Spanish soldiers compare to those of the Catholic missionaries? What accounts for the differences and similarities?

3. How did the religious convictions of Jayme and Serra influence their reports? What might Spanish soldiers or Indians have said about these events? What might they have said about missionaries like Jayme and Serra?

culty developing relations of trust and respect with influential colonists because their terms of office averaged just five years and could be terminated at any time. Colonial governors controlled few patronage positions to secure political friendships in the colonies. The officials who administered the colonial customs service, for example, received their positions through patronage networks centered in England rather than in the hands of colonial governors. In obedience to England, colonial governors fought incessantly with the colonial assemblies. They battled over governors' vetoes of colonial legislation, removal of colonial judges, creation of new courts, dismissal of the representative assemblies, and other local issues. Some governors developed a working relationship with the assemblies. But during the eighteenth century, the assemblies gained the upper hand.

British policies did not clearly define the powers and responsibilities of colonial assemblies. In effect, the assemblies made many of their own rules and established a strong tradition of representative government analogous, in their eyes, to the English Parliament. Voters often returned the same representatives to the assemblies year after year, building continuity in power and leadership that far exceeded that of the governor. By 1720, colonial assemblies had won the power to initiate legislation, including tax laws and authorizations to spend public funds. Although all laws passed by the assemblies (except in Maryland, Rhode Island, and Connecticut) had to be approved by the governor and then by the Board of Trade in England, the difficulties in communication about complex subjects over long distances effectively ratified the assemblies' decisions. Years often passed before laws were repealed, and in the meantime the assemblies' laws prevailed.

The heated political struggles between royal governors and colonial assemblies that occurred throughout the eighteenth century taught colonists a common set of political lessons. They learned to employ traditionally British ideas of representative government to defend their own interests. They learned that power in the British colonies rarely belonged to the British government.

Conclusion: The Dual Identity of British North American Colonists

During the eighteenth century, a society that was both distinctively colonial and distinctively British emerged in British North America. Tens of thousands of immigrants and slaves gave the colonies an unmistakably colonial complexion

and contributed to the colonies' growing population and expanding economy. People of different ethnicities and faiths sought their fortunes in the colonies, where land was cheap, labor was dear, and—as Benjamin Franklin preached—work promised to be rewarding. Indentured servants and redemptioners risked a temporary period of bondage for the potential reward of better opportunities than on the Atlantic's eastern shore. Slaves endured lifetime servitude that they neither chose nor desired but from which their masters greatly benefited.

Identifiably colonial products from New England, the middle colonies, and the southern colonies flowed across the Atlantic. Back came unquestionably British consumer goods along with fashions in ideas, faith, and politics. The bonds of the British Empire required colonists to think of themselves as British subjects and, at the same time, encouraged them to consider their status as colonists.

People of European origin in the North American colonies of Spain and France did not share in the emerging political identity of the British colonists. They also did not participate in the cultural, economic, social, and religious changes experienced by their counterparts in British North America. Unlike the much more numerous colonists in British North America, North American Spanish and French colonists did not develop societies that began to rival the European empires that sponsored and supported them.

By 1750, British colonists in North America could not imagine that their distinctively dual identity—as British and as colonists—would soon become a source of intense conflict. But by 1776, colonists in British North America had to choose whether they were British or American.

For additional firsthand accounts of this period, see Chapter 5 in Michael Johnson, ed., *Reading the American Past*, Third Edition.

To assess your mastery of the material in this chapter, see the Online Study Guide at bedfordstmartins.com/roark.

For Web links related to topics in this chapter, see "HistoryLinks," "DocLinks," and "PlaceLinks" at bedfordstmartins.com/roark.

CHRONOLOGY

1702 • Queen Anne's War triggers large German migration to British North American colonies.

1711 • North Carolina founded.

1715 • Yamasee War pits South Carolina colonists against Yamasee and Creek Indians.

1717 • Scots-Irish immigration to American colonies begins to increase.

1721 • *New England Courant* begins publication.

1723 • Benjamin Franklin arrives in Philadelphia.

1730s • Jonathan Edwards leads New England religious revival known as "Great Awakening."

1732 • Georgia founded.

1733 • Benjamin Franklin begins to publish *Poor Richard's Almanack.*

1737 • Penn family exploits "Walking Purchase" to claim extra land from Indians.

1739 • Slave insurrection occurs and is suppressed at Stono, South Carolina.

1740s • George Whitefield preaches revival of religion throughout England and British North America.

• Majority of southern slaves are born in the colonies rather than in Africa.

1741 • New York City officials suspect slave conspiracy and execute 31 slaves.

1745 • Olaudah Equiano born in present-day Nigeria.

1750s • British colonists from Pennsylvania begin to move down Shenandoah Valley into southern back-country.
• Colonists increasingly become indebted to English merchants.

1754 • Seven Years' War begins in North America pitting France, Britain, and their respective colonists and Indian allies against one another in a military contest for dominance in North America.

1769 • American Philosophical Society founded in Philadelphia.

1770 • Gaspar de Portolá and Junípero Serra establish Mission San Carlos Borroméo de Carmelo and presidio at Monterey, California.
• British North American colonists number over 2 million, almost ten times more than in 1700.

1775 • Indians revolt and destroy San Diego mission.

BIBLIOGRAPHY

Please consult the bibliographies of chapters 2, 3, and 4 for more readings on related topics.

General Works

Douglas Anderson, *The Radical Enlightenment of Benjamin Franklin* (1997).

Richard Aquila, *The Iroquois Restoration: Iroquois Diplomacy on the Colonial Frontier, 1701–1754* (1997).

Bernard Bailyn, *Voyagers to the West: A Passage in the Peopling of America on the Eve of the Revolution* (1986).

Linda Baumgarten, *What Clothes Reveal: The Language of Clothing in Colonial and Federal America* (2002).

Ira Berlin, *Generations of Captivity: A History of African-American Slaves* (2003).

Richard D. Brown, *Knowledge Is Power: The Diffusion of Information in Early America, 1700–1865* (1989).

Jon Butler, *Becoming America: The Revolution before 1776* (2000).

Colin G. Calloway, *New Worlds for All: Indians, Europeans, and the Remaking of Early America* (1997).

A. Roger Ekirch, *Bound for America: The Transportation of British Convicts to the Colonies, 1718–1775* (1987).

Jack P. Greene, *Peripheries and Center: Constitutional Development in the Extended Polities of the British Empire and the United States, 1607–1788* (1986).

Jack P. Greene, *The Intellectual Construction of America: Exceptionalism and Identity from 1492 to 1800* (1993).

Patrick Griffin, *The People with No Name: Ireland's Ulster Scots, America's Scots Irish, and the Creation of a British Atlantic World, 1689–1764* (2001).

Timothy D. Hall, *Contested Boundaries: Itineracy and the Reshaping of the Colonial American Religious World* (1994).

Robert H. Jackson, *Race, Caste, and Status: Indians in Colonial Spanish America* (1999).

Nancy F. Koehn, *The Power of Commerce: Economy and Governance in the First British Empire* (1994).

Frank Lambert, *"Pedlar in Divinity": George Whitefield and the Transatlantic Revivals, 1723–1770* (1994).

Frank Lambert, *Inventing the "Great Awakening"* (1999).

Michael N. McConnell, *A Country Between: The Upper Ohio Valley and Its People, 1724–1774* (1997).

Kerby A. Miller et al., eds., *Irish Immigrants in the Land of Canaan: Letters and Memoirs from Colonial and Revolutionary America, 1675–1815* (2003).

Robert D. Mitchell, *Appalachian Frontiers: Settlement, Society, and Development in the Preindustrial Era* (1991).

Edmund S. Morgan, *Benjamin Franklin* (2002).

Gregory H. Nobles, *American Frontiers: Cultural Encounters and Continental Conquest* (1997).

Mary Beth Norton, *Founding Mothers and Fathers: Gendered Power and the Forming of American Society* (1996).

Alison Gilbert Olson, *Making the Empire Work: London and American Interest Groups, 1690–1790* (1992).

A. G. Roeber, *Palatines, Liberty, and Property: German Lutherans in Colonial British America* (1993).

Sharon V. Salinger, *Taverns and Drinking in Early America* (2002).

Martha Saxton, *Being Good: Women's Moral Values in Early America* (2003).

Michael Schudson, *The Good Citizen: A History of American Civic Life* (1998).

Carole Shammas, *The Pre-Industrial Consumer in England and America* (1990).

David S. Shields, *Civil Tongues and Polite Letters in British America* (1997).

Nancy L. Struna, *People of Prowess: Sport, Leisure, and Labor in Early Anglo-America* (1996).

Laurel Thatcher Ulrich, *The Age of Homespun: Objects and Stories in the Creation of an American Myth* (2001).

Marianne E. Wokeck, *Trade in Strangers: The Beginnings of Mass Migration to North America* (1999).

Stephanie Grauman Wolf, *As Various as Their Land: The Everyday Lives of Eighteenth-Century Americans* (1993).

New England

John L. Brooke, *The Heart of the Commonwealth: Society and Political Culture in Worcester County, Massachusetts, 1713–1861* (1989).

Richard Bushman, *From Puritan to Yankee: Character and the Social Order in Connecticut, 1690–1765* (1967).

David W. Conroy, *In Public Houses: Drink and the Revolution of Authority in Colonial Massachusetts* (1995).

Jay Coughtry, *The Notorious Triangle: Rhode Island and the African Slave Trade, 1700–1807* (1981).

Elaine Forman Crane, *Ebb Tide in New England: Women, Seaports, and Social Change, 1630–1800* (1998).

Christopher Grasso, *A Speaking Aristocracy: Transforming Public Discourse in Eighteenth-Century Connecticut* (1999).

Christine Leigh Heyrman, *Commerce and Culture: The Maritime Communities of Colonial Massachusetts, 1690–1750* (1984).

Phyllis Whitman Hunter, *Purchasing Identity in the Atlantic World: Massachusetts Merchants, 1670–1780* (2001).

Douglas Lamar Jones, *Village and Seaport: Migration and Society in Eighteenth-Century Massachusetts* (1981).

Daniel R. Mandell, *Behind the Frontier: Indians in Eighteenth-Century Eastern Massachusetts* (1996).

George M. Marsden, *Jonathan Edwards: A Life* (2003).

Carolyn Merchant, *Ecological Revolutions: Nature, Gender, and Science in New England* (1989).

Gregory H. Nobles, *Divisions throughout the Whole: Politics and Society in Hampshire County, Massachusetts, 1740–1775* (1983).

Lisa Norling, *Captain Ahab Had a Wife: New England Women and the Whale Fishery, 1720–1870* (2000).

William D. Piersen, *Black Yankees: The Development of an Afro-American Subculture in Eighteenth-Century New England* (1988).

Patricia J. Tracy, *Jonathan Edwards, Pastor: Religion and Society in Eighteenth-Century Northampton* (1979).

Lynne Withey, *Urban Growth in Colonial Rhode Island: Newport and Providence in the Eighteenth Century* (1984).

Middle Colonies

Randall H. Balmer, *A Perfect Babel of Confusion: Dutch Religion and English Culture in the Middle Colonies* (1989).

Thomas J. Davis, *A Rumor of Revolt: The "Great Negro Plot" in Colonial New York* (1985).

Thomas M. Doerflinger, *A Vigorous Spirit of Enterprise: Merchants and Economic Development in Revolutionary Philadelphia* (1986).

Aaron Spencer Fogelman, *Hopeful Journeys: German Immigration, Settlement, and Political Culture in Colonial America, 1717–1775* (1996).

J. William Frost, *A Perfect Freedom: Religious Liberty in Pennsylvania* (1990).

Leslie M. Harris, *In the Shadow of Slavery: African Americans in New York City, 1626–1863* (2003).

Eric Hinderaker, *Elusive Empires: Constructing Colonialism in the Ohio Valley, 1673–1800* (1997).

Peter Charles Hoffer, *The Great New York Conspiracy of 1741: Slavery, Crime, and Colonial Law* (2003).

Jessica Kross, *The Evolution of an American Town: Newtown, New York, 1642–1775* (1983).

Ned C. Landsman, *Scotland and Its First American Colony, 1683–1765* (1985).

Hartmut Lehmann et al., eds. *In Search of Peace and Prosperity: New German Settlements in Eighteenth-Century Europe and America* (2000).

Stephen L. Longenecker, *Piety and Tolerance: Pennsylvania German Religion, 1700–1850* (1994).

Peter C. Mancall, *Valley of Opportunity: Economic Culture along the Upper Susquehanna, 1700–1800* (1991).

Brendan J. McConville, *These Darling Disturbers of the Public Peace: The Struggle for Property and Power in Early New Jersey* (1999).

James H. Merrell, *Into the American Woods: Negotiators on the Pennsylvania Frontier* (1999).

Jane T. Merritt, *At the Crossroads: Indians and Empires on a Mid-Atlantic Frontier, 1700–1763* (2003).

Gary B. Nash and Jean R. Soderlund, *Freedom by Degrees: Emancipation in Pennsylvania and Its Aftermath* (1991).

Benjamin H. Newcomb, *Political Partisanship in the American Middle Colonies, 1700–1776* (1995).

Simon P. Newman, *Embodied History: The Lives of the Poor in Early Philadelphia* (2003).

Sharon V. Salinger, *"To Serve Well and Faithfully": Labor and Indentured Servitude in Pennsylvania, 1682–1800* (1987).

Sally Schwartz, *"A Mixed Multitude": The Struggle for Toleration in Colonial Pennsylvania* (1987).

Mary M. Schweitzer, *Custom and Contract: Household, Government, and the Economy in Colonial Pennsylvania* (1987).

Timothy J. Shannon, *Indians and Colonists at the Crossroads of Empire: The Albany Congress of 1754* (2000).

Beverly Prior Smaby, *The Transformation of Moravian Bethlehem: From Communal Mission to Family Economy* (1988).

Billy G. Smith, *The "Lower Sort": Philadelphia's Laboring People, 1750–1800* (1990).

Merrill D. Smith, *Breaking the Bonds: Marital Discord in Pennsylvania, 1730–1830* (1991).

Jean R. Soderlund, *Quakers and Slavery: A Divided Spirit* (1985).

Peter Thompson, *Rum Punch and Revolution: Taverngoing and Public Life in Eighteenth-Century Philadelphia* (1999).

Alan Tully, *William Penn's Legacy: Politics and Social Structure in Provincial Pennsylvania, 1726–1755* (1977).

Southern Colonies

Gary Clayton Anderson, *The Indian Southwest, 1580–1830: Ethnogenesis and Reinvention* (1999).

Richard R. Beeman, *The Evolution of the Southern Backcountry: A Case Study of Lunenburg County, Virginia, 1746–1832* (1984).

Trevor G. Burnhard, *Creole Gentlemen: The Maryland Elite, 1691–1776* (2002).

Edward J. Cashin, *Lachlan McGillivray, Indian Trader: The Shaping of the Southern Colonial Frontier* (1992).

Edward J. Cashin, *Governor Henry Ellis and the Transformation of British North America* (1994).

David R. Chesnutt, *South Carolina's Expansion into Colonial Georgia, 1720–1765* (1989).

Paul G. E. Clemons, *The Atlantic Economy and Colonial Maryland's Eastern Shore: From Tobacco to Grain* (1980).

Peter A. Coclanis, *The Shadow of a Dream: Economic Life and Death in the South Carolina Low Country, 1670–1920* (1989).

Harry W. Crosby, *Antigua California: Mission and Colony on the Peninsular Frontier, 1697–1768* (1994).

Harold E. Davis, *The Fledgling Province: Social and Cultural Life in Colonial Georgia, 1733–1776* (1976).

A. Roger Ekirch, *Poor Carolina: Politics and Society in Colonial North Carolina, 1729–1776* (1981).

David Hackett Fischer and James C. Kelly, *Bound Away: Virginia and the Westward Movement* (2000).

Sylvia R. Frey and Betty Wood, *Come Shouting to Zion: African American Protestantism in the American South and British Caribbean to 1830* (1998).

Allan Gallay, *The Formation of a Planter Elite: Jonathan Bryan and the Southern Colonial Frontier* (1989).

Michael Angelo Gomez, *Exchanging Our Country Marks: The Transformation of African Identities in the Colonial and Antebellum South* (1998).

Ramón A. Gutiérrez and Richard J. Orsi, eds., *Contested Eden: California before the Gold Rush* (1998).

Gwendolyn Midlo Hall, *Africans in Colonial Louisiana: The Development of Afro-Creole Culture in the Eighteenth Century* (1992).

Rhys Isaac, *The Transformation of Virginia, 1740–1790* (1982).

Robert H. Jackson and Edward Castillo, *Indians, Franciscans, and Spanish Colonization: The Impact of the Mission System on California Indians* (1995).

George Johnson, *The Frontier in the Colonial South: South Carolina Backcountry, 1736–1800* (1997).

Alan L. Karras, *Sojourners in the Sun: Scottish Migrants in Jamaica and the Chesapeake, 1740–1800* (1992).

Marvin L. Michael Kay, *Slavery in North Carolina, 1748–1775* (1995).

Cynthia A. Kierner, *Beyond the Household: Women's Place in the Early South, 1700–1835* (1998).

John Gilman Kolp, *Gentlemen and Freeholders: Electoral Politics and Political Commentary in Colonial Virginia* (1998).

Allan Kulikoff, *Tobacco and Slaves: The Development of Southern Cultures in the Chesapeake, 1680–1800* (1986).

Hugo Prosper Leaming, *Hidden Americans: Maroons of Virginia and the Carolinas* (1995).

Jan Lewis, *The Pursuit of Happiness: Family and Values in Jeffersonian Virginia* (1983).

Philip D. Morgan, *Slave Counterpoint: Black Culture in the Eighteenth-Century Chesapeake and Low Country* (1998).

Michael P. Morris, *The Bringing of Wonder: Trade and the Indians of the Southeast, 1700–1783* (1999).

Michael Mullin, *Africa in America: Slave Acculturation and Resistance in the American South and the British Caribbean, 1736–1831* (1992).

John K. Nelson, *A Blessed Company: Parishes, Parsons, and Parishioners in Anglican Virginia, 1690–1776* (2002).

Robert Olwell, *Masters, Slaves, and Subjects: The Culture of Power in the South Carolina Low Country, 1740–1790* (1998).

Anthony S. Parent, *The Formation of a Slave Society in Virginia, 1660–1740* (2003).

Michael J. Rozbicki, *The Complete Colonial Gentleman: Cultural Legitimacy in Plantation America* (1998).

Jon F. Sensbach, *A Separate Canaan: The Making of an Afro-Moravian World in North Carolina, 1763–1840* (1997).

Marc Simmons, *Hispanic Albuquerque, 1706–1846* (2003).

Daniel Blake Smith, *Inside the Great House: Planter Family Life in Eighteenth-Century Chesapeake Society* (1980).

Mechal Sobel, *The World They Made Together: Black and White Values in Eighteenth-Century Virginia* (1987).

Donna Spindel, *Crime and Society in North Carolina, 1663–1776* (1989).

Daniel B. Thorp, *The Moravian Community in Colonial North Carolina: Pluralism on the Southern Frontier* (1989).

Lorena S. Walsh, *From Calabar to Carter's Grove: The History of a Virginia Slave Community* (1997).

Betty Wood, *The Origins of American Slavery: Freedom and Bondage in the English Colonies* (1997).

PATRICK HENRY'S MAP DESK

Like many of the leading gentry of 1760s Virginia, Patrick Henry pursued land speculation as a way to gain wealth. From 1767 to 1773, he engaged in a half-dozen land ventures, buying up thousands of acres of frontier land in regions now part of Kentucky—purchases that would soon figure in the emerging crisis of empire. This odd little table was Henry's map desk. Its fold-out extensions provided support for the large maps required to represent Virginia's vast western land claims, and its light weight allowed Henry to position it near the best light source in his law office. As is often the case with speculative purchases, Henry's land deals entailed risk: Many of his properties were occupied by the Cherokee, who did not recognize his claim of ownership. The British government, fearing war between Indians and settlers, tried to choke off risky land speculation in 1763 by establishing an imaginary line along the crest of the Appalachian Mountains beyond which settlement was prohibited. But men like Henry continued to buy land cheap in the hopes of selling dear at a later time. As a leading planter and powerful orator, Patrick Henry quickly became a spokesman in the growing imperial struggle with Britain. When he gained election to the Virginia House of Burgesses in 1765, he skillfully maneuvered that assembly into the startling repudiation of British power known as the Virginia Resolves. By 1775 he favored independence from England, a position that eventually would unleash settlers looking to buy land in the West. In 1776, he was elected the first governor of the Commonwealth of Virginia. Patrick Henry ultimately had seventeen children, fourteen of whom survived to adulthood. Through astute land purchases, he managed to establish each with a landed estate.

Courtesy of Scotchtown, photo by Katherine Wetzel.

6

The British Empire and the Colonial Crisis

1754–1775

I N 1771, THOMAS HUTCHINSON became the royal governor of the colony of Massachusetts. Unlike most royal governors, who were British aristocrats sent over by the king for short tours of duty, Hutchinson was a fifth-generation American. A Harvard-educated member of the Massachusetts elite, from a family of successful merchants, Hutchinson had served two decades in the Massachusetts general assembly. In 1758 he was appointed lieutenant governor, and in 1760 he also became chief justice of the colony's highest court. He lived in the finest mansion in Boston. Wealth, power, and influence were his in abundance. He was proud of his connection to the British empire and loyal to his king.

Hutchinson had the misfortune to be a loyal colonial leader during the two very tumultuous decades leading up to the American Revolution. He worked hard to keep the British and colonists aligned in interests, even promoting a plan to unify the colonies into a single defensive unit (the Albany Plan of Union) to ward off Indian wars. The plan of union failed, and a major war ensued—the Seven Years' War, pitting the British and colonists against the French and their Indian allies in the backcountry of the American colonies. When the war ended and the British government began to think about taxing colonists to pay for it, Hutchinson had no doubt that the new British policies were legitimate. Unwise, perhaps, in their specific formulation, but certainly legitimate.

Not everyone in Boston shared his opinion. Fervent, enthusiastic crowds protested against a succession of British taxation policies enacted after 1763—the Sugar Act, the Stamp Act, the Townshend duties, the Tea Act, all landmark events on the road to the American Revolution. But Hutchinson maintained his steadfast loyalty to England. His love of order and tradition inclined him to unconditional support of the British empire, and he was, by nature, a measured and cautious man. "My temper does not incline to enthusiasm," he once wrote.

Privately, he lamented the stupidity of the British acts that provoked trouble, but his sense of duty required him to defend the king's policies, however misguided. Quickly, he became an inspiring villain to the emerging revolutionary movement. Governor Hutchinson came to personify all that was wrong with British and colonial relations. The man not inclined to enthusiasm unleashed popular enthusiasm all around him. He never appreciated that irony.

In another irony, Thomas Hutchinson was actually one of the first Americans to recognize the difficulties of maintaining full rights and privileges

Thomas Hutchinson

The only formal portrait of Thomas Hutchinson still in existence shows an assured young man in ruffles and hair ribbons. Decades of turmoil in Boston failed to puncture his self-confidence. Doubtless he sat for several portraits, as did all the Boston leaders in the 1760s to 1780s, but no other likeness has survived. One portrait hung in his summer house outside Boston, but a revolutionary crowd mutilated it and stabbed out the eyes. In 1775, Hutchinson fled to England, the country he had regarded as his cultural home, only to realize how very American he was.

Courtesy of the Massachusetts Historical Society.

for colonists so far from their supreme government, the king and Parliament in England. In 1769, when British troops occupied Boston in an effort to provide civil order, he wrote privately to a friend in England, "There must be an abridgement of what are called English liberties. . . . I doubt whether it is possible to project a system of government in which a colony three thousand miles distant from the parent state shall enjoy all the liberty of the parent state." What he could not imagine was the possibility of giving up the parent state altogether and creating an independent government closer to home.

Thomas Hutchinson was a loyalist; in the 1750s, most English-speaking colonists were affectionately loyal to England. But the Seven

Years' War, which England and its colonies fought together as allies, shook that affection, and imperial policies in the decade following the war (1763–1773) shattered it completely. Over the course of that decade, colonists insistently and repeatedly raised serious questions about American liberties and rights, especially over the issues of taxation and representation. Many came to believe what Thomas Hutchinson could never credit, that a tyrannical Britain had embarked on a course to enslave the colonists by depriving them of their traditional English liberties.

The opposite of **liberty** was slavery, a condition of nonfreedom and of coercion. Political rhetoric about liberty, tyranny, and slavery heated up emotions of white colonists during the many crises of the 1760s and 1770s. But this rhetoric turned out to be a two-edged sword. The call for an end to tyrannical slavery meant one thing when sounded by Boston merchants whose commercial shipping rights had been revoked; the same call meant something quite different in 1775 when sounded by black Americans locked in the bondage of slavery.

All of this was set in motion by the Seven Years' War. The British victory at first fortified loyalty to England, but its aftermath, taxation, stirred up discussions of rights, fueled white colonists' fear of enslavement by king and Parliament, and produced a potent political vocabulary with unexpected consequences.

The Seven Years' War, 1754–1763

For nearly half of the first fifty years of the eighteenth century, England was at war intermittently with France or Spain. Often the colonists in America experienced reverberations from these conflicts, most acutely along the **frontier** in northern New England, which bumped up against New France, an area of French settlement along the St. Lawrence River with population centers at Montreal and Quebec. (New France was also called *Canada* by the French, a borrowed Indian word meaning "settlement.") In the 1750s, international tensions mounted again, but this time over events originating in America. The conflict centered on contested land in the Ohio Valley, variously claimed by Virginians, by Pennsylvanians, by the French in Canada, and by the Indians already living on the land. The result was the costly Seven Years' War, which spread in 1756 to encompass much of Europe, the Caribbean, and even India; in its global reach, the war has justly been called by some the first world war. In its American setting, the war actually ran for nine years, not seven, during which British and American soldiers shared the hardships of battle and the glory of victory over the French and their Indian allies. (The conflict in North America is also known as the French and Indian War.) But the immense costs of the war—in money, in deaths, in desires for revenge by losers and even winners—laid the groundwork for the imperial crisis of the 1760s between British leaders and American colonists.

French-English Rivalry in the Ohio Country

In 1753, French soldiers advanced from Canada south into Indian territory in the Ohio Country, a frontier region encompassing present-day western Pennsylvania and eastern Ohio. For several decades, French traders had cultivated alliances with the Indian tribes there, cementing their relationships with gifts in order to facilitate a profitable trade of manufactured goods for beaver furs. Then in the late 1740s, aggressive Pennsylvania traders had pushed into the Ohio Valley and begun to poach on their business, underselling French goods and threatening to reorient Indian loyalties. In response, the French built a series of forts, hoping to create a western barrier to British-American expansion. Their goal was to secure their trade routes, not to open land for French colonial settlement.

The same region was also claimed by Virginia, and in 1747 a group of wealthy Virginians, including the brothers Lawrence and Augustine Washington, formed the Ohio Company and obtained a large **land grant** from the English king. Unlike the French, the Virginians were interested primarily in land acquisition, not fur trading; the exploding English-American population fueled their hopes of profitable resale of

Ohio River Valley, 1753

British fort
French fort

the western land in the near future. But now a small trading post built by the enterprising Virginians at the forks of the Ohio River (at present-day Pittsburgh) was under threat as an ideal site for a French fort. The royal governor of Virginia, Robert Dinwiddie, himself a shareholder in the Ohio Company, sent a messenger to warn the French that they were trespassing on Virginia land.

The messenger on this dangerous mission was George Washington, younger half-brother of the Ohio Company leaders. Although he was only twenty-one, Washington was an ambitious youth whose imposing height (six feet two) and air of silent competence convinced the governor he could do the job. The middle child in a family of eight, Washington did not stand to inherit great wealth, so he sought to gain public reputation and impress the Virginia elite by volunteering for this perilous duty. Accompanied by six other Virginians (one of whom spoke French), Washington delivered Dinwiddie's message to a French outpost near Lake Erie in late 1753 and returned from his assignment with crucial intelligence about French military strength.

Impressed, Dinwiddie appointed the youth to lead a small military expedition west to assert and, if need be, defend Virginia's claim. Dinwiddie acted with explicit backing from imperial officials in London, who were concerned by the French fortifications and who authorized the Virginia governor "to repell force by force," but only if Virginia troops were attacked first. By early 1754, the French had laid claim to the land at the forks of the Ohio River and had built Fort Duquesne there. Washington's assignment was somehow to chase the French away without being the aggressor and without provoking a larger war.

In spring of 1754, Washington returned to the Ohio Country, this time with 160 armed Virginians aided by Indian allies of the Mingo tribe led by its chief, Tanaghrisson. On an early morning in May, Tanaghrisson and a group of Mingos led a detachment of Washington's soldiers to a small French encampment in the woods. A brief skirmish ensued and fourteen Frenchmen were wounded; who fired the first shot was later a matter of dispute. While Washington struggled to communicate with the

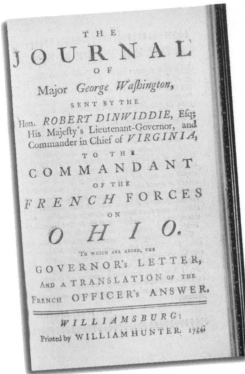

Washington's Journal, 1754
When George Washington returned from his first mission to the French, Governor Dinwiddie asked him to write a full report of what he had seen of the western countryside, of the Indians, and of French troop strength. Washington obliged, writing about 7,000 words in less than two days (about equivalent to a 25-page double-spaced paper). He coolly narrated scenes of personal danger: of traveling in deep snow and freezing temperatures, of falling off a raft into an icy river, of being shot at by a lone Indian. Dinwiddie printed Washington's report, along with his own letter and the French commander's defiant answer, in a 32-page pamphlet; shortly thereafter it was reprinted in London. The governor's aim was to inform Virginians and British leaders about the French threat to the west. But the pamphlet suited Washington's aims as well: At age twenty-two, he became known on both sides of the Atlantic for resolute and rugged courage.
The Huntington Library and Art Collections, San Marino, California.

sumed were on their side. After a third of the fort's occupants were killed or wounded, Washington surrendered, and the victors sent him back to his governor carrying a message of defeat: The French had no intention of departing from the disputed territory.

The Albany Congress and Intercolonial Defense

Even as Virginians, Frenchmen, and Indians fought and died in the Ohio Country, British imperial leaders were hoping to prevent the

George Washington, **by Charles Willson Peale**
In 1772, George Washington posed for the artist Charles Willson Peale in his splendid vintage uniform from the Seven Years' War, by then fifteen years in the past. It looks a tight fit. Notice the ornamental gorget hung around his neck, a miniature version of the throat-piece of a medieval suit of armor. Both English and Indian leaders in the eighteenth century often sported gorgets. Peale captured Washington's grandeur in his clothes but not his face, which appears plain, simple, and still very youthful. Washington wrote a friend that he was "in so grave—so sullen a mood" and often so sleepy during the portrait sitting "that I fancy the skill of this gentleman's pencil will be hard put to it, in describing to the world what manner of man I am."
Washington/Custis/Lee Collection, Washington and Lee University, Lexington, Virginia.

injured French commander, Tanaghrisson and his men intervened to kill and then scalp the wounded men, including the commander, probably with the aim of enflaming hostilities between the French and colonists.

This sudden massacre violated Washington's instructions to avoid being the aggressor and raised the stakes considerably. Washington, understandably anxious about French retaliation, ordered his men to fortify their position. They dubbed the flimsy structure that they built "Fort Necessity." Reinforcements amounting to several hundred more Virginians arrived; but the Mingos, sensing disaster and displeased by Washington's style of command over them, abandoned the Virginians. (Tanaghrisson later said: "The Colonel was a good-natured man, but had no experience; he took upon him to command the Indians as his slaves, [and] would by no means take advice from the Indians.") In early July, over 600 French soldiers attacked Fort Necessity, aided by tribes the Virginians had as-

Chief Hendrick and John Caldwell

What might it mean when a Mohawk chief dresses in English clothes and a British soldier goes native, and each of them poses for a portrait in attire adopted from the other culture? Dress is a symbol system that conveys status and self-presentation to viewers. Might it also change the way the dresser thinks about himself or herself? Chief Hendrick worked closely with the British in New York to maintain the trade alliance known as the Covenant Chain. In 1740, when he was sixty, he traveled to England, was presented at the royal court, and sat for this portrait. His blue coat, ruffled shirt, three-cornered hat, and cravat are all signs of the well-dressed British gentleman; but he holds a tomahawk in one hand and wampum in the other, and his long white hair is conspicuously uncurled, unlike an eighteenth-century gent's wig. John Caldwell also holds a tomahawk, which goes with his Indian garb: feather headdress, blankets, leggings, and moccasins. During the Revolutionary War, Caldwell was stationed at Fort Detroit, a British garrison that provided aid to tribes in the Ohio Valley battling Americans. Caldwell acquired this Indian outfit for a formal diplomatic mission to the Shawnee in 1780; he took the clothes back to England and wore them for this portrait. Do you think these instances of imitation indicate a willingness to cross cultural boundaries and try to be like, think like, or experience the other culture? Is the co-opting just play or a sign of something deeper?

Hendrick: Courtesy of the John Carter Brown Library at Brown University; Caldwell: The Board of Trustees of the National Museums & Galleries on Merseyside (King's Regiment Collection).

struggle from turning into a larger war. One obvious strategy was to strengthen British alliances with powerful and seemingly neutral Indian tribes who might otherwise support the French. To this end, British authorities directed the governor of New York to convene a conference drawing delegates from all colonies from Virginia northward.

In June and July of 1754, twenty-four delegates from seven colonies met in Albany, New York; also attending were Iroquois Indians of the Six Nations, a political confederacy of six large tribes inhabiting the central and western parts of what is now the state of New York. Albany had long been the site of periodic meetings that affirmed a trade alliance called the Covenant

Chain, first created in 1692 between New York leaders and Mohawk Indians, the most easterly of the Six Nations tribes. In 1753, the aged and venerable Mohawk leader, Hendrick, accused the English of breaking the Covenant Chain. A prime goal of the Albany Congress was thus to repair trade relations with the Mohawk and enlist their help—or at least their neutrality—against the French threat.

Two delegates at the congress had more ambitious plans. Benjamin Franklin of Pennsylvania and Thomas Hutchinson of Massachusetts, both rising political stars in their home colonies, coauthored the Albany Plan of Union, a document that proposed to provide for colonial defense by instituting a unified but limited government over all the colonies. In the course of the meeting, the Albany delegates learned of George Washington's defeat at Fort Necessity and understood instantly the escalating risk of war with France; they approved the plan. Key features included a president general appointed by the crown, together with a grand council of 48 colonial representatives, which would meet annually to consider questions of war, peace, and trade with the Indians. The writers of the Albany Plan humbly reaffirmed Parliament's authority; this was no bid for enlarged autonomy of the colonies.

> To Franklin's surprise, not a single colony approved the Albany Plan. The Massachusetts assembly feared it was "a Design of gaining power over the Colonies," especially the power of taxation.

To Franklin's surprise, not a single colony approved the Albany Plan. The Massachusetts assembly feared it was "a Design of gaining power over the Colonies," especially the power of taxation. Others objected that it would be impossible to agree on unified policies toward scores of quite different Indian tribes. The British government never backed the Albany Plan either, which perplexed both Franklin and Hutchinson. Instead, British authorities chose to centralize dealings with the Indians by appointing in 1755 two superintendents of Indian affairs, one for the northern and another for the southern colonies, each with exclusive powers to negotiate treaties, trade, and land sales. The superintendent of the northern district was William Johnson, a longtime trading partner and friend of the Mohawk people. This good news for the Mohawks was not welcomed by other tribes of the Iroquois confederacy; they had left the Albany Congress without pledging to help the English battle the French. At this very early point in the Seven Years' War, the Iroquois nations in western New York concluded that the French military presence around the Great Lakes and in the frontier west would help discourage the westward push of American colonists and therefore served their interests.

The War and Its Consequences

By 1755, Washington's frontier skirmish had turned into a major mobilization of British and American troops against the French. At first, the British hoped for quick victory by throwing armies at the French in three strategic places. A large force led by General Edward Braddock, recently arrived from England, was to attack the French at Fort Duquesne in western Pennsylvania; accompanying them would be George Washington's Virginia militia. In Massachusetts, Governor William Shirley aimed his soldiers at Fort Niagara, critically located between Lakes Erie and Ontario. And forces under William Johnson of New York, the new Indian affairs superintendent for the northern colonies, moved north toward Lake Champlain, intending to push the French back to Canada (Map 6.1).

Unfortunately for the British, the French were prepared to fight and had cemented respectful alliances with many Indian tribes from Canada down through the Great Lakes region and into the Ohio Country. In July 1755, General Braddock's large and well-armed force of 2,000 British and Virginia troops (joined by just eight Oneida Indians) marched toward Fort Duquesne, expecting an easy victory with their big guns and overwhelming numbers. One day short of their target, they were encircled in the woods and ambushed by 250 French soldiers and 640 Indian warriors, including Ottawas, Ojibwas, Potawatomis, Shawnees, and Delawares. In the bloody Battle of the Monongahela, named for a nearby river, nearly a thousand on the British side were killed or wounded. Washington was unhurt, though two horses in succession were shot out from under him; General Braddock was killed. Despite the humiliation of defeat, Washington's bravery in battle caused the governor of Virginia to promote him to commander of the Virginia army. At age twenty-two, Washington was beginning to realize his ambitions.

News of Braddock's defeat alarmed the other two British armies, then hacking their way through the dense forests of northern New York, and they retreated from action. For the next two years, the British stumbled badly on the American front. They lacked adequate numbers of soldiers

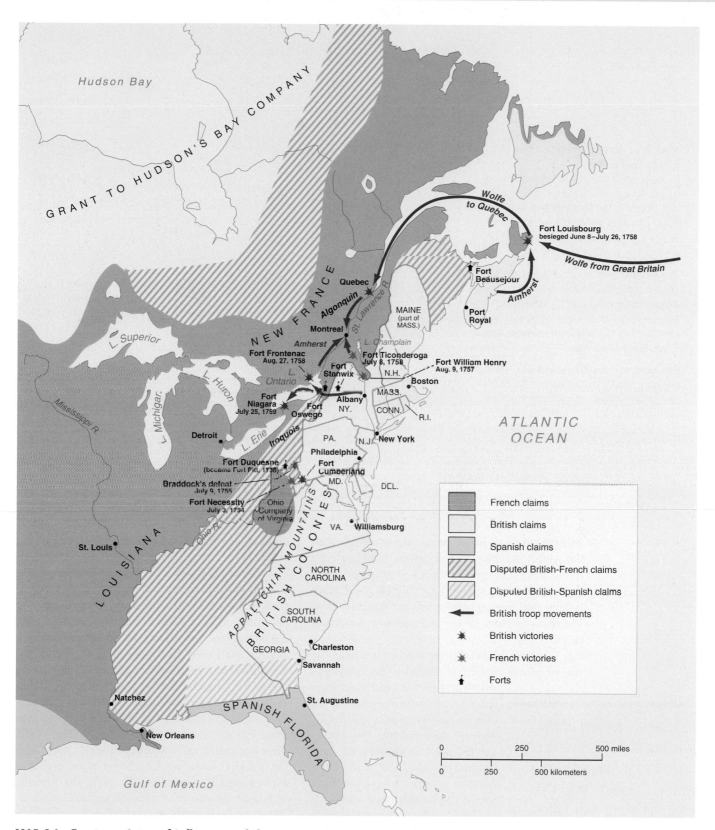

MAP 6.1 European Areas of Influence and the Seven Years' War, 1754–1763
In the mid-eighteenth century, France, England, and Spain claimed vast areas of North America, many of them already inhabited by various Indian peoples. The early flash points of the Seven Years' War were in regions of disputed claims where the French had allied with powerful native groups—the Iroquois and the Algonquian—to put pressure on the westward-moving English.

MAP 6.2 North America after the Seven Years' War

In the peace treaty of 1763, France ceded its interior lands but retained fishing rights and islands in the far north and several sugar islands in the Caribbean. Much of France's claim to land called Louisiana went not to England but to Spain.

READING THE MAP: How did European land claims change from 1750 to 1763?

CONNECTIONS: What was the goal of the Proclamation Act of 1763? What was the eventual fate of Louisbourg following the Seven Years' War?

FOR MORE HELP ANALYZING THIS MAP, see the map activity for this chapter in the Online Study Guide at **bedfordstmartins .com/roark**.

England's version of the victory of 1763 awarded all credit to the mighty British army. Colonists read the lessons of the war differently.

and supplies, and they received scant help from the American colonial assemblies. Nearly all the Indian tribes allied themselves with the French, figuring that the sparsely populated fur-trading French settlements were much to be preferred to the fast-growing, westward-pushing American colonies.

What finally turned the war around was the rise to power in 1757 of William Pitt, England's prime minister, a man willing to commit massive resources to an all-out war to ensure England's victory over France. His strategy led to the capture of Fort Duquesne in 1758 and Forts Niagara and Ticonderoga in 1759. When the British navy sailed up the St. Lawrence River, the French cities of Montreal and Quebec were isolated from help. The decisive victory on the North American continent was the capture of the seemingly invincible fortress city of Quebec in

September 1759 by the young British general James Wolfe.

The fall of Quebec broke the backbone of the French in North America. The victory was completed by the surrender of the French at Montreal in late 1760. American colonists rejoiced, but the worldwide war was not over yet. Battles continued in the Caribbean, where the French sugar islands Martinique and Guadeloupe fell to the English. Battles raged in Europe, and fighting extended to India. In 1762, the British laid siege to Spanish Cuba because Spain was France's ally in the global conflict. The costly water invasion of Havana required some four thousand colonial soldiers from New York and New England. By the end of 1762, the fighting was over. France and Spain capitulated, and the Treaty of Paris was signed in 1763.

The triumph of victory was sweet but short-lived. The complex peace negotiations reorganized the map of North America but stopped short of providing England with the full spoils of victory. England gained control of Canada, eliminating the French threat from the north and west. English and American title to the eastern half of North America, precisely what England had claimed before the war, was confirmed. But all French territory west of the Mississippi River, including New Orleans, was transferred to Spain as compensation for Spain's assistance to France during the war. Stranger still, Cuba was returned to Spain, and Martinique and Guadeloupe were returned to France (Map 6.2).

In truth, the French islands in the Caribbean were hardly a threat to Americans, for they provided a profitable trade in smuggled molasses. The main threat to the safety of colonists came instead from Indians dismayed by England's victory. The Treaty of Paris completely ignored the Indians and assigned their lands to English rule. With the French gone, the Indians lost the advantage of having two opponents to play off against each other, and they now had to cope with the westward-moving Americans. Indian policy would soon become a serious point of contention between the British government and the colonists.

England's version of the victory of 1763 awarded all credit to the mighty British army. According to this version, ungrateful colonists had provided inadequate support for a war fought to save them from the French. In defiance of British law, the colonists had engaged in smuggling—notably a lively trade in beaver pelts with French fur traders and an illegal molasses trade in the Caribbean. American traders, grumbled the British leaders, were really traitors. William Pitt was convinced that the illegal trade "principally, if not alone, enabled France to sustain and protract this long and expensive war."

Colonists read the lessons of the war differently. American colonial soldiers had turned out in force, they claimed, but the troops had been relegated to grunt work by arrogant British military leaders. Worse yet, they experienced unexpectedly harsh military discipline at British hands, ranging from floggings to executions. One soldier recalled watching three New England soldiers endure whippings of 800 lashes for some "trifling offense" at the hands of the British. At 300 lashes, "the flesh appeared to be entirely whipped from their shoulders, and they hung as mute and motionless as though they had been long since deprived of life." Then a British doctor revived them with "a vial of sharp stuff," saying, "'D__mn you, you can bear it yet'—and then the whipping would commence

again." Americans bristled at stories of British disdain, such as the remark of the impetuous General Wolfe, the British hero of Quebec, who said the American soldiers were "contemptible dogs." General Braddock had foolishly bragged to Benjamin Franklin that "these savages may, indeed, be a formidable enemy to your raw American militia, but upon the king's regular and disciplined troops, sir, it is impossible they should make any impression." Braddock's defeat "gave us Americans," Franklin wrote, "the first suspicion that our exalted ideas of the prowess of British regulars had not been well founded."

The human costs of the war were etched especially sharply in the minds of New England colonists, who had contributed many troops. About one-third of all Massachusetts men between ages fifteen and thirty had seen service. Many families lost loved ones, and this cost would not soon be forgotten. The assault on Havana in Cuba, for example, took the lives of

The Seven Years' War

1692–1750s	English and Iroquois create and affirm the Covenant Chain alliance in western New York.
1700–1740s	French settlers enjoy exclusive trade with Indians in Ohio Valley.
1747	Ohio Company receives land grant from king of England.
1753	Mohawk chief Hendrick accuses English of breaking the Covenant Chain.
	French soldiers advance from Canada into Ohio Country.
	George Washington delivers a message telling the French that they are trespassing.
1754	French build Fort Duquesne.
	Washington returns to Ohio Country with troops and Mingo allies.
	May. Washington, guided by Mingo chief Tanaghrisson, attacks the French.
	July. French and Indian soldiers defeat Washington at Fort Necessity.
	June–July. Albany Congress convenes.
1755	British authorities appoint two superintendents of Indian affairs.
	July. Braddock defeated in the Battle of Monongahela.
1756	William Pitt becomes leader of England's House of Commons.
1758	British capture Fort Duquesne.
1759	British capture Forts Niagara and Ticonderoga.
	British capture Quebec.
1760	British capture Montreal.
1762	British capture Cuba.
1763	Treaty of Paris signed.

some 2,000 Americans, half the colonial soldiers who had been sent there.

The enormous expense of the war caused by Pitt's no-holds-barred military strategy cast another huge shadow over the victory. By 1763, England's national debt, double what it had been when Pitt took office, posed a formidable challenge to the next decade of leadership in England.

British Leadership, Indians, and the Proclamation of 1763

In 1760, in the middle of the Seven Years' War, twenty-two-year-old George III came to the British throne, underprepared for his monarchical duties. Timid and insecure, the new king trusted only his tutor, the Earl of Bute, a Scotsman who was an outsider to power circles in London. George III immediately installed Bute as head of his cabinet of ministers. Bute made blunders and did not last long, but in his short time in office he made one very significant decision—to keep a standing army in the mainland colonies even though the last battles there were over in 1760. In both financial and political terms, this was a costly move.

> The ostensible reason for keeping several thousand British troops in America was to maintain the peace between the colonists and the Indians. This was not a misplaced concern.

The ostensible reason for keeping several thousand British troops in America was to maintain the peace between the colonists and the Indians. This was not a misplaced concern. The defeat and withdrawal of the French from North America had left their Indian allies—who did not accept defeat—in a state of alarm. Just three months after the Treaty of Paris was signed in 1763, Pontiac, chief of the Ottawa tribe in the northern Ohio region, attacked the British garrison near Detroit. Six more attacks on forts quickly followed; American settlements were also hit. Joining the Ottawa were tribes from western New York, the Ohio Valley, and the Great Lakes region: the Chippewa, Huron, Potawatomi, Miami, Kickapoo, Mascouten, Wea, Shawnee, Mingo, Delaware, and Seneca. By fall, these tribes had captured every fort west of Detroit,

Pontiac's Uprising, 1763

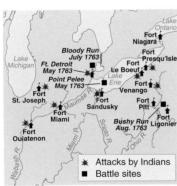

more than 400 British soldiers were dead, and another 2,000 colonists had been killed or taken captive. Pontiac's uprising was quelled in December 1763 by the combined efforts of British and colonial soldiers, but the potential for continued frontier warfare was hardly diminished. (See "Historical Question," page 184.)

To minimize violence, the British government that fall issued an order called the Proclamation of 1763, forbidding colonists to settle west of an imaginary line drawn along the crest of the Appalachian Mountains from Canada in the north to Georgia in the south. The Proclamation chiefly aimed to separate Indians and settlers, but it also was intended to limit trade with Indians to traders licensed by colonial governors, and it forbade private sales of Indian land. The Proclamation's language took care not to identify western lands as belonging to the Indians. Instead, it spoke of Indians "who live under our protection" on "such parts of our Dominions and Territories as, not having been ceded to or purchased by Us, are reserved to them, as their Hunting Grounds." Other parts of the Proclamation of 1763 referred to American colonists and even to the French inhabitants of now-British Canada as "our loving subjects" who could enjoy the blessings of English rights and privileges. In contrast, Indians were clearly rejected as British subjects, described more vaguely as "Tribes of Indians with whom We are connected." Of course, the English were not really well connected with the Indians, nor did they wish connections to form among the tribes. As William Johnson, the superintendent of northern Indian affairs, advised in 1764, "It will be expedient to treat with each nation separately . . . for could they arrive at a perfect union, they must prove very dangerous Neighbours." In Johnson's view, "As long as they Quarrell with one another, we shall be well with them all. And when they are all at Peace, It's the Signal for us to have a good Look out."

The 1763 proclamation line proved nearly impossible to enforce. Surging American population growth had already sent many hundreds of settlers west of the line, and land speculators, such as those of Virginia's Ohio Company, had no desire to lose opportunities for profitable resale of the lands they had been granted more than a decade earlier. Bute's decision to post a standing army in the colonies was thus a cause for concern for western settlers, eastern speculators, and Indian tribes alike.

Silver Medal to Present to Indians
After Pontiac's uprising ended, the British attempted to mend relations with Indian tribes by honoring them with gifts. This silver medal, minted in 1766, displays a profile of King George III on the front and a cozy depiction on the back of an Indian and Briton sharing a smoking peace pipe. The Latin words on the front announce George's name, title, and kingly dominions; the English words on the back would have been equally unintelligible to the recipients of the gift. Imagine a conversation between an Indian chief and an English translator who tries to explain what the slogan "HAPPY WHILE UNITED" might mean. The scene depicted—two men with relaxed, friendly body language—illustrates "HAPPY" and "UNITED." The "WHILE," rooted in a sense of time, temporariness, and contingency, might be tricky to explain. Why?
The American Numismatic Society.

The Sugar and Stamp Acts, 1763–1765

Lord Bute lost power in 1763, and the young King George turned to a succession of leaders throughout the 1760s, searching for a prime minister he could trust. Nearly half a dozen ministers in seven years took their turns formulating policies designed to address one basic, underlying British reality: A huge war debt, amounting to £123 million and growing because of interest due on the loans, needed to be serviced, and the colonists, as British subjects, should help to pay it off. To many Americans, however, that proposition seemed in deep violation of what they perceived to be their rights and liberties as British subjects, and it created resentment that grew and eventually erupted in rebellion. The first provocative revenue acts were the work of Sir George Grenville, prime minister from 1763 to 1765.

Grenville's Sugar Act

To find revenue, George Grenville scrutinized the customs service, a division of the British government responsible for monitoring the flow of ships and collecting duties on specified trade items in both England and America. Grenville found that the salaries of customs officers cost the government four times what was collected in revenue. The shortfall was due in part to bribery and smuggling, so Grenville began to insist on rigorous attention to paperwork and a strict accounting of collected duties.

The hardest duty to enforce was the one imposed by the Molasses Act of 1733—a stiff tax of six pence per gallon on any molasses purchased from non-British sources. The purpose of the tax was to discourage trade with French Caribbean islands and redirect the molasses trade to British sugar islands. But it did not work: French molasses remained cheap and abundant because French **planters** on Martinique and Guadeloupe had no use for it. A by-product of sugar production, molasses was a key ingredient in rum, a drink the French scorned. Rum-loving Americans were eager to buy French molasses, and they had ignored the tax law for decades.

Grenville's ingenious solution to this problem was the Revenue Act of 1764, popularly dubbed the "Sugar Act." It lowered the duty on French molasses to three pence, making it more attractive for shippers to obey the law, and at the same time raised penalties for smuggling. The act appeared to be in the tradition of navigation acts meant to regulate trade, but Grenville's actual intent was to raise revenue. He was using an established form of law for new ends, and he was doing it by the novel means of lowering a duty.

The Sugar Act toughened enforcement policies. From now on, all British naval crews could act as impromptu customs officers, boarding suspicious ships and seizing cargoes found to be in violation. Smugglers caught without proper paperwork would be prosecuted, not in a friendly civil court with a local jury but in a vice-admiralty court located in Halifax, Nova Scotia, where a single judge presided. The implication was that justice would be sure and severe.

How Long Did the Seven Years' War Last in Indian Country?

France was defeated on the North American continent in 1760, and the Treaty of Paris officially ended the global war between France and England in 1763. But there was no lasting peace for the Indian nations of the Ohio Valley and Great Lakes region. In 1761, a Chippewa chief named Minavavana clearly explained why in an ominous speech delivered to a British trader at Fort Michilimackinac, a British outpost guarding the straits of Mackinaw where Lakes Huron and Michigan meet: "Englishman, although you have conquered the French, you have not yet conquered us! We are not your slaves. These lakes, these woods and mountains were left to us by our ancestors. They are our inheritance; and we will part with them to none." Furthermore, Minavavana pointedly noted, "your king has never sent us any presents, nor entered into any treaty with us, wherefore he and we are still at war; and until he does these things we must consider that we have no other father, nor friend, among the white men than the King of France."

Minavavana and other Indians of the region had cause to be alarmed. With the exit of the French, British regiments took over the French-built forts all over the Northwest. Fort Duquesne, renamed Fort Pitt in honor of the British leader who authorized the war-winning strategy, underwent two years of fortification. No one could mistake the new walls—

sixty feet thick at their base, ten at the top—for the external facade of a friendly fur trading post. Nonmilitary Americans were moving into Fort Pitt's neighborhood too, just as Indians had feared they would, crowding out native inhabitants and relying on the military protection of the fort.

Minavavana's complaint about the lack of British presents was a far more serious problem than the British military leaders figured. Gifts exchanged in Indian culture cemented social relationships; they symbolized honor and established obligation. The French over many decades had mastered the subtleties of gift exchange, distributing clothing, textiles, and hats, and receiving calumets (ornamented ceremonial pipe stems) as symbols of friendship. New to the practice, British military leaders often discarded the calumets as trivial trinkets, thereby insulting the givers. Major General Jeffrey Amherst was sometimes willing to offer gifts to particular Indian leaders, positioning the "gift" as a bribe in the British frame of reference. But Amherst saw extensive gift exchange as demeaning to the British, forcing them to pay tribute to people whom he considered inferior. "It is not my intention ever to attempt to gain the friendship of Indians by presents," Amherst declared. The Indian view was the opposite: Generous givers expressed dominance and protection, not subordination, in the act of giving. William Johnson, superintendent of northern

Indian affairs, warned Amherst that he was insulting the Indians, but the imperious Amherst did not listen.

A religious revival in 1760–1761, fueled by the prophetic visions of an Indian leader named Neolin, greatly enhanced the prospects of frontier war in the Northwest. Neolin, of the Delaware tribe, predicted a swift decline for all tribes unless they altered their ways, gave up quarreling with each other, shunned trade in guns, alcohol, and other trade goods, and curbed their overkill of animals for the pelt trade. His preachings spread quickly, gaining credence as the British bungled diplomacy and American settlers continued to penetrate western lands.

A renewal of commitment to Indian ways and the formation of tribal alliances led to open warfare in 1763, called (by the British) Pontiac's Rebellion. (The Indians would not have credited Pontiac with sole leadership; the coordination of the war was the work of many men.) Jeffrey Amherst, never a shrewd observer of Indian relations, flatly declared in April 1763 that reports of impending attack were "Meer Bugbears." But by mid-May, the British commander at Detroit knew the threat was real. Pontiac, chief of the Ottawa, along with Potawatomi and Huron warriors, attacked Fort Detroit and laid siege for two months. In late May, within two weeks of Pontiac's first move, Indians captured four more forts in Ohio, through ruses in which Indians pretending to have peaceful business gained entry to the garrisons. A fifth fort, at Michilimackinac, fell to Ojibwas who seemed to be playing a game of lacrosse near the fort. After several hours of strenuous play, the ball landed near the fort's open gate, and the enthralled British spectators realized too late that the convergence of players on the ball was really a rush

Plan of the New Fort at Pittsburgh

The French Fort Duquesne sat at the strategic forks of the Ohio River on a triangle of land formed by the Allegheny and Monongahela rivers rushing together to create the mighty Ohio. Built in 1754, Fort Duquesne provided a supply depot and a meeting place for the Indian allies of the French. It was the intended target of General Braddock's English army in 1755, but Braddock was forced into battle and soundly defeated a day before his planned attack. In 1758, the British captured an English-speaking man named Johnson along with some Indians taken prisoner. Johnson, an apparent traitor, saved his life by yielding information that Fort Duquesne was greatly undermanned and an easy hit. British and colonial troops sped to attack it; once taken, the fort was blown into rubble. In 1759, this plan for a new fort, named for Prime Minister William Pitt, showed the grand and imposing stronghold with room enough to house 1,000 soldiers inside the thick protective walls. By 1762, the fort was finished, fulfilling Pitt's mandate to "maintain His Majesty's subjects in undisputed possession of the Ohio."

of warriors into the fort. The players seized tomahawks that had been hidden under blankets worn by Indian women on the sidelines. The Ojibwas took the fort.

By the end of June, thirteen British garrisons had either fallen or been evacuated under threat of attack. Yet the British managed to hold on to the three most important forts— Detroit, Niagara, and Pitt—besieged by Indians. At Fort Pitt, two ostensibly friendly Delaware Indians showed up at the end of May to suggest that the British leave to avoid attack. Pitt's commander thanked them but declined their suggestion and sent them on their way with his idea of a gift: two blankets and a handkerchief used by British smallpox patients in the fort. "We hope it will have the desired effect," wrote a militiaman in his diary. Two months later, Jeffrey Amherst suggested to a subordinate that spreading smallpox—a practice akin to later germ warfare—should be considered as a method of war: "We must use Every Strategem in our Power to Reduce them." There is no evidence that the infected blankets ac-

tually propagated smallpox or that Amherst's war strategem was put into greater practice.

From late summer of 1763 into the early months of 1764, Indian country was the scene of tremendous bloodshed. Indians targeted British supply routes and civilian settlements, resulting in several thousand deaths. Two thousand British troops were moved west from points in upper New York and Canada to join the fray. In December, Pennsylvania civilians went on the offensive. Some fifty vigilantes known as the Paxton Boys decided to make war on any Indians they could find. They descended on a peaceful village of friendly Conestoga Indians and murdered and scalped twenty of them. The vigilantes, numbers swelling to 500, next marched on Philadelphia to try to capture and murder some Christian Indians held in protective custody. British troops prevented that, but the unruly Paxton Boys escaped all punishment for their murderous attack on the Conestoga.

In 1764, the rebellion faded. The Indians were short on ammunition;

the British were tired and broke. Amherst's superiors in Britain blamed him for mishandling the conflict, and when he was recalled home, his own soldiers toasted his leaving. Thomas Gage took command and soon distributed gifts profusely among the Indians.

Was the Seven Years' War finally over for the Indians, ten years after it started? If 1764 represents an end, it was only a brief one. Periodic raids and killings punctuated the rest of the 1760s and early 1770s, climaxing in the late 1770s as Indians joined the British to fight the Americans in the Revolutionary War. Warfare and massacres occurred in New England and New York, down to South Carolina and Georgia, and especially in the Ohio Country. The American Revolution eventually ended as well, but the frontier war between Americans and Indians continued on and off— mostly on—until 1815, the end of the War of 1812. Perhaps the Seven Years' War could be called the Sixty-One Years' War, from the Indian point of view.

Paper Currency of the 1750s to 1770s

Colonists generally used coins of valued metal for money (British shillings, Spanish doubloons) or else engaged in barter. But during the upheaval of the Seven Years' War, several colonies printed paper money. The currency shown here is laden with words stipulating the legality and value of the money. To discourage counterfeiting, each paper had an elaborate design, a unique handwritten number, and the signature of some authority who vouched for its authenticity. London merchants did not like accepting colonial paper money and prevailed on Parliament to pass a Currency Act in 1764 prohibiting the colonies from printing any, which put a crimp in the colonial economy, always short of coinage. In 1775, the newly established Continental Congress began printing paper money to finance the war. Notice the three-dollar paper at the lower left.

Courtesy of the Decorative & Industrial Arts Collection of the Chicago Historical Society.

Grenville hoped that his tightening of the customs service and the lowered duties of the Sugar Act would reform American smugglers into law-abiding shippers and in turn generate income for the empire. Unfortunately, the decrease in duty was not sufficient to offset the attractions of smuggling. The vigilant customs officers made bribery harder to accomplish, and several ugly confrontations occurred in port cities such as Newport, Rhode Island, and New York City. Reaction to the Sugar Act foreshadowed questions about England's right to tax Americans, but in 1764 objections to the act came principally from Americans in the shipping trades inconvenienced by the law.

From the British point of view, the Proclamation of 1763 and the Sugar Act seemed to be reasonable efforts to administer the colonies. To the Americans, however, the British supervision appeared to be a disturbing intrusion into colonial practices, by which taxes were raised by colonial assemblies composed of elected representatives. Philadelphian Benjamin Franklin, living in London as the agent for Pennsylvania, warned that "two distinct Jurisdictions or Powers of Taxing cannot well subsist together in the same country. If a Tax is propos'd with us, how dare we venture to lay it, as the next Ship perhaps may bring us an Account of some heavy Tax propos'd by you?"

The Stamp Act

By his second year in office, Grenville had made almost no dent in the national debt. Continued evasion prevented the Sugar Act from becoming the moneymaker he had hoped it would be. So in February 1765, he escalated his revenue program with the Stamp Act, precipitating a major conflict between England and the colonies over Parliament's right to tax. The Stamp Act imposed a tax on all paper used for various colonial documents—newspapers, pamphlets, court documents, licenses, wills, ships' bills of lading—and required that a special stamp be affixed to the paper proving that the tax had been paid. Unlike the Sugar Act, which regulated trade, the Stamp Act was designed plainly and simply to raise money. It affected nearly everyone who used any taxed paper—newspaper readers, for example—but it fell heaviest on the business and legal communities, heavily reliant on official documents.

Thomas Hutchinson, lieutenant governor of Massachusetts, had warned Grenville that the stamp tax posed difficulties. Aside from the navigation acts, which were intended primarily to regulate trade, Parliament had levied no previous taxes on the colonists. Hutchinson warned that the colonies could reasonably conclude that Parliament had conceded to them the right to tax themselves. On practical grounds, he also urged the British officials to consider whether trade disruptions caused by the Stamp Act might cost more than the revenue the act generated. Instead of heeding Hutchinson's fears, Grenville merely delegated the administration of the act to Americans, to avoid the problem of hostility to British enforcers. In each colony, local stamp distributors would be hired at a handsome salary of 8 percent of the revenue collected.

English tradition held that taxes were a gift of the people to their monarch, granted by the people's representatives. This view of taxes as a freely given gift preserved an essential concept of English political theory—the idea that citizens have the liberty to enjoy and use their property without fear of confiscation. The king could not demand money; only the House of Commons could grant it. Grenville quite agreed with the notion of taxation by consent, but he argued that the colonists were already "virtually" represented in Parliament. The House of Commons, he insisted, represented all British subjects, wherever they were.

Colonial leaders emphatically rejected this British view, arguing that **virtual representation** could not withstand the stretch across the Atlantic. The stamp tax itself, levied by a distant Parliament on unwilling colonies, illustrated the problem. "The MINISTER'S virtual representation in Support of the TAX on us is fantastical and frivolous," Maryland inhabitants complained. Daniel Dulany, a Maryland lawyer, wrote a best-selling pamphlet explaining that virtual representation was "a mere cob-web, spread to catch the unwary, and entangle the weak."

Resistance Strategies and Crowd Politics

The Stamp Act was scheduled to take effect on November 1, 1765. News of its passage arrived in the colonies in April 1765, so colonial leaders had seven months to contemplate a response. Governors were unlikely to challenge the law, for most of them owed their office to the king. Instead, the colonial assemblies took the lead; eight of them held discussions on objections to the Stamp Act.

Virginia's assembly, the House of Burgesses, was the first to object. At the very end of its May 1765 session, after two-thirds of the members had gone home, Patrick Henry, a twenty-nine-year-old lawyer and political newcomer, presented a series of resolutions on the Stamp Act that were debated and passed, one by one. They became known as the Virginia Resolves.

Henry's resolutions inched the assembly toward radical opposition to the Stamp Act. The first three stated the obvious: that Virginians were British citizens, that they enjoyed the same rights and privileges as Britons, and that self-taxation was one of those rights. The fourth resolution noted that Virginians had always taxed themselves, through their representatives in the House of Burgesses. The fifth took a radical leap by pushing the other four unexceptional statements to one logical conclusion—that the Virginia assembly alone had the right to tax Virginians.

> The traditional English view of taxes as a gift of the people to their monarch preserved an essential concept of English political theory—the idea that citizens have the liberty to enjoy and use their property without fear of confiscation.

Tax Assessment Book

American colonists routinely paid property taxes to local authorities. This 1772 tax book from Rowley, Massachusetts, records amounts due in pounds, shillings, and pence. The several entries for each name indicate assessments on real estate, personal property, and a poll (head) tax. Notice that two women identified as "Mrs." owe taxes. Since married women by law owned no property, we can conclude that these were widows. What do you think the seven large X marks meant? Why might "Capt Samuel Pike" lack one? Chicago Historical Society.

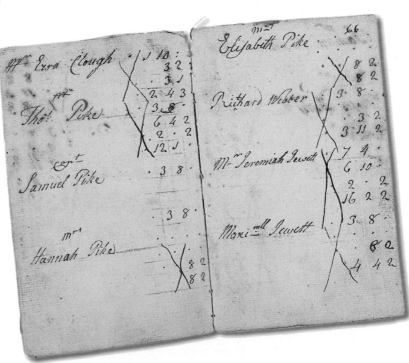

Two more fiery resolutions were debated, but majority support eroded as Henry pressed the logic of his case to the extreme. The sixth resolution denied legitimacy to any tax law originating outside Virginia, and a seventh boldly called anyone who disagreed with these propositions an enemy of Virginia. This was too much for the other representatives. They backed away from resolutions six and seven and later rescinded their vote on number five as well.

Their caution hardly mattered, however, because newspapers in other colonies printed all seven Virginia Resolves, creating the impression that a daring first challenge to the Stamp Act had taken place. As a result, other assemblies were willing to consider even more radical questions, such as: By what authority could Parliament legislate for the colonies without also taxing them? No one disagreed, in 1765, that Parliament had legislative power over the colonists, who were, after all, British subjects. Several assemblies advanced the argument that there was a distinction between *external* taxes, imposed to regulate trade, and *internal* taxes, such as a stamp tax or a property tax, which could only be self-imposed.

Reaction to the Stamp Act ran far deeper than political debate in assemblies. Every person whose livelihood required the use of official paper had to decide whether to comply with the act. Local communities strategized their responses. Should they boycott all paper use? A boycott would keep noncompliance within the law but would be inconvenient; if enough people ceased using stamped paper, the information network dependent on newspapers, the legal system, and business and commerce might grind to a halt. Should communities defy the law and conduct business as usual on unstamped paper, running the risk of fines or jail? A third strategy promised the surest success: destroying the stamped paper or preventing its distribution at the source, before the law took effect, thus ensuring universal noncompliance.

The first organized resistance to the Stamp Act began in Boston, port city and capital of Massachusetts, under the leadership of Samuel Adams, a town politician with a history of opposition to Lieutenant Governor Thomas Hutchinson. Unlike Hutchinson, Adams cared nothing for status, high office, or fine material goods. He was the Harvard-educated son of a Boston brewer, a man with shrewd political instincts and a gift for organizing. He mobilized shopkeepers, master craftsmen, dockworkers, and

Samuel Adams, by John Singleton Copley
Samuel Adams consented to pose for Boston artist John Singleton Copley in 1770. The portrait highlights Adams's face, which projects a dramatic intensity and dominates the bulky body, subdued by dark clothes. Adams stares thoughtfully and silently at the viewer and points to important legal documents before him, including the Massachusetts Charter of 1689. Wealthy merchant John Hancock commissioned the portrait, which hung in his house. Copley painted scores of Boston's leaders in the 1760s, both loyalists and patriots. He maintained neutrality until 1773, when his father-in-law became an official East India tea distributor. Copley's home was threatened by a crowd, and he left for England in 1774. Deposited by the City of Boston, Museum of Fine Arts, Boston.

laborers into a group of protesters who called themselves—and anyone who joined them—Sons of Liberty.

The plan hatched by the Boston Sons of Liberty called for a large street demonstration highlighting a ritualized mock execution designed to convince Andrew Oliver, the stamp distributor, that his personal safety would best be served by resigning. With no stamp distributor, no stamps could be sold. On the morning of August 14, 1765, an effigy of Oliver was found hanging from a tree. In an effort to keep tensions under control, the royal governor of Massachusetts, Francis Bernard, took no action. By evening, a crowd of two to three thousand people paraded Oliver's effigy around town, using it as a prop in short plays demonstrating the dangers of selling stamps, before finally be-heading and burning it. The crowd also pulled down a small building on Oliver's dock, re-ported to be the future stamp office. The flesh-and-blood Oliver stayed in hiding; the next day he resigned his office in a well-publicized an-nouncement.

The demonstration provided lessons for everyone. Oliver learned that stamp distributors would be very unpopular people. Bernard and Hutchinson learned the limitations of their own powers to govern, with no police to call on. The demonstration's leaders learned that street ac-tion was very effective. And hundreds of labor-ers, sailors, and apprentices not only learned what the Stamp Act was all about but also gained pride in their ability to have a decisive impact on politics.

Twelve days later, another crowd action showed how well some of these lessons had been learned. On August 26, a crowd visited the houses of four detested officials. One was a cus-toms officer; two of the others were officers of the admiralty courts, where smugglers were tried; the crowd broke windows and raided wine cellars. The fourth house was the finest dwelling in Massachusetts, owned by the stiff-necked Thomas Hutchinson. Rumors abounded that Hutchinson had urged Grenville to adopt the Stamp Act. Although he had done the opposite, Hutchinson refused to set the record straight, saying curtly, "I am not obliged to give an an-swer to all the questions that may be put me by every lawless person." The crowd attacked his house, and by daybreak only the exterior walls were standing.

The destruction of Hutchinson's house brought a temporary halt to crowd activities in Boston. The Boston town meeting issued a state-ment of sympathy, but a reward of £300 for the arrest and conviction of riot organizers failed to produce a single lead. The Sons of Liberty denied planning the event.

Essentially, the opponents of the Stamp Act in Boston had triumphed; no one volunteered

Andrew Oliver

This portrait shows Bostonian Andrew Oliver at age twenty-two, just a few years after his graduation from Harvard College. The powdered wig and stern look add years to his face; the blousy clothing adds substance to his body. He was fifty-nine and probably even more im-posing in appearance when he ran afoul of the Stamp Act rioters in Boston in 1765.

Collection of the Oliver Family, photo by Clive Russ.

Seal of Andrew Oliver, Lieutenant Governor of Massachusetts Bay

This amethyst seal sug-gests that important business was a routine event for its owner, An-drew Oliver. Long before he became the unfortunate stamp distributor in 1765, Oliver held a succession of offices—overseer of the poor, collector of taxes, member of the provincial council, and secretary of Massachusetts. He thus had many occasions to press the seal into melted wax to authenticate documents. The stone bears the tough-minded motto *Pax Quareritur Bello* (Peace Is Obtained by War), an appropriate maxim for the man willing to become the royal lieutenant governor of Massachusetts in 1770. He re-placed his brother-in-law Thomas Hutchinson, who had moved up to be royal governor.

Collection of the Oliver Family, photo by Clive Russ.

to replace Oliver as distributor. When the Stamp Act took effect on November 1, customs officers were unable to prevent ships lacking properly stamped clearance papers from passing through the harbor. Hutchinson, as chief justice of the Massachusetts court, could not tolerate this defiance of the law, but he could not bring the lawbreakers to justice in his court. So he did the only thing he could do as a principled man: He resigned his judgeship. He remained lieutenant governor, however, and within five years he would agree to become the royal governor.

Liberty and Property

Boston's crowd actions of August sparked similar eruptions by groups calling themselves Sons of Liberty in nearly fifty towns throughout the colonies, and stamp distributors everywhere hastened to resign. One Connecticut distributor was forced by a crowd to throw his hat and powdered wig in the air while shouting a cheer for "Liberty and property!" This man fared better than another Connecticut stamp agent, who was nearly buried alive by Sons of Liberty. Only when the thuds of dirt sounded on his coffin did he have a sudden change of heart, shouting out his resignation to the crowd above. Luckily, he was heard. In Charleston, South Carolina, the stamp distributor resigned after crowds burned effigies and chanted "Liberty! Liberty!"

> The rallying cry "Liberty and property" made perfect sense to many white Americans of all social ranks, who feared that the Stamp Act threatened their traditional right to liberty as British subjects.

Some colonial leaders, disturbed about the riots, hastened to mount a more moderate challenge to parliamentary authority. Twenty-seven delegates representing nine colonial assemblies met in New York City in October 1765 as the Stamp Act Congress. For two weeks, the men hammered out a petition about taxation addressed to the king and Parliament. Their statement closely resembled the first five Virginia Resolves, claiming taxes were "free gifts of the people" that only the people's representatives could give. They dismissed virtual representation: "The people of these colonies are not, and from their local circumstances, cannot be represented in the House of Commons." But the delegates also took great care to affirm their subordination to Parliament and monarch in deferential language. Nevertheless, the Stamp Act Congress, by the mere fact of its meeting, advanced a radical potential, the notion of intercolonial political action.

The rallying cry of "Liberty and property" made perfect sense to many white Americans of all social ranks, who feared that the Stamp Act threatened their traditional right to liberty as British subjects. In this case the liberty in question was the right to be taxed only by representative government. "Liberty and property" came from a trinity of concepts—"life, liberty, property"—that had come to be regarded as the birthright of freeborn British subjects since at least the seventeenth century. A powerful tradition of British political thought invested representative government with the duty to protect individual lives, liberties, and property (possessions or money) against potential abuse by royal authority. Up to 1765, Americans consented to accept Parliament as a body that in some way represented them. But now, in this matter of taxation via stamps, Parliament seemed a distant body that had failed to protect Americans' liberty and property against royal authority.

Alarmed, some Americans began to speak and write about a plot by British leaders to enslave them. The opposite of liberty was slavery, the condition of being under the control of someone else. A Maryland writer warned that if the colonies lost "the right of exemption from all taxes without their consent," that loss would "deprive them of every privilege distinguishing freemen from slaves." In Virginia, a group of planters headed by Richard Henry Lee issued a document called the Westmoreland Resolves, claiming that the Stamp Act was an attempt "to reduce the people of this country to a state of abject and detestable slavery." The opposite meanings of *liberty* and *slavery* were utterly clear to white Americans, but they stopped short of applying similar logic to the half million black Americans they held in bondage. Many blacks, however, could see the contradiction. When a crowd of Charleston blacks paraded with shouts of "Liberty!" just a few months after white Sons of Liberty had done the same, the town militia turned out to break up the demonstration.

Politicians and merchants in England reacted with alarm to the American demonstrations and petitions. Merchants particularly feared trade disruptions and pressured Parliament to repeal the Stamp Act. By late 1765, yet another new minister, the Marquess of Rockingham, headed the king's cabinet. His dilemma was to find a dignified way for Parliament to repeal the act without losing face. George Grenville, author of the Stamp Act, defended his policy and roundly condemned American ingratitude: "When they want the protection of this kingdom, they are always ready to ask for it. . . . The nation has run itself into an immense debt to give them their protection; and now [when] they are called upon to contribute a small share towards the public expence, an expence arising from themselves, they renounce your authority, insult your officers, and break out, I might almost say, into open rebellion."

No doubt many in the British government shared Grenville's anger, but economic considerations won out. In March 1766, Parliament repealed the Stamp Act but passed the Declaratory Act, which asserted Parliament's right to legislate for the colonies "in all cases whatsoever." Perhaps the stamp tax had been inexpedient, but the power to tax—one prime case of a legislative power—was stoutly upheld.

The Townshend Acts and Economic Retaliation, 1767–1770

Rockingham did not last long as prime minister. By the summer of 1766, George III had persuaded William Pitt to resume that position. Pitt appointed Charles Townshend to be chancellor of the exchequer, the chief financial minister. Facing both the old war debt problem and the continuing cost of stationing British troops in America, Townshend turned again to taxation. But his knowledge of the changing political climate in the colonies was limited, and his simple idea to raise revenue turned into a major mistake. In 1768 and 1769, the American colonies were agitated by boycotts of British goods and demonstrations against British policies, even to the point of politicizing women, self-styled "Daughters of Liberty." Boston led the uproar, causing the British to send peacekeeping soldiers to arrest the royal governor. The stage was thus set for the first fatalities in the brewing revolution.

The Townshend Duties

Townshend proposed new taxes in the old form of a navigation act. Officially called the Revenue Act of 1767, it established new duties on tea, glass, lead, paper, and painters' colors imported into the colonies, to be paid by the importer but passed on to consumers in the retail price. A year before, the duty on French molasses had been reduced from three pence to one pence per gallon, and finally the Sugar Act was pulling in a tidy revenue of about £45,000 annually. So it was not unreasonable to suppose that duties on additional trade goods might also improve the cash flow. Townshend assumed that external taxes—that is, duties levied on the transatlantic trade—would be more acceptable to Americans than internal taxes, such as the stamp tax.

The Townshend duties were not especially burdensome, but the principle they embodied—taxation through trade duties—looked different to the colonists in the wake of the Stamp Act crisis. Although Americans once distinguished between external and internal taxes, that distinction was wiped out by an external tax meant only to raise money. John Dickinson, a Philadelphia lawyer, articulated this view in a series of articles titled *Letters from a Farmer in Pennsylvania*, widely reprinted in the winter of 1767–68. "We are taxed without our consent. . . . We are therefore—SLAVES," Dickinson wrote, calling for "a total denial of the power of Parliament to lay upon these colonies any 'tax' whatever."

A controversial provision of the Townshend duties directed that some of the revenue generated would be used to pay the salaries of royal governors. Before 1767, local assemblies set the salaries of their own officials, giving them significant influence over crown-appointed officeholders. Townshend wanted to strengthen the governors' position as well as to curb the growing independence of the assemblies.

In New York, for example, the assembly had refused to enforce a British rule of 1765 called the Quartering Act, which directed the colonies to furnish shelter and provisions for the British army. The assembly argued that the Quartering Act was really a tax measure because it required New Yorkers to pay money by order of Parliament. Townshend came down hard on the New York assembly: He orchestrated a parliamentary order, the New York Suspending Act, which declared all the assembly's acts null and void until it met its obligations to the army. Both measures—

> "We are taxed without our consent. . . . We are therefore—SLAVES," wrote Philadelphia lawyer John Dickinson, calling for "a total denial of the power of Parliament to lay upon these colonies any 'tax' whatever."

the new way to pay royal governors' salaries and the suspension of the governance functions of the New York assembly—struck a chill throughout the colonies. Many wondered if legislative government was at all secure.

The Massachusetts assembly took the lead in protesting the Townshend duties. Samuel Adams, now a member from Boston, argued that any form of parliamentary taxation was unjust because Americans were not represented in Parliament. Further, he argued that the new way to pay governors' salaries subverted the proper relationship between the people and their rulers. The assembly circulated a letter with Adams's arguments to other colonial assemblies and urged their endorsement. As with the Stamp Act Congress of 1765, colonial assemblies were starting to coordinate their protests.

In response to Adams's letter, the new man in charge of colonial affairs in Britain, Lord Hillsborough, instructed the Massachusetts governor, Francis Bernard, to dissolve the assembly if it refused to repudiate the letter. The assembly refused, by a vote of 92 to 17, and Governor Bernard carried out his instruction. In the summer of 1768, Boston was in an uproar.

Nonconsumption and the Daughters of Liberty

The Boston town meeting had already passed resolutions, termed "nonconsumption agreements," calling for a boycott of all British-made goods. Dozens of other towns passed similar resolutions in 1767 and 1768. For example, prohibited purchases in the town of New Haven, Connecticut, included carriages, furniture, hats, clothing, shoes, lace, iron plate, clocks, jewelry, toys, textiles, malt liquors, and cheese. The idea was to encourage home manufacture of such items and to hurt trade with Britain, causing London merchants to pressure Parliament for repeal of the duties.

The nonconsumption agreements were very hard to enforce. With the Stamp Act, there was one hated item, a stamp, and a limited number of official distributors. In contrast, an agreement to shun the purchase of all British goods required attention on many fronts. It also required great personal sacrifice, from buyers and sellers both. Some merchants were wary of nonconsumption because it hurt their pocketbooks, and a few continued to import in readiness for the end of nonconsumption (or to sell on the side to people choosing to ignore nonconsumption). In Boston,

Edenton Tea Ladies
American women in many communities renounced British apparel and tea during the early 1770s. Women in Edenton, North Carolina, publicized their pledge and drew hostile fire in the form of a British cartoon. The cartoon's message is that brazen women who meddle in politics will undermine their femininity. Neglected babies, urinating dogs, wanton sexuality, and mean-looking women are some of the dire consequences, according to the artist. The cartoon works as humor for the British because of the gender inversions it predicts and because of the insult it poses to American men.
Library of Congress.

such merchants found themselves blacklisted in newspapers and broadsides.

A more direct blow to trade came from nonimportation agreements, but getting merchants to agree to stop importing British goods proved even more difficult than enforcing nonconsumption. There was always the risk that merchants in other colonies might continue to trade and thus receive handsome profits if neighboring colonies prohibited trade. Not until late 1768 could Boston merchants agree to suspend trade through a nonimportation agreement lasting from January 1, 1769, to January 1, 1770. Sixty signed the agreement. New York merchants soon followed suit, as did Philadelphia and Charleston merchants in 1769.

Doing without British products, whether luxury goods, tea, or textiles, no doubt was a hardship. But it also presented an opportunity, for many of the British products specified in nonconsumption agreements were household goods traditionally under the control of the "ladies." By 1769, male leaders in the patriot cause clearly understood that women's cooperation in nonconsumption and home manufacture was beneficial to their cause. The Townshend duties thus provided an unparalleled opportunity for encouraging female patriotism. During the Stamp Act crisis, Sons of Liberty took to the streets in protest. During the difficulties of 1768–69, the concept of "Daughters of Liberty" emerged to give shape to a new idea—that women might play a role in public affairs.

Any woman could express affiliation with the colonial protest through conspicuous boycotts of British-made goods. In Boston, over three hundred women signed a petition to abstain from tea, "sickness excepted," in order to "save this abused Country from Ruin and Slavery." A Philadelphia woman inscribed some "patriotic poesy" in praise of women boycotters in her notebook in 1768, ending with the lines, "Stand firmly resolved and bid Grenville to see, That rather than Freedom, we'll part with our Tea." More direct action was taken by a nine-year-old girl visiting the royal governor's house in New Jersey. She took the tea she was offered, curtsied, and tossed the beverage out a nearby window.

Homespun cloth became a prominent symbol of patriotism. A young Boston girl learning to spin called herself "a daughter of liberty," noting that "I chuse to wear as much of our own manufactory as pocible." A stylish matron in Massachusetts who pieced together a patchwork petticoat sewn from dozens of old remnants was deemed exemplary and therefore newsworthy to a Boston newspaper. In the boycott period of 1768–1770, newspapers reported on spinning matches or bees in some sixty New England towns, in which women came together in public to make yarn. Nearly always, the bee was held at the local minister's house, and the yarn produced was charitably handed over to him for distribution to the poor. Newspaper accounts variously called the spinners "Daughters of Liberty" or "Daughters of Industry."

This surge of public spinning was related to the politics of the boycott, which infused traditional women's work with new political purpose. But it is clear that the women spinners were not direct equivalents of the Sons of Liberty. The Sons marched in streets, burned effigies, threatened hated officials, and celebrated anniversaries of their major successes with raucous drinking and feasting in taverns. The Daughters manifested their patriotism

> During the difficulties of 1768–69, the concept of "Daughters of Liberty" emerged to give shape to a new idea—that women might play a role in public affairs.

Spinning Wheel
A lot of skill was needed to spin high-quality thread and yarn. This wheel was used for spinning flax (a plant with a long fibrous stem) into linen thread; it is likely the type used in the politicized 1769 spinning bees in which "Daughters of Liberty" proclaimed their boycott of British textiles. A foot treadle controls the turning of the wheel, and a spindle holds the thread produced. The art of spinning was all in the spinster's hand, which controlled the tension on the thread and the speed of the twisting. The spinning Daughters of Liberty were praised for their virtuous industry. Responding to such praise, one young woman complained, in a Rhode Island newspaper, that young male patriots were deficient in virtue: "Alas! We hear nothing of their working matches, nothing of their concern for the honor of their King or for the safety or liberties of their country"; instead the news is of "nocturnal Carousals and Exploits; of their drinking, gaming & whoring matches; and how they disturb the quiet of honest people."
Smithsonian Institution, Washington, D.C.

quietly, in ways marked by piety, industry, and charity. The difference was due in part to cultural ideals of gender, which prized masculine self-assertion but feminine selflessness. It also was due to class: The Sons were a cross-class alliance, with leaders from the middling orders reliant on men and boys of the lower ranks to fuel their crowds. The Daughters, dusting off spinning wheels and shelving their teapots, were genteel ladies used to buying British goods. The difference between the Sons and Daughters also speaks to two views of how best to challenge authority. Was resistance to British policy most effectively communicated through violent threats and street actions—actions that might border on anarchy? Or were self-discipline and self-sacrifice the better strategies?

On the whole, the anti-British boycotts were a success. Imports fell by more than 40 percent; British merchants felt the pinch and let Parliament know it. In Boston, Lieutenant Governor Hutchinson and his merchant family, prevented from importing or selling goods, also felt the economic pinch. Even more alarming to the rigid man of order and principle was the fact that Boston seemed overrun with anti-British sentiment. The Sons of Liberty staged annual rollicking celebrations of the first Stamp Act riot, and Hutchinson along with Governor Bernard concluded that British troops were necessary to restore order.

The Bloody Massacre Perpetrated in King Street, Boston, on March 5, 1770

This mass-produced engraving by Paul Revere sold for six pence a copy. In this patriot version of events, British soldiers fire on an unarmed crowd under orders of their captain. The tranquil dog is an artistic device to signal the crowd's peaceful intent. Crispus Attucks, a black sailor, was among the five killed, but Revere shows only whites among the casualties.

Anne S. K. Brown Military Collection, Brown University Library.

FOR MORE HELP ANALYZING THIS IMAGE, see the visual activity for this chapter in the Online Study Guide at bedfordstmartins.com/roark.

Military Occupation and "Massacre" in Boston

In the fall of 1768, three thousand uniformed troops arrived to occupy Boston. The soldiers drilled conspicuously on the Common, played loud music on the Sabbath, and in general grated on the nerves of Bostonians. Although the situation was frequently tense, no major troubles occurred during that winter and through most of 1769. But as January 1, 1770, approached, marking the end of the nonimportation agreement, it was clear that some merchants would no longer engage in the boycott. Thomas Hutchinson's two sons, for example, were both importers hostile to the boycott, and they had already ordered new goods from England. The early months of 1770 were thus bound to be conflict-ridden.

Serious troubles began in January. The shop of the Hutchinson brothers was visited by a crowd that smeared "Hillsborough paint," a potent mixture of human excrement and urine, on the door. In mid-February, a crowd surrounded the house of Ebenezer Richardson, a cranky, low-level customs official. When Richardson panicked and fired his musket to scare off the crowd, he accidentally killed a young boy passing on the street. Although the boy had not been a participant in the demonstration, the Sons of Liberty mounted a massive funeral procession to mark this first instance of violent death in the struggle with England.

For the next week, heightened tensions gripped Boston, and frequent brawls occurred. The climax came on Monday evening, March 5, 1770, when a small crowd taunted a British soldier guarding the customs house. Among other things, he was called a "damned rascally

Scoundrel Lobster Son of a Bitch" (the red uniforms of the British were often likened to lobsters). Captain Thomas Preston sent a seven-man guard to join the lone sentry. Meanwhile, the hostile crowd grew, and the nervous soldiers raised their loaded muskets. Onlookers threw snowballs and sticks, heckling and daring the soldiers to fire. Finally one of the soldiers, hit by some object, pulled his trigger. After a short pause, during which someone yelled "Fire!", the other soldiers fired as well. Eleven men in the crowd were hit, five of them fatally.

The Boston Massacre, as the event quickly became known, was over in minutes. In the immediate aftermath, Hutchinson (now acting governor after Bernard's recall to England) showed courage in addressing the crowd from the balcony of the statehouse. By daybreak the next day, he ordered the removal of all the regiments to an island in the harbor to prevent further bloodshed. Hutchinson also jailed Preston and the eight soldiers, as much for their own protection as to appease the townspeople, and promised they would be held for trial.

The Sons of Liberty made sure that the five victims had funerals befitting heroic martyrs. Their bodies lay in state in the town's meeting hall (Faneuil Hall) and then were buried with honors in a cemetery in the center of Boston. (See "American Places," page 197.) Significantly, the one nonwhite victim shared equally in the public's veneration: Crispus Attucks, a sailor and ropemaker in his forties, son of an African man and a Natick Indian woman, a slave in his youth but at the time of his death a free laborer around the Boston docks. Attucks was possibly the first American partisan to die in the American Revolution, and certainly the first African American.

The trial of the eight soldiers was held in the fall of 1770. They were defended by two young Boston attorneys, Samuel Adams's cousin John Adams and Josiah Quincy. Because Adams and Quincy had direct ties to the leadership of the Sons of Liberty, their decision to defend the British soldiers at first seems odd. But John Adams was deeply committed to the idea that even unpopular defendants deserve a fair trial. Samuel Adams respected his cousin's decision to take the case, for there was a tactical benefit as well. It showed that the Boston leadership was not lawless but could be seen as defenders of British liberty and law.

The five-day trial, with dozens of witnesses, resulted in acquittal for Preston and for all but two of the soldiers, who were convicted of manslaughter, branded on the thumbs, and released. Nothing materialized in the trial to indicate a conspiracy or concerted plan, either by the British or by the leaders of the Sons of Liberty, to provoke trouble. To this day, the question of who was responsible for the Boston Massacre remains obscure.

> Among other things, the lone British sentry was called a "damned rascally Scoundrel Lobster Son of a Bitch."

The Tea Party and the Coercive Acts, 1770–1774

In the same week as the Boston Massacre, yet another new British prime minister, Frederick North, acknowledged the decrease in trade caused by the Townshend duties and recommended repeal. A skillful politician, Lord North took office in 1770 and kept it for twelve years; at last King George had stability at the helm. North sought peace with the colonies and prosperity for British merchants, so he persuaded Parliament to remove all the Townshend duties, except the tax on tea, a pointed reminder of Parliament's ultimate power. North hoped to cool tensions without sacrificing principles.

Those few Americans who could not abide the symbolism of the tea tax turned to smuggled Dutch tea. The renewal of trade and the return of cooperation between England and the colonies gave men like Thomas Hutchinson hope that the worst of the crisis was behind them. For nearly two years, peace seemed possible, but signal incidents in 1772 followed by a renewed struggle over the tea tax in 1773 precipitated a full-scale crisis that by 1775 resulted in war.

The Calm before the Storm

Sons of Liberty celebrated the repeal of the Townshend duties, which came not a moment too soon because the political will to maintain nonimportation could not have been sustained much longer. Pent-up demand caused trade to boom in 1770 and 1771. Moreover, the leaders of the popular movement seemed to be losing their power. Samuel Adams, for example, ran for a minor local office in Boston and lost to a conservative merchant.

Then in 1772, several incidents again brought the conflict with England into sharp focus. One was the attacking and burning of the *Gaspée*, a Royal Navy ship pursuing suspected smugglers off the coast of Rhode Island. A royal investigating commission failed to arrest anyone but announced that it would send suspects, if any were found, to England for trial on charges of high treason. This ruling seemed to fly in the face of the traditional English right to trial by a jury of one's peers.

When news of the *Gaspée* investigation spread, it was greeted with disbelief in other colonies. Patrick Henry, Thomas Jefferson, and Richard Henry Lee in the Virginia House of Burgesses proposed that a network of standing committees be established to link the colonies and pass along alarming news. By mid-1773, every colonial assembly except Pennsylvania had such a "committee of correspondence."

Another British action in 1772 furthered the spread of the communications network. Lord North proposed to pay the salaries of superior court justices out of the tea revenue, in a move parallel to Townshend's plan for paying royal governors. The Boston town meeting, alarmed that judges would now be in the pockets of their new paymasters, established a committee of correspondence and urged other towns to do likewise. The first vital message, circulated in December 1772, attacked the judges' salary policy as the latest proof of a British plot to undermine traditional "liberties": unjust taxation, military occupation, massacre, now capped by the subversion of justice. By spring 1773, half the towns in Massachusetts had set up their own committees of correspondence, providing local forums for debate. These committees politicized ordinary townspeople and bypassed the official flow of power and information through the colony's royal government.

> The Boston Sons of Liberty were slower than their compatriots in other cities to act, but their action ultimately provoked alarm as well as alarming reprisals from England.

The third and final incident that irrevocably shattered the relative calm of the early 1770s was the Tea Act of 1773. Americans had been drinking moderate amounts of English tea and paying the duty without objection, but they were also smuggling large quantities of Dutch tea, cutting into the sales of Britain's East India Company. So Lord North proposed special legislation giving favored status to the East India Company, allow-ing it to sell its tea through special government agents rather than through public auction to independent merchants. The hope was that the price of the East India tea, even with the duty, would then fall below that of the smuggled Dutch tea, motivating Americans to obey the law as well as boosting sales for the East India Company.

Tea in Boston Harbor

In the fall of 1773, news of the Tea Act reached the colonies. Parliamentary legislation to make tea inexpensive struck many colonists as an insidious plot to trick Americans into buying large quantities of the dutied tea. The real goal, some argued, was the increased revenue, which would be used to pay the royal governors and judges. The Tea Act was thus a sudden and painful reminder of Parliament's claim to the power to tax and legislate for the colonies.

As with the Stamp Act and the Townshend duties, the colonists' strategy was crucial. Nonimportation was not a viable option, because the tea trade was too lucrative to expect colonial merchants to give it up willingly. Consumer boycotts of tea had proved ineffective since 1770, chiefly because it was impossible to distinguish between dutied tea (the object of the boycott) and smuggled tea (illegal but politically clean) once the tea was in the teapot. Like the Stamp Act, the Tea Act mandated special agents to handle the tea sales, and that requirement pointed to the solution for anti-tea activists. In every port city, revived Sons of Liberty pressured tea agents to resign.

The Boston Sons of Liberty were slow to act at first, but their action—more direct and illegal than actions anywhere else—ultimately provoked alarm as well as alarming reprisals from England. Three ships bearing tea arrived in Boston in late November 1773. They cleared customs and unloaded their other cargoes but not the tea. Sensing the extreme tension, the captains wished to return to England, but because the ships had already entered the harbor, they could not get clearance to leave without first paying the tea duty. Also, there was a time limit on the stay allowed in the harbor. After twenty days, the duty had to be paid or local authorities would confiscate the tea and sell it.

For the full twenty days, pressure built in Boston. Daily mass meetings energized citizens not only from Boston but also from surrounding towns, alerted by the committees of correspon-

AMERICAN PLACES

The Freedom Trail, Boston, Massachusetts

Visitors to Boston today can relive many of the events leading up to the American Revolution through a walk along the Freedom Trail, a 2.5-mile urban route starting at Boston Common, where British soldiers encamped in 1768. The trail, marked with a red line on the sidewalk, winds around and through the old downtown, passing more than a dozen historic and preserved sites of the Revolutionary era. Among these are the Old Granary Burying Ground, where victims of the Boston Massacre are interred, and the Old State House, in front of which the Massacre took place and where Governor Thomas Hutchinson addressed the distraught crowds from the balcony. The trail also passes the Old South Church, where Samuel Adams spoke right before British tea was dumped in Boston harbor. The last half of the route passes by Paul Revere's home in the North End, as well as the Old North Church from whence Revere got the famous signal for his midnight ride. The trail then crosses a bridge over the Charles River and passes by Bunker Hill, the site of the second battle in the Revolutionary War, and ends at the old Charlestown wharf, where a 1790s sailing ship—the U.S.S. *Constitution*—is open for tours.

Although the Freedom Trail has been in existence since 1952, the city it traverses continues to change. Boston has expanded far beyond its 1760s boundaries. Hills were leveled, and the dirt was used to fill in watery bays, creating the neighborhood known as Back Bay. But despite skyscrapers, a train system for public transportation (the "T"), and the "Big Dig" submerging an interstate highway underground, the core of the old city still preserves the footprint of Samuel Adams's town in its narrow curving streets and tiny alleyways.

A hike on the Freedom Trail can trigger the historical imagination. Costumed interpreters lead tours along the path and help re-create the past. The one in this picture kneels in front of Faneuil Hall, the building where Boston's town meetings were held in the 1760s and 1770s and where Samuel Adams and others debated responses to the Sugar Act, the Stamp Act, and other flash points of the pre-Revolutionary decade. Faneuil Hall was built in 1742 and rebuilt after a fire in 1761. It has street-level shops and markets and, on the second floor, a great hall that throughout the nineteenth and twentieth centuries has remained a lecture hall for famous speakers. Its most famous speaker, Adams himself, now stands guard by the building as a large statue—a powerful reminder of the important role Boston and its inhabitants played in the colonial crisis.

FOR WEB LINKS TO THIS SITE AND OTHER AMERICAN PLACES, see "PlaceLinks" at bedfordstmartins.com/roark.

The Freedom Trail
Courtesy Freedom Trail Foundation.

Tossing the Tea
This colored engraving appeared in an English book published in 1789, recounting the history of North America from its earliest settlement to "becoming united, free, and independent states." Men on the ship break into the chests and dump the contents; a few are depicted in Indian disguise, with feathers on their heads or topknots of hair. A large crowd on the shore looks on. The red rowboat is clearly stacked with tea chests, suggesting that some of the raiders were stealing rather than destroying the tea. However, the artist, perhaps careless, shows the rowboat heading toward the ship instead of away. This event was not dubbed the "Tea Party" until the 1830s when a later generation celebrated the illegal destruction of the tea and made heroes out of the few surviving participants, by then men in their eighties and nineties.
Library of Congress.

dence. On the final day, December 16, a large crowd gathered at Old South Church to learn whether Governor Hutchinson would bend the rules. When word arrived that he would not, Samuel Adams declared, "This meeting can do nothing more to save the country." This was a signal to adjourn to the harbor, where between 100 and 150 men, thinly disguised as Indians, their faces darkened with coal, boarded the ships and dumped thousands of pounds of tea into the water while a crowd of 2,000 watched. (See "Documenting the American Promise," page 200.)

The Coercive Acts

Lord North's response was swift and stern. Within three months he persuaded Parliament to issue the first of the Coercive Acts, four laws meant to punish Massachusetts for the destruction of the tea. In America those laws, along

with a fifth one—the Quebec Act—not aimed at Massachusetts alone, were soon known as the Intolerable Acts.

The Boston Port Act closed Boston harbor to all shipping as of June 1, 1774, until the destroyed tea was paid for. England's objective was to bring to a halt the commercial life of the city. The Massachusetts Government Act altered the colony's charter, underscoring Parliament's claim to supremacy over Massachusetts. The royal governor's powers were greatly augmented. The council became an appointive, not elective, body. No town meeting beyond the annual spring election of town selectmen could be held unless the governor expressly permitted it. Not only Boston but every Massachusetts town felt the punitive sting.

The third Coercive Act, the Impartial Administration of Justice Act, stipulated that any royal official accused of a capital crime—for example, Captain Preston and his soldiers at the Boston Massacre—would be tried in a court in England. It did not matter that Preston had gotten a fair trial in Boston. What this act ominously suggested was that down the road more Captain Prestons and soldiers might be firing into unruly crowds.

The Dangers of Neutrality

Reverend Eli Forbes was nearly fifty when his townsmen's revolutionary fervor cost him his job in the central Massachusetts town of Brookfield. In February and March 1775, Forbes's dedication to the anti-British cause was suspect, and despite his twenty-three years of service to the town and a heroic ministry in Canada with wounded troops during the Seven Years' War, his parishioners wanted him out. Forbes thought that ministers should not "meddle much with civil Power," but his congregation thought he meddled on the wrong side. One night, townsmen followed his carriage in the street and hurled stones and epithets at him and his wife. Next, he discovered a bag of feathers and a pot of tar on his doorstep. A church trial and vote at first failed to dismiss him. But when he took the podium to lecture the disciplinary proceedings, a majority to dismiss quickly materialized. Forbes and his wife fled to Boston, to the protection of the British army, and then to Gloucester, a town north of Boston where a married daughter lived. There Forbes eventually resumed the ministry and lived another quarter century in peace. Either Gloucester was a more tolerant town, or Reverend Forbes moderated his political opinions to avoid trouble.

Courtesy of the Society for the Preservation of New England Antiquities, Gift of Bertram K. and Nina Fletcher Little.

The fourth act amended the 1765 Quartering Act and permitted military commanders to lodge soldiers wherever necessary, even in private households. In a related move, Lord North appointed General Thomas Gage, commander of the Royal Army in New York, governor of Massachusetts. Thomas Hutchinson was out, relieved at long last of his duties. Military rule, including soldiers, returned once more to Boston.

Ill-timed, the fifth act—the Quebec Act—had nothing to do with the four Coercive Acts, but it fed American fears. It confirmed the continuation of French civil law, government form, and Catholicism for Quebec—all an affront to **Protestant** New Englanders denied their own representative government. The act also gave Quebec control of disputed lands (and control of the lucrative fur trade) throughout the Ohio Valley, lands also claimed by Virginia, Pennsylvania, Connecticut, and a number of Indian tribes.

The five Intolerable Acts spread alarm among all the colonies. If England could step on Massachusetts and change its charter, suspend government, inaugurate military rule, and on top of that give Ohio to Catholic Quebec, then what liberties were secure? Fearful royal governors in a half-dozen colonies suspended the sitting assemblies, adding to the sense of urgency. Some of the suspended assemblies defiantly continued to meet in new locations. Via the committees of correspondence, colonial leaders arranged to meet in Philadelphia in the fall of 1774 to respond to the crisis.

The First Continental Congress

Most of the statesmen who assembled in Philadelphia in September 1774 in what was later called the First Continental Congress were leaders of the anti-British cause in their home colonies, and many were meeting each other for the first time. The gathering included notables such as Samuel Adams and John Adams from Massachusetts and George Washington and Patrick Henry from Virginia. A few colonies purposely sent men who were cool to provoking a crisis with England, such as Pennsylvania's Joseph Galloway, out of recognition that the best way to keep a foot on the brakes of impending revolt was to not ignore the gathering.

Two difficult tasks confronted the congress: The delegates wanted to agree on exactly what liberties they claimed as English subjects and

The Destruction of the Tea

O n the night of December 16, 1773, over 100 men disguised as Indians threw 342 chests of tea into Boston harbor. Here are three accounts by participants close to the action.

DOCUMENT 1
Governor Hutchinson's Account, Published in 1828

In exile in England, Thomas Hutchinson wrote a long history of Massachusetts, which was first published in 1828, decades after his death. In narrating Boston events of the 1760s and 1770s, Hutchinson referred to himself in the third person, but his point of view was definitely weighted toward self-vindication. Here he describes the consequences of his final rejection of a demand by the town meeting that he permit the ship to leave port without paying the tea tax.

It was not expected the governor would comply with the demand; and, before it was possible for the owner of the ship to return . . . with an answer, about fifty men had prepared themselves, and passed by the house where the people were assembled, to the wharf where the vessels lay, being covered with blankets, and making the appearance of Indians. The body of the people remained until they had received the governor's answer; and then, after it had been observed to them, that, every thing else in their power having been done, it now remained to proceed in the only way left . . . the meeting was declared to be dissolved, and the body of the people repaired to the wharf, and sur-

rounded the immediate actors, as a guard and security, until they finished their work. In two or three hours, they hoisted out of the holds of the ships, three hundred and forty-two chests of tea, and emptied them into the sea. The governor was unjustly censured by many people in the province, and much abused by the pamphlet and newspaper writers in England, for refusing his pass, which, it was said, would have saved the property thus destroyed; but he would have been justly censured, if he had granted it. He was bound, as all the king's governors were, by oath, faithfully to observe the acts of trade. . . . His granting a pass to a vessel which had not cleared at the custom-house, would have been a direct violation of his oath, by making himself an accessory in the breach of those laws which he had sworn to observe. It was out of his power to have prevented this mischief, without the most imminent hazard of much greater mischief. The tea could have been secured in the town in no other way than by landing marines from the men of war, or bringing to town the regiment which was at the castle, to remove the guards from the ships, and to take their places. This would have brought on a greater convulsion than there was any danger of in 1770, and it would not have been possible . . . for so small a body of troops to have kept possession of the town. Such a measure the governor had no reason to suppose would have been approved of in England. He was not sure of support from any one person in authority. The house of representa-

tives openly avowed principles which implied complete independency. The council, appointed by charter to be assisting to him, declared against any advice from which might be inferred an acknowledgment of the authority of parliament in imposing taxes. . . . There was not a justice of peace, sheriff, constable, or peace officer in the province, who would venture to take cognizance of any breach of law, against the general bent of the people.

SOURCE: Thomas Hutchinson, *The History of the Colony and Province of Massachusetts-Bay* (Cambridge, Mass.: Harvard University Press, 1936), 3:311–14.

DOCUMENT 2
George Robert Twelves Hewes's Recollection, Transcribed in 1834

George Robert Twelves Hewes, a thirty-one-year-old Boston shoemaker, was first stirred to political action by witnessing the Boston Massacre. During the struggle over tea, he joined the "Indian" boarding party and found himself thrust into a leadership role, a singular moment of glory that he proudly recounted when he was in his nineties. As one of the last surviving participants of that famous event, he enjoyed enormous celebrity in the 1830s. His life came to symbolize the Revolution's power to lift up the common man and endow him with a sense of political significance.

The commander of the division to which I belonged, as soon as we were on board the ship, appointed me boatswain, and ordered me to go to the captain and demand of him the keys to the hatches and a dozen candles. I made the demand accordingly, and the captain promptly replied, and delivered the articles; but requested me at the same time to do no damage to the ship or rigging. We then were ordered by our commander to open the hatches, and take out all the chests of tea and throw them overboard, and we immediately proceeded to execute his orders; first cutting and splitting the chests with our tomahawks, so as thoroughly to expose them to the effects of the water. In about three hours from the time we went on board, we had thus broken and thrown overboard every tea chest to be found in the ship; while those in the other ships were disposing of the tea in the same way, at the same time. We were surrounded by British armed ships, but no attempt was made to resist us. We then quietly retired to our several places of residence, without having any conversation with each other, or taking any measures to discover who were our associates.

SOURCE: [James Hawkes], *A Retrospect of the Boston Tea-Party, with a Memoir of George R. T. Hewes, a Survivor of the Little Band of Patriots Who Drowned the Tea in Boston Harbour in 1773* (New York, 1834), reprinted in Alfred F. Young, *The Shoemaker and the Tea Party: Memory and the American Revolution* (Boston: Beacon Press, 1999), 44.

DOCUMENT 3
John Adams's Diary Entry of December 17, 1773

John Adams reveled in the bold destruction of the tea in his diary the day after the event. He also gave thought to the legal consequences that might follow, rehearsing the justifications that motivated "the People."

Last Night 3 Cargoes of Bohea Tea were emptied into the Sea. This Morning a Man of War sails.

This is the most magnificent Movement of all. There is a Dignity, a Majesty, a Sublimity, in this last Effort of the Patriots, that I greatly admire. . . . This Destruction of the Tea is so bold, so daring, so firm, intrepid and inflexible, and it must have so important Consequences, and so lasting, that I cant but consider it as an Epocha in History.

This however is but an Attack upon Property. Another similar Exertion of popular Power, may produce the destruction of Lives. Many Persons wish, that as many dead Carcasses were floating in the Harbour, as there are Chests of Tea:—a much less Number of Lives however would remove the Causes of all our Calamities.

The malicious Pleasure with which Hutchinson the Governor, the Consignees of the Tea, and the officers of the Customs, have stood and looked upon the distresses of the People, and their Struggles to get the Tea back to London, and at last the destruction of it, is amazing. Tis hard to believe Persons so hardened and abandoned.

What Measures will the Ministry take, in Consequence of this?—Will they resent it? will they dare to resent it? will they punish Us? How? By quartering Troops upon Us?—by annulling our Charter?—by laying on more duties? By restraining our Trade? By Sacrifice of Individuals, or how.

The Question is whether the Destruction of this Tea was necessary? I apprehend it was absolutely and indispensably so.—They could not send it back, the Governor, Admiral, and Collector and Comptroller would not suffer it. It was in their Power to have saved it—but in no other. It could not get

by the Castle, the Men of War &c. Then there was no other Alternative but to destroy it or let it be landed. To let it be landed, would be giving up the Principle of Taxation by Parliamentary Authority, against which the Continent have struggled for 10 years, it was loosing all our labour for 10 years and subjecting ourselves and our Posterity forever to Egyptian Taskmasters—to Burthens, Indignities, to Ignominy, Reproach and Contempt, to Desolation and Oppression, to Poverty and Servitude.

SOURCE: L. H. Butterfield, ed., *Diary and Autobiography of John Adams* (Cambridge, Mass.: Harvard University Press, 1961), 2:85–86.

QUESTIONS FOR ANALYSIS AND DEBATE

1. Does Thomas Hutchinson persuade you that he had no other option than to refuse to let the ship either leave or land? Why did he reject the use of troops to guard the tea?

2. How might men like Hewes be politicized by hacking open chests of tea?

3. John Adams says that Hutchinson took a malicious pleasure in forcing the tea crisis to its conclusion. Was he right or wrong in your judgment? Why?

4. What is at stake, for John Adams, in the showdown over tea, when he speaks of ten years of struggle by "the Continent" and of poverty and servitude to "Egyptian Taskmasters"? How does he feel about the possibility of deaths in the building struggle?

what powers Parliament held over them, and they needed to make a unified response to the Coercive Acts. Some delegates wanted a total ban on trade with England to force a repeal of the Coercive Acts. Others—especially those from southern colonies heavily dependent on the export of tobacco and rice—opposed halting trade. Samuel Adams and Patrick Henry were eager for a ringing denunciation of all parliamentary control. The conservative Joseph Galloway proposed a plan (quickly defeated) to create a secondary parliament in America to assist the British Parliament in ruling the colonies.

The congress met for seven weeks in Carpenter's Hall in Philadelphia and produced a declaration of rights couched in traditional language: "We ask only for peace, liberty and security. We wish no diminution of royal prerogatives, we demand no new rights." But, from England's point of view, the rights assumed already to exist were in fact radical. Chief among them was the claim that because Americans were not represented in Parliament, each colonial government had the sole right to legislate for and tax its own people. The one slight concession to England was a carefully worded agreement that the colonists would "cheerfully consent" to trade regulations for the larger good of the empire—so long as trade regulation was not a covert means of raising revenue.

To put pressure on England, the delegates agreed to a staggered and limited boycott of trade—imports prohibited this year, exports the following, and rice totally exempted (to keep South Carolinians happy). To enforce the boycott, they called for a Continental Association, with chapters in each town variously called committees of public safety or of inspection, to monitor all commerce and punish suspected violators of the boycott (sometimes with a bucket of tar and a bag of feathers). Its work done, the congress disbanded in October 1774, with agreement to reconvene the following May.

Many towns and localities heeded the call and established committees of public safety and committees of correspondence. British-authorized government was beginning to break down, being challenged and supplanted by local committees, by the reconstituted colonial assemblies, and by the Continental Congress itself. All these became functioning political bodies without any formal constitutional authority. British officials did not recognize them as legitimate, but many Americans who supported the patriot cause instantly accepted them. A key reason for the stability of such unauthorized bodies throughout the Revolutionary period was that they were composed of the same men, by and large, who had composed the official bodies that were now disbanded.

England's severe reaction to Boston's destruction of the tea finally succeeded in making many colonists from New Hampshire to Georgia realize that the problems of British rule went far beyond questions of taxation. The Coercive Acts infringed on liberty and denied self-government; they could not be ignored. With one colony already subordinated to military rule and a British army at the ready in Boston, the threat of a general war was at the doorstep.

Tarring and Feathering Cartoon

In 1774, a Boston crowd tarred and feathered customs collector John Malcolm as punishment for extorting money from shippers. This ritualized humiliation involved stripping a man, painting him with hot tar, and dipping him in chicken feathers. Local committees of public safety often used threats of this treatment as a weapon to enforce boycotts; actual tarring and feathering was not a common occurrence. This cartoon, of English origin, is hostile to Americans, who are shown with cruelly gleeful faces, forcing tea down Malcolm's throat. The Liberty Tree has become a gallows; posted to it is the Stamp Act, upside down. The dumping of tea in the harbor is shown in the background.
Courtesy of the John Carter Brown Library at Brown University.

Domestic Insurrections, 1774–1775

Before the Second Continental Congress could meet, war broke out in Massachusetts. General Thomas Gage, military commander and the new royal governor, at first thought he faced a domestic insurrection that could be quieted with only a show of force. But the rebels saw things differently: They were defending their homes and liberties against an intrusive power bent on enslaving them. To the south, a different and inverted version of the same story began to unfold, as thousands of enslaved black men and women seized an unprecedented opportunity to mount a different kind of insurrection—against planter-patriots who looked over their shoulders uneasily whenever they called out for liberty from the British.

Lexington and Concord

Over the winter of 1774–75 Americans pressed on with boycotts. Optimists hoped to effect a repeal of the Coercive Acts; pessimists started stockpiling arms and ammunition. In Massachusetts, gunpowder and shot were secretly stored, and militia units known as minutemen prepared to respond on a minute's notice to any threat from the British troops in Boston.

Thomas Gage soon realized how desperate the British position was. The people, Gage wrote Lord North, were "numerous, worked up to a fury, and not a Boston rabble but the freeholders and farmers of the country." Gage requested twenty thousand reinforcements. He also strongly advised repeal of the Coercive Acts. Leaders in England, however, could not bring themselves to admit failure. Instead, they ordered Gage in mid-April 1775 to arrest the troublemakers immediately, before the Americans got better organized.

Gage quickly planned a surprise attack on a suspected ammunition storage site at Concord, a village about eighteen miles west of Boston (Map 6.3). Near midnight on April 18, 1775, British soldiers moved west across the Charles River. Boston silversmith Paul Revere and William Dawes, a tanner, raced ahead to alert the

MAP 6.3   Lexington and Concord, April 1775
Under pressure from England, some 900 British forces at Boston staged a raid on a suspected rebel arms supply in Concord, Massachusetts, starting the first battle of the Revolutionary War. The routes of two early warning scouts are marked. Paul Revere went by boat from Boston to Charlestown and then continued by horse through Medford to Lexington, while William Dawes casually passed British sentries guarding the only land route out of Boston, a land bridge called the Neck, and then rode his horse full speed to Lexington. Revere and Dawes reached Samuel Adams and John Hancock, guests in a Lexington home, and urged them to flee to avoid capture. The two then went on to Concord, to warn residents of the impending attack.

READING THE MAP: William Dawes was, like Paul Revere, a messenger who raced ahead of British troops to warn the minutemen of British plans for raiding their supply of weapons. How did Dawes's route differ from Revere's? What kinds of terrain and potential dangers did each man face during his ride, according to the map?

CONNECTIONS: Why might it matter who shot first on the Lexington Green? What is at stake for each side in claiming the other shot first?

FOR MORE HELP ANALYZING THIS MAP, see the map activity for this chapter in the Online Study Guide at bedfordstmartins.com/roark.

minutemen. When the soldiers got to Lexington, a village five miles east of Concord, they were met by some seventy armed men assembled on the village green.

The British commander barked out, "Lay down your arms, you damned rebels and disperse." The militiamen hesitated and began to comply, turning to leave the green. Then someone—nobody knows who—fired. In the next two minutes, more firing left eight Americans dead and ten wounded.

The British units continued their march to Concord, any pretense of surprise gone. Three companies of minutemen nervously occupied the center of Concord but offered no challenge to the British as they searched in vain for the ammunition. Finally, at Old North Bridge in Concord, troops and minutemen exchanged shots, killing two Americans and three British soldiers.

By now both sides were very apprehensive. The British had failed to find the expected arms storage, and the Americans had failed to stop their raid. As the British returned to Boston along a narrow road, militia units in hiding attacked from the sides of the road in the bloodiest fighting of the day. In the end, 273 British soldiers were wounded or dead; the toll for the Americans stood at about 95. It was April 19, 1775, and the war had begun.

Rebelling against Slavery

News of the battles of Lexington and Concord spread rapidly. Within eight days, Virginians had heard of the fighting, and, as Thomas Jefferson reflected, "A phrenzy of revenge seems to have seized all ranks of people." The royal governor of Virginia, Lord Dunmore, removed a large quantity of gunpowder from the Williamsburg powder house and put it on a ship in the dead of

British Troops in Concord Center

In this contemporary engraving by Amos Doolittle, based on a painting done on the spot by Ralph Earl, two British officers seek the high ground of the cemetery in Concord, Massachusetts, to orient themselves to the unfamiliar town at around 9 A.M. on April 19, 1775. Their troops march in formation, fresh from the skirmish at Lexington. American militiamen had amassed at the Old North Bridge, off to the right about a mile from the town center. The officer with the telescope is undoubtedly scanning for them.

Miriam and Ira D. Wallah Division of Art, Prints and Photographs, The New York Public Library. Astor, Lenox and Tilden Foundations.

night, out of reach of any frenzied Virginians. Next, he threatened to arm slaves, if necessary, to ward off attacks by colonists.

This was an effective threat; Dunmore understood full well how to produce panic among the planters. He did not act on his warning until November 1775, when he issued an official proclamation promising freedom to defecting slaves who would fight for the British. His offer was limited to able-bodied men. Although Dunmore wanted to scare the planters, he had no intention of liberating all slaves or of starting a real slave rebellion. Female, young, and elderly slaves were not welcome behind British lines, and many were sent back to face irate masters. Astute blacks noticed that Dunmore neglected to free his own slaves. A Virginia barber named Caesar declared that "he did not know any one foolish enough to believe him [Dunmore], for if he intended to do so, he ought first to set his own free."

Not surprisingly, Lord Dunmore's proclamation was not reported in southern newspapers. Blacks, however, did not depend on newspapers for their information. John Adams was assured by southern delegates to the Continental Congress that Dunmore's decree would quickly draw 20,000 slaves in South Carolina because "the Negroes have a wonderful art of communicating Intelligence among themselves; it will run several hundreds of miles in a week or fortnight." White planters sped the news along themselves by publicizing Dunmore's inflammatory decree as a means of unifying anti-British sentiment and recruiting whites into the militia. A South Carolina planter foresaw that the proclamation would "more effectively . . . work an eternal separation between Great Britain and the Colonies,—than any other expedient, which could possibly be thought of."

By December 1775, around 2,000 slaves in Virginia had fled to Lord Dunmore, who armed them and called them his "Ethiopian Regiment." Camp diseases quickly set in: dysentery, typhoid fever, and worst of all, smallpox. When Dunmore sailed for England in mid-1776, he took just 300 black survivors with him. But the association of freedom with the British authorities had been established, and throughout the war, thousands more southern slaves made bold to run away as soon as they heard the British army was approaching.

In the northern colonies as well, slaves clearly recognized the evolving political struggle with England as an ideal moment to bid for freedom. A twenty-one-year-old Boston domestic

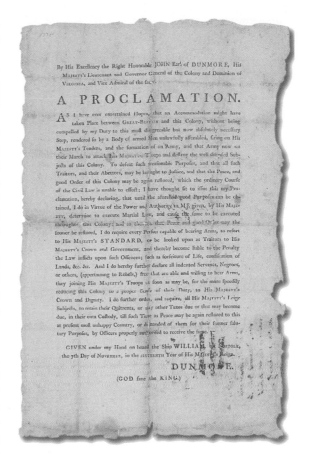

Lord Dunmore's Proclamation
In November 1775, Lord Dunmore of Virginia offered freedom to "all indented Servants, Negroes, or others (appertaining to Rebels)" who would help put down the rebellion. Dunmore issued multiple printed copies in broadside form from the safety of a ship anchored at Norfolk, Virginia.
Special Collections, University of Virginia, Alderman Library.

slave employed biting sarcasm in a 1774 newspaper essay to call attention to the hypocrisy of local slave owners: "How well the Cry for Liberty, and the reverse Disposition for exercise of oppressive Power over others agree,— I humbly think it does not require the Penetration of a Philosopher to Determine." This extraordinary young woman, Phillis Wheatley, had already gained international recognition through a book of poems, endorsed by Governor Thomas Hutchinson and Boston merchant John Hancock and published in London in 1773. Possibly neither man fully appreciated the irony of his endorsement, however, for Wheatley's poems spoke of "Fair Freedom" as the "Goddess long desir'd" by Africans enslaved in America.

Slaves clearly recognized the evolving political struggle with England as an ideal moment to bid for freedom.

At the urging of his wife, Wheatley's master freed the young poet in 1775.

Wheatley's poetic ideas about freedom found concrete expression among other discontented groups. Some slaves in Boston petitioned Thomas Gage, promising to fight for the British if he would liberate them. Gage turned them down. In Ulster County, New York, along the Hudson River, two blacks were overheard discussing gunpowder, and thus a plot unraveled that involved at least twenty slaves in four villages discovered to have ammunition stashed away.

In Maryland, soon after the news of the Lexington battle arrived, blacks exhibited impatience with their status as slaves, causing one Maryland planter to report that "the insolence of the Negroes in this county is come to such a height, that we are under a necessity of disarming them. . . . We took about eighty guns, some bayonets, swords, etc." In North Carolina, a planned uprising was uncovered and scores of slaves were arrested; ironically, it was the revolutionary committee of public safety that ordered the whippings to punish this quest for liberty.

By 1783, when the Revolutionary War ended, as many as 80,000 blacks had voted against slavery with their feet by seeking refuge with the British army. (As a percentage of all slaves in the thirteen colonies, the number might very roughly have been 10 percent.) Most failed to achieve the liberation they were seeking. The British generally used them for menial labor; and disease, especially smallpox, devastated encampments of runaways. But several thousand persisted through the war and later, under the protection of the British army, left America to start new lives of freedom in Canada's Nova Scotia or Africa's Sierra Leone.

Conclusion: How Far Does Liberty Go?

The Seven Years' War set the stage for the imperial crisis of the 1760s and 1770s by creating distrust between England and its colonies and by running up a huge deficit in the British treasury. The years from 1763 to 1775 brought repeated attempts by the British government to subordinate the colonies into taxpaying partners in the larger scheme of empire. The Sugar and Stamp Acts, the Townshend duties, the Tea Act, which culminated in the Coercive Acts, all demonstrated the British view that Americans were subject to parliamentary control.

American resistance grew slowly but steadily over those years. In 1765, loyalist Thomas Hutchinson shared with patriot Samuel Adams the belief that it was exceedingly unwise for England to assert a right to taxation, because Parliament did not adequately represent Americans. But by temperament and office, Hutchinson had to uphold British policy; Adams, in contrast, protested the policy and made political activists out of thousands in the process. Through crowd actions, congresses, and petitions to Britain by colonial assemblies, many Americans gravitated to the Adams position and became radicals in a struggle against British authority.

By 1775, events propelled many Americans to the conclusion that a concerted effort was afoot to deprive them of all their liberties, the most important of which were the right to self-taxation, the right to live free of an occupying army, and their right to self-rule. Hundreds of minutemen converged on Concord, prepared to die for these American liberties. April 19 marked the start of their rebellion.

Another rebellion under way in 1775 was doomed to be short-circuited. Black Americans who had experienced actual slavery listened to shouts of "Liberty!" from white crowds and appropriated the language of revolution swirling around them that spoke to their deepest needs and hopes. Defiance of authority was indeed contagious.

The emerging leaders of the patriot cause were mindful of a delicate balance they felt they had to strike. To energize the American public about the crisis with England, they had to politicize masses of men—and eventually women too—and infuse them with a keen sense of their rights and liberties. But in so doing, they became fearful of the unintended consequences of teaching a vocabulary of rights and liberties. They worried that the rhetoric of enslavement might go too far.

The question of how far the crisis could be stretched before something snapped was largely unexamined in 1765. Patriot leaders in that year wanted a correction, a restoration of an ancient liberty of self-taxation that Parliament seemed to be ignoring. But events from 1765 to 1775 convinced many that a return to the old ways was impossible. Challenging Parliament's right to tax had led, step by step, to challenging Parliament's right to legislate over the colonies in any matter. If Parliament's sovereignty was set aside, then who actually had authority over the American colonies? By 1775, with the outbreak of fighting and the specter of slave rebellions, American leaders turned to the king for the answer to that question.

For additional firsthand accounts of this period, see Chapter 6 in Michael Johnson, ed., *Reading the American Past*, Third Edition.

To assess your mastery of the material in this chapter, see the Online Study Guide at bedfordstmartins.com/roark.

For Web links related to topics in this chapter, see "HistoryLinks," "DocLinks," and "PlaceLinks" at bedfordstmartins.com/roark.

CHRONOLOGY

1747 • Ohio Company of Virginia formed, raising hopes of colonist land speculation in territory controlled by French and Indians.

1754 • Seven Years' War begins in North America.
• Albany Congress proposes Plan of Union and courts Iroquois support; the plan is never implemented.

1755 • French and Indians defeat General Braddock in western Pennsylvania.

1756 • William Pitt, prime minister in Britain, fully commits to war effort against France.

1759 • Quebec falls to British.

1760 • Montreal falls to British in the last Seven Years' War battle in North America.
• George III becomes British king.

1763 • Treaty of Paris ends Seven Years' War; hostilities between British and Indians in Ohio Valley and Great Lakes region continue.
• Pontiac's uprising brings destruction to western forts and frontier settlements.
• Paxton Boys massacre friendly Indians in Pennsylvania.
• Proclamation of 1763 forbids colonial settlement west of Appalachians.

1764 • Parliament enacts Revenue (Sugar) Act, lowering tax on foreign molasses to promote compliance with trade duty.

1765 • Parliament enacts Stamp Act, imposing tax on documents and other papers in colonies and raising complaints of taxation without representation.
• Patrick Henry presents Virginia Resolves, opposing Stamp Act.
• Crowd actions fomented by Sons of Liberty intimidate local stamp distributors into resignations.
• Stamp Act Congress meets in New York City.

1766 • Parliament repeals Stamp Act and passes Declaratory Act, which asserts Parliament's right to pass laws affecting the colonies.

1767 • Parliament enacts Townshend duties, imposing revenue-raising taxes on tea, paper, glass, and other products imported to the colonies; colonists respond with boycotts.

1768 • British station troops in Boston to restore order.

1769 • Merchants in Boston and other cities sign nonimportation agreements.
• "Daughters of Liberty" formed.

1770 • Boston Massacre ignites outrage among Sons of Liberty.
• Parliament repeals Townshend duties.

1772 • British navy ship *Gaspée* attacked and burned, an action considered treason by British authorities.
• Committees of correspondence formed to speed communication between colonies.

1773 • Parliament passes Tea Act, lowering price of tea to encourage Americans to purchase legal English rather than smuggled Dutch tea.
• Dumping of tea in Boston harbor.

1774 • As punishment for destruction of tea, Parliament passes Coercive Acts (Intolerable Acts): Boston Port Act; Massachusetts Government Act; Impartial Administration of Justice Act; an amendment to the 1765 Quartering Act; and Quebec Act.
• Alarm about the attack on liberties in Massachusetts spreads throughout colonies.
• First Continental Congress meets; Continental Association formed.

1775 • Battles of Lexington and Concord spark the Revolutionary War.
• Virginia's Lord Dunmore promises freedom to defecting slaves.

BIBLIOGRAPHY

General Works

John R. Alden, *A History of the American Revolution* (1989).

Edward Countryman, *The American Revolution* (1985).

Marc Egnal, *A Mighty Empire: The Origins of the American Revolution* (1988).

Francis Jennings, *The Creation of America through Revolution to Empire* (2000).

Merrill Jensen, *The Founding of a Nation: A History of the American Revolution, 1763–1776* (1968).

A. J. Langguth, *Patriots: The Men Who Started the American Revolution* (1989).

James Kirby Martin, *In the Course of Human Events: An Interpretive Exploration of the American Revolution* (1979).

Robert Middlekauff, *The Glorious Cause: The American Revolution, 1763–1789* (1982).

Edmund S. Morgan, *The Challenge of the American Revolution* (1976).

Gordon Wood, *The Radicalism of the American Revolution* (1992).

Alfred F. Young, *The American Revolution: Explorations in the History of American Radicalism* (1976).

Native Americans and the Seven Years' War

Fred Anderson, *A People's Army: Massachusetts Soldiers and Society in the Seven Years' War* (1984).

Fred Anderson, *Crucible of War: The Seven Years' War and the Fate of Empire in British North America, 1754–1766* (2000).

Colin G. Calloway, ed., *The World Turned Upside Down: Indian Voices from Early America* (1994).

Greg Evans Dowd, *War under Heaven: Pontiac, the Indian Nations and the British Empire* (2002).

Francis Jennings, *Empire of Fortune: Crowns, Colonies, and Tribes in the Seven Years' War in America* (1988).

Douglas E. Leach, *Roots of Conflict: British Armed Forces and Colonial Americans, 1677–1763* (1986).

Daniel Martson, David Martson, and Robert O'Neill, *The Seven Years' War* (2001).

Michael N. McConnell, *A Country Between: The Upper Ohio Valley and Its Peoples, 1724–1774* (1992).

James H. Merrell, *Into the American Woods: Negotiators on the Pennsylvania Frontier* (1999).

Jane T. Merritt, *At the Crossroads: Indians and Empires on a Mid-Atlantic Frontier, 1700–1763* (2003).

Timothy J. Shannon, *Indians and Colonists at the Crossroads of Empire: The Albany Congress of 1754* (1999).

Ian K. Steele, *Warpaths: Invasions of North America* (1994).

Richard White, *The Middle Ground: Indians, Empires, and Republics in the Great Lakes Region, 1650–1815* (1991).

The British View of Empire

Bernard Bailyn, *The Origins of American Politics* (1968).

John L. Bullion, *A Great and Necessary Measure: George Grenville and the Genesis of the Stamp Act, 1763–1765* (1983).

Don Cook, *The Long Fuse: How England Lost the American Colonies, 1760–1785* (1996).

Jack P. Greene, *Peripheries and Center: Constitutional Development in the Extended Politics of the British Empire and the United States, 1607–1788* (1986).

James A. Henretta, *"Salutary Neglect": Colonial Administration under the Duke of Newcastle* (1972).

Michael Kammen, *A Rope of Sand: Colonial Agents, British Politics, and the American Revolution* (1968).

Michael Kammen, *Empire and Interest: The American Colonies and the Politics of Mercantilism* (1970).

Philip Lawson, *George Grenville: A Political Life* (1984).

Alison Gilbert Olson, *Making the Empire Work: London and American Interest Groups, 1690–1790* (1992).

Alan Rogers, *Empire and Liberty: American Resistance to British Authority, 1755–1763* (1974).

The Revolutionary Crisis of the 1760s and 1770s

David Ammerman, *In the Common Cause: American Response to the Coercive Acts of 1774* (1975).

Bernard Bailyn, *The Ideological Origins of the American Revolution* (1967).

Bernard Bailyn, *The Ordeal of Thomas Hutchinson* (1974).

Bernard Bailyn, *Faces of Revolution: Personalities and Themes in the Struggle for American Independence* (1990).

Richard R. Beeman, *Patrick Henry* (1974).

Ruth H. Bloch, *Visionary Republic: Millennial Themes in American Thought, 1775–1800* (1985).

John L. Brooke, *The Heart of the Commonwealth: Society and Political Culture in Worcester County, Massachusetts, 1713–1861* (1989).

John E. Ferling, *The First of Men: A Life of George Washington* (1988).

David Hackett Fischer, *Paul Revere's Ride* (1994).

Jay Fliegelman, *Prodigals and Pilgrims: The American Revolution against Patriarchal Authority, 1750–1800* (1982).

Dirk Hoerder, *Crowd Action in Revolutionary Massachusetts, 1765–1780* (1977).

Woody Holton, *Forced Founders: Indians, Debtors, Slaves, and the Making of the American Revolution in Virginia* (1999).

Marjoleine Kars, *Breaking Loose Together: The Regulator Rebellion in Pre-Revolutionary North Carolina* (2002).

Thomas A. Lewis, *For King and Country: The Maturing of George Washington, 1748–1760* (1993).

Pauline Maier, *From Resistance to Revolution: Colonial Radicals and the Development of American Opposition to Britain, 1765–1776* (1972).

Pauline Maier, *The Old Revolutionaries: Political Lives in the Age of Samuel Adams* (1980).

Edmund S. Morgan, *The Genius of George Washington* (1980).

Edmund S. Morgan, *Inventing the People: The Rise of Popular Sovereignty in England and America* (1988).

Edmund S. Morgan, *Benjamin Franklin* (2002).

Edmund S. Morgan and Helen M. Morgan, *The Stamp Act Crisis: Prologue to Revolution* (1962).

Gary B. Nash, *The Urban Crucible: Social Change, Political Consciousness, and the Origins of the American Revolution* (1979).

Peter Shaw, *American Patriots and the Rituals of Revolution* (1981).

John W. Tyler, *Smugglers and Patriots: Boston Merchants and the Advent of the American Revolution* (1986).

Ann Fairfax Withington, *Toward a More Perfect Union: Virtue and the Formation of American Republics* (1991).

Alfred F. Young, *The Shoemaker and the Tea Party: Memory and the American Revolution* (1999).

Hiller B. Zobel, *The Boston Massacre* (1970).

Women

Richard Buel and Joy Day Buel, *The Way of Duty: A Woman and Her Family in Revolutionary America* (1984).

Joan Gundersen, *To Be Useful to the World: Women in Revolutionary America, 1740–1790* (1996).

Ronald Hoffman and Peter J. Albert, eds., *Women in the Age of the American Revolution* (1989).

Linda Kerber, *Women of the Republic: Intellect and Ideology in Revolutionary America* (1980).

Mary Beth Norton, *Liberty's Daughters: The Revolutionary Experience of American Women, 1750–1800* (1980).

Slavery

Ira Berlin and Ronald Hoffman, *Slavery and Freedom in the Age of the American Revolution* (1983).

Jeffrey Crow, *The Black Experience in Revolutionary North Carolina* (1977).

David Brion Davis, *The Problem of Slavery in the Age of Revolution, 1770–1823* (1975).

Sylvia Frey, *Water from the Rock: Black Resistance in a Revolutionary Age* (1991).

Winthrop D. Jordan, *White over Black: American Attitudes toward the Negro, 1550–1812* (1968).

Sidney Kaplan and Emma Nogrady Kaplan, *The Black Presence in the Era of the American Revolution* (1989).

Duncan J. Macleod, *Slavery, Race, and the American Revolution* (1974).

Philip Morgan, *Slave Counterpoint: Black Culture in the Eighteenth-Century Chesapeake and Low Country* (1998).

Donald L. Robinson, *Slavery in the Structure of American Politics, 1765–1820* (1971).

Regional Studies

Richard R. Beeman, *The Evolution of the Southern Backcountry: A Case Study of Lunenburg County, Virginia, 1746–1832* (1984).

T. H. Breen, *Tobacco Culture: The Mentality of the Great Tidewater Planters on the Eve of the American Revolution* (1985).

Richard D. Brown, *Revolutionary Politics in Massachusetts: The Boston Committee of Correspondence and the Towns, 1772–1774* (1970).

Edward Countryman, *A People in Revolution: The American Revolution and Political Society in New York, 1760–1790* (1981).

A. Roger Ekirch, *"Poor Carolina": Politics and Society in North Carolina, 1729–1776* (1981).

Paul Gilje, *Road to Mobocracy: Popular Disorder in New York City, 1763–1834* (1987).

Robert A. Gross, *The Minutemen and Their World* (1976).

Ronald Hoffman, *A Spirit of Dissension: Economics, Politics, and the Revolution in Maryland* (1973).

Rhys Isaac, *The Transformation of Virginia, 1740–1790* (1982).

Stephen E. Lucas, *Portents of Rebellion: Rhetoric and Revolution in Philadelphia, 1765–1776* (1976).

William Pencak, *Politics and Revolution in Provincial Massachusetts* (1981).

Bruce A. Ragsdale, *A Planters' Republic: The Search for Economic Independence in Revolutionary Virginia* (1996).

Steven Rossman, *Arms, Country, and Class: The Philadelphia Militia and the "Lower Sort" during the American Revolution* (1987).

Albert H. Tillson, *Gentry and Common Folk: Political Culture on a Virginia Frontier, 1740–1789* (1991).

CONTINENTAL ARMY UNIFORM WORN AT THE SIEGE OF FORT STANWIX, 1777

In 1775, the Continental Congress faced the daunting prospect of fielding an army to fight the largest military force in the world. Money was scarce, soldiers were hastily trained and short of equipment, and uniforms were hard to come by. (Many were purchased from France.) At the start of the war, ordinary enlisted men often wore brown work clothes, and while this gave them a unified look, it did not allow for easy categorization of soldiers by their unit. When Washington finally issued dress specifications, he chose the color already preferred by many officers—dark blue— and then specified the variety of colors to be used for the facings and linings of the coat to establish the rank and the unit of each soldier. Officers especially needed distinctive clothing, to distinguish them from ordinary soldiers and also from other officers, so that military hierarchy could be maintained at all times. The coat pictured here belonged to a brigadier general, Peter Gansevoort Jr., who was twenty-eight in 1777 and in command of Fort Stanwix in the Mohawk River valley of New York. The coat has a buff-colored lining (seen inside the coattails) and bright red facings on the collar, the lapel, and the cuffs, marking him as a New York soldier. The color of the shoulder ribbons reveals Gansevoort's rank; the ribbons could be easily replaced with a new color, enabling a man to ascend in rank without having to get a new coat.

National Museum of American History, Smithsonian Institution, Washington, D.C.

The War for America
1775–1783

ABIGAIL ADAMS WAS IMPATIENT for American independence. While her husband, John, was away in Philadelphia as a member of the Second Continental Congress, Abigail tended house and farm in Braintree, Massachusetts, just south of British-occupied Boston. She had four young children to look after, and in addition to her feminine duties, such as cooking, sewing, and making soap, she also had to shoulder masculine duties in her husband's absence—hiring farm help, managing rental property, selling the crop. John wrote to her often, approving of the fine "Farmeress" who was conducting his business so well. She replied, conveying news of the family along with shrewd commentary on revolutionary politics. In December 1775, she chastised the congress for being too timid and urged that independence be declared. A few months later, she astutely observed to John that southern slave owners might shrink from a war in the name of **liberty**: "I have sometimes been ready to think that the passion for Liberty cannot be Equally strong in the Breasts of those who have been accustomed to deprive their fellow Creatures of theirs."

"I long to hear that you have declared an independency," she wrote in March 1776. "And by the way in the new Code of Laws which I suppose it will be necessary for you to make I desire you would Remember the Ladies, and be more generous and favourable to them than your ancestors." If Abigail was politically precocious in favoring independence and questioning slave owners' devotion to liberty, she was positively visionary in this extraordinary plea to her husband to "Remember the Ladies." "Do not put such unlimited power into the hands of the Husbands," she advised. "Remember all Men would be tyrants if they could." Abigail had put her finger on another form of tyranny that was rarely remarked on in her society: that of men over women. "If particular care and attention is not paid to the Ladies," she jokingly threatened, "we are determined to foment a Rebellion, and will not hold ourselves bound by any Laws in which we have no voice, or Representation."

John Adams dismissed his wife's provocative idea as a "saucy" suggestion: "As to your extraordinary Code of Laws, I cannot but Laugh." The Revolution had perhaps unleashed discontent among other dependent groups, he allowed; children, apprentices, students, Indians, and blacks had grown "disobedient" and "insolent." "But your Letter was the first Intimation that another Tribe more numerous and powerful than all the rest were grown discontented." Men were too smart to repeal their "Masculine Systems," John assured her, for otherwise they would find themselves living under a "despotism of the petticoat."

This clever exchange between husband and wife in 1776 says much about the cautious, limited radicalism of the American Revolution. Both John and

Abigail Adams
Abigail Smith Adams was twenty-two when she sat for this pastel portrait in 1766. A wife for two years and a mother for one, Adams exhibits a steady, intelligent gaze. Pearls and a lace collar anchor her femininity, while her facial expression projects a confidence and maturity not often credited to young women of the 1760s.
Courtesy of the Massachusetts Historical Society ©.

Abigail Adams understood (Abigail probably far more than John) that ungluing the hierarchical bond between the king and his subjects potentially unglued other kinds of social inequalities. John was surely joking in listing the groups made unruly in the spirit of a challenge to authority, for children, apprentices, and students were hardly rebellious in the 1770s. But it would soon prove to be an uncomfortable joke, because Indians and blacks did take up the cause of their own liberty during the Revolution, and the great majority of them saw their liberty best served by joining the British side in the war.

Though Abigail Adams was impatient for independence, many other Americans feared sepa-

ration from Britain. What kind of civilized country had no king? Who, if not Britain, would protect Americans from the French and Spanish? How could the colonies possibly win a war against the most powerful military machine on the globe? Reconciliation, not independence, was favored by many.

Members of the Continental Congress, whether they were pro-independence like John Adams or more cautiously hoping for reconciliation, had their hands full in 1775 and 1776. The war had already begun, and it fell to the congress to raise an army, finance it, and explore diplomatic alliances with foreign countries. In part a classic war with professional armies and textbook battles, the Revolutionary War was also a civil war in America, at times even a brutal **guerrilla war**, of committed rebels versus loyalists.

In one glorious moment, the congress issued a ringing statement about how social hierarchy would be rearranged in America after submission to the king was undone. That was on July 4, 1776, when the Declaration of Independence asserted that "all men are created equal." But this striking phrase went completely unremarked in the two days of congressional debate spent tinkering with the language of the Declaration. The solvent to dissolve social inequalities in America was created at that moment, but none of the men at the congress, or even Abigail Adams up in Braintree, fully realized it at the time.

The Second Continental Congress

On May 10, 1775, nearly one month after the fighting at Lexington and Concord, the Second Continental Congress assembled in Philadelphia. The congress immediately set to work on two crucial and seemingly contradictory tasks: to raise and supply an army and to explore reconciliation with England. To do the former, they needed soldiers and a commander to come to the aid of the Massachusetts militiamen, they needed money, and they needed to work out a declaration of war. To do the latter, however, they needed diplomacy to approach the king. But the king was not receptive, and by 1776, as the war progressed and hopes of reconciliation faded, delegates at the congress began to ponder the treasonous act of declaring independence— said by some to be plain common sense.

Assuming Political and Military Authority

Like members of the First Continental Congress (see chapter 6), the delegates to the second were well-established figures in their home colonies, but they still had to learn to know and trust each other; they did not always agree. The Adams cousins John and Samuel defined the radical end of the spectrum, favoring independence. John Dickinson of Pennsylvania, no longer the eager revolutionary who had dashed off *Letters from a Farmer* back in 1767, was now a moderate, seeking reconciliation with England. Benjamin Franklin, fresh off a ship from an eleven-year residence in England, was feared by some to be a British spy. Mutual suspicions flourished easily when the undertaking was so dangerous, opinions were so varied, and a misstep could spell disaster.

Most of the delegates were not yet prepared to break with England. Several legislatures instructed their delegates to oppose independence. Some felt that government without a monarchical element was unworkable, while others feared it might be suicidal to lose England's protection against the traditional enemies, France and Spain. Colonies that traded actively with England feared undermining their economies. Nor were the vast majority of ordinary Americans able to envision independence from the British monarchy. From the Stamp Act of 1765 to the Coercive Acts of 1774 (see chapter 6), the constitutional struggle with England had turned on the issue of parliamentary power. During that decade, almost no one had questioned the legitimacy of the monarchy.

In mid-1775, the few men at the Continental Congress who did think that independence was desirable were, not surprisingly, from Massachusetts. Their colony had been stripped of civil government under the Coercive Acts, and their capital was occupied by the British army. Even so, those men knew that it was premature to push for a break with England. John Adams wrote to Abigail in June 1775: "America is a great, unwieldy body. Its progress must be slow. It is like a large fleet sailing under convoy. The fleetest sailors must wait for the dullest and slowest."

As slow as the American colonies were in sailing toward political independence, they needed to take swift action to coordinate a military defense, for the Massachusetts countryside was under threat of further attack. Even the hesitant moderates in the congress agreed that a military buildup was necessary. Around the country, militia units from New York to Georgia collected arms and drilled on village greens in anticipation. (See "The Promise of Technology," page 214.) On June 14, the congress voted to create the Continental army. Choosing the commander in chief offered an opportunity to demonstrate that this was no local war of a single rebellious colony. The congress bypassed Artemas Ward from Massachusetts, a veteran of the Seven Years' War, who was already commanding the soldiers massed around Boston. The congress instead chose George Washington, also an experienced war veteran but preferable precisely because he was from a colony five hundred miles to the south of the fighting. His appointment sent the clear message to England that there was widespread commitment to war beyond New England.

Next the congress drew up a document titled "A Declaration on the Causes and Necessity of Taking Up Arms," which rehearsed familiar arguments about the tyranny of Parliament and the need to defend traditional English liberties. This declaration was first drafted by a young Virginia **planter**, Thomas Jefferson, a newcomer to the congress and a radical on the question of independence. The moderate John Dickinson, fearing that the declaration would offend England and rule out reconciliation, was allowed to rewrite it; however, he still left much of Jefferson's highly charged language about choosing "to die freemen rather than to live slaves." Even a man as reluctant for independence as Dickinson acknowledged the necessity of military defense against an invading army.

To pay for the military buildup, the congress authorized a currency issue of $2 million. The Continental dollars were merely paper; they did not represent gold or silver, for the congress owned no precious metals. The delegates somewhat naively expected that the currency would be accepted as valuable on trust as it spread in the population through the hands of soldiers, farmers, munitions suppliers, and beyond.

In just two months, the Second Continental Congress had created an army, declared war, and issued its own currency. It had taken on the major functions of a legitimate government, both

> From the Stamp Act of 1765 to the Coercive Acts of 1774, the constitutional struggle with England had turned on the issue of parliamentary power. Almost no one had questioned the legitimacy of the monarchy.

Arming the Soldiers: Muskets and Rifles

How combat-ready was the American side in the Revolutionary War? Were there adequate numbers of firearms along with men trained in their use? These lively and important questions have recently generated sharp debate among historians. A book published in 2000 argued that gun ownership was surprisingly rare in the 1770s, occurring in only one out of seven households. This finding did not square with historians' largely untested assumption that a militia-based defense system implied that virtually all households contained a gun. The ensuing controversy quickly became a firestorm, involving activists on both sides of the modern gun-control debate as well as historians. In consequence, the examination of evidence and methods to evaluate gun ownership has been considerably sharpened.

What were eighteenth-century guns like? There were guns called fowling pieces that fired shot (small pellets), useful for hunting ducks and wild turkeys as food and small game such as raccoons and squirrels. For larger game, and for warfare purposes, muskets were the preferred weapon. Muskets were a sixteenth-century invention, featuring by the mid-eighteenth century an improved flinklock ignition system in which the trigger released a spring-held cock that caused a hammer to strike a flint, creating sparks. The sparks set off a small charge in a priming pan leading directly to a larger explosion in the barrel. To load the gun, a shooter first put it on half-cock to prevent an accidental firing. He next put a small quantity of powder (carried in a powder horn) in the priming pan and closed it, poured more powder down the smooth gun barrel, dropped in the projectile—usually a one-ounce lead ball—and then wadded paper down the barrel with a ramrod to hold the loose ball in place. He then raised the gun to firing position, put it on full cock, and fired. The whole procedure took highly experienced shooters from 45 to 90 seconds.

The range of muskets extended only about 50 to 100 yards. They were notoriously inaccurate, because of the poor fit between ball and barrel and the considerable kick produced by firing, which interfered with aiming. Far more accurate were longer-barreled rifles, used in frontier regions where big-game hunting was more common. The interior of a rifle barrel carried spiral grooves that imparted spin to the ball as it traversed the barrel, stabilizing and lengthening its flight, and enabling expert marksmen to hit small targets at 150 or 200 yards. Yet for militia use, muskets were preferred over rifles. Rifles took twice as long to load and fire, and their longer barrels made them unwieldy for soldiers on the march. Inaccurate muskets were quite deadly enough when fired by a group of soldiers in unison at targets 50 yards away.

How many American men actually owned fowling pieces, muskets, or rifles? A partial answer can be gleaned from probate inventories, many thousands of which exist in state archives. Inventories listed a decedent's possessions, to facilitate inheritance practice and to make sure creditors were paid off. Yet these sources are fraught with thorny problems. For one thing, they are often not complete: If few inventories itemized clothing, can we conclude the decedents went nude? If no firearm is listed, can we conclude the decedent *never* owned a gun? Clearly not. Probate inventories were made only for a subset of dead property owners, primarily for the use of creditors and heirs, so they are biased by age (older), sex (male), and wealth (more).

Despite complexities, scholars have worked with probate inventories to establish a baseline figure for gun ownership. It takes sophistication with statistical sampling technique as well as ability to read old handwriting to use the evidence, since the thousands of inventories cannot all be read. Recent careful studies based on this source yield estimates on overall gun ownership that range from 40 to 50 percent of all probated estates in the 1770s.

A second way to assess gun ownership is to look at the arms procurement experiences of state legislatures and the Continental Congress as they geared up for war. In the early months of 1775, New England patriot leaders had a keen interest to know how many armed soldiers could be mobilized in the event of war. One scholar has located militia returns from thirty towns in Massachusetts, New Hampshire, and Rhode Island. Scattered returns from other states exist in archives. At their most complete, these records form a census of soldiers and equipment taken on a militia training day. A particularly detailed list from Salem,

Massachusetts, notes against each man's name his ownership of a firelock, a bayonet, a sword, a pouch, a cartouche box, a cartridge, a flint, lead balls, gunpowder, a knapsack, and priming wires. Salem's list appears to support the conclusion that 100 percent of adult men owned guns, yet the scholar seeking to calculate gun ownership must ask: Who is not on this list? Who failed to report to the muster exercise? This careful study concludes that in 1775, roughly three quarters of all men age sixteen to sixty in New England owned guns.

These high rates of ownership are not matched by a final kind of evidence: reports from militia officers to state legislatures complaining of being underarmed. A New Hampshire captain complained of his unit's plight in June 1775: "We are in want of both arms and ammunition. There is but very little, nor none worth mentioning—perhaps one pound of powder to twenty men, and not one-half our men have arms." A militia officer in Pennsylvania noted that men who owned high-quality muskets and rifles were often reluctant to report for active duty with them unless assured they would be reimbursed in the event of loss of the valuable possession. A Prussian general who volunteered his expertise to the Continental army arrived at Valley Forge in 1778 and was shocked to find "muskets, carbines, fowling pieces, and rifles" all in the same company of troops. Lack of uniformity in guns posed considerable problems for supplying appropriate ammunition. While this evidence seems to point to an underarmed soldiery, the opposite evidence— militia captains who failed to register complaints—did not leave a corresponding paper trail for historians. Historians must take care not to be misled by stray documents or quotations that may be atypical.

The Continental Congress knew more guns were needed, certainly. Before 1774, American artisans imported British-made gunlocks, the central firing mechanism, and added the wooden stock and iron barrel to produce muskets. But in October 1774, the British Parliament, anticipating trouble, prohibited all gunlock and firearm exports to the colonies. Congress then turned to French and Dutch suppliers to purchase gunlocks, gunpowder, and finished muskets.

Muskets and even fowling pieces worked well enough for the Revolutionary War, where similarly armed combatants engaged in massed, synchronized firing at close range. In individual use, however, muskets were clumsy, inaccurate, and hence not highly lethal. High rates of musket ownership did not translate to high rates of successful homicide or accidental deaths by shooting. But sixty years after the Revolution, all that changed with the advent of machine-tooled firearms such as the Colt revolver and the Remington rifle. These new repeat-fire weapons were cheaper, more accurate, and far more deadly. Comparing ownership rates of muskets with that of revolvers—or assault weapons—across time may not be the most meaningful path to understanding this country's historic relationship with guns.

Powder Horn

James Pike, a twenty-three-year-old New England militiaman, made and then personalized this powder horn, a hollow cow's horn capped on both ends with leather. The stopper was designed to be pulled off by the teeth, so the hands of the user would be free to hold the musket barrel and pour the powder. Pike's carvings suggest his motivation for fighting. Above his name he depicts a scene dated April 19, 1775, in which British soldiers, labeled "the Aggressors," fire through the Liberty Tree at "Provincials, Defending." Pike was not at Lexington or Concord; his first combat experience came two months later at the battle of Bunker Hill, where he saw his brother killed and was himself wounded in the shoulder.

Chicago Historical Society.

Committee of Safety Musket

This gun was one of the small number of American-made muskets produced in 1775 in a German region of Pennsylvania where blacksmith shops were numerous. The smithy forged and fashioned the gun barrel and attached it to an imported gunlock, the mechanism over the trigger. A wooden stock completed the design.

York County Historical Society.

military and financial, without any legal basis for its authority, for it had not—and would not for a full year—declare independence from the authority of the king.

Pursuing Both War and Peace

The battle of Bunker Hill was a British victory, but an expensive one. As General Clinton later remarked, "It was a dear bought victory; another such would have ruined us."

Three days after the congress voted to raise the Continental army, one of the bloodiest battles of the Revolution occurred. The British commander in Boston, Thomas Gage, had recently received troop reinforcements, three talented generals (William Howe, John Burgoyne, and Henry Clinton), and new instructions to root out the rebels around Boston. But before Gage could take the offensive, the Americans fortified the hilly terrain of Charlestown, a peninsula just north of Boston, on the night of June 16, 1775.

The British generals could have nipped off the peninsula where it met the mainland, to box in the Americans. But General Howe insisted on a bold frontal assault, sending his 2,500 soldiers across the water and up the hill in an intimidating but potentially costly attack. The American troops, 1,400 strong, listened to the British drummers pacing the uphill march and held their fire until the British were about twenty yards away. At that distance, the musket volley was sure and deadly, and the British turned back. Twice more General Howe sent his men up the hill and received the same blast of firepower; each time they had to step around the bodies of men felled in the previous attempts.

On the third assault, the British took the hill, mainly because the American ammunition supply gave out, and the defenders quickly retreated. The battle of Bunker Hill was thus a British victory, but an expensive one. The dead numbered 226 on the British side, with more than 800 wounded; the Americans suffered 140 dead, 271 wounded, and 30 captured. As General Clinton later remarked, "It was a dear bought victory; another such would have ruined us."

Instead of pursuing the fleeing Americans, Howe pulled his army back to Boston, unwilling to risk more raids into the countryside. If the British had had any grasp of the basic instability of the American units gathered around Boston, they might have pushed westward and perhaps decisively defeated the core of the Continental army in its infancy. Instead they hung back in Boston, dependent on British naval vessels for their food and supplies, abandoning the town without a fight nine months later. Howe used the time in Boston to inoculate his army against smallpox, because a new epidemic of the deadly disease was spreading in port cities along the Atlantic. Inoculation worked by producing a light but real (and therefore risky) case of smallpox, followed by lifelong immunity. Howe's instinct here was right: From 1775 to 1782, the years coinciding with the American Revolution, some 130,000 people on the American continent, most of them Indians, died of smallpox.

A week after Bunker Hill, General Washington arrived to take charge of the new Continental army. He found enthusiastic but undisciplined troops. Sanitation was an unknown concept, with inadequate latrines fouling the campground. Drunkenness on duty was common. Soldiers apparently came and went at will. The amazed general attributed the disarray to the New England custom of letting militia units elect their own officers, a custom he felt undermined deference. A captain from a Connecticut regiment was spotted shaving one of his own men, an inappropriate gesture of personal service by a superior officer. But in civilian life the captain was a barber; he had been elected an officer by the men of his town, who saw nothing strange in his practicing his trade in the camp. Washington quickly imposed more hierarchy and authority. "Discipline is the soul of the army," he stated.

While military plans moved forward, the Second Continental Congress pursued its second, contradictory objective, reconciliation with England. Delegates from the middle colonies (Pennsylvania, Delaware, and New York), whose merchants depended on trade with England, urged that channels for negotiation remain open. In July 1775, congressional moderates led by John Dickinson engineered an appeal to the king called the Olive Branch Petition. The petition affirmed loyalty to the monarchy and blamed all the troubles on the king's ministers and on Parliament. It proposed that the American colonial assemblies be recognized as individual parliaments, under the umbrella of the monarchy. That Dickinson himself could write both the

The Battle of Bunker Hill, 1775

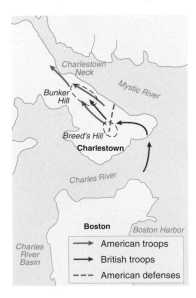

Charlestown Neck

Mystic River

Bunker Hill

Breed's Hill

Charlestown

Charles River

Boston

Boston Harbor

Charles River Basin

→ American troops

→ British troops

--- American defenses

An Exact View of the Late Battle at Charlestown, June 17th 1775

This dramatic panorama is the earliest visual representation of the battle of Bunker Hill. On sale to the public six weeks after the battle, the engraving shows Charlestown in flames (center back) and British and American soldiers in fixed formation firing muskets at each other. The Americans, to the left, are dug in along the crest of the hill; British casualties have begun to mount up. The artist, Bernard Romans, was a noted cartographer, military engineer, linguist, and mathematician. Born in the Netherlands, he came to America as a British-paid surveyor, but he took the American side in the Revolution. His maps of war zones were bought by Americans eager to track the geography of war. His large depiction of Bunker Hill, produced in multiple copies, some of which were hand-colored like this one, likely decorated many a patriot's wall. It was advertised for sale in newspapers in Philadelphia and Virginia, and a half-size copy was engraved and inserted in an issue of *The Pennsylvania Magazine*, a monthly periodical edited by Thomas Paine. One ad for the picture promised that "Every well-wisher to this country cannot but delight in seeing a plan of the ground on which our brave American Army conquered the British Ministerial Forces." Technically the British won the battle by taking the hill, but that was not the story told by this picture.

Colonial Williamsburg Foundation.

George Washington's Camp Chest

This portable camp chest (or mess kit) belonged to George Washington during the Revolutionary War. The wooden box, covered in leather and lined with wool fabric, held an elaborate setup neatly collapsed into a small space: four tin pots with detached handles, five tin plates, three tin platters, two tin boxes, two knives, three forks, eight glass bottles with cork stoppers, salt and pepper shakers, and a woolen sack with six compartments. The chest also contained a tinder box, which held kindling and a flint for starting a fire, and a gridiron (or grate) with collapsed legs for cooking over the fire. Washington—or, more likely, a subordinate preparing his food—would have used this chest when the army was on the move. It was an officer's chest, presented to the general by a Philadelphia merchant in 1776; enlisted men would have had something much more basic, if anything. Washington saved the chest for two decades after the war. After his death it was auctioned off and donated to the federal government by the new owner. It is now owned by the Smithsonian Institution in Washington, D.C.

National Museum of American History, Smithsonian Institution, Behring Center.

"Declaration on the Causes and Necessity of Taking Up Arms" and the Olive Branch Petition within a few days of each other shows how ambivalent the American position was in the summer of 1775.

By late fall 1775, however, reconciliation was out of the question. King George rejected the Olive Branch Petition and heatedly condemned the Americans, calling them rebels and traitors. Thereafter it was hard to maintain the illusion that ministers and not the king himself were to blame for the conflict.

Thomas Paine and the Case for Independence

Pressure for independence started to mount in January 1776, when a pamphlet titled *Common Sense* appeared in Philadelphia. Thomas Paine, its author, was an English **artisan** and coffeehouse intellectual who had befriended Benjamin Franklin in London. He came to America in the fall of 1774 with letters of introduction from Franklin to several Philadelphia printers. He landed a job with *The Pennsylvania Magazine* and

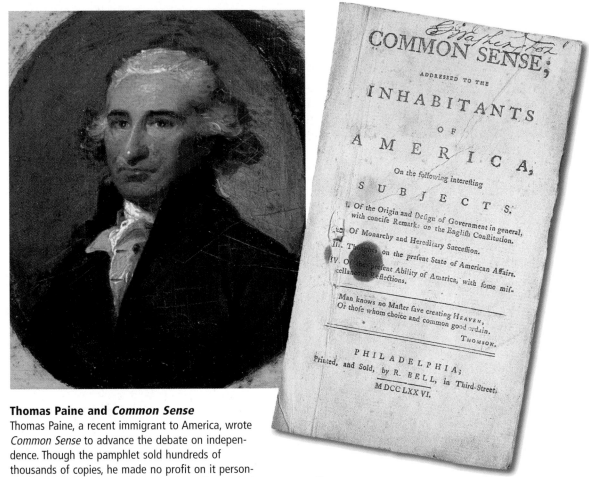

Thomas Paine and *Common Sense*

Thomas Paine, a recent immigrant to America, wrote *Common Sense* to advance the debate on independence. Though the pamphlet sold hundreds of thousands of copies, he made no profit on it personally but instead donated the proceeds to the revolutionary cause. Shown here is George Washington's personal copy with his name inscribed at the top. Paine became a soldier during the early part of the Revolution; he then worked as a clerk for the Continental Congress and the Pennsylvania assembly. He returned to Europe in 1787 and quickly became involved in the French Revolution, defending it in a major pamphlet called *The Rights of Man*. Paine was imprisoned for a time in France in the 1790s for having opposed the beheading of the king, and during his sentence he wrote *The Age of Reason*, a book that among other things seemed to avow atheism. In 1802, he returned to the United States, welcomed by Thomas Jefferson but spurned by nearly everyone else because of his reputation for infidel ideas. He died in obscurity in 1809 in New Rochelle, New York, and a Manhattan newspaper unfairly summarized his life by saying, "He had lived long, did some good and much harm."

Book: Boston Athenaeum; portrait: Monticello/Thomas Jefferson Memorial Foundation, Inc.

soon met delegates from the Second Continental Congress. With their encouragement, he wrote *Common Sense* to lay out a lively and compelling case for complete independence.

In simple yet forceful language, Paine elaborated on the absurdities of the British monarchy. Why should one man, by accident of birth, claim extensive power over others? he asked. A king might be foolish or wicked. "One of the strongest natural proofs of the folly of hereditary right in kings," Paine wrote, "is that nature disapproves it; otherwise she would not so frequently turn it into ridicule by giving mankind *an ass for a lion.*" Calling the king of England an ass broke through the automatic deference most Americans still had for the monarchy. To replace monarchy, Paine advocated **republican** government, based on the consent of the people. Rulers, according to Paine, were only representatives of the people, and the best form of government relied on frequent elections to achieve the most direct **democracy** possible.

Paine's pamphlet sold more than 150,000 copies in a matter of weeks. Newspapers reprinted it; men read it aloud in taverns and coffeehouses; John Adams sent a copy to Abigail Adams, who passed it around to neighbors. Another of John Adams's correspondents wrote him in late February that many New Englanders desired an official declaration of independence. Middle and southern colonies, under no immediate threat of violence, remained cautious.

One factor hastening official independence was the prospect of an alliance with France, Britain's archrival. France was willing to provide military supplies as well as naval power, but not without firm assurance that the Americans would separate from England. News that the British were negotiating for German mercenary soldiers further solidified support for independence. By May, all but four colonies were agitating for a declaration. The holdouts were Pennsylvania, Maryland, New York, and South Carolina, the latter two containing large loyalist populations. An exasperated Virginian wrote to his friend in the congress, "For God's sake, why do you dawdle in the Congress so strangely? Why do you not at once declare yourself a separate independent state?" But a more pessimistic southerner feared that independence

Jefferson's Laptop Writing Desk
On a long stagecoach ride from Virginia to Philadelphia in May 1776, thirty-three-year-old Thomas Jefferson sketched out a design for a portable laptop writing desk. On arrival, he hired a Philadelphia cabinetmaker to produce it in mahogany. The adjustable book rest shown here (notice the notches) could also unfold on its hinges to create a large writing surface. Pens, quills, ink, and paper were stored below; the desk weighed five pounds. Here Jefferson penned rough drafts of the Declaration of Independence. Near the end of his life, he gave the desk to his granddaughter's husband, expressing the hope that it might become esteemed for its connection to the Declaration. The man replied that he would revere the desk as something "no longer inanimate, and mute, but as something to be interrogated and caressed." In 1876, it was a featured exhibit at a centennial exhibition in Philadelphia honoring the independence of the nation.
National Museum of American History, Smithsonian Institution, Washington, D.C.

was "in truth a delusive bait which men inconsiderably snatch at, without knowing the hook to which it is affixed."

In early June, Richard Henry Lee of the Virginia delegation introduced a resolution calling for independence. The moderates still commanded enough support to postpone a vote on the measure until July, so they could go home and consult about this extreme step. In the meantime, the congress appointed a committee, with Thomas Jefferson and others, to draft a longer document setting out the case for independence.

On July 2, after intense politicking, all but one state voted for independence; New York abstained. The congress then turned to the document drafted by Thomas Jefferson and his committee. Jefferson began with a preamble that articulated philosophical principles about natural rights, equality, the right of revolution, and the consent of the governed as the only true basis for government. He then listed more than two dozen grievances against King George. The congress merely glanced at the political philosophy, finding nothing exceptional in it; the ideas about natural rights and the consent of the governed were seen as "self-evident truths," just as the document claimed. In itself, this absence of comment showed a remarkable transformation in political thinking since the end of the Seven Years' War. The single phrase declaring the natural equality of "all men" was also passed over without comment; no one elaborated on its radical implications.

For two days, the congress wrangled over the list of grievances, especially the issue of slavery. Jefferson had included an impassioned statement blaming the king for slavery, which delegates from Georgia and South Carolina struck out. They had no intention of denouncing their labor system as an evil practice. But the congress let stand another of Jefferson's fervent grievances, blaming the king for mobilizing "the merciless Indian Savages" into bloody **frontier** warfare.

On July 4, the amendments to Jefferson's text were complete and the congress formally adopted the document. (See appendix, page A-1.) Nearly a month later, on August 2, the delegates gathered to sign the official parchment copy, handwritten by an exacting scribe. Four men, including John Dickinson, declined to sign; several others "signed with regret . . . and with many doubts," according to John Adams. The document was then printed, widely distributed, and read aloud in celebrations everywhere. A crowd in New York listened to a public reading of it and then toppled a lead statue of George III on horseback to melt it down for bullets. On July 15, the New York delegation switched from abstention to endorsement, making the vote on independence truly unanimous.

Printed copies of the Declaration of Independence did not include the signers' names, for they had committed treason, a crime punishable by death. On the day of signing, they indulged in gallows humor. When Benjamin Franklin paused before signing to look over the document, John Hancock of Massachusetts teased him, "Come, come, sir. We must be unanimous. No pulling different ways. We must all hang together." Franklin replied, "Indeed we must all hang together. Otherwise we shall most assuredly hang separately."

> Printed copies of the Declaration of Independence did not include the signers' names, for they had committed treason, a crime punishable by death.

The First Year of War, 1775–1776

Both sides had cause to approach the war for America with uneasiness. The Americans, with only inexperienced and undertrained militias, opposed the mightiest military power in the world, and many thought it was foolhardy to expect victory. Further, pockets of loyalism remained strong; the country was not united. But the British faced serious obstacles as well. Their utter disdain for the fighting abilities of the Americans had to be reevaluated in light of their costly Bunker Hill victory. The logistics of supplying an army with food across three thousand miles of water were daunting. And since the British goal was to regain allegiance, not to destroy and conquer, the army was often constrained in its actions. These patterns—undertrained American troops and British troops strangely unwilling to press their advantage—played out repeatedly in the first year of war when the Americans invaded Canada, the British invaded New York, and the two sides chased each other up and down the length of New Jersey.

The American Military Forces

Americans claimed that the initial months of war were purely defensive, triggered by the British army's invasion. But quickly the war also became a rebellion, an overthrowing of long-established authority. As both defenders and rebels, Americans were generally highly motivated to fight, and the potential manpower that could be mobilized was in theory very great.

From the earliest decades of settlement, local defense in the colonies rested with a militia requiring participation from nearly every able-bodied man over age sixteen. When the main threat to public safety was the occasional Indian attack, the local militia made sense. But such attacks were now mostly limited to the frontier. Southern militias trained with potential slave rebellions in mind, but these too were rare. The annual muster day in most communities had evolved into a holiday of drinking, marching, and perhaps shooting practice with small fowling guns or muskets.

Militias were best suited to limited engagements, when a local community was under immediate attack. They were not appropriate for extended wars requiring military campaigns far from home. In forming the Continental army, the congress set enlistment at one year, but army leaders soon learned that that was not enough time to train soldiers and carry out campaigns. A three-year enlistment earned a new soldier a $20 bonus, while men who committed for the duration of the war were promised a postwar **land grant** of one hundred acres. To make this in-

Black Revolutionary War Sailor
The fledgling American navy recruited blacks from the beginning of the war, because there was a pool of experienced black sailors to draw from. They were mainly hired as ordinary seamen, though a few were pilots of ships. Their names are preserved in crew lists; rarely, however, were their likenesses preserved. This 1780 portrait by an unknown artist shows an unnamed man in dress uniform, sword and scabbard at hand, with a ship in view to establish his naval connection.
Collection of A. A. McBurney.

ducement effective, of course, recruits had to believe that the Americans would win. By early 1777, the army was the largest it would ever be. Over the course of the war, some 231,000 men spent time in military service, amounting to roughly one-quarter of the white male population over age sixteen.

Women also served in the Continental army. They were needed to do the daily cooking and washing, and after battle they nursed the wounded. The British army established a ratio of one woman to every ten men; in the Continental army, the ratio was set at one woman to fifteen men. Close to 20,000 women served during the war, probably most of them wives of men in service. Children tagged along as well, and babies were born in the camps and on the road.

Black Americans were at first excluded from the Continental army, a rule that slave owner George Washington made as commander in chief. But as manpower needs increased, the northern states began to welcome free blacks into service; even slaves could serve, with their masters' permission. About 5,000 black men served in the Revolutionary War on the rebel side, nearly all from the northern states. Black Continental soldiers sometimes were segregated into separate units; two battalions from Rhode Island were entirely black. Just under three hundred blacks joined regiments from Connecticut. While some of these were **draftees**, others were clearly inspired by the ideals of freedom being voiced in a war against tyranny. For example, twenty-three blacks gave "Liberty," "Freedom," or "Freeman" as their surname at the time of enlistment. (Southern slaves did not join the Continental army; in large numbers they chose to run to the British instead.)

Military service helped to politicize Americans during the early stages of the war. In early 1776, independence was a risky idea, potentially treasonous. But as the war heated up and recruiters demanded commitment, some Americans discovered that apathy had its dangers as well. Anyone who refused to serve ran the risk of being called a traitor to the cause. Military service established one's credentials as a patriot; it became a prime way of defining and demonstrating political allegiance.

The American army was at times raw and inexperienced and much of the time woefully undermanned. It never had the precision and discipline of European professional armies. But it was never as bad as the British continually assumed. The British were to learn that it was a serious mistake to underrate the enemy.

> Close to 20,000 women served during the war. Children tagged along as well, and babies were born in the camps and on the road.

The British Strategy

The American strategy was relatively straightforward—to repulse and defeat an invading army. The British strategy was not nearly so clear. England wanted to put down a rebellion and restore monarchical power in the colonies, but the question was how to accomplish this. A decisive defeat of the Continental army was essential but not sufficient to end the rebellion, for the British would still have to contend with an armed and highly motivated insurgent population.

Furthermore, there was no single political nerve center whose capture would spell certain victory. The Continental Congress moved from place to place, staying just out of reach of the British. During the course of the war, the British captured and for a time occupied every major port city—Boston, New York, Newport, Philadelphia, and Charleston—essential for receiving their constant caravan of supply ships. But capturing them brought no serious loss to the Americans, 95 percent of whom lived in the countryside.

England's delicate task was to restore the old governments, not to destroy an enemy country. Hence, the British generals were usually reluctant to ravage the countryside, confiscate food, or burn villages and towns. There were thirteen distinct political entities to capture, pacify, and then restore to the crown, and they stretched in a long line from New Hampshire to Georgia. Clearly a large land army was required for the job. Without the willingness to seize food from the locals, such an army needed hundreds of supply ships that could keep several months' worth of food in storage. Another ingredient of the British strategy was the untested assumption that many Americans remained loyal to the king and would come to their aid. Without substantial numbers of loyal subjects, the plan to restore old royal governments made no sense.

The overall British plan was a divide-and-conquer approach, focusing first on New York, the state judged to harbor the greatest number of loyal subjects. New York offered a geographic advantage as well: Control of the Hudson River would allow the British to isolate those troublesome New Englanders. British armies could descend from Canada and move up from New York City along the Hudson River into western Massachusetts. Squeezed between a naval blockade on the eastern coast and army raids in the west, Massachusetts could be driven to surrender. New Jersey and Pennsylvania would fall in line, the British thought, due to loyalist strength. Virginia was a problem, like Massachusetts, but the British were confident that the Carolinas would help them isolate and subdue Virginia.

Quebec, New York, and New Jersey

In late 1775, an American expedition was swiftly launched to capture the British cities Montreal and Quebec before British reinforcements could arrive. This offensive was a clear sign that the war was not purely a reaction to the invasion of

Massachusetts. The two cities were symbolic as well as strategic goals, having been sites of bloody contest in the French-British wars of the 1740s and 1750s (see chapter 6). A force of New York Continentals commanded by General Richard Montgomery took Montreal easily in September 1775 and then advanced on Quebec. Meanwhile, a second contingent of Continentals led by Colonel Benedict Arnold moved north through Maine to Quebec, a punishing trek through mountainous country drenched in late fall freezing rain with woefully inadequate supplies; many men died. Arnold's determination to get to Quebec was heroic, but in human costs the campaign was a tragedy. Arnold and Montgomery jointly attacked Quebec in December but failed to take the city (Map 7.1). Worse yet, they encountered smallpox, which killed more men than had been felled by the British.

The main action of the first year of war came not in Canada, however, but in New York, so crucial to England. In August 1776, some 45,000 British troops (including 8,000 German mercenaries, called Hessians) landed south of New York City, under the command of General Howe. General Washington had anticipated that New York would be Howe's target and had moved his army, numbering about 20,000, south from Massachusetts. The Battle of Long Island, in late August 1776, pitted the well-trained British redcoats (common slang referring to the red British uniforms) against a very green Continental army. Howe attacked, inflicting many casualties

---

MAP 7.1   The War in the North, 1775–1778 ▶
After the early battles in Massachusetts in 1775, rebel forces invaded Canada but failed to capture Quebec. A large British army landed in New York in August 1776, turning New Jersey into a continual site of battle in 1777 and 1778. Burgoyne arrived to secure Canada and made his attempt to pinch off New England along the Hudson River line, but he was stopped at Saratoga in 1777 in the key battle of the early war years.

READING THE MAP: Which general's troops traveled the farthest in each of these years: 1775, 1776, and 1777? How did the availability of water routes affect British and American strategy?

CONNECTIONS: Why did the French wait until early 1778 to join American forces against the British? What did they hope to gain from participating in the war?

FOR MORE HELP ANALYZING THIS MAP, see the map activity for this chapter in the Online Study Guide at bedfordstmartins.com/roark.

(1,500 dead and wounded) and spreading panic among the American soldiers, who fled under fire to the eastern edge of Long Island. Howe failed to press forward, however, perhaps re-membering the costly victory of Bunker Hill, and in the meantime Washington evacuated his troops to Manhattan Island in the dead of a foggy night.

A View of the Attack against Fort Washington and Rebel Redouts near New York on the 16 of November 1776 by the British and Hessian Brigades Drawn on the Spot by Thos Davies Cap.n R.R. of Artillery.

"A View of the Attack against Fort Washington"

An eyewitness sketched this scene of British troops attacking Fort Washington in mid-November 1775. The fort, manned by 3,000 American soldiers, sat on well-secured high ground over the Hudson River; it was matched by Fort Lee on the New Jersey side, also a Continental stronghold. (The modern-day George Washington Bridge connects the approximate sites of the two forts.) A British lieutenant colonel at the scene wrote home that "we could not be masters of York Island or indeed secure of New York" while the Americans held the fort. Yet taking it was dangerous. The boatloads of soldiers could not land under protective cover of their own fire because of "the shortness of artillery," and the open boats and steep hillside denuded of leaves allowed American gunners easy pickings. "So smart was the fire that the Sailors abandoned their oars & hid themselves in the bottom of the Boats," the British officer wrote. The British prevailed, however, and the fort finally surrendered, prompting the officer to note, "This secures all York Island to us. We took a number of cannons, stores of all kinds with two Months provisions & likewise took the heart of the rebels."

The Phelps Stokes Collection, Miriam and Ira D. Wallach Division of Art, Prints, and Photographs, The New York Public Library. Astor, Lenox, and Tilden Foundations.

Washington knew it would be hard to hold Manhattan against British attack. One of his generals recommended burning the city; two-thirds of the buildings belonged to loyalists anyway, and burning it would prevent the British from housing troops there. Washington vetoed this idea, preferring instead to strip it of ammunition and supplies. He left quickly, moving north to two critical forts on either side of the Hudson River.

For two months, the armies engaged in limited skirmishing, but in November, Howe finally captured Fort Washington and Fort Lee, taking thousands of prisoners. Washington retreated quickly across New Jersey into Pennsylvania. The British army followed him; at one point, Howe was only one hour behind Washington, but he rested his men for a day and widened the gap. As Howe moved through New Jersey, the Continental Congress, meeting in Philadelphia, fled to Baltimore.

Yet again, Howe unaccountably failed to press his advantage. Had he attacked Washington's army at Philadelphia, he probably would have taken the city. Instead he parked his German troops in winter quarters along the Delaware River. Perhaps he knew that many of the Continental soldiers' enlistment periods ended on December 31, so he felt confident that the Americans would not attack him. But he was wrong. On December 25 near midnight, as a storm of sleet and hail rained down, Washington stealthily moved his large army across the icy Delaware River and in the early morning made a quick capture of the unsuspecting German soldiers encamped at Trenton. This impressive victory did much to restore the sagging morale of the patriot side. For the next two weeks, Washington remained on the offensive, capturing supplies in a clever attack on British units at Princeton on January 3. Soon he was safe in Morristown, in northern New Jersey, where he settled his troops for the winter, a season when eighteenth-century armies in snowy climates generally stayed put, out of harm's way. Finally Washington had time enough to do as Howe had done, to administer mass smallpox inoculations and see his men through the abbreviated course of the disease. Future recruits would also face inoculation.

All in all, in the first year of declared war, the rebellious Americans had a few isolated moments to feel proud of but also much to worry about. The very inexperienced Continental army had barely hung on in the New York campaign. Washington had shown exceptional daring as well as admirable restraint, but what really saved the Americans may have been the repeated reluctance of the British to follow through militarily when they had the advantage.

The Home Front

Battlefields alone did not determine the outcome of the war. Struggles on the home front were equally important. In 1776, each community contained small numbers of highly committed people on both sides and far larger numbers who were uncertain about whether independence was worth a war. The contest for the allegiance of the many neutrals thus was a major factor, and both persuasion and force were used. Revolutionaries who took control of local government often used it to punish loyalists and intimidate neutrals. On their side, loyalists worked to reestablish British authority. The struggle to secure political allegiance was complicated greatly by the wartime instability of the economy. The creative financing of the fledgling government brought hardships as well as opportunities, forcing Americans to confront new manifestations of virtue and corruption.

Patriotism at the Local Level

Committees of correspondence, of public safety, and of inspection dominated the political landscape in patriot communities. These committees took on more than customary local governance; they enforced boycotts, picked army draftees, and policed suspected traitors. They sometimes invaded homes to search for contraband goods such as British tea or textiles.

Loyalists were dismayed by what seemed to them to be arbitrary power taken on by patriots. A man in Westchester, New York, described his response to intrusions by committees: "Choose your committee or suffer it to be chosen by a half

Rhode Island Regiment Flag

In the absence of an official American flag, regiments often commissioned their own symbolic banners. Almost certainly the elaborate stitchery and even the design work of this Rhode Island artillery company flag came from female hands wielding needle and thread. There were thus dozens, not just one, "Betsy Ross," the legendary Philadelphia woman credited with designing the prototype of the Stars and Stripes. A popular 1770s flag theme portrayed a coiled rattlesnake paired with the slogan "Don't Tread on Me." Such a flag conveyed a dire warning and a clear point of view about who had started the war in America: the rattler, uniquely American, was deadly only when aroused or provoked. This 1775 flag offers an unusual variant, using the more formal "do not" instead of "don't." The slogan endures today, showing up on state license plates and as lyrics in popular songs. Notice as well another nearly familiar motto: "In God We Hope." It precedes by almost a century the Civil War–era origins of the modern day motto on U.S. coinage, "In God We Trust."
Collection of Mr. and Mrs. Boleslaw Mastai.

dozen fools in your neighborhood—open your doors to them—let them examine your tea-cannisters and molasses-jugs, and your wives' and daughters' petty coats—bow and cringe and tremble and quake—fall down and worship our sovereign lord the mob. . . . Should any prag-matical committee-gentleman come to my house and give himself airs, I shall show him the door, and if he does not soon take himself away, a good hickory cudgel shall teach him better man-ners." Oppressive or not, the local committees of safety and of in-spection were rarely challenged. Their persuasive powers con-vinced many middle-of-the-road citizens that neutrality was not a comfortable option.

> Local committees of safety and of inspection convinced many middle-of-the-road citizens that neutrality was not a comfortable option.

Another group new to politi-cal life—white women—increas-ingly demonstrated a capacity for patriotism at the local level as wartime hardships dramatically altered their work routines. Like Abigail Adams on her Braintree farm, many wives with hus-bands away on military or political service took on masculine duties. Their increased compe-tence to tend farms and make business decisions encouraged some to assert competence in politi-cal matters as well. Eliza Wilkinson managed a plantation on the South Carolina coast and talked revolutionary politics with her women friends. "None were greater politicians than the several knots of ladies who met together," she re-marked, alert to the unusual turn female conver-sations had taken. "We commenced perfect statesmen."

Women from prominent Philadelphia fami-lies went a step beyond political talk to action. In 1780, they formed the Ladies Association, going door to door collecting a substantial sum of money to help support the Continental soldiers. A published broad-side, "The Sentiments of an American Woman," defended their female patrio-tism. "The time is arrived to display the same sentiments which animated us at the beginning of the Revolution, when we re-nounced the use of teas [and] when our republi-can and laborious hands spun the flax."

The Loyalists

Between 20 and 30 percent of the American pop-ulation remained openly loyal to the British monarchy in 1776, and another 20 to 40 percent could be described as neutral. Such a large pop-ulation base could have sustained the British empire in America, if only the British army lead-ers had known how to use it (Map 7.2). In gen-eral, loyalists were people who still felt strong cultural and economic ties to the British empire and who believed that American prosperity and stability depended on British rule and on a gov-ernment anchored by monarchy and aristocracy. Perhaps most of all, they feared democratic tyranny. Like Abigail Adams, they understood that dissolving the automatic respect that sub-jects had for their king could lead to a society in which hierarchy came unglued. Adams wel-

Joseph Brant

The Mohawk leader Thayendanegea, called Joseph Brant by Americans, had been educated in English ways at Eleazar Wheelock's New England school (which became Dartmouth College in 1769). In 1775, the thirty-four-year-old Brant traveled to England with another warrior to ne-gotiate Mohawk support for the British. While there, he had his portrait painted by the English artist George Romney. Notice that Brant wears a metal gorget around his neck over his English shirt, along with Indian arm-bands, sash, and headdress. A gorget was a symbolic piece of armor, a shrunken version of a throatpiece from the feudal days of metal-clad knights. Many military men, both white and Indian, wore gorgets when they dressed formally for portraits—or for war.
National Gallery of Canada.

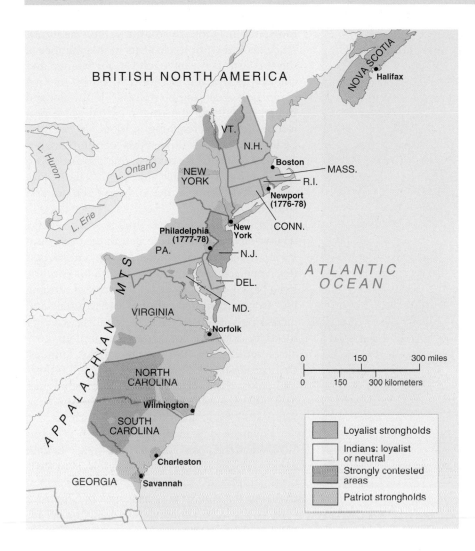

BRITISH NORTH AMERICA

MAP 7.2 Loyalist Strength and Rebel Support
The exact number of loyalists can never be known. No one could have made an accurate count at the time; in addition, political allegiance often shifted with the winds. This map shows the regions of loyalist strength on which the British relied—most significantly the lower Hudson valley and the Carolina Piedmont.

READING THE MAP: Which forces were stronger, those loyal to Britain or those rebelling? (Consider size of areas, centers of population, and vital port locations.) What areas were contested? If the contested areas ultimately sided with the British, how would the balance of power change?

CONNECTIONS: Who was more likely to be a loyalist, and why? How many loyalists left the United States? Where did they go?

FOR MORE HELP ANALYZING THIS MAP, see the map activity for this chapter in the Online Study Guide at bedfordstmartins.com/roark.

comed this chance to identify tyranny in unequal power relations, as between men and women; loyalists feared it. Patriots seemed to them to be unscrupulous, violent, self-interested men who simply wanted power for themselves.

The most visible and dedicated loyalists (also called Tories by their enemies) were royal officials, not only top officeholders like Thomas Hutchinson in Massachusetts but also local judges and customs officers. Wealthy merchants with commercial ties to England gravitated toward loyalism to maintain the trade protections of navigation acts and the British navy. Conservative urban lawyers admired the stability of British law and order. Some colonists chose loyalism simply to oppose traditional adversaries. For example, backcountry farmers in the Carolinas tended to be loyalists out of resentment over the political and economic power of the lowlands gentry, who were largely on the

patriot side. And of course southern slaves had their own resentments against the white slave-owning class and looked to Britain for hope of freedom.

Many Indian tribes attempted to maintain neutrality at the start of the war, seeing the conflict as a civil war between English and American brothers. But eventually most were drawn in, many taking the British side. The powerful Iroquois confederacy divided: Mohawk, Cayuga, Seneca, and Onondaga peoples lined up with the British; the Oneida and Tuscarora aided the Americans. One young literate and Christianized Mohawk leader, Thayendanegea (known also by his English name, Joseph Brant), had worked closely with the British Indian agent William Johnson in the 1760s; Brant's sister Molly was for some years Johnson's domestic partner (an acknowledged common-law wife but without the formalities of British marriage).

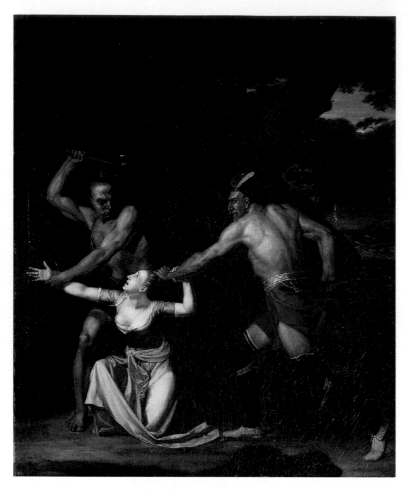

Death of Jane McCrea

This 1804 painting by John Vanderlyn memorializes the martyr legend of Jane McCrea. McCrea lived with her patriot family in northern New York, and in July 1777 she fled to join her fiancé, a loyalist fighting with Burgoyne's army. She was murdered en route, allegedly by Iroquois allies of the British. The American general Horatio Gates sent Burgoyne an accusatory letter. "The miserable fate of Miss McCrea was particularly aggravated by her being dressed to meet her promised husband," Gates wrote, "but she met her murderers employed by you." Gates skillfully used the story of the vulnerable, innocent maiden dressed in alluring clothes as propaganda to inspire his soldiers' drive for victory at Saratoga. Vanderlyn's work, and other similar pictorial representations, emphasized McCrea's helplessness and sexuality. Had McCrea been a man, her flight would have been traitorous. Why this different treatment of a woman?

Wadsworth Atheneum, Hartford.

Johnson died in 1774, and Brant traveled from New York to England in 1775 to meet King George to complain about American settlers cheating his people of their land. "It is very hard when we have let the King's subjects have so much of our lands for so little value," he wrote, "they should want to cheat us in this manner of the small spots we have left for our women and children to live on. We are tired out in making complaints & getting no redress." Brant pledged Indian support for the king in exchange for protection from encroaching settlers. In western Pennsylvania and Ohio, parts of the Shawnee and Delaware tribes started out pro-American but shifted to the British side by 1779 in the face of repeated betrayals by American settlers and soldiers.

Pockets of loyalism thus existed everywhere—in the middle colonies, in the backcountry of the southern colonies, and out beyond the Appalachian Mountains in Indian country. Even New England towns at the heart of turmoil, like Concord, Massachusetts, had a small and increasingly silenced core of loyalists who refused to countenance armed revolution. Loyalists could even lurk within patriot families: On occasion, husbands and wives, fathers and sons disagreed completely on the war. (See "Documenting the American Promise," page 230.)

Loyalists were most vocal between 1774 and 1776, when the possibility of a full-scale rebellion against England was still uncertain. Loyalists used pamphlets, broadsides, and newspapers to challenge the emerging patriot side. In New York City, 547 loyalists signed and circulated a broadside titled "A Declaration of Dependence," in rebuttal to the congress's July 4 declaration, denouncing this "most unnatural, unprovoked Rebellion that ever disgraced the annals of Time."

Speeches delivered by ministers in the pulpit and others at open-air meetings bolstered the loyalist cause. At a backcountry rally in South Carolina in 1775, a loyalist warned listeners of the superior might of the British army and of the damage to trade that war would bring. Most effectively, he played on white farmers' resentment of coastal planters' wealth and political power: It is ironic, he said, that "the charge of our intending to enslave you should come oftenest from the mouths of those lawyers who in your southern provinces, at least, have long made you slaves to themselves."

Who Is a Traitor?

The rough treatment that loyalists experienced at the hands of the revolutionaries seemed to substantiate their worst fears. In June 1775, the First

Continental Congress passed a resolution declaring loyalists to be traitors. Over the next year, state laws defined as treason acts such as joining or provisioning the British army, saying or printing anything that undermined patriot morale, or discouraging men from enlisting in the Continental army. Punishments ranged from house arrest and suspension of voting privileges to confiscation of property and deportation. And sometimes self-appointed committees of Tory-hunters bypassed the judicial niceties and terrorized loyalists, raiding their houses or tarring and feathering them.

A question rarely asked in the heat of the revolutionary moment was whether the wives of loyalists were traitors as well. When loyalist families fled the country, property held in the name of the family patriarch was then confiscated. But what if the wife stayed? One Connecticut woman brought witnesses to testify that she was "a steady and true and faithful friend to the American states in opposition to her husband, who has been of quite a different character." In such cases, the court typically allowed the woman to keep one-third of the property, the amount she was due if widowed, and confiscated the rest. But even when the wife fled with her husband, was she necessarily a traitor? If he insisted, was she not obligated to go? Such questions came up in several lawsuits after the Revolution, when descendants of refugee loyalists sued to regain property that had entered the family through the mother's inheritance. In one well-publicized Massachusetts case in 1805, the outcome confirmed the traditional view of women as political blank slates. The American son of loyalist refugee Anna Martin recovered her property on the grounds that she had no independent will to be a loyalist.

Tarring and feathering, property confiscation, deportation, terrorism—to the loyalists, such denials of liberty of conscience and of freedom to own private property proved that democratic tyranny was more to be feared than the monarchical variety. A Boston loyalist, Mather Byles, aptly expressed this point: "They call me a brainless Tory, but tell me . . . which is better—to be ruled by one tyrant three thousand miles away, or by three thousand tyrants not a mile away?" Byles was soon sentenced to deportation.

Throughout the war, probably 7,000 to 8,000 loyalists fled to England, and 28,000 found closer haven in Canada. But many chose to remain in the new United States and tried to swing with the changing political winds. In some instances, that proved difficult. In New Jersey, for example, 3,000 Jerseyites felt protected (or scared) enough by the occupying British army in 1776 to swear an oath of allegiance to the king. But then General Howe drew back to New York City, leaving them to the mercy of local patriot committees. British strategy depended on using loyalists to hold occupied territory, but the New Jersey experience showed just how poorly that strategy was carried out.

Financial Instability and Corruption

Wars cost money—for arms and ammunition, for food and uniforms, for soldiers' pay. The Continental Congress printed money, but its value quickly deteriorated because the congress held no reserves of gold or silver to back the currency. In practice, it was worth only what buyers and sellers agreed it was worth. When the dollar eventually bottomed out at one-fortieth of its face value, a loaf of bread that once sold for two and a half cents then sold for a dollar. States too were printing their own paper money to pay for wartime expenses, further complicating the economy.

Soon the congress had to resort to other means to procure supplies and labor. One method was to borrow **hard money** (gold or silver coins, not paper) from wealthy men in exchange for certificates of debt (public securities) promising repayment with interest. The certificates of debt were similar to present-day **government bonds**. To pay soldiers, the congress issued land grant certificates, written promises of acreage usually located in frontier areas such as central Maine or eastern Ohio. Both the public securities and the land grant certificates quickly became forms of negotiable currency. A soldier with no cash, for example, could sell his land grant certificate to get food for his family. These certificates fluctuated in value, mainly depreciating.

Depreciating currency inevitably led to rising prices, as sellers compensated for the falling value of the money. The wartime economy of the late 1770s, with its unreliable currency and price inflation, was extremely demoralizing to Americans everywhere. In 1778, in an effort to impose some stability, local committees of public

> The wartime economy of the late 1770s, with its unreliable currency and price inflation, was extremely demoralizing to Americans everywhere.

Families Divide over the Revolution

Generalizing about rebels versus loyalists is a complex historical task. Sometimes categorizing by class, race, and geographical descriptors helps explain the split. But beyond economic interests or cultural politics, sometimes the loyalist-patriot split cut across families—and cut deeply. These documents reveal men and women divided with loved ones over wartime allegiance.

DOCUMENT 1
A Loyalist Wife Writes to Her Patriot Husband, 1778

Mary Gould Almy, wife and mother, lived in Newport, Rhode Island, an island town occupied by the British army in 1778. She was a Quaker and loyalist, in contrast to her Anglican husband, Benjamin Almy, who joined the American army. Mary wrote to Benjamin in September 1778, sending him her account of the month-long siege of the town by the French fleet and American troops.

September 02, 1778. Once more, my dear Mr. Almy, I am permitted to write you. . . . I am to give you an account of what passes during the siege; but first let me tell you, it will be done with spirit, for my dislike to the nation that you call your friends, is the same as when you knew me, knowing there is no confidence to be placed in them. . . .

[The 1st day]: At nine in the morning a signal was made for a fleet in sight; at ten o'clock was discovered the number to be eleven large ships . . . the French fleet. . . .

With a distressed heart, I endeavor to comfort my poor children by saying, that they would not come in till morning, and then began to secure my papers and plate in the ground.

[The 9th day]: Heavens! what a scene of wretchedness before this once happy and flourishing island. . . . Neither sleep to my eyes, nor slumber to my eyelids, this night; but judge you, what preparation could I make, had I been endowed with as much presence of mind as ever woman was; six children hanging around me, the little girls crying out, "Mamma, will they kill us?" The boys endeavor to put on an air of manliness, and strive to assist, but slip up to the girls, in a whisper, "Who do you think will hurt you? Ain't your papa coming with them?" Indeed this cut me to the soul.

[The 18th day]: Still carting, still fortifying; your people encroaching nearer, throwing up new works every night. Our people beholding it every morning, with wonder and astonishment. And really, Mr. Almy, my curiosity was so great, as to wish to behold the entrenchment that I supposed you were behind; . . . Believe me, my dear friend, never was a poor soul more to be pitied, such different agitations as by turns took hold upon me. Wishing most ardently to call home my wanderer, at the same time, filled with resentment against those he calls his friends.

[The 24th day]: They kept up a smart firing till two o'clock, and then they began to bury the dead and bring in the wounded. . . . The horrors of that day will never be quite

out of my remembrance. I quitted company and hid myself to mourn in silence, for the wickedness of my country. Never was a heart more differently agitated than mine. Some of my good friends in the front of the battle here; and Heaven only knows how many of the other side. . . . At last I shut myself from the family, to implore Heaven to protect you, and keep you from imprisonment and death.

SOURCE: *Mrs. Almy's Journal: Siege of Newport, R.I., August 1778* (Newport, R.I.: Newport Historical Pub. Co., 1881, pp. 19–31). Available online in select college libraries in the electronic database *North American Women's Letters and Diaries,* Alexander Street Press.

DOCUMENT 2
Patriot Benjamin Franklin and Loyalist Son William Correspond, 1784

Benjamin Franklin was a member of the Continental Congress and a special envoy to France on behalf of the American rebels. Franklin's son, William, stayed loyal to the crown. William was Benjamin's illegitimate son; the mother's identity has never been known. Franklin raised him from infancy in his own family in Philadelphia and took William to England in 1757 for four years when he was a colonial agent for Pennsylvania. Thanks to his father, William acquired connections at court and in 1762, at age thirty-one, was appointed the royal governor of New Jersey, a post he held until 1776. When the war began, he was declared a traitor to the patriot cause and placed under house arrest. Father and son did not communicate for the next nine years, even when William was confined in a Connecticut prison for eight months. During this time, Benjamin took charge of William's oldest son, himself an illegitimate child born before William's legal marriage. In 1783 William returned to England. In 1784 he wrote to his father, then in Paris, asking for a meeting of reconciliation. He did not apologize for his loyalism.

Dear and honored Father,
Ever since the termination of the unhappy contest between Great Britain and America, I have been anxious to write to you, and to endeavor to revive that affectionate intercourse and connection which, until the commencement of the late troubles, had been the pride and happiness of my life. . . . There are narrow illiberal Minds in all Parties. In that which I took, and on whose Account I have so much suffered, there have not been wanting some who have insinuated that my Conduct has been founded on Collusion with you, that one of us might succeed whichever Party should prevail. Similar Collusions, they say, were known to have existed between Father and Son during the civil Wars in England and Scotland. The Falsity of such Insinuation in our Case you well know, and I am happy that I can with Confidence appeal not only to you but to my God, that I have uniformly acted from a strong Sense of what I conceived my Duty to my King, and Regard to my Country, required. If I have been mistaken, I cannot help it. It is an Error of Judgment what the maturest Reflection I am capable of cannot rectify; and I verily believe were the same Circumstances to occur again Tomorrow, my Conduct would be exactly similar to what it was heretofore.

The father replied:

Dear Son,
I received your letter of the 22nd past, and am glad to find that you desire to revive the affectionate Intercourse, that formerly existed between us. It will be very agreeable to me; indeed nothing has ever hurt me so much and affected me with such keen Sensations, as to find myself deserted in my old age by my only Son; and not only deserted, but to find him taking up Arms against me, in a Cause, wherein my good Fame, Fortune and Life were all at Stake. You conceived, you say, that your Duty to your King and regard for your Country requir'd this. I ought not to blame you for differing in Sentiment with me in Public Affairs. We are Men, all subject to errors. Our opinions are not in our own Power; they are form'd and govern'd much by Circumstances, that are often as inexplicable as they are irresistible. Your Situation was such that few would have censured your remaining Neuter, *tho' there are Natural Duties which preceded political ones, and cannot be extinguish'd by them.*

This is a disagreeable Subject. I drop it. And we will endeavor, as you propose mutually to forget what has happened relating to it, as well as we can. I send your Son over to pay his Duty to you. You will find him much improv'd. He is greatly esteem'd and belov'd in this Country, and will make his Way anywhere. It is my Desire, that he should study the Law, as the necessary Part of Knowledge for a public Man, and profitable if he should have occasion to practise it. . . . I shall be glad to see you when convenient, but would not have you come here at present. You may confide to your son the Family Affairs you wished to confer upon with me, for he is discreet. And I trust, that you will prudently avoid introducing him to Company, that it may be improper for him to be seen with. . . . Wishing you Health, and more happiness than it seems you have lately experienced, I remain your affectionate father,

B. Franklin

SOURCE: Courtesy of the American Philosophical Society, <www.amphilsoc.org>.

DOCUMENT 3
Two Oneida Brothers Confront Their Different Allegiances, 1779

Mary Jemison is the source for this story of two Oneida brothers on different sides of the war. Jemison was captured as a girl during the Seven Years' War and adopted into the Seneca tribe of western New York, where she remained for life. When she was eighty, her narrative was taken down and published. In this story, some Oneida warriors siding with the British capture two Indians guiding General Sullivan's 1779 campaign of terror in central New York. One of the conquerors recognizes his own brother.

Envy and revenge glared in the features of the conquering savage, as he advanced to his brother (the prisoner) in all the haughtiness of Indian pride, heightened by a sense of power, and addressed him in the following manner:

"Brother, you have merited death! The hatchet or the war-club shall finish your career! When I begged of you to follow me in the fortunes of war, you was deaf to my cries—you spurned my entreaties!

"Brother! You have merited death and shall have your deserts! When the rebels raised their hatchets to fight their good master, you sharpened your knife, you brightened your rifle and led on our foes to the fields of our fathers! You have merited

(continued)

death and shall die by our hands! When those rebels had drove us from the fields of our fathers to seek out new homes, it was you who could dare to step forth as their pilot, and conduct them even to the doors of our wigwams, to butcher our children and put us to death! No crime can be greater! But though you have merited death and shall die on this spot, my hands shall not be stained in the blood of a brother! *Who will strike?*"

Little Beard, who was standing by, as soon as the speech was ended, struck the prisoner on the head with his tomahawk, and dispatched him at once.

SOURCE: James E. Seaver, *A narrative of the life of Mrs. Mary Jemison, who was taken by the Indians, in the year 1755, when only about twelve years of age, and has continued to reside amongst them to the present time* (1824), chapter VII, Project Gutenberg, <http://www.ibiblio.org/gutenberg/etext04/jemsn10.txt> (accessed January 14, 2004).

DOCUMENT 4
Petition from a Wife Deserted by a Tory Husband, 1783

Margaret Brisbane's husband James, of Charleston, South Carolina, was a loyalist throughout the war. The state legislature banished him and confiscated his estate; her petition of 1783 was an effort to recover some property to support herself and her children. Her petition was rejected, but three years later her sons recovered their father's property.

The Petition of Margerett Brisbane Humbly Sheweth

That she . . . intermarried with Mr. James Brisbane, formerly of this State; A Gentleman, whose political sentiments differed from those of his fellow Citizens, which, induced him to quit this Country, at a very early period, in this unhappy Contest. The part he has taken, has, unfortunately, drawn on him the heavy displeasure of the Legislature. . . . And your petitioner, apprehensive least this honorable House, under an Idea of Retaliation, or, from political motives, may think proper, to send away from this Country, the Unfortunate & distressed Wives & Children of those persons who have become so obnoxious, has taken the Liberty of requesting that she may be considered, not only in the view of a wife, but that of a Mother. . . .

[She] flatters herself with hopes, that when the House reflects on the weak and Defenceless Situation of woman & children, who are not the promoters of the War, nor, from their Sphere in Life, can possibly be disadvantageous to the contest; and whose Opinions seldom avail, and do not frequently operate on the Judgment of Men; when they recollect this, and are informed that her Sentiments *with regard to the present Contest* never coincided with, but were always contrary to her Husbands. . . . That they will take into Consideration the facts above set forth, and extend its benevolence

towards her, by permitting her to remain in this Country . . . and by granting some part of that property, which she once considered, as, in some degree, her own, and ultimately, as the inheritance of her now destitute Children.

SOURCE: Cynthia A. Kierner, *Southern Women in Revolution, 1776–1800: Personal and Political Narratives* (Columbia: University of South Carolina Press, 1998), 174–75.

QUESTIONS FOR ANALYSIS AND DEBATE

1. Why is Mary Almy "cut to the soul" by the remarks of her sons? She is frightened for her husband's safety. Is she also angry with him? Why or why not?

2. What does Benjamin Franklin mean by the emphasized words "*Natural Duties*"? Do you think Franklin really believed his son was entitled to his own political opinions on the Revolutionary War? What factors help explain why William remained loyal to the crown?

3. Why does the Oneida warrior believe his brother merits death?

4. Is Margaret Brisbane's claim of allegiance to the American cause compelling? Can you imagine what a more successful petition might contain?

---

safety began to fix prices on goods such as flour, bread, and other essentials for short periods. Inevitably, some Americans turned this unstable situation to their advantage. Money that fell fast in value needed to be spent quickly; being in debt was suddenly advantageous because the debt could be repaid in devalued currency. A brisk black market sprang up in prohibited luxury imports, such as tea, sugar, textiles, and wines, even though these items came from Britain. A New Hampshire delegate to the congress denounced the extravagance that flew in the face of the virtuous homespun association agreements of just a few years before: "We are a crooked and perverse generation, longing for the fineries and follies of those Egyptian task masters from whom we have so lately freed ourselves."

The Campaigns of 1777–1779: The North and West

In early 1777, the Continental army had a bleak road ahead. General Washington had shown considerable skill in avoiding outright defeat, but the minor victories in New Jersey lent only faint optimism to the American side. The British moved large numbers of soldiers into Quebec, readying their plan to isolate New England from the rest of the colonies by taking control of the Hudson River. Their attack moving down from the north drew the American Continental army up into central New York, polarizing Indian tribes of the Iroquois nation and turning the Mohawk Valley into a bloody war zone. By 1779, tribes in western New York and in Indian country in the Ohio Valley were fully involved in the Revolutionary War; most sided with the British and against the Americans. The Americans had some success in this period, such as the victory at Saratoga, but the involvement of Indians and the continuing strength of the British forced the American government to look toward France for help.

Burgoyne's Army and the Battle of Saratoga

In 1777, General John Burgoyne assumed command of a British army of 7,800 soldiers in Canada and began the northern squeeze on the Hudson River valley. His goal was to capture Albany, a town 150 miles north of New York City near the intersection of the Hudson and Mohawk rivers (see Map 7.1). Traveling with Burgoyne and his soldiers were a thousand assorted "camp followers" (cooks, laundresses, musicians) and some 400 Indian warriors and scouts. This large force did not travel light, requiring food supplies not only for 9,200 people but also for the more than 400 horses needed to haul heavy artillery. Burgoyne also carted thirty trunks of personal belongings, including fine wines and elegant clothing.

In July, Burgoyne captured Fort Ticonderoga with ease. Some 3,000 American troops stationed there spotted the approaching British and, low on food and supplies, abandoned the fort without a fight. The British continued to move south, but the large army moved slowly on primitive roads through heavily forested land. Burgoyne

A Soldier's Canteen
This wooden canteen belonged to Noah Allen, whose name and regiment number are carved into the side. Allen was from the Sixth Continental Regiment from Massachusetts. Almost no piece of equipment surpassed in importance the soldier's canteen.
Fort Ticonderoga Museum.

lost a month hacking his way down the road, and meanwhile his supply lines back to Canada were severely stretched. Soldiers sent out to forage for food were beaten back by local militia units.

The logical second step in isolating New England should have been to advance troops up the Hudson from New York City to meet Burgoyne. American surveillance indicated that General Howe in Manhattan was readying his men for a major move in August 1777. George Washington, watching from New Jersey, was astonished to see Howe's men sail south; Howe had decided to try to capture Philadelphia.

The third prong of the British strategy involved bringing troops—regular British soldiers along with German mercenary soldiers hired by England—from Montreal to the Great Lakes and thence east along the Mohawk River in central New York. The 800 troops were joined by some 800 Mohawks and Senecas of the Iroquois confederacy, and these in turn were aided by loyalists native to the Mohawk Valley who had taken up arms for the king. The British believed that a large enclave of Palatine Germans living in the Mohawk Valley would be heavily loyalist, so they expected little trouble getting to Albany. These Germans were descendants of some 10,000 migrants who came to New York around 1710 from the Palatinate, a region of Germany near the Rhine River.

A hundred miles west of their goal, in August 1777, the British encountered American Continental army soldiers at Fort Stanwix, reinforced by hundreds of Palatine German militiamen and their Oneida Indian allies. Led by the Mohawk Joseph Brant, the Senecas and Mohawks ambushed the Germans and the Oneidas in a narrow ravine called Oriskany and inflicted extremely heavy losses: 500 out of 800 men on the American side were killed or mortally wounded. On Brant's side, about 90 warriors were killed. But Fort Stanwix held back the

British regulars and Seneca and eventually sent them into retreat (see Map 7.1). The Oriskany and Fort Stanwix battles were very deadly; they were also complexly multiethnic, pitting Indians against Indians, German Americans against German mercenaries, New York patriots against neighboring New York loyalists, and English Americans against the British.

The British retreat at Fort Stanwix deprived General Burgoyne of the additional troops he expected to carry out his Hudson River strategy. Camped at a small village called Saratoga, he was isolated with food supplies dwindling and men deserting. His adversary at Albany, General Horatio Gates, began moving 7,000 Continental soldiers toward him. Burgoyne decided to attack first because every day his army was weakening. In this first attack, the British prevailed, but at the great cost of 600 dead or wounded redcoats. Three weeks later, an American attack on Burgoyne's forces at Saratoga cost the British another 600 men and most of their cannons. Burgoyne finally surrendered to the American forces at Saratoga on October 17, 1777.

Americans on the side of the rebellion were jubilant. After Saratoga, the first decisive victory for the Continental army, a popular dance called "General Burgoyne's Surrender" swept through the country, and bookies in the major cities set odds at five to one that the war would be won in six months.

General Howe, meanwhile, had succeeded in occupying Philadelphia in September 1777. Figuring that the Saratoga loss was balanced by the capture of Philadelphia, the British government proposed a negotiated settlement—not including independence—to end the war. The American side refused.

American optimism in the winter of 1777–78 was not well founded. Spirits ran high, but supplies of arms and food ran precariously low. Washington moved his troops into winter quarters at Valley Forge, a day's march west of occupied Philadelphia, where they stayed from December to June. (See "American Places," page 235.) Quartered in drafty huts, the men lacked blankets, boots, and stockings. Washington complained to the congress that nearly 3,000 of his men were "unfit for duty because they are bare foot and otherwise naked"; without blankets, large numbers were forced to "set up all Night by fires, instead of taking comfortable rest in a natural way." Food was also scarce. Local farms had produced adequate grain that year, but Washington was sure that the farmers were selling it to the British, who could pay with the king's silver.

Evidence of corruption and profiteering was abundant. Army suppliers too often provided defective food, clothing, and gunpowder. Washington's men unfolded a shipment of blankets only to discover that they were a quarter of their customary size. Teamsters who hauled barrels of preserved salted meat might drain out the brine to lighten their load and then refill the barrels later, allowing the meat to rot in transit. Selfishness and greed seemed to infect the American side. As one Continental officer said, "The people at home are destroying the Army by their conduct much faster than Howe and all his army can possibly do by fighting us."

The War in the West: Indian Country

Burgoyne's defeat in the fall of 1777 and Washington's long stay at Valley Forge up to June 1778 might suggest that the war paused for a time; and it did, on the Atlantic coast. But in the interior western areas—the Mohawk Valley, the Ohio Valley, and Kentucky—the war of Indians against the American pro-independence side was heating up. For native tribes, the war was not about taxation, representation, or monarchical rule; it was about independence, freedom, and land.

The ambush and slaughter at Oriskany in August 1777 marked the beginning of three years of near-constant terror for all the inhabitants of the Mohawk Valley. Loyalists and Indians together engaged in many small raids on farms and villages throughout the spring and summer of 1778, killing and capturing the residents. In retaliation, American militiamen destroyed the Indian village of Joseph Brant, called Onaquaga, thought to be the headquarters for many hundreds of Iroquoian warriors. Most of the village residents fled the day before the at-

The Battle of Saratoga, 1777

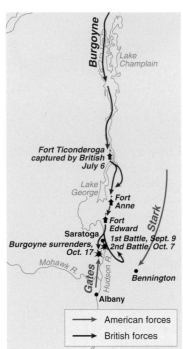

American forces →
British forces →

For native tribes, the war was not about taxation, representation, or monarchical rule; it was about independence, freedom, and land.

AMERICAN PLACES

Valley Forge National Historical Park, Valley Forge, Pennsylvania

From December 1777 to June 1778, 12,000 Continental army soldiers camped at Valley Forge, 18 miles northwest of British-occupied Philadelphia. The soldiers felled trees and built a thousand rough huts, like the one pictured here, for winter quarters. Wood for huts and firewood was plentiful, but nothing else was. Severe hardship afflicted the army, making Valley Forge famous to future generations as a glorious symbol of American sacrifice and patriotic determination. At the time it did not seem at all glorious. Washington had to conceal his troops' hardships for fear of letting the British know how weakened his army really was.

Food was always inadequate. Standard rations dwindled for a time to "firecake," a tasteless pancake made of flour and water. In one week in February there were no food rations at all. Clothing was even harder to procure, and men went barefoot and in rags in the cold winter months. Disease flourished. Some 2,000 men died of dysentery, pneumonia, and other contagious illnesses. Not everyone could cope with such sacrifice. Official records show that 8 or 10 men deserted every day, totaling 2,000 desertions over the six months. Yet 8,000 men did not desert or die; they stayed and suffered, out of dedication to the cause.

Spring finally came, as did Baron Friedrich von Steuben, a Prussian general who arrived from Europe to begin formal training of the troops. American officers did not inspire their men to obey; the baron sharply corrected that. He inaugurated constant drill parades, overseeing the men himself, gaining their respect through his competence and authority. He worked a near miracle, transforming both officers and men into a model of military discipline. Before the baron's arrival, ran a common joke, an enlisted man might call his commanding officer "a Chuckleheaded Son of a bitch" if he disliked an order. After training by von Steuben, the soldier would instead say "Damn your orders sir." Clearly, neither the Prussian baron nor the severe winter drained all the spunk out of the American recruits.

Valley Forge was preserved as a historical park in 1893 and became part of the National Park Service in 1977. Visitors can tour Washington's headquarters and several re-created log huts. If their visit is well timed, they can experience the snow and bone-chilling cold that created misery in February 1778. The Park Service wisely does not try to re-create all of the harsh conditions of the camp, but it provides ample information to help visitors tap their own imagination.

For Web links related to this site and other American Places, see "PlaceLinks" at bedfordstmartins.com/roark.

Reenactors in Winter at Valley Forge
Courtesy Valley Forge National Historical Park.

tack, but some children in hiding were killed. A month later, in November, Brant's warriors attacked the town of Cherry Valley, killing 32 townspeople and 16 soldiers and taking 71 people captive.

The following summer, General Washington authorized a campaign to wreak "total destruction and devastation" on all the Iroquoian villages of central New York. Some 4,500 Continental army troops under the command of General John Sullivan carried out a deliberate campaign of terror in late summer and fall of 1779. Forty Indian towns met with total obliteration; the soldiers looted and torched the dwellings, then burned cornfields and fruit orchards. In a few towns, women and children were slaughtered; but in most, the inhabitants managed to escape, fleeing to the British at Fort Niagara. Thousands of Indian refugees, sick and starving, camped around the fort in one of the most miserable winters on record.

Much farther to the west, beyond Fort Pitt, another complex story unfolded, of alliances and betrayals between American militiamen and Indians. Some 150,000 native peoples lived between the Appalachian Mountains and the Mississippi River. By 1779, it was clear to the multitudes of Indian tribes that neutrality was not a viable option. Most sided with the British, who maintained a major garrison at Fort Detroit. But a portion of the Shawnee and Delaware tribes for a time actively sought peace with the Americans.

In mid-1778, a Delaware leader named White Eyes negotiated a treaty with the Americans at Fort Pitt, pledging Indian support in the war in exchange for supplies and trade goods. But supplies and goods were not forthcoming, and escalating violence began to undermine the agreement. That fall, American soldiers in Ohio captured and killed two friendly Shawnee chiefs, Cornstalk and Red Hawk. The Continental Congress hastened to apologize, as did the governors of Pennsylvania and Virginia, but the soldiers who stood trial for the murders were acquitted. Two months later, White Eyes, still nominally an ally and informant for the Americans, died under mysterious circumstances, almost certainly murdered by militiamen. Despite Indian professions of support, American military leaders repeatedly had trouble honoring distinctions between allied and enemy Indians.

The frontier war zone extended from western North Carolina into the area later called Tennessee, where in 1779 militias attacked Cherokee settlements, destroying thirty-six villages and burning fields and livestock. In Kentucky, Indian raiders from north of the Ohio River who had allied with the British stationed at Fort Detroit repeatedly attacked white settlements, such as Boonesborough, that had sprouted up in defiance of the Proclamation of 1763 (Map 7.3; see also chapter 6). In retaliation, a young Virginian, George Rogers Clark, led Kentucky militiamen into what is now Illinois, his men attacking and taking the British (formerly French) fort at Kaskaskia. Clark's men wore hunting shirts and breech cloths, native clothing, but their native dress was not a sign of solidarity with Indians. When they attacked British-held Fort Vincennes, in 1779, Clark's troops tomahawked Indian captives and threw their still-live bodies in the river in a gory spectacle witnessed by the redcoats. "To excel them in barbarity is the only way to make war upon Indians," Clark announced. And, he might have added, a good way to terrorize the British soldiers as well.

By 1780, very few Indians remained neutral. Clark's and other violent raids drove Indians into the hills, into starvation, and into the arms of the British at Detroit and Niagara, or into the arms of the Spanish, who still held much of the land west of the Mississippi River. Said one officer on the Sullivan campaign, "Their nests are destroyed but the birds are still on the wing." For those who stayed near their native lands, chaos and confusion prevailed.

Rare as it was, Indian support for the American side occasionally emerged out of a strategic sense that the Americans were unstoppable in their westward pressure and that it was better to work out an alliance than to lose in a war. But American treatment of even friendly Indians showed that there really was no winning strategy to be had for the Indians.

The French Alliance

On their own, the Americans could not have defeated England, and the western pressure from hostile Indians magnified their task. Essential help arrived as a result of the victory at Saratoga, which convinced the French to enter the war; a formal alliance was signed in February 1778. France recognized the United States as an independent nation and promised full military and commercial support throughout the war. Most crucial was the French navy, which could chal-

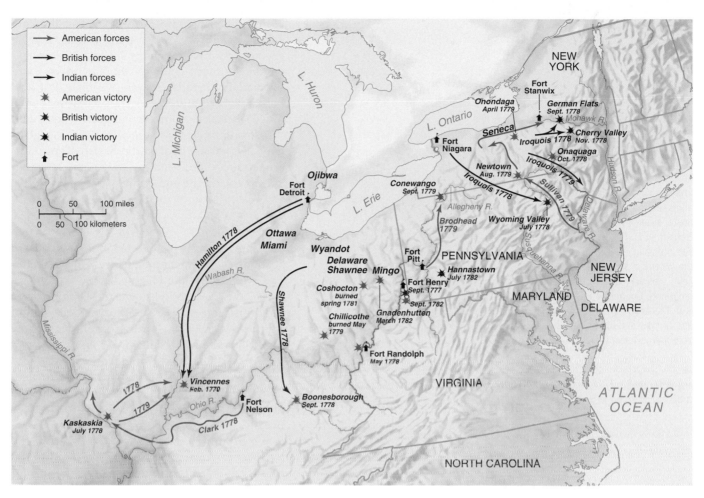

Legend:
- → American forces
- → British forces
- → Indian forces
- ✳ American victory
- ✳ British victory
- ✳ Indian victory
- ⚑ Fort

MAP 7.3   The War in the West, 1778–1782

The American Revolution involved many Indian tribes, most of them supporting the British side. Iroquois with British aid attacked American towns in New York's Mohawk Valley throughout 1778. In 1779 the Continental army marched on 40 Iroquois villages in central New York and destroyed them. Shawnee and Delaware to the west of Fort Pitt tangled with American militia units in 1779, while tribes supported by the British at Fort Detroit conducted raids on Kentucky settlers who hit back with raids of their own. George Rogers Clark led Kentucky militiamen against Indians in the Illinois region. Sporadic fighting continued in the West through 1782, ending with Indian attacks on Hannastown, Pennsylvania, and Fort Henry on the Ohio River. By the late 1780s, occasional fighting resumed, sparked by American settlers pressing west onto Indian lands.

lenge England's transatlantic shipment of supplies and troops.

Although France had been waiting for a promising American victory to justify a formal declaration of war, since 1776 the French had been providing aid to the Americans in the form of cannons, muskets, gunpowder, and highly trained military advisers. Still, monarchical France was understandably cautious about endorsing a democratic revolution attacking the principles of kingship. For France, the main attraction of an alliance was the opportunity it provided to defeat England, its archrival. A victory would also open pathways to trade and perhaps result in France acquiring the coveted British West Indies. Even American defeat would not be a full disaster for France if the war lasted many years and drained England of men and money.

French support materialized slowly. The navy arrived off the coast of Virginia in July 1778 but then went south to the West

> On their own, the Americans could not have defeated England. The victory at Saratoga convinced the French to enter the war.

Pulpit of the Reverend Samuel Cooper

From this pulpit in the Brattle Street Congregational Church in Boston, the Reverend Samuel Cooper departed from his customary apolitical sermons one day in 1778 to announce that a letter from his friend Benjamin Franklin in Paris declared that France had officially entered the war on the American side. This long-awaited news was very welcome to his congregation. Cooper had deep sympathies with the American side. Like many Bostonians, he had fled his city while the British army occupied it, returning when they left in 1776. Cooper's church had been taken over as a temporary barracks for British soldiers. The elegant mahogany pulpit was spared any defacement by the redcoats because it was covered in a wooden casing.

Courtesy of the Society for the Preservation of New England Antiquities.

Indies to defend the French sugar-producing islands. French help would prove indispensable to the American victory, but the alliance's first months brought no dramatic victories, and some Americans grumbled that the partnership would prove worthless.

The Southern Strategy and the End of the War

When France joined the war, some British officials wondered whether the fight was worth continuing. A troop commander, arguing for an immediate negotiated settlement, shrewdly observed that "we are far from an anticipated peace, because the bitterness of the rebels is too widespread, and in regions where we are masters the rebellious spirit is still in them. The land is too large, and there are too many people. The more land we win, the weaker our army gets in the field." The commander of the British navy argued for abandoning the war, and even Lord

> White southerners feared that all-out war might unleash violence from slaves seizing the moment to claim freedom.

North, the prime minister, agreed. But the king was determined to crush the rebellion, and he encouraged a new strategy for victory focusing on the southern colonies, thought to be more persuadably loyalist. It was a brilliant but desperate plan, and ultimately unsuccessful, as the king learned that southern colonists were not all that loyal and in fact were willing to engage in guerrilla warfare against the British. The southern strategy thus led to a British defeat at Yorktown and the end of the war.

Georgia and South Carolina

The new strategy called for British forces to abandon New England and focus on the South. The southern region had valuable crops—tobacco, rice, and indigo—worth keeping under the British flag. Also, the large slave population was a powerful destabilizing factor from which the British hoped to benefit. White southerners feared that all-out war might unleash violence from slaves seizing the moment to claim freedom. Living in Georgia and the Carolinas were large numbers of loyalists likely to support Britain's war effort. The British hoped to recapture the southern colonies one by one, restore the loyalists to power, and then move north to the more problematic middle colonies, saving prickly New England for last.

Georgia, the first target, fell at the end of December 1778 (Map 7.4). A small army of British soldiers occupied Savannah and Augusta, and a new royal governor and loyalist assembly were quickly installed. Taking Georgia was easy because the bulk of the Continental army was in New York and New Jersey, keeping an eye on General Henry Clinton, Howe's replacement as commander in chief, and the French were in the West Indies. The British in Georgia quickly organized twenty loyal militia units, and 1,400 Georgians swore an oath of allegiance to the king. So far, the southern strategy looked as if it might work.

The next target was South Carolina. General Clinton moved British troops south from New York by sea, while the Continental army raised 2,500 soldiers from southern states and 2,000 local militiamen and put them in Charleston to defend it. For five weeks in early 1780, the British laid siege to the city, which finally surrendered in mid-May 1780, sending 3,300 American soldiers, a tremendous loss, into British captivity. Again, the king's new strategy seemed to be on target.

Clinton returned to New York, leaving the task of pacifying the rest of South Carolina to General Charles Cornwallis and 4,000 troops. The boldest of all the British generals in the war for America, Lord Cornwallis quickly moved into action. He chased out the remaining Continental army units and established military control of South Carolina by midsummer 1780. He purged rebels from government office and disarmed potential rebel militias. The export of South Carolina's main crop, rice, resumed, and as in Georgia, pardons were offered to Carolinians who swore loyalty oaths to the crown and then proved their loyalty by taking up arms for the British.

In August 1780, the Continental army was ready to strike back at Cornwallis. General Gates, the hero of the Battle of Saratoga, arrived in South Carolina with more than 3,000 troops, some of them experienced army units and others

militiamen with little battlefield experience. They met Cornwallis's army at Camden, South Carolina, on August 16 (see Map 7.4). Gates put the militiamen into the center of the battle. At the sight of the approaching enemy cavalry, they panicked; men threw down unfired muskets and ran. When regiment leaders tried to regroup the next day, only 700 showed up; the rest were dead, captured, or still in flight. Camden was a devastating defeat; prospects seemed very grim for the Americans.

Britain's southern strategy succeeded in 1780 in part because of information about American troop movements secretly passed on to the British by an American traitor: Benedict Arnold. The hero of several American battles, Arnold was a brilliant military talent but also a deeply insecure man who never felt he got his due, in either honor or financial reward. Sometime in 1779, he opened secret negotiations

MAP 7.4   The War in the South, 1780–1781

After taking Charleston in May 1780, the British advanced into South Carolina and the foothill region of North Carolina, leaving a bloody civil war in their wake. When the American general Horatio Gates and his men fumbled and fled from the humiliating Battle of Camden, Gates was replaced by General Nathaniel Greene and General Daniel Morgan, who pulled off major successes at King's Mountain and Cowpens. The British general Cornwallis then moved north and invaded Virginia but was bottled up and finally overpowered at Yorktown in the fall of 1781.

of turncoat southern Tories, panic like that of the terrified soldiers at Camden. But instead of symbolizing all that was troubling about the American side of the war, the treachery of Arnold was publically and ritually denounced—in parades, broadsides, and cartoons—in a kind of displacement of the anxieties of the moment. Vilifying Arnold allowed Americans to stake out a wide distance between themselves and dastardly conduct. It inspired a renewal of patriotism at a particularly low moment.

The Other Southern War: Guerrillas

Shock over Gates's defeat at Camden and Arnold's treason revitalized rebel support in western South Carolina, an area that Cornwallis believed to be pacified and loyal. The backcountry of the South soon became the site of guerrilla warfare. In hit-and-run attacks, both sides burned and ravaged not only opponents' property but the property of anyone claiming to be neutral. Loyalist militia units organized by the British were met by fierce rebel militia units who figured they had little to lose. In South Carolina, some six thousand men became active partisan fighters, and they entered into at least twenty-six engagements with loyalist units. Some were classic battles, but on other occasions the fighters were more like bandits than soldiers. Guerrilla warfare soon spread to Georgia and North Carolina. Both sides committed murders and atrocities and plundered property, clear deviations from standard military practice.

The success of Britain's southern strategy depended on sufficient loyalist strength to hold reconquered territory as Cornwallis's army moved north. The backcountry guerrilla war proved that loyalist support was far weaker than the British had supposed. The Americans won few major battles in the South, but they ultimately succeeded by harassing the British forces and thus preventing them from foraging for food. Cornwallis moved into North Carolina in the fall of 1780, not because he thought South Carolina was secure—it was not—but because the North Carolinians were supplying the South Carolina rebels with arms and men (see Map 7.4). Then news of a massacre on October 7 of loyalist units in western South Carolina at King's Mountain, at the hands of 1,400 frontier riflemen, sent him hurrying back. The British were stretched too thin to hold on to even two of their onetime colonies.

Benedict Arnold
This portrait shows Benedict Arnold in 1776, when he was the hero of the Quebec campaign. Probably the final straw for Arnold came when he failed to earn a promotion while men he considered inferior were elevated to higher rank.
Anne S. K. Brown Military Collection, Providence, R.I.

with General Clinton in New York, trading information for money and hinting that he could deliver far more of value. When General Washington made him commander of West Point, a new fort sixty miles north of New York City on the Hudson River, Arnold's plan crystallized. West Point controlled the Hudson; its easy capture by the British might well have meant victory in the war.

Arnold's plot to sell a West Point victory to the British was foiled when Americans captured the man carrying plans of the fort's defense from Arnold to Clinton. News of Arnold's treason created shock waves. Arnold represented all of the patriots' worst fears about themselves: greedy self-interest like that of the war profiteers, the unprincipled abandonment of war aims like that

A French Officer's View of the French Blockade
Pierre Joseph Jeunot, a young naval officer, sketched the lines of British and French ships shortly before they clashed at the Battle of the Chesapeake Capes, at the entrance to Chesapeake Bay on September 5, 1781. More than two dozen French ships sealed the bay and the York River, preventing the escape of Cornwallis's army at Yorktown. Jeunot showed some ships in action, totally obscured by the impenetrable smoke of the fired cannons.
The Huntington Library & Arts Collections, San Marino, California.

Surrender at Yorktown

In early 1781, the war was going very badly for the British. Their defeat at King's Mountain was quickly followed by a second major defeat, the Battle of Cowpens in South Carolina in January 1781, where local militia units backed by Continental soldiers bested the British army. Meanwhile, Cornwallis had pushed further north into Virginia, where he captured Williamsburg in June and sent a raiding party to Charlottesville, the town hosting Virginia's revolutionary government. The British seized members of the Virginia assembly but failed to capture Governor Thomas Jefferson, who escaped the soldiers by a mere ten minutes. (More than a dozen of Jefferson's slaves chose this moment to seek refuge with the British.) These minor victories allowed Cornwallis to imagine that he was gaining the upper hand in Virginia. On instructions from General Henry Clinton in New York City,

Cornwallis took over Yorktown, Virginia, near Chesapeake Bay, to prepare for the arrival of British ships.

What tipped the balance of power in the war was the arrival, finally, of French military support. A large French army under the command of the Comte de Rochambeau had joined General Washington in Rhode Island in mid-1780. News that a fleet of warships had sailed from France in the spring of 1781 set in motion Washington's plan to defeat the British. The fleet, commanded by the Comte de Grasse, was bound for the Chesapeake Bay, so Washington and Rochambeau fixed their attention on Virginia. Bypassing New York (where Clinton had been expecting an attack), thousands of American and French soldiers headed south in August 1781, traveling on four separate roads to confuse the British.

When British navy ships arrived to defend the Chesapeake, they found that the French navy had already taken control of it. A five-day naval battle in early September sent the British ships limping away and left the French navy in clear control of the Virginia and North Carolina coasts. This proved to be the decisive factor in ending the war, because it eliminated the possibility of reinforcements for Cornwallis's army, dug in at Yorktown, and made rescue by the British navy impossible.

On land, General Cornwallis and his 7,500 troops faced a combined French and American army numbering over 16,000. For twelve days, the Americans and French bombarded the British fortifications at Yorktown; Cornwallis ran low on food and ammunition. An American observer keeping a diary noted that "the enemy, from want of forage, are killing off their horses in great numbers. Six or seven hundred of these valuable animals have been killed, and their carcasses are almost continually floating down the river." Realizing escape was impossible, Cornwallis signaled his intention to surrender. On October 19, 1781, he formally capitulated.

What began as a promising southern strategy in 1778 turned into a discouraging defeat by 1781. British attacks in the South had energized American resistance, as did the timely exposure of Benedict Arnold's treason. The arrival of the French fleet sealed the fate of Cornwallis at Yorktown, and the military war quickly came to a halt.

Siege of Yorktown, 1781

The Losers and the Winners

The surrender at Yorktown proved to be the end of the war with England, but it took some time for the principal combatants to realize that. Frontier areas in Kentucky, Ohio, and Illinois still blazed with battles and sieges. The peace treaty was nearly two years in the making, and in the meantime both American and British armies remained in the field in case the treaty fell through. King George clung to the idea of pursuing the war, but sentiment favoring a formal peace was growing in Parliament. The war had become unpopular among the British citizenry in general, and support for it dwindled until finally the king had to realize it was over.

It took six months for the American commissioners—Benjamin Franklin, John Adams, and John Jay of New York—and their British and French counterparts to negotiate the three-way settlement in Paris. In November 1782, eighty-two articles of peace were agreed to. The first article went to the heart of the matter: "His Britannic Majesty acknowledges the said United States to be free Sovereign and independent States." Other articles set the western boundary of the new country at the Mississippi River and guaranteed that creditors on both sides could collect debts owed them in sterling money, a provision especially important to British merchants. England agreed to withdraw its troops quickly; more than a decade later, this promise still had not been fully kept. The final, official peace treaty—the Treaty of Paris—was signed on September 2, 1783.

Like the Treaty of Paris at the end of the Seven Years' War, this Treaty of Paris failed to recognize the Indians as players in the conflict. As one American told the Shawnee people, "Your Fathers the English have made Peace with us for themselves, but forgot you their Children, who Fought with them, and neglected you like Bastards." Indian lands were assigned to the victors as though they were uninhabited. Some Indian refugees fled west into present-day Missouri and Arkansas, and others, such as Joseph Brant's Mohawks, relocated to Canada. But significant numbers remained within the new United States, occupying their traditional homelands in areas west and north of the Ohio River. For them, the Treaty of 1783 brought no peace at all; their longer war against the Americans would extend at least until 1795 and for some, to 1813. Their ally, Britain, conceded defeat, but the Indians did not.

When the treaty was finally signed, the British began their evacuation of New York, Charleston, and Savannah, a process complicated by the sheer numbers involved—soldiers, fearful loyalists, and runaway slaves by the thousands. In New York City, more than 27,000 soldiers and 30,000 loyalists sailed on hundreds of ships for England in late fall 1783. In a final act of mischief, on the November day when the last ships left, the losing side raised the British flag at the southern tip of Manhattan, cut away the ropes used to hoist it, and greased the flagpole.

The first article of the peace treaty went to the heart of the matter: "His Britannic Majesty acknowledges the said United States to be free Sovereign and independent States."

"The Ballance of Power," 1780

This cartoon was published in England soon after Spain and the Netherlands declared an alliance with France to support the war in America. On the left, Britannia, a female figure representing Great Britain, cannot be moved by all the lightweights combined on the right side of the scale. France wears a ruffled shirt, Spain has a feather in his hat, and a Dutch boy has just hopped on, saying, "I'll do anything for money." The forlorn Indian maiden, the standard icon representing America in the eighteenth century, sits on the scale, head in hand, wailing, "My Ingratitude is Justly Punished." The poem printed below the cartoon predicts that "The Americans too will with Britons unite." This fanciful prediction was punctured nine months after it appeared, when the British surrendered to the Americans and the French at Yorktown in 1781.

Print Collection, Miriam and Ira D. Wallach Division of Art, Prints, and Photographs, the New York Public Library. Astor, Lenox and Tilden Foundations.

For more help analyzing this image, see the visual activity for this chapter in the Online Study Guide at **bedfordstmartins.com/roark.**

Conclusion: Why the British Lost

The British began the war for America convinced that they could not lose. They had the strongest and best-trained army and navy in the world; they were familiar with the American landscape from the Seven Years' War; they outnumbered their opponents in uniform; they had the willing warrior-power of most of the native tribes of the backcountry; and they easily captured every port city of consequence in America. Probably one-fifth of the population was loyalist, and another two-fifths were undecided. Why, then, did the British lose?

One continuing problem the British faced was the uncertainty of supplies. Unwilling to ravage the countryside, the army depended on a steady stream of supply ships from home. Insecurity about food helps explain the repeated reluctance of Howe and Clinton to pursue the Continental army aggressively.

A second obstacle to British success was their continual misuse of loyalist energies. Any plan to repacify the colonies required the cooperation of the loyalists as well as new support from the many neutrals. But again and again, the British failed to back the loyalists, leaving them to the mercy of vengeful rebels. In the South, they allowed loyalist militias to engage in vicious guerrilla warfare that drove away potential converts among the rest of the population.

The French alliance looms large in any explanation of the British defeat. The artillery and ammunition the French supplied even before 1778 were critical necessities for the Continental army. In 1780, the French army brought a fresh infusion of troops to a war-weary America, and the French navy made the Yorktown victory possible. The major naval defeat in the Chesapeake, just before the Yorktown siege, dissolved the pro-war spirit in England and forced the king to concede defeat.

Finally, the British abdicated civil power in the colonies in 1775 and 1776, when royal officials were forced to flee to safety, and they never really regained it. For nearly seven years, of necessity the Americans created their own government structures, from the Continental Congress to local committees and militias. Staffed by many who before 1775 had been the political elites, these new government agencies had remarkably little trouble establishing their authority to rule. The basic British goal—to turn back the clock to imperial rule—receded into impossibility as the war dragged on.

The war for America had taken five and a half years to fight, from Lexington to Yorktown; negotiations and the evacuation took two more. It profoundly disrupted the lives of Americans everywhere. It was a war for independence from England, but it was more. It was a war that required men and women to think about politics and the legitimacy of authority. The precise disagreement with England about representation and political participation had profound implications for the kinds of governance the Americans would adopt, both in the moment of emergency and in the longer run of the late 1770s and early 1780s when states began to write their constitutions. The rhetoric employed to justify the revolution against England put words such as *liberty, tyranny, slavery, independence,* and *equality* into common usage. These words carried far deeper meanings than a mere complaint over taxation without representation. As Abigail Adams and others saw, the Revolution unleashed a dynamic of equality and liberty. That it was largely unintended and unwanted by the revolutionary leaders of 1776 made it all the more potent a force in American life in the decades to come.

For additional firsthand accounts of this period, see Chapter 7 in Michael Johnson, ed., *Reading the American Past,* Third Edition.

To assess your mastery of the material in this chapter, see the Online Study Guide at bedfordstmartins.com/roark.

For Web links related to topics in this chapter, see "HistoryLinks," "DocLinks," and "PlaceLinks" at bedfordstmartins.com/roark.

CHRONOLOGY

1775 • Second Continental Congress convenes in Philadelphia and creates Continental army.

• British win Battle of Bunker Hill, though at a great cost.
• Congress offers Olive Branch Petition to King George; he rejects it.

1776 • American forces assault Quebec and lose.
• Thomas Paine's *Common Sense* creates sensation over idea of independence from Britain.
• British evacuate Boston to avoid entrapment and further dangerous encounters with American troops.
• **July 4.** Congress adopts Declaration of Independence.
• Massive British forces land on Long Island and take Manhattan.

1777 • American army winters at Morristown, New Jersey, and gets inoculated against smallpox.
• General Burgoyne takes Fort Ticonderoga for British.
• Ambush by Mohawk, Seneca, and British at Oriskany inflicts heavy losses on Americans.
• Americans hold Fort Stanwix, depriving Burgoyne's army of additional troops.
• General Howe and the British occupy Philadelphia
• Burgoyne surrenders at Saratoga; France encouraged to enter war.
• General Washington camps Contiental army for six months in Valley Forge, Pennsylvania, where army endures extreme hardship.

1778 • France enters war on American side.
• Terrorizing warfare strikes both sides in Mohawk Valley of New York.
• American militiamen destroy Mohawk Joseph Brant's village.
• Delaware leader White Eyes negotiates a treaty with the Americans at Fort Pitt.
• Americans murder Shawnee chiefs Cornstalk and Red Hawk; Delaware chief White Eyes mysteriously dies.
• Savannah, Georgia, falls to British.

1779 • Militias attack Cherokee settlements in North Carolina and Tennessee.

• Skirmishes in South Carolina and Georgia.
• General Sullivan's campaign destroys 40 Indian towns in New York.
• George Rogers Clark's militia takes Forts Kaskaskia and Vincennes in the West.
• British evacuate Newport.

1780 • Philadelphia Ladies Association raises money for soldiers.
• Charleston, South Carolina, falls to British.
• Comte de Rochambeau arrives at Newport, bringing much-needed French army.
• British victory at Battle of Camden, South Carolina, dims hopes for Americans.
• Benedict Arnold's treasonous plot to betray West Point to the British exposed.

• Guerrilla warfare between loyalists and rebels starts in South Carolina and spreads to Georgia and North Carolina.
• American victory at Battle of King's Mountain, South Carolina, results in heavy loyalist casualties.

1781 • American victory at Battle of Cowpens, South Carolina.
• British forces led by General Cornwallis push into Virginia and capture Williamsburg.
• Cornwallis occupies Yorktown, Virginia.
• French fleet blockades Chesapeake Bay.
• Cornwallis surrenders at Yorktown and concedes British defeat in the Revolutionary War.

1783 • Treaty of Paris ends war.
• United States gains all land to the Mississippi River from British; Indians living on much of that land not consulted.

BIBLIOGRAPHY

General Works

Benson Bobrick, *Angel in the Whirlwind: The Triumph of the American Revolution* (1997).

Edward Countryman, *The American Revolution* (1985).

Don Higginbotham, *The War of Independence: Military Attitudes, Policies, and Practices, 1763–1789* (1983).

Don Higginbotham, *War and Society in Revolutionary America: The Wider Dimensions of Conflict* (1988).

Ronald Hoffman and Peter J. Albert, *Arms and Independence: The Military Character of the American Revolution* (1984).

Mark V. Kwasny, *Washington's Partisan War, 1775–1783* (1996).

Piers Mackesy, *The War for America, 1775–1783* (1964).

Ray Raphael, *A People's History of the American Revolution: How Common People Shaped the Fight for Independence* (2001).

Charles Royster, *A Revolutionary People at War: The Continental Army and American Character, 1775–1783* (1979).

Geoffrey Scheer, *Rebels and Redcoats: The American Revolution through the Eyes of Those Who Fought and Lived It* (1988).

John Shy, *A People Numerous and Armed: Reflections on the Military Struggle for American Independence* (rev. ed., 1990).

James L. Stokesbury, *A Short History of the American Revolution* (1991).

The Wartime Confederation

John Alden, *George Washington* (1984).

H. W. Brands, *The First American: The Life and Times of Benjamin Franklin* (2000).

Joseph J. Ellis, *Passionate Sage: The Character and Legacy of John Adams* (1993).

John E. Ferling, *John Adams: A Life* (1992).

John E. Ferling, *Setting the World Ablaze: Washington, Adams, Jefferson, and the American Revolution* (2000).

Jay Fliegelman, *Declaring Independence: Jefferson, Natural Language, and the Culture of Performance* (1993).

Eric Foner, *Tom Paine and Revolutionary America* (1976).

Edith Gelles, *Portia: The World of Abigail Adams* (1992).

James H. Hutson, *John Adams and the Diplomacy of the American Revolution* (1980).

Allen Jayne, *Jefferson's Declaration of Independence: Origins, Philosophy and Theology* (1998).

Pauline Maier, *American Scripture: Making the Declaration of Independence* (1997).

Jackson Turner Main, *The Sovereign States, 1775–1783* (1973).

David McCullough, *John Adams* (2001).

Edmund S. Morgan, *Benjamin Franklin* (2002).

Jack N. Rakove, *The Beginnings of National Politics: An Interpretive History of the Continental Congress* (1979).

Sheila L. Skemp, *William Franklin, Son of a Patriot, Servant of a King* (1990).

Henry Wiencek, *An Imperfect God: George Washington, His Slaves, and the Creation of America* (2003).

Garry Wills, *Inventing America: Jefferson's Declaration of Independence* (1978).

Lynne Withey, *Dearest Friend: A Life of Abigail Adams* (1981).

The Loyalists

Wallace Brown, *The Good Americans: The Loyalists in the American Revolution* (1969).

Robert M. Calhoon, *The Loyalists of Revolutionary America* (1973).

Robert M. Calhoon, *The Loyalist Perception and Other Essays* (1989).

John E. Ferling, *The Loyalist Mind: Joseph Galloway and the American Revolution* (1977).

Malcolm Frieberg, *Prelude to Purgatory: Thomas Hutchinson in Provincial Massachusetts Politics, 1760–1770* (1990).

Adele Hast, *Loyalism in Revolutionary Virginia* (1982).

William N. Nelson, *The American Tory* (1961).

Mary Beth Norton, *The British-American: The Loyalist Exiles in England, 1774–1789* (1972).

William Pencak, *America's Burke: The Mind of Thomas Hutchinson* (1982).

Janice Potter, *The Liberty We Seek: Loyalist Ideology in Colonial New York and Massachusetts* (1983).

James W. St. G. Walker, *The Black Loyalists: The Search for a Promised Land in Nova Scotia and Sierra Leone, 1783–1870* (1976).

The War in the North

Michael A. Bellesiles, *Revolutionary Outlaws: Ethan Allen and the Struggle for Independence on the Early American Frontier* (1993).

W. Jeffrey Bolster, *Black Jacks: African American Seamen in the Age of Sail* (1998).

Clare Brandt, *The Man in the Mirror: A Life of Benedict Arnold* (1994).

Richard Buel Jr., *Dear Liberty: Connecticut's Mobilization for the Revolutionary War* (1980).

E. Wayne Carp, *To Starve the Army at Pleasure: Continental Army Administration and American Political Culture, 1775–1783* (1984).

Edward Countryman, *A People in Revolution: The American Revolution and Political Society in New York, 1760–1790* (1981).

John C. Dann, ed., *The Revolution Remembered: Eyewitness Accounts of the War for Independence* (1980).

William M. Fowler Jr., *Rebels under Sail: The American Navy during the Revolution* (1976).

Francis S. Fox, *Sweet Land of Liberty: The Ordeal of the American Revolution in Northampton County, Pennsylvania* (2000).

Sylvia Frey, *The British Soldier in America: A Social History of Military Life in the Revolutionary Period* (1965).

Robert Gross, *The Minutemen and Their World* (1976).

Ira D. Gruber, *The Howe Brothers and the American Revolution* (1972).

Richard J. Hargrove Jr., *General John Burgoyne* (1983).

Sidney Kaplan and Emma Nogrady Kaplan, *The Black Presence in the Era of the American Revolution* (1989).

Richard M. Ketchum, *Saratoga: Turning Point of America's Revolutionary War* (1997).

Arthur S. Lefkowitz, *The Long Retreat: The Calamitous American Defense of New Jersey, 1776* (1999).

Donald R. Lennon and Charles E. Bennett, *A Quest for Glory: Robert Howe and the American Revolution* (1991).

David G. Martin, *The Philadelphia Campaign: June 1777–1778* (2003).

James Kirby Martin, *Benedict Arnold, Revolutionary Hero: An American Warrior Reconsidered* (1997).

James Kirby Martin and Edward Mark Lender, *A Respectable Army: The Military Origins of the Republic, 1763–1789* (1982).

David B. Mattern, *Benjamin Lincoln and the American Revolution* (1995).

Holly A. Mayer, *Belonging to the Army: Camp Followers and Community during the American Revolution* (1996).

Dave R. Palmer, *The Way of the Fox: American Strategy in the War for America, 1775–1783* (1975).

Gary A. Puckrein, *The Black Regiment in the American Revolution* (1978).

Ray Raphael, *The First American Revolution, before Lexington and Concord* (2002).

John Shy, *Toward Lexington: The Role of the British Army in the Coming of the American Revolution* (1965).

Evan Thomas, *John Paul Jones: Sailor, Hero, Father of the American Navy* (2003).

John A. Tilley, *The British Navy and the American Revolution* (1987).

John E. Walsh, *The Execution of Major André* (2001).

Donald Wallace White, *A Village at War: Chatham, New Jersey, and the American Revolution* (1979).

Robert K. Wright Jr., *The Continental Army* (1983).

The War in Indian Country

Colin G. Calloway, *The American Revolution in Indian Country: Crisis and Diversity in Native American Communities* (1995).

Gregory E. Dowd, *A Spirited Resistance: The North American Indian Struggle for Unity, 1745–1815* (1992).

Joseph R. Fischer, *A Well-Executed Failure: The Sullivan Campaign against the Iroquois, July–September 1779* (1997).

Barbara Graymont, *The Iroquois in the American Revolution* (1972).

Lowell Hayes Harrison, *George Rogers Clark and the War in the West* (2001).

Isabel T. Kelsay, *Joseph Brant, 1743–1807* (1984).

Diplomacy

Jonathan R. Dull, *A Diplomatic History of the American Revolution* (1985).

R. Ernest Dupuy et al., *The American Revolution: A Global War* (1977).

Ronald Hoffman and Peter Albert, eds., *Peace and the Peacemakers: The Treaty of 1783* (1986).

Reginald Horsman, *The Diplomacy of the New Republic, 1776–1815* (1985).

James H. Hutson, *John Adams and the Diplomacy of the American Revolution* (1980).

Lee Kennett, *The French Forces in America, 1780–1783* (1977).

The Southern Strategy

Lawrence E. Babits, *A Devil of a Whipping: The Battle of Cowpens* (1998).

W. Arthur Bowler, *Logistics and the Failure of the British Army in America, 1775–1783* (1975).

Jeffrey J. Crow and Larry Tise, eds., *The Southern Experience in the American Revolution* (1978).

John Ferling, ed., *The World Turned Upside Down: The American Victory in the War of Independence* (1988).

M. Thomas Hatley, *The Dividing Paths: Cherokees and South Carolinians through the Era of Revolution* (1993).

W. Robert Higgins, ed., *The Revolutionary War in the South* (1979).

Ronald Hoffman, Thad W. Tate, and Peter J. Albert, eds., *An Uncivil War: The Southern Backcountry during the American Revolution* (1985).

Marjoleine Kars, *Breaking Loose Together: The Regulator Rebellion in Pre-Revolutionary North Carolina* (2002).

Henry Lumpkin, *From Savannah to Yorktown* (1981).

Jerome J. Nadelhaft, *The Disorders of War: The Revolution in South Carolina* (1981).

James H. O'Donnell III, *Southern Indians in the American Revolution* (1973).

John S. Pancake, *This Destructive War: The British Campaign in the Carolinas, 1780–1782* (1985).

Hugh Rankin, *The North Carolina Continentals* (1971).

John E. Selby, *The Revolution in Virginia, 1775–1783* (1988).

Timothy Silver, *A New Face on the Countryside: Indians, Colonists, and Slaves in South Atlantic Forests, 1500–1800* (1990).

Russell F. Weigley, *The Partisan War: The South Carolina Campaign of 1780–1782* (1970).

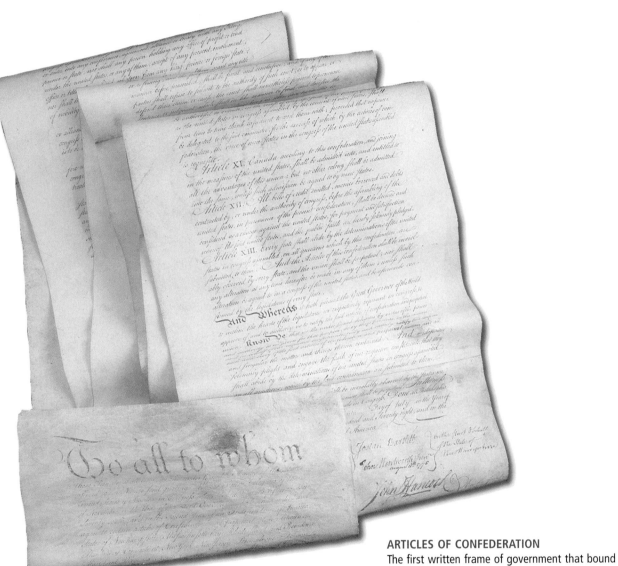

ARTICLES OF CONFEDERATION

The first written frame of government that bound together the thirteen rebelling colonies was called the Articles of Confederation. Delegates to the Second Continental Congress hammered out the plan over many months in 1776 and 1777, working on it when there was time free from the more pressing problems of pursuing the war. Once the congress agreed on it, the plan was printed and distributed to state legislatures for ratification, a process that took nearly five years because it required the assent of all thirteen. After ratification, in February 1781, this parchment copy became the official original version. As was often done with significant manuscript documents, a professional scribe wrote the opening words of the Articles in very large print, to proclaim the news. How does "To all to whom" compare with such famous opening words as "In Congress, July 4, 1776" (the start of the Declaration of Independence) and "We the people" (the start of the U.S. Constitution, which replaced the Articles in 1788)? Do you think "To all to whom" would have become a slogan or catchphrase had the Articles persisted as the country's sacred text? Why or why not?

National Archives.

Building a Republic
1775–1789

JAMES MADISON GRADUATED from Princeton College in New Jersey in 1771, not knowing what to do next with his life. Certainly the twenty-year-old had an easy fallback position. As the firstborn son of a wealthy plantation owner, he could return home to the foothills of Virginia and wait to inherit substantial land and a large force of slaves. But James was an intensely studious young man, uninterested in farming and reluctant to leave the collegiate environment. Five years at boarding school had given him fluency in Greek, Latin, French, and mathematics, and three years at Princeton acquainted him with the great thinkers, both ancient and modern. Driven by a thirst for learning, young Madison slept only five hours a night, perhaps undermining his health. Protesting that he was too ill to travel, he hung around Princeton six months after graduation.

In 1772, he returned home, still adrift. He tried studying law, but his unimpressive oratorical talents discouraged him. Political theory greatly attracted him, and he swapped reading lists and ideas about political theory by letter with a Princeton classmate, prolonging his student life. While Madison struggled for direction, the powerful winds before the storm of the American Revolution swirled through the colonies; the youth's drifting would abruptly end. In May 1774, Madison traveled north to deliver his brother to boarding school and was in Philadelphia when the startling news broke that Britain had closed the port of Boston in retaliation for the destruction of the tea. Turbulent protests over the Coercive Acts turned him into a committed revolutionary.

Back in Virginia, Madison joined his father on the newly formed committee of public safety. For a few days in early 1775, the twenty-four-year-old took up musket practice, but his continued poor health ruled out the soldier's life, and he quickly gave it up. His special contribution to the Revolution lay along a different path. In spring 1776, Madison was elected to the Virginia Convention, an extra-legal assembly replacing the defunct royal government. The convention's main task was to hammer out a state constitution featuring revolutionary goals such as frequent elections and a limited executive power. Shy, self-effacing, and still learning the ropes, Madison mostly stayed on the sidelines. Still, Virginia's elder statesmen noted the young man's logical, thoughtful contributions. When his county failed to return him to the assembly in the next election, he was appointed to the governor's council, where he spent two years gaining experience helping to manage a wartime government.

In early 1780, Madison represented Virginia in the Continental Congress. Not quite twenty-nine, unmarried, and supported by his father's money, Madison was free of the burdens that made distant political service difficult for so many others. He stayed in the North for three years, working with men such as Alexander Hamilton of New York and Robert Morris of Pennsylvania as the congress wrestled with the chaotic economy and the ever-precarious war effort. In one crisis Madison's negotiating skills proved crucial: He broke the deadlock over the ratification of the Articles of Confederation by arranging for the cession of Virginia's vast western lands. Those lands would soon appear on maps as the Northwest Territory, calling forth a series of western land ordinances planned out by Madison's friend Thomas Jefferson that were the shining example of promise and high hopes for the future of the new confederation government. But more often, service in the congress proved frustrating to Madison because the confederation government seemed to lack essential powers, chief among them the power to tax.

Madison resumed a seat in the Virginia state assembly in 1784. But he did not retreat to a local point of view, as so many other state politicians of the decade did. The difficult economic times and hardships created by heavy state taxation programs—which in Massachusetts led to a full-fledged rebellion against state government—spurred Madison to pursue means to strengthen the government of the thirteen new states. He worked hard to bring about an all-state convention in Philadelphia in the late spring of 1787, where he took the lead in steering the delegates to a complete rewrite of the structure of the na-tional government, investing it with considerably greater powers. True to form, Madison spent the months before the convention in fever-ish study of the great thinkers he had read in college, searching out the best way to constitute a government on **republican** principles. His life-long passion for scholarly study, seasoned by a dozen years of energetic political experience, paid off handsomely. The United States Constitution was the result.

By the end of the 1780s, James Madison had had his finger in every kind of political pie, on the local, state, confederation, and finally national level. He had transformed himself from a directionless and solitary youth into one of the leading political thinkers of the Revolutionary period. His personal history over the 1780s was deeply entwined with the path of the emerging United States.

The Articles of Confederation

For five years after declaring independence, the Second Continental Congress continued to meet in Philadelphia and other cities without any formal constitutional basis. Delegates first had to work out a plan of government that embodied Revolutionary principles. With monarchy gone, where would sovereignty lie? What would be the nature of representation? Who would hold the power of taxation? Who should vote; who

***James Madison*, by Charles Willson Peale**

A short and slight man, James Madison appeared younger than he was. This minia-ture portrait, made in 1783 when he was thirty-two, shows him with natural hair (no wig) and a boyishly smooth face. Madison commissioned the portrait on the occasion of his first serious romance. The Philadelphia artist Charles Willson Peale painted matching miniatures of Madison and his fiancée, Kitty Floyd, the six-teen-year-old daughter of a New York delegate in the Continental Congress. Madison and his Virginia friend Thomas Jefferson both boarded with the Floyd family while the congress met in Philadelphia. Jefferson, a very recent widower, encouraged the shy Madison and assured him that Kitty "will render you happier than you can possibly be in a single state." Madison's portrait was mounted in a brooch (note the pin sticking out on the right) so that his lady love might wear it on her person; the back of the brooch held a neatly plaited lock of Madison's hair. The companion miniature of Kitty no longer holds a lock of her hair, if it ever did, for Kitty soon jilted Madison for a suave younger man and returned the Madison miniature to the grieving bachelor. Eleven years later, Madison tried ro-mance again when New York congressman Aaron Burr introduced him to a Virginia widow named Dolley Payne Todd, seventeen years his junior. Madison was forty-three and Dolley was twenty-six; they married four months after meeting.
Library of Congress.

should rule? And exactly who were "the people" anyway? The resulting plan, called the Articles of Confederation, proved to be surprisingly difficult to implement, mainly because the thirteen states had serious disagreements about how to manage lands to the west whose political ownership was contested. Once the Articles were finally ratified and the confederation was formally constituted, that arena of government seemed to many to be far less relevant or interesting than the state governments.

Congress and Confederation

The Second Continental Congress assumed power in May 1775, when the British attack on Lexington and Concord required a unified colonial response (see chapter 7). Only as the delegates fashioned the Declaration of Independence a year later did they consider the need for a written document that would specify what powers the congress had and by what authority it existed. It finally fell to John Dickinson, the moderate conciliator from Pennsylvania, to chair the committee entrusted with the important task of drafting such a document.

Dickinson's draft of the Articles of Confederation reveals that the delegates, unified by their opposition to England, agreed on key government powers: pursuing war and peace, conducting foreign relations, regulating trade, and running a postal service. But there was serious disagreement about the powers of congress over the western boundaries of the states. Virginia and Connecticut, for example, had old colonial charters that located their western boundaries many hundreds of miles to the west. States without extensive land claims wanted to redraw those colonial boundaries. Dickinson's draft granted the congress final authority on this and many other matters.

For over a year, the congress tinkered with the Articles; its energies were far more consumed by the war. A final version of the document emerged only in November 1777, departing from the Dickinson draft in defining the Union as a loose confederation of states. Gone was the provision giving the congress control of state boundaries and western lands. Each state retained all powers and rights not expressly delegated to the congress, and the Union was characterized as "a firm league of friendship" existing mainly to foster a common defense. There was no national executive (that is, no president) and no national judiciary.

The structure of the government paralleled that of the existing Continental Congress. The congress was composed of two to seven delegates from each state, selected annually by the state legislatures and prohibited from serving more than three years out of any six. The actual number of delegates was not critical, since each state delegation cast a single vote.

> With monarchy gone, where would sovereignty lie? What would be the nature of representation? And exactly who were "the people" anyway?

Routine decisions in the congress required a simple majority of seven states; for momentous decisions, such as declaring war, nine states needed to agree. To approve or amend the Articles required the unanimous consent both of the thirteen state delegations and of the thirteen state legislatures. The congressional delegates undoubtedly thought they were guaranteeing that no individual state could be railroaded by the other twelve in fundamental constitutional matters. But what this requirement really did was to hamstring the government. One state could—and did—hold the rest of the country hostage to its demands.

On the delicate question of deriving revenue to run the government, specifically to finance the war, the Articles provided an ingenious but ultimately troublesome solution. Each state was to contribute in proportion to the property value of the state's land. Large and populous states would give more than small or sparsely populated states. The actual taxes would be levied by the state legislatures, not by the congress, to preserve the Revolution's principle of taxation only by direct representation. However, no mechanism was created to compel states to contribute their fair share.

The lack of centralized authority in the confederation government was exactly what many state leaders wanted in the late 1770s. A league of states with rotating personnel, no executive branch, no power of taxation, and a requirement of unanimity for any major change seemed to be a good way to avoid the potential tyranny of government. But right away, the inherent weaknesses of these features became apparent.

The Problem of Western Lands

Once approved by the congress in 1777, the Articles of Confederation had to be approved unanimously by the state legislatures. Newspapers published the plan, but there was

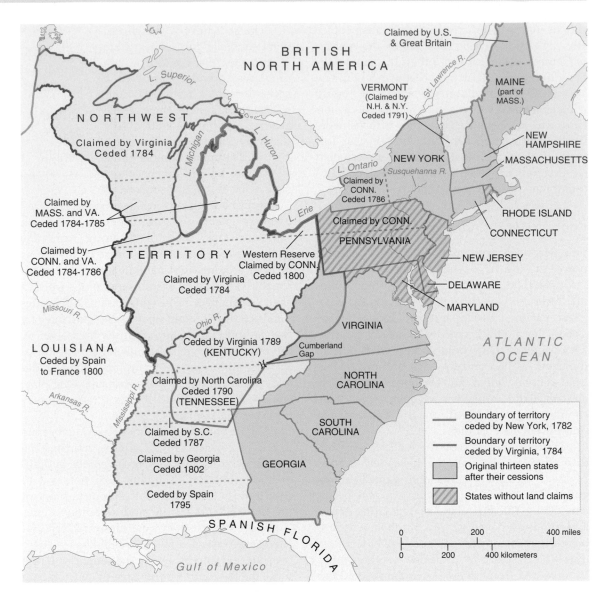

MAP 8.1   Cession of Western Lands, 1782–1802
The thirteen new states found it hard to ratify the Articles of Confederation without settling their conflicting land claims in the west, an area larger than the original states and occupied by Indian tribes. The five states objecting to the Articles' silence over western lands policy were Maryland, Delaware, New Jersey, Rhode Island, and Pennsylvania.

READING THE MAP: Which states had the largest claims on western territory? What disputed territory became the fourteenth state?
CONNECTIONS: In what context did the first dispute regarding western lands arise? How was it resolved? Does the map suggest a reason why Pennsylvania, a large state, joined the four much smaller states on this issue?

FOR MORE HELP ANALYZING THIS MAP, see the map activity for this chapter in the Online Study Guide at
bedfordstmartins.com/roark.

---

little public discussion because the war monopolized the news.

The approval process stalled for five years, principally due to sharply conflicting ideas about how to deal with lands west of the existing states and east of the Mississippi River. Five states, all lacking prior land claims—Maryland,

Delaware, New Jersey, Rhode Island, and Pennsylvania—insisted that the congress control those lands as a national domain that would eventually constitute new states. The other eight states refused to yield their colonial-era claims and opposed giving the congress power to alter boundaries (Map 8.1). In all the heated debate, few seemed to remember that those same western lands were inhabited by many thousands of Indians not party to the disputes.

The eight land-claiming states were ready to sign the Articles of Confederation in 1777. Rhode Island, Pennsylvania, and New Jersey eventually capitulated and signed, "not from a Conviction of the Equality and Justness of it," said a New Jersey delegate, "but merely from an absolute Necessity there was of complying to save the Continent." But Delaware and Maryland continued to hold out, insisting on a national domain policy. In 1779, the disputants finally compromised: Any land a state volunteered to relinquish would become the national domain. The logjam finally broke in 1781, when congressmen James Madison and Thomas Jefferson ceded all of Virginia's huge land claim, except the area that later became West Virginia. The compromise undercut Virginia's economic interests but made sense in terms of republican principles. Both Madison and Jefferson recognized that such a large area as Virginia claimed could not really be governed successfully because the seat of state government would be too far from its citizens to represent them adequately. With Virginia's concession, the Articles were at last unanimously approved.

The western lands issue demonstrated that powerful interests divided the thirteen new states. The apparent unity of purpose inspired by fighting the war against England papered over sizable cracks in the new confederation.

Running the New Government

No fanfare greeted the long-awaited inauguration of the new government. The congress continued to sputter along, its problems far from solved by the signing of the Articles. The lack of a quorum often hampered day-to-day activities. The Articles required representation from seven states to conduct business, and a minimum of two men from each state's delegation. But some days, fewer than fourteen men in total showed up. State legislatures were slow to select delegates, and many of those appointed were reluctant to attend, especially if they had wives and children at home. Absenteeism was a constant problem. Consequently, some of the most effective and committed delegates were young bachelors like James Madison and men in their fifties and sixties whose families were grown, like Samuel Adams. Other delegates came for very short terms, barely learning the business of the congress before they were on their way home.

Many active politicians preferred to devote their energies to their state governments, especially when the congress seemed deadlocked or, worse, irrelevant. It also did not help that the congress had no permanent home. During the war, when the British army threatened Philadelphia, the congress relocated to small Pennsylvania towns such as Lancaster and York and then to Baltimore. After hostilities ceased, the congress moved from Trenton to Princeton to Annapolis to New York City.

To address the difficulties of an inefficient congress, executive departments of war, finance, and foreign affairs were created to handle purely administrative functions. When the department heads were ambitious—as was Robert Morris, a wealthy Philadelphia merchant who served as superintendent of finance—they could exercise considerable executive power. The Articles of Confederation had deliberately refrained from setting up an executive branch, but a modest one was being invented by necessity.

Because of the pressing needs of running a war machine, the confederation government got a slow start on writing its plan of government, and then the difficulties over ownership of western lands slowed ratification for years. By the time the Articles were fully functioning, yet another problem emerged. Much more exciting political work was going on at the state level, especially during the creative burst of state constitution writing in the late 1770s. Before 1776, the cream of political talent in the country was attracted to the Continental Congress, but between 1776 and 1780 the talent flowed instead to the state governments.

> No fanfare greeted the long-awaited inauguration of the new government. The congress continued to sputter along, its problems far from solved by the signing of the Articles.

The Sovereign States

In the first decade of independence, the states were sovereign and all-powerful. Relatively few functions, like that of declaring war and peace, had been transferred to the confederation government. As Americans discarded their English identity, they thought of themselves instead as Virginians or New Yorkers or Rhode Islanders. Familiar and close to home, state government claimed the allegiance of citizens and became the arena in which the Revolution's innovations would first be tried. States defined who was a voter, and they also defined who would be free. The question of slavery quickly became a front-burner issue, as all the states were forced to grapple with squaring revolutionary ideals with lifelong bondage for African Americans. Northern states had more success with this than did the southern, where slavery was deeply entrenched in the economy.

The State Constitutions

In May 1776, the congress in Philadelphia recommended that all states draw up constitutions based on "the authority of the people." By 1778, ten had produced documents spelling out the **liberties,** rights, and obligations of citizens and rulers, and three more (Connecticut, Massachusetts, and Rhode Island) adopted and updated their original colonial charters. Americans felt they had been injured by the unwritten nature of British political traditions; liberties they had assumed were theirs had been denied them. They wanted a written contract whose basic principles could not be easily altered by the government in power at the moment. Having been denied unwritten British liberties, Americans wanted written contracts that guaranteed basic principles.

A shared feature of all the state constitutions was the conviction that government ultimately rests on the consent of the governed. Political writers in the late 1770s embraced the concept of republicanism as the underpinning of the new governments. Republicanism meant more than popular elections and representative institutions. For some, republicanism invoked a way of thinking about who leaders should be—autonomous, virtuous citizens who placed civic values above private interests. For others, it suggested direct **democracy,** with nothing standing in the way of the will of the people. For all, it meant government that promoted the people's welfare.

Widespread agreement about the virtues of republicanism went hand in hand with the idea that republics could succeed only in relatively small units. A government run for and by the people had to be near at hand, so the people could make sure their interests were being served. Distant governments could easily become tyrannical; that was the lesson of the 1760s.

It followed, then, that the best form of government was one that allowed maximum voice to the people. Nearly every state continued the colonial practice of a two-chamber assembly but greatly augmented the powers of the lower house. Two states, Pennsylvania and Georgia, did away with the upper house altogether, believing—as had Thomas Paine in *Common Sense*—that an upper house usually was an aristocratic and therefore undesirable check on the powers of the democratic lower house. Virtually all of the state constitutions severely limited the powers of the governor, identified in most people's minds with the royal governor of colonial days. Governors could no longer convene or dismiss legislatures at will, veto legislation, or buy loyalty through land grants or job patronage. Most states also restricted the governor's term to one year and limited eligibility for reelection. Pennsylvania and Georgia went so far as to abolish the office of governor.

Daily governance of each state rested with the lower house, whose most important decisions were economic: printing, borrowing, taxing, and spending money to finance each state's war effort. Most states made their lower houses very responsive to popular majorities, with annual elections and guaranteed rotation in office. If a representative displeased his constituents, he could be out of office in a matter of months. James Madison's second attempt to win election to the Virginia assembly offers an example. After only one year in office, the fledgling politician was defeated in 1777; he was sure he lost because he failed to campaign in the traditional style with the abundant liquor and glad-handing that his constituents had come to expect. Shy and retiring, Madison was not capable of electioneering in this manner. His series of increasingly significant political posts from 1778 to 1787 all came as a result of appointment, not popular election.

Six of the state constitutions included bills of rights, lists of basic individual liberties that governments could not abridge. Virginia debated and passed the first bill of rights in June 1776, and many of the other states borrowed from it. Its language also bears a close resemblance to the wording of the Declaration of Independence, which Thomas Jefferson was drafting that same June in Philadelphia: "That all men are by nature equally free and independent, and have certain inherent rights, of which, when they enter into a state of society, they cannot by any compact deprive or divest their posterity; namely, the enjoyment of life and liberty, with the means of acquiring and possessing property, and pursuing and obtaining happiness and safety." Along with these inherent rights went more specific rights to freedom of speech, freedom of the press, and trial by jury.

Who Are "the People"?

When the Continental Congress called for state constitutions based on "the authority of the people," and when the Virginia bill of rights granted "all men" certain rights, who was meant by "the people"? Who exactly were the citizens of this new country, and how far would the principle of democratic government extend? Different people answered these questions differently, but in the 1770s certain limits to full political participation by all Americans were widely agreed upon.

One limit was defined by property. The idea prevailed everywhere that the propertied classes were the only legitimate participants in government. In nearly every state, candidates for the highest offices—the governorship and membership in the upper house—needed to meet substantial property qualifications. In Maryland, for example, a candidate for governor had to be worth £5,000, quite a large sum of money. Voters in Maryland had to own fifty acres of land or £30, a sum that screened out perhaps one-third of adult white males. In the most democratic state, Pennsylvania, voters and candidates alike needed only to be taxpayers—that is, to own enough property to owe taxes.

The justification for restricting political participation to property owners was so widely accepted that it rarely needed to be explained. Only property owners were presumed to possess the necessary independence of mind to make wise political choices. Are not propertyless men, asked John Adams, "too little acquainted with public affairs to form a right judgment, and too dependent upon other men to have a will of their own?" Adams and others assumed that only property owners would feel a keen sense of community and thus be able to think clearly about the public interest. Besides, it did not seem right to give a propertyless man a voice in decisions to levy taxes if he was not going to be paying taxes himself.

Property qualifications probably disfranchised from one-quarter to one-half of adult white males in all the states. Not all of them took their nonvoter status quietly. One Maryland man wondered what was so special about being worth £30: "Every poor man has a life, a personal liberty, and a right to his earnings; and is in danger of being injured by government in a variety

of ways." Why then restrict such a man from voting for his representatives? Others pointed out that propertyless men were fighting and dying in the Revolutionary War; surely they were expressing an active concern about politics. A very few radical voices challenged the notion that owning property transformed men into good citizens. Perhaps it did the opposite: The richest men might well be greedy and selfish and therefore bad citizens. But ideas like this were clearly outside the mainstream. The writers of the new constitutions, themselves men of property, viewed the Revolution as an effort to guarantee people the right to own property and to prevent unjust governments from appropriating it through taxation.

Another exclusion from voting—women—was so ingrained that very few stopped to question it. Yet the logic of allowing propertied females to vote did occur to at least two well-placed women, who raised the issue with their male relatives. Abigail Adams wrote to John in 1782 that "Even in the freest countrys our property is subject to the controul and disposal of our partners, to whom the Laws have given a sovereign Authority. Deprived of a voice in Legislation, obliged to submit to those Laws which are imposed upon us, is it not sufficient to make us indifferent to the publick Welfare?" A wealthy Virginia widow named Hannah Corbin wrote to her brother, Richard Henry Lee, to complain of her taxation without the corresponding representation. Her letter no longer exists, but his reply does: "You complain that widows are not represented, and that being temporary possessors of the estates, ought not to be liable to the tax." Yet, he continued, women would be "out of character . . . to press into those tumultuous assemblies of men where the business of choosing representatives is conducted."

Only three states bothered to specify that voters had to be male, so powerful was the unspoken assumption that only men could vote. Still, in one state, small numbers of women began to turn out at the polls in the 1780s. New Jersey's constitution of 1776 enfranchised all free inhabitants worth over £50, language that in theory opened the door to free blacks as well as unmarried women who met the property requirement. (Married women owned no property, for by law their husbands held title to

> Who exactly were the citizens of this new country, and how far would the principle of democratic government extend? Different people answered these questions differently.

A Possible Voter in Essex County, New Jersey
Mrs. Elizabeth Alexander Stevens was married to John Stevens, a New Jersey delegate to the Continental Congress in 1783. Widowed in 1792, she would have then been eligible to vote in state elections according to New Jersey's unique enfranchisement of property-holding women. Mrs. Stevens's family was a prominent one. Her father had been surveyor general of New Jersey and New York; her husband was active in politics and was secretary to the governor of New York. Her son, John Stevens, was the inventor of steamboat and locomotive innovations; her daughter Mary married Robert R. Livingston of New York, also a delegate to the Continental Congress and a man who later built a fortune in steamboating. Essex County, where Elizabeth Stevens lived, was said to be the place where female suffrage was exercised most actively. This portrait, done around 1793–1794, represents the most likely face of that rare bird, the eighteenth-century female voter. The widow Stevens died in 1799, before suffrage was redefined to be the exclusive right of males.
New Jersey Historical Society.

everything; few free blacks would meet the property qualification.) Little fanfare accompanied this radical shift, and some historians have inferred that the inclusion of unmarried women and blacks was an accidental oversight. Yet other parts of the **suffrage** clause pertaining to residency and property were extensively debated when it was put in the state constitution, and no

objections were raised at that time to its gender- and race-free language. Thus other historians have concluded that the law was intentionally inclusive. In 1790, a revised election law used the words *he or she* in reference to voters, thus making woman suffrage explicit. As one New Jersey legislator declared, "Our Constitution gives this right to maids or widows *black or white*."

In 1790, only about 1,000 free black adults of both sexes lived in New Jersey, a state with a population of 184,000. The number of unmarried adult white women was probably also small, and most of them probably were widows. In view of the property requirement, the voter bloc enfranchised under this law could not have been decisive in elections. Still, this highly unusual situation lasted until 1807, when a new state law specifically disfranchised both blacks and women. Henceforth, independence of mind, that essential precondition of voting, was redefined to be sex- and race-specific.

In the 1780s, voting everywhere was class-specific. John Adams urged the framers of the Massachusetts constitution not even to discuss the scope of suffrage but simply to adopt the traditional colonial property qualifications. If suffrage is brought up for debate, he warned, "there will be no end of it. New claims will arise; women will demand a vote; lads from twelve to twenty-one will think their rights not enough attended to; and every man who has not a farthing, will demand an equal voice with any other." Adams was astute enough to anticipate complaints about excluding women, youth, and poor men from political life, but it did not even occur to him to worry about another group: slaves.

Equality and Slavery

Restrictions on political participation did not mean that propertyless people enjoyed no civil rights and liberties. The various state bills of rights applied to all individuals who had, as the Virginia bill so carefully phrased it, "enter[ed] into a state of society." No matter how poor, a free person was entitled to life, liberty, property, and freedom of conscience. Unfree people, however, were another matter. Their status was legally controlled by the states, and with thirteen of them, variation was possible.

The author of the Virginia bill of rights was George Mason, a plantation owner with 118 slaves. When he penned the sentence "all men are by nature equally free and independent," he did not have his slaves in mind; he meant that Americans were the equals of the British and could not be denied the liberties of British citizens. Other Virginia legislators, however, worried that the words could be construed to apply to slaves. These aristocratic slaveholders were finally put at ease by the addition of the phrase that rights belonged only to people who had entered civil society. As one wrote, with relief, "Slaves, not being constituent members of our society, could never pretend to any benefit from such a maxim."

One month later, the Declaration of Independence used essentially the same phrase about equality, this time without the modifying

Paul Cuffe's Silhouette

Captain Paul Cuffe of Martha's Vineyard, off the Massachusetts coast, was the son of a Wampanoag Indian woman and an African man who had purchased his own freedom from a Quaker owner. Cuffe studied navigation and went to sea at age sixteen during the American Revolution, enduring several months of imprisonment by the British. After the war, he and his brother petitioned for tax relief, a move that foreshadowed Cuffe's life of dedication to racial issues. In his thirty-year career as a shipbuilder and master mariner, Cuffe traveled extensively. By 1812, when this engraving with silhouette was made, Cuffe had explored the African country of Sierra Leone as a possible site for resettlement of American blacks and had met with African kings, English dukes, and an American president. Library of Congress.

clause about entering society. Two state constitutions, for Pennsylvania and Massachusetts, also included the inspiring language about equality, again without limiting it as in Virginia. In Massachusetts, where the state constitution was sent around to be ratified town by town, the town of Hardwick suggested that the sentence on equality be reworded to read "All men, whites and blacks, are born free and equal." The suggestion fell on deaf ears.

The only other state to draft language about equality was Vermont, whose 1777 constitution explicitly made slavery illegal and based its logic on the equality phrase. (Vermont had almost no slaves within its borders. Its statehood was not recognized until 1791 because New York and New Hampshire, each of which claimed the Vermont land as its own, had many friends in the Continental Congress.) Reluctance to include equality language in other state bills of rights and constitutions probably means that its radical implication for the institution of slavery was beginning to be recognized.

Yet inevitably, after 1776, the ideals of the Revolution about natural equality and liberty began to erode the institution of slavery. Sometimes enslaved blacks led the challenge. (See "Documenting the American Promise," page 258.) In 1777, several Massachusetts slaves petitioned the state legislature, claiming a "natural & unalienable right to that freedom which the great Parent of the Universe hath bestowed equally on all mankind." They modestly asked for freedom for their children at age twenty-one and were turned down. In 1779, similar petitions in Connecticut and New Hampshire met with no success. Seven Massachusetts freemen, including the mariner brothers Paul and John Cuffe, refused to pay taxes for three years on the grounds that they could not vote and so were not represented. The Cuffe brothers landed in jail in 1780 for tax evasion, but their petition to the state

> Reluctance to include equality language in state bills of rights and constitutions probably means that its radical implication for the institution of slavery was beginning to be recognized.

BRITISH NORTH AMERICA

MAINE (MASS.)

L. Ontario

VT. 1777

N.H. 1783

N.Y. 1799

MASS. 1783

CONN. 1784

R.I. 1784

PA. 1780

N.J. 1804

MD. 1790

DEL. 1787

ATLANTIC OCEAN

VA. 1782

N.C.

Abolished slavery

Gradual emancipation

Individual cases of emancipation

Legal Changes to Slavery, 1777–1804

Blacks Petition for Freedom and Rights

In the 1780s, a language of rights and liberty was in the air and on many lips. Extraordinary times encouraged extraordinary actions, and enslaved as well as newly freed African Americans everywhere felt emboldened to make bids to enlarge their own liberty. Brand-new state governments held out the potential for revolutionary change in legal and social relations, encouraging some blacks to take up their pens to petition for various freedoms. To be effective, petitions generally needed to beg or persuade rather than assert. Notice the kinds of argument made by these three sets of petitioners, the ways they describe themselves, and the promises they make about how they will use their hoped-for freedom.

DOCUMENT 1
Four Men Petition the Massachusetts Assembly for Their Freedom, 1773

Massachusetts law in the 1770s allowed even slaves to present petitions to the government. These four enslaved men arranged for a printing of their petition so they could send a separate copy to each town representative instead of submitting a single copy to the assembly. (The document was entirely set in type except the last word—Thompson—which was written in by hand.) Making a separate appeal to each representative was perhaps a way to maximize the impact of the petition.

Boston, April 20th, 1773
Sir, The efforts made by the legislative of this province in their last sessions to free themselves from slavery, gave us, who are in that deplorable state, a high degree of satisfaction. We expect great things from men who have made such a noble stand against the designs of their fellow-men to enslave them. We cannot but wish and hope Sir, that you will have the same grand object, we mean civil and religious liberty, in view in your next session. The divine spirit of freedom, seems to fire every humane breast on this continent, except such as are bribed to assist in executing the execrable plan.

We are very sensible that it would be highly detrimental to our present masters, if we were allowed to demand all that of right belongs to us for past services; this we disclaim. Even the Spaniards, who have not those sublime ideas of freedom that English men have, are conscious that they have no right to all the services of their fellow-men, we mean the Africans, whom they have purchased with their money; therefore they allow them one day in a week to work for themselves, to enable them to earn money to purchase the residue of their time, which they have a right to demand in such portions as they are able to pay for (a due appraizement of their services being first made, which always stands at the purchase money). We do not pretend to dictate to you Sir, or to the Honorable Assembly, of which you are a member. We acknowledge our obligations to you for what you have already done, but as the people of this province seem to be actuated by the principles of equity and justice, we cannot but expect your house will again take our deplorable case into serious consideration, and give us that ample relief which, as men, we have a natural right to.

But since the wise and righteous governor of the universe, has permitted our fellow men to make us slaves, we bow in submission to him, and determine to behave in such a manner as that we may have reason to expect the divine approbation of, and assistance in, our peaceable and lawful attempts to gain our freedom.

We are willing to submit to such regulations and laws, as may be made relative to us, until we leave the province, which we determine to do as soon as we can, from our joynt labours procure money to transport ourselves to some part of the Coast of Africa, where we propose a settlement. We are very desirous that you should have instructions relative to us, from your town, therefore we pray you to communicate this letter to them, and ask this favor for us.

In behalf of our fellow slaves in this province, and by order of their Committee.

Peter Bestes,
Sambo Freeman,
Felix Holbrook,
Chester Joie.
For the Representative of the town of Thompson.

SOURCE: Herbert Aptheker, ed., *A Documentary History of the Negro People in the United States* (New York: Citadel Press, 1968), 1:7–8. Copyright © by Citadel Press. Reprinted with permission.

DOCUMENT 2
Paul and John Cuffe Protest Taxation in Massachusetts, 1780

After judicial emancipation in Massachusetts, Paul and John Cuffe, together with five other freed men from the town of Dartmouth, sent this petition to the Massachusetts legislature.

To the Honouerable Councel and House of Representatives in General Court assembled for the State of the Massachusetts Bay in New England—March 14th AD 1780—

The petition of several poor Negroes & molattoes who are Inhabitant of the Town of Dartmouth Humbly Sheweth—That we being Chiefly of the African Extract and by Reason of Long Bondag and hard Slavery we have been deprived of Injoying the Profits of our Labouer or the advantage of Inheriting Estates from our Parents as our Neighbouers the white peopel do haveing some of us not long Injoyed our own freedom & yet of late, Contrary to the invariable Custom & Practice of the Country we have been & now are Taxed both in our Polls and that small Pittance of Estate which through much hard Labour & Industry we have got together to Sustain our selves & families withal—We apprehand it therefore to be hard usag and will doubtless if Continued will Reduce us to a State of Beggary whereby we shall become a Berthan to others if not timely prevented by the Interposition of your Justice & power & yor Petitioners farther sheweth that we apprehand ourselves to be Aggreeved, in that while we are not allowed the Privilage of freemen of the State having no vote or Influence in the Election of those that Tax us yet many of our Colour (as is well known) have cheerfully Entered the field of Battle in the defence of the Common Cause and that (as we conceive) against a similar Exertion of Power (in Regard to taxation) too well Known to need a recital in this place—

That these the Most honouerable Court we Humbley Beseech they would take this into Considerration and Let us aside from Paying tax or taxes or cause us to Be Cleaired for we ever have Been a people that was fair from all these thing ever since the days of our four fathers and therefore we take it as aheard ship that we should be so delt By now in these Difficulty times for there is not to exceed more then five or six that hath a cow in this town and theirfore in our Distress we send unto the peaceableness of thee people and the mercy of God that we may be Releaved for we are not alowed in voating in the town meating in nur to chuse an oficer Neither their was not one ever heard in the active Court of the General Asembly the poor Dispised miserable Black people, & we have not an equal chance with white people neither by Sear nur by Land therefore we take it as a heard ship that poor old Negroes should be Rated which have been in Bondage some thirty some forty and some fifty years and now just got their Liberty some by going into the serviese and some by going to Sea and others by good fortan and also poor Distressed mungrels which have no larning and no land. . . . Neither where to put their head but some shelter them selves into an old rotten hut which thy dogs would not lay in.

Therefore we pray that these may give no offence at all By no means But that thee most Honouerable Court will take it in to consideration as if it were their own case for we think it as to be a heard ship that we should be assessed and not be a lowed as we may say to Eat Bread therefore we Humbley Beg and pray thee to plead our Case for us with thy people O God; that those who have the rule in their hands

may be mercyfull unto the poor and needy give unto those who ask of thee and he that would Borrow of thee turn not away empty. . . . Neither with lieing Lips therefore we think that we may be clear from being called tories tho some few of our Colour hath Rebelled and Done Wickedly however we think that there is more of our Collour gone into the wars according to the Number of them into the Respepiktive towns then any other nation here. . . . We most humbley Request therefore that you would take our unhappy Case into your serious Consideration and in your wisdom and Power grant us Relief from Taxation while under our Present depressed Circumstances and your poor Petioners as in duty bound shall ever pray &c.

SOURCE: Herbert Aptheker, ed., *A Documentary History of the Negro People in the United States* (New York: Citadel Press, 1968), 1:15–16. Copyright © 1968 by Citadel Press. Reprinted with permission.

DOCUMENT 3
The Connecticut Assembly Answers a Petition from a Husband and Wife, 1789

Fifteen years after their loyalist owner fled the country, this black couple petitioned the state assembly to clarify their legal status. After a hearing, the assembly reviewed the evidence and granted them and their children freedom.

Upon the Petition of Cesar a Negro and Lowis his Wife both of Hebron in the County of Tolland Shewing to this Assembly that by the Laws of this State they were Slaves to the Revd Samuel Peters lateof said Hebron but now of the City of

(continued)

(continued)

London in Great Britain who left Said Hebron in Septembr 1774 and hath ever since remained in the Kingdom of Great Britain, and that the Petitioners have during the absence of the said Peters been at Liberty to provide for themselves, and that the Petitioners now have eight Children, which they have by their Industry maintained in a decent Manner, and the Petitioners in April 1784, wrote to the said Peters then at London requesting that he would give to the Petitioners and their Children their Freedom. And that the said Peters in answer to the request of the Petitioners on the 26th Day of July 1784 Wrote a Letter to the Petitioners declaring his willingness to grant the request of the Petitioners if it was in his Power, but supposed that the Petitioners were Claimed by the State of Connecticut as forfeited by the said Peters to said State, and that some Persons have lately been endeavouring to sell the Petitioners and their Children out of this State, and that the Petitioners are in continual fear of being secretly taken with their Children and sold out of this State to some foreign Country. Praying that they and their said eight Children may be emancipated and declared free from the said Peters as per Petition on File, And upon the Tryal of said Cause and a full hearing of the said Petition and the Evidence produced to support the same, it appears that the said Peters by his Letter dated at London the 26th Day of July 1784, to the Petitioners in answer to their request that he has in said Letter declared that he is willing to emancipate the Petitioners and their Children, and that he would do all in his Power to effect the same.

Whereupon it is Resolved by this Assembly that the Petitioners and their said eight Children be and they are hereby emancipated and declared free from the said Peters and all others from by or under his former Claim to the Petitioners and their said eight Children as Slaves.

SOURCE: Herbert Aptheker, ed., *A Documentary History of the Negro People in the United States* (New York: Citadel Press, 1968), 1:21–22. Copyright © 1968 by Citadel Press. Reprinted with permission.

QUESTIONS FOR ANALYSIS AND DEBATE

1. What do the four Massachusetts petitioners mean when they congratulate the state legislators for their recent efforts "to free themselves from slavery"? Are they contradictory when they claim a natural right "as men" to relief from slavery but then also "bow in submission" to the "governor of the universe" who has allowed their slavery? What is it they "disclaim" out of consideration to their present masters? Why do they raise the case of a Spanish version of slavery?

2. Is the Cuffe petition essentially a call for "no taxation without representation"? Does it differ from the revolutionaries' stand on taxation in relation to Britain? Do the petitioners want representation—or relief from taxation? Why do they mention their military service?

3. Why do you think the Connecticut couple waited until 1784 to contact their former owner, who had left in 1774? Who might be scaring the family with threats to sell them out of state? What is the basis of their petition to the state government? On what grounds were they finally freed? How might you account for the assembly's additional five-year delay to arrive at this decision in 1789?

4. What can you conclude about the options available to northern blacks to secure freedom or rights under law? Are the petitioners confident about their rights, or about the outcome they expect? How have they had to shape their petitions to appeal to an all-white legislature? Do you see instances of subtle irony or sarcasm employed?

legislature spurred the extension of suffrage to taxpaying free blacks in that state.

Another way to bring the issue before lawmakers was to sue in court. In 1781, a Massachusetts slave named Quok Walker charged his master with assault and battery, arguing that he was a free man under the state constitution's assertion that "all men are born free and equal." Walker won and was set free, a decision confirmed in an appeal to the state's superior court in 1783. Several similar cases followed, and by 1789 slavery had been effectively abolished by judicial decision in Massachusetts.

In other northern states, untold numbers of blacks simply ran away from owners and claimed their freedom, sometimes with the help of sympathetic whites. One estimate holds that more than half of young slave men in Philadelphia took flight in the 1780s and joined the ranks of free blacks. By 1790, free blacks outnumbered slaves in Pennsylvania by nearly a factor of two.

Pennsylvania was the first state to legislate an end to slavery by statute, in 1780. Yet the law provided for very gradual **emancipation:** Only infants born to a slave mother on or after March 1, 1780, would be freed, but not until age twenty-eight. That meant that no current slave in Pennsylvania would gain freedom until 1808, and that well into the nineteenth century some blacks—those born before 1780—would still be slaves. (Not until 1847 did Pennsylvania fully abolish slavery.) Rhode Island and Connecticut adopted gradual emancipation laws in 1784. In 1785, New York expanded the terms under which individual owners could free slaves, but only in 1799 did the state adopt a gradual emancipation law; New Jersey followed suit in 1804. These were the two northern states with the largest number of slaves: New York in 1800 with 20,000 and New Jersey, more than 12,000. In contrast, Pennsylvania had just 1,700. Gradual emancipation illustrates the tension between radical and conservative implications of republican ideology. Republican government protected people's liberties and property, yet slaves were both people and property. Gradual emancipation balanced the civil rights of blacks and the property rights of their owners by delaying the promise of freedom.

South of Pennsylvania, in Delaware, Maryland, and Virginia, where slavery was so important to the economy, general emancipation bills were rejected. All three states, however, eased legal restrictions and allowed individual acts of emancipation for adult slaves below the age of forty-five, under new manumission laws passed in 1782 (Virginia), 1787 (Delaware), and 1790 (Maryland). By 1790, close to 10,000 newly freed Virginia slaves had formed local free black communities complete with schools and churches.

In the deep South—the Carolinas and Georgia—freedom for slaves was unthinkable for whites. Yet more than 10,000 slaves from South Carolina achieved freedom in 1783 by leaving with the British army from Charleston, and another 6,000 set sail under the British flag from Savannah, Georgia. This was by far the largest emancipation of blacks in the entire country. Some went to Canada, some to England, and a small number to Sierra Leone, on the west coast of Africa. In addition, many hundreds of ex-slaves took refuge with Seminole and Creek Indians, becoming permanent members of their communities in Spanish Florida and western Georgia.

Black Loyalists in Canada
This rare sketch from 1788 shows an ordinary day laborer: a black woodcutter who came to Nova Scotia in the migration of black loyalists. Over 3,000 black refugees from the American Revolution arrived in northeastern Canada between 1783 and 1785. Very few were able to acquire land, and after 1786 the British authorities stopped provisioning them. Most, like the man pictured here, were forced to become servants or day laborers for whites. Low wages created dissatisfaction, and racial tensions broke loose in a riot. In 1791–1792, nearly a third of the black refugees in Nova Scotia left for Sierra Leone in west Africa, where British officials promised them land ownership and opportunities for self rule. In 1798, a refugee from South Carolina named Boston King published a memoir of his experiences joining the British during the Revolution, living in Nova Scotia, and traveling on to Sierra Leone; his rich account is one of the few existing personal narratives of black loyalism.
William Booth, National Archives of Canada C-401621.

Although emancipation affected fewer blacks in the North than in the South, simply because there were far fewer of them there to begin with, its symbolic importance was enormous. Every state from Pennsylvania northward acknowledged that slavery was fundamentally inconsistent with revolutionary ideology; "all men are created equal" was beginning to acquire real force as a basic principle. On some level, southerners also understood this, but their inability to imagine a free biracial society prevented them from taking much action. George Washington owned 390 slaves and freed not one of them in the 1780s, even when his friend the French general Lafayette urged him to do so as a model for others. In his will, written in 1799, the now guilt-stricken Washington provided for the eventual freedom of his slaves—but only after his wife, Martha, died. (One year after his death, Martha Washington freed them all, preferring loss of income to the uneasy situation of her life being her slaves' only barrier to freedom.) From the 1780s on, the North was associated with freedom and the South with slavery. This geographical pattern would have profound consequences for the next two centuries of American history.

The Critical Period

From 1781 to 1786, a sense of crisis gripped some of the revolutionary leaders who feared the Articles of Confederation were too weak. But others defended the Articles as the best guarantee of individual liberty, because real governance occurred at the state level, closer to the people. Political theorizing about the proper relation among citizen, state, and confederation remained active and controversial throughout the decade as Americans confronted questions of finance, territorial expansion, and civil disorder.

Financial Chaos and Paper Money

Seven years of war produced a chaotic economy in the 1780s. The confederation and the individual states had run up huge war debts, financed by printing paper money and borrowing from private sources.

Some $400 to $500 million in paper currency had been injected into the economy, and prices and wages fluctuated wildly. Private debt and rapid expenditure flourished, as people quickly bought what goods they could with the depreciating currency. Newspapers bemoaned the rampant spending on imported items—hats, silks, china, tea—indulged in even by ordinary people. In many localities, legal suits between debtors and creditors quadrupled over prewar levels. A laborer in central Massachusetts, William Manning, described the economic trouble brewing: "With the prices of labor and produce falling very fast, creditors began calling for old debts and saying that they would not take payment in paper money. . . . Property was selling almost every day by execution [court-ordered foreclosures] for less than half its value. The jails were crowded with debtors." A serious postwar depression settled in by the mid-1780s and did not lift until the 1790s.

The confederation government itself was in a terrible financial fix. Continental dollars had lost almost all value: It took 146 of them to buy what one dollar had bought in 1775. Desperate times required desperate measures. The congress turned to Robert Morris, a merchant and newly reelected delegate from Pennsylvania, appointing him superintendent of finance. Six years earlier, the wealthy Morris had procured from Europe much-needed muskets for the army, which were shipped to his private firm in crates disguised as routine merchandise. Morris had resigned from the congress in 1778 under suspicion that he had unfairly profited from his public service efforts; indeed, he had left public life many thousands of dollars richer than he had entered it. Nevertheless, the congress called on him from 1781 to 1784 to apply his considerable talent to the confederation's economic problems.

To augment the government's revenue, Morris first proposed a 5 percent import tax (called an impost). Since there was no authority in the Articles of Confederation for such a tax, Morris's plan required an amendment to the Articles approved unanimously by the thirteen states. But unanimous agreement was impossible. States with bustling ports already collected taxes on imports and were loath to share that income. Rhode Island, with its active wharves at Newport and Providence, absolutely refused. When Morris pushed the impost amendment again late in 1783, it was New York (whose premier port had just been freed from British occupation) that refused.

Morris's next idea was the creation of the Bank of North America. This private bank, located in Philadelphia, would enjoy a special relationship with the confederation, holding the government's **hard money** (insofar as there was any) as well as private deposits, and providing the government with short-term loans. The bank's contribution to economic stability came in the form of banknotes, pieces of paper inscribed with a dollar value. Unlike the Continental dollars of the early war days, these banknotes were backed by hard money in the bank's vaults and thus would not depreciate. Morris hoped this form of money would retain value; Congress agreed and voted to approve the bank in 1781.

But the bank had limited success curing the confederation's economic woes. In the short run, the bank supplied the government with currency that held its value, but it issued so little that the impact was very small. The bank mainly en-

Philadelphia Almshouse

The city almshouse occupied a block on Spruce Street between Tenth and Eleventh Streets in Philadelphia. Built in 1767 to provide greater capacity than the prior almshouse, it was run by a city board called the Guardians of the Poor and financed by a city poor tax. It offered temporary housing and care for indigents unable to support themselves, many of whom were children, unwed mothers, or mentally disturbed people. A neighboring building named the House of Employment sheltered able-bodied poor who were forced to work in exchange for food and shelter.

Rare Book Department, The Free Library of Philadelphia.

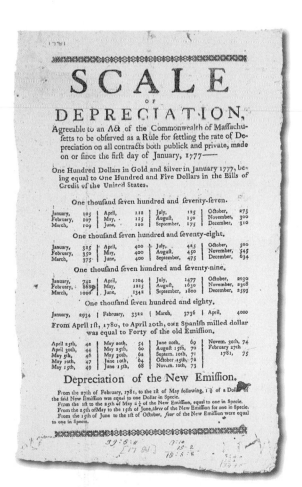

riched Morris and three close associates, who owned a large part of the bank's stock.

If Morris could not resuscitate the economy in the 1780s, probably no one could have done it. Because the Articles of Confederation reserved most economic functions to the states, the congress was helpless to tax trade, control inflation, curb the flow of state-issued paper money, or pay the mounting public debt. But the confederation had acquired one source of enormous potential wealth: the huge territory ceded by

Scale of Depreciation

This chart shows the monthly value of U.S. Continental dollars from January 1777 to February 1781, as stipulated by the government of Massachusetts. For example, in March 1780, 3,736 Continental dollars equaled the buying power of $100 in gold or silver based on values of the dollar in January 1777. By April 1780, the same value of hard money required $4,000 Continentals. Such a chart was needed when debtors and creditors settled accounts contracted at one time and paid off later in greatly depreciated dollars. How easy would you find it to keep your head above water in an economy with such fast currency depreciation? What level of arithmetic and chart-reading skills were required? Notice the handwritten figuring at the bottom of the chart. Do these arithmetic operations look familiar to you?

Courtesy, American Antiquarian Society.

Virginia, which in 1784 became the national domain. With American settlers resuming their westward pressure at the end of the Revolutionary War, there was need to plan for the orderly sale and distribution of that land.

Land Ordinances and the Northwest Territory

Jefferson's aim was to encourage rapid and democratic settlement, to build a nation of freeholders, and to avoid speculative frenzy.

The Continental Congress appointed Thomas Jefferson to draft a national domain policy. Jefferson proposed dividing the territory north of the Ohio River and east of the Mississippi—called the Northwest Territory—into ten new states, each divided into townships ten miles square. He at first advocated giving the land to settlers, rather than selling it, on the grounds that the improved lands would so enrich the country through future property taxes that there was no need to make the settlers pay twice. Jefferson's aim was to encourage rapid and democratic settlement of the land, to build a nation of freeholders (as opposed to renters), and to avoid speculative frenzy. Jefferson also insisted that the new states have representative governments equal in status to those of the original states once they reached a certain population. Most boldly of all, Jefferson's draft prohibited slavery in the ten new states.

The congress adopted parts of Jefferson's plan in the Ordinance of 1784: the rectangular grid, the ten states, and the guarantee of self-government and eventual statehood. What the congress found too radical was the proposal to give away the land; the national domain was the confederation's only source of independent wealth. The slavery prohibition also failed, by a vote of seven to six states.

A year later, the congress refined and revised the legislation to set up procedures for surveying, mapping, and selling the land. The Ordinance of 1785 called for a rectilinear survey of the national domain (Map 8.2). On paper, the plan seemed to guarantee precision: There were to be walkable townships six miles square, each containing thirty-six perfect one-mile-square sections. Each section was to contain 640 acres, enough for four family farms, and one lot in each township was to be set aside for educational purposes. The 1785 ordinance reduced Jefferson's plan for ten rectangular states down to a less specific three to five states with boundaries conforming to natural geographic features such as the Great Lakes and major rivers instead of to abstractly drawn survey lines. But within the future states, the unrelentingly rectilinear survey lines ran straight over hills and mountains and through rivers and lakes, reducing all property to mappable squares.

***Thomas Jefferson,* by John Trumbull**

This miniature shows Thomas Jefferson at age forty-five, during his years as a diplomat in Paris. The American artist John Trumbull visited France in 1788 and painted Jefferson's likeness in this five-by-four-inch format so he could later copy it into his planned large canvas depicting the signing of the Declaration of Independence. Jefferson requested three replicas of the miniature to bestow as gifts. One went to his daughter Martha, another to an American woman in London, and the third to Maria Cosway, a British artist with whom Jefferson shared an intense infatuation during his stay in France. A widower, Jefferson never remarried, but a scandal over his private life erupted in 1802, when a journalist charged that he had fathered several children by his slave Sally Hemings. In 1998, a careful DNA study concluded that uniquely marked Jefferson Y-chromosomes were common to male descendants in both the Hemings and Jefferson lines. The DNA evidence, when combined with historical evidence about Jefferson's whereabouts at the start of each of Hemings's six pregnancies, makes it extremely likely that Jefferson fathered some or perhaps all of her children. What cannot be known is the nature of the relationship between the two. Was it coerced or voluntary, or somewhere in between? In all his voluminous writings, Jefferson left no comment about Sally Hemings, and the record on her side is entirely mute.

Monticello/Thomas Jefferson Memorial Foundation, Inc.

Jefferson's Map of the Northwest Territory
Thomas Jefferson sketched out borders for ten new states in his initial plan for the Northwest Territory in 1784. Straight lines and right angles held a strong appeal for him. But such regularity ignored inconvenient geographic features such as rivers and even more inconvenient political features such as Indian territorial claims, most unlikely to be ceded by treaty in orderly blocks. Jefferson also submitted ten distinctive names for the states. Number 9, for example, was Polypotamia, "land of many rivers" in Greek.
William L. Clements Library.

FOR MORE HELP ANALYZING THIS IMAGE, see the visual activity for this chapter in the Online Study Guide at **bedfordstmartins.com/roark**.

The 1785 ordinance decreed that land sales would occur by public auction. The minimum price was set at one dollar an acre, but market forces could drive up the prices of the most desirable land. Two further restrictions applied: Land was to be sold in minimum parcels of 640 acres each, and payment had to be in hard money or in certificates of debt from Revolutionary days. This effectively meant that the land's first owners would be prosperous speculators, men who had the large sum of $640 on hand or who had bought up quantities of certificates of debt at bargain prices. The grid of invariant squares further enhanced speculation, because owners could buy and sell exactly mapped parcels of land without ever setting foot on the acreage. The commodification of land had been taken to a new level.

Speculators usually held the land for resale rather than inhabiting it. Thus they avoided direct contact with the most serious obstacle to settlement: the dozens of Indian tribes that claimed the land as their own. Treaties signed at Fort Stanwix in 1784 and Fort McIntosh in 1785 coerced partial cessions of land from Iroquois, Delaware, Huron, and Miami tribes. Then in 1786, a united Indian meeting near Detroit issued an ultimatum: No cession would be valid without unanimous consent. The Indians advised the United States to "prevent your surveyors and other people from coming upon our side

MAP 8.2 The Northwest Territory and Ordinance of 1785
Surveyors mapping the eastern edge of the Northwest Territory followed the Ordinance of 1785, using the stars as well as poles and chains (standard surveying equipment) to run long boundary lines. The result was a blanket of six-mile-square townships, subdivided into one-mile squares each containing sixteen 40-acre farms.

of the Ohio river." For two more decades, violent Indian wars in Ohio and Indiana would continue to impede white settlement (see chapter 9).

In 1787, a third land act, called the Northwest Ordinance, went well beyond the first two to specify the exact mechanism by which settled territories would advance to statehood, "on an equal footing with original states." Three stages of development were identified. First, a sparsely settled territory would be gov-

erned by officials appointed by the congress, and they in turn could adopt a legal code and appoint local magistrates as needed to administer justice. When the white male population of voting age and landowning status (fifty acres) reached 5,000, the territory could elect its own legislature and send a nonvoting delegate to the congress. When the population of voting citizens reached 60,000, they could write a state constitution and apply for full admission to the Union.

At all three territorial stages, the inhabitants were subject to taxation to support the Union, in the same manner as were the original states.

The Northwest Ordinance of 1787 was one of the most important pieces of legislation passed by the confederation government. It ensured that the new United States, so recently released from colonial dependency, would not itself become a colonial power—at least not with respect to white citizens. The mechanism it established allowed for the successful and orderly expansion of the United States across the continent in the next century.

Nonwhites were not forgotten or neglected in the 1787 ordinance. The brief document acknowledged the Indian presence in the Northwest Territory and promised that "the utmost good faith shall always be observed towards the Indians; their lands and property shall never be taken from them without their consent; and, in their property, rights, and liberty, they shall never be invaded or disturbed, unless in just and lawful wars authorized by Congress." The 1787 ordinance further pledged that "laws founded in justice and humanity, shall from time to time be made for preventing wrongs being

A Survey Plat of William Few's Land in Georgia

An anonymous artist illustrates the traditional metes-and-bounds surveying technique in this charming land plat (or map) drawn in 1784, in which chains and compasses measured out the boundaries of property. These 887 acres along a river bottom in Georgia were owned by the wealthy William Few. Two surveyors pictured at the upper right measure out land with chains of standard length; compass readings (such as N30 W50) indicate the direction of the lines being measured from one fixed point to the next. Note that the fixed points are not actually permanent; they are poplar, oak, hickory, and maple trees. In the metes-and-bounds technique, large stones might also serve that function. In contrast, Jefferson's 1785 plan to map out the Northwest Territory in perfect squares represented a revolutionary approach to land measurement. His rectilinear system called for surveying by the stars to run long baseline or meridian lines over hundreds of miles; subdivisions of land, defined by straight lines and right angles, could then be drawn on maps with a ruler and protractor, irrespective of rivers, trees, rocks, or steep hillsides. William Few of Georgia could buy a rich river bottom with the metes-and-bounds system of property division; Jefferson's plan aimed to democratize and simplify land measurement, which meant that valuable geographic features might well be divided.

Georgia Division of Archives and History, Office of Secretary of State.

done to them, and for preserving peace and friendship with them." These promises were full of noble intentions, but they were not generally honored in the decades to come.

Jefferson's original suggestion to prohibit slavery in the Northwest Territories resurfaced in the 1787 ordinance, and it passed this time without debate. But the document acknowledged and supported slavery's existence in the South, in the assurance that fugitive southern slaves caught north of the Ohio River would be returned to their owners. Southerners could thus vote for the prohibition on slavery, secure in the knowledge that it applied only north of the Ohio; plenty of territory south of the river and west of Georgia and the Carolinas was still available for the spread of slavery. Still, the prohibition of slavery in the Northwest Territory perpetuated the dynamic of gradual emancipation in the North: A North-South sectionalism, based on slavery, was slowly taking shape.

Shays's Rebellion, 1786–1787

Without an impost amendment, and with the land sales of the Northwest Territory projected but not yet realized, the confederation turned to the states in the 1780s to contribute revenue voluntarily. Struggling with their own war debts, most state legislatures were reluctant to tax their constituents too heavily. Massachusetts, however, had a tough-minded, fiscally conservative legislature, dominated by the coastal commercial centers, which wanted to retire the state debt by raising taxes. Worse yet, it insisted that taxes be paid in hard money, not cheap paper. For four years, the state legislature exacted property and poll (or head) taxes; farmers in the western two-thirds of the state found it increasingly difficult to comply.

Western farmers had learned from the American Revolution how to resist oppressive taxation.

Western farmers had learned from the American Revolution how to resist oppressive taxation. From 1782, they sent petitions to the state legislature, voicing their grievances. In July 1786, when the legislature adjourned yet again without addressing the farmers' complaints, a series of conventions was quickly organized. At one such convention, representing fifty towns, dissidents called for revisions to the state constitution that would promote democracy, eliminate the elite upper house, and move the capital farther west in the state.

Still not being heard in Boston, the dissidents targeted the most visible symbol of state authority in their regions, the county courts. In the fall of 1786, armed men numbering two or three thousand marched on courthouses in six Massachusetts counties and closed them down. Bewildered judges were forced to sign agreements not to hold court until the state constitution was revised or replaced. Sympathetic local militias did little or nothing to stop these activities. The insurgents were not predominantly poor or debt-ridden farmers; they included veteran soldiers and officers in the Continental army as well as leaders of their towns, men who thought the state government had fallen into the hands of a tyrannical few and ceased to be responsive to the interests of the many. One of several leaders was a farmer and one-time captain in the army, Daniel Shays, from the town of Pelham.

The governor of Massachusetts, James Bowdoin, who had once organized protests against British taxes, now characterized the western dissidents as illegal rebels. He villified Shays as the chief leader, and a Boston newspaper claimed Shays planned to burn Boston to the ground and overthrow the government, clearly an overreaction. Another former radical, Samuel Adams, took the extreme position that "the man who dares rebel against the laws of a republic ought to suffer death." These aging revolutionaries had given little thought to the possibility that popular majorities, embodied in a state legislature, could seem to be just as oppressive as monarchs. The dissidents challenged the assumption that popularly elected governments would always be fair and just.

Members of the Continental Congress grew worried that the situation in Massachusetts was spinning out of control. In October, the congress issued plans to triple the size of the federal army, calling for 660 new recruits from Massachusetts and another 560 from New England; but fewer than 100 enlisted in the troubled state. So Governor Bowdoin raised a private army, gaining the services of some 3,000 by paying them bounties provided by donations from a small wealthy circle of Boston merchants (who were later repaid by the state).

In January 1787, the insurgents learned of the private army marching their way, and 1,500 of them moved swiftly to capture a federal armory in Springfield to gain weapons. But a militia band loyal to the state government beat them to the weapons facility and met their attack with gunfire; four rebels were killed and another

Silver Bowl for an Anti-Shays General
Members of the militia of Springfield in western Massachusetts presented their leader, General William Shepard, with this silver bowl to honor his victory over the insurgents in Shays's Rebellion. Presentational silver conveyed a double message. It announced gratitude and praise in engraved words, and it transmitted considerable monetary value in the silver itself. General Shepard could display his trophy on a shelf, use it as a punch bowl, will it to descendants to keep his famous moment alive in memory, or melt it down in hard times. Shepard's is not the only name commemorated on the bowl; Shays's name appears in the last line, there for the ages to remember.
Yale University Art Gallery, Mabel Brady Garvan Collection.

tion's ability to handle civil disorder. Massachusetts newspapers made it seem that bloody mob rule had nearly succeeded; perhaps, some feared, similar "combustibles" in other states were awaiting the spark that would set off a dreadful political conflagration. New York lawyer and diplomat John Jay wrote to George Washington, "Our affairs seem to lead to some crisis, some revolution—something I cannot foresee or conjecture. I am uneasy and apprehensive; more so than during the war." Benjamin Franklin, in his eighties, shrewdly observed that in 1776 Americans had feared "an excess of power in the rulers," but now the problem was "a defect of obedience" in the subjects. Among such leaders, the sense of crisis in the confederation had greatly deepened.

The United States Constitution

Shays's Rebellion provoked an odd mixture of fear and hope that the government under the Articles of Confederation was losing its grip on power. A small circle of Virginians decided to try one last time to augment the powers granted to the government by the Articles. Their call for a meeting to discuss trade regulation led, more quickly than they could have imagined in 1786, to a total reworking of the national government.

twenty wounded. The final and bloodless encounter came at Petersham, where Bowdoin's army surprised the rebels on a freezing February morning and took 150 prisoners; the others fled into the woods. Shays took off for Canada and other leaders left the state, but more than 1,000 dissidents were rounded up and jailed.

In the end, only two men were executed for rebellion; sixteen more were sentenced to hang but were reprieved, sometimes at the last moment on the gallows. Some 4,000 men gained leniency by confessing their misconduct and swearing an oath of allegiance to the state. A special Disqualification Act prohibited the penitent rebels from voting, holding public office, serving on juries, working as schoolmasters, or operating taverns for up to three years, a period shortened to a year for those demonstrating good behavior.

Shays's Rebellion caused leaders throughout the country to worry about the confedera-

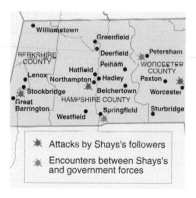

Shays's Rebellion, 1786–1787

From Annapolis to Philadelphia

The Virginians took their lead from James Madison, now thirty-five and a member of the Virginia assembly. Madison convinced the congress of the confederation government to allow a meeting of delegates at Annapolis, Maryland, in September 1786, to try again to revise the trade regulation powers of the Articles. But only five states participated. Like Madison, the dozen men who attended sensed an impending crisis, and they rescheduled the meeting for Philadelphia in May 1787. (See "American Places," page 271.) The congress reluctantly endorsed the Philadelphia meeting and tried to limit its scope to "the sole and express purpose of revising the Articles of

Confederation." But at least one representative at the Annapolis meeting had far more ambitious plans. Alexander Hamilton of New York hoped the Philadelphia meeting would do whatever was necessary to strengthen the federal government.

Alexander Hamilton by character was suited for such bold steps. The illegitimate son of

City Tavern

Philadelphia's City Tavern, built in 1773, became a favorite gathering place for political delegates who traveled to that city for continental congresses. Taverns provided important public meeting spaces for business and social functions; they were critical nodes on the information network of the day, the place to learn news from travelers, newspapers, or local gossip. John Adams called the City Tavern "the most genteel one in America." Here, in the Long Room on the second floor, delegates toasted each other on the anniversary of the Declaration of Independence on July 4, 1777. The men who wrote the Constitution in the summer of 1787 took meals and drinks there. This engraving and others like it aided in the complete reconstruction of the tavern on its original site in the 1970s; today it is open to the public as a period restaurant, complete with staff in costume.

Rare Book Department, The Free Library of Philadelphia.

a poor mother in the West Indies, Hamilton trained as a bookkeeper and prospered under the intellectual mentorship of a local minister. In 1773, the bright lad greatly impressed an American trader, who sent him to New York City for a college education. Hamilton soon got swept up in the military enthusiasm of 1776 and by 1777 had joined George Washington's staff, serving at the general's side through much of the Revolution. After the war, he studied law, married into a New York merchant family, and sat in the Continental Congress for two years. Despite his stigmatized and impoverished childhood, the aspiring Hamilton identified with the elite classes and their fear of democratic disorder.

The fifty-five men who assembled at Philadelphia in May 1787 to consider the shortcomings of the Articles of Confederation were generally those most concerned about weaknesses in the present government. Few attended who were opposed to revising the Articles. Patrick Henry, author of the Virginia Resolves in 1765 and more recently state governor, refused to go, saying he "smelled a rat." Rhode Island refused to send delegates. Two New York representatives left in dismay in the middle of the convention, leaving Hamilton as the sole New York delegate.

This gathering of white men included no **artisans** or day laborers or even farmers of middling wealth. Two-thirds of the delegates were lawyers. The majority had served in the confederation congress and knew its strengths and weaknesses; fully half had been officers in the Continental army. Seven men had been governors of their states and knew firsthand the frustrations of thwarted executive power. A few elder statesmen attended, such as Benjamin Franklin and George Washington, but on the whole, the delegates were young, like Madison and Hamilton.

The Virginia and New Jersey Plans

The convention worked in secrecy, so the men could freely explore alternatives without fear that their honest opinions would come back to haunt them. The Virginia delegation first laid out a fifteen-point plan for a complete restructuring of the government. This Virginia Plan was a total repudiation of the principle of a confederation of states. Largely the work of Madison, the plan set out a three-branch government composed of a two-chamber legislature, a powerful executive, and a judiciary. It practically eliminated the

AMERICAN PLACES

Independence Park, Philadelphia, Pennsylvania

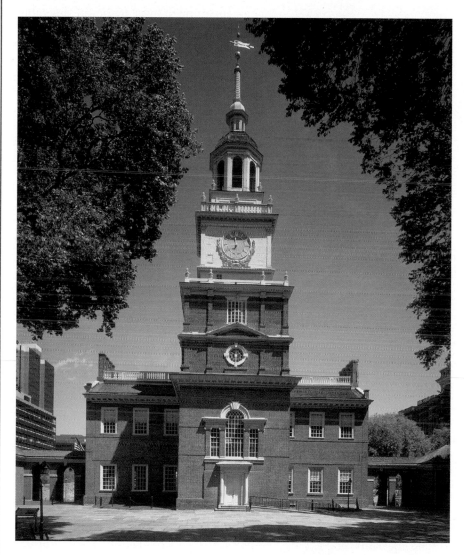

Philadelphia Independence Park
Independence National Historic Park.

In the 1780s, Philadelphia was the largest city in America, with over 30,000 inhabitants. With many hotels and taverns and a convenient location (equidistant from Boston and Williamsburg, each 300 miles away), there is little wonder that it became the preferred meeting site for Revolutionary-era congresses.

Nine eighteenth-century buildings in downtown Philadelphia are open to visitors at the 45-acre Independence National Historical Park, established in 1948. The main attraction is Independence Hall (shown here), where both the Declaration of Independence and the U.S. Constitution were debated and signed.

Nearby is Carpenter's Hall, built as a meeting hall for a trade guild (a skilled labor union), where the First Continental Congress met in 1774. Congress Hall, built in 1787, housed the U.S. House and Senate through the 1790s.

Although the focus at Independence Park is understandably on those important congresses, the site reveals much more about Revolutionary-era life. Typical of late-eighteenth-century cities, the neighborhood around Independence Hall was both commercial and residential and mixed by class. A mansion owned by the financier Robert Morris became the residence of Presidents Washington and John Adams in the 1790s; it no longer exists. A more modest house (open for tours) was home to Dolley Payne Todd (future wife of James Madison), whose first husband and child died in the yellow fever epidemic that killed over 4,000 Philadelphians in 1793. Much smaller houses once lined the streets around Independence Hall and were home and shop to working-class shoemakers, potters, and at least two African American women who peddled fruit tarts.

Today, nearly a million visitors each year stroll the grounds of this historic park, perhaps without realizing that until the 1940s the grassy areas were crowded with structures. **Archaeological** digs have produced upwards of 30,000 items—pieces of pottery, bones, buttons, household utensils, toys, and chamber pots, even a shoe with leather still flexible after two centuries, preserved by moisture at the bottom of a buried well. These **artifacts** help remind historians and tourists that even at a time of momentous political change, most Americans still went about their daily lives.

FOR WEB LINKS RELATED TO THIS SITE AND OTHER AMERICAN PLACES, see "PlaceLinks" at bedfordstmartins.com/roark.

The Pennsylvania Statehouse
The constitutional convention assembled at the Pennsylvania statehouse to sweat out the summer of 1787. Despite the heat, the delegates nailed the windows shut to eliminate the chance of being heard by eavesdroppers, so intent were they on secrecy. The statehouse, built in the 1740s to house the colony's assembly, accommodated the Continental Congress at various times in the 1770s and 1780s. The building is now called Independence Hall, in honor of the signing of the Declaration of Independence within its walls in 1776.
Historical Society of Pennsylvania.

voices of the smaller states by pegging representation in both houses of the congress to population. The theory was that government operated directly on people, not on states. Among the breathtaking powers assigned to the congress were the rights to veto state legislation and to coerce states militarily to obey national laws. To prevent the congress from having absolute power, the executive and judiciary could jointly veto its actions.

In mid-June, delegates from New Jersey, Connecticut, Delaware, and New Hampshire— all small states—unveiled an alternative proposal. The New Jersey Plan, as it was called, maintained the existing single-house congress of the Articles of Confederation in which each state had one vote. Acknowledging the need for an executive, it created a plural presidency to be shared by three men elected by the congress

from among its membership. Where it sharply departed from the existing government was in the sweeping powers it gave to the congress: the right to tax, to regulate trade, and to use force on unruly state governments. In favoring national power over **states' rights,** it aligned itself with the Virginia Plan. But the New Jersey Plan retained the confederation principle that the national government was to be an assembly of states, not of people.

For two weeks, delegates debated the two plans, focusing on the key issue of representation. The small-state delegates conceded that one house in a two-house legislature could be apportioned by population, but they would never agree that both houses could be. Madison was equally vehement about bypassing representation by state, which he viewed as the fundamental flaw in the Articles.

The debate seemed deadlocked, and for a while the convention was "on the verge of dissolution, scarce held together by the strength of a hair," according to one delegate. Only in mid-July did the so-called Great Compromise break the stalemate and produce the basic structural features of the emerging United States Constitution. Proponents of the competing plans agreed on a bicameral legislature. Representation in the lower house, the House of Representatives, would be apportioned by population, and representation in the upper house, the Senate, would come from all the states equally. Instead of one vote per state in the upper house, as in the New Jersey Plan, the compromise provided two senators who voted independently.

Representation by population turned out to be an ambiguous concept once it was subjected to rigorous discussion. Who counted? Were slaves, for example, people or property? As people, they would add weight to the southern delegations in the House of Representatives, but as property they would add to the tax burdens of those states. What emerged was the compromise known as the three-fifths clause: All free persons plus "three-fifths of all other Persons" constituted the numerical base for the apportionment of representatives.

Using "all other Persons" as a substitute for "slaves" indicates the discomfort delegates felt in acknowledging in the Constitution the existence of slavery. The words *slave* and *slavery* appear nowhere in the document, but slavery figured in two other places besides the three-fifths clause. Trade regulation, for example, a power of the new House of Representatives, naturally included regulation of the slave trade. In euphemistic language, a compromise between southern and northern states specified that "the Migration or Importation of such Persons as any of the States now shall think proper to admit, shall not be prohibited by the Congress prior to the Year one thousand eight hundred and eight." A third provision guaranteed the return of fugitive slaves: "No person, held to Service or Labour in one State, under the Laws thereof, escaping into another, shall, in Consequence of any Law or Regulation therein, be discharged from such Service or Labour but shall be delivered up on Claim of the party to whom such Service or Labour may be due." Slavery was nowhere named, but it was recognized, guaranteed, and thereby perpetuated by the U.S. Constitution.

Plenty of fine-tuning followed the Great Compromise of mid-July, but the most difficult problem, representation, had been solved. The small states worked to consolidate power in the Senate, where their weight would be proportionately greater than in the lower house, and Madison slowly recovered from his initial crushing sense of defeat. He had entered the convention convinced that the major flaw in the old government was that it had relied on unreliable states, and he feared that the Great Compromise perpetuated that flaw. But as the respective powers of the House and Senate were hammered out, he lent his support to the package as the most reasonable of political outcomes.

Democracy versus Republicanism

The delegates in Philadelphia made a distinction between *democracy* and *republicanism* new to American political vocabulary. Pure democracy was now taken to be a dangerous thing. As a Massachusetts delegate put it, "the evils we experience flow from the excess of democracy." The delegates still favored republican institutions, but they created a government that gave direct voice to the people only in the House and that granted a check on that voice to the Senate, a body of men elected not by direct popular vote but by the state legislatures. Senators served for six years, with no limit on reelection; they were protected from the whims of democratic majorities, and their long terms fostered experience and maturity in office.

Similarly, the presidency evolved into a powerful office out of the reach of direct democracy. The delegates devised an electoral college whose only function was to elect the president and vice president. Each state's legislature would choose the electors, whose number was the sum of representatives and senators for the state, an interesting melding of the two principles of representation. The president thus would owe his office not to the Congress, the states, or the people, but to a temporary assemblage of distinguished citizens who could vote their own judgment on the candidates.

The framers had developed a far more complex form of federal government than that provided by the Articles of Confederation. To curb the excesses of democracy, they devised a government with limits and checks on all three branches of government. They set forth a powerful president who could veto Congress, but they gave Congress power to override presidential vetoes. They set up a national judiciary to settle disputes between states and citizens of different states. They made the other branches of government as independent from the other branches as they could, by basing election on different universes of voters—voting citizens, state legislators, the electoral college.

> The words *slave* and *slavery* appear nowhere in the document, but slavery was recognized, guaranteed, and thereby perpetuated by the U.S. Constitution.

The convention carefully listed the powers of Congress and of the president. The president could initiate policy, propose legislation, and veto acts of Congress; he could command the military and direct foreign policy; and he could appoint the entire judiciary, subject to Senate approval. Congress held the purse strings: the power to levy taxes, to regulate trade, and to coin money and control the currency. States were expressly forbidden to issue paper money. Two more powers of Congress—to "provide for the common defence and general Welfare" of the country and "to make all laws which shall be necessary and proper" for carrying out its powers—provided elastic language that came closest to Madison's wish to grant sweeping powers to the new government.

The Constitution was a product of lengthy debate and compromise; no one was entirely satisfied with every line. Madison himself, who soon became its staunchest defender, remained unsure that the most serious flaws of the Articles had been expunged. But when the final vote was taken at the Philadelphia convention in September 1787, only three dissenters refused to endorse the document. The thirty-nine who signed it (thirteen others had gone home early) no doubt wondered how to sell this plan, with its powerful executive and Congress and its deliberate limits on pure democracy, to the American public. The Constitution specified a mechanism for ratification that avoided the dilemma faced earlier by the confederation government: Nine states, not all thirteen, had to ratify it, and special ratifying conventions elected only for that purpose, not state legislatures, would make the crucial decision.

Ratification of the Constitution

Had a popular vote been taken on the Constitution in the fall of 1787, it would probably have been rejected. In the three most populous states—Virginia, Massachusetts, and New York—substantial majorities opposed a powerful new national government. North Carolina and Rhode Island refused to call ratifying conventions. Seven of the eight re-

---

MAP 8.3 Ratification of the Constitution, 1788–1790
Populated areas cast votes for delegates to state ratification conventions. This map shows Antifederalist strength generally concentrated in backcountry, noncoastal, and nonurban areas, but with significant exceptions (for example, Rhode Island).

READING THE MAP: Where was Federalist opinion concentrated? How did the distribution of Federalist and Antifederalist sentiment affect the order of state ratifications of the Constitution?
CONNECTIONS: What objections did Antifederalists have to the new United States Constitution? How did their locations affect their view of the Federalist argument?

FOR MORE HELP ANALYZING THIS MAP, see the map activity for this chapter in the Online Study Guide at
bedfordstmartins.com/roark.

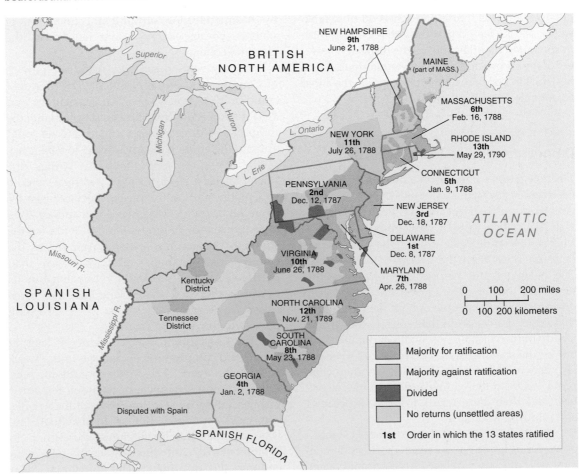

maining states were easy victories for the Constitution, but securing the approval of the ninth proved difficult. Pro-Constitution forces, called Federalists, had to strategize very shrewdly to defeat anti-Constitution forces, who were called Antifederalists.

The Federalists

Proponents of the Constitution moved into action swiftly. To silence the criticism that they had gone beyond their charge (which indeed they had), they sent the document to the congress. Congress withheld explicit approval but resolved to send the Constitution to the states for their consideration. The pro-Constitution forces shrewdly secured another advantage by calling themselves "Federalists." By all logic, this label was more suitable for the backers of the confederation concept, because the Latin root of the word *federal* means "league." Their opponents became known as "Antifederalists," a label that made them sound defensive and negative, lacking a program of their own.

The Federalists targeted the states most likely to ratify quickly, to gain momentum. Delaware provided unanimous ratification by early December, before the Antifederalists had even begun to campaign. Pennsylvania, New Jersey, and Georgia followed within a month (Map 8.3). In the latter two states, voter turnout was extremely low; apathy favored the Federalists. Delaware and New Jersey were small states surrounded by more powerful neighbors; a government that would regulate trade and set taxes according to population was an attractive proposition. Georgia sought the protection that a stronger national government would afford against hostile Indians and Spanish Florida to the south. "If a weak State with the Indians on its back and the Spaniards on its flank does not see the necessity of a General Government there must I think be wickedness or insanity in the way," said Federalist George Washington.

Another three easy victories came in Connecticut, Maryland, and South Carolina. As in Pennsylvania, merchants, lawyers, and urban artisans in general favored the new Constitution, as did large landowners and slaveholders. This tendency for the established political elite to be Federalist enhanced the prospects of victory, for Federalists already had power disproportionate to their numbers. Antifederalists in these states

Bed Curtain
This fabric, made into a bed curtain, was manufactured in England for sale in the American market around 1785. In repeating pattern it depicts two heroes of the new young country. One row shows George Washington standing majestically at the front of a chariot drawn by panthers. The alternate row depicts Benjamin Franklin dressed in a humble fur cap (his trademark) leading Miss Liberty forward. The British government may have lost the war, but the British textile industry was determined not to lose business.
Colonial Williamsburg Foundation.

tended to be rural, western, and noncommercial, men whose access to news was limited and whose participation in state government was tenuous. (See "Historical Question," page 276.)

Was the New United States a Christian Country?

Rebecca Samuel, a Jewish resident of Virginia, conveyed her excitement about the new U.S. Constitution when she wrote her German parents in 1791 that finally "Jew and Gentile are as one" in the realm of politics and citizenship. Other voices were distinctly less approving. An Antifederalist pamphlet warned that the pope could become president; another feared that "a Turk, a Jew, a Roman Catholic, and what is worse than all, a Universalist, may be President."

The document that produced such wildly different readings was indeed remarkable in its handling of religion. The Constitution did not invoke Christianity as a state religion. It made no reference to an almighty being, and it specifically promised, in Article 6, section 3, that "no religious test shall ever be required as a qualification to any office or public trust under the United States." The six largest congregations of Jews—numbering about two thousand and located in Newport, New York, Philadelphia, Baltimore, Charleston, and Savannah—were delighted with this nearly unprecedented statement of political equality and wrote George Washington to express their hearty thanks.

But more than a few Christian leaders were stunned at the Constitution's near silence on religion. It seemed to represent a complete turnabout from the state constitutions of the 1770s and 1780s. A New Yorker warned that "should the Citizens of America be as irreligious as her Constitution, we will have reason to tremble, lest the Governor of the universe . . . crush us to atoms." A delegate to North Carolina's ratifying convention played on anti-immigrant fears by predicting that the Constitution was "an invitation for Jews and pagans of every kind to come among us." A concerned Presbyterian minister asked Alexander Hamilton why religion was not in the Constitution. Hamilton reportedly quipped, "Indeed, Doctor, we forgot it."

Measured against the practices of state governments, Hamilton's observation is hardly credible. The men who wrote and debated the state and federal constitutions from 1775 to 1787 actively thought about principles of inclusion and exclusion when they defined citizenship, voting rights, and officeholding. They carefully considered property ownership, race, gender, and age in formulating rules about who could participate. And they also thought about religious qualifications.

Most leaders of the 1780s took for granted that Christianity was the one true faith and the essential foundation of morality. All but two state constitutions assumed the primacy of **Protestantism,** and one-third of them collected public taxes to support Christian churches. Every state but New York required a Christian oath as a condition for officeholding. Every member of Pennsylvania's legislature swore to "acknowledge the Scripture of the Old and New Testament to be given by divine inspiration." North Carolina's rule was even more restrictive, since it omitted Catholics: "No person who shall deny the being of God or the truth of the Protestant religion, or the divine authority of the Old or New Testaments" could hold office. In South Carolina all voters had to be Protestants.

Other common political practices affirmed that the United States was a Christian country. Governors proclaimed days of public thanksgiving in the name of the Holy Trinity. Chaplains led legislatures in Christian prayer. Jurors and witnesses in court swore Christian oaths. New England states passed Sabbath laws prohibiting all work or travel on Sunday. Blasphemy laws punished people who cursed the Christian God or Jesus.

Close to half the state constitutions included the right to freedom of religion as an explicit guarantee. But freedom of religion meant only that difference would be tolerated; it did not guarantee political equality. How then did the U.S. Constitution come to be such a break from the im-

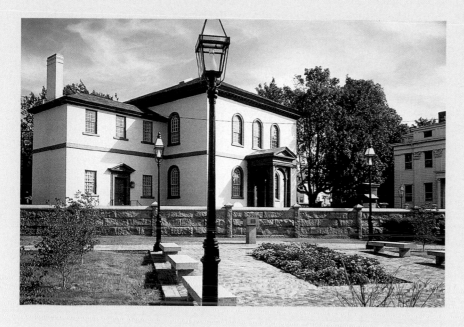

Touro Synagogue
A Jewish community inhabited the coastal shipping city of Newport, Rhode Island, as early as the 1650s. In 1759, the thriving group built a synagogue, the oldest Jewish house of worship still standing in the United States. The building blends a Georgian brick exterior with elements of Sephardic Jewish origin. It is sited diagonally on its property so that worshippers face east, the direction of Jerusalem. President Washington visited Newport in 1790 and wrote to "the Hebrew Congregation" a few days later: "It is now no more that toleration is spoken of, as if it was by the indulgence of one class of people, that another enjoyed the exercise of their inherent natural rights."

Touro Synagogue/photo John T. Hopf.

mediate past? Had the framers really just forgotten about religion?

Not James Madison of Virginia. Madison arrived at the 1787 convention fresh from a hard-won victory in Virginia to establish religious liberty. At the end of 1786, he had finally secured passage of a bill written by Thomas Jefferson seven years earlier called the Virginia Statute of Religious Freedom. "All men shall be free to profess, and by argument to maintain, their opinions in matters of religion, and that the same shall in no wise diminish, enlarge, or affect their civil capacities," the bill read. Madison had convinced both the Episcopalians and the Baptist dissenters, at war with each other over state support, that to grant either or both churches tax money would be to concede to the state the authority to endorse one religion—and by implication to crush another. The statute separated church from state

to protect religion. Further, it went beyond mere toleration to guarantee that religious choice was independent of civil rights.

In Madison's judgment, it was best for the U.S. Constitution to say as little as possible about religion, especially since state laws reflected a variety of positions. When Antifederalists demanded a bill of rights, Madison drew up a list for the first Congress to consider. Two items dealt with religion, but only one was approved. One became part of the First Amendment: "Congress shall make no law respecting an establishment of religion, or prohibiting the free exercise thereof." In a stroke, Madison set religious worship and the privileging of any one church beyond Congress's power. Significantly, his second proposal failed to pass: "No State shall violate the equal rights of conscience." Evidently, the states wanted to be

able to keep their Christian-only rules without federal interference. Different faiths would be tolerated—but not guaranteed equal standing. And the very same session of Congress proceeded to hire Christian chaplains and proclaim days of thanksgiving.

Gradually, states deleted restrictive laws, but as late as 1840 Jews still could not hold public office in four states. Into the twentieth century, some states maintained Sunday laws that forced business closings on the Christian Sabbath, working enormous hardship on those whose religion required Saturday closings. The guarantee of freedom of religion was embedded in state and federal founding documents in the 1770s and 1780s, but it has taken many years to fulfill Jefferson's vision of what true religious liberty means: the freedom for religious belief to be independent of civil status.

Massachusetts was the only early state that gave the Federalists difficulty. The vote to select the ratification delegates decidedly favored the Antifederalists, whose strength lay in the western areas of the state, home to Shays's Rebellion. One rural delegate from Worcester County voiced widely shared suspicions: "These lawyers and men of learning and money men that talk so finely, and gloss over matters so smoothly, to make us poor illiterate people swallow down the pill, expect to get into Congress themselves; they expect to be the managers of the Constitution and get all the power and all the money into their own hands, and then they will swallow up all us little folks." Nevertheless, the Antifederalist lead was slowly eroded by a vigorous newspaper campaign. In the end, the Federalists won by a very slim margin and only with promises that amendments to the Constitution would be taken up in the first Congress.

By May 1788, eight states had ratified; only one more was needed. North Carolina and Rhode Island were hopeless for the Federalist cause, and New Hampshire seemed nearly as bleak. More worrisome was the failure to win over the largest and most important states, Virginia and New York.

The Antifederalists

Antifederalists were a composite group, united mainly in their desire to block the Constitution. Although much Antifederalist strength came from backcountry areas long suspicious of eastern elites, many Antifederalist leaders came from the same social background as Federalist leaders; economic class alone did not differentiate them. Antifederalism also drew strength in states already on sure economic footing, like New York, that could afford to remain independent. Probably the biggest appeal of antifederalism lay in the long-nurtured fear that distant power might infringe on people's liberties. The language of the earlier revolutionary movement was not easily forgotten.

But by the time eight states had ratified, the Antifederalists faced a far harder task than they had once imagined. First, they were no longer defending the status quo, now that the momentum lay with the Federalists. Second, it was dif-

> Probably the biggest appeal of antifederalism lay in the long-nurtured fear that distant power might infringe on people's liberties. The language of the Revolution was not easily forgotten.

ficult to defend the confederation government with its admitted flaws. Even so, they remained genuinely fearful that the new government would be too distant from the people and could thus become corrupt or tyrannical. "The difficulty, if not impracticability, of exercising the equal and equitable powers of government by a single legislature over an extent of territory that reaches from the Mississippi to the western lakes, and from them to the Atlantic ocean, is an insuperable objection to the adoption of the new system," wrote one articulate Antifederalist in a compelling and much-read political pamphlet by "A Columbia Patriot." The Columbia Patriot was the alias for Mercy Otis Warren, a Massachusetts woman whose father, brother, and husband had all been active leaders in the revolutionary movement in Boston.

The new government was indeed distant. In the proposed House of Representatives, the only directly democratic element of the Constitution, one member represented some 30,000 people. How could that member really know or communicate with his whole constituency, the Antifederalists wondered. In contrast, one wrote, "The members of our state legislatures are annually elected—they are subject to instructions—they are chosen within small circles—they are sent but a small distance from their respective homes. Their conduct is constantly known to their constituents. They frequently see, and are seen, by the men whose servants they are."

The Antifederalists also worried that elected representatives would always be members of the elite. Such men "will be ignorant of the sentiments of the middling and much more of the lower class of citizens, strangers to their ability, unacquainted with their wants, difficulties, and distress," worried a Maryland man. None of this would be a problem under a confederation system, according to the Antifederalists, because real power would continue to reside in the state governments.

The Federalists generally agreed that the elite would be favored for election to the House of Representatives, not to mention the Senate and the presidency. That was precisely what they hoped. Federalists wanted power to flow to intelligent, virtuous, public-spirited leaders like themselves. They did not envision a government constituted of every class of people. "Fools and knaves have voice enough in government already," argued a New York Federalist, without being guaranteed representation in proportion to the total population of fools. Alexander Hamilton claimed that mechanics and laborers preferred to have their social betters represent them. Antifederalists challenged the notion that any class could be sufficiently selfless to rule disinterestedly for others. One, calling himself "Brutus" in a newspaper article, complained that "in reality, there will be no part of the people represented, but the rich, even in that branch of the legislature, which is called the democratic. . . . It will literally be a government in the hands of the few to oppress and plunder the many."

Antifederalists fretted over many specific features of the Constitution. It prohibited state-issued paper money. It regulated the time and place of congressional elections, leading to fears that only one inconvenient polling place might be authorized, to disfranchise rural voters. The most widespread objection to the Constitution was its lack of any guarantees of individual liberties in a bill of rights, like those contained in many state constitutions. This glaring omission made many Antifederalists exceedingly uneasy.

Despite Federalist campaigns in the large states, it was a small state—New Hampshire—that provided the decisive ninth vote for ratification, on June 21, 1788. Federalists there succeeded in getting the convention postponed from February to June and in the interim conducted an intense and successful lobbying effort on specific delegates.

The Big Holdouts: Virginia and New York

Four states still remained outside the new union, and a glance at a map demonstrated the necessity of pressing the Federalist case in the two largest, Virginia and New York (see Map 8.2). Though Virginia was home to Madison and Washington, an influential Antifederalist group led by Patrick Henry and George Mason made the outcome uncertain. Mason had been present throughout the Philadelphia convention and was one of the three delegates who refused to sign the Constitution; this made him an especially effective opponent. The Federalists finally won his support by proposing twenty specific amendments—some of which would protect individual liberties—that the new government would promise to consider. By a 10-vote margin, out of 168 votes cast, the Federalists got their ratification in Virginia.

New York voters tended to antifederalism out of a sense that a state so large and powerful need not relinquish so much authority to the new federal government. But New York was also home to some of the most persuasive Federalists. Starting in October 1787, Alexander Hamilton collaborated with James Madison and New York lawyer John Jay on a series of eighty-five essays on the political philosophy of the new Constitution, published in New York newspapers and later republished as *The Federalist*. The essays brilliantly set out the failures of the Articles of Confederation and offered an analysis of the complex nature of federalism. In one of the most compelling essays, number 10, Madison challenged the Antifederalists' heartfelt conviction that republican government had to be small-scale. Madison argued that a large and diverse population was itself a guarantee of liberty. In a national government, no single faction could ever be large enough to subvert the freedom of other groups. "Extend the sphere, and you take in a greater variety of parties and interests; you make it less probable that a majority of the whole will have a common motive to invade the rights of other citizens," Madison asserted. He called it "a republican remedy for the diseases most incident to republican government."

At New York's ratifying convention, Antifederalists predominated, some fearful that an extended republic would fail, others worried that individual liberties were endangered. But impassioned debate and lobbying—plus the dramatic news of Virginia's ratification—finally tipped the balance to the Federalists. Still, the Antifederalists' approval of the document was delivered with a list of twenty-four individual rights they hoped would be protected and thirty-three structural changes they hoped to see in the Constitution. New York's ratification assured the solidity and legitimacy of the new government. It took another year and a half for Antifederalists in North Carolina to come around. Fiercely independent Rhode Island held out until May 1790, and even then it ratified by only a two-vote margin.

In less than twelve months, the U.S. Constitution was both written and ratified. (See appendix, page A-4.) An amazingly short time by twentieth-century standards, it is even more remarkable for the late eighteenth century, with its horse-powered transportation and hand-printed communications. The Federalists had faced a formidable task, but by building momentum and assuring consideration of a **Bill of Rights,** they did indeed carry the day.

Conclusion:
The "Republican Remedy"

Thus ended one of the most intellectually tumultuous and creative decades in American history. American leaders experimented with ideas and drew up plans to embody their evolving and conflicting notions of how a society and a government ought to be formulated. There was widespread agreement that government should derive its power and authority from the people, but there was fierce disagreement over the degree of democracy—the amount of direct control of government by the people—that would be workable in American society.

The decade began in 1776 with a confederation government that could barely be ratified because of its requirement of unanimity, but there was no reaching unanimity on the western lands, on the impost amendment, or on the proper way to respond to unfair taxation in a republican state. The new Constitution offered a different approach to these problems by loosening the grip of impossible unanimity and by embracing the ideas of a heterogeneous public life and a carefully balanced government that together would prevent any one part of the public from tyrannizing another. The genius of James Madison was to anticipate that diversity of opinion was not only an unavoidable reality but a hidden strength of the new society beginning to take shape. This is what he meant in his tenth Federalist essay when he spoke of the "republican remedy" for the troubles most likely to befall a government where the people are the source of authority.

Despite Madison's optimism, political differences remained keen and worrisome to many. The Federalists still hoped for a society in which leaders of exceptional wisdom would discern the best path for public policy. They looked backward to a society of hierarchy, rank, and benevolent rule by an aristocracy of talent, but they created a government with forward-looking **checks and balances** as a guard against corruption, which they figured would most likely emanate from the people. The Antifederalists also looked backward, but to an old order of small-scale direct democracy and local control, where virtuous people kept a close eye on potentially corruptible rulers. Antifederalists feared a national government led by distant, self-interested leaders who needed to be held in check. In the 1790s, these two conceptions of republicanism and of leadership would be tested in real life.

FOR ADDITIONAL FIRSTHAND ACCOUNTS OF THIS PERIOD, see Chapter 8 in Michael Johnson, ed., *Reading the American Past,* Third Edition.

TO ASSESS YOUR MASTERY OF THE MATERIAL IN THIS CHAPTER, see the Online Study Guide at bedfordstmartins.com/roark.

FOR WEB LINKS RELATED TO TOPICS IN THIS CHAPTER, see "HistoryLinks," "DocLinks," and "PlaceLinks" at bedfordstmartins.com/roark.

CHRONOLOGY

1775 • Second Continental Congress meets and takes over direction of the war.

1776 • Virginia adopts state bill of rights.

1777 • Congress approves final draft of Articles of Confederation and sends it to states; controversies over western lands hold up ratification for five years.

1778 • State constitutions completed.

1780 • Pennsylvania institutes gradual emancipation.

• Cuffe brothers' petition to Massachusetts legislature results in extension of suffrage in Massachusetts to taxpaying free blacks.

1781 • Articles of Confederation ratified.

• Creation of executive departments; Robert Morris appointed superintendent of finance.

• Congress charters Bank of North America in an attempt to create stable currency, but bank has only a small impact.

• Slave Quok Walker successfully sues for freedom in Massachusetts.

1782 • Virginia relaxes state manumission law.

1783 • Treaty of Paris signed, ending the Revolutionary War.

1784 • Gradual emancipation laws passed in Rhode Island and Connecticut.

• Treaty of Fort Stanwix cedes Iroquois land to U.S. confederation government.

1786 • Virginia adopts Statute of Religious Freedom.

• Daniel Shays and fellow rebels challenge Massachusetts government, spreading fears that neither state nor central government can put down rebellions.

• Annapolis meeting proposes convention to revise Articles of Confederation.

1787 • Shays's Rebellion crushed in Massachusetts.

• Northwest Ordinance allows self-government and prohibits slavery in Northwest Territory.

• Delaware provides manumission law.

• Constitutional convention meets in Philadelphia.

1788 • U.S. Constitution ratified after vigorous campaign by Federalists.

1790 • Maryland provides manumission law.

1799 • Gradual emancipation law passed in New York.

1804 • Gradual emancipation law passed in New Jersey.

BIBLIOGRAPHY

General Works

Lance Banning, *The Sacred Fire of Liberty: James Madison and the Founding of the Federal Republic* (1995).

Jacob E. Cooke, *Alexander Hamilton* (1982).

Joseph J. Ellis, *After the Revolution: Profiles of Early American Culture* (1979).

Merrill Jensen, *The New Nation: A History of the United States during the Confederation, 1781–1789* (1950).

Ralph Ketcham, *James Madison: A Biography* (1971).

Edmund S. Morgan, *Inventing the People: The Rise of Popular Sovereignty in England and America* (1988).

Richard B. Morris, *The Forging of the Union, 1781–1789* (1987).

Peter S. Onuf and Cathy D. Matson, *A Union of Interests: Political and Economic Thought in Revolutionary America* (1990).

John Phillip Reid, *The Concept of Liberty in the Age of the American Revolution* (1988).

Robert E. Shalhope, *The Roots of Democracy: American Thought and Culture, 1760–1800* (1990).

Gordon Wood, *The Creation of the American Republic, 1776–1787* (1969).

Alfred F. Young, ed., *Beyond the American Revolution: Explorations in the History of American Radicalism* (1993).

The Confederation Government

Joseph L. Davis, *Sectionalism in American Politics, 1774–1787* (1977).

Daniel M. Friedenberg, *Life, Liberty, and the Pursuit of Land: The Plunder of Early America* (1992).

J. James Henderson, *Party Politics in the Continental Congress* (1974).

Merrill Jensen, *The Articles of Confederation: An Interpretation of the Social-Constitutional History of the American Revolution, 1774–1781* (1940).

Jackson Turner Main, *Political Parties before the Constitution* (1973).

Peter S. Onuf, *Statehood and Union: A History of the Northwest Ordinance* (1987).

Jack N. Rakove, *The Beginnings of National Politics: An Interpretive History of the Continental Congress* (1979).

Rosemarie Zagarri, *The Politics of Size: Representation in the United States, 1776–1850* (1987).

The Sovereign States

Willi Paul Adams, *The First American Constitutions: Republican Ideology and the Making of the State Constitutions in the Revolutionary Era* (1980).

Van Beck Hall, *Politics without Parties: Massachusetts, 1780–1791* (1972).

Ronald Hoffman and Peter J. Albert, eds., *Sovereign States in an Age of Uncertainty* (1981).

Marc W. Kruman, *Between Authority and Liberty: State Constitution Making in Revolutionary America* (1997).

Jackson Turner Main, *The Sovereign States, 1775–1783* (1973).

Richard P. McCormick, *Experiment in Independence: New Jersey in the Critical Period, 1781–1789* (1950).

Alfred Young, *The Democratic-Republicans of New York: The Origins, 1763–1797* (1967).

Citizenship

Ira Berlin, *Many Thousands Gone: The First Two Centuries of Slavery in North America* (1998).

Robert Dinkin, *Voting in Revolutionary America* (1982).

Linda K. Kerber, *Women of the Republic: Intellect and Ideology in Revolutionary America* (1980).

Linda K. Kerber, *No Constitutional Right to Be Ladies: Women and the Obligations of Citizenship* (1998).

James H. Kettner, *The Development of American Citizenship, 1608–1870* (1978).

Joanne Pope Melish, *Disowning Slavery: Gradual Emancipation and "Race" in New England, 1780–1860* (1998).

Gary B. Nash and Jean R. Sonderlund, *Freedom by Degrees: Emancipation in Pennsylvania and Its Aftermath* (1991).

Marylynn Salmon, *Women and the Law of Property in Early America* (1986).

Rogers M. Smith, *Civic Ideals: Conflicting Visions of Citizenship in U.S. History* (1997).

Rosemarie Zagarri, *A Woman's Dilemma: Mercy Otis Warren and the American Revolution* (1995).

The Critical Period

William G. Anderson, *The Price of Liberty: The Public Debt of the American Revolution* (1983).

Robert A. Becker, *Revolution, Reform, and the Politics of American Taxation, 1763–1783* (1980).

John L. Brooke, *The Heart of the Commonwealth: Society and Political Culture in Worcester County, Massachusetts, 1713–1861* (1989).

E. James Ferguson, *The Power of the Purse: A History of American Public Finance, 1776–1790* (1961).

Robert A. Gross, ed., *In Debt to Shays: The Bicentennial of an Agrarian Rebellion* (1993).

James R. Morrill, *The Practice and Politics of Fiat Finance: North Carolina in the Confederation, 1783–1789* (1969).

Leonard L. Richards, *Shays's Rebellion: The American Revolution's Final Battle* (2002).

David P. Szatmary, *Shays' Rebellion: The Making of an Agrarian Insurrection* (1980).

Alan Taylor, *Liberty Men and Great Proprietors: The Revolutionary Settlement on the Maine Frontier, 1760–1820* (1990).

The Constitution and Ratification

John K. Alexander, *The Selling of the Constitutional Convention: A History of News Coverage* (1990).

Lance Banning, *The Sacred Fire of Liberty: James Madison and the Founding of the Federal Republic* (1995).

Charles Beard, *An Economic Interpretation of the Constitution* (1913).

Richard Beeman, Stephen Botein, and Edward C. Carter II, eds., *Beyond Confederation: Origins of the Constitution and American National Identity* (1987).

Herman Belz, Ronald Hoffman, and Peter J. Albert, eds., *To Form a More Perfect Union: The Critical Ideas of the Constitution* (1992).

Richard B. Bernstein and Kym S. Rice, *Are We to Be a Nation? The Making of the Constitution* (1987).

Stephen R. Boyd, *The Politics of Opposition: Antifederalists and the Acceptance of the Constitution* (1979).

M. E. Bradford, *Original Intentions: On the Making and Ratification of the United States Constitution* (1993).

Richard Brookhiser, *Gentleman Revolutionary: Gouverneur Morris, the Rake Who Wrote the Constitution* (2003).

Robert E. Brown, *Charles Beard and the Constitution* (1956).

Roger H. Brown, *Redeeming the Republic: Federalists, Taxation, and the Origins of the Constitution* (1993).

Christopher Collier and James Lincoln Collier, *Decision in Philadelphia: The Constitutional Convention of 1787* (1987).

Patrick T. Conley and John P. Kaminski, eds., *The Bill of Rights and the States: The Colonial and Revolutionary Origins of American Liberties* (1992).

Saul Cornell, *The Other Founders: Anti-Federalism and the Dissenting Tradition in America, 1788–1828* (1999).

Linda Grant DePauw, *The Eleventh Pillar: New York State and the Federal Constitution* (1966).

Michael Allen Gillespie and Michael Lienesch, eds., *Ratifying the Constitution* (1989).

John P. Kaminski and Richard Leffler, *Federalists and Antifederalists: The Debate over the Constitution* (1998).

Michael Kammen, *A Machine That Would Go of Itself: The Constitution in American Culture* (1986).

Cecelia M. Kenyon, *Men of Little Faith: Selected Writings by Cecelia Kenyon* (2003).

Ralph Ketcham, *Framed for Posterity: The Enduring Philosophy of the Constitution* (1993).

Peter B. Knupfer, *The Union as It Is: Constitutional Unionism and Sectional Compromise, 1787–1861* (1991).

Leonard W. Levy and Dennis J. Mahoney, eds., *The Framing and Ratification of the Constitution* (1987).

Jackson Turner Main, *The Antifederalists: Critics of the Constitution, 1781–1788* (1961).

Elizabeth P. McCaughey, *Government by Choice: Inventing the United States Constitution* (1987).

Forrest McDonald, *We the People: The Economic Origins of the Constitution* (1958).

William Lee Miller, *The Business of May Next: James Madison and the Founding* (1992).

Richard B. Morris, *Witnesses at the Creation: Hamilton, Madison, Jay, and the Constitution* (1985).

Ellen Franken Paul and Howard Dickman, eds., *Liberty, Property, and the Foundations of the American Constitution* (1989).

Jack N. Rakove, *James Madison and the Creation of the American Republic* (1990).

Jack N. Rakove, *Original Meanings: Politics and Ideas in the Making of the Constitution* (1996).

John Phillip Reid, *Constitutional History of the American Revolution: The Authority of Rights* (1986).

William H. Riker, *The Strategy of Rhetoric: Campaigning for the American Constitution* (1996).

Robert A. Rutland, *The Ordeal of the Constitution: The Antifederalists and the Ratification Struggle of 1787–1788* (1966).

Stephen L. Schechter, *The Reluctant Pillar: New York and the Adoption of the Federal Constitution* (1985).

Bernard Schwartz, *The Great Rights of Mankind: A History of the American Bill of Rights* (1992).

Garry Wills, *Explaining America: The Federalist* (1981).

Religion

Ruth H. Bloch, *Visionary Republic: Millennial Themes in American Thought, 1756–1800* (1985).

Morton Borden, *Jews, Turks, and Infidels* (1984).

Thomas E. Buckley, *Church and State in Revolutionary Virginia, 1776–1787* (1977).

Jon Butler, *Awash in a Sea of Faith: Christianizing the American People* (1990).

Naomi W. Cohen, *Jews in Christian America: The Pursuit of Religious Equality* (1992).

Thomas J. Curry, *The First Freedoms: Church and State in America to the Passage of the First Amendment* (1986).

Nathan O. Hatch, *The Sacred Cause of Liberty: Republican Thought and the Millennium in Revolutionary New England* (1977).

Nathan O. Hatch, *The Democratization of American Christianity* (1989).

Ronald Hoffman and Peter Albert, eds., *Religion in a Revolutionary Age* (1994).

Rhys Isaac, *The Transformation of Virginia, 1740–1790* (1982).

Leonard W. Levy, *The Establishment Clause: Religion and the First Amendment* (1994).

Jacob Marcus, *United States Jewry, 1776–1985* (1989).

William G. McLoughlin, *New England Dissent, 1630–1833: The Baptists and the Separation of Church and State* (1971).

William Lee Miller, *The First Liberty: Religion and the American Republic* (1986).

Sally Schwartz, *A Mixed Multitude: The Struggle for Toleration in Colonial Pennsylvania* (1987).

WASHINGTON STANDS OUTSIDE OF TIME
A French clockmaker and artist produced this piece of Washington memorabilia after the death of the president. Washington's trim figure, rendered in gilt bronze, sports a spiffy uniform complete with fringed epaulets. One gloved hand rests on a sword; the other holds a rolled parchment, offered up in front of an eagle, the symbol of America's strength. Below the eagle a familiar motto is inscribed: "E Pluribus Unum"—"Out of many, one"—a reference to the political unity of the sovereign states. Below the clock is a motto about Washington that was first uttered in his funeral eulogy: "First in War, First in Peace, and First in the Hearts of his Countrymen." Death elevated Washington to celebrity status, and Americans immortalized him in many souvenirs.

The Warner Collection of Gulf States Paper Corporation.

CHAPTER 9

The New Nation Takes Form

1789–1800

ALEXANDER HAMILTON, the first secretary of the United States Treasury, faced a challenge in June 1790. The new Constitution provided powers of taxation and an explicit promise to honor the large debt dating from the Revolutionary War, but it fell to the bright young treasury secretary to propose a concrete plan to finance the debt. Hamilton's idea was to roll over the old and nearly worthless federal debt certificates into new, valuable certificates that carried the same dollar amounts but paid guaranteed interest and were backed by the new government. That much had proved somewhat controversial, but Hamilton went a step further and proposed adding all the states' debts still outstanding to the federal debt. Such large-scale debt consolidation (called *assumption* at the time) struck some other politicians as expensive, unnecessary, plainly unfair, and, worst of all, possibly a power grab by the new government to subordinate the states. Hamilton's bold plan was deadlocked in Congress.

Hamilton's chief opponent on the debt question was his onetime ally James Madison, now a member of the first federal Congress, which had convened in New York City. Together, these two had created the intellectual underpinnings of federalism by writing the *Federalist* essays during the ratification of the Constitution. But now the collaborators took opposite sides; the trust between them had eroded. Madison feared that Virginians, who had responsibly paid down the debt of their own state, would be taxed to pay the debts of other states. He also had strong misgivings about the whole debt plan because of the way it rewarded speculators who had bought the old debt at a steep discount in anticipation of its being fully repaid. Greedy speculators, Madison claimed, "are still exploring the interior & distant parts of the Union in order to take advantage of the holders." Through strenuous politicking, Madison had stalled out Hamilton's plan.

At this first crisis point—one of many to come in the 1790s—a solution arrived thanks to the hospitality of Thomas Jefferson, the secretary of state. Deeply worried about the stability of the Union, Jefferson invited Hamilton and Madison to dinner at his New York residence, and over good food and candlelight Hamilton secured the reluctant Madison's promise to restrain his opposition. In return, Hamilton pledged to back efforts to locate the nation's new capital city in the South, along the Potomac River, an outcome that was sure to please Virginians. In early July, Congress voted for the Potomac site, and in late July, Congress passed the debt package, assumption and all.

Alexander Hamilton
Alexander Hamilton was brash, confident, handsome, and audacious. Through force of personality, he had overcome what was for his era and culture a double obstacle in life, being born in obscurity and bastardy on the small West Indies island of Nevis. His mother died when he was thirteen, and five years later he had made his way to the mainland colony of New York and managed to charm his way into elite circles. He attended college, served in the Continental army, earned George Washington's uncommon admiration, and helped to write and ratify the Constitution. Along the way, he married Betsey Schuyler, whose father was one of the richest men in New York. He posed for this portrait by John Trumbull in 1792, at the age of thirty-seven and at the height of his power.
Yale University Art Gallery.

Far from being a cozy agreement-by-handshake, this momentous political deal points up the fears and fragility that haunted the new government in its first years of existence. Jefferson and Madison feared that Hamilton's funding plan would not only reward the wrong sort of men but bind them by financial ties to the government. Jefferson later wrote that the deal he and Madison struck "was unjust, and was acquiesced in merely from a fear of disunion, while our government was still in its infant state." They feared "disunion" when they heard fellow Virginians comparing Hamilton's assumption plan to the unjust parliamentary taxation that had started the Revolutionary War. Their solution was to do what it took to get the capital city situated in their own region, the better to watch it and influence it.

From 1790 to 1800, the "Founding Fathers" of the Revolution and Constitution era became keen competitors and sometimes bitter rivals. Part of the problem arose from clashing personalities. Hamilton's charm no longer worked with Madison, and it had never worked with John Adams, the new vice president, who privately called Hamilton "the bastard brat of a Scotch pedlar," and worse, a brat characterized by "disappointed Ambition and unbridled malice and revenge." Abigail Adams thought Hamilton a second Napoleon Bonaparte, an uncomplimentary reference to the belligerent leader of war-torn France. Late in his life, Madison was asked why he deserted Hamilton, his onetime ally, and Madison replied, "Colonel Hamilton deserted me."

Some of the rivalry stemmed from serious differences in political philosophy. Hamilton assumed that government was safest when in the hands of "the rich, the wise, and the good," three words that to him summarized one group: America's commercial elite. For Hamilton, economic and political power naturally belonged together, creating an energetic force for economic growth. Jefferson and Madison, in contrast, assumed the country's future lay with those whose wealth was tied to the land. Agrarian values ran deep with them, and they were suspicious of get-rich-quick speculators and financiers.

And finally, the breakup of the old Federalist alliance arose out of different loyalties and orientations toward Europe. Hamilton was an unabashed admirer of everything British, while Jefferson was enchanted by France, where he had lived in the 1780s. These loyalties governed foreign relations in the late 1790s, when the United States was in a war or near war with both of these overseas rivals.

The personal and political antagonisms of this first generation of American leaders left their marks on the young country. No one was prepared for the intense and passionate polarization that emerged over economic and foreign policy. The disagreements were articulated around particular events and policies: taxation and the public debt, a new farmers' rebellion in a western region, economic policies favoring commercial development, a treaty with England, a rebellion in Haiti, and a quasi-war with France that led to severe strictures on ideas of sedition and free speech. But at their heart, these disagreements arose out of opposing ideological stances on the value of **democracy**, the nature of leadership, and the limits of federal power. About the only major policy development that did not replicate or intensify these antagonisms among political leaders was Indian policy in the new republic.

By 1800, the oppositional politics ripening between Hamiltonian and Jeffersonian politicians would begin to crystallize into political parties, the Federalists and the Republicans. To the men of that day, this appeared to be an unhappy development.

The Search for Stability

Political parties were not part of the Constitution's plan for government. James Madison had argued in *The Federalist* in 1788 that a superior feature of the national government was precisely that the country's extensive size would prevent small, selfish factions from becoming dangerously dominant. Parties were thought of as destructive political forces, and their development was unanticipated and unwelcome. Only in future decades would American politicians come to realize that parties serve to organize conflict, legitimize disagreement, and mediate among competing political strategies.

Leaders in the early 1790s instead sought ways to heal divisions of the 1780s and bring unity to the country. Widespread veneration for President Washington provided one powerful source of stability. People trusted him to initiate the untested and perhaps elastic powers of the presidency. Congress quickly agreed on passage of the **Bill of Rights** in 1791, which pleased many Antifederalist critics. And the private virtue of women was mobilized to bolster the public virtue of male citizens; **republicanism** was forcing a rethinking of women's relation to the state.

Washington Inaugurates the Government

The election of George Washington in February 1789 was quick work, the tallying of the unanimous votes by the electoral college a mere formality. Washington, everyone's first choice, perfectly embodied the republican ideal of disinterested, public-spirited leadership. Indeed, he cultivated that image through such astute ceremonies as the dramatic surrender of his sword to the Continental Congress at the end of the war, symbolizing the subservience of military power to the law.

With attractive modesty, Washington at first feigned reluctance to accept the presidency. He wrote his wartime confidant, Alexander

> George Washington perfectly embodied the republican ideal of disinterested, public-spirited leadership.

Liverpool Souvenir Pitcher, 1789
A British pottery manufacturer produced this commemorative pitcher for the American market to capture sales at the time of George Washington's inauguration in 1789. The design shows Liberty as a woman dressed in a golden gown, her liberty cap on a pole, holding a laurel wreath (signifying classical honors) over Washington's head. Fifteen labeled links encircle the scene, representing the states. Yet in 1789, only eleven states had ratified the Constitution. No doubt the Liverpool manufacturer hoped to improve sales by maximizing the territory included. What two states are named beyond the original thirteen? Commemorative pitchers, jugs, and mugs were a commonplace article of consumer culture produced in Britain for specialized markets.
Smithsonian Institute, Washington, D.C.

Hamilton, for advice: Could he hesitate to accept but then ultimately take the office, without seeming to be too ambitious? Hamilton replied that he must accept the office; public sentiment was universally for it.

Once in the presidency, Washington carefully calculated his moves, knowing that with every step he was setting a precedent and any misstep could be dangerous for the fragile new government. How kingly should a president be? Congress debated the proper form of address, and the various options under consideration reveal a range of thought about how lofty executive leadership should be. Suggestions included such titles as "His Highness, the President of the United States of America and Protector of Their Liberties" and "His Majesty, the President"; Washington was known to favor "His High Mightiness." But in the end, republican simplicity prevailed. The final version was simply "President of the United States of America," and the established form of address became "Mr. President," a subdued yet dignified title in a society where only property-owning adult white males could presume to be called "Mister."

Washington's genius in establishing the presidency lay in his capacity for implanting his own reputation for integrity into the office itself. He was not a brilliant thinker, nor was he a shrewd political strategist. He was not even a particularly congenial man. In the political language of the day, he was virtuous. He remained aloof, resolute, and dignified, to the point of appearing wooden at times. He really preferred being a farmer, home at Mount Vernon, his Virginia plantation. (See "American Places," page 289.) But as president, he encouraged pomp and ceremony to create respect for the office, traveling with no fewer than six horses drawing his coach, hosting formal balls, and surrounding himself with servants in livery. He even held weekly levees, as European monarchs did, hour-long audiences granted to distinguished visitors (and including women), at which Washington appeared attired in black velvet, with a feathered hat and a polished sword. The president and his guests bowed, avoiding the egalitarian familiarity of handshakes. But he always managed, perhaps just barely, to avoid the extreme of royal splendor.

Washington chose talented and experienced men to preside over the newly created departments of war, treasury, and state. Yet deep philosophical differences separated key appointees. For the Department of War,

Washington chose General Henry Knox, former secretary of war in the confederation government. For the Treasury—an especially tough job in view of revenue conflicts during the Confederation (see chapter 8)—the president picked Alexander Hamilton of New York, known for his general brilliance and financial astuteness. To lead the Department of State, the foreign policy arm of the executive branch, Washington chose Thomas Jefferson, a master of the intricacy of diplomatic relations, who was then serving as minister to France. For attorney general Washington picked Edmund Randolph, a Virginian who had attended the Constitutional Convention but had turned Antifederalist during ratification. For chief justice of the Supreme Court, Washington designated John Jay, the New York lawyer who, along with Madison and Hamilton, had vigorously defended the Constitution in *The Federalist.*

Washington liked and trusted all these men, and by 1793, in his second term, he was meeting regularly with them, thereby establishing the precedent of a presidential cabinet. (Vice President John Adams did not join these meetings; his only official duty was to preside over the Senate, a job he found "a punishment" because he could not actually participate in legislative debates. He complained to his wife, Abigail, "My country has in its wisdom contrived for me the most insignificant office.") No one anticipated that two decades of party turbulence would emerge from the brilliant but explosive mix of Washington's first cabinet.

The Bill of Rights

An early order of business in the First Congress was the passage of a Bill of Rights. Seven states had ratified the Constitution on the condition that guarantees of individual liberties and limitations to federal power be incorporated into the founding document. James Madison and other Federalists of 1787 had thought an enumeration of rights unnecessary, but in 1789 Madison, now a member of Congress, understood that healing the divisions of the 1780s was of prime importance. "It will be a desirable thing to extinguish from the bosom of every member of the community," Madison said in his speech proposing his list of amendments, "any apprehensions that there are those among his countrymen who wish to deprive them of the liberty for which they valiantly fought and honorably bled."

AMERICAN PLACES

Mount Vernon, Virginia

When George Washington became president in 1789, he left his rural Virginia home for New York, the capital city, feeling like "a culprit who is going to the place of his execution, so unwilling am I, in the evening of a life nearly consumed in public cares, to quit a peaceful abode for an Ocean of difficulties." Washington had spent over thirty years improving that peaceful abode, Mount Vernon, along the Potomac River, and during his presidency he retreated to it whenever he could.

Washington had inherited the 2,000-acre plantation (a farm with a modest house) from a half-brother in the late 1750s, and as soon as his duties in the Seven Years' War were concluded, he set to work transforming the property. He designed another story to give the house two and a half floors, and he directed workers to renovate the exterior walls using pine boards spackled with sand and painted to look like stone. He also altered the entrance road, creating a dramatic vista down a long grassy mall for a visitor's first glimpse of the house; at that distance, the pine board really looked like the stones of a British manor.

When Martha Dandridge Custis, a young widow, married Washington in 1759, she brought to Mount Vernon two small children, a large fortune, and many slaves. The new money allowed Washington to enhance the building and decorating plans. Consulting a British architectural design book, he chose paint colors and wood paneling that reflected upper-class taste from England, a country he never visited. When the remodel was finally finished, the house contained 9,000 square feet, with nine bedrooms and plenty of space for the constant visits of friends, relations, and political dignitaries.

The mansion's grounds also were carefully planned, with formal gardens and practical kitchen gardens. There were the ordinary outbuildings: kitchen, storehouse, smokehouse, icehouse, privies, washhouse, and stable. More unusual was a large greenhouse, still standing, where exotic plants such as orange trees could be nurtured in a controlled climate. Two brick wings off the greenhouse were slave quarters, housing a portion of the several hundred slaves Washington owned.

When he was not a soldier or a statesman, George Washington preferred to think of himself as a farmer—up at dawn, surveying his acreage, his overseers, and his slaves. Farming it was, but on a grand scale. Washington aspired to, and achieved, the life of a country gentleman. Today one can glimpse Washington's life as gentleman farmer by visiting the accurately restored buildings and grounds, which are maintained by the Mount Vernon Ladies' Association.

FOR WEB LINKS RELATED TO THIS SITE AND OTHER AMERICAN PLACES, see "PlaceLinks" at bedfordstmartins.com/roark.

A Reenactor at Mount Vernon
Courtesy of Mount Vernon Ladies' Association.

Madison pulled much of his wording of rights directly from the language of various state constitutions with bills of rights. He enumerated guarantees of freedom of speech, press, and religion; the right to petition and assemble, the right to be free from unwarranted searches and seizures. One amendment asserted the right to keep and bear arms in support of a "well-regulated militia," to which Madison added, "but no person religiously scrupulous of bearing arms, shall be compelled to render military service in person." That provision for what a later century would call "conscientious objector" status failed to gain acceptance in Congress.

In September 1789, Congress approved a set of twelve amendments and sent them to the states for approval; ten were eventually ratified. Amendments One through Eight dealt with individual liberties, and Nine and Ten concerned the boundary between federal and state authority. (See the amendments to the U.S. Constitution in the appendix, page A-12.) One of the proposed amendments that failed of passage suggested a formula for fine-tuning the ratio of representation as population grew; the other required that any congressional pay raise voted in would not take effect until after the next election (not until 1992 did this amendment—the Twenty-seventh—pass). The process of state ratification took another two years, but there was no serious doubt about the outcome.

Still, not everyone was entirely satisfied. State ratifying conventions had submitted some eighty proposed amendments. Congress never considered proposals to change the structural details of the new government, and Madison had no intention of reopening debates about the length of the president's term or the power to levy excise taxes.

Significantly, no one complained about one striking omission in the Bill of Rights: the right to vote. Only much later was voting seen as a fundamental **liberty** requiring protection by constitutional amendment—indeed, by four amendments. The 1788 Constitution deliberately left definition of voters to the states, which set differing property qualifications. Any uniform federal voting law would run the double risk of excluding—or including—people who could already vote in some state elections with unusual voting statutes: for example, the unmar-

> Republican ideals cast motherhood in a new light by claiming significant maternal influence on the future male citizenry.

ried women worth over £50 who were allowed to vote in New Jersey, at first perhaps by oversight but in 1790 by an explicit election statute using *he or she* (see chapter 8, page 256). Voter qualification remained a state decision, and no other state followed New Jersey's lead.

The Republican Wife and Mother

The general exclusion of women from political activity did not mean they had no civic role or responsibility. A flood of periodical articles of the 1790s by both male and female writers reevaluated courtship, marriage, and motherhood in light of republican ideals and found ways to enlist white, literate women in the cause of the republican experiment in government. Tyrannical power in the ruler, whether king or husband, was now declared a thing of the past. Affection, not duty, bound wives to their husbands and citizens to their government. In republican marriages, the writers claimed, women had the capacity to reform the morals and manners of men. A male commencement speaker at a girl's school promised the graduates that "the solidity and stability of the liberties of your country rest with you; since Liberty is never sure, 'till Virtue reigns triumphant. . . . While you thus keep our country virtuous, you maintain its independence."

Until the 1790s, public virtue was strictly a masculine quality. But another sort of virtue loomed in importance: sexual chastity, a private asset prized as a feminine quality. Essayists of the 1790s explicitly advised young women to use sexual virtue to increase public virtue in men. "Love and courtship . . . invest a lady with more authority than in any other situation that falls to the lot of human beings," one male essayist proclaimed. A young woman at boarding school wrote in an essay, "Were all women rational, unaffected, and virtuous, coxcombs, flatterers and libertines would no longer exist." If women spurned selfish suitors, they could promote good morals more than any social institution could, essayists promised.

Republican ideals also cast motherhood in a new light. Throughout the 1790s, advocates legitimized female education, still a controversial proposition, through the claim of significant maternal influence on the future male citizenry. Benjamin Rush, a Pennsylvania physician and educator, called for female education because "our ladies should be qualified . . . in instructing their sons in the principles of liberty and government." A series of published essays by Judith

Republican Womanhood: Judith Sargent Murray
The twenty-one-year-old in this portrait became known eighteen years later as America's foremost public spokeswoman for the idea of woman's equality to man. Judith Sargent Murray frequently wrote essays for the *Massachusetts Magazine* under the pen name "Constantia." In "On the Equality of the Sexes," published in 1790, she confidently asserted that women had "natural powers" of mind fully the equal of men's. Murray, the wife of a Universalist minister, wrote plays that were performed on the Boston stage, and in 1798 she published her collected "Constantia" essays in a book titled *The Gleaner;* George Washington and John Adams each bought a copy. Murray is the only woman of her era to keep an indexed letter book, containing copies of nearly two thousand of her own letters written over her lifetime.

John Singleton Copley, *Portrait of Mrs. John Stevens* (Judith Sargent, later Mrs. John Murray), 1770–1772, oil on canvas, 50 × 40 inches, Terra Foundation for the Arts, Daniel J. Terra Art Acquisition Endowment Fund, 2000.6; photograph courtesy of Terra Foundation for the Arts, Chicago.

Sargent Murray of Massachusetts favored education that would remake women into self-confident, competent, rational beings, poised to become the equals of men. Her first essay, published in 1790, was boldly titled "On the Equality of the Sexes." A subsequent essay on education asserted that educated women "will accustom themselves to reflection; they will investigate accurately, and reason will point their conclusion; Yet they will not be assuming; the characteristic trait [sweetness] will still remain." Even Murray had to dress her advanced ideas in the cloak of republican motherhood, assuring that female education would not destroy women's compliant, domestic character.

Although women's obligations as wives and mothers were now infused with political meaning, traditional gender relations remained unaltered. (For the relatively few American voices that raised questions about what rights women might have, see "Beyond America's Borders," page 292.) The analogy between marriage and civil society worked precisely because of the self-subordination inherent in the term *virtue*. Men should put the public good first, before selfish desires, just as women must put their husbands and families first, before themselves. Women might gain literacy and knowledge, but only in the service of improved domestic duty. Many of the essayists took care to caution wives that they must still defer to their husbands. In Federalist America, wives and citizens alike should feel affection for and trust in their rulers; neither should ever rebel.

Hamilton's Economic Policies

The new government had the lucky break to be launched in flush economic times. Compared to the severe financial instability of the 1780s, the 1790s brimmed with opportunity and prosperity, as seen in increased agricultural trade, transportation, and banking improvements. In 1790, the federal government moved from New York City to Philadelphia, a more central location with a substantial mercantile class. There, Alexander Hamilton, the secretary of the treasury, embarked on his innovative and controversial programs designed to solidify the government's economic base.

Agriculture, Transportation, and Banking

Dramatic increases in the international price of grain in the 1790s motivated American farmers to boost agricultural production for the export trade. Europe's rising population needed grain, and the French Revolutionary and Napoleonic Wars that engulfed Europe for some dozen years after 1793 severely compromised production there. From the Connecticut River valley to the Chesapeake,

France, England, and Woman's Rights in the 1790s

During the 1770s and 1780s in America, only rarely did anyone wonder about rights for women. Abigail Adams's letter to husband John in 1776, asking him to "remember the ladies" when writing new laws, stayed a private document for a century. Boycotts by Daughters of Liberty did not challenge gender hierarchy, nor did New Jersey's handful of women voters. Simply replacing a monarchy with a republic did not, in America, lead to an immediate or substantial challenge to women's subordinate status. It was influence from abroad, not at home, that initially sparked Americans' ideas about women's place in society.

In France between 1789 and 1793, the revolution against monarchy enlarged ideas about citizenship and led some women to argue for the concept of the *citoyenne,* the female citizen. Women's political clubs such as the Society of Republican Revolutionary Women in Paris sent petitions and gave speeches to the National Assembly, demanding education, voting rights, and a curbing of the paternal and marital powers of men over women. In 1791, Frenchwoman Olympe de Gouges rewrote the male revolutionaries' document *The Rights of Man* into *The Rights of Woman,* asserting that "All women are born free and remain equal to men in rights." Another prominent woman, Théroigne de Méricourt, held a feminist salon, marched around Paris in masculine riding attire, and took part in an attack on a palace. Her vision went beyond political rights to the social customs that dictated women's subordination: "It is time for women to break out of the shameful incompetence in which men's ignorance, pride, and injustice have so long held us captive."

While voting rights for French women never passed in that era, the male National Assembly reformed French civil and family law in the early 1790s. Marriage was removed from the control of the church, divorce was legalized, and the age of majority for women was lowered. A far-reaching advance in inheritance law *required* division of a patriarch's estate among all his children, regardless of age, sex, and even legitimacy. Henceforth daughters could inherit along with sons; no longer did a woman from a family of means need to marry money—or indeed, to marry at all. In contrast, most American states imported traditional English family law virtually unchanged into their lawbooks.

French **feminism** traveled across the channel to England and directly inspired a talented woman named Mary Wollstonecraft. In 1792 she published *A Vindication of the Rights of Woman,* arguing for the intellectual equality of the sexes, economic independence for women, and participation in representative government. Most radically, she called marriage legalized prostitution.

Wollstonecraft's book created a sensation in America. Excerpts appeared immediately in Philadelphia and Boston periodicals, bookstores stocked the London edition, and by 1795 there were three American reprints. Some women readers were cautious. A sixty-year-old Philadelphian, Elizabeth Drinker, reflected in her diary that "In very many of her sentiments, she, as some of our friends say, *speaks my mind;* in some others, I do not altogether coincide with her. I am not for quite so much independence." Other women embraced Wollstonecraft's ideas. A woman much younger than Drinker, Priscilla Mason, gave a biting commencement address at the new Young Ladies' Academy in Philadelphia in 1794 and took Wollstonecraft as her departure for a rousing speech condemning "the high and mighty lords"—men—who had denied women education and professional opportunities in church, law, and politics. "Happily, a more liberal way of thinking begins to prevail. . . . Let us by suitable education, qualify ourselves for those high departments," and, she concluded with unwarranted optimism, "they will open before us." Many women's letters report lively debates stimulated by *A Vindication of the Rights of Woman.*

Male readers' responses were varied as well. Aaron Burr, a senator from New York, called the book "a work of genius." A Fourth of July speaker in New Jersey in 1793 proclaimed that "the Rights of Woman are no longer strange sounds to an American ear," and he hoped they would soon be embedded in state law codes. A more negative orator on that same holiday in New York argued that woman's rights really meant a woman's duty "to submit to the control of that government she has voluntarily chosen," namely the government of a husband. And a New Hampshire July Fourth orator advanced this tart joke: "Every man, by the Constitution, is born with an equal right to be elected to the highest office. And every woman is born with an equal right to be the wife of the most eminent man." For some, it was clearly hard to think seriously about gender equality.

The notion of equal rights for women had a long incubation period in the United States. In the 1790s, ideas of equality were too closely associated with the radicalism of the French Revolution, a divisive topic in America; and soon revelations of Wollstonecraft's unconventional personal life as an unwed mother dampened enthusiasm for her pioneering book. Not until the 1830s and 1840s would there be a new generation of women, led by Sarah Grimké, raising questions of sex equality anew (see chapter 11, page 377, and chapter 12, page 428). Most Americans of the 1790s preferred a moderate stance, praising women's contribution to civil society through their influence on family—the "Republican motherhood" concept, histo-

rians have called it. While this fell far short of an egalitarian claim to rights, it did justify—and this was no small gain—women's formal education. A young woman speaker at a Fourth of July picnic in Connecticut in 1799 summed it up perfectly to her all-female audience: "As mothers, wives, sisters, and daughters, we may all be important, [and] teach our little boys, the inestimable value of Freedom, how to blend and harmonize the natural and social rights of man, and as early impressions are indelible, thus assist our dear country, to be as glorious in maintaining, as it was great in gaining her immortal independence."

BIBLIOGRAPHY

Jane Abray, "Feminism in the French Revolution," *American Historical Review* 80 (1975).

Harriet Branson Applewhite and Darline G. Levy, eds. *Women and Politics in the Age of the Democratic Revolution* (1990).

Susan Branson, *These Fiery Frenchified Dames: Women and Political Culture in Early National Philadelphia* (2001).

Linda Kerber, *Women of the Republic: Intellect and Ideology in Revolutionary America* (1980).

Barbara Taylor, *Mary Wollstonecraft and the Feminist Imagination* (2003).

Rosemarie Zagarri, "The Rights of Man and Woman in Post-Revolutionary America," *William and Mary Quarterly* 55 (1998).

FRONTISPIECE.

Publish'd at Philad.ª Dec.ʳ 1ˢᵗ 1792.

Woman's Rights in the *Lady's Magazine* of 1792

This frontispiece, appearing in the first volume of the Philadelphia periodical the *Lady's Magazine and Repository of Entertaining Knowledge*, accompanied excerpts from Mary Wollstonecraft's *Vindication*. (The editor was a literary man, Charles Brockden Brown.) The caption identified the kneeling figure as "the Genius of the *Lady's Magazine*," accompanied by "the Genius of Emulation" carrying a trumpet and a laurel wreath. (*Genius* here meant a spirit; *emulation* meant ambition to excel, now an obsolete usage. Thus the genius of emulation was the spirit of ambition—women's ambition in this case.) The spirit representing the *Lady's Magazine* kneels before Liberty, identified by her liberty cap on a poll, and presents a paper titled "RIGHTS OF WOMAN." Study the objects below Liberty: two books, a musical instrument, artist's paints, a globe, and a page of geometrical shapes. The kneeling figure seems to gesture toward them. What do they suggest about the nature of the "rights of woman" this picture endorses?

Library Company of Philadelphia.

farmers responded by planting more wheat. The increase in overseas grain trade generated a host of new jobs in related areas as the number of millers, coopers, dockworkers, and ship and wagon builders expanded.

Cotton production in the southern states also underwent a boom, spurred by market demand and a mechanical invention. Limited amounts of smooth-seed cotton had long been grown in the low-lying coastal areas of the South, but this variety of cotton did not prosper in the drier, inland regions. Green-seed cotton grew well inland, but it contained many rough seeds that adhered tenaciously to the cotton fibers, making it very labor-intensive to clean. In 1793, a Yale graduate named Eli Whitney, visiting a Georgia plantation, invented the cotton gin, a device to separate out the seeds. Use of the gin increased cotton production, from 138,000 pounds in 1792 to 35 million in 1800. Most of it was shipped to English factories to be made into textiles.

Major Roads in the 1790s

A surge of road building helped propel the prosperous economy. Only one continuous and improved road existed before 1790, the Post Road running for 1,600 miles from Maine to Georgia near the coast. This was joined, in 1794, by the Lancaster Turnpike, the first private toll road in the nation, connecting Philadelphia with Lancaster, Pennsylvania. Soon another turnpike connected Boston with Albany, New York, and continued west. Private companies chartered by state governments financed and built these and other turnpikes and collected fees from all vehicles. Farther inland, a major road extended southwest down the Shenandoah Valley, while another road linked Richmond, Virginia, with the Tennessee towns of Knoxville and Nashville.

By 1800, a dense network of dirt, gravel, or plank roadways connected cities and towns in southern New England and the Middle Atlantic states, while isolated roadways and old Indian trails fanned out to the west. Commercial stage lines connected major eastern cities, offering four-day travel time between New York and Boston and an exhausting but speedy one-and-one-half-day trip between New York and Philadelphia (Map 9.1). In 1790, only three stage-coach companies operated out of Boston, but by 1800 there were twenty-four. Transport of goods by road was still expensive per mile compared to water transport on navigable rivers or along the coast, but at least it was possible.

A third development signaling economic resurgence was the growth of commercial banking. During the 1790s, the number of banks nationwide multiplied tenfold, from three to twenty-nine in 1800. Banks drew in money chiefly through the sale of stock. They then made loans in the form of banknotes, paper currency backed by the gold and silver paid in by stockholders. Because they issued two or three times as much money in banknotes as they held in **hard money**, banks were really creating new money for the economy.

Bridge Toll Sign, 1796

This sign lists an amazing variety of tolls charged for crossing a bridge over the Connecticut River between Cornish, New Hampshire, and Windsor, Vermont, in 1796. Owners of bridges and toll roads collected fees from users of their privately built right-of-ways. Can you deduce any principle of pricing in this list? Is the list exhaustive? What if a boy with a dog attempted to cross the bridge? Do you imagine there were traffic jams at the tollgate?
New Hampshire Historical Society.

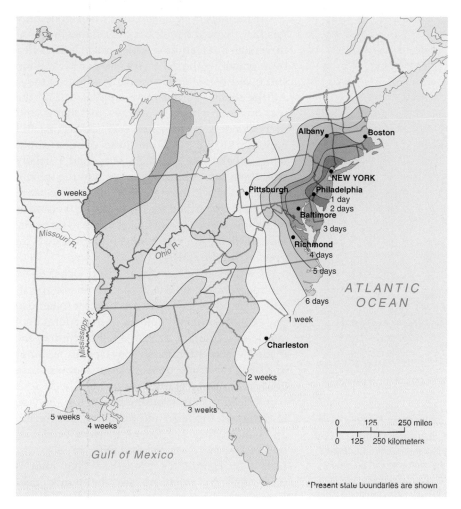

MAP 9.1   Travel Times from New York City in 1800

Notice that travel out of New York extends over a much greater distance in the first week than in subsequent weeks. River corridors in the West and East speeded up travel—but only if one were going downriver. Also notice that travel by sea (north and south along the coast) was much faster than land travel.

READING THE MAP: Compare this map to the map of "Major Roads in the 1790s" (page 294) and to Map 9.2. What physical and cultural elements account for the slower travel times west of Pittsburgh?

CONNECTIONS: Why did Americans in the 1790s become so interested in traveling long distances? How did travel times affect the American economy?

FOR MORE HELP ANALYZING THIS MAP, see the map activity for this chapter in the Online Study Guide at bedfordstmartins.com/roark.

The Public Debt and Taxes

The upturn in the economy, plus the new taxation powers of the government, suggested that the government might soon be able to repay its debts, amounting to some $52 million owed to foreign and domestic creditors. The debt dated from the difficult war years, when the government needed supplies and manpower but had no independent source of revenue. Many of the certificates of debt had been issued to soldiers as their pay. In the 1780s, those certificates had fallen in value, reflecting the widespread belief that the confederation government could never make good on them. The Constitution promised that "all debts contracted and engagements entered into, before the adoption of this Constitution, shall be as valid against the United States" under the new government as under the old. But how valid, exactly, would that be?

Alexander Hamilton's answer, elaborated in his *Report on Public Credit* in January 1790, was that the debt be funded—but not repaid immediately—at full value. This meant that old certificates of debt would be rolled over into new bonds, which would earn interest until retired several years later. There would still be a public debt, but it would be secure, supported by citizens' confidence in the new government. The bonds would circulate, injecting new valuable money into the economy. "A national debt if not excessive will be to us a national blessing; it will be a powerfull cement of our union," Hamilton wrote to a financier.

A large part of the old debt had been bought up cheaply by speculators in the late 1780s, and Hamilton's report touched off more rapid purchasing by men in the know. (Hamilton held none of the debt personally, but his father-in-law, Philip Schuyler, held $60,000 worth at face

The Return for SOUTH CAROLINA having been made since the foregoing Schedule was originally printed, the whole Enumeration is here given complete, except for the N. Western Territory, of which no Return has yet been published.

DISTRICTS	Free white Males of 16 years and upwards, including heads of families	Free white Males under 16 years	Free white Females, including heads of families	All other free persons	Slaves	Total
Vermont	22435	22328	40505	255	16	85539
N. Hampshire	36086	34851	70160	630	158	141885
Maine	24384	24748	46870	538	NONE	96540
Massachusetts	95453	87289	190582	5463	NONE	378787
Rhode Island	16019	15799	32652	3407	948	68825
Connecticut	60523	54403	117448	2808	2764	237946
New York	83700	78122	152320	4654	21324	340120
New Jersey	45251	41416	83287	2762	11423	184139
Pennsylvania	110788	106948	206363	6537	3737	434373
Delaware	11783	11143	22384	3899	8887	59094
Maryland	55915	51339	101395	8043	103036	319728
Virginia	110936	116135	215046	12866	292627	747610
Kentucky	15154	17057	28922	114	12430	73677
N. Carolina	69988	77506	140710	4975	100572	393751
S. Carolina	35576	37722	66880	1801	107094	249073
Georgia	13103	14044	25739	398	29264	82548
	807094	791850	1541263	59150	694280	3893635

Total number of Inhabitants of the United States exclusive of S. Western and N. Territory.	Free white Males of 21 years and upwards	Free Males under 21 years	Free white Females	All other persons	Slaves	Total
S.W. territory N. Ditto	6271	10277	15365	361	3417	35691

1790 Census Page

This page provides a published tally of the final results of the first federal census of 1790, mandated by the U.S. Constitution as a means by which representation in Congress and proportional taxation on the states would be determined. Notice the choice of 5 classifications for the count: free white males over 16, free white males under 16, free white women, all other free persons, and slaves. To implement the Constitution's three-fifths clause (counting slaves as three-fifths of a person), slaves had to be counted separately from all free persons. Separating white males into two broad age groups at 16 allows for a measure of military strength, surely something important for the government to gauge at a time of continuing and threatened Indian wars. Why separate males from females? Who does "all other free persons" mean? Which northern states still have slaves? Which state is the largest in population? Which largest in white population?

U.S. Census Bureau.

If the *Report on Public Credit* had gone only this far, it would have been only somewhat controversial. But Hamilton took a much bolder step by augmenting the debt with another $25 million still owed by state governments to individuals. All the states had obtained supplies during the war by issuing IOUs to farmers, merchants, and moneylenders. Some states, such as Virginia and New York, had paid off these debts entirely, while others, like Massachusetts, had partially paid them through heavy taxation of the inhabitants. About half the states had made little headway. Hamilton called for the federal government to assume these state debts and add them to the federal debt, in effect consolidating federal power over the states.

Congressman James Madison objected to putting windfall profits in the pockets of speculators. He proposed instead a complex scheme to pay both the original holders of the federal debt and the speculators, each at a fair fraction of the total. He also strenuously objected to assumption of all the states' debts. A large debt was dangerous, Madison warned, especially because it would lead to high taxation. But he lost the vote in Congress. Madison and Hamilton, so recently allies in writing *The Federalist,* were becoming opponents. Secretary of State Jefferson also was fearful of Hamilton's proposals. "No man is more ardently intent to see the public debt soon and sacredly paid off than I am. This exactly marks the difference between Colonel Hamilton's views and mine, that I would wish the debt paid tomorrow; he wishes it never to be paid, but always to be a thing where with to corrupt and manage the legislature." Eventually, Madison and Jefferson compromised with Hamilton on the assumption of state debts; in exchange, a decision favoring Virginians was reached to locate the nation's capital on the banks of the Potomac River, on the border shared by Virginia and Maryland. (See "Historical Question," page 298.)

The First Bank of the United States and the *Report on Manufactures*

The second and third major elements of Hamilton's economic plan were his proposal for a national Bank of the United States and his program to encourage domestic manufacturing. Believing that banks were the "nurseries of national wealth," Hamilton modeled his plan on the Bank of England, a private corporation that worked primarily for the public good. In

value.) These investors would now have a direct financial stake in the new government, support that Hamilton regarded as essential to the country's stability. He was also providing those same men with more than $40 million released for new investment, a distinct improvement over the old depreciated bonds, which had circulated in daily transactions at a fraction of their face value.

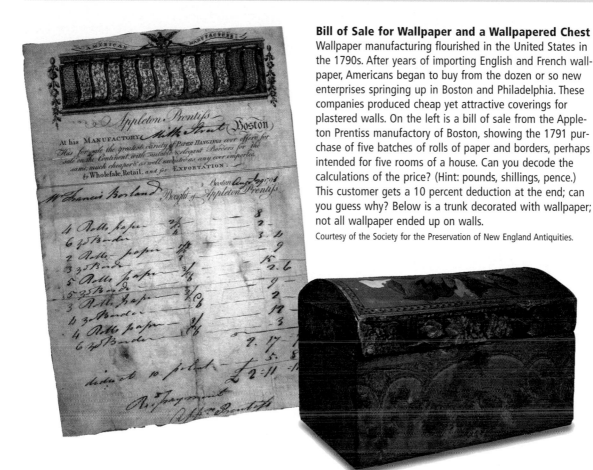

Bill of Sale for Wallpaper and a Wallpapered Chest
Wallpaper manufacturing flourished in the United States in the 1790s. After years of importing English and French wallpaper, Americans began to buy from the dozen or so new enterprises springing up in Boston and Philadelphia. These companies produced cheap yet attractive coverings for plastered walls. On the left is a bill of sale from the Appleton Prentiss manufactory of Boston, showing the 1791 purchase of five batches of rolls of paper and borders, perhaps intended for five rooms of a house. Can you decode the calculations of the price? (Hint: pounds, shillings, pence.) This customer gets a 10 percent deduction at the end; can you guess why? Below is a trunk decorated with wallpaper; not all wallpaper ended up on walls.
Courtesy of the Society for the Preservation of New England Antiquities.

Hamilton's plan, 20 percent of the bank's stock would be bought by the federal government. In effect, the bank would become the fiscal agent of the new government, holding and handling its revenues derived from import duties, land sales, and various other taxes. The other 80 percent of the bank's capital would come from private investors, who could buy stock in the bank with either hard money (silver or gold) or federal securities. Because of its size and the privilege of being the only national bank, the bank would help stabilize the economy by exerting prudent control over credit, interest rates, and the value of the currency. The bank had twenty-five directors, five appointed by the government and the other twenty chosen from the bank's stockholders, sure to be merchants from the world of high finance.

Concerned that the bank would give a handful of rich men undue influence over the economy, Madison tried but failed to stop the plan in Congress. Jefferson advised Washington that the Constitution did not permit Congress to charter banks. Hamilton, however, argued that the Constitution listed certain powers to regulate commerce ending with a broad grant of the right "to make all laws which shall be necessary and proper for carrying into execution the foregoing powers." Washington agreed with Hamilton and signed the Bank of the United States into law in February 1791, providing it with a charter to operate for twenty years. When the bank's privately held stock went on sale in New York City in July, it sold out in a few hours, touching off an immediate mania of speculation in resale. A discouraged Madison reported that "the Coffee House is an eternal buzz with the gamblers," some of them self-interested congressmen intent on "public plunder."

The third component of Hamilton's plan was issued in December 1791 in the *Report on Manufactures,* a proposal to encourage the production of American-made goods. Manufacturing was in its infancy in 1790, the result of years of dependence on British imports. Hamilton recognized that a balanced and self-reliant economy required the United States to produce its own cloth and iron products. His plan mobilized the new powers of the federal government to impose tariffs and grant subsidies to encourage the

How Did Washington, D.C., Become the Federal Capital?

Why didn't Boston, Philadelphia, or New York City become the capital of the United States? The great cities of London and Paris were great precisely because political power was situated at the heart of commerce and culture in those European countries. Although much smaller in scale, several American cities boasted elegant houses, cultural institutions, lively economies, newspapers, food markets, taverns, coffeehouses, and stagecoach and shipping lines—nearly everything necessary to accommodate the political elites who would be running the new government. Instead, the infant United States chose marshy, vacant acreage along the Maryland shore of the Potomac River for its permanent capital.

While the choice of that particular site was by no means inevitable, the country's leaders agreed that there should be only one site. During the war years, the Continental Congress had jumped around many times, from Philadelphia, Lancaster, and York in Pennsylvania to Princeton and Trenton in New Jersey, and down to Baltimore, often on the run from the British army. Even after the war, the Congress continued to circulate, meeting in Trenton, in Annapolis and Georgetown in Maryland, and finally in New York City. When the confederation government commissioned an equestrian statue of George Washington to inspire and dignify its meetings, a humorist suggested that the marble horse be fitted with wheels so it could be towed from place to place.

For some, a floating capital symbolized the precarious status of the confederation. But the alternative, a fixed location, put the federal government at the mercy of the particular state it sat in. If irate citizens stormed the congress, as had happened once in Philadelphia in 1783, could the local state militia always be counted on to protect it? The writers of the Constitution thus came up with a novel solution. They decided to locate the capital on land not controlled by any state. The 1788 Constitution specified a square district, not exceeding ten miles on a side, where Congress would have sole jurisdiction; but it deferred the complicated choice of the exact site to the First Congress.

In 1790, more than forty cities and towns clamored for consideration, from Kingston and Newburgh in New York's Hudson River valley down to Richmond and Williamsburg in Virginia. Eleven contenders clustered along the Delaware River between New Jersey and Pennsylvania, roughly the demographic center of the country. Six more sites fell in the interior of Pennsylvania, along the Susquehanna River, each claiming to be the future geographic center as the country grew westward. Another eleven locations dotted the Potomac River from Chesapeake Bay to the Appalachians. Clearly, river transportation figured heavily in all these plans, and investors in canal and river navigation companies took special notice.

The First Congress struggled to reconcile private interests, regional jealousies, and genuine dilemmas of citizen access. A Pennsylvania proposal naming a Susquehanna River site finally passed the House but not the Senate. Virginians held out for the Potomac, drawing objections from New Englanders fearful of disease-laden southern swamps. Philadelphians insisted that their city, the premier cultural and economic center of America, was the only logical choice. In short, the situation was at a stalemate.

Another, unrelated stalemate obstructed Congress in early 1790. Alexander Hamilton presented Congress with his controversial plan to fund the public debt by assuming state debts. James Madison objected and wrested the necessary votes from Hamilton—at first.

Hamilton approached Robert Morris of Pennsylvania to propose a deal: If Morris would deliver votes for Hamilton's assumption plan, the influential Hamilton would back a capital site in Pennsylvania. But Morris could not command enough congressional votes, so Hamilton next approached Thomas Jefferson, secretary of state, who invited him to dinner with James Madison. There the three reached agreement:

enough southern votes for assumption in exchange for a Potomac River site. Madison could not bring himself to vote for assumption, but he rounded up the necessary votes from men representing districts along the river. In the final bill, Philadelphia was named the interim capital until 1800, by which time a site on the Potomac River, to be selected by President Washington, would be constructed and open for business. Robert Morris gloated that the Virginians had been tricked; he felt sure that Philadelphia's charms would ensnare the government permanently. Assumption quickly passed, by six votes.

Washington, drawing on his surveying expertise, took another year to select the hill banked plain east of Georgetown, after scouting far up the river. No matter what location he chose, the Potomac Company—a canal-building enterprise of which Washington himself was president and principal investor—stood to benefit, but this was not considered a conflict of interest in the 1790s. Indeed, Washington had extensive landholdings up the Potomac and into the Ohio Valley, so the decision to site the capital on the Potomac River was much to his personal benefit. What made the Potomac advantageous both for a capital site and for investment in navigation was that it penetrated the farthest inland of any East Coast river, traversing the lowest point in the Appalachian Mountains. Washington's scouting trips convinced him that with short portages, water routes

Plan for Washington, D.C., on a Handkerchief

In 1791 and 1792, the pressure was high to get a detailed map of the proposed capital city into circulation so that prospective land buyers could be lined up. Finally a Philadelphia engraving firm produced this plan of the future city with each block numbered. It was reproduced on large handkerchiefs in an early marketing strategy to entice buyers. The actual site in 1792 consisted of fields and marshes.
Library of Congress.

could connect Chesapeake Bay to western Pennsylvania and beyond to the Ohio and Mississippi rivers.

Next, the rural site had to be purchased from the Maryland farmers who owned it. Washington and Jefferson purposely deployed surveyors in widely scattered locations up and down the river, to keep local owners from guessing where the government center would finally rest within the district—and thus to keep a lid on land prices. The president also deputized friends to pur-

chase the land, "as if for yourselves, and to conduct your propositions so as to excite no suspicion that they are on behalf of the public."

Washington then hired a French-born master designer to plan the capital. Pierre L'Enfant, an architect living in New York City, mapped out a grid of streets slashed dramatically by wide diagonal boulevards. L'Enfant envisioned a mall surrounded by grand government buildings. The rest of his map showed small lots intended for private buyers, who, it was hoped, would provide housing and services for the government population. The proceeds of the land sales would fund construction, so that a city could be built without having to draw on the U.S. Treasury at all.

In the end, the capital landed in the South because a major east-west river was there and because the South had crucial votes to trade on the assumption bill. Washington, D.C., represented the geographic but not the demographic center of the thirteen states. Its placement exerted a southern tug on the federal government, augmented by the fact that five of the first seven presidents were southerners. In all the political horse trading over choosing the site, nobody thought it worthy to note that the capital of the Republic sat in the heart of a slave society. But it would turn out to be of major significance some sixty years later, when the capital of President Abraham Lincoln's Union was surrounded by slavery, with many of its inhabitants of doubtful loyalty to the Union.

growth of local manufacturing. Hamilton had to be careful not to undercut his important merchant allies who traded with England and generated over half the government's income. A high tariff would either seriously dampen that trade or force merchants into smuggling. So Hamilton favored a moderate tariff, with extra bounties paid to American manufacturers to encourage production. The *Report on Manufactures* was the one Hamiltonian plan that was not approved by Congress.

The Whiskey Rebellion

Hamilton's plan to restore public credit required new taxation measures to meet the interest payments on a national debt swollen to some $77 million. Hamilton did not propose raising import duties, in deference to the merchant class, whose favor he sought; nor did he propose land taxes, which would have put the biggest burden on the nation's wealthiest landowners. Instead, he convinced Congress in 1791 to pass a 25 percent excise tax on whiskey, to be paid by farmers when they brought their grain to the distillery, then passed on to individual whiskey consumers in the form of higher prices. Members of Congress from eastern areas favored the tax—especially those from New England, where the favorite drink was rum, an imported beverage already taxed under the import laws. A New Hampshire representative pointed out that the country would be "drinking down the national debt," an idea he evidently found acceptable.

Not surprisingly, the new excise tax proved very unpopular with cash-short grain farmers in the western regions and whiskey drinkers everywhere. In 1791, farmers in the western parts of Pennsylvania, Virginia, Maryland, and the Carolinas and throughout Kentucky forcefully conveyed to Congress their resentment of Hamilton's tax. One farmer complained that he already paid half his grain to the local distillery for distilling his rye, and now the distiller was taking the new whiskey tax out of the farmer's remaining half. This "reduces the balance to less than one-third of the original quantity. If this is not an oppressive tax, I am at a loss to describe what is so." Congress responded with modest modifications to the tax in 1792; but even so, discontent was rampant.

> The Whiskey Rebellion presented an opportunity for the new federal government to flex its muscles and stand up to civil disorder.

Simple evasion of the law was the most common response; the tax proved hard to collect. Renewing painful humiliation rituals of revolutionary days, crowds tarred and feathered federal tax collectors, while some distilleries underreported their production. Four counties in Pennsylvania established committees of correspondence and held assemblies to carry their message to Congress. President Washington issued a warning that the protests had to stop, and for a time things cooled down. Still, noncompliance continued, and an embarassed Hamilton had to admit that the revenue was far less than anticipated. But rather than abandon the law, he tightened up the prosecution of tax evaders.

In western Pennsylvania, Hamilton had one ally, a stubborn tax collector named John Neville, who refused to quit even after a group of spirited farmers burned him in effigy. In May 1794, Neville filed charges against seventy-five farmers and distillers for tax evasion. In July, he and a federal marshal were ambushed in Allegheny County by a group of forty men, and then Neville's house was burned to the ground by a crowd estimated at five hundred; one man in the crowd was killed. At the end of July, 7,000 farmers planned a march—or perhaps an attack, some thought—on Pittsburgh to protest the hated tax.

The governor of Pennsylvania refused to call out the militia, preferring to allow arrests and judicial authority to handle illegal acts. In response, Washington nationalized the Pennsylvania militia and set out, with Hamilton at his side urging him on, at the head of 13,000 soldiers. (This event remains the only time in the country's history when a president in military uniform has led an army in anticipated action.) A worried Philadelphia newspaper criticized the show of force: "Shall Pennsylvania be converted into a human slaughter house because the dignity of the United States will not admit of conciliatory measures? Shall torrents of blood be spilled to support an odious excise system?" But in the end, no blood was spilled. By the time the army arrived in late September, the demonstrators had evaporated. No battles were fought, and no fire was exchanged. Twenty men were rounded up as rebels and charged with high treason, but only two were convicted, and both were soon pardoned by Washington.

Had the government overreacted? Thomas Jefferson thought so; he saw the event as a replay of Shays's Rebellion of 1786, when a protest against government taxation had been met with unreasonable government force (see chapter 8).

Americans offered $25,000 worth of treaty goods (calico shirts, axes, knives, blankets, kettles, mirrors, ribbons, thimbles, and abundant wine and liquor casks) and promised additional shipments every year. The government's idea was to create a dependency on American goods to keep the Indians friendly. In exchange, the Indians ceded most of Ohio to the Americans; only the northwest region of the territory was reserved solely for the Indians.

The treaty brought peace to the region, but it did not bring back a peaceful life to the Indians. The annual allowance from the United States too often came in the form of liquor. "More of us have died since the Treaty of Greenville than we lost by the years of war before, and it is all owing to the introduction of liquor among us," said Chief Little Turtle in 1800. "This liquor that they introduce into our country is more to be feared than the gun and tomahawk."

Across the Atlantic: France and England

While Indian battles engaged the American military, another war overseas had to be closely watched. Since 1789, a violent revolution had been raging in France. At first, the general American reaction was positive, for it was flattering to think that the American Revolution had inspired imitation in France. Monarchy and privilege were overthrown in the name of republicanism; towns throughout America celebrated the victory of the French people with civic feasts and public festivities.

But news of the beheading of King Louis XVI quickly dampened the uncritical enthusiasm for everything French. Those who fondly remembered the excitement and risk of the American Revolution were still likely to regard France with optimism. However, the reluctant revolutionaries of the 1770s and 1780s, who had worried about excessive democracy and social upheaval in America, deplored the far greater violence occurring in the name of republicanism as France in 1793 moved into the Reign of Terror, characterized by a bloody surge of executions of counterrevolutionaries.

In the United States, support for the French Revolution could remain a matter of personal conviction until 1793, when England and France fell to fighting in what were called the Napoleonic Wars and loyalty to France versus loyalty to England became a critical foreign policy question. France had helped America substantially during the American Revolution, and the confederation government had signed an alliance in 1778 promising aid if France were ever under attack. Americans optimistic about the eventual outcome of the French Revolution wanted to deliver on that promise. But others, including those shaken by the guillotining of thousands of French people as well as those with strong commercial ties to England, sought ways to stay neutral.

In May 1793, President Washington issued a Neutrality Proclamation with friendly assurances to both sides. But tensions at home flared in response to official neutrality. "The cause of France is the cause of man, and neutrality is desertion," wrote H. H. Brackenridge, a western Pennsylvanian, voicing the sentiments of thousands. Dozens of pro-French political clubs called Democratic or Republican Societies sprang up around the country. The societies mobilized farmers and mechanics, issued circular letters, injected pro-French and anti-British feelings into local elections, and in general heightened popular participation and public interest in foreign policy. The activities of these societies disturbed Washington and Hamilton intensely, for they encouraged opposition to the policies of the president.

The Neutrality Proclamation was in theory a fine idea, in view of Washington's goal of staying out of European wars. Yet American ships continued to trade between the French West Indies and France, and in late 1793 and early 1794, the English expressed their displeasure by halting more than three hundred of these vessels near the West Indies, capturing their cargoes and impressing (illegally seizing) their crews. Clearly, something had to be done to assert American power.

President Washington sent John Jay, the chief justice of the Supreme Court and a man of strong pro-British sentiments, to England to negotiate commercial relations in the British West Indies, secure compensation for the seized cargoes, and stop the impressment of sailors. In addition, Jay was supposed to resolve several long-standing problems dating from the end of the Revolution. Southern **planters** wanted reimbursement for the slaves lured away by the British army during the war, and western settlers wanted England to vacate the western forts still

> Support for the French Revolution could remain a matter of personal conviction until 1793, when England and France went to war.

occupied—twelve years after the end of the Revolution—because of their strategic proximity to the Indian fur trade.

Jay returned from his diplomatic mission in 1795 with a treaty that no one could love. First, the treaty made no direct provision for the captured cargoes, impressed seamen, or the lost property in slaves. Second, it granted the British eighteen more months to withdraw from the western forts while guaranteeing them continued rights in the fur trade. (Even with the delay, the provision disheartened the Indians just then negotiating the Treaty of Greenville out in Ohio; it was a significant factor in their decision to make peace.) Finally, the Jay Treaty called for repayment with interest of the debts that some American planters still owed to British firms dating from the Revolutionary War. In exchange for such generous terms, Jay secured limited trading rights in the West Indies and agreement that some issues—boundary disputes with Canada, the damage and loss claims of the shipowners—would be decided later by arbitration commissions.

The Senate debated the treaty in secrecy, knowing how explosive its terms would be, and passed it by a vote of twenty to ten. President Washington signed it, but with misgivings. When newspapers published the terms of the treaty, powerful opposition emerged from Maine to Georgia. In Massachusetts, graffiti appeared on a wall: "Damn John Jay! Damn everyone who won't damn John Jay! Damn everyone who won't stay up all night damning John Jay!" Bonfires in many places burned effigies of Jay and copies of the treaty. A newspaper in New Jersey used accessible gender imagery to explain to its readers the implications of the Jay Treaty:

> The nation has been secretly, I will not say treacherously, divorced from France, and most clandestinely married to Great Britain: we are taken from the embraces of a loving wife, and find ourselves in the arms of a destestable and abandoned whore, covered with crimes, rottenness, and corruption.

When Alexander Hamilton appeared at a public meeting in New York City to defend the treaty, he was hissed and booed, and several stones were thrown at him. Within days he was challenging opponents to fights, but no one took up his challenge.

Some representatives in the House, led by Madison, tried to undermine the Senate's approval by insisting on a separate vote on the funding provisions of the treaty, on the grounds that the House controlled all money bills. Finally, in 1796, the House approved funds to implement the various commissions mandated by the treaty, but by only a three-vote margin. The cleavage of votes in both houses of Congress divided along the same lines as the Hamilton-Jefferson split on economic policy. This was the most bitter political split yet in the country's short history.

To the South: The Haitian Revolution

In addition to the Indian wars in Ohio and the European wars across the Atlantic, a third bloody conflict to the south polarized and even terrorized many Americans in the 1790s. The western third of the large Caribbean island of Hispaniola, just to the east of Cuba, became engulfed in revolution starting in 1791. The eastern portion of the island was a Spanish colony called Santo Domingo; the western part, in bloody conflagration, was the French Saint Domingue.

Haitian Revolution, 1790–1804

War raged there for over a decade, resulting in the birth of the Republic of Haiti in 1804, distinguished as the first and only independent black state to arise out of a successful slave revolution.

The Haitian Revolution was a complex event involving many participants, including the diverse local population and, eventually, three European countries. Some 30,000 whites ruled the island in 1790, running sugar and coffee plantations with close to half a million slaves, two-thirds of them of African birth. The white French colonists were not the only plantation owners, however. About 28,000 free coloreds (*gens de couleur*) of mixed race also lived in Saint Domingue; they owned one-third of the island's plantations and nearly a quarter of the slave labor force. Despite their economic status, the free coloreds were barred from political power; but they aspired to it.

The French Revolution of 1789 was the immediate catalyst for rebellion in this already tense society. First, white colonists challenged the white royalist government in an effort to link Saint Domingue with the new revolutionary government in France. Next the free coloreds rebelled in 1791, demanding equal civil rights with the whites. No sooner was this revolt viciously suppressed than another part of the island exploded as thousands of slaves armed with machetes and torches wreaked devastation and slaughter. In 1793, the civil war escalated to include French, Spanish, and British troops fighting the inhabitants and also each other. Slaves led by Toussaint L'Ouverture in alliance with Spain occupied the northern regions of the island, leaving a thousand plantations in ruins and tens of thousands of people dead. Thousands of whites and free coloreds, along with some of their slaves, fled to Spanish Louisiana and southern cities of the United States.

White Americans followed the revolution in fascinated horror through newspapers and refugees' accounts. A few sympathized with the impulse for liberty, but many more shuddered at the violent atrocities. White refugees were welcomed in Charleston, Norfolk, and Richmond; but French-speaking blacks, whether free or slave, were eventually barred from entry in all southern states except Virginia. White Southerners clearly feared that violent black insurrection might be imported from Haiti into their own society.

Many black American slaves also followed the revolution, hearing about it from dockworkers, from black sailors, from anxious whites who spoke of it over dinner or at the tavern, where blacks waited on table, and from the French blacks themselves, arriving in Virginia ports in significant numbers after 1793. Amazing news—the success of a first ever, massive revolution by slaves—traveled quickly in this oral culture. Whites complained of behaviors that might prefigure plots and conspiracies, such as increased insolence and higher runaway rates among slaves.

The Haitian Revolution provoked naked fear of race war in white southern Americans. Jefferson, agonizing over the contagion of liberty in 1797, wrote another Virginia slaveholder that "if something is not done, and soon done, we shall be the murderers of our own children . . . ; the revolutionary storm, now sweeping the globe, will be upon us, and happy if we make timely provision to give it an easy passage over our land. From the present state of things in Europe and America, the day which brings our combustion must be near at hand; and only a single spark is wanting to make that day to-morrow." Jefferson's cataclysmic fears were not shared by New Englanders. Timothy Pickering of Massachusetts, in Washington's cabinet since 1795, chastised the inconsistent Jefferson for supporting French revolutionaries while condemning black Haitians fighting for freedom, just because they had "a skin not colored like our own." Not that Pickering supported either type of violent revolutionary—he did not. But he and his political allies, soon to be called the Federalists, were far more willing to contemplate trade and diplomatic relations with the emerging black republic of Haiti.

> White Southerners clearly feared that violent black insurrection might be imported from Haiti into their own society.

Federalists and Republicans

By the mid-1790s, the polarization of opinions on the French Revolution, on Haiti, on the Jay Treaty, and on Hamilton's economic plans had led to two distinct and consistent rival political groups: Federalists and Republicans. Politicians and newspapers adopted these labels, words that summarized conflicting ideologies and principles; they did not yet describe full-fledged political parties, which were still thought to be a sign of failure of the experiment in government. Washington's decision not to seek a third term opened the floodgates to serious partisan electioneering in the presidential and congressional elections of 1796. Although Federalist John Adams emerged the victor, his single term in office was very acrimonious as party strife accelerated over failed diplomacy in France, which brought the United States to the brink of war. Pro-war and antiwar antagonism created a major crisis in the young country over political free speech, militarism, and fears of sedition and treason.

The Election of 1796

Washington struggled to appear to be above party politics, and in his farewell address of September 1796 he stressed the need to maintain a "unity of government" reflecting a unified body politic. He also urged the country to "steer

Washington's Farewell Address Printed on a Textile, 1806

This small square of fabric, suitable for framing or tacking to the wall, was one of many items that served to immortalize Washington as the benevolent savior of the young Republic. Known well by close associates as a man with ordinary human failings—one Federalist member of his last cabinet complained that he was "vain and weak and ignorant"—Washington in death became a demigod, a genius of inspired leadership and faultless integrity. This 1806 textile features the final paragraph of Washington's 1796 farewell address, one highlighting his modesty and self-deprecation. At the bottom, the American eagle and the British lion flank two sailing ships (one close, one far off) under the words "Commercial Union." The textile picture, then, was an implicit criticism of the new president, Thomas Jefferson, whose leadership was producing deteriorating relations with Britain that would finally result in the War of 1812.

Collection of Janice L. and David J. Frent.

persuasion and intrigue. Bruised by his conflicts with Hamilton, Jefferson had resigned as secretary of state in 1793 and retreated to Monticello, his home in Virginia. Adams's job as vice president kept him closer to the political action, but his personality often put people off. He was temperamental, thin-skinned, and quick to take offense.

The leading Federalists and Republicans informally caucused to choose candidates. The Federalists picked Thomas Pinckney of South Carolina to run with Adams; the Republicans settled on Aaron Burr of New York to pair with Jefferson. The Constitution did not anticipate parties and tickets. Instead, each electoral college voter could cast two votes for any two candidates, but on only one ballot. The top vote-getter became president and the next highest assumed the vice presidency. (This procedural flaw was corrected by the Twelfth Amendment, adopted in 1804.) With only one ballot, careful maneuver-

John Adams

In 1793, a year after the youthful secretary of the treasury Alexander Hamilton posed for him (see page 286), John Trumbull painted Vice President John Adams, then age fifty-eight. A friend once listed Adams's shortcomings as a politician: "He can't dance, drink, game, flatter, promise, dress, swear with gentlemen, and small talk and flirt with the ladies."

National Portrait Gallery, Smithsonian Institution/Art Resources, NY.

clear of permanent alliances with any portion of the foreign world." The leading contenders for his position, John Adams of Massachusetts and Thomas Jefferson of Virginia, in theory agreed with him, but around them raged a party contest split along pro-English versus pro-French lines.

Adams and Jefferson were not adept politicians in the modern sense, skilled in the arts of ing was required to make sure the chief rivals for the presidency did not land in the top two spots.

Into that maneuverable moment stepped Alexander Hamilton. No longer in the cabinet, Hamilton had returned to his law practice in 1795, but he kept a firm hand on political developments. Hamilton did not trust Adams; he preferred Pinckney, and he tried to influence electors to throw their support to the South Carolinian. But his plan backfired: Adams was elected president with 71 electoral votes, and Jefferson came in second with 68 and thus became vice president. Pinckney got 59 votes, while Burr trailed with 30.

Adams's inaugural speech pledged neutrality in foreign affairs and respect for the French people, which made Republicans hopeful. To please Federalists, Adams retained three cabinet members from Washington's administration—the secretaries of state, treasury, and war. But the three were Hamilton loyalists, passing on Hamilton's judgments and advice as their own to the unwitting Adams. Vice President Jefferson extended a conciliatory arm to Adams when the two old friends met in Philadelphia, still the capital. They even took temporary lodging in the same boardinghouse as if expecting to work closely together. But the Hamiltonian cabinet ruined the honeymoon. Jefferson's advice was spurned, and he withdrew from active counsel of the president.

The XYZ Affair

Foreign policy lay at the heart of the rift between Adams and Jefferson and between Federalists and Republicans. If the Jay Treaty heated American tempers initially, the French response in 1797 was like oil added to the fire. Adams's one-term presidency was a perpetual crisis.

France read the Jay Treaty as the Republicans did: as a document giving so many concessions to the British that it made the United States a British satellite. In retaliation, France abandoned the terms of its 1778 wartime alliance with the United States and allowed French privateers—armed private vessels—to detain American ships carrying British goods. By March 1797, more than 300 American vessels had been seized. In a related move, in the winter of 1796–97, France refused to recognize a new minister sent by President Washington, Charles Cotesworth Pinckney.

To avenge these insults, Federalists started murmuring openly about war with France.

"The Ladies Patriotic Song," 1799
This sheet music invests women with the power to inspire soldiers and sailors in the undeclared war with France. The second verse begins: "What Hero will Beauty's soft influence disprove / What Sword will not start, urg'd by Honour and Love / Columbia's fair Daughters will bless with their charms / The generous in Peace—The Triumphant in Arms." The song was published in Boston, a staunchly Federalist city in the heart of New England federalism. Would you expect to see a song like this published in Charlottesville, Virginia, Thomas Jefferson's home town? Chicago Historical Society.

Adams preferred negotiations and dispatched a three-man commission to France in the fall of 1797. At the same time, the president recommended new expenditures for military defense; negotiations needed to be backed by military preparedness. Congress agreed and approved the construction of three new naval frigates. When the three commissioners arrived in Paris, French officials would not receive them. Finally the French minister of foreign affairs, Talleyrand, sent three French agents, unnamed and later known to the American public as X, Y, and Z, to the American commissioners with the recommendation that $250,000 might grease the wheels of diplomacy and that a $12 million loan to the French government would be the price of a peace treaty. Incensed by Talleyrand's suggestion of a bribe, the three American commissioners departed to inform the president.

> Foreign policy lay at the heart of the rift between Adams and Jefferson and between Federalists and Republicans. If the Jay Treaty heated American tempers initially, the XYZ affair was like oil added to the fire.

Cartoon of the Matthew Lyon Fight in Congress
The political tensions of 1798 were not merely intellectual. A February session in Congress degenerated from name-calling to a brawl. Roger Griswold, a Connecticut Federalist, called Matthew Lyon, a Vermont Republican, a coward. Lyon responded with some well-aimed spit, the first departure from the gentleman's code of honor. Griswold responded by raising his cane to Lyon, whereupon Lyon grabbed nearby fire tongs to beat back his assailant. Madison wrote to Jefferson that the two should have dueled: "No man ought to reproach another with cowardice, who is not ready to give proof of his own courage" by negotiating a duel, the honorable way to avenge insults in Virginia's planter class. But Lyon, a Scots-Irish immigrant, did not come from a class or culture that cultivated the art of the duel; rough-and-tumble fighting was his first response to insult. What is the picture on the wall of the House chambers?
Library of Congress.

FOR MORE HELP ANALYZING THIS IMAGE, see the visual activity for this chapter in the Online Study Guide at **bedfordstmartins.com/roark**.

Americans reacted to the XYZ affair with shock and anger. Even staunch pro-French Republicans began to reevaluate their allegiance. The Federalist-dominated Congress appropriated money for an army of 10,000 soldiers. It repealed all prior treaties with France, and in 1798 twenty naval warships launched the United States into its first undeclared war, now called the Quasi-War by historians to underscore its uncertain legal status. The main scene of action was the Caribbean, where more than 100 French privateers were captured.

There was no home-front unity in this time of undeclared war; antagonism only intensified between Federalists and Republicans. Because there seemed to be very little chance of a land invasion by France, leading Republicans feared, with some justification, that the Federalists' real aim might be to raise the army to threaten domestic dissenters. Some claimed that Hamilton had masterminded the army buildup and was lobbying to be second in command, behind the aging Washington. President Adams was increasingly mistrustful, but his cabinet backed the military buildup, and Adams was too weak politically to prevail. He was, moreover, beginning to suspect that his cabinet was more loyal to Hamilton than to the presidency.

Republican newspapers heaped abuse on Adams. Pro-French mobs roamed the capital city, and Adams, fearing for his personal safety, stocked weapons in his presidential quarters. Federalists too went on the offensive. In Newburyport, Massachusetts, they lit a huge bonfire, burning issues of the state's Republican newspapers. One Federalist editor ominously declared that "he who is not for us is against us." Officers in a New York militia unit drank a menacing toast on July 4, 1798: "One and but one party in the United States."

The Alien and Sedition Acts

With tempers so dangerously high, and fears that political dissent was perhaps akin to treason, Federalist leaders moved to muffle the opposition. In mid-1798, Congress hammered out a Sedition Act that mandated a heavy fine or a jail sentence for anyone engaged in conspiracies or revolts or convicted of speaking or writing anything that defamed the president or Congress. Criticisms of government leaders were now criminal utterances. (See "Documenting the American Promise," page 312.)

Congress also passed two Alien Acts. The first extended the waiting period for an alien to achieve citizenship from five to fourteen years and required all aliens to register with the federal government. The second empowered the president in time of war to deport or imprison without trial any foreigner suspected of being a danger to the United States. The clear intent of the alien laws was to harass French immigrants already in the United States and discourage others from coming.

The main targets of the Sedition Act were Republican newspaper editors who were free and abusive in their criticism of the Adams administration. One Federalist in Congress justified his vote for the law: "Let gentlemen look at certain papers printed in this city and elsewhere, and ask themselves whether an unwarrantable and dangerous combination does not exist to overturn and ruin the government by publishing the most shameless falsehoods against the representatives of the people." In all, twenty-five men, almost all newspaper editors, were charged with sedition; twelve were convicted.

Republicans strongly opposed the Alien and Sedition Acts on the grounds that they were in conflict with the Bill of Rights, but they did not have the votes to revoke the acts in Congress, nor could the federal judiciary, dominated by Federalist judges, be counted on to challenge them. Jefferson and Madison turned to the state legislatures, the only other competing political arena, to press their opposition. Each man drafted a set of resolutions condemning the acts and had the legislatures of Virginia and Kentucky present them to the federal government in late fall 1798. The Virginia and Kentucky Resolutions tested the novel argument that state legislatures have the right to judge the constitutionality of federal laws and to **nullify** laws that infringe on the liberties of the people as defined in the Bill of Rights. The resolutions made little dent in the Alien and Sedition Acts, but the idea of a state's right to nullify federal law did not disappear. It surfaced several times in decades to come, most notably in a major tariff dispute in 1832 and in the sectional arguments that led to the Civil War.

> Republicans strongly opposed the Alien and Sedition Acts on the grounds that they were in conflict with the Bill of Rights.

Amid all the war hysteria and sedition fears in 1798, President Adams regained his balance. He was uncharacteristically restrained in pursuing opponents under the Sedition Act, and he finally refused to declare war on France, despite the wishes of extreme Federalists. No doubt he was beginning to realize how much he had been the dupe of Hamilton. He also shrewdly realized that France was not in fact eager for war and that a peaceful settlement might be close at hand. In January 1799, a peace initiative from France arrived in the form of a letter assuring Adams that diplomatic channels were open again and that new commissioners would be welcomed in France. Adams accepted this overture and appointed a new negotiator. By late 1799, the Quasi-War with France had subsided; but in responding to the French initiative, Adams lost the support of a significant part of his own party and sealed his fate as the first one-term president of the United States.

The election of 1800 was openly organized along party lines. The self-designated national leaders of each group met to handpick their candidates for president and vice president. Adams's chief opponent was Thomas Jefferson. When the election was finally over, President Jefferson mounted the inaugural platform to

The Crisis of 1798: Sedition

As President John Adams inched toward an undeclared war with France, criticism of his foreign policy reached an all-time high. Newspaper editors and politicians favorable to France blasted him with such intemperate language that his supporters feared the United States could be pushed to the brink of civil war. Federalists in Congress tried to muffle the opposition by criminalizing seditious words, believing it the only path to preserve the country. Republicans just redoubled their opposition.

DOCUMENT 1
Abigail Adams Complains of Sedition, 1798

Throughout the spring of 1798, a beleaguered Abigail Adams complained repeatedly in confidential letters to her sister Mary Cranch about the need for a sedition law to put a stop to the political criticisms of her husband, the president, by Benjamin Bache, pro-French editor of the Philadelphia Aurora.

(April 26): . . . Yet dairingly do the vile incendaries keep up in Baches paper the most wicked and base, voilent & caluminiating abuse—It was formerly considerd as leveld against the Government, but now it . . . insults the Majesty of the Sovereign People. But nothing will have an Effect untill congress pass a Sedition Bill. . . . (April 28): . . . we are now wonderfully popular except with Bache & Co who in his paper calls the President old, querilous, Bald, blind, cripled, Toothless

Adams. (May 10): . . . This Bache is cursing & abusing daily. If that fellow . . . is not surpressd, we shall come to a civil war. (May 26): . . . I wish the Laws of our Country were competant to punish the stirer up of sedition, the writer and Printer of base and unfounded calumny. This would contribute as much to the Peace and harmony of our Country as any measure. . . . (June 19): . . . in any other Country Bache & all his papers would have been seazd and ought to be here, but congress are dilly dallying about passing a Bill enabling the President to seize suspisious persons, and their papers. (June 23): . . . I wish our Legislature would set the example & make a sedition act, to hold in order the base Newspaper calumniators. In this State, you could not get a verdict, if a prosecution was to be commenced.

SOURCE: Stewart Mitchell, ed., *New Letters of Abigail Adams, 1788–1801* (Boston: Houghton Mifflin, 1947), 165, 167, 172, 179, 193, 196.

DOCUMENT 2
The Sedition Act of 1798

On July 14, 1798, Congress approved a bill making sedition with malicious intent a crime.

SECTION 1. . . . if any persons shall unlawfully combine or conspire together, with intent to oppose any measure or measures of the government of the United States . . . , or to impede the operation of any law of the United States, or to intimidate

or prevent any person holding . . . office in or under the government of the United States, from undertaking, performing or executing his trust or duty, and if any person or persons, with intent as aforesaid, shall counsel, advise or attempt to procure any insurrection, riot, unlawful assembly, or combination . . . , he or they shall be deemed guilty of a high misdemeanor, and on conviction . . . shall be punished by a fine not exceeding five thousand dollars, and by imprisonment during a term not less than six months nor exceeding five years. . . .

SEC. 2. . . . if any person shall write, print, utter or publish, or shall cause or procure to be written, printed, uttered or published . . . , any false, scandalous and malicious writing or writings against the government of the United States, or either house of the Congress of the United States, or the President of the United States, with intent to defame the said government . . . or to bring them . . . into contempt or disrepute; or to excite against them . . . the hatred of the good people of the United States . . . , or to aid, encourage or abet any hostile designs of any foreign nation against the United States . . . , then such person, being thereof convicted thereof . . . shall be punished by a fine not exceeding two thousand dollars, and by imprisonment not exceeding two years.

DOCUMENT 3
Matthew Lyon Criticizes John Adams, 1798

Matthew Lyon, a member of Congress from Vermont, published this criticism of President Adams in a letter to the editor of Spooner's Vermont Journal (July 31, 1798). It became the first of three counts against him in a sedition *trial. Lyon drew a four-month sentence and a fine of $1,000. From jail he ran for reelection to Congress—and won.*

As to the Executive, when I shall see the efforts of that power bent on the promotion of the comfort, the happiness, and the accommodation of the people, that Executive shall have my zealous and uniform support. But when I see every consideration of the public welfare swallowed up in a continual grasp for power, in an unbounded thirst for ridiculous pomp, foolish adulation, or selfish avarice; when I shall behold men of real merit daily turned out of office for no other cause but independence of sentiment; when I shall see men of firmness, merit, years, abilities, and experience, discarded on their application for office, for fear they possess that independence; and men of meanness preferred for the ease with which they take up and advocate opinions, the consequence of which they know but little of; when I shall see the sacred name of religion employed as a State engine to make mankind hate and persecute one another, I shall not be their humble advocate.

SOURCE: Matthew Lyon, Letter in *Spooner's Vermont Journal*, July 31, 1798. Quoted in Aleine Austin, *Matthew Lyon: New Man of the Democratic Revolution, 1749–1822* (University Park: Pennsylvania State University Press, 1981), 108–09.

DOCUMENT 4
James Bayard Defends the Law, 1799

James Bayard, a Federalist representative from Delaware, led the charge in the House to expel Matthew Lyon from his seat in Congress. Bayard argued that Lyon was guilty of subverting the government.

This Government . . . depends for its existence upon the good will of the people. That good will is maintained by their good opinion. But, how is that good opinion to be preserved, if wicked and unprincipled men, men of inordinate and desperate ambition, are allowed to state facts to the people which are not true, which they know at the time to be false, and which are stated with the criminal intention of bringing the Government into disrepute among the people? This was falsely and deceitfully stealing public opinion; it was a felony of the worst and most dangerous nature.

SOURCE: *Annals of Congress* (1799). Quoted in Richard Buel, *Securing the Revolution: Ideology in American Politics* (Ithaca, N.Y.: Cornell University Press, 1972), 256.

DOCUMENT 5
The Virginia Resolution, December 24, 1798

James Madison drafted the Virginia Resolution and had a trusted ally present it to the Virginia legislature, which was dominated by Republicans. (Jefferson did the same for Kentucky.) The Virginia document denounces the Alien and Sedition Acts and declares that states have the right to "interpose" to stop unconstitutional actions by the federal government.

RESOLVED . . . That this assembly most solemnly declares a warm attachment to the Union of the States, to maintain which it pledges all its powers; and that for this end, it is their duty to watch over and oppose every infraction of those principles which constitute the only basis of that Union, because a faithful observance of them, can alone secure its existence and the public happiness.

That this Assembly doth explicitly and peremptorily declare, that it views the powers of the federal government, as resulting from the compact, to which the states are parties; as limited by the plain sense and intention of the instrument constituting the compact; as no further valid that they are authorized by the grants enumerated in that compact; and that in case of a deliberate, palpable, and dangerous exercise of other powers, not granted by the said compact, the states who are parties thereto, have the right, and are in duty bound, to interpose for arresting the progress of the evil, and for maintaining within their respective limits, the authorities, rights and liberties appertaining to them. . . .

That the General Assembly doth particularly protest against the palpable and alarming infractions of the Constitution, in the two late cases of the "Alien and Sedition Acts" . . . ; the first of which exercises a power no where delegated to the federal government . . ; and the other of which acts, exercises in like manner, a power not delegated by the constitution, but on the contrary, expressly and positively forbidden by one of the amendments thereto; a power, which more than any other, ought to produce universal alarm, because it is levelled against that right of freely examining public characters and measures, and of free communication among the people thereon, which has ever been justly deemed, the only effectual guardian of every other right.

SOURCE: Avalon Project, Yale Law School, 1996, <www.yale.edu/lawweb/avalon/virres.htm>.

(continued)

(continued)

QUESTIONS FOR ANALYSIS
AND DEBATE

1. Why did Federalists believe a Sedition Act was necessary? What exactly was the threat, according to Abigail Adams? According to James Bayard? What threat is implied by the wording of the act?

2. Does Matthew Lyon's criticism of President Adams rise to the level of threat that Federalists feared? How do you explain his guilty verdict? His reelection to Congress?

3. What might Madison have meant by "interpose" as the desired action by states? What could states actually do?

4. How would Adams and Bayard square the Sedition Act with the First Amendment's protection of free speech? Did critics of the law invoke freedom of speech and press?

5. Which side had the stronger argument in 1798–1799? Do you think there should be limits on what can be said publicly about high government officials? Why or why not?

announce, "We are all republicans, we are all federalists," an appealing rhetoric of harmony appropriate to an inaugural address. But his formulation perpetuated a denial of the validity of party politics, a denial that ran deep in the founding generation of political leaders.

Conclusion: Parties Nonetheless

American political leaders began operating the new government in 1789 with great hopes to unify the country and to overcome selfish factionalism. The enormous popularity of, and trust in, President Washington was the central foundation for that hope, and Washington did not disappoint, becoming a model Mr. President with a good blend of integrity and authority. Stability was further aided by easy passage of the Bill of Rights (to appease Antifederalists) and by attention to cultivating a virtuous citizenry of upright men supported and rewarded by republican womanhood. Yet the hopes of the honeymoon period soon turned to worries and then fears as major political disagreements flared up.

At the core of the conflict was a group of talented men—Hamilton, Madison, Jefferson, and Adams—so recently allies but now opponents. They diverged over Hamilton's economic program, over relations with the British and the Jay Treaty, over the French and Haitian revolutions, and over preparedness for war abroad and free speech rights at home. Hamilton was perhaps the driving force in these conflicts, but the antagonism was not about mere personality. Parties were taking shape, not around individuals but around principles, such as ideas about what constitutes enlightened leadership, how powerful should the federal government be, who is the best ally in Europe, and when does oppositional political speech turn into treason. The Federalists were pro-British, pro-commerce, and ever alarmed about the potential excesses of democracy. The Republicans celebrated, up to a point, the radical republicanism of France and found the Sedition Act an alarming example of the old Antifederalists' worst nightmare.

When Jefferson, then, in his inaugural address of 1800 offered his conciliatory assurance that Americans were at the same time "all republicans" and "all federalists," he probably mystified some listeners. Possibly he meant to suggest that both groups shared two basic ideas—the value of republican government, in which power derived from the people, and the value of the unique federal system of shared governance structured by the Constitution. But by 1800, these two words defined competing philosophies of government. Jefferson's speech was spoken aloud; his listeners could not hear the presence or absence of capital letters. To at least some of his listeners, Jefferson's assertion of harmony across party lines could only have seemed bizarre. For the next two decades, these two parties would battle each other, both fearing that the success of the other might bring the demise of the country. And for the next two decades, leaders continued to worry that party spirit itself was a bad thing.

FOR ADDITIONAL FIRSTHAND ACCOUNTS OF THIS PERIOD, see Chapter 9 in Michael Johnson, ed., *Reading the American Past,* Third Edition.

TO ASSESS YOUR MASTERY OF THE MATERIAL IN THIS CHAPTER, see the Online Study Guide at bedfordstmartins.com/ roark.

FOR WEB LINKS RELATED TO TOPICS IN THIS CHAPTER, see "HistoryLinks," "DocLinks," and "PlaceLinks" at bedfordstmartins.com/roark.

CHRONOLOGY

1789
- George Washington inaugurated first president.
- French Revolution begins, causing celebration in America.
- First Congress meets in New York City.
- Fort Washington erected in western Ohio as command post for invasions of Indian country.

1790
- Alexander Hamilton issues his *Report on Public Credit,* and Congress approves his plan for funding the federal debt and assuming states' debts.
- Congress approves Potomac River site for U.S. capital.
- Federal government moves from New York to Philadelphia.
- Judith Sargent Murray publishes "On the Equality of the Sexes."
- New Jersey election law specifically refers to state voters as *he or she.*
- General Josiah Harmar's defeat by Shawnee and Miami Indians in Ohio leads to his recall and court-martial.

1791
- Bill of Rights ratified by states.
- Hamilton proposes and Congress charters the Bank of the United States.
- General Arthur St. Clair's forces defeated by Ohio Indians in worst loss ever by Americans in Indian wars.
- Congress passes whiskey tax.
- Haitian Revolution begins and raises fears of race wars in U.S. South.
- Hamilton issues his *Report on Manufactures,* proposing tariffs to encourage American manufacturing.

1793
- Washington's second term begins.
- Napoleonic Wars break out between France and England.
- Washington issues Neutrality Proclamation over war between France and England.
- Reign of Terror in France throws deep chill over American admiration of French Revolution.
- Eli Whitney invents cotton gin, leading to large rise in agricultural production of cotton in the South.

1794
- Farmers stage Whiskey Rebellion in western Pennsylvania, causing President Washington to lead U.S. army west to break it up.
- Lancaster Turnpike, first private toll road, constructed in Pennsylvania.

1795
- Treaty of Greenville cedes most Indian land in Ohio to United States.
- Jay Treaty settles little with England and causes much popular protest in the United States.

1796
- Federalist John Adams elected second president, Thomas Jefferson vice president.

1797
- XYZ affair in France insults U.S. honor and leads to preparations for war with France.

1798
- Quasi-War with France erupts, resulting in capture of French ships in the Caribbean.
- Congress passes Alien and Sedition Acts to suppress pro-French, anti-Adams sentiments.
- Virginia and Kentucky Resolutions press for states' rights in judging constitutionality of federal laws.

1800
- Republican Thomas Jefferson elected third president.

BIBLIOGRAPHY

General Works

Bernard Bailyn, *To Begin the World Anew: The Genius and Ambiguities of the American Founders* (2003).

Doron Ben-Atar and Barbara B. Oberg, eds., *Federalists Reconsidered* (1998).

Richard Buel, *Securing the Revolution: Ideology in American Politics, 1789–1815* (1972).

William Nisbet Chambers, *Political Parties in a New Nation: The American Experience, 1776–1809* (1963).

David P. Currie, *The Constitution in Congress: The Federalist Period, 1789–1801* (1997).

Stanley Elkins and Eric McKitrick, *The Age of Federalism: The Early American Republic, 1788–1800* (1993).

Joseph J. Ellis, *Founding Fathers: The Revolutionary Generation* (2000).

John E. Ferling, *A Leap in the Dark: The Struggle to Create the American Republic* (2003).

Marshall Foletta, *Coming to Terms with Democracy: Federalist Intellectuals and the Shaping of an American Culture* (2001).

Joanne B. Freeman, *Affairs of Honor: National Politics in the New Republic* (2001).

John F. Hoadley, *Origins of American Political Parties, 1789–1803* (1986).

Ronald Hoffman and Peter J. Albert, eds., *Launching the "Extended Republic": The Federalist Era* (1996).

Donald R. Kennon, ed., *A Republic for the Ages: The United States Capitol and the Political Culture in the Early Republic* (1999).

Ralph Ketcham, *Presidents above Party: The First American Presidency, 1789–1829* (1984).

David McCullough, *John Adams* (2001).

John R. Nelson, *Liberty and Property: Political Economy and Policymaking in the New Nation, 1789–1812* (1987).

James Rogers Sharp, *American Politics in the Early Republic: The New Nation in Crisis* (1993).

Larry E. Tise, *The American Counterrevolution: A Retreat from Liberty, 1783–1800* (1999).

David Waldstreicher, *In the Midst of Perpetual Fetes: The Making of American Nationalism, 1776–1820* (1997).

Washington's Administration

Carl Abbott, *Political Terrain: Washington, D.C., from Tidewater Town to Global Metropolis* (1999).

Akhil Reed Amar, *The Bill of Rights: Creation and Reconstruction* (2000).

Bob Arnebeck, *Through a Fiery Trial: Building Washington, 1790–1800* (1991).

Kenneth R. Bowling, *Politics in the First Congress, 1789–1791* (1990).

Kenneth R. Bowling, *The Creation of Washington, D.C.: The Idea and Location of the American Capital* (1991).

Steven R. Boyd, ed., *The Whiskey Rebellion: Past and Present Perspectives* (1985).

Jerry A. Clouse, *The Whiskey Rebellion: Southwestern Pennsylvania's Frontier People Test the American Constitution* (1995).

James T. Flexner, *George Washington and the New Nation, 1783–1793* (1970).

James T. Flexner, *George Washington: Anguish and Farewell, 1793–1799* (1972).

Robert F. Jones, *George Washington: Ordinary Man, Extraordinary Leader* (2002).

Forrest McDonald, *The American Presidency: An Intellectual History* (1994).

Robert A. Rutland, *The Birth of the Bill of Rights, 1776–1791* (1991).

Thomas P. Slaughter, *The Whiskey Rebellion: Frontier Epilogue to the American Revolution* (1986).

Henry Wiencek, *An Imperfect God: George Washington, His Slaves, and the Creation of America* (2003).

The Economy and Hamilton's Program

Joyce Appleby, *Capitalism and a New Social Order: The Republican Vision of the 1790s* (1984).

Richard Brookhiser, *Alexander Hamilton, American* (2000).

Christopher Clark, *The Roots of Rural Capitalism: Western Massachusetts, 1780–1860* (1990).

Jacob E. Cooke, *Alexander Hamilton* (1982).

Paul A. Gilje, ed., *Wages of Independence: Capitalism in the Early American Republic* (1997).

James A. Henretta, *The Origins of American Capitalism: Collected Essays* (1991).

Joan Jensen, *Loosening the Bonds: Mid-Atlantic Farm Women, 1750–1850* (1986).

Lawrence S. Kaplan, *Alexander Hamilton: Ambivalent Anglophile* (2002).

Allan Kulikoff, *The Agrarian Origins of American Capitalism* (1992).

James Lemon, *The Best Poor Man's Country: A Geographical Study of Early Southeastern Pennsylvania* (1972).

Forrest McDonald, *Alexander Hamilton: A Biography* (1982).

Winifred Rothenberg, *From Market-Places to a Market Economy: The Transformation of Rural Massachusetts, 1750–1850* (1992).

Herbert E. Sloan, *Principle and Interest: Thomas Jefferson and the Problem of Debt* (1995).

Society and Culture

Richard D. Brown, *Knowledge Is Power: The Diffusion of Information in Early America, 1700–1865* (1989).

Patricia Cline Cohen, *A Calculating People: The Spread of Numeracy in Early America* (1999).

Nancy Cott, *The Bonds of Womanhood: Women's Sphere in New England, 1780–1835* (1977).

Cathy N. Davidson, *Revolution and the Word: The Rise of the Novel in America* (1986).

Emory Elliott, *Revolutionary Writers: Literature and Authority in the New Republic, 1725–1810* (1982).

Richard R. John, *Spreading the News: The American Postal System from Franklin to Morse* (1996).

Richard B. Kielbowicz, *News in the Mail: The Press, the Post Office, and Public Information, 1700–1860* (1989).

Sheila L. Skemp, *Judith Sargent Murray: A Brief Biography with Documents* (1998).

Indians and the Frontier

Robert F. Berkhofer Jr., *Salvation and the Savage: An Analysis of Protestant Missions and American Indian Response, 1787–1862* (1965).

Colin G. Calloway, *Crown and Calumet: British-Indian Relations, 1783–1815* (1987).

Andrew R. L. Cayton, *Frontier Republic: Ideology and Politics in the Ohio Country, 1780–1825* (1989).

Gregory E. Dowd, *A Spirited Resistance: The North American Indian Struggle for Unity, 1745–1815* (1992).

R. Douglas Hurt, *The Ohio Frontier: Crucible of the Old Northwest, 1720–1830* (1998).

Francis Paul Prucha, *American Indian Policy in the Formative Years: The Indian Trade and Intercourse Acts, 1780–1834* (1962).

Malcolm J. Rohrbough, *The Transappalachian Frontier: People, Societies, and Institutions, 1775–1850* (1978).

Wiley Sword, *President Washington's Indian War: The Struggle for the Old Northwest, 1790–1795* (1985).

Richard White, *The Middle Ground: Indians, Empires, and Republics in the Great Lakes Region, 1650–1815* (1991).

Foreign Relations

Albert H. Bowman, *The Struggle for Neutrality: Franco-American Diplomacy during the Federalist Era* (1974).

Jerald A. Combs, *The Jay Treaty: Political Battleground of the Founding Fathers* (1970).

Alexander DeConde, *The Quasi-War: The Politics and Diplomacy of the Undeclared War with France, 1797–1801* (1966).

Carolyn E. Fick, *The Making of Haiti: The Saint Domingue Revolution from Below* (1991).

David Barry Gaspar and David Patrick Geggus, eds., *A Turbulent Time: The French Revolution and the Greater Caribbean* (1997).

Peter P. Hill, *French Perceptions of the Early American Republic, 1783–1793* (1988).

Daniel G. Lang, *Foreign Policy in the Early Republic* (1985).

Martin Ros, *Night of Fire: The Black Napoleon and the Battle for Haiti* (1993).

William Stinchcombe, *The XYZ Affair* (1981).

Richard J. Twomey, *Jacobins and Jeffersonians: Anglo-American Radicalism in the United States, 1790–1820* (1989).

Federalists and Republicans

Ralph A. Brown, *The Presidency of John Adams* (1975).

Noble Cunningham, *The Jeffersonian Republicans: The Formation of Party Organization, 1789–1801* (1957).

Larry D. Eldridge, *A Distant Heritage: The Growth of Free Speech in Early America* (1994).

Joseph J. Ellis, *Passionate Sage: The Character and Legacy of John Adams* (1993).

John Ferling, *John Adams: A Life* (1992).

Richard Hofstadter, *The Idea of a Party System: The Rise of Legitimate Opposition in the United States, 1780–1840* (1969).

Richard H. Kohn, *Eagle and Sword: The Federalists and the Creation of the Military Establishment in America, 1783–1802* (1975).

Leonard Levy, *The Emergence of a Free Press* (1985).

Drew McCoy, *The Elusive Republic: Political Economy in Jeffersonian America* (1980).

Jeffrey L. Pasley, *The Tyranny of Printers: Newspaper Politics in the Early American Republic* (2001).

James Morton Smith, *Freedom's Fetters: The Alien and Sedition Laws and American Civil Liberties* (1966).

John Zvesper, *Political Philosophy and Rhetoric: A Study of the Origins of American Party Politics* (1977).

State Histories

Richard R. Beeman, *The Old Dominion and the New Nation, 1788–1801* (1972).

Andrew R. L. Cayton, *Frontier Indiana* (1996).

Paul Goodman, *The Democratic-Republicans of Massachusetts* (1964).

Christopher Grasso, *A Speaking Aristocracy: Transforming Public Discourse in Eighteenth-Century Connecticut* (1999).

Norman Risjord, *Chesapeake Politics, 1781–1800* (1978).

Charles Steffen, *The Mechanics of Baltimore: Workers and Politics in the Age of Revolution, 1763–1812* (1984).

Alan Taylor, *Liberty Men and Great Proprietors: The Revolutionary Settlement on the Maine Frontier, 1760–1820* (1990).

Alfred Young, *The Democratic-Republicans of New York: The Origins, 1763–1797* (1967).

A JEFFERSON FAN

Ladies' fans became increasingly popular fashion accessories in the late eighteenth and early nineteenth centuries, equally useful for communication and cooling. This folding fan of vellum and carved ivory, made in the early 1800s, features a medallion portrait of President Thomas Jefferson. Carried by the ribbon on a woman's wrist, the fan could be flicked open to announce a partisan political statement. Fans and other handheld articles such as parasols and handkerchiefs expanded the repertoire of nonverbal expression for women, who by the custom and training of the time were expected to be less assertive than men in mixed-sex conversation. Many emotions and messages—from modesty, coyness, and flirtatiousness to anger, irritability, and boredom—could be communicated by the expert deployment of this delicate emblem of femininity. Women learned the conventions of fluttering the fan by close observation and perhaps by explicit training.

Collection of David J. and Janice L. Frent.

Republicans in Power

1800–1824

THE NAME TECUMSEH translates to "Shooting Star," a fitting name for the Shawnee chief who reached meteoric heights of fame among Indians during Thomas Jefferson's presidency. From Canada to Georgia and west to the Mississippi, Tecumseh was accounted a charismatic leader. White Americans praised (and feared) him as a would-be Moses of the Indians. Graceful, eloquent, compelling, magnetic, astute: Tecumseh was all these and more, a gifted natural leader, equal parts politician and warrior.

Tecumseh was born in 1768 into a family of six sons and one daughter in the Ohio Country. His parents had migrated there around 1760 from the South along with hundreds of Shawnees. The Northwest Territory had become home to some dozen Indian tribes, several of them recent migrants from points east and south. But now Ohio was a battleground in the struggle with the Big Knives, as the Shawnee people called the Americans, producing perpetual conflict from the Revolution to the 1790s Indian wars. Tecumseh's childhood was marked by repeated violence and the loss of his father and two brothers in battle. Five times between 1774 and 1782 the boy fled raids by American soldiers that left his homes in flames and his villages destroyed. When he was ten, his widowed mother returned to the South, leaving her remaining children in the care of an aunt.

The establishment of the United States government brought no peace to the Indians' country. George Washington's administration could not stem the flow of eager but foolhardy American settlers floating down the Ohio River on flatboats, and the youthful Tecumseh honed his warrior skills by ambushing those pioneers. He did not take part in the Indians' 1791 dramatic victory over General St. Clair's army, but he fought at the Battle of Fallen Timbers, a major Indian defeat. He avoided the 1795 negotiations of the Treaty of Greenville, in which a half dozen dispirited tribes ceded much of Ohio to the Big Knives. With frustration he watched as seven additional treaties between 1802 and 1805 whittled away more Indian land.

Some Indians, resigned and tired, looked for ways to accommodate to new realities, taking up farming, trade, and even intermarriage with the Big Knives. Others spent their treaty payments on deadly alcohol. Tecumseh's younger brother Tenskwatawa led an embittered life of idleness and drink. But Tecumseh rejected assimilation and inebriation and embarked on a campaign to return his people to their ancient ways. Donning traditional animal-skin garb, he traveled around the Great Lakes area, persuading tribes to join his pan-Indian confederacy. The American territorial governor of Indiana, William Henry Harrison, reported, "For four years he has been in constant motion. You see him today on the Wabash, and in a short time hear of him on the shores of Lake Erie or Michigan, or on the banks of the Mississippi, and

Tecumseh

Several portraits of Tecumseh exist, but they all present a different visage, and none of them enjoys verified authenticity. This one perhaps comes closest: It is an 1848 engraving adapted from an earlier drawing that no longer exists, sketched by a French trader in Indiana named Pierre Le Dru in a live sitting with the Indian leader in 1808. The engraver has given Tecumseh a British army officer's uniform, showing that he fought on the British side in the War of 1812. Notice the head covering and the medallion around the neck, marking Tecumseh's Indian identity.

Library of Congress.

wherever he goes he makes an impression favorable to his purpose." In 1811, he toured the South, visiting tribes from Mississippi to Georgia while an especially brilliant comet illuminated the night sky. The human Shooting Star understood that only a powerful alliance of Indians could block the path of the westward-moving Big Knives.

Tecumseh's once-dissolute brother joined his campaign after a close brush with death in 1805. Tenskwatawa miraculously revived and recounted a startling vision, a meeting with the Master of Life. Renaming himself the Prophet, Tenskwatawa urged Indians everywhere to return to tradition. He preached that the white Americans were children of the Evil Spirit, des-

tined to be destroyed. Headquartered at a new village called Prophetstown, located in present-day Indiana along Tippecanoe Creek, Tecumseh and his brother pledged a potent blend of spiritual regeneration and political unity that attracted thousands of followers. Governor Harrison admired and feared Tecumseh, calling him "one of those uncommon geniuses which spring up occasionally to produce revolutions."

President Jefferson worried about Tecumseh as well. Although his first term in office was marked by notable successes, such as the Louisiana Purchase and the Lewis and Clark expedition, Jefferson's second term brought the storm clouds of impending war generated by a worrisome Indian-English alliance. That war eventually came in 1812, during President Madison's term. It was partly fought over issues similar to those of the late 1790s: insults over international shipping rights, the capture of vessels, and impressment of sailors. But it was also a product of tensions with Indians in the West in renewed coalition with England, occupying land coveted by westward-moving Americans.

Tecumseh's confederacy delivered 800 warriors to augment British military strength in Canada. Unfortunately for the Indians, the British concentrated on protecting Canada, not the Indians' country. Tecumseh died on Canadian soil at the Battle of the Thames in the fall of 1813, defending Canada against an army led by American general William Henry Harrison. In the end, the War of 1812 settled little between the Americans and the British, but it was tragically conclusive for the Indians. No Indian leader with the star power of Tecumseh would emerge again east of the Mississippi.

The briefly unified Indian confederacy under Tecumseh had no counterpart in the young Republic's confederation of states, where widespread unity and enthusiasm behind a single leader proved impossible to achieve. Republicans did battle with Federalists during the Jefferson and Madison administrations, but then Federalists doomed their party by opposing the War of 1812 and after 1815 ceased to be a major force in political life. The next two presidents, James Monroe and John Quincy Adams, congratulated themselves on the Federalists' demise and Republican unity, but in fact divisions within their party were extensive. Wives of politicians increasingly inserted themselves into this dissonant mix, managing men's politicking and jockeying for power in the Capitol, enabling their husbands to appear above the fray and maintain the fiction of a non-factionalized state. That it was a fiction became sharply apparent in the most serious political crisis of this period, the Missouri Compromise of 1820.

Jefferson Assumes Power, 1800–1801

The nerve-wracking election of 1800, decided in the House of Representatives, enhanced fears that party divisions born in the 1790s would ruin the country. A panicky Federalist newspaper in Connecticut predicted that Jefferson's victory would produce civil war and usher in an immoral reign of "murder, robbery, rape, adultery and incest," leading to a "nation black with crimes," its "soil soaked with blood."

Nothing nearly so drastic or revolutionary occurred. Jefferson later called his election the "revolution of 1800," by which he meant his thorough yet peaceful repudiation of the monarchical power of the Federalists. He first had to deal with a set of midnight appointments made by John Adams as he vacated office, an instance demonstrating keen Federalist mistrust but also leading to the important legal principle of judicial review. Meanwhile, quite a different "revolution of 1800" nearly materialized when a literate Virginia slave named Gabriel followed the scurrilous rhetoric of the presidential campaign and plotted his own rebellion, figuring it might succeed when white men were so badly divided. Gabriel was wrong, but his plot added greatly to the turbulence of 1800–1801.

Jefferson indeed did radically transform the presidency, away from the Federalists' vision of a powerful, even regal, executive branch to republican simplicity and limited government. Yet even Jefferson found that circumstances sometimes required him to draw on the expansive powers of the presidency.

Election by the House

Jefferson's election in 1800 was a cliff-hanger. It was no surprise that his Federalist opponent, John Adams, lost. Adams's diplomatic overtures to France had angered many in his own party, and Alexander Hamilton's abusive scorn of Adams doomed him to defeat. But the Republican voters in the electoral college slipped up, giving equal numbers of votes to Jefferson and his run-

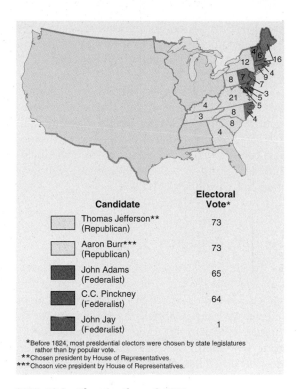

Candidate	Electoral Vote*
Thomas Jefferson** (Republican)	73
Aaron Burr*** (Republican)	73
John Adams (Federalist)	65
C.C. Pinckney (Federalist)	64
John Jay (Federalist)	1

*Before 1824, most presidential electors were chosen by state legislatures rather than by popular vote.
**Chosen president by House of Representatives.
***Chosen vice president by House of Representatives.

MAP 10.1   The Election of 1800

ning mate, Senator Aaron Burr of New York, an outcome possible because of the single balloting to choose both president and vice president (Map 10.1). (The Twelfth Amendment to the Constitution, adopted four years later, provided for distinct ballots for the two offices to fix this problem.) Burr, driven by ambition and vanity, declined to concede the presidency to Jefferson. So the election moved to the Federalist-dominated House of Representatives for decision.

In February 1801, the House met to choose. Each state delegation commanded one vote, and the winner needed nine votes. Some Federalists preferred Burr, believing his character flaws made him more susceptible to Federalist pressure. "His very selfishness prevents his entertaining any mischievous predilections for foreign nations," wrote one senator privately. But Hamilton, although no friend to Jefferson, recognized that the high-strung and arrogant Burr would be more dangerous in the presidency than Jefferson, with his hated but steady habits of **republicanism**. Jefferson was a fanatic and a "contemptible hypocrite" in Hamilton's opinion, but at least he was not corrupt. Jefferson had the votes of eight states on the first ballot; it took thirty-six more ballots and six days to get a ninth vote (and also a tenth) in his column. In the end, anti-Burr Federalist representatives in three states abstained from voting to allow Jefferson the victory without actually having to cast a ballot for him.

The election of 1800 demonstrated a remarkable feature of the new constitutional government. No matter how hard fought the campaign, this election showed that leadership of the nation could shift from one group to a distinctly different group in a peaceful transfer of power effected by ballots, not bullets.

Gabriel's Rebellion

As the country struggled over its white leadership crisis, a twenty-four-year-old blacksmith named Gabriel plotted his own revolution of 1800 in Virginia. Gabriel, the slave of Thomas Prosser, recruited hundreds of co-conspirators from five counties. Inspired by the Haitian Revolution (see chapter 9), and perhaps directly informed of it by French slaves new to the Richmond area, Gabriel and his followers planned to march on the state capitol at Richmond, set diversionary fires, capture an arsenal, and take the governor, James Monroe, hostage. Gabriel intended to spare Methodists and Quakers, known to hold antislavery views, and he also expected Indians and "the poor white people" of Richmond to join him. Taking seriously the Federalist rhetoric about Republican Francophiles, Gabriel assumed that the pro-French (and thus **liberty**-loving) Republican governor Monroe might prove sympathetic to the rebels' cause.

Gabriel's revolt never materialized. A massive thunderstorm scuttled it on the appointed day in August, and a few nervous slaves spilled the secret. Within days, scores of implicated conspirators were jailed and brought to trial. One of the accused, Jack Ditcher, declared in court, "We have as much right to fight for our liberty as any men." Another jailed rebel compared himself to the most venerated icon of the early Republic: "I have nothing more to offer than what General Washington would have had to offer, had he been taken by the British and put to trial by them." Such talk invoking the specter of a black George Washington worried James Monroe and Thomas Jefferson.

> As the country struggled over its white leadership crisis, a twenty-four-year-old blacksmith named Gabriel plotted his own revolution of 1800 in Virginia.

Persistent rumors implicated two white Frenchmen in the plot. If that connection had been established, it would have strengthened Federalist claims that the slave insurrections were a logical outcome of Republican slogans about liberty and equality. Meanwhile, Virginia judges were keeping the Richmond gallows busy. Over September and October, 27 black men were hanged for contemplating rebellion. Finally, Jefferson advised Monroe that the hangings had gone far enough and that deportation was a better alternative. "The world at large will forever condemn us if we indulge a principle of revenge," Jefferson wrote Monroe.

Gabriel's near-rebellion failed, but it scared Virginia politicians into a serious—but secret—effort to identify a site to which future troublesome slaves could be deported. In 1801, the Virginia legislature pressed the federal government for help because deportation required cooperation with a foreign power. Though sympathetic to this effort, Jefferson let the idea drop. Deporting insubordinate slaves to Sierra Leone in Africa or to some Spanish colony west of the Mississippi would perhaps reduce tensions in Virginia, but it might also encourage defiance because the eventual payoff was freedom.

The Jeffersonian Vision of Republican Simplicity

Jefferson sidestepped the problem of slavery and turned his attention to establishing a mode of governing that presented a clear contrast to that of the Federalists. On inauguration day, held for the first time in the village optimistically called Washington City, he walked to the new Capitol building to be sworn in, shunning the pageantry of a horse-drawn carriage and an entourage of attendants. His clothes were rustic, not dressy: green breeches and gray woolen stockings. A disdainful Federalist later remarked, "Everyone knew, of course, that he had a fine French wardrobe of damask waistcoats, frilled shirts, and silk stockings." But Jefferson's aim was to strike the tone of republican simplicity.

Once in office, he continued to emphasize unfussy frugality. He scaled back on Federalist building plans for Washington City and cut the government budget. He continued to wear plain clothes, appearing "neglected but not slovenly," according to one onlooker. He cultivated a casual style, wearing slippers to greet important guests, avoiding the formality of state parties and liveried servants. Jefferson's studied carelessness was very deliberate.

Martha Washington and Abigail Adams had received the wives of government figures at formal weekly teas, thereby helping to create and cement social relations in the governing class. But Jefferson, a long-term widower, abolished female gatherings and avoided the women of Washington City. He abandoned George Washington's tradition of weekly levees, scaling back open-house receptions to just two a year, on New Year's Day and July 4. His preferred social event was the small dinner party with carefully chosen politicos seated at one round table, a table shape that guaranteed nonhierarchical seating plus the certainty that no conversation could escape the president's ears. Generally his guest list was either entirely Republican or entirely Federalist, and in both cases usually entirely male. At these intimate dinners, the president demonstrated his version of statecraft, exercising influence and strengthening informal relationships that would help him to govern.

Jefferson's paramount goal was to scale back the federal exercise of power and promote policies that would foster the independence of ordinary American citizens. Jefferson was no Antifederalist. He had supported the Constitution in 1788, although he had qualms about the unrestricted reelection allowed to the president. But events of the 1790s had caused him to worry about the stretching of powers in the executive branch. Jefferson had watched with distrust as Hamilton led the Federalists to fund the public debt, establish a national bank, and secure commercial ties with England (see chapter 9). The Hamiltonian program seemed to Jefferson to be promoting the interests of money-hungry speculators at the expense of the rest of the country. Jefferson was not at all anticommerce. But financial schemes that seemed merely to allow rich men to become richer, without enhancing the vast and natural productivity of America, were corrupt and worthless, he believed, and their promotion had no authority under the Constitution. In Jefferson's vision, the source of true liberty in America was the independent farmer, someone who owned and worked his land both for himself and for the market.

Jefferson set out to dismantle Federalist innovations. He reduced the size of the army by a third, leaving only three thousand soldiers, and he cut back the navy from twenty-five to seven ships. Peacetime defense, he felt, should rest with "a well-disciplined militia," not a standing army. With the consent of Congress, he abolished all federal internal taxes based on population or on whiskey. A national tax on population had been tried just once, in 1798, and proved as burdensome and expensive as taking a census. It was far more feasible to derive government revenue solely from customs duties and from the sale of west-

> In Jefferson's vision, the source of true liberty in America was the independent farmer, someone who owned and worked his land both for himself and for the market.

Jefferson's Red Waistcoat

During his presidency, Jefferson often wore this red silk waistcoat as informal daywear. The garment had a velvet collar, woolen sleeves, and a thick lining made from recycled cotton and wool stockings. The thrifty Jefferson preferred to conserve firewood by wearing layers of warm clothes. A senator visiting in 1802 reported in dismay that the president was "dressed, or rather undressed, with an old brown coat, red waistcoat, old corduroy small clothes, much soiled, woolen hose, and slippers without heels." Another guest in 1804 found him wearing the red waistcoat, green velveteen breeches with pearl buttons, and "slippers down at the heels" that made him look like an ordinary farmer. Such colorful clothing in silk and velveteen carries dressy or feminine connotations in the twenty-first century, but it did not in 1800. Jefferson put on silk stockings and clean linen for fancy dinner parties; and when he lived in Paris in the 1780s, he wore an elaborately embroidered silk waistcoat under a greatcoat trimmed with gold lace. But in the 1800s, he used simple, colorful clothes to make a point about republican manners.

Courtesy of Monticello. Photo by Colonial Williamsburg.

Jefferson's Duplicating Machine

Jefferson wrote tens of thousands of letters over his lifetime. For some years he kept copies of his work by using a patented slow-drying ink and special tissue paper obtained in England. The very thin tissue could be pressed against a manuscript page whose ink was still wet and then carefully peeled off to create a copy. In 1804, Jefferson acquired his first polygraph or duplicating machine, which could produce four identical copies of a handwritten page. No doubt the stepped-up business of the presidency (and his small clerical staff) made this machine very useful. Patented by an Englishman and a Philadelphian in 1803, the polygraph linked up to five pens using rods in three dimensions. The motion of the first pen, held in Jefferson's hand, was perfectly mimicked by the rest of the pens poised over tautly held paper.

National Museum of American History, Smithsonian Institution, Behring Center.

ern lands. This maneuver was of particular benefit to the South, because the three-fifths clause of the Constitution counted slaves for both representation and taxation. Now the South could enjoy its extra weight in the House of Representatives without the threat of extra taxes. By the end of his first term, Jefferson had deeply reduced Hamilton's cherished national debt.

A properly limited federal government, according to Jefferson, was responsible merely for running a postal system, maintaining the federal courts, staffing lighthouses, collecting customs duties, and conducting a census once every ten years. Government jobs were kept to a minimum. The president had just one private secretary, a young man named Meriwether Lewis, to help with his correspondence, and Jefferson paid him out of his own pocket. (Another 14 servants performed domestic and valet chores for the president, and they were also paid—or owned—by Jefferson.) The Department of State employed only 8 people: Secretary James Madison, 6 clerks, and a messenger. The Treasury Department was by far the largest unit, with 73 revenue commissioners, auditors, and clerks, plus 2 watchmen. The entire payroll of the executive branch amounted to a mere 130 people in 1801.

The Judiciary and the Midnight Judges

There was one set of government workers not under Jefferson's control to appoint. His predecessor, John Adams, seized the short time between his election defeat and Jefferson's inauguration to appoint 217 Federalist men to various judicial, diplomatic, and military posts.

Most of this windfall of appointments came to Adams as a result of the Judiciary Act of 1801, passed in the final month of his presidency. Its predecessor, the Judiciary Act of 1789, had established a six-man Supreme Court and six circuit courts. The new law authorized sixteen circuit courts, each headed by a new judge. The fast-acting Adams could appoint sixteen judges with lifetime tenure, plus dozens more state attorneys, marshals, and clerks for each court. The 1801 act also reduced the Supreme Court from six to five justices. Adams had recently appointed solidly Federalist Virginian John Marshall to a vacant sixth seat, but once the 1801 act became law, a future president would not be able to fill the next empty seat.

In the last weeks of February 1801, Adams and Marshall worked feverishly to secure agreements from the new appointees. In view of the slowness of mail, achieving 217 acceptances was astonishing. The two men were at work until 9 P.M. on the last night Adams was president, signing and delivering commissions (appointment papers) to the new officeholders.

The hasty selection of Federalist "midnight judges" infuriated the Republicans. Jefferson, upon taking office, immediately canceled the nonjudicial appointments that lacked tenure and refused to honor the few appointments that had not yet been delivered. One of them was addressed to William Marbury, who soon decided to sue the new secretary of state, James Madison, for failure to make good on the appointment.

This action gave rise to a landmark Supreme Court case, *Marbury v. Madison,* decided in 1803. The Court, presided over by John Marshall, ruled that although Marbury's commission was valid and the new president should have delivered it, the Court could not compel him to do so. What made the case significant was little noted at the time: The Court found that the grounds of Marbury's suit, resting in the Judiciary Act of 1789, were in conflict with the Constitution. For the first time, the Court acted to disallow a law on the grounds that it was unconstitutional. John Marshall quietly established the concept of judicial review; the Supreme Court in effect assumed the legal authority to **nullify** acts judged in conflict with the Constitution.

Jefferson's Presidency

The reach of the *Marbury* decision went largely unnoticed in 1803 because the president and Congress were preoccupied with foreign policy problems. The rise of Napoleon to power in France brought France and England into open warfare again in 1803, and these renewed foreign tensions created unexpected opportunities and challenges for Jefferson's administration. On the opportunity side, Jefferson's envoys in France negotiated the spectacular purchase of the Louisiana Territory, and explorers Meriwether Lewis and William Clark set out on a cross-country expedition to the Pacific Northwest coast. On the challenge side, pirates threatened American ships off the north coast of Africa, and British and French naval forces nipped at American ships—and American honor—in the Atlantic Ocean.

The Promise of the West: The Louisiana Purchase and the Lewis and Clark Expedition

Up through the Seven Years' War (see chapter 6), France claimed but only lightly settled a large expanse of land west of the Mississippi River, then lost it to Spain in the 1763 Treaty of Paris. Spain never sent adequate forces to control or settle the land, and Spanish power in North America remained precarious everywhere outside New Orleans.

In the 1770s to 1790s, American farming families were settling Kentucky and Tennessee, along rivers emptying into the upper Mississippi. For a time, the Spanish governor of New Orleans granted free navigational rights on that major river to the Americans, who shipped their agricultural produce south for sale in New Orleans and points beyond. Spain even encouraged American settlements on the western side of the river, in Spanish territory, in an effort to augment the population. By 1801, Americans made up a sizable minority of the population around the lower Mississippi. Publicly, Jefferson protested the luring of Americans into Spanish territory, but privately he welcomed it as a first move in a potential appropriation of territory immediately west of the Mississippi. He wrote, "I wish a hundred thousand of our inhabitants would accept the invitation; it will be the means of delivering to us peaceably, what may otherwise cost us a war."

Jefferson's fears of war were not unrealistic. In 1802, the Spanish governor revoked American shipping privileges through or past New Orleans. Congressmen began muttering about taking the city by force. Talk of war, especially in Federalist newspapers, became commonplace.

In the same year, rumors reached Jefferson that Spain had struck a secret bargain with France to hand over a large part of Spain's trans-Mississippi territory to Napoleon in exchange for some land in Italy. Spain had proved a weak western neighbor, but France was another story. Jefferson was so alarmed that he instructed Robert R. Livingston, America's minister in France, to try to buy New Orleans. At first the French denied they owned the city, but when Livingston hinted that the United States might simply seize it if buying was not an option, the French negotiator suddenly asked him to name his price for the entire Louisiana Territory, from the Gulf of Mexico north to Canada. Livingston stalled, and the Frenchman made suggestions: $125 million? $60 million? Livingston shrewdly stalled some more, and within days the French sold the entire territory for the bargain price of $15 million (Map 10.2). The French, motivated sellers, needed cash because of impending war with England and the recent failure, despite twenty thousand troops, to prevent Haitian independence.

Jefferson and most of Congress were delighted with the outcome of the diplomatic mission. Still, Jefferson had some qualms about the Louisiana Purchase. The price was right, and the enormous territory fulfilled Jefferson's dream of abundant farmland for future generations. But by what authority in the Constitution could he justify the purchase? His frequent criti-

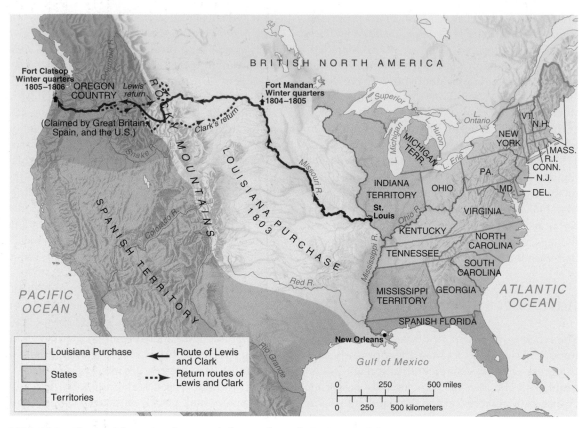

MAP 10.2   The Louisiana Purchase and the Lewis and Clark Expedition
Robert Livingston's bargain buy of 1803 far exceeded his initial assignment, to acquire the city of New Orleans. New England Federalists, worried that their geographically based power in the federal government would someday be eclipsed by the West, voted against the purchase. The Indians who inhabited the vast region, unaware that their land had been claimed by either the French or the Americans, got their first look at Anglo-American and African American men when the Lewis and Clark expedition came exploring in 1804–1806.

READING THE MAP: What natural boundaries defined the Louisiana Purchase? How did the size of the newly acquired territory compare to the existing land area of American states and territories?
CONNECTIONS: What political events in Europe created the opportunity for the Jefferson administration to purchase Louisiana? What constitutional obstacles to expansion did Jefferson have to contend with? How did the American acquisition of the Louisiana territory affect Spain's hold on North America?

FOR MORE HELP ANALYZING THIS MAP, see the map activity for this chapter in the Online Study Guide at bedfordstmartins.com/roark.

> Even before the Louisiana Purchase, Jefferson had eyed the trans-Mississippi West with intense curiosity.

cism of the Hamiltonian stretching of the Constitution came back to haunt him. His legal reasoning told him he needed a constitutional amendment to authorize the addition of territory; more expedient minds told him the treaty-making powers of the president were sufficient. Expediency won out. In late 1803, the American army took formal control of the Louisiana Territory, and the United States was now 828,000 square miles larger.

Even before the Louisiana Purchase, Jefferson had eyed the trans-Mississippi West with intense curiosity. In early 1803, he had arranged congressional funding for a secret scientific and military mission into Spanish and Indian territory. Jefferson appointed twenty-eight-year-old Meriwether Lewis, his personal secretary, to head the expedition, instructing him to investigate Indian cultures, to collect plant and animal specimens, and to chart the geography of the West.

Grizzly Bear Claw Necklace

Lewis and Clark collected hundreds of Indian artifacts on their expedition, but until December 2003 only six were known to still exist. Then this grizzly bear claw necklace unexpectedly turned up at Harvard University's Peabody Museum of Archaeology and Ethnology, stored by mistake in a South Pacific collection. Curators instantly recognized it as a necklace missing since 1899 that had been part of a Lewis and Clark museum exhibit in the mid-nineteenth century. In their expedition journal, the famed explorers noted seeing bear claw necklaces on Shoshone warriors in the Rocky Mountains; possibly one of these warriors gave his necklace to the travelers. The 38 impressive claws, each 3 to 4 inches long, are strung together by rawhide thongs; the necklace required at least two grizzly bears. Male grizzlies are large—6 to 7 feet tall, 500 to 900 pounds—and aggressive. What would it be like to wear this necklace? Whether spiritual or physical, it seems certain that a sense of power was bestowed on the wearer.

Peabody Museum of Archaeology and Ethnology, Harvard University.

Congress had more traditional goals in mind: The expedition was to scout locations for military posts, open commercial agreements for the fur trade, and locate any possible waterway between the east and west coasts.

For his co-leader, Lewis chose Kentuckian William Clark, a fellow veteran of the 1790s Indian wars. Together they handpicked a crew of forty-five, including expert rivermen, gunsmiths, hunters, interpreters, a cook, and a slave named York, who belonged to Clark. The explorers left St. Louis in the spring of 1804, working their way northwest up the Missouri River. They camped for the winter at a Mandan village in what is now central North Dakota. (See "American Places," page 329.) The Mandan Indians were familiar with British and French traders from Canada, but the black man York created a sensation. Reportedly, Indians rubbed moistened fingers over the man's skin to see if the color was painted on.

The following spring, the explorers headed west, aided by a French trapper accompanied by his wife, a sixteen-year-old Indian woman named Sacajawea, and their baby. Sacajawea's presence was to prove unexpectedly helpful. Indian tribes encountered en route withdrew their suspicion that the Americans were hostile because, as Lewis wrote in his journal, "no woman ever accompanies a war party of Indians in this quarter."

The Lewis and Clark expedition reached the Pacific Ocean at the mouth of the Columbia River in November 1805. When Lewis and Clark returned home the following year, they were greeted as national heroes. They had established favorable relations with dozens of Indian tribes; they had collected invaluable information on the peoples, soils, plants, animals, and geography of the West; and they had inspired a nation of restless explorers and solitary imitators.

Challenges Overseas: The Barbary Wars

The inspiring opportunity of westward exploration was matched at the same time by a frustrating challenge overseas. From 1801 to 1805, the United States was drawn into belligerent exchanges off the north coast of Africa that featured hijacked ships and captured crews. For well over a century, four Arabic settlements on the Barbary coast—Morocco, Algiers, Tunis, and Tripoli—controlled shipping traffic through the Mediterranean by means of privateering. Swift vessels overtook merchant ships, plundered the cargoes, and captured the crews for ransom. Most European states spared their ships by paying tribute—an annual sum of money—to secure safe passage. When American ships flew under the British flag, up to 1776, they were protected. But once independent, the United States also began to pay tribute, by the mid-1790s, on the order of $50,000 to the leader of each state.

In 1801, the pasha (military head) of Tripoli demanded a large increase in his tribute. Jefferson had long thought such payments were extortion, and his response was to send four warships to Tripoli. A rallying slogan backed Jefferson: "Millions for defense, not one cent for

The Burning of the Frigate Philadelphia in Tripoli Harbor

The American frigate *Philadelphia* went down in flames in the harbor of Tripoli on the North African coast in 1804. The man responsible became an instant hero in America: a young naval commander named Stephen Decatur, who pulled off a stealth mission into the Tripoli harbor at night in order to destroy the ship. North African sailors, called "Barbary pirates" in the United States, had captured the American warship and planned to refurbish it as their own vessel of war, but Decatur foiled that plan. Nicolino Calyo, an Italian-born American, made this painting several decades after the 1804 event.

The Mariners Museum, Newport News, Virginia.

tribute." In response, the pasha declared war on the United States.

From 1801 to 1803, American ships blockaded Tripoli and Tunis with only partial success and offered escort protection to passing American merchant ships. Only a few skirmishes ensued. Then, in late 1803, the first major action by the United States floundered: the USS *Philadelphia,* a large frigate, ran aground near the Tripoli harbor. Its 300-man crew was captured, along with the ship, which greatly augmented Tripoli's naval strength.

Several months later, the Americans retaliated. Seventy men led by the young navy lieutenant Stephen Decatur sailed into the harbor after dark with an Arabic-speaking pilot to fool harbor sentries. They drew up to the

Philadelphia, boarded it, set it on fire, and escaped. Decatur was an instant hero in America.

In summer of 1804, the U.S. forces attacked Tripoli, destroying enemy vessels, firing on the city, and also offering ransom for the captured *Philadelphia* sailors. The pasha resisted, holding out for more money, until he learned that fresh U.S. forces, aided by Egyptian and Turkish mercenaries, were headed toward Tripoli. The pasha then entered treaty negotiations, accepting $60,000 for the prisoners and agreeing to forgo tribute. One significant clause of the treaty stipulated that "no pretext arising from Religious Opinions" should interrupt good relations since the United States has "no character of enmity against the Laws, Religion or Tranquility of Musselmen" (that is, Muslims).

AMERICAN PLACES

Fort Mandan, Washburn, North Dakota

Along the upper Missouri River, the Lewis and Clark expedition arrived at a major center of Indian trade composed of five Mandan and Hidatsa villages with a population of over 4,000. An early snowfall signaled a long winter for 1804–05, so the men built rough wooden cabins surrounded by a palisade (a fence of pointed stakes). The fort provided some degree of protection against the frigid air of a northern plains winter, but it fell far short of the dwellings of the local Indians, who were warmer in their round earth lodges with central fireplaces.

The expedition rested at the fort for five months. To develop a reliable map for the projected journey west, Meriwether Lewis "separately and carefully" interviewed many Indian traders arriving at the Mandan villages. New members joined the expedition at Mandan: the French Canadian trader Toussaint Charbonneau, his young wife Sacajawea, and their baby, born in one of these cabins in February 1805. The new mother was a Shoshone Indian captured by Hidatsas at about age ten from her tribe five hundred miles to the west. Lewis anticipated that her language skill would prove helpful when they reached the Rocky Mountains. Still, the translation chain was tenuous: Sacajawea rendered Shoshone into Hidatsa to Charbonneau, who trans-lated it into French to a bilingual expedition member, who then delivered it in English to Lewis and Clark.

The long winter wait at Fort Mandan allowed for sociability with the locals. The Americans had a fiddle, and Indians attending a New Year's Day party were "much pleased at the Danceing of our men," wrote William Clark; "I ordered my black Servent to Dance which amused the Croud Verry much, and somewhat astonished them, that So large a man should be active." Social events like these at Fort Mandan helped to restore the spirits of Lewis and Clark's men, something that proved useful as they set off to continue their re-markable journey in the spring.

Today visitors to the Fort Mandan site can relive the past through a fully reconstructed replica of the original fort, complete with furnished rooms adorned with the type of equipment and other trappings members of the expedition would have brought with them. Run by the North Dakota Lewis & Clark Bicentennial Foundation, the site, located on the Lewis & Clark National Historic Trail in Washburn, North Dakota, includes a visitors' center showcasing a variety of related exhibits and on-site interpreters who provide educational programs and tours of the fort year round.

FOR WEB LINKS RELATED TO THIS SITE AND OTHER AMERICAN PLACES, see "PlaceLinks" at bedfordstmartins.com/roark.

Reconstruction of Lewis and Clark's Winter Quarters
Lewis & Clark National Historic Trail.

Although the tribute system with other Barbary states would not end until 1812, when frigates returned to the Mediterranean for further skirmishes, none of this affected the election of 1804, which proved an easy triumph for Jefferson. The Federalist candidate, Charles Cotesworth Pinckney of South Carolina, secured only 14 votes in the electoral college, in contrast to 162 for the president. Just months before the election, the Federalists had lost their shrewdest statesman: Alexander Hamilton, called by some "the brains of the Federalist Party," was tragically killed in a duel with Aaron Burr. (See "Historical Question," page 332.) Republicans would hold the presidency for another twenty years.

More Maritime Troubles: Impressment and Embargo

The Barbary coast was not the only trouble spot for Americans. When France and England resumed war in 1803, each warned America not to aid the other. Britain acted on these threats in 1806, stopping American ships, inspecting cargoes for military aid to France, and seizing suspected deserters from the British navy, along with not a few Americans. Ultimately, 2,500 sailors were swept up—impressed—by the British. Jefferson and the American public were outraged.

One incident made the usually cautious Jefferson nearly belligerent. In June 1807, an American ship, the *Chesapeake*, harboring some British deserters, was ordered to stop by a British frigate, the *Leopard*. The *Chesapeake* refused, and the *Leopard* opened fire, killing three Americans—right at the mouth of Chesapeake Bay, well within U.S. territory. Before this incident, Jefferson had convinced Congress to pass nonimportation laws banning a select list of British-made goods as a strategy for putting pressure on Britain. But now Jefferson and Secretary of State James Madison pushed the idea of total embargo, prohibiting American ships from engaging in trade with any foreign port. The Embargo Act passed by Congress in December 1807 was surely a drastic measure but one meant to forestall a

greater crisis, all-out war. The goal was to make England suffer, and all trade to foreign ports was banned to make sure no ships could engage in secret trading with England through secondary ports. Jefferson was convinced that England needed America's agricultural products far more than America needed British goods. He also was wary of Federalist shipowners who might circumvent the ban.

The Embargo Act of 1807 was a total disaster. From 1790 to 1807, U.S. exports had increased fivefold; the new law brought commerce to a standstill. In New England, the heart of the shipping industry, unemployment rose. Grain plummeted in value, river traffic halted, tobacco rotted in the South, and cotton went unpicked. Protest petitions flooded Washington. The federal government suffered too, for import duties were a significant source of revenue. Jefferson's Republicans paid political costs as well. The Federalist Party, in danger of fading away after its weak showing in 1804, began to revive.

The Madisons in the White House

In mid-1808, Jefferson indicated that he would not run for a third term. Secretary of State James Madison got the nod from Republican caucuses—informal political groups that orchestrated the selection of candidates for state and local elections. Federalist caucuses chose Charles Cotesworth Pinckney again. Pinckney did much better than in 1804; he received 47 electoral votes, nearly half Madison's total. Support for the Federalists remained centered in the New England states, but Republicans still held the balance of power nationwide.

As president, Madison continued Jefferson's policy of economic pressure on England and France with a modified embargo, but he broke new ground in the domestic management of the executive office, with the aid of his astute and talented wife, Dolley Madison. Under her leadership, the president's house became the White House—something close to a palace, but a palace many Americans were welcome to visit. Under his leadership, the country went to war in 1812 with England and with Tecumseh's warrior confederacy. In 1814, British forces burned the White House and Capitol building nearly to the ground.

The *Chesapeake* Incident, June 22, 1807

Women in Washington City

In her first eight years in Washington as wife of the highest-ranked cabinet officer, Dolley Madison had developed elaborate social networks that, in the absence of any Mrs. Jefferson, constituted the uppermost level of female politicking in the highly political city. Though women could not vote and supposedly left politics to men, the women of Washington took on several critical and overtly political functions that greased the wheels of the affairs of state. Through dinners, balls, receptions, and the intricate custom of "calling," in which men and women paid brief visits or left calling cards at each other's houses, a regularized social network developed that facilitated cohesion among

Dolley Madison

The "presidentress" of the Madison administration sat for this official portrait in 1804. Mrs. Madison here wears an empire-style dress, at the height of French fashion in 1804 and worn by many women at the coronation of the emperor Napoleon in Paris. The hallmarks of an empire dress were light fabric in muslin or chiffon, short sleeves, a high waistline from which the fabric fell straight to the ground, and usually a low open neckline as shown here. The artist, Gilbert Stuart, made a companion likeness of James Madison, and the two portraits hung in the drawing room of Madison's Virginia estate, Montpelier.

Courtesy of the Pennsylvania Academy of the Fine Arts, Philadelphia.

the governing classes and provided avenues of preferment for jobs and for advancement. It was not uncommon for women in this social set to write letters of introduction or recommendation for men seeking government work. Hostessing was therefore no trivial or leisured business: Washington women mediated the webs of personal connections (as well as the gossip networks) that influenced the patronage system of the federal government.

Upon her husband's election, Dolley Madison, called by some the "presidentress," struck a balance between queenliness and republican openness. She dressed the part in resplendent clothes, choosing a plumed velvet turban for her headdress at her husband's inauguration. She swiftly redesigned three large and newly elegant rooms in the executive mansion and opened them to evening parties once a week. George and Martha Washington's levees had been stiff, brief affairs with few guests accomplishing little more than bows and curtsies. In contrast, the Madisons' drawing-room parties went on for hours with scores and even hundreds of guests standing, milling about, talking, and eating. Nicknamed "Mrs. Madison's crush" or "squeeze," the weekly party required an invitation or letter of introduction to attend, if one did not already know the Madisons. Evidently this was not a highly restrictive requirement. Members of Congress, cabinet officers, distinguished guests, envoys from foreign countries, important travelers, all these and their womenfolk attended with regularity. Even those who hated parties—or this party in particular—still attended. Mrs. Madison's "squeeze" was an essential event for gaining political access, trading information, and establishing the kinds of informal channels that smooth the governing process.

In 1810–1811, Dolley Madison's house acquired the unofficial nickname "White House," probably a reference to the building's light sandstone exterior. The fact that the house received a nickname is significant: This was not a palace named after a royal family or duchy, nor was it an unnamed private residence meant simply to shelter a president when off duty and out of sight. It was the people's house, and, said a Baltimore newspaper in 1810, "'White house' may be considered the 'people's name.'" People came in very large numbers to the weekly parties, experiencing simultaneously the splendor of the executive mansion and the atmosphere of republicanism that made it accessible to so many. Dolley Madison, ever an enormous political

How Could a Vice President Get Away with Murder?

On July 11, 1804, the vice president of the United States, Aaron Burr, shot Alexander Hamilton, the architect of the Federalist Party, in a duel on a narrow ledge below the cliffs of Weehawken, New Jersey, across the Hudson River from New York City. The pistol blast tore through a rib, demolished Hamilton's liver, and splintered his spine. The forty-seven-year-old Hamilton died the next day, in agonizing pain.

How could it happen that a sitting vice president and a prominent political leader could put themselves at such risk? Why did men who made their living by the legal system go outside the law and turn to the centuries-old ritual of the duel? Here were two eminent attorneys, skilled in the legalistic negotiations meant to substitute for violent resolution of disputes, firing .54-caliber hair-trigger weapons at ten paces. Did anyone try to stop them? How did the public react? Was Hamilton's death a criminal act? How could Burr continue to fulfill his federal office, presiding over the U.S. Senate?

Burr challenged Hamilton in late June after learning from a newspaper report that Hamilton "looked upon Mr. Burr to be a dangerous man, and one who ought not be trusted with the reins of government." Burr knew that Hamilton had long held a very low opinion of him and had never hesitated to say so in private, but now his private disparagement had made its way into print. Compounding the insult were political consequences: Burr was sure that Hamilton's remark had cost him election to the governorship of New York.

Quite possibly he was right. Knowing that Jefferson planned to dump him from the federal ticket in the 1804 election, Burr decided to run for New York's highest office; his opponent was an obscure Republican judge. Burr's success depended on the support of the old Federalist leadership in the state. Up to the eve of the election, he appeared to have it—until Hamilton's remark was circulated.

So on June 18, Burr challenged Hamilton to a duel if he did not disavow his comment. Over the next three weeks, the men exchanged several letters clarifying the nature of the insult that aggrieved Burr. Hamilton the lawyer evasively quibbled over words, causing Burr finally to rail against his focus on syntax and grammar. At heart, Hamilton could not deny the insult, nor could he spurn the challenge without injury to his reputation for integrity and bravery. Both Burr and Hamilton were locked in a highly ritualized procedure meant to uphold a gentleman's code of honor.

In accordance with the code of dueling, each man had a trusted "second" who helped frame and deliver the letters and finally assisted at the duel site. Only a handful of close friends knew of the challenge, and no one tried to stop it. Hamilton did not tell his wife. He wrote her a tender farewell letter the night before, to be opened in the event of his death. He knew full well the pain dueling brought to loved ones, for three years earlier, his nineteen-year-old son Philip had been killed in a duel at the same ledge at Weehawken, as a result of hotheaded words exchanged at a New York theater. Even when Hamilton's wife was called to her husband's deathbed, she was first told he had terrible spasms from an illness. Women were completely shut out of the masculine world of dueling.

News of Hamilton's death spread quickly in New York and then throughout the nation. On the day of the funeral, church bells tolled continuously and New York merchants shut down all business. Thousands joined the procession, and the city council declared a six-week mourning period. Burr fled to Philadelphia, fearing retribution by the crowd.

Response in the South was subdued. Dueling was fully accepted there as an extralegal remedy for insult, and Burr's grievance fit perfectly the sense of violated honor that legitimated duels. In addition, Southerners had never been particularly fond of the Federalist Hamilton.

Northern newspapers, in contrast, expressed indignation over the illegal duel and the tragic death of so prominent a man. Many northern states had criminalized dueling recently, treating a challenge as a misdemeanor and a dueling death as a homicide. After death, the body of the loser of an illegal duel could be subjected to one final indignity—being buried without a coffin, having a stake driven through the body, being strung up in public until the body rotted, or (more horrible still at that time) being donated to medical students for dissection. Such prescribed mutilation of the dead showed that northern lawmakers themselves participated in the code of honor by using threats of postmortem humiliation to discourage dueling. Hamilton's body was spared such a fate. But two ministers in succession refused to administer Holy Communion to him in his dying hours because he was a duelist; finally, one relented.

The public demanded to know the reasons for the duel, so the seconds prepared the correspondence between the principals for publication. A coroner's jury in New York soon indicted the vice president on misdemeanor charges for issuing a challenge; a grand jury in New Jersey indicted him for murder. By that time, Burr was a fugitive from justice, hiding out with sympathetic friends in South Carolina.

But not for long. Amazingly, he returned to Washington, D.C., in November 1804 to resume presiding over the Senate, a role he continued to assume until his vice presidential term ended in March 1805. Federalists snubbed him, but eleven Republican senators petitioned New Jersey to drop its indictment on the grounds that "civilized nations" do not treat dueling deaths as "common murders." New Jersey did not pursue the murder charge. Burr freely visited New Jersey and New York for three more decades, paying no penalty for killing Hamilton.

Few would doubt that Burr was a scoundrel, albeit a brilliant one. A few years later, he was indicted for treason against the U.S. government in a presumed plot to break off part

***Aaron Burr,* by John Vanderlyn**
Aaron Burr was fifty-three years old when the New York artist John Vanderlyn painted this portrait in 1809, five years after the Burr-Hamilton duel.
Collection of The New-York Historical Society.

of the United States and start his own country in the Southwest. (He dodged that bullet too, in a spectacular trial presided over by John Marshall, chief justice of the Supreme Court.) Hamilton certainly thought Burr a scoundrel, and when that opinion reached print, Burr had cause to defend his honor under the etiquette of dueling. The accuracy of Hamilton's charge was of absolutely no account. Dueling redressed questions of honor, not questions of fact.

Dueling continued to be a feature of southern society for many more decades, but in the North the custom became extremely rare by the 1820s, helped into obscurity by the disrepute of Hamilton's death and by the rise of a legalistic society that preferred evidence, interrogation, and monetary judgments to avenge injury.

Pistols from the Burr-Hamilton Duel
Alexander Hamilton's brother-in-law John B. Church purchased this pair of dueling pistols in London in 1797. Church used them once in a duel with Aaron Burr, occasioned by Church's calling Burr a scoundrel in public; neither man was hurt. Hamilton's son Philip borrowed them for his own fatal duel. When Burr challenged Hamilton, the latter also turned to John Church for the weapons. The guns stayed in the Church family until 1930, when they were given to the Chase Manhattan Bank in New York City, chartered in 1799 as the Manhattan Company. (Burr, Church, and Hamilton all served on the bank's board of directors.) When the pistols were cleaned in 1874, a hidden hair trigger came to light. Each gun could be cocked by moving the trigger forward one-eighth inch; then only a half-pound pull, instead of ten pounds, was needed to fire each gun. Hamilton gained no advantage from the hair trigger, if he knew of it.
Courtesy of Chase Manhattan Archives.

asset to her rather shy husband, understood well the symbolic function of inventing this new White House to create power and legitimacy for the presidency.

Indian Troubles in the West

While the Madisons cemented alliances at home, difficulties with England and France overseas and Indians in the old Northwest continued to increase. The Shawnee chief Tecumseh actively solidified his confederacy, while far northern tribes renewed ties with supportive British agents and fur traders in Canada, a potential source of food and weapons. If the United States embarked on a war with England, there would clearly be serious repercussions on the **frontier**.

> A fundamental part of Tecumseh's message was the assertion that all Indian lands were held in common by all the tribes.

Tenskwatawa

Tenskwatawa, the Shawnee Prophet, and his brother Tecumseh led the spiritual and political efforts of a number of Indian tribes to resist land-hungry Americans moving west in the decade before the War of 1812. The Prophet is shown in a portrait by George Catlin with beaded necklaces, metal arm- and wristbands, and earrings. Compare the metal gorget here with the one worn by Joseph Brant (page 226).

National Museum of American Art, Washington, D.C./Art Resource, NY.

Shifting demographics raised the stakes for both sides. The 1810 census counted some 230,000 Americans living in Ohio, only seven years after statehood. Another 40,000 Americans inhabited the territories of Indiana, Illinois, and Michigan. The Indian population of the entire region (the old Northwest Territory) was much smaller, probably about 70,000, a number unknown (because uncounted) to the Americans but certainly gauged by Tecumseh during his extensive travels.

Up to 1805, Indiana's territorial governor, William Henry Harrison, had negotiated a series of treaties in a divide-and-conquer strategy extracting Indian lands for paltry payments. But with the rise to power of Tecumseh and his brother Tenskwatawa, the Prophet, Harrison's strategy became harder to carry out. A fundamental part of Tecumseh's message was the assertion that all Indian lands were held in common by all the tribes:

> No tribe has the right to sell, even to each other, much less to strangers. . . . Sell a country! Why not sell the air, the great sea, as well as the earth? Didn't the Great Spirit make them all for the use of his children? The way, the only way to stop this evil is for the red man to unite in claiming a common and equal right in the land, as it was first, and should be now, for it was never divided.

Taking advantage of Tecumseh's absence on a recruiting trip, Harrison assembled leaders of the Potawatomi, Miami, and Delaware tribes to negotiate the Treaty of Fort Wayne in 1809. As required, Harrison first sought approval from President Madison, who authorized negotiations so long as all "who have or pretend right to these lands" were party to the agreement. Harrison sidestepped that requirement, working instead with chiefs who in some cases had no pretense of claims to the land in question, along the Wabash River in southern Indiana. After promising (falsely) that this was the last cession of land the United States would seek, Harrison secured three million acres at about two cents per acre (Map 10.3).

When he returned, Tecumseh was furious with both Harrison and the tribal leaders. Leaving his brother in charge at Prophetstown on Tippecanoe Creek, the Shawnee chief left on a trip to seek alliances in the South. Harrison then decided to attack Prophetstown with one thousand men. The two-hour battle resulted in the deaths of 62 Americans and 40 Indians before the

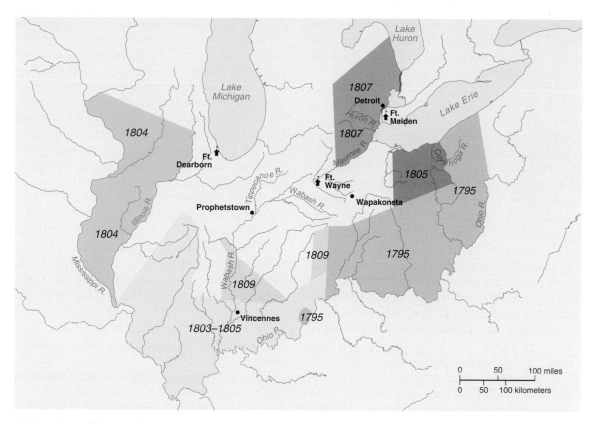

MAP 10.3   Indian Lands Ceded by Treaties in the Old Northwest Territory, 1795–1809
The Treaty of Greenville (1795) transferred two-thirds of Ohio to the Americans. For more than a decade thereafter, by negotiating with Indians whose authority to speak for their tribes was often unclear or dubious, officials
such as William Henry Harrison managed to acquire vast tracts along the Ohio and up the Mississippi rivers.
"Land Cessions in the Old Northwest, 1795–1809." From *Tecumseh: A Life* by John Sugden. Copyright 1997 by John Sugden. Reprinted with the
permission of Henry Holt and Company LLC.

Prophet's forces fled the town, which Harrison's men set on fire. The November 1811 Battle of Tippecanoe was heralded as a glorious victory for the Americans; the Prophet Tenskwata-wa's magical powers were sharply diminished among his people and he lost influ-ence. But Tecumseh was now more determined than ever to unite Indians to hold back the Americans.

The War of 1812

The Indian conflicts in the Northwest Territory in 1811 soon merged into the wider conflict with England now known as the War of 1812.

Battle of Tippecanoe, 1811

Between 1809 and 1812, President Madison teetered between declar-ing England or France the prime enemy, as attacks by both countries on American ships continued. In 1809, Congress had replaced Jef-ferson's stringent embargo with the Non-Intercourse Act, which pro-hibited trade only with England and France and their colonies, thus opening up other trade routes to di-minish the anguish of shippers, farmers, and **planters**. In 1810, the Non-Intercourse Act expired, and Congress replaced it with a law that permitted direct trade with ei-ther France or England, whichever first promised to stop harassing American ships. Napoleon seized the initiative and declared that France would comply. Madison too hastily accepted this offer, reopened trade with France, and notified England that he intended to reinstate the embargo in the spring of 1811 unless England rescinded its search-and-seizure policy.

Unfortunately for Madison, the duplicitous French continued to seize American ships and sailors. Furthermore, the British made no move to stop impressments or to repeal trade restrictions, and Madison was forced to reactivate the embargo, much to the great displeasure of the New England shipping industry. In 1811, the country was seriously divided and in a deep quandary. To some, the United States seemed, appropriately, on the verge of war—though with France or England was not clear. To others, war with either meant disaster for commerce.

A new Congress, elected in the fall of 1810, arrived in Washington in March 1811 as Madison's embargo took effect. Several dozen of the new and much younger Republican members were eager to avenge the insults from abroad. In particular, Henry Clay, thirty-four, from Kentucky, and John C. Calhoun, twenty-nine, from South Carolina, became the center of a group informally known as the **War Hawks**. They saluted Harrison's Tippecanoe victory and urged the country to war. Mostly lawyers by profession, they came from the West and South, and they welcomed a war with England both to legitimize attacks on the Indians and to bring an end to impressment. Many were also expansionists, looking to occupy Florida and threaten Canada. And they captured prominent posts in Congress from which to wield influence. Henry Clay was elected Speaker of the House, an extraordinary honor for a young newcomer. John C. Calhoun won a seat on the Foreign Relations Committee. The War Hawks approved major defense expenditures; the army, for example, quadrupled in size.

In June 1812, Congress declared war on Great Britain in a vote that divided on sectional lines: New England and some Middle Atlantic states opposed the war, while the South and West were strongly for it. Ironically, Great Britain had just announced it would stop the search and seizure of American ships. But the war momentum would not be slowed. The Foreign Relations Committee issued an elaborate justification titled *Report on the Causes and Reasons for War*, written mainly by Calhoun and containing extravagant language about Britain's "lust for power," "unbounded tyranny," and "mad ambition." These were fighting words in a war that was in large measure about insult and honor.

The War Hawks proposed an invasion of Canada, confidently predicting victory in four weeks. Instead, the war lasted two and a half years, and Canada never fell. The northern invasion turned out to be a series of strategic blunders that revealed the grave unpreparedness of the United States for war. The combined British and Indian forces were unexpectedly powerful, and the United States made no attempt at the outset to create a naval presence on the Great Lakes. Detroit quickly fell, as did Fort Dearborn (site of the future Chicago). By the fall of 1812, the outlook was grim.

Worse, the New England states dragged their feet in raising troops, while New England merchants carried on illegal trade with Great Britain. Britain encouraged friendly overtures with New England, hoping to create dissension among the Americans. New Englanders drank India tea in Liverpool cups while President Madison fumed in Washington about Federalist disloyalty.

The presidential election in 1812 solidified Federalist discontent with the war. Madison was opposed by DeWitt Clinton of New York, nominally Republican but able to attract the Federalist vote. He picked up all of New England's electoral votes, with the exception of Vermont's, and also took New York, New Jersey, and part of Maryland. Madison won in the electoral college, 128 to 89, but his margin of victory was considerably smaller than in 1808.

In late 1812 and early 1813, the tide began to turn in the Americans' favor. First came some reassuring victories at sea. Then Americans attacked York (now Toronto), the capital of Upper Canada, and burned it in April 1813. A few months later, Commodore Oliver Hazard Perry defeated the British fleet at the western end of Lake Erie. Emboldened, General Harrison drove an army into Canada from Detroit and in October 1813 defeated the British and Indians at the Battle of the Thames, where Tecumseh met his death (Map 10.4).

Indians in the South who had allied with Tecumseh's confederacy were also plunged into all-out war. Some fifty villages containing around 10,000 Creek Indians in the southern region of Mississippi Territory put up a spirited fight against American militia troops for ten months in 1813–1814. Even without Tecumseh's recruitment trip of 1811 or the War of 1812, the Creeks had grievances aplenty, sparked by American settlers moving into their territory along the rivers of the future Alabama. Aided by

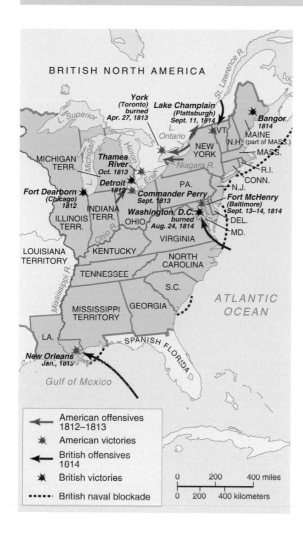

MAP 10.4   The War of 1812
During the War of 1812, battles were fought along the border of Canada and in the Chesapeake region. The most important American victory came in New Orleans, two weeks after peace had been agreed to in England.

worker removed the Declaration of Independence to safety. Dolley Madison, with dinner for guests on the fire (see "The Promise of Technology," page 338), fled with her husband's papers and a portrait of George Washington. Five thousand British troops entered the city and began torching government buildings. British commanders ate Mrs. Madison's meal before burning her house; they also burned the Capitol, a newspaper office, some dockyards, and a well-stocked arsenal. August 24 was a very low moment for the American side.

Instead of trying to hold the city, the British headed north for Baltimore and attacked it on September 11, 1814. A fierce defense by the Maryland militia and a steady barrage of gunfire from Fort McHenry in the harbor kept them at bay. The firing continued until midnight, motivating Francis Scott Key to compose a poem he called "The Star-Spangled Banner" the next day. The British pulled back, unwilling to try to take the city.

September 1814 brought another powerful British offensive. Marching from Canada into New York State, the British seemed to have every advantage—trained soldiers, superior artillery, cavalry. But a series of mistakes cost them a naval skirmish at Plattsburgh on Lake Champlain and also cost them their nerve, and they retreated to Canada. The withdrawal was a decisive military event, for British leaders in England, hearing of the retreat, concluded that incursions by land into the United States would be expensive and difficult.

This point was confirmed when a large British army landed in lower Louisiana and encountered General Andrew Jackson and his militia just outside New Orleans in early January 1815. Jackson's forces dramatically carried the day. The British suffered between 2,000 and 3,000 casualties, the Americans fewer than 80. Jackson became an instant hero. The Battle of New Orleans was the most glorious and decisive victory the

guns provided by Spanish agents living in the panhandle of Spanish Florida, the Creeks mounted a strong defense. But the Creek War was suddenly over in March 1814, when a general named Andrew Jackson led 2,500 Tennessee militiamen in a bloody attack called the Battle of Horseshoe Bend. Jackson's militia killed more than 550 Indians, and several hundred more died trying to escape across a river. Later that year, General Jackson extracted a treaty from the defeated Creeks relinquishing thousands of square miles of their land to the United States.

Washington City Burns: The British Offensive

In August 1814, British ships sailed into Chesapeake Bay, throwing the capital into a panic. Families evacuated, banks hid their money, and government clerks carted away boxes of important papers. One State Department

> The Battle of New Orleans was the most glorious and decisive victory the Americans had experienced. Ironically, negotiators in Europe had already signed a peace agreement.

Stoves Transform Cooking

The cookstove, one of the most underrated achievements of the technology of daily life, fundamentally changed the way men and women labored to put food on the table. Its slow development can be traced in the nearly one thousand patents registered between 1815 and 1850 by inventors tinkering to control heat, devise convenient cooking surfaces, and improve fuel efficiency.

Before 1815, nearly all household cooking was accomplished in wood-burning fireplaces. Daily fires used for cooking and heating consumed immense amounts of wood; in cold climates, a household might require 40 cords of wood per year. Supplying each cord (a pile measuring 4-by-4-by-8 feet) was laborious men's work; the difficult and dangerous tasks of cooking and maintaining the fire fell to women. Great skill was needed to time the peak heat to coordinate with the varying temperature needs of baking, stewing, and roasting. Muscles and stamina were required to hoist 20-pound iron pots and cauldrons onto the hooks that suspended them over the fire. Cooks worked dangerously close to open flames when tending a roasting joint of meat on a spit or raking smaller fires out of the large one to heat frying skillets set on trivets on the hearth. Women wearing long skirts risked clothing fires, and children running about sometimes collided with hot pots and burning logs at floor level. The heavy lifting and exposure to the blasting heat, especially uncomfortable on hot summer days, exacted a toll on every cook.

In 1744, Benjamin Franklin developed a heating stove that enclosed a wood fire on three sides in a small cast-iron box, which radiated heat to the room. (The open fourth side allowed a pleasing view of the dancing flames.) The Franklin stove cut fuel costs, but it did not catch on for another half century as an alternative to heating by fireplace. Its inadequate venting of smoke was one problem, not fixed until the 1790s. Further, cast iron was expensive and wood was cheap, and the Franklin stove offered no provision for cooking. As long as wood remained affordable, Americans preferred the look of a log fire and the taste of food cooked over one.

Then, between 1800 and 1815, a serious fuel shortage driven by the depletion of forests caused wood prices to double along the eastern coast. At the same time, domestic iron manufacturing started to flourish, encouraged by Jefferson's shipping embargo and the War of 1812.

With wood rising and iron falling in price, the conditions were right for the start of serious cookstove manufacture. Many inventors got to work.

The cast iron contraptions advertised around 1815 were larger than the Franklin stove and had a flat surface on top where pots and pans could be heated by the fire burning below. One challenge was to find a simple way to modulate the fire by varying the amount of air feeding it, through better design of the damper system. Dampers were valves or movable plates that controlled the draft of air to the fire and hence the rate of combustion. A related challenge was to manage the temperatures of the cooking spaces and surfaces. This could be done by moving pots around, by raising and lowering the grate that held the logs inside the firebox, or even by using cranks to rotate the fire.

Most of the new stoves raised the cooking surface nearly to waist level, offering relief from the back-breaking labor required by fireplace cookery. They fully enclosed the fire, minimizing the risk of clothing fires; they prevented sparks from jumping on floors and carpets; and they piped sooty air with combustion pollutants out of the house. For all these reasons, stove cooking was a great advance in safety.

New stoves changed not only the way people cooked but the way they ate. On a hearth, separate dishes

Americans had experienced. Ironically, negotiators in Europe had signed a peace agreement two weeks earlier.

The Treaty of Ghent, signed in December 1814, settled few of the surface issues that had led to war. Neither country could claim victory, and no land changed hands. Instead, the treaty reflected a mutual agreement to give up certain goals. The Americans yielded on impressment and gave up any claim to Canada; and the

An Early Cookstove

A stove of the 1820s, patented by W. T. James, sits in this reconstructed historical site adjacent to the fireplace it has replaced. A stovepipe vents combustion fumes out the old chimney; a large flat surface over the fire provides a cooktop, shown here with a copper pot and a teakettle whose extremely large base speeds water to a boil. The round container on the lower ledge of the stove is a reflector oven, called a "tin kitchen," first used with fireplaces and then adapted for cookstoves. A spit inside held meat, and a crank (visible on the end) was used to turn the food. Put against the fire, the tin oven cooked its contents by direct and reflected heat, while the round bottom preserved the meat juices. In this scene, the old fireplace is bricked up and used for storing wood for the stove. Householders of the 1820s would have seen this setup as a highly modern convenience, with improvements in safety, fuel efficiency, and heat control.

Old Sturbridge Village.

---

required separate fires, so cooks generally limited meals to one-pot stews. Using the new stoves, cooks could prepare several different dishes with just one fire, and meals became more varied. However, not everyone was pleased. Many complained that the convenience of stoves came at the price of food quality. Oven-baked meat was nearly universally regarded as less savory than meat roasted over a fire, and in flavor and crustiness oven-baked bread did not measure up to bread baked in the brick chamber of a fireplace wall. Nonetheless, convenience triumphed.

The cookstove changed home labor for both men and women. It shrank men's role in meal preparation by curtailing the work of procuring wood. No such reduction occurred for women, however. Replacing the hours of careful fire-tending that women had once done were hours spent maintaining and cleaning stoves—removing ashes, cleaning soot from flues and dampers, and blacking the entire stove weekly with a thick paste to keep it from rusting.

From 1815 to the mid-nineteenth century, the cookstove was a work in progress; the many imperfections in the initial designs sent inventors back to the workbench again and again to try to perfect this new cooking system. Nonetheless, women wanted stoves for their safety and convenience, and men liked them for their fuel efficiency. In the late 1840s, the widespread popularity of cookstoves became evident along wagon trails heading west. Many families had packed up their stoves for the trip—evidence they embraced the new style of cooking—but had to abandon them along the way when forced to lighten their loads. One traveling teenager wrote that "we heard great talk of things being thrown away on the road but we saw little that was any good excepting stoves and there were plenty of them." Cookstoves had become America's first popular "consumer durable."

British agreed to abandon aid to Indians. Nothing was said about shipping rights. The most concrete result was a plan for a commission to determine the exact boundary between the United States and Canada.

Antiwar New England Federalists did not feel triumphant at the war's ambiguous conclusion. Instead they felt disgrace because of a meeting convened in Hartford, Connecticut, in December 1814. Politicians at the Hartford Convention

Remains of the President's House

This watercolor sketch documents the burning of the White House in Washington in August 1814, when the British attacked the city. The light-colored walls still stand, but the interior has been gutted by the fire. Some British engaged in plundering that night. Shown here is James Madison's personal medicine chest, taken by a British soldier back to England. A descendent of his returned the wartime souvenir in 1939 to President Franklin D. Roosevelt.

Watercolor: Library of Congress; medicine chest: FDR Library.

its grip, and within a few years its presence even in New England was reduced to a shadow.

No one really won the War of 1812. Americans celebrated as though they had, however, with parades and fireworks. The war gave rise to a new spirit of **nationalism**. The paranoia over British tyranny evident in the 1812 declaration of war was laid to rest, replaced by pride in a more equal relationship with the old mother country. Indeed, in 1817 the two countries signed the Rush-Bagot disarmament treaty (named after its two negotiators), which limited each country to a total of four naval vessels, each with just a single cannon, to patrol the vast watery border between them. The Rush-Bagot treaty was perhaps the most successful disarmament treaty for a century to come.

The biggest winners in the War of 1812 were the young men, once called War Hawks, who took up the banner of the Republican Party and carried it in new, expansive directions. These young politicians favored trade, western expansion, internal improvements, and the energetic development of new economic markets. The biggest losers of the war were the Indians. Tecumseh was dead, the Prophet discredited, the prospects of an Indian confederacy dashed, the Creeks' large homeland seized, and the British protectors gone.

discussed the possible secession of New England from the Union. They also proposed amending the Constitution to abolish the three-fifths clause as a basis of representation; to specify that congressional powers to pass embargoes, admit states, or declare war should require a two-thirds vote instead of a simple majority; and to limit the president to one term and prohibit successive presidents from the same state. The cumulative effect of these proposals would have been to reduce the South's political power and break the lock of the Virginia dynasty on national office. New England wanted to assure that no one sectional party could again lead the country into war against the clear interests of another. Coming just as peace was achieved, however, the Hartford Convention suddenly looked very unpatriotic. The Federalist Party never recovered

Women's Status in the Early Republic

With the model of Dolley Madison, the able "presidentress," so prominently before the public, and the memory of the 1790s debate over education for motherhood not yet erased (see chapter 9), it might be expected that the first three decades of the nineteenth century would provide new arenas of social change for women. One that definitely did permit tangible advancement was that of female schooling, which continued to expand. The spread of basic public education for children up to age twelve, so vital to the production of citizens in a **democratic** state, routinely included girls as well as boys; by

1830, female literacy and numeracy were rapidly rising. Further, between 1790 and 1830, some 400 female academies were founded, providing the opportunity for adolescent girls of genteel families to move beyond the rudiments of reading and writing to such subjects as history, rhetoric, natural philosophy, arithmetic, and French. But other arenas and institutions central to the shaping of women's lives—laws, marriage, and church—showed either no change or only incremental change. State legislatures and the courts grappled with the legal dependency of married white women in a country whose defining characteristic was independence, while religious organizations struggled to redefine the role of women in church governance. If, in the end, there was no giant step forward for women in these decades, it is still significant that these questions were raised at all.

Women and the Law

The Anglo-American view of women, implanted in British common law, was that wives had no independent legal or political personhood. The legal doctrine of *feme covert* (covered woman) held that a wife's civic life was completely subsumed by her husband's. A wife was obligated to obey her husband; her property was his, her domestic and sexual services were his, and even their children were legally his. Women had no right to keep their wages, to make contracts, or to sue or be sued. Any crime committed by a wife in the presence of her husband was chargeable to him, with two exceptions: treason against the state and keeping a brothel. The fundamental assumption of coverture was that husbands did—and ought to—control their wives.

State legislatures generally passed up the opportunity to rewrite the laws of domestic relations even though they redrafted other British laws in light of republican principles. The standard treatise on family law, published in 1816 and consulted by lawyers everywhere as a summary of the best legal thinking on marriage, was titled *The Law of Baron and Feme*—that is "lord and woman." The title perfectly captured how lawyers framed husband-wife power relations. Lawyers never paused to defend, much less to challenge, the assumption that unequal power relations lay at the heart of marriage. An occasional woman offered a challenge in print, as in this 1801 example from an anonymous Connecticut author writing *The Female Advocate:*

Home and Away: The New Boarding School
These two engravings show "before" and "after" pictures of a young woman circa 1820 whose family enrolled her in one of the new female academies that were springing up by the scores in the decades after 1800. What seem to be the family's expectations as they send her off? How is she changed when she returns? Did she acquire a practical or an ornamental education? Notice the various emblems of women's household work. What do these pictures reveal about the options for young women in this period? Is the artist, John Lewis Krimmel, making a joke? Or does this picture betray anxieties about women's education? Krimmel himself was a Philadelphia painter who worked as a drawing master at a girls' academy.
Library Company of Philadelphia.

"Must woman have no law but her husband? Has she not a rational nature, as well as the man? And is she not equally accountable for the improvement or misuse of her judgment?"

The one aspect of family law that did change in the early Republic was divorce. Before the Revolution, only New England jurisdictions recognized a limited right to divorce; by 1820, every state except South Carolina did so. This was a major symbolic crack in the traditional assumption that marriage was lifelong and indissoluble. However, divorce was uncommon and difficult and in many states could be obtained only by petition to the state's legislature, a daunting obstacle for many ordinary people. A mutual wish to terminate a marriage was never sufficient grounds for legal divorce. A New York judge affirmed that "it would be aiming a deadly blow at public morals to decree a dissolution of the marriage contract merely because the parties requested it. Divorces should never be allowed, except for the protection of the innocent party, and for the punishment of the guilty." States upheld the institution of marriage both to protect persons they thought of as naturally dependent (women and children) and to regulate the use and inheritance of property. (Unofficial self-divorce, desertion, and bigamy were remedies that ordinary people sometimes chose to get around the strictness of marriage law. But powerful social sanctions against such behavior usually prevailed.) Legal enforcement of marriage as an unequal relationship played a major role in maintaining gender inequality in the nineteenth century.

Single adult women could own and convey property, make contracts, initiate suits, and pay taxes. They could not vote (except in New Jersey before 1807), serve on juries, or practice law, so their civil status was limited. Single women's economic status was often limited as well, by custom as much as by law. Unless they had inherited adequate property or could live with married siblings, single adult women in the early Republic were very often poor.

None of the legal institutions that structured white gender relations applied to black slaves. As property themselves, slaves could not freely consent to any contractual obligations, including marriage. The protective features of state-sponsored unions were thus denied to black men and women in slavery, who were controlled by a more powerful authority, the slave owner. But this also meant that slave unions did not establish unequal power relations between partners, backed by the force of law, as did marriages among the free.

Women and Church Governance

In most **Protestant** denominations around 1800, white women made up the majority of congregants, as they had for some time. Yet the church hierarchy—ordained ministers and elders—was exclusively male, and the governance of most denominations rested in men's hands.

There were some exceptions, however. In several small **evangelical** groups, notably Baptist congregations in New England that had been strongly affected by the **Great Awakening**, women served along with men on church governance committees, where they decided admission of new members, voted on the hiring of ministers, and even debated doctrinal points.

Women and the Church: Jemima Wilkinson
Jemima Wilkinson, the "Publick Universal Friend," in an early woodcut, wears a clerical collar and body-obscuring robe, in keeping with the claim that the former Jemima was now a person without sex or gender. Her hair is pulled back tight on her head and curled at the neck in a masculine style of the 1790s. Did she become masculinized, or did she truly transcend gender?
Rhode Island Historical Society.

Quakers, too, had a history of recognizing women's spiritual talents. Quaker women who felt a special call were accorded the status of minister, which meant they were capable of leading and speaking in Quaker meetings. Separate men's and women's committees heard disciplinary cases and formulated Quaker policy.

Between 1790 and 1820, a small and highly unusual set of women emerged who actively engaged in open preaching. Most were from Freewill Baptist groups centered in New England and upstate New York. Some were from small Methodist sects, and others rejected any formal religious affiliation. Probably fewer than a hundred such women existed, but several dozen traveled beyond their local communities, creating converts and controversy. They spoke from the heart, without prepared speeches, often exhibiting trances and claiming to exhort (counsel or warn) rather than to preach. None of these women were ordained ministers with official credentials to preach or perform baptisms.

Perhaps the most well-known exhorting woman was Jemima Wilkinson, who called herself the "Publick Universal Friend." After a near-death experience from high fever in 1776, Wilkinson proclaimed her body no longer female *or* male but the incarnation of the "Spirit of Light." She dressed in men's clothes, wore her hair in a masculine style, shunned gender-specific pronouns, and preached openly in Rhode Island and Philadelphia. In the early nineteenth century, Wilkinson withdrew with more than 250 followers, to a settlement called New Jerusalem in western New York. Her fame was sustained by periodic newspaper articles that fed public curiosity about her lifelong transvestism and her unfeminine forcefulness.

As more women exhorters cropped up, their behavior came under increasing fire. A Baptist periodical in Massachusetts printed frequent reminders of the biblical prohibition "Let your women learn to keep silence in the churches" (1 Corinthians 14:34). Female preachers well knew such scriptural passages and were ready with biblical interpretations of their own, as in Deborah Peirce's 1820 pamphlet *A Scriptural Vindication of Female Preaching, Prophesying, or Exhortation.*

The decades from 1790 to the 1820s marked a period of unusual confusion, ferment, and creativity in American religion. New denominations blossomed, new styles of religiosity gripped adherents, and an extensive periodical press devoted to religion popularized all manner of theological and institutional innovations. Congregations increasingly attracted vibrant female participation, often eclipsing the percentage of male congregants. In such a climate, the age-old tradition of gender subordination came into question here and there among the most radically democratic of the churches. But the presumption of male authority over women was deeply entrenched in American culture. Even denominations that had allowed women to participate in church governance began to pull back, and most churches reinstated patterns of hierarchy along gender lines. In church as in state, top leadership remained completely in male hands.

Monroe and Adams

With the elections of 1816 and 1820, Virginians continued their long hold on the presidency. In 1816, James Monroe beat Federalist Rufus King of New York by 183 electoral votes to 34. When Monroe was reelected in 1820 with all but one electoral vote, the national presence of the Federalists was fully eclipsed. The unanimity of the 1820 election did not necessarily reflect voter satisfaction with the status quo, however, for barely one-quarter of eligible voters bothered to cast ballots.

The collapse of the Federalist Party led one over-optimistic newspaper to dub Monroe's first term the "Era of Good Feelings," as though a one-party government would of course be harmonious. The harmony turned out to be very short-lived. Monroe and his aloof wife Elizabeth sharply curtailed regular social affairs in the White House and returned to a 1790s style of high formality in the events that remained. Mrs. Monroe even shunned the practice of formal calling. But instead of closing down the avenues for social cohesion that Dolley Madison had enlarged, the Monroes' chilliness drove the hard work of social network building into different channels. Ill feelings were further displayed in a major sectional crisis over the admission of Missouri to the Union, and foreign policy questions animated sharp disagreements as well. The election of 1824 brought forth an abundance of candidates, all claiming to be Republicans; the winner was John Quincy Adams, in an election decided by the House of Representatives—and, many believed, maybe by a backroom bargain. A one-party political system was put to the test of practical circumstances; it failed and then fractured.

The Missouri Compromise

In February 1819, Missouri applied for statehood. Since 1815, four other states had joined the Union (Indiana, Mississippi, Illinois, and Alabama), following the blueprint laid out by the Northwest Ordinance of 1787. But Missouri posed a problem. Although much of its area was on the same latitude as Illinois, its territorial population was already one-sixth slave, consisting of 10,000 African Americans brought there by southern white planters.

> Just as southern economic power rested on slave labor, southern political power drew extra strength from the slave population, which was counted as three-fifths of the free population for purposes of representation.

Missouri's unusual combination of geography and demography led a New York representative in Congress, James Tallmadge Jr., to propose two amendments to the statehood bill. The first stipulated that slaves born in Missouri after statehood would be free at age twenty-five, and the second declared that no new slaves could be imported into the state. Tallmadge modeled the first amendment on New York's gradual **emancipation** law of 1799. It did not strip slave owners of their current property, and it allowed them full use of the labor of newborn slaves well into their prime productive years. Still, Southerners in Congress loudly protested the amendments. Although gradual emancipation protected slave owners from immediate financial loss, in the long run it made Missouri a free state, tipping the national balance of power between free and slave states. Just as southern economic power rested on slave labor, southern political power drew extra strength from the slave population, when three-fifths of all slaves were added to the count of all whites to determine representation in Congress. In 1820, the South had seventeen additional seats in the House of Representatives based on slave population.

Both of Tallmadge's amendments passed in the House, but by a close and sharply sectional vote of North against South (with a few northern Republicans taking the side of the South). The ferocious debate led a Georgia representative to observe that the question had started "a fire which all the waters of the ocean could not extinguish. It can be extinguished only in blood." The Senate, with an even number of slave and free states, voted down the amendments; some free border states joined the proslavery line. Missouri statehood was postponed for the next congressional term.

In 1820, a compromise emerged in the Senate. Maine, once a part of Massachusetts, applied for statehood, balancing against Missouri as a slave state. The Senate further agreed that

Eli Terry's Pillar and Scroll Clock

Before the 1790s, sundials and church bells answered most timekeeping needs; clocks were objects of art, not utility. The Connecticut clockmaker Eli Terry realized that affordable clocks might change all that. First he switched from brass to wood for the clock's internal movement, and then he designed machinery to mass-produce the parts, achieving the first successful system of "interchangeable parts" and turning out thousands of clocks a year. In 1814, Terry developed this inexpensive compact clock and sold tens of thousands over the next dozen years. Affordable clocks revolutionized timekeeping, enabling workers to arrive before the factory bell and travelers to make stagecoach and canal boat departure times. Employers could demand punctuality, a moral virtue made possible by the pervasiveness of clocks. For good or ill, clocks did not merely measure time; they helped speed up the pace of life.

American Clock & Watch Museum, Bristol, CT. Photo by C. R. Lang Photography.

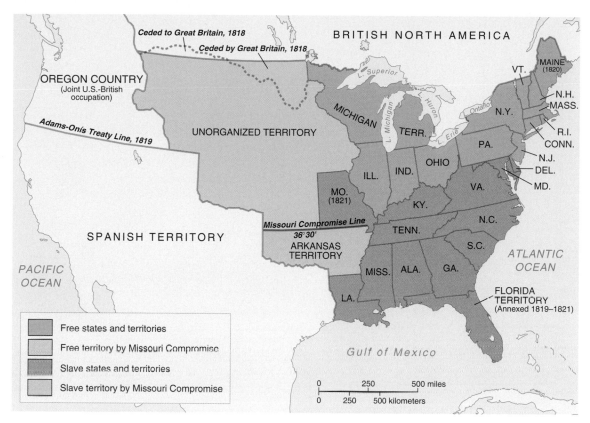

MAP 10.5   The Missouri Compromise, 1820
After a difficult battle in Congress, Missouri entered the Union in 1821 as part of a package of compromises. Maine was admitted as a free state to balance slavery in Missouri, and a line drawn at latitude 36°30′ put most of the rest of the Louisiana Territory off limits to slavery in the future.

READING THE MAP: How many free and how many slave states were there prior to the Missouri Compromise? What did the admission of Missouri as a slave state threaten to do?
CONNECTIONS: Who precipitated the crisis over Missouri, what did he propose, and where did the idea come from? Who proposed the Missouri Compromise, and who benefited from it?

FOR MORE HELP ANALYZING THIS IMAGE, see the map activity for this chapter in the Online Study Guide at bedfordstmartins.com/roark.

the southern boundary of Missouri—latitude 36°30′—extended west, would become the permanent line dividing slave from free states (Map 10.5). The House also approved the compromise, thanks to expert deal brokering by Kentucky's Henry Clay, who earned the nickname the "Great Pacificator" for his superb negotiating skills. The North secured a large area where federal prohibition of slavery was guaranteed and also got Maine as a counterbalance to Missouri. The South got Missouri without any interference with slavery. The whole package passed only because seventeen northern representatives in the House decided that minimizing sectional con-

flict was in the best interests of the United States and so voted with the South.

President Monroe and Thomas Jefferson at first worried that the Missouri crisis would reinvigorate the Federalist Party as the party of the North. But even ex-Federalists agreed that the split between free and slave states was too dangerous a fault line to be permitted to become a shaper of national politics. When new parties did develop in the 1830s, they took pains to bridge geography, each party developing a presence in both North and South. Monroe and Jefferson also worried about the future of slavery. Each understood slavery to be deeply

A View of St. Louis from an Illinois Town, 1835
Just fifteen years after the Missouri Compromise, St. Louis was already a booming city, having gotten its start in the eighteenth century as a French fur-trading village. It was incorporated as a town in 1809 and chartered as a city in 1822. In this 1835 view, commercial buildings and steamships line the riverfront; a ferry on the Illinois shore prepares to transport travelers across the Mississippi River. Black laborers (in the foreground) handle loading tasks. The Illinois side is a free state; Missouri, where the ferry lands, is a slave state.
A View of St. Louis from an Illinois Town, 1835: Private collection.

For more help analyzing this image, see the visual activity for this chapter in the Online Study Guide at
bedfordstmartins.com/roark.

problematic, but, as Jefferson said, "We have the wolf by the ears, and we can neither hold him, nor safely let him go. Justice is in one scale, and self-preservation in the other."

The Monroe Doctrine

New foreign policy challenges arose even as Congress struggled with the slavery issue. In 1816, American troops led by General Andrew Jackson invaded Spanish Florida in search of Seminole Indians welcoming and harboring escaped slaves. Once there, Jackson declared himself the commander of northern Florida, demonstrating his power in 1818 by executing two British men who he claimed were dangerous enemies. In asserting rule over the territory, and surely in executing the two British subjects on Spanish land, Jackson had gone too far. Privately, President Monroe was distressed and pondered court-martialing Jackson, prevented only by Jackson's immense popularity as the hero of the Battle of New Orleans. Instead, John Quincy Adams, the secretary of state, negotiated with Spain the Adams-Onís Treaty, which delivered Florida to the United States in 1819. In exchange, the Americans agreed to abandon any claim to Texas or Cuba; Southerners viewed this as a large concession, having eyed both places as potential acquisitions for future slave states.

Spain at that moment was preoccupied with its colonies in South America. One after another—Chile, Colombia, Peru, and finally

Mexico—declared itself independent in the early 1820s. To discourage Spain or France from reconquering these colonies, Monroe formulated a declaration of principles on South America. Incorporated into his annual message to Congress in December 1823, the declaration became known in later years as the **Monroe Doctrine**. The president warned that "the American Continents, by the free and independent condition which they have assumed and maintain, are henceforth not to be considered as subjects for future colonization by any European power." Any attempt to interfere in the Western Hemisphere would be regarded as "the manifestation of an unfriendly disposition towards the United States." In exchange for noninterference by Europeans, Monroe pledged that the United States would stay out of European struggles. He articulated these policy goals without any real force to back them up. Realistically, the American navy could not defend Chile or Peru against Spain or France. Monroe did not even have the backing of Congress for his statement; it was merely his idea of a sound policy laid out in a public message.

The Election of 1824

Monroe's attempt at a nonpartisan administration was the last of its kind, a fitting throwback to eighteenth-century ideals, led by the last president to wear a powdered wig and knee breeches. Monroe's cabinet contained men of sharply different philosophies, all calling themselves Republicans. Secretary of State John Quincy Adams represented the urban Northeast; South Carolinian John C. Calhoun spoke for the planter aristocracy as secretary of war; and William H. Crawford of Georgia, secretary of the treasury, was a proponent of Jeffersonian **states' rights** and limited federal power. Even before the end of Monroe's first term, these men and others began to maneuver for the election of 1824.

Election Sewing or Trinket Boxes from 1824

Women could mark their partiality to a presidential candidate by purchasing a sewing box emblazoned with the face of their choice. On the left is a box with John Quincy Adams's picture inside the cover, created with a lithographic process just coming into wide use in the 1820s that made possible the production of thousands of pictures from a single master stone plate. (Wood and copper plates, the earlier technology, produced prints numbering only in the hundreds before deteriorating under pressure.) The top of the Adams box carries a velvet pincushion printed with the slogan "BE FIRM FOR ADAMS." A competing box on the right puts Andrew Jackson's likeness under glass on the top of the cover. The lithographic portrait is hand colored with watercolors. Notice that Jackson is shown in his military uniform with the title of general and a rather younger-looking face than he actually had in 1824.
Collection of Janice L. and David J. Frent.

Crucially helping them to maneuver were their wives, who accomplished some of the work of modern campaign managers through assiduous courting of men—and women—of influence. The parties not thrown by Mrs. Monroe were now thrown all over town by women whose husbands were jockeying for political favor. Louisa Catherine Adams, for example, remodeled her house and had parties every Tuesday night for guests numbering in the hundreds. (At one party she learned before her husband did that the Adams-Onís Treaty he had negotiated had been formally approved by Spain.) Adams lacked charm—"I am a man of reserved, cold, austere, and forbidding manners" he once wrote—but his abundantly charming (and hardworking) wife more than made up for that. She attended to the etiquette of social calls, sometimes making two dozen in one morning, and counted sixty-eight members of Congress as her regular Tuesday guests.

Since 1800, the congressional caucus of each party had met to identify and lend its considerable but still informal support to its party's leading candidate. In 1824, with only one party alive—and alive with five serious candidates—the caucus system splintered. Since such a large number of candidates reduced the chance of anyone securing a majority in the electoral college, many expected that the final election would be decided by the House of Representatives. Having sixty-eight members of the House on one's regular guest list was thus smart politics.

> The 1824 election was the first presidential contest in which candidates' popularity with ordinary voters could be measured.

John Quincy Adams (and Louisa Catherine) very much wanted the presidency, an ambition fed by John's sense of rising to his father's accomplishment. Furthermore, since 1800 every president had once been secretary of state; Adams was the heir apparent, or so he thought. Henry Clay, Speaker of the House, also was a declared candidate. A man of vast congressional experience, he had engaged in high-level diplomacy, having accompanied Adams to Ghent to negotiate the 1814 peace treaty with Britain. The Kentuckian put forth a set of policies he called the American System, a package of protective tariffs to promote manufacturing and federal expenditures for extensive internal improvements, such as roads and canals. William Crawford, of the Treasury Department, was a favorite of Republicans from the big states of Virginia and New York; despite suffering an incapacitating stroke in mid-1824, he remained their favorite. South Carolinian John C. Calhoun, a lawyer as well as a planter, was another serious contender, having served in Congress and in several cabinets. Like Clay, he favored internal improvements and protective tariffs, which he figured would gain him support in northern states.

The final candidate was an outsider and a latecomer: General Andrew Jackson of Tennessee. Jackson had much less national political experience than the others, having served one year in the House and two in the Senate. His fame rested on his reputation as a military leader, but that was sufficient to gain him a huge following, much to the surprise of the experienced politicians. In early 1824, on the anniversary of the Battle of New Orleans, the Adamses had thrown a spectacular ball with five hundred guests in honor of General Jackson. No doubt John Quincy Adams hoped that some of Jackson's charisma would rub off on him; he was not yet thinking of Jackson as a rival for office. But later in 1824, Jackson supporters put his name in play, and voters in the West and South reacted with enthusiasm. Calhoun soon dropped out of the race and shifted his attention to winning the vice presidency.

The 1824 election was the first presidential contest in which candidates' popularity with ordinary voters could be measured. Recent changes in state constitutions gave voters in all but six states the power to choose electors for the electoral college. (Before, state legislatures had held this power.) Jackson was by far the most popular candidate with voters. He won more than 153,000 votes, while Adams was second with 109,000; Clay won 47,000 votes, and the debilitated Crawford garnered 46,600. This was not a large voter turnout, probably amounting to only a quarter of adult white males. Many more voters participated regularly in local and state elections, where the real political action generally lay.

In the electoral college, Jackson received 99 votes, Adams 84, Crawford 41, and Clay 37 (Map 10.6). Jackson did not have a majority, so the election was thrown into the House of Representatives, for the second (and last) time in American history. Each state delegation had one vote; according to the Twelfth Amendment to the Constitution, passed in 1804, only the top three candidates could enter the runoff. Thus Henry Clay was out of the race and in a position to bestow his support on another candidate.

Jackson's supporters later characterized the election of 1824 as the "corrupt bargain." Clay backed Adams, and Adams won by one vote in the House. Clay's support made sense on several levels. Despite strong mutual dislike, he and Adams agreed on issues such as federal support to build roads and canals, and Clay was uneasy with Jackson's volatile temperament and unstated political views and with Crawford's diminished capacity. What made Clay's decision look "corrupt" was that immediately after the election, Adams offered to appoint Clay secretary of state—and Clay accepted.

In the weeks before the vote in the House, rumors of such a deal had been denied by Adams and Clay supporters, confident that the two archenemies could never cooperate. There probably was no concrete bargain; Adams's subsequent cabinet appointments demonstrated his lack of political astuteness. But Andrew Jackson felt that the election had been stolen from him, and he wrote bitterly that "the Judas of the West has closed the contract and will receive the thirty pieces of silver."

Candidate*	Electoral Vote	Popular Vote	Percent of Popular Vote**
John Q. Adams	84	108,740	30.5
Andrew Jackson	99	153,544	43.1
Henry Clay	37	47,136	13.2
W.H. Crawford	41	46,618	13.1

*No distinct political parties
**Approximate

Note: Because no candidate garnered a majority in the electoral college, the election was decided in the House of Representatives. Although Clay was eliminated from the running, as Speaker of the House he influenced the final decision in favor of Adams.

MAP 10.6 The Election of 1824

The Adams Administration

John Quincy Adams, like his father, was a one-term president. His career had been built on diplomacy, not electoral politics, and, despite his wife's deft experience in the art of political influence, his own political horse sense was not well developed. His cabinet choices welcomed his opposition into his inner circle. He asked Crawford to stay on in the Treasury, and he retained an openly pro-Jackson postmaster general, even though that position controlled thousands of nationwide patronage appointments. Most amazingly, he asked Jackson to become secretary of war. With Calhoun as vice president (elected without opposition by the electoral college) and Clay at the State Department, the whole argumentative crew would have been thrust into the executive branch. Crawford and Jackson had the good sense to decline the appointments.

Adams had lofty ideas for federal action during his presidency, and the plan he put before Congress was so sweeping that it took Henry Clay aback. Adams called for federally built roads, canals, and harbors. He proposed a national university in Washington as well as government-sponsored scientific research. He wanted to build observatories to advance astronomical

knowledge and to promote precision in time-keeping, and he backed a decimal-based system of weights and measures. In all these endeavors, Adams believed he was continuing the Jefferson and Madison legacy, using the powers of government to advance knowledge. But his opponents feared he was too Hamiltonian, using federal power inappropriately to advance commercial interests.

Whether he was more truly Federalist or Republican was a moot point, however. Lacking the give-and-take political skills required to gain congressional support, Adams was unable to implement much of his program. He scorned the idea of courting voters to gain support and using the patronage system to enhance his power. He often made appointments (to posts such as customs collectors) to placate enemies rather than reward friends. A story of a toast offered to the president may well have been mythical, but as humorous folklore it made the rounds during his term and came to summarize Adams's precarious hold on leadership. A dignitary raised a glass and pledged, "May he strike confusion to his foes . . . ," to which another voice scornfully chimed in, "as he has already done to his friends."

Conclusion: Republican Simplicity Becomes Complex

The nineteenth century opened with the Jeffersonian Republicans in power, trying to undo much of what Federalists had created in the 1790s. But Jefferson's promise of a simpler government—limited in size, scope, and power—quickly gave way to the lure of the West. The Lewis and Clark expedition excited armchair travelers and real travelers alike, and the sudden acquisition of the Louisiana Purchase promised land and opportunity to settlers. But Southerners and Northerners moving into Missouri, the second state after Louisiana carved out of the Louisiana Purchase, brought differing ideas about slavery (along with a large number of slaves), greatly complicating the country's political future with the burning issues central to the crisis over Missouri statehood.

Jeffersonian simplicity also gave way in the face of increasing antagonism both from foreign nations and from Indian nations. Jefferson and his successor Madison met it with a combination of embargoes, treaties, and military action. Battles with Indians blended into the major engagement with England, the War of 1812—a war motivated less by concrete economic or political issues than by questions of honor. Its conclusion at the Battle of New Orleans allowed Americans the illusion that they had fought a second war of independence.

If the War of 1812 seemed a second war of independence for the whites, how much more so was it for the Indians, who lost both times. Tecumseh's vision of an unprecedentedly large confederacy of Indian tribes that would halt western expansion by white Americans was cut short by the war and by his death. Without British support, the Indians probably could not have successfully challenged for long the westward dynamic of American settlement. But British support came at a time when Canada was under attack, and the British valued their own defense more than they valued their promises to help the Indians.

The war elevated to national prominence General Andrew Jackson, whose sudden popularity with voters in the 1824 election surprised traditional politicians—and their politically astute wives—and threw the one-party rule of Republicans into a tailspin. John Quincy Adams barely occupied his office in 1825 before the election campaign of 1828 was off and running. Appeals to the people—the mass of white male voters—would be the hallmark of all elections after 1824. It was a game Adams could not easily play.

Politics in this entire period was a game that women could not play either. Except for the political wives of Washington, women, whether white or free black, had no place in government. While male legislatures maintained women's *feme covert* status, keeping wives dependent on husbands, a few women found a pathway to greater personal autonomy through religion. Meanwhile, the routine inclusion of girls in public schools and the steady spread of female academies planted seeds that would blossom into a major transformation of gender in the 1830s and 1840s.

The War of 1812 started another chain of events that would prove momentous in later decades. Jefferson's long embargo and Madison's wartime trade stoppages gave strong encouragement to American manufacturing, momentarily protected from competition with English factories. When peace returned in 1815, the years of independent development burst forth into a period of sustained economic growth that continued nearly unabated into the mid-nineteenth century.

FOR ADDITIONAL FIRSTHAND ACCOUNTS OF THIS PERIOD, see Chapter 10 in Michael Johnson, ed., *Reading the American Past*, Third Edition.

TO ASSESS YOUR MASTERY OF THE MATERIAL IN THIS CHAPTER, see the Online Study Guide at bedfordstmartins.com/roark.

FOR WEB LINKS RELATED TO TOPICS IN THIS CHAPTER, see "HistoryLinks," "DocLinks," and "PlaceLinks" at bedfordstmartins.com/roark.

CHRONOLOGY

1789 • Judiciary Act establishes six Supreme Court justices, who preside over six circuit courts.

1800 • Thomas Jefferson and Aaron Burr tie in electoral college.
• Gabriel's slave rebellion in Virginia tries but fails to exploit white electoral crisis.

1801 • Judiciary Act reduces Supreme Court justices to five and allows for sixteen circuit courts and circuit court judges.
• House of Representatives elects Jefferson president after 36 ballots.

1803 • Supreme Court in *Marbury v. Madison* establishes concept of judicial review.
• England and France place embargoes on American shipping.
• United States purchases Louisiana Territory from France for $15 million.

1804 • Jefferson elected to a second term.
• Burr-Hamilton duel ends in Alexander Hamilton's death.

1804–1806
• Lewis and Clark expedition goes to the Pacific and inspires ideas of western expansion.

1807 • New Jersey revises the law to exclude women and blacks from voting.
• British attack and search *Chesapeake* in Chesapeake Bay.
• Embargo Act forbids American ships from engaging in trade with any foreign port.

1808 • James Madison elected president; Dolley Madison soon dubbed "presidentress."

1809 • Treaty of Fort Wayne cedes 3 million acres of Indian land in Indiana Territory to United States.
• Non-Intercourse Act forbids American trade with England, France, and their colonies.

1811 • William Henry Harrison's troops win Battle of Tippecanoe, destroying Prophetstown in Indiana Territory and breaking Tenskwatawa's power.

1812 • United States declares war on Great Britain.
• Madison elected to a second term.

1813 • Tecumseh dies at Battle of the Thames.

1814 • British attack Washington, D.C., burning White House and Capitol.
• Treaty of Ghent ends War of 1812.
• New England Federalists at Hartford Convention consider secession and look unpatriotic.

1815 • Andrew Jackson's forces win Battle of New Orleans.

1816 • James Monroe elected president.

1819 • Spain cedes Florida to United States in Adams-Onís Treaty.

1820 • Missouri Compromise admits Missouri as slave state and Maine as free state, ending the most serious North-South political crisis in the early Republic.
• Monroe elected to a second term.

1823 • Monroe Doctrine asserts independence of Western Hemisphere from European intervention.

1824 • John Quincy Adams becomes president in "corrupt bargain" election.

BIBLIOGRAPHY

General Works

Lance Banning, *The Jeffersonian Persuasion: Evolution of a Party Ideology* (1978).

Saul Cornell, *The Other Founders: Anti-Federalism and the Dissenting Tradition in America, 1788–1828* (1999).

Noble E. Cunningham, *In Pursuit of Reason: The Life of Thomas Jefferson* (1987).

Ralph Ketcham, *Presidents above Party: The First American Presidency, 1789–1829* (1984).

David Waldstreicher, *In the Midst of Perpetual Fetes: The Making of American Nationalism, 1776–1820* (1997).

Stephen Watts, *The Republic Reborn: War and the Making of Liberal America, 1790–1820* (1987).

Republicans and Federalists

Doron S. Ben-Atar, *The Origins of Jeffersonian Commercial Policy and Diplomacy* (1993).

James Broussard, *The Southern Federalists, 1800–1816* (1978).

Noble E. Cunningham, *The Jeffersonian Republicans in Power: Party Operations, 1801–1809* (1963).

Alexander DeConde, *This Affair of Louisiana* (1976).

Joseph J. Ellis, *American Sphinx: The Character of Thomas Jefferson* (1997).

Richard E. Ellis, *The Jeffersonian Crisis: Courts and Politics in the Young Republic* (1971).

David Hackett Fischer, *The Revolution of American Conservatism: The Federalist Party in the Era of Jeffersonian Democracy* (1965).

Marshall Fotella, *Coming to Terms with Democracy: Federalist Intellectuals and the Shaping of an American Culture* (2001).

Joanne B. Freeman, *Affairs of Honor: National Politics in the New Republic* (2001).

Annette Gordon-Reed, *Thomas Jefferson and Sally Hemings: An American Controversy* (1997).

Morton J. Horwitz, *The Transformation of American Law, 1780–1860* (1977).

Herbert A. Johnson, *The Chief Justiceship of John Marshall, 1801–1835* (1997).

Lawrence S. Kaplan, *"Entangling Alliances with None": American Foreign Policy in the Age of Jefferson* (1987).

Jon Kukla, *A Wilderness So Immense: The Louisiana Purchase and the Destiny of America* (2003).

Jan Ellen Lewis and Peter S. Onuf, eds., *Sally Hemings and Thomas Jefferson: History, Memory, and Civic Culture* (1999).

Milton Lomask, *Aaron Burr* (1982).

Dumas Malone, *Jefferson the President: First Term, 1801–1805* (1970).

Dumas Malone, *Jefferson the President: Second Term, 1805–1809* (1974).

Richard K. Matthews, *The Radical Politics of Thomas Jefferson: A Revisionist View* (1984).

Drew R. McCoy, *The Elusive Republic: Political Economy in Jeffersonian America* (1980).

Drew R. McCoy, *The Last of the Fathers: James Madison and the Republican Legacy* (1989).

R. Kent Newmyer, *The Supreme Court under Marshall and Taney* (1986).

Peter Onuf, ed., *Jeffersonian Legacies* (1993).

Merrill Peterson, *Thomas Jefferson and the New Nation: A Biography* (1970).

Arnold A. Rogow, *A Fatal Friendship: Alexander Hamilton and Aaron Burr* (1998).

Robert A. Rutland, *The Presidency of James Madison* (1990).

Thomas C. Shevory, ed., *John Marshall's Achievement: Law, Politics, and Constitutional Interpretations* (1989).

Jack M. Sosin, *The Aristocracy of the Long Robe: The Origins of Judicial Review in America* (1989).

Francis N. Stites, *John Marshall: Defender of the Constitution* (1981).

Robert W. Tucker, *Empire of Liberty: The Statecraft of Thomas Jefferson* (1990).

G. E. White, *The Marshall Court and Cultural Change, 1815–1835* (1988).

Lewis and Clark and the West

Stephen E. Ambrose, *Undaunted Courage: Meriwether Lewis, Thomas Jefferson, and the Opening of the American West* (1996).

Albert Furtwangler, *Acts of Discovery: Visions of America in the Lewis and Clark Journals* (1993).

David Freeman Hawke, *Those Tremendous Mountains: The Story of the Lewis and Clark Expedition* (1980).

James P. Ronda, *Lewis and Clark among the Indians* (1984).

Foreign Policy and the War of 1812

James M. Banner, *To the Hartford Convention: The Federalists and the Origins of Party Politics in Massachusetts, 1789–1815* (1969).

Carl Benn, *The Iroquois in the War of 1812* (1998).

Pierre Berton, *The Invasion of Canada* (1980).

Harry L. Coles, *The War of 1812* (1965).

Ronald L. Hatzenbuehler and Robert L. Ivie, *Congress Declares War: Rhetoric, Leadership, and Partisanship in the Early Republic* (1983).

Donald R. Hickey, *The War of 1812: A Forgotten Conflict* (1989).

Reginald Horsman, *The Causes of the War of 1812* (1962).

Linda K. Kerber, *Federalists in Dissent: Imagery and Ideology in Jeffersonian America* (1970).

C. Edward Skeen, *Citizen Soldiers in the War of 1812* (1999).

Burton Spivak, *Jefferson's English Crisis: Commerce, Embargo, and the Republican Revolution* (1979).

J. C. A. Stagg, *Mr. Madison's War: Politics, Diplomacy, and Warfare in the Early American Republic, 1783–1830* (1983).

Slavery

David Brion Davis, *The Problem of Slavery in the Age of Revolution, 1770–1823* (1975).

Douglas Egerton, *Gabriel's Rebellion* (1993).

Sylvia Frey, *Water from the Rock* (1991).

James Oliver Horton and Lois E. Horton, *In Hope of Liberty: Culture, Community, and Protest among Northern Free Blacks, 1700–1860* (1997).

Robert McColley, *Slavery and Jeffersonian Virginia* (1964).

Gary B. Nash, *Forging Freedom: The Formation of Philadelphia's Black Community, 1720–1840* (1988).

Donald L. Robinson, *Slavery in the Structure of American Politics, 1765–1820* (1971).

James Sidbury, *Ploughshares into Swords: Race, Rebellion, and Identity in Gabriel's Virginia* (1997).

Shane White, *Somewhat More Independent: The End of Slavery in New York City, 1710–1810* (1991).

Native Americans

Henry Warner Bowden, *American Indians and Christian Missions: Studies in Cultural Conflict* (1981).

Christopher Densmore, *Red Jacket: Iroquois Diplomat and Orator* (1999).

Gregory E. Dowd, *A Spirited Resistance: The North American Indian Struggle for Unity, 1745–1815* (1992).

R. David Edmunds, *The Shawnee Prophet* (1983).

R. David Edmunds, *Tecumseh and the Quest for Indian Leadership* (1984).

Bil Gilbert, *God Gave Us This Country: Tekamthi and the First American Civil War* (1989).

H. S. Halbert and T. H. Ball, *The Creek War of 1813 and 1814* (1969).

William G. McLoughlin, *Cherokees and Missionaries, 1789–1839* (1984).

James Merrell, *The Indians' New World: Catawbas and Their Neighbors from European Contact through the Era of Removal* (1989).

Paul Francis Prucha, *The Great Father: The United States Government and the American Indians* (1984).

Bernard W. Sheehan, *Seeds of Extinction: Jeffersonian Philanthropy and the American Indians* (1973).

John Sugden, *Tecumseh: A Life* (1997).

Richard White, *The Middle Ground: Indians, Empires, and Republics in the Great Lakes Region, 1650–1815* (1991).

Women, Marriage, and Religion

Catherine Allgor, *Parlor Politics: In Which the Ladies of Washington Help Build a City and a Government* (2000).

Norma Basch, *In the Eyes of the Law: Women, Marriage, and Property in Nineteenth-Century New York* (1982).

Norma Basch, *Framing American Divorce: From the Revolutionary Generation to the Victorians* (1999).

Catherine A. Brekus, *Strangers and Pilgrims: Female Preaching in America, 1740–1845* (1998).

Jon Butler, *Awash in a Sea of Faith: Christianizing the American People* (1990).

Nancy Cott, *Public Vows: A History of Marriage and the Nation* (2001).

Philip Greven, *The Protestant Temperament: Patterns of Child-Rearing, Religious Experience, and the Self in Early America* (1977).

Michael Grossberg, *Governing the Hearth: Law and the Family in Nineteenth-Century America* (1985).

Hendrik Hartog, *Man and Wife in America: A History* (2000).

Nathan Hatch, *The Democratization of American Christianity* (1989).

Nancy Isenberg, *Sex and Citizenship in Antebellum America* (1998).

Susan Juster, *Disorderly Women: Sexual Politics and Evangelicalism in Revolutionary New England* (1994).

Linda Kerber, *Women of the Republic* (1980).

Jan Lewis, *The Pursuit of Happiness: Family and Values in Jefferson's Virginia* (1983).

Carla Pestana, *Quakers and Baptists in Colonial Massachusetts* (1991).

Marylynn Salmon, *Women and the Law of Property in Early America* (1986).

Suzanne R. Thurman, *"O Sisters Ain't You Happy?": Gender, Family, and Community among the Harvard and Shirley Shakers, 1781–1918* (2002).

Laurel Thatcher Ulrich, *A Midwife's Tale: The Life of Martha Ballard, Based on Her Diary, 1786–1812* (1990).

Monroe and Adams Presidencies

Harry Ammon, *James Monroe: The Quest for National Identity* (1971).

Noble E. Cunningham Jr., *The Presidency of James Monroe* (1996).

George Dangerfield, *The Era of Good Feelings* (1952).

Don E. Fehrenbacher, *The South and Three Sectional Crises* (1980).

Mary W. M. Hargreaves, *The Presidency of John Quincy Adams* (1986).

Shaw Livermore, *The Twilight of Federalism: The Disintegration of the Federalist Party, 1815–1830* (1962).

Ernest R. May, *The Making of the Monroe Doctrine* (1975).

Paul C. Nagel, *John Quincy Adams: A Public Life, a Private Life* (1997).

SHIP'S FIGUREHEAD OF ANDREW JACKSON

Carved in 1834 and affixed to the bow of the revered navy frigate *Constitution,* this figurehead of Andrew Jackson symbolized national pride by putting "the image of the most popular man of the West upon the favorite ship of the East," according to the commodore who commissioned it. But when Jackson introduced a new, strict banking policy, his popularity in the urban East quickly plummeted. In Boston, where the *Constitution* was docked, protesters complained that the figurehead of a tyrant corrupted their ship. On the night of July 3, 1834, the eve of the national holiday, a twenty-seven-year-old mariner and ardent Whig stole on board and decapitated the figurehead, sawing it through just below the ears. Jackson deflected the insult with humor, declaring, "I never did like that image! Give the man a postmaster's job." The commodore, himself alert to symbolic actions, wrapped the headless statue in a flag and sent it to New York City, where woodworkers fashioned a new head in 1835. The figurehead was reattached to the ship in another port: Jackson's banking policies still rankled in urban financial centers, and naval authorities did not want to risk a second mutilation of the president's image. In 1990, the original head was recovered from a private collector in France and restored to view in the museum that now owns the figurehead.

Museum of the City of New York, Gift of the Seawanhaka Corinthian Yacht Club.

11

The Expanding Republic

1815–1840

PRESIDENT ANDREW JACKSON was the dominant figure of his age, yet his precarious childhood little foretold the fame, fortune, and influence he would enjoy in the years after 1815. Jackson was born in the Carolina backcountry in 1767. His Scots-Irish father had recently died, leaving a poor, struggling mother to support three small boys. During the Revolution, Andrew followed his brothers into the militia, where both died of disease, as did his mother. Orphaned at fourteen, Jackson drifted around, drinking, gambling, and brawling.

But at seventeen, his prospects improved. He studied under a lawyer for three years and then moved to Nashville, a **frontier** community full of opportunities for a young man with legal training and an aggressive temperament. He became a public prosecutor, married into a leading family, and acquired land and slaves. When Tennessee became a state in 1796, Jackson, then twenty-nine, was elected to Congress for a single term.

Jackson captured national attention in 1815 by leading the victory at the Battle of New Orleans. With little else to celebrate about the War of 1812, many Americans seized on the Tennessee general as the champion of the day. Songs, broadsides, and an admiring biography set him up as the original self-made man, the parentless child magically responsible for his own destiny. Jackson seemed to have created himself, a gritty, forceful personality extracting opportunities from the dynamic, turbulent frontier.

Jackson was more than a man of action, however. He was also strong-willed, reckless, and quick to anger, impulsively challenging men to duels, sometimes on slight pretexts. In one legendary fight in 1806, Jackson deliberately let his opponent, an expert marksman, shoot first. The bullet hit him in a rib, but Jackson masked all sign of injury under a loose cloak and immobile face. He then took careful aim at the astonished man and killed him. Such steely courage chilled his political opponents.

Jackson's image as a tough frontier hero set him apart from the learned and privileged gentlemen from Virginia and Massachusetts who had occupied the presidency up to 1828. When he lost the 1824 election to John Quincy Adams, an infuriated Jackson vowed to fight a rematch. He won in 1828 and again in 1832, capturing large majorities. His appeal stretched across the urban working classes of the East, frontier voters of the West, and slaveholders in the South, who all saw something of themselves in Jackson. Once elected, he brought a combative style to politics and enlarged the powers of the presidency.

The confidence and even recklessness of Jackson's personality mirrored the new confidence of American society in the years after 1815. An entrepreneurial spirit gripped the country, producing a market revolution of unprecedented scale. Old social hierarchies eroded; ordinary men dreamed of moving high on the ladder of success, just as Jackson had done. Stunning advances in transportation and economic productivity fueled such dreams and propelled thousands to move west or to cities. Urban growth and technological change fostered the diffusion of a distinctive and vibrant public culture, spread through newspapers and the spoken word. The development of rapid print allowed popular opinions to coalesce and intensify; Jackson's sudden nationwide celebrity was a case in point.

Expanded communication transformed politics dramatically. Sharp disagreements over the best way to promote individual **liberty**, economic opportunity, and national prosperity in the new market economy defined key differences between Jackson and Adams and the parties they gave rise to in the 1830s. The process of party formation brought new habits of political participation and party loyalty to many thousands more adult white males. Religion became democratized as well: A nationwide **evangelical** revival brought its adherents the certainty that salvation and perfection were now available to all.

As president from 1829 to 1837, Jackson presided over all these changes, fighting some and supporting others in his vigorous and volatile way. As with his own stubborn person-

MAP 11.1   Routes of Transportation in 1840

By the 1830s, transportation advances had cut travel times significantly. Goods and people could move from New York City to Buffalo, New York, in four days by way of the Erie Canal, a trip that took two weeks by road in 1800. A trip from New York to New Orleans that took four weeks in 1800 could be accomplished in less than half that time on steamboats in the western rivers.

READING THE MAP: In what parts of the country were canals built most extensively? Were most of them within a single state's borders, or did they encourage interstate travel and shipping?

CONNECTIONS: What impact did the Erie Canal have on the development of New York City? How did improvements in transportation affect urbanization in other parts of the country?

FOR MORE HELP ANALYZING THIS MAP, see the map activity for this chapter in the Online Study Guide at bedfordstmartins.com/roark.

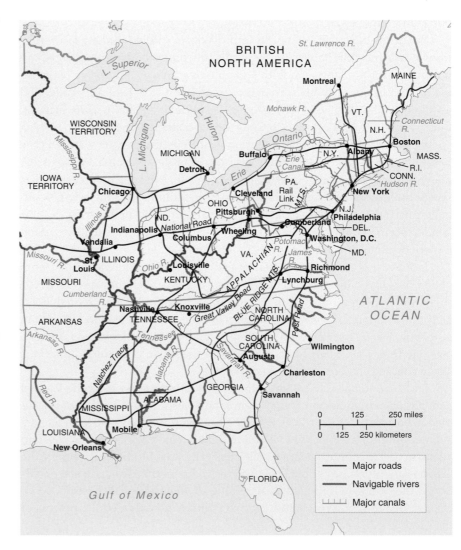

ality, there was a dark underside to the confidence and expansiveness of American society. Steamboats blew up, banks and businesses periodically collapsed, alcoholism rates soared, Indians were killed or relocated farther west, and slavery continued to expand. The brash confidence that turned some people into rugged, self-promoting, Jackson-like individuals inspired others to think about the human costs of rapid economic expansion and thus about reforming society in dramatic ways. The common denominator was a faith that people and societies can shape their own destinies.

The Market Revolution

The return of peace in 1815 unleashed powerful forces that revolutionized the organization of the economy. Spectacular changes in transportation facilitated the movement of commodities, information, and people, while textile mills and other factories created many new jobs, especially for young unmarried women. Innovations in banking, legal practices, and tariff policies promoted swift economic growth.

This was not yet an industrial revolution but a market revolution, fueled by traditional sources—water, wood, beasts of burden, and human muscle. What was new was the accelerated pace of economic activity and the scale of distribution of goods. Men and women were drawn out of old patterns of rural self-sufficiency into the wider realm of national market relations. At the same time, the nation's money supply enlarged considerably, leading to speculative investments in commerce, manufacturing, transportation, and land. The new nature and scale of production and consumption changed Americans' economic behavior, leading to raised expectations of material improvement. But in 1819 and again in 1837, serious crashes of the economy punctured those optimistic expectations.

Improvements in Transportation

Before 1815, transportation in the United States was slow and expensive; it cost as much to ship freight over thirty miles of domestic roads as it did to send the same cargo across the Atlantic Ocean. The fastest stagecoach trip from Boston to New York took an uncomfortable four days. But between 1815 and 1840, networks of roads, canals, steamboats, and finally railroads dramatically raised the speed and lowered the cost of travel (Map 11.1). Andrew Jackson spent weeks walking and riding west to Nashville in the 1790s along old Indian trails, but when he returned east in 1829, the new president traveled by steamboat and turnpike to Washington, D.C., in a matter of days.

Improved transportation moved goods and products into much wider markets. It moved people too, broadening the horizons of passengers on business and pleasure trips and allowing youth to take up new employment in cities or factory towns. Transportation also facilitated the flow of political and other information through heavy traffic in newspapers, periodicals, and books.

Enhanced public transport was expensive and produced uneven economic benefits, so administrations from Jefferson to Monroe were reluctant to fund it with federal dollars. Only the National Road, begun in 1806, was government sponsored. By 1818, it extended from Baltimore to Wheeling, in western Virginia. Instead, private investors pooled resources and chartered stagecoach, canal, steamboat, and railroad companies, receiving significant aid from state governments in the form of subsidies and guarantees of **monopoly** rights. Turnpike and roadway mileage dramatically increased after 1815, reducing the cost of land shipment of goods. Stagecoach lines proliferated in an extensive network of passenger corridors dense in the populated East and fanning out to the Mississippi River. Travel time on main routes was cut in half; Boston to New York now took two days.

Water travel was similarly transformed. In 1807, Robert Fulton's steam-propelled boat, the *Clermont,* churned upstream on the Hudson River from New York City to Albany in thirty-two hours, touching off a steamboat craze. In 1820, a dozen boats left New York City daily, and scores more operated on midwestern rivers and the Great Lakes. A voyager on one of the first steamboats to go down the Mississippi reported that the Chickasaw Indians called the vessel a "fire canoe" and considered it "an omen of evil." By the early 1830s, steamboat travel in the East was routine, and more than seven hundred steamboats were in operation on the Ohio and Mississippi rivers. A journey upriver from New Orleans to Louisville, Kentucky, took only one week.

Steamboats were not benign advances, however. The urgency to cut travel time led to

> The new nature and scale of production and consumption changed Americans' behavior, attitudes, and expectations.

Early Steamboats

Steamboats revolutionized travel in the early nineteenth century. The basic technology consisted of an engine powered by the steam from a boiler heated by a wood-burning furnace. The steam first collected in a cylinder and then cooled and condensed to create a vacuum that drove a piston, which in turn propelled a paddlewheel mounted at the side or the stern of the boat. From the 1780s to 1807, several inventors sought the ideal combination of engine size, boat size, and paddlewheel type. Robert Fulton's *Clermont* of 1807 was not the first American steamboat, but it was the first long-distance, commercially successful endeavor.

Two advantages marked Fulton's effort: He imported a superior British-made engine, a low-pressure model built with many precision parts, and he formed a partnership with New York businessman Robert R. Livingston. Livingston had acquired from the New York state legislature in 1798 the right to a twenty-year monopoly on all steam transportation on the Hudson River, on the condition that he produce a boat capable of traveling four miles per hour upriver. The *Clermont* met that test.

In 1811, Fulton and Livingston launched the first steamboat on the Mississippi River. Their low-pressure engine, operating at about two pounds per square inch of pressure in the cylinder, failed to maneuver against the river's shifting currents and many obstructions. A high-pressure steam engine developed by Delaware entrepreneur Oliver Evans proved far more suitable. Generating pressures from eighty to one hundred pounds per square inch, it required 30 percent more fuel, but at that time wood was plentiful along western waterways. By the 1830s, there were many hundreds of boats on the Mississippi, the Ohio, and the lower Missouri rivers, run by companies competing to reduce travel time. An upriver trip from New Orleans to Louisville that took nearly a month in the 1810s took less than a week in the 1830s. The American traveling public fell in love with steamboats for their speed and power.

Steamboats offered luxury as well as speed. They often were floating palaces, carrying several hundred passengers and providing swank accommodations to ladies and gentlemen paying first-class fares. A few boats had private cabins, but most often there were two large rooms, one for each sex, filled with chairs that converted to beds. (The separation of sexes answered an important need in addition to bodily modesty: Women travelers often expressed their disgust over the spit-drenched carpets in the men's cabin.) Dining rooms with elegant appointments served elaborate meals. Many steamboats had gambling rooms as well. Low-fare passengers, typically men, occupied the lower decks, finding sleeping space out in the open or in crowded berths in public rooms. Often these men were pressed into service loading wood at the frequent fueling stops.

The fire and smoke of a steamboat proved awesome and even terrifying to many. An older gent making his first trip in 1836 wrote that "I went on board, and passing the fireroom, where they were just firing up, I stopped, with unfeigned horror, and asked myself if, indeed, I was prepared to die!" But many others were enthralled by the unprecedented power represented by the belching smoke. Impromptu boat racing became a popular sport. A German traveler identified a competitive streak in American passengers: "When two steamboats happen to get alongside each other, the passengers will encourage the captains to run a race. . . . The boilers intended for a pressure of only 100 pounds per square inch, are by the accelerated generation of steam, exposed to a pressure of 150, and even 200 pounds, and this goes sometimes so far, that the trials end with an explosion."

Steamboats were far from safe. Between 1811 and 1851, accidents destroyed nearly 1,000 boats—a third of all steam vessels built in that period. More than half the sinkings resulted from underwater debris that penetrated hulls. Fires, too, were fearsome hazards in wooden boats that commonly carried highly combustible cargoes, such as raw cotton in burlap bags. The development of overstoked furnaces, sudden boiler explosions, and terrible mass fatalities. (See "The Promise of Technology," on this page.) Another huge cost, to the environment, was the deforestation brought by steamboats, which had to load fuel—"wood up"—every twenty miles or so. By the 1830s the banks of main rivers were denuded of trees, and forests miles in from the rivers fell to the ax.

"The Awful Conflagration of the Steamboat _Lexington_ in Long Island Sound," 1840

The _Lexington_ was six years old in 1840 and equipped with many extra safety features, such as a fire engine and pump, but with only three lifeboats. The lifeboats could accommodate only half of the passengers; they were quickly swamped in the emergency and rendered useless. Only four people survived; many of the 139 victims froze to death in the icy January waters. Consider this lithograph as a commodity made for sale in many thousands of copies: Who would buy this kind of artistic production?

The Mariners Museum, Newport News, VA.

pal cause human error—reckless or drunk pilots (none of them licensed) or captains bent on breaking speed records?

And who was responsible for public safety? When the three-week-old _Moselle_ blew up near Cincinnati in 1838, with the loss of 150 lives, a citizen's committee fixed blame on the twenty-eight-year-old captain, who had ordered the fires stoked with pitch and the safety valves shut to build up a bigger head of steam. "Such disasters have their foundation in the present mammoth evil of our country, an inordinate love of gain," said the committee. "We are not satisfied with getting rich, but we must get rich in a day. We are not satisfied with traveling at a speed of ten miles an hour, but we must fly. Such is the effect of competition that everything must be done cheap; boiler iron must be cheap, traveling must be done cheap, freight must be cheap, yet everything must be speedy. A steamboat must establish a reputation of a few minutes 'swifter' in a hundred miles than others, before she can make fortunes fast enough to satisfy the owners."

In 1830, the federal government awarded a grant to the Franklin Institute of Philadelphia to study the causes of boiler explosions. But not until 1852 did public safety become a federal responsibility with the passage of regulations by Congress mandating steamboat inspections. After the Civil War, affordable sheet steel and the development of new welding techniques produced boilers that were much stronger and safer.

sheet metal, which strengthened hulls and protected wooden surfaces near the smokestacks from sparks, was a major safety advance.

Boiler explosions were the most horrifying cause of accidents. By far the greatest loss of life came from scalding steam, flying wreckage, and fire, which could engulf a boat in a matter of minutes. In the 1830s alone, 89 boiler explosions caused 861 deaths and many more injuries. The cause of explosion was often mysterious: Was it excessive steam pressure or weak metal? Exactly how much pressure could plate iron fastened with rivets really withstand? Did a dangerous or explosive gas develop in the boiler when the water level fell too low? Or was the princi-

Steamboats burned large amounts of wood, transferring the carbon stored in trees into the atmosphere, creating America's first signficant air pollution.

Canals were another major innovation of the transportation revolution. These shallow highways of water (sometimes just four feet deep) allowed passage for barges and boats pulled by

View of the Erie Canal at Lockport
The Erie Canal struck many as the eighth wonder of the world when it was completed in 1825, not only for its length of 350 miles but also for its impressive elevation. Eighty-three locks were required to move canal boats over the combined ascent and descent of 680 feet. The biggest challenge of the entire route came at Lockport, 20 miles northeast of Buffalo, where the canal had to traverse a steep escarpment of rocky slate. Work crews—mostly immigrant Irishmen—used gunpowder and grueling physical labor to blast out a deep artificial gorge into the cliff; note the raw cut rock on the left. Next, five double locks were constructed to move boats in stages up and down the 60-foot elevation. Pedestrians would take the stairs that separate the locks, while barge animals would take the towpath on the far side. Even with double locks, this passage surely created bottlenecks in traffic on the canal. So, not surprisingly, a village grew here to service waiting passengers and crews; its name, Lockport, was probably an obvious choice.
Library of Congress.

horses or mules trudging on a towpath beside the canal. Travel speed was slow, under five miles per hour, but the economy came from increased loads. The low-friction water allowed one horse to pull a fifty-ton barge. In winter, canals froze over and became smooth stump- and rock-free highways for sleighs.

Pennsylvania in 1815 and New York in 1817 commenced major state-sponsored canal enterprises. Pennsylvania's Schuylkill Canal stretched from Philadelphia 108 miles west into the state when it was completed in 1826. It was overshadowed by the impressive Erie Canal in New York, finished in 1825, stretching 350 miles between Albany on the Hudson River and Buffalo on Lake Erie. The canal was a waterbridge linking the port of New York City with the entire Northwest Territory. Wheat and flour moved east, textiles and other goods moved west, and passengers went in both directions. By the 1830s, the cost of shipping by canal fell to less than a tenth of the cost of overland transport, and New York City quickly blossomed into the premier commercial city in the United States.

In the 1830s, private railroad companies began to give canals stiff competition, and by the mid-1840s the canal-building era was over. (However, use of the canals for freight continued well into the twentieth century.) The nation's first railroad, the Baltimore and Ohio, laid thirteen miles of track in 1829. During the 1830s, three thousand more miles of track materialized nationwide, the result of a speculative fever in railroad construction master-minded by bankers, locomotive manufacturers, and state legislators, who provided subsidies, charters, and land rights-of-way. Rail lines in the 1830s were generally short, on the order of twenty to one hundred miles; they were not yet an efficient distribution system for goods. But passengers flocked to experience the marvelous travel speeds of fifteen to twenty miles per hour, enduring the frightful noise and cascades of cinders that rained on them.

Taken together, the advances in transportation by the 1830s were little short of revolutionary. They made possible an economic and cultural unification of the United States, connecting far-flung rural outposts with the broader currents of social change.

Factories, Workingwomen, and Wage Labor

Transportation advances promoted a rapid expansion of manufacturing after 1815. Teamsters and bargemen hauled consumer products such as shoes, textiles, clocks, and books into nationwide distribution. Some of the gain in manufacturing, especially in the textile industry, came from the development of water-driven machinery, built near fast-coursing rivers. (The steam power harnessed for steamboats and railroads had limited application in industry until the 1840s.) Much of the new manufacturing involved a reorganization of production, still using the power and skill of human hands, as well as improved mechanical devices. Both mechanized and manual manufacturing pulled young women into the labor market for the first time and greatly enlarged the segment of the population earning a living by selling labor for hourly wages.

The earliest factory, built by British immigrant Samuel Slater in Pawtucket, Rhode Island, in the 1790s, featured a mechanical spinning machine that produced thread and yarn. By 1815, nearly 170 spinning mills dotted lower New England, along streams and rivers. Unlike English

manufacturing cities, where entire families worked in low-wage, health-threatening factories, American factories targeted young women as employees, cheap to hire because of their limited employment options. Mill girls would retire to marriage, replaced by fresh recruits earning a beginner's wage. There would thus be no class of permanent poor clustered around factories, and factory labor would remain cheap.

In 1821, a group of Boston entrepreneurs founded the town of Lowell, on the Merrimack River, where all aspects of cloth production—carding, fulling, spinning, weaving, and dyeing—were centralized. By 1830, the eight mills in Lowell employed more than 5,000 young women, most of them sixteen to twenty-three years old. A key innovation was the close moral supervision of the female workers, who lived in company-owned boardinghouses with housemothers, four to six girls per bedroom. Corporation rules required regular church attendance and prohibited card playing, drinking, and unsupervised courtship; dorm lockdown came at 10 P.M. Typical mill workers averaged $2 to $3 for a seventy-hour workweek, more than a seamstress or domestic servant could earn but less than a young man's wages. The job consisted of tending noisy power looms in large rooms kept hot and humid, ideal for thread but not for people. (See "American Places," page 363.)

> The mill workers welcomed the unprecedented if still limited personal freedom of living in an all-female social space, away from parents and domestic tasks and with pay in their pockets.

Despite the discomforts, young women left farms and flocked to factory towns in the hope of gaining more autonomy. They welcomed the unprecedented if still limited personal freedom of living in an all-female social space, away from parents and domestic tasks and with pay in their pockets. In Lowell, the women could engage in evening self-improvement activities, such as attending lectures or writing for the company's periodical, *The Lowell Offering*.

In the mid-1830s, worldwide changes in the cotton market impelled mill owners to speed up

Cotton Textile Industry, 1839

L. Champlain

Penobscot R.

Connecticut R.

MAINE

Kennebec R.

N.H.

VT.

Merrimack

Lowell

MASS.   • Boston

Pawtucket

Housatonic

R.I.

CONN.

ATLANTIC OCEAN

N.Y.

Largest circle represents 3,000 employees

Mill Worker Tending a Power Loom, 1850
This daguerreotype—the earliest form of photograph (see page 482)—shows a young woman weaver tending a power loom in a textile mill. Her main task was to replace the spindle of thread when it ran out, by reloading a new spindle into the shuttle. The close-up shows a shuttle next to spindles of pink and blue thread. The factory operative also had to be constantly alert for sudden breaks in the wrap yarn which then required a fast shut-down of the loom and a quick repair of the thread. In the 1830s, women weavers generally tended two machines at a time; in the 1840s, some companies increased the workload to four.
Mill worker: American Textile History Museum; shuttle with spindle: Picture Research Consultants & Archives.

work and lower wages. The workers protested, emboldened by their communal living arrangements and by their relative independence from the job as temporary employees. In 1834 and again in 1836, hundreds of women at Lowell went out on strike. All over New England, female mill workers led strikes and formed unions. Women at a mill in Dover, New Hampshire, in 1834 denounced their owners for trying to turn them into "slaves": "However freely the epithet of 'factory slaves' may be bestowed upon us, we will never deserve it by a base and cringing submission to proud wealth or haughty insolence." Their assertiveness surprised many; but ultimately their easy replaceability undermined their bargaining power, and owners in the 1840s began to shift to immigrant families as their labor source.

Other manufacturing enterprises of the 1820s and 1830s, such as shoemaking, employed women in ever larger numbers. New modes of organizing the work allowed the manufacturers to step up production, control wastage and quality, and lower wages by subdividing the tasks and by hiring women, including wives. Male workers cut leather and made soles. The stitching of the upper part of the shoe, called shoebinding, became women's work, performed at home so that it could mesh with domestic chores. Although their wages were lower than men's, shoebinder wives contributed earned cash to family income.

In the economically turbulent 1830s, the new shoe entrepreneurs cut shoebinder wages. Unlike the mill workers in factories, women shoebinders worked in isolation, a serious hindrance to organized protest. In Lynn, Massachusetts, a major shoemaking center, women turned to other female networks, mainly churches, as sites for

AMERICAN PLACES

Lowell National Historic Park, Lowell, Massachusetts

Lowell was America's first planned factory town. Eight large textile mills and hundreds of boardinghouses provided work and housing for the unprecedented concentration of 5,000 female factory operatives who lived there in the 1830s. These mill girls pioneered several experiences entirely new to young American women. Freed from the watchful scrutiny (as well as kindly protection) of parents, they slept in dormitories, lived by the clock backed up by the insistent factory bell, and worked very long hours in deafening machine rooms. They also earned cash wages, escaped domestic drudgery, and made new friends. Little wonder that Lowell quickly became a showcase city, to which European and American tourists flocked to see water-powered manufacturing free of smoke and a novel labor force seemingly free of poverty and vice.

In the twenty-first century, tourists still arrive at Lowell to experience the historic restoration of several of the old mills. The Boott Cotton Mills Museum features a room with eighty-eight power looms. In the 1830s, similar looms were driven by the power of the coursing Merrimack River diverted into nearly six miles of canals that threaded their way around and under the manufacturing buildings. A few of the power looms in Boott Mills stay in operation as tourists walk through the room, experiencing the incredible din and roar of that early machinery. National Park Service rangers hand out earplugs—something that mill workers of the 1830s must have improvised somehow. But the discomfort went beyond noise: Workers spoke of the constant vibration of the work rooms.

Next to Boott Mills is a restored boardinghouse where crowded tables are set for a swift midday meal. Factory timetables show that a mere 35 minutes was allowed for this break, including travel time to and from the boardinghouse and bathroom time. This was the only official break of what was a 12-hour workday yearlong. In upstairs bedrooms, two double beds accommodated four to six roommates per room.

Lowell remained an active textile town until the 1930s, but the labor force changed over time. As wages fell and other occupations (such as teaching) opened to women, fewer New England girls came to Lowell. Their places were taken by Irish girls and then by entire Irish families in the 1850s, then by Poles and other immigrant groups. Aging mills were not modernized, and in the early twentieth century, textile producers moved operations to the South, where labor tended to be nonunion and thus cheaper. In the 1920s and 1930s, the Lowell factories started to close, and urban decay set in, accelerated by the Great Depression. The gritty Lowell of the mid-twentieth century has now come back to a semblance of its former self, as a scrubbed-up stop on the circuit of early American historical sites.

FOR WEB LINKS RELATED TO THIS SITE AND OTHER AMERICAN PLACES, see "PlaceLinks" at bedfordstmartins.com/roark.

Boott Mills
Kevin Harkins.

**Fancy Wedding Shoes
Made in Lynn, Massachusetts**
Emily Lucinda Alden wore these shoes when she married Addison Davis in 1840. The soles are flat, with no heel, and the upper part of the shoe is hand-stitched white satin. Nothing except the ankle lacing distinguishes the right from the left shoe (most footwear from the period was made with identical rights and lefts). An extraordinary clue about women and marriage is revealed in the bride's name-to-be affixed to the shoe box. Etiquette books of the 1840s uniformly decreed that the correct public name would be Mrs. Addison Davis. We might surmise that Emily, on the verge of marriage, had not entirely internalized the eclipse of her own public and legal personage that marriage would soon impose on her. When Elizabeth Cady married Henry Stanton in 1840, she had to do battle to be called Mrs. Elizabeth Cady Stanton when she became a leader of the emerging women's rights movement in 1848 (see page 428).
Lynn Historical Society.

meetings and to religious newspapers as forums for communication. The Lynn shoebinders who demanded higher wages in 1834 built on a collective sense of themselves as women even though they did not share daily work lives. "Equal rights should be extended to all—to the weaker sex as well as the stronger," they wrote in a document forming the Female Society of Lynn.

In the end, the Lynn shoebinders' protests failed to achieve wage increases. Isolated workers all over New England continued to accept low wages, and even in Lynn, many women shied away from organized protest, preferring to situate their work in the context of family duty (helping their menfolk to finish shoes) instead of market relations.

Bankers and Lawyers

Entrepreneurs like the Lowell factory owners relied on innovations in the banking system to finance their ventures. The number of state-chartered banks in the United States more than doubled in the boom years 1814–1816, from fewer than 90 to 208; by 1830, there were 330, and hundreds more by 1840. Banks stimulated the economy by making loans to merchants and manufacturers and by enlarging the money supply. Borrowers were issued loans in the form of banknotes—certificates unique to each bank.

Borrowers used the notes exactly as they used money, for all transactions. Neither federal nor state governments issued paper money, so banknotes became the currency of the country.

In theory, a note could always be traded in at a bank for its **hard-money** equivalent in gold or silver (a transaction known as "specie payment"). A note from a solid local bank might be worth exactly what it was written for, but if a note came from a distant or questionable bank, its value would be discounted by a fraction. Buying and selling banknotes in Jacksonian America surely required knowledge and caution. Not surprisingly, counterfeiting flourished under these conditions.

Bankers exercised great power over the economy, deciding who would get loans and what the discount rates would be. The most powerful bankers sat on the board of directors for the second Bank of the United States, headquartered in Philadelphia. (The first Bank of the United States, chartered in 1791, had lapsed in 1811.) The second Bank of the United States, with eighteen branches throughout the country, opened for business in 1816 under a twenty-year charter. The rechartering of this bank would prove to be a major issue in Andrew Jackson's reelection campaign in 1832.

Accompanying the market revolution was a revolution in commercial law, fashioned by politicians to enhance the prospects of private investment. By 1820, most representatives in the U.S. Congress were lawyers, and a similar wave of legal professionals moved into state politics. Starting in 1811, states rewrote laws of incorporation (the chartering of businesses by states), and the number of corporations expanded rapidly, from about twenty in 1800 to eighteen hundred by 1817. Incorporation protected individual investors from being held liable for corporate financial debts. State lawmakers also wrote laws of eminent domain, empowering states to buy land for roads and canals, even from unwilling sellers. They drafted legislation on contributory negligence, relieving employers from responsibility for workplace injuries. In such ways, entrepreneurial lawyers of the 1820s and 1830s created the legal foundation for an economy that gave priority to ambitious individuals interested in maximizing their own wealth.

Not everyone applauded these developments. Andrew Jackson, himself a skillful lawyer-turned-politician, spoke for a large and mistrustful segment of the population when he warned about the abuses of power "which the moneyed interest derives from a paper currency which they are able to control, from the multitude of corporations with exclusive privileges which they have succeeded in obtaining in the different states, and which are employed altogether for their benefit." Jacksonians believed that ending government-granted privileges was the way to maximize individual liberty and economic opportunity.

Booms and Busts

One aspect of the economy that the lawyer-politicians could not control was the threat of financial collapse. The boom years from 1815 to 1818 exhibited a volatility that resulted in the first sharp, large-scale economic downturn in U.S. history, a depression that Americans called a "panic"; the pattern was repeated in the 1830s. Rapidly rising consumer demand stimulated rising prices for goods, and speculative investment opportunities with high payoffs abounded—in bank stocks, western land sales, urban real estate, and commodities markets. Steep inflation made some people wealthy but created hardships for workers on fixed incomes.

When the bubble burst in 1819, the overnight rich suddenly became the overnight poor. Some suspected that a precipitating cause of the panic of 1819 was the second Bank of the United States. For too long, the bank had neglected to exercise control over state banks, many of which had suspended specie payments—the exchange of gold or silver for banknotes—in their eagerness to make loans and expand the economic bubble. Then, in mid-1818, the Bank of the United States started to call in its loans and insisted that state banks do likewise. The contraction of the money supply created tremors throughout the economy, a foretaste of the catastrophe to come.

What made the crunch worse was a parallel financial crisis in Europe in the spring of 1819. Overseas prices of cotton, tobacco, and wheat plummeted by more than 50 percent. Now when the Bank of the United States and state banks tried to call in their outstanding loans, debtors involved in the commodities trade could not pay. The number of business and personal bankruptcies skyrocketed. The intricate web of credit and debt relationships meant that almost everyone with even a toehold in the new commercial economy was affected by the panic of 1819. Thousands of Americans lost their savings and property, and unemployment estimates suggest that a half million people lost their jobs.

Recovery from the panic of 1819 took several years. Unemployment rates fell, but bitterness lingered, ready to be mobilized by politicians in the decades to come. The dangers of a system dependent on extensive credit were now clear: In one memorable, folksy formulation that circulated around 1820, a farmer was said to compare credit to "a man pissing in his breeches on a cold day to keep his arse warm—very comfortable at first but I dare say . . . you know how it feels afterwards."

By the mid-1820s, the booming economy was back on track, driven by increases in productivity and consumer demand for goods, an accelerating international trade, and a restless and calculating people moving goods, human labor, and investment capital in expanding circles of commerce. But an undercurrent of anxiety about rapid economic change continued to shape the political views of many Americans.

> Jacksonians believed that ending government-granted privileges was the way to maximize individual liberty and economic opportunity.

The Spread of Democracy

Just as the market revolution held out the promise, if not the reality, of economic opportunity for anyone who worked hard, the political transformation of the 1830s held out the promise of political opportunity for hundreds of thousands of new voters. Between 1829 and 1837, the years of Andrew Jackson's presidency, the second American party system took shape, although not until 1836 would the parties have distinct names and consistent programs that transcended the particular personalities running for office. Over those years, more men could and did vote, responding to new methods of arousing voter interest. In 1828, Jackson's charismatic personality defined his party, and the election against

> Just as the market revolution held out the promise, if not the reality, of economic opportunity for anyone who worked hard, the political transformation of the 1830s held out the promise of political opportunity for hundreds of thousands of new voters.

John Quincy Adams was particularly personal, fought over questions of moral character. Once in office, Jackson identified his supporters as the ordinary citizens arrayed against the special power elite, or **democracy** versus aristocracy in Jackson's terminology. A lasting contribution of the Jackson years was the notion that politicians had to appear to have the common touch in an era when popularity with voters drove the electoral process.

Popular Politics and Partisan Identity

The election of 1828 was the first presidential contest in which popular votes determined the outcome. In twenty-two out of twenty-four states, voters—not state legislatures—chose the electors in the electoral college; each elector was committed in advance to a particular candidate. More than a million voters participated, three times the number in 1824 and nearly half the electorate, reflecting the high stakes that voters perceived in the Adams-Jackson rematch. Throughout the 1830s, the number of voters rose to all-time highs. This increase resulted partly from relaxed voting restrictions; by the mid-1830s, all but three states allowed universal white male **suffrage,** without property qualifications. But the higher turnout—over 70 percent in some states—also indicated increased political interest.

The 1828 election inaugurated new campaign styles as well. State-level candidates routinely gave speeches to woo the voters, appearing at rallies, picnics, and banquets. Adams and Jackson still declined such activities as too undignified; but Henry Clay of Kentucky, campaigning for Adams, earned the nickname "Barbecue Orator." Campaign rhetoric, under the necessity to create popular appeal, became more informal and even blunt. The Jackson camp established many Hickory Clubs, trading on Jackson's popular nickname, "Old Hickory," from a common Tennessee tree suggesting resilience and toughness. (Jackson was the first presidential candidate to have an affectionate and widely used nickname.)

Partisan newspapers defined issues and publicized political personalities as never before. Party leaders judiciously dispensed subsidies and other favors to secure the loyalties of papers,

> The campaign of 1828 was the first national election in which scandal and character questions reigned supreme.

even in remote towns and villages. In New York State, where party development was most advanced, a pro-Jackson group called the Bucktails controlled fifty weekly publications. Stories from the leading Jacksonian paper in Washington, D.C., were reprinted two days later in a Boston or Cincinnati paper, as fast as the mail stage could carry them. Presidential campaigns were now coordinated in a national arena.

Parties declined to adopt official names in 1828, still honoring the fiction of Republican Party unity. Instead, they called themselves the Jackson party or the Adams party. By the 1832 election, labels began to appear. Adams's political heir, Henry Clay, represented the National Republicans; Jackson's supporters called themselves Democratic Republicans. The National Republicans favored federal action to promote commercial development; the Democratic Republicans promised to be responsive to the will of the majority. By 1834, a few state-level National Republicans had changed their name to the Whig Party, a term that was in common use by 1836, the same year that Jackson's party became simply the Democrats. Thus, Whig and Democrat crystallized as names only at the end of an eight-year evolution.

The Election of 1828 and the Character Issue

The campaign of 1828 was the first national election in which scandal and character questions reigned supreme. John Quincy Adams was vilified by his opponents as an elitist, bookish academic, perhaps even a monarchist. Critics pointed to Adams's White House billiard table and ivory chess set as symbols of his aristocratic degeneracy along with the "corrupt bargain" of 1824, the alleged election deal between Adams and Henry Clay (see chapter 10). The Adams men returned fire with fire. They played on Jackson's fatherless childhood to portray him as the bastard son of a prostitute. Worse, the cloudy circumstances around his marriage to Rachel Donelson Robards in 1791 gave rise to the story that Jackson was a seducer and an adulterer, having married a woman whose divorce from her first husband was not entirely legal. Pro-Adams newspapers howled that Jackson was sinful and impulsive, while portraying Adams as pious, learned, and virtuous.

Editors in favor of Adams played up Jackson's notorious violent temper, evidenced by the many duels, brawls, and canings they

Campaign Posters from 1828

The campaign poster on the left praises Andrew Jackson as a war hero and "man of the people" and reminds readers that Jackson, who won the largest popular vote in 1824, did not stoop to bargain for the presidency, as presumably John Q. Adams did in his dealing with Henry Clay. (What "two wars" does the poster refer to?) The campaign poster at right, with ominous tombstone and coffin graphics, accuses Jackson of the unjustified killing of a Kentucky militiaman (one of six executed) during the Creek War in 1815. The text implores readers to think of the "hero" as a man capable of "bloody deeds."

Pro-Jackson broadside: © Collection of the New-York Historical Society; anti-Jackson broadside: Smithsonian Institute, Washington, D.C.

could recount. Jackson men used the same stories to project Old Hickory as a tough frontier hero who knew how to command obedience. As for learning, Jackson's rough frontier education gave him a "natural sense," wrote a Boston editor, which "can never be acquired by reading books—it can only be acquired, in perfection, by reading men."

These stories were not smoke screens to obscure the "real" issues in the election. They became real issues themselves because voters used them to comprehend the kind of public officer each man would make. Character issues conveyed in shorthand larger questions about morality, honor, and discipline; Jackson and Adams presented two radically different styles of masculinity.

Jackson won a sweeping victory, with 56 percent of the popular vote and 178 electoral votes, compared with Adams's 83 (Map 11.2).

MAP 11.2   The Election of 1828

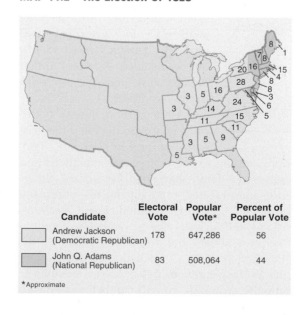

Candidate	Electoral Vote	Popular Vote*	Percent of Popular Vote
Andrew Jackson (Democratic Republican)	178	647,286	56
John Q. Adams (National Republican)	83	508,064	44

*Approximate

President Jackson's Kitchen Cabinet

Early in his administration, Jackson fell out with most of his official cabinet—largely over a social crisis provoked by the wives of cabinet officers. So Jackson turned to a set of close friends, quickly dubbed the Kitchen Cabinet by the press, for advice, for patronage decisions, and even for the drafting of official papers. Several were newspapermen; one was an old Tennessee friend, William B. Lewis, who moved into the White House with Jackson. Martin Van Buren was also in this inner circle. This cartoon purports to show a meeting of the Kitchen Cabinet: raucous, argumentative, violently employing the tools of women's work. How does its pointed message reflect the new partisan politics of the time?

Granger Collection.

> The courteous Jackson, committed to his image as the president of the "common man," held audience with unannounced visitors throughout his two terms.

The victor took most of the South and West and carried Pennsylvania and New York as well. Jackson's vice president was John C. Calhoun, who had just served as vice president under Adams but had broken with Adams's policies.

After 1828, national politicians no longer deplored the existence of political parties. They were coming to see that parties mobilized and delivered voters, sharpened candidates' differences, and created party loyalty that surpassed loyalty to individual candidates and elections. Adams and Jackson clearly symbolized and defined for voters the competing ideas of the emerging parties: a moralistic, top-down party (the Whigs) ready to make major decisions to promote economic growth competing against a contentious, energetic party (the Democrats) ready to embrace liberty-loving individualism.

Jackson's Democratic Agenda

Before the inauguration in March 1829, Rachel Jackson died. The president, certain that the ugly campaign had hastened her death, went into deep mourning. His depression was worsened by constant pain from the 1806 bullet still lodged in his chest and by mercury poisoning from the medicines he took. Sixty-two years old, he carried only 140 pounds on his six-foot-one frame. His adversaries doubted he would make it to a second term. His supporters, however, went wild at the inauguration. Thousands cheered his ten-minute inaugural address, the shortest in history. An open reception at the White House turned into a near riot as well-wishers jammed the premises, used windows as doors, stood on furniture for a better view of the great man, and broke thousands of dollars' worth of china and glasses.

During his presidency, Jackson continued to offer unprecedented hospitality to the public. Twenty spittoons newly installed in the East Room of the White House accommodated the tobacco spit of the throngs that arrived daily to see the president. The courteous Jackson, committed to his image as the president of the "common man," held audience with unannounced visitors throughout his two terms.

Jackson's cabinet appointments marked a departure. Past presidents had tried to lessen party conflict by including men of different factions in their cabinets, but Jackson would have only Jackson loyalists, a political tactic followed by most later presidents. The most important position, secretary of state, he offered to Martin Van Buren, one of the shrewdest politicians of the day and newly elected governor of New York.

Jackson put new stress on party allegiance throughout the federal government. As a candidate he promised to remove corrupt federal appointees; as president he went further and removed competent civil servants as well on a newly asserted principle of rotation in office. There were some ten thousand civil servants on the federal payroll: ambassadors, judges, auditors, customs collectors, land office registrars, and thousands of local postmasters, clerks, and deputy clerks. In the end, Jackson removed fewer than one-tenth of these employees, so there was no clean sweep of the federal bureaucracy. But when he made replacement appointments, he made sure to reward party loyalists. "To the victor belong the spoils," said a Democratic senator from New York, expressing approval of patronage-driven appointments. Jackson's approach to civil service employment got tagged the **spoils system**; it was a concept the president strenuously defended.

Jackson's agenda quickly emerged once he was in office. Like Jefferson, he favored a limited federal government. Fearing that intervention in the economy inevitably favored some groups at the expense of others, he opposed federal support of transportation and grants of monopolies and charters that privileged wealthy investors. Like Jefferson, he anticipated rapid settlement of the country's interior, where land sales would spread economic democracy to settlers. Thus, establishing a federal policy to remove the Indians had high priority. Unlike Jefferson, however, Jackson exercised full presidential powers over Congress; a limited government did not mean a limited presidency. In 1830, he vetoed a highway project in Maysville, Kentucky— Henry Clay's home state—that Congress had voted to support with federal dollars. The Maysville Road veto articulated Jackson's principled stand that citizens' federal tax dollars could only be spent on projects of a "general, not local" character. In all, Jackson used the veto twelve times; all previous presidents had exercised that right a total of nine times.

Cultural Shifts

Despite differences on the best or fairest way to enhance commercial development, Jackson's Democratic Republicans and Henry Clay's National Republicans shared enthusiasm for the outcome—a growing, booming economy. For increasing numbers of families, especially in the highly commercialized Northeast, the standard of living rose, consumption patterns changed, and the nature and location of work altered.

All of these changes had a direct impact on the roles and duties of men and women and on the training of youth for the economy of the future. New ideas about gender relations in a commercial economy surfaced in printed material and in public behavior. In Jacksonian America, a widely shared public culture came into being, originating within the new commercial classes and spreading rapidly through rising levels of literacy and an explosion of print.

The Family and Separate Spheres

The centerpiece of new ideas about gender relations was the notion that husbands found their status and authority in the new world of work, leaving wives to tend the hearth and home. Sermons, advice books, periodicals, and novels reinforced the idea that men and women inhabited **separate spheres** and had separate duties. "To woman it belongs . . . to elevate the intellectual character of her household [and] to kindle the fires of mental activity in childhood," wrote Mrs. A. J. Graves in a popular book titled *Advice to American Women*. For men, in contrast, "the absorbing passion for gain, and the pressing demands of business, engross their whole attention." In particular, the home, now the exclusive domain of women, was sentimentalized as the source of intimacy, love, and safety, a refuge from the cruel and competitive world of market relations.

> The home, now the exclusive domain of women, was sentimentalized as a refuge from the cruel and competitive world of market relations.

Some new aspects of society gave substance to this formulation of separate spheres. Men's work was undergoing profound change after 1815, especially in the manufacturing Northeast and in urban areas both large—Boston, New York, Cincinnati— and small—Buffalo, Cleveland, Chicago. Increasingly, men's jobs brought cash to the household. Farmers and tradesmen sold products in a market, and bankers, bookkeepers, shoemakers, and canal diggers got pay envelopes. Furthermore, many men performed jobs outside of the home, at an office or store. For men who were not farmers, work indeed seemed newly disconnected from the home.

A woman's domestic role was more complicated than the cultural prescriptions indicated. Although the vast majority of married white women did not hold paying jobs, the home continued to be a site of time-consuming labor. But

Sheet Music Cover from 1840
Popular songs in the early nineteenth century circulated in the form of sheet music, usually consisting of a cover picture and three pages of music scored for the piano. This lithographed cover illustrates a sentimental ballad called "The Old Arm Chair." A sad woman in black with handkerchief in hand stands behind an empty chair of a departed family member who has in all likelihood just died. (Note the piano behind her.) The armchair with open book (to suggest a very recent and perhaps somehow *temporary* departure) appeared in cemeteries as a sentimentalized stone monument over graves. Online sheet music collections allow a new form of downloading music: A pianist can print the scores and play hundreds of mawkish pop tunes from the 1830s and 1840s. The Library of Congress maintains a large collection at <http://memory.loc.gov/ammem/sm2html/sm2home.html>.
Collection of Lynn Wenzel.

for shoebinding, hatmaking, or needlework done at home. Even among the most comfortable classes, the market intruded whenever wives hired domestic servants to perform the heavy household tasks no true lady would consider doing, such as laundry. Most middle- and upper-income families hired servants; households striving to meet a respectable level of class display simply could not be run on the labor of one woman. Wives in the poorer classes of society, including most free black wives, did not have the luxury of husbands earning adequate wages; for them, work as servants or laundresses helped augment family income.

These idealized notions about the sentimental, noncommercial, feminine home and the masculine world of work gained acceptance in the 1830s (and well beyond) because of the cultural dominance of the middle and upper classes of the Northeast, expressed through books and periodical publications. The doctrine of separate spheres unambiguously defined masculinity and femininity: Men were to achieve a sense of manhood through work and pay; women established a sense of femininity through duty to the home and family and service to others. The convenient fiction of this formulation of gender difference helped smooth the path for the first generation of Americans experiencing the market revolution. The doctrine of separate spheres ordained that men would absorb and display the values appropriate to the market economy—competition, acquisitiveness—and women would exemplify and foster traditional, noncommercial values of virtuous service to family and community. Both men and women of the middle classes benefited from this bargain: Men were set free to pursue wealth, and women gained moral authority within the home. Beyond white families of the middle and upper classes, however, these new gender ideals had limited applicability. Despite their apparent dominance in printed material of the period, they were never all-pervasive.

The Education and Training of Youth

The market economy with its new expectations for men and women required fresh methods of training youth of both sexes. The generation that came of age in the 1820s and 1830s had opportunities for education and work unparalleled in previous eras, at least for white children in the middling classes and above. Northern states

the advice books treated household tasks as loving familial duties; housework as *work* was thereby rendered invisible in an economy that evaluated work by how much cash it generated.

In reality, wives directly contributed to family income in many ways. Some took in boarders, while others engaged in outwork, earning pay adopted public schooling between 1790 and the 1820s, and in the 1820s and 1830s southern states followed suit. The curriculum produced pupils who were able, by age twelve or fourteen, to read, write, and participate in marketplace calculations. Remarkably, girls usually received the same basic education as boys. Literacy rates for white females climbed dramatically, rivaling the rates for white males for the first time.

The fact that taxpayers paid for children's education created an incentive to seek an inexpensive teaching force. By the 1830s, school districts began replacing male teachers with young females. Like mill workers, teachers were in their late teens and regarded the work as temporary. Often these female teachers had attended private female academies, hundreds of which were

spread over all states of the Union. Starting in the 1830s, states from Massachusetts to Kentucky began to open teacher training schools ("normal" schools) exclusively for women students, because, as a Massachusetts report put it, "females can be educated cheaper, quicker, and better, and will teach cheaper after they are qualified." With the exception of Oberlin College in Ohio, no other colleges admitted women until after the Civil War, but a handful of private "female seminaries" established a rigorous curriculum that rivaled that of the best men's colleges. Three of the most prominent were the Troy Seminary in New

> The generation that came of age in the 1820s and 1830s had opportunities for education and work unparalleled in previous eras.

Women Graduates of Oberlin College, Class of 1855

Oberlin College was founded in Ohio by evangelical and abolitionist activists in the 1830s. It admitted white and black men and women, although in the early years the black students were all male and the women students were all white. Admission was not exactly equal: The women entered a separate Ladies' Department. By 1855, as this daguerreotype shows, black women had integrated the Ladies' Department. The two older women with bonnets were the principal and a member of the board. The students wear the latest fashion: dark taffeta dresses with sloping shoulders and a tight bodice topped by detachable white lace collars. Hair fashions were similarly uniform for women of all ages throughout the 1850s: a central part, hair dressed with oil and lustrously coiled over the ears. Compare these women with the mill woman pictured on page 362. What differences do you see?
Oberlin College Archives, Oberlin, Ohio.

York, founded by Emma Willard in 1821; the Hartford Seminary in Connecticut, founded by Catharine Beecher in 1822; and Mount Holyoke in Massachusetts, founded by Mary Lyon in 1837. These women educators argued that women made better teachers than men: "If men have more knowledge, they have less talent at communicating it. Nor have they the patience, the long-suffering, and gentleness necessary to superintend the formation of character," said the author Harriet Beecher Stowe, who taught at her sister's Hartford school.

Male youths leaving public school faced two paths. A small percentage continued at private boys' academies (numbering in the several hundreds nationwide), and a far smaller number entered the country's two dozen colleges. More typically, boys left school at fourteen to apprentice to a specific trade or to seek business careers in entry-level clerkships, abundant in the growing urban centers. Young girls also headed for mill towns or for the cities in unprecedented numbers, seeking work in the expanding service sector as seamstresses and domestic servants.

Changes in patterns of youth employment and training meant that large numbers of youngsters in the 1830s and later escaped the watchful eyes of their families. Moralists fretted about the dangers of unsupervised youth, and, following the lead of the Lowell mill owners, some established apprentices' libraries and uplifting lecture series to keep young people honorably occupied. Advice books published by the hundreds instructed youth in the virtues of hard work and delayed gratification.

Public Life, the Press, and Popular Amusements

Many new forms of inexpensive reading matter and public entertainment competed with the moralistic messages for youth. Innovations in printing technology as well as rising literacy rates created a brisk market in the 1830s for publications appealing to popular tastes: adventure and mystery pamphlets, romance novels, and penny press newspapers. In cities, theaters were nightly magnets for audiences in the thousands.

In the 1790s, fewer than ninety newspapers, each printing a few thousand copies per issue, provided news of current events. By 1830, there were eight hundred papers, sixty-five of them urban dailies, and in the 1830s the most successful of these, the innovative penny press papers, gained circulations of ten to twenty thousand copies daily. Such huge print runs were made possible by the development of steam-driven rotary presses with automatic paper feed devices replacing the old-style handpresses. Six-cent papers covered politics, banking, and shipping news; the one-cent ("penny") papers featured breezy political coverage, irreverent editorializing on current events, and crime reporting. Issued in eastern cities, the penny papers extended their influence throughout the nation, facilitated by a regular system of newspaper exchange by means of the postal system. Town and village papers reprinted the snappy political editorials and sensationalized crime stories, putting very undeferential ideas into the heads of readers new to politics.

Newspapers were not the only new medium for spreading a shared American culture. Starting in the 1820s, traveling lecturers crisscrossed the country, bringing entertainment and instruction to small-town audiences. Speakers gave dramatic readings of plays or poetry or lectured on history, current events, popular science, or controversial topics such as advanced female education or anatomy and physiology. Theater also blossomed in the 1830s, providing urban Americans with their most common form of shared entertainment, featuring Shakespearean plays, melodramas, and the newly popular minstrelsy, a musical comedy first performed in 1831 by white performers with blackened faces.

The popularity of theaters exemplified a general cultural turn toward the celebration of brilliant public speech. In this golden age of oration, actors, lawyers, politicians, and ministers could hold crowds spellbound for hours with their flawless elocution and elegant turns of phrase. Criminal trials, for example, were very short by modern standards, but the lawyers' closing arguments might consume many hours, with crowds of spectators hanging on every word. Senator Daniel Webster of Massachusetts was the acknowledged genius of political oration. At a Webster speech commemorating the Pilgrims' arrival, one man in a crowd of

TABLE 11.1	THE GROWTH OF NEWSPAPERS, 1820–1840			
	1820	*1830*	*1835*	*1840*
U.S. population (in millions)	9.6	12.8	15.0	17.1
Number of newspapers published	500	800	1,200	1,400
Daily newspapers	42	65	——	138

Lurid Cover of a Crime Pamphlet, New York
Cheap and easy printing in the early nineteenth century gave rise to new genres of popular reading matter, including a large pamphlet literature detailing horrific murder stories that invited readers to contemplate the nature of evil. This woodcut cover from 1836 promises to reveal the "interesting particulars" of the murder of Ellen Jewett, a New York City prostitute axed to death in her brothel bed. The pamphlet claims to constitute "an impressive warning" to youth about the tragedies of "dens of infamy." But the crude picture of the female corpse, with bare legs and breasts fully exposed, suggests that alternative, less moralistic readings of the same material were certainly possible for the purchasers.
William L. Clements Library.

Democracy and Religion

Oratorically gifted ministers had work aplenty in the 1820s and 1830s. An unprecedented revival of evangelical religion peaked in that period, after gathering two decades of momentum in states across the North and the Upper South. Known as the **Second Great Awakening**, the outpouring of religious fervor changed the shape of American **Protestantism**. The heart of the evangelical message was that salvation was available to anyone willing to eradicate individual sin and accept faith in God's grace. Just as universal male suffrage allowed all white men to vote, democratized religion offered salvation to all who chose to embrace it.

Among the most serious adherents of evangelical Protestantism were men and women of the new merchant classes whose self-discipline in pursuing market ambitions meshed well with the message of self-discipline in pursuit of spiritual perfection. Not content with individual perfection, many of these men and women sought to perfect society as well, by defining excessive alcohol consumption, nonmarital sex, and slavery as the three major evils of modern life in need of correction.

> Just as universal male suffrage allowed all white men to vote, democratized religion offered salvation to all who chose to embrace it.

The Second Great Awakening

The earliest manifestations of fervent piety marking the start of the Second Great Awakening appeared in 1801 in Kentucky. A crowd of ten thousand people camped out on a hillside at Cane Ridge for a revival meeting that lasted several weeks. By the 1810s and 1820s, "camp meetings" had spread to the Atlantic seaboard states, finding especially enthusiastic audiences in western New York and Pennsylvania. The outdoor settings permitted huge attendance, which itself intensified the emotional impact of the experience. "For more than a half mile, I could see people on their knees before God in humble prayer," recalled one Cane Ridge worshipper.

The gatherings attracted women and men hungry for a more immediate access to spiritual peace, one not requiring years of soul-searching. Ministers adopted an emotional style and invited an immediate experience of conversion and salvation. One eyewitness at a revival reported that

fifteen hundred recalled that "three or four times I thought my temples would burst with the gush of blood." Ministers with gifted tongues could in the space of an evening transform crowds of skeptics into believers. Skillful speakers demanded and generally got attentive listeners.

Charles G. Finney and His Broadway Tabernacle

The Reverend Charles G. Finney (shown here in a portrait done in 1834) took his evangelical movement to New York City in the early 1830s, operating first out of a renovated theater. In 1836, the Broadway Tabernacle was built for his pastorate. In its use of space, the tabernacle resembled a theater more than a traditional church, but in one respect it departed radically from one very theaterlike tradition of churches—the custom of charging pew rents. In effect, most churches required worshippers to purchase their seats. Finney, in contrast, insisted that all seats in his house were free, unreserved, and open to all.

Oberlin College Archives, Oberlin, Ohio.

FOR MORE HELP ANALYZING THIS IMAGE, see the visual activity for this chapter in the Online Study Guide at bedfordstmartins.com/roark.

"some of the people were singing, others praying, some crying for mercy. . . . At one time I saw at least five hundred swept down in a moment as if a battery of a thousand guns had been opened upon them, and then immediately followed shrieks and shouts that rent the very heavens."

From 1800 to 1820, church membership doubled in the United States, much of it among the evangelical groups. Methodists, Baptists, and Presbyterians formed the core of the new movement; Episcopalians, Congregationalists, Unitarians, Dutch Reformed, Lutherans, and Catholics maintained strong skepticism about the emotional enthusiasm. Women more than men were attracted to the evangelical movement, and wives and mothers typically recruited husbands and sons to join them.

The leading exemplar of the Second Great Awakening was a lawyer-turned-minister. Charles Grandison Finney lived in western New York, where the completion of the Erie Canal in 1825 fundamentally altered the social and economic landscape overnight. Towns swelled with new inhabitants who brought in remarkable prosperity along with other, less admirable side effects, such as prostitution, drinking, and gaming. Finney saw New York canal towns as especially ripe for evangelical awakening. In Rochester, New York, he sustained a six-month revival through the winter of 1830, generating thousands of new converts.

Finney's message was directed primarily at women and men of the business classes, and, true to his training, he couched it in legal metaphors. "The world is divided into two great political parties," he announced—the party of Satan and the party of Jehovah. "Ministers should labor with sinners, as a lawyer does with a jury . . . ; and the sinner should weigh his arguments, and make up his mind as upon oath and for his life, and give a verdict upon the spot." Finney's sermons reached national distribution through the religious press. He argued that a reign of Christian perfection loomed, one that required a public-spirited outreach to the less than perfect to foster their salvation. Evangelicals promoted Sunday schools to bring piety to children; they battled to end mail delivery, to stop public transport, and to close shops on Sundays to honor the Sabbath. Many women formed missionary societies, which distributed millions of Bibles and religious tracts. Through such avenues, evangelical religion offered women expanded spheres of influence.

In 1832, Finney moved to New York City and renovated a disreputable theater into a Free Presbyterian church. His dynamic, theatrical performances were taken down by scribes and published in the *New York Evangelist,* a weekly paper of national distribution. Finney adopted tactics of Jacksonian-era politicians—publicity, argumentation, rallies, and speeches—to sell his cause. His object, he said, was to get Americans to "vote in the Lord Jesus Christ as the governor of the Universe."

The Temperance Movement and the Campaign for Moral Reform

The evangelical disposition—a combination of faith, energy, self-discipline, and righteousness—animated vigorous campaigns to eliminate alcohol abuse and eradicate sexual sin. Millions of Americans took the temperance pledge to abstain from strong drink, and thousands became involved in efforts to end prostitution.

Alcohol consumption had risen steadily in the decades up to 1830, when the average person over age thirteen consumed an astonishing 9 gallons of hard liquor plus around 30 gallons of hard cider, beer, and wine per year. To a degree, consumption of bottled, fermented drinks made sense in view of unsafe urban water sources and the lack of reliable refrigeration. However, alcohol abuse was on the rise.

All classes imbibed. A lively saloon culture fostered masculine camaraderie along with extensive alcohol consumption among laborers, and a new style of binge drinking alarmed older proponents of moderate consumption. In elite homes, the after-dinner whiskey or sherry was commonplace. Colleges before 1820 routinely served students a pint of ale with meals, and the army and navy included rum in the standard daily ration.

Organized opposition to drinking first surfaced in the 1810s among health and religious re-

formers. In 1826, Lyman Beecher, a Connecticut minister of an "awakened" church, founded the American Temperance Society, which held that drinking led to poverty, idleness, crime, and family violence. Adopting the methods of evangelical ministers, temperance lecturers traveled the country expounding the damage of drink; by 1833, some six thousand local affiliates of the American Temperance Society boasted more than a million members. Middle-class drinking began a steep decline. One powerful tool of persuasion was the temperance pledge, which many manufacturers and business owners began to require of employees.

In 1836, leaders of the **temperance movement** regrouped into a new society, the American Temperance Union, which demanded total abstinence of its adherents. The intensified war against alcohol moved beyond individual moral suasion into the realm of politics, as reformers sought to deny taverns liquor licenses. By 1845, temperance advocates had put an impressive dent in alcohol consumption, which diminished to one-quarter of the per capita consumption of 1830. In 1851, Maine became the first state to ban entirely the manufacture and sale of all alcoholic beverages.

More controversial than temperance was a social movement called "moral reform," which first aimed at public morals in general but quickly narrowed to a campaign to eradicate sexual sin, **especially** prostitution. In 1833, a group of Finneyite women started the New York Female Moral Reform Society. Its members insisted that uncontrolled male sexual expression posed a serious threat to society

The Cold Water Army Fan
This fan was a keepsake for children enlisted in the Reverend Thomas Hunt's Cold Water Army of 1836, which advocated abstinence from alcohol. Hunt, a Presbyterian, figured that preventing children from beginning to drink would be an effective strategy against future alcoholism: "Prevention is better than cure" was his motto.
Museum of American Political Life.

in general and to women in particular. The society's nationally distributed newspaper, the *Advocate of Moral Reform,* was the first major paper in the country that was written, edited, and typeset by women. Columns were devoted to first-person tales of woe and to advice about curbing sexual sin. The women reformers condemned men who visited brothels or who seduced innocent victims. Within five years, more than four thousand auxiliary groups of women members had sprung up, mostly in New England, New York, Pennsylvania, and Ohio.

In its analysis of the causes of licentiousness and its conviction that women had a duty to speak out about unspeakable things, the Moral Reform Society pushed the limits of what even the men in the evangelical movement could tolerate. Yet they did not regard themselves as radicals. They were simply pursuing the logic of a gender system that defined home protection and morality as women's special sphere and a religious conviction that called for the eradication of sin.

Organizing against Slavery

> Even more radical than temperance and moral reform was the movement in the 1830s to abolish the sin of slavery.

More radical still was the movement in the 1830s to abolish the sin of slavery. The only previous antislavery organization, the American Colonization Society, had been founded in 1817 by some Maryland and Virginia **planters** to promote gradual individual **emancipation** of slaves followed by **colonization** in Africa (see page 430). By the early 1820s, several thousand ex-slaves had been transported to Liberia on the West African coast. But not surprisingly, newly freed men and women were often not eager to emigrate; their African roots were three or more generations in the past. Emigration to Africa proved to be so gradual (and expensive) as to have a negligible impact on American slavery.

At the end of the 1820s, northern challenges to slavery surfaced with increasing frequency and resolve, beginning in the free black communities of Boston, Philadelphia, and New York. In 1829, a Boston printer named David Walker published *Appeal . . . to the Coloured Citizens of the World,* which condemned racism, invoked the egalitarian language of the Declaration of Independence, and hinted at racial violence if whites did not change their prejudiced ways. In 1830, a ten-day National Negro Convention met in Philadelphia, the first of

three decades of such meetings. At that inaugural event, forty blacks from nine states met to discuss the racism of American society and to found the "American Society of Free People of Colour for improving their condition in the United States; for purchasing lands; and for the establishment of a settlement in the Province of Canada." In 1832, a twenty-eight-year-old black woman, Maria Stewart, delivered public lectures for black audiences in Boston on slavery and racial prejudice. While her arguments against slavery were welcomed, her voice—that of a woman—created problems even among her sympathetic audiences. Few American-born women had yet engaged in public speaking beyond theatrical performances or religious prophesizing. (See "Documenting the American Promise," page 378.) Stewart was breaking a social taboo, an offense made worse by her statements suggesting black women should rise above housework: "How long shall the fair daughters of Africa be compelled to bury their minds and talents beneath a load of iron pots and kettles?" She retired from the platform in 1833 but took up writing and published her lectures in a national publication called the *Liberator,* giving them much wider circulation.

The *Liberator,* founded in 1831 in Boston, took antislavery agitation to new heights. Its founder and editor, an uncompromising twenty-six-year-old white printer named William Lloyd Garrison, advocated immediate abolition of slavery:

> On this subject, I do not wish to think, or speak, or write, with moderation. No! No! Tell a man whose house is on fire to give a moderate alarm; tell him to moderately rescue his wife from the hands of the ravisher; tell the mother to gradually extricate her babe from the fire into which it has fallen;—but urge me not to use moderation in a cause like the present.

In 1832, Garrison supporters started the New England Anti-Slavery Society; Philadelphia and New York started similar groups in 1833. Soon there were a dozen antislavery newspapers, along with scores of antislavery lecturers spreading the word and inspiring the formation of new local societies, which grew to number 1,300 by 1837. Entirely confined to the North, their membership totaled a quarter of a million men and women.

Many white Northerners were not prepared to embrace the abolitionist call for emancipation, immediate or gradual. They might oppose slavery as a blot on the country's ideals or as a rival to the **free-labor** system of the North, but at the same time most white Northerners remained antiblack and therefore antiabolition. From 1834 to 1838, there were more than a hundred eruptions of serious mob violence against abolitionists or free blacks. On one occasion, antislavery headquarters in Philadelphia and a black church and orphanage were burned to the ground; in another incident, Illinois abolitionist editor Elijah Lovejoy was killed by a rioting crowd attempting to destroy his printing press.

Women played a prominent role in abolition, just as they did in moral reform and evangelical religion. (See "Beyond America's Borders," page 380.) They formed women's auxiliaries and engaged in fund-raising to support lecturers in the field. They circulated antislavery petitions, presented to the U.S. Congress with tens of thousands of signatures. Garrison particularly welcomed women's activity. When a southern plantation daughter named Angelina Grimké wrote him about her personal repugnance for slavery, Garrison published the letter in the *Liberator* and brought her overnight fame. Grimké and her older sister Sarah quickly became lecturers for the antislavery movement and started a speaking tour to women's groups in Massachusetts in 1837. The Grimkés' powerful eyewitness speeches attracted men as well, causing leaders of the Congregational Church in Massachusetts to warn all Congregational ministers not to let the Grimké sisters use their pulpits. Like Maria Stewart, the Grimkés had violated a gender norm by presuming to instruct men.

In the late 1830s, the cause of abolition divided the nation as no other issue did. Even among the abolitionists, significant divisions emerged. The Grimké sisters, radicalized by the public reaction to their speaking tour, began to write and speak about woman's rights. They were opposed by moderate abolitionists who were unwilling to mix a new and controversial issue about women with their first cause, the rights of blacks. A few radical men, like Garrison, embraced women's rights fully, working to get women leadership positions in the national antislavery group.

The many men and women active in reform movements in the 1830s found their initial inspiration in evangelical Protestantism's dual mes-

Abolitionist Purses
Female antislavery societies raised many thousands of dollars to support the abolitionist cause by selling handcrafted items at giant antislavery fairs. Toys, infant clothes, quilts, caps and collars, purses, needlebooks, wax flowers, inlaid boxes: The list was endless. Items were often emblazoned with abolitionist mottoes, such as "Let My People Go," "Liberty," and "Loose the Bonds of Wickedness." These pink silk drawstring bags were decorated with pictures of the hapless slave woman, an object of compassion. Dollars raised at these fairs supported the travels of abolitionist speakers as well as the publication and distribution of many antislavery books and articles.
The Daughters of the American Revolution Museum, Washington, D.C. Gift of Mrs. Erwin L. Broecker.

sage: Salvation was open to all, and society needed to be perfected. Their activist mentality squared well with the interventionist tendencies of the party forming in opposition to Andrew Jackson's Democrats. On the whole, reformers gravitated to the Whig Party.

Jackson Defines the Democratic Party

In his eight years in office, Andrew Jackson worked to implement his vision of a politics of opportunity for all white men. He also greatly enhanced the power of the presidency. To open more land east of the Mississippi River for white settlement, he favored the relocation of all the eastern Indian peoples. He had a dramatic confrontation with John C. Calhoun and South Carolina when that state tried to nullify the tariff of 1828. Disapproving of all government-granted privilege, Jackson challenged what he called the "monster" Bank of the United States and took it

American Women Speak Out in Public

Public speaking was strictly a masculine prerogative up to the 1830s. Only actresses on the stage and a handful of religious women who claimed to be passive instruments of God's voice escaped criticism for breaking this firm gender barrier, thought to have ancient biblical sanction in 1 Corinthians 14:33–39, which commands women to keep silent in the church. Maria Stewart, a young African American widow in Boston, was probably the first American woman to lecture on social issues. A few years later, Angelina Grimké and her sister Sarah staged a lecture tour on abolition, paving the way for Mary S. Gove a year later to offer a lecture series on women's health. All these women endured stiff criticism, but the barrier was broken, leading to a cascade of women speakers in the 1840s and 1850s.

DOCUMENT 1
Maria Stewart Addresses the Afric-American Female Intelligence Society of America, 1832

In 1832 Maria Stewart commenced public lecturing to black audiences of both sexes in Boston. She stressed racial uplift through Christian values, diligent parenting, education, discipline, and ambition. In this speech to an audience of black women, Stewart acknowledged criticism of her lectures and justified her course of action as one inspired by religion.

The frowns of the world shall never discourage me, nor its smiles flatter me; for with the help of God, I am resolved to withstand the fiery darts of the devil, and the assaults of wicked men. . . . The only motive that has prompted me to raise my voice in your behalf, my friends, is because I have discovered that religion is held in low repute among some of us. . . . I am a strong advocate for the cause of God, and for the cause of freedom. . . . Suffer me, then, to express my sentiments but this once . . . and then hereafter let me sink into oblivion, and let my name die in forgetfulness.

. . . my soul has been so discouraged within me, that I have almost been induced to exclaim, "Would to God that my tongue hereafter might cleave to the roof of my mouth, and become silent forever!" and then I have felt that the Christian has no time to be idle, and I must be active, knowing that the night of death cometh, in which no man can work.

O woman, woman! upon you I call; for upon your exertions almost entirely depends whether the rising generation shall be any thing more than we have been or not. O woman, woman! your example is powerful, your influence great; it extends over your husbands and over your children, and throughout the circle of your acquaintance. Then let me exhort you to cultivate among yourselves a spirit of Christian love and unity. . . . And O, my God, I beseech thee to grant that the nations of the earth may hiss at us no longer!

SOURCE: Maria Stewart lectures, African American History, 1 March 2004, <http://afroamhistory.about.com/library/blmaria_stewart_intelligencesociety.htm>

DOCUMENT 2
Angelina Grimké Writes a Friend about Speaking to a "Mixed" Audience, 1837

The Grimké sisters' speaking tour of 1837 caused a sensation in Massachusetts. Raised in a South Carolina slave-owning family, the white sisters abhorred slavery and fled north. Their firsthand experience of the system made them especially compelling abolitionist speakers. By June, men as well as women were coming to their public talks, giving them a "mixed" or "promiscuous" audience. Grimké writes her friend Jane Smith about stage fright.

In the evening of the same day [June 21], addressed our first large mixed audience [in Lynn]. about 1000 present. Great openness to hear & ease in speaking. 22d. Held another in Lynn, but in a smaller house, so that it was crowded to excess. About 600 seated. Many went away, about 100 stood around the door, & we were told that on each window on the outside stood three men with their heads above the lowered sash. Very easy speaking indeed. 23d. held a meeting here [Danvers]. About 200 out—a few of the brethren. Very hard speaking. . . . And now thou will want to know how we feel about all these things. . . . Whilst in the act of speaking I am favored to forget little "I" entirely & to feel altogether hid behind the great cause I am pleading. Were it not for this feeling, I know not how I could face such audiences without embarrassment.

It is wonderful to us how the way has been opened for us to address mixed audiences, for most sects here are greatly opposed to public speaking for women, but curiosity in many & real interest in the AS [anti-slavery] cause in others induce the attendance of our meetings. When they are over, we feel as if we had nothing to do with the results. We cast our burden upon the Lord, & feel an inexpressible relief until the approach of another meeting produces an exercise & sense of responsibility which becomes at times almost insupportable. At some meetings I have really felt sick until I rose to speak. But our health has been good & we bear the exertion of body & exercise of mind wonderfully. Our compass of voice has astonished us, for we can fill a house containing 1000 persons with ease. . . .

SOURCE: Kathryn Kish Sklar, *Women's Rights Emerges within the Antislavery Movement, 1830–1870: A Brief History with Documents* (Boston: Bedford/St. Martin's, 2000), 115–16.

DOCUMENT 3
A Massachusetts Minister Rebukes the Grimkés, July 1837

Jonathan Stearns, a Presbyterian minister in Newburyport, Massachusetts, devoted a sermon to female public speaking. His ideas accorded with a "Pastoral Letter" issued also in July by the leadership of the Massachusetts Congregational Association, warning ministers not to open their pulpits for antislavery meetings featuring the Grimké sisters. Stearns outlined woman's rightful spheres of influence—home, benevolence and charity work, religion—and argued that women were not *inferior to men but rather* different. *He then rehearsed the biblical prohibitions that forbade women from speaking in church or instructing their husbands— prohibitions that, he argued, elevated women, gave them influence over men, and kept them modest and delicate.*

Let her lay aside delicacy, and her influence over our sex is gone. And for what object would she make such sacrifices? That she may do good more extensively? Then she sadly mistakes her vocation. But why then? That she may see her name blazoned on the rolls of fame, and hear the shouts of delighted assemblies, applauding her eloquence? That she may place her own sex on a fancied equality with men, obtain the satisfaction of calling herself independent, and occupy a station in life which she can never adorn? For this would she sacrifice the almost magic power, which, in her own proper sphere she now wields over the destinies of the word? . . . That there are ladies who are capable of public debate, who could make their voice heard from end to end of the church and the senate house, that there are those who might bear a favorable comparison with others as eloquent orators, and who might speak to better edification than most of those on whom the office has hitherto devolved, I am not disposed to deny. The question is not in regard to *ability,* but to *decency,* to order, to Christian *propriety.*

SOURCE: Jonathan F. Stearns, "Female Influence, and the True Christian Mode of Its Exercise: A Discourse Delivered in the First Presbyterian Church in Newburyport, July 30, 1837," in Aileen S. Kraditor, ed., *Up from the Pedestal. Selected Writings in the History of American Feminism* (Chicago: University of Chicago Press, 1968), 47–50.

DOCUMENT 4
Mary Gove Lectures on Health Reform and Sex, 1838

The Grimké lecture tour of 1837 emboldened other women to take up public speaking. Mary S. Gove, a self-trained medical practitioner from Lynn, Massachusetts, launched her career as a lecturer on women's anatomy and physiology in 1838. Her lectures on corsets and on sex were particularly controversial, even though she restricted her audience for the latter lecture to married women only. In this letter, Anna Breed, a Quaker woman from Lynn, writes Abigail Kelley about the local reaction to Gove's first series. The lecture on tight lacing drew 2,000 listeners in Boston.

Thou has probably heard of M. S. Gove's success in her new sphere. I have attended three of her lectures which were both edifying and interesting. The first that I heard was upon the formation of bones—the 2nd upon their situations, number, and wonderful use—3d The evils of tight lacing—an excellent lecture—she has according to my estimation, very correct views of the effects of that horrid practice. I think Abby, thou would be much interested in her lectures; she appears better than I ever saw her in any other situation. She is censured, ridiculed, and misrepresented, of course; but as she has a pretty good share of independence, I think she will not be much affected by the [sa]rcasms inflicted upon her. I have never before seen so intelligent looking a company of women together in this place as we met there. She is giving a second course to a large audience in Boston.

SOURCE: Anna Breed to Abigail Kelley, November 1838, Abigail Kelley Foster Papers, American Antiquarian Society, Worcester, MA.

QUESTIONS FOR ANALYSIS AND DEBATE

1. What did Reverend Stearns identify as the chief social ill that would follow if women were allowed to lecture in public? What would women lose? What might men lose?

2. Stearns condemns female ambition and ego. Do you think Stewart, Grimké, or Gove exhibit female ambition? What do you think motivated each one to lecture?

3. How much do you think the *subject matter* of the lectures would influence the degree of criticism each woman experienced? Can you discern strategies that any of these speakers adopted to try to ward off criticism?

Transatlantic Abolition

Lucretia Coffin Mott

Lucretia Coffin was born in 1793 in a Quaker community of Nantucket, Massachusetts. She later recalled the influence of British abolitionists in her formative years: "My sympathy was early enlisted for the poor slave by the class books read in our schools, and the pictures of the slave-ships as presented by [Thomas] Clarkson." She married James Mott of Philadelphia in 1811, and by the mid-1820s both Motts endorsed boycotts of slave products (sugar, cotton), a particular hardship for James, a cloth merchant, who only sold wool thereafter. Lucretia Mott was a prime mover in the Philadelphia Female Anti-Slavery Society, founded in 1833, and she gave her first public lecture on slavery to an all-female audience in May 1837. In 1840 she was one of eight American women chosen to attend the World Antislavery Convention, presided over by the octogenarian Clarkson, whose work had early inspired her. Though the women were rejected as delegates on account of their sex, Mott made the most of the meeting's networking opportunities. For years after 1840, she was a steady correspondent with English and Irish abolitionists.

Chicago Historical Society.

Abolitionism blossomed in the United States in the 1830s, but its roots stretched back to the 1780s, both in the northern states and in Europe. Developments on both sides of the Atlantic reinforced each other, leading to a transatlantic antislavery movement with shared ideas and strategies, shared activists, shared songs, and, eventually, shared victories.

An important source of antislavery sentiment derived from the Quaker religion, with its deep convictions of human equality, so, not surprisingly, antislavery activism first spread along established Quaker networks in England, Ireland, and the United States, propelled by traveling ministers and religious pamphlet literature. In Pennsylvania, Quakers launched the Pennsylvania Society for Promoting the Abolition of Slavery, which non-Quakers Benjamin Franklin and Thomas Paine also joined. Founded in 1784, the Society worked to end slavery in that state and also petitioned the confederation congress—unsuccessfully—to put an end to American participation in the international slave trade. Quaker counterparts in the British cities of London and Plymouth formed antislavery societies that same year and embarked on a drive to ban England's transatlantic traffic in humans. A French group, the Société des Amis des Noirs (Society of the Friends of Blacks) sprang up in Paris in 1788. All three groups agreed that ending the overseas commerce was the critical first step in ending slavery.

The English Quakers were initially the most successful in mounting a public campaign. From 1787 to 1791, the Society for Effecting the Abolition of the Slave Trade amassed thousands of signatures on petitions and organized a boycott of slave-produced sugar from the British West Indies, a boycott said to have involved 300,000 Britons. Women, the traditional cooks of English families, were essential to that effort. In 1789, the Society scored a publicity coup by publishing two chilling illustrations of cross-sectioned slaving ships stacked with human cargo, the dark, near-naked bodies packed like sardines in each ship's hold. These images, reprinted by the thousands, created a sensation. The Reverend Thomas Clarkson of the Society distributed them in Paris and in northern U.S. cities along with a book he wrote detailing the shipboard tortures inflicted on slaves by the use of shackles, handcuffs, whips, and branding irons. The Society mobilized the resulting groundswell of antislavery sentiment to pressure Parliament. A sympathetic member of that body, the Methodist William Wilburforce, brought the anti–slave trade issue to a debate and vote in 1791; it lost.

American Quakers approached the first federal Congress, meeting in New York in 1790, with petitions requesting an immediate end to the slave trade. This caused some puzzlement at first, because the U.S. Constitution contained a clause prohibiting the federal government from banning the "Importation of Such Persons as any of the States now existing shall think proper to admit" (that is, slaves) before the year 1808. Congressmen banished the Quaker petitions to a committee. The next day, a bolder Quaker petition, endorsed by the venerated Benjamin Franklin, arrived requesting an end to slavery as well as to the slave trade and suggesting how to accomplish it.

The petitioners urged Congress to invoke the constitutional provision that empowered the government to make all laws "necessary and proper" to ensure the "general welfare" of the country, arguing that "Liberty for all Negroes" was crucial to the general welfare. This petition triggered the first debate in the new government on slavery. As in England, the outcome did not bode well for slaves: By a close vote (29 to 25), Congress not only rejected this move for emancipation but also clarified its view—in a precedent-setting resolution—that slavery was under the sole regulation of the states where it existed.

Over the next three decades, the antislavery cause in Britain and in America moved forward in piece-meal fashion. Efforts to ban the slave trade in England came to parliamentary votes in 1805 and again in 1807, when a law forbidding English ships to carry Africans into slavery finally passed. (The British law was not perfect, however; it levied a fine of £100 per slave on any English captain caught with illegal cargo, creating a grim incentive for captains to shove people overboard if they faced challenge by the British navy.) A year later, in 1808, the United States also banned the slave trade, meeting the constitutional time limit. What made for relatively easy passage at this time was the burgeoning natural increase of the African American population. Older slave states supported the international ban because it increased the value of their native-born slave population, which could be sold and transported to points west in the interstate slave trade.

British antislavery opinion took a new tack in the 1820s, when women became active and pushed beyond the ban on trade. Quaker widow Elizabeth Heyrick authored *Immediate not Gradual Abolition* in 1824, triggering the formation of scores of all-women societies. A massive petition campaign again bombarded Parliament, and of the 1.3 million signatures submitted in 1833, 30 percent were women's. In 1833, Parliament finally passed the Abolition of Slavery Act, which freed all slave children under age six and gradually phased out slavery for everyone older during a four-year apprenticeship. The act also provided financial compensation for owners (£20 million), a key proviso made possible by the relatively small number of slaveowners in the British slaveholding colonies.

Description of a Slave Ship

This powerful and often-reprinted image combined a precise technical rendering of a British ship (normally evoking pride in Britons) with the horrors of a crowded mass of dark human flesh.

Peabody Essex Museum, Salem, MA.

DESCRIPTION OF A SLAVE SHIP.

(continued)

(continued)

American abolitionists were also heating up the struggle in the 1830s, and as in Britain, women's involvement was accelerating. The Grimké sisters were only the most visible part of women's new activism. Many hundreds of women joined Female Anti-Slavery organizations and held fairs where they sold handmade goods to raise money to promote the abolitionist cause. Both women and men abolitionists from both sides of the Atlantic traveled overseas to meet their counterparts abroad. In one worrisome moment, a Boston crowd threatened to lynch British abolitionist George Thompson and his host, William Lloyd Garrison, the editor of the *Liberator*.

British and American abolitionists came together in full force at the World Antislavery Convention, held in London in 1840. Among the 409 delegates were Clarkson, who presided, Garrison, and Philadelphia Quaker Lucretia Mott, a lifelong antislavery activist. A half dozen French delegates attended, 53 others were Americans, and the rest were from Britain and the West Indies. Only about a quarter of the attendees were Quakers. Ten days of meetings produced speeches and fact-finding reports on slavery worldwide, captured in a 600-page book detailing the proceedings. Economic and religious strategies were debated, and a plan was hatched to inform America about how British emancipation had worked. Memorials were sent to governments, and each governor of a southern U.S. state was targeted with a letter condemning the interstate slave trade. The delegates closed their meeting, exhilarated by the idea of their international congress to move toward international solutions to an international problem.

BIBLIOGRAPHY

David Brion Davis, *The Problem of Slavery in the Age of Revolution, 1770–1823* (1975).

Seymour Drescher, *The Mighty Experiment: Free Labor versus Slavery in British Emancipation* (2002).

Julie Roy Jeffrey, *The Great Silent Army of Abolition: Ordinary Women in the Antislavery Movement* (1998).

James Stewart, *Holy Warriors: The Abolitionists and American Slavery* (1976).

David Turley, *The Culture of English Anti-Slavery, 1780–1860* (1991).

Marcus Wood, *Blind Memory: Visual Representations of Slavery in England and America, 1780–1865* (2000).

down to defeat. Jackson's legacy to his successor, Martin Van Buren, was a Democratic Party strong enough to withstand the passing of the Old Hickory. But another of his legacies was the most severe economic contraction yet to hit the U.S. economy, the panic of 1837. Although the panic was not solely Jackson's doing, it was a fitting ending to a decade of rambunctious speculation and expansion.

Indian Policy and the Trail of Tears

Jackson declared in his first annual message that removing Indians to territory west of the Mississippi was the only way to save them.

Probably nothing defined Jackson's presidency more than his efforts to "solve" what he saw as the Indian problem. Many thousands of Indians lived in the South and the old Northwest; indeed, not a few lived in New England and New York. Jackson, who had gained his national reputation fighting the Creek in 1814 and the Seminole in 1816–1817, declared in 1829 in his first annual message to Congress that removing Indians to territory west of the Mississippi was the only way to save them. White civilization destroyed Indian resources and thus doomed the Indians: "That this fate surely awaits them if they remain within the limits of the states does not admit of a doubt. Humanity and national honor demand that every effort should be made to avert so great a calamity." Jackson never publicly wavered from this seemingly noble theme, returning to it in his next seven annual messages.

Prior administrations had tried different policies. Starting in 1819, Congress granted $10,000 a year to various missionary associations eager to "civilize" native peoples by converting them to Christianity. The assimilationist program also included teaching Indians English literacy and agricultural practices. Missionaries also promoted white gender customs, but Indian women were reluctant to embrace practices that accorded them less power than their tribal system did. The federal government had also pursued aggressive treaty making with many tribes, dealing with the Indians as if they were foreign nations. (See chapter 10, pages 334–35.)

Privately, Andrew Jackson thought it was "absurd" to treat the Indians as foreigners. In his view, they were subjects of the United States. Jackson also did not approve of assimilation; that way lay extinction, he said. In his 1833 annual message to Congress he wrote, "They have neither the intelligence, the industry, the moral habits, nor the desire of improvement which are essential. . . . Established in the midst of a superior race . . . they must necessarily yield to the force of circumstances and ere long disappear." Congress backed Jackson's goal and passed the Indian Removal Act of 1830, appropriating $500,000 to relocate eastern tribes to land west of the Mississippi River. About 100 million acres of eastern land would be vacated for eventual white settlement under this act authorizing ethnic expulsion (Map 11.3).

For northern tribes, their numbers diminished by years of war, gradual removal was already well under way. But not all the Indians went quietly. In 1832 in western Illinois, Black Hawk, a leader of the Sauk and Fox Indians who had fought with Tecumseh in the War of 1812 (see chapter 10, page 336), resisted. Volunteer militias attacked and chased the Indians into

---

MAP 11.3 Indian Removal and the Trail of Tears

The federal government under President Andrew Jackson pursued a vigorous policy of Indian removal in the 1830s. Tribes were forcibly moved west to land known as Indian Territory (in present-day Oklahoma). As many as a quarter of the Cherokee Indians died in 1838 on the route known as the Trail of Tears.

READING THE MAP: From which states were most of the Native Americans removed? Through which states did the Trail of Tears go?

CONNECTIONS: Before Jackson's presidency, how did the federal government view Native Americans, and what policy initiatives were undertaken by the government and private groups? How did Jackson change the government's Native American policies?

FOR MORE HELP ANALYZING THIS MAP, see the map activity for this chapter in the Online Study Guide at bedfordstmartins.com/roark.

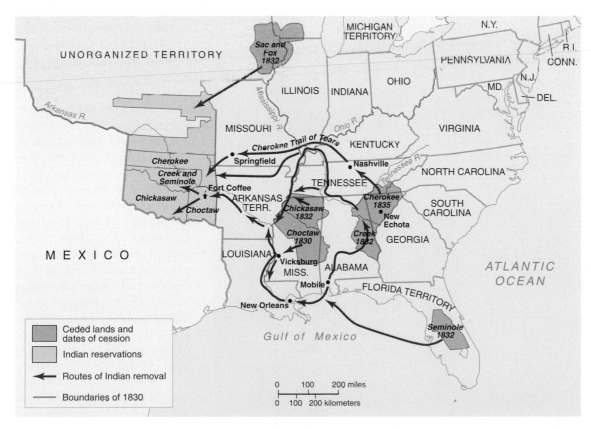

southern Wisconsin, where, after several skirmishes and a deadly battle, Black Hawk was captured and some 400 of his people were massacred.

Southern tribes proved even more resistant to removal. The powerful Creek, Chickasaw, Choctaw, and Cherokee tribes refused to relocate. A second Seminole War in Florida broke out as the Indians there—a mixture of Seminoles and escaped black slaves who had intermarried with the tribe—took up arms against relocation in 1836–1837.

The Cherokee of Georgia responded with a unique legal challenge to being treated as subjects. More than any other southern tribe, the 17,000 Cherokee had incorporated white political and economic practices into their tribal life. Spurred by dedicated missionaries, they had adopted written laws, culminating in 1827 in

a constitution closely modeled on the U.S. Constitution. Some two hundred of the wealthiest Cherokees had intermarried with whites and had adopted white styles of housing, dress, and cotton agriculture, including the ownership of more than a thousand slaves. They had developed a written alphabet and published a newspaper as well as Christian prayerbooks in their language.

In 1831, after Georgia announced it would subject the Indians to state law and seize their property, the Cherokee tribe appealed to the U.S. Supreme Court to restrain Georgia. Chief Justice John Marshall found for Georgia on the grounds that the Cherokee did not have standing to sue. When Georgia jailed two missionaries under an 1830 state law forbidding missionary aid to Indians without permission, the Cherokee brought suit again, fronting one of the missionaries as plaintiff. In the 1832 case, *Worcester v. Georgia,* the Supreme Court upheld the territorial sovereignty of the Cherokee, recognizing their existence as "a distinct community, occupying its own territory, in which the laws of Georgia can have no force." Ignoring the Supreme Court's decision, an angry President Jackson pressed the Cherokee for removal west. "If they now refuse to accept the liberal terms offered, they can only be liable for whatever evils and difficulties may arise. I feel conscious of having done my duty to my red children."

The Cherokee tribe remained in Georgia for two more years without significant violence. Then in 1835, a small, unauthorized part of the tribe signed a treaty ceding all the tribal land—a large piece of northern Georgia— to the state in exchange for $5 million and equal acreage west of Arkansas. Georgia rapidly sold the land to whites. Cherokee chief John Ross, backed by several thousand Cherokees, petitioned the U.S. Congress to ignore the bogus treaty. "By the stipulations of this instrument," he wrote, "we are stripped of every attribute of freedom and eligibility for legal self-defence. Our property may be plundered before our eyes; violence may be committed on our persons; even our

Cherokee Phoenix

Around 1820, Sequoyah, about forty-five years old and nephew of a Cherokee chief, invented written symbols to convey the Cherokee language. Each symbol represented a syllable of sound. In 1828, the Cherokees in New Echota, Georgia, ordered custom-made type embodying the new symbols and began printing a newspaper, the *Cherokee Phoenix,* the first newspaper published by Native Americans, printed in both English and Cherokee.

Special Collections Division, Georgetown University Library, Washington, D.C.

Choctaw Indian Sash, 1820s

The pattern of beadwork on wool marks this sash as Choctaw handiwork. A sash like this one, which is 46 inches long, was worn diagonally across the chest. Its sharply contrasting colors and vivid design could be seen at a distance, allowing for quick identification of tribal members. The Choctaw lived in Mississippi and were one of the five southern Indian nations that were subjected to Andrew Jackson's removal policy in the 1830s.

Peabody Essex Museum, Salem, MA.

lives may be taken away. . . . We are denationalized; we are disfranchised."

Most Cherokees refused to move, so in May 1838, the deadline for voluntary evacuation, federal troops sent by Jackson's successor, Martin Van Buren, arrived to deport them. Under armed guard, the Cherokees embarked on a 1,200-mile journey that came to be called the Trail of Tears. A newspaperman in Kentucky described the forced march: "Even aged females, apparently, nearly ready to drop into the grave, were travel-

ing with heavy burdens attached to the back. . . . They buried fourteen to fifteen at every stopping place." Nearly a quarter of the Cherokees died en route from the hardship. Survivors joined the fifteen thousand Creek, twelve thousand Choctaw, five thousand Chickasaw, and several thousand Seminole Indians also forcibly relocated to "Indian Territory" (which became, in 1907, the state of Oklahoma).

In his farewell address to the nation in 1837, Jackson again professed his belief about the benefit of Indian removal: "This unhappy race . . . are now placed in a situation where we may well hope that they will share in the blessings of civilization and be saved from the degradation and destruction to which they were rapidly hastening while they remained in the states." Possibly Jackson genuinely believed that exile to the West was necessary to save Indian cultures from destruction. But for the forcibly removed tribes, the costs of relocation were high.

The Tariff of Abominations and Nullification

Jackson's Indian policy happened to harmonize with the principle of **states' rights**: The president supported Georgia's right to ignore the Supreme Court decision in *Worcester v. Georgia*. But in another pressing question of states' rights, Jackson contested South Carolina's attempt to ignore federal tariff policy.

Federal tariffs as high as 33 percent on imports such as textiles and iron goods had been passed in 1816 and again in 1824, in an effort to favor new American manufactures and shelter them from foreign competition as well as to raise federal revenue. Some southern congressmen opposed the steep tariffs, fearing they would decrease overseas shipping and hurt the South's cotton export. During John Quincy Adams's administration (1825–1829), tariff policy generated heated debate. In 1828, Congress passed a revised tariff that came to be known as the Tariff of Abominations. A bundle of conflicting duties— some as high as 50 percent—the legislation had provisions that pleased and angered every economic and sectional interest. Assembled mostly by southern congressmen, who loaded it with duties on raw materials needed by New England, it also contained protectionist elements favored by northern manufacturers.

South Carolina in particular suffered from the Tariff of Abominations. Worldwide prices for cotton were already in sharp decline in the late

1820s, and the further depression of shipping caused by the high tariffs hurt the South's export market. In 1828, a group of South Carolina politicians headed by John C. Calhoun drew up a statement outlining a doctrine called **nullification**. The Union, they argued, was a confederation of states that had yielded some but not all power to the federal government. When Congress overstepped its powers, states had the right to nullify Congress's acts; as precedents they pointed to the Virginia and Kentucky Resolutions of 1798, which had attempted to invalidate the Alien and Sedition Acts (see chapter 9). Congress had erred in using tariff policy as an instrument to benefit specific industries, the South Carolinians claimed; tariffs should be used only to raise revenue.

On assuming the presidency in 1829, Jackson ignored the South Carolina statement of nullification and shut out Calhoun, his new vice president, from influence or power. Tariff revisions in early 1832 brought little relief to the South. Sensing futility, Calhoun resigned from the vice presidency in 1832 and accepted election by the South Carolina legislature to a seat in the U.S. Senate, where he could better argue his state's antitariff stance. Strained to their limit, the South Carolina leaders took the radical step of declaring the federal tariffs to be null and void in their state as of February 1, 1833. Finally, the constitutional crisis was out in the open.

Opting for a dramatic confrontation, Jackson sent armed ships to Charleston's harbor and threatened to invade the state. He pushed through Congress a bill, called the Force Bill, defining the Carolina stance as treason and authorizing military action to collect federal tariffs. At the same time, Congress moved quickly to pass a revised tariff more acceptable to the South. The conciliating Senator Henry Clay rallied support for a moderate bill that gradually reduced tariffs down to the 1816 level. On March 1, 1833, Congress passed both the new tariff and the Force Bill. South Carolina responded by withdrawing its nullification of the old tariff—and then nullifying the Force Bill. It was a symbolic gesture, since Jackson's show of muscle was no longer necessary. Both sides were satisfied with the immediate outcome. Federal power had prevailed over a dangerous assertion of states' rights, and South Carolina got the lower tariff it wanted.

Yet the question of federal power versus states' rights was far from settled. The implied threat behind nullification was secession, a position articulated in 1832 by some South Carolinians whose concerns went beyond tariff policy. The growing voice of antislavery activism in the North threatened the South's economic system. If and when a northern-dominated federal government decided to end slavery, the South Carolinians thought, the South must have the right to remove itself from the Union.

The Bank War and the Panic of 1837

Along with the tariff and nullification, President Jackson had another political battle on his hands, over the Bank of the United States. After riding out the panic of 1819, the bank finally prospered. It handled the federal government's deposits, extended credit and loans, and issued banknotes—by 1830 the most stable currency in the country. Now having twenty-nine branches, it benefited the whole nation. Jackson, however, did not find the bank's functions sufficiently valuable to offset his criticism of the concept of a national bank. In his first two annual messages to Congress, in 1829 and 1830, Jackson claimed that the bank concentrated undue economic power in the hands of a few.

National Republican (Whig) senators Daniel Webster and Henry Clay decided to force the issue. They convinced the bank to apply for charter renewal in 1832, well before the fall election, even though the existing charter ran until 1836. They fully expected that Congress's renewal would force Jackson to follow through on his rhetoric with a veto, that the unpopular veto would cause Jackson to lose the election, and that the bank would survive on an override vote from a new Congress swept into power on the anti-Jackson tide.

At first the plan seemed to work. The bank applied for rechartering, Congress voted to renew, and Jackson, angry over being manipulated, issued his veto. But it was a brilliantly written veto, full of fierce language about the privileges of the moneyed elite who oppress the democratic masses in order to enrich themselves. "Many of our rich men have not been content with equal protection and equal benefits, but have besought us to make them richer by act of Congress," Jackson wrote.

Clay and his supporters found Jackson's economic ideas so absurd and his language of class antagonism so shocking that they distributed thousands of copies of the bank veto as campaign material for their own party. A confident Henry Clay headed his party's ticket for the presidency. But the plan backfired. Jackson's

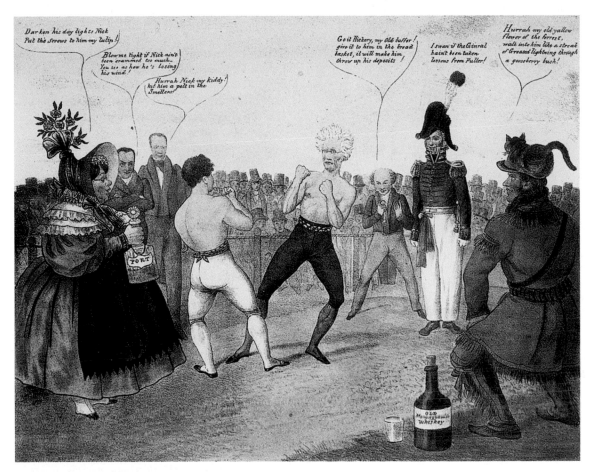

Fistfight between Old Hickory and Bully Nick
This 1834 cartoon represents President Andrew Jackson squaring off to fight Nicholas Biddle, the director of the Bank of the United States. Pugilism as a semiprofessional sport gained great popularity in the 1830s. The joke here is that the aged Jackson and the aristocratic Biddle would strip to revealing tight pants and engage in open combat. To Biddle's left are his seconds, Daniel Webster and Henry Clay; behind the president is his vice president, Martin Van Buren. Whiskey and port wine lubricate the action.
The Library Company of Philadelphia.

translation of the bank controversy into a language of class antagonism and egalitarian ideals strongly resonated with many Americans. Old Hickory won the election easily, gaining 55 percent of the popular vote and a lopsided electoral college vote of 219 to 49. The Jackson party still controlled Congress, so no override was possible. The second Bank of the United States would cease to exist after 1836.

Jackson, however, wanted to destroy the bank sooner. Calling it a "monster," he ordered the sizable federal deposits to be removed from its vaults and redeposited into favored "pet banks," Democratic-leaning state banks throughout the country. In retaliation, the Bank of the United States raised interest rates and called in loans. This action caused a brief decline

in the economy in 1833 and actually enhanced Jackson's claim that the bank was too powerful for the good of the country.

Unleashed and unregulated, the economy in 1834 went into high gear. Perhaps only a small part of the problem arose from irresponsible banking practices. Just at this moment, an excess of silver from Mexican mines made its way into American banks, giving bankers license to print ever more banknotes. Inflation soared from 1834 to 1837; prices of basic goods rose more than 50 percent. States quickly chartered many hundreds of new private banks. Each bank issued its own banknotes and set

> Jackson's translation of the bank controversy into a language of class antagonism and egalitarian ideals strongly resonated with many Americans.

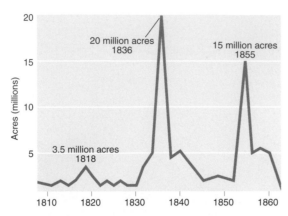

FIGURE 11.1 Western Land Sales, 1810–1860
Land sales peaked in the 1810s, 1830s, and 1850s as Americans rushed to speculate in western lands sold by the federal government. The surges in 1818 and 1836 demonstrate the volatile, speculative economy that suddenly collapsed in the panics of 1819 and 1837.

interest rates as high as the market would bear. Entrepreneurs borrowed and invested money, much of it funneled into privately financed railroads and canals.

The market in western land sales heated up. In 1834, about 4.5 million acres of the public domain had been sold, the highest annual volume since the peak year 1819; by 1836, the total reached an astonishing 20 million acres (Figure 11.1). Some of this was southern land in Mississippi and Louisiana, which slave owners rushed to bring under cultivation, but much more was in the North, where land offices were deluged with buyers. The Jackson administration worried that the purchasers were overwhelmingly eastern capitalists, land speculators instead of self-reliant **yeoman** farmers who intended to settle on the land.

In one respect, the economy attained an admirable goal: The national debt disappeared, and, for the first and only time in American history, from 1835 to 1837, the government had a monetary surplus. But much of it consisted of questionable bank currencies— "bloated, diseased" currencies, in Jackson's vivid terminology.

Jackson decided to restrain the economy. In 1836, the Treasury Department issued the Specie Circular, an order that public land could be purchased only with hard money, federally coined gold and silver. In response, bankers started to reduce their loans, fearing a general contraction of the economy. Compounding the difficulty, the Bank of England also now insisted on hard-money payments for American loans, which had grown large since 1831 because of a trade imbalance. Failures in various crop markets, a downturn in cotton prices on the international market, and the silver glut, all unrelated to Jackson's fiscal policies, fed the growing economic crisis.

The familiar events of the panic of 1819 unfolded again, with terrifying rapidity. In April 1837, a wave of bank and business failures ensued, and the credit market tumbled like a house of cards. The Specie Circular was only one precipitating cause, but the Whig Party held it and Jackson responsible for the depression. For more than five years after the panic of 1837, the United States suffered from economic hard times.

Van Buren's One-Term Presidency

The election of 1836, which preceded the panic by six months, demonstrated the transformation of the Democrats from coalition to party. Jackson's personality had stamped the elections of 1824, 1828, and 1832. By 1836, the party apparatus was sufficiently developed to support itself. Local and state committees existed throughout the country. Democratic candidates ran in every state election, succeeding even in old Federalist states like Maine and New Hampshire. More than four hundred newspapers declared themselves Democratic. In 1836, the Democrats repeated an innovation begun in 1832: holding a national convention. They nominated Vice President Martin Van Buren of New York for president.

Sophisticated party organization was Martin Van Buren's specialty. Nicknamed the "Little Magician" for his consummate political skills, the New Yorker had built his career by pioneering many of the loyalty-enhancing techniques the Democrats used in the 1830s. After serving as senator and then governor, he became Jackson's secretary of state in 1828. Four years later he replaced Calhoun as Jackson's running mate. His eight years in the volatile Jackson administration required the full measure of his political deftness as he sought repeatedly to save Jackson from both his enemies and his own obstinacy.

Van Buren was a backroom politician, not a popular public figure, and the Whigs hoped that he might be defeatable. In many states, Whigs had captured high office in 1834, shedding the awkward National Republican label and developing statewide organizations to rival those of the Democrats. However, no figure commanded nationwide support. The result was that three candidates opposed Van Buren in 1836, each with a solid regional base. Senator Daniel Webster of Massachusetts could deliver New England; Senator Hugh Lawson White of Tennessee attracted proslavery, pro-Jackson, but anti–Van Buren voters in the South; and the aging General William Henry Harrison of Indiana, memorable for his Indian war heroics in 1811, pulled in the western, anti-Indian vote. Not one of the three candidates could have won the presidency, but together they came close to denying Van Buren a majority vote. Their combined strength drew many Whigs into office at the state level. In the end, Van Buren had 170 electoral votes, while the other three received a total of 113.

Van Buren took office in March 1837, and a month later the panic hit. The new president called a special session of Congress to consider creating an independent treasury system to fulfill some of the functions of the defunct Bank of the United States. Such a system, funded by government deposits, would deal only in hard money, forcing commercial banks to restrict their issuance of paper currency. Equally important, the new system would not make loans and would thus avoid the danger of speculative meddling in the economy. In short, an independent treasury system could exert a powerful moderating influence on inflation and the credit market without itself being directly involved in the market. But Van Buren encountered strong resistance in Congress, even from Democrats. The treasury system finally won approval in 1840; by then, however, Van Buren's chances of a second term in office were virtually nil. With federal bank policy at a stalemate, the four years had proved to be tumultuous for the economy.

In 1840, the Whigs settled on William Henry Harrison, sixty-seven, to oppose Van Buren. The campaign drew on voter involvement as no presidential campaign ever had. The Whigs borrowed tricks from the Democrats: Harrison was touted as a common man born in a log cabin (in reality he was born on a Virginia plantation), and raucus campaign parades featured toy log cabins held aloft. His Indian-fighting days, now thirty years behind him, were played up to give him a Jacksonian aura. Whigs staged festive rallies all over the country, drumming up mass appeal with candlelight parades and song shows. Women partici-

pated in Whig campaign rallies as never before. Some 78 percent of eligible voters cast ballots— the highest percentage ever in American history. Harrison took 53 percent of the popular vote and won a resounding 234 electoral college votes to Van Buren's 60. A Democratic editor lamented, "We have taught them how to conquer us!"

Conclusion: The Age of Jackson or the Era of Reform?

Harrison's election marked the close of a decade that brought the common man and democracy into the forefront of American politics. The same forces that propelled Jacksonian politics also laid the groundwork for the first large wave of American reform activity cresting in the 1830s. Jacksonian Democrats and reform-minded Whigs were on opposite sides of politics, but both were products of vast and important changes marking the 1830s.

One of the most significant of those changes was the economic transformation of the period. Revolutionary advances in transportation put goods and people in circulation, drawing the rural backcountry to the densely settled East Coast and propelling the growth of urban centers. Entrepreneurs figured out new ways to harness the power of water to drive manufacturing. Trade and banking mushroomed, and western lands once occupied by Indians were auctioned off in a landslide of sales. As one religious periodical put it, the country was marked by the "overstrained pursuit of wealth." Two economic downturns, the panics of 1819 and 1837, offered sobering but easily forgotten lessons about where speculative fever can lead.

With increased economic opportunity came increased public involvement in politics. Andrew Jackson symbolized the age for many. His fame as an aggressive general, Indian fighter, champion of the common man, and defender of slavery attracted voters to an emergent Democratic Party that championed personal liberty, free competition, and egalitarian opportunity for all white men.

Jackson's constituency was challenged by a small but vocal segment of the population troubled by serious moral problems that Jacksonians preferred to ignore. Reformers drew sustenance from the message of the Second

Great Awakening: that all men and women are free to choose salvation, and that personal *and* societal sins can be overcome. Reformers targeted personal vices (illicit sex, intemperance) and social problems (prostitution, poverty, and slavery), confident that a perfect world was attainable. Reformers who could vote tended to vote Whig. But of course a lot of reformers—women imbued with a combined sense of benevolence and urgent duty—could not vote at all. Reformers joined forces with evangelicals and wealthy lawyers and merchants North or South who appreciated a national bank and protective tariffs. The Whig Party was the party of activist moralism and state-sponsored entrepreneurship.

National politics in the 1830s were more heated and divisive than at any other time since the 1790s. The new party system of Democrats and Whigs cut far deeper into the electorate than had the previous system of Federalists and Republicans. Stagecoaches and steamboats carried newspapers with their political coverage from the city to the backwoods, politicizing voters who now understood what they might gain or lose under the competing economic policies of the two parties. Politics acquired immediacy and excitement, causing four out of five white men to cast ballots in 1840.

High rates of voter participation would continue into the 1840s and 1850s because politics remained the arena where difficult choices about economic development and social change were contested. Unprecedented urban growth, westward expansion, and early industrialism marked those decades, sustaining the Jacksonian-Whig split in the electorate. But other new challenges not easily dealt with by those two parties—critiques of slavery, concerns for free labor, and an emerging protest against women's second-class citizenship—complicated the political scene of the 1840s, leading to third-party movements that splintered from the two parties of the 1830s. One of these third parties, called the Republican Party, would achieve dominance in 1860 with the election of an Illinois lawyer, Abraham Lincoln, to the presidency.

For additional firsthand accounts of this period, see Chapter 11 in Michael Johnson, ed., *Reading the American Past*, Third Edition.

To assess your mastery of the material in this chapter, see the Online Study Guide at bedfordstmartins.com/roark.

For Web links related to topics in this chapter, see "HistoryLinks," "DocLinks," and "PlaceLinks" at bedfordstmartins.com/roark.

CHRONOLOGY

1807 • Robert Fulton develops first commercially successful steamboat, *Clermont.*

1816 • Congress charters second Bank of the United States for twenty years.
• Congress imposes high import tariff on foreign textiles to stimulate American textile manufacturing.

1817 • American Colonization Society founded to promote gradual emancipation and removal of African Americans to Liberia.

1818 • National Road links Baltimore and Wheeling, in western Virginia.

1819 • Economic panic grips nation—the first major short depression.

1821 • Boston entrepreneurs start to build mills with power looms at Lowell, Massachusetts.

1824 • Congress increases tariff on foreign imports.

1825 • Erie Canal spans 350 miles in New York State, in effect linking New York City with Great Lakes.

1826 • American Temperance Society, founded in Connecticut, encourages temperance pledges from working-class laborers as condition of employment.
• Schuylkill Canal—108 miles long—opens in Pennsylvania.

1828 • Congress passes Tariff of Abominations, setting the stage for South Carolina's nullification of federal law.

- Democrat Andrew Jackson elected president.

1829
- David Walker's *Appeal . . . to the Coloured Citizens of the World* published in Boston.
- Baltimore and Ohio Railroad, the first U.S. railroad, lays 13 miles of track.

1830
- Indian Removal Act appropriates money to relocate Indian tribes west of Mississippi River.
- First National Negro Convention meets in Philadelphia to discuss status of free blacks in the North; such conventions continue for three decades.

1831
- William Lloyd Garrison begins publishing abolitionist newspaper the *Liberator.*
- Charles G. Finney stages evangelical revival in Rochester, New York, taking Second Great Awakening mainstream to the new business classes.
- U.S. Supreme Court fails to prevent Georgia from subjecting Cherokee Indians to state laws.

1832
- Chief Black Hawk and Sauk and Fox Indians lose war against American militias in Illinois and Wisconsin.
- U.S. Supreme Court in *Worcester v. Georgia* recognizes Cherokees as distinct community outside legal jurisdiction of Georgia.
- Jackson vetoes Bank of the United States charter, gaining greater popularity and momentum for victory in the fall election; Henry Clay greatly surprised.

- Maria Stewart of Boston becomes one of the first American women to speak in public lectures on social issues.
- New England Anti-Slavery Society founded—the start of an organized and sustained antislavery movement.
- Andrew Jackson elected to a second term.

1833
- Nullification crisis: South Carolina declares federal tariffs void in the state.
- New York and Philadelphia antislavery societies founded.
- New York Female Moral Reform Society founded, with goal to curb male sexual excess.

1834–1836
- Female mill workers strike in Lowell, Massachusetts, protesting wage cuts and work speedups—the first major labor strike in U.S. history.

1836
- Jackson issues Specie Circular, requiring use of hard money to purchase public lands; start of contraction of the economy.
- Democrat Martin Van Buren elected president.

1837
- Economic panic.

1838
- Trail of Tears—Cherokees forced to relocate west.

1840
- Whig William Henry Harrison elected president.

BIBLIOGRAPHY

General Works

Daniel Feller, *The Jacksonian Promise: America, 1815–1840* (1995).
Michael F. Holt, *Political Parties and American Political Development from the Age of Jackson to the Age of Lincoln* (1992).
Merrill D. Peterson, *The Great Triumvirate: Webster, Clay, and Calhoun* (1987).
Charles G. Sellers, *The Market Revolution: Jacksonian America, 1815–1846* (1991).
Harry L. Watson, *Liberty and Power: The Politics of Jacksonian America* (1990).
Robert H. Wiebe, *The Opening of American Society: From the Adoption of the Constitution to the Eve of Disunion* (1984).

The Market Revolution

Elizabeth Blackmar, *Manhattan for Rent, 1785–1850* (1989).
Mary H. Blewett, *Men, Women, and Work: Class, Gender, and Protest in the New England Shoe Industry, 1780–1910* (1988).

Jeanne Boydston, *Home and Work: Housework, Wages, and the Ideology of Labor in the Early Republic* (1990).
Christopher Clark, *The Roots of Rural Capitalism: Worcester, Massachusetts, 1780–1860* (1990).
Alan Dawley, *Class and Community: The Industrial Revolution in Lynn* (1976).
Thomas Dublin, *Women at Work: The Transformation of Work and Community in Lowell, Massachusetts, 1826–1860* (1979).
Thomas Dublin, *Transforming Women's Work: New England Lives in the Industrial Revolution* (1994).
Tony A. Freyer, *Producers versus Capitalists: Constitutional Conflict in Antebellum America* (1994).
Paul A. Gilje, ed., *Wages of Independence: Capitalism in the Early Republic* (1997).
Jonathan A. Glickstein, *Anxiety: Wages, Competition, and Degraded Labor in the Antebellum United States* (2002).
Erik F. Haites, James Mak, and Gary M. Walton, *Western River Transportation: The Era of Early Internal Development, 1800–1860* (1975).

Morton J. Horwitz, *The Transformation of American Law, 1780–1860* (1977).

Bruce Laurie, *Artisans into Workers: Labor in Nineteenth-Century America* (1989).

John D. Majewski, *A House Dividing: Economic Development in Pennsylvania and Virginia before the Civil War* (2000).

Otto Mayr and Robert C. Post, eds., *Yankee Enterprise: The Rise of the American System of Manufactures* (1981).

Lawrence A. Peskin, *Manufacturing Revolution: The Intellectual Origins of Early American Industry* (2003).

Ronald E. Shaw, *Erie Water West: A History of the Erie Canal, 1792–1854* (1990).

Carol Sheriff, *The Artificial River: The Erie Canal and the Paradox of Progress, 1817–1862* (1996).

Richard B. Stott, *Workers in the Metropolis: Class, Ethnicity, and Youth in Antebellum New York City* (1990).

Christopher L. Tomlins, *Law, Labor, and Ideology in the Early American Republic* (1993).

Barbara Tucker, *Samuel Slater and the Origins of the American Textile Industry, 1790–1860* (1984).

The Spread of Democracy

Andrew Burstein, *The Passions of Andrew Jackson* (2003).

Marshall Foletta, *Coming to Terms with Democracy: Federalist Intellectuals and the Shaping of an American Culture* (2001).

Ronald P. Formisano, *The Birth of Mass Political Parties: Michigan, 1827–1861* (1971).

Paul Goodman, *Towards a Christian Republic: Antimasonry and the Great Transition in New England, 1826–1836* (1988).

Daniel W. Howe, *The Political Culture of the American Whigs* (1980).

Lawrence Frederick Kohl, *The Politics of Individualism: Parties and the American Character in the Jacksonian Era* (1989).

Robert V. Remini, *Andrew Jackson and the Course of American Freedom, 1822–1832* (1981).

Robert V. Remini, *The Life of Andrew Jackson* (2001).

Alexander Saxton, *The Rise and Fall of the White Republic: Class Politics and Mass Culture in Nineteenth-Century America* (1990).

Sean Wilentz, *Chants Democratic: New York City and the Rise of the American Working Class, 1788–1850* (1984).

Culture and Society

Gerald J. Baldasty, *The Commercialization of News in the Nineteenth Century* (1992).

Stuart M. Blumin, *The Emergence of the Middle Class: Social Experience in the American City, 1760–1900* (1989).

Richard L. Bushman, *The Refinement of America: Persons, Houses, Cities* (1992).

Kenneth Cmiel, *Democratic Eloquence: The Fight over Popular Speech in Nineteenth-Century America* (1990).

Patricia Cline Cohen, *The Murder of Helen Jewett: The Life and Death of a Prostitute in Nineteenth-Century New York* (1998).

Faye E. Dudden, *Women in the American Theatre: Actresses and Audiences, 1790–1870* (1994).

Ann Fabian, *Card-Sharps, Dream Books, and Bucket Shops: Gambling in Nineteenth-Century America* (1990).

Timothy J. Gilfoyle, *City of Eros: New York City, Prostitution, and the Commercialization of Sex, 1790–1920* (1992).

Karen Halttunen, *Confidence Men and Painted Women: A Study of Middle-Class Culture in America, 1830–1870* (1982).

Shawn Johansen, *Family Men: Middle-Class Fatherhood in Early Industrializing America* (2001).

Richard R. John, *Spreading the News: The American Postal System from Franklin to Morse* (1995).

Carl F. Kaestle, *Pillars of the Republic: Common Schools and American Society, 1780–1860* (1983).

John F. Kasson, *Rudeness and Civility: Manners in Nineteenth-Century America* (1990).

Lawrence W. Levine, *Highbrow/Lowbrow: The Emergence of Cultural Hierarchy in America* (1988).

Louis P. Masur, *1831: Year of Eclipse* (2001).

Lewis Perry, *Boats against the Current: American Culture between Revolution and Modernity, 1820–1860* (1993).

E. Anthony Rotundo, *American Manhood: Transformations in Masculinity from the Revolution to the Modern Era* (1993).

Mary P. Ryan, *Women in Public: Between Banners and Ballots, 1825–1880* (1990).

Carroll Smith-Rosenberg, *Disorderly Conduct: Visions of Gender in Victorian America* (1985).

Christine Stansell, *City of Women: Sex and Class in New York, 1789–1860* (1986).

Richard B. Stott, *Workers in the Metropolis: Class, Ethnicity, and Youth in Antebellum New York City* (1990).

Alan Taylor, *William Cooper's Town: Power and Persuasion on the Frontier of the Early American Republic* (1995).

Ronald J. Zboray, *A Fictive People: Antebellum Development and the American Reading Public* (1993).

Reform and Religion

Robert Abzug, *Cosmos Crumbling: American Reform and the Religious Imagination* (1994).

R. J. M. Blackett, *Building an Antislavery Wall: Black Americans in the Atlantic Abolitionist Movement, 1830–1860* (1983).

Ellen Eslinger, *Citizens of Zion: The Social Origins of Camp Meeting Revivalism* (1999).

Lawrence J. Friedman, *Gregarious Saints: Self and Community in American Abolitionism, 1830–1870* (1982).

Lori D. Ginzberg, *Women and the Work of Benevolence: Morality, Politics, and Class in the Nineteenth-Century United States* (1990).

Charles E. Hambrick-Stowe, *Charles G. Finney and the Spirit of American Evangelicalism* (1996).

Stanley Harrold, *The Abolitionists and the South, 1831–1861* (1995).

Stanley Harrold, *Subversives: Antislavery Community in Washington, D.C., 1828–1865* (2003).

Nathan O. Hatch, *The Democratization of American Christianity* (1989).

Nancy A. Hewitt, *Women's Activism and Social Change: Rochester, New York, 1822–1872* (1984).

Christine Leigh Heyrman, *Southern Cross: The Beginnings of the Bible Belt* (1997).

Donald M. Jacobs, ed., *Courage and Conscience: Black and White Abolitionists in Boston* (1993).

Julie Roy Jeffrey, *The Great Silent Army of Abolitionism: Ordinary Women in the Antislavery Movement* (1998).

Paul E. Johnson, *A Shopkeeper's Millennium: Society and Revivals in Rochester, New York, 1815–1837* (1978).

Paul E. Johnson and Sean Wilentz, *The Kingdom of Matthias* (1994).

Katharine Du Pré Lumpkin, *The Emancipation of Angelina Grimké* (1974).

Steven Mintz, *Moralists and Modernizers: America's Pre–Civil War Reformers* (1995).

Richard S. Newman, *The Transformation of American Abolitionism: Fighting Slavery in the Early Republic* (2002).

Jane and William H. Pease, *They Who Would Be Free: Blacks' Search for Freedom, 1830–1861* (1990).

Benjamin Quarles, *Black Abolitionists* (1969).

Mary P. Ryan, *Cradle of the Middle Class: The Family in Oneida County, New York, 1790–1865* (1981).

Ian Tyrrell, *Sobering Up: From Temperance to Prohibition in Antebellum America, 1800–1860* (1979).

Jean Fagan Yellin and John C. Van Horne, eds., *The Abolitionist Sisterhood: Women's Political Culture in Antebellum America* (1994).

Jacksonian Politics

Irving H. Bartlett, *John C. Calhoun: A Biography* (1993).

Maurice G. Baxter, *Henry Clay and the American System* (1995).

Hendrik Booraem, *Young Hickory: The Making of Andrew Jackson* (2001).

Donald B. Cole, *The Presidency of Andrew Jackson* (1993).

Richard E. Ellis, *The Union at Risk: Jacksonian Democracy, States' Rights, and the Nullification Crisis* (1987).

Daniel Feller, *The Public Lands in Jacksonian Politics* (1984).

William W. Freehling, *Prelude to Civil War: The Nullification Controversy in South Carolina, 1816–1836* (1965).

Michael F. Holt, *The Rise and Fall of the American Whig Party: Jacksonian Politics and the Onset of the Civil War* (1999).

Peter B. Knupfer, *The Union as It Is: Constitutional Unionism and Sectional Compromise, 1787–1861* (1991).

Richard B. Latner, *The Presidency of Andrew Jackson: White House Politics, 1829–1837* (1979).

John Niven, *Martin Van Buren: The Romantic Age of American Politics* (1983).

John Niven, *John C. Calhoun and the Price of Union: A Biography* (1988).

Lynn Hudson Parsons, *John Quincy Adams* (1998).

Robert V. Remini, *Henry Clay: Statesman for the Union* (1991).

Robert V. Remini, *Daniel Webster: The Man and His Time* (1997).

Leonard Richards, *The Life and Times of Congressman John Quincy Adams* (1986).

Native Americans

William H. Anderson, *Cherokee Removal: Before and After* (1991).

John A. Andrew, *From Revivals to Removal: Jeremiah Evarts, the Cherokee Nation, and the Search for the Soul of America* (1992).

Black Hawk, *Black Hawk's Autobiography* (1999).

John Drinnan, *Facing West: The Metaphysics of Indian Hating and Empire Building* (1981).

John Ehle, *Trail of Tears: The Rise and Fall of the Cherokee Nation* (1997).

David S. Heidler and Jeanne T. Heidler, *Old Hickory's War: Andrew Jackson and the Quest for Empire* (1996).

Roger L. Nichols, *Black Hawk and the Warrior's Path* (1992).

Sean Michael O'Brien, *In Bitterness and in Tears: Andrew Jackson's Destruction of the Creeks and Seminoles* (2003).

Theda Perdue, *Cherokee Women: Gender and Culture Change, 1700–1835* (1998).

Theda Perdue and Michael D. Green, eds., *The Cherokee Removal: A Brief History with Documents* (1995).

Robert V. Remini, *Andrew Jackson and His Indian Wars* (2001).

Michael Paul Rogin, *Fathers and Children: Andrew Jackson and the Subjugation of the American Indian* (1975).

Anders Stephanson, *Manifest Destiny: American Expansionism and the Empire of Right* (1996).

Anthony F. C. Wallace, *The Long, Bitter Trail: Andrew Jackson and the Indians* (1993).

Philip Weeks, *Farewell, My Nation: The American Indian and the United States, 1820–1890* (1990).

J. Leitch Wright, *The Only Land They Knew: The Tragic Story of the American Indians in the Old South* (1981).

GOLD NUGGETS
Gold! Nuggets like these scooped from a California river drove
Easterners crazy with excitement. A quarter of a million people joined
the great rush for western riches in the five years after gold's discovery in 1848. Men from the East and around the world sought to escape
routine jobs and mundane lives by "making their pile" in California.
The carnival that was the gold rush fulfilled the hopes of only a
few, but the rest participated in one of the great adventures of the
nineteenth-century and rarely regretted their experiences.
The Oakland Museum.

The New West and Free North

1840–1860

E ARLY IN NOVEMBER 1842, Abraham Lincoln and his new wife, Mary, moved into their first home in Springfield, Illinois, a rented room measuring eight by fourteen feet on the second floor of the Globe Tavern, the nicest place Abraham had ever lived. A busy blacksmith shop next door filled the Lincolns' room with the clanging of iron being pounded into horseshoes, hinges, and other useful shapes. Mary Todd Lincoln had grown up in Lexington, Kentucky, attended by slaves in the elegant home of her father, a prosperous merchant, banker, and politician. The small, noisy room above the Globe Tavern was the worst place she had ever lived. Fewer than twenty years later, in March 1861, the Lincolns moved into what would prove to be their last home, the presidential mansion in Washington, D.C. Abraham Lincoln climbed from the Globe Tavern to the White House by relentless work, unslaked ambition, and immense talent, traits he had honed since boyhood.

Born in a Kentucky log cabin in 1809, Lincoln grew up on small, struggling farms as his family moved westward. His father, Thomas, moved to Kentucky from Virginia, where he had been born, and he never learned to read or, as Abraham explained, "never did more in the way of writing than to bunglingly sign his own name." Lincoln's mother, Nancy, could neither read nor write. In December 1816, Thomas Lincoln moved his young family out of Kentucky, crossing the Ohio River to the Indiana wilderness. They lived for two frozen months in a crude lean-to only partially enclosed by limbs and bushes while Thomas, a skilled carpenter, built a new cabin. On the Indiana farmstead, Abraham learned the arts of agriculture practiced by families throughout the nation. Although only eight years old, Abraham "had an axe put into his hands at once" and used it "almost constantly" for the next fifteen years, he recalled. He worked for neighbors for twenty-five cents a day and gave the money to his father. When he could be spared from work, the boy attended school, less than a year in all. "There was absolutely nothing to excite ambition for education," Lincoln recollected. In contrast, Mary Todd, his future wife, received ten years of schooling in Lexington's best academies for young women.

By 1830, Thomas Lincoln decided to move farther west and start over again. The Lincolns hitched up the family oxen and headed two hundred miles west to central Illinois, and there they built another log cabin. The next spring Thomas Lincoln moved once again, and this time Abraham stayed behind and set out on his own, a "friendless, uneducated, penniless boy," as he described himself.

Abraham Lincoln's Hat
Abraham Lincoln wore this stovepipe hat, made of beaver pelt, during his years as president of the United States. Stovepipe hats were worn by established, respectable, middle-class men in the 1850s. Workingmen and farmers would have felt out of place wearing such a hat, except perhaps on special occasions like weddings or funerals. Growing up in Kentucky, Indiana, and Illinois, Lincoln may have seen stovepipe hats on the leading men of his community, but he probably never owned one until he became an aspiring Illinois lawyer and politician. Wearing such a hat was a mark that one had achieved a certain success in life, in Lincoln's case the enormous social distance he had traveled from his backwoods origins to the White House. But even as president he continued a backwoods practice he had begun as a young postmaster in New Salem, Illinois, using his hat as a place to store letters and papers. Lincoln's law partner William Herndon termed Lincoln's hat "an extraordinary receptacle [that] served as his desk and memorandum book."
Smithsonian Institution, Washington, D.C.

> By 1850, the boundaries of the United States stretched to the Pacific, and the nation had more than doubled its size.

By dogged striving, Lincoln gained an education and the respect of his Illinois neighbors, although a steady income eluded him for years. He and Mary received help from her father. Shortly after their marriage, he gave the young couple eighty acres of land and promised them a yearly allowance of about $1,100 for six years, helping them to move out of their room above the Globe Tavern. Lincoln eventually built a thriving law practice in Springfield and served in the Illinois legislature and then in Congress. His political activity and hard-driving ambition ultimately catapulted him into the White House, the first president to be born west of the Appalachian Mountains.

Like Lincoln, millions of Americans believed they could make something of themselves, whatever their origins, so long as they were willing to work. Individuals who refused to work—who were lazy, improvident, or foolish—had only themselves to blame if they failed. Work was a prerequisite for success, not a guarantee. The promise of rewards from hard work spurred efforts that shaped the contours of America, pushing the boundaries of the nation south to the Rio Grande, north to the Great Lakes, and ever westward from Indiana, Illinois, Iowa, and Kansas to Texas, Oregon, California, and the Pacific Ocean. During his presidency, Lincoln himself talked about moving to California at the end of his term. The economic, political, and geographic expansion that Lincoln exemplified raised anew the question of whether slavery should also move west, the question that Lincoln and other Americans confronted again and again following the Mexican War, yet another outgrowth of the nation's ceaseless westward movement.

The Westward Movement

Westward expansion was nothing new in American history, but the 1840s ushered in a new era of rapid westward movement. Until then, the overwhelming majority of Americans lived east of the Mississippi River. To the west, Native Americans inhabited the plains, prairies, and deserts to the rugged coasts of the Pacific. The British claimed Oregon Country, and the Mexican flag flew over the vast expanse of the Southwest. But by 1850, the boundaries of the United States stretched to the Pacific, and the nation had more than doubled its size. By 1860, the great migration had carried four million Americans west of the Mississippi River.

Thomas Jefferson, John Quincy Adams, and other government officials had helped clear the way for the march across the continent by aggressively acquiring territory in the west. The nation's revolution in transportation and communication, its swelling population, and its booming economy propelled the westward surge. But the emigrants themselves conquered the continent. Shock troops of the American empire, **frontier** settlers craving land took the soil and then, with the exception of the Mormons in Deseret, lobbied their government to follow them with the flag. The human cost of westward expansion was high. The young Mexican nation suffered a humiliating defeat and the loss of half its territory. Two centuries of Indian wars east of the Mississippi ended during the 1830s, but the old, fierce struggle between native inhabitants and invaders continued for another half century in the West.

Manifest Destiny

Most Americans believed that the superiority of their institutions and white culture bestowed on them a God-given right to spread their civilization across the continent. They imagined the West as a howling wilderness, empty and undeveloped. If they recognized Indians and Mexicans at all, they dismissed them as primitive drags on progress who would have to be redeemed, shoved aside, or exterminated. The sense of uniqueness and mission was as old as the Puritans, but by the 1840s the conviction of superiority had been bolstered by the United States's amazing success. The West needed the civilizing power of the hammer and plow, the ballot box and pulpit, that had transformed the East, most Americans believed.

In 1845, New York journalist John L. O'Sullivan coined the term **manifest destiny** as the latest justification for white settlers to take the land they coveted. Although O'Sullivan was only an armchair expansionist, he took second place to no one in his passion for conquest of the West. He called on Americans to resist any foreign power—British, French, or Mexican—that attempted to thwart "the fulfillment of our manifest destiny to overspread the continent allotted

In the Mountains, **Albert Bierstadt, 1867**
Born and trained in Germany, Albert Bierstadt visited the American West for the first time in 1859 with a U.S. government expedition searching for shortcuts along the Oregon Trail. The Rocky Mountains captured his imagination. He portrays a new Eden, an epic landscape of spectacular beauty that silently beckons a restless, questing young nation. Bountiful, empty, lacking any marks of civilization, Bierstadt's West shimmers in a golden light, a kind of divine sanction of manifest destiny. The writer Mark Twain claimed that Bierstadt's landscapes were more beautiful than even the Creator's, but he lamented that the artist strayed from factual accuracy. Indeed, Bierstadt painted his dramatic images back in his New York studio (or even in Europe), where he was less interested in accuracy than in creating a romantic visual metaphor for America's national potential.
The Wadsworth Atheneum, Hartford. Gift of John J. Morgan in memory of his mother, Juliet Pierpont Morgan.

by Providence for the free development of our yearly multiplying millions . . . [and] for the development of the great experiment of liberty and federative self-government entrusted to us." Almost overnight, the magic phrase *manifest destiny* swept the nation and provided an ideological shield for conquering the West.

As important as national pride and racial arrogance were to manifest destiny, economic gain made up its core. Land hunger drew hundreds of thousands of average Americans westward. Some politicians, moreover, had become convinced that national prosperity depended on capturing the rich trade of the Far East. To trade with Asia, the United States needed the Pacific coast ports that stretched from San Francisco to Puget Sound. No one was more eager to extend American trade in the Pacific than Missouri's Senator Thomas Hart Benton. "The sun of civilization must shine across the sea: socially and commercially," he declared. The United States and Asia must "talk together, and trade together. Commerce is a great civilizer." In the 1840s, American economic expansion came wrapped in the rhetoric of uplift and civilization.

Oregon and the Overland Trail

Oregon Country—a vast region bounded on the west by the Pacific, on the east by the Rockies, on the south by the forty-second parallel, and on the north by Russian Alaska—caused the pulse of American expansionists to race (Map 12.1). But Americans were not alone in hungrily eyeing the Pacific Northwest. The British traced their interest—and their rights—to the voyage of Sir Francis Drake, who, they argued, discovered the Oregon coast in 1579. Americans matched the British assertion with historic claims of their own. Unable to agree on ownership, the United States and Great Britain decided in 1818 on "joint occupation" that would leave Oregon "free and open" to settlement by both countries. A handful of American fur traders and "mountain men" roamed the region in the 1820s, but in the 1830s and 1840s expansionists made Oregon Country an early target of manifest destiny.

By the late 1830s, settlers began to trickle along the Oregon Trail, following a path blazed

Plains Indians and Trails West in the 1840s and 1850s

by the mountain men. The first wagon trains hit the trail in 1841, and by 1843 about 1,000 emigrants a year set out from Independence, Missouri. By 1869, when the first transcontinental railroad was completed, something like 350,000 migrants had traveled west to the Pacific in wagon trains.

Emigrants encountered Plains Indians, whose cultures differed markedly from those of the Eastern Woodland tribes (see chapter 1). The quarter of a million Native Americans who populated the area between the Rocky Mountains and the Mississippi River defy easy generalization. Some were farmers who lived peaceful, sedentary lives, but a majority of Plains Indians—the Sioux, Cheyenne, Shoshone, and Arapaho of the central Plains and the Kiowa, Wichita, Apache, and Comanche in the Southwest—were horse-mounted, nomadic, nonagricultural peoples whose warriors symbolized the "savage Indian" in the minds of whites.

Horses, which had been brought to North America by Spaniards in the sixteenth century, permitted the Plains tribes to become highly mobile hunters of buffalo. In time, they came to depend on buffalo for most of their food, clothing, shelter, and fuel. As they followed the huge herds over the plains, these peoples bumped into one another. Competition and warfare became crucial components of their way of life. Young men were introduced to the art of war early, learning to ride ponies at breakneck speed while firing off arrows and, later, rifles with astounding accuracy. "A Comanche on his feet is out of his element," observed George Catlin, an artist of the West, "but the moment he lays his hands upon his horse, his *face* even becomes handsome, and he gracefully flies away like a different being."

Plains Indians struck fear in the hearts of whites on the wagon trains. But Native Americans had far more to fear from whites. Indians killed fewer than 400 emigrants on the trail between 1840 and 1860, while whites proved to be deadly to the Indians. Even though

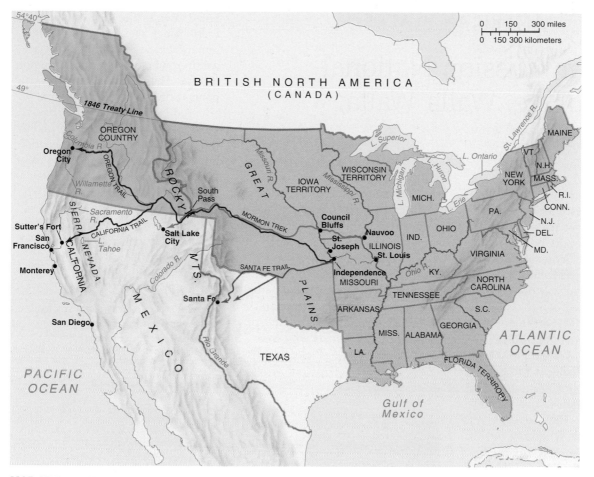

MAP 12.1 Trails to the West
In the 1830s, wagon trains began snaking their way to the Southwest and the Pacific coast. Deep ruts, some of which can still be seen today, soon marked the most popular routes.

they were usually just passing through on their way to the Pacific Slope, whites brought alcohol and disease, especially epidemics of smallpox, measles, cholera, and scarlet fever. Moreover, whites killed the buffalo, often slaughtering them for sport. Buffalo still numbered some twelve million in 1860, but the herds were shrinking rapidly, intensifying conflict among the Plains Indians.

As the number of wagon trains increased, emigrants insisted that the federal government provide them more protection. The government responded by constructing a chain of forts along the Oregon Trail. More important, the United States adopted a new Indian policy: "concentration." The government rescinded the "permanent" buffer it had granted the Indians west of the ninety-fifth meridian, which was only two or three hundred miles west of the Mississippi River. Then, in 1851, it called the Plains tribes to a

conference at Fort Laramie, Wyoming. Some ten thousand Dakota, Sioux, Arapaho, Cheyenne, Crow, and other Indians showed up, hopeful that something could be done to protect them from the ravages of the wagon trains. Instead, U.S. government negotiators persuaded the chiefs to sign agreements that cleared a wide corridor for wagon trains by restricting Native Americans to specific areas that whites promised they would never violate. This policy of concentration became the seedbed for the subsequent policy of reservations. But whites would not keep out of Indian territory, and Indians would not easily give up their traditional ways of life. (See "American Places," page 400.) Competition meant warfare for decades to come.

> Whites would not keep out of Indian territory, and Indians would not easily give up their traditional ways of life.

AMERICAN PLACES

Whitman Mission National Historic Site, Walla Walla, Washington

In 1836, Marcus and Narcissa Whitman, Presbyterian missionaries from New York, joined a group of fur trappers bound for Oregon Country. Scores of other missionaries would follow, but Narcissa Whitman was one of the first two white women to cross the continent overland. Settling among the Cayuse Indians near present-day Walla Walla, Washington, the Whitmans established a mission station to promote Christianity and "civilization." Their efforts created tensions with the Cayuse, especially in the 1840s when the mission became a stop for wagon trains traveling the Oregon Trail. The newcomers slaughtered game, took Indian land, and inadvertently brought disease. When a measles outbreak in 1847 killed nearly half of the local Cayuse, the survivors blamed the whites and attacked the mission, killing the Whitmans and eleven others. News of the murders shocked the nation and prompted Congress to make Oregon a U.S. territory. It also reinforced in easterners' imaginations links between Indians, heathenism, violence, and the West.

Since 1936, the National Park Service has managed the 98-acre Whitman Mission site. Visitors can walk a portion of the old Oregon Trail, which runs through the property. The foundations of the original buildings are visible, and outdoor exhibits revive for visitors the feel of the mission in the 1840s. The Cayuse called the area Waiilatpu, "Place of the Rye Grass," and the Park Service has restored the natural grasses to the site. The Whitman Mission also preserves the grave of the thirteen individuals who were killed. Two of the thirteen, John and Frank Sager, were members of the remarkable Sager family of seven children who arrived at the mission in 1844. The children were orphaned on the Oregon Trail and adopted by Marcus and Narcissa Whitman. The 1847 attack orphaned the five surviving Sagers a second time. The Sager story reminds us of the risks families took when they struck out on the Oregon Trail. The Whitman site exemplifies the violence that so often accompanied the clash of cultures and interests between U.S. citizens and Native Americans in the West.

FOR WEB LINKS RELATED TO THIS SITE AND OTHER AMERICAN PLACES, see "PlaceLinks" at bedfordstmartins.com/roark.

Whitman Mission Reenactors on the Oregon Trail
Whitman Mission National Historic Site.

Still, Indians threatened emigrants less than life on the trail did. The men, women, and children who headed west each spring could count on at least six months of grueling travel. With nearly two thousand miles to go and traveling no more than fifteen miles a day, the pioneers endured parching heat, drought, treacherous rivers, disease, physical and emotional exhaustion, and, if the snows closed the mountain passes before they got through, freezing and starvation. Women sometimes faced the dangers of trailside childbirth. It was said that a person could walk from Missouri to the Pacific stepping only on the graves of those who had died heading west.

Everyone experienced hardships on the trail, but no one felt the burden quite as much as the women. Because husbands usually made the decision to pull up stakes and go west, many wives went involuntarily. One miserable woman, trying to keep her children dry in a rainstorm and to calm them as they listened to Indian shouts, wondered "what had possessed my husband, anyway, that he should have thought of bringing us away out through this God forsaken country." Men viewed the privation as a necessary step to land of their own and an independent life; women tended to judge it by the homes, kin, and friends they had left behind to take up what one called "this wild goose chase."

When men reached Oregon, they usually liked what they found. Oregon is "one of the greatest countries in the world," Richard R. Howard declared. From "the Cascade mountains to the Pacific, the whole country can be cultivated." When women reached Oregon, they found a wilderness. "I had all I could do to keep from asking George to turn around and bring me back home," one woman wrote to her mother in Missouri. Neighbors were few and far between, and the isolation weighed heavily. Moreover, things were in a "primitive state." One young wife set up housekeeping with her new husband with only one stew kettle and three knives. Necessity blurred the traditional division between men's and women's work. "I am maid of all traids," one busy woman remarked in 1853. Work seemed unending. "I am a very old woman," remarked twenty-nine-year-old Sarah Everett. "My face is thin sunken and wrinkled, my hands bony withered and hard." As another settler observed, "A woman that can not endure almost as much as a horse has no business here."

***Kee-O-Kuk, the Watchful Fox, Chief of the Tribe*, George Catlin, 1835**
In the 1830s, Pennsylvania-born artist George Catlin traveled the West painting Native American portraits, rituals, and landscapes. Although not the first artist to paint Indians, he was the first to portray them in their own environments and one of the few to present them as human beings, not savages. Convinced that western Indian cultures would soon disappear, Catlin sought to document Indian life through hundreds of paintings and prints. Keokuk, chief of the Sac and Fox, struggled with the warrior Black Hawk about the proper strategy for dealing with whites. Black Hawk fought American expansion; Keokuk believed war was fruitless and signed over land in Illinois, Missouri, and Wisconsin.
Smithsonian American Art Institution, Washington, D.C. Gift of Mrs. Joseph Harrison Jr.

Despite the ordeal of the trail and the difficulties of starting from scratch, emigrants kept coming. By 1845, Oregon counted 5,000 American settlers. And from the beginning, they clamored for the protection of the U.S. government.

The Mormon Exodus

Not every wagon train heading west was bound for the Pacific Slope. One remarkable group of religious emigrants chose to settle in the heart of the arid West. Halting near the Great Salt Lake in what was then Mexican territory, the Mormons deliberately chose the remote site as a refuge. After years of persecution in the East, they fled west to find religious freedom and communal security.

In 1830, Joseph Smith Jr., who was only twenty-four, published *The Book of Mormon* and founded the Church of Jesus Christ of Latter-Day Saints (the Mormons). A decade earlier, the upstate New York farm boy had begun to have visions and revelations that were followed, he

Pioneer Family on the Trail West

In 1860, W. G. Chamberlain photographed these unidentified travelers momentarily at rest by the upper Arkansas River in Colorado. We do not know their fates, but we can hope that they fared better than the Sager family: Henry, Naomi, and their six children, who set out from St. Joseph, Missouri, in 1844. "Father," one of Henry and Naomi's daughters remembered, "was one of those restless men who are not content to remain in one place long at a time. [He] had been talking of going to Texas. But mother, hearing much said about the healthfulness of Oregon, preferred to go there." Still far from Oregon, Henry Sager died of fever; twenty-six days later, Naomi died, leaving seven children, the last delivered on the trail. The Sager children, under the care of other families in the wagon train, pressed on. After traveling 2,000 miles in seven months, the migrants arrived in Oregon, where Marcus and Narcissa Whitman, whose own daughter had drowned, adopted all seven of the Sager children.

Denver Public Library, Western History Division # F3226.

FOR MORE HELP ANALYZING THIS IMAGE, see the visual activity for this chapter in the Online Study Guide at bedfordstmartins.com/roark.

said, by a visit from an angel who led him to golden tablets buried near his home. With the aid of magic stones, Smith translated the mysterious language on the tablets. What was revealed was *The Book of Mormon*. It told the story of an ancient Christian civilization in the New World and predicted the appearance of an American prophet who would reestablish Jesus Christ's undefiled kingdom in America. Converts, attracted to the promise of a pure faith in the midst of **antebellum** America's social turmoil and rampant materialism, flocked to the new church.

Neighbors branded Mormons heretics, and persecution drove Smith and his followers from New York to Ohio, then to Missouri, and finally in 1839 to Nauvoo, Illinois, where they built a prosperous community of fifteen thousand. But dissenters within the church accused Smith of advocating plural marriage (polygamy) and published an exposé of the practice. Non-Mormons caught wind of the controversy and eventually arrested Smith and his brother. On June 27, 1844, a mob stormed the jail and shot both men dead.

The embattled church turned to an extraordinary new leader, Brigham Young, who immediately began to plan the exodus of his people from Illinois. In 1846, traveling in 3,700 wagons, 12,000 Mormons made their way to eastern Iowa; the following year they arrived at their new home beside the Great Salt Lake. Young described the region as a barren waste, "the paradise of the lizard, the cricket and the rattlesnake." Within ten years, however, the Mormons developed an extensive irrigation system and made the desert bloom. They accomplished the feat through cooperative labor, not the individualistic and competitive enterprise common among most emigrants. Under the stern leadership of Young and other church leaders, the Mormons built a thriving community.

In 1850, only three years after its founding, Deseret, as the Mormons called their kingdom, became annexed to the United States as Utah Territory. But what focused the nation's attention on the Latter-Day Saints was the announcement by Brigham Young in 1852 that many Mormons practiced polygamy. Although only one Mormon man in five had more than one wife (Young had twenty-three), Young's public statement caused an outcry that forced the U.S. government to establish its authority in Utah. In 1857, 2,500 U.S. troops invaded Salt Lake City in what was known as the Mormon War. The bloodless occupation illustrates that most Americans viewed the Mormons as a threat to American morality, law, and institutions. The invasion did not dislodge the Mormon Church from its central place in Utah, however, and for years to come most Americans perceived the Mormon settlement as a strange and suitably isolated place.

The Mexican Borderlands

In the Mexican Southwest, westward-moving Anglo-American pioneers confronted northern-moving Spanish-speaking frontiersmen. On this frontier of brush country, deserts, and mountains, as elsewhere, national cultures, interests, and aspirations collided. Since 1821, when Mexico won its independence from Spain, the Mexican flag had flown over the vast expanse that stretched from the Gulf of Mexico to the Pacific and from Oregon Country to Guatemala (Map 12.2). Mexico's borders remained ill defined, and its northern provinces were sparsely populated. Moreover, severe problems plagued the young nation: civil wars, economic crises, quarrels with the Roman Catholic Church, and devastating raids by the Comanche, Apache, and Kiowa. Mexico

found it increasingly difficult to defend its borderlands, especially when faced with a northern neighbor convinced of its superiority and bent on territorial acquisition.

The American assault began quietly. In the 1820s, Anglo-American trappers, traders, and settlers drifted into Mexico's far northern provinces and discovered that their newly independent neighbor was eager for American business. Santa Fe, a remote outpost in the province of New Mexico, became a magnet for American enterprise. Each spring, American traders gathered at Independence, Missouri, for the long trek southwest along the Santa Fe Trail (see Map 12.1). They crammed their wagons with inexpensive American manufactured goods and returned home with Mexican silver, furs, and mules.

The Mexican province of Texas attracted a flood of Americans who had settlement, not long-distance trade, on their minds (see Map 12.2). The Mexican government, which wanted

> In the Mexican Southwest, Anglo-American pioneers confronted Spanish-speaking frontiersmen. On this frontier as elsewhere, cultures, interests, and aspirations collided.

MAP 12.2 Texas and Mexico in the 1830s

As Americans spilled into lightly populated and loosely governed northern Mexico, Texas and then other Mexican provinces became contested territory.

Surveying Texas Land, **Theodore Gentilz, c. 1844**
Land has always bred conflict in Texas. The new republic (1836–1845) wrestled with a confusing variety of Spanish, Mexican, and Texas claims, surveys, and titles. In this painting, Theodore Gentilz portrays the efforts of surveyor John James to settle thorny landownership issues. Five years later, Texas governor P. H. Bell could still observe: "There is no subject which addresses itself more forcibly . . . than that of settling upon a secure and permanent basis the land titles of the country."
Courtesy Mr. Larry Sheerin.

to populate and develop its northern territory, granted the American Stephen F. Austin a huge tract of land along the Brazos River, and in the 1820s he became the first Anglo-American *empresario* (colonization agent) in Texas. Land was cheap—only ten cents an acre—and thousands of farmers poured across the border. Most of the migrants were Southerners, who brought cotton and slaves with them. By 1835, the American settlers had established a thriving plantation economy and numbered—free and slave—thirty-five thousand, while the *Tejano* (Spanish-speaking) population was less than eight thousand. Most Anglo-American settlers were not Roman Catholic, did not speak Spanish, and cared little about assimilating into a culture that

was so different from their own. In 1829, the Mexican government sought to halt further immigration by outlawing slavery, which it hoped would make Texas less attractive. The settlers sidestepped the decree by calling their slaves servants, but settlers had other grievances, most significantly the puny voice they had in local government. General Antonio López de Santa Anna all but extinguished that voice when he seized political power and concentrated authority in Mexico City.

Faced with what they considered tyranny, the Texan settlers rebelled and declared the independent Republic of Texas. Santa Anna ordered the Mexican army northward and in February 1836 arrived at the outskirts of San Antonio.

The rebels, who included the Tennessee frontiersman David Crockett and the Louisiana adventurer James Bowie, as well as a number of Tejanos, took refuge in a former Franciscan mission known as the Alamo. When Santa Anna's siege failed, he sent wave after wave of his 4,000-man army crashing against the walls until the attackers finally broke through and killed all 187 defenders. A few weeks later in the small town of Goliad, Mexican forces surrounded and captured a garrison of Texans. Following orders from Santa Anna, Mexican firing squads executed more than 300 of the men as "pirates." Then in April 1836 at San Jacinto, General Sam Houston's army adopted the massacre at Goliad as a battle cry and produced a crushing defeat of Santa Anna's troops. Texans had succeeded in establishing their Lone Star Republic, and the following year the United States recognized the independence of Texas from Mexico.

Texas War for Independence, 1836

The distant Mexican province of California also caught the eye of a few Anglo-Americans. In 1824, in an effort to increase Mexican migration to thinly settled California, the Mexican government granted *ranchos*—huge estates devoted to cattle raising—to new settlers. *Rancheros* ruled over near-feudal empires worked by Indians whose condition sometimes approached that of slaves. Not satisfied, *rancheros* coveted the vast lands controlled by the Franciscan missions. In 1834, they persuaded the Mexican government to confiscate the missions and make their lands available to new settlement, a development that accelerated the decline of California Indians. Devastated by disease, the Indians, who numbered approximately 300,000 when the Spanish arrived in 1769, declined to half that number by 1846.

Despite the efforts of the Mexican government, California in 1840 counted a population of only 7,000 Mexican settlers. Non-Mexican settlers numbered only 380, but among them were Americans who championed manifest destiny. Thomas O. Larkin, a prosperous merchant, John Marsh, a successful *ranchero* in the San Joaquin Valley, and others became boosters who sought to attract Americans from Oregon Country to California. The first overland party arrived in California in 1841. Thereafter, wagon after wagon followed the California Trail, which forked off from the Oregon Trail near the Snake River and led through the Sierra Nevada at Lake Tahoe (see Map 12.1). As the trickle of Americans became a river, Mexican officials grew alarmed, for as a New York newspaper put it in 1845, "Let the tide of emigration flow toward California and the American population will soon be sufficiently numerous to play the Texas game." Only a few Americans in California looked forward to separatist war, but many dreamed of living again under the American flag.

The U.S. government made no secret of its desire to acquire California. In 1835, President Andrew Jackson tried to purchase it. In 1842, Commodore Thomas Catesby Jones, hearing a rumor that the United States and Mexico were at war, seized the port of Monterey and ran up the American flag. The red-faced officer promptly ran it down again when he learned of his error, but his actions left no doubt about Washington's intentions. In 1846, American settlers in the Sacramento Valley took matters into their own hands. Prodded by John C. Frémont, a former army captain and explorer who had arrived in December 1845 with a party of sixty buckskin-clad frontiersmen spoiling for a fight, the Californians raised an independence movement known as the Bear Flag Revolt. By then, James K. Polk, a champion of expansion, sat in the White House.

Expansion and the Mexican-American War

Although emigrants acted as the advance guard of American empire, there was nothing automatic about the U.S. annexation of territory in the West. Acquiring territory required political action, and in the 1840s the difficult problems of Texas, Oregon, and the Mexican borderlands intruded into national politics. The politics of expansion became entangled with sectionalism and the slavery question and thrust the United States into dangerous diplomatic crises with Great Britain and Mexico.

Aggravation between Mexico and the United States escalated to open antagonism in 1845 when the United States annexed Texas. Absorbing territory still claimed by Mexico ruptured diplomatic relations between the two countries and set the stage for war. But it was President James K. Polk's insistence on having Mexico's other northern provinces that made war certain. The war was not as easy as Polk anticipated, but it ended in American victory and the acquisition of a new American West.

The Politics of Expansion

The complicated issues of westward expansion and the nation's boundaries ended up on the desk of John Tyler when he became president in April 1841. The Whig William Henry Harrison had been elected president in 1840 but died one month after taking office. Tyler, nominally a Whig but actually a Democrat in his political convictions, spent much of his administration beating back Henry Clay's efforts to turn the Whig Party's American System—protective tariffs, a national bank, and internal improvements—into law. But the issue that stirred Tyler's blood, and that of much of the nation, was Texas. Texans had sought admission to the Union almost since winning their independence from Mexico in 1836. Tyler, an ardent expansionist, understood that Texas was a dangerous issue: Any suggestion of adding another slave state to the Union would bring many Northerners to a boil. Annexing Texas also risked precipitating war because Mexico had never relinquished its claim to its lost province.

Cold-shouldered by the United States, Texans explored Great Britain's interest in recognition. Britain was eager to keep Texas independent. In Britain's eyes, Texas provided a buffer against American expansion and also a new market for English manufactured goods. American officials worried that Britain's real objective was to add Texas to the British Empire. Southerners knew that if Britain, the leading abolitionist power in the world, gained Texas, the westward expansion of slavery would end. This volatile mix of threat, fear, and opportunity convinced Tyler to risk negotiations with Texas, and he worked vigorously to annex the republic before his term expired. His efforts pushed Texas and the slavery issue to the center of national politics.

In April 1844, after months of secret negotiations between Texas and the Tyler administration, Secretary of State John C. Calhoun laid an annexation treaty before the Senate. But when Calhoun linked annexation to the defense of slavery, he doomed the treaty. Howls of protest erupted across the North. Michigan politician Lewis Cass described Calhoun's proposal as an "avalanche." In Massachusetts, future senator Charles Sumner deplored the "insidious" plan to annex Texas and carve from it "great slaveholding states." The Senate soundly rejected the treaty, and it appeared that Tyler had succeeded only in inflaming sectional conflict.

The issue of Texas had not died down by the 1844 elections. Henry Clay looked forward to receiving the Whig presidential nomination and waging his campaign on the old Whig economic principles that Tyler had frustrated. In an effort to appeal to northern voters, Clay came out against the immediate annexation of Texas. "Annexation and war with Mexico are identical," he declared. When news of Clay's statement reached Andrew Jackson at his plantation in Tennessee, he chuckled, "Clay [is] a dead political Duck." In Jackson's shrewd judgment, no man who opposed annexation could be elected president. Nevertheless, the Whig Party nominated Clay.

The Democrats chose Tennessean James K. Polk, who was as strong for the annexation of Texas as Clay was against it. To make Texas annexation palatable to Northerners, the Democrats shrewdly yoked Texas to Oregon, thus tapping the desire for expansion in the free states of the North as well in the slave states of the South. The Democratic platform called for the "reannexation of Texas" and the "reoccupation of Oregon." The suggestion that the United States was merely reasserting existing rights was poor history but good politics. According to the Democratic formula, the annexation of Texas would not give an advantage to slavery and the South; instead, linked to Oregon, Texas would expand America to the advantage of the entire nation.

> Texas was a dangerous issue: Any suggestion of adding another slave state to the Union would bring many Northerners to a boil.

During the campaign, Clay finally recognized the groundswell for expansion, and he waffled, hinting that under certain circumstances he might accept annexation. His retreat won little support in the South and succeeded only in alienating antislavery opinion in the North. James G. Birney, the candidate of the fledgling Liberty Party, picked up the votes of thousands of disillusioned Clay supporters. In the November election, Polk received 170 electoral votes and Clay 105. New York's 35 electoral votes proved critical to Clay's defeat. A shift of just one-third of Birney's 15,000 votes to Clay would have given Clay the state and the presidency.

On March 4, 1845, James K. Polk, at age forty-nine, became the youngest president in the nation's history. In his inaugural address, he offered a ringing reaffirmation of aggressive **nationalism** and manifest destiny. "This heaven-favored land," Polk declared, enjoyed the "most admirable and wisest system of well-regulated self-government . . . ever devised by human minds." And he asked, "Who shall assign limits to the achievements of free minds and free hands under the protection of this glorious Union?"

The nation did not have to wait for Polk's inauguration to see results from his victory. One month after the election, President Tyler announced that the triumph of the Democratic Party provided a mandate for the annexation of Texas "promptly and immediately." In February 1845, after a fierce debate between antislavery and proslavery forces, Congress approved a joint resolution offering the Republic of Texas admission to the United States. Texas entered as the fifteenth slave state.

Tyler delivered Texas, but Polk had promised Oregon, too. Westerners particularly demanded that the new president make good on the Democrats' pledge—"Fifty-four Forty or Fight"—that is, all of Oregon, right up to Alaska (54°40' was the southern latitude of Russian Alaska). But Polk was close to war with Mexico and could not afford a simultaneous war with Britain over U.S. claims in Canada. After the initial bluster, therefore, Polk muted the all-of-Oregon refrain and renewed an old offer to divide Oregon along the forty-ninth parallel. When Britain accepted the compromise, some cried betrayal, but most Americans celebrated the agreement that gave the nation an enormous territory peacefully. Besides, when the Senate finally approved the treaty in June 1846, the United States and Mexico were already at war.

Polk and Dallas Banner, 1844

In 1844, Democratic presidential nominee James K. Polk and vice presidential nominee George M. Dallas campaigned under this cotton banner. The extra star spilling over into the red and white stripes symbolizes Polk's vigorous support for annexing the huge slave republic of Texas, which had declared independence from Mexico eight years earlier. Henry Clay, Polk's Whig opponent, ran under a banner that was similar but conspicuously lacked the additional star. Collection of Janice L. and David J. Frent.

The Mexican-American War, 1846–1848

From the day he entered the White House, Polk craved Mexico's remaining northern provinces: California and New Mexico, land that today makes up California, Nevada, and Utah, most of New Mexico and Arizona, and parts of Wyoming and Colorado. Polk hoped to buy the territory, but the Mexicans refused to sell. Furious, Polk concluded that military force would be needed to realize the United States's manifest destiny.

Polk had already ordered General Zachary Taylor to march his 4,000-man army of occupation of Texas from its position on the Nueces River, the southern boundary of Texas according to the Mexicans, 150 miles south, to the banks of the Rio Grande, the boundary claimed by Texans (Map 12.3). Viewing the American advance as aggression, the Mexican general in Matamoros ordered Taylor back to the Nueces. Taylor refused, and on April 25 Mexican cavalry attacked a party of American soldiers, killing or wounding sixteen and capturing the rest. Even before news of the battle arrived in Washington, Polk had already obtained his cabinet's approval of a war message.

On May 11, 1846, the president told Congress, "Mexico has passed the boundary of the United States, has invaded our territory, and shed American blood upon American soil." Thus "war exists, and, notwithstanding all our efforts to avoid it, exists by the act of Mexico herself." Two days later, Congress passed a declaration of war and began raising an army. Despite years of saber rattling toward Mexico and Britain, the U.S. army was pitifully small, only 8,600 soldiers. Faced with the nation's first foreign war, against a Mexican army that numbered more than 30,000, Polk called for volunteers. Of the men who rushed to the colors, 40 percent were immigrants and a third of them were illiterate. Eventually, more than 112,000 white Americans (blacks were banned) joined the army to fight in Mexico.

> Despite the outpouring of support, the Mexican-American War divided the nation.

Despite the outpouring of support, the war divided the nation. Northern Whigs in particular loudly condemned the war as the unwarranted bullying of a weak nation by its greedy expansionist neighbor. The Massachusetts legislature declared that the war was being fought for the "triple object of extending slavery, of strengthening the slave power, and of obtaining control of the free states." On January 12, 1848, a gangly freshman Whig representative from Illinois rose from his back-row seat in the House of Representatives to deliver his first important speech in Congress. Before Abraham Lincoln sat down, he had questioned Polk's intelligence, honesty, and sanity. The president simply ignored the upstart representative, but antislavery, antiwar Whigs kept up the attack throughout the conflict. In their effort to undercut national support, they labeled it "Mr. Polk's War."

Since most Americans backed the war, it was not really Polk's war, but the president acted as if it were. Although he had no military experience, he directed the war personally. Working eighteen hours a day, Polk established overall strategy and oversaw the details of military campaigns. He planned a short war in which U.S. armies would occupy Mexico's northern provinces and defeat the Mexican army in a decisive battle or two, after which Mexico would sue for peace and the United States would keep the territory its armies occupied.

At first, Polk's strategy seemed to work. In May 1846, Zachary Taylor's troops drove south from the Rio Grande and routed the Mexican army, first on the plain of Palo Alto and then in vicious hand-to-hand fighting in a palm-filled ravine known as Resaca de la Palma (see Map 12.3). "Old Rough and Ready," as Taylor was af-

Shako Hat

American soldiers fighting in the Mexican-American War were a colorful lot. U.S. army regulars wore as a dress uniform a dark blue wool tailcoat and sky-blue wool trousers, topped with the shako, a full-dress cap made of leather, crowned with black feathers, and adorned with a decorative plate showing the eagle spreading its wings—the symbol of manifest destiny.

One veteran criticized the army for "dressing up men within an inch of their lives, until they looked more like a flock of eastern flamingos . . . than the descendants of the race of men who fought and bled to establish civil liberty and republican simplicity in our country." General Winfield Scott—his men nicknamed him "Old Fuss and Feathers"—expected his troops to follow "regulations of dress, hair, whiskers, and so forth." Other commanders, most notably General Zachary Taylor, were notoriously lax, especially for volunteer troops, who were required to furnish their own uniforms. One junior officer serving under Taylor observed: "We wear all kinds of uniforms here, each one to his taste, some shirtsleeves, some white, some purple, some fancy jackets and all colors of cottonelle pants, some straw and some Quaker hats, and that is just the way, too, that our fellows went into battle."
Chicago Historical Society.

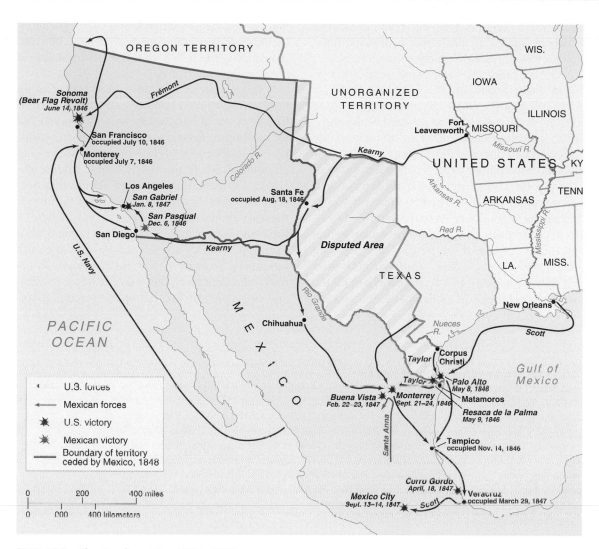

MAP 12.3 The Mexican War, 1846–1848
American and Mexican soldiers skirmished across much of northern Mexico, but the major battles took place between the Rio Grande and Mexico City.

fectionately known among his adoring troops, became an instant war hero. Polk rewarded Taylor for his victories by making him commander of the Mexican campaign.

A second prong of the campaign to occupy Mexico's northern provinces centered on Colonel Stephen Watts Kearny, who led a 1,700-man army from Missouri into New Mexico. Without firing a shot, U.S. forces took Santa Fe in August 1846. Kearny promptly proclaimed New Mexico U.S. territory. Polk ordered him on to California. On the trail, Kearny met Kit Carson, part of John C. Frémont's buckskin army. Carson mistakenly informed him that California was al-

ready secured. Pushing on with only 300 troops, Kearny three months later marched into San Diego and into a major Mexican rebellion against American rule. In January 1847, after several clashes and severe losses, the U.S. forces occupied Los Angeles. California and New Mexico were in American hands.

By then, Taylor had driven deep into the interior of Mexico. In September 1846, after a five-day siege and house-to-house fighting, he took the fortified city of Monterrey. With reinforcements and fresh supplies, Taylor pushed his 5,000 troops southwest, where the Mexican hero of the Alamo, General Antonio López de Santa

Anna, was concentrating an army of 21,000, which he hoped would strike a decisive blow against the numerically inferior invaders.

On February 23, 1847, Santa Anna's troops began their assault at Buena Vista. Superior American artillery and accurate musket fire won the day, but the Americans suffered heavy casualties, including Henry Clay Jr., the son of the man who had opposed Texas annexation for fear it would precipitate war. The Mexicans suffered even greater losses (some 3,400 dead, wounded, and missing compared with 650 Americans), and during the night Santa Anna withdrew his battered army from the battlefield, much to the "profound disgust of the troops," one Mexican officer remembered. "They are filled with grief that they were going to lose the benefit of all the sacrifices that they had made; that the conquered field would be abandoned, and that the victory would be given to the enemy." Retreat, he complained, fed the belief "that it was impossible to conquer the Americans."

The series of uninterrupted victories in northern Mexico certainly fed the American troops' sense of superiority and very nearly led to a feeling of invincibility. "No American force has ever thought of being defeated by any amount of Mexican troops," one soldier declared. The Americans worried about other hazards, however. "I can assure you that fighting is the least dangerous & arduous part of a soldier's life," one young man said. Letters home told of torturous marches across arid wastes alive with tarantulas, scorpions, and rattlesnakes. Others recounted dysentery, malaria, smallpox, cholera, and yellow fever. One out of every ten U.S. sol-

---

Battala del Sacramento, Michaud y Thomas

Most images of the Mexican-American War were created by artists from the United States, but Mexicans also recorded the war. In this hand-colored lithograph, Mexican artist Michaud y Thomas offers his interpretation of the battle that took place in February 1847 when 1,100 American troops engaged 3,000 Mexicans on the banks of the Sacramento River in northern Mexico. Thomas accurately portrays the first moments of the bold Mexican cavalry charge at the American center, but he neglects to finish the story. American artillery forced the Mexican lancers to retreat, with "great confusion in their ranks." When the fighting ended, 700 Mexicans had been killed, wounded, or captured. American forces lost one man killed and six wounded. The battle made a national hero of the American commander, Colonel Alexander Doniphan, who watched the battle with one leg hooked around his saddle horn, whittling a stick in full view of the enemy.

Yale Collection of Western Americana, Beinecke Rare Book and Manuscript Library.

diers died while in Mexico. Of the 13,000 American soldiers who died (some 50,000 Mexicans died), fewer than 2,000 fell to Mexican bullets and shells. Disease killed most of the others. Medicine was so primitive and conditions so harsh that army doctors could do little. As a Tennessee man observed, "nearly all who take sick die."

Victory in Mexico

Although Americans won battle after battle, President Polk's strategy misfired. Despite its loss of territory and men, Mexico determinedly refused to trade land for peace. One American soldier captured the Mexican mood: "They cannot submit to be deprived of California after the loss of Texas, and nothing but the conquest of their Capital will force them to such a humiliation." Polk had arrived at the same conclusion. Zachary Taylor had not proved decisive enough for Polk, and the president tapped another general to carry the war to Mexico City. While Taylor occupied the north, General Winfield Scott would land his army on the Gulf coast of Mexico and march 250 miles inland to the capital. Polk's plan entailed enormous risk; it meant that Scott would have to cut himself off from supplies and lead his men deep into enemy country against a much larger army.

After months of careful planning and the skillful coordination of army and navy, an amphibious landing on March 9, 1847, near Vera Cruz put some 10,000 American troops ashore by midnight without the loss of a single life. After eighty-eight hours of furious shelling, Vera Cruz surrendered. Scott immediately began preparations for the march west. Transportation alone posed enormous problems. His army required 9,300 wagons and 17,000 pack mules, 500,000 bushels of oats and corn, and 100 pounds of blister ointment before it could begin the mountainous journey. In early April 1847, the army moved out, following the path that had been trodden more than three centuries earlier by Hernán Cortés to "the halls of the Montezumas" (see chapter 2).

Meanwhile, after the frightful defeat at Buena Vista, Santa Anna had returned to Mexico City. He rallied his ragged troops and marched them east to set a trap for Scott in the mountain pass at Cerro Gordo. Knifing through Mexican lines, the Americans almost captured Santa Anna, who fled the field on foot. So complete was the victory that Scott gloated to Taylor,

Mexican Family

This family had its portrait taken in 1847, in the middle of the war. Where were the adult males? Mexican civilians were vulnerable to atrocities committed by the invading army. Volunteers, a large portion of American troops, received little training and resisted discipline. The "lawless Volunteers stop at no outrage," Brigadier General William Worth declared. "Innocent blood has been basely, cowardly, and barbarously shed in cold blood." Generals Zachary Taylor and Winfield Scott gradually tamed the volunteers with stern military justice.

Amon Carter Museum of Western Art.

"Mexico no longer has an army." But Santa Anna, ever resilient, again rallied the Mexican army. Some 30,000 troops took up defensive positions on the outskirts of Mexico City. They hurriedly began melting down church bells to cast new cannon.

In August, Scott began his assault on the Mexican capital. The fighting proved the most brutal of the war. Santa Anna backed his army into the city, fighting each step of the way. At the Battle of Churubusco, the Mexicans took 4,000 casualties in a single day and the Americans more than 1,000. At the castle of Chapultepec, American troops scaled the walls and fought the Mexican defenders hand to hand. After Chapultepec, Mexico City officials persuaded Santa Anna to evacuate the city to save it from destruction, and on September 14, 1847, General Winfield Scott rode in triumphantly. The ancient capital of the Aztecs had fallen once again to an invading army.

With Mexico City in U.S. hands, Polk sent Nicholas P. Trist, the chief clerk in the State Department, to Mexico to negotiate the peace. On February 2, 1848, Trist and Mexican officials signed the Treaty of Guadalupe Hidalgo. Mexico agreed to give up all claims to Texas north of the Rio Grande and to cede the provinces of New Mexico and California—more than 500,000 square miles—to the United States (see Map 12.3). The United States agreed to pay Mexico $15 million and to assume $3.25 million in claims that American citizens had against Mexico. Some Americans clamored for all of Mexico, others for less, but in March 1848 the Senate ratified the treaty by a vote of thirty-eight to fourteen. The last American soldiers left Mexico a few months later.

Golden California

The American triumph in the war had enormous consequences for both Mexico and the United States. Less than three-quarters of a century after its founding, the United States had achieved its self-proclaimed manifest destiny to stretch from the Atlantic to the Pacific (Map 12.4). The United States would enter the industrial age with vast new natural resources and a two-ocean economy, while Mexico suffered sharply diminished economic opportunities. Moreover, with the northern half of Mexico in American hands, California gold poured into American and not Mexican pockets.

On a cold January morning in 1848, just weeks before the formal transfer of territory, James Marshall discovered gold in the American River in the foothills of the Sierra Nevada. The flakes he found set off the California gold rush, one of the wildest mining stampedes in the world's history. Between 1849 and 1852, more than 250,000 "forty-niners," as the would-be miners were known, descended on the Golden State. In less than two years, Marshall's discovery transformed California from foreign territory to statehood.

Americans did not find it surprising that the discovery coincided with American acquisition. "God kept that coast for a people of the Pilgrim blood," one minister intoned. "He would not permit any other to be fully developed there." But news of gold quickly spread around the world. Soon a polyglot swirl of races and nationalities bent on getting rich arrived in California, where the forty-niners remade the quiet world of Mexican ranches into a raucous, roaring mining and town economy. (See "Historical Question," page 414.)

Forty-niners rarely had much money or mining experience, but as one witness observed, "No capital is required to obtain this gold, as the laboring man wants nothing but his pick, shovel, and tin pan, with which to dig and wash the gravel; and many frequently pick gold out of the crevices of rock with their butcher knives in pieces from one to six ounces." But life in the gold fields was nasty, brutish, and often short. Men faced abysmal living conditions, some living in holes and brush lean-tos. They also faced diseases such as cholera and scurvy, exorbitant prices for food and services (eggs sold for a dollar apiece), deadly encounters with claim jumpers, and endless backbreaking labor. Still, an individual with gold in his pocket could find temporary relief in the saloons, card games, dog fights, gambling dens, and brothels that flourished in the mining camps.

At first, news of the gold strike turned the city of San Francisco, on the coast, into a ghost town as men raced to the foothills. New arrivals, who sailed into the port by the thousands, abandoned five hundred ships when passengers and crews struck out for the gold fields. "The whole country from San Francisco to Los Angeles, and from the seashore to the base of the Sierra Nevada, resounds to the sordid cry *gold*! GOLD!! **GOLD**!!!" observed one newspaper, "while the field is left half planted, the house half built, and everything neglected but the manufacture of shovels and pickaxes." By 1853, however, San Francisco had grown into a raw, booming urban settlement of 50,000 and depended as much on gold as did the mining camps inland. The city suffered from overcrowding, fire, crime, and violence, like all the towns that dotted the San Joaquin and Sacramento valleys, but enterprising individuals had learned that there was money to be made tending to the needs of the miners. Hotels, saloons, restaurants, laundries, and shops and stores of all kinds exchanged services for miners' gold.

As wild as the mining camps were, San Francisco was no tamer. In 1851, an association called the Committee of Vigilance determined to bring order to the city. Members pledged that "no thief, burglar, incendiary or assassin shall escape punishment, either by the quibbles of the

> The American triumph in the Mexican-American War had enormous consequences. Less than three-quarters of a century after its founding, the United States stretched from the Atlantic to the Pacific.

law, the insecurity of prisons, the carelessness or corruption of the police, or a laxity of those who pretended to administer justice." Lynchings soon proved that the Committee meant business. In time, merchants, **artisans,** and professionals made the city their home and brought their families from back east. Theaters sprouted and gunfights in the streets declined, but many years would pass before anyone tamed San Francisco.

Establishing civic order on a turbulent frontier was made more difficult by the welter of nationalities, ethnicities, and races drawn to California and by Anglo bigotry. The Chinese attracted special scrutiny from the white majority. By 1851, there were 25,000 Chinese in California, and their religion, language, dress, queues (long pigtails), eating habits, and opium convinced

many Anglos that they were not fit citizens of the Golden State. As early as 1852, opponents demanded a halt to Chinese immigration. Chinese leaders in San Francisco fought back. While admitting deep cultural differences, they insisted that "in the important matters we are good men. We honor our parents; we take care of our children; we are industrious and peaceable; we trade much; we are trusted for small and large sums; we pay our debts; and are honest, and of course must tell the truth." Their protestations, however, offered little protection, and racial violence braided with forty-niner optimism and energy.

Westward expansion did not stop at the California shore. By midcentury, California's ports were connected to a vast trade network in the Pacific, where American seafarers and

MAP 12.4 Territorial Expansion by 1860

Less than a century after its founding, the United States had spread from the Atlantic seaboard to the Pacific Ocean. War, purchase, and diplomacy had gained a continent.

READING THE MAP: List the countries from which the United States acquired land. Which nation lost the most land because of U.S. expansion?

CONNECTIONS: Who coined the phrase *manifest destiny*? When? What does it mean? What areas targeted for expansion were the subjects of debate during the presidential campaign of 1844?

FOR MORE HELP ANALYZING THIS MAP, see the map activity for this chapter in the Online Study Guide at bedfordstmartins.com/roark.

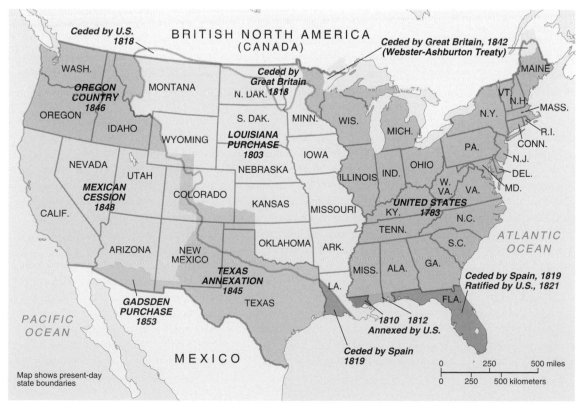

Who Rushed for California Gold?

When news of John Marshall's discovery reached the East in the fall of 1848, gold proved irresistible. Newspapers went crazy with stories about prospectors who extracted half a pan of gold from every pan of gravel they scooped from western streams. Soon, cities reverberated with men singing:

Oh Susannah, don't you cry for me;
I'm gone to California with my
wash-bowl on my knee.

Scores of ships sailed from East Coast ports, headed either around South America to San Francisco or across the Gulf of Mexico to Panama, where the passengers made their way by foot and canoe to the Pacific coast and waited for a ship to carry them north. Even larger numbers of gold seekers took riverboats to the Missouri River and then set out in wagons, on horseback, or by foot for the West.

Young men everywhere contracted gold fever. As stories of California gold circled the globe, Chinese and Germans, Mexicans and Irish, Australians and French, Chileans and Italians, and people of dozens of other nationalities set out to strike it rich. Louisa Knapp Clappe, wife of a minister and one of the few women in gold country, remarked that when she walked through Indian Bar, the little mining town where she lived, she heard English, French, Spanish, German, Italian, Kanaka (Hawaiian), Asian Indian, and American Indian languages. Hangtown, Hell's Delight, Gouge Eye, and a hundred other crude mining camps became temporary home to a diverse throng of nationalities and peoples.

One of the largest groups of new arrivals was the Chinese. Between 1848 and 1854, Chinese men numbering 45,000 (but almost no Chinese women) arrived in California. Most considered themselves "sojourners," temporary residents who planned to return home as soon as their savings allowed. The majority came under a Chinese-controlled contract labor system in which each immigrant worked out the cost of his transportation. In the early years, most became wage laborers in mining. By the 1860s, they dominated railroad construction in the West. Ninety percent of the Central Pacific Railroad's 10,000 workers were Chinese. The Chinese also made up nearly half of San Francisco's labor force, working in the shoe, tobacco, woolen, laundry, and sewing trades. By 1870, the Chinese population had grown to 63,200, including 4,500 women. They constituted nearly 10 percent of the state's people and 25 percent of its wage-earning force.

The presence of peoples from around the world shattered the Anglo-American dream of a racially and ethnically homogeneous West, but ethnic diversity did nothing to increase the tolerance of Anglo-American prospectors. In their eyes, no "foreigner" had a right to dig for gold. In 1850, the California legislature passed the Foreign Miners' Tax Law, which levied high taxes on non-Americans to drive them from the gold fields, except as hired laborers working on claims owned by Americans. Stubborn foreign miners were sometimes hauled before "Judge Lynch." Among the earliest victims of lynching in the gold fields were a Frenchman and a Chilean.

Anglo-Americans considered the Chinese devious and unassimilable. They also feared that hardworking, self-denying Chinese labor would undercut white labor and drive it from the country. As a consequence, the Chinese were segregated residentially and occupationally and made ineligible for citizenship. Along with blacks and Indians, Chinese were denied public education and the right to testify in court. In addition to exclusion, they suffered from violence. Mobs drove them from Eureka, Truckee, and other mining towns.

American prospectors swamped the *Californios*, Spanish and Mexican settlers who had lived in California for generations. Soon after the American takeover, raging prejudice and discriminatory laws pushed Hispanic *rancheros*, professionals,

Gold Mountain

This hardworking young man is wearing the typical dress of Chinese laborers, a blue cotton shirt and baggy pants. We cannot tell if a queue is hanging down his back. He bears the heavy tools of his trade of placer (surface) mining but still manages a smile. Although he probably did not strike it rich in Gum Sam (Gold Mountain), he did find a new world and a new way of life.

Nevada Historical Society.

merchants, and artisans into the ranks of unskilled labor. Americans took their land even though the U.S. government had pledged to protect Mexican and Spanish land titles after the cession of 1848. Anglo forty-niners branded Spanish-speaking miners, even native-born Californios, "foreigners" and drove them from the diggings. Mariano Vallejo, a leading Californio, said of the forty-niners: "The good ones were few and the wicked many."

For Native Americans, the gold rush was a catastrophe. Numbering about 150,000 in 1848, the Indian population of California fell to 25,000 in 1856. Californios had exploited the native peoples, but the forty-niners wanted to eradicate them. Starvation, disease, and a declining birthrate took a heavy toll. Indians

also fell victim to wholesale murder. "That a war of extermination will continue to be waged between the two races until the Indian race becomes extinct must be expected," declared California governor Peter W. Burnett in 1851. The nineteenth-century historian Hubert Howe Bancroft described white behavior toward Indians during the gold rush as "one of the last human hunts of civilization, and the basest and most brutal of them all." To survive, Indians moved to the most remote areas of the state and tried to stay out of the way.

The forty-niners created dazzling wealth—in 1852, 81 million ounces of gold, nearly half of the world's production. Only a few prospectors—of whatever race and nationality—struck it rich, however.

The era of the prospector panning in streams quickly gave way to corporate-owned deep-shaft mining. The larger the scale of mining operations became, the smaller were the opportunities for individual miners. Most forty-niners eventually took up farming or opened small businesses or worked for wages for the corporations that pushed them out. But because of gold, an avalanche of people had roared into California. Anglo-Americans were most numerous, and Anglo dominance developed early. But the gold rush also brought a rainbow of nationalities. Anglo-American ascendancy *and* ethnic and racial diversity in the West both count among the most significant legacies of the gold rush. But because Anglo-Americans made the rules, not everyone shared equally.

merchants traded furs, hides and tallow, and lumber and participated in whaling and the China trade. But as California's first congressional representative observed, the state was separated "by thousands of miles of plains, deserts, and almost impossible mountains" from the rest of the Union. Dreamers talked about a railroad that would someday connect the Golden State with the booming agriculture and thriving industry of the East.

Economic and Industrial Evolution

During the 1840s and 1850s, Americans lived amid profound economic transformation that had been under way since the start of the nineteenth century. By 1860, the nation's population numbered over 31 million. Since 1800, the total output of the U.S. economy had multiplied twelvefold. Four fundamental changes in American society fueled this phenomenal economic growth.

First, millions of Americans—Abraham Lincoln among them—left their farms, swelling the urban population, although farmers still made up 80 percent of the nation's population by 1860. Second, more and more Americans were working in factories, almost 20 percent of the labor force by 1860. This trend contributed to the nation's economic growth because, in general, factory workers were twice as productive (in output per unit of labor input) as agricultural workers.

A third fundamental change was the shift from water to steam as a source of energy, which permitted factories to be more productive. Beginning around 1840, steam became harnessed to manufacturing, but the transition was slow, delayed by the continued effectiveness of water and animal power. By 1850, for example, animal and human muscles still provided thirty-three times more energy for manufacturing than steam. During the 1830s, extensive mining began in Pennsylvania coal fields, and massive quantities of coal became available for industrial fuel. Coal provided heat to power steam engines in factories, railroads, and ships.

> While cities, factories, and steam engines multiplied throughout the nation—especially in the North and West—the roots of the United States's economic growth lay in agriculture.

A fourth fundamental change propelling America's industrial development was the rise in agricultural productivity (defined as crop output per unit of labor input), which nearly doubled during Lincoln's lifetime. More than any other single factor, this dramatic increase spurred the economic growth of the era. While cities, factories, and steam engines multiplied throughout the nation—especially in the North and West—the roots of the United States's economic growth lay in agriculture.

This cascade of interrelated developments—steam, coal, factories, cities, railroads, and farms—was beginning to transform the American economy by the 1850s. Historians often refer to this transformation as an industrial revolution. However, the profound changes occurring in these years did not cause a revolutionary discontinuity in the economy or society. The United States remained overwhelmingly agricultural. Old methods of production continued alongside the new. The process that the American economy underwent before 1860 might best be termed "industrial evolution."

Agriculture and Land Policy

It may seem odd to consider an ax a basic agricultural tool, like a hoe or a shovel, yet farmers needed axes. A French traveler observed that Americans had "a general feeling of hatred against trees" and taught their children "at an early age to use the axe against the trees, their enemies." Although the traveler exaggerated, his observation contained an important truth. Forests impeded agriculture. With axes—Lincoln termed them "that most useful instrument"—farmers leveled trees, cleared land for planting, and built cabins, fences, and barns.

The amount of physical labor required to convert unimproved land to cultivated fields limited agricultural productivity. Energy that might have gone to growing crops went instead to clearing land. But as farmers pushed westward, they encountered thinner forests and eventually the Midwest's comparatively treeless prairie, where they could spend less time with an ax and more time with a plow or hoe. Rich prairie soils gave somewhat higher crop yields than eastern farms, and farmers migrated to the Midwest by the tens of thousands between 1830 and 1860. The population of Indiana, Illinois, Michigan, Wisconsin, and Iowa exploded tenfold, growing from 500,000 in 1830 to more than 5 million by 1860, four times faster than the

Harvesting Grain with Cradles
This late-nineteenth-century painting shows the grain harvest during the mid-nineteenth century at Bishop Hill, Illinois, a Swedish community where the artist, Olof Krans, and his parents settled in 1850. The men swing cradles, slowly cutting a swath through the grain; the women gather the cut grain into sheaves to be hauled away later for threshing. Bishop Hill, a well-organized community, could call upon the labor of a large number of men and women at harvest time. Most farmers had only a few family members and a hired hand or two to help with the harvest. Notice that although the grain field appears level enough to be ideal for a mechanical reaper, all the work is done by hand; no machine is in sight.
Bishop Hill State Historic Site, Illinois Historic Preservation Agency.

growth of the nation as a whole. During the 1850s, Illinois added more people than any other state in the Union.

Labor-saving improvements in farm implements also hiked agricultural productivity. The cast-iron plow in use since the 1820s proved too weak for the thick turf and dense soil of the midwestern prairie. In 1837, John Deere patented a strong, smooth steel plow that sliced through prairie soil so cleanly that farmers called it the "singing plow." Deere's company became the leading plow manufacturer in the Midwest, turning out more than ten thousand plows a year by the late 1850s. By 1860, the energy for plowing still came from two- and four-legged animals, but better plows permitted that energy to break more ground and plant more crops.

Improvements in wheat harvesting also multiplied farmers' productivity. In 1850, most farmers harvested wheat by hand, cutting two or three acres a day with backbreaking labor. Tinkerers throughout the nation tried to fashion a mechanical reaper that would make the wheat harvest easier and quicker. Cyrus McCormick and others experimented with designs until the late 1840s, when mechanical reapers began to appear in American wheat fields. A McCormick reaper that cost between $100 and $150 allowed a farmer to harvest up to twelve acres a day. By 1860, about eighty thousand reapers had been sold. Although reapers represented the cutting edge of agricultural technology, they still had to be powered by a horse or an ox. Most farmers continued to cut their grain by hand. Neither reapers nor plows increased the yield of a given acre of cultivated land. Instead, they allowed more land to be brought into cultivation: The labor that farmers saved could be used to plow and plant more land. Access to fresh, uncultivated land allowed farmers to double the corn and wheat harvests between 1840 and 1860.

The agricultural productivity that fueled the nation's economy was an outgrowth of federal land policy. Up to 1860, the United States continued to be land-rich and labor-poor. During the nineteenth century, the nation became a great deal richer in land, acquiring more than a billion acres with the Louisiana Purchase (see chapter 10) and the annexation of Florida, Oregon, and vast territories following the Mexican War. The federal government made the land available for purchase to attract settlers and to generate revenues. Although federal land cost only $1.25 an acre, millions of Americans could not afford to pay $50 for a forty-acre farm. They squatted on unclaimed federal land and carved out a farm that they neither rented nor owned. Many poor farmers never accumulated enough money to purchase the land on which they squatted, and eventually they moved elsewhere, often to squat again on unclaimed federal land.

In addition to aiding small farmers, government land policy enriched wily speculators who found ways to claim large tracts of the most desirable plots and sell them to settlers at a generous markup. Nonetheless, by making land available to millions of ordinary people, the federal government achieved the goal of attracting settlers to the new territories in the West, which in due course joined the Union as new states. Above all, federal land policy created the basic precondition for the increase in agricultural productivity that underlay the nation's impressive economic growth.

Manufacturing and Mechanization

Changes in manufacturing arose in the context of the nation's land-rich, labor-poor economy. England and other European countries had land-poor, labor-rich economies; there, meager opportunities in agriculture kept factory laborers plentiful and wages low. In the United States, western expansion and government land policies buoyed agriculture, keeping millions of people on the farm and thereby limiting the supply of workers for manufacturing and elevating

Railroads captured Americans' imaginations because they seemed to break the bonds of nature.

wages. Because of this relative shortage of workers, manufacturers searched constantly for ways to save labor.

Mechanization marched forward as quickly as manufacturers could turn innovative ideas into workable combinations of gears, levers, screws, and pulleys. Outside the textile industry (see chapter 11), homegrown machines set the pace. The practice of manufacturing and then assembling interchangeable parts spread from gun making to other industries and became known as the "American system." Clock makers used it; sewing machine makers used it; even ax makers used it. Mechanization became so integral to American manufacturing that some machinists specialized in what was called the machine tool industry, which made machines that made parts for other machines.

Manufacturing and agriculture meshed into a dynamic national economy. New England led the nation in manufacturing, shipping products such as clocks, guns, and axes west and south, while commodities such as wheat, pork, whiskey, tobacco, and cotton moved north and east. Manufacturers specialized in producing for the gigantic domestic market rather than for export. British goods dominated the international market and, on the whole, were cheaper and better than American-made products. U.S. manufacturers supported tariffs to minimize British competition, but their best protection from British competitors was to strive harder to please their American customers, the vast majority of whom were farmers.

Throughout American manufacturing, hand labor continued to be essential despite advances in mechanization. Even in heavily mechanized industries, factories remained fairly small; few had more than twenty or thirty employees. The industrial evolution under way before 1860 would quicken later in the nineteenth century; railroads were a harbinger of that future.

Railroads: Breaking the Bonds of Nature

Railroads incorporated the most advanced developments of the age. A Swedish visitor in 1849 noticed that American schoolboys constantly doodled sketches of locomotives, always belching smoke and steam, always in motion. Why did railroads capture Americans' imaginations? They seemed to break the bonds of nature. When

Railroad Travel

In addition to carrying people and goods more quickly and reliably than ever before, railroads also brought many Americans face-to-face for the first time with machinery that was much larger and more powerful than any human being. This painting of a train leaving Rochester, New York, in 1852 contrasts the size and power of human beings and machines. The huge, lovingly portrayed, steam-belching locomotive is barely held back by some unseen brake against which the massive engine strains, ready to pull the long train through the columns of the station, out of the past and into the future. The people, in contrast, appear indistinct, passive, and dependent. Except for the two women and child in the foreground, the people face backward, and all of them avoid looking directly at the locomotive. The painting evokes the way the almost incomprehensible power of the railroads dwarfed human effort.

Rochester Historical Society.

canals and rivers froze in winter or became impassable during summer droughts, trains steamed ahead. When becalmed sailing ships went nowhere, locomotives kept on chugging, averaging over twenty miles an hour during the 1850s. Above all, railroads offered cities not blessed with canals or navigable rivers a way to compete for the trade of the countryside.

By 1850, trains steamed along nine thousand miles of track, almost two-thirds of it in New England and the Middle Atlantic states. By 1860, several railroads had crossed the Mississippi River to link frontier farmers to the nation's 30,000 miles of track, approximately as much as in all the rest of the world combined (Map 12.5). (In 1857, for example, France had

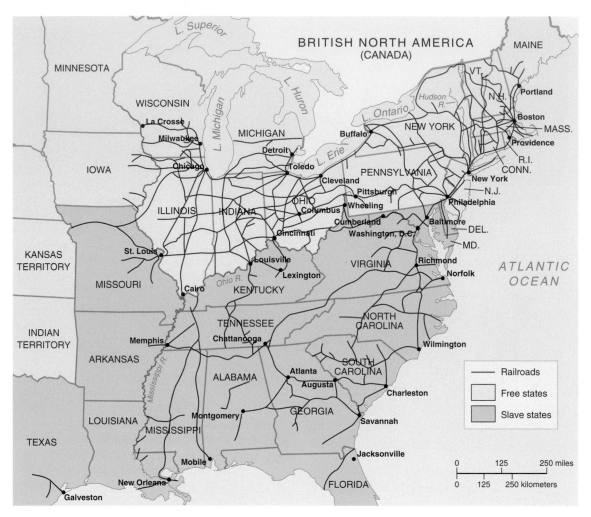

MAP 12.5   Railroads in 1860

Railroads were a crucial component of the revolutions in transportation and communications that transformed nineteenth-century America. The railroad system reflected the differences that had developed in the economies of the North and South.

READING THE MAP: In which sections of the country were most of the railroad tracks laid by the middle of the nineteenth century? What cities served as the busiest railroad hubs?

CONNECTIONS: How did the expansion of railroad networks affect the American economy? Why was the U.S. government willing to grant more than twenty million acres of public land to the private corporations that ran the railroads?

FOR MORE HELP ANALYZING THIS MAP, see the map activity for this chapter in the Online Study Guide at bedfordstmartins.com/roark.

3,700 miles of track; England and Wales had a total of 6,400 miles.) Chicago stood at the hub of eleven railroads, including the Illinois Central, the longest railroad anywhere. This massive expansion of railroads helped the United States catapult into position as the world's second leading industrial power, behind Great Britain.

In addition to speeding transportation, railroads propelled the growth of the iron and coal industries, both vital to railroad construction and operation. Iron production grew five times faster than the population during the decades up to 1860, in part to meet the demand for rails, wheels, axles, locomotives, and heavy, gravity-defying iron bridges. Railroads also stimulated the fledgling telegraph industry (see "The Promise of Technology," page 422). In 1844, Samuel F. B. Morse persuasively demonstrated the potential of his telegraph by transmitting a series of dots and dashes that instantly conveyed an electronic message along forty miles of wire strung between Washington and Baltimore. By 1861, more than fifty thousand miles of wire stretched across the continent to the Pacific, often alongside railroad tracks. Telegraphy made railroads safer and more efficient, swiftly signaling whether tracks were clear.

Almost all railroads were built and owned by private corporations rather than by governments. Undergirding these private investments was massive government aid, especially federal **land grants**. Up to 1850, the federal government had granted a total of seven million acres of federal land to various turnpike, highway, and canal projects. In that year, Illinois senator Stephen A. Douglas obtained congressional approval for a precedent-setting grant to railroads of 6 square miles of federal land for each mile of track laid. Railroad companies quickly lined up congressional support for other lucrative land deals. By 1860, Congress had granted railroads more than twenty million acres of federal lands, establishing a generous policy that would last for decades.

The railroad boom of the 1850s signaled the growing industrial might of the American economy. But railroads, like other industries, succeeded because they served farms as well as cities. And older forms of transportation remained significant. By 1857, for example, trains carried only about one-third of the mail; most of the rest still went by stagecoach or horseback. In 1860, most Americans were still far more familiar with four-legged horses than with iron horses.

The economy of the 1840s and 1850s linked an expanding, westward-moving population by muscles, animals, and farms as well as machines, steam, railroads, and cities. Abraham Lincoln split rails as a young man and defended railroad corporations as a successful attorney. His upward mobility illustrated the direction of economic change and the opportunities that change offered to enterprising individuals.

Free Labor: Promise and Reality

The nation's impressive economic performance did not reward all Americans equally. Native-born white men tended to do better than immigrants. With few exceptions, women were excluded from the opportunities open to men. Tens of thousands of women worked as seamstresses, laundresses, domestic servants, factory hands, and teachers but had little opportunity to aspire to higher-paying jobs. In the North and West, slavery was slowly eliminated in the half century after the American Revolution, but most free African Americans there found themselves relegated to dead-end jobs as laborers and servants. Discrimination against immigrants, women, and free blacks did not trouble most white men. With certain notable exceptions, they considered it proper and just.

The Free-Labor Ideal: Freedom plus Labor

During the 1840s and 1850s, leaders throughout the North and West emphasized a set of ideas that seemed to explain why the changes under way in their society benefited some more than others. They referred again and again to the advantages of what they termed **free labor**. (The word *free* referred to laborers who were not slaves; it did not mean laborers who worked for nothing.) By the 1850s, free-labor ideas described a social and economic ideal that accounted for both the successes and the shortcomings of the economy and society taking shape in the North and West.

Free-labor spokesmen celebrated hard work, self-reliance, and independence. They proclaimed that the door to success was open not just to those who inherited wealth or status but also to self-made men like Abraham Lincoln. Lincoln himself declared, "Free labor—the just and generous, and prosperous system, which opens the way for all—gives hope to all, and energy, and progress, and improvement of condition to all." The free-labor system, Lincoln argued, permitted farmers and artisans to enjoy the products of their own labor and also benefited wage workers. Ultimately, the free-labor system made it possible for hired laborers to become independent property owners, proponents argued. "The prudent, penniless beginner in the world," Lincoln asserted, "labors for wages awhile, saves a surplus with which to buy tools or land, for himself; then labors on his own account another while, and at length hires another new beginner to help him." Wage labor was the first rung on the ladder toward self-employment and, eventually, to hiring others.

> Free-labor spokesmen proclaimed that the door to success was open not just to those who inherited wealth or status but also to self-made men like Abraham Lincoln.

The Telegraph: The "Wonder Working Wire"

The telegraph played as important a role as the railroad in opening the West and uniting the nation. Telegraph wires often paralleled railroad lines, and the two developments were allies in the nineteenth-century communications revolution. Both delivered what nineteenth-century Americans craved—speed and efficiency and the ability to overcome vast distances.

Samuel F. B. Morse is credited with inventing the telegraph because of his patent of June 20, 1840, but, as is the case with many inventions, the assumption of "one man, one invention" exaggerates the contribution of a single individual. The telegraph grew out of scientific knowledge gradually acquired in the eighteenth and nineteenth centuries by a number of scientists, especially André Ampère of France, Alessandro Volta of Italy, and Joseph Henry of the United States, who pioneered in the field of electromagnetism and experimented with sending electrical signals through wires.

Morse was no scientist—he was an acclaimed painter—but beginning in the early 1830s he devoted himself to creating a machine that transmitted messages electrically. As one contemporary observed, Morse's talent consisted of "combining and applying the discoveries of others in the invention of a particular instrument and process for telegraphic purposes." This was no small achievement. In addition, Morse's system depended on a code he devised that represented each letter and number with dots and dashes. With a series of taps on a telegraph key, operators sent short and long pulses of electricity—a dash was three times as long as a dot. At the receiver's end, the code was originally written out by an electrically activated stylus on a moving strip of paper and then read off. But soon skilled operators found that by listening to the taps they could interpret the message and write it down. The Morse code became the universal language of the telegraph.

The breakthrough moment for Morse's invention came in 1842 when Congress voted $30,000 to build an experimental line between Washington and Baltimore. Four years earlier, a congressional report had declared that if Morse's invention succeeded, "space will be, to all practical purposes of information, completely annihilated between the States of the Union," and Congress was eager to find out if it would work. With the federal subsidy, Morse strung the line, and from the Supreme Court in Washington on May 22, 1844, he tapped out a biblical phrase. In Baltimore, forty-one miles away, a receiver transcribed: "What hath God wrought!" The trial was a stunning technical success, and it was also a public relations coup, for the entire nation stood awed by the speed and precision of the "wonder working wire."

The telegraph spread almost as swiftly as news of its existence. By 1846, most eastern cities were connected by telegraph. By 1850, of the states east of the Mississippi River, only Florida remained without it. More than fifty thousand miles of wires webbed the nation by 1861 when the telegraph reached California. Despite the cost—initially, an astronomical $1 a word—the line between San Francisco and the East chattered with dots and dashes.

The telegraph obliterated distance, and cheap, efficient, and fast communication changed American businesses, newspapers, government, and everyday life. Telegraphs made it possible to synchronize clocks, which in turn allowed railroads to run safely according to precise schedules. Businesses of every kind could send and receive information and orders almost instantaneously. Investors from across the country could learn the latest stock

---

The free-labor ideal affirmed an egalitarian vision of human potential. Lincoln and other spokesmen stressed the importance of universal education to permit "heads and hands [to] cooperate as friends." Throughout the North and West, communities supported public schools to make the rudiments of learning available to young children. By 1860, many cities and towns boasted that up to 80 percent of children ages seven to thirteen attended school at least for a few weeks each year. In rural areas, where the labor of children was more difficult to spare,

Telegraph Transmitter
This is Samuel Morse's telegraph key, the one that sent the first telegraph in 1844.
Division of Political History, Smithsonian Institution, Washington, D.C.

Telegraph Receiver
Early receivers pressed dots and dashes into a moving paper strip attached to the machine.
Division of Political History, Smithsonian Institution, Washington, D.C.

prices from the New York Stock Exchange. In 1852, an English visitor reported:

> If, on the arrival of an European mail at one of the northern ports, the news from Europe report that the supply of cotton or of corn is inadequate to meet the existing demand, almost before the vessel can be moored intelligence is spread by the Electric Telegraph, and the merchants and shippers of New Orleans are busied in the preparation of freights, or the corn-factors of St. Louis and Chicago, in the far west, are emptying their granaries and forwarding their contents by rail or by canal to the Atlantic ports.

Newspapers could gather information from around the country and have it in the headlines within hours.

As early as 1848, Americans followed the war in Mexico not from reports brought by messengers on horseback or on ships but by the magical wire. After 1866, when an underwater transatlantic cable linked Europe and the United States, the federal government used the telegraph to monitor international affairs and to respond swiftly to crises. On a personal level, families scattered across the continent could communicate more quickly than letter writing allowed. The telegraph met the needs of the vigorous, sprawling nation.

It is one thing to conceive of and build an innovative device. It is another to develop the idea into a profitable business. Unlike Eli Whitney, the unlucky inventor of the cotton gin, Morse was a skilled entrepreneur who grew rich from his invention. Patent rights, which he defended vigorously and successfully, allowed the Morse telegraph to dominate the United States and most of the non-British world. Morse's technology made him wealthy and worked powerfully to draw the far-flung young nation together, even as it began to pull apart politically.

schools typically enrolled no more than half the school-age children. Lessons included more than arithmetic, penmanship, and a smattering of other subjects. Teachers—most of whom were young women—and textbooks drummed into students the virtues of the free-labor system: self-reliance, discipline, and, above all, hard work. "Remember that all the ignorance, degradation, and misery in the world is the result of indolence and vice," one textbook intoned. Free-labor ideology, whether in school or out, emphasized labor as much as freedom.

Miner with Pick, Pan, and Shovel
This young man exhibits the spirit of individual effort that was the foundation of free labor ideals. Posing with a pick and shovel to loosen gold-bearing deposits and a pan to wash away debris, the man appears determined to succeed as a miner by his own muscle and sweat. Hard work with these tools, the picture suggests, promises deserved rewards and maybe riches.
Collection of Matthew Isenburg.

Economic Inequality

The free-labor ideal made sense to many Americans, especially in the North and West, because it seemed to describe their own experience. Lincoln frequently referred to his humble beginnings as a hired laborer and implicitly invited his listeners to consider how far he had come. In 1860, his wealth of $17,000 easily placed him in the top 5 percent of the population. The opportunities presented by the expanding economy made a few men much, much richer. In 1860, the nation had about forty millionaires, including Cyrus McCormick, whose wealth exceeded $2 million. Most Americans, however, measured success in far more modest terms. The average wealth of adult white men in the North in 1860 barely topped $2,000. Only about a quarter of American men possessed that much.

Nearly half had no wealth at all; about 60 percent owned no land. It is difficult to estimate the wealth of adult white women because property possessed by married women was normally considered to belong to their husbands, but certainly women had less wealth than men. Free African Americans had still less; 90 percent were propertyless.

Free-labor spokesmen considered these economic inequalities a natural outgrowth of freedom, the inevitable result of some individuals being more able, more willing to work, and luckier. These inequalities suggest, however, the gap between the promise and the performance of the free-labor ideal. Economic growth permitted many men to move from being landless squatters to landowning farmers and from being hired laborers to independent, self-employed producers. But many more Americans remained behind, landless and working for wages. Even those who realized their aspirations had a precarious hold on their independence; bad debts, crop failure, sickness, or death could quickly eliminate a family's gains.

Seeking out new opportunities in pursuit of free-labor ideals created restless social and geographic mobility. Commonly up to two-thirds of the residents of a rural area moved every decade, and the population turnover in cities was even greater. Such constant comings and goings weakened community ties to neighbors and friends and threw individuals even more on their own resources for help in times of trouble. Abraham Lincoln managed to get out of the log cabin in which he grew up, but memories of his life in that log cabin—with its economic insecurities and educational deficiencies, with his illiterate mother and semiliterate father—remained with him, reminding him how far he had come and how few were able to come so far.

Immigrants and the Free-Labor Ladder

The risks and uncertainties of free labor did not deter millions of immigrants from entering the United States during the 1840s and 1850s. Almost 4.5 million immigrants arrived between 1840 and 1860, six times more than had come during the previous two decades (Figure 12.1). The half-million immigrants who came in 1854 accounted for nearly 2 percent of the entire U.S. population, a higher proportion than in any other single year of the nation's history. By 1860, foreign-born residents made up about one-

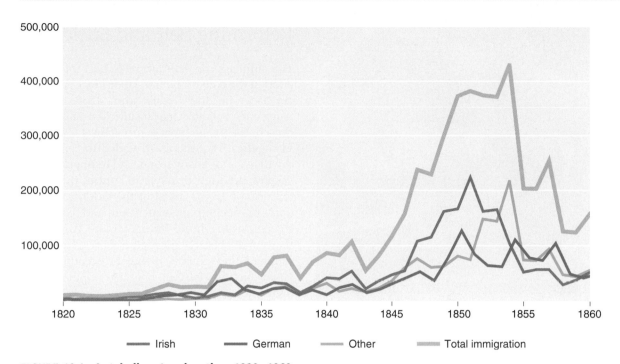

FIGURE 12.1 Antebellum Immigration, 1820–1860
After increasing gradually for several decades, immigration shot up in the mid-1840s. Between 1848 and 1860, nearly 3.5 million immigrants entered the United States.

eighth of the U.S. population, a fraction that held steady well into the twentieth century.

Nearly three out of four of the immigrants who arrived between 1840 and 1860 came from Germany or Ireland. The vast majority of the 1.4 million Germans who entered the United States during these years were skilled tradesmen and their families. They left Germany to escape deteriorating economic conditions and to seize opportunities offered by the expanding American economy. Skilled artisans had little difficulty finding work in the United States. German butchers, bakers, beer makers, carpenters, shopkeepers, machinists, and others tended to congregate in cities, particularly in the Midwest. Roughly a quarter of German immigrants were farmers, most of whom scattered throughout the Midwest, although some settled in Texas. On the whole, German Americans settled into that middle stratum of sturdy independent producers celebrated by free-labor spokesmen; relatively few Germans occupied the bottom rung of the free-labor ladder as wage laborers or domestic servants.

Irish immigrants, in contrast, entered at the bottom of the free-labor ladder and had difficulty climbing up. Nearly 1.7 million Irish immigrants arrived between 1840 and 1860, nearly all of them desperately poor and often weakened by hunger and disease. Potato blight struck Ireland in 1845 and returned repeatedly in subsequent years, spreading a catastrophic famine throughout the island. Many of the lucky ones, half-starved, crowded into the holds of ships and set out for America, where they congregated in northeastern cities. As one immigrant group declared, "All we want is to get out of Ireland; we must be better anywhere than here." Death trailed after them. So many died crossing the Atlantic that ships from Ireland were often termed "coffin ships."

Roughly three out of four Irish immigrants worked as laborers or domestic servants. Irish men dug canals, loaded ships, laid railroad track, and took what other work they could find. Irish women hired out to cook, wash and iron, mind children, and clean house. Almost all Irish immigrants were Catholic, a fact that set them apart from the overwhelmingly **Protestant** native-born residents. Many natives regarded the Irish as hard-drinking, obstreperous,

The risks and uncertainties of free labor did not deter millions of immigrants from entering the United States during the 1840s and 1850s.

Eviction of Irish Tenant

An Irish tenant (the seated man with crossed arms) and his family (two barefoot boys are shown) are evicted; their few pieces of furniture have been piled outside the cottage. The landlord or his agent (the man near the doorway) has brought four armed police to force the tenant to leave. Evictions like this were common in Ireland in the mid-nineteenth century. Poverty and human suffering pushed many Irish immigrants to the United States.

Lawrence Collection, National Library of Ireland.

half-civilized folk. Such views lay behind the discrimination that often excluded Irish immigrants from better jobs. Job announcements commonly stated, "No Irish need apply." Despite such prejudices, native residents hired Irish immigrants because they accepted low pay and worked hard.

In America's labor-poor economy, Irish laborers could earn in one day wages that would require several weeks' work in Ireland, if work could be found there. In America, one immigrant explained in 1853, there was "plenty of work and plenty of wages plenty to eat and no land lords thats enough what more does a man want." But some immigrants wanted more, especially respect and decent working conditions. One immigrant complained that he was "a slave for the Americans as the generality of the Irish . . . are."

Such testimony illustrates that the free-labor system, whether for immigrants or native-born laborers, often did not live up to the optimistic vision outlined by Abraham Lincoln and others. Many wage laborers could not realistically aspire to become independent, self-sufficient property holders, despite the claims of free-labor proponents.

Reforming Self and Society

The emphasis on self-discipline and individual effort at the core of the free-labor ideal pervaded America in the 1840s and 1850s. Many Americans believed that insufficient self-control caused the major social problems of the era. **Evangelical** Protestants struggled to control individuals' propensity to sin, and **temperance** advocates exhorted drinkers to control their urge for alcohol. In the midst of the worldly disruptions of geographic expansion and economic change, evangelicals brought more Americans than ever before into churches. Historians estimate that church members accounted for about one-third of the American population by midcentury. Most Americans remained outside churches, as did Abraham Lincoln. But the influence of evangelical religion reached far beyond those who belonged to churches. The evangelical temperament—a conviction of righteousness coupled with energy, self-discipline, and faith that the world could be improved—animated most reformers.

A few activists pointed out that certain fundamental injustices lay beyond the reach of individual self-control. Transcendentalists and utopians believed that perfection could be attained only by rejecting the competitive values of the larger society. Women's rights activists and abolitionists sought to reverse the subordination of women and to eliminate the enslavement of blacks by changing laws and social institutions as well as attitudes and customs. They confronted the daunting challenge of repudiating widespread assumptions about male supremacy and white supremacy and somehow subverting the entrenched institutions that reinforced those assumptions: the family and slavery.

The Pursuit of Perfection: Transcendentalists and Utopians

A group of New England writers that came to be known as transcendentalists believed that individuals should conform neither to the dictates of the materialistic world nor to the dogma of formal religion. Instead, people should look within themselves for truth and guidance. The leading transcendentalist, Ralph Waldo Emerson—an essayist, poet, and lecturer—proclaimed that the power of the solitary individual was nearly limitless. Henry David Thoreau, Margaret Fuller, and other transcendentalists agreed with Emerson that "if the single man plant himself indomitably on his instincts, and there abide, the huge world will come round to him." In many ways, transcendentalism represented less an alternative to the values of mainstream society than an exaggerated form of the rampant individualism of the age.

Unlike transcendentalists who sought to turn inward, a few reformers tried to change the world by organizing utopian communities as alternatives to prevailing social arrangements. Although these communities never attracted more than a few thousand people, the activities of their members demonstrated both dissatisfaction with the larger society and their efforts to realize their visions of perfection. Some communities functioned as retreats for those who did not want to sever ties with the larger society. Brook Farm, organized in 1841 in West Roxbury, Massachusetts, briefly provided a haven for a few literary and artistic New Englanders trying to balance bookish pursuits with manual labor.

Other communities set out to become models of perfection that they hoped would point the way toward a better life for everyone. During the 1840s, more than two dozen communities—principally in New York, New Jersey, Pennsylvania, and Ohio—organized around the ideas of Charles Fourier, a French critic of contemporary society. Members of Fourierist phalanxes, as these communities were called, believed that individualism and competition were evils that denied the basic truth that "men . . . are brothers and not competitors." Fourierist phalanxes tried to replace competition with harmonious cooperation based on communal ownership of property. Members were supposed to work not because they had to but because their work was satisfying and fulfilling. One former member recalled that "there was plenty of discussion, and an abundance of variety, which is called the spice of life. This spice however constituted the greater part of the fare, as we sometimes had scarcely anything to eat." Such complaints signaled the failure of the Fourierist communities to achieve their ambitious goals. Few survived more than two or three years.

The Oneida community went beyond the Fourierist notion of communalism. John Humphrey Noyes, the charismatic leader of Oneida, believed that individuals who had achieved salvation were literally without sin but the larger society's commitment to private property made even saints greedy and selfish. Noyes believed that the root of private property lay in marriage, in men's conviction that their wives were their exclusive property. Drawing from a substantial inheritance, Noyes organized the Oneida community in New York in 1848 to practice what he called "complex marriage." Sexual intercourse was permitted between any man and woman in the community who had been saved. Noyes usually reserved for himself the duties of "first husband," introducing sanctified young virgins to

Mary Cragin, Oneida Woman

A founding member of the Oneida community, Mary Cragin had a passionate sexual relationship with John Humphrey Noyes even before the community was organized. Within the bounds of complex marriage as practiced by the Oneidans, Cragin's magnetic sexuality made her a favorite partner of many men. In her journal, she confessed that "every evil passion was very strong in me from my childhood, sexual desire, love of dress and admiration, deceit, anger, pride." Oneida, however, transformed evil passion to holy piety. Cragin wrote, "In view of [God's] goodness to me and of his desire that I should let him fill me with himself, I yield and offer myself, to be penetrated by his spirit, and desire that love and gratitude may inspire my heart so that I shall sympathize with his pleasure in the thing, before my personal pleasure begins, knowing that it will increase my capability for happiness." Oneida's sexual practices were considered outrageous and sinful by almost all other Americans. Even Oneidans did not agree with all of Noyes's ideas about sex. "There is no reason why [sex] should not be done in public as much as music and dancing," he declared. It would display the art of sex, he explained, and watching "would give pleasure to a great many of the older people who now have nothing to do with the matter." Nonetheless, public sex never caught on among Oneidans.

Oneida Community Mansion House.

Elizabeth Cady Stanton
Women's rights leader Elizabeth Cady Stanton, pictured here with her sons, knew firsthand the joys and frustrations of domestic life. Like other women's rights activists, she sought to expand women's political, moral, and social responsibilities beyond the confines of hearth and home.
Collection of Rhoda Jenkins.

In 1848, about one hundred reformers led by Elizabeth Cady Stanton and Lucretia Mott gathered at Seneca Falls, New York, for the first national women's rights convention in the United States.

complex marriage. To prevent a population explosion and to promote health and self-control, Noyes insisted that Oneida men practice "male continence," sexual intercourse without ejaculation. Noyes also required all members to relinquish their economic property to the community, which developed a lucrative business manufacturing animal traps. Oneida's sexual and economic communalism attracted several hundred members, but most of their neighbors considered Oneidans adulterers, blasphemers, and worse. Yet the practices

that set Oneida apart from its mainstream neighbors strengthened the community, and it survived long after the Civil War.

Women's Rights Activists

Women participated in the many reform activities that grew out of evangelical churches. Women church members outnumbered men two to one and worked to put their religious ideas into practice by joining peace, temperance, antislavery, and other societies. Involvement in reform organizations gave a few women activists practical experience in such political arts as speaking in public, running a meeting, drafting resolutions, and circulating petitions. Along with such experience came confidence. The abolitionist Lydia Maria Child pointed out in 1841 that "those who urged women to become missionaries and form tract societies . . . have changed the household utensil to a living energetic being and they have no spell to turn it into a broom again."

In 1848, about one hundred reformers led by Elizabeth Cady Stanton and Lucretia Mott gathered at Seneca Falls, New York, for the first national women's rights convention in the United States. The Seneca Falls Declaration of Sentiments proclaimed that "the history of mankind is a history of repeated injuries and usurpations on the part of man toward woman, having in direct object the establishment of an absolute tyranny over her." In the style of the Declaration of Independence (see appendix, page A-1), the Seneca Falls Declaration listed the ways in which women had been discriminated against. Through the tyranny of male supremacy, men "endeavored in every way that [they] could to destroy her confidence in her own powers, to lessen her self-respect, and to make her willing to lead a dependent and abject life." The Declaration demanded that women "have immediate admission to all the rights and privileges which belong to them as citizens of the United States," particularly the "inalienable right to the elective franchise."

Nearly two dozen other women's rights conventions assembled before 1860, repeatedly calling for **suffrage**. But they had difficulty receiving a respectful hearing, much less obtaining legislative action. No state came close to permitting women to vote. Politicians and editorialists hooted at the idea. Everyone knew, they sneered, that a woman's place was in the home, rearing her children and civilizing her man. Nonetheless, the Seneca Falls Declaration served as a pathbreaking manifesto of dissent against male supremacy and of support for woman suffrage, which would become the focus of the women's rights movement during the next seventy years.

Abolitionists and the American Ideal

During the 1840s and 1850s, abolitionists continued to struggle to draw the nation's attention to the plight of slaves and the need for emancipation. Former slaves such as Frederick Douglass, Henry Bibb, and Sojourner Truth lectured to reform audiences throughout the North about the cruelties of slavery. Abolitionists published newspapers, held conventions, and petitioned Congress. But they never attracted a mass following among white Americans. Many white Northerners became convinced that slavery was wrong, but they still believed that blacks were inferior. Many other white Northerners shared the common view of white Southerners that slavery was necessary and even desirable. The geographic expansion of the nation during the 1840s offered abolitionists an opportunity to link their unpopular ideal to a goal that many white Northerners found much more attractive—limiting the geographic expansion of slavery, an issue that moved to the center of national politics during the 1850s (see chapter 14).

Black leaders rose to prominence in the abolitionist movement during the 1840s and 1850s. African Americans had actively opposed slavery for decades, but a new generation of leaders came to the forefront in these years. Frederick Douglass, Henry Highland Garnet, William Wells Brown, Martin R. Delany, and others became impatient with white abolitionists' appeals to the conscience of the white majority. Garnet proclaimed in 1843 that slaves should rise in insurrection against their masters, an idea that alienated almost all white people. To express their own uncompromising ideas, black abolitionists founded their own newspapers and held their own antislavery conventions, although they still cooperated with sympathetic whites.

The commitment of black abolitionists to battling slavery grew out of their own experiences with white supremacy. The 250,000 free African Americans in the North and West constituted less than 2 percent of the total population. They confronted the humiliations of racial discrimination in virtually every arena of daily life: at work, at school, at church, in shops, in the streets, on

Abolitionist Meeting
This rare daguerreotype was made by Ezra Greenleaf Weld in August 1850 at an abolitionist meeting in Cazenovia, New York. Frederick Douglass, who had escaped from slavery in Maryland twelve years earlier, is seated on the platform next to the woman at the table. One of the nation's most brilliant and eloquent abolitionists, Douglass also supported equal rights for women. The man immediately behind Douglass gesturing with his outstretched arm is Gerrit Smith, a wealthy New Yorker and militant abolitionist whose funds supported many reform activities. Notice the two black women in similar clothing on either side of Smith and the white woman next to Douglass. Most white Americans considered such voluntary racial proximity scandalous and promiscuous. What messages did abolitionists attempt to convey by attending such protest meetings?
Collection of the J. Paul Getty Museum, Malibu, CA.

trains, in hotels. Only four states (Maine, Massachusetts, New Hampshire, and Vermont) permitted black men to vote; New York imposed a special property-holding requirement on black—but not white—voters, effectively excluding most black men from the **franchise**. The pervasive racial discrimination both handicapped and energized black abolitionists. Some

Back to Africa: The United States in Liberia

In the first half of the nineteenth century, thousands of free African Americans returned to Africa. In Liberia, they established a beachhead for American culture, one that clearly remains alive today. American-sounding names (the county of Maryland), American institutions (Masonic lodges), a red, white, and blue flag patterned on the Stars and Stripes, and a restaurant that advertises Maryland-style fried chicken make it impossible to forget the American origins of this modern-day West African nation.

In 1817, white men with a range of motives founded the American Colonization Society to transport black Americans to Africa. Some colonizationists sympathized with America's oppressed blacks and urged them to return to Africa, their "natural home," to escape racism, improve their lot in life, and help "civilize" an entire continent. Other colonizationists wanted to rid the United States of what they considered a "useless, pernicious, and dangerous" people. Whatever their motivation, colonizationists agreed that the two races could not live together and that blacks should leave. Aware that British antislavery forces had founded Sierra Leone in West Africa as a haven for freed slaves a generation earlier, the Society purchased land to the south from African chiefs. They named it Liberia, after **liberty**, and its capital Monrovia, after President James Monroe.

Between 1820, when it shipped the first settlers to Liberia, and the start of the American Civil War in 1861, the Society sent approximately 12,000 African Americans to Africa. Some 7,000 were slaves whose masters freed them (often because they were favorites or kin) on the condition that they leave America, and some 5,000 were free blacks who chose to go because they had lost hope of achieving equality in the United States. John Russwurm was one such free black who accepted the Society's invitation because he concluded that blacks in America could never overcome "the odium of [an] inferior and degraded caste." The overwhelming majority of free blacks claimed America as their country and decided to make their stand at home. Frederick Douglass spoke for them in 1849 when he denounced colonizationists: "Shame upon the guilty wretches that dare propose . . . such a proposition. We live here—have lived here—have a right to live here, and mean to live here."

American settlers in Liberia found life even harder there than at home. Land along the coast was swampy, covered with forests, and often lacked fresh water. The Society never had enough funds to support the settlers adequately, and even though former masters provided some assistance, the newcomers faced shortages of basic necessities. Moreover, settlers and Africans clashed as the Americans pushed inland, taking land, killing game, and attacking slave traders who kidnapped or bought people to ship as laborers to Cuba and Brazil. The outpost somehow managed to survive, but many emigrants did not. In the first two decades of settlement, "African fever," most likely malaria, killed about one-quarter of the settlers.

In time, the settlers established a foothold, and life grew a little less precarious. They learned to farm without their horses and mules, which could not survive African diseases, and they began trading coffee, sugar, and palm oil. They stabilized the boundaries of the colony, controlling some 250 miles of coastline to a depth of 40 or 50 miles. But by the 1840s, the American Colonization Society was nearly bankrupt. When the U.S. government refused to assume sovereignty of the private colony, the Society demanded that the settlers proclaim independence. In 1847, a few thousand North American immigrants announced the Republic of Liberia and took control of a substantial piece of Africa and several hundred thousand Africans.

The settlers had fled America, but rather than cast off American culture, they clung to it, straining every muscle to rebuild American lives, without slavery and white supremacy, in Africa. As far as possible, they retained American habits in food, dress, manners, and housing. Liberia produced abundant crops of millet, yams, cassava, and pawpaw, but the settlers maintained a taste for flour, pork, and dried fruit, which they imported when they could. Settlers established American institutions, including public schools, fraternal organizations, and temperance societies. Most important, they promoted their evangelical Christian faith by building Methodist and Baptist churches everywhere they settled. Most newcomers felt a profound missionary urge to carry "the blessed Gospel" to the land of their forefathers.

Despite their African heritage, settlers felt little kinship with Africans. The newcomers displayed a strong sense of superiority and engaged in what they considered a

Liberian Crowds Await the U.S. President
In April 1978, Americans and Liberians await the arrival of President Jimmy Carter at the airport outside Monrovia. Flying side by side, the two national flags offer dramatic evidence of the American origins and continuing influence of the United States on Liberian history.
© Wally McNamee/Corbis.

providential effort to "civilize and uplift." "It is something to think that these people are calld [sic] our ancestors," Peyton Skipwith, an ex-slave from Virginia, declared. "In my present thinking if we have any ancestors they could not have been like these hostile tribes . . . for you may . . . do all you can for them and they still will be your enemy." Settlers labored to maintain the distinctions between themselves and the Gola, Kru, and Vai peoples who surrounded them. Africa was populated, Matilda Skipwith insisted, with "the most savage, & blud thirsty people I ever saw." But opposition to Africans did not mean that the African American settler community was united. Settlers carried with them old tensions and divisions, especially those between the free-born and slave-born. Light-skinned free-born African Americans often arrived with more money, education, and skills, and they quickly enjoyed greater wealth and political power.

The settlers did, however, agree that they had found in Africa what they had primarily come for— dignity and freedom. Despite the continuing heartache of leaving family behind and the stubborn reality of physical hardship, they refused to return to America. In 1848, one African American declared, "I will never consent to leave the country . . . for this is the only place where a colored person can enjoy his liberty, for there exists no prejudice of color in this country, and every man is free and equal."

In the second half of the nineteenth century, when European powers sliced Africa into colonies, Liberia managed to retain its political independence. But in the 1920s an American corporation, the Firestone Rubber Company, made Liberia a kind of economic colony. Today, Liberians of American descent comprise only about 5 percent of Liberia's population, but they continue to wield disproportionate power. Only in 1946 did the dominant Americo-Liberians allow indigenous people to vote.

In 1980, the African majority rose up in bloody rebellion against the still-Americanized Liberian elite. Years of civil war have largely wrecked the country, trapping its people in fear and starvation.

Contemporary Liberia

Liberians have implored the United States, which some call "big brother," to recognize its historic connections with the African nation and fulfill what they see as its continuing responsibilities by intervening with peacekeeping forces. Black Americans in the twentieth century developed a close sense of kinship with Africa, particularly in the 1950s and 1960s when they sensed the interconnectedness of freedom struggles on both sides of the Atlantic, but the U.S. government has been slower to acknowledge historic ties. In August 2003, following a bloody uprising in Liberia and intense pressure from the international community for swift action, the Bush administration successfully pressured President Charles Taylor into resigning his office, and sent in a token handful of troops to keep the peace. Nevertheless, the U.S. government continues to resist the argument that the United States has a special relationship with Liberia.

BIBLIOGRAPHY

David Eltis, *Economic Growth and the Ending of the Transatlantic Slave Trade* (1987).

James H. Meriwether, *Proudly We Can Be Africans: Black Americans and Africa, 1935–1961* (2002).

Floyd J. Miller, *The Search for a Black Nationality: Black Emigration and Colonization, 1787–1863* (1975).

Randall M. Miller, ed., *Dear Master: Letters of a Slave Family* (1978).

Tom W. Shick, *Behold the Promised Land: A History of Afro-American Settler Society in Nineteenth-Century Liberia* (1977).

Philip J. Staudenraus, *The African Colonization Movement, 1816–1865* (1961).

Richard West, *Back to Africa: A History of Sierra Leone and Liberia* (1970).

Bell I. Wiley, ed., *Slaves No More: Letters from Liberia, 1833–1869* (1980).

cooperated with the American Colonization Society's efforts to send freed slaves and other black Americans to Liberia in west Africa (see "Beyond America's Borders," page 430). Other black American leaders organized campaigns against segregation, particularly in transportation and education. Their most notable success came in 1855 when Massachusetts integrated public schools. Elsewhere white supremacy continued unabated.

Outside the public spotlight, free African Americans in the North and West contributed to the antislavery cause by quietly aiding fugitive slaves. Harriet Tubman escaped from slavery in Maryland in 1849 and repeatedly risked her freedom and her life to return to the South to escort slaves to freedom. When the opportunity arose, free blacks in the North provided fugitive slaves with food, a safe place to rest, and a helping hand. This "underground railroad" ran mainly through black neighborhoods, black churches, and black homes, an outgrowth of the antislavery sentiment and opposition to white supremacy that unified nearly all African Americans in the North.

Conclusion: Free Labor, Free Men

In the 1840s, diplomacy and war handed the United States 1.2 million square miles and more than 1,000 miles of Pacific coastline. California almost immediately rewarded its new owners with mountains of gold. To most Americans, vast geographical expansion seemed to be the natural companion of a stunning economic transformation. A cluster of interrelated developments—steam power, railroads, and the growing mechanization of agriculture and manufacturing—resulted in greater productivity, a burst of output from farms and factories, and prosperity for many.

To Northerners, industrial evolution confirmed the choice they had made to eliminate slavery and to promote free labor as the key to independence, equality, and prosperity. Millions of Northerners, like Abraham Lincoln, could point to personal experience as evidence of the practical truth of the free-labor ideal. But millions of others had different stories to tell. Rather than producing economic equality, the free-labor system saw wealth and poverty continue to rub shoulders. Instead of social independence, more than half of the nation's free-labor workforce toiled for someone else by 1860. Free-labor enthusiasts denied that the problems were built into the system. They argued that most social ills—including poverty and dependency—sprang from individual deficiencies. Consequently, reformers usually focused on the lack of self-control and discipline, on sin and alcohol. They denied that free labor meant exploitation. They argued that slaves, not free workers, suffered. White Southerners, in contrast, pitied northern free workers, not slaves.

By the 1840s, the nation was half slave and half free, and each region was animated by economic interests, cultural values, and political aims that were antithetical to those of the other. Not even the victory over Mexico could bridge the deepening differences between North and South.

For additional firsthand accounts of this period, see Chapter 12 in Michael Johnson, ed., *Reading the American Past*, Third Edition.

To assess your mastery of the material in this chapter, see the Online Study Guide at bedfordstmartins.com/roark.

For Web links related to topics in this chapter, see "HistoryLinks," "DocLinks," and "PlaceLinks" at bedfordstmartins.com/roark.

CHRONOLOGY

1836 • Texas declares independence from Mexico.

1837 • John Deere patents his steel plow.

1840s • Americans begin harnessing steam power to manufacturing.
• Cyrus McCormick and others create practical mechanical reapers.

1841 • First wagon trains head west on Oregon Trail.
• Vice President John Tyler becomes president when William Henry Harrison dies in office after one month.

1844 • Democrat James K. Polk elected president on platform calling for annexation of Texas and Oregon.
• Samuel F. B. Morse invents telegraph.

1845 • Term *manifest destiny* coined by New York journalist John L. O'Sullivan; used as justification for Anglo-American settlers to take land in West.
• United States annexes Texas, which enters Union as slave state.

1846 • Bear Flag Revolt, independence movement to secede from Mexico, takes place in California.
• Congress declares war on Mexico.

• United States and Great Britain agree to divide Oregon Country at forty-ninth parallel.

1847 • Brigham Young leads advance party of Mormons to Great Salt Lake in Utah.

1848 • Treaty of Guadalupe Hidalgo ends Mexican War: Mexico gives up all claims to Texas north of Rio Grande and cedes provinces of New Mexico and California to United States.
• Oneida community organized in New York.
• First U.S. women's rights convention takes place at Seneca Falls, New York.

1849 • California gold rush begins.
• Harriet Tubman escapes from slavery in Maryland.

1850 • Mormon community of Deseret annexed to United States as Utah Territory.

1851 • Conference in Laramie, Wyoming, between U.S. government and Plains tribes marks beginning of government policy of forcing Indians onto reservations.

1855 • Massachusetts integrates public schools as result of campaigns led by African Americans.

BIBLIOGRAPHY

General Works

Glenn C. Altschuler and Stuart M. Blumin, *Rude Republic: Americans and Their Politics in the Nineteenth Century* (2000).

Stuart Bruchey, *Enterprise: The Dynamic Economy of a Free People* (1990).

David B. Danbom, *Born in the Country: A History of Rural America* (1995).

David Herbert Donald, *Lincoln* (1995).

John Mack Faragher, *Sugar Creek: Life on the Illinois Frontier* (1986).

Lori D. Ginzberg, *Women and the Work of Benevolence: Morality, Politics, and Class in the Nineteenth-Century United States* (1990).

Jon Gjerde, *The Minds of the West: Ethnocultural Evolution in the Rural Middle West, 1830–1917* (1997).

Nathan O. Hatch, *The Democratization of American Christianity* (1991).

Helen Lefkowitz Horowitz, *Rereading Sex: Battles over Sexual Knowledge and Suppression in Nineteenth-Century America* (2002).

Bruce Laurie, *Artisans into Workers: Labor in Nineteenth-Century America* (1989).

Patricia Nelson Limerick, *The Legacy of Conquest: The Unbroken Past of the American West* (1987).

Malcolm Rohrbough, *Days of Gold: The California Gold Rush and the American Nation* (1997).

Mark Voss-Hubbard, *Beyond Party: Cultures of Antipartisanship in Northern Politics before the Civil War* (2002).

Richard White, *"It's Your Misfortune and None of My Own": A New History of the American West* (1993).

Kenneth J. Winkle, *The Young Eagle: The Rise of Abraham Lincoln* (2001).

Politics and Expansion

Leonard J. Arrington and Davis Bitton, *The Mormon Experience: A History of the Latter-Day Saints* (1979).

Richard A. Bartlett, *The New Country: A Social History of the American Frontier, 1776–1890* (1974).

William A. Bowen, *The Willamette Valley: Migration and Settlement on the Oregon Frontier* (1978).

Gene Brack, *Mexico Views Manifest Destiny, 1821–1846: An Essay on the Origins of the Mexican War* (1975).

Mark M. Carroll, *Homesteads Ungovernable: Families, Sex, Race, and Law in Frontier Texas, 1823–1860* (2001).

Tom Chaffin, *Pathfinder: John Charles Frémont and the Course of American Empire* (2002).

Donald E. Chipman, *Spanish Texas, 1519–1821* (1992).

Arnoldo De Leon, *The Tejano Community, 1836–1900* (1982).

William Dusinberre, *Slavemaster President: The Double Career of James Polk* (2003).

John Mack Faragher, *Women and Men on the Overland Trail* (1979).

James R. Gibson, *Farming the Frontier: The Agricultural Opening of the Oregon Country, 1786–1846* (1985).

William H. Goetzmann, *New Lands, New Men: America and the Second Great Age of Discovery* (1986).

Thomas R. Hietala, *Manifest Design: Anxious Aggrandizement in Late Jacksonian America* (rev. ed., 2002).

Reginald Horsman, *Race and Manifest Destiny: The Origins of American Racial Anglo-Saxonism* (1981).

Stephen G. Hyslop, *Bound for Santa Fe: The Road to New Mexico and the American Conquest, 1806–1848* (2002).

Julie Roy Jeffrey, *Frontier Women: The Trans-Mississippi West, 1840–1880* (1979).

D. W. Meinig, *The Shaping of America: A Geographical Perspective on 500 Years of History*, vol. 2, *Continental America, 1800–1867* (1993).

Frederick Merk, *Manifest Destiny and Mission in American History: A Reinterpretation* (1963).

David Montejano, *Anglos and Mexicans in the Making of Texas, 1836–1986* (1987).

Gregory H. Nobles, *American Frontiers: Cultural Encounters and Continental Conquest* (1997).

David M. Pletcher, *The Diplomacy of Annexation: Texas, Oregon, and the Mexican War* (1973).

Glenda Riley, *The Female Frontier: A Comparative View of Women on the Prairie and the Plains* (1988).

Randy Roberts and James L. Olson, *A Line in the Sand: The Alamo in Blood and Memory* (2001).

Malcolm J. Rohrbough, *The Trans-Appalachian Frontier* (1978).

Joel H. Silbey, *The American Political Nation, 1838–1915* (1991).

John D. Unruh, *The Plains Across: The Overland Emigrants and the Trans-Mississippi West, 1840–1860* (1979).

David J. Weber, *The Mexican Frontier, 1821–1846: The American Southwest under Mexico* (1982).

Sanford Wexler, ed., *Westward Expansion: An Eyewitness History* (1991).

The Mexican War and California Gold

Jajia Aarim-Heriot, *Chinese Immigrants, African Americans, and Racial Anxiety in the United States, 1848–82* (2003).

K. Jack Bauer, *The Mexican War, 1846–1848* (1974).

Peter J. Blodgett, *Land of Golden Dreams: California in the Gold Rush Decade, 1848–1858* (1999).

H. W. Brands, *The Age of Gold: The California Gold Rush and the New American Dream* (2002).

Yong Chen, *Chinese San Francisco, 1850–1943: A Trans-Pacific Community* (2000).

Seymour V. Conner and Odie B. Faulk, *North America Divided: The Mexican War, 1846–1848* (1971).

John S. D. Eisenhower, *So Far from God: The U.S. War with Mexico, 1846–1848* (1989).

Donald S. Frazier, ed., *The United States and Mexico at War: Nineteenth-Century Expansionism and Conflict* (1998).

William S. Greever, *Bonanza West: The Story of the Western Mining Rushes, 1848–1900* (1963).

Albert L. Hurtado, *Indian Survival on the California Frontier* (1988).

Albert L. Hurtado, *Intimate Frontiers: Sex, Gender, and Culture in Old California* (1999).

Robert H. Jackson and Edward Castillo, *Indians, Franciscans, and Spanish Colonization: The Impact of the Mission System on California Indians* (1995).

Robert W. Johannsen, *To the Halls of the Montezumas: The Mexican War in the American Imagination* (1985).

David Alan Johnson, *Founding the Far West: California, Oregon, and Nevada, 1840–1890* (1992).

Susan Lee Johnson, *Roaring Camp: The Social World of the California Gold Rush* (2000).

Ernest M. Lander Jr., *Reluctant Imperialists: Calhoun, the South Carolinians, and the Mexican War* (1980).

Rudolph M. Lapp, *Blacks in Gold Rush California* (1977).

Ward McAfee and J. Cordell Robinson, eds., *Origins of the Mexican War: A Documentary Source Book*, 2 vols. (1982).

James M. McCaffrey, *Army of Manifest Destiny: The American Soldier in the Mexican War, 1846–1848* (1992).

Charles J. McClain, *In Search of Equality: The Chinese Struggle against Discrimination in Nineteenth-Century America* (1994).

Kenneth N. Owens, *Riches for All: The California Gold Rush and the World* (2002).

Rodman W. Paul, *Mining Frontiers of the Far West, 1848–1880* (1963).

Ramón Eduardo Ruiz, ed., *The Mexican War: Was It Manifest Destiny?* (1963).

Richard Bruce Winders, *Mr. Polk's Army: The American Military Experience in the Mexican War* (1997).

The Economy and Free Labor

Edward J. Balleisen, *Navigating Failure: Bankruptcy and Commercial Society in Antebellum America* (2001).

Howard Bodenhorn, *A History of Banking in Antebellum America: Financial Markets and Economic Development in an Era of Nation Building* (2000).

James Dilts, *The Great Road: The Building of the Baltimore and Ohio, the Nation's First Railroad, 1828–1853* (2003).

J. Matthew Gallman, *Receiving Erin's Children: Philadelphia, Liverpool, and the Irish Famine Migration, 1854–1855* (2000).

Jonathan A. Glickstein, *Concepts of Free Labor in Antebellum America* (1991).

Jonathan A. Glickstein, *American Exceptionalism, American Anxiety: Wages, Competition, and Degraded Labor in the Antebellum United States* (2002).

Brooke Hindle and Steven Lubar, *Engines of Change: The American Industrial Revolution, 1790–1860* (1986).

Donald R. Hoke, *Ingenious Yankees: The Rise of the American System of Manufactures in the Private Sector* (1990).

David A. Hounshell, *From the American System to Mass Production, 1800–1932: The Development of Manufacturing Technology in the United States* (1984).

Reeve Huston, *Land and Freedom: Rural Society, Popular Protest, and Party Politics in Antebellum New York* (2000).

Paul Israel, *From Machine Shop to Industrial Laboratory: Telegraphy and the Changing Context of American Invention, 1830–1920* (1992).

Allan Kulikoff, *The Agrarian Origins of American Capitalism* (1992).

Amy Schrager Lang, *Syntax of Class: Writing Inequality in Nineteenth-Century America* (2003).

Edward Laxton, *The Famine Ships: The Irish Exodus to America* (1998).

Robert A. Margo, *Wages and Labor Markets in the United States, 1820–1860* (2000).

Jonathan Prude, *The Coming of Industrial Order: Town and Factory Life in Rural Massachusetts, 1810–1860* (1983).

W. J. Rorabaugh, *The Craft Apprentice: From Franklin to the Machine Age in America* (1986).

Antebellum Culture and Reform

Norman Basch, *In the Eyes of the Law: Women, Marriage, and Property in Nineteenth-Century New York* (1982).

Stuart Blumin, *The Emergence of the Middle Class: Social Experience in the American City, 1790–1900* (1989).

Jeanne Boydston, *Home and Work: Housework, Wages, and the Ideology of Labor in the Early Republic* (1990).

Bruce Dorsey, *Reforming Men and Women: Gender in the City* (2002).

Ellen Carol DuBois, *Feminism and Suffrage: The Emergence of an Independent Women's Suffrage Movement in America, 1848–1869* (1978).

David F. Ericson, *The Debate over Slavery: Antislavery and Proslavery Liberalism in Antebellum America* (2001).

Robert Fanuzzi, *Abolition's Public Sphere* (2003).

Joseph P. Ferrie, *Yankeys Now: Immigrants in the Antebellum United States, 1840–1860* (1999).

Lawrence Foster, *Women, Family, and Utopia: Communal Experiments of the Shakers, the Oneida Community, and the Mormons* (1991).

Rhoda Golden Freeman, *The Free Negro in New York City in the Era before the Civil War* (1994).

Kathryn Grover, *The Fugitives' Gibraltar: Escaping Slaves and Abolition in New Bedford, Massachusetts* (2001).

Paul Goodman, *Of One Blood: Abolitionism and the Origins of Racial Equality* (1998).

Karen Halttunen, *Confidence Men and Painted Women: A Study of Middle-Class Culture in America, 1830–1870* (1982).

Debra Gold Hansen, *Strained Sisterhood: Gender and Class in the Boston Female Anti-Slavery Society* (1993).

Stephen John Hartnett, *Democratic Dissent and the Cultural Fictions of Antebellum America* (2002).

David Henkin, *City Reading: Written Words and Public Spaces in Antebellum New York* (1999).

Nancy A. Hewitt, *Women's Activism and Social Change: Rochester, New York, 1822–1872* (1984).

Leo P. Hirrel, *Children of Wrath: New School Calvinism and Antebellum Reform* (1998).

Sylvia D. Hoffert, *When Hens Crow: The Women's Rights Movement in Antebellum America* (1995).

James O. Horton and Lois E. Horton, *In Hope of Liberty: Culture, Community, and Protest among Northern Free Blacks, 1700–1860* (1998).

Nancy Isenberg, *Sex and Citizenship in Antebellum America* (1998).

Julie Roy Jeffrey, *The Great Silent Army of Abolitionism: Ordinary Women in the Antislavery Movement* (1998).

Joan M. Jensen, *Loosening the Bonds: Mid-Atlantic Farm Women, 1750–1850* (1986).

Carl F. Kaestle, *Pillars of the Republic: Common Schools and American Society, 1780–1860* (1983).

Spencer Klaw, *Without Sin: The Life and Death of the Oneida Community* (1993).

Isabelle Lehuu, *Carnival on the Page: Popular Print Media in Antebellum America* (2000).

Timothy Mahoney, *Provincial Lives: Middle-Class Experience in the Antebellum Middle West* (1999).

Henry Mayer, *All on Fire: William Lloyd Garrison and the Abolition of Slavery* (1998).

William J. McFeely, *Frederick Douglass* (1991).

Kerby A. Miller, *Emigrants and Exiles: Ireland and the Irish Exodus to North America* (1985).

Steven Mintz, *Moralists and Modernizers: America's Pre–Civil War Reformers* (1995).

Richard S. Newman, *The Transformation of American Abolitionism: Fighting Slavery in the Early Republic* (2002).

John W. Quist, *Restless Visionaries: The Social Roots of Antebellum Reform in Alabama and Michigan* (1998).

Patrick Rael, *Black Identity and Black Protest in the Antebellum North* (2002).

Mary P. Ryan, *Civic Wars: Democracy and Public Life in the American City during the Nineteenth Century* (1998).

Susan M. Ryan, *The Grammar of Good Intentions: Race and the Antebellum Culture of Benevolence* (2003).

Mark S. Schantz, *Piety in Providence: Class Dimensions of Religious Experience in Antebellum Rhode Island* (2000).

John Stauffer, *The Black Hearts of Men: Radical Abolitionists and the Transformation of Race* (2002).

Daniel W. Stowell, *In Tender Consideration: Women, Families, and the Law in Abraham Lincoln's Illinois* (2002).

Albert J. Von Frank, *The Trials of Anthony Burns: Freedom and Slavery in Emerson's Boston* (1998).

Edward L. Widmer, *Young America: The Flowering of Democracy in New York City* (1998).

Shirley Yee, *Black Women Abolitionists: A Study in Activism, 1828–1860* (1992).

Jean Fagan Yellin, *Women and Sisters: The Antislavery Feminists in American Culture* (1989).

Susan Zaeske, *Signatures of Citizenship: Petitioning, Antislavery, and Women's Political Identity* (2003).

CLAY JUG

This ceramic water cooler, made in about
1840, is attributed to Thomas Chandler, a
famous potter of Edgefield District, South
Carolina. The relatively fine clothes of the
African American man and woman portrayed on
the vessel suggest that they are house servants.
On the wall of the home of Alexander Stephens in
Crawfordsville, Georgia, an intriguing letter from
Stephens states that two of his favorite slaves are
getting married and orders the plantation manager to
butcher a hog for their wedding. This cooler, with its
portrait of a couple, a hog, and a jug, way have been
commissioned by Stephens to commemorate the union.

Potters made vessels to be used—to hold water and food.
Analysis of the form, decoration, and glazes of southern pottery suggests a blend of European, African, and
Native American ceramic traditions. Some pottery went beyond the utilitarian and became art. The most
renowned slave potter was an Edgefield man named Dave, who skillfully fashioned huge vessels, inscribed poems on their surfaces, and proudly and boldly signed them "Dave the potter."

The Slave South

1820–1860

NAT TURNER WAS BORN A SLAVE in Southampton County, Virginia, in October 1800. People in his neighborhood claimed that he had always been different. His parents noticed special marks on his body, which they said were signs that he was "intended for some great purpose." His master said that he learned to read without being taught. As an adolescent, he adopted an austere lifestyle of Christian devotion and fasting. In his twenties, he received visits from the "Spirit," the same spirit, he believed, that had spoken to the ancient prophets. In time, Nat Turner began to interpret these things to mean that God had appointed him an instrument of divine vengeance for the sin of slaveholding.

In the early morning of August 22, 1831, he set out with six trusted friends—Hark, Henry, Sam, Nelson, Will, and Jack—to punish slave owners and free their suffering slaves. Turner struck the first blow, an ax to the head of his master, Joseph Travis. The rebels killed all of the white men, women, and children they encountered in each household they attacked. By noon, they had visited eleven farms and slaughtered fifty-seven whites and, along the way, added fifty or sixty men to their army. Word spread quickly, however, and soon the militia and hundreds of local whites gathered. By the next day, whites had captured or killed all of the rebels, except Nat Turner, who successfully hid out for about ten weeks before being captured in nearby woods. Within a week, he was tried, convicted, and executed. By then, forty-five slaves had stood trial, twenty had been convicted and hanged, and another ten had been transported from Virginia. Frenzied whites had killed another hundred or more blacks—insurgents and innocent bystanders—in their counterattack against the rebellion.

Virginia's governor John Floyd asked how Turner's band of "assassins and murderers" could have assaulted the "unsuspecting and defenseless" citizens of "one of the fairest counties in the Commonwealth." White Virginians prided themselves on having the "mildest" slavery in the South, but sixty black rebels on a rampage challenged the comforting theory of the contented slave. Nonetheless, whites found explanations that allowed them to feel safer. They placed the blame on outside agitators. In 1829, David Walker, a freeborn black man living in Boston, had published his *Appeal . . . to the Coloured Citizens of the World*, an invitation to slaves to rise up in bloody rebellion, and copies had fallen into the hands of Virginia slaves. Moreover, on January 1, 1831, in Boston, William Lloyd Garrison, the Massachusetts abolitionist, had published the first issue of *Liberator*, his fiery newspaper. White Virginians also dismissed the rebellion's leader, Nat Turner, as insane. "He is a complete fanatic, or plays his part admirably," wrote Thomas R. Gray, the lawyer who was assigned to defend Turner.

Nat Turner
There are no known contemporary images of Nat Turner. This imagined portrait comes from William Still's *The Underground Railroad* (1872). Meeting secretly at night deep in a forest and thus well out of earshot of whites, an intense Turner passionately tries to convince four other slaves to join him in rebellion. What do their faces reveal? What considerations do you suppose entered their calculations about whether to join Turner? Significantly perhaps, they are holding work tools, not arms.
Library of Congress.

labor, Southerners spread slavery, cotton, and plantations. Geographic expansion meant that slavery became more vigorous and profitable than ever, embraced more people, and increased the South's political power. **Antebellum** Southerners included diverse peoples who at times found themselves at odds with one another—not only slaves and free people, but also women and men; Indians, Africans, and Europeans; and aristocrats and common folk. Nevertheless, beneath this diversity of Southerners, there was also forming a distinctively southern society and culture. The South became a slave society, and most white Southerners were proud of it.

The Growing Distinctiveness of the South

From the earliest settlements, inhabitants of southern colonies had shared a great deal with northern colonists. Most whites in both sections were British and **Protestant**, and they spoke a common language, even if a regional twang or drawl flavored their speech. They shared an exuberant pride in their victorious revolution against British rule. The creation of the new nation under the Constitution in 1789 forged strong political ties that bound all Americans. In the nineteenth century, the beginnings of a national economy fostered economic interdependence and communication across regional boundaries. White Americans everywhere celebrated the achievements of the prosperous young nation, and they looked forward to its seemingly boundless future.

Despite these national similarities, Southerners and Northerners grew increasingly different. The French political observer Alexis de Tocqueville believed he knew why. "I could easily prove," he asserted in 1831, "that almost all the differences which may be noticed between the character of the Americans in the Southern and Northern states have originated in slavery." Slavery made the South different, and it was the differences between the North and the South, not the similarities, that came to shape antebellum American history.

In the months following the insurrection, white Virginians debated the future of slavery in their state. While some expressed substantial doubts, the Virginia legislature reaffirmed the state's determination to beat back threats to white supremacy. Delegates passed a raft of laws strengthening the institution of slavery and further restricting free blacks. A thirty-year-old professor at the College of William and Mary, Thomas R. Dew, published a vigorous defense of slavery that became the bible of Southerners' proslavery arguments. More than ever, the nation was divided along the "Mason-Dixon line," the surveyors' mark that in colonial times had established the boundary between Maryland and Pennsylvania but half a century later divided the free North and slave South.

Black slavery increasingly dominated the South and shaped it into a distinctive region. In the decades after 1820, Southerners, like Northerners, raced westward, but unlike Northerners who spread small farms and free

> Slavery made the South different, and it was the differences between the North and the South, not the similarities, that came to shape antebellum American history.

Cotton Kingdom, Slave Empire

In the first half of the nineteenth century, legions of Americans migrated west. In the South, the stampede began after the Creek War of 1813–14, which divested the Creek Nation of 24 million acres and initiated the government campaign to remove Indian people living east of the Mississippi River to the West (see chapters 10 and 11). Eager slaveholders seeking virgin acreage for new plantations, struggling farmers looking for patches of good land for small farms, herders and drovers pushing their hogs and cattle toward fresh pastures—anyone who was restless and ambitious felt the pull of Indian land. Southerners pushed westward relentlessly, until by mid-century the South encompassed nearly a million square miles, much of it planted in cotton.

The South's climate and geography were ideally suited for the cultivation of cotton. As Southerners advanced nearly a thousand miles west from the Atlantic, they encountered a variety of terrain, soil, and weather, but the cotton seeds they carried with them proved very adaptable. They grew in the sandy plains of the tidewater along the Atlantic, in the red clay of the piedmont east of the Blue Ridge and Appalachian Mountains, and especially in the rich soils of the black belt (named for the dark color of the soil in Georgia and Alabama) and of the alluvial deltas of the Mississippi Valley. Cotton requires two hundred frost-free days from planting to picking and prefers rains that are plentiful in spring and lighter in fall, conditions found in much of the South. By the 1830s, cotton fields stretched from southern Virginia to central Texas. Heavy westward migration led to statehood for Arkansas in 1836 and for Texas and Florida in 1845. Production soared, from 300,000 bales in 1830 to nearly 5 million in 1860, and by 1860 the South produced three-fourths of the world's supply. The South—especially that tier of states from

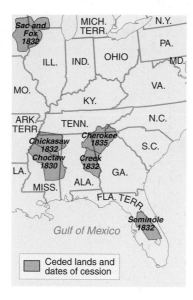

Frontier Land Opened by Indian Removal, 1830s

South Carolina west to Texas known as the Lower South—had become the cotton kingdom (Map 13.1).

The cotton kingdom was also a slave empire. The South's cotton boom rested on the backs of slaves, who grew 75 percent of the crop on plantations, toiling in gangs in broad fields under the direct supervision of whites. As cotton agriculture expanded westward, whites shipped more than 300,000 slaves out of the old seaboard states. Some slaves accompanied masters who were leaving behind worn-out, eroded plantations, but at least two-thirds were victims of a brutal but thriving domestic slave trade. Traders advertised for slaves who were "hearty and well made" and marched black men, women, and children hundreds of miles to the new plantation regions of the Lower South. Cotton, slaves, and plantations moved west together.

Slave Traders: Sold to Tennessee

Slave trading—or "Negro speculation," as it was called by contemporaries—was a booming business in the antebellum South. This color drawing by Lewis Miller portrays slaves walking from Virginia to Tennessee under the watchful eyes of professional slave traders. A few children accompany the adults, some of whom may be their parents. Forced migrations almost always resulted in the separation of black family members. Abby Aldrich Rockefeller Folk Art Center, Williamsburg, VA.

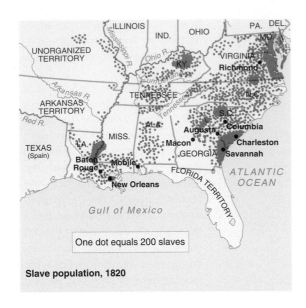

Slave population, 1820

One dot equals 200 slaves

Slave population, 1860

One dot equals 200 slaves

Cotton production, 1820

One dot equals 1,000 bales

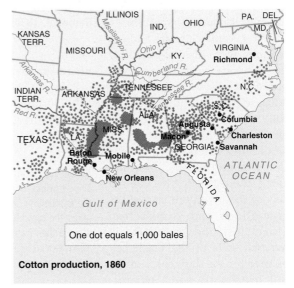

Cotton production, 1860

One dot equals 1,000 bales

MAP 13.1   Cotton Kingdom, Slave Empire: 1820 and 1860
As the production of cotton soared, the slave population increased dramatically. Slaves continued to toil in tobacco and rice fields along the Atlantic seaboard, but increasingly they worked on cotton plantations in Alabama, Mississippi, and Louisiana.

READING THE MAP: Where was slavery most prevalent in 1820? In 1860? How did the spread of slavery compare with the spread of cotton?
CONNECTIONS: How much of the world's cotton was produced in the American South in 1860? While most slaves worked in agriculture, how else were slaves employed?

FOR MORE HELP ANALYZING THESE MAPS, see the map activity for this chapter in the Online Study Guide at bedfordstmartins.com/roark.

The slave population grew enormously. Southern slaves numbered fewer than 700,000 in 1790, about 2 million in 1830, and over 4 million by 1860, an increase of almost 600 percent in seven decades. By 1860, the South contained more slaves than all the other slave societies in the New World combined. The extraordinary growth was not the result of the importation of slaves, which was outlawed in 1808. Instead, the slave population grew through natural reproduction. By the nineteenth century, most slaves were native-born Southerners.

The South in Black and White

By 1860, one in every three Southerners was black (more than 4 million blacks and 8 million whites). In the Lower South, the proportion was higher, for whites and blacks lived there in almost equal numbers. In Mississippi and South Carolina, blacks were the majority (Figure 13.1). The contrast with the North was striking: In 1860, only one Northerner in 76 was black (about 250,000 blacks to 19 million whites).

The presence of large numbers of African Americans had profound consequences for the South. Southern culture—language, food, music, religion, and even accents—was in part shaped by blacks. But the most direct consequence of the South's biracialism was the response it stimulated in the region's white majority. Southern whites were dedicated to white supremacy. Northern whites believed in racial superiority, too, but they lived in a society in which blacks made up barely more than 1 percent of the population. Their commitment to white supremacy lacked the intensity and urgency increasingly felt by white Southerners. White Southerners lived among millions of blacks, whom they simultaneously despised and feared. They despised blacks because they considered them members of an inferior race, further degraded by their status as slaves. They feared blacks because they realized that slaves had every reason to hate them and to seek to end their oppression, as Nat Turner had, by any means necessary.

Attacks on slavery after 1820—from blacks and a handful of white antislavery advocates within the South and from abolitionists without—jolted southern slaveholders into a distressing

> The presence of large numbers of African Americans had profound consequences for the South. Southern culture—language, food, music, religion, and even accents—was in part shaped by blacks.

FIGURE 13.1 Black and White Populations in the South, 1860
Blacks represented a much larger fraction of the population in the South than in the North, but considerable variation existed from state to state. Only one Missourian in ten, for example, was black, while Mississippi and South Carolina had black majorities. States in the Upper South were "whiter" than states in the Lower South, despite the Upper South's greater number of free blacks.

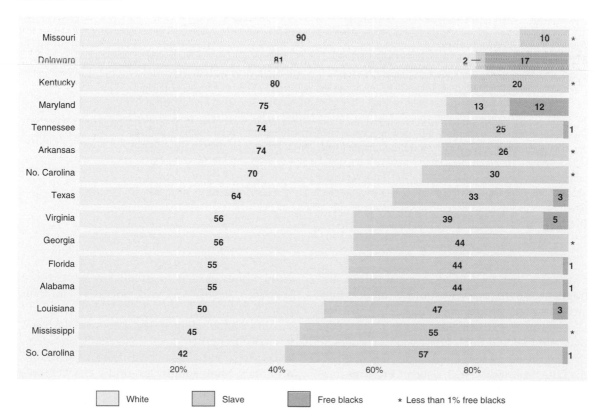

State	White	Slave	Free blacks
Missouri	90	10	*
Delaware	81	2	17
Kentucky	80	20	*
Maryland	75	13	12
Tennessee	74	25	1
Arkansas	74	26	*
No. Carolina	70	30	*
Texas	64	33	3
Virginia	56	39	5
Georgia	56	44	*
Florida	55	44	1
Alabama	55	44	1
Louisiana	50	47	3
Mississippi	45	55	*
So. Carolina	42	57	1

20%   40%   60%   80%

■ White   ■ Slave   ■ Free blacks   * Less than 1% free blacks

The Fruits of Amalgamation

White Southerners and Northerners alike generally agreed that giving blacks equal rights would lead to miscegenation (also known as "amalgamation"). In this lithograph from 1839, Edward W. Clay of Philadelphia attacked abolitionists by imagining the outcome of their misguided campaign. He drew a beautiful white woman with her two black children, one suckling at her breast while her dark-skinned, ridiculously overdressed husband, resting his feet in his wife's lap, reads an abolitionist newspaper. The couple is attended by a white servant. Another interracial couple—perhaps the man is abolitionist William Lloyd Garrison himself—has come calling. Hanging on the wall is a picture entitled *Othello & Desdemona*, based on the popular play *Othello*, a tragic tale about a couple who crossed the color line. A black and a white dog play indiscriminately on the floor. Abolitionists denied the charge of amalgamation and pointed to the lasciviousness of southern slaveholders as the true source of miscegenation in antebellum America.

Courtesy, American Antiquarian Society.

awareness that they lived in a dangerous and fragile world. In response, southern leaders initiated fresh efforts to strengthen slavery. State legislatures constructed elaborate slave codes that required the total submission of slaves to their masters and to white society in general. As the Louisiana code stated, a slave "owes his master . . . a respect without bounds, and an absolute obedience." The laws underlined the authority of all whites, not just masters. Any white could "correct" slaves who did not stay "in their place."

Intellectuals joined legislators in the campaign to strengthen slavery. The South's academics, writers, and clergy constructed a proslavery argument that sought to unify the region's whites around slavery and provide ammunition for the emerging war of words with northern abolitionists. Under the intellectuals' tutelage, the white South gradually moved away from defending slavery as a "necessary evil"—the halfhearted argument popular in Jefferson's day—and toward a full-throated, aggressive defense of slavery as a "positive good." John C. Calhoun declared that in the states where slavery had been abolished "the condition of the African, instead of being improved, has become worse," while in the slave states the Africans "have improved greatly in every respect."

Slavery's champions employed every imaginable defense. The law protected slavery, they declared, for slaves were legal property. And wasn't the security of property the bedrock of American **liberty**? They also used historical evidence to endorse slavery. Weren't the great civilizations—such as those of the Hebrews, Greeks, and Romans—slave societies? They argued that the Bible, properly interpreted, also sanctioned slavery. Old Testament patriarchs owned slaves, they observed, and in the New Testament Paul returned the runaway slave Onesimus to his master. Some proslavery spokesmen went on the offensive and attacked the economy and society of the North. George Fitzhugh of Virginia argued that behind the North's grand slogans—**free labor**, individualism, and egalitarianism—lay a heartless philosophy: "Every man for himself, and the devil take the hindmost." Gouging capitalists exploited wage workers unmercifully, Fitzhugh said, and he contrasted the vicious capitalist-laborer relationship with the humane relations that he claimed prevailed between masters and slaves because slaves were valuable capital that masters sought to protect.

Since slavery was a condition that white southerners reserved exclusively for African Americans, the heart of the defense of slavery slavon claims of black inferiority. Black enbellun t was both necessary and proper, antebellum inferior nders argued, because Africans were was a mass gs. Rather than exploitative, slavery lifted lowly ilizing effort by caring whites that taught them d iplined work, and converted them to soul-sav g Christianity. According to Virginian Thomas R. Dew, most slaves were grateful. He declared that "the slaves of a good master are his warmest, most constant, and most devoted friends."

Black slavery encouraged whites to unify around race rather than to divide by class. The grubbiest, most tobacco-stained white man

could proudly proclaim his superiority to all blacks and his equality with the most refined southern patrician. Because slaves were not recognized as citizens in the South, Georgia attorney Thomas R. R. Cobb observed, every white Southerner "feels that he belongs to an elevated class. It matters not that he is no slaveholder; he is not of the inferior race; he is a freeborn citizen." Consequently, the "poorest meets the richest as an equal; sits at his table with him; salutes him as a neighbor; meets him in every public assembly, and stands on the same social platform." In the South, Cobb boasted, "there is no war of classes."

In reality, slavery did not create perfect harmony among whites or ease every strain along class lines. But by providing every antebellum white Southerner symbolic membership in the ruling class, racial slavery helped whites bridge differences in wealth, education, and culture. Slavery meant white dominance, white superiority, and white equality.

The Plantation Economy

As important as slavery was in unifying white Southerners, only about one-quarter of the white population lived in slaveholding families. A majority of slaveholders owned fewer than five slaves. Only about 12 percent of slave owners owned twenty or more, the number of slaves that historians consider necessary to distinguish a **planter** from a farmer. Although hugely outnumbered, planters nevertheless dominated the southern economy. In 1860, 52 percent of the South's slaves lived and worked on plantations. Plantation slaves produced more than 75 percent of the South's export crops, the backbone of the region's economy. Although slavery was dying elsewhere in the New World, slave plantations increasingly dominated southern agriculture.

The South's major cash crops—tobacco, sugar, rice, and cotton—grew on plantations (Map 13.2). Tobacco was the original plantation crop in North America, but by the nineteenth century tobacco had shifted westward from the Chesapeake to Tennessee and Kentucky. Work in the tobacco fields was labor-intensive. Most phases of the process—planting, transplanting, thinning, picking off caterpillars, cutting, drying, packing—required field hands to stoop or bend down in painful labor.

Large-scale sugar production began in 1795, when Étienne de Boré built a modern sugar mill in what is today New Orleans. Labor on sugarcane

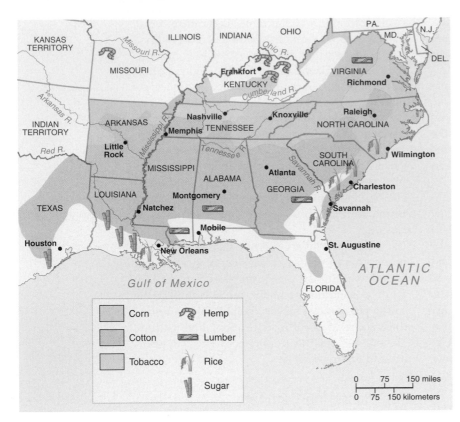

MAP 13.2   The Agricultural Economy of the South, 1860
Cotton dominated the South's agricultural economy, but the region grew a variety of crops and was largely self-sufficient in foodstuffs.

READING THE MAP: In what type of geographical areas were rice and sugar grown in 1860? After cotton, what crop commanded the greatest agricultural area in the South? In which region of the South was this crop predominantly found?

CONNECTIONS: What role did the South play in the U.S. economy in 1860? How did the economy of the South differ from that of the North?

FOR MORE HELP ANALYZING THIS MAP, see the map activity for this chapter in the Online Study Guide at bedfordstmartins.com/roark.

---

plantations was reputed to be the most physically demanding in the antebellum South. During the fall, slaves worked eighteen hours a day to cut the cane and haul it to the sugar mill, where they would grind and boil it. So hard was the slaves' task that one visitor concluded that "nothing but 'involuntary servitude' could go through the toil and suffering required to produce sugar." Sugar plantations were confined almost entirely to Louisiana.

Commercial rice production began in the seventeenth century, and like sugar, rice was confined to a small geographic area, a narrow strip of coast stretching from the Carolinas into Georgia. For slaves, rice

> If tobacco, sugar, and rice were the princes of plantation agriculture, cotton was king.

meant danger and extreme discomfort. Working in water and mud in the heat of a Carolina summer regularly threatened slaves with malaria, yellow fever, and other diseases. Rice cultivation required huge numbers of slaves to plant, cultivate, and harvest rice, as well as to maintain the canals, dikes, and gates necessary to flood the fields with water and then drain them. As a consequence, blacks accounted for 90 percent of the population in the coastal area.

If tobacco, sugar, and rice were the princes of plantation agriculture, cotton was king. Cotton became commercially significant after the advent of Eli Whitney's cotton gin in 1793. (See "The Promise of Technology," page 448.) By the early years of the nineteenth century, cotton had begun to dominate the southern economy. Cotton was relatively easy to grow and took little capital to get started—just enough for land, seed, and simple tools. Thus, small farmers as well as planters grew the white fluffy stuff. While hardscrabble Mississippi farmer Jessup Snopes grew half a bale of cotton in 1859, fellow Mississippian Frederick Stanton, who owned a plantation of more than 15,000 prime acres and hundreds of slaves, produced 3,054 bales. Although farmers far outnumbered planters, slave labor meant that plantations were responsible for producing three-quarters of the South's cotton.

For major slaveholders, then, the Old South's economy was productive and profitable. Further, plantation slavery benefited the national economy. By 1840, cotton alone accounted for more than 60 percent of the nation's exports. Soaring international demand meant eager buyers for every pound the southern cotton growers produced. Much of the profit from sales of cotton overseas went to planters, but some went to northern middlemen who bought, sold, insured, warehoused, and shipped cotton to the mills in Great Britain and elsewhere. As one New York merchant observed, "Cotton has enriched all through whose hands it has passed." As middlemen invested their profits in the burgeoning northern economy, industrial development received a burst of much-needed capital. Furthermore, southern plantations benefited northern industry by providing an important market for textiles, agricultural tools, and other manufactured goods.

The economies of the North and the South steadily diverged. While the North developed a mixed economy—agriculture, commerce, and manufacturing—the South remained overwhelmingly agricultural. Since planters were earning healthy profits, they saw little reason to diversify. Moreover, planters knew that if the South followed the path blazed by the North, manufacturing would mean the rise of a southern urban, industrial working class without direct ties to slavery or the plantation. Would city-dwelling factory workers accept rural planter rule and give their hearty support to slavery, or would they view slaves as unfair competition and favor free labor, as northern workers did? Planters did not want to find out. Year after year, they funneled the profits they earned from land and slaves back into more land and slaves.

With its capital flowing into agriculture, the South did not develop many factories. By 1860, only 10 percent of the nation's industrial workers lived in the South. Indiana and Illinois, two midwestern states known for agriculture, had more capital invested in industry than the seven Lower South states, including Louisiana with its sugar mills. Some cotton mills sprang up, but the region that produced 100 percent of the nation's cotton manufactured less than 7 percent of its cotton textiles.

Without significant economic diversification, the South developed fewer cities than the North (Map 13.3). In 1860, it was the least urban region in the country. While nearly 37 percent of New England's population lived in cities, less than 12 percent of Southerners were urban dwellers. That figure would have been dramatically smaller without Maryland's 34 percent urban population (because of Baltimore) and Louisiana's 26 percent (because of New Orleans). In fact, nine southern states counted 5 percent or fewer of their people in cities.

Not only were cities less common in the South, but they were also different from those in the North. They were mostly port cities on the

The *Henry Frank*, New Orleans
The steamboat *Henry Frank* sits dangerously overloaded with cotton bales at the New Orleans levee in 1854. The banner flying from the flagstaff indicates that captains boasted about the number of bales their boats carried. The magnitude of the cotton trade in the South's largest city and major port is difficult to capture. Six years earlier, a visitor, Solon Robinson, had expressed awe: "It must be seen to be believed; and even then, it will require an active mind ' ompre- hend acres of cotton bales standing upon the levee, while miles of drays [carts]   ly taking it off to the cotton presses. . . . Boats are constantly arriving, so piled '   , that the lower tier of bales on deck are in the water." Amid the mountains of c   .erners doubted that cotton was king.
Historic New Orleans Collection.

periphery of the region and busy principally with exporting the agricultural products of plantations in the interior. Urban merchants provided agriculture with indispensable services, such as hauling, insuring, and selling cotton, rice, and sugar, but as the tail on the plantation dog, southern cities did not become nationally significant manufacturing centers or important independent centers of social and economic innovation. Southern cities could also claim something no northern city desired—140,000 slaves in 1860. Urban slaves sometimes made up half of a southern city's population, and they worked in nearly every conceivable occupation, helping the southern economy thrive.

Because the South had so few cities and industrial jobs, it attracted relatively small numbers of European immigrants. Seeking economic

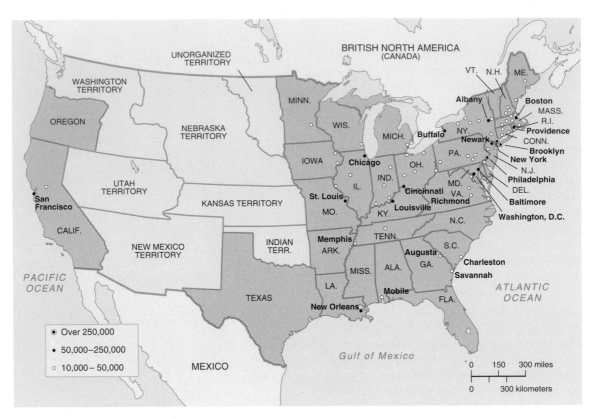

MAP 13.3 Major Cities in 1860
By 1860, northern cities were more numerous and larger than southern cities. In the slave states, cities were usually seaports or river ports that served the needs of agriculture, especially cotton.

opportunity, not competition with slaves (whose labor would keep wages low), immigrants steered well north of the South's slave-dominated, agricultural economy. In 1860, 13 percent of all Americans were foreign-born. But in nine of the fifteen slave states, only 2 percent or fewer were born abroad. Immigrants who did venture below the Mason-Dixon line concentrated in cities, just as they did in the North.

Not every Southerner celebrated the region's plantation economy. Critics railed against the excessive commitment to cotton and slaves and bemoaned what one called the "deplorable scarcity" of factories. Diversification, reformers promised, would make the South not only economically independent but more prosperous as well. State governments encouraged economic diversifica-

tion and development by helping to create banking systems that supplied credit for a wide range of projects, industrial as well as agricultural. Alabama constructed its first railroad in 1830 just five years after Englishmen built the world's first modern railroad and only three years after the inauguration of the first railroad in America. Thirty years later, 9,280 miles of track spanned the South.

But encouragement of a diversified economy had clear limits. State governments failed to create some of the essential services modern economies require. By midcentury, for example, no southern legislature had created a statewide public school system. Consequently, the South's illiteracy rate for whites topped 20 percent. Dominant slaveholders failed to see any benefit in educating the region's labor force, especially with their tax money. Despite the flurry of railroad building, the South's mileage in 1860 was less than half that of the North. Moreover, while railroads crisscrossed the North carrying manufactured goods as well as agricultural products, most railroads in the South ran from port cities

Immigrants as a Percentage of State Populations, 1860

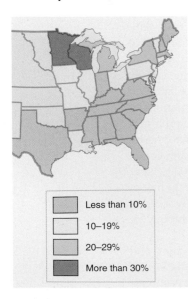

Less than 10%

10–19%

20–29%

More than 30%

back into farming areas and were built to export staple crops (see Map 12.5, page 420).

Northerners claimed that slavery was an outmoded and doomed labor system, but few Southerners perceived economic weakness in their region. In fact, the planters' pockets were never fuller than at the end of the 1850s. Compared with Northerners, Southerners invested less of their capital in industry, transportation, and public education. Planters' decisions to reinvest in staple agriculture ensured the momentum of the plantation economy and the political and social relationships rooted in it.

Masters, Mistresses, and the Big House

Nowhere was the contrast between northern and southern life more vivid than on the plantations of the South. Located on a patchwork of cleared fields and dense forests, a plantation typically included a "big house" and slave quarters. Scattered about were numerous outbuildings, each with a special function. Near the big house were the kitchen, storehouse, smokehouse (for curing and preserving meat), and hen coop. More distant were the barns, toolsheds, **artisans'** workshops, and overseer's house. Large plantations sometimes had additional buildings such as an infirmary and a chapel for slaves. Depending on the crop, there was a tobacco shed, a rice mill, a sugar refinery, or a cotton gin house. Lavish or plain, plantations everywhere had an underlying similarity (Figure 13.2).

The plantation was the home of masters, mistresses, and slaves. Slavery shaped the lives of all the plantation's inhabitants, from work to leisure activities, but it affected each differently. A hierarchy of rigid roles and duties governed relationships. Presiding was the master, who ruled his wife, children, and slaves, none of whom had many legal rights and all of whom were designated by the state as dependents under his dominion and protection.

Plantation Masters

The work relationship between plantation master and slave was organized quite simply. While smaller planters supervised the labor of their slaves themselves, larger planters often hired overseers who went to the fields with the slaves, leaving planters free to concentrate on marketing,

FIGURE 13.2 A Southern Plantation
Slavery determined how masters laid out their plantations, where they situated their "big houses" and slave quarters, and what kinds of buildings they constructed. This model of the Hermitage, the mansion built in 1830 for Henry McAlpin, a Georgia rice planter, shows the overseer's house poised in the grove of oak trees halfway between the owner's mansion and the slave huts. The placement of the mansion at the end of an extended road leading up from the river underscored McAlpin's affluence and authority.

Adapted from *Back of the Big House: The Architecture of Plantation Slavery* by John Michael Vlach. Copyright © 1993 by the University of North Carolina Press. Original illustration property of the Historic American Buildings Survey, a division of the National Park Service.

finance, and general plantation affairs. Planters also found time to escape to town to discuss the weather, to the courthouse and legislature to debate politics, and to the woods to hunt and fish.

The Cotton Gin: Engine of the South

In 1792, a young New Englander accepted a position as tutor to the children of a Georgia planter. The teaching post did not work out, but Eli Whitney stayed on at the Savannah River plantation of Mrs. Catherine Greene, widow of Nathanael Greene, hero of the American Revolution. On September 11, 1793, Whitney wrote his sister: "I have . . . heard much said of the extreme difficulty of ginning cotton. That is, separating it from its seed." He had met "a number of respectable Gentlemen at Mrs Greene's who all agreed that if a machine could be invented which would clean the cotton with expedition, it would be a great thing both to the country and the inventor." Whitney was a Yale graduate who could read Latin, but he was also a practical man, and he turned his attention to the problem.

Cotton gins (the word *gin* is short for *engine*) already existed in 1793. One model in which cotton was fed between two rollers to squeeze out the seeds operated efficiently on the sea-island cotton that grew on the South Carolina and Georgia coasts. But the variety of cotton that grew inland—green seed, or short staple—was filled with seeds that clung to the fiber like ticks to the skin. Many a pioneer family spent long winter evenings seated around the fire tediously plucking the fluff from each seed. The little cotton produced by evenings of handpicking got made up into homespun on family spinning wheels and handlooms.

The problem of sticky seeds attracted the attention of mechanics from India to Santo Domingo, but it was Whitney who succeeded in building a simple little device for separating cotton from the seeds—wire teeth set in a wooden cylinder that, when rotated, reached through narrow slats to pull cotton fibers away from the seeds while a brush swept the fibers from the revolving teeth. It was crude, but news of the invention spread like wildfire. Just days later, the South Carolina planter Pierce Butler wrote a friend, "There is a young Man at Mrs Greene's in Georgia, who has made a Cotton Ginn that with two Boys cleans of the green seed cotton 64 pds of clean cotton in about 9 hours." Planters understood that Whitney's invention would break the bottleneck in the commercial production of cotton. They also understood that his invention would allow them to produce vast amounts of clean cotton and satisfy the cotton-hungry English market. Eager to cash in on his invention, Whitney rushed back to

Increasingly in the nineteenth century, planters characterized their mastery in terms of what they called "Christian guardianship" and what historians have called **paternalism**. The concept of paternalism denied that the form of slavery practiced in the South was brutal and exploitative. Instead, it defined slavery as a set of reciprocal obligations between masters and slaves. In exchange for the slaves' labor and obedience, masters provided basic care and necessary guidance. To northern claims that they were tyrants and exploiters, slaveholders responded that they were stewards and guardians. As owners of blacks, masters argued, they had the heavy responsibility of caring for a childlike, dependent people. In 1814, Thomas Jefferson captured the essence of the advancing ideal: "We should endeavor, with those whom fortune has thrown on our hands, to feed & clothe them well, protect them from ill usage, require such reasonable labor only as is performed voluntarily by freemen, and be led by no repugnancies to abdicate them, and our duties to them." A South Carolina rice planter insisted, "I manage them as my children."

Paternalism was part propaganda and part self-delusion. But it was more. Slavery in the South reached its zenith in the nineteenth cen-

Connecticut, where he took out a patent and began manufacturing cotton gins.

Planters clamored for the machines, and southern craftsmen who understood Whitney's basic design could reproduce it (and enlarge and improve it) without looking at a model or drawing. No mere patent could stop them, and nothing could force them to pay Whitney royalties. The Patent Act of 1793 stressed that proof of invention and proof of infringement were the burden of the inventor. Although Whitney's gin was pirated time and again, he found that it was difficult and costly to gain proof. At one time Whitney had more than sixty lawsuits pending, and the revenue from his gin factory in New Haven could scarcely keep up with his legal bills.

While Whitney made little money from the cotton gin, planters profited hugely. Cotton quickly pushed out indigo, then tobacco, as

The Cotton Gin
By the 1790s, the English had succeeded in mechanizing the manufacture of cotton cloth, but they were unable to get enough raw cotton. The South could grow cotton in unimaginable quantities, but cotton stuck to seeds was useless in English textile mills. In 1793, Eli Whitney, a Northerner who was living on a Savannah River plantation, built a simple device for separating the cotton from the seed. Widespread use of the cotton gin broke the bottleneck in the commercial production of cotton and eventually bound millions of African Americans to slavery.
Smithsonian Institution, Washington, D.C.

the southern interior's major cash crop. In just a few years, the gin helped transform the entire economy of the South. The commercial production of cotton bound millions of African Americans to perpetual slavery. For them, the promise of this particular piece of technology proved tragically hollow. Whitney's invention also spawned a cotton industry that changed the face of northern Britain and New England as mill towns sprang up everywhere. The cotton mills of Lancashire and Lowell brought cotton cloth within reach of everyone. Before the gin, the world was clothed in flax and wool, and cotton fabrics were luxury items. After the gin, cotton soon became the poor people's cloth.

The great nineteenth-century British historian Lord Macaulay hardly exaggerated when he declared: "What Peter the Great did to make Russia dominant, Eli Whitney's invention of the cotton gin has more than equaled in relation to the power and progress of the United States."

tury, after the nation closed its external slave trade. Masters increasingly recognized slaves as valuable assets to be maintained, and they realized that the expansion of the slave labor force could come only from natural reproduction. The rising price of slaves led one planter to declare in 1849 that "it behooves those who own them to make them last as long as possible." Another planter instructed his overseer to pay attention to "whatever tends to promote their health and render them prolific."

One consequence of this paternalism and economic self-interest was a small improvement in slaves' welfare. Diet improved, although nineteenth-century slaves still mainly ate fatty pork and cornmeal. Housing improved, although the cabins still had cracks large enough, slaves said, for cats to slip through. Clothing improved, although slaves seldom received much more than two crude outfits a year and perhaps a pair of cheap shoes. In the fields, workdays remained sunup to sundown, but planters often provided a rest period in the heat of the day. And most owners ceased the colonial practices of punishing slaves by branding and mutilation.

Paternalism should not be mistaken for "Ol' Massa"'s kindness and goodwill. It encouraged

Southern Man with Children and Their Mammy
Obviously prosperous and looking like a man accustomed to giving orders and being obeyed, this patriarch poses around 1848 with his young daughters and their nurse. The black woman is clearly a servant, a status indicated by her race and her attire. Why does she appear in the daguerreotype? The absent mother may be dead. Her death might account for the inclusion of the African American woman in the family circle. In any case, her presence signals her importance in the household. Fathers left the raising of children to mothers and nurses.
Collection of the J. Paul Getty Museum, Malibu, CA.

better treatment because it made economic sense to provide at least minimal care for valuable slaves. Nor did paternalism require that planters put aside their whips. They could flail away and still claim that they were only fulfilling their responsibilities as guardians of their naturally lazy and at times insubordinate dependents. The law in southern states gave masters nearly "uncontrolled authority over the body" of the slave, according to the North Carolina judge Thomas Ruffin. Paternalism offered slaves some protection against the most brutal punishments, but whipping remained the planters' essential coercion. (See "Historical Question," page 452.)

Paternalism never won universal acceptance among planters, but by the nineteenth century it had become a kind of communal standard. With its notion that slavery imposed on masters a burden and a duty, paternalism provided slaveholders with a means of legitimizing their rule. But it also provided some slaves with leverage over the conditions of their lives. Slaves learned to

manipulate a slaveholder's need to see himself as a good and decent master. To avoid a reputation as a cruel tyrant, planters sometimes negotiated with slaves, rather than just resorting to the whip. Small garden plots in which they could work for themselves after their day in the fields or a few days off and a dance when they had gathered the last of the cotton were among the concessions slaves sometimes won from masters who were seeking to confirm their status as benevolent paternalists.

The Virginia statesman Edmund Randolph argued that slavery created in white southern men a "quick and acute sense of personal liberty" and a "disdain for every abridgement of personal independence." Indeed, prickly individualism and aggressive independence became crucial features of the southern concept of honor. Social standing, political advancement, and even self-esteem rested on an honorable reputation. Defending honor became a male passion. Andrew Jackson's mother reportedly told her son, "Never tell a lie, nor take what is not your own, nor sue anybody for slander or assault and battery. *Always settle them cases yourself.*" Southern boys were expected to master the "manly" arts, and among planters such advice sometimes led to duels. Dueling arrived from Europe in the eighteenth century. It died out in the North, but in the South, even after legislatures banned it, gentlemen continued to defend their honor with pistols at ten paces.

Southerners also expected an honorable gentleman to be a proper patriarch. Nowhere in America was masculine power more accentuated. Slavery buttressed the power of husbands and fathers. Planters described plantations as households that incorporated both their "white and black families." And planters brooked no opposition from any of their dependents. The master's absolute dominion sometimes led to **miscegenation**, the sexual mixing of the races. Laws prohibited interracial sex, and some masters practiced self-restraint. Others merely urged discretion. How many trips masters and their sons made to slave cabins is impossible to tell, but as long as slavery gave white men extraordinary power, slave women were forced to submit to the sexual appetites of the men who ruled them.

Individualistic impulses were strong among planters, but duty to family was paramount. In time, as the children of one elite family married the children of another, ties of blood and kinship as well as ideology and economic interest linked

AMERICAN PLACES

Middleton Place, Charleston, South Carolina

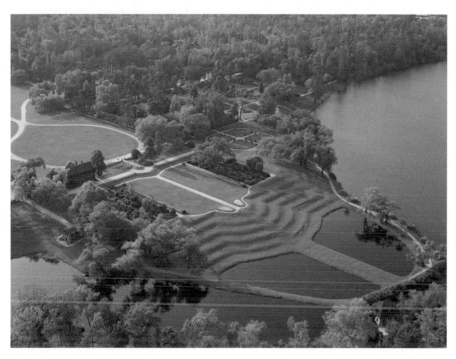

The Grounds of Middleton Place
The Middleton Place Foundation, Charleston, South Carolina.

Situated a few miles north of Charleston on the Ashley River, Middleton Place exemplifies the taste, pride, and wealth of eighteenth-century South Carolina planters. Like many plantation homes of that era, the main house faces the river, the highway for shipping rice, South Carolina's principal crop. Visitors arriving by boat were certain to be impressed by the spectacular view of the house and grounds from the water.

In 1741, Henry Middleton married Mary Williams, who brought as her dowry the house and plantation that became Middleton Place. One of the wealthiest and most politically powerful men in the colony of South Carolina, in 1774 Henry Middleton was elected president of the First Continental Congress. Between 1741 and the Civil War, four generations of Middletons sustained the family's economic and political standing by producing

tons of rice and a host of political leaders, including a signer of the Declaration of Independence, a governor of the state, and a signer of South Carolina's ordinance of secession.

Soon after Henry Middleton acquired the property in 1741, he began constructing lavish formal gardens, laid out in the grand classic European style that emphasized geometry and symmetry. According to family lore, it took a hundred slaves ten years to complete the sixty-five acres of broad terraces, walkways, artificial ponds, and sweeping vistas of the river and marshlands beyond. In 1857, a visitor observed: "In its natural and artificial beauty and elegance, Middleton Place comes nearer than any place I have seen in America to the Italian villas, which I visited, or saw, near Rome."

During the Civil War, federal troops burned much of the brick, three-story main residence, and in 1886 an earthquake largely completed the destruction, leaving only one wing of the elegant old home standing. The twentieth-century restoration of the remaining structure and the extensive gardens gives visitors a stunning impression of how the eighteenth-century South's plantation gentry lived. Missing, however, are the cabins of the generations of slaves who labored their lives away producing rice and maintaining the beauty of Middleton Place.

For Web links related to this site and other American Places, see "PlaceLinks" at bedfordstmartins.com/roark.

planters to one another. Conscious of what they shared as slaveholders, planters worked together to defend their common interests. The values of the big house—slavery, honor, male domination—washed over the boundaries of plantations and flooded all of southern life.

Plantation Mistresses

Like their northern counterparts, southern ladies were expected to possess feminine virtues of piety, purity, chastity, and obedience within the context of marriage, motherhood, and domesticity.

How Often Were Slaves Whipped?

As important as this question is to historians, and obviously was to slaves, we have very little reliable evidence on the frequency of whipping. We know from white sources that whipping was the prescribed method of physical punishment on most antebellum plantations. Masters' instructions to overseers authorized whippings and often set limits on the number of strokes an overseer could administer. Some planters allowed fifteen lashes, some fifty, and some one hundred. But slave owners' instructions, as revealing as they are, tell us more about the severity of beatings than their frequency.

Remembrances of former slaves confirm that whipping was widespread and frequent. In the 1930s, a government program gathered testimony from more than 2,300 elderly African Americans about their experiences as slaves. Their accounts offered grisly evidence of the cruelty of slavery. "You say how did our Master treat his slaves?" asked one woman. "Scandalous, they treated them just like dogs." She was herself whipped "till the blood dripped to the ground." A few slaves remembered kind masters and never personally felt the sting of the lash. Bert Strong was one such slave, but he also recalled hearing slaves on other

farms "hollering when they get beat." He said, "They beat them till it a pity." Beatings occurred often, but how often?

A remarkably systematic record of whippings over a sustained period of time comes from the diary of Bennet H. Barrow, the master of Highland plantation in West Feliciana Parish, Louisiana. For a twenty-three-month period in 1840–1841, Barrow meticulously recorded every whipping he administered or ordered. On most large plantations, overseers handled the business of day-to-day management, but in 1838 Barrow concluded that overseers were "good for nothing" and "a perfect nuisance." He dismissed his white overseer and, assisted only by a black driver, began managing his own plantation.

What does the Barrow evidence show? In 1840, according to the federal census, Barrow owned 129 slaves. In the twenty-three-month period, Barrow recorded 160 whippings. That means that, on the average, a slave was whipped every four and a half days. Sixty of the 77 slaves who worked in the fields were whipped at least once. Most of the 17 field slaves who escaped being beaten were children and pregnant women. Eighty percent of male cotton pickers and 70 percent of female cotton pickers were

whipped at least once in this period. Dave Barley received eight floggings, more than any other Barrow slave, and Patience received six whippings, more than any other female slave.

In most instances, Barrow recorded not only the fact of a whipping but also its cause. All sorts of "misconduct," "rascality," and "disorderly acts" made Barrow reach for his whip. The provocations included family quarrels in the slave quarters, impudence, running away, and failure to keep curfew. But nearly 80 percent of the acts he recorded were related to poor work. Barrow gave beatings for "not picking as well as he can," for picking "very trashy cotton," and for failing to pick the prescribed weight of cotton. One slave claimed to have lost his eyesight and for months refused to work until Barrow "gave him 25 cuts yesterday morning & ordered him to work Blind or not."

Whippings should not be mistaken for spankings. Some planters used whips that raised welts, caused blisters, and bruised. Others resorted to rawhide and cowhide whips that broke the skin, caused scarring, and sometimes permanently maimed. Occasionally, slaves were beaten to death. Whipping was not Barrow's only means of inflicting pain. His diary mentions confining slaves to a plantation jail, putting them in chains, shooting them, breaking a "sword cane" over one slave's head, having slaves mauled by dogs, placing them in stocks, "staking down" slaves for hours, "hand sawing" them, holding their heads under water, and a variety of punishments intending to ridicule

---

Southerners also expected ladies to exemplify all that was best in plantation society. Countless toasts praised the southern lady as the perfect complement to her husband, the patriarch. She was physically weak, "formed only for the less laborious occupations," and thus dependent on male protection. To gain this protection, she was

naturally modest and delicate, possessed beauty and grace, and cultivated refinement and charm.

But for women, the image of the lady, which rigidly prescribed proper character and behavior, was no blessing. Chivalry—the South's romantic ideal of male-female relationships—glorified the lady while it subordinated her. Chivalry's and to shame, including making men wear women's clothing and do "women's work," such as the laundry. Still, Barrow's preferred instrument of punishment was the whip.

On the Barrow plantation, as on many others, whipping was public. Victims were often tied to a stake in the quarters, and the other slaves were made to watch. In a real sense, the entire slave population on the plantation experienced a whipping every four and a half days. Even though some never felt the lash personally, all were familiar with its terror and agony.

Was whipping effective? Did it produce a hardworking, efficient, and conscientious labor force? Not according to Barrow's own record. No evidence indicates that whipping changed the slaves' behavior. What Barrow considered bad work continued. Unabated whipping is itself evidence of the failure of punishment to achieve the master's will. Slaves knew the rules. Yet they continued to act "badly." And they continued to suffer. It was a gruesome drama—the master seeking from his slaves hard labor and slaves denying their master what he most wanted, day after day.

Did Barrow whip with the same frequency as other planters? We simply do not know. As much as we would like to answer the question precisely, because of the lack of quantifiable evidence we will never know exactly how often whippings occurred. Still, the Barrow evidence allows us to speculate profitably on the frequency of whipping by large planters. We do know that Barrow

Gordon
This photograph of Gordon, a runaway slave from Baton Rouge, Louisiana, was taken on April 2, 1863, and sent home from the Civil War by Frederick W. Mercer, an assistant surgeon with the Forty-seventh Massachusetts Regiment. Mercer examined four hundred other runaways and found many "to be as badly lacerated." Masters claimed that they whipped only when they had to and only as hard as they had to, but slave testimony and photographic evidence refute their defense of slavery as a benign institution.
Courtesy of the Massachusetts Historical Society.

did not consider himself a cruel man. He bitterly denounced his neighbor as "the most cruel Master i ever knew of" for castrating three of his slaves. Moreover, Barrow had dispensed with the overseers in part because of their "brutal feelings" toward slaves. Like most whites, he believed that the lash was essential to get work done. He used it no more than he believed absolutely necessary.

Most masters, including Barrow, tried to encourage work with promises of small gifts and brief holidays, but punishment was their most important motivator. We will never know if the typical slave was beaten

once a year as on the Barrow plantation, but the admittedly scanty evidence suggests that on large plantations the whip fell on someone's back every few days.

And former slaves remembered. More than a half century after emancipation, their sharpest recollections usually involved punishment. They remembered the pain, the injustice, and their bitter resentment. They evaluated their former masters according to how frequently they reached for the whip. According to one former slave, "some was good and some was bad, and about the most of them was bad."

underlying assumptions about the weakness of women and the protective authority of men resembled the paternalistic defense of slavery. Indeed, the most articulate spokesmen for slavery also vigorously defended the subordination of women. George Fitzhugh, for example, insisted that "a woman, like children, has but one right and that is the right to protection. The right to protection involves the obligation to obey. A husband, a lord and master, nature designed for every woman. . . . If she be obedient she stands little danger of maltreatment." Just as the slaveholder's mastery was written into law, so too were the paramount rights of husbands.

453

Once married, women found divorce almost impossible.

Daughters of planters confronted chivalry's demands at an early age. Their educations aimed at fitting them to become southern ladies. At their private boarding schools they read literature, learned languages, and struggled to master the requisite drawing-room arts. Elite women began courting at a young age and married early. Kate Carney exaggerated only slightly when she wrote in her diary: "Today, I am seventeen, getting quite old, and am not married." Elizabeth Ruffin, who was about the same age, complained of being pushed into a wedding. Everyone, she said, seemed determined to "deter me from all the anticipated horrors of *old-maidenhood*." Some young women hesitated, realizing that marriage meant turning their fates over to their husbands. One mother warned her daughter: "A single life has fewer troubles; but then it is not the one for which our maker designed us." When they married, elite women made enormous efforts to live up to their region's lofty ideal.

Proslavery ideologues claimed that slavery freed white women from drudgery. Surrounded "by her domestics," declared Thomas Roderick

Bird Store, 626 Royal Street, New Orleans

Most elite white women in the antebellum South lived isolated existences on rural plantations. But some lived in cities, where others visited them from time to time, and going shopping was a prominent feature of such visits. Teenager Gertrude Clanton, who lived in Augusta, Georgia, wore store-bought clothes that she described endlessly in letters to her friends. Here a wealthy mother and daughter shop for a pet in a New Orleans bird store. The attentive proprietor and attractive shop provide everything they need—birds, cages, bird food, even an inviting couch and blanket in case they want to rest before moving on. Elite white women themselves were, in a way, like birds kept in golden cages. Could it be that they were attracted to the thought of owning birds of their own, something they could care for, train, and control?

Historic New Orleans Collection.

Tools of a Plantation Mistress: Key Basket and Keys
Almost every plantation mistress supervised the big house's storerooms and oversaw the distribution of the supplies kept there. To protect the goods from sticky-fingered house servants, each mistress kept the supplies under lock and key and carried the keys with her. The large five-inch key would have opened a door, and the four smaller keys on a ring would have opened boxes that held valuable foodstuffs such as sugar and tea. Throughout the day, slaves came to the mistress for access to household goods: "I keep all the keys and if anything is wanted they are obliged to come to me," one white woman declared.
Basket: Courtesy June Lambert; Keys: Valentine Museum, Cook Collection.

Dew, "she ceases to be a mere beast of burden" and "becomes the cheering and animating center of the family circle." In fact, however, the ideal of the southern lady clashed with the daily reality of the plantation mistress. Rather than being freed from labor by servants, she discovered that having servants required her to work long hours. Like her husband, the mistress had managerial responsibilities. She managed the big house, directly supervising as many as a dozen servants. But unlike her husband, the mistress had no overseer. All house servants answered directly to her. She assigned them tasks each morning, directed their work throughout the day, and punished them when she found fault. In addition to supervising a complex household, she had responsibility for the henhouse and dairy. And on some plantations, she directed the slave hospital and nursery and rationed supplies for the slave quarters. Women also bore the dangers of childbearing and responsibilities of child rearing. Southern ladies did not often lead lives of leisure.

Whereas masters used their status as slaveholders as a springboard into public affairs, the mistress's life was circumscribed by the plantation. Masters left the plantation when they pleased, but plantation mistresses needed chaperones to travel. When they could, they went to church, but women spent most days on the plantation, where they often became lonely. In 1853, Mary Kendall wrote how much she enjoyed her sister's letter: "For about three weeks I did not have the pleasure of seeing one white female face, there being no white family except our own upon the plantation." In their few leisure hours, plantation mistresses read and wrote letters, but they preferred the company of friends. Grand parties and balls occasionally broke the daily routine, but the burden of planning and supervising the preparation of the food and drink fell to the mistress.

As members of slaveholding families, mistresses lived privileged lives. But they also had significant grounds for discontent, and a few independent-minded women protested. No feature of plantation life generated more rage and anguish among mistresses than miscegenation. Mary Boykin Chesnut of Camden, South Carolina, wrote in her diary, "ours is a monstrous system, a wrong and iniquity. Like the patriarchs of old, our men live all in one house with their wives and their concubines; and the mulattos one sees in every family partly resemble the white children. Any lady is ready to tell you who is the father of all the mulatto children in everybody's household but her own. Those, she seems to think drop from the clouds."

Out of eyesight and
earshot of the big house,
slaves drew together and
built lives of their own.

But most planters' wives, including Mary Boykin Chesnut, found ways to accept slavery. After all, the mistress's world rested on slaves, just as the master's did. By acknowledging the realities of male power, mistresses enjoyed the rewards of their class and race. These rewards came at a price. Still, the heaviest burdens of slavery fell not on those who lived in the big house but on those who toiled to support it.

Slaves and the Quarters

On most plantations, only a few hundred yards separated the big house and the slave quarters. The distance was short enough to assure whites easy access to the labor of blacks. Yet the distance was great enough to provide slaves with some privacy. Out of eyesight and earshot of the big house, slaves drew together and built lives of their own. They created families, worshipped God, and developed an African American community.

The Price of Blood

This 1868 painting by T. S. Noble depicts a transaction between a slave trader and a rich planter. The trader nervously pretends to study the contract, while the planter waits impatiently for the completion of the sale. The planter's mulatto son, who is being sold, looks away. The children of white men and slave women were property and could be sold by the father/master. The tragedy of miscegenation, however, extended beyond the son shown here. Who is absent from the painting? Whose marriage has been betrayed? Who else's son is being sold away?
Morris Museum of Art, Augusta, GA.

FOR MORE HELP ANALYZING THIS IMAGE, see the visual activity for this chapter in the Online Study Guide at bedfordstmartins.com/roark.

Despite the rise of plantations, a substantial minority of slaves lived and worked elsewhere. Most labored on small farms, where they wielded a hoe alongside another slave or two and perhaps their master. But by 1860, almost half a million slaves (one in eight) did not work in agriculture at all. Some were employed in towns and cities as domestics, day laborers, bakers, barbers, tailors, and more. Others, far from urban centers, toiled as fishermen, lumbermen, railroad workers, and deckhands and stokers on riverboats. Slavery was a flexible labor system, and slaves could be found in virtually every skilled and unskilled occupation throughout the South, including the region's factories. Nevertheless, a majority of slaves (52 percent) counted plantations as their homes and workplaces.

Work

Slaves understood clearly the motive for their enslavement. As ex-slave Albert Todd recalled, "Work was a religion we was taught." Indeed, all slaves who were capable of productive labor worked. Young children were introduced to the world of work as early as age five or six. Ex-slave Carrie Hudson recalled that children who were "knee high to a duck" were sent to the fields to carry water to thirsty workers or to protect ripening crops from hungry birds. Others helped in the slave nursery, caring for children even younger than themselves, or in the big house, where they swept floors or shooed flies in the dining room. When slave boys and girls reached the age of eleven or twelve, masters sent most of them to the fields, where they learned farmwork by laboring alongside their parents. After a lifetime of labor, old women left the fields to care for the small children and spin yarn and old men moved on to mind livestock and clean stables.

The overwhelming majority of all plantation slaves in 1860 were field hands. Planters sometimes assigned men and women to separate gangs, the women working at lighter tasks and the men doing the heavy work of clearing and breaking the land. But women also did heavy work. "I had to work hard," Nancy Boudry remembered, and "plow and go and split wood just like a man." Although the daily tasks of slaves differed according to the crop, the backbreaking labor and the monotonous year-round routines made for grim similarity. As one ex-slave observed, on the plantation the "history of one day is the history of every day."

Nancy Fort, House Servant
This rare portrait of a slave woman at the turn of the nineteenth century depicts a strong and dignified person. Some individuals who worked in domestic service took pride in their superior status and identified more with the master than with their fellow slaves. "Honey, I wan't no common eve'day slave," one former servant recalled proudly. "I [helped] de white folks in de big house." But intense interaction with whites did not necessarily breed affection. Most domestic servants remained bound to the slave quarters by ties of kinship and friendship as well as by common oppression.
Courtesy of Georgia Department of Archives and History.

A few slaves (only one or two in every ten) became house servants. And nearly all of those who did (nine of ten) were women. There, under the critical eye of the white mistress, they cooked, cleaned house, babysat, washed clothes, and did the dozens of other tasks the master and mistress required. House servants enjoyed certain advantages over field hands, such as somewhat less physically demanding work and better food, but working in the big house had significant drawbacks. House servants were constantly on call, with no time that was entirely their own. Since no servant could please constantly, most bore the brunt of white frustration and rage. Ex-slave Jacob Branch of Texas remembered, "My poor mama! Every washday old Missy give her a beating."

Even rarer than house servants were skilled artisans. In the cotton South, no more than one slave in twenty (almost all men) worked in a skilled trade. Most were blacksmiths and carpenters, but slaves also worked as masons, mechanics, millers, and shoemakers. When a slave artisan's labor was not needed on the plantation, masters would often send the slave to work in the neighborhood as hired help. Slave craftsmen took pride in their skills and often exhibited the independence of spirit that caused slaveholder James H. Hammond of South Carolina to declare in disgust that when a slave became a skilled artisan, "he is more than half freed." Skilled slave fathers often taught their crafts to their sons. "My pappy was one of the black smiths and worked in the shop," John Mathews remembered. "I had to help my pappy in the shop when I was a child and I learnt how to beat out the iron and make wagon tires, and make plows."

Rarest of all slave occupations was that of slave driver. Probably no more than one male slave in a hundred worked in this capacity. These men were well named, for their primary task was driving other slaves to work harder in the fields. In some drivers' hands, the whip never rested. Ex-slave Jane Johnson of South Carolina called her driver the "meanest man, white or black, I ever see." But other drivers showed all the restraint they could. "Ole Gabe didn't like that whippin' business," West Turner of Virginia remembered. "When Marsa was there, he would lay it on 'cause he had to. But when old Marsa wasn't lookin', he never would beat them slaves."

Normally, slaves worked from what they called "can to can't," from "can see" in the morning to "can't see" at night. Even with a break at noon for a meal and rest, it made for a long day. For slaves, Lewis Young recalled, "work, work, work, 'twas all they do."

Family, Religion, and Community

From dawn to dusk, slaves worked for the master, but at night, when the labor was done, and all day Sundays and usually Saturday afternoons, slaves were left largely to themselves. Bone tired perhaps, they nonetheless used the time and space to develop and enjoy what mattered most: family, religion, and community.

In the quarters, slaves lived lives that their masters were hardly aware of. Temporarily leaving the master-slave relationship at their cabin doors, slaves became husbands and wives, mothers and fathers, sons and daughters, preachers and singers, storytellers and conjurers. Over the generations, they created a community and a culture of their own that buoyed them up during long hours in the fields and brought them joy and hope in the few hours they had to themselves.

One of the most important consequences of the slaves' limited autonomy was the preservation and persistence of the family. Perhaps the most serious charge abolitionists leveled against slavery was that it wrecked black family life, a telling indictment in a society that put family at the heart of decent society. Slaveholders sometimes agreed that blacks had no family life, but they placed the blame on the slaves themselves, claiming that blacks chose to lead licentious, promiscuous lives.

Contrary to both abolitionists' and slaveholders' claims, the black family survived slavery. Indeed, family was the chief fact of life in the quarters. Although owners increasingly encouraged the creation and maintenance of families, slave family life grew primarily from slaves'

Haywood Dixon, Slave Carpenter
In this 1854 daguerreotype, Dixon (1826–c. 1889), a slave carpenter who worked in Greene County, North Carolina, poses with a symbol of his craft, the carpenter's square. When work was slow on the home plantation, masters could hire out their skilled artisans to neighbors who needed a carpenter, blacksmith, or mason.
Collection of William L. Murphy.

own commitment. No laws recognized slave marriage, and therefore no master or slave was legally obligated to honor the bond. Nevertheless, plantation records show that slave marriages were often long-lasting. Young men and women in the slave quarters fell in love, married, and set up housekeeping in cabins of their own. The primary cause of the ending of slave marriages was death, just as it was in white families. But the second most frequent cause of the end of slave marriages was the sale of the husband or wife, something no white family ever had to fear. Precise figures are unavailable, but one scholar estimates that in the years 1820 to 1860, sales destroyed 300,000 slave marriages.

In 1858, a South Carolina slave named Abream Scriven wrote a letter to his wife, who lived on a neighboring plantation. "My dear wife," he began, "I take the pleasure of writing you . . . with much regret to inform you I am Sold to man by the name of Peterson, a Treader and Stays in New Orleans." Scriven promised to send some things when he got to his new home in Louisiana, but he admitted that he was not sure how he would "get them to you and my children." He asked his wife to "give my love to my father and mother and tell them good Bye for me. And if we shall not meet in this world I hope to meet in heaven. . . . My dear wife for you and my children my pen cannot express the griffe I feel to be parted from you all." Finally, he closed with words that no master would have permitted in a slave's marriage vows: "I remain your truly husband until Death." While there can be no doubt about Abream Scriven's love for the family he was forced to leave behind, it remains clear that slavery represented a massive assault on family life in the quarters.

Not all fathers could live with their children—some men like Scriven married women on neighboring plantations—but plantation records reveal that slave fathers often managed to create significant roles for themselves within their families. Despite their inability to fulfill the traditional roles of provider and protector, they gained status by doing what they could to help

Slave Quarter, South Carolina

On large plantations, several score of African Americans lived in cabins that were often arranged along what slaves called "the street." The dwellings in this image by Civil War photographer George N. Barnard of a South Carolina plantation were better built than the typical rickety, one-room, dirt-floored slave cabin. Almost certainly posed, this photograph shows the inhabitants of the slave quarter—little children playing in the dirt, girls and women sitting on the steps talking and working at something, older boys and men driving carts and wagons. During the daylight hours of the workweek, when most men and women labored in the fields, the quarter was mostly empty. At night and on Sundays, it was a busy place. Collection of the New York Historical Society.

their families. Slave fathers and mothers divided responsibilities in the quarters along traditional gender lines: Women cooked, sewed, and cleaned, while men hunted, raised hogs, cultivated a garden, and made furniture for the cabin. Slaves held both their mothers and their fathers in high esteem, grateful for the small bits of refuge their parents provided from the rigors of slavery when they were children.

Like families, religion also provided slaves with a refuge and a reason for living. Beginning about the time of the American Revolution, Protestant **evangelical** sects, particularly the

Baptists and Methodists, began trying to convert slaves from their African beliefs. Evangelicals offered an emotional "religion of the heart" to which blacks (and many whites as well) responded enthusiastically. By the mid-nineteenth century, perhaps as many as one-quarter of all slaves claimed church membership, and many of the rest would not have objected to being called Christians.

Planters began promoting Christianity in the quarters because they came to see the slaves' salvation as part of their obligation and to believe that religion made slaves more obedient. Certainly, the Christianity that masters broadcast to slaves emphasized the meeker virtues and admonished them to obey their masters. South Carolina slaveholder Charles Colcock Jones, the leading missionary to the slaves, published his *Catechism for Colored Persons* in 1834. In it, he instructed slaves "to count their Masters 'worthy of all honour,' as those whom God has placed over them in this world." But slaves laughed up their sleeves at such messages. "That old white preacher just was telling us slaves to be good to our masters," one ex-slave chuckled. "We ain't cared a bit about that stuff he was telling us 'cause we wanted to sing, pray, and serve God in our own way."

> Slaves created a Christianity that served their needs, not the masters'. Rather than obedience, their faith emphasized justice. They believed that God kept score and that the accounts of this world would be settled in the next.

Meeting in their cabins or secretly in the woods, slaves created an African American Christianity that served their needs, not the masters'. Beginning in the 1830s, laws prohibited teaching slaves to read, but a few slaves could read enough to struggle with the Bible. With the help of black preachers, they interpreted the Christian message themselves. Rather than obedience, their faith emphasized justice. Nat Turner felt himself to be an avenging angel who would punish whites and end bondage. More often, slaves believed that God kept score and that the accounts of this world would be settled in the next. "The idea of a revolution in the conditions of the whites and blacks is the cornerstone" of the slaves' religion, recalled ex-slave Charles Ball. But the slaves' faith also spoke to their experiences in this world. In the Old Testament they discovered Moses, who delivered his people from slavery, and in the New Testament they found Jesus, who offered salvation to all and thereby established the equality of all people. Jesus' message of equality provided a potent antidote to the planters' claim that blacks were an inferior people whom God condemned to slavery, and it became a crucial buttress to the slaves' self-esteem.

Christianity did not entirely drive out traditional African beliefs. Even slaves who were Christians sometimes continued to believe that conjurers, witches, and spirits possessed the power to injure and protect. Moreover, their Christian music, preaching, and rituals showed the influence of Africa, as did many of the slaves' secular activities, such as wood carving, quilt making, and storytelling. But by the mid-nineteenth century, black Christianity had assumed a central place in slaves' quest for freedom. In the words of one spiritual: "O my Lord delivered Daniel/O why not deliver me too?"

Gourd Fiddle

Found in St. Mary's County, Maryland, this slave-made gourd fiddle is an example of the many musical instruments that African Americans crafted and played throughout the South. Henry Wright, an ex-slave from Georgia, remembered: "I made a fiddle out of a large sized gourd—a long wooden handle was used as a neck, and the hair from a horse's tail was used for the bow. The strings were made of catgut." A hybrid of African and European elements, this fiddle offers material evidence of the cultural transformation of African slaves. Although Africans lost much in their forced journey to the Americas, Africa remained in their cultural memory. Black men and women drew on the traditions of their homeland and the South to create something new—an African American culture. Music, a crucial component of that sustaining culture, provided slaves with a creative outlet and relief from the rigors of slavery.

Smithsonian Institution/Aldo Tutino/Folio, Inc.

Resistance and Rebellion

Slaves did not suffer slavery passively. They were, as whites said, "troublesome property." Slaves understood that accommodation to what they could not change was the price of survival, but in a hundred ways they protested their bondage. Theoretically, the master was all-powerful and the slave powerless. But sustained by their families, religion, and community, slaves engaged in day-to-day resistance against their enslavers.

The spectrum of slave resistance ranged from mild to extreme. Telling a pointed story by the fireside in a slave cabin was probably the mildest form of protest. But when the weak got the better of the strong, as they did in tales of Br'er Rabbit and Br'er Fox (*Br'er* is a contraction of *Brother*), listeners could enjoy the thrill of a vicarious victory over their masters. Protest in the fields was more active than that around firesides. Slaves were particularly inventive in resisting their master's demand that they work. They dragged their feet getting to the fields, put rocks in their cotton bags before putting them on the scale to be weighed, feigned illness, and pretended to be so thickheaded that they could not understand the simplest instruction. Slaves broke so many handles on their hoes that owners outfitted the hoes with oversized handles. Slaves so mistreated the work animals that masters switched from horses to mules, which could absorb more abuse. While slaves worked hard in the master's fields, they also sabotaged his interests.

Running away, a widespread form of protest, particularly angered masters. By escaping the plantation, runaways denied masters what they wanted most from their slaves—work. Sometimes runaways sought the ultimate prize: freedom in the North or in Canada. Over the decades, thousands of slaves, almost all from the Upper South, made it. But escape from the Lower South was almost impossible, except in Texas, where several hundred slaves found freedom by slipping across the Mexican border. But the overwhelming majority of runaways could hope only to escape for a few weeks. They usually stayed close to their plantation, keeping to the deep woods or swamps and slipping back into the quarters at night to get food. "Lying out," as it was known, usually ended when the runaway, worn out and ragged, gave up or was finally chased down by slave-hunting dogs.

"$50 Reward"

Runaway slaves were as common as thunderstorms in the South. Slave owners often employed notices—reward posters like this one and newspaper advertisements—to recover their property. Typically, notices provide precise information about the runaway's physical appearance—size, age, color, build, scars, and hairstyle—and clothing, since slaves often fled with only the clothes on their backs. Notices frequently mentioned the slave's personality and speech habits as well. Here, according to her owner, prominent rice planter Louis Manigault, Dolly was slow to repond when spoken to. Manigault apparently could not accept that a trusted house servant would flee on her own, and thus he suggests that "some white man" had enticed her away. But Manigault also notes that Dolly was new to Augusta, which may suggest that she was seeking to reunite with her family on the coast after Manigault had moved his white family and house servants inland seeking safety during the Civil War. What distinguishes this runaway notice from almost all others is Dolly's photograph. Manigault had apparently rewarded this favorite servant with a photograph, and then he used it to track her down.

Manigault Papers, Southern Historical Collection, North Carolina Collection, The Library of the University of North Carolina, Chapel Hill, collection #P484.

While resistance was common, outright rebellion—a violent assault on slavery by large numbers of slaves—was very rare. The scarcity of revolts is not evidence of the slaves' content-edness, however. Rather, conditions gave rebels almost no chance of success. By 1860, whites in the South outnumbered blacks two to one and were heavily armed. Moreover, communication between plantations was difficult, and the South provided little protective wilderness into which rebels could retreat and defend themselves. Organized rebellion in the American South, as Nat Turner's experience showed, was virtual suicide.

Despite the rarity of slave revolts, whites believed that they were surrounded by conspir-acies to rebel. In 1822, whites in Charleston ac-cused Denmark Vesey, a free black carpenter, of conspiring with plantation slaves to storm the city arsenal, capture its weapons, kill any white who stood in the way, and set fire to the city. The authorities rounded up scores of suspects, who, prodded by torture and the threat of death, implicated others in the plot "to riot in blood, outrage, and rapine." Although the city fathers never found any weapons and Vesey and most of the accused steadfastly denied the charges of conspiracy, officials hanged thirty-five black men, including Denmark Vesey, and banished another thirty-seven blacks from the state.

Although masters often boasted that their slaves were "instinctively contented," steady re-sistance and occasional rebellion proved other-wise. Slaves did not have the power to end their bondage, but by asserting themselves, they affirmed their humanity and worth. By resisting their masters' will, slaves became actors in the plantation drama, helping to establish limits beyond which planters and overseers hesitated to go.

It would be false to the historical record to minimize what the lack of freedom meant to slaves. Because the essence of slavery was the in-ability to shape one's own life, slavery blunted and thwarted African Americans' hopes and aspirations. Slavery broke some and crippled others. But slavery's destructive power had to contend with the resiliency of the human spirit. Slaves fought back physically, culturally, and spiritually. They not only survived bondage, but they created in the quarter a vibrant African American culture and community that sustained them through more than two centuries of slavery and after.

Black and Free: On the Middle Ground

Not every black Southerner was a slave. In 1860, some 260,000 (approximately 6 percent) of the re-gion's 4.1 million African Americans were free (see Figure 13.1). What is surprising is not that their numbers were small but that they existed at all. "Free black" seemed increasingly a contra-diction to most white Southerners. According to the emerging racial thinking, blacks were sup-posed to be slaves; only whites were supposed to be free. Blacks who were free did not fit neatly into the South's idealized social order. They stood out, and whites made them more and more objects of scrutiny and scorn. Free blacks realized that they stood precariously between slavery and full freedom, on what a young free black artisan in Charleston in 1848 characterized as "a middle ground." But they made the most of their freedom, and some managed significant success despite the restrictions placed on them by southern society.

Precarious Freedom

Free blacks were rare in the colonial era, but their numbers swelled after the Revolution, when the natural rights philosophy of the Declaration of Independence and the egalitarian message of evangelical Protestantism joined to challenge slavery. Although probably not more than one slaveholder in a hundred freed his slaves, a brief flurry of **emancipation** visited the Upper South, where the ideological assault on slavery coin-cided with a deep depression in the tobacco economy. Other planters permitted favorite slaves to work after hours to accumulate money with which to buy their freedom. By 1810, free blacks numbered more than 100,000 and had be-come the fastest-growing element of the south-ern population. Burgeoning numbers of free blacks worried white Southerners, who, because of the cotton boom, wanted desperately to see more slaves, not more free blacks.

In the 1820s and 1830s, state legislatures acted to stem the growth of the free black popu-lation and to shrink the liberty of those blacks who had already gained their freedom. Laws de-nied masters the right to free their slaves. Other laws humiliated and restricted free blacks by subjecting them to special taxes, requiring them to register annually with the state or to choose a white guardian, prohibiting them from interstate travel, denying them the right to have schools and to participate in politics, and requiring them to carry "freedom papers" to prove they were not slaves. Increasingly, whites subjected free blacks to many of the same laws as slaves. They could not testify under oath in a court of law or serve on juries. They were liable to punishment meted out to slaves such as whipping and the treadmill. Like slaves, free blacks were forbidden to strike whites, even to defend themselves. "Free negroes belong to a degraded caste of society," a South Carolina judge summed up in 1848. "They are in no respect on a perfect equality with the white man. . . . They ought, by law, to be compelled to demean themselves as inferiors."

The elaborate system of regulations confined most free African Americans to a constricted life of poverty and dependence. Typically, free blacks were rural, uneducated, unskilled agricultural laborers and domestic servants, scrambling to find work and eke out a living. Opportunities of all kinds—for work, education, community—were slim. Planters looked on free blacks as degraded parasites, likely to set a bad example for slaves. They believed that free blacks subverted the racial subordination that was the essence of slavery.

Achievement despite Restrictions

Despite increasingly harsh laws and stepped-up persecution, free African Americans made the most of the advantages their status offered. Unlike slaves, free blacks could legally marry. They could protect their families from arbitrary disruption and pass on their heritage of freedom to their children. Freedom also meant that they could choose occupations and own property. For most, these economic rights proved only theoretical, for whites allowed most free blacks few opportunities. Unlike whites, a majority of the antebellum South's free blacks remained propertyless.

Still, some free blacks escaped the poverty and degradation whites thrust on them. Particularly in urban areas—especially the cities of Charleston, Mobile, and New Orleans—a small elite of free blacks developed and even flourished. Urban whites enforced many of the restrictive laws only sporadically, allowing free blacks room to maneuver. The elite consisted overwhelmingly of light-skinned African Americans who worked at skilled trades, as tailors, carpenters, mechanics, and the like. Their

Freedom Paper
This legal document attests to the free status of the Rev. John F. Cook of Washington, D.C., his daughter Mary, and his son George. Cook was a free black man who kept his "freedom paper" in this watertight tin, which he probably carried with him at all times. Free blacks had to be prepared to prove their free status any time a white man challenged them, for southern law presumed that a black person was a slave unless he or she could prove otherwise. Without such proof, blacks risked enslavement.
Moorland-Spingarn Research Center, Howard University, Washington, D.C.

customers were prominent whites—planters, merchants, and judges—who appreciated their able, respectful service. The free black elite operated schools for their children and traveled in and out of their states, despite laws forbidding both activities. They worshipped with whites (in separate seating) in the finest churches and lived scattered about in white neighborhoods, not in ghettos. And like elite whites, some owned slaves. Blacks could own blacks because, despite all of the restrictions whites placed on free African Americans, whites did not deny them the right to own property, which in the South included human property. Of the 3,200 black slaveholders (barely 1 percent of the free black population), most owned only a few slaves, who were sometimes family members whom they could not legally free. But others owned slaves in large numbers and exploited them for labor.

One such free black slave owner was William Ellison of South Carolina. Ellison was born a slave in 1790, but in 1816 he bought his freedom and moved to a thriving plantation district about one hundred miles north of Charleston. He set up business as a cotton gin maker, a trade he had learned as a slave, and by 1835 he was prosperous enough to purchase the home of a former governor of the state. By the time of his death in 1861, he had become a cotton planter, with sixty-three slaves and an 800-acre plantation.

Most free blacks neither became slaveholders like Ellison nor sought to raise a slave rebellion, as whites accused Denmark Vesey of doing. Rather, most free blacks simply tried to preserve their freedom, which was under increasing attack from planters who wanted to eliminate or enslave them and from white artisans who coveted their jobs. For their part, free blacks clung to their precarious freedom by seeking to impress whites with their reliability, economic contribution, and good behavior.

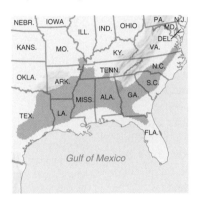

The Cotton Belt

The Plain Folk

Like most free blacks, most whites in the South did not own slaves, not even one. In 1860, more than 6 million of the South's 8 million whites lived in slaveless households. Some slaveless whites lived in cities and worked as artisans, mechanics, and traders. Others lived in the country but worked outside agriculture as storekeepers, parsons, and schoolteachers. But the majority of "plain folk" were small farmers. Perhaps three out of four were **yeomen**, small farmers who owned their own land. As in the North, farm ownership provided a family with an economic foundation, social respectability, and political standing. Unlike their northern counterparts, however, southern yeomen lived in a region whose economy and society were increasingly dominated by unfree labor.

In an important sense, the South had more than one white yeomanry. The huge southern landscape provided space enough for two yeoman societies, separated roughly along geographical lines. Yeomen throughout the South

had a good deal in common, but the life of a small farm family in the plantation belt—the flatlands that spread from South Carolina to east Texas—differed from the life of one in the upcountry—the area of hills and mountains. And some rural slaveless whites were not yeomen; they owned no land at all and were often desperately poor.

Plantation Belt Yeomen

Plantation belt yeomen lived within the orbit of the planter class. Small farms actually outnumbered plantations in that great arc of fertile cotton land that spread from South Carolina to east Texas, but they were dwarfed in importance. Small farmers grew food crops, particularly corn, but like planters, yeomen devoted a significant portion of their land to growing cotton. With only family labor to draw upon, however, they produced only a few 400-pound bales each year, whereas large planters measured their crop in hundreds of bales. The small farmers' cotton tied them to planters. Unable to afford cotton gins or baling presses of their own, they relied on helpful neighborhood slave owners to gin and bale their small crops. With no link to merchants in the port cities, plantation belt yeomen turned to better-connected planters to ship and sell their cotton.

A dense network of relationships laced small farmers and planters together in patterns of reciprocity and mutual obligation. A planter might send his slaves to help a newcomer build a house or a sick farmer get in his crop. He hired out surplus slaves to ambitious yeomen who wanted to expand cotton production. He sometimes chose his overseers from among the sons of local farm families. Plantation mistresses sometimes nursed ailing neighbors. Family ties could span class lines, making rich and poor kin as well as neighbors. Yeomen shared the planters' commitment to white supremacy and actively defended black subordination. Rural counties required adult white males to ride in slave patrols, which nightly scoured country roads to make certain that no slaves were moving about without permission. On Sundays, plantation dwellers and plain folk came together

***Gathering Corn in Virginia*, c. 1870**
In this romanticized agricultural scene, painter Felix O. C. Darley depicts members of a white farm family gathering its harvest by hand. A young black drover, who before the Civil War would have been the property of the white man or would have been rented by him from a neighboring planter, steadies the team of oxen while another man fills the wagon. Sitting before the bundled stalks, the couple shucks the ripened ears of corn. The happy moment is made complete by playful and dozing children and a sleeping dog. In reality, growing corn was hard work. Even yeomen who grew considerable cotton also grew lots of corn, usually producing about twice the corn they needed for their families and livestock and marketing the rest. The artist, however, is less concerned with realism than with extolling rural family labor as virtuous and noble. Darley surrounds the southern yeomen with an aura of republican independence, dignity, and freedom.
Warner Collection of Gulf States Paper Corporation.

in church to worship and afterward lingered to gossip and to transact small business.

Plantation belt yeomen may have envied, and at times even resented, wealthy slaveholders, but in general small farmers learned to accommodate. Planters made accommodation easier by going out of their way to provide necessary services, behave as good neighbors, and avoid direct exploitation of slaveless whites in their community. As a consequence, rather than raging at the oppression of the planter regime, the typical plantation belt yeoman sought entry into it. He dreamed of adding acreage to his farm, buying a few slaves of his own, retiring from fieldwork, and perhaps even joining his prosperous neighbors on their shady verandas for a cool drink.

Upcountry Yeomen

By contrast, the hills and mountains of the South resisted the penetration of slavery and plantations. In the western parts of Virginia, North Carolina, and South Carolina, northern Georgia and Alabama, and eastern Tennessee and Kentucky, the higher elevation, colder climate,

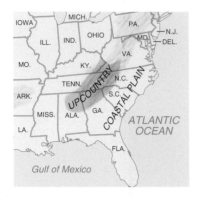

Upcountry of the South

rugged terrain, and poor transportation made it difficult for commercial agriculture to make headway. As a result, yeomen dominated these isolated areas, and planters and slaves were scarce.

At the core of this distinctive upcountry society was the independent farm family working its own patch of land; raising hogs, cattle, and sheep; and seeking self-sufficiency and independence. Toward that end, all members of the family worked, their tasks depending on their sex and age. Husbands labored in the fields, and with their sons they cleared, plowed, planted, and cultivated primarily food crops—corn, wheat, sweet potatoes, and perhaps some fruit. Although pressed into field labor at harvest time, wives and daughters of upcountry yeomen, like those of plantation belt yeomen, worked in and about the cabin most of the year. One upcountry farmer remembered that his mother "worked in the house cooking, spinning, weaving [and doing] patchwork." Women also tended the vegetable garden, kept a cow and some chickens, preserved foods, cleaned their homes, fed their families, and cared for their children. Male and female tasks were equally crucial to the farm's success, but as in other white southern households, the domestic sphere was subordinated to the will of the male patriarch.

The typical upcountry yeoman also grew a little cotton or tobacco, but production for home consumption was more important than production for the market. Not much currency changed hands in the upcountry. Credit was common, as was barter. A yeoman might trade his small cotton or tobacco crop to a country storeowner for a little salt, lead shot, needles, and nails. Or he might swap extra sweet potatoes with the blacksmith for a plow or with the tanner for leather. Networks of exchange and mutual assistance tied individual homesteads to the larger community. Farm families also joined together in logrolling, house- and barn-raising, and cornhusking.

Yeomen did not have the upcountry entirely to themselves. Even the hills had some plantations and slaves. But they existed in much smaller numbers than in the plantation belt. Most upcountry counties were less than a quarter black, whereas counties in the plantation belt were more than half black. The few upcountry folks who owned slaves usually had only two or three. As a result, slaveholders had much less direct social and economic power, and yeomen had more. But yeoman domination did not mean that the upcountry opposed slavery. As long as they were free to lead their own lives, upcountry plain folk defended slavery and white supremacy just as staunchly as did other white Southerners.

Poor Whites

The South's white majority constituted a sturdy yeomanry—hardworking, landholding small farmers. But Northerners believed that slavery had produced a misshapen society that condemned all slaveless whites to poverty, brutality, and backwardness. The British antislavery advocate J. E. Cairnes charged that the South harbored "three classes . . .—the slaves on whom devolves all the regular industry, the slaveholders who reap all its fruits, and an idle and lawless rabble who live dispersed over vast plains little removed from absolute barbarism." Critics called this third class a variety of derogatory names: hillbillies, crackers, rednecks, and poor white trash. Poor whites were not just whites who were poor, according to these claims. The label carried a moral as well as a material meaning. Poor whites were supposedly ignorant and inbred, sick in body, and degenerate in culture. Even slaves were known to chant: "I'd rather be a nigger an' plow ol' Beck/Than a white hillbilly with a long red neck."

A fraction of the white population of the South was poor, rather than the majority, as the critics of the South's social structure claimed. Perhaps one in four white farmers was landless. Some lived as tenants, renting land and struggling to make a go of it. Others scratched out a living by herding pigs and cattle. And still others worked for wages—ditching, mining, logging, and laying track for railroads. A Georgian remembered that his "father worked by the day when ever he could get work." Poor white men gained a reputation for unruly behavior and spontaneous violence. One visitor claimed that a "bowie-knife was a universal, and a pistol a not at all unusual, companion." But unlike the planter class, with its carefully delineated rules for dueling, poor whites were more likely to en-

> At the core of this distinctive upcountry society was the independent farm family working its own patch of land and seeking self-sufficiency and independence.

gage in ear-biting, eye-gouging free-for-alls to preserve their masculine honor. Observers also claimed that poor whites were lazy, but visitors often mistook physical disability for laziness, for in the South's warm, wet climate, barefooted people sometimes contracted hookworm, pellagra, and other debilitating diseases.

Although impoverished, most poor white Southerners were not degenerate. They sat at the bottom of the white pecking order, but they had not lost heart or ambition. Most were ambitious people scratching to survive and aspiring to climb into the yeomanry. The Lipscomb family illustrates the possibility of upward mobility. In 1845, Smith and Sally Lipscomb and their children abandoned their tired land in South Carolina for Benton County, Alabama. "Benton is a mountainous country but ther is a heep of good levil land to tend in it," Smith wrote back to his brother. Alabama, Smith said, "will be better for the rising generation if not for ourselves but I think it will be the best for us all that live any length of time." Indeed, primitive living conditions made life precarious. All of the Lipscombs fell ill, but all recovered, and the entire family went to work. Because they had no money to buy land, they squatted on seven unoccupied acres. With the help of neighbors, they built a 22-by-24-foot cabin, a detached kitchen, and two stables. From daylight to dark, Smith and his sons worked the land. Nature cooperated, and they produced enough food for the table and several bales of cotton. The women worked as hard in the cabin, and Sally contributed to the family's income by selling homemade shirts and socks. In time, the Lipscombs bought land of their own and joined the Hebron Baptist Church, completing their transformation to respectable yeomen.

Many poor whites succeeded in climbing the economic ladder, but in the 1850s upward mobility slowed. The cotton boom of that decade caused planters to expand their operations, driving the price of land beyond the reach of poor families. Whether they gained their own land or not, however, most poor whites shared a great deal in common with yeomen, including their culture.

The Culture of the Plain Folk

Situated on scattered farms and in tiny villages, rural plain folk lived isolated, local lives. Bad roads and a lack of newspapers meant that everyday life revolved around family, a handful of neighbors, the local church, and perhaps a country store. Work occupied most hours, but plain folk still found time for pleasure. "Dancing they are all fond of," a visitor to the backcountry of North Carolina discovered, "especially when they can get a fiddle, or bagpipe." They also loved their tobacco. One visitor complained that the "use of tobacco is almost universal." Men smoked and chewed (and spat), while women dipped snuff. Some plain folk also showed a fondness for liquor, especially whiskey. But the truly universal pastimes among men and boys were fishing and hunting. A traveler in Mississippi recalled that his host sent "two of his sons, little fellows that looked almost too small to shoulder a gun," for food. "One went off towards the river and the other struck into the forest, and in a few hours we were feasting on delicious venison, trout and turtle."

Plain folk did not usually associate "book learning" with the basic needs of life. A northern woman visiting the South in the 1850s observed, "Education is not extended to the masses here as at the North." Private academies charged fees that yeomen could not afford, and public schools were scarce. Even where public schools existed, terms were short, only about 50 or 60 days a year compared with 100 to 150 days in the North. Although most people managed to pick up a basic knowledge of the "three R's," approximately one southern white man in five was illiterate in 1860, and the rate for white women was even higher. "People here prefer talking to reading," a Virginian remarked. Telling stories, reciting ballads, and singing hymns were important activities in yeoman culture.

Plain folk everywhere spent more hours in revival tents than in classrooms. By no means were all rural whites religious, but many were, and the most characteristic feature of their evangelical Christian faith was the revival. The greatest of the early-nineteenth-century revivals occurred in 1801 at Cane Ridge, Kentucky, where some 20,000 people gathered to listen to a host of evangelical preachers who spoke day and night for a week. Ministers sought to convert and save souls by bringing individuals to a personal conviction of sin. Revivalism crossed denominational

> Although impoverished, most poor white Southerners were ambitious people scratching to survive and aspiring to climb into the yeomanry.

A Baptising on the South Branch of the Potomac near Franklin, Virginia (detail), 1844
In 1844, noted painter William Thompson Russell Smith undertook a geological expedition to Virginia, and there he encountered a rural baptism. Primarily a landscape painter, Smith portrayed the human figures as minor characters. If one of the participants had sketched the baptism, he or she might have emphasized the human drama, the emotional pitch of what was for evangelical Christians throughout the South a profound religious moment.
The Charleston Renaissance Gallery, Robert M. Hicklin Jr., Inc., Charleston, South Carolina.

lines; Baptists and Methodists adopted it wholeheartedly and by midcentury had become the South's largest religious groups. By emphasizing free choice and individual worth, the plain folk's religion was hopeful and affirming. Hymns and spirituals provided guides to right and wrong—praising humility and steadfastness, condemning drunkenness and profanity. Above all, hymns spoke of eventual release from worldly sorrows and the assurance of eternal salvation.

The Politics of Slavery

By the mid-nineteenth century, all southern white men—aristocrats and plain folk alike—had gained access to the arena of politics. Like every other significant feature of southern society, politics reflected slavery's power. Even after the South's politics became **democratic** in form for the white male population, political power remained unevenly distributed. The nonslaveholding white majority wielded less political power than their numbers indicated. The slaveholding white minority wielded more. Self-conscious, cohesive, and with a well-developed sense of class interest, slaveholders busied themselves with party politics, campaigns, and officeholding and made demands of state governments. As a result, they received significant benefits. Nonslaveholding whites were concerned mainly with preserving their liberties and keeping their taxes low. Collectively, they asked government for little of an economic nature, and they received little.

> By the early 1850s, southern politics became democratic politics—for white men.

Slaveholders sometimes worried about nonslaveholders' loyalty to slavery, but since the eighteenth century, the mass of whites had accepted the planters' argument that the existing social order served *all* Southerners' interests. Slavery compensated every white man—no matter how poor—with membership in the South's white ruling class. It also provided the means by which nonslaveholders might someday advance into the ranks of the planters. White men in the South fought furiously about many things, but the majority agreed that they should take land from Indians, promote agriculture, uphold white supremacy and masculine privilege, and defend slavery from its enemies.

The Democratization of the Political Arena

The political reforms that swept the nation in the first half of the nineteenth century reached deeply into the South. Southern politics became democratic politics—for white men. Southerners eliminated the wealth and property requirements that had once restricted political participation. By the early 1850s, every state had extended **suffrage** to all white males who were at least twenty-one years of age. Most southern states also removed the property requirements for holding state offices. In addition, increasing numbers of local and state officials—justices of the peace, judges, militia officers, and others—were chosen by the voters. To be sure, undemocratic features lingered. Plantation districts still wielded disproportionate power in several state legislatures. Nevertheless, southern politics took place within an increasingly democratic political structure.

White male suffrage ushered in an era of vigorous electoral competition. Eager voters rushed to the polls to exercise their new rights. In South Carolina, for example, in the 1810 election—the last election with voting restrictions in place—only 43 percent of white men cast ballots. In 1824, a remarkable 76 percent of white men voted. High turnouts became a hallmark of southern electoral politics. Candidates crisscrossed their electoral districts, speaking to voters who demanded stirring oratory and also good entertainment—barbecues and bands, rum and races. In the South, it seemed, "everybody talked politics everywhere," even the "illiterate and shoeless."

As politics became aggressively democratic in the South and across the nation, it also grew fiercely partisan. From the 1830s to the 1850s, Whigs and Democrats battled for the electorate's favor. In the South, both parties presented themselves as the plain white folk's best friend. All candidates declared their fervent commitment to **republican** equality and pledged to defend the people's liberty. Each party sought to portray the other as a collection of rich, snobbish, selfish men who had antidemocratic designs up their silk sleeves. Each, in turn, claimed for itself the mantle of humble "servant of the people."

The Whig and Democratic parties sought to serve the people differently, however. Southern Whigs tended, as Whigs did elsewhere in the nation, to favor government intervention in the economy, and Democrats tended to oppose it. Whigs generally backed state support of banks, railroads, and corporations, arguing that government aid would stimulate the economy, enlarge opportunity, and thus increase the general welfare. Democrats emphasized the threat to individual liberty that government intervention posed, claiming that granting favors to special economic interests would result in concentrated power, which would in turn jeopardize the common man's opportunity and equality. Beginning with the panic of 1837, the parties clashed repeatedly on concrete economic and financial issues.

Planter Power

Whether Whig or Democrat, southern officeholders were likely to be slave owners. The power slaveholders exerted over slaves did not translate directly into political authority over whites, however. In the nineteenth century, political power could be won only at the ballot box, and almost everywhere nonslaveholders were in the majority. Yet year after year, proud and noisily egalitarian common men elected wealthy slaveholders.

Over time, slaveholders increased their power in state legislatures. By 1860, the percentage of slave owners in state legislatures ranged from 41 percent in Missouri to nearly 86 percent in North Carolina (Table 13.1). Legislators not only tended to own slaves—they often owned large numbers. The percentage of planters (indi-viduals with twenty or more slaves) in southern legislatures in 1860 ranged from 5.3 percent in Missouri to 55.4 percent in South Carolina. In North Carolina, where only 3 percent of the state's white families belonged to the planter class, 36.6 percent of the legislature were planters. The democratization of politics in the nineteenth century meant that more ordinary citizens participated in elections, but yeomen and artisans remained rare sights in the halls of southern legislatures.

Upper-class dominance of southern politics reflected the elite's success in persuading the white majority that what was good for slaveholders was also good for them. The South had, on the whole, done well by the plain folk. Most had farms of their own. They participated as equals in a democratic political system. They enjoyed an elevated social status, above all blacks and in theory equal to all other whites. They commanded patriarchal authority over their households. And as long as slavery existed, they could dream of joining the planter class, of rising above the drudgery of field labor. Slaveless white men found much to celebrate in the slave South.

Most slaveholders took pains to win the plain folk's trust and to nurture their respect. In the plantation districts especially, where slaveholders and nonslaveholders lived side by side,

TABLE 13.1	PERCENT OF SLAVEHOLDERS AND PLANTERS IN SOUTHERN LEGISLATURES, 1860	
Legislature	Slaveholders	Planters*
Virginia	67.3%	24.2%
Maryland	53.4	19.3
North Carolina	85.8	36.6
Kentucky	60.6	8.4
Tennessee	66.0	14.0
Missouri	41.2	5.3
Arkansas	42.0	13.0
South Carolina	81.7	55.4
Georgia	71.6	29.0
Florida	55.4	20.0
Alabama	76.3	40.8
Mississippi	73.4	49.5
Louisiana	63.8	23.5
Texas	54.1	18.1

*Planters: Owned 20 or more slaves.

Source: Adapted from Ralph A. Wooster, *The People in Power: Courthouse and Statehouse in the Lower South, 1850–1860* (1969), 41; Wooster, *Politicians, Planters, and Plain Folks: Courthouse and Statehouse in the Upper South* (1975), 40. Courtesy of the University of Tennessee Press.

planters learned that flexing their economic muscle was a poor way to win the political allegiance of common men. Instead, they developed a lighter touch, fully attentive to their own interests but aware of the personal feelings of poorer whites. One South Carolinian told his wealthy neighbor that he had a bright political future because he never thought himself "too good to sit down & talk to a poor man." South Carolinian Mary Boykin Chesnut complained about the fawning attention her slaveholding husband showed to poor men, including one who had "mud sticking up through his toes."

Smart candidates found ways to convince wary plain folk of their democratic convictions and egalitarian sentiments, whether they were genuine or not. When young John A. Quitman ran for a seat in the Mississippi legislature, he amazed a boisterous crowd of small farmers at one campaign stop by not only entering but winning contests in jumping, boxing, wrestling, and sprinting. For his finale he outshot the area's champion marksman. Then, demonstrating his deft political touch, he gave his prize, a fat ox, to the defeated rifleman. The electorate showed its approval by sending Quitman to the state capital. When Walter L. Steele ran for a seat in the North Carolina legislature in 1846, he commented sarcastically to a friend that he was "busily engaged in proving to the people, the soundness of my political faith, and the purity of my personal character & playing fool to a considerable extent, as you know, all candidates are obliged to do." He detested pandering to the electorate, but he had learned to speak with "a candied tongue."

The massive representation of slaveholders ensured that southern legislatures would make every effort to preserve their interests. Georgia politics show how well planters protected themselves in the political struggle. In 1850, about half of the state's revenues came from taxes on slave property, the characteristic form of planter wealth. However, the tax rate on slaves was trifling, only about one-fifth the rate on land. Moreover, planters benefited far more than other social groups from public spending: Financing railroads—which carried cotton to market—was the largest state expenditure. The legislature also established low tax rates on land, the characteristic form of yeoman wealth, which meant that the typical yeoman's annual tax bill was small. Still, relative to their wealth, large slaveholders paid less than did other whites. Relative to their numbers, they got more in return. A sym-

pathetic slaveholding legislature protected planters' interests and gave the impression of protecting the small farmers' interests as well.

The South's elite protected slavery in other ways. In the 1830s, whites decided that slavery was too important to debate. "So interwoven is [slavery] with our interest, our manners, our climate and our very being," one man declared in 1833, "that no change can ever possibly be effected without a civil commotion from which the heart of a patriot must turn with horror." To end free speech on the slavery question, slavery's critics were dismissed from college faculties, driven from pulpits, and hounded from political life. Sometimes they fell victim to vigilantes and mob violence. One could defend slavery; one could even delicately suggest mild reforms. But no Southerner could safely call slavery evil or advocate its destruction.

In the antebellum South, therefore, the rise of the common man occurred alongside the continuing, even growing, power of the planter class. Rather than pitting slaveholders against nonslaveholders, elections remained an effective means of binding the region's whites together. Elections affirmed the sovereignty of white men, whether planter or plain folk, and the subordination of African Americans. Those twin themes played well among white women as well. Although unable to vote, white women supported equality for whites and slavery for blacks. In the antebellum South, the politics of slavery helped knit together all of white society.

Conclusion: A Slave Society

By the early nineteenth century, northern states had either abolished slavery or put it on the road to extinction while southern states were aggressively building the largest slave society in the New World. Regional differences increased over time, not merely because the South became more and more dominated by slavery, but also because developments in the North rapidly propelled it in a very different direction.

In 1860, one-third of the South's population was enslaved. Bondage saddled blacks with enormous physical and spiritual burdens: hard labor, poor treatment, broken families, and most important, the denial of freedom itself. Although degraded and exploited, they were not defeated. Out of African memories and New World realities, blacks created a life-affirming African

American culture that sustained and strengthened them. Their families, religion, and community provided antidotes to white racist ideas and even to white power. Defined as property, they refused to be reduced to things. Perceived as inferior beings, they rejected the notion that they were natural slaves. Slaves engaged in a war of wills with masters who sought their labor while the slaves sought to live dignified, autonomous lives.

Much more than racial slavery contributed to the South's distinctiveness and to the loyalty and regional identification of its whites. White Southerners felt strong attachments to local communities, to extended families, to personal, face-to-face relationships, to rural life, to evangelical Protestantism, and to codes of honor and chivalry, among other things. But slavery was crucial to the South's economy, society, culture, and politics, as well as to its developing sectional consciousness. After the 1830s, the South was not merely a society with slaves; it was a slave society. Little disturbed the white consensus south of the Mason-Dixon line that racial slavery was necessary and just. By making all blacks a pariah class, all whites gained a measure of equality and harmony.

Racism did not erase stress along class lines. Nor did the other features of southern life that helped confine class tensions: the wide availability of land, rapid economic mobility, the democratic nature of political life, patriarchal power among white men, the shrewd behavior of slaveholders toward poorer whites, kinship ties between rich and poor, and rural traditions. Anxious slaveholders continued to worry that yeomen would defect from the proslavery consensus. But during the 1850s, a far more ominous division emerged—between the "slave states" and the "free states."

FOR ADDITIONAL FIRSTHAND ACCOUNTS OF THIS PERIOD, see Chapter 13 in Michael Johnson, ed., *Reading the American Past*, Third Edition.

TO ASSESS YOUR MASTERY OF THE MATERIAL IN THIS CHAPTER, see the Online Study Guide at bedfordstmartins.com/roark.

FOR WEB LINKS RELATED TO TOPICS IN THIS CHAPTER, see "HistoryLinks," "DocLinks," and "PlaceLinks" at bedfordstmartins.com/roark.

CHRONOLOGY

1808 • External slave trade outlawed.

1813–1814
  • Creek War opens 24 million acres of Indian land to southern settlement in the West.

1810s–1850s
  • Suffrage gradually extended throughout South to white males over twenty-one years of age.

1820s–1830s
  • Southern legislatures enact slave codes to strengthen slavery.
  • Southern legislatures enact laws to restrict growth of free black population and to limit freedom of free blacks.
  • Southern intellectuals begin to fashion systematic defense of slavery.

1820–1860
  • Cotton production soars from about 300,000 bales to nearly 5 million bales.

1822 • Denmark Vesey executed for conspiring to lead a slave rebellion in South Carolina.

1829 • David Walker publishes *Appeal . . . to the Coloured Citizens of the World.*

1830 • U.S. Census reveals southern slaves number approximately 2 million.

1831 • Nat Turner's slave rebellion occurs in Virginia.
  • William Lloyd Garrison publishes the first issue of *Liberator*, his abolitionist newspaper, in Boston.

1834 • Charles Colcock Jones publishes *Catechism for Colored Persons.*

1836 • Arkansas admitted to the Union as a slave state.

1840 • Cotton accounts for more than 60 percent of the nation's exports.

1845 • Texas and Florida admitted to the Union as slave states.

1860 • U.S. Census reveals that southern slaves number more than 4 million, one-third of the South's population.

BIBLIOGRAPHY

General Works

John B. Boles, *The South through Time: A History of an American Region* (2nd ed., 1999).

W. J. Cash, *The Mind of the South* (1941).

William J. Cooper Jr. and Thomas E. Terrill, *The American South: A History* (2nd ed., 1996).

Carl N. Degler, *Place over Time: The Continuity of Southern Distinctiveness* (1977).

Peter Kolchin, *A Sphinx on the American Land: The Nineteenth-Century South in Comparative Perspective* (2003).

James Oakes, *Slavery and Freedom: An Interpretation of the Old South* (1990).

The Economy

Fred Bateman and Thomas Weiss, *A Deplorable Scarcity: The Failure of Industrialization in the Slave Economy* (1981).

David L. Carlton and Peter A. Coclanis, *The South, the Nation, and the World: Perspectives on Southern Economic Development* (2003).

Daniel S. Dupre, *Transforming the Cotton Frontier: Madison County, Alabama, 1800–1840* (1997).

Robert W. Fogel, *Without Consent or Contract: The Rise and Fall of American Slavery* (1989).

Sam B. Hilliard, *Atlas of Antebellum Southern Agriculture* (1984).

John Majewski, *A House Dividing: Economic Development in Pennsylvania and Virginia before the Civil War* (2000).

Joseph P. Reidy, *From Slavery to Agrarian Capitalism in the Cotton Plantation South: Central Georgia, 1800–1880* (1992).

Larry Schweikart, *Banking in the American South from the Age of Jackson to Reconstruction* (1987).

Harold D. Woodman, *King Cotton and His Retainers: Financing and Marketing the Cotton Crop of the South, 1800–1925* (1968).

Gavin Wright, *The Political Economy of the Cotton South: Households, Markets, and Wealth in the Nineteenth Century* (1978).

Slaveholders

Jane T. Censer, *North Carolina Planters and Their Children, 1800–1860* (1984).

Catherine Clinton, *The Plantation Mistress: Woman's World in the Old South* (1982).

Drew G. Faust, *James Henry Hammond and the Old South: A Design for Mastery* (1982).

Elizabeth Fox-Genovese, *Within the Plantation Household: Black and White Women of the Old South* (1988).

Eugene D. Genovese, *The World the Slaveholders Made: Two Essays in Interpretation* (1969).

James David Miller, *South by Southwest: Planter Emigration and Identity in the Slave South* (2002).

James Oakes, *The Ruling Race: A History of American Slaveholders* (1982).

Anne F. Scott, *The Southern Lady: From Pedestal to Politics, 1830–1930* (1970).

Steven M. Stowe, *Intimacy and Power in the Old South: Ritual in the Lives of the Planters* (1987).

Michael Tadman, *Speculators and Slaves: Masters, Traders, and Slaves in the Old South* (1989).

Marli F. Weiner, *Mistresses and Slaves: Plantation Women in South Carolina, 1830–1880* (1998).

Jeffrey Robert Young, *Domesticating Slavery: The Master Class in Georgia and South Carolina, 1670–1837* (1999).

Slaves, Slavery, and Race Relations

GENERAL WORKS

Ira Berlin, *Generations of Captivity: A History of African-American Slaves* (2003).

John W. Blassingame, *The Slave Community: Plantation Life in the Antebellum South* (1972).

Carl N. Degler, *Neither Black nor White: Slavery and Race Relations in Brazil and the United States* (1971).

George M. Fredrickson, *The Black Image in the White Mind: The Debate on Afro-American Character and Destiny, 1817–1914* (1971).

George M. Fredrickson, *The Arrogance of Race: Historical Perspectives on Slavery, Racism, and Social Inequality* (1988).

Eugene D. Genovese, *Roll, Jordan, Roll: The World the Slaves Made* (1974).

Peter Kolchin, *American Slavery, 1619–1877* (1993).

Elise Lemire, *"Miscegenation": Making Race in America* (2002).

George P. Rawick, ed., *The American Slave: A Composite Autobiography*, 41 vols. (1972–1979).

Willie Lee Rose, ed., *A Documentary History of Slavery in North America* (1976).

Kenneth M. Stampp, *The Peculiar Institution: Slavery in the Antebellum South* (1956).

Sterling Stuckey, *Slave Culture: Nationalist Theory and the Foundations of Black America* (1987).

IMPORTANT ASPECTS OF SLAVERY

Wilma A. Dunaway, *The African-American Family in Slavery and Emancipation* (2002).

Sharla M. Fett, *Working Cures: Healing, Health, and Power on Southern Slave Plantations* (2002).

John Hope Franklin and Loren Schweninger, *Runaway Slaves: Rebels on the Plantation* (1999).

David Barry Gaspar and Darlene Clark Hine, eds., *More Than Chattel: Black Women and Slavery in the Americas* (1996).

Eugene D. Genovese, *From Rebellion to Revolution: Afro-American Slave Revolts in the Making of the Modern World* (1979).

Kenneth S. Greenberg, ed., *Nat Turner: A Slave Rebellion in History and Memory* (2002).

Herbert G. Gutman, *The Black Family in Slavery and Freedom, 1750–1925* (1976).

Walter Johnson, *Soul by Soul: Life inside the Antebellum Slave Market* (1999).

Ann Patton Malone, *Sweet Chariot: Slavery, Family, and Household Structure in Nineteenth-Century Louisiana* (1992).

Thomas D. Morris, *Southern Slavery and the Law, 1619–1860* (1996).

Dylan C. Penningroth, *The Claims of Kinfolk: African American Property and Community in the Nineteenth-Century South* (2003).

Albert J. Raboteau, *Slave Religion: The "Invisible Institution" in the Antebellum South* (1978).

Judith Kelleher Schafer, *Becoming Free, Remaining Free: Manumission and Enslavement in New Orleans, 1846–1862* (2002).

Marie Jenkins Schwartz, *Born in Bondage: Growing Up Enslaved in the Antebellum South* (2000).

Brenda E. Stevenson, *Life in Black and White: Family and Community in the Slave South* (1996).

William L. Van Deburg, *The Slave Drivers: Black Agricultural Labor Supervisors in the Antebellum South* (1979).

Richard C. Wade, *Slavery in the Cities: The South, 1820–1860* (1964).

Deborah G. White, *Ar'n't I a Woman? Female Slaves in the Plantation South* (1985).

STATE AND LOCAL STUDIES

Edward E. Baptist, *Creating an Old South: Middle Florida's Plantation Frontier before the Civil War* (2002).

Randolph B. Campbell, *An Empire for Slavery: The Peculiar Institution in Texas, 1821–1865* (1989).

Margaret W. Creel, *"A Peculiar People": Slave Religion and Community-Culture among the Gullahs* (1988).

Charles B. Dew, *Bond of Iron: Master and Slave at Buffalo Forge* (1994).

Barbara J. Fields, *Slavery and Freedom on the Middle Ground: Maryland during the Nineteenth Century* (1985).

John C. Inscoe, *Mountain Masters, Slavery, and the Sectional Crisis in Western North Carolina* (1989).

Charles W. Joyner, *Down by the Riverside: A South Carolina Slave Community* (1984).

Melton A. McLaurin, *Celia, a Slave* (1991).

SOCIETY AND CULTURE

Edward L. Ayers, *Vengeance and Justice: Crime and Punishment in the Nineteenth-Century American South* (1984).

Peter W. Bardaglio, *Reconstructing the Household: Families, Sex, and the Law in the Nineteenth-Century South* (1995).

Ira Berlin, *Slaves without Masters: The Free Negro in the Antebellum South* (1974).

Charles C. Bolton and Scott P. Culclasure, eds., *The Confessions of Edward Isham: A Poor White Life of the Old South* (1998).

Orville Vernon Burton, *In My Father's House Are Many Mansions: Family and Community in Edgefield, South Carolina* (1985).

Victoria E. Bynum, *Unruly Women: The Politics of Social and Sexual Control in the Old South* (1992).

Bruce Collins, *White Society in the Antebellum South* (1985).

John Patrick Daly, *When Slavery Was Called Freedom: Evangelicalism, Proslavery, and the Causes of the Civil War* (2002).

Susanna Delfino and Michele Gillespie, eds., *Neither Lady nor Slave: Working Women of the Old South* (2002).

Neil Foley, *The White Scourge: Mexicans, Blacks, and Poor Whites in Texas Cotton Culture* (1997).

Sally E. Hadden, *Slave Patrols: Law and Violence in Virginia and the Carolinas* (2001).

Steven Hahn, *The Roots of Southern Populism: Yeoman Farmers and the Transformation of the Georgia Upcountry, 1850–1890* (1983).

J. William Harris, *Plain Folk and Gentry in a Slave Society: White Liberty and Black Slavery in Augusta's Hinterlands* (1985).

Christine Leigh Heyrman, *Southern Cross: The Beginnings of the Bible Belt* (1997).

Samuel C. Hyde Jr., ed., *Plain Folk of the South Revisited* (1997).

Michael P. Johnson and James L. Roark, *Black Masters: A Free Family of Color in the Old South* (1984).

Robert C. Kenser, *Kinship and Neighborhood in a Southern Community: Orange County, North Carolina, 1849–1881* (1987).

Suzanne Lebsock, *The Free Women of Petersburg: Status and Culture in a Southern Town, 1784–1860* (1984).

Stephanie McCurry, *Masters of Small Worlds: Yeoman Households, Gender Relations, and the Political Culture of the Antebellum South Carolina Low Country* (1995).

Christopher Morris, *Becoming Southern: The Evolution of a Way of Life, Warren County and Vicksburg, Mississippi, 1770–1860* (1995).

John Solomon Otto, *The Southern Frontiers, 1607–1860* (1989).

Christopher H. Owen, *The Sacred Flame of Love: Methodism and Society in Nineteenth-Century Georgia* (1998).

Nicolas W. Proctor, *Bathed in Blood: Hunting and Mastery in the Old South* (2002).

Mark M. Smith, *Mastered by the Clock: Time, Slavery, and Freedom in the American South* (1997).

Mitchell Snay, *Gospel of Disunion: Religion and Separatism in the Antebellum South* (1993).

Randy J. Sparks, *On Jordan's Stormy Banks: Evangelicalism in Mississippi, 1773–1876* (1994).

Christopher Waldrep, *Roots of Disorder: Race and Criminal Justice in the American South, 1817–80* (1998).

Bertram Wyatt-Brown, *Southern Honor: Ethics and Behavior in the Old South* (1982).

POLITICS AND POLITICAL CULTURE

Anthony Gene Carey, *Parties, Slavery, and the Union in Antebellum Georgia* (1997).

William J. Cooper Jr., *Liberty and Slavery: Southern Politics to 1860* (1983).

Lacy K. Ford Jr., *Origins of Southern Radicalism: The South Carolina Upcountry, 1800–1860* (1988).

Robert E. May, *John A. Quitman: Old South Crusader* (1985).

John N. Sacher, *A Perfect War of Politics: Parties, Politicians, and Democracy in Louisiana, 1824–1861* (2003).

Craig M. Simpson, *A Good Southerner: The Life of Henry A. Wise of Virginia* (1985).

J. Mills Thornton III, *Politics and Power in a Slave Society: Alabama, 1800–1860* (1978).

Elizabeth R. Varon, *We Mean to Be Counted: White Women and Politics in Antebellum Virginia* (1998).

Peter Wallenstein, *From the Slave South to New South: Public Policy in Nineteenth-Century Georgia* (1987).

Ralph A. Wooster, *The People in Power: Courthouse and Statehouse in the Lower South, 1850–1860* (1969).

Ralph A. Wooster, *Politicians, Planters, and Plain Folks: Courthouse and Statehouse in the Upper South, 1850–1860* (1975).

JOHN BROWN'S PIKES

Scorning what he called "milk-and-water" abolitionists who only talked about slavery, John Brown favored "action!" In 1859 when he brought his abolitionist war to Virginia, he carried with him 950 pikes, handsome but deadly spears made by a Connecticut blacksmith, which he expected to put into the hands of rebelling slaves. Bloody pikes, he thought, would end slavery in America. After Brown's failure at Harpers Ferry, townspeople sold many of the weapons as souvenirs.

Chicago Historical Society.

The House Divided

1846–1861

OTHER THAN TWENTY CHILDREN, John Brown did not have much to show for his life in 1859. Grizzled, gnarled, and fifty-nine years old, he had for decades lived like a nomad, hauling his large family back and forth across six states as he tried desperately to better himself. He turned his hand to farming, raising sheep, running a tannery, and selling wool, but failure followed failure. The world had given John Brown some hard licks, but it had not budged his conviction that slavery was wrong and ought to be destroyed. He had learned to hate slavery at his father's knee, and in the wake of the fighting that erupted over the issue in Kansas in the 1850s, his beliefs turned violent. On May 24, 1856, he led an eight-man antislavery posse in the midnight slaughter of five allegedly proslavery men at Pottawatomie, Kansas. He told Mahala Doyle, whose husband and two oldest sons he killed, that if a man stood between him and what he thought right, he would take that man's life as calmly as he would eat breakfast.

After the killings, Brown slipped out of Kansas and reemerged in the East. More than ever, he was a man on fire for abolition. He spent thirty months begging money from New England abolitionists to support his vague plan for military operations against slavery. He captivated the genteel easterners, particularly the Boston elite. They were awed by his iron-willed determination and courage, but most could not accept violence. "These men are all talk," Brown declared. "What is needed is action—action!" But the hypnotic-eyed Brown convinced a handful that God had touched him for a great purpose, and they donated enough for him to gather a small band of antislavery warriors.

On the night of October 16, 1859, John Brown took his war against slavery into the South. With only twenty-one men, including five African Americans, he invaded Harpers Ferry, Virginia. His band quickly seized the town's armory and rifle works, but the invaders were immediately surrounded, first by local militia and then by Colonel Robert E. Lee, who commanded the U.S. troops in the area. When Brown refused to surrender, federal soldiers charged with bayonets. Seventeen men, two of whom were slaves, lost their lives. Although a few of Brown's raiders escaped, federal forces killed ten (including two of his sons) and captured seven, among them Brown.

"When I strike, the bees will begin to swarm," Brown told Frederick Douglass a few months before the raid. As slaves rushed to Harpers Ferry, Brown planned to arm them with the pikes he carried with him and with weapons stolen from the armory. They would then fight a war of liberation. Brown, however, neglected to inform the slaves that he had arrived in Harpers Ferry, and the few who knew of his arrival wanted nothing to do

John Brown
In this 1859 photograph, John Brown appears respectable, even statesmanlike, but contemporaries debated his mental state and moral character, and the debate has raged ever since. Critics argue that he was a bloody terrorist, a religious fanatic who believed that he was touched by God for a great purpose, one for which he was willing to die. Admirers see a resolute and selfless hero, a rare white man who believed that black people were the equals of whites, a reformer who recognized that moral suasion would not end slavery in America.
National Portrait Gallery, Smithsonian Institution/Art Resource, NY.

with his enterprise. "It was not a slave insurrection," Abraham Lincoln observed. "It was an attempt by white men to get up a revolt among slaves, in which the slaves refused to participate. In fact, it was so absurd that the slaves, with all their ignorance, saw plainly enough it could not succeed."

Although Brown's raid ended in utter defeat, white Southerners viewed it as proof of their growing suspicion that Northerners actively sought to incite slaves in bloody rebellion. For more than a decade, Northerners and Southerners had accused one another of hostile intentions, and by 1859, emotions were raw. Sectional tension was as old as the United States, but hostility had escalated to unprecedented heights with the outbreak of war with Mexico in May 1846, provoked by President Polk's desire to add northern Mexican lands to U.S. territory in the West (see chapter 12). Only three months after the war began, national expansion and the slavery issue intersected when Representative David Wilmot introduced a bill to prohibit slavery from any territory that might be acquired as a result of the war. After that, the problem of slavery in the territories became the principal wedge that divided the nation.

"Mexico is to us the forbidden fruit," South Carolina senator John C. Calhoun declared at the war's outset. "The penalty of eating it [is] to subject our institutions to political death." For a decade and a half, the slavery issue intertwined with the fate of former Mexican land, poisoning national political debate. Slavery proved powerful enough to transform party politics into sectional politics. Rather than Whigs and Democrats confronting one another across party lines, Northerners and Southerners eyed one another hostilely across the Mason-Dixon line. Sectional politics encouraged the South's separatist impulses. A fitful tendency before the Mexican War, southern separatism gained strength with each confrontation. As the nation lurched from crisis to crisis, southern disaffection and alienation mounted, and support for compromise and conciliation eroded. The era began with a crisis of Union and ended with the Union in even graver peril. As Abraham Lincoln predicted in 1858, "A house divided against itself cannot stand."

The Bitter Fruits of War

Between 1846 and 1848, the nation grew by 1.2 million square miles, an incredible two-thirds. By 1850, the gold rush had transformed the sleepy **frontier** of California into a booming, thriving economy (see chapter 12). The 1850s witnessed new "rushes," for gold in Colorado and silver in Nevada's Comstock Lode. Hundreds of thou-

Vischer's Views of California
This illustrated title page from *Vischer's Views of California*, a book intended for curious Easterners, dramatizes (and exaggerates) the gargantuan size of California's redwoods by portraying microscopic individuals walking on the stump of a cut tree. Some Easterners were awed by nature's bounty in the West; others calculated the board feet in a single tree. Images such as this inspired hundreds of thousands of individuals to dream of life in the West.
Yale Collection of American Literature, Beinecke Rare Book Room and Manuscript Library, Yale University.

sands of people from around the world flocked west, particularly to the Pacific Slope, where they produced a vibrant agriculture as well as tons of gold and silver. The phenomenal dynamism of the West demanded the attention of the federal government. It quickly became clear that Northerners and Southerners had very different visions of the West, particularly the place of slavery in its future. As slavery in the western territories became the preeminent issue in national politics, Americans came to understand that the nation's fate rested on finding a solution.

Congress had faced the question of slavery in the national territories before the Mexican-American War, but history provided contradictory precedents. In 1787, Congress passed the Northwest Ordinance, which banned slavery in territory north of the Ohio River. In 1803, when the United States acquired the Louisiana Territory, where slavery was already legal, Congress allowed slavery to remain. As part of the Missouri Compromise of 1820, Congress voted to prohibit slavery in part of the territory and allow it in the rest. In 1846, when it appeared that the war with Mexico would mean new territory for the United States, politicians put on the table a variety of different plans; but when the war ended in 1848, Congress had made no headway in solving the great issue of slavery in the western territories. In 1850, after four years of strife, Congress patched together a settlement, one that Americans hoped would be permanent.

The Wilmot Proviso and the Expansion of Slavery

In the years leading up to the Civil War, Americans focused not on slavery where it existed but on the possibility that slavery might expand into areas where it did not exist. Except for a few abolitionists who strove to uproot slavery wherever they found it, most Americans agreed that the Constitution had left the issue of slavery to the individual states to decide. Northern states had done away with slavery, while southern states had retained it. But what about slavery in the nation's territories? The Constitution stated that "Congress shall have power to . . . make all needful rules and regulations respecting the territory . . . belonging to the United States." The debate between North and South about slavery, then, turned toward Congress and the definition of its authority over western lands.

The spark for the national debate was provided in August 1846 by a young Democratic

representative from Pennsylvania, David Wilmot, who proposed that Congress bar slavery from all lands acquired in the war with Mexico. Wilmot explained that the Mexicans had already abolished slavery in their country, adding, "God forbid that we should be the means of planting this institution upon it."

Regardless of party affiliation, Northerners lined up behind Wilmot's effort to stop the spread of slavery. Some supported **free soil**, by which they meant territory from which slavery would be prohibited, on the basis of principle. They denounced slavery as a sin and quoted Scripture as proof. But not all Northerners who opposed slavery's extension did so out of moral outrage or sympathy for slaves. Support also came from those who were not so much antislavery as they were anti-South. New slave territories would eventually mean new slave states, and they opposed any act that would magnify the political power of Southerners. From experience, they knew that proslavery Southerners in Congress backed economic policies radically different from those favored by Northerners, especially in banking, internal improvements, and the tariff (see chapters 11 and 12). Wilmot himself said he saw his proposal as a means of blunting "the *power* of slaveholders" in the national government.

Further support for "free soil" came from Northerners who were hostile to African Americans and wanted to reserve new lands for whites. Wilmot understood what one Indiana man put bluntly: "The American people are emphatically a *Negro-hating* people." Wilmot himself had blatantly encouraged racist support when he declared, "I would preserve for free white labor a fair country, a rich inheritance, where the sons of toil, of my own race and own color, can live without the disgrace which association with negro slavery brings upon free labor." It is no wonder that some called the Wilmot Proviso the White Man's Proviso.

While the specter of new slave territory alarmed most Northerners, the thought that slavery might be excluded outraged almost all white Southerners. **Yeoman** and **planter** alike regarded the West as a ladder for economic and social opportunity. In addition, they agreed that

Mexican Cession, 1848

the exclusion of slavery was a slap in the face. An Alabaman observed that at least half of the American soldiers in Mexico were Southerners. "When the war-worn soldier returns home," he asked, "is he to be told that he cannot carry his property to the country won by his blood?"

Southern leaders also approached the territorial issue with an eye on political clout. They understood the need for political parity with the North to protect the South's interests, especially slavery. The need never seemed more urgent than in the 1840s, when the North's population and wealth were booming. James Henry Hammond of South Carolina predicted that ten new states would be carved from the acquired Mexican land. If free soil won, the North would "ride over us rough shod" in Congress, he claimed. "Our only safety is in *equality* of POWER."

In the nation's capital, the two sides squared off. Because Northerners had a majority in the House, they easily passed the Wilmot Proviso over the united opposition of Southerners. In the Senate, John C. Calhoun of South Carolina denied that Congress had constitutional authority to exclude slavery from the nation's territories. He argued in 1847 that the territories were the "joint and common property" of all the states, that Congress could not justly deprive any state of equal rights in the territories, and that Congress therefore could not bar citizens of one state from migrating with their property (including slaves) to the territories. Whereas Wilmot demanded that Congress slam shut the door to slavery, Calhoun called on Congress to hold the door wide open. Because slave states in the Senate outnumbered free states fifteen to fourteen, southern senators successfully stopped the proviso.

Senator Lewis Cass of Michigan offered a compromise between these extremes. He proposed the doctrine of **popular sovereignty**, by which he meant letting the people who actually settled the territories decide for themselves slavery's fate. This solution, Cass argued, sat squarely in the American tradition of **democracy** and local self-government. It had the added attraction of removing the incendiary issue of the expansion of slavery from the nation's capital and lodging it in distant, sleepy territorial legislatures, where it would excite fewer passions.

The plan's most attractive feature was its ambiguity about the precise moment when settlers could determine slavery's fate. Northern advocates believed that the decision on slavery could be made as soon as the first territorial legislature assembled. With free-soil majorities likely because of the North's greater population, they would shut the door to slavery almost before the first slave arrived. Southern supporters declared that popular sovereignty guaranteed that slavery would be unrestricted throughout the entire settlement period. Only at the very end, when settlers in the territory drew up a constitution and applied for statehood, could they decide the issue of slavery or freedom. By then, slavery would have sunk deep roots. As long as the matter of timing remained vague, popular sovereignty provided some Northerners and some Southerners with common ground.

When Congress ended its session in 1848, no plan had won a majority in both houses. Northerners who demanded no new slave territory anywhere, ever, and Southerners who demanded free entry for their slave property into all territories, or else, staked out their extreme positions. Unresolved in Congress, the territorial question naturally became an issue in the presidential election of 1848.

The Election of 1848

The Democratic and Whig parties were both hurting in 1848. The territorial debate revealed free-soil factions in both parties. Antislavery northern Democrats challenged Democratic President Polk and the dominant southern element of their party. Northern Whigs split between an antislavery group called Conscience Whigs and a more **conservative** group called Cotton Whigs (many of them were textile mill owners), who sought compromise to hold the party together. Conscience Whigs denounced the evil alliance of northern "lords of the loom" and southern "lords of the lash" and threatened to bolt the party.

When President Polk—worn out, ailing, and unable to unite the Democratic Party—chose not to seek reelection, the Democratic convention nominated Lewis Cass of Michigan, the man most closely associated with popular sovereignty. But, in an effort to keep peace between the proslavery and antislavery factions within the party, the Democrats adopted a platform that avoided a firm position on slavery in the territories. The Whigs followed a different strategy in their effort to patch the fissure within their party over slavery. They nominated a Mexican War hero, General Zachary Taylor. The Whigs bet that the combination of a military hero and total silence on the central issue facing the country would carry the day, so they declined to adopt a

General Taylor Cigar Case

This papier-mâché cigar case portrays General Zachary Taylor, Whig presidential candidate in 1848, in a colorful scene from the Mexican War. Shown here as a dashing, elegant officer, Taylor was in fact a short, thickset, and roughly dressed Indian fighter who had spent his career commanding small frontier garrisons. The inscription reminds voters that Taylor was a victor in the first four battles fought in the war and directs attention away from the fact that in politics he was a rank amateur.

Collection of Janice L. and David J. Frent.

party platform. Taylor, who owned more than 100 slaves on plantations in Mississippi and Louisiana, was hailed by Georgia politician Robert Toombs as a "Southern man, a slave-holder, a cotton planter."

Antislavery Whigs balked and looked for an alternative. The time seemed ripe for a major political realignment. Senator Charles Sumner called for "one grand Northern party of Freedom," and in the summer of 1848 antislavery Whigs and antislavery Democrats founded the Free-Soil Party. Nearly 15,000 noisy Free-Soilers gathered in Buffalo, New York, where they welded the factions together by nominating a Democrat, Martin Van Buren, for president and a Whig, Charles Francis Adams, for vice president. The platform boldly proclaimed, "Free soil, free speech, free labor, and free men."

The November election dashed the hopes of the Free-Soilers. Although they succeeded in making slavery the campaign's central issue, they did not carry a single state. The major parties went through contortions to present their candidates favorably in both North and South, and their evasions succeeded. As one disappointed Free-Soiler observed: "During the last Presidential canvas, it was hard to find in the free States an opponent of slavery prohibition." Taylor won the all-important electoral vote, 163 to 127, carrying eight of the fifteen slave states and seven of the fifteen free states (Map 14.1). (Wisconsin had entered the Union earlier in 1848 as the fifteenth free state.) Northern voters proved they were not yet ready for Sumner's "one grand Northern party of Freedom," but the struggle over slavery in the territories had shaken the major parties badly.

Debate and Compromise

Zachary Taylor entered the White House in March 1849 and almost immediately shocked the nation. The slaveholding Southerner championed a free-soil solution to the problem of western land. The discovery of gold and the rush of 1849 made the existing military rule of California and New Mexico pitifully inadequate and the need for competent civil government urgent. Believing that he could avoid further sectional strife if California and New Mexico skipped the territorial stage, he sent agents west to persuade the settlers to frame constitutions and apply for admission to the Union as states. Predominately antislavery, the settlers began writing free-state constitutions. "For the first time," Mississippian Jefferson Davis lamented, "we are about permanently to destroy the balance of power between the sections."

MAP 14.1 The Election of 1848

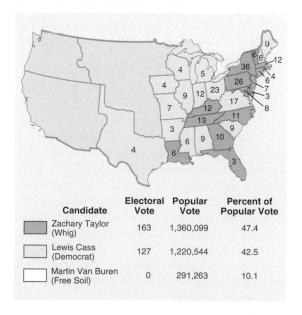

Candidate	Electoral Vote	Popular Vote	Percent of Popular Vote
Zachary Taylor (Whig)	163	1,360,099	47.4
Lewis Cass (Democrat)	127	1,220,544	42.5
Martin Van Buren (Free Soil)	0	291,263	10.1

When Congress convened in December 1849, anxious citizens packed the galleries, eager for the "Great Debate." They witnessed what proved to be one of the longest, most contentious, and most significant sessions in the history of Congress.

When Congress convened in December 1849, anxious citizens packed the galleries, eager for the "Great Debate." They witnessed what proved to be one of the longest, most contentious, and most significant sessions in the history of Congress. Foremost was the territorial issue. President Taylor urged Congress to admit California as a free state immediately and to admit New Mexico, which lagged behind a few months, as soon as it applied. Southerners exploded. In their eyes, Taylor had betrayed his region. Southerners who would "consent to be thus degraded and enslaved," a North Carolinian declared, "ought to be whipped through their fields by their own negroes."

Into this rancorous scene stepped Henry Clay, recently returned to the Senate by his home state of Kentucky. His reputation preceded him: the "Great Pacificator," master of accommodation, architect of Union-saving compromises in the Missouri and **nullification** crises. "Mr. President," Clay declared when he took the floor on January 29, 1850, "I hold in my hand a series of resolutions which I desire to submit to the consideration of this body. Taken together, in combination, they propose an amicable arrangement of all questions in controversy between the free and slave states, growing out of the subject of slavery." Clay's comprehensive plan sought to balance the interests of the slave and free states. Admit California as a free state, he proposed, but organize the rest of the Southwest without restrictions on slavery. Require Texas to abandon its claim to parts of New Mexico, but compensate it by assuming its preannexation debt. Abolish the domestic slave trade in Washington, D.C., but confirm slavery itself in the nation's capital. Reassert Congress's lack of authority to interfere with the interstate slave trade. And enact a more effective fugitive slave law.

Antislavery advocates and "fire-eaters" (as radical Southerners who urged secession from the Union were called) savaged Clay's plan. Senator Salmon Chase of Ohio ridiculed it as "sentiment for the North, substance for the South." Senator Henry S. Foote of Mississippi denounced it as more offensive to the South than the speeches of abolitionists William Lloyd Garrison, Wendell Phillips, and Frederick Douglass combined. The most ominous response came from Calhoun, who rose from his sickbed to charge that unending northern agitation on the slavery question had "snapped" many of the "cords which bind these states together in one common Union . . . and has greatly weakened all the others." Calhoun argued that the fragile political unity of North and South depended on continued equal representation in the Senate, which Clay's plan for a free California destroyed. "As things now stand," he said in February 1850, the South "cannot with safety remain in the Union."

After Clay and Calhoun had spoken, it was time for the third member of the "great triumvirate," Senator Daniel Webster of Massachusetts, to address the Senate. Like Clay, Webster sought to build a constituency for compromise. Admitting that the South had complaints that required attention, he argued forcefully that secession from the Union would mean civil war.

John C. Calhoun
Hollow-cheeked and dark-eyed in this 1850 daguerreotype by Mathew Brady, Calhoun had only months to live. Still, his passion and indomitable will come through. British writer Harriet Martineau once described the champion of southern rights as "the cast-iron man who looks as if he had never been born and could never be extinguished."
National Portrait Gallery, Smithsonian Institution/Art Resource, NY.

He appealed for an end to reckless proposals and, to the dismay of many Northerners, mentioned by name the Wilmot Proviso. A legal ban on slavery in the territories was unnecessary, he said, because the harsh climate effectively prohibited the expansion of cotton and slaves into the new American Southwest.

Free-soil forces recoiled from what they saw as Webster's desertion. In Boston, the clergyman and abolitionist Theodore Parker could only conclude that "the Southern men" must have offered Webster the presidency. In Washington, Senator William H. Seward of New York responded that Webster's and Clay's compromise with slavery was "radically wrong and essentially vicious." He flatly rejected Calhoun's argument that Congress lacked constitutional authority to exclude slavery from the territories. In any case, Seward said, in the most sensational moment in his address, there was a "higher law than the Constitution"—the law of God—to ensure freedom in all the public domain. Claiming that God was a Free-Soiler did nothing to cool the superheated atmosphere of Washington or to quiet rumblings across the nation.

In May, a Senate committee (with the tireless Clay at its head) reported a bill that joined Clay's resolutions into a single comprehensive package, known as the Omnibus Bill because it was a vehicle on which "every sort of passenger" could ride. Clay bet that a majority of Congress wanted compromise and that even though the omnibus contained items that individuals disliked, each would vote for the package to gain an overall settlement of sectional issues. But the omnibus strategy backfired. Free-Soilers and proslavery Southerners would support separate parts of Clay's bill, but they would not endorse the whole. After making seventy speeches to defend his plan, Clay saw it go down to defeat.

Fortunately for those who favored a settlement, Senator Stephen A. Douglas, a rising Democratic star from Illinois, stepped into Clay's shoes. Rejecting the omnibus strategy, he broke the bill into its various parts and skillfully ushered each through Congress. The agreement Douglas won in September 1850 was very much the one Clay had proposed in January. California entered the Union as a free state. New Mexico and Utah became territories in which the ques-

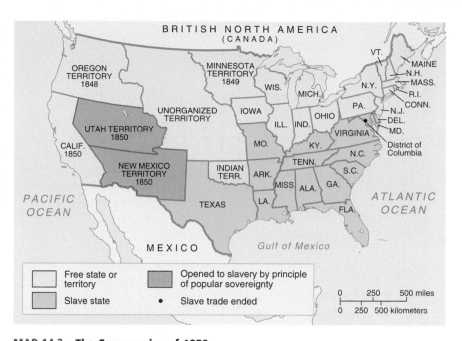

MAP 14.2   The Compromise of 1850
The patched-together sectional agreement was both clumsy and unstable. Few Americans—in either the North or South—supported all five parts of the Compromise.

tion of slavery would be decided by popular sovereignty. Texas accepted its present-day boundary with New Mexico and received $10 million from the federal government. Congress ended the slave trade in the District of Columbia but enacted a more stringent fugitive slave law. In September, Millard Fillmore, who had become president when Zachary Taylor died suddenly in July, signed each bill, collectively known as the Compromise of 1850, into law (Map 14.2; see also "The Promise of Technology," page 482).

Actually, the Compromise of 1850 was not a true compromise at all. Douglas's parliamentary skill, not a spirit of conciliation, led to legislative success. Only by nimbly allying a small group of true compromisers with larger blocs of Northerners and Southerners who voted along sectional lines did Douglas gain a majority for each separate measure. Still, the nation breathed a sigh of relief, for the Compromise preserved the Union and peace for the moment. Daniel Webster declared, "we have gone through the most important crisis that has occurred since the foundation of the Government." But others recognized that the Compromise scarcely touched the deeper conflict over slavery. Free-Soiler Salmon Chase correctly observed, "The question of slavery in the territories has been avoided. It has not been settled."

Daguerreotypes: The "Sunbeam Art"

Early in the nineteenth century, several Europeans working separately discovered that the shadow of an object falling on a chemically treated surface remained after the light source was removed. In the late 1830s, Frenchman Louis Daguerre learned how to keep the "shadow" from fading. News of Daguerre's success in fixing an image arrived in New York City in the spring of 1839.

As Americans found, photography was not for amateurs. The daguerreotype photographic process was cumbersome and messy. Initially, a photographer's equipment included a large wooden box, glass lens, copper plates coated with silver, vials of chemicals, and fire for heat. Because picture taking required several minutes of exposure, candid shots were impossible. To ease the strain of sitting immobile for so long while facing the camera, an American photographer invented a vise to clamp the sitter's head from behind. The process tested patience and often led to photographs that captured grimaces and pained scowls.

Despite their considerable shortcomings, daguerreotypes were an instant success. Samuel Morris, the first American to see a daguerreotype, exclaimed, "The exquisite minuteness of the delineation cannot be conceived. No painting or engraving ever approached it." Another awed observer declared that the daguerreotype was a "perfect transcript of the thing itself." The hyperrealism of the images spooked country people, some of whom suspected magic. But by the early 1840s, photography was a booming business. Itinerant photographers rode the rural and small-town circuit, while in the cities photographic galleries sprang up. In 1850, one observer declared, "In our great cities a Daguerreotypist is to be found in almost every square; and there is scarce a county in the states that has not one or more of those industrious individuals busy at work catching 'the shadow' ere the 'substance fade.'"

Ordinary citizens could not afford to have their portraits painted, and thus few working people owned personal likenesses. Compared to paintings, daguerreotypes were cheap, and at midcentury one reporter claimed that "it is hard to find a man who has not gone through the operator's hands from once to half-a-dozen times, or who has not the shadowy faces of his wife & children done up in purple morocco and velvet. . . . Truly the sunbeam art is a most wonderful one, and the public feel it a great benefit." In the 1850s, the rage for photographs meant that Americans were buying millions of images each year. The new technology met the needs of a culture undergoing vast and rapid change. People kept their precious daguerreotypes in safe places, thankful that this "camera magic" preserved families so often parted by distance or death.

No early American photographer was more important than Mathew Brady. In 1844, he opened the Daguerrean Miniature Gallery at Broadway and Fulton Street in New York City. He sought to bend photography from merely personal to political ends. Brady declared that "from the first, I regarded myself as under obligation to my country to preserve the faces of its historic men and mothers." Seeing himself as a kind of historian of the nation, he shot portraits of distinguished citizens—presidents, congressmen, senators, and statesmen—as well as everyday people who walked into his gallery. Likenesses of illustrious Americans reflected Brady's devotion to the country, and he hoped that they would inspire patriotism in others.

The Sectional Balance Undone

With the words "final settlement" still resounding through the halls of Congress like a magical phrase, the Compromise of 1850 began to come apart. The thread that unraveled the Compromise was not slavery in the Southwest, the crux of the original disagreement, but runaway slaves in New England, a part of the settlement that had previously received relatively little attention. Instead of restoring calm, the Compromise brought the horrors of slavery into the North.

The Palmer Family
Although sitters had to remain still for long periods, early masters of the daguerreotype managed to create memorable photographic portraits. This 1845 photograph by Marcus Aurelius Root is obviously posed and formal but is not painfully somber and stiff. Instead, it captures the conviviality of the family—the Palmers, Quaker abolitionists of Philadelphia—and reaches beyond mere likeness to delve into individual character and personality.
Wm. B. Becker Collection/American Museum of Photography.

His elegant establishment was renowned as a meeting place where people of all classes mingled freely. "People used to stroll in there in those days," a writer remembered, "to see what new celebrity had been added to the little collection, and the last new portrait at Brady's was a standing topic of conversation."

In 1850, Brady sought to extend the public-spirited message of his photographs beyond his shop. He published *The Gallery of Illustrious Americans*—twelve portraits of famous statesmen, including John C. Calhoun, Daniel Webster, and Henry Clay. Anxiety framed the project. At that moment, Washington was embroiled in bitter sectional controversy, and the United States stood on the brink of disintegration. Accurate, realistic images of eminent public men, Brady figured, would capture the "genius" of the nation and rally citizens to their beleaguered Republic. The *Gallery* was a nonpartisan, nonsectional gesture that sought to embrace Whigs and Democrats, Northerners and Southerners, and to urge them to overcome the disuniting elements in American life. The magic of daguerreotypes, Brady thought, would help bind citizens more directly, more personally to living statesmen and to the country they symbolized.

Technology, even technology married to art, could not save the nation. But such was the promise of early photography that some believed it might. Like Webster and Clay, the *Gallery* pleaded for compromise and national unity. Brady hoped that the new technology of photography would serve as a moral agent furthering political reconciliation and peace. By 1860, however, daguerreotypes had all but disappeared from American life, replaced by more efficient photographic processes, and the Union remained imperiled.

Millions of Northerners who had never seen a runaway slave confronted slavery in the early 1850s. Harriet Beecher Stowe's *Uncle Tom's Cabin*, a novel that vividly depicted the brutality and heartlessness of the South's "peculiar institution," aroused passions so deep that many found goodwill toward white Southerners nearly impossible. But no popular uprising forced Congress to reopen the slavery controversy: Politicians did it themselves. Four years after Congress delicately stitched the sectional compromise together, it ripped the threads out. Once again it posed the question of slavery in the territories, the deadliest of all sectional issues.

The Fugitive Slave Act

The Fugitive Slave Act proved the most explosive of the Compromise measures. The issue of runaways was as old as the Constitution, which contained a provision for the return of any "person held to service or labor in one state" who escaped to another. In 1793, a federal law gave muscle to the provision by authorizing slave owners to enter other states to recapture their slave property. Proclaiming the 1793 law a license to kidnap free blacks, northern states in the 1830s began passing "personal liberty laws" that provided fugitives with some protection.

Some northern communities also formed vigilance committees to help runaways and to obstruct white Southerners who came north to reclaim them. Each year, a few hundred slaves escaped into free states and found friendly northern "conductors" who put them aboard the "underground railroad," which was not a railroad at all but a series of secret "stations" (hideouts) on the way to Canada. Harriet Tubman, an escaped slave from Maryland, returned to the South more than a dozen times and guided more than 300 slaves to freedom.

Furious about northern interference, Southerners in 1850 insisted on the stricter fugitive

---

The Modern Medea

In 1855, a slave family—Robert Garner, his twenty-two-year-old wife Margaret, their four children, and his parents—fled Kentucky. Archibald Gaines, Margaret's owner, tracked them to a cabin in Ohio. Thinking that all was lost and that her children would be returned to slavery, Margaret seized a butcher knife and cut the throat of her two-year-old daughter. She was turning on her other children when slave catchers burst in and captured her. Garner's child-murder electrified the nation. Abolitionists claimed that the act revealed the horror of slavery and the tragic heroism of slave mothers. Defenders of slavery argued that the deed proved that slaves were savages. In 1867, Thomas Satterwhite Noble painted a defiant Margaret Garner standing over the bodies of two boys. Noble's departure from history was demanded by his allusion to Greek myth about Medea killing her two children to spite her husband. In 1988, Toni Morrison's novel *Beloved*, drawing on the Garner tragedy, was awarded a Pulitzer Prize.

Harper's Weekly, May 18, 1867/Picture Research Consultants & Archives.

slave law that was passed as part of the Compromise. To seize an alleged slave, a slaveholder or his agent simply had to appear before a commissioner and swear that the runaway was his. The commissioner earned $10 for every black returned to slavery but only $5 for those set free. Most galling to Northerners, the law stipulated that all citizens were expected to assist officials in apprehending runaways.

Theodore Parker, the clergyman and abolitionist, denounced the law as "a hateful statute of kidnappers" and headed a Boston vigilance committee that openly violated it. In February 1851, an angry crowd overpowered federal marshals and snatched a runaway named Shadrach from a courtroom, put him on the underground railroad, and whisked him off to Montreal, Canada. Three years later when another Boston crowd rushed the courthouse in a failed attempt to rescue Anthony Burns, who had recently fled slavery in Richmond, a guard was shot dead. A judge sentenced Burns to be returned to slavery in Virginia. Martha Russell was among the angry crowd that observed him being escorted to the ship. "Did you ever feel every drop of blood in you boiling and seething, throbbing and burning, until it seemed you should suffocate?" she asked. "I have felt all this today. I have seen that poor slave, Anthony Burns, carried back into slavery!"

To white Southerners, it seemed that fanatics of the "higher law" creed had whipped Northerners into a frenzy of massive resistance. Actually, the overwhelming majority of fugitives claimed before federal commissioners were reenslaved and shipped south peacefully. Spectacular rescues such as the one that saved Shadrach and tried to save Burns were rare. But brutal enforcement of the unpopular law had a radicalizing effect in the North, particularly in New England. And to Southerners it seemed that Northerners had betrayed the Compromise. "The continued existence of the United States as one nation," warned the *Southern Literary Messenger*, "depends upon the full and faithful execution of the Fugitive Slave Bill."

Uncle Tom's Cabin

The spectacle of shackled African Americans being herded south seared the conscience of every Northerner who witnessed such a scene. But even more Northerners were turned against slavery by a fictional account, a novel. Harriet Beecher Stowe, a Northerner who had never

Uncle Tom's Cabin
The cover drawing on this early illustrated edition of Harriet Beecher Stowe's novel shows a runaway slave mother racing across ice floes to escape dogs and slave catchers. During the 1850s, at least ten individuals, including Harriet Beecher Stowe herself, dramatized the novel. Stowe's moral indictment of slavery translated well to the stage. Scenes of Eliza crossing the ice with bloodhounds in pursuit, the cruelty of Simon Legree, and Little Eva borne to heaven on puffy clouds gripped the imagination of audiences in America and Britain and fueled the growing antislavery crusade.
Picture Research Consultants & Archives.

seen a plantation, made the South's slaves into flesh-and-blood human beings almost more real than life.

The daughter of evangelist Lyman Beecher and member of a famous clan of preachers, teachers, and reformers, Stowe despised the slave catchers and wrote to expose the sin of slavery. Serialized in a leading magazine in 1851 and then published as a book in 1852, *Uncle Tom's Cabin, or Life among the Lowly* became a blockbuster hit and sold 300,000 copies in its first year and more than 2 million copies within ten years. Her characters leaped from the page. Here was the gentle slave Uncle Tom, a Christian saint who forgave those who beat him to death; the courageous slave Eliza, who fled with her child across the frozen Ohio River; and the fiendish overseer Simon Legree, whose Louisiana plantation was a nightmare of torture and death. Herself the mother of seven children, Stowe aimed her most powerful blows at slavery's destructive impact on the family. Her character Eliza succeeds in keeping her son from being sold away, but other mothers are not so fortunate. When told that her infant has been sold, Lucy drowns herself. Driven half mad by the sale of a son and daughter, Cassy decides "never again [to] let a child live to grow up!" She gives her third child an opiate and watches as "he slept to death."

Responses to *Uncle Tom's Cabin* depended on geography. What Northerners accepted as truth, Southerners denounced as slander.

Responses to *Uncle Tom's Cabin* depended on geography. In the North, common people and literary giants alike shed tears and sang its praises. The poet John Greenleaf Whittier sent "ten thousand thanks for thy immortal book"; the poet Henry Wadsworth Longfellow judged it "one of the greatest triumphs recorded in literary history." What Northerners accepted as truth, Southerners denounced as slander. Virginian George F. Holmes proclaimed Stowe a member of the "Woman's Rights" and "Higher Law" schools and dismissed the novel as a work of "intense fanaticism." Unfortunately, he said, this "maze of misinterpretation" had filled those who knew nothing about slavery "with hatred for that institution and those who uphold it." Although it is impossible to measure precisely the impact of a novel on public opinion, *Uncle Tom's Cabin* clearly helped to crystallize northern sentiment against slavery and to confirm white Southerners' suspicion that they no longer had any sympathy in the free states.

Other writers—ex-slaves who knew life in slave cabins firsthand—also produced stinging indictments of slavery. Solomon Northup's compelling *Twelve Years a Slave* (1853) sold 27,000 copies in two years, and the powerful *Narrative of the Life of Frederick Douglass, as Told by Himself* (1845) eventually sold more than 30,000 copies. But no work touched the North's conscience like the novel by the woman who had never set foot on a plantation. A decade after its publication, when Stowe visited Abraham Lincoln at the White House, he reportedly said, "So you are the little woman who wrote the book that made this great war."

The Kansas-Nebraska Act

As national elections approached in 1852, Democrats and Whigs sought to close the sectional rifts that had opened within their parties. For their presidential nominee, the Democrats turned to Franklin Pierce of New Hampshire. Pierce's most valuable asset was his well-known sympathy with southern views on public issues. His leanings caused northern critics to include

him among the "doughfaces," northern men malleable enough to champion southern causes. The Whigs were less successful in bridging differences. Adopting the formula that had proved successful in 1848, they chose another Mexican War hero, General Winfield Scott of Virginia. But the Whigs were hopelessly divided between their northern and southern factions and suffered a humiliating defeat. The Democrat Pierce carried twenty-seven states to Scott's four, 254 electoral votes to 42 (Table 14.1). In the afterglow of the Compromise of 1850, the Free-Soil Party lost almost half of the voters who had turned to it in the tumultuous atmosphere of 1848.

Eager to leave the sectional controversy behind, the new president turned swiftly to foreign expansion. **Manifest destiny** remained robust. (See "Beyond America's Borders," page 490.) Pierce's major objective was Cuba, which was owned by Spain and in which slavery flourished, but Pierce's clumsy diplomatic efforts galvanized antislavery Northerners, who blocked Cuba's acquisition to keep more slave territory from entering the Union. Pierce's fortunes improved in Mexico. In 1853, he sent diplomat James Gadsden to negotiate a $15 million purchase of some 30,000 square miles of territory south of the Gila River in present-day Arizona and New Mexico. The Gadsden Purchase stemmed from the dream of a transcontinental railroad to California and Pierce's desire for a southern route through Mexican territory. The booming population of the Pacific coast made it obvious that the vast, loose-jointed republic needed a railroad to bind it together. Talk of a railroad ignited rivalries in cities from New Orleans to Chicago as they maneuvered to become the eastern terminus. Thus, the desire for a transcontinental railroad evolved into a sectional contest, which by the 1850s inevitably involved slavery.

No one played the railroad game more enthusiastically than Illinois's Democratic senator Stephen A. Douglas, who was an energetic spokesman for western economic development. He badly wanted the transcontinental railroad for Chicago and his home state, and his chairmanship of the Senate Committee on Territories provided him with an opportunity. Any railroad that ran west from Chicago would pass through

Gadsden Purchase of 1853

a region that Congress in 1830 had designated a "permanent" Indian reserve. Douglas proposed giving this vast area between the Missouri River and the Rocky Mountains an Indian name, Nebraska, and then nullifying Indian titles and throwing the Indians out. Once the region achieved territorial status, whites could survey and sell the land, establish civil government, and build a railroad.

Congress's promise to the Indians did not cause Douglas to hesitate, but another of its promises did. Nebraska lay within the Louisiana Purchase north of latitude 36°30′ and, according to the Missouri Compromise of 1820, was closed to slavery (see chapter 10). Since Douglas could not count on New England to back western economic development, he needed southern votes

TABLE 14.1	THE ELECTION OF 1852		
Candidate	Electoral Vote	Popular Vote	Percent of Popular Vote
Franklin Pierce (Democrat)	254	1,601,117	50.9
Winfield Scott (Whig)	42	1,385,453	44.1
John P. Hale (Free-Soil)	0	155,825	5.0

to pass his Nebraska legislation. But Southerners had no incentive to create another free territory or to help a northern city win the transcontinental railroad. Southerners, however, agreed to help organize Nebraska for a price: nothing less than repeal of the Missouri Compromise. Southerners insisted that Congress organize Nebraska according to popular sovereignty. That meant giving slavery a chance in the Nebraska Territory and reopening the dangerous issue of slavery expansion, which Douglas himself had so ably helped to resolve only four years earlier.

In January 1854, Douglas introduced his bill to organize the Nebraska Territory, leaving to the settlers themselves the decision about slavery. At southern insistence, and even though he knew it would "raise a hell of a storm," Douglas added an explicit repeal of the Missouri Compromise. Indeed, the Nebraska bill raised a storm of controversy. Free-Soilers branded Douglas's plan "a gross violation of a sacred pledge" and an "atrocious plot" to transform free land into a "dreary region of despotism, inhabited by masters and slaves."

Undaunted, Douglas skillfully shepherded the explosive bill through Congress in May 1854. Nine-tenths of all southern members (Whigs and Democrats) and half of the northern Democrats cast votes in favor. Like Douglas, most northern Democrats believed that popular sovereignty would make Nebraska free territory. Ominously, however, half of the northern Democrats broke with their party and opposed the bill. In its final form, the Kansas-Nebraska Act divided the huge territory in two: Nebraska west of the free state of Iowa and Kansas west of the slave state of Missouri (Map 14.3). With this act, the government pushed the Plains Indians farther west, making way for railroads and farmers.

Papago Indians

Major William Emory's Mexican boundary survey of the early 1850s provided Americans with glimpses of a little-known southwestern frontier. In this drawing, Papago Indian women in Arizona Territory use sticks to knock down cactus fruit.

The Center for American History, The University of Texas at Austin.

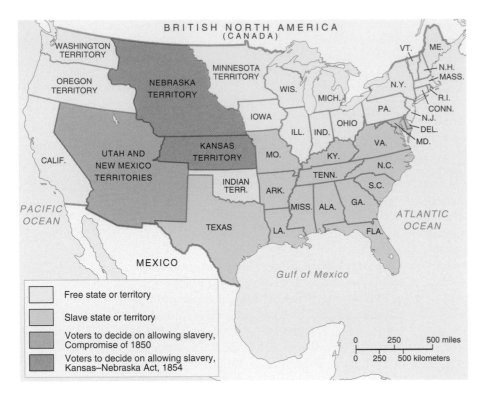

MAP 14.3   The Kansas-Nebraska Act, 1854

Americans hardly thought twice about dispossessing the Indians of lands guaranteed them by treaty, but many worried about the outcome of repealing the Missouri Compromise and opening up lands to slavery.

READING THE MAP: How many slave states and how many free states does the map show? Estimate the percentage of territory likely to be settled by slaveholders.

CONNECTIONS: Who would be more likely to support changes in government legislation to discontinue the Missouri Compromise, slaveholders or free-soil advocates? Why?

FOR MORE HELP ANALYZING THIS MAP, see the map activity for this chapter in the Online Study Guide at bedfordstmartins.com/ roark.

Realignment of the Party System

The Kansas-Nebraska Act marked a fateful escalation of the sectional conflict. Douglas's controversial measure had several consequences, none more crucial than the realignment of the nation's political parties. Since the rise of the Whigs in the early 1830s, Whigs and Democrats had organized and channeled political conflict in the nation. This party system dampened sectionalism and strengthened the Union. To achieve national political power, Whigs and Democrats had to retain strength in both North and South. Strong northern and southern wings required that each party compromise and find positions acceptable to both wings.

The Kansas-Nebraska controversy shattered this stabilizing political system. In place of two national parties with bisectional strength, the mid-1850s witnessed the development of one party heavily dominated by one section and another party entirely limited to the other section. Rather than "national" parties, the country had what one critic disdainfully called "geographic" parties. Parties now had the advantage of sharpening ideological and policy differences between the sections; they no longer muffled moral issues, like slavery. But the new party system also thwarted political compromise and instead promoted political polarization and further jeopardized the Union.

The Old Parties: Whigs and Democrats

Distress signals could be heard from the Whig camp as early as the Mexican-American War, when members clashed over the future of slavery in annexed Mexican lands. But the disintegration of the party dated from 1849–1850, when southern Whigs watched in stunned amazement as Whig president Zachary Taylor sponsored a plan for a free California. Thereafter, Southerners left the party in droves. The slavery issue also confounded northern Whigs, but antislavery forces were clearly dominant in the North. By 1852, the Whig Party could please its southern wing or its northern wing but not both. The Whigs' miserable showing in the election of 1852 made clear that they were no longer a strong national party. By 1856, after more than two decades of contesting the Democrats, they were hardly a party at all (Map 14.4).

The decline and eventual collapse of the Whig Party left the Democrats as the country's only national party. Although the Democrats were not immune to the disruptive pressures of the territorial question, they discovered in

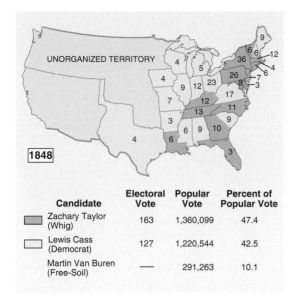

Candidate	Electoral Vote	Popular Vote	Percent of Popular Vote
Zachary Taylor (Whig)	163	1,360,099	47.4
Lewis Cass (Democrat)	127	1,220,544	42.5
Martin Van Buren (Free-Soil)	—	291,263	10.1

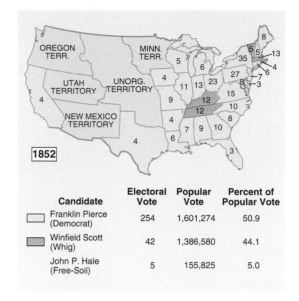

Candidate	Electoral Vote	Popular Vote	Percent of Popular Vote
Franklin Pierce (Democrat)	254	1,601,274	50.9
Winfield Scott (Whig)	42	1,386,580	44.1
John P. Hale (Free-Soil)	5	155,825	5.0

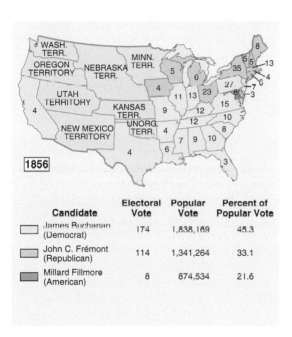

Candidate	Electoral Vote	Popular Vote	Percent of Popular Vote
James Buchanan (Democrat)	174	1,838,169	45.3
John C. Frémont (Republican)	114	1,341,264	33.1
Millard Fillmore (American)	8	874,534	21.6

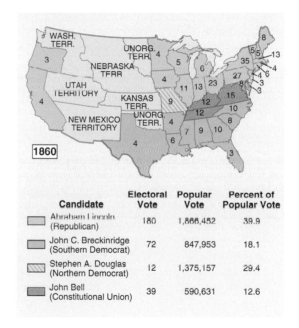

Candidate	Electoral Vote	Popular Vote	Percent of Popular Vote
Abraham Lincoln (Republican)	180	1,866,452	39.9
John C. Breckinridge (Southern Democrat)	72	847,953	18.1
Stephen A. Douglas (Northern Democrat)	12	1,375,157	29.4
John Bell (Constitutional Union)	39	590,631	12.6

MAP 14.4   Political Realignment, 1848–1860

In 1848, slavery and sectionalism began hammering the country's party system. The Whig Party was an early casualty. By 1860, national parties—those that contended for votes in both North and South—had been replaced by regional parties.

READING THE MAP: Which states did the Democrats pick up in the 1852 election over the previous election? Which of the states won in 1852 were lost to the Democrats in 1856? Describe the general geographical location of the states won by the Republicans in 1860 over the 1856 election.

CONNECTIONS: In the 1860 election, which party benefited the most from the addition of western and midwestern states added to the Union since 1848? Why would these states choose to back the Republicans over the Democrats?

FOR MORE HELP ANALYZING THIS MAP, see the map activity for this chapter in the Online Study Guide at bedfordstmartins.com/roark.

Filibusters: The Underside of Manifest Destiny

Each year the citizens of Caborca, Mexico, a small town in the northern state of Sonora, celebrate the defeat there in 1857 of an American army. The invaders did not wear the uniform of the U.S. army but marched as a private army, the "Arizona Colonization Company." Their commander, Henry A. Crabb, a Mississippian who followed the gold rush to California, saw fresh opportunity in the civil disorder that reigned south of the border. Fierce fighting between Mexicans and Apache and Yaqui Indians made life precarious in Sonora and prompted division among the Mexicans. When the governor of Sonora faced an insurrection, he invited Crabb, who was married to a Sonoran woman, to help him repress his enemies in exchange for mineral rights and land.

Crabb marched his band of sixty-eight heavily armed ex-miners south from Los Angeles into Mexico. But by the time the Americans arrived, the governor had put down the insurgency, and he turned on the invaders. Every American except one died either in battle or at the hands of Mexican firing squads. Crabb's head was preserved in alcohol and placed on display as a symbol of victory.

Henry Crabb was one of thousands of American adventurers, known as "filibusters" (from Spanish *filibustero*, meaning "freebooter" or "pirate"), who in the mid-nineteenth century joined private armies that invaded foreign countries in North America, Central America, South America, and the Caribbean. Although these expeditions were illegal and violated the U.S. Neutrality Act of 1818, private American armies attacked Canada, Mexico, Ecuador, Honduras, Cuba, and Nicaragua and planned invasions of places as far away as the Hawaiian kingdom. The federal government occasionally winked at the actions of filibusters, but more often it cracked down, fearful that private invasions would jeopardize legitimate diplomatic efforts to promote trade and acquire territory.

Filibusters joined invading armies for a variety of reasons ranging from personal gain to validating manhood. Many saw themselves as carrying on the work of manifest destiny, extending America's reach beyond Texas, California, and Oregon, the prizes of the 1830s and 1840s. In addition, during the 1840s and 1850s when Northerners grew increasingly intent on containing slavery's spread to the North and West, Southerners joined filibustering expeditions to expand slavery to the south beyond U.S. borders. Although filibusters came from all regions of the country, their greatest numbers and support came from the proslavery forces of the South. The leading proslavery ideologue, George Fitzhugh, sought to blunt criticism of filibustering by defending it through historical comparison: "They who condemn the modern filibuster, to be consistent, must also condemn the discoverers and settlers of America, of the East Indies of Holland, and of the Indian and Pacific Oceans." Such arguments, deeply rooted in manifest destiny, failed to convince many, including the ambassador from Costa Rica, who called filibustering America's "social cancer." Northerners claimed (with some justification) that filibustering was a southern campaign to extend "the empire of the lash."

One of the most vigorous filibusters to appeal to southern interests was not an American: Narciso Lopez was a Venezuelan-born Cuban who dedicated himself to the liberation of Cuba from Spanish rule. In his first attempt in 1849, he recruited an army of several hundred would-be liberators but got no farther than New York harbor, where U.S. marshals intercepted his fleet. Thereafter, he resolved to "rest his hopes on the men of the bold West and chivalric South." Lopez claimed that Spain was planning to free Cuba's slaves, and he told Southerners that "self-preservation" demanded that they seize the island. When Governor John Quitman of Mississippi joined his scheme, Lopez shifted his headquarters to New Orleans. Early in 1850, Lopez and an army of more than 500 landed on the northwest coast of Cuba, but Spanish troops quickly drove them off. Two months later, with 450 troops, he tried again. This time, the Spanish crushed the invasion, killing 200 filibusters, shipping 160 prisoners to Spain, executing 50 invaders by firing squad, and publicly garroting Lopez. John Quitman gathered another army of several thousand, but federal authorities seized one of his ships and ended the threat to Cuba.

Filibustering in Nicaragua
In this image of a pitched battle in Nicaragua in 1856, Costa Ricans on foot fight American filibusters on horseback. Costa Rican soldiers and their Central American allies defeated William Walker's *filibusteros* in 1857, but before then the Pierce administration had extended diplomatic recognition to Walker's regime, and white Southerners had cheered Walker's attempt to "introduce civilization" in Nicaragua and to develop its rich resources "with slave labor."

London Illustrated Times, May 24, 1856.

The most successful of all filibusters was William Walker of Tennessee, a restless dreamer who longed for an empire of his own south of the border. Walker cut his filibustering teeth with expeditions to Baja California and Sonora, but when they failed, he turned to Central America. He believed that Southerners paid too much attention to Kansas and that instead they should expand slavery in tropical America. In May 1855, Walker and an army of fifty-six men sailed from San Francisco to the west coast of Nicaragua. Two thousand reinforcements and a civil war in Nicaragua gave Walker his victory. He had himself proclaimed president, legalized slavery, and called on Southerners to come raise cotton, sugar, and coffee in "a magnificent country." Hundreds of Southerners took up **land grants**, but Walker's regime survived only until 1857, when a coalition of Central American countries allied with the Nicaraguans and sent Walker packing. Walker doggedly launched four other attacks on Nicaragua; then in 1860, Honduran forces captured and shot him.

Filibustering had lost steam by 1861, but the battle-hardened adventurers found new employment in the armies of the Civil War, particularly in the service of the Confederate military. The Confederacy paid a diplomatic price for its association with filibustering, however. The Guatemalan minister Antonio Jose de Irisarri declared that there was "no foreign Nation which can have less cause for sympathy with the enemies of the American Union, than the Republics of Central America, because from the Southern States were set on foot those filibustering expeditions." No Central American state recognized Confederate independence.

A century and more later, the peoples of Central America and the Caribbean, like the inhabitants of Sonora, harbor bitter memories of filibusters' private wars of **imperialism** and honor those who fought off American advances. When U.S. marines occupied Nicaragua in the 1920s, insurgents found inspiration in their country's defeat of William Walker's army of freebooters eighty years earlier. In 1951, on the centennial of Lopez's invasion, Cubans erected a monument at the very spot where his ill-fated army came ashore. Costa Ricans celebrate Juan Santamaria as their national martyr for his courage in battling William Walker. Memories of the invasions by nineteenth-century filibusters set the stage for anti-American sentiment in Latin America that lingers to this day.

BIBLIOGRAPHY

Charles H. Brown, *Agents of Manifest Destiny: The Lives and Times of the Filibusters* (1980).

John Hope Franklin, *The Militant South, 1800–1861* (1956).

Robert E. May, *The Southern Dream of a Caribbean Empire, 1854–1861* (1973).

Robert E. May, *Manifest Destiny's Underworld: Filibustering in Antebellum America* (2002).

Frank L. Owsley, *Filibusters and Expansionists: Jeffersonian Manifest Destiny, 1800–1821* (1997).

William Walker, *The War in Nicaragua* (1860).

popular sovereignty a doctrine that many Democrats could support. Even so, popular sovereignty very nearly undid the party as well. When Stephen Douglas applied the doctrine to the part of the Louisiana Purchase where slavery had been barred, he divided northern Democrats and destroyed the dominance of the Democratic Party in the free states. After 1854, the Democrats became a southern-dominated party.

Nevertheless, the Democrats, unlike the Whigs, remained a national political organization throughout the 1850s. Gains in the South more than balanced Democratic losses in the North. During the decade, Democrats elected two presidents and won majorities in Congress in almost every election. But holding on to national power required the party to maintain northern and southern wings, which in turn required the Democrats to avoid the issue of the expansion of slavery.

The breakup of the Whigs and the disaffection of significant numbers of northern Democrats set many Americans politically adrift. As they searched for new political harbors, Americans found that the death of the old party system created a multitude of fresh political alternatives. The question was which party would attract the drifters.

Know-Nothing Banner

Convinced that the incendiary issue of slavery had blinded Americans to the greater dangers of uncontrolled immigration and foreign influence, the Know-Nothing Party in 1856 ran Millard Fillmore for president. There is more than a little irony in this banner's appeal to "Native Americans" to stem the invasion from abroad. Know-Nothings meant native-born Americans, but bona fide Native Americans, American Indians, also faced an invasion and to them it made little difference whether the aggressors were fresh off the boat or born in the U.S.A.

Milwaukee County Historical Society.

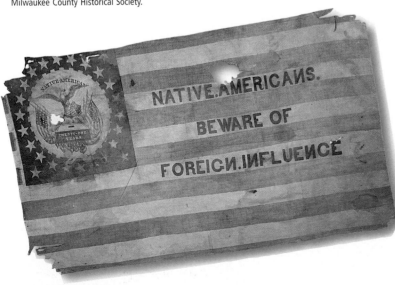

The New Parties: Know-Nothings and Republicans

Dozens of new political organizations vied for voters' attention. Out of the confusion two emerged as true contenders. One grew out of the slavery controversy, a spontaneous coalition of indignant antislavery Northerners. The other arose from an entirely different split in American society, between Roman Catholic immigrants and native **Protestants**.

The tidal wave of immigrants that broke over America from 1845 to 1855 produced a nasty backlash among Protestant Americans, who believed that the American Republic was about to drown in a sea of Roman Catholics from Ireland and Germany (see Figure 12.1, page 425). The new arrivals encountered economic prejudice, ethnic hostility, and religious antagonism. Most immigrants who entered American politics became Democrats because they perceived that party as more tolerant of newcomers than were the Whigs. But in the 1850s they met sharp political opposition when **nativists** (individuals who were anti-immigrant) began to organize, first into secret fraternal societies and then into a political party. Recruits swore never to vote for either foreign-born or Roman Catholic candidates and not to reveal any information about the organization. When questioned, they said: "I know nothing." Officially, they were named the American Party, but most Americans called them Know-Nothings.

The Know-Nothings exploded onto the political stage in 1854 and 1855 with a series of dazzling successes. They captured state legislatures in the Northeast, West, and South and claimed dozens of seats in Congress. Their greatest triumph came in Massachusetts, a favorite destination for the Irish. Know-Nothings elected the Massachusetts governor, all of the state senators, all but two of the state representatives, and all of the congressmen. The American Party attracted both Democrats and Whigs, but with their party crumbling, more Whigs responded to the attraction. Members of both traditional parties described the phenomenal success of the Know-Nothings as a "tornado," a "hurricane," or "a freak of political insanity." By 1855, an observer might reasonably have concluded that the Know-Nothings had emerged as the successor to the Whigs.

Know-Nothings were not the only new party making noise. One of the new antislavery organizations provoked by the Kansas-Nebraska Act called itself Republican. Republicans attempted to unite under their banner all the dissidents and political orphans—Whigs, Free-Soilers, anti-Nebraska Democrats, even Know-Nothings—who opposed the extension of slavery into any territory of the United States.

The Republican creed tapped into the basic beliefs and values of the northern public. Slave labor and free labor, Republicans argued, had spawned two incompatible civilizations. In the South, slavery degraded the dignity of white labor by associating work with blacks and servility. Three-quarters of the South's white population, claimed one Republican, "retire to the outskirts of civilization, where they live a semi-savage life, sinking deeper and more hopelessly into barbarism with every succeeding generation." Republicans argued that slavery repressed every Southerner except planter aristocrats. They warned that those insatiable slave lords, whom antislavery Northerners called the "Slave Power"—were conspiring through their control of the Democratic Party to expand slavery, subvert liberty, and undermine the Constitution. Only if slavery were restricted to the South, Republicans believed, could the system of **free labor** flourish elsewhere. The ideal of free labor respected the dignity of work and provided anyone willing to toil an opportunity for a decent living and for advancement (see chapter 12).

In the North, one Republican declared in 1854, "every man holds his fortune in his own right arm, and his position in society, in life, is to be tested by his own individual character." Free of slavery, the western territories would provide vast economic opportunity for free men. These powerful images of **liberty** and free labor attracted a wide range of Northerners to the Republican cause.

The Election of 1856

By the mid-1850s, the Know-Nothings had emerged as the principal champions of nativism, the Republicans as the primary advocates of the antislavery position. But the election of 1856 revealed that the Republicans had become the Democrats' main challenger and slavery in the territories the election's only issue. The Know-Nothings came apart when party leaders insisted on a platform that endorsed the Kansas-Nebraska Act. Most Northerners walked out. The Know-Nothings who remained nominated ex-president Millard Fillmore.

The Republicans, in contrast, adopted a platform that focused almost exclusively on "making

The Realignment of Political Parties

Whig Party

1848 Whig Party divides into two factions over slavery; Whigs adopt no platform and nominate war hero Zachary Taylor, who is elected president.

1852 Whigs nominate war hero General Winfield Scott for president; deep divisions in party result in humiliating loss.

1856 Shattered by sectionalism, Whig Party fields no presidential candidate.

Democratic Party

1848 President Polk declines to run again. Democratic Party nominates Lewis Cass, the man most closely associated with popular sovereignty, but the party avoids firm platform position on expansion of slavery.

1852 To bridge the rift in the party, Democrats nominate a northern war veteran with southern views, Franklin Pierce, for president; he wins with 50.9 percent of popular vote.

1856 Democrat James Buchanan elected president on an ambiguous platform; his prosouthern actions in office alienate northern branch of the party.

1860 Democrats split into northern Democrats and southern Democrats, and each group fields its own presidential candidate.

Free-Soil Party

1848 Breakaway antislavery Democrats and antislavery Whigs found Free-Soil Party. Free-Soil presidential candidate takes 10.1 percent of popular vote, mainly from Whigs.

1852 Support for Free-Soil Party ebbs in wake of Compromise of 1850; Free-Soil presidential candidate wins only 5 percent of popular vote.

American (Know-Nothing) Party

1851 The anti-immigrant American (Know-Nothing) Party formed.

1854–1855 American Party succeeds in state elections and attracts votes from northern and southern Whigs in congressional elections.

1856 Know-Nothing presidential candidate wins only the state of Maryland and subsequently disbands.

Republican Party

1854 Republican Party formed to oppose the expansion of slavery in the territories; it attracts northern Whigs, northern Democrats, and Free-Soilers.

1856 Republican presidential candidate wins all but five of the northern states, establishing the Republicans as the main challenger to the Democrats.

1860 Republican Abraham Lincoln wins all of the northern states except New Jersey and is elected president in four-way race against the divided Democrats and the southern Constitutional Union Party.

every territory free." When they labeled slavery a "relic of barbarism," Republicans signaled that they had written off the South. For president, they nominated the dashing soldier and California adventurer John C. Frémont, "Pathfinder of the West." Frémont lacked political credentials, but political know-how resided in his wife, Jessie, who, as a daughter of Senator Thomas Hart Benton of Missouri, knew the political map as well as her husband knew western trails. Although careful to maintain a proper public image, the vivacious young mother and antislavery zealot helped draw ordinary women into electoral politics. (See "Documenting the American Promise," page 498.)

The Democrats, successful in 1852 in bridging sectional differences by nominating a northern man with southern principles, chose another "doughface," James Buchanan of Pennsylvania. The Democrats took refuge in the ambiguity of popular sovereignty and portrayed Republicans as extremists ("Black Republican Abolitionists") whose support for the Wilmot Proviso risked pushing the South out of the Union.

The Democratic strategy helped carry the day for Buchanan, but Frémont did astonishingly well. Buchanan won 174 electoral votes against Frémont's 114 and Fillmore's 8. Campaigning under the banner "Free soil, Free men, Fremont," the Republican carried all but five of the states north of the Mason-Dixon line. The election made clear that the Whigs had disintegrated, that the Know-Nothings would not ride nativism to national power, and that the Democrats were badly strained (see Map 14.4). But the big news was what the press called the "glorious defeat" of the Republicans. Despite being a brand-new party and purely sectional, Republicans seriously challenged other parties for national power. Sectionalism had fashioned a new party system, one that spelled danger for the Republic (Figure 14.1). Indeed, war had already broken out between proslavery and antislavery forces in distant Kansas Territory.

Freedom under Siege

The "glorious defeat" of the Republicans meant that the second party in the new two-party system was entirely sectional. Without a southern wing, the Republican Party had no need to compromise, to conciliate, to keep Southerners happy. Indeed, Republicans organized around the premise that the slaveholding South provided a profound threat to "free soil, free labor, and free men."

Events in Kansas Territory in the mid-1850s provided the young Republican organization with an enormous boost and help explain its strong showing in the election of 1856. Kansas reeled with violence between settlers with northern and settlers with southern sympathies. Republicans argued that the violence was southern in origin. They claimed that the Kansas frontier opened a window to southern values and intentions. Republicans also pointed to the brutal beating by a Southerner of a respected northern senator on the floor of Congress. Even the Supreme Court, in the Republicans' view, reflected the South's drive toward tyranny and minority rule. Then, in 1858, the issues dividing North and South received an extraordinary airing

John and Jessie Frémont Poster
The election of 1856 marked the first time a candidate's wife appeared on campaign items. Smart and ambitious, Jessie Benton Frémont made the breakthrough. In this poster—made from paper letters and figures cut from an English hunting print—Jessie and her husband, John C. Frémont, Republican Party presidential nominee, ride spirited horses. The scene emphasizes their youth (John was 43 and Jessie 31), their vigor, and their outdoor exuberance. Jessie helped plan Frémont's campaign, coauthored his election biography, and drew northern women into political activity as never before. "What a shame that women can't vote!" declared abolitionist Lydia Maria Child. "We'd carry 'our Jessie' into the White House on our shoulders, wouldn't we." Critics of Jessie's violation of women's traditional sphere ridiculed both Frémonts. A man who met the couple in San Francisco pronounced her "the better man of the two." Jessie Frémont was, as Abraham Lincoln observed ambivalently, "quite a female politician."
Museum of American Political Life.

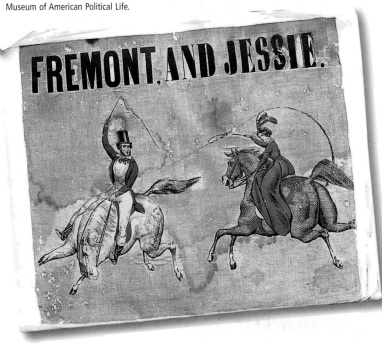

in a senatorial contest in Illinois, when the nation's foremost Democrat debated a resourceful Republican.

"Bleeding Kansas"

Three days after the House of Representatives approved the Kansas-Nebraska Act in 1854, Senator William H. Seward of New York boldly challenged the South. "Come on then, Gentlemen of the Slave States," he cried, "since there is no escaping your challenge, I accept it in behalf of the cause of freedom. We will engage in competition for the virgin soil of Kansas, and God give the victory to the side which is stronger in numbers as it is in right." Because of Stephen Douglas, popular sovereignty would determine whether Kansas became slave or free. No one really expected New Mexico and Utah, with their harsh landscapes, to become slave states when Congress instituted popular sovereignty there in 1850. But many believed Kansas could go either way. Free-state and slave-state settlers each sought majorities at the ballot box, claimed God's blessing, and kept their rifles ready. In theory, popular sovereignty meant an orderly tallying of ballots. In Kansas, however, elections became violent events.

In the North, emigrant aid societies sprang up to promote settlement from the free states. The most famous, the New England Emigrant Aid Company, sponsored some 1,240 settlers in 1854 and 1855. In the South, tiny rural communities from Virginia to Texas raised money to support proslavery settlers. Missourians, already bordered on the east by the free state of Illinois and on the north by the free state of Iowa, especially thought it important to secure Kansas for slavery.

Thousands of hell-for-leather frontiersmen from Missouri, egged on by Missouri senator David Rice Atchison, invaded Kansas. "There are eleven hundred coming over from Platte

---

Fraudulent Voting in Kansas

This drawing is a northern indictment of the corruption of popular sovereignty by Missourians. Rough frontier types, with pistols and knives tucked into their belts, rush to get free whiskey and then line up at the polling place, whose sign, DOWN WITH THE ABOLITIONISTS, indicates that they voted the proslavery ticket.

Kansas State Historical Society.

FOR MORE HELP ANALYZING THIS IMAGE, see the visual activity for this chapter in the Online Study Guide at bedfordstmartins.com/roark.

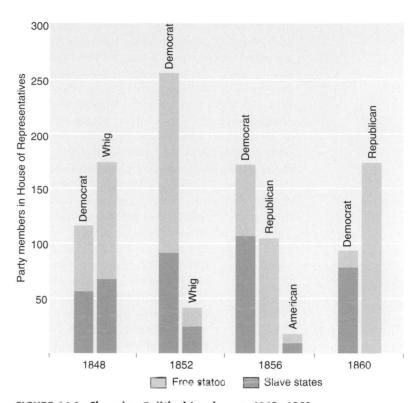

FIGURE 14.1 Changing Political Landscape, 1848–1860
The polarization of American politics between the free states and slave states occurred in little more than a decade.

County to vote," Atchison reported, "and if that ain't enough we can send five thousand—enough to kill every God-damned abolitionist in the Territory." Not surprisingly, proslavery candidates swept the elections in November 1854. When Kansas's first territorial legislature met, it enacted some of the most severe proslavery laws in the nation. Antislavery men, for example, were barred from holding office or serving on juries. Assisting a runaway became a capital offense. Ever-pliant President Pierce endorsed the work of the fraudulently elected proslavery legislature. Free-soil Kansans did not. They elected their own legislature, which promptly banned both slaves and free blacks from the territory. Organized into two rival governments and armed to the teeth, Kansans verged on civil war.

Fighting broke out on the morning of May 21, 1856, when a mob of several hundred proslavery men entered the town of Lawrence, the center of free-state settlement. Only one man died—a proslavery raider who was killed when a burning wall collapsed—but the "Sack of Lawrence," as free-soil forces called it, inflamed northern opinion. Elsewhere in Kansas, news of events in Lawrence provoked John Brown, a free-soil settler, to "fight fire with fire." Announcing that "it was better that a score of bad men should die than that one man who came here to make Kansas a Free State should be driven out," he led the posse that massacred five allegedly proslavery settlers along the Pottawatomie Creek. After that, **guerrilla war** engulfed the territory.

By providing graphic evidence of a dangerously aggressive Slave Power, "Bleeding Kansas" further hardened opinions in the antislavery North and West and gave the fledgling Republican Party fresh ammunition. The Republicans received additional encouragement from an event that occurred in the national capital. On May 19 and 20, 1856, Senator Charles Sumner of Massachusetts delivered a scathing speech entitled "The Crime against Kansas." He damned the administration, the South, and proslavery Kansans. He also indulged in a scalding personal attack on the elderly South Carolina senator Andrew P. Butler, whom Sumner de-

"Bleeding Kansas," 1850s

scribed as a "Don Quixote" who had taken as his mistress "the harlot, slavery."

Preston Brooks, a young South Carolina member of the House and a kinsman of Butler, felt compelled to defend the honor of both his aged relative and his state. On May 22, armed with a walking cane, Brooks entered the Senate, where he found Sumner working at his desk. He began beating Sumner over the head with his cane, and within a minute, Sumner lay bleeding and unconscious on the Senate floor. Brooks resigned his seat in the House, only to be promptly reelected. In the North, the southern hero became an archvillain. Like "Bleeding Kansas," "Bleeding Sumner" provided the Republican Party with a potent symbol of the South's twisted and violent "civilization."

The *Dred Scott* Decision

Political debate over slavery in the territories became so heated in part because the Constitution lacked precision on the issue. Only the Supreme Court speaks definitively about the meaning of the Constitution; in 1857, in the case of *Dred Scott v. Sandford,* the Court announced its judgment of the matter, but its decision demonstrated that it enjoyed no special immunity from the sectional and partisan passions that convulsed the land.

In 1833, John Emerson, an army doctor, bought the slave Dred Scott in St. Louis, Missouri, and took him as his personal servant to Fort Armstrong, Illinois. Two years later, Scott accompanied Emerson when he was transferred to Fort Snelling in Wisconsin Territory. Emerson eventually returned Scott to St. Louis, where in 1846, Scott, with the help of white friends, sued to prove that he, his wife Harriet, and their two daughters, Eliza and Lizzie, were legally entitled to their freedom. Scott based his claim on his travels and residences. He argued that living in Illinois, a free state, and Wisconsin, a free territory according to the Missouri Compromise of 1820, had made his family free. And they remained free even after returning to Missouri, a slave state.

In 1857, eleven years after the Scotts first sued for freedom, the U.S. Supreme Court ruled in the case. The Court saw the case as an opportunity to settle once and for all the vexing question of slavery in the territories. Chief Justice Roger B. Taney hated Republicans and detested

The Dred Scott Family

The *Dred Scott* case in 1857 not only produced a fierce political storm but also fueled enormous curiosity about the family suing for freedom. The correspondent for the popular *Frank Leslie's Illustrated* met Dred Scott in St. Louis and reported: "We found him on examination to be a pure-blooded African, perhaps fifty years of age, with a shrewd, intelligent, good-natured face, of rather light frame, being not more than five feet six inches high." Northerners wanted to see all of the Scotts: Harriet, who was a slave when Dred Scott married her in Wisconsin Territory in about 1836; daughter Eliza, who was born in 1838 on board a ship traveling in free territory north of Missouri; and daughter Lizzie, born after the Scotts returned to St. Louis.

Library of Congress.

Women's Politics

Although women could not vote before the Civil War, they nevertheless participated in public political activity. Hundreds of thousands of women exercised their right of petition and sought through petition campaigns to influence Congress and exert political influence. Uncle Tom's Cabin, Harriet Beecher Stowe's searing indictment of slavery, galvanized support for the Republican Party's campaign against the extension of slavery. Throughout her life, Jessie Benton Frémont sought unabashedly to affect politics, even as she sought to fulfill her domestic roles as wife and mother. She, like many other women, wrote to men of influence on behalf of her husband. "Do not suppose Sir, that I lightly interfere in a matter properly belonging to men," she began a letter to President James Polk, "but in the absence of Mr. Frémont I attend to his affairs at his request." During the 1850s, she became one of her husband's principal political analysts and advisers.

DOCUMENT 1
Jessie Benton Frémont's Letter to Elizabeth Blair Lee, 1856

On October 20, 1856, Jessie Frémont offered a clear-eyed interpretation of the significance of the Republican Party's paper-thin but devastating loss in the October 14 Pennsylvania state election.

I heartily regret the defeat we have met and do not look for things to change for the better. The Democrats will follow up their advantage with the courage of success & our forces are unorganized and just now surprised and inactive. I wish the cause had triumphed. I do wish Mr. Frémont had been the one to administer the bitter dose of subjection to the South for he has the coolness & nerve to do it just as it needs to be done—without passion & without sympathy—as coldly as a surgeon over a hospital patient would he have cut off their right hand Kansas from the old unhealthy southern body. . . . Tell your Father he must come to us for example & comfort in November for I don't think we will wear any but black feathers this year.

SOURCE: Pamela Herr and Mary Lee Spence, eds., *The Letters of Jessie Benton Frémont* (Urbana: University of Illinois Press, 1993), 140.

DOCUMENT 2
Harriot K. Hunt's Letter "to . . . [the] Treasurer, and the Assessors, and other Authorities of the city of Boston, and the Citizens generally," 1852

Some activist women challenged the domesticity that Stowe and Frémont honored, arguing that women's equality depended on their liberation from tradition. These women attended women's rights conventions, signed petitions asking legislators to change laws that discriminated against women, and worked to put the ideas of equal rights into practice in their personal lives. Harriot K. Hunt protested having to pay taxes when she was prohibited from voting. A physician who had practiced medicine in Boston since 1835, Hunt had been refused admission to Harvard Medical School and finally received her medical degree in 1853 from the Female Medical College of Philadelphia.

Harriot K. Hunt, physician, a native and permanent resident of the city of Boston, and for many years a taxpayer therein, in making payment of her city taxes for the coming year, begs leave to protest against the injustice and inequality of levying taxes upon women, and at the same time refusing them any voice or vote in the imposition and expenditure of the same. The only classes of male persons required to pay taxes, and not at the same time allowed the privilege of voting, are aliens and minors. The objection in the case of aliens is their supposed want of interest in our institutions and knowledge of them. The objection in the case of minors, is the want of sufficient understanding. These objections can not apply to women, natives of the city, all of whose property interests are here, and who have accumulated, by their own sagacity and

racial equality, and the Court's majority decision, which he wrote, reflected those prejudices. First, the Court ruled that Dred Scott could not legally claim violation of his constitutional rights because he was not a citizen of the United States. In 1787, when the Constitution was written, Taney said, blacks "had for more than a century before been regarded as beings of an inferior order . . . so far inferior, that they had no rights which the white man was bound to respect." Second, the laws of Dred Scott's home state, Missouri, determined his status, and thus his travels in free areas did not make him free. Third, Congress's power to make "all needful rules and regulations" industry, the very property on which they are taxed. But this is not all; the alien, by going through the forms of naturalization, the minor on coming of age, obtain the right of voting; and so long as they continue to pay a mere poll-tax of a dollar and a half, they may continue to exercise it, though so ignorant as not to be able to sign their names, or read the very votes they put into the ballot-boxes. Even drunkards, felons, idiots, and lunatics, if men, may still enjoy that right of voting to which no woman, however large the amount of taxes she pays, however respectable her character, or useful her life, can ever attain. Wherein, your remonstrant would inquire, is the justice, equality, or wisdom of this?

SOURCE: Elizabeth Cady Stanton, Susan B. Anthony, and Matilda Joslyn Gage, eds., *History of Woman Suffrage*, vol. 1 (New York: Fowler & Wells, 1881), 259.

DOCUMENT 3
Lucy Stone–Henry B. Blackwell Marriage Agreement, 1855

Marriage typically made women legally inferior to their husbands, but women's rights activists refashioned marriage vows to honor equality rather than subordination. When women's rights leader Lucy Stone married Henry B. Blackwell in 1855, both signed the following statement.

While acknowledging our mutual affection by publicly assuming the re-

lationship of husband and wife, yet in justice to ourselves and a great principle, we deem it a duty to declare that this act on our part implies no sanction of, nor promise of voluntary obedience to such of the present laws of marriage, as refuse to recognize the wife as an independent, rational being, while they confer upon the husband an injurious and unnatural superiority, investing him with legal powers which no honorable man would exercise, and which no man should possess. We protest especially against the laws which give to the husband:

1. The custody of the wife's person.
2. The exclusive control and guardianship of their children.
3. The sole ownership of her personal [property], and use of her real estate. . . .
4. The absolute right to the product of her industry.
5. Also against laws which give to the widower so much larger and more permanent an interest in the property of his deceased wife, than they give to the widow in that of the deceased husband.
6. Finally, against the whole system by which "the legal existence of the wife is suspended during marriage," so that in most States, she neither has a legal part in the choice of her residence, nor can she make a will, nor sue or be sued in her own name, nor inherit property.

We believe that personal independence and equal human rights can never be forfeited, except for crime; that marriage should be an equal and permanent partnership, and so recognized by law; that until it is so recognized, married partners should provide against the radical injustice of present laws, by every means in their power. . . .

Thus reverencing law, we enter our protest against rules and customs which are unworthy of the name, since they violate justice, the essence of law.

(signed) Henry B. Blackwell
Lucy Stone

SOURCE: Elizabeth Cady Stanton, Susan B. Anthony, and Matilda Joslyn Gage, eds., *History of Woman Suffrage*, vol. 1 (New York: Fowler & Wells, 1881), 260–61.

QUESTIONS FOR ANALYSIS AND DEBATE

1. Jessie Frémont did not interpret the Republican defeat in Pennsylvania in 1856 as a "glorious defeat." Can you suggest possible reasons why she did not?
2. On what grounds, according to Harriot Hunt, should women be accorded the vote? Do you agree with her argument? Why or why not?
3. What legal disabilities for women was the marriage contract of Henry Blackwell and Lucy Stone designed to overcome?

for the territories did not include the right to prohibit slavery. The Court then explicitly declared the Missouri Compromise unconstitutional, even though it had already been voided by the Kansas-Nebraska Act.

Republicans exploded in rage at the Taney Court's extreme proslavery position. By declar-

ing the Missouri Compromise unconstitutional, the decision nullified the underlying precept of federal exclusion of slavery in the territories and cut the ground out from under the Republican Party. Moreover, as the *New York Tribune* lamented, the decision cleared the way for "all our Territories . . . to be ripened into Slave States."

Particularly frightening to African Americans in the North was the Court's declaration that blacks were not citizens and had no rights. Black leader Frederick Douglass predicted that "the National Conscience" would soon overturn this dangerous and undemocratic ruling.

The Republican rebuttal to the *Dred Scott* ruling relied heavily on the brilliant dissenting opinion of Justice Benjamin R. Curtis. Scott *was* a citizen of the United States, Curtis argued. At the time of the writing of the Constitution, free black men could vote in five states and participated in the ratification process. Scott *was* free: Because slavery was prohibited in Wisconsin, the "involuntary servitude of a slave, coming into the Territory with his master, should cease to exist." And the Missouri Compromise *was* constitutional. The Founders had meant exactly what they said: Congress had the power to make "*all needful rules and regulations*" for the territories, including barring slavery.

Rejecting such arguments, a seven-to-two majority of the justices validated the most extreme statement of the South's territorial rights. John C. Calhoun's claim that Congress had no authority to exclude slavery became the law of the land. While southern Democrats cheered, northern Democrats feared that the *Dred Scott* decision would annihilate not just the Missouri Compromise but popular sovereignty as well. If Congress itself lacked the authority to exclude slavery, how could a mere territorial government assume that right? The Kansas-Nebraska Act had opened the territory to popular sovereignty, and now, contrary to Stephen A. Douglas's promise, it appeared that Free-Soilers would not be able to keep slavery out, and that no one could legally exclude slavery until the moment of statehood. By draining nearly the last drop of ambiguity out of popular sovereignty, the *Dred Scott* decision jeopardized the ability of the Democratic Party to hold its northern and southern wings together.

The *Dred Scott* decision actually strengthened the young Republican Party. That "outrageous" decision, one Republican said, was "the best thing that could have happened." It gave evidence for the Republicans' claim that a hostile Slave Power conspired against northern liberties. Only the capture of the Supreme Court by

> While southern Democrats cheered, northern Democrats feared that the *Dred Scott* decision annihilated not just the Wilmot Proviso but popular sovereignty as well.

the "slavocracy," Republicans argued, could explain the tortured and historically inaccurate *Dred Scott* decision. As for Dred Scott, although the Court rejected his suit, he did in the end gain his freedom. In May 1857, Taylor Blow, the son of his first owner, purchased and freed Scott and his family. On September 17, 1858, Dred Scott died in obscurity. Nevertheless, his case played a key role in changing the political landscape and bringing new Republican politicians to the fore.

Prairie Republican: Abraham Lincoln

The re-igniting of sectional flames provided Republican politicians, including Abraham Lincoln of Illinois, with fresh challenges and fresh opportunities. Lincoln had long since put behind him his hardscrabble log-cabin beginnings in Kentucky and Indiana. At the time of the *Dred Scott* decision, he lived in a fine two-story house in Springfield. (See "American Places, page 503.) He brought in enough business from the Illinois Central Railroad to be known as the "railroad lawyer," and by virtue of his marriage into a well-to-do family and his successful law practice, he associated with men and women of reputation and standing.

The law provided Lincoln's living, but politics was his life. "His ambition was a little engine that knew no rest," observed his law partner William Herndon. At age twenty-six, he served his first term in the Illinois state legislature. Between 1847 and 1849, he enjoyed his only term in the House of Representatives, where he fired away at "Mr. Polk's War" and cast dozens of votes for free soil but otherwise served inconspicuously. When he returned to Springfield, he pitched into his law practice but kept his eye fixed on public office.

But, like Whigs everywhere in the mid-1850s, Lincoln had no political home. His credo—opposition to "the *extension* of slavery"—made the Democrats an impossible choice. Because the Republicans chose free soil as their principal tenet, in 1856 Lincoln joined the party. Convinced that slavery was a "monstrous injustice," a "great moral wrong," and an "unqualified evil to the negro, the white man, and the State," Lincoln condemned Douglas's Kansas-Nebraska Act of 1854 for giving slavery a new life. He accepted that the Constitution permitted slavery in those states where it existed, but he believed that the Founders had planned to contain its spread. Penned in, Lincoln believed, plantation slavery would exhaust southern soil,

Discussing the News
Newspapers permitted midwesterners to keep up-to-date. Here a farmer takes a break from cutting firewood to debate the latest news with his friends. He is so engrossed that he ignores the little girl tugging at his pants leg and trying to get him to notice the woman waving in the doorway. Men like these increasingly accepted Lincoln's portrait of the Republican Party as the guardian of the common people's liberty and economic opportunity. When Lincoln claimed that southern slaveholders threatened free labor and democracy, the midwestern farmers listened.

Copyright © 1971, The R. W. Norton Art Gallery, Shreveport, LA. Used by permission. Painting by Arthur F. Tait.

and in time Southerners would have no choice but to end slavery themselves. In Lincoln's opinion, by providing fresh land in the territories, Douglas had put slavery "on the high road to extension and perpetuity."

Just as Lincoln staked out the middle ground of antislavery opinion, he held what were, for his times, moderate racial views. Like a majority of Republicans, Lincoln defended black humanity without challenging white supremacy. He denounced slavery as immoral and believed that it should end, but he also viewed black equality as impractical and unachievable. "Negroes have natural rights . . . as other men have," he said, "although they cannot enjoy them here." Insurmountable white prejudice made it

impossible to extend full citizenship and equality to blacks in America, he believed. Freeing blacks and allowing them to remain in this country would lead to race war. In Lincoln's mind, social stability and black progress required that slavery end and that blacks leave the country.

Lincoln envisioned the western territories as "places for poor people to go to, and better their conditions." The "*free* labor system," he said, "opens the way for all—gives hope to all, and energy, and progress, and improvement of condition to all." Lincoln believed that the expansion of slave labor threatened free men's basic freedom to succeed. He became persuaded that slaveholders were engaging in an aggressive and dangerous conspiracy to nationalize slavery. As evidence, he pointed both to the Kansas-Nebraska Act, which repealed the restriction on slavery's advance in the territories, and to the *Dred Scott* decision, which denied Congress the right to impose fresh restrictions. The next step, Lincoln warned, would be "another Supreme Court decision, declaring that the Constitution of the United States does not permit a State to exclude slavery from its limits." Unless the citizens of Illinois woke up, he warned, the Supreme Court would make "Illinois a slave State."

In Lincoln's view, the nation could not "endure, permanently half slave and half free." Either opponents of slavery would arrest its spread and place it on the "course of ultimate extinction," or its advocates would push it forward until it became legal in "*all* the States, *old* as well as *new*—*North* as well as *South*." Lincoln's convictions that slavery was wrong, that Congress must stop its spread, and that it must be put on the road to extinction formed the core of the Republican ideology. Although Lincoln had not held public office in the 1850s, by 1858 he had so impressed his fellow Republicans in Illinois with his speeches and other statements about major national issues that they chose him to challenge the nation's premier Democrat, who was seeking reelection to the U.S. Senate.

The Lincoln-Douglas Debates

When Stephen Douglas learned that the Republican Abraham Lincoln would be his opponent for the Senate, he confided in a fellow Democrat: "He is the strong man of the party—full of wit, facts, dates—and the best stump speaker, with his droll ways and dry jokes, in the West. He is as honest as he is shrewd, and if I beat him my victory will be hardly won."

Not only did Douglas have to contend with a formidable foe, but he also carried the weight of a burden not of his own making. The previous year, the nation's economy experienced a sharp downturn. Prices plummeted, thousands of businesses failed, and unemployment rose. Although Illinois suffered less than the Northeast, Douglas the Democrat had to go before the voters in 1858 as a member of the party whose policies stood accused of causing the "panic" of 1857.

Lincoln and Douglas debated, often brilliantly, the central issue before the country: slavery and freedom.

Douglas's response to another crisis in 1857, however, helped shore up his standing with his constituents. Proslavery forces in Kansas met in the town of Lecompton, drafted a proslavery constitution, and applied for statehood. Everyone knew that Free-Soilers outnumbered proslavery settlers by at least two to one, but President Buchanan instructed Congress to admit Kansas as the sixteenth slave state. Republicans denounced the "Lecompton swindle." Douglas broke with the Democratic administration and came out against the proslavery constitution, not because it accepted slavery but because it violated the principle of democratic rule. Congress killed the Lecompton bill. (When Kansans reconsidered the Lecompton constitution in an honest election, they rejected it six to one. Kansas entered the Union in 1861 as a free state.) In coming out against the Lecompton constitution, Douglas declared his independence from the South and, he hoped, made himself acceptable at home.

A relative unknown and a decided underdog in the Illinois election, Lincoln challenged the incumbent Douglas to debate him face-to-face. Douglas agreed, and the two met in seven communities for what would become a legendary series of debates. To the thousands who stood straining to see and hear, they must have seemed an odd pair. Douglas was five feet four inches tall, broad, and stocky; Lincoln was six feet four inches tall, angular, and lean. Douglas was in perpetual motion, darting across the platform, shouting, and jabbing the air. Lincoln stood still and spoke deliberately. Douglas wore the latest fashion and dazzled audiences with his flashy vests. Lincoln wore good suits but managed to look rumpled anyway. Their differences in physical appearance and style, however, were of little importance. They showed the citizens of Illinois (and much of the nation because of widespread press coverage) the difference between an anti-Lecompton Democrat and a true Republican. They debated, often brilliantly, the central issue before the country: slavery and freedom.

Lincoln badgered Douglas with the question of whether he favored the spread of slavery. He tried to force Douglas into the damaging admission that the Supreme Court had repudiated Douglas's own territorial solution, popular sovereignty. In the debate at Freeport, Illinois, Douglas admitted that settlers could not now pass legislation barring slavery, but he argued

AMERICAN PLACES

Lincoln Home National Historic Site, Springfield, Illinois

Abraham Lincoln's Home In Springfield, Illinois
Lincoln Home National Historic Site.

In 1844, Abraham Lincoln, who was born in a one-room, dirt-floored log cabin, and Mary Todd Lincoln, who was born in a fourteen-room southern mansion, moved into this Springfield, Illinois, home. It was the only home that Lincoln ever owned, and today visitors can easily imagine Lincoln's domestic life while he was still the "railroad lawyer" from Illinois.

Three of the Lincolns' four sons were born here, and one, Eddie, died here. When Lincoln was elected president in 1860, he and Mary decided to rent rather than to sell their house, expecting to return after the presidency. After Lincoln's assassination, however, Mary said that she "could not bear to return to the scenes of the happiest times in my life without my family," and she never lived in the house again. In 1887, Lincoln's only surviving son, Robert, gave the house to the state of Illinois, which in time donated it to the nation.

The National Park Service restored the house to its 1860 appearance. Springfield had become the capital of Illinois only in 1839, and pigs, chickens, and cattle still roamed the streets in Lincoln's time. Improvements during the seventeen years the Lincolns lived in the house reflected both their growing family and his rising income. The nicest room is the formal parlor, where the Lincolns entertained and where on May 19, 1860, Republican leaders asked Lincoln to run for the presidency. Family members spent most of their time in the sitting room. At six foot four inches, Lincoln found the furniture uncomfortable and often sprawled on the floor with the children, dog, and cats. One visitor described the rooms as "elegantly and comfortably furnished." Another said that the home was "handsome, but not pretentious." As long as he lived here, Lincoln chopped wood, lit the fires in the morning, brushed the horse, and milked the cow. Although the Lincolns employed servants, the successful railroad lawyer had obviously not entirely forgotten his hardscrabble beginnings.

For Web links related to this site and other American Places, see "PlaceLinks" at bedfordstmartins.com/roark.

---

that they could ban slavery just as effectively by not passing protective laws. Without "appropriate police regulations and local legislation," such as those found in slave states, he explained, slavery could not live a day, an hour. Southerners condemned Douglas's "Freeport Doctrine" and charged him with trying to steal the victory they had gained with the *Dred Scott* decision. Lincoln chastised his opponent for his "don't care" atti-

tude about slavery, for "blowing out the moral lights around us."

Douglas worked the racial issue. He called Lincoln an abolitionist and an egalitarian enamored with "our colored brethren." Put on the defensive, Lincoln came close to staking out positions on abolition and race that were as conservative as Douglas's. Lincoln reiterated his belief that slavery enjoyed constitutional protection where it existed. He also reaffirmed his faith in white rule: "I will say, then, that I am not, nor ever have been, in favor of bringing about in any way the social and political equality of the white and black race." But unlike Douglas, who told racist jokes and spit out racial epithets, Lincoln was no negrophobe. He always tried to steer the debate back to what he considered the true issue: the morality and future of slavery. "Slavery is wrong," Lincoln repeated, because "a man has the right to the fruits of his own labor."

As Douglas predicted, the election was hard-fought. It was also closely contested. Until the adoption of the Seventeenth Amendment in 1911, citizens voted for state legislators, who in turn selected U.S. senators. Since Democrats won a slight majority in the Illinois legislature, the members returned Douglas to the Senate. But the debates thrust Lincoln, the prairie Republican, into the national spotlight.

The Union Collapses

Lincoln's thesis that the "slavocracy" conspired to make slavery a national institution now seems exaggerated. But from the northern perspective, the Kansas-Nebraska Act, the Brooks-Sumner affair, the *Dred Scott* decision, and the Lecompton constitution amounted to irrefutable evidence of the South's aggressiveness. Southerners, of course, saw things differently. They were the ones who were under siege and had grievances, they declared. Signs were everywhere, they argued, that the North planned to use its numerical advantage to attack slavery, and not just in the territories. Republicans had loudly denounced the *Dred Scott* decision and made it clear that they were unwilling to accept the Supreme Court's ruling as the last word on the issue of slavery expansion. After John Brown attempted to incite a slave insurrection in Virginia in 1859, Southerners argued that Northerners had also proved themselves unwilling to be bound by Christian decency and reverence for life.

Threats of secession increasingly laced the sectional debate. Talk of leaving the Union had been heard for years, but until the final crisis, Southerners had used secession as a ploy to gain concessions within the Union, not to destroy it. Then the 1850s delivered powerful blows to Southerners' confidence that they could remain Americans and protect slavery. And when the Republican Party won the White House in 1860, many Southerners concluded that they would have to leave.

The Aftermath of John Brown's Raid

If John Brown had been killed during his raid on Harpers Ferry in 1859, his impact on history would probably have been minor. But he lived and stood trial for treason, murder, and incitement of slave insurrection. "To hang a fanatic is to make a martyr of him and fledge another brood of the same sort," cautioned one newspaper, but on December 2, 1859, the state of Virginia executed Brown. In life, Brown was a ne'er-do-well, but he died with courage, dignity, and composure. At his trial, he told the court: "If it is deemed necessary that I should forfeit my life for the furtherance of the ends of justice, and mingle my blood further with the blood of . . . millions in this slave country whose rights are disregarded by wicked, cruel, and unjust enactments, I say, let it be done." When he left his cell the morning of his hanging, he passed a message to one of his guards. "I John Brown am now quite *certain*," it read, "that the crimes of this *guilty land will* never be purged *away*; but with Blood."

Northerners had at first denounced Brown's raid at Harpers Ferry as dangerous fanaticism and perhaps even the work of a madman. But after Brown's heroic death, denunciation gave way to grudging respect. Some Northerners even celebrated John Brown. The abolitionist author Lydia Maria Child declared, "What a splendid martyrdom. The scaffold will be as glorious as the Cross of Calvary." Writer and philosopher Henry David Thoreau also likened Brown to Christ and concluded, "he is an angel of light." Some abolitionists went beyond canonizing Brown to explicitly endorse Brown's resort to violence. Abolitionist William Lloyd Garrison, who usually professed pacifism, announced, "I am prepared to say 'success to every slave insurrection at the South and in every country.'"

Most Northerners did not advocate bloody rebellion, however. Like Lincoln, they concluded that Brown's noble antislavery ideals could not "excuse violence, bloodshed, and treason." Still, when many in the North marked the day of John Brown's execution with tolling bells, hymns, and prayer vigils, white Southerners were beside themselves with rage.

***John Brown Going to His Hanging*, Horace Pippin, 1942**

The grandparents of Horace Pippin, a Pennsylvania artist, were slaves. His grandmother witnessed the hanging of John Brown, and here Pippin recalls the scene she so often described to him. He uses a muted palette to establish the bleak setting and to tell the grim story, but he manages to convey a striking intensity nevertheless. Historically accurate, the painting depicts Brown tied and sitting erect on his coffin, passing resolutely before the silent, staring white men. The black woman in the lower right corner is presumably Pippin's grandmother.

Romare Bearden, a leading twentieth-century African American artist, recalled the central place of John Brown in black memory: "Lincoln and John Brown were as much a part of the actuality of the Afro-American experience, as were the domino games and the hoe cakes for Sunday morning breakfast. I vividly recall the yearly commemorations for John Brown and see my grandfather reading Brown's last speech to the court, which was a regular part of the ceremony at Pittsburgh's Shiloh Baptist Church."

Pennsylvania Academy of Fine Arts, Philadelphia. John Lambert Fund.

In Philadelphia, more than 250 medical students from the South were so appalled by what they witnessed that they marched to the railroad station and boarded a train to Richmond. In Mississippi, a planter disgusted with northern sympathy denounced Brown as a bloodthirsty fiend whose mission was "to incite slaves to murder helpless women and children." Southerners everywhere contemplated what they had in common with people who "regard John Brown as a martyr and a Christian hero, rather than a murderer and robber." Many Southerners concluded that, like Brown, Northerners were eager to see slavery washed away in a river of blood. Georgia senator Robert Toombs announced solemnly that Southerners must "never permit this Federal government to pass into the traitorous hands of the black Republican party." At that moment, the presidential election was only months away.

Republican Victory in 1860

Anxieties provoked by John Brown's raid flared for months as southern whites feverishly searched for abolitionists and whipped, tarred and feathered, and sometimes hanged those they suspected. Moreover, other events in the eleven months between Brown's hanging and the presidential election heightened sectional hostility and estrangement. A southern business convention meeting in Nashville shocked the country (including many Southerners) by calling for the reopening of the African slave trade, closed since 1808 and considered an abomination everywhere in the Western world. Chief Justice Taney provoked new indignation when the Supreme Court ruled northern personal liberty laws unconstitutional and reaffirmed the Fugitive Slave Act.

Then, in February 1860, the normally routine business of electing a Speaker of the House threatened to turn bloody as Democrats and Republicans battled over control of the office. After two months of acrimonious debate left the House deadlocked, one congressman observed that the "only persons who do not have a revolver and a knife are those who have two revolvers." The House averted a shootout when a few Know-Nothings finally joined the Republicans to elect an old Whig. Finally, Mississippian Jefferson Davis demanded that the Senate adopt a federal slave code for the territories, a goal of extreme proslavery Southerners for several years. Not only was Congress powerless to block slavery's spread, he argued, but it was obligated to offer slavery all "needful protection."

When Democrats converged on Charleston for their convention in April 1860, Southerners gave notice that they intended to make their extreme position on the territories binding party doctrine. Southern fire-eaters denounced Stephen Douglas and demanded a platform that included federal protection of slavery in the territories. But northern Democrats knew that northern voters would not stomach a federal slave code. When two platforms—one with a federal slave code and one with popular sovereignty—came before the delegates, popular sovereignty won. Representatives from the entire Lower South and Arkansas stomped out of the convention. The remaining delegates adjourned to meet a few weeks later in Baltimore, where they nominated Douglas for president and adopted a platform that advocated little beyond congressional noninterference in the territories.

When southern Democrats met, they nominated Vice President John C. Breckinridge of Kentucky for president and approved a platform with a federal slave code. But southern moderates refused to support Breckinridge and the fire-eaters. Senator John J. Crittenden of Kentucky and others formed a new party to provide voters a Unionist choice. Instead of adopting a platform and confronting the slavery question, the Constitutional Union Party merely approved a vague resolution pledging "to recognize no political principle other than *the Constitution . . . the Union . . . and the Enforcement of the Laws.*" For president they picked former senator John Bell of Tennessee.

The Republicans smelled victory. Four years earlier they had enjoyed "glorious defeat" by a Democratic Party that had since broken up. Still, Republicans estimated that they needed to carry nearly all the free states to win. In 1856, they were essentially a one-idea party. In 1860, the Republicans expanded their platform beyond antislavery opinion. They hoped that free homesteads, a protective tariff, a transcontinental railroad, and a guarantee of immigrant political rights would provide an economic and social agenda broad enough to unify the North. While recommitting themselves to stopping the spread of slavery, they also denounced John Brown's raid as "among the gravest of crimes" and confirmed the security of slavery in the South.

Republicans cast about for a moderate candidate to go with their evenhanded platform. The foremost Republican, William H. Seward, had made enemies with his radical "higher law" doctrine and "irrepressible conflict" speech. Lincoln, however, since bursting onto the national scene in 1858 had demonstrated his clear purpose, good judgment, and solid Republican credentials. That, and his residence in Illinois, a crucial state, made him attractive to the party. Masterful maneuvering by Lincoln's managers converted his status as the second choice of many convention delegates into a majority on the third ballot. Defeated by Douglas in a state contest less than two years earlier, Lincoln now stood ready to take him on for the presidency.

The election of 1860 was like none other in American politics. It took place in the midst of the nation's severest crisis. Four major candidates crowded the presidential field. Rather than a four-cornered contest, however, the election

Abraham Lincoln
Lincoln actively sought the Republican presidential nomination in 1860. When in New York City to give a political address, he had his photograph taken by Mathew Brady. "While I was there I was taken to one of the places where they get up such things," Lincoln explained, sounding more innocent than he was, "and I suppose they got my shadow, and can multiply copies indefinitely." Multiply they did. Copies of the dignified photograph of Lincoln soon replaced the less flattering drawings. Later, Lincoln credited his victory to his New York speech and to Mathew Brady.
The Lincoln Museum, Fort Wayne, Indiana. Photo: #0-17; drawing: #2024.

broke into two contests, each with two candidates. In the North, Lincoln faced Douglas; in the South, Breckinridge confronted Bell. Southerners did not even permit Lincoln's name to appear on the ballot in ten of the fifteen slave states, so outrageous did they consider the Republican Party.

An unprecedented number of voters cast ballots on November 6, 1860. Approximately 82 percent of eligible northern men and nearly 70 percent of eligible southern men went to the polls. Lincoln swept all of the eighteen free states except New Jersey, which split its electoral votes between him and Douglas. While Lincoln received only 39 percent of the popular vote, he won easily in the electoral balloting, gaining 180 votes, 28 more than he needed for victory. Lincoln did not win because his opposition was

splintered. Even if the votes of his three opponents had been combined, Lincoln would still have won. He won because 99 percent of his votes were concentrated in the free states, which contained a majority of electoral votes. Ominously, however, Breckinridge, running on a southern-rights platform, won the entire Lower South plus Delaware, Maryland, and North Carolina. Two fully sectionalized parties swept their regions, but the northern one won the presidency (Map 14.5).

Secession Winter

The telegraphs had barely stopped tapping out the news of Lincoln's victory when anxious Southerners began reappraising the value of the

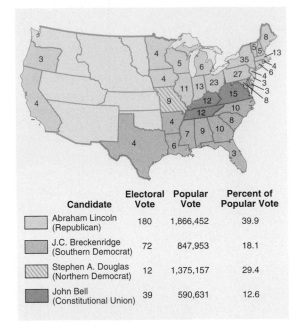

Candidate	Electoral Vote	Popular Vote	Percent of Popular Vote
Abraham Lincoln (Republican)	180	1,866,452	39.9
J.C. Breckenridge (Southern Democrat)	72	847,953	18.1
Stephen A. Douglas (Northern Democrat)	12	1,375,157	29.4
John Bell (Constitutional Union)	39	590,631	12.6

MAP 14.5   The Election of 1860

started than controlled," he warned. "I consider slavery much more secure in the Union than out of it."

Secessionists emphasized the urgency of the moment and the dangers of delay. No Southerner should mistake Republican intentions, they argued. "Mr. Lincoln and his party assert that this doctrine of equality applies to the negro," former Georgia governor Howell Cobb declared, "and necessarily there can exist no such thing as property in our equals." Lincoln's election without a single electoral vote from the South meant that Southerners were unable to defend themselves within the Union, Cobb argued. Why wait, he asked, for Lincoln to appoint Republican judges, marshals, customs collectors, and postmasters to federal posts throughout the South? Each would become an abolitionist emissary, he warned. As for war, there would be none. The Union was a voluntary compact, and Lincoln would not coerce patriotism. If Northerners did resist with force, secessionists argued, the conflict would be brief, for one southern woodsman could whip five of Lincoln's greasy mechanics.

For all their differences, southern whites were generally united in their determination to defend slavery, to take slave property into the territories, and to squeeze from the North an admission that they were good and decent people. They disagreed about whether the mere presence of a Republican in the White House made it necessary to exercise what they considered a legitimate right to secede.

The debate about what to do was briefest in South Carolina. It seceded from the Union on December 20, 1860. By February 1861, the six other deep South states marched in South Carolina's footsteps. Only South Carolinians voted overwhelmingly in favor of secession, however; elsewhere, the vote was close. In general, the nonslaveholding inhabitants of the Piedmont and mountain counties, where slaves were relatively few, displayed the greatest attachment to the Union. Slaveholders spearheaded secession. On February 4, representatives from South Carolina, Georgia, Florida, Alabama, Mississippi, Louisiana, and Texas met in Montgomery, Alabama, where three days later they celebrated the birth of the Confederate States of America. Jefferson

Union. Although Breckinridge had carried the South, a vote for "southern rights" was not necessarily a vote for secession. In fact, Breckinridge steadfastly denied that he was a secession candidate. Besides, slightly more than half of the Southerners who had voted cast ballots for Douglas and Bell, two stout defenders of the Union. During the winter of 1860–61, Southerners debated what to do.

Southern Unionists tried to calm the fears that Lincoln's election triggered. Let the dust settle, they pleaded. Extremists in both sections, they argued, had created the crisis. Former congressman Alexander Stephens of Georgia eloquently defended the Union. He asked what Lincoln had done to justify something as extreme as secession. Had he not promised to respect slavery where it existed? In Stephens's judgment, the fire-eater cure would be worse than the Republican disease. Secession might lead to war, which would loosen the hinges of southern society, possibly even open the door to slave insurrection or a revolt by nonslaveholding whites. "Revolutions are much easier

Secession of the Lower South, December 1860–February 1861

"The Union Is Dissolved!"
On December 20, 1860, the *Charleston Mercury* put out this special edition of the paper to celebrate South Carolina's secession from the Union. Six weeks earlier, upon hearing the news that Lincoln had won the presidency, it had predicted as much. "The tea has been thrown overboard," the *Mercury* announced. "The revolution of 1860 has been initiated."
Chicago Historical Society.

Davis became president, and Alexander Stephens, who had spoken so eloquently about the dangers of revolution, became vice president.

Lincoln's election had split the Union. Now secession split the South. Seven slave states seceded during the winter, but eight did not. Citizens of the Upper South debated just as furiously whether the South could defend itself better inside or outside the Union, but they came down opposite the Lower South, at least for the

moment. The fact was that the Upper South had a smaller stake in slavery. Just over half as many white families in the Upper South held slaves (21 percent) as did those in the Lower South (37 percent). Slaves represented twice as large a percentage of the population in the Lower South (48 percent) as in the Upper South (23 percent). Consequently, whites in the Upper South had fewer fears that Republican ascendancy meant economic catastrophe, racial war, and social chaos. Lincoln would need to do more than just be elected to provoke them into secession.

The nation had to wait until March 4, 1861, when Lincoln took office to see what he would do. (Presidents-elect waited four months to take office until 1933, when the Twentieth Amendment to the Constitution shifted the inauguration forward to January 20.) After his election, Lincoln chose to stay in Springfield and to say nothing. "Lame-duck" president James Buchanan sat in Washington and did nothing. Buchanan firmly denied the constitutionality of secession but also denied that he had power to resist it. Buchanan demonstrated, William H. Seward said mockingly, that "it is the President's duty to enforce the laws, unless somebody opposes him." In Congress, efforts at cobbling together a peace-saving compromise came to nothing.

In his inaugural address, Lincoln began with reassurances to the South. He had "no lawful right" to interfere with slavery where it existed, he said again, adding for emphasis that he had "no inclination to do so." There would be "no invasion—no using of force against or among the people anywhere." In filling federal posts, he would not "force obnoxious strangers" on the South. Conciliatory toward Southerners, Lincoln proved inflexible about the Union. The Union, he declared, is "perpetual." Secession was "anarchy" and "legally void." The Constitution required him to execute the law "in all the States." He would hold federal property, collect federal duties, and deliver the mails.

The decision for civil war or peace rested in the South's hands, Lincoln warned. "You can have no conflict, without being yourselves the aggressors. *You* have no oath registered in Heaven to destroy the government, while *I* shall have the most solemn one to 'preserve, protect, and defend' it." What Southerners in Charleston held in their hands at that very moment were the cords for firing the cannons aimed at the federal garrison at Fort Sumter.

Lincoln's election had split the Union. Now secession split the South.

Conclusion: Slavery, Free Labor, and the Failure of Political Compromise

As their economies, societies, and cultures diverged in the nineteenth century, Northerners and Southerners increasingly expressed different concepts of the American promise and the role of slavery within it. Their differences crystallized into political form in 1846 when David Wilmot proposed banning slavery in any territory won in the Mexican-American War. "As if by magic," a Boston newspaper observed, "it brought to a head the great question that is about to divide the American people." Discovery of gold and other precious metals in the West added urgency to the controversy over slavery in the territories. Although Congress attempted to address the issue with the Compromise of 1850, the Fugitive Slave Act provision quickly brought discontent and mistrust of the compromise in both free and slave states. Matters worsened with the 1852 publication of *Uncle Tom's Cabin*, which further hardened northern sentiments against slavery and confirmed southern suspicions of northern ill will. The bloody violence that erupted in Kansas in 1856 and the incendiary *Dred Scott* decision in 1857 further eroded hope for a solution to this heated question.

During the extended crisis of the Union that stretched from 1846 to 1861, the slavery question braided with national politics. As the traditional Whig and Democratic parties struggled with fallout from the slavery issue, new parties, most notably the Republican Party, emerged. Although the nation fixed its attention on the expansion of slavery, from the beginning both Northerners and Southerners recognized that the controversy had less to do with slavery in the territories than with the future of slavery in America.

For more than seventy years, imaginative statesmen had found compromises that accepted slavery and preserved the Union. Citizens on both sides of the Mason-Dixon line took enormous pride in the national experiment in **republican** democracy and few gave up the experiment easily. But as each section grew increasingly committed to its labor system and the promise it provided, Americans discovered that accommodation had limits. In 1859, John Brown's militant antislavery had pushed white Southerners to the edge. In 1860, Lincoln's election convinced whites in the deep South that slavery and the society they had built on it were at risk in the Union, and they seceded. In his inaugural, Lincoln pleaded, "We are not enemies but friends. We must not be enemies." By then, however, the deep South had ceased to sing what he called "the chorus of the Union." It remained to be seen whether disunion would mean war.

FOR ADDITIONAL FIRSTHAND ACCOUNTS OF THIS PERIOD, see Chapter 14 in Michael Johnson, ed., *Reading the American Past,* Third Edition.

TO ASSESS YOUR MASTERY OF THE MATERIAL IN THIS CHAPTER, see the Online Study Guide at bedfordstmartins.com/ roark.

FOR WEB LINKS RELATED TO TOPICS IN THIS CHAPTER, see "HistoryLinks," "DocLinks," and "PlaceLinks" at bedfordstmartins.com/roark.

CHRONOLOGY

1820 • Missouri Compromise divides Louisiana Purchase between slave and free territory.

1846 • Wilmot Proviso proposes barring slavery from all lands acquired in Mexican War.

1847 • Senator John C. Calhoun challenges Wilmot Proviso on constitutional grounds, stating that Congress has no power to exclude slavery from territories.

• Senator Lewis Cass offers compromise of "popular sovereignty," allowing people of territories to determine fate of slavery.

1848 • Opponents of expansion of slavery found Free-Soil Party.

• Whig General Zachary Taylor elected president.

1849 • California Gold Rush leads thousands to the West, further fueling the debate over slavery in the territories.

1850 • Vice President Millard Fillmore becomes president upon death of Zachary Taylor.

• Senator Stephen Douglas's compromise bills (Compromise of 1850) become law: California admitted to the Union as a free state, Utah and New Mexico organized as territories with the status of slavery deliberately left uncertain; fugitive slave law strengthened.

1850s • Vigilance committees in North resist Fugitive Slave Act.

1852 • Harriet Beecher Stowe's *Uncle Tom's Cabin* published in book form.

• Democrat Franklin Pierce elected president.

1853 • Gadsden Purchase adds 30,000 square miles of territory in present-day Arizona and New Mexico.

1854 • American Party (Know-Nothings) emerges, advocating nativist positions.

• Kansas-Nebraska Act becomes law: repeals Missouri Compromise, opens Kansas and Nebraska territories to popular sovereignty, deprives Indians of land and forces them to move farther west.

• Republican Party emerges, opposing extension of slavery into territories.

1856 • Proslavery and antislavery forces clash in "Bleeding Kansas."

• Preston Brooks of South Carolina assaults Charles Sumner of Massachusetts on Senate floor.

• John Brown leads massacre of proslavery men in Pottawatomie, Kansas.

• Democrat James Buchanan elected president; Republicans suffer "glorious defeat."

1857 • In *Dred Scott* decision, U.S. Supreme Court rules that African Americans have no constitutional rights, that Congress cannot exclude slavery in the territories, and that the Missouri Compromise is unconstitutional.

• Congress rejects Kansas's proslavery Lecompton constitution.

• Nation experiences economic downturn—the panic of 1857.

1858 • Abraham Lincoln and Stephen A. Douglas debate slavery; Douglas defeats Lincoln for Illinois Senate seat.

1859 • John Brown's attempt to foment slave uprising in Harpers Ferry, Virginia, further alienates South and moves nation toward war.

1860 • Republican Abraham Lincoln elected president in four-way race that divides electorate along sectional lines.

• South Carolina secedes from Union.

1861 • Six other deep South states secede.

• The seven seceded states form the Confederate States of America.

• Lincoln takes office.

BIBLIOGRAPHY

General Works

John Ashworth, *Slavery, Capitalism, and Politics in the Antebellum Republic* (1995).

Don E. Fehrenbacher, *The Slaveholding Republic: An Account of the United States Government's Relations to Slavery* (2001).

Eric Foner, *Politics and Ideology in the Age of the Civil War* (1980).

Michael F. Holt, *Political Parties and American Political Development from the Age of Jackson to the Age of Lincoln* (1992).

Michael F. Holt, *The Rise and Fall of the American Whig Party: Jacksonian Politics and the Onset of the Civil War* (1999).

Bruce C. Levine, *Half Slave and Half Free: The Roots of Civil War* (1992).

John D. Majewski, *A House Dividing: Economic Development in Pennsylvania and Virginia before the Civil War* (2000).

James M. McPherson, *Ordeal by Fire: The Civil War and Reconstruction* (1982).

Allan Nevins, *Ordeal of the Union*, 2 vols. (1947).

Allan Nevins, *The Emergence of Lincoln*, 2 vols. (1950).

Roy F. Nichols, *Disruption of American Democracy* (1948).

Merrill D. Peterson, *The Great Triumvirate: Webster, Clay, and Calhoun* (1987).

David M. Potter, *The Impending Crisis, 1848–1861* (1976).

Leonard Richards, *The Slave Power: The Free North and Southern Domination, 1780–1860* (2000).

Richard Sewell, *A House Divided: Sectionalism and Civil War, 1848–1865* (1988).

Kenneth M. Stampp, ed., *The Imperiled Union: Essays on the Background of the Civil War* (1980).

Kenneth M. Stampp, ed., *The Causes of the Civil War* (rev. ed., 1991).

Mark W. Summers, *The Plundering Generation: Corruption and the Crisis of the Union, 1849–1861* (1987).

Slavery in the Territories

Paul H. Bergeron, *The Presidency of James K. Polk* (1987).

Eugene H. Berwanger, *The Frontier against Slavery: Western Anti-Negro Prejudice and the Slavery Extension Controversy* (1967).

Don E. Fehrenbacher, *The Dred Scott Case: Its Significance in American Law and Politics* (1978).

Paul Finkelman, *An Imperfect Union: Slavery, Federalism, and Comity* (1981).

Holman Hamilton, *Prologue to Conflict: The Crisis and Compromise of 1850* (1964).

Robert W. Johannsen, *The Frontier, the Union, and Stephen A. Douglas* (1989).

Chaplain W. Morrison, *Democratic Politics and Sectionalism: The Wilmot Proviso Controversy* (1967).

James A. Rawley, *Race and Politics: "Bleeding Kansas" and the Coming of the Civil War* (1969).

Kenneth M. Stampp, *America in 1857: A Nation on the Brink* (1990).

Gerald W. Wolff, *The Kansas-Nebraska Bill: Party, Section, and the Coming of the Civil War* (1977).

Northern Sectionalism

Richard H. Abbott, *Cotton and Capital: Boston Businessmen and Antislavery Reform, 1854–1868* (1991).

Tyler Anbinder, *Nativism and Slavery: The Northern Know Nothings and the Politics of the 1850s* (1992).

Jean H. Baker, *Affairs of Party: The Political Culture of Northern Democrats in the Mid-Nineteenth Century* (1983).

Dale Baum, *The Civil War Party System: The Case of Massachusetts, 1848–1876* (1984).

R. J. M. Blackett, *Building an Antislavery Wall: Black Americans in the Atlantic Abolitionist Movement, 1830–1860* (1983).

Frederick J. Blue, *The Free Soilers: Third Party Politics, 1848–1854* (1973).

Stanley W. Campbell, *The Slave Catchers: Enforcement of the Fugitive Slave Law, 1850–1860* (1970).

Tom Chaffin, *Pathfinder: John Charles Frémont and the Course of American Empire* (2002).

Gary Lee Collison, *Shadrach Minkins: From Fugitive Slave to Citizen* (1997).

Robert F. Dalzell Jr., *Daniel Webster and the Trial of American Nationalism, 1843–1852* (1972).

David H. Donald, *Charles Sumner and the Coming of the Civil War* (1960).

Robert R. Dykstra, *Bright Radical Star: Black Freedom and White Supremacy on the Hawkeye Frontier* (1993).

Don E. Fehrenbacher, *Prelude to Greatness: Lincoln in the 1850s* (1962).

Eric Foner, *Free Soil, Free Labor, Free Men: The Ideology of the Republican Party before the Civil War* (1970).

George B. Forgie, *Patricide in the House Divided: A Psychological Interpretation of Lincoln and His Age* (1979).

Ronald P. Formisano, *The Birth of Mass Political Parties: Michigan, 1827–1861* (1971).

William E. Gienapp, *The Origins of the Republican Party, 1852–1856* (1987).

Thomas F. Gossett, *"Uncle Tom's Cabin" and American Culture* (1985).

Len Gougeon, *Virtue's Hero: Emerson, Antislavery, and Reform* (1990).

Susan-Mary Grant, *North over South: Northern Nationalism and American Identity in the Antebellum Era* (2000).

David Grimsted, *American Mobbing, 1828–1865: Toward Civil War* (1998).

Stanley Harrold, *Subversives: Antislavery Community in Washington, D.C., 1828–1865* (2002).

Joan D. Hedrick, *Harriet Beecher Stowe: A Life* (1994).

Pamela Herr, *Jessie Benton Frémont: A Biography* (1987).

Pamela Herr and Mary Lee Spence, eds., *The Letters of Jessie Benton Frémont* (1993).

Nancy Isenberg, *Sex and Citizenship in Antebellum America* (1998).

Robert W. Johannsen, *Lincoln, the South, and Slavery: The Political Dimension* (1991).

Bruce C. Levine, *The Spirit of 1848: German Immigrants, Labor Conflict, and the Coming of the Civil War* (1992).

William S. McFeely, *Frederick Douglass* (1991).

John R. McKivigan, *The War against Proslavery Religion: Abolitionism and the Northern Churches, 1830–1865* (1984).

Thomas D. Morris, *Free Men All: The Personal Liberty Laws of the North, 1780–1861* (1974).

Stephen B. Oates, *To Purge This Land with Blood: A Biography of John Brown* (2nd ed., 1984).

Merrill D. Peterson, *John Brown: The Legend Revisited* (2002).

James A. Rawley, *Race and Politics: "Bleeding Kansas" and the Coming of the Civil War* (1969).

Richard H. Sewell, *Ballots for Freedom: Antislavery Politics in the United States, 1837–1860* (1976).

Thomas P. Slaughter, *Bloody Dawn: The Christiana Riot and Racial Violence in the Antebellum North* (1991).

James Brewer Stewart, *Holy Warriors: The Abolitionists and American Slavery* (1976).

James Brewer Stewart, *Wendell Phillips, Liberty's Hero* (1986).

Hans L. Trefousse, *The Radical Republicans: Lincoln's Vanguard for Racial Justice* (1969).

Wendy Hamand Venet, *Neither Ballots nor Bullets: Women Abolitionists and the Civil War* (1991).

Albert J. Von Frank, *The Trials of Anthony Burns: Freedom and Slavery in Emerson's Boston* (1998).

Ronald G. Walters, *The Antislavery Appeal: American Abolitionism after 1830* (1976).

Douglas L. Wilson, *Honor's Voice: The Transformation of Abraham Lincoln* (1998).

Susan Zaeske, *Signatures of Citizenship: Petitioning, Antislavery, and Women's Political Identity* (2003).

David Zarefsky, *Lincoln, Douglas, and Slavery: In the Crucible of Public Debate* (1990).

Southern Sectionalism

William L. Barney, *The Road to Secession: A New Perspective on the Old South* (1972).

Irving H. Bartlett, *John C. Calhoun: A Biography* (1993).

Tom Chaffin, *Fatal Glory: Narciso López and the First Clandestine U.S. War against Cuba* (1996).

William J. Cooper Jr., *The South and the Politics of Slavery, 1828–1856* (1978).

John Patrick Daly, *When Slavery Was Called Freedom: Evangelicalism, Proslavery, and the Causes of the Civil War* (2002).

Drew Gilpin Faust, *James Henry Hammond and the Old South: A Design for Mastery* (1982).

Don E. Fehrenbacher, *The South and Three Sectional Crises* (1980).

Lacy K. Ford Jr., *Origins of Southern Radicalism: The South Carolina Upcountry, 1800–1860* (1988).

William W. Freehling, *The Road to Disunion*, vol. 1, *Secessionists at Bay, 1776–1854* (1990).

Vicki Vaughn Johnson, *The Men and the Vision of the Southern Commercial Conventions, 1845–1871* (1992).

Robert E. May, *The Southern Dream of a Caribbean Empire, 1854–1861* (1973).

John Niven, *John C. Calhoun and the Price of Union: A Biography* (1988).

Christopher J. Olsen, *Political Culture and Secession in Mississippi: Masculinity, Honor, and the Antiparty Tradition, 1830–1860* (2002).

David M. Potter, *The South and the Sectional Conflict* (1968).

Manisha Sinha, *The Counterrevolution of Slavery: Politics and Ideology in Antebellum South Carolina* (2000).

Mitchell Snay, *Gospel of Disunion: Religion and Separatism in the Antebellum South* (1993).

J. Mills Thornton III, *Politics and Power in a Slave Society: Alabama, 1800–1860* (1978).

Eric H. Walther, *The Fire-Eaters* (1992).

Secession

William L. Barney, *The Secessionist Impulse: Alabama and Mississippi in 1860* (1974).

Walter L. Buenger, *Secession and the Union in Texas* (1984).

Steven A. Channing, *Crisis of Fear: Secession in South Carolina* (1970).

Daniel W. Crofts, *Reluctant Confederates: Upper South Unionists in the Secession Crisis* (1989).

Charles B. Dew, *Apostles of Disunion: Southern Secession Commissioners and the Causes of the Civil War* (2001).

James L. Huston, *The Panic of 1857 and the Coming of the Civil War* (1987).

Michael P. Johnson, *Toward a Patriarchal Republic: The Secession of Georgia* (1977).

William A. Link, *Roots of Secession: Slavery and Politics in Antebellum Virginia* (2002).

David M. Potter, *Lincoln and His Party in the Secession Crisis* (1942).

Lorman A. Ratner and Dwight L. Teeter Jr., *Fanatics and Fire Eaters: Newspapers and the Coming of the Civil War* (2003).

Kenneth M. Stampp, *And the War Came: The North and the Secession Crisis, 1860–61* (1960).

James M. Woods, *Rebellion and Realignment: Arkansas's Road to Secession* (1987).

Ralph A. Wooster, *The Secession Conventions of the South* (1962).

FORT SUMTER STARS AND STRIPES
This U.S. flag flew over Fort Sumter throughout the Confederate bombardment that initiated the Civil War on April 12, 1861. Shrapnel from thirty-three hours of cannon fire shredded the flag, but when the Union major Robert Anderson surrendered on April 13, he and his men marched out of the fort under this tattered banner. The governor of South Carolina cheered what he called the humbling of the flag of the United States. Northerners bridled at this insult, and within days flags sprouted across the Union. The Civil War stitched the flag and American nationalism together and made the Stars and Stripes the powerful symbol it is today. When Anderson returned to Fort Sumter in April 1865, he triumphantly raised this very flag.

Confederate Museum, United Daughters of the Confederacy.

The Crucible of War

1861–1865

ON THE RAINY NIGHT OF SEPTEMBER 21, 1862, in Wilmington, North Carolina, twenty-four-year-old William Gould and seven other black men crowded into a small boat on Cape Fear River and quietly pushed away from the dock. Knowing that the authorities would sound the alarm for eight runaway slaves at daybreak, they rowed hard throughout the night. By dawn, the runaways had traveled twenty-eight miles to where the river flowed into the Atlantic Ocean. No longer concerned about being detected, they raised their sail and plunged into the swells. They made for the Union navy patrolling offshore to disrupt the flow of goods in and out of Wilmington, a major Confederate port. At 10:30 that morning, the U.S.S. *Cambridge* spied the sail and took the men aboard.

Astonishingly, on the same day that Gould reached the federal ship, President Abraham Lincoln announced to his cabinet in Washington, D.C., that he intended to issue a proclamation of **emancipation** freeing slaves in the Confederate states. Because the proclamation would not take effect until January 1863, Gould was not legally free in the eyes of the U.S. government. But the U.S. navy, suffering from a shortage of sailors, cared little about the formal status of runaway slaves. And within days of setting foot on the *Cambridge*, all eight runaways became sailors "for three years," Gould said, "first taking the Oath of Allegiance to the Government of Uncle Samuel."

Unlike most slaves, William Gould could read and write, and he began making almost daily entries in a remarkable diary, apparently the only diary kept during the war by a sailor who had been a slave. Much of Gould's naval experience was indistinguishable from that of white sailors. He found duty on a ship in the blockading squadron both boring and exhilarating. He often recorded "All hands painting, cleaning," and "Cruised as usual." But long days of tedious work were sometimes interrupted by the sighting of a ship on the horizon and a frantic "period of daring exploit" as enemies locked in combat. When the *Cambridge* closed on one Confederate vessel, Gould declared that "we told them good morning in the shape of a shot." In one five-day period in 1862, his ship and two other blockaders captured four blockade runners and ran another aground.

In October 1863, Gould transferred to the U.S.S. *Niagara* and sailed for European waters to search for Confederate cruisers abroad. "We are expecting a fight," he confided, "but who will be the victors remains to be seen." The *Niagara* did not engage the enemy in Europe, but when a sister ship, the U.S.S. *Kearsarge,* caught up with and sent to the bottom the *Alabama,* an infamous Confederate raider, Gould declared that his crew was "as delighted and as proud of the deed as if they had done it themselves."

Newly Recruited Contrabands, 1862
The U.S. navy recruited men with little regard for status or color. Blacks initially served only as coal heavers, cooks, and stewards, but within a year, some black sailors joined their ships' gun crews. As this photograph of newly recruited ex-slaves reveals, naval service was not limited to young men.
Courtesy of the New Hampshire Historical Society.

Despite having much in common with white sailors, Gould's Civil War experience was shaped by his race. Most whites fought to preserve their government and society, but most black men in the Union military saw service as an opportunity to fight slavery. From the beginning, Gould linked freedom and Union, which he called "the holiest of all causes."

Even though the navy treated black sailors better than the army treated black soldiers, Gould witnessed a number of racial incidents. "There was A malee [melee] on Deck between the white and colard men," he declared. Later, when a black regiment came aboard, "they were treated verry rough by the crew." White sailors "refused to let them eat off the mess pans and calld them all kinds of names[;] . . . in all they was treated shamefully." Recording another incident, Gould stated, "This Morning four or fiv[e] white fellows beat Jerry Jones (co[lored]). He was stabd in his left shoulder. Verry bad."

Still, Gould was proud of his service in the navy and carefully traced the progress of racial equality during the war. On shore leave in 1863, he cheered the "20th Regmt of U.S. (collard [colored]) Volunteers, the first collard Regement raised in New York pronounce[d] by all to be A splendid Regement." In March 1865, he celebrated the "passage of an amendment of the Con[sti]tution prohibiting slavery througho[ut] the United States." And a month later, he thrilled to the "Glad Tidings that the Stars and Stripe[s] had been planted over the Capital of the D—nd Confederacy by the invincible Grant." He added, we must not forget the "Mayrters to the cau[se] of Right and Equality."

Many slaves like the eight runaways from Wilmington took the first steps toward making the war a contest for freedom. Early in the war, black abolitionist Frederick Douglass challenged the friends of freedom to "*be up and doing;—now is your time.*" Although Southerners believed that the North threatened slavery, few Northerners agreed that their fight against disunion marked the beginning of the end of slavery. For eighteen months, Union soldiers fought solely to uphold the Constitution and preserve the nation. But in 1863, the northern war effort took on a dual purpose: to save the Union and to free the slaves.

Even if the Civil War had not touched slavery, the conflict still would have transformed America. As the world's first modern war, it mobilized the entire populations of North and South, harnessed the productive capacities of both economies, and produced battles that fielded 200,000 soldiers and created casualties in the tens of thousands. The carnage lasted four years and cost the nation an estimated 633,000 lives, nearly as many as in all of its other wars before and after combined. The war helped mold the modern American nation-state. The federal government emerged with new power and responsibility over national life. War furthered the emergence of a modern industrializing nation. It tore families apart and pushed women into new work and roles. But because the war to preserve the Union also became a war to destroy slavery, the northern victory had truly revolutionary meaning. Defeat and emancipation destroyed the slave society of the Old South and gave birth to a different southern society.

Years later, remembering the Civil War years, Frederick Douglass said, "It is something to couple one's name with great occasions." It *was* something—for William Gould and millions of other Americans. Whether they fought for the Confederacy or the Union, whether they labored behind the lines to supply Yankee or rebel soldiers, whether they prayed for the safe return of Northerners or Southerners, all Americans experienced the crucible of war. But the war affected no group more than the four million African Americans who saw its beginning as slaves and emerged as free people.

"And the War Came"

New to high office, Abraham Lincoln faced the worst crisis in the history of the nation: the threat of disunion. Lincoln revealed his strategy on March 4, 1861, in his inaugural address, which he carefully crafted to combine firmness and conciliation. First, he sought to stop the contagion of secession. Eight of the fifteen slave states had said "no" to disunion, but they remained suspicious and skittish. Lincoln wanted to avoid any act that would push the Upper South (North Carolina, Virginia, Maryland, Delaware, Kentucky, Tennessee, Missouri, and Arkansas) into leaving. Second, he sought to buy time so that emotions could cool in the deep South. By reassuring South Carolina, Georgia, Florida, Alabama, Mississippi, Louisiana, and Texas that the Republicans would not abolish slavery, Lincoln believed that Unionists there would assert themselves and overturn the secession decision. Always, Lincoln expressed his uncompromising will to oppose secession and to uphold the Union.

His counterpart, Jefferson Davis, fully intended to establish the Confederate States of America as an independent republic. To achieve permanence, Davis had to sustain the secession fever that had carried the deep South out of the Union. Even if the deep South held firm, however, the Confederacy would remain weak without additional states. Davis watched for opportunities to add new stars to the Confederate flag.

Neither man sought war. Both wanted to achieve their objectives peacefully. But as Lincoln later observed, "Both parties deprecated war, but one of them would *make* war rather than let the nation survive, and the other would *accept* war rather than let it perish. And the war came."

Attack on Fort Sumter

Fort Sumter's thick brick walls rose forty feet above the tiny island on which it perched at the entrance to Charleston harbor. Major Robert Anderson and some eighty U.S. soldiers occupied what Confederates claimed as their property. The fort with its American flag became a hated symbol of the nation that Southerners had abandoned, and they wanted federal troops out. Sumter was also a symbol to Northerners, a beacon affirming federal sovereignty in the seceded states.

The situation at Fort Sumter presented Lincoln with hard choices. Ordering the fort's evacuation would play well in the Upper South, whose edgy slave states threatened to bolt to the Confederacy if Lincoln resorted to military force to resolve the secession crisis. But yielding the fort would make it appear that Lincoln accepted the Confederacy's existence. He decided to hold Fort Sumter. But to do so, he had to provision it, for Anderson was running dangerously short of food. In the first week of April 1861, Lincoln authorized a peaceful expedition to bring supplies, but not military reinforcements, to the fort. The president understood that he risked war, but his plan honored his inaugural promises to defend federal property and to avoid using military force unless first attacked. Masterfully, Lincoln had shifted the fateful decision of war or peace to Jefferson Davis.

On April 9, Jefferson Davis and his cabinet met to consider the situation in Charleston harbor. The territorial integrity of the Confederacy demanded the end of the federal presence, Davis argued. But his secretary of state, Robert Toombs of Georgia, pleaded against military action. "Mr. President," he declared, "at this time it is suicide, murder, and will lose us every friend at the North. You will wantonly strike a hornet's nest which extends from mountain to ocean, and legions now quiet will swarm out and sting us to death." Davis rejected Toombs's prophecy and sent word to General Pierre Gustave T. Beauregard, the Louisianan commanding Confederate troops in Charleston, to take the fort before the relief expedition arrived. Thirty-three hours of bombardment on April 12 and 13 reduced the fort to rubble. Miraculously, not a single Union soldier died. On April 14, with the fort ablaze, Major Anderson offered his surrender and lowered the U.S. flag. The Confederates had Fort Sumter, but they also had war.

The response of the free states was thunderous. On April 15, Lincoln called for 75,000 militiamen to serve for ninety days to put down the rebellion, but several times that number rushed to defend the flag. Democrats responded as fervently as Republicans. Stephen A. Douglas, the recently defeated Democratic candidate for president, pledged his support. "There are only two sides to the question," he told a massive crowd in Chicago. "Every man must be for the United States or against it. There can be no

> The fort with its American flag became a hated symbol of the nation that Southerners had abandoned. Sumter was also a symbol to Northerners, a beacon affirming federal sovereignty in the seceded states.

Fort Sumter after the Bombardment
Located on an artificial island inside the entrance to Charleston harbor, Fort Sumter had walls eight to twelve feet thick. The fort was so undermanned that when Confederate shells began raining down on April 12, U.S. troops could answer back with only a few of the fort's forty-eight guns. Confederate artillery lobbed more than 4,000 rounds. Cannonballs pulverized the walls, while hot shot ignited the wooden buildings inside.
Minnesota Historical Society.

neutrals in this war, *only patriots—or traitors.*" No one faced more acutely the dilemma of loyalty than the men and women of the Upper South.

The Upper South Chooses Sides

The Upper South faced a horrendous choice: either to fight against the Lower South or to fight against the Union. Many who only months earlier had rejected secession now embraced the Confederacy. To oppose southern independence was one thing; to fight fellow Southerners another. Thousands felt betrayed, believing that Lincoln had promised to achieve a peaceful reunion by waiting patiently for Unionists to retake power in the seceding states. One man furiously denounced the conflict as a "politician's war," conceding that "this is no time now to discuss the causes, but it is the duty of all who regard Southern institutions of value to side with the South, make common cause

> Throughout the border states, but especially in Kentucky, the Civil War was truly a "brother's war."

with the Confederate States and sink or swim with them."

Some found the choice excruciating. Robert E. Lee, a career military officer and the son of one of Virginia's oldest families, denounced secession in the deep South as the work of cotton-state hotheads. "I can anticipate no greater calamity for the country than a dissolution of the Union," he told his son in January 1861. Still, he said, "a Union that can only be maintained by swords and bayonets . . . has no charm for me." When Virginia left the Union in April, Lee went with his state and resigned from the U.S. army and declared, "Save in defense of my native State, I never desire again to draw my sword." But his beloved state offered no sanctuary for his tortured allegiences. Richmond would soon be the capital of the Confederacy; Virginia would be a battlefield, and Lee would again command military forces.

One by one the other states of the Upper South jumped off the fence. Within weeks, Arkansas, Tennessee, and North Carolina had followed Virginia's lead (Map 15.1). But in the border states of Delaware, Maryland, Kentucky, and Missouri, Unionism triumphed. Only in Delaware, where slaves accounted for less than 2 percent of the population, was the victory easy. In Maryland, Unionism needed a helping hand. Rather than allow the state to secede and make Washington, D.C., a federal island in a Confederate sea, Lincoln suspended the writ of habeas corpus, essentially setting aside constitutional guarantees that protect citizens from illegal and arbitrary arrest and detention, and he ordered U.S. troops into Baltimore, essentially placing the city under military arrest. Maryland's legislature, frightened by the federal invasion and aware of the strength of Union sentiment in the state's western counties, rejected secession.

The struggle turned violent in the West. In Missouri, Unionists won a narrow victory, but southern-sympathizing **guerrilla** bands roamed the state for the duration of the conflict, wreaking bloody havoc on civilians and soldiers alike. In Kentucky as in Missouri, Unionists barely defeated secession, and a prosouthern minority claimed that the state had severed ties with the Union. The Confederacy was not particularly fastidious in counting votes and eagerly made Missouri and Kentucky the twelfth and thirteenth stars on the Confederate flag.

Throughout the border states, but especially in Kentucky, the Civil War was truly a "brother's war." Seven of Henry Clay's grandsons fought: four for the Confederacy and three for the

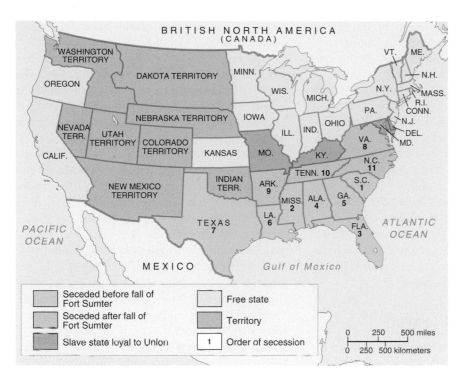

BRITISH NORTH AMERICA
(CANADA)

MAP 15.1   Secession, 1860–1861
After Lincoln's election, the fifteen slave states debated what to do. Seven states quickly left the Union, four left after the firing on Fort Sumter, and four remained loyal to the Union.

Union. Lincoln understood that the border states—particularly Kentucky—not only contained indispensable resources, population, and wealth but also controlled major rivers and railroads. "I think to lose Kentucky is nearly the same as to lose the whole game," Lincoln said. "Kentucky gone, we can not hold Missouri, nor, as I think, Maryland. These all against us, . . . we would as well consent to separation at once."

In the end, only eleven of the fifteen slave states joined the Confederate States of America. Moreover, the four seceding Upper South states contained significant numbers of people who felt little affection for the Confederacy. Dissatisfaction was so rife in the western counties of Virginia that in 1863 citizens there voted to create the separate state of West Virginia, loyal to the Union. Still, the acquisition of four new Confederate states greatly strengthened the cause of southern independence.

The Combatants

Although fierce struggle continued in the border states and in some areas within the seceding states, most whites in the South chose to defend the Confederacy. Only slaveholders had a direct economic stake in preserving slavery (estimated at some $3 billion in 1860), but most whites de-

fended the institution and the way of life they had built on it. The degraded and subjugated status of blacks was the basis of elevated status for even the most humble whites. "It matters not whether slaves be actually owned by many or by few," one Southerner declared. "It is enough that one simply belongs to the superior and ruling race, to secure consideration and respect." Moreover, Yankee "aggression" was no longer a secessionist's abstraction; it was real, and it was at the South's door. Most southern whites equated the secession of 1861 with the declaration of independence from tyrannical British rule in 1776. As one Georgia woman observed, Southerners wanted "nothing from the North but—*to be let alone*—and *they*, a people like ourselves whose republican independence was won by a rebellion, whose liberty was achieved by a secession, to think that they should attempt to coerce us—the idea is preposterous."

For Northerners, rebel "treason" threatened to destroy the best government on earth. The South's failure to accept the **democratic** election of a president and its firing on the nation's flag challenged the rule of law, the authority of the Constitution, and the ability of the people to govern themselves. As an Indiana soldier told his wife, a "good government is the best thing on earth. Property is nothing without it, because it is not protected; a family is nothing without it, because they cannot be educated." Lincoln captured the special magnetism of the Union cause when he called it "a People's contest," one in which America's promise "to elevate the condition of man" hung in the balance.

Men rallied behind their separate battle flags, fully convinced that they were in the right and that God was on their side. While both sides claimed the lion's share of virtue, no one could argue that the South's resources and forces equaled the North's. A glance at the census figures contradicted such a notion. Yankees took heart at their superior power, but the rebels believed they had advantages that nullified every northern strength. Both sides mobilized swiftly in the spring and summer of 1861, and each devised what it believed would be a winning military and diplomatic strategy.

How They Expected to Win

The balance sheet of northern and southern resources reveals enormous advantages for the Union (Figure 15.1). The twenty-three states remaining in the Union had a population of 22.3

million; the eleven Confederate states had a population of only 9.1 million, of whom 3.67 million (40 percent) were slaves. The North's economic advantages were even more overwhelming. The North manufactured more than 90 percent of the nation's industrial goods. It produced 13 times as much textiles as the South, 16 times as much iron, 32 times as many firearms, and so on. So mismatched were North and South that the question becomes why the South made war at all. Was not the South's cause lost before Confederates lobbed the first rounds at Fort Sumter? The answer quite simply is "no." Southerners expected to win—for some good reasons—and they came very close to doing so.

Southerners believed that they would triumph because of their region's just cause, superior civilization, and unsurpassed character. They bucked the military odds, but hadn't the **liberty**-loving colonists in 1776 also done so? "Britain could not conquer three million," a Louisianan proclaimed, and "the world cannot conquer the South." How could anyone doubt the outcome of a contest between lean, hard, country-born rebel warriors defending family, property, and liberty, and soft, flabby, citified Yankee mechanics waging an unconstitutional war of aggression and subjugation?

The South's confidence also rested on its estimation of the economic clout of its principal crop, cotton. Southerners believed that northern prosperity depended on the South's cotton. It followed then that without cotton, New England textile mills would stand idle. And without southern **planters** purchasing northern manufactured goods, northern factories would drown in their own unsold goods. And without the foreign exchange earned by the overseas sales of cotton, the financial structure of the entire Yankee nation would collapse. A Virginian spoke for most Confederates when he declared that in the South's ability to "withhold the benefits of our trade, we hold a power over the North more powerful than a powerful army in the field."

Cotton would also make Europe a powerful ally of the Confederacy, Southerners reasoned. After all, they said, England's economy (and to a lesser degree France's) depended on cotton. Of the 900 million pounds of cotton

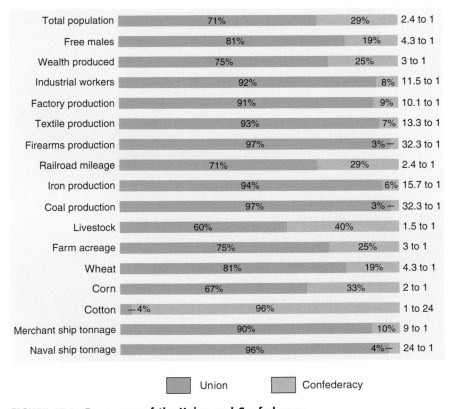

	Union	Confederacy	
Total population	71%	29%	2.4 to 1
Free males	81%	19%	4.3 to 1
Wealth produced	75%	25%	3 to 1
Industrial workers	92%	8%	11.5 to 1
Factory production	91%	9%	10.1 to 1
Textile production	93%	7%	13.3 to 1
Firearms production	97%	3%—	32.3 to 1
Railroad mileage	71%	29%	2.4 to 1
Iron production	94%	6%	15.7 to 1
Coal production	97%	3%—	32.3 to 1
Livestock	60%	40%	1.5 to 1
Farm acreage	75%	25%	3 to 1
Wheat	81%	19%	4.3 to 1
Corn	67%	33%	2 to 1
Cotton	—4%	96%	1 to 24
Merchant ship tonnage	90%	10%	9 to 1
Naval ship tonnage	96%	4%—	24 to 1

FIGURE 15.1 Resources of the Union and Confederacy
The Union's enormous statistical advantages failed to convince Confederates that their cause was doomed.

Bridge on the Orange and Alexandria Railroad
Confederate forces burned southern railroads and bridges to slow Union advances, cut federal supply lines, and protect Confederate retreats. West Point–trained Herman Haupt, seen here inspecting a rebuilt bridge, was in charge of the Union's efforts at railroad construction and repair. Although railroads were used as an instrument of war in the Crimea in the 1850s, it was during the Civil War that railroads took on revolutionary importance. Railroads helped set new standards of overland mobility, rapid maneuver, and concentration of forces.
Library of Congress.

England imported annually, more than 700 million came from the South. If the supply were interrupted, sheer economic need would make England (and perhaps France) a Confederate ally. And because the British navy ruled the seas, the North would find Britain a formidable foe.

Southerners' confidence may seem naive today, but even tough-minded European military observers picked the South to win. Offsetting the North's power was the South's expanse. The North, Europeans predicted, could not conquer the vast territory (750,000 square miles) extending from the Potomac to the Rio Grande, with rugged terrain and bad roads. To defeat the South, the Union would need to raise a massive invading army, supply it with huge quantities of provisions and arms, and protect supply lines that would stretch farther than any in modern history.

Indeed, the South enjoyed major advantages, and the Confederacy devised a military strategy to exploit them. Jefferson Davis called it an "offensive-defensive" strategy. It recognized that a Union victory required the North to defeat and subjugate the South but a Confederate victory required only that the South stay at home, blunt invasions, avoid battles that risked annihilating its army, and outlast the North's will to fight. When an opportunity presented itself, the South would strike the invaders. Like the American colonists, the South could win independence by not losing the war.

If the North did nothing, the South would by default establish

> The Confederacy devised an "offensive-defensive" strategy. Victory required only that the South stay at home, blunt invasions, avoid battles that risked annihilating its army, and outlast the North's will to fight.

itself as a sovereign nation. The Lincoln administration therefore adopted an offensive strategy. On April 19, four days after the president issued the proclamation calling for a militia to put down the rebellion, he issued another proclamation declaring a naval blockade of the Confederacy. He sought to deny the Confederacy the advantages offered by its most valuable commodity—cotton. Without the sale of cotton abroad, the South would have far fewer dollars to pay for war goods. Even before the North could mount an effective blockade, however, Jefferson Davis decided voluntarily to cease exporting cotton. He wanted to create a cotton "famine" that would enfeeble the northern economy and precipitate European intervention. But the cotton famine Davis created devastated the South, not the North, and left Europe on the diplomatic sidelines.

Southerners were not the only ones with illusions. Lincoln's call-up of 75,000 men for ninety days illustrates his inability to foresee the magnitude and duration of the war. He and most other Americans thought of war in terms of their most recent experience, the Mexican-American War of the 1840s. In Mexico, fighting had taken place between relatively small armies, had cost relatively few lives, and had inflicted only light damage on the countryside. Americans on the eve of the Civil War could not know that four ghastly years of bloodletting lay ahead.

Lincoln and Davis Mobilize

Mobilization required effective political leadership, and at first glance the South appeared to have the advantage. A gentleman from a Mississippi planter family, Jefferson Davis brought to the Confederate presidency a distinguished political career, including experience in the U.S. Senate. He was also a West Point graduate, a combat veteran and authentic hero of the Mexican-American War, and a former secretary of war. Dignified and erect, with "a jaw sawed in steel," Davis appeared to be everything a nation could want in a wartime leader.

In contrast, Abraham Lincoln brought to the White House one lackluster term in the House of Representatives and almost no administrative experience, and his sole brush with anything

> In Lincoln, the North got far more than met the eye. He proved himself a master politician and a superb leader.

military was as a captain in the militia in the Black Hawk War, a brief struggle in Illinois in 1832 in which whites expelled the last Indians from the state. Lincoln later joked about his service in the Black Hawk War as the time when he survived bloody encounters with mosquitoes and led raids on wild onion patches. The lanky, disheveled Illinois lawyer-politician looked anything but military or presidential in his bearing, and even his friends feared that he was in over his head.

Davis, however, proved to be less than he appeared. Although he worked hard and was fervently dedicated to the Confederate cause, Davis possessed little capacity for broad military strategy yet intervened often in military affairs. He was an even less able political leader. Quarrelsome and proud, he had an acid tongue that made enemies the Confederacy could ill afford. He insisted on dealing with every scrap of paper that came across his desk, and he grew increasingly unbending and dogmatic. The Confederacy's intimidating problems might have defeated an even more talented leader, however. For example, **state sovereignty**, which was enshrined in the Confederate constitution, made Davis's task of organizing a new nation and fighting a war difficult in the extreme.

With Lincoln, in contrast, the North got far more than met the eye. He proved himself a master politician and a superb leader. He never allowed personal feelings to get in the way of his objectives. When forming his cabinet, for example, Lincoln shrewdly appointed representatives of every Republican faction, men who were often his chief rivals and critics. He appointed Salmon P. Chase secretary of the treasury, knowing that Chase had presidential ambitions. As secretary of state, he chose his chief opponent for the Republican nomination in 1860, William H. Seward, who mistakenly expected to twist Lincoln around his little finger and formulate policy himself. Despite his civilian background, Lincoln displayed an innate understanding of military strategy. In time, no one was more crucial in mapping the Union war plan. Further, Lincoln wrote beautifully and through letters and speeches reached out to the North's people, helping to galvanize them in defense of the nation he called "the last best hope of earth."

Guided by Lincoln and Davis, the North and South began gathering their armies. Southerners had to build almost everything from scratch, and Northerners had to mobilize their superior numbers and industrial resources for war. In 1861,

Minié Ball

The Union army was one of the best equipped armies in history. None of its weaponry proved more vital than a French innovation: Captain Claude Minié's new bullet. In 1848, Minié created an inch-long slug that was

rammed down a rifled barrel and would spin at great speed as it left the muzzle. The spin gave the bullet greater distance and accuracy than bullets fired from smoothbore weapons. When the war began, most soldiers carried smoothbore muskets; but by 1863, infantry on both sides fought with rifles. Bullets caused more than 90 percent of battle wounds, and minié balls proved extremely destructive to human bodies on impact.

Picture Research Consultants & Archives.

---

before the war, the puny federal army numbered only 16,000 men, most of them scattered over the West subjugating Indians. One-third of the officers followed the example of the Virginian Robert E. Lee, resigning their commissions and heading south. The U.S. navy was in better shape. Forty-two ships were in service, and a large merchant marine would in time provide more ships and sailors for the Union cause. The Confederate navy was never a match for the Union fleet, and thus the South pinned its hopes on its armies.

From the beginning, the South exhibited more enthusiasm than ability to provide its soldiers with supplies and transportation. The Confederacy made prodigious efforts to build new factories to produce tents, blankets, shoes, and its gray uniforms, but many rebel soldiers slept in the open air without proper clothes and sometimes without shoes. Even when factories managed to produce what the soldiers needed, southern railroads—constructed to connect plantations with ports—often could not deliver the goods. And in each year of the war, more railroads were captured, destroyed, or left in disrepair. Food production proved less of a problem, but food sometimes rotted before it reached the soldiers. The one bright spot was the Confederacy's Ordnance Bureau, headed by Josiah Gorgas, a near miracle worker when it came to manufacturing gunpower, cannon, and rifles. In April 1864, Gorgas proudly observed:

"Where three years ago we were not making a gun, a pistol nor a sabre, no shot nor shell . . . — a pound of powder—we now make all these in quantities to meet the demands of our large armies."

Recruiting and supplying huge armies required enormous public spending. Before the war, the federal government's tiny income had come primarily from tariff duties and the sale of public lands. Massive wartime expenditures made new revenues imperative. At first, both North and South sold war bonds, which essentially were loans from patriotic citizens. In addition, both Union and Confederacy turned to taxes. The North raised one-fifth of its wartime revenue from taxes; the South raised only one-twentieth. Eventually, both sides began printing paper money. Inflation soared, but the South suffered more because it financed a greater part of its wartime costs through the printing press. Prices in the North rose by about 80 percent during the war, while inflation in the South topped 9,000 percent.

Within months of the bombardment of Fort Sumter, both sides had found men to fight and people to supply and support them. But the underlying strength of the northern economy gave the Union the decided advantage. With their military and industrial muscles beginning to ripple, Northerners became itchy for action. They wanted an invasion that once and for all would smash the rebellion. Horace Greeley's *New York Tribune* began to chant: "Forward to Richmond! Forward to Richmond!"

Battling It Out, 1861–1862

During the first year and a half of the war, armies fought major campaigns in both East and West. Because the rival capitals—Richmond and Washington, D.C.—were only ninety miles apart and each was threatened more than once with capture, the eastern campaign was especially dramatic and commanded public attention. But the battles in the West proved more decisive. As Yankee and rebel armies pounded each other on land, the navies of each side fought on the seas and in the rivers of the South, and Confederate and U.S. diplomats competed for advantage in the corridors of power in Europe. All the while, casualty lists in both South and North reached appalling lengths.

Stalemate in the Eastern Theater

Lincoln appointed Mexican-American War veteran Irvin McDowell to be commanding general of the Union army assembling outside Washington. McDowell had no thought of taking his raw recruits into battle during the summer of 1861, but Lincoln ordered him to prepare his 35,000 greenhorn troops for an attack on the 20,000 Confederates defending Manassas, a railroad junction in Virginia about thirty miles southwest of Washington.

On July 21, the Union army forded Bull Run, a branch of the Potomac River, and engaged the southern forces effectively (Map 15.2). But fast-moving southern reinforcements blunted the Union attack and then counterattacked. What began as an orderly Union retreat turned

MAP 15.2   The Civil War, 1861–1862

While eyes focused on the eastern theater, especially the 90-mile stretch of land between the U.S. capital at Washington and the Confederate capital at Richmond, Union troops were winning strategic victories in the West.

READING THE MAP: In which states did the Confederacy and the Union each win the most battles in this period? Which side used or followed water routes most for troop movements and attacks?

CONNECTIONS: Which major cities in the South and West fell to Union troops in 1862? Which strategic area did those Confederate losses place in Union hands? How did this outcome affect the later movement of troops and supplies?

FOR MORE HELP ANALYZING THIS MAP, see the visual activity for this chapter in the Online Study Guide at bedfordstmartins.com/roark.

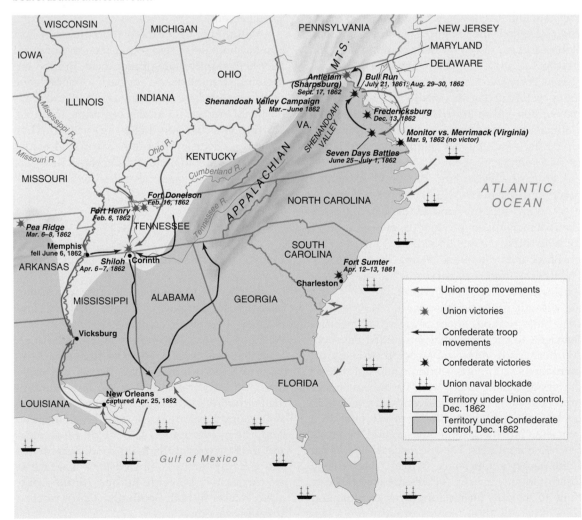

C.S.S. *H. L. Hunley:* The First Successful Submarine

The Confederacy had no navy when it came into being in 1861, and without major shipyards, it could not build a naval fleet to match that of the Union. As the federal blockade of southern ports gradually began to strangle Confederate shipping, Southerners were forced to innovate in naval technology: the ironclad, floating mines called torpedoes, and, most spectacular of all, the submarine.

On the bone-chilling night of February 17, 1864, a lookout aboard the U.S.S. *Housatonic,* the largest ship among the Union blockaders off Charleston, noticed something in the water. It might have been a log or a porpoise, but he was jumpy because of rumors of a Confederate secret weapon roaming the ocean, something Union sailors called the "infernal machine." The lookout sounded the alarm. The *Housatonic*'s cannons could not target something so low in the water, and the ship's crew soon discovered that rifle and revolver rounds would not stop it.

Just below the surface of the Atlantic, eight sweating men at hand cranks propelled their peculiar vessel—a submarine named C.S.S. *H. L. Hunley*—toward the Union blockader. The *Hunley* rammed a 135-pound explosive, which was lashed to a spar protruding from its bow, into the *Housatonic* below the waterline, then quickly backed away as a 150-foot detonation rope played out. Within seconds, an explosion ripped the big Union ship. The *Housatonic* quickly sank, the first ship ever sunk by a submarine. Five sailors lost their lives. The *Hunley* then surfaced, and crew members flashed a light to their comrades on the shore to signal a successful mission. Minutes later, the *Hunley* and its crew vanished without a trace.

Three years of trial-and-error experimentation and wartime innovation produced the *Hunley.* Shortly after the war began, a group of New Orleans engineers and investors, including H. L. Hunley, imagined a new kind of ship: an underwater vessel that would defend the city from assault by the U.S. navy. First, they built the *Pioneer,* a cigar-shaped submarine with a crew of two, but in April 1862, Admiral David Farragut's fleet captured New Orleans before the *Pioneer* could go into action. Hunley and his partners moved their operations to Mobile, where they built a second underwater ship, the *American Diver,* with a four-man crew. The builders experimented with propelling the submarine with an electromagnetic engine, but when the device failed to generate enough power, they returned to the hand-crank design. Stormy seas sank the *American Diver* in February 1863. Within weeks, the civilian builders, now joined by the Confederate military, began work on a third submarine, the *H. L. Hunley.*

A sleek, 40-foot version of previous efforts, the *Hunley* was an engineering marvel that exhibited both sophisticated technology and primitive features. Ballast tanks at each end of the hull could be flooded to submerge the vessel and emptied to raise it to the surface. Two lateral fins, or adjustable dive planes, regulated the ship's underwater depth. The captain steered the sub with a vertical rod attached to the rudder. A 4,000-pound keel ensured that the ship would remain upright as it slipped through the water. Eight men, squeezed into a space no more than four feet high, turned a crankshaft connected to a propeller. The ship had two towers with manholes secured by hatch covers fitted with watertight rubber gaskets that the crew secured from inside. Each

---

fugitives back. But Union armies needed laborers, and some officers accepted the runaways and put them to work. At Fort Monroe, Virginia, General Benjamin F. Butler not only refused to turn them over to their owners but also provided them with a new status. He called them "contraband of war," meaning "confiscated property."

Congress made Butler's practice national policy in March 1862 when it forbade the practice of returning fugitive slaves to their masters. Slaves were still not legally free, but there was a tilt toward emancipation.

Gradually, Lincoln's policy of noninterference with slavery crumbled. To calm Northerners'

From Slaves to Contraband

Personally, Lincoln detested human bondage, but as president he felt compelled to act prudently in the interests of the Union. He doubted his right under the Constitution to tamper with the "domestic institutions" of any state, even states in rebellion. An astute politician, Lincoln worked within the limits of public opinion, and in 1861 he believed those limits were tight. The issue of black freedom was particularly explosive in the loyal border states, where slaveholders threatened to jump into the arms of the Confederacy at even the hint of emancipation. Black freedom also raised alarms in the free states. The Democratic Party gave notice that emancipation would kill the bipartisan alliance and make the war strictly a Republican affair. Democrats were as passionate for union as Republicans, but they marched under the banner "The Constitution As It Is, the Union As It Was."

Moreover, many white Northerners were not about to risk their lives to satisfy abolitionist "fanaticism." "We Won't Fight to Free the Nigger," one popular banner read. They feared that emancipation would propel "two or three million semi-savages" northward, where they would crowd into white neighborhoods, compete for white jobs, and mix with white "sons and daughters." A surge of anti-emancipation, antiblack sentiment, then, threatened to dislodge the loyal slave states from the Union, alienate the Democratic Party, deplete the armies, and perhaps even spark race warfare.

Yet proponents of emancipation pressed Lincoln as relentlessly as the anti-emancipation forces. Abolitionists argued that by seceding, Southerners had forfeited their right to the protection of the Constitution, and that Lincoln could—as the price of their treason—legally confiscate their property in slaves. When Lincoln refused, abolitionists scalded him. Frederick Douglass labeled him "the miserable tool of traitors and rebels." Abolitionists won increasing numbers of converts during the war, especially among the radical faction of the Republican Party.

The Republican-dominated Congress refused to leave slavery policy entirely in Lincoln's hands. In August 1861, Congress approved the Confiscation Act, which allowed the seizure of any slave employed directly by the Confederate military. The House and the Senate also fulfilled the **free-soil** dream of prohibiting slavery in the territories and abolished slavery in Washington, D.C. Democrats and border-state representatives voted against even these mild measures, but little by little, Congress displayed a stiffening of attitude as it cast about for a just and practical slavery policy.

Slaves, not politicians, became the most insistent force for emancipation. By escaping their masters by the tens of thousands and running away to Union lines, they forced slavery on the North's wartime agenda. Union officials could not ignore the flood of fugitives, and runaways precipitated a series of momentous decisions by the army, Congress, and the president. Were the runaways really free, or were they still slaves who, according to the fugitive slave law, had to be returned to their masters? At first, most Yankee military officers believed that administration policy required them to send the

> Slaves, not politicians, became the most insistent force for emancipation. By escaping their masters by the tens of thousands and running away to Union lines, they forced slavery on the North's wartime agenda.

Contrabands

These refugees from slavery crossed the Rappahannock River in Virginia in August 1862 to seek sanctuary with a federal army. Most slaves fled with little more than the clothes on their backs, but not all escaped slavery empty-handed. The oxen, wagon, and goods seen here could have been procured by a number of means—purchased during slavery, "borrowed" from the former master, or gathered during flight. Refugees who possessed draft animals and a wagon had much more economic opportunity than those who had only their labor to sell.
Library of Congress.

ports nearly at will. Taking on cargoes in the Caribbean, the sleek, fast blockade runners brought in vital supplies—guns and medicine—and also small quantities of luxury goods such as tea and liquor. But with the U.S. navy commissioning a new blockader almost weekly, the naval fleet eventually numbered 150 ships on duty, and the Union navy dramatically improved its score.

Unable to build a conventional navy equal to the expanding U.S. fleet, the Confederates experimented with a radical new maritime design: the ironclad warship. At Norfolk, Virginia, they layered the wooden hull of the frigate *Merrimack* with two-inch-thick armor plate. Rechristened *Virginia*, the ship steamed out in March 1862 to engage the wooden ships enforcing the federal blockade (see Map 15.2). Within a few hours, it sank two large federal ships, killing at least 240 Union sailors. The following morning, when the *Virginia* returned to finish off the federal blockaders, it was challenged by the *Monitor*, a federal ironclad that had arrived from Brooklyn during the night. The *Monitor*, a ship of even more radical design than the *Virginia*, was topped with a revolving turret containing two eleven-inch guns. On March 9, the two ships hurled shells at each other for two hours, but neither could penetrate the other's armor and the battle ended in a draw.

The Confederacy never found a way to break the Union blockade, despite exploring many naval innovations, including a new underwater vessel—the submarine. (See "The Promise of Technology," page 532.) Each month the Union fleet tightened its noose. By 1863, the South had abandoned its embargo policy and desperately wanted to ship cotton to pay for imports of the arms, bullets, shoes, and uniforms it needed to fight the war. But the growing effectiveness of the federal blockade, a southern naval officer observed, "shut the Confederacy out from the world, deprived it of supplies, weakened its military and naval strength." By 1865, the blockaders were intercepting about half of the southern ships attempting to break through.

What Confederates could not achieve on saltwater, they sought to achieve through foreign policy. According to their theory of King Cotton, cotton-starved European nations had no choice but to break the Union blockade and recognize the

> According to the theory of King Cotton, cotton-starved European nations had no choice but to break the Union blockade and recognize the Confederacy.

Confederacy. Britain and France briefly discussed joint action to lift the blockade in 1862 but rejected the notion. Some European nations granted the Confederacy "belligerent" status, which enabled it to buy goods and build ships in European ports, but none recognized the Confederate States of America as a nation, a bold act that probably would have drawn them into war with the United States.

King Cotton diplomacy failed for several reasons. A bumper cotton crop in 1860 meant that the warehouses of British textile manufacturers bulged with surplus cotton throughout 1861. In 1862, when Europe began to feel the pinch of a cotton shortage, manufacturers found new sources in Egypt and India. In addition, the development of a brisk trade between the Union and Britain—British war materiel for American grain and flour—helped offset the decline in textiles and encouraged Britain to remain neutral.

Europe's temptation to intervene disappeared for good in 1862. Union military successes on the rivers of the West made Britain and France think twice about linking their fates to the Confederacy. And in September 1862, five days after the northern victory at Antietam, Lincoln announced a new policy that made an alliance with the Confederacy an alliance with slavery, an alliance the French and British were not willing to make.

Union *and* Freedom

For a year and a half, Lincoln insisted that the abolition of slavery was not a northern war aim; the war, he said, was strictly to save the Union. But despite Lincoln's repeated pronouncements, the war for union became a war for African American freedom. Each month the conflict dragged on, it became clearer that the Confederate war machine depended heavily on slavery. Rebel armies used slaves to build fortifications, haul materiel, tend horses, and perform camp chores. On the home front, slaves labored in ironworks and shipyards, and they grew the food that fed both soldiers and civilians. Slavery undergirded the Confederacy as certainly as it had the Old South. In the field among Union military commanders, in the halls of Congress, and in the White House, the truth gradually came into focus: To defeat the Confederacy, the North would have to destroy slavery. "I am a slow walker," Lincoln said, "but I never walk back."

Colorado miners ambushed and crushed southern forces at Glorieta Pass, outside Santa Fe. One rebel soldier described the Unionists as "regular demons, that iron and lead had no effect upon, in the shape of Pike's Peakers from the Denver City Gold mines." (The Coloradans were commanded by Colonel John M. Chivington, who later shocked the nation in November 1864 when his volunteers massacred some 500 Cheyenne and Arapaho—primarily women and children—peacefully camped at Sand Creek, Colorado.) Confederate military failures in the far West in 1862 meant that there would be no Confederate empire beyond Texas.

Battle of Glorieta Pass, 1862

The principal western battles took place in Tennessee, where General Ulysses S. Grant emerged as the key northern commander. Grant had graduated from West Point and served bravely in Mexico. When the Civil War began, he was a thirty-nine-year-old dry-goods clerk in Galena, Illinois. Gentle at home, he became pugnacious on the battlefield. "The art of war is simple," he said. "Find out where your enemy is, get at him as soon as you can and strike him as hard as you can, and keep moving on." Grant's philosophy of war as annihilation would take a huge toll in human life, but it played to the North's strength: superiority in manpower. In his old uniform and slouch hat, with his tired, sad, nondescript face, Grant did not look much like a general. But Lincoln, who did not look much like a president, learned his worth. Later, to critics who wanted the president to sack Grant because of his drinking, Lincoln would say: *"I can't spare this man. He fights."*

In February 1862, operating in tandem with U.S. navy gunboats, Grant captured Fort Henry on the Tennessee River and Fort Donelson on the Cumberland (see Map 15.2). Defeat forced the Confederates to withdraw from all of Kentucky and most of Tennessee. Grant pushed after the retreating rebels. On April 6, General Albert Sidney Johnston's army surprised him at Shiloh Church in Tennessee. Grant's troops were badly mauled the first day, but Grant remained cool and brought up reinforcements throughout the night. The next morning, the Union army counterattacked, driving the Confederates before it. The Battle of Shiloh was terribly costly to both

sides; there were 20,000 casualties, among them General Johnston. Grant later said that after Shiloh he "gave up all idea of saving the Union except by complete conquest."

Although no one knew it at the time, Shiloh inflicted a mortal wound to the Confederacy's bid to control the theater of operations in the West. In short order, the Yankees captured the strategic town of Corinth, Mississippi, the river city of Memphis, and the South's largest city, New Orleans. By the end of 1862, the far West and most—but not all—of the Mississippi valley lay in Union hands. At the same time, the outcome of the struggle in another theater of war was also becoming clearer.

War and Diplomacy in the Atlantic Theater

At the beginning of the war, with a blockade fleet of only about three dozen ships and more than 3,500 miles of southern coastline to patrol, the U.S. navy faced an impossible task. At first, rebel merchant ships slipped in and out of southern

Major Battles of the Civil War, 1861–1862

April 12–13, 1861	Attack on Fort Sumter
July 21, 1861	First Battle of Bull Run (Manassas)
February 6, 1862	Battle of Fort Henry
February 16, 1862	Battle of Fort Donelson
March 9, 1862	Battle of the *Merrimack* (the *Virginia*) and the *Monitor*
March 26, 1862	Battle of Glorieta Pass
March 28, 1862	Battle of Pea Ridge
May–July 1862	McClellan's peninsula campaign
April 6–7, 1862	Battle of Shiloh
June 6, 1862	Fall of Memphis
June 25–July 1, 1862	Seven Days Battles
August 29–30, 1862	Second Battle of Bull Run (Manassas)
September 17, 1862	Battle of Antietam
December 13, 1862	Battle of Fredericksburg

Union Victories in the Western Theater

While most eyes focused on events in the East, the decisive early encounters of the war were taking place to the west, between the Appalachian Mountains and the Ozarks (see Map 15.2). The West's rivers—the Mississippi, the Tennessee, and the Cumberland—became the keys to the military situation. Looking northward along the three rivers, Southerners spied Missouri and Kentucky, states they claimed but did not control. Looking southward, Northerners saw that they would split Arkansas, Louisiana, and Texas from the Confederacy if they controlled the Mississippi River. The Cumberland and Tennessee rivers penetrated Tennessee, one of the Confederacy's main producers of food, mules, and iron—all vital resources.

> While most eyes focused on events in the East, the decisive early encounters of the war were taking place to the West between the Appalachian Mountains and the Ozarks.

Before the Federals could march on Tennessee, they needed to secure Missouri to the west. Union troops commanded by General Samuel R. Curtis swept across Missouri to the northwestern border of Arkansas. There, in March 1862 at Pea Ridge, they encountered General Earl Van Dorn's 16,000-man Confederate army, which included three regiments of Indians from the Five Civilized Nations in Indian Territory. Although Native Americans fought on both sides during the war, in this battle the Indians, mostly Cherokees, sided with the South because they hoped that the Confederacy would grant them more independence than had the United States. Curtis's victory at the Battle of Pea Ridge left Missouri free of Confederate troops and opened much of Arkansas to federal advance. But Missouri was not free of Confederate guerrillas. Guerrilla bands led by the notorious William Clarke Quantrill and "Bloody Bill" Anderson burned, tortured, scalped, and murdered Union civilians and soldiers until the final year of the war.

Farther west, Confederate armies sought to fulfill Jefferson Davis's vision of a slaveholding empire stretching all the way to the Pacific and even into Mexico. Both the Confederacy and the Union recognized the immense value of the gold and silver mines of California, Nevada, and Colorado. A quick strike by Texas troops had taken Sante Fe, New Mexico, in the winter of 1861–62. Then in March 1862, a band of

Native American Recruits
Both the Union and the Confederacy sought soldiers from tribes in Indian Territory. Here a Union recruiter swears in Indian recruits, but it was the Confederacy that signed treaties with the so-called Five Civilized Tribes—the Choctaw, Chickasaw, Creek, Seminole, and Cherokee—in 1861. Confederates promised to assume the financial obligations of the old treaties with the United States, guarantee slavery, respect the independence of the tribes, and permit the tribes to send delegates to Richmond. John Ross, chief of the Cherokee Nation, prayed that he had chosen the right side. "We are in the situation of a man standing upon a low naked spot of ground," he said, "with the water rising all around him. . . . The tide carries by him, in its mad course, a drifting log. . . . By refusing it he is a doomed man. By seizing hold of it he has a chance for his life." Several thousand Indians fought in blue and in gray uniforms. In some battles in Arkansas, Indians fought Indians.
Wisconsin Historical Society.

AMERICAN PLACES

Antietam National Battlefield, Sharpsburg, Maryland

Bloody Lane
Antietam National Battlefield.

Fresh from their victory at Second Manassas, General Robert E. Lee's troops reached Sharpsburg, Maryland, on September 15 and took up positions on the low ridge that runs along the western side of Antietam Creek. General George McClellan's army arrived on the east side of the creek that same day. On the morning of September 17, McClellan's troops attacked Lee's lines.

General Joseph "Fighting Joe" Hooker's men rushed forward, pouring into a cornfield, "loading and firing with demoniacal fury and shouting and laughing hysterically." So intense was the firing, Hooker remembered, that quickly "every stalk of corn in the . . . field was cut as closely as could have been done with a knife." Rival soldiers surged back and forth. According to some accounts, the field changed hands fifteen times before the Yankees prevailed.

A little to the south of Miller's Cornfield, Confederate troops concentrated in a 800-yard sunken road, worn down over the years by heavy wagons hauling grain. The well-protected rebels repelled four Union assaults. "For three hours and thirty minutes," a Union officer remembered, "the battle raged incessantly, without either party giving way." In the early afternoon, northern troops finally routed the rebels, but by then some 6,400 killed and mortally wounded soldiers lay along the sunken road, known thereafter as Bloody Lane.

South of Bloody Lane, Union general Ambrose E. Burnside's 12,000 men struggled to cross a 12-foot-wide bridge over Antietam Creek while 450 Georgia sharpshooters in a wooded bluff overlooking the bridge poured down lethal fire. Late in the day, Burnside's troops forced their way across and cleared out the Georgia defenders.

The fighting ended when night fell. The next morning, a Pennsylvania soldier wrote: "No tongue can tell, no mind can conceive, no pen portray the horrible sights I witnessed." Antietam proved to be one of the critical turning points in the Civil War. The U.S. army stopped the Confederacy's first invasion of the North, and the victory provided Lincoln an opportunity to transform the war for Union into a crusade for freedom. A national site since 1890, the Antietam battlefield offers visitors access to Miller's Cornfield, Bloody Lane, and "Burnside's Bridge," killing fields that silently testify to the fighting on that awful day.

For Web links related to this site and other American Places, see "PlaceLinks" at **bedfordstmartins.com/roark**.

ground separated the armies. "A chicken could not live on that field when we open on it," a Confederate artillery officer predicted. Yet Burnside ordered a frontal assault. Wave after wave of Union soldiers crashed against impregnable defenses. When the shooting finally ceased, the Federals counted nearly 13,000 casualties, the Confederates fewer than 5,000. The Battle of Fredericksburg was one of the Union's worst defeats. As 1862 ended, the North seemed no nearer to ending the rebellion than it had been when the war began. Rather than checkmate, military struggle in the East had reached stalemate.

Peninsula Campaign, 1862

holding the line at Manassas, and James E. B. (Jeb) Stuart, a dashing twenty-nine-year-old cavalry commander who rode circles around Yankee troops.

Lee's assault initiated the Seven Days Battle (June 25–July 1) and began McClellan's march back down the peninsula. By the time McClellan reached the water and the safety of the Union navy, 30,000 men from both sides had died or been wounded. Although Southerners suffered twice the casualties of Northerners, Lee had saved Richmond and achieved a strategic success. Lincoln wired McClellan to abandon the peninsula campaign and replaced him with General John Pope.

In August, north of Richmond, Pope had his own rendezvous with Lee. At the Second Battle of Bull Run, Lee's smaller army battered Pope's forces and sent them scurrying back to Washington. Lincoln ordered Pope to Minnesota to pacify Indians and again put McClellan in command. Lincoln had not changed his mind about McClellan's capacity as a warrior. But he reluctantly acknowl-

edged that "If he can't fight himself, he excels in making others ready to fight."

Lee could fight, and sensing that he had the enemy on the ropes, he sought to land the knockout punch. Lee pushed the Army of Northern Virginia across the Potomac and invaded Maryland. A victory on northern soil would dislodge Maryland from the Union, Lee reasoned, and might even cause Lincoln to sue for peace. On September 17, 1862, McClellan's forces finally engaged Lee's army at Antietam Creek (see Map 15.2). (See "American Places," page 527.) Earlier, a Union soldier had found a copy of Lee's orders to his army wrapped around some cigars dropped by a careless Confederate officer, so McClellan had a clear picture of Lee's position. McClellan's characteristic caution, however, cost him the opportunity to destroy the opposing army. Still, he did severe damage. With "solid shot . . . cracking skulls like eggshells," according to one observer, the armies went after each other. By nightfall, 6,000 men lay dead or dying on the battlefield, and 17,000 more had been wounded. The Battle of Antietam would be the bloodiest day of the war. Instead of being the war-winning fight Lee had anticipated when he came north, Antietam sent the battered Army of North Virginia limping back home. McClellan claimed to have saved the North, but Lincoln again removed him from command of the Army of the Potomac and appointed General Ambrose Burnside.

Although bloodied, Lee remained alert for an opportunity to punish the enemy. In December, Burnside provided that chance. At Fredericksburg, Virginia, Burnside's 122,000 Union troops faced 78,500 Confederates dug in behind a stone wall on the heights above the Rappahannock River. Half a mile of open

The Dead of Antietam

In October 1862, Mathew Brady opened at his New York gallery an exhibition that shocked the nation. Entitled "The Dead of Antietam," the exhibition consisted of ninety-five photographs and presented the battlefield as the soldiers saw it. This photograph shows the bodies of Confederate troops lined up for burial. Among the thousands of visitors to the exhibit was a reporter for the *New York Times*, who observed: "Mr. Brady has done something to bring to us the terrible reality and earnestness of the war. If he has not brought bodies and laid them in our door-yards and along [our] streets, he has done something very like it."

Library of Congress.

into a panicky stampede. Demoralized federal troops ran over shocked civilians as the soldiers raced back to Washington.

By Civil War standards, casualties (wounded and dead) at Bull Run (or Manassas, as Southerners called the battle) were light: about 2,000 Confederates and 1,600 Federals. The significance of the battle lay in the lessons Northerners and Southerners drew from it. For Southerners, it confirmed the superiority of rebel fighting men and the inevitability of Confederate nationhood. Manassas was *"one of the decisive battles of the world,"* a Georgian proclaimed. It *"has* secured our independence." While victory elevated southern pride, defeat sobered Northerners. It was a major setback, admitted the *New York Tribune*, but "Let us go to work, then, with a will." Bull Run taught Lincoln that victory would be neither quick nor easy. Within four days of the disaster, the president signed bills authorizing the enlistment of one million men for three years.

Lincoln also found a new general, replacing McDowell with young George B. McClellan. Born in Philadelphia of well-to-do parents, educated in the best schools before graduating from West Point second in his class, the thirty-four-year-old McClellan believed that he was a great soldier and that Lincoln was a dunce, the "original Gorilla." A superb administrator and organizer, McClellan came to Washington as commander of the newly named Army of the Potomac. In the months following his appointment, McClellan energetically whipped his dispirited army into shape but was reluctant to send his soldiers into battle. For all his energy, McClellan lacked decisiveness. Lincoln wanted a general who would advance, take risks, and fight, but McClellan went into winter quarters without budging from the banks of the Potomac. "If General McClellan does not want to use the army I would like to *borrow* it," Lincoln declared in frustration.

The Battle of Savage's Station, Robert Knox Sneden, 1862
In 1862, thirty-year-old Robert Sneden joined the Fortieth New York Volunteers and soon found himself in Virginia, part of George McClellan's peninsula campaign. A gifted artist in watercolor as well as an eloquent writer, Sneden captures here an early Confederate assault in what became known as the Seven Days Battle. "The immense open space in front of Savage's [house] was densely thronged with wagon trains, artillery, caissons, ammunition trains, and moving troops," Sneden observed. The "storm of lead was continuous and deadly on the approaching lines of the Rebels. They bravely rushed up, however, to within twenty feet of our artillery, when bushels of grape and canister from the cannon laid them low in rows." Over the next three years, Sneden produced hundreds of vivid drawings and eventually thousands of pages of remembrance, providing one of the most complete accounts of a Union soldier's Civil War experience.
© 1996, Lora Robbins Collection of Virginia Art, Virginia Historical Society.

Finally, in May 1862, McClellan launched his long-awaited offensive. He transported his highly polished army, now 130,000 strong, down the Chesapeake Bay to the mouth of the James River and began moving up the Yorktown peninsula toward Richmond. McClellan took two and a half months to advance a mere sixty-five miles. When he was within six miles of the Confederate capital, the Confederate general Joseph Johnston hit him like a hammer. In the assault, Johnston was wounded and was replaced by Robert E. Lee, the reluctant Confederate, who would become the South's most celebrated general. Lee named his command the Army of Northern Virginia.

The contrast between Lee and McClellan could hardly have been greater. McClellan brimmed with conceit and braggadocio; Lee was courteous and reserved. On the battlefield, McClellan grew timid and irresolute, and Lee became audaciously, even recklessly, aggressive. And Lee had at his side in the peninsula campaign military men of real talent: General Thomas J. Jackson, nicknamed "Stonewall" for

The C.S.S. H. L. Hunley *at Charleston, 6 December 1863,* Conrad Wise Chapman
This striking image of the *Hunley* makes clear why General P. G. T. Beauregard felt compelled to explain to men who were considering volunteering for its crew the "desperately hazardous nature of the service required." The artist contrasts the grim reality of the submarine with the beautiful (and safe) sailboat in the distance.
Museum of the Confederacy.

teen men, including H. L. Hunley himself. The sinkings were apparently caused by accidents, not design flaws. After the second accident, however, Beauregard declared, "I can have nothing more to do with that submarine boat. It is more dangerous to those who use it than the enemy." But Charleston's plight caused him to raise the sub and man it with an all-volunteer crew. The *Hunley* did no more damage after its destruction of the *Housatonic* in 1864, when it sank for a third and final time for unknown reasons. No submarine would sink an enemy ship until World War I, more than a half century later.

Much of what we know about the world's first successful submarine comes from discovery of the *Hunley* in May 1995, four miles off Sullivan's Island, South Carolina, in thirty feet of water and under three feet of sand. One marine **archaeologist** described it as the "find of the century." Raised in August 2000 and deposited in a large steel tank filled with 55,000 gallons of cold fresh water to protect it from further deterioration, the *Hunley* is today the object of intensive investigation; scientists and historians are successfully teasing evidence of its past from its remains. Essentially a time capsule, the *Hunley* has not yet given an answer to the question of why it did not return safely to Charleston harbor, but investigators are closing in on the answer.

tower had small round windows. The vessel was equipped with a kind of snorkel for air, but because it never worked, the sub had to surface every half hour or so for fresh air. The *Hunley* also was outfitted with a mercury depth gauge, a compass, and a single wax candle, which provided not only light but a warning when the oxygen level became dangerously low.

Desperate to break the Union blockade in Charleston, General P. G. T. Beauregard ordered the *Hunley* loaded on a train and shipped from Mobile to Charleston harbor. Test runs began immediately, and the sub sank twice, with the loss of thir-

racial fears, which he considered the chief obstacle to Union acceptance of emancipation, Lincoln offered **colonization**, the deportation of African Americans from the United States to Haiti, Panama, or elsewhere. (For earlier colonization efforts in Liberia, see pages 430–31.) In the summer of 1862, he defended colonization to a delegation of black visitors to the White House. He told them that deep-seated racial prejudice made it impossible for blacks to achieve equality in this country. An African American from Philadelphia spoke for the group when he told the president, "This is our country as much as it is yours, and we will not leave it." Congress voted a small amount of money to underwrite colonization, but after one miserable experiment on a small island in the Caribbean, practical limitations and black opposition sank further efforts.

While Lincoln was developing his own initiatives, he snuffed out actions that he believed would jeopardize northern unity. He was particularly alert to Union commanders who tried to dictate slavery policy from the field. In August 1861, when John C. Frémont, former Republican presidential nominee and now commander of federal troops in Missouri, impetuously freed the slaves belonging to Missouri rebels, Lincoln forced the general to revoke his edict and then removed him from command. The following May, when General David Hunter issued a proclamation freeing the slaves in Georgia, South Carolina, and Florida, Lincoln countermanded his order. Events moved so rapidly, however, that Lincoln found it impossible to control federal policy on slavery.

> Lincoln described emancipation as an "act of justice," but it was the lengthening casualty lists that finally brought him around.

From Contraband to Free People

On August 22, 1862, Lincoln replied to an angry abolitionist who demanded that he go after slavery. "My paramount objective in this struggle *is* to save the Union," Lincoln said deliberately, "and is *not* either to save or destroy slavery. If I could save the Union without freeing *any* slave I would do it, and if I could save it by freeing *all* the slaves I would do it; and if I could save it by freeing some and leaving others alone I would also do that." At first glance, it seemed a restatement of his old position: that union was the North's sole objective. But what marked it as a radical departure was Lincoln's refusal to say that slavery was untouchable. Instead, he said that he would emancipate every slave if doing so would preserve the Union.

By the summer of 1862, events were tumbling rapidly toward emancipation. On July 17, Congress adopted a second Confiscation Act. The first had confiscated slaves employed by the Confederate military; the second declared all slaves of rebel masters "forever free of their servitude." In theory, this breathtaking measure freed most of the slaves in the Confederacy, for slaveholders formed the backbone of the rebellion. Congress had traveled far since the war began. Lincoln had too. On July 21, the president informed his cabinet that he was ready "to take some definitive steps in respect to military action and slavery." The next day, he read a draft of a preliminary emancipation proclamation that promised to free *all* slaves in the seceding states on January 1, 1863.

Lincoln described emancipation as an "act of justice," but it was the lengthening casualty lists that finally brought him around. Emancipation, he declared, was "a military necessity, absolutely essential to the preservation of the Union." Only freeing the slaves would "strike at the heart of the rebellion." His cabinet favored Lincoln's plan but advised him to wait for a military victory before announcing it so that critics would not call it an act of desperation. On September 22, after Antietam, he promised freedom to all slaves in all areas still in rebellion on January 1, 1863.

The limitations of the proclamation—it exempted the loyal border states and Union-occupied areas of the Confederacy—caused some to ridicule the act. The *London Times* observed cynically, "Where he has no power Mr. Lincoln will set the negroes free, where he retains power he will consider them as slaves." But Lincoln had no power to free slaves in loyal states, and invading Union armies would liberate slaves in the Confederacy as they advanced.

By presenting emancipation as a "military necessity," Lincoln hoped he had disarmed his **conservative** critics. Emancipation would deprive the Confederacy of valuable slave laborers, shorten the war, and thus save lives. Democrats, however, exploded with rage. They charged that the "shrieking and howling abolitionist faction" had captured the White House and made it "a nigger war." The fall 1862 congressional elections were only weeks away, and Democrats sought to make political hay out of Lincoln's action. War-weariness probably had as much to do with the results as emancipation, but Democrats gained thirty-four congressional seats. House Democrats quickly proposed a resolution branding emancipation "a high crime against the Constitution." The Republicans, who maintained narrow majorities in both houses of Congress, beat it back.

As promised, on New Year's Day 1863, Lincoln issued the final Emancipation Proclamation. In addition to freeing the slaves in the states that were in rebellion, the edict also committed the federal government to the fullest use of African Americans to defeat the Confederate enemy.

War of Black Liberation

Even before Lincoln proclaimed freedom a Union war aim, African Americans in the North had volunteered to fight. But the War Department, doubtful of their abilities and fearful of white reaction to serving side by side with them, refused to make black men soldiers. Instead, the army employed black men as manual laborers; black women sometimes found employment as laundresses and cooks. The navy, however, from the outset accepted blacks, including runaway slaves like William Gould, as sailors. They usually served in noncombatant roles, but within months a few blacks served on gun crews.

As the Union experienced manpower shortages, Northerners gradually and reluctantly turned to African Americans to fill the Union army's blue uniforms. With the Militia Act of July 1862, Congress authorized enrolling blacks in "any military or naval service for which they may be found competent." Lingering resistance to black military service largely disappeared in 1863. After the Emancipation Proclamation, whites—like it or not—were fighting and dying for black freedom, and few were likely to insist that blacks remain out of harm's way behind the lines. Indeed, rather than resist black military participation, whites insisted that blacks share the danger, especially after March 1863, when Congress resorted to the **draft** to fill the Union army.

Black soldiers discovered that the military was far from color-blind. The Union army established segregated black regiments, paid black soldiers $10 per month rather than the $13 it paid to whites, refused blacks the opportunity to become commissioned officers, punished blacks as if they were slaves, and assigned blacks to labor battalions rather than to combat units. But nothing deterred black recruits. When the war ended, 179,000 African American men had served in the Union military, approximately 10 percent of the army total. An astounding 71 percent of black men ages eighteen to forty-five in the free states wore Union blue, a participation rate that was substantially higher than that of white men. More than 130,000 black soldiers came from the slave states, perhaps 100,000 of them ex-slaves.

In time, whites allowed blacks to put down their shovels and to shoulder rifles. At the battles of Port Hudson and Milliken's Bend on the Mississippi River and at Fort Wagner in Charleston harbor, black courage under fire

Guard Detail of the 107th U.S. Colored Infantry, Arlington, Virginia, 1865

A white man's war when it began, the Civil War eventually gained color, as this photograph of the soldiers of the 107th U.S. Colored Infantry attests. The Lincoln administration was slow to accept black soldiers, in part because of lingering doubts about their ability to fight. Colonel Thomas W. Higginson, a white Massachusetts clergyman and abolitionist, commanded the First South Carolina Infantry, which was made up of former slaves. After his regiment's first skirmish with Confederate troops, Higginson celebrated his men's courage: "No officer in this regiment now doubts that the key to the successful prosecution of this war lies in the unlimited employment of black troops. . . . Instead of leaving their homes and families to fight they are fighting for their homes and families." After the spring of 1863, the federal government did all it could to maximize the number of black soldiers. Eventually, ex-slaves and free blacks filled 145 Union regiments. Throughout the war, however, policy required that blacks serve under white commissioned officers.

© Bettmann/Corbis.

finally dispelled notions that African Americans could not fight. More than 38,000 black soldiers died in the Civil War, a mortality rate that was higher than that of white troops. Blacks played a crucial role in the triumph of the Union and the destruction of slavery in the South.

The South at War

By seceding, Southerners brought on themselves a firestorm of unimaginable fury. Monstrous losses on the battlefields nearly bled the Confederacy to death. White Southerners on the home front also suffered, even at the hands of their own government. Efforts by the Davis administration in Richmond to centralize power to fight the war effectively convinced some men and women that the Confederacy had betrayed them. Wartime economic changes hurt everyone, some more than others. By 1863, planters and

yeomen who had stood together began to drift apart. Most disturbing of all, slaves became open participants in the destruction of slavery and the Confederacy.

Revolution from Above

As one Confederate general observed, Southerners were engaged in a total war "in which the whole population and the whole production . . . are to be put on a war footing, where every institution is to be made auxiliary to war." When Jefferson Davis became president of the Confederacy in 1861, he faced the task of building an army and navy from scratch, supplying them from factories that were scarce and anemic, and paying for it all from a treasury that did not exist. Building the army proved easiest. Hundreds of officers defected from the U.S. army, and hundreds of thousands of eager young rebels volunteered to follow them. Very quickly, the Confederacy developed formidable striking power.

The Confederacy's economy and finances proved tougher. Because of the Union blockade, the government had no choice but to build an industrial sector itself. Government-owned clothing and shoe factories, mines, arsenals, and powder works "sprung up almost like magic," according to one Mississippian. In addition, the government harnessed private companies, such as the huge Tredegar Iron Works in Richmond, to the war effort. The financial task proved most difficult because Southerners had invested their capital in land and slaves, which Confederate officials found difficult to tap for the war effort. Richmond came up with a mix of bonds, taxes, and paper money to finance the war.

Despite its bold measures, however, the Davis administration failed to transform the slave-labor, staple-producing agricultural economy into a modern industrial one. The Confederacy manufactured much more than most people imagined possible, but it never produced all that the South needed. Each month, the gap between the North's and the South's production widened. Moreover, the flood of paper money coming from Richmond caused debilitating inflation. By 1863, Charlestonians paid ten times more for food than they had paid at the start of the war. By Christmas 1864, a Confederate soldier's monthly pay no longer bought a pair of socks.

Richmond's war-making effort meant that government intruded in unprecedented ways into the private lives of Confederate citizens. In April 1862, the Confederate Congress passed the first **conscription** (draft) law in American history. All able-bodied white males between the ages of eighteen and thirty-five (later seventeen and fifty) were liable to serve in the rebel army for three years. The Confederate government adopted a policy of impressment, which allowed officials to confiscate food, horses, wagons, and whatever else they wanted from private citizens and to pay for them at below-market rates. After March 1863, the Confederacy also legally impressed slaves, employing them as military laborers. In addition, Richmond took control of the South's railroads and shipping.

The war necessitated much of the government's unprecedented behavior, but citizens found it arbitrary and inequitable. Richmond's

Confederate Soldiers and Their Slaves
Soldiers of the Seventh Tennessee Cavalry pose with their slaves. Many slaveholders took "body servants" with them to war. These slaves cooked, washed, and cleaned for the white soldiers. In 1861, James H. Langhorne reported to his sister: "Peter . . . is charmed with being with me & 'being a soldier.' I gave him my old uniform overcoat & he says he is going to have his picture taken . . . to send to the servants." Do you think Peter was "puttin' on ol' massa" or just glad to be free of plantation labor?
Daguerreotype courtesy of Tom Farish. Photographed by Michael Latil.

FOR MORE HELP ANALYZING THIS IMAGE, see the visual activity for this chapter in the Online Study Guide at bedfordstmartins.com/roark.

centralizing efforts ran head-on into the South's traditional values of **states' rights** and unfettered individualism. The states lashed out at what Georgia governor Joseph E. Brown denounced as the "dangerous usurpation by Congress of the reserved right of the States." Richmond and the states struggled for control of money, supplies, and soldiers, with damaging consequences for the war effort. Individual citizens also remembered that Davis had promised to defend southern "liberty" against Republican "despotism." In time, Southerners named Jefferson Davis as the politician they hated most, after Lincoln.

Hardship Below

Hardships were widespread, but they fell most heavily on the poor. Inflation, for example, threatened the poor with starvation. Salt— necessary for preserving meat—shot up from $2 to $60 a bag during the first year of the war. Flour that cost three or four cents a pound in 1861 cost thirty-five cents in 1863. The draft depopulated yeoman farms of men, leaving the women and children to grow what they ate. A rampaging army, a drought, a sickness, a lame mule—any one calamity could cost a family a vital crop. When farm wives succeeded in bringing in a harvest, government agents took 10 percent of it as a "tax-in-kind" on agriculture. Like inflation, shortages also afflicted the entire population, but the rich lost luxuries while the poor lost necessities. In the spring of 1863, bread riots broke out in a dozen cities and villages across the South. In Richmond, a mob of nearly a thousand hungry women broke into shops and took what they needed.

Severe deprivation had powerful consequences. One southern leader observed in November 1862, "Men cannot be expected to fight for the Government that permits their wives & children to starve." A few wealthy individuals shared their bounty, the Confederacy

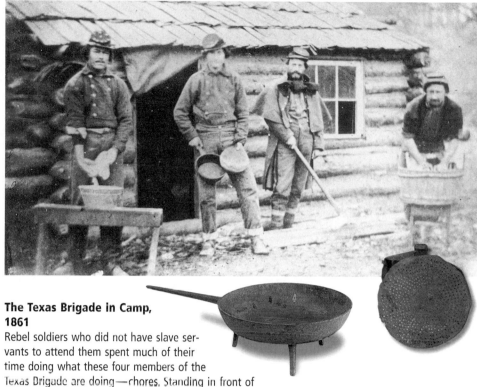

The Texas Brigade in Camp, 1861
Rebel soldiers who did not have slave servants to attend them spent much of their time doing what these four members of the Texas Brigade are doing—chores. Standing in front of their winter quarters near Dumfries, Virginia, the Texans are busy washing dishes, washing clothes, chopping firewood, and cooking. The soldier with the skillet displays the cornbread he has just cooked. Confederate troops ate salted meat and cornbread more than anything else. A federal officer marching through an abandoned rebel camp near Sharpsburg, Maryland, in 1862 recalled that "huge corn cakes, 2 inches thick and 12 to 15 inches wide, lay in piles and were kicked along the road by our men." Southerners learned to appreciate anything on their plates, but soldiers grew very tired of the old standbys. "If any person offers me cornbread after this war comes to a close," a Louisianan declared just before Lee's surrender, "I shall probably tell him to— go to hell!" Atlanta History Center, Austin Public Library, Museum of the Confederacy.

made some efforts at social welfare, and the states did even more; but every effort fell short. In late 1864, one desperate farm wife told her husband: "I have always been proud of you, and since your connection with the Confederate army, I have been prouder of you than ever before. I would not have you do anything wrong for the world, but before God, Edward, unless you come home, we must die." By some estimates, when the war ended, one-third of the soldiers had already gone home. A Mississippi deserter explained, "We are poor men and are willing to defend our country but our families [come] first." (See "Documenting the American Promise," page 538.)

The Confederacy also failed to persuade the suffering white majority that the war's burdens were being shared equally. Instead, yeomen saw a profound inequality of sacrifice. They called it

Home and Country

Husbands fighting for the Confederacy and wives back home exchanged countless letters during the war. They wrote movingly of family, hardships, and battles, and they shared their deepest loves and fears. Their letters, which were uncensored, often revealed the conflicting tugs of home and country.

Christian Marion Epperly and his wife, Mary Epperly, lived in the Blue Ridge Mountains of Virginia. Although neither was an ardent secessionist, Marion entered the army as a private early in 1862. He saw action in the eastern and western theaters of the war. He hated army life and longed for his wife and children. Mary was equally heartsick without Marion. The couple's letters reveal their limited schooling, but more important they show how plain folks wrestled with the tangled issues of personal and political loyalties and obligations.

DOCUMENT 1
Letter from Chickahominy Creek, Virginia, May 16, 1862

During the peninsula campaign in Virginia, as Union general George B. McClellan was approaching the Confederate capital of Richmond, Marion wrote to Mary from near the action.

I think the people will be bound to suffer for something to eat[;] the grain is all destroid and nearly all the fenses is burnt up from yorktown to Richmond: it looks distressing just to travel along the road: the wheat up waist hi some of it and horses and cattle has eat the most of it to the ground and I think the yankees will make a finish of the ballans [balance] that is left but the[y] cant doo much more damage than our army did[;] our own men killed all the cattle and hogs & sheep that the farmers had[,] even took ther chickens[;] every thing is totally destroid in this part of the State[.] I don't think the yankeys could doo much wors if they had a chanse[.]

I hope and pray this awful war will soon come to a close some way or another[,] any way to get pease in the world wonst more[;] it seems to me I had drather be at home and live on bred and water than to have this war hanging over us but I pray god pease will soon be made[.] I dont think the war can last long.

DOCUMENT 2
Letter from Camp near Bells Bridge, Tennessee, August 15, 1863

By the summer of 1863, Marion's regiment had moved to Tennessee, where he notices increasing war weariness, desertions, and disillusionment with the Confederacy.

You don't know how glad I would be if I was just thar with you this morning to see the sun rise over the hills in Virginia again[,] for everry thing seames so sad and desolate here this morning; it seames like the absens of dear friends and the present condition of things has brought deep refletion and sadnes upon everry heart, and [men] are growing weary and getting out of heart and leaving the Army everry day. I cant tell wheather it will be for the better or wheather it will make things wors: but I hope it is a way god has provided to bring this war and time of sorrow to an end and to give us pease in our land again: Thoug I believe the south first started on a just course but our own wickedness and disobedians has brought us to what we are and I firmly believe wee will be bound to give up to subjugation[.] I don't think the south will stand much longer, and I am sorrow to say it for wee will be a ruined people while time ma [may] last, but wee ought to submit to any thing to have this awwful war ended.

DOCUMENT 3
Letter from Floyd County, Virginia, August 16, 1863

Mary longs for peace and argues that desertion will end the war.

Oh how much beter satisfied would I be if you was just hear with me this beatiful Sabath morning. I feel as if my troubles on earth would all be over if you was just at home to stay wonst more[,] but god sent it upon us and we will have to bear with it the best we can but I do pray that he may soon end this destressing time some way[.] I would be willing for it to end most any way just so it would end[.] Dear Marion I think if the head men dont soon end this war that the soldiers will for they are runing way from down east by hundreds[;] they was five hundard went though hear last weak and well armed and they say they wont go back any more and I dont blame them for it[.] I wish they would all runaway and these head men would be oblige to fight it out but as long as they can stay at home and speculate off of the poor soulders they dont care how long the war lasts[.] Serious Smith wrote a leter the 9 of this month and he wrote that they had to pay 15 dolars for a bushel of taters . . . how can the poor soulders make out and only get a leven [eleven] dolars a month[?] He wrote that they sawd very hard times down thare and had a heap of hard fighting to do[;] they had a fight the 1 and 4 of this month and he wrote that thare was five wounded and more killed and they was expecting a fight every hour.

DOCUMENT 4
Letter from Floyd County, Virginia, December 4, 1863

Mary tells Marion that the Confederacy's new conscription law has thrown their neighborhood into turmoil.

It seams like things [are in] such a uproar that I cant keep my mind together long a nuff to write a leter as it aut to be wrote[;] people has never bin in such a uproar and confusion hear since the war as they are now[;] thare is orders now to take up every man between the age of 17 and 50 that hasent reported and if they hant [aren't] able to walk they have to hall them. . . . Dear Husban I expect they will pass a law yet to take the wimen for they have taken all the men and children almost ded and alive and the next I read I recon will be for the wiman. Dear Marion hour Country has got in a turable fix[;] thare is nothing but sorow and destress in this world any more[;] when I set and study about it and think if I could just take you and my dear litle children with me to heaven I would be willing to do to day but Dear Husban wee was born in this world to see trouble and wee will have to put up with it the best wee can and pray for a beter day to come which I hope is not fare off.

DOCUMENT 5
Letter from Outskirts of Dalton, Georgia, March 25, 1864

As his regiment is backing toward Atlanta, trying to fend off Sherman, Marion considers what has gone wrong with the Confederacy.

I dont think it will last much longer if the souldiers doo what they say they will doo[;] they are all verry tired of this war and the way it is carried on[.] I think wee all have stud it about as long as we can unless our leading men dos a heap better than they ever have yet: if they wer God fearing men I would think wee would prosper but so long as they [seek] the Bottom of a Whiskey Barl and frolick around bad places just so long we will hafto fight and suffer. . . . we was all Born in a free land and I think wee ought to stil be free and not be bound down wors than slaves[;] we wonst had a union and was living happy and had all man can wish for[;] now we are cut off from that union and what are wee nothing but a ruend people as long as we shal live . . . dissatisfaction and wickedness all over the south[;] may God show us our errors and put us in the rite way and Bring us Back to our old union again.

DOCUMENT 6
Letter from Floyd County, Virginia, March 24, 1865

Mary expects a Yankee victory and says again that Confederate soldiers can end the war by deserting. Despite his doubts about the Confederacy and continued affection for the Union, Marion left the army without authorization only once, and after a few weeks at home in 1863, he returned to his regiment. Like many

disillusioned soldiers, he fought in the rebel army to the very end.

Dear Marion they are looking every day for the yankees to take Richmond and Linchburg and I do wish from my hart that they had it now for I am not afrade of the yankeys treating us any worse nor not half as bad as our own men dos for they have taking all the men or tride to take all that is any acout [account] and are now taking the horses. . . . How much worse could the yankeys do than that[?] . . . It lais in the souldires hands now to make pease and I do wish that they may make it soon[;] our strongest sesess [secessionists] hear say that wee are whiped and they have nown [known] it for some time but was ashame to own it.

Source: Christian M. Epperly Correspondence, Gilder Lehrman Collection, Pierpont Morgan Library, New York.

QUESTIONS FOR ANALYSIS AND DEBATE

1. For Marion and Mary Epperly, what explains the suffering of the South in the Civil War? How do they each see the matter differently?

2. How does Marion contrast life in the Union with life in the Confederacy?

3. In what ways does the Epperlys' perspective on the Confederacy reflect their social position as plain folk in Virginia society?

4. Marion makes clear why he had such affection for his home; he is much less clear about why he fought for the Confederacy. What might some of his reasons have been?

Yeomen saw a profound inequality of sacrifice. They called it "a rich man's war and a poor man's fight," and they had evidence.

"a rich man's war and a poor man's fight," and they had evidence. The original draft law permitted a man who had money to hire a substitute to take his place. Moreover, the "twenty-Negro law" exempted one white man on every plantation with twenty or more slaves. The government intended this law to provide protection for white women and to see that slaves tended the crops, but yeomen perceived it as rich men evading military service. A slaveless Mississippian complained to his governor about stay-at-home planters who sent their slaves into the fields to grow cotton while in plain view "poor soldiers' wives are plowing with *their own* hands to make a subsistence for themselves and children—while their husbands are suffering, bleeding and dying for their country." In fact, most slaveholders went off to war, but the extreme suffering of common folk and the relative immunity of planters fueled class animosity.

The Richmond government hoped that the crucible of war would mold a region into a nation. Officials and others worked tirelessly to promote a vibrant southern **nationalism** that, as one Confederate politician said, would "excite in our citizens an ardent and enduring attachment to our Government and its institutions." Clergymen assured their congregations that God had blessed slavery and the new nation. Jefferson Davis asked citizens to observe national days of fasting and prayer. Patriotic songwriters, poets, authors, and artists extolled southern culture. But it proved difficult to create a united slave republic in the midst of all-out war. Efforts to build consensus never succeeded in winning over thousands of die-hard Unionists. And friction between yeomen and planters increased rather than decreased. The war also threatened to rip the southern social fabric along its racial seam.

The Disintegration of Slavery

The legal destruction of slavery was the product of presidential proclamation, congressional legislation, and eventually constitutional amendment, but the practical destruction of slavery was the product of war, what Lincoln called war's "friction and abrasion." War exposed the flimsy nature of planter **paternalism** and the illusion of slave contentment. Rather than laboring faithfully, protecting their white folks, and

Maria Isabella ("Belle") Boyd, Spy
Most white southern women, in addition to keeping their families fed and safe, served the Confederate cause by sewing uniforms, knitting socks, rolling bandages, and nursing the sick and wounded. But Belle Boyd became a spy. Only seventeen when the war broke out, she became in the words of a northern journalist "insanely devoted to the rebel cause." Her first act for the Confederacy came on July 3, 1861, when she shot a drunken federal soldier who barged into her Virginia home and insulted her mother. Her relations with occupying northern troops improved, and soon this compelling young woman was eavesdropping on officers' conversations and slipping messages to Confederate armies. Boyd's information handed Stonewall Jackson an easy victory at Front Royal, Virginia, in May 1862. "I thank you," the general wrote Boyd, ". . . for the immense service that you have rendered your country today." Imprisoned several times for spying, Boyd took up a theatrical career when the war ended.
Courtesy Warren Rifles Confederate Museum, Front Royal, VA.

hiding the mistress's silver from marauding Yankees, slaves took advantage of the upheaval to reach for freedom. Some half a million of the South's four million slaves ran away to northern military lines. More than 100,000 men fled bondage, took up arms as federal soldiers and sailors, and attacked slavery directly. Other men and women stayed in the slave quarters, where they staked their claim to more freedom.

In dozens of ways, the war disrupted the routine, organization, and discipline of bondage. Almost immediately, for example, it called the master away, leaving white women to assume additional managerial responsibilities. But neither plantation mistresses nor masters could maintain traditional standards of slave discipline in wartime.

In large parts of the South, the balance of power between master and slave gradually shifted. Slaveholders complained about the slaves' "demoralization" and "betrayal." Slaves got to the fields late, worked indifferently, and quit early. Some slaveholders responded violently; most saw no alternative but to strike bargains—offering gifts or part of the crop—to keep slaves at home and at work. An Alabama woman reported that she "begged . . . what little is done." Changes in slave behavior shocked slaveholders. They had prided themselves on "knowing" their slaves, and they learned that they did not know them at all. When the war began, a North Carolina woman praised her slaves as "diligent and respectful." When it ended, she said, "As to the idea of a *faithful servant, it is all a fiction.*"

As military action increasingly sliced through the South's farms and plantations, some slaveholders fled, leaving behind their slaves. Many more took their slaves with them, but flight meant additional chaos and offered slaves new opportunities to resist bondage. Whites' greatest fear—retaliatory violence—rarely occurred. Instead, slaves undermined white mastery and expanded control over their own lives.

The North at War

Because rebel armies generally operated within the Confederate borders, most of the North was untouched by fighting. But Northerners could not avoid being touched by war. Almost every family had a son, a husband, a brother in uniform. Moreover, this war—a total war—blurred the distinction between home front and battlefield. As in the South, men marched off to fight, but preserving the country, either Union or Confederacy, was also women's work. For civilians as well as soldiers, for women as well as men, war was transforming.

The need to build and fuel the Union war machine boosted the northern economy. The North sent nearly 2 million men into the military and still increased production in almost every area. But because the rewards and burdens of patriotism were not evenly distributed, the North experienced sharp, even violent, divisions. Workers confronted employers, whites confronted blacks, and Democrats confronted Republicans. Still, Northerners on the home front remained fervently attached to the ideals of **free labor** and the Union.

The Government and the Economy

When the war began, the United States had no national banking system, no national currency, and no federal income or excise taxes. But the secession of eleven slave states cut the Democrats' strength in Congress in half and destroyed their capacity to resist Republican economic programs. The Legal Tender Act of February 1862 created a national currency, paper money that Northerners called "greenbacks." With passage of the National Banking Act in February 1863, Congress created a system of national banks that by the 1870s had largely replaced the **antebellum** system of decentralized state banks. Congress also enacted a series of sweeping tax laws that encompassed everything from incomes to liquor to billiard tables. The Internal Revenue Act created the Bureau of Internal Revenue to collect taxes. In addition, Congress enacted a higher tariff to increase revenues and protect manufacturers against foreign competition. By revolutionizing the country's banking, monetary, and tax structures, the Republicans generated enormous economic power.

> The secession of eleven slave states cut the Democrats' strength in Congress in half and destroyed their capacity to resist Republican economic programs.

Some of the Republicans' wartime legislation was designed to integrate the West more thoroughly into the Union. In May 1862, Congress approved the Homestead Act, which offered public land—limited to 160 acres to prevent the spread of plantations—to settlers who would live and labor on it. The Homestead Act bolstered western loyalty and in time resulted in more than a million new farms. The passage of the Pacific Railroad Act in July 1862 provided massive federal assistance for building a transcontinental railroad that ran from Omaha to San Francisco when completed in 1869. Congress

Union Ordnance, Yorktown, Virginia
As the North successfully harnessed its enormous industrial capacity to the needs of war, cannon, mortars, and shells poured out of its factories. A fraction of that abundance is seen here in 1862 at Yorktown, ready for transportation to Union troops in the field. Two years later, Abraham Lincoln observed that the Union was "gaining strength, and may if need be maintain the contest indefinitely. . . . Material resources are now more complete and abundant than ever. . . . The national resources are unexhausted, and, as we believe, inexhaustible." Library of Congress.

FOR MORE HELP ANALYZING THIS IMAGE, see the visual activity for this chapter in the Online Study Guide at bedfordstmartins.com/roark.

further bound East and West by subsidizing the Pony Express mail service and a transcontinental telegraph.

Two additional initiatives had long-term consequences for agriculture and industry. Congress created a Department of Agriculture and passed the Land-Grant College Act (also known as the Morrill Act after its sponsor, Representative Justin Morrill of Vermont), which set aside public lands to support universities that emphasized "agriculture and mechanical arts." Republicans defended their wartime legislation by arguing that additional economic muscle meant increased military might. Initiatives from

the Lincoln administration in Washington immeasurably strengthened the North's effort to win the war, but they were also permanently changing the nation.

Women and Work on the Home Front

More than a million farm men were called to the military, so farm women added men's chores to their own. "I met more women driving teams on the road and saw more at work in the fields than men," a visitor to Iowa reported in the fall of 1862. Rising production figures testified to their success in plowing, planting, and harvesting. Rapid mechanization assisted farm women in their new roles. Cyrus McCormick sold 165,000 of his reapers during the war years. The combination of high prices for farm products and increased production ensured that war and prosperity joined hands in the rural North.

A few industries, such as textiles (which depended on southern cotton), declined during the war, but many more grew. Huge profits prompted one Pennsylvania ironmaster to remark, "I am in no hurry for peace." With orders pouring in and a million nonfarm workers siphoned off into the military, unemployment declined and wages often rose. The boom proved friendlier to owners than to workers, however. Inflation and taxes cut so deeply into their paychecks that workers' standard of living actually fell.

Women in cities also stepped into jobs vacated by men, particularly in manufacturing, and also into essentially new occupations such as government secretaries and clerks. Many had no choice because they could not make ends meet on their husbands' army pay. Women made up about one-quarter of the manufacturing workforce when the war began and one-third when it ended. As more and more women entered the workforce, employers cut wages. By 1864, New York seamstresses working fourteen-hour days earned only an average of $1.54 a week. Cincinnati seamstresses complained to Abraham Lincoln that their wages were not enough "to sustain life." Urban workers resorted increasingly to strikes to wrench decent salaries from their employers, but their protests rarely succeeded. Nevertheless, tough times failed to undermine the patriotism of most workers, who took pride in their contribution to northern victory.

Middle-class white women were expected to be homebodies, and hundreds of thousands of them contributed to the war effort in traditional ways. Like southern white women, they sewed, wrapped bandages, and sold homemade goods at local fairs to raise money to aid the soldiers. Other women expressed their patriotism in an untraditional way—as wartime nurses. Thousands of women on both sides defied prejudices about female delicacy and volunteered to nurse the wounded. Many of the northern female volunteers worked through the U.S.

Sanitary Commission, a civilian organization that bought and distributed clothing, food, and medicine and recruited doctors and nurses. Nursing meant working in the midst of unspeakable sights, sounds, and smells, but it often brought profound satisfaction. Katherine Wormeley of Rhode Island, who served three months as a volunteer nurse on a hospital ship in 1862, recorded in her diary, "We all know in our hearts that it is thorough enjoyment to be here—it is life."

Some volunteers went on to become paid military nurses. For example, Dorothea Dix, well known for her efforts to reform insane asylums, was named superintendent of female nurses in April 1861. Eventually, some 3,000 women served under her. Most nurses worked in hospitals behind the battle lines, but some, like Clara Barton, who later founded the American Red Cross, worked in battlefield units. At Antietam, as Barton was giving a wounded man a drink, a bullet ripped through her sleeve, striking and killing the soldier. Women who served in the war went on to lead the postwar movement to establish training schools for female nurses.

Politics and Dissent

At first, the bustle of economic and military mobilization seemed to silence politics; Democrats supported the Union as fervently as Republicans. But bipartisan unity did not last. Within a year, Democrats were labeling the Republican administration a "reign of terror," and Republicans were calling Democrats the party of "Dixie, Davis, and the Devil." Year by year, Republican policy pushed the Democrats toward a dangerous alienation. Republicans emancipated the slaves, subsidized private business, and expanded federal power at every turn. The Lincoln administration argued that the war required a loose interpretation of the Constitution, to which the Democrats countered, "The Constitution is as binding in war as in peace."

> At first, the bustle of economic and military mobilization seemed to silence politics. But bipartisan unity did not last.

In September 1862, in an effort to stifle opposition to the war, Lincoln placed under military arrest any person who discouraged enlistments, resisted the draft, or engaged in "disloyal" practices. Before the war ended, his administration had imprisoned nearly 14,000 individuals, most in the border states. The campaign fell short of a reign of terror, for the majority of the prisoners

---

U.S. Sanitary Commission, Brandy Station, Virginia, 1863

The burden of caring for millions of Union soldiers was more than the government could shoulder. Private initiative in the form of the U.S. Sanitary Commission brought additional medical attention to the Union wounded and boosted the comfort and morale of soldiers in the camps. Volunteers like these northern women standing in front of the Commission's headquarters in Brandy Station, Virginia, offered soldiers some of the comforts of home—clean socks, new blankets, and fresh fruit. Do you suppose that the freshly painted white picket fence surrounding their building had symbolic value? If so, what did it symbolize? National Archives.

were not northern Democratic opponents but Confederates, blockade runners, and citizens of foreign countries, and most of those arrested gained quick release. Still, the administration's heavy-handed tactics did suppress free speech.

When the Republican-dominated Congress enacted the draft law in March 1863, Democrats had another grievance. Grim news from the battlefields had dried up the stream of volunteers, and the North, like the South a year earlier, turned to military conscription to fill the ranks. The law required that all men between the ages of twenty and forty-five enroll and make themselves available for a lottery, which would decide who went to war. What poor men found particularly galling were provisions that allowed a draftee to hire a substitute or simply to pay a $300 fee and get out of his military obligation. As in the South, common folk could be heard chanting, "A rich man's war and a poor man's fight."

Linking the draft and emancipation, Democrats argued that Republicans employed an unconstitutional means (the draft) to achieve an unconstitutional end (emancipation). In the summer of 1863, antidraft, antiblack mobs went on rampages in northern cities. In July, New York City experienced an explosion of unprecedented proportions. Solidly Democratic Irish workingmen—crowded into stinking, disease-ridden tenements, gouged by inflation, enraged by the inequities of the draft, and dead set against fighting to free blacks—erupted in four days of rioting. By the time police and soldiers restored order, at least 105 people, most of them black, lay dead, and the Colored Orphan Asylum was a smoking ruin.

The riots stunned black Northerners, but the racist mobs failed to achieve their purpose: the subordination of African Americans. Free black leaders had lobbied aggressively for emancipation, and after Lincoln's proclamation they fanned out over the North agitating for equality. They won some small wartime successes. Illinois and Iowa overturned laws that had excluded blacks from entering those states. Illinois and Ohio began permitting blacks to testify in court. But defeat was more common. Indiana, for example, continued to forbid blacks to vote, testify, and attend public schools, and additional blacks were not allowed to enter the state. Significant progress toward black equality would have to wait until the war ended.

Grinding Out Victory, 1863–1865

In the early months of 1863, the Union's prospects looked bleak, and the Confederate cause stood at high tide. Then in July 1863, the tide began to turn. The military man most responsible for this shift was Ulysses S. Grant. Lifted from obscurity by his successes in the West in 1862 and 1863, Grant became the "great man of the day," one man observed in July 1864, "perhaps of the age." Elevated to supreme command, Grant knit together a powerful war machine that integrated a sophisticated command structure, modern technology, and complex logistics and supply systems. But the arithmetic of this plain man remained unchanged: Killing more of the enemy than he kills of you equaled "the complete overthrow of the rebellion."

The North ground out the victory, battle by bloody battle. The balance tipped in the Union's favor in 1863, but if the Confederacy was beaten, Southerners clearly did not know it. The fighting reached new levels of ferocity in the last two years of the war. As national elections approached in the fall of 1864, a discouraged Lincoln expected a war-weary North to make him a one-term president. Instead, northern voters declared their willingness to continue the war in the defense of the ideals of union and freedom.

Vicksburg and Gettysburg

Perched on the bluffs above the eastern bank of the Mississippi River, Vicksburg, Mississippi, bristled with cannons and dared Yankee ships to try to pass. This Confederate stronghold stood between Union forces and complete control of the river. Impenetrable terrain made the city impossible to take from the north. To get his army south of

Vicksburg Campaign, 1863

MISSISSIPPI

Yazoo R.

Big Black R.

LA.

Siege of Vicksburg May 22–July 4

Champion's Hill May 16

J. E. Johnston

Grant

Pemberton

Jackson May 14

Mississippi R.

Grant

Grand Gulf

Port Gibson May 1

Pearl R.

← Union troops
← Confederate troops
←--- Confederate retreat
✳ Union victories

Why Did So Many Soldiers Die?

From 1861 to 1865, Americans killed Americans on a scale never before seen. Not until the First World War, a half century later, would the world match (and surpass) the killing fields at Shiloh, Antietam, and Gettysburg (Figure 15.2). Why were the Civil War totals so horrendous? Why did 260,000 rebel soldiers and 373,000 Union soldiers die?

By the mid-nineteenth century, the balance between the ability to kill and the ability to save lives had tipped disastrously toward death. The sheer size of the armies—some battles involved more than 200,000 soldiers—ensured that battlefields would turn red with blood. Moreover, armies fought with antiquated strategy. In the generals' eyes, the ideal soldier remained the veteran of Napoleonic warfare, a man trained to advance with his comrades in a compact, close-order formation. Theory also emphasized frontal assaults. In classrooms at West Point and on the high plains of Mexico in the 1840s, men who would one day be officers in rival armies learned that infantry advancing shoulder to shoulder, supported by artillery, carried the day.

By the 1860s, modern technology had made such strategy appallingly deadly. Weapons with rifled barrels (that is, with spiral grooves cut into the bore) were replacing smoothbore muskets and cannon. Whereas muskets had an effective range of only about eighty yards, rifles propelled spinning bullets four times as far. The rifle's greater range and accuracy, and rifled cannons firing canisters filled with flesh-ripping, bone-breaking steel shot, made sitting ducks of charging infantry units and gave an enormous advantage to entrenched defensive forces. As a result, battles took thousands of lives in a single day. On July 2, 1862, the morning after the battle at Malvern Hill in eastern Virginia, a Union officer surveyed the scene: "Over 5,000 dead and wounded men were on the ground . . . enough were alive and moving to give to the field a singular crawling effect."

Wounded soldiers often lay on battlefields for hours, sometimes days, without water or care of any kind. When the Civil War began, no one anticipated casualty lists with thousands of names. Union and

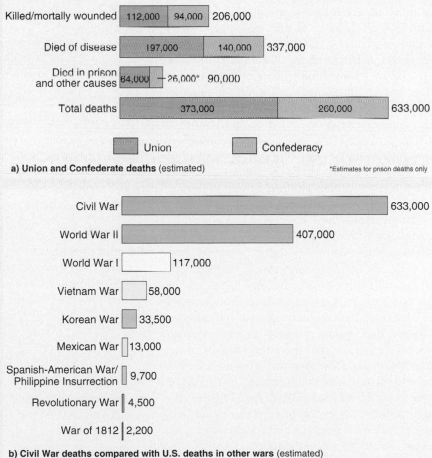

a) **Union and Confederate deaths** (estimated)

*Estimates for prison deaths only

b) **Civil War deaths compared with U.S. deaths in other wars** (estimated)

FIGURE 15.2 Civil War Deaths
The loss of life in the Civil War was almost equal to the losses in all other American wars.

The victory at Chattanooga on November 25 had immense strategic value. It opened the door to Georgia. It also confirmed Lincoln's estimation of Grant. In March 1864, the president asked Grant to come east to become the general in chief of all Union armies.

In Washington, Grant implemented his grand strategy for a war of annihilation. He ordered a series of simultaneous assaults from Virginia to Louisiana. Two actions proved more significant than the others. In one, General William Tecumseh Sherman, whom Grant appointed his successor to command the western armies, plunged southeast toward Atlanta. In the other, Grant, who took control of the Army of the Potomac, went head-to-head with Lee for almost four straight weeks in Virginia.

Grant and Lee met in the first week of May 1864 in northern Virginia at the Wilderness, a dense tangle of scrub oaks and small pines that proved to be Lee's ally, for it helped offset the Yankees' numerical superiority. Often unable to see more than ten paces, the armies pounded away at each other until approximately 18,000 Yankees and 11,000 rebels had fallen. The savagery of the Battle of the Wilderness did not compare with that at Spotsylvania Court House a few days later. Frenzied men fought hand to hand for eighteen hours in the rain. One veteran remembered men "piled upon each other in some places four layers deep, exhibiting every ghastly phase of mutilation." Spotsylvania cost Grant another 18,000 casualties and Lee 10,000, but the Yankee bulldog would not let go. Grant kept moving and tangled with Lee again at Cold Harbor, where he suffered 13,000 additional casualties to Lee's 5,000. (See "Historical Question," page 548.)

Twice as many Union soldiers as rebel soldiers died in four weeks of fighting in Virginia in May and June. Yet Grant did not consider himself defeated. Because Lee had only half the number of troops, he lost proportionally as many men as Grant. Grant knew that the South could not replace the losses. Moreover, the campaign carried Grant to the outskirts of Petersburg, just south of Richmond, the Confederate capital. Most of the major railroad lines supplying Richmond ran through Petersburg, so Lee had little choice but to defend the city. Grant abandoned the costly tactic of the frontal assault and began a siege that immobilized both armies and dragged on for nine months.

There was no pause in Sherman's invasion of Georgia. Grant had instructed Sherman to

Grant at Cold Harbor
Seated next to his chief of staff, John A. Rawlins, at his Cold Harbor, Virginia, headquarters, Ulysses S. Grant plots his next move against Robert E. Lee. On June 3, 1864, Grant ordered frontal assaults against entrenched Confederate forces, resulting in enormous Union losses. "I am disgusted with the generalship displayed," young Brigadier General Emory Upton exclaimed. "Our men have, in many cases, been foolishly and wantonly slaughtered." Years later, Grant said that he regretted the assault at Cold Harbor, but in 1864 he kept pushing toward Richmond.
Chicago Historical Society.

"get into the interior of the enemy's country as far as you can, inflicting all the damage you can against their War resources." In early May, Sherman moved 100,000 men south against the

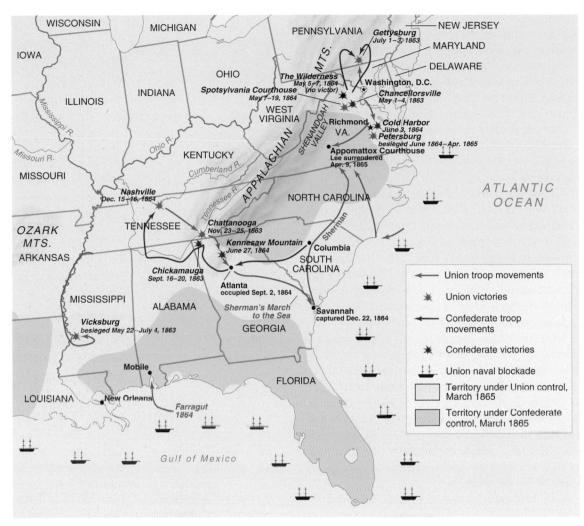

MAP 15.3   The Civil War, 1863–1865

Ulysses S. Grant's victory at Vicksburg divided the Confederacy at the Mississippi River. William Tecumseh Sherman's march from Chattanooga to Savannah divided it again. In northern Virginia, Robert E. Lee fought fiercely, but Grant's larger, better-supplied armies prevailed.

READING THE MAP: Describe the difference between Union and Confederate naval capacity. Were the battles shown on the map fought primarily in Union-controlled or Confederate-controlled territory (look at the land areas on the map)?

CONNECTIONS: Did former slaves serve in the Civil War? If so, on which side, and what did they do?

FOR MORE HELP ANALYZING THIS MAP, see the map activity for this chapter in the Online Study Guide at bedfordstmartins.com/roark.

back on the defensive in Virginia, still had a vicious sting. War-weariness threatened to erode the North's will to win before Union armies could destroy the Confederacy's ability to go on.

Grant Takes Command

Toward the end of September 1863, Union general William Rosecrans placed his army in a dangerous situation in Chattanooga, Tennessee, where he had retreated after taking a whipping at the Battle of Chickamauga earlier in the month (see Map 15.3). Rebels surrounded the disorganized bluecoats and threatened to starve them into submission. Ulysses S. Grant, whom Lincoln had made commander of Union forces between the Mississippi River and the Appalachians, arrived in Chattanooga in October. Within weeks, he opened an effective supply line, broke the siege, and then (largely because Union troops disobeyed orders and charged wildly up Missionary Ridge) routed the Confederate army.

Vicksburg, Grant marched it down the swampy western bank of the Mississippi. Union forces crossed the Mississippi River, marched north more than one hundred miles, and attacked the city. The Confederates beat back the assault, and in May, Grant decided to lay siege to the city and starve out the enemy. Civilian residents of Vicksburg moved into caves to escape the incessant Union bombardment, and as the siege dragged on, they had to eat mules and rats to survive.

After six weeks, the siege had the desired effect. On July 4, 1863, nearly 30,000 rebels marched out of Vicksburg, stacked their arms, and surrendered unconditionally. A Yankee captain wrote home to his wife: "The backbone of the Rebellion is this day broken. The Confederacy is divided. . . . Vicksburg is ours. The Mississippi River is opened, and Gen. Grant is to be our next President."

On the same Fourth of July that a grateful nation received the news of Vicksburg, word arrived that Union forces had crushed General Lee at Gettysburg, Pennsylvania (Map 15.3). Lee's triumph in early May at Chancellorsville, Virginia, over Joseph "Fighting Joe" Hooker had revived his confidence, even though the battle cost him his favorite commander, the incomparable Stonewall Jackson, accidentally shot in the dark by his own troops.

Emboldened by the victory at Chancellorsville and hoping to relieve Virginia of the burden of the fighting, Lee and his 75,000-man Army of Northern Virginia invaded Pennsylvania in June. On June 28, the Army of the Potomac, under its new commander, General George G. Meade, moved quickly to intercept the Confederate force. Advance units of both armies met at the small town of Gettysburg, where Union forces occupied the high ground. Three days of furious fighting involving 165,000 soldiers could not dislodge the Federals from the ridges and hills. Lee ached for a decisive victory, and on July 3 he ordered a major assault against the

Major Battles of the Civil War, 1863–1865

May 1–4, 1863	Battle of Chancellorsville
July 1–3, 1863	Battle of Gettysburg
July 4, 1863	Fall of Vicksburg
September 16–20, 1863	Battle of Chickamauga
November 23–25, 1863	Battle of Chattanooga
May 5–7, 1864	Battle of the Wilderness
May 7–19, 1864	Battle of Spotsylvania Court House
June 3, 1864	Battle of Cold Harbor
June 27, 1864	Battle of Kennesaw Mountain
September 2, 1864	Fall of Atlanta
November–December 1864	Sheridan sacks Shenandoah Valley Sherman's March to the Sea
December 15–16, 1864	Battle of Nashville
December 22, 1864	Fall of Savannah
April 2–3, 1865	Fall of Petersburg and Richmond
April 9, 1865	Lee surrenders at Appomattox Court House

Union center on Cemetery Ridge. Open, rolling fields provided the dug-in Yankees with three-quarters of a mile of clear vision, and they raked the mile-wide line of Confederate soldiers under General George E. Pickett with cannon and rifle fire. Time and again, the rebels closed ranks and raced forward, until finally their momentum failed. Gettysburg cost Lee more than one-third of his army—28,000 casualties. "It's all my fault," he lamented. In a drenching rain on the night of July 4, 1863, he marched his battered army back to Virginia.

The twin disasters at Vicksburg and Gettysburg proved to be the turning point of the war. The Confederacy could not replace the nearly 60,000 soldiers who were captured, wounded, or killed. Lee never launched another major offensive north of the Mason-Dixon line. It is hindsight, however, that permits us to see the pair of battles as decisive. At the time, the Confederacy still controlled the heartland of the South, and Lee,

Battle of Gettysburg, July 1–3, 1863

UNION
— Earlier position
— Later position
◄— Retreat

CONFEDERATE
— Earlier position
— Later position
◄— Advance

Wounded Men at Savage's Station
Misery did not end when the cannon ceased firing. This heap of mangled humanity was but a fraction of the cost of General George McClellan's campaign on the Virginia peninsula in 1862.
Library of Congress.

Confederate medical departments could not cope with skirmishes, much less large-scale battles. They had no ambulance corps to remove the wounded from the scene. They had no field hospitals. Early in the war, someone in the U.S. Quartermaster Department, which was responsible for constructing Union hospitals, responded to demands that it do something to improve the care of the wounded by saying: "Men need guns, not beds." Only the shock of massive casualties compelled reform. A lack of resources meant that the South lagged behind the North, but gradually both North and South organized effective ambulance corps, built hospitals, and hired trained surgeons and nurses.

Soldiers did not always count speedy transportation to a field hospital as a blessing. As one Union soldier said, "I had rather risk a battle than the Hospitals." Real danger lurked behind the lines. While the technology of killing advanced to very high standards, medicine remained primitive. Physicians gained a reputation as butchers, and soldiers dreaded the operating table more than they did entrenched riflemen. Serious wounds to a leg or an arm usually meant amputation, the

Doctor's Surgical Kit
With simple instruments like these, not unlike the tools of the butcher's trade, northern and southern surgeons performed approximately 60,000 amputations. Approximately 45,000 of the amputees survived.
Chicago Historical Society.

best way doctors knew to save lives. After major battles, surgeons worked among piles of severed limbs.

(continued)

A wounded man's real enemy was not doctors' callousness but medical ignorance. Physicians had almost no knowledge of the cause and transmission of disease or the benefits of antiseptics. Not aware of basic germ theory, they spread infection almost every time they operated. Doctors wore the same bloody smocks for days and washed their hands and their scalpels and saws in buckets of dirty water. When they had difficulty threading their needles, they wet the thread with their own saliva. Soldiers often did not survive amputations, not because of the operation but because of the infection that inevitably followed. Of the Union soldiers whose legs were amputated above the knee, more than half died. A Union doctor discovered in 1864 that bromine (previously used in combination with other elements as a sedative) arrested gangrene, but the best that most amputees could hope for was maggots, which ate dead flesh on the stump and thus inhibited the spread of infection. During the Civil War, nearly one of every five wounded rebel soldiers died, and one of every six Yankees. A century later, in Vietnam, the proportion of deaths was one wounded American soldier in four hundred.

Soldiers who avoided battlefield wounds and hospital infections still faced sickness. Deadly diseases swept through crowded army camps, where latrines were often dangerously close to drinking-water supplies. The principal killers were dysentery and typhoid, but pneumonia and malaria also cut down thousands. Doctors did what they could, but often their treatments only added to the misery. They prescribed doses of turpentine for patients with typhoid, they fought respiratory problems with mustard plasters, and they attacked intestinal disorders by blistering the skin with sulfuric acid.

Thousands of female nurses, including Dorothea Dix, Clara Barton, and Juliet Ann Opie Hopkins, improved the wounded men's odds and alleviated their suffering. Civilian relief agencies, such as the U.S. Sanitary Commission and the Women's Relief Society of the Confederacy, promoted hygiene in army camps and made some headway. Nevertheless, as Figure 15.2 shows, disease killed nearly twice as many soldiers as did combat. Many who died of disease were prisoners of war. Approximately 30,000 Northerners died in Confederate prisons, and approximately 26,000 Southerners died in Union prisons. No northern prison, however, could equal the horror of Andersonville in southern Georgia. In August 1864, about 33,000 emaciated men lived in unspeakable conditions in a 26-acre barren stockade with no shelter except what the prisoners were able to construct. More than 13,000 perished.

In the end, 633,000 northern and southern soldiers died, a staggering toll.

65,000 rebels in the rugged mountains of northern Georgia. Skillful maneuvering, constant skirmishing, and one pitched battle, at Kennesaw Mountain at the end of June, brought Sherman to Atlanta, which fell on September 2.

Sherman was only warming up. Intending to "make Georgia howl," he marched out of Atlanta on November 15 with 62,000 battle-hardened veterans, heading for Savannah, 285 miles away on the Atlantic coast. Federal troops cut a swath from twenty-five to sixty miles wide. One veteran remembered, "[We] destroyed all we could not eat, stole their niggers, burned their cotton & gins, spilled their sorghum, burned & twisted their R. Roads and raised Hell generally." Sherman's "March to the Sea" aimed at destroying the will of the southern people. A few weeks earlier, General Philip H. Sheridan had carried out his own scorched-earth campaign in the Shenandoah Valley, complying with Grant's order to turn the valley into "a barren waste . . . so that crows flying over it for the balance of this season will have to carry their provender [food] with them." When Sherman's troops entered an undefended Savannah in the third week of December, the general telegraphed Lincoln that he had "a Christmas gift" for him. A month earlier, Union voters had bestowed on the president an even greater gift.

The Election of 1864

In the fall, white men in the Union states turned to the election of a president. Never before had a nation held general elections in the midst of war. "We can not have free government without elections," Lincoln explained, "and if the rebellion could force us to forgo or postpone a national

R. K. Sneden's Shanty at Andersonville Prison, GA, Robert Knox Sneden, July 15, 1864
The train carrying prisoner-of-war Robert Sneden arrived at Andersonville on the last day of February
1864 as the Confederates were completing the stockade that surrounded their newest prison. Soon the
sixteen and a half acres in southwestern Georgia were crammed with humanity. By June, the prison area
had to be extended to 26.5 acres. Its 33,000 Union prisoners made Andersonville the fifth largest city in
the Confederacy. A talented watercolorist, Sneden sketched this scene while a captive and touched it up
later. Smallpox, dysentery, scurvy, malnutrition, and infections took the lives of thousands. "The flies are
now here in millions," Sneden observed. "Everything is covered with them, dense swarms like a cloud
settle on the pile of dead which are daily seen near the gates. The ground in the thickest part settled in
the camp is fairly alive and moves with maggots or lice! The filthy swamp undulates like small waves
with them, while the insufferable stench nearly takes away one's breath!"
© 1996, Lora Robbins Collection of Virginia Art, Virginia Historical Society.

election, it might fairly claim to have already conquered and ruined us." Lincoln's determination to hold elections is especially noteworthy because the Democratic Party smelled victory. With Sherman temporarily checked outside Atlanta and Grant bogged down in the siege of Petersburg, the Union war effort had stalled during the summer, and frustration had settled over the North. Rankled by inflation, the draft, the attack on civil liberties, and the commitment to blacks, Northerners appeared ready for a change. Lincoln himself concluded in the gloomy summer of 1864, "It seems exceedingly probable that this administration will not be re-elected."

Democrats were badly divided, however. "Peace" Democrats insisted on an armistice, while "war" Democrats supported the conflict but opposed Republican means of fighting it. The party tried to paper over the chasm by nominating a war candidate, General George McClellan, but adopting a peace platform that demanded that "immediate efforts be made for a cessation of hostilities." Republicans denounced the peace plank as a sellout that "virtually proposed to surrender the country to the rebels in arms against us."

Lincoln was no shoo-in for renomination, much less reelection. Conservatives believed he had acted precipitously in emancipating the slaves, and radicals criticized him for moving too slowly to free them and for failing to champion black equality. But frightened by the strength of the peace Democrats, the Republican

> "We can not have free government without elections," Lincoln explained, "and if the rebellion could force us to forgo or postpone a national election, it might fairly claim to have already conquered and ruined us."

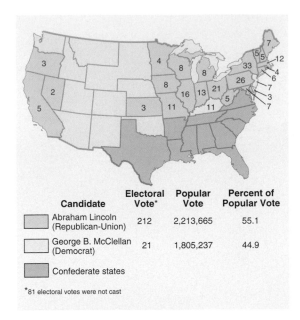

Candidate	Electoral Vote*	Popular Vote	Percent of Popular Vote
Abraham Lincoln (Republican-Union)	212	2,213,665	55.1
George B. McClellan (Democrat)	21	1,805,237	44.9
Confederate states			

*81 electoral votes were not cast

MAP 15.4 The Election of 1864

Party stuck with Lincoln. In an effort to reach out to the largest number of voters, however, the Republicans made two changes. First, they chose the new name, the Union Party, making it easier for prowar Democrats to embrace Lincoln. Second, they chose a new vice presidential candidate, Andrew Johnson of Tennessee, a Southerner who was an uncompromising Unionist.

The capture of Atlanta on September 2 turned the political tide in favor of the Republicans. Lincoln received 55 percent of the popular vote, but his electoral margin was a whopping 212 to McClellan's 21 (Map 15.4). The Republicans also stormed back in the congressional elections, gaining large margins over the Democrats in the Senate and the House. The Union Party bristled with factions, but they united for a resounding victory, one that gave Lincoln a mandate to continue the war until slavery and the Confederacy were dead.

The Confederacy Collapses

As 1865 dawned, military disaster littered the Confederate landscape. With the destruction of John B. Hood's army at Nashville in December 1864, the interior of the Confederacy lay in Yankee hands (see Map 15.3). Sherman's troops, resting momentarily in Savannah, eyed South Carolina hungrily. Farther north, Grant had Lee's army pinned down in Petersburg, just a

Ruins of Richmond
A Union soldier and a small boy wearing a Union cap contemplate the silence and devastation of the Confederacy's capital. On their way out of the city on the evening of April 2, 1865, Confederate demolition squads set fire to tobacco warehouses and ammunition dumps. Huge explosions tore holes in the city, and windswept fires destroyed much of what was left standing. As one Confederate observed, "The old war-scarred city seemed to prefer annihilation to conquest."
Library of Congress.

few miles from Richmond. Southerners took out their frustration and bitterness on their president. Kinder than most, Alexander Stephens, vice president of the Confederacy, likened Jefferson Davis to "my poor old blind and deaf dog."

In the final months of the war, more and more Confederates turned their backs on the rebellion. News from the battlefields made it difficult not to conclude that the Yankees had beaten them. Soldiers' wives begged their husbands to return home to keep their families from starving, and the stream of deserters became a flood. In most cases, white Southerners lost the will to continue, not so much because they lost faith in independence but because they had been battered into submission. Despite all the divisions and conflicts within the Confederacy and the loss of heart in the final months, white Southerners had shown remarkable endurance for their cause. Half of the 900,000 Confederate soldiers had been killed or wounded, and ragged, hungry women and children had sacrificed for four years. Confederates exhibited astounding staying power through the bloodiest war then known to history.

The end came with a rush. On February 1, 1865, Sherman's troops stormed out of Savannah into South Carolina, the "cradle of the Confederacy." Before Sherman could push through North Carolina and arrive at the rear of Lee's army at Petersburg, where he expected to crush the Confederates between his hammer and Grant's anvil, Lee abandoned the city. Davis fled Richmond, and the capital city of the Confederacy fell a few days later. Grant pursued Lee for one hundred miles, until Lee surrendered on April 9, 1865, in a farmhouse near the village of Appomattox Court House, Virginia. The beaten general arrived wearing an immaculate full-dress uniform, complete with sash and sword; the victor wore his usual mud-splattered private's outfit. Grant offered generous peace terms. He allowed Lee's men to return home and to keep their horses to help "put in a crop to carry themselves and their families through the next winter." With Lee gone, the remaining Confederate armies lost hope and gave up within two weeks. After four years, the war was over.

The day after Lee's surrender, a brass band led a happy crowd of three thousand to the White House, where they pleaded with Lincoln for a speech. He begged off and asked the band to strike up "Dixie." He knew that the rebels had claimed the tune as their own, he said, but it was one of his favorites, and now he was taking it back. The crowd roared its approval, and the band played "Dixie," following it with "Yankee Doodle." No one was more relieved than Lincoln that the war was over, but his celebration was re-

Robert E. Lee and Friends, Mathew Brady, 1865
One week after the surrender at Appomattox Court House, Robert E. Lee, again wearing his uniform, sat for this portrait by Mathew Brady, the country's most famous photographer. Lee is joined by his eldest son, Major General George Washington Custis Lee, left, and Lieutenant Colonel Walter H. Taylor, a longtime aide. Lee's sober, worn expression reflects four hard years of war and his final defeat. Already a matchless hero to white Southerners, Lee was well on his way toward saintly immortality. In 1868, one woman described Lee as "bathed in the white light which falls directly upon him from the smile of an approving and sustaining God."
Museum of the Confederacy.

strained. He told his cabinet that his postwar burdens would weigh almost as heavily as those of wartime.

Seeking distraction, Lincoln attended Ford's Theatre on the evening of Good Friday, April 14, 1865. While he and his wife, Mary, enjoyed *Our American Cousin*, a British comedy, John Wilkes Booth, an actor with southern sympathies, slipped into the president's box and shot Lincoln in the head. He died at 7:22 the following morning. Vice President Andrew Johnson became president. The man who had led the nation through the war would not lead it during the postwar search for a just peace.

Conclusion: The Second American Revolution

A transformed nation emerged from the crucible of war. Antebellum America was decentralized politically and loosely integrated economically. To bend the resources of the country to a Union victory, Congress enacted legislation that reshaped the nation's political and economic character. It created national currency and banking systems, and turned to free land, a transcontinental railroad, and miles of telegraph lines to bind the West to the rest of the nation. Congress also adopted policies that established the sovereignty of the federal government and permanently increased its power. To the average citizen before the war, Washington meant the post office and little more; during the war years, the federal government drafted, taxed, and judged Americans in unprecedented ways. The massive changes brought about by war—the creation of a national government, a national economy, and a national spirit—led one historian to call the American Civil War the "Second American Revolution."

The Civil War also had a profound effect on individual lives. When the war began in 1861, millions of men dropped their hoes, hammers, and pencils, put on blue or gray uniforms, and fought and suffered for what they passionately believed was right. The war disrupted families, leaving most women at home with additional responsibilities while offering new opportunities to others for wartime work in factories, offices, and hospitals. It offered blacks new and more effective ways to resist slavery and agitate for equality; for nearly 200,000 black men it provided the opportunity to fight for their freedom, as William Gould did.

The war also devastated the South. Three-fourths of southern white men of military age served in the Confederate army, and at least half of them were captured, wounded, or killed or died of disease. The war destroyed two-fifths of the South's livestock, wrecked half of the farm machinery, and blackened dozens of cities and towns. The immediate impact of the war on the North was more paradoxical. Putting down the slaveholders' rebellion cost the North a heavy price: 373,000 lives. But rather than devastating the land, war set the countryside and cities humming with business activity. The radical shift in power from South to North signaled a new direction in American development: the long decline of agriculture and the rise of industrial capitalism.

Most revolutionary of all, the war ended slavery. Ironically, the South's war to preserve slavery killed it. Ex-slaves like William Gould dedicated their wartime service to its destruction. Because slavery was both a labor and a racial system, the institution was entangled in almost every aspect of southern life. Slavery's uprooting inevitably meant fundamental change. But the full meaning of abolition remained unclear in 1865. Determining the new economic, political, and social status of four million ex-slaves would be the principal task of reconstruction.

FOR ADDITIONAL FIRSTHAND ACCOUNTS OF THIS PERIOD, see Chapter 15 in Michael Johnson, ed., *Reading the American Past*, Third Edition.

TO ASSESS YOUR MASTERY OF THE MATERIAL IN THIS CHAPTER, see the Online Study Guide at bedfordstmartins.com/roark.

FOR WEB LINKS RELATED TO TOPICS IN THIS CHAPTER, see "HistoryLinks," "DocLinks," and "PlaceLinks" at bedfordstmartins.com/roark.

CHRONOLOGY

1861
- **April.** Confederate attack on Fort Sumter opens the Civil War.

- Union nurse Dorothea Dix named superintendent of female nurses.
- **April–May.** Four Upper South states secede and join Confederacy.
- **July.** Union forces routed in First Battle of Bull Run at Manassas, Virginia, the first major clash of war.
- **August.** Congress approves first Confiscation Act, which allows seizure of any slave employed by Confederate military.

1862
- **February.** Legal Tender Act creates first national currency—paper money called "greenbacks."
- Union forces under General Grant capture Fort Henry and Fort Donelson and drive Confederates from Kentucky and most of Tennessee.
- **March.** Defeat at Glorieta Pass helps convince Confederates to abandon their dream of a southwestern slaveholding empire.

- Union victory at Battle of Pea Ridge clears Missouri of Confederate troops and opens Arkansas to federal advance.
- **April.** Battle of Shiloh in Tennessee ends Confederate bid to control Mississippi Valley.
- Confederate Congress passes first draft law in American history.
- **May.** Homestead Act offers western land to people willing to live and labor on it.
- **May–July.** General McClellan's Union forces defeated during Virginia peninsula campaign.
- **July.** Congress approves second Confiscation Act, freeing all slaves of rebel masters.

- Congress passes Militia Act, authorizing enrollment of blacks in Union military.

- **September.** Battle of Antietam stops General Lee's advance into Maryland.
- Lincoln announces preliminary emancipation proclamation.

1863
- **January.** Emancipation Proclamation becomes law, freeing slaves in areas still in rebellion.

- **February.** National Banking Act creates system of national banks.
- **March.** Congress authorizes draft.
- **July.** Vicksburg falls to Union forces, effectively cutting Confederacy in two along Mississippi River.
- Battle of Gettysburg costs Lee more than one-third of his army.
- Antidraft riots sweep New York City.

1864
- **March.** Grant appointed general in chief of all Union forces.
- **May–June.** Grant's forces engage Confederates in Virginia in bloodiest fighting of war, from Wilderness campaign to beginnings of siege of Petersburg.

- **September.** Atlanta falls to Union forces under General Sherman.
- **November.** Lincoln elected to a second term.
- **December.** General Sherman occupies Savannah after scorched-earth campaign in Georgia.

1865
- **April 9.** Lee surrenders to Grant at Appomattox Court House, Virginia, bringing Civil War to an end.
- **April 14.** John Wilkes Booth shoots Lincoln at Ford's Theatre in Washington.
- **April 15.** Lincoln dies.
- Vice President Andrew Johnson becomes president.

BIBLIOGRAPHY

General Works

Jean Harvey Baker, David Herbert Donald, and Michael F. Holt, *The Civil War and Reconstruction* (2001).

James M. McPherson, *Battle Cry of Freedom: The Civil War Era* (1988).

James M. McPherson and William J. Cooper Jr., *Writing the Civil War: The Quest to Understand* (1998).

Allan Nevins, *The War for the Union*, 4 vols. (1959–1971).

Roger L. Ransom, *Conflict and Compromise: The Political Economy of Slavery, Emancipation, and the American Civil War* (1989).

Russell F. Weigley, *A Great Civil War: A Military and Political History, 1861–1865* (2000).

LeeAnn Whites, *The Civil War as a Crisis in Gender* (2000).

The Combatants

Michael Barton, *Goodmen, the Character of Civil War Soldiers* (1981).

Richard E. Beringer et al., *Why the South Lost the Civil War* (1986).

Stephen W. Berry II, *All That Makes a Man: Love and Ambition in the Civil War South* (2003).

Gabor S. Boritt, ed., *Why the Confederacy Lost* (1992).

Catherine Clinton and Nina Silber, eds., *Divided Houses: Gender and the Civil War* (1992).

Richard Nelson Current, *Lincoln's Loyalists: Union Soldiers from the Confederacy* (1992).

David Herbert Donald, *Lincoln* (1995).

David Herbert Donald, ed., *Why the North Won the Civil War* (1960).

Lesley J. Gordon, *General George E. Pickett in Life and Legend* (1998).

William B. Gould IV, ed., *Diary of a Contraband: The Civil War Passage of a Black Sailor* (2002).

Gerald F. Linderman, *Embattled Courage: The Experience of Combat in the American Civil War* (1987).

John F. Marszalek, *Sherman: A Soldier's Passion for Order* (1993).

James Marten, *The Children's Civil War* (1998).

William S. McFeely, *Grant: A Biography* (1981).

James M. McPherson, *What They Fought For, 1861–1865* (1994).

Randall M. Miller, Harry S. Stout, and Charles Reagan Wilson, eds., *Religion and the American Civil War* (1998).

Reid Mitchell, *Civil War Soldiers: Their Expectations and Their Experiences* (1988).

Reid Mitchell, *The Vacant Chair: The Northern Soldier Leaves Home* (1993).

Mark E. Neely Jr., *The Last Best Hope of Earth: Abraham Lincoln and the Promise of America* (1993).

Alan T. Nolan, *Lee Considered: General Robert E. Lee and Civil War History* (1991).

Stephen B. Oates, *A Woman of Valor: Clara Barton and the Civil War* (1994).

James I. Robertson Jr., *Soldiers Blue and Gray* (1988).

Stephen W. Sears, *George B. McClellan: The Young Napoleon* (1988).

Brooks D. Simpson, *Ulysses S. Grant: Triumph over Adversity, 1822–1865* (2000).

Emory M. Thomas, *Robert E. Lee: A Biography* (1995).

Bell I. Wiley, *The Life of Johnny Reb: The Common Soldier of the Confederacy* (1943).

Bell I. Wiley, *The Life of Billy Yank: The Common Soldier of the Union* (1952).

C. Vann Woodward, ed., *Mary Chesnut's Civil War* (1981).

Military History

Gabor S. Boritt, ed., *Lincoln's Generals* (1994).

Robert M. Browning Jr., *Success Is All That Was Expected: The South Atlantic Blockading Squadron during the Civil War* (2002).

Bruce Catton, *The Centennial History of the Civil War*, 3 vols. (1961–1965).

Michael Fellman, *Inside War: The Guerrilla Conflict in Missouri during the American Civil War* (1989).

Joseph T. Glatthaar, *The March to the Sea and Beyond: Sherman's Troops in the Savannah and Carolinas Campaigns* (1985).

Mark Grimsley, *The Hard Hand of War: Union Military Policy toward Southern Civilians, 1861–1865* (1995).

Herman Hattaway and Archer Jones, *How the North Won: A Military History of the Civil War* (1983).

Archer Jones, *Civil War Command and Strategy: The Process of Victory and Defeat* (1992).

Alvin M. Josephy Jr., *The Civil War in the American West* (1991).

George C. Rable, *Fredericksburg! Fredericksburg!* (2002).

Charles Royster, *The Destructive War: William Tecumseh Sherman, Stonewall Jackson, and the Americans* (1991).

Stephen W. Sears, *Landscape Turned Red: The Battle of Antietam* (1983).

Steven E. Woodworth, *Davis and Lee at War* (1995).

Union and Freedom

Herman Belz, *Emancipation and Equal Rights: Politics and Constitutionalism during the Civil War Era* (1978).

Ira Berlin et al., eds., *Freedom: A Documentary History of Emancipation, 1861–1867*, 4 vols. (1982–1993).

David W. Blight, *Frederick Douglass's Civil War: Keeping Faith in Jubilee* (1989).

Dudley Taylor Cornish, *The Sable Arm: Black Troops in the Union Army, 1861–1865* (1987).

LaWanda Cox, *Lincoln and Black Freedom: A Study in Presidential Leadership* (1981).

Louis S. Gerteis, *From Contraband to Freedman: Federal Policy toward Southern Blacks, 1861–1865* (1973).

Joseph T. Glatthaar, *Forged in Battle: The Civil War Alliance of Black Soldiers and White Officers* (1990).

Waldo E. Martin Jr., *The Mind of Frederick Douglass* (1984).

William S. McFeely, *Frederick Douglass* (1991).

James M. McPherson, *Abraham Lincoln and the Second American Revolution* (1990).

Clarence L. Mohr, *On the Threshold of Freedom: Masters and Slaves in Civil War Georgia* (1986).

Steven J. Ramold, *Slaves, Sailors, Citizens: African Americans in the Union Navy* (2002).

Edwin S. Redkey, ed., *A Grand Army of Black Men: Letters from African-American Soldiers in the Union Army, 1861–1865* (1992).

C. Peter Ripley, *Slaves and Freedmen in Civil War Louisiana* (1976).

C. Peter Ripley, ed., *Witness for Freedom: African American Voices on Race, Slavery, and Emancipation* (1993).

The South at War

Stephen V. Ash, *When the Yankees Came: Conflict and Chaos in the Occupied South, 1861–1865* (1995).

William A. Blair, *Virginia's Private War: Feeding Body and Soul in the Confederacy, 1861–1865* (1998).

William J. Cooper, *Jefferson Davis, American* (2000).

Mary A. DeCredico, *Patriotism for Profit: Georgia's Urban Entrepreneurs and the Confederate War Effort* (1990).

Charles B. Dew, *Ironmaker to the Confederacy: Joseph R. Anderson and the Tredegar Iron Works* (1966).

Wayne K. Durrill, *War of Another Kind: A Southern Community in the Great Rebellion* (1990).

Paul D. Escott, *After Secession: Jefferson Davis and the Failure of Confederate Nationalism* (1978).

Drew Gilpin Faust, *The Creation of Confederate Nationalism: Ideology and Identity in the Civil War South* (1988).

Drew Gilpin Faust, *Mothers of Invention: Women of the Slaveholding South in the American Civil War* (1996).

Noralee Frankel, *Freedom's Women: Black Women and Families in Civil War Era Mississippi* (1999).

William W. Freehling, *The South vs. the South: How Anti-Confederate Southerners Shaped the Course of the Civil War* (2001).

Ernest B. Furgurson, *Ashes of Glory: Richmond at War* (1996).

Gary W. Gallagher, *The Confederate War* (1997).

Charles M. Hubbard, *The Burden of Confederate Diplomacy* (1998).

John C. Inscoe and Gordon B. McKinney, *The Heart of Confederate Appalachia: Western North Carolina in the Civil War* (2000).

Ervin L. Jordan Jr., *Black Confederates and Afro-Yankees in Civil War Virginia* (1995).

Mark E. Neely Jr., *Southern Rights: Political Prisoners and the Myth of Confederate Constitutionalism* (1999).

John Solomon Otto, *Southern Agriculture during the Civil War Era, 1860–1880* (1994).

Philip Shaw Paludan, *Victims: A True Story of the Civil War* (1981).

George C. Rable, *Civil Wars: Women and the Crisis of Southern Nationalism* (1989).

George C. Rable, *The Confederate Republic: A Revolution against Politics* (1994).

James L. Roark, *Masters without Slaves: Southern Planters in the Civil War and Reconstruction* (1977).

Daniel E. Sutherland, *Seasons of War: The Ordeal of a Confederate Community, 1861–1865* (1995).

Emory M. Thomas, *The Confederate Nation, 1861–1865* (1979).

Steven Elliott Tripp, *Yankee Town, Southern City: Race and Class Relations in Civil War Lynchburg* (1997).

Stephen R. Wise, *Lifeline of the Confederacy: Blockade Running during the Civil War* (1988).

The North at War

Iver Bernstein, *The New York City Draft Riots: Their Significance for American Society and Politics in the Age of the Civil War* (1990).

George M. Fredrickson, *The Inner Civil War: Northern Intellectuals and the Crisis of the Union* (1965).

Judith Ann Giesberg, *Civil War Sisterhood: The U.S. Sanitary Commission and Women's Politics in Transition* (2000).

Earl J. Hess, *Liberty, Virtue, and Progress: Northerners and Their War for the Union* (1988).

Howard Jones, *Abraham Lincoln and a New Birth of Freedom: The Union and Slavery in the Diplomacy of the Civil War* (1999).

Theodore J. Karamanski, *Rally 'Round the Flag: Chicago and the Civil War* (1993).

Ernest A. McKay, *The Civil War and New York City* (1990).

James H. Moorhead, *American Apocalypse: Yankee Protestants and the Civil War, 1860–1869* (1978).

Mark E. Neely Jr., *The Fate of Liberty: Abraham Lincoln and Civil Liberties* (1991).

Philip Shaw Paludan, *"A People's Contest": The Union and Civil War, 1861–1865* (1988).

Philip Shaw Paludan, *The Presidency of Abraham Lincoln* (1994).

Heather Cox Richardson, *The Greatest Nation of the Earth: Republican Economic Policies during the Civil War* (1997).

Joel H. Silby, *A Respectable Minority: The Democratic Party in the Civil War Era, 1860–1868* (1977).

Amy Dru Stanley, *From Bondage to Contract: Wage Labor, Marriage, and the Market in the Age of Slave Emancipation* (1998).

CARPETBAG

A carpetbag was a nineteenth-
century suitcase made from carpet, often brightly
colored. Applied first to wildcat bankers on the western frontier, "carpetbagger" was a derogatory name for rootless and penniless adventurers
who could carry everything they owned in a single carpetbag. Critics of Republican administrations in the South hurled the name "carpetbaggers" at white Northerners who
moved South during reconstruction and became active in politics. According to white
Southerners, carpetbaggers exploited gullible ex-slaves to gain power and wealth. In
fact, many Northerners who came to the South joined with blacks and some southern
whites to form Republican state and local governments that were among the most
progressive anywhere in the nineteenth century.

16

Reconstruction
1863–1877

"**Y**ORK DISAPPEARED on yesterday morning," David Golightly Harris noted in his journal on June 6, 1865. "I suppose that he has gone to the yankey. I wish they would give him a good whipping & hasten him back." York, a black field hand, had once belonged to Harris, a white slaveholder in Spartanburg District, South Carolina. When York disappeared, the war had been over for two months, and York was a free man. In Harris's mind, however, simply declaring York free did not make him so. In July, Harris noted that another field hand, Old Will, had left "to try to enjoy the freedom the Yankey's have promised the negroes." Two weeks later, black freedom still seemed in doubt. "There is much talk about freeing the negroes. Some are said already to have freed them," Harris declared. But Harris had not freed anyone. He did not inform his former slaves of their freedom until federal military authorities required him to. "*Freed the Negroes*," he declared on August 16, four months after Appomattox and more than two and a half years after the Emancipation Proclamation.

Like many ex-slaveholders, Harris had trouble coming to grips with **emancipation**. "Family well, Horses well, Cattle well, Hogs well & everything else are well so far as I know, if it was not for the free negroes," Harris wrote on September 17. "On their account everything is turned upside down. So much so that we do not know what to do with our land, nor who to hire if we want it worked. . . . We are in the midst of troublesome times & do not know what will turn up." Harris had owned ten slaves, and now he faced what seemed to him an insoluble problem. He needed blacks to cultivate his farm, but like most whites he did not believe that African Americans would work much when free. Some kind of compulsion would be needed. But slavery was gone, leaving the South upside down. White men in Harris's neighborhood sought to set it straight again. "In this district several negroes have been badly whipped & several have been hung by some unknown persons," he noted in November. "This has a tendency to keep them in their proper bounds & make them more humble." But the violence did not keep ex-slaves from acting like free people. On Christmas Day 1865, Harris recorded, "The negroes leave today to hunt themselves a new home while we will be left to wait upon ourselves."

Across the South, ex-masters predicted that emancipation would mean economic collapse and social anarchy. Carl Schurz, a Union general who undertook a fact-finding mission to the former Confederate states in the summer of 1865, encountered this dire prediction often enough to conclude that the Civil War was a "revolution but half accomplished." Northern victory had freed the slaves, but it had not changed former slaveholders' minds about the need for slavery. Left to themselves, Schurz believed, whites would "introduce some new system of forced labor, not perhaps exactly slavery in its old form but something similar to it." To defend their freedom, blacks would need federal protection, land of their own, and voting rights, Schurz concluded. Until whites "cut loose from the past, it will be a dangerous experiment to put Southern society upon its own legs." Schurz discovered that the end of the war did not mean the beginning of peace. Instead, the nation entered one of its most chaotic and conflicted eras—Reconstruction, an era that would define the status of the defeated South within the Union and the meaning of freedom for ex-slaves.

The status of the South and the contours of black freedom were determined in the nation's capital, where the federal government played an active role, but also in the state legislatures and county seats of the South and through the active participation of blacks themselves. On farms and plantations from Virginia to Texas, ex-slaves like York and Old Will struggled to become free people, while whites like David Golightly Harris clung to the Old South. In the midst of the racial flux and chaos, a small band of crusading women sought to achieve gender equality. The years of reconstruction witnessed an enormous struggle to determine the consequences of Confederate defeat and emancipation. In the end, white Southerners prevailed. Their **New South** was a very different South from the one to which whites like David Golightly Harris wished to return.

Wartime Reconstruction

Reconstruction did not wait for the end of war. As the odds of a northern victory increased, thinking about reunification quickened. Immediately, a question arose: Who had authority to devise a plan for reconstructing the Union? Lincoln believed firmly that reconstruction was a matter of executive responsibility. Congress just as firmly asserted its jurisdiction. Fueling the argument about who had authority to set the terms of reconstruction were significant differences about the terms themselves. Lincoln's primary aim was the restoration of national unity, which he sought through a program of speedy, forgiving political reconciliation. Congress feared that the president's program amounted to restoring the old southern ruling class to power. It wanted greater assurances of white loyalty and greater guarantees of black rights.

Black Woman in Cotton Fields, Thomasville, Georgia

Few images of everyday black women during the Reconstruction era survive. This photograph was taken in 1895, but it nevertheless goes to the heart of the labor struggle after the Civil War. Before emancipation black women worked in the fields, and after emancipation white landlords wanted them to continue working there. Freedom allowed some women to escape field labor, but not this Georgian, who probably worked to survive. The photograph reveals a strong person with a clear sense of who she is. Though worn to protect her head and body from the fierce heat, her intricately wrapped headdress dramatically expresses her individuality. Her bare feet also reveal something about her life.
William Gladstone.

In their eagerness to formulate a plan for political reunification, neither Lincoln nor Congress gave much attention to the South's land and labor problems. But as the war rapidly eroded slavery and traditional plantation agriculture, Yankee military commanders in the Union-occupied areas of the Confederacy had no choice but to oversee the emergence of a new labor system.

"To Bind Up the Nation's Wounds"

On March 4, 1865, President Abraham Lincoln delivered his second inaugural address. He surveyed the history of the long, deadly war and then looked ahead to peace. "With malice toward none; with charity for all; with firmness in the right, as God gives us to see the right," Lincoln said, "let us strive on to finish the work we are in; to bind up the nation's wounds . . . to do all which may achieve and cherish a just, and a lasting peace." Lincoln had contemplated reunion for nearly two years. Deep compassion for the enemy guided his thinking about peace. But kindness is not the key to understanding Lincoln's program. His reconstruction plan aimed primarily at shortening the war and ending slavery.

In his Proclamation of Amnesty and Reconstruction, issued in December 1863, Lincoln offered a full pardon to rebels willing to renounce secession and to accept the abolition of slavery. (Pardons were valuable because they restored all property, except slaves, and full political rights.) His offer excluded several groups of Confederates, such as high-ranking civilian and military officers. When only 10 percent of the men who had been qualified voters in 1860 had taken an oath of allegiance, they could organize a new state government. Lincoln's plan did not require ex-rebels to extend social or political rights to ex-slaves, nor did it anticipate a program of long-term federal assistance to freedmen. Clearly, the president sought to restore the broken Union, not to reform it.

Lincoln's easy terms enraged abolitionists like Bostonian Wendell Phillips, who charged that the president "makes the negro's freedom a mere sham." He "is willing that the negro should be free but seeks nothing else for him," Phillips declared. He compared Lincoln to the most passive of the Civil War generals: "What McClellan was on the battlefield—'Do as little hurt as possible!'—Lincoln is in civil affairs—'Make as little change as possible!'" Phillips and other northern radicals called instead for a thorough overhaul of southern society. Their ideas proved to be too drastic for most Republicans during the war years, but Congress agreed that Lincoln's plan was inadequate. In July 1864, Congress put forward a plan of its own.

Congressman Henry Winter Davis of Maryland and Senator Benjamin Wade of Ohio jointly sponsored a bill that threw out Lincoln's "10 percent plan" and demanded that at least half of the voters in a conquered rebel state take the oath of allegiance before reconstruction could begin. Moreover, the Wade-Davis bill banned ex-Confederates from participating in the drafting of new state constitutions. Finally, the bill guaranteed the equality of freedmen before the law. Congress's reconstruction would be neither as quick nor as forgiving as Lincoln's. Still, the Wade-Davis bill angered radicals because it did not include a provision for black **suffrage**. When Lincoln exercised his right not to sign the bill and let it die instead, Wade and Davis published a manifesto charging the president with usurpation of power. They warned Lincoln to confine himself to "his executive duties—to obey and execute, not make the laws—to suppress by arms armed rebellion, and leave political organization to Congress."

Undeterred, Lincoln continued to nurture the formation of loyal state governments under his own plan. Four states—Louisiana, Arkansas, Tennessee, and Virginia—fulfilled the president's requirements, but Congress refused to seat representatives from the "Lincoln states." In his last public address in April 1865, Lincoln defended his plan but for the first time expressed publicly his endorsement of suffrage for southern blacks, at least "the very intelligent, and . . . those who serve our cause as soldiers." The announcement demonstrated that Lincoln's thinking about reconstruction was still evolving. Four days later, he was dead.

> Clearly, the president sought to restore the broken Union, not to reform it.

Land and Labor

Lincoln's thinking about how to deal with the South's systems of land and labor was still undeveloped when he died, but of all the problems raised by emancipation, none proved more critical. As federal armies proceeded to invade and occupy the Confederacy during the war, hundreds of thousands of slaves became free workers. Northern occupation also meant that Union armies controlled vast territories where legal title to land had become unclear. The wartime Confiscation Acts punished "traitors" by taking away their property. The question of what to do with federally occupied land and how to organize labor on it engaged former slaves, former slaveholders, Union military commanders, and federal government officials long before the war ended.

Up and down the Mississippi Valley, occupying federal troops announced a new labor code. The code required slaveholders to sign contracts with ex-slaves and to pay wages. It also obligated employers to provide food, housing, and medical care. It outlawed whipping, but it reserved to the army the right to discipline blacks who refused to work. The code required black laborers to enter into contracts, work diligently, and remain subordinate and obedient. Military leaders clearly had no intention of promoting a social or economic revolution. Instead, they sought with wage labor to restore plantation agriculture. The effort resulted in a hybrid system that one contemporary called "compulsory free labor," something that satisfied no one. Depending on one's point of view, it provided either too little or too much of a break with the past.

> The wartime system of "compulsory free labor" satisfied no one. Depending on one's point of view, it provided either too little or too much of a break with the past.

Planters complained because the new system fell short of slavery. Blacks could not be "transformed by proclamation," a Louisiana sugar planter warned. Yet under the new system, blacks "are expected to perform their new obligations without coercion, & without the fear of punishment which is essential to stimulate the idle and correct the vicious." Without the right to whip, he argued, the new labor system did not have a chance.

African Americans found the new regime too reminiscent of slavery to be called **free labor**. Of its many shortcomings, none disappointed ex-slaves more than the failure to provide them land of their own. "What's the use of being free if you don't own land enough to be buried in?" one man asked. Freedmen believed they had a moral right to land because they and their ancestors had worked it without compensation for more than two centuries. Moreover, several wartime developments led them to believe that the federal government planned to undergird black freedom with landownership.

In January 1865, General William T. Sherman set aside part of the coast south of Charleston for black settlement. He devised the plan to relieve himself of the burden of thousands of impoverished blacks who trailed desperately after his army. By June 1865, some 40,000 freedmen sat on 400,000 acres of "Sherman land." In addition, in March 1865, Congress passed a bill establishing the Bureau of Refugees, Freedmen, and Abandoned Lands. The Freedmen's Bureau, as it was called, distributed food and clothing to destitute Southerners and eased the transition of blacks from slaves to free persons. Congress also authorized the agency to divide abandoned and confiscated land into 40-acre plots, to rent them to freedmen, and eventually to sell them "with such title as the United States can convey." By June 1865, the bureau had situated nearly 10,000 black families on a half million acres abandoned by fleeing planters. Hundreds of thousands of other ex-slaves eagerly anticipated farms of their own.

Despite the flurry of activity, wartime reconstruction settled nothing. Two years of controversy failed to produce agreement about whether the president or Congress had the authority to devise and direct policy or what proper policy should be. Clearly, the nation faced dilemmas almost as trying as those of the war.

The African American Quest for Autonomy

Ex-slaves never had any doubt about what they wanted freedom to mean. They had only to contemplate what they had been denied as slaves. (See "Documenting the American Promise," page 564.) Slaves had to remain on their plantations; freedom allowed blacks to go wherever they pleased. Thus, in the first heady weeks after emancipation, freedmen often abandoned their plantations just to see what was on the other side of the hill. Slaves had to be at work in the fields by dawn; freedom permitted blacks to taste the formerly forbidden pleasure of sleeping through a sunrise. Freedmen also tested the etiquette of racial subordination. "Lizzie's maid passed me today when I was coming from church *without speaking to me*," huffed one plantation mistress.

To whites, emancipation looked like pure anarchy. Without the discipline of slavery, they said, blacks reverted to their natural condition: lazy, irresponsible, and wild. Actually, these former slaves were experimenting with freedom, but they could not long afford to roam the countryside, neglect work, and casually provoke whites. Soon, most were back on plantations, at work in the fields and kitchens.

But other items on ex-slaves' agenda of freedom endured. Freedmen did not easily give up their quest for economic independence. "The way we can best take care of ourselves is to have land," a delegation of South Carolina blacks told General Sherman in 1865, "and turn it and till it by our own labor." Another group of former slaves from South Carolina declared that they wanted land, "not a Master or owner[,] Neither a driver with his Whip." In addition, slavery had deliberately kept blacks illiterate, and freedmen emerged from slavery eager to read and write. "I wishes the Childern all in School," an ex-slave and Union army veteran asserted. "It is beter for them then to be their Surveing a mistes [mistress]."

Moreover, bondage had denied slaves secure family lives, and the restoration of their families became a persistent black aspiration. As a consequence, thousands of black men and women took to the roads in 1865 to look for relations who had been sold away or to free those who were being held illegally as slaves. A black soldier from Missouri wrote his daughters that he was coming for them. "I will have you if it cost me my life," he declared. "Your Miss Kitty said that I tried to steal you," he told them. "But I'll let her know that god never intended for a man to steal his own flesh and blood." And he swore that "if she meets me with ten thousand soldiers, she [will] meet her enemy."

Another hunger that freedom permitted African Americans to satisfy was independent worship. Under slavery, blacks had often prayed with whites in biracial churches. Intent on religious independence, blacks greeted freedom with a mass exodus from white churches. Some joined the newly established southern branches of all-black northern churches, such as the African Methodist Episcopal Church. Others formed black versions of the major southern denominations, Baptists and Methodists. Slaves had comprehended their tribulations through the lens of their deeply felt Christian faith, and freedmen continued to interpret the events of the Civil War and reconstruction as people of faith. One black woman

Washington Miller and Family
After the Civil War, thousands of ex-slaves whose marriages had no legal standing under slavery rushed to formalize their unions. Natchez, Mississippi, home of cotton millionaires before the war, became the home of many black families after the war. Most ex-slaves worked as house servants, laundresses, gardeners, cooks, and day laborers, but some gained real economic independence. The proud and respectable Washington Miller family represents the achievement of middle-class African Americans. This sensitive photograph is the work of Henry C. Norman, a white Georgian who arrived in Natchez about 1870. Over the next four decades, Norman made thousands of photographs of the black and white citizens who visited his studio.
Collection of Thomas H. Gandy and Joan W. Gandy.

thanked Lincoln for the Emancipation Proclamation, declaring, "When you are dead and in Heaven, in a thousand years that action of yours will make the Angels sing your praises I know it."

Presidential Reconstruction

Abraham Lincoln died on April 15, 1865, just hours after John Wilkes Booth shot him at a Washington, D.C., theater. Chief Justice Salmon P. Chase immediately administered the oath of office to Vice President Andrew Johnson of Tennessee. Congress had adjourned in March, which meant that legislators were away from

The Meaning of Freedom

On New Year's Day 1863, President Abraham Lincoln issued the Emancipation Proclamation. It states that "all persons held as slaves" within the states still in rebellion "are, and henceforward shall be, free." Although the Proclamation in and of itself did not free any slaves, it transformed the character of the war. Despite often intolerable conditions, black people focused on the possibilities of freedom.

DOCUMENT 1
Letter from John Q. A. Dennis to Edwin M. Stanton, July 26, 1864

John Q. A. Dennis, formerly a slave in Maryland, wrote to ask Secretary of War Edwin M. Stanton for help in reuniting his family.

Boston
Dear Sir I am Glad that I have the Honour to Write you afew line I have been in troble for about four yars my Dear wife was taken from me Nov 19th 1859 and left me with three Children and I being a Slave At the time Could Not do Anny thing for the poor little Children for my master it was took me Carry me some forty mile from them So I Could Not do for them and the man that they live with half feed them and half Cloth them & beat them like dogs & when I was admitted to go to see them it use to brake my heart & Now I say again I am Glad to have the honour to write to you to see if you Can Do Anny thing for me or for my poor little Children I was keap in Slavy untell last Novr 1863. then the Good

lord sent the Cornel borne [federal Colonel William Birney?] Down their in Marland in worsester Co So as I have been recently freed I have but letle to live on but I am Striveing Dear Sir but what I went too know of you Sir is it possible for me to go & take my Children from those men that keep them in Savery if it is possible will you pleas give me a permit from your hand then I think they would let them go. . . .

Hon sir will you please excuse my Miserable writeing & answer me as soon as you can I want get the little Children out of Slavery, I being Criple would like to know of you also if I Cant be permited to rase a Shool Down there & on what turm I Could be admited to Do so No more At present Dear Hon Sir

SOURCE: Ira Berlin, Joseph P. Reidy, and Leslie S. Rowland, eds., *Freedom: A Documentary History of Emancipation, 1861–1867*, ser. 1, vol. 1, *The Destruction of Slavery* (Cambridge: Cambridge University Press, 1985), 386.

DOCUMENT 2
Report from Reverend A. B. Randall, February 28, 1865

Freedom prompted ex-slaves to seek legal marriages, which under slavery had been impossible. Writing from Little Rock, Arkansas, to the adjutant general of the Union army, A. B. Randall, the white chaplain of a black regiment, affirmed the importance of marriage to freed slaves and emphasized their conviction that emancipation was only the first step toward full freedom.

Weddings, just now, are very popular, and abundant among the Colored People. They have just learned, of the Special Order No. 15. of Gen Thomas [Adjutant General Lorenzo Thomas] by which, they may not only be lawfully married, but have their Marriage Certificates, Recorded; in a book furnished by the Government. This is most desirable. . . . Those who were captured . . . at Ivy's Ford, on the 17th of January, by Col Brooks, had their Marriage Certificates, taken from them; and destroyed; and then were roundly cursed, for having such papers in their posession. I have married, during the month, at this Post; Twenty five couples; mostly, those, who have families; & have been living together for years. I try to dissuade single men, who are soldiers, from marrying, till their time of enlistment is out: as that course seems to me, to be most judicious.

The Colord People here, generally consider, this war not only; their exodus, from bondage; but the road, to Responsibility; Competency; and an honorable Citizenship—God grant that their hopes and expectations may be fully realized.

SOURCE: Ira Berlin, Joseph P. Reidy, and Leslie S. Rowland, eds., *Freedom: A Documentary History of Emancipation, 1861–1867*, ser. 2, *The Black Military Experience* (Cambridge: Cambridge University Press, 1982), 712.

DOCUMENT 3
Petition "to the Union Convention of Tennessee Assembled in the Capitol at Nashville," January 9, 1865

Early efforts at political reconstruction prompted petitions from former slaves

demanding civil and political rights. In January 1865, black Tennesseans petitioned a convention of white Unionists debating the reorganization of state government.

We the undersigned petitioners, American citizens of African descent, natives and residents of Tennessee, and devoted friends of the great National cause, do most respectfully ask a patient hearing of your honorable body in regard to matters deeply affecting the future condition of our unfortunate and long suffering race.

First of all, however, we would say that words are too weak to tell how profoundly grateful we are to the Federal Government for the good work of freedom which it is gradually carrying forward; and for the Emancipation Proclamation which has set free all the slaves in some of the rebellious States, as well as many of the slaves in Tennessee. . . .

We claim freedom, as our natural right, and ask that in harmony and co-operation with the nation at large, you should cut up by the roots the system of slavery, which is not only a wrong to us, but the source of all the evil which at present afflicts the State. For slavery, corrupt itself, corrupted nearly all, also, around it, so that it has influenced nearly all the slave States to rebel against the Federal Government, in order to set up a government of pirates under which slavery might be perpetrated.

In the contest between the nation and slavery, our unfortunate people have sided, by instinct, with the former. We have little fortune to devote to the national cause, for a hard fate has hitherto forced us to live in poverty, but we do devote to its success, our hopes, our toils, our whole heart, our sacred honor, and our lives. We will work, pray, live, and, if need be, die for the Union, as cheerfully as ever a white patriot died for his country. The color of our skin does not lessen in the least degree, our love either for God or for the land of our birth. . . .

We know the burdens of citizenship, and are ready to bear them. We know the duties of the good citizen, and are ready to perform them cheerfully, and would ask to be put in a position in which we can discharge them more effectually. . . .

This is a democracy—a government of the people. It should aim to make every man, without regard to the color of his skin, the amount of his wealth, or the character of his religious faith, feel personally interested in its welfare. Every man who lives under the Government should feel that it is his property, his treasure, the bulwark and defence of himself and his family, his pearl of great price, which he must preserve, protect, and defend faithfully at all times, on all occasions, in every possible manner.

This is not a Democratic Government if a numerous, law-abiding, industrious, and useful class of citizens, born and bred on the soil, are to be treated as aliens and enemies, as an inferior degraded class, who must have no voice in the Government which they support, protect and defend, with all their heart, soul, mind, and body, both in peace and war. . . .

The possibility that the negro suffrage proposition may shock popular prejudice at first sight, is not a conclusive argument against its wisdom and policy. No proposition ever met with more furious or general opposition than the one to enlist colored soldiers in the United States army. The opponents of the measure exclaimed on all hands that the negro was a coward; that he would not fight; that one white man, with a whip in his hand could put to flight a regiment of them; that the experiment would end in the utter rout and ruin of the Federal army. Yet the colored man has fought so well, on almost every occasion, that the rebel government is prevented, only by its fears and distrust of being able to force him to fight for slavery as well as he fights against it, from putting half a million of negroes into its ranks.

The Government has asked the colored man to fight for its preservation and gladly has he done it. It can afford to trust him with a vote as safely as it trusted him with a bayonet.

Source: Ira Berlin, Joseph P. Reidy, and Leslie S. Rowland, eds., *Freedom: A Documentary History of Emancipation, 1861–1867,* ser. 2, *The Black Military Experience* (Cambridge: Cambridge University Press, 1982), 811–16.

Questions for Analysis and Debate

1. How does John Q. A. Dennis interpret his responsibility as a father?

2. Why do you think ex-slaves wanted their marriages legalized?

3. Why, according to petitioners to the Union Convention of Tennessee, did blacks deserve voting rights?

Washington when Lincoln was killed. They would not reconvene until December. Throughout the summer and fall, therefore, the "accidental president" made critical decisions about the future of the South without congressional input. Like Lincoln, Johnson believed that responsibility for restoring the Union lay with the president. With dizzying speed, he drew up and executed a plan of reconstruction.

Congress returned to the capital in December to find that, as far as the president and former Confederates were concerned, reconstruction was already decided. To most Republicans, Johnson's modest demands of ex-rebels made a mockery of the sacrifice of Union soldiers. Instead of honoring the dead by providing the nation with "a new birth of freedom," as Lincoln had promised in the 1863 speech at Gettysburg, Johnson had acted as midwife to the rebirth of the Old South. He had achieved political reunification at the cost of black **liberty**. To let his program stand, Republican legislators said, would mean that the North's dead had indeed died in vain. They proceeded to dismantle it and substitute a program of their own, one that southern whites found ways to resist.

Johnson's Program of Reconciliation

Born in 1808 in Raleigh, North Carolina, Andrew Johnson was the son of poor, illiterate parents. Unable to afford to send her son to school, Johnson's widowed mother apprenticed him to a tailor. Self-educated and ambitious, he later worked as a tailor in Tennessee, accumulated a fortune in land, acquired five slaves, and built a career in politics championing the South's common white people and assailing its "illegitimate, swaggering, bastard, scrub aristocracy." The only senator from a Confederate state to remain loyal to the Union, Johnson held the planter class responsible for secession. Less than two weeks before he became president, he made it clear what he would do to planters if he ever had the chance: "I would arrest them—I would try them—I would convict them and I would hang them."

Despite such statements, Johnson was no friend of northern radicals. A southern Democrat all his life, Johnson occupied the White House only because the Republican Party in 1864 had needed to broaden its appeal to loyal, Union-supporting Democrats. Johnson favored traditional Democratic causes, vigorously defending **states' rights** (but not secession) and opposing Republican efforts to expand the power of the federal government. He voted against almost every federal appropriation, including a bill to pave the streets of Washington.

Mount Zion Baptist Church, San Antonio, Texas, 1877
Freedom from bondage permitted blacks to flee white ministers and white churches, to "come out from under the yoke," as one ex-slave put it. Former slave Nancy Williams recalled: "Ole white preachers used to talk wid dey tongues widdout sayin' nothin', but Jesus told us slaves to talk wid our hearts." When slavery ended, African Americans worshipped as their hearts dictated. This large, well-dressed congregation standing in front of its substantial church building in San Antonio, Texas, demonstrates how successful some freedmen were in building churches of their own.
Institute of Texas Cultures, San Antonio, Texas.

Johnson had also been a steadfast defender of slavery. He had owned slaves until 1862, when Tennessee rebels, angry at his Unionism, confiscated them. He only grudgingly accepted emancipation. When he did, it was more because he hated planters than sympathized with slaves. "Damn the negroes," he said. "I am fighting those traitorous aristocrats, their masters." At a time when the nation faced its moment of truth regarding black Americans, the new president harbored unshakable racist convictions. Africans, Johnson said, were "inferior to the white man in point of intellect—better calculated in physical structure to undergo drudgery and hardship."

Johnson presented his plan of reconstruction as a continuation of Lincoln's plan, and in some ways it was. Like Lincoln, he stressed reconciliation between the Union and the defeated Confederacy and rapid restoration of civil government in the South. Like Lincoln, he offered to pardon most, but not all, ex-rebels. Johnson recognized the state governments created by Lincoln but set out his own requirements for restoring the rebel states to the Union. All that the citizens of a state had to do was to renounce the right of secession, deny that the debts of the Confederacy were legal and binding, and ratify the Thirteenth Amendment abolishing slavery, which became part of the Constitution in December 1865. Johnson's plan ignored Lincoln's acceptance near the end of his life of some form of limited black voting.

Johnson's eagerness to normalize relations with southern states and his lack of sympathy for blacks also led him to instruct military and government officials to return to pardoned ex-Confederates all confiscated and abandoned land, even if it was in the hands of freedmen. Reformers were shocked. They had expected the president's vendetta against planters to mean the permanent confiscation of the South's plantations and the distribution of the land to loyal freedmen. Instead, his instructions canceled the promising beginnings made by General Sherman and the Freedmen's Bureau to settle blacks on land of their own. As one freedman observed, "Things was hurt by Mr. Lincoln getting killed."

Southern Resistance and Black Codes

In the summer of 1865, delegates across the South gathered to draw up the new state constitutions required by Johnson's plan of reconstruction.

The Black Codes

Titled "Selling a Freeman to Pay His Fine at Monticello, Florida," this 1867 drawing from a northern magazine equates the black codes with the reinstitution of slavery. The laws stopped short of reenslavement but sharply restricted blacks' freedom. In Florida, as in other southern states, certain acts, such as breaking a labor contract, were made criminal offenses, the penalty for which could be involuntary plantation labor for a year.

Library of Congress.

Although they had been defeated, whites clearly had not been subdued. Rather than take their medicine, delegates choked on even the president's mild requirements. Refusing to declare their secession ordinances null and void, the South Carolina and Georgia conventions merely "repudiated" their ordinances, preserving in principle their right to secede. In addition, South Carolina and Mississippi refused to disown their Confederate war debts. Finally, Mississippi rejected the Thirteenth Amendment outright, and Alabama rejected it in part. Despite these defiant acts, Johnson did not demand that Southerners comply with his lenient terms. By failing to draw a hard line, he rekindled southern resistance. White Southerners began to think that by standing up for themselves they—not victorious Northerners—would shape the transition from slavery to freedom. In the fall of 1865, newly elected southern legislators set out to reverse what they considered the "retreat into barbarism" that followed emancipation.

State governments across the South adopted a series of laws known as *black codes*. Emancipation had brought freedmen important rights that they had lacked as slaves—to own property, make contracts, marry legally, and sue and be sued in court. The black codes made a travesty of freedom. They sought to keep blacks subordinate to whites by subjecting blacks to every sort of discrimination. Several states made it illegal for blacks to own a gun. Mississippi made insulting gestures and language by blacks a criminal offense. The codes barred blacks from jury duty. Not a single southern state granted any black—no matter how educated, wealthy, or refined—the right to vote.

> Emancipation had brought freedmen important rights that they had lacked as slaves—to own property, to make contracts, to marry legally. The black codes made a travesty of freedom.

At the core of the black codes, however, lay the matter of labor. Faced with the death of slavery and the disintegration of plantations, legislators sought to hustle freedmen back into traditional roles to restore the old plantation economy. South Carolina attempted to limit blacks to either farmwork or domestic service by requiring them to pay annual taxes of $10 to $100 to work in any other occupation. Mississippi declared that blacks who did not possess written evidence of employment could be declared vagrants and be subject to fines or involuntary plantation labor. Most states allowed judges to bind certain black children—orphans and others whose parents they deemed unable to support them—to white employers. Under these so-called apprenticeship laws, courts bound thousands of black children to work for planter "guardians."

Johnson refused to intervene decisively. A staunch defender of states' rights, he believed that the citizens of every state, even those citizens who had attempted to destroy the Union, should be free to write their own constitutions and laws. Moreover, since Johnson was as eager as other white Southerners to restore white supremacy and black subordination, the black codes did not offend him.

But Johnson also followed the path that he believed would offer him the greatest political return. A **conservative** Tennessee Democrat at the head of a northern Republican Party, he began to look southward for political allies. Despite tough talk about punishing traitors, he personally pardoned 14,000 wealthy or high-ranking ex-Confederates. By pardoning planters and Confederate officials, by acquiescing in the South's black codes, and by accepting the new southern governments even when they failed to satisfy his minimal demands, he won useful friends.

If Northerners had any doubts about the mood of the South, they evaporated in the elections of 1865. To represent them in Congress, white Southerners chose former Confederates, not loyal Unionists. Of the eighty senators and representatives they sent to Washington, fifteen had served in the Confederate army, ten of them as generals. Another sixteen had served in civil and judicial posts in the Confederacy. Nine others had served in the Confederate Congress. One—Alexander Stephens—had been vice president of the Confederacy. In December, this remarkable group arrived on the steps of the nation's Capitol building to be seated in Congress. As one Georgian remarked: "It looked as though Richmond had moved to Washington."

Expansion of Federal Authority and Black Rights

Southerners had blundered monumentally. They had assumed that what Andrew Johnson was willing to accept, the northern public and Congress would accept as well. But southern intransigence compelled even moderate Republicans to conclude that ex-rebels were a "generation of vipers," still dangerous and untrustworthy. So angry were northern Republicans with the rebels that the federal government refused to supply artificial limbs to disabled Southerners, as they did for Union veterans (see "The Promise of Technology," page 570).

The black codes in particular soured moderate Republicans on the South. The codes became a symbol of southern intentions not to accept the verdict of the battlefields but instead to "restore all of slavery but its name." Northerners were hardly saints when it came to racial justice, but black freedom had become a hallowed war aim. "We tell the white men of Mississippi," the *Chicago Tribune* roared, "that the men of the North will convert the State of Mississippi into a frog pond before they will allow such laws to disgrace one foot of the soil in which the bones of our soldiers sleep and over which the flag of freedom waves."

Moderates represented the mainstream of the Republican Party and wanted only assurance that slavery and treason were dead. They did not champion black equality or the confiscation of plantations or black voting, as did the Radicals, a minority faction within the Republican Party. In December 1865, however, when Congress convened in Washington, it became clear that southern obstinacy had succeeded in forging unity (at least temporarily) among Republican factions. Exercising Congress's right to determine the qualifications of its members, Republicans refused to seat the southern representatives. Rather than accept Johnson's claim that the "work of restoration" was done, Congress challenged his executive power. Congressional Republicans enjoyed a three-to-one majority over the Democrats, and if they could agree on a program of reconstruction, they could easily pass legislation and even override presidential vetoes.

The moderates took the initiative. Senator Lyman Trumbull of Illinois declared that the president's policy of trusting southern whites proved that the ex-slave would "be tyrannized over, abused, and virtually reenslaved without some legislation by the nation for his protection." Early in 1866, the moderates produced two bills that strengthened the federal shield. The first, the Freedmen's Bureau bill, prolonged the life of the agency established by the previous Congress. Since the end of the war, it had distributed food, supervised labor contracts, and sponsored schools for freedmen. Arguing that the Constitution never contemplated a "system for the support of indigent persons," President Andrew Johnson vetoed the Freedmen's Bureau bill. Congress failed by a narrow margin to override the president's veto.

Johnson's veto galvanized nearly unanimous Republican support for the moderates' second measure, the Civil Rights Act. Designed to nullify the black codes, it affirmed the rights of blacks to enjoy "full and equal benefit of all laws and proceedings for the security of person and property as is enjoyed by white citizens." The act boldly required the end of legal discrimination in state laws and represented an extraordinary expansion of black rights and federal

Confederate Flag Dress
While politicians in Washington, D.C., debated the future of the South, white Southerners were coming to grips with the meaning of Confederate defeat. They began to refer to their failure to secede from the Union as the "Lost Cause." They enshrined the memory of certain former Confederates, especially Robert E. Lee, whose nobility and courage represented the white South's image of itself, and they made a fetish of the Confederate flag. White Southerners incorporated symbols of the Lost Cause into their daily lives. This dress, made from material embossed with the rebel flag, did double duty. It both memorialized the Confederacy and, through the sale of the cloth, raised funds for the Confederate Soldiers' Home in Richmond, Virginia.
Valentine Museum, Cook Collection.

authority. The president argued that the civil rights bill amounted to an "unconstitutional invasion of states' rights" and vetoed it. In essence, he denied that the federal government possessed authority to protect the civil rights of blacks.

The president did not have the final word. In April 1866, an incensed Republican Party again pushed the civil rights bill through Congress and overrode the presidential veto. In July, it passed another Freedmen's Bureau bill and overrode Johnson's veto. For the first time in American history, Congress had overridden presidential vetoes of major legislation. As a worried South Carolinian observed, Johnson had succeeded in uniting the Republicans and probably touched off "a fight this fall such as has never been seen."

Congressional Reconstruction

By the summer of 1866, President Andrew Johnson and Congress had dropped their gloves and stood toe to toe in a bare-knuckled contest

Filling the "Empty Sleeve": Artificial Limbs

Industrial and technological developments that made the Civil War so destructive also came to the aid of maimed veterans during national reconstruction. The minié ball, a new kind of ammunition used in the war, proved extremely destructive to human flesh. In attempts to save lives, northern and southern surgeons performed approximately 60,000 amputations. Confederate nurse Kate Cummings observed that in her hospital amputations were so common that they were "scarcely noticed." Approximately 45,000 of the amputees survived, and as the nation began reconstructing the Union, it also sought the literal reconstruction of disabled veterans.

Once their wounds had healed, most amputees were eager to fill an empty sleeve or pant leg with an artificial limb. The federal government provided limbs to those who had fought for the Union, and individual southern states provided limbs for Confederate veterans. Innovations in design and production began during the war and accelerated sharply as the enormous demand produced a surge of interest in prosthetic tech-

nology. In the 15 years before the war, 34 patents were issued for artificial limbs and assisting devices; in the 12 years from the beginning of the war to 1873, 133 patents for limbs were issued, nearly a 300 percent increase. As Oliver Wendell Holmes Jr., an army veteran and future Supreme Court justice, observed, if "war unmakes legs," then "human skill must supply their places."

The search for a functional, lightweight, artificial limb drew on a number of advancing fields, including photography, physiology, physics, mathematics, and psychology. For example, in 1859 photographers in Edinburgh and New York succeeded in taking a rapid succession of fast-speed pictures of pedestrians and breaking their strides down into minute parts. Photographs of individuals frozen in midstep provided new information about human movement that helped make better artificial limbs.

The application of photography is but one example of the growing application of science and technology to the alleviation of human suffering in the second half of the

nineteenth century. As excited designers sought to overcome problems of noise, weight, appearance, and discomfort, artificial limbs advanced quickly from crude peg legs to hollow willow legs with movable ankles that simulated the natural motions of the foot. Newly invented vulcanized rubber (called India rubber) increased strength and flexibility and allowed disabled veterans to dispense with metal bolts and springs in their new limbs. Limb makers sought to erase the line between nature and technology, to merge "bodies with machines," as one manufacturer promised. One doctor boasted: "In our time, limb-making has been carried to such a state of perfection that both in form and function they so completely resemble the natural extremity that those who wear them pass unobserved and unrecognized in walks of business and pleasure." He exaggerated, for the artificial limbs of the 1860s were crude by today's standards, but they did represent significant technological advances.

Less than two years after the war, the manufacture of artificial limbs was, according to Oliver Wendell Holmes Jr., "a great and active branch of history." Before the war, locksmiths, gunsmiths, toolmakers, harness makers, and cabinetmakers had made peg legs and artificial arms individually as sidelines to their principal tasks. After the war, the great demand for

unprecedented in American history. Johnson made it clear that he would not budge on either constitutional issues or policy. Moderate Republicans made a major effort to resolve the dilemma of reconstruction by amending the Constitution. But the obstinacy of Johnson and white Southerners pushed Republican moderates ever closer to the Radicals and to acceptance of additional federal intervention in the South. In time, white men in Congress debated whether to give the ballot to black men. Outside of Congress, blacks raised their voices on behalf of color-blind voting rights, while women argued to make voting sex-blind as well.

artificial limbs prompted businesses to apply industrial manufacturing processes to limbs. Soon American factories—high-volume, mechanized, and uniform—were producing untold numbers of sewing machines, bicycles, and typewriters—as well as artificial limbs.

The postwar business of prosthesis was highly competitive. With the federal and state governments placing large, lucrative orders, dozens of manufacturers entered the market. Very quickly, buyers could choose from among English, French, German, and American models. With so many choices, men had to be persuaded that one leg was better than another. Aggressive advertising campaigns announced the new products. Northern manufacturers used government military and pension registration rolls to mail brochures directly to the homes of Union veterans. Manufacturers in New York, Philadelphia, and Boston established dazzling showrooms on major shopping streets and sponsored "cripple races" to test and promote their products.

Politics sometimes affected opinions about artificial limbs and about which product to choose. Southern manufacturers proclaimed that they

"Before and After"
These photographic images of a veteran showing the results of two amputations and wearing his artificial legs come from the back of an A. A. Marks business card in about 1878. This manufacturer of artificial limbs sent a clear message: Marks legs make maimed men whole again. Marks promised that, thus restored, the wounded man would be the "equal of his fellowmen in every employment of life."
Warshaw Collection, National Museum of American History, Smithsonian Institution.

were "a home manufacturer" and were more deserving of contracts from former Confederate states than were their northern competitors. Former Confederate general John B. Hood made a controversial admission when he declared that his "Yankee leg was the best of all." Another disabled Southerner, however, disliked his northern-manufactured leg, which, he concluded, "like the majority of Yankee inventions proved to be a 'humbug.'"

Disabled veterans were likely to find their postwar struggle to obtain work, to overcome stigma, and to regain their confidence almost as difficult as their battlefield experiences. Some manufacturers of prosthetics attempted, through a combination of technology and psychology, to help them. Each year in New York City, for example, manufacturers sponsored a left-handed penmanship contest to encourage men who had lost their right arms to learn to write with their left hands. Well into the twentieth century, veterans' "empty sleeve" remained both a badge of courage and a sign of permanent loss, a wound national reconstruction could never heal.

The Fourteenth Amendment and Escalating Violence

In April 1866, Republican moderates introduced the Fourteenth Amendment to the Constitution. Congress passed it in June, and two years later it gained the necessary ratification of three-fourths of the states. The most important provisions of this complex amendment made all native-born or naturalized persons American citizens and prohibited states from abridging the "privileges and immunities" of citizens, depriving them of "life, liberty, or property without due process of law," and denying them "equal protection of the laws."

By making blacks national citizens, the Fourteenth Amendment provided a national guarantee of equality before the law. In essence, it protected the rights of citizens against violation by their own state governments.

By making blacks national citizens, the amendment nullified the *Dred Scott* decision of 1857 and provided a national guarantee of equality before the law. In essence, it protected the rights of citizens against violation by their own state governments.

The Fourteenth Amendment also dealt with voting rights. Rather than explicitly granting the vote to black men, as Radicals wanted, the amendment gave Congress the right to reduce the congressional representation of states that withheld suffrage from some of its adult male population. In other words, white Southerners could either allow black men to vote or see their representation in Washington slashed.

The Republicans drafted the Fourteenth Amendment to their benefit. If southern whites granted voting rights to freedmen, the Republican Party, entirely a northern party, would gain valuable black votes, establish a wing in the South, and secure its national power. But if whites refused, representation of southern Democrats would plunge, and Republicans would still gain political power. Although whites in the North were largely hostile to voting rights for blacks too, northern states could continue to withhold suffrage and not suffer in Washington, for the black populations in the North were too small to count in figuring representation. To Radicals, the Fourteenth Amendment's voting provision was "hypocritical" and a "swindle."

The suffrage provisions in the amendment completely ignored the small band of politicized and energized women who had emerged from the war demanding "the ballot for the two disenfranchised classes, negroes and women." Founding the American Equal Rights Association in 1866, Susan B. Anthony and Elizabeth Cady Stanton lobbied for "a government by the people, and the whole people; for the people and the whole people." They felt betrayed when their old antislavery allies, who now occupied positions of national power, proved to be fickle and refused to work for their goals. "It was the Negro's hour," Frederick Douglass later

The Fourteenth Amendment's suffrage provisions completely ignored the small band of politicized and energized women who had emerged from the war demanding "the ballot for two disenfranchised classes, negroes and women."

explained. The Republican Party had to avoid anything that might jeopardize black gains, Charles Sumner declared. He suggested that woman suffrage could be "the great question of the future."

The Fourteenth Amendment dashed women's expectations. It provided for punishment of any state that excluded voters on the basis of race but not on the basis of sex. The amendment also introduced the word *male* into the Constitution when it referred to a citizen's right to vote. Stanton had predicted that "if that word 'male' be inserted, it will take us a century at least to get it out."

Despite women's objections, Tennessee approved the Fourteenth Amendment in July, and Congress promptly welcomed the state's representatives and senators back. Had Johnson counseled other southern states to ratify this relatively mild amendment and warned them that they faced the fury of an outraged Republican Party if they refused, they might have listened. Instead, Johnson advised Southerners to reject the Fourteenth Amendment and to rely on him to trounce the Republicans in the fall congressional elections.

Johnson had decided to make the Fourteenth Amendment the overriding issue of the 1866 congressional elections and to gather its white opponents into a new conservative party, the National Union Party. In August, his supporters met in Philadelphia. Democrats came, but most Republicans did not. Johnson was unable to draw disgruntled Republicans; his previous actions had united the Republican Party against him.

The president's strategy had suffered a setback two weeks earlier when whites in several southern cities went on rampages against blacks. It was less an outbreak of violence than an escalation of the violence that had never ceased. In New Orleans, a mob assaulted delegates to a black suffrage convention, and 34 blacks died. In Memphis, white mobs hurtled through the black sections of town and killed at least 46 people. The slaughter shocked Northerners and renewed skepticism about Johnson's claim that southern whites could be trusted. "Who doubts that the Freedmen's Bureau ought to be abolished forthwith," a New Yorker observed sarcastically, "and the blacks remitted to the paternal care of their old masters, who 'understand the nigger, you know, a great deal better than the Yankees can.'"

The 1866 election resulted in an overwhelming Republican victory in which the party re-

Memphis Riots, May 1866

On May 1, 1866, two carriages, one driven by a white man and the other by a black man, collided on a busy Memphis street. This minor incident spiraled into three days of bloody racial violence in which dozens of blacks and two whites died. Racial friction was common in postwar Memphis, and white newspapers routinely heaped abuse on black citizens. "Would to God they were back in Africa, or some other seaport town," the *Memphis Argus* shouted two days before the riot erupted, "anywhere but here." South Memphis, pictured in this lithograph from *Harper's Weekly*, was a shantytown where the families of black soldiers stationed at nearby Fort Pickering lived. The army commander refused to send troops to protect soldiers' families and property, and white mobs ran wild.

Library of Congress.

tained its three-to-one congressional majority over Democrats. Johnson had bet that Northerners would not support federal protection of black rights. He expected a racist backlash to blast the Republican Party. But the Fourteenth Amendment was not radical enough to drive Republican voters into Johnson's camp, and the war was still fresh in northern minds. As one Republican explained, southern whites "with all their intelligence were traitors, the blacks with all their ignorance were loyal."

Radical Reconstruction and Military Rule

The elections of 1866 should have taught southern whites the folly of relying on Andrew Johnson as a guide through the thicket of reconstruction. But when Johnson continued to urge Southerners toward rejection of the Fourteenth Amendment, every southern state except

Tennessee voted it down. "The last one of the sinful ten," thundered Representative James A. Garfield of Ohio, "has flung back into our teeth the magnanimous offer of a generous nation." In the void created by the South's rejection of the moderates' program, the Radicals seized the initiative.

Each act of defiance by southern whites had boosted the standing of the Radicals within the Republican Party. At the Radical core was a small group of men who had cut their political teeth on the **antebellum** campaign against slavery, who had goaded Lincoln toward making the war a crusade for freedom, and who had carried into the postwar period the conviction that only federal power could protect the rights of the freedmen. Except for freedmen themselves, no one did more to make freedom the "mighty moral question of the age." Men like Senator Charles Sumner, that pompous but sincere Massachusetts crusader, and Thaddeus Stevens, the caustic representative from Pennsylvania, did not speak with a single voice, but they united in calling for civil and political equality. They insisted on extending to ex-slaves the same opportunities that northern working people enjoyed under the free-labor system. The southern states were "like clay in the hands of the potter," Stevens declared in January 1867, and he called on Congress to begin reconstruction all over again.

In March 1867, moderates joined the Radicals to overturn the Johnson state governments and initiate military rule of the South. The Military Reconstruction Act (and three subsequent acts) divided the ten unreconstructed Confederate states into five military districts. Congress placed a Union general in charge of each district and instructed him to "suppress insurrection, disorder, and violence" and to begin political reform. After the military had completed voter registration, which would include black men and exclude all those barred by the Fourteenth Amendment from holding public office, voters in each state would elect delegates to conventions that would draw up new state constitutions. Each constitution would guarantee black suffrage. When the voters of each state had approved the constitution and the state legislature had ratified the Fourteenth Amendment, the state could submit its work to Congress. If Congress approved, the state's senators and representatives could be seated, and political reunification would be accomplished.

Radicals proclaimed the provision for black suffrage "a prodigious triumph." The doggedness of the Radicals and of African Americans, and the pigheadedness of Johnson and the white South, swept the Republican Party far beyond the limited suffrage provisions of the Fourteenth Amendment. Republicans finally agreed with Sumner that only the voting power of ex-slaves could bring about a permanent revolution in the South. Indeed, suffrage provided blacks with a powerful instrument of change and self-protection. When combined with

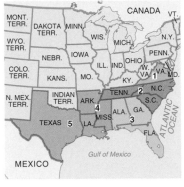

Reconstruction Military Districts, 1867

the disfranchisement of thousands of ex-rebels, it promised to cripple any neo-Confederate resurgence and guarantee Republican state governments in the South.

Despite its bold suffrage provision, the Military Reconstruction Act of 1867 disappointed those who advocated the confiscation and redistribution of southern plantations to ex-slaves. Among the most distressed was Thaddeus Stevens, who believed that at bottom reconstruction was an economic problem. He agreed wholeheartedly with the ex-slave who said, "Give us our own land and we take care of ourselves, but without land, the old masters can hire us or starve us, as they please." But most Republicans believed they had already provided blacks with the critical tools: equal legal rights and the ballot. If blacks were to get forty acres, they would have to gain the land themselves.

Declaring that he would rather sever his right arm than sign such a formula for "anarchy and chaos," Andrew Johnson vetoed the Military Reconstruction Act. Congress overrode his veto the very same day, dramatizing the shift in power from the executive to the legislative branch of government. With the passage of the Reconstruction Acts of 1867, congressional reconstruction was virtually completed. Congress had left whites owning most of the South's land but, in a radical departure, had given black men the ballot. More than any other provision, black suffrage justifies the term "radical reconstruction." In 1867, the nation began an unprecedented experiment in interracial democracy—at least in the South, for Congress's plan did not touch the North. Soon the former Confederate states would become the primary theater for political struggle. But before the spotlight swung away from Washington, the president and Congress had one more scene to play.

Impeaching a President

Despite his defeats, Andrew Johnson had no intention of yielding control of reconstruction. In a dozen ways he sabotaged Congress's will and encouraged white belligerence and resistance. He issued a flood of pardons to undermine efforts at political and economic change. He

The doggedness of the Radicals and of African Americans, and the pigheadedness of Johnson and the white South, swept the Republican Party far beyond the limited suffrage provisions of the Fourteenth Amendment.

waged war against the Freedmen's Bureau by removing officers who sympathized too fully with ex-slaves. And he replaced Union generals eager to enforce Congress's Reconstruction Acts with conservative men eager to defeat them. Johnson claimed that he was merely defending the "violated Constitution." At bottom, however, the president subverted congressional reconstruction to protect southern whites from what he considered the horrors of "Negro domination."

When Congress realized that overriding Johnson's vetoes did not ensure that Congress got its way, it attempted to tie the president's hands. Congress required that all orders to field commanders pass through the General of the Army, Ulysses S. Grant, who Congress believed was sympathetic to southern freedmen, southern Unionists, and Republicans. It also enacted the Tenure of Office Act in 1867, which required the approval of the Senate for the removal of any government official who had been appointed with Senate consent. Congress intended the Tenure of Office Act to protect Secretary of War Edwin M. Stanton, the last remaining friend of radical reconstruction in Johnson's cabinet. Some Republicans, however, believed that nothing less than getting rid of Johnson could save reconstruction, and they initiated a crusade to impeach the president and remove him from office.

As long as Johnson refrained from breaking a law, **impeachment** remained a faint hope. According to the Constitution, the House of Representatives can impeach and the Senate can try any federal official for "treason, bribery, or other high crimes and misdemeanors." Radicals argued that Johnson's abuse of constitutional powers and his failure to fulfill constitutional obligations were impeachable offenses, but moderates interpreted the constitutional provision to mean violation of criminal statutes. Then in August 1867, Johnson suspended Secretary of War Stanton from office. As required by the Tenure of Office Act, the president requested the Senate to consent to the dismissal. When the Senate balked, Johnson removed Stanton anyway. "Is the President crazy, or only drunk?" asked a dumbfounded Republican moderate. "I'm afraid his doings will make us all favor impeachment."

News of Johnson's open defiance of the law convinced every Republican in the House to vote for a resolution impeaching the president. Supreme Court Chief

Andrew Johnson, with Additions
This dignified portrait by Currier and Ives of President Andrew Johnson appeared in 1868, the year of his impeachment trial. The portrait was apparently amended by a disgruntled citizen. Johnson's vetoes of several reconstruction measures passed by Congress caused his opponents to charge him with arrogant monarchical behavior. Johnson preferred the unamended image—that of a plain and sturdy statesman.
Museum of American Political Life.

Justice Salmon Chase presided over the Senate trial, which lasted from March until May 1868. Chase refused to allow Johnson's opponents to raise broad issues of misuse of power and forced them to argue their case exclusively on the narrow legal grounds of Johnson's removal of Stanton. Johnson's lawyers argued that he had not committed a criminal offense, that the Tenure of Office Act was unconstitutional, and that in any case it did not apply to Stanton, who had been appointed by Lincoln. When the critical vote came, seven moderate Republicans broke with their party and joined the Democrats in voting not guilty. With 35 in favor and 19 opposed, the impeachment forces fell one vote short of the two-thirds needed to convict.

Johnson survived but did not come through the ordeal unscathed. After his trial he called a truce, and for the remaining ten months of his term congressional reconstruction proceeded unhindered by presidential interference. Without interference from Johnson, Congress revisited the suffrage issue.

The Fifteenth Amendment and Women's Demands

In February 1869, Republicans passed the Fifteenth Amendment to the Constitution. The amendment prohibited states from depriving any citizen of the right to vote because of "race, color, or previous condition of servitude." The Reconstruction Acts of 1867 already required black suffrage in the South; the Fifteenth Amendment extended black voting to the entire

nation. Partisan advantage played an important role in the amendment's passage. Gains by northern Democrats in the 1868 elections worried Republicans, and black voters now represented the balance of power in several northern states. By giving ballots to northern blacks, Republicans could lessen their political vulnerability. As one Republican congressman observed, "Party expediency and exact justice coincide for once."

Some Republicans, however, found the final wording of the Fifteenth Amendment "lame and halting." Rather than absolutely guaranteeing the right to vote, the amendment merely prohibited exclusion on grounds of race. The distinction would prove to be significant. In time, inventive white Southerners would devise tests of literacy and property and other apparently nonracial measures that would effectively disfranchise blacks yet not violate the Fifteenth Amendment. But an amendment that fully guaranteed the right to vote courted defeat outside the South. Rising antiforeign sentiment—against the Chinese in California and against European immigrants in the Northeast—caused states to resist giving up total control of suffrage requirements. The limits of the proposed amendment made it appealing. In March 1870, after three-fourths of the states had ratified it, the Fifteenth Amendment became part of the Constitution. Republicans generally breathed a sigh of relief, confident that black suffrage was "the last great point that remained to be settled of the issues of the war."

Woman suffrage advocates, however, were sorely disappointed with the Fifteenth Amendment's failure to extend voting rights to women. Although women fought hard to include the word *sex* (as they had fought hard to keep the word *male* out of the Fourteenth Amendment), the amendment denied states the right to forbid suffrage only on the basis of race. Elizabeth Cady Stanton and Susan B. Anthony condemned the Republicans' "negro first" strategy and concluded that woman "must not put her trust in man."

The Fifteenth Amendment severed the early **feminist** movement from its abolitionist roots. Over the next several decades, women would establish an independent suffrage crusade that drew millions of women into political life. But in 1869 northern Republicans took enough satisfaction in the Fifteenth Amendment to promptly scratch the "Negro question" from the agenda of national politics. Even that steadfast crusader for

Major Reconstruction Legislation, 1865–1875

1865	
Thirteenth Amendment (ratified 1865)	Abolishes slavery.
1865 and 1866	
Freedmen's Bureau Acts	Establish the Freedmen's Bureau to distribute food and clothing to destitute Southerners and help freedmen with labor contracts and schooling.
Civil Rights Act of 1866	Affirms the rights of blacks to enjoy "full and equal benefit of all laws and proceedings for the security of person and property as is enjoyed by white citizens" and effectively requires the end of legal discrimination in state laws.
Fourteenth Amendment (ratified 1868)	Makes native-born blacks citizens and guarantees all citizens "equal protection of the laws." Threatens to reduce representatives of a state that denies suffrage to any of its male inhabitants.
1867	
Military Reconstruction Acts	Impose military rule in the South, establish rules for readmission of ex-Confederate states to the Union, and require those states to guarantee the vote to black men.
1869	
Fifteenth Amendment (ratified 1870)	Prohibits racial discrimination in voting rights in all states in the nation.
1875	
Civil Rights Act of 1875	Outlaws racial discrimination in transportation, public accommodations, and juries.

Susan B. Anthony

Like many outspoken suffragists, Anthony, depicted here in 1852, began her public career working on behalf of temperance and abolition. But she grew tired of laboring under the direction of male clergymen—"white orthodox little saints," she called them—who controlled the reform movements and who routinely dismissed the opinions of women. Anthony's continued passion for other causes—improving working conditions for labor, for example—led some conservatives to oppose women's political rights because they equated the suffragist cause with radicalism in general. Women could not easily overcome such views, and the long struggle for the vote eventually drew millions of women into public life.

Susan B. Anthony House, Inc.

equality, Wendell Phillips, concluded that the black man now held "sufficient shield in his own hands. . . . Whatever he suffers will be largely now, and in future, his own fault." Reformers like Phillips had no idea of the violent struggles that lay ahead.

The Struggle in the South

Northerners believed they had discharged their responsibilities with the Reconstruction Acts and the amendments to the Constitution, but Southerners knew that the battle had just begun. Black suffrage and large-scale rebel disfranchise-ment that came with congressional reconstruction had destroyed traditional southern politics and established the foundation for the rise of the Republican Party in the South. Gathering together outsiders and outcasts, southern Republicans won elections, wrote new state constitutions, and formed new state governments.

Challenging the established class for political control was dangerous business. Equally dangerous were the confrontations that took place on farms and plantations across the South. In the countryside, blacks sought to give practical, everyday meaning to their newly won legal and political equality. But ex-masters like David Golightly Harris and other whites had their own ideas about the social and economic arrangements that should replace slave labor and the old plantation economy. Freedom remained contested territory, and Southerners fought pitched battles with one another to determine the contours of their postemancipation world.

Freedmen, Yankees, and Yeomen

African Americans made up the majority of southern Republicans. Freedmen realized that without the ballot they were almost powerless, and they threw themselves into the suffrage campaign. Southern black men gained voting rights in 1867, and within months nearly every eligible black man had registered to vote. Almost all registered as Republicans, grateful to the party that had freed them and given them the **franchise**. Black women, like white women, remained disfranchised but mobilized along with black men. They attended political rallies and parades and in the 1868 presidential election bravely wore buttons supporting the Republican candidate, former Union general Ulysses S. Grant. Southern blacks did not have identical political priorities, but they united in their desire for education and equal treatment before the laws.

Northern whites who decided to make the South their home after the war were a second element of the South's Republican Party. Conservative white Southerners called any northern migrant a "carpetbagger," a man so poor that he could pack all his earthly belongings in a single carpet-sided suitcase and swoop southward like a buzzard to "fatten on our misfortunes." But most Northerners who moved south were restless, relatively well-educated young men, often former Union officers and Freedmen's Bureau agents who looked upon the South as they did the West—as a promising place to make a living. They expected that a South without slavery would prosper, and they wanted to be part of it. Northerners in the southern Republican Party consistently supported programs that encouraged vigorous economic development along the lines of the northern free-labor model.

Southern whites made up the third element of the Republican Party in the South. Approximately one out of four white Southerners voted Republican. The other three cursed those who did. They condemned southern-born white Republicans as traitors to their region and their race and called them "scalawags," a term for runty horses and low-down, good-for-nothing rascals. **Yeoman** farmers accounted for the vast majority of white Republicans in the South. Some were Unionists who emerged from the war with bitter memories of Confederate persecution. Others were small farmers who welcomed the Republican Party because it promised to end favoritism toward the interests of plantation owners who had dominated southern politics before the war. Yeomen usually supported initiatives for public schools and for expanding economic opportunity in the South.

The Republican Party in the South, then, was made up of freedmen, Yankees, and yeomen—an improbable coalition. The mix of races, regions, and classes inevitably meant friction as each group maneuvered to define the party. But Reconstruction represents an extraordinary moment in American politics: Through the Republican Party, blacks and whites joined together to pursue political change. Formally, of course, only men participated in politics—casting ballots and holding offices—but women also played parts in the political struggle by joining in parades and rallies, attending stump speeches, and even campaigning.

Reconstruction politics was not for cowards. Activity on behalf of Republicans in particular took courage. Most whites in the South condemned the entire political process as illegitimate and felt justified in doing whatever they could to stamp out Republicanism. Violence against blacks—the "white terror"—took brutal institutional form in 1866 with the formation in Tennessee of the Ku Klux Klan, a social club of Confederate veterans that quickly developed into a paramilitary organization armed against Republicans. The Klan went on a rampage of whipping, hanging, shooting, burning, and throat-cutting to defeat reconstruction and restore white supremacy. (See "Historical Question," page 580.) Rapid demobilization of the Union army after the war left only 20,000 troops to patrol the entire South, a vast territory. Without effective military protection, southern Republicans had to take care of themselves.

Republican Rule

The Reconstruction Acts required southern states to draw up new constitutions before they could be readmitted to Congress. Beginning in the fall of 1867, southern states held elections for delegates to state constitutional conventions. About 40 percent of the white electorate stayed home because they had been disfranchised or because they had decided to boycott politics. Republicans won three-fourths of the seats. About 15 percent of the Republican delegates to the conventions were Northerners who had moved south, 25 percent were African Americans, and 60 percent were white Southerners. As a British visitor observed, the delegate elections reflected "the mighty revolution that had taken place in America." But Democrats described the state conventions as zoos of "baboons, monkeys, mules . . . and other jackasses." In fact, the conventions brought together serious, purposeful men who hammered out the legal framework for a new order.

The reconstruction constitutions introduced two broad categories of changes in the South: those that reduced aristocratic privilege and increased **democratic** equality and those that expanded the state's responsibility for the general welfare. In the first category, the constitutions adopted universal male suffrage, abolished property qualifications for holding office, and made more offices elective and fewer appointed. In the second category, they enacted prison reform; made the state responsible for caring for orphans, the insane, and the deaf and mute; and aided debtors by exempting their homes from seizure.

These forward-looking state constitutions provided blueprints for a new South but stopped short of the specific reforms advocated by some southern Republicans. Despite the wishes of virtually every former slave, no southern constitution confiscated and redistributed land. And despite the prediction of Unionists that unless all

> Reconstruction represents an extraordinary moment in American politics: Through the Republican Party, blacks and whites joined together to pursue political change.

Congressman John R. Lynch
Although whites almost always maintained control of reconstruction politics, over 600 blacks served in legislatures in the South. Ex-slaves made up the majority of the black legislators. The Union army freed John R. Lynch of Mississippi, and he gained an education at a Natchez freedmen's school. Lynch (1847–1939) was only twenty-four when he became speaker of Mississippi's house of representatives. In 1872, he joined six other African Americans in Congress in Washington, D.C., where in support of civil rights legislation he described his personal experience of being forced to occupy railroad smoking cars with gamblers and drunks. After reconstruction ended, Lynch practiced law and wrote a history of the reconstruction legislatures, which, he argued, were the "best governments those States ever had." Natchez photographer Henry C. Norman took this powerful photograph, probably in the early 1870s.
Collection of Thomas H. Gandy and Joan W. Gandy.

former Confederates were banned from politics they would storm back and wreck reconstruction, no state constitution disfranchised ex-rebels wholesale.

Democrats, however, were blind to the limits of the Republican program. They thought they faced wild revolution. According to Democrats, Republican victories initiated "black and tan" (ex-slave and mulatto) governments across the South. But the claims of "Negro domination" had almost no validity. While four out of five

Republican voters were black men, more than four out of five Republican officeholders were white. Southerners sent fourteen black congressmen and two black senators to Washington, but only 6 percent of Southerners in Congress during reconstruction were black (Figure 16.1). With the exception of South Carolina, where blacks briefly held a majority in one house of the legislature, no state experienced "Negro rule," despite black majorities in the populations of three states.

In almost every state, voters ratified the new constitutions and swept Republicans into power. After ratifying the Fourteenth Amendment, the former Confederate states were readmitted to Congress. Southern Republicans then turned to a staggering array of problems. Wartime destruction—burned cities, shattered bridges, broken levees—still littered the landscape. The South's share of the nation's wealth had fallen from 30 to only 12 percent. Manufacturing limped along at a fraction of prewar levels, agricultural production remained anemic, and the region's railroads had hardly advanced from the devastated condition in which Union armies had left them. Without the efforts of the Freedmen's Bureau, black and white Southerners would have starved. Making matters worse, racial harassment and reactionary violence dogged Southerners who sought reform. In this desperate

FIGURE 16.1 Southern Congressional Delegations, 1865–1877
The statistics contradict the myth of black domination of congressional representation during Reconstruction.

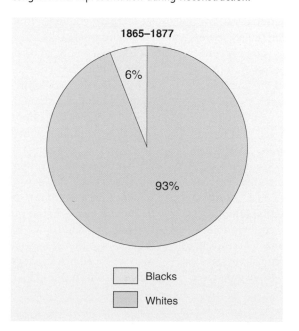

1865–1877

6%

93%

☐ Blacks
☐ Whites

What Did the Ku Klux Klan Really Want?

In the summer of 1866, six Confederate veterans in Pulaski, Tennessee, founded the Ku Klux Klan. Borrowing oaths and rituals from a college fraternity, the young men innocently sought fun and fellowship in a social club. But they quickly tired of playing pranks on one another and shifted to more serious matters. By the spring of 1868, when congressional reconstruction went into effect, new groups, or "dens," of the Ku Klux Klan had sprouted throughout the South.

According to former Confederate general and Georgia Democratic politician John B. Gordon, the Klan owed its popularity to the "instinct of self-preservation . . . the sense of insecurity and danger, particularly in those neighborhoods where the Negro population largely predominated." Everywhere whites looked, he said, they saw "great crime." Republican politicians organized ignorant freedmen and marched them to the polls, where they blighted honest government. Ex-slaves drove overseers from plantations and claimed the land for themselves. Black robbers and rapists made white women cower behind barred doors. It was necessary, Gordon declared, "in order to protect our families from outrage and preserve our own lives, to have something that we could regard as a brotherhood—a combination of the best men of the country, to act purely in self-defense." According to Gordon and other conservative white Southerners, Klansmen were

good men who stepped forward to do their duty—men who wanted nothing more than to guard their families and defend decent society from the assaults of degraded ex-slaves and a vindictive Republican Party.

Behind the Klan's high-minded and self-justifying rhetoric, however, lay another agenda, revealed in members' actions. Klansmen embarked on a campaign to reverse history. Garbed in robes and hoods, Klansmen engaged in hit-and-run **guerrilla warfare** against free labor, civil equality, and political democracy. They aimed to terrorize their enemies—ex-slaves and white Republicans—into submission. As the South's chief terrorist organization between 1868 and 1871, the Klan whipped, burned, and shot in the name of white supremacy. Changes in four particular areas of southern life proved flash points for Klan violence: racial etiquette, education, labor, and politics.

Klansmen punished blacks and whites whom they considered guilty of breaking the Old South's racial code. The Klan considered "impudence" a punishable offense. Asked to define "impudence" before a congressional investigating committee, one white opponent of the Klan responded: "Well, it is considered impudence for a negro not to be polite to a white man—not to pull off his hat and bow and scrape to a white man, as was done formerly." Klansmen whipped blacks for crimes that ranged from speaking disrespectfully

and refusing to yield the sidewalk to raising a good crop and dressing well. Black women who "dress up and fix up like ladies" risked a midnight visit from the Klan. The Ku Klux Klan sought to restore racial subordination in every aspect of private and public life.

Klansmen also took aim at black education. White men, especially those with little schooling, found the sight of blacks in classrooms hard to stomach. Schools were easy targets, and scores of them went up in flames. Teachers, male and female, were flogged, or worse. Klansmen drove northern-born teacher Alonzo B. Corliss from North Carolina for "teaching niggers and making them like white men." In Cross Plains, Alabama, the Klan hanged an Irish-born teacher along with four black men. But not just ill-educated whites opposed black education. Planters wanted ex-slaves back in the fields, not at desks. Each student meant one less laborer. In 1869, an Alabama newspaper reported the burning of a black school and observed that it should be "a warning for them to stick hereafter to 'de shovel and de hoe,' and let their dirty-backed primers go."

Planters turned to the Klan as part of their effort to preserve plantation agriculture and restore labor discipline. An Alabama white admitted that in his area, the Klan was "intended principally for the negroes who failed to work." Masked bands "punished Negroes whose landlords had complained of them." Sharecroppers who disputed their share at "settling up time" risked a visit from the night riders. Klansmen murdered a Georgia blacksmith who refused to do additional work for a white man until he was paid for a previous job. It was dangerous for freedmen to consider changing employers. "If we got out looking for some other place to go," an ex-slave from Texas remembered, "them KKK they would tend to Mister negro good and plenty." In Marengo County, Alabama, when the Klan heard that some local blacks were planning to leave, "the disguised men went to them and told them if they undertook it they would be killed on their way." Whites had decided that they would not be "deprived of their labor."

Above all, the Klan terrorized state and local Republican leaders and voters. Klansmen became the military arm of the Democratic Party. They drove blacks from the polls on election day and terrorized black officeholders. Klansmen gave Andrew Flowers, a black politician in Chattanooga, a brutal beating and told him that they "did not intend any nigger to hold office in the United States." Jack Dupree, president of the Republican Club in Monroe County, Mississippi, a man known to "speak his mind," had his throat cut and was disemboweled while his wife was forced to watch.

Between 1868 and 1871, political violence reached astounding levels. Arkansas experienced nearly 300 political killings in the three months before the fall elections in 1868. Little Rock's U.S. congressman, J. M. Hinds, was one of the victims. Louisiana was even bloodier. Between the local elections in the spring of 1868 and the presidential election in the fall, Louisiana experienced more than 1,000 killings. Political violence often proved effective. In Georgia, Republican presidential candidate Ulysses S. Grant received no votes at all in 1868 in eleven counties, despite black majorities. The Klan murdered three

Ku Klux Klan Robe and Hood

The white robes that we associate with the Ku Klux Klan are a twentieth-century phenomenon. In the Reconstruction era, Klansmen donned robes of various designs and colors. Joseph Boyce Stewart of Lincoln County, Tennessee, wore this robe of brown and white linen. The robe's fancy trimming and the elaborate hat make it highly unlikely that Stewart sewed the costume himself. Women did not participate in midnight raids, but mothers, wives, and daughters of Klansmen often shared their reactionary vision and did what they could to bring about the triumph of white supremacy.

Photograph courtesy of the Chicago Historical Society, Hope B. McCormick Costume Center. Worn by Joseph Boyce Stewart, Lincoln County, TN, c. 1866. Gift of W. G. Dithmer.

scalawag members of the Georgia legislature and drove ten others from their homes. As one Georgia Republican commented after a Klan attack: "We don't call them Democrats, we call them southern murderers."

It proved hard to arrest Klansmen and harder still to convict them. "If a white man kills a colored

man in any of the counties of this State," observed a Florida sheriff, "you cannot convict him." By 1871, the death toll had reached thousands. Federal intervention—in the Ku Klux Klan Acts of 1870 and 1871—signaled an end to much of the Klan's power but not to counter-revolutionary violence in the South. Other groups continued the terror.

context, Republicans struggled to breathe life into their new state governments.

Republican activity focused on three areas—education, civil rights, and economic development. Every state inaugurated a system of public education and began building schools and training teachers. Before the Civil War, whites had deliberately kept slaves illiterate, and planter-dominated governments rarely spent tax money to educate the children of yeomen. By 1875, half of Mississippi's and South Carolina's eligible children (the majority of whom were black) were attending school. Despite underfunding and dilapidated facilities, literacy rates rose sharply. Although public schools were racially segregated, education remained for many blacks a tangible, deeply satisfying benefit of freedom and Republican rule. Freedmen looked upon schools as "first proof of their *independence.*"

State legislatures also attacked racial discrimination and defended civil rights. Republicans especially resisted efforts to segregate blacks from whites in public transportation. Mississippi levied fines of up to $1,000 and three years in jail for railroads, steamboats, hotels, and theaters that denied "full and equal rights" to all citizens. But passing color-blind laws was one thing; enforcing them was another. Despite the law, segregation—later called **Jim Crow**—developed at white insistence and became a feature of southern life long before the end of the Reconstruction era.

Republican governments also launched ambitious programs of economic development. They envisioned a South of diversified agriculture, roaring factories, and booming towns. Republican legislatures chartered scores of banks and industrial companies, appropriated funds to fix ruined levees and to drain swamps, and went on a railroad-building binge. These efforts fell far short of solving the South's economic troubles, however. Republican spending to stimulate economic growth also meant rising taxes and enormous debt that drained funds from schools and other programs.

The southern Republicans' record, then, was mixed. To their credit, the biracial Republican coalition had taken up an ambitious agenda to change the South under trying circumstances. Money was scarce, the Democrats kept up a constant drumbeat of harassment, and factionalism threatened the Republican Party from within. However, corruption infected Republican governments in the South. Public morality reached new lows everywhere in the nation after the Civil War, and the chaos and disruption of the postwar South proved fertile soil for bribery, fraud, and influence peddling. Despite problems and shortcomings, however, the Republican Party made headway in its efforts to purge the South of aristocratic privilege and racist oppression. Republican governments had less success in overthrowing the long-established white oppression of black farm laborers in the rural South.

> Despite the law, segregation developed at white insistence and became a feature of southern life long before the end of the Reconstruction era.

One-Cent Primer

"The people are hungry and thirsty after knowledge," a former slave observed after the Civil War. Future African American leader Booker T. Washington remembered "a whole race trying to go to school. Few were too young, and none too old, to make the attempt to learn." Inexpensive elementary textbooks (this eight-page primer cost a penny) offered ex-slaves the basic elements of literacy. For people long forbidden to learn to read and write, literacy symbolized freedom and allowed the deeply religious to experience the joy of Bible reading. It also permitted African Americans to understand labor agreements, sign contracts, and participate knowledgeably in politics. Gladstone Collection.

White Landlords, Black Sharecroppers

In the countryside, clashes occurred daily between ex-slaves who wished to take control of their working lives and ex-masters who wanted to reinstitute old ways. Except for having to put down the whip and pay subsistence wages, planters had not been required to offer many concessions to emancipation. They continued to believe that African Americans were inherently lazy and would not work without coercion. Whites moved quickly to restore the antebellum world of work gangs, white overseers, field labor for black women and children, clustered cabins, minimal personal freedom, and even whipping whenever they could get away with it.

Ex-slaves resisted every effort to roll back the clock. They argued that if any class could be described as "lazy," it was the planters, who, as one ex-slave noted, "lived in idleness all their lives on stolen labor." Land of their own would anchor their economic independence, they believed, and do much to end planters' interference in their personal lives. They could then, for example, make their own decisions about whether women and children would labor in the fields. Indeed, within months after the war, perhaps one-third of black women abandoned field labor to work on chores in their own cabins just as poor white women did. With freedom to decide how to use family time, hundreds of thousands of black children enrolled in school. But landownership proved to be beyond the reach of most blacks once the federal government abandoned plans to redistribute Confederate property. Without land, ex-slaves had little choice but to work on plantations.

Although they were forced to return to the planters' fields, freedmen resisted efforts to restore slavelike conditions. In his South Carolina neighborhood, David Golightly Harris discovered that few freedmen were "willing to hire by the day, month or year." Instead of working for wages, "the negroes all seem disposed to rent land," which would increase their independence from whites. By rejecting wage labor, by striking, and by abandoning the most reactionary employers, blacks sought to force concessions. Out of this tug-of-war between white landlords and black laborers emerged a new system of southern agriculture.

Sharecropping was a compromise that offered both ex-masters and ex-slaves something but satisfied neither. Under the new system,

Black Family, 1870s

"If a man got to go crost de riber, and he can't git a boat, he take a log," a South Carolina freedman declared after President Andrew Johnson allowed planters to repossess their land. "If I can't own de land, I'll hire or lease land, but I won't contract." Determined to "set up for himself," almost every freedman in the cotton South preferred the economic independence and personal freedom of sharecropping to the dependency of wage labor. The members of this black family posed in front of their dilapidated home are clearly proud and undefeated, but optimism was hard to sustain in the postwar rural South. "We thought we was goin' to be richer than the white folks," recalled a former slave in Texas, "cause we was stronger and knowed how to work, and the whites didn't and they didn't have us to work for them anymore. But it didn't turn out that way."
Roll, Jordan, Roll by Doris Ullman 1933.

planters divided their cotton plantations into small farms of twenty-five to thirty acres that freedmen rented, paying with a share of each year's crop, usually two-thirds. Sharecropping gave blacks more freedom than the system of wages and labor gangs and released them from the day-to-day supervision of whites. Black families abandoned the old slave quarters and scattered over plantations, building separate cabins for themselves on the patches of land they rented (Map 16.1). Black families now decided who would work, for how long, and how hard. Still, most blacks remained dependent on white landlords, who had the power to expel them at the end of each growing season. For planters, sharecropping offered a way to resume agricultural production, but it did not allow them to restore the old plantation system or to administer whatever discipline they considered necessary.

> Sharecropping was a compromise that offered both ex-masters and ex-slaves something but satisfied neither.

MAP 16.1   A Southern Plantation in 1860 and 1881

These maps of the Barrow plantation in Georgia illustrate some of the ways in which ex-slaves expressed their freedom. Freed men and women deserted the clustered living quarters behind the master's house, scattered over the plantation, built family cabins, and farmed rented land. The former Barrow slaves also worked together to build a school and a church.

READING THE MAP: Compare the number and size of the slave quarters in 1860 with the homes of the former slaves in 1881. How do they differ? Which buildings were prominently located along the road in 1860, and which could be found along the road in 1881?

CONNECTIONS: How might the former master feel about the new configuration of buildings on the plantation in 1881? In what ways did the new system of sharecropping replicate the old system of plantation agriculture? In what ways was it different?

FOR MORE HELP ANALYZING THIS MAP, see the map activity for this chapter in the Online Study Guide at bedfordstmartins.com/roark.

Sharecropping introduced a new figure—the country merchant—into the agricultural equation. Landlords supplied sharecroppers with land, mules, seeds, and tools, but blacks also needed credit so they could obtain essential food and clothing before they harvested their crops. Thousands of merchants at small crossroads stores sprang up to offer credit. Under an arrangement called a crop lien, a local merchant would advance goods to a sharecropper in exchange for a *lien*, or legal claim, on the farmer's future crop. Some merchants charged exorbitant rates of interest, as much as 60 percent, on the goods they sold. At the end of the growing season, after the landlord had taken two-thirds of the farmer's crop for rent, the merchant would consult his ledger to see how much the sharecropper owed him. Often, the farmer's debt to the merchant exceeded the income he received from his remaining one-third of the crop. Empty-handed, the farmer would have no choice but to borrow more from the merchant and begin the cycle all over again.

An experiment at first, sharecropping spread quickly and soon dominated the cotton South. By 1870, the work gang system, direct white supervision, and clustered black living quarters were fading memories. Sharecropping quickly ensnared small white farmers as well as black farmers. Lien merchants forced tenants to plant cotton, which was easy to sell, instead of food crops. The result was excessive production of cotton and a disastrous decline in food production in the South after the Civil War. The new sharecropping system of agriculture took shape just as the political power of Republicans in the South began to buckle under Democratic pressure.

Reconstruction Collapses

By 1870, after a decade of engagement with the public issues of war and reconstruction, Northerners wanted to turn to their own affairs and put "the southern problem" behind them. Increasingly, practical, business-minded men came to the forefront of the Republican Party, replacing the band of reformers and idealists who had been prominent in the 1860s. While northern commitment to defend black freedom eroded, southern commitment to white supremacy intensified. Without northern protection, southern Republicans were no match for the Democrats' economic coercion, political corruption, and bloody violence. One by one, Republican state governments fell in the South. The election of 1876 both confirmed and completed the collapse of reconstruction.

Grant's Troubled Presidency

In 1868, the Republican Party's presidential nomination went to Ulysses S. Grant, the man who at the start of the Civil War was a clerk in his father's general store and at the end was the nation's leading general. As the republic's foremost hero and a supporter of congressional reconstruction, Grant was the obvious choice. His Democratic opponent, Horatio Seymour of New York, ran on a platform that blasted congressional reconstruction as "a flagrant usurpation of power . . . unconstitutional, revolutionary, and void." The Republicans answered by "waving the **bloody shirt**"; that is, they reminded voters that the Democrats were "the party of rebellion," the party that stubbornly resisted a just peace. During the campaign, the Ku Klux Klan erupted in a reign of terror, murdering hundreds of southern Republicans. Violence in the South cost Grant votes, but he gained a narrow 309,000-vote margin in the popular vote and a substantial victory (214 votes to 80) in the electoral college (Map 16.2).

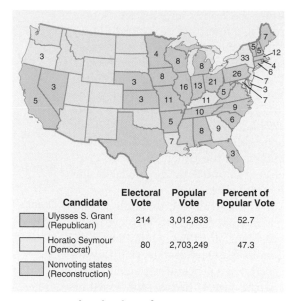

Candidate	Electoral Vote	Popular Vote	Percent of Popular Vote
Ulysses S. Grant (Republican)	214	3,012,833	52.7
Horatio Seymour (Democrat)	80	2,703,249	47.3
Nonvoting states (Reconstruction)			

MAP 16.2   The Election of 1868

Grant hoped to forge a policy that secured both sectional reconciliation and justice for blacks. But he took office at a time when a majority of white Northerners had grown weary of the "Southern Question" and were increasingly willing to let southern whites manage their own affairs. Moreover, Grant was not as good a president as he was a general. The talents he had demonstrated on the battlefield—decisiveness, clarity, and resolution—were less obvious in the White House. Able advisers might have helped, but he surrounded himself with fumbling kinfolk and old cronies from his army days. He also made a string of dubious appointments that led to a series of damaging scandals. Charges of corruption tainted his vice president, Schuyler Colfax, and brought down his secretary of war and secretary of the navy as well as his private secretary. Grant's dogged loyalty to liars and cheats only compounded the damage. While never personally implicated in any scandal, Grant was aggravatingly naive and his administration filled with rot.

Anti-Grant Republicans grew increasingly disgusted and in 1872 bolted and launched the Liberal Party. The Liberals condemned the Grant regime of graft and corruption. To clean up the mess, they proposed ending the **spoils system**, by which victorious parties rewarded loyal workers with public office, and replacing it with a nonpartisan **civil service** commission that would oversee competitive examinations for appointment to office. Moreover, they demanded that the federal government remove its troops from the South and restore "home rule" (southern white control). Democrats especially liked the Liberals' southern policy, and the Democratic Party endorsed the Liberal presidential candidate, Horace Greeley, the longtime editor of the *New York Tribune*. However, the nation still felt enormous affection for the man who had saved the Union and in 1872 reelected Grant with 56 percent of the popular vote.

Grant was not without accomplishments during his eight years as president. In 1872, Hamilton Fish, Grant's secretary of state, skillfully orchestrated a peaceful settlement of the U.S. claim against Great Britain for wartime damages caused by British-built Confederate ships. But Grant's great passion in foreign affairs—

Grant's Proposed Annexation of Santo Domingo

annexation of Santo Domingo in the Caribbean—ended in failure. Grant argued that the acquisition of this tropical land would permit the United States to expand its trade and simultaneously provide a new home for the South's blacks, who were so desperately harassed by the Klan. Aggressive foreign policy had not originated with the Grant administration. Lincoln and Johnson's secretary of state, William H. Seward, had thwarted French efforts to set up a puppet empire under Maximilian in Mexico, and his purchase of Alaska ("Seward's Ice Box") from Russia in 1867 for only $7 million had fired Grant's **imperialist** ambition. But in the end, Grant could not marshal the votes needed in Congress to approve the treaty of annexation of Santo Domingo. Issues closer to home preoccupied Congress and undermined Grant's initiatives.

Northern Resolve Withers

Grant understood that most Northerners had grown weary of reconstruction. Northern businessmen who wanted to invest in the South believed that recurrent federal intrusion was itself a major cause of instability in the region. A growing number of northern Republican leaders began to question the wisdom of their party's alliance with the South's lower classes—its small farmers and sharecroppers. Grant's secretary of the interior, Jacob D. Cox of Ohio, proposed allying with the "thinking and influential native southerners . . . the intelligent, well-to-do, and controlling class."

Northerners increasingly wanted to shift their attention from reconstruction to other issues, especially after the nation slipped into a devastating economic depression in 1873. More than eighteen thousand businesses collapsed, and more than a million workers lost their jobs. The old issues of reconstruction, however, would not go away. When southern Republicans pleaded for federal protection from Klan violence, Congress enacted three laws in 1870 and 1871 that were intended to break the back of white terrorism. The severest of the three, the Ku Klux Klan Act (1871), made interference with

Grant and Scandal
In this anti-Grant cartoon, Thomas Nast, the nation's most celebrated political cartoonist, shows the president falling headfirst into the barrel of fraud and corruption that tainted his administration. During Grant's eight years in the White House, many members of his administration failed him. Sometimes duped, sometimes merely loyal, Grant stubbornly defended wrongdoers, even to the point of perjuring himself to keep an aide out of jail.
Library of Congress.

For more help analyzing this image, see the visual activity for this chapter in the Online Study Guide at bedfordstmartins.com/roark.

voting rights a felony and authorized the use of the army to enforce it. Intrepid federal marshals arrested thousands of Klansmen suspected of violently depriving citizens of the right to vote. The government came close to destroying the Klan but did not end terrorism against blacks. Congress also passed the Civil Rights Act of 1875, which boldly outlawed racial discrimination in transportation, public accommodations, and juries. But federal authorities did little to enforce the law, and segregated facilities remained the rule throughout the South.

The retreat from reconstruction had begun in 1868 with Grant's election. Grant genuinely wanted to see blacks' civil and political rights protected, but he felt uneasy about an open-ended commitment that seemed to ignore constitutional limitations on federal power. In May 1872, Congress restored the right of officeholding to all but three hundred ex-rebels. By the early 1870s, reform had lost its principal spokesmen to death or defeat at the polls. Many Republicans concluded that the quest for black equality was mistaken or hopelessly naive. In the opinion of many, traditional white leaders offered the best hope for honesty, order, and prosperity in the South.

Underlying the North's abandonment of reconstruction was unyielding racial prejudice. During the war, Northerners had learned to accept black freedom, but deep-seated prejudice prevented many from equating freedom with equality. Even the actions they took on behalf of blacks often served partisan political advantage. Northerners generally supported Indiana senator Thomas A. Hendricks's declaration that "this is a white man's Government, made by the white man for the white man."

The U.S. Supreme Court also did its part to undermine reconstruction. In the 1870s, a series of Court decisions significantly weakened the federal government's ability to protect black Southerners under the Fourteenth and Fifteenth Amendments. In the *Slaughterhouse* Cases (1873), the Court distinguished between national and state citizenship and ruled that the Fourteenth Amendment protected only those rights that stemmed from the federal government, such as voting in federal elections and interstate travel. Since the Court decided that most rights derived from the states, it sharply curtailed the federal government's authority to protect black citizens. Even more devastating, the *United States v. Cruikshank* ruling (1876) said that the reconstruction amendments gave Congress power to leg-

islate against discrimination only by states, not by individuals. The "suppression of ordinary crime," such as assault, remained a state responsibility. The Supreme Court did not declare reconstruction unconstitutional but gradually undermined its legal foundation.

The mood of the North had found political expression in the election of 1874, when for the first time in eighteen years the Democrats gained control of the House of Representatives. As one Republican observed, the people had grown tired of the "negro question, with all its complications, and the reconstruction of Southern States, with all its interminable embroilments." Reconstruction had come apart. Congress gradually abandoned it. President Grant grew increasingly unwilling to enforce it. The Supreme Court busily denied the constitutionality of significant

---

Is This a Republican Form of Government?
In this powerful 1876 drawing, Thomas Nast depicts the end of reconstruction as the tragedy it was. As white supremacists in the South piled up more and more bodies, supporters of civil rights accused the Grant administration of failing to protect black Southerners and legitimately elected governments. They pointed specifically to the constitutional requirement that "the United States shall guarantee to every State in this Union a republican form of government, and shall protect each of them . . . against domestic violence" (Article IV, section 4).
Library of Congress.

parts of it. And the people sent unmistakable messages that they were tired of it. Rather than defend reconstruction from its southern enemies, Northerners steadily backed away from the challenge. After the early 1870s, southern blacks faced the forces of reaction largely on their own.

White Supremacy Triumphs

Republican state and local governments in the South attracted more bitterness and hatred than any other political regimes in American history. In the eyes of the majority of whites, each day of Republican rule produced fresh insults: Black militiamen patrolled town streets, black laborers negotiated contracts with former masters, black maids stood up to former mistresses, black voters cast ballots, and black legislators enacted laws. The northern retreat from reconstruction permitted southern Democrats to harness this white rage to politics. Taking the name "Redeemers," they promised to replace "bayonet rule" (some federal troops continued to be stationed in the South) with "home rule." They branded Republican governments a carnival of extravagance, waste, and fraud and promised that honest, thrifty Democrats would supplant the irresponsible tax-and-spend Republicans. Above all, Redeemers swore to save southern civilization from a descent into African "barbarism" and "negro rule." As one man put it, "We must render this either a white man's government, or convert the land into a Negro man's cemetery."

By the early 1870s, Democrats understood that race was their most potent weapon. They adopted a two-pronged racial strategy to overthrow Republican governments. First, they sought to polarize the parties around color; then they relentlessly intimidated black voters. They went about gathering all the South's white voters into the Democratic Party, leaving the Republicans to depend on blacks. The "straight-out" appeal to whites promised great advantage because whites made up a majority of the population in every southern state except Mississippi, South Carolina, and Louisiana.

Democrats employed several devices to dislodge whites from the Republican Party. First and foremost, they fanned the flames of racial

> Redeemers swore to save southern civilization from a descent into African "barbarism" and "negro rule."

"White Man's Country"
White supremacy emerged as a central tenet of the Democratic Party before the Civil War, and Democrats kept up a vicious racist attack on Republicans as long as reconstruction lasted. On this silk ribbon from the 1868 presidential election between Republican Ulysses S. Grant and his Democratic opponent, New York governor Horatio Seymour, the Democrats openly declare their racial goal. During the campaign, Democratic vice presidential nominee Francis P. Blair Jr. promised that a Seymour victory would restore "white people" to power by declaring the reconstruction governments in the South "null and void." The Democrats' promotion of white supremacy reached new levels of shrillness in the 1870s, when northern support for reconstruction began to waver.
Collection of Janice L. and David J. Frent.

prejudice. In South Carolina, a Democrat crowed that his party appealed to the "proud Caucasian race, whose sovereignty on earth God has proclaimed." Ostracism also proved effective. Local newspapers published the names of whites who kept company with blacks. So complete was the ostracism that one of its victims said, "No white man can live in the South in the future and act with any other than the Democratic party unless he is willing and prepared to live a life of social isolation."

In addition, Democrats exploited the severe economic plight of small white farmers by blaming it on Republican financial policy. Government spending soared during reconstruction, and small farmers saw their tax burden skyrocket. When cotton prices fell by nearly 50 percent in the 1870s, yeomen farmers found cash in short supply. In South Carolina, David Golightly Harris observed, "This is tax time. We are nearly all on our head about them. They are so high & so little money to pay with." Golightly and other farmers without enough cash to pay their taxes began "selling every egg and chicken they can get." In 1871, Mississippi reported that one-seventh of the state's land—3.3 million acres—had been forfeited for nonpayment of taxes. The small farmers' economic distress had a racial dimension. Because few freedmen succeeded in acquiring land, they rarely paid taxes. In Georgia in 1874, blacks made up 45 percent of the population but paid only 2 percent of the taxes. From the perspective of a small white farmer, Republican rule meant not only that he was paying more taxes but that he was paying them to aid blacks. Democrats asked whether it was not time for hard-pressed yeomen to join the white man's party.

If racial pride, social isolation, and Republican financial policies proved insufficient to drive yeomen from the Republican Party, Democrats turned to terrorism. "Night riders" targeted white Republicans as well as blacks for murder and assassination. "A dead Radical is very harmless," South Carolina Democratic leader Martin Gary told his followers. By the early 1870s, then, only a fraction of southern whites any longer professed allegiance to the party of Lincoln. Racial polarization became a reality as rich and poor whites united against southern Republicanism.

The second prong of Democratic strategy—intimidation of black voters—proved equally devastating. Antiblack political violence escalated to unprecedented levels. In 1873 in Louisiana, a clash between black militiamen and gun-toting whites killed two white men and an estimated seventy black men. Ruthless whites slaughtered half of the black men after they surrendered. Although the federal government indicted more than one hundred white men, local juries failed to convict a single one of them. This regime of violent intimidation prompted some blacks to move to the North and West in search of a better life (see "American Places," page 590).

Even before adopting the all-out white supremacist tactics of the 1870s, Democrats had already taken control of the governments of Virginia, Tennessee, and North Carolina. The new campaign brought fresh gains. The Redeemers retook Georgia in 1871, Texas in 1873, and Arkansas and Alabama in 1874. In 1876, Mississippi fell. Mississippi was a scene of open, unrelenting, and often savage intimidation of black voters and their few re-

maining white allies. As the state election approached in 1876, Governor Adelbert Ames appealed to Washington for federal troops to control the violence, only to hear from the attorney general that the "whole public are tired of these annual autumnal outbreaks in the South." Abandoned, Mississippi Republicans succumbed to the Democratic onslaught in the fall elections. By 1876, only three Republican state governments—in Florida, Louisiana, and South Carolina—survived (Map 16.3).

An Election and a Compromise

The centennial year of 1876 witnessed one of the most tumultuous elections in American history. Its chaos and confusion provided a fitting conclusion to the experiment known as Reconstruction. The election took place in November, but not until March 2 of the following year, at 4 A.M., did the nation know who would be

---

MAP 16.3 The Reconstruction of the South
Myth has it that Republican rule of the former Confederacy was not only harsh but long. In most states, however, conservative southern whites stormed back into power in a few months or a very few years. By the election of 1876, Republican governments could be found in only three states. And they soon fell.

READING THE MAP: List in chronological order the readmission of the former Confederate states to the Union. Which states reestablished conservative governments most quickly?
CONNECTIONS: What did the former Confederate states need to do in order to be readmitted to the Union? How did reestablished conservative governments react to reconstruction?

FOR MORE HELP ANALYZING THIS MAP, see the map activity for this chapter in the Online Study Guide at bedfordstmartins.com/roark.

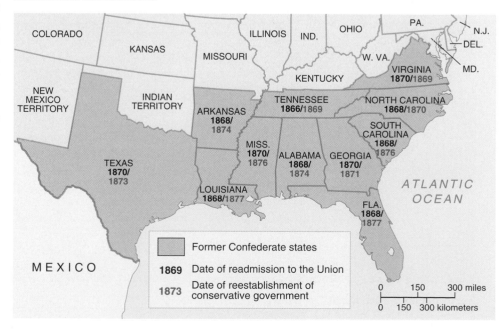

AMERICAN PLACES

Nicodemus National Historic Site, Nicodemus, Kansas

Former slaves hoped that emancipation would usher in an age of equal rights and bountiful opportunity in the South. But when racial violence and oppression overwhelmed the promises of freedom, some African Americans concluded that to find security and prosperity they would have to leave.

Town and land promoters lured millions of Americans westward after the Civil War, and southern blacks particularly were drawn to Kansas, the land of the fiery abolitionist John Brown, where there was ample free or cheap federal land and, they hoped, a fresh start. In 1877 thirty blacks from Kentucky founded the town of Nicodemus, and within a year another 550 settlers joined them. For a "Promised Land," the treeless and apparently desolate Kansas prairie did not look very promising. Willina Hickman, who arrived in 1878, remembered that the men in her party began shouting when they approached Nicodemus: "Where is Nicodemus? I don't see it yet." Hickman recalled, "My husband pointed out various smokes coming out of the ground and said, 'That is Nicodemus.' The families lived in dugouts. . . . The scenery was not at all inviting, and I began to cry."

Briefly living "like prairie dogs," by the mid-1880s the strong-willed settlers had built a prosperous town. They could boast of two newspapers, two pharmacies, three general stores, several churches, a number of small hotels, a school, an ice cream parlor, a bank, a livery stable, a blacksmith shop, and many homes. But only a railroad could assure long-term economic success. When the Union Pacific bypassed Nicodemus in 1887, the town's fate was sealed. Population dwindled, until the town had only sixteen inhabitants in 1950. In 1996, Congress established Nicodemus National Historic Site, and today the National Park Service preserves the town's five remaining historic structures—First Baptist Church, the African Methodist Episcopal Church, the St. Francis Hotel, the school, and the town hall.

Nicodemus is the only remaining western town planned and settled by African Americans during the Reconstruction era. Visitors to Nicodemus today can learn more about the town and the history of blacks in the West through interpretative exhibits at the visitors' center. Walking tours of the five historic buildings offer physical testament to the mainstays of this community—religion, business, education, and government. In addition, every July, descendants from around the nation return to celebrate "Homecoming" and to remember their southern ancestors who went west.

For Web links related to this site and other American Places, see "PlaceLinks" at bedfordstmartins.com/roark.

Homecoming in Nicodemus
Nicodemus National Historic Site.

inaugurated president on March 4. For four months the country suffered through a constitutional and political crisis. Sixteen years after Lincoln's election, Americans feared that a presidential contest would again precipitate civil war.

The Democrats had nominated New York's reform governor, Samuel J. Tilden, who immediately targeted the corruption of the Grant administration and the despotism of Republican reconstruction. The Republicans put forward a reformer of their own, Rutherford B. Hayes, governor of Ohio. Privately, Hayes considered "bayonet rule" a mistake but concluded that waving the "bloody shirt"—that is, reminding voters that the Democrats were the "party of rebellion"—remained the Republicans' best political strategy.

On election day, Tilden tallied 4,300,000 votes to Hayes's 4,036,000. But in the all-important electoral college, Tilden fell one vote short of the majority required for victory. The electoral votes of three states—South Carolina, Louisiana, and Florida, the only remaining Republican governments in the South—remained in doubt because both Republicans and Democrats in those states claimed victory and submitted electoral votes supporting their candidates. To win, Tilden needed only one of the nineteen contested votes. Hayes had to have all of them.

Congress had to decide who had actually won the elections in the three southern states and thus who would be president. The Constitution provided no guidance for this situation. Moreover, Democrats controlled the House, and Republicans controlled the Senate. To break the deadlock, Congress created a special electoral commission to arbitrate the disputed returns. A cumbersome compromise, the commission was made up of five representatives (two Republicans, three Democrats), five senators (two Democrats, three Republicans), and five justices of the Supreme Court (two Republicans, two Democrats, and David Davis, who was considered an independent). Before the commission could meet, the Illinois legislature elected Davis to the Senate, and his place on the commission was filled with a Republican. All of the commissioners voted the straight party line, giving every state to the Republican Hayes and putting him over the top in electoral votes (Map 16.4).

Some outraged Democrats vowed to resist Hayes's victory. Rumors flew of an impending coup and renewed civil war. But the impasse was broken when negotiations behind the scenes between Hayes's lieutenants and some moderate southern Democrats resulted in an informal understanding, known as the Compromise of 1877. In exchange for a Democratic promise not to block Hayes's inauguration and to deal fairly with the freedmen, Hayes vowed not to use the army to uphold the remaining Republican regimes in the South. The South would also gain substantial federal subsidies for internal

"Reading Election Bulletin by Gaslight"
Throughout the nation in November 1876, eager citizens gathered on street corners at night to catch the latest news about the presidential election. When Democrats and Republicans disputed the returns, anxiety and anger mounted. With Samuel J. Tilden well ahead in the popular count, some Democrats began chanting "Tilden or War." Tilden received letters declaring that thousands of "well armed men" stood ready to march on Washington. In Columbia, Ohio, a bullet shattered a window in the home of Rutherford B. Hayes as his family sat down to dinner. Violent rhetoric and action badly frightened a nation with fresh memories of a disastrous civil war, and for four long months it remained unclear whether the nation would peacefully inaugurate a new president.
Granger Collection.

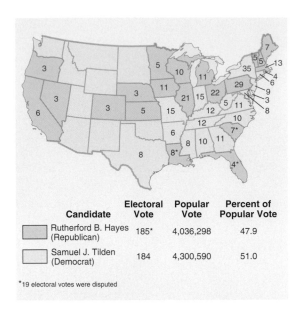

Candidate	Electoral Vote	Popular Vote	Percent of Popular Vote
Rutherford B. Hayes (Republican)	185*	4,036,298	47.9
Samuel J. Tilden (Democrat)	184	4,300,590	51.0

*19 electoral votes were disputed

MAP 16.4   The Election of 1876

improvements. Two days later, the nation celebrated Hayes's peaceful inauguration.

Stubborn Tilden supporters bemoaned the "stolen election" and damned "His Fraudulency," Rutherford B. Hayes. Old-guard Radicals such as William Lloyd Garrison denounced Hayes's bargain as a "policy of compromise, of credulity, of weakness, of subserviency, of surrender." But the nation as a whole celebrated, for the Republic had weathered a grave crisis. The last three Republican state governments in the South fell quickly once Hayes abandoned them and withdrew the U.S. army. Reconstruction came to an end.

Conclusion: "A Revolution But Half Accomplished"

In 1865, when General Carl Schurz visited the South, he discovered "a revolution but half accomplished." War and defeat had not prepared the South for an easy transition from slavery to free labor, from white racial despotism to equal justice, and from white political **monopoly** to biracial democracy. Ex-masters like David Golightly Harris had trouble seeing former slaves like York and Old Will as free people. The old elite wanted to get "things back as near to slavery as possible," Schurz reported, while ex-slaves and whites who had lacked power in the slave regime were eager to exploit the revolutionary implications of defeat and emancipation.

The northern-dominated Republican Congress pushed the revolution along. Although it refused to provide an economic underpinning to black freedom, through constitutional amendments Congress required defeated Confederates to accept legal equality and share political power with black men. Congress was not willing to extend such power to women. Conservative whites fought ferociously to recover their power and privilege. When they regained control of politics through the Democratic Party, they used the power of the state, along with private violence, to wipe out many of the gains of reconstruction. So successful were the reactionaries that one observer concluded that the North had won the war but the South had won the peace.

The Redeemer counterrevolution, however, did not mean a return to slavery. Northern victory in the Civil War ensured abolition, and ex-slaves gained the freedom to not be whipped or sold, to send their children to school, to worship in their own churches, and to work independently on their own rented farms. The lives of impoverished sharecroppers overflowed with hardships, but even sharecropping provided more autonomy and economic welfare than bondage had. It was limited freedom, to be sure, but it was not slavery.

The Civil War and emancipation set in motion the most profound upheaval in the nation's history, and nothing whites did entirely erased its revolutionary impact. War destroyed the richest and largest slave society in the New World, and abolition overturned the social and economic order that had dominated the region for nearly two centuries. The world of masters and slaves succumbed to that of landlords and sharecroppers, a world in which old lines of racial dominance continued, though with greater freedom for blacks. War also served as midwife for the birth of a modern nation-state. For the first time sovereignty rested uncontested in the federal government, and Washington increased its role in national affairs. When the South returned to the Union, it did so as a junior partner. The victorious North now possessed the power to establish the nation's direction, and the North set the nation's compass toward the expansion of industrial capitalism.

Still, despite massive changes, the Civil War remained only a "half accomplished" revolution. The nation did not fulfill the promises that it seemed to hold out to black Americans at war's end, and thus Reconstruction represents a tragedy of enormous proportions. Southern Democrats bludgeoned Republican governments just as northern interest in reconstruction faded. The failure to protect blacks and guarantee their rights had enduring consequences. Almost a century after Reconstruction, the nation would embark on what one observer called a "second reconstruction," another effort to fulfill nineteenth-century promises. The solid achievements of the Thirteenth, Fourteenth, and Fifteenth Amendments to the Constitution would provide a legal foundation for the renewed commitment. It is worth remembering, though, that it was only the failure of the first reconstruction that made a modern civil rights movement necessary.

For additional firsthand accounts of this period, see Chapter 16 in Michael Johnson, ed., *Reading the American Past,* Third Edition.

To assess your mastery of the material in this chapter, see the Online Study Guide at bedfordstmartins.com/roark.

For Web links related to topics in this chapter, see "HistoryLinks," "DocLinks," and "PlaceLinks" at bedfordstmartins.com/roark.

CHRONOLOGY

1863
- President Lincoln issues Proclamation of Amnesty and Reconstruction.

1864
- Wade-Davis bill offers more stringent plan for reconstruction.

1865
- General William T. Sherman sets aside land in South Carolina for black settlement.
- Congress establishes Freedmen's Bureau.
- Lincoln sworn in for second term as president.
- Lincoln shot, dies on April 15, succeeded by Vice President Andrew Johnson.
- Johnson presents his plan of reconstruction to restore ex-Confederate states to the Union; terms include restoration of confiscated lands, thus canceling distribution of land to freedmen.
- Southern state legislatures enact discriminatory black codes.
- Thirteenth Amendment, which abolishes slavery, becomes part of Constitution.

1866
- Congress approves Fourteenth Amendment, making native-born blacks American citizens and guaranteeing all American citizens "equal protection of the laws" (amendment becomes part of Constitution in 1868).
- Overriding presidential veto, Congress passes Civil Rights Act prohibiting discrimination by states.
- Susan B. Anthony and Elizabeth Cady Stanton found Equal Rights Association to lobby for the vote for women.

- Overriding presidential veto, Congress extends Freedmen's Bureau.
- Ku Klux Klan founded in Tennessee.
- Republicans triumph over Johnson's Democrats in congressional elections.

1867
- Overriding presidential veto, Congress passes Military Reconstruction Act, imposing military rule on South and requiring southern states to guarantee the vote to black men.
- Congress passes Tenure of Office Act, requiring Senate approval for removal of officials appointed with Senate consent.

1868
- Senate impeachment trial of President Johnson results in acquittal.
- Ulysses S. Grant elected president.

1869
- Congress approves Fifteenth Amendment, prohibiting racial discrimination in voting rights in all states (amendment becomes part of Constitution in 1870).

1871
- Congress enacts Ku Klux Klan Act in effort to end white terrorism in South.

1872
- Anti-Grant Republicans form Liberal Party and demand an end to government corruption.
- President Grant elected to a second term.

1873
- Economic depression sets in for remainder of decade.
- Supreme Court decision in *Slaughterhouse* cases limits government authority to protect black citizens.

1874
- Elections return Democratic majority to House of Representatives.

1875
- Civil Rights Act outlaws racial discrimination; federal authorities do little to enforce it.

1876
- Supreme Court in *United States v. Cruikshank* rules Congress may legislate against discrimination by states, not by individuals, thus weakening federal ability to protect black citizens.

1877
- Special congressional commission awards disputed electoral votes to Republican Rutherford B. Hayes, making him president of United States. Hayes agrees to pull military out of South, ending Reconstruction.

BIBLIOGRAPHY

General Works

David Herbert Donald, Jean H. Baker, and Michael F. Holt, *The Civil War and Reconstruction* (2000).

W. E. B. Du Bois, *Black Reconstruction, 1860–1880* (1935).

Eric Foner, *Reconstruction: America's Unfinished Revolution* (1988).

John Hope Franklin, *Reconstruction after the Civil War* (1961).

Susan-Mary Grant and Peter J. Parish, *Legacy of Disunion: The Enduring Significance of the American Civil War* (2003).

James M. McPherson, *Ordeal by Fire: The Civil War and Reconstruction* (3rd ed., 2000).

Paul A. Shackel, *Memory in Black and White: Race, Commemoration, and the Post-Bellum Landscape* (2003).

Kenneth M. Stampp, *The Era of Reconstruction, 1865–1877* (1965).

Wartime Reconstruction

Richard H. Abbott, *The Republican Party and the South, 1855–1877: The First Southern Strategy* (1986).

Herman Belz, *Emancipation and Equal Rights: Politics and Constitutionalism in the Civil War Era* (1978).

Louis S. Gerteis, *From Contraband to Freedman: Federal Policy toward Southern Blacks, 1861–1865* (1973).

William S. McFeely, *Yankee Stepfather: General O. O. Howard and the Freedmen* (1968).

James M. McPherson, *The Struggle for Equality: Abolitionists and the Negro in the Civil War and Reconstruction* (1964).

Willie Lee Rose, *Rehearsal for Reconstruction: The Port Royal Experiment* (1964).

Brooks D. Simpson, *Let Us Have Peace: Ulysses S. Grant and the Politics of War and Reconstruction, 1861–1868* (1991).

The Meaning of Freedom

James D. Anderson, *The Education of Blacks in the South, 1860–1935* (1988).

Ira Berlin et al., eds., *Freedom: A Documentary History of Emancipation, 1861–1867*, 4 vols. to date (1982–).

Edmund L. Drago, *Black Politicians and Reconstruction in Georgia: A Splendid Failure* (1982).

Russell Duncan, *Freedom's Shore: Tunis Campbell and the Georgia Freedmen* (1986).

Barbara J. Fields, *Slavery and Freedom on the Middle Ground: Maryland during the Nineteenth Century* (1985).

Michael W. Fitzgerald, *The Union League Movement in the Deep South: Politics and Agricultural Change during Reconstruction* (1989).

Eric Foner, *Nothing but Freedom: Emancipation and Its Legacy* (1983).

Janet Sharp Hermann, *The Pursuit of a Dream* (1981).

Thomas C. Holt, *Black over White: Negro Political Leadership in South Carolina during Reconstruction* (1977).

Peter Kolchin, *First Freedom: The Responses of Alabama's Blacks to Emancipation and Reconstruction* (1972).

Leon F. Litwack, *Been in the Storm So Long: The Aftermath of Slavery* (1979).

William E. Montgomery, *Under Their Own Vine and Fig Tree: The African-American Church in the South, 1865–1900* (1992).

Lynda J. Morgan, *Emancipation in Virginia's Tobacco Belt, 1850–1870* (1992).

Robert Morris, *Reading, 'Riting and Reconstruction* (1981).

Howard N. Rabinowitz, *Race Relations in the Urban South, 1865–1890* (1978).

Roger L. Ransom and Richard Sutch, *One Kind of Freedom: The Economic Consequences of Emancipation* (1977).

C. Peter Ripley, *Slaves and Freedmen in Civil War Louisiana* (1976).

Julie Saville, *The Work of Reconstruction: From Slave to Wage Laborer in South Carolina, 1860–1870* (1994).

Clarence E. Walker, *A Rock in a Weary Land: The African Methodist Episcopal Church during the Civil War and Reconstruction* (1982).

Joel Williamson, *After Slavery: The Negro in South Carolina during Reconstruction, 1861–1877* (1965).

Joel Williamson, *The Crucible of Race: Black/White Relations in the American South since Emancipation* (1984).

The Politics of Reconstruction

Michael Les Benedict, *The Impeachment and Trial of Andrew Johnson* (1973).

Michael Les Benedict, *A Compromise of Principle: Congressional Republicans and Reconstruction* (1974).

Richard F. Bensel, *Yankee Leviathan: The Origins of Central State Authority in America, 1859–1877* (1990).

Michael Kent Curtis, *No State Shall Abridge: The Fourteenth Amendment and the Bill of Rights* (1986).

David H. Donald, *Charles Sumner and the Rights of Man* (1970).

Ellen Carol DuBois, *Feminism and Suffrage: The Emergence of an Independent Women's Movement in America* (1978).

William Gillette, *The Right to Vote: Politics and the Passage of the Fifteenth Amendment* (1965).

Victor B. Howard, *Religion and the Radical Republican Movement, 1860–1870* (1990).

Harold M. Hyman, *A More Perfect Union: The Impact of the Civil War and Reconstruction on the Constitution* (1973).

Michael L. Lanza, *Agrarianism and Reconstruction Politics: The Southern Homestead Act* (1990).

William S. McFeely, *Grant: A Biography* (1981).

Eric L. McKitrick, *Andrew Johnson and Reconstruction* (1960).

James C. Mohr, ed., *Radical Republicans in the North: State Politics during Reconstruction* (1976).

David Montgomery, *Beyond Equality: Labor and the Radical Republicans, 1862–1872* (1967).

William E. Nelson, *The Fourteenth Amendment: From Political Principle to Judicial Doctrine* (1988).

James E. Sefton, *Andrew Johnson and the Uses of Constitutional Power* (1980).

Joel H. Sibley, *A Respectable Minority: The Democratic Party in the Civil War Era, 1860–1868* (1977).

Hans L. Trefousse, *Andrew Johnson: A Biography* (1989).

The Struggle in the South

Stephen V. Ash, *Middle Tennessee Society Transformed, 1860–1870: War and Peace in the Upper South* (1988).

James Alex Baggett, *The Scalawags: Southern Dissenters in the Civil War and Reconstruction* (2003).

Dwight B. Billings Jr., *Planters and the Making of a "New South": Class, Politics, and Development in North Carolina, 1865–1900* (1979).

Randolph B. Campbell, *A Southern Community in Crisis: Harrison County, Texas, 1850–1880* (1983).

Dan T. Carter, *When the War Was Over: The Failure of Self-Reconstruction in the South, 1865–1867* (1985).

Jane Turner Censer, *The Reconstruction of White Southern Woman-hood, 1865–1895* (2003).

Paul A. Cimbala, *Under the Guardianship of the Nation: The Freed-men's Bureau and the Reconstruction of Georgia, 1865–1870* (1997).

Barry A. Crouch, *The Freedmen's Bureau and Black Texans* (1992).

Richard N. Current, *Those Terrible Carpetbaggers: A Reinterpreta-tion* (1988).

Jane E. Dailey, *Before Jim Crow: The Politics of Race in Post-Eman-cipation Virginia* (2000).

Laura F. Edwards, *Gendered Strife and Confusion: The Political Cul-ture of Reconstruction* (1997).

W. McKee Evans, *Ballots and Fence Rails: Reconstruction on the Lower Cape Fear* (1966).

Gaines Foster, *Ghosts of the Confederacy: Defeat of the Lost Cause and the Emergence of the New South, 1865 to 1913* (1987).

Steven Hahn, *The Roots of Southern Populism: Yeoman Farmers and the Transformation of the Georgia Upcountry, 1850–1890* (1983).

William C. Harris, *Day of the Carpetbagger: Republican Reconstruc-tion in Mississippi* (1979).

Elizabeth Jacoway, *Yankee Missionaries in the South: The Penn School Experiment* (1980).

Jacqueline Jones, *Soldiers of Light and Love: Northern Teachers and Georgia Blacks, 1865–1873* (1980).

Robert C. Kenzer, *Kinship and Neighborhood in a Southern Commu-nity: Orange County, North Carolina, 1849–1881* (1987).

Richard G. Lowe, *Republicans and Reconstruction in Virginia, 1865–1870* (1991).

Scott Reynolds Nelson, *Iron Confederacies: Southern Railways, Klan Violence, and Reconstruction* (1999).

Donald G. Nieman, *To Set the Law in Motion: The Freedmen's Bureau and the Legal Rights of Blacks, 1865–1868* (1979).

Michael Perman, *Reunion without Compromise: The South and Reconstruction, 1865–1868* (1973).

Michael Perman, *The Road to Redemption: Southern Politics, 1869–1879* (1984).

Lawrence N. Powell, *New Masters: Northern Planters during the Civil War and Reconstruction* (1980).

George C. Rable, *But There Was No Peace: The Role of Violence in the Politics of Reconstruction* (1984).

Philip N. Racine, ed., *Piedmont Farmer: The Journals of David Golightly Harris, 1855–1870* (1990).

James L. Roark, *Masters without Slaves: Southern Planters in the Civil War and Reconstruction* (1977).

John C. Rodrigue, *Reconstruction in the Cane Fields: From Slavery to Free Labor in Louisiana's Sugar Parishes, 1862–1880* (2001).

Crandall A. Shifflett, *Patronage and Poverty in the Tobacco South: Louisa County, Virginia, 1860–1900* (1982).

James M. Smallwood, Barry A. Crouch, and Larry Peacock, *Mur-der and Mayhem: The War of Reconstruction in Texas* (2003).

Mark W. Summers, *Railroads, Reconstruction, and the Gospel of Pros-perity: Aid under the Radical Republicans, 1865–1877* (1984).

Allen Trelease, *White Terror: The Ku Klux Klan Conspiracy and Southern Reconstruction* (1971).

Ted Tunnell, *Crucible of Reconstruction: War, Radicalism, and Race in Louisiana, 1862–1877* (1984).

Peter Wallenstein, *From Slave South to New South: Public Policy in Nineteenth-Century Georgia* (1987).

Michael Wayne, *The Reshaping of Plantation Society: The Natchez District, 1860–1880* (1983).

Jonathan M. Wiener, *Social Origins of the New South, 1860–1885* (1978).

Sara Woolfolk Wiggins, *The Scalawag in Alabama Politics, 1865–1881* (1977).

Gavin Wright, *Old South, New South: Revolutions in the Southern Economy since the Civil War* (1986).

The Collapse of Reconstruction

William Gillette, *Retreat from Reconstruction, 1869–1879* (1979).

Otto H. Olsen, ed., *Reconstruction and Redemption in the South: An Assessment* (1980).

Ian Polakoff, *The Politics of Inertia: The Election of 1876 and the End of Reconstruction* (1973).

Terry L. Seip, *The South Returns to Congress: Men, Economic Mea-sures, and Intersectional Relationships, 1868–1879* (1983).

John G. Sproat, *"The Best Men": Liberal Reformers in the Gilded Age* (1968).

Mark W. Summers, *The Era of Good Stealings* (1993).

Margaret S. Thompson, *The "Spider Web": Congress and Lobbying in the Age of Grant* (1985).

C. Vann Woodward, *Reunion and Reaction: The Compromise of 1877 and the End of Reconstruction* (1951).

CLEVELAND AND BLAINE CAMPAIGN PINS, 1884
These gilt campaign pins from the election of 1884 show Republican candidate James G. Blaine, on the right, thumbing his nose at Democratic candidate Grover Cleveland. Considered "one of the vilest campaigns ever waged," the 1884 race pitted Cleveland, who had made his political reputation on his honest dealings, against Blaine, who was tainted with charges of corruption. However, when the *Buffalo Telegraph* revealed that the bachelor Cleveland had fathered an illegitimate child, the tables turned, and Cleveland and his followers lost the high moral ground. Perhaps this is why Blaine is portrayed in this mechanical pin as thumbing his nose at Cleveland. His gesture proved premature; Cleveland squeaked past Blaine in a close race. The gilt pins are a good symbol for Gilded Age politics, when corruption and party strife typified the nation's political life.

Collection of Janice L. and David J. Frent.

Business and Politics in the Gilded Age

1870–1895

ONE NIGHT OVER DINNER, the humorist and author Mark Twain and his friend Charles Dudley Warner, editor of the *Hartford Courant*, teased their wives about the popular novels they read. When the two women challenged them to write something better, they set to work. Warner supplied the sentimental melodrama, while Twain "hurled in the facts." The result was a runaway best seller, uneven as fiction but offering a savage satire of the "get rich quick" era that forever after would be known by the book's title, *The Gilded Age* (1873).

Twain left no one unscathed in the novel—political hacks, Washington lobbyists, Wall Street financiers, small-town boosters, wildcat miners, and the "great putty-hearted public" that tolerated being plundered by greedy and self-interested politicians and promoters. Underneath the glitter of the Gilded Age, as Twain's title implied, lurked much baser stuff. The booming economy of the postwar era set off a reckless rush for riches, devil take the hindmost.

Twain had witnessed up close the corrupt partnership of business and politics in the administration of Ulysses S. Grant. Drawing on this experience, he described how a lobbyist could get an appropriation bill through Congress:

> Why the matter is simple enough. A Congressional appropriation costs money. Just reflect, for instance. A majority of the House Committee, say $10,000 apiece—$40,000; a majority of the Senate Committee, the same each—say $40,000; a little extra to one or two chairmen of one or two such committees, say $10,000 each—$20,000; and there's $100,000 of the money gone, to begin with. Then, seven male lobbyists, at $3,000 each—$21,000; one female lobbyist, $3,000; a high moral Congressman or Senator here and there—the high moral ones cost more, because they give tone to a measure—say ten of these at $3,000 each, is $30,000; then a lot of small fry country members who won't vote for anything whatever without pay—say twenty at $500 apiece, is $10,000 altogether; lot of jimcracks for Congressmen's wives and children—those go a long way—you can't spend too much money in that line—well, those things cost in a lump, say $10,000—along there somewhere;—and then comes your printed documents. . . . Oh, my dear sir, printing bills are destruction itself. Ours, so far amount to—let me see— . . . well, never mind the details, the total in clean numbers foots up $118,254.42 thus far!

In Twain's satire, Congress is for sale to the highest bidder. Indeed, the Grant administration witnessed scandals like the Crédit Mobilier scheme, in which an entrepreneurial congressman named Oakes Ames set up a company

Mark Twain and *The Gilded Age*
Popular author Mark Twain (Samuel Langhorne Clemens)
wrote acerbically about the excesses of the Gilded Age in
his novel of that name written with Charles Dudley Warner
and published in 1873. No one knew the meretricious lure
of the era better than Twain, who succumbed to a get-
rich-quick scheme that left him bankrupt.
Left: Beinecke Rare Book and Manuscript Library, Yale University; right:
Newberry Library.

riverboat pilot. Taking the pen name Mark Twain, he moved west and gained fame chronicling mining booms in California and Nevada. In 1866 he came east to launch a career as an author, public speaker, and itinerant humorist.

Twain played to packed houses, but his work was judged too vulgar for the genteel tastes of the time because he wrote about common people and used common language. *The Adventures of Huckleberry Finn*, his masterpiece of American realistic fiction, was banned in Boston when it appeared in 1884.

Huck Finn's creator eventually stormed the citadels of polite society, hobnobbing with the wealthy and living in increasingly expensive and elegant style. He built an ornate Victorian mansion in Hartford, Connecticut, and maintained a townhouse off Fifth Avenue in New York City. Succumbing without much of a struggle to the money fever of his age, Twain plunged into one scheme after another in the hope of making millions. The Paige typesetting machine proved his downfall. Twain invested heavily in this elaborate invention (it had more than eighteen thousand parts), which promised to mechanize typesetting, replacing human labor. The idea was a good one; a competing invention, the Linotype, developed by German-born inventor Ottmar Mergenthaler and adopted by the *New York Tribune*, eventually set the new standard in typesetting. The Paige machine, in comparison, proved too temperamental to be practical. Despite much retooling, which required new infusions of capital, the Paige machine never performed reliably. By the 1890s, Twain faced bankruptcy. Only the help of Standard Oil millionaire Henry H. Rogers enabled him to begin his dogged climb out of debt.

Twain's tale was a common one in an age when the promise of wealth led as many to ruin as to riches. In the Gilded Age, great fortunes were made and lost with dizzying frequency. Wall Street panics, like those in 1873 and 1893, periodically interrupted the boom times and led to nationwide depressions. But with railroads to be built, cities demanding bridges, buildings, and mass transportation, and industry expanding on every level, the mood of the country remained buoyant.

(Crédit Mobilier) that plundered $44 million from the Union Pacific Railroad with the help of prominent politicians, including future U.S. president James Garfield. The unseemly intimacy between government and business (the concept of "conflict of interest" did not yet exist) meant that more often than not senators, representatives, and even members of the executive branch were on the payroll of business interests, if not in their pockets. This often corrupt interplay of business and politics raised serious questions about the health of American democracy.

The Gilded Age seemed to tarnish all who touched it. No one would learn that lesson better than Twain, who, even as he attacked it as an "era of incredible rottenness," fell prey to its enticements. Born Samuel Langhorne Clemens, he grew up in a rough Mississippi River town where he first became a journeyman printer and then a

The rise of industrialism in the United States and the interplay of business and politics strike the key themes in the Gilded Age, the period from the 1870s through the 1890s. In these three decades, the transition from a rural, agricultural economy to urban industrialism transformed American society. The growth of old industries and the creation of new ones, along with the rise of big business, signaled the coming of age of industrial capitalism. With new times came new economic and political issues. Old divisions engendered by sectionalism and slavery still influenced politics. But increasingly with the rise of industrialism and big business new economic issues such as the tariff and monetary policy shaped party politics. And as concern grew over the power of big business and the growing chasm between the rich and the poor, many Americans looked to the government for solutions.

Perhaps nowhere were the hopes and fears that industrialism inspired more evident than in the public's attitude toward the great business moguls of the day, men like Jay Gould, Andrew Carnegie, John D. Rockefeller, and J. P. Morgan. These larger-than-life figures not only dominated business but also sparked the popular imagination as the heroes and villains in the high drama of industrialization. At no other period in U.S. history would the industrial giants and the businesses they built (and sometimes wrecked) loom so large in American life.

Old Industries Transformed, New Industries Born

In the years following the Civil War, the scale and scope of American industry expanded dramatically. Old industries like iron transformed into the modern steel industry, while discovery and invention stimulated new industries such as oil and electric power. The rise of the railroad played the key role in the transformation of the American economy, creating a national market that enabled businesses to expand from a regional to a nationwide scale. The railroads were America's first big business.

Jay Gould, Andrew Carnegie, John D. Rockefeller, and other business leaders pioneered new strategies to seize markets and consolidate power in the rising railroad, steel, and oil industries. Always with an eye to the main chance, these business tycoons set the tone in the get-rich-quick era of freewheeling capitalism that came to be called the Gilded Age.

Railroads: America's First Big Business

In the decades following the Civil War, the United States built the greatest railroad network in the world. The first transcontinental railroad was completed in 1869 when the tracks of the Union Pacific and Central Pacific railroads came together at Promontory Point, Utah, linking new markets in the West to the nation's economy. Between 1870 and 1880, the amount of track in the country doubled, and it nearly doubled again in the following decade. By 1900, the nation boasted over 193,000 miles of railroad track, more than in all of Europe and Russia combined (Map 17.1).

> By 1900, the nation boasted over 193,000 miles of railroad track, more than in all of Europe and Russia combined.

To understand how the railroads developed and came to dominate American life, there is no better place to start than the career of Jay Gould, who came to personify the Gilded Age. Jason "Jay" Gould bought his first railroad before he turned twenty-five. It was only sixty-two miles long, in bad repair, and on the brink of failure, but within two years he sold it at a profit of $130,000. Thus began the career of the man who would pioneer the development of America's railway system and become the era's most notorious speculator.

Gould, by his own account, knew little about railroads and cared less about their operation. Nevertheless, as a result of his mania for speculation, he became a master of corporate expansion, the architect of the vast railway systems that developed in the 1880s. The secretive Gould operated in the stock market like a shark, looking for vulnerable railroads, buying enough stock to take control, and threatening to undercut his competitors until they bought him out at a high profit. The railroads that fell into his hands fared badly and often went bankrupt; Gould's genius lay in cleverly buying and selling railroad stock, not in providing transportation. He was a speculator first and only incidentally a builder. Yet in his single-minded search for profit Gould laid the foundations for the nation's railroad system. In the 1880s, he moved to put together a second transcontinental railroad. To defend their interests, his competitors had little choice but to adopt his strategy of expansion and consolidation, which in turn encouraged railroad growth.

The dramatic growth of the railroads created the country's first big business.

JUSTICE IN THE WEB.

Jay Gould as a Spider

In this 1885 political cartoon titled "Justice in the Web," artist Fredrick Burr Opper portrays Jay Gould as a hideous spider whose web, formed by Western Union telegraph lines, has entrapped "justice" through its monopoly of the telegraph industry. Gould, who controlled Western Union as well as the Erie Railroad, made his fortune by stock speculation. Images like this one fueled the public's distaste for him and made Gould, in his own words, "the most hated man in America."

Granger Collection.

Before the Civil War even the largest textile mill in New England employed no more than 800 workers. In contrast, the Pennsylvania Railroad by the 1870s boasted a payroll of more than 55,000 workers spread out over six thousand miles of track. Capitalized at over $400 million, the Pennsylvania Railroad constituted the largest private enterprise in the world.

A similar revolution in communications accompanied and supported the growth of the railroads. The telegraph, developed by Samuel F. B. Morse, marched across the continent alongside the railroad. By transmitting coded messages across electrical wire, the telegraph formed the nervous system of the new industrial order. Telegraph service replaced the Pony Express mail carriers in the West and transformed business by providing instantaneous communication. Again Jay Gould took a leading role. By 1879, through stock manipulation, he seized control of Western Union, the company that monopolized the telegraph industry.

The power and success Gould enjoyed underscored the haphazard development of the American railway system. To encourage railroad building, the federal and state governments provided the railroad companies with generous cash subsidies and **land grants**. States and local communities clamored to offer inducements to railroad builders, knowing that towns and villages along the tracks would grow and flourish. The federal government held vast tracts of public land in the West, and Congress did not hesitate to give it away to promote railroad building. The railroads received not only land for rights-of-way but also liberal sections of land on alternating sides of the track. The giveaway diminished the amount of public land available to homesteaders and allowed the railroads to increase their profits by selling the land to the settlers who followed the railroads west. Over the years, the federal government granted the railroad builders 180 million acres, an area larger than Texas. But the lion's share of capital for the railroads came from private investors.

Lack of planning led to overbuilding. Already by the 1870s, the railroads competed fiercely for business on the eastern seaboard. A manufacturer who needed to get goods to market and who was fortunate enough to be in an area served by competing railroads could get substantially reduced shipping rates in return for promises of steady business. Because railroad owners lost money through this kind of competition, they tried to set up agreements, or "pools," to end cut-throat competition by dividing up territory and setting rates. These informal agreements invariably failed because men like Jay Gould, intent on undercutting all competitors to gain business for themselves, refused to honor the agreements.

Not all the early railroad builders were as unscrupulous as Gould. James J. Hill built the Great Northern Railroad and built it well. Entering the railroad business too late to benefit from land grants or subsidies, Hill had to plan carefully and calculate which areas would best be served by the railroad in order to maximize returns to his investors. As a result, the Great Northern, completed in 1893, became one of the few major railroads able to weather the depression that began that same year. In contrast, speculators like Gould and his partners Daniel Drew and James Fisk could more accurately be called wreckers than builders. Through speculation, they ruined the Erie Railroad by gambling with its stock on Wall Street, profiting from its losses to line their own pockets. Novelist Charles Dudley Warner described how they operated:

> [They fasten upon] some railway that is prosperous, pays dividends, pays a liberal interest on its bonds, and has a surplus. They contrive to buy, no matter at what cost, a controlling interest in it, either in its stock or its management. Then they absorb its surplus; they let it run down so that it pays no dividends, and by-and-by cannot even pay its interest; then they squeeze the bondholders, who may be glad to accept anything that is offered out of the wreck, and perhaps then they throw the property into the hands of a receiver, or consolidate it with some other road at a value enormously greater than it cost them in stealing it. Having in one way or another sucked it dry, they look around for another road.

Even when unprincipled magnates did not wreck the railroads, their enormous power made them a menace. In the West, the Big Four railroad builders—Collis P. Huntington, Charles Crocker, Leland Stanford, and Mark Hopkins—became so powerful that critics claimed the Southern Pacific Railroad held California in the grip of an "octopus."

MAP 17.1 Railroad Expansion, 1870–1890

Railroad mileage nearly quadrupled between 1870 and 1890; the greatest growth occurred in the trans-Mississippi West. New transcontinental lines—the Great Northern, the Northern Pacific, the Southern Pacific, and the Atlantic and Pacific—were completed in the 1880s. Small feeder lines like the Oregon Short Line and the Atchison, Topeka, and Santa Fe fed into the great transcontinental systems, knitting the nation together.

READING THE MAP: Where were most of the railroad lines located in 1870? What cities were the major railroad centers? What was the end point of the only western route?

CONNECTIONS: Why were so many rails laid between 1870 and 1890? How did the railroads affect the nation's economy?

FOR MORE HELP ANALYZING THIS MAP, see the map activity for this chapter in the Online Study Guide at bedfordstmartins.com/roark.

"The Curse of California"
This political cartoon drawn by G. Frederick Keller appeared in 1882 in *The Wasp*, a periodical edited by Ambrose Bierce, whose vituperative wit and acerbic political commentary made him one of the premier journalists of his day. Bierce had a special animus for the Southern Pacific Railroad and the "Big Four" who controlled it. Here the railroad monopoly is pictured as an octopus, its many tentacles controlling such financial areas as San Francisco's Nob Hill elite, farmers, lumber interests, shipping, fruit growers, stage lines, mining, and the wine industry. Novelist Frank Norris later expanded on the theme in his 1901 best-selling novel *The Octopus*.
University of California at Berkeley, Bancroft Library.

The public's alarm at the control wielded by the new railroad magnates provided a barometer of attitudes toward big business itself. When Jay Gould died in 1892, the press described him as "the world's richest man," estimating his fortune at over $100 million. His competitor "Commodore" Cornelius Vanderbilt, who built the New York Central Railroad, judged Gould "the smartest man in America." But to the public, who found in Gould a symbol of all that most troubled them about the rise of big business, he was, as he himself admitted shortly before his death, "the most hated man in America."

Andrew Carnegie, Steel, and Vertical Integration

If Jay Gould was the man Americans loved to hate, Andrew Carnegie, the leader in the transition from iron to steel, became one of America's heroes. Unlike Gould, for whom speculation was the game and wealth the goal, Carnegie turned his back on speculation and worked to build something enduring—Carnegie Steel, the biggest steel business in the world during the Gilded Age.

The growth of the steel industry proceeded directly from railroad building. The first railroads ran on iron rails, which cracked and broke with alarming frequency. Steel, both stronger and more flexible than iron, remained too expensive for use in rails until the 1850s, when an Englishman named Henry Bessemer developed a way to make steel more cheaply from pig iron. After the Civil War, with the discovery of rich iron ore deposits near the Great Lakes, the Bessemer process came into use in America. Andrew Carnegie, among the first to champion the new "King Steel," came to dominate the emerging industry.

Carnegie, a Scottish immigrant, landed in New York in 1848 at the age of twelve. He rose from a job cleaning bobbins in a textile factory to become one of the richest men in America. Before he died, he gave away more than $300 million of his fortune, most notably to public libraries. His generosity, combined with his own rise from poverty, bolstered his public image. But Carnegie had another side: He was a harsh taskmaster who made nearly inhuman demands on his employees.

When Carnegie was still a teenager, his skill as a telegraph operator caught the attention of Tom Scott, superintendent of the Pennsylvania Railroad. Scott hired Carnegie, soon promoted him, and lent him the money for his first foray into Wall Street investment. A millionaire before his thirtieth birthday, Carnegie turned away from speculation and struck out on his own to reshape the iron and steel industry. "My prefer-

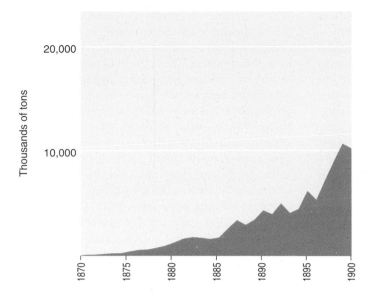

FIGURE 17.1 Iron and Steel Production, 1870–1900

Iron and steel production in the United States grew from nearly none to 10 million tons a year by 1900. In steel production, the secrets to the great increase were the use of the Bessemer process and the vertical integration pioneered by Andrew Carnegie. By 1900, Carnegie's mills alone produced more steel than all of Great Britain. With corporate consolidation after 1900, the rate of growth in iron and steel production was even more spectacular.

ence was always manufacturing," he wrote. "I wished to make something tangible." By applying the lessons of cost accounting and efficiency that he had learned from twelve years with the Pennsylvania Railroad, Carnegie turned steel into the nation's first manufacturing big business.

In 1872 Andrew Carnegie acquired 100 acres in Braddock, Pennsylvania, on the outskirts of Pittsburgh, convenient to two railroad lines and fronted by the Monongahela River, a natural highway up to Pittsburgh and the Ohio River and the coal fields farther north. There Carnegie built the most up-to-date Bessemer steel plant in the world and began turning out steel at a furious rate. At that time, steelmakers produced about 70 tons a week (Figure 17.1). Within two decades, Carnegie's blast furnaces poured out an incredible 10,000 tons a week. He soon cut the cost of making rails by more than half, from $58 to $25 a ton. Carnegie's formula for success was simple: "Cut the prices, scoop the market, run the mills full; watch the costs and profits will take care of themselves." And they did. By 1900, Carnegie Steel earned $40 million a year.

Andrew Carnegie as a Young Man

Andrew Carnegie, shown here in 1861, made a small fortune as a young man. In 1868, he totaled his assets. "Thirty three and an income of $50,000 per annum," he recorded. "Beyond this never earn—make no effort to increase fortune, but spend the surplus each year for benevolent [sic] purposes." Carnegie didn't stick to his plan. In 1872, he founded Carnegie Steel and went on to become one of the richest men in America. Before his death in 1919 he gave away an estimated $300 million to charitable causes.

Carnegie Library of Pittsburgh.

To guarantee the lowest costs and the maximum output, Carnegie pioneered a system of business organization called **vertical integration**. All aspects of the business were under Carnegie's control—from the mining of iron ore, to its transport on the Great Lakes, to the production of steel. Vertical integration, in the words of one observer, meant that "from the moment these crude stuffs were dug out of the earth until they flowed in a stream of liquid steel in the ladles, there was never a price, profit, or royalty paid to any outsider."

Always Carnegie kept his eyes on the account books, looking for ways to cut costs. The great productivity Carnegie encouraged came at a high price. He deliberately pitted his managers against one another, firing the losers and rewarding the winners with a share in the company. Workers achieved the output Carnegie demanded by enduring long hours, low wages, and dangerous working conditions. They toiled twelve hours a day, seven days a week in his plants, and when the shift changed every other week, they worked twenty-four hours straight. One worker, commenting on the contradiction between Carnegie's generous philanthropy in endowing public libraries and his tight-fisted labor policy, observed, "After working twelve hours, how can a man go to a library?"

By 1900, Andrew Carnegie had become the best-known manufacturer in the nation, and the age of iron had yielded to an age of steel. Carnegie Steel, now expanded to include several plants, stood as an industrial giant, the largest steel producer in the world. Steel from Carnegie's mills supported the elevated trains in New York and Chicago, formed the skeleton of the Washington Monument, supported the first steel bridge to span the Mississippi, and girded America's first skyscrapers. As a captain of industry Carnegie had no rival but the titan of the oil industry, John D. Rockefeller.

> As the largest refiner in Cleveland, Rockefeller demanded secret rebates from the railroads in exchange for his steady business.

John D. Rockefeller, Standard Oil, and the Trust

Edwin Drake's discovery of oil in Pennsylvania in 1859 sent thousands rushing to the oil fields in search of "black gold." In the days before the automobile and gasoline, crude oil was refined into lubricating oil for machinery and kerosene for lamps, the major source of lighting in nineteenth-century houses before the invention of gas lamps or electric lighting. The amount of capital needed to buy or build an oil refinery in the 1860s and 1870s remained relatively low: less than $25,000, or roughly what it cost to lay one mile of railroad track. With investment cost so low, the new petroleum industry experienced riotous competition among many small refineries. Ultimately, John D. Rockefeller and his Standard Oil Company succeeded in controlling nine-tenths of the oil-refining business.

Rockefeller grew up the son of a shrewd Yankee who peddled quack cures for cancer. Under his father's rough tutelage, he learned how to drive a hard bargain. "I trade with the boys and skin 'em and just beat 'em every time I can," Big Bill Rockefeller boasted. "I want to make 'em sharp." John D. learned his lessons well. In 1865, at the age of twenty-five, he controlled the largest oil refinery in Cleveland. Like a growing number of business owners, Rockefeller abandoned partnership or single proprietorship to embrace the corporation as the business structure best suited to maximize profit and minimize personal liability. In 1870, he incorporated his oil business, founding the Standard Oil Company, a precursor of today's ExxonMobil Corporation.

As the largest refiner in Cleveland, Rockefeller demanded secret rebates, or refunds, from the railroads in exchange for his steady business. These rebates enabled Standard Oil to undercut its competitors. The railroads wanted Rockefeller's business so badly that they not only gave him rebates on his own shipping fares but also granted him a share of the rates that his competitors paid. A Pennsylvania Railroad official later confessed that Rockefeller extracted such huge rebates that the railroad, which could not risk losing his business, sometimes ended up paying him to transport Standard's oil. Using this kind of leverage, Rockefeller pressured competing refiners to sell out or face ruin.

To gain legal standing for Standard Oil's secret deals, Rockefeller in 1882 pioneered a new form of corporate structure—the **trust**. The trust differed markedly from Carnegie's vertical approach in steel. Instead of attempting to control all aspects of the oil business, from the well to the consumer, Rockefeller moved horizontally to control only the refining process. Several trustees held stock in various refinery companies "in trust" for Standard's stockholders. This elabo-

"What a Funny Little Government"

The power wielded by John D. Rockefeller and the Standard Oil Company is captured in this political cartoon, which appeared in the January 22, 1900, issue of *The Verdict*. Rockefeller is pictured holding the White House and the Treasury Department in the palm of his hand, while in the background the U.S. Capitol has been converted into an oil refinery. Standard Oil epitomized the gigantic trusts that many feared were threatening democracy in the Gilded Age.

Collection of The New-York Historical Society.

FOR MORE HELP ANALYZING THIS IMAGE, see the visual activity for this chapter in the Online Study Guide at bedfordstmartins.com/roark.

rate stock swap allowed the trustees to coordinate policy among the refineries, ensuring that they could act in concert. The new enterprise, valued at $70 million, gave Rockefeller a virtual **monopoly** of the oil-refining business and the unsuspecting public knew nothing about it.

When the federal government threatened to outlaw the trust as a violation of free trade, Standard Oil changed tactics and reorganized as a **holding company**. Instead of stockholders in competing companies acting through trustees to set prices and determine territories, the holding company simply brought competing companies under one central administration. No longer technically separate businesses, they could act in concert without violating antitrust laws that forbade competing companies from forming "combinations in restraint of trade."

Rockefeller began to integrate vertically, while continuing to expand Standard Oil horizontally. As the company's empire grew, central control became essential. Rockefeller ended the independence of the refinery operators and closed inefficient plants. Next he moved to control sources of crude oil and took charge of the transportation and marketing of petroleum products. By the 1890s, Standard Oil ruled more than 90 percent of the oil business, employed 100,000 people, and was the biggest, richest, most feared, and most admired business organization in the world.

John D. Rockefeller enjoyed enormous success in business, but he was not well liked by the public. Before he died in 1937 at the age of ninety-eight, Rockefeller had become the country's first billionaire. But despite his modest

Ida Tarbell

Ida M. Tarbell served as managing editor of *McClure's Magazine*, where her "History of the Standard Oil Company" ran in serial form for three years. Her revelations of the ruthless practices John D. Rockefeller used to seize control of the oil-refining industry convinced readers that it was time for economic and political reforms to curb the power of big business. Tarbell grew up in the Pennsylvania oil region and knew firsthand how Standard Oil forced out competitors.

Library of Congress.

her "Miss Tarball." "If I step on that worm I will call attention to it," he explained. "If I ignore it, it will disappear." Yet by the time Tarbell finished publishing her story, Rockefeller slept with a loaded revolver by his bed in fear of would-be assassins. Standard Oil and the man who created it had become the symbol of heartless monopoly. (See "Documenting the American Promise," page 608.)

New Inventions: The Telephone and Electricity

Although many Americans disliked industrial giants like Rockefeller, they admired inventors. The second half of the nineteenth century witnessed an age of invention. Men like Thomas Alva Edison and Alexander Graham Bell became folk heroes. But no matter how dramatic the inventors or the inventions themselves, the new electric and telephone industries pioneered by Edison and Bell soon eclipsed their inventors and fell under the control of bankers and industrialists.

Alexander Graham Bell came to America from Scotland at the age of twenty-four with a

habits, his pious Baptist faith, and his many charitable gifts, he never shared in the public affection that Carnegie enjoyed. Editor and journalist Ida M. Tarbell's *History of the Standard Oil Company*, which ran for three years (1902–1905) in serial form in *McClure's Magazine*, largely shaped the public's harsh view of Rockefeller. Tarbell had grown up in the Pennsylvania oil region, and her father had owned one of the small refineries gobbled up by Standard Oil. Her devastatingly thorough history chronicled the methods Rockefeller used to take over the oil industry. Publicly Rockefeller refused to respond, although in private he dubbed

Notable American Inventions, 1865–1899

1865	Railroad sleeping car
1867	Typewriter
1867	Barbed wire
1868	Railroad refrigerator car
1870	Stock ticker
1876	Telephone
1877	Phonograph
1879	Cash register
1882	Electric fan
1885	Adding machine
1886	Coca-Cola
1888	Kodak camera
1889	Kinetoscope
1890	Electric chair
1891	Zipper
1895	Safety razor
1896	Electric stove
1896	Ice cream cone
1899	Tape recorder

passion to find a way to teach the deaf to speak (his wife and mother were deaf). Instead, he developed a way to transmit voice over wire—the telephone. Bell's invention astounded the world when he demonstrated it at the Philadelphia Centennial Exposition in 1876. Dumbfounded by the display, the emperor of Brazil cried out, "My God, it talks!" In 1880 American Bell, the company formed by the inventor, began to market the telephone under the skilled direction of Theodore N. Vail, a professional manager. Vail pioneered "long lines" (long-distance telephone service), creating American Telephone and Telegraph (AT&T) as a subsidiary of American Bell. In 1900, AT&T became the parent company of the system as a whole, controlling Western Electric, which manufactured and installed the equipment, and coordinating the Bell regional divisions. This complicated organizational structure meant that Americans could communicate not only locally but across the country. Providing both private and instantaneous communication, the telephone eventually replaced the telegraph for high-speed communication.

Even more than Alexander Graham Bell, inventor Thomas Alva Edison embodied the old-fashioned virtues of Yankee ingenuity and rugged individualism that Americans most admired. A self-educated dynamo, he worked twenty hours a day in his laboratory in Menlo Park, New Jersey, vowing to turn out "a minor invention every ten days and a big thing every six months or so." (See "American Places," page 614.) He almost made good on his promise. At the height of his career, he averaged a patent every eleven days and invented such "big things" as the phonograph, the motion picture camera, and the filament for the incandescent lightbulb.

Edison, in competition with George W. Westinghouse, went on to pioneer the use of electricity as an energy source. By the late nineteenth century, electricity had become a part of American urban life. It powered trolley cars, subways, and factory machinery. It lighted homes, apartments, factories, and office buildings. Indeed, electricity became so prevalent in urban life that it symbolized the city, whose bright lights contrasted with rural America, left largely in the dark. As late as the 1930s, only 10 percent of the nation's farms had electricity, because private enterprise judged it not profitable enough to run electric lines to America's farms and ranches.

While Americans thrilled to the new electric cities and the changes wrought by inventors, the day of the inventor quietly yielded to the heyday of the corporation. In 1892 the electric industry

The Telephone in the Home

The telephone achieved spectacular success, despite the daunting technical and marketing problems posed by a new technology that called for the linking of towns and cities by electrical wires to transmit voice. The number of phones soared from 310,000 in 1895 to over 1.5 million by 1900.
Corbis.

Rockefeller and His Critics

No one inspired the nation's fear of industrial consolidation more than John D. Rockefeller, creator of the Standard Oil trust. To many Americans Rockefeller and "the sovereign state of Standard Oil" came to represent a danger to **democracy** *itself because of the underhanded methods and enormous political influence of the corporation and its founder.*

DOCUMENT 1
"The Smokeless Rebate," from Henry Demarest Lloyd's *Wealth against Commonwealth*, 1894

As early as 1881 Henry Demarest Lloyd introduced Rockefeller to a national audience by attacking Standard Oil and its founder in "The Story of a Great Monopoly," published in the February issue of Atlantic Monthly. *The public eagerly snapped up the exposé—the issue went through six printings. Lloyd embarked on a full-scale exposé of the company, published in 1894 under the title* Wealth against Commonwealth. *To avoid charges of libel, Lloyd used no names, but readers knew he referred to Rockefeller and Standard Oil when he spoke of the "oil combination." Here Lloyd describes how Rockefeller used illegal railroad rebates to best his competitors and take control of the oil-refining industry.*

With searching intelligence, indomitable will, and a conscience which makes religion, patriotism, and the domestic virtues but subordinate paragraphs in a ritual of money worship, the mercantile mind flies its air-line to business supremacy. That entirely modern social arrange-

ment—the private ownership of [railroads]—has introduced a new weapon into business warfare which means universal dominion to him who will use it with an iron hand.

This weapon is the rebate, smokeless, noiseless, invisible, of extraordinary range, and the deadliest gun known to commercial warfare. It is not a lawful weapon. . . . It has to be used secretly. All the rates he got were a secret between himself and the railroads. "It has never been otherwise," testified one of the oil combination.

The smokeless rebate makes the secret of success in business to be not manufacture, but manufacture—breaking down with a strong hand the true makers of things. To those who can get the rebate it makes no difference who does the digging, building, mining, making, producing the million forms of wealth they covet for themselves. They need only get control of the roads. . . . To succeed, ambitious men must make themselves refiners of freight rates, distillers of discriminations, owners not of lands, mines, and forests—not in the first place, at least—but of the railway officials through whose hands the produce must go to market. Builders, not of manufactories, but of privileges; inventors only of schemes . . . , contrivers, not of competition, but of ways to tax the property of their competitors into their pockets. They need not make money; they can take it from those who have made it.

SOURCE: Henry Demarest Lloyd, *Wealth against Commonwealth* (New York: Harper & Brothers, 1894), 474–75, 488.

Editor and journalist Ida Minerva Tarbell, whose "History of the Standard Oil Company" ran for three years (1902–1905) in serial form in McClure's Magazine, *proved Rockefeller's most damaging critic. Tarbell grew up in the Pennsylvania oil region; her father had owned a small refinery gobbled up by Standard Oil. In a devastatingly thorough history, she chronicled the underhanded methods Rockefeller used to gain control of the oil-refining industry. Here she portrays a critical chapter in the history of Standard Oil. In 1879, Rockefeller's first attempt to consolidate the oil industry through the use of illegal rebates had failed.*

If Mr. Rockefeller had been an ordinary man the outburst of popular contempt and suspicion which suddenly poured on his head would have thwarted and crushed him. But he was no ordinary man. He had the powerful imagination to see what might be done with the oil business if it could be centered in his hands—the intelligence to analyze the problem into its elements and to find the key to control. He had the essential element to all great achievement, a steadfastness to a purpose once conceived which nothing can crush. The Oil Regions might rage, call him a conspirator and those who sold to him traitors; the railroads might withdraw their contracts and the legislature annul his charter; undisturbed and unresting he kept at this great purpose. . . .

He got a rebate. . . . How much less a rate than $1.25 Mr. Rockefeller had before the end of April the writer does not know. Of course the rate was secret and he probably understood now, as he had not two months before, how essential it was that he keep it secret. His task was more difficult now, for he had an enemy active, clamorous, contemptuous, whose suspicions had reached that acute point where they could believe nothing but evil of him—the producers and independents of the Oil Regions. It was utterly impossible that he should ever silence his enemy, for their points of view were diametrically opposed.

They believed in independent effort—every man for himself and fair play for all. They wanted competition, loved open fight. They considered that all business should be done openly—that railways were bound as public carriers to give equal rates—that any combination which favored one firm or one locality at the expense of another was unjust and illegal. . . .

Those theories which the body of oil men held as vital and fundamental Mr. Rockefeller and his associates either did not comprehend or were deaf to. This lack of comprehension by many men of what seems to other men to be the most obvious principles of justice is not rare. Many men who are widely known as good, share it. Mr. Rockefeller was "good." There was no more faithful Baptist in Cleveland than he. Every enterprise of that church he had supported liberally from youth. He gave to its poor. He visited its sick. He wept with its suffering. Moreover, he gave unostentatiously to many outside charities of whose worthiness he was satisfied. He was simple and frugal in his habits. He never went to the theater, never drank wine. He was a devoted husband, and he gave much time to the training of his children, seeking to develop in them his own habits of economy and of charity. Yet he was willing to strain every nerve to obtain for himself special and illegal privileges from the railroads which were bound to ruin every man in the oil business not sharing them with him. Religious emotion and sentiments of charity, propriety and self-denial seem to have taken the place in him of notions of justice and regard for the rights of others.

SOURCE: Ida M. Tarbell, "The Oil War of 1872," in Ellen F. Fitzpatrick, ed., *Muckraking: Three Landmark Articles* (Boston: Bedford/St. Martin's, 1994), 77–79.

DOCUMENT 3
Matthew Josephson, *The Robber Barons*, 1934

The historian Matthew Josephson, writing in 1934 in the trough of the Great Depression, took a dim view of the capitalists of the Gilded Age in his book The Robber Barons. *Noting that Rockefeller, Gould, and Morgan had avoided fighting in the Civil War by hiring substitutes, Josephson described them as follows.*

But besides the young men who marched to Bull Run, there were other young men of '61 whose instinctive sense of history proved to be unerring. Loving not the paths of glory they slunk away quickly bent upon business of their own. They were warlike enough and pitiless yet never risked their own skin: they fought without military rules or codes of honor or any tactics or weapons familiar to men: they were the strange, new mercenary soldiers of economic life. The plunder and trophies of victory would go neither to the soldier nor the statesman, but to these other young men of '61, who soon figured as "massive interests moving obscurely in the background" of wars. Hence these, rather than the military captains or tribunes, are the subject of this history.

Josephson's portrait of the young John D. Rockefeller is a caricature of the bloodless miser.

In his first position, bookkeeper to a produce merchant at the Cleveland docks, when he was sixteen, he distinguished himself by his composed orderly habits. Very carefully he examined each item on each bill before he approved it for payment. Out of a salary which began at $15 a month and advanced ultimately to $50 a month, he saved $800 in three years, the lion's share of his total earnings! This was fantastic parsimony. . . .

He was given to secrecy; he loathed all display. When he married a few years afterward, he lost not a day from his business. His wife, Laura Spelman, proved an excellent mate. She encouraged his furtiveness, he relates, advising him always to be silent, to say as little as possible. His composure, his self-possession was excessive. . . . He was a hard man to best in a trade, he rarely smiled and almost never laughed, save when he struck a good bargain. Then he might clap his hands with delight, or he might even, if the occasion warranted, throw up his hat, kick his heels, and hug his informer. One time he was so overjoyed at a favorable piece of news that he burst out: "I'm bound to be rich! Bound to be rich!"

SOURCE: Excerpt (pp. 4, 48–49) from *The Robber Barons* by Matthew Josephson. Copyright © 1934 Harcourt, Brace and Company. Reprinted with permission.

QUESTIONS FOR ANALYSIS AND DEBATE

1. Henry Demarest Lloyd and Ida Tarbell agree that Rockefeller gained control of the oil industry through illegal methods. What was his primary weapon, and how did it operate?

(continued)

(continued)

2. Compare Henry Demarest Lloyd's style to that of Ida Tarbell. Which is the more effective and why? Was either of these journalists an impartial observer?

3. Rockefeller never responded to his critics. Do you think Rockefeller's silence was a good strategy? Why or why not?

4. By the time Matthew Josephson wrote his unflattering portrait of Rockefeller in *The Robber Barons*, Rockefeller was long retired, Standard Oil had been broken up by an edict from the Supreme Court, and oil discoveries in Texas and Oklahoma had eclipsed the oil regions in Pennsylvania and Ohio. What do you think motivated Josephson's attack on the "robber barons" in 1934?

AN UNRESTRAINED DEMON.

Fears of Electricity

Electricity was by no means easy to sell, as this 1889 cartoon shows. Innocent pedestrians are electrocuted by the wires, a woman swoons, presumably as a result of the buzzing current, a horse and driver have collapsed, and a policeman runs for help. The skull in the wires attached to the electric lightbulb warns that this new technology is deadly. Both an urban sophisticate in a top hat and a cowboy in boots have succumbed to the deadly wires. Edison had to develop an entirely new system of marketing that relied on skilled engineers to sell electric light and power.

Granger Collection.

consolidated. Reflecting a nationwide trend in business, Edison General Electric dropped the name of its inventor, becoming General Electric, a behemoth that soon dominated the market.

From Competition to Consolidation

Even as Rockefeller and Carnegie built their empires, the era of the robber baron was coming to a close. Business increasingly developed into the anonymous corporate world of the twentieth century as the corporation became the dominant form of business organization and as corporate mergers restructured American industry.

Banks and financiers played such a key role in this consolidation that individual entrepreneurship yielded to finance capitalism—investment sponsored by banks and bankers. During these years, a new social philosophy based on the theories of naturalist Charles Darwin helped to justify consolidation and to inhibit state or federal regulation of business. A **conservative** Supreme Court further frustrated attempts to control business by consistently declaring unconstitutional legislation designed to regulate railroad rates or to outlaw trusts and monopolies.

J. P. Morgan and Finance Capitalism

John Pierpont Morgan, the preeminent finance capitalist of the late nineteenth century, loathed competition and sought whenever possible to eliminate it by substituting consolidation and central control. Morgan's hatred of competition and passion for order made him the architect of

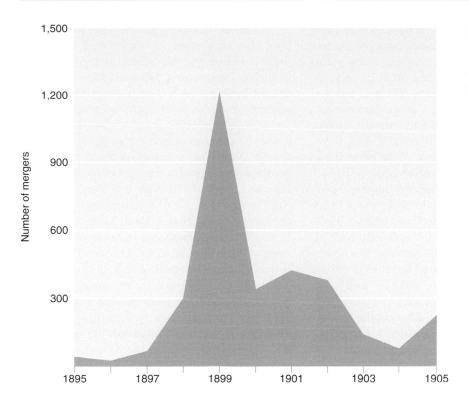

1,500

1,200

900

600

300

Number of mergers

1895   1897   1899   1901   1903   1905

FIGURE 17.2 Merger Mania, 1895–1905
The depression that began with the panic of 1893 fueled a "merger mania," as businesses consolidated and reorganized, often at the prompting of finance capitalists like J. P. Morgan. The number of mergers peaked in 1899, but high rates of consolidation continued into the first decade of the twentieth century.

business consolidation (Figure 17.2). Aloof and silent, Morgan looked down on the climbers and the speculators with a haughtiness that led his rivals to call him "Jupiter," after the ruler of the Roman gods. At the turn of the twentieth century, J. P. Morgan dominated American banking, exerting an influence so powerful that his critics charged he controlled a vast "money trust."

Morgan acted as a power broker in the reorganization of the railroads and the creation of industrial giants like General Electric and U.S. Steel. When the railroads fell on hard times in the 1890s, Morgan, with his passion for order and his access to capital, emerged as rescuer of embattled, wrecked, and ruined companies. One contemporary observer hailed the change, remarking, "Railroad 'wreckers' have . . . for a long period been a blight upon all progress. Now it appears that in Mr. Morgan and his co-laborers, conservators instead of destructionists, have the control." Morgan quickly moved to eliminate competition by creating what he called "a community of interest" among the managers he handpicked. By the time Morgan finished reorganizing the railroads, he had spawned a network of interlocking directorates and holding companies that concentrated the nation's railroads in the hands of a few directors who controlled two-thirds of the nation's track.

Banker control of the railroads rationalized, or coordinated, the industry. But stability came at a high price. To keep investors happy and to guarantee huge profits from the sale of stock, Morgan heavily "watered" the stock of the railroads, issuing more shares than the assets of the company warranted. J. P. Morgan & Co. made millions of dollars from commissions and from blocks of stock acquired through reorganization. The flagrant overcapitalization created by the watered stock hurt the railroads in the long run, saddling them with enormous debts. Equally harmful was the management style of the Morgan directors who ran the railroads. They were bankers, not railroad men, and they saw the railroads as little more than "a set of books." Their conservative approach aimed at short-term profit and discouraged the continued technological and organizational innovation needed to run the railroads effectively.

In 1898, Morgan moved into the steel industry, directly challenging Andrew Carnegie. Morgan supervised the mergers of several smaller steel companies, which soon expanded from the manufacture of finished goods into steel

At the turn of the twentieth century, J. P. Morgan dominated American banking, exerting an influence so powerful that his critics charged he controlled a vast "money trust."

production. Carnegie, who for decades had controlled the production of steel, countered by invading Morgan's domain and creating a new plant for the manufacture of finished products such as tubing, nails, wire, and hoops. The pugnacious Carnegie cabled his partners in the summer of 1900: "Action essential: crisis has arrived . . . have no fear as to the result; victory certain."

The press trumpeted news of the impending fight between the feisty Scot and the haughty Wall Street banker, but what the papers called the "battle of the giants" in the end proved little more than the wily maneuvering of two businessmen so adept that even today it is difficult to say who won. For all his belligerence, the sixty-six-year-old Carnegie yearned to retire to Skibo Castle, his home in Scotland, and may well have invited Morgan's bid for power, knowing that only Morgan could command the capital to buy him out. Morgan, who disdained haggling,

J. P. Morgan, Photograph by Edward Steichen
Few photographs of J. P. Morgan exist. Morgan, who suffered from a skin condition that left him with a misshapen strawberry of a nose, rarely allowed his picture to be taken. But it was his eyes that people remembered—eyes so piercing that Edward Steichen, who took this photograph, observed that "meeting his gaze was a little like confronting the headlights of an express train."
George Eastman House. Reprinted with permission of Joanna T. Steichen.

agreed to pay Carnegie's asking price, $480 million (the equivalent of about $9.6 billion in today's currency). According to legend, when Carnegie later teased Morgan, saying that he should have asked $100 million more, Morgan replied: "You would have got it if you had."

Morgan's acquisition of Carnegie Steel signaled the passing of one age and the arrival of another. Carnegie represented the old entrepreneurial order, Morgan the new corporate world. He quickly moved to pull together Carnegie's chief competitors to form a huge new steel corporation, United States Steel, known today as USX. Capitalized (some said grossly overcapitalized) at $1.4 billion, U.S. Steel was the largest corporation in the world. Yet for all its size, it did not hold a monopoly in the steel industry. Significant small competitors, such as Bethlehem Steel, remained independent, creating a competitive system called an **oligopoly**, in which several large companies control production. Instead of competing head-to-head, the smaller steel manufacturers simply followed the lead of giants like U.S. Steel in setting prices and dividing the market so that each company held a comfortable share. Many other industries, such as meatpacking, also functioned as oligopolies. Although oligopoly did not entirely eliminate competition, it did effectively blunt it.

When J. P. Morgan died in 1913, his estate totaled $68 million, not counting an estimated $50 million in art treasures. Andrew Carnegie, who gave away more than $300 million before his death six years later, is said to have quipped, "And to think he was not a rich man!" But Carnegie's gibe missed the mark. The quest for power, not wealth, had motivated J. P. Morgan, and his power could best be measured not in the millions he owned but in the billions he controlled. Even more than Carnegie or Rockefeller, Morgan left his stamp on the twentieth century and formed the model for corporate consolidation that economists and social scientists soon justified with a new social theory known as **social Darwinism**.

Social Darwinism and the Gospel of Wealth

John D. Rockefeller Jr., the son of the founder of Standard Oil, once remarked to his Baptist Bible class that the Standard Oil Company, like the American Beauty rose, resulted from "pruning the early buds that grew up around it." The elimination of smaller, inefficient units, he said, was

Homestead Steelworks
The Homestead steelworks, outside Pittsburgh, Pennsylvania, is pictured shortly after J. P. Morgan bought out Andrew Carnegie and created U.S. Steel, the precursor of today's USX. Try to count the smokestacks in the picture. Air pollution on this scale posed a threat to the health of citizens and made for a dismal landscape. Workers complained that trees would not grow in Homestead.
Hagley Museum & Library.

"merely the working out of a law of nature and a law of God." The comparison of the business world to the natural world formed the backbone of a theory of society based on the law of evolution formulated by British naturalist Charles Darwin. In his monumental work *On the Origin of Species* (1859), Darwin theorized that in the struggle for survival, the process of adaptation to environment triggered a natural selection process among species that led to evolutionary progress. Drawing on Darwin's work, Herbert Spencer in Britain and William Graham Sumner in the United States developed the theory of social Darwinism. Crudely applying Darwin's theory to human society, the social Darwinists concluded that progress came about as a result of relentless competition in which the strong survived and the weak died out.

In social terms, the idea of the survival of the fittest had profound significance, as Sumner, a professor of political economy at Yale University, made clear in his 1883 book, *What Social Classes Owe to Each Other*. "The drunkard in the gutter is just where he ought to be, according to the fitness and tendency of things," Sumner insisted. Conversely, "millionaires are the product of natural selection," and although "they get high wages and live in luxury," Sumner claimed, "the bargain is a good one for society." Social Darwinists equated wealth and power with "fitness" and believed that the unfit, like the poor drunkard, should be allowed to die off to advance the progress of humanity. Any efforts by the rich to aid the poor would only tamper with the rigid laws of nature and slow evolution. Social Darwinism acted to curb social reform while at the same time it glorified great wealth. Not surprisingly, the wealthy widely subscribed to this idea. In an age when Rockefeller and Carnegie amassed hundreds of millions of

AMERICAN PLACES

Edison National Historic Site, West Orange, New Jersey

In 1887, Thomas Edison moved his laboratory from Menlo Park, New Jersey, to West Orange. There he oversaw the creation of what he called "the best equipped and largest laboratory extant, [its] facilities incomparably superior to any other for rapid and cheap development of an invention." In this giant complex, Edison employed as many as 200 chemists, machinists, engineers, and experimenters, all working under his direction. Here he perfected his invention of the phonograph, invented the incandescent lightbulb and the motion picture camera and projector, and conducted experiments that resulted in over 500 patents.

The National Park Service now manages Edison's laboratory and nearby estate. Visitors can wander through the buildings, most of which are preserved much as they were in Edison's day. Jar-lined shelves, scientific equipment, and machinery fill the laboratories. Remaining buildings at this site include the main laboratory, which held Edison's library, a stockroom, two machine shops, and approximately thirty experiment rooms. Four other small laboratory buildings housed facilities for physics, chemistry, metallurgy, and a chemical storage and pattern shop. The site also contains a replica of Edison's motion picture studio and the remains of outbuildings that supported the laboratories.

Edison's home, Glenmont, is located in the adjoining community of Llewellyn Park, about a mile from the laboratory. Edison purchased the 29-room Queen Anne–style house in 1886 as a wedding gift for his new bride, twenty-year-old Mina Miller. A thirty-nine-year-old widower, Edison already had three children when he married Mina, and the couple had three more children while living at Glenmont. The estate's close proximity to the laboratory complex made it possible for Edison, always preoccupied with his work, to stay late in the lab but come home for dinner. Although he was obliged by his reputation to entertain, he didn't relish company and sometimes feigned illness to avoid dinner parties. Mina Edison managed the home, with its 13.5 acres, including a barn and a greenhouse, calling herself "the home executive." She planned the meals, served as hostess, and oversaw the staff, which included a cook, a laundress, a nurse, maids, a butler, a gardener, a personal secretary, and later a liveried chauffeur. The domestic life of the household comes to life for visitors through the numerous mementos and the period furnishings that adorn the home.

FOR WEB LINKS RELATED TO THIS SITE AND OTHER AMERICAN PLACES, see "PlaceLinks" at bedfordstmartins.com/roark.

Edison's Chemistry Lab
Edison National Historic Site.

dollars (billions in today's currency) and the average worker earned $500 a year (about $8,800), social Darwinism justified economic inequality. (See "Historical Question," page 618.)

Andrew Carnegie softened some of the harshness of social Darwinism in his essay "The Gospel of Wealth," published in 1889. The millionaire, Carnegie wrote, acted as a "mere trustee and agent for his poorer brethren, bringing to their service his superior wisdom, experience, and ability to administer, doing for them better than they could or would do for themselves." Carnegie preached philanthropy and urged the rich to "live unostentatious lives" and "administer surplus wealth for the good of the people." His **gospel of wealth** earned much praise but won few converts. Most millionaires followed the lead of J. P. Morgan, who contributed to charity but amassed private treasures in his marble library rather than living the unostentatious, philanthropic life Carnegie counseled.

Social Darwinism nicely suited an age in which the gross inequalities accompanying industrialization seemed to cry out for action. Assuaging the nation's conscience, social Darwinism justified neglect of the poor in the name of "race progress." Because the poor were often of a different race or ethnicity, social Darwinism smacked of racism. Indeed, racism was part and parcel of social Darwinist ideology, which judged Anglo-Saxons superior to all other groups. In an era noted for greed and crass materialism, social Darwinism reassured comfortable Americans that all was as it should be. Even the gospel of wealth, which mitigated the harshest dictates of social Darwinism, insisted that Americans lived in the best of all possible worlds and that the rich should be left in charge.

Laissez-faire and the Supreme Court

Social Darwinism, with its emphasis on the free play of competition and survival of the fittest, encouraged the economic theory of **laissez-faire** (French for "let it alone"). Business argued that the government should not meddle in economic affairs, except to protect private property. The conservative Supreme Court agreed and used its power to protect business interests. During the 1880s and 1890s, the Court increasingly reinterpreted the Constitution to protect business from taxation, regulation, labor organization, and antitrust legislation.

In a series of landmark decisions, the Court used the Fourteenth Amendment, originally intended to protect freed slaves from state laws violating their rights, to protect corporations. The Fourteenth Amendment declares that no state can "deprive any person of life, liberty, or property, without due process of law." By defining corporations as "persons" under the law, the Court determined that legislation designed to regulate corporations deprived them of "due process." Using this reasoning, the Court struck down state laws regulating railroad rates, declared income tax unconstitutional, and judged labor unions a "conspiracy in restraint of trade." Faced with the economic and social dislocations caused by industrialism, the Court insisted on elevating the rights of property over all other rights. According to Justice Stephen J. Field, the Constitution "allows no impediments to the acquisition of property." Field, born into a wealthy New England family, spoke with the bias of the privileged class to whom property rights were sacrosanct. Imbued with this ideology, the Court refused to impede corporate consolidation and did nothing to curb the excesses of big business. Only in the arena of politics did Americans tackle the issues raised by corporate capitalism.

> In an age when Rockefeller and Carnegie amassed hundreds of millions of dollars while the average worker earned $500 a year, social Darwinism justified economic inequality.

Politics and Culture

One could easily argue that politics, not baseball, constituted America's pastime in the Gilded Age. For many Americans politics provided a source of identity, a means of livelihood, and a ready form of entertainment. No wonder voter turnout averaged a hefty 77 percent, in contrast to voter participation of 51 percent in 2000 (Figure 17.3). A variety of factors contributed to the complicated interplay of politics and culture. Patronage provided an economic incentive for voter participation, but ethnicity, religion, sectional loyalty, race, and gender all influenced the political life of the period.

Political Participation and Party Loyalty

Patronage—the **spoils system**—proved a strong motivation for party loyalty among many voters. Political parties in power doled out federal, state, and local government jobs to their loyal

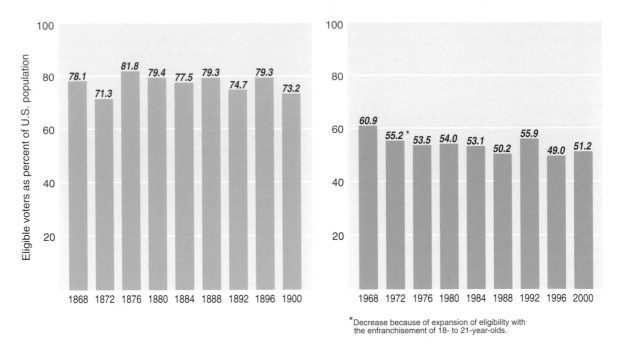

FIGURE 17.3 Voter Turnout, 1868–1900 and 1968–2000
Despite the weakness of the presidency and the largely undistinguished men who filled the office, voters turned out in record numbers to vote in late-nineteenth-century elections. Compare the robust rate of voter participation to the anemic turnout in late-twentieth-century elections. What factors do you think account for the change?

> Politics provided entertainment and spectacle for voters and nonvoters alike in an age before mass recreation and amusement, particularly in rural areas.

supporters. With hundreds of thousands of jobs to be filled, the choice of party affiliation could mean the difference between a paycheck or an empty pocket. Money greased the wheels of the spoils system. Party bosses expected jobholders to kick back from 2 to 4 percent of their salaries to support the party's electoral campaigns. With their livelihoods tied to their party identity, government employees in particular had an incentive to vote in great numbers during the Gilded Age.

Even without patronage as a prod, political affiliation provided a powerful sense of group identity for many voters, proud of their loyalty to the Democrats or the Republicans. Being a Republican or a Democrat helped define an individual. Democrats, who traced the party's roots back to Thomas Jefferson, called theirs "the party of the fathers." The Republican Party, founded in the 1850s, still claimed strong loyalties as a result of its alignment with the Union during the Civil War. Often regional loyalty as well as personal identity was at stake. In the Midwest, known for strong Republican ties during the Civil War, one faithful party member promised, "Iowa will go Democratic when Hell goes Methodist." Both Republicans in the North and Democrats in the South played to regional sentiments by a tactic called "waving the **bloody shirt**"—reminding voters which side they had fought for in the Civil War.

Politics also provided entertainment and spectacle for voters and nonvoters alike in an age before mass recreation and amusement, particularly in rural areas. Political parties sponsored parades, rallies, speeches, picnics, torchlight processions, and Fourth of July fireworks, attracting millions of Americans. Outside the big cities, only religious revivals and traveling shows could compete.

Religion and ethnicity also played a significant role in politics. In the North, **Protestants** from the old-line denominations, particularly Presbyterians and Methodists, flocked to the

Hayes Campaign Lantern, 1876
Republicans carried this lantern in the campaign of 1876. Designed for nighttime rallies, the lantern featured paper transparencies that allowed light to shine through the stars and illuminate the portrait of the candidate, Rutherford B. Hayes. Marching men with lighted lanterns held aloft must have been a dramatic sight in small towns across the country. Politics constituted a major form of entertainment in nineteenth-century life.
Collection of Janice L. and David J. Frent.

Republican Party, which championed a series of moral reforms, including local laws requiring businesses to close in observance of the Sabbath. In the burgeoning cities, the Democratic Party courted immigrants and working-class Catholic and Jewish voters by consistently opposing Sunday closing laws that shut down taverns and other businesses on the only day workers had off. Democrats charged, rightly, that Republican moral crusades often masked attacks on immigrant culture.

Sectionalism and the New South

After the end of Reconstruction, voters in the former Confederate states remained loyal Democrats, voting for Democratic candidates in every presidential election for the next seventy years. Labeling the Republican Party the agent of "Negro rule," Democrats urged white Southerners to "vote the way you shot." Yet the so-called solid South proved far from solid on the state and local levels. The economic plight of the South led to shifting political alliances and to third-party movements that challenged Democratic attempts to define politics along race lines and maintain the Democratic Party as the white man's party.

The South's economy, devastated by the war, foundered at the same time the North experienced an unprecedented industrial boom. Soon an influential group of Southerners called for a **New South** modeled on the industrial North. Henry Grady, the ebullient young editor of the *Atlanta Constitution*, used his paper's substantial influence (it boasted the largest circulation of any weekly in the country) to extol the virtues of a new industrial South. Part bully, part booster, Grady exhorted the South to use its natural advantages—cheap labor and abundant natural resources—to go head-to-head in competition with northern industry.

Grady's message fell on receptive ears. Many Southerners, men and women, black and white, joined the national migration from farm to city, leaving the old plantations to molder and decay. With the end of military rule in 1877, southern Democrats took back state governments, calling themselves "Redeemers." Yet they did not look back to the values and beliefs of the old **planter** class. Instead, they enthusiastically embraced northern promoters who promised prosperity and profits.

The railroads came first, opening up the region for industrial development. Southern railroad mileage grew fourfold from 1865 to 1890 (see Map 17.1). The number of cotton spindles also soared, as textile mill owners abandoned New England in search of the cheap labor and proximity to raw materials promised in the South. By 1900 the South had become the nation's leading producer of cloth, and more than 100,000 Southerners, many of them women and children, worked in the region's textile mills.

The New South was proudest of its iron and steel industry, which grew up in the area surrounding Birmingham, Alabama. During this era the smokestack replaced the white-pillared plantation as the symbol of the South. Andrew Carnegie toured the region in 1889 and observed, "The South is Pennsylvania's most formidable industrial enemy." But as long as control of southern industry remained in the hands of northern investors, Pennsylvania had nothing to fear. Whatever the South's natural advantages, northern bankers and investors had no intention of letting the South beat the North at its own game. Elaborate mechanisms rigged the price of southern steel, inflating it, as one northern insider confessed, "for the purpose of protecting the Pittsburgh mills and in turn the Pittsburgh steel users." Similarly, in the extractive industries—lumber

> The solid South proved far from solid on the state and local levels. The economic plight of the South led to shifting political alliances and to third-party movements that challenged Democratic attempts to define politics along race lines.

Social Darwinism—Did Wealthy Industrialists Practice What They Preached?

Darwinism, with its emphasis on survival of the fittest and tooth-and-claw competition, seemed ideally suited to the get-rich-quick mentality of the Gilded Age. By placing the theory of evolution in an economic context, social Darwinism argued against government intervention in business while at the same time insisting that reforms to ameliorate the evils of urban industrialism would only slow evolutionary progress. Although most of the wealthy industrialists of the day probably had never read Charles Darwin or the exponents of social Darwinism, the catchphrase "survival of the fittest" nevertheless larded the rhetoric of business in the Gilded Age.

Andrew Carnegie, alone among the American business moguls, not only championed social Darwinism but avidly read the works of its primary exponent, British social philosopher Herbert Spencer. Carnegie spoke of his indebtedness to Spencer in terms usually reserved for religious conversion: "Before Spencer, all for me had been darkness, after him, all had become light—and right." In his *Autobiography* Carnegie wrote, "I had found the truth of evolution. 'All is well since all grows better' became my motto, my true source of comfort."

Not content to worship Spencer from afar, Carnegie assiduously worked to make his acquaintance

and then would not rest until he had convinced the reluctant Spencer to come to America. In Pittsburgh, Carnegie promised, Spencer could best view his evolutionary theories at work in the world of industry. Clearly, Carnegie viewed his steelworks as the apex of America's new industrial order, a testimony to the playing out of evolutionary theory in the economic world.

In 1882 Spencer undertook an American tour. Carnegie personally invited him to Pittsburgh, squiring him through the Braddock steel mills. But Spencer failed to appreciate Carnegie's achievement. The heat, noise, and pollution of Pittsburgh reduced Spencer to near collapse, and he could only choke out, "Six months' residence here would justify suicide." Carnegie must have been devastated by Spencer's reaction to America's new industrial order, but he never let on.

How well Carnegie actually understood the principles of social Darwinism is debatable. In his 1900 essay "Popular Illusions about Trusts," Carnegie spoke of the "law of evolution that moves from the heterogeneous to the homogeneous," citing Spencer as his source. Spencer, however, had written of the movement "from an indefinite incoherent

and mining—investors in the North and abroad, not Southerners, reaped the lion's share of the profits.

In only one industry did the South truly dominate—tobacco. Capitalizing on the invention of a machine for rolling cigarettes, the American Tobacco Company founded by the Duke family of North Carolina eventually dominated the industry. The new popularity of cigarettes, which replaced chewing tobacco at

the turn of the twentieth century, provided a booming market for Duke's "ready mades." Soon the company was selling 400,000 cigarettes a day.

In practical terms, the industrialized New South proved an illusion. Much of the South remained agricultural, caught in the grip of the insidious crop lien system (see chapter 16). White Southern farmers, desperate to get out of debt, often joined with African Americans to pursue their goals politically. Southerners used this homogeneity to a definite coherent heterogeneity." Instead of acknowledging that the history of human evolution moved from the simple to the more complex, Carnegie seemed to insist that evolution moved from the complex to the simple. This confusion of the most basic evolutionary theory calls into question Carnegie's grasp of Spencer's ideas or indeed Darwins'. Other business leaders less well read than Carnegie no doubt understood even less about the working of evolutionary theory and social Darwinism, which they so often claimed as their own.

The distance between preachment and practice is also boldly evident in the example of William Graham Sumner, America's foremost social Darwinist. Ironically, Sumner, who so often sounded like an apologist for the rich, was attacked by the very group he supposedly supported. The problem was that strict social Darwinists like Sumner insisted absolutely that the government ought not to meddle in the economy. The purity of Sumner's commitment to laissez-faire led him to adamantly oppose the protective tariffs by which the government artificially inflated the prices of foreign manufactured goods so that U.S. businesses could compete against

foreign rivals. Sumner outspokenly attacked the tariff and firmly advocated free trade from his chair in Political Economy at Yale University. In 1890, the same year the Congress passed the nation's highest tariff, Sumner's fulminations so angered Yale's wealthy alumni that they mounted a campaign (unsuccessful) to have him fired.

Sumner's theoretical consistency did not seem to trouble Andrew Carnegie, who never acknowledged a contradiction between his worship of Spencer and his strong support

Herbert Spencer
British writer and philosopher Herbert Spencer became a hero to Andrew Carnegie, who orchestrated Spencer's trip to America in 1882. The sage of social Darwinism proved a great disappointment to Carnegie. A cautious hypochondriac, Spencer guarded himself zealously against any painful contact with that teeming competitive world that he extolled. Once on American soil, Spencer spurned Carnegie's offers of hospitality during his visit to Pittsburgh and insisted on staying in a hotel. And when Carnegie eagerly demonstrated the wonders of the world's most modern steel mill to his guest, the tour reduced Spencer to a state of near collapse.
Hulton Archives / Getty Images.

for the tariff. The comparison of Carnegie's position and Sumner's underscores the reality that although in theory laissez-faire constrained the government from playing an active role in business affairs, in practice industrialists fought for government favors—whether tariffs, land grants, or subsidies—that worked to their benefit. Only when the issue was taxes or regulation were they quick to cry foul and invoke the "natural laws" of social Darwinism and its corollary, laissez-faire.

strategy in a variety of ways. Between 1865 and 1900, voters in every state south of the Mason-Dixon line experimented with political alliances that crossed the color line. In Virginia the "Readjusters," a coalition of blacks and whites determined to "readjust" (lower) the state debt and spend more money on public education, captured state offices from 1879 to 1883. In Southern politics, the interplay of race and gender made coalitions like the Readjusters a potent threat to the status quo.

Gender, Race, and Politics

Gender—society's notion of what constitutes acceptable masculine or feminine behavior—influenced politics throughout the nineteenth century. From the early days of the Republic, citizenship had been defined in male terms. Citizenship and its prerogatives (voting and officeholding) served as a badge of manliness and rested on its corollary, patriarchy—the power and authority men exerted over their wives and families. With the advent of universal (white) male **suffrage** in the early nineteenth century, gender eclipsed class as the defining feature of citizenship; men's dominance over women provided the common thread that knit all white men, regardless of class, into one political fraternity. The concept of **separate spheres** dictated political participation for men only. Once the public sphere of political participation became equated with manhood, women found themselves increasingly restricted to the private sphere of home and hearth.

Gender permeated politics in other ways, especially in the tangled skein of the New South. Cross-racial alliances like the Readjusters rested on the belief that universal political rights (voting, officeholding, patronage) could be extended to black males in the public sphere without eliminating racial barriers in the private sphere. Democrats, for their part, fought back by trying to convince voters that black voting would inevitably lead to **miscegenation** (racial mixing). Black male political power and sexual power, they warned, went hand in hand. Ultimately their arguments prevailed, and many whites returned to the Democratic fold to protect "white womanhood" and with it white supremacy.

The notion that black men threatened white Southern womanhood reached its most vicious form in the practice of lynching—the killing and mutilation of black men by white mobs. By 1892 the practice had become so prevalent that a courageous black woman, Ida B. Wells, launched an antilynching movement. That year a white mob lynched a friend of Wells's whose only transgression was that his grocery store competed too successfully with a white-owned store. Wells shrewdly concluded that lynching served "as an excuse to get rid of Negroes who were acquiring wealth and property and thus keep the race terrorized." Determined to do something, she began systematically to collect data on lynching. In the decade between 1882 and 1892, she discovered, lynching rose in the South by an overwhelming 200 percent; more than 241 people were killed. The vast increase in lynching testified to the retreat of the federal government following Reconstruction and to white Southerners' determination to maintain supremacy through terrorism and intimidation.

As the first salvo in her attack, Wells put to rest the "old threadbare lie that Negro men assault white women." As she pointed out, violations of black women by white men, which were much more frequent than black attacks on white

Ida B. Wells

Ida B. Wells began her antilynching campaign at the age of thirty after a friend's murder in 1892 led her to examine the extent of lynching in the South. She spread her message in lectures and pamphlets like this one distributed for fifteen cents. Wells brought the horror of lynching to a national and international audience and mobilized other African American women to undertake social action under the auspices of the National Association of Colored Women.

Manuscript, Archives and Rare Books Division, Schomburg Center for Research in Black Culture, The New York Public Library, Astor, Lenox, and Tilden.

women, went unnoticed and unpunished. Wells articulated lynching as a problem of race and gender. She insisted that the myth of black attacks on white southern womanhood masked the reality that mob violence had more to do with economics and the shifting social structure of the South than with rape. She demonstrated in a sophisticated way how the southern patriarchal system, having lost its control over blacks with the end of slavery, used its control over women to circumscribe the liberty of black men.

Wells's strong stance immediately resulted in reprisal. While she was traveling in the North, her office in Tennessee was ransacked and her printing equipment destroyed. Yet the warning that she would be killed on sight if she ever returned to Memphis only stiffened her resolve. As she wrote in her autobiography, *Crusade for Justice*, "Having lost my paper, had a price put on my life and been made an exile . . . , I felt that I owed it to myself and to my race to tell the whole truth now that I was where I could do so freely." Antilynching became a lifelong commitment that took Wells twice to Britain, where she placed lynching on the international agenda. As a reporter, first for the *New York Age* and later for the *Chicago Inter-Ocean*, she used every opportunity to hammer home her message.

Wells's activities mobilized other black women, including Victoria Earle Matthews and Maritcha Lyons, who were already engaged in social reform and self-improvement. They hosted a testimonial dinner for Wells in New York in 1892 that led to the organization of a black women's club, the Women's Loyal Union. The club became a spearhead for the creation of the National Association of Colored Women (NACW) in 1896. The organization's first president, Mary Church Terrell of Washington, D.C., urged her followers to "promote the welfare of our race, along all the lines that tend to its development and advancement." Taking as their motto "Lifting as we climb," the women of the NACW attacked myriad issues including health care, housing, education, and the promotion of a positive image of the Negro race. The NACW played a critical role in Wells's antilynching campaign by lobbying for legislation that would make lynching a federal crime. Beginning in 1894 and continuing for decades, antilynching bills were introduced in Congress only to be defeated by southern opposition.

Lynching did not end during Ida B. Wells's lifetime, nor did antilynching legislation gain passage in Congress; but Wells's forceful voice brought the issue to national prominence. At her funeral in 1931, black leader W. E. B. Du Bois eulogized Wells as the woman who "began the awakening of the conscience of the nation." Wells's determined campaign against lynching provided just one example of women's political activism during the Gilded Age. The suffrage and **temperance** movements also demonstrated how women refused to be relegated to a "separate sphere" that kept them out of politics by gendering it male.

Women's Politics: The Origins of the Suffrage and Temperance Movements

No one better recognized the potency of the gendered notion of political rights than Elizabeth Cady Stanton, who lamented the introduction of the word *male* into the Fourteenth Amendment (see chapter 16). The explicit linking of manhood with citizenship and voting rights in the Constitution marked a major setback for women who supported the vote for women. In 1869 Stanton, along with Susan B. Anthony, who was jailed in New York state for attempting to vote, formed the National Woman's Suffrage Association (NWSA), the first independent women's rights organization in the United States.

The NWSA's political activity on behalf of woman suffrage illustrates the active political role that women played despite their inability to vote or hold office. Women found ways to act politically long before they voted, as evidenced not only in the campaign for the vote but also in the temperance movement (the movement to end drunkenness). Temperance women adopted a new approach during the winter of 1873–74. Armed with Bibles and singing hymns, they marched on taverns and saloons and refused to leave until the proprietors signed a pledge to quit selling liquor. Known as the Woman's Crusade, the movement spread like a prairie fire through small towns in Ohio, Indiana, Michigan, and Illinois and soon moved east into New York, New England, and Pennsylvania. Before it was over, more than 100,000 women marched in over 450 cities and towns.

> The NWSA's political activity on behalf of woman suffrage points to the active political role women played despite their inability to vote or hold office.

The women's tactics may have been new, but the temperance movement dated back to the 1820s. Originally, the movement had been led by Protestant men who organized clubs to pledge voluntary abstinence from liquor. The Woman's Crusade marked a distinct change in strategy, as women moved into leadership and increasingly turned to political action to end the sale of alcohol. Temperance proved an especially explosive issue, one that divided communities, pitting middle class against working class, native-born against immigrant, Protestant against Catholic, and women against men. By the 1850s, temperance advocates had won significant victories when states, starting with Maine, passed laws to prohibit the sale of liquor (known as "Maine laws"). But by the late 1860s and 1870s the liquor business was on the rise, with about one saloon for every fifty males over the age of fifteen. Willing to spend as much money as it took, the liquor interests mounted a powerful lobby to fight temperance. Most "drys," as temperance advocates were dubbed, stayed in the Republican Party, although a Prohibition Party emerged in 1869. Democrats, with strength in the big cities of the North, won the support of the "wets," often

WCTU Flyer

This Woman's Christian Temperance Union flyer shows the wife pitted against the saloon keeper for her husband's pay. The economic consequences to the family of a drinker were a serious matter. At a time when the average worker made only $500 a year, money spent on alcohol meant less to eat for the family. As the poster indicates, thirty cents a day over a year paid for a substantial amount of family staples. Beer and liquor lobbyists worked hard not only to counter the WCTU but to fight woman suffrage because they feared that when women got the vote they would enact prohibition.

Culver Pictures.

working-class immigrants who sought recreation in saloons and beer gardens. To avoid the divisive issue, both parties preferred to leave to counties and towns (local option) the decision of whether to ban the sale of liquor.

The Woman's Crusade dramatically brought the issue of temperance back into the national spotlight and led to the formation of a new organization, the Woman's Christian Temperance Union (WCTU) in 1874. Composed entirely of women, the WCTU advocated total abstinence from alcohol (see chapter 20). When the women of the WCTU joined with the Prohibition Party (formed by a group of **evangelical** clergymen), one wag observed that "politics is a man's game, an' women, chidlhern, and prohyibitionists do well to keep out iv it." By sharing power with women, the Prohibitionist men violated the old political rules and risked such attacks on their honor and manhood.

Women in the Gilded Age enlisted in a variety of political projects. Antilynching, suffrage, and temperance constituted only a few of women's political causes. Even though they could not yet vote, women found ways to organize to affect the political process. Like men, they displayed strong party loyalties and rallied around traditional Republican and Democratic candidates. Third parties courted women, recognizing that although they could not vote, their volunteer labor and support could be key assets in party building. Nevertheless, despite the political power women exerted, politics, particularly presidential politics, remained—like chewing tobacco—an exclusively male prerogative.

Presidential Politics in the Gilded Age

Why do the great industrialists—Rockefeller, Morgan, Carnegie—jump vividly from the pages of the past while the presidents of that period remain so pallid? The presidents from Rutherford B. Hayes (1877–1881) to William McKinley (1897–1901) are indeed forgotten men, largely because so little was expected of them. Until the 1890s, few Americans thought the president or the national government had any role to play in addressing the problems accompanying the industrial transformation of the nation. The dominant creed of laissez-faire, coupled with the dictates of social Darwinism, warned government to leave business alone. This crippling view of government's rights and responsibilities in the economy and in society reduced the federal government to something of a sideshow. The real action took place elsewhere—in the boardrooms of business and industry and in party politics on the local and state levels. Nevertheless, the presidents grappled with corruption and party strife and struggled toward the creation of new political ethics that would replace patronage with a **civil service** system. This system promised to award jobs on the basis of merit, not party loyalty.

Corruption and Party Strife

The political corruption and party factionalism that characterized the administration of Ulysses S. Grant (1869–1877) continued to trouble the nation in the 1880s. The spoils system—awarding jobs for political purposes—remained the driving force in party politics at all levels of government in the Gilded Age. Reformers eager to replace the spoils system with civil service faced an uphill battle.

A small but determined group of reformers, not only distressed by the spoils system but also sickened by the graft and corruption rampant at all levels of government, championed a new ethics that would preclude politicians from getting rich from public office. The selection of U.S. senators particularly concerned them. Under the Constitution, senators were selected by state legislatures, not directly elected by the voters. Powerful business interests often contrived to control state legislatures and through them U.S. senators. As journalist Henry Demarest Lloyd observed, Standard Oil "had done everything to the Pennsylvania legislature except to refine it." The "oil combination," he charged, practically owned Pennsylvania's two senators. Nothing prevented a senator from collecting a paycheck from any of the great corporations. So many did that political cartoonists often portrayed senators as huge moneybags labeled with the names of the corporations they served. Nelson Aldrich, the powerful Republican from Rhode Island whose daughter married John D. Rockefeller Jr., did not object to being called "the senator from Standard Oil." In this climate, a constitutional amendment calling for the direct election of senators faced opposition from entrenched interests.

Republican president Rutherford B. Hayes, whose disputed election in 1876 signaled the end of Reconstruction in the South, tried to steer a middle course between spoilsmen and reformers. A hardworking, well-informed executive, Hayes wanted peace, prosperity, and an end to party strife. The Democratic press ridiculed him as "Rutherfraud" and "His Fraudulency" because he had not been elected by the people, but Hayes proved to be a figure of honesty and integrity well suited to his role as a national leader. His was not an easy task. The Republican Party remained divided into factions led by strong party bosses who boasted that they could make or break a president.

Fiery and dynamic party bosses dominated politics on the national scene. Foremost among them stood Senator Roscoe Conkling of New York, a master spoilsman, who ridiculed civil service as "snivel service" and tried his best to get the Republicans to run Grant again for president in 1880. He and his followers were known as "Stalwarts." Conkling's archrival, Senator James G. Blaine of Maine, led a faction called the "Half Breeds." Not as openly corrupt as the Grant wing of the party, the Half Breeds and their champion were also tainted with charges of corruption. Blaine had his own presidential ambitions and worked in 1880 to block Grant and oust Hayes. A third group, called the Mugwumps, consisting primarily of reform-minded Republicans from Massachusetts and New York, deplored the spoils system and advocated civil service reform. The name "Mugwump" came from the Algonquian word for *chief*, but critics used the term derisively, punning that the Mugwumps straddled the fence on issues of party loyalty, "with their mug on one side and wump on the other."

Despite his virtues, President Hayes soon managed to alienate all factions in his party. He used federal patronage to build Republican strength by filling government jobs with, if not the best men, the best Republicans he could find. To the Stalwarts, who wanted more positions, his action constituted betrayal; to the Mugwumps his appointments smacked too much of the spoils system. Blaine and the Half Breeds, coveting the presidency, offered no support. Hayes soon found himself a president without a party and announced that he would not seek reelection in 1880.

> The spoils system—awarding jobs for political purposes—remained the driving force in party politics at all levels of government during the Gilded Age.

The Republicans did not nominate Blaine in 1880 as the Half Breeds had hoped. To avoid choosing among its factions, the Republican Party nominated a "dark-horse" candidate, Representative James A. Garfield from Ohio. To appease Conkling, they picked Stalwart Chester A. Arthur as the vice presidential candidate. The Democrats made an attempt to overcome sectionalism and establish a national party by selecting as their presidential standard-bearer an old Union general, Winfield Scott Hancock. But as one observer noted, "It is a peculiarly constituted party that sends rebel brigadiers to Congress because of their rebellion, and then nominates a Union General as its candidate for president because of his loyalty." Hancock won only lukewarm support. Although the popular vote was close, Garfield won 214 electoral votes to Hancock's 155.

Garfield's Assassination and Civil Service Reform

"My God," Garfield swore after only a few months in office, "what is there in this place that a man should ever want to get into it?" Garfield, like Hayes, faced the difficult task of remaining independent while pacifying the party bosses and placating the reformers. As the federal bureaucracy grew to nearly 150,000 jobs, thousands of office seekers swarmed to the nation's capital, each clamoring for a position. In the days before Secret Service protection, the White House door stood open to all comers. Garfield took a fatalistic view. "Assassination," he told a friend, "can no more be guarded against than death by lightning, and it is best not to worry about either."

On July 2, 1881, less than four months after taking office, Garfield was shot in the back and mortally wounded at a Washington, D.C., railroad station while catching a train. His assassin, Charles Guiteau, though clearly insane, turned out to be a disappointed office seeker who claimed to be motivated by political partisanship. He told the police officer who arrested him, "I did it; I will go to jail for it; Arthur is president, and I am a Stalwart." Garfield lay on his deathbed through the hot summer. He finally died on September 19, 1881.

The press almost universally condemned Republican factionalism, if not for inspiring Guiteau, then for creating the political climate that produced him. Stalwart Roscoe Conkling saw his hopes for the White House dashed as a result. Attacks on the spoils system increased, and the public joined the chorus calling for reform. But though Garfield's death crystallized the desire for civil service reform, the debate was long and hard. Many who opposed reform recognized that civil service had built-in class and ethnic biases. At a time when few men achieved more than a grammar school education, written civil service examinations threatened to undo political advances made by Irish Americans and turn government back over to an educated Yankee elite. As one opponent argued, "George Washington could not have passed examination for a clerkship," noting that "in his will written by his own hand, he spells clothes, cloathes."

Reform came with the passage of the Pendleton Civil Service Act in 1883, after more than a year of congressional debate and compromise. Both parties claimed credit for the act, which established a permanent Civil Service Commission of three members, appointed by the president. Some fourteen thousand jobs were placed under a merit system that required examinations for office and made it impossible to remove jobholders for political reasons. Half of the postal jobs and most of the customhouse jobs, the largest share of the spoils system's bounty, passed to the control of the Civil Service Commission. The new law also prohibited federal jobholders from contributing to political campaigns, thus drying up the major source of the party bosses' revenue. Soon business interests stepped in to replace officeholders as the nation's chief political contributors. Ironically, civil service reform thus gave business an even greater influence in political life.

Reform and Scandal: The Campaign of 1884

With Conkling's downfall, James G. Blaine assumed leadership of the Republican Party and at long last captured the presidential nomination in 1884. A magnetic Irish American politician, Blaine inspired such devotion that his supporters called themselves Blainiacs. But to many reformers, Blaine personified corruption. Led by Mugwump Carl Schurz, who insisted that Blaine "wallowed in spoils like a rhinoceros in an African pool," Republican reformers bolted the party and embraced the Democrats' presidential nominee, the stolid Grover Cleveland, reform governor of New York. The burly, beer-drinking Cleveland distinguished himself from an entire

Civil Service Exams

In this 1890s photograph, prospective police officers in Chicago take the written civil service exam. Civil service meant that politicians and party bosses could no longer use jobs in the government to reward the party faithful. Many people worried that merit examinations would favor the educated elite at the expense of immigrant groups like the Irish, who had made a place for themselves in the political system by the late nineteenth century. The political cartoon (inset) underscores the point by showing an applicant sweating over the exam while in his pocket he carries a recommendation from his alderman. The cartoon implies that in the past this man would have received a job even though he couldn't answer simple questions.

Photo: Chicago Historical Society; inset: Chicago Historical Society.

generation of politicians by the simple motto "A public office is a public trust." First as mayor of Buffalo and later as governor of New York, he built a reputation for honesty, economy, and administrative efficiency. The Democrats, who had not won the presidency since 1856, had high hopes for his candidacy, especially after the Mugwumps supported Cleveland, insisting "the paramount issue this year is moral rather than political."

The Mugwumps soon regretted their words. The 1884 contest degenerated so far into scandal and nasty mudslinging that one disgusted journalist styled it "the vilest campaign ever waged."

In July, Cleveland's hometown paper, the *Buffalo Telegraph*, dropped the bombshell that the bachelor candidate had fathered an illegitimate child in an affair with a local widow. Crushed by the scandal, the Mugwumps tried to argue the difference between public and private morality. But robbed of their moral righteousness, they lost much of their enthusiasm. "Now I fear it has resolved itself into a choice of two evils," one weary reformer confessed.

At public rallies, Blaine's partisans taunted Cleveland, chanting, "Ma, Ma, where's my Pa?" The stoic Cleveland accepted responsibility for the child, who may in fact have been fathered by his business partner. Some said Cleveland, a bachelor, took the blame to spare his partner's reputation because he had fallen in love with the man's daughter. Silent but fuming, Cleveland waged his campaign in the traditional fashion by staying home while Blaine broke precedent by making a national tour.

A campaign misstep by Blaine quickly revived Cleveland's chances. On a last-minute stop in New York City, the exhausted candidate overlooked a remark by a local clergyman that eventually cost him many votes. While introducing Blaine, the Reverend Samuel Burchard blasted the Democrats as the party of "Rum, Romanism, and Rebellion." An Associated Press correspondent recognized the blunder and hurriedly filed his story, crying, "If anything will elect Cleveland, these words will do it." By linking drinking (rum) and Catholicism (Romanism), Burchard cast a slur on Irish Catholic voters, who had been counted on to desert the Democratic Party and support Blaine because of his Irish background.

The reporter proved right. With less than a week to go until the election, Blaine had no chance to recover from the negative publicity. He lost New York State by fewer than 1,200 votes and with it the election. In the final tally, Cleveland defeated Blaine by a scant 29,214 votes nationwide but won 219 electoral votes to 182 (Map 17.2). After twenty-five years of Republican rule, Cleveland and the Democrats withstood the mudslinging to win the presidency. Cleveland's followers had the last word. To the chorus of "Ma, Ma, where's my Pa?" they retorted, "Going to the White House, ha, ha, ha."

Anti-Cleveland Card, 1888

In this early example of negative campaign advertising, Republicans pillory Democratic president Grover Cleveland as an advocate of free trade, while dredging up the image of his illegitimate child, which had proved such a scandal in the 1884 campaign. The bottom lines echo the earlier campaign ditty "Ma, Ma, Where's My Pa?" In this election the tariff became a potent issue, winning support from business and labor and helping elect Republican Benjamin Harrison.

Collection of David J. and Janice L. Frent.

Economic Issues and Shifting Political Alliances

Four years later, in the election of 1888, fickle voters turned Cleveland out, electing Republican Benjamin Harrison, the grandson of President William Henry Harrison (1841–1845). Then, in the only instance in America's history when a president once defeated at the polls returned to office, the voters brought Cleveland back in the election of 1892. What factors account for such a surprising turnaround? The strengths and weaknesses of the men themselves partially determined the outcome. The stubborn Cleveland, newly married to Frances Folson, his partner's daughter, resented demands on his time and refused to campaign in 1888. Although he won more popular votes than Harrison, he lost in the electoral college. Once in office, Harrison proved to be a cold and distant leader, prompting critics to call him "the human iceberg."

But new issues as well as personalities increasingly swayed the voters. The 1880s wit-

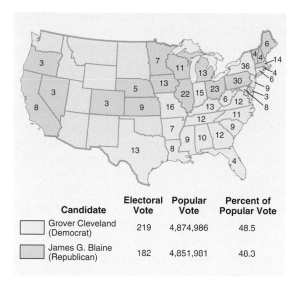

Candidate	Electoral Vote	Popular Vote	Percent of Popular Vote
Grover Cleveland (Democrat)	219	4,874,986	48.5
James G. Blaine (Republican)	182	4,851,981	48.3

MAP 17.2   The Election of 1884

nessed a remarkable political realignment as a new set of economic concerns replaced appeals to Civil War sectional loyalties. The tariff, federal regulation of the railroads and trusts, and the campaign for **free silver** restructured American politics.

The Tariff and the Politics of Protection

The tariff became a potent political issue in the 1880s. The concept of a protective tariff to raise the price of imported goods and stimulate American industry dated back to Alexander Hamilton in the founding days of the Republic. Congress enacted the first tariff following the War of 1812. The Republicans turned the tariff to political ends in 1861 by enacting a measure that both raised revenues for the Civil War and rewarded their industrial supporters, who wanted protection from foreign competition. After the war, the Republicans continued to revise and enlarge the tariff at the prompting of northeastern industrialists. By the 1880s, the tariff was so high it posed a threat to prosperity. The huge surplus created by the tariff sat in the Treasury's vaults, depriving the country of money that might otherwise have been invested to create jobs and products, while the government argued about how (or even whether) to spend it.

To many Americans, particularly southern and midwestern farmers who sold their crops in a world market yet had to buy goods priced artificially high because of the protective tariff, the answer was simple: Reduce the tariff. Advocates of free trade and moderates agitated for tariff reform. But those who benefited from the tariff—industrialists insisting that America's "infant industries" needed protection and some westerners producing protected raw materials such as wool, hides, and lumber—firmly opposed lowering the tariff. Many workers, too, believed that the tariff protected American wages by giving American products a competitive edge over goods imported from other countries.

The Republican Party seized on the tariff question to forge a new national coalition. Blaine shrewdly recognized the potent political uses of the tariff in allying the Midwest, West, and East. "Fold up the bloody shirt and lay it away," he advised a colleague in 1880. "It's of no use to us. You want to shift the main issue to protection." By encouraging an alliance among industrialists, labor, and western producers of raw materials—groups who benefited from the tariff—Blaine hoped to solidify the North, Midwest, and West against the solidly Democratic South. Although the tactic failed for Blaine in the election of 1884, it worked for the Republicans four years later. Cleveland, who had straddled the tariff issue in the election of 1884, startled the nation in 1887 by calling for tariff reform. The Republicans countered by arguing that "tariff tinkering" would only unsettle prosperous industries, drive down wages, and shrink the farmers' home market. Republican Benjamin Harrison, who supported the high tariff, ousted Cleveland from the White House in 1888, carrying all the western and northern states except Connecticut and New Jersey.

Back in power, the Republicans demonstrated their new commitment to economics over ideology by abandoning their principled support for freed slaves while currying favor with the new industrialists. Massachusetts senator Henry Cabot Lodge's 1890 Force Bill, a federal election law to restore the vote to African Americans who faced intimidation and disfranchisement in the South, died in the same Republican Congress that passed the highest tariff in the nation's history. The new tariff, sponsored by Republican representative William McKinley of Ohio and signed into law by Harrison, stirred a hornet's nest of protest across the United States. The American people had elected Harrison to preserve protection but not to enact a higher tariff.

Democrats condemned the McKinley tariff and labeled the Republican Congress that passed it the "Billion Dollar Congress" for its carnival of spending that depleted the nation's surplus by enacting a series of pork barrel programs shamelessly designed to bring federal money to congressmen's own constituents. In the congressional election of 1890, angry voters swept the hapless Republicans, including tariff sponsor McKinley, out of office. Two years later, Harrison himself was defeated. Grover Cleveland, whose call for tariff revision had lost him the election in 1888, triumphantly returned to the White House vowing to lower the tariff. Such were the changes in the political winds whipped up by the tariff issue.

Railroads, Trusts, and the Federal Government

American voters may have divided on the tariff, but increasingly they agreed on the need for federal regulation of the railroads and federal legislation against the "trusts" (a term loosely applied to all large business combinations). As early as the 1870s, angry farmers in the Midwest who suffered from the unfair shipping practices of the railroads organized to fight for railroad regulation. The Patrons of Husbandry, or the Grange, founded in 1867 as a social and educational organization for farmers, soon became an independent political movement. By electing Grangers to state office, farmers made it possible for several midwestern states to pass laws in the 1870s and 1880s regulating the railroads. At first the Supreme Court ruled in favor of state regulation (*Munn v. Illinois*, 1877). But in 1886, the Court reversed itself, ruling that because railroads crossed state boundaries, they fell outside state jurisdiction (*Wabash v. Illinois*). With more than three-fourths of railroads crossing state lines, the Supreme Court's decision effectively quashed the states' attempts at railroad regulation.

Anger over the *Wabash* decision finally led to the first federal law regulating the railroads, the Interstate Commerce Act, passed in 1887 during Cleveland's first administration. The act established the nation's first federal regulatory agency, the Interstate Commerce Commission

> American voters may have divided on the tariff, but increasingly they agreed on the need for federal regulation of the railroads and federal legislation against the trusts.

(ICC), to oversee the railroad industry. In its early years, the ICC was never strong or sure enough to pose a serious threat to the railroads. It could not, for example, end rebates to big shippers. In its early decades it proved more important as a precedent than effective as a watchdog.

Concern over the growing power of the trusts led Congress to pass the Sherman Antitrust Act in 1890. The act outlawed pools and trusts, ruling that businesses could no longer enter into agreements to restrict competition. It did nothing to restrict huge holding companies like Standard Oil, however, and proved to be a weak sword against the trusts. In the decade after passing the Sherman Antitrust Act, the government successfully struck down only six trusts. And rather than acting solely as a check on big business, the act was used four times against labor by outlawing

The Corruption of Government by Big Business
In this *Puck* cartoon, a gullible Uncle Sam is being led by trusts and monopolies satirically styled as "his philanthropic friends." Concern over the power of big business led in 1890 to the passage of the Sherman Antitrust Act, the first attempt to regulate business by making it illegal to restrict competition.
Picture Research Consultants & Archives.

unions as a "conspiracy in restraint of trade." In 1895, the Supreme Court dealt the antitrust law a crippling blow in *United States v. E. C. Knight Company*. In its decision the Court ruled that "manufacture" did not constitute "trade." This semantic quibble drastically narrowed the law, in this case allowing the American Sugar Refining Company, which had bought out a number of other sugar companies (including E. C. Knight) and controlled 98 percent of the production of sugar, to continue its virtual monopoly.

Both the ICC and the Sherman Antitrust Act testified to the nation's concern about corporate abuses of power and to a growing willingness to use federal measures to intervene on behalf of the public interest. As corporate capitalism became more and more powerful, public pressure grew toward political intervention. Yet not until the twentieth century would more active presidents sharpen and use these weapons effectively against the large corporations.

The Fight for Free Silver

While the tariff and regulation of the trusts gained many backers, the silver issue stirred passions like no other issue of the day. On one side stood those who believed that gold constituted the only honest money. Although other forms of currency circulated, notably paper money like banknotes and greenbacks, the government's support of the **gold standard** meant that all currency could be redeemed for gold. Many who supported the gold standard were eastern creditors who did not wish to be paid in devalued dollars. On the opposite side stood a coalition of western silver barons and poor farmers from the West and South. The mining interests, who had seen the silver bonanza in the West drive down the price of precious metals, wanted the government to buy silver and mint silver dollars. Farmers from the West and South who had suffered economically during the 1870s and 1880s hoped that increasing the money supply with silver dollars, thus causing inflation, would give

U.S. Currency

Gold remained the nation's standard currency, but silver supporters, including farmers and western mining interests, demanded the minting of silver dollars and the issuance of silver certificates. In the center is a dollar gold piece.

The American Numismatic Assn.; Picture Research Consultants & Archives.

them some relief by enabling them to pay off their debts with cheaper dollars.

Advocates of silver pointed out that until 1873 the country had enjoyed a system of bimetalism—the minting of both silver and gold into coins. In that year, at the behest of those who favored gold, Congress voted to stop buying and minting silver, an act advocates of bimetalism denounced as the "crime of '73." In 1878 and again in 1890 with the Sherman Silver Purchase Act, Congress took steps to appease advocates of silver by passing legislation that required the government to buy silver and issue silver certificates. While good for the mining interests, the laws did little to promote the inflation desired by the farmers. Soon they began to call for "the free and unlimited coinage of silver," a plan whereby nearly all the silver mined in the West would be minted into coins circulated at the rate of sixteen ounces of silver to one ounce of gold.

The silver issue crossed party lines, but the Democrats hoped to use it to achieve a union between western and southern voters. Unfortunately for them, Grover Cleveland, a Democrat who was a staunch conservative in money

> The silver issue stirred passions like no other issue of the day. On one side stood Easterners who believed that gold constituted the only honest money. On the opposite side stood a coalition of silver barons and poor farmers from the West and South.

matters and a strong supporter of the gold standard, sat in the White House. After a panic on Wall Street touched off a major depression in the spring of 1893, Cleveland called a special session of Congress and bullied the legislature into repealing the 1890 Silver Purchase Act. But repeal did not bring prosperity; it only divided the country. Angry farmers warned Cleveland not to travel west of the Mississippi River if he valued his life.

Panic and Depression

President Cleveland had scarcely begun his second term in office in 1893 when the nation fell into a deep economic depression, the worst the country had yet seen. In the winter of 1894–95, Cleveland walked the floor of the White House, sleepless over the prospect that the United States might go bankrupt. The Treasury's gold reserves had dipped so low that unless gold could be purchased abroad, the unthinkable might happen: The U.S. Treasury might not be able to meet its obligations.

At this juncture J. P. Morgan stepped in and suggested a plan. A group of bankers would purchase gold abroad and supply it to the Treasury. Cleveland knew only too well that such a scheme would unleash a thunder of protest from citizens and politicians already suspicious of the power the influential banker wielded. Yet to save the gold standard, the president had no choice but to turn to Morgan for help. A storm of controversy erupted over the deal. The press claimed that Cleveland had lined his own pockets and rumored that Morgan had made $8.9 million. Neither allegation was true. Cleveland had not profited a penny, and Morgan made about $300,000 on the deal—far less than the millions his critics claimed.

Yet the passions stirred by Cleveland's action cannot be dismissed lightly. Undoubtedly Morgan saved the gold reserves. But if President Cleveland's action managed to salvage the gold standard, it did not save the country from hardship. The winter of 1894–95 was one of the hardest in American history. People faced unemployment, cold, and hunger. A firm believer in limited government, Cleveland insisted that nothing could be done to help. "I do not believe that the power and duty of the General Government ought to be extended to the relief of individual suffering which is in no manner properly related to the public service or benefit." Nor did it occur to Cleveland that his great faith in the gold standard prolonged the depression, favored creditors over debtors, and caused immense hardship for millions of Americans. Their discontent would touch off a **Populist** revolt and lead to one of the most hotly contested elections in the nation's history in 1896 (see chapter 20).

Conclusion: Business Dominates an Era

The deal between J. P. Morgan and Grover Cleveland underscored a dangerous reality: The federal government was so weak that its solvency depended on a private banker. This lopsided power relationship signaled the dominance of business in the era Mark Twain satirically but accurately characterized as the Gilded Age. Perhaps no other era in American history spawned greed, corruption, and vulgarity on so grand a scale—an era when speculators like Jay Gould not only built but wrecked businesses to turn paper profits; an era when business boasted openly of buying politicians, who in turn lined their pockets at the public's expense.

Nevertheless, the Gilded Age was not without its share of solid achievements. In these years, America made the leap into the industrial age. Factories and refineries poured out American steel and oil at unprecedented rates. Businessmen like Carnegie, Rockefeller, and Morgan developed new strategies to consolidate American industry. By the end of the nineteenth century, the country had achieved industrial maturity. It boasted the largest, most innovative, most productive economy in the world. Its citizens enjoyed the highest standard of living on the globe. No other era in the nation's history witnessed such a transformation.

Yet the changes that came with these developments worried many Americans and gave rise to much of the era's political turmoil. Race and gender profoundly influenced American politics, leading to new political alliances. Fearless activist Ida B. Wells fought racism in its most brutal form—lynching. Women's organizations championed suffrage and temperance, challenging prevailing views of woman's proper sphere. Reformers fought corruption by instituting civil service. And new issues—the tariff, the regulation of the trusts, and currency reform—restructured the nation's politics.

During the Gilded Age the country expanded west across the continent, displacing the

Indians. Eight new states entered the Union, leaving only three territories in the continental United States. The problems and issues facing the nation—the growing power of corporations, corruption in business and politics, ethnic and racial animosities, and the exploitation of labor and natural resources—all had their western variations. Chapter 18 explores the way these themes played out in the West in the Gilded Age.

For additional firsthand accounts of this period, see Chapter 17 in Michael Johnson, ed., *Reading the American Past,* Third Edition.

To assess your mastery of the material in this chapter, see the Online Study Guide at bedfordstmartins.com/roark.

For Web links related to topics in this chapter, see "HistoryLinks," "DocLinks," and "PlaceLinks" at bedfordstmartins.com/roark.

CHRONOLOGY

1869 • Completion of first transcontinental railroad connects the East to markets in the West.

1870 • John D. Rockefeller incorporates Standard Oil Company in Cleveland.

1872 • Andrew Carnegie builds nation's largest Bessemer process steel plant near Pittsburgh.

1873 • U.S. government stops minting silver dollars.
• Panic on Wall Street leads to major economic depression.
• Mark Twain and Charles Dudley Warner publish *The Gilded Age.*

1873– 1874 • Woman's Crusade mounts attack on saloons across the country.

1874 • Woman's Christian Temperance Union founded.

1876 • Alexander Graham Bell demonstrates telephone at Philadelphia Centennial Exposition.

1877 • Republican Rutherford B. Hayes sworn in as president after disputed election.
• Democratic "Redeemers" come to power in the South.
• Supreme Court upholds right of states to regulate railroads in *Munn v. Illinois.*

1879 • Thomas Alva Edison perfects filament for incandescent lightbulb.

1880 • Dark-horse Republican candidate James A. Garfield elected president.

1880s • Jay Gould becomes architect of a transcontinental railway system.

1881 • Garfield assassinated; Vice President Chester A. Arthur becomes president.

1882 • Standard Oil develops the trust.

1883 • Congress passes Pendleton Act, establishing civil service reform.

1884 • Grover Cleveland becomes first Democrat elected president since before the Civil War.
• Mark Twain's *Adventures of Huckleberry Finn* banned in Boston.

1886 • In *Wabash v. Illinois,* Supreme Court reverses itself and disallows state regulation of railroads that cross state lines.

1887 • Congress passes Interstate Commerce Act, creating the first federal agency to regulate railroads.

1888 • Republican Benjamin Harrison elected president.

1890 • Senate defeats Force Bill intended to protect African American voting rights in the South.
• Congress passes McKinley tariff.
• Congress passes Sherman Antitrust Act.

1892 • Ida B. Wells launches antilynching campaign.

1893 • Panic devastates financial markets and touches off national depression.

1895 • J. P. Morgan bails out U.S. Treasury and saves country's gold reserves.

BIBLIOGRAPHY

General Works

Charles W. Calhoun, ed., *The Gilded Age: Essays on the Origins of Modern America* (1996).

Sean Dennis Cashman, *America in the Gilded Age: From the Death of Lincoln to the Rise of Theodore Roosevelt* (1993).

Alan Dawley, *Struggles for Justice: Social Responsibility and the Liberal State* (1991).

Vincent P. DeSantis, *The Shaping of Modern America, 1877–1920* (2nd ed., 1989).

Nell Irwin Painter, *Standing at Armageddon: The United States, 1877–1919* (1987).

Business

David Haward Bain, *Empire Express: Building the First Transcontinental Railroad* (1999).

Kathleen Brady, *Ida Tarbell: Portrait of a Muckraker* (1984).

Stuart Bruchey, *Growth of the Modern American Economy* (1975).

Vincent P. Carosso, *The Morgans: Private International Bankers, 1854–1913* (1987).

Edward Chancellor, *Devil Take the Hindmost: A History of Financial Speculation* (1999).

Alfred D. Chandler Jr., *The Visible Hand: The Managerial Revolution in American Business* (1977).

Alfred D. Chandler Jr., *Scale and Scope: The Dynamics of Industrial Capitalism* (1990).

Alfred D. Chandler Jr., ed., *The Railroads, the Nation's First Big Business: Sources and Readings* (1965).

Ron Chernow, *The House of Morgan: An American Banking Dynasty and the Rise of Modern Finance* (1990).

Ron Chernow, *Titan: The Life of John D. Rockefeller, Sr.* (1998).

John Steele Gordon, *The Scarlet Woman of Wall Street: Jay Gould, Jim Fiske, Cornelius Vanderbilt, the Erie Railway Wars, and the Birth of Wall Street* (1988).

David Freeman Hawke, *John D.: The Founding Father of the Rockefellers* (1980).

Jonathan Hughes, *The Vital Few: The Entrepreneur and American Economic Progress* (1986).

Thomas P. Hughes, *American Genesis: A Century of Invention and Technological Enthusiasm, 1870–1970* (1989).

Edward C. Kirkland, *Industry Comes of Age: Business, Labor, and Public Policy, 1860–1897* (1961).

Maury Klein, *The Life and Legend of Jay Gould* (1987).

Harold C. Livesay, *Andrew Carnegie and the Rise of Big Business* (1975).

James Mackay, *Little Boss: A Life of Andrew Carnegie* (1997).

Albro Martin, *James J. Hill and the Opening of the Northwest* (1991).

Albro Martin, *Railroads Triumphant: The Growth, Rejection, and Rebirth of a Vital American Force* (1992).

Carol Marvin, *When Technologies Were New* (1988).

Andre Millard, *Edison and the Business of Invention* (1990).

Glenn Porter, *The Rise of Big Business, 1860–1910* (1973).

Martin J. Sklar, *The Corporate Reconstruction of American Capitalism, 1890–1916* (1988).

Jean Strouse, *Morgan: American Financier* (1999).

William G. Thomas, *Lawyering for the Railroad: Business, Law, and Power in the New South* (1999).

Joseph Frazier Wall, *Andrew Carnegie* (1970).

Thomas Weiss and Donald Schaefer, eds., *American Economic Development in Historical Perspective* (1994).

David O. Whitten, *The Emergence of Giant Enterprise, 1860–1914* (1983).

Elmus Wicker, *Banking Panics of the Gilded Age* (2000).

John Hoyt Williams, *The Great and Shining Road: The Epic Story of the Transcontinental Railroad* (1988).

Viviana A. Zelizer, *The Social Meaning of Money* (1994).

Law

William E. Forbath, *Law and the Shaping of the American Labor Movement* (1991).

Morton J. Horowitz, *The Transformation of American Law, 1870–1960* (1992).

Paul Kens, *Justice Stephen Field: Shaping Liberty from the Gold Rush to the Gilded Age* (1997).

Robert Green McCloskey, *American Conservatism in the Age of Enterprise, 1865–1910* (1951).

John V. Orth, *Due Process of Law* (2003).

Arnold M. Paul, *Conservative Crisis and the Rule of Law: Attitudes of the Bar and Bench, 1887–1895* (1965).

Charles E. Rosenberg, *The Trial of the Assassin Guiteau: Psychiatry and the Law in the Gilded Age* (1968).

Politics

Paula Baker, *The Moral Framework of Public Life* (1991).

Jack S. Blocker Jr., *"Give to the Winds Thy Fears": The Women's Temperance Crusade, 1873–1874* (1985).

Ruth Bordin, *Woman and Temperance, The Quest for Power and Liberty, 1873–1900* (1990).

Alyn Brodsky, *Grover Cleveland: A Study in Character* (2000).

Jane Dailey, *Before Jim Crow: The Politics of Race in Postemancipation Virginia* (2000).

Jane Dailey, Glenda Elizabeth Gilmore, and Bryant Simon, eds., *Jumpin' Jim Crow: Southern Politics from the Civil War to Civil Rights* (2000).

John M. Dobson, *Politics in the Gilded Age: A New Perspective on Reform* (1972).

Rebecca Edwards, *Angels in the Machinery: Gender in American Party Politics from the Civil War to the Progressive Era* (1997).

Barbara Leslie Epstein, *The Politics of Domesticity: Women, Evangelism, and Temperance in Nineteenth Century America* (1981).

Glenda Elizabeth Gilmore, *Gender and Jim Crow: Women and the Politics of White Supremacy in North Carolina, 1896–1920* (1996).

Michael L. Goldberg, *An Army of Women: Gender and Politics in Gilded Age Kansas* (1997).

Lewis L. Gould, *William McKinley: A Biography* (1988).

Darlene Clark Hine and Kathleen Thompson, *A Shining Thread of Hope: The History of Black Women in America* (1998).

Ari Hoogenboom, *Rutherford B. Hayes: Warrior and President* (1995).

David H. Howard, *People, Pride, and Progress: 125 Years of the Grange in America* (1992).

H. Paul Jeffers, *An Honest President: The Life and Presidencies of Grover Cleveland* (2000).

David M. Jordan, *Roscoe Conkling of New York: Voice in the Senate* (1986).

James A. Kehl, *Boss Rule in the Gilded Age: Matt Quay of Pennsylvania* (1980).

Linda Kerber, *No Constitutional Right to Be Ladies* (1998).

Alexander Keyssar, *The Right to Vote: The Contested History of Democracy in the United States* (2000).

Paul Kleppner, *The Cross of Culture: A Social Analysis of Midwestern Politics, 1850–1900* (1970).

Robert D. Marcus, *Grand Old Party: Political Structure in the Gilded Age, 1880–1896* (1971).

John F. Marszalek, *Grover Cleveland* (1988).

Donald B. Marti, *Women of the Grange* (1991).

Carol Mattingly, *Well-Tempered Women, Nineteenth Century Temperance Rhetoric* (1998).

Gerald W. McFarland, *Mugwumps, Morals and Politics, 1884–1920* (1975).

Michael E. McGerr, *The Decline of Popular Politics: The American North, 1865–1928* (1986).

Louise Michele Newman, *White Women's Rights: The Racial Origins of Feminism in the United States* (1999).

D. Sven Nordin, *Rich Harvest: A History of the Grange, 1867–1900* (1974).

Ross Evans Paulson, *Women's Suffrage and Prohibition: A Comparative Study of Equality and Social Control* (1973).

Ross Evans Paulson, *Liberty, Equality and Justice: Civil Rights, Women's Rights and the Regulation of Business, 1865–1932* (1997).

Allan Peskin, *Garfield: A Biography* (1998).

Thomas C. Reeves, *Gentleman Boss: The Life of Chester Alan Arthur* (1991).

Joanne R. Reitano, *The Tariff Question in the Gilded Age* (1994).

Jacqueline Jones Royster, *Southern Horrors and Other Writings: The Anti-Lynching Campaign of Ida B. Wells, 1892–1900* (1996).

Milton Rugoff, *America's Gilded Age: Intimate Portraits from an Era of Extravagance and Change, 1850–1890* (1989).

Dorothy Salem, *To Better Our World: Black Women in Organized Reform, 1890–1920* (1990).

John G. Sproat, *The Best Men: Liberal Reformers in the Gilded Age* (1968).

Mark Wahlgren Summers, *Rum, Romanism, and Rebellion: The Making of a President, 1884* (1999).

John Tomsich, *A Genteel Endeavor: American Culture and Politics in the Gilded Age* (1971).

David M. Tucker, *Mugwumps: Public Moralists of the Gilded Age* (1998).

Ian Tyrell, *Woman's World, Woman's Empire: The Woman's Christian Temperance Union in International Perspective, 1880–1930* (1991).

Lynette Boney Wrenn, *Crisis and Commission Government in Memphis: Elite Rule in a Gilded Age City* (1998).

Culture

Louis Auchincloss, *The Vanderbilt Era: Profiles of a Gilded Age* (1989).

Mary Warner Blanchard, *Oscar Wilde's America: Counterculture in the Gilded Age* (1998).

Sarah Burns, *Inventing the Modern Artist: Art and Culture in Gilded Age America* (1996).

Ballard C. Campbell, ed., *The Human Tradition in the Gilded Age and Progressive Era* (2000).

John G. Cawelti, *Apostles of the Self-Made Man: Changing Concepts of Success in America* (1965).

John Foreman, *The Vanderbilts and the Gilded Age* (1991).

Judy Arlene Hilkey, *Character Is Capital: Success Manuals and Manhood in Gilded Age America* (1997).

Jane H. Hunter, *How Young Ladies Became Girls: The Victorian Origins of American Girlhood* (2002).

Wilbert Jenkins, *Seizing the Day: African Americans in Post–Civil War Charleston* (1998).

Justin Kaplan, *Mr. Clemens and Mark Twain* (1966).

Paulette D. Kilmer, *The Fear of Sinking: The American Success Formula in the Gilded Age* (1996).

Gloria Moldow, *Women Doctors in Gilded-Age Washington: Race, Gender and Professionalization* (1987).

Frederick Platt, *America's Gilded Age: Its Architecture and Decoration* (1976).

John Tomsich, *A Genteel Endeavor: American Culture and Politics in the Gilded Age* (1971).

Alan Trachtenberg, *The Incorporation of America: Culture and Society in the Gilded Age* (1982).

LAKOTA VEST
This Lakota vest belonged to Thomas American Horse, a member of the Oglala band of Lakota Sioux who lived on the Pine Ridge Reservation in South Dakota at the end of the nineteenth century. His initials are worked in beads across the shoulders. Made of tanned hide, with glass beads and tanned leather binding and lining, the vest shows how Native Americans adopted Euro-American articles of clothing and decorative motifs while employing materials that perpetuated native traditions. On the vest two mounted Indians in feathered headdresses face each other under American flags. The American flag as a decorative motif appeared frequently in Indian bead art and testifies to some of the great changes taking place in the Gilded Age West.

18

The West in the Gilded Age
1870–1900

T O CELEBRATE INDIAN CITIZENSHIP DAY in 1892, Native American students at the Indian boarding school at Hampton Institute in Virginia staged a pageant honoring the four hundredth anniversary of the "discovery" of the New World. Indian students appeared dressed as the nation's heroes— among them Christopher Columbus, Miles Standish, and George Washington. Not until halfway through the program did the pageant honor any Indian heroes and then the Indians selected—Samoset, Pocahontas—all came from the distant past in lands east of the Appalachians. There was no mention of Crazy Horse, Sitting Bull, Red Cloud, or Geronimo—Indians who resisted white encroachment and appropriation of their lands in the West. Only two years earlier, the massacre of over 200 Miniconjou Sioux at Wounded Knee, South Dakota, marked the end of three decades of war against the Indians in the trans-Mississippi West. The Indian wars left the Native American popula- tion in the continental United States at 250,000, down from estimates as high as 15 million at the time of first contact with Europeans. Not only had the Indian population been decimated, but Indian lands had shrunk so that by 1890 Euro-Americans controlled 97.5 percent of the territory formerly occupied by Native Americans.

The Hampton pageant could not entirely ignore a catastrophe of this magnitude. Yet it managed to end on a note of reconciliation as one student proclaimed:

> You have taken our rivers and fountains
>   And the plains where we loved to roam,—
> Banish us not to the mountains
>   And the lonely wastes for home!
> Our clans that were strongest and bravest,
>   Are Broken and powerless through you:
> Let us join the great tribe of the white men,
>   As brothers to dare and to do!

How the actors felt about the lines they spoke we cannot know. But the pageant clearly reflected the values and beliefs that Indian boarding schools hoped to inculcate in their pupils at the end of the nineteenth century.

Indian schools constituted the cultural battleground of the Indian wars in the West, their avowed purpose "to destroy the Indian and save the man." In 1877 Congress appropriated funds for Indian education, reasoning that "it was less expensive to educate Indians than to kill them." Hampton Institute,

Hampton Pageant, 1892

The Indian students in this picture are dressed for Columbia's Roll Call, a pageant at Hampton Institute honoring the nation's heroes on Indian Citizen Day, 1892. *Front row, left to right*—Thomas Last, Sioux, as Samoset, an Indian friend to the Pilgrims; David Hill, Onondaga, as Pilgrim Miles Standish. *Middle row, left to right*—Harry Kingman, Sioux, as White Mingo, an Iroquois killed by white settlers; Laura Face, Sioux, as Pocahontas, who saved the life of Captain John Smith; James Enouff, Potawatomi, as Christopher Columbus; Juanita Espinosa, Piegan, as Columbia, symbol of the Republic; Addie Stevens, Winnebago, as Puritan Priscilla Alden; Lucy Trudell, Sioux, as a Quakeress. *Back row, left to right*—Frank Bazhaw, Potawatomi, as Pilgrim leader Captain John Smith; Ebenezer Kingsley, Winnebago, as Puritan John Eliot; William Moore, Sac and Fox, as the Herald of Fame; Frank Hubbard, Penobscot, as President George Washington; Adam Metoxen, Oneida, as William Penn, founder of Pennsylvania; Joseph Redhorse, Sioux, as Tamimend, an Indian friend of William Penn.

Courtesy of Hampton University Archives.

them away in camp, and the police had to chase and capture them like so many wild rabbits," the agent observed. "This unusual proceeding created quite an outcry. The men were sullen and muttering, the women loud in their lamentations, and the children almost out of their wits with fright."

Once at school, the children were stripped and scrubbed, their clothing and belongings confiscated, their hair hacked off and doused with kerosene to kill lice. Issued stiff new uniforms, shoes, and what one boy recalled as the "torture" of woolen long underwear, the children often lost not only their possessions but their names—Hehakaavita (Yellow Elk) became Thomas Goodwood, Polingaysi Qoyawayma became Elizabeth White.

The curriculum offered agriculture and manual arts for boys and domestic skills for girls, training designed to make Indians economically self-sufficient and no longer a burden on the government. The Carlisle Indian School in Pennsylvania, founded in 1879, became the model for later institutions. To encourage assimilation, the Carlisle school pioneered the "outing system" under which Indian students lived with white families during summer vacations. The policy reflected the school's slogan, "To civilize the Indian, get him into civilization. To keep him civilized, let him stay." Yet despite their education and acculturation, graduating students rarely found a promising future. Many of them entered a dismal netherworld—never accepted in white society as equals but no longer at home on the reservation.

Merrill Gates, a member of the Board of Indian Commissioners, summed up a key goal of Indian education: "To get the Indian out of the blanket and into trousers,—and trousers with a pocket in them, and with a *pocket that aches to be filled with dollars!*" Gilded Age preoccupation with the pursuit of the almighty dollar clearly did not stop at the Mississippi. In fact, it might be more accurate to say that the get-rich-quick mentality of the California gold fields produced a society addicted to gambling and speculation. In 1871, two years before penning *The Gilded Age*, Mark Twain published *Roughing It*, his chronicle of days spent in mining towns in California and Nevada. There he found the same corrupt politics, vulgar display, and mania for speculation that he later skewered in his satire of life in the nation's capital.

The settlement of the West and the ensuing clash of cultures among Anglos, Native

created in 1868 to school newly freed slaves, accepted its first Indian students in 1878. While some Indian schools operated on the reservations, authorities much preferred boarding facilities that isolated students from the "contamination" of home and tribal values.

Parents resisted sending their children away. When all else failed, the military or Indian police kidnapped the children and put them on the trains taking them to Indian schools. An agent at the Mescalero Apache agency in Arizona Territory reported in 1886 how "it became necessary to visit the camps unexpectedly with a detachment of police, and seize such children as were proper and take them away to school, willing or unwilling." The parents put up a struggle. "Some hurried their children off to the mountains or hid

Americans, Hispanics, and others who followed the promise of land and riches into the West created many of the key issues facing Americans in the Gilded Age. Nor can the problems confronting the nation in the waning decades of the nineteenth century be fully understood without paying attention to the way they played out under western skies. The West witnessed the consolidation of business in mining, ranching, and commercial farming; corruption and cupidity in territorial government; vicious ethnic and racial animosity whether in the form of Indian wars or Chinese exclusion; and the exploitation of labor and natural resources that led to the decimation of the great bison herds, the pollution of rivers with mining wastes, and pitched battles between workers and bosses. The major themes of the era all had western variants, making the Gilded Age a truly national phenomenon.

Gold Fever and the Mining West

Western mining in nineteenth-century America began with the rush for California gold in 1849 (see chapter 12). The next four decades witnessed equally frenzied rushes for gold and other metals, most notably on the Comstock Lode in Nevada and later in New Mexico, Colorado, the Dakotas, Montana, Idaho, Arizona, and Utah. Each new rush built upon the last, producing new technologies and innovations in financing as hordes of miners, eager to strike it rich, moved from one boomtown to the next. (See "The Promise of Technology," page 638.) Mining in the Gilded Age West, however, was a story not only of boom and bust but also of community building and the development of territories into states as miners and settlers followed the promise of a better life into places like Cripple Creek, Colorado; Virginia City, Nevada; and Coeur d'Alene, Idaho (Map 18.1). At first glance, the mining West may seem much different from the East, but by the 1870s "urban industrialism" described Virginia City as accurately as it did Pittsburgh or Cleveland. A close look at mining on the Comstock Lode indicates some of the patterns and paradoxes of western mining. And a look at territorial government uncovers striking parallels with Gilded Age politics east of the Mississippi.

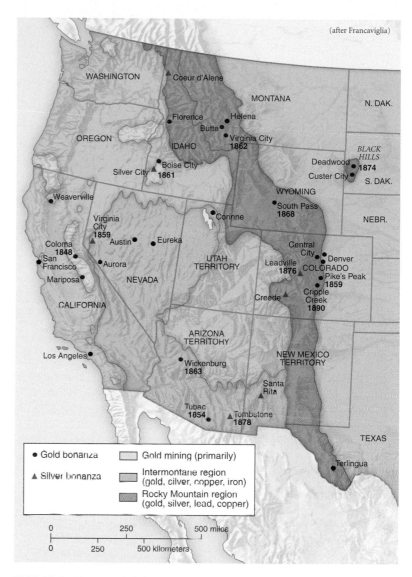

MAP 18.1 Western Mining, 1848–1890
Rich deposits of gold, silver, copper, lead, and iron larded the mountains of the West, from the Sierras of California to the Rockies of Colorado and the Black Hills of South Dakota. Beginning with the gold strike on Sutter's Creek in California in 1848 and continuing through the rush for gold in Cripple Creek, Colorado, in 1890, miners from all over the world flocked to the West in search of riches. Few struck it rich. Many more stayed on as paid workers in the increasingly mechanized corporate mines.

Mining on the Comstock Lode

California's forty-niners proved a restless lot. By 1859, refugees from California's played-out mines flocked to the Washoe basin in Nevada. There they found the gold they sought mired in blackish sand that they called "that blasted blue stuff." Eventually an enterprising miner had the blue stuff assayed, and it turned out that miners on the Washoe had stumbled on the richest vein

Hydraulic Mining

Individual prospectors who made the first gold strikes in California in 1849 employed a simple process known as placer mining. "No capital is required to obtain this gold, as the laboring man wants nothing but his pick and shovel and tin pan with which to dig and wash the gravel." But when the easy pickings along the rivers and streams gave out, a good deal of gold still remained trapped in quartz or buried deep in the earth, extractable only by methods far beyond the means and capacity of the average prospector.

Soon technology and capital invaded the diggings. As early as 1853 a French Canadian sail maker, Antoine Chabot, hoping to avoid the cost and labor of digging a long feeder ditch to get water to his claim, stitched together heavy strips of canvas and made a 100-foot length of hose. Building on this invention, a Connecticut forty-niner named Edward Matteson marveled at the power of the new technology he called "hydraulicking." "Ten men who own a claim are enabled . . . by directing streams of water against the base of a high bank to cut away such an extent as to cause immense slides of earth which often bring with them large trees and heavy boulders." Tons of fallen earth "are carried away through the sluices with almost as much rapidity as if they were a bank of [melting] snow."

The speed and efficiency of hydraulic mining promised more gold in less time for less work. With water doing the labor formerly provided by pick and shovel, prospectors who came to the gold fields to make a fortune often ended up working for the big mines for $3 a day, a decent wage for the time but no way to get rich quick.

Hydraulic mining industrialized gold mining, introducing what amounted to a form of mass production that involved all the features of modern, capital-intensive industry: corporations trading shares on an international market, engineers installing large and expensive works and equipment, and wage laborers replacing prospectors. By the 1880s, the Army Corps of Engineers estimated that some $100 million had been spent to build California's hydraulic mining system. The results proved worthwhile for the mine owners. Hydraulic mining produced 90 percent of California's gold.

Eager to make a quick profit, the purveyors of this new technology gave little thought to its impact on the environment. Hydraulic mining used prodigious amounts of water—two large nozzles could shoot out 1.7 million gallons a day. These huge water cannons washed away entire mountains, clogging streambeds and creating heaps of rubble. Thomas Starr King, a young Unitarian minister visiting hydraulic mining operations near Nevada City, California, was appalled by the sight that greeted him. Enormous nozzles blasted water, "tearing all the beauty out of the landscape and setting up 'the abomination of desolation' in its place." He grimly predicted, "If the hydraulic mining method is to be infinitely used, without restraint, upon all the surface that will yield a good return, then California of the future will be a waste more repulsive than any denounced in prophecy."

---

of silver ore on the continent—the legendary Comstock Lode, named for prospector Henry Comstock.

Silver mining, much more complicated than mining gold, presented new challenges to miners hoping to get rich quick. To exploit even potentially valuable claims required capital and expensive technology well beyond the means of the prospector. An active San Francisco stock market sprang up to finance operations on the Comstock. The shrewdest businessmen soon recognized that the easiest way to get rich from the boom was not to mine at all but to sell their claims or to form mining companies and sell shares of stock. The most unscrupulous mined the wallets of gullible investors by selling shares in bogus mines to stockholders to whom the very word *Comstock* conjured up images of riches. Speculation, misrepresentation, and outright thievery ran rampant in the mining West of the Gilded Age. And, although the mines produced no symbol of

Angry farmers protested that hydraulic mines discharged tailings (debris) that filled channels and forced rivers out of their banks, causing devastating floods. Farms were swept away and cattle drowned. Millions of cubic yards of silt from the hydraulic tailings washed down and covered farms with a muddy sand (slickens) two to seven feet deep, destroying all hopes of vegetation. Orchards and fields disappeared each year under new layers of mining debris.

In 1875, farmers organized to stop the destruction. But after four years of litigation, the California Supreme Court ruled in favor of the miners. Gold remained king in California. Not until the mid-1880s, when California's economy tilted from mining to agriculture and wheat became California's new gold, did farmers finally succeed in winning a court injunction against hydraulic mining. Renegade miners continued to use hydraulic methods until the 1890s, when more aggressive enforcement finally silenced the great hoses. The sounds of nature eventually returned to the California foothills, and the rivers began to run clear.

Hydraulic Mining and the Environment
Hydraulic mining of California's gold ripped up the landscape, creating waterfalls, as seen in this picture. The pipes connected to huge hoses capable of washing away entire hills. The debris clogged rivers and caused devastating floods that wiped out entire farms.
California History Section, California State Library.

greed as powerful as the arch speculator Jay Gould (see chapter 17), they did spawn their own share of robber barons. In twenty years, more than $300 million poured from the earth in Nevada alone. A little stayed in Virginia City, but a great deal more went to speculators in California, some of whom got rich without ever leaving Nob Hill in San Francisco. A small group of men—including George Hearst, Daniel Mackay, and Adolph Sutro—monopolized much of the Comstock's riches.

The promise of gold and silver drew thousands of men to the mines of the West, the honest as well as the unprincipled. As Mark Twain observed from his position as a writer on the *Territorial Enterprise* in Virginia City, the Comstock attracted an international array of immigrants. "All the peoples of the earth had representative adventures in the Silverland," he wrote. Irish, Chinese, Germans, English, Scots, Welsh, Canadians, Mexicans, Italians, Scandinavians, French, Swiss, Chileans, and other South and Central Americans came to share in the bonanza. With them came a sprinkling of Russians, Poles, Greeks, Japanese, Spaniards, Hungarians, Portuguese, Turks, Pacific Islanders, Moroccans, and Caribbeans, as well as other North Americans, African Americans, and American Indians. This polyglot population, typical of mining boomtowns, made Virginia City more cosmopolitan than New York or Boston. In the part of Utah Territory that would later become Nevada, as many as 30 percent of the people came from other countries, compared to 25 percent in New York and 21 percent in Massachusetts.

Irish immigrants formed the largest ethnic group in the mining district. In Virginia City, fully one-third of the population claimed at least one parent from Ireland. Irish and Irish American women constituted the largest group of women on the Comstock. Irish servants, boardinghouse owners, and washerwomen made up a significant part of the workforce. In contrast, the Chinese community, composed of 642 men in 1870, remained overwhelmingly male. Virulent anti-Chinese sentiment barred the men from work in the mines, but despite the violent anti-Asian rhetoric, the mining community came to depend on Chinese labor. Even the most prejudiced observed that the Chinese worked hard and did not gossip, making them ideal servants. Many boardinghouses and affluent homes employed a Chinese cook or servant along with the Irish parlor maid.

As was so often the case in the West, where white American ambitions clashed with Native American ways, the discovery of precious metals on the Comstock spelled disaster for the Native American population. No sooner had the miners struck pay dirt than they demanded army troops be dispatched to "hunt Indians" and establish forts to protect transportation to and from the diggings. This sudden and dramatic intrusion left Nevada's native tribes—Northern Paiute and Bannock Shoshone—exiles in their own land even as it was rapidly being despoiled. Comstock miners cut down acres of piñon groves for shelter and firewood—trees that produced the pine nuts local tribes relied on for survival in the winter. Mining communities also ruined the habitat for game and overhunted the remaining animals. Soon the Indians faced starvation. At first they resisted, but eventually they

> The "Big Bonanza" in 1873 speeded the transition from small-scale industry to corporate oligopoly, creating a radically new social and economic environment.

made peace with the invaders. Over time, Native Americans proved resourceful in finding ways to adapt and preserve their culture and identity despite the havoc wrought by western mining and settlement.

In 1873, Comstock miners uncovered a new vein of ore, a veritable cavern of gold and silver. This "Big Bonanza" speeded the transition from small-scale industry to corporate **oligopoly**, creating a radically new social and economic environment. The Comstock became a laboratory for new mining technology, a place of industry and engineers. Huge stamping mills pulverized rock with pistonlike hammers driven by steam engines. Enormous engines, known as Cornish pumps, sucked water from the mine shafts. Huge ventilators circulated air in the underground chambers. Many of the mines were large, industrial operations. The Gould and Curry Mine covered sixty acres, running forty stamping mills and employing sixty workers. No backwoods mining camp, Virginia City was an industrial center, with more than 1,200 stamping mills working on average a ton of ore every day. Almost 400 men worked in milling, nearly 300 in manufacturing industries, and roughly 3,000 laborers worked in the mines. Most of the miners who came to the Comstock ended up as laborers for the big companies. Although they sometimes worked their own small "rat hole" mines on their time off, still hoping to strike it rich, they generally subsisted on wages.

The miner's job was filled with peril. Descending deep into the earth, down 1,500 to 3,000 feet where temperatures rose to 120 degrees, stripped-down miners on the Comstock Lode worked only a few minutes at a time before retreating to "cooling off rooms" where the company provided barrels of ice water to bring down body temperature. Death stalked the mines and came in many forms—fires, floods, cave-ins, bad air, falling timbers, and misfired explosives.

Ross Moudy worked as a miner in Cripple Creek, Colorado, where gold was discovered in 1890. (See "American Places," page 642.) According to Moudy, "dangers do not seem so great to a practiced miner, who is used to climbing hundreds of feet on . . . braces put about six feet apart . . . and then walking the same distance on a couple of poles sometimes not larger than fence rails, where a misstep would mean a long drop." When a group of stockholders came to tour the mine, Moudy recounted how one man, terrified after a near fall, told the miner beside

"Mining on the Comstock"

This illustration, made at Gold Hill, Nevada, in 1876, shows a sectional view of a mine, including the tunnels, incline, cooling room, blower, and air shaft, along with a collection of miner's tools. Mines like the one pictured here honeycombed the hills of Gold City and neighboring Virginia City on the Comstock Lode in Nevada.

University of California at Berkeley, Bancroft Library.

him that "instead of being paid $3 per day they ought to have all the gold they could take out."

New technology eliminated some dangers but often created new ones. Machinery could maim and kill. In the hard-rock mines of the West in the 1870s, accidents annually disabled one out of every thirty miners and killed one in eighty. Moudy's biggest worry was carbon dioxide, which often filled the tunnels because of poor ventilation. "Many times," he confessed, "I have been carried out unconscious and not able to work for two or three days after." Those who avoided accidents still breathed air so dangerous that respiratory diseases eventually disabled them. After a year on the job, Moudy joined a labor union "because I saw it would help me to keep in work and for protection in case of accident or sickness." The union provided good sick benefits and hired nurses, "so if one is alone and sick he is sure to be taken care of." Indeed, labor

unions, by providing funds for injured workers and the widows of miners, relieved the mining companies of these responsibilities. In Nevada, because of the difficulty of obtaining skilled labor, the richness of the ore, and the need for a stable workforce, labor unions formed early and held considerable bargaining power. Comstock miners commanded $4 a day, the highest wage in the mining West.

The mining towns of the "Wild West" are often portrayed as lawless outposts, filled with saloons and rough gambling dens and populated almost exclusively by men, except for the occasional dance-hall floozy. The truth is more complex. Virginia City provides a clear example of an urban, industrialized western community. Sprawling uphill, clinging to the steep slope that followed the ore body, serenaded day and night by the crash of the stamping mill and hiss and boom of the steam engines, the "Queen of the

AMERICAN PLACES

Cripple Creek, Colorado

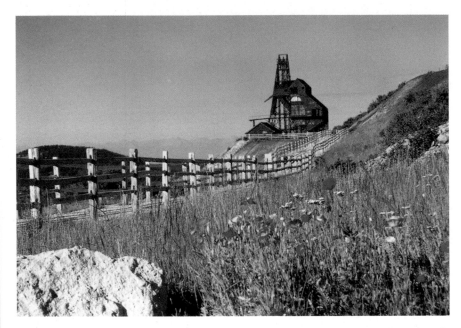

Cripple Creek, Colorado
Zstudios, Victor, CO.

In October 1890, after twelve years of searching, a hard-drinking ranchhand named Bob Womack struck gold while prospecting near Cripple Creek in Colorado. Too poor to develop his claim, he sold it for $500 and soon a gold rush was on. In a decade the town of Cripple Creek grew from a scraggly village of nomadic cowboys to a mining boomtown with over 35,000 inhabitants and 25,000 more living in outlying areas. Styling itself the "World's Greatest Gold Camp," Cripple Creek produced more than $65 million in gold during its first decade.

By 1900 the city's main drag, Bennett Avenue, boasted four department stores, two dance schools, and a business college. Myers Avenue, legendary for its astonishing variety of gambling dens, saloons, and dance halls, meandered eastward toward Poverty Gulch, named by the despairing Womack before his big strike. The National Hotel rose five stories high and had 150 guest rooms. Dozens of restaurants offered a good dinner for thirty-five cents. The city's sixteen churches preached morality, but five times that number of saloons made Cripple Creek a wide-open town. Fire destroyed the downtown in 1896, but it was quickly rebuilt. Among the new buildings stood an Opera House that seated over 800 people. Although Cripple Creek boasted such refined amenities, it remained a workingman's town. Most of the wealthy mine owners lived in nearby Colorado Springs.

The Western Federation of Miners (WFM) formed in 1893 and immediately organized the Cripple Creek miners. After winning a strike in 1894, the WFM dominated the mines, ensuring workers a minimum wage of $3 for an eight-hour day. A decade of working-class power ended in 1904, when military occupation of Cripple Creek broke the back of the union.

Today, visitors can explore Cripple Creek's past by strolling through the Historic District, visiting the Cripple Creek District Museum, and touring the Mollie Kathleen Mine, named for the first woman to file a gold claim in her own name. The Old Homestead Museum preserves a prominent 1890s brothel, and the Gold Camp Trail leads past a mix of contemporary mining sites and those from the first gold rush, giving visitors a good sense of the community, which continues to thrive.

FOR WEB LINKS RELATED TO THIS SITE AND OTHER AMERICAN PLACES, see "PlaceLinks" at bedfordstmartins.com/roark.

Comstock" was no fickle boomtown. When fire destroyed the downtown in 1875, the city rose like a phoenix from the ashes, more stately than before as brick and stone buildings replaced the burned-out wooden structures. An established community built to serve an industrial giant, Virginia City in its first decade boasted churches, schools, theaters, an opera house, and hundreds of families. By 1870 women composed 30 percent of the population, and 75 percent of the women listed their occupation in the census as housekeepers. Women in Virginia City also found opportunities to earn money. Because of the disproportionate number of men to women, many housekeepers made money on the side providing domestic services such as lodging, cooking, sewing, and laundry for the miners. Mary McNair Mathews, a widow from Buffalo, New York, who lived on the Comstock in the 1870s, worked as a teacher, nurse, seamstress, laundress, and lodging-house operator and later published a book on her adventures.

By 1875 Virginia City boasted a population of 25,000 people, making it one of the largest cities between St. Louis and San Francisco. A "must see" stop on the way West, the Queen of the Comstock hosted Presidents Ulysses S. Grant and Rutherford B. Hayes as well as legions of lesser dignitaries. No rough outpost of the Wild West, Virginia City represented in the words of its most recent chronicler, Ronald M. James, "the distilled essence of America's newly established course—urban, industrial, acquisitive, and materialistic, on the move, 'a living polyglot' of cultures that collided and converged." In short, Virginia City was an integral part of an America transformed in the Gilded Age.

Territorial Government

The federal government practiced a policy of benign neglect when it came to territorial government in the West. Washington did little more than provide a governor, a secretary, and two to four judges appointed by the president, along with an attorney and a marshal. In Nevada Territory that meant that a handful of officials governed an area the size of New England. Originally a part of the larger Utah Territory, Nevada moved on the fast track to statehood, entering the Union in 1864, long before its population or its development merited statehood. There as elsewhere in the West, gold and silver influenced politics, propelling Nevada to statehood.

More typical were the territories extant in 1870—New Mexico, Utah, Washington, Colorado, Dakota, Arizona, Idaho, Montana, and Wyoming. These areas remained territories for inordinate periods ranging from twenty-three to sixty-two years. While awaiting statehood, they were subject to territorial governments that were underpaid, often unqualified, and largely ignored in Washington. The vast majority of territorial appointments made by the president fell under the **spoils system**. Most of the loyal party men

who became governors and secretaries had no knowledge of the areas they served, little notion of their duties, and limited ability to perform them.

In theory, territorial governors received adequate salaries, as high as $3,500 in an era when the average working man earned less than $500 a year. In practice, the funds rarely arrived in a timely fashion, and more than one governor found he had to pay the expenses of government out of his own pocket. As one cynic observed, "Only the rich or those having 'no visible means of support,' can afford to accept office." John C. Frémont, the governor of Arizona Territory, was so poor that he complained to Washington that he could not afford to travel within the territory and inspect the Grand Canyon because he didn't have enough money to keep a horse.

> The vast majority of territorial appointments made by the president fell under the spoils system. Most of the loyal party men who became governors and secretaries had no knowledge of the areas they served.

Many territorial officials increased their incomes by private enterprise. Lew Wallace, for example, wrote the novel *Ben Hur* in his spare time while serving as governor of New Mexico. Territorial governors with fewer scruples accepted money from special-interest groups like mine owners or ranchers. The situation was even worse for judges. In private practice, the best legal talent commanded many times the territorial salary, so men who accepted territorial judicial appointments immediately came under suspicion. "The men who have been appointed as our judges," wrote one observer in 1876, "have only too often either been broken-down politicians or men without capacity or integrity." Nearly all territorial appointees tried to make ends meet by maintaining business connections with the East or by taking advantage of investment opportunities in the West. Special interests whether in mining, lumber, or cattle found they could easily control the new territorial appointees once they arrived in the West.

Conflict of interest and financial scandal in the territories rarely came to the attention of either the White House or the Department of the Interior, which oversaw the territories after 1873. Distance and the lack of funds to pay for travel made it difficult if not impossible to summon officers to Washington to answer to charges of corruption or incompetence. And Washington officials who went west to look into charges of malfeasance felt intimidated by gun-packing westerners. In 1871, a judge dispatched to New Mexico to investigate corruption, according to one account, "stayed three days, made up his mind that it would be dangerous to do any investigating, became demoralized, and returned to his home without any action."

Underfunded and overlooked, a victim of the spoils system and a prey to local interests, territorial government was rife with conflicts of interest and corruption. In short, territorial government in the West mirrored the political and economic values (or lack thereof) of the rest of Gilded Age America even as increasing numbers of settlers flocked to the region.

> Two factors stimulated the land rush in the trans-Mississippi West: the Homestead Act of 1862 and the transcontinental railroads.

Land Fever

After the Civil War, Americans by the hundreds of thousands packed up and moved west, goaded not by the hope of striking gold but by the promise of owning their own land. In the three decades following 1870, this westward stream swelled into a torrent, spilling across the prairies, moving on to the Pacific coast, and eventually flooding back onto the Great Plains.

Admission of States in the Trans-Mississippi West

Year	State	Year	State
1812	Louisiana	1876	Colorado
1821	Missouri	1889	North Dakota
1836	Arkansas	1889	South Dakota
1845	Texas	1889	Montana
1846	Iowa	1889	Washington
1850	California	1890	Idaho
1858	Minnesota	1890	Wyoming
1859	Oregon	1896	Utah
1861	Kansas	1907	Oklahoma
1864	Nevada	1912	New Mexico
1867	Nebraska	1912	Arizona

During this brief span of time, more land was settled than in all the previous history of the country. Between 1876 and 1900, eight new states entered the Union—Colorado, Montana, North and South Dakota, Washington, Idaho, Wyoming, and Utah—leaving only three territories—Oklahoma, New Mexico, and Arizona—in the continental United States. The agrarian West shared with the mining West a persistent American restlessness, an equally pervasive addiction to speculation, and a penchant for exploiting virgin natural resources and labor.

Two factors stimulated the land rush in the trans-Mississippi West. The Homestead Act of 1862 promised 160 acres free to any citizen or prospective citizen, male or female, who settled on the land for five years. And transcontinental railroads opened up new areas and actively recruited settlers. To New England farmers working rocky fields, immigrants pursuing the dream of owning their own land, city workers tired of mean streets and grim tenements, and Southerners on the played-out soil of old plantations, the West often proved irresistible. In the 1870s, the promise of land lured hundreds of thousands west across the plains in covered wagons, a hard journey that took many months and cost many lives. With the completion of a transcontinental railroad system in the 1880s, settlers could choose from four competing rail lines and make the trip in less than a week.

Although the country was rich in land and resources, not all who wanted to own land were able to do so. A growing number of Americans found themselves forced to work for wages on land they would never own. During the transition from the family farm to large commercial farming, small farms gave way to vast spreads worked by migrant labor or paid farmworkers. Just as industry corporatized and consolidated in the East, the period from 1870 to 1900 witnessed the emergence of an industrial West.

Moving West: Homesteaders and Speculators

A Missouri homesteader remembered packing as her family pulled up stakes and headed west to Oklahoma in 1890. "We were going to God's Country," she wrote. "You had to work hard on that rocky country in Missouri. I was glad to be leaving it. We were going to God's Country. . . . We were going to a new land and get rich."

People who ventured west searching for "God's country" faced hardship, loneliness, and deprivation. To carve a farm from the raw prairie of Iowa, the plains of Nebraska, or the forests of the Pacific Northwest took more than fortitude and backbreaking toil. It took luck. Homesteaders, as much as miners, gambled on the future. (See "Documenting the American Promise," page 646.) Blizzards, tornadoes, grasshoppers, hailstorms, drought, prairie fires, accidental death, and disease were only a few of the catastrophes that could befall even the best farmer. Homesteaders on free land needed as much as $1,000 for a house, a team of farm animals, a well, fencing, and seed. Poor farmers called "sodbusters" did without even these basics, living in dugouts carved into the sod of hillsides and using muscle instead of machinery.

"Father made a dugout and covered it with willows and grass," one Kansas girl recounted. When it rained, the dugout flooded and "we carried the water out in buckets, then waded around in the mud until it dried." Rain wasn't the only problem. "Sometimes the bull snakes would get in the roof and now and then one would lose his hold and fall down on the bed, then off on the floor. Mother would grab the hoe . . . and after the fight was over Mr. Bull Snake was dragged outside." The sod house, a step up from the dugout, had walls cut from blocks of sod and roofs of sod, lumber, or tin. In the Dakotas homesteaders often erected claim shacks, some as small as eight feet by ten. The government did not stipulate a specific size or manner of construction. It simply required homesteaders to establish a "permanent residence."

For women on the frontier, obtaining simple daily necessities such as water and fuel meant backbreaking labor. Out on the plains, where water was scarce, women often had to trudge to the nearest creek or spring. "A yoke was made to

Railroad Locomotive
In the years following the Civil War, the locomotive replaced the covered wagon, enabling settlers to travel from Chicago or St. Louis to the West Coast in two days. By the 1890s, more than 72,000 miles of track stretched west of the Mississippi River. The first transcontinental railroad, completed in 1869, soon led to the creation of competing systems so that by the 1880s travelers going into the West could choose from four competing lines. In this photograph, men and women perched on a locomotive celebrate the completion of a section of track. Library of Congress.

Our Home
A mother and her children pose in front of their dugout near McCook, Nebraska, in the 1890s. With its real roof, glass windowpanes, and solid door, their dugout was more substantial than most. On the plains, where trees were scarce and lumber was often prohibitively expensive, settlers built with materials at hand. The dugout was the most primitive dwelling, carved into a hillside. The sod hut, made from blocks of sod cut from the earth, provides another example of how homesteaders adapted to their new environment by using native materials to build homes.
Nebraska State Historical Society.

Young Women Homesteaders and the Promise of the West

"*Young men! Poor men! Widows! Resolve to have a home of your own!*" urged New York editor Horace Greeley. "*If you are able to buy and pay for one in the East, very well; if not, make one in the broad and fertile West!*" In his exhortation to go west, Greeley did not speak to men alone. Many women, and not just widows, heeded the call. The Homestead Act of 1862 allowed unmarried women and female heads of households to claim free land. Many did. The number of women establishing homesteads in the West ranged from 5 percent of homesteaders in the early settlements to over 20 percent after 1900.

Among the women homesteaders were Clara and Mary Troska and their two cousins, Helen and Christine Sonnek, who headed to North Dakota. "*Mary, Helen, Cristine and I packed our suitcases,*" Clara wrote. "*I took my mandolin, Christine took hers and her rifle. . . . We were on our way to Minot.*" Young women like Clara between the ages of twenty-one and twenty-five constituted the largest percentage of women (53 percent) taking up claims in the Dakotas. Like Christine Sonnek, who took her mandolin along with her rifle, homesteading women prepared to enjoy their new environment despite its challenges. Their letters, diaries, and reminiscences reveal not only the hardships they faced but also the sense of promise that lured them west.

Adventurous, resourceful, and exuberant, many of these young homesteading women of the West seemed to relish their experience.

DOCUMENT 1
The Varied Activities of a Woman Homesteader

Dakota homesteader Bess Cobb's letter to a friend reveals the optimism and high spirits that energized the young women who filed homesteading claims.

Suppose you girls are saying "poor Bess" and feeling dreadfully sorry for me out here in the wild and wooly uncivilized regions of America. But really time just seems to fly. I haven't done half I had planned and I am afraid winter will be here before we are ready for it. I've sewed some, done a little fancywork and lots of darning and mending but most of my time has been spent out of doors digging in the garden and riding. . . . You can see a team miles away—up one valley we can see ten miles, up to the Cannon Ball river—so when any one starts to our shack, if we see them in time we can comb our hair, change our gowns and get a good meal in running order before they arrive. You see Dakota has some redeeming qualities. Wish you could come out, but I suppose you think I am too far away. I have the neatest little shack I've ever seen and "my crops" are tip top. I know you would enjoy our camp life for a short time.

SOURCE: "Excerpts from a letter written by Bess Cobb, Guide to Manuscripts 1364, State Historical Society, North Dakota Heritage Center, Bismarck," in H. Elaine Lindgren, *Land in Her Own Name: Women as Homesteaders in North Dakota* (Norman: University of Oklahoma Press, 1996), 140–41.

DOCUMENT 2
A Hard Winter

Lucy Goldthorpe, a young schoolteacher, came from Iowa to Dakota in 1905. Here she describes to a reporter her survival during the winter and contrasts her childhood fantasies with homestead reality.

There were many long, cold days and nights in my little homestead shack that winter! The walls were only single board thickness, covered with tar paper on the outside. I'd spent money sparingly, because I didn't have much, but I had worked hard all during summer and fall in an effort to winterize the structure. Following the pattern used by many of the settlers, I covered the interior walls with a blue building paper. Everything was covered, including the ceiling, and the floor. To help seal out the cold I'd added layers of gunny sacks over the paper on the floor and then the homemade wool rugs I'd shipped from home.

Regardless of what I did the cold crept in through the thin walls. With no storm entry at the door and only single windows my little two-lid laundry stove with oven attached to the pipe had a real struggle to keep the place livable. . . .

A neighbor family returning to their claim "from the outside" brought me fresh vegetables. They were such a prized addition to my meals that I put the bag in bed with me at night to keep them from freezing. Night after night I stored food and my little alarm clock in the stove pipe oven; that was the only way I could keep the clock running and be sure of a non-frozen breakfast.

Each day brought new, unexpected challenges and at times I wondered if I would be able to stay with it until the land was mine. Could any land be worth the lonely hours and hardships? The howling wind and driving snow, the mournful wail of coyotes searching the tormented land for food did nothing to make the winter any more pleasant. . . .

As a child I had enjoyed hearing my father tell of the hardships of the early days. They seemed so exciting to me as I listened in the warmth and security of our well built, fully winterized Iowa home. Like most youngsters I'd wished for the thrill of those other days. Little did I think that an opportunity for just that would come through homesteading alone, far out in the windswept, unsettled land. Believe me, it wasn't nearly as glamorous as the imagination would have it!

SOURCE: Roberta M. Starry, "Petticoat Pioneer," *The West* 7, no. 5 (October 1967), 48.

DOCUMENT 3
Socializing and Entertainment

Homesteading wasn't all hard times. Young, single homesteaders found time for fun. Here Effie Vivian Smith describes a "shack party" during the winter of 1906 on her Dakota claim.

I never enjoyed myself better in my life than I have this winter. We go some place or some one is here from 1 to 4 times a week. A week ago last Fri. a load of 7 drove out to my claim. Cliff, Clara, David, and I had gone out the Wed. before and such a time as we had. My shack is 10×16 and I have only 2 chairs and a long bench for seats, a table large enough for 6, a single bed, and only 3 knives so 2 of them ate with paring knives & 1 with the butcher knife. We had two of them sit on the bed and moved the table up to them. . . . We played all the games we could think of both quiet and noisy and once all but Clara went out & snowballed. They brought a bu[shel] of apples, & a lot of nuts, candy, & gum & we ate all night. . . .

We have just started a literary society in our neighborhood. I had our first debate last Fri. The question was Resolved that city life is better than country life. All the judges decided in the negative. . . . Tomorrow our crowd is going to a literary 6 or 7 miles from here, and the next night to a dance at the home of one of our bachelor boys. We always all go in our sleigh. I am learning to dance this winter but don't attend any except the ones we get up ourselves and they are just as nice & just as respectable as the parties we used to have at Ruthven [Iowa]. I just love to dance. . . .

SOURCE: "Letter to her cousin, written on January 9, 1906," in H. Elaine Lindgren, *Land in Her Own Name: Women as Homesteaders in North Dakota* (Norman: University of Oklahoma Press, 1996), 177–78.

DOCUMENT 4
Homesteading Pays Off

Homesteading proved rewarding for many women, not only economically but also because of the sense of accomplishment they experienced. Here Theona Carkin tells how the sale of her Dakota homestead helped finance her university degree.

Life in general was dotted with hardships but there were many good times also. I have always felt that my efforts on my homestead were very worthwhile and very rewarding, and I have always been proud of myself for doing it all.

By teaching off and on . . . and upon selling the homestead, I was able to pay all my own college expenses.

SOURCE: "99-year-old U graduate recalls early childhood," *Alumni Review*, University of North Dakota, Grand Forks (June 1985), 5.

QUESTIONS FOR ANALYSIS AND DEBATE

1. What sorts of hardships do the young women homesteaders encounter in the Dakotas?

2. How does their youth affect how these women react to hardship?

3. What do the young women find particularly appealing about their new experiences as homesteaders?

4. What do they wish to convey about their experiences?

5. How did homesteading benefit women who chose not to remain on the land?

place across [Mother's] shoulders, so as to carry at each end a bucket of water," one daughter recollected, "and then water was brought a half mile from spring to house." Gathering fuel was another heavy chore. Without ready sources of coal or firewood, settlers on the prairies and plains turned to what substitutes they could scavenge. Anything that would burn—twigs, tufts of grass, old corncobs, sunflower stalks—was used for fuel. By far the most prevalent fuel used for cooking and heating was "chips"—chunks of dried cattle and buffalo dung found in abundance on the plains and grasslands.

Despite the hardships, many homesteaders and settlers succeeded in building comfortable lives. The sod hut made way for a more substantial house; the log cabin yielded to a white clapboard home with a porch and a rocking chair. And the type and quality of the family diet improved. "Our living at first was very scanty," recalled one Kansas woman, "mostly corn coarsely ground and made into hominy." Then the family raised a crop of wheat and ground it into flour. "We would invite the neighbors proudly telling them we have 'flour doings.'" When the farm wife began to raise chickens, the family added "chicken fixings" to its diet, "and when we could have 'flour doings' and 'chicken fixings' at the same meal we felt we were on the road to prosperity."

For others the promise of the West failed to materialize. Already by the 1870s, much of the best land had been taken, given to the railroads as **land grants** or to the states to finance education. Too often, homesteaders found that only the least desirable tracts were left—poor land, far from markets, transportation, and society. Speculators took the lion's share of the land. "There is plenty of land for sale in California," one migrant complained in 1870, but "the majority of the available lands are held by speculators, at prices far beyond the reach of a poor man."

> Many farmers who went west to homestead on government land ended up buying land from the railroads or from speculators.

The railroads were the biggest winners in the scramble for western land. To encourage railroad building after the Civil War, the federal government and the states gave public lands to the railroads. Together the land grants totaled approximately 180 million acres—an area almost one-tenth the size of the United States (Map 18.2). Many farmers who went west to homestead on government land ended up buying land from the railroads or from the speculators and land companies that quickly followed the railroads into the West. Of the 2.5 million farms established between 1860 and 1900, homesteading accounted for only one in five; the vast majority of farmland sold for a profit.

As land for homesteading grew scarce on the prairie in the 1870s, farmers began to push farther west, moving into western Kansas, Nebraska, and eastern Colorado—the region called the Great American Desert by settlers who had passed over it on their way to California and Oregon. Many agricultural experts warned that the semiarid land (where less than twenty inches of rain fell annually) would not support a farm on the 160 acres allotted to homesteaders, but their words of caution were drowned out by the extravagant claims of western promoters, many employed by the railroads to sell off their land grants. "Rain follows the plow" became the slogan of western boosters, who insisted that cultivation would alter the climate of the region and bring more rainfall.

It would have been more accurate to say that drought followed the plow. Droughts at roughly twenty-year intervals were a fact of life on the Great Plains. Plowed up, the dry topsoil blew away in the wind. A period of relatively good rainfall in the early 1880s encouraged farming; then a protracted drought in the late 1880s and early 1890s sent starving farmers reeling back from the plains. Hundreds of thousands retreated from western Kansas and Nebraska, some in wagons carrying the slogan "In God we trusted, in Kansas we busted." A popular ballad bitterly summed up the plight of the worst off, those too poor to leave:

> But here I am stuck and here I must stay
> My money's all gone and I can't get away;
> There's nothing will make a man hard and profane
> Like starving to death on a government claim.

The fever for fertile land set off a series of spectacular land runs in Oklahoma. When the

Map

(Map showing area from Dakota Territory south to Texas)

0   150   300 miles
0   150   300 kilometers

DAKOTA TERRITORY
MINN.
WIS.
NEBRASKA TERRITORY
IOWA
KANSAS
MO.
INDIAN TERRITORY
ARK.
TEXAS
LA.

Western extent of settlement before Homestead Act of 1862

Areas Settled before 1862

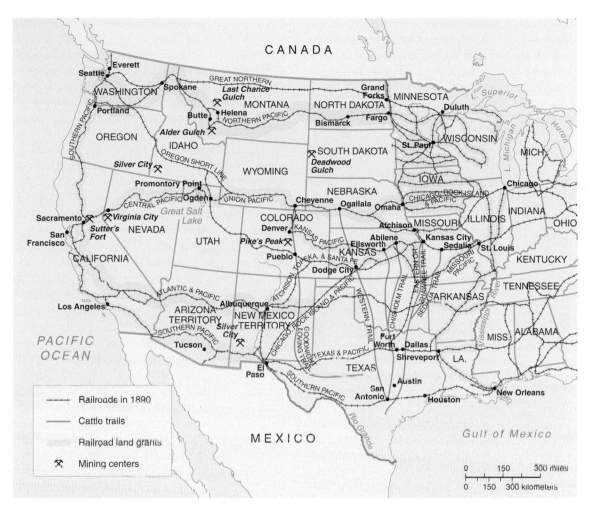

MAP 18.2   Federal Land Grants to Railroads and the Development of the West, 1850–1900
Generous federal land grants meant that railroads could sell the desirable land next to the track at a profit or hold it for speculation. Railroads received more than 180 million acres, an area as large as Texas. Notice how the cattle trails connect with major railroads in Dodge City, Abilene, and Kansas City and to mines in Montana, Nevada, Colorado, and New Mexico.

READING THE MAP: Which mining cities and towns were located directly on a railroad line? Which towns were located at the junction of more than one line or railroad branch? Which five railroads were granted the widest stretches of land on either side of the track?
CONNECTIONS: In what ways did the growth of the railroad affect the population of the West? What western goods and products did the railroads help bring east and to ports for shipping around the world during the Gilded Age?

FOR MORE HELP ANALYZING THIS MAP, see the map activity for this chapter in the Online Study Guide at bedfordstmartins.com/roark.

U.S. government took over two million acres of what had formerly been Indian Territory and opened it to settlement in 1889, thousands rushed to grab a piece. As the official opening of the land drew near, federal troops kept order while homesteaders massed on the border. On April 22 at noon, pistol shots signaled the opening and the would-be homesteaders took off. "Along the line as far as the eye could reach, with a shout and a yell the swift riders shot out, then followed the light buggies or wagons and last the lumbering prairie schooners and freighters' wagons," a reporter wrote. "Above all a great cloud of dust hover[ed] like smoke over a battlefield." In one day, thousands staked their claims, and by nightfall Oklahoma boasted two tent cities with more than 10,000 residents. Four years later in the last frenzied land rush, on

Oklahoma's Cherokee strip, several settlers were killed in the stampede, and nervous men guarded their claims with rifles. As public lands grew scarce, the hunger for land grew fiercer for both farmers and ranchers.

Ranchers and Cowboys

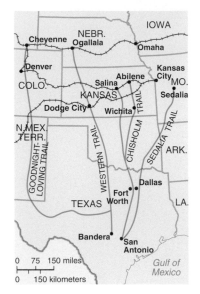

Cattle Trails, 1860–1890

Cattle ranchers followed the railroads onto the plains, establishing between 1865 and 1885 a cattle kingdom from Texas to Wyoming. Cowboys drove huge herds, as many as 3,000 head of cattle that grazed on public lands as they followed cattle tracks like the Chisholm Trail from Texas to railheads in Kansas. From there the cattle traveled by boxcar to Chicago, where they sold for as much as $45 a head. Over a million and a half Texas longhorns went to market in this way before the range began to close in the 1880s.

Cattle ranchers grazed their herds on free range until barbed wire made it possible for ranchers to fence in cattle. Barbed wire revolutionized the cattle business. In 1874 Joseph F. Glidden, an Illinois sheriff, invented and successfully patented barbed wire, although he had

to go to court to fight off a host of copycats. The real promoter of barbed wire, however, was gambler and promoter John "Bet a Million" Gates, who in 1879 set up a corral in the center of San Antonio to prove that the flimsy wire could contain Texas longhorns. Gates's demonstration paid off, and he made his fortune in barbed wire before he moved on to oil.

As the largest ranches in Texas began to fence, nasty fights broke out between the large ranchers and "fence cutters," who resented the end of the free range. One old-timer observed, "Those persons, Mexicans and Americans, without land but who had cattle were put out of business by fencing." Fencing eliminated those cattle and sheep ranchers who had grazed their herds on the open range, and it forced small-time ranchers who could not afford to buy barbed wire or sink wells to sell out for the best price they could get. The displaced ranchers, many of them Mexican, ended up as wageworkers on the huge spreads owned by Anglos or by European syndicates.

On the range, the cowboy gave way to the cattle king and, like the miner, became a wage laborer. Many cowboys were African Americans (as many as 5,000 in Texas alone), some of whom had gone west after the Civil War. Writers of western literature chose to ignore black cowboys like Deadwood Dick (Nat Love) who was portrayed as a white man in the dime novels of the era. Though the cowboy was more colorful than

Barbed Wire Machine and Soothing Liniment
The original working model of Joseph Glidden's barbing machine consisted of an old-fashioned coffee mill with its casing cut away and its grinder altered to cut and coil small lengths of wire. The barbs were strung by hand between strands of plain wire. Despite its flimsiness, barbed wire could contain cattle, as master promoter John "Bet a Million" Gates demonstrated by corralling a herd of Texas longhorns in downtown San Antonio in 1879. With the invention of barbed wire, medicine makers cashed in by marketing products like the liniment shown in the photograph to soothe the cuts and scrapes made on man and beast by the barbed wire.
Barbed wire machine: Ellwood House Museum, De Kalb, Illinois. Photo by Charles Philips; liniment: Kansas Barbed Wire Museum.

his eastern counterparts in the factory, his life was no easier. Like many other dissatisfied workers, cowboys organized labor unions in the 1880s and mounted strikes in both Texas and Wyoming.

By 1886, cattle overcrowded the range. Severe blizzards during the winters of 1886–87 and 1887–88 decimated the herds. "A whole generation of cowmen," wrote one chronicler, "went dead broke." Fencing worsened the situation. During blizzards, cattle stayed alive by keeping on the move. But when they ran up against the barbed wire fences, they froze to death. In the aftermath of the "Great Die Up," new forms of cattle ranching, more labor-intensive, replaced the Texas model of free-roaming longhorns.

Tenants, Sharecroppers, and Migrants

Many who followed the American promise into the West prospered, but landownership proved an elusive goal for many others—freed slaves, immigrants from Europe and Asia, and Mexicans in California and on the Texas border. In the post–Civil War period, as agriculture became a big business tied to national and global markets, an increasing number of laborers worked land that they would never own.

In the southern United States, farmers labored under particularly heavy burdens (see chapter 16). The Civil War wiped out much of the region's capital, which had been invested in slaves, and crippled the plantation economy. Newly freed slaves rarely managed to obtain land of their own. Instead, they soon found themselves reduced to propertyless farm laborers. "The colored folks stayed with the old boss man and farmed and worked on the plantations," a black Alabama sharecropper observed bitterly. "They were still slaves, but they were free slaves." Some freed people did manage to pull together enough resources to go west. In 1879, over 15,000 black "Exodusters" moved from Mississippi and Louisiana to take up land in Kansas. They were among the lucky few.

In California, Mexicans who held land grants from the Spanish or Mexican governments found themselves in the aftermath of the Mexican-American War in the new state of California (1850), which demanded that they prove their claims in court. The process took on average seventeen years, and many *rancheros* (Mexican ranchers), discouraged by the wait, sold out to Anglos. Skilled horsemen,

California's Mexican cowboys—*vaqueros*—commanded decent wages until the 1870s, when the coming of the railroads ended the long cattle drives in the state. The vaqueros lost their skilled status and became migrant laborers, often on land their families had once owned.

After the heyday of cattle ranching ended in the late 1880s, cotton production rose in the southeastern regions of Texas. Ranchers turned their pastures into sharecroppers' plots and hired displaced cowboys, most of them Mexican, as seasonal laborers for as little as seventy-five cents a day. Within the space of ten years, ranch life in southern Texas gave way to a growing army of agricultural wageworkers.

In California, a pattern of land **monopoly** and large-scale farming fostered tenancy and migratory labor. By the 1870s, less than 1 percent of the population owned half the state's available agricultural land. The rigid economics of large-scale commercial agriculture and the seasonal nature of the crops spawned a ragged army of migratory agricultural laborers. Derisively labeled "blanket men" or "bindle stiffs," these homeless and landless transients worked the fields in the growing season and wintered in the flophouses of San Francisco. Wheat farming in California in the 1870s and 1880s exhausted the land and was replaced, with the introduction of irrigation, by fruit and sugar beet farming. Most of the California farm laborers were Chinese immigrants until the Chinese Exclusion Act of 1882 forced big growers to look to other groups, primarily Mexicans, Filipinos, and Japanese, for farm labor.

> Many who followed the American promise into the West prospered, but landownership proved an elusive goal for many others—freed slaves, immigrants from Europe and Asia, and Mexicans.

Commercial Farming and Industrial Cowboys

In the late nineteenth century, America's population remained overwhelmingly rural. The 1870 census showed that nearly 80 percent of the nation's people lived on farms and in villages of fewer than 8,000 inhabitants. By 1900, the figure had dropped to 66 percent (Figure 18.1). But while the percentage of rural inhabitants fell, the number of farms rose. Rapid growth in the West increased the number of the nation's farms from 2 million in 1860 to over 5.7 million in 1900.

FIGURE 18.1 Changes in Rural and Urban Populations, 1870–1900

Between 1870 and 1900, not only did the number of urban dwellers increase but, even as the number of rural inhabitants fell, the number of farms increased. Mechanization made it possible to farm with fewer hands, fueling the exodus from farm to city throughout the second half of the nineteenth century.

Mechanical Corn Planter

The Farmers Friend Manufacturing Company of Dayton, Ohio, advertised its lever and treadle corn planter in this colorful advertisement in the early 1880s. Mechanical planters came into use in the 1860s. Although the 1880 planter featured attachments for grain drilling and fertilizing, it appears designed to be drawn by farm animals. Steam-powered farm implements would soon replace animal power. Notice how the idealized, bucolic farm life pictured in the advertisement gets a dose of reality in the illustration of the company's impressive factory in Dayton. Ohio Historical Society.

Despite the hardships that individual farmers experienced, farming itself thrived as new technology and farming techniques revolutionized American farm life. New plows and reapers halved the time and labor cost of production and made it possible to cultivate vast tracts of land. Industrialization and urbanization provided farmers with expanding markets for their produce, and railroads carried crops to markets thousands of miles away. The diversified family farm of the past began to give way to huge specialized commercial farms. Even before the opening of the twentieth century, American agriculture had entered the era of what would come to be called **agribusiness**—farming as a big business.

Business became the order of the day. Instead of extolling the virtues of the self-sufficient farmer, farm journals, agricultural societies, and educators pushed farmers to act more like businessmen, to specialize and consolidate. Together they helped to create a striking new image of what constituted successful farming. "Farming for business, not for a living—this is the motif of the New Farmer," announced one agricultural writer. The message was clear: The job of the up-to-date farmer was to produce money, not just crops.

As farming moved onto the prairies and plains, mechanization took command. Steel plows, reapers, mowers, harrows, seed drills, combines, and threshers replaced human muscle on the farm. Horse-drawn implements gave way to steam-powered machinery. By 1880, a new harvester could reap and shock twenty acres of wheat in a day, and a single combine could do the work of twenty men. Machines enabled farmers to vastly increase their acreage. Two men with one machine could cultivate 250 acres of wheat. Production soared. Mechanization spurred the growth of huge wheat farms, some

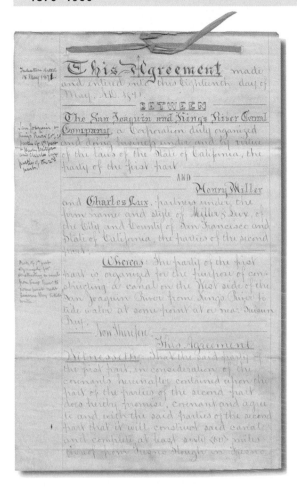

Miller & Lux Contract

This handwritten agreement dated May 18, 1871, provides for the construction of a canal in California's San Joaquin Valley. Reclamation projects such as canals and irrigation systems constituted one branch of business for the firm of Miller & Lux, which industrialized agriculture and eventually controlled 1.25 million acres of land in California, Nevada, and Oregon. Canals and irrigation ditches transformed the landscape, making vast tracts available for huge bonanza wheat farms.

University of California at Berkeley, Bancroft Library.

over 100,000 acres, in California and the Red River Valley of North Dakota and Minnesota. This agricultural revolution meant that Americans raised more than four times the corn, five times the hay, and seven times the wheat and oats they had before the Civil War. Much of this new production went to feed people as far away as England and Germany.

Like the cotton farmer in the South, western grain and livestock farmers increasingly depended on foreign markets for their livelihood. A fall in market prices meant that a farmer's entire harvest went to pay off debts. In the de-

pression that followed the panic of 1893, many heavily mortgaged farmers lost their land to creditors. As a Texas cotton farmer complained, "By the time the World Gets their Liveing out of the Farmer as we have to Feed the World, we the Farmer has nothing Left but a Bear Hard Liveing."

Commercial farming, along with mining, represented another way in which the West developed its own brand of Gilded Age industrialism. The far West's industrial economy sprang initially from California gold and the vast lands that came under American control following the Mexican-American War. In the ensuing rush on land and resources, environmental factors interacted with economic and social forces to produce enterprises as vast in scale and scope as anything found in the East. At the same time Carnegie consolidated the steel industry and Rockefeller monopolized oil refining, two Alsatian immigrants, Henry Miller and Charles Lux, pioneered the West's mix of agriculture and industrialism.

> Commercial farming represented another way in which the West developed its own brand of Gilded Age industrialism.

Beginning as meat wholesalers, Miller and Lux quickly expanded their business to encompass cattle, land, and land reclamation projects such as dams and irrigation systems. With a labor force of migrant workers, a highly coordinated corporate system, and large sums of investment capital, the firm of Miller & Lux became one of America's industrial behemoths. Already by 1870, Miller & Lux owned well over 300,000 acres of grazing land in California's central San Joaquin Valley, over half of it derived from former Mexican land grants. Its industrial-sized wheat operations in California bore little resemblance to any previous form of agriculture. Eventually these "industrial cowboys" grazed a herd of 100,000 cattle on 1.25 million acres of company land in three western states (California, Oregon, and Nevada) and employed over 1,200 migrant laborers on their corporate ranches. By 1900, Miller & Lux controlled capital and labor to a degree far surpassing most eastern manufacturing firms.

Miller & Lux developed remarkably dynamic investment strategies and corporate structures to control not only California land but water rights as well. The state's largest land speculators, Miller & Lux employed an army of lobbyists to serve its interests in Sacramento. Although the specific environmental components of the Miller

& Lux business may have differed from those in the nation's more celebrated industries east of the Mississippi, the company nonetheless shared the main characteristics of other modern enterprises: corporate consolidation, **vertical integration**, and schemes to minimize labor costs and stabilize the workforce. Miller & Lux accomplished the latter by offering free meals to migratory laborers, thus winning goodwill and discouraging property damage while recruiting an army of unemployed who competed for work and kept wages low. When the company's Chinese cooks rebelled at washing more dishes from the free meals, the migrant laborers were forced to eat after the ranch hands and use their dirty plates. By the 1890s, over 800 migrants followed what came to be known as the "Dirty Plate Route," on Miller & Lux ranches throughout California.

Since the days of Thomas Jefferson, farming had been linked with the highest ideals of a democratic society. Now agrarianism itself had been transformed. The farmer was no longer the self-sufficient **yeoman** but a businessman on the one hand or a wage laborer on the other, each tied to a global market. And even as farm production soared, industrialization outstripped it. More and more farmers left the fields for urban factories or found work in the "factories in the fields" of the new industrialized agribusiness. Now that the future seemed to lie not with the small farmer but with industrial enterprises, was **democracy** itself at risk? This question would ignite a farmers' revolt in the 1880s and dominate political debate in the 1890s.

A Clash of Cultures

In the movies, the American West is often portrayed in mythic terms as a picturesque landscape where strong-jawed heroes square off against villains. The good guys are always white, even their hats. Often the bad guys are Indians—the name that Columbus mistakenly gave to Native Americans. In this masculine tableau, the setting is so timeless it is easy to forget that the action takes place at roughly the same time that waves of new immigrants sailed past the Statue of Liberty, engineers built the Brooklyn Bridge, and men like John D. Rockefeller consolidated their empires in emerging industrial America. The mythical West seems to exist away from all of this, out of time. But once the West is situated within its historical context and seen as a particular place at a particular time, reality supersedes myth, and the West appears to be not so different from the rest of the country after all. The same racial antagonisms that marked the Gilded Age in the South and East flared up dramatically in the West and led to the exclusion of Chinese immigrants, the dispossession of Mexicans, and the decimation of Native Americans.

The Diverse Peoples of the West

"West" has always been a relative term. Until the gold rush of 1849 focused attention on California, the West for settlers lay beyond the Appalachians, east of the Mississippi in the lands drained by the Ohio River. But by 1870, "West" increasingly referred to the land across the Mississippi, from the Great Plains to the Pacific Ocean. The West of the late nineteenth century was a polyglot place, as much so as the big cities of the East. An illustrator on his way to the California gold fields deftly depicted the mix: "The stranger as he ascends the mountains towards the mining towns . . . notices the contrast in the scenes around him to anything he ever saw before. Indians are met in groups. . . . Strings of Chinamen pass, and greet you in broken English. . . . Next comes a Negro, with a polite 'good morning, sar' or Chileno, Mexican, or Kanaka [Hawaiian]."

The parade of peoples who came to the West included immigrants from Europe, Asia, and Canada, not to mention New Englanders, Mormons, African Americans, Mexicans, Latinos, and numerous Indian tribes removed by the government. The sheer number of peoples who came together and mingled in the West produced a complex blend of racism and prejudice. One historian has noted, not entirely facetiously, that there were at least eight oppressed "races" in the West—Indians, Latinos, Chinese, Japanese, blacks, Mormons, strikers, and radicals.

African Americans who ventured out to the territories faced hostile settlers determined to keep the West "for whites only." Often they formed all-black communities like Nicodemas, Kansas, a settlement founded by thirty black Kentuckians in 1877, which grew to a community

---

One historian has noted, not entirely facetiously, that there were at least eight oppressed "races" in the West—Indians, Latinos, Chinese, Japanese, blacks, Mormons, strikers, and radicals.

Buffalo Soldiers

Members of the African American Tenth Cavalry pause for lunch near St. Mary's, Montana, in 1894. In 1866 the army formed two cavalry regiments of African American soldiers under white officers to serve in the Indian wars. Called "buffalo soldiers" by Comanche and Cheyenne Indians, the soldiers adopted the title and wore it proudly. Over 25,000 African American soldiers fought in the West. In the face of discrimination, poor treatment, and harsh conditions, the Buffalo Soldiers served with distinction and had the lowest desertion rate in the army. Twenty members of the Ninth and Tenth Cavalry regiments received the coveted Congressional Medal of Honor.

Hayes Foundation Collection, Montana Historical Society.

of 700 by 1880. (See "American Places" in chapter 16.) Isolated and often separated by great distances, small black settlements grew up throughout the West, in Nevada, Utah, and the Pacific Northwest as well as in Kansas. Black westerners weren't only former slaves from the South. Some were soldiers who served in the West during the Indian wars that followed the Civil War. Called "buffalo soldiers" because Native Americans thought their hair resembled that of the buffalo, these black troops numbered up to 25,000. They fought the Apaches in Arizona Territory and helped subdue the Sioux in the Dakotas.

Hispanic peoples had lived in Texas and the Southwest since Juan de Oñate led pioneer settlers up the Rio Grande in 1598. Hispanics had occupied the Pacific coast since San Diego was founded in 1769. Overnight they were reduced to a "minority" after the United States annexed Texas in 1845 and took lands stretching to California after the Mexican-American War ended in 1848. At first, the Hispanic owners of large *ran-*

chos in California, New Mexico, and Texas, greeted conquest as an economic opportunity— new markets for their livestock and buyers for their lands. But racial prejudice soon ended their optimism. Californios (Mexican residents of California), who had been granted American citizenship by the Treaty of Guadalupe Hidalgo (1848), faced discrimination by Anglos who sought to keep them out of California's mines and commerce. Whites illegally squatted on *rancho* lands while protracted litigation over Spanish and Mexican land grants forced the *rancheros* into court. Although the U.S. Supreme Court eventually validated most of their claims, it took so long that many Californios sold their property to pay taxes and legal bills. The city of Oakland, California, sits on what was once a 19,000-acre ranch owned by the Peralta family, who lost the land to Anglos. Swindle, chicanery, and intimidation dispossessed scores of Californios. Many ended up segregated in urban barrios (neighborhoods) in their own homeland. Their percentage of California's population

Peralta Family

Don Antonio Peralta, grandson of Don Luis Peralta, whose vast landholdings once included most of Alameda County, California, is shown here in a 1870 photograph with his two sons, Nelson (left) and Vincente (right). The Peraltas and many other Californio families lost their land in protracted legal proceedings trying to prove the validity of their ancestors' Spanish land grants, which had gone unchallenged when Mexico ruled Alta California. The city of Oakland now sits on what was once the Peralta *rancho*.

The Oakland Tribune.

declined from 82 in 1850 to 19 percent by 1880 as Anglos pushed them aside. A similar fate befell Hispanic people in New Mexico and Texas. In these states, they remained a majority of the population but became increasingly impoverished as Anglos dominated business and commerce and took the best jobs.

Another among the West's oppressed groups was the Mormons. The followers of Joseph Smith, the founder and prophet of the Church of Jesus Christ of Latter-Day Saints, fled west to avoid religious persecution. They believed that they had a divine right to the land, and their messianic militancy contributed to making them outcasts. The Mormons' polygamy (men taking more than one wife) became a con-

venient point of attack for those who hated and feared the group. After Smith was killed by an Illinois mob in 1844, Brigham Young led the flock, which numbered more than 20,000, over the Rockies to the valley of the Great Salt Lake in Utah Territory. The Utah land that they settled was a desert, but the Mormons quickly set to work irrigating it. Lacking foreign or eastern capital to back them, they relied on cooperation and communalism, which not coincidentally worked to exclude competition from those outside the faith. The church established and controlled water supplies, stores, insurance companies, and later factories and mining smelters. By 1882, the Mormons had built a thriving city of more than 150,000 residents— Salt Lake City. Not until 1896, however, when the church renounced the traditional polygamy and gave women the right to vote, did Congress grant Utah statehood.

The Chinese suffered brutal treatment at the hands of employers and other laborers. In the 1850s California gold exerted a powerful pull as far away as China. By 1852 over 20,000 *gam san haak* (travelers to the gold mountain) joined the gold rush. Miners determined to keep "California for Americans" succeeded in passing prohibitive foreign license laws that for the most part kept the Chinese out of the mines. But Chinese immigration continued. In the 1860s when white workers rushed to find riches in the bonanza mines of Nevada, Chinese laborers filled the gap. Railroad magnate Charles Crocker hired Chinese gangs to work on the Central Pacific, reasoning that the race that built the Great Wall could lay tracks across the treacherous Sierras. Some 12,000 Chinese, representing 90 percent of Crocker's workforce, completed America's first transcontinental railroad in 1869.

By 1870, over 63,000 Chinese immigrants lived in America, 77 percent of them in California. A 1790 federal statute that limited naturalization to "white persons" was revised in 1870 during Reconstruction to extend naturalization to persons of African descent, but the Chinese continued to be denied access to citizenship. As perpetual aliens they constituted a reserve army of transnational industrial laborers that many saw as a threat to American labor. For the most part, the Chinese did not displace white workers but instead found work as railroad laborers, cooks, servants, and farmhands while white workers sought out more lucrative fields (including the gold and silver fields of the West) In the 1870s, when California and the rest of the nation weathered a major economic depression, the Chinese became easy scapegoats. California workingmen rioted and fought to keep the Chinese out of the state, claiming they were "coolie labor"—involuntary contract laborers recruited by business interests determined to keep wages at rock bottom.

In 1876 the Workingmen's Party formed to fight for Chinese exclusion. Racial and cultural animosities stood at the heart of anti-Chinese agitation. Denis Kearney, the fiery San Francisco leader of the movement, made clear this racist bent when he urged legislation to "expel every one of the moon-eyed lepers." Nor was California alone in its anti-Asian **nativism**. As the country confronted growing ethnic and racial diversity with the rising tide of immigration, many in the nation questioned the principle of racial equality at the same time they argued against the assimilation of "nonwhite" groups. In this climate a Chinese Exclusion Act gained passage in 1882, effectively barring further Chinese immigration. The Exclusion Act led to a sharp drop in the Chinese population—from 105,465 in 1880 to 89,863 by 1900, because the Chinese immigrants, overwhelmingly male, did not have families to sustain their population. Eventually Japanese immigrants replaced the Chinese, particularly in agriculture. The prohibition of naturalization did not affect Japanese immigrants, who included women as well as men. As "nonwhite" immigrants, the Japanese, like the Chinese, could not become naturalized citizens, but Japanese children born in the United States could claim the rights of citizenship. Japanese parents seeking to own land were able to purchase it in the names of their children, who as citizens could not be barred from owning property. Although anti-Asian prejudice remained strong in California and elsewhere in the West, Asian immigrants formed an important part of the economic fabric of the western United States.

The American West in the nineteenth century witnessed more than its share of conflict and bloodshed. Violent prejudice against the Chinese and other Asian immigrants remained common. But violence also broke out between cattle ranchers and sheep ranchers, between ranchers and farmers, between striking miners and their bosses, among rival Indian groups, and between whites and Indians. At issue was who would control the vast resources of the emerging region. Each group claimed the public domain as its own, and many were prepared to fight for it. In the ensuing struggle, the biggest losers were

Chinese Cook

This young Chinese cook and his helper prepare a meal in their woks for lumberjacks in a western lumber camp in the late 1880s. Barred from the mines, Chinese found work as cooks throughout the West. In the male enclave of a lumber or mining camp, a Chinese cook reinforced race and gender hierarchies. By giving Chinese men tasks such as cooking, laundry, and other domestic work, native white males feminized the Chinese, excluding them from men's work. Anti-Asian groups insisted that the Chinese drove down the pay of male workers, but the Chinese actually competed more directly with women, particularly in the laundry business, where in many places they replaced the Irish washerwoman. University of California at Berkeley, Bancroft Library.

those with the first and best claim to the land: the Native Americans, who had been living in the West before the arrival of European explorers, Spanish missionaries, or American settlers.

The Final Removal of the Indians

From the early days of the Republic, Americans had advocated a policy of Indian removal. In the 1830s, President Andrew Jackson pushed the Cherokee, Choctaw, Chickasaw, Creek, and Seminole tribes off their lands in the southern United States. Jackson's Indian removal forced thousands of men, women, and children to leave their homes in Georgia and Tennessee and walk hundreds of miles to lands across the Mississippi River. So many died of hunger, exhaustion, and disease along the way that the Cherokee called their path "the trail on which we cried." At the end of this trail of tears stood the Great Plains. Here, the government promised the Indians, they could remain "as long as grass shall grow."

But in the 1840s, Oregon land fever, the Mexican War, and the gold rush in California put an end to the promise. Settlers repeatedly trespassed onto Indian land and then were surprised when they encountered hostility. Indignantly, they demanded protection from the U.S. army. The result was thirty years of Indian wars that culminated in a final removal of the Indians.

The Indian wars on the plains lasted from 1861 until 1890. To Americans filled with theories of racial superiority, the Indian constituted, in the words of a Colorado militia major, "an obstacle to civilization." Testifying before a congressional commission in 1864, the major concluded that they "should be exterminated." The federal government, acting through the army, adopted a different policy, succinctly summed up by General William T. Sherman: "Remove all to a safe place and then reduce them to a helpless condition." The government herded the Indians onto reservations where the U.S. Bureau of Indian Affairs—a badly managed, weak agency, often acting through corrupt agents—supposedly ministered to their needs (Map 18.3).

> To Americans filled with theories of racial superiority, the Indian constituted, in the words of a Colorado militia major, "an obstacle to civilization."

Sevara, Ute Chieftain

Sevara, identified as a Ute chieftain, poses with three generations of his family in this photograph. Pictures like this one depict a way of life that by the end of the nineteenth century was already becoming extinct. Only in posed photographs carefully crafted for public consumption did the proud history of Native Americans seem able to survive.

From "Birth of a Century," KEA Publishing Services Ltd.

On the plains, the Sioux, Cheyenne, Arapaho, Nez Perce, Comanche, Kiowa, Ute, Apache, and Navajo nations put up a determined resistance. The Indian wars (which more accurately might be called settlers' wars since most frequently they began with "peaceful settlers," often miners, overrunning Native American lands) involved violence and atrocities on both sides. In 1864, Colonel John M. Chivington and his local Colorado militia slaughtered an entire village of Cheyenne, mostly women and children peacefully camped along the Sand Creek. An upright Methodist elder, Chivington watched as his men mutilated their hapless victims and later justified the killing of Indian children with the terse remark "Nits make lice." The city of Denver treated Chivington and his men as heroes, but after a congressional inquiry revealed the shocking details of the Sand Creek massacre, he was forced to resign his commission to avoid court martial.

The fever for gold fueled conflict with the Indians as whites encroached on Indian lands. In 1866, the Cheyenne united with the Sioux in Wyoming, where they fought to protect their lands from the building of the Bozeman Trail, connecting Fort Laramie with the gold fields in Montana. Captain William Fetterman, who had boasted that with eighty men he could ride through the Sioux Nation, died in an Indian attack along with all of his troops. The Sioux's impressive victories led to the Treaty of Fort Laramie in 1868, in which the United States agreed to abandon the Bozeman Trail and guaranteed Indians control of their sacred lands in the Black Hills. The government induced the Plains tribes to accept reservation lands, and the great chief Red Cloud led many of his people onto the new reservation. But several young Sioux chiefs, among them Crazy Horse of the Oglala band and Sitting Bull of the Hunkpapa, refused to go. Crazy Horse said that he wanted no part of the "piecemeal penning" of his people. The army launched a series of campaigns to round up tribes who refused to accept confinement. Fights between the U.S. military and the Indians persisted into the 1870s, as bands of Sioux continued to roam the plains, hunting buffalo.

Forces more powerful than the military eventually ended the traditional world of the Plains Indians. The coming of the transcontinental railroads and the eastern demand for buffalo hides led to the decimation of the great bison herds, spelling disaster for Native Americans. To

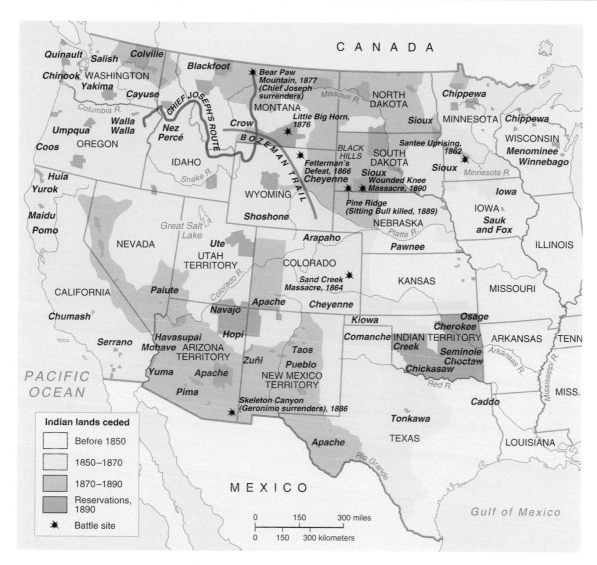

MAP 18.3 The Loss of Indian Lands, 1850–1890
By 1890, western Indians were isolated on small, scattered reservations. Native Americans had struggled to retain their land in major battles, from the Santee uprising in Minnesota in 1862 to the massacre at Wounded Knee, South Dakota, in 1890.

READING THE MAP: Where was the largest reservation located in 1890? Which states on this map show no reservations in 1890? Compare this map to Map 18.2, Federal Land Grants to Railroads and the Development of the West. Where do the contours of Indian lands ceded from 1850 to 1890 parallel the placement of the railroads?

CONNECTIONS: Why did the federal government force Native Americans onto reservations? What developments prompted these changes?

FOR MORE HELP ANALYZING THIS MAP, see the map activity for this chapter in the Online Study Guide at bedfordstmartins.com/roark.

the Sioux and the Kiowa, the buffalo (American bison) constituted a way of life—the source of food, fuel, and shelter and a central part of religion and ritual. To the railroads, the buffalo were a nuisance, at best a target for sport and a source of cheap meat for their workers. In 1870 buffalo hunters hired by the railroads began to decimate the great herds; sport hunters fired at random from railroad cars just for the thrill of it. Trade in buffalo hides, popular in the East, led to a heyday of buffalo hunting in the 1880s. Hunters sold as many as 50,000 hides at a time to tanneries in the East. In thirty years, more than sixty million animals were slaughtered. By 1895

Bison Slaughter, 1895

In this 1895 photograph a man stands atop a hill of buffalo (bison) skulls. After the buffalo had been slaughtered for their hides, the skulls shown here were shipped to Michigan to make fertilizer. By 1895, fewer than a thousand bison survived on a range that once supported over 50 million. Sport shooting and easterners' desire for buffalo robes fueled the slaughter at the same time that the introduction of cattle ranching meant the bison faced increasing competition for forage on the range.

Courtesy Burton Historical Collection, Detroit Public Library.

fewer than a thousand bison survived. The army took credit for subduing the Indians, but their victory came about more as a result of the decimation of the great bison herds. General Philip Sheridan acknowledged as much when he applauded the hunters for "destroying the Indians' commissary." With their food supply gone, Indians had to choose between starvation and the reservations.

In 1874, gold fever once again jeopardized the delicate peace established by the Treaty of Fort Laramie. The discovery of gold in the Black Hills of the Dakotas led the government to break its promise to Red Cloud to preserve the Black Hills as land sacred to the Indians. Miners began pouring into the area, and the Northern Pacific Railroad made plans to lay track. By 1875 over a thousand prospectors swarmed into Dakota territory. Lieutenant Colonel George Armstrong Custer, whose troopers first struck gold in the area, had fed the fever by trumpeting news of the gold strike. At first the government offered to purchase the Black Hills, but the Indians refused

to sell. The United States responded by ordering all Lakota Sioux and Northern Cheyenne bands onto the Pine Ridge Reservation. Under the leadership of Crazy Horse and Sitting Bull, the Sioux tribes massed to resist. In June 1876, Custer led 265 men of the Seventh Cavalry into the Indian camp. At the Little Bighorn River in Montana Territory, perhaps as many as 2,000 Sioux warriors set upon Custer and his troops. No federal soldier lived to tell the story, but Crazy Horse, Sitting Bull, and others recounted the killing of Pahuska, or "Long Hair," as the Indians called the dashing Custer.

Their victory, however, proved short-lived. Within six years, the Indians suffered a series of defeats. Crazy Horse was killed and Sitting Bull surrendered. The government took the Black Hills and confined the Lakota to the Great Sioux Reservation. Chief Joseph of the Nez Perce resisted removal and fled toward Canada. Federal troops caught up with his band just forty miles from freedom. With his people cold and starving, the chief surrendered. His speech stands as an eloquent statement of the plight of the Indians:

> I am tired of fighting. Our chiefs are killed. . . . It is cold and we have no blankets. The little children are freezing to death. My people, some of them, have run away to the hills, and have no blankets, no food; no one knows where they are—perhaps freezing to death. I want to have time to look for my children and see how many I can find. Maybe I shall find them among the dead. Hear me, my chiefs, I am tired; my heart is sick and sad. From where the sun now stands, I will fight no more forever.

The Sioux never accepted the loss of the Black Hills. In 1923 they filed suit, demanding compensation for lands illegally taken from them. After a protracted court battle, the U.S. Supreme Court ruled in 1980 that the government had illegally abrogated the Treaty of Fort Laramie, and upheld an award of $122.5 million in compensation to the tribes.

The Dawes Act and Indian Land Allotment

The practice of rounding up Indians and herding them onto reservations lost momentum in the 1880s in favor of allotment—a new policy designed to encourage assimilation through farming and the ownership of private property. Indian rights groups, often led by white Americans, mounted a campaign to dismantle the reservations, which in their judgment impeded full assimilation by preserving tribal culture. Believing they acted in the best interests of native peoples, Indian rights groups called for a policy that would grant Indians full citizenship and give them farms. In 1887 Congress passed the Dawes Allotment Act to abolish reservations and allot lands to individual Indians as private property. By eliminating reservations (and along with them Indian tribes), reformers hoped to push Indians toward individualism and self-sufficiency. Each Indian household received 160 acres of land from reservation property. To prevent the Indians from being fleeced by land speculators, the government held title to the land in trust for twenty-five years. Only those Indians who took allotments earned citizenship. Since Indian lands far surpassed the acreage needed for allotments, the government reserved the right to sell the "surplus" land. Well-meaning Americans viewed the Dawes Act as a positive initiative, but the act effectively reduced Indian lands from 138 million acres to a scant 48 million. The legislation, in the words of one critic, worked "to despoil the Indians of their lands and to make them vagabonds on the face of the earth." The opening of the "surplus" to white settlement set off the great land rushes in Oklahoma Territory. Although the Indian Reorganization Act of 1934 restored the right of Native Americans to own land communally (see chapter 24), the Dawes Act dealt a damaging blow to traditional tribal culture.

The Last Acts of Indian Resistance

Faced with the extinction of their entire way of life, different groups of Indians responded in different ways in the waning decades of the nineteenth century. Apaches in the Southwest resorted to outright violence, while the Ghost Dance, a form of nonviolent resistance, swept across the Plains in 1889–1890. Both triggered brutal military repression by the U.S. army.

The Apache tribes who roamed the Sonoran desert of southern Arizona and northern Mexico never combined as the Plains Indians had done so successfully at the Little Bighorn. Instead they operated in small raiding parties, perfecting a hit-and-run **guerrilla warfare** that terrorized white settlers and bedeviled the army in the 1870s and 1880s. General George Crook, a skilled Indian fighter, combined a policy of dogged pursuit with judicious diplomacy. Convinced that white troops could not fight the Apache on their home ground, Crook relied on Indian scouts, recruiting nearly two hundred, including some Apaches along with Navajos and Paiutes. Trained to a life of hunting, tracking, and raiding, the Indian scouts welcomed a release from the boredom of reservation life. By 1882 Crook succeeded in persuading most of the Apaches to settle on the San Carlos Reservation in Arizona Territory. A desolate piece of desert inhabited by scorpions and rattlesnakes, San Carlos, in the words of one Apache, was "the worst place in all the great territory stolen from the Apaches." There was no grass, no game, only withering heat, venomous snakes and insects, and terrible water. With bitter humor one Apache remarked that San Carlos "was considered a good place for the Apaches—a good place for them to die."

Reservation life proved particularly difficult for the nomadic Apaches. Geronimo, a respected shaman (medicine man) of the fierce Chiricahua Apaches, repeatedly led raiding parties in the 1880s. His Apache warriors attacked ranches to resupply ammunition and horses, killing the ranchers and burning their homesteads. Among Geronimo's band was Lozen, a woman who rode with the male warriors, armed with a rifle and a cartridge belt. The sister of a great chief who described her as "Strong as a man, braver than most, and cunning in strategy," Lozen never married and remained a warrior in Geronimo's band even after her brother's death. In the spring of 1885, Lozen, along with Geronimo, went on a ten-month offensive, moving from the Apache sanctuary in the Sierra Madre to raid and burn ranches and towns on both sides of the Mexican border. General Crook caught up with Geronimo in the fall and persuaded him to return to San Carlos, only to have him slip away with a small band on the way back to the reservation. Chagrined, Crook resigned his post. General Nelson Miles, Crook's replacement, determined to put an end to Geronimo once and for all by adopting a policy of hunt and destroy.

Only thirty-three Apaches remained at large, thirteen of them women, when Miles took command, but they managed to elude Miles's troops for more than five months. Throughout the blistering summer, the Indians, constantly on

> Well-meaning Americans viewed the Dawes Act as a positive initiative, but the act effectively reduced Indian lands from 138 million acres to a scant 48 million.

the move, kept one step ahead of the army. In the end, this small band of Apaches fought two thousand soldiers to a stalemate. Miles, who believed in the superiority of white troops, watched as his spit-and-polish cavalry, after months of tracking the elusive Apaches, became barely recognizable as soldiers. Lieutenant Leonard Wood, one of only two white soldiers who rode with the Indian scouts, discarded his horse and most of his clothes. Reduced to wearing nothing "but a pair of canton flannel drawers, and an old blue blouse, a pair of moccasins and a hat without a crown," Wood had trouble convincing one Indian party that he was actually a U.S. soldier.

Eventually, the scouts tracked down Geronimo and his band. Caught between Mexican regulars and the U.S. army, in 1886 Geronimo agreed to march north with the soldiers and negotiate a settlement. "We have not slept for six months," Geronimo admitted, "and we are worn out." He met with General Miles to negotiate a peace, but, as in the past, the Indians did not get what they were promised. Fewer than three dozen Apaches had been hostile when General Miles induced them to surrender, yet the government gathered up nearly five hundred Apaches and sent them as prisoners to Florida, including the scouts who had helped track Geronimo. By 1889, more than a quarter of them had died, some by illness contracted in the damp, lowland climate and some by suicide. Their plight roused public opinion and eventually, in 1892, they were moved to Fort Sill in Oklahoma and later to New Mexico.

Geronimo lived to become something of a celebrity. He appeared at the St. Louis Exposition in 1904, where he sold pictures of himself for twenty-five cents apiece, and he rode in President Theodore Roosevelt's inaugural parade in 1905. In a newspaper interview he confessed, "I want to go to my old home before I die. . . . Want to go back to the mountains again. I asked the Great White Father to allow me to go back, but he said no." None of the Apache were permitted to return to Arizona; when Geronimo died in 1909, he was buried in Oklahoma.

On the plains many different tribes turned to a nonviolent form of resistance—a compelling new religion, the Ghost Dance. The Paiute shaman Wovoka, drawing on a cult that had developed in the 1870s, combined elements of Christianity and traditional Indian religion to found the Ghost Dance religion in 1889. Wovoka claimed that he had received a vision in which the Great Spirit spoke through him to all Indians, urging them to unite and prophesying that whites would be destroyed in an apocalypse. The shaman promised that Indian warriors slain in battle would return to life and that buffalo once again would roam the land unimpeded. This religion of despair with its message of hope spread like wildfire over the plains. It was danced in Idaho, Montana, Utah, Wyoming, Colorado, Nebraska, Kansas, the Dakotas, and Oklahoma Territory by tribes as diverse as the Arapaho, Cheyenne, Pawnee, and Shoshone. Various tribes developed different forms of the dance, but all dances were held in a circle. Often dancers went into hypnotic trances. Some danced until they dropped from exhaustion.

Ghost Dances were generally nonviolent, but among the Sioux, especially the Oglala, Blackfeet, and Hunkpapa, the dance took on a more militant flavor. Sioux disciples of the Ghost Dance religion taught that wearing white ghost shirts made Indians immune to the bullets of the soldiers. Their message frightened whites, who began to fear an uprising. "Indians are dancing in the snow and are wild and crazy," wrote the Bureau of Indian Affairs agent at the Pine Ridge

Ghost Dance Dress

An Arapaho woman wore this deerskin dress during the Ghost Dance fervor of 1889–1890 in Oklahoma. Decorated with stars and eagles, it was intended to protect its wearer. Ghost dancers believed that the clothing they wore made them impervious to army bullets. The symbols and the decoration on the garments evoked powerful magic. The men wore white Ghost Dance shirts; women and children dressed in more colorful garments like the one pictured here.

Division of Political History, Smithsonian Institution, Washington, D.C.

Reservation in South Dakota. Frantic, he pleaded for reinforcements. "We are at the mercy of these dancers. We need protection, and we need it now." President Benjamin Harrison dispatched several thousand federal troops to Sioux country to handle any outbreak.

In December 1890 when Sitting Bull joined the Ghost dancers, he was arrested and later shot and killed by Indian police at the Pine Ridge Reservation. His people, fleeing the scene, were apprehended by the Seventh Cavalry, Custer's old regiment, near Wounded Knee Creek, South Dakota. As the Indians laid down their arms, a shot rang out and the army opened fire. In the ensuing melee, Indian men, women, and children were mowed down in minutes by the army's brutally efficient Hotchkiss machine guns. More than 200 Sioux lay dead or dying in the snow. Settler Jules Sandoz surveyed the scene the day after the massacre. "Here in ten minutes an entire community was as the buffalo that bleached on the plains," he wrote. "There was something loose in the world that hated joy and happiness as it hated brightness and color, reducing everything to drab agony and gray."

Although the massacre at Wounded Knee did not end the story of Native Americans, it ended a way of life. The Indian population would gradually recover; the 2000 census showed 2.4 million Native Americans, compared to a scant 250,000 in 1890. But their culture sustained a crushing blow. In the words of the visionary Black Elk, "The nation's hoop is broken and scattered. There is no center any longer, and the sacred tree is dead." Not until the 1960s did Indians mount a protest movement to fight for tribal lands and rights and to recover Native American identity and cultural pride (see chapter 28).

The West of the Imagination

Even as the Old West was dying, the myth of the "Wild West" was being born. The dime novel, a precursor to today's paperback, capitalized on gun-slinging cowboy heroes like Kit Carson, Wild Bill Hickok, Calamity Jane, and Deadwood Dick to entertain readers seeking escapist fare. Published in the East and sometimes written by tenderfeet who had never ventured beyond the Hudson River, dime novels sold at a prodigious rate.

The prince of the dime novel heroes was Buffalo Bill, featured in more than two hundred titles. Born William F. Cody, the real-life Buffalo Bill had panned for gold, ridden for the Pony Express, scouted for the army, and earned his nickname hunting buffalo for the railroad. A masterful showman, he capitalized on his success and formed a touring Wild West company in 1883. Part circus, part theater, the Wild West extravaganza featured exhibitions of riding, shooting, and roping and presented dramatic reenactments of great moments in western U.S. history. The star of the show, Annie Oakley (Phoebe Moses), dubbed "Little Miss Sure Shot," delighted the crowd by shooting a dime out of her husband's hand. The centerpiece of Buffalo Bill's Wild West show was a reenactment of Custer's Last Stand, in which Indians wearing war paint and feathered headdresses massacred the hapless Custer and his men. At the end, Buffalo Bill galloped in through a cloud of dust and dramatically mouthed the words "Too late!" The Wild West that Buffalo Bill presented indiscriminately mixed the authentic with the romantic until reality itself blurred in the popular mind. Cody had not been at the Little Bighorn, but some of the Indians in his troupe, like Sitting Bull, who toured with the show in 1885, had been there and knew their parts firsthand. As history the Wild West show was dubious, but as spectacle it was unbeatable.

> The Wild West that Buffalo Bill presented indiscriminately mixed the authentic with the romantic until reality itself blurred in the popular mind.

The rapid demise of the Wild West that Buffalo Bill enshrined in his show may perhaps best be comprehended if we juxtapose Cody with historian Frederick Jackson Turner. At the 1893 Columbian Exposition in Chicago, Turner addressed the American Historical Association on "The Significance of the Frontier in American History." The **frontier**, Turner posited, had shaped the character of Americans and the nation. Prompted by the U.S. Census Bureau's 1890 declaration that a clear frontier line no longer existed, Turner's message was elegiac. He feared that without a frontier, the United States might lose the character that made it unique. The sense of an old world passing summed up in Turner's talk was perhaps nowhere better demonstrated than across the Chicago fairground in the spectacle of Buffalo Bill's Wild West Show performing to sellout crowds in the bleachers. The high drama of the struggle for the West had become by 1893 little more than a thrilling but harmless entertainment.

Buffalo Bill Poster
Buffalo Bill Cody used colorful posters to publicize his Wild West Show during the 1880s and 1890s. One of his most popular features was the reenactment of Custer's Last Stand, which he performed for Queen Victoria in London and at the World's Columbian Exposition in Chicago. Cody hired Native Americans for his troop, including Sitting Bull, who had fought at the Battle of the Little Bighorn. Sitting Bull toured with the company in 1885 and traveled to England with the show.
Buffalo Bill Historical Center, Cody, Wyoming.

For more help analyzing this image, see the visual activity for this chapter in the Online Study Guide at **bedfordstmartins.com/roark**.

Conclusion: The West, an Integral Part of Gilded Age America

Between 1870 and 1900, the United States filled out the map of the continent all the way to the Pacific Ocean as miners and settlers pushed into the trans-Mississippi West. Native Americans who resisted met defeat in the bloody Indian wars that raged from 1861 to 1890 and left the Indians dispossessed, forced onto reservations, and later put out to farm on 160-acre plots. At the same time, Indian boarding schools worked to erase tribal identity and force assimilation.

By 1900 eight new states had entered the Union, leaving only three territories. As settlers moved onto the plains, agriculture became increasingly mechanized and commercial; huge farms totaling thousands of acres were tilled by machine, not muscle. With its huge mining companies and burgeoning agribusiness, the West developed its own industrialism, paralleling industrial development in the East.

In the decades following the Civil War the American West, as much as the urban East, confronted the new problems of the Gilded Age that had replaced the old issues of slavery and sectionalism. The growing power of big business, the exploitation of labor and natural resources, corruption in politics, and ethnic and racial tensions exacerbated by unparalleled immigration dominated the debates of the day, in both East and West. Industrialism changed the nature of the American promise, which for decades had been dominated by Jeffersonian agrarian ideals. Could such a promise exist in the new world of corporations, wage labor, and burgeoning cities?

As the nineteenth century ended, Americans had more questions than answers. But one thing was certain: The West with its mining companies and huge commercial farms, its displaced cowboys and migratory laborers, its corporate buccaneers and corrupt territorial officials, and the racial and ethnic tensions that beset its polyglot population was as much a part of the Gilded Age as any region east of the Mississippi. Neither out of place nor out of time, the West constituted an important part of Gilded Age America, tied to the rest of the nation not only by the get-rich-quick ethos and speculative mania of the era but by the reality of the thousands of miles of rail-way tracks crisscrossing the continent, linking the growing cities of the East to the mining towns of Nevada, the orange groves of California, and the cotton fields and cattle ranches of Texas—an integral part of an increasingly urban and industrial nation spanning the continent from sea to sea.

FOR ADDITIONAL FIRSTHAND ACCOUNTS OF THIS PERIOD, see Chapter 18 in Michael Johnson, ed., *Reading the American Past*, Third Edition.

TO ASSESS YOUR MASTERY OF THE MATERIAL IN THIS CHAPTER, see the Online Study Guide at bedfordstmartins.com/ roark.

FOR WEB LINKS RELATED TO TOPICS IN THIS CHAPTER, see "HistoryLinks," "DocLinks," and "PlaceLinks" at bedfordstmartins.com/roark.

CHRONOLOGY

1862 • Homestead Act promises 160 acres of western land to anyone who settles on land for five years.

1868 • Treaty of Fort Laramie promises land, including Black Hills, to Indians.

1870 • Hunters begin to decimate bison herds.

1873 • Miners discover "Big Bonanza" on Comstock Lode.

1874 • Barbed wire patented.
• Lt. Col. George Armstrong Custer announces discovery of gold in Black Hills.

1875 • Virginia City, Nevada, reports 25,000 population.

1876 • Indians kill Custer's cavalry forces near Little Bighorn River in Montana Territory.

1877 • Chief Joseph surrenders.
• Crazy Horse surrenders and later is arrested and killed.

1878 • First Indian students enroll at Hampton Institute in Virginia.

1879 • Carlisle Indian School opens in Pennsylvania.
• Over 15,000 Exodusters move to Kansas.

1881 • Sitting Bull surrenders.

1882 • Chinese Exclusion Act bars Chinese immigration to United States.

1883 • Buffalo Bill Cody begins to tour with his Wild West Company.

1886 • Geronimo surrenders.

1886–1888
• Severe blizzards in Dakota Territory devastate cattle ranching.

1887 • Congress passes Dawes Act, breaking up Indian lands.

1889 • Rise of Ghost Dance religion among Native Americans frightens whites and leads to repression of Indians.
• Government opens 2 million acres of former Indian Territory in Oklahoma to settlement.

1890 • U.S. soldiers kill Sitting Bull at Pine Ridge Reservation.
• U.S. troops massacre Indians at Wounded Knee, South Dakota.
• Gold discovered in Cripple Creek, Colorado.

1893 • Last frenzied land rush takes place on Cherokee strip in Oklahoma Territory.

1900 • Census finds 66 percent of population lives in rural areas, compared to 80 percent in 1870.

BIBLIOGRAPHY

General Works

William Cronon, George Miles, and Jay Gitlin, *Under an Open Sky: Rethinking America's Western Past* (1992).

Elizabeth Jameson and Susan Armitage, *Writing the Range: Race, Class and Culture in the Women's West* (1997).

Patricia Nelson Limerick, *The Legacy of Conquest: The Unbroken Past of the American West* (1987).

Patricia Nelson Limerick, Clyde A. Milner II, and Charles E. Rankin, eds., *Trails: Toward a New Western History* (1991).

Valerie Matsumoto and Blake Allmendinger, eds., *Over the Edge: Remapping the American West* (1999).

Page Stegner, *Winning the Wild West: The Epic Saga of the American Frontier, 1800–1899* (2002).

Richard White, *"It's Your Misfortune and None of My Own": A History of the American West* (1991).

The Mining West

J. S. Holliday, *Rush for Riches, Gold Fever and the Making of California* (1999).

Ronald M. James, *The Roar and the Silence: The History of Virginia City and the Comstock Lode* (1998).

Ronald M. James and C. Elizabeth Raymond, eds., *Comstock Women: The Making of a Mining Community* (1998).

Elizabeth Jameson, *All That Glitters: Class, Conflict, and Community in Cripple Creek* (1998).

Rodman Wilson Paul, *Mining Frontiers of the Far West, 1848–1880* (rev. ed., 2001).

Paula Petrik, *No Step Backward: Women and Family on the Rocky Mountain Mining Frontier* (1987).

Earl S. Pomeroy, *The Territories and the United States, 1861–1890* (1969).

Farming and Ranching

James H. Beckstead, *Cowboying: A Tough Job in a Hard Land* (1991).

Sucheng Chan, *This Bittersweet Soil: The Chinese in California Agriculture, 1860–1910* (1986).

Cletus E. Daniel, *Bitter Harvest: A History of Farmworkers, 1870–1941* (1981).

David Dary, *Cowboy Culture* (1981).

Sarah Deutsch, *No Separate Refuge* (1987).

Deborah Fink, *Agrarian Women, Wives and Mothers in Rural Nebraska, 1880–1940* (1992).

Deborah Fitzgerald, *Every Farm a Factory: The Industrial Ideal in American Agriculture* (2003).

Paul W. Gates, *A History of Public Land Law Development* (1987).

Florence C. Gould and Patricia N. Pando, *Claiming Their Land: Women Homesteaders in Texas* (1991).

Kenneth L. Holmes, ed., *Covered Wagon Women: Diaries and Letters from the Western Trails, 1879–1903* (2000).

David Igler, *Industrial Cowboys: Miller & Lux and the Transformation of the Far West, 1850–1920* (2001).

Julie Roy Jeffrey, *Frontier Women: The Trans-Mississippi West, 1840–1880* (1979).

Terry G. Jordan, *North American Cattle-Ranching Frontiers* (1993).

H. Elaine Lindgren, *Land in Her Own Name: Women as Homesteaders in North Dakota* (1996).

Gerald McFarland, *A Scattered People: An American Family Moves West* (1985).

Sally McMurry, *Families and Farmhouses in Nineteenth Century America: Vernacular Design and Social Change* (1988).

Karen R. Merrill, *Public Lands and Political Meaning: Ranchers, the Government, and the Property between Them* (2002).

Eric H. Monkkonen, ed., *Walking to Work: Tramps in America, 1790–1935* (1984).

Sandra J. Myres, *Westering Women and the Frontier Experience, 1800–1915* (1982).

Nell Irvin Painter, *Exodusters: Black Migration to Kansas after Reconstruction* (1976).

Rodman W. Paul, *The Far West and the Great Plains in Transition, 1859–1900* (1988).

Glenda Gates Riley, *Women and Nature: Saving the "Wild" West* (1999).

William G. Robbins, *Colony and Empire: The Capitalist Transformation of the American West* (1994).

Virginia Scharff, *Twenty Thousand Roads: Women, Movement, and the West* (2003).

Lillian Schlissel, Byrd Gibbens, and Elizabeth Hampsten, *Far from Home: Families of the Westward Journey* (1989).

Richard Slatta, *Cowboys of the Americas* (1990).

Paul F. Starrs, *Let the Cowboy Ride: Cattle Ranching in the American West* (1998).

Ted Steinberg, *Down to Earth: Nature's Role in American History* (2002).

Steven Stoll, *Larding the Lean Earth: Soil and Society in Nineteenth-Century America* (2002).

Joanna L. Stratton, *Pioneer Women: Voices from the Kansas Frontier* (1981).

Don D. Walker, *Clio's Cowboys: Studies in the Historiography of the Cattle Trade* (1981).

Michael Wallis, *The Real Wild West: The 101 Ranch and the Creation of the American West* (1999).

Donald Worster, *Under Western Skies* (1992).

William Wyckoff, *Creating Colorado: The Making of a Western American Landscape, 1860–1940* (1999).

Native Americans, Mexicans, and Asians

Najia Aarin-Heriot, *Chinese Immigrants, African Americans, and Racial Anxiety in the United States, 1848–82* (2003).

David Wallace Adams, *Education for Extinction: American Indians and the Boarding School Experience, 1875–1928* (1995).

Tomas Almaguer, *Racial Fault Lines: The Historical Origins of White Supremacy in California* (1994).

Margaret L. Archuleta, Brenda J. Child, and K. Tsianina Lomawaima, eds., *Away from Home: American Indian Boarding School Experiences, 1879–2000* (2000).

Colin G. Calloway, *First Peoples: A Documentary Survey of American Indian History* (2nd ed., 2003).

Colin G. Calloway, ed., *Our Hearts Fell to the Ground: Plains Indian Views of How the West Was Lost* (1996).

Leonard A. Carlson, *Indians, Bureaucrats, and Land: The Dawes Act and the Decline of Indian Farming* (1981).

Ward Churchill, *A Little Matter of Genocide: Holocaust and Denial in the Americas, 1492 to the Present* (1997).

Roger Daniels, *Asian America: Chinese and Japanese in the United States since 1850* (1997).

Richard Drinnon, *Facing West: The Metaphysics of Indian-Hating and Empire Building* (1980).

T. R. Fehrenbach, *Comanches: The Destruction of a People* (1974).

Neil Foley, *The White Scourge: Mexicans, Blacks, and Poor Whites in Texas Cotton Culture* (1999).

Manuel G. Gonzales, *Mexicanos: A History of Mexicans in the United States* (1999).

Andrew Gyory, *Closing the Gate: Race, Politics, and the Chinese Exclusion Act* (1999).

Andrew C. Isenberg, *The Destruction of the Bison: An Environmental History, 1740–1920* (2000).

Peter Iverson, *Dine: A History of the Navajos* (2002).

Huping Ling, *Surviving on the Gold Mountain: A History of Chinese American Women and Their Lives* (1998).

Valerie Sherer Mathes, *Helen Hunt Jackson and Her Indian Reform Legacy* (1990).

Larry McMurtry, *Crazy Horse* (1999).

Dusanka Miscevic and Peter Kwong, *Chinese Americans: The Immigrant Experience* (2000).

David Montejano, *Anglos and Mexicans in the Making of Texas, 1836–1986* (1989).

Harry W. Paige, *Land of the Spotted Eagle: A Portrait of the Reservation Sioux* (1987).

Lynn Pan, *Sons of the Yellow Emperor: The Story of the Overseas Chinese* (1990).

Theda Perdue, ed., *Sifters: Native American Women's Lives* (2001).

Francis Paul Prucha, *American Indian Policy in Crisis: Christian Reformers and the Indian, 1865–1900* (1976).

Charles M. Robinson III, *A Good Year to Die: The Story of the Great Sioux War* (1995).

Lucy Salyer, *Laws as Harsh as Tigers: Chinese Immigrants and the Shaping of Modern Immigration Law* (1995).

Alexander Saxon, *The Indispensable Enemy: Labor and the Anti-Chinese Movement in California* (1971).

Sherry L. Smith, *Reimagining Indians: Native Americans through Anglo Eyes, 1880–1940* (2000).

H. Henrietta Stockel, *Survival of the Spirit: Chiricahua Apaches in Captivity* (1993).

Ronald Takaki, *Strangers from a Different Shore: A History of Asian Americans* (1989).

Russell Thornton, *American Indian Holocaust and Survival: A Population History since 1492* (1987).

Dan L. Thrapp, *The Conquest of Apacheria* (1967).

Robert M. Utley, *The Indian Frontier of the American West, 1846–1890* (1984).

Robert M. Utley, *The Lance and the Shield: The Life and Times of Sitting Bull* (1993).

Frank Waters, *Brave Are My People: Indian Heroes Not Forgotten* (1993).

Elliott West, *The Contested Plains: Indians, Goldseekers, and the Rush to Colorado* (1998).

James Wilson, *The Earth Shall Weep: A History of Native America* (1998).

The West of the Imagination

Sarah J. Blackstone, *Buckskins, Bullets, and Business: A History of Buffalo Bill's Wild West* (1986).

Bobby Bridger, *Buffalo Bill and Sitting Bull: Inventing the Wild West* (2002).

Paul H. Carlson, ed., *The Cowboy Way: An Exploration of History and Culture* (2000).

Robert A. Carter, *Buffalo Bill Cody: The Man behind the Legend* (2000).

David T. Courtwright, *Violent Land: Single Men and Social Disorder from the Frontier to the Inner City* (1996).

Robert Heide, *Box-Office Buckaroos: The Cowboy Hero from the Wild West Show to the Silver Screen* (1989).

James David Horan, *The Authentic Wild West* (1980).

Joy S. Kasson, *Buffalo Bill's Wild West: Celebrity, Memory, and Popular History* (2000).

Jules David Prown et al., *Transforming Visions of the American West* (1992).

Paul Reddin, *Wild West Shows* (1999).

Isabelle S. Sayers, *Annie Oakley and Buffalo Bill's Wild West* (1981).

Jane Tompkins, *West of Everything: The Inner Life of Westerns* (1992).

Alf H. Walle, *The Cowboy Hero and Its Audience: Popular Culture as Market Derived Art* (2000).

David M. Wrobel, *Promised Lands: Promotion, Memory, and the Creation of the American West* (2002).

BROOKLYN BRIDGE FAN

This commemorative fan celebrates the opening of the Brooklyn Bridge on May 24, 1883. A testament in stone and steel to the growing importance of urban America, the great bridge stood as a symbol not only of New York but of the era. The lithograph on the fan depicts a view of the bridge over the East River with ships in the foreground and the Manhattan skyline as well as commerce along the quays illustrated in detail in the background. Printed on the back are several facts about the design and construction of the bridge. Americans, proud of the great bridge, used it in advertising as a recurring motif. This fan doubles as an advertisement for the Cowperthwaits Furniture Company. The firm's sign is visible among the buildings on the front of the fan, and an image of the company's building, along with its address and telephone number, is printed on the back.

Museum of the City of New York.

The City and Its Workers

1870–1900

"**A** TOWN THAT CRAWLED now stands erect, and we whose backs were bent above the hearths know how it got its spine," boasted an immigrant steelworker surveying New York City. Where once wooden buildings stood rooted in the mire of unpaved streets, cities of stone and steel sprang up in the last decades of the nineteenth century. The labor of millions of workers, many of them immigrants, laid the foundations for urban America.

No symbol better represented the new urban landscape than the Brooklyn Bridge, opened in May 1883 and quickly hailed as "one of the wonders of the world." The great bridge soared over the East River in a single mile-long span connecting Brooklyn and Manhattan. Begun in 1869, the bridge was the dream of builder John Roebling, who did not live to see it completed.

The building of the Brooklyn Bridge took fourteen years and cost the lives of twenty men. Nearly 300 workers labored around the clock in three shifts, six days a week, most for $2 a day. To sink the foundation deep into the riverbed, common laborers tunneled down through mud and debris, working in reinforced wooden boxes called caissons, which were open at the bottom and pressurized to keep the water from flooding in. Before long the workers experienced a mysterious malady they called "bends" because it left them doubled over in pain after they came to the surface. (Scientists later discovered that nitrogen bubbles trapped in the bloodstream caused the condition and that it could be prevented if the men came up slowly to allow for decompression.) The first death occurred when the caisson reached a depth of seventy-one feet. On April 22, 1872, a heavy-set German immigrant named John Meyers complained he did not feel well and headed home to his boardinghouse. Before he could reach his bed, he collapsed and died. Eight days later another man dropped dead, and the entire workforce in the caissons went out on strike. Conditions had become so dangerous, so terrifying, that the workers demanded a higher wage for fewer hours of work.

One worker, Frank Harris, remembered the men's fear working in the caisson. As a scrawny, sixteen-year-old from Ireland, Harris started to work a few days after landing in America. He described how the men went into a coffin-like "air-lock" to acclimate to the pressure of the compressed air in the caissons:

> When the air was fully compressed, the door of the air-lock opened at a touch and we all went down to work with pick and shovel on the gravelly

bottom. My headaches soon became acute. The six of us were working naked to the waist in the small iron chamber with the temperature of about 80 degrees Fahrenheit: In five minutes the sweat was pouring from us, and all the while we were standing in icy water that was only kept from rising by the terrific pressure. No wonder the headaches were blinding.

Harris recalled the big Swede who headed the work gang saying to him that "I could stay as long as I liked, but he advised me to leave at the end of a month: it was too unhealthy." By the fifth day, Harris experienced terrible shooting pains in his ears, and fearing he might go deaf, he quit. Like Harris, many immigrant workers walked off the job, often as many as a hundred a week. But a ready supply of immigrants meant that the work never slowed or stopped; new workers eagerly entered the caissons, where they could earn in a day more than they made in a week in Ireland or Italy.

Workers in the Caisson

In 1870 *Leslie's Illustrated Weekly* ran an article on the construction of the Brooklyn Bridge, including illustrations showing the work that went on inside the caissons below the surface of the East River. Here a work crew wields sledgehammers to break up rock. Boulders on the river bottom, some the size of boxcars, led eventually to the use of explosives—a dangerous undertaking in the cramped caissons.

Leslie's Illustrated Weekly, October 15, 1870. "Views of the interior of the Brooklyn Bridge Caisson" #3.

Washington Roebling, who took over as chief engineer after his father's death, routinely worked twelve to fourteen hours, six days a week. Soon he too fell victim to the bends and ended up an invalid, directing the completion of the bridge from his window in Brooklyn Heights through a telescope. His wife, Emily Warren Roebling, acted as site superintendent and general engineer of the project. At the dedication of the bridge, Roebling turned to his wife and said, "I want the world to know that you, too, are one of the Builders of the Bridge."

Arching 130 feet above the East River, the bridge carried a roadway for vehicles and above it a pedestrian walkway. Together they pierced massive granite towers at each end through two huge Gothic arches. Roebling intended the bridge to stand as "a great work of art" as well as "a successful specimen of advanced Bridge engineering." Generations of artists and poets have testified to his success.

At the end of the nineteenth century the Brooklyn Bridge stood as a symbol of many things: the industrial might of the United States; the labor of the nation's immigrants; the ingenuity and genius of its engineers and inventors; the rise of iron and steel; and most of all, the ascendancy of urban America. Poised on the brink of the twentieth century, the nation was shifting inexorably from a rural, agricultural society to an urban, industrial nation. Immigrants, political bosses, middle-class managers, poor laborers, and the very rich populated burgeoning cities, crowding the streets, laboring in the stores and factories, and taking their leisure at the ballparks, amusement parks, dance halls, and municipal parks that dotted the urban landscape. As the new century dawned, the city and its workers moved to center stage in American life.

The Rise of the City

"We cannot all live in cities, yet nearly all seem determined to do so," New York editor Horace Greeley complained. The last three decades of the nineteenth century witnessed an urban explosion. Cities and towns grew more than twice as rapidly as the total population, far outstripping rural growth. The emergence of the modern metropolis marked the most dramatic demographic development of the period. Among the fastest-growing cities, Chicago expanded at a meteoric rate, from 100,000 in 1860 to over a million by 1890, doubling its population each decade. By 1900, the number of cities with more than 100,000 inhabitants had jumped from eighteen in 1870 to thirty-eight. Most of the nation's largest cities were east of the Mississippi, although St. Louis and San Francisco both ranked among the top ten urban areas in 1900. And in the far West, Los Angeles exploded from a sleepy village of 5,000 in 1870 to a metropolis of more than 100,000 a scant thirty years later. By the dawn of the new century, the United States boasted three cities with more than a million inhabitants—New York, Chicago, and Philadelphia.

Patterns of global migration contributed to the rise of the city. In the port cities of the East Coast, over 14 million people arrived, many from southern and eastern Europe, and huddled together in dense urban ghettos. The word *slum* entered the American vocabulary and with it growing concern over the rising tide of newcomers. With immigration, the widening gap between the rich and the poor became more visible, a gap exacerbated by changes in the city landscape brought about by transportation and technology.

The Urban Explosion, a Global Migration

The United States grew up in the country and moved to the city, or so it seemed by the end of the nineteenth century. Hundreds of thousands of farm boys and girls ran away to the city looking for jobs and adventure. But rural migrants to the cities were by no means limited to American farmers. Worldwide in scope, the movement from rural areas to urban industrial centers attracted millions of immigrants to American shores in the waning decades of the nineteenth century.

America's industrial growth in the years following the Civil War brought about a massive redistribution of population. Burgeoning industrial centers such as Pittsburgh, Chicago, New York, and Cleveland acted like giant magnets, attracting workers from the countryside (Map 19.1). Farm boys who left for the mills of Pittsburgh or Chicago were part of a global migration that included rural people from Ireland, southern Italy, Russia, Japan, and China. As economies shifted around the world, so too did the demands for labor, prompting rural immigrants to become urban workers.

Immigrant Couple
Wearing the clothing of the old country (cap and collarless shirt, apron, and shawl), this immigrant couple carries their meager possessions—bedding in his bundle, food and utensils in her basket, and two umbrellas tied together. Notice how the man gazes confidently, almost defiantly, into the camera, while the woman, looking miserable, averts her eyes. What do their postures tell about who made the decision to come to America and about their individual hopes and apprehensions?
Wide World Photos.

By the 1870s, the world could be conceptualized as three interconnected geographic regions (Map 19.2). At the center stood an industrial core bounded by Chicago and St. Louis in the west; Toronto, Glasgow, and Berlin in the north; Warsaw in the east; and Milan, Barcelona, Richmond, and Louisville in the south. Surrounding this industrial core lay a vast agricultural domain encompassing Canada, much of Scandinavia, Russia and Poland, Hungary, Greece, Italy and Sicily, southern Spain, the South and the western plains of America, central and northern Mexico, the hinterlands of northern China, and the southern islands of Japan. Capitalist development in the late nineteenth century shattered

> Farm boys who left for the mills of Pittsburgh or Chicago were part of a global migration that included rural people from Ireland, Italy, Russia, Japan, and China.

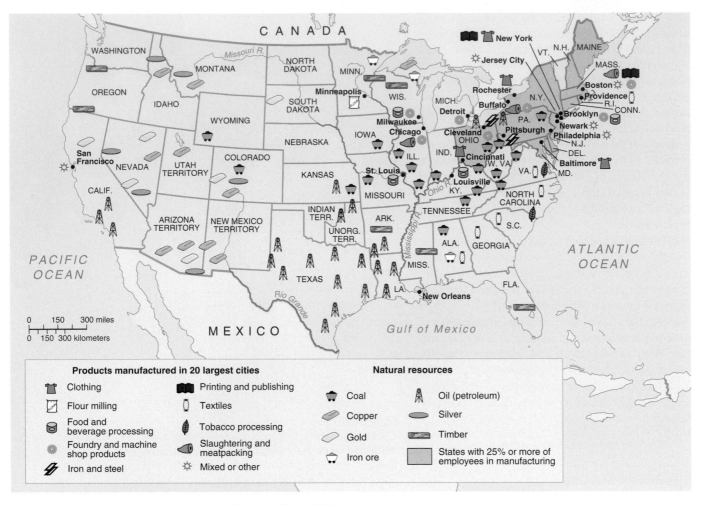

MAP 19.1   Industrialization, 1865–1900

Between 1865 and 1900, industry clustered in the Northeast and Great Lakes states; only in those regions did industry employ 25 percent or more of the labor force. The West supplied raw materials—oil, minerals, and timber—while in the South and Midwest agriculture and attendant industries such as tobacco processing and meatpacking dominated. Notice, however, the concentration of textile manufacturing in the South.

traditional patterns of economic activity in this rural periphery. As old patterns broke down, these rural areas exported, along with other raw materials, new recruits for the industrial labor force.

Beyond this second circle lay an even larger area including the Caribbean, Central and South America, the Middle East, Africa, India, and most of Asia. Ties between this part of the world and the industrial core strengthened in the late nineteenth century, but most of the people living there stayed put. They worked on plantations and railroads, in mines and ports, as part of a huge export network managed by foreign powers that staked out spheres of influence and colonies in this vast region.

In the 1870s, railroad expansion and low steamship fares gave the world's peoples a newfound mobility that enabled industrialists to draw on a global population for cheap labor. When Andrew Carnegie opened his first steel mill in 1872, his superintendent hired workers he called "buckwheats"—young American boys just off the farm. By the 1890s, however, Carnegie's workforce was liberally sprinkled with other rural boys—Hungarians and Slavs who had migrated to the United States, willing to work for low wages.

European immigration to the United States in the nineteenth century came in two distinct waves that have been called the "old" and "new" immigration. Before 1880, the majority of immigrants came from northern and western Europe, with the Germans, Irish, English, and Scandinavians making up approximately 85 percent of the newcomers. After 1880, the pattern shifted, with more and more ships carrying passengers from southern and eastern Europe. Italians, Hungarians, eastern European Jews, Turks, Armenians, Poles, Russians, and other Slavic peoples accounted for more than 80 percent of all immigrants by 1896 (Figure 19.1). Alongside the tide of new European immigrants streamed French Canadians flowing south to work in New England's mill towns and Mexicans and other Latin Americans heading north to settle in California and the Southwest,

as well as Japanese and Chinese coming across the Pacific from Asia to ports on the West Coast (Map 19.3).

The "new" immigration resulted from a number of factors. Improved economic conditions in western Europe, as well as immigration to Australia and Canada, lessened the flow of immigrants from northern and western Europe. At the same time, a protracted economic depression in southern Italy, the religious persecution of Jews in eastern Europe, and a general desire to avoid **conscription** into the Russian army led many people from southern and eastern Europe to move to the United States. Economic factors in the United States also played a role. The need of

---

MAP 19.2 **Economic Regions of the World, 1890s**

The global nature of the world economy at the turn of the twentieth century is indicated by three interconnected geographic regions. At the center stands the industrial core—western Europe and the northeastern United States. The second region—the agricultural periphery—supplied immigrant laborers to the industries in the core. Beyond these two regions lay a vast area tied economically to the industrial core by colonialism.

READING THE MAP: What types of economic regions were contained in the United States in this period? Which held most of the industrial core—the Northern or Southern Hemisphere? Which hemisphere held the most of the agricultural rural domain? Which held the greatest portion of the third region?

CONNECTIONS: Which of these three areas provided the bulk of immigrant workers to the United States? What major changes prompted the global migration at the end of the nineteenth century?

FOR MORE HELP ANALYZING THIS MAP, see the map activity for this chapter in the Online Study Guide at bedfordstmartins.com/roark.

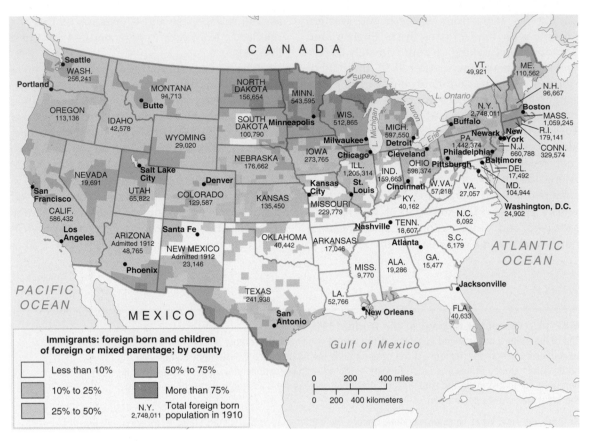

MAP 19.3   The Impact of Immigration, to 1910
Immigration flowed in all directions—south from Canada, north from Mexico, east from Asia to Seattle and San Francisco, and west from Europe to port cities like Boston and New York.

READING THE MAP: Which states have high percentages of immigrants? Which cities attracted the most immigrants? Which cities the fewest?
CONNECTIONS: Why did most immigrants gravitate toward the cities? Why do you think the South drew such a low percentage of immigrants?

FOR MORE HELP ANALYZING THIS MAP, see the map activity for this chapter in the Online Study Guide at bedfordstmartins.com/roark.

America's industries for cheap, unskilled labor stimulated immigration during good times. In the depressions following the economic panics of 1873 and 1893, immigration slowed, only to pick up again when prosperity returned. Although the U.S. government did not offer direct inducements, steamship companies courted immigrants—a highly profitable, self-loading cargo. Agents from the large lines traveled throughout Europe drumming up business. Colorful pamphlets and posters mingled fact with fantasy to advertise America as the land of promise.

Would-be immigrants eager for information about the United States relied on letters, adver-

tisements, and word of mouth—sources that were not always dependable or truthful. Even photographs proved deceptive: Workers dressed in their Sunday best looked more prosperous than they actually were to relatives in the old country, where only the very wealthy wore white collars or silk dresses. As one Italian immigrant recalled, "Everything emanating from America reached [Italy] as a distortion. . . . News was colored, success magnified, comforts and advantages exaggerated beyond all proportions." No wonder people left for America believing, as the Italian immigrant observed, "that if they were ever fortunate enough to reach America, they would fall into a pile of manure and get up brushing the diamonds out of their hair."

While the old immigrants had spread throughout the country, most of the new remained in the cities. By 1900, almost two-thirds of the nation's immigrant population resided in cities, drawn by the availability of jobs there and too poor to buy land in the West. Although rarely did the foreign-born outnumber the native-born population, taken together immigrants and their American-born children did constitute a majority, particularly in the nation's largest cities— Philadelphia, 55 percent; Boston, 66 percent; Chicago, 75 percent; and an amazing 80 percent in New York City by 1900.

Not all the newcomers came to stay. Perhaps eight million of the fourteen million European immigrants—most of them young men— worked for a year or a season and then returned to their homelands. Immigration officers called these young male immigrants, many of them Italians, "birds of passage" because they followed a regular pattern of migration to and from the United States. By 1900, almost 75 percent of the new immigrants were single young men. Intent on making money as quickly as possible, they were willing to accept conditions that other workers regarded as intolerable. They showed little interest in labor unions and organized only when the dream of returning home faded, as it did for millions who ultimately remained in the United States.

Jews from eastern Europe most often came with their families and came to stay. In the 1880s,

FIGURE 19.1   The Old and the New Immigration, 1870–1910
Before 1880, over 85 percent of immigrants came from western Europe—Germany, Ireland, England, and the Scandinavian countries. After 1880, 80 percent of the new arrivals came from Italy, Turkey, Hungary, Armenia, Poland, Russia, and other Slavic countries.

Knife and Scissors Sharpener Pushcart
Joseph Antonucci, an Italian immigrant, used this knife and scissor sharpener cart on Chicago's West Side in 1900. After a day's work, Antonucci usually parked the cart in a fire station or a customer's stable, then took the train home. He sometimes pushed his cart for miles to ply his trade beyond the city limits in towns like Hammond, Indiana. For poor immigrants who could not afford rent, pushcarts provided a cheap and portable means of livelihood. The cries of street peddlers, vendors, and scissors sharpeners like Antonucci added to the cacophony of the urban streets.
Chicago Historical Society.

a wave of violent pogroms, or persecutions, in Russia and Poland prompted the departure of more than a million Jews in the next two decades. Mary Antin, a Jew leaving Poland for America, recalled her excitement: "So, at last I was going to America! Really going, at last! The boundaries burst. The arch of heaven soared. . . . 'America! America!'" Most of the Jewish immigrants settled in the port cities of the East. New York City's Lower East Side soon replicated the Jewish ghettos of eastern Europe, teeming with street peddlers and pushcarts. Hester Street, at the heart of New York's Jewish section, rang with the calls of vendors hawking their wares, from pickles to feather beds.

Racism and the Cry for Immigration Restriction

Ethnic diversity and racism played a role in dividing skilled workers (those with a craft or specialized ability) from the unskilled (those who supplied muscle or tended machines). As industrialists mechanized to replace skilled workers with lower-paid, unskilled labor, they drew on immigrants from southern and eastern Europe

who had come to the United States in the hope of bettering their lives. (See "Historical Question," page 678.) Skilled workers, usually members of older immigrant groups from northern or western Europe, criticized the newcomers. As one Irish worker complained, "There should be a law . . . to keep all the Italians from comin' in and takin' the bread out of the mouths of honest people."

The Irish worker's resentment of the new Italian immigrants brings into focus the impact of racism on America's immigrant laborers. Throughout the nineteenth century and into the twentieth, members of the educated elite as well as workers viewed ethnic and even religious differences as racial characteristics—referring to the Polish "race" or the Jewish "race." Each wave of newcomers was seen as being somehow inferior to the established residents. The Irish who judged the Italians so harshly had themselves been seen as a lesser race a generation earlier. Immigrants not only brought their own religious and racial prejudices to the United States but also absorbed the popular prejudices of American culture. **Social Darwinism,** with its strongly racist overtones, decreed that whites stood at the top of the evolutionary ladder. But who was "white"? The social construction of race is nowhere more apparent than in the testimony of an Irish dockworker who boasted that he hired only "white men" to load cargo, a category that he insisted excluded "Poles and Italians." For the new immigrants, Americanization and assimilation proved inextricably part of becoming "white."

Racism took its most blatant form in the treatment of African Americans and Asians. Like other migrants from the rural periphery, African American men in the South—former slaves and the children of slaves—found work as "human machines." The labor gang system used in many industries reached brutal extremes in the South, where private employers contracted prison labor, mostly African Americans jailed for such minor crimes as vagrancy. Shackled together in chains as they worked under the watchful eyes of armed guards, these men stood on the bottom rung of labor's ladder. A Georgia man who escaped the brutal chain gang system remarked, "Call it slavery, peonage, or what not, the truth is we lived in a hell on earth." Eager to escape such brutal conditions, some African Americans looked to the North.

For African Americans, the cities of the North promised not just economic opportunity but an end to segregation and persecution. **Jim Crow** laws—restrictions that segregated blacks—became common throughout the South in the decades following Reconstruction. Intimidation and lynching, excused by white Southerners as necessary to "keep the Negro in his place," terrorized blacks throughout the South (see chapter 17). "To die from the bite of frost is far more glorious than at the hands of a mob," proclaimed the *Defender*, Chicago's largest African American newspaper. In the 1890s, many blacks agreed and moved north, settling for the most part in the growing cities. In 1900, New York, Philadelphia, and Chicago contained the largest black communities in the nation. Although the largest African American migration out of the South would occur during and after World War I, the great exodus was already under way.

On the West Coast, Asian immigrants soon became the scapegoats of the changing economy. After the California gold rush, Chinese who had come to work "on the gold mountain" found jobs on the country's transcontinental railroads. When the railroad boom ended, Chinese found work as agricultural laborers, cooks, and laundrymen. Prohibited from owning land, many migrated to the cities. By 1870, San Francisco's Chinatown housed a population estimated at 12,022, and it continued to grow until passage of the Chinese Exclusion Act in 1882 slowed immigration from China to a trickle (see chapter 18). Some Chinese continued to come to America, using a loophole that allowed relatives to join their families. But pressures to keep them out led in 1910 to the creation of an immigration station at Angel Island in San Francisco Bay. There Chinese immigrants were detained, sometimes for months, and many were deported as "undesirables." Their sad stories can be read in the graffiti on the barrack walls. One immigrant from Heungshan (Macao) wrote:

> There are tens of thousands of poems
> on these walls.
> They are all cries of suffering
> and sadness.

In sheer numbers, the new immigration from Europe that began in the 1880s proved unprecedented. In 1888 alone, more than a half million Europeans landed in America, 75 percent of them arriving in New York City. The Statue of Liberty, a gift from the people of France erected in 1886, stood sentinel in the harbor. A young Jewish girl named Emma Lazarus penned the verse inscribed at, Liberty's base:

> Give me your tired, your poor,
> Your huddled masses yearning to breathe free,
> The wretched refuse of your teeming shore,
> Send these, the homeless, tempest-tost to me,
> I lift my lamp beside the golden door!

The tide of immigrants to New York City soon swamped the immigration office at Castle Garden in lower Manhattan. An imposing new brick facility opened on Ellis Island in New York harbor in 1900. Able to handle 5,000 immigrants a day, it was already inadequate by the time it opened. Nonetheless, its overcrowded halls became the gateway to the United States for millions.

As the numbers of new immigrants swelled, scrutiny of the newcomers increased. To many Americans, men and women from southern and eastern Europe seemed uneducated, backward, and outlandish in appearance—impossible to assimilate. "These people are not Americans," editorialized the popular journal *Public Opinion*, "they are the very scum and offal of Europe." Terence Powderly, head of the Knights of Labor, complained that the newcomers "herded together like animals and lived like beasts." Convinced that the new immigrants were undesirable, groups began to call for measures to limit immigration.

Blue-blooded Yankees such as Senator Henry Cabot Lodge of Massachusetts formed an unlikely alliance with organized labor to press for immigration restriction. Lodge and his old-stock followers championed a literacy test, knowing that the vast majority of Italian and Slavic peasants were unable to read. In 1896, Congress approved a literacy test for immigrants, but President Grover Cleveland promptly vetoed it. "It is said," the president reminded Congress, "that the quality of recent immigration is undesirable. The time is quite within recent memory when the same thing was said of immigrants, who, with their descendants, are now numbered among our best citizens." Cleveland's veto forestalled immigration restriction but did not stop the forces seeking to close the gates. They would continue to press for restriction until they achieved their goal in the 1920s (see chapter 23).

> Ethnic diversity and racism played a role in dividing skilled workers (those with a craft or specialized ability) from the unskilled (those who supplied muscle or tended machines).

From Rags to Riches: What Is "Making It" in America?

The rags-to-riches fables of Horatio Alger and other writers fueled the dreams of countless young people at the end of the nineteenth century. Alger's formulaic novels feature fatherless young men who through the right combination of "pluck and luck" move ahead in the world. Yet despite the myth, few Americans rose from rags to riches. Even Alger's heroes, like his popular Ragged Dick, more often traded rags for respectability, not for great wealth.

Without exception, Alger's characters came from old stock and were not the new immigrants who poured through the "golden door" into the United States at the turn of the century. What were their chances of success? Literature written by the immigrants tells different stories. Abraham Cahan, in *The Rise of David Levinsky* (1917), describes the experience of an eastern European Jewish immigrant who, as the story's title indicates, achieves material success. Although the theme of success is distinctively American, Cahan's treatment of it is not. The author laments that Levinsky's "rise" is paralleled by spiritual loss. "I cannot escape from my old self," Levinsky confesses at the end of the novel. "David, the poor lad swinging over a Talmud volume at the Preacher's Synagogue, seems to have more in common with my inner identity than David Levinsky the well-known cloak manufacturer." Having sacrificed all for

material gain, David Levinsky confesses, "At the height of my business success I feel that if I had my life to live over again I should never think of a business career."

Mike Gold tells a darker story of immigrant life in *Jews without Money* (1930), an autobiographical tale of the implacable economic forces that devastate Gold's fictional family and turn its young protagonist to communism. Gold's characters inhabit a world of grinding poverty and ignorance, a landscape so bleak that one character comes to doubt the existence of a benevolent God, asking plaintively, "Did God make bedbugs?" Determined to "write a truthful book of Poverty," Gold pledged, "I will mention bedbugs":

> It wasn't a lack of cleanliness in our home. My mother was as clean as any German housewife; she slaved, she worked herself to the bone keeping us fresh and neat. The bedbugs were a torment to her. She doused the beds with kerosene, changed the sheets, sprayed the mattresses in an endless frantic war with the bedbugs. What was the use; nothing could help. It was Poverty; it was the Tenement.

Gold's own success belied the grim economic determinism of his fiction. He made it out of the ghetto and into the world of literature and social activism.

Fascinated by the subject of "making it" in America, historians repeatedly have attempted to measure economic and social mobility, from colonial times to the twentieth century. Looking at the lives of common folk, scholars have struggled to determine who made it, who did not, and why. Was America a land of boundless opportunity where the poor could rise? Or did the rich stay rich and the poor stay poor-to-middling, as pioneering studies of social mobility in the 1950s indicated?

By the 1960s, quantitative methods made possible by advances in computer technology promised to move history away from the "impressionistic," anecdotal evidence of fiction and memoirs and provide a statistical framework in which to measure success. But what could historians measure with their new tools? Comparing Jewish and Italian immigrants in New York City at the turn of the century, one historian concluded that the Jews had done a better job of making it. By employing a table that categorized occupations—ranking them from professional, white-collar jobs to unskilled labor—the historian duly noted the movement from one category to another, concluding from his data that Jews moved more quickly than Italians into the white-collar class.

Studies of occupational mobility, however, contained major flaws. Census data, the staple of quantitative studies, provide information on occupation but not on income. Quantitative historians' use of occupational categories and not income as a yardstick of mobility is misleading in a country where money has been and continues to be the common measure of success. Even occupational mobility proved difficult to measure accurately. For example, in the study cited, peddlers somewhat

RAGGED DICK.

Rags to Riches

Horatio Alger's novels like *Ragged Dick* (1868) invariably end with the young hero on the road to success. Contrast Alger's cheerful message with the bathos of the 1900 song "No One Cares for Me," in which the young newsboy in his rags replicates Alger's hero. Instead of getting ahead, the newsboy is portrayed as a victim of cruel neglect. Which portrait is more accurate? Historians for decades have wrestled with the question of social mobility and success.

Book cover: Private collection; sheet music: Picture Research Consultants & Archives.

arbitrarily ranked at low-white-collar status because they were self-employed. Yet the pushcart peddler and the Italian street vendor could hardly be said to have enjoyed white-collar status in the larger society in which they moved. Students must look carefully at what historians measure, recognizing that occupational mobility may not equate with social mobility or economic success.

The larger questions remain: What is "making it" in America? How best can it be measured—in dollars and cents, job satisfaction, occupational status, comparison with the lives of one's parents or neighbors? And what of the immigrants themselves? How did they define it? If becoming a bricklayer spelled success to the Italian immigrant and his family, do studies of occupational mobility based on statisticians' categories and job rankings distort his lived reality? In dealing with the issue of "making it" in America, historians have increasingly come to recognize that each immigrant group had its own definition of success. Not all immigrants sought upward mobility, whether economic or occupational. Cultural factors, such as the value Italians placed on loyalty to the family, also played key roles. Ultimately, questions of success and mobility cannot easily be quantified, and they direct attention to the larger cultural context that shaped individuals' economic and occupational choices.

The Social Geography of the City

During the Gilded Age, cities experienced demographic and technological changes that greatly altered the social geography of the city. Cleveland, Ohio, provides a good example. In the 1870s, Cleveland was a small city, in both population and area. Oil magnate John D. Rockefeller could, and often did, walk from his large brick house on Euclid Avenue to his office downtown. On his way he passed the small homes of his clerks and other middle-class families. Behind these homes ran miles of alleys crowded with the dwellings of Cleveland's working class. Farther out, on the shores of Lake Erie, close to the factories and foundries, clustered the shanties of the city's poorest laborers.

Within two decades, the Cleveland that Rockefeller knew no longer existed. The coming of mass transit transformed the walking city. In its place emerged a central business district surrounded by concentric rings of residences organized by ethnicity and income. First the horsecar in the 1870s and then the electric streetcar in the 1880s made it possible for those who could afford the five-cent fare to work downtown and flee after work to the "cool green rim" of the city with its single-family homes, lawns, gardens, and trees. By the early twentieth century, more than half of Cleveland's residents rode streetcars to work. Unable to afford even a few cents for streetcar fare, the city's poor crowded into the inner city or lived "back of the yards" near the factories where they worked. This pattern of development repeated throughout the country as urban congestion and suburban sprawl forever altered the social geography of the city. Social segregation—the separation of rich and poor, and of ethnic and old-stock Americans—was one of the major social changes engendered by the rise of the industrial metropolis and was evident not only in Cleveland but also in cities across the nation.

Race and ethnicity affected the way cities evolved. Newcomers to the burgeoning cities sought out their kin and country folk and struggled to maintain their culture in distinct neighborhoods often formed around a synagogue or church. Blacks typically experienced the greatest residential segregation, but every large city had ethnic enclaves—Little Italy, Chinatown,

> Jacob Riis's audience shivered at his revelations about the "other half." But middle-class Americans worried equally about the excesses of the wealthy.

Bohemia Flats, Germantown—where English was rarely spoken.

In 1890, Jacob Riis, a young police reporter, took his notebook and camera into the tenements of New York's Lower East Side; the result was the best-selling book *How the Other Half Lives*. Riis invited his readers into a Cherry Street tenement:

> Be careful please! The hall is dark and you might stumble over the children pitching pennies back there. . . . Close? Yes! What would you have? All the fresh air that ever enters these stairs comes from the hall door and it is forever slamming, and from the windows of dark bedrooms that in turn receive from the stairs their sole supply of the elements God meant to be free, but man deals out with such niggardly hand.

As Riis discovered, poverty, crowding, dirt, and disease constituted the daily reality of New York City's immigrant poor. Riis's book, like his photographs, presented a world of black and white. There were many layers to the population Riis labeled the "other half," distinctions deepened by ethnicity, religion, race, and gender. Although *How the Other Half Lives* must be read as a social reformer's call to action rather than as an entirely accurate portrayal, the book for the first time opened the nation's eyes to conditions in the tenements. (See "American Places," page 681.)

Jacob Riis's audience shivered at his revelations about the "other half." But middle-class Americans worried equally about the excesses of the wealthy. They feared the class antagonism fueled by the growing chasm between rich and poor so visible in the nation's cities. Many people shared Riis's view that "the real danger to society comes not only from the tenements, but from the ill-spent wealth which reared them."

The excesses of the Gilded Age's newly minted millionaires were nowhere more visible than in the lifestyle of the Vanderbilts. "Commodore" Cornelius Vanderbilt, the uncouth ferryman who built the New York Central Railroad, died in 1877, leaving his son $90 million. William Vanderbilt doubled that sum, and his two sons proceeded to spend it on Fifth Avenue mansions and "cottages" in Newport, Rhode Island, which, with their marble and gold leaf, sought to rival the palaces of Europe. In 1883, Alva Vanderbilt (Mrs. William K. Vanderbilt I) launched herself in New York society by throwing a costume party so lavish that

AMERICAN PLACES

The Lower East Side Tenement Museum, New York City, New York

New York City's Lower East Side was home to many of the city's Jewish immigrants at the turn of the twentieth century. The Lower East Side Tenement Museum gives visitors an opportunity to see what life was like for the poor, largely immigrant residents from the 1870s to the 1930s. The museum occupies a tenement at 97 Orchard Street built in 1863 by Lucas Glockner, an immigrant tailor who lived in the building with his family. The tenement contained 20 three-room apartments, arranged four to a floor, two in front and two in the rear. Reached by an unlighted wooden staircase that ran through the center of the building, each apartment included a "front room" (11′-by-12′6″), the only room that received light and ventilation. Behind it were the kitchen and one tiny bedroom, about 8 feet square, shut off from fresh air and light with only one window opening onto the hall. An entire apartment, which often housed seven or more people, totaled about 325 square feet. Tenements like this one made the Lower East Side more crowded than the streets of Calcutta. More than 240,000 individuals per square mile crowded together in lower Manhattan at the turn of the century.

There was no toilet, no shower, no bath in these apartments when they were built—in fact no running water at all. The building's privies stood in the rear yard. Tenement reform laws requiring toilets connected to municipal sewers and providing for more light and air passed in the late nineteenth century but were rarely enforced. Not until the Tenement Act of 1901 did New York City require improved sanitary arrangements and access to light and air. The law mandated one flush toilet for every two families.

From 1935 through 1987, the structure at 97 Orchard Street was boarded up. During the restoration that created the tenement museum, over 1,500 artifacts were unearthed in the building, including kitchenware, toys, cosmetic products, documents, bottles, newspapers, buttons, and old coins. Some of them are displayed in the museum's exhibits.

Restored apartments at the museum show how residents lived in the 1870s, 1890s, 1910s, and 1930s. The Levine apartment, shown in the picture, belonged to Harris Levine and his family in the 1890s. Levine ran a small dressmaking factory, or sweatshop, in his home, demonstrating how the distinction between home and work life blurred in the tenement.

For Web links related to this site and other American Places, see "PlaceLinks" at bedfordstmartins.com/roark.

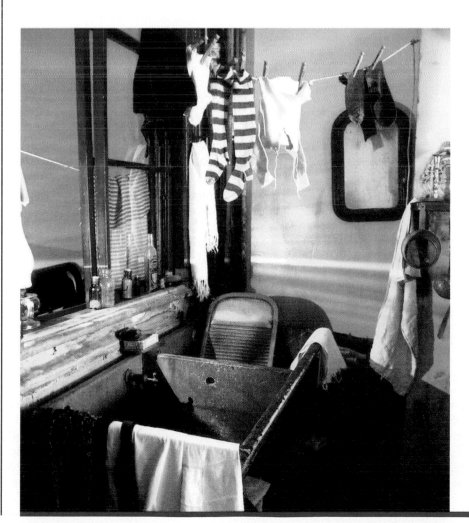

The Levine Apartment
Lower East Side Tenement Museum.

Such ostentatious displays of wealth became especially alarming when they were coupled with disdain for the well-being of ordinary people. When a reporter in 1882 asked William Vanderbilt whether he considered the public good in running his railroads, he shot back, "The public be damned." The fear that America had become a plutocracy—a society ruled by the rich—gained credence from the fact that the wealthiest 1 percent of the population owned more than half the real and personal property in the country (a century later, the top 1 percent controlled less than a quarter). As the new century dawned, reformers would form a **progressive** movement to address the problems of urban industrialism and the substandard living and working conditions it produced.

How the Wealthy Lived

Shown here is Alice Vanderbilt, as she appeared at the Vanderbilt costume ball in 1883 dressed as the "Spirit of Electricity." Her gown, by the French design house of Worth, was no doubt inspired by Thomas Edison's triumphant lighting of lower Manhattan six months earlier. Made of silk satin and trimmed with velvet, gilt metallic bullion, and diamonds, the gown epitomized what political economist Thortstein Veblen would call conspicuous consumption.

Collection of the New-York Historical Society.

For more help analyzing this image, see the visual activity for this chapter in the Online Study Guide at bedfordstmartins.com/roark.

not even old New York society, which turned up its nose at the *nouveau riche* (new rich), could resist an invitation. Dressed as a Venetian princess, the hostess greeted her twelve hundred guests. But her sister-in-law capped the evening, appearing as that miraculous new invention, the electric light, resplendent in a white satin evening dress studded with diamonds. Many costumes cost as much as $1,500 apiece, three times the average yearly wage of a worker. The *New York World* speculated that Mrs. Vanderbilt's party cost over a quarter of a million dollars, more than $4 million in today's dollars.

At Work in the City

Throughout the nineteenth century, America's urban industrial workers toiled in a variety of settings. Many skilled workers and **artisans** still earned a living in small workshops or were self-employed. But with the rise of corporate capitalism, large factories, mills, and mines increasingly dotted the landscape. Sweatshops and outwork, the contracting of piecework to be performed in the home, provided work experiences different from those of factory operatives (machine tenders) and industrial workers. Pick-and-shovel labor, whether on the railroads or in the building trades, constituted yet another kind of work. Managers and other white-collar employees as well as women "typewriters" and salesclerks formed a new white-collar segment of America's workforce. The best way to get a sense of the diversity of workers and workplaces is to look at the industrial nation at work.

America's Diverse Workers

Common laborers formed the backbone of the American labor force. They built the railroads and subways, tunneled under New York's East River to anchor the Brooklyn Bridge, and helped to lay the foundation of industrial America. These "human machines" stood at the bottom of the country's economic ladder and generally came from the most recent immigrant groups. Initially the Irish wielded the picks and shovels that built American cities, but by the turn of the century, as the Irish bettered their lot, Slavs and Italians took up their tools.

At the opposite end of the labor hierarchy stood skilled craftsmen like iron puddler James J. Davis, a Welsh immigrant. Using brains along with brawn, puddlers took the melted pig iron in the heat of the furnace and, with long poles, formed the cooling metal into 200-pound balls, relying on eye and intuition to make each ball uniform. Davis compared the task to baking bread: "I am like some frantic baker in the inferno kneading a batch of iron bread for the devil's breakfast. My spoon weighs twenty-five pounds, my porridge is pasty iron, and the heat of my kitchen is so great that if my body was not hardened to it, the ordeal would drop me in my tracks."

Possessing such a skill meant earning good wages, up to $7 a day, when there was work. But often no work could be found. Much industry and manufacturing in the nineteenth century remained seasonal; few workers could count on year-round pay. In addition, two major depressions only twenty years apart, beginning in 1873 and 1893, spelled unemployment and hardship for all workers. In an era before unemployment insurance, workers' compensation, or old-age pensions, even the best worker could not guarantee security for his family. "The fear of ending in the poor house is one of the terrors that dog a man through life," Davis confessed.

As the century wore on, employers attempted to limit workers' autonomy by replacing people with machinery, breaking down skilled work into ever smaller tasks, and replacing skilled workers with unskilled factory operatives, often immigrant laborers or young women working for low wages. Although such efficiencies made a greater variety of goods at lower prices available to American consumers, workers lost out in the bargain.

New England's textile mills provide a classic example of the effects of mechanized factory labor in the nineteenth century. Mary, a weaver at the mills in Fall River, Massachusetts, told her story to the *Independent* magazine. She went to work in the 1880s at the age of twelve. By then, mechanization of the looms had reduced the job of the weaver to watching for breaks in the thread. "At first the noise is fierce, and you have to breathe the cotton all the time, but you get used to it," Mary told her interviewer. "When the bobbin flies out and a girl gets hurt, you can't hear her shout—not if she just screams, you can't. She's got to wait, 'till you see her. . . . Lots of us is deaf."

The majority of factory operatives in the textile mills were young unmarried women like Mary. They worked from six in the morning to six at night, six days a week, and they took home about $1 a day. The seasonal nature of the work also drove wages down. "Like as not your mill will 'shut down' three months," and "some weeks you only get two or three days' work," Mary recounted. After twenty years of working in the mill, Mary's family had not been able to scrape together enough money to buy a house: "We saved some, but something always comes."

Mechanization transformed the garment industry as well. With the introduction of the foot-pedaled sewing machine in the

Sweatshop Worker

Sweatshop workers endured crowded and often dangerous conditions. Most were young women, like the one shown here sewing pants in New York City. Young working girls earned little money but prided themselves on their independence. Notice the young woman's stylish hairdo, white shirtwaist, and necklace—indications that she did not turn over all the money in her pay envelope to her father, as was sometimes the case. Because most white women quit working when they married, spending money on finery to attract a husband could turn out to be a good investment in the long run.

George Eastman House.

1850s and the use of mechanical cloth-cutting knives in the 1870s, independent tailors were replaced with workers hired by contractors to sew pieces of cloth into clothing. Working in sweatshops, small rooms hired for the season or even the contractor's own tenement, women and children formed an important segment of garment workers.

Sadie Frowne, a sixteen-year-old Polish Jew, went to work in a Brooklyn sweatshop in the 1890s. Frowne sewed for eleven hours a day in a room twenty feet long and fourteen feet wide containing fourteen machines. "The machines go like mad all day, because the faster you work the more money you get," she recalled. Paid by the piece, she earned about $4.50 a week and, by rigid economy, tried to save $2. Young and single, Frowne typified the woman wage earner in the late nineteenth century. In 1890, the aver-

age working woman was twenty-two and had been working since the age of fifteen, laboring twelve hours a day, six days a week, and earning less than $6 a week. Discriminated against in the marketplace, where they earned less than men, and largely ignored by the labor unions, women generally worked only eight to ten years, until they married. These young working women formed a unique subculture. Their youth, high spirits, and camaraderie made their hard, repetitive work bearable, and after hours they relished the "cheap amusements" of the day—the dance halls, social clubs, and amusement parks.

The Family Economy: Women and Children

The buying power of wages rose by 15 percent between 1873 and 1893, but workers did not share equally in the improvement. African American men, immigrant laborers, and women and children continued to be paid at much lower rates than white men. And the economic depressions following the panics of 1873 and 1893 undercut many workers' gains. In 1890, the average male worker earned $500 a year, about $8,000 in today's dollars. Many working-class families, whether native-born or immigrant, lived in poverty or near poverty; their economic survival depended on the contributions of all family members, regardless of sex or age. One statistician estimated that in 1900 as many as 64 percent of working-class families relied on income other than the husband's wages to make ends meet. The paid and unpaid work of women and children proved essential for family survival and economic advancement.

In the cities, boys young as six years old plied their trades as bootblacks and newsboys. Often working under an adult contractor, these children earned as little as fifty cents a day. Many of them were homeless—orphaned or cast off by their families. "We wuz six, and we ain't got no father," a child of twelve told reporter Jacob Riis. "Some of us had to go." And so he went, to make a living on the street selling newspapers. In New York City the Children's Aid Society tried to better the situation of these, the city's youngest workers, by establishing lodging houses. To encourage "self sufficiency and self respect," the boys were expected to pay their way—six cents for a bed, six for a breakfast of bread and coffee, and six for a supper of pork and beans. Lodged in dormitories that sometimes held more than a

Bootblacks

The faces and hands of the two bootblacks posed here with a third boy on a New York City street in 1896 testify to their grimy trade. Boys as young as six years old found work on the city streets as bootblacks and newsboys. Often they worked for contractors who took a cut of their meager earnings. When families could no longer afford to feed their children, boys often headed out on their own at a young age. For these child workers, education was a luxury they could not afford.
Alice Austin photo, Staten Island Historical Society.

hundred berths, the boys had to be on good behavior. A sign at the entrance admonished, "Boys who swear and chew tobacco cannot sleep here."

Child labor increased decade by decade; the percentage of children under fifteen engaged in paid labor did not drop until after World War I. The 1900 census estimated that 1,750,178 children aged ten to fifteen were employed, an increase of more than a million since 1870. Children in this age range constituted over 18 percent of the industrial labor force. Many younger children not counted by the census worked in mills, in factories, and on the streets.

In the late nineteenth century, the number of women workers also rose sharply, with their most common occupation changing slowly from domestic service to factory work and then to office work. In 1870, the census listed 1.5 million women working for wages in nonagricultural occupations. By 1890, more than 3.7 million women earned wages (Figure 19.2). Women's working patterns varied considerably according to race and ethnicity. White married women,

even among the working class, rarely labored outside the home. In 1890, only 3 percent were employed for wages. Nevertheless, married women found ways to contribute to the family economy. Families often took in boarders or lodgers, which meant extra housework. In many Italian families, piecework such as making artificial flowers allowed married women to contribute to the family economy without leaving their homes. Black women, married and unmarried, worked for wages in much greater numbers than white women. The 1890 census showed that 25 percent of African American married women worked for wages, often as domestics in the houses of white families.

> Many working-class families, whether native-born or immigrant, lived in poverty or near poverty; their economic survival depended on the contributions of all family members, regardless of sex or age.

Managers and White Collars

In the late nineteenth century, business expansion and consolidation led to a managerial revolution, creating a new class of managers. As skilled workers saw their crafts replaced by mechanization, some moved into management positions. "The middle class is becoming a salaried class," a writer for the *Independent* magazine observed, "and is rapidly losing the economic and moral independence of former days." As large business organizations consolidated, corporate development separated management from ownership, and the job of directing the firm became the province of salaried executives and managers, the majority of whom were white men drawn from the 8 percent of Americans who held high school diplomas. In 1880, the middle managers at the Chicago, Burlington, and Quincy Railroad earned between $1,500 and $4,000 a year; senior executives, generally recruited from the college-educated elite, took home $4,000 or more; and the company's general manager made $15,000 a year, approximately thirty times what the average worker earned.

Until late in the century, when engineering schools began to supply recruits, many skilled workers moved from the shop floor to positions of considerable responsibility. The career of Captain William "Billy" Jones provides a glimpse of a skilled ironworker turned manager. Jones, the son of a Welsh immigrant, grew up in the heat of the blast furnaces, where he started working as an apprentice at the age of

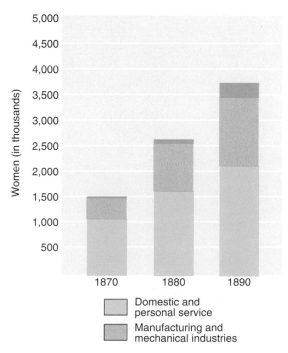

FIGURE 19.2 Women and Work, 1870–1890
In 1870 close to 1.5 million women worked in nonagricultural occupations. By 1890, that number had more than doubled to 3.7 million. More and more women sought work in manufacturing and mechanical industries, although domestic and service jobs still constituted the largest employment arena for women.

Women (in thousands)

- Domestic and personal service
- Manufacturing and mechanical industries

ten. During the Civil War, he served in the Union army and earned the rank of captain, a title he used for the rest of his life. When Andrew Carnegie opened his steelworks on the outskirts of Pittsburgh in 1872, he hired Jones as his plant superintendent. By all accounts, Jones was the best steel man in the industry. "Good wages and good workmen" was his motto. Carnegie constantly tried to force down workers' pay, but Jones fought for his men: He succeeded in shortening the shift from twelve to eight hours a day by convincing Carnegie that shorter hours would reduce absenteeism and accidents. Jones himself demanded and received a "hell of a big salary." Carnegie paid him $25,000—the same salary as the president of the United States—a stupendous sum in the 1870s, which made Jones perhaps the most successful manager to move up from the shop floor.

> Far from viewing their jobs as dehumanizing, women "typewriters" took pride in their work and relished the economic independence it afforded them.

"Typewriters" and Salesclerks

In the decades after the Civil War, as businesses became larger and more far-flung, the need for more elaborate and exact records as well as the greater volume of correspondence led to the hiring of more office workers. Mechanization transformed business as it had industry and manufacturing. The adding machine, the cash register, and the typewriter came into general use in the 1880s. Employers seeking literate workers soon turned to women. Educated men had many other career choices, but for middle-class white women, secretarial work constituted one of very few areas where they could put their literacy to use for wages.

Sylvie Thygeson was typical of the young women who went to work as secretaries. Thygeson grew up in an Illinois prairie town. When her father died in 1884, she went to work as a country schoolteacher at the age of sixteen, immediately after graduating high school. Quickly learning that teaching school did not pay a living wage, she mastered typing and stenography and found work as a secretary to help support her family. According to her account, she made "a fabulous sum of money." Nevertheless, she gave up her job after a few years when she met and married her husband.

Called "typewriters," women workers like Thygeson were seen as indistinguishable from the machines they operated. Far from viewing their jobs as dehumanizing, women typewriters took pride in their work and relished the economic independence it afforded them. By the 1890s, secretarial work was the overwhelming choice of white, native-born women, who consti-

Clerical Worker
A stenographer takes dictation in an 1890s office. Notice that the apron, a symbol of feminine domesticity, has accompanied the woman into the workplace. In the 1880s, with the invention of the typewriter, many women put their literacy skills to use for wages in the nation's offices. Brown Brothers.

tuted over 90 percent of the female clerical force. Not only considered more genteel than factory work or domestic labor, office work also meant more money for shorter hours. Boston's clerical workers made more than $6 a week in 1883, compared with less than $5 for women working in manufacturing. For thousands of women like Sylvie Thygeson, office work provided a welcome opportunity.

As a new consumer culture came to dominate American urban life in the late nineteenth century, department stores offered another employment opportunity for women in the cities. Boasting ornate facades, large plate-glass display windows, and marble and brass fixtures, stores like Macy's in New York, Wanamaker's in Philadelphia, and Marshall Field in Chicago stood as monuments to the material promise of the era. Within these palaces of consumption, cash girls, stock clerks, and wrappers earned as little as $3 a week while, at the top of the scale, buyers like Belle Cushman of the fancy goods department at Macy's earned $25 a week, an unusually high salary for a woman in the 1870s.

Typically, the gender segregation that kept women's wages low in the office and the factory also prevailed in the department stores. Male supervisors called floorwalkers commanded salaries of $10 to $16 per week at a time when the typical Macy's saleswoman received $5 to $6. In all stores, saleswomen were subject to harsh and arbitrary discipline. Sitting was forbidden, and conversation with other clerks led to instant dismissal. Yet salesclerks counted themselves a cut above factory workers. Their work was neither dirty nor dangerous, and even when they earned less than factory workers, they felt a sense of superiority.

Workers Organize

By the late nineteenth century, industrial workers were losing ground in the workplace. In the fierce competition to lower prices and cut costs, industrialists like Andrew Carnegie invested heavily in new machinery that enabled managers to replace skilled workers with unskilled labor. The erosion of skill and the redefinition of labor as mere "machine tending" left the worker with a growing sense of individual helplessness that served as a spur to collective action. In the 1870s and 1880s labor unions grew, and the Knights of Labor and the American Federation

The Lure of the Department Store
Grand department stores like Marshall Field in Chicago, pictured here in the 1890s, became monuments to the new art of mass consumption. Occupying an entire city block and featuring as many as ten floors overflowing with goods, not counting the main floor and the bargain basement, department stores used lavishly decorated display windows to attract shoppers. In this photograph, men in straw "boaters" and women in elaborate hats are drawn like magnets to Marshall Field's displays, where they indulge in a favorite new pastime—window shopping.
Chicago Historical Society.

of Labor attracted many workers. The inflammatory rhetoric of some radical groups caused many comfortable Americans to equate the labor movement with the specter of violence and **anarchism**. In 1877, in the midst of a depression that left many workers destitute, labor flexed its muscle in the Great Railroad Strike and showed the power of collective action.

The Great Railroad Strike of 1877

Economic depression following the panic of 1873 threw as many as 3 million people out of work. Those who were lucky enough to keep their jobs watched as pay cuts eroded their wages until they could no longer feed their families. In the summer of 1877 the Baltimore and Ohio (B&O) Railroad announced a 10 percent wage reduction and at the same time declared a 10 percent dividend to its stockholders. Angry brakemen in West Virginia, whose wages had already fallen from $70 to $30 a month, walked out on strike. One B&O worker described the hardship that drove him to take such desperate action: "We eat our hard bread and tainted meat two days old on the sooty cars up the road, and when we come home, find our children gnawing bones and our wives complaining that they cannot even buy hominy and molasses for food."

The West Virginia brakemen's strike touched off the Great Railroad Strike of 1877, a nationwide uprising that spread rapidly to Pittsburgh and Chicago, St. Louis, and San Francisco (Map 19.4). Within a few days, nearly 100,000 railroad workers walked off the job. The spark of rebellion soon fired other workers to action. An estimated 500,000 laborers joined the striking train workers. Steelworkers, longshoremen, workers from other industries, often with their wives and children, made common cause with the railroad strikers. In Reading, Pennsylvania, militiamen refused to fire on the strikers, saying, "We may be militiamen, but we are workmen first." Rail traffic ground to a halt; the nation lay paralyzed.

Violence erupted as the strike spread. In Pittsburgh, strikers clashed with militia brought in from Philadelphia, who arrogantly boasted they would clean up "the workingmen's town." Opening fire on the crowd, the militia killed twenty people. Angry workers retaliated by reducing an area two miles long beside the tracks to smoldering rubble. Before the day ended, twenty more workers had been shot, and the railroad had sustained property damage totaling $2 million.

Destruction from the Great Railroad Strike of 1877

Pictures of the devastation caused in Pittsburgh during the strike shocked many Americans. When militiamen fired on striking workers, killing more than 20 strikers, the mob retaliated by destroying a two-mile area along the track, reducing it to the smoldering rubble shown here. Property damage totaled $2 million. Curious pedestrians came out to view the destruction.

Carnegie Library of Pittsburgh.

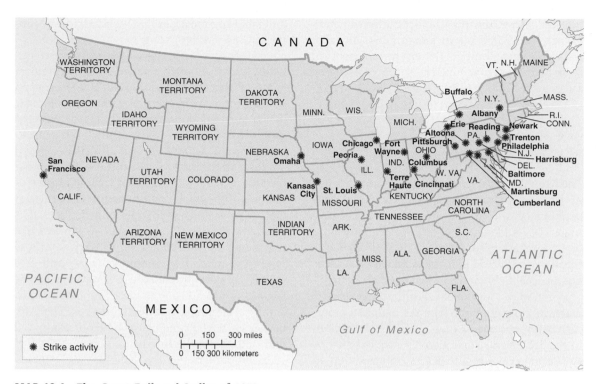

MAP 19.4 The Great Railroad Strike of 1877
Starting in West Virginia and Pennsylvania, the strike spread as far north as Buffalo and as far west as San Francisco, bringing rail traffic to a standstill.

Within eight days, the governors of nine states, acting at the prompting of the railroad owners and managers, defined the strike as an "insurrection" and called for federal troops. President Rutherford B. Hayes, after hesitating briefly, called out the army. By the time the troops arrived, the violence had run its course. Federal troops did not shoot a single striker in 1877. But they struck a blow against labor by acting as strikebreakers—opening rail traffic, protecting nonstriking "scab" train crews, and maintaining peace along the line.

Although the Great Railroad Strike was spontaneous and unorganized, it frightened the authorities and upper classes like nothing before in U.S. labor history, making them hostile to labor organization. They quickly tried to blame the tiny, radical Workingman's Party for the strike and predicted a bloody uprising. "Any hour the mob chooses it can destroy any city in the country—that is the simple truth," wrote future secretary of state John Hay to his wealthy father-in-law. The *New York Times* editorialized about the "dangerous classes," and the *Independent* magazine urged the use of violence to subdue the "rioters": "If the club of a policeman, knocking out the brains of the rioter, will answer, then well and good," an editor opined. "But if it does not . . . then bullets and bayonets, canister and grape[shot] . . . constitutes the one remedy."

In three weeks the strike was over. "The strikes have been put down by force," President Hayes noted in his diary on August 5. "But now for the real remedy. Can't something be done by education of the strikers, by judicious control of the capitalists, by wise general policy to end or diminish the evil? The railroad strikers, as a rule, are good men, sober, intelligent, and industrious." While Hayes acknowledged the workers' grievances, most businessmen and industrialists did not and fought the idea of labor unions, arguing that workers and employers entered into contracts as individuals and denying the right of unions to bargain collectively for their workers. For their part, workers

> Although the Great Railroad Strike of 1877 was spontaneous and unorganized, it frightened the authorities and upper classes like nothing before in U.S. labor history, making them hostile to labor organization.

quickly recognized they held little power individually and flocked to join unions. As labor leader Samuel Gompers noted, the strike served as an alarm bell to labor "that sounded a ringing message of hope to us all."

The Knights of Labor and the American Federation of Labor

The Knights of Labor, the first mass organization of America's working class, proved the chief beneficiary of labor's newfound consciousness. The Noble and Holy Order of the Knights of Labor had been founded in 1869 by Uriah Stephens, a Philadelphia garment cutter. A secret but peaceable society of workers, the Knights envisioned a "universal brotherhood" of all workers, from common laborers to master craftsmen. Although the Knights played no active role in the 1877 strike, membership swelled as a result of the growing interest in unionism that accompanied the strike. In 1878, the organization dropped the trappings of secrecy and launched an ambitious campaign to organize workers regardless of skill, sex, race, or nationality.

Under the direction of Grand Master Workman Terence V. Powderly, the Knights of Labor became the dominant force in labor during the 1880s. The Knights advocated a kind of workers' democracy that embraced reforms including public ownership of the railroads, an income tax, equal pay for women workers, and the abolition of child labor. The Knights sought to remove class distinctions and encouraged local assemblies to welcome all comers, employees and employers alike. "I hate the word 'class' and would drive it from the English language if I could," Powderly stated. Only the "parasitic" members of society—gamblers, stockbrokers, lawyers, bankers, and liquor dealers—were denied membership.

In theory, the Knights of Labor opposed strikes. Powderly championed arbitration and preferred to use boycotts. But in practice, much of the organization's appeal came from a successful strike the Knights mounted in 1885 against three railroads controlled by Jay Gould. The Knights won a sweeping victory, including the revocation of a 15 percent pay cut. Despite the reservations of its leadership, the Knights of Labor became a militant labor organization that won passionate support from working people.

The Knights of Labor was not without rivals. Other trade unionists disliked the broad reform goals of the Knights and sought to focus on workplace issues. Samuel Gompers, a cigar maker born in London of Dutch Jewish ancestry, promoted what he called "pure and simple" unionism. Gompers founded the Organized Trades and Labor Unions in 1881 and reorganized it in 1886 into the American Federation of Labor (AFL), which coordinated the activities of craft unions throughout the United States. His plan was simple: Organize skilled workers like machinists and locomotive engineers—those with the most bargaining power—and use strikes to gain immediate objectives such as higher pay and better working conditions. Gompers at first drew few converts. The AFL had only 138,000 members in 1886, compared with 730,000 for the Knights of Labor. But events soon brought down the Knights and enabled Gompers to take control of the labor movement.

Haymarket and the Specter of Labor Radicalism

While the AFL and the Knights of Labor competed for members, radical socialists and anarchists offered different visions of labor's true path. The radicals, many of whom were immigrants steeped in the tradition of European **socialism**, believed that reform was futile; they called instead for social revolution. Anarchists, too, wanted revolutionary change but along with it an end to the power of the state. Both groups, sensitive to criticism that they preferred revolution in theory to improvements here and now, rallied around the popular issue of the eight-hour day.

Since the 1840s, labor had sought to end the twelve-hour workday, which was standard in industry and manufacturing. By the mid-1880s, it seemed clear to many workers that labor shared too little in the new prosperity of the decade, and pressure mounted for the eight-hour day. The radicals seized on the popular issue and launched major rallies in cities across the nation. Supporters of the movement set May 1, 1886, as the date for a nationwide general strike in support of the eight-hour day.

All factions of the nascent labor movement came together in Chicago on May Day for what was billed as the largest demonstration to date. A group of radicals led by anarchist Albert

> By the mid-1880s, it seemed clear to many workers that labor shared too little in the new prosperity of the decade, and pressure mounted for the eight-hour day.

Parsons, a *Mayflower* descendant, and August Spies, a German immigrant, spearheaded the eight-hour movement in Chicago. Chicago's Knights of Labor rallied to the cause even though Powderly and the union's national leadership, worried by the increasing activism of the rank and file, refused to champion the movement for shorter hours. Samuel Gompers was on hand, too, to lead the city's trade unionists, although he privately urged the AFL assemblies not to participate in the general strike.

Gompers's skilled workers were labor's elite. Many still worked in small shops where negotiations between workers and employers took place in an environment tempered by personal relationships. Well dressed in their Prince Albert coats and starched shirts, the AFL's skilled workers stood in sharp contrast to the dispossessed workers out on strike across town at Chicago's huge McCormick reaper works. There strikers watched helplessly as the company brought in strikebreakers to take their jobs and marched the "scabs" to work under the protection of the Chicago police and security guards supplied by the Pinkerton Detective Agency. Cyrus McCormick Jr., son of the inventor of the mechanical reaper, viewed labor organization as a threat to his power as well as to his profits; he was determined to smash the union.

During the May Day rally, 45,000 workers paraded peacefully down Michigan Avenue in support of the eight-hour day, many singing the song that had become the movement's anthem:

> We mean to make things over;
>   we're tired of toil for naught
> But bare enough to live on: never
>   an hour for thought.
> We want to feel the sunshine; we
>   want to smell the flowers;
> We're sure that God has willed it,
>   and we mean to have eight hours.
> We're summoning our forces from
>   shipyard, shop, and mill:
> Eight hours for work, eight hours for rest,
>   eight hours for what we will!

Trouble came two days later, when strikers attacked scabs outside the McCormick works and police opened fire, killing or wounding six men. Angry radicals rushed out a circular urging workers to "arm yourselves and appear in full force" at a rally in Haymarket Square.

On the evening of May 4, the turnout at Haymarket was disappointing. No more than two or three thousand gathered in the drizzle to hear Spies, Parsons, and the other anarchist speakers. Mayor Carter Harrison, known as a friend of labor, mingled conspicuously in the crowd, pronounced the meeting peaceable, and went home to bed. A short time later, police captain John "Blackjack" Bonfield, who had made his reputation cracking skulls, marched his men into the crowd, by now fewer than three hundred people, and demanded that it disperse. Suddenly, someone threw a bomb into the police ranks. After a moment of stunned silence, the police drew their revolvers. "Fire and kill all you can," shouted a police lieutenant. When the melee ended, seven policemen and an unknown number of others lay dead. An additional sixty policemen and thirty or forty civilians suffered injuries.

News of the "Haymarket riot" provoked a nationwide convulsion of fear, followed by blind rage directed at anarchists, labor unions, strikers, immigrants, and the working class in general. The hysteria ran deepest in Chicago. The police rounded up Spies and the other Haymarket speakers and jailed hundreds of radicals. Parsons managed to escape but later turned himself in to stand trial with his fellows.

Eight men went on trial in Chicago, although witnesses testified that none of them had thrown the bomb. From the start it was clear that the men were on trial for their ideas, not their actions. "Convict these men," thundered the state's attorney Julius S. Grinnell, "make examples of them, hang them, and you save our institutions." Although the state could not link any of the defendants to the Haymarket bomb, the jury nevertheless found them all guilty. Four were executed, one committed suicide, and three received prison sentences. On the gallows, August Spies spoke for the Haymarket martyrs: "The time will come when our silence will be more powerful than the voices you throttle today."

In 1893, Governor John Peter Altgeld, after a thorough investigation, pardoned the three remaining Haymarket anarchists. He denounced the trial as a shameless travesty of justice and concluded that Captain Bonfield was "the man really responsible for the death of the police officers." The governor's action brought on a storm of protest and cost him his political career.

The bomb blast at Haymarket had lasting repercussions. To commemorate the death of the Haymarket martyrs, labor made May 1 an annual international celebration of the worker. But the Haymarket bomb, in the eyes of one observer, proved "a godsend to all enemies of the

"The Chicago Riot"
Inflammatory pamphlets like this one published in the wake of the Haymarket bombing presented a one-sided view of the incident and stirred public passion. In this charged atmosphere the anarchist speakers were tried and convicted for the bombing even though witnesses testified that none of them had thrown the bomb. The identity of the bomb thrower remains uncertain.
Chicago Historical Society.

At Home and at Play

The growth of urban industrialism not only dramatically altered the workplace but also transformed home and family life and gave rise to new forms of commercialized leisure. Industrialization redefined the very concepts of work and home. Increasingly, men went out to work for wages, while most white married women stayed home, either working in the home without pay—cleaning, cooking, and rearing children—or supervising paid domestic servants who did the housework.

Domesticity and "Domestics"

The separation of the workplace and the home that marked the shift to industrial society redefined the home as a "haven in the heartless world," presided over by a wife and mother who made the household her **separate sphere**. The growing separation of workplace and home led to a new ideology, one that sentimentalized the home and women's role in it. The cultural ideology that dictated woman's place in the home has been called the **cult of domesticity**, a phrase used to prescribe an ideal of middle-class, white womanhood that dominated the period from 1820 to the end of the nineteenth century (see chapter 11).

In the decades after the Civil War, the typical middle-class dwelling became more embellished architecturally and its interiors more cluttered. Ownership of such a home, indeed of any home, marked the gulf between the working poor and the middle class. Homeowners constituted only 36 percent of the U.S. housing population in 1900, compared with 69 percent today.

The gap between working-class austerity and the trappings associated with middle-class respectability becomes evident in a comparison of two households. In *The Gilded Age* (1873) authors Mark Twain and Charles Dudley Warner describe an ideal middle-class home:

> Every room had its book-cases or book-shelves, and was more or less a litter of new books, fresh periodicals and daily newspapers. There were plants in the sunny windows and some choice engravings on the walls, with bits of color in oil or watercolors; the piano was sure to be open and strewn with music; and there were photographs and little souvenirs here and there of foreign travels.

labor movement." It effectively scotched the eight-hour-day movement and dealt a fatal blow to the Knights of Labor.

With the labor movement everywhere under attack, many skilled workers turned to the American Federation of Labor. Gompers's narrow economic strategy made sense at the time and enabled one segment of the workforce—the skilled—to organize effectively and achieve tangible gains. But the nation's unskilled workers remained untouched by the AFL's brand of trade unionism. The vast majority of America's workers would have to wait another forty years before a mainstream labor union, the Congress of Industrial Organizations (CIO), moved to organize the unskilled (see chapter 24).

This interior stands in stark contrast to the household of a working-class immigrant family that reformer Margaret Byington visited in Homestead, the Carnegie mill town outside of Pittsburgh. A Slavic worker and his family lived in a two-room tenement where Byington found the young mother doing the laundry in a big washtub set on a chair in the middle of one room, struggling to keep her two babies from tumbling into the scalding water. In *Homestead: The Households of a Mill Town* (1910) Byington describes the sparse furnishings:

> On one side of the room was a huge puffy bed, with one feather tick to sleep on and another for covering; near the window stood a sewing machine; in the corner, an organ,—all these, besides the inevitable cook stove upon which, in the place of honor, was simmering the evening's soup. Upstairs in a second room, a boarder and the man of the house were asleep. Soon they would get up and turn their beds over to two more boarders, who were out at work.

To middle-class eyes, the Slavs' crowded tenement, with its boarders and lack of privacy, scarcely merited the name home. Yet for all the obvious differences between the two households, one can see in the working family's two feather ticks, sewing machine, and organ the same urge for comfort and sociability apparent in the middle-class home. Nor was the Slavic wife cooking dinner and doing the laundry any less domestic than her middle-class counterpart, although the latter more likely supervised the laundry and the cooking rather than doing it herself.

The cult of domesticity and the elaboration of the middle-class home led to a major change in patterns of hiring household help. The live-in servant, or domestic, became a fixture in the North, replacing the hired girl of the previous century. (The South continued to rely on black female labor, first slave and later free.) In American cities by 1870, from 15 to 30 percent of all households included live-in domestic servants, more than 90 percent of them women. By the mid-nineteenth century, native-born women increasingly took up other work and left domestic service to immigrants. In the East the maid was so often Irish that "Bridget" became a generic term for female domestics.

Servants by all accounts resented their long hours and lack of privacy. "She is liable to be rung up at all hours," one study reported. "Her very meals are not secure from interruption, and even her sleep is not sacred." Furthermore, going into service carried a social stigma. As one young woman observed, "If a girl goes into the kitchen she is sneered at and called 'the Bridget,' but if she goes behind the counter she is escorted by gentlemen." Domestic service became the occupation of last resort, a "hard and lonely life" in the words of one servant girl.

For women of the white middle class, domestics were a boon, freeing them from household drudgery and giving them more time to spend with their children or to pursue club work or reform. Thus, while domestic service supported the cult of domesticity, it created for those women who could afford it opportunities that expanded their horizons outside the home.

> The cult of domesticity and the elaboration of the middle-class home led to a major change in patterns of hiring household help. The live-in servant replaced the hired girl of the previous century.

Cheap Amusements

Growing class divisions manifested themselves in patterns of leisure as well as in work and home life. The poor and working class took their leisure, when they had any, in the cities' streets, dance halls, music houses, ballparks, and amusement arcades, which by the 1890s formed a familiar part of the urban landscape. Recreation varied according to ethnicity, religion, gender, and age. For many new immigrants social life revolved around the family; weddings, baptisms, birthdays, and bar mitzvahs constituted the chief celebrations. Generally, American men spent more time away from home in neighborhood clubs, saloons, and fraternal orders than did their new immigrant counterparts. German beer gardens, for example, entertained the whole family. But more often, men and women of all backgrounds took their leisure separately, except during youth and courtship.

The growing anonymity of urban industrial society posed a challenge to traditional rituals of courtship. Adolescent working girls no longer met prospective husbands only through their families. Fleeing crowded tenements, the young sought each other's company in dance halls and other commercial retreats. Scorning proper introductions, working-class youth "picked up" partners at the dance halls, where drinking was part of the evening's entertainment. Young working women, who rarely could afford more than across the nation, and Mark Twain hailed baseball as "the very symbol, the outward and visible expression, of the drive and push and rush and struggle of the raging, tearing, booming nineteenth century."

The increasing commercialization of entertainment in the late nineteenth century can best be seen at Coney Island. A two-mile stretch of sand close to Manhattan by trolley or steamship, Coney Island in the 1870s and 1880s attracted visitors to its beaches, dance pavilions, and penny arcades—all connected by its famous boardwalk. In the 1890s, Coney Island was transformed into the site of some of the largest and most elaborate amusement parks in the country. Promoter George Tilyou built Steeplechase Park in 1897, advertising "10 hours of fun for 10 cents." With its mechanical thrills and funhouse laughs, the amusement park encouraged behavior that one schoolteacher aptly described as "everyone with the brakes off." By 1900 as many as a half million New Yorkers flocked to Coney Island on any given weekend, making the New York amusement park the unofficial capital of a new mass culture.

Luna Park at Coney Island
Coney Island became a pleasure resort in the 1870s, but not until the turn of the century, with the development of elaborate amusement parks like Luna Park—pictured here with its elaborate tower, electric lights, flags, and "Helter Skelter" chute—did Coney Island come into its own as the capital of commercialized leisure. The official guide shown on the right outlined highlights for visitors, including the beach, the vaudeville hall, and the midway with its rides and its risqué harem dancers.
Photo: Library of Congress; booklet: Brooklyn Historical Society.

trolley fare when they went out, counted on being "treated" by men, a transaction that often implied sexual payback. Young women's need to negotiate sexual encounters if they wished to participate in commercial amusements blurred the line between respectability and promiscuity and made the dance halls a favorite target for reformers who feared they lured girls into prostitution.

For men, baseball became a national pastime in the 1870s—then, as now, one force in urban life capable of uniting a city across class lines. Cincinnati mounted the first entirely paid team, the Red Stockings, in 1869. Soon professional teams proliferated in cities

City Growth and City Government

Private enterprise, not planners, built the cities of the United States. Boosters, builders, businessmen, and politicians all had a hand in creating the modern metropolis. With a few notable exceptions, such as Washington, D.C., and Savannah, Georgia, there was no such thing as a comprehensive city plan. Cities simply mushroomed, formed by the dictates of private enterprise and the exigencies of local politics. With the rise of the city came the need for public facilities, transportation, and services that would tax the imaginations of America's architects and engineers and set the scene for the rough-and-tumble of big-city government, politics, and politicians.

Building Cities of Stone and Steel

Skyscrapers and mighty bridges dominated the imagination and the urban landscape. Less imposing but no less significant were the paved streets, the parks and public libraries, and the subways and sewers. In the late nineteenth century, Americans rushed to embrace new technology of all kinds, making their cities the most modern in the world.

Structural steel made enormous advances in building possible. A decade after the completion of the Brooklyn Bridge, engineers used the new technology to construct the Williamsburg Bridge less than one mile to the north. More prosaic and utilitarian than its neighbor, the new bridge was never as acclaimed, but it was longer by four feet and completed in half the time. It became the model for future building as the age of steel supplanted the age of stone and iron.

Skyscrapers forever changed the cityscape. Competition for space in Manhattan pushed the city up into the air even before the use of steel. The invention of Elisha Otis's elevator (called a "safety hoister") in the 1850s led to the construction of cast-iron buildings with elevators that carried passengers as high as ten stories. (See "The Promise of Technology," page 696.) But until the advent of structural steel in the 1880s, no building in Manhattan topped the spire of Wall Street's Trinity Church. In 1890, the Pulitzer Building climbed to 349 feet, the tallest office building in the world.

Chicago, not New York, gave birth to the modern skyscraper. Rising from the ashes of the Great Fire of 1871, which destroyed three square miles and left 18,000 homeless, Chicago offered a generation of skilled architects and engineers the chance to experiment with new technologies. Commercial architecture became an art form at the hands of a skilled group of architects who together constituted the "Chicago school." Men of genius such as Louis Sullivan and John Wellborn Root gave Chicago some of the world's finest commercial buildings. Employing the dictum "Form follows function," they built startlingly modern structures. The massive commercial buildings, in Root's words, "carried out the ideas of modern business life, simplicity, breadth, dignity." A fitting symbol of modern America, the skyscraper expressed and exalted the domination of corporate power.

Alongside the skyscrapers rose new residential apartments for the rich and middle class. The "French flat"—apartments with the latest plumbing and electricity—gained popularity in the 1880s as affluent city dwellers overcame their distaste for multifamily housing (which carried the stigma of the tenement) and gave in to "flat fever." Fashionable new apartments boasted modern luxuries such as telephones, central heating, and elevators. The convenience of apartment living appealed particularly to women. "Housekeeping isn't fun," cried one New York woman. "Give us flats!" In 1883 alone, more than 1,000 new apartments went up in Chicago.

The flush toilets, bathtubs, and lavatories of the new apartments would not have been pos-

> Until the advent of structural steel in the 1880s, no building in Manhattan topped the spire of Wall Street's Trinity Church.

Chicago Skyscraper Going Up

With the advent of structural steel, skyscrapers like this one in progress in Chicago in 1894 became a feature of the American urban landscape. Once the frame was up, the walls could simply "hang" on the outside of the building because they no longer had to support the structure.
Culver Pictures.

The Elevator

In 1890 for the first time a building in New York City reached higher than the spire of Trinity Church in lower Manhattan. The new Church Building gave New York its first skyscraper, a feat that would have been impossible without the development of vertical transport—the elevator.

The concept of the elevator was not new. As early as the Renaissance, Leonardo da Vinci had drawn up plans for one. By the mid-nineteenth century, power elevators operated by steam carried materials in factories, mines, and warehouses. But not until Elisha Graves Otis perfected the "safety hoister" and patented it in the 1860s was the elevator judged safe enough to carry people. A master mechanic in a bed factory, Otis was an ambitious inventor who pioneered the safety elevator in a warehouse in Yonkers, New York, in 1854. He devised an ingenious mechanism consisting of two metal pieces fastened to the elevator platform. If the rope or cable supporting the elevator broke, the metal pieces would spring out and stop the downward motion. In a dramatic demonstration in the Crystal Palace Exposition in New York in 1854, Otis cut the cable and proved the safety of his elevator.

Otis designed his first elevators to carry freight, but it was as people movers that the elevator came into its own. The Otis elevator transformed the value of urban real es-

Otis Elevator
A 1893 catalog for the Otis Elevator Company showed this hydraulic model. With its "birdcage" cab, fancy grillwork, and elaborate interior, complete with a bench for lady passengers, it was probably intended for use in an apartment house.
Archive United Technologies Corporation, Hartford, CT 06101.

tate, making it possible to build into the air. In the 1870s, steam elevators gave way to hydraulic mechanisms powered by water operating under the force of gravity. Movement up and down was smooth, fast, and economical—but also dangerous: The car was controlled only by its brake, which could (and sometimes did) fail. As buildings pushed higher into the sky, the risk increased. In 1896, an elevator in the 23-story American Tract Society Building dropped from the nineteenth floor to the bottom of the shaft, killing both occupants. The accident underscored the necessity of employing highly trained technical personnel in the maintenance of elevators, and the necessity for routine inspection to ensure safety.

As Elisha Otis's son Charles later wrote, "I do not suppose that my father had the slightest conception at the time of what the outcome of his invention would be." Otis died in 1861 before his invention made a fortune. His sons, who proved to be astute businessmen as well as skilled mechanics, founded the Otis Elevator Company and continued to pioneer vertical transportation, developing the escalator in 1900. Otis Elevator, capitalized at $11 million, formed in 1898 after a merger of eight competing elevator companies. The company went on to become one of the major industrial enterprises in America as well as one of the first multinational corporations.

sible without major improvements in city sewers and water mains. In the absence of proper sewage disposal, contaminated water wreaked havoc in big cities. In 1882 an outbreak of typhoid fever caused by the city's polluted water killed over 20,000 in Chicago. To end this scourge, enlightened city engineers created and expanded municipal sewage systems and de-

Central Park Lake, 1896
Looking south across Central Park Lake, this photograph shows boaters and well-dressed New Yorkers
with their bowler hats and parasols taking their leisure on Bethesda Terrace. Its centerpiece, the bronze
figure *Angel of the Waters*, was the work of sculptor Emma Stebbins. Calvert Vaux, who along with Frederick Law Olmsted designed the landscaping, considered Bethesda Terrace the "drawing room of the
park." By the 1870s the broad plaza had become one of the most popular gathering places in the city,
especially on Sundays. All ages, from children floating toy sailboats on the pond to grandparents out for
a stroll and young couples boating, found something to enjoy in the park.
Photo: Culver Pictures; boat: Picture Research Consultants & Archives.

vised ingenious ways to bring clean water to the
urban population. By the 1890s, the residents of
American cities demanded and received, at the
twist of a faucet, water for their
bathtubs, toilets, and even their
lawn sprinklers. Those who could
afford it enjoyed a standard of living that was the envy of civilization.

Across the United States municipal governments undertook public works on a scale never
before seen. They paved streets, built sewers and
water mains, replaced gas lamps with electric
lights, ran trolley tracks on the old horsecar
lines, and dug underground to build subways,
tearing down the unsightly elevated tracks that
had clogged the city streets. In San Francisco,
Andrew Smith Hallidie mastered the city's
hills, building a system of cable cars in 1873.
Montgomery, Alabama, became the first city in
the country to install a fully electrified streetcar
system in 1886. Boston completed the nation's

first subway system in 1897, and New York and
Philadelphia soon followed.

Cities became more beautiful with the creation of urban public parks to complement the
new buildings that quickly filled city lots. Much
of the credit for America's greatest parks goes to
one man—landscape architect Frederick Law
Olmsted. The indefatigable Olmsted designed
parks in Atlanta, Boston, Brooklyn, Hartford,
Detroit, Chicago, and Louisville, as well as the
grounds for the U.S. Capitol. But he is best remembered for the creation of New York City's
Central Park. Completed in 1873, it became the
first landscaped public park in the United States.
Olmsted and his partner, Calvert Vaux, directed
the planting of more than five million trees,
shrubs, and vines to transform the eight hundred
acres between 59th and 110th Streets into an
oasis for urban dwellers. "We want a ground to
which people may easily go after their day's
work is done," he wrote, "where they may stroll

for an hour, seeing, hearing, and feeling nothing of the bustle and jar of the streets."

American cities did not overlook the mind in their efforts at improvement. They created a comprehensive free public school system that educated everyone from the children of the middle class to the sons and daughters of immigrant workers. The exploding urban population strained the system and led to crowded and inadequate facilities. In 1899, more than 544,000 pupils attended school in New York's five boroughs. Schools in Boston, New York, Chicago, and San Francisco as well as other cities and towns provided the only classrooms in the world where students could attend secondary school free of charge.

In addition to schools, the cities built libraries to educate their citizens. In the late nineteenth century, American cities created the most extensive free public library system in the world. In 1895, the Boston Public Library opened its bronze doors under the inscription "Free to All." Designed in the style of a Renaissance palazzo, with more than 700,000 books on the shelves ready to be checked out, the library earned the description "a palace of the people."

Despite the Boston Public Library's legend "Free to All," the poor did not share equally in the advantages of city life. The parks, the libraries, and even the subways and sewers benefited some city dwellers more than others. Few library cards were held by Boston's laborers, who worked six days a week and found the library closed on Sunday. And in the 1890s, there was nothing central about New York's Central Park. It was a four-mile walk from the tenements of Hester Street to the park's entrance at 59th Street and Fifth Avenue. Cities spent more money on plumbing improvements for affluent apartment dwellers than on public baths and lodging houses for the down-and-out. Even the uniform subway fare, which enabled Boston and New York riders to travel anywhere in the system for five cents, worked to the advantage of the middle-class commuter and not the downtown poor. Then, as now, the comfortable majority, not the indigent minority, reaped a disproportionate share of the benefits in the nation's big cities.

Any story of the American city, it seems, must be a tale of two cities—or, given the cities' great diversity, a tale of many cities within each metropolis. At the turn of the twentieth century a central paradox emerged: The enduring monuments of America's cities—the bridges, skyscrapers, parks, and libraries—stood as the undeniable achievements of the same system of municipal government that reformers dismissed as boss ridden, criminal, and corrupt.

City Government and the "Bosses"

The physical growth of the cities required the expansion of public services and the creation of entirely new facilities: streets, subways, elevated trains, bridges, docks, parks, sewers, and public utilities. There was work to be done and money to be made. The professional politician—the colorful big-city boss—became a phenomenon of urban growth. Though corrupt and often criminal, the boss saw to the building of the city and provided needed social services for the new residents. Yet not even the big-city boss could be said to rule the unruly city. The governing of America's cities resembled more a tug-of-war than boss rule.

The most notorious of all the city bosses was William Marcy Tweed of New York. At midcentury, Boss Tweed's Democratic Party "machine" held sway. A machine was really no more than a political party organized at the grassroots level. Its purpose was to win elections and reward its followers with jobs on the city's payroll. New York's citywide Democratic machine, Tammany Hall, commanded an army of party functionaries. At the bottom were district captains. In return for votes, they provided services for their constituents, everything from a scuttle of coal in the winter to housing for an evicted family. At the top were powerful ward bosses who distributed lucrative franchises for subways and streetcars. They formed a shadow government, more powerful than the city's elected officials. The only elected office Tweed ever held was alderman. But as chairman of the Tammany general committee, he wielded more power than the mayor. Through the use of bribery and graft, he kept the Democratic Party together and ran the city. "As long as I count the votes," he shamelessly boasted, "what are you going to do about it?"

The cost of Tweed's rule was staggering. The construction of New York City's courthouse, budgeted at $250,000, ended up costing the taxpayers $14 million. The inflated sum represented bribery, kickbacks, and the greasing of many palms. The excesses of the Tweed ring soon led to a clamor for reform and cries of "Throw the rascals out." Cartoonist Thomas Nast pilloried

Tweed in the pages of *Harper's Weekly*. His cartoons, easily understood even by those who could not read, did the boss more harm than hundreds of outraged editorials. Tweed fled to Europe in 1871 to avoid prosecution, but eventually he was tried and convicted and died in jail.

New York was not the only city to experience bossism and corruption. The British visitor James Bryce concluded in 1888, "There is no denying that the government of cities is the one conspicuous failure of the United States." More than 80 percent of the nation's thirty largest cities experienced some form of boss rule in the decades around the turn of the twentieth century.

Infighting among powerful ward bosses was more typical than domination by one big-city boss. Chicago's "Bathhouse" John Coughlin and Michael "Hinky Dink" Kenna exemplified the breed. Their colorful nicknames signaled their distance from respectable society and hinted at unsavory connections with an underworld of crime and vice. The power they wielded belied the charge that any single boss enjoyed hegemony in the big cities.

Urban reformers and proponents of good government (derisively called "goo goos" by their rivals) challenged machine rule and sometimes succeeded in electing reform mayors. But the reformers rarely managed to stay in office for long. Their detractors called them "mornin' glories," observing that they "looked lovely in

Tammany Bank

This cast-iron bank, a campaign novelty, is named after the New York City Democratic machine. It tells its political reform message graphically: When you put a penny into the politician's hand, he puts it in his pocket. Tammany Hall dominated city politics for more than a century, dispensing contracts and franchises worth millions of dollars. Some of those dollars invariably found their way into the pockets of Tammany politicians.

Collection of Janice L. and David J. Frent.

the mornin' and withered up in a short time." The bosses enjoyed continued success for one reason: The urban political machine helped the cities' immigrants and poor. In return for votes, the machine provided legal aid, jobs, fuel, temporary shelter, and a host of small favors. The ability to combine philanthropy and politics was a hallmark of the urban boss. "What tells in holding your district is to go right down among the poor and help them in the different ways they need help," a Tammany ward boss observed. "It's philanthropy, but it's politics, too—mighty good politics." For the social services they received (and not because they were ignorant or undemocratic, as critics charged), the urban poor remained the bosses' staunchest allies.

Some reform mayors managed to achieve success and longevity. Hazen S. Pingree of Detroit exemplified the successful reform mayor. A businessman who went into politics in the 1890s, Pingree, like most good-government candidates, promised to root out dishonesty and inefficiency. He did, but he also tangled with business interests when he sought to lower streetcar fares and utility rates. When the depression of 1893 struck, Pingree emerged as a champion of the working class and the poor. He hired the unemployed to build schools, parks, and public baths. By providing jobs and needed services, he built a powerful political organization based on working-class support. Detroit's voters kept him in the mayor's office for four terms and then helped elect him governor twice.

While most good-government candidates harped on the Sunday closing of saloons and attacked vice and crime, Pingree demurred. "The most dangerous enemies to good government are not the saloons, the dives, the dens of iniquity and the criminals," but "the temptations which are offered to city officials when franchises are sought by wealthy corporations, or contracts are to be let for public works."

As Pingree shrewdly observed, not only the urban poor but also the business class benefited from bossism and

Not only the urban poor but also the business class benefited from bossism and corruption. The boss could rig tax assessments for property owners and provide lucrative franchises for city businessmen.

corruption. The boss could rig tax assessments for property owners and provide lucrative franchises for city businessmen. Through the skillful orchestration of rewards, an astute political operator could exert powerful leverage and line up support for his party from a broad range of constituents, from the urban poor to wealthy industrialists. In 1902, when journalist Lincoln Steffens began "The Shame of the Cities," a series of articles exposing city corruption, he found that business leaders who fastidiously refused to mingle socially with the bosses nevertheless struck deals with them. "He is a self-righteous fraud, this big businessman," Steffens concluded. "I found him buying boodlers [bribers] in St. Louis, defending grafters in Minneapolis, originating corruption in Pittsburgh, sharing with bosses in Philadelphia, deploring reform in Chicago, and beating good government with corruption funds in New York."

The complexity of big-city government, apparent in the many levels of corruption that Steffens uncovered, pointed to one conclusion: For all the color and flamboyance of the big-city boss, he was simply one of many actors in the drama of municipal government. The successful boss was not an autocratic ruler but a power broker. Old-stock aristocrats, new professionals, saloonkeepers, pushcart peddlers, and politicians all fought for their interests in the hurly-burly of city government. They didn't much like each other, and they sometimes fought savagely. But they learned to live with one another. Compromise and accommodation—not boss rule—best characterized big-city government by the turn of the twentieth century, although the cities' reputation for corruption left an indelible mark on the consciousness of the American public.

White City or City of Sin?

Americans in the late nineteenth century, like Americans today, were of two minds about the city. They liked to boast of its skyscrapers and bridges, its culture and sophistication, and they prided themselves on its bigness and bustle. At the same time they feared it as the city of sin, the home of immigrant slums, the center of vice and crime. Nowhere did the divided view of the American city take form more graphically than in Chicago in 1893.

In that year Chicago hosted the Columbian Exposition, the grandest world's fair in the nation's history. The fairground, called the White City and built on the shores of Lake Michigan to honor the four hundredth anniversary of Columbus's first voyage to America, offered a lesson in what Americans on the eve of the twentieth century imagined a city might be. Only five miles down the shore from Chicago, the White City seemed light-years away. Its very name celebrated a harmony, a uniformity, and a pristine beauty unknown in Chicago, with its stockyards, slums, and bustling terminals. Frederick Law Olmsted and architect Daniel Burnham supervised the transformation of a swampy wasteland into a paradise of lagoons, fountains, wooded islands, gardens, and imposing buildings. "Here," wrote the novelist Theodore Dreiser, "hungry men, raw from the shops and fields, idylls and romances in their minds, builded them an empire crying glory in the mud."

"Sell the cookstove and come," the novelist Hamlin Garland wrote to his parents on the farm. And come they did, in spite of the panic and depression that broke out only weeks after the fair opened in May 1893. In six months fairgoers purchased more than 27 million tickets, turning a profit of nearly a half million dollars for promoters. Visitors from home and abroad strolled the elaborate grounds, visited the exhibits—everything from a model of the Brooklyn Bridge carved in soap to the latest goods and inventions. (See "Beyond America's Borders," page 702.) A Denver attorney wrote home, "I am dazzled, captivated and bewildered, and return to my room, tired in mind, eyes, ears and body, so much to think about, so much to entice you on from place to place, until your knees clatter and you fall into a chair completely exhausted." Half carnival, half culture, the great fair offered something for everyone. On the Midway Plaisance, crowds thrilled to the massive wheel built by Mr. Ferris and watched agog as Little Egypt danced the hootchy-kootchy.

In October the fair closed its doors in the midst of the worst depression the country had yet seen. During the winter of 1894, Chicago's unemployed and homeless took over the grounds, vandalized the buildings, and frightened the city's comfortable citizens out of their wits. When reporters asked Daniel Burnham what should be done with the moldering remains of the White City, he responded, "It should be torched." And it was. In July 1894, in a clash between federal troops and striking railway workers, incendiaries set fire and leveled the fairgrounds.

In the end, the White City remained what it had always been, a dreamscape. Buildings that looked like marble were actually constructed of staff, a plaster of paris substance that began to crumble even before fire destroyed the fairgrounds. The White City was a fantasy never destined to last. Perhaps it was not so strange, after all, that the legacy of the White City could be found on Coney Island, where two new amusement parks, Luna and Dreamland, sought to combine, albeit in a more tawdry form, the beauty of the White City and the thrill of the Midway Plaisance. More enduring than the White City itself was what it represented—the emergent industrial might of the United States with its inventions, manufactured goods, and growing **consumer culture**.

Chicago's White City, 1894

This painting by H. D. Nichols captures the monumental architecture of the White City built for the World's Columbian Exposition in 1893. The picture shows the Court of Honor viewed from the balcony of the Administration building, with Frederick MacMonnies's fountain featuring Columbus at the prow of his ship in the foreground. To the left is the huge Manufactures and Liberal Arts building, at over one million square feet the largest building in the world. To the right stands the Agriculture building. In the distance Daniel Chester French's 60-foot gilded statue *Republic* raises her arms in front of the the columned Peristyle. Monumental, harmonious, and pristine, the White City was designed by its creators, John Burnham and Frederick Law Olmsted, to awe and overwhelm fairgoers. And so it did, drawing millions of visitors from America and abroad who eagerly snapped up souvenirs to commemorate their visit.

Chicago Historical Society.

The World's Columbian Exposition and Nineteenth-Century World's Fairs

Dedicated as much to commerce as to culture, the 1893 World's Columbian Exposition in Chicago and the other great world's fairs of the nineteenth century represented a unique phenomenon of industrial capitalism and a testament to the expanding global market economy. The Chicago fair, named to celebrate the four hundredth anniversary of Columbus's arrival in the New World, offered a cornucopia of international exhibits testifying to growing international influences ranging from cultural to technological exchange. Such a celebration of global commerce and influence seemed an appropriate way to honor Columbus, whose voyage in 1492 initiated one of the world's most significant international exchanges.

Beginning with London's Great Exhibition in 1851 with its famous Crystal Palace and continuing through the age of Western commercial and cultural expansion in the late nineteenth century, international exhibitions proliferated and flourished. By the time Chicago secured the right to host its celebration, world's fairs had evolved into monumental extravaganzas that showcased the products of the host country and city along with impressive international displays. Great cities vied to play host to world's fairs, as much to promote

commercial growth as to demonstrate their cultural refinement. Each successive fair sought to outdo its predecessor. Chicago's fair followed upon the great success of the 1889 Universal Exposition in Paris commissioned to celebrate the hundredth anniversary of the French Revolution. The Paris Exposition featured as its crowning glory the 900-foot steel tower constructed by Alexander Gustav Eiffel. What could Chicago, a prairie upstart, do to top that?

The answer was the creation of the White City with its monumental architecture, landscaped grounds, and first Ferris wheel. Itself a tribute to the international style of architecture, the White City celebrated the classicism of the French Beaux Arts school, which borrowed heavily from the massive geometric styling and elaborate detailing of Greek and Renaissance architecture. With the exception of Louis Sullivan's Transportation Building, nothing hinted of the clean and simple lines of indigenous American design soon to be celebrated with the advent of Frank Lloyd Wright.

Beneath its Renaissance façade, the White City acted as an enormous emporium dedicated to the unabashed materialism of the Gilded Age. Participants from more than 100 states, territories, countries, and

colonies, as well as thousands of concessionaires—from small businesses to the largest corporations—mounted exhibits to demonstrate their wares and compete for international attention. Fairgoers could view virtually every kind of manufactured product in the world inside the imposing Manufactures and Liberal Arts Building: Swiss glassware and clocks, Japanese laquerware and bamboo ornaments, British woolen products, and French perfumes and linens. The German pavilion included fine wooden furniture as well as tapestries, porcelain, and jewelry belonging to the ruling family. As suited an industrial age, manufactured products and heavy machinery received privileged status, drawing the largest crowds. Displays introduced visitors to the latest mechanical and technological innovations, many the result of international influences. For five cents, fairgoers could put two hard rubber tubes into their ears and listen for the first time to a Gramophone playing the popular tune "The Cat Came Back." The Gramophone, which signaled the beginning of the recorded music industry, was itself the work of a German immigrant, Emile Berliner (although Thomas Edison later claimed credit for a similar invention, calling it the phonograph).

Such international influences were evident throughout the Columbian Exposition. At the Tiffany pavilion, one of the most popular venues at the fair, visitors oohed and aahed over the display of lamps, ornamental metalwork, and fine jewelry that Louis Comfort Tiffany credited to the influence of Japanese art forms. Juxtaposed with Tiffany's finery stood a display of firearms in the Colt gallery. Colt had been an international company since

"All Nations Are Welcome"

Uncle Sam, flanked by the city of Chicago, welcomes representatives carrying the flags of many nations to the World's Columbian Exposition in 1893. In the background are the fairgrounds on the shores of Lake Michigan. Over one hundred nations participated in the fair by sending exhibits and mounting pavilions to showcase their cultures and products. Chicago Historical Society.

1851 when it opened a factory in England. The company's revolvers enjoyed an international reputation—the best-known firearms not only in America but in Canada, Mexico, and many Europen countries. And Colt's new automatic weapon, the machine gun, would soon play a major role on the world stage in both the Boxer uprising in China and the Spanish-American War.

All manner of foodstuffs—teas from India, Irish whiskey, and pastries and other confectionery from Germany and France—tempted fairgoers. American food products like Shredded Wheat, Aunt Jemima syrup, and Juicy Fruit gum debuted at the fair, where they competed for ribbons. Winners like Pabst "Blue Ribbon" Beer used the award in advertisements. And the fair introduced two new foods—carbonated soda and the hamburger—destined to become America's best-known contributions to international cuisine.

The Columbian Exposition also served as a testimony to American technological achievement and progress. By displaying technology in action, the White City tamed it and made it accessible to American and world consumers. The fair helped develop positive reactions to new technology, particularly electric light and power. With 90,000 electric lights, 5,100 arc lamps, electric fountains, an electric elevated railroad, and electric launches plying the lagoons, the White City provided a glowing advertisement for electricity. Indeed, an entire building was devoted to it. In the Electricity Building fairgoers visited the Bell Telephone Company exhibit, marveled at General Electric's huge dynamo (electric generator), and gazed into the future at the all-electric home and model demonstration kitchen.

Consumer culture received its first major expression and celebration at the Columbian Exposition. Not only did this world's fair anticipate the mass marketing, packaging, and advertising of the twentieth century, the vast array of products on display cultivated the urge to consume. Thousands of concessionaires with products for sale sent a message that tied enjoyment inextricably to spending money and purchasing goods, both domestic and foreign. The Columbian Exposition set a pattern for the twentieth-century world's fairs that followed it, making a powerful statement about the possibilities of urban life in an industrial age and encouraging the rise of a new middle class consumer culture. As G. Brown Goode, head of the Smithsonian Institution in 1893, observed, the Columbian Exposition was in many ways "an illustrated encyclopedia of civilization."

BIBLIOGRAPHY

Reid Badger, *The Great American Fair: The World's Columbian Exposition and American Culture* (1979).

Julie K. Brown, *Contesting Images: Photography and the World's Columbian Exposition* (1994).

Carolyn Kinder Carr and George Gurney, organizers, *Revisiting the White City: American Art at the 1893 World's Fair* (1993).

Dennis B. Downey, *A Season of Renewal: The Columbian Exposition and Victorian America* (2002).

Neil Harris, *Cultural Excursions: Marketing Appetites and Cultural Tastes in Modern America* (1990).

Robert W. Rydell, *All the World's a Fair: Visions of Empire at American International Expositions, 1876–1916* (1984).

Conclusion: Who Built the Cities?

As much as the great industrialists and financiers, as much as eminent engineers like John and Washington Roebling, common workers, most of them immigrants, built the nation's cities. The unprecedented growth of urban, industrial America resulted from the labor of millions of men, women, and children who toiled in workshops and factories, in sweatshops and mines, on the railroads and construction sites across America.

It is no coincidence that in urban America mass transportation and the development of the skyscraper transformed the cityscape at the same time that millions of new immigrants arrived on the shores. Not all immigrants worked as common laborers, but the "human machines" who laid the groundwork for the great cities with pick and shovel came disproportionately from among the immigrants—first the Irish, later Italians and eastern Europeans.

America's cities in the late nineteenth century teemed with life. Immigrants and blue bloods, poor laborers and millionaires, middle class managers and corporate moguls, secretaries, salesgirls, sweatshop laborers, and society matrons lived in the cities and contributed to their growth. Townhouses, tenements, and new apartment buildings jostled for space with skyscrapers and great department stores, while parks, ball fields, amusement arcades, and public libraries provided the city masses with recreation and entertainment.

Municipal governments, straining to build the new cities, experienced the rough-and-tumble of machine politics as bosses and their constituents looked to profit from city growth. Reformers deplored the graft and corruption that accompanied the rise of the cities. But they were rarely able to oust the party bosses for long because they failed to understand the services the political machines provided for their largely immigrant and poor constituents as well as the ties between the politicians and wealthy businessmen who sought to benefit from franchises and contracts.

For America's workers, urban industrialism along with the rise of big business and corporate consolidation drastically changed the workplace. Industrialists replaced skilled workers with new machinery that could be operated by cheaper, unskilled labor. And during hard times employers did not hesitate to cut workers' already meager wages. As the Great Railroad Srike of 1877 demonstrated, when labor united it could bring the nation to attention. Organization offered the best hope for the working man, and unions—first the Knights of Labor and later the American Federation of Labor—won converts among the nation's workers.

The rise of urban industrialism challenged the American promise, which for decades had been dominated by Jeffersonian agrarian ideals. Could such a promise exist in the changing world of cities, tenements, immigrants, and huge corporations? In the great depression that came in the 1890s, mounting anger and frustration would lead workers and farmers to join forces and create a grassroots movement to fight for change under the banner of a new People's Party.

FOR ADDITIONAL FIRSTHAND ACCOUNTS OF THIS PERIOD, see Chapter 19 in Michael Johnson, ed., *Reading the American Past*, Third Edition.

TO ASSESS YOUR MASTERY OF THE MATERIAL IN THIS CHAPTER, see the Online Study Guide at bedfordstmartins.com/roark.

FOR WEB LINKS RELATED TO TOPICS IN THIS CHAPTER, see "HistoryLinks," "DocLinks," and "PlaceLinks" at bedfordstmartins.com/roark.

CHRONOLOGY

1869
- Uriah Stephens founds Knights of Labor.
- Cincinnati mounts first paid baseball team, the Red Stockings.

1871
- Political boss William Marcy Tweed's rule in New York ends.
- Fire ravages Chicago and leads to architectural innovation.

1872
- Andrew Carnegie opens steelworks outside Pittsburgh.

1873
- Panic on Wall Street touches off depression.
- San Francisco's cable car system opens.

1877
- Great Railroad Strike paralyzes nation and inspires workers to join unions.

1878
- Knights of Labor campaigns to organize workers regardless of skill, sex, or race.

1880s
- Immigration patterns shift as more people arrive from southern and eastern Europe.

1881
- Samuel Gompers founds Organized Trades and Labor Unions to organize skilled craftsworkers.

1882
- Chinese Exclusion Act bars immigration of Chinese to United States.

1883
- Brooklyn Bridge opens.
- Mrs. William K. Vanderbilt throws a $4 million party.

1886
- Gomper's Organized Trades and Labor Unions reorganizes as American Federation of Labor (AFL).

- Statue of Liberty, a gift from France, dedicated in New York harbor.

- Massive rally in support of eight-hour workday takes place in Chicago; Haymarket bombing three days later raises fear of anarchy and deals a blow to labor movement.
- Montgomery, Alabama, completes nation's first electric streetcar system.

1890s
- First wave of African American migration from the South begins.

1890
- Jacob Riis publishes *How the Other Half Lives*.
- Average male worker earns $500 per year.

1893
- Columbian Exposition opens in Chicago.
- Panic on Wall Street touches off major economic depression.

1895
- Boston Public Library opens under the slogan "Free to All."

1896
- Congress passes literacy test for immigrants; President Grover Cleveland vetoes it.

1897
- Steeplechase amusement park opens on Coney Island.
- Nation's first subway system opens in Boston.

1900
- Ellis Island in New York harbor opens to process newly arrived immigrants.
- Three cities—New York, Chicago, and Philadelphia—top 1 million inhabitants.

BIBLIOGRAPHY

General

William Cronin, *Nature's Metropolis: Chicago and the Great West* (1991).

Allan Dawley, *Struggles for Justice: Social Responsibility and the Liberal State* (1991).

David Montgomery, *The Fall of the House of Labor: The Workplace, the State, and American Labor Activism, 1865–1925* (1987).

Nell Irvin Painter, *Standing at Armageddon: The United States, 1877–1919* (1984).

The Rise of the City

Gunther Barth, *City People: The Rise of Modern City Culture in Nineteenth-Century America* (1980).

Edwin G. Burrows and Mike Wallace, *Gotham: A History of New York City to 1898* (1999).

Sarah Deutsch, *Women and the City: Gender, Space, and Power in Boston, 1870–1940* (2000).

David C. Hammack, *Power and Society: Greater New York at the Turn of the Century* (1982).

Donald L. Miller, *City of the Century: The Epic of Chicago and the Making of America* (1996).

Raymond A. Mohl, *The New City: Urban America in the Industrial Age, 1860–1920* (1985).

Eric H. Monkkonen, *America Becomes Urban* (1988).

Immigrants

Glenn C. Altschuler, *Race, Ethnicity, and Class in American Social Thought, 1865–1919* (1982).

John Bodnar, *The Transplanted: A History of Immigration in Urban America* (1985).

Roger Daniels, *Coming to America: A History of Immigration and Ethnicity in American Life* (1991).

Hasia R. Diner, *Lower East Side Memories: A Jewish Place in America* (2000).

Leonard Dinnerstein and David M. Reimers, *Ethnic Americans: A History of Immigration* (1999).

Donna Gabaccia, *From the Other Side: Women, Gender, and Immigrant Life in the U.S., 1820–1990* (1994).

William D. Griffin, *The Book of Irish Americans* (1990).

John Higham, *Send These to Me: Jews and Other Immigrants in Urban America* (1975).

Matthew Frye Jacobson, *Whiteness of a Different Color: European Immigrants and the Alchemy of Race* (1998).

Alan M. Kraut, *The Huddled Masses: The Immigrant in American Society, 1880–1921* (1982).

Gwendolyn Mink, *Old Labor and New Immigrants in American Political Development* (1986).

Humbert S. Nelli, *The Italians in Chicago, 1860–1920* (1970).

Thomas M. Pitkin, *Keepers of the Gate: A History of Ellis Island* (1975).

David M. Reimers, *Unwelcome Strangers* (1998).

Ronald Takaki, *Strangers from a Different Shore: A History of Asian Americans* (1998).

Mark Wyman, *Round-Trip to America: The Immigrants Return to Europe, 1880–1930* (1993).

Work and Workers

Karen Anderson, *Changing Woman: A History of Racial Ethnic Women in America* (1996).

Eric Arnesen, *Waterfront Workers in New Orleans: Race, Class, and Politics, 1863–1923* (1991).

Cindy Sondik Aron, *Ladies and Gentlemen of the Civil Service: Middle Class Workers in Victorian America* (1987).

James R. Barrett, *Work and Community in the Jungle: Chicago's Packinghouse Workers, 1894–1922* (1987).

Henry F. Bedford, ed., *Their Lives and Numbers: The Condition of Working People in Massachusetts, 1870–1900* (1995).

Susan Porter Benson, *Counter Cultures: Saleswomen, Managers, and Customers in American Department Stores, 1890–1940* (1986).

Mary H. Blewett, *Men, Women, and Work: Class, Gender, and Protest in the New England Shoe Industry, 1870–1910* (1988).

John Bodnar, *Workers' World* (1982).

Paul Boyer, *Urban Masses and Moral Order in America, 1820–1920* (1978).

Patricia A. Cooper, *Once a Cigar Maker: Men, Women, and Work Culture in American Cigar Factories* (1987).

Margery W. Davies, *Woman's Place Is at the Typewriter: Office Work and Office Workers, 1870–1930* (1982).

Faye E. Dudden, *Serving Women: Household Service in Nineteenth-Century America* (1983).

Nan Enstad, *Ladies of Labor, Girls of Adventure: Working Women, Popular Culture, and Labor Politics at the Turn of the Twentieth Century* (1999).

Philip S. Foner, *Women and the American Labor Movement: From the First Trade Unions to the Present* (1979).

Michael H. Frisch and Daniel J. Walkowitz, eds., *Working-Class America: Essays on Labor, Community, and American Society* (1983).

David M. Gordon, Richard Edwards, and Michael Reich, eds., *Segmented Work, Divided Workers: The Historical Transformation of Labor in the United States* (1982).

Herbert C. Gutman, *Work, Culture, and Society in Industrializing America: Essays in American Working-Class and Social History* (1976).

William H. Harris, *The Harder We Run: Black Workers since the Civil War* (1982).

Jacqueline Jones, *Labor of Love, Labor of Sorrow: Black Women, Work, and the Family from Slavery to the Present* (1985).

Jacqueline Jones, *The Dispossessed: America's Underclasses from the Civil War to the Present* (1992).

Jacqueline Jones, *American Work: Four Centuries of Black and White Labor* (1998).

David M. Katzman, *Seven Days a Week: Women and Domestic Service in Industrializing America* (1978).

David M. Katzman and William M. Tuttle Jr., eds., *Plain Folk: The Life Stories of Undistinguished Americans* (1982).

Alice Kessler-Harris, *Out to Work: The History of Wage-Earning Women in the United States* (1982).

Alexander Keyssar, *Out of Work* (1986).

S. J. Kleinberg, *The Shadow of the Mills: Workingclass Families in Pittsburgh, 1870–1907* (1989).

A. T. Lane, *Solidarity or Survival? American Labor and European Immigrants, 1830–1924* (1987).

Susan Levine, *Labor's True Women: Carpet Weavers, Industrialization, and Labor Reform in the Gilded Age* (1984).

Julie A. Matthaei, *An Economic History of Women in America: Women's Work, the Sexual Division of Labor, and the Development of Capitalism* (1982).

Joanne J. Meyerowitz, *Women Adrift: Independent Wage Earners in Chicago, 1880–1930* (1988).

Ruth Milkman, ed., *Women, Work, and Protest: A Century of U.S. Women's Labor History* (1985).

Daniel Nelson, *Farm and Factory: Workers in the Midwest, 1880–1900* (1995).

Marilyn D. Rhinehart, *A Way of Work and a Way of Life* (1992).

Richard B. Rice, William A. Bullough, and Richard J. Orsi, *The Elusive Eden: A New History of California* (1988).

Roy Rosenzweig, *Eight Hours for What We Will: Workers and Leisure in an Industrial City, 1870–1920* (1983).

Leon Stein and Philip Taft, eds., *Workers Speak* (1971).

Dorothy Sterling, ed., *We Are Your Sisters: Black Women in the Nineteenth Century* (1984).

Sharon Hartman Strom, *Beyond the Typewriter: Gender, Class, and the Origins of Modern American Office Work, 1900–1930* (1992).

Leslie Woodcock Tentler, *Wage-Earning Women: Industrial Work and Family Life in the United States, 1900–1930* (1979).

Carole Turbin, *Working Women of Collar City: Gender, Class, and Community in Troy, New York, 1864–1886* (1992).

Jules Tygiel, *Workingmen in San Francisco, 1880–1901* (1992).

Viviana A. Zelizer, *Pricing the Priceless Child: The Changing Social Value of Children* (1985).

The Labor Movement

Paul Avrich, *The Haymarket Tragedy* (1984).

Robert V. Bruce, *1877: Year of Violence* (1959).

Paul Buhle, *From the Knights of Labor to the New World Order: Essays on Labor and Culture* (1997).

Henry David, *The History of the Haymarket Affair* (1963).

Leon Fink, *Workingman's Democracy: The Knights of Labor and American Politics* (1983).

Philip S. Foner, *The Great Labor Uprising of 1877* (1977).

William E. Forbath, *Law and the Shaping of the American Labor Movement* (1991).

Stuart B. Kaufman, *Samuel Gompers and the Origins of the American Federation of Labor* (1973).

John Laslett, *Labor and the Left: A Study of Socialist and Radical Influences in the American Labor Movement, 1881–1924* (1970).

Harold Livesay, *Samuel Gompers and Organized Labor in America* (1978).

David O. Stowell, *Streets, Railroads, and the Great Strike of 1877* (1999).

Christopher L. Tomlins, *The State and the Unions: Labor Relations, Law, and the Organized Labor Movement in America, 1880–1960* (1985).

Robert Weil, *Beyond Labor's Veil: The Culture of the Knights of Labor* (1996).

Robert E. Weir, *Knights Unhorsed: Internal Conflict in a Gilded Age Social Movement* (2000).

Home and Leisure

Judith Adams, *The American Amusement Park Industry: A History of Technology and Thrills* (1991).

David T. Courtwright, *Violent Land: Single Men and Social Disorder from the Frontier to the Inner City* (1996).

Lewis A. Erenberg, *Steppin' Out: New York Nightlife and the Transformation of American Culture, 1890–1930* (1981).

Michael Kammen, *American Culture, American Tastes* (1999).

John Kasson, *Amusing the Million: Coney Island at the Turn of the Century* (1978).

William Leach, *Land of Desire: Merchants, Power, and the Rise of a New American Culture* (1993).

David Nasaw, *Going Out: The Rise and Fall of Public Amusements* (1993).

Kathryn J. Oberdeck, *The Evangelist and the Impresario: Religion, Entertainment, and Cultural Politics in America, 1884–1914* (1999).

Kathy Peiss, *Cheap Amusements: Working Women and Leisure in Turn-of-the-Century New York* (1986).

Ellen M. Plante, *Women at Home in Victorian America: A Social History* (1997).

Steven Pope, *Patriotic Games: Sporting Traditions in the American Imagination, 1876–1926* (1996).

Benjamin G. Rader, *Baseball: A History of America's Game* (2002).

Thomas J. Schlereth, *Victorian America: Transformations in Everyday Life, 1876–1915* (1992).

Daphne Spain, *Gendered Spaces* (1992).

Daniel E. Sutherland, *The Expansion of Everyday Life, 1860–1876* (1989).

Jules Tygiel, *Past Time: Baseball as History* (2000).

City Building and City Government

Reid Badger, *The Great American Fair: The World's Columbian Exposition and American Culture* (1979).

Charles W. Cheape, *Moving the Masses: Urban Public Transport in New York, Boston, and Philadelphia, 1880–1912* (1980).

Elizabeth Collins Cromley, *Alone Together: A History of New York's Early Apartments* (1990).

Mona Domosh, *Invented Cities: The Creation of Landscape in Nineteenth-Century New York and Boston* (1996).

Dennis B. Downey, *A Season of Renewal: The Columbian Exposition and Victorian America* (2002).

Elizabeth Hawes, *New York, New York: How the Apartment House Transformed Life in the City, 1869–1930* (1993).

Melvin G. Holli, *The American Mayor* (1999).

Erik Larson, *The Devil in the White City: Murder, Magic, and Madness at the Fair That Changed America* (2003).

David E. Nye, *Electrifying America: Social Meanings of a New Technology, 1880–1940* (1990).

Henry Petroski, *Engineers of Dreams* (1994).

Harold L. Platt, *The Electric City: Energy and Growth of the Chicago Area, 1880–1930* (1991).

Roy Rosenzweig and Elizabeth Blackmar, *The Park and the People: A History of Central Park* (1992).

Witold Rybczynski, *A Clearing in the Distance: Frederick Law Olmsted and America in the Nineteenth Century* (1999).

Robert W. Rydell, *All the World's a Fair: Visions of Empire at American International Expositions, 1876–1916* (1984).

Luc Sante, *Low Life: Lures and Snares of Old New York* (1991).

Carl Smith, *Urban Disorder and the Shape of Belief* (1995).

John R. Stilgoe, *Borderland: Origins of the American Suburb, 1820–1939* (1988).

Jon C. Teaford, *City and Suburb: The Political Fragmentation of Metropolitan America, 1850–1970* (1979).

John Emerson Todd, *Frederick Law Olmsted* (1982).

David B. Tyack, *The One Best System: A History of American Urban Education* (1974).

Oliver Zunz, *The Changing Face of Inequality* (1982).

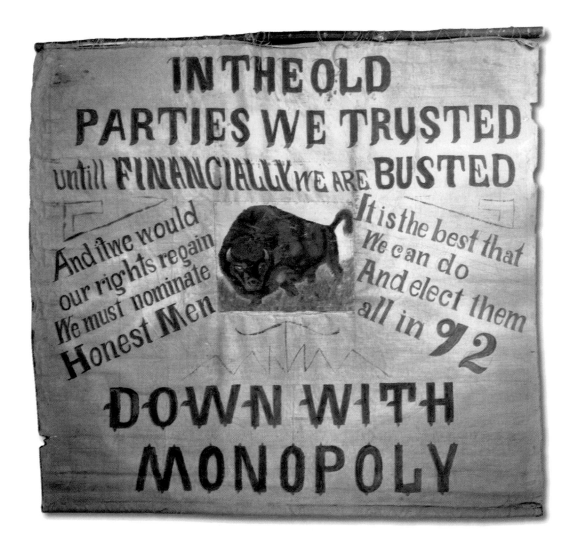

BUFFALO BANNER FROM THE 1892 POPULIST CONVENTION
This flag graphically declares the frustration with the Democratic and Republican parties that led angry Americans, particularly farmers, to gather in St. Louis in 1892 to create a new People's Party. Featuring the buffalo (American bison) as a symbol, the flag urged the election of "honest men" and proclaimed as its motto "Down with Monopoly." The buffalo was perhaps a poor choice as a mascot, for just as the great herds on the western plains had been decimated during the 1880s, the People's (or Populist) Party would not survive the '90s.
Nebraska State Historical Society.

Dissent, Depression, and War

1890–1900

S

T. LOUIS IN FEBRUARY 1892 played host to one of the most striking political gatherings of the century. Thousands of farmers, laborers, reformers, and common people flocked to Missouri to attend a meeting, in the words of one reporter, "different from any other political meeting ever witnessed in St. Louis." The cigar-smoking politicians who generally worked the convention circuit were nowhere to be found. In their place "mostly grayhaired, sunburned and roughly clothed men" assembled under a banner that proclaimed, "We do not ask for sympathy or pity. We ask for justice."

Exposition Music Hall presented a colorful spectacle. "The banners of the different states rose above the delegates throughout the hall, fluttering like the flags over an army encamped," wrote one reporter. Ignatius Donnelly, a fiery orator, attacked the money kings of Wall Street. Mary Elizabeth Lease, a veteran campaigner from Kansas known for exhorting farmers to "raise less corn and more hell," added her powerful voice to the cause. Terence V. Powderly, head of the Knights of Labor, called on workers to join hands with farmers against the "nonproducing classes." And Frances Willard of the Woman's Christian Temperance Union argued against liquor and for woman **suffrage**. Between speeches the crowd sang labor songs like "Hurrah for the Toiler" and "All Hail the Power of Laboring Men."

In the course of the next few days, delegates hammered out a series of demands, breathtaking in their scope. They tackled the tough questions of the day—the regulation of business, the need for banking and currency reform, the right of labor to organize and bargain collectively, and the role of the federal government in regulating business, curbing **monopoly**, and guaranteeing **democracy**. The convention ended its work amid a chorus of cheers. According to one eyewitness,

> Hats, paper, handkerchiefs, etc., were thrown into the air; wraps, umbrellas and parasols waved; cheer after cheer thundered and reverberated through the vast hall reaching the outside of the building where thousands who had been waiting the outcome joined in the applause till for blocks in every direction the exultation made the din indescribable.

What was all the shouting about? People were building a new political party, officially named the People's Party. Dissatisfied with the Democrats and Republicans, a broad coalition of groups came together in St. Louis to fight for change. They determined to reconvene in Omaha in July to nominate candidates for the upcoming presidential election.

People's Party 1892 Convention Ribbon

The People's Party standard-bearer, General James B. Weaver, and his running mate are pictured on a ribbon promising "HOMES FOR THE TOILERS" and "EQUAL RIGHTS TO ALL, SPECIAL PRIVILEGES TO NONE." Populist issues are clearly proclaimed—"MONEY, LAND, AND TRANSPORTATION." The Populists' hope that these economic issues would replace sectional loyalties is evident in the symbolism of the blue Union and gray Confederate hands shaking.

Collection of Janice L. and David J. Frent.

The St. Louis gathering marked a milestone in one of the most turbulent decades in U.S. history. Unrest, agitation, agrarian revolt, labor strikes, a severe financial panic and depression, and a war of expansion shook the 1890s. While the two major political parties continued to do business as usual, Americans flocked to organizations like the Farmers' Alliance, the American Federation of Labor, and the Woman's Christian Temperance Union, and they worked together to create the political alliance that gave rise to the People's (or **Populist**) Party. In a decade of unrest and uncertainty, the People's Party challenged **laissez-faire** economics by insisting that the federal government play a more active role to ensure greater economic equity in industrial America. This challenge to the status quo culminated in 1896 in one of the most hotly contested presidential elections in the nation's history. At the close of the tumultuous decade, the Spanish-American War helped to bring the country together as Americans rallied to support the troops. But disagreement over American **imperialism** and expansion raised questions about the nation's role on the world stage as the United States stood poised to enter the twentieth century.

Nebraska Farm Family

A Nebraska farm family poses in front of their sod house. Their shriveled corn testifies to the drought conditions they faced. Drought and falling crop prices devastated farmers in the 1880s. Midwestern farmers lost their land to bank foreclosure when they could not make mortgage payments. By 1894 nearly half the farms in Kansas had been foreclosed. Many farmers retreated from the plains in covered wagons carrying the slogan, "In God we Trusted, In Kansas we Busted." Growing discontent among farmers in the Midwest and the South led to the growth of the Farmers' Alliance in the 1880s and the People's Party in the 1890s.

Nebraska State Historical Society.

The Farmers' Revolt

Farmers counted themselves among the most disaffected Americans, and hard times in the 1880s created a groundswell of agrarian revolt. Farmers in all regions of the country saw themselves as victims of rules, such as the **gold standard** and the protective tariff, that worked to the advantage of big business. Across the United States angry farmers raised a chorus of protest and in the process created new political alliances.

The Farmers' Alliance

Farm prices fell decade after decade. Wheat that sold for a dollar a bushel in 1870 dropped to sixty cents in the 1890s. Cotton plummeted from fifteen cents to five cents a pound. Corn started at forty-five cents and fell to thirty cents a bushel by the 1890s. At the same time, consumer prices soared (Figure 20.1). By 1894, in Kansas alone almost half the farms had fallen into the hands of the banks because poor farmers could not make enough money to pay their mortgages.

In the West, farmers rankled under a system that allowed railroads to charge them exorbitant freight rates while granting rebates to large shippers (see chapter 17). Also, the railroads' policy of charging higher rates for short hauls than for long hauls meant that large grain elevator companies could ship their wheat from Chicago to New York and across the ocean to England for less money than it cost a Dakota farmer to send his crop to mills in nearby Minneapolis. In the South, lack of currency and credit drove farmers to the stopgap credit system of the crop lien: In order to pay for seed and supplies, farmers pledged their crops to local creditors (furnishing merchants). All together, the southern states had less money in circulation than the state of Massachusetts. At the heart of the problem stood a banking system dominated by eastern commercial banks committed to the gold standard, a railroad rate system capricious and unfair, and rampant speculation that drove up the price of land.

Farm protest was not new. In the 1870s, farmers supported the Grange and the Greenback Labor Party. And as the farmers' situation grew more desperate, the 1880s witnessed spontaneous outbreaks as farmers organized into regional alliances. The Farmers' Alliance movement had begun when a group of farmers gathered at a Lampasas County farm in Texas and banded together to fight "landsharks and horse

thieves." During the 1880s the movement spread rapidly. In **frontier** farmhouses in Texas, in log cabins in backwoods Arkansas, in the rural parishes of Louisiana, separate groups of farmers formed similar alliances for self-help.

As the movement grew, farmers' groups consolidated into two regional alliances: The Northwestern Farmers' Alliance was active in Kansas, Nebraska, and other midwestern Granger states. The more radical Southern Farmers' Alliance, which got its start in Texas, soon spread to Georgia, Louisiana, and Arkansas. By 1890, the Southern Alliance counted more than three million members.

Determined to reach black farmers as well as whites, the Southern Alliance worked with the Colored Farmers' Alliance, an African American group founded in Texas in the 1880s. Richard Manning Humphrey, a white Baptist minister, served as general superintendent of the organization and traveled through the South organizing black farmers. By 1891, Humphrey claimed a membership of 1.2 million. The Colored Alliance published its own weekly newspaper, raised funds for schools, and provided help for sick and disabled members. Although the Colored Farmers' Alliance did not always agree with the Southern Alliance, blacks and whites attempted

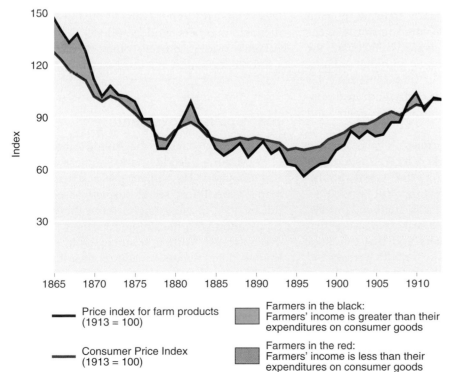

FIGURE 20.1 Consumer Prices and Farm Income, 1865–1910
Around 1870, consumer prices and farm income were about equal. During the 1880s and 1890s, however, farmers suffered great hardships as prices for their crops declined steadily and the cost of consumer goods continued to rise.

The First Farmers' Alliance Flag
In 1878 a "Grand State Farmers' Alliance" formed in Texas as a self-help organization. Growing out of a meeting in Lampasas a year earlier, the group was part of a spontaneous Farmers' Alliance movement that spread rapidly during the 1880s. By 1900 the Alliance boasted over 3 million members in the South alone. This flag commemorates the organization's founding and spells out what the Alliance stood for—"FREE TRADE," "The most good for the most PEOPLE," and "Wisdom, Justice, & Moderation." The last claim many would view skeptically, seeing the Alliance not as a moderate group, but as a force for sweeping change.
Torreyson Library, University of Central Arkansas.

their cotton—that is, selling it together—farmers could negotiate a better price. And by setting up trade stores and exchanges, they sought to escape the grasp of the merchant/creditor. Soon alliances in a dozen states competed to pioneer new purchasing cooperatives. Through the cooperatives, the Farmers' Alliance promised to change the way farmers lived. "We are going to get out of debt and be free and independent people once more," exulted one Georgia farmer. But the Alliance failed in its attempt to replace the southern furnishing merchant with cooperative stores. Opposition by merchants, bankers, wholesalers, and manufacturers made it impossible for the cooperatives to get credit. The Texas exchange survived only one season. Farmers soon realized that the cooperatives stood little chance of working unless fundamental changes were made in the money and credit system of the United States.

As the cooperative movement died, the Farmers' Alliance, which had begun as an organization for self-help, moved toward direct political action. Texas farmers drafted a set of demands in 1886 and pressured political candidates to endorse them. These demands became the basis of a platform proposed by the Southern Alliance in 1890 calling for railroad regulation, laws against land speculation, and currency and credit reform. But it proved easier to get politicians to make promises than to force them to follow through. Confounded by the failure of the Democrats and Republicans to break with commercial interests and support the farmer, Alliance leaders moved, often reluctantly, toward the formation of a third party.

> Although the Colored Farmers' Alliance did not always agree with the Southern Alliance, blacks and whites attempted to make common cause.

to make common cause. As Georgia's Tom Watson, a Southern Alliance stalwart, pointed out, "The colored tenant is in the same boat as the white tenant, the colored laborer with the white laborer, and . . . the accident of color can make no difference in the interests of farmers, croppers, and laborers."

The Farmers' Alliance reached out to workers as well as to farmers. During the Great Southwestern Strike against Jay Gould's Texas and Pacific Railroad in 1886, the Alliance supported the strikers, insisting that farmers, too, were workers and that the labor question was a crucial issue for both farmers and wage laborers. The Southern Farmers' Alliance rushed food and supplies to the strikers and issued a proclamation in support of the Knights of Labor, calling on farmers to boycott Gould's railroad.

At the heart of the Alliance movement stood a series of farmers' cooperatives. By "bulking"

The Populist Movement

In the earliest days of the Alliance movement, C. W. Macune, a leader in the Southern Alliance, had insisted, "The Alliance is a strictly white man's nonpolitical, secret business association." But by 1892, it was none of those things, as its cooperation with the Colored Farmers' Alliance demonstrated. Although some white southern leaders, like Macune, made it clear that they would never threaten the unity of the white vote in the South by leaving the Democratic Party, advocates of a third party carried the day at the convention of laborers, farmers, and common folk in St. Louis in 1892. There, the Farmers' Alliance gave birth to the People's Party and launched the Populist movement.

On the Way to a Populist Meeting in Kansas
Populism was more than a political movement; it was a culture unto itself. For farmers in sparsely settled regions, the movement provided reassurance that they were not alone, that others shared their problems, and that solutions could be found. When the Populists called a meeting, wagons came from miles around, as in this gathering in Dickinson County, Kansas.
Kansas State Historical Society.

The Populists mounted a critique of industrial society and a call for action. Convinced that the money and banking systems worked to the advantage of the wealthy few, they demanded economic democracy. To help farmers get the credit they needed at reasonable rates, southern farmers hit on the ingenious idea of a subtreasury—a plan that would allow farmers to store nonperishable crops in government storehouses until market prices rose. At the same time, borrowing against their crops, farmers would receive commodity credit from the federal government to enable them to buy needed supplies and seed for the coming year. The subtreasury became an article of faith in the South, where it promised to eliminate the crop lien system once and for all. Although the idea would be enacted piecemeal in **progressive** and **New Deal** legislation in the twentieth century, **conservatives** in the 1890s dismissed it as far-fetched and communistic.

For the western farmer, the enemy was not the merchant but the speculator and the railroad.

Populism promised land reform, championing a plan that would reclaim excessive lands granted to railroads or sold to foreign investors. The Populists' boldest proposal called for government ownership of the railroads and telegraph system to put an end to discriminatory rate practices. With the powerful railroads dominating politics and effectively nullifying the Interstate Commerce Act of 1887, Populists did not shrink from advocating what their opponents called state **socialism**.

Money joined transportation and land as the third major focus of the Populist movement. Farmers in all sections rallied to the cry for cheaper currency, endorsing platform planks calling for **free silver** and greenbacks—attempts to increase the nation's tight money supply and thus make credit easier to obtain. Because they

> The Populists mounted a critique of industrial society and a call for action. Convinced that the money and banking systems worked to the advantage of the wealthy few, they demanded economic democracy.

shared common cause with labor against corporate interests, Populists supported the eight-hour workday and an end to contract labor. To empower the common people, the Populist platform called for the direct election of senators and electoral reforms including the secret ballot and the right to initiate legislation, to recall elected officials, and to submit issues to the people by means of a referendum. More than just a response to hard times, Populism presented an alternative vision of American economic democracy. (See "Documenting the American Promise," page 716.)

The Labor Wars

While farmers united to fight for change, industrial laborers fought their own battles in a series of bloody strikes so fiercely waged on both sides that historians have called them the "labor wars." Coal miners struck to fight the use of convict labor in the mines of eastern Tennessee. Miners in Coeur d'Alene, Idaho, battled the bosses and gave rise to the militant Western Federation of Miners (WFM). Railroad switchmen went on strike in Buffalo, New York, and a general strike closed down the port of New Orleans. Industrial workers of all kinds felt increasingly threatened and in the 1890s made their stand. At issue was the right of labor to organize and speak through unions to bargain collectively and fight for better working conditions, higher wages, shorter hours, and greater worker control in the face of increased mechanization.

Three major conflicts of the period, the lockout of steelworkers in Homestead, Pennsylvania, in 1892, the miners' strike in Cripple Creek, Colorado, in 1894, and the Pullman strike in Illinois that same year raised fundamental questions about the rights of labor and the sanctity of private property.

The Homestead Lockout

In 1892, steelworkers in Pennsylvania squared off against Andrew Carnegie in a decisive struggle over the right to organize in the Homestead steel mills. At first glance it seemed ironic that Carnegie became the adversary in the workers' fight for the right to unionize. Andrew Carnegie was unusual among industrialists as a self-styled

friend of labor. In 1886 he had written, "The right of the workingmen to combine and to form trades unions is no less sacred than the right of the manufacturer to enter into associations and conferences with his fellows." Yet six years later at Homestead, Carnegie set out to crush a union in one of labor's legendary confrontations.

As much as he cherished his **liberal** beliefs, Carnegie cherished his profits more. Labor unions had worked to his advantage during the years when he was building his empire. Labor strife at Homestead during the 1870s had enabled Carnegie to buy the plant from his competitors at cost and to take over the steel industry. And during the 1880s, strong national craft unions ensured that competing mills could not undercut his labor costs. But by the 1890s, Carnegie had beat out his competitors, and the only thing standing in the way of his control of the industry was the Amalgamated Association of Iron and Steel Workers, one of the largest and richest of the craft unions that made up the American Federation of Labor (AFL).

In 1892, when the Amalgamated attempted to renew its contract at Carnegie's Homestead mill, its leaders were told that since "the vast majority of our employees are Non union, the Firm has decided that the minority must give place to the majority." While it was true that only 800 skilled workers belonged to the elite Amalgamated, the union had long enjoyed the support of the plant's 3,000 nonunion workers. Slavs, who did much of the unskilled work, made common cause with the Welsh, Scots, and Irish skilled workers who belonged to the union. Never before had the Amalgamated been denied a contract.

As the situation built toward a showdown, Carnegie sailed to Scotland in the spring. No doubt aware of his hypocrisy, he preferred not to be directly involved in the union busting that lay on the horizon. He left Henry Clay Frick, the toughest antilabor man in the industry, in charge of the Homestead plant. By summer, a strike looked inevitable. Frick prepared by erecting a fifteen-foot fence around the plant and topping it with barbed wire. Workers aptly dubbed it "Fort Frick." To defend his fort, Frick hired 316 mercenaries from the Pinkerton Detective Agency at the rate of $5 per day, more than double the wage of the average Homestead worker.

The Pinkerton National Detective Agency, founded before the Civil War, came into its own in the 1880s as businessmen like Frick used Pinkerton agents as a private security force. They

FRANK LESLIE'S
ILLUSTRATED
HOMESTEAD TROUBLES.
WEEKLY

NEW YORK, JULY 14, 1892.

Homestead Workers Attack the Pinkertons

The nation's attention was riveted on labor strife at Homestead in the summer of 1892. *Frank Leslie's Illustrated Weekly* ran a cover story on the violence that Pinkerton agents faced from a crowd of men, women, and children armed with clubs, guns, and ax handles. The workers, who had been locked out by Henry Clay Frick, were enraged that Frick had hired the Pinkertons to bring in strikebreakers. In a standoff with workers, the Pinkertons fired into the crowd, killing three men and wounding scores. A truce was negotiated, but when the Pinkertons came ashore, the crowd could not contain its rage and viciously attacked the hated "Pinks." The illustration shows a boy with a gun in the foreground. Although the mob was armed, none of the Pinkertons were shot as they ran the gantlet. Almost all, however, were beaten. How does the cover illustration portray the crowd? Can you tell whose side the magazine was on?

The New-York Society Library.

young Irishman who led the union, vowed to prevent strikebreakers from entering the plant. On July 6 at four in the morning, a lookout spotted two barges moving up the Monongahela River in the fog. Frick was attempting to smuggle his Pinkertons into Homestead. Workers sounded the alarm, and within minutes a crowd of more than a thousand, hastily armed with rifles, hoes, and fence posts, rushed to the riverbank to meet the enemy. When the Pinkertons attempted to come ashore, gunfire broke out, and more than a dozen Pinkertons and some thirty strikers fell, killed or wounded. The Pinkertons retreated to the barges.

For twelve hours, the workers (joined by their family members) threw everything they had at the barges. Finally, the Pinkertons hoisted a white flag and arranged with O'Donnell to surrender. With three workers dead and scores wounded, the crowd, numbering perhaps 10,000, was in no mood for conciliation. As the hated "Pinks" came up the hill, they were forced to run a gantlet of screaming, cursing men, women, and children. When a young guard dropped to his knees, weeping for mercy, a woman used her umbrella to poke out his eye. One Pinkerton had been killed in the siege on the barges. In the grim rout that followed their surrender, not one avoided injury.

The "battle of Fort Frick" ended in a dubious victory for the workers. They took control of the plant and elected a council to run the community. At first, public opinion favored their cause. Newspapers urged Frick to negotiate or submit to arbitration. A congressman castigated Carnegie for "skulking in his castle in Scotland," and the Populists, meeting in St. Louis, condemned the use of "hireling armies."

But the action of the Homestead workers struck at the heart of the capitalist system, pitting the workers' right to their jobs against the rights of private property. The workers' insistence that "We are not destroying the property of the company—merely protecting our rights" did not prove as compelling to the courts and the state as the rights of private property. Four days after the confrontation, Pennsylvania's governor, who sympathized with the workers, nonetheless yielded to pressure from Frick and ordered 8,000 National Guard troops into Homestead to protect

> The action of the Homestead workers struck at the heart of the capitalist system, pitting the workers' right to their jobs against the rights of private property.

were a motley crew, recruited from all levels of society, from urban thugs to college boys on vacation. The "Pinks" earned the hatred of workers by protecting strikebreakers and acting as company spies.

On June 28, Frick locked the workers out of the mills. They immediately rallied to the support of the Amalgamated. Hugh O'Donnell, the

Voices of Protest

Populists spoke with passion and fire, documenting the plight of farmers, workers, and the nation's dispossessed. Intending to educate as well as to agitate, Populist speakers larded their speeches with statistics, but the speeches were never dull. The sense of a new day dawning when the people would rule brought apocalyptic vision and religious fervor to their rhetoric.

DOCUMENT 1
Mary Elizabeth Lease,
Address to the WCTU, 1890

Populist orator Mary Elizabeth Lease, born in Pennsylvania in 1850, moved to Kansas in 1868, where she became a schoolteacher, studied law, and gained admittance to the bar. Lease spent ten years trying to make a living farming, then gave up and moved with her husband, a pharmacist, to Wichita in 1883. She lent her voice to many causes, including temperance, and spoke in support of the Knights of Labor and the Farmers' Alliance. She earned her greatest fame in the 1890s when she spoke in support of Populist causes. Her charismatic speaking style led Kansas editor William Allen White to observe, "she could recite the multiplication table and set a crowd hooting and harrahing at her will." In a speech given before the WCTU in 1890, Lease explained why women supported the Farmers' Alliance.

. . . You wonder, perhaps, at the zeal and enthusiasm of the Western woman in this reform movement. Let me tell you why they are inter-ested. Turn to your school-maps and books of a quarter of a century ago, and you will find that what is now a teeming and fruitful West was then known as the Treeless Plain, the Great American Desert. To this sterile and remote region, infested by savage beasts and still more savage men, the women of the New England states, the women of the cultured East, came with husbands, sons and brothers to help them build up a home upon the broad and vernal prairies of the West. We came with roses of health on our cheek, the light of hope in our eyes, the fire of youth and hope burning in our hearts. . . . We endured hardships, dangers and privations; hours of loneliness, fear and sorrow; our little babes were born upon these wide, unsheltered prairies; and there, upon the sweeping prairies beneath the cedar trees our hands have planted to mark the sacred place, our little ones lie buried. We toiled in the cabin and in the field; we planted trees and orchards; we helped our loved ones to make the prairie blossom as the rose. The neat cottage took the place of the sod shanty, the log-cabin and the humble dug-out.

Yet, after all our years of toil and privation, dangers and hardships upon the Western frontier, monopoly is taking our homes from us by the infamous system of mortgage foreclosure, the most infamous that has ever disgraced the statutes of a civilized nation. It takes from us at the rate of five hundred a month the homes that represent the best years of our life, our toil, our hopes, our happiness. How did it happen? The government, at the bid of Wall Street, repudiated its contracts with the people; the circulating medium was contracted . . . from $54 per capita to less than $8 per capita; or, . . . as grand Senator [William Morris] Stewart [of Nevada] put it, "For twenty years the market value of the dollar has gone up and the market value of labor has gone down, till to-day the American laborer, in bitterness and wrath, asks which is the worst—the black slavery that has gone or the white slavery that has come?"

Do you wonder the women are joining the [Farmers'] Alliance? I wonder if there is a woman in all the broad land who can afford to stay out of the Alliance. . . .

SOURCE: Joan M. Jensen, *With These Hands: Women Working on the Land* (New York: McGraw-Hill, 1981), 154–60.

DOCUMENT 2
Ignatius Donnelley,
Address to the People's
Party Convention, 1892

An Irish immigrant, Ignatius Donnelley practiced law in Philadelphia before moving to St. Paul in Minnesota Territory in 1856. By turns a liberal Republican and a member of the Greenback Party, Donnelley became a leader in the midwest Populist movement in the 1890s. His hellfire rhetoric earned him the spot as keynote speaker at the Populist convention in St. Louis in 1892, where he delivered a speech (excerpted below), which later became the preamble to the platform of the People's Party.

We meet in the midst of a nation brought to the verge of moral, political, and material ruin. Corruption dominates the ballot-box, the legislatures, the Congress, and touches even the ermine of the bench. The people are demoralized; most of the States have been compelled to isolate the voters at the polling-places to prevent universal intimidation or bribery. The newspapers are largely subsidized or muzzled; public opinion silenced; business prostrated; our homes covered with mortgages; labor impoverished; and the land concentrating in the hands of the capitalists. The urban workmen are denied the right of organization for self-protection, imported pauperized labor beats down their wages; a hireling standing army, unrecognized by our laws, is established to shoot them down, and they are rapidly degenerating into European conditions. The fruits of the toil of millions are boldly stolen to build up colossal fortunes for a few, unprecedented in the history of mankind; and the possessors of these, in turn, despise the republic and endanger liberty. From the same prolific womb of governmental injustice we breed the two great classes—tramps and millionaires. . . .

SOURCE: Norman Pollack, ed., *The Populist Mind* (Indianapolis: Bobbs-Merrill, 1967), 59–60.

DOCUMENT 3
Lorenzo Lewelling,
Inaugural Address, 1893

By turns a schoolteacher, newspaper reporter, and farmer, Lorenzo Lewelling moved to Wichita, Kansas, in 1887 and soon became active in the Farmers' Alliance and later the Populist Party. Elected governor on the People's Party ticket in 1893, he used his inaugural address to attack social Darwinism and define a new role for government as the champion of the people.

The survival of the fittest is the government of brutes and reptiles, and such philosophy must give place to a government which recognizes human brotherhood. It is the province of government to protect the weak, but the government of to-day is resolved into a struggle of the masses with the classes for supremacy and bread, until business, home, and personal integrity are trembling in the face of possible want in the family. Feed a tiger regularly and you tame and make him harmless, but hunger makes tigers of men. If it be true that the poor have no right to the property of the rich let it also be declared that the rich have no right to the property of the poor. . . .

The problem of to-day is how to make the State subservient to the individual, rather than to become his master. . . . What is the State to him who toils, if labor is denied him and his children cry for bread? What is the State to the farmer, who wearily drags himself from dawn till dark to meet the stern necessities of the mortgage on the farm? What is the State to him if it sanctions usury and other legal forms by which his home is destroyed and his innocent ones become a prey to the fiends who lurk in the shadow of civilization? What is the State to the business man, early grown gray, broken in health and spirit by successive failures; anxiety like a bod-ing owl his constant companion by day and the disturber of his dreams by night? How is life to be sustained, how is liberty to be pursued under such adverse conditions as the State permits if it does not sanction? Is the State powerless against these conditions?

This is the generation which has come to the rescue. Those in distress who cry out from the darkness shall not be heard in vain. Conscience is in the saddle. We have leaped the bloody chasm and entered a contest for the protection of home, humanity, and the dignity of labor. . . .

SOURCE: Norman Pollack, ed., *The Populist Mind* (Indianapolis: Bobbs-Merrill, 1967), 51–54.

QUESTIONS FOR ANALYSIS AND DEBATE

1. According to Mary Elizabeth Lease, what accounts for the high rate of foreclosures on Kansas farms?

2. When Ignatius Donnelley refers to "a hireling army, unrecognized by our laws" in his 1892 keynote speech at the St. Louis convention of the People's Party, what current event is he referencing?

3. Kansas governor Lorenzo Lewelling's inaugural address in 1893 states, "If it be true that the poor have no right to the property of the rich let it also be declared that the rich have no right to the property of the poor." What does he mean by the "property of the poor"? What does he want the state to do?

Carnegie's mills. The strikers, thinking they had nothing to fear from the militia, welcomed the troops with a brass band. But they soon understood the reality. The troops' 95-day occupation not only protected Carnegie's property but also enabled Frick to reopen the mills using strikebreakers. "We have been deceived," one worker bitterly complained. "We have stood idly by and let the town be occupied by soldiers who come here, not as our protectors, but as the protectors of non-union men. . . . If we undertake to resist the seizure of our jobs, we will be shot down like dogs."

Then, in a misguided effort to ignite a general uprising, Alexander Berkman, a Russian immigrant and **anarchist**, attempted to assassinate Frick. Berkman bungled his attempt. Shot twice and stabbed with a dagger, Frick survived and showed considerable courage, allowing a doctor to remove the bullets but refusing to leave his desk until the day's work was completed. "I do not think that I shall die," Frick remarked coolly, "but whether I do or not, the Company will pursue the same policy and it will win."

After the assassination attempt, public opinion turned against the workers. Berkman was quickly tried and sentenced to prison. Although the Amalgamated and the AFL denounced his action, the incident linked anarchism and unionism, already associated in the public mind as a result of the Haymarket bombing in 1886 (see chapter 19). Hugh O'Donnell later wrote that "the bullet from Berkman's pistol, failing in its foul intent, went straight through the heart of the Homestead strike."

In the end, the workers capitulated after four and a half months. The Homestead mill reopened in November and the men returned to work, except for the union leaders, now blacklisted in every steel and iron mill in the country. With the owners firmly in charge, the company slashed wages, reinstated the twelve-hour day, and eliminated five hundred jobs.

In the drama of events at Homestead, the significance of what occurred often remained obscured: The workers at Homestead had been taught a lesson. They would never again, in the words of the National Guard commander, "believe the works are their's [sic] quite as much as Carnegie's." Another forty-five years would pass before steelworkers, unskilled as well as skilled, successfully unionized. In the meantime, Carnegie's production tripled, even in the midst of a depression. "Ashamed to tell you profits these days," Carnegie wrote a friend in 1899. And no wonder: Carnegie's profits had grown from $4 million in 1892 to $40 million in 1900.

The Cripple Creek Miners' Strike

Less than a year after the Homestead lockout, a stock market crash on Wall Street in the spring of 1893 touched off a bitter economic depression. In the West, silver mines fell on hard times. Looking for work, many miners left for the goldfields of Cripple Creek, Colorado. There, because of the demand for gold, miners enjoyed relatively high wages—$3 a day. When conservative mine owners moved to lengthen the workday from eight to ten hours, the newly formed Western Federation of Miners (WFM) vowed to hold the line and demanded an eight-hour day. On February 2, 1894, the WFM threatened to strike all mines working more than eight-hour shifts. The mine owners divided. Some held firm for ten hours; others quickly settled with the WFM. Fewer than half of the town's mines stood against the union, provoking a strike.

The striking miners received help from many quarters. Working miners paid $15 a month to a strike fund, and miners in neighboring districts sent substantial contributions. Because so many of the mine owners lived in nearby Colorado Springs, Cripple Creek styled itself a workers' town. The miners enjoyed the support and assistance of local businesses and grocers, who provided credit to the strikers. With these advantages, the Cripple Creek strikers could afford to hold out for their demands.

Even more significant was the solidarity of local officials. The mine owners controlled the county sheriff and used him as their tool, but when he called up deputies to put down the strike, local officials intervened. In nearby Altman, Colorado, the mayor, city marshal, and police magistrate all belonged to the WFM. When sheriff's deputies arrived, Altman officials promptly arrested them for disturbing the peace and carrying concealed weapons. The sheriff then appealed to Governor Davis H. Waite to send troops. But Waite, a Populist elected in 1892, also had strong ties to the miners and refused to use the power of the state against the peaceful strikers. Desperate, the sheriff deputized over a thousand men and in May sent them to occupy the mines. The strikers, entrenched on Bull Hill outside of Cripple Creek, prepared for a showdown. Kathleen Welch Chapman recalled her mother's story of one confrontation where the miners managed to trick the militia and avoid bloodshed.

> There wasn't too many people up there, you know—and the men went out and they had their wives with them. And Mama said she wrapped Tom in a blanket and went along. And the men took their coats off, and their hats, and put them up in a tree and put the guns up in there . . . and oh, they just thought that the *world* was up there, this militia [sheriff's deputies] did, when they seen them.

After several confrontations at Bull Hill, pressure mounted for a settlement. Governor Waite asked the strikers to lay down their arms and demanded that the mine owners disperse their hired deputies. The miners agreed to arbitration and selected Waite their sole arbitrator. By May, the recalcitrant mine owners capitulated, and the union won an eight-hour day.

But the settlement did not end the conflict. In June, the sheriff and his twelve hundred deputies, defying the governor's order to disperse, advanced on Bull Hill. Waite immediately called out the state militia. Before the troops arrived, deputies exchanged shots with the strikers. Finally, the militia marched in and camped between the miners and the deputies. When the deputies advanced on Bull Hill, the militia's commander threatened to fire on them. The sheriff agreed to withdraw the deputies, but he managed to arrest thirty-seven union men and jail them on assorted charges.

Governor Waite's intervention demonstrated the pivotal power of the state in the nation's labor wars. At Cripple Creek, the WFM's union organization, divisions among the mine owners, and support from local officials combined with the restraint of Governor Waite to bring about the miners' success. Having a Populist in power made a difference. A decade later, the miners were defeated in another strike. In 1904, with the help of state troops, mine owners took back control of the mines on their own terms, blacklisting all WFM members. In retrospect, the Cripple Creek miner's strike of 1894 proved the exception to the rule of state intervention on the side of private property. When the Populist governor of Colorado used troops in 1894 to keep the peace and not to put down the strike, the outcome proved very different from what occurred in Homestead, Pennsylvania, or what was taking place across the country in Pullman, Illinois.

Eugene V. Debs and the Pullman Strike

The economic depression swelled the ranks of the unemployed to 3 million by 1894, almost half of the working population. "A fearful crisis is upon us," wrote a labor publication. "Countless thousands of our fellow men are unemployed; men, women and children are suffering the pangs of hunger." Nowhere were workers more demoralized than in the model town of Pullman on the outskirts of Chicago.

In the wake of the Great Railroad Strike of 1877 George M. Pullman, the builder of Pullman railroad cars, had moved his plant and workers away from the "snares of the great city." In 1880 he purchased forty-three hundred acres nine miles south of Chicago on the shores of Lake Calumet and built a model town. Like the Pullman Palace cars that made his fortune, he intended the company town to be orderly, clean, and with the appearance of luxury. It was "to the employer's interest," he determined, "to see that his men are clean, contented, sober, educated and happy." The town of Pullman boasted parks, fountains, playgrounds, an auditorium, a library, a hotel, shops, and markets along with eighteen hundred units of housing. Noticeably absent was a saloon.

The housing in Pullman was clearly superior to that in neighboring towns, but workers who chose to live in Pullman paid a high price. George M. Pullman insisted the town support itself and expected a 6 percent return on his investment. As a result, Pullman's rents ran 10 to 20 percent higher than housing costs in nearby communities. And a family in Pullman could never own its own home. George Pullman refused to "sell an acre under any circumstances." As long as he controlled the town absolutely, he held the powerful whip of eviction over his employees and could quickly get rid of "troublemakers." Although observers at first praised the beauty and orderliness of the town, critics by the 1890s compared Pullman's model town to a "gilded cage" for workers. (See "American Places," page 720.)

The depression brought hard times to Pullman. Workers saw their wages slashed five times between May and December 1893, with cuts totaling at least 28 percent. At the same time, Pullman refused to lower the rents in his model town, insisting that "the renting of the dwellings and the employment of workmen at Pullman are in no way tied together." When

AMERICAN PLACES

Pullman Historic District, Chicago, Illinois

Hotel Florence, Pullman, Illinois
Historic Pullman Foundation.

Visitors to the Pullman Historic District in Chicago can see much of the model town built by George M. Pullman for workers at the Pullman Palace Car Company. Between 1880 and 1884, architect Solon Spencer Beman and landscape architect Nathan Barrett oversaw the construction of Pullman's model town, which included over 900 residences, primarily row houses built of solid brick. Some housed single families; others contained apartments. The company built several public buildings, including the Arcade and Market Hall, where private businesses could rent space for meat markets, bakeries, and other retail shops. Pullman included a bank, library, theater, post office, church, parks, and a hotel. An imposing clock tower and administration building dominated the large industrial complex at the center of the town.

George M. Pullman died in 1897. The following year the Illinois Supreme Court ruled that the company had to sell its nonindustrial buildings to private homeowners. By 1907 all the homes had been sold. In 1889 the expanding metropolis of Chicago annexed the town of Pullman, and it has been part of Chicago ever since. Pullman became a state landmark district in 1969, a national landmark district in 1971, and a city of Chicago landmark district in 1972. Over 95 percent of the original buildings are still standing, owned by private individuals. Guided walking tours of the Pullman Historic District include a visit to an 1880s row house for a glimpse at what today's residents are doing to preserve the historic architecture.

Among the remaining prominent buildings is the Hotel Florence. Named for George M. Pullman's favorite daughter, it is an imposing Queen Anne–style building in Indiana red pressed brick. During Pullman's heyday in the 1880s it was the only place in town where visiting businessmen and dignitaries could buy a drink. One worker lamented that he frequently walked by and "looked at but dared not enter Pullman's hotel with its private bar." In his eagerness to inculcate what he referred to as the "habits of respectability," George Pullman failed to provide a saloon for his workers. Today the hotel is open for touring, and the second floor houses a museum and gift shop.

FOR WEB LINKS RELATED TO THIS SITE AND OTHER AMERICAN PLACES, see "PlaceLinks" at bedfordstmartins.com/roark.

workers went to the bank to cash their paychecks, they found the rent had been taken out. One worker discovered only forty-seven cents in his pay envelope for two weeks' work. When the bank teller asked him whether he wanted to apply it to his back rent, he retorted, "If Mr. Pullman needs that forty-seven cents worse than I do, let him have it." At the same time Pullman continued to pay his stockholders an 8 percent dividend, and the company accumulated a $25 million surplus.

At the heart of the labor problems at Pullman lay not only economic inequity but the company's attempt to control the work process, substituting piecework for day wages and undermining skilled craftsworkers. The Pullman workers rebelled. During the spring of 1894, Pullman's desperate workers, seeking help, flocked to the ranks of the American Railway Union (ARU), led by the charismatic Eugene Victor Debs. The ARU, unlike the skilled craft unions of the AFL, pledged to organize all railway workers—from engineers to engine wipers.

A Pullman Craftsworker

Pullman Palace cars were known for their luxurious details. Here a painter working in the 1890s applies elaborate decoration to the exterior of a Pullman car. In the foreground is an intricately carved door, an example of fine hand detailing. The Pullman workers' strike in 1894 stemmed in part from the company's efforts to undermine the status of craftsworkers by reducing them to low-paid piecework. Control of the workplace, as much as issues related to wages and hours, fueled the labor wars of the 1890s.

Chicago Historical Society.

George Pullman responded to union organization at his plant by firing three of the union's leaders the day after they led a delegation to protest wage cuts. Angry men and women walked off the job in disgust. What began as a spontaneous protest in May 1894 quickly blossomed into a strike that involved more than 90 percent of Pullman's thirty-three hundred workers. "We do not know what the outcome will be, and in fact we do not much care," one worker confessed. "We do know that we are working for less wages than will maintain ourselves and families in the necessaries of life, and on that proposition we refuse to work any longer." Pullman countered by shutting down the plant.

In June, the Pullman strikers appealed to the ARU to come to their aid. Debs hesitated to commit his fledgling union to a major strike in the midst of a depression. He pleaded with the workers to find another solution. When George Pullman adamantly refused arbitration, the ARU membership, brushing aside Debs's call for caution, voted to boycott all Pullman cars. Beginning on June 29, switchmen across the United States refused to handle any train that carried Pullman cars.

The conflict escalated quickly. The General Managers Association (GMA), an organization of managers from twenty-four different railroads, acted in concert to quash the boycott. Determined to kill the ARU, they recruited strikebreakers and fired all the protesting switchmen. Their tactics set off a chain reaction. Entire train crews walked off the job in a show of solidarity with the Pullman workers and the ARU. In a matter of days the boycott/strike spread to more than fifteen railroads and affected twenty-seven states and territories. By July 2, rail lines from New York to California lay paralyzed. Even the GMA was forced to concede that the railroads had been "fought to a standstill."

The boycott remained surprisingly peaceful. Mobs stopped trains carrying Pullman cars and forced train crews to uncouple the cars and leave them on the sidings. In contrast to the Great Railroad Strike of 1877, no major riots broke out, and no serious property damage occurred. Debs, in a whirlwind of activity, fired off telegrams to all parts of the country advising his followers to

> At the heart of the labor problems at Pullman lay not only economic inequity but the company's attempt to control the work process, substituting piecework for day wages and undermining skilled craftsworkers.

National Guard Occupying Pullman, Illinois
After President Grover Cleveland called out the troops to put down the Pullman strike in 1894, the National Guard occupied the town of Pullman to protect George M. Pullman's property. Here the guard rings the Arcade building, the town shopping center, while curious men and women look on. The intervention of troops in Homestead and Pullman enabled the owners to bring in strikebreakers and defeat the unions. In Cripple Creek, Colorado, where a Populist governor used militia only to maintain the peace and not against the strikers, striking miners won the day in 1894.
Chicago Historical Society.

avoid violence, to use no force to stop trains, and to respect law and order. But the nation's newspapers, fed press releases by the GMA, distorted the issues and misrepresented the strike. Across the country, papers ran headlines like "Wild Riot in Chicago" and "Mob Is in Control." Editors rushed to denounce "Dictator Debs."

In Washington, Attorney General Richard B. Olney, a lawyer with strong ties to the railroads, determined to put down the strike. In his way stood the governor of Illinois, John Peter Altgeld, who, observing that the boycott remained peaceful, refused to call out troops. To get around Altgeld, Olney convinced President Grover Cleveland that federal troops had to intervene even without the governor's request, in order to protect the mails. To further cripple the boycott, two conservative Chicago judges issued an injunction so sweeping that it prohibited Debs from speaking in public. By issuing the injunction, the court made the boycott a crime punishable by jail sentence for contempt of court, a civil process that did not require trial by jury. Even the conservative *Chicago Tribune* judged the injunction "a menace to liberty . . . a weapon ever ready for the capitalist." Furious, Debs risked jail by refusing to honor it.

Olney's strategy worked. With the strikers violating a federal injunction and with the mails in jeopardy (the GMA made sure that Pullman cars were put on every mail train), Cleveland called out the army. On July 5, nearly 8,000 troops marched into Chicago. Violence immediately erupted. In one day, more than $340,000 worth of property was destroyed, 25 workers were shot, and more than 60 were wounded. In the face of bullets and bayonets, the strikers held firm. "Troops cannot move trains," Debs reminded his followers, a fact that was borne out as the railroads remained paralyzed despite the military intervention. But if the army could not put down the boycott, the injunction could and did. Debs was arrested and imprisoned for contempt of court. With its leader in jail, its headquarters raided and ransacked, and its members demoralized, the ARU was defeated along with the boycott. Pullman reopened his factory, hiring new workers to replace many of the strikers and leaving 1,600 workers without jobs and without the means to relocate.

In the aftermath of the strike, a special commission investigated the events at Pullman, taking testimony from 107 witnesses, from the lowliest workers to George M. Pullman himself. Stubborn and self-righteous, Pullman spoke for the business orthodoxy of his era, steadfastly affirming the right of business to safeguard its interests through confederacies like the GMA and at the same time denying labor's right to organize. "If we were to receive these men as representatives of the union," he stated, "they could probably force us to pay any wages which they saw fit."

From his jail cell, Eugene Debs reviewed the events of the Pullman strike. With the courts and the government ready to side with industrialists in the interest of defending private property, Debs realized that labor had little recourse. Strikes seemed futile and unions remained helpless; workers would have to take control of the state itself. Debs went into jail a trade unionist and came out six months later a socialist. At first he turned to the Populist Party, but after its demise he formed the Socialist Party in 1900 and ran for president on its ticket five times. Debs's dissatisfaction with the status quo was shared by another group even more alienated from the political process—women.

Women's Activism

"Do everything," Frances Willard urged her followers in 1881. The new president of the Woman's Christian Temperance Union (WCTU) meant what she said. The WCTU followed a trajectory that was common for women in the late nineteenth century. As women organized to deal with issues that touched their homes and families, they moved into politics, lending new urgency to the cause of woman suffrage. Urban industrialism dislocated women's lives no less than men's. Like men, women sought political change and organized to promote issues central to their lives, from temperance and suffrage to antilynching (see chapter 17).

THE GENERAL OFFICERS OF THE WORLD'S W. C. T. U.

Frances Willard and the Officers of the Woman's Christian Temperance Union
This photograph of the general officers of the Woman's Christian Temperance Union shows Frances Willard seated in the center. Willard, who came to the presidency in 1879, led the organization in a turn from a religious toward a reform agenda. Her advocacy of the "home protection ballot" helped recruit supporters for woman suffrage.
The Beautiful Life of Frances E. Willard by Anna A. Gordon, 1898.

Frances Willard and the Woman's Christian Temperance Union

Frances Willard, the visionary leader of the WCTU, spoke for a group left almost entirely out of the U.S. electoral process—women. In 1890, only one state, Wyoming, allowed women to vote in national elections. But lack of the **franchise** did not mean that women were apolitical. The WCTU demonstrated the breadth of women's political activity in the late nineteenth century.

Women supported the **temperance movement** because they felt particularly vulnerable to the effects of drunkenness. Dependent on men's wages, women and children suffered when money went for drink. They also suffered at the hands of drunken husbands and fathers who beat and abused them. The drunken, abusive husband epitomized the evils of a nation in which women remained second-class citizens. The temperance movement provided women with a respectable outlet for their increasing resentment of women's inferior status and their growing recognition of women's capabilities. Composed entirely of women, the WCTU viewed all women's interests as essentially the same—crossing class, ethnic, and racial lines—and therefore did not hesitate to use the singular *woman* to emphasize gender solidarity. Although mostly white and middle class, WCTU members resolved to speak for their entire sex.

In its first five years, under the leadership of Annie Wittenmyer, the WCTU relied on education and persuasion to achieve its goal of total abstinence from alcohol. But when Frances Willard became president in 1879, she radically changed the direction of the organization. Moving away from a religious approach, the WCTU began to view alcoholism as a disease rather than a sin, and poverty as a cause rather than a result of drink. Accordingly, social action replaced prayer as women's answer to the threat of drunkenness. Willard, along with other reformers in this period, viewed many social ills as the result of urban industrialism and took a variety of steps to improve the lives of American women. By the 1890s the WCTU worked to establish women's reformatories, promoted the hiring of female police officers, and sponsored day nurseries, industrial training schools for women, missions for the homeless, medical dispensaries, and lodging houses for the poor. At the same time, the WCTU became involved in labor issues, joining with the Knights of Labor to press for better working conditions for women workers. Describing factory operatives in a textile mill, a WCTU member wrote in the *Union Signal*, the WCTU monthly magazine, "It is dreadful to see those girls stripped almost to the skin, wearing only [a] kind of loose wrapper, and running like racehorses from the beginning to the end of the day." "The hard slavish work," she concluded, "is drawing the girls into the saloon."

Willard capitalized on the **cult of domesticity** as a shrewd political tactic to move women into public life and gain power to ameliorate social problems. Using "home protection" as her watchword, she argued as early as 1884 that women needed the vote to protect home and family. By the 1890s, the WCTU's grassroots network of local unions had spread to all but the most isolated rural areas of the country. Strong and rich, with over 150,000 dues-paying members, the WCTU was a formidable group.

Willard worked to create a broad reform coalition in the 1890s, embracing the Knights of Labor, the People's Party, and the Prohibition Party. Until her death in 1898, she led, if not a women's rights movement, then the first organized mass movement of women united around a women's issue. By 1900, thanks largely to the WCTU, women could claim a generation of experience in political action—speaking, lobbying, organizing, drafting legislation, and running private charitable institutions. As Willard observed, "All this work has tended more toward the liberation of women than it has toward the extinction of the saloon."

Elizabeth Cady Stanton, Susan B. Anthony, and the Movement for Woman Suffrage

Unlike the WCTU, the organized movement for woman suffrage remained small and relatively weak in the late nineteenth century. The women's rights movement, begun by Elizabeth Cady Stanton at Seneca Falls in 1848 (see chapter 12), split in 1867 over whether the Fourteenth and Fifteenth Amendments, which granted voting rights to African American men, should have extended the vote to women as well. Stanton and her ally, Susan B. Anthony, launched the National Woman Suffrage Association (NWSA) in 1869, demanding the vote for women (see chapter 17). A more conservative group, the American Woman Suffrage Association (AWSA), formed the same year. Composed of men as well as women, the AWSA believed that women should vote in local but not national elections.

By 1890 the split had healed and the newly united National American Woman Suffrage Association (NAWSA) launched campaigns on the state level to gain the vote for women. Twenty years had made a great change. Woman suffrage, though not yet generally supported, was no longer considered a crackpot idea. Thanks to the WCTU's support of the "home protection ballot," suffrage had become accepted as a means to an end even when it was not embraced as woman's natural right. The NAWSA honored Elizabeth Cady Stanton by electing her

> Thanks to the WCTU's support of the "home protection ballot," suffrage had become accepted as a means to an end even when it was not supported as a woman's natural right.

Campaigning for Woman Suffrage

In 1896 women voted in only four states—Wyoming, Colorado, Idaho, and Utah. The West led the way in the campaign for woman suffrage, partially because of demographics, as in the case of Wyoming, where only 16 votes were needed in the state's tiny legislature to obtain passage of the vote for women. This poster calls on Nebraska to join the suffrage column while the flag illustrates the number of states where women voted.

Poster: Nebraska State Historical Society; flag: Smithsonian Institution, Washington, D.C.

its first president, but Susan B. Anthony, who took the helm in 1892, emerged as the leading figure in the new united organization.

Stanton and Anthony, both in their seventies, were coming to the end of their public careers. Since the days of the Seneca Falls Woman's Rights Convention they had worked for reforms for their sex, including property rights, custody rights, and the right to education and gainful employment. Some of these goals they had achieved. But the prize of woman suffrage still eluded them. Suffragists won victories in Colorado in 1893 and Idaho in 1896. One more state joined the suffrage column in 1896 when Utah entered the Union. But women suffered a bitter defeat in a California referendum on woman suffrage that same year. Never losing faith, Susan B. Anthony remarked in her last public appearance in 1906, "Failure is impossible." Although it would take another two decades for all women to gain the vote with the ratification of the Nineteenth Amendment in 1920, the unification of the two woman suffrage groups in 1890 signaled a new era in women's fight for the vote, just as Frances Willard's place on the platform in 1892 at the founding of the People's Party in St. Louis symbolized women's growing role in politics and reform.

Depression Politics

The depression that began in the spring of 1893 and lasted for more than four years put nearly half of the labor force out of work, a higher percentage of unemployed than that experienced even in the Great Depression of the 1930s. The country swarmed with people looking for jobs. They rode the rails, slept in barns, and begged for work; when they could get no work, they begged for food. Towns and cities rushed to clamp down on vagrancy by imposing fines and jail terms on the hapless wanderers, dismissed by those better off as tramps and hoboes. But for the most part the unemployed sought jobs, not handouts. Populist governor Lorenzo Lewelling of Kansas, one of the few public officials to sympathize with their plight, issued his "tramp circular" in December 1893. In it he lashed out at vagrancy laws that imprisoned "thousands of men, guilty of no crime but poverty."

The human cost of the depression was staggering. "I Take my pen in hand to let you know that we are Starving to death," a Kansas farm woman wrote to the governor in 1894. "Last cent gone," wrote a young widow in her diary. "Children went to work without their breakfasts." The destitute turned where they could for

Coxey's Army
This contingent of Coxey's army on the way to Washington, D.C., is led by Carl Browne, Coxey's principal aide, on horseback. A "petition in boots," Coxey's followers were well dressed—notice the men in white shirts, vests, neckties, and bowler hats in the foreground. The marchers insisted on their right to petition Congress for relief. Their action stirred the fears of many conservative Americans, who predicted an uprising of the unemployed. Most members of Congress wished to see the marchers halted, but Populist senator William V. Allen of Nebraska argued that their grievances should be heard by a congressional committee. Instead, Coxey was arrested and jailed when he reached Washington, D.C., for "walking on the grass."
Library of Congress.

relief. The burden of feeding and sheltering the unemployed and their families fell to private charity, city government, and some of the stronger trade unions. Following the harsh dictates of **social Darwinism** and laissez-faire, the majority of America's elected officials believed that it was inappropriate for the government to intervene. But the scope of the depression made it impossible for local agencies to supply sufficient relief, and increasingly Americans called on the federal government to take action. Armies of the unemployed marched on Washington to demand relief, and the Populist Party experienced a surge of support as the election of 1896 approached.

Coxey's Army

Masses of unemployed Americans marched to Washington, D.C., in the spring of 1894 to call attention to their plight and to urge Congress to

enact a public works program to end unemployment. From as far away as Seattle, San Francisco, Los Angeles, and Denver, hundreds joined the march. Jacob S. Coxey of Massilon, Ohio, led the most publicized contingent. Coxey, a millionaire with a penchant for racehorses and high living, seemed an unlikely champion of the unemployed. Convinced that men could be put to work building badly needed roads for the nation, he proposed a scheme to finance public works through non-interest-bearing bonds. "What I am after," he maintained, "is to try to put this country in a condition so that no man who wants work shall be obliged to remain idle." His plan won the support of the AFL and the Populists.

Starting out from Ohio with one hundred men, Coxey's "army," as it was dubbed by journalists, swelled as it marched east through the spring snows of the Alleghenies. In Pennsylvania, Coxey recruited several hundred from the ranks of those left unemployed by the

Homestead lockout. Called by Coxey the Commonweal of Christ, the army advanced to the tune of "Marching through Georgia":

> We are not tramps nor vagabonds,
>   that's shirking honest toil,
> But miners, clerks, skilled artisans,
>   and tillers of the soil
> Now forced to beg our brother worms
>   to give us leave to toil,
> While we are marching with Coxey.
> Hurrah! hurrah! for the unemployed's appeal
> Hurrah! hurrah! for the marching commonweal!

On May 1, Coxey's army arrived in Washington. Given permission to parade but forbidden to speak from the Capitol, Coxey defiantly marched his men onto the Capitol grounds. Police set upon the demonstrators with nightsticks, cracking skulls and arresting Coxey and his lieutenants. Coxey went to jail for twenty days and was fined $5 for "walking on the grass."

Mass demonstrations of the unemployed served only to frighten comfortable Americans, who saw the specter of insurrection and rebellion everywhere in 1894. Those who had trembled for the safety of the Republic heaved a sigh of relief after Coxey's arrest, hoping that it would halt the march on Washington. But other armies of the unemployed, totaling possibly as many as 5,000 people, were still on their way. Too poor to pay for railway tickets, they rode the rails as "freeloaders." The more daring contingents commandeered entire trains, stirring fears of revolution. Nervous midwestern governors put trains at the marchers' disposal to speed them quickly out of state. Journalists who covered the march did little to quiet the nation's fears. They delighted in military terminology, describing themselves as "war correspondents." To boost newspaper sales, they gave to the episode a tone of urgency and heightened the sense of a nation imperiled.

By August, the leaderless, tattered armies dissolved. Although the "On to Washington" movement proved ineffective in forcing federal relief legislation, Coxey's army dramatized the plight of the unemployed and acted, in the words of one participant, as a "living, moving object lesson." Like the Populists, Coxey's army called into question the underlying values of the new industrial order and demonstrated how ordinary citizens turned to means outside the regular party system to influence politics in the 1890s.

The People's Party and the Election of 1896

Even before the depression of 1893 gave added impetus to their cause, the Populists had railed against the status quo. "We meet in the midst of a nation brought to the verge of moral, political, and material ruin," Ignatius Donnelly had declared in his keynote address at the creation of the People's Party in St. Louis in 1892.

> Corruption dominates the ballot-box, the legislatures, the Congress, and touches even the ermine of the bench. . . . The fruits of the toil of millions are boldly stolen to build up colossal fortunes for a few. . . . From the same prolific womb of governmental injustice we breed the two great classes—tramps and millionaires.

The fiery rhetoric frightened many who saw in the People's Party a call not to reform but to revolution. Throughout the country, the press denounced the Populists as "cranks, lunatics, and idiots." When one righteous editor dismissed them as "calamity howlers," Populist governor Lorenzo Lewelling of Kansas shot back, "If that is so I want to continue to howl until those conditions are improved." And Mary Elizabeth Lease, accused of being a Communist because of Populists' advocacy of government ownership of railroads, responded unperturbed, "You may call me an anarchist, a socialist, or a communist, I care not, but I hold to the theory that if one man has not enough to eat three times a day and another man has $25 million, that the last man has something that belongs to the first."

The People's Party captured more than a million votes in the presidential election of 1892, a respectable showing for a new party (Map 20.1). The Populists might have done better, but on the eve of the convention they lost their standard-bearer when Leonidis L. Polk, president of the Southern Farmers' Alliance, died suddenly. Scrambling to find a replacement, the convention nominated General James B. Weaver of Iowa, a former Union general who had run for president on the Greenback Labor ticket in 1880. Many southern Populists could not bring themselves to vote for a Yankee general and stayed away from the polls.

Increasingly, sectional and racial animosities threatened party unity. More than their alliance

> Even before the depression of 1893 gave added impetus to their cause, the Populists had railed against the status quo.

Mary Elizabeth Lease
This photograph of Lease, taken in 1895 at the height of her political activities in Kansas, shows a well-dressed, mild-eyed woman—belying her reputation as a hell-raiser who supposedly exorted Kansas farmers to "raise less corn and more hell." Lease brought her considerable oratorical skills to the causes of temperance, suffrage, and the Populist Party. Her admirers styled her "The People's Joan of Arc." But in the eyes of her detractors, who attacked not only her speeches but the propriety of a woman who dared a career as public speaker, she appeared "a lantern-jawed, google-eyed nightmare" and "a petticoated smut-mill."
Kansas State Historical Society.

The People's Party fared better in the 1894 congressional elections, when, unencumbered by a Union general, the Populists added half a million voters to their column. With the depression swelling the ranks of the disaffected, the Populists looked forward to the election of 1896.

As the presidential election approached, the depression intensified cries for reform not only from the Populists but throughout the electorate. Depression worsened the tight money problem caused by the deflationary pressures of the gold standard. Once again, proponents of free silver (the unlimited coinage of silver in addition to gold) stirred rebellion in the ranks of both the Democratic and the Republican parties. When the Republicans nominated Ohio governor William McKinley on a platform pledging the preservation of the gold standard, western advocates of free silver representing miners and farmers walked out of the convention. Open rebellion also split the Democratic Party as vast segments in the West and South repudiated President Grover Cleveland because of his support of the gold standard. In South Carolina, Benjamin Tillman won his race for Congress by promising, "Send me to Washington and I'll stick my pitchfork into [Cleveland's] old ribs!"

The spirit of revolt animated the Democratic National Convention in Chicago in the summer of 1896. "Pitchfork Ben" Tillman set the tone by attacking the party's president, denouncing the Cleveland administration as "undemocratic and tyrannical." But the man of the hour was

with the Yankee North, it was the Populists' willingness to form common cause with black farmers that made them anathema in the white South. Tom Watson of Georgia had tackled the "Negro question" head-on in 1892. Realizing that race prejudice obscured the common economic interests of black and white farmers, Watson openly courted African Americans, appearing on platforms with black speakers and promising "to wipe out the color line." When angry Georgia whites threatened to lynch a black Populist preacher, Watson rallied two thousand gun-toting Populists to the man's defense. Although many Populists remained racist in their attitude toward African Americans, the spectacle of white Georgians riding through the night to protect a black man from lynching was nevertheless symptomatic of the enormous changes the Populist Party promised in the South.

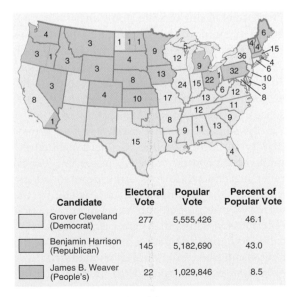

Candidate	Electoral Vote	Popular Vote	Percent of Popular Vote
Grover Cleveland (Democrat)	277	5,555,426	46.1
Benjamin Harrison (Republican)	145	5,182,690	43.0
James B. Weaver (People's)	22	1,029,846	8.5

MAP 20.1 The Election of 1892

William Jennings Bryan of Nebraska, the thirty-six-year-old "boy orator from the Platte," who whipped the convention into a frenzy with his passionate call for free silver. In his keynote address, Bryan masterfully cataloged the grievances of farmers and laborers, closing his dramatic speech with the ringing exhortation "Do not crucify mankind upon a cross of gold." Pandemonium broke loose as delegates stampeded to nominate Bryan, the youngest candidate ever to run for the presidency.

The juggernaut of free silver rolled out of Chicago and on to St. Louis, where the People's Party met a week after the Democrats adjourned. Smelling victory, many western Populists urged the party to ally with the Democrats and endorse Bryan. A major obstacle in the path of fusion, however, was Bryan's running mate, Arthur M. Sewall. A Maine railway director and bank president, Sewall had been placed on the ticket to appease conservative Democrats. To the Populists, Sewall as an easterner, a banker, and a railroad director, symbolized everything they opposed.

Populism's regional constituencies remained as divided on tactics as they were uniform in their call for change. Western Populists, including a strong coalition of farmers and miners in states like Idaho and Colorado, championed free silver as a way to put the ailing Rocky Mountain silver industry back on its feet and restore prosperity to the region. In these largely Republican states, Populists had joined forces with Democrats in previous elections and saw no problem with becoming "Popocrats" once Bryan led the Democratic ticket on a free-silver platform. Similarly in the Midwest, a Republican stronghold, Populists who had used fusion with the Democrats as a tactic to win elections had little trouble backing Bryan. But in the South, where Democrats had resorted to fraud and violence to steal elections from the Populists in 1892 and 1894, support for a Democratic ticket proved especially hard to swallow. Although both southern Democrats and Populists subscribed to the same principles, they split on whether the ruling Democrats could effectively lead the crusade for change. Diehard southern Populists wanted no part of fusion.

All of these tactical differences emerged as Populists met in St. Louis in 1896 to nominate a candidate for president. To show that they remained true to their principles, delegates first voted to support all the planks of the 1892 plat-

form, added to it a call for public works projects for the unemployed, and only narrowly defeated a plank for woman suffrage. To deal with the problem of fusion, the convention selected the vice presidential candidate first. The nomination of Tom Watson undercut opposition to Bryan's candidacy. And, although Bryan quickly wired to protest that he would not drop Sewall as his running mate to run on a Populist ticket with Watson, mysteriously, his message never reached the convention floor. Fusion triumphed. Watson's vice presidential nomination paved the way for the selection of Bryan by a lopsided vote. The Populists did not know it, but their cheers for Bryan signaled not a chorus of victory but the death knell of the People's Party.

Few contests in the nation's history have been as fiercely fought and as full of emotion as the presidential election of 1896. On one side stood Republican William McKinley, backed by the wealthy industrialist and

> The Populists did not know it, but their cheers for Bryan in St. Louis signaled not a chorus of victory but the death knell of the People's Party.

Gold Elephant Campaign Button and Silver Ribbon from St. Louis, 1896

Mechanical elephant badges that opened to show portraits of William McKinley and his running mate, Garret Hobart, were popular campaign novelties in the election of 1896. The elephant, the mascot of the Republican Party, is gilded to indicate the party's support of the gold standard. The delegate ribbon from the St. Louis National Silver Convention in 1896 testifies to the power of free silver as a campaign issue. Democrats nominated William Jennings Bryan on a free-silver platform and Populists meeting in St. Louis put him on their ticket as well.

Pin: Collection of Janice L. and David J. Frent; ribbon: Nebraska State Historical Society.

party boss Mark Hanna. Hanna played on the business community's fears of Populism to raise more than $4 million for the Republican war chest, double the amount of any previous campaign. On the other side, William Jennings Bryan, with few assets beyond his silver tongue, struggled to make up in energy and eloquence what his party lacked in campaign funds. He set a new style for presidential campaigning, crisscrossing the country in a whirlwind tour, traveling more than eighteen thousand miles and delivering more than six hundred speeches in three months. According to his own reckoning, he visited twenty-seven states and spoke to more than five million Americans.

As election day approached, the silver states of the Rocky Mountains lined up solidly for Bryan. In Nevada, Idaho, and Colorado, miners and their bosses came together in the hope that free silver would shore up the mining industry, which had seen the price of silver drop from $1.32 an ounce in the heyday of the Comstock Lode to 87 cents in 1892. The Northeast stood solidly for McKinley. Much of the South, with the exception of the border states, abandoned the Populists and returned to the Democratic fold, leaving Tom Watson to lament that "[Populists] play Jonah while [Democrats] play the whale." The Midwest hung in the balance. Bryan intensified his campaign in Illinois, Michigan, Ohio, and Indiana. But midwestern farmers proved less receptive than western voters to the blandishments of free silver. In the cities, Democrats charged the Republicans with mass intimidation. "Men, vote as you please," the head of New York's Steinway Piano Company reportedly announced to his workers on the eve of the election, "but if Bryan is elected tomorrow the whistle will not blow Wednesday morning."

Intimidation alone did not explain the failure of urban labor to rally to Bryan in 1896. Republicans repeatedly warned workers that if the Democrats won, the inflated silver dollar would be worth only fifty cents. However much farmers and laborers might insist that they were united as producers against the nonproducing bosses, it was equally true that inflation did not offer the boon to urban laborers that it did to western debtors. For while debtors benefited from the inflated currency, which allowed them to pay off their debts with cheaper, more plentiful dollars, inflation promised no real gain to city workers and in fact might worsen their situation by resulting in higher prices for food and rent. Populism's alliance of West and South also wor-

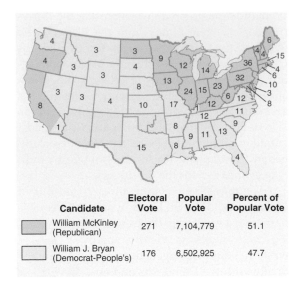

Candidate	Electoral Vote	Popular Vote	Percent of Popular Vote
William McKinley (Republican)	271	7,104,779	51.1
William J. Bryan (Democrat-People's)	176	6,502,925	47.7

MAP 20.2   The Election of 1896

ried workers who read daily in the eastern press that the Populist Party threatened not only the industrial East but industrialism itself. While industrial workers in the West and South, particularly miners, voted Populist, eastern workers failed to rally to Bryan.

On election day, four out of every five voters went to the polls in an unprecedented turnout. In the critical midwestern states, as many as 95 percent of the eligible voters cast their ballots. In the end, the election outcome hinged on from 100 to 1,000 votes in several key states. Although McKinley won twenty-three states to Bryan's twenty-two, the electoral vote showed a lopsided 271 to 176 in McKinley's favor (Map 20.2).

The biggest losers in 1896 turned out to be the Populists. On the national level, they polled fewer than 300,000 votes, over a million fewer than in 1894. In the clamor to support Bryan, Populists in the South drifted back to the Democratic Party. The People's Party was crushed, and with it died the agrarian revolt.

But if Populism proved unsuccessful at the polls, it nevertheless set the domestic political agenda for the United States in the next decades, highlighting issues such as banking and currency reform, electoral reforms, and an enlarged role for the federal government in the economy. Meanwhile, as the decade ended, the bugle call to arms turned America's attention to foreign affairs and effectively drowned out the trumpet of reform. The struggle for social justice gave way to a war for empire as the United States asserted its power on the world stage.

The United States and the World

Throughout much of the last half of the nineteenth century, U.S. interest in foreign policy took a backseat to domestic developments. Intent on its own continental expansion, the United States stood aloof while the European powers—Great Britain, France, Germany, Spain, and Belgium—as well as an increasingly powerful Japan, competed for empires abroad, gobbling up what they liked to call the great "empty spaces" in Asia, Africa, Latin America, and the Pacific. Between 1870 and 1900, European nations **colonized** more than 20 percent of the world's landmass and 10 percent of the world's population.

At the turn of the twentieth century, American foreign policy consisted of two currents—**isolationism** and expansionism. The determination to remain aloof from European politics had been a hallmark of U.S. foreign policy since President George Washington, in his farewell address, warned Americans to "steer clear" of permanent alliances. Simultaneously, Americans believed in **manifest destiny**—the "obvious" right to expand the nation from ocean to ocean and possibly on a continental scale, taking in Canada and Mexico. The United States's determination to protect its sphere of influence in the Western Hemisphere at the same time it expanded its trading in Asia moved the nation away from isolationism and toward a more active role on the world stage. The push for commercial expansion joined with a sense of Christian mission to refocus the nation's attention abroad and led both to the strengthening of the **Monroe Doctrine** in the Western Hemisphere and to a new Open Door policy in Asia.

Markets and Missionaries

The depression of the 1890s provided a powerful impetus to American commercial expansion. As markets weakened at home, American businesses looked abroad for profits. As early as 1890, Captain Alfred Thayer Mahan, leader of a growing group of American expansionists, prophesied, "Whether they will or not, Americans must now begin to look outward. The growing production of the country requires it." Although not all U.S. business leaders thought it advantageous to undertake adventures abroad,

the logic of acquiring new markets to absorb the nation's growing capacity for production proved convincing to many. As the depression deepened, one diplomat warned that Americans "must turn [their] eyes abroad, or they will soon look inward upon discontent."

Exports of cloth, kerosene, flour, and steel already constituted a small but significant percentage of the profits of American business in the 1890s. And where American interests led, businessmen expected American power and influence to follow to protect their investments (Figure 20.2). Companies like Standard Oil actively sought to use the government as their agent, often putting foreign service employees on the payroll. "Our ambassadors and ministers and consuls," wrote John D. Rockefeller appreciatively, "have aided to push our way into new markets to the utmost corners of the world." Whether by "our" he meant the United States or Standard Oil remained ambiguous; in practice, the distinction was of little importance in late-nineteenth-century foreign policy.

America's foreign policy often appeared little more than a sidelight to business development. In Hawaii (first called the Sandwich Islands), American sugar interests fomented a rebellion in 1893, toppling the increasingly anti-American Queen Liliuokalani. They pushed Congress to annex the islands, which would allow planters to avoid the high McKinley tariff on sugar. When President Cleveland learned that Hawaiians opposed annexation, he withdrew the proposal from Congress. But expansionists still coveted the islands and continued to look for an excuse to push through annexation.

However compelling the economic arguments about overseas markets proved, business interests alone did not account for the new expansionism that seized the nation during the 1890s. As Mahan confessed, "Even when material interests are the original exciting cause, it is the sentiment to which they give rise, the moral tone which emotion takes that constitutes the greater force." Much of that moral tone was set by American missionaries intent on spreading the gospel of Christianity to the "heathen." No area on the globe constituted a greater challenge than China. In 1858, the Tientsin treaty admitted foreign missionaries. Roman Catholics from

> The United States' determination to protect Its sphere of influence in the Western Hemisphere at the same time it expanded its trading in Asia moved the nation away from isolationism.

France and Protestants from Britain, Germany, and the United States rushed to China.

Increased missionary activity and Western enterprise touched off a series of antiforeign outbreaks in China that culminated in the Boxer uprising of 1900. Although for the most part Christian missionaries proved unsuccessful in their endeavors, converting only 100,000 in a population of 400 million, the Chinese nevertheless resented the interference of missionaries in village life and the preference and protection they afforded their Christian converts. Opposition to foreign missionaries took the form of antiforeign secret societies, most notably the Boxers, whose Chinese name translated to "Righteous Harmonious Fist." The Boxers believed that through ritual they could induce a trance that would make them invincible to Western weapons. Their virulent anti-Christian, antimissionary, and

Women Missionaries

Methodist women missionaries in China's Szechuan Province relied on traditional means of transportation, in this case "back chairs." The independence enjoyed by women missionaries stood in marked contrast to the restrictions placed on young, unmarried women of their class at home. Perhaps the opportunity for autonomy as well as missionary zeal explains why by 1890 women constituted 60 percent of America's foreign missionaries. Special Collections, Yale Divinity School Library.

antiforeign beliefs soon led the Boxers to violence. No simple boxing club, in 1899 the Boxers began to terrorize Chinese Christians and missionaries in northwestern Shandong Province. Men and women were hacked to death with swords, burned alive in their houses, and dragged by howling mobs to their execution. With the tacit support of China's Dowager Empress, the Boxers became bolder. Under the slogan "Uphold the Ch'ing Dynasty, Exterminate the Foreigners," they attacked railroads and telegraph lines, the twin symbols of Western imperialism, and marched on the cities. Their rampage eventually led to the massacre of some 30,000 Chinese converts and 250 foreign nuns, priests, and missionaries along with their families.

As the Boxers spread terror throughout northern China, some 800 Americans and Europeans sought refuge in the foreign legation buildings in Beijing (then called Peking). Along with missionaries from the countryside came thousands of their Chinese converts, fleeing the Boxers. Unable to escape and cut off from outside aid and communication, the Americans and Europeans in Beijing mounted a defense to face the Boxer onslaught. One American described the scene as 20,000 Boxers stormed the walls in June 1900:

> Their yells were deafening, while the roar of gongs, drums, and horns sounded like thunder. . . . They waved their swords and stamped on the ground with their feet. They wore red turbans, sashes, and garters over blue cloth. [When] they were only twenty yards from our gate, . . . three volleys from the rifles of our sailors left more than fifty dead upon the ground.

For two months the Europeans and Americans held out under siege, eating mule and horse meat and losing 76 men in battle. American missionary Luella Miner wrote sadly, "We are isolated here as if we were on a desert island. . . . Are our Christians everywhere being slaughtered?" And Sarah Conger, the wife of the U.S. minister (ambassador) wrote wearily, "[The siege] was exciting at first, but night after night of this firing, horn-blowing, yelling, and whizzing of bullets has hardened us to it."

Americans back home who learned of the fate of their countrymen and women at the hands of the Chinese showed little toleration for the cautious diplomatic approach favored by Secretary of State John Hay. In August 1900, 2,500 U.S. troops joined an international force

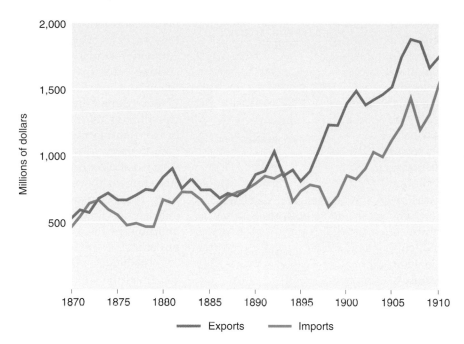

FIGURE 20.2   Expansion in U.S. Trade, 1870–1910

Between 1870 and 1910, American exports nearly tripled. Imports generally rose, but they were held in check by the high protective tariffs championed by Republican presidents from Ulysses Grant to William Howard Taft. A decline in imports is particularly noticeable after passage of the prohibitive McKinley tariff in 1890.

sent to rescue the foreigners besieged in Beijing. After routing the Boxers, the troops looted the Forbidden City, home of the imperial court, forcing the Dowager Empress to flee disguised as a peasant. In 1901 the European powers imposed the humiliating Boxer Protocol, giving them the right to maintain military forces in the Chinese capital and requiring the Chinese government to pay an indemnity of $333 million for the loss of life and property resulting from the Boxer uprising.

In the aftermath of the uprising, missionaries voiced no concern at the paradox of bringing Christianity to China at gunpoint. "It is worth any cost in money, worth any cost in bloodshed," argued one bishop, "if we can make millions of Chinese true and intelligent Christians." Merchants and missionaries alike shared such moralistic reasoning. Indeed, they worked hand in hand; trade and Christianity marched into Asia together. "Missionaries," admitted the American clergyman Charles Denby, "are the pioneers of trade and commerce. . . . The missionary, inspired by holy zeal, goes everywhere and by degrees foreign commerce and trade follow."

The Monroe Doctrine and the Open Door Policy

The emergence of the United States as a world power pitted the nation against the colonial powers, particularly Germany and Japan, which posed a threat to the twin pillars of America's expansionist foreign policy—one dating back to President James Monroe in the 1820s, the other formalized in 1900 under President William McKinley. The first, the Monroe Doctrine, proclaimed the Western Hemisphere an American "sphere of influence" and warned European powers to stay away or risk war. The second, the Open Door, dealt with maintaining market access to China.

American diplomacy actively worked to buttress the Monroe Doctrine, with its assertion of American hegemony (domination) in the Western Hemisphere. In the 1880s, Republican secretary of state James G. Blaine promoted hemispheric peace and trade through Pan-American cooperation but at the same time used American troops to intervene in Latin American border disputes. In 1895 Americans risked war with Great Britain to enforce the Monroe Doctrine. When a conflict developed between Venezuela and British Guiana over lands where gold had been discovered, President Cleveland asserted the U.S. prerogative to step in and mediate, reducing Venezuela to the role of mere onlooker in its own affairs. At first, Britain refused to accept U.S. mediation and conflict seemed imminent. "Let the fight come if it must," wrote Republican neophyte Theodore Roosevelt, always itching to do

> Merchants and missionaries worked hand in hand; trade and Christianity marched into Asia together.

battle. "I don't care whether our sea coast cities are bombarded or not." Seeing war with Britain as an opportunity to fulfill a long-held goal of extending manifest destiny to the north as well as to the west, Roosevelt promised that "we would take Canada." A less bellicose Cleveland wished only to see America's presence in the hemisphere respected and its solution for peace accepted. He was relieved when the British, who feared the possibility of war in Europe and as a consequence wished to avoid conflict in Latin America, accepted the terms of U.S. mediation.

In Central America, where the United States kept a watchful eye on European adventures, American business triumphed in a bloodless takeover that saw French and British interests routed by behemoths like the United Fruit Company of Boston. United Fruit virtually dominated the Central American nations of Costa Rica and Guatemala, while an importer from New Orleans turned Honduras into a "banana republic" (a country run by U.S. business interests). Thus, by 1895, the Venezuelan crisis signaled the extent to which the United States, through business as well as diplomacy, had successfully achieved hegemony in Latin America and the Caribbean, forcing even the British to concur with the secretary of state that "the infinite resources [of the United States] combined with its isolated position render it master of the situation and practically invulnerable as against any or all other powers."

At the same time that American foreign policy warned European powers to stay out of the Western Hemisphere, the United States competed with the colonial powers for trade in the Eastern Hemisphere. As American interests in China grew, the United States became more aggressive in defending its presence in Asia and the Pacific. The United States risked war with Germany in 1889 to guarantee the U.S. navy access to a port for refueling on the way to Asia. The United States

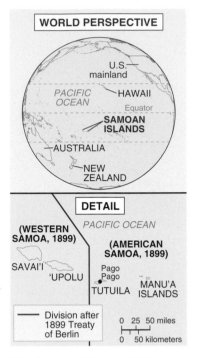

The Samoan Islands, 1889

held treaty rights to the harbor at Pago Pago in the Samoan Islands. Germany, seeking dominance over the islands, challenged the United States by sending warships to the region. But before fighting broke out, a great typhoon destroyed the German and American ships. Acceding to the will of nature, the potential combatants later divided the islands amicably in the 1899 Treaty of Berlin.

The biggest prize in Asia remained the China market. In the 1890s, China, weakened by years of warfare, looked as if it might be partitioned into spheres of influence by England, Japan, Germany, France, and Russia. Concerned about the integrity of China and not coincidentally about American trade, Secretary of State John Hay in 1899–1900 hastily wrote a series of notes calling for an "open door" policy that would ensure trade access to all and maintain the semblance of Chinese sovereignty. The notes—sent to Britain, Germany, and Russia and later to France, Japan, and Italy—were greeted by the major powers with polite evasions. Nevertheless, Hay skillfully managed to maneuver the powers into doing his bidding and boldly announced in 1900 the Open Door as international policy. By insisting on an Open Door policy, the United States managed to secure access to Chinese markets, expanding its economic power while avoiding the problems of maintaining a far-flung colonial empire on the Asian mainland. But as the Spanish-American War demonstrated, Americans found it hard to resist the temptations of empire.

War and Empire

The Spanish-American War began as a humanitarian effort to free Cuba from Spain's colonial grasp and ended with the United States itself becoming a colonial power and fighting a dirty **guerrilla war** with Filipino nationalists, who, like the Cubans, sought independence. Yet be-

> At the same time that American foreign policy warned European powers to stay out of the Western Hemisphere, the United States competed with the colonial powers for trade in the Eastern Hemisphere.

The Open Door
The trade advantage gained by the United States through the Open Door policy, enunciated by Secretary of State John Hay in 1900, is portrayed graphically in this political cartoon. Uncle Sam stands prominently in the "open door" while representatives of the other great powers seek admittance to the "Flowery Kingdom" of China. Great Britain is symbolized by the stocky figure of John Bull; czarist Russia is portrayed by the bearded figure with the hat sporting the imperial double eagle. Other imperialist powers variously represented have yielded to Uncle Sam, who holds the golden key of "American Diplomacy" while the Chinese beam with pleasure. In fact, the Open Door policy promised equal access for all powers to the China trade, not U.S. preeminence as the cartoon implies.
Culver Pictures.

FOR MORE HELP ANALYZING THIS IMAGE, see the visual activity for this chapter in the Online Study Guide at bedfordstmartins.com/roark.

hind the contradiction stood the twin pillars of American foreign policy: The Monroe Doctrine made Spain's presence in Cuba unacceptable, and U.S. determination to keep open the door to Asia made the Philippines attractive as a stepping-stone to China.

"A Splendid Little War"

Looking back on the Spanish-American War of 1898, Secretary of State John Hay judged it "a splendid little war; begun with the highest motives, carried on with magnificent intelligence and spirit, favored by that fortune which loves the brave." At the close of a decade marred by bitter depression, social unrest, and political upheaval, the war offered Americans a chance to wave the flag and march in unison. War fever proved as infectious as the tune of a John Philip Sousa march. Few argued the merits of the conflict until it was over and the time came to divide the spoils.

The war began with moral outrage over the treatment of Cuban revolutionaries, who had launched a fight for independence against the Spanish colonial regime in 1895. In an attempt to isolate the guerrillas, Spanish general Valeriano Weyler herded Cubans into crowded and unsanitary concentration camps, where thousands died of hunger, disease, and exposure. Starvation soon spread to the cities. Tens of thousands of Cubans died, and countless others were left without food, clothing, or shelter. By 1898, fully a quarter of the island's population had perished in the Cuban revolution.

As the Cuban rebellion dragged on, pressure for American intervention mounted. American newspapers fueled public outrage at Spain. A fierce circulation war raged in New York City between William Randolph Hearst's *Journal* and Joseph Pulitzer's *World*. Their competition provoked what came to be called "yellow journalism," named for the colored ink Hearst used in the popular comic strip *The Yellow Kid*. Practitioners of yellow journalism pandered to the public's appetite for violence and sensationalism and found in the Cuban war a wealth of dramatic copy. Newspapers fed the American people a daily diet of "Butcher" Weyler and Spanish atrocities. Hearst sent artist Frederic Remington to document the horror, and when Remington wired home, "There is no trouble here. There will be no war," Hearst shot back, "You furnish the pictures and I'll furnish the war."

American interests in Cuba were, in the words of the U.S. minister to Spain, more than "merely theoretical or sentimental." American business had more than $50 million invested in Cuban sugar, and American trade with Cuba, a

> At the close of a decade marred by bitter depression, social unrest, and political upheaval, the Spanish-American War offered Americans a chance to wave the flag and march in unison.

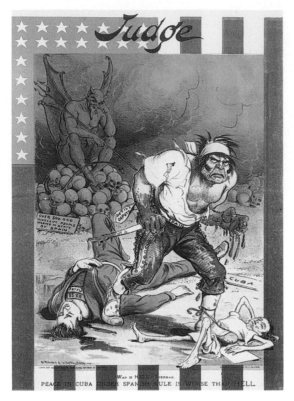

Yellow Journalism

Most cartoonists followed the lead of Hearst-Pulitzer "yellow journalism" in promoting war with Spain. Cartoonist Grant Hamilton drew this cartoon for *Judge* magazine in March 1898. It shows a brutish Spain (the "Devil's Deputy") with bloody hands trampling on a sailor from the *Maine*. Cuba is prostrate, and skulls represent civilians "starved to death" by Spain. Such vicious representations of Spain became common in the American press in the weeks leading up to the Spanish-American War. What does the cartoon say about American attitudes toward race?

Collection of the New-York Historical Society.

preparedness whenever his boss's back was turned. During the hot summer while Navy Secretary John D. Long vacationed, Roosevelt took the helm in his absence and audaciously ordered the U.S. fleet to Manila in the Philippines. In the event of conflict with Spain, he put the navy in a position to capture the islands and gain an entry point to China.

President McKinley slowly moved toward intervention. In a show of American force, he dispatched the battleship *Maine* to Cuba. On the night of February 15, 1898, a mysterious explosion destroyed the *Maine*, killing 267 crew members. The source of the explosion remained unclear, but inflammatory stories in the press enraged Americans, who immediately blamed the Spanish government. (See "Historical Question," page 738.) Rallying to the cry "Remember the *Maine*," Congress declared war on Spain in April. In the surge of patriotism that followed, more than 235,000 men enlisted. War brought with it a unity of purpose and national harmony

Old Glory Banner

Colorful cotton bandanna handkerchiefs like the one pictured here were intended for display and not necessarily to be worn. This bandanna commemorating the Spanish-American War shows President William McKinley in the upper right corner along with the military heroes of the war—Admiral George Dewey, General Nelson Miles, and Rear Admiral William T. Sampson. With an American eagle at the top and an American naval vessel pictured in the middle, the Old Glory motif makes for a colorful display. Who might have displayed this bandanna and why?

Collection of Janice L. and David J. Frent.

brisk $100 million a year before the rebellion, had dropped to near zero. Nevertheless, the business community balked, wary of a war with Spain. When industrialist Mark Hanna, the Republican kingmaker and senator from Ohio, urged restraint, a hot-headed Theodore Roosevelt exploded, "We will have this war for the freedom of Cuba, Senator Hanna, in spite of the timidity of commercial interests."

To expansionists like Roosevelt, more than Cuban independence was at stake. War with Spain opened up the prospect of expansion into Asia as well, since Spain controlled not only Cuba and Puerto Rico but also Guam and the Philippine Islands. Appointed assistant secretary of the navy in April 1897, Roosevelt worked for

The Battle of San Juan Hill

This 1898 lithograph portrays a highly romantic version of the Battle of San Juan Hill. The famous charge was much less glamorous than pictured here. Theodore Roosevelt, whose Rough Riders had taken nearby Kettle Hill, called to his men to charge the next line of Spanish trenches in the San Juan hills. But in the excitement of the battle, they didn't hear him and Roosevelt found himself charging virtually alone. He had to go back and rally the Rough Riders, who then charged the hill on foot. The illustration does get one thing right: The nearsighted Theodore Roosevelt led the charge wearing his spectacles. Fearing that he might lose his glasses in battle, Roosevelt insisted that Brooks Brothers custom-make his uniforms to include a dozen pockets for extra eyeglasses.
Library of Congress.

that ended a decade of political dissent and strife. "In April, everywhere over this good fair land, flags were flying," wrote the Kansas editor William Allen White. "At the stations, crowds gathered to hurrah for the soldiers, and to throw hats into the air, and to unfurl flags."

Soon they had something to cheer about. Five days after McKinley signed the war resolution, a U.S. navy squadron commanded by Admiral George Dewey destroyed the Spanish fleet in Manila Bay (Map 20.3). Dewey's stunning victory caught the United States by surprise. Although naval strategists including Theodore Roosevelt had been orchestrating the move for some time, few Americans had ever heard of the Philippines. Even McKinley con-

fessed that he could not immediately locate the archipelago on the map. He nevertheless recognized the strategic importance of the Philippines and dispatched U.S. troops to secure the islands.

The war in Cuba ended almost as quickly as it began. The first troops landed on June 22, and after a handful of battles the Spanish surrendered on July 17. The war lasted just long enough to elevate Theodore Roosevelt to the status of bona fide war hero. Roosevelt, sensitive to charges that he and his friends were no more than "armchair or parlor **jingoes**," resigned his navy post and formed the Rough Riders, a regiment composed about equally of Ivy League polo players and cowboys who knew of Roosevelt from his stint as a cattle rancher in the Dakotas.

Did Terrorists Sink the *Maine*?

At 9:40 p.m. on the evening of February 15, 1898, the U.S. battleship *Maine* blew up in Havana harbor. Eyewitness accounts differed, but most reported hearing a small concussion followed by a ferocious blast. An American who witnessed the explosion from the wharf reported, "The shock threw us backward. From the deck forward of amidships shot a streak of fire as high as the tall buildings on Broadway. Then the glare of light widened out like a funnel at the top, and down through this bright circle fell showers of wreckage and mangled sailors." Two hundred sixty-seven sailors drowned or burned to death in one of the worst naval catastrophes during peacetime.

Captain Charles Dwight Sigsbee, the last man to leave the burning ship, filed a terse report saying the *Maine* had blown up and "urging [that] public opinion should be suspended until further report." Within two days, however, the yellow press led by William Randolph Hearst's *New York Journal* carried banner headlines announcing, "The War Ship *Maine* Was Split in Two by an Enemy's Secret Infernal Machine!" Such sensational headlines more than doubled the *Journal*'s circulation in the weeks following the disaster.

Public opinion quickly divided between those who suspected foul play and those who believed the explosion had been an accident. Foremost among the accident theorists was the Spanish government, but U.S. business interests who hoped to avoid war with Spain also favored this view. Among the jingoes, as proponents of war were called, there was no doubt who was to blame. Assistant Secretary of the Navy Theodore Roosevelt wrote even before the details were known, "The *Maine* was sunk by an act of dirty treachery on the part of the Spaniards I believe; though we shall never find out definitely, and officially it will go down as an accident."

In less than a week, the navy formed a court of inquiry, and divers inspected the wreckage. The panel reported on March 25 that a mine had exploded under the bottom of the ship, igniting gunpowder in the forward magazine. The navy named no guilty party since the panel could not determine whether the mine had been planted by the Spanish government or by recalcitrant followers of Valeriano Weyler, the Spanish general recalled after the American press dubbed him "the Butcher" for his harsh treatment of the Cubans. The U.S. Senate carried on its own investigation, concluding that whether by intent or by negligence the Spanish government bore responsibility for the catastrophe.

As time passed, however, more people came to view the explosion of the *Maine* as an accident. European naval authorities analyzed the U.S. naval court inquiry and proved that it had made a gross error: The explosion had not occurred at the location named in the report. The European experts concluded that the *Maine* had exploded accidentally, from a fire in the coal bunker adjacent to the reserve gunpowder and shell magazine. Many came to believe that poor design, not treachery, had sunk the *Maine*.

In 1910, the *Maine* still lay in the mud of Havana harbor, a sunken tomb containing the remains of many sailors. The Cuban government asked for the removal of the wreck, and veterans demanded a decent burial for the sailors. With so many questions about the naval court of inquiry's report, American public opinion urged further investigation. New York congressman William Sultzer put it succinctly, "The day after the ship was sunk, you could hardly find an American who did not believe that she had been foully done to death by a treacherous enemy. Today you can

---

While the troops languished in Tampa awaiting their orders, Roosevelt and his men staged daily rodeos for the press, with the likes of New York blueblood William Tiffany busting broncs in competition with Dakota cowboy Jim "Dead Shot" Simpson. When the Rough Riders shipped out to Cuba, journalists fought for a berth with the colorful regiment. Roosevelt's charge up Kettle Hill and his role in the decisive Battle of San Juan Hill made front-page news. Overnight, Roosevelt became the most famous man in America. By the time he sailed home from Cuba, a coalition of independent Republicans was already plotting his political future.

The *Maine* Sunk in Havana Harbor
This photograph of the *Maine*, sunk in the mud of Havana harbor, ran in New York newspapers on February 16, 1898, the morning after the blast. The extent of the destruction and the consequent death of 267 sailors fueled war fever. The yellow press in short order ran eight-inch headlines proclaiming "THE MAINE WAS DESTROYED BY TREACHERY," although there was no evidence to back up the assertion.
National Archives.

hardly find an American who believes Spain had anything to do with it." So in March 1910, Congress voted to raise the *Maine* and reinvestigate.

The "Final Report on Removing the Wreck of Battleship *Maine* from the Harbor of Habana, Cuba" appeared in April 1913. This report confirmed that the original naval inquiry was in error about the location of the initial explosion, but it did not endorse the accident theory. According to the "Final Report," the destruction of the *Maine* resulted from "the explosion of a charge of a low form of explosive exterior to the ship," which led to a massive explosion as the ship's magazine ignited. The nature of the initial explosion indicated a homemade bomb, not a Spanish naval mine—casting suspicion on Weyler's fanatic followers.

After the investigation and removal of human remains, the wreckage of the *Maine* was towed out to sea and, with full funeral honors, sunk in six hundred fathoms of water. But the controversy over the *Maine* proved harder to sink. In the Vietnam era, when faith in the "military establishment" reached an all-time low, Admiral Hyman Rickover launched yet another investigation. Many critics had come to believe that the 1913 "Final Report" was little more than a cover-up; they complained that the ship had been sunk so deep "that there will be no chance of the true facts being revealed." Rickover, a maverick who held the naval brass in low esteem, hired experts to pore over the evidence from previous investigations. He noted that "the warlike atmosphere in Congress and the press, and the natural tendency to look for reasons for the loss that did not reflect on the Navy," made the earlier findings highly suspect. Self-ignition in the coal bunker, he concluded, had triggered an explosion in the reserve magazine. Reading the past in the jaundiced light of the early 1970s, Rickover warned, "We must make sure that those in 'high places' do not without more careful consideration of the consequences, exert our prestige and might," presumably in unnecessary and immoral wars. Published in book form in 1976, Rickover's report, entitled *How the Battleship* Maine *Was Destroyed*, became for a time the accepted version of the event.

Nearly twenty years later, the pendulum swung back. A 1995 study of the *Maine* published by the Smithsonian Institution concluded that zealot followers of General Weyler sank the battleship. "They had the opportunity, the means, and the motivation, and they blew up the *Maine* with a small low-strength mine they made themselves." According to this theory, the terrorists' homemade bomb burst the *Maine*'s hull, triggering a massive explosion.

Today, only one thing seems certain: The lessons of the *Maine* have changed with the times and may continue to be redrawn as each new generation questions history.

The Debate over American Imperialism

After a few brief campaigns in Cuba and Puerto Rico brought the Spanish-American War to an end, the American people woke up in possession of an empire that stretched halfway around the globe. As part of the spoils of war, the United States acquired Cuba, Puerto Rico, Guam, and the Philippines. Yielding to pressure from American sugar growers, McKinley expanded the empire farther, annexing Hawaii in July 1898.

Cuba, freed from Spanish rule, still had not gained full autonomy. Contemptuous of the

Cubans, whom General William Shafter, commander of U.S. troops, declared "no more fit for self-government than gun-powder is for hell," the U.S. government dictated a Cuban constitution. It included the so-called Platt Amendment—a series of provisions that granted the United States the right to intervene to protect Cuba's "independence" as well as the power to oversee Cuban debt so that European creditors could not find an excuse for intervention. For good measure, the United States gave itself a ninety-nine-year lease on a naval base at Guantánamo. In return, McKinley promised to implement an extensive sanitation program to clean up the island, making it more attractive to American investors.

The formal Treaty of Paris ending the war with Spain ceded the Philippines to the United States along with Spain's former colonies in Puerto Rico and Guam (Map 20.4). Empire did not come cheap. When Spain balked, the United States agreed to pay an indemnity of $20 million for the islands. Nor was the cost measured in money alone. Filipino revolutionaries under Emilio Aguinaldo, who had greeted U.S. troops as liberators, bitterly fought the new masters. It would take seven years and 4,000 American dead—almost ten times the number killed in Cuba—not to mention an estimated 20,000 Filipino casualties, to defeat Aguinaldo and secure American control of the Philippines, America's coveted stepping-stone to China.

MAP 20.3   The Spanish-American War, 1898

The Spanish-American War was fought in two theaters, the Philippine Islands and Cuba. Five days after President William McKinley called for a declaration of war, Admiral George Dewey captured Manila without the loss of a single American sailor. The war lasted only eight months. Troops landed in Cuba in mid-June and by mid-July had taken Santiago and Havana and destroyed the Spanish fleet.

READING THE MAP: Which countries held imperial control over countries and territories immediately surrounding the Philippine Islands and Cuba? Which imperial power provided the launching point for the U.S. fleet before Dewey captured Manila?

CONNECTIONS: What role did American newspapers play in the start of the war? How did the results of the war with Spain serve American aims in both Asia and the Western Hemisphere?

FOR MORE HELP ANALYZING THIS MAP, see the map activity for this chapter in the Online Study Guide at bedfordstmartins.com/roark.

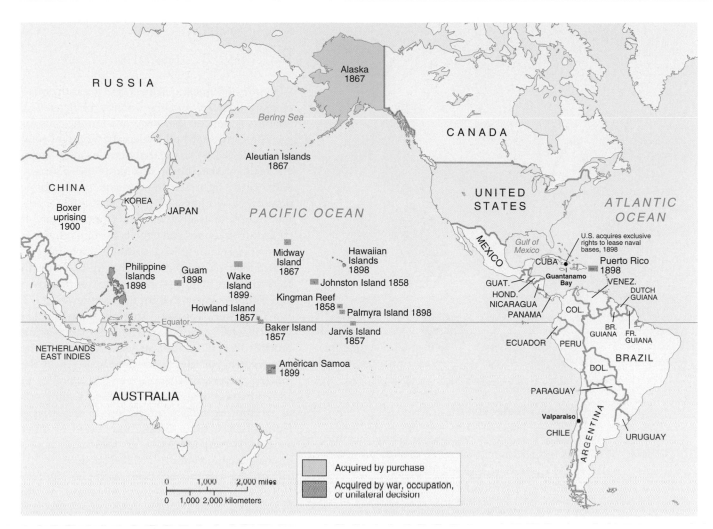

MAP 20.4 U.S. Territorial Expansion through 1900
The United States extended its interests abroad with a series of territorial acquisitions. Although Cuba was granted independence, the Platt Amendment kept the new nation firmly under U.S. control. In the wake of the Spanish-American War, the United States woke up to find that it held an empire extending halfway around the globe.

READING THE MAP: Does the map indicate that more territory was acquired by (1) purchase or (2) war, occupation, or unilateral decision? How many purchases of land outside the continental United States did the government make?
CONNECTIONS: What foreign policy developments occurred in the 1890s? How did American political leaders react to them? Where was U.S. expansion headed, and why?

FOR MORE HELP ANALYZING THIS MAP, see the map activity for this chapter in the Online Study Guide at bedfordstmartins.com/roark.

At home, a vocal minority, mostly Democrats and former Populists, resisted the country's foray into empire, judging it unwise, immoral, and unconstitutional. William Jennings Bryan, who enlisted in the army but contracted typhoid fever and never saw action, came to the conclusion that American expansionism served only to distract the nation from its real problems at home. What did imperialism offer the ordinary American, Bryan asked. His answer: "Heavier taxes, Asiatic emigration and an opportunity to furnish more sons for the army." Mark Twain, lending his bitter eloquence to the cause of anti-imperialism, lamented that the United States had indeed become "yet another Civilized Power, with its banner of the Prince of Peace in one hand and its loot-basket and its butcher-knife in the other."

Columbia's Easter Bonnet
The United States, symbolized by the female figure of Columbia, tries on World Power in this cartoon from *Puck*, which appeared in 1901 after the Spanish-American War left the United States in control of Spain's former colonies in Guam, the Philippines, and Puerto Rico. The bonnet, in the shape of an American battleship, indicates the key role the U.S. navy, under the command of Admiral George Dewey, played in the U.S. victory in Manila that secured the Philippines for the United States. "Expansion," spelled out in the smoke from the ship's smokestack, points to the new direction for American foreign policy at the turn of the twentieth century.
Library of Congress.

Conclusion: Rallying around the Flag

A decade of domestic strife ended amid the blare of martial music and the waving of flags. The Spanish-American War drowned out the calls for social reform that had fueled the Populist politics of the 1890s. During that decade, angry farmers facing hard times looked to the Farmers' Alliance to fight for their vision of economic democracy, workers staged bloody battles across the country to assert their rights, and women attacked drunkenness and the conditions that fostered it and mounted a suffrage movement to secure their basic political rights. In St. Louis in 1892 disaffected groups came together to form a new People's Party to fight for change.

The bitter depression that began in 1893 led to increased labor strife. The Pullman boycott brutally dramatized the power of property and the conservatism of the laissez-faire state. Even the miners' victory in Cripple Creek, Colorado, in 1894 proved short-lived. But workers' willingness to confront capitalism on the streets of Chicago, Homestead, Cripple Creek, and a host of other sites across America eloquently testified to labor's growing determination, unity, and strength.

As the depression deepened, the sight of Coxey's army of unemployed marching on Washington to demand federal intervention in the economy signaled a growing shift in the public mind against the stand-pat politics of laissez-faire. The call for the government to take action to better the lives of workers, farmers, and the dispossessed manifested itself in the fiercely fought presidential campaign of William Jennings Bryan in 1896. With the outbreak of the Spanish-American War in 1898, the decade ended on a harmonious note with patriotic Americans rallying around the flag and cheering America's foray into empire. The United States took its place on the world stage, buttressing its hemispheric domination with the Monroe Doctrine and employing the Open Door policy, which promised access to the riches of China. But even though Americans basked in patriotism and contemplated empire, old grievances had not been laid to rest. The People's Party had been beaten, but the Populists' call for greater government involvement in the economy, expanded opportunities for direct democracy, and a more equitable balance of profits and power between the people and the big corporations, sounded the themes that would be taken up by a new generation of

The anti-imperialists were soon drowned out by cries for empire. The moral tone of the age, set by social Darwinism with its emphasis on survival of the fittest and Anglo-Saxon racial superiority, proved ideally suited to imperialism. Congregational minister Josiah Strong revealed the mixture of racism and missionary zeal that fueled American adventurism abroad when he remarked, "It seems to me that God, with infinite wisdom and skill, is training the Anglo Saxon race for an hour sure to come in the world's future." The *Washington Post* trumpeted, "The taste of empire is in the mouth of the people," thrilled at the prospect of "an imperial policy, the Republic renascent, taking her place with the armed nations."

progressive reformers in the first decades of the twentieth century.

FOR ADDITIONAL FIRSTHAND ACCOUNTS OF THIS PERIOD, see Chapter 20 in Michael Johnson, ed., *Reading the American Past*, Third Edition.

TO ASSESS YOUR MASTERY OF THE MATERIAL IN THIS CHAPTER, see the Online Study Guide at bedfordstmartins.com/roark.

FOR WEB LINKS RELATED TO TOPICS IN THIS CHAPTER, see "HistoryLinks," "DocLinks," and "PlaceLinks" at bedfordstmartins.com/roark.

CHRONOLOGY

1884 • Woman's Christian Temperance Union (WCTU) under Frances Willard calls for woman suffrage (the "home protection ballot").

1886 • Southern Farmers' Alliance reaches out to labor during Great Southwestern Strike.

1889 • Typhoon averts hostilities between German and U.S. ships contesting rights to Pago Pago harbor in the Samoan Islands.

1890 • National American Woman Suffrage Association (NAWSA) forms and elects Elizabeth Cady Stanton president.

• Wyoming enters Union with woman suffrage.

• Southern Farmers' Alliance numbers 3 million members.

1892 • People's Party (Populist Party) founded in St. Louis.

• Homestead lockout pits Carnegie steelworkers against hired Pinkertons.

• Pennsylvania National Guard takes over the Homestead mills, ending the workers' strike.

• Anarchist Alexander Berkman's attempt to assassinate Henry Clay Frick links anarchism with unionism and turns public opinion against Homestead workers.

• People's Party wins more than 1 million votes in presidential election.

• Susan B. Anthony becomes president of NAWSA.

1893 • Panic on Wall Street touches off severe economic depression.

• President Grover Cleveland nixes attempt to annex Hawaii after Americans foment overthrow of Queen Liliuokalani.

1894 • Miners mount a successful strike in Cripple Creek, Colorado, to gain an 8-hour workday.

• Coxey's "army" marches to Washington, D.C. to dramatize plight of unemployed.

• Federal troops crush Pullman strike.

• Union leader Eugene V. Debs jailed for violating court injunction.

1895 • People's Party scores victories in congressional elections.

• President Grover Cleveland risks war with Great Britain to defend Monroe Doctrine in border dispute between British Guiana and Venezuela.

1896 • Democrats support William Jennings Bryan for president on free-silver platform; People's Party also nominates Bryan but substitutes Populist Tom Watson as vice presidential nominee.

• Republican William McKinley defeats Democrat William Jennings Bryan for presidency.

1898 • U.S. battleship *Maine* mysteriously explodes in Havana harbor.

• Congress declares war on Spain.

• Admiral George Dewey destroys Spanish fleet in Manila Bay, the Philippines.

• U.S. troops defeat Spanish forces in Cuba.

• Treaty of Paris ends Spanish-American War; United States acquires Puerto Rico, Guam, and the Philippines.

• United States annexes Hawaii.

• Platt Amendment gives United States oversight of liberated Cuba.

1899 • Treaty of Berlin resolves conflict between Germany and the United States over rights to the Samoan Islands.

1899–1900

• Secretary of State John Hay enunciates Open Door policy in China to guarantee trade access.

• Boxer uprising in China leads to deaths of more than 250 foreign Christian priests, nuns, and missionaries along with 30,000 of their converts.

1901 • Boxer Protocol forces Chinese government to pay $333 million indemnity for loss of life and property resulting from Boxer uprising.

BIBLIOGRAPHY

General

H. W. Brands, *The Reckless Decade: America in the 1890s* (1995).

Alan Dawley, *Struggles for Justice: Social Responsibility and the Liberal State* (1991).

Steven Hahn, *A Nation under Our Feet: Black Political Struggles in the Rural South from Slavery to the Great Migration* (2003).

David Montgomery, *The Fall of the House of Labor: The Workplace, the State, and American Labor Activism, 1865–1925* (1987).

Nell Irvin Painter, *Standing at Armageddon: The United States, 1877–1919* (1987).

The Farmers' Revolt

Edward L. Ayers, *The Promise of the New South: Life after Reconstruction* (1992).

Donna A. Barnes, *Farmers in Rebellion: The Rise and Fall of the Southern Farmers Alliance and People's Party in Texas* (1984).

Marion K. Barthelme, ed., *Women in the Texas Populist Movement* (1997).

William Joseph Gaboury, *Dissension in the Rockies: A History of Idaho Populism* (1988).

Gerald H. Gaither, *Blacks and the Populist Revolt: Ballots and Bigotry in the "New South"* (1977).

Lawrence Goodwyn, *The Populist Moment: A Short History of the Agrarian Revolt in America* (1978).

David B. Griffiths, *Populism in the Western United States, 1890–1900*, vols. 1 and 2 (1992).

Steven Hahn, *The Roots of Southern Populism: Yeoman Farmers and the Transformation of the Georgia Upcountry, 1850–1890* (1983).

Stephen Kantrowitz, *Ben Tillman and the Reconstruction of White Supremacy* (2000).

Michael Kazin, *The Populist Persuasion: An American History* (1998).

Robert W. Larson, *Populism in the Mountain West* (1986).

Robert C. McMath Jr., *American Populism: A Social History, 1877–1898* (1993).

Scott G. McNall, *The Road to Rebellion: Class Formation and Kansas Populism, 1865–1900* (1988).

Theodore R. Mitchell, *Political Education in the Southern Farmers' Alliance, 1887–1900* (1987).

Jane Taylor Nelsen, ed., *A Prairie Populist: The Memoirs of Luna Kellie* (1992).

Jeffrey Ostler, *Prairie Populism: The Fate of Agrarian Radicalism in Kansas, Nebraska, and Iowa, 1880–1892* (1993).

Norman Pollack, *The Just Polity: Populism, Law, and Human Welfare* (1987).

Norman Pollack, *The Humane Economy: Populism, Capitalism, and Democracy* (1990).

Elizabeth Sanders, *Roots of Reform: Farmers, Workers, and the American State, 1877–1917* (1999).

Barton Shaw, *The Wool-Hat Boys: Georgia's Populist Party* (1984).

Lala Carr Steelman, *The North Carolina Farmers' Alliance* (1985).

C. Vann Woodward, *Tom Watson: Agrarian Rebel* (1963).

The Labor Wars

Stanley Buder, *Pullman: An Experiment in Industrial Order and Community Planning* (1976).

Elizabeth Jameson, *All That Glitters: Class, Conflict, and Community in Cripple Creek* (1998).

Paul Krause, *The Battle for Homestead, 1880–1892* (1992).

Nick Salvatore, *Eugene V. Debs: Citizen and Socialist* (1982).

Carl Smith, *Urban Disorder and the Shape of Belief: The Great Chicago Fire, the Haymarket Bomb, and the Model Town of Pullman* (1995).

Leon Stein, ed., *The Pullman Strike* (1969).

Joseph Frazier Wall, *Andrew Carnegie* (1970).

Alice Wexler, *Emma Goldman: An Intimate Life* (1984).

Women's Activism

Jean H. Baker, ed., *Votes for Women: The Struggle for Suffrage Revisited* (2002).

Jack S. Blocker Jr., *"Give to the Winds Thy Fears": The Women's Temperance Crusade, 1873–1874* (1985).

Ruth Bordin, *Women and Temperance: The Quest for Power and Liberty, 1873–1900* (1981).

Ruth Bordin, *Frances Willard: A Biography* (1986).

Ellen Carol DuBois, *Feminism and Suffrage: The Emergence of an Independent Women's Movement in America, 1848–1869* (1978).

Barbara Leslie Epstein, *The Politics of Domesticity: Women, Evangelism, and Temperance in Nineteenth-Century America* (1981).

Michael Lewis Goldberg, *An Army of Women: Gender and Politics in Gilded Age Kansas* (1997).

Gayle Anne Gullett, *Becoming Citizens: The Emergence and Development of the California Women's Movement, 1880–1911* (2000).

Anne Firor Scott, *Natural Allies: Women's Associations in American History* (1991).

Kathryn Kish Sklar, *Florence Kelley and the Nation's Work: The Rise of Women's Political Culture, 1830–1900* (1995).

Ian Tyrell, *Woman's World, Woman's Empire: The Woman's Christian Temperance Union in International Perspective, 1880–1930* (1991).

Depression Politics

Robert A. Allen, *Reluctant Reformers: Racism and Social Reform Movements in the United States* (1974).

Robert W. Cherny, *A Righteous Cause: The Life of William Jennings Bryan* (1985).

Gene Clanton, *Populism: The Humane Preference in America, 1890–1900* (1991).

Robert F. Durden, *The Climax of Populism: The Election of 1896* (1969).

Lewis L. Gould, *The Presidency of William McKinley* (1981).

Stephen Kantrowitz, *Ben Tillman and the Reconstruction of White Supremacy* (2000).

Louis W. Koenig, *Bryan: A Political Biography of William Jennings Bryan* (1971).

Kenneth L. Kusmer, *Down and Out, on the Road: The Homeless in American History* (2002).

Samuel McSeveney, *The Politics of Depression* (1972).

Gretchen Ritter, *Goldbugs and Greenbacks: The Antimonopoly Tradition in the Politics of Finance in America* (1997).

Carol A. Schwantes, *Coxey's Army: An American Odyssey* (1985).

Douglas Steeples and David O. Whitten, *Democracy in Desperation: The Depression of 1892* (1998).

American Foreign Policy

David Anderson, *Imperialism and Idealism: American Diplomacy in China, 1861–1898* (1985).

William Becker, *The Dynamics of Business-Government Relations* (1982).

Robert Beisner, *From the Old Diplomacy to the New, 1865–1900* (1975).

Charles Campbell, *The Transformation of American Foreign Relations, 1865–1900* (1976).

Kendrick A. Clements, *William Jennings Bryan, Missionary Isolationist* (1982).

Edward P. Crapol, *James G. Blaine: Architect of Empire* (1999).

John Dobson, *America's Ascent: The United States Becomes a Great Power, 1880–1914* (1978).

Willard Gatewood Jr., *Black Americans and the White Man's Burden* (1975).

Kenneth Hagen, *American Gun-Boat Diplomacy* (1973).

Patricia R. Hill, *The World Their Household: The American Woman's Foreign Mission Movement and Cultural Transformation, 1870–1920* (1985).

Kristin Hoganson, *Fighting for American Manhood* (1998).

Michael H. Hunt, *The Making of a Special Relationship: The United States and China to 1914* (1983).

Jane Hunter, *The Gospel of Gentility: American Women Missionaries in Turn-of-the-Century China* (1984).

Matthew Frye Jacobson, *Barbarian Virtues: The United States Encounters Foreign Peoples at Home and Abroad, 1876–1917* (2000).

Walter LaFeber, *The American Search for Opportunity, 1865–1913* (1993).

Walter LaFeber, *Inevitable Revolutions: The United States in Central America* (2nd rev. ed., 1993).

Hazel M. McFerson, *The Racial Dimension of American Overseas Colonial Policy* (1997).

Ivan Musicant, *The Banana Wars: A History of U. S. Military Intervention from the Spanish-American War to the Invasion of Panama* (1990).

Thomas J. Osborne, *Annexation Hawaii* (1998).

Diana Preston, *Besieged in Peking: The Story of the 1900 Boxer Rising* (1999).

Emily S. Rosenberg, *Spreading the American Dream: American Economic and Cultural Expansion, 1890–1945* (1982).

James C. Thompson Jr., Peter W. Stanley, and John Curtis Perry, *Sentimental Imperialists: The American Experience in East Asia* (1981).

Richard Turk, *The Ambiguous Relationship: Theodore Roosevelt and Alfred Thayer Mahan* (1987).

The Spanish-American War

H. W. Brands, *Bound to Empire: The United States and the Philippines* (1992).

Stan Cohen, *Images of the Spanish-American War, April–August 1898* (1997).

John A. Corry, *1898: Prelude to a Century* (1998).

Brian P. Damiani, *Advocates of Empire: William McKinley, the Senate, and American Expansion, 1898–1899* (1987).

Philip S. Foner, *The Spanish-Cuban-American War and the Birth of American Imperialism,* 2 vols. (1972).

Lewis W. Gould, *The Spanish-American War and President McKinley* (1982).

Louis J. Halle, *The United States Acquires the Philippines: Consensus vs. Reality* (1985).

Stanley Karnow, *In Our Image: America's Empire in the Philippines* (1989).

Gerald F. Linderman, *The Mirror of War: American Society and the Spanish-American War* (1974).

Bryan Linn, *The Philippine War, 1899–1902* (2000).

Stuart Creighton Miller, *"Benevolent Assimilation": The American Conquest of the Philippines, 1899–1903* (1982).

Joyce Milton, *The Yellow Kids: Foreign Correspondents in the Heyday of Yellow Journalism* (1989).

Ivan Musicant, *Empire by Default: The Spanish-American War and the Dawn of the American Century* (1998).

Albert A. Nofi, *The Spanish-American War, 1898* (1997).

John L. Offner, *An Unwanted War: The Diplomacy of the United States and Spain over Cuba, 1895–1898* (1992).

George J. A. O'Toole, *The Spanish War: An American Epic—1898* (1986).

Louis A. Perez Jr., *The War of 1898: The United States and Cuba in History and Historiography* (1998).

John D. Seelye, *War Games: Richard Harding Davis and the New Imperialism* (2003).

Lars Shoultz, *Beneath the United States* (1998).

David F. Trask, *The War with Spain in 1898* (1981).

David Traxel, *1898: The Birth of the American Century* (1999).

THE PROGRESSIVE PARTY

BORN 1912

PROGRESSIVE PARTY CAMPAIGN SOUVENIR
This colorful cotton bandana, a campaign novelty from the 1912 presidential race, celebrates the Progressive Party and its candidate Theodore Roosevelt. The progressive reform movement, growing out of the crises of the 1890s, emerged full-blown in the first decades of the twentieth century. Progressives challenged laissez-faire liberalism and argued for government action to counter the power of big business and ensure greater social justice. Theodore Roosevelt, whose presidency set the tone for the era, became so closely associated with progressivism that when he failed to win the Republican nomination in 1912, his followers formed a new Progressive Party proclaiming, as the bandana notes, "We Want Our Teddy Back." Accepting the nomination, Roosevelt announced that he felt "as fit as a bull moose," giving the new party a mascot. But progressivism was more than one man or one party. A movement that ran from the grass roots to the White House, it included not only members of the short-lived Progressive Party, but Democrats and Republicans as well, who had in common a belief in government activism that would reshape the liberal state of the twentieth century.

Collection of Janice L. and David J. Frent.

Progressivism from the Grass Roots to the White House

1890–1916

IN THE SUMMER OF 1889, a young woman leased the upper floor of a dilapidated mansion on Chicago's West Side in the heart of a burgeoning immigrant population of Italians, Russian Jews, and Greeks. Watching the preparations, neighbors scratched their heads, wondering why the well-dressed woman, who surely could afford a better house in a better neighborhood, chose to live on South Halsted Street. Yet the house built by Charles Hull precisely suited the needs of Jane Addams.

For Addams, personal action marked the first step in the search for solutions to the social problems fostered by urban industrialism. Her object was twofold: She wanted to help her immigrant neighbors, and she wanted to offer an opportunity for educated women like herself to find meaningful work. As she later wrote in her autobiography, *Twenty Years at Hull-House* (1910), "I gradually became convinced that it would be a good thing to rent a house in a part of the city where many primitive and actual needs are found, in which young women who had been given over too exclusively to study might restore a balance of activity along traditional lines and learn of life from life itself." Addams's emphasis on the reciprocal relationship between the social classes made Hull House different from other philanthropic enterprises. She wished to do things with, not just for, Chicago's poor.

In the next decade, Hull House expanded from one rented floor in the old brick mansion to some thirteen buildings housing a remarkable variety of activities. Bathrooms in the basement were converted into public baths, a coffee shop and restaurant sold take-out food to working women too tired to cook after their long shifts, and a nursery and kindergarten provided care for neighborhood children. Hull House offered classes, lectures, art exhibits, musical instruction, and college extension courses. It boasted a gymnasium, a theater, a manual training workshop, a labor museum, and the first public playground in Chicago.

But Hull House was more than a group of buildings. From the first, it attracted an extraordinary set of reformers. Some stayed for decades, as did Julia Lathrop before she went to Washington, D.C., in 1912 to head the Children's Bureau. Others, like Gerard Swope, who later became president of the General Electric Company, came for only a short while. Most had jobs, paid room and board, and devoted time to research and reform. The people

Jane Addams

Jane Addams was twenty-nine years old when she founded Hull House on South Halsted Street in Chicago. Graduates of the Rockford Female Seminary, she and her college roommate, Ellen Gates Starr, established America's premier social settlement. Her desire to live among the poor and her insistence that settlement house work benefited educated women like herself as well as her immigrant neighbors separated her from the charity workers who had come before her and marked the distance from philanthropy to progressive reform.

Jane Addams Memorial Collection, Special Collection, University Library, University of Illinois at Chicago.

who lived at Hull House were among the first to investigate the problems of the city with scientific precision. Armed with statistics, they launched campaigns to improve housing, end child labor, fund playgrounds, mediate between labor and management, and lobby for protective legislation.

Addams quickly learned that it was impossible to deal with urban problems without becoming involved in political action. Her determination to clean up the garbage on Halsted Street led her into politics. Piles of decaying garbage overflowed the street's wooden trash bins, breeding flies and disease. Investigation revealed that the contract to pick up the trash was a political plum awarded by the local ward boss to a contractor who felt under no obligation to provide adequate service. To end the graft, Addams got herself appointed garbage inspector. Out on the streets at six in the morning, she rode atop the garbage wagon to make sure it made its rounds. When the ward boss removed her, she squared off against him. After backing several unsuccessful political campaigns to oust the boss, Addams realized that bossism was a symptom and not the cause of urban blight. Recognizing that bosses stayed in power by providing jobs and services to their constituents, she moved instead to sponsor legislation to help her neighbors. Eventually her struggle to aid the urban poor led her not only to city hall but on to the state capitol and to Washington, D.C. Addams became a strong advocate of woman **suffrage**, arguing that city women needed the ballot, not the broom, to keep their neighborhoods clean.

Under Jane Addams's leadership, Hull House, the premier settlement house in the United States, became a "spearhead for reform," part of a broader movement that contemporaries called **progressivism**. The transition from personal action to political activism that Addams personified became one of the hallmarks of this reform period, which lasted from the 1890s to World War I.

By the 1890s it had become clear to many Americans that the **laissez-faire** approach of government toward business no longer worked. The classical **liberalism** of the nation's Founders, with its emphasis on opposition to the tyranny of centralized government, had not reckoned on the enormous private wealth and power of the Gilded Age's Rockefellers and Morgans. The injunction that government stay out of the marketplace made it impossible to curb the excesses of the huge corporations. As the gap between rich and poor widened in the 1890s, issues of social justice also challenged traditional notions of laissez-faire liberalism. The violence and militance of the 1890s—labor strikes, farmers' revolt, suffrage rallies, the antilynching campaign—eloquently testified to the growing polarities in society. Yet a laissez-faire state only exacerbated the inequalities of class, race, and gender. With women denied basic political and economic rights, southern blacks threatened by lynching and intimidation, and courts privileging private property over personal rights, laissez-faire liberalism effectively prevented the country from addressing issues of social justice and ameliorating the inequities of urban industrial capitalism. A generation of progressive reformers demanded government intervention to guarantee a more equitable society. The willingness to use the government to promote change and to counterbalance the power of private interests redefined liberalism in the twentieth century.

Faith in activism in both the political and the private realms formed a common thread that

Hull House Playground

Settlement houses worked hard to provide opportunities for neighborhood youth. Hull House opened Chicago's first children's playground, shown here, in 1894 to provide supervised recreation in a safe, clean alternative to filthy tenement alleys. Reformers believed that access to playgrounds and parks would instill qualities of morality and citizenship in the city's children. As Jacob Riis testified, "A boy robbed of his chance to play will not be an honest and effective citizen."

Jane Addams Memorial Collection, Special Collection, University Library, University of Illinois at Chicago.

Grassroots Progressivism

Much of progressive reform began at the grassroots level and percolated upward into local, state, and eventually national politics as reformers attacked the social problems fostered by urban industrialism. While reform flourished in many different settings across the country, urban problems inspired the progressives' greatest efforts. In their zeal to "civilize the city," reformers founded settlement houses, professed a new Christian **social gospel**, and campaigned against vice and crime in the name of "social purity." Allying with the working class, they sought to better the lot of sweatshop garment workers and to end child labor. Their reform efforts often began on the local level but ended up being debated in state legislatures, in Congress, and in the Oval Office. From Hull House to the White House, progressivism became a major political force in the first decade of the twentieth century.

Civilizing the City

Progressives attacked the problems of the city on many fronts. The settlement house movement attempted to bridge the distance between the classes. The social gospel called for the churches to play a new role in social reformation. And the **social purity movement** campaigned to clean up vice, particularly prostitution.

The settlement house movement, begun in England, came to the United States in 1886 with the opening of the University Settlement House in New York City. The needs of poor urban neighborhoods provided the impetus for these social settlements. In 1893, Lillian Wald, a nurse attending medical school in New York, went to care for a woman living in a dilapidated tenement. The experience led Wald to leave medical school and recruit several other nurses to move to New York City's Lower East Side "to live in the neighborhood as nurses, identify ourselves with it socially, and . . . contribute to it our citizenship." Expanded in 1895, the Henry Street settlement pioneered public health nursing. Although Wald herself was Jewish, she insisted that the Henry Street settlement remain independent of religious ties, making it different from the avowedly religious English settlements.

Women, particularly college-educated women like Jane Addams and Lillian Wald, formed the backbone of the settlement house movement. Eager to use their knowledge, educated women

united an otherwise diverse group of progressive reformers with a variety of schemes for the betterment of society. A sense of Christian mission inspired some. Others, frightened by the political tensions of the 1890s, feared social upheaval and sought to remove some of the worst evils of urban industrialism—tenements, child labor, and harsh working conditions. Progressives shared a growing concern about the power of wealthy individuals and corporations and a strong dislike of the **trusts**. But often they feared the new immigrants at the opposite end of the economic ladder and sought to control and Americanize them. Along with moral fervor, a belief in technical expertise and scientific principles infused progressivism and made the cult of efficiency part and parcel of the movement. All of these elements—uplift and efficiency, social justice and social control—came together in the Progressive Era and characterized the progressive movement both at the grassroots level in the cities and states and in the presidencies of Theodore Roosevelt and Woodrow Wilson.

AMERICAN PLACES

Jane Addams Hull-House Museum, Chicago, Illinois

The Jane Addams Hull-House Museum, administered by the University of Illinois at Chicago, is located at 800 South Halsted Street in Chicago. Built by Charles J. Hull in 1856, the two-story brick mansion is decorated with a white wooden cupola and classic Greek columns. After the Chicago fire of 1871, the "better classes" moved to other parts of the city, and the area attracted a large population of Italian, Greek, and Jewish immigrants. The run-down mansion sat in the midst of factories and tenements in 1889 when Jane Addams and her college roommate, Ellen Gates Starr, leased the drawing room and the upper floor to found the Hull House social settlement.

From the first, Jane Addams put her personal stamp on the social settlement, or settlement house, movement. Hull House attracted women who sought to put their education to work for the betterment of society, and it became the first social settlement in which residents of both sexes lived under one roof.

Addams intended Hull House to serve as a living room for her tenement neighbors. Its educative function worked in both directions: for the benefit of her poor neighbors, who used it as a clubhouse, day nursery, union meeting hall, and a place to relax; but also to educate the privileged classes who came to live at Hull House or attended lectures by prominent speakers who stopped by on their trips to Chicago. In this way Hull House functioned as a bridge between the classes, introducing the well-off to the poor in a personal, homelike setting.

With no set program or political theory to advance, Addams sought to help her neighbors where she could. In the process, she and other Hull House workers pioneered an impressive list of firsts for Chicago: the first public playground, the first public baths, the first public gymnasium, the first citizenship preparation classes, the first public kitchen, the first community theater, the first college extension courses, the first free art exhibits, the first public swimming pool, and the first Boy Scout troop.

Residents at Hull House paid their own way and put their talents to work in the service of their neighbors by investigating urban problems—truancy, poor sanitation, infectious diseases, drug traffic, and infant mortality. Their meticulous research led to the first factory laws in Illinois and to Chicago's first model tenement code. Illinois' first factory inspector, Florence Kelley, came from Hull House, as did Alzina Stevens, Chicago's first probation officer, and Julia Lathrop, the head of the federal government's Children's Bureau.

By grounding their investigations in concern for the lives of their immigrant neighbors, the residents of Hull House put a human face on urban statistics. Their work helped

---

Settlement houses gave college-educated women a place to use their talents in the service of society. In the process, settlement house women created a new profession—social work.

found themselves blocked from medicine, law, and the clergy (fewer than 1,500 women practiced law in 1900, and women constituted only 6 percent of the medical profession). Settlement houses gave college-educated women a place to use their talents in the service of society. Largely due to women's efforts, settlements like Hull House grew in number from six in 1891 to more than four hundred in 1911. (See "American Places," above.) In the process, settlement house women created a new profession—social work.

Some churches along with the settlement houses confronted urban social problems by enunciating a new social gospel, one that saw its mission not simply to reform individuals but to reform society. The social gospel offered a powerful corrective to the **gospel of wealth**, as outlined by Andrew Carnegie, with its belief that riches somehow signaled divine favor. Washington Gladden, a prominent social gospel minister, challenged that view when he urged Congregationalists to turn down a gift from John D. Rockefeller, arguing that it was "tainted money." In place of the gospel of wealth, the clergy exhorted their congregations to put Christ's teachings to work in their daily lives. For Walter Rauschenbusch, a Baptist minister change public attitudes about poverty, challenging the notion that the poor were drunken, vicious, or lazy and turning the private troubles of the urban poor into public issues. Hull House became a "spearhead for reform," an integral part of the progressive movement, championing the belief that the nation had a responsibility to address poverty, living conditions, and the health and welfare of working people.

By 1907, the Hull House settlement included a two-block complex of thirteen buildings. Jane Addams lived at Hull House until her death in 1935. During her lifetime, she worked to advance the cause of social justice, writing ten books and over 200 articles and delivering hundreds of speeches. She fought for women's right to vote, helped found the National Association for the Advancement of Colored People (NAACP), organized labor unions, and presided over the Women's International League for Peace and Freedom. In 1931, Addams received the Nobel Peace Prize. Thousands of mourners attended her funeral in the Hull House courtyard in 1935 to pay their respects to "Saint Jane." Hull House continued to function as a

The Jane Addams Hull-House Museum
Jane Addams Hull-House Museum.

social settlement until 1963, when the University of Illinois purchased the property. Plans to demolish Hull House set off a public protest that led to its designation as a National Historic Landmark in 1967.

Today the Jane Addams Hull-House Museum includes two of the original buildings, the Hull Mansion and the Residents' Dining Hall.

The mansion contains furnishings, paintings, and photographs—many belonging to Addams—as well as exhibits that re-create the history of this world-famous settlement and the work of its residents.

FOR WEB LINKS RELATED TO THIS SITE AND OTHER AMERICAN PLACES, see "PlaceLinks" at bedfordstmartins.com/roark.

working in New York's tough Hell's Kitchen neighborhood, the social gospel grew out of the depression of the 1890s, which left thousands of people unemployed. "They wore down our threshold and they wore away our hearts," he later wrote. "One could hear human virtue cracking and crumbling all around." In *Christianity and the Social Crisis* (1907), Rauschenbusch called for the church to play a new role in promoting social justice.

Ministers also played an active role in the social purity movement, the campaign to attack vice. To end the "social evil," as reformers euphemistically called prostitution, the social purity movement brought together ministers who wished to stamp out sin, doctors concerned

about the spread of venereal disease, and women reformers determined to fight the double standard that made it acceptable for men to engage in premarital and extramarital sex but punished women who strayed. Together, they waged campaigns to close red-light districts in cities across the country and lobbied for the Mann Act, passed in 1910, which made it illegal to transport women across state lines for "immoral purposes." On the state level, they struck at venereal disease by securing legislation to require a blood test for syphilis before marriage.

Attacks on alcohol went hand in hand with the push for social purity. The **temperance** campaign launched by the Woman's Christian

Temperance Union (WCTU) heated up in the early twentieth century. The Anti-Saloon League, formed in 1895 under the leadership of **Protestant** clergy, campaigned for an end to the sale of liquor. Reformers pointed to links between drinking, prostitution, wife and child abuse, unemployment, and industrial accidents. The powerful liquor lobby fought back, spending liberally in election campaigns, fueling the charge that liquor corrupted the political process.

An element of **nativism** (dislike of foreigners) ran through the movement for prohibition, as it did in a number of progressive reforms. The Irish, the Italians, and the Germans were among the groups stigmatized by temperance reformers for their drinking. Progressives often failed to see the important role the tavern played in many ethnic communities. Unlike the American saloon, an almost exclusively male domain, the tavern was often a family retreat. German

Americans of all ages socialized at beer gardens after church on Sunday. Even though most workers toiled six days a week and had only Sunday for recreation and relaxation, some progressives campaigned on the local level to enforce the Sunday closing of taverns. To deny the working class access to alcohol, these progressives pushed for state legislation to outlaw the sale of liquor; by 1912, seven states were "dry."

Progressives' efforts to civilize the city, whether by launching social settlements or campaigning against prostitution and alcohol, demonstrated their willingness to take action, their belief that environment, not heredity alone, determined human behavior, and their optimism that conditions could be corrected through government action without radically altering America's economy or institutions. All of these attitudes characterized the progressive movement.

Progressives and the Working Class

Day-to-day contact with their neighbors made settlement house workers particularly sympathetic to labor unions. When Mary Kenney O'Sullivan complained that her bookbinders' union met in a dirty, noisy saloon, Jane Addams invited the union to meet at Hull House. And during the Pullman strike in 1894, Hull House residents organized strike relief and lent their

prestige and financial resources. "Hull-House has been so unionized," grumbled one Chicago businessman, "that it has lost its usefulness and become a detriment and harm to the community." But to the working class, the support of middle-class reformers marked a significant gain.

Attempts to forge a cross-class alliance became institutionalized in 1903 with the creation of the Women's Trade Union League (WTUL). The WTUL brought together women workers and middle-class "allies." Its goal was to organize working women into unions under the auspices of the American Federation of Labor (AFL). However, the AFL provided little more than lip service to the organization of women workers. As one working woman confided, "The men think that the girls should not get as good work as the men and should not make half as much money as a man." When it came to women, the AFL's main concern seemed to be to protect men from female competition. Samuel Gompers, president of the AFL, endorsed the principle of equal pay for equal work, shrewdly observing that it would help male workers more than women, since many employers hired women precisely because they could be paid less and otherwise would hire men. Given the AFL's attitude, it was not surprising that the money and leadership to organize women came largely from wealthy allies in the WTUL.

The league's most notable success came in 1909 in the "uprising of twenty thousand." In November, hundreds of women employees of the Triangle Shirtwaist Company in New York City went on strike to protest low wages, dangerous and demeaning working conditions, and management's refusal to recognize their union, the International Ladies' Garment Workers Union (ILGWU). In support of the walkout, the ILGWU called for a general strike of all garment workers. An estimated 20,000 workers, most of them teenage girls and many of them Jewish and Italian immigrants, walked off the job and stayed out on strike through the winter, picketing in the bitter cold. More than 600 were arrested, and many were sent to jail for "streetwalking," a move by the authorities to try to break the strike by impugning the morals of the striking women. By the time the strike ended in February 1910, the workers had won important demands in many shops. But they lost their bid to gain recognition for their union. The solidarity shown by the women workers proved to be the strike's greatest achievement. As Clara Lemlich, one of the strike's leaders, exclaimed, "They used to say that you couldn't even organize women. They wouldn't come to union meetings. They were 'temporary' workers. Well we showed them!"

The WTUL made enormous contributions to the strike. The league provided volunteers for the picket lines, posted more than $29,000 in bail, protested police brutality, organized a parade of 10,000 strikers, took part in the arbitration conference, arranged mass meetings, appealed for funds, and generated publicity for the strike. Under the leadership of the WTUL, women from every class of society, from J. P. Morgan's daughter Anne to **socialists** on New York's Lower East Side, joined the strikers in a dramatic demonstration of cross-class alliance.

But despite its demonstration of solidarity, the uprising of the twenty thousand failed to change the dangerous conditions faced by women workers. In March 1911, a little over a year after the shirtwaist makers' strike ended, fire alarms sounded at the Triangle Shirtwaist factory. The building, full of lint and combustible cloth, went up in flames in minutes and burned to rubble in half an hour. A WTUL member described the scene below on the street: "Two young girls whom I knew to be working in the vicinity came rushing toward me, tears were running from their eyes and they were white and shaking as they caught me by the arm. 'Oh,' shrieked one of them, 'they are jumping. Jumping from ten stories up! They are going through the air like bundles of clothes.'"

The terrified Triangle workers had little choice but to jump. One door was blocked by flames, and the other had been locked so that workers leaving the building could be searched to prevent pilfering. The lucky ones made it out on the elevator or by climbing to the roof where they escaped to a neighboring building. For the rest, the building proved a deathtrap. The flimsy, rusted fire escape collapsed under the weight of fleeing workers, killing dozens. Trapped, 54 workers jumped from the ninth-floor windows, only to smash to their deaths on the sidewalk. Of 500 workers, 146 died and scores of others were injured. The owners of the Triangle firm were later tried for negligence, but they avoided conviction when authorities determined that the fire had been started by a careless smoker. The Triangle Shirtwaist Company reopened in another firetrap within weeks.

Outraged and overwhelmed by the catastrophe, Rose Schneiderman, a leading WTUL organizer, made a bitter speech at the memorial service for the dead Triangle workers. "I would

Women Strikers
The "uprising of the 20,000" pitted garment workers against their employers in a strike that lasted throughout the bitter winter of 1909–10. The strikers, primarily young women from the Jewish and Italian immigrant communities, joined the International Ladies' Garment Workers Union and proved that women could be unionized and mount an effective strike. The Women's Trade Union League, a cross-class alliance of working women and middle-class "allies," contributed money and offered moral support to the strikers.
ILGWU Archives, Labor-Management Documentation Center, Cornell University.

be a traitor to those poor burned bodies if I came here to talk good fellowship," she told her audience. "We have tried you good people of the public and we have found you wanting. . . . I know from my experience it is up to the working people to save themselves . . . by a strong working class movement."

The Triangle fire tested severely the bonds of the cross-class alliance. Along with Schneiderman, WTUL leaders experienced a growing sense of futility. It seemed not enough to organize and to strike. Increasingly, the WTUL turned its efforts to lobbying for protective legislation—laws that would limit hours and regulate working conditions for women workers.

> By the time the strike ended in February 1910, the workers had won important demands in many shops. The solidarity shown by the women proved to be the strike's greatest achievement.

14. Viewing the unfortunates at the M...

Triangle Fire Morgue
After the Triangle fire on March 26, 1911, New York City set up a makeshift morgue at the end of Manhattan's Charities Pier. There the remains of more than a hundred young women and two dozen young men were laid out in coffins for their friends and relatives to identify. Victims who had jumped to their deaths from the ninth-floor windows or leaped down the elevator shaft could be easily recognized. Those trapped in the building were burned beyond recognition. A ring, a charred shoe, a melted hair comb often provided the only clues to the identity of a sister, a daughter, or a sweetheart. In the *New York Evening Journal* (right), a survivor recounted the horror inside when the girls discovered that one of the two doors leading out of the building was locked, barring their escape. In the trial that followed the fire, the owners of the Triangle Shirtwaist Company avoided penalty when their skillful lawyer challenged the credibility of witnesses like the woman in the news story, who testified that one door had been locked to keep girls from pilfering.
UNITE Archives, Kheel Center, Cornell University, Ithaca, NY 14853-3901.

Advocates of protective legislation won a major victory in 1908 when the U.S. Supreme Court, in *Muller v. Oregon,* reversed its previous rulings and upheld an Oregon law that limited to ten the hours women could work in a day. A mass of sociological evidence put together by Florence Kelley of the National Consumers' League and Josephine Goldmark of the WTUL and presented by Goldmark's brother-in-law, lawyer Louis Brandeis, demonstrated the ill effects of long hours on the health and safety of women. The "Brandeis brief" convinced the Court that long hours endangered women and therefore the entire race. The Court's ruling set a precedent, but one that separated the well-being of women workers from that of men by arguing that women's reproductive role justified special treatment. Later generations of women fighting

for equality would question the effectiveness of this strategy and argue that it ultimately closed good jobs to women. But the WTUL greeted protective legislation as a first step in the attempt to ensure the safety not just of women but of all workers.

The National Consumers' League (NCL), like the WTUL, fostered cross-class alliance. Its work also extended beyond the United States (see "Beyond America's Borders," page 756). When Florence Kelley took over the leadership of the NCL in 1899, she urged middle-class women to boycott stores and exert pressure for decent wages and working conditions for women employees, primarily saleswomen. But like the WTUL, the National Consumers' League turned increasingly to protective legislation to achieve its goals. Frustrated by the reluctance of the private sector to respond to the need for reform, progressives turned to government at all levels. Critics would later charge that the progressives assumed too easily that government regulation could best solve social problems.

Progressivism: Theory and Practice

Progressive reformers developed a theoretical basis for their activist approach by countering **social Darwinism** with a dynamic new **reform Darwinism** and by championing the uniquely American philosophy of pragmatism. Progressives emphasized action and experimentation. No longer was the universe seen as a massive, slow-moving machine, but as a system amenable to tinkering by human intelligence. Unchecked admiration for speed and productivity also inspired enthusiasm for **scientific management** and a new cult of efficiency. These varied strands of progressive theory found practical application in state and local politics, where reformers challenged traditional laissez-faire government.

Reform Darwinism, Pragmatism, and Social Engineering

The active, interventionist approach of the progressives directly challenged social Darwinism, with its insistence that the world operated on the principle of survival of the fittest and that human beings stood powerless in the face of the law of natural selection. Without abandoning the evolutionary framework of Darwinism, a new group of sociologists argued that evolution could be advanced more rapidly if men and women used their intellects to alter the environment. Dubbed "reform Darwinism," the new sociological theory condemned laissez-faire, insisting that the liberal state should play a more active role in solving social problems. Reform Darwinism provided a rationale for attacking social ills and became the ideological basis for progressive reform.

In their pursuit of reform, progressives were influenced by the work of two philosophers, William James and John Dewey, who argued for a new test for truth. They insisted that there were no eternal truths and that the real worth of any idea lay in its consequences. They called their relativistic philosophy pragmatism. Dewey put his theories to the test in the classroom of his laboratory school at the University of Chicago. A pioneer in American education, he emphasized process rather than content and encouraged child-centered schools where students would learn by doing. By championing social experimentation, the American pragmatists provided an important impetus for progressive reform.

Efficiency and *expertise* became watchwords in the progressive vocabulary. The journalist and critic Walter Lippmann, in *Drift and Mastery* (1914), a classic statement of the progressive agenda, called for skilled technocrats to use scientific techniques to control social change, substituting social engineering for aimless drift. Progressive reformers' emphasis on expertise inevitably fostered a kind of elitism. Whereas **Populists** had called for a greater voice for the masses, progressivism, for all its emphasis on social justice, insisted that experts be put in charge.

At its extreme, the application of expertise and social engineering took the form of scientific management, which by elevating productivity and efficiency alienated the working class. Frederick Winslow Taylor pioneered "systematized shop management." After dropping out of Harvard after a nervous breakdown, Taylor went to work as a machinist at Midvale Steel in Philadelphia in the 1880s. Obsessed with making men and machines produce more and faster, he carefully timed workers with his stopwatch and attempted to break their work down into its simplest components, one repetitious action after another, on the theory that productivity would increase if tasks were reduced to their simplest parts. Workers hated the monotony of systematized shop management and argued that it led to the speedup—pushing workers to produce more in less time and for less pay. But advocates of "Taylorism" included progressives like Louis Brandeis, who applauded the increased productivity and efficiency of Taylor's system.

> Whereas Populists had called for a greater voice of the masses, progressivism, for all its emphasis on social justice, insisted that experts be put in charge.

Progressive Government: City and State

The politicians who became premier progressives were generally the followers, not the leaders, in a movement already well advanced at the grassroots level. Yet they left their stamp on the movement. Tom Johnson made Cleveland, Ohio,

Protecting the World's Workers: The National Consumers' League

The United States was not alone in wrestling with the problems accompanying urban industrialism. In western Europe, particularly Germany and England where industrial development occurred even more rapidly than in the United States, concern for the welfare of the industrial workforce led beginning in the 1890s to the elaboration of statutes designed to protect workers' safety and general welfare. America lagged behind. "In no country of the first rank is this legislation so weak as in the United States," observed John Graham Brooks, the first president of the National Consumers' League. Compared to European workers, he concluded, American workers' lives were barely touched by protective legislation. But progressive associations in the United States slowly began to work on issues of protection, and with the help of their cross-Atlantic connections eventually inspired the formation of additional groups in Europe to fight for similar measures.

The National Consumers' League (NCL) that Brooks headed drew on European models of factory inspection and legislation that sought to promote better working conditions for laborers. Like the social settlement movement, another significant European import, the consumers' league movement in the United States soon outstripped its European counterparts, largely thanks to the college-educated women who also gave the American settlement house movement its unique stamp. While Brooks and other men served as its officers (largely honorific posts), women formed the backbone of the National Consumers' League.

The league began on the grassroots level. In 1888, New York City garment worker and union organizer Leonora O'Reilly invited some of the city's prominent women to a meeting of the New York Working Women's Society, where they heard an appeal to help their "toiling and down-trodden sisters." The group appointed a committee to make and circulate a list of "such shops as deal justly with their employees" so that women consumers could patronize shops that met minimum standards. Begun as a genteel boycott among New York City women alarmed at the conditions of women in the garment trades, the Consumers' League of New York took shape in 1891, led by philanthropist Josephine Shaw Lowell. Lowell liked to portray the league's work as part of a historical continuum in women's activism, tracing its roots back to colonial women's patriotic refusal to buy British goods in the Revolutionary War era.

Taking as its motto "Investigate, agitate, legislate," the New York league affixed a "white label" to goods made in shops that met its standards for wages, work hours, and safety. Women shoppers were urged to "look for the white label" before buying. To determine which shops merited the label, consumers' league inspectors explored working conditions in cramped sweatshops, canneries, laundries, and department stores. They collected masses of data on women's wages, budgets, health, employment, and living standards. And they used the tactics of exposure and muckraking to bring to the nation's attention the grim realities of women's working conditions.

The movement spread rapidly. By 1896, 64 consumers' leagues had formed in 20 states, primarily in the Northeast and Midwest. In 1898 the national scope of the movement was recognized with the founding of the National Consumers' League. Membership in the NCL peaked in 1916, when it claimed 15,000 members in 43 states.

The most prominent woman in the NCL was Florence Kelley, who left Hull House in 1899 to become a model of progressive reform; Robert La Follette turned Wisconsin into a laboratory for progressivism; and Hiram Johnson ended the domination of the Southern Pacific Railroad in California politics.

Progressivism burst forth at every level of government in 1900, but nowhere more forcefully than in Cleveland, Ohio, with the election of Thomas Lofton Johnson mayor. A self-made millionaire by age forty, Johnson had made his the salaried executive secretary of the newly formed NCL, a post she held for two decades. Kelley grew up in Philadelphia the daughter of a Republican congressman nicknamed William "Pig Iron" Kelley because of his support for the protective tariff benefiting Pennsylvania's iron and steel industry. When she was a young girl her father reportedly told her, "My generation has created industry, and your generation must humanize it." Kelley along with other highly educated and public-spirited women of the Progressive period eagerly took on the task of civilizing capitalism.

After graduating from Cornell University in 1882, Kelley traveled to Europe to study law and government at the University of Zurich. There she became an ardent socialist, married a Russian medical student, and had three children. In 1891 she left her abusive husband and moved into Chicago's Hull House. She soon established herself as an expert on tenement labor. In 1893, reform governor John Peter Altgeld named Kelley Illinois's chief factory inspector, making her the first woman in the United States to head a state labor department. Kelley developed a formidable reputation as a champion of better working conditions. And, as an active member of Chicago's consumers' league, she spearheaded the campaign against sweatshops.

At the NCL, Kelley helped propel the league from consumer pressure tactics to political action, sometimes with influence from

Florence Kelley, 1905
Florence Kelley left Hull House in 1899 to become the salaried executive secretary of the National Consumers' League headquartered in New York City. While men like John Graham Brooks held offices (largely honorific) in the organization, Kelley and other highly educated women made up the backbone of the NCL, demonstrating the significant role women played in international progressive reform. Until her death in 1932, Kelley used the NCL to campaign for shorter hours and better working conditions for America's workingwomen.
Rare Books & Manuscripts, Columbia University in the City of New York.

abroad. By 1902, the league maintained a separate lobbying agency to fight for an end to child labor. After hearing convincing arguments from British delegates at the 1908 international consumers league congress in Geneva, Kelley led the NCL to push for minimum wage legislation. Working with women like Maud Nathan (a prominent figure in international women's circles), Mary

Kingsbury Simkhovitch of New York's Greenwich House, and Pauline and Josephine Goldmark and their brother-in-law Louis Brandeis, the NCL also mounted a legal defense campaign on behalf of state statutes limiting the maximum hours of women wage earners. Their efforts paid off in 1908 when in *Muller v. Oregon* the Supreme Court ruled constitutional the regulation of women's working hours—a landmark decision in which, for the first time, the Court acknowledged that an individual's right to form contracts did not rule out setting limits on working hours.

Such successes, along with the international ties of many NCL activists, helped the league spin off a number of European sister organizations. By 1910, league-inspired affiliates had formed in France, Belgium, Germany, and Switzerland. Reversing the trend for progressive reform measures to cross the Atlantic from Europe to America, the National Consumers' League reached beyond America's borders as European consumer organizations borrowed American tactics to help protect workers.

BIBLIOGRAPHY

Josephine Goldmark, *Impatient Crusader: Florence Kelley's Life Story* (1976).
Daniel T. Rodgers, *Atlantic Crossings: Social Politics in a Progressive Age* (1998).
Kathryn Kish Sklar, *Florence Kelley and the Nation's Work: The Rise of Women's Political Culture, 1830–1900* (1995).
Landon R.Y. Storrs, *Civilizing Capitalism: The National Consumers' League, Women's Activism, and Labor Standards in the New Deal Era* (2000).

money in the street railroad business in Detroit, where he had clashed frequently with reform mayor Hazen Pingree. Johnson turned his back on business in 1899 and moved to Cleveland, where he determined to seek election as a reform mayor. "I embarked on this new field for purely selfish motives," he later wrote. A flamboyant man who craved power and acclaim, Johnson pledged during the campaign to reduce the streetcar fare from five cents to three cents. His

Tom Johnson
Tom Johnson, the reform mayor of Cleveland, Ohio, from 1901 to 1909, is shown here campaigning in Cleveland's Wade Park in 1908. For more than seven years, Mayor Johnson fought for a three-cent streetcar fare, winning the support of the working class and angering the business interests who ran the city's streetcars. To get this low fare, Johnson finally instituted municipal ownership of the transit system. The three-cent token was a campaign novelty distributed during Johnson's bid for reelection in 1907.
The Western Reserve Historical Society, Cleveland, Ohio.

election touched off a seven-year war between advocates of the lower fare, who believed that workers paid a disproportionate share of their meager earnings for transportation, and the streetcar moguls, who argued that they couldn't meet costs with the lower fare. When Johnson responded by building his own streetcar line, his foes tore up the tracks and blocked him with court injunctions and legal delays. At the prompting of his opponents, the Ohio legislature sought to limit Johnson's mayoral power by revoking the charters of every city in the state, replacing home rule with central control from the state capital, Columbus.

During his tenure as mayor, Johnson fought for home rule and fair taxation even as he called for greater **democracy** through the use of the initiative, referendum, and recall—devices that allowed voters to have a direct say in legislative and judicial matters. Frustrated in his attempt to bring the streetcar industry to heel, he successfully championed municipal ownership of street railways and public utilities, a tactic that progressives called "gas and water socialism." The city bought the streetcar system and instituted the three-cent fare. Under Johnson's administration, Cleveland became, in the words of journalist Lincoln Steffens, the "best governed city in America."

In Wisconsin, Robert M. La Follette, who as a young congressional representative had supported William McKinley, converted to the progressive cause early in the 1900s. An astute politician, La Follette capitalized on the grassroots movement for reform to launch his long political career, first as governor (1901–1905) and later as a U.S. senator (1906–1925). A graduate of the University of Wisconsin, La Follette brought scientists and professors into his administration and used the university, only a few blocks from the statehouse in Madison, as a resource in drafting legislation. As governor he lowered railroad rates, raised railroad taxes, improved education, preached conservation, established factory regulation and workers' compensation, instituted the first direct primary in the country, and inaugurated the first state income tax. Under his leadership, Wisconsin earned the title "laboratory of democracy."

A fiery orator, "Fighting Bob" La Follette united his supporters around issues that transcended party loyalties. This emphasis on reform characterized progressivism, which attracted followers from both major parties. Democrats like Tom Johnson and Republicans like Robert La Follette could lay equal claim to the label "progressive."

West of the Rockies, progressivism arrived somewhat later and found a champion in Hiram Johnson of California, who served as governor from 1911 to 1917 and as U.S. senator from 1917 to 1945. Since the 1870s, California politics had been dominated by the Southern Pacific Railroad, a corporation so rapacious that novelist Frank Norris called it "the Octopus." Johnson ran for governor in 1910 on the promise to "kick the Southern Pacific out of politics." With the support of the reform wing of the Republican Party, he handily won. *Efficiency* and *rationalization* became the watchwords of Hiram Johnson's administration. He promised to "return the government to the people"—to give them honest public service untarnished by corruption and corporate influence. As governor he introduced the direct primary; supported the initiative, referendum, and recall; strengthened the state's railroad commission; supported conservation; and signed an employer's liability law.

Who benefited most from Johnson's progressivism? California's entrepreneurs—large farmers, independent oil producers, and other rising businessmen who could make money more easily once Johnson curtailed the influence of the Southern Pacific. A vigorous, compelling personality with a reputation for a towering temper, Hiram Johnson proved an able governor. In 1912 he could boast that by regulating the Southern Pacific Railroad he had saved shippers more than $2 million.

Progressivism Finds a President: Theodore Roosevelt

On September 6, 1901, President William McKinley was shot twice by Leon Czolgosz, an **anarchist**, while attending the Pan-American Exposition in Buffalo, New York. Eight days later, McKinley died. When news of his assassination reached his friend and political mentor Mark Hanna, Hanna is said to have growled, "Now that damned cowboy is president." He was speaking of Vice President Theodore Roosevelt, the colorful hero of San Juan Hill, who had indeed punched cattle in the Dakotas in the 1880s.

At age forty-two, Roosevelt was the youngest man ever to move into the White House. A patrician by birth and an activist by temperament, Roosevelt brought to the job enormous talent and energy. As president he would use that energy to strengthen the power of the federal government, putting business on notice that it could no longer count on laissez-faire to give it free rein.

The Square Deal

The "absolutely vital question" facing the country, Roosevelt wrote to a friend in 1901, was "whether or not the government has the power to control the trusts." The Sherman Antitrust Act of 1890 had been badly weakened by a conservative Supreme Court and by attorneys general more willing to use it against labor unions than against **monopolies**. To determine if the law had any teeth left, Roosevelt, in one of his first acts as president, ordered his attorney general to begin a secret antitrust investigation of the Northern Securities Company. He chose a good target. Northern Securities, formed by a controversial merger, monopolized railroad traffic in the

> The "absolutely vital question" facing the country, Roosevelt wrote a friend in 1901, was "whether or not the government has the power to control the trusts."

Northwest and to many small investors and farmers symbolized corporate high-handedness.

Five months later, in February 1902, Wall Street rocked with the news that the government had filed an antitrust suit against Northern Securities. As one newspaper editor sarcastically observed, "Wall Street is paralyzed at the thought that a President of the United States would sink so low as to try to enforce the law." An indignant J. P. Morgan, who had created Northern Securities, demanded to know why he had not been consulted. "If we have done anything wrong," he told the president, "send your man to my man and they can fix it up." Roosevelt, amused, later noted that Morgan "could not help regarding me as a big rival operator." In a sense, that was just what Roosevelt intended. Roosevelt's thunderbolt put Wall Street on notice that the money men were dealing with a president who demanded to be treated as an equal and who was willing to use government to control business. Perhaps sensing the new mood, the Supreme Court, in a significant turnaround, upheld the Sherman Act and called for the dissolution of Northern Securities in 1904.

"Hurrah for Teddy the Trustbuster," cheered the papers. Roosevelt went on to use the Sherman Act against forty-three trusts, including such giants as the American Tobacco Company, Du Pont, and Standard Oil. Always the moralist, he insisted on a "rule of reason." He would punish "bad" trusts (those that broke the law) and leave "good" ones alone. In practice, he preferred regulation to antitrust suits. In 1903, he pressured Congress to pass the Elkins Act, outlawing railroad rebates (money returned to a shipper to guarantee repeat business). And he created the new cabinet-level Department of Commerce and Labor with a subsidiary Bureau of Corporations to act as a corporate watchdog.

In his handling of the anthracite coal strike in 1902,

Roosevelt as a Giant Killer
In this political cartoon from 1904, President Theodore Roosevelt is "Jack the Giant Killer," taking on the Wall Street titans. To the right of the president looms J. P. Morgan with his hand out. To the left stands James J. Hill, builder of the Great Northern Railroad. The cartoon was published after Roosevelt brought antitrust proceedings against the Northern Securities Company, a railroad combination put together by Morgan that included Hill's Great Northern Railroad. Roosevelt's unprecedented action earned him a reputation as a "trustbuster," but in fact he favored government regulation of big business. His activist presidency used government to counter the power of big business. As the cartoonist clearly shows, the government was seen as small indeed when Roosevelt took his stand. Library of Congress.

Roosevelt again demonstrated his willingness to assert the moral and political authority of the presidency, this time to mediate between labor and management. In May, 147,000 coal miners in

Theodore Roosevelt
Described aptly by a contemporary observer as "a steam engine in trousers," Theodore Roosevelt at forty-two was the youngest president to occupy the White House. He brought to the office energy, intellect, and activism in equal measure. Roosevelt boasted that he used the presidency as a "bully pulpit"—a forum from which he advocated reforms ranging from trust-busting to conservation.
Library of Congress.

Pennsylvania went out on strike. Most of the miners were Slavic immigrants organized by the United Mine Workers (UMW) under the leadership of a young Irishman, John Mitchell. The UMW demanded a reduction in the workday from twelve to ten hours, an equitable system of weighing each miner's output, and a 10 percent wage increase, along with recognition of the union.

When asked about the appalling conditions in the mines that had led to the strike, George Baer, the mine operators' spokesman, scoffed, "The miners don't suffer, why they can't even speak English." Buttressed by social Darwinism, Baer observed that "God in his infinite wisdom" had placed "the rights and interests of the laboring man" in the hands of the capitalists, not "the labor agitators." His Olympian confidence rested on the fact that six eastern railroads owned over 70 percent of the anthracite mines. With the power of the railroads behind them, Baer and the mine owners refused to budge.

The strike dragged on through the summer and into the fall. Hoarding and profiteering drove the price of coal from $2.50 to $6.00 a ton. Coal heated nearly every house, school, and hospital in the Northeast, and as winter approached, coal shortages touched off near riots in the nation's big cities. In the face of mounting tension, Roosevelt did what no president had ever done. He stepped in to mediate, issuing a personal invitation to representatives from both sides to meet in Washington in October. At the meeting, Baer and the mine owners refused to talk with the union representatives, insulting both the president and the attorney general. Angered by the "wooden-headed obstinacy and stupidity" of management, Roosevelt threatened to seize the mines and run them with federal troops. This was a powerful bluff that called into question not only the supremacy of private property but also the rule of law. The specter of federal troops being used to operate the mines quickly brought management around. At the prompting of J. P. Morgan, the mine owners agreed to arbitration. In the end, the miners won a reduction in hours and a wage increase, but the owners succeeded in preventing formal recognition of the UMW.

Taken together, Roosevelt's actions in the Northern Securities case and the anthracite coal strike marked a dramatic departure from the presidential passivity of his predecessors in the Gilded Age. Roosevelt demonstrated conclusively that government intended to act as a force independent of big business. Pleased with his role in the anthracite strike, he announced that all he had tried to do was give labor and capital a "square deal."

The phrase "Square Deal" became his slogan in the 1904 election campaign. To win the presidency in his own right, Roosevelt moved to wrest control of the Republican Party from party boss Mark Hanna, the only man who stood between him and the nomination. Roosevelt adroitly used patronage to win supporters. Even before Hanna died of typhoid fever in 1904, Roosevelt was the undisputed leader of the party. In the presidential election of 1904, he swept into office with the largest popular majority—57.9 percent—any candidate had polled to that time.

Breaker Boys

When anthracite miners declared a strike in 1902, child labor was common in the mines of Pennsylvania. "Breaker boys," some as young as seven years old, picked over coal moving on a conveyor belt to remove rock and stone. The boys in this photograph are taking a short rest during their twelve-hour workday. Their unsmiling faces bear testimony to the difficulty and danger of their work. A committee investigating child labor found more than 10,000 children illegally employed in the Pennsylvania coalfields.

Brown Brothers.

Roosevelt the Reformer

"Tomorrow I shall come into my office in my own right," Roosevelt is said to have remarked on the eve of his election. "Then watch out for me!" Roosevelt's stunning victory gave him a mandate for reform. He would need all the popularity and political savvy he could muster, however, to guide his reform measures through Congress. The Senate remained controlled by a staunchly **conservative** Republican "old guard," with many senators on the payrolls of the corporations Roosevelt sought to curb. Roosevelt's pet project remained railroad regulation. The Elkins Act prohibiting rebates had not worked. No one could stop big shippers like Standard Oil from wringing concessions from the railroads. The Interstate Commerce Commission (ICC), created in 1887 to regulate the railroads, had been largely stripped of its powers by the Supreme Court. In the face of a widespread call for railroad reform, Roosevelt determined that the only solution lay in giving the ICC real power to set rates and prevent discriminatory practices. But the right to determine the price of goods or services was an age-old prerogative of private enterprise, and one that business had no intention of yielding to government.

To ensure passage of the Hepburn Act, which would increase the power of the ICC, Roosevelt worked skillfully behind the scenes. At first, he allied himself with insurgent progressives; then, when they could not muster the needed votes, he switched sides and succeeded in getting the Republican old guard to accept a compromise. In its final form, the Hepburn Act, passed in May 1906, gave the ICC power to set rates subject to court review. Committed progressives like La Follette judged the law a defeat for reform.

Die-hard conservatives branded it a "piece of populism." Both sides exaggerated. The law left the courts too much power and failed to provide adequate means for the ICC to determine rates, but its passage was a landmark in federal control of private industry. For the first time, a government commission had the power to investigate private business records and to set rates.

Passage of the Hepburn Act marked the high point of Roosevelt's presidency. In a serious political blunder, Roosevelt had announced on the eve of his election in 1904 that he would not run again. By 1906, his term was starting to run out and his influence on Congress and his party was waning. He became a "lame duck" at the very moment he was enjoying his greatest public popularity and was eager to press for more reform.

Always an apt reader of the public temper, Roosevelt witnessed a growing appetite for reform fed by the revelations of corporate and political wrongdoing and social injustice that filled the papers and boosted the sales of popular periodicals. (See "The Promise of Technology," page 764.) Roosevelt, who wielded publicity like a weapon in his pursuit of reform, counted many of the new investigative journalists, such as Jacob Riis, among his friends. But he warned them against going too far like the allegorical character in *Pilgrim's Progress* who was so busy raking muck that he took no notice of higher things. Roosevelt's criticism gave the American vocabulary a new word, *muckraker*, which journalists soon appropriated as a title of honor.

Muckraking, as Roosevelt was keenly aware, had been of enormous help in securing progressive legislation. In the spring of 1906, publicity generated by the muckrakers about poisons in patent medicines goaded the Senate, with Roosevelt's backing, into passing a pure food and drug bill. Opponents in the House of Representatives hoped to keep the legislation locked up in committee. There it would have

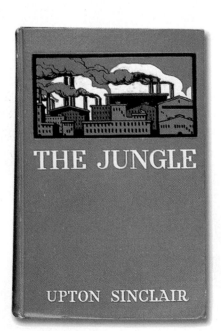

The Jungle

Novelist Upton Sinclair, a lifelong socialist, wrote *The Jungle* to expose the evils of capitalism. But readers were more horrified by the unsanitary conditions he described in the meatpacking industry, where the novel's hapless hero saw rats, filth, and diseased animals processed into potted beef. It was rumored that after reading the book, President Theodore Roosevelt could no longer stomach sausage for breakfast. The president immediately ordered a thorough study of conditions in the meatpacking industry. The public outcry surrounding *The Jungle* contributed to the enactment of pure food and drug legislation and a federal meat inspection law. Sinclair ruefully remarked, "I aimed at the public's heart, but I hit them in the stomach."

By permission of the Houghton Library, Harvard University.

died, were it not for publication of Upton Sinclair's novel *The Jungle* (1906), with its sensational account of filthy conditions in meatpacking plants. A massive public outcry led to the passage of a tough Pure Food and Drug Act and a Meat Inspection Act.

In the waning years of his administration, Roosevelt moved farther to the left, allying with the more progressive elements of the Republican Party. In speech after speech, he attacked "malefactors of great wealth." Styling himself a "radical," he claimed credit for leading the "ultra conservative" party of McKinley to a position of "progressive conservatism and conservative radicalism."

When an economic panic developed in the fall of 1907, business interests quickly blamed the president. The panic of 1907 proved to be severe but short. As he had done in 1895, J. P. Morgan stepped in to avert disaster, this time switching funds from one bank to another to prop up weak institutions. For his services, he claimed the Tennessee Coal and Iron Company, an independent steel business that had long been coveted by his U.S. Steel Corporation. Morgan dispatched his lieutenants to Washington, where they told Roosevelt that the sale of the company would aid the economy "but little benefit" U.S. Steel. Willing to take the word of a gentleman, Roosevelt tacitly agreed not to institute antitrust proceedings against U.S. Steel. But, as Roosevelt later learned, Morgan and his men had been less than candid. The acquisition of Tennessee Coal and Iron for a price below market value greatly strengthened U.S. Steel and undercut the economy of the Southeast. This episode later gave rise to the charge that Roosevelt had acted as a tool of the Morgan interests.

The charge of collusion between business and government underscored the extent to which business leaders like Morgan and his partner George W. Perkins found federal regulation preferable to unbridled competition or harsher state measures. During the Progressive Era, enlightened business leaders cooperated with government in the hope of avoiding antitrust prosecution. Convinced that regulation and not trust-busting offered the best way to deal with big business, Roosevelt never acknowledged that his regulatory policies fostered an alliance between business and government that today is called corporate liberalism. Despite his harsh attacks on "malefactors of great wealth," Roosevelt's actions in the panic of 1907 demonstrated the president's indebtedness to Morgan,

who still functioned as the national bank and would continue to do so until passage of the Federal Reserve Act six years later.

Roosevelt and Conservation

In at least one area, Roosevelt was well ahead of his time. Robert La Follette, who thought Roosevelt a lukewarm progressive and found much to criticize in his presidency, hailed as Roosevelt's "greatest work" his efforts in the conservation of natural resources. When Roosevelt took office, some 45 million acres of land remained as government reserves. He more than tripled that number to 150 million acres, buying land and creating national parks and wildlife preserves by executive order. To conserve natural resources, he fought not only western cattle barons, lumber kings, and mining interests but also powerful leaders in Congress, including Speaker of the House Joseph Cannon, who was determined to spend "not one cent for scenery."

As the first president to have lived and worked in the West—as a rancher in the Dakotas—Roosevelt came to the White House convinced of the need for better management of the nation's rivers and forests. During the 1890s, concern for the wanton exploitation of natural resources led Congress to pass legislation giving the president the power to "reserve" forest land from commercial development by executive proclamation. During his presidency, Roosevelt did not hesitate to wield that power. He placed the nation's conservation policy in the hands of scientifically trained experts like his chief forrester, Gifford Pinchot. Pinchot fought for the principle of managed use. He desired not so much to remove land from commercial use, but to use the power of the federal government to effect long-term planning and the rational management of the nation's resources. Unlike preservationists, who wished to leave the land in its natural state, Roosevelt, Pinchot,

> Roosevelt's regulatory policies fostered an alliance between business and government that today is called corporate liberalism.

and the conservationists advocated efficient use of natural resources. Willing to permit grazing, lumbering, and the development of hydroelectric power, conservationists fought private interests only when they felt business acted irresponsibly or threatened to monopolize water and electric power.

Flash Photography and the Birth of Photojournalism

The camera was not new at the turn of the twentieth century. Americans had eagerly imported the technology developed by Frenchman L. J. M. Daguerre to make portraits called daguerreotypes as early as the 1840s. By the 1880s, the invention of dry plates had simplified photography, and by the 1890s, Americans could purchase a Kodak camera marketed by George Eastman. But for Jacob Riis, who wished to document the horrors of tenement life, photography was useless because it required daylight or careful studio lighting. Riis, a progressive reformer and journalist who covered the police beat for the *New York Tribune*, never thought of buying a camera. He could only rudely sketch the dim hovels, the criminal nightlife, and the windowless tenement rooms of New York. Then came the breakthrough. "One morning scanning my newspaper at the breakfast table," he wrote, "I put it down with an outcry. . . . There it was, the thing I had been looking for all these years. . . . A way had been discovered . . . to take pictures by flashlight. The darkest corner might be photographed that way."

The new technology involved a pistol lamp that fired magnesium cartridges to provide light for instantaneous photography. Armed with the new flash pistols, Riis and a band of amateur photographers soon set out to shine light in the dark corners of New York. "Our party carried terror wherever it went," Riis later recounted. "The spectacle of strange men invading a house in the midnight hours armed with [flash] pistols which they shot off recklessly was hardly reassuring . . . and it was not to be wondered at if the tenants bolted through the windows and down fire-escapes."

Unhappy with the photographers he hired to follow him on his nighttime forays into the slums, Riis determined to try his own hand at taking pictures and laid out $25 for his first photographic equipment in 1888. It consisted of a four-by-five-inch wooden box camera, glass plates, a tripod, a safety lantern, flash pistols, developing trays, and a printing frame. He soon replaced the pistols with a newer flash technology developed in 1887 that used magnesium powder blown through an alcohol flame. Riis carried a frying pan in which to ignite the powder, observing, "It seemed more homelike."

Flash photography was dangerous. The pistol lamp cartridges contained highly explosive chemicals that could seriously burn the photographer. The newer technology employing magnesium powder also proved risky. Riis once blew the flash into his own eyes, and only his glasses saved him from being blinded. Nor was Riis the only one in peril. When he photographed the residents of a tenement on "Blind Man's Alley," he set the place on fire when he ignited the flash. He later claimed the tenement, nicknamed the "Dirty Spoon," was so filthy it wouldn't burn. He was able to douse the flames without his blind subjects ever realizing their danger.

Riis turned his photographs into slides that he used to illustrate his lectures on tenement life. They helped spread his message, but not until *Scribner's* magazine printed his story entitled "How the Other Half Lives" in December 1889 did he begin to develop a mass audience. The article, illustrated with line drawings of Riis's photographs, became the basis for his best-selling book of the same title published in 1890.

Preservationists like John Muir, the founder of the Sierra Club, believed the wilderness needed to be protected from all commercial exploitation. Muir soon clashed with Roosevelt. After a devastating earthquake in 1906, San Francisco sought federal approval for a project that would supply fresh water and electric power to the city. The plan called for building a dam that would flood the spectacular Hetch Hetchy Valley in Yosemite National Park. Muir, who had played a central role in establishing Yosemite as a national park, fiercely opposed

Jacob Riis and Baxter Court

Jacob Riis (to the right), a Danish immigrant who knew the squalor of New York's lodging houses and slums from his early days in the city, vigorously campaigned for tenement reform. He warned slumlords (some of them prominent New Yorkers) that their greed bred crime and disease and might provoke class warfare. Flash photography enabled Riis to expose the dark alleys and tenements of New York. He took his camera (much like the one pictured in the inset) into Baxter Street Court, then recorded these observations: "I counted the other day the little ones, up to ten years old in a . . . tenement that for a yard has a . . . space in the center with sides fourteen or fifteen feet long, just enough for a row of ill-smelling [water] closets . . . and a hydrant. . . . There was about as much light in the 'yard' as In the average cellar. . . . I counted one hundred twenty eight [children] In forty families."

Riis portrait: National Portrait Gallery, Smithsonian Institution/Art Resource, NY; Baxter Street courtyard: The Jacob A. Riis Collection, #108 Museum of the City of New York; camera: George Eastman House.

How the Other Half Lives made photographic history. It contained, along with Riis's text and the line drawings that had appeared in *Scribner's,* seventeen halftone prints of Riis's photographs. Riis's text and pictures shined the light on New York's darkest corners—vagrants in filthy lodging houses; "street arabs," homeless boys who lived by their wits on the streets; the saloons and dives of lower New York; evil-smelling tenement yards; stifling sweatshops.

For the first time, unposed action pictures taken with a flash documented social conditions. Riis's pioneering photojournalism shocked the nation and led not only to tenement reform but also to the development of city playgrounds, neighborhood parks, and child labor laws.

Roosevelt and Pinchot, who saw the Hetch Hetchy project as a progressive victory because it would place control of the water supply in the hands of the municipal government and not private developers. After a protracted publicity battle, Roosevelt and the conservationists prevailed, although preservationists won many converts to the cause of saving the vanishing wilderness and launched what would become the modern environmentalist movement.

The Newlands Reclamation Act of 1902 also drew criticism. It established a Reclamation

Bureau within the Department of the Interior and provided federal funding for irrigation projects. Rather than aiding small farmers, as the act's framer originally intended, the legislation encouraged the growth of large-scale farming. Yet the growing involvement of the federal government in the management of water resources, a critical issue in the West, marked another victory for the policy of federal intervention that characterized progressivism and marked the end of laissez-faire liberalism.

In 1907, Congress put the brakes on Roosevelt's conservation program through a law limiting his power to create forest reserves in six western states. In the days leading up to the law's passage, Roosevelt feverishly created twenty-one new reserves and enlarged eleven more. And when Congress denied Pinchot the right to withdraw hydroelectric power sites from private use, he managed to save 2,500 by designating them "ranger stations." Roosevelt backed him up, even though the subterfuge involved stretching the law considerably. Firm in his commitment to conservation, Roosevelt never wavered. Today, the six national parks, sixteen national monuments, and fifty-one wildlife refuges that he created stand witness to his substantial accomplishments as a conservationist (Map 21.1).

Roosevelt the Diplomat

Roosevelt took a keen interest in shaping foreign policy and worked to buttress the United States's newly won place among world leaders. A fierce proponent of America's interests abroad, he believed that Congress was inept in foreign affairs, and he relied on executive power to effect a vigorous foreign policy, sometimes stretching the powers of the presidency beyond legal limits in his pursuit of American interests. A man who relished military discipline and viewed life as a constant conflict for supremacy, Roosevelt believed that "civilized nations" should police the world and hold "backward" countries in line. In

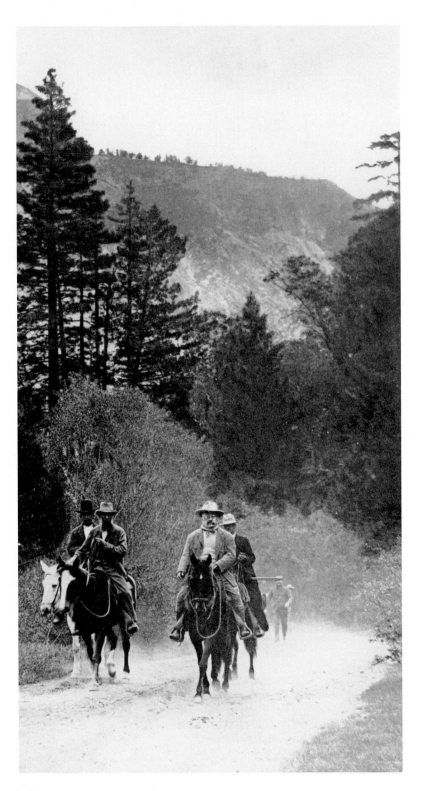

Roosevelt and Muir in Yosemite
In 1903, President Roosevelt took a camping trip to Yosemite, California, with John Muir, naturalist and founder of the Sierra Club. Roosevelt's experience as a rancher in the Dakotas made him the first president to have experienced firsthand the trans-Mississippi West. As president, he acted vigorously to protect the beauty and resources of the West for posterity, using executive power to set aside more than a hundred million acres in government reserves and to create six national parks. Roosevelt and Muir later clashed over the flooding of the Hetch Hetchy Valley in Yosemite. Muir upheld the preservationist position; Roosevelt, a conservationist, advocated managed use.
Theodore Roosevelt Collection, Harvard College Library.

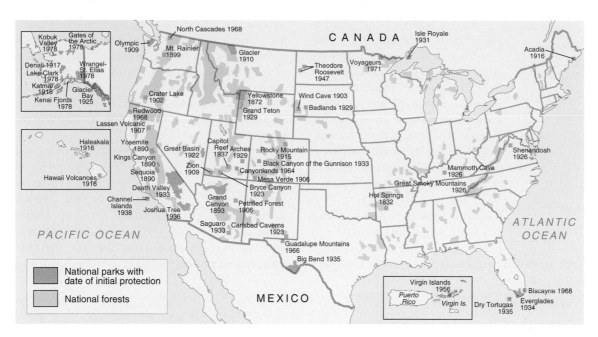

MAP 21.1   National Parks and Forests

The national park system in the West began with Yellowstone in 1872. Grand Canyon, Yosemite, Kings Canyon, and Sequoia followed in the 1890s. During his presidency, Theodore Roosevelt added six parks — Crater Lake, Wind Cave, Petrified Forest, Lassen Volcanic, Mesa Verde, and Zion.

READING THE MAP: Collectively, do national parks or national forests contain larger tracts of land? According to the map, how many national parks were created before 1910? How many were created after 1910?

CONNECTIONS: How do conservation and preservation differ? Why did Theodore Roosevelt believe conservation was important? What principle guided the national land use policy of the Roosevelt administration?

FOR MORE HELP ANALYZING THIS MAP, see the map activity for this chapter in the Online Study Guide at bedfordstmartins.com/roark.

---

his relations with the European powers, he relied on military strength and diplomacy, a combination he aptly described with the aphorism "Speak softly but carry a big stick."

In the Caribbean, Roosevelt jealously guarded the U.S. sphere of influence defined in the **Monroe Doctrine**. In 1902, he risked war to keep Germany from intervening in Venezuela when that country's dictator borrowed money in Europe and could not repay it. Roosevelt issued an ultimatum to the German kaiser, warning him to stay out of Latin American affairs or face war with the United States. The matter was eventually settled by arbitration.

Roosevelt's proprietary attitude toward the Western Hemisphere became evident in the case of the Panama Canal. A firm advocate of naval power and an astute naval strategist, Roosevelt had long been a supporter of a canal linking the Caribbean and the Pacific, which, by enabling ships to move quickly from the Atlantic to the

Pacific, would effectively double the navy's power. Having decided on a route across the Panamanian isthmus (a narrow strip of land connecting North and South America), then a part of Colombia, Roosevelt in 1902 offered the Colombian government a one-time sum of $10 million and an annual rent of $250,000. When the government in Bogotá refused to accept the offer, Roosevelt became incensed at what he called the "homicidal corruptionists" in Colombia for trying to "blackmail" the United States. The result was an uprising in Panama in 1903 arranged by New York investors. The U.S. government aided and protected the "revolution" by placing the warship *Nashville* off the isthmus, and the State Department recognized the new government of Panama within twenty-four hours. The Panamanians promptly accepted the $10 million, and the building got under way (Map 21.2). The canal would take eleven years and $375 million to complete; it opened in 1914.

The Roosevelt Corollary in Action

In the wake of the Panama affair, the confrontation with Germany over Venezuela, and yet another default on a European debt, this time in the Dominican Republic, Roosevelt announced in 1904 what became known as the Roosevelt Corollary to the Monroe Doctrine: The United States would not intervene in Latin America as long as nations there conducted their affairs with "decency." But the United States would step in if any Latin American nation proved guilty of "brutal wrongdoing," such as defaulting on debts owed to European nations. The Roosevelt Corollary in effect made the United States the policeman of the Western Hemisphere and served notice to the European powers to keep out. To ensure the payment of debts, Roosevelt immediately put the corollary into practice by intervening in Costa Rica and by taking over the customhouse in the Dominican Republic.

In Asia, Roosevelt inherited the Open Door policy initiated by Secretary of State John Hay in 1899, which was designed to ensure U.S. commercial entry into China. As Britain, France, Russia, Japan, and Germany raced to secure Chinese trade and territory, Roosevelt was tempted to use force to enter the fray and gain economic or possibly territorial concessions. As a

Theodore Roosevelt and the Big Stick
In this political cartoon from 1904, President Theodore Roosevelt, dressed in his Rough Rider uniform and carrying his "big stick," turns the Caribbean into a Yankee pond. The Roosevelt Corollary to the Monroe Doctrine did exactly that.
Granger Collection.

FOR MORE HELP ANALYZING THIS IMAGE, see the visual activity for this chapter in the Online Study Guide at
bedfordstmartins.com/roark.

THE BIG STICK IN THE CARIBBEAN SEA

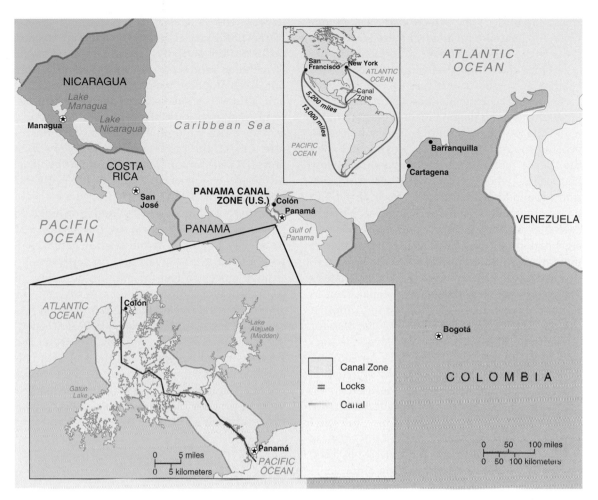

MAP 21.2   The Panama Canal, 1914

The Panama Canal, completed in 1914, bisected the isthmus in a series of massive locks and dams. As Theodore Roosevelt had planned, the canal greatly strengthened the navy by allowing ships to move from the Atlantic to the Pacific in a matter of days.

READING THE MAP: How long was the trip from New York to San Francisco before the Panama Canal was built? And after? Geographically, why is Panama a likely site for a canal?

CONNECTIONS: How did Roosevelt's desire for a canal lead to independence for Panama? How did canal benefit the U.S. navy?

FOR MORE HELP ANALYZING THIS MAP, see the map activity for this chapter in the Online Study Guide at bedfordstmartins.com/roark.

result of victory in the Spanish-American War, the United States already enjoyed a foothold in the region by virtue of its control of the Philippines. Realizing that Americans would not support an aggressive Asian policy, Roosevelt sensibly held back.

In his relations with Europe, Roosevelt sought to establish the United States, fresh from its victory over Spain, as a rising force in world affairs. When tensions flared between France

and Germany in Morocco in 1905, Roosevelt was invited to mediate at a conference in Algeciras, Spain, where he worked to maintain a balance of power that helped neutralize German ambitions. His skillful mediation of the dispute gained him a reputation as an astute player on the world stage and demonstrated the United States's new presence in world affairs.

Roosevelt earned the Nobel Peace Prize in 1906 for his role in negotiating an end to the

Russo-Japanese War, which had broken out when the Japanese invaded Chinese Manchuria, threatening Russia's sphere of influence in the area. Once again, Roosevelt sought to maintain a balance of power, in this case working to curb Japanese expansionism. Roosevelt admired the Japanese, judging them "the most dashing fighters in the world," but he did not want Japan to become too strong in Asia. He presided over the peace conference at Portsmouth, New Hampshire, where he was able to prevent Japan from dominating Manchuria. However, he had no qualms about initiating the Taft-Katsura agreement, granting Japan control of the sovereign nation of Korea in exchange for a pledge that Japan would not threaten the Philippines.

Roosevelt fumed when the United States's good relations with Japan were jeopardized in 1906 by discriminatory legislation in California calling for segregated public schools for "Orientals." Roosevelt smoothed over the incident by negotiating a "Gentleman's Agreement" in 1907 whereby he reversed the segregation order in exchange for voluntary restrictions on Japanese immigration to the United States. This informal arrangement allowed the Japanese to save face while also placating nativist sentiment in California.

To demonstrate America's naval power and counter Japan's growing bellicosity, Roosevelt dispatched the Great White Fleet, sixteen of the navy's most up-to-date battleships, on a "goodwill mission" around the world. U.S. relations with Japan improved, and in the 1908 Root-Takahira agreement the two nations pledged to maintain the Open Door and support the status quo in the Pacific. Roosevelt's show of American force constituted a classic example of his dictum "Speak softly but carry a big stick." Political cartoonists delighted in caricaturing the president wielding a cudgel in foreign affairs, and the American public seemed to relish the image.

> Once in office, Taft proved a perfect tool in the hands of Republicans who yearned for a return to the days of a less active executive.

Progressivism Stalled

Roosevelt retired from the presidency in 1909 at age fifty and went on safari to shoot big game in Africa. He turned the White House over to his handpicked successor, William Howard Taft, a lawyer who had served as governor general of the Philippines. In the presidential election of 1908, Taft soundly defeated the perennial Democratic candidate, William Jennings Bryan. But Taft's popular majority amounted to only half of Roosevelt's record win in 1904. On the eve of his inauguration, Taft showed little enthusiasm about his triumph and little zest for the future. In fact, the presidency for Taft proved an ordeal. As a symptom of his discomfort in office, his weight ballooned from an already hefty 297 pounds to over 350 pounds.

Any man would have found it difficult to follow in Roosevelt's footsteps, but Taft proved hopelessly ill suited to the task. A genial man with a talent for law, Taft had no experience in elective office, no feel for politics, no ability to compromise, and no nerve for controversy. His ambitious wife coveted the office and urged him to seek it. He would have been better off listening to his mother, who warned, "Roosevelt is a good fighter and enjoys it, but the malice of politics would make you miserable." Her words proved prophetic. Taft's presidency was marked by a progressive stalemate, a bitter break with Roosevelt, and a schism in the Republican Party.

The Troubled Presidency of William Howard Taft

Once in office, Taft proved a perfect tool in the hands of Republicans who yearned for a return to the days of a less active executive. A lawyer by training and instinct, Taft believed that it was up to the courts, not the president, to arbitrate social issues. Roosevelt had carried presidential power to a new level, often castigating the judiciary and flouting the separation of powers. Taft the legalist found it difficult to condone such actions. Wary of the progressive insurgents in his own party and without Roosevelt to guide him, Taft relied increasingly on conservatives in the Republican Party. As a progressive senator lamented, "Taft is a ponderous and amiable man completely surrounded by men who know exactly what they want."

Taft's troubles began on the eve of his inaugural when he called a special session of Congress to deal with the tariff, which had grown unconscionably high under Republican rule. Roosevelt had been too politically astute to tackle the troublesome tariff issue, even though he knew that rates needed to be lowered. Taft, with his stubborn courage, blundered into the fray. The House of Representatives passed a modest downward revision and, to make up for lost revenue, imposed a small inheritance tax. Led by Senator Nelson Aldrich of Rhode Island, the conservative Senate struck down the tax and added more than eight hundred crippling amendments to the tariff. The Payne-Aldrich bill that emerged actually raised the tariff, benefiting big business and trusts at the expense of consumers. As if paralyzed, Taft neither fought for changes nor vetoed the measure. On a tour of the Midwest in 1909, he was greeted with jeers when he claimed, "I think the Payne bill is the best bill that the Republican Party ever passed." In the eyes of a growing number of Americans, his praise of the tariff made him either a fool or a liar.

Taft's legalism got him into hot water in the area of conservation as well. He refused to endorse his predecessor's methods of bending the law to protect the nation's resources. He undid Roosevelt's work to preserve hydroelectric power sites when he learned that they had been improperly designated as ranger stations. And when Gifford Pinchot publicly denounced Taft's secretary of the interior, Richard Ballinger, as a tool of western land-grabbers, Taft fired Pinchot, touching off a storm of controversy that damaged Taft and alienated Roosevelt.

Talk of substituting Roosevelt on the ticket in 1912 grew as Republican progressives became increasingly dissatisfied with Taft's policies. In June 1910, Roosevelt returned to New York, where he received a hero's welcome and attracted a stream of visitors and reporters seeking his advice and opinions. Hurt, Taft kept his distance. By late summer, Roosevelt had taken sides with the progressive insurgents in his party. "Taft is utterly hopeless as a leader," Roosevelt confided to his son as he set out on a speaking tour of the West. Reading the mood of the country, Roosevelt began to sound more and more like a candidate.

With the Republican Party divided, the Democrats swept the congressional elections of 1910. Branding the Payne-Aldrich tariff "the mother of trusts," they captured a majority in the House of Representatives and won several key governorships. The revitalized Democratic Party could look to new leaders, among them the progressive governor of New Jersey, Woodrow Wilson.

The new Democratic majority in the House, working with progressive Republicans in the Senate, achieved a number of key reforms, including legislation to regulate mine and railroad safety, to create a Children's Bureau in the

William Howard Taft
William Howard Taft had little aptitude for politics. When Theodore Roosevelt tapped him as his successor in 1908, Taft had never held an elected office. A legalist by training and temperament, Taft moved congenially in the conservative circles of the Republican Party. His actions dismayed progressives and eventually led Roosevelt to challenge him for the presidency in 1912. The break with Roosevelt saddened and embittered Taft, who heartily disliked the presidency and was glad to leave it.
Library of Congress.

Department of Labor, and to establish an eight-hour day for federal workers. Two significant constitutional amendments—the Sixteenth Amendment, which provided for a modest graduated income tax, and the Seventeenth Amendment, which called for the direct election of senators (formerly chosen by state legislatures)—went to the states, where they would later win ratification in 1913. While Congress rode the high tide of progressive reform, Taft sat on the sidelines.

In foreign policy, too, Taft had a difficult time following in Roosevelt's footsteps. In the

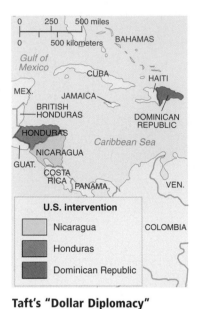

Taft's "Dollar Diplomacy"

Caribbean, he pursued a policy of "dollar diplomacy," championing commercial goals rather than the strategic aims that Roosevelt had advocated. He provoked anti-American feeling by attempting to force commercial treaties on Nicaragua and Honduras and by dispatching the U.S. marines to Nicaragua and the Dominican Republic in 1912.

In Asia, Taft's foreign policy proved equally inept. He openly avowed his intent to promote in China "active intervention to secure for . . . our capitalists opportunity for profitable investment." Lacking Roosevelt's understanding of power politics, Taft naively believed that he could substitute "dollars for bullets." He never recognized that an aggressive commercial policy could not exist without military might. As a result, dollar diplomacy was doomed to failure.

Taft was forced to recognize the limits of dollar diplomacy when revolution broke out in Mexico in 1911. Under pressure to protect American investment, which amounted to more than $4 billion, he mobilized troops along the border. But in the end, with no popular support for a war with Mexico, he fell back on diplomatic pressure to salvage American interests.

Always a legalist at heart, Taft hoped to encourage world peace through the use of a world court and arbitration. He unsuccessfully sponsored a series of arbitration treaties that Roosevelt, who prized national honor more than international law, vehemently opposed. By 1910, Roosevelt had become a vocal critic of Taft's foreign policy, which he dismissed as "maudlin folly."

The final breach between Taft and Roosevelt came in 1911, when Taft's attorney general filed an antitrust suit against U.S. Steel. In its brief against the corporation, the government cited Roosevelt's agreement with the Morgan interests in the 1907 acquisition of Tennessee Coal and Iron by the steel giant. The incident greatly embarrassed Roosevelt by making it clear that he either had been hoodwinked or had acted as a tool of Wall Street. Thoroughly enraged, Roosevelt lambasted Taft's "archaic" antitrust policy and hinted that he might be persuaded to run for president again.

Progressive Insurgency and the Election of 1912

In February 1912, Roosevelt challenged Taft for the Republican nomination, announcing, "My hat is in the ring." But for all his popularity, Roosevelt no longer controlled the party machinery. Taft, with uncharacteristic strength, refused to step aside. As he bitterly told a journalist, "Even a rat in a corner will fight." Roosevelt took advantage of newly passed primary election laws and ran in thirteen states, winning 278 delegates to Taft's 48. But at the Chicago convention, Taft's bosses refused to seat the Roosevelt delegates. Fistfights broke out on the convention floor as Taft won renomination on the first ballot. Crying robbery, Roosevelt's supporters bolted the party.

Seven weeks later, in the same Chicago auditorium, the hastily organized Progressive Party met to nominate Roosevelt. Few Republican officeholders joined the new party, but the advance guard of progressivism turned out in full force. Amid a thunder of applause, Jane Addams seconded Roosevelt's nomination. Full of reforming zeal, the delegates chose Roosevelt and Hiram Johnson to head the new party and approved the most ambitious platform since the Populists' in 1892. Planks called for woman suffrage, the direct election of senators, presidential primaries, conservation of natural resources, an end to child labor, minimum wages for women, workers' compensation, social security, and a federal income tax.

Roosevelt arrived in Chicago to accept the nomination and announced that he felt "as strong as a bull moose," giving the new party a nickname and a mascot. But for all the excitement and the cheering, the new Progressive Party was doomed, and the candidate knew it. The people may have supported the party, but the politicians, even insurgents like La Follette, stayed within the Republican fold. "I am under no illusion about it," Roosevelt confessed to a friend. "It is a forlorn hope." But he had gone too far to turn back. He led the Bull Moose Party into the fray, exhorting his followers in ringing biblical tones, "We shall not falter, we stand at Armageddon and do battle for the Lord."

The Democrats, delighted at the split in the Republican ranks, smelled victory for the first time since 1892. Their convention turned into a bitter fight for the nomination. After forty-six ballots, Woodrow Wilson became the party's nominee. Wilson's career in politics was nothing

Wilson Ribbon

Woodrow Wilson's political career was meteoric, propelling him from the presidency of Princeton University to the presidency of the United States in three years. As governor of New Jersey from 1910 to 1912, Wilson turned against the Democratic machine that had backed him and made a reputation as a champion of progressive reform. With the Republicans divided in 1912, the Democrats turned to Wilson to lead their party, nominating him on the forty-sixth ballot. In those days, prospective candidates generally did not attend the nominating convention. The ribbon in the photograph belonged to a member of the Democratic National Committee who traveled to Wilson's summer home in Sea Girt, New Jersey, on August 7, 1912, to inform Wilson officially of his nomination for president.

Collection of Janice L. and David J. Frent.

short of meteoric. Elected governor of New Jersey in 1910, after only eighteen months in office the former professor of political science and president of Princeton University found himself running for president of the United States.

Voters in 1912 could choose among three candidates, each claiming to be a progressive. That the term could stretch to cover all three underscored major disagreements in progressive thinking about the relation between business and government. Taft, in spite of his trust-busting, was generally viewed as the candidate of the old guard. The real contest for the presidency was between Roosevelt and Wilson and the two political philosophies summed up in their respective campaign slogans: "The New Nationalism" and "The New Freedom."

The New Nationalism expressed Roosevelt's belief in federal planning and regulation. He accepted the inevitability of big business but demanded that government act as "a steward of the people" to regulate the giant corporations. Roosevelt called for an increase in the power of the federal government, a decrease in the power of the courts, and an active role for the president. As political theorist Herbert Croly pointed out in his influential book *The Promise of American Life* (1909), Roosevelt hoped to use an active federal government to promote social justice and democracy, replacing the laissez-faire policies of the old liberal state with a new form of liberalism.

Wilson, schooled in the Democratic principles of limited government and **states' rights**, set a markedly different course with his New Freedom. Tutored in economics by *Muller v. Oregon* lawyer Louis Brandeis, who railed against the "curse of bigness," Wilson promised to use antitrust legislation to get rid of big corporations and to give small businesses and farmers better opportunities in the marketplace.

Wilson and Roosevelt fought it out, and the energy and enthusiasm of the Bull Moosers made the race seem closer than it really was. In the end, the Republican vote was split while the Democrats remained united. No candidate claimed a majority in the race. Wilson captured a bare 42 percent of the popular vote, polling fewer votes than Bryan had received when he lost to Taft in 1908. Roosevelt and his Bull Moose Party won 27 percent of the vote, an unprecedented tally for a new party. Taft came in third with 23 percent. But in the electoral college, Wilson won a decisive 435, with 88 going to Roosevelt and only 8 to Taft (Map 21.3). The

MAP 21.3   The Election of 1912

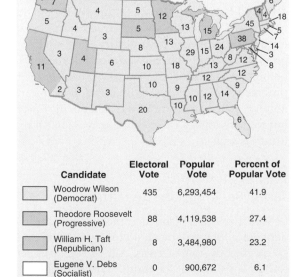

Candidate	Electoral Vote	Popular Vote	Percent of Popular Vote
Woodrow Wilson (Democrat)	435	6,293,454	41.9
Theodore Roosevelt (Progressive)	88	4,119,538	27.4
William H. Taft (Republican)	8	3,484,980	23.2
Eugene V. Debs (Socialist)	0	900,672	6.1

Novelty Postcards of the Election of 1912

These postcards picture the mascot of each party with a moving spring for a tail—the Democrats' donkey, the Progressives' bull moose, and the Republicans' elephant. The hat shown with Roosevelt comes from his phrase "My hat is in the ring," signifying his challenge to incumbent William Howard Taft. Taft's Grand Old Party (GOP) elephant is shown with a steamroller. Many critics charged that Taft won the Republican nomination from Roosevelt in 1912 by steamrolling the party's convention. The caption asks "Has He Got Enough Steam?" In a more obscure reference, Woodrow Wilson is pictured with "The New Jersey Mosquito," and the caption asks "Will He Get Stung?" Collection of Janice L. and David J. Frent.

Bull Moose Party essentially collapsed after Roosevelt's defeat. It had always been, in the words of one astute observer, "a house divided against itself and already mortgaged."

Woodrow Wilson and Progressivism at High Tide

Born in Virginia and raised in Georgia, Woodrow Wilson became the first southerner to be elected president since James K. Polk in 1844 and only the second Democrat to occupy the White House since Reconstruction. Democrats who anticipated a wild celebration when Wilson took office soon had their hopes dashed. The son of a Presbyterian minister, Wilson was a teetotaler more given to Scripture than to celebration. He called instead for a day of prayer.

This lean, ascetic man with an otherworldly gaze was, as one biographer conceded, a man whose "political convictions were never as fixed as his ambition." Although he owed his governorship to the Democratic machine, he quickly turned his back on the bosses and put New Jersey in the vanguard of progressivism. A year into his term, Wilson had his eye on the presidency. Always able to equivocate, Wilson proved rarely able to compromise. He brought to the White House a gift for oratory, a stern will, and a set of fixed beliefs. His tendency to turn differences of opinion into personal hatreds would impair his leadership and damage his presidency. Fortunately for Wilson, he came to power with a Democratic Congress eager to do his bidding.

Although he opposed big government in his campaign, Wilson viewed himself as the only leader who could speak for the country. He was prepared to work on the base built by Roosevelt to strengthen presidential power, exerting leadership and working through his party in Congress to accomplish the Democratic agenda. Before he was finished, Wilson presided over progressivism at high tide and lent his support not only to the platform of the Democratic Party but to many of the Progressive Party's social reforms as well.

Wilson's Reforms: Tariff, Banking, and the Trusts

In March 1913, Wilson became the first president since John Adams to go to Capitol Hill and speak directly to Congress, calling for tariff reform. "The object of the tariff," Wilson told Congress, "must be effective competition." Eager to topple the high tariff, the Democratic House of Representatives hastily passed the Underwood tariff, which lowered rates by 15 percent. To compensate for lost revenue, Congress approved a moderate federal income tax, made possible by ratification of the Sixteenth Amendment a month earlier. In the Senate, lobbyists for industries quietly went to work to get the tariff raised, but Wilson rallied public opinion by attacking the "industrious and insidious lobby." In the harsh glare of publicity, the Senate passed the Underwood tariff, which earned praise as "the most honest tariff since the Civil War."

Wilson next turned his attention to banking. The panic of 1907 dramatically testified to the failure of the banking system. That year, Roosevelt, like President Grover Cleveland before him, had to turn to J. P. Morgan to avoid economic catastrophe. But by the time Wilson came to office, Morgan's legendary power was coming under close scrutiny. In 1913, Arsène Pujo, a Democratic senator from Louisiana, headed a committee to investigate the "money trust," calling J. P. Morgan himself to testify. The Pujo committee uncovered an alarming concentration of banking power. J. P. Morgan and Company and its affiliates held 341 directorships in 112 corporations, controlling assets of more than $22 billion. The sensational findings created a mandate for banking reform.

The Federal Reserve Act of 1913 marked the most significant piece of domestic legislation of Wilson's presidency. It established a national banking system composed of twelve regional banks, privately controlled but regulated and supervised by a Federal Reserve Board appointed by the president. It gave the United States its first efficient banking and currency system and, at the same time, provided for a larger degree of government control over banking than had ever existed. The new system made currency more elastic and credit adequate for the needs of business and agriculture. It did not, however, attempt to take control of the boom and bust cycles in the U.S. economy, which would produce another major depression in the 1930s.

Wilson, flushed with success, tackled the trust issue next. When Congress reconvened in January 1914, Wilson supported the introduction of the Clayton Antitrust Act to outlaw "unfair competition"—practices such as price discrimination and interlocking directorates (directors from one corporation sitting on the board of another). By spelling out which practices were unfair, Wilson hoped to guide business activity

back to healthy competition without resorting to regulation. Despite a grandiose preamble that stated, "The labor of human beings is not a commodity or article of commerce," the Clayton Act did not improve labor's position. Although AFL president Samuel Gompers hailed the act as the "Magna Carta of labor," the conservative courts continued to issue injunctions and to use antitrust legislation against labor unions.

In the midst of the fight for the Clayton Act, Wilson, at the prompting of Louis Brandeis, changed course and threw his support behind the creation of the Federal Trade Commission (FTC), precisely the kind of federal regulatory agency that Roosevelt had advocated in his New Nationalism platform. The FTC, created in 1914, had not only wide investigatory powers but the authority to prosecute corporations for "unfair trade practices" and to enforce its judgments by issuing "cease and desist" orders. Along with the Clayton Act, Wilson's antitrust program worked to regulate rather than to break up big business.

> Before he was finished, Wilson presided over progressivism at high tide and championed not only the platform of the Democratic Party but many of the Progressive Party's social reforms as well.

By the fall of 1914, Wilson had exhausted the stock of ideas that made up the New Freedom. He alarmed progressives by declaring that the progressive movement had fulfilled its mission and that the country needed "a time of healing." Disgruntled progressives also disapproved of Wilson's conservative appointments. Having fought provisions in the Federal Reserve Act that would give bankers control, Wilson promptly named a banker, Paul Warburg, as the first chief of the Federal Reserve Board. Appointments to the new FTC also went to conservative businessmen. The progressive penchant for efficiency and expertise helps explain Wilson's choices. Believing that experts in the field could best understand the complex issues at stake, Wilson appointed bankers to oversee the banks and businessmen to regulate business.

Wilson, Reluctant Progressive

Progressives watched in dismay as Wilson repeatedly obstructed or obstinately refused to endorse further progressive reforms. He failed to support labor's demand for an end to court injunctions against labor unions. He twice threatened to veto legislation providing for farm credits on nonperishable crops. He refused to

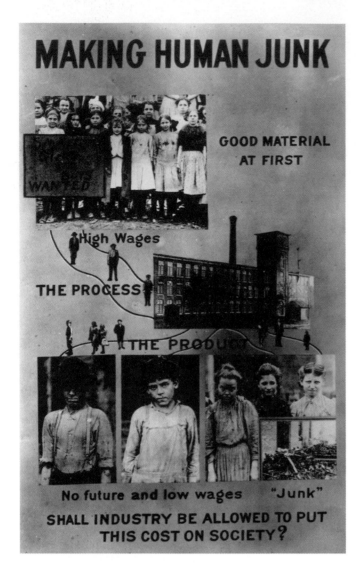

Progressive Poster Condemning Child Labor
This poster attacks child labor, borrowing the convention of the business flowchart to portray graphically how industries employing children are "making human junk." Progressives' concern for the plight of poor children won them the label "child savers." Although activists worked hard to enact federal legislation prohibiting child labor in 1916, the Supreme Court declared the law unconstitutional two years later on the grounds that Congress had no right to regulate manufacturing within states. What does this poster emphasize most in its appeal to end child labor—concern for children or for society?
Library of Congress.

In the face of Wilson's obstinacy, reform might have ended in 1913 had not politics intruded. In the congressional elections of 1914, the Republican Party, no longer split by Roosevelt's Bull Moose faction, won substantial gains. Democratic strategists, with their eyes on the 1916 presidential race, recognized that Wilson needed to pick up support in the Midwest and the West by capturing votes from former Bull Moose progressives.

Wilson responded belatedly to this political pressure by lending his support to reform in the months leading up to the election of 1916. In a sharp about-face, he cultivated union labor, farmers, and social reformers. To please labor, he appointed Louis Brandeis to the Supreme Court. To woo farmers, he threw his support behind legislation to obtain rural credits. And he won support from advanced progressives like Jane Addams by supporting workers' compensation and the Keating-Owen child labor law, which outlawed the regular employment of children younger than sixteen. When a railroad strike threatened in the months before the election, Wilson practically ordered Congress to establish an eight-hour day at ten-hour pay on the railroads. He had moved a long way from his position in 1912 to embrace many of the social reforms championed by Theodore Roosevelt. (See "Documenting the American Promise," page 777.) As Wilson boasted, the Democrats had "opened their hearts to the demands of social justice" and had "come very near to carrying out the platform of the Progressive Party." Wilson's shift toward reform, along with his claim that he had kept the United States out of the war in Europe, helped him win reelection in 1916.

The Limits of Progressive Reform

While progressivism called for a more active role for the liberal state, at heart it was a movement that sought reforms designed to preserve American institutions and stem the tide of more radical change. Its basic conservatism can be seen by comparing it to more radical movements of the era—socialism, radical labor, and birth control—and by looking at the groups progressive reform left behind, including women and African Americans.

support child labor legislation or woman suffrage. Wilson used the rhetoric of the New Freedom to justify his actions, claiming that his administration would condone "special privileges to none." But in fact his stance often reflected the interests of his small-business constituency.

The Issue of Child Labor

By the early years of the twentieth century, as many as four million children between the ages of ten and fifteen toiled long hours for little pay. They worked in the depths of coal mines, in the searing heat of glass factories, in canneries and textile mills, in cotton fields—wherever employers coveted small size and nimble fingers. Progressive reformers, often called "child savers," attempted to curb exploitation of children under the age of fourteen in sweatshops, mines, and mills across America. But they ran into solid opposition not only from employers, who had a vested interest in the cheap labor children performed, but also from parents, who counted on the meager wages of their children. In rural America, no one questioned parents' right to put children to hard tasks in the fields and on the farm. Similarly, immigrants from rural Italy, Germany, or Russia could see no harm in putting children to work in factories or sweatshops in America's industrial cities and viewed it as the parents' prerogative to command their children's wages. Progressives found themselves up against stiff opposition.

DOCUMENT 1
Lewis W. Parker, Testimony before the Congressional Committee on Labor, 1914

Not just immigrants but old-stock Americans relied on child labor, particularly in the South, where entire families of poor whites left the land to work side by side in the textile mills. On May 22, 1914, a South Carolina mill owner testified before the House of Representatives Committee on Labor on why child labor was necessary in the South.

It is not possible for a man who has been working on a farm who is an adult—after the age of 21 years, for instance—to become a skilled employee in a cotton mill. His fingers are knotted and gnarled; he is slow in action, whereas activity is required in working in the cotton mills. Therefore, as a matter of necessity, the adult of the family had to come to the cotton mill as an unskilled employee, and it was the children of the family who became the skilled employees in the cotton mills. For that reason it was the children who had to support the families for the time being. I have seen instances in which a child of 12 years of age, working in the cotton mills, is earning one and one-half times as much as his father of 40 or 50 years of age.

DOCUMENT 2
Florence Kelley, Testimony before the Congressional Committee on Labor, 1914

Progressives countered these arguments with poignant testimony about the plight of young workers and the failure of the states to enforce the law. At the same 1914 committee hearings, reformer Florence Kelley described her experiences investigating child labor practices in Illinois.

. . . I was at one time chief inspector of factories and workshops in the State of Illinois. I found great numbers of children working at night—working illegally. The superintendent of a glass-bottle company told me himself that this occurred once when he was rushed with work: A widow had come to him bringing two little boys, one still in kilts [baby skirts worn by small boys] and one in knee breeches. She told him that their father had just been killed on the railroad, and that they were penniless; and she wanted the older little boy to go to work in the glassworks, where he would get 40 cents a day. The superintendent was pressed for boys, and said, "I won't take the bigger fellow alone, but if you will take the baby back home and put him into knee pants, and then bring them both back in trousers, I will take them both." She did so, and those two little fellows, aged 9 and 7 years, began their work on the night shift.

DOCUMENT 3
Lowell Mellett, Interview with Reuben Dagenhart, 1923

Despite heavy odds against them, progressives achieved victory in 1916 when the National Child Labor Committee finally convinced Congress and President Woodrow Wilson to enact the Keating-Owen bill forbidding the regular employment of children under sixteen. The child savers' victory proved short-lived, however. Powerful business interests and a Supreme Court sympathetic to their views took advantage of the waning fervor for reform, and in 1918 in Hammer v. Dagenhart, the Court struck down the child labor law on the grounds that Congress could not regulate manufacturing within states. This decision made it legal for the chief plaintiff in the case, Roland Dagenhart, to continue having his young sons, aged thirteen and seven, work in a North Carolina cotton mill. It also protected the boys' "constitutional right" to continue to work at the mill, where they put in

(continued)

twelve-hour days and sometimes worked night shifts as well.

Ironically, one of the plaintiffs in the Dagenhart case had a very negative view of its outcome. In 1923, reporter Lowell Mellett tracked down Reuben Dagenhart, one of the boys in whose favor the Supreme Court had ruled six years earlier. In an article published in Labor *in November 1923, Mellett recounted his meeting with Dagenhart.*

I found him at his home in Charlotte. He is about the size of the office boy—weighs 105 pounds, he told me. But he is a married man with a child. He is 20 years old.

"What benefit," I asked him, "did you get out of the suit which you won in the United States Supreme Court?"

"You mean the suit the Fidelity Manufacturing Company won? (It was the Fidelity Company for which the Dagenharts were working.) I don't see that I got any benefit. I guess I'd been alot better off if they hadn't won it. . . .

"Look at me! A hundred and five pounds, a grown man and no education. I may be mistaken, but I think the years I've put in in the cotton mills have stunted my growth. They kept me from getting any schooling. I had to stop school after the third grade and now I need the education I didn't get."

"How was your growth stunted?"

"I don't know—the dust and the lint, maybe. But from 12 years old on, I was working 12 hours a day—from 6 in the morning till 7 at night, with time out for meals. And sometimes I worked nights besides. Lifting a hundred pounds and I only weighed 65 pounds myself."

He explained that he and his sister worked together, "on section," spinning. They each made about a dollar a day, though later he worked up to where he could make $2. His father made $15 a week and infant John, at the time the suit was brought, was making close to $1 a day.

"Just what did you and John get out of that suit, then?"

"Why, we got some automobile rides when them big lawyers from the North was down here. Oh, yes, and they brought both of us a coca-cola! That's all we got out of it."

"What did you tell the judge when you were in court?"

"Oh, John and me never was in court! Just Paw was there. John and me was just little kids in short pants. I guess we wouldn't have looked like much in court. We were working in the mill while the case was going on. But Paw went up to Washington."

Reuben hasn't been to school, but his mind has not been idle.

"It would have been a good thing for all the kids in this state if that law they passed had been kept. . . . I know one thing. I ain't going to let them put my kid sister in the mill. . . . She's only 15 and she's crippled and I bet I stop that!"

Despite the efforts of committed reformers, child labor persisted into the 1920s, immune from federal law and condoned by states reluctant to exercise their authority against the force of private money and growing public indifference.

SOURCE: Documents 1 and 2, House of Representatives Hearings before the Committee on Labor (1914), 93, 35–36; document 3, *Labor*, November 17, 1923.

Radical Alternatives

The year 1900 marked the birth of the Social Democratic Party in America, later called simply the Socialist Party. Like the progressives, the socialists were middle class and native-born. They had broken with the older, more militant Socialist Labor Party precisely because of its dogmatic approach and immigrant constituency. The new group of socialists proved eager to appeal to a broad mass of Americans.

The Socialist Party chose as its standard-bearer Eugene V. Debs, whose experience in the Pullman strike of 1894 convinced him that "there is no hope for the toiling masses of my country-men, except by the pathways mapped out by Socialism." Debs's brand of socialism, which owed as much to the social gospel as to the theories of Karl Marx, advocated cooperation over competition and urged men and women to liberate themselves from "the barbarism of private ownership and wage slavery." Roosevelt labeled Debs a "mere inciter to murder and preacher of applied anarchy." Debs, for his part, pointed to the conservatism that underlay Roosevelt's fiery rhetoric. In the 1912 election, Debs indicted both old parties as "Tweedledee and Tweedledum," each dedicated to the preservation of capitalism and the continuation of the wage system. The Socialist Party alone, he argued, was the "revolutionary party of the working class." Debs would run for president five times, in every election (except 1916) from 1900 to 1920. His best showing came in 1912, when he polled 6 percent of the popular vote, capturing almost a million votes.

Farther to the left of the socialists stood the Industrial Workers of the World (IWW), nicknamed the Wobblies. In 1905, Debs, along with Western Federation of Miners leader William Dudley "Big Bill" Haywood, created the IWW, "one big union" dedicated to organizing the most destitute segment of the workforce, the unskilled workers disdained by Samuel Gompers's AFL—western miners, migrant farmworkers, lumbermen, and immigrant textile workers. Haywood, a craggy-faced miner with one eye (he had lost the other in a childhood accident), was a charismatic leader and a proletarian intellectual. Debs in-

sisted that change could come from ballots, not bullets, but the IWW unhesitatingly advocated direct action, sabotage, and the general strike—tactics designed to trigger a workers' uprising. The IWW never had more than 10,000 members at any one time, although possibly as many as 100,000 workers belonged to the union at one time or another in the early twentieth century. Nevertheless, the IWW's influence on the country extended far beyond its numbers.

The movement for birth control during the Progressive Era was another example of a cross-class alliance in which middle-class women made common cause with the working class. The leading advocates of birth control from 1914 to 1920 came from the ranks of anarchists, **feminists**, and socialists. Radicals such as the anarchist Emma Goldman were among the first to champion birth control, which they saw as a way to improve the plight of the workers, urging

"We Want Debs"

Eugene Victor Debs, shown in the train window wearing a bow tie, poses with Socialist Party campaign workers on a whistle-stop tour during the presidential campaign of 1912. Arguing that Roosevelt and Wilson were as alike as "Tweedledee and Tweedledum," Debs saw the Socialist Party as the only hope for the working class. Over a million voters agreed and cast their votes for him in 1912.

Photo: Brown Brothers; button: Collection of Janice L. and David J. Frent.

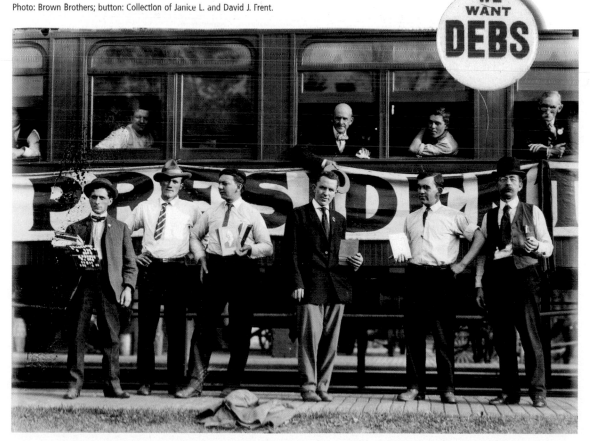

working-class women to quit producing recruits for the factory and the army.

Margaret Sanger, a nurse and social activist, promoted birth control as a movement for social change. Sanger, the daughter of a radical Irish father and a mother who died at age fifty after bearing eleven children, coined the term *birth control* in 1915 and launched a movement with broad social implications. Sanger and her followers saw birth control not only as a sexual and medical reform but also as a means to alter social and political power relationships and to alleviate human misery.

Although birth control became a public issue only in the early twentieth century, the birthrate in the United States had been falling consistently throughout the nineteenth century. The average number of children per family dropped from 7.0 in 1800 to 3.6 by 1900. The desire for family limitation was widespread, and in this sense, birth control was nothing new. But the open advocacy of *contraception*, the use of artificial means to prevent pregnancy, seemed to many people both new and shocking. Theodore Roosevelt fulminated against birth control as "race suicide," warning that the "white" population was declining while immigrants and "undesirables" continued to breed.

Convinced that women needed to be able to control their pregnancies but unsure of the best

Margaret Sanger's Brownsville Birth Control Clinic

Margaret Sanger opened the first birth control clinic in the United States in the Brownsville section of Brooklyn in 1916. During the nine days it operated before police shut it down, more than four hundred women visited the clinic. Here they are shown waiting patiently in line with their baby carriages. Sanger published her flyers in English, Yiddish, and Italian, and her clinic attracted immigrant women, proving that Italian Catholics and Russian Jews wanted birth control information as much as their middle- and upper-class Protestant counterparts did. What does the picture say about which women sought birth control, married or single women?

Sophia Smith Collection, Smith College.

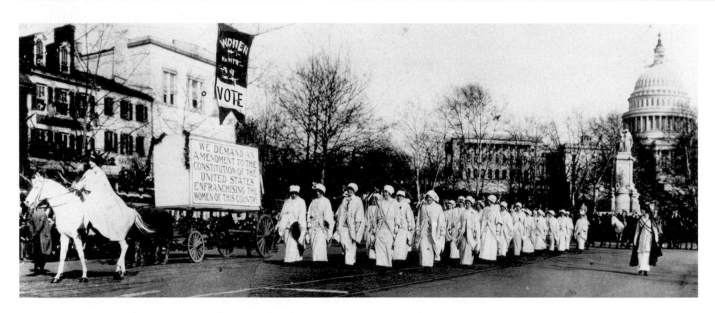

Inez Mullholland Leads Washington Suffrage Parade
In 1913 when women marched on Washington, D.C., to demand the vote, the mass march was a novel tactic. Many worried that women would not be physically able to march the full distance. Ambulances stood by to tend to any who fainted along the way. Led by Inez Hayes Mullholland riding a white horse, the women proved neither faint nor faint-hearted. Incoming president Woodrow Wilson refused even to acknowledge their protest in his inaugural address the following day.
Brown Brothers.

methods to do so, Sanger traveled to Europe in 1913 to learn more about contraceptive techniques. On her return, she promoted birth control in her newspaper, *The Woman Rebel*. Social purity laws passed in the 1870s made it illegal to distribute either information on birth control or contraceptive devices, classing both as "obscene." The post office confiscated Sanger's magazine and brought charges against her. Facing arrest, she fled to Europe only to return in 1916 something of a national celebrity. In her absence, birth control had become linked with free speech and had been taken up as a liberal cause. Under public pressure, the government dropped the charges against Sanger, who undertook a nationwide tour to publicize the birth control cause.

Sanger then turned to direct action, opening the nation's first birth control clinic in the Brownsville section of Brooklyn, New York, in October 1916. Located in the heart of a Jewish and Italian immigrant neighborhood, the clinic attracted 464 clients in the nine days it remained open. On the tenth day, police shut down the clinic and threw Sanger in jail. By then she had become a national figure, and the cause she championed had gained legitimacy, if not legal-

ity. After World War I, the birth control movement would become much less radical as Sanger turned to medical doctors for support and mouthed the racist theories of the eugenics movement. But in its infancy, the movement Sanger led was part of a radical vision for reforming the world that made common cause with the socialists and the IWW in challenging the limits of progressive reform.

Progressivism for White Men Only

The day before President Woodrow Wilson's inauguration in March 1913, more than five thousand demonstrators marched in Washington to demand the vote for women. A rowdy crowd on hand to celebrate the Democrats' triumph heckled the marchers, as did the police. "If my wife were where you are," a burly cop told one suffragist, "I'd break her head." But for all the marching, Wilson, who didn't believe that a "lady" should vote, pointedly ignored woman suffrage in his inaugural address the next day.

The march served as a reminder that the political gains of progressivism were not spread equally in the population. As the twentieth century dawned, women still could not vote in most states. Increasingly, however, woman suffrage had become an international movement. In Great Britain, Emmeline Pankhurst and her daughters Cristabel and Sylvia promoted a new, militant suffragism. They seized the spotlight in a series of marches, mass meetings, and acts of civil disobedience, which sometimes escalated into riots, violence, and arson.

Alice Paul, a Quaker social worker who had visited England and participated in suffrage activism there, returned to the United States in 1910 in time to plan the mass march on the eve of Wilson's inauguration and to lobby for a federal amendment to give women the vote. Paul's dramatic tactics alienated many in the National American Woman Suffrage Association (NAWSA). In 1916, Paul founded the militant National Woman's Party (NWP), which became the radical voice of the suffrage movement, advocating direct action such as mass marches and civil disobedience. Paul and her followers rejected the state-by-state strategy of the NAWSA and continued to press for a constitutional suffrage amendment, called by its supporters the Susan B. Anthony amendment.

The NAWSA, spurred by the actions of Paul and her followers, gained new direction after Carrie Chapman Catt became president in 1915. Catt revitalized the organization with a carefully crafted "winning plan" designed to achieve suffrage in six years. While Paul and her NWP held a six-month vigil outside the White House— holding banners that read "Mr. Wilson, What Will You Do for Woman Suffrage?"—Catt led a centrally directed effort that worked on several levels. In states where women already voted, Catt lobbied for a federal constitutional amendment. Where state referenda could be won, she launched campaigns to maintain the suffrage momentum. Catt's strategy was to "keep so much 'suffrage noise' going all over the country that neither the enemy [n]or friends will discover where the real battle is." Catt's "winning plan" worked effectively, taking only four years instead of the six Catt had predicted to ratify a constitutional amendment for woman suffrage.

World War I would provide the final impetus for woman suffrage. Paul and the NWP refused to work for the war, insisting "democracy should begin at home." In contrast, Catt seized the mantle of pa-

> Progressivism, as it was practiced in the West and South, was tainted with racism and sought to limit the rights of African and Asian Americans.

triotism, arguing that there was no conflict between fighting for suffrage and aiding the war effort. When the Nineteenth Amendment became part of the U.S. Constitution in August 1920, the victory belonged both to Catt and to Paul. For without the militancy of the NWP, the NAWSA would not have seemed so moderate and respectable.

Women weren't the only group left out in progressive reform. Progressivism, as it was practiced in the West and South, was tainted with racism and sought to limit the rights of African and Asian Americans. Anti-Asian bigotry in the West had led to a renewal of the Chinese Exclusion Act in 1902. At first, California governor Hiram Johnson stood up against the strong anti-Asian prejudice of his state; then in 1913 he caved in to near unanimous pressure and signed the Alien Land Law, which barred Japanese immigrants from purchasing land in California. His support of the legislation amounted to little more than cynical demagoguery. As Johnson well knew, the law was largely symbolic—ineffectual in practice because Japanese children born in the United States were U.S. citizens and property could be purchased in their names. Progressive politicians like Johnson, dedicated to democracy and opposed to special interests, proved willing to lay aside their principles and condone nativism and racism in order to maintain their popularity with voters.

South of the Mason-Dixon line, the progressives' racism targeted African Americans. Progressives preached the disfranchisement of black voters as a "reform." During the bitter electoral fights that had pitted Populists against Democrats in the 1890s, the party of white supremacy held on to power by means of votes purchased or coerced from African Americans. Southern progressives proposed to "reform" the electoral system by eliminating black voters. Beginning in 1890 with Mississippi, southern states curtailed the African American vote through devices such as poll taxes (fees required for voting) and literacy tests. Not coincidentally, these measures also denied access to poor, illiterate whites likely to vote Populist. The racist intent of southern voting legislation became especially clear after 1900. With the Populist threat gone, states resorted to the grandfather clause, a legal provision that allowed men who failed a literacy test to vote if their grandfathers had cast a ballot. Grandfathering permitted nearly all southern white men to vote and excluded nearly all blacks, whose grandparents had most likely been slaves and never voted.

The Progressive Era also witnessed the rise of **Jim Crow** laws to segregate public facilities (Jim Crow was the name of a character in a popular minstrel song). The new railroads precipitated segregation in the South where it had rarely existed before, at least on paper. Blacks traveling by train were restricted to Jim Crow coaches even when they paid the first-class fare. Soon separate waiting rooms, separate bathrooms, and separate dining facilities for blacks sprang up across the South. In courtrooms in Mississippi, blacks were even required to swear on a separate Bible.

In the face of this growing repression, Booker T. Washington, the preeminent black leader of the day, urged caution and restraint. A former slave, Washington had opened the Tuskegee Institute in Alabama in 1881 to teach vocational skills to African Americans. He emphasized education and economic progress for his race and urged African Americans to put aside issues of political and social equality. In an 1895 speech in Atlanta, which came to be known as the "Atlanta Compromise," he stated, "In all things that are purely social we can be as separate as the fingers, yet one as the hand in all things essential to mutual progress." Washington's accommodationist policy appealed to whites in all sections, who elevated "the wizard of Tuskegee" to the role of national spokesman for African Americans.

The year after Washington proclaimed the Atlanta Compromise, the Supreme Court upheld the legality of racial segregation, affirming in *Plessy v. Ferguson* (1896) the constitutionality of the doctrine of "separate but equal." Blacks could be segregated in separate schools, restrooms, and other facilities, as long as the facilities were "equal" to those provided for whites. In actuality, facilities for blacks rarely proved equal. In the North, where racism of a different sort led to a clamor for legislation to restrict immigration, support for African American equality found few advocates. And with anti-Asian bigotry strong in the West, the doctrine of "white

DINNER GIVEN AT THE WHITE HOUSE BY PRESIDENT ROOSEVELT TO BOOKER T. WASHINGTON, OCTOBER 17th, 1901

Booker T. Washington and Theodore Roosevelt Dine at the White House
When Theodore Roosevelt invited Booker T. Washington to the White House in 1901, he stirred up a hornet's nest of controversy that continued into the election of 1904. This Republican campaign piece gives the meeting a positive slant, showing Roosevelt and Washington sitting under a portrait of Abraham Lincoln, a symbol of the party's historic commitment to African Americans. Can you tell from this illustration that Washington is African American? Democrats portrayed the meeting in a very different light; their campaign buttons pictured Washington with darker skin and implied that Roosevelt favored "race mingling."
Collection of Janice L. and David J. Frent.

supremacy" found increasing support in all sections of the country.

When Theodore Roosevelt invited Booker T. Washington to dine at the White House in 1901, a storm of racist criticism erupted. One southern editor fumed that the White House "had been painted black." But Roosevelt summoned Washington to talk politics and patronage, not African American rights. Busy tearing apart Mark Hanna's Republican machine, Roosevelt wanted Washington's counsel in selecting black Republicans for party posts in the South. The president remained more interested in his own political fortunes than in those of African Americans. His attitude became obvious in the Brownsville incident in 1906, when he dishonorably discharged three companies of black soldiers because he suspected (although there was no proof) that they were shielding the murderer of a white saloonkeeper killed in a shootout in the Texas town.

When Woodrow Wilson became president, he brought with him southern attitudes toward race and racial segregation. At the prompting of his wife, he instituted segregation in the federal workforce, especially the post office, and approved segregated drinking fountains and restrooms in the nation's capital. When critics attacked the policy, Wilson insisted that segregation was "in the interest of the Negro."

Faced with intolerance and open persecution, educated blacks in the North rebelled against the conservative leadership of Booker T. Washington. In *The Souls of Black Folk* (1903), Harvard graduate W. E. B. Du Bois attacked the "Tuskegee Machine," comparing Booker T. Washington to a political boss who used his influence to silence his critics and reward his followers. Du Bois founded the Niagara movement in 1905, calling for universal male suffrage, civil rights, and leadership by a black intellectual elite. In 1909, the Niagara movement helped found the National Association for the Advancement of Colored People (NAACP), a coalition of blacks and whites who sought legal and political rights for African Americans through the courts. Like many progressive reform coalitions, the NAACP attracted a diverse group—social workers, socialists, and black intellectuals. In the decades that followed, the NAACP came to represent the future for African Americans, while Booker T. Washington, who died in 1915, represented the past.

Conclusion: The Transformation of the Liberal State

Progressivism was never a radical movement. Its goal remained the reform of the existing system—by government intervention if necessary, but without uprooting any of the traditional American political, economic, or social institutions. As Theodore Roosevelt, the bellwether of the movement, insisted, "The only true conservative is the man who resolutely sets his face toward the future." Roosevelt was such a man, and progressivism was such a movement. But although progressivism was never radical, neither was it the laissez-faire liberalism of the previous century. Progressives' willingness to use the power of the federal government to regulate business and achieve a measure of social justice redefined liberalism in the twentieth century, tying it to the expanded power of the state.

Progressivism contained many paradoxes. A diverse coalition of individuals and interests, the progressive movement began at the grass roots but left as its legacy a stronger presidency and unprecedented federal involvement in the economy and social welfare. A movement that believed in social justice, progressivism often promoted social control. And while progressives called for greater democracy, they worshipped experts and efficiency.

But whatever its inconsistencies and limitations, progressivism took action to deal with the problems posed by urban industrialism. Progressivism saw grassroots activists address social problems on the local and state levels and search for national solutions to the problems of urban industrialism. By increasing the power of the presidency and expanding the power of the state, progressives worked to bring about greater social justice and to achieve a better balance between government and business. Jane Addams and Theodore Roosevelt could lay equal claim to the movement that redefined liberalism and launched the liberal state of the twentieth century. War on a global scale would provide progressivism with yet another challenge even before it had completed its ambitious agenda.

For additional firsthand accounts of this period, see Chapter 21 in Michael Johnson, ed., *Reading the American Past*, Third Edition.

To assess your mastery of the material in this chapter, see the Online Study Guide at bedfordstmartins.com/roark.

For Web links related to topics in this chapter, see "HistoryLinks," "DocLinks," and "PlaceLinks" at bedfordstmartins.com/roark.

CHRONOLOGY

1889 • Jane Addams opens Hull House in Chicago.

1895 • Booker T. Washington enunciates "Atlanta Compromise," supporting separation of blacks and whites.
• Protestant clergy found Anti-Saloon League.

1896 • U.S. Supreme Court upholds doctrine of "separate but equal" in *Plessy v. Ferguson*.

1899 • Florence Kelley heads National Consumers' League (NCL).

1900 • Socialist Party founded with Eugene V. Debs as standard-bearer.
• Tom Johnson elected mayor of Cleveland, Ohio.
• Robert M. La Follette elected governor of Wisconsin.

1901 • Theodore Roosevelt succeeds to presidency following assassination of William McKinley.

1902 • U.S. government files antitrust lawsuit against Northern Securities Company.
• Roosevelt brings labor and management to bargaining table in anthracite coal strike.
• Dispute between United States and Germany over Venezuelan debt ends in arbitration.

1903 • Women's Trade Union League (WTUL) founded, bringing together women workers and middle-class "allies."
• United States begins construction of Panama Canal.
• Congress passes Elkins Act, outlawing railroad rebates.
• W. E. B. Du Bois challenges Booker T. Washington in his book *The Souls of Black Folk*.

1904 • Roosevelt wins presidential election in landslide.
• Roosevelt Corollary to Monroe Doctrine effectively makes the United States "policeman" of the Western Hemisphere.

1905 • Big Bill Haywood, calling for labor to adopt radical measures in its struggle against capitalism, founds Industrial Workers of the World (IWW).
• W. E. B. Du Bois founds the Niagara movement, calling for suffrage and civil rights for blacks.
• Roosevelt mediates dispute between Germans and French over access to trade in Morocco at the Algeciras conference in Spain.
• Taft-Katsura Agreement gives Japan control over Korea.

1906 • Congress passes Pure Food and Drug Act and Meat Inspection Act.

• Roosevelt urges investigative reporters not to resort to "muckraking." Journalists appropriate the term for exposé writing, calling themselves *muckrakers*.
• Congress passes Hepburn Act to regulate railroads and strengthen Interstate Commerce Commission.
• Roosevelt dishonorably discharges three companies of African American soldiers in Brownsville, Texas, without proof of their guilt.
• Roosevelt receives Nobel Peace Prize for mediating Russo-Japanese War.

1907 • Panic on Wall Street.
• Barred by Congress from creating any more federal reserves in six western states, Roosevelt hastily adds 21 before law goes into effect.
• Roosevelt signs "Gentleman's Agreement" with Japan restricting immigration.
• Social gospel minister Walter Rauschenbusch publishes *Christianity and the Social Crisis*.

1908 • In *Muller v. Oregon*, U.S. Supreme Court upholds Oregon state law limiting women's working hours to ten a day.
• In the Root-Takahira agreement, the United States and Japan agree to maintain Open Door policy in the Pacific.
• William Howard Taft elected president.

1909 • "Uprising of twenty thousand" in New York City, a garment workers' strike, backed by the WTUL.
• Herbert Croly publishes *The Promise of American Life*.
• National Association for the Advancement of Colored People (NAACP) formed.
• Taft defends Payne-Aldrich tariff.

1910 • Hiram Johnson elected governor of California.
• Woodrow Wilson elected governor of New Jersey.
• Congress passes Mann Act to limit traffic in women across state lines.
• Jane Addams publishes *Twenty Years at Hull-House*.

1911 • Triangle fire in New York City kills 146 workers.
• Taft launches antitrust suit against U.S. Steel.

1912 • Taft sends marines into Nicaragua and the Dominican Republic.
• Republicans nominate incumbent William Howard Taft.
• Theodore Roosevelt runs for president on Progressive Party ticket.
• Democrat Woodrow Wilson elected president.

- Socialist Eugene V. Debs garners 6 percent of the presidential vote.

1913
- Suffragists march on eve of Wilson's inauguration to demand the vote.
- Congress passes Federal Reserve Act, establishing national banking system under government control.
- Sixteenth Amendment (income tax) and Seventeenth Amendment (direct election of senators) ratified.

1914
- Wilson signs legislation establishing Federal Trade Commission (FTC).
- Congress passes Clayton Antitrust Act, outlawing "unfair competition."
- Panama Canal opens.

- Walter Lippmann publishes *Drift and Mastery*, statement of progressive belief in scientific expertise.

1915
- Carrie Chapman Catt takes over leadership of national woman suffrage movement.

1916
- Alice Paul launches National Woman's Party.
- Margaret Sanger opens first U.S. birth control clinic, in Brooklyn, New York.
- Congress passes Keating-Owen bill, outlawing child labor.
- Woodrow Wilson elected to a second term.

1918
- In *Hammer v. Dagenhart*, U.S. Supreme Court strikes down Keating-Owen child labor law.

BIBLIOGRAPHY

General

Sean Dennis Cashman, *America in the Age of the Titans: The Progressive Era and World War I* (1988).

Alan Dawley, *Struggles for Justice: Social Responsibility and the Liberal State* (1991).

Vincent P. DeSantis, *The Shaping of Modern America, 1877–1920* (2nd ed., 1989).

Steven Diner, *A Very Different Age: Americans of the Progressive Era* (1998).

Glenda Elizabeth Gilmore, ed., *Who Were the Progressives?* (2002).

Linda K. Kerber, Alice Kessler-Harris, and Katherine Kish Sklar, *U.S. History as Women's History* (1995).

Nell Irvin Painter, *Standing at Armageddon: The United States, 1877–1919* (1987).

Daniel Rogers, *Atlantic Crossings: Social Politics in a Progressive Age* (1998).

Grassroots Progressivism

Joyce Antler, *Lucy Sprague Mitchell* (1987).

Karen J. Blair, *The Clubwoman as Feminist: True Womanhood Redefined, 1868–1914* (1980).

Paul Boyer, *Urban Masses and Moral Order in America, 1820–1920* (1978).

Mina Carson, *Settlement Folk: Social Thought and the American Settlement Movement, 1885–1930* (1990).

Robert M. Crunden, *Ministers of Reform: The Progressive Achievement in American Civilization, 1889–1920* (1982).

Doris Groshen Daniels, *Always a Sister: The Feminism of Lillian D. Wald* (1989).

Allen F. Davis, *American Heroine: The Life and Legend of Jane Addams* (1973).

Nancy Schrom Dye, *As Equals and as Sisters: Feminism, Unionism, and the Women's Trade Union League of New York* (1980).

John H. Ehrenreich, *The Altruistic Imagination: A History of Social Work and Social Policy in the United States* (1985).

Jean Bethke Elshtain, *Jane Addams and the Dream of American Democracy* (2002).

Ellen Fitzpatrick, *Endless Crusade: Women, Social Scientists, and Progressive Reform* (1990).

Lynn D. Gordon, *Gender and Higher Education in the Progressive Era* (1989).

Alice Kessler Harris, *Out to Work: A History of Wage-Earning Women in the United States* (1982).

Melvin Holli, *The American Mayor: The Best and Worst Big-City Leaders* (1999).

Michael B. Katz, *In the Shadow of the Poorhouse: A Social History of Welfare in America* (1986).

Seth Koven and Sonya Michel, eds., *Mothers of a New World: Maternalist Politics and the Origins of the Welfare State* (1993).

Rivka Lissak, *Pluralism and Progressives: Hull House and the New Immigrants, 1890–1919* (1989).

Kathleen McCarthy, ed., *Lady Bountiful Revisited: Women, Philanthropy, and Power* (1990).

Robyn Muncy, *Creating a Female Dominion in American Reform* (1991).

Elizabeth Payne, *Reform, Labor, and Feminism: Margaret Dreier Robins and the Women's Trade Union League* (1988).

David Pivar, *The Purity Crusade: Sexual Morality and Social Control* (1973).

Anne Firor Scott, *Natural Allies: Women's Associations in American History* (1991).

Peter R. Shergold, *Working-Class Life: The "American Standard" in Comparative Perspective, 1899–1913* (1982).

Beatrice Siegel, *Lillian Wald of Henry Street* (1983).

Kathryn Kish Sklar, *Florence Kelley and the Nation's Work: The Rise of Women's Political Culture, 1830–1900* (1995).

Barbara Miller Solomon, *In the Company of Educated Women* (1985).

Landon R. Y. Storre, *Civilizing Capitalism: The National Consumers' League, Women's Activism, and Labor Standards in the New Deal Era* (2000).

David Stradling, *Smokestacks and Progressives: Environmentalists, Engineers, and Air Quality in America, 1881–1951* (1999).

David Von Drehle, *Triangle: The Fire That Changed America* (2003).

Barbara Mayer Wertheimer, *We Were There: The Story of Working Women in America* (1977).

Harold S. Wilson, *"McClure's Magazine" and the Muckrakers* (1970).

Progressive Politics and Diplomacy

Donald E. Anderson, *William Howard Taft* (1973).

Norman Birnbaum, *After Progress: American Social Reform and European Socialism in the Twentieth Century* (2001).

John Morton Blum, *The Republican Roosevelt* (2nd ed., 1977).

H. W. Brands, *T. R.: The Last Romantic* (1997).

John D. Buenker, *Urban Liberalism and Progressive Reform* (1973).

David Mark Chalmers, *The Muckrake Years* (1980).

James Chace, *1912: Wilson, Roosevelt, Taft and Debs—the Election that Changed the Country* (2004).

Kendrick A. Clements, *The Presidency of Woodrow Wilson* (1992).

Michael L. Collins, *That Damned Cowboy: Theodore Roosevelt and the American West, 1883–1898* (1989).

John Milton Cooper Jr., *The Warrior and the Priest: Woodrow Wilson and Theodore Roosevelt* (1983).

Louis Filler, *Muckraking and Progressivism in the American Tradition* (rev. ed., 1996).

Lewis L. Gould, *Reform and Regulation: American Politics from Roosevelt to Wilson* (2nd ed., 1986).

Lewis L. Gould, *The Presidency of Theodore Roosevelt* (1991).

William H. Harbaugh, *The Life and Times of Theodore Roosevelt* (rev. ed., 1982).

Samuel P. Hays, *Conservation and the Gospel of Efficiency* (1959).

Matthew Frye Jacobson, *Barbarian Virtues: The United States Encounters Foreign Peoples at Home and Abroad, 1876–1917* (2000).

James Kloppenberg, *Uncertain Victory: Social Democracy and Progressivism in European and American Thought, 1870–1920* (1986).

Gabriel Kolko, *The Triumph of Conservatism* (1963).

William A. Link, *The Paradox of Southern Progressivism, 1880–1930* (1992).

Richard Coke Lower, *A Bloc of One: The Political Career of Hiram W. Johnson* (1993).

Richard L. McCormick, *From Realignment to Reform: Political Change in New York State* (1981).

Richard L. McCormick, *The Party Period and Public Policy* (1986).

Edmund Morris, *Theodore Rex* (2001).

Spencer Olin Jr., *California's Prodigal Sons: Hiram Johnson and the Progressives, 1911–1917* (1968).

Eric Rauchway, *Murdering McKinley: The Making of Theodore Roosevelt's America* (2003).

Emily S. Rosenberg, *Spreading the American Dream: American Economic and Cultural Expansion, 1890–1945* (1982).

Alan R. Sadovnik and Susan F. Semel, eds., *Founding Mothers and Others: Women Educational Leaders during the Progressive Era* (2002).

Judith Sealander, *Grand Plans: Business Progressivism and Social Change in Ohio's Miami Valley, 1890–1919* (1988).

Ted Steinberg, *Down to Earth: Nature's Role in American History* (2002).

Phillipa Strum, *Louis D. Brandeis* (1984).

David P. Thelen, *Robert M. La Follette and the Insurgent Spirit* (1985).

Nancy C. Unger, *Fighting Bob La Follette: The Righteous Reformer* (2000).

Michael A. Weatherson and Hal W. Bochin, *Hiram Johnson, Political Revivalist* (1995).

James Weinstein, *The Corporate Ideal in the Liberal State, 1900–1918* (1969).

Robert H. Wiebe, *The Search for Order, 1877–1920* (1967).

James Wright, *The Progressive Yankees* (1987).

Clarence E. Wunderlin Jr., *Visions of a New Industrial Order: Social Science and Labor Theory in America's Progressive Era* (1992).

James Harvey Young, *Securing the Federal Food and Drug Act of 1906* (1989).

Radical Alternatives

Mary Jo Buhl, *Women and American Socialism, 1870–1920* (1981).

Ellen Chesler, *Woman of Valor: Margaret Sanger and the Birth Control Movement in America* (1993).

Melvyn Dubofsky, *"Big Bill" Haywood* (1987).

Melvyn Dubofsky, *We Shall Be All: A History of the Industrial Workers of the World* (2nd ed., 1988).

Leslie Fishbein, *Rebels in Bohemia: The Radicals of the Masses, 1911–1917* (1982).

David J. Goldberg, *A Tale of Three Cities: Labor Organization and Protest in Paterson, Passaic, and Lawrence, 1916–1921* (1988).

Anthony Lukas, *Big Trouble: A Murder in a Small Western Town Sets Off a Struggle for the Soul of America* (1998).

Janice Jacqueline Miller, *Challenge from the Left: The Socialist Press and the Progressive Reform Movement, 1900–1917* (1989).

Bruno Ramirez, *When Workers Fight: The Politics of Industrial Relations in the Progressive Era, 1898–1916* (1978).

Salvatore Salerno, *Red November, Black November: Culture and Community in the Industrial Workers of the World* (1989).

Nick Salvatore, *Eugene V. Debs: Citizen and Socialist* (1982).

Ann Huber Tripp, *The IWW and the Paterson Silk Strike of 1913* (1987).

Alice Wexler, *Emma Goldman: An Intimate Life* (1984).

Race Relations and Woman Suffrage

Sara M. Evans, *Born for Liberty: A History of Women in America* (1989).

Kevin K. Gaines, *Uplifting the Race: Black Leadership, Politics, and Culture in the Twentieth Century* (1996).

Glenda Elizabeth Gilmore, *Gender and Jim Crow: Women and the Politics of White Supremacy in North Carolina, 1896–1920* (1996).

Louis R. Harlan, *Booker T. Washington: The Making of a Black Leader, 1856–1901* (1972).

Louis R. Harlan, *Booker T. Washington: The Wizard of Tuskegee, 1901–1915* (1983).

Evelyn Higginbotham, *Righteous Discontent: The Women's Movement in the Black Baptist Church, 1880–1920* (1993).

Charles F. Kellogg, *NAACP: A History of the National Association for the Advancement of Colored People, 1909–1920* (1967).

Jack Temple Kirby, *Darkness at the Dawning: Race and Reform in the Progressive South* (1972).

Elisabeth Lasch-Quinn, *Black Neighbors: Race and the Limits of Reform in the American Settlement House Movement, 1890–1945* (1993).

David Levering Lewis, *W. E. B. Du Bois: Biography of a Race, 1868–1919* (1993).

Alessandra Lorini, *Rituals of Race: American Public Culture and the Search for Racial Democracy* (1999).

Christine Lunardini, *From Equal Suffrage to Equal Rights: Alice Paul and the National Woman's Party, 1910–1928* (1986).

Neil R. McMillen, *Dark Journey: Black Mississippians in the Age of Jim Crow* (1989).

Joel Williamson, *The Crucible of Race* (1984).

GAS MASK

Prior to World War I, poison gas was considered uncivilized. But desperate fighting eroded old moral boundaries. On April 22, 1915, the Germans used poison gas for the first time in battle, and after that soldiers faced death by chemical weapons as well as by artillery, rifles, mortars, machine guns, hand grenades, tanks, airplanes, bayonets, and flamethrowers. The Allies condemned the German innovation as diabolic, but they quickly developed research programs of their own, and for the remainder of the fighting poison gas warfare increased. Gas caused a large number of casualties early on, but the growing use of improved gas masks meant deaths from gas declined sharply. Despite the crude appearance of this gas mask, filter respirators (using charcoal or antidote chemicals) proved highly effective. While some 50,300 American soldiers were killed in action during the war, fewer than 1,500 died from gas. But those who were gassed and survived were often disabled and likely to die young.

Collection of Colonel Stuart S. Corning Jr./Picture Research Consultants & Archives.

22

World War I: The Progressive Crusade at Home and Abroad

1914–1920

WHEN THE UNITED STATES entered World War I against Germany and its allies in 1917, it had neither a grand army nor a commander to lead one. But President Woodrow Wilson quickly tapped Major General John "Black Jack" Pershing, a ramrod-straight West Point graduate, to command the American Expeditionary Force (AEF) on the battlefields of France. Pershing had much to recommend him: He fought Apaches in the West in the 1880s, led a company of African American soldiers up San Juan Hill in 1898 (hence his nickname "Black Jack"), overcame fierce resistance in the Philippine jungles in the first decade of the twentieth century, and headed Wilson's Punitive Expedition into Mexico in 1916 and 1917 in pursuit of the revolutionary bandit Pancho Villa. Pershing's courage and resilience had been severely tested in 1915 when he suffered the irretrievable loss of his wife and three daughters in a fire at their home in San Francisco.

On June 13, 1917, Pershing and his officer corps arrived in France, where huge crowds shouted "Vive l'Amérique!" and greeted the Americans as saviors. Three years of savage warfare had bled France white and pushed the war-weary nation to the breaking point. But Pershing knew that it would be months before America's disorganized war effort succeeded in supplying a steady stream of "doughboys," as American troops would be called. Pershing, who was responsible for organizing, training, and supplying this inexperienced force that eventually numbered more than 2 million, sought to put his own stamp on the AEF. "The standards for the American Army will be those of West Point," he declared. "The upright bearing, attention to detail, uncomplaining obedience to instruction required of the cadet will be required of every officer and soldier of our armies in France." Hard and relentless, Pershing more than once chewed out an exhausted soldier for having mud on his boots and his collar unbuttoned.

Pershing found himself waging two wars, one against the Germans and the other against America's allies, as he constantly rebuffed French and British efforts to siphon off his soldiers into their badly depleted divisions on the front lines. Having seen too much of Europe's trench warfare, where enemies dug in, pounded one another with artillery, and squandered thousands of lives in hopeless assaults, Pershing insisted on keeping American soldiers under his own command. He believed that the Americans could break

Pershing Button

A steely-eyed and determined General John J. Pershing stares out at the viewer while surrounded by the flags of the Allied nations. The words circling the button declare that the Allies fight in the "cause of liberty," echoing President Woodrow Wilson's insistence that American democratic ideals were universal and could be achieved internationally through U.S. participation in the war.
Collection of Janice L. and David J. Frent.

the impasse by relying on the rifle and rapid movement tactics taught at West Point to create "open warfare," an American style of warfare. But as a disgusted British journalist observed, "After eight months . . . you haven't really fired a damned shot!"

By the summer of 1918, Americans had still seen only limited action, and when the Allied armies began preparing a massive attack against the Germans, Ferdinand Foch, head of the French army, rushed to Pershing's headquarters to "insist" once again that American troops merge with his decimated divisions. Pershing responded: "Marshal Foch, you may insist all you please, but . . . our army will fight . . . only as an independent American Army." Foch stormed out, and Pershing readied his army to strike at the German forces dug in at Saint-Mihiel and to begin what he was certain would be a victory march to Berlin. Assembling his officers, Pershing praised them for what they were about to do—break the stalement of trench warfare. But American troops would be attacking fortifications the German army had spent years constructing. Indeed, American troops met a storm of machine-gun and artillery fire, and it took forty days and 100,000 casualties for the Americans to reach the German border, something Pershing had thought his soldiers could do in a few days. Nevertheless, fresh American troops helped destroy the German will to continue the war. In November 1918, Berlin asked for an immediate armistice, and the "Great War," as participants called the conflict, ended.

Pershing's stubborn effort to protect the autonomy of his army was only part of America's tortuous struggle to identify its interests in World War I and to maintain its national independence. When Wilson entered the White House, he believed that war was an affliction that modern diplomacy would eventually eradicate. He proclaimed America's absolute neutrality when war erupted in Europe in 1914. By standing apart, Wilson explained, America could offer "impartial mediation" and broker a healing peace. But trade and principle soon entangled the United States in Europe's troubles. When the nation was finally drawn into the war in 1917, Wilson sought to rescue America's grand purpose. Clinging to his battered ideals, he hoped that America's participation would uplift both the United States and the entire world.

At home, the war helped reformers finally achieve their goals of national prohibition and woman **suffrage**, but war also promoted a vicious attack on Americans' civil liberties. Hyperpatriotism meant intolerance, repression, and vigilante violence. Overseas, American troops under Pershing helped win the war in 1918, and in 1919 Wilson sailed for Europe to secure a just peace. Unable to dictate a settlement to the victors, Wilson accepted disappointing compromises. Upon his return to the United States he met a crushing defeat that marked the end of Wilsonian internationalism. Crackdowns on dissenters, immigrants, racial and ethnic minorities, and unions signaled the end of the **Progressive** Era at home.

Woodrow Wilson and the World

Shortly after winning election to the presidency in 1912, Woodrow Wilson confided to a friend: "It would be an irony of fate if my administration had to deal with foreign affairs." Indeed, Wilson had based his life and career on domestic concerns, seldom venturing far from home and traveling abroad only on brief vacations. As president of Princeton University and then governor of New Jersey, he had remained rooted in local affairs. In his campaign for the presidency, Wilson spoke passionately about domestic reform but hardly mentioned foreign affairs.

But Wilson could not avoid the world and the rising tide of militarism, **nationalism**, and violence that beat against American shores. America's own economic needs also compelled the nation outward. Moreover, Wilson was drawn abroad by his own progressive political principles. He believed that the United States had a moral duty to set an example in international affairs by championing national self-determination, peaceful free trade, and political **democracy**. "We have no selfish ends to serve," he proclaimed. "We desire no conquest, no dominion. . . . We are but one of the champions of the rights of mankind." Yet, as president Wilson revealed, he was as ready as any American president to apply military solutions to problems of foreign policy.

Taming the Americas

When he took office, Wilson sought to distinguish his foreign policy from that of his Republican predecessors. To Wilson, Theodore Roosevelt's "big stick" and William Howard Taft's "dollar diplomacy" appeared a crude flexing of military and economic muscle. To counter such arrogance, Wilson appointed William Jennings Bryan as secretary of state. A pacifist on religious grounds, Bryan immediately turned his attention to making agreements with thirty nations for the peaceful settlement of disputes.

But Wilson and Bryan, like Roosevelt and Taft, also believed that the **Monroe Doctrine** gave the United States special rights and responsibilities in the Western Hemisphere. Issued in 1823 to warn Europeans not to attempt to **colonize** the New World again, the doctrine had become a cloak for American domination. Wilson thus authorized the 1912 occupation of Nicaragua by U.S. marines to thwart a radical revolution that threatened American property. In 1915, he sent marines into Haiti to quell lawlessness and to protect American interests, and in 1916 he followed a similar course in the Dominican Republic. Almost everywhere in the Western Hemisphere, U.S. military intervention paved the way for the firm financial control of American banks and corporations. All the while, Wilson believed that American actions were promoting order and democracy. "I am going to teach the South American Republics to elect good men!" he declared. He did not mention protecting the Panama Canal and American investments (Map 22.1).

Wilson's most serious and controversial involvement in Latin America came in Mexico. Just weeks before Wilson was elected, General Victoriano Huerta seized power by violent means. Most European nations promptly recognized Huerta as the new Mexican president, but Wilson balked, declaring that he would not support a "government of butchers." In April 1914,

"Pancho" Villa and General Pershing
In 1914, Mexican revolutionary Francisco "Pancho" Villa (center) and American general John J. Pershing (right) posed genially as allies in the struggle to overthrow the dictatorial ruler of Mexico, Victoriano Huerta. Soon afterward, Villa and Pershing became adversaries. After Villa's raid across the New Mexico border in 1915 to punish Americans for aiding his revolutionary rivals, Pershing pursued Villa into Mexico.
© Bettmann/Corbis.

when Huerta refused to apologize for briefly detaining American sailors in Tampico, Wilson sent 800 marines to seize the port of Veracruz to prevent the unloading of a large shipment of arms for Huerta, who was by then involved in a civil war of his own. After brief resistance, Huerta fled to Spain, and the United States welcomed a more compliant government.

Wilson was not able to subdue Mexico that easily, however. A rebellion erupted among desperately poor farmers who believed that the new government, aided by American business interests, had betrayed the revolution's promise to help the common people. In January 1916, the rebel army, commanded by Francisco "Pancho" Villa, seized a train carrying gold to Texas from an American-owned mine deep within Mexico and killed the seventeen American engineers aboard. Another band of Villa's men crossed the border on March 9 for a predawn raid on

U.S. Intervention in Mexico, 1916–1917

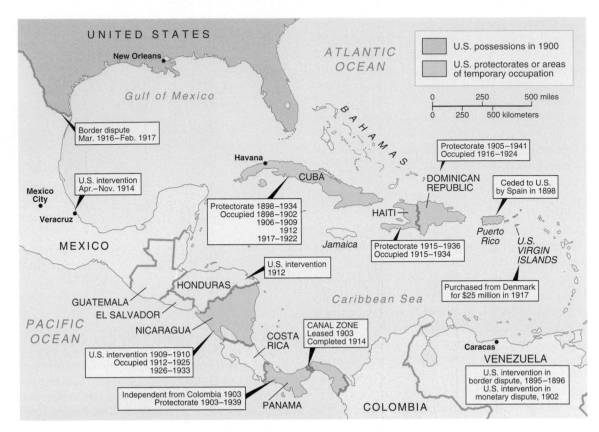

MAP 22.1   U.S. Involvement in Latin America and the Caribbean, 1895–1941
Victory against Spain in 1898 made Puerto Rico an American possession and Cuba a protectorate. The United States also gained control over the Panama Canal. The nation proved quick to protect expanding economic interests with military force by propping up friendly, though not necessarily democratic, governments.

Columbus, New Mexico, that cost several more lives and left the town in flames. (See "American Places," page 793.) Wilson promptly dispatched 12,000 troops, led by General John J. Pershing, who years earlier had chased the Apache chief Geronimo through the same Mexican desert. Unlike Geronimo, the wily Villa avoided capture, and in January 1917 Wilson recalled Pershing so that he might prepare the army for the possibility of fighting in the Great War.

The European Crisis

Before 1914, Europe had enjoyed decades of peace, but just beneath the surface lay the potentially destructive forces of nationalism and **imperialism**. The consolidation of the German and Italian states into unified nations and the similar ambition of Russia to create a "Pan-Slavic" union initiated new rivalries throughout Europe. As the conviction spread that colonial possessions were a mark of national greatness, competition expanded onto the world stage. Most ominously, Germany's efforts under Kaiser Wilhelm II to challenge Great Britain's world supremacy by creating an empire abroad, industrial muscle at home, and a mighty navy threatened the balance of power and thus the peace.

European nations sought to avoid an explosion with a complex web of military and diplomatic alliances. By 1914, Germany, Austria-Hungary, and Italy (the Triple Alliance) stood opposed to Great Britain, France, and Russia (the Triple Entente, also known as "the Allies"). But in their effort to prevent war through a balance of power, Europeans had actually magnified the possibility of large-scale conflict by creating trip wires along the boundaries of two heavily armed power blocs (Map 22.2). Treaties, some of them secret, obligated members of the alliances to come to the aid of another member if attacked.

The fatal sequence started in southeastern Europe, in the Balkans. On June 28, 1914, in the

AMERICAN PLACES

Pancho Villa State Park, Columbus, New Mexico

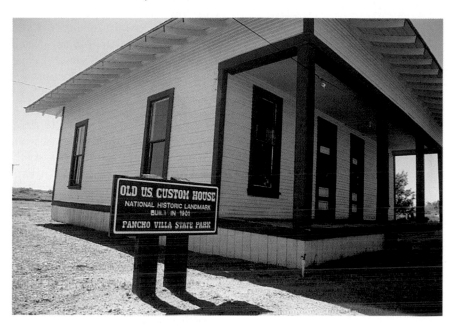

Old U.S. Custom House, Pancho Villa State Park
Courtesy of Pancho Villa State Park, New Mexico Energy, Minerals, and Natural Resources Department.

Before dawn on March 9, 1916, General Francisco "Pancho" Villa and some 400 to 500 troops ("Villistas") raced across the Mexican border on horseback and attacked the village and U.S. military camp at Columbus, New Mexico. At the time, Villa was locked in a fierce civil war in Mexico. Between 1913 and 1917, Woodrow Wilson meddled almost continuously in Mexican affairs, first supporting the wild revolutionary Villa, and then by 1916 Villa's chief rival,

the dignified Venustiano Carranza. Villa figured that his raid would draw U.S. troops across the border and that an American invasion of Mexico would weaken Carranza's claim to authority. The Villistas stayed in Columbus for less than two hours, but they burned much of the village and killed 18 Americans before disappearing into the vastness of the Mexican interior. Wilson took Villa's bait, and General "Black Jack" Pershing, who would later command American forces

in France during World War I, launched his fruitless eleven-month chase of Villa into Mexico.

Pancho Villa State Park in Columbus, New Mexico, sits in the Chihuahuan Desert just east of the Continental Divide, only three miles from the border with Mexico. Several buildings dating from the time of Villa's raid still stand in Columbus. The adobe Hoover Hotel was the site of some of the fiercest fighting. American troops set up a machine gun on the street in front of the hotel and both Villistas and U.S. citizens died fighting there. The Columbus railroad depot has been restored and today houses a private museum. Within the park, the old 1901 U.S. Customs House serves as the visitor center and contains exhibits describing the colorful histories of Pancho Villa, the Columbus raid of 1916, and Pershing's Punitive Expedition. Although Camp Furlong lies in ruins, visitors to Columbus can get a feel for the camp through the park's display of vehicles similar to those employed by Pershing and his men: a 1916 four-wheel-drive truck, a 1915 Jeffery Quad armored personnel carrier, and two Dodge touring cars — a 1916 model that was Pershing's choice for a personal staff car and a 1915 model that was sprayed by gunfire as one Columbus family fled the Villistas. The park also contains nature trails and a botanical garden with more than 30 kinds of cacti.

FOR WEB LINKS RELATED TO THIS SITE AND OTHER AMERICAN PLACES, see "PlaceLinks" at bedfordstmartins.com/roark.

Bosnian city of Sarajevo, a Bosnian Serb terrorist assassinated Archduke Franz Ferdinand, heir to the Austro-Hungarian throne. The next day, Austria declared war on Serbia, holding it accountable for the killing. The elaborate **alliance system** meant that the war could not

remain local. Russia announced that it would back the Serbs. Compelled to support Austria-Hungary, Germany on August 6 declared war on Russia and on France. In response, Great Britain, upholding its pact with France, declared war on Germany. Within weeks, Europe was engulfed in

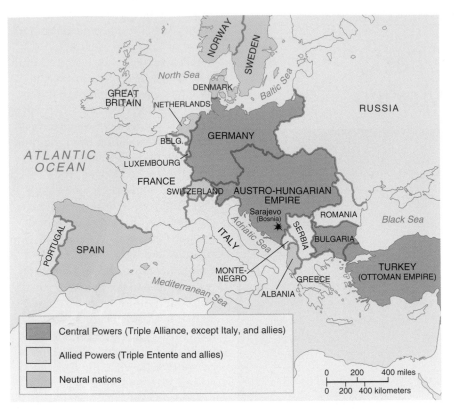

MAP 22.2   European Alliances after the Outbreak of World War I
With Germany and the Austro-Hungarian Empire wedged between their Entente rivals, and all parties fully armed, Europe was poised for war when the Archduke Franz Ferdinand of Austria was assassinated in Sarajevo in July 1914.

> When news of the outbreak of war reached the United States, Woodrow Wilson announced that it was a European matter that had nothing to do with America.

war. The conflict became a world war when Japan, seeing an opportunity to rid itself of imperialist competition in China, joined the cause against Germany.

Recognizing that the war would devastate the civilization he knew, England's foreign secretary, Edward Grey, announced: "The lamps are going out all over Europe. We shall not see them lit again in our lifetime." Indeed, the evenly matched alliances would fight a long, exhausting, and bloody war lasting more than four years, at a cost of 8.5 million soldiers' lives—an entire generation of young men. A war that started with a solitary murder proved impossible to stop.

The Ordeal of American Neutrality

When news of the outbreak of war reached the United States, Woodrow Wilson announced that it was a European matter that had

nothing to do with America. "Again and ever," he declared, "I thank heaven for the Atlantic Ocean." Because the war engaged no vital American interest and involved no significant principle, Wilson said, the United States would remain neutral and continue normal relations with the warring nations. The United States had traditionally insisted on the broadest possible definition of neutral rights. In the American view, "free ships made free goods"—that is, neutral nations were entitled to trade freely with all nations at war, to send their ships safely through the open seas, and to demand the safe passage of their citizens on the merchant and passenger ships of all belligerents. More was involved than just this belief. In the year before Europe went to war, the American economy had started to slide into a recession that wartime disruption of European trade could drastically worsen.

Although Wilson proclaimed neutrality, his sympathies, like those of many Americans, lay with Great Britain and France. Americans shared with the English a language, a culture, and a commitment to **liberty**. Germany, in contrast, was a monarchy with strong militaristic traditions. The German ruler, Kaiser Wilhelm II, proved a cartoonist's dream. The British portrayed him as personally responsible for the war's atrocities, and before long American newspapers were labeling him "the Mad Dog of Europe" and "the Beast of Berlin." Still, Wilson insisted on neutrality, in part because he feared the conflict's effects on the United States as a nation of immigrants, millions of whom had only recently come from countries now at war. As he told the German ambassador, "We definitely have to be neutral, since otherwise our mixed populations would wage war on each other."

Great Britain was the first to test America's neutrality. Britain's powerful fleet controlled the seas and quickly set up a blockade of Germany. The United States vigorously protested, but Britain refused to give up its naval advantage. Although the blockade bruised American feelings, it had little economic impact on the United States. Between 1914 and the spring of 1917, while trade with Germany dwindled to the vanishing point, war-related exports to Britain— food, clothing, steel, and munitions—escalated by some 400 percent, enough to pull the American economy out of its prewar slump. Although the British blockade of German ports clearly violated American neutrality, the Wilson administration gradually and reluctantly acquiesced, thus beginning the fateful process of alienation from Germany.

Germany retaliated with a submarine blockade of British ports. This terrifying new form of combat by *Unterseebooten*, or U-boats, threatened traditional rules of war. Unlike surface warships that could harmlessly stop and search freighters and prevent them from entering a war zone, submarines relied on surprising and sinking their quarry. And once they sank a ship, the tiny, cramped U-boats could not possibly pick up any survivors. Britain portrayed the

Sinking of the *Lusitania*, 1915

submarine as an outlaw weapon that violated notions of how a "civilized" nation should fight. Nevertheless, in February 1915, Germany announced that it intended to sink on sight enemy ships en route to the British Isles. On May 7, 1915, a German U-boat torpedoed the British passenger liner *Lusitania*, killing 1,198 passengers, 128 of them U.S. citizens.

The attack seemed to confirm what anti-German propaganda claimed: that the Germans

were by nature barbaric and uncivilized. American newspapers featured drawings of drowning women and children, and some editorials demanded war. Most Americans, however, did not want to break relations with Germany. Some pointed out that the German embassy had warned prospective passengers that the *Lusitania* carried millions of rounds of ammunition and so was a legitimate target. Secretary of State Bryan resisted the hysteria and declared that a ship carrying war materiel "should not rely on passengers to protect her from attack—it would be like putting women and children in front of an army." He argued that Wilson should instead warn American citizens that they traveled on ships of belligerent countries at their own risk.

Wilson sought a middle course that would retain his commitment to peace and neutrality without condoning German attacks on passenger ships. On May 10, he distanced himself from the proponents of American intervention by declaring that "there is such a thing as a man being too proud to fight," which caused former president Theodore Roosevelt, who urged war, to label him a "flub dub and mollycoddle." But Wilson also rejected Bryan's position. Any further destruction of ships, Wilson warned, would be regarded as "deliberately unfriendly" and might lead the United States to break diplomatic relations with Germany. Wilson essentially demanded that Germany abandon unrestricted submarine warfare. Rather than support the president, Bryan resigned, predicting that he had placed the United States on a colli-

Construction of a German U-boat
Even in drydock, this German submarine looks menacing. Deadly and stealthy, U-boats became known as "Assassins of the Seas." German submarines reached their peak of power in the summer of 1917, when nearly 150 patrolled the Atlantic, seeking both Allied warships and merchant vessels. But predator turned prey when the Allies developed SONAR (a kind of underwater radar), the depth-charge (a container filled with explosives that detonates deep under the sea), mines (used in the relatively confined English Channel), and the convoy system. One consequence of Allied advances against the menace of the U-boat was that the entire American Expeditionary Force arrived in Europe with the loss of only one ship.
Bibliothek fur Zeitgeschichte Stuttgart.

sion course with Germany. Wilson's replacement for Bryan was far from neutral. Two weeks after taking over the State Department, Robert Lansing announced that "the German Government is utterly hostile to all nations with democratic institutions." Because of Germany's "ambition for world dominance," it "must not be permitted to win this war or even to break even."

When Germany, anxious not to provoke the United States any further, apologized for the civilian deaths on the *Lusitania* and offered an indemnity, tensions momentarily subsided. After the sinking of the English steamer *Sussex* in 1916, at the cost of two more American lives, the German government quickly acted to head off war by promising no more submarine attacks without warning and without provisions for the safety of civilians. Observers celebrated the success of Wilson's middle-of-the-road strategy that steered a course between Roosevelt's aggressiveness and Bryan's pacifism.

Wilson's diplomacy proved helpful in his bid for reelection in 1916. Still, he was no shoo-in, for controversies over neutrality, intervention in Mexico, and the government's role in regulating the economy gave Wilson's able Republican opponent, Charles Evans Hughes—an associate justice of the Supreme Court and former governor of New York—a good chance. The Democratic Party ran Wilson under the slogan "He kept us out of war," but Wilson shied away from the claim, recognizing that any "little German lieutenant can push us into the war at any time by some calculated outrage." Ultimately, Wilson's case for neutrality appealed to the majority in favor of peace. Wilson won, but only by the razor-thin margins of 600,000 popular and 23 electoral votes.

The United States Enters the War

Step by step, the United States backed away from "absolute neutrality" and grew more forthrightly pro-Allied (that is, pro–Triple Entente). The consequence of protesting the German blockade of Great Britain but accepting the British blockade of Germany was that by 1916 the United States was supplying the Allies with 40 percent of their war material. When France and Britain ran short of money to pay for American goods and asked for loans, some Americans objected.

> Step by step, the United States backed away from "absolute neutrality" and grew more forthrightly pro-Allied.

Wilson himself argued that "Loans by American bankers to any foreign government which is at war are inconsistent with the true spirit of neutrality." But rather than jeopardize America's wartime prosperity, Wilson relaxed his objections, and billions of dollars in loans kept American goods flowing to Britain and France.

In January 1917, the German military high command persuaded the kaiser that the country could no longer afford to allow neutral shipping to reach Great Britain while the enemy blockade gradually starved Germany. The German government chose to resume unrestricted submarine warfare and sink without warning any ship, enemy and neutral, found in the waters off Great Britain. The German military understood that the decision would probably bring the United States into the war but gambled that the submarines would strangle the British economy and allow the kaiser's armies to win a military victory in France before American troops began arriving in Europe.

Theodore Roosevelt and most of Wilson's advisers demanded an immediate declaration of war, but Wilson continued to hope for a negotiated peace and only broke off diplomatic relations with Germany. Then on February 25, 1917, British authorities informed Wilson of a secret telegram sent by the German foreign secretary, Arthur Zimmermann, to the German minister in Mexico. It promised that in the event of war between Germany and the United States, Germany would see that Mexico regained its "lost provinces" of Texas, New Mexico, and Arizona if Mexico would declare war against the United States. Wilson angrily responded to the Zimmermann telegram by asking Congress to approve a policy of "armed neutrality" that would allow merchant ships to fight back against any attackers. Wilson stated privately that this wicked attempt to penetrate the Western Hemisphere finally convinced him that the war was, indeed, a defense of democracy against autocratic German aggression.

In March, German submarines sank five American vessels in the sea lanes to Britain, killing 66 Americans. After agonizing over the probable consequences, on April 2 the president asked Congress to issue a declaration of war. No longer too proud to fight, Wilson accused Germany of "warfare against all mankind." Still, he called for a "war without hate" and insisted that the destruction of Germany was not the goal of the United States. Rather, America fought to "vindicate the principles of peace and justice";

he promised that in a world made "safe for democracy," a reconstructed Germany would find its proper place. On April 6, 1917, by majorities of 373 to 50 in the House and 82 to 6 in the Senate, Congress voted to declare war.

Wilson did not overlook the tragic difference between those lofty aims and the brutal means chosen to achieve them. He spoke despairingly to a friend just prior to his appearance before Congress: "Once lead this people into war, and they'll forget there ever was such a thing as tolerance. To fight you must be brutal and ruthless, and the spirit of ruthless brutality will infect Congress, the courts, the policeman on the beat, the man in the street."

Over There

The American Expeditionary Force that eventually carried 2 million troops to Europe, by far the largest military venture the United States had ever undertaken on foreign soil, was trained to be morally upright as well as fiercely effective. Imbued with a sense of democratic mission, some doughboys found the adventure exhilarating and maintained their idealism to the end. The majority, however, saw little that was gallant in rats, lice, and poison gas, and—despite the progressives' hopes—little to elevate the human soul in a landscape of utter destruction and death.

"Men Wanted for the United States Army"
The exuberant soldiers swarming over this overloaded truck are so thrilled with their task of recruiting new men that they managed to display the flag backward. Their urgency reflects the fact that when America declared war in April 1917 its army numbered barely 120,000, roughly the size of the army of Chile. Unwilling to trust voluntary enlistments, Wilson's war message to Congress included an endorsement of "the principle of universal liability to service," in other words, a draft. Congress quickly obliged with a conscription bill, and within months, nearly 10 million American men had registered for the draft. When the war ended, 2 million men had volunteered for military service and 3 million had been drafted.
Brown Brothers.

The Call to Arms

When America entered the war, Britain and France were nearly exhausted after almost three years of conflict. Hundreds of thousands of soldiers had perished; morale and food supplies were dangerously low. One of the Allied powers, Russia, was in turmoil. In March 1917, a revolution had forced Czar Nicholas II to abdicate, and eight months later in a separate peace with Germany the Bolshevik revolutionary government removed Russia from the war. On May 18, 1917, to meet the demand for fighting men, Wilson signed a sweeping Selective Service Act, authorizing a **draft** of all young men into the armed forces. In contrast to the Civil War, this draft prohibited enlistment bounties and personal substitutes, while it sanctioned deferments on the basis of family responsibility. **Conscription** soon transformed a tiny volunteer armed force of 80,000 men, spread thinly around the United States and in outposts from the Caribbean to China, into a vast army and navy. Although almost 350,000 inductees either failed to report or claimed conscientious objector status, the draft boards eventually inducted 2.8 million men into the armed services, in addition to the 2 million who volunteered.

Progressives in the government were determined that the training camps that transformed raw recruits into fighting men would have the highest moral and civic purposes. Medical examinations, along with recently developed sociological and psychological testing, took the measure of American youth. The shocking news that almost 30 percent of those drafted were rejected on physical grounds acted as a stimulus to the public health and physical education movements. Secretary of War Newton D. Baker, whose outlook had been shaped by reform crusades as progressive mayor of Cleveland, created a Commission on Training Camp Activities staffed by YMCA workers and veterans of the settlement house and playground movements. The Military Draft Act of 1917 prohibited prostitution and alcohol near training camps. An army pamphlet asked soldiers to stop thinking about sex, explaining that a "man who is thinking below the belt is not efficient." Instead, military training included games, singing, and college extension courses. Baker de-

> The shocking news that almost 30 percent of those drafted were rejected on physical grounds acted as a stimulus to the public health and physical education movements.

scribed military camps as "national universities—training schools to which the flower of American youth is being sent" to provide them with an "invisible armor" of education, comradeship, and moral fitness.

Wilson's selection of Pershing to command the AEF recognized the need for hard professionalism in the leadership, not the sort of romantic patriotism that had given amateurs like Theodore Roosevelt the chance to command combat troops in the Spanish-American War. Pershing, described by one observer as "lean, clean, keen," gave progressives confidence that he would carry out his duties with the level-headed efficiency required of modern war on a vast scale. When Pershing and the wide-eyed troops of the AEF marched through Paris on the Fourth of July 1917, just a week after the first troopship landed, grateful French citizens showered them with flowers. At the statue of the hero who symbolized France's aid to the American Revolution, an officer stepped out and proclaimed in an inspired phrase that summed up the spirit of the occasion, "Lafayette, we are here!"

The War in France

At the front, the AEF discovered a desperate situation. The three-year-old war had degenerated into a stalemate of armies dug defensively into hundreds of miles of trenches across France. Huddling in the mud among the corpses and rats, soldiers were separated from the enemy by only a few hundred yards of "no-man's-land." When ordered "over the top," troops raced desperately toward the enemy's trenches, only to be entangled in barbed wire, enveloped in poison gas, and mowed down by machine guns. Commanders were slow to recognize the futility of their tactics even after the deadly stand-off at the Battle of the Somme in 1916, the bloodiest battle of the war. After a three-day assault in which French and British forces lost 600,000 dead and wounded and the Germans 500,000, the Allies were able to advance their trenches only a few meaningless miles across devastated land.

Still, American troops hurried to France only to wait while Pershing assessed the situation, and they saw almost no combat in 1917. Instead, they continued to train and used much of their free time to explore places that most of them otherwise could never have hoped to see. True to the crusader image, American officials allowed only uplifting tourism. Paris temptations were off-limits, and French premier Georges Clemenceau's offer to supply American troops with licensed prostitutes was declined with the half-serious remark that if Wilson found out he would stop the war.

The sightseeing ended abruptly in March 1918. The Brest-Litovsk treaty signed that month by Germany and the Bolsheviks officially took Russia out of the war, and the Germans launched a massive offensive aimed at French ports on the Atlantic. After six thousand cannons let loose the heaviest barrage in history, a million German soldiers smashed a hole in the French and British lines at a cost of 250,000 casualties on each side. Paris became gripped by the greatest terror of the war when shells fired eighty miles away by "Big Bertha" cannons began falling on the city. Pershing, who believed the right moment for U.S. action had finally come, visited Foch to ask for the "great honor" of becoming "engaged in the greatest battle in history." Foch agreed to Pershing's terms of a separate American command and in May assigned a combined army and marine force to the central sector.

Once committed, the Americans remained true to their way of war. In May and June, at Cantigny and then at Château-Thierry, the eager but green Americans checked the German advance with a series of dashing assaults (Map 22.3). Then they headed toward the forest stronghold of Belleau Wood. The American force, with the Fifth and Sixth Marine Regiments in the lead, made its way against streams of refugees and retreating Allied soldiers who cried that the Germans had won: "La guerre est finie!" (The war is over!) A French officer commanded the marines to turn and retreat with them, but the American commander replied sharply, "Retreat, hell. We just got here." After charging through a wheat field against withering machine-gun fire, the marines plunged into a hand-to-hand forest battle of stalking and ambush. Victory came hard, but a German report praised the enemy's spirit, noting that "the Americans' nerves are not yet worn out." Indeed, it was German morale that was on the verge of cracking.

MAP 22.3   The American Expeditionary Force, 1918
In the last year of the war, the AEF joined the French army on the western front to counter-attack the final German offensive and pursue the retreating enemy until surrender.

READING THE MAP: Across which rivers did the Germans advance in 1918? Where did the armistice line of November 11, 1918, lie in relation to the stabilized front of 1915–1917? Through which countries did the armistice line run?
CONNECTIONS: What events paved the way for the American Expeditionary Force to join the combat in 1918? What characteristic(s) differentiated American troops from other Allied forces and helped them achieve victory?

FOR MORE HELP ANALYZING THIS MAP, see the map activity for this chapter in the Online Study Guide at bedfordstmartins.com/roark.

In the summer of 1918, the Allies launched a massive counteroffensive that would end the war. A quarter of a million American troops joined in the rout of German forces along the Marne River. In September, more than a million Americans took part in the assault that threw the Germans back from positions along the Meuse River. By November, German survivors were

Life in the Trenches

These U.S. soldiers in a rat-infested trench either tensely look out for danger or slump in exhausted sleep. They offer a glimpse of the reality of the Great War, minus the noise, stench, and danger. This trench is dry for the moment, but with the rains came mud so deep that wounded men drowned in it. By the time American doughboys arrived in Europe, troops had faced one another for more than three years, burrowed into a double line of trenches, protected by barbed wire, machine gun nests, and mortars, backed by heavy artillery. Trenches with millions of inhabitants stretched from French ports on the English channel all the way to Switzerland. Nothing could make living in such holes anything better than miserable, but a decent shave with a Gillette safety razor, a pair of dry boots, and a set of checkers offered doughboys temporary relief. Inevitably, however, whistles would blow that ended the boredom, fatigue, and discomfort of trench life and sent soldiers "over the top," streaming toward enemy lines.

For more help analyzing this image, see the visual activity for this chapter in the Online Study Guide at bedfordstmartins.com/roark.

Photo: Imperial War Museum; shaving kit and boots: Collection of Colonel Stuart S. Corning Jr./Picture Research Consultants, Inc.

---

trudging northward. Soon, a revolt against the German government sent Kaiser Wilhelm II fleeing to Holland. On November 11, 1918, a delegation from the newly established German republic met with the French high command in a railroad car in Compiègne to sign an armistice that brought the fighting to an end.

The adventure of the AEF was brief, bloody, and victorious. When Germany had resumed unrestricted U-boat warfare in 1917, it was gambling that it could defeat Britain and France before the Americans could raise and train an army and ship it to France. The German military had miscalculated. Of the 2 million American troops in Europe, 1.3 million saw at least some action. By the end, 112,000 soldiers of the AEF had perished from wounds and disease. Another 230,000 Americans suffered casualties but survived, many of them with permanent physical and psychological disabilities. Poison gas accounted for almost 30 percent of all AEF casualties. Only the Civil War, which lasted much longer, had been more costly in American lives. European nations, however, suffered much greater losses: 2.2 million Germans, 1.9 million Russians, 1.4 million French, and 900,000 Britons. Where they had fought, the landscape was as blasted and barren as the moon.

The Crusade for Democracy at Home

Despite Wilson's fears that entering the war would lead to brutal intolerance at home, many progressives hoped that war would improve the quality of American life as well as free Europe from its bondage to tyranny and militarism. Progressive enthusiasm powered the mobilization of industrial and agricultural production behind the war effort. Moreover, labor shortages caused by workers entering the military provided new opportunities in the booming wartime economy. With labor at a premium, unionized workers gained higher pay and shorter hours. They were joined by women taking jobs formerly reserved for men. To instill loyalty in a public whose ancestry was rooted in all the belligerent nations, Wilson launched a campaign to foster patriotism. The campaign included the creation of a government agency to promote official propaganda, indoctrination in the schools, and parades, rallies, films, and other forms of patriotic expression. But with stimulation of patriotism also came suppression of dissent. When the government launched a harsh assault on civil liberties, mobs gained license to attack those whom they considered disloyal. Increasingly, the progressive ideals of rational progress and free expression took a beating as the nation undertook its crusade for democracy.

The Progressive Stake in the War

The idea of the war as an agent of social improvement fanned the old zeal of the progressive movement. The Wilson administration realized that Washington would have to assert greater control to mobilize the nation's human and physical resources. The nation's capital soon bristled with hastily created agencies charged with managing the war effort. Bernard Baruch headed the central planning authority, the War Industries Board (WIB), created to stimulate and direct industrial production. At once a wealthy southern gentleman, a Jewish Wall Street stockbroker, and a reform Democrat, Baruch could speak to many constituencies. Shrewdly, he brought industrial management and labor together into a team that produced everything from boots to bullets and made American troops the best equipped soldiers in the world.

Herbert Hoover, a self-made millionaire engineer, headed the Food Administration.

Sober and tireless, he led remarkably successful "Hooverizing" campaigns for "meatless" Mondays and "wheatless" Wednesdays and other means of conserving resources. Guaranteed high prices, the American heartland not only supplied the needs of U.S. citizens and armed forces but also became the breadbasket of America's allies. Even the First Family, including Wilson's second wife, Edith Galt, did its part with a White House "victory garden" and sheep put to graze on the White House lawn in the absence of the gardeners, who had moved on to new work in the war effort.

Other wartime agencies abounded: The Railroad Administration directed railroad traffic, the Fuel Administration coordinated the coal industry and other fuel suppliers, the Shipping Board organized the merchant marine, and the National War Labor Policies Board resolved labor disputes. Their successes gave progressives reason to believe that the Wilson administration would mediate between business and government and encourage harmony in the public interest. Buoyed by these developments, influential voices like those of philosopher-educator John Dewey and journalist-critic Walter Lippmann cheered the war as a means of promoting progressive reform. Some progressives, however, stubbornly refused to accept the argument that war and reform marched together. Wisconsin senator Robert La Follette kept up a steady drumbeat of opposition to the war and claimed that Wilson's promises of peace and democracy were a case of "the blind leading the blind," at home and abroad.

Industrial leaders were encouraged that, in achieving feats of production and efficiency, wartime agencies helped corporate profits triple. Some working people also had cause to celebrate. Mobilization meant high prices for farmers and plentiful jobs in the new war industries (Figure 22.1). Aware that increased industrial production required peaceful labor relations and the avoidance of strikes, the National War Labor Policies Board and other agencies enacted the eight-hour day, a living minimum wage, and **collective bargaining** rights in some industries that had long resisted them. Wages rose sharply during the war (as did prices), and the American Federation of Labor (AFL) saw its membership soar from 2.7 million to more than 5 million.

> The idea of the war as an agent of social improvement fanned the old zeal of the progressive movement.

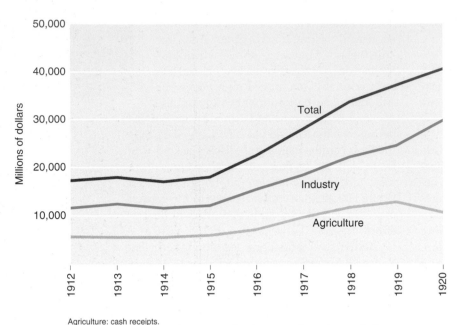

Agriculture: cash receipts.
Industry: includes mining, electric power, manufacturing, construction, and communications.

FIGURE 22.1   Industrial Wages, 1912–1920
With help from unions and progressive reformers, wage workers gradually improved their economic condition. The entry of millions of young men into the armed forces caused labor shortages and led to a rapid surge in wages.

After long insisting that health was a private matter, Congress bowed to the patriotic cause of providing death and disability insurance for the armed forces.

The war also provided a huge boost to the stalled moral crusade to ban alcohol. Before the war, prohibitionists had campaigned to ban the manufacture and sale of alcoholic beverages, and by 1917, nineteen states had gone dry. Liquor's opponents could now cite the war as a reason for national prohibition, for banning alcohol would make the cause of democracy powerful and pure. At the same time, shutting down the distilleries would save millions of bushels of grain that could feed the United States and its allies. "Shall the many have food or the few drink?" the drys asked. Prohibitionists added a patriotic twist by arguing that closing breweries with German names like Schlitz, Pabst, and Anheuser-Busch would deal a blow to the kaiser and the German cause. Swept along by these arguments, Congress in December 1917 passed the Eighteenth Amendment, which banned the manufacture, transportation, and sale of alcohol; after swift ratification by the states, the amendment went into effect on January 1, 1920.

Women, War, and the Battle for Suffrage

Women had made real strides during the Progressive Era, but war presented new opportunities. When Theodore Roosevelt told young men that the war was the "Great Adventure" of the age, young women listened too. More than 25,000 women served in France. About half were nurses; the others drove ambulances, ran canteens for the Red Cross and YMCA, worked with French civilians in devastated areas, and acted as war correspondents. Like men, women struggled against disillusionment and depression. One

U.S. Army Medical Corps Contract Surgeon's Uniform
Before the war ended, some 25,000 American women made it to France, all as volunteers. Ex-president Theodore Roosevelt proclaimed war the "Great Adventure," and some women were eager to share in it. About half became nurses, where as one said, they dealt with "a sea of stretchers, a human carpet." Women also drove ambulances, acted as social workers, and ran canteens for the Red Cross and the YMCA. One YMCA worker, Mary Baldwin, hoped that a few hours in her canteen would "make life, and even death, easier 'out there.'" A handful of female physicians worked as contract surgeons for the U.S. army. Dr. Loy McAfee wore this uniform in France.
National Museum of American History, Smithsonian Institution, Washington, D.C.

woman explained: "Over in America, we thought we knew something about the war . . . but when you get here the difference is [like the one between] studying the laws of electricity and being struck by lightning."

At home, long-standing barriers against hiring women fell when millions of working men became soldiers and few new immigrant workers made it across the Atlantic. The new Women's Bureau of the Department of Labor along with the Women's Trade Union League (WTUL) helped open jobs to women, often against the opposition of the major trade organization, the AFL. For the first time, tens of thousands of women found work with the railroads and in defense plants as welders, metalworkers, and heavy machine operators, jobs traditionally reserved for men. Between 1910 and 1920, the number of women clerks doubled. Before the war ended, more than a million women found work in war industries. "This is the women's age," exaggerated Margaret Dreier Robins, president of the WTUL. "At last . . . women are coming into the labor and festival of life on equal terms with men."

The most dramatic advance for women came in the political arena. Since the Seneca Falls convention of 1848, where women voiced their first formal demand for the ballot, the struggle for woman suffrage had inched forward. Adopting a state-by-state approach, suffragists had achieved some success in the West; but by 1910, only four small western states had adopted woman suffrage (Map 22.4). Elsewhere, voting rights for women met strong hostility and defeat. After 1910, suffrage leaders added a federal campaign to amend the Constitution to the traditional state-by-state strategy for suffrage. Their powerful and well-organized federal campaign targeted Congress and the president.

The radical wing of the suffragists, led by the indomitable Alice Paul, picketed the White House, where they unfurled banners that proclaimed: "America Is Not a Democracy. Twenty Million Women Are Denied the Right to Vote." They chained themselves to fences and went to jail, where many engaged in hunger strikes. "They seem bent on making their cause as obnoxious as possible," Woodrow Wilson declared. His wife, Edith, detested the idea of "masculinized" voting women. But membership in the mainstream organization, the National American Woman Suffrage Association, led by Carrie

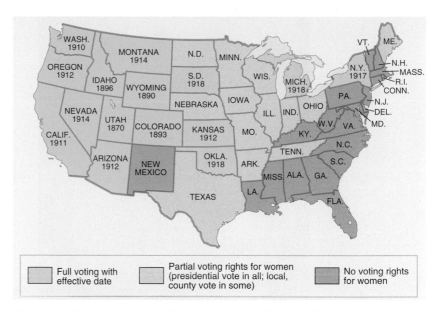

MAP 22.4 **Women's Voting Rights before the Nineteenth Amendment**
The long campaign for women's voting rights reversed the pioneer epic that ran from east to west. Suffrage rolled eastward from its first successes in the new democratic West toward the entrenched, male-dominated public life of the Northeast and the South.

READING THE MAP: What was the first state to grant woman suffrage? How many states extended full voting rights to women before the World War I years (1914–1918)? During World War I?
CONNECTIONS: Suffragists redirected their focus during World War I. What strategies did they use during the war? In which states was the struggle for woman suffrage fiercest, and why?

FOR MORE HELP ANALYZING THIS MAP, see the map activity for this chapter in the Online Study Guide at bedfordstmartins.com/roark.

Chapman Catt, soared to some 2 million members. NAWSA even accepted African American women in its ranks, although not on an equal basis. Seeing the handwriting on the wall, the Republican and Progressive parties endorsed woman suffrage in time for the 1916 election.

In 1918, Wilson gave his support to suffrage, calling the amendment "vital to the winning of the war." He praised women's wartime contributions and conceded that it would be wrong not to reward the "partnership of suffering and sacrifice" with a "partnership of privilege and right." By linking the drive for a constitutional amendment to the wartime emphasis on national unity, the advocates of woman suffrage finally triumphed. In 1919, Congress passed the Nineteenth Amendment, granting women the vote, and by August 18, 1920, it was ratified by the required

> By linking the drive for a constitutional amendment to the wartime emphasis on national unity, the advocates of woman suffrage finally triumphed.

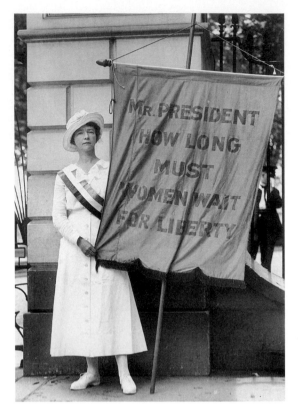

Picketing the White House for the Vote
Here Mrs. William L. Colt pickets Woodrow Wilson's home to demand women's right to vote. Because of such direct pressure and in recognition of women's service in the defense industry at home and in France as nurses and Red Cross workers, Wilson finally pledged support for the suffrage amendment. A gentleman from the old school, he believed women could tame men's aggressive tendencies, and he hoped that women's moderating influence would help make the Great War the war to end all wars.
© Bettmann/Corbis.

two-thirds of the states. As Carrie Chapman Catt later recalled, "to get that word, male, out of the Constitution, cost the women of the country fifty-two years of campaigning." But rather than woman suffrage being the end of the long road to women's full equality, as some suffragists contended, it proved to be only the beginning.

The Struggle over National Purpose

When Congress finally committed the nation to war, most peace advocates rallied around the flag. Several business and civic leaders who had been antiwar created the League to Enforce Peace in support of Wilson's insistence that military force had become the only means to peaceful ends. In a similar shift in view, the Carnegie

Endowment for International Peace adopted new stationery with the heading "Peace through Victory" and issued a resolution saying that "the most effectual means of promoting peace is to prosecute the war against the Imperial German Government."

Only a handful of reformers resisted the tide of conversion from pacifism to patriotism. Soon after the guns began booming in 1914, a group of professional women, led by settlement house leader Jane Addams and economics professor Emily Greene Balch, denounced what Addams described as "the pathetic belief in the regenerative results of war." The Women's Peace Party that emerged in 1915 and its foreign affiliates in the Women's International League for Peace and Freedom (WILPF) led the struggle to persuade governments to negotiate peace and spare dissenters from harsh punishment. It proved to be discouraging, unpopular work, and after America entered the conflict, advocates for peace were routinely labeled cowards and traitors, their efforts crushed by the steamroller of conformity.

Wilson's major strategy for fending off criticism of the war was to stir up patriotic fervor. In 1917, the president created the Committee on Public Information (CPI) under the direction of George Creel, a muckraking journalist who thumped for the war like a cheerleader at the big game. He sent "Four-Minute Men," a squad of 75,000 volunteers, around the country to give brief pep talks and distribute millions of press releases that described successes on the battlefields and in the factories. (See "Documenting the American Promise," page 806.) Everywhere, posters, pamphlets, and cartoons depicted brave American soldiers and sailors defending freedom and democracy against the "evil Hun." (The derogatory nickname "Hun" was often applied to Germans, particularly German soldiers, during both world wars.)

America turned out to help Creel's campaign. The film industry cranked out reels of melodrama about battle-line and home-front heroes and induced audiences to hiss at the German kaiser. A musical, *The Kaiser: The Beast of Berlin*, opened on Broadway in 1918. Colleges and universities generated war propaganda in the guise of scholarship, and some added courses depicting the war as a culmination of the age-old struggle for civilization. When Professor James McKeen Cattell of Columbia University in New York urged that America should seek peace with Germany short of victory, university president Nicholas Murray Butler fired him on the grounds that "what had been folly is now treason."

A firestorm of anti-German passion swept the nation. Campaigns with the slogan "100% American" enlisted ordinary people to sniff out disloyalty. German, the most widely taught foreign language in 1914, practically disappeared from the high school and college curriculum. Anger mounted against German-born Americans, including Karl Muck, conductor of the Boston Symphony Orchestra, and the renowned violinist Fritz Kreisler, who were driven from the concert stage. *The Saturday Evening Post*, one of America's most popular magazines, declared that it was time to rid the country of "the scum of the melting pot." The rabid attempt to

D. W. Griffith's *Hearts of the World*

Hollywood joined in the government's efforts to work up war rage against the "brutal Huns," as Germans were often called. In a film made for the British and French governments by America's leading filmmaker, D. W. Griffith, a hulking German is about to whip a defenseless farm woman (Lillian Gish, one of the nation's favorite stars) innocently carrying potatoes from a field. When the film premiered in Washington, D.C., in 1918, Mrs. Woodrow Wilson wrote Griffith pleading with him to cut or soften the violent whipping scene. Her plea was one of the few acts coming from the nation's capital that sought to moderate the hate campaign.

Library of Congress.

punish Germans reached its extreme with the lynching of Robert Prager, a baker in Collinsville, Illinois. In the atmosphere of mob rule, it was enough that Prager was German-born and had **socialist** leanings, even though he had not opposed American participation in the war. Persuaded by the defense lawyer who praised what he called a "patriotic murder," the jury at the trial of the killers took only twenty-five minutes to acquit.

As hysteria increased, absurdity mingled with cruelty. In Montana, a school board barred a history text that had good things to say about medieval Germany. Menus across the nation changed German toast to French toast and sauerkraut to liberty cabbage. In Milwaukee, vigilantes mounted a machine gun outside the Pabst Theater to prevent the staging of Schiller's *Wilhelm Tell*, a powerful protest against tyranny. One vigilant citizen claimed to see a periscope in the Great Lakes, and the fiancée of one of the war's leading critics, caught dancing on the dunes of Cape Cod, was held on suspicion of signaling to German submarines.

The Wilson administration's zeal in suppressing dissent contrasted sharply with its war aims of defending democracy. Undermining the First Amendment, in the name of self-defense, the Espionage Act (June 1917), the Trading with the Enemy Act (October 1917), and the Sedition Act (May 1918) gave the government sweeping powers to punish any opinion or activity it considered "disloyal, profane, scurrilous, or abusive" to the American flag or uniform. When Postmaster General Albert Burleson blocked mailing privileges for publications he considered disloyal, a number of independent-minded journals were forced to close down, including the leading literary magazine *Seven Arts*. Of the fifteen hundred individuals eventually charged with sedition, all but a dozen had merely spoken words the government found objectionable. One of them was Eugene V. Debs, the leader of the Socialist Party, who was convicted under the Espionage Act for speeches condemning the war as a capitalist plot and sent to the Atlanta penitentiary.

The president hoped that national commitment to the war would subdue partisan politics. He could not legitimately repress his Republican rivals, however, and they found many opportunities to use the war as a weapon against the Democrats. The trick was to oppose Wilson's conduct of the war but not the war itself. For example, Republicans outshouted Wilson on the

For and Against World War I

World War I became a battle-ground of loyalties as well as of guns. Through the Committee on Public Information (CPI), the Wilson administration developed the art of propaganda far beyond anything known before. The CPI promoted the war by organizing rallies and parades, blanketing the country with posters and cartoons, publishing a daily official bulletin, and mobilizing 75,000 volunteers to give speeches to hometown audiences. Only a few conscientious objectors, socialists, and disillusioned idealists were left to argue that war could not produce democracy but would instead destroy many lives and perhaps cherished values of progress and reform as well.

DOCUMENT 1
A "Four-Minute Man" Speech

The Committee on Public Information recruited volunteers in local communities to carry the official version of the war directly to their neighbors. Called "Four-Minute Men" because their speeches were supposed to last only four minutes, these enthusiasts spoke from carefully crafted scripts. The following example indicates how the speakers encouraged audiences to buy war bonds by rousing their indignation against the Germans.

While we are sitting here tonight enjoying a picture show, do you realize that thousands and thousands of Belgians, people just like ourselves, are languishing in slavery under Prussian masters? . . .

Prussian "Schrecklichkeit" (the deliberate policy of terrorism) leads to almost unbelievable besotten brutality. The German soldiers—their letters are reprinted—were often forced against their wills, they themselves weeping, to carry out unspeakable orders against defenseless old men, women, and children, so that "respect" might grow for German "efficiency." For instance, at Dinant the wives and children of 40 men were forced to witness the execution of their husbands and fathers.

Now, then, do you want to take the slightest chance of meeting Prussianism here in America?

If not, then you'll have to help in summoning all the resources of this country for the giant struggle. For resources will win the war.

Here's the way you can help save our resources. Instead of throwing money away on unnecessary things, buy Thrift Stamps, 25 cents, and War-Savings-Stamps, $4.12, worth $5 in five years, 4 percent compound interest. They're good as government money; like a mortgage on the U.S.A.

SOURCE: James R. Mock and Cedric Larson, excerpt (pp. 123–24) from *Words That Won the War.* Copyright © 1939 by Princeton University Press. Reprinted with permission of Princeton University Press. All rights reserved.

DOCUMENT 2
John S. P. Tatlock, "Why America Fights Germany," 1918

To influence public opinion, the War Department enlisted journalists and professors to write a series of "war information pamphlets." In the following example, history professor John S. P. Tatlock of Stanford University describes the sort of invasion that could be expected if the German hordes were not checked.

Now let us picture what a sudden invasion of the United States by these Germans would mean; sudden, because their settled way is always to attack suddenly. First they set themselves to capture New York City. While their fleet blockades the harbor and shells the city and the forts from far at sea, their troops land somewhere near and advance toward the city in order to cut its rail communications, starve it into surrender and then plunder it. One body of from 50,000 to 100,000 men lands, let us suppose, at Barnegat Bay, New Jersey, and advances without meeting resistance, for the brave but small American army is scattered elsewhere. They pass through Lakewood, a station on the Central Railroad of New Jersey. They first demand wine for the officers and beer for the men. Angered to find that an American town does not contain large quantities of either, they pillage and burn the post office and most of the hotels and stores. Then they demand $1,000,000 from the residents. One feeble old woman tries to conceal $20 which she has been hoarding in her desk drawer; she is taken out and hanged (to save a cartridge). Some of the teachers in two district schools meet a fate which makes them envy her. The Catholic priest and Methodist minister are thrown into a pig-sty, while the German soldiers look on and laugh. Some of the officers quarter themselves in a handsome house on the edge of the town, insult the ladies of the family, and destroy and defile the contents of the house. By this time some of the soldiers have managed to get drunk . . .

and then hell breaks loose. Robbery, murder and outrage run riot. Fifty leading citizens are lined up against the First National Bank building, and shot. Most of the town and the beautiful pinewoods are burned, and then the troops move on to treat New Brunswick in the same way—if they get there.

This is not just a snappy story. It is not fancy. The general plan of campaign against America has been announced repeatedly by German military men. And every horrible detail is just what the German troops have done in Belgium and France.

SOURCE: John S. P. Tatlock, "Why America Fights Germany," War Information Series pamphlet no. 15, War Department, 1918.

DOCUMENT 3
Jane Addams,
Address at Carnegie Hall,
New York City, July 9, 1915

True to her belief in reason, not force, the leader of the settlement house movement, Jane Addams, helped form the Women's Peace Party in 1915. Soon afterward, she participated in the Hague Conference of Women in Holland and then, with a group of the delegates, visited the capitals of six warring nations to urge the leaders of those countries to seek peaceful resolution of the conflict. In this address to a New York City audience, Addams spoke about the conclusions she had drawn from her tour of Europe.

The first thing which was striking is this, that the same causes and reasons for the war were heard everywhere. Each warring nation solemnly assured you it is fighting under the impulse of self-defense. . . .

In each of the warring nations there is this other point of similarity.

Generally speaking, we heard everywhere that this war was an old man's war; that the young men who were dying, the young men who were doing the fighting, were not the men who wanted the war, and were not the men who believed in the war; that somewhere in church and state, somewhere in the high places of society, the elderly people, the middle-aged people, had established themselves and had convinced themselves that this was a righteous war. . . .

I quote a letter published in the *Cambridge Magazine* at Cambridge University and written by a young man who had gone to the front. . . .

". . . Just when the younger generation was beginning to take its share in the affairs of the world, and was hoping to counteract the Victorian influences of the older generation, this war has come to silence us,—permanently or temporarily as the case may be. Meanwhile, the old men are having field days on their own. In our name, and for our sakes as they pathetically imagine, they are doing their very utmost, it would seem, to perpetuate, by their appeals to hate, intolerance and revenge, those very follies which have produced the present conflagration." . . .

It seemed to me . . . that the older men believed more in abstractions, shall I say; that when they talked of patriotism, when they used certain theological or nationalistic words, these meant more to them than they did to the young men; that the young men had come to take life much more from the point of view of experience . . . and when they went to the trenches and tested it out, they concluded that it did not pay, that it was not what they wanted to do with their lives.

Perhaps the most shocking impression left upon one's mind is this, that in the various countries the tem-

per necessary for continuing the war is worked up and fed largely by the things which have occurred in the war itself. . . .

Let us say that there are two groups of boys in a boys' club, and I have much experience of that sort in boys' clubs to draw upon. If one says, "We did this because the other fellows did that," you will simply have to say, "I won't go into the rights and wrongs of this, but this thing must stop, because it leads nowhere and gets nowhere." . . .

. . . And what it needs, it seems to me, and to many of us, is a certain touch of human nature. . . . When you find that you can't talk to a woman on any subject, however remote from the war, without finding at once that she is in the deepest perplexity,—that while she is carrying herself bravely and going on with her accustomed activities because she thinks thereby that she is serving her country, her heart is being torn all the time,—it is borne in upon you that at last human nature must revolt. . . . Then men must see the horrible things which have happened; they will have to soberly count up the loss of life, and the debt they have settled upon themselves for years to come.

SOURCE: Jane Addams, "The Revolt against War," *Survey,* July 17, 1915.

DOCUMENT 4
Diary of an Anonymous
American Soldier, 1918

Encouraged by civilian and military officials to make their crusade in Europe an enlightening experience, many soldiers recorded their impressions in diaries and letters. In the case of one anonymous

(continued)

(continued)

soldier, the task became so absorbing that it eventually found its way into print as Wine, Women, and War: A Diary of Disillusionment *(1926). As time in combat dragged on, the diarist changed his tone and looked critically at war aims and their probable outcome.*

25 August 1918: Base Hospital at Neuilly. Has the Lord ordained that from hideous mangling of flesh beautiful things should come? . . . Can't evade it—there is sublimity in war. Man made in mold of divinity, and more than a flavor of his origin still clinging to his soul. The cheer of these lads, their quiet grave resignation, too beautiful for marring touch of praise. . . .

One comes away from this eddy of human wreckage, a little sick at heart. But one presently forgets the bodies shattered, the faces marred, the freshness of lives become stale and useless, and remembers only that "God fulfills himself in many ways." The singular evangelism of blood. . . .

18 October 1918: Three hundredth day from Hoboken! Damned cold. Shivering, fingers numb as lead, and not even November yet. . . . Race between Kaiser and my pants still on. Vital interest in early termination of conflict! Each day another seam opens or another button drops from fatigue—and can't keep pants up by merely gritting teeth. Each morning,

scan communiques first—then breeches. Strain beginning to tell.

After the war problems of readjustment, hitherto kept in background, going to make all sorts of trouble. League of Nations, not mere imaginative sentimental Utopia, but only practicable solution of world in chaos. . . . The real victors in this war will be determined 10 or 20 years afterwards, and they will be the nation who will be the best able to face the growing discontent of a disillusioned people, to ward off impending famine, and to save their people from the appalling consequences of the universal bankruptcy to which Europe is speeding every day with increasing pace.

Vast amount of nonsense about Germany. Silly idea of demanding huge indemnities, and in same breath refusing to allow access to raw material, i.e., ask tree to give fruit, but shut off sun and air. . . . Either slaughter entire Teutonic race, or take them back and try to make something of them. No middle ground. No sense hating Germans. Only proper object for hate, to anyone with brains God gave little snails, is an idea. And can't destroy ideas, or crush them, or punish them. Can only substitute good ideas for bad ones.

This life hard on illusions. Not many left. A hell of a way from best

of all possible worlds, and man certainly a son-of-a-bitch when he puts his mind to it. But hope not to travel too far along road on which so many realists stub their silly toes, of believing there is no angel worth mentioning in poor, complex human heart. Heaven and hell both there.

SOURCE: Anonymous, *Wine, Women, and War: A Diary of Disillusionment* (New York, 1926).

QUESTIONS FOR ANALYSIS AND DEBATE

1. What did the Committee on Public Information mean by "Prussianism"? In what ways did the committee suppose it might be present in American life?

2. How likely were Americans to be convinced by Professor Tatlock's warning of a German invasion? What estimate does Tatlock seem to be making of the general awareness and intelligence of the American public?

3. How plausible is Jane Addams's contention that war is the disastrous result of old men's abstractions that are later refuted by young men's experience?

4. Does the anonymous diarist become more at peace with the world, or less, as a result of his war experience? Why?

---

nation's need to mobilize for war but then complained that Wilson's War Industries Board was a tyrannical agency that crushed free enterprise. Such attacks appealed to widely diverse business, labor, and patriotic groups. As the war progressed, Republicans gathered power against the coalition of Democrats and progressives that had narrowly reelected Wilson in 1916.

Wilson erred when he attempted to make the off-year congressional elections of 1918 a referendum on his leadership. Instead, amid criticism of the White House for playing politics with the war, Republicans gained a narrow majority in both House and Senate. The end of Democratic control of Congress not only suspended any possibility of further domestic reform but also meant that the United States would advance toward military victory with authority divided between a Democratic presidency and a Republican Congress likely to contest Wilson's plans for international cooperation.

A Compromised Peace

Wilson decided to reaffirm his noble war ideals by announcing his peace aims before the end of hostilities was in sight. He hoped the victorious Allies would rally around his generous ideas, but he soon discovered that his plan for international democracy did not receive eager acceptance. The leaders of England, France, and Italy understood that Wilson's principles jeopardized their own postwar plans for the acquisition of enemy territory, new colonial empires, and reparations. He also faced strong opposition at home from those who feared that his ardor for international cooperation would undermine American sovereignty.

Wilson's Fourteen Points

On January 8, 1918, nine months after the United States entered the war, President Wilson delivered a speech to Congress that revealed his vision of a liberal peace. Wilson's Fourteen Points provided a blueprint for a new democratic world order. The first five points affirmed basic liberal ideals: "open covenants of peace, openly arrived at," that is, an end to secret treaties; freedom of the seas in war and peace; removal of economic barriers to free trade; reduction of weapons of war; and recognition of the rights of colonized peoples. The next eight points supported the right to self-determination of European peoples who had been dominated by Germany or its allies. Wilson's final point called for a "general association of nations"—a League of Nations—to provide "mutual guarantees of political independence and territorial integrity to great and small states alike." The insistence on a League of Nations reflected Wilson's lifelong dream of a "parliament of man." Only such an organization, he believed, could justify the war and secure a lasting peace. Wilson concluded his speech by pledging that the United States would welcome Germany into the family of "peace-loving nations" if it would renounce its militarism and imperialism.

The Fourteen Points roused popular enthusiasm in the United States and every Allied country. Armed with such public support, Wilson felt confident that he could prevail against undemocratic forces at the peace table. During the final year of the war, he pressured the Allies to accept the Fourteen Points as the basis of the settlement. If necessary, Wilson was willing to speak over the heads of government leaders directly to the people and so expand his role as spokesman for American citizens to the champion of all the world's people. The Allies had won the war; Wilson would win the peace.

The Paris Peace Conference

From January 18 to June 28, 1919, the eyes of the world focused on Paris. There, powerful men wrestled with difficult problems. Inspired by his sense of mission, Wilson decided to attend the peace conference in person, as head of the U.S. delegation. No other American president had ever gone to Europe while in office, but Wilson believed he owed it to the American soldiers. "It is now my duty," he announced, "to play my full part in making good what they gave their life's blood to obtain." A dubious British diplomat retorted that Wilson was drawn to Paris "as a debutante is entranced by the prospect of her first ball." The decision to leave the country at a time when his political opponents were sharply contesting his leadership was risky enough, but his stubborn refusal to include prominent Republicans in the delegation proved foolhardy and eventually cost him his dream of a new world order with America at its center.

The peace venture began well. Huge crowds cheered the American president's motorcade on its way to Paris. After four terrible years of war, Europeans looked on Wilson as someone who would create a safer, more decent world. However, when the conference convened at Louis XIV's magnificent palace at Versailles, Wilson encountered a very different reception. Representing the Allies were the decidedly unidealistic David Lloyd George of Britain, Georges Clemenceau of France, and Vittorio Orlando of Italy. To the Allied leaders, Wilson was a naive and impractical moralist whose desire to reconcile former foes within a new international democratic order showed how little he understood hard European realities. The French premier claimed that Wilson "believed you could do everything by formulas" and "empty theory." Disparaging the Fourteen Points, he added, "God himself was con-

> Wilson's Fourteen Points provided a blueprint for a new democratic world order.

> To the Allied leaders, Wilson was a naive and impractical moralist whose desire to reconcile former foes within a new international democratic order showed how little he understood hard European realities.

Leaders of the Paris Peace Conference
The three leaders in charge of putting the world back together after the Great War—from left to right, David Lloyd George, prime minister of Great Britain; Georges Clemenceau, premier of France; and U.S. president Woodrow Wilson—amiably and confidently stride toward the peace conference at the palace of Versailles. Clemenceau is caught offering animated instruction to Wilson, whom he considered naively idealistic. Indeed, in an unguarded moment, Clemenceau expressed his contempt for the entire United States as a country that was unique in having passed directly from barbarism to decadence without an intervening period of civilization. Walking silently alongside, Lloyd George maintains the poker face that helped keep his views carefully guarded throughout the conference.
Gamma Liaison.

tent with ten commandments." The Allies wanted to fasten blame for the war on Germany, totally disarm it, and make it pay so dearly that it would never threaten its neighbors again. The French demanded retribution in the form of territory containing some of Germany's richest mineral resources. And the British made it clear that they were not about to give up the powerful weapon of naval blockade for the vague principle of the freedom of the seas.

Wilson was forced to make drastic compromises. In return for French moderation of territorial claims, he agreed to support Article 231 of the peace treaty, assigning war guilt to Germany. Though saved from permanently losing Rhineland territory to the French, Germany was outraged at being singled out as the instigator of the war and saddled with more than $33 billion in damages. Many Germans felt that their nation had been betrayed. After agreeing to an armistice on the belief that peace terms would be based on Wilson's generous Fourteen Points, they faced hardship and humiliation instead.

Wilson had better success in establishing the principle of self-determination. But from the beginning, he had been vague about what self-determination actually meant. "When I gave utterance to those words," he admitted, "I said them without the knowledge that nationalities existed, which are coming to us day after day." Secretary of State Robert Lansing knew that the "phrase is simply loaded with dynamite." Lansing wondered, "What unit has he in mind? Does he mean a race, a territorial area, or a community?" Lansing believed that the notion of self-determination "will raise hopes which can never be realized. It will, I fear, cost thousands of lives. In the end it is bound to be discredited, to be called the dream of an idealist who failed to realize the danger until it was too late."

Yet on the basis of self-determination, the conference redrew the map of Europe and parts of the rest of the world. Portions of the Austro-Hungarian Empire were ceded to Italy, Poland, and Romania, and the remainder was reassembled into Austria, Hungary, Czechoslovakia, and Yugoslavia—independent republics with boundaries determined according to concentrations of ethnic groups. More arbitrarily, the Ottoman Empire was carved up into small mandates (including Palestine) run by local leaders but under the control of France and Great Britain. The conference reserved the mandate system for those regions it deemed insufficiently "civilized" or advanced to have full independence. Thus, with varying degrees of danger from ethnic and nationalist rivalries, each reconstructed nation faced the challenge of making a new democratic government work (Map 22.5). Many of today's bitterest disputes—in the Balkans and Iraq, between Greece and Turkey, between Arabs and Jews—have roots in the decisions made in Paris in 1919.

Wilson hoped that self-determination would also be the fate of Germany's colonies in Asia and Africa. But the Allies who had taken over the colonies during the war would go no further than allowing the League of Nations a mandate to administer them. Technically, the mandate system rejected imperialism, but in reality it was an attempt to avoid outright imperialism while

MAP 22.5 Europe after World War I
The post–World War I settlement redrew boundaries to create new nations based on ethnic groupings. This left within defeated Germany and Russia bitter peoples who resolved to recover territory that the new arrangements took from their homelands.

still allowing Europeans to maintain control. While denying Germany its colonies, the Allies retained their own colonial empires.

The cause of democratic equality suffered another setback when the peace conference refused to endorse Japan's proposal for a clause in the treaty proclaiming the principle of racial equality. Wilson's belief in the superiority of whites, as well as his apprehension about how white Americans would respond to such a declaration, led him to oppose the clause. To soothe hurt feelings, Wilson agreed to grant Japan a mandate over the Shantung Peninsula in northern China, which had formerly been controlled by Germany. The gesture mollified Japan's moderate leaders, but the military faction preparing to take over the country used bitterness toward racist Western colonialism to build support for expanding Japanese power throughout Asia.

The issue that was closest to Wilson's heart was finding a new way of managing international relations, an idea sketched out in his Fourteen Points. In Wilson's view, war had finally discredited the old strategy of balance of power. Instead, he proposed a League of Nations that would provide **collective security** and order. The League would establish rules of international conduct and resolve conflicts between

nations through rational and peaceful means. When the Allies agreed to the League, Wilson was overjoyed. He believed that the League would rectify the errors his colleagues had forced on him in Paris. The League would solidify and extend the noble work he had begun.

To many Europeans and Americans whose hopes had been stirred by Wilson's lofty aims, the Versailles treaty came as a bitter disappointment. Wilson's admirers were shocked that the president dealt in compromise like any other politician. But without Wilson's presence, the treaty that was signed on June 28, 1919, surely would have been more vindictive. Wilson returned home in July 1919 consoled that, despite his many frustrations, he had gained what he most wanted—creation of the League of Nations. In Wilson's judgment, "We have completed in the least time possible the greatest work that four men have ever done."

The Fight for the Treaty

The tumultuous reception Wilson received when he arrived home persuaded him, probably correctly, that the American people supported the treaty. On July 10, 1919, the president submitted the treaty to the Senate, warning that failure to ratify it would "break the heart of the world." By then, however, criticism of the treaty was mounting, especially from Americans convinced that their countries of ethnic origin had not been given fair treatment. Irish Americans, Italian Americans, and German Americans launched especially sharp attacks. Even Wilson's supporters worried that the president's concessions at Versailles had jeopardized the treaty's capacity to provide a generous plan for rebuilding Europe and to guarantee world peace.

Some of the most potent critics were found in the Senate. Bolstered by a slight Republican majority in Congress, a group of Republican "irreconcilables," which included such powerful **isolationist** senators as Hiram Johnson of California and William Borah of Idaho, condemned the treaty for entangling the United States in world affairs. A larger group of Republicans did not object to American participation in world politics but feared that membership in the League of Nations would jeopardize the nation's independence. No Republican, in any case, was eager to hand Wilson and the Democrats a foreign policy victory with the 1920 presidential election little more than a year away.

At the center of Republican opposition was Wilson's archenemy, Senator Henry Cabot Lodge of Massachusetts. Lodge's hostility was in part purely personal. "I never thought I could hate a man as much as I hate Wilson," he once admitted. But in addition to seeking Wilson's personal humiliation and defeat, Lodge raised cogent objections to the treaty and the League. Lodge was no isolationist, but he thought that too much of the Fourteen Points was a "general bleat about virtue being better than vice." Like his friend Theodore Roosevelt, who died in January 1919, Lodge expected the United States's economic might and strong army and navy to propel the nation into a major role in world affairs. But he insisted that membership in the League of Nations, which would require collective action to maintain peace, threatened the nation's freedom of choice in foreign relations.

To undermine public support for Wilson, Lodge used his position as chairman of the Senate Foreign Relations Committee to air every sort of complaint. Out of the committee hearings came several amendments, or "reservations," that sought to limit the consequences of American membership in the League. For example, several reservations required approval of both House and Senate before the United States could participate in League-sponsored economic sanctions or military action.

Eventually, it became clear that ratification of the treaty depended on acceptance of the Lodge reservations. Democratic senators, who overwhelmingly supported the treaty, urged Wilson to accept Lodge's terms, arguing that they left the essentials of the treaty intact. Wilson, however, insisted that the reservations cut "the very heart out of the treaty." He expressed personal hatred as well. "*Lodge* reservations?" he thundered. "Never! I'll never consent to adopt any policy with which that impossible name is so prominently identified."

With the treaty about to be reported from the Foreign Relations Committee to the full Senate with reservations attached, Wilson decided to take his case directly to the people. On

Pro-League Poster

Woodrow Wilson's faith in international cooperation through the League of Nations struck a chord among a majority of Americans. To them, the League represented an extension of progressivism's conviction that humans could achieve democracy, human rights, and peace through just and effective government. In this poster announcing a rally to support the League, the victorious international community employs the League to lock up German militarism and end the threat of world war.

By Special Permission of Manuscripts Division, University of Minnesota Libraries, Minneapolis.

September 3, 1919, he set out by train on the most ambitious speaking tour ever undertaken by a president. Already exhausted by the peace conference and further debilitated by his fight with Lodge, Wilson went despite the objections of his doctors. He enjoyed some early success, but on September 25 in Pueblo, Colorado, Wilson collapsed and had to return to Washington. There he suffered a massive stroke that partially paralyzed him. From his bedroom, Wilson sent messages through his wife and cabinet instructing Democrats in the Senate to hold firm against any and all reservations. If the Senate approved the treaty with reservations, he said, he would not sign it. In the end, Wilson commanded enough loyalty to ensure a vote against the Lodge reservations. But when the treaty without reservations came before the Senate in March 1920, the combined opposition of the Republican irreconcilables and Republican reservationists left Wilson six votes short of the two-thirds majority needed for passage.

The nations of Europe went about organizing the League of Nations at Geneva, Switzerland, but the United States never became a member. Whether American membership could have prevented the world war that began in Europe in 1939 is highly unlikely, but America's failure to join certainly weakened the League from the start. In refusing to accept relatively minor compromises with Senate moderates, Wilson lost his treaty and American membership in the League. Would the Europeans have accepted reservations by the Americans? Lloyd George claimed later that they had always expected that they might have to. Brought low by their feud, Woodrow Wilson and Henry Cabot Lodge both died in 1924, never seeing international order or security, never knowing the whirlwind of resentment and violence that would eventually follow the Great War's failure to make the world safe for democracy.

Democracy at Risk

The defeat of Wilson's idealistic hopes for international democracy was the crowning blow to those progressives who had hoped that the war could serve as a vehicle for reform at home. The reaction that followed included an urge to demobilize swiftly. In the process, servicemen, defense workers, and farmers lost their war-related jobs and much of their economic security. The combination of displaced veterans returning home, a stalled economy, and leftover wartime patriotism looking for a new cause was so volatile that it could hardly fail to explode. Wartime anti-German passion was quickly succeeded by antiradicalism, a fevered campaign broad enough to ensnare unionists, socialists, dissenters, and African Americans and Mexicans who had committed no offense but to seek to escape rural poverty.

> Wartime anti-German passion was quickly succeeded by antiradicalism, a fevered campaign broad enough to ensnare unionists, socialists, dissenters, African Americans, and Mexicans.

Economic Hardship and Labor Upheaval

With the armistice came an urgent desire to return the United States to a peacetime economy. In response, the government abruptly abandoned its wartime controls on the economy and almost overnight canceled millions of dollars in orders for war materiel. In a matter of months, more than three million soldiers were mustered out of the military with only $60 and a one-way ticket home. When war production ceased and veterans flooded the job market, unemployment rose sharply. At the same time, consumers went on a postwar spending spree and inflation soared. In 1919, prices rose an astonishing 75 percent over prewar levels, and in 1920, though inflation slowed, prices rose another 28 percent.

Most of the gains workers had made during the war evaporated. Freed from wartime control, business turned against the eight-hour day and attacked labor unions. Workers fought back rather than sitting back and watching inflation eat up their paychecks and bosses destroy their unions. The year 1919 witnessed nearly 3,600 strikes involving 4 million workers. The most spectacular strike occurred in February 1919 in Seattle, where shipyard workers had been put out of work by demobilization. When a coalition of the radical International Workers of the World (IWW) and the moderate American Federation of Labor (AFL) called a general strike, the largest work stoppage in American history shut down the city. Newspapers across the nation echoed claims in the *Seattle Times* that the walkout was "a Bolshevik effort to start a revolution" engineered by "Seattle labor criminals." An effort to deport strike leaders failed because they were citizens, not aliens, but the suppression of the strike by Seattle's anti-union mayor, Ole Hanson, cost the AFL much of the support it had gained during the war and contributed to the destruction of the IWW soon afterward.

A strike by Boston policemen in the fall of 1919 brought out postwar hostility toward labor militancy in the public sector. Though they were paid less than pick-and-shovel laborers and had received no raise since before the war, the police won little sympathy. Once the officers stopped walking their beats, looters sacked the city. After two days of near anarchy only slightly tamed by a volunteer police force of Harvard students and recently discharged soldiers, Massachusetts governor Calvin Coolidge called in the National Guard to restore order. The public, yearning for peace and security in the wake of war, welcomed Coolidge's anti-union assurance that "there is no right to strike against the public safety by anybody, anywhere, any time."

Labor strife climaxed in the grim steel strike of 1919. Steelworkers had serious grievances, but for decades the industry had succeeded in beating back all their efforts to unionize. In 1919, however, the AFL, still led by its founding father, Samuel Gompers, decided it was time to try again. It had little choice given the industry's plan to revert to seven-day weeks, twelve-hour days, and weekly wages of about $20. Having loyally backed the government's war effort, the AFL expected federal support for unionization. When Gompers began to recruit union members, however, he learned that he faced the steel barons alone. Following the refusal of U.S. Steel and Bethlehem Steel to negotiate, Gompers called for a strike; 350,000 workers in fifteen states walked out in September 1919. The steel industry hired 30,000 strikebreakers (many of them African Americans) and convinced the public that the strikers were radicals bent on subverting the Republic. State and federal troops protected scabs who crossed picket lines. In January 1920, after eighteen striking workers had been killed, the strike collapsed. That devastating defeat initiated a sharp decline in the fortunes of the labor movement, a trend that would continue for almost twenty years.

"The Warrior's Return"

About 16,000 Native Americans served in the U.S. armed forces during World War I. This magazine cover offers a romanticized reconstruction of one homecoming. The young soldier, still in uniform and presumably fresh from France, rides his painted pony to the tepee of his parents, where they proudly welcome the brave warrior. Their tepee even has a star, a national symbol that families with sons in the military displayed on their homes. The painting sought to demonstrate that all Americans, even those on the margins of national life, were sufficiently assimilated and loyal to join the national sacrifice to defeat the enemy.

Picture Research Consultants & Archives.

The Red Scare

Suppression of labor strikes was one manifestation of a general fear of internal subversion that swept the nation in 1919. The "Red scare" (*red* refers to the color of the Bolshevik flag), which far outstripped the assault on civil liberties during the war, had homegrown causes: the postwar recession, labor unrest, and the difficulties of reintegrating millions of returning veterans. But unsettling events abroad also added to Americans' anxieties. Russian bolshevism became even more menacing in March 1919 when the new Soviet leaders created the Comintern, a worldwide association of **Communist** leaders intent on fomenting revolution in capitalist countries. (See "Beyond America's Borders," page 816.) A Communist revolution in the United States was extremely unlikely, but a flurry of isolated terrorist acts in 1919, most notably thirty-eight bombs mailed to prominent Americans, convinced edgy Americans that revolutionaries were at the door. Fear, anger, and uncertainty led swiftly to a hunt for terrorists. Arguing that "there could be no nice distinctions

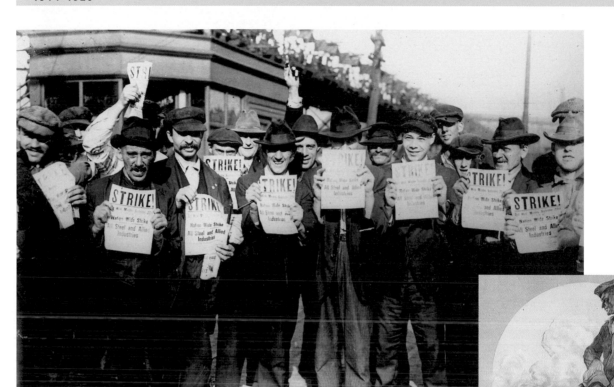

Returning Veterans and Work

After the triumphal parades ended, attention turned to the question of what the heroes would do at home. The Department of Labor poster tries to convey a strong image of purposefulness and prosperity by portraying a soldier in front of a booming industrial landscape. The U.S. Employment Service had little to offer veterans beyond posters, however, and unions were unprepared to cope with the massive numbers of former soldiers who needed retraining. As workplace conditions deteriorated, the largest number of strikes in the nation's history broke out in 1919.

Library of Congress, © Bettmann/Corbis.

After the Welcome Home— a JOB!

U.S. EMPLOYMENT SERVICE *Dep't of Labor*

drawn between the theoretical ideals of the radicals and their actual violations of our national laws," Attorney General A. Mitchell Palmer led an assault on alleged conspirators. Targeting men and women who harbored what Palmer considered ideas that could lead to violence, even though they may not have done anything illegal, the Justice Department sought to purge the supposed enemies of America.

In January 1920, Palmer ordered a series of raids that netted 6,000 alleged subversives. Though the revolutionary conspiracies he expected to uncover did not turn up, and the three pistols he confiscated did not amount to an armory, Palmer nevertheless ordered 500 noncitizen suspects deported. His action came in the midst of a campaign against the most notorious radical alien, Russian-born Emma Goldman. Before the war, Goldman's passionate support of labor strikes, women's rights, and birth control had made her a leading symbol of outspoken disrespect for mainstream opinion. Finally, after a stay in prison for attacking military conscription, she was ordered deported by the fervent young director of the Radical Division of the Justice Department, J. Edgar Hoover. In December 1919, as Goldman and 250 others boarded a ship for exile in Russia, the defiant

Bolshevism

One month before Woodrow Wilson asked Congress for a declaration of war against Germany, revolutionary forces in Russia overthrew Czar Nicolas II and installed a democratic government. The March 1917 revolution removed the last despot among the Allies fighting Germany and bolstered Wilson's confidence that the war really was a clear-cut fight between "democracy and autocracy." The American president embraced the revolution, declaring that Russia "is a fit partner for a league of honour."

In November 1917, however, Russia experienced a second revolution. Marxist radicals calling themselves Bolsheviks seized control and made their leader, Vladimir Ilyich Lenin, ruler of Russia, which after 1922 was known as the Soviet Union. Lenin scoffed at the idea that the Allies were fighting for democracy and insisted that greedy capitalists were waging war for international dominance. In March 1918, Lenin shocked Wilson and the Allies when Russia signed a separate peace with Germany and withdrew from the war. The Allies, still locked in a desperate struggle with Germany, cried betrayal and feared that vast numbers of German soldiers fighting on the eastern front would turn to confront exhausted Allied troops on the western front.

Britain and France, prodded by British leader Winston Churchill who declared that "the Bolshevik infant should be strangled in its cradle," urged the United States to join them in sending troops to Russia where they would support Russian democrats against the new revolutionary socialist regime. Wilson hesitated before committing troops to a civil war in Russia. He told his trusted advisor, Colonel House, "I've been sweating blood over the question of what is right and feasible to do in Russia." Several prominent Americans spoke out against American intervention. Senator William Borah of Idaho declared: "The Russian people have the same right to establish a Socialist state as we have to establish a republic." But Wilson concluded that the Bolsheviks were a dictatorial party that came to power through a violent coup that denied Russians political choice. Moreover, if anti-Bolshevik forces succeeded, Wilson figured, they might bring Russia back into the war against Germany. By September 1918, on the pretext of helping 60,000 trapped Czechoslovakians return to the West to fight the Germans, Wilson had ordered 14,000 American troops to Russia to join British and French forces there. When the Allies defeated Germany in November 1918, the continued presence of Western troops in Russia could no longer be defended as part of the war with Germany. Clearly, American, British, and French troops were fighting to overthrow Lenin and annul the Bolshevik Revolution. But the Bolsheviks (who by this time called themselves Communists) prevailed, and American troops withdrew from Russia in June 1919, after the loss of more than 200 American lives.

The Bolshevik regime dedicated itself not only to ending capitalism in Russia but also to overthrowing capitalist and imperialist regimes everywhere. Clearly, Lenin's imagined future jeopardized Wilson's proposed liberal new world order. Wilson withheld diplomatic recognition from the Soviet Union (a policy that persisted until 1934) and joined the Allies in an economic boycott to bring down the Bolshevik government. Unbowed, Lenin promised that his party would "incite rebellion among all the peoples now oppressed," and revolutionary agitation became central to Soviet foreign policy. Communist revolutions erupted in Bavaria and Hungary following the end of World War I. Although short-lived, the Communist regimes sent shock waves throughout the West. In 1919, moreover, a Russian official claimed that monies sent to Europe to foment rebellion were "nothing compared to the funds transmitted to New York for the purpose of spreading bolshevism in the United States." American attention shifted from revolutionaries in Europe to revolutionaries at home. The Red scare was on.

Having failed to make the world "safe for democracy," the Wilson administration set out to make democracy safe in America. Attorney General A. Mitchell Palmer perceived a "blaze of Revolution sweeping over every American institution of law and order . . . licking the altars of churches . . . crawling into the sacred corners of American homes." The government launched an all-out attack on the Communist ("Red") menace (see page 814). But rather than looking on the Bolshevik success as monstrous, a few Americans saw Russia as the world's best hope, especially after the Versailles treaty shattered Wilson's grand plans for the peace. Some traveled to Russia and wrote rapturously about the society that promised economic and social justice and the end of the exploitation of workers by capitalist bosses.

Nevertheless, the vast majority of Americans were no more drawn to communism than to czarism. When disgruntled socialists founded the American Communist Party in 1919, the new party attracted only a handful of members. And they spent most of their time arguing the fine points of doctrine, not manufacturing bombs. But in 1919, a few radicals did resort to bombs. "Bolshevism means chaos, wholesale murder, the complete destruction of civilization," one observer declared, and the nation responded by bullying and terrorizing even mild dissenters. Workers seeking better wages and conditions, women and African Americans demanding equal rights, and others who pushed for change found the government hurling the epithet "Red" at anyone who opposed the status quo. Beatings, jailings, and deportation often followed. But with the sailing of the "Soviet Ark" that deported Emma Goldman and other radicals out of the country on December 21, 1919, the hysteria subsided.

The Bolshevik Revolution in Russia had endless consequences. It initiated a brutal reign of terror in the Soviet Union that lasted more than seven decades. It also set up a polarity in international politics that lasted nearly as long. In a very real sense, the cold war that set the United States and the Soviet Union at each others' throats after World War Two began in 1917. America's abortive military intervention against the

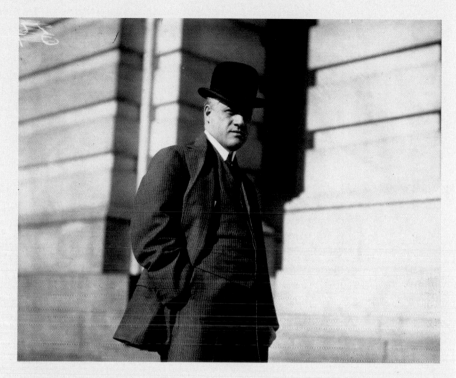

Attorney General A. Mitchell Palmer
On January 2, 1920, Attorney General A. Mitchell Palmer ordered hundreds of federal agents to 33 American cities to smash the alleged Bolshevik conspiracy. Led by J. Edgar Hoover, the agents arrested more than 6,000 individuals on charges of plotting to overthrow the government. Palmer revealed much more about himself than about those arrested when he said, "Out of the sly and crafty eyes of many of them leap cupidity, cruelty, insanity, and crime; from their lopsided faces, sloping brows, and misshapen features may be recognized the unmistakable criminal type."
Library of Congress.

Bolshevik regime and the Bolsheviks' call for worldwide revolution convulsed relations from the very beginning. In the United States, the Red scare's rabid antiradicalism did significant damage to American values. Commitment to the protection of dissent succumbed to irrational anticommunism. Even mild reform became tarred with the brush of Bolshevism. Although the Red scare withered as quickly as it sprouted, the habit of crushing dissent in the name of security lived on. Years later, when Americans' anxiety mounted and confidence waned once again,

witch hunts against radicalism would again haunt American democracy.

BIBLIOGRAPHY

Peter G. Boyle, *American-Soviet Relations: From the Russian Revolution to the Fall of Communism* (1993).

Gordon A. Craig, *Europe since 1815* (1961).

Thomas Fleming, *The Illusion of Victory: America in World War I* (2003).

John Gaddis, *Russia, the Soviet Union, and the United States* (1978).

N. Gordon Levin Jr., *Woodrow Wilson and World Politics: America's Response to War and Revolution* (1968).

Ted Morgan, *Reds: McCarthyism in Twentieth-Century America* (2004).

rebel turned on the gangplank to thumb her nose at a jeering crowd and disappeared onto the deck. Anticipating timid conformity in the next decade, one observer remarked, "With Prohibition coming in and Emma Goldman goin' out, 'twill be a dull country."

The effort to rid the country of alien radicals was matched by efforts to crush troublesome citizens. Law enforcement officials and vigilante groups joined hands in several cities and towns to rid themselves of so-called Reds. On Armistice Day, November 11, 1919, events reached their grimmest in Centralia, Washington, a rugged lumber town home to one of only two IWW halls left in the state. Intimidated by a menacing crowd gathered in front of the hall, nervous IWW members opened fire, killing three people. Three IWW members were arrested and later convicted of murder, but another, an ex-soldier, was carried off by a mob who castrated him and then, after hanging him from a bridge, riddled his body with bullets. His death was officially ruled a suicide.

Public institutions joined the attack on civil liberties. Local libraries removed dissenting books. Schools and colleges fired unorthodox teachers. Police shut down radical newspapers. State legislatures refused to seat elected representatives who professed socialist ideas, and in 1919, Congress removed its lone socialist representative, Victor Berger, on the grounds that he was a threat to national safety. That same year, the Supreme Court provided a formula for restricting free speech. In upholding the conviction of socialist Charles Schenck for publishing a pamphlet urging resistance to the draft during wartime (*Schenck v. United States*), Justice Oliver Wendell Holmes, writing for the Court, established a "clear and present danger" test. Such utterances as Schenck's during a time of national peril, Holmes wrote, were equivalent to shouting "Fire!" in a crowded theater. But Schenck's pamphlet spoke softly in the open air, not in a crowded theater, and had little power to provoke a public firmly opposed to its message.

In time, the Red scare lost credibility. The lack of any real radical menace became clear after newspaper headlines carried Attorney General Palmer's warning that radicals were planning to celebrate the Bolshevik Revolution with a nationwide wave of violence on May 1, 1920. Officials responded by calling out state militia, fortifying public buildings and churches, mobilizing bomb squads, even placing machine-gun nests at major city intersections. When May 1 came and went without a single disturbance, the public mood turned from fear to scorn. The Red scare collapsed in its excesses.

The Great Migrations of African Americans and Mexicans

Before the Red scare lost steam, the government raised alarms about the loyalty of African Americans. A Justice Department investigation concluded that Reds were fomenting racial unrest among blacks. While the report was wrong about Bolshevik influence, it was correct in identifying a new stirring among African Americans, a new assertiveness borne of participation in the war effort and in a massive migration out of the South.

In 1900, nine of every ten blacks still lived in the South, where disfranchisement, segregation, and violence dominated their lives. Thirty-five years after **emancipation**, African Americans had made little progress toward full citizenship. The majority of black men continued to toil in agriculture as dirt-poor tenants or sharecroppers, or they worked for wages of sixty cents a day. Black women worked in the homes of

Emma Goldman Is Deported

In the fall of 1919, federal agents arrested hundreds of "Bolsheviks" they considered a "menace to law and order." On December 6, 1919, anarchist Emma Goldman, seen here hiding her face, was escorted to detention on Ellis Island, which had welcomed millions of immigrants over the years. Two weeks later, Goldman and 248 others were put on the aging troopship *Buford* and deported to Soviet Russia. Some of this crowd (and much of America) was happy to see "Red Emma" and her friends sent, as the State Department said, "whence they came."
© Bettmann / Corbis.

If You are a Stranger in the City

If you want a job   If you want a place to live
If you are having trouble with your employer
If you want information or advice of any kind
CALL UPON
The CHICAGO LEAGUE ON URBAN
CONDITIONS AMONG NEGROES
3719 South State Street
Telephone Douglas 9098   T. ARNOLD HILL, Executive Secretary
No charges—no fees. We want to help YOU

SELF-HELP

1. Do not loaf. Get a job at once.
2. Do not live in crowded rooms. Others can be obtained.
3. Do not carry on loud conversations in street cars and public places.
4. Do not keep your children out of school.
5. Do not send for your family until you get a job.
6. Do not think you can hold your job unless you are industrious, sober, efficient and prompt.

Cleanliness and fresh air are necessary for good health. In case of sickness send immediately for a good physician. Become an active member in some church as soon as you reach the city.

Issued by

African Americans Migrate North

In 1912, this southern family arrived in its new home in an unnamed northern city. Dressed in their Sunday best, they carried the rest of what they owned in two suitcases. Several factors combined to prompt the massive African American migration out of the South. To the burden of racism was added the steady erosion of opportunities to make a living. In the 1920s, many rural blacks lost work when boll weevils drastically reduced the cotton crop. Then mechanization and government programs to support crop prices by reducing acreage drove many more people off the land.

In Chicago, the young Urban League sought to ease the transition of southern blacks to life in the North. As the card suggests, new arrivals—mostly rural, agricultural people—faced a raft of difficulties, including finding work in factories, places to live in a confusing, congested city, and getting along with their northern employers. Other Urban League cards advised hard work, sobriety, cleanliness, finding a church, getting children into school, and speaking softly in public places.

Photograph: Photographs and Prints Division, Schomburg Center for Research in Black Culture, New York Public Library, Astor, Lenox and Tilden Foundations; card: Special Collections, The University Library, University of Illinois at Chicago.

whites as domestics for $2 or less a week. Whites remained committed to keeping blacks down. "If we own a good farm or horse, or cow, or bird-dog, or yoke of oxen," a black Mississippian observed in 1913, "we are harassed until we are bound to sell, give away, or run away, before we can have any peace in our lives."

The First World War provided African Americans with the opportunity to escape the South's cotton fields and kitchens. Just as production demands in northern factories were increasing, the war deprived companies of their traditional sources of labor—immigrants and white male workers. War caused the number of European immigrants to fall from more than a million in 1914 to 31,000 in 1918. In addition, war channeled some 5 million American workers into military service. When acute labor shortages caused northern industries to turn to black labor, labor recruiters, newspapers, and word of mouth spread the news that north-

> The First World War provided African Americans with the opportunity to escape the South's cotton fields and kitchens.

ern factories had jobs for African Americans. Young black men, who made up the bulk of the early migrants, found work in steel mills, ship-yards, munitions plants, railroad yards, and mines. From 1915 to 1920, a half million blacks (approximately 10 percent of the South's black population) boarded trains bound for Philadelphia, Detroit, Cleveland, Chicago, St. Louis, and other industrial cities.

Opportunities differed from city to city. In Detroit, for example, blacks found work in automobile factories. Ford and other companies established strong relations with urban black churches, which acted as recruiters for the labor-strapped industry. Workers at Ford wore badges to get in the gates, and black men were so proud of their jobs that they wore their badges to church on Sunday. Thousands of migrants wrote home to tell family and friends about their experiences in the North. One man announced proudly that he had recently been promoted to "first assistant to the head carpenter." He added, "I should have been here twenty years ago. I just begin to feel like a man. . . . My children are going to the same school with the whites and I don't have to [h]umble to no one. I have registered—will vote the next election and there ain't any 'yes sir'—it's all yes and no and Sam and Bill."

But the North was not the promised land. Black men stood on the lowest rungs of the labor ladder. Jobs of any kind proved scarce for black women. Limited by both race and sex, most worked as domestic servants as they did in the South. The existing black middle classes sometimes shunned the less educated, less sophisticated rural Southerners crowding into northern cities. Many whites, fearful of losing jobs and status, lashed out against the new migrants. Savage race riots ripped through two dozen northern cities. The worst occurred on a hot July night in 1917 when a mob of whites invaded a section of East St. Louis, Illinois, crowded with blacks who had been recruited to help break a strike. The mob murdered at least thirty-nine people and left most of the black district in flames. In 1918, the nation witnessed ninety-six lynchings of blacks, some of them returning war veterans still in uniform.

African Americans in the military also suffered from racial violence. The most disastrous episode occurred in August 1917 when a group of armed black soldiers went to Houston, Texas, to avenge incidents of harassment by the police. In the clash that followed, thirteen whites, including several policemen, and one black soldier were killed. With vengeful swiftness that denied any appeal, a military court had thirteen of the black soldiers hanged and sentenced forty-one others to life imprisonment. (See "Historical Question," page 822.)

While the North was not the promised land, it was better than the South. Most migrants stayed and encouraged friends and family to follow. By 1940, more than one million blacks had left the South, profoundly changing their own lives and the course of the nation's history. The rising black population in the North led to the emergence of black enclaves, "cities within cities," such as Harlem in New York and the South Side of Chicago. These assertive communities provided a solid foundation for black protest and political organization in the years ahead. Indeed, drawing strength from these black urban communities, the NAACP evolved from an interracial organization to a largely black organization, funded by its growing black membership.

At virtually the same moment that black Americans streamed into northern cities, another migration was under way in the American Southwest. Between 1910 and 1920, the Mexican-born population in the United States soared from 222,000 to 478,000. Mexican immigration was the result of developments on both sides of the border. At the turn of the century the Mexican dictator Porfirio Díaz initiated land policies that decimated poor farmers. When the Mexicans revolted against Díaz in 1910, initiating a ten-year civil war that eventually claimed the lives of one to two million people, the trickle of migration became a flood. North of the border, the Chinese Exclusion Act of 1882, then the disruption of World War I, cut off the supply of cheap foreign labor and caused western employers in the expanding rail, mining, construction, and agricultural industries to look south to Mexico for workers.

As a result of Americans' racial stereotyping of Mexicans—a U.S. government economist described them as "docile, patient, usually orderly in camp, fairly intelligent under competent supervision, obedient and cheap"—Mexicans were considered excellent prospects for manual labor but not for citizenship. Employers tried to dampen racial fears by stressing that the immigrants were only temporary residents, no lasting

> By 1940, more than one million blacks had left the South, profoundly changing their own lives and the course of the nation's history.

threat. "Like a pigeon," a spokesman for the California Farm Bureau Federation said, "he goes back to roost." Even after the revelation of the Zimmermann telegram, when the *Los Angeles Times* denounced Germany's "proposed alliance with Mexico" and accused recent Mexican migrants of "treason and sedition within our own gates," the need for laborers trumped **nativist** sentiment. And in 1917, when anti-immigration advocates convinced Congress to do something about foreigners coming into the United States, the restrictive legislation bowed to southwestern industry and exempted Mexicans. By 1920, ethnic Mexicans made up some three-fourths of California's farm laborers. They were also crucial to the Texas economy, comprising 75 percent of laborers in the cotton fields and in construction.

Like immigrants from Europe and black migrants from the South, Mexicans in the American Southwest dreamed of a better life. And like the others, they found both opportunity and disappointment. Wages were better than in Mexico, but life in the fields, mines, and factories was hard, and living conditions—in box cars or labor camps or urban barrios—often dismal. Signs that read "No Mexicans Allowed" increased rather than declined. Mexicanas nurtured families, but many women also worked for wages. Thousands of women, for example, picked cotton, sometimes dragging hundred-pound cotton sacks with a baby perched on top. *Los recien llegados* (the recent arrivals) encountered mixed reactions among Mexican Americans, some of whom had lived in the Southwest for a century or more. One Mexican American expressed the ambivalence: "We are all Mexicans anyway because the *gueros* [Anglos] treat us all alike," he declared, but he also called for immigration quotas because the recent arrivals drove down wages and incited white prejudice that affected all ethnic Mexicans. *Los recien llegados* also harbored mixed feelings, sometimes calling Mexican Americans *pochos* (faded or bleached ones).

Despite this friction, large-scale immigration into the Southwest meant a resurgence of the Mexican cultural presence, which in time became the basis for greater solidarity and political action for the ethnic Mexican population. Shortly after World War I, Mexican Americans began organizing, a development that culminated with the formation of the League of United Latin American Citizens (LULAC) in Texas in 1929.

> Like immigrants from Europe and black migrants from the South, Mexicans in the American Southwest dreamed of a better life.

Mexican Women Arriving in El Paso, 1911

These new arrivals, carrying bundles and wearing traditional shawls, try to get their bearings on arriving in El Paso, Texas—the Ellis Island for Mexican immigrants. Perhaps they are looking for a family member who preceded them, or perhaps they are alone and calculating their next step. In any case, these women were part of the first modern wave of Mexican immigration to the United States. Women like these found work at home taking in sewing, laundry, and boarders and in the cotton and sugar-beet fields, canneries, and restaurants of the Southwest. Whatever their work, their journey across the border proved life changing.

Courtesy of the Rio Grande Historical Collections, New Mexico State University Library, Las Cruces, New Mexico.

Postwar Politics and the Election of 1920

Two thousand miles away in Washington, D.C., President Woodrow Wilson, bedridden and paralyzed, stubbornly ignored the mountain of domestic troubles—labor strikes, the Red scare, race riots, immigration backlash—and insisted that the 1920 election would be a "solemn referendum" on the League of Nations. Dutifully, the Democratic nominees for president, James M. Cox, three-time governor of Ohio, and for vice president, the New York aristocrat Franklin

What Did the War Mean to African Americans?

When the United States entered the First World War, some black leaders remembered the crucial role of African American soldiers in the Civil War. They rejoiced that military service would again offer blacks a chance to demonstrate their patriotism and prove themselves as citizens. Others believed that black Americans had long ago demonstrated their worth. They instead saw the war as an opportunity to force the nation to pay its debt to African Americans.

A month after America entered the war, the National Association for the Advancement of Colored People (NAACP) approved a series of resolutions, most of them written by W. E. B. Du Bois, known for his bold dissent against the white power structure. The NAACP demanded that the principle of consent of the governed be extended "not only to the smaller nations of Europe but among the natives of Asia and Africa, the Western Indies, and the Negroes of the United States." It declared that black Americans would support the war but added, "absolute loyalty in arms and civil duties need not for a moment lead us to abate our just complaints and just demands." Still, Du Bois in an editorial in the NAACP's journal *Crisis* urged blacks to "close ranks" and to temporarily "forget our special grievances" until the nation had won the war. The enemy of the moment, Du Bois insisted, was German "military despotism." Unchecked, that despotism "spells death to the aspirations of Negroes and all darker races for equality, freedom, and democracy."

While African Americans remained skeptical about President Wilson's claim that the United States was fighting to make the world safe for democracy, most nevertheless followed Du Bois's advice and supported the war effort. On the first day of registration for military service, more than 700,000 black men signed in at their draft boards. By war's end, 370,000 blacks had been inducted, some 31 percent of the total number of blacks registered. The figure for whites was 26 percent.

During training, black recruits suffered the same prejudices that they had encountered in civilian life. Rigidly segregated, they were usually assigned to labor battalions. They faced crude abuse and miserable conditions. One base in Virginia that trained blacks as cargo handlers quartered troops in tents without floors or stoves and provided no changes of clothes, no blankets for the winter, and no facilities for bathing. Only several deaths from disease and exposure moved the authorities to make conditions barely tolerable.

When black soldiers began arriving in Europe, white commanders made a point of maintaining racial distinctions. A special report from the headquarters of the American commander, General John J. Pershing, advised the French that their failure to draw the color line threatened Franco-American relations. They should resist the urge, the report declared, to accept blacks as equals or to thank them for their efforts, for fear of "spoiling the Negroes."

Under such circumstances, German propagandists raised some painful questions. One leaflet distributed by the Germans to black troops reminded them that they lacked the rights that whites enjoyed and that they were segregated and often lynched. "Why, then, fight the Germans," the leaflet asked, "only for the benefit of the Wall Street robbers and to protect the millions they have loaned to the British, French, and Italians?" Why, indeed?

Black soldiers hoped to prove a point. While at first they worked mainly as laborers and stevedores, before long they had their chance to fight. In February 1918, General Pershing received an urgent call from the French for help on the front lines. Determined not to lose command over the white troops he valued the most, Pershing sent black soldiers—the 369th, 370th, 371st, and 372nd Regiments of the 92nd Division—to the front, where they were integrated into units of the French army. In 191 days spent in battle—longer than the time spent by any other American outfit—the

Delano Roosevelt, campaigned on Wilson's international ideals. The Republican Party chose a very different sort of candidate: handsome, gregarious Warren Gamaliel Harding, senator from Ohio. Harding's rise in Ohio politics was a tribute to his amiability and ability to connect with the common folk rather than to any political commitment. On the two most heated domestic political issues of the day—woman suffrage and prohibition—Harding showed little knowledge

African American Machine Gun Company
The members of this company from the 370th Regiment of the Illinois National Guard, shown early in their training, exemplify the proud determination of black soldiers to prove their worth in battle. Once in France, the 370th encountered resistance from American commanders reluctant to use combat-ready black troops for anything but hard labor behind the lines. When desperation in the face of a German offensive in the spring of 1918 gave them the chance to fight with French units, the 370th showed its mettle by receiving more medals for valor than any other unit in the American armed forces. Black soldiers recognized the irony of having to gain respect as Americans by serving with the French.
William Gladstone.

369th Regiment won the most medals of any American combat unit, more than one hundred Croix de Guerre, crosses given by the French for gallantry in war. In June 1918, the French high command paid its highest respect by asking the Americans to send all the black troops they could spare.

When the battle-scarred survivors of the 92nd Division returned home, they marched proudly past cheering crowds in Manhattan and Chicago. Black spokesmen proclaimed a new era for black Americans. In May 1919, Du Bois argued that it was time for African Americans to collect what was due them. "We return *from fighting*," Du Bois declared. "We *return fighting*. Make way for Democracy. We saved it in France, and by the Great Jehovah, we will save it in the U.S.A., or know the reason why."

Reasons soon presented themselves. Segregation remained entrenched, and its defenders continued to hold power in Congress and in the White House. Postwar recession left blacks "the last hired, the first fired." Whites scapegoated blacks and launched race riots across the nation. The willingness of blacks to stand their ground demonstrated a new resolve, but it also meant more suffering from escalating violence. Nor did the armed services continue to offer new opportunities. Until the late 1940s, after the next world war, the American military remained not only segregated but also almost devoid of black officers. Discrimination extended even beyond the ultimate sacrifice. When the organizers of a trip to France for parents of soldiers lost in the First World War announced that the boat would be segregated, black mothers felt honor bound to decline the offer to visit the cemeteries where their sons lay.

It took decades for the nation to recognize the sacrifice and heroism of black soldiers in France. In 1991, as the nation cheered U.S. success in the Gulf War, a Defense Department investigating team, though insisting it had found no evidence of discrimination in the fact that none of the 127 Medals of Honor awarded during World War I had gone to blacks, declared that the time had come to correct an "administrative oversight." For leading a charge on September 28, 1918, up a German-held hill that cost him and 40 percent of his company their lives, Corporal Freddie Stowers would receive the Medal of Honor—until then the only one attained by an African American in the world wars. The slain soldier's elderly sister, who had survived seventy-three years to accept the award for her hero brother, could take solace that recognition came under the command of General Colin Powell, the first black chairman of the Joint Chiefs of Staff.

or conviction, but eventually he voted for them in a nod to grassroots sentiment.

Harding found the winning formula when he declared that "America's present need is not heroics, but healing; not nostrums [questionable remedies] but normalcy." But what was "normalcy"? Harding explained: "By 'normalcy' I don't mean the old order but a regular steady order of things. I mean normal procedure, the natural way, without excess." The urbane *New*

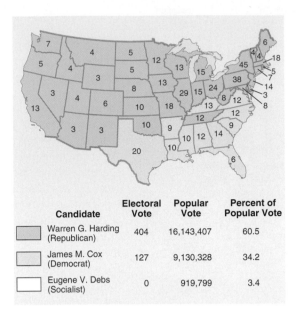

Candidate	Electoral Vote	Popular Vote	Percent of Popular Vote
Warren G. Harding (Republican)	404	16,143,407	60.5
James M. Cox (Democrat)	127	9,130,328	34.2
Eugene V. Debs (Socialist)	0	919,799	3.4

MAP 22.6 The Election of 1920

York Times understood the word's appeal, observing, "Mr. Harding is not writing for the super-fine weighers of verbs and adjectives but for the men and women who see in his expressions their own ideas."

Eager to put wartime crusades and postwar strife behind them, voters responded by giving Harding the largest presidential victory ever: 60.5 percent of the popular vote and 76 percent of the electoral vote (Map 22.6). On his coattails rode Republican majorities in both houses of Congress. Once in office, the Hardings threw open the White House gates, which had been closed since the declaration of war in 1917. Their welcome brought throngs of visitors and lifted the national pall, signaling a new era of easygoing good cheer.

Conclusion: Troubled Crusade

America's experience in the war that raged from 1914 to 1918 was exceptional. For much of the world, the Great War produced great destruction, acres of blackened fields and ruined facto-

ries and millions of casualties. But in the United States, war and prosperity marched hand in hand. America emerged from World War I with the strongest economy in the world and a position of international preeminence.

Still, the nation paid a heavy price both at home and abroad. American soldiers and sailors encountered unprecedented horrors—submarines, poison gas, machine guns—and more than 100,000 died. General Pershing recognized and honored their sacrifice. "I pay supreme tribute to our officers and soldiers of the line. When I think of their heroism, their patience under hardships, their unflinching spirit of offensive action, I am filled with emotions which I am unable to express." Rather than redeeming their sacrifice, however, as Wilson promised, the peace that followed the armistice tarnished it. At home, war brought prosperity, but rather than permanently improving working conditions, advancing public health, and spreading educational opportunity, as progressives had hoped, the war threatened to undermine the achievements of the previous two decades. Moreover, rather than promoting American democracy, the war bred fear, intolerance, and repression that led to a crackdown on dissent and a demand for conformity. Reformers could count only woman suffrage as a permanent victory.

Woodrow Wilson had promised more than anyone could deliver. Progressive hopes of extending democracy and **liberal** reform nationally and internationally were dashed. In 1920, a bruised and disillusioned society stumbled into a new decade. The era coming to an end had called on Americans to crusade and sacrifice. Now whoever could promise them peace, prosperity, and a good time would have the best chance to win their hearts.

FOR ADDITIONAL FIRSTHAND ACCOUNTS OF THIS PERIOD, see Chapter 22 in Michael Johnson, ed., *Reading the American Past,* Third Edition.

TO ASSESS YOUR MASTERY OF THE MATERIAL IN THIS CHAPTER, see the Online Study Guide at bedfordstmartins.com/roark.

FOR WEB LINKS RELATED TO TOPICS IN THIS CHAPTER, see "HistoryLinks," "DocLinks," and "PlaceLinks" at bedfordstmartins.com/roark.

CHRONOLOGY

1914
- **April.** Attempting to impose democracy on Mexico, President Woodrow Wilson sends marines to occupy the port of Veracruz.
- **June 28.** Assassination of Archduke Franz Ferdinand of Austria in Sarajevo starts chain of events leading to World War I.
- **July 28.** Austria declares war on Serbia.
- **August 6.** All-out conflict erupts when Germany declares war on Russia and France; in response, Great Britain declares war on Russia.

1915
- German submarine sinks British liner *Lusitania*, with loss of 1,198 lives, including 128 Americans.

- Settlement house reformer Jane Addams helps form Women's Peace Party to seek peaceful resolution of war.

1916
- General John J. Pershing leads military expedition into Mexico in pursuit of rebel leader Francisco "Pancho" Villa.
- Wilson wins reelection by narrow margin.

1917
- Intercepted telegram from German foreign secretary, Arthur Zimmermann, promising aid to Mexico for war against the United States prompts Wilson to ask Congress to approve "armed neutrality" policy.
- **April 6.** Congress votes to declare war on Germany.
- Wilson creates Committee on Public Information to promote U.S. war aims.
- Selective Service Act authorizes military draft that brings 2.8 million men into armed services; in addition, 2 million volunteer.

- Congress passes Espionage Act, first of three laws limiting First Amendment rights.
- Resentment against blacks migrating northward in search of work ignites race riot in East St. Louis, Illinois.
- **August.** Armed action by black soldiers against racial discrimination in Houston results in execution of 13 of the soldiers and life sentences for 41 more.

- Bolshevik revolutionary government ends Russian participation in war by arranging for a separate peace with Germany.

1918
- **January 8.** President Wilson gives Fourteen Points speech, outlining his plan for peace.
- **May–June.** U.S. marines succeed in their first major combat with Germans at Cantigny and Château-Thierry.

- **September.** American forces deployed to support Russian efforts to undo Bolshevik Revolution.
- **November 11.** Armistice signed ending World War I.

1919
- **January.** Paris peace conference begins; President Wilson heads the U.S. delegation.
- **June.** Versailles peace treaty signed.
- **September.** Wilson undertakes speaking tour to rally support for ratification of Versailles treaty and League of Nations; his ill health in Colorado ends the tour.

- Postwar recession and end of wartime support for labor unions lead to wave of strikes.

1919–1920
- As part of the Red scare, Attorney General A. Mitchell Palmer leads effort to rid country of radicals and aliens.

1920
- **January 1.** Prohibition begins, following ratification of Eighteenth Amendment.
- Steel strike ends without settlement, dealing organized labor its greatest blow.
- Senate votes against ratification of Versailles peace treaty.
- **August 18.** Nineteenth Amendment ratified, granting women the vote.

- **November.** Warren G. Harding elected president.

BIBLIOGRAPHY

General Works

Byron Farwell, *Over There: The United States in the Great War, 1917–1918* (1999).

Niall Ferguson, *The Pity of War: Explaining World War I* (1999).

Thomas Fleming, *The Illusion of Victory: America in World War I* (2003).

Paul Fussell, *The Great War and Modern Memory* (1975).

Ellis W. Hawley, *The Great War and the Search for a Modern Order: A History of the American People and Their Institutions, 1917–1933* (1979).

Derek Heater, *National Self-Determination: Woodrow Wilson and His Legacy* (1994).

John Keegan, *The First World War* (1999).

David Kennedy, *Over Here: The First World War and American Society* (1980).

Nell Painter, *Standing at Armageddon: The United States, 1877–1919* (1987).

Robert D. Schulzinger, *American Diplomacy in the Twentieth Century* (1984).

David Steigerwald, *Wilsonian Idealism in America* (1994).

David Stevenson, *The First World War and International Politics* (1988).

J. M. Winter, *The Experience of World War I* (1989).

Neil A. Wynn, *From Progressivism to Prosperity: World War I and American Society* (1986).

Robert H. Zieger, *America's Great War: World War I and the American Experience* (2000).

Woodrow Wilson and the World

Kendrick A. Clement, *Woodrow Wilson, World Statesman* (1987).

Patrick Devlin, *Too Proud to Fight: Woodrow Wilson's Neutrality* (1974).

Modris Eksteins, *Rites of Spring: The Great War and the Birth of the Modern Age* (1990).

John S. D. Eisenhower, *Intervention! The United States and the Mexican Revolution, 1913–1917* (1993).

Lloyd C. Gardner, *Safe for Democracy: The Anglo-American Response to Revolution, 1913–1923* (1987).

James Joll, *The Origins of the First World War* (1992).

Friedrich Katz, *The Life and Times of Pancho Villa* (1998).

Burton I. Kaufman, *Efficiency and Expansion: Foreign Trade Organization in the Wilson Administration, 1913–1921* (1974).

Thomas Knock, *To End All Wars: Woodrow Wilson and the Quest for a New World Order* (1992).

Gordon N. Levin, *Woodrow Wilson and World Politics: America's Response to War and Revolution* (1970).

Margaret Olwen Macmillan, *Paris 1919: Six Months That Changed the World* (2002).

Charles L. May Jr., *The End of Order: Versailles, 1919* (1980).

George L. Mosse, *Fallen Soldiers: Reshaping the Memory of the World Wars* (1991).

Mary A. Renda, *Taking Haiti: Military Occupation and the Culture of U.S. Imperialism, 1915–1940* (2001).

Emily S. Rosenberg, *Financial Missionaries to the World: The Politics and Culture of Dollar Diplomacy, 1890–1930* (1999).

Martin J. Sklar, *The United States as a Developing Country: Studies in U.S. History in the Progressive Era and the 1920s* (1992).

Ralph A. Stone, *The Irreconcilables: The Fight against the League of Nations* (1970).

Barbara W. Tuchman, *The Guns of August* (1962).

Arthur Walworth, *Wilson and His Peacemakers: American Diplomacy at the Paris Peace Conference, 1919* (1986).

William C. Widenor, *Henry Cabot Lodge and the Search for an American Foreign Policy* (1980).

Over There

Michael C. C. Adams, *The Great Adventure: Male Desire and the Coming of World War I* (1990).

Gerald Astor, *The Right to Fight: A History of African Americans in the Military* (1998).

Arthur E. Barbeau and Florette Henri, *The Unknown Soldiers: Black American Troops in World War I* (1974).

Thomas A. Britten, *American Indians in World War I: At Home and at War* (1997).

John Whiteclay Chambers II, *To Raise an Army: The Draft Comes to Modern America* (1987).

Edward M. Coffman, *The War to End All Wars: The American Military Experience in World War I* (1968).

Kenneth J. Hagan, *This People's Navy: The Making of American Sea Power* (1990).

Lee Kennett, *The First Air War, 1914–1918* (1990).

Albert Marrin, *The Yanks Are Coming* (1986).

Bernard C. Nalty, *Strength for the Fight: A History of Black Americans in the Military* (1986).

Gerald Wilson Patton, *War and Race: The Black Officer in the American Military, 1915–1941* (1981).

G. Kurt Piehler, *Remembering War the American Way* (1995).

Gene Smith, *Until the Last Trumpet Sounds: The Life of General of the Armies John J. Pershing* (1998).

Donald Smythe, *Pershing, General of the Armies* (1986).

David F. Trask, *The AEF and Coalition Warmaking, 1917–1918* (1993).

William S. Triplet, *A Youth in the Meuse-Argonne: A Memoir, 1917–1918* (2000).

Frank E. Vandiver, *Black Jack: The Life and Times of John J. Pershing*, 2 vols. (1977).

Russell F. Weigley, *The American Way of War: A History of United States Military Strategy and Policy* (1977).

Stanley Weintraub, *A Stillness Heard round the World: The End of the Great War, November 1918* (1985).

The Crusade for Democracy at Home

Daniel Beaver, *Newton D. Baker and the American War Effort, 1917–1919* (1966).

William T. Breen, *Uncle Sam at Home: Civilian Mobilization, Wartime Federalism, and the Council of National Defense, 1917–1919* (1984).

Jean Conner, *The National War Labor Board: Stability, Social Justice, and the Voluntary State in World War I* (1983).

Richard Cork, *The Bitter Truth: Avant-Garde Art and the Great War* (1994).

Nancy F. Cott, *The Grounding of American Feminism* (1987).

Robert D. Cuff, *The War Industries Board: Business-Government Relations during World War I* (1973).

Leslie Midkiff DeBauche, *Reel Patriotism: The Movies and World War I* (1997).

Marc A. Eisner, *From Warfare State to Welfare State: World War I, Compensatory State Building, and the Limits of the Modern Order* (2000).

Carrie A. Foster, *The Women and the Warriors: The U.S. Section of the Women's International League for Peace and Freedom, 1915–1946* (1995).

Maurine Weiner Greenwald, *Women, War, and Work: The Impact of World War I on Women Workers in the United States* (1980).

Margaret Randolph Higonnet, Jane Jenson, Sonya Michel, and Margaret Collins Weitz, eds., *Behind the Lines: Gender and the Two World Wars* (1987).

C. Roland Marchand, *The American Peace Movement and Social Reform* (1973).

John F. McClymer, *War and Welfare: Social Engineering in America, 1890–1925* (1980).

Marian J. Morton, *Emma Goldman and the American Left* (1992).

Paul L. Murphy, *World War I and the Origin of Civil Liberties in the United States* (1979).

George H. Nash, *The Life of Herbert Hoover*, vol. 2, *The Humanitarian, 1914–1917*, vol. 3, *Master of Emergences, 1917–1918* (c. 1983–c. 1996).

Ronald Schaffer, *America in the Great War: The Rise of the War Welfare State* (1991).

Barbara J. Steinson, *American Women's Activism in World War I* (1982).

Cass Sunstein, *Democracy and the Problem of Free Speech* (1993).

Rosalyn Terborg-Penn, *African American Women in the Struggle for the Vote, 1850–1920* (1998).

Stephen Vaughn, *Holding Fast the Inner Lines: Democracy, Nationalism, and the Committee for Public Information* (1980).

Susan Zeiger, *In Uncle Sam's Service: Women with the AEF, 1917–1919* (1999).

Disappointment and Reaction

Casey N. Blake, *Beloved Community: The Cultural Criticism of Randolph Bourne, Van Wyck Brooks, Waldo Frank and Lewis Mumford* (1990).

Peter G. Boyle, *American-Soviet Relations: From the Russian Revolution to the Fall of Communism* (1993).

David Brody, *Labor in Crisis: The Steel Strike of 1919* (1965).

Elizabeth Clark-Lewis, *Living In, Living Out: African American Domestics in Washington, D.C., 1910–1940* (1994).

Melvyn Dubofsky, *We Shall Be All: A History of the Industrial Workers of the World* (1969, 1988).

Melvyn Dubofsky, *The State and Labor in Modern America* (1994).

Mario T. Garcia, *Mexican Americans: Leadership, Ideology, and Identity, 1930–1960* (1989).

James R. Grossman, *Land of Hope: Chicago, Black Southerners, and the Great Migration* (1989).

David G. Gutierrez, *Walls and Mirrors: Mexican Americans, Mexican Immigrants, and the Politics of Ethnicity* (1995).

David Levering Lewis, *W. E. B. Du Bois: Biography of a Race, 1868–1919* (1993).

Carole Marks, *Farewell—We're Good and Gone: The Great Black Migration* (1989).

Joseph A. McCartin, *Labor's Great War: The Struggle for Industrial Democracy and the Origins of Modern American Labor Relations, 1912–1921* (1977).

Robert K. Murray, *Red Scare: A Study in National Hysteria, 1919–1920* (1955).

William Pencak, *For God and Country* (1989).

Richard Polenberg, *Fighting Faiths: The Abrams Case, the Supreme Court, and Free Speech* (1987).

William G. Ross, *Forging New Freedoms: Nativism, Education, and the Constitution, 1917–1927* (1994).

Vicki Ruiz, *From out of the Shadows: Mexican Women in Twentieth-Century America* (1998).

Francis Russell, *A City in Terror: 1919, the Boston Police Strike* (1975).

George J. Sanchez, *Becoming Mexican American: Ethnicity, Culture, and Identity in Chicano Los Angeles, 1900–1945* (1993).

Richard Severo and Lewis Milford, *The Wages of War: When America's Soldiers Came Home—from Valley Forge to Vietnam* (1989).

Joe William Trotter Jr., ed., *The Great Migration in Historical Perspective* (1991).

William Tuttle Jr., *Race Riot: Chicago and the Red Summer of 1919* (1970).

MODEL T FORD

Nothing symbolized the 1920s more than automobiles. Americans drove millions of them—Briscoes, Dodges, Lexingtons, Cadillacs, Maxwells, and especially Model T Fords. When Henry Ford introduced the Model T in 1908, Americans thought of automobiles as toys of the rich, far too costly for average people. By the 1920s, millions of Americans owned Fords, and their lives were never the same. Oklahoma humorist Will Rogers claimed that Henry Ford "changed the habits of more people than Caesar, Mussolini, Charlie Chaplin, Clara Bow, Xerxes, Amos 'n Andy, and Bernard Shaw." One of novelist Booth Tarkington's characters expressed some reservation about automobiles: "With all their speed forward, they may be a step backward in civilization." But most Americans loved their automobiles and sped away into the future.

National Museum of American History, Smithsonian Institution, Behring Center.

23

From New Era to Great Depression

1920–1932

MERICANS IN THE 1920s cheered Henry Ford as an authentic American folk hero. When the decade began, he had already produced 6,000,000 automobiles; by 1927, the figure reached 15,000,000. In 1920, one car rolled off the Ford assembly line every minute; in 1925, one appeared every ten seconds. In 1920, a Ford car cost $845; in 1928, the price was less than $300, within range of most of the country's skilled workingmen. Henry Ford put America on wheels, and in the eyes of most Americans he was a good and honest man whose simple virtues were reflected in the car he made: basic, inexpensive, and reliable. He became the embodiment of American industry and free enterprise, the greatest example of its promise and achievement. But like the age in which he lived, Henry Ford was many-sided, more complex and contradictory than this simple image suggests.

Born in 1863 on a farm in Dearborn, Michigan, Ford hated the drudgery of farmwork and loved tinkering with machines. At sixteen, he fled rural life for Detroit, where he became a journeyman machinist and experimented with internal combustion engines. In 1893, he put together one of the first successful gasoline-driven carriages in the United States. His ambition, he said, was to "make something in quantity." The product he chose reflected American restlessness, the desire to be on the move. "Everybody wants to be someplace he ain't," Ford declared. "As soon as he gets there he wants to go right back." In 1903, with $28,000 from a few backers, Ford gathered twelve workers in a 250-by-50-foot shed and created the Ford Motor Company.

Ford's early cars were custom-made one at a time. By 1914, his cars were being built along a continuously moving assembly line; workers bolted on parts brought to them by cranes and conveyor belts. Ford made only one kind of car, the Model T, which became synonymous with mass production. Ford conceived of his product as the "universal car," a boxlike black vehicle that was cheap, easy to drive, and simple to repair. His reward was dominance over the market. Throughout the rapid expansion of the automotive industry, the Ford Motor Company remained the industry leader, peaking in 1925 when it outsold all its rivals combined (Map 23.1).

Nobody entertained grander or more contradictory visions of the new America he had helped to create than Henry Ford himself. When he began his rise, **progressive** critics were vilifying the industrial giants of the nineteenth century as "robber barons" who lived in luxury while reducing their workers to wage slaves. Ford, however, identified with the common folk and sought to claim his place as benefactor of Americans yearning to be free and mobile.

Henry and Edsel

In this 1924 photograph, Henry Ford looks fondly at his first car while his son, Edsel, stands next to the ten millionth Model T. Edsel, the Fords' only child, remained unspoiled by his father's enormous wealth. Forsaking college, he entered the family business out of high school. Serious, disciplined, and an acute observer, he realized by the mid-1920s that General Motors's more advanced Chevrolet was about to surpass the Model T. Henry Ford stubbornly refused to change his automobile, insisting that the "Model T is the most perfect car in the world." Under Edsel's leadership, however, the Ford Motor Company moved beyond the plain, boxy, black, and fabulously successful Model T.

Henry Ford Museum and Greenfield Village.

farm and the small town. Although the nation prospered as a whole, the new wealth widened the gap between rich and poor. While millions admired urban America's sophisticated new style and consumer products, others condemned postwar society for its vulgar materialism. A great outpouring of artistic talent led, ironically, to incessant critiques of America's artistic barrenness. The Ku Klux Klan and some other champions of an idealized older America resorted to violence and harassment as well as words when they chastised the era's "new women," "new Negroes," and surging immigrant populations.

The public, disillusioned with the outcome of World War I, no longer thrilled to the Christian moralism and idealism that had fueled the crusades of progressives. In the twenties, Ford and businessmen like him replaced political reformers such as Theodore Roosevelt and Woodrow Wilson as the exemplars of progress. The U.S. Chamber of Commerce crowed, "The American businessman is the most influential person in the nation." Social justice gave way to individual advancement. At the center of it all, President Calvin Coolidge spoke in praise of those in power when he declared, "The business of America is business." The fortunes of the era rose, and then crashed, according to the values and practices of the business community.

Ford's automobile plants made him a billionaire, but their highly regimented assembly lines reduced Ford workers to near robots. On the cutting edge of modern technology, Ford nevertheless remained nostalgic about rural values. His pet project was to revive the past in Greenfield Village, a museum outside Detroit, where he relocated buildings from a bygone era, including his parents' farmhouse. With its exhibits of homespun family life and crafts, Greenfield Village contrasted poignantly with the roaring, racing Ford plant farther along the Detroit River at River Rouge. In the factory toiled the African American and immigrant workers left out of Ford's village idyll. Yet all would be well, Ford insisted, if Americans remained loyal to the virtues of an agrarian past and somehow managed to be modern and scientific at the same time.

Tension between traditional values and modern conditions lay at the heart of the conflicted 1920s. For the first time, according to the census of 1920, more Americans lived in urban than in rural areas, yet nostalgia idealized the

The New Era

The rejection of the progressive call for government intervention and regulation in favor of the revival of free-enterprise individualism was one of several factors that made the 1920s a time of contradiction and ambivalence. Once Woodrow Wilson left the White House, the energy generated by the crusade in Europe flowed away from civic reform and toward private economic endeavor and personal creativity. The rise of a free-wheeling economy and a heightened sense of individualism caused Secretary of Commerce Herbert Hoover to declare that America had entered a "New Era." But the complexity of the 1920s finds expression in other labels attached to the age. Some terms focus on the decade's high-spirited energy and cultural changes: Roaring Twenties, Jazz Age, Flaming Youth, Age of the Flapper. Others echo the rising importance of money—Dollar Decade, Golden Twenties, Prosperity Decade—or reflect the sinister side of

MAP 23.1 Auto Manufacturing

By the mid-1920s, the massive coal and steel industries of the Midwest had made the region the center of the new automobile industry. A major road-building program by the federal government carried the thousands of new cars produced each day to every corner of the country.

READING THE MAP: How many states had factories involved with the manufacture of automobiles? In what regions was auto manufacture concentrated?

CONNECTIONS: On what related industries did auto manufacture depend? How did the integration of the automobile into everyday life affect American society?

FOR MORE HELP ANALYZING THIS MAP, see the map activity for this chapter in the Online Study Guide at bedfordstmartins.com/roark.

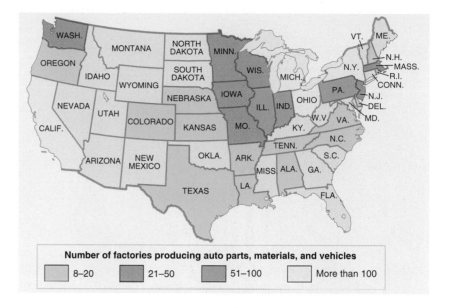

Number of factories producing auto parts, materials, and vehicles

8–20	21–50	51–100	More than 100

gangster profiteering—Lawless Decade. Still others emphasize the lonely confusion of a Lost Generation and the stress and anxiety of the Aspirin Age.

America in the twenties was many things, but there was no getting around the truth of Calvin Coolidge's insight: The business of America was business. Politicians and diplomats tipped their hats to businessmen and proclaimed business the heart of American civilization. Average men and women bought into the idea that business and its wonderful products were what made America great, as they snatched up the unprecedented flood of new consumer items American factories sent forth.

A Business Government

Republicans controlled the White House from 1921 to 1933. The first of the three Republican presidents was Warren Gamaliel Harding, the Ohio senator who in his 1920 campaign called for a "return to normalcy," by which he meant the end of public crusades and a return to private pursuits. Harding, who had few qualifications for the presidency, promised a government run by the best minds, and he chose some men of real stature for his cabinet. Charles Evan Hughes, former associate justice of the Supreme Court and Republican presidential candidate in 1916, became secretary of state. Henry C. Wallace, the leading champion of scientific agriculture,

was tapped for secretary of agriculture. Herbert Hoover, the self-made millionaire and former head of the wartime Food Administration, became secretary of commerce and, according to one wag who testified to Hoover's ambition and energy, assistant secretary of everything else. But wealth also counted. Most significantly, Harding answered the call of **conservatives** to name Andrew Mellon, one of the richest men in America, secretary of the treasury. And friendship counted, too. Harding loyally handed out jobs to his old "Ohio gang" for whom friendship was their only qualification. This curious combination of merit and cronyism made for a disjointed administration in which a few "best minds" debated national needs, while much less qualified men looked for ways to advance their own interests.

When Harding was elected in 1920 in a landslide over Democratic opponent James Cox (see chapter 22, Map 22.6), the national unemployment rate hit 20 percent, the highest ever suffered up to that point. Farmers fared the worst, as their bankruptcy rate increased tenfold and real farm income fell far below wartime levels. Seeking to return the country to prosperity, Harding pushed several measures to aid American enterprise—high tariffs to protect American businesses (the Fordney-McCumber

> Politicians and diplomats tipped their hats to businessmen and proclaimed business the heart of American civilization.

Republican Campaign Decal

Stern and determined, these 1920 Republican candidates seek to persuade voters that they can put an end to radical and alien disruption and restore old-fashioned American values. Warren G. Harding, the Washington insider from the traditional Republican stronghold of Ohio, promises to get the country "back to normal." His running mate, Calvin Coolidge, the Massachusetts governor who gained national fame by crushing the Boston police strike, appears as the exemplar of "law and order."

Collection of Janice L. and David J. Frent.

tariff in 1922 raised duties to unprecedented heights), price supports for agriculture, and the dismantling of wartime government control over industry in favor of unregulated private business. "Never before, here or anywhere else," the U.S. Chamber of Commerce said proudly, "has a government been so completely fused with business."

Harding's policies to boost American enterprise made him a very popular president, but ultimately the small-town congeniality and trusting ways that had made his career possible did him in. The affable Harding resisted admitting for as long as he could that certain of his friends in the "Ohio gang" were involved in lawbreaking. In the end, three of Harding's appointees would go to jail and others would be indicted. When Interior Secretary Albert Fall was convicted of accepting bribes of more than $400,000 for leasing oil reserves on public land in Teapot Dome, Wyoming, "Teapot Dome" became a lasting label for political corruption.

Baffled about how to deal with "my God-damned friends," Harding in the summer of 1923 set off on a trip to Alaska to escape his troubles. But the president found no rest and his health declined. On August 2, 1923, a shocked nation learned of the fifty-eight-year-old Harding's sudden death from a heart attack.

Vice President Calvin Coolidge was vacationing at his family's farmhouse in Plymouth Notch, Vermont, when he was wakened during the night with the news of Harding's death. The family gathered in the parlor where, by the flickering light of an oil lamp, Coolidge's father, a justice of the peace, swore his son in as president. This rustic drama had the intended effect of calming a nation confronting the death of a president and continuing scandal in Washington. A spare, solemn man, steeped in old-fashioned Yankee morality, the new president basked in the public's acceptance of him as a savior.

Coolidge once expressed his belief that "the man who builds a factory builds a temple, the man who works there worships there." Reverence for free enterprise meant that Coolidge rarely stirred in the White House and discouraged others in his administration from taking initiatives that would expand government. With his approval, Secretary of the Treasury Andrew Mellon concentrated on reducing the government's control over the economy. Tax cuts for corporations and wealthy individuals reduced government tax revenue by about half. New rules for the Federal Trade Commission severely limited its power to regulate business. Even the most active cabinet member, Secretary of Commerce Herbert Hoover, shied away from exerting governmental authority over the economy, preferring instead to encourage trade associations that would keep business honest and efficient through voluntary cooperation.

Coolidge found a staunch ally in the Supreme Court. For many years the Court had opposed federal regulation of hours, wages, and working conditions on the grounds that such legislation was the proper concern of the states. Early in the Coolidge years, the Court found ways to curtail a state's ability to regulate business as well. The Court showed its partiality toward management by ruling against **closed shops**, businesses where only union members could be employed, while confirming the right of owners to form exclusive trade associations. In 1923, the Court declared unconstitutional the District of Columbia's minimum-wage law for women, asserting that the law interfered with the freedom of employer and employee to make labor contracts. On a broad front, the Court and the president attacked government intrusion in the free market, even when the prohibition of government regulation threatened the welfare of workers.

The election of 1924 confirmed the defeat of the progressive principle that the state should take a leading role in ensuring the general welfare. To oppose Coolidge, the Democrats nominated John W. Davis, a corporate lawyer whose conservative views differed little from Republican principles. Only the Progressive Party and its presidential nominee, Senator Robert La Follette of Wisconsin, offered a genuine alternative. In the showdown, the Republicans, who focused their attack on "Fighting Bob" La Follette, coined the slogan "Coolidge or Chaos." La Follette's fervent pledges to champion the progressive tradition of support for labor unions, regulation of business, and protection of civil liberties failed to rouse the public. By this time, most Americans had turned their backs on what they considered labor radicalism and reckless reform. Coolidge managed to capture more votes than his two opponents put together, and conservative Republicans strengthened their majorities in both houses of Congress. The 1924 election proved that Coolidge was right when he declared, "This is a business country, and it wants a business government." What was true of the government's relationship to business at home was also true abroad.

Promoting Prosperity and Peace Abroad

After directing the Senate's successful effort to deny American membership in the League of Nations, Henry Cabot Lodge boasted, "We have torn Wilsonism up by the roots." But repudiation of Wilsonian internationalism and rejection of **collective security** offered through the League of Nations did not mean that the United States retreated into **isolationism**. The United States emerged from World War I with its economy intact and enjoyed a decade of stunning growth. Deep economic involvement in the world and the continuing chaos in Europe made withdrawal impossible. Corporate chieftain Owen Young observed: "Whether the United States will sit in the court of great economic movements throughout the world is not a question which the Senate, or even all of our people combined can decide. We are there . . . inescapably there." New

Coolidge Posing as a Farmer
After the labor wars subsided, the image of Coolidge as the enforcer of law and order gave way to the softer image of "Silent Cal." Though he knew the ways of farming from his youth, the hay and pitchfork are mere props for playing the political game. Coolidge's gleaming dress shoes and the official car with Secret Service men in the background give the game away and show that traditional rural imagery had become nostalgic window dressing for the New Era of wealth and power.
Brown Brothers.

York replaced London as the center of world finance, and the United States became the world's chief creditor. American banks poured billions into war-torn Europe's economic recovery. Europe not only absorbed American loans and products but encountered a flood of American popular culture in the form of fashion, style, and Hollywood motion pictures.

One of the Republicans' most ambitious foreign policy initiatives was the Washington Disarmament Conference that convened in 1921 to establish a global balance of naval power. Secretary of State Charles Evans Hughes shaped the Five-Power Naval Treaty, which was signed in 1922, that committed Britain, France, Japan, Italy, and the United States to a proportional reduction of naval forces. The treaty resulted in the scrapping of more than two million tons of warships, by far the world's greatest success in disarmament. This effort gained President Harding

> The election of 1924 confirmed the defeat of the progressive principle that the state should take a leading role in ensuring the general welfare.

popular acclaim for safeguarding the peace without reopening the contentious issue of whether the United States should join the League. By fostering international peace, he also helped make the world a safer place for American trade.

A second major effort on behalf of world peace came in 1928 when American secretary of state Frank Kellogg joined French foreign minister Aristide Briand to produce the Kellogg-Briand pact. Eventually, nearly fifty nations signed the solemn pledge to renounce war and settle international disputes peacefully. The nation's signature, most Americans hoped, would inoculate it from the foolishness of Wilson's notion of a progressive, uplifting war.

But Republican administrations preferred private sector diplomacy to state action. With the blessing of the White House, a team of American financiers led by the Chicago banker Charles Dawes swung into action when Germany suspended its war reparation payments in 1923. Impoverished, Germany was staggering under the massive bill of $33 billion presented by the victorious Allies in the Versailles treaty. When Germany failed to meet its annual payment, France sought to enforce the treaty by occupying Germany's industrial Ruhr Valley, creating the worst international crisis since the war. In 1924, American corporate leaders produced the Dawes Plan, which halved Germany's annual reparation payments, initiated fresh American loans to Germany, caused the French to retreat from the Ruhr, and got money flowing again in Germany's financial markets. Although the United States failed to join the League and rarely participated in big-power politics, it continued to exercise significant economic and diplomatic influence abroad. These Republican successes overseas helped to fuel prosperity at home.

Automobiles, Mass Production, and Assembly-Line Progress

The automobile industry emerged as the largest single manufacturing industry in the nation. Aided by the federal government's decision to spend more on roads than on anything else, cars, trucks, and buses surged past the railroads by the end of the 1920s as the primary haulers of passengers and freight. Henry Ford made a shrewd decision when he located his company

Detroit and the Automobile Industry in the 1920s

in Detroit. Key materials for the automobile—steel, oil, glass, and rubber— were manufactured in Pennsylvania, Ohio, Indiana, and Illinois, making transportation of these goods convenient (see Map 23.1). The keystone of the American economy, the automobile industry not only employed hundreds of thousands of workers directly but also brought whole industries into being —filling stations, garages, fast-food restaurants, and "guest cottages" (motels). The need for tires, glass, steel, highways, oil, and refined gasoline for automobiles provided millions of related jobs (see "American Places," page 836). By 1929, one American in four found employment directly or indirectly in the automobile industry. "Give us our daily bread" was no longer addressed to the Almighty, one commentator quipped, but to Detroit.

Automobiles altered the face of America. Cars changed where people lived, what work they did, how they spent their leisure, even how they thought. Hundreds of small towns declined or died within the decade, largely because the automobile enabled rural people to bypass them in favor of more distant cities and towns. The one-room schoolhouse and the crossroads church began to vanish from the landscape. Urban streetcars began to disappear as workers moved from the cities to the suburbs and commuted to work along crowded highways. Nothing shaped modern America more than the automobile. And efficient mass production made the automobile revolution possible.

Mass production by the assembly-line technique had become standard in almost every factory, from automobiles to meatpacking to cigarettes. Moreover, Ford's assembly-line success also renewed interest in the **scientific management** movement, pioneered by steel industry engineer Frederick Winslow Taylor at the end of the nineteenth century (see chapter 21). In an effort to improve efficiency, corporations reduced assembly-line work to the simplest, most repetitive tasks. They also established specialized divisions—procurement, production, marketing, and employee relations—each with its own team of professionally trained managers. Such changes on the assembly line and in manage-

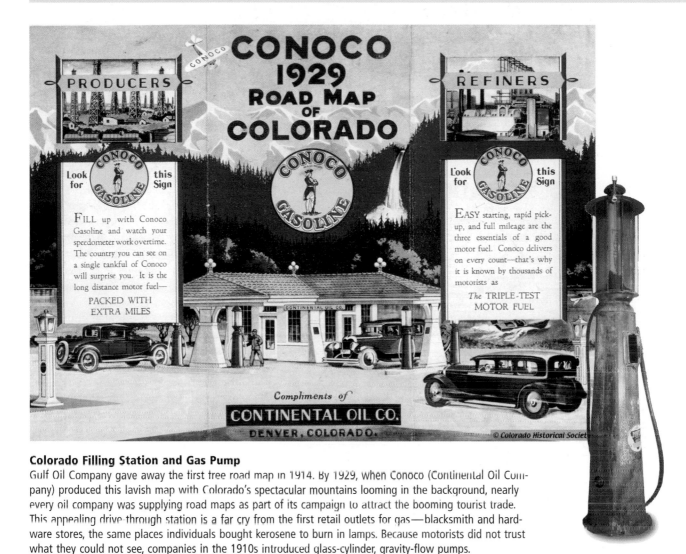

Colorado Filling Station and Gas Pump

Gulf Oil Company gave away the first free road map in 1914. By 1929, when Conoco (Continental Oil Company) produced this lavish map with Colorado's spectacular mountains looming in the background, nearly every oil company was supplying road maps as part of its campaign to attract the booming tourist trade. This appealing drive-through station is a far cry from the first retail outlets for gas—blacksmith and hardware stores, the same places individuals bought kerosene to burn in lamps. Because motorists did not trust what they could not see, companies in the 1910s introduced glass-cylinder, gravity-flow pumps.
Courtesy, Colorado Historical Society.

FOR MORE HELP ANALYZING THIS IMAGE, see the visual activity for this chapter in the Online Study Guide at bedfordstmartins.com/roark.

ment, along with technological advances, significantly boosted overall efficiency. Between 1922 and 1929, productivity in manufacturing increased 32 percent. Average wages, however, increased only 8 percent. As assembly lines became standard, laborers lost many of the skills in which they had once taken pride, but corporations reaped great profits from these changes.

Scientific management also led industries to develop programs beneficial to workers that came to be called **welfare capitalism**. With the help of industrial psychologists and labor consultants, some businesses improved safety and sanitation inside factories and instituted paid va-

cations and contributory pension plans. Welfare capitalism purposely encouraged loyalty to the company and discouraged traditional labor unions. Not wanting to relive the chaotic strikes of 1919, industrialists sought to eliminate reasons for workers to join unions. One labor organizer in the steel industry bemoaned the success of welfare capitalism. "So many workmen here had been lulled to sleep by the company union, the welfare plans, the social organizations fostered by the employer," he declared, "that they had come to look upon the employer as their protector, and had believed vigorous trade union organization unnecessary for their welfare."

AMERICAN PLACES

East Texas Oil Museum, Kilgore, Texas

Re-created Kilgore Street in the East Texas Oil Museum

East Texas Oil Museum.

The automobile revolution of the 1920s ran on petroleum. Wildcatters (individuals who drilled for oil in unlikely areas) fanned out over the Southwest seeking to fill the urgent need. In 1930, they found oil in East Texas, an oil field that became the largest in the lower forty-eight states. The town of Kilgore stands at the center of the vast East Texas Oil Field, and within months of oil's discovery there, wells began sprouting up all over town. By 1931, Kilgore looked like a pin cushion with more than 1,100 wells within the city limits. One oil-crazy Kilgore citizen even drilled a well through the floor of the town's bank. East Texas's most successful wildcatter was H. L. Hunt, who brought in more than 900 successful wells and thus became one of the country's richest men.

The East Texas Oil Museum, which stands on the campus of Kilgore College in Kilgore, Texas, re-creates the discovery of oil and its production in the early 1930s. Visitors can walk down a re-created street of Kilgore and relive the lives of wildcatters and roughnecks (oilfield workers) who swarmed into the area. A roadster is mired in knee-high mud on Main Street, and a mule-drawn wagon struggles to get through. Along the street are the businesses that catered to the tough oilmen. The museum also depicts the process of drilling for oil with a simulated 3,800-foot elevator ride through multiple layers of rock to the rich deposits deep inside the earth. A film shows historical footage of the chaotic early days of oil drilling—gushers like that at Hunt's Daisy Bradford #3; the building boom that occurred when more than 10,000 people rushed to the tiny town of 500; and the day when the governor ordered the National Guard out to keep peace between the roughnecks, oil speculators, and town folks. Outside the museum an old drilling rig stands as a monument to the courage and fortitude of East Texas's oil pioneers and to the East Texas Oil Field, which continues to produce oil today.

FOR WEB LINKS RELATED TO THIS SITE AND OTHER AMERICAN PLACES, see "PlaceLinks" at bedfordstmartins.com/roark.

Consumer Culture

Mass production's success fueled corporate profits and national economic prosperity. Despite a brief postwar recession, the economy grew spectacularly during the 1920s. Per capita income increased by a third, the cost of living stayed the same, and unemployment remained low. But the rewards of the economic boom were not evenly distributed. Americans who labored with their hands inched ahead, while white, urban Americans in the middle and upper classes enjoyed significantly more spending money and more leisure time to spend it (Figure 23.1). Mass production of a broad range of wonderful new products—automobiles, radios, refrigerators, electric irons, washing machines—produced a consumer goods revolution. (See "The Promise of Technology," page 838.)

In this new era of abundance, more people than ever conceived of the American dream in terms of the things they could acquire. No better guide exists to how the business boom and business values of the 1920s affected average Americans than the classic *Middletown* (1929). Sociologists Robert and Helen Lynd visited the small city of Muncie, Indiana, to compile data on its secular and spiritual life. At the end of five years of study, the Lynds determined that Muncie was, above all, "a culture in which everything hinges on money." Faced with technological and organizational change beyond their comprehension, many citizens had lost confidence in their ability to play an effective role in civic affairs. Instead, they deferred to the supposed expertise of leaders in politics and economics and even in child rearing and so found themselves relegated to the role of more passive consumers.

The pied piper of these disturbing changes, according to the Lynds, was the rapidly expanding business of advertising, which stimulated the desire for new products and "pounded away" at the traditional values of thrift and saving. Newspapers, magazines, radios, and billboards told Americans what they had to have in order to be popular, secure, and successful. The advertising industry linked the possession of material goods to the fulfillment of every spiritual and emotional

> Mass production of a broad range of new products—automobiles, radios, refrigerators, electric irons, washing machines—produced a consumer goods revolution.

FIGURE 23.1   Production of Consumer Goods, 1920–1930

Transportation, communications, and entertainment changed the lives of consumers in the 1920s. Labor-saving devices for the home were popular, but the vastly greater sales of automobiles and radios showed that consumerism was powerful in moving people's attention beyond their homes.

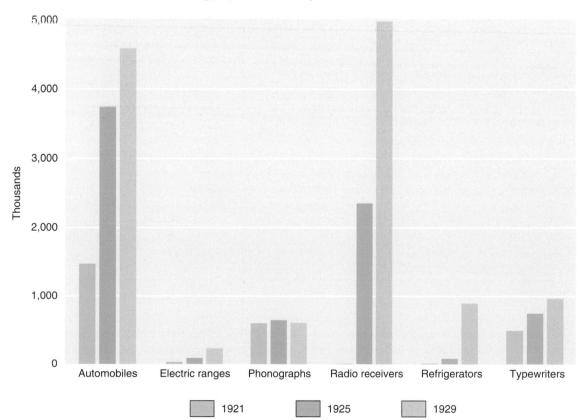

Better Living through Electricity

In the 1920s, after forty years of technical development, prophecies that electricity would be a bearer of leisure and culture seemed about to come true. Thomas Edison, America's greatest inventor of electric marvels, cheerfully predicted that electrified homes would free women from household drudgery. Warming to his subject, Edison suggested that some women might then be able to develop their minds as highly as men. Perpetual light might eliminate the need for sleep. Perhaps, he concluded, someone might even invent electrical means for communicating with the dead.

Edison's hard-driving protégé Samuel Insull led in expanding electricity from commercial to domestic use. Insull's Chicago-based Commonwealth Edison Company, with General Electric and Westinghouse close behind, provided the power to increase the number of homes with electricity from 14 percent in 1910 to 70 percent in 1930. Now the lights that had shown exclusively on the privileged could also shine on average Americans and their aspirations—as long as they lived in the cities.

A barrage of advertising— General Electric alone raised its annual budget from $2 million to $12 million between 1922 and 1930— fanned Americans' expectations of a better life. Without sooty gaslights, their houses would be easier to maintain, and electric vacuum cleaners would lessen whatever toil was still necessary. Electric refrigerators would keep a wide array of food available for elegant entertaining, electric washers and irons would facilitate high fashion, and radios would bring knowledge and music into comfortable, air-conditioned homes. One General Electric ad cheerily announced that, nowadays, "nobody works but ol' man river." Chiding foolish backwardness, other ads insisted that "any woman who turns the wringer [on a hand-operated clothes washer] . . . who cooks in a hot stuffy kitchen is doing work which electricity will do for a few cents per day." Rather than struggling with wringers and scrub boards, women could relax and listen to the radio "soap operas" sponsored by the makers of the laundry detergents foaming in their automatic washers.

Yet, despite $555 million in utility revenues by 1928, the promise of an idyllic electric future was hard to keep. Because electric companies saw little profit in running lines into sparsely settled rural areas, country folk lacked access. And the urban poor could not afford to buy into the fully wired paradise. Most city homes, for example, stayed with iceboxes until the late 1930s because they were considerably cheaper to buy and use than electric refrigerators. Freezers were so much more expensive that, although the advantages of frozen food were known in the 1920s, their use was limited to hotels and ocean liners until the late 1940s. Television, another invention of the 1920s, remained undeveloped for lack of financial support, and air conditioning was rarely used because the very people in the hottest parts of the country who needed it most were least able to afford it.

To the extent that electric appliances found a place in American homes, they did not bear out utopian dreams of leisure. The gleaming new devices fostered expectations of higher standards of cleanliness that housewives could meet only by operating their appliances early and often. In some affluent homes, the burden was lightened by servants who used the appliances. But the number of domestic servants was declining because the booming 1920s economy offered better-paying work

need. Americans increasingly defined and measured their social status, and indeed their personal worth, on the yardstick of material possessions. Happiness itself rode on owning a car and choosing the right cigarettes and toothpaste.

By the 1920s, the United States had achieved the physical capacity to satisfy Americans' material wants. The economic problem shifted from production to consumption: Who would buy the goods flying off American assembly lines? One solution was to expand America's markets in in offices and factories—including those that manufactured electric appliances. Electricity boosters, however, remained unfazed until the end of the decade.

The gap between technology's promises and real life was magnified by the 1929 stock market crash and ensuing depression, which shattered many consumer dreams. While the means to pay for electricity dwindled, the collapse of Insull's electric empire revealed a tangle of fraud and corruption. Insull was indicted and vilified as the bearer of technology's false hopes. Ironically, in the face of such woes, one of the most popular electric inventions, the radio, provided old-fashioned reassurance. In the 1930s, families that had been lured from their traditional closeness around the hearth by central heating and electric light in every room huddled around technology's electronic hearth—the radio—to hear President Franklin Roosevelt pledge protection of their homes and basic values in his fireside chats (see chapter 24). Once prosperity returned, they were assured, the promise of a bright electric future would be renewed.

Hard times eventually eased, and sales of new appliances soared again. But surveys showed that the hours people spent taking care of their households remained essentially the same as before the advent of electricity. Only in the boom years after World War II would electricity begin to deliver on its promise.

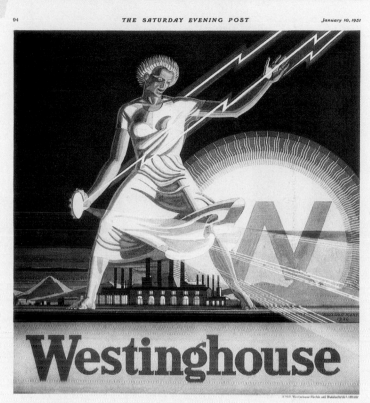

Westinghouse

Advertisements like this one from a 1931 issue of *The Saturday Evening Post* often presented the promise of electricity in terms of its almost magical powers. The illustrator, Rockwell Kent, makes the generating plant in the background puny in comparison with the superhuman reflector of lightning and the fireball next to her. As a result, the "completely balanced" electric refrigerator seems a marvel created out of nature by divine genius. Still, scientists and managers at the corporate giant Westinghouse gladly accepted credit.

Picture Research Consultants & Archives.

foreign countries, and government and business joined in that effort. Another solution to the problem of consumption was to expand the market at home.

Henry Ford had realized early on what became accepted truth in the 1920s: "Mass production requires mass consumption." Understanding that automobile workers not only produced cars but would buy them if they made enough money, Ford in 1914 raised wages in his factories to $5 a day, more than twice the going rate. High wages made for workers who were more loyal

Lucky Strike

Smoking cigarettes promised instant maturity, sophistication, and worldlinesss—and, as revealed in this 1929 advertisement for the popular brand Lucky Strike, a svelte figure. Any woman seeking to remain attractive by avoiding matronly extra pounds could just reach for her Luckies. In the 1920s, Americans smoked billions of cigarettes each year, and they could puff Luckies confident that because they were "toasted," they were "purified." How did smokers know that they ran no health risk? Because precisely 20,679 physicians said so! How has cigarette advertising changed? How has it remained the same?

Gaslight Advertising Archives.

and more exploitable, and high wages returned as profits when workers bought Fords.

Not all industrialists were as far-seeing as Ford. The wages of many workers barely edged upward; many people's incomes were too puny to satisfy the growing addiction to consumer goods. Business supplied the solution: Americans could realize their dreams through credit. Installment buying—a little money down, a payment each month—allowed people to purchase expensive items they could not otherwise afford or purchase items before saving the necessary money. As one newspaper announced, "The first

responsibility of an American to his country is no longer that of a citizen, but of a consumer." During the 1920s, America's motto became spend, not save, and replace, rather than make do. American culture had shifted.

The Roaring Twenties

By the beginning of the decade, psychoanalyst Sigmund Freud had become a household name. Most Americans were spared the complexity of his pioneering work in the psychology of the unconscious by learning about his therapies in popular magazines that stressed self-fulfillment. Still, people realized that Freud offered a way of looking at the world that was as radically different and important to the twentieth century as Charles Darwin's theory of evolution had been to the century before.

In the twenties, much to Freud's disgust, the American media turned his therapeutic wisdom about the sexual origins of behavior on its head. If it is wrong to deny that we are sexual beings, some reasoned, then the key to health and fulfillment must lie in following impulse freely. Those who doubted this reasoning were simply "repressed."

The new ethic of personal freedom excited a significant number of Americans to seek pleasure without guilt in a whirl of activity that earned the decade the name "Roaring Twenties." Prohibition made lawbreakers of millions of otherwise decent folks. Flappers and "new women" challenged traditional gender boundaries. Other Americans, inhibited by conscience or concern for appearances, enjoyed the "Roaring Twenties" at a safe distance through the words and images of vastly expanded mass communication. Motion pictures, radio, and magazines marketed celebrities. In the freedom of America's big cities, particularly New York, a burst of creativity produced a "New Negro," who confounded and disturbed white Americans. And a "lost generation" of writers, profoundly disillusioned with mainstream America's cultural direction, fled the country.

Prohibition

Republicans generally sought to curb the powers of government and liberate private initiative, but the twenties witnessed a great exception to this rule when the federal government implemented one of the last reforms of the Progressive Era, the Eighteenth Amendment, which banned the manufacture and sale of alcohol and took effect in January 1920 (see chapter 22, page 802). Drying up the rivers of liquor that Americans consumed, supporters of prohibition declared, would boost production, eliminate crime, and lift the nation's morality. Women particularly lent support to prohibition because heavy drinking was closely associated with domestic violence and poverty. Charged with enforcing prohibition, the Treasury Department put more than 3,000 agents in the field, and in 1925 alone, they smashed more than 172,000 illegal stills.

Treasury agents succeeded in lowering the consumption of alcohol, but they faced a staggering task. Local resistance was intense. In 1929, an agent in Indiana reported, "Conditions in most important cities very bad. Lax and corrupt public officials great handicap . . . prevalence of drinking among minor boys and the . . . middle or better class of adults." (See "Historical Question," page 842.) The "speakeasy," a place where men (and, increasingly, women) drank publicly, became a common feature of the urban landscape. There, bootleggers, so named a century before because they put bottles in their tall boots to sneak past tax collectors, provided whiskey smuggled from Canada, tequila from Mexico, and liquor concocted in makeshift stills. Otherwise upright people discovered the thrill of breaking the law. One dealer, trading on common knowledge that whiskey still flowed in the White House, distributed cards advertising himself as the "President's Bootlegger."

Eventually, serious criminals took over the liquor trade. They made bootlegging a highly organized big business. Although Alphonse "Al" Capone's business cards listed his occupation as "secondhand furniture dealer," Capone became the era's most notorious gang lord by establishing a bootlegging empire in Chicago that reputedly grossed more than $60 million in a single year. During the first four years of prohibition, Chicago witnessed over 200 gang-related killings as rival mobs struggled for control of the lucrative liquor trade. The most notorious event came on St. Valentine's Day, 1929, when Capone's Italian-dominated mob machine-gunned seven members of a rival Irish gang. Federal authorities finally sent Capone to prison for income tax evasion, but by then he had achieved hero status in the eyes of some immigrant youth eager to escape poor ethnic ghettos as Capone had done. Capone was a gangster, but

he was also a resourceful entrepreneur and successful businessman.

Gang-war slayings generated by enforcement of the Eighteenth Amendment prompted demands for its repeal. In 1931, a panel of distinguished experts reported to President Hoover that prohibition, which Hoover had once called "a great social and economic experiment," had failed. The social and political costs of prohibition outweighed the benefits. Prohibition caused ordinary citizens to disrespect the law, corrupted the police, and demoralized the judiciary. In 1933, after thirteen years, the nation ended prohibition.

The New Woman

Of all the changes in American life in the 1920s, none sparked more heated debates than the alternatives offered to the traditional roles of women. Increasing numbers of women worked and went to college. Older gender hierarchies and norms shook under the onslaught of the changes in American society. Even mainstream magazines like *Ladies' Home Journal* and *Saturday Evening Post* offered radical challenges to Victorian notions of female propriety. The *Post* began publishing stories early in the decade about young, college educated women who drank gin cocktails, smoked cigarettes, wore skimpy dresses and dangly necklaces, daringly rolled their stockings at the knee, swore like sailors, and enjoyed sex. Before the Great War, the "new woman" dwelt in New York City's bohemian Greenwich Village, but afterward the mass media brought her into middle-class America's living rooms.

Politically, women entered uncharted territory in the 1920s. The Nineteenth Amendment, ratified in 1920, granted women the vote and set off wild speculation about how women would exercise their new right. **Feminists** expected women to reshape the political landscape. Women quickly began pressuring Congress to pass laws that especially concerned women, including measures to protect women in factories, grant federal aid to schools, and promote disarmament. Black women activists lobbied particularly for federal courts to assume jurisdiction over the crime of lynching, but white Southerners crushed the effort. Women achieved a measure of victory in 1921 when Congress enacted the Sheppard-Towner Act, which extended federal assistance to states seeking to reduce shockingly high infant mortality rates. Rather

Was Prohibition a Bad Idea?

Americans have always been fond of alcohol. By the 1830s, the average adult was consuming a yearly total of 14 gallons of hard liquor, mostly whiskey and rum. Alarm over what one historian has called the "alcoholic republic" eventually produced two unique developments. First, the United States became the world's only society ever to outlaw its most popular intoxicant. Second, to accomplish that feat, Americans passed the only constitutional amendment to be subsequently repealed.

At the end of the nineteenth century, prohibitionists challenged the thousands of saloons that were springing up alongside factories and in immigrant neighborhoods. Prominent dry champion Reverend Mark Matthews raged against the saloon, "the most fiendish, corrupt and hell-soaked institution that ever crawled out of the slime of the eternal pit." To back up such claims, the Anti-Saloon League produced statistics and scientific studies of drunkenness, vividly portraying horror stories of its destructive results. A powerful coalition against alcohol

emerged. Because saloons were mostly male preserves—awash with gambling and prostitution as well as beer—they roused strong resistance from advocates for women and children, who suffered most of the saloons' bad side effects. Prohibition also became linked to nativism and anti-Catholicism when old-line Yankees and old-time Protestants backed efforts to ban saloons frequented by Irish and German Catholics. Mobilization for World War I added another boost when the army insisted soldiers remain pure in spirit and free of drink. Many industrialists advocated prohibition because efficiency experts advised that alcohol was the enemy of a productive workplace and thus of a successful war effort. With such broad support, the prohibition amendment was easily ratified in 1919.

Prohibition enjoyed some success. At the start of the Jazz Age, saloons disappeared from American street corners, and Americans emerged from prohibition drinking less than before. The annual per person consumption of alcoholic beverages declined from 2.60 gallons per

capita just before prohibition to 0.97 gallons in 1934, the year after prohibition ended. Down as well were arrests for drunken disorder, along with alcohol-related deaths and psychoses.

Nonetheless, the "noble experiment," as Herbert Hoover called prohibition, became the butt of jokes. To critics, prohibition was a ridiculous violation of human nature by puritanical busybodies. H. L. Mencken, a cynical journalist who appreciated the German beer halls in his native Baltimore, jeered that given the depth of human depravity, society would be safer if people were drunk all the time.

An avalanche of other objections helped overthrow prohibition. As gangsters moved into bootlegging and bodies began to pile up, the public became convinced that prohibition was more about crime than about redemption. Believers in individual and **states' rights** joined the clamor by opposing the federal government's attempt to control private behavior. And even the most committed "drys" found it difficult to claim that prohibition was a noble experiment once the Ku Klux Klan used it as a justification for a brutal campaign against minorities. At the head of the parade to repeal the Eighteenth Amendment marched a group of practical businessmen. By 1930, several of them pushed for repeal of prohibition, convinced that

---

than the beginning of women's political success, however, the act marked the high tide of women's influence in the 1920s.

A number of factors helped to dilute women's political influence. Most important, women, like men, held a wide range of political views. In addition, male domination of both political parties, the rarity of female candidates, and lack of

experience in voting, especially among recent immigrants, kept many women away from the polls. In the South, poll taxes, residency requirements, literacy tests, as well as outright terrorism, continued to decimate the vote of African Americans, men and women alike. Some women, deeply anxious about shifting gender roles, refused to join in political activity at all.

banning alcohol was more likely to produce an unruly lower class, angry over losing their saloons, than a sober and docile workforce as they had once believed.

The repeal of prohibition in 1933 set off a rush of profit seekers, including gangsters who converted their bootlegging empires into legitimate businesses. Heavy advertising campaigns, along with story lines on radio and in the movies, promoted drinking and smoking as signs of sophistication and success. Making the old vices respectable and glamorous helped reverse the decline in drinking; by the 1970s, Americans had reached the pre-prohibition levels of consumption. By 1996, 52 percent of the population, or 111 million persons, used alcohol; of these, 32 million were part of a new binge-drinking trend and about 11 million were alcoholics. A quarter of the alcoholics also abused drugs.

Alarm over substance abuse in the latter part of the twentieth century led to sharply divided action. Memory of the prohibition fiasco prevented any serious consideration of outlawing alcohol use except by minors; rescue of the expanding number of alcoholics was left mainly to the self-help of Alcoholics Anonymous (AA), a private group founded in 1935, two years after prohibition

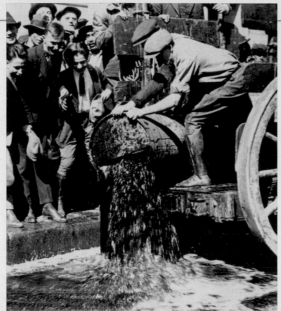

Prohibition Action
Prohibition agents sometimes entertained appreciative audiences. The wastefulness of pouring 900 gallons of perfectly good wine down a drain in Los Angeles amuses some spectators and troubles others. Of course, those who had an interest in drinking despite the law could witness the disposal of bootleg alcohol serenely confident that they could easily find more.
Corbis.

ended. Other drugs, however, were strictly prohibited. Efforts culminated in the Anti–Drug Abuse Acts of 1986 and 1988, which set mandatory minimum sentences for using as well as dealing controlled substances and established the nation's first "drug czar" to coordinate several federal agencies in a "war on drugs."

This new approach to the drug problem created problems of its own.

Ten years after passage of the first Anti–Drug Abuse Act, the United States stood out in the world as the country with the largest proportion of its population in jail. The number of newly admitted prisoners, most of them in on drug charges, rose by 120 percent between 1986 and 1996, bringing the total incarcerated to a record 1 million, at an estimated increase in cost from $45.6 billion to $93.8 billion. By 2000, the number of persons behind bars in America for nonviolent drug offenses alone, a disproportionate percentage of them black and Hispanic, exceeded the prison population of all European nations combined. Yet, despite the crackdown and a corresponding wave of antidrug propaganda, an estimated 25 million Americans continued to use hard drugs, and double that number smoked marijuana.

The unwelcome ghost of prohibition has hovered confusingly around subsequent efforts to crack down on the abuse of drugs. The Eighteenth Amendment was repealed on the grounds that outlawing drink had been a spectacular failure that bred disrespect for the law. America today, however, has suffered an even greater defeat, for unlike prohibition the current war on drugs has not produced a decline in the use of forbidden substances.

Moreover, rather than forming a solid voting bloc, feminists divided. Some argued for women's right to special protection; others demanded equal protection. The radical National Woman's Party fought for an Equal Rights Amendment, which the party put before Congress in 1923. The amendment made all forms of discrimination against women illegal: "Men and women shall have equal rights throughout the United States. . . ." The more moderate League of Women Voters feared that the amendment's wording threatened state laws that provided women special protection, such as barring women from night work and preventing them from working on certain machines. The Equal Rights Amendment went down to defeat, and

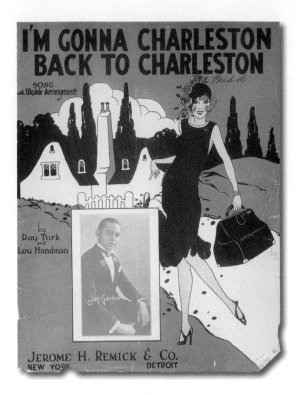

Charleston Flapper
The music to this popular 1920s tune portrays the kind of postadolescent girl who was making respectable families frantic. Flappers scandalized their middle-class parents by ripping up the old moral codes. This saucy young woman wears the latest fashion and clearly suffers from what one critic called "the intoxication of rouge." She's kicking up her high heels in anticipation of doing the Charleston, one of those modern dances the *Catholic Telegraph* of Cincinnati denounced: "The music is sensuous, the embracing of partners—the female only half dressed—is absolutely indecent; and the motions—they are such as may not be described, with any respect for propriety, in a family newspaper."
Picture Research Consultants & Archives.

> Rather than forming a solid voting block, feminists divided. Some argued for women's right to special protection; others demanded equal protection.

women who stuck with a progressive agenda were forced to act within a network of private agencies and reform associations to advance the causes of birth control, legal equality for minorities, and the end of child labor.

Economically, women's relationship to paid work changed. More women worked for pay—approximately one in four by 1930—but they clustered in "women's jobs." The proportion of women working in manufacturing fell, while the number of women working as secretaries, stenographers, typists, and office clerks skyrocketed. Women almost monopolized the occupations of librarian, nurse, elementary school teacher, and telephone operator. Women also represented 40 percent of salesclerks by 1930. More female white-collar workers meant fewer women were interested in protective legislation for women; "new women" wanted salaries and opportunities equal to men's.

Increased earnings gave working women more buying power and a special relationship with the new **consumer culture**. A stereotype of the new earning and spending young women soon emerged in which women spent freely on clothes and cosmetics. The flapper, so called because of the short-lived fad of wearing unbuckled galoshes, was a woman who had short "bobbed" hair and wore lipstick and rouge. She favored the latest styles—dresses with short skirts and drop waists, bare arms, and no petticoats—and she danced all night to wild jazz.

The new woman both reflected and propelled the modern birth control movement as well. Margaret Sanger, the crusading pioneer for contraception during the Progressive Era, restated her principal conviction in 1920: "No woman can call herself free until she can choose consciously whether she will or will not be a mother." By shifting strategy in the twenties, Sanger successfully courted the conservative American Medical Association, linked birth control with the eugenics movement, which advocated limiting reproduction among "undesirable" groups, and thus made contraception a respectable subject for discussion.

Flapper style and values spread from coast to coast through films, novels, magazines, and advertisements. New women challenged older American certainties of **separate spheres** for women and men, the double standard of sexual conduct, and Victorian ideas of proper female appearance and behavior. While the majority of American women in the 1920s were decidedly not radical new women, all women, even those who remained at home, felt the great changes of the era. The greater availability of birth control, for example, meant that married couples could be sexually active and still control family size.

The New Negro

The 1920s witnessed the emergence not only of a "new woman" but of a "New Negro" as well. And both new identities riled conservatives and reactionaries. African Americans who challenged the caste system that confined dark-skinned Americans to the lowest levels of society confronted whites who insisted that race relations would not change. Cheers for black soldiers quickly faded after their return from the First World War, and African Americans soon faced grim days of race riots and economic hardship (see chapter 22).

Still, a sense of optimism remained strong among African Americans. In New York City, hope and talent came together to form an exceptionally dynamic moment in black history. Poor blacks from the South, as well as sophisticated immigrants from the West Indies, poured into Harlem in uptown Manhattan. New York City's black population increased 115 percent (from 152,000 to 327,000) in the 1920s, while white population increased only 20 percent. Similar demographic changes occurred on a smaller scale throughout the urban North. Overcrowding and unsanitary housing accompanied this black population explosion, but so too did a new self-consciousness and self-confidence that fed into political activity.

During the 1920s, the prominent African American intellectual W. E. B. Du Bois and the National Association for the Advancement of Colored People (NAACP) aggressively pursued the passage of a federal antilynching law to counter mob violence against blacks in the South. Many poor urban blacks, however, disillusioned with mainstream politics, turned for new leadership to a Jamaican-born visionary named Marcus Garvey. Garvey regularly mounted a soapbox at 135th Street and Lenox Avenue in New York City to urge African Americans to rediscover the heritage of Africa, take pride in their own culture and achievements, and maintain racial purity by avoiding **miscegenation**. He denounced the NAACP for its reliance on white funding, its acceptance of white members, and the prominence of light-skinned blacks like Du Bois within its membership. In 1917, Garvey launched the Universal Negro Improvement Association (UNIA) to help African Americans gain economic and political independence entirely outside white society. After the war, the UNIA gained thousands of new members and in 1919 created its own shipping company, the Black Star Line, to support the migration of black Americans to Africa (a movement known as "Back to Africa"). Garvey knew how to inspire followers, but he was no businessman, and the enterprise was a massive economic failure. In 1927, the federal government pinned charges of illegal practices on Garvey and deported him to

Jamaica. Nevertheless, the issues Garvey raised about racial pride, black identity, and the search for equality persisted, and his legacy remains at the center of **black nationalist** thought.

During this active time, an extraordinary mix of black artists, sculptors, novelists, musicians, and poets made Harlem their home. They introduced to the world a "New Negro," as Howard University scholar Alain Locke put it in 1925 in a book by that name, who rose from the ashes of slavery and segregation to proclaim African Americans' creative genius. The emergence of the New Negro came to be known as the Harlem Renaissance. Harlem became home to African American intellectuals, artists, and social leaders who deliberately set out to create a distinctive African American culture that drew on their identities as Americans and Africans. Building on the independence and pride displayed by black soldiers during the war, they sought to defeat the fresh onslaught of racial discrimination and violence with poems, paintings, and plays. "We younger Negro artists . . . intend to express our individual dark-skinned selves without fear or shame," Langston Hughes, a determined young black poet, said of the Harlem Renaissance. "If white people are pleased, we are glad. If they are not, it doesn't matter. We know we are beautiful. And ugly, too."

The Harlem Renaissance produced dazzling talent. Black writer James Weldon Johnson, who in 1903 had written the Negro national anthem, "Lift Every Voice," wrote "God's Trombones" (1927), in which he expressed the wisdom and beauty of black folktales from the South. Zora Neale Hurston focused on those tales as an anthropology student at Barnard College. Her masterpiece, a novel called *Their Eyes Were Watching God* (1937), explores the complex passions of black people in a southern community. Langston Hughes, Claude McKay, and Countee Cullen wrote poetry conveying the vitality of life in Harlem. Black painters, led by Aaron Douglas, linked African art, from which European modernist artists had begun taking inspiration, to the concept of the New Negro. In bold, colorful scenes, Douglas combined biblical and African myths in ways that expressed a powerful

> Harlem became home to African American intellectuals, artists, and social leaders who deliberately set out to create a distinctive African American culture that drew on their identities as Americans and Africans.

Noah's Ark

Kansas-born painter Aaron Douglas expressed the Harlem Renaissance visually. When Douglas arrived in New York City in 1925, he quickly attracted the attention of W. E. B. Du Bois, who believed that the arts could manifest the African American soul. At Du Bois's urging, Douglas sought ways of integrating the African cultural heritage with American experience. This depiction of an African Noah commanding the loading of the ark displays a technique that became closely associated with African American art: strong silhouetted figures awash in misty color, indicating a connection between Christian faith and the vital, colorful origins of black Americans in a distant, mythologized African past.

Fisk University Art Galleries.

> Thousands of movie palaces sprang up in cities across the country. Admission was cheap, and in the dark, Americans of all classes could savor the same ideal of the good life.

cultural heritage for African Americans.

Despite such vibrancy, for most whites, Harlem remained a separate black ghetto known to them only for its lively nightlife. Fashionable whites crowded into Harlem's nightclubs, the most famous of which was the Cotton Club, a gangster-owned speakeasy. There, whites believed, they could hear "real" jazz, a relatively new musical form, in its "natural" surroundings. In reality, black performers hired to entertain strictly white audiences had to enter the Cotton Club through delivery doors and could not use the restrooms, which were for whites only. The vigor and optimism of the Harlem Renaissance left a powerful legacy for black Americans, but the creative burst did little in the short run to dissolve the prejudice of a white society not yet prepared to allow African Americans equal opportunities.

Mass Culture

By the late 1920s, jazz had captured the nation. Americans who clung to symphonic music as the epitome of high culture might still call jazz "jungle music," but jazz giants such as Louis Armstrong, Jelly Roll Morton, Duke Ellington, and King Oliver, accompanied by singers such as Ma Rainey, Bessie Smith, and Ethel Waters, entertained huge audiences. Jazz was only one of the entertainment choices of Americans, however. In the twenties, popular culture, like consumer goods, was mass-produced and -consumed. Since politics was undemanding and uninteresting, Americans looked elsewhere for excitement. The proliferation of movies, radios, music, and sports meant that they found plenty to do, and in doing the same things, they helped create a national culture.

Nothing offered such escapist delights as the movies. Starting with the construction of the Regent Theatre in New York City in 1913, thousands of movie palaces, some of them larger and more ornate than European opera houses, sprang up in cities across the country. Admission was cheap, and in the dark, Americans of all classes could savor the same ideal of the good life. Blacks and whites, however, still entered theaters through separate entrances and sat separately.

The center of the film industry moved in the 1920s from makeshift sound stages in New York City to Hollywood, California, where producers found open space and endless sunshine. A new breed of entrepreneur, the movie mogul, soon discovered the successful formula of combining opulence, sex, and adventure. By 1929, Hollywood was drawing more than 80 million people to the movies in a single week, as many as lived in the entire country. Rudolph Valentino, described as "catnip to women," and Clara Bow, the "It Girl" (everyone knew what *it* was), became household names. "America's Sweetheart," Mary Pickford, and her real-life husband, Douglas Fairbanks, offered more wholesome adventure. Comedy made the closest connection

Heroes and Heroines

Two kinds of women look up adoringly at two kinds of 1920s heroes. A wholesome image is seen to the left on this 1927 cover of *People Popular Monthly* magazine. The healthy outdoor girl, smartly turned out in her raccoon coat and pennant, flatters a naive college football hero but remains in control. At the right, the pale, sensitive Vilma Banky kneels imploringly before the hypnotic gaze of the movies' greatest heartthrob, Rudolph Valentino. The 1926 movie poster titillates with ambivalence: Is the pale heroine beseeching her kidnapper to release her? Or is she swooning with desire as the sheik begins to disrobe?

Magazine: Picture Research Consultants & Archives; poster: Billy Rose Theatre Collection, The New York Public Library at Lincoln Center.

with audiences, however, especially in calling sympathetic attention to the pitfalls and absurdity ordinary people experienced. Most loved of all the comics was Charlie Chaplin, whose famous character, the wistful tramp, showed an endearing inability to cope with the rules and complexities of modern life.

Americans also found heroes in sports. Baseball, professionalized since 1869 and segregated into white and black leagues, solidified its place as the national pastime in the 1920s (Figure 23.2). It remained essentially a game played by and for the working class, an outlet for raw energy with a tinge of rebelliousness. In George

Herman "Babe" Ruth, baseball had the most cherished free spirit of the time. An incorrigible whose parents sent him to reform school at age eight, Ruth mixed his record-setting home runs with rowdy escapades, satisfying the view that sports offered a way to break out of the ordinariness of everyday life.

The public also fell in love with a young boxer from the grim mining districts of Colorado. As a teenager, Jack Dempsey had made his living hanging around saloons betting he could beat anyone in the house. When he took the heavyweight crown just after World War I, he was revered as America's equalizer, a stand-in for the average American who felt increasingly confined by bureaucracy and machine-made culture. In Philadelphia in 1926, a crowd of 125,000 fans saw challenger Gene Tunney carve up and defeat the people's champ.

Football, essentially a college sport, held greater sway with the upper classes. The most famous coach, Knute Rockne of Notre Dame, celebrated football for its life lessons of hard work and teamwork. Let the professors make learning as interesting and significant as football, Rockne advised, and the problem of getting youth to learn would disappear. But in keeping with the times, football moved toward a more commercial spectacle. The gridiron's greatest hero, Harold "Red" Grange, the "Galloping Ghost," a quiet, straitlaced son of the prairies, led the way by going from stardom at the University of Illinois to the Chicago Bears in the new professional football league.

The decade's hero worship reached its zenith in the celebration of Charles Lindbergh, a young pilot who set out on May 20, 1927, from Long Island in his specially built single-engine plane, *The Spirit of St. Louis*, to become the first person to fly nonstop across the Atlantic. Thirty-three hours later, Lindbergh landed in the midst of a wildly cheering crowd at the Paris airport. Newspapers tagged Lindbergh the "Lone Eagle"—the perfect hero for an age that celebrated individual accomplishment. "Charles Lindbergh," one journalist proclaimed, "is the stuff out of which have been made the pioneers that opened up the wilderness. His are the qualities which we, as a people, must nourish." Lindbergh realized, however, that technical and organizational complexity was fast reducing chances for solitary achievement. To make the point about a new sort of heroism, he entitled his book about the flight *We* (1927) to include the machine that made it all possible.

Another machine—the radio—became important to mass culture in the 1920s. The nation's first licensed radio station, KDKA in Pittsburgh, began broadcasting in 1920, and soon American airwaves buzzed with news, sermons, soap operas, sports, comedy, and music. Americans isolated in the high plains laughed at the latest jokes from New York. For the first time, citizens were able to listen to the voices of political candidates without leaving home. Because they could now reach prospective customers in their own homes, advertisers bankrolled the new medium's rapid growth. Between 1922 and 1929,

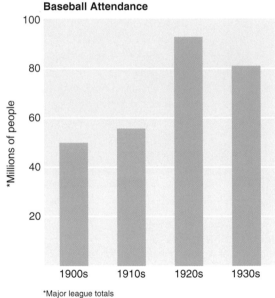

FIGURE 23.2 Movie and Baseball Attendance
America's favorite pastimes, movies and baseball, served as a fever chart for the economy. The percentage of national income spent by spectators of movies and major league baseball remained nearly constant during the interwar years; the rise and fall of weekly movie attendance and seasonal baseball attendance mirrored the rise and fall of prosperity.

the number of radio stations in the United States increased from 30 to 606. In those seven short years, homes with radios jumped from 60,000 to a staggering 10,250,000.

Radio added to the spread of popular music, especially jazz. Young people particularly welcomed jazz's energetic style and its suggestion of freedom and sexual openness. Jazz provided the sounds for the rebellious mood of youth, who for the first time in the 1920s became a social class distinct in itself. As the traditional bonds of community, religion, and family loosened, the young felt less pressure to imitate their elders and more freedom to develop their own culture. An increasing number of college students helped the "rah-rah" style of college life become a fad, promoted in movies, songs, and advertisements. The collegiate set was the vanguard of the decade's "flaming youth."

The Lost Generation

Some writers and artists felt alienated from America's mass-culture society, which they found shallow, anti-intellectual, and materialistic. Adoration of silly movie stars and other favorites of popular culture disgusted them. Moreover, they believed that business culture and business values blighted nearly every aspect of American life. To their minds, Henry Ford made a poor hero. Young, white, and mostly college educated, these expatriates, as they came to be called, felt embittered by the war and renounced the progressives who had promoted it as a crusade. For them, Europe—not Hollywood or Harlem—seemed the place to seek their renaissance.

The American-born writer Gertrude Stein, long established in Paris, remarked famously as the young exiles gathered around her, "They are the lost generation." Most of the expatriates, however, believed to the contrary that they had finally found themselves. The cost of living in Paris was low and the culture receptive to free expression. Far from the complications of home and steady work, the expatriates helped launch the most creative period in American art and literature in the twentieth century.

The novelist whose spare, clean style best exemplified the expatriate efforts to make art mirror basic reality was Ernest Hemingway. Hemingway's experience in the war convinced him that the world in which he was raised, with its Christian moralism and belief in progress, was bankrupt. His code of honor dismissed creeds, ideologies, and patriotism as pious attempts to cover up the fact that life is a losing battle with death. Hemingway expressed his ideal of macho courage, "grace under pressure," with unflinching directness in his novel *The Sun Also Rises* (1926). The central characters discover little to sustain them on a journey through Spain and France except their own animal ability to appreciate sensual experience and endure suffering. Admirers found the novel's terse language

and hard lessons perfect expressions of a world stripped of illusions.

Many writers who remained in America were exiles in spirit. Before the war, intellectuals had eagerly joined progressive, even radical, reform movements that sought social uplift and regeneration. Afterward, they were more likely to act as lonely critics of American cultural barrenness and vulgarity. With prose dripping with scorn for conventional values, novelist Sinclair Lewis in *Main Street* (1920) and *Babbitt* (1922) satirized his native Midwest as a cultural wasteland. Humorists like James Thurber created outlandish characters to poke fun at American stupidity and inhibitions. And southern writers, led by William Faulkner, railed against the South's reputation as a literary desert by exploring the dark undercurrents of that region's grim class and race heritage. But worries about alienation surfaced as well. Although he gained fame and wealth as chronicler of flaming youth, F. Scott Fitzgerald spoke sadly in *This Side of Paradise* (1920) of a disillusioned generation "grown up to find all Gods dead, all wars fought, all faiths in man shaken."

Resistance to Change

Large areas of the country did not share in the wealth of the 1920s and had little confidence that they would anytime soon. By the end of the decade, 40 percent of the nation's farmers were landless, and 90 percent of rural homes had no indoor plumbing, gas, or electricity. Rural America had known a troubled relationship with urban America since the nineteenth century, but wariness and distrust turned to despair in 1920s when the census reported that the majority of the population had shifted from the country to the city (Map 23.2). Urban domination over the nation's political and cultural life and sharply rising economic disparity drove rural Americans in often ugly, reactionary directions.

The cities seemed to stand for everything rural areas stood against. Rural America imagined itself as solidly Anglo-Saxon (despite the presence of millions of African Americans in the South and Mexican Americans, Native Americans, and Asian Americans in the West), and the cities seemed to be filling up with immigrants—swarthy, different, and potentially dangerous foreigners. Rural America was the home

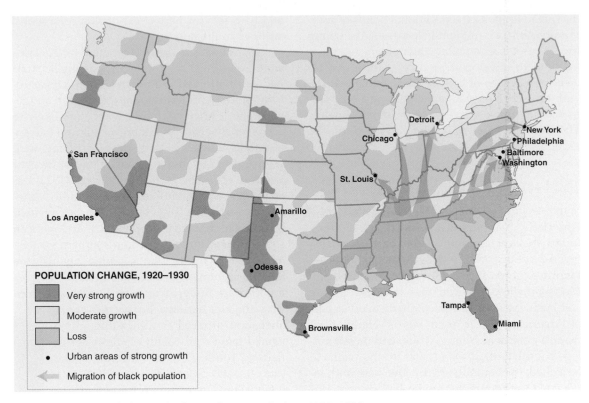

POPULATION CHANGE, 1920–1930

Very strong growth

Moderate growth

Loss

• Urban areas of strong growth

⟵ Migration of black population

MAP 23.2   The Shift from Rural to Urban Population, 1920–1930
The movement of whites and Hispanics toward urban and agricultural opportunity made Florida, the West, and the Southwest the regions of fastest population growth. In contrast, large numbers of blacks left the rural South to find a better life in the North. Because almost all migrating blacks went from the countryside to cities in distant parts of the nation, while white and Hispanic migrants tended to move shorter distances toward familiar places, the population shift brought more drastic overall change to blacks than to whites and Hispanics.

READING THE MAP: Which states held the areas of strongest growth? To which cities did southern blacks predominantly migrate?
CONNECTIONS: What conditions in the countryside made the migration to urban areas appealing to many rural Americans? In what social and cultural ways did rural America view itself as different from urban America?

FOR MORE HELP ANALYZING THIS MAP, see the map activity for this chapter in the Online Study Guide at bedfordstmartins.com/roark.

of old-time **Protestant** religion, and the cities teamed with Catholics, Jews, liberal Protestants, and atheists. Rural America championed old-fashioned moral standards—abstinence, self-denial, and regenerative suffering—while the cities spawned every imaginable vice. America had changed. Once the "backbone of the republic," rural Americans had become poor country cousins. In the 1920s, frustrated rural people sought to regain their country by helping to push through prohibition, dam the flow of immigrants, revive the Ku Klux Klan, defend the

Bible as literal truth, and defeat an urban Roman Catholic for president.

Rejecting the "Huddled Masses"

Before the war, when about a million immigrants arrived each year, some Americans warned that the nation was about to drown in an "invasion" of unassimilable foreigners. War against Germany and its allies expanded **nativist** and antiradical sentiment. After the war, large-scale immigration resumed (another 800,000 immigrants arrived in

1921) at a moment when industrialists no longer needed new factory laborers. African American and Mexican migration had relieved labor shortages. Moreover, union leaders feared that millions of poor immigrants would undercut their efforts to organize American workers. Rural America's God-fearing Protestants were particularly alarmed that most of the immigrants were Catholic, Jewish, or atheist. In 1921, Congress responded by very nearly slamming shut the open door to immigrants.

In 1924, Congress passed an even tougher immigrant restriction measure, the Johnson-Reid Act. The 1924 law limited the number of immigrants to no more than 161,000 a year and gave each European nation a quota based on 2 percent of the number of people from that country listed in the U.S. census of 1890. The act revealed the fear and bigotry that fueled anti-immigration legislation. It cut immigration by more than 80 percent, but it squeezed some nationalities more than others. Backers of Johnson-Reid openly declared that America had become the "garbage can and the dumping ground of the world," and they manipulated quotas to ensure entry only to "good" immigrants. By basing quotas on the 1890 census, in which western Europeans predominated, the law effectively reversed the trend toward immigration from southern and eastern Europe, which by 1914 had amounted to 75 percent of the yearly total. For example, the Johnson-Reid Act allowed Great Britain 62,458 entries, but Russia could send only 1,992.

Rural Americans, who had most likely never laid eyes on a Polish packing-house worker, a Slovak coal miner, or an Armenian sewing-machine operator, strongly supported the 1924 law, as did industrialists and labor leaders. The immigrants' few defenders were congressmen who represented urban, ethnic ghettos. No one championed immigrants more fiercely than New York City representative (and later mayor) Fiorello La Guardia, who had an Italian father and a Jewish mother and was an Episcopalian.

The 1924 law reaffirmed the 1880s legislation barring Chinese immigrants and added Japanese and other Asians to the list of the excluded. But it left open immigration from the Western Hemisphere, and during the 1920s, some 500,000 Mexicans crossed the border. Farm interests preserved Mexican immigration because of their value in southwestern agriculture. The immigration restriction laws of the 1920s provided the basic framework for immigration policy until the 1960s. They marked the end of an

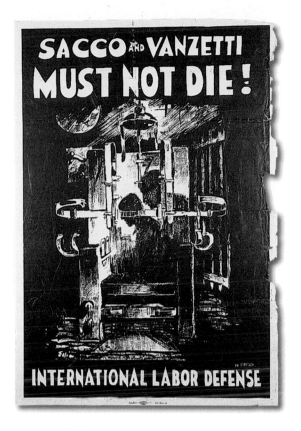

Sacco and Vanzetti Poster
This grim poster sought to galvanize support for pardoning the shoemaker Nicola Sacco and the fish peddler Bartolomeo Vanzetti. The shadows of the convicted men are cast on the electric chair, the sinister device that summoned the two men to their doom. In the 1920s, Sacco and Vanzetti became symbols of the suffering of immigrants, the working class, and political radicals. On August 23, 1927, the state of Massachusetts executed them both. Deportation and mob violence were the typical weapons used against alien radicals and others deemed dangerously un-American.
Collection of Janice L. and David J. Frent.

era, the denial of the Statue of Liberty's open-armed welcome to Europe's "huddled masses yearning to breathe free."

Antiforeign hysteria climaxed in the trial of two **anarchist** immigrants from Italy, Nicola Sacco and Bartolomeo Vanzetti. Arrested in 1920 for robbery and murder in South Braintree, Massachusetts, the men were sentenced to death by a judge who openly referred to them as "anarchist bastards." In response to doubts about the fairness of the verdict, the governor of Massachusetts named a review committee of establishment notables, including the presidents of Harvard University and Massachusetts Institute of Technology. The panel found the trial judge guilty of a "grave breach of official decorum" but refused to recommend a motion for retrial. When Massachusetts executed Sacco and Vanzetti on August 23, 1927, 50,000 mourners followed the caskets in the rain, convinced that the men had died because they were immigrants and radicals, not because they were murderers.

> The Klan's secrecy, uniforms, and rituals helped counter a sense of insignificance among people outside the new world of cities and corporations.

The Rebirth of the Ku Klux Klan

The nation's sour, antiforeign mood struck a responsive chord in members of the Ku Klux Klan. The Klan first appeared in the South during Reconstruction to thwart black freedom and expired with the reestablishment of white supremacy. In 1915, the Klan revived soon after D. W. Griffith's blockbuster film *Birth of a Nation* celebrated earlier Klan racist violence as heroic and necessary. Launched at Stone Mountain, Georgia, the new Klan swiftly spread beyond the South and extended its targets beyond black Americans. Under a banner proclaiming "100 percent Americanism," the new Klan organized a network of local societies across the country. The Klan promised to defend family, morality, and traditional American values against the threat posed by blacks, immigrants, radicals, feminists, Catholics, and Jews.

So widespread was the sense of cultural dislocation in rural America that the Klan quickly attracted some 3 to 4 million members—women as well as men. Women members worked for prohibition, strong public schools, and traditional morality. By the mid-1920s, the Klan had spread throughout the nation, virtually controlling Indiana and influencing politics in Illinois, California, Oregon, Texas, Louisiana, Oklahoma, and Kansas. The Klan's secrecy, uniforms, and rituals helped counter a sense of insignificance among people outside the new world of cities and corporations. At the same time, the Klan appealed to the vengeful and brutal side of human nature, enabling its hooded members to beat and intimidate their victims anonymously with little fear of consequences. The Klan offered a certain counterfeit dignity for old-stock, Protestant, white Americans who felt passed over.

Eventually, social changes, along with lawless excess, brought the Klan down. Immigration restrictions eased the worry about invading foreigners, and sensational wrongdoing by Klan leaders cost it the support of traditional moralists. Grand Dragon David Stephenson of Indiana, for example, went to jail for the kidnap and rape of a woman who subsequently committed suicide. Yet the social grievances, economic problems, and religious anxieties of the countryside and small towns remained, ready to be ignited by other incidents.

The Scopes Trial

In 1925 in a steamy Tennessee courtroom, old-time religion and the new spirit of science went head to head. The confrontation occurred after several southern states passed legislation in the early twenties against the teaching of Charles Darwin's theory of evolution in the public schools. **Fundamentalist** Protestants insisted that the Bible's creation story be taught as the literal truth. In answer to a clamor from scientists and civil liberties organizations for a challenge to the law, John Scopes, a young biology teacher in Dayton, Tennessee, offered to test his state's ban on teaching evolution. When the state of Tennessee brought Scopes to trial in the summer of 1925, Clarence Darrow, a brilliant defense lawyer from Chicago, volunteered to defend him. Darrow, an avowed agnostic, took on the prosecution's William Jennings Bryan, three-time Democratic nominee for president, symbol of rural America, and fervent fundamentalist, who was eager to defeat the proposition that humans had evolved from apes.

The Scopes trial quickly degenerated into a media circus, despite the serious issues it raised.

WKKK Badge
Some half a million women were members of Women of the Ku Klux Klan (WKKK). Young girls could join the female youth auxiliary, the Tri-K for Girls. Klanswomen fit perfectly within the organization because it proclaimed itself the defender of the traditional virtues of pure womanhood and decent homes. This badge from Harrisburg, Pennsylvania, advertises the local WKKK's support for a home for needy and orphan children. Klanswomen also joined in boycotts of businesses owned by Jews and others whom they did not consider "100% American."
Collection of Janice L. and David J. Frent.

The first trial to be covered live on radio, it attracted an avid nationwide audience. Most of the reporters from big-city papers who converged on Dayton were hostile to Bryan, none more so than the cynical H. L. Mencken, who painted Bryan as a sort of Darwinian missing link ("a sweating anthropoid," a "gaping primate"). When, under relentless questioning by Darrow, Bryan declared on the witness stand that he did indeed believe the world was created in six days and that Jonah had lived in the belly of a whale, his humiliation in the eyes of most urban observers was complete. Nevertheless, the Tennessee court upheld the law in defiance of modern intellectual consensus and punished Scopes with a $100 fine. Although fundamentalism won the battle, it lost the war. Mencken had the last word in a merciless obituary for Bryan, who died just weeks after the trial ended. Portraying the "monkey trial" as a battle between the country and the city, Mencken flayed Bryan as a "charlatan, a mountebank, a zany without shame or dignity," motivated solely by "hatred of the city men who had laughed at him for so long."

As Mencken's acid prose indicated, Bryan's humiliation was not purely a victory of reason and science. It also revealed the disdain urban people felt for country people and the values they clung to. The Ku Klux Klan revival and the Scopes trial dramatized and inflamed divisions between city and country, intellectuals and the unlettered, the privileged and the poor, the scoffers and the faithful.

Al Smith and the Election of 1928

The presidential election of 1928 brought many of the most significant developments of the 1920s—prohibition, immigration, religion, and the clash of rural and urban values—into sharp focus. Republicans emphasized the economic success of their party's pro-business government. But both parties generally agreed that the American economy was basically sound, so the campaign turned on social issues that divided Americans. Tired of the limelight, Calvin Coolidge chose not to seek reelection, and the Republicans turned to Herbert Hoover, the energetic secretary of commerce and the leading public symbol of 1920s prosperity.

The Democrats nominated four-time governor of New York, Alfred E. Smith. A New Yorker by birth, bearing, and accent, Smith adopted "The Sidewalks of New York" as a campaign theme song and seemed to represent all that rural Americans feared and resented. A child of immigrants, Smith got his start in politics with the help of Tammany Hall, New York City's Irish-dominated political machine, the epitome of big-city corruption in many minds. He believed that immigration quotas were wrong, and he spoke out against restriction. He signed New York State's anti-Klan bill and condemned the decade's growing intolerance. Smith also opposed prohibition, believing that it was a nativist attack on immigrant customs. When Smith supposedly asked reporters in 1922, "Wouldn't you like to have your foot on the rail and blow the foam off some suds?" prohibition forces dubbed him "Alcohol Al."

> The presidential election of 1928 brought prohibition, immigration, religion, and the clash of rural and urban values into sharp focus.

Hoover Campaign Poster

Herbert Hoover's 1928 campaign poster effectively illustrated his message: Republican administrations in the 1920s had produced middle-class prosperity, complete with a house in the suburbs and the latest automobile. To remind voters that Hoover as secretary of commerce had promoted industry that made the suburban dream possible, the poster displays smoking chimneys at a discrete distance. The poster gives no hint that this positive message would give way to outright religious bigotry in the campaign against the Democrat (and Catholic) Al Smith. Collection of Janice L. and David J. Frent.

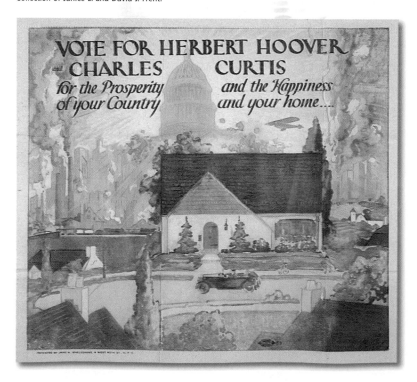

VOTE FOR HERBERT HOOVER
and CHARLES CURTIS
for the Prosperity of your Country and the Happiness and your home....

Smith's greatest vulnerability in the heartland, however, was his religion. He was the first Catholic to run for president. A Methodist bishop in Virginia denounced Roman Catholicism as "the Mother of ignorance, superstition, intolerance and sin" and begged Protestants not to vote for a candidate who represented "the kind of dirty people that you find today on the sidewalks of New York." An editorial in the *Baptist and Commoner* argued that the election of Smith "would be granting the Pope the right to dictate to this government what it should do." The editorial further claimed that edicts from the White House would proclaim that "Protestants are now living in adultery because they were not married by a priest."

Hoover, who neatly combined the images of morality, efficiency, service, and prosperity, won the election by a landslide (Map 23.3). He received 58 percent of the vote, taking all but eight states, and gained 444 electoral votes to Smith's 87. The Republicans' most notable success came in the previously solid Democratic South, where Smith's religion, views on prohibition, and big-city persona allowed them to take four states. Smith carried the deep South, where the Democratic Party's identification with white supremacy prevailed. The only dark cloud over the Republican victory was the party's reduced support in the cities and among discontented farmers. The nation's largest cities voted Democratic in a striking reversal of 1924, indicating the rising strength of ethnic minorities, including Smith's fellow Catholics.

The Great Crash

At his inauguration in 1929, Herbert Hoover told the American people, "given a chance to go forward with the policies of the last eight years, we shall soon with the help of God be in sight of the day when poverty will be banished from this nation." Those words came back to haunt Hoover, for in eight short months the Roaring Twenties came to a crashing halt. The prosperity Hoover touted collapsed with the stock market, and the nation ended nearly three decades of barely interrupted economic growth and fell into the most serious economic depression of all time. Hoover and his reputation were among the first casualties, along with the reverence for business that had been the hallmark of the New Era.

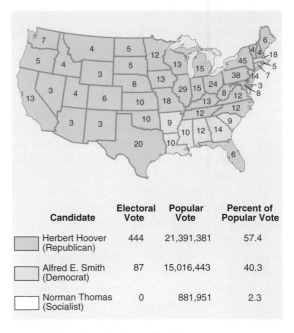

Candidate	Electoral Vote	Popular Vote	Percent of Popular Vote
Herbert Hoover (Republican)	444	21,391,381	57.4
Alfred E. Smith (Democrat)	87	15,016,443	40.3
Norman Thomas (Socialist)	0	881,951	2.3

MAP 23.3 The Election of 1928

Herbert Hoover: The Great Engineer

When Herbert Hoover became president in 1929, he possessed credentials that seemed perfect for the leader of a prosperous business nation. He personified America's rags-to-riches ideal, having risen from poor Iowa orphan to one of the world's most successful mining engineers by the time he was thirty. His success in managing efforts to feed civilian victims of the fighting during World War I won him acclaim as the "Great Humanitarian" and led Woodrow Wilson to name him head of the Food Administration once the United States entered the war. During the 1920s, Hoover's reputation soared even higher when he proved himself an especially effective secretary of commerce in the Harding and Coolidge administrations.

But Hoover was no old-fashioned pro-business advocate like most of the men who gathered in Washington during the 1920s. He belonged to the progressive wing of his party, and as early as 1909 he declared, "The time when the employer could ride roughshod over his labor is disappearing with the doctrine of '*laissez-faire*' on which it is founded." He urged a limited business-government partnership that would actively manage the sweeping changes Americans experienced. "A new era and new forces have come into our economic life and our setting among nations of the world," he declared in 1928. "These forces demand of us constant study and effort if prosperity, peace, and contentment shall be maintained." In his thoughtful book *American Individualism* (1922), Hoover sketched a picture of individualism that was as much cooperative, mutual, and responsible as it was "rugged." He candidly described flaws in American capitalism and turned to his cooperative brand of individual effort to address them. When Hoover entered the White House, he brought a reform agenda: "We want to see a nation built of home owners and farm owners. We want to see their savings protected. We want to see them in steady jobs. We want to see more and more of them insured against death and accident, unemployment and old age. We want them all secure."

But Hoover also had ideological and political liabilities. Principles that appeared to most observers as strengths in the prosperous 1920s—individual self-reliance, industrial self-management, and a limited federal government—became straitjackets when economic catastrophe struck at the end of the decade. Moreover, Hoover had never held an elected public office, he had a poor political touch, and he seemed overly stiff in his starched white color and was too thin-skinned to be an effective politician. Hoover realized that despite these shortcomings most Americans considered him "a sort of superman" able to solve any problem. Prophetically, he confided to a friend his fear that "If some unprecedented calamity should come upon the nation . . . I would be sacrificed to the unreasoning disappointment of a people who expected too much." The distorted national economy set the stage for the calamity Hoover so feared.

The Distorted Economy

In the spring of 1929, the United States basked in the sunshine of a false paradise. Although America had become the world's leading economy, it had done little to help the international economic community after the First World War. European countries, devastated by the war, could not get the aid they needed for full recovery. Rather than stepping in to help rebuild Europe's shattered economy, the Harding and Coolidge administrations demanded that European nations repay their war loans. In addition, to further boost American business, the United States enacted tariffs that prevented

other nations from selling their goods to Americans. Foreign nations thus had less money to buy American goods, which were pouring out in record abundance. In a move that could work only in the short run, American banks propped up the nation's export trade by extending credit to foreign customers. Debt piled onto debt in an absurd pyramid. By the end of the decade, the United States had acquired most of the world's gold in return for its exports.

The domestic economy was also in trouble. The distribution of wealth was badly skewed. Farmers continued to suffer from low prices and chronic indebtedness; the average income of families working the land amounted to only $240 per year during the 1920s. Industrial workers, though enjoying a slight rise in wages during the decade, failed to keep up with productivity and corporate profits. Overall, nearly two-thirds of all American families lived on less than the $2,000 per year that economists estimated would "supply only basic necessities." In sharp contrast, the top 1 percent received 15 percent of the nation's income, an amount equal to that received by the bottom 42 percent of the population. The Coolidge administration worsened the deepening inequality by cutting taxes on the wealthy.

> Ideological principles that appeared as strengths in the prosperous 1920s—individual self-reliance, industrial self-management, and a limited federal government—became straitjackets when economic catastrophe struck.

By 1929, the inequality of wealth produced a serious problem in consumption. The rich, brilliantly portrayed in F. Scott Fitzgerald's novel *The Great Gatsby* (1925), gave the era much of its eye-popping glitter with their lavish spending; but they could absorb only a tiny fraction of the nation's output. Ordinary folk, on whom the system ultimately depended, were unable to take up the slack. For a time, the new device of installment buying—buying on credit—kept consumer demand up; by the end of the decade, four out of five automobiles and two out of three radios were bought on credit. But personal indebtedness rose to an all-time high that could not be sustained.

Signs of economic trouble began to appear at mid-decade. A slowdown of new construction after 1925 indicated that the rate of business expansion had decreased. Faltering automobile sales signaled that, with nearly 30 million cars already on the road, demand had been met and producers would begin to cut back production and lay off workers. Banks followed suit. Between 1921 and 1928, as investment and loan opportunities faded, 5,000 banks failed. Still, the boom seemed to roar on, muffling the sounds of economic distress just beneath the surface.

The Crash of 1929

Even as the economy faltered, America's faith in it remained unshaken. Hoping for yet bigger slices of the economic pie, Americans speculated wildly in the stock market on Wall Street. Between 1924 and 1929, the values of stocks listed on the New York Stock Exchange increased by more than 400 percent. Buying stocks on margin—that is, putting up only part of the money at the time of purchase—grew rampant. Many people got rich this way, but those who bought on credit could finance their loans only if their stock increased in value. Thus, the stock market became dependent on uninterrupted expansion. Speculators could not imagine that the market might fall and they would be forced to meet their margin loans with cash they did not have.

> The stock market became dependent on uninterrupted expansion. Speculators could not imagine that the market might fall and they would be forced to meet their margin loans with cash they did not have.

When stock purchased on margin rose to about 20 percent of the total by the summer of 1929, Hoover urged Richard Whitney, the head of the New York Stock Exchange, to tighten requirements. But Whitney, who later went to prison for embezzlement, gave only empty promises. Spokesmen from prestigious banks and investment houses assured Hoover that all was well. The prudent Hoover, however, rejected the optimistic advice and decided to sell some of his own stocks, saying: "The only trouble with capitalism is capitalists. They're too damned greedy."

Finally, in the autumn of 1929, the market hesitated. Sniffing danger, investors nervously began to sell their overvalued stock. The dip quickly became a rush, building to panic on October 24, the day that came to be known as Black Thursday. Brokers jammed the stock exchange and overflowed into the street. Stirred by the cries of "Sell! Sell!" outside their windows, the giants of finance gathered in the offices of J. P. Morgan Jr., son of the nineteenth-century Wall Street lion, to plot ways of restoring confidence. They injected $100 million of their assets to bolster the market and issued brave declara-

Black Friday

Edward Laning, a mural painter who lost his personal fortune in the stock market crash, gained a measure of revenge in this melodramatic version of panic on the floor of the New York Stock Exchange. The painting shows Exchange president Richard Whitney standing in the center as stock prices fall and brokers collapse around him. A few years later, Whitney went to prison for stealing from other people's accounts to cover his own losses. Why do you suppose the painter placed an American flag so prominently in this mural? Laning later achieved fame for the murals he painted to adorn buildings on Ellis Island and the New York Public Library.

Collection of John P. Axelrod.

tions of faith. But more panic selling came on Black Tuesday, October 29, the day the market suffered a greater fall than ever before. In the next six months, the stock market lost six-sevenths of its total value.

It was once thought that the crash alone caused the Great Depression. It did not. In 1929, the national and international economies were already riddled with severe problems. But the dramatic losses in the stock market crash and the fear of risking what was left acted as a great brake on economic activity. The collapse on Wall Street shattered the New Era's aggressive confidence that America would enjoy perpetually expanding prosperity.

Hoover and the Limits of Individualism

At first, Americans expressed relief that Herbert Hoover resided in the White House when the "bright bubble broke." One observer declared that no previous president "would have been so well prepared as Hoover." Hoover had no use for conservative wisdom that preached that the government should do nothing during economic downturns. He believed that "we should use the powers of government to cushion the situation" by preventing future financial panics and mitigating the hardships of farmers and the unemployed. Hoover was no do-nothing president, but there were limits to his activism.

To keep the stock market collapse from ravaging the entire economy, Hoover in November 1929 called a White House conference of business and labor leaders and urged them to join in a voluntary plan for recovery: Businesses would forge ahead with their pre-crash investment plans, maintain production, and keep their workers on the job; labor would accept the status quo and withdraw demands for improvements in wages, hours, or conditions. Within a few months, however, the bargain fell apart. As demand for their products declined, industrialists cut production, sliced wages, and laid off workers. Poorly paid or unemployed workers could not buy much, and their decreased spending led to further cuts in production and further loss of jobs. Thus began the terrible spiral of economic decline.

To deal with the problems of rural America, Hoover got Congress in 1929 to pass the Agricultural Marketing Act. The act created the Farm Board, which used its budget of $500 million to buy up agricultural surpluses and thus, it was hoped, raise prices. Although the Farm Board bought one-third of the nation's wheat supply in 1930, conditions worsened. To help end the decline, Hoover joined conservatives in urging protective tariffs on agricultural goods, and, with his approval, the Hawley-Smoot tariff of 1930 established the highest rates in history. In early 1930, Congress authorized $420 million for public works projects to give the unemployed jobs and create more purchasing power. In three years, the Hoover administration nearly doubled federal public works expenditures.

But with each year of Hoover's term, the economy declined. Tariffs did not end the suffering of farmers because foreign nations retaliated with increased tariffs of their own that further crippled American farmers' ability to sell abroad. Hoover's response to hard-pressed industry was more generous. In keeping with his previous efforts to promote cooperation between business and government, in 1932 Hoover sponsored the Reconstruction Finance Corporation (RFC), a federal agency empowered to lend government funds to endangered banks and corporations. The theory was **trickle-down economics**: Pump money into the economy at the top, and in the long run the people at the bottom would benefit. Or as one wag put it, "feed the sparrows by feeding the horses." In the end, very little of what critics of the RFC called a "millionaires' dole" trickled down to the poor.

And the poor multiplied. Hundreds of thousands of additional workers lost their jobs each month. By 1932, an astounding one-quarter of the American workforce—more than 12 million men and women—were unemployed. There was no direct federal assistance, and state services and private charities were swamped. Cries grew louder for the federal government to give hurting people relief.

In responding, Hoover revealed the limits of his conception of government's proper role. He compared direct federal aid to the needy to the "dole" in England, which he thought destroyed the moral fiber of the chronically unemployed. In 1931, he called on the Red Cross to distribute government-owned agricultural surpluses to the hungry. In 1932, he relaxed his principles further to offer small federal loans, not gifts, to the states to help them in their relief efforts. But these concessions were no more than Band-Aids on deep wounds. Hoover's circumscribed philosophy of legitimate government action proved vastly inadequate to the problems of restarting the economy and ending human suffering.

Life in the Depression

In 1930, the nation realized that prosperity would not soon return. Suffering on a massive scale set in, and despair settled over the land. Men and women hollow-eyed with hunger grew increasingly bewildered and angry in the face of cruel contradictions. They saw agricultural surpluses pile up in the countryside and knew that their children were going to bed hungry. They saw factories standing idle and knew that they and millions of others were willing to work. The gap between the American people and leaders who failed to resolve these contradictions widened as the depression deepened. By 1932, America's economic problems had created a dangerous social crisis.

The Human Toll

Statistics only hint at the human tragedy of the Great Depression. When Herbert Hoover took office in 1929, the American economy stood at its peak. When he left in 1933, it had reached its twentieth-century low (Figure 23.3). In 1929, national income was $88 billion. By 1933, it had declined to $40 billion. In 1929, unemployment was 3.1 percent, one and a half million workers. By 1933, unemployment stood at 25 percent, twelve and a half million workers. By 1932, more than nine thousand banks had shut their doors, and depositors had lost more than $2.5 billion. The nation's steel industry operated at only 12 percent of capacity.

> Jobless, homeless victims wandered in search of work, and the tramp, or hobo, became one of the most visible figures of the decade.

Jobless, homeless victims wandered in search of work, and the tramp, or hobo, became one of the most visible figures of the decade. Young men and women unable to land their first job made up about half of the million-strong army of hoboes. Riding the rails or hitchhiking, the vagabonds tended to move southward and westward, toward the sun and opportunities, they hoped, for seasonal agricultural work. Other unemployed men and women, sick or less hopeful, huddled in doorways. Scavengers haunted alleys behind restaurants and picked over garbage dumps in search of food. In describing what he called the "American Earthquake," the writer Edmund Wilson told of an elderly woman who always took off her glasses to avoid seeing the maggots crawling over the garbage she ate. Starvation claimed its victims, but enervating, rampant malnutrition posed the greater threat. The Children's Bureau announced that one in five schoolchildren did not get enough to eat.

Rural poverty was most acute. Landless tenant farmers and sharecroppers, mainly in the South, came to symbolize how poverty crushed the human spirit. In 1930, eight and a half million people, three million of them black, lived in tenant and sharecropping families—amounting to one-quarter of the total southern population. Often illiterate, usually without cash incomes, they crowded into two- and three-room cabins lacking screens or even doors, without plumbing, electricity, running water, or sanitary wells. They subsisted—just barely—on salt pork, cornmeal, molasses, beans, peas, and whatever they could hunt or fish. All the diseases of dietary and vitamin deficiencies wracked them. When economist John Maynard Keynes was

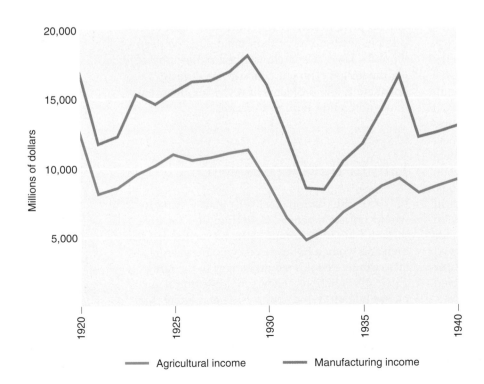

FIGURE 23.3 Manufacturing and Agricultural Income, 1920–1940
After economic collapse, recovery in the 1930s began under New Deal auspices. The sharp declines in 1937–1938, when federal spending was reduced, indicated that New Deal stimuli were still needed to restore manufacturing and agricultural income.

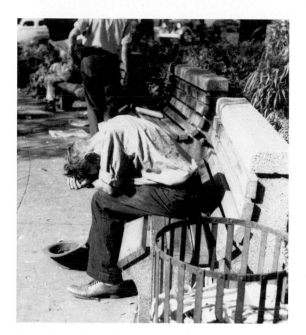

Unemployed Youth
Joblessness was frightening and humiliating. Brought up to believe that if you work hard, you get ahead, the unemployed had difficulty seeing failure to find work as anything other than personal failure. Many slipped into despair and depression. We can only imagine this young man's story. Utterly alone, sitting on a bench that might be his bed, his hat on the ground and his head in his hands, he looks emotionally battered and perhaps defeated. Whether he found work, joined the throngs of beggars and panhandlers on the streets, or cast his lot with the army of hoboes who rode the rails looking for something better is unknown.
Library of Congress

asked whether anything like this degradation had existed before, he replied, "Yes, it was called the Dark Ages and it lasted four hundred years."

There was no federal assistance to meet this human catastrophe, only a patchwork of strapped charities and destitute state and local agencies. For a family of four without any income, the best the city of Philadelphia could do was provide $5.50 per week. That was not enough to live on but still comparatively generous. New York City, where the greatest number of welfare cases gathered, provided only $2.39 per week; and Detroit, devastated when the bottom fell out of the auto industry, allotted sixty cents a week before the city ran out of money altogether.

The deepening crisis roused old fears and caused some Americans to look for scapegoats. Among the most thoroughly scapegoated were

Mexican Americans. During the relatively prosperous years of the 1920s, cheap agricultural labor from Mexico flowed legally across the U.S. border, welcomed by the large farmers. In the 1930s, however, public opinion turned on the newcomers, denouncing them as dangerous aliens who took jobs from Americans. Government officials, most prominently those in Los Angeles County, targeted all Mexican residents for deportation regardless of citizenship status. As many as half a million Mexicans and Mexican Americans were deported or fled to Mexico. Among them were children born in the United States, American citizens from the start who had never lived outside the country.

The depression deeply affected the American family. Young people postponed marriage; when they did marry, they produced so few children that demographers warned that, for the first time, the United States was on the verge of losing population. White women, who generally worked in light industry or low-paying service areas, did not lose their jobs as often as men who worked in steel, automobile, and other heavy in-

Deportation to Mexico
On March 9, 1932, 1,400 Mexicans and Mexican Americans crowded into this Los Angeles train station en route to Mexico. Men, women, and children, with their blankets, bundles, and suitcases, wait for the four trains that Los Angeles County chartered to carry them away. County officers estimated that transportation would cost $15,000, a sum that "would be recovered within six weeks in savings on charity." Perhaps sensitive to criticism, officials promised that "many of the Mexicans will be taken back to their home towns." Some of the deportees were American-born citizens who had never been south of the border.
Security Pacific National Bank Photograph Collection, Los Angeles Public Library.

Unemployed men resented women workers, yet necessity drove women into the marketplace.

dustries. Unemployed men resented women workers. To lose one's job in America's business culture was devastating. After a decade of rising consumption and conflating consumption with self-worth, idle men fell prey to guilt and loss of self-respect. Both government and private employers discriminated against married women workers, but necessity continued to drive women into the marketplace during the depression. As a result, by 1940, some 25 percent more women were employed for wages than in 1930.

Denial and Escape

Under scrutiny, those who had presided over the economic collapse and now sought to lead the nation back to prosperity showed how little they knew about ordinary American society. Chief among the offenders was President Hoover himself. To express his confidence in prosperity, he favored formal dress and manners in the White House, and at dinner, with or without guests, a retinue of valets and waiters attended him. No one was starving, he calmly assured the American people. Contradicting the president's message were makeshift shantytowns, called "Hoovervilles," that sprang up on the edges of America's cities. Newspapers used as cover by those sleeping on the streets were "Hoover blankets." An empty pocket turned inside out was a "Hoover flag," and jackrabbits caught for food were "Hoover hogs." Innumerable bitter jokes circulated about the increasingly unpopular president. One told of Hoover asking for a nickel to telephone a friend. Flipping him a dime, an aide said, "Here, call them both."

While Hoover practiced denial, other Americans sought refuge from reality at the movies. Throughout the depression, between sixty and seventy-five million people (nearly two-thirds of the nation) managed to scrounge up enough change to fill the movie palaces every week. Box office successes typically capitalized on the hope that renewed prosperity lay just around the corner. Leading musicals— *Forty-Second Street* and *Gold Diggers of 1933*, for example—offered a variation on the old rags-to-riches story of the chorus girl who makes the most of her big break.

Grim conditions moved a few filmmakers to grapple with depression woes rather than escape them. Films such as King Vidor's *Our Daily*

Bread (1932) expressed compassion for the down-and-out. Gangster films such as *The Public Enemy* (1931) taught hard lessons about ill-gotten gains. Indeed, under the new production code of 1930, designed to protect public morals, all movies had to find some way to show that crime does not pay.

Despite Hollywood's efforts to keep Americans on the right side of the law, crime increased in the early 1930s. Away from the movie palaces, out in the countryside, the plight of people who had lost their farms to bank foreclosures led to the romantic idea that bank robbers were only getting back what banks had stolen from the poor. Woody Guthrie, the populist folk singer from Oklahoma, captured the public's tolerance for outlaws in his widely admired tribute to a murderous bank robber with a choirboy face, "The Ballad of Pretty Boy Floyd":

Yes, as through this world I ramble,
I see lots of funny men,
Some will rob you with a six-gun,
Some will rob you with a pen.
But as through your life you'll travel,
Wherever you may roam,
You won't never see an outlaw drive
A family from their home.

Working-Class Militancy

Members of the nation's working class—both employed and unemployed—bore the brunt of the economic collapse. In Chicago, working women received less than twenty-five cents an hour. Sawmill workers in the West got a nickel. Still, the labor movement, including the dominant American Federation of Labor (AFL), was slow to respond. During the 1920s, court injunctions curtailing the right of unions to organize and strike had hobbled organized labor. Early in the depression, William Green, head of the AFL, echoed Hoover when he argued that a dole would turn the worker into "a ward of the state." But by 1931, Green had turned militant. "I warn the people who are exploiting the workers," he shouted at the AFL's annual convention, "that they can drive them only so far before they will turn on them and destroy them. They are taking no account of the history of nations in which governments have been overturned. Revolutions grow out of the depths of hunger."

Like the labor leaders, the American people were slow to anger, then strong in protest. On the morning of March 7, 1932, several thousand unemployed autoworkers massed at the gates of Henry Ford's River Rouge factory in Dearborn, Michigan, to demand work. Ford sent out his private security forces, who told the demonstrators to disperse. The workers refused and began hurling rocks. Ford's army responded with tear gas and freezing water but quickly turned to gunfire, killing four demonstrators and wounding dozens more. An outraged public—forty thousand strong—turned out for the unemployed men's funerals, while editorials and protest rallies across the country denounced Ford's callous resort to violence.

Farmers, who desperately needed relief, mounted uprisings of their own. When Congress refused to guarantee farm prices that would at least equal the cost of production, some three thousand farmers, led by the charismatic Milo Reno, created the National Farmers' Holiday Association, so named because its members planned to force farmers to take a "holiday" from delivering produce to the public. Reno and his followers barricaded roads around Sioux City, Iowa, turned back farmers heading for market, and dumped thousands of gallons of milk in the ditches. Although the 1932 rebellion was short-lived and did not force a critical shortage of food, it raised general awareness of farm grievances. Farm militants had greater success with what they called "penny sales." When farmers defaulted on their mortgages and farms were put up for auction, neighbors packed the auctions and, after warning others not to bid, bought the foreclosed property for a few pennies and returned it to the bankrupt owners. Under this kind of pressure, some states suspended debts or reduced mortgages.

Resistance also took root in the fields of California. When landowners cut their laborers' already substandard wages, more than 50,000 farmworkers, most of them Mexicans, went on strike in 1933. About half of the workers won small wage increases. Surveying the strife mounting nationwide, John Simpson, president of the National Farmers Union, observed that "the biggest and finest crop of revolutions you ever saw is sprouting all over the country right now."

Hard times revived the left in America. The Great Depression—the massive failure of Western capitalism—brought **socialism** back to life and propelled the **Communist Party** to its greatest size and influence in American history. Eventually, some 100,000 Americans—workers, intellectuals, college students—joined the Communist Party in the belief that only an overthrow of the capitalist system could save the victims of depression. In 1931, the party, through its National Miners Union, carried its convictions into Harlan County, Kentucky, to support a strike by brutalized coal miners. Newspapers and newsreels riveted the attention of the public with their graphic portrayals of the violence unleashed by mine owners' thugs against the strikers. Eventually, the owners beat the miners down, but the Communist Party emerged from the coalfields with a reputation as the most dedicated and fearless champion of the union cause.

The left also led the fight against racism. While both major parties refused to challenge the system of segregation in the South, the

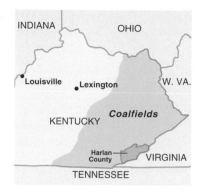

Harlan County Coal Strike, 1931

"Scottsboro Boys"

Nine black youths, ranging in age from thirteen to twenty-one, stand in front of rifle-bearing National Guard troops called up by Alabama governor B. M. Miller, who feared a mob lynching after two white women accused the nine of rape in March 1931. In less than two weeks, an all-white jury heard flimsy evidence, convicted the nine of rape, and sentenced them to death. Although none was executed, all nine spent years in jail. Eventually, the state dropped charges against the youngest four and granted paroles to others. The last "Scottsboro Boy" left jail in 1950.

© Bettmann/Corbis.

Socialist Party, led by Norman Thomas, attacked the system of sharecropping that left many African Americans in poverty and near servitude. The Communist Party also took action. When nine young black men in Scottsboro, Alabama, were arrested on trumped-up rape charges in 1931, a team of lawyers sent by the party saved the defendants from the electric chair. The party also opposed the efforts of Alabama plantation owners to evict their black tenants. Although Communists were unable to force much change on the deeply entrenched southern way of life, their efforts briefly attracted new recruits to the party. From only about 50 black members in 1930, party totals rose to 10,000 by the end of the decade.

Radicals on the left often sparked action, but protests by moderate workers and farmers occurred on a far greater scale. Breadlines, soup kitchens, foreclosures, unemployment, and cold despair drove patriotic men and women to question American capitalism. "I am as conservative as any man could be," a Wisconsin farmer explained, "but any economic system that has in its power to set me and my wife in the streets, at my age—what can I see but red?"

Conclusion: Dazzle and Despair

In the aftermath of World War I, America turned its back on progressive crusades and embraced conservative Republican politics, the growing influence of corporate leaders, and business values. Changes in the nation's industrial economy—Henry Ford's automobile revolution, advertising, mass production—propelled fundamental change throughout society. Living standards rose, economic opportunity increased, and Americans threw themselves into private pleasures—gobbling up the latest household goods and fashions, attending baseball and football games and boxing matches, gathering around the radio, and going to the movies. As big cities came to dominate American life, the culture of youth and flappers became the leading edge of what one observer called a "revolution in manners and morals." The twenties were also a wildly creative and vital moment in American novels, art, and music. At home in Harlem and abroad in Paris, American high culture flourished.

For many Americans, however, none of the glamour and vitality had much meaning. Instead of seeking thrills at speakeasies, plunging into speculation on Wall Street, or escaping abroad, the vast majority struggled just to earn a decent living. Blue-collar America did not participate fully in white-collar prosperity. Rural America was almost entirely left out of the Roaring Twenties. Country folks, deeply suspicious and profoundly discontented, championed prohibition, revived the Klan, attacked immigration, and defended old-time Protestant religion.

Just as the dazzle of the Roaring Twenties hid divisions in society, extravagant prosperity masked structural flaws in the economy. The crash of 1929 and the depression that followed starkly revealed the economy's crises of consumption and international trade. Economic hard times swept high living off the front pages of the nation's newspapers. Different images emerged: hoboes hopping freight trains, strikers confronting police, malnourished sharecroppers staring blankly into the distance, empty apartment buildings alongside cardboard shantytowns, and mountains of food rotting in the sun while guards with shotguns chased away the hungry.

The depression shook up all quarters of American society. Everyone was hurt, but the poor were hurt most. As the laboring ranks sank into aching hardship, businessmen rallied around Herbert Hoover to proclaim that private enterprise would get the country moving again. But things fell apart, and Hoover faced increasingly determined and more radical opposition. Membership in the Socialist and Communist parties surged, and more and more Americans contemplated desperate measures. By 1932, the depression had nearly brought the nation to its knees. America faced its greatest crisis since the Civil War, and citizens demanded new leaders who would save them from the "Hoover Depression."

FOR ADDITIONAL FIRSTHAND ACCOUNTS OF THIS PERIOD, see Chapter 23 in Michael Johnson, ed., *Reading the American Past*, Third Edition.

TO ASSESS YOUR MASTERY OF THE MATERIAL IN THIS CHAPTER, see the Online Study Guide at bedfordstmartins.com/roark.

FOR WEB LINKS RELATED TO TOPICS IN THIS CHAPTER, see "HistoryLinks," "DocLinks," and "PlaceLinks" at bedfordstmartins.com/roark.

CHRONOLOGY

1920
- Eighteenth Amendment, prohibiting sale of liquor, goes into effect.
- Nineteenth Amendment, granting women the vote, ratified.
- Station KDKA in Pittsburgh begins first regular commercial radio broadcasts.
- Membership in Marcus Garvey's Universal Negro Improvement Association surges.
- Republican Warren G. Harding elected president.

1921
- Congress passes Sheppard-Towner Act, providing federal funds to states to help reduce infant mortality.
- Congress passes immigration restriction law.

1922
- Fordney-McCumber Act sets protective tariffs at record heights.
- Five-Power Naval Treaty sharply reduces the number of warships in British, French, Japanese, Italian, and U.S. navies.

1923
- Equal Rights Amendment introduced in Congress.
- Calvin Coolidge succeeds to presidency when Harding dies in office.

1924
- Dawes Plan temporarily saves Europe from economic collapse and renewed military conflict.
- Calvin Coolidge elected president.
- Congress passes Johnson-Reid Act, limiting immigration to small annual quotas.

1925
- John Scopes convicted for violating Tennessee statute forbidding teaching of evolution.
- Alain Locke expresses cultural aspirations of Harlem Renaissance in *The New Negro*.

1926
- Ernest Hemingway publishes his novel *The Sun Also Rises*.

1927
- Charles Lindbergh becomes America's most famous hero by flying nonstop alone across Atlantic Ocean.
- Massachusetts executes Italian anarchist immigrants Nicola Sacco and Bartolomeo Vanzetti.
- Ford Motor Company produces its 15,000,000th automobile.

1928
- Kellogg-Briand pact renounces war as an instrument of foreign policy.
- Herbert Hoover defeats Alfred E. Smith in presidential election.

1929
- St. Valentine's Day massacre claims seven lives in Chicago as rival gangs seek control of the illegal liquor trade.
- Robert and Helen Lynd publish *Middletown*, their study of an average American small city.
- Congress passes the Agricultural Marketing Act to support prices of farm products.
- Stock market collapses in panicked selling of stock on Black Thursday, October 24, and on Black Tuesday, October 29.

1930
- Congress authorizes $420 million for public works projects to relieve the unemployed.
- Hawley-Smoot tariff passes, protecting agricultural goods from foreign competition.
- Farm Board buys one-third of the nation's wheat to support prices.

1931
- Communist Party lawyers ardently defend nine black men arrested in Scottsboro, Alabama.
- Communist Party gains reputation as defender of labor by championing coal miners' strike in Harlan County, Kentucky.

1932
- Thousands of demonstrators at Ford plant protest unemployment; security forces fire on crowd, killing four.
- Congress establishes the Reconstruction Finance Corporation to lend government funds to industries and banks.
- National Farmers' Holiday Association blocks roads and pours milk on ground to protest falling prices.

BIBLIOGRAPHY

General Works

Frederick Lewis Allen, *Only Yesterday: An Informal History of the Nineteen-Twenties* (1930).

Michael Bernstein, *The Great Depression* (1987).

Dorothy Brown, *Setting a Course: American Women in the 1920s* (1987).

Stanley Coben, *Rebellion against Victorianism: The Impetus for Cultural Change in 1920s America* (1991).

Nancy Cott, *The Grounding of Modern Feminism* (1987).

Robert Crunden, *From Self to Society: Transition in American Thought, 1919–1941* (1972).

Alan Dawley, *Struggles for Justice: Social Responsibility and the Liberal State* (1991).

Lynn Dumenil, *The Modern Temper: American Culture and Society in the 1920s* (1995).

David J. Goldberg, *Discontented America: The United States in the 1920s* (1999).

David M. Kennedy, *Freedom from Fear: The American People in Depression and War, 1929–1945* (1999).

William E. Leuchtenburg, *The Perils of Prosperity, 1914–1932* (1958).

Michael Parrish, *Anxious Decades: America in Prosperity and Depression, 1920–1941* (1992).

Mainstream Politics, 1920–1933

Kristi Andersen, *After Suffrage: Women in Partisan and Electoral Politics before the New Deal* (1996).

David Burner, *Herbert Hoover: A Public Life* (1979).

Kendrick A. Clements, *Hoover, Conservation, and Consumerism: Engineering the Good Life* (2000).

Warren I. Cohen, *Empire without Tears: America's Foreign Relations, 1921–1933* (1987).

Frank Costigliola, *Awkward Dominion: American Political, Economic, and Cultural Relations with Europe, 1919–1933* (1984).

Paula Elder, *Governor Alfred E. Smith: The Politician as Reformer* (1983).

Robert H. Ferrell, *The Strange Deaths of Warren Harding* (1996).

Donald R. McCoy, *Calvin Coolidge* (1967).

Frances Fox Piven and Richard A. Cloward, *Why Americans Don't Vote* (1988).

Emily S. Rosenberg, *Spreading the American Dream: American Economic and Cultural Expansion, 1890–1945* (1982).

Martin J. Sklar, *The United States as a Developing Country: Studies in U.S. History in the Progressive Era and the 1920s* (1992).

Joan Hoff Wilson, *Herbert Hoover: Forgotten Progressive* (1975).

Technology and Consumption

Susan Porter Benson, *Counter Cultures* (1986).

Douglas Brinkley, *Wheels for the World: Henry Ford, His Company, and a Century of Progress, 1903–2003* (2003).

Ruth Schwartz Cowan, *More Work for Mother: The Ironies of Household Technology from the Open Hearth to the Microwave* (1983).

James J. Flink, *The Automobile Age* (1988).

Louis Galambos and Joseph Pratt, *The Rise of the Corporate Commonwealth: U.S. Business and Public Policy in the Twentieth Century* (1988).

Kenneth T. Jackson, *Crabgrass Frontier: The Suburbanization of the United States* (1985).

Jill Jonnes, *Empires of Light: Edison, Tesla, and Westinghouse, and the Race to Electrify the World* (2003).

T. J. Jackson Lears, *Fables of Abundance: A Cultural History of Advertising in America* (1994).

Roland Marchand, *Advertising the American Dream: Making Way for Modernity, 1920–1940* (1985).

John Margolies, *Pump and Circumstances: Glory Days of the Gas Station* (1993).

David F. Noble, *America by Design: Science, Technology, and the Rise of Corporate Capitalism* (1977).

Labor

Irving Bernstein, *The Lean Years: A History of the American Worker, 1920–1933* (1960).

Lizabeth Cohen, *Making a New Deal: Industrial Workers in Chicago, 1919–1939* (1990).

Colin Gordon, *New Deals: Business, Labor, and Politics in America, 1920–1935* (1994).

Sanford M. Jacoby, *Employing Bureaucracy: Managers, Unions, and the Transformation of Work in American Industry, 1900–1945* (1985).

Stephen Meyer, *The Five Dollar Day* (1981).

John A. Salmond, *Gastonia 1929: The Story of the Loray Mill Strike* (1995).

Winifred Wandersee, *Women's Work and Family Values, 1920–1940* (1981).

Gerald Zahavi, *Workers, Managers, and Welfare Capitalism* (1988).

Robert H. Zieger, *Republicans and Labor, 1919–1929* (1969).

Rural and Small-Town Life

Michael L. Berger, *The Devil Wagon in God's Country: The Automobile and Social Change in Rural America, 1893–1929* (1979).

James N. Gregory, *American Exodus: The Dust Bowl Migration and Okie Culture in California* (1989).

Jack Temple Kirby, *Rural Worlds Lost: The American South, 1920–1960* (1987).

Donald Worster, *Dust Bowl: The Southern Plains in the 1930s* (1979).

Popular Culture

Thomas Cripps, *Slow Fade to Black: The Negro in American Film, 1900–1942* (1977).

Ann Douglas, *Mongrel Manhattan in the 1920s* (1994).

Ronald Edsforth, *Popular Culture and Political Change in Modern America* (1991).

Lewis Erenberg, *Steppin' Out: New York City Nightlife and the Transformation of American Culture, 1890–1930* (1981).

Paula S. Fass, *The Damned and the Beautiful: American Youth in the 1920s* (1977).

Jill Jonnes, *Hep-Cats, Narcs, and Pipe Dreams: A History of America's Romance with Illegal Drugs* (1996).

Lary May, *The Big Tomorrow: Hollywood and the Politics of the American Way* (2000).

Ray Robinson, *Rockne of Notre Dame: The Making of a Football Legend* (1999).

Steven J. Ross, *Working-Class Hollywood: Silent Film and the Shaping of Class in America* (2000).

Arnold Shaw, *The Jazz Age: Popular Music in the 1920s* (1987).

Susan Smulyan, *Selling Radio: The Commercialization of American Broadcasting, 1920–1934* (1994).

Education and Art

Charles C. Alexander, *Here the Country Lies: Nationalism and the Arts in Twentieth-Century America* (1980).

Malcolm Cowley, *Exile's Return* (1934).

Helen Lefkowitz Horowitz, *Campus Life: Undergraduate Cultures from the End of the Eighteenth Century to the Present* (1987).

Lary May, *Outside In: Minorities and the Transformation of American Education* (1989).

Elizabeth Hutton Turner, *American Artists in Paris, 1919–1929* (1988).

Resistance to Change

David H. Bennett, *The Party of Fear: From Nativist Movements to the New Right in American History* (1988).

Kathleen M. Blee, *Women of the Klan: Racism and Gender in the 1920s* (1991).

Roger Daniels, *Guarding the Golden Door: American Immigration Policy and Immigrants since 1882* (2004).

Lyle W. Dorsett, *Billy Sunday and the Redemption of Urban America* (1991).

Ray Ginger, *Six Days or Forever? Tennessee v. John Thomas Scopes* (1958).

Nancy MacLean, *Behind the Mask of Chivalry: The Making of the Second Ku Klux Klan* (1994).

George M. Marsden, *Fundamentalism and American Culture* (1980).

David M. Reimers, *Unwelcome Strangers: American Identity and the Turn against Immigration* (1998).

Daniel Joseph Singal, *The War Within: From Victorian to Modernist Thought in the South, 1919–1945* (1982).

Reform and Dissent

James R. Barrett, *William Z. Foster and the Tragedy of American Radicalism* (1999).

Milton Cantor, *The Divided Left: American Radicalism, 1900–1975* (1978).

Clarke Chambers, *Seedtime of Reform, 1918–1933* (1956).

John P. Diggins, *The Rise and Fall of the American Left* (1992).

Alex Keyssar, *Right to Vote: The Contested History of Democracy in the United States* (2000).

Davis Levering Lewis, *W. E. B. Du Bois: The Fight for Equality and the American Century, 1919–1963* (2000).

Thomas R. Pegram, *Battling Demon Rum: The Struggle for a Dry America, 1800–1933* (1998).

Nick Salvatore, *Eugene V. Debs: Citizen and Socialist* (1982).

David Thelen, *Robert M. La Follette and the Insurgent Spirit* (1976).

Race and Minorities

Rodolfo Acuna, *Occupied America: A History of Chicanos* (1980).

Francisco E. Balderrama and Raymond Rodriguez, *Decade of Betrayal: Mexican Repatriation in the 1930s* (1995).

William B. Barlow, *"Looking Up at Down": The Emergence of Blues Culture* (1989).

Dan T. Carter, *Scottsboro: A Tragedy of the Modern South* (1969).

Angela Davis, *Blues Legacies and Black Feminism: Gertrude "Ma" Rainey, Bessie Smith, and Billie Holiday* (1999).

George Hutchinson, *The Harlem Renaissance in Black and White* (1995).

David Levering Lewis, *When Harlem Was in Vogue* (1989).

Manning Marable, *W. E. B. Du Bois: Black Radical Democrat* (1986).

Donald L. Parman, *Indians and the American West in the Twentieth Century* (1994).

Judith Stein, *The World of Marcus Garvey* (1986).

Cheryl A. Wall, *Women of the Harlem Renaissance* (1995).

Henry Yu, *Thinking Orientals: Migration, Contact, and Exoticism in Modern America* (2001).

The Crash and Response

William J. Barber, *From New Era to New Deal: Herbert Hoover, the Economists, and American Economic Policy, 1921–1933* (1985).

John Kenneth Galbraith, *The Great Crash, 1929* (1961).

Robert McElvaine, *The Great Depression in America* (1984).

David P. Peeler, *Hope Among Us Yet: Social Criticism and Social Thought in the Depression Years* (1987).

Studs Terkel, *Hard Times: An Oral History of the Great Depression* (1979, 1986).

Tom Terrill and Jerrold Hirsch, *Such as Us* (1978).

T. H. Watkins, *The Hungry Years: America in an Age of Crisis, 1929–1939* (1999).

FRANKLIN ROOSEVELT'S MICROPHONE

President Roosevelt used this microphone to broadcast his famous fireside chats explaining New Deal programs to ordinary Americans. These chats traveled on airwaves into homes throughout the nation, reassuring listeners that Washington cared about the suffering the Great Depression was spreading across the land. Shortly after the first chat in March 1933, a New Yorker, "a citizen of little or no consequence" as he called himself, wrote the White House in gratitude for "the President's broadcast. I felt that he walked into my home, sat down and in plain and forceful language explained to me how he was tackling the job I and my fellow citizens gave him. . . . Such forceful, direct and honest action commands the respect of all Americans, it is certainly deserving of it."

National Museum of American History, Smithsonian Institution, Behring Center.

The New Deal Experiment

1932–1939

IN THE DEPTHS OF THE GREAT DEPRESSION, a Pennsylvania mother with three small children appealed to the Hoover administration for help for her husband "who is a world war Veteran and saw active service in the trenches, became desperate and applied for Compensation or a pension from the Government and was turned down." With a weekly income of only $15.60, she declared, there ought to be "enough to pay all world war veterans a pension . . . and there by relieve a lot of suffering, and banish resentment that causes Rebellions and Bolshevism." She asked questions murmured by millions of other desperate Americans: "Oh why is it that it is always a bunch of overley rich, selfish, dumb ignorant money hogs that persist in being Senitors, legislatures, representitives? Where would they and their possessions be if it were not for the Common Soldier, the common laborer that is compelled to work for a starvation wage[?] . . . Right now our good old U.S.A. is sitting on a Seething Volcano."

This mother's plea echoed in the demands of tens of thousands of World War I veterans who gathered in Washington, D.C., during June and July 1932 to lobby for immediate payment of the pension (known as a "bonus"). The veterans came from every state and by nearly every means of transportation. The throng that congregated in a huge camp on the outskirts of Washington appeared "dusty, weary, and melancholy" to a Washington reporter who noted that the veterans included jobless "truck drivers and blacksmiths, steel workers and coal miners, stenographers and common laborers," in all "a fair cross section" of the nation: immigrants and natives; whites, blacks, and Indians. The "one absentee," a black civil rights leader observed, was "James Crow." Beneath the veterans' social and geographic diversity lay their shared economic suffering. They were all, one journalist wrote, "down at the heel."

Calling themselves Bonus Marchers or the Bonus Army, the veterans hoped their numbers, solidarity, and poverty would persuade Congress to give them the bonus they had been promised in 1924: $1 for every day they had been in uniform and a bit extra for time served overseas. Instead of cash payments, Congress decided to hand out promissory notes that veterans could not convert to cash until 1945. Bonus Marchers condemned this "tombstone bonus" that would not be paid until many of them were dead. As veterans from Utah and California emblazoned their truck, "We Done a Good Job in France, Now You Do a Good Job in America—We Need the Bonus."

The veterans had supporters in Congress but not in the White House. President Hoover opposed the payment of an expensive bonus that would require the government to go into debt. Hoover refused to meet with representatives of the Bonus Army, who, his press secretary charged, were "communists or bums." The House of Representatives, controlled by Democrats, voted to pay the promised bonus of $2.4 billion, but the Senate, dominated by Hoover's fellow Republicans, rejected the bonus. Upon hearing of their defeat in the Senate, the Bonus Marchers did not confirm Republican fears of an enraged mob led by **Communists**. Instead, the disap-

pointed but patriotic veterans joined in singing "America," then slowly drifted back to their camp.

About 20,000 veterans remained in Washington, determined, as one of them proclaimed, "to stay here until 1945 if necessary to get our bonus." While the Bonus Army hunkered down in their shanties, Hoover feared the veterans would riot and spark uprisings throughout the country. He ordered General Douglas MacArthur to evict the Bonus Marchers from the city, but not to invade their camp.

On July 28, MacArthur led an attack force of five tanks and 500 soldiers armed with loaded weapons and fixed bayonets through the streets of Washington. Exceeding Hoover's orders, MacArthur pushed the Bonus Marchers back into their camp, where his soldiers torched the veterans' humble dwellings. While their camp burned, the Bonus Marchers raced away. MacArthur boasted that without his victory over the veterans, "I believe the institutions of our Government would have been severely threatened."

MacArthur's expulsion of the Bonus Army undermined public support for the beleaguered, fearful Hoover. When the Democrats' recently nominated presidential candidate, Franklin Delano Roosevelt, heard about the attack, he predicted that it "will elect me." Roosevelt's political instincts proved correct. Voters rejected Hoover, who seemed unsympathetic to the suffering the Great Depression inflicted on millions

Attack on the Bonus Marchers

Washington police, spearheaded by 500 army soldiers commanded by General Douglas MacArthur, participated in the attack on the Bonus Marchers. Soldiers lobbed tear gas grenades toward the Bonus Marchers, quickly breaking up skirmishes like the one shown here, then advanced into the veterans' camp and torched it. At the head of the mounted cavalry attacking the veterans was George S. Patton, who became a famous general in World War II. MacArthur's chief aide was Dwight D. Eisenhower, who subsequently commanded the Allied assault on Nazi Germany and became president. Eisenhower recalled later that he "told that dumb son-of-a-bitch [MacArthur] he had no business going down there" to destroy the Bonus Marchers' camp, in violation of Hoover's orders. Hoover, however, did not discipline MacArthur for his insubordination.

National Archives.

For more help analyzing this image, see the visual activity for this chapter in the Online Study Guide at bedfordstmartins.com/roark.

of Americans. In his inaugural address in March 1933, barely seven months after the expulsion of the Bonus Army, Roosevelt proclaimed a central theme of his personal style, his political temperament, and his public appeal by saying, "The only thing we have to fear is fear itself." Instead of succumbing to fear and suspicion, Roosevelt said, Americans should roll up their sleeves and find some way out of their present difficulties. Roosevelt's confidence that the government could somehow improve the lives of citizens energized **New Deal** policies and his presidency, the longest in American history.

When several thousand veterans reassembled in Washington to lobby again for the bonus a few months after Roosevelt's inauguration, the new president's hospitality contrasted with Hoover's hostility. Roosevelt arranged for the veterans to be housed in abandoned military barracks and fed at government expense while they lobbied for the bonus. He invited a delegation of veterans to the White House, where he chatted casually with them, explaining that he could not support the bonus because it was too expensive, although he was determined to help them and other victims of the depression. And, to the veterans' surprise and delight, Eleanor Roosevelt slogged through rain and mud to talk personally with the veterans, to express her sympathy, and to lead them in singing their favorite songs. As the veterans voluntarily left their encampment in Washington, one remarked, "Hoover sent the Army; Roosevelt sent his wife."

Unlike the Bonus Marchers, the tens of millions of other Americans suffering from the Great Depression did not flock to Washington to lobby the government. But like the Bonus Marchers, they appreciated Roosevelt's optimism and expressions of concern. Even more, they welcomed government help from Roosevelt's New Deal initiatives to provide relief for the needy, to speed economic recovery, and to reform basic economic and governmental institutions. Roosevelt's New Deal elicited bitter opposition from critics on the right and left and failed to satisfy fully its own goals of relief, recovery, and reform. But within the Democratic Party the New Deal energized a powerful political coalition that helped millions of Americans withstand the privations of the Great Depression and, in the process, made the federal government a major presence in the daily lives of most American citizens.

Franklin D. Roosevelt: A Patrician in Government

Unlike the millions of Americans in 1932 who had no work, little food, and still less hope, Franklin Roosevelt came from a wealthy and privileged background that contributed to his sunny optimism, self-confidence, and vitality. He constantly drew upon these personal qualities in his political career to bridge the economic, social, and cultural chasm that separated him from the struggles of ordinary Americans. During the twelve years he served as president (1933–1945), many elites came to hate him as a traitor to his class, while millions more Americans, especially the hardworking poor and dispossessed, revered him because he cared about them and their problems.

The Making of a Politician

Born in 1882, Franklin Delano Roosevelt grew up on his father's leafy estate at Hyde Park on the Hudson River, north of New York City. Insulated from the privations, uncertainties, and conflicts experienced by working people, Roosevelt was steeped at home and school in high-minded doctrines of public service and Christian duty to help the poor and weak. He prepared for a career in politics, hoping to follow in the political footsteps of his fifth cousin, Theodore Roosevelt. In 1905, when he married his distant cousin Eleanor Roosevelt, the president of the United States, Theodore Roosevelt, gave the bride away—an indication of Franklin Roosevelt's gilt-edged political and familial connections.

Unlike cousin Teddy, Franklin Roosevelt sought his political fortune in the Democratic Party. After a two-year stint in the New York legislature, he ascended to national office when Woodrow Wilson appointed him assistant secretary of the navy. In 1920, he catapulted to the second spot on the national Democratic ticket, as the vice presidential candidate of presidential nominee James M. Cox. Although the Republicans' Warren G. Harding trounced Cox in the general election (see chapter 23), Roosevelt's energetic campaigning convinced Democratic leaders that he had a bright future in national politics.

In the summer of 1921, however, his life took a painful detour. He became infected with the polio virus, which paralyzed both his legs. For the rest of his life, he could stand only with his legs encased in heavy steel braces and could walk a few awkward steps only by leaning on another person. Tireless physical therapy helped him regain his vitality and intense desire for high political office. But he had to recapture his political momentum mostly from a sitting position, although he studiously avoided being photographed in the wheelchair he used routinely.

After his polio attack, Roosevelt frequently visited a polio therapy facility at Warm Springs, Georgia. There, Roosevelt combined the health benefits of the soothing waters with political overtures to southern Democrats, which helped make him a rare political creature: a New Yorker from the Democratic Party's urban and immigrant wing with whom whites from the Democratic Party's entrenched southern wing felt comfortable.

Roosevelt's chance to return to political office came in 1928. New York's Democratic governor, Al Smith, decided to run for president and hoped to secure the state's electoral votes by encouraging Roosevelt to campaign to succeed him as governor. Smith lost both New York and the general election (see chapter 23), but Roosevelt squeaked out a narrow victory. As the newly elected governor of the nation's most populous state, Roosevelt was poised to showcase his leadership and his suitability for a presidential bid of his own. His activist policies following the 1929 stock market crash and the cascading economic woes of the Great Depression made his governorship a dress rehearsal for his subsequent actions as president.

Governor Roosevelt took immediate action. He believed government should intervene to protect citizens from economic hardships, rather than standing passively on the sidelines and waiting for the blind laws of supply and demand to improve the economy. Roosevelt's sympathy for the underdog contrasted with the traditional **laissez-faire** views of many **conservatives**— both Republicans and Democrats—that the depression represented the hard hand of the market winnowing the strong from the weak. For government to help the needy, according to conservatives, was wrong on at least two counts: It sapped individual initiative, the source of self-respect and economic hope for the poor; and it impeded the self-correcting forces of the market by rewarding the losers in the economic struggle

> Roosevelt's activist policies following the 1929 stock market crash made his governorship a dress rehearsal for his subsequent actions as president.

Roosevelt's Common Touch
In his campaign for reelection as governor of New York in 1930, Franklin Roosevelt boosted his vote total by 700,000 over his slender victory margin of 25,000 in 1928, and he became the first Democratic candidate for governor to win the vote outside New York City. Sensing that his presentation of himself as a good neighbor was responsible for much of his popularity, Roosevelt arranged to have a friendly chat outside polls in his hometown of Hyde Park with working-class voter Ruben Appel. In this photograph, Appel seems unaware that Roosevelt's standing was itself a feat of stagecraft. His legs rendered useless by polio, Roosevelt could remain upright only by using the strength he had developed in his arms and shoulders to prop himself up on his cane. Rare photos like this and a taboo against showing Roosevelt in his wheelchair kept the public from thinking of Roosevelt as a "cripple" and unfit for office, or in many cases from even realizing that he was disabled.
Franklin D. Roosevelt Library.

to survive. Roosevelt lacked a full-fledged counterargument to these conservative qualms, but he refused to allow them to hobble his government's efforts to provide short-term aid to the jobless and the hungry. "To these unfortunate citizens," he proclaimed, "aid must be extended by governments, not as a matter of charity but as a matter of social duty. . . . [No one should go] unfed, unclothed, or unsheltered."

The highlight of Roosevelt's efforts to relieve the economic hardships of New Yorkers was the Temporary Emergency Relief Administration (TERA), created in 1931. Until then, no state had ever provided so much help for the poor, some $20 million. TERA and Roosevelt's other initiatives as governor earned the gratitude of New Yorkers and the attention of national politicians.

To his supporters, Roosevelt seemed to be a leader determined to use the resources of government to attack the economic crisis without deviating from **democracy**—unlike **fascist** parties gaining strength in Europe—or from capitalism—unlike Communists in power in the Soviet Union. Roosevelt's ideas about precisely how to revive the economy were vague. A prominent journalist characterized Roosevelt in 1931 as "a kind of amiable boy scout . . . a pleasant man who, without any important qualifications for the office, would very much like to be president." Such sneering assessments did not much concern Roosevelt's numerous supporters, who appreciated his energy, his activism, and his belief that, as he put it, "The duty of the state towards its citizens is the duty of the servant to its master." Roosevelt's conviction that government could and should do something to help Americans climb out of the economic abyss propelled him into the front ranks of the national Democratic Party.

The Election of 1932

The Democrats who convened in Chicago in July 1932 to nominate their presidential candidate knew they had a good chance to recapture the White House. Many Americans blamed President Hoover, just then confronting the Bonus Marchers in Washington, for the nation's economic distress. Hoover's unpopularity gave the Democrats a historic opportunity. In 56 of the 72 years since Abraham Lincoln's election, the White House had been a Republican preserve. Now, with the nation gripped by the worst depression

in its history, Democrats might reverse generations of Republican rule if they chose the right nominee.

Opposition to Republicans and hunger for office, but little else, united Democrats. Warring factions divided Democrats by region, religion, culture, and commitment to the status quo. Southern Democrats chaired powerful committees in Congress thanks to their continual reelection in the one-party South devoted to white supremacy. This southern, native-born, white, rural, **Protestant**, conservative wing of the Democratic Party found little common ground with the northern, immigrant, urban, disproportionately Catholic, **liberal** wing. Rural and small-town drys (supporters of prohibition) clashed with urban and foreign-born wets (opponents of prohibition). Eastern-establishment Democratic dignitaries shared few goals with angry farmers and factory workers. Nonetheless, this unruly coalition of constituencies finally agreed to nominate Franklin Roosevelt as their presidential candidate.

Roosevelt signaled his break with tradition as well as his energy and activism by flying to Chicago to appear before the Democratic conventioneers and accepting their nomination in person. He pledged his commitment to "the forgotten man at the bottom of the pyramid" and promised "bold, persistent experimentation" to find ways to help. Highlighting his differences with Hoover and Republicans, he proposed to lead the nation toward "liberal thought, . . . planned action, . . . enlightened international outlook, and . . . the greatest good to the greatest number of our citizens." He summarized his determination to govern decisively without being bound by "foolish traditions" by announcing, "I pledge you, I pledge myself, to a new deal for the American people."

Few details about what Roosevelt meant by a "new deal" emerged in the presidential campaign. He declared that "the people of America want more than anything else . . . two things; work . . . with all the moral and spiritual values that go with work . . . and a reasonable measure of security . . . for themselves and for their wives and children." He encouraged Americans to go into voting booths asking themselves one simple question: Should Hoover be reelected, or was it time for a change, a new deal? Voters answered that question in no uncertain terms.

Roosevelt won in a historic landslide (Map 24.1). He received 57 percent of popular votes, the first Democratic popular-vote majority since the election of Franklin Pierce in 1852. In the electoral college, Roosevelt amassed an 89 percent majority, carrying state after state that had voted Republican for years (Map 24.2). Roosevelt's coattails also swept Democrats into control of Congress by large margins. Voters' mandate for change could hardly have been more emphatic.

Roosevelt's victory represented the emergence of what came to be known as the New Deal coalition. Attracting support from farmers, factory workers, immigrants, city folk, African Americans, women, and **progressive** intellectuals, Roosevelt launched a realignment of the nation's political loyalties. The New Deal coalition dominated American politics throughout Roosevelt's presidency and remained powerful long after his death in 1945. United less by ideology or support for specific policies, voters in the New Deal coalition instead expressed their faith in Roosevelt's promise of a government that would, somehow, change things for the better. Nobody, including Roosevelt, knew exactly what the New Deal would change or whether the changes would revive the nation's ailing economy and improve Americans' lives. But Roosevelt and many others knew that the future of American capitalism and democracy was at stake.

> Attracting support from farmers, factory workers, immigrants, city folk, African Americans, women, and progressive intellectuals, Roosevelt launched a realignment of the nation's political loyalties.

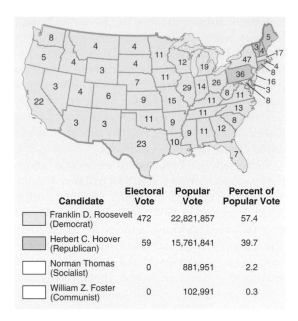

Candidate	Electoral Vote	Popular Vote	Percent of Popular Vote
Franklin D. Roosevelt (Democrat)	472	22,821,857	57.4
Herbert C. Hoover (Republican)	59	15,761,841	39.7
Norman Thomas (Socialist)	0	881,951	2.2
William Z. Foster (Communist)	0	102,991	0.3

MAP 24.1   The Election of 1932

Launching the New Deal

At noon on March 4, 1933, Americans gathered around their radios to hear the inaugural address of the newly elected president. Roosevelt began by asserting his "firm belief that the only thing we have to fear is fear itself—nameless, unreasoning, unjustified terror which paralyzes needed efforts to convert retreat into advance." Roosevelt promised "direct, vigorous action" in order "to wage war against the emergency" cre-

MAP 24.2   Electoral Shift, 1928–1932

Democratic victory in 1932 signaled the rise of a New Deal coalition within which women and minorities, many of them new voters, made the Democrats the majority party for the first time in the twentieth century.

READING THE MAP: How many states voted Democratic in 1928? How many states voted Republican in 1932? How many states shifted from Republican to Democratic between 1928 and 1932?

CONNECTIONS: What did Franklin Roosevelt's campaign slogans call for? What past programs did Roosevelt cite as influences? What factions within the Democratic Party opposed his candidacy in 1932, and why?

FOR MORE HELP ANALYZING THIS MAP, see the map activity for this chapter in the Online Study Guide at bedfordstmartins.com/roark.

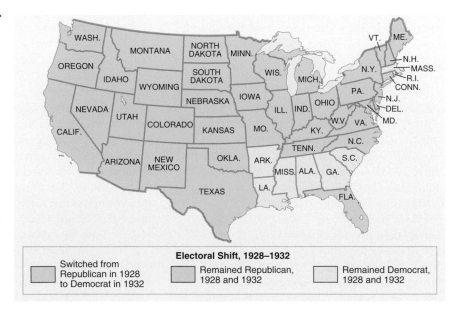

Electoral Shift, 1928–1932

Switched from Republican in 1928 to Democrat in 1932   Remained Republican, 1928 and 1932   Remained Democrat, 1928 and 1932 ated by "the dark realities" confronting "a stricken Nation in the midst of a stricken world." The first months of Roosevelt's administration, termed "the Hundred Days," fulfilled that promise in a whirlwind of government initiatives that launched the New Deal.

Roosevelt and his advisers had three interrelated objectives: to provide relief to the destitute, especially the one out of four Americans who were unemployed; to foster the economic recovery of farms and businesses, thereby creating jobs and reducing the need for relief; and to reform the government and economy in ways that would reduce the risk of devastating consequences in future economic slumps. The New Deal never fully achieved these goals of relief, recovery, and reform. But by aiming for them, Roosevelt's experimental programs enormously expanded government's role in the nation's economy and society.

The New Dealers

To design and implement the New Deal, Roosevelt needed ideas and people. As governor of New York, he frequently hosted private, informal conversations about social and economic policy with a small group of professors from Columbia University. Dubbed the "Brains Trust," these men and others continued to advise the new president about the problems faced by the nation and how to deal with them.

Hundreds of other reformers rushed to join the Roosevelt administration. Among the most important were two veterans of Roosevelt's New York governorship: Harry Hopkins and Frances Perkins. Hopkins, a tough-talking, soft-hearted social worker devoted to the **social gospel** of moral and material uplift of the downtrodden, administered New Deal relief efforts and served as one of the president's loyal confidants. Perkins, like Hopkins, embraced the social gospel tradition, having worked for a time in Jane Addams's Hull House in Chicago. Perkins also had extensive experience trying to improve working conditions in shops and factories, including directing New York's investigation of the 1911 Triangle Shirtwaist Factory fire that killed 146 women (see chapter 21). Roosevelt tapped Perkins to serve as secretary of labor, the first woman cabinet member in American history—an indication of her expertise and of the growing strength of women in the Democratic Party, which had an organized and active Women's Division.

No New Dealers were more important than the president and his wife, Eleanor. The gregarious president radiated charm and good cheer, giving the New Deal's bureaucratic regulations a benevolent human face. During his frequent informal news conferences, Roosevelt bantered with reporters and skillfully broadcast his plans and policies. Eleanor Roosevelt became the New Deal's unofficial ambassador. She served as her husband's eyes and ears—and legs—as she traveled throughout the nation connecting the corridors of power in Washington to Americans of all colors and creeds in church basements, meeting halls, and front parlors.

As Roosevelt's programs swung into action, many Americans benefited directly through jobs and relief or indirectly from economic improvements. In time, the millions of beneficiaries of the New Deal became grassroots New Dealers who expressed their appreciation by voting Democratic on election day. A signal success of the New Deal was to create a durable political coalition of Democrats that stretched from the Oval Office to the nation's fields and factories and that would reelect Roosevelt in 1936, 1940, and 1944.

As Roosevelt and his advisers developed plans to meet the economic emergency, their watchwords were *action, experiment*, and *improvise*. Without a sharply defined template for how to provide relief, recovery, and reform, they moved from ideas to policies as quickly as possible, hoping to identify ways to help people and to boost the economy. But underlying New Dealers' experimentation and improvisation were four guiding ideas.

First, Roosevelt and his advisers sought capitalist solutions to the economic crisis. They believed that the depression resulted from basic imbalances in the nation's capitalist economy, imbalances they wanted to correct. They had no desire to eliminate private property or impose **socialist** programs, such as public ownership of productive resources. Instead, they hoped to save the capitalist economy by remedying its flaws.

Second, Roosevelt's Brains Trust persuaded him that the greatest flaw of America's capi-

> The New Deal never fully achieved the goals of relief, recovery, and reform. But by aiming for them, Roosevelt's experimental programs enormously expanded government's role in the nation's economy and society.

> A signal success of the New Deal was to create a durable political coalition of New Deal Democrats that stretched from the Oval Office to the nation's fields and factories and re-elected Roosevelt in 1936, 1940, and 1944.

talist economy was underconsumption, the root cause of the current economic paralysis. Underconsumption, New Dealers argued, resulted from the gigantic productive success of capitalism. Factories and farms produced more than they could sell to consumers, causing factories to lay off workers and farmers to lose money on bumper crops. Workers without wages and farmers without profits shrank consumption and choked the economy. Somehow, the balance between consumption and production needed to be restored.

Third, New Dealers believed that the immense size and economic power of American corporations needed to be counterbalanced by government and by organization among workers and small producers. Unlike progressive trustbusters in Woodrow Wilson's administration, New Dealers did not seek to splinter big businesses. Huge businesses had developed for good economic reasons and were here to stay. Roosevelt and his advisers hoped to counterbalance big economic institutions and their quest for profits with government programs focused on protecting individuals and the public interest.

Fourth, New Dealers felt that government must somehow moderate the imbalance of wealth created by American capitalism. Wealth concentrated in a few hands reduced consumption by most Americans and thereby contributed to the current economic gridlock. In the long run, government needed to find a way to permit ordinary working people to share more fully in the

Eleanor Roosevelt Meeting Women Reporters

Even though about 80 percent of newspaper owners opposed the president and his wife, both Franklin and Eleanor Roosevelt had close rapport with the working press. Making the point that women had something important to contribute to public affairs and that the First Lady could be more than simply a White House hostess, Eleanor Roosevelt wrote a daily column, "My Day," and held regular news conferences to which only women reporters were admitted. She used the occasions to reinvigorate the commitment women had expressed in the Progressive Era to education, equal rights, decent working conditions, and child welfare.

Stock Montage.

Soup Kitchen
Chicago gangster Al Capone sponsored this soup kitchen for the unemployed in 1931. Before the New Deal, most relief for the jobless came from private sources, although very little came from mobsters like Capone. Notice that the people in line are all men, that they include both whites and blacks, and that they appear comparatively well dressed, suggesting that they had lost their jobs relatively recently. Why might a gangster like Capone offer free soup to the jobless?
National Archives.

fruits of the economy. In the short term, New Dealers sought to lend a helping hand to poor people who suffered from the maldistribution of wealth.

Roosevelt had outlined these guiding ideas during the presidential campaign, and they served as a creed among New Dealers. "Our task now," Roosevelt declared, "is . . . meeting the problem of underconsumption, . . . adjusting production to consumption, . . . [and] distributing wealth and products more equitably." Once Roosevelt took office, the New Dealers' creed guided their actions.

Banking and Finance Reform

Roosevelt wasted no time making good on his inaugural pledge for "action now." As he took the oath of office on March 4, the nation's banking system was on the brink of collapse. Since 1930 more than 5,000 banks had failed. Depositors who feared losing their savings withdrew their money from surviving banks, making them so shaky that the nation's governors had suspended almost all states' banking operations. Roosevelt immediately declared a four-day "bank holiday" in order to devise a plan to shore up banks and restore depositors' confidence. Working round the clock, New Dealers drafted the Emergency Banking Act, which gave the secretary of the treasury the power to decide which banks could be safely reopened and to release funds from the Reconstruction Finance Corporation (RFC) to bolster banks' assets. To secure the confidence of depositors, Congress passed the Glass-Steagall Banking Act, setting up the Federal Deposit Insurance Corporation (FDIC), which guaranteed bank customers that the federal government would reimburse them for deposits if their banks failed.

On Sunday night March 12, while the banks were still closed, Roosevelt broadcast the first of what became a series of "fireside chats." Speaking in a friendly, informal manner, Roosevelt addressed the millions of Americans who tuned their radios to hear the president explain these first New Deal initiatives. The new banking legislation, he said, made it "safer to keep your money in a reopened bank than under the mattress." With such plain talk, Roosevelt translated complex matters into common sense. This and subsequent fireside chats forged a direct connection—via radio waves—between Roosevelt and millions of Americans. Evidence of their link to Roosevelt piled up in the White House mail room: During Roosevelt's first week in office, Americans sent him almost half a million personal letters, an avalanche of correspondence from ordinary people that persisted throughout his presidency. Millions shared the views of a man from Paris, Texas, who wrote Roosevelt, "you are the one & only President that ever helped a Working Class of People. . . . Please help us some way I Pray to God for relief."

The banking legislation and fireside chat worked. Within a few days, most of the nation's major banks reopened, and they remained solvent as reassured depositors switched funds from their mattresses to their accounts (Figure 24.1). Some radical critics of the New Deal believed Roosevelt should have nationalized

the banks and made them a cornerstone of economic planning by the federal government. Instead, these first New Deal measures propped up the private banking system with federal funds and subjected banks to federal regulation and oversight. One adviser correctly identified the New Deal's goal, claiming, "Capitalism was saved in eight days," although the rescue operation took much longer to succeed.

In his inaugural address Roosevelt criticized financiers for their greed and incompetence. To prevent the fraud, corruption, insider trading, and other abuses that had tainted Wall Street and contributed to the crash of 1929, Roosevelt pressed Congress to regulate the stock market—like banks, a fundamental institution of American capitalism. Legislation in 1934 created the Securities and Exchange Commission (SEC) to oversee financial markets by licensing investment dealers, monitoring all stock transactions, and requiring corporate officers to make full disclosures about their companies. To head the SEC, Roosevelt named an abrasive and ravenously ambitious Wall Street trader, Joseph P. Kennedy, whose reputation had been clouded by questionable stock manipulations. When critics complained about Kennedy's selection, Roosevelt replied shrewdly, "Set a thief to catch a thief."

Kennedy proved to be a tough administrator who faced down threats by stockbrokers, some of them with things to hide. Cleaned up and regu-

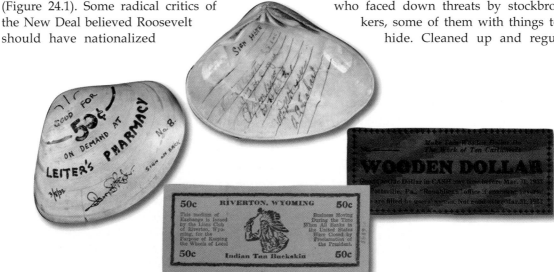

Emergency Money
When bank failures in 1933 caused prudent depositors to withdraw their money from their accounts and hide it away, the resulting scarcity of currency paralyzed businesses. Store owners, service clubs, and communities created "emergency money" to keep the wheels of local commerce turning. Leiter's Pharmacy in Pismo Beach, California, for example, used clamshells for currency; other places issued buckskin and wooden dollars. Such improvisation demonstrates the collapse of the banking system and the creative solutions of some of its victims.
National Museum of American History, Smithsonian Institution, Behring Center.

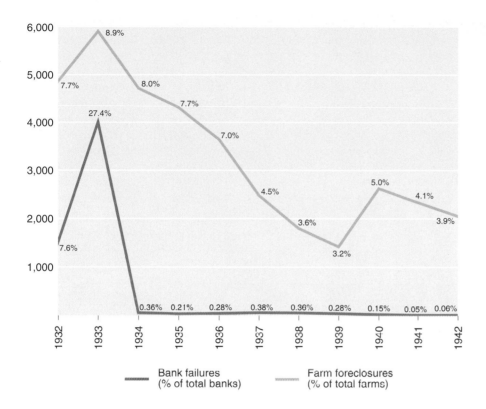

FIGURE 24.1   Bank Failures and Farm Foreclosures, 1932–1942
New Deal legislation to stabilize the economy had its most immediate and striking effect in preventing banks, along with their depositors, from going under and farmers from losing their land.

Bank failures
(% of total banks)

Farm foreclosures
(% of total farms)

lated, Wall Street slowly recovered, but the stock market stayed well below its frothy heights of the 1920s.

Relief and Conservation Programs

Patching up the nation's financial structure provided little relief for the hungry and unemployed. A poor man from Nebraska asked Eleanor Roosevelt "if the folk who was borned here in America . . . are this Forgotten Man, the President had in mind, [and] if we are this Forgotten Man then we are still Forgotten." Since its founding, the federal government had never assumed responsibility for needy people, except in moments of natural disaster or emergencies such as the Civil War. Instead, churches, private charities, county and municipal governments, and occasionally states assumed the burden of poor relief, usually with meager payments. To persuade Americans that the depression necessitated unprecedented federal relief efforts, Harry Hopkins dispatched investigators throughout the nation to describe the plight of impoverished Americans. Reports of families surviving on "bull-dog gravy"—a thin paste of lard, flour, and water—and of many others who lacked even that filtered back to Washington, along with news that working hours of tens of thou-

sands of workers had been cut back, reducing their wages to about $1.50 a day. As one New Yorker wrote the government, "We work, ten hours a day for six days. In the grime and dirt of a nation [for] . . . low pay [making us] . . . slaves—slaves of the depression!"

Such reports galvanized support for the Federal Emergency Relief Administration (FERA), which provided $500 million to feed the hungry and create jobs. Established in May 1933, FERA supported 4 to 5 million households with $20 or $30 a month. FERA also created jobs for the unemployed on thousands of public works projects, organized by Hopkins into the Civil Works Administration (CWA), which siphoned funds from other government agencies. Earning wages between forty and sixty cents an hour, laborers renovated schools, dug sewers, and rebuilt roads and bridges. In the five months it existed, CWA put paychecks worth over $800 million into the hands of previously jobless workers. FERA extended the scope of relief to include health and education, providing vaccinations and immunizations for millions and funding literacy classes.

The most popular work relief program was the Civilian Conservation Corps (CCC), established in March 1933. It offered unemployed young men a chance to earn wages while working

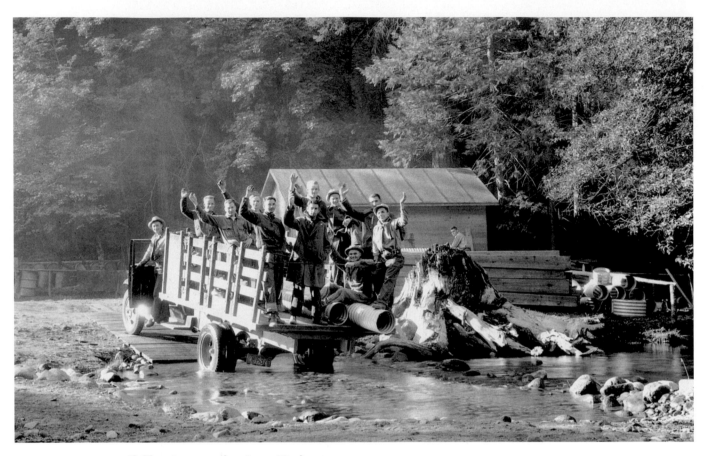

Civilian Conservation Corps Workers
No New Deal program was more popular among its participants and the general public than the Civilian Conservation Corps. It offered young men healthy outdoor work that got them out of the cities and eased their unemployment blues. To the public it showed that the New Deal would act against the depression in a way that would repair neglect of America's natural resources.
Forest Service Photo Collection.

> The CCC, CWA, and other work relief efforts replaced the stigma of welfare with the dignity of jobs.

to conserve natural resources, a long-standing interest of Roosevelt. Like the 3 million other young men who enlisted with CCC, Blackie Gold had been out of work and had to "beg for coal, [and] buy bread that's two, three days old" in order to help support his large family. After he joined the CCC, he earned $30 a month and was required to send all but $5 home to his family. By the end of the program in 1942, CCC workers had checked soil erosion, tamed rivers, and planted more than 2 billion trees. In the process, the CCC left a legacy of vast new recreation areas, along with roads that made them accessible to millions of people. Just as important, CCC, CWA, and other work relief efforts replaced the stigma of welfare with

the dignity of jobs. As one woman said, "We aren't on relief anymore. My husband is working for the Government."

The New Deal also sought to harness natural resources for hydroelectric power. Continuing a project begun under Hoover, the New Deal completed the colossal Hoover Dam across the Colorado River in Nevada, providing not only electricity but also flood control and irrigation water for Arizona and southern California (see "American Places," page 879).

The New Deal's most ambitious and controversial natural resources development project was the Tennessee Valley Authority (TVA), created in May 1933 to build dams along the Tennessee River to supply impoverished rural communities with cheap electricity (Map 24.3). TVA planned model towns for power station

AMERICAN PLACES

Hoover Dam, Nevada

When President Franklin Roosevelt dedicated the just-completed Boulder Dam in Nevada in September 1935, he noted that only four years earlier "the mighty waters of the Colorado [River] were running unused to the sea" but now the dam "translate[s] them into a great national possession." The massive dam—then the largest in the world—tamed the river to provide public services of flood control, hydroelectric power, and water for crops and people throughout the Southwest. From the neon glare of the Las Vegas strip to the suburban expanses of Phoenix and Los Angeles, Americans today switch on lights, water their lawns, and eat irrigated crops all made possible by the enormous concrete monolith that turned the wild river into a great national possession.

Construction began in 1931, when the project was called the Hoover Dam in honor of the president who was instrumental in pushing the long-contemplated dream into reality. By 1933, when Roosevelt became president, the first of some 4.3 million cubic yards of concrete had been poured, enough to pave a highway from San Francisco to New York. Before construction could begin, however, loose rock from the canyon walls had to be stripped away. This physically demanding and dangerous work was done by men called "high-scalers." Climbing with ropes, the high-scalers—many of them former sailors and circus acrobats, plus some Native Americans—used jackhammers and dynamite to remove the loose rock. When they were finished, welders, "greasemen," blacksmiths, pipefitters, electricians, cement finishers, and others built the dam.

On-the-job accidents killed 96 of the dam workers. Others perished from heat exhaustion, pneumonia, or heart trouble. After falling debris caused several deaths, workers took steps to protect their heads. They smeared coal tar on their cloth hats and let it harden, creating an early precursor to the hard hats now routinely worn at construction sites.

By 1933, New Dealers had officially renamed the dam Boulder Dam, and so it remained until 1947 when it was officially renamed Hoover Dam. At a cost of less than $200 million, the construction project provided jobs for over 4,000 men and inspired Americans with dramatic evidence of the creative potential of ambitious public works.

Today, a million people a year visit what Roosevelt called this "twentieth century marvel." They listen to the roar of water jetting

through the spillway outlets and wander among the giant turbines that generate power for western homes and businesses. Admiring the modernist design, they can contemplate the human brains and brawn responsible for erecting such a massive structure—two years ahead of schedule—to turn the rampaging Colorado River into Lake Mead, which stretches over 100 miles. Tours conducted through the visitor center and exhibits at the nearby Boulder City/Hoover Dam Museum bring to life the history of the dam and the many people who helped harness the river's power.

For Web links related to this site and other American Places, see "PlaceLinks" at bedfordstmartins.com/roark.

Hoover Dam
Hoover Dam National Historic Landmark.

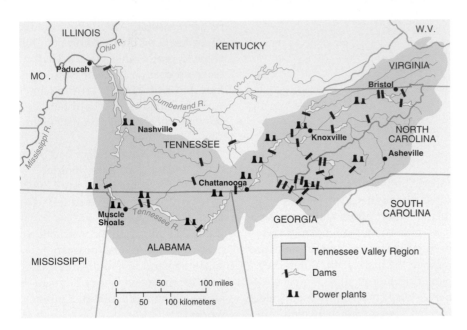

MAP 24.3 The Tennessee Valley Authority

The New Deal created the Tennessee Valley Authority to modernize a vast impoverished region with hydroelectric power dams and, at the same time, to reclaim eroded lands and preserve old folkways.

READING THE MAP: How many states were affected by the TVA? How many miles of rivers (approximately) were affected?

CONNECTIONS: What kinds of benefits—economic as well as social and cultural—did TVA programs bring to the region? How might the lives of a poor farming family in Alabama or Tennessee have changed after the mid-1930s owing to these programs?

FOR MORE HELP ANALYZING THIS MAP, see the map activity for this chapter in the Online Study Guide at bedfordstmartins.com/roark.

workers and new homes for farmers, who would benefit from electricity and flood control. The TVA also sought to preserve the region's culture with programs to encourage local crafts and folkways. The most ambitious example of New Deal enthusiasm for planning, TVA set out to demonstrate that a partnership between the federal government and local residents could overcome barriers of state governments and of private enterprises to make efficient use of abundant natural resources and break the ancient cycle of poverty. TVA never fully realized these utopian ends, especially because of bitter resistance from competing private power companies. It did, however, succeed in improving the lives of millions in the region with electric power, flood protection, soil reclamation, and jobs.

Agricultural Initiatives

Farmers had been mired in depression since the end of World War I. New Dealers diagnosed farmers' plight as a classic case of overproduction and underconsumption. Following age-old practices, farmers tried to compensate for low crop prices by growing more crops, hoping to boost their earnings by selling larger quantities. Instead, producing more pushed prices lower still. Farm income sank from a disastrously low $6 billion in 1929 to a catastrophically low $2 billion in 1932. The median annual income among farm families plunged to $167, barely one-tenth of the national average.

New Dealers sought to cut agricultural production, thereby raising crop prices and farmers' income. With more money in their pockets, farm families—who made up one-third of all Americans—would then buy more goods and thereby lift consumption in the entire economy. To reduce production, the Agricultural Adjustment Act (AAA) authorized the "domestic allotment plan," which paid farmers not to grow crops: Individual farmers who agreed not to plant crops on a portion of their fields (their "allotment") would receive a government payment compensating them for the crops they did not plant. Since crops were already in the ground by the time AAA passed in May 1933, drastic measures were necessary to reduce production immediately. While millions of Americans went to bed hungry, farmers slaughtered millions of cattle, hogs, sheep, and other livestock and destroyed millions of acres of crops in order to qualify for their allotment payments.

With the formation of the Commodity Credit Corporation, the federal government allowed farmers to hold their harvested crops off the market and wait for a higher price. In the meantime, the government stored the crop and gave farmers a "commodity loan" based on a favorable price. If the market price rose above that level, the farmer could repay the loan, sell the crop, and pocket the difference. If the market price never rose above the loan level, the farmer simply took the loan as payment, and the government kept the crop. In effect, commodity loans addressed the problem of underconsumption by making the federal government a major consumer of agricultural goods and reducing farmers' vulnerability to low prices. New Dealers also sponsored the Farm Credit Act (FCA) to provide long-term credit on mortgaged farm property, allowing debt-ridden farmers to avoid foreclosures that were driving thousands off their land.

Crop allotments, commodity loans, and mortgage credit made farmers major beneficiaries of the New Deal. Crop prices rose impressively, farm income jumped 50 percent by 1936, and FCA loans financed 40 percent of farm mortgage debt by the end of the decade. These gains were distributed fairly equally among farmers in the corn, hogs, and wheat region of the Midwest. In the South's cotton belt, however, landlords controlled the distribution of New Deal agricultural benefits and shamelessly rewarded themselves while denying benefits to many sharecroppers and tenant farmers—blacks and whites—by taking the land they had worked out of production and assigning it to the allotment program. Many such tenants and sharecroppers could no longer find work, and their privation worsened. (See "The Promise of Technology," page 882.)

The New Deal also brought the wonders of electric power to country folk, fulfilling an old progressive dream. When Roosevelt became president, 90 percent of rural Americans lacked electricity. Private electric companies refused to build transmission lines into the sparsely settled countryside when they had a profitable market in more accessible and densely populated urban areas. Beginning in 1935, the Rural Electrification Administration (REA) made low-cost loans available to local cooperatives for power plants and transmission lines to serve rural communities. Within ten years, the REA delivered electricity to nine out of ten farms, giving rural Americans access for the first time to modern conveniences that urban people had enjoyed for decades.

Industrial Recovery

Unlike farmers, industrialists cut production with the onset of the depression. Between 1929 and 1933, industrial production fell more than 40 percent. In a sense, industrialists voluntarily adopted the general strategy that the New Dealers used in agriculture: cutting production to balance low demand with low supply and

Sketch for a Federal Arts Program Mural

This sketch for a mural commissioned for Lenoir City, Tennessee, is typical of the Federal Arts Program's goal to memorialize significant moments of achievement in every region of the country. For rural folk, the sight of Rural Electrification Authority (REA) workers extending power lines was an exciting symbol of the New Deal. When the REA came into existence in 1935, less than 10 percent of the nation outside the cities had electricity. Ten years later the figure had risen to 90 percent, and the gulf of silence and darkness between town and country was successfully bridged.

Public Buildings Service, General Services Administration.

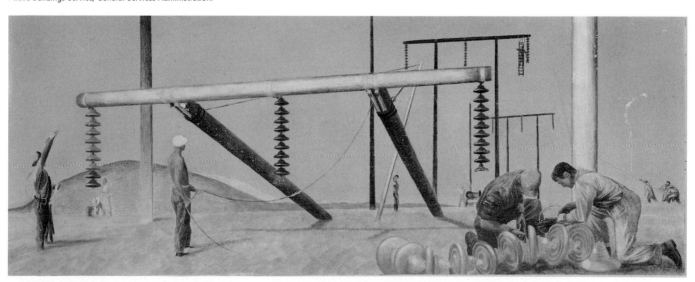

Mechanized Cotton Picking Waits Out the Depression

Cotton Picker
Courtesy of the Fogg Art Museum, Harvard University Art Museums. Gift of Bernarda Bryson Shahn.

In 1935, the Farmall tractor and the Rust cotton picker cut through a field of cotton, showing how mechanization could eliminate the backbreaking work of harvesting cotton by hand. Within ten years, tractors would displace horses as the main means of doing heavy farmwork. Success for mechanical cotton pickers, however, was longer in coming. Since the invention of the cotton gin in 1793, inventors had been trying to create a device that would make picking cotton as efficient as ginning it. The first patent for a crude mechanical picker was granted in 1850, and nearly two thousand more patents were issued before John Rust in 1931 demonstrated a machine that could pick more bales of cotton in a day than the average farmer in the deep South grew in a year.

Although the technology of mechanized cotton agriculture was available during the 1930s, few farmers used it. Why? One reason was the availability of ample cheap labor from poor tenants and sharecroppers. Another was landowning farmers' lack of money to invest in machinery during the hard times of the 1930s. By 1931, cotton prices had plunged to six cents a bale from a high of thirty-five cents in 1919, and New Deal agricultural policies were designed to reduce crop production, not increase it.

Not until the depression lifted during World War II, as the nation geared up for maximum production with a labor force reduced by millions of men and women in uniform, did economic circumstances begin to favor the widespread purchase and use of mechanical cotton pickers. During the 1940s and 1950s, large farms using the new mechanical cotton picker became dominant, shifting most cotton growing from the South to the West, where vast agricultural holdings were the rule. Displaced by the decline of King Cotton in the South, thousands of sharecroppers like the woman shown here migrated to the North in search of new jobs and a new life.

Cotton-Picking Machine
Mississippi State University Libraries.

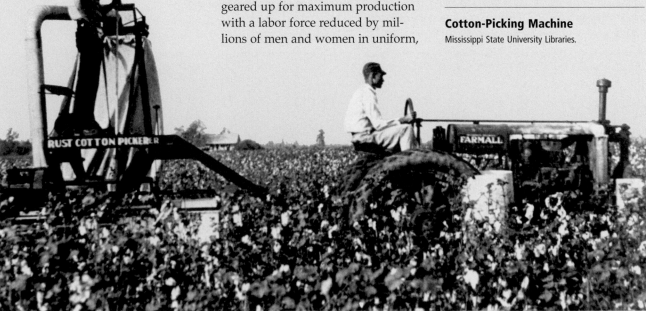

thereby maintaining prices. But the industrialists' strategy created major economic and social problems for Roosevelt and his advisers, for declining industrial production meant that millions of working people lost their jobs. Unlike farmers, most working people lived in towns and cities and did not grow their own food—they literally needed jobs to eat. Mass unemployment also reduced consumer demand for industrial products, contributing to a downward spiral in both production and jobs, with no end in sight. Industries responded by reducing wages for employees who still had jobs, further depressing demand—a trend made worse by competition among industrial producers. New Dealers struggled to find a way to break this cycle of unemployment and underconsumption, a way consistent with corporate profits and capitalism.

The New Deal's National Industrial Recovery Act (NIRA) opted for a government-sponsored form of industrial self-government through the National Recovery Administration (NRA), established in June 1933. The NRA encouraged industrialists in every part of the economy to agree on rules—known as codes—to define fair working conditions, to set prices, and to minimize competition. The idea behind codes was to stabilize existing industries and maintain their workforces while avoiding what both industrialists and New Dealers termed "destructive competition" that forced employers to cut both wages and jobs. Industry after industry wrote elaborate codes addressing detailed features of production, pricing, and competition. In exchange for relaxing federal antitrust regulations that prohibited such business agreements, the NRA received a promise from participating businesses that they would recognize the right of working people to organize and engage in **collective bargaining**. To encourage consumers to patronize businesses participating in NRA codes, the New Deal mounted a public relations campaign that displayed the NRA's Blue Eagle in shop windows and on billboards throughout the nation.

New Dealers hoped that NRA codes would yield businesses with a social conscience, ensuring fair treatment for workers and consumers and promotion of the general economic welfare. Instead, NRA codes tended to strengthen conventional business practices. Large corporations wrote codes that served primarily the interests of corporate profits rather than the needs of workers or the welfare of the national economy. Many

Major Legislation of the New Deal's First Hundred Days

	Name of Act	Basic Provisions
March 9, 1933	Emergency Banking Act	Provided for reopening stable banks and authorizing RFC to supply funds
March 31, 1933	Civilian Conservation Corps Act	Provided jobs for unemployed youth
May 12, 1933	Agricultural Adjustment Act	Provided funds to pay farmers for not growing surplus crops
May 12, 1933	Federal Emergency Relief Act	Provided relief funds for the destitute
May 18, 1933	Tennessee Valley Authority Act	Set up authority for development of electric power and conservation
June 16, 1933	National Industrial Recovery Act	Specified cooperation among business, government, and labor in setting fair prices and working conditions
June 16, 1933	Glass-Steagall Banking Act	Created Federal Deposit Insurance Corporation (FDIC) to insure bank deposits

business leaders criticized NRA codes as heavy-handed government regulation of private enterprise. Some even claimed the NRA was a homegrown version of Benito Mussolini's corporate fascism taking shape in Italy. In reality, however, compliance with NRA codes was voluntary, and government enforcement efforts were weak to nonexistent. The NRA did little to reduce unemployment, raise consumption, or relieve the depression. In effect, the NRA represented a peace offering to business leaders by Roosevelt and his advisers, conveying the message that the New Deal did not intend to wage war against profits or private enterprise. The peace offering failed, however. Most corporate leaders became active and often bitter opponents of Roosevelt and the New Deal.

National Recovery Administration Quilt
The Blue Eagle of the National Recovery Administration, fiercely clutching a machine gear and lightning bolts, symbolized the government's determination to bring American industry around to a coordinated plan for recovery. The attempt to balance the interests of producers, workers, and consumers proved too much for the Blue Eagle. Yet, as this backcountry quilt indicates, the Blue Eagle was sometimes able to carry the spirit of cooperation far from the centers of industrial turmoil.
Franklin D. Roosevelt Library.

> Having enjoyed a long era of public adoration and political deference from Republicans, business leaders fulminated against New Deal efforts to reform or regulate what they considered their private concerns.

Challenges to the New Deal

The first New Deal initiatives engendered fierce criticism and political opposition. From the right, Republicans and business people charged that New Deal programs were too radical, undermining private property, economic stability, and democracy. Critics on the left faulted the New Deal for its failure to allay the human suffering caused by the depression and for its timidity in attacking corporate power and greed.

Resistance to Business Reform

Although New Deal programs rescued capitalism, business leaders criticized Roosevelt even though their prospects improved more steadily during the depression than did those of most other Americans. The hierarchical structure of concentrated corporate power that had developed during the boom years at the turn of the century avoided reform. The greatest wounds business leaders suffered were to their pride and political control. Resentful and fearful of regulation, taxes, and unions, they mounted stridently anti–New Deal campaigns. One editor called the president "Stalin Delano Roosevelt" and insisted that the New Deal was a "Raw Deal." Having enjoyed a long era of public adoration and political deference from Republicans, business leaders fulminated against New Deal efforts to reform or regulate what they considered their private concerns.

By 1935, two major business organizations, the National Association of Manufacturers and the Chamber of Commerce, had become openly anti–New Deal. Their critiques were amplified by the American Liberty League, founded in 1934, which decried the New Deal for betraying basic constitutional guarantees of freedom and individualism. To them, the AAA was a "trend toward fascist control of agriculture," relief programs marked "the end of democracy," and the NRA was a plunge into the "quicksand of visionary experimentation." Although the Liberty League's membership never exceeded 125,000, its well-financed publicity campaign widened the rift between Roosevelt and business people.

Economic planners who favored rational planning in the public interest and labor leaders who sought to influence wages and working conditions by organizing unions attacked the New Deal from the left. In their view, the NRA stifled enterprise by permitting **monopolistic** practices. They pointed out that industrial trade associations twisted NRA codes to suit their aims, thwarted competition, and engaged in price gouging. Labor leaders especially resented the NRA's willingness to allow businesses to form company-controlled unions while blocking workers from organizing genuine grassroots unions to bargain for themselves.

The Supreme Court stepped into this crossfire of criticisms in May 1935 and declared that the NRA unconstitutionally conferred powers reserved to Congress on an administrative agency staffed by government appointees. The

NRA lingered briefly, but its codes lost their authority. The failure of the NRA demonstrated the depth of many Americans' resistance to economic planning and the stubborn refusal of business leaders to yield to government regulations or reforms.

Casualties in the Countryside

The AAA weathered critical battering by champions of the old order better than the NRA. Allotment checks for keeping land fallow and crop prices high created loyalty among farmers with enough acreage to participate. As a white farmer in North Carolina declared, "I stand for the New Deal and Roosevelt. . . . The NRA, the AAA . . . and crop control." Agricultural processors and distributors, however, criticized the AAA. They objected that the program reduced the volume of crop production—the only source of their profits—while they paid a tax on processed crops that funded the very program that disadvantaged them. In 1936, the Supreme Court agreed with their contention that they were victims of an illegal attempt to tax one group (processors and distributors) to enrich another (farmers). Down but not out, the AAA rebounded from the Supreme Court ruling by eliminating the offending tax and funding allotment payments from general government revenues.

Protests stirred, however, among those who did not qualify for allotments. The Southern Farm Tenants Union argued passionately that the AAA enriched large farmers and impoverished small farmers who rented rather than owned their land. Landlords took out of production the land that tenants farmed, simultaneously qualifying themselves for government subsidies and relieving themselves of the need to employ tenants. One black sharecropper explained why only $75 a year from New Deal agricultural subsidies trickled down to her: "De landlord is landlord, de politicians is landlord, de judge is landlord, de shurf [sheriff] is landlord,

Black Sharecroppers
An unintended consequence of the New Deal plan to maintain farm prices by reducing acreage in production was the eviction of tenant farmers when the land they worked was unused. Champions of the tenant farmers, most notably the Southern Farm Tenants Union, protested in vain that federal crop subsidies should be shared between owners and those who usually worked the land. Often, however, sharecroppers like these were simply cast adrift, and lobbies for farm owners thwarted any governmental challenge. Tenant farmers' sad state continued until World War II provided opportunities for displaced tenants to escape to the cities. Corbis.

ever'body is landlord, en we [sharecroppers] ain' got nothin'!" Such testimony showed that the AAA, like the NRA, tended to help most those who least needed help. Roosevelt's political dependence on southern Democrats caused him to avoid confronting such economic and racial inequities in the South's entrenched order.

Displaced tenants often joined the army of migrant workers who straggled across rural America during the 1930s, some to flee Plains dust storms. Many migrants came from Mexico to work Texas cotton, Michigan beans, Idaho sugar beets, and California crops of all kinds. But since people willing to take agricultural jobs usually

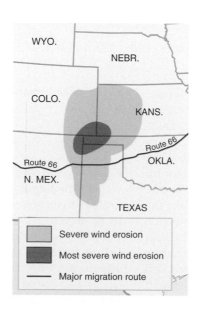

The Dust Bowl

Map labels: WYO. NEBR. COLO. KANS. Route 66 OKLA. Route 66 N. MEX. TEXAS

Legend:
- Severe wind erosion
- Most severe wind erosion
- Major migration route

Okie Family
This tenant farmer worked land near Eagleton, Oklahoma, but became sick with pneumonia and lost his farm. The county he had lived in for fifteen years refused to give him WPA benefits because he briefly left the county after recovering from his illness. Accompanied by his five children, he pulled his earthly possessions in a toy wagon along a highway, looking for work. Such poor, jobless migrants were common along America's roads during the 1930s.
Library of Congress.

exceeded the jobs available, wages fell and native-born white migrants fought to reserve even these low-wage jobs for themselves. Hundreds of thousands of "Okie" migrants streamed out of the Dust Bowl of Oklahoma, Kansas, Texas, and Colorado, where chronic drought and harmful agricultural practices blasted crops and hopes. Parched, poor, and windblown, Okies—like the Joad family immortalized in John Steinbeck's novel *The Grapes of Wrath*—migrated to the lush fields and orchards of California, congregating in labor camps and hoping to find work and a future. But migrant laborers seldom found steady or secure work. As one Okie said, "When they need us they call us migrants, and when we've picked their crop, we're bums and we got to get out."

Politics on the Fringes

Politically, the New Deal's staunchest opponents were in the Republican Party—organized, well-heeled, mainstream, and determined to challenge Roosevelt at every turn. But from the political fringes the New Deal also faced challenges, fueled by the hardship of the depression and the hope for a cure-all.

Socialists and Communists accused the New Deal of being the handmaiden of business elites and of rescuing capitalism from its self-inflicted crisis. Socialist author Upton Sinclair ran for governor of California in 1934 on a plan he called "End Poverty in California." Sinclair demanded that the state take ownership of idle factories and unused land and give them to cooperatives of working people, a first step toward what he envisioned as a "Cooperative Commonwealth" that would put the needs of people above profits. Although Sinclair received endorsements from intellectuals and labor leaders and considerable popular support, he lost the election, ending the most serious socialist electoral challenge to the New Deal.

Many other intellectuals and artists decided the time was ripe to advance the cause of more radical change, and they joined left-wing organizations, including the American Communist Party. The Communists eventually claimed about 30,000 members, the large majority of them immigrants, especially Scandinavians in the Midwest and eastern European Jews in major cities. Individual Communists worked to organize labor unions, protect the civil rights of black people, and help the destitute, but the party preached the overthrow of "bourgeois democracy" and the destruction of capitalism in favor of Soviet-style communism. Party spokesmen termed the NRA a "fascist slave program" and likened Roosevelt and the New Deal to Hitler and the Nazis. But heated talk about proletarian workers breaking their chains and rising in revolution against their bosses attracted few followers among the nation's millions of poor and unemployed. They wanted jobs and economic security within American capitalism and democracy, not violent revolution to establish a dictatorship of the Communist Party.

More powerful radical challenges to the New Deal sprouted from homegrown roots. Many Americans felt overlooked by New Deal programs that concentrated on finance, agriculture, and industry but did little to produce jobs or aid the poor. The merciless reality of the depression also continued to erode the security of people who still had a job but worried constantly about when they too might be pushed into the legions of the unemployed and penniless.

A Catholic priest in Detroit named Charles Coughlin spoke to, and for, many worried Americans in his weekly radio broadcasts, which reached a nationwide audience of 40 million. Father Coughlin expressed outrage at the suffering and inequities that he blamed on Communists, bankers, and "predatory capitalists" who, he claimed, were mostly Jews. In 1932,

Coughlin applauded Roosevelt's election and declared, "The New Deal is Christ's deal." But frustrated by Roosevelt's refusal to grant him influence, Coughlin turned against the New Deal for its failure to "drive the moneychangers from the temple" and end "want in the midst of plenty." Coughlin's message resonated with his radio audience, who inundated him with even more mail than Roosevelt received. Encouraged, Coughlin founded the National Union for Social Justice, or the Union Party, in 1935 and invited other dissidents to join him in a third-party challenge to Roosevelt in the 1936 presidential election. Tapping the popular appeal of anti-Semitism, Coughlin's Union Party called for an expanded money supply backed by silver so that the poor could be rescued from the "international bankers" responsible for the depression and coddled by Roosevelt.

Among those who answered Father Coughlin's call was Dr. Francis Townsend in Long Beach, California. Angry that many of his retired patients lived in misery, Townsend proposed in 1934 the creation of an Old Age Revolving Pension that would pay every American over age sixty a pension of $200 a month. In order to receive the pension, senior citizens had to agree to spend the entire amount within thirty days, thereby stimulating the economy. Townsend organized pension clubs with more than 2 million paying members and petitioned the federal government to enact his scheme. Had Townsend's plan been adopted, it would have required doubling taxes and spending half the nation's income to support the elderly, who comprised less than 10 percent of the population. When the major political parties rebuffed his impractical plan, Townsend merged his forces with Coughlin's Union Party in time for the 1936 election.

A more formidable challenge to the New Deal came from the ranks of the Democratic Party and from the region of its greatest strength. Huey Long, son of a backcountry Louisiana farmer, was elected governor of the state in 1928 with his slogan "Every man a king, but no one wears a crown." As governor, Long delivered on his promises to provide jobs and build roads, schools, and hospitals. Swaggering and bullying to get his way, Long delighted his grateful supporters, who elected him to the U.S. Senate in 1932 (see "Historical Question," page 888). As a freshman senator, Long introduced a sweeping "soak the rich" tax bill that would outlaw personal incomes of more than $1 million and in-

Huey Long: Demagogue or Champion of the Dispossessed?

From the time he was a small child, Huey Pierce Long was what one exasperated neighbor called a "pesterance." Defiant at school, artful at avoiding any disagreeable chores, ruthlessly driven to be the center of attention, Long got ahead with his intelligence and willingness to flout conventional rules. Though he spent only brief periods studying law at the University of Oklahoma and Tulane University, he cajoled a judge to convene a special bar examination, which he passed easily at the age of twenty-one. Declaring that he came out of that examination "running for office," Long rose swiftly from election as state railroad commissioner in 1918 to governor ten years later, dazzling the public with his brash style.

Louisiana's established leaders made white supremacy the cornerstone of their rule. Out of step with majority opinion on race, Long advanced his fortunes by appealing to class division—poor against rich, rural against urban, the humble against the elite—rather than white against black. He focused his reform program on a more equitable distribution of income and opportunity. At St. Martinsville, deep in swampy Cajun country, he asked, "Where are the schools that you have waited for your children to have, that have never come? Where are the roads and the highways that you sent your money to build . . . ? Where are the institutions to care for the sick and disabled?" When Long became governor, Louisiana had only 331 miles of paved roads outside the cities. It was also the most illiterate state in the nation. In 1893, when Long was born, 45 percent of those above the age of ten could not read; by 1920, the rate of illiteracy was still 22 percent, including 38 percent of all blacks.

Long articulated the grievances and hopes of the poor people of Louisiana. He also behaved ruthlessly to achieve his goals. After overcoming an **impeachment** effort in 1929, Long moved to consolidate his power. "I used to try to get things done by saying 'please,'" he said. "That didn't work and now I'm a dynamiter. I dynamite 'em out of my path." By 1930, Long completely dominated the state. Journalists around the country routinely referred to him as the "dictator of Louisiana." He made no effort to hide his power. Once an angry opponent thrust a volume in his face and shouted, "Maybe you've heard of this book. It's the constitution of the state of Louisiana." Long shrugged and said, "I'm the constitution here now." He bullied and bribed the state legislature into a rubber-stamp body that passed a series of laws giving him the power to count ballots and thus determine the outcome of elections. Every state employee knew that his or her job depended on loyalty to "the Kingfish," as Long liked to call himself.

His grasp on Louisiana firm, Long leaped into the national limelight by winning election to the U.S. Senate in 1932, where he quickly introduced a sweeping "soak-the-rich" tax bill that would have outlawed annual personal incomes of more than $1 million and inheritances of more than $5 million. Swift rejection by the Senate triggered his long-range strategy of becoming president by mobilizing the vast numbers of low-income Americans into a Share Our Wealth protest movement. Long's plan was to mount a presidential campaign in 1936 that would

heritances of more than $5 million. When the Senate summarily rejected his proposal, Long decided to run for president, mobilizing more than 5 million Americans behind his "Share Our Wealth" plan. Like Townsend's scheme, Long's program promised far more than it could deliver. Even if all wealth over a million dollars could have been converted to cash and confiscated, it would have paid for no more than 1 or 2 percent of the awards Long promised. Long did not linger over such troublesome details, predicting instead that he would become "your next President." Although the Share Our Wealth campaign died when Long was assassinated in 1935, his constituency and the wide appeal of a more equitable distribution of wealth persisted.

The challenges to the New Deal from Republicans as well as from more radical groups take enough votes from Roosevelt to tip the election to the Republican candidate. After four years of Republican failure to alleviate the depression with conservative policies, Long planned to sweep into the presidency in 1940, the savior of a suffering people.

The electoral showdown never came, however. On September 8, 1935, Carl Austin Weiss, a young physician enraged by the dishonor Long had visited on his family by removing his father from the Louisiana bench and suggesting black ancestry, fatally shot Long in a corridor of the Louisiana State House and was immediately gunned down by Long's bodyguards. The long lines of worn and ragged people passing by Long's coffin in the capitol and the smaller number of better-dressed mourners at Weiss's funeral testified to the split in Louisiana along class lines.

Long always answered charges that he was a dictator rather than a man of the people by insisting that the polite ways of conventional democratic rules could never cure the nation's deepest ills. Only forceful means, he insisted, could finally break the hold of the privileged and extend opportunity to everyone. He could point to real achievements in Louisiana. As promised, he taxed the oil companies and utilities that had run Louisiana for decades, and

Huey Long

Huey Long's ability to adapt his captivating stump-speech style to the radio made him the one rival politician who gave Roosevelt serious concern in the mid-1930s. Here Long is shown in 1932 campaigning in Arkansas in support of Hattie Carraway's bid for election to the U.S. Senate. Stigmatized as both a woman and a populist reformer, Carraway seemed a sure loser until Long crossed the border from Louisiana on her behalf. In a mere two weeks of speaking and pressing the flesh, Long brushed aside criticism that he was an interloper and boosted Carraway to victory as part of his crusade to share the wealth.

Corbis.

he funneled the revenue into programs to benefit those who had been left out. While he built monuments to his own vanity, Long also addressed many of the state's genuine social needs. At one time, Louisiana's road-building program was the biggest in the nation, and by 1935 the state had ten times more paved roads than when Long became governor. He made Louisiana State University a major institution of higher learning. He greatly expanded the state's pitiful public health facilities. For children, he provided free schoolbooks and new schools. For adults, he started night schools to combat illiteracy.

Disdainful both of Long and of those who turned to him, critics labeled Long a homegrown fascist and called him the "Messiah of the Rednecks." They compared him to Mussolini and Hitler and expressed relief that his life, and thus the damage he and the "rabble" who supported him could do, was cut short. Roosevelt recognized that the New Deal had to reach out to the "forgotten man," but Long reached farther to connect with neglected citizens. He gave Americans the only chance they ever had, for better or worse, to vote for a candidate with a broad national following who offered sweeping change comparable to that of parties on the radical right and left in other countries during the 1930s.

stirred Democrats to solidify their winning coalition. In 1934, in the midterm congressional elections—normally a time when a seated president loses support—Roosevelt sought to distance the New Deal from critics on the right and left. In the election, voters gave New Dealers a landslide victory. Democrats increased their majority in the House of Representatives and gained a two-thirds majority in the Senate.

Toward a Welfare State

The popular mandate for the New Deal revealed by the congressional elections persuaded Roosevelt to press ahead with bold new efforts of relief, recovery, and reform. Despite the initiatives of the Hundred Days, the depression still strangled the economy. Rumbles of discontent from Father Coughlin, Huey Long, and their

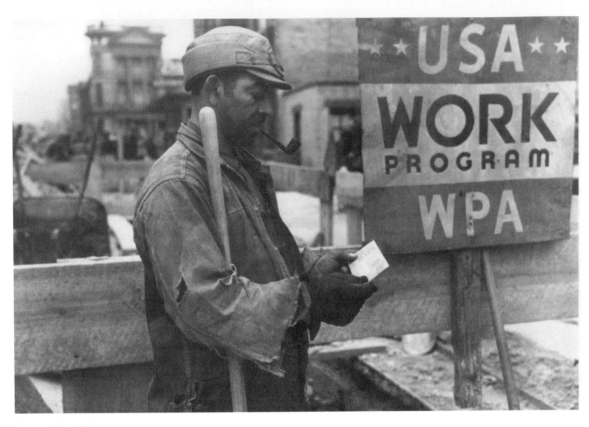

WPA Paycheck
WPA projects gave jobs and paychecks to millions of Americans who, like this man in Washington, D.C., dug ditches. Workers on New Deal public works projects also built the San Francisco–Oakland Bay Bridge, the Lincoln Tunnel in New York, and the Overseas Highway in the Florida Keys, as well as thousands of other bridges, roads, and buildings still in use today.
National Archives.

supporters showed that New Deal programs had fallen far short of their goals. In 1935, Roosevelt capitalized on his congressional majorities to enact major new programs that signaled the emergence of an American **welfare state**.

Taken together, these New Deal efforts stretched a safety net under the lives of ordinary Americans. Although many citizens remained unprotected, New Deal programs helped millions with jobs, relief, and government support. Knitting together the safety net was the idea that the federal government bore responsibility for the welfare of individual Americans. When individuals suffered because of economic and social forces beyond their control—as in the Great Depression—the federal government had the duty to provide them a measure of support and protection. The safety net of welfare programs tied the political loyalty of working people to the New Deal and the Democratic Party. As a North Carolina mill worker said, "Mr. Roosevelt is the only man we ever had in the White House who would understand that my boss is a sonofabitch."

Relief for the Unemployed

First and foremost, Americans still needed jobs. Since the private economy left 8 million people jobless by 1935, Roosevelt and his advisers launched a massive work relief program. Government handouts, Roosevelt declared, crippled recipients by inducing "spiritual and moral disintegration . . . destructive to the human spirit." Work relief—jobs—bolstered individuals' "self-respect, . . . self-confidence, . . . courage, and determination." With a congressional appropriation of nearly $5 billion—more than all government revenues in 1934—the New Deal created the Works Progress Administration (WPA) to give unemployed Americans government-funded jobs on public works projects. The WPA put millions of jobless citizens to work on roads, bridges, parks, public buildings, and more—projects that served public needs not otherwise being met. WPA paychecks pumped billions of dollars into the economy, boosting consumption along with what Roosevelt termed "the human spirit" of working people. In addition, Congress passed—over Roosevelt's veto—the bonus long-sought by the Bonus Marchers, giving veterans an average of $580, further stimulating the economy.

By 1936, WPA funds provided jobs for 7 percent of the nation's labor force. In effect, the WPA made the federal government the employer of last resort, creating useful jobs when the capitalist economy failed to do so. By the time the WPA ended in 1943—because mobilization for World War II created full employment—it had made major contributions to both relief and recovery. WPA jobs put 13 million men and women to work and gave them paychecks worth $10 billion.

About three out of four WPA jobs involved construction and renovation of the nation's physical infrastructure. WPA workers built 572,000 miles of country roads, 78,000 bridges, 67,000 miles of city streets, 40,000 public buildings, 8,000 parks, 350 airports, and much else. In addition to work with picks, shovels, hammers, nails, bricks, and mortar, the WPA gave jobs to 6,000 artists, musicians, actors, journalists, poets, and novelists. Artists painted murals in post offices and courthouses while writers penned travel guides and interviewed elderly former slaves. Actors in WPA theater groups attracted 60 million people to their performances, and more than 50 million Americans listened to concerts by WPA musicians. The WPA reached the most isolated corners of the nation; for example, WPA-funded librarians delivered books on horseback to remote cabins in Appalachia. WPA projects throughout the nation displayed tangible evidence of the New Deal's commitment to public welfare.

Empowering Labor

During the Great Depression, factory workers who managed to keep their jobs worried constantly about being laid off while their wages and working hours were cut. When workers tried to organize labor unions to protect themselves, municipal and state governments usually sided with employers. Since the Gilded Age, the state and federal governments had been far more effective at busting unions than busting **trusts**. The New Deal dramatically reversed the federal

government's stance toward unions. With legislation and political support, the New Deal encouraged an unprecedented wave of union organizing among the nation's working people. When the head of the United Mine Workers, John L. Lewis, told coal miners that "the President wants you to join a union," he exaggerated only a little. New Dealers believed unions would counterbalance the organized might of big corporations by defending working people, maintaining wages, and replacing the bloody violence that often accompanied strikes with economic peace and commercial stability.

Violent battles on the nation's streets and docks showed the determination of militant labor leaders to organize unions that would protect jobs as well as wages. In 1934, striking workers in Toledo, Minneapolis, San Francisco, and elsewhere were beaten and shot by police and the National Guard. In Congress, labor leaders lobbied for the National Labor Relations Act (NLRA), a bill sponsored by Senator Robert Wagner of New York that authorized the federal government to intervene in labor disputes and supervise the organization of labor unions. Justly considered a "Magna Carta for labor," the Wagner Act, as it came to be called, guaranteed workers the right to organize unions, putting the might of federal law behind the appeals of labor leaders. The Wagner Act created the National Labor Relations Board (NLRB) to sponsor and oversee elections for union representation. If the majority of workers at a company voted for a union, then the union became the sole bargaining agent for the entire workplace, and the employer was required to negotiate with the elected union leaders. Roosevelt signed the Wagner Act in July 1935, providing for the first time federal support for labor organization—the most important New Deal reform of the industrial order.

The achievements that flowed from the Wagner Act and renewed labor militancy were impressive. When Roosevelt became president in 1933, union membership—almost entirely composed of skilled workers in trade unions affiliated with the American Federation of Labor

> In addition to work with picks, shovels, hammers, nails, bricks, and mortar, the WPA gave jobs to 6,000 artists, musicians, actors, journalists, poets, and novelists.

> Justly considered a "Magna Carta for labor," the Wagner Act guaranteed workers the right to organize unions, putting the might of federal law behind the appeals of labor leaders.

Sit-Down Strikers

In 1937, workers occupied General Motors's Fisher Body plant in Flint, Michigan, demanding recognition of the United Auto Workers (UAW) as the sole bargaining agent for all GM workers. With nearly 250,000 workers producing about half of all American automobiles, General Motors fought the union with what a government committee termed an "industrial Cheka [Cheka was the Soviet Union's network of spies, later known as the KGB] . . . the most colossal supersystem of spies yet devised in any American corporation." Nonetheless, the Flint plant was a crucial choke point in the production of many popular GM cars, allowing the sit-down strikers to outmaneuver the spies and cut production to a trickle. After 44 days, the strikers won General Motors's recognition of the UAW, a landmark victory in industrial unionism.
Library of Congress.

(AFL)—stood at 3 million, down by half since the end of World War I. With the support of the Wagner Act, union membership expanded almost fivefold, to 14 million by the time of Roosevelt's death in 1945. By then, 30 percent of the workforce was unionized, the highest union representation in American history.

Most of the new union members were factory workers and unskilled laborers, many of them immigrants and African Americans. For decades, established AFL unions had no desire to organize factory and unskilled workers, who struggled along without unions. In 1935, under the aggressive leadership of the mine workers' John L. Lewis, and the head of the Amalgamated Clothing Workers, Sidney Hillman, a coalition of unskilled workers formed the Committee for Industrial Organization (CIO; later the Congress

of Industrial Organizations). The CIO, helped by the Wagner Act, mobilized organizing drives in major industries. The exceptional courage and organizing skill of labor militants, a few of them Communists, earned the CIO the leadership role in the campaign to organize the bitterly anti-union automobile and steel industries.

The bloody struggle by the CIO-affiliated United Auto Workers (UAW) to organize workers at General Motors climaxed in January 1937 when striking workers occupied the main assembly plant in Flint, Michigan, in a "sit-down" strike that slashed the plant's production of 15,000 cars a week to a mere 150. In desperation, General Motors obtained court injunctions against the sit-down strikers. But neither Roosevelt nor the Michigan governor would act to enforce the injunction. Stymied, General

Motors surrendered and agreed to make the UAW the sole bargaining agent for all the company's workers and to refrain from interfering with union activity. Having subdued the auto industry's leading producer, the UAW expanded its campaign until, after much violence, the entire industry was unionized when the Ford Motor Company capitulated to the union in 1941.

The CIO hoped to ride organizing success in auto plants to victory in the steel mills. But after unionizing the industry giant U.S. Steel, the CIO ran up against fanatic opposition from smaller steel firms. The climax came in May 1937 when a crowd of strikers gathered in a field outside Chicago to organize a picket line around Republic Steel. Without warning, police who had been sent to keep order charged the crowd, swinging clubs and firing their weapons, killing ten strikers and injuring scores. Following this debacle, the battered steelworkers halted their organizing campaign. In steel and other major industries, such as the stridently anti-union southern textile mills, organizing efforts stalled until after 1941, when military mobilization created labor shortages that gave workers greater bargaining power.

Social Security and Tax Reform

The single most important feature of the New Deal's emerging welfare state was Social Security. An ambitious, far-reaching, and permanent reform, Social Security was designed to provide a modest income to relieve the poverty of elderly people. Only about 15 percent of older Americans had private pension plans, and during the depression corporations and banks often failed to pay the meager pensions they had promised. Prompted by the popular but impractical panaceas of Dr. Townsend, Father Coughlin, and Huey Long, Roosevelt became the first president to advocate protection for the elderly.

The political struggle for Social Security highlighted class differences among Americans. Support for the measure came from a coalition of advocacy groups for the elderly and the poor, traditional progressives, leftists, social workers, and labor unions. Arrayed against them were economic conservatives, including the Liberty League, the National Association of Manufacturers, the Chamber of Commerce, and the American Medical Association. Enact the Social Security system, these conservatives and their representatives in the Republican Party warned, and the government will gain a whip hand over private property, destroy initiative, and reduce proud individuals to spineless loafers.

The large New Deal majority in Congress carried the day in August 1935. Yet the strong objections to federal involvement in matters traditionally left to individuals and local charities persuaded the framers of Social Security to strike an awkward balance among federal, state, and personal responsibility. The Social Security Act required that pensions for the elderly be funded not by direct government subsidies but instead by tax contributions from workers and their employers. Although this provision subtracted money from consumption—hindering economic recovery—it gave contributing workers a personal stake in the system and made it politically invulnerable. Social Security also created unemployment insurance, paid for by employers' contributions, that provided modest benefits for workers who lost their jobs. In a bow to traditional beliefs about local governments' responsibility for public assistance, Social Security also issued multi-million-dollar grants to the states to use to support dependent mothers and children, public health services, and the blind, providing desperately needed

Social Security Card
The Social Security Act required each working American who participated in the system to register with the government and obtain a unique number—the "SSN" familiar to every citizen today—inscribed on an identity card, making benefits portable from one job and one state to another. For the first time in the nation's history, millions of ordinary citizens were numbered, registered, and identified by a government bureaucracy, creating a personal, individualized connection between people and the federal government. Administering the massive agency needed to collect, monitor, and regulate this information and distribute the benefits that flowed from it gave government jobs to tens of thousands, providing security for government workers as well as for Social Security beneficiaries.
Picture Research Consultants & Archives.

Millions of Americans—women, children, old folks, the unorganized, unskilled, uneducated, and unemployed—often fell through the New Deal's safety net.

relief. After a Supreme Court decision in 1937 upheld the right of Congress to require all citizens to pay for Social Security through federal taxes, the program was expanded to include benefits for dependent survivors of deceased recipients. Although the first Social Security check (for $41.30) was not issued until 1940, the system gave working people assurance that in the future, when they became too old to work, they would receive income from the government. This safety net protected ordinary working people from fears of a penniless and insecure old age.

Fervent opposition to Social Security struck New Dealers as evidence that the rich had learned little from the depression. Roosevelt had long felt contempt for the moneyed elite who ignored the sufferings of the poor. He looked for a way to redistribute wealth that would weaken conservative opposition, advance the cause of social equity, and defuse political challenges from Huey Long and Father Coughlin. In June 1935, as the Social Security Act was being debated, Roosevelt delivered a message to Congress outlining comprehensive tax reform. Charging that large fortunes put "great and undesirable concentration of control in [the hands of] relatively few individuals," Roosevelt urged a graduated tax on corporations, an inheritance tax, and an increase in maximum personal income taxes. Congress endorsed Roosevelt's basic principle by taxing those with higher incomes at a somewhat higher rate.

Neglected Americans and the New Deal

While the WPA and other work relief programs aided working people, the average unemployment rate for the 1930s stayed high—17 percent, about one of every six workers. Even many working people remained more or less untouched by New Deal benefits. Workers in industries that resisted unions received little help from the Wagner Act or the WPA. Tens of thousands of women in southern textile mills, for example, commonly received wages of less than ten cents an hour and were fired if they protested. Domestic workers—almost all of them women—and agricultural workers—many of them African, Hispanic, or Asian

Americans—were neither unionized nor eligible for Social Security. The safety net of New Deal programs provided the best protection for unionized workers in major industries, neglecting millions of other, less fortunate Americans. The patchwork of New Deal reforms erected a two-tier welfare state. In the top tier, organized workers were the greatest beneficiaries of New Deal initiatives. In the bottom tier, millions of neglected Americans—women, children, old folks, the unorganized, unskilled, uneducated, and

Mary McLeod Bethune
At the urging of Eleanor Roosevelt, Mary McLeod Bethune, a southern educational and civil rights leader, became director of the National Youth Administration's Division of Negro Affairs. The first black woman to head a federal agency, Bethune used her position to promote social change. Here Bethune takes her mission to the streets to protest the discriminatory hiring practices of the Peoples Drug Store chain in the nation's capital.
Moorland-Spingarn Research Center, Howard University.

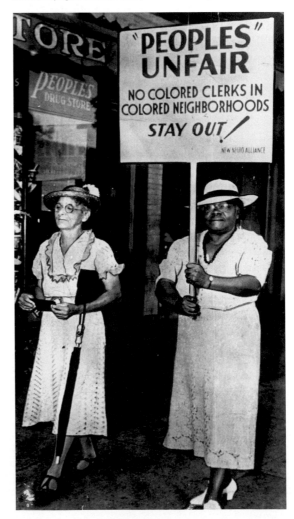

Hispanic-American Alliance Banner

Between 1910 and 1940, when refugees from the Mexican revolution poured across the American border, the Hispanic-American Alliance and other such organizations sought to protect Mexican Americans' rights against nativist fears and hostility. In the years between the world wars, many alliance banners such as this one flew in opposition to the deportation of Mexican aliens, an attempt in 1926 to bar Mexican Americans from city jobs in Los Angeles, and the disproportionately high use of the death penalty against Mexicans convicted of crimes. Throughout these and other trials, the alliance steadfastly emphasized the desire of Mexican Americans to receive permanent status in the United States.

The Oakland Museum.

unemployed—often fell through the New Deal safety net.

The New Deal neglected few citizens more than African Americans. About half of black Americans in cities were jobless, double the unemployment rate among whites. In the rural South, where the vast majority of African Americans lived, conditions were worse. New Deal agricultural policies like the AAA favored landowners and often resulted in black sharecroppers and tenants being pushed off land they farmed. Disfranchisement by intimidation and legal subterfuge prevented southern blacks from protesting their plight at the ballot box. Protest risked vicious retaliation from local whites. After years of decline, lynching increased during the 1930s. In Alabama, the black "Scottsboro Boys" faced the death penalty in 1931 for a rape they did not commit (see chapter 23); in Georgia, radical black unionist Angelo Herndon received a sentence to the chain gang for trying to organize black workers. Only 11 of more than 10,000 WPA supervisors in the South were black, even though African Americans comprised about a third of the region's population. Up north, a riot in 1935 that focused on white-owned businesses in Harlem dramatized blacks' resentment and despair. Bitter critics charged that the New Deal's NRA stood for "Negro Run Around" or "Negroes Ruined Again."

Roosevelt responded to such criticisms with great caution since New Deal reforms required the political support of powerful conservative, segregationist, southern Democrats, who would be alienated by programs that aided blacks. A white Georgia relief worker expressed the common view that "Any Nigger who gets over $8 a week is a spoiled Nigger, that's all." Stymied by the political clout of entrenched white racism, New Dealers tried to attract political support from black leaders. Roosevelt's overtures to African Americans prompted northern black voters to shift in the 1934 elections from the Republican to the Democratic Party, helping elect New Deal Democrats.

Eleanor Roosevelt sponsored the appointment of Mary McLeod Bethune—the energetic cofounder of the National Council on Negro Women—as head of the Division of Negro Affairs in the National Youth Administration. The highest ranking black official in Roosevelt's administration, Bethune used her position to guide a small number of black professionals and civil rights activists to posts within New Deal agencies. Nicknamed the "Black Cabinet," these men and women comprised the first sizable representation of African Americans in white-collar posts in the federal government, and they ultimately helped about one in four African Americans get access to New Deal relief programs.

Despite these gains, by 1940 African Americans still suffered severe handicaps. Most of the 13 million black workers toiled at low-paying menial jobs, unprotected by the New Deal safety net. Infant mortality was 50 percent greater than for whites, and life expectancy was twelve years shorter. Making a mockery of the "separate but equal" doctrine, segregated black schools had less money and worse facilities than those of whites, and only 1 percent of black students earned college degrees. In southern states, there were no black police officers or judges and hardly any black lawyers, and vigilante violence against blacks went unpunished. To these problems of black Americans, the New Deal offered few remedies.

Hispanic Americans did no better. About a million Mexican Americans lived in the United States in the 1930s, most of them first- or second-generation immigrants who worked at stoop labor tending crops throughout the West. During the depression, field workers saw their low wages plunge lower still to about a dime an hour. Ten thousand Mexican American pecan shellers in San Antonio, Texas, earned only a nickel an hour. To preserve scarce jobs for U.S. citizens, the federal government choked off immigration from Mexico while state and local officials prohibited employment of aliens on work relief projects and summarily deported tens of

thousands of Mexican Americans, many with their American-born children. Local white administrators of many New Deal programs throughout the West discriminated against Hispanics and other people of color. Even when Mexican Americans managed to join government work projects, they often received lower pay than their white counterparts, and less aid when out of a job. A New Deal study concluded that "The Mexican is . . . segregated from the rest of the community as effectively as the Negro . . . [by] poverty and low wages."

Asian Americans had similar experiences. Asian immigrants were still excluded from U.S. citizenship and in many states were not permitted to own land. Although by 1930 more than half of Japanese Americans had been born in the United States, they were still liable to discrimination. Even college-educated Asian Americans worked in family shops, restaurants, and laundries. One young Asian American expressed frustrations felt by many others: "I am a fruit-stand worker. I would much rather it were doctor or lawyer . . . but my aspirations [were] frustrated long ago by circumstances [and] I am only what I am, a professional carrot washer."

Native Americans—like blacks, Hispanics, and Asian Americans—suffered neglect from New Deal agencies. As a group, they remained the poorest of the poor. Since the Dawes Act of 1887, the federal government had encouraged Native Americans to assimilate, to abandon their Indian identities and adopt the cultural norms of the majority society. Under the leadership of the New Deal's commissioner of Indian affairs, John Collier, the New Deal's Indian Reorganization Act (IRA) of 1934 largely reversed that policy. Collier claimed that "the most interesting and important fact about Indians" was that they "do not expect much, often they expect nothing at all; yet they are able to be happy." Given such views, the IRA provided little economic aid to Native Americans, but it did restore their right to own land communally and to have greater control over their own affairs, including the right to vote on whether they should live under the IRA. In special elections in 1934 and 1935, 172 tribes with about 132,000 members opted to accept the IRA, and 73 tribes with about 63,000 members voted to reject it. The IRA brought little immediate benefit to Native Americans and remained a divisive issue for decades, but it did provide an important foundation for Indians' economic, cultural, and political resurgence a generation later.

John Collier Meets with Navajo Representatives

Commissioner of Indian Affairs John Collier receives a Navajo delegation protesting restrictions in the Indian Reorganization Act of 1934. The Navajos display a blanket made from the wool of their own sheep to protest limits on the number of sheep they could raise. Collier had crafted the act to revive Native American society by granting tribes an independent land base and many self-governing powers. However, his attempt to make the reservations economically viable through conservation measures, including restrictions on grass-devouring sheep, roused resistance by Indians who chose traditional ways of using resources. The tension between federal benevolence and Indian views of their own way of life has remained a painful issue.

Wide World Photos, Inc.

New Deal Needle Book

In the 1936 presidential campaign, Democrats distributed this sewing-needle book to celebrate New Deal achievements during Roosevelt's first term. Evoking Roosevelt's 1932 campaign theme song, "Happy Days Are Here Again," the illustrations on the needle book emphasize the return of harmony in agriculture, of booming factories providing plenty of jobs, and above all of "happiness restored" at home around the well-appointed dinner table. Notice that the working people in factories are faceless but the white-collar worker and the family are individualized sympathetically. The needle book signifies Democrats' attempt to mobilize women to vote in gratitude for the happiness supplied by Roosevelt and the New Deal. Like most campaign material, the needle book's claims for New Deal success exaggerated greatly.

Collection of Janice L. and David J. Frent.

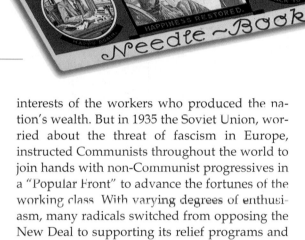

The troubadour of working people, singer and songwriter Woody Guthrie, traveled the nation for eight years during the 1930s "by the thumb route . . . no job, no money, no home . . . no nothing." At night, he recalled, other rambling men told him "the story of their life, how it used to be," giving voice to experiences especially common among Americans neglected by the New Deal: "how the home went to pieces, how the young wife died or left, how the mother died in the insane asylum, how Dad tried twice to kill himself, and lay flat on his back for 18 months and then crops got to where they wouldn't bring nothing, work in factories would kill a dog . . . work in the steel mills burned your system up . . . and—always, always [you] had to fight and argue and cuss and swear . . . to try to get a nickel more out of the rich bosses."

interests of the workers who produced the nation's wealth. But in 1935 the Soviet Union, worried about the threat of fascism in Europe, instructed Communists throughout the world to join hands with non-Communist progressives in a "Popular Front" to advance the fortunes of the working class. With varying degrees of enthusiasm, many radicals switched from opposing the New Deal to supporting its relief programs and encouragement of labor unions.

Roosevelt's conservative opponents reacted to the massing of New Deal force by intensifying their opposition to the welfare state. To Roosevelt, the situation seemed part of a drama that had played out since the nation's beginning, pitting a Hamiltonian faction of wealth and privilege against the heirs of Jefferson who, like Roosevelt himself, favored a more equitable distribution of wealth and opportunity.

The New Deal from Victory to Deadlock

To accelerate the sputtering economic recovery, Roosevelt shifted the emphasis of the New Deal in the mid-1930s. Instead of seeking cooperation from conservative business leaders, he decided to rely on the growing New Deal coalition to enact reforms over the strident opposition of Republicans and corporate interests.

Added to New Deal strength in farm states and big cities were some new allies on the left. Throughout Roosevelt's first term, socialists and Communists denounced the slow pace of change and accused the New Deal of failing to serve the

The Election of 1936

Roosevelt believed that the presidential election of 1936 would test his leadership and progressive ideals. The depression still had a stranglehold on the economy. Nearly 8 million remained jobless, and millions more were stuck in poverty. Conservative leaders believed that the New Deal's failure to lift the nation out of the depression indicated that Americans were ready for a change. Left-wing critics insisted that the New Deal had missed the opportunity to displace capitalism with a socialist economy and would lose votes to candidates who recommended more radical remedies.

Faces of the Depression

New Deal agencies dispatched dozens of photographers to document the lives of Americans during the 1930s. In thousands of pictures, the photographers captured the faces of the depression. Their photographs, the sources of the portraits shown here, demonstrate that, unlike the people shown on the New Deal sewing book, working Americans were not faceless drones but human individuals struggling to survive—whether dispossessed black sharecroppers in the South, Japanese American mothers and daughters in California produce fields, Mexican laborers in the Southwest, farmers in the Tennessee mountains, or Okie grannies, mothers, and children in California labor camps. As these portraits suggest, working people knew that, while the New Deal might provide welcome aid, they depended in the end on their own resourcefulness and the support of family and friends.

Library of Congress.

Republicans turned to the Kansas heartland to select Governor Alfred (Alf) Landon as their presidential nominee. A moderate who had supported some New Deal measures, Landon stressed mainstream Republican proposals to achieve a balanced federal budget and to ease the perils of illness and old age with old-fashioned neighborliness instead of faceless government bureaucracies like Social Security.

Roosevelt put his faith in the growing coalition of New Deal supporters, who he believed shared his conviction that the New Deal was the nation's liberator from a long era of privilege and wealth for a few and "economic slavery" for the rest. At the end of the campaign, Roosevelt struck a defiant pose before a thunderous crowd at Madison Square Garden, calling "the roll of honor of those who stood with us in 1932 and still stand with us today . . . men who never had a chance, women in sweatshops, [and] children at looms." Assailing his "old enemies . . . business and financial monopoly, speculation, reckless banking, [and] class antagonism," he proclaimed, "Never before in all our history have these forces been so united against one candidate as they stand today. They are unanimous in their hate for me—and I welcome their hatred." When the crowd's roar subsided, Roosevelt concluded: "I should like to have it said of my first Administration that in it the forces of selfishness and of lust for power met their match. I should like to have it said of my second Administration that in it these forces met their master."

Roosevelt triumphed spectacularly. He won 60.8 percent of the popular vote, 11 million more votes than Landon, the widest presidential margin to date. He carried the electoral votes of every state except Maine and Vermont. Third parties—including the Socialists and the Communists—fell pitifully short of the support they expected and never again mounted a significant challenge to the New Deal. Congressional results were equally lopsided, with Democrats outnumbering Republicans more than three to one in both houses.

Roosevelt's victory testified to the New Deal's mobilization of voters. For example, in nineteen northern cities where more than half the population was composed of first- and second-generation immigrants, Democratic votes more than doubled compared to 1932, while Republican voters increased by less than a third. In his inaugural address, Roosevelt pledged to use his mandate to help all citizens achieve a decent standard of living. He announced, "I see one third of a nation ill-housed, ill-clad, [and] ill-nourished," and he promised to devote his second term to alleviate their wants.

Court Packing

In the afterglow of his reelection triumph, Roosevelt pondered how to remove the remaining obstacles to New Deal reforms. He decided to target the Supreme Court. Laden with conservative justices appointed by Republican presidents, the Court had invalidated eleven New Deal measures as unconstitutional interferences with free enterprise. Now, Social Security, the Wagner Act, the Securities and Exchange Commission, and other New Deal innovations were moving toward an ominous rendezvous with the justices.

Roosevelt concluded that he must do something to ensure that the Supreme Court's "horse and buggy" notions did not dismantle the New Deal. He proposed that one new justice be added for each existing judge who had already served for ten years and was over the age of seventy. In effect, the proposed law would give Roosevelt the power to pack the Court with up to six New Dealers who could outvote the elderly, conservative, Republican justices.

But the president had not reckoned with Americans' deeply rooted deference to the independent authority of the Supreme Court. More than two-thirds of Americans believed the Court should be free from political interference. Even New Deal supporters were disturbed by the "court-packing" scheme. The suggestion that individuals over seventy had diminished mental capacity also offended many elderly members of Congress. Although Roosevelt insisted that the bill was intended to improve the efficiency of an "overworked" Court, the real purpose was to make room for supporters of New Deal initiatives. A storm of public protest whipped up by conservatives prompted the heavily Democratic Senate to defeat the bill.

Although Roosevelt's court-packing plan failed, Supreme Court justices nonetheless got Roosevelt's message. After the furor abated, Chief Justice Charles Evans Hughes and fellow moderate Owen Roberts moderated their views enough to keep the Court from invalidating the Wagner Act and Social Security. Then the most

> To ensure that the Supreme Court did not dismantle the New Deal, Roosevelt proposed that one new justice be added for each existing judge who had already served for ten years and was over the age of seventy.

conservative of the elderly justices—the "four horsemen of reaction," one New Dealer called them—retired. Roosevelt eventually named eight justices to the Court—more than any other president. His choice of liberals to fill vacancies on the Court ultimately gave safe passage to New Deal laws through the shoals of judicial review.

Reaction and Recession

Emboldened by their defeat of the court-packing plan, Republicans and southern Democrats rallied around their common conservatism to obstruct additional reforms. Arguments over whether the New Deal needed to be expanded and, if so, how, undermined consensus among reformers and sparked antagonism between Congress and the White House. The ominous rise of belligerent regimes in Germany, Italy, Japan, and elsewhere slowed reform as some Americans began to worry more about defending the nation than changing it. These developments impeded reform despite Roosevelt's 1936 landslide.

Roosevelt himself favored slowing the pace of the New Deal. He believed that existing New Deal measures had steadily boosted the economy and largely eliminated the depression crisis. In fact, the gross national product in 1937 briefly equaled the 1929 level, before drooping lower for the rest of the decade. Unemployment declined to 14 percent in 1937 but quickly spiked upward and stayed higher until 1940. Roosevelt's unwarranted optimism about the economic recovery persuaded him that additional deficit spending by the federal government was no longer necessary. He also worried that pump-priming deficits would cause inflation and reduce the value of hard-earned savings. Accordingly, Roosevelt moved cautiously toward a balanced budget by cutting funds for relief projects. He also urged the Federal Reserve to raise interest rates to discourage speculators from borrowing on easy terms.

Roosevelt's retrenchment soon backfired. Rather than preventing inflation, the reduction in deficit spending reversed the improving economy. Anxious about inflation, Roosevelt failed to consider how far the economy had to go before it would reach inflationary levels. Even at

> Roosevelt's unwarranted optimism about the economic recovery persuaded him that additional deficit spending by the federal government was no longer necessary.

the high-water mark of recovery in the summer of 1937, 7 million people lacked jobs. In the next few months, national income and production slipped backward so steeply that almost two-thirds of the economic gains since 1933 were lost by June 1938. Farm prices dropped 20 percent, and unemployment rose by more than 2 million.

This economic reversal hurt the New Deal politically. Conservatives argued that this recession proved New Deal measures produced only an illusion of progress. The way to weather the recession was to tax and spend less and wait for the natural laws of supply and demand to restore prosperity. Many New Dealers believed instead that the recession demonstrated anew the failure of free-enterprise orthodoxies. They insisted that the continuing depression showed the necessity of government intervention in the economy. They demanded that Roosevelt revive federal spending and redouble efforts to stimulate the economy. In 1938, Congress heeded such pleas and enacted a massive new program of federal spending.

The New Deal's ad hoc methods received support from new economic ideas advanced by the brilliant British economist John Maynard Keynes. In his influential work *The General Theory of Employment, Interest, and Money* (1936), Keynes made a sophisticated, theoretical argument in favor of practices that New Deal relief agencies had developed in a commonsense way. A nation's economy, Keynes declared, could not automatically reach its full potential in the complex, interdependent modern world. The depression had painfully illustrated that economic activity could become stalled at a level far short of a society's true potential. When that happened, only government intervention could pump enough money into the system to revive production, boost consumption, and restore prosperity.

Roosevelt never had the inclination or the time to follow his economic advisers into the thicket of **Keynesian** theory. But the recession scare of 1938 taught the president the Keynesian lesson that economic growth had to be carefully nurtured. Escape from the depression required a plan for large-scale spending to alleviate distress and stimulate economic growth.

The Last of the New Deal Reforms

From the moment he was sworn in, Roosevelt sought to expand the powers of the presidency. He believed that the president needed more authority to meet emergencies such as the depression and to administer the sprawling federal bureaucracy. Arguing the need for "efficiency," Roosevelt submitted an ambitious plan of executive reorganization to Congress in 1937. The bill failed, but in September 1938 Congress passed the Administrative Reorganization Act, which gave Roosevelt part of what he desired. With a Democratic majority in Congress, a now friendly Supreme Court, and the revival of deficit spending, the newly empowered White House seemed to be in a good position to move ahead with a revitalized New Deal.

Resistance to further reform was also on the rise, however. Conservatives argued that the New Deal had pressed government centralization too far and was bent on creating what later came to be known as the "imperial presidency." Even the New Deal's friends became weary of one emergency program after another, especially while economic woes still shadowed New Deal achievements. By the midpoint of Roosevelt's second term, restive members of Congress balked at new initiatives. Clearly, the New Deal was losing momentum, but enough energy remained for one last burst of reform.

The farm sector still had strong claims on New Deal attention in the face of drought, declining prices, and impoverished sharecroppers and tenants. In 1937, the Agriculture Department created the Farm Security Administration (FSA) to provide housing and loans to help tenant farmers become independent. But the FSA was starved for funds and ran up against the major farm organizations intent on serving their own interests. With only minor successes to show, the FSA petered out in the early 1940s. For those who owned farms, the New Deal offered renewed prosperity with a second Agricultural Adjustment Act (AAA) in 1938. To moderate price swings by regulating supply, the plan combined production quotas on five staple crops—cotton, tobacco, wheat, corn, and rice—with storage loans through its Commodity Credit Corporation. The most prosperous farmers benefited most, but the act's Federal Surplus Commodities Corporation added an element of charity by issuing food stamps so that the poor could obtain surplus food. The AAA of 1938 brought stability to American agriculture and ample food to most—but not all—tables.

Advocates for the urban poor also made modest gains after decades of neglect. New York senator Robert Wagner convinced Congress to pass the National Housing Act in 1937. By 1941, some 160,000 residences had been made available to poor people at affordable rents. The project did not come close to meeting the need for affordable housing, but for the first time the federal government took an active role in providing decent urban housing.

The last major piece of New Deal labor legislation, the Fair Labor Standards Act of June 1938, reiterated the New Deal pledge to provide workers with a decent standard of living. After lengthy haggling and compromise that revealed the waning strength of the New Deal, Congress finally agreed to intervene in the long-sacrosanct realm of worker contracts. The new law set wage and hours standards and at long last curbed the use of child labor. The minimum-wage level was modest—twenty-five cents an hour for a maximum of forty-four hours a week. And, in order to attract enough conservative votes, the act exempted merchant seamen, fishermen, domestic help, and farm laborers from these minimal wage and hours standards—relegating most white women and most African Americans to lower wages. Nevertheless, the Fair Labor Standards Act advanced Roosevelt's inaugural promise to improve the living standards of the poorest Americans.

The final New Deal reform effort failed to make much headway against the hidebound system of racial segregation. Although Roosevelt denounced lynching as murder, he would not jeopardize his vital base of southern political support by demanding antilynching legislation. In 1934 and 1935, Congress voted down attempts to make lynching a federal crime, and in 1938 the last antilynching bill of the decade died in a Senate filibuster. Laws to eliminate the poll tax—used to deny blacks the opportunity to vote—encountered the same overwhelming resistance. Although some African Americans received benefits from employment opportunities in northern relief projects and federal agencies, the New Deal refused to confront the injustice of racial segregation with the same vigor it brought to bear on economic hardship.

By the end of 1938, the New Deal had lost steam and encountered stiff opposition. As leg-

> Conservatives argued that the New Deal had pressed government centralization too far and was bent on creating what later came to be known as the "imperial presidency."

> The Fair Labor Standards Act reiterated the New Deal pledge to provide workers with a decent standard of living, setting wage and hours standards and at long last curbing the use of child labor.

islative initiative waned and programs played themselves out, the conservative tide rose. In the congressional elections of 1938, Republicans picked up seven seats in the Senate and eighty in the House, giving them more congressional influence than they had enjoyed since 1932. New Dealers could claim unprecedented and resounding achievements since 1933, but nobody needed reminding that those achievements had not ended the depression. In his annual message to Congress in January 1939, Roosevelt signaled a halt to New Deal reforms by speaking about preserving the progress already achieved, rather than extending it. He pointed to the threat posed by fascist aggressors in Europe and Asia, and he proposed defense expenditures that surpassed New Deal appropriations for relief and economic recovery.

Conclusion: Achievements and Limitations of the New Deal

The New Deal replaced the fear symbolized by Hoover's expulsion of the Bonus Army with Roosevelt's confidence, optimism, and energetic pragmatism. A growing majority of Americans agreed with Roosevelt that the federal government should help those in need, thereby strengthening the political coalition that propelled the New Deal. In the process of seeking relief for victims of the depression, recovery of the general economy, and basic reform of major economic institutions, the New Deal vastly expanded the size and influence of the federal government and changed the way the American people viewed Washington. New Dealers achieved significant victories such as Social Security, labor's right to organize, and guarantees that farm prices would be maintained through controls on production and marketing. New Deal measures marked the emergence of a welfare state, but its limited, two-tier character left many needy Americans with little aid.

Full-scale relief, recovery, and reform eluded New Deal programs. Even though millions of Americans benefited directly from the New Deal's alphabet soup of agencies and programs, both relief and recovery were limited and temporary. By 1940 the depression still proved distressingly durable. The most durable achievements of the New Deal were reforms that stabilized agriculture, encouraged the organization of labor unions, and created the safety net of Social Security and fair labor standards. But perhaps the most impressive achievement of the New Deal was what did not happen: Authoritarian governments and anticapitalist policies were common during the 1930s outside the United States, but they were shunned by the New Deal. The greatest economic crisis the nation had ever faced did not cause Americans to abandon democracy, as happened in Germany, where Adolf Hitler seized dictatorial power. Nor did the nation turn to radical alternatives such as socialism or communism.

Republicans and other conservatives claimed that the New Deal amounted to a form of socialism that threatened democracy and capitalism. But as Frances Perkins said, Franklin Roosevelt took capitalism as much for granted as he did his family. Rather than attack capitalism, he sought to save it, and he succeeded. That success also marked the limits of the New Deal's achievements. Like his cousin Teddy, Franklin Roosevelt understood that a strengthened national government was necessary to curb the destructive tendencies of concentrated economic power. A shift of authority toward the federal government, both Roosevelts believed, would allow capitalist enterprises to be balanced by the nation's democratic tradition. The New Deal stopped far short of challenging capitalism either by undermining private property or by imposing strict national planning.

New Dealers repeatedly described their programs as a kind of warfare against the economic adversities of the 1930s. In the next decade, with the depression only partly vanquished, the Roosevelt administration had to turn from the New Deal's war against economic crisis at home to participate in a worldwide conflagration to defeat the enemies of democracy abroad.

For additional firsthand accounts of this period, see Chapter 24 in Michael Johnson, ed., *Reading the American Past,* Third Edition.

To assess your mastery of the material in this chapter, see the Online Study Guide at bedfordstmartins.com/roark.

For Web links related to topics in this chapter, see "HistoryLinks," "DocLinks," and "PlaceLinks" at bedfordstmartins.com/roark.

CHRONOLOGY

1932 • Bonus Army marches on Washington and is routed by federal troops.

1933 • Democrat Franklin D. Roosevelt assumes presidency.

• **March–June.** New Deal established through passage of reform legislation of the Hundred Days.

• Roosevelt closes nation's banks for four-day "holiday" to allow time to stabilize banking system.

• Federal Emergency Relief Administration (FERA) provides relief for unemployed.

1934 • Securities and Exchange Commission (SEC) licenses and regulates stock exchanges.

• Upton Sinclair loses bid for governorship of California and the chance to enact his End Poverty in California work relief program.

• Wealthy conservatives of American Liberty League oppose New Deal.

• Dr. Francis Townsend devises Old Age Revolving Pension scheme to provide money to impoverished elderly.

• Congress passes Indian Reorganization Act.

1935 • Louisiana senator Huey Long assassinated.

• Legislation creates Works Progress Administration (WPA).

• Congress passes Wagner Act to guarantee workers the right to organize unions and bargain collectively.

• Committee for Industrial Organization (CIO) founded to provide union representation for unskilled workers.

• Social Security Act provides supplementary income for aged and retired persons.

• "Radio Priest" Father Charles Coughlin begins National Union for Social Justice.

1936 • John Maynard Keynes publishes *The General Theory of Employment, Interest, and Money,* providing theoretical justification for government deficit financing.

• Franklin Roosevelt elected to a second term by a landslide over Republican Alfred Landon.

1937 • CIO stages successful sit-down strike at General Motors plant in Flint, Michigan.

• Roosevelt's court-packing legislation defeated in Senate.

1937–1938
• Economic recession slows recovery from depression.

1938 • Second Agricultural Adjustment Act and Fair Labor Standards Act bring New Deal legislation to an end.

• Congress rejects administration's antilynching bill.

• Administrative Reorganization Act enlarges scope and power of presidency.

BIBLIOGRAPHY

General Works

Anthony Badger, *The New Deal: The Depression Years, 1933–1940* (1989).

Gary Dean Best, *The Retreat from Liberalism: Collectivists versus Progressives in the New Deal Years* (2002).

Alan Brinkley, *The End of Reform: New Deal Liberalism in Recession and War* (1995).

Laura Browder, *Rousing the Nation: Radical Culture in Depression America* (1998).

William H. Chafe, ed., *The Achievement of American Liberalism: The New Deal and Its Legacies* (2003).

Kenneth S. Davis, *FDR*, 4 vols. (1985–1993).

Ronald Edsforth, *The New Deal: America's Response to the Great Depression* (2000).

Steve Fraser and Gary Gerstle, eds., *The Rise and Fall of the New Deal Order* (1988).

David M. Kennedy, *Freedom from Fear: The American People in Depression and War, 1929–1945* (1999).

Alice Kessler-Harris, *In Pursuit of Equity: Women, Men, and the Quest for Economic Citizenship in Twentieth-Century America* (2001).

William E. Leuchtenburg, *The FDR Years: On Roosevelt and His Legacy* (1995).

Suzanne Mettler, *Dividing Citizens: Gender and Federalism in New Deal Public Policy* (1998).

Sidney M. Milkis and Jerome M. Mileur, eds., *The New Deal and the Triumph of Liberalism* (2002).

Harvard Sitkoff, ed., *Fifty Years Later: The New Deal Evaluated* (1985).

Gene Smiley, *Rethinking the Great Depression* (2002).

G. Edward White, *The Constitution and the New Deal* (2000).

The Roosevelt Leadership

Philip Abbott, *The Exemplary Presidency: Franklin D. Roosevelt and the American Political Tradition* (1990).

Blanche Wiesen Cook, *Eleanor Roosevelt*, 2 vols. (1992, 1999).

Matthew J. Dickinson, *Bitter Harvest: FDR, Presidential Power, and the Growth of the Presidential Branch* (1997).

Frank Friedel, *Franklin D. Roosevelt: A Rendezvous with Destiny* (1990).

Alonzo L. Hamby, *For the Survival of Democracy: Franklin Roosevelt and the World Crisis of the 1930s* (2004).

Davis W. Houk and Amos Kiewe, *FDR's Body Politics: The Rhetoric of Disability* (2003).

Marian C. McKenna, *Franklin Roosevelt and the Great Constitutional War: The Court-Packing Crisis of 1937* (2002).

Albert U. Romasco, *The Politics of Recovery: Roosevelt's New Deal* (1983).

Sean J. Savage, *Roosevelt: The Party Leader, 1932–1945* (1991).

Richard W. Steele, *Propaganda in an Open Society: The Roosevelt Administration and the Media, 1933–1941* (1985).

Geoffrey C. Ward, *A First-Class Temperament: The Emergence of Franklin Roosevelt* (1989).

Susan Ware, *Beyond Suffrage: Women in the New Deal* (1981).

Susan Ware, *Partner and I: Molly Dewson, Feminism, and New Deal Politics* (1987).

Economics and Planning

William J. Barber, *From New Era to New Deal: Herbert Hoover, the Economists, and American Economic Policy, 1921–1933* (1985).

Donald R. Brand, *Corporatism and the Rule of Law: A Study of the National Recovery Administration* (1988).

Mark Gelfand, *A Nation of Cities: The Federal Government and Urban America, 1933–1945* (1975).

Erwin C. Hargrove, *Prisoners of Myth: The Leadership of the Tennessee Valley Authority, 1933–1990* (1990).

Ellis Hawley, *The New Deal and the Problem of Monopoly: A Study in Economic Ambivalence* (1966).

Susan Estabrook Kennedy, *The Banking Crisis of 1933* (1973).

Mark Leff, *The Limits of Symbolic Reform: The New Deal and Taxation, 1933–1939* (1984).

Dean May, *From New Deal to New Economics* (1981).

Michael Parrish, *Securities Regulation and the New Deal* (1970).

Patrick D. Reagan, *Designing a New America: The Origins of New Deal Planning, 1890–1936* (1999).

Theodore Rosenof, *Economics in the Long Run: New Deal Theorists and Their Legacies, 1933–1993* (1997).

Landon R. Y. Stors, *Civilizing Capitalism: The National Consumers' League, Women's Activism, and Labor Standards in the New Deal Era* (2000).

Michael J. Webber, *New Deal Fat Cats: Business, Labor, and Campaign Finance in the 1936 Presidential Election* (2000).

Reform and Welfare

W. Andrew Achenbaum, *Shades of Gray: Old Age, American Values and Federal Policies since 1920* (1983).

Edward D. Berkowitz, *America's Welfare State: From Roosevelt to Reagan* (1991).

William R. Brock, *Welfare, Democracy, and the New Deal* (1987).

Floris Barnett Cash, *African American Women and Social Action: The Clubwomen and Volunteerism from Jim Crow to the New Deal, 1896–1936* (2001).

John A. Clausen, *Looking Back at the Children of the Great Depression* (1993).

Phoebe Cutler, *The Public Landscape of the New Deal* (1986).

Linda Gordon, *Pitied but Not Entitled: Single Mothers and the History of Welfare* (1994).

William Graebner, *A History of Retirement: The Meaning and Function of an American Institution, 1885–1978* (1980).

Kenneth J. Heineman, *A Catholic New Deal: Religion and Reform in Depression Pittsburg* (1999).

Roy Lubove, *The Struggle for Social Security, 1900–1935* (1968).

Paul E. Mertz, *New Deal Policy and Southern Rural Poverty* (1978).

James T. Patterson, *America's Struggle against Poverty, 1900–1980* (1981).

John Salmond, *The Civilian Conservation Corps, 1933–1942* (1967).

Bonnie Fox Schwartz, *The Civil Works Administration, 1933–1934* (1984).

Challenges to the New Deal

Alan Brinkley, *Voices of Protest: Huey Long, Father Coughlin, and the Great Depression* (1983).

Cecilia Bucki, *Bridgeport's Socialist New Deal, 1915–1936* (2001).

William Ivy Hair, *The Kingfish and His Realm* (1991).

Harvey Klehr, *The Heyday of American Communism* (1984).

Donald J. Lisio, *The President and Protest: Hoover, Conspiracy, and the Bonus Riot* (1974).

Leo P. Ribuffo, *The Old Christian Right: The Protestant Far Right from the Great Depression to the Cold War* (1983).

Clyde P. Weed, *The Nemesis of Reform: The Republican Party during the New Deal* (1994).

George Wolfskill, *The Revolt of the Conservatives: A History of the American Liberty League, 1934–1940* (1962).

Agriculture

David E. Conrad, *The Forgotten Farmers: The Story of the Share-Croppers in the New Deal* (1965).

Cletus E. Daniel, *Bitter Harvest: A History of California Farmworkers, 1870–1941* (1981).

David E. Hamilton, *From New Day to New Deal: American Farm Policy from Hoover to Roosevelt, 1928–1933* (1991).

Michael R. Grey, *New Deal Medicine: The Rural Health Programs of the Farm Security Administration* (1999).

Jack Temple Kirby, *Rural Worlds Lost: The American South, 1920–1960* (1987).

Richard Lowitt, *The New Deal and the West* (1984).

Labor

John Barnard, *Walter Reuther and the Rise of the Auto Workers* (1983).

Irving Bernstein, *A Caring Society: The New Deal, the Worker, and the Great Depression* (1985).

Lizbeth Cohen, *Making a New Deal: Industrial Workers in Chicago, 1919–1939* (1990).

Sidney Fine, *Sitdown: The General Motors Strike of 1936–1937* (1969).

Steve Fraser, *Labor Will Rule: Sidney Hillman and the Rise of American Labor* (1991).

Gary Gerstle, *Working-Class Americanism: The Politics of Labor in a Textile City, 1914–1960* (1989).

Colin Gordon, *New Deals: Business, Labor, and Politics in America, 1920–1935* (1994).

James A. Hodges, *New Deal Labor Policy and the Southern Cotton Textile Industry, 1933–1941* (1986).

Janet Irons, *Testing the New Deal: The General Textile Strike of 1934 in the American South* (2000).

August Meier and Elliott Rudwick, *Black Detroit and the Rise of the UAW* (1979).

David Milton, *The Politics of United States Labor: From the Great Depression to the New Deal* (1980).

Julie Novkov, *Constituting Workers, Protecting Women: Gender, Law, and Labor in the Progressive Era and New Deal Years* (2001).

Judith Sealander, *As Minority Becomes Majority: Federal Reaction to the Phenomenon of Women in the Work Force, 1920–1963* (1983).

Robert H. Zieger, *John L. Lewis: Labor Leader* (1988).

Neglected Americans

Rodolfo Acuna, *Occupied America: A History of Chicanos* (1988).

Christine Bolt, *American Indian Policy and American Reform* (1987).

Karen Ferguson, *Black Politics in New Deal Atlanta* (2002).

Donald L. Fixico, *The Invasion of Indian Country in the Twentieth Century: American Capitalism and Tribal Natural Resources* (1998).

Camille Guerin-Gonzales, *Mexican Workers and the American Dream: Immigration, Repatriation, and California Farm Labor, 1900–1939* (1994).

Robin D. G. Kelley, *Hammer and Hoe: Alabama Communists during the Great Depression* (1990).

John B. Kirby, *Black Americans in the Roosevelt Era: Liberalism and Race* (1980).

Doug McAdam, *Political Process and the Development of Black Insurgency, 1920–1970* (1982).

Harvard Sitkoff, *A New Deal for Blacks: The Emergence of Civil Rights as a National Issue*, vol. 1, *The Depression Decade* (1978).

Graham D. Taylor, *The New Deal and American Indian Tribalism: The Administration of the Indian Reorganization Act, 1935–1945* (1980).

Public Culture

E. Quita Craig, *Black Drama of the Federal Theatre Era: Beyond the Formal Horizons* (1980).

Jonathan Harris, *Federal Art and National Culture: The Politics of Identity in New Deal America* (1995).

Karal Ann Marling, *Wall-to-Wall America: A Cultural History of Post-Office Murals in the Great Depression* (1982).

Jane DeHart Matthews, *The Federal Theatre, 1935–1939: Plays, Relief, and Politics* (1967).

Richard McKinzie, *The New Deal for Artists* (1973).

GI WEB GEAR

Millions of American GIs strapped on web belts hooked with canteens, knives, and other military gear as they went into battle. Navy medical corpsman Leo H. Scheer wore this belt when Allied forces stormed the Normandy beaches on D Day, June 6, 1944. Scheer's landing craft sank as it approached Omaha Beach, and he swam ashore wearing this web gear. Once on land, he grabbed unused bandages from the belts of dead soldiers to bind the wounds of the living. The pockets of this belt are still stuffed with the bandages Scheer collected while Americans and their allies secured the beach and launched the great western offensive against Nazi Germany.

Jackson Hill / The National D-Day Museum.

The United States and the Second World War

1939–1945

O N A SUN-DRENCHED FLORIDA AFTERNOON in January 1927, Paul Tibbets took his first airplane ride. Twelve-year-old Tibbets cinched on a leather helmet, clambered into the front seat of the open cockpit of a cloth-covered red, white, and blue biplane, and sailed aloft over Miami. While the barn-storming pilot sitting behind him brought the plane in low over the Hialeah race track, Tibbets pitched Baby Ruth candy bars tethered to small paper parachutes to racing fans in the grandstands below. After two more candy bar drops over the race track, the pilot raced to the beach and swooped down to 200 feet as Tibbets tossed out the remaining candy bars and watched the bathers scramble for chocolate from heaven. After Tibbets and the pilot repeated their stunt for a week, sales of Baby Ruths soared for Tibbets's father's candy business, and Tibbets was hooked on flying.

Born in Quincy, Illinois, in 1915, Tibbets moved to Florida when he was nine, then migrated back and forth to the Midwest. He entered the University of Florida in 1933 and took flying lessons at the Gainesville airport. After transferring to the University of Cincinnati, he continued to fly in his spare time and in 1937 decided to join the Army Air Corps to become a military pilot.

Shortly after the Japanese attack on Pearl Harbor, Tibbets led a squadron of airplanes flying antisubmarine patrol against German U-boats lurking along the East Coast. When the heavily armored B-17 Flying Fortress bombers began to come off American assembly lines early in 1942, Tibbets took a squadron of the new planes from the United States to England. On August 17, 1942, Tibbets led the first American daytime bombing raid on German-occupied Europe, releasing 1,100 pounds of bombs from his B-17, nicknamed "Butcher Shop," on the railroad yards of Rouen in northern France—the first of some 700,000 tons of explosives dropped by over 330,000 American bombers during the air war in Europe.

After numerous raids over Europe, Tibbets was reassigned to the North African campaign, where his duties included ferrying the American commander, General Dwight D. Eisenhower, into the battle zone. Following eight months of combat missions, Tibbets returned to the United States and was ordered to test the new B-29 Super Fortress being built in Wichita, Kansas. The B-29 was much bigger than the B-17 and could fly higher and faster, making it ideal for the campaign against Japan. Tibbets's mastery of the B-29 caused him to be singled out in September 1944 to command a top-secret unit training for a special mission.

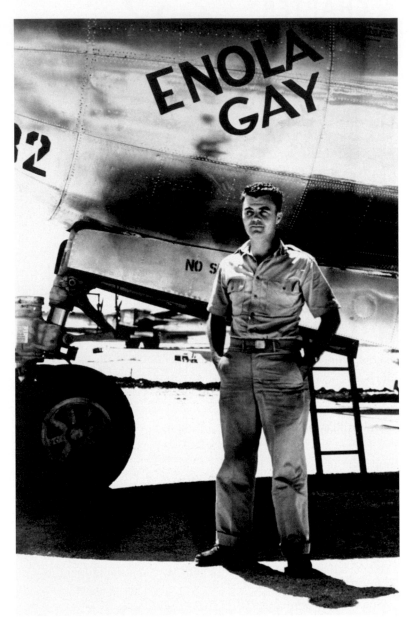

Colonel Paul Tibbets
Before taking off to drop the world's first atomic bomb on Hiroshima, Colonel Paul Tibbets posed on the tarmac next to his customized B-29 Super Fortress bomber, named *Enola Gay* in honor of his mother. A crew of eleven handpicked airmen accompanied Tibbets in the *Enola Gay* on their top-secret mission. After the war, President Harry S. Truman invited Tibbets to the White House and told him, "Don't you ever lose any sleep over the fact that you planned and carried out that mission. It was my decision. You had no choice."
© Bettmann/Corbis.

The mission, officials confided to Tibbets, was to be ready to drop on Japan a bomb that was so powerful it might bring the war to an end. Although no such bomb yet existed, American scientists and engineers were working around the clock to build one. Tibbets kept this secret from his men but took them and his B-29s to Utah to develop a way to drop such a powerful weapon without getting blown up by it. Tibbets trained his pilots to fly at 31,000 feet, then execute a dangerous, sharp, diving turn of 155 degrees that tested the limits of the aircraft but moved it beyond the range of the expected blast.

In May 1945, Tibbets took his B-29s and men to Tinian Island and trained for their secret mission by flying raids over Japanese cities and dropping ordinary bombs. The atomic bomb arrived on Tinian aboard the cruiser *Indianapolis* on July 26, just ten days after the successful test explosion in the New Mexico desert. Nicknamed "Little Boy," the bomb was twelve feet long and weighed 9,000 pounds. The explosive force of its nuclear core packed the equivalent of 40 million pounds of TNT or 200,000 of the 200-pound bombs Tibbets and other American airmen dropped on Europe.

At 2:30 A.M. on August 6, 1945, Tibbets and his crew of eleven and their atomic payload took off in the B-29 bomber *Enola Gay* and headed for Japan. Less than seven hours later, over the city of Hiroshima, Tibbets and his crew released Little Boy from the *Enola Gay*'s bomb bay. The plane bucked upward after dropping the 4.5-ton explosive, while Tibbets banked the plane sharply to the right and struggled to maintain control as the shock wave from the explosion blasted past and a purple cloud mushroomed nearly ten miles into the air. For an hour and a half as Tibbets and his crew flew back toward Tinian, they could see the mushroom cloud of the atomic destruction they had unleashed. Three days later, Tibbets's men dropped a second atomic bomb on Nagasaki, and in five days Japan surrendered.

Paul Tibbets's experiences traced an arc followed by millions of his fellow Americans during World War II, from the innocence of bombarding Miami with candy bars to the deadly nuclear firestorms that rained down on Japan. Like Tibbets, Americans joined their allies to fight the Axis powers in Europe and Asia. Like his *Enola Gay* crewmen—who hailed from New York, Texas, California, New Jersey, New Mexico, Maryland, North Carolina, Pennsylvania, Michigan, and Nevada—Americans from all regions united to defeat the **fascist** aggressors. American industries mobilized to produce advanced bombers—like the ones Tibbets piloted over Europe, North Africa, and Japan—along with enough other military equipment to supply the American armed forces and their allies. At enormous cost in human life and suffering, the war brought full employment and prosperity to Americans at home, ending the depression, providing new opportunities for women, and ushering the nation into the postwar world as a triumphant economic and—on the wings of Paul Tibbets's *Enola Gay*—atomic superpower.

Peacetime Dilemmas

The First World War left a dangerous and ultimately deadly legacy. The victors—especially Britain, France, and the United States—sought to avoid future wars at almost any cost. The defeated nations as well as those who felt humiliated by the Versailles peace settlement—particularly Germany, Italy, and Japan—aspired to reassert their power and avenge their losses by means of renewed warfare. Japan invaded the northern Chinese province of Manchuria in 1931 with ambitions to expand throughout Asia. Italy, led by the fascist Benito Mussolini since 1922, hungered for an empire in Africa. In Germany, National Socialist Adolf Hitler rose to power as chancellor in 1933 in a grandiose quest to dominate Europe and the world. These aggressive, militaristic, antidemocratic regimes seemed a smaller threat to most people in the United States during the 1930s than the economic crisis at home. Shielded from external threats by the Atlantic and Pacific oceans, Americans hoped to avoid entanglement in foreign woes and to concentrate on climbing out of the nation's economic abyss.

Roosevelt and Reluctant Isolation

Like most Americans during the 1930s, Franklin Roosevelt believed that the nation's highest priority was to attack the domestic causes and consequences of the depression. But unlike most Americans, Roosevelt had long advocated an active role for the United States in international affairs. As assistant secretary of the navy in Woodrow Wilson's administration, he championed the significance of naval strength in the global balance of power. After World War I, Roosevelt embraced Wilson's vision that the United States should take the lead in making the world "safe for democracy," and he continued to advocate American membership in the League of Nations during the **isolationist** 1920s. When he ran for governor of New York in 1928,

Roosevelt criticized Republican isolationists for undermining domestic prosperity by setting high tariffs and for subverting international peace by demanding that battered European nations pay off their wartime loans and reparations in full and on time.

The depression forced Roosevelt to retreat from his previous internationalism. He came to believe that energetic involvement in foreign affairs diverted resources and political support from domestic recovery. During his 1932 presidential campaign, he pulled back from his endorsement of the League of Nations and reversed his previous support for forgiving European war debts. Once in office, Roosevelt sought to combine domestic economic recovery with a low-profile foreign policy that encouraged free trade and disarmament. "Foreign markets must be regained if America's producers are to rebuild a full and enduring domestic prosperity," he explained in 1935. In turn, free trade required international peace, the goal of disarmament.

In pursuit of international amity, Roosevelt was constrained by economic circumstances and American popular opinion. After an opinion poll demonstrated popular support for recognizing the Soviet Union—an international pariah since the Bolshevik Revolution in 1917—Roosevelt established formal diplomatic relations in 1933. But when the League of Nations condemned Japanese and German aggression, Roosevelt did not enlist the nation in the League's attempts to keep the peace because he feared jeopardizing isolationists' support for **New Deal** measures in Congress. America watched from the sidelines when Japan withdrew from the League and ignored the limitations on its navy imposed after World War I. Likewise, the United States looked the other way when Hitler rearmed Germany and recalled its representative to the League in 1933, declaring that the peace-seeking body sought to thwart Germany's legitimate ambitions. Roosevelt worried that the League's inability to curb German and Japanese violations of League sanctions and the Versailles settlement threatened world peace. But he reassured Americans that the nation would not "use its armed forces for the settlement of any [international] dispute anywhere."

> Shielded from external threats by the Atlantic and Pacific oceans, Americans hoped to avoid entanglement in foreign woes and to concentrate on climbing out of the nation's economic abyss.

The Good Neighbor Policy

In his 1933 inaugural address, Franklin Roosevelt announced that the United States would pursue "the policy of the good neighbor" in international relations. A few weeks later, he emphasized that the good neighbor policy applied specifically to Latin America, where previous presidents had routinely sent U.S. military forces to intervene in local affairs. Now, Roosevelt said, the old policy of arrogant intervention would be replaced by a "helping hand" extended in a desire for friendly cooperation to create "more order in this hemisphere and less dislike." In December 1933 at the Inter-American Conference in Montevideo, Uruguay, Secretary of State Cordell Hull formalized the good-neighbor pledge that no nation had the right to intervene in the internal or external affairs of another.

This commitment to nonintervention did not indicate a U.S. retreat from empire in Latin America. Instead, the good neighbor policy declared that the United States would not depend on military force to exercise its influence in the region. When Mexico nationalized American oil holdings and revolution boiled over in Nicaragua, Guatemala, and Cuba during the 1930s, Roosevelt refrained from sending in the marines to defend the interests of American corporations. In 1934, Roosevelt even withdrew American marines from Haiti, which they had occupied since 1916. While nonintervention honored the principle of national self-determination, it also permitted the rise of dictators like Anastasio Somoza in Nicaragua and Fulgencio Batista in Cuba, who exploited and terrorized their nations with private support from U.S. businesses and the hands-off policy of Roosevelt's administration.

Military nonintervention also did not prevent the United States from exerting its economic influence in Latin America. In 1934, Congress passed the Reciprocal Trade Agreements Act, which gave the president power to reduce tariffs on goods imported into the United States from nations that agreed to lower their own tariffs on U.S. exports. By 1940, twenty-two nations had agreed to reciprocal tariff reductions, helping U.S. exports to Latin America double during Roosevelt's first two terms and contributing to the New Deal's goal of boosting the domestic economy through free trade. Although the economic power of the United States continued to overshadow that of its neighbors, the nonintervention policy planted seeds of friendship and hemispheric solidarity that grew in importance while events in Europe and Asia continued to erode international peace.

> The good neighbor policy declared that the United States would not depend on military force to exercise its influence in Latin America.

The Price of Noninvolvement

In Europe, fascist governments in Italy and Germany spouted belligerent rhetoric and threatened military aggression. Italian dictator Benito Mussolini proclaimed, "War is to the man what maternity is to the woman. . . . Peace [is] . . . depressing and a negation of all the fundamental virtues of man." In Germany, Hitler combined similar pronouncements with vigorous rebuilding of the nation's military strength. Although German rearmament openly defied the terms of the Versailles peace treaty, neither Britain nor France did more than register verbal protests. The overpowering desire to avoid conflict led Britain in 1935 to permit Germany to begin rebuilding its fleet of surface ships and submarines. Emboldened, Hitler plotted to avenge defeat in World War I by recapturing territories with German inhabitants, all the while accusing Jews of polluting the purity of the Aryan master race. The virulent anti-Semitism of Hitler and his Nazi Party unified non-Jewish Germans and attracted sympathizers among many other Europeans, even in France and Britain, thereby weakening support for opposing Hitler or defending Jews.

In Japan, a stridently militaristic government planned to follow the invasion of Manchuria in 1931 with conquests extending throughout Southeast Asia. The Manchurian invasion bogged down in a long and vicious war when Chinese Nationalists rallied around their leader Chiang Kai-shek to fight against the Japanese. Preparations for new conquests continued, however. Early in 1936, Japan openly violated naval limitation treaties it had agreed to and began to build a battle-ready fleet to achieve naval superiority in the Pacific.

In the United States, the hostilities in Asia and Europe reinforced isolationist sentiments. Popular disillusionment with the failure of Woodrow Wilson's idealistic goals caused many Americans to question the nation's participation in World War I. In 1933, Gerald Nye, a Republican from North Dakota, chaired a Senate committee that investigated why the United States had gone to war in 1917. The Nye committee concluded

The Quest for Disarmament

With startling swoops, a little white plane that evokes the dove of peace is covered by a blood-red hawk of a fighter plane, gun ablaze. The shouted cry "Disarm!" at the bottom of the poster expresses the view of peace advocates at the beginning of the 1930s that the way to make the world safe was to take weapons away from the strong, not to arm the weak. Soon after the poster appeared, the march of fascist aggression began to shift opinion toward the belief that nations could better attain collective security by using force to counter the enemies of peace.
Private Collection.

that greedy "merchants of death"—American weapons makers, bankers, and financiers—dragged the nation into the war to line their own pockets. The Nye committee persuaded many Americans that war profiteers might once again push the nation into a world war.

International tensions and the Nye committee report prompted Congress to pass a series of neutrality acts between 1935 and 1937, to avoid the circumstances that, they believed, had caused the nation to abandon its isolationism and become a combatant in World War I. The neutrality acts prohibited making loans and selling arms to nations at war and authorized the president to warn Americans about traveling on ships belonging to belligerent countries.

By 1937, as the nation continued to struggle with the depression, intensifying conflicts overseas caused some Americans to call for a total embargo, not just on munitions but on all trade with warring countries. Roosevelt and Congress worried that such an embargo would hurt the nation's economy by limiting production and boosting unemployment. The Neutrality Act of 1937 sought to allow trade but prevent foreign entanglements by requiring warring nations to pay cash for nonmilitary goods and transport them in their own ships. This "cash-and-carry" policy seemed to reconcile the nation's desire for both peace and foreign trade. Although such trade benefited the domestic economy, it also helped foreign aggressors and thereby undermined peace. In short, by strenuously seeking to avoid war, American isolationism encouraged German and Japanese militarists, who concluded that the United States posed little threat to them.

The desire for peace in France, Britain, and the United States led Germany, Italy, and Japan to launch offensives on the assumption that the western democracies lacked the will to oppose them. In March 1936, Nazi troops marched into the industry-rich Rhineland on Germany's western border, in blatant violation of the Treaty of Versailles, which had ceded the region to France. One month later, Italian armies completed their conquest of Ethiopia, projecting fascist power into Africa. In December 1937, Japanese invaders captured Nanking and celebrated their triumph in a deadly rampage of murder, rape, and plunder that killed 200,000 Chinese civilians.

In Spain, a bitter civil war broke out in 1936 when fascist rebels led by General Francisco Franco attacked the democratically elected Republican government. Both Germany and Italy reinforced Franco with soldiers, weapons, and aircraft, while the Soviet Union provided much less aid to the Republican Loyalists. The Spanish civil war seemed to many observers a dress rehearsal for a coming worldwide conflict, but it did not cause European democracies or the U.S. government to help the Loyalists, despite sympathizing with their cause.

Spanish Civil War, 1936–1939

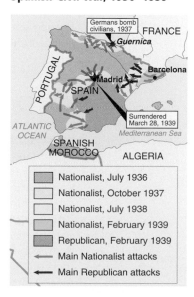

More than 3,000 individual Americans enlisted in the Russian-sponsored Abraham Lincoln Brigade to fight for the Loyalists. But, abandoned by western nations, Loyalists and their allies were defeated in 1939 by the fascists. Germany and Italy welcomed Franco's victory, which created a fascist bulwark in southern and western Europe.

Hostilities in Europe, Africa, and Asia alarmed Roosevelt and other Americans. He sought to persuade most Americans to moderate their isolationism and find a way to support the victims of fascist aggression. Speaking in Chicago, the heartland of isolationism, in October 1937, Roosevelt declared that the "epidemic of world lawlessness is spreading" and warned that "mere isolation or neutrality" offered no remedy for the "contagion" of war. Instead, the president proposed that the United States "quarantine" aggressor nations and arrest the spread of war's contagion.

Roosevelt's speech ignited a storm of protest from isolationists. The *Chicago Tribune* accused the president of seeking to replace "Americanism" with "internationalism." Chastened by the popular outcry and by the failure of congressional leaders to echo his concerns, Roosevelt did not pursue the quarantine proposal. "It's a terrible thing," he remarked to an aide, "to look over your shoulder when you are trying to lead and find no one there." The strength of isolationist sentiment convinced Roosevelt that he needed to maneuver carefully if the United States were to help prevent fascist aggressors from conquering Europe and Asia, leaving the United States an isolated and imperiled island of **democracy**.

> Hostilities abroad alarmed Roosevelt and other Americans. He sought to persuade most Americans to moderate their isolationism and find a way to support the victims of fascist aggression.

The Onset of War

Between 1939 and 1941, fascist victories overseas eventually eroded American isolationism and engulfed the nation in a worldwide conflagration. But initially, fascist anti-Semitism, boastful saber-rattling, and military conquests in China, Ethiopia, and Spain failed to arouse many Americans. Trying to work their way out of the depression and refusing to be diverted by conflicts on the far shores of the Atlantic and Pacific, most Americans hoped to stay out of the seemingly endless conflicts that embroiled Europe and Asia. By 1939, however, continuing German and Japanese aggression caused more and more Americans to believe that it was time for the nation to take a stand. At first, taking a stand was limited to providing material support to the enemies of Germany and Japan, principally Britain, China, and the Soviet Union. But Japan's surprise attack on Pearl Harbor eliminated that restraint, and the nation began to mobilize for an all-out assault on foreign foes.

Nazi Aggression and War in Europe

Under the spell of isolationism, Americans passively watched Hitler's relentless campaign to dominate Europe. Under the ruse of uniting all German peoples regardless of the nation they happened to inhabit, Hitler bullied Austria in 1938 into accepting incorporation—*Anschluss*—into the Nazi Third Reich, expanding the territory under Germany's control. Having whetted his appetite for conquest, Hitler turned his attention to the German-speaking Sudetenland, granted to Czechoslovakia by the Versailles treaty. Although the Czechs were prepared to fight rather than surrender their territory, Britain and France hoped to avoid war by making a deal with Hitler. British prime minister Neville Chamberlain went to Munich, Germany, and offered Hitler terms of "appeasement," as he called it, that would give the Sudetenland to Germany if Hitler agreed to leave the rest of Czechoslovakia alone. On September 29, 1938, Hitler accepted Chamberlain's offer, solemnly promising that he would make no more territorial claims in Europe. Chamberlain returned to Britain proclaiming that his diplomacy had achieved "peace in our time." But since peace depended on Hitler keeping a promise he never intended to honor, Chamberlain's attempt at appeasement was doomed from the outset. In March 1939, Hitler boldly marched the German army into Czechoslovakia and conquered it without firing a shot (Map 25.1).

In April 1939, hardly pausing for breath, Hitler demanded that Poland return the German territory it had been awarded after World War I. Britain and France finally recognized that appeasement had failed and that Hitler would continue his aggression unless he was defeated by military might. Both Britain and France assured Poland that they would go to war with Germany if Hitler launched an eastward offensive across the Polish border. In turn, Hitler negotiated with

MAP 25.1 Axis Aggression through 1941
For different reasons, Hitler and Mussolini launched a series of surprise military strikes. Mussolini sought to re-create the Roman Empire in the Mediterranean. Hitler struck to reclaim German territories occupied by France after World War I and to annex Austria. When the German dictator began his campaign to rule "inferior" peoples beyond Germany's border by attacking Poland, World War II broke out.

his bitter enemy, the Soviet premier Joseph Stalin, offering him concessions in order to prevent the Soviet Union from joining Britain and France in opposing a German attack on Poland. Despite the enduring hatred between fascist Germany and the **Communist** Soviet Union, the two powers signed the Nazi-Soviet treaty of nonaggression in August 1939, exposing Poland to an onslaught by the German Wehrmacht (army).

At dawn on September 1, 1939, Hitler unleashed the attack on Poland, exhorting his generals to "close your hearts to pity! Act brutally!"

in a *blitzkrieg* (literally, "lightning war") attack led by tanks and airplanes that gave lethal mechanized support to the invading infantry. The attack triggered declarations of war from France and Britain two days later, igniting a conflagration that raced around the globe, killing over 60 million people and maiming untold millions more until it finally ended after Paul Tibbets's historic flight in August 1945. But in September 1939, Germany seemed invincible as its armies sped across Poland, causing many people to wonder if any nation could stop the Nazi war machine or if, sooner or later, all of Europe would

German Panzer
German Panzers, supported by well-coordinated aircraft of the German Luftwaffe, contributed speed, maneuverability, and firepower to blitzkrieg attacks. Hitler's mechanized army stunned foes with the lethal combination of tanks and airplanes racing west into France and east into Poland and the Soviet Union.
U.S. Army Ordnance Museum Foundation, Inc.

share Poland's fate: defeat, German occupation, and vicious authoritarian government enforced by merciless repression and unblinking terror.

After the Nazis overran Poland, Hitler paused for a few months before launching a westward blitzkrieg. In April 1940, German forces smashed through Denmark and Norway. In May, Germany invaded the Netherlands, Belgium, and Luxembourg, and then France. The French believed that their Maginot Line, a concrete fortification built after World War I and stretching from the Swiss border to the forested Ardennes region on the edge of Belgium, would halt the German attack (see Map 25.1). Designed to stop the plodding advance of foot soldiers in World War I–style trench warfare, the Maginot Line proved little more than a detour for Hitler's mechanized divisions, which wheeled around the fortification's northern end and raced south toward Paris.

The speed of the German attack trapped more than 300,000 British and French soldiers, who retreated to the port of Dunkirk, where an improvised armada of English vessels of every size and shape hurriedly ferried them to safety across the English Channel, leaving the Dunkirk beaches strewn with thousands of tons of military gear. By mid-June 1940, France had surrendered the largest army in the world, signed an armistice that gave Germany control of the entire French coastline and nearly two-thirds of the countryside, and installed a collaborationist government at Vichy in southern France headed by Philippe Pétain, and Hitler had strolled the

boulevards of Paris in triumph. With an empire that stretched across Europe from Poland to France, Hitler seemed poised to vault the English Channel and attack Britain.

The new British prime minister, Winston Churchill, vowed that Britain, unlike France, would never accept a humiliating surrender to Hitler. "We shall fight on the seas and oceans [and] . . . in the air," he proclaimed, "whatever the cost may be, we shall fight on the beaches, . . . on the landing grounds, . . . in the fields and in the streets . . . [and] we shall never surrender." Churchill's defiance stiffened British resolve for a last-ditch defense against Hitler's attack, which began in mid-June 1940 with wave after wave of German bombers targeting British military installations and cities, killing tens of thousands of civilians. The undermanned and outgunned Royal Air Force, fighting as doggedly as Churchill had predicted, finally won the Battle of Britain by November, clearing German bombers from British skies and handing Hitler his first frustrating defeat. Churchill lauded the valiant British pilots, proclaiming, "Never . . . was so much owed by so many to so few." Churchill left unspoken the pilots' advance knowledge of German plans made possible by British use of the new technology of radar and the ability to decipher Germany's top-secret military codes. But battered and exhausted, Britain could not hold out forever without American help, as Churchill repeatedly wrote Roosevelt in private.

From Neutrality to the Arsenal of Democracy

When the Nazi attack on Poland ignited the war in Europe, Roosevelt issued an official proclamation of American neutrality. Although most Americans strongly condemned German aggression and favored Britain and France, Roosevelt had to steer a political course that tacked between placating isolationists at home and helping the antifascist cause abroad. Roosevelt feared that if Congress did not repeal the arms embargo mandated by the Neutrality Act of 1937, France and Britain would soon succumb to the Nazi onslaught. The president's request for repeal of the arms embargo provoked isolationists to protest that the United States had no business interfering in a European conflict that did not threaten American shores. After heated debate, Congress voted in November 1939 to revise the neutrality legislation and allow belligerent nations to buy arms, as well as nonmilitary supplies, on a cash-and-carry basis.

In practice, the revised neutrality law permitted Britain and France to purchase American war materials and carry them across the Atlantic in their own ships. America could help the antifascist Allies at a distance, selling them war goods without exposing American ships to the German submarines lurking in the Atlantic. Such half-hearted efforts in support of the antifascist cause troubled Roosevelt. He wrote a friend, "What worries me is that public opinion . . . is patting itself on the back every morning and thanking God for the Atlantic Ocean (and the Pacific Ocean)," greatly underestimating "the serious implications" of the European war for "our own future."

Roosevelt knew that the serious implications for America included the possibility of British defeat and Nazi supremacy on the high seas, and he resolved to find some way to aid Britain short of entering a formal alliance or declaring war against Germany. Privately, Churchill pleaded for American destroyers, aircraft, and munitions but had no money to buy them under the prevailing cash-and-carry neutrality law. In May 1940, Roosevelt asked Congress for almost $1.3 billion in defense spending to expand the navy and multiply the

production of airplanes to 50,000 a year. By late summer, as the Battle of Britain raged in the skies over England, Roosevelt concocted a scheme to deliver fifty old destroyers to Britain in exchange for American access to British bases in the Western Hemisphere. Claiming the constitutional power to strengthen America's defenses by swapping destroyers for bases, Roosevelt took the first steps toward building a firm Anglo-American alliance against Hitler.

While Luftwaffe pilots bombed Britain, German officers lingered over leisurely meals in France, and Nazi officials administered their new territories in Poland, Austria, Czechoslovakia, and elsewhere, Roosevelt decided to run for an unprecedented third term as president in 1940. He hoped to woo voters away from their complacent isolationism to back the nation's international interests as well as New Deal reforms. But the presidential election, which Roosevelt won handily, provided no clear mandate for American involvement in the European war. The

The County of London Orchestra
The gallant resistance of the British to the bombing of their cities captured Americans' sympathy and helped to build support for U.S. entry into the war. Here in the Chelsea section of London in 1942, the County of London Orchestra and an audience of mostly children demonstrate how to carry on in the ruins with poise and a stiff upper lip. Getty Images.

Republican candidate, Wendell Willkie, a former Democrat who generally favored New Deal measures and Roosevelt's foreign policy, attacked Roosevelt as a warmonger. Willkie's accusations caused the president to promise voters, "Your boys are not going to be sent into any foreign wars," a pledge counterbalanced by his repeated warnings about the threats to America posed by Nazi aggression.

> Empowered by the voters for another presidential term, Roosevelt maneuvered to support Britain in every way short of war.

Empowered by the voters for another presidential term, Roosevelt maneuvered to support Britain in every way short of war. In a fireside chat shortly after Christmas 1940, Roosevelt called Britain "the spearhead of resistance to [Nazi] world conquest" and proclaimed that it was incumbent on the United States to become "the great arsenal of democracy" and send "every ounce and every ton of munitions and supplies that we can possibly spare to help the defenders who are in the front lines." Events of the last year had proved, he said solemnly, "that no nation can appease the Nazis. . . . There can be no appeasement with ruthlessness."

In January 1941, Roosevelt proposed the Lend-Lease Act, which allowed the British to obtain arms from the United States without paying cash but with the promise to reimburse the United States when the war ended. The purpose of Lend-Lease, Roosevelt proclaimed, was to defend democracy and human rights throughout the world, specifically the Four Freedoms: "freedom of speech and expression . . . freedom of every person to worship God in his own way . . . freedom from want . . . [and] freedom from fear." Congress passed the Lend-Lease Act in March 1941, starting a flow of support to Britain that totaled more than $50 billion during the war, far more than all federal expenditures combined since Roosevelt had become president in 1933.

Lend-Lease placed the United States on a collision course with Germany. Nazi U-boats (submarines) prowled the Atlantic, preying on ships laden with supplies for Britain, making it only a matter of time before American citizens and American property would be attacked. While German U-boats sank British shipping at an alarming pace, Roosevelt provided naval escorts for Lend-Lease supplies and gave his commanders orders to "shoot on sight" any menacing German submarine they spotted, edging the nation ever closer to all-out combat.

Stymied in his plans for an invasion of England, Hitler turned his massive army eastward and on June 22, 1941, sprang a surprise attack on the Soviet Union, his erstwhile ally in the 1939 Nazi-Soviet nonaggression pact. Neither Roosevelt nor Churchill had any love for Joseph Stalin or communism, but they both welcomed the conversion of the Soviet Union to the anti-Nazi cause. Both western leaders understood that Hitler's attack on Russia would divert his divisions toward the eastern front and provide relief for the hard-pressed British. Roosevelt quickly persuaded Congress to extend Lend-Lease to the Soviet Union, beginning the shipment of millions of tons of trucks, jeeps, locomotives, and other equipment that, in all, supplied about 10 percent of Russian war materiel.

As Hitler's Wehrmacht raced across the Russian plains and Nazi U-boats tried to choke off supplies to Britain and the Soviet Union, Roosevelt met with Churchill aboard a ship near Newfoundland to cement the Anglo-American alliance. In August 1941, the two leaders issued the Atlantic Charter, pledging the two nations to freedom of the seas and free trade, as well as the right of national self-determination. Roosevelt told Churchill privately that the United States would continue to serve as the arsenal of democracy and that he would be on the lookout for some incident that might trigger public support for full-scale American entry into the war against Germany.

Japan Attacks America

Although the likelihood of war with Germany preoccupied Roosevelt, Hitler exercised a measure of restraint in directly provoking America, even though he boasted that "America is not dangerous to us." Japanese ambitions in Asia clashed more openly with American interests and commitments, especially in China and the Philippines. And unlike Hitler, the Japanese high command planned to attack the United States if necessary to pursue their aspirations to rule an Asian empire they termed the Greater East Asia Co-Prosperity Sphere. Appealing to widespread Asian bitterness toward white colonial powers like the British in India and Burma, the French in Indochina (now Vietnam), and the Dutch in the East Indies (now Indonesia), the Japanese campaigned to preserve "Asia for the Asians." Japan's invasion of China—which had lasted for ten years by 1941—proved that Japan's true goal was Asia for the Japanese (Map 25.2). Japan cov-

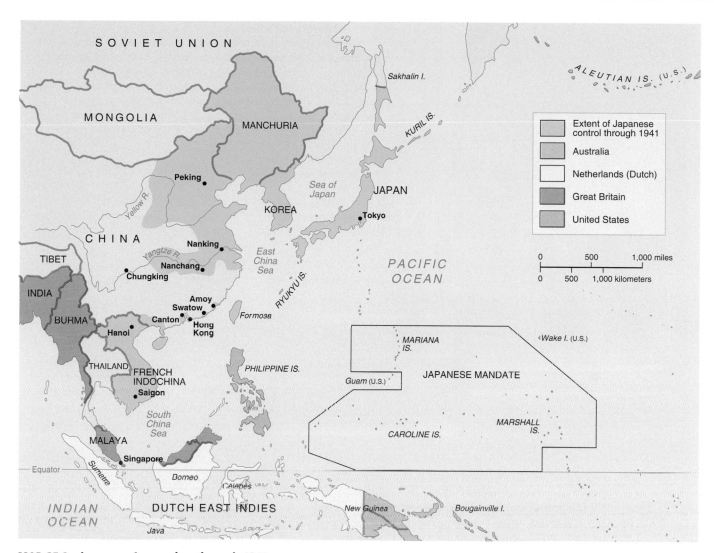

MAP 25.2 Japanese Aggression through 1941
Beginning with the invasion of Manchuria in 1931, Japan sought to force its imperialist control over most of East Asia. Japanese aggression was driven by the need for raw materials for the country's expanding industries and by the military government's devotion to martial honor.

eted China's raw materials and hoped to combine them with additional resources extracted from the nations forced into the Greater East Asia Co-Prosperity Sphere. Although the United States demanded that Japan pull out of China and retreat from its ambitions for a grand empire, the toothless rebukes did not deter the Japanese.

In 1940, Japan signaled a new phase of its imperial designs by entering a defensive alliance with Germany and Italy—the Tripartite Pact—and by receiving permission from the Vichy government in France to build airfields and station soldiers in northern Indochina. By 1941, U.S. naval intelligence cracked the Japanese secret

code and learned that Tokyo also planned to invade the resource-rich Dutch East Indies. To thwart these plans, in July 1941 Roosevelt announced a trade embargo that denied Japan access to oil, scrap iron, and other goods essential for its war machines. Roosevelt hoped the embargo would strengthen factions within Japan who opposed the militarists and sought to restore relations with the United States.

The American embargo played into the hands of Japanese militarists headed by General Hideki Tojo, who seized control of the government in October 1941 and persuaded other leaders, including Emperor Hirohito, that swift destruction of American naval bases in the

Pearl Harbor Victims

Brothers Wesley and Edward Heidt from Los Angeles, California—shown here posing in their navy uniforms—were two of 34 pairs of brothers killed when Japanese warplanes attacked and sank the battleship *Arizona* in the surprise attack on Pearl Harbor on December 7, 1941. The life preserver and pennant from the *Arizona* were salvaged a few days after the attack. The official telegram informed the Heidt brothers' mother that her sons "lost their life in the service of their country," a tragic message received by hundreds of thousands of other American parents during the next four years.

U.S.S. Arizona Memorial, Hawaii, National Park Service/photos by Douglas Peebles.

Bombing of Pearl Harbor, December 7, 1941

Pacific would leave Japan free to follow its destiny. Decoded Japanese messages alerted American officials that an attack on U.S. forces was imminent somewhere in the Pacific, but exactly where and when, no American knew until it was too late. Early on the morning of December 7, 1941, 183 attack aircraft lifted off six Japanese carriers that had secretly steamed within striking range of the U.S. Pacific Fleet at Pearl Harbor on the Hawaiian island of Oahu. About 8 o'clock on this sleepy Sunday morning, the Japanese planes streaked from the sky, bombing and torpedoing the American fleet riding serenely at anchor in the harbor and destroying hundreds of aircraft parked in neat rows on the runways of Hickam Field. The devastating surprise attack sank or disabled 18 ships, including all of the fleet's battleships, killed more than 2,400 Americans, and wounded over 1,000, almost crippling U.S. war-making capacity in the Pacific. Luckily for the United States, Japanese pilots failed to destroy the vital machine shops and oil storage facilities at Pearl Harbor, and none of the nation's aircraft carriers was in port at the time of the attack.

The Japanese scored a stunning tactical success at Pearl Harbor, but in the long run the attack proved a colossal blunder. The victory infected many Japanese commanders with dangerous overconfidence about their military prowess. Worse for the Japanese, Americans instantly united in their desire to fight and avenge the attack, which Roosevelt termed "dastardly and unprovoked," vowing that "this form of treachery shall never endanger us again." On December 8, Congress unanimously endorsed the president's call for a declaration of war, except for pacifist Republican congresswoman Jeannette Rankin, of Montana, who had also opposed U.S. entry into World War I. Although neither Hitler nor Mussolini knew about the Japanese attack in advance, both Germany and Italy declared war against America on December 11, bringing the United States into all-out war with Axis powers in both Europe and Asia.

Mobilizing for War

The time had come, Roosevelt announced, for the prescriptions of "Dr. New Deal" to be replaced by the stronger medicines of "Dr. Win-the-War." Military and civilian leaders rushed to secure the nation against possible attacks by its enemies, causing Americans of Japanese descent to be stigmatized and sent to internment camps. Roosevelt and his advisers lost no time enlisting millions of Americans in the armed forces to bring the isolationist-era military to fighting strength for a two-front war. The war emergency also required economic mobilization unparalleled in the nation's history. As Dr. Win-the-War, Roosevelt set aside New Deal goals of reform and plunged headlong into transforming the American economy into the world's greatest military machine, thereby achieving full employment and economic recovery, goals that had eluded the New Deal.

Home-Front Security

Shortly after declaring war against the United States, Hitler dispatched German submarines to hunt American ships along the Atlantic coast from Maine to Florida, where Paul Tibbets and other American pilots tried to destroy them. But the U-boats had devastating success for about eight months, sinking hundreds of U.S. ships and threatening to disrupt the Lend Lease lifeline to Britain and the Soviet Union. The submarines benefited from the failure of port cities such as New York and Miami to observe the rules requiring blackouts, making it easier for the U-boats to spot vulnerable ships against the lighted horizon.

As hulks of destroyed vessels littered Atlantic beaches, blackouts became more rigorously enforced, and by mid-1942 the U.S. navy had chased German submarines away from the coast and into the mid-Atlantic, reducing the direct threat to the nation's homeland. Naval ships patrolled the nation's coasts, and fortifications were built to defend against seaborne assaults. While these and other security measures raised popular awareness of the possibility of an attack on the U.S. mainland, no such attack occurred. Within the continental United States, Americans remained sheltered by the Atlantic and Pacific oceans from the chaos and destruction the war brought to hundreds of millions in Europe and Asia.

The Road to War: The United States and World War II

1931	Japan invades Manchuria.
1933	Franklin D. Roosevelt becomes U.S. president.
	Adolf Hitler becomes German chancellor.
1935–1937	Congress passes series of Neutrality Acts to protect United States from involvement in world conflicts.
1936	**March.** Nazi troops invade Rhineland, violating Treaty of Versailles.
	July. Civil war breaks out in Spain.
	Mussolini's Fascist Italian regime conquers Ethiopia.
	November. Roosevelt reelected president.
1937	**December.** Japanese troops capture Nanking, China.
1938	Hitler annexes Austria.
	September 29. Hitler accepts offer of "appeasement" in Munich from British prime minister Neville Chamberlain.
1939	**March.** Hitler invades Czechoslovakia.
	August. Hitler and Stalin sign Nazi-Soviet nonaggression pact.
	September 1. Germany invades Poland, beginning World War II.
	United States and Britain conclude cash-and-carry agreement for arms sales.
1940	**Spring.** German blitzkrieg smashes through Denmark, Norway, Belgium, Holland, and into northern France.
	Japan signs Tripartite Pact with Germany and Italy.
	May–June. German armies flank the Maginot Line. France surrenders. British evacuation at Dunkirk.
	Summer/Fall. German bombing campaign against England.
	November. Roosevelt wins third term as president. Royal Air Force wins Battle of Britain.
1941	**March.** Congress approves Lend-Lease Act, making arms available to Britain.
	June 22. Hitler invades Soviet Union.
	August. Roosevelt and Churchill sign Atlantic Charter.
	October. Militarists led by Hideki Tojo take over Japan.
	December 7. Japanese bomb Pearl Harbor. United States declares war on Japan.
	December 11. Germany and Italy declare war on United States.

The government still worried constantly about espionage and internal subversion. Billboards and posters warned Americans that "Loose lips sink ships" and "Enemy agents are always near; if you don't talk, they won't hear." The campaign for patriotic vigilance focused on German and Japanese foes, but Americans of Japanese descent became targets of official and popular persecution.

About 320,000 people of Japanese descent lived in the United States in 1941, two-thirds of them in Hawaii, where they largely escaped wartime persecution because they were essential and valued members of society. On the mainland, in contrast, Japanese Americans were a tiny minority—even along the West Coast, where most of them worked on farms and in small businesses—subject to frenzied wartime suspicions and persecution. A prominent newspaper columnist echoed the widespread sentiment that "The Japanese . . . should be under armed guard to the last man and woman right now and to hell with habeas corpus until the danger is over." Although an official military survey concluded that Japanese Americans posed no danger, popular hostility fueled a campaign to round up all mainland Japanese Americans—two-thirds of them U.S. citizens. "A Jap's a Jap. . . . It makes no difference whether he is an American citizen or not," one official declared.

FBI Searching Japanese American Home

When President Roosevelt informed military commanders that they might "from time to time" remove persons deemed dangerous, he had reason to suspect that nearly all Japanese Americans would be affected. An army "expert" on Asian culture had already advised the War Department that "as you cannot . . . penetrate the Oriental thinking . . . the easiest course is to remove them all from the West Coast and place them . . . under guard." Intent on getting to the bottom of one Japanese American family's allegiance, an FBI agent in 1942 scrutinizes a picture album while family members whose home has been invaded look on helplessly.

Los Angeles Daily News Photographic Archive, Department of Special Collections, Charles E. Young Research Library, UCLA.

On February 19, 1942, Roosevelt issued Executive Order 9066, which authorized sending all Americans of Japanese descent to ten makeshift prison camps located in remote areas of the West, euphemistically termed "relocation centers" (Map 25.3). Allowed little time to secure or sell their properties, Japanese Americans lost homes and businesses worth about $400 million and lived out the war penned in by barbed wire and armed guards. (See "Documenting the American Promise," page 922.) Although several thousand Japanese Americans served with distinction in the U.S. armed forces and no case of subversion by Japanese Americans was ever uncovered, the Supreme Court, in its 1944 *Korematsu* decision, upheld Executive Order 9066's blatant violation of constitutional rights as justified by "military necessity."

Building a Citizen Army

In 1940, Roosevelt encouraged Congress to pass the Selective Service Act to register men of military age who would be subject to **draft** into the armed forces if the need arose. More than 6,000 local draft boards registered over 30 million men and, when war came, rapidly inducted them into military service. In all, more than 16 million men and women served in uniform during the war, two-thirds of them draftees, mostly young men between the ages of 18 and 26. Although only about one family in five had a family member in the military, nearly everybody had friends and neighbors who had gone off to war. Relatively few young, single men received exemptions. By the time the war ended, over 10 million had served in the army, nearly 4 million in the navy, 600,000 in the marines, and 240,000 in the coast guard. In addition, 350,000 women joined the Nurse's Corps and women's military units such as the Women's Army Corps, the navy's Women Accepted for Volunteer Emergency Service, and the Women's Marine Corps. Though barred from combat duty, these women worked at nearly every noncombatant assignment, eroding traditional barriers to women's military service.

The Selective Service Act prohibited discrimination "on account of race or color," and almost a million African American men and women donned uniforms, as did half a million Mexican Americans, 25,000 Native Americans, and 13,000 Chinese Americans. The racial insults and discrimination suffered by all people of color made some soldiers ask, as a Mexican American GI said on his way to the European

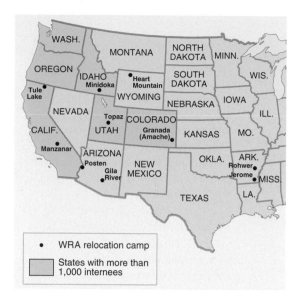

MAP 25.3 Western Relocation Authority Centers
Responding to prejudice and fear of sabotage, in 1942 President Roosevelt authorized the roundup and relocation of all Americans of Japanese descent. Taken from their homes in the cities and fertile farms of the far West, Japanese Americans were confined in desolate areas scattered as far east as the Mississippi River.

front, "Why fight for America when you have not been treated as an American?" Only black Americans were trained in segregated camps, confined in segregated barracks, and assigned to segregated units. The Red Cross even segregated the blood it supplied to treat battlefield casualties, thereby supposedly protecting wounded whites from being contaminated by black blood—needless to say, a practice without scientific merit. Secretary of War Henry Stimson opposed any change in the segregation of blacks, declaring that the military effort should not serve as a "sociological laboratory." Accordingly, most black Americans were consigned to manual labor positions, and relatively few served in combat until late in 1944, when the need for military manpower in Europe intensified. Then, as General George Patton told black soldiers in a tank unit in Normandy, "I don't care what color you are, so long as you go up there and kill those Kraut sonsabitches." Combat service slowly weakened the official military policy of racial segregation, and it was officially banned from the armed forces in 1948 by order of President Harry Truman, although genuine integration was delayed until the Korean War.

Homosexuals also served in the armed forces, although in much smaller numbers than black Americans. Secretary of War Stimson reminded commanding generals that they were expected to prosecute cases of sodomy, but in reality most officers, under pressure to field an army, followed the traditional policy of looking the other way. Lesbians volunteered for the newly formed women's branches of service. Allowed to serve, gay Americans, like other minorities, sought to demonstrate their worth under fire. "I was superpatriotic," a gay combat veteran recalled. Another gay GI remarked, "Who in the hell is going to worry about [homosexuality]" in the midst of the life-or-death realities of war?

Conversion to a War Economy

In 1940, the American economy remained mired in depression. Nearly one worker in seven was still without a job, factories operated far below their productive capacity, and the total federal budget was under $10 billion. Shortly after the attack on Pearl Harbor, Roosevelt announced the goal of converting the economy to produce "overwhelming . . . crushing superiority of equipment in any theater of the world war." In a rush to produce military supplies, factories were converted from producing passenger cars to assembling tanks and airplanes, and production of everything from bullets to shoes was ramped up to record levels. By the end of the war, there were more jobs than workers, plants were operating at full capacity, and the federal budget topped $100 billion.

To organize and oversee this tidal wave of military production, Roosevelt called upon business leaders to come to Washington and, for the token payment of a dollar a year, head new government agencies such as the War Production Board, which among other things, set production priorities and pushed for maximum output. Contracts flowed to large corporations such as General Electric, Ford, and U.S. Steel, often on a basis that guaranteed their profits. During the first half of 1942, the government issued contracts worth over $100 billion, a sum greater than the entire gross national product in 1941.

Booming wartime employment swelled union membership. To speed production, the government asked unions to pledge not to strike. Despite the relentless pace of work, union mem-

> By the end of the war, there were more jobs than workers, plants were operating at full capacity, and the federal budget topped $100 billion.

Japanese Internment

Determined that the bombing of Pearl Harbor would not be followed by more sneak attacks, military and political leaders on the West Coast targeted persons of Japanese descent—alien and citizen alike—as potential saboteurs.

DOCUMENT 1
Final Recommendations of the Commanding General, Western Defense Command and Fourth Army, Submitted to the Secretary of War

Early in 1942, General John DeWitt, commander of the Western Defense Command, persuaded President Franklin Roosevelt to issue an executive order authorizing the removal of the Japanese living in the United States. Subsequently, 110,000 Japanese Americans were confined to relocation camps for the duration of the war. DeWitt's recommendation expressed concern for military security by appealing to racist conceptions long used to curb Asian immigration. Japanese Americans and their supporters fought the internment order in the courts as a violation of fundamental constitutional rights, an argument rejected during the war by the U.S. Supreme Court. Long after the war ended, the U.S. government officially apologized for Japanese internment and issued modest monetary payments to survivors.

February 14, 1942
Memorandum for the Secretary of War.
Subject: Evacuation of Japanese and Other Subversive Persons from the Pacific Coast.

1. In presenting a recommendation for the evacuation of Japanese and other subversive persons from the Pacific Coast, the following facts have been considered:

a. Mission of the Western Defense Command and Fourth Army.
   (1) Defense of the Pacific Coast of the Western Defense Command, as extended, against attacks by sea, land, or air;
   (2) Local protection of establishment and communications vital to the National Defense for which adequate defense cannot be provided by local civilian authorities.

b. Brief Estimate of the Situation.
   (1) . . . The following are possible and probable enemy activities: . . .
      (a) Naval attack on shipping on coastal waters;
      (b) Naval attack on coastal cities and vital installations;
      (c) Air raids on vital installations, particularly within two hundred miles of the coast;
      (d) Sabotage of vital installations throughout the Western Defense Command.

Hostile Naval and air raids will be assisted by enemy agents signaling from the coastline and the vicinity thereof; and by supplying and otherwise assisting enemy vessels and by sabotage.

In the war in which we are now engaged racial affinities are severed by migration. The Japanese race is an enemy race and while many second and third generation Japanese born on United States soil, possessed of United States citizenship, have become "Americanized," the racial strains are undiluted. To conclude otherwise is to expect that children born of white parents on Japanese soil sever all racial affinity and become loyal Japanese subjects, ready to fight and, if necessary, to die for Japan in a war against the nation of their parents. . . .

It, therefore, follows that along the vital Pacific Coast over 112,000 potential enemies, of Japanese extraction, are at large today. There are indications that these are organized and ready for concerted action at a favorable opportunity. The very fact that no sabotage has taken place to date is a disturbing and confirming indication that such action will be taken.

SOURCE: *Final Recommendations*, report by General John Lesesne DeWitt to the United States Secretary of War, February 14, 1942.

DOCUMENT 2
An Oral History of Life in the Japanese American Detention Camps

Imprisoned in bleak surroundings far from home, Japanese internees sometimes succumbed to despair and bitterness. Looking back after forty years, Kazue Yamane recalled her confinement as a disturbing and baffling experience.

In April 1942, my husband and I and our two children left for camp, and my mother-in-law and father-in-law came about a month later. I wasn't afraid, but I kept asking in my mind, how could they? This is impossible. Even today I still think it was a nightmarish thing. I cannot reconcile myself to the fact that I had to go, that I was interned, that I was segregated, that I was taken away, even though it goes back forty years. . . .

I was separated from my husband; he went to the Santa Fe, New

Mexico, camp. All our letters were censored; all our letters were cut in parts and all that. So we were not too sure what messages was getting through and not getting through, but I do know that I informed him many times of his mother's condition. He should have been allowed to come back to see her, because I thought she wouldn't live too long, but they never did allow him to come back, even for her funeral. They did not allow that. I learned that a lot of the messages didn't get to him; they were crossed out. I now have those letters with me.

In 1944 I was left with his parents and our kids. But I had no time to think of what was going to happen because my child was always sick and I had been quite sick. . . .

My son knew what was going on, and he too had many times asked me why . . . you know, why? why? Of course, I had no explanation why this was happening to us.

SOURCE: Excerpt from *And Justice for All*, by John Tateishi. Copyright © 1999 by John Tateishi. Reprinted by permission of the University of Washington Press.

DOCUMENT 3
The Kikuchi Diary

Forcibly removed from his life as a student at the University of California at Berkeley, Charles Kikuchi sought in his prison camp diary to make sense of the internment and to judge where it would lead.

December 7, 1941, Berkeley, California
Pearl Harbor. We are at war! Jesus Christ, the Japs bombed Hawaii and the entire fleet has been sunk. I just can't believe it. I don't know what in the hell is going to happen to us, but we will all be called into the Army right away.

. . . The next five years will determine the future of the Nisei

[Japanese American citizens]. They are now at the crossroads. Will they be able to take it or will they go under? If we are ever going to prove our Americanism, this is the time. The Anti-Jap feeling is bound to rise to hysterical heights, and it is most likely that the Nisei will be included as Japs. I wanted to go to San Francisco tonight, but Pierre says I am crazy. He says it's best we stick on campus. In any event, we can't remain on the fence, and a positive approach must be taken if we are to have a place in fulfilling the Promise of America. I think the U.S. is in danger of going Fascist too, or maybe Socialist. . . .

I don't know what to think or do. Everybody is in a daze.

April 30, 1942, Berkeley
Today is the day that we are going to get kicked out of Berkeley. It certainly is degrading. . . .

I'm supposed to see my family at Tanforan as Jack told me to give the same family number. I wonder how it is going to be living with them as I haven't done this for years and years? I should have gone over to San Francisco and evacuated with them, but I had a last final to take. I understand that we are going to live in the horse stalls. I hope that the Army has the courtesy to remove the manure first. . . .

July 14, 1942
Marie, Ann, Mitch, Jimmy, Jack, and myself got into a long discussion about how much democracy meant to us as individuals. Mitch says that he would even go in the army and die for it, in spite of the fact that he knew he would be kept down. Marie said that although democracy was not perfect, it was the only system that offered any hope for a future, if we could fulfill its destinies. Jack was a little more skeptical. He even

suggested that we [could] be in such grave danger that we would then realize that we were losing something. Where this point was he could not say. I said that this was what happened in France and they lost all. Jimmy suggested that the colored races of the world had reason to feel despair and mistrust the white man because of the past experiences. . . .

In reviewing the four months here, the chief value I got out of this forced evacuation was the strengthening of the family bonds. I never knew my family before this and this was the first chance that I have had to really get acquainted.

SOURCE: Excerpts (pp. 43, 51, 183, 252) from *The Kikuchi Diary: Chronicle from an American Concentration Camp*, edited by John Modell. Copyright © 1973 by the Board of Trustees of the University of Illinois. Used with the permission of the University of Illinois Press and the author.

QUESTIONS FOR ANALYSIS AND DEBATE

1. What explains General DeWitt's insistence on evacuating the Japanese after he received the report of military investigators that no acts of sabotage had occurred?

2. How do the Kikuchi diary and the oral histories of life in the camps reveal the meaning of internment for the detainees?

3. Despite the internment of their families and friends in concentration camps, the Japanese American army unit in Italy earned a larger number of citations for combat heroism than any comparable army group. What hints in the documents here might help explain this combat record?

4. How did the internment camp experience influence the detainees' attitudes about their identity as Americans of Japanese descent?

Tank Production Line
The General Motors plant shown here assembled automobiles until Roosevelt
called for American factories to covert to wartime production as rapidly as possible. This and other plants built tens of thousands of armored vehicles destined
principally for American and Allied soldiers in the European theater, where they
dueled with Hitler's Panzers.

General Motors Corp. Used with permission, GM Media Archives.

lions of shoes, socks, shirts, pants, and much
more—in all more than double the combined
production of Germany, Japan, and Italy. In the
last 18 months of war, for example, every
American in the Pacific theater could draw upon
8,000 pounds of military supplies, in stark contrast with each Japanese soldier's access to two
pounds. Giving tangible meaning to the term
"arsenal of democracy," this outpouring of military goods supplied not only U.S. forces but also
sizable portions of the military needs of the
Allies.

Fighting Back

The United States confronted a daunting military challenge in December 1941. The attack on
Pearl Harbor destroyed much of its Pacific fleet,
crippling the nation's ability to defend against
Japan's massive offensive throughout the southern Pacific. In the Atlantic, Hitler's U-boats
sank American ships, while German armies occupied most of western Europe and relentlessly
advanced eastward into the Soviet Union.
Roosevelt and his military advisers believed defeating Germany took top priority. To achieve
that victory required preventing Hitler from defeating America's allies, Britain and the Soviet
Union. If they fell, Hitler would command all the
resources of Europe in a probable assault on the
United States. To fight back effectively against
Germany and Japan, the United States had to coordinate military and political strategy with its
allies and muster all its human and economic assets. But in 1941, nobody knew if that would be
enough.

Turning the Tide in the Pacific

In the Pacific theater, Japan's leading military
strategist, Admiral Isoroku Yamamoto, ordered
an all-out offensive throughout the southern
Pacific. He believed that if his forces did not
quickly conquer and secure the territories they
targeted, Japan would eventually lose the war
to America's far greater resources. Swiftly, the
Japanese assaulted American airfields in the
Philippines and captured U.S. outposts on Guam
and Wake Island. Singapore, the great British
naval base in Malaya, surrendered to the
Japanese in February 1942, and most of Burma
had fallen by March. All that stood in the way of
Yamamoto's plan for Japan's domination of the

bers kept their no-strike pledge, with the important exception of the United Mine Workers, who
walked out of the coal mines in 1943 behind their
leader John L. Lewis, demanding a pay hike and
earning the enmity of many Americans.

Overall, conversion to war production
achieved Roosevelt's ambitious goal of "overwhelming . . . , crushing superiority" in military
goods. At a total cost of $304 billion during the
war, the nation produced an avalanche of military equipment, including 300,000 airplanes,
88,000 tanks, 7,000 ships, 3 million vehicles, as
well as billions of bullets, not to mention mil-

southern Pacific was the American stronghold in the Philippines.

The Japanese unleashed a withering assault against Philippine defenses in January 1942, causing the American commander General Douglas MacArthur to retreat to fortifications on the Bataan Peninsula across the harbor from Manila. Unsuccessful in repelling the Japanese attack, MacArthur slipped away to Australia in March, leaving General Jonathan Wainwright to hold out in the Corregidor fortress as long as possible. Wainwright finally surrendered in May 1942, and Japanese soldiers marched the weak and malnourished survivors sixty-five miles to a concentration camp. Hundreds of Americans and as many as 10,000 Filipinos died during the Bataan Death March, and 16,000 more perished within weeks from disease and brutality in the prison camp. By summer 1942, the Japanese war machine had swooped from its Philippine successes to conquer the oil-rich Dutch East Indies and was poised to strike Australia and New Zealand.

Reeling from Japanese assaults, Americans had learned that the soldiers of the Rising Sun were tough, fearless, and prepared to fight to the death for honor and their emperor. The Japanese had larger, faster, and more heavily armed ships than the United States, and their airplanes outperformed anything the Americans could send up against them. The unbroken series of Japanese victories caused Americans at home to worry about their own safety. A false report that Japanese fighter planes had been spotted near Los Angeles set off an antiaircraft barrage and inspired the commander of West Coast defenses to announce that "death and destruction [from enemy planes] are likely to come at any moment." But a daring raid on Tokyo in April 1942 by a squadron of carrier-based B-25 bombers led by Lieutenant Colonel James Doolittle boosted American morale and demonstrated that even the Japanese imperial capital lay within reach (barely) of American might.

In the spring of 1942, U.S. forces launched a major two-pronged counteroffensive that military officials hoped would reverse the Japanese advance. Forces led by General MacArthur moved north from Australia and attacked the Japanese in the Philippines. Far more decisively, Admiral Chester W. Nimitz sailed his battle fleet west from Hawaii to retake Japanese-held islands in the mid-Pacific. On May 7–8, 1942, in the Coral Sea just north of Australia, the American fleet and carrier-based warplanes de-

feated a Japanese armada that was sailing around the coast of New Guinea.

After victory in the Coral Sea, Nimitz learned from an intelligence intercept that the Japanese were massing an invasion force aimed at Midway Island, an outpost guarding the Hawaiian Islands. Nimitz maneuvered his carriers and cruisers into the Central Pacific to surprise the Japanese. In a furious battle that raged from June 3 to June 6, American naval ships and planes delivered a punishing blow, sinking a heavy cruiser, two destroyers, and four of Japan's six carriers, while the American armada lost only one carrier and a destroyer. The Battle of Midway reversed the balance of naval power in the Pacific and put the Japanese at a disadvantage for the rest of the war. Although Japan still wielded formidable naval firepower, it managed

Japanese Pilot's Flag

Japanese pilots often carried small flags covered with admonitions to fight hard and well. This flag belonged to a pilot named Imano, whose relatives sent him aloft with inscriptions that read "Let your divine plane soar in the sky. We who are left behind pray only for your certain success in sinking an enemy ship." Notably, the inscription emphasized harming Japan's enemies rather than returning home safe and sound.

U.S. Naval Academy Museum/photo by Richard D. Bond Jr.

to build only six more large carriers during the war while the U.S. fleet launched an additional seventeen large carriers and ninety-six smaller carriers, a disparity that proved the wisdom of Yamamoto's fear of America's vast human and material resources. The Battle of Midway turned the tide of Japanese advance in the Pacific but did little to dislodge Japan from the many places it had conquered and now stoutly defended.

The Campaign in Europe

In the dark months after Pearl Harbor, Hitler's eastern-front armies marched ever deeper into the Soviet Union while his western forces prepared to invade Britain. As in World War I, the Germans attempted to starve the British into submission by destroying their seaborne lifeline.

Radar Screen

The new technology of radar gave American military commanders unprecedented information about the location and power of their foes. The radar operator shown here aboard an American aircraft carrier in the Pacific is charting air strikes against Japan in 1945.

© Bettmann/Corbis.

Technological advances made German U-boats much more effective than they had been in World War I, and for month after month in 1941 and 1942 they sank Allied ships faster than new ones could be built. The fearsome toll of the U-boat campaign eventually reached more than 4,700 merchant ships, almost 200 warships, and 40,000 Allied seamen.

Until mid-1943, the outcome of the war in the Atlantic remained in perilous doubt. Then, newly invented radar detectors and production of sufficient destroyer escorts for merchant vessels allowed the Allies to convert the lurking U-boats from predators into vulnerable prey. After suffering a 75 percent casualty rate among U-boat crews, Hitler withdrew German submarines from the North Atlantic in late May 1943. In the next four months, more than 3,500 American supply ships crossed the Atlantic without a single loss. Winning the battle of the Atlantic allowed the United States to continue to supply its British and Soviet allies for the duration of the war and to reduce the imminent threat of a German invasion of Britain.

The most important strategic question confronting the United States and its allies was when and where to open a second front against the Nazis. Stalin demanded that America and Britain mount an immediate and massive assault across the English Channel into western France. A cross-channel invasion would force Hitler to divert his armies from the eastern front and relieve the pressure on the Soviet Union, which was fighting alone against the full strength of the German Wehrmacht. Churchill and Roosevelt were willing to delay opening a second front, allowing the Germans and the Soviets to slug it out, weakening both the Nazis and the Communists, and making an eventual Allied attack on western France more likely to succeed. Both Churchill and Roosevelt promised Stalin that they would open a second front, but they decided to strike first in southern Europe and the Mediterranean, which Churchill termed Europe's "soft under-belly." Roosevelt worried that this plan that would merely "peck on the periphery" of Nazi power and Stalin vehemently agreed, but Roosevelt ultimately backed Churchill's desire for an invasion of North Africa as a first step toward a second front.

The plan targeted a region of long-standing British influence in the eastern Mediterranean. In October 1942, British forces at El-Alamein in Egypt halted German general Erwin Rommel's drive to capture the Suez Canal, Britain's lifeline to the oil of the Middle East and to British colonies in India and South Asia. In November, an American army under General Dwight D. Eisenhower landed far to the west, in French Morocco. Propelled by American tank units commanded by General George Patton, the Allied armies caught the Germans in North Africa in a giant vise that finally squeezed shut in May 1943. The North African campaign killed and captured 350,000 Axis soldiers, pushed the Germans out of Africa, made the Mediterranean safe for Allied shipping, and opened the door for an Allied invasion of Italy.

In January 1943, while the North African campaign was still under way, Roosevelt traveled to the Moroccan city of Casablanca to confer with Churchill and other Allied leaders. Stalin, preoccupied with the Soviet army's last-ditch defense of Stalingrad against massive German assault, did not attend the meeting but urged his allies to keep their promise of opening a major second front in western Europe. Roosevelt and Churchill announced that they would accept nothing less than the "unconditional surrender" of the Axis powers, ruling out peace negotiations. But Churchill and Roosevelt concluded that they needed more time to amass sufficient forces for the cross-channel invasion of France that Stalin demanded. In the meantime, they planned to capitalize on their success in North Africa and strike against Italy, consigning the Soviet Union to bear the brunt of the Nazi war machine for another year.

On July 10, 1943, combined American and British amphibious forces landed 160,000 troops in Sicily. The badly equipped Italian defenders quickly withdrew to the mainland. Soon afterward, Mussolini was deposed in Italy, ending the reign of Italian fascism. Quickly, the Allies invaded the mainland, and the Italian government surrendered unconditionally. The Germans responded by rushing reinforcements to Italy and seizing control of Rome, turning the Allies' Italian campaign into a series of battles to liberate Italy from German occupation.

German troops dug into strong fortifications and fought to defend every inch of Italy's rugged terrain. Only after a long, deadly, and frustrating campaign up the Italian peninsula did the Allies finally liberate Rome in June 1944. Allied forces continued to push into northern Italy against stubborn German defenses for the remainder of the war, making the Italian campaign the war's deadliest for American infantrymen. One soldier

wrote that his comrades died "like butchered swine" in attacks on German defenses that ended in death, not triumph.

While the Italian campaign occupied numerous German divisions that Hitler might otherwise have deployed on the Russian front, no German forces were in fact taken away from the ongoing attack on the Soviet Union. Stalin denounced the Allies' Italian campaign because it left "the Soviet Army, which is fighting not only for its country, but also for its Allies, to do the job alone, almost single-handed." The campaign exacted a high cost from the Americans and the British, consuming men and material that might have been reserved for a second front in France and bringing the Nazis no closer to unconditional surrender.

> The most important strategic question confronting the United States and its allies was when and where to open a second front against the Nazis.

The Wartime Home Front

The war effort mobilized Americans as never before. Factories strained to churn out ever more bombs, bullets, tanks, ships, and airplanes, which workers rushed to assemble, leaving farms and small towns to congregate in cities. Women took jobs with wrenches and welding torches, boosting the nation's workforce and fraying traditional notions that women's place was in the home rather than on the assembly line. Despite rationing and shortages, unprecedented government expenditures for war production brought prosperity to many Americans after years of depression-era poverty (Figure 25.1). While Americans in uniform risked their lives on battlefields in Europe and Asia, where millions of civilians suffered bombing, strafing, and all-out military assaults, Americans on the mainland enjoyed complete immunity from foreign attack—in sharp contrast to their Soviet and British allies. The wartime ideology of human rights provided justification for the many sacrifices Americans were required to make in support of the military effort, as well as establishing a standard of basic human equality that became a potent weapon in the campaign for equal rights at home.

> Despite rationing and shortages, unprecedented government expenditures for war production brought prosperity to many Americans after years of depression-era poverty.

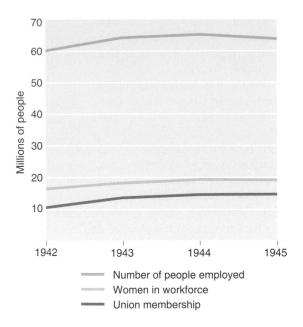

FIGURE 25.1   World War II and the Economy, 1942–1945

The end of the depression followed by war mobilization sent employment and union membership to high levels that continued into peacetime. Women lost many jobs in heavy industry after the war, but their increased numbers in the total workforce were sustained by the strong economy that followed.

"If you've sewed on buttons, or made buttonholes, on a [sewing] machine, you can learn to do spot welding on airplane parts. If you've used an electric mixer in your kitchen, you can learn to run a drill press. If you've followed recipes exactly in making cakes, you can learn to load a shell." Millions of women responded, and by the end of the war, women working outside the home numbered eighteen million, 50 percent more than in 1939. Contributing to the war effort also paid off in wages that averaged $31 for a forty-eight-hour week, more than the typical steelworker earned in 1941. A Kentucky woman remembered her job at a munitions plant where she earned "the fabulous sum of $32 a week. To us it was an absolute miracle. Before that, we made nothing." Although men got paid an average of $54 for comparable wartime work, women accepted the pay differential and welcomed their chance to earn wages and help win the war at the same time. (See "American Places," page 929.)

Female Defense Worker

The war effort brought persons and activities together in unlikely ways, leading to unexpected outcomes. This photo appearing in the army magazine *Yank* sought to boost morale by presenting a defense worker as pinup girl. No one could know that the young propeller technician, nineteen-year-old Norma Jean Baker Dougherty, would later remake herself as the most glamorous of movie stars, Marilyn Monroe.

David Conover Images; © Norma Jean Enterprises, a division of 733548 Ontario Limited.

Women and Families, Guns and Butter

> Wartime mobilization of the economy and the siphoning of millions of men into the armed forces left factories begging for women workers.

Millions of American women gladly left home toting a lunch pail and changed into overalls and work gloves to take their places on assembly lines in defense industries. At the start of the war, about a quarter of adult women worked outside the home, most as teachers, nurses, social workers, or domestic servants. Few women worked in factories, except for textile mills and sewing industries, because employers and male workers often discriminated against them. But wartime mobilization of the economy and the siphoning of millions of men into the armed forces left factories begging for women workers.

Government advertisements urged women to take industrial jobs by assuring them that their household chores had prepared them for work on the "Victory Line." One billboard proclaimed,

AMERICAN PLACES

Rosie the Riveter/World War II Home Front National Historical Park, Richmond, California

On the eve of World War II, Richmond, California, on the San Francisco Bay, was a backwater town of some 20,000. By 1943, its population had skyrocketed to more than 100,000, and it had become the site of Kaiser Shipyards, the largest and most productive shipyards anywhere. Work never stopped during the war. Three shifts a day working seven days a week produced 747 cargo and troop-carrying Liberty and Victory ships.

With millions of men in uniform, tens of thousands of women were recruited to fill what were previously considered "men's jobs"—welders, riveters, ship fitters, heavy equipment operators. Any woman who worked in the defense industry was known as "Rosie the Riveter." Putting on coveralls, hard hats, and heavy gloves, women—including black, Hispanic, and Asian women—made up nearly one-third of Kaiser Shipyards' 90,000 workers at the height of the war. Women arrived from all parts of the country, but most came from the deep South and the Midwest, and most had never before held a job. One Richmond "Rosie" remembered, "We didn't care about the money. We all did what we could do for the war effort."

The park site sprawls over nearly five miles of shoreline and includes many historic buildings, most of them not yet open to the public. Already in place, however, is the Rosie the Riveter Memorial, an abstract rendition of a 441-foot-long Liberty ship. The Keel Walk leads visitors from the water's edge along a time line of facts about the home front during the war and past large panels holding photographs and quotations from "Rosies." One welder's memory is inscribed in granite: "It was hard to convince your lead man that you could do the work. When he assigned jobs, I used to follow him around and say, 'I could do that, I could do that.' He got sick of me and said, 'Okay, do it!' And of course, I could. I could do it." This is the only American memorial that honors women's labor during World War II.

The cargo ship S.S. *Red Oak Victory* is moored a short distance from the memorial. Built in Richmond and commissioned in December 1944, the ship saw service in the South Pacific. Barely saved from the scrap heap, *Red Oak Victory* is today a rusty hulk, but each day it welcomes dozens of dedicated volunteers who are laboring to preserve and restore the old ship.

For Web links related to this site and other American Places, see "PlaceLinks" at bedfordstmartins.com/roark.

Rosie the Riveter Memorial
Rosie the Riveter/WWII Home Front National Historic Park/photo by Lew Watts.

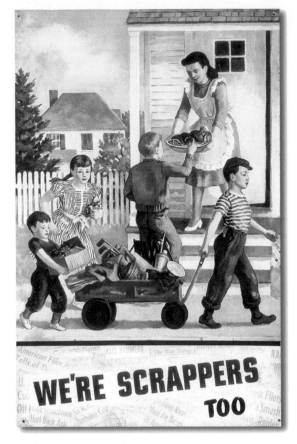

Pitching in at Home

This poster adapts the standard children's book illustration style of the period to the war effort. White and middle class all, mother and children collect old golf clubs, cocktail shakers, and trophies—which dad, away at war, will never miss—so that these symbols of the American way of life can be recycled into armaments for defense.
Chicago Historical Society.

For more help analyzing this image, see the visual activity for this chapter in the Online Study Guide at bedfordstmartins.com/roark.

The majority of married women remained at home, occupied with domestic chores and child care. But they, too, pitched in to the war effort, planting Victory Gardens of home-grown vegetables, saving tin cans and newspapers for recycling into war materials, and hoarding pennies and nickels to buy war bonds. Many families scrimped to cope with the 30 percent inflation during the war. But families supported by men and women in manufacturing industries enjoyed wages that grew twice as fast as inflation.

The war influenced how all families spent their earnings. Buying a new washing machine or car was out of the question since factories that used to build them now made military goods. Many other consumer goods—such as tires, gasoline, shoes, and meat—were rationed at home to sustain military needs overseas. But most Americans had more money in their pockets than ever before, and they readily found things to spend it on, including movie tickets, cosmetics, recordings of music, and so much more that spending for personal consumption rose by 12 percent during the war.

The wartime prosperity and abundance enjoyed by most Americans contrasted with the experiences of their hard-pressed allies: Personal consumption fell by 22 percent in Britain; and in the Soviet Union food output plummeted to just one-third of prewar levels, creating widespread hunger and even starvation. Few went hungry in the United States, however. The government lifted the New Deal's restraints on agricultural production, and farm output grew by 25 percent every year during the war, providing an astonishing cornucopia that allowed surplus food to be exported to nourish the Allies.

The Double V Campaign

Fighting against Nazi Germany and its ideology of Aryan racial supremacy confronted Americans with the extensive racial prejudice in their own society. Roosevelt declared that black Americans were in the war "not only to defend America but . . . to establish a universal freedom under which a new basis of security and prosperity can be established for all—regardless of station, race, or creed." The *Pittsburgh Courier*, a leading black newspaper, seized upon such statements and asserted that the wartime emergency called for a "Double V" campaign seeking "victory over our enemies at home and victory over our enemies on the battlefields abroad." It was time, the *Courier* proclaimed, "to persuade, embarrass, compel and shame our government and our nation . . . into a more enlightened attitude."

In 1941, black organizations barraged Congress and the White House with petitions demanding that the federal government require companies receiving defense contracts to integrate their workforces. A. Philip Randolph, head of the Brotherhood of Sleeping Car Porters, promised that 100,000 African American marchers would descend on Washington if the president did not eliminate discrimination in defense industries. Roosevelt decided to risk offending his white allies in the South and in unions and issued Executive Order 8802 in mid-1941. It authorized a Committee on Fair Employment Practices to investigate and prevent race discrimination in employment. Civil rights champions hailed the act, and Randolph triumphantly called off the march.

Progress came slowly, however. In 1940, nine out of ten black Americans lived below the federal poverty line, and those who worked earned on average 39 percent of whites' wages. In search of better jobs and living conditions, five and a half million black Americans migrated from the South during the war to centers

A Plea for Inclusion

This illustration, drawn by black artist E. Simms Campbell for the cover of *Opportunity*, the journal of the National Urban League, advances a goal that was important to the League: the full inclusion of African Americans in the nation's economic life. To press home the extreme absurdity of restraining black potential in times of crisis, Campbell depicted a mob of puny bigots preventing John Henry, the fabled black laborer, from using his strength for liberation and service in the creation of weapons to defeat Nazism. John Henry was the perfect symbol of the war as a struggle for democracy against oppression and prejudice.
Yale University Library.

of industrial production in the North and West, making a majority of African Americans city dwellers for the first time in U.S. history. Many discovered that although laboring jobs were available, unions and employers often barred blacks from skilled jobs. At least eighteen major unions—including the machinists, ironworkers, shipbuilders, and railway workers—explicitly prohibited black members. Severe labor shortages and government fair employment pressures opened assembly-line jobs in defense plants to African American workers, causing black unemployment to drop by 80 percent during the war. But more jobs did not mean equal pay for black working people. Although the income of black families rose during the war, by the end of the conflict it still stood at half of white families' income.

Blacks' migration to defense jobs intensified racial antagonisms, which boiled over in the hot summer of 1943 when 242 race riots erupted in 47 cities. In Los Angeles, hundreds of white servicemen, claiming they were punishing draft dodgers, chased and beat young Chicano men who dressed in distinctive broad-shouldered, peg-legged zoot suits. The worst mayhem occurred in Detroit, where conflict between whites and blacks at a city park ignited a race war. Whites with clubs smashed through black neighborhoods, and blacks retaliated by destroying and looting white-owned businesses. In two days of violence, 25 blacks and 9 whites were killed, and scores more were injured.

Racial violence created impetus for the Double V campaign, officially supported by the National Association for the Advancement of Colored People (NAACP), which asserted black Americans' demands for the rights and privileges enjoyed by all other Americans—demands reinforced by the Allies' wartime ideology of freedom and democracy. While the NAACP focused on court challenges to segregation, other civil rights activists who wanted more direct confrontations founded a new organization in 1942, the Congress of Racial Equality (CORE), which organized picketing and sit-ins against **Jim Crow** restaurants and theaters. The Double V campaign greatly expanded membership in the NAACP, but achieved only limited success against racial discrimination at home during the war.

> The Double V campaign asserted black Americans' demands for the rights and privileges enjoyed by all other Americans—demands reinforced by the Allies' wartime ideology of freedom and democracy.

Wartime Politics and the 1944 Election

Americans rallied around the war effort in unprecedented unity. Despite the consensus on war aims, the strains and stresses of the nation's massive wartime mobilization made it difficult for Roosevelt to maintain his political coalition. Whites often resented blacks who migrated to northern cities, took jobs, and made themselves at home. Many Americans complained about government price controls and the rationing of scarce goods, while the war dragged on with no end in sight and casualties mounted. Magnifying the Democrats' problems, service overseas kept many Democratic voters from casting ballots in the 1942 congressional elections, and the low turnout helped Republicans gain congressional seats.

> In the 1944 presidential election, voters gave Roosevelt a 53.5 percent majority, his narrowest presidential victory, ensuring his continued leadership as Dr. Win-the-War.

Republicans seized the opportunity to roll back New Deal reforms. A **conservative** coalition of Republicans and southern Democrats succeeded in abolishing several New Deal agencies in 1942 and 1943, including the Work Projects Administration and the Civilian Conservation Corps. But the Democratic administration fought back. By persuading states to ease residency requirements and Congress to guarantee absentee ballots for servicemen, Democrats brought scattered members of the New Deal coalition back to the voting booth in 1944.

In June 1944, Congress unanimously approved the landmark GI Bill of Rights, promising to give veterans government funds for education, housing, and health care, and to provide loans to start businesses and buy homes when they returned from overseas. The GI Bill put the financial resources of the federal government behind the abstract goals of freedom and democracy for which veterans were fighting, and it empowered millions of GIs to better themselves and their families after the war.

After twelve turbulent years in the White House, Roosevelt was exhausted and gravely ill with heart disease. But he was determined to remain president until the war ended. "All that is within me cries out to go back to my home on the Hudson River," he declared. "But as a good soldier . . . I will accept and serve" if reelected president. Roosevelt's poor health made the selection of a vice presidential candidate unusually important. Convinced that many Americans had soured on **liberal** reform, Roosevelt dumped Vice President Henry Wallace, an outspoken **progressive**, and chose Senator Harry S. Truman of Missouri as his running mate. A reliable party man from a southern border state, Truman satisfied urban Democratic leaders while not worrying white southerners who were nervous about challenges to racial segregation.

The Republicans, confident of a strong conservative upsurge in the nation, nominated as their presidential candidate the governor of New York, Thomas E. Dewey, who had made his reputation as a tough crime fighter. In the 1944 presidential election, Roosevelt's failing health alarmed many observers, but his frailty was outweighed by Americans' unwillingness to change presidents in the midst of the war and by Dewey's failure to persuade most voters that the New Deal was a creeping **socialist** menace. The Germans and the Japanese seemed far greater menaces than four more years of President Roosevelt. Voters gave Roosevelt a 53.5 percent majority, his narrowest presidential victory, ensuring his continued leadership as Dr. Win-the-War.

Reaction to the Holocaust

The political cross-currents in the United States were tame in comparison with Hitler's vicious campaign to exterminate Jews. Since the 1930s, Nazis had persecuted Jews in Germany and every German-occupied territory, causing many Jews to seek asylum beyond Hitler's reach. (See "Beyond America's Borders," page 934.) Millions of Jews from southern and eastern Europe had arrived in the United States during the late nineteenth and early twentieth centuries. But after the immigration restriction laws of the 1920s, the open door slammed shut except for a small quota of immigrants from each nation. Some Americans sought to make exceptions to the quotas for Jews fleeing the Nazis' wrath, but many Americans resisted. Roosevelt sympathized with the refugees' pleas for help, but he did not want to jeopardize his foreign policy or offend American voters. After Hitler's Anschluss in 1938, thousands of Austrian Jews sought to immigrate to the United States, but 82 percent of Americans opposed admitting them, and they were turned away. Roosevelt tried to persuade countries in Latin America and Africa to accept refugees, but none complied. Friends of the refugees introduced legislation in Congress in 1939 that would have granted asylum to 20,000 German refugee children, most of them Jewish. The bill was defeated, in large measure because of American anti-Semitism; in 1940, refugee English children—few of whom were Jewish—were welcomed into the United States without delay.

In 1942, numerous reports filtered out of German-occupied Europe that Hitler was implementing a "final solution": Jews and other "undesirables"—such as Gypsies, religious and political dissenters, and homosexuals—were being sent to concentration camps. Old people, children, and others deemed too weak to work were systematically slaughtered and cremated while the able-bodied were put to work at slave labor until they died of starvation and abuse. Despite such reports, skeptical U.S. State Department officials refused to set aside quotas and grant asylum to refugees. The U.S. Office of War Information worried that charging the Germans with crimes against humanity might incite them to greater resistance and prolong the war. Most Americans, including top officials, believed the reports of the killing camps were exaggerated, and they clung to the conviction that such an inhumane nightmare could not be true. Only 152,000 of Europe's millions of Jews managed to gain refuge in the United States prior to America's entry into the war; thereafter, the number of refugees dropped steadily to a mere 2,400 in 1944. Those trapped in Europe could hope only for rescue by Allied armies.

The nightmare of the Holocaust was all too real. When Russian troops arrived at Auschwitz in Poland in February 1945, they found emaciated prisoners, many too weak to survive their liberation. Skeletal corpses, half burned, lay around them. Nearby were pits filled with the ashes of those who had been cremated. The Russians discovered sheds filled with loot the Nazis had stripped from the dead—clothing, gold fillings, false teeth, even cloth made from human hair. At last, the truth about the Nazis' Holocaust began to be known beyond the Germans who perpetrated and tolerated these atrocities and the men,

women, and children who succumbed to genocide. But by then it was too late for the nine million victims—mostly Jews—of the Nazis' crimes against humanity. (See "Historical Question," page 936.)

Toward Unconditional Surrender

By February 1943, Soviet defenders had finally defeated the massive German offensive against Stalingrad, turning the tide of the war in Europe. After gargantuan sacrifices in fighting that had lasted for eighteen months and killed more than 95 percent of the Russian soldiers and noncommissioned officers engaged at Stalingrad, the Red Army forced Hitler's Wehrmacht to turn back toward the west. Now the Soviets and their western allies faced the task of driving the Nazis out of eastern and western Europe and crushing them until they could fight no longer. It was long past time, Stalin proclaimed, for Britain and the United States to open a second front in France, but that offensive was postponed for more than a year after the Red Army's victory at Stalingrad. In the Pacific, the Allies had halted the expansion of the Japanese empire but now had the deadly task of dislodging Japanese defenders from the far-flung outposts they still occupied. Military planners in the United States maneuvered millions of soldiers, sailors, marines, and airmen in a strategy designed to annihilate Axis resistance by taking advantage of America's industrial superiority.

The Holocaust, 1933–1945

Principal German
• concentration and
extermination camp

From Bombing Raids to Berlin

While the Allied campaigns in North Africa and Italy depended heavily on foot soldiers, tanks, and heavy artillery, British and American pilots flew bombing missions from England to the continent as an airborne substitute for the delayed second front on the ground. Because of the vulnerability of British bombers to the German Luftwaffe, British pilots flew raids at night; and because they could not hit

Nazi Anti-Semitism and the Atomic Bomb

During the 1930s, Jewish physicists fled Adolf Hitler's fanatical anti-Semitic persecutions and came to the United States, where they played a leading role in the research and development of the atomic bomb. In this way, Nazi anti-Semitism contributed to making the United States the first atomic power.

One of Germany's greatest scientists, Albert Einstein, won the Nobel Prize for physics in 1921. Among other things, Einstein's work demonstrated that the nuclei of atoms of physical matter stored almost inconceivable quantities of energy. A fellow scientist praised Einstein's discoveries as "the greatest achievements in the history of human thought."

Einstein was born in Germany in 1879, grew up in Munich, and by 1914 headed the Kaiser Wilhelm Institute for Physics in Berlin. But he was a Jew, and his ideas were ridiculed by German anti-Semites. A German physicist who had won the Nobel Prize in 1905 attacked Einstein for his "Jewish nonsense" that was "hostile to the German spirit." Einstein wrote to a friend, "Anti-Semitism is strong here [in Berlin] and political reaction is violent." In 1922, anti-Semitic extremists assassinated the German foreign minister, Walter Rathenau, a Jewish chemist and friend of Einstein. Einstein's associates warned him that he, too, was targeted for assassination.

By 1921, when Einstein won the Nobel Prize, Adolf Hitler, a former corporal in the German infantry, had already organized the Nazi Party and recruited a large private army to intimidate his opponents—Jews foremost among them. Jailed in 1923 for attempting to overthrow the German government, Hitler wrote his Nazi manifesto, *Mein Kampf*, which proclaimed that Jews and Communists had betrayed Germany in the First World War and needed to be eliminated. Jews, Hitler insisted, were "a foreign people," "inferior beings," the "personification of the devil," "a race of dialectical liars," "parasites," and "eternal blood-suckers" who had the "clear aim of ruining the . . . white race." Hitler's rantings attracted a huge audience in Germany, and his personal Nazi army, which numbered 400,000 by 1933, terrorized and murdered anyone who got in the way.

In January 1933, just weeks before Franklin Roosevelt's inauguration as president of the United States, Hitler became chancellor of Germany on a tidal wave of popular support for his Nazi Party. Within months, he abolished freedom of speech and assembly, outlawed all political opposition, and exercised absolute dictatorial power. On April 7, Hitler announced the Law for the Restoration of the Professional Civil Service, which stipulated that "civil servants of non-Aryan descent must retire." A non-Aryan was defined as any person "descended from non-Aryan, especially Jewish, parents or grandparents." The law meant that scientists of Jewish descent who worked for state institutions, including universities, no longer had jobs. About 1,600 intellectuals in Germany immediately lost their livelihood and their future in Hitler's Reich. Among them were about a quarter of the physicists in Germany, including Einstein and ten other Nobel Prize winners. The Nazis' anti-Semitism laws forced many leading scientists to leave Germany. Between 1933 and 1941, Einstein and about 100 other Jewish physicists joined hundreds of Jewish intellectuals in an exodus from Nazi Germany to the safety of the United States.

The refugee physicists scrambled to find positions in American universities and research institutes that would allow them to continue their studies. The accelerating pace of research in physics during the 1930s raised the possibility that a way might exist to release the phenomenal energy bottled up in atomic nuclei, perhaps even to create a superbomb. Einstein and other scientists considered that possibility remote. But many worried that if scientists loyal to Germany discovered a way to harness nuclear energy, then Hitler would have the power to spread Nazi terror throughout the globe.

The refugee physicists asked Einstein to write a letter to President Roosevelt explaining the military

specific targets, they bombed general areas, hoping to hit civilians, create terror, and undermine morale. Beginning with Paul Tibbets's flight in August 1942, American pilots flew heavily armored B-17s from English airfields in daytime raids on industrial targets vital for the German war machine, especially oil refineries and ball bearing factories.

German air defenses took a fearsome toll on Allied pilots and aircraft. In 1943, two-thirds of and political threats posed by the latest research in nuclear physics. In early October 1939, as Hitler's blitzkreig swept through Poland, Roosevelt received Einstein's letter and immediately grasped the central point, exclaiming, "what you are after is to see that the Nazis don't blow us up." Roosevelt quickly convened a small group of distinguished American scientists, who convinced the president to authorize an all-out effort to learn whether an atomic bomb could be built and, if so, to build it. Only weeks before the

Japanese attack on Pearl Harbor, Roosevelt decided to launch the Manhattan Project, the top-secret atomic bomb program.

Leading scientists from the United States and Britain responded to the government's appeal: "No matter what you do with the rest of

your life, nothing will be as important to the future of the World as your work on this Project right now." Many of the most creative, productive, and irreplaceable scientists involved in the Manhattan Project were physicists who had fled Nazi Germany. Their efforts had brought the possibility of an atomic bomb to Roosevelt's attention. Having personally experienced Nazi anti-Semitism, they understood what was at stake—a world in which Hitler had the atomic bomb or his enemies did.

In the end, Hitler's scientists failed to develop an atomic bomb, and Germany surrendered before the American bomb was ready to go. But the Manhattan Project succeeded, as Paul Tibbets proved over Hiroshima, Japan, on August 6, 1945. After the war, Leo Szilard, a leader among the refugee physicists, remarked, "If Congress knew the true history of the atomic energy project . . . it would create a special medal to be given to meddling foreigners for distinguished services."

Einstein Becomes U.S. Citizen

Nazi laws that prohibited Jewish scientists from working in universities and research institutes also excluded Jews from public places such as shops, parks, and theaters—as proclaimed by signs like the one shown here. Nazi anti-Semitism caused Albert Einstein to renounce his German citizenship, emigrate to the United States, and—in the naturalization ceremony recorded in this photo—officially become an American citizen in 1940, along with his secretary Helen Dukas and his stepdaughter Margot Einstein.

Photo: Courtesy, American Institute of Physics Emilio Segré Visual Archives; sign: Arnold Kramer/United States Holocaust Memorial Museum.

BIBLIOGRAPHY

John Cornwell, *Hitler's Scientists: Science, War, and the Devil's Pact* (2003).

Daniel J. Kevles, *The Physicists: The History of a Scientific Community in Modern America* (1995).

Richard Rhodes, *The Making of the Atomic Bomb* (1986).

Paul Lawrence Rose, *Heisenberg and the Nazi Atomic Bomb Project* (1998).

S. S. Schweber, *In the Shadow of the Bomb: Bethe, Oppenheimer, and the Moral Responsibility of the Scientist* (2000).

Brian VanDeMark, *Pandora's Keepers: Nine Men and the Atomic Bomb* (2003).

American airmen did not survive to complete their 25-mission tour of duty. In all, 85,000 American airmen were killed in the skies over Europe. The arrival in February 1944 of America's durable and deadly P-51 Mustang fighter gave Allied bomber pilots superior protection and slowly began to sweep the Luftwaffe from the skies, allowing bombers to penetrate deep into Germany and pound civilian and military targets around the clock. In

Why Did the Allies Refuse to Bomb the Death Camps?

The Dead at Buchenwald
In this stark moment, all distance between official Washington and the Holocaust is breached. Soldiers and civilians pause somberly in the background as Senator Alben Barkley of Kentucky, stooped in sadness, tries to comprehend the incomprehensible.
Pentagon, U.S. Army Signal Corps.

Only a few days after the German blitzkrieg swept into Poland in September 1939, Adolf Hitler instructed military commanders to begin, as swiftly as possible, to make room for Germans in captured Polish territory by eliminating clergymen, aristocrats, intellectuals, and, above all, Jews. Soon Nazi soldiers began machine-gunning groups of unarmed, defenseless men, women, and children who stood in burial pits they had been forced to dig. Later, seeking more efficient means of annihilation, Nazi engineers devised airtight vans that roamed the countryside suffocating the condemned with carbon monoxide fumes.

To achieve the "final solution" to what Hitler and other Germans considered the Jewish menace to Aryan racial purity, the Nazis built death camps to slaughter millions in gas chambers and cremate their remains in gas ovens. Although the Nazis tried to keep the final solution a secret from the outside world, news that they were systematically killing millions of Jews at Auschwitz in Poland and in other locations leaked out in the summer of 1942. The World Jewish Congress appealed to the Allies to bomb the death camps and the railroad tracks leading to them in order to hamper the killing operation and block further shipments of victims.

The proposals to bomb the death camps got no farther than the desks of Assistant Secretary of War

April 1944, pilots began to target bridges and railroads in northwestern Europe in order to isolate German troops in northern France from reinforcements and prepare for the Allies' cross-channel invasion.

In November 1943, Churchill, Roosevelt, and Stalin met in Teheran, Iran, to plan the Allies' next step. Roosevelt conceded to Stalin that the Soviet Union would exercise de facto control of the eastern European countries that

John J. McCloy in Washington and British Foreign Secretary Anthony Eden in London. Both men were seasoned members of foreign service elites, which routinely discriminated against Jews. Intent on achieving military victory as soon as possible, they repeatedly turned aside bombing requests, arguing that the air forces could not spare resources from their military missions. There was an element of moral indifference as well. An eloquent plea from Jewish leader Chaim Weizmann elicited a rejection letter from Eden's Foreign Office that ended with tragic understatement: "I understand that this decision will be a disappointment to you, but be sure that the matter was considered exhaustively."

Tactically, however, the Allies had little reason to hesitate after 1943. The German air force could no longer muster much resistance. The Allies had sufficient planes to bomb the death camps without hindering the military campaign against Germany. And Allied refusal to commit heavy bombers to the mission because they would inevitably kill innocent people in the camps overlooked the reality that if nothing was done, all the inmates would die anyway. Auschwitz survivors recalled that they fervently prayed that Allied planes would bomb their hell into oblivion.

The U.S. Office of War Information avoided publicizing the death

Tragic Booty
In a shed not far from the bodies confounding Senator Barkley were these thousands of wedding rings. Nazis insisted that racial purity was their ideal goal. But the greed of jackals led them to strip these last marks of human affection from their victims.
National Archives.

camps, fearing that public accusations of genocide might inspire the Germans to prolong the war and cause more American casualties. Deprived of authoritative information to dispel widespread skepticism that death camps really existed, American newspapers relegated news of the Holocaust to the back pages. Even Supreme Court Justice Felix Frankfurter, a Jew and a veteran of fights against anti-Semitism, found the truth incomprehensible. After a member of the Polish underground gave him a detailed account of mass murder in Poland, Frankfurter denied the information as beyond the realm of possibility. "I did not say

this young man is lying," he explained. "I said I cannot believe him. There is a difference." At least once, though, the will to disbelieve wavered. Leon Kubowitski of the World Jewish Congress, after repeatedly being rebuffed by false arguments masquerading as "technical reasons" for not intervening, had a tense meeting with Assistant Secretary McCloy in December 1944. Kubowitski recalled that McCloy took him aside and asked anxiously, "Tell me the truth. Do you really believe that all those horrible things happened?"

By then it was too late. The death camps and their skeletal survivors were finally liberated by Allied armies in the spring of 1945. The Nazi captors fled after trying to hide their crimes against humanity by wrecking the gas chambers and crematoria. Before then, the only destruction of the camps' killing equipment had been carried out by the prisoners themselves. In the fall of 1944, four women prisoners smuggled dynamite from the munitions plant at Auschwitz to men assigned to remove ashes from the crematoria. The men managed to blow up one of the furnaces and kill several Nazi guards. Immediately, the Germans hanged the women and had the men shot. Their heroic acts were unknown to the Allied officials who chose not to send bombers to aid the doomed victims of Nazi mass murder.

the Red Army occupied as it rolled back the still-potent German Wehrmacht. Stalin agreed to enter the war against Japan once Germany finally surrendered, in effect promising to open a second front in the Pacific theater. Roosevelt and Churchill promised that they would at last launch a massive second-front assault in northern France. Code-named Overlord, the offensive was scheduled to begin in May 1944 with the combined manpower of four million Americans massed in England along with fourteen divisions from Britain, three from Canada, and one each from Poland and France.

General Eisenhower was assigned overall command of Allied forces, who assembled mountains of supplies that allowed each American GI to fight in Europe supported by 45 pounds of supplies a day, compared to 20 pounds per day for British soldiers and about 4 or 5 pounds for German combatants. German defenders, directed by General Erwin Rommel, fortified the cliffs and mined the beaches of northwestern France. But the huge deployment of Hitler's armies in the east trying to halt the Red Army's westward offensive left too few German troops to stop the millions of Allied soldiers waiting in England. More decisive, years of Allied air raids had decimated the German Luftwaffe, which could send aloft only 300 fighter planes against 12,000 Allied aircraft.

Diversionary bombing and false radio messages about armies that in fact did not exist encouraged the Germans to expect an Allied invasion at the Pas de Calais area, where the English Channel is narrowest. The actual invasion site was 300 miles away on the beaches of Normandy (Map 25.4). After frustrating delays caused by stormy weather, Eisenhower launched the largest amphibious assault in world history on D Day, June 6, 1944. After paratroopers dropped behind German lines, Allied landing craft hit the Normandy beaches under cover of ferocious naval and air

D Day Invasion

"Taxi to Hell—and Back" is what Robert Sargent called his photograph of the D Day invasion of Normandy on June 6, 1944. Amid a dense fleet of landing craft, men lucky enough to have made it through rough seas and enemy fire struggle onto the beach to open a second front in Europe. The majority of soldiers in this first wave were cut down by enemy fire from the high cliffs beyond the beach.
Library of Congress.

MAP 25.4   The European Theater of World War II, 1942–1945

Russian reversal of the German offensive by breaking the sieges of Stalingrad and Leningrad, combined with Allied landings in North Africa and Normandy, placed Germany in a closing vise of armies from all sides.

READING THE MAP: By 1942, what nations or parts of nations in Europe were under Axis control? What nations had been absorbed before the war? What nations remained neutral, and what nations were members of the Allies?

CONNECTIONS: What were the three fronts in the European theater? When did the Allies initiate actions in each of them, and why did Churchill, Stalin, and Roosevelt disagree on the timing of the opening of these fronts?

FOR MORE HELP ANALYZING THIS MAP, see the map activity for this chapter in the Online Study Guide at bedfordstmartins.com/roark.

bombardment. Rough seas and deadly fire from German machine guns slowed the assault, but Allied paratroopers attacked German defenses from the rear, and rangers scaled the beachfront cliffs to knock out enemy gun emplacements and finally secure the beachhead.

Within a week, an avalanche of soldiers, tanks, and other military equipment rolled across the Normandy beaches and propelled Allied forces toward Germany. On August 25, the Allies liberated Paris from four years of Nazi occupation. Allied forces entered Germany on September 12, and in October they captured the city of Aachen. As the giant pincers of the Allied and Soviet armies closed on Germany in December 1944, Hitler ordered a counterattack to capture the Allies' essential supply port at Antwerp, Belgium. In the Battle of the Bulge (December 16, 1944–January 31, 1945), as the Allies termed it, German forces drove fifty-five miles into Allied lines before being stopped at Bastogne. More than 70,000 Allied soldiers were killed, including more Americans than in any other battle of the war. But the Nazis lost 100,000 men and hundreds of tanks, fatally depleting Hitler's reserves.

> Within a week of D Day, an avalanche of soldiers, tanks, and other military equipment rolled across the Normandy beaches and propelled Allied forces toward Germany.

In February 1945, while Allied armies relentlessly pushed German forces backward, Churchill, Stalin, and Roosevelt met secretly at Yalta, a Russian resort town on the Black Sea, to discuss the plans for the postwar future. Seriously ill and noticeably frail, Roosevelt managed to secure Stalin's promise to permit votes of self-determination by people in the eastern European countries occupied by the Red Army. The Allies pledged to support Chiang Kai-shek as the leader of China. The Soviet Union obtained a role in the postwar government of Korea and Manchuria in exchange for entering the war against Japan after the defeat of Germany.

The "Big Three" also agreed on the creation of a new international peacekeeping organization, the United Nations (UN). All nations would have a place in the UN's General Assembly, but the Security Council would wield decisive power, and its permanent representatives from the Allied powers—China, France, Great Britain, the Soviet Union, and the United States—would possess a veto over UN actions. American response to the creation of the UN reflected the triumph of internationalism during the nation's mobilization for war. The Senate ratified the United Nations Charter in July 1945 by a vote of 89 to 2.

While Allied armies sped toward Berlin, Allied war planes bombed German roads, bridges, rail lines, war plants, and cities, dropping more bombs after D Day than in all previous European bombing raids combined. In February 1945, Allied bombers rained a firestorm of death and destruction on Berlin and Dresden, killing 60,000 civilians. By April 11, Allied armies sweeping in from the west reached the banks of the Elbe River, the agreed-upon rendezvous with the Red Army, and paused while the Soviets smashed into Berlin. In three weeks of vicious house-to-house fighting, the Red Army pulverized German defenses and captured Berlin on May 2. Hitler committed suicide on April 30, and on May 7 a provisional German government surrendered unconditionally. The war in Europe was finally over, for which 135,576 American soldiers, nearly 250,000 British troops, and 9 million Russian combatants had sacrificed their lives.

Roosevelt did not live to witness the end of the war. On April 12, while resting in Warm Springs, Georgia, the president suffered a fatal stroke. Americans grieved for the man who had led them through years of depression and world war, and they worried aloud about his successor, Vice President Harry Truman, who would have to steer the nation to victory over Japan and protect American interests in the postwar world.

The Defeat of Japan

At the outset of the war, Japan intended to use its navy to shield its economic empire in China and Southeast Asia. Instead, after the punishing defeats in the Coral Sea and at Midway, Japan had to quell renewed resistance on the Asian mainland and to fend off Allied naval and air attacks. In 1943 British and American forces, along with Indian and Chinese allies, launched an offensive against Japanese outposts in southern Asia, pushing through Burma and into China, where the armies of Chiang Kai-shek continued to resist conquest. In the Pacific, Americans and their allies attacked Japanese strongholds by sea, air, and land, moving island by island toward the Japanese homeland (Map 25.5).

> In the Pacific, Americans and their allies attacked Japanese strongholds by sea, air, and land, moving island by island toward the Japanese homeland.

Yalta Conference
In February 1945, President Roosevelt and British prime minister Winston Churchill met with Russian leader Joseph Stalin at the Black Sea resort of Yalta to plan the postwar reconstruction of Europe. Roosevelt, near the end of his life, and Churchill, soon to suffer reelection defeat, look weary next to the resolute "Man of Steel." Controversy would later arise over whether a stronger stand by the American and British leaders could have prevented the Soviet Union from imposing Communist rule on Eastern Europe.
U.S. Army.

The island-hopping campaign began in August 1942 when American marines landed on Guadalcanal in the southern Pacific, where the Japanese were constructing an airfield. For the next six months, a savage battle raged for control of the strategic area. Finally, during the night of February 7, 1943, Japanese forces withdrew. The terrible losses on both sides indicated to the marines how costly it would be to defeat Japan.

In mid-1943, American, Australian, and New Zealand forces launched offensives in New

Guinea and the Solomon Islands that gradually secured the South Pacific. In the Central Pacific, amphibious forces conquered the Gilbert and Marshall Islands, which served as forward bases for decisive air assaults on the Japanese home islands. As the Allies attacked island after island, Japanese soldiers were ordered to refuse to surrender no matter how hopeless their plight. At Tarawa, a barren coral island of less than three square miles, three thousand Japanese defenders battled American marines for three days, killing

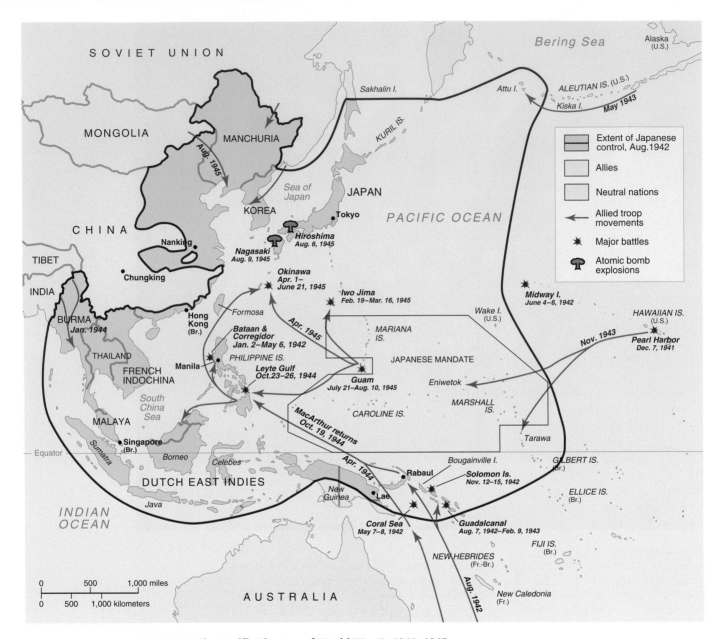

MAP 25.5   The Pacific Theater of World War II, 1941–1945
To drive the Japanese from their far-flung empire, the Allies launched two combined naval and military offensives—one to recapture the Philippines and then attack Japanese forces in China, the other to hop from island to island in the Central Pacific toward the Japanese mainland.

READING THE MAP: What was the extent of Japanese control up until August 1942? Which nations in the Pacific theater sided with the Allies? Which nations remained neutral?

CONNECTIONS: Describe the economic and military motivations behind the Japanese domination of the region. How and when did they achieve this dominance? Judging from this map, what strategic and geographic concerns might immediately have prompted Truman and his advisers to consider using the atomic bomb against Japan?

FOR MORE HELP ANALYZING THIS MAP, see the map activity for this chapter in the Online Study Guide at bedfordstmartins.com/roark.

a thousand marines and wounding two thousand until the seventeen Japanese survivors finally succumbed. Such fierce Japanese resistance spurred remorseless Allied attacks on Japanese-occupied islands, usually begun with air and naval bombardment, followed by amphibious landings by marines, and grinding, inch-by-inch combat to root Japanese fighters out of bunkers and caves with grenades, flamethrowers, and anything else at hand.

While the island-hopping campaign kept pressure on Japanese forces, the Allies invaded the Philippines in the fall of 1944. In the three-day Battle of Leyte Gulf, the greatest naval encounter in world history, the American fleet crushed the Japanese armada, clearing the way for Allied victory in the Philippines. While the Philippine campaign was under way, American forces captured two crucial islands from which they planned to launch an attack on the Japanese homeland—Iwo Jima, 750 miles from Japan, and Okinawa, only 370 miles from Tokyo. To defend Okinawa and prevent the American invaders from getting within close bombing range of their home islands, Japanese leaders ordered thousands of suicide pilots, known as *kamikaze*, to crash their bomb-laden planes into Allied ships. Like airborne torpedoes, kamikaze dived into American ships, causing fearsome destruction. But instead of destroying the American fleet, the

Marine Pinned Down on Saipan

Over 100,000 American GIs assaulted the Japanese garrison of 32,000 on Saipan in the Mariana Island chain in mid-June 1944. The Japanese fought to their deaths against overwhelming odds, prolonging the battle for nearly a month and inflicting 14,000 casualties on the American troops. The intensity of the fighting is visible on the face of the marine shown here. More than a thousand Japanese civilians, mostly women and children, rushed to the edge of a 200-foot cliff and committed suicide by leaping onto the rocks below to avoid surrendering. The suicidal defenses of the Japanese on Saipan persuaded American military planners that the final assault on the Japanese homeland would cause hundreds of thousands of American casualties.

Marine Corps Photo, National Archives.

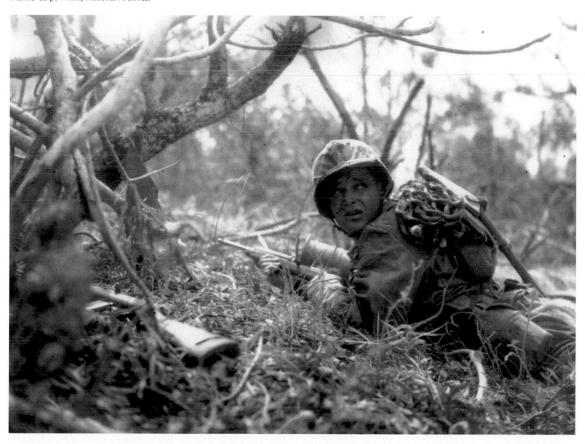

Major Campaigns and Battles of World War II, 1939–1945

September 1, 1939	Germany attacks Poland.
September 3, 1939	Britain and France declare war on Germany.
April 1940	Germany attacks Denmark and Norway.
May 1940	Germany invades Netherlands, Belgium, Luxembourg, and France.
June 1940	Italy joins Germany in the war against the Allies.
June–November 1940	Battle of Britain.
June 22, 1941	Germany invades Soviet Union.
December 7, 1941	Japan attacks Pearl Harbor.
December 8, 1941	U.S. Congress declares war on Japan.
December 11, 1941	Germany and Italy declare war on the United States.
January 2–May 6, 1942	Battles of Bataan and Corregidor.
May 7–8, 1942	Battle of the Coral Sea.
June 3–6, 1942	Battle of Midway.
August 21, 1942–January 31, 1943	Battle of Stalingrad.
August 1942–February 1943	Battle for Guadalcanal.
October 1942	British halt Germans at Battle of El-Alamein.
November 1942–May 1943	Allies mount North African campaign.
July 10, 1943	Allies begin Italian invasion through Sicily.
June 1944	Allies liberate Rome from German occupation.
June 6, 1944	D Day—Allied forces invade Normandy.
August 25, 1944	Allies liberate Paris.
September 12, 1944	Allies enter Germany.
October 23–26, 1944	Battle for Leyte Gulf.
December 16, 1944–January 31, 1945	Battle of the Bulge.
February 19–March 16, 1945	Battle of Iwo Jima.
April 1–June 21, 1945	Battle of Okinawa.
May 2, 1945	Soviet forces capture Berlin.
August 6, 1945	United States drops atomic bomb on Hiroshima.
August 9, 1945	United States drops atomic bomb on Nagasaki.

kamikaze demolished the last vestige of the Japanese air force. By June 1945, the Japanese were nearly defenseless on sea and in the air. Still, their leaders prepared to fight to the death for their homeland.

Atomic Warfare

In mid-July 1945, as Allied forces were preparing for the final assault on Japan, American scientists tested a secret weapon at an isolated desert site near Los Alamos, New Mexico. In 1942, Roosevelt had authorized the top-secret Manhattan Project to find a way to convert nuclear energy into a superbomb before the Germans added such a weapon to their arsenal. More than 100,000 Americans, led by scientists, engineers, and military officers at Los Alamos, worked frantically at thirty-seven secret locations across the country to win the fateful race for an atomic bomb. Germany surrendered two and a half months before the first test on July 16, 1945, when scientists witnessed an awesome explosion equivalent to hundreds of tons of TNT that sent a mushroom cloud of debris eight miles into the atmosphere.

A delegation of scientists and officials, troubled by the bomb's destructive force, secretly proposed that the United States give a public demonstration of the bomb's cataclysmic power, hoping to persuade Japan's leaders to surrender. With the Japanese incapable of offensive action and blockaded by the Allied fleet, proponents of a demonstration were encouraged because Japanese emissaries were already putting out feelers about peace negotiations. But U.S. government officials quickly rejected such a demonstration: Americans had enough nuclear material for only three bombs, the demonstration bomb might fail to explode, and the Japanese might not surrender even if it did. Also, despite numerous defeats, Japan still had more than 6 million reserves at home fortified by over 5,000 kamikaze aircraft stockpiled for a last-ditch defense against the anticipated Allied assault, which U.S. military advisers estimated would cost the lives of at least 250,000 Americans.

President Truman heard about the successful bomb test at Los Alamos when he was in Potsdam, Germany, negotiating with Stalin about postwar issues. Truman vaguely mentioned to Stalin that the United States had a powerful new weapon, but, Truman wrote later, "The Russian premier showed no special interest. All he said was that he was glad to hear it and hoped we would make 'good use of it against the Japanese.'" Truman realized that the atomic bomb could hasten the end of the war with Japan, perhaps before the Russians could attack the Japanese in Korea and Manchuria, as Stalin pledged at Yalta to do. Within a few months after the defeat of Germany, Truman also recognized that the bomb gave the United States a devastating atomic **monopoly** that could be used to counter Soviet ambitions and advance American interests in the postwar world.

Truman, who had been a commander of combat troops on the ground in World War I, saw no reason not to use the atomic bomb against Japan if doing so would save American lives. But first he issued an ultimatum: Japan must surrender unconditionally or face utter ruin. When the Japanese failed to respond by the deadline, Truman ordered that a bomb be dropped on a Japanese city not already heavily damaged by American raids. On August 6, Colonel Paul Tibbets piloted the *Enola Gay* over Hiroshima and released an atomic bomb, leveling the city and incinerating 78,000 people. Three days later, after the Japanese government still refused to surrender, Tibbets-trained airmen dropped a second atomic bomb on Nagasaki, killing more than 100,000 civilians.

At last, a peace faction took control of the Japanese government, and with American assurance that the emperor could retain his throne

Hiroshima Bombing
This rare shot taken by a news photographer in Hiroshima immediately after the atomic bomb exploded on August 6, 1945, suggests the shock and incomprehension that survivors later described as their first reaction. On August 9, another atomic bomb created similar devastation in Nagasaki.
UN photo.

after the Allies took over, Japan surrendered on August 14. On a troop ship departing from Europe for what would have been the final assault on Japan, an American soldier spoke for millions of others when he heard the wonderful news that the killing was over: "We are going to grow to adulthood after all."

Conclusion: Allied Victory and America's Emergence as a Superpower

Shortly after Pearl Harbor, Hitler pronounced America "a decayed country" without "much future," a country "half Judaized, and the other half Negrified," a country "where everything is built on the dollar" and bound to fall apart. American mobilization for World War II disproved Hitler's arrogant prophecy, as Paul Tibbets's historic flight dramatized. At a cost of 405,399 American lives, the nation united with its allies to battle Axis aggressors in Europe and Asia and eventually to crush them into unconditional surrender. Almost all Americans believed they had won a "good war" against totalitarian evil. The Allies saved Asia and Europe from enslavement and finally halted the Nazis' genocidal campaign against Jews and others whom the Nazis considered inferior. To secure human rights and protect the world against future wars, the Roosevelt administration took the lead in creating the United Nations.

Wartime production lifted the nation out of the Great Depression. The gross national product soared to four times what it had been when Roosevelt became president in 1933. Jobs in defense industries eliminated chronic unemployment, provided wages for millions of women workers and African American migrants from southern farms, and boosted Americans' prosperity. Ahead stretched the challenge of maintaining that prosperity while reintegrating millions of uniformed men and women coming home from overseas.

By the end of the war, the United States had emerged as a global superpower. Wartime mobilization made the American economy the strongest in the world, buttressed by the military clout of the nation's nuclear monopoly. While the war left much of the world a smoldering wasteland, the American mainland enjoyed immunity from attack. The Japanese occupation of China left 50 million people without homes and millions more dead, maimed, and orphaned. The German offensive against the Soviet Union killed more than 26 million Russian soldiers and civilians. Germany and Japan lay in ruins, their economies as shattered as their military forces. The Allies killed more than 4 million Nazi soldiers and over 1.2 million Japanese combatants, as well as hundreds of thousands of civilians. But in the gruesome balance sheet of war, the Axis powers inflicted far more grief, misery, and destruction upon the global victims of their aggression than they suffered in return.

As the dominant western nation in the postwar world, the United States asserted leadership in the reconstruction of Europe while occupying Japan and overseeing its economic and political recovery. America soon confronted new challenges in the tense aftermath of the war, as Soviets seized political control of Eastern Europe, a Communist revolution swept China, and national liberation movements emerged in the colonial empires of Britain and France. The surrender of the Axis powers ended the battles of World War II, but the forces unleashed by the war shaped the United States and the rest of the world for decades to come.

FOR ADDITIONAL FIRSTHAND ACCOUNTS OF THIS PERIOD, see Chapter 25 in Michael Johnson, ed., *Reading the American Past*, Third Edition.

TO ASSESS YOUR MASTERY OF THE MATERIAL IN THIS CHAPTER, see the Online Study Guide at bedfordstmartins.com/roark.

FOR WEB LINKS RELATED TO TOPICS IN THIS CHAPTER, see "HistoryLinks," "DocLinks," and "PlaceLinks" at bedfordstmartins.com/roark.

CHRONOLOGY

1933
- Adolf Hitler becomes chancellor of Germany.
- United States formally recognizes Soviet Union.

1935–1937
- Congress seeks to shield America from world conflicts with neutrality acts.

1936
- Nazi Germany occupies Rhineland.
- Mussolini's fascist Italian regime conquers Ethiopia.
- Civil war breaks out in Spain.

1937
- Japanese troops capture Nanking.
- Roosevelt delivers speech urging U.S. "quarantine" against aggressor nations.

1938
- Hitler annexes Austria.
- British prime minister Neville Chamberlain meets with Hitler in Munich and agrees to German seizure of Sudetenland in Czechoslovakia.

1939
- German troops occupy remainder of Czechoslovakia without resistance.
- Nazi Germany and Soviet Union sign nonaggression pact.
- **September 1.** Germany's attack on Poland begins World War II.
- United States and Great Britain conclude cash-and-carry agreement for arms sales.

1940
- **May–June.** British troops evacuated at Dunkirk, France.
- **June.** German occupation of France begins.
- Roosevelt elected to a third term; defeats Wendell Willkie.

1941
- Lend-Lease Act enables Britain to obtain war materiel from United States on credit.
- **June.** Germany invades Soviet Union.
- **August.** Atlantic Charter devised by Roosevelt and Allies to guarantee human and international freedoms after war.

- **December 7.** Japanese launch surprise attack on Pearl Harbor; United States declares war on Japan.

1942
- Japan captures Philippines.
- Civil rights activists found Congress of Racial Equality (CORE).
- U.S. navy scores its first major victories in Battle of Coral Sea and at Midway.
- Roosevelt authorizes top-secret Manhattan Project.
- **November.** U.S. forces invade North Africa.
- Roosevelt authorizes internment of Japanese Americans.

1943
- Allied leaders agree that war will end only with unconditional surrender of Axis forces.
- "Zoot suit" riots occur in Los Angeles.
- U.S. forces invade Sicily.

1944
- **June 6.** Combined Allied army stages successful D Day landing at Normandy.
- Roosevelt elected to a fourth term; defeats Thomas E. Dewey.

1945
- Churchill, Roosevelt, and Stalin meet at Yalta to plan reconstruction of Europe after defeat of Germany.
- **April 12.** Roosevelt dies, and Vice President Harry Truman becomes president.
- **April 30.** Hitler commits suicide.
- **May 7.** Germany surrenders.
- **July.** U.S. Senate ratifies United Nations Charter, and U.S. tenure as a permanent member of the Security Council begins.
- **August 6.** United States drops atomic bomb on Hiroshima.

- **August 9.** United States drops atomic bomb on Nagasaki.
- **August 14.** Japan surrenders, ending World War II.

BIBLIOGRAPHY

General Works

Michael Beschloss, *The Conquerors: Roosevelt, Truman, and the Destruction of Hitler's Germany, 1941–1945* (2002).

Kenneth S. Davis, *FDR: Into the Storm, 1937–1940* (1993).

Kenneth S. Davis, *FDR: The War President, 1940–1943* (2000).

Thomas Fleming, *The New Dealers' War: Franklin D. Roosevelt and the War within World War II* (2001).

Martin Folly, *The U.S. and World War II: The Awakening Giant* (2002).

Paul Fussell, *Wartime* (1989).

Akira Iriye, *The Origins of the Second World War in Asia and the Pacific* (1987).

John Keegan, *The Second World War* (1989).

David M. Kennedy, *Freedom from Fear: The American People in Depression and War, 1929–1945* (1999).

Richard Ketchum, *The Borrowed Years, 1938–1941: America on the Way to War* (1989).

Eric Larrabee, *Commander in Chief: Franklin Delano Roosevelt, His Lieutenants, and Their War* (1987).

Jon Meacham, *Franklin and Winston: An Intimate Portrait of an Epic Friendship* (2003).

Michael S. Sherry, *In the Shadow of War: The United States since the 1930s* (1995).

Studs Terkel, *"The Good War": An Oral History of World War II* (1984).

Paul W. Tibbets Jr., *The Tibbets Story* (1978).

Gerhard Weinberg, *World at Arms: A Global History of World War II* (1994).

Foreign Policy

Tokomo Akami, *Internationalizing the Pacific: The U.S., Japan, and the Institute of Pacific Relations in War and Peace, 1919–1945* (2002).

Wayne S. Cole, *Roosevelt and the Isolationists, 1932–1945* (1983).

Thomas Connell, *America's Japanese Hostages: The World War II Plan for a Japanese-Free Latin America* (2002).

Robert Dallek, *Franklin D. Roosevelt and American Foreign Policy, 1932–1945* (1979).

Robert A. Divine, *The Illusion of Neutrality* (1982).

Max Paul Friedman, *Nazis and Good Neighbors: The U.S. Campaign against the Germans of Latin America in World War II* (2003).

Erwin F. Gellman, *Good Neighbor Diplomacy: United States Policies in Latin America, 1933–1945* (1979).

Waldo Heinrichs, *Threshold of War: Franklin D. Roosevelt and American Entry into World War II* (1988).

Robert Hilderbrand, *Dumbarton Oaks: The Origins of the United Nations and the Search for Postwar Security* (1990).

Akira Iriye, *The Globalizing of America, 1913–1945* (1995).

Walter LaFeber, *Inevitable Revolutions* (1983).

Robert Franklin Maddox, *The War within World War II: The U.S. and International Cartels* (2001).

Frederick W. Marks, *Wind over Sand: The Diplomacy of Franklin Roosevelt* (1988).

James McAllister, *No Exit: America and the German Problem, 1943–1954* (2002).

J. Robert Moskin, *Mr. Truman's War: The Final Victories of World War II and the Birth of the Postwar World* (2002).

David Reynolds, *From Munich to Pearl Harbor: Roosevelt's America and the Origins of the Second World War* (2001).

David F. Schmitz, *The United States and Fascist Italy, 1922–1944* (1988).

Gaddis Smith, *American Diplomacy during the Second World War, 1941–1945* (1985).

Geoffrey S. Smith, *To Save a Nation: American "Extremism," the New Deal, and the Coming of WW II* (1992).

Jonathan Utley, *Going to War with Japan, 1937–1942* (1985).

Andrew J. Whitfield, *Hong Kong, Empire, and the Anglo-American Alliance at War, 1941–1945* (2001).

Mobilization and the Home Front

Karen Anderson, *Wartime Women: Sex Roles, Family Relations, and the Status of Women during World War II* (1981).

D'Ann Campbell, *Women at War with America: Private Lives in a Patriotic Era* (1984).

Stephanie A. Carpenter, *On the Farm Front: The Women's Land Army in World War II* (2003).

Steven Casey, *Cautious Crusade: FDR, American Public Opinion and the War against Nazi Germany* (2001).

Michael Dobbs, *The Saboteurs: The Nazi Raid on America* (2004).

Daniel R. Ernst and Victor Jew, *Total War and the Law: The American Home Front in World War II* (2002).

Mark Jonathan Harris, Franklin D. Mitchell, and Steve J. Schechter, *The Home Front: America during World War II* (1985).

Susan Hartmann, *The Home Front and Beyond: American Women in the 1940s* (1982).

John Earl Haynes and Harvey Klehr, *Verona: Decoding Soviet Espionage in America* (1999).

John W. Jeffries, *Wartime America: The World War II Home Front* (1996).

Nelson Lichtenstein, *Labor's War at Home: The CIO in World War II* (1983).

Gerald D. Nash, *The American West Transformed: The Impact of the Second World War* (1985).

William L. O'Neill, *A Democracy at War: America's Fight at Home and Abroad in World War II* (1993).

Geoffrey Perret, *Days of Sadness, Years of Triumph: The American People, 1939–1945* (1985).

Ruth Sarles, *A Story of America First: The Men and Women Who Opposed U.S. Intervention in World War II* (2003).

William Tuttle, *Daddy's Gone to War: The Second World War in the Lives of America's Children* (1993).

Brian Waddell, *The War against the New Deal: World War II and American Democracy* (2001).

Military Organization and Campaigns

Gar Alperovitz, *The Decision to Use the Atomic Bomb and the Architecture of an American Myth* (1995).

Stephen E. Ambrose, *D-Day, June 6, 1944* (1994).

Anthony Beevor, *Stalingrad* (1998).

Anthony Beevor, *The Fall of Berlin, 1945* (2002).

Allan Berube, *Coming Out under Fire: The History of Gay Men and Women in World War Two* (1990).

Paul S. Boyer, *By the Bomb's Early Light: American Thought and Culture at the Dawn of the Atomic Age* (1985).

Richard Breitman, *Official Secrets: What the Nazis Planned, What the British and Americans Knew* (1998).

John Costello, *Virtue under Fire: How World War II Changed Our Social and Sexual Attitudes* (1986).

Gavan Daws, *Prisoners of the Japanese: POWs of World War II* (1992).

John Dower, *War without Mercy: Race and Power in the Pacific War* (1986).

Gordon A. Harrison, *Cross-Channel Attack* (2002).

D. Clayton James, *A Time for Giants: The Politics of the American High Command in World War II* (1987).

Dan Kurzman, *Day of the Bomb: Countdown to Hiroshima* (1986).

Robert Leckie, *Delivered from Evil: The Saga of World War II* (1987).

Gerald F. Linderman, *The World within War: America's Combat Experience in World War II* (1997).

Tim Maga, *America Attacks Japan: The Invasion That Never Was* (2002).

Evelyn M. Monahan and Rosemary Neidel-Greenlee, *And If I Perish: Frontline U.S. Army Nurses in World War II* (2003).

Michael Neufeld and Michael Berenbaum, *The Bombing of Auschwitz: Should the Allies Have Attempted It?* (2000).

Mark P. Parillo, *We Were in the Big One: Experiences of the World War II Generation* (2002).

Geoffrey Perret, *Winged Victory: The Army Air Forces in World War II* (1993).

Joseph Persico, *Roosevelt's Secret War: FDR and World War II Espionage* (2001).

Gordon W. Prange, *At Dawn We Slept* (1981).

Richard Rhodes, *The Making of the Atomic Bomb* (1986).

Ronald Schaffer, *Wings of Judgment: American Bombing in World War II* (1988).

Michael Schaller, *Douglas MacArthur: The Far Eastern General* (1989).

Peter Schrijvers, *The GI War against Japan: American Soldiers in Asia and the Pacific during World War II* (2002).

Michael S. Sherry, *The Rise of American Air Power: The Creation of Armageddon* (1987).

Ronald H. Spector, *Eagle against the Sun: The American War with Japan* (1985).

Murray Williamson and Allan R. Millett, *A War to Be Won: Fighting the Second World War, 1937–1945* (2000).

Thomas W. Zeiler, *Unconditional Defeat: Japan, America and the End of World War II* (2004).

Race and Minorities

Gerald Astor, *The Right to Fight: A History of African Americans in the Military* (1998).

Alison R. Bernstein, *American Indians and World War II: Toward a New Era in Indian Affairs* (1991).

Jeffrey F. Burton et al., *Confinement and Ethnicity: An Overview of World War II Japanese American Relocation Sites* (2002).

David P. Colley, *Blood for Dignity: The Story of the First Integrated Combat Unit in the U.S. Army* (2003).

Roger Daniels, *Concentration Camps: North American Japanese in the United States and Canada during World War II* (1971, 1989).

Jere Bishop Franco, *Crossing the Pond: The Native American Effort in World War II* (1999).

Peter H. Irons, *Justice at War: The Story of the Japanese American Internment Cases* (1983).

Daniel Kryder, *Divided Arsenal: Race and the American State during World War II* (2000).

Steven F. Lawson, *Running for Freedom: Civil Rights and Black Politics in America since 1941* (1991).

Brenda L. Moore, *Serving Our Country: Japanese American Women in the Military during World War II* (2003).

Bernard C. Nalty, *Strength for the Fight: A History of Black Americans in the Military* (1989).

Wendy Ng, *Japanese American Internment during World War II* (2002).

Page Smith, *Democracy on Trial: The Japanese American Evacuation and Relocation in World War II* (1995).

Ronald Takaki, *Strangers from a Different Shore: A History of Asian Americans* (1989).

Depicting the War

M. Joyce Baker, *Images of Women on Film: The War Years* (1981).

Thomas Doherty, *Projections of War: Hollywood, American Culture, and World War II* (1993).

Gerd Horten, *Radio Goes to War: The Cultural Politics of Propaganda during World War II* (2002).

Karal Ann Marling and John Wetenhall, *Iwo Jima: Monuments, Memories, and the American Hero* (1991).

Peter Maslowski, *Armed with Cameras: The American Military Photographers of World War II* (1993).

George H. Roeder Jr., *The Censored War: American Visual Experience during World War II* (1993).

Emily S. Rosenberg, *A Day Which Will Live: Pearl Harbor in American Memory* (2003).

Holly Cowan Shulman, *The Voice of America: Propaganda and Democracy, 1941–1945* (1991).

Michael S. Sweeney, *Secrets of Victory: The Office of Censorship and the American Press and Radio in World War II* (2001).

Frederick S. Voss, *Reporting the War: The Journalistic Coverage of World War II* (1994).

America and the Holocaust

Robert Abzug, *Inside the Vicious Heart: Americans and the Liberation of Nazi Concentration Camps* (1987).

Richard Breitman and Alan Kraut, *American Refugee Policy and European Jewry* (1987).

Lucy Dawidowicz, *The War against the Jews, 1933–1945* (1986).

Leonard Dinnerstein, *America and the Survivors of the Holocaust* (1982).

Deborah E. Lipstadt, *Beyond Belief: The American Press and the Coming of the Holocaust, 1933–1945* (1986).

Verne W. Newton, *FDR and the Holocaust* (1995).

Peter Novick, *The Holocaust in American Life* (1999).

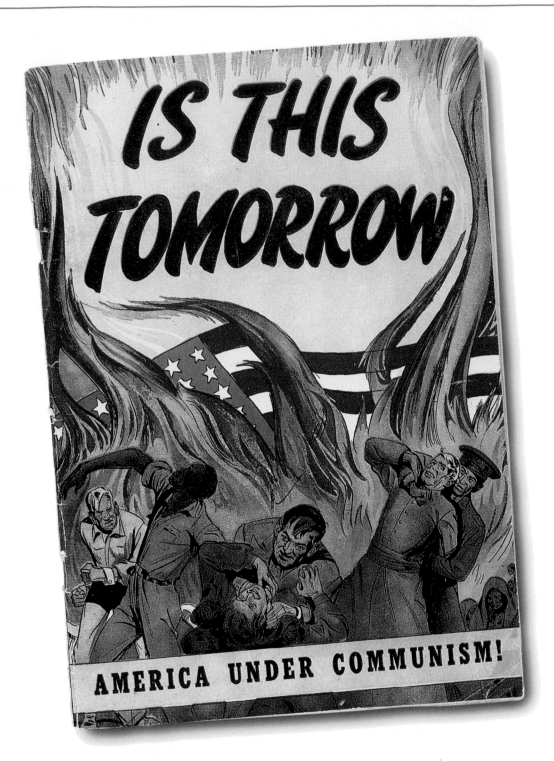

COLD WAR COMIC BOOK
Americans barely had time to celebrate the Allied victory in World War II when they perceived a
new threat, posed by the Soviet Union. Fear of communism dominated much of postwar American
life and politics, even invading popular culture. Four million copies of this comic book, published by
a religious organization in 1947, painted a terrifying picture of what would happen to Americans if
the Soviets took over the country. Such takeover stories appeared in movies, cartoons, and magazines as well as in other comic books.

Collection of Charles H. Christensen.

Cold War Politics in the Truman Years

1945–1953

O N NOVEMBER 5, 1946, President Harry S. Truman, his wife, and his daughter boarded the train back to Washington from Truman's hometown, Independence, Missouri, where they had gone to vote in the congressional elections. During the campaigns, Republicans had blasted Truman as incapable of dealing with economic problems and the threat of **communism**. Campaign slogans had jeered, "To Err is Truman," while the president's approval rating sank to a mere 32 percent. Many Democratic candidates had avoided mentioning his name and instead used recordings of the late Franklin Roosevelt's voice to stir voters. Playing poker with reporters on the train as the returns came in, Truman appeared unconcerned. But the results were devastating: The Republicans captured both the House and the Senate by substantial majorities, dominating Congress for the first time since 1932.

When Truman arrived in Washington at the lowest point of his presidency, only one member of his administration showed up to greet him, Undersecretary of State Dean Acheson. Acheson's gesture signaled a developing relationship of central importance to the two men and to postwar history. The fifty-three-year-old Acheson shared most of Truman's political principles, though their backgrounds differed sharply. Acheson had enjoyed an upper-class education at a private prep school, Yale University, and Harvard Law School. After clerking for Supreme Court Justice Louis Brandeis, he earned a comfortable living as a corporate lawyer. In contrast, Truman, the son of a Missouri farmer, had not attended college and had failed in a business venture before entering local politics in the 1920s.

Despite his wealth and privilege, Acheson supported much of the **New Deal** and staunchly defended organized labor. He spoke out against **isolationism** in the 1930s, and in 1941 he accepted President Roosevelt's offer of a job at the State Department. Shortly after Truman became president, the supremely confident Acheson wrote privately about shortcomings in Truman's "judgment and wisdom that the limitations of his experience produce," but he also found the fledgling president "straightforward, decisive, simple, entirely honest," a man who "will learn fast and will inspire confidence." In June 1947, Acheson left the State Department, but Truman lured him back in 1949 to be secretary of state during the president's second term. Acheson appreciated Truman's willingness to make tough decisions and admiringly noted that Truman's "ego never came between him and his job." Truman cherished Acheson's abiding loyalty, calling him "my good right hand."

Truman needed all the help he could get. The "accidental president" lacked the charisma, experience, and political skills with which Roosevelt had transformed both foreign and domestic policy, won four presidential elections, and forged a Democratic Party coalition that dominated national politics. Initially criticized and abandoned by many Roosevelt loyalists, Truman faced a resurgent Republican Party as well as revolts from within his own party. Besides addressing domestic problems that the New Deal had not solved—how to sustain economic growth and avoid another depression without the war to fuel the economy—Truman had to redefine the nation's foreign policy goals in a new international context.

Dean Acheson was instrumental in forging that foreign policy. As early as 1946, Acheson became convinced that the Soviet Union posed a major threat to U.S. security. With other officials, he helped to shape a policy designed to contain and thwart Soviet power wherever it threatened to spread. By 1947, a new term had been coined to describe the intense rivalry between the superpowers—**cold war**. The **containment** policy worked in Western Europe with the enunciation of the **Truman Doctrine**, implementation of the Marshall Plan, and creation of **NATO**; but communism spread in Asia, and at home a wave of anti-Communist hysteria erupted that harmed many Americans and stifled dissent and debate about U.S. policies.

As the preeminent foreign policy official, Acheson too reaped abuse from Republicans for being "soft on communism." At the height of the anti-Communist frenzy, Acheson received so much hate mail that guards were posted at his house. Yet he kept both his job and his sense of humor. When cab drivers asked him, "Aren't you Dean Acheson?" he would reply, "Yes. Do I have to get out?"

From the Grand Alliance to Containment

With victory over Japan in August 1945, Americans besieged the government for the return of their loved ones. Baby booties arrived at the White House with a note, "Please send my daddy home." Americans looked forward to the end of international crises and the dismantling of the large military establishment. They expected the Allies, led by the United States and working within the United Nations, to cooperate in the management of international peace. Postwar realities quickly dashed these expectations. A dangerous new threat seemed to arise as the wartime alliance forged by the United States, Great Britain, and the Soviet Union crumbled, and the United States began to develop the military and diplomatic means to contain the spread of Soviet power around the globe.

Dean Acheson
No individual had more to do with transforming America's role in the world after World War II than Dean Acheson, President Truman's closest foreign policy adviser. Acheson, shown here with Truman in 1945, criticized those who saw the cold war in black-and-white terms and communism as an evil that the United States could expel from the earth. Rather, he advocated that American leaders learn "to limit objectives, to get ourselves away from the search for the absolute, to find out what is within our powers."
Harry S. Truman Library.

The Cold War Begins

"The guys who came out of World War II were idealistic," reported Harold Russell, a young paratrooper who lost both hands in a training accident. "We felt the day had come when the wars were all over." Public opinion polls echoed the veterans' confidence in the promise of peace. But political leaders were less optimistic, especially Winston Churchill, who had always distrusted the Soviets. Once the Allies had overcome a common enemy, the prewar mistrust and antagonism between the Soviet Union and the West resurfaced over their very different visions of the postwar world.

The Western Allies' delay in opening a second front in Western Europe aroused Soviet suspicions during the war. The Soviet Union made supreme wartime sacrifices, losing more than twenty million citizens and vast portions of its agricultural and industrial capacity. At the war's end, Soviet leader Joseph Stalin wanted to make Germany pay for the rebuilding of the Soviet economy and to expand Soviet influence in the world. Above all, he wanted governments friendly to the Soviet Union on its borders in Eastern Europe, especially in Poland, through which Germany had attacked the Soviet Union twice within twenty-five years.

In contrast, enemy fire had never touched the mainland of the United States, and its 405,000 dead amounted to just 2 percent of the Soviet loss. With a vastly expanded productive capacity and a monopoly on atomic weapons, the United States emerged from the war the most powerful nation on the planet. That sheer power, along with U.S. economic interests, policymakers' understandings of how the recent war might have been avoided, and a sense that the United States had the best institutions and best intentions in the world, all affected how its leaders approached the Soviet Union in the aftermath of World War II.

Fearing a return of the depression, U.S. officials believed that a healthy economy depended on opportunities abroad. The United States needed access to raw materials, markets for its goods, and security for American investments overseas. These needs could be met best in countries with economic and political systems resembling its own, not in those where government controls interfered with the free flow of products and dollars. As Truman put it in 1947, "The American system can survive in America only if it becomes a world system."

Yet both leaders and citizens regarded their foreign policy not as a self-interested campaign to guarantee economic interests, but as the means to preserve national security and bring freedom, **democracy**, and capitalism to the rest of the world. Laura Briggs spoke for many Americans who believed "it was our destiny to prove that we were the children of God and that our way was right for the world."

Recent history also shaped postwar foreign policy. Americans believed that Britain, France, and the United States might have prevented World War II had they resisted rather than appeased Hitler's initial aggression. Secretary of the Navy James V. Forrestal, for example, argued against trying to "buy [the Soviets'] understanding and sympathy. We tried that once with Hitler." This "appeasement" analogy would be invoked time and again when the United States faced challenges to the international status quo.

> Once the Allies had overcome a common enemy, the prewar mistrust and antagonism between the Soviet Union and the West resurfaced over their very different visions of the postwar world.

The man with ultimate responsibility for U.S. policy was a keen student of history but came to the White House with little experience in international affairs. When Germany attacked the Soviet Union in 1941, then-senator Truman expressed his hope that the two would kill each other off. As president he envisioned Soviet-American cooperation, as long as the Soviet Union conformed with U.S. plans for the postwar world and restrained its expansionist impulses. Proud of his ability to make quick decisions, Truman was determined to be firm with the Soviets, knowing well that America's nuclear monopoly gave him the upper hand.

Soviet and American interests clashed first in Eastern Europe. Stalin insisted that the Allies' wartime agreements gave him a free hand in the countries defeated or liberated by the Red Army, just as the United States was unilaterally reconstructing governments in Italy and Japan. The Soviet dictator used harsh methods to install Communist governments in neighboring Poland and Bulgaria. Elsewhere, the Soviets initially tolerated non-Communist governments in Hungary and Czechoslovakia. And in the spring of 1946, Stalin responded to pressure from the West and removed troops from Iran on the Soviet Union's southwest border, allowing United States access to rich oil fields there.

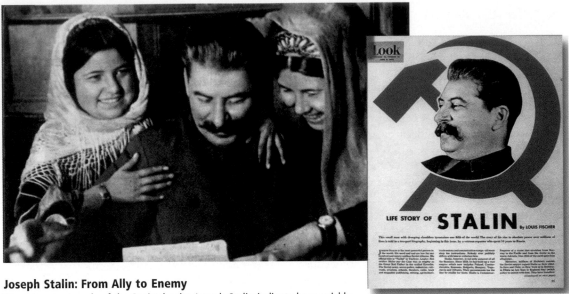

Joseph Stalin: From Ally to Enemy
These two portrayals of the Soviet leader Joseph Stalin indicate how quickly
the World War II alliance disintegrated into the cold war. On the left in a
1944 issue of the popular magazine *Look,* Stalin is photographed with adoring schoolchildren.
The accompanying article depicts Stalin as an effective leader but also a sensitive man who
wrote poetry and loved literature. Only four years later, in 1948, *Look* published Stalin's life
story. The photo frames his face with communism's emblem, the hammer and sickle, which
symbolizes the alliance of workers and peasants. Whereas the 1944 piece had called Stalin a
"man of trenchant speech, indomitable will and extraordinary mental capacity [and] lover of
literature," the 1948 article emphasized his "rise to absolute power over millions of lives" and
depicted him as a "small man with drooping shoulders [who] tyrannizes one-fifth of the
world." What do these two items suggest about the role of the press in American society?
The Michael Barson Collection/Past Perfect; Collection of Janice L. and David J. Frent.

Stalin considered U.S. officials hypocritical in demanding democratic elections in Eastern Europe while supporting dictatorships friendly to U.S. interests in Cuba and other Latin American countries. The United States clung to its own sphere of influence while opposing Soviet efforts to create its own. But the Western Allies were unwilling to match tough words with military force; and their sharp protests failed to prevent the Soviet Union from establishing satellite countries in most of Eastern Europe.

In 1946, the wartime Allies contended over Germany's future. American policymakers wanted to strip the nation of its military capacity, but they also desired a rapid industrial revival in Germany to foster European economic recovery and thus America's own long-term prosperity. By contrast, the Soviet Union wanted Germany weak militarily and economically, and it sought heavy reparations that could be used to rebuild the devastated Soviet economy. Unable to settle their differences, the Allies divided Germany. The Soviet Union installed a puppet Communist government in the eastern section, and in December 1946, Britain, France, and the United States unified their occupation zones and began the process that established the Federal Republic of Germany—West Germany—in 1949 (Map 26.1).

The war of words escalated early in 1946. Boasting of the superiority of the Soviet system, Stalin told a Moscow audience in February that capitalist economies inevitably produced war. One month later, Truman traveled with Winston Churchill to Fulton, Missouri, where the former prime minister denounced Soviet suppression of the popular will in Eastern and central Europe. "From Stettin in the Baltic to Trieste in the Adriatic, an iron curtain has descended across the Continent," Churchill said. (See "Documenting the American Promise," page 956.) Although Truman did not officially endorse Churchill's **iron curtain** speech, his presence implied agreement with the idea of joint British-American strength to combat Soviet aggression. Stalin regarded the speech as "a call to war against the USSR."

In February 1946, career diplomat George F. Kennan, who had served in U.S. embassies in Eastern Europe and Moscow, wrote a comprehensive rationale for hard-line foreign policy. He downplayed the influence of Communist ideology in Soviet policy. Instead, Kennan stressed the Soviets' insecurity and their need to maintain authority at home, which prompted Stalin to exaggerate threats from abroad and to expand

Soviet power. All of these circumstances, Kennan argued, made it impossible to negotiate with Stalin, a conclusion shared by Secretary of State James F. Byrnes, Undersecretary Acheson, and other key Truman advisers.

Kennan predicted that the Soviet Union would retreat from efforts to expand its influence worldwide "in the face of superior force." Therefore, the United States should respond with "unalterable counterforce," making Russia "face frustration indefinitely," an approach that came to be called containment. Kennan expected that containment would eventually end in

---

MAP 26.1 The Division of Europe after World War II

The "iron curtain," a term coined by Winston Churchill to refer to the Soviet grip on Eastern and central Europe, divided Europe for nearly fifty years. Communist governments controlled the countries along the Soviet Union's western border. The only exception was Finland, which remained neutral.

READING THE MAP: Is the division of Europe between NATO, Communist, and neutral countries about equal? Why would the location of Berlin pose a problem for the Western allies?

CONNECTIONS: When was NATO founded, and what is its purpose? How did the postwar division of Europe compare with the wartime alliances?

FOR MORE HELP ANALYZING THIS MAP, see the map activity for this chapter in the Online Study Guide at bedfordstmartins.com/roark.

The Emerging Cold War

Although antagonism between the Soviet Union and the West stretched back to the Russian Revolution of 1917, the United States, the Soviet Union, Britain, and other powers had cooperated to win World War II and managed to reach compromises at the Yalta and Potsdam summits in 1945. Early in 1946, however, officials in both the Soviet Union and the West publicly expressed distrust and attributed hostile motivations to each other. Within the United States, disagreement developed about how to deal with the Soviet Union.

DOCUMENT 1
Joseph Stalin Addresses an Election Rally in Moscow, February 9, 1946

At an election rally in early 1946 ("election" in name only since there was just one Communist Party candidate for each position), Premier Joseph Stalin called on the Soviet people to support his program for economic development and postwar recovery. Although Stalin did not address cold war issues, leaders in the West viewed his comments about communism and capitalism, as well as his boasts about the strength of the Red Army, as a threat to peace.

It would be incorrect to think that the [Second World] war arose accidentally or as the result of the fault of some of the statesmen. Although these faults did exist, the war arose in reality as the inevitable result of the development of the world economic and political forces on the basis of monopoly capitalism.

Our Marxists declare that the capitalist system of world economy conceals elements of crisis and war, that the development of world capitalism does not follow a steady and even course forward, but proceeds through crises and catastrophes. The uneven development of the capitalist countries leads in time to sharp disturbances in their relations and the group of countries which consider themselves inadequately provided with raw materials and export markets try usually to change this situation and to change the position in their favor by means of armed force. As a result of these factors, the capitalist world is split into two hostile camps and war follows. . . .

Now victory [in World War II] means, first of all, that our Soviet social system has won, that the Soviet social system has successfully stood the test in the fire of war and has proved its complete vitality. . . .

The war has shown that the Soviet social system is a truly popular system, issued from the depths of the people and enjoying its mighty support. . . . The Soviet social system has proved to be more capable of life and more stable than a non-Soviet social system. . . .

Our victory implies that it was the Soviet armed forces that won. . . . The Red Army heroically withstood all the adversities of the war, routed completely the armies of our enemies and emerged victoriously from the war. This is recognized by everybody—friend and foe.

Now a few words on the plans for the work of the Communist Party in the near future. . . . The fundamental task of the new Five-Year Plan consists in restoring the areas of the country which have suffered, restoring the prewar level in industry and agriculture, and then exceeding this level.

Apart from the fact that in the very near future the rationing system will be abolished, special attention will be focused on expanding the production of goods for mass consumption, on raising the standard of life of the working people by consistent and systematic reduction of the costs of all goods, and on wide-scale construction of all kinds of scientific research institutes to enable science to develop its forces. I have no doubt that if we render the necessary assistance to our scientists they will be able not only to overtake but also in the very near future to surpass the achievements of science outside the boundaries of our country. [Stalin then announced goals for production of key materials.] Only under such conditions will our country be insured against any eventuality.

SOURCE: Excerpts from Joseph Stalin, *Vital Speeches of the Day*, February 9 (1946). Reprinted with permission.

DOCUMENT 2
Winston Churchill Delivers His "Iron Curtain" Speech at Westminster College, in Fulton, Missouri, March 5, 1946

Winston Churchill, former prime minister of Britain, stated that he spoke for himself alone, but President Harry Truman's presence on the platform at Westminster College suggested his approval of Churchill's assessment of Soviet actions. After reading Churchill's words, Stalin justified Soviet action in Eastern Europe as the means to "ensure its security," drew parallels between Hitler and Churchill, and called Churchill's words "a call to war with the Soviet Union."

The United States stands at this time at the pinnacle of world power. It is a solemn moment for the American democracy. With primacy in power is also joined an awe-inspiring accountability to the future. [Churchill then spoke of the need to support the United Nations.]

It would nevertheless be wrong and imprudent to intrust the secret knowledge or experience of the atomic bomb, which the United States, Great Britain and Canada now share, to the world organization [the United Nations], while it is still in its infancy. It would be criminal madness to cast it adrift in this still agitated and ununited world. No one in any country has slept less well . . . because this knowledge and the method and the raw materials to apply it are at present largely retained in American hands. I do not believe we should all have slept so soundly had the positions been reversed and some Communist or neo-Fascist state monopolized, for the time being, these dread agencies. The fear of them alone might easily have been used to enforce totalitarian systems upon the free democratic world. . . . God has willed that this shall not be, and we have at least a breathing space before this period has to be encountered, and even then, if no effort is spared, we should still possess so formidable superiority as to impose effective deterrents upon its employment or threat of employment by others. . . .

A shadow has fallen upon the scenes so lately lighted by the Allied victory. Nobody knows what Soviet Russia and its Communist international organization intends to do in the immediate future, or what are the limits, if any, to their expansive and proselytizing tendencies. I have a strong admiration and regard for the valiant Russian people and for my war-time comrade, Marshal Stalin. . . . We understand the Russians need to be secure on her western frontiers from all renewal of German aggression. . . . It is my duty, however, to place before you certain facts. . . .

From Stettin in the Baltic to Trieste in the Adriatic, an iron curtain has descended across the Continent. Behind that line lie all the capitals of the ancient states of central and eastern Europe. Warsaw, Berlin, Prague, Vienna, Budapest, Belgrade, Bucharest and Sofia, all these famous cities and the populations around them lie in the Soviet sphere and all are subject in one form or another, not only to Soviet influence but to a very high and increasing measure of control from Moscow. . . . The Communist parties, which were very small in all these eastern states of Europe, have been raised to pre-eminence and power far beyond their numbers and are seeking everywhere to obtain totalitarian control. Police governments are prevailing in nearly every case, and so far, except in Czechoslovakia, there is no true democracy. . . .

In front of the iron curtain which lies across Europe are other causes for anxiety. . . . In a great number of countries, far from the Russian frontiers and throughout the world, Communist fifth columns are established and work in complete unity and absolute obedience to the directions they receive from the Communist center.

I do not believe that Soviet Russia desires war. What they desire is the fruits of war and the indefinite expansion of their power and doctrines. . . . Our difficulties and dangers will not be removed by closing our eyes to them. They will not be removed by mere waiting to see what happens; nor will they be relieved by a policy of appeasement. . . .

From what I have seen of our Russian friends and allies during the war, I am convinced that there is nothing they admire so much as strength, and there is nothing for which they have less respect than for military weakness.

SOURCE: Excerpts from Winston Churchill, *Vital Speeches of the Day*, March 5 (1946). Reprinted with permission.

DOCUMENT 3
Henry A. Wallace Addresses an Election Rally at Madison Square Garden, New York, September 12, 1946

Throughout 1946, Henry A. Wallace, Franklin D. Roosevelt's vice president from 1941 to 1945, and Harry S. Truman's secretary of commerce, urged the president to take a more conciliatory approach toward the Soviet Union, a position reflected in a speech Wallace gave to a rally of leftist and other liberal groups in New York City. Compared with the more pro-Soviet speeches given that night, Wallace's speech was moderate and drew criticism from the U.S. Communist Party's newspaper. Nevertheless, Wallace's words in the context in which he delivered them seemed to the president to undermine his foreign policy. One week later, Truman asked for Wallace's resignation.

Tonight I want to talk about peace—and how to get peace. Never have the common people of all lands so longed for peace. Yet, never in a time of comparative peace have they feared war so much. . . .

During the past year or so, the significance of peace has been increased immeasurably by the atomic bomb, guided missiles and airplanes which soon will travel as fast as

(continued)

sound. . . . We cannot rest in the assurance that we invented the atom bomb—and therefore that this agent of destruction will work best for us. He who trusts in the atom bomb will sooner or later perish by the atom bomb—or something worse. . . .

To prevent war and insure our survival in a stable world, it is essential that we look abroad through our own American eyes and not through the eyes of either the British Foreign Office or a pro-British or anti-Russian press. . . . We must not let British balance-of-power manipulations determine whether and when the United States gets into war. . . .

To achieve lasting peace, we must study in detail just how the Russian character was formed—by invasions of Tartars, Mongols, Germans, Poles, Swedes, and French; by the czarist rule based on ignorance, fear and force; by the intervention of the British, French and Americans in Russian affairs from 1919 to 1921; by the geography of the huge Russian land mass situated strategically between Europe and Asia; and by the vitality derived from the rich Russian soil and the strenuous Russian climate. Add to all this the tremendous emotional power which Marxism and Leninism gives to the Russian leaders—and then we can realize that we are reckoning with a force which cannot be handled successfully by a "Get tough with Russia" policy. "Getting tough" never bought anything real and lasting—whether for schoolyard bullies or businessmen or world

powers. The tougher we get, the tougher the Russians will get. . . .

We most earnestly want peace with Russia—but we want to be met half way. We want cooperation. And I believe that we can get cooperation once Russia understands that our primary objective is neither saving the British Empire nor purchasing oil in the Near East with the lives of American soldiers. . . .

On our part we should recognize that we have no more business in the political affairs of Eastern Europe than Russia has in the political affairs of Latin America, Western Europe and the United States. . . . The Russians have no more business in stirring up native communists to political activity in Western Europe, Latin America and the United States than we have in interfering in the politics of Eastern Europe and Russia. We know what Russia is up to in Eastern Europe, for example, and Russia knows what we are up to. We cannot permit the door to be closed against our trade in Eastern Europe any more than we can in China. But at the same time we have to recognize that the Balkans are closer to Russia than to us—and that Russia cannot permit either England or the United States to dominate the politics of that area. . . .

Russian ideas of social-economic justice are going to govern nearly a third of the world. Our ideas of free enterprise democracy will govern much of the rest. The two ideas will endeavor to prove which can deliver the most satisfaction to the common

man in their respective areas of political dominance. . . . Under friendly peaceful competition the Russian world and the American world will gradually become more alike. The Russians will be forced to grant more and more of the personal freedoms; and we shall become more and more absorbed with the problems of social-economic justice.

SOURCE: Excerpts from Henry A. Wallace, *Vital Speeches of the Day*, September 12 (1946). Reprinted with permission.

QUESTIONS FOR ANALYSIS AND DEBATE

1. What lessons do these three leaders draw from World War II? What do they see as the most critical steps to preventing another war?

2. How do these three men describe the political and economic system of the Soviet Union? What differences do they see between the systems of the Soviet Union on the one hand and the United States and Western Europe on the other? How do their predictions about these systems differ?

3. What motives do these three men ascribe to Soviet actions? How do Churchill and Wallace differ in their proposals for the Western response to the Soviet Union?

4. Which leader do you think was most optimistic about the prospects for good relationships between Russia and the West? Which was most correct? Why?

"either the breakup or the gradual mellowing of Soviet power." This message reached a larger audience when, as "Mr. X," Kennan published an article in *Foreign Affairs* magazine in July 1947. Kennan later displayed dismay at the use of his ideas to justify what he considered an indiscriminate American response wherever communism seemed likely to succeed. But his analysis marked a critical turning point in the development of the cold war, providing a powerful rationale for using U.S. power throughout the world.

Not all public figures accepted the toughening line. In an election campaign speech in September 1946, Secretary of Commerce Henry A. Wallace, Truman's predecessor as vice president, urged greater understanding of the Soviets' concerns about their nation's security, insisting that "we have no more business in the political affairs of Eastern Europe than Russia has in the political affairs of Latin America." (See "Documenting the American Promise," page 956.) State Department officials were furious. When Wallace refused to be muzzled on foreign policy topics, Truman fired him.

The Truman Doctrine and the Marshall Plan

In 1947, the United States moved from tough words to action, implementing the doctrine of containment that would guide foreign policy for the next four decades. It was not an easy transition; despite public approval of a verbal hard line, Americans wanted to keep their soldiers and tax dollars at home. In addition to selling containment to the public, Truman had to gain the support of a Republican-controlled Congress, which included a forceful bloc, led by Ohio senator Robert A. Taft, opposed to a strong U.S. presence in Europe.

Crises in two Mediterranean countries triggered the implementation of containment. In February 1947, Britain informed the United States that its crippled economy could no longer sustain military assistance to Greece and Turkey. Turkey was trying to resist Soviet pressures, and Greece's government faced a challenge from internal leftists. Truman promptly sought congressional authority to send military and economic missions, along with $400 million in aid, to the two countries. At a meeting with congressional leaders, Undersecretary of State Acheson predicted that if Greece and Turkey fell, communism would soon consume three-fourths of the planet. After a stunned silence, Michigan senator Arthur Vandenberg, the Republican foreign policy leader and a recent convert from isolationism, warned that to get approval Truman would have to "scare hell out of the country."

Truman did just that. Outlining what would later be called the **domino theory**, he warned that if Greece fell to the rebels, "confusion and disorder might well spread throughout the entire Middle East . . . and would have a profound effect upon . . . Europe." Failure to step in, he said, "may endanger the peace of the world—and shall surely endanger the welfare of the nation." According to what came to be called the Truman Doctrine, the United

The Marshall Plan in Greece
Greece was one of sixteen European nations that participated in the European Recovery Program. In this photograph taken in December 1949, a parade through Athens marks the one-millionth ton of supplies sent to Greece as part of Marshall Plan aid. This truck carries wheat flour. Why would such a parade be staged? What effect might it have on the Greek people?
Library of Congress.

States must not just resist Soviet military power but must "support free peoples who are resisting attempted subjugation by armed minorities or by outside pressures." Congressional authorization of aid for Greece and Turkey did not entail formal acceptance of the Truman Doctrine. Yet the assumption that American security depended on rescuing any anti-Communist government from internal rebels or outside pressure became the cornerstone of U.S. foreign policy from 1947 until the end of the 1980s.

A much larger assistance program for Europe followed aid to Greece and Turkey. In May 1947, Dean Acheson described a war-ravaged Western Europe, with "factories destroyed, fields impoverished, transportation systems wrecked, populations scattered and on the borderline of starvation." American citizens were sending generous amounts of private aid, amounting to some $2 billion in the first six years

> In 1947, the United States moved from tough words to action, implementing the doctrine of containment that would guide foreign policy for the next four decades.

after the war, but Europe needed large-scale assistance. It was "a matter of national self-interest," Acheson argued, for the United States to provide aid. Only economic recovery could halt the growth of **socialist** and Communist parties in France and Italy and confine Soviet influence to Eastern Europe.

In March 1948, Congress approved the European Recovery Program—more commonly known as the Marshall Plan, after retired general George C. Marshall, then serving as secretary of state—and over the next five years the United States spent $13 billion to restore the economies of Western Europe. Marshall invited all European nations and the Soviet Union to cooperate in a request for aid, but as administration officials expected, the Soviets refused to meet the American terms of free trade and financial disclosure and ordered their East European satellites likewise to reject the offer. Sixteen nations became beneficiaries of Marshall Plan aid, which marked the first step toward the European Union. The assistance program was also good business for the United States, because the European nations spent most of the dollars to buy American products carried on American ships, and Europe's economic recovery expanded the realm of raw materials, markets, and investment opportunities available to American capitalists.

While Congress debated the Marshall Plan, in February 1948 the Soviets staged a brutal coup against the government of Czechoslovakia and installed a Communist regime. Next, Soviet leaders threatened Western access to Berlin. The former capital of Germany lay within Soviet-controlled East Germany, but all four Allies jointly occupied Berlin, dividing it into separate administrative units. As the Western Allies moved to organize West Germany as a separate nation, the Soviets retaliated by blocking roads and rail lines that connected West Germany to the Western-held sections of Berlin, cutting off food, fuel, and other essentials to two million inhabitants.

"We stay in Berlin, period," Truman insisted. Yet he wanted to avoid a confrontation with Soviet troops. So for nearly a year U.S. and British pilots airlifted 2.3 million tons of goods to sustain the West Berliners. Stalin hesitated to shoot down these cargo planes, and in 1949 he lifted the blockade. The city was then divided into East

Berlin Divided, 1948

The Berlin Airlift

These Germans living in West Berlin are greeting a U.S. plane carrying food, fuel, and other necessities to Berlin during the Soviet blockade that began in June 1948. Truman and his advisers were "prepared to use any means that may be necessary to stay in Berlin," and the president confided to his diary that "we are very close to war." To reduce that risk, Truman chose to supply the city with an airlift rather than sending ground convoys to shoot their way through Soviet lines. Apparently impressed with American resolve and resources, Stalin backed down and lifted the blockade in May 1949. The vulnerability of Germans like these helped to ease hostile feelings that other Europeans felt toward their former enemy.
© Bettmann/Corbis.

Berlin, under Soviet control, and West Berlin, which became part of West Germany. For many Americans, the Berlin airlift confirmed the wisdom of containment: When challenged, the Russians backed down, as Kennan had predicted.

Building a National Security State

The new policy of containment quickly acquired a military capacity to back it up. During the Truman years, the United States fashioned a five-pronged defense strategy: (1) development of atomic weapons, (2) strengthening traditional military power, (3) military alliances with other nations, (4) military and economic aid to friendly nations, and (5) an espionage network and secret means to subvert Communist expansion.

In September 1949, the United States lost its nuclear monopoly when officials confirmed that the Soviets had detonated an atomic bomb. Within months, Truman approved development of an even deadlier weapon, a hydrogen bomb based on a thermonuclear explosion equivalent to five hundred atomic bombs. By 1954, the United States had the capacity to deliver the "super bomb," but its advantage was brief. In November 1955, the Soviets exploded their own hydrogen bomb.

From the 1950s through the 1980s, **deterrence** formed the basis of American nuclear strategy. To deter the Soviet Union from attacking, the United States strove to maintain a more powerful nuclear force than the Soviets. Because the Russians pursued a similar policy, the superpowers became locked in an ever-escalating race for nuclear dominance. Albert Einstein, whose mathematical discoveries had laid the foundations for nuclear weapons, commented grimly on the enormous destructive force now possessed by the superpowers. The war that came after World War III, he said, would be fought with stones.

The United States also beefed up its conventional military power to deter Soviet threats that might not warrant nuclear retaliation. To streamline defense planning, Congress passed the National Security Act in 1947, uniting the military branches under a single secretary of defense and creating the National Security Council (NSC) to advise the president. As the Berlin crisis simmered in 1948, Congress stepped up military appropriations and enacted a peacetime **draft**. Congress also granted permanent status to the women's military branches, though it limited them to low numbers and rank and banned them from combat. With about 1.5 million men and women in uniform in 1950, the military strength of the United States had quadrupled since the 1930s, and defense expenditures claimed one-third of the federal budget.

Collective security, the third prong of postwar military strategy and the sharpest break from America's past, also developed during the Berlin showdown. In June 1948, the Senate approved the general principle of regional military alliances. One year later, the United States joined Canada and Western European nations in its first peacetime military alliance, the North Atlantic Treaty Organization (NATO), designed to counter a Soviet threat to Western Europe (see Map 26.1). For the first time in its history, the United States pledged to go to war if one of its allies were attacked.

The fourth element of defense strategy involved foreign assistance programs to strengthen friendly countries, such as aid to Greece and Turkey in 1947 and the Marshall Plan. In addition, in 1949 Congress approved $1 billion of military aid to its NATO allies and began economic assistance to nations in other parts of the world.

The fifth element of the national security state was development of the government's espionage capacities and the means to deter communism through covert activities. The National Security Act of 1947 created the Central Intelligence Agency (CIA) to gather information and to perform any "functions and duties related to intelligence affecting the national security" that the NSC might authorize. Eventually,

---

Cold War Spying

"Intelligence," the gathering of information to determine the capabilities and intentions of the enemy, was as old as human warfare, but it took on new importance with the onset of the cold war. Created by the National Security Act of 1947, the Central Intelligence Agency (CIA) became one of the most important tools for obtaining Soviet secrets, deceiving the enemy about U.S. plans, countering subversive activities on the part of Communists, and assisting local forces against leaders that the United States wanted to oust. While much of the CIA's intelligence function took place in Washington, where analysts combed through Communist newspapers, official reports, and leaders' speeches, agents behind the iron curtain performed the most dramatic work, gathering information with a variety of bugs and devices, such as this camera hidden inside a pack of cigarettes. Spying soon gained a prominent place in popular culture, most notably in more than a dozen movies featuring James Bond, British agent 007, created by former British naval intelligence agent Ian Fleming in 1952 and first appearing on screen in *Dr. No* in 1962.
Jack Naylor Collection.

CIA agents conducted secret operations that toppled legitimate foreign governments and violated the rights of U.S. citizens. In many respects, the CIA was virtually unaccountable to Congress or the public.

By 1950, the United States had abandoned age-old tenets of foreign policy. Isolationism and neutrality had given way to a peacetime military alliance and economic and military efforts to control events far beyond U.S. borders. Short of war, the United States could not stop the descent of the iron curtain, but it aggressively and successfully promoted economic recovery and a military shield for the rest of Europe.

Superpower Rivalry around the Globe

Efforts to implement containment moved beyond Europe. In Africa, Asia, and the Middle East, World War II furthered a tide of national liberation movements against war-weakened **imperial** powers. Between 1945 and 1960, forty countries, with more than a quarter of the world's people, won their independence. These nations came to be referred to collectively, along with Latin America, as the **third world**, a term denoting countries outside the Western (first world) and Soviet (second world) orbits that had not yet developed industrial economies. Like Woodrow Wilson during World War I, Roosevelt and Truman promoted the ideal of self-determination: The United States granted independence to its own dominion, the Philippines, in 1946; applauded the British withdrawal from India; and encouraged France to relinquish its empire in Indochina. At the same time, both the United States and the Soviet Union cultivated governments in emerging nations that were friendly to their own interests.

Leaders of many liberation movements, impressed with the rapid economic growth of Russia, adopted socialist or Communist ideas, although few had formal ties with the Soviet Union. But American leaders insisted on viewing these movements as a threatening extension of Soviet power. Seeking to hold communism at bay by fostering economic development and political stability, in 1949 the Truman administration initiated the Point IV Program, providing technical aid to developing nations. Reflecting the Truman administration's cold war priorities, the modest amounts of such aid contrasted sharply with the huge sums provided to Europe.

In Asia, civil war raged in China, where the Communists, led by Mao Zedong (Mao Tsetung), fought the official Nationalist government under Chiang Kai-shek. While the Communists gained support among the peasants for their land reforms and valiant stand against the Japanese, Chiang's corrupt and incompetent government alienated much of the population. The so-called China bloc, a lobby that included Republican members of Congress and religious groups with missionary ties to China, pressured the Truman administration to save that nation from the Communists. Failing in its effort to promote negotiations between Chiang and Mao, the United States provided almost $3 billion in aid to the Nationalists during the civil war. Yet Truman and his advisers believed that to divert further resources from Europe to China would be futile, given the ineptness of Chiang's government.

In October 1949, Mao established the People's Republic of China (PRC), and the Nationalists fled to the island of Taiwan. The United States refused to recognize the existence of the PRC, blocked its admission to the United Nations, and sent aid to the Nationalist government in Taiwan. Nothing less than a massive U.S. military commitment could have stopped the Chinese Communists, but some Republicans cried that Truman and "the pro-Communists in the State Department" had "lost"

The Chinese Communist Movement

The leaders of the young Communist movement in China in 1937 exude confidence as they stand in a doorway to one of the cave dwellings where they lived and worked in Yan'an, in northwest China. Bo Gu (right) died in a plane crash in 1946. Zhou Enlai (left) and Mao Zedong (center) led the revolutionary forces to victory and the establishment of the People's Republic of China in 1949.

Peabody Museum, Harvard University.

China. Thus, China became a political albatross for the Democrats, who resolved never again to be vulnerable to charges of being soft on communism.

As it became clear that China would not be a stable capitalist ally in Asia, the administration reconsidered its plans for postwar Japan. Initially, the U.S. military occupation had aimed to reform the Japanese government, purge militarists from official positions, and decentralize the economy. But by 1948, U.S. policy had shifted to concentrate on economic recovery. The new goals were to help Japan rapidly reindustrialize and secure access to food, markets, and natural resources in Asia, and in a short time the Japanese economy was flourishing. American soldiers remained on military bases in Japan, but the official occupation ended when the two nations signed a peace treaty and a mutual security pact in September 1951. Like West Germany, Japan now sat squarely within the American orbit, ready to serve as an economic hub in a vital area.

The one area where cold war considerations did not control American policy was Palestine. In 1943, then-Senator Harry Truman spoke passionately about Nazi Germany's systematic extermination of Jews, asserting, "This is not a Jewish problem, it is an American problem—and we

CYPRUS
SYRIA
Mediterranean Sea
LEBANON
ISRAEL
Jerusalem
Dead Sea
JORDAN
EGYPT
SAUDI ARABIA

Jewish state
Palestinian territories

Israel, 1948

must . . . face it squarely and honorably." As president, he had the opportunity to make good on his words. Jews had been migrating to Palestine, their biblical homeland, since the nineteenth century, resulting in tension and hostilities between Palestinian Arabs and Jews. After World War II, as hundreds of thousands of European Jews sought refuge and creation of a national homeland in Palestine, fighting devolved into brutal terrorism on both sides.

Truman's foreign policy experts saw American-Arab friendship as a critical barrier against Soviet influence in the Middle East and as a means to secure access to Arabian oil. Uncharacteristically defying his advisers, the president responded instead to pressure from Jewish organizations, his moral commitment to Holocaust survivors, and his interest in the American Jewish vote for the 1948 elections. When Jews in Palestine declared the state of Israel in May 1948, Truman quickly recognized the new country and made its defense the cornerstone of U.S. policy in the Middle East.

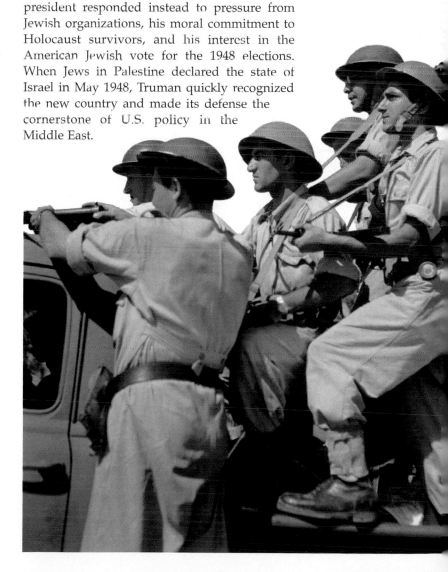

Haganah Troops Mobilize in Palestine

The Haganah originated in the 1910s as a paramilitary group to defend Jewish settlers in Palestine as they struggled with Arabs hostile to the growing presence of Zionists committed to building a Jewish state there. Because Palestine was governed by the British under a League of Nations mandate, Haganah was an illegal, underground organization, yet it gathered substantial numbers and weapons by the end of World War II. After Israel declared itself a nation in 1948, Haganah became the core of the Israel Defense Forces, Israel's main military organization. In this photo, Haganah troops are mobilizing in July 1948 to defend the new state from the armies of the surrounding nations of Syria, Jordan, Egypt, Lebanon, and Iraq. The Israelis won the war, but the consolidation of the state of Israel created 700,000 Arab refugees and an issue that would fuel turmoil in the area for decades to come.
© Bettmann/Corbis.

Truman and the Fair Deal at Home

Referring to the Civil War general who coined the phrase "War is hell," Truman said in December 1945, "Sherman was wrong. I'm telling you I find peace is hell." Challenged by crises abroad, Truman also faced shortages, strikes, inflation, and other problems attending the reconversion of the economy to peacetime production. At the same time, he tried to expand New Deal reform, with his own "Fair Deal" agenda, which proposed initiatives in civil rights, housing, education, and health care. In sharp contrast to his success with Congress in foreign policy, however, Truman achieved but a modest slice of his domestic agenda.

Reconversion and the Postwar Economic Boom

Despite deprivations during World War II, most Americans had enjoyed a higher standard of living than ever before. Economic experts as well as ordinary citizens worried about both sustaining that standard and providing jobs for millions of returning soldiers. Truman wasted no time

unveiling his plan, asking Congress to enact a twenty-one-point program of social and economic reforms. "Not even President Roosevelt ever asked for as much at one sitting," exploded Republican leader Joseph W. Martin Jr.

Congress approved only one of Truman's key proposals—full-employment legislation—and even that was watered down. The Employment Act of 1946 invested the federal government with responsibility "to promote maximum employment, production, and purchasing power," thereby formalizing what had been implicit in Roosevelt's actions to counter the depression—government's responsibility for maintaining a healthy economy. The law created a Council of Economic Advisors to assist the president, but it authorized no new powers to translate the government's obligation into effective action.

Inflation, not unemployment, turned out to be the most severe problem in the early postwar years. Unable to buy civilian goods during the war, in 1945 consumers had $30 billion of savings that they now itched to spend. But shortages of meat, automobiles, housing, and a host of other items persisted. Six million people wanted new cars in 1946, twice as many as the industry managed to produce. Housing was so scarce that returning veterans lived in basements and garages. Until industry could convert fully to civilian production and make more goods available, consumer demand would continue to drive up prices.

Labor relations were another thorn in Truman's side. Organized labor survived the war stronger than ever, its 14.5 million members making up 35 percent of the civilian workforce. "The workers felt they were in a good bargaining position," recalled Henry Fiering, an organizer for the United Electrical Workers, "so they went after some more things." Union members feared erosion of wartime gains. With wages frozen during the war, the rising incomes enjoyed by working-class families had come largely from the availability of higher-paying jobs and the chance to work longer hours than before. The end of overtime meant a 30 percent cut in take-home pay for most workers.

Women who had flocked into wartime jobs also saw their earnings decline. Some were ready to return to their homes, but polls indicated that as many as 68 to 85 percent wanted to keep their jobs. Most who remained in the workforce had to settle for relatively low-paying jobs in light industry or the service sector (Figure 26.1). Displaced from her shipyard work, Marie

FIGURE 26.1 Women Workers in Selected Industries, 1940–1950
Women demolished the idea that some jobs were "men's work" during World War II, but they failed to maintain their gains in the manufacturing sector after the war.

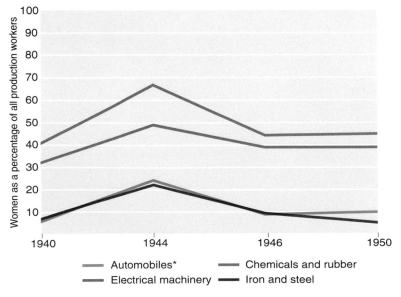

*During World War II, this industry did not produce cars, but rather military transportation such as jeeps, tanks, aircraft, etc.

Schreiber found work as a cashier. "You were back to women's wages, you know . . . practically in half," she recalled. (See "Historical Question," page 966.)

Paying scant attention to the problems of women workers, unions sought to preserve wartime gains with the weapon they had relinquished during the war. More strikes took place in 1946 than at any other time in U.S. history, with five million workers disrupting production in nearly every major industry. Workers saw corporate executives profiting at their expense. Shortly before his union voted to strike, a former marine and the men he carpooled with calculated that a lavish party given by a company executive had cost more than they earned for a whole year's work in the steel mill. "That sort of stuff made us realize, hell we *had* to bite the bullet . . . the bosses sure didn't give a damn for us."

Veterans Go to College

So many World War II veterans wanted to use their GI benefits for higher education that colleges were overwhelmed; many had to turn away students. These veterans, sprinting out of the building where they just registered, express their joy at having been admitted to Indiana University in 1947.

Indiana University.

Although most Americans approved of unions in principle, they became fed up with labor stoppages, blamed unions for rising prices and shortages of consumer goods, and called for more government restrictions on organized labor. Truman shared the public's exasperation and expressed dismay that the wartime unity and sense of sacrifice had given way to greed and selfishness. In a letter to his mother in October 1945, he spread the blame around: "The Congress [is] balking, labor has gone crazy, and management isn't far from insane in selfishness." In May 1946, after coal miners rejected government recommendations for a settlement, Truman placed the mines under federal control. When the massive wave of strikes subsided at the end of 1946, workers had won wage increases of about 20 percent, but the loss of overtime along with rising prices left their purchasing power only slightly higher than in 1942.

"The conversion period was not as traumatic as everybody was afraid it was going to be," Henry Fiering remembered. By 1947, the nation had survived the strains of reconversion and avoided a postwar depression. Wartime profits enabled businesses to invest in new plants and equipment. Consumers used their wartime savings to buy the houses, cars, and appliances that had lain beyond their reach during the depression and war. Both defense spending and the $38 billion in grants and loans that enabled war-stricken countries to purchase American products also stimulated the economy. A soaring birthrate, 25 percent higher in 1949 than in 1940, further sustained consumer demand. The United States entered into a remarkable economic boom that lasted through the 1960s and flooded the American people with new consumer goods. (See chapter 27.)

The nation's gratitude to its returning warriors provided yet another economic boost, resulting in the only large welfare measure passed after the New Deal. The Servicemen's Readjustment Act (the GI Bill), enacted in 1944, offered 16 million veterans job training and education; unemployment compensation while they looked for jobs; and low-interest loans to purchase homes, farms, and small businesses. By 1948, some 1.3 million veterans had bought houses with government loans, and by 1956 veterans had used $14.5

> Paying scant attention to the problems of women workers, unions sought to preserve wartime gains with the weapon they had relinquished during the war. More strikes took place in 1946 than at any other time in U.S. history.

What Happened to Rosie the Riveter?

Although studies have been made of the postwar lives of World War II soldiers, we know much less about another group of veterans—the women who helped fight the war on the domestic front and who were recognized in the popular song "Rosie the Riveter." Statistics show that women's employment fell by more than 2 million between 1945 and 1947. But gross statistics do not reveal which women left the labor force and why, and they obscure the experiences of women who continued to work but in different jobs.

We do know what public officials and business and labor leaders expected of women who had taken up men's work during the war. With the shadow of the depression still hovering, Americans doubted that the economy could accommodate the 6 million new women workers along with millions of returning veterans once wartime production had ceased. A nearly universal response to anxieties about unemployment pushed a big part of the responsibility onto women: Their wartime duty to produce the goods needed for victory was replaced with their postwar obligation to withdraw from the labor force.

The message that they should quit their jobs "for the sake of their homes as well as the labor situation" overwhelmed women. The company newspaper at Kaiser shipyards in the Pacific Northwest proclaimed in May 1945, "The Kitchen—Women's Big Post-War Goal." Putting words into the mouths of Kaiser's female employees, the article asserted, "Brothers, the tin hat and welder's torch will be yours! . . . The thing we want to do is take off these unfeminine garments and button ourselves into something starched and pretty." A General Electric ad predicted that women would welcome a return to "their old housekeeping routine" because GE intended to transform housework with new appliances. Some experts connected married women's employment to their obligations to help their husbands readjust to civilian life. A psychiatrist warned that women's economic independence might "raise problems in the future," urging women to realize that "reunion means relin-

Sisters under the apron—Yesterday's war worker becomes today's housewife.

What's Become of Rosie the Riveter?

Women's Postwar Future
This photograph headed a *New York Times Magazine* article in June 1946. Written by the director of the Women's Division of the Department of Labor, the article discussed the needs of women workers, stressing their right to work and to equal pay, but also assumed that women would all but vanish from heavy manufacturing.
Ellen Kaiper Collection, Oakland.

quishing [independence]—to some extent at any rate."

Other evidence suggests that many women did not have to be told to give up their wartime jobs. Skyrocketing marriage rates and birthrates from that period reveal the attraction of home and family life to people compelled to postpone marriage and childbearing. Thanks to the accumulation of wartime savings, veterans' benefits, and favorable opportunities for men in the postwar economy, many families found it possible to rely on a single earner.

The double burdens placed on married women who took wartime jobs suggest another reason for women's voluntary withdrawal from the workforce. The wartime scarcity of goods had made housekeeping much more difficult, especially for women who typically worked forty-eight hours a week with one day off. Shopping became a problem: Stores often sold out of goods early in the day, and few shops kept evening or Sunday hours. Washing machines, refrigerators, vacuum cleaners, and other labor-saving appliances were not produced at all during the war. Child care centers accommodated only about 10 percent of the children of employed mothers. Employed women with families to care for were simply worn out.

Yet surveys reported that 75 percent of women in wartime jobs wanted—and usually needed—to keep working. As two women employed at a Ford plant in Memphis put it, "Women didn't stop eating when the war stopped." Those who struggled to remain in the workforce experienced the most wrenching changes. The vast majority were able to find jobs; in fact, women's workforce participation began growing again in 1947 and equaled the wartime peak by 1950. But women lost the traditionally male, higher-paying jobs in durable goods industries (such as iron and steel, automobile, and machinery production) and were pushed back into the lower-paying light manufacturing and service industries that had customarily welcomed them. In the words of one historian, "Rosie the Riveter had become a file clerk."

Statistics tell part of the story of this displacement. Women virtually disappeared from shipbuilding, and their share of jobs in the auto industry fell from 25 percent in 1944 to 10 percent in 1950. In the burgeoning Los Angeles aircraft industry, the proportion of women plunged from 40 percent at its wartime height to 12 percent in 1948, rising to just 25 percent in the 1950s. Even in light manufacturing, such as the electrical goods industry, where women had claimed one-third of the prewar jobs, women maintained their numbers but were bumped down to lower-paying work. During the war, women had narrowed the wage gap between men and women, but in 1950, women earned only 53 percent of what men did.

How women reacted to their displacement can be pieced together to some extent from what they were willing to say to reporters and oral history interviewers and what they wrote to government agencies and labor unions. "Women do not expect or want to hold jobs at the expense of returning soldiers," proclaimed a resolution passed by the Women's Trade Union League, expressing its members' overwhelming support for veterans' claims to jobs based on seniority awarded for the years of their wartime service. Tina Hill, a black worker at North American Aircraft in Los Angeles, said, "[Being laid off] didn't bother me much. I was just glad that the war was over . . . [and] my husband had a job." Nonetheless, after doing domestic work, she accepted readily when North American called her back: "Was I a happy soul!"

When management violated women's seniority rights by hiring nonveterans, some women protested bitterly. According to one automobile worker, "We have women laid off with seniority . . . and every day they hire in new men off the street. They hire men, they say, to do the heavy work. . . . During the war they didn't care what kind of work we did." When Ford laid off women with as much as twenty-seven years' seniority, 150 women picketed with signs that read, "The Hand That Rocks the Cradle Can Build Tractors, Too." A worker infuriated by her union's failure to protect women's seniority rights told a reporter, "We are making the bullets now, and we will give the [union executive] board members a blast that will blow them out of their shoes."

Protests from a minority of women workers could not save the jobs that the "Rosies" had held during the war. Despite women's often exemplary performance, most employers still saw women and men as different species fit for different roles and deserving of different rewards. Most labor unions paid lip service to representing all their members, but even the most progressive unions gave low priority to protecting women's seniority rights. In the absence of a feminist movement that could have given both visibility and credibility to their claims for equal treatment, most Rosie the Riveters resigned themselves to "women's work."

million in education benefits. Helping 2.2 million ex-soldiers attend college, the subsidies sparked a boom in higher education. A drugstore clerk before his military service, Don Condren was able to get an engineering degree and to buy his first house. "I think the GI Bill gave the whole country an upward boost economically," he said.

Yet prosperity was not universal. The real gains came during the war, and while wages and salaries increased by 23 percent from 1945 to 1950, prices went up by 36.2 percent. A recession in 1949 threw 7 percent of the labor force out of work, abating only when the Korean War sparked economic recovery. Moreover, despite the return to peacetime production, one-third of all Americans still lived in poverty.

Black and Mexican American Protest and the Politics of Civil Rights

"I spent four years in the army to free a bunch of Frenchmen and Dutchmen," an African American corporal declared, "and I'm hanged if I'm going to let the Alabama version of the Germans kick me around when I get home." Black men and women filled 16 percent of military positions in World War II; they as well as civilians resolved that the return to peace would not be a return to the racial injustices of prewar America. Their political clout had grown with the migration of two million African Americans to northern and western cities, where they could vote and their ballots could make a difference. Even in the South, the proportion of blacks who were allowed to vote inched up from 2 percent to 12 percent in the 1940s. Pursuing civil rights through the courts and Congress, the National Association for the Advancement of Colored People (NAACP) counted half a million members.

> Black men and women filled 16 percent of military positions in World War II; they as well as civilians resolved that the return to peace would not be a return to the racial injustices of prewar America.

In the postwar years, individual African Americans broke through the color barrier, achieving several "firsts." Jackie Robinson integrated major league baseball when he started at first base for the Brooklyn Dodgers in 1947, braving abuse from fans and players to win the Rookie of the Year Award. In 1950, Ralph J. Bunche received the Nobel Peace Prize for his contributions to the United Nations, and Gwendolyn Brooks was awarded the Pulitzer Prize for poetry.

Still, in most respects little had changed, especially in the South, where violence greeted African Americans' attempts to assert their rights. Armed white men turned back Medgar Evers (who would become a key civil rights leader in the 1960s) and four other veterans trying to vote in Mississippi. A mob lynched Isaac Nixon for voting in Georgia, and an all-white jury acquitted the men accused of his murder. In the South, governors, U.S. senators, and other politicians routinely intimidated potential black voters with threats of economic retaliation and violence.

The cold war heightened American leaders' sensitivity to racial issues, as the United States and Soviet Union competed for the allegiance of

Jackie Robinson

John Roosevelt Robinson slides into home plate in a game against the Philadelphia Phillies in 1952. Before becoming the first African American to play modern major league baseball in 1947, Robinson had excelled in track and football as well as baseball at UCLA and had been an army officer in World War II. Even his brilliant play for the Brooklyn Dodgers did not save him from fans' and players' racist taunts or exclusion from restaurants and hotels that catered to his white teammates. Having paved the way for other black players, Robinson competed until 1956.

The Michael Barson Collection/Past Perfect.

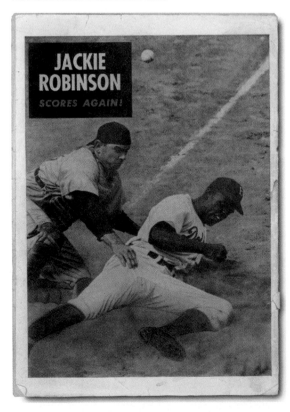

new nations with nonwhite populations emerging in Asia and Africa. How could the United States counter Soviet propaganda about its treatment of blacks when that propaganda reflected reality and African Americans themselves were petitioning the United Nations to pressure the government on their behalf? Even Dean Acheson, far from a champion of racial equality, recognized the costs of discrimination and segregation to national interests abroad, noting that "hostile reaction [to such practices] among normally friendly peoples . . . is growing in alarming proportions," endangering "our moral leadership of the free and democratic nations of the world."

"My very stomach turned over when I learned that Negro soldiers just back from overseas were being dumped out of army trucks in Mississippi and beaten," wrote Truman, shaken by the violence and under pressure to act by civil rights leaders and **liberals**. Wrestling with the Democrats' need for northern black and liberal votes as well as white southern votes, Truman acted more boldly on civil rights than had any previous president. In 1946, he created a Committee on Civil Rights, and in February 1948 he asked Congress to enact the committee's recommendations. The first president to address the NAACP, in June 1947, Truman asserted that all Americans should have equal rights to housing, education, employment, and the ballot.

As with much of his domestic program, the president failed to follow up aggressively on his bold words. In the throes of the 1948 election campaign and pressured by civil rights activists, Truman did issue an executive order to desegregate the armed services, but it lay unimplemented until the Korean War. A large gap loomed between what Truman said about civil rights and what his government accomplished, yet desegregation of the military and the administration's support of civil rights cases in the Supreme Court contributed to far-reaching changes, while his Civil Rights Committee set an agenda for years to come. Breaking sharply with the past, Truman used his office to set a moral agenda for the nation's longest unfulfilled promise.

Although discussion of race and civil rights initiatives were usually linked to African Americans, Mexican Americans endured similar injustices, and they too raised their voices after

Segregation

Signs like this one in Mobile, Alabama, were a normal feature of life in the South from the late nineteenth century until the 1960s. State and local laws mandated segregation in every aspect of life, literally from the cradle to the grave. African Americans could not use white hospitals, cemeteries, schools, libraries, swimming pools, playgrounds, restrooms, or drinking fountains. They were relegated to balconies in movie theaters and kept apart from whites in all public meetings. This scene was captured by the self-trained Gordon Parks, an African American who was one of the most notable photographers of the twentieth century as well as a filmmaker, composer, and author.

© Gordon Parks.

World War II. In 1929, Mexican Americans had formed the League of United Latin-American Citizens (LULAC) to combat discrimination and segregation in the Southwest. Like black soldiers, Mexican American veterans believed, as one of them insisted, "We had earned our credentials as American citizens. We had paid our dues. . . . We were not about to take any crap." Responding to difficulties Mexican Americans encountered in trying to obtain veterans' benefits, in 1948 a group in Corpus Christi, Texas, led by Dr. Héctor Peréz García, a combat surgeon decorated with the Bronze Star, formed the American GI Forum. The organization took off when the wife of Felix Longoria, who had given his life in the Philippines, was refused the use of a funeral chapel in Three Rivers, Texas, "because the whites wouldn't like it" and was told that her husband would be buried in the Mexican section of the cemetery. With the help of Senator Lyndon Johnson, they arranged to lay him to rest in Arlington National Cemetery, and the GI Forum went on to become a key national organization battling discrimination and electing sympathetic officials.

The routine segregation of children in the public schools also energized Mexican Americans.

Truman's Whistle-Stop Campaign

Harry Truman rallies a crowd from his campaign train at a stop in Bridgeport, Pennsylvania, in October 1948. His campaign theme song, "I'm Just Wild about Harry," was borrowed, with the words slightly changed, from the 1921 musical *Shuffle Along*. This was the last presidential election in which the pollsters predicted the wrong winner. They stopped taking polls in mid-October, after which many voters apparently changed their minds. One commentator praised the American citizenry, who "couldn't be ticketed by the polls, knew its own mind and had picked the rather unlikely but courageous figure of Truman to carry on its banner." In what ways have presidential campaigns changed since Harry Truman's time?

Photo: Truman Library; Sheet music: Collection of Janice L. and David J. Frent.

FOR MORE HELP ANALYZING THIS IMAGE, see the visual activity for this chapter in the Online Study Guide at bedfordstmartins.com/roark.

Parents filed a class action suit in Orange County, California, winning a federal circuit court decision in 1947 that outlawed the practice of separating Mexican American and white children in the schools. In 1948, LULAC and the GI Forum cooperated in a suit producing a federal court verdict that prohibited any Texas school district from segregating Mexican American students in separate schools or classes. Such projects, which paralleled the efforts of the NAACP on behalf of African Americans that would culminate in the *Brown* decision in 1954 (see chapter 27), along with challenges to discrimination in employment and other areas and efforts for political representation, demonstrated a growing mobilization of Mexican Americans in the Southwest.

The Fair Deal Flounders

Republicans capitalized on public frustrations with economic reconversion in the 1946 congressional elections, accusing the administration of "confusion, corruption, and communism."

Capturing Congress for the first time in fourteen years, Republicans looked eagerly to the 1948 presidential campaign. Many Republicans campaigned against New Deal "bureaucracy" and "radicalism" in 1946, and the Eightieth Congress weakened some reform programs and enacted tax cuts favoring higher-income groups over Truman's veto.

Organized labor took the most severe attack, when Congress passed the Taft-Hartley Act over Truman's veto in 1947. Called a "slave labor" law and "Tuff-Heartless" by unions, the law reduced the power of organized labor and made it more difficult to organize workers. For example, states could now pass "right-to-work" laws, which banned the practice of requiring all workers to join a union once a majority had voted for it. Many states, especially in the South and West, rushed to enact such laws, encouraging the relocation of industry there. Taft-Hartley also compelled union leaders to swear that they were not Communists and to make public annual financial reports. It maintained the New Deal principle of government protection for **collective bargaining**, but it put the government more squarely between labor and management and between unions and individual workers.

As the 1948 elections approached, Truman faced not only a resurgent Republican Party headed by its nominee Thomas E. Dewey, but also two revolts within his own party. On the left, Henry A. Wallace, whose foreign policy views had cost him his cabinet seat, led a new Progressive Party. On the right, South Carolina governor J. Strom Thurmond headed the States' Rights Party—the Dixiecrats—formed by southern Democrats who had walked out of the 1948 Democratic Party convention when it passed a liberal civil rights plank.

Almost alone in believing he could win, Truman crisscrossed the country by train, answering supporters' cries of "Give 'em hell, Harry." So bleak were Truman's prospects that the confident Dewey ran a low-key campaign and, on election night, the *Chicago Daily Tribune* printed its next day's issue with the headline DEWEY DEFEATS TRUMAN. But Truman took 303 electoral votes to Dewey's 189, as his party regained control of Congress (Map 26.2). His unexpected victory attested to his skills as a campaigner, broad support for his foreign policy, the enduring popularity of New Deal reform, and the booming economy. Yet Thurmond's capture of 39 electoral votes signaled a break in the traditionally solid Democratic South, foreshad-

owing the political realignment that would result in a two-party region in the 1970s.

Truman failed to turn his victory into success for his Fair Deal agenda. Congress made modest improvements in Social Security and raised the minimum wage, but it passed only one significant reform measure. The Housing Act of 1949 authorized 350,000 units of government-constructed housing over the next fifteen years. Although it fell far short of actual need, the legislation represented a landmark commitment by the government to address the housing needs of the poor.

With southern Democrats often joining the Republicans, Congress rejected Truman's civil rights measures and proposals for a federal health care program, federal aid to education, and a new agriculture program to benefit small farmers and consumers. His efforts to revise immigration policy produced the McCarran-Walter Act of 1952, ending the outright ban on immigration and citizenship for Japanese and other Asians. But the law also authorized the government to bar immigration of suspected Communists and homosexuals and maintained the discriminatory quota system established in the 1920s. Truman denounced that provision as "unworthy of our traditions and our ideals . . . and a slur on the patriotism, the capacity, and the decency of a such a large part of our citizenry," but Congress passed the bill over his veto.

MAP 26.2   The Election of 1948

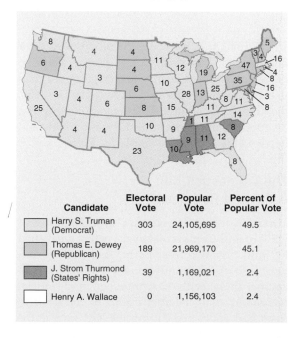

Candidate	Electoral Vote	Popular Vote	Percent of Popular Vote
Harry S. Truman (Democrat)	303	24,105,695	49.5
Thomas E. Dewey (Republican)	189	21,969,170	45.1
J. Strom Thurmond (States' Rights)	39	1,169,021	2.4
Henry A. Wallace	0	1,156,103	2.4

The Red Scare
This map, titled "The Bear Grows and Grows," appeared in the Sunday magazine section of the *New York News* in November 1947. What impact might such an image have on newspaper readers?
The Michael Barson Collection/Past Perfect.

Although he blamed political opponents for defeating his Fair Deal, in fact Truman chose to devote much more energy to foreign policy than to his domestic proposals. Moreover, by late 1950, the Korean War embroiled Truman in controversy, diverted his attention from domestic affairs, and depleted his power as a legislative leader.

The Domestic Chill: A Second Red Scare

Truman's domestic program also suffered from a wave of anti-Communist hysteria that weakened left and liberal forces. Both "Red-baiting" (attempts to discredit individuals or ideas by associating them with Communists) and official retaliation against leftist critics of the government had flourished during the Red scare at the end of World War I. A second Red scare convulsed the nation after World War II, born of partisan political maneuvering, collapse of the Soviet-American alliance, setbacks in U.S. foreign policy, and disclosures of Soviet espionage.

Warnings about subversion and attacks on Communists and other radicals went back to the 1920s, but the cold war greatly intensified them. Republicans jumped on cold war setbacks, such as the Communist triumph in China, to accuse Democrats of fostering internal subversion. Wisconsin senator Joseph R. McCarthy, the leading crusader, avowed that "the Communists within our borders have been more responsible for the success of Communism abroad than Soviet Russia." Revelations of Soviet espionage furnished some credibility to such charges. For example, a number of ex-Communists, including

Whittaker Chambers and Elizabeth Bentley, tes-tified that they and others had provided secret documents to the Soviets. In 1950, a British physicist working on the atomic bomb project confessed that he was a spy and implicated sev-eral Americans, including a couple, Ethel and Julius Rosenberg. The Rosenbergs pleaded inno-cent but were convicted of conspiracy to commit espionage and electrocuted in 1953.

Records opened in the 1990s showed that the Soviet Union did receive secret documents from Americans, such as Alger Hiss and Julius Rosenberg, but at most such information may have marginally hastened Soviet development of nuclear weapons. At the peak of the hysteria, the

Senator Joseph R. McCarthy

Although the Wisconsin senator made his reputation from anticommunism, he seized that issue more from the need to have a platform for his 1950 reelection campaign than from genuine concern grounded in real evidence. McCarthy had loved politics from his high school days in Appleton, Wisconsin, and easily distorted the truth to promote his political ambitions. The 1946 campaign poster in this photograph highlights his World War II career, which he presented as one involving dangerous combat missions as a tail-gunner. In fact, he spent his time as an intelligence officer debriefing combat pilots; his only missions were flights over islands already evacuated by the Japanese.

© Bettmann/Corbis.

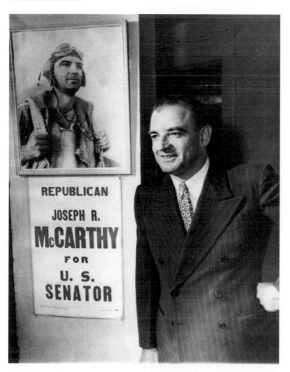

U.S. Communist Party counted only about 20,000 members, some of them undercover FBI agents. The vast majority of individuals prose-cuted in the Red scare were guilty of nothing more than having joined the Communist Party, associated with Communists, or supported radi-cal causes. And most of the charges involved ac-tivities that took place long before the cold war had made the Soviet Union an enemy. Red-hunters cared little for such distinctions, how-ever. For more than ten years following World War II, congressional committees and a host of other official bodies ordered citizens to testify about their past and present political associa-tions. If they refused, anti-Communists charged that silence was tantamount to confession, and these "unfriendly witnesses" lost their jobs and suffered public ostracism.

Senator McCarthy's influence was so great that **McCarthyism** became a term synonymous with the anti-Communist crusade. Attacking in-dividuals recklessly, in 1950 McCarthy claimed to have a list of 205 "known Communists" em-ployed in the State Department. Dean Acheson, "a pompous diplomat in striped pants, with a phony British accent," he charged, said that Jesus Christ "endorsed communism, high trea-son, and betrayal of a sacred trust." Even though most of his charges were absurd—such as the al-legation that retired general George C. Marshall belonged to a Communist conspiracy—the press covered McCarthy avidly.

Not all Republicans joined McCarthy, nor did the party have a monopoly on the politics of anticommunism. Shortly after being stung with charges of com-munism in the 1946 midterm elec-tions, in March 1947, President Truman issued Executive Order 9835 requiring investigation of every federal employee. In effect, Truman's "loyalty program" vio-lated the principles of American justice by allowing anonymous in-formers to make charges and plac-ing the burden of proof on the accused. More than two thousand civil service employees lost their jobs, and another ten thousand resigned while the program continued into the mid-1950s. "A nightmare from which there [was] no awak-ening" was how State Department employee Esther Brunauer described it when she and her husband, a chemist in the navy, both lost their jobs. Years later, Truman admitted that the loy-alty program had been a mistake.

> Senator McCarthy's influence was so great that "McCarthyism" became a term synonymous with the anti-Communist crusade.

The administration also went directly after the Communist Party, prosecuting its leaders under the Smith Act, passed in 1940, which made it a crime to "advocate the overthrow and destruction of the Government of the United States by force and violence." Although civil libertarians argued that the guilty verdicts violated First Amendment rights to freedom of speech, press, and association, the Supreme Court ruled in 1951 (*Dennis v. United States*) that the Communist threat overrode constitutional guarantees.

The domestic cold war spread beyond the nation's capital. State and local governments undertook investigations, demanded loyalty oaths, fired individuals suspected of disloyalty, banned books from public libraries, and more. In addition, a 1950 Senate report claimed that "moral turpitude" and susceptibility to blackmail made homosexuals unfit for government jobs. A 1950s tabloid attempted to shock readers with the news that "more than ninety twisted twerps had been swished out of the State department" and "at least 6,000 homosexuals [were still] on the government payroll." Fired from civil service jobs and drummed out of the military, gay men and women also underwent surveillance and harassment at the hands of the FBI and local police forces. Rutgers, Harvard, Michigan, and other universities dismissed professors, and public school teachers lost their jobs in New York, Philadelphia, Los Angeles, and elsewhere. The House Un-American Activities Committee (HUAC) took on the movie industry in 1947. When ten writers and directors refused to testify, they went to prison and later were blacklisted from Hollywood jobs. Because the Communist Party had helped organize unions and championed racial justice, labor and civil rights activists, too, fell prey to McCarthyism. As African American activist Jack O'Dell remembered, "The segregationists defended segregation by saying they weren't against . . . equal rights for blacks— they were against communism. But their interpretation of Communist was anybody who supported the right of blacks to have civil rights."

McCarthyism caused untold economic and psychological harm to individuals innocent of breaking any law. Thousands of people found themselves humiliated and discredited, hounded from their jobs, even in some cases imprisoned. The anti-Communist crusade violated fundamental constitutional rights of freedom of speech and association, stifled expression of dissenting ideas, and removed unpopular causes from public contemplation.

The Cold War Becomes Hot: Korea

The cold war erupted into a shooting war in June 1950, when troops from Communist North Korea invaded South Korea. For the first time, Americans went into battle to implement containment. Confirming the global reach of the Truman Doctrine, U.S. involvement in Korea also marked the militarization of American foreign policy. The United States, in concert with the United Nations, ultimately held the line in Korea, but at a great cost in lives, dollars, and domestic unity.

Korea and the Military Implementation of Containment

The war grew out of the artificial division of Korea after World War II. Having expelled the Japanese, who had controlled Korea since 1904, the United States and the Soviet Union divided Korea at the thirty-eighth parallel into two occupation zones (Map 26.3). The Soviets supported the Korean Communist Party in the north, while the United States backed the Korean Democratic Party in the south. With Moscow and Washington unable to agree on a unification plan, in July 1948 the United Nations sponsored elections in South Korea. The American-favored candidate, Korean nationalist Syngman Rhee, was elected president, and the United States withdrew most of its troops. In the fall of 1948, the Soviets established the People's Republic of North Korea under Kim Il-sung and also withdrew. U.S. Defense and State Department officials did not consider Korea to be of vital strategic interest, and many doubted that Rhee's repressive government could sustain popular support. But because Rhee was staunchly anti-Communist, Truman authorized a small amount of economic and military aid to South Korea.

Skirmishes between North and South Korean troops had occurred since 1948, with both sides crossing the thirty-eighth parallel. In June 1950, however, 90,000 North Koreans swept into South Korea. Truman's advisers immediately assumed that the Soviet Union, China, or both had instigated the attack. Revelations decades later indicated that both the Russians and the Chinese had acquiesced, but with little enthusiasm, in North Korean plans. Kim wanted to bolster his position by championing Korean

MAP 26.3 The Korean War, 1950–1953
After each side had plunged deep into its enemy's territory, the Korean War ended in 1953 with the dividing line between North and South Korea being nearly the same as it had been before the war.

READING THE MAP: How far south did the North Korean forces progress at the height of their invasion? How far north did the UN forces get? What countries border Korea?

CONNECTIONS: What dangers did the forays of MacArthur's forces to within forty miles of the Korean-Chinese border pose? Why did Truman forbid MacArthur to approach that border? What political considerations on the home front influenced Truman's policy and military strategy regarding Korea?

FOR MORE HELP ANALYZING THIS MAP, see the map activity for this chapter in the Online Study Guide at bedfordstmartins.com/roark.

unification, and the substantial opposition to the Rhee government, including a guerrilla insurgency, suggested that many South Koreans would support the North Korean army.

On June 30, six days after learning of the attack, Truman decided to commit ground troops, believing that Korea was "the Greece of the

Far East" and that the United States must "put up a fight [against communism] right now." Moreover, a non-Communist South Korea was a key element in U.S. plans to revive Japan economically and to make that nation the core of its defense strategy in Asia. Because the Soviet Union was boycotting the UN Security Council for its refusal to seat a delegate from the People's Republic of China, the U.S. representative was able to obtain UN sponsorship of a collective effort to repel the attack. Authorized to appoint a commander for the UN force, Truman named General Douglas MacArthur, hero of the American World War II victory in the Pacific and head of the postwar occupation of Japan.

> Truman decided to commit ground troops, believing that Korea was "the Greece of the Far East."

Sixteen nations, including many NATO allies, sent troops to Korea, but the United States furnished most of the personnel and weapons, deploying almost 1.8 million troops and essentially dictating military strategy. By failing to ask Congress for a declaration of war, Truman violated at least the spirit if not the letter of the Constitution. Moreover, although Congress authorized the mobilization of troops and appropriated funds to fight the war, the president's political opponents called it "Truman's war" when the military situation worsened.

The first American soldiers rushed to Korea unprepared and ill equipped. The North Koreans took the capital of Seoul and drove deep into the south between June and September, forcing UN troops to retreat south to Pusan. Then, in September, General MacArthur launched a bold counteroffensive at Inchon, 180 miles behind North Korean lines. By mid-October, UN forces had pushed the North Koreans back to the thirty-eighth parallel. Now came the momentous decision of whether to invade North Korea and seek to unify Korea under UN supervision.

From Containment to Rollback to Containment

"Troops could not be expected . . . to march up to a surveyor's line and stop," remarked Dean Acheson, now secretary of state, reflecting sentiment among the public and most government officials to transform the military objective from containment to elimination of the enemy and unification of Korea. Pennsylvania congressman Hugh D. Scott and other Republicans in fact insisted that stopping at the thirty-eighth parallel would be "to subvert our military victory." Thus, for the only time during the cold war, the United States tried to roll back communism. With UN approval, on September 27, 1950, Truman ordered MacArthur to move beyond the thirty-eighth parallel if necessary to destroy North Korean forces. Concerned about possible intervention by China and the Soviet Union, Truman directed the general to keep UN troops away from the Korean-Chinese border. Yet MacArthur sent UN forces to within forty miles of China, whereupon more than 150,000 Chinese troops crossed the Yalu River into Korea. With Chinese help, by December 1950, the North Koreans had recaptured Seoul.

Then, under the leadership of General Matthew B. Ridgway, the Eighth Army turned the tide again. After three months of grueling battle, UN forces worked their way back to the thirty-

eighth parallel. At that point, Truman decided to seek a negotiated settlement. When the goal of the war reverted to containment, MacArthur was furious. To him, a holding action against communism represented defeat. Truman and his advisers, however, adamantly opposed a wider war in Asia. According to General Omar Bradley, chairman of the Joint Chiefs of Staff, MacArthur wanted to wage "the wrong war, at the wrong place, at the wrong time, with the wrong enemy."

MacArthur took his case public, in effect challenging the president's authority to make foreign policy and violating the principle of civilian control over the military. Fed up with MacArthur's insubordination, Truman fired him in April 1951. Many Americans, however, sided with MacArthur and castigated Truman. "Quite an explosion. . . . Letters of abuse by the dozens," Truman recorded in his diary. The general came

---

POWs in Korea
These demoralized U.S. soldiers reflect the grim situation for U.S. forces during the early months of the Korean War. Their North Korean captors forced them to march through Seoul in July 1950, carrying a banner proclaiming the righteousness of the Communist cause and attacking U.S. intervention.
Wide World Photos, Inc.

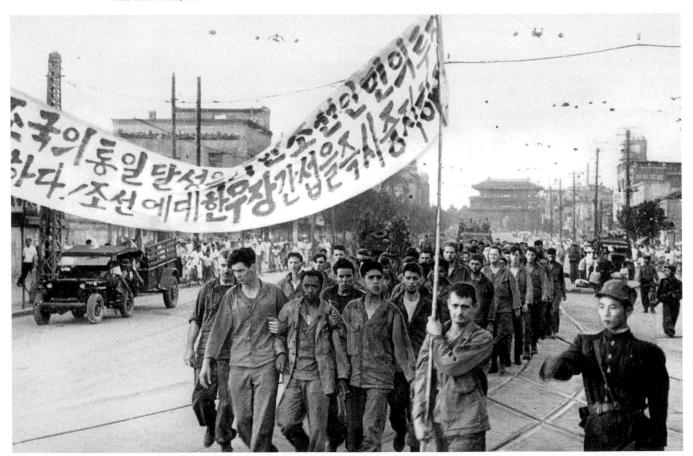

AMERICAN PLACES

The Harry S. Truman Library, Independence, Missouri

Entrance to the Harry S. Truman Library and Museum
Harry S. Truman Library.

W hen he left office in 1953, Truman said that the two things he most wanted were to become a grandfather (which he did) and to have a library established to document the history of his presidency. His was not the first presidential library. Franklin Roosevelt had donated his personal and official papers to the federal government; he also bestowed part of his estate at Hyde Park, New York, for a library and a museum. Truman's friends and associates helped him raise money, and in 1957 the Truman Library was dedicated on a site in Independence, Missouri, down the street from the house where Truman and his wife Bess had lived since their wedding.

From childhood, Truman avidly read history, believing passionately that effective public action depended on knowledge of the past. "There is nothing new in the world

except the history you do not know," he said. His desire for a place to house the raw materials that scholars would used to reconstruct the history of his own life and administration helped to ensure that Roosevelt's initiative would not be a singular phenomenon; every president thereafter has followed suit. The federal government administers the presidential libraries through the National Archives and Records Administration.

In addition to letters, memos, reports, films, correspondence from the public, and other documents that Truman donated, he also encouraged family members, friends, and officials in his administration, such as Dean Acheson, to deposit their own papers. Scholars from all over the world visit the library in Independence to conduct research on the history of the Truman period. Some of the most important

of these documents, including Truman's thoughts on dropping the atomic bomb and his decision to go to war in Korea, are available on the library's Web site.

The Truman Library also houses a museum containing thousands of objects, such as the footlocker Truman used as a soldier in France during World War I; political cartoons; gifts from foreign dignitaries and ordinary Americans; the cabinet chairs Truman and Acheson used; campaign paraphernalia; and gowns worn by the First Lady. A permanent interactive exhibit provides a close-up view of key events and decisions, such as the use of the atomic bomb, the recognition of Israel, the cold war, and the election of 1948. Visitors can walk through a replica of the Oval Office in the museum, and from time to time special exhibits have featured Truman's letters to Bess, NATO at 50, and desegregation of the armed services. Several of these exhibits are available online at the library's Web site, along with pages from Truman's diary and other key documents, photographs, and audio clips of Truman speaking on such topics as the United Nations, NATO, and Korea.

Harry and Bess Truman are buried in the library's courtyard, their gravestones displaying epitaphs that Truman wrote. His own simply provides the dates of his birth and death, notes the birth of their daughter, and lists the public offices that he held, reflecting his characteristic unpretentiousness. Truman's down-to-earth nature and his small-town, Midwest roots come to life in many of the displays and documents throughout the library; at the same time visitors are struck by how this ordinary man led the nation through extraordinary times and made extraordinary decisions.

FOR WEB LINKS RELATED TO THIS SITE AND OTHER AMERICAN PLACES, see "PlaceLinks" at bedfordstmartins.com/roark.

home to a hero's welcome, while baseball fans booed Truman when he appeared at Griffith Stadium on opening day.

The adulation of MacArthur reflected American frustrations with containment. Why should Americans die simply to preserve the status quo rather than destroy the enemy once and for all? Siding with MacArthur enabled Americans to hold on to their belief that the United States was all-powerful and to pin the Korean stalemate on the government's ineptitude or willingness to shelter subversives. Moreover, Truman's earlier success in "scaring the hell" out of the American people over the threat of communism in the Mediterranean came back to haunt him. If communism was so evil, why not stamp it out as MacArthur wanted? When Congress investigated MacArthur's firing, all of the top military leaders supported the president, yet Truman never recovered from the political fallout. Nor was he able to end the war in Korea. Cease-fire negotiations began in July 1951, but peace talks dragged on for two more years, while twelve thousand more U.S. soldiers died.

> Siding with MacArthur enabled Americans to hold on to their belief that the United States was all-powerful and to pin the Korean stalemate on the government's ineptitude or willingness to shelter subversives.

Korea, Communism, and the 1952 Election

Popular discontent with Truman's war gave the Republicans a decided edge in the election battles of 1952. Their presidential candidate, General Dwight D. Eisenhower, enjoyed immense stature for his role in World War II. Reared in modest circumstances in Abilene, Kansas, Eisenhower attended West Point and rose steadily through the army ranks. As supreme commander in Europe, he won widespread acclaim for leading the Allied armies to victory over Germany. After the war, he served as army chief of staff and then as president of Columbia University. In 1950, Truman appointed Eisenhower the first supreme commander of NATO forces.

Both Republicans and Democrats had courted Eisenhower for the presidency in 1948. Although he believed that civilian control over the military worked best when professional soldiers kept out of politics, he found compelling reasons to run in 1952. Eisenhower agreed with the broad scope of Democratic foreign policy, but he deplored the Democrats' efforts to solve domestic problems with costly new federal programs. He equally disliked the foreign policy views of the leading Republican presidential contender, Senator Robert A. Taft, who attacked containment and sought to cut defense spending. Eisenhower decided to run as much to stop Taft and the **conservative** wing of the party as to turn the Democrats out of the White House.

Eisenhower defeated Taft for the nomination, but the old guard prevailed on the party platform. It excoriated containment as "negative, futile, and immoral" and charged the Truman administration with shielding "traitors to the Nation in high places." Eisenhower's choice of thirty-nine-year-old Senator Richard M. Nixon for his running mate helped to appease the Republican right wing and ensured that anticommunism would be a major theme of the campaign.

Richard Milhous Nixon grew up in southern California, raised by a Quaker mother and father who operated a grocery store. After working his way through college and law school, he served in the navy and briefly practiced law. In 1946, he entered politics, helping the Republicans recapture Congress by defeating a liberal incumbent for a seat in the House of Representatives. Nixon quickly made a name for himself as a member of HUAC and a key anti-Communist. In his 1950 bid for the Senate, he ran an effective smear campaign against the liberal congresswoman Helen Gahagan Douglas, charging her with being "pink [Communist] right down to her underwear."

Having decided not to run for another term, Truman persuaded Adlai E. Stevenson, governor of Illinois, to seek the Democratic nomination. A popular governor and acceptable to both liberals and southern Democrats, Stevenson easily won the nomination. He could not escape the domestic fallout from the Korean War, however, nor could he match the popular appeal of Eisenhower, the World War II hero.

The Republican campaign stumbled just once, over the last item of its "Korea, Communism, and Corruption" campaign. A newspaper reported that Nixon had accepted $18,000 from supporters in California. Although such gifts were then common in politics, Democrats leaped to attack Nixon. As newspaper editorials called for Nixon to withdraw from the ticket, most of Eisenhower's advisers urged him to dump his running mate.

Nixon saved himself by exploiting the new medium of television. In an emotional nationwide appeal, he disclosed his finances and documented his modest standard of living.

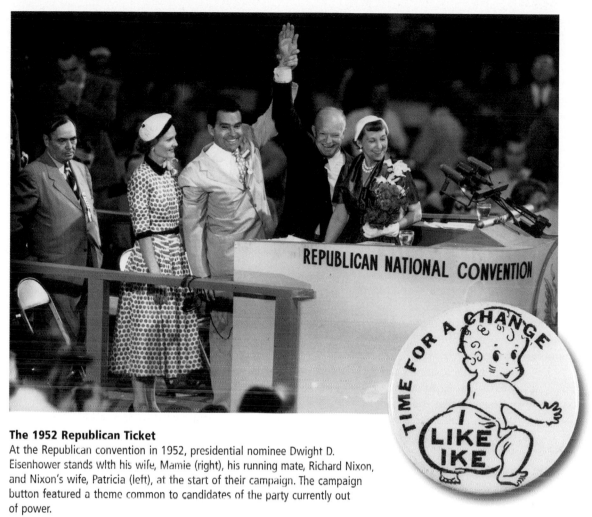

The 1952 Republican Ticket

At the Republican convention in 1952, presidential nominee Dwight D. Eisenhower stands with his wife, Mamie (right), his running mate, Richard Nixon, and Nixon's wife, Patricia (left), at the start of their campaign. The campaign button featured a theme common to candidates of the party currently out of power.

© Bettmann/Corbis; Collection of Janice L. and David J. Frent.

Conceding that the family pet, Checkers, could be considered an illegal gift, he vowed that he would not break his daughters' hearts by returning the cocker spaniel. The overwhelming popular response to the "Checkers speech" turned the tide for Nixon and convinced Eisenhower to keep him on the ticket.

With the issue of corruption neutralized, the Republicans harped on communism at home and failure to achieve victory in Korea. Less than two weeks before the election, Eisenhower announced dramatically, "I shall go to Korea," and voters registered their confidence in his ability to end the war. Cutting sharply into traditional Democratic territory, Eisenhower won several southern states and, overall, 55 percent of the popular vote. His coattails carried a narrow Republican majority to Congress.

An Armistice and the War's Costs

Eisenhower made good on his pledge to end the Korean War. In July 1953, the two sides reached an armistice that left Korea divided just as it had been three years earlier (see Map 26.3). The war took the lives of 36,000 Americans and wounded more than 100,000. Nick Tosques, among thousands of U.S. soldiers who were taken prisoners of war, spent two and a half years in a POW camp. "They interrogated us every day, and also at night," he recalled. "You never knew when they were coming for you. . . . Pretty soon I was telling them anything, just to keep from getting hit. . . . There were times when I did lose hope of ever getting back." South Korea lost more than 1 million people to war-related causes, and more than 1.8 million North Koreans and Chinese were killed or wounded.

The nature of the war and the unpopularity of the Rhee government made it difficult for soldiers to distinguish between friends and enemies, since civilian populations sometimes harbored North Korean agents. Consequently, as one journalist reported, the situation "forced upon our men in the field, acts and attitudes of the utmost savagery . . . the blotting out of villages where the enemy might be hiding, the shooting and shelling of refugees who may be North Koreans."

The Truman administration judged the war a success for its containment policy, since the United States had supported its promise to help nations that were resisting communism. Both Truman and Eisenhower managed to contain what amounted to a world war—involving twenty nations altogether—within a single country. Moreover, despite the presidents' threats to use nuclear bombs, they limited the Korean War to a conflict fought with conventional weapons.

The war had an enormous effect on defense policy and spending. In April 1950, two months before the Korean War began, the National Security Council completed a top-secret report on the nation's military strength. NSC 68, as the document was called, warned that the survival of the nation required a massive military buildup. Truman took no immediate action on its recommendations to triple the defense budget. Nonetheless, the Korean War brought about nearly all of the military buildup called for in NSC 68, vastly increasing U.S. capacity to act as a global power. Using the Korean crisis to expand American might elsewhere, Truman persuaded Congress to approve the rearming of West Germany and the commitment of troops to NATO. Military spending shot up from $14 billion in 1950 to $50 billion in 1953 and remained above $40 billion thereafter. By 1953, defense spending claimed 60 percent of the federal budget, and the size of the armed forces had tripled.

To General Matthew Ridgway, who succeeded MacArthur as commander of the UN forces, Korea taught the lesson that U.S. forces should never again fight a land war in Asia. Eisenhower concurred. Nevertheless, the Korean War induced the Truman administration to expand its role in Asia by increasing aid to the French, who were fighting to hang on to their colonial empire in Indochina. As U.S. marines retreated from a battle against Chinese soldiers in 1950, they sang, prophetically, "We're Harry's police force on call,/So put back your pack on,/ The next step is Saigon,/Cheer up, me lads, bless 'em all."

Conclusion: The Cold War's Costs and Consequences

Dean Acheson titled his memoir about the Truman years *Present at the Creation*, aptly capturing the magnitude of change that marked the aftermath of World War II. More than any development in the postwar world, the cold war defined American politics and society for decades to come. Truman's decision to oppose communism throughout the world marked the most momentous foreign policy initiative in the nation's history. It transformed the federal government, shifting its priorities from domestic to external affairs, greatly expanding its budget, and substantially increasing the power of the president. Military spending helped transform the nation itself, as defense contracts encouraged economic and population booms in the West and Southwest. The nuclear arms race attending the cold war put the people of the world at risk, consumed resources that might have been used to improve living standards, and skewed the economy toward dependence on military projects. While debate about who was responsible for the cold war and whether it could have been avoided persisted, no one could doubt its impact on American society or the world.

In sharp contrast to foreign policy, the domestic policies of the postwar years reflected continuity with the past. Preoccupied with foreign policy, Truman failed to mobilize support for his ambition to assist the disadvantaged with new initiatives in education, health, agriculture, and civil rights, but he successfully defended most New Deal reforms. Although the poor and minorities suffered from the inattention to domestic problems, the boost to industry from cold war spending and the reconstruction of Western Europe and Japan contributed to an economic boom that lifted the standard of living for a majority of Americans.

Many Americans had difficulty accepting the terms of the cold war, not accustomed to paying sustained attention to the rest of the world or to fighting wars without total defeat of the enemy. Consequently, another high cost of the cold war was the anti-Communist hysteria, which silenced the left, stifled debate, and narrowed the range of ideas acceptable for political discussion. Partisan politics and the Truman administration's constant rhetoric about the Communist menace fueled McCarthyism, but the obsession with subversion also fed on popular frustrations over the failure of containment to produce clear-cut victories. Convulsing the nation in bitter disunity, McCarthyism reflected a loss of confidence in American power. It would be a major challenge of the next administration to restore that unity and confidence.

For additional firsthand accounts of this period, see Chapter 26 in Michael Johnson, ed., *Reading the American Past,* Third Edition.

To assess your mastery of the material in this chapter, see the Online Study Guide at bedfordstmartins.com/ roark.

For Web links related to topics in this chapter, see "HistoryLinks," "DocLinks," and "PlaceLinks" at bedfordstmartins.com/roark.

CHRONOLOGY

1945
- Harry S. Truman becomes president of United States upon death of Franklin D. Roosevelt.

1946
- Postwar labor unrest erupts throughout United States.
- Truman creates Committee on Civil Rights.
- United States grants independence to Philippines.
- Congress passes Employment Act, signifying government's responsibility for healthy economy.
- Congressional elections result in Republican control of 80th Congress.

1947
- George F. Kennan's article on policy of containment appears in *Foreign Affairs.*
- National Security Act unifies military services under secretary of defense and creates National Security Council (NSC) and Central Intelligence Agency (CIA).
- Truman asks Congress for aid to Greece and Turkey to counter communism and announces Truman Doctrine.
- Truman establishes by executive order a loyalty and security program designed to eliminate Communists and their sympathizers from the federal government.

1948
- Congress approves Marshall Plan, providing massive aid to stimulate European recovery.
- Congress makes women permanent part of armed services.
- Truman issues executive order to desegregate armed services.
- Mexican American veterans found the American GI Forum to fight discrimination.
- United States recognizes state of Israel.

- Truman defeats Thomas E. Dewey to win full term as president.

1948–1949
- Soviets block access to West Berlin, setting off Berlin crisis and eleven-month Western airlift.

1949
- Communists under Mao Zedong win Chinese civil war and take over mainland China; Nationalists under Chiang Kai-shek retreat to Taiwan.
- North Atlantic Treaty Organization (NATO) forms to counter Soviet threat to Western Europe.
- Truman administration initiates Point IV technical aid program to assist third world nations.
- Soviet Union explodes atomic bomb.

1950
- Senator Joseph McCarthy begins campaign against alleged Communists in United States, ushering in the period of anti-Communist hysteria known as McCarthyism.
- Truman approves development of hydrogen bomb.
- United States sends troops to South Korea to repel North Korean assault.

1951
- Truman relieves General Douglas MacArthur of command in Korea for insubordination.
- United States ends postwar occupation of Japan; the two nations sign peace treaty and mutual security pact.

1952
- Republican Dwight D. Eisenhower elected president.

1953
- Armistice halts Korean War.

BIBLIOGRAPHY

General Works

John Patrick Diggins, *The Proud Decades: America in War and Peace, 1941–1960* (1988).

Alonzo L. Hamby, *Man of the People: A Life of Harry S. Truman* (1995).

Melvyn Leffler, *A Preponderance of Power: National Security, the Truman Administration, and the Cold War* (1992).

David McCullough, *Truman* (1992).

Steve Neal, *Harry and Ike: The Partnership That Remade the Postwar World* (2001).

William L. O'Neill, *American High: The Years of Confidence, 1945–1960* (1986).

James T. Patterson, *Grand Expectations: The United States, 1945–1974* (1996).

William E. Pemberton, *Harry S. Truman: Fair Dealer and Cold Warrior* (1989).

Lisle A. Rose, *The Cold War Comes to Main Street: America in 1950* (1999).

Michael S. Sherry, *In the Shadow of War* (1995).

Stephen Whitfield, *The Culture of the Cold War* (1990).

Domestic Politics and Policies

Kevin Boyle, *The UAW and the Heyday of American Liberalism, 1945–1968* (1995).

John C. Culver and John Hyde, *American Dreamer: The Life and Times of Henry A. Wallace* (2000).

Richard M. Dalfiume, *Desegregation of the U.S. Armed Forces: Fighting on Two Fronts* (1969).

Richard O. Davies, *Housing Reform during the Truman Administration* (1966).

Gary A. Donaldson, *Truman Defeats Dewey* (1998).

John Egerton, *Speak Now against the Day: The Generation before the Civil Rights Movement in the South* (1994).

Kari Frederickson, *The Dixiecrat Revolt and the End of the Solid South, 1932–1968* (2001).

Michael R. Gardner, *Harry Truman and Civil Rights: Moral Courage and Political Risks* (2002).

Susan M. Hartmann, *Truman and the 80th Congress* (1971).

Zachary Karabell, *The Last Campaign: How Harry Truman Won the 1948 Election* (2000).

R. Alton Lee, *Truman and Taft-Hartley* (1966).

Nelson Lichtenstein, *The Most Dangerous Man in Detroit: Walter Reuther and the Fate of American Labor* (1996).

Norman D. Markowitz, *The Rise and Fall of the People's Century: Henry A. Wallace and American Liberalism, 1941–1948* (1973).

Allen J. Matusow, *Farm Policies and Politics in the Truman Years* (1967).

Keith W. Olson, *The G.I. Bill, the Veterans, and the Colleges* (1974).

James Patterson, *Mr. Republican: A Biography of Robert A. Taft* (1974).

William B. Pickett, *Eisenhower Decides to Run: Presidential Politics and Cold War Strategy* (2000).

Monte M. Poen, *Harry S. Truman versus the Medical Lobby: The Genesis of Medicare* (1979).

Jules Tygiel, *Baseball's Great Experiment: Jackie Robinson and His Legacy* (1997).

Robert Zieger, *The CIO, 1935–1955* (1995).

Origins of the Cold War

Gar Alperovitz, *Atomic Diplomacy* (rev. ed., 1994).

Carolyn Eisenberg, *Drawing the Line: The American Decision to Divide Germany, 1944–1949* (1996).

John Fousek, *To Lead the Free World: American Nationalism and the Cultural Roots of the Cold War* (2000).

John L. Gaddis, *The United States and the Origins of the Cold War* (rev. ed., 2000).

James L. Gormly, *The Collapse of the Grand Alliance, 1945–1948* (1987).

Fraser J. Harbut, *The Iron Curtain: Churchill, America, and the Origins of the Cold War* (1986).

Michael Hogan, *A Cross of Iron: Harry S. Truman and the Origins of the National Security State* (1998).

Bruce R. Kuniholm, *The Origins of the Cold War in the Near East* (1980).

Ernest R. May, ed., *American Cold War Strategy: Interpreting NSC 68* (1993).

Wilson D. Miscamble, *George F. Kennan and the Making of Foreign Policy, 1947–1950* (1992).

Arnold A. Offner, *Another Such Victory: President Truman and the Cold War, 1945–1953* (2002).

Chester J. Pach Jr., *Arming the Free World: The Origins of the United States Military Assistance Program, 1945–1950* (1990).

Robert A. Pollard, *Economic Security and the Origins of the Cold War* (1985).

Michael Schaller, *The American Occupation of Japan: The Origins of the Cold War in Asia* (1985).

Randall B. Woods and Howard Jones, *Dawning of the Cold War: The United States' Quest for Order* (1994).

Daniel Yergin, *Shattered Peace: The Origins of the Cold War and the National Security State* (1977).

Foreign Policy

Dean Acheson, *Present at the Creation* (1969).

Carol Anderson, *Eyes Off the Prize: The United Nations and the African American Struggle for Human Rights, 1944–1955* (2003).

William S. Borden, *The Pacific Alliance: United States Foreign Economic Policy and Japanese Trade Recovery, 1947–1955* (1984).

James Chace, *Acheson: The Secretary of State Who Created the American World* (1998).

Gordon H. Chang, *Friends and Enemies: The United States, China, and the Soviet Union, 1948–1972* (1990).

Michael J. Cohen, *Truman and Israel* (1990).

Peter L. Hahn, *The United States, Great Britain, and Egypt: Strategy and Diplomacy in the Early Cold War* (1991).

Gary R. Hess, *The United States' Emergence as a Southeast Asian Power, 1940–1950* (1987).

Walter L. Hixon, *George F. Kennan: Cold War Iconoclast* (1989).

Michael J. Hogan, *The Marshall Plan: America, Britain, and the Reconstruction of Western Europe, 1947–1952* (1987).

Walter Isaacson and Evan Thomas, *The Wise Men: Six Friends and the World They Made: Acheson, Bohlen, Harriman, Kennan, Lovett, McCloy* (1986).

Lawrence S. Kaplan, *The United States and NATO: The Formative Years* (1984).

Stuart W. Leslie, *The Cold War and American Science* (1993).

Thomas J. McCormick, *America's Half-Century: United States Foreign Policy in the Cold War* (1989).

Brenda Gayle Plummer, *Rising Wind: Black Americans and U.S. Foreign Affairs, 1935–1960* (1996).

Richard Rhodes, *Dark Sun: The Making of the Hydrogen Bomb* (1995).

David Rudgers, *Creating the Secret State: The Origins of the Central Intelligence Agency, 1943–1947* (2000).

Michael Schaller, *Altered States: The United States and Japan since the Occupation* (1997).

Nancy B. Tucker, *Patterns in the Dust: Chinese-American Relations and the Recognition Controversy, 1949–1950* (1983).

Evan M. Wilson, *Decision on Palestine: How the U.S. Came to Recognize Israel* (1979).

Lawrence S. Wittner, *American Intervention in Greece, 1943–1949* (1982).

McCarthyism

Michael R. Belknap, *Cold War Political Justice: The Smith Act, the Communist Party, and American Civil Liberties* (1977).

Larry Ceplair and Steven Englund, *The Inquisition in Hollywood: Politics in the Film Community* (1980).

Richard M. Freeland, *The Truman Doctrine and the Origins of McCarthyism: Foreign Policy, Domestic Politics, and International Security, 1946–1948* (1972).

Richard M. Fried, *Nightmare in Red: The McCarthy Era in Perspective* (1990).

John Earl Haynes, *Red Scare or Red Menace: American Communism and Anticommunism in the Cold War Era* (1990).

John Earl Haynes and Harvey Klehr, *Venona: Decoding Soviet Espionage in America* (1999).

Stanley I. Kutler, *The American Inquisition* (1982).

David Oshinsky, *A Conspiracy So Immense: The World of Joe McCarthy* (1983).

Richard Gid Powers, *Not without Honor: The History of American Anticommunism* (1995).

Ronald Radosh and Joyce Milton, *The Rosenberg File: A Search for the Truth* (1983).

Ellen W. Schrecker, *No Ivory Tower: McCarthyism and the Universities* (1986).

Ellen W. Schrecker, *Many Are the Crimes: McCarthyism in America* (1998).

Peter L. Steinberg, *The Great "Red" Menace: United States Persecution of American Communists, 1947–1952* (1984).

Sam Tannenhaus, *Whittaker Chambers* (1997).

Allen Weinstein, *Perjury: The Hiss-Chambers Case* (1978).

Allen Weinstein and Alexander Vassiliev, *The Haunted Wood: Soviet Espionage in America* (1999).

Korea

Jian Chen, *China's Road to the Korean War* (1996).

Bruce Cumings, *The Origins of the Korean War*, 2 vols. (1981, 1990).

Rosemary Foot, *The Wrong War: American Policy and the Dimensions of the Korean Conflict, 1950–1953* (1984).

Burton I. Kaufman, *The Korean War: Challenges in Crisis, Credibility, and Command* (1986).

Paul J. Pierpaoli Jr., *Truman and Korea: The Political Culture of the Early Cold War* (1999).

Stanley Sandler, *The Korean War: No Victors, No Vanquished* (1999).

William Stueck, *The Korean War: An International History* (1995).

William Stueck, *Rethinking the Korean War: A New Diplomatic and Strategic History* (2002).

Richard C. Thornton, *Odd Man Out: Truman, Stalin, Mao and the Origins of the Korean War* (2000).

John Toland, *In Mortal Combat: Korea, 1950–1953* (1992).

Stanley Weintraub, *MacArthur's War: Korea and the Undoing of an American Hero* (2000).

Richard Whelan, *Drawing the Line: The Korean War, 1950–1953* (1990).

1956 CADILLAC CONVERTIBLE
The automobile reflected both corporate and family prosperity in the 1950s. This car was manufactured by General Motors, the biggest and richest corporation in the world and the first to sell a billion dollars' worth of products. Costing about $5,000, the Cadillac was GM's top-of-the-line car, one of the first purchases the McDonald brothers made when they struck it rich with their hamburger stand in California. Even the cheaper models that average Americans could afford featured the gas-guzzling size and space-age style of this Cadillac. A massive interstate highway system begun in 1956 boosted automobile travel, and widespread car ownership went hand in hand with Americans' move to the suburbs.

Ron Kimball Photography.

The Politics and Culture of Abundance

1952–1960

TRAILED BY REPORTERS, U.S. vice president Richard M. Nixon led Soviet premier Nikita Khrushchev through the American National Exhibition in Moscow in July 1959. The display of American consumer goods followed an exhibition of Soviet products in New York, part of a cultural exchange between the two superpowers that reflected a slight thaw in the **cold war**. Both Khrushchev and Nixon seized on the propaganda potential of the moment. As they made their way through the display, their verbal sparring turned into a slugfest of words and gestures that reporters dubbed "the kitchen debate."

Showing off a new color television set, Nixon told Khrushchev that the Soviet Union "may be ahead of us . . . in the thrust of your rockets for . . . outer space," but the United States outstripped the Soviets in consumer goods. "Any steelworker could buy this house," Nixon boasted, as they walked through a six-room ranch-style model. Khrushchev retorted that in the Soviet Union, "you are entitled to housing," whereas in the United States the poor were reduced to sleeping on the pavement.

While the two men inspected appliances in the model kitchen, Nixon declared, "These are designed to make things easier for our women." Khrushchev responded that his country did not have "the capitalist attitude toward women" and appreciated women's contributions to the economy, not their domesticity. The Soviet leader found many of the items on display interesting, he said, but he added that "they are not needed in life. . . . They are merely gadgets." In reply, Nixon insisted, "Isn't it far better to be talking about washing machines than machines of war?" Khrushchev agreed, yet he affirmed the persistence of cold war tensions when he later blustered, "We too are giants. You want to threaten—we will answer threats with threats."

The Eisenhower administration in fact had begun with threats to the Soviet Union. Republican campaigners vowed to roll back **communism** and liberate "enslaved" peoples under Soviet rule. In practice, however, Eisenhower settled for a **containment** policy much like that of his predecessor, Harry S. Truman, though Eisenhower relied more on nuclear weapons and on secret actions by the Central Intelligence Agency (CIA). Yet, as Nixon's visit to Moscow demonstrated, Eisenhower took advantage of political changes in the Soviet Union to reduce tensions in Soviet-American relations.

Continuity with the Truman administration also characterized domestic policy. Although Eisenhower favored the business community with tax cuts and opposed strong federal efforts in health care, education, and race relations, he did not propose to roll back **New Deal** programs. A majority of

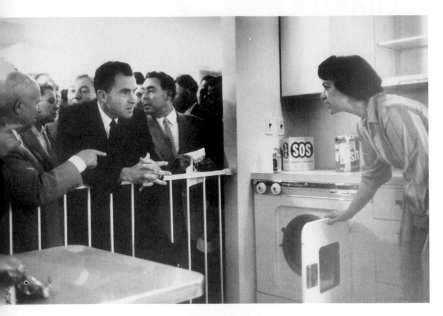

The Kitchen Debate
Soviet premier Nikita Khrushchev (left) and Vice President Richard M. Nixon (center) debate the relative merits of their nations' economies at the American National Exhibition held in Moscow in 1959.

Howard Sochurek/TimePix/Getty.

Americans enjoyed astounding material gains under the immensely popular president and seemed content with his "moderate Republicanism."

Cold war weapons production spurred the economy, whose vitality stimulated suburban development, contributed to the burgeoning populations and enterprise in the West and Southwest, and enabled millions of Americans to buy the products on display in Moscow. As new homes, television sets, and household appliances transformed their patterns of living, Americans took part in a dominant **consumer culture** that also celebrated marriage, family, and traditional gender roles, even as more and more married women took jobs outside their homes.

The cold war and the economic boom helped African Americans mount a strong challenge to tradition in the 1950s. Large numbers of African Americans took direct action against segregation and disfranchisement, developing the institutions, leadership, and strategies to mount a civil rights movement of unprecedented size and power.

> Although Eisenhower deplored McCarthy's methods, he made little effort to silence him.

Eisenhower and the Politics of the "Middle Way"

Moderation was the guiding principle of Eisenhower's domestic agenda and leadership style. Favoring in 1953 a "middle way between untrammeled freedom of the individual and the demands for the welfare of the whole Nation," he pledged that his administration would "avoid government by bureaucracy as carefully as it avoids neglect of the helpless." Claiming that Democrats appealed to divisive class interests, Eisenhower presented himself as a leader above partisan politics and interest groups who would govern by compromise and consensus. Nicknamed "Ike" by his friends and the public, the confident war hero remained popular throughout his presidency.

The President and McCarthy

The new president attempted to distance himself from the anti-Communist fervor that had plagued the Truman administration. Eisenhower shared Senator Joseph McCarthy's goal of eliminating communism from American life, and though he deplored McCarthy's methods, he made little effort to silence him, privately explaining that he would not demean the presidency by getting into "a pissing contest with that skunk." Eisenhower feared that denouncing McCarthy would alienate powerful **conservative** Republicans in Congress, and many Republicans realized the benefits from McCarthy's attacks on Democrats. While one senator called McCarthy an "SOB," he shrewdly observed that "sometimes it's useful to have SOB's around to do the dirty work." Even under a Republican administration, McCarthy continued his allegations of Communists in the government, and thousands of federal employees lost their jobs.

Eisenhower correctly predicted that McCarthy would ultimately destroy himself. With the end of the Korean War, popular frustrations over containment abated, and the anti-Communist hysteria subsided. In 1954, McCarthy tightened his own noose when he went after the army. As he hurled reckless charges of communism against military personnel during weeks of televised hearings, public opinion turned against him. "Have you left no sense of decency?" demanded the army's lawyer. A Senate vote to condemn him in December 1954 marked the end of his influence, but Eisenhower's inaction had allowed the senator to spread his poison longer than he might otherwise have done.

Modern Republicanism

In contrast to the Old Guard conservatives in his party who wanted to repeal much of the New Deal and preferred a unilateral approach to foreign policy, Eisenhower preached "modern Republicanism." This meant resisting additional federal intervention in economic and social life, but it did not mean turning the clock back to the 1920s. Democratic control of Congress after the elections of 1954 further contributed to the moderate approach of the Eisenhower administration (1953–1961), whose record overall maintained the course charted by the New Deal and Fair Deal.

Despite his claim to be above interest-group politics, Eisenhower turned for advice almost exclusively to business leaders and chose wealthy executives and attorneys for his cabinet. When he appointed Martin Durkin, president of the plumbers union, as secretary of labor, a liberal journal quipped that Eisenhower had "picked a cabinet of eight millionaires and one plumber." Eisenhower also sought advice from his "gang," a group of wealthy businessmen with whom he socialized.

Eisenhower sometimes echoed the conservative old-guard Republicans' conviction that government was best left to the states and economic decisions to private business. "If all Americans want is security, they can go to prison," Eisenhower commented about social welfare in 1949. Yet, although **liberals** scorned the president's conservatism by calling him "Eisenhoover," the **welfare state** actually grew during his administration, and the federal government took on new projects. The "middle way" applied the brakes, but it did not reduce federal responsibility for economic development and for assistance to poor Americans.

In 1954, Eisenhower signed laws expanding Social Security and continuing the federal government's modest role in financing public housing. He enlarged the government by obtaining congressional approval for a Department of Health, Education, and Welfare, naming former Women's Army Corps commander and Texas publisher Oveta Culp Hobby to head it, the second female appointed to a cabinet post. And

Polio Vaccine Distribution in the South
In 1954, American children lined up to be inoculated with the new vaccine to prevent polio. But as this scene from Blytheville, Arkansas, shows, children waiting to receive the vaccine stood in strictly segregated lines.
Charles Bell, *Memphis Commercial Appeal.*

when the spread of polio neared epidemic proportions in the 1950s, Eisenhower obtained funds from Congress to distribute a vaccine, even though conservatives preferred that states assume that responsibility.

Eisenhower's greatest domestic initiative was the Interstate Highway and Defense System Act of 1956. Promoted as essential to the nation's cold war defense strategy and an impetus to economic growth, the act authorized construction of a national highway system, with the federal government paying most of the costs through increased fuel and vehicle taxes. Millions of Americans benefited from the greater ease of travel and improved transportation of goods, and the new highways also spurred growth in the fast-food and motel industries as well as the development of shopping malls. The most substantial gains went to the trucking, construction, and automobile industries, which had lobbied hard for the law. The monumental highway project eventually exacted severe costs, unforeseen at the time, in the form of air pollution, energy consumption, declining railroads and other forms of mass transportation, and decay in central cities (Map 27.1).

Eisenhower's "middle way" applied the brakes, but it did not reverse federal responsibility for economic development and for assistance to poor Americans.

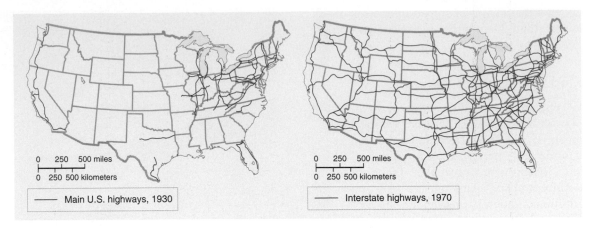

Main U.S. highways, 1930

Interstate highways, 1970

MAP 27.1   The Interstate Highway System, 1930 and 1970
Built with federal funds authorized in the Interstate Highway Act of 1956, superhighways soon crisscrossed the nation. Trucking, construction, gasoline, and travel were among the industries that prospered, but railroads suffered from the subsidized competition.

READING THE MAP: What regions of the United States had main highways in 1930? What regions did not? How had the situation changed by 1970?
CONNECTIONS: What impact did the growth of the interstate highway system have on migration patterns in the United States? What benefits did the new interstate highways bring to Americans and at what costs?

FOR MORE HELP ANALYZING THIS MAP, see the map activity for this chapter in the Online Study Guide at bedfordstmartins.com/roark.

> Most urban Indians remained in or near poverty, and even many who had welcomed relocation eventually determined that they needed to resist "assimilation to the degree that we would . . . lose our culture and our [way] of living."

In other areas, Eisenhower restrained federal activity in favor of state governments and private enterprise. His large tax cuts, for example, directed most benefits to business and the wealthy, and he stubbornly resisted a larger federal role in health care, education, and civil rights. Moreover, whereas Democrats sought to keep nuclear power in government hands, Eisenhower signed legislation authorizing the private manufacture and sale of nuclear power. Workers broke ground at Shippingport, Pennsylvania, for the first commercial nuclear power plant in 1954.

Termination and Relocation of Native Americans

The Eisenhower administration's efforts to restrict federal activity also helped shape a new direction in Indian policy, reversing the emphasis on strengthening tribal governments and pre-

serving Indian culture established in the Indian Reorganization Act of 1934 (see chapter 24). After World War II, when some 25,000 Indians had left their homes for military service and another 40,000 for work in defense industries, policymakers began to push harder for assimilating Native Americans and ending their special relationships with government. To some officials, who reflected the cold war emphasis on conformity and national unity, the communal practices of Indians resembled socialism and stifled individual initiative. Commissioner of Indian Affairs Glenn Emmons expressed the pragmatic view that tribal lands could not produce sufficient income to lift Indians from poverty, but he also revealed the ethnocentrism of policymakers when he insisted that Indians wanted to "work and live like Americans."

By the 1950s, the government had implemented a three-part program of compensation, termination, and relocation. In 1946, Congress established a commission to discharge once and for all any claims by Native Americans for lands taken from them by the government. When it closed in 1978, the Indian Claims Commission had settled 285 cases with compensation

Indian Relocation

As part of its new emphasis on assimilation in the late 1940s and 1950s, the Bureau of Indian Affairs distributed this leaflet to entice Native Americans to move from their reservations to cities. Either with government assistance or on their own, thousands of Indians relocated in the years after World War II. In 1950, just 13.4 percent of Indians lived in urban areas; by 1970, 44 percent did so, and by 1990 the figure had reached 63 percent. Which of the features on this leaflet do you think would be most appealing to Native Americans living on reservations? Which might evoke little interest?

National Archives.

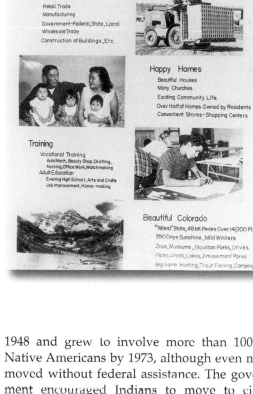

exceeding $800 million. The second policy—termination—began during the Truman administration under Dillon S. Myer, who had managed the internment of Japanese Americans during World War II and who became commissioner of Indian affairs in 1950. Believing that the Bureau of Indian Affairs should "not do anything which others can do as well or better" and "nothing for Indians which Indians can do for themselves," Myer proposed to end the special relationship between Indians and the federal government and to eliminate health and educational services to Indian tribes, initiatives that were carried out under his successor.

Beginning in 1953, Eisenhower signed bills transferring jurisdiction over tribal lands in several states to state and local governments. The loss of federal hospitals, schools, and other special arrangements devastated some tribes. As had happened after passage of the Dawes Act in 1887 (see chapter 18), some corporate interests and individuals took advantage of the opportunity to purchase Indian lands cheaply. According to one Indian leader, some of his people saw termination as "severing of ties already loose and ineffective," but to the great majority it was "like the strike of doom." Decades later the Menominees and the Klamaths secured restoration of their tribal status, and the government abandoned termination in the 1960s.

Relocation, the third piece of Native American policy, began with a pilot program in

Selected Indian Relocations, 1950–1970

1948 and grew to involve more than 100,000 Native Americans by 1973, although even more moved without federal assistance. The government encouraged Indians to move to cities, providing one-way bus tickets and, at their destinations, relocation centers to help with housing, job training, and medical care. To make it difficult to return home, officials sent them to cities far away from their reservations—South Dakota Sioux to California, for example, and Alaskan Natives to Chicago. Yet about one-third of those relocated went back to the reservation, and most of those who stayed faced great difficulties: racism, lack of adequately paying jobs for which they had skills, poor housing in what became Indian ghettos, and above all the loss of their traditional culture. "I wish we had never left home," sighed one woman. "It's dirty and noisy, and people all around, crowded. . . . It seems like I never see the sky or trees." Her sons were headed for reform school, and her husband was out of work and drinking.

Some who overcame these obstacles applauded the program. One man did not mind that his grandchildren did not consider themselves Indians; he contrasted the urban job and educational opportunities with the reservation where "I see no jobs, nothing to do, everyone just drinks." But most urban Indians remained in or near poverty, and even many who had welcomed relocation eventually determined that they needed to resist "assimilation to the degree that we would lose our identity as Indian people, lose our culture and our [way] of living." Within two decades, when a national pan-Indian movement emerged to do just that and demand much more for Indians, that new militancy was very much the product of the urbanization of Native Americans (see chapter 28).

The 1956 Election and the Second Term

While not all people in the United States were living the American dream, with the nation at peace and the economy booming, Eisenhower easily defeated Adlai Stevenson in 1956, losing only seven states. But two years later, the Democrats all but wiped out the Republican Party, gaining a 64–34 majority in the Senate and a 282–135 advantage in the House. Though Ike captured voters' hearts, a majority of voters remained wedded to the programs and policies of the Democrats.

In part because of the Democratic resurgence, Eisenhower faced more serious leadership challenges in his second term. The economy plunged into a recession, and unemployment rose to 7 percent. Eisenhower fought with Congress over the budget and vetoed bills providing for expanded public works projects, a high level of price supports for farmers, and housing and urban development. The president and Congress did reach agreement in two key areas: enacting the first, though largely symbolic, civil rights legislation in a century and establishing a new role for the government in education.

In the end, the first Republican administration after the New Deal left the size and functions of the federal government intact, though it tipped policy somewhat more in favor of corporate interests. Unparalleled prosperity graced the Eisenhower years, and inflation was kept low. The late-1957 recession was one of two in the 1950s, but the economy recovered without putting to a test the president's aversion to substantial federal intervention.

Liberation Rhetoric and the Practice of Containment

At his 1953 inauguration, Eisenhower warned that "forces of good and evil are massed and armed and opposed as rarely before in history." Like Truman, he saw communism as a threat to the nation's security and economic interests. Eisenhower's foreign policy differed from Truman's, though, in three areas: its rhetoric, its means, and—after Stalin's death in 1953—its movement toward accommodation with the Soviet Union.

Republican rhetoric—voiced most prominently by Secretary of State John Foster Dulles—deplored containment as "negative, futile, and immoral" because it accepted the existing Soviet sphere of control. Yet, despite promises to roll back Soviet power, the Eisenhower administration continued the containment policy, actively intervening at the margins of Communist power in Asia, the Middle East, and Latin America, but not at its core in Europe.

The "New Look" in Foreign Policy

To meet his goals of balancing the federal budget and cutting taxes, Eisenhower determined to control military expenditures. Moreover, he feared that massive defense spending would threaten the economic strength of the nation. A state based on warfare could destroy the very society it was intended to protect. As he declared in 1953, "Every gun that is made, every warship launched, every rocket fired signifies, in the final sense, a theft from those who hunger and are not fed, those who are cold and not clothed."

Reflecting Americans' confidence in technology and opposition to a large peacetime army, Eisenhower's defense strategy concentrated U.S. military strength in nuclear weapons along with planes and missiles to deliver them. By 1955, one U.S. bomber carried more force than all the explosives ever detonated in the history of humankind. Instead of spending huge amounts for large ground forces of its own, the United States would give friendly nations American weapons and back them up with an ominous nuclear arsenal.

This was Eisenhower's "New Look" in foreign policy. Airpower and nuclear weapons provided, in Secretary of State Dulles's words, a "maximum deterrent at bearable cost" or, as Defense Secretary Charles Wilson put it, a

The Nuclear Arms Race
This *Newsweek* cover of Soviet leader Nikita Khrushchev and President Dwight D. Eisenhower balanced on the head of a nuclear missile suggests the precarious world created by the nuclear arms race. The table on which the two men sit refers to the arms limitation negotiations under way when the magazine came off the press in 1959.

"bigger bang for the buck." Dulles believed that America's willingness to "go to the brink" of war with its intimidating nuclear superiority—a strategy called **brinksmanship**—would block any Soviet efforts to expand.

Nuclear weapons could not stop a Soviet nuclear attack, but, in response to one, they could inflict enormous destruction on the USSR. The certainty of "massive retaliation" was meant to deter the Soviets from launching an attack. Because the Soviet Union could respond similarly to an American first strike, this nuclear standoff became known as mutually assured destruction, or MAD. Winston Churchill called it a "mutual balance of terror." Yet leaders of each nation sought not just balance, but nuclear superiority, and pursued an ever-escalating arms race.

Nuclear weapons were useless, however, in rolling back the **iron curtain**, because they would destroy the very peoples whom the United States promised to liberate. When a re-

volt against the Soviet-controlled government began in Hungary in 1956, Dulles's liberation rhetoric proved to be empty. A radio plea from the Hungarian Freedom Fighters cried, "SOS! They just brought us a rumor that the American troops will be here within one or two hours." But help did not come. Eisenhower was unwilling to risk U.S. soldiers and possible nuclear war, and Soviet troops soon suppressed the insurrection, killing thirty thousand Hungarians.

Applying Containment to Vietnam

A major challenge to the containment policy came in Southeast Asia, where in 1945 a nationalist coalition called the Vietminh, led by Ho Chi Minh, had proclaimed Vietnam's independence from France. When France fought to maintain its colony, Ho fought back, and the area plunged into war (see Map 29.2 in chapter 29). Because Ho declared himself a Communist, the Truman administration quietly began to provide aid to the French.

Eisenhower viewed communism in Vietnam much as Truman had regarded it in Greece and Turkey, a view that became known as the **domino theory**. "You have a row of dominoes," Eisenhower explained, and "you knock over the first one, and what will happen to the last one is the certainty that it will go over very quickly." A Communist victory in Southeast Asia, he warned, could trigger the fall of Japan, Taiwan, and the Philippines. By 1954, the United States was contributing 75 percent of the cost of France's war, but Eisenhower resisted a larger role. When the French asked for troops and airplanes from the United States in order to avert almost certain defeat at Dien Bien Phu, Eisenhower firmly said no. Conscious of U.S. losses in the Korean War, he would not commit troops to another ground war in Asia.

Dien Bien Phu fell in May 1954 and with it the French colony of Vietnam. Two months later in Geneva, France signed a truce. The Geneva accords temporarily partitioned Vietnam at the seventeenth parallel, separating the Vietminh in the north from the puppet government established

Geneva Accords of 1954

by the French in the south and prohibiting both from joining a military alliance or permitting foreign bases on their soil. Within two years, the Vietnamese people were to vote in elections for a unified government. The United States promised to support free elections but did not sign the accords.

Some officials warned against U.S. involvement in Vietnam. An intelligence study, for example, predicted that even with American assistance, the chances of securing a viable government in the South were "poor." Defense Secretary Wilson could "see nothing but grief in store for us if we

Fidel Castro Triumphs in Cuba

Fidel Castro came from a privileged family and earned a law degree at the University of Havana, but he spent his youth working for the overthrow of Cuban dictator Fulgencio Batista. After leading an assault on Batista's soldiers in 1953, he spent two years in prison and then slowly built up an army of guerrilla fighters. "I began revolution with 82 men," he said. "If I had [to] do it again, I do it with 10 or 15 and absolute faith. It does not matter how small you are if you have faith and plan of action." He is shown at the city hall of Santa Clara just before his triumphal march to Havana in January 1959.

Andrew St. George/Magnum Photos, Inc.

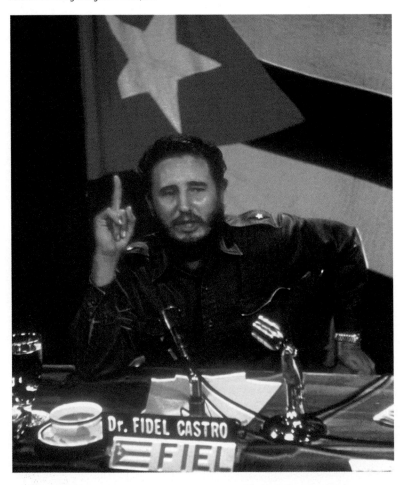

remained in that area." Eisenhower and Dulles, however, believed that a Communist Vietnam would threaten all of Asia and moved to prop up the dominoes with a new alliance. In September 1954, the United States joined with Britain, France, Australia, New Zealand, Thailand, Pakistan, and the Philippines in the Southeast Asia Treaty Organization (SEATO), committed to the defense of Cambodia, Laos, and South Vietnam. The ink was barely dry on the treaty when the United States began to send weapons and military advisers to South Vietnam and put the CIA to work infiltrating and destabilizing North Vietnam. Fearing that the popular vote mandated by the Geneva accords would result in a Communist victory, the United States supported South Vietnamese prime minister Ngo Dinh Diem's refusal to hold the election.

Between 1955 and 1961, the United States provided $800 million to the South Vietnamese army (ARVN). Yet even with U.S. dollars, the ARVN was grossly unprepared for the **guerrilla warfare** that began in the late 1950s. In 1959, Ho Chi Minh's government in Hanoi began sending military assistance to Vietminh rebels in the south, who stepped up their guerrilla attacks on the Diem government. The insurgents gained control over villages not only through sheer military power but also because the largely rural and Buddhist peasants were alienated from the Catholic, Westernized, French-speaking Diem and outraged by his repressive regime. Unwilling to abandon containment, Eisenhower handed over the deteriorating situation—along with a firm commitment to defend South Vietnam against communism—to his successor.

Interventions in Latin America and the Middle East

While buttressing friendly governments in Asia, the Eisenhower administration also worked to topple unfriendly ones in Latin America and the Middle East. The CIA became an important arm of foreign policy in the 1950s, as Eisenhower relied on behind-the-scenes efforts and covert activities against governments that appeared too leftist and threatened U.S. economic interests. Increasingly, the administration conducted foreign policy behind the back of Congress.

The Eisenhower administration employed clandestine activities in Guatemala, where the government was not Communist or Soviet controlled but accepted support from the local Communist Party (see Map 29.1 in chapter 29).

In 1954, when the reformist president Jacobo Arbenz sought to nationalize land owned but not used by a U.S. corporation, the United Fruit Company, Eisenhower authorized the CIA to carry out covert operations destabilizing Guatemala's economy and assisting a coup. A military dictatorship friendly to United Fruit replaced Arbenz's popularly elected government.

"We're going to take care of Castro just like we took care of Arbenz," promised a CIA agent when Cubans' desire for political and economic autonomy erupted in 1959. American companies had long controlled major Cuban resources—especially sugar, tobacco, and mines—and decisions made in Washington directly influenced the lives and livelihoods of the Cuban people. An uprising in 1959 led by Fidel Castro drove out the U.S.-supported dictator Fulgencio Batista and led the CIA to warn Eisenhower that "Communists and other extreme radicals appear to have penetrated the Castro movement." When the United States denied Castro's requests for loans, he turned for help to the Soviet Union. And when U.S. companies refused Castro's offer to purchase them at their assessed value, he began to nationalize their property. Many anti-Castro Cubans fled to the United States and reported his atrocities, including the execution of hundreds of Batista's supporters. Before leaving office, Eisenhower broke off diplomatic relations with Cuba and authorized the CIA to train Cuban exiles for an invasion.

In the Middle East, as in Guatemala, the CIA intervened to support an unpopular dictatorship and help American corporations (see Map 31.2 in chapter 31). In 1951, the left-leaning prime minister of Iran, Mohammed Mossadegh, had nationalized oil fields and refineries, thereby threatening Western oil interests. While accepting support from the Iranian Communist Party, Mossadegh also challenged the power of the shah, Mohammad Reza Pahlavi, Iran's hereditary leader, who favored foreign oil interests and the Iranian wealthy classes.

For all of these reasons, Eisenhower authorized CIA agents to instigate a coup against Mossadegh by bribing army officers and paying

Iranians to demonstrate against the government. In August 1953, army officers took Mossadegh prisoner and reestablished the shah's power, whereupon Iran renegotiated oil concessions, giving U.S. companies a 40 percent share. Although the intervention worked in the short run, Americans in the 1970s and 1980s would feel the full fury of Iranian opposition to the repressive government that the United States had helped to reinstall.

Elsewhere in the Middle East, the Eisenhower administration shifted from Truman's all-out support for Israel to fostering friendships with Arab nations. Hindering such efforts, however, were U.S. demands that smaller nations take the American side in the cold war, even when those nations preferred neutrality and the opportunity for assistance from both Western and Communist nations. In 1955, Secretary of State Dulles began talks with Egypt about American support to build the Aswan Dam on the Nile River. But in 1956, Egypt's leader, Gamal Abdel Nasser, sought arms from Communist Czechoslovakia, formed a military alliance with other Arab nations, and recognized the People's Republic of China.

Unwilling to tolerate such independence, Dulles called off the deal for the dam. On July 26, 1956, Nasser responded by seizing the Suez Canal, then owned by Britain and France. Taking the canal advanced Nasser's prestige and power in the region, because it coincided with **nationalist** aspirations in the Arab world, and revenue from the canal could provide capital for constructing the dam. In response to the seizure, Israel, whose forces had been skirmishing with Egyptian troops along their common border since 1948, attacked Egypt, with military help from Britain and France.

Eisenhower opposed the intervention, recognizing that the Egyptians had claimed their own territory and recognizing that Nasser "embodie[d] the emotional demands of the people . . . for independence." He put economic pressure on

> While buttressing friendly governments in Asia, the Eisenhower administration also worked to topple unfriendly ones in Latin America and the Middle East.

The Suez Crisis, 1956

Anglo-French landings
Invasion force bombardment and landings
Mediterranean Sea
Gaza
Port Said
Al Arish
Beersheba
Tanta
Qantara
Abu Agheila
ISRAEL
Al Auja
Ismailia
Al Quseima
Bir Hasne
Suez Canal
Bir Gafgafa
Kuntilla
Suez
Nakhl
Israeli paratroop drop
Ras al Naqb
JORDAN
Gulf of Suez
SINAI PENINSULA
Gulf of Aqaba
SAUDI ARABIA
EGYPT
Al Tor
Ras Nasrani
Sharm al Sheikh

The Suez Crisis, 1956
Oct. 29th–Nov. 5th
Israeli troop movements
0   25   50 miles
0   50 kilometers

Britain and France while calling on the United Nations to arrange a truce. Lacking U.S. support, the French and British soon pulled back, forcing Israel to retreat from territory it had captured in the Sinai peninsula of Egypt.

Although staying out of the Suez crisis, Eisenhower made clear that the United States would actively combat communism in the Middle East. In March 1957, Congress passed a joint resolution approving economic and military aid to any Middle Eastern nation "requesting assistance against armed aggression from any country controlled by international communism." The president invoked this "Eisenhower Doctrine" to send aid to Jordan in 1957 and troops to Lebanon in 1958 to counter anti-Western pressures on those governments.

The Nuclear Arms Race

While Eisenhower's foreign policy centered on countering perceived Communist inroads abroad, a number of events encouraged the president to seek reduction of superpower tensions and accommodation with the Soviet Union. After Stalin's death in 1953, a more moderate leadership under Nikita Khrushchev emerged. The Soviet Union signed a peace treaty with Austria guaranteeing Austrian neutrality and removed its troops. Like Eisenhower, who remarked privately that the arms race would lead "at worst to atomic warfare, at best to robbing every people and nation on earth of the fruits of their own toil," Khrushchev worried about the domestic costs of the cold war and wanted to reduce defense spending and the threat of nuclear devastation.

> American nuclear superiority did not guarantee security, because the Soviet Union possessed sufficient nuclear weapons to devastate the United States.

Eisenhower and Khrushchev met in Geneva in 1955 at the first summit conference since the end of World War II. Though it produced no significant agreements, the meeting symbolized a lessening of tensions—in Eisenhower's words, "a new spirit of conciliation and cooperation." In 1959, Khrushchev visited the United States, and Nixon went to the Soviet Union, where he engaged in the famous kitchen debate. By 1960, the two sides were within reach of a ban on nuclear testing, and Khrushchev and Eisenhower agreed to meet again in Paris in May.

To avoid jeopardizing the summit, Eisenhower decided to cancel espionage flights over the Soviet Union, but his order came one day too late. On May 1, 1960, a Soviet missile shot down a U-2 spy plane over Soviet territory. The State Department first denied that U.S. planes had been violating Soviet air space, but then the Soviets produced the pilot and the photos taken on his flight. Eisenhower met with Khrushchev briefly in Paris, but the U-2 incident dashed all prospects for a nuclear arms agreement.

Eisenhower's "more bang for the buck" defense budget enormously increased the U.S. nuclear capacity, more than quadrupling the stockpile of nuclear weapons. By the time he left office in 1961, the United States had installed seventy-two intercontinental ballistic missiles (ICBMs) in the United States and Britain and was prepared to deploy more in Italy and Turkey. The first Polaris submarine carrying nuclear missiles was launched in November 1960.

In August 1957, the Soviets test-fired their first ICBM and two months later beat the United States into space by launching *Sputnik*, the first artificial satellite to circle the earth. Senate majority leader Lyndon Johnson called the Soviet success a scientific Pearl Harbor, and other leaders warned that the United States lagged behind not only in missile development and space exploration but also in science and education. When the United States tried to launch a response to *Sputnik*, its satellite exploded, prompting news headlines calling it a "Stayputnik" and a "Flopnik." A successful satellite launch came finally in January 1958.

Eisenhower insisted that the United States possessed nuclear superiority, but in 1957 he could not reveal the evidence for his confidence, the top-secret U-2 surveillance of the Soviet Union. He tried to diminish public panic, establishing the National Aeronautics and Space Administration (NASA) in July 1958 and approving a gigantic budget increase for space research and development. In addition, he signed the National Defense Education Act, providing loans and scholarships for students in math, foreign languages, and science.

American nuclear superiority did not guarantee security because the Soviet Union possessed sufficient nuclear weapons to devastate the United States. Instructed to "duck and cover," American schoolchildren dove under their desks or crouched on the floor during regular drills to prepare for a nuclear attack. Most Americans did not follow Civil Defense Administration recommendations to construct home bomb shelters, and few could respond to real estate ads that offered "good bomb immunity," but

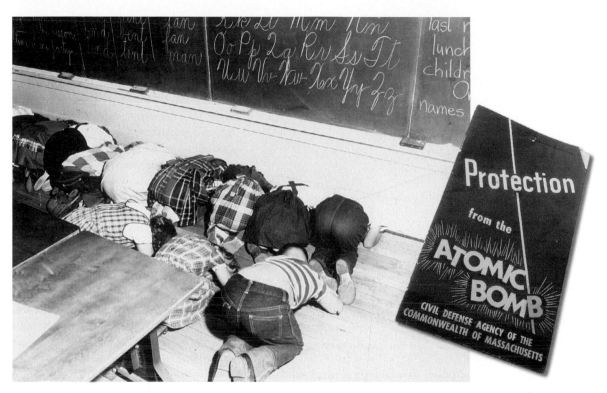

The Age of Nuclear Anxiety

Within just five years after World War II, governments throughout the United States were educating the public about the nuclear threat and urging them to prepare. As schools routinely held drills to prepare for possible Soviet attacks, children directly experienced the anxiety and insecurity of the 1950s nuclear arms race. This pamphlet about how to survive an atomic attack was published by the federal government and distributed to the general public. How effective do you think the strategy pictured here would have been in the event of a nuclear attack?

Archive Photos; Lynn Historical Society.

FOR MORE HELP ANALYZING THIS IMAGE, see the visual activity for this chapter in the Online Study Guide at bedfordstmartins.com/roark.

---

they did realize how precarious nuclear weapons had made their lives. "Facing a Danger Unlike Any Danger That Has Ever Existed," headlined an ad placed by the Committee for a Sane Nuclear Policy, an organization founded to oppose the nuclear arms race, with 130 chapters by 1958.

As he left office, Eisenhower warned about the growing influence of the **military-industrial complex** in American government and life. To contain the defense budget, Eisenhower had struggled against persistent pressures from defense contractors who, in tandem with the military, sought more dollars for newer, more powerful weapons systems. In his farewell address, he warned that the "conjunction of an immense military establishment and a large arms industry . . . exercised a total influence . . . in every city, every state house, every office of the federal government." The cold war had created a warfare state.

New Work and Living Patterns in an Economy of Abundance

American military spending helped stimulate domestic prosperity. Economic productivity increased enormously in the 1950s (Figure 27.1), a multitude of new items came on the market, consumption became the order of the day, and millions of Americans enjoyed new homes in the suburbs. Prosperity enabled young people to stay in school longer, as higher education became the norm for the middle class. Although every section of the nation enjoyed the new abundance,

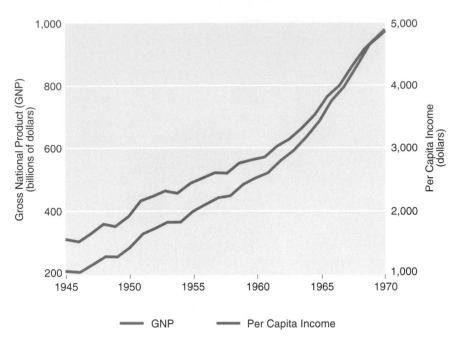

FIGURE 27.1 The Postwar Economic Boom: GNP and Per Capita Income, 1945–1970
American dominance of the worldwide market, innovative technologies that led to new industries such as computers and plastics, population growth, and increases in worker productivity all contributed to the enormous economic growth of the United States after World War II.

the West and Southwest especially boomed in production, commerce, and population.

Work itself changed: Fewer people labored on farms; service sector employment overtook manufacturing jobs; and women's employment grew. These economic shifts disadvantaged some Americans, and some forty million people—20 percent of the population—lived in poverty. Most Americans, however, enjoyed a higher standard of living, leading the economist John Kenneth Galbraith to call the United States "the affluent society."

Technology Transforms Agriculture and Industry

Between 1940 and 1960, the output of American farms mushroomed, while the number of farm-workers declined by nearly one-third. Farmers achieved nearly miraculous productivity through greater crop specialization, more intensive use of fertilizers, and, above all, mechanization. Tractors, mechanical pickers, and other machines increasingly substituted for human and animal power. A single mechanical cotton picker replaced fifty people and cut the cost of harvesting a bale of cotton from $40 to $5.

The decline of family farms and the growth of large commercial farming, or **agribusiness**, were both causes and consequences of mechanization. Larger farmers benefited handsomely from federal price supports begun in the New Deal, and they could afford technological improvements, whereas smaller producers lacked capital to invest in the machinery necessary to compete. Consequently, average farm size more than doubled between 1940 and 1964, while the farm population sank from thirty million to thirteen million, and the number of farms fell by more than 40 percent.

Many small farmers who hung on constituted a core of rural poverty often overlooked in the celebration of affluence. Southern landowners replaced sharecroppers with machines, forcing them off the land. Hundreds of thousands of African Americans joined an exodus to cities, where racial discrimination and a lack of jobs for which they could qualify mired many in urban poverty. A Mississippi woman whose family had worked on a plantation since slavery reported that most of her relatives headed for Chicago when they heard that "it was going to be machines now that harvest the crops." Worrying that "it might be worse up there," she agonized, "I'm afraid to leave and I'm afraid to stay, and whichever I do, I think it might be real bad for my boys and girls."

As in agriculture, new technology increased industrial production. Between 1945 and 1960, for example, the automobile industry cut in half the number of labor-hours needed to manufacture a car. Technology also transformed such industries as electronics, chemicals, and air transportation and promoted the growth of television, plastics, computers, and other newer industries. American businesses enjoyed access to cheap oil, and the nation's dominance in the international economy guaranteed ample markets abroad and little foreign competition. Moreover, even with Eisenhower's conservative fiscal policies, government spending reached $80 billion annually and created new jobs.

Labor unions enjoyed their greatest success during the 1950s, and real earnings for production workers shot up 40 percent. The merger in 1955 of the American Federation of Labor (AFL) and the Congress of Industrial Organizations (CIO) lessened internal conflicts and improved labor's bargaining position. As one worker put it, "We saw continual improvement in wages, fringe benefits like holidays, vacation, medical plans . . . all sorts of things that provided more security for people." Such benefits became a staple of most union contracts, though workers in heavy industries such as steel and automobiles did much better than those in food processing, garment making, and other light manufacturing. Unlike most industrial nations, where government provided most of the benefits, the United States developed a mixed system in which company-funded programs won by unions through **collective bargaining** played a larger role. This system resulted in wide disparities among workers, severely disadvantaging those not represented by unions.

While the absolute number of organized workers continued to increase, union membership peaked at 27.1 percent of the labor force in 1957. Technological advances chipped away at jobs in heavy industry, reducing the number of workers in the steel, copper, and aluminum industries by 17 percent. "You are going to have trouble collecting union dues from all of these machines," commented a Ford manager at a newly automated engine plant to union leader Walter Reuther. Moreover, the economy as a whole was shifting from production to service. Instead of making products, more and more workers distributed goods, performed services, kept records, provided education, or carried out government work. Unions made some headway in these fields—union membership among local, state, and federal government employees became especially strong in the next few decades—but most service industries resisted unionization, and many of the workers—such as janitors, food servers, and domestics—performed hard manual labor for low wages.

The growing clerical and service occupations swelled the demand for female workers. By

Poverty in an Era of Abundance

The Whiteheads, a coal-mining family in Kentucky, represented the hidden side of the affluent post-war era. Mrs. John Whitehead, shown here, lived with her husband, their six children, and their six grandchildren in this three-room house. It had neither running water nor electricity, and the only access to the house was over a mountain trail.
National Archives.

Technology Transforms Agriculture
A mechanical cotton picker was patented as early as 1850, but the abundant supply of slave labor
and then sharecroppers delayed its widespread use until after World War II. In 1950, machines harvested
just 5 percent of cotton in the South, but ten years later mechanization accounted for 50 percent
of the crop. This kind of technological advance was both cause and effect of the movement of African
Americans out of the rural South. In this photo, cotton harvesters munch their way through a North
Carolina cotton field in the 1950s.
United States Department of Agriculture.

the end of the 1950s, 35 percent of all women over age sixteen worked outside the home—twice as many as in 1940—and women held more than one-third of all jobs. Women entered a sharply segregated workplace. The vast majority worked in clerical jobs, light manufacturing, domestic service, teaching, and nursing, and because these were female occupations, wages were relatively low. In 1960, the average full-time female worker earned just 60 percent of the average male worker's wages. At the bottom of the employment ladder, black women took home only 42 percent of what white men earned.

Burgeoning Suburbs and Declining Cities

Although suburbs had existed since the nineteenth century, nothing symbolized the affluent society more than their tremendous expansion in the 1950s: Eleven million of the thirteen million new homes were built in the suburbs, and by 1960, one in four Americans lived there. As Vice President Nixon boasted to Khrushchev during the kitchen debate, the suburbs were accessible to families with modest incomes. Builder William J. Levitt modified the factory assembly-line process, planning nearly identical units so that individual construction work-

> Nothing symbolized the affluent society more than the tremendous expansion of suburbs.

ers could move from house to house and perform the same single operation in each, such as caulking windows or installing bathtubs. In 1949, families could purchase these mass-produced houses in his 17,000-home development called Levittown, on Long Island, New York, for just under $8,000. Developments similar to Levittown, as well as more luxurious ones, quickly went up throughout the country.

While private industry built the suburbs, the government subsidized home ownership with low-interest mortgage guarantees through the Federal Housing Administration and the Veterans Administration and by making interest on mortgages tax deductible. A veteran could buy a house in Levittown with payments of just $58 per month for twenty-five years. Moreover, thousands of interstate highway miles ran through urban areas, indirectly subsidizing suburban development. Without the automobile and the freeway, the suburban explosion could not have occurred.

Suburban culture was not without detractors. Social critic Lewis Mumford blasted the suburbs as "a multitude of uniform, unidentifiable houses, lined up inflexibly, at uniform distances, on uniform roads, in a treeless communal wasteland, inhabited by people of the same class, the same income, the same age group." By the 1960s, suburbs came under attack for bulldozing the natural environment, leveling hills and trees, creating groundwater contamination, and disrupting wildlife patterns. Moreover, the growing suburbs contributed to a more polarized society, especially along racial lines. Each Levittown homeowner signed a contract pledging that "no dwelling shall be used or occupied by members of other than the Caucasian race." Although the Supreme Court declared such covenants unenforceable in 1948, suburban America remained dramatically segregated.

As white residents joined the suburban migration, blacks moved to cities in search of economic opportunity, increasing their numbers in most cities by 50 percent during the 1950s. Black migrants to the North and East, however, came to cities that were already in decline, losing not only population but also commerce and industry to the suburbs or to southern and western states. "Detroit is in the doldrums," commented social welfare worker Mary Jorgensen in 1952; indeed, the city lost more than 100,000 manufacturing jobs in the 1950s. New business facilities began to ring central cities, and shoppers gradually chose suburban malls over downtown department stores. Many of the new jobs lay beyond the reach of the recent black arrivals to the inner cities.

The Rise of the Sun Belt

Americans were on the move westward as well as to the suburbs. Architect Frank Lloyd Wright quipped that the nation itself seemed to tip westward: Everything not bolted down was sliding toward California. No regions experienced the postwar economic and population booms more intensely than the West and Southwest. Americans had been moving westward, of course, since the nineteenth century, and the depression and Dust Bowl had sent more. After World War II, California's inhabitants more than doubled, and it overtook New York as the most populous state. Sports franchises followed fans: In 1958, the Brooklyn Dodgers moved to Los Angeles, joined by the Minneapolis Lakers three years later.

A warm climate and a pleasant natural environment drew new residents to the West and Southwest, but no magnet proved stronger than the promise of economic opportunity (Map 27.2). As

railroads had fueled western growth in the nineteenth century, the automobile and airplane spurred the post– World War II surge, providing efficient transportation for people and products. The technology of air-conditioning made possible industrial development in the so-called **Sun Belt**, which stretched from Florida to California. Crucial to the region's population explosion, air-conditioning cooled nearly eight million Sun Belt homes by 1960. (See "The Promise of Technology," page 1001.)

So important was the cold war defense industry to the South and West that it was later referred to as the "Gun Belt." The aerospace industry boomed in Seattle–Tacoma, Los Angeles, Tucson, and Dallas–Fort Worth, and military bases helped underwrite prosperity in such cities as San Diego and San Antonio (Table 27.1).

> A warm climate and a pleasant natural environment drew new residents to the West and Southwest, but no magnet proved stronger than the promise of economic opportunity.

An African American Suburb

The pioneer of mass-produced suburban housing, William J. Levitt, reflected the racism that kept blacks out of suburbia when he said, "We can solve a housing problem, or we can try and solve a racial problem, but we cannot combine the two." These African Americans developed their own suburb, a planned community for middle-class blacks in Richmond, California, which welcomed the first families in 1950.
Richmond Public Library.

Although defense dollars benefited other regions, the Sun Belt captured the lion's share of cold war spending for research and production of bombers and missiles, other weapons, and satellites. In California alone, the federal government spent more than $100 billion for defense between 1945 and 1965. By the 1960s, nearly one of every three California workers held a defense-related job.

The surging populations and industries brought with them needs that soon raised environmental concerns. Providing sufficient water and power to cities and to agribusiness meant replacing free-flowing rivers in the West with a series of dams and reservoirs. Five dams along the Missouri inundated Indian tribal lands in violation of treaty rights. Sprawling urban and suburban settlement without efficient public transportation contributed to blankets of smog over cities like Los Angeles. Development began to degrade the very environment that people came to enjoy, and inhabitants became less hospitable to newcomers. "Come and visit again and again," Oregon's governor told conventioneers in 1971, "but for heaven's sake, don't come here to live."

The high-technology basis of postwar economic development drew well-educated, highly skilled workers to the West. But the economic promise also attracted the poor. "We see opportunity all around us here. . . . We smell freedom here, and maybe soon we can taste it," commented a black mother in California. Between 1945 and 1960, more than one-third of the African Americans who left the South moved west, and more blacks moved to California than to any other state.

MAP 27.2 The Rise of the Sun Belt, 1940–1980

The growth of defense industries, a nonunionized labor force, and the spread of air-conditioning all helped spur economic development and population growth, which made the Sun Belt the fastest-growing region of the nation between 1940 and 1980.

READING THE MAP: What states experienced an over 20 percent growth in population? What states experienced the largest population growth?

CONNECTIONS: What stimulated the population boom in the Southwest? What role did the cold war play in this boom? What role did African Americans play in the western population boom?

FOR MORE HELP ANALYZING THIS MAP, see the map activity for this chapter in the Online Study Guide at bedfordstmartins.com/roark.

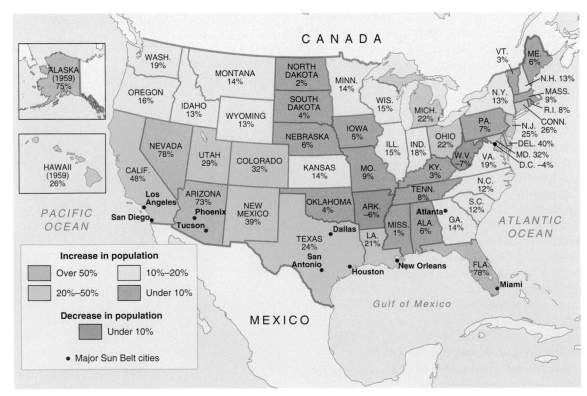

Air-Conditioning

Combining two technological advances of the late nineteenth century, refrigeration and electricity, air-conditioning developed primarily in response to the needs of industry. In 1902, Willis Haviland Carrier, a twenty-six-year-old American engineer who formulated basic theories of air-conditioning, designed the first system to control temperature and humidity and installed it in a Brooklyn printing plant. In 1915, he founded the Carrier Corporation to manufacture air-conditioning equipment.

Because fibers are sensitive to moisture, the textile industry provided an early and important market for air-conditioning. The process also helped to popularize movie theaters by making them a cool as well as an entertaining retreat during hot summer months. Room air conditioners began to appear in the 1930s. This 1950 Carrier ad promoted the clean air in homes and offices that would come with purchase of a room air conditioner. Fewer than a million homes had room air conditioners in 1950, but nearly eight million did in

1960, and more than half of all homes had some form of air-conditioning by 1975, as its status changed from a luxury to a necessity. By the end of the twentieth century, more than 80 percent of

EXCUSE MY DUST

Carrier   AIR CONDITIONING · REFRIGERATION

"That's Modern Air Control!"
Ads like this one for the Carrier room air conditioner promised consumers that homes could be cool as well as clean.
Courtesy Carrier Corporation.

households had air-conditioning, and it had become standard equipment on automobiles.

Air-conditioning was a mixed blessing. On the one hand, companies no longer had to shut down and send workers home when heat and humidity became unbearable, and air quality inside businesses, homes, and cars improved. On the other hand, air conditioners consumed large amounts of energy and contributed to outdoor air pollution. Like other technologies such as television and, more recently, the Internet, air-conditioning had an isolating effect as people deserted front porches and backyards for closed-up houses and thus curtailed their interactions with neighbors. Perhaps its greatest impact on the nation was to make possible the population explosion in the Sun Belt. By facilitating the movement of commerce, industry, and tourism to the South and Southwest, air-conditioning made that region more like the rest of the nation. One historian of the South, referring disparagingly to the transformation worked by air-conditioning on that region, proclaimed that "[General Electric] has proved a more devastating invader than even General Sherman."

The Mexican American population also grew, especially in California and Texas. To supply California's vast agribusiness industry, the government continued the *bracero* program begun during World War II (see chapter 25). Until the program ended in 1964, more than 100,000 Mexicans entered the United States each year to labor in the fields—and many of them stayed, legally or illegally. But while the government encouraged the use of Mexican labor, it reflected white Americans' opposition to permanent Mexican immigration, launching a series of raids in 1954 called "Operation Wetback." Designed to ferret out and deport illegal

TABLE 27.1	THE GROWING SUN BELT CITIES, 1920–1980			
	1920	1940	1960	1980
Los Angeles	879	2,916	6,039	7,478
Houston	168	529	1,418	2,905
Dallas	185	527	1,084	2,430
Atlanta	249	559	1,017	2,030
San Diego	74	289	1,033	1,862
Miami	30	268	935	1,626
Phoenix	29	186	664	1,509
New Orleans	398	552	907	1,256
San Antonio	191	338	716	1,072
Tucson	20	37	266	531

Population in thousands.

immigrants, the operation made U.S. citizens of Mexican descent feel unwelcome and threatened them with incidents of mistaken identity.

At the same time, Mexican American citizens gained a small victory in their ongoing struggle for civil rights in *Hernandez v. Texas*. When a Texas jury convicted Pete Hernandez of murder, lawyers from the American GI Forum and the League of United Latin-American Citizens (see chapter 26) appealed on the grounds that persons of Mexican origin had been systematically excluded from jury service for decades. In the first Mexican American civil rights case of the post–World War II era, the Supreme Court ruled unanimously that Hispanics represented a distinct group and that their systematic exclusion from juries violated the constitutional guarantee of equal protection.

Free of the discrimination faced by minorities, white Americans reaped the fullest fruits of prosperity in the West. In April 1950, California developers advertised the opening of Lakewood, a large housing development in Los Angeles County. On the first day of sales, 30,000 people lined up to purchase tract houses for $8,000 to $10,000. Many of the new homeowners were veterans, blue-collar and lower-level white-collar workers whose defense-based jobs at McDonnell Douglas and other aerospace corporations or at the Long Beach naval base enabled them to fulfill the American dream of the 1950s. A huge shopping mall, Lakewood Center, offered myriad products of the consumer culture. And California implemented a tremendous expansion of higher education. Their children had access to community colleges, four campuses of California State University, and two campuses of the University of California system— all within easy reach of Lakewood.

Rounding Up Undocumented Migrants

Not all Mexican Americans who wanted to work in the United States were accommodated by the bracero program. In 1953, Los Angeles police arrested these men who did not have legal documents and were hiding in a freight train. Americans used the crude term "wetback" to refer to illegal immigrants because many of them swam across the Rio Grande, at the border between the United States and Mexico. © Bettmann/Corbis.

The Democratization of Higher Education

California's system was only the largest element in a spectacular transformation of higher education. Between 1940 and 1960, enrollments leaped from 1.5 million to 3.6 million; and more than

Moving into the Suburbs

In 1953, Leo Ferguson responded to an ad in a St. Louis newspaper calling for engineers to work at North American Aviation and moved his family from Alton, Illinois, to Lakewood, California. Using cash and installment payments, the Fergusons purchased their $10,290 house and $6,800 worth of additional products. What does the photograph tell us about the kinds of items that fueled the consumer economy?

J. B. Eyerman/TimePix/Getty.

40 percent of young Americans attended college by the mid-1960s, in contrast to 15 percent in the 1940s. More families could afford to keep their children in school longer, and the federal government subsidized the education of more than two million World War II and Korean War veterans. The cold war also sent millions of federal dollars to universities for defense-related research. Total tax dollars spent for higher education more than doubled from 1950 to 1960, as state governments vastly expanded the number of four-year colleges and universities, and municipalities began to build two-year junior or community colleges.

The GI Bill made college possible for thousands of African Americans, the majority of whom attended black institutions. College enrollments of blacks surged from 37,000 in 1941 to 90,000 in 1961. Yet African Americans constituted only about 5 percent of all college students, less than half their percentage in the general population. Unlike their white counterparts, among whom women received just 33 percent of college degrees in 1960, black men and women attended college in nearly equal numbers.

For a time, the democratization of higher education increased the educational gap between white men and women. The numbers of college women grew, but they did not keep pace relative to those of men. In 1940, women earned 40 percent of undergraduate degrees, but as veterans flocked to college campuses, women's proportion fell to 25 percent in 1950. Even by 1960, women constituted just 33 percent of college graduating classes.

The large veteran enrollments also introduced a new feature of college life—the married student. Colleges that had previously forbidden students to marry relaxed the rule to accommodate the mature, war-tempered population.

Unlike men, however, women dropped out of college upon marriage, taking jobs to enable their husbands to stay in school and earning their own "Ph.T's" by "putting hubby through." Reflecting gender-role norms of the 1950s, most college women responding to a survey agreed that "it is natural for a woman to be satisfied with her husband's success and not crave personal achievement." Yet just a decade later, many of these same women would express resentment at their second-class status by joining the **feminist** movement.

Some observers in the 1950s termed college students a "silent generation," pointing to their apparent passivity, caution, and conformity. Students seemed too eager to suspend independent, critical thinking in favor of pleasing their professors and getting good grades to launch them on profitable careers. Those who remembered favorably the student generation of the 1930s found students in the 1950s apolitical or safely conservative.

The Culture of Abundance

With increased prosperity in the 1950s, more people married and the birthrate soared. Religious observance expanded even as Americans sought satisfaction in material possessions. Television entered the homes of most Americans, helping to promote a consumer culture. Dominant values favored family life and traditional gender roles, consumption, and conformity. Undercurrents of rebellion, especially among youth, defied some of the dominant norms but did not greatly disrupt the complacency of the 1950s.

A Consumer Culture

"If you grew up in the 1950s," journalist Robert Samuelson remembered, "you were a daily witness to the marvels of affluence . . . [to] a seemingly endless array of new gadgets and machines." Scorned by Khrushchev during the kitchen debate as worthless gadgets, consumer items flooded American society in the 1950s. Although the purchase and display of consumer goods had always been part of American life (see chapter 23), by the 1950s consumption had become a reigning value, vital for economic prosperity and essential to individuals' identity and status. While not altogether disappearing, the work ethic competed with a newer norm that stressed satisfaction and joy through the purchase and use of new products. The man who designed Ford automobiles captured this emphasis on happiness and also the corporate strategy of obsolescence when he remarked, "We design a car to make a man unhappy with his 1957 Ford 'long about the end of 1958."

The consumer culture rested on a firm material base. Between 1950 and 1960, the gross national product (the value of all goods and services produced during a year) as well as median family income grew by 25 percent in constant dollars. Alongside a 20 percent poverty rate, economists claimed that 60 percent of Americans enjoyed middle-class incomes in 1960. By the late 1950s, four of every five families owned television sets and washing machines, nearly all had refrigerators, and the majority owned at least one car.

Several forces spurred this unparalleled abundance. A population surge—from 152 million in 1950 to 180 million in 1960—expanded demand for products and boosted industries ranging from housing to baby goods to music. Consumer borrowing also fueled the economic boom, as people increasingly bought houses, cars, and appliances on installment plans. Diner's Club issued the first credit card in 1951, and American Express followed in 1958. Private debt, which more than doubled during the decade to reach $263 billion by 1960, was a key element of the consumer culture. Shopping itself changed as the number of shopping centers quadrupled between 1957 and 1963. Instead of taking a bus or streetcar downtown to the city center, suburbanites could drive to malls now accessible along new highways.

To encourage more and more consumption, corporate executives tripled the dollars they spent on advertising between World War II and 1959. By then, large advertising companies earned more than half their revenues from TV, which soon began to target specific markets. "For toys and games we go right to children audiences. For a household product to women," reported a media advertising director. Nor did television's support of consumption stop with commercials. Its programs also tantalized viewers with things to buy, especially the quiz shows. For example, women with the most pitiful personal stories won fur coats, vacuum cleaners, and other merchandise on *Queen for a Day*. To win on another popular show, *The Price Is Right*, required consumer skills, as contestants had to guess the retail prices of such items as cameras, appliances, furniture, and vacations.

Although the sheer need to support themselves and their families accounted for most of women's presence in the labor force, a desire to secure some of the new abundance for their families pulled increasing numbers of women out of the home. Married women working part-time filled many of the sales positions in the new shopping malls. In fact, married women experienced the largest increases in employment in the 1950s. As one woman remarked, "My Joe can't put five kids through college . . . and the washer had to be replaced, and Ann was ashamed to bring friends home because the living room furniture was such a mess, so I went to work." Increasingly families needed a second income to meet the standards for happiness imposed by the consumer culture.

The Revival of Domesticity and Religion

Even though married women took jobs in unprecedented numbers, a dominant ideology celebrated traditional family life and conventional gender roles. Despite the fact that more than one-third of mothers with school-age children left the home for work, the family ideal defined by popular culture and public figures persisted: a male breadwinner, a full-time homemaker, and three or four children in a new suburban home.

The emphasis on home and family life reflected to some extent anxieties about the cold war and nuclear menace. Not unlike Nixon in the kitchen debate, one government official saw women's role in cold war terms, charging that the Soviet Union viewed women "first as a source of manpower, second as a mother," and insisting that "the highest calling of a woman's sex is the home." *Life* magazine echoed the sentiment: "Of all the accomplishments of the American woman, the one she brings off with the most spectacular success is having babies."

Writer and feminist Betty Friedan gave a name to the idealization of women's domestic roles in her book *The Feminine Mystique*, published in 1963. Friedan criticized advertisers, social scientists, educators, women's magazines, and public officials for pressuring women to seek fulfillment in serving others. According to the feminine mystique that they promulgated, biological differences fitted men and women for entirely different roles in life. The ideal woman kept a spotless house, raised perfect children, served her husband's career, and provided him emotional and sexual satisfaction. The feminine mystique reinforced the notion that strong men and subservient women were as important to the survival of the nuclear family as virile political leadership was to the survival of the nation. Not many women then directly challenged the feminine mystique, but Edith Stern, a college-educated writer, maintained that "many arguments about the joys of housewifery have been advanced, largely by those who have never had to work at it," while she deplored the "incalculable skilled services" that were "buried in the homemade cakes the family loves and sunk in the suds of the week's wash."

Although the glorification of domesticity clashed with married women's increasing participation in the labor force, the lives of many Americans did embody the family ideal. Postwar prosperity enabled people to marry earlier and to have more children. Whereas its general trend over the twentieth century was downward, the American birthrate soared during the period 1945 to 1965, reaching a peak in 1957 with 4.3 million births and producing the "baby boom" generation (see appendix, page A-49). The norms for child rearing were more demanding than ever before. Dr. Benjamin Spock's best-selling *Common Sense Book of Baby and Child Care* (1946) advocated a permissive approach requiring mothers' full-time involvement instead of the traditional emphasis on strictness and rigid schedules. Experts also urged fathers to cultivate family "togetherness" and spend more time with their children.

Along with a renewed emphasis on family life, the 1950s witnessed a surge of interest in religion. By 1960, about 63 percent of Americans belonged to churches and synagogues, up from 50 percent in 1940. Polls reported that 95 percent of all Americans believed in God. Evangelism took on new life, most notably in the nationwide crusades of Baptist minister Billy Graham, whose powerful oratory moved mass audiences to accept Christ. Congress linked religion more closely to the state by adding "under God" to the pledge of allegiance in 1954 and by requiring in 1955 that "In God We Trust" be printed on all currency.

> Even though married women took jobs in unprecedented numbers, a dominant ideology celebrated traditional family life and conventional gender roles.

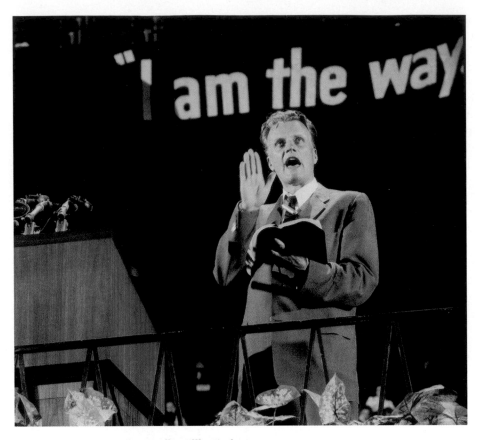

Evangelist Billy Graham

A young Baptist minister from North Carolina, Billy Graham electrified mass audiences across the country, entreating them to find salvation in Jesus Christ and to uphold Christian moral standards. Perhaps reflecting their ambivalence about their avid participation in a consumer society, Americans flocked to hear him even as he condemned their sinfulness in being "materialistic, worldly, secular, greedy, and covetous." So large were his audiences that Graham extended his 1957 New York crusade from eight to sixteen weeks. Here he preaches in Madison Square Garden.

Gjon Mili/TimePix/Getty.

Eisenhower's pastor attributed the renewed interest in religion to the prosperous economy that "provided the leisure, the energy, and the means for a level of human and spiritual values never before reached." Religion also offered reassurance and peace of mind in the nuclear age, while ministers like Graham turned the cold war into a holy war, labeling communism "a great sinister anti-Christian movement masterminded by Satan." Some critics questioned the depth of the religious revival, attributing the growth in church membership to a desire for conformity and a need for social outlets. One commentator, for example, noted that 53 percent of Americans could not name any book of the New Testament.

Television Transforms Culture and Politics

Just as family life and religion offered a respite from cold war anxieties, so too did the new medium of television. In 1950, fewer than 10 percent of American homes boasted a television set, but by 1960 about 87 percent of all households owned one. On average, Americans spent more than five hours each day in front of the screen.

Television kept people at home more but did not necessarily enhance family relationships, since parents and children focused their attention on the screen, not each other. The new medium altered eating habits; in 1954, the frozen dinner appeared, a complete meal in a portable tray that enabled families to spend the dinner hour in front of the TV. Noticing that the heaviest water consumption took place on the hour and half hour, civil engineers in Toledo, Ohio, realized that television regulated even trips to the bathroom.

Viewers especially tuned in to situation comedies, which projected the family ideal and the feminine mystique into millions of homes. On TV, married women did not work outside the home and deferred to their husbands, though they often got the upper hand through subtle manipulation. In the most popular television show of the early 1950s, *I Love Lucy*, the husband-and-wife team of Lucille Ball and Desi Arnaz played the couple Lucy and Ricky Ricardo. In step with the trends, they moved from an apartment in the city to a house in suburbia. Ricky would not let Lucy get a job, and many plots depicted her zany attempts to thwart his objections.

Television began to affect politics in the 1950s. Richard Nixon's "Checkers speech" reached a nationwide audience and kept him on the Republican ticket in 1952. Senator McCarthy's reckless attacks on army members televised nationwide contributed to his downfall. Eisenhower's 1952 presidential campaign used TV ads for the first time, and by 1960, television played a key role in election campaigns. Reflecting on his narrow victory in 1960, president-elect John F. Kennedy remarked, "We wouldn't have had a prayer without that gadget."

Television transformed politics in other ways. Money played a much larger role in elections because candidates needed to raise huge sums for expensive TV spots. The ability to appeal directly to voters in their living rooms put a premium on personal attractiveness and encouraged candidates to build their own campaign organizations, relying less on political parties. The declining strength of parties and the growing power of money in elections were not new trends, but television did much to accelerate them.

Unlike government-financed television in Europe, American TV was paid for by private enterprise. What NBC called a "selling machine in every living room" became the major vehicle for hawking the products of the affluent society and creating a consumer culture. In the mid-1950s, advertisers spent $10 billion to push their goods on TV, and the soap manufacturer Procter & Gamble spent more than 90 percent of its advertising budget on the new medium. Advertisers did not hesitate to interfere with shows that might jeopardize the sale of their products. The cigarette company that sponsored the *Camel News Caravan*, for example, banned any news film clips showing "No Smoking" signs.

In 1961, Newton Minow, chairman of the Federal Communications Commission, called television a "vast wasteland." While acknowledging some of TV's great achievements, particularly documentaries and drama, Minow depicted it as "a procession of game shows, . . . formula comedies about totally unbelievable families, blood and thunder, mayhem, violence, sadism, murder . . . and cartoons." But viewers kept tuning in. In little more than a decade, television came to dominate Americans' leisure time, influence their consumption patterns, and shape their perceptions of the nation's leadership.

Countercurrents

Pockets of dissent underlay the complacency of the 1950s. Some intellectuals took exception to the politics of consensus and to the materialism and conformity celebrated in popular culture. In *The Lonely Crowd* (1950), sociologist David Riesman lamented a shift from the "inner-directed" to the "other-directed" individual. In contrast to the independent thinking that had characterized earlier Americans, Riesman found a regrettable eagerness to adapt to external standards of behavior and belief. Sharing that distaste for the importance of "belonging," William H. Whyte Jr., in his popular book *The Organization Man* (1956), blamed the modern corporation. When employees had to tailor their behavior and ideas to those of the group, these "organization men" sacrificed risk taking and independence to dull conformity. And Vance Packard's 1959 best seller, *The Status Seekers*, decried "the vigorous merchandising of goods as status-symbols," while arguing that in this era of abundance "class lines in several areas of our national life appear to be hardening."

Less direct challenges to mainstream standards appeared in the everyday behavior of large numbers of Americans, especially youth. "Roll over Beethoven and tell Tchaikovsky the news!" belted out Chuck Berry in his 1956 hit record celebrating a new form of music. White teenagers lionized Elvis Presley, who shocked their parents with his tight pants, hip-rolling gestures, and sensuous

> In little more than a decade, television came to dominate Americans' leisure time, influence their consumption patterns, and shape their perceptions of the nation's leadership.

The Made-for-TV Family
This scene is from the popular television sitcom *Father Knows Best*, which ran from 1954 to 1963. Along with shows such as *Ozzie and Harriet* and *Leave It to Beaver*, it idealized white family life. In these shows, no one got divorced or became gravely ill, no one took drugs or seriously misbehaved, fathers held white-collar jobs, mothers did not work outside the home, and husbands and wives slept in twin beds. In what ways do today's sitcoms differ from those of the 1950s?

Culver Pictures/Picture Research Consultants.

music, a blend of country and western and black rhythm and blues. "Before there was Elvis . . . I started going crazy for 'race music,'" recalled a white man of his teenage years. "It had a beat. I loved it. . . . That got me into trouble with my parents and the schools." His experience illustrated African Americans' contributions to rock and roll as well as the rebellion expressed by white youths' attraction to black music.

Just as rock and roll's sexual suggestiveness violated norms of middle-class respectability, Americans' sexual behavior often departed from the family ideal of the postwar era. Two books published by Alfred Kinsey and other researchers at Indiana University, *Sexual Behavior in the Human Male* (1948) and *Sexual Behavior in the Human Female* (1953), uncovered a surprising range of sexual conduct. Surveying more than 16,000 individuals, Kinsey found that 85 percent of the men and 50 percent of the women had had sex before marriage; half of the husbands and a quarter of the wives had engaged in adultery; and one-third of the men and one-seventh of the women reported homosexual experiences.

Although Kinsey's sampling procedures later cast doubt on his ability to generalize across the population, the books became best sellers. They also drew a firestorm of outrage, especially because Kinsey refused to make moral judgments. Evangelist Billy Graham protested "the damage this book will do to the already deteriorating morals of America," and the Rockefeller Foundation stopped funding Kinsey's work.

The most blatant revolt against conventionality came from the self-proclaimed Beat generation, a small group of literary figures based in

Elvis Presley
Young people seeking escape from white middle-class conformity thrilled to Elvis Presley's pulsating music, long sideburns and ducktail haircut, colorful clothing, and suggestive movements. His gyrating hips, illustrated in these 1957 photographs, led to the appellation "Elvis the Pelvis." Adult viewers complained about his "grunt and groin antics" and "unnecessary bump and grind routine."
© Bettmann/Corbis.

New York City's Greenwich Village and in San Francisco. Rejecting nearly everything in mainstream culture—patriotism, consumerism, technology, conventional family life, discipline—the Beats celebrated spontaneity and absolute personal freedom, including drug consumption and freewheeling sex. In his landmark poem *Howl* (1956), Allen Ginsberg inveighed against "Robot apartments! invisible suburbs! skeleton treasuries! blind capitals! demonic industries! . . . monstrous bombs!" and denounced the social forces that "frightened me out of my natural ecstasy!" In 1957, Jack Kerouac, who gave the Beat generation its name, published the bestselling novel *On the Road* (1957), whose energetic, bebop-style prose narrated the restless and impetuous cross-country traveling of two young men. The Beats' rebelliousness would provide a model for a much larger movement of youthful dissidents in the 1960s.

Bold new styles in the visual arts also showed the 1950s to be more than a decade of bland conventionality. An artistic revolution that flowered in New York City, known as "action painting," "abstract expressionism," or the "New York school," rejected the idea that painting should represent recognizable forms. Jackson Pollock and other abstract expressionists, emphasizing energy and spontaneity, poured, dripped, and threw paint on canvases or substituted sticks and other implements for brushes. Reflecting the sweep of anticommunism in the 1950s, one conservative congressman condemned abstract art as part of "a sinister conspiracy conceived in the black heart of Russia." Yet the new form of painting so captivated and redirected the Western art world that New York replaced Paris as its center.

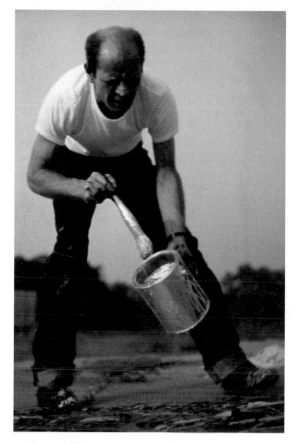

Jackson Pollock
The leading artist in the post–World War II revolution in painting, Jackson Pollock, illustrates his technique of pouring and splattering paint onto the canvas. He worked with the canvas on the floor because, he said, "I feel nearer, more a part of the painting. . . . I can walk around it, work from the four sides and be literally 'in' the painting."
Hans Namuth ©1990 Hans Namuth Estate. Courtesy Center for Creative Photography, the University of Arizona.

Emergence of a Civil Rights Movement

African Americans conducted the most dramatic challenge to the status quo of the 1950s as they sought to break the chains that had replaced the literal bonds of slavery. Every southern state mandated rigid segregation in public settings from hospitals and schools to drinking fountains and restrooms. Southern voting laws and practices disfranchised the vast majority of African Americans; employment discrimination kept them at the bottom of the economic ladder.

Although black protest was as old as American racism, in the 1950s a grassroots movement arose that attracted national attention and the support of white liberals. The Supreme Court delivered significant institutional reforms, but blacks themselves directed the most important changes. Ordinary African Americans in substantial numbers sought their own liberation, building a movement that would transform race relations in the United States.

African Americans Challenge the Supreme Court and the President

A number of factors spurred black protest in the 1950s. Between 1940 and 1960, more than three million African Americans moved from the South into areas where they could vote and exert pressure on politicians. The cold war raised white leaders' concern that its poor treatment of minorities handicapped the United States in competing with the Soviet Union. In the South, the system of segregation itself meant that African Americans controlled certain resources essential to a movement, such as churches and colleges, where leadership skills could be honed and a mass base and organizational network developed.

The legal strategy of the major civil rights organization, the National Association for the Advancement of Colored People (NAACP), reached its crowning achievement with the Supreme Court decision in *Brown v. Board of Education* in 1954. *Brown* was actually a consolidation of five separate suits that reflected the growing determination of black Americans to fight for their rights. Oliver Brown, a welder in Topeka, Kansas, filed suit because his eight-year-old daughter had to pass by a white school just seven blocks from their home to attend a black school more than a mile away. In Virginia, sixteen-year-old Barbara Johns, angered at the wretched conditions in her black high school, came home from school one day and declared, "I walked out of school this morning and carried 450 students with me." "Took my breath away," her grandmother recalled. That strike resulted in another of the suits joined together in *Brown*. The lead lawyer for the NAACP, future Supreme Court justice Thurgood Marshall, urged the Court to overturn the precedent established in *Plessy v. Ferguson* (1896), which had made "separate but equal" the law of the land (see chapter 17). A unanimous Court, headed by Chief Justice Earl Warren, declared, "Separate educational facilities are inherently unequal" and thus violated the Fourteenth Amendment.

It was one thing to issue a decision, another matter entirely to see it enforced. The Court called for desegregation "with all deliberate speed" but established no deadlines or guidelines. Ultimate responsibility for enforcement lay with President Eisenhower, but he refused to endorse *Brown*, just as he kept silent in 1955 when whites lynched Emmett Till, a fourteen-

> Ordinary African Americans in substantial numbers sought their own liberation, building a movement that would transform race relations in the United States.

year-old black boy who had allegedly whistled at a white woman in Mississippi. Reflecting his own racial prejudice, preference for a limited federal government, and a leadership style that favored consensus and gradual progress, Eisenhower would not urge the South to comply with desegregation. Such inaction fortified southern resistance to school desegregation and contributed to the gravest constitutional crisis since the Civil War.

The crisis came in Little Rock, Arkansas, in September 1957. Local officials dutifully prepared for the integration of Central High School, but Governor Orval Faubus sent Arkansas National Guard troops to block the enrollment of nine black students, claiming that their presence would cause public disorder. Later, Faubus agreed to allow the black students to enter, but he withdrew the National Guard, leaving the students to face an angry mob of whites. "During those years when we desperately needed approval from our peers," Melba Patillo Beals remembered, "we were victims of the most harsh rejection imaginable." As television cameras transmitted the ugly scene across the nation, Eisenhower was forced to send regular army troops to take federal control of the Arkansas National Guard, the first federal military intervention in the South since Reconstruction.

Escorted by paratroopers, the black students stayed in school, and Eisenhower withdrew the army in November. Other southern cities avoided integration by closing public schools and using tax dollars to support private, white-only schools. In 1961—nearly seven years after *Brown*—only 6.4 percent of southern black students attended integrated schools. (See "Documenting the American Promise," page 1012.)

Eisenhower did order the integration of public facilities in Washington, D.C., and on military bases, and he supported the first federal civil rights legislation since Reconstruction. Yet the Civil Rights Acts of 1957 and 1960 lacked effective enforcement mechanisms, leaving southern blacks still unprotected in the exercise of basic rights. Baseball star Jackie Robinson spoke for many African Americans when he wired Eisenhower, "We disagree that half a loaf is better than none. Have waited this long for bill with meaning—can wait a little longer." Eisenhower did appoint the first black professional to the White House staff, but E. Frederick Morrow confided to his diary, "I feel ridiculous . . . trying to defend the administration's record on civil rights."

Montgomery and Mass Protest

From slave revolts and individual acts of defiance through the legal and lobbying efforts of the NAACP, black protest had a long tradition in American society. What set the civil rights movement of the 1950s and 1960s apart were the masses of people involved, their willingness to confront white institutions directly, and the use of nonviolence and passive resistance to bring about change. The Congress of Racial Equality (CORE) and other groups had experimented with these tactics in the 1940s, and African Americans had boycotted the segregated bus system in Baton Rouge, Louisiana, in 1953, but the first sustained protest to claim national attention began in Montgomery, Alabama, on December 1, 1955.

On that day, police arrested a black woman, Rosa Parks, for violating a local segregation ordinance. Riding a crowded bus home from her job as a seamstress in a department store, she refused to give up her seat so that a white man could sit down. "People always say that I didn't give up my seat because I was tired, but that isn't true," Parks recalled. "I was not tired physically . . . I was not old . . . I was forty-two. No, the only tired I was, was tired of giving in." The bus driver called the police, who promptly arrested her.

Parks had long been active in the local NAACP, headed by E. D. Nixon, who was also president of the local Brotherhood of Sleeping Car Porters. They and others had already talked about challenging bus segregation. A possible boycott had engaged another group, the Women's Political Council (WPC), composed of black professional women and led by Jo Ann Robinson, an English professor at Alabama State College who had been humiliated by a bus driver when she had inadvertently sat in the white section. Such local individuals and organizations, long committed to improving conditions for African Americans, laid critical foundations for the black freedom struggle throughout the South.

School Integration in Little Rock, Arkansas

The nine African American teenagers who integrated Central High School in Little Rock, Arkansas, endured nearly three weeks of threats and hateful taunts before they even got through the doors. Here Elizabeth Eckford tries to ignore the angry students and adults as she approaches the entrance to the school only to be blocked by the Arkansas National Guard troops. Even after Eisenhower intervened to enable the "Little Rock Nine" to attend school, they were called names, tripped, spat upon, and otherwise harassed by some white students. When Minnijean Brown, one of the black students, could take no more, she dumped a bowl of chili on a white boy who had taunted her. After she was expelled for that, cards circulated among white students reading, "One Down . . . Eight to Go."
Francis Miller/TimePix/Getty.

The *Brown* Decision

Brown v. Board of Education of Topeka *was the principal Supreme Court decision in the transformation of African Americans' legal and political status during the 1950s and 1960s. Responding to lawsuits argued by NAACP lawyers, the* Brown *ruling was the culmination of a series of Supreme Court rulings between 1938 and 1950 that chipped away at an earlier Court's decision in* Plessy v. Ferguson *(1896) permitting "separate but equal" public facilities.*

DOCUMENT 1
Brown v. Board of Education of Topeka, May 1954

In 1954, Chief Justice Earl Warren delivered the unanimous opinion of the Supreme Court in Brown v. Board of Education of Topeka, *declaring racial segregation in public education unconstitutional and explaining why.*

In these days, it is doubtful that any child may reasonably be expected to succeed in life if he is denied the opportunity of an education. Such an opportunity, if the state has undertaken to provide it, is a right that must be made available to all on equal terms. . . .

We come then to the question presented: Does segregation of children in public schools solely on the basis of race, even though the physical facilities and other "tangible" factors may be equal, deprive the children of the minority group of equal educational opportunities? We believe that it does. . . .

In *McLaurin* [a 1950 case], the Court, in requiring that a Negro ad-

mitted to a white graduate school be treated like all other students, again resorted to intangible considerations: ". . . his ability to study, to engage in discussions and exchange views with other students, and, in general, to learn his profession." Such considerations apply with added force to children in grade and high schools. To separate them from others of similar age and qualifications solely because of their race generates a feeling of inferiority as to their status in the community that may affect their hearts and minds in a way unlikely ever to be undone.

We conclude that in the field of public education the doctrine of "separate but equal" has no place. Separate educational facilities are inherently unequal.

SOURCE: *Brown,* 347 U.S. 483 (1954).

DOCUMENT 2
Southern Manifesto on Integration, March 1956

The Brown *decision, along with a second Supreme Court ruling in 1955 about implementing desegregation, outraged many southern whites. In 1956, more than one hundred members of Congress signed a manifesto pledging resistance to the rulings.*

We regard the decision of the Supreme Court in the school cases as a clear abuse of judicial power. It climaxes a trend in the Federal judiciary undertaking to legislate . . . and to encroach upon the reserved rights of the states and the people.

The original Constitution does not mention education. Neither does

the Fourteenth Amendment nor any amendment. . . . The Supreme Court of the United States, with no legal basis for such action, undertook to exercise their naked judicial power and substituted their personal political and social ideas for the established law of the land.

This unwarranted exercise of power by the court, contrary to the Constitution, is creating chaos and confusion in the states principally affected. It is destroying the amicable relations between the white and negro races that have been created through ninety years of patient effort by the good people of both races. It has planted hatred and suspicion where there has been heretofore friendship and understanding. . . .

We pledge ourselves to use all lawful means to bring about a reversal of this decision which is contrary to the Constitution and to prevent the use of force in its implementation.

SOURCE: "Southern Manifesto on Integration" (1956).

In the face of white hostility, black children carried the burden of implementing the Brown *decision. The following accounts by black students reflect varied experiences, but even those who entered white schools fairly easily found obstacles to their full participation in school activities. Nonetheless, they cherished the new opportunities, favoring integration for reasons different from those given by the Supreme Court.*

DOCUMENT 3
A High School Boy in Oak Ridge, Tennessee, 1957

I like it a whole lot better than the colored school. You have a chance to learn more and you have more sports. I play forward or guard on the basketball team, only I don't get to participate in all games. Some teams don't mind my playing. Some teams object not because of the fellows on the team, but because of the people in their community. Mostly it's the fans or the board of education that decides against me. . . . The same situation occurs in baseball. I'm catcher, but the first game I didn't get to participate in. A farm club of the major league wrote the coach that they were interested in seeing me play so maybe I'll get to play the next time.

SOURCE: Dorothy Sterling, *Tender Warriors* (New York: Hill and Wang, 1958), 83. Copyright © 1958 by Dorothy Sterling. Reprinted with permission.

DOCUMENT 4
A High School Girl in Louisville, Kentucky, 1957

I'm accepted now as an individual rather than as a person belonging to the Negro race. People say to me, "I'm glad I met you because if I met someone else I might not have liked them." I don't think it's fair, this individual acceptance. I feel like I was some ambassador from some foreign country.

I couldn't go out for any extracurricular activities. Cheerleading, band, drum majorettes, the people who are members of these organizations, they go to camps in the summer which are segregated. Well, what can you do? It just leaves me out. It's not the school, it's the community.

SOURCE: Dorothy Sterling, *Tender Warriors* (New York: Hill and Wang, 1958), 83. Copyright © 1958 by Dorothy Sterling. Reprinted with permission.

DOCUMENT 5
A High School Girl in the Deep South, May 1966

The first day a news reporter rode the bus with us. All around us were state troopers. In front of them were federal marshals. When we got to town there were lines of people and cars all along the road. A man without a badge or anything got on the bus and started beating up the newspaper reporter. . . . He was crying and bleeding. When we got to the school the students were all around looking through the windows. The mayor said we couldn't come there because the school was already filled to capacity [and] if six of us came in it would be a fire hazard. He told us to turn around and go back. We turned around and the students started yelling and clapping. When we went back [after obtaining a court order] there were no students there at all. There were only two teachers left so they had to bring a couple of teachers from other places. [The white students did not return, so the six black students finished the year by themselves.] The shocking thing was during the graduation ceremonies. All six of the students got together to make a speech. After we finished, I looked around and saw three teachers crying. The principal had tears in his eyes and he got up to make a little speech about us. He said at first he didn't think he would enjoy being around us. You could see in his face that he was really touched. We said something like we really enjoyed school together and that we were glad they stuck it out and all that kind of stuff.

SOURCE: *In Their Own Words: A Student Appraisal of What Happened after School Desegregation* (Washington, D.C.: Department of Health, Education, and Welfare, Office of Education, 1966), 17–18.

DOCUMENT 6
A High School Girl in the Deep South, May 1966

I chose to go because I felt that I could get a better education here. I knew that the [black] school that I was then attending wasn't giving me exactly what I should have had. As far as the Science Department was concerned, it just didn't have the chemicals we needed and I just decided to change. When I went over the students there weren't very friendly and when I graduated they still weren't. They didn't want us there and they made that plain, but we went there anyway and we stuck it out. The lessons there were harder, lots harder, but I studied and I managed to pass all my subjects.

SOURCE: *In Their Own Words: A Student Appraisal of What Happened after School Desegregation* (Washington, D.C.: Department of Health, Education, and Welfare, Office of Education, 1966), 44.

QUESTIONS FOR ANALYSIS AND DEBATE

1. What reasons did the Supreme Court give in favor of desegregation? What reasons did black students give for wanting to attend integrated schools? How did these reasons differ?

2. What arguments did the southern legislators make against the Supreme Court decision? Did they question its power to make the decision or the content of the decision itself?

3. What obstacles remained for African American students to confront once they had been admitted to integrated schools?

4. What conditions do you feel would be worth enduring to obtain a better education?

When word came of Parks's arrest and her decision to fight the case, WPC leaders immediately mobilized teachers and students to distribute flyers calling for Montgomery blacks to stay off the buses. E. D. Nixon called a mass meeting for December 5 at the Holt Street Baptist Church, where so many gathered that a crowd of people stretched for blocks outside. Those assembled founded the Montgomery Improvement Association (MIA) to organize a bus boycott among the African American community. The MIA ran a system of volunteer car pools and marshaled more than 90 percent of the black community to sustain the year-long boycott. It held mass meetings to keep up the spirits of those who had to depend on the car pool to get to work and back, brave bad weather on foot to keep a job or get to the grocery store, or face harassment from policemen. Jo Ann Robinson, though a cautious

> Montgomery demonstrated that blacks could sustain a lengthy protest and would not be intimidated.

driver, got seventeen traffic tickets in the space of two months.

Elected to head the MIA was Martin Luther King Jr., a newcomer to Montgomery and pastor at the Dexter Avenue Baptist Church. At only twenty-six, King had a doctorate in theology from Boston University. A captivating speaker before blacks who gathered regularly at churches throughout the boycott, King inspired their courage and commitment by linking racial justice to the redeeming power of Christian love. He promised, "If you will protest courageously and yet with dignity and Christian love . . . historians will have to pause and say, 'There lived a great people—a black people—who injected a new meaning and dignity into the veins of civilization.' This is our challenge and our overwhelming responsibility." (See "American Places," page 1015.)

Montgomery blacks summoned their courage and determination in abundance. They walked miles to get to work, contributed their meager financial resources, and stood up with dignity to

Montgomery Civil Rights Leaders

During the Montgomery bus boycott, local white officials sought to intimidate African Americans with arrests and lawsuits. Here Rosa Parks, one of ninety-two defendants, ascends the steps of the Montgomery County courthouse in March 1956, accompanied by longtime civil rights leader E. D. Nixon. He felt that Parks would be a perfect plaintiff in a suit against segregation, and Parks agreed. "The white people couldn't say that there was anything I had done to deserve such treatment except to be born black." Wide World Photos.

AMERICAN PLACES

Martin Luther King Jr. National Historic Site, Atlanta, Georgia

On January 15, 1929, Martin Luther King Jr. was born in his parents' bedroom on the second floor of a house on 501 Auburn Street in Atlanta, Georgia. King's maternal grandfather, the Reverend A. D. Williams, had bought the Queen Anne–style house in 1909, and King lived there with his parents, grandparents, older sister, and younger brother until he was twelve years old. Just two blocks away stood Ebenezer Baptist Church, a three-story red brick and stucco Gothic revival–style building, where King's father, his grandfather, and eventually King himself all served as pastors.

The house and church were part of the larger Sweet Auburn district, just east of downtown Atlanta and the center of a vibrant and achieving African American community during King's youth. At the age of thirteen, he took a segregated bus to the west side of the city to attend the only black public high school in Atlanta. Segregation restricted black Atlantans, but—as in most cities—at the same time it made possible flourishing black-owned businesses in the Auburn neighborhood, including banks, insurance companies, barber shops, laundries, drugstores, and restaurants. King remembered his neighborhood as a "wholesome community," though none of the residents were of the "upper upper

Martin Luther King Jr. Birthplace
Martin Luther King Jr. National Historic Site.

class." Yet he grew up in an environment with substantial class and occupational diversity. Black teachers, doctors, ministers, and business owners called the Auburn district home, as did domestic workers, laundry workers, and laborers. Solid Victorian houses, like the one where King was born, were interspersed with small cottages, boardinghouses, and businesses. African Americans in such neighborhoods as Auburn Street developed close community ties and a sense of collective identity that nourished the civil rights struggle.

Today visitors can walk through King's birth home, Ebenezer Baptist

Church, and the Auburn neighborhood, which have been preserved and restored as part of the Martin Luther King Jr. National Historic Site, an urban park of about thirty-eight acres established in 1980. Sweet Auburn continues as a "real" neighborhood, but along with King's house and church, several buildings have been restored to their 1930s appearance. The historic site also includes the Martin Luther King Jr. Center for Nonviolent Social Change, Inc., established in 1968 by Coretta Scott King to preserve and advance her husband's work in civil rights and human rights. Completed in 1981, the King Center complex includes a museum with artifacts from King's life, a library and archives that house his papers, and a conference center as well as King's tomb.

A visit to the Web site offers a virtual tour through the rooms of the King house and photographs and information about Ebenezer Church and the neighborhood. The Web site also contains many of King's writings, including a speech he wrote as a high school junior, "The Negro and the Constitution," which won first place in an oratorical contest sponsored by the black Elks. Exploring such documents and the streets of Sweet Auburn provides an understanding of the solid, middle-class, church-oriented community that produced Martin Luther King Jr. and fired his lifelong sense of injustice and the possibility of redemption.

FOR WEB LINKS RELATED TO THIS SITE AND OTHER AMERICAN PLACES, see "PlaceLinks" at bedfordstmartins.com/roark.

legal, economic, and physical intimidation. One older woman insisted, "I'm not walking for myself, I'm walking for my children and my grandchildren." Authorities arrested several leaders, and whites firebombed King's house. Yet the

movement persisted, and in November 1956, the Supreme Court finally declared unconstitutional Alabama's laws requiring bus segregation. Although the Montgomery movement's victory came from Washington rather than the local power structure, it had demonstrated that blacks could sustain a lengthy protest and would not be intimidated.

In January 1957, black clergy from across the South met to coordinate local protests against segregation and to secure the ballot for blacks. They founded the Southern Christian Leadership Conference (SCLC) and chose King to head it. Although dominated by ministers, the SCLC owed much of its success to Ella Baker, a seasoned activist who came from New York to set up and run its office.

King's face on the cover of *Time* magazine in February 1957 marked his rapid rise to national and international fame. He crisscrossed the nation and the world, speaking to large audiences, raising funds, and meeting with other activists. In June 1958, Eisenhower extended his first invitation to black leaders, and King and three others met with the president. Meanwhile, in the late 1950s, the SCLC, NAACP, and CORE developed centers in several southern cities, paving the way for a mass movement that would revolutionize the racial system of the South.

Martin Luther King Jr. in Montgomery

Martin Luther King Jr. preaches at the First Baptist Church during the Montgomery bus boycott. First Baptist was the congregation of Ralph D. Abernathy, the man who would become King's close associate in the crusades to come. The importance of churches as inspiration for and organizing centers in the black freedom struggle was not lost on white racists, who bombed First Baptist and three other black churches in Montgomery during the boycott.

Dan Weiner, courtesy Sandra Weiner.

Conclusion: Peace and Prosperity Mask Unmet Challenges

At the American National Exhibition in Moscow in 1959, the consumer goods that Nixon proudly displayed to Khrushchev and the cold war competition that crackled through their dialogue reflected two dominant themes of the 1950s: the prosperity of the U.S. economy and the superpowers' success in keeping cold war competition within the bounds of peace. The tremendous economic growth of the 1950s, which raised the standard of living for most Americans, resulted in part from the cold war: One of every ten American jobs depended directly on defense spending.

Affluence helped to change the very landscape of the United States. Suburban housing developments sprang up, interstate highways began to divide cities and connect the country, farms declined in number but grew in size, and population and industry moved south and west. Daily habits and even values of ordinary people changed as the economy became more service oriented and the opportunity to buy a host of new products intensified the growth of a culture based on consumption.

The general prosperity and seeming conformity, however, masked a number of developments and problems that Americans would face head-on in later years: rising resistance to an unjust racial system, a 20 percent poverty rate, the movement of married women into the labor force, and the emergence of a self-conscious youth generation. Although the federal government's defense spending and housing, highway, and education subsidies played a large role in the economic boom, in general Eisenhower tried to curb domestic programs and let private enterprise have its way. His administration maintained the welfare state inherited from the Democrats but opposed further reforms.

In global affairs, Eisenhower exercised restraint on large issues, recognizing the limits of U.S. power. In the name of **deterrence**, he promoted development of more destructive atomic weapons, but he resisted pressures for even larger defense budgets. Still, Eisenhower took from Truman the assumption that the United

States must fight communism everywhere, and when movements in Iran, Guatemala, Cuba, and Vietnam seemed too radical, too friendly to communism, or too inimical to American economic interests, he tried to undermine them, often with secret operations.

Thus, although Eisenhower presided over eight years of peace and prosperity, his foreign policy inspired anti-Americanism, established dangerous precedents for the expansion of executive power, and forged commitments that future generations would deem unwise. As Eisenhower's successors took on the struggle against communism and grappled with the domestic challenges of race, poverty, and urban decay that he had avoided, the tranquillity and consensus of the 1950s would give way to the turbulence and conflict of the 1960s.

FOR ADDITIONAL FIRSTHAND ACCOUNTS OF THIS PERIOD, see Chapter 27 in Michael Johnson, ed., *Reading the American Past*, Third Edition.

TO ASSESS YOUR MASTERY OF THE MATERIAL IN THIS CHAPTER, see the Online Study Guide at bedfordstmartins.com/roark.

FOR WEB LINKS RELATED TO TOPICS IN THIS CHAPTER, see "HistoryLinks," "DocLinks," and "PlaceLinks" at bedfordstmartins.com/roark.

CHRONOLOGY

1952
- Dwight D. Eisenhower elected president of United States.
- *I Love Lucy* becomes number-one television show.

1953
- Government implements policy of termination of special status of American Indians and relocates thousands off reservations.
- CIA engineers coup against government of Mohammed Mossadegh in Iran.

1954
- CIA stages coup against government of Jacobo Arbenz in Guatemala.
- France signs Geneva accords, withdrawing from Vietnam.
- United States organizes Southeast Asia Treaty Organization (SEATO) in wake of French defeat in Vietnam; Eisenhower administration begins aid program to government of South Vietnam.
- Government launches Operation Wetback, a series of raids designed to seek out and deport illegal immigrants from Mexico.
- Ground broken in Pennsylvania for first commercial nuclear power plant.
- In *Hernandez v. Texas*, U.S. Supreme Court declares exclusion of Mexican Americans from jury service a violation of constitutional rights.
- In *Brown v. Board of Education*, U.S. Supreme Court declares segregation in public schools unconstitutional.
- Senate condemns Senator Joseph McCarthy, effectively ending his four-year campaign of Red-baiting.

1955
- Eisenhower and Khrushchev meet in Geneva for first superpower summit since end of World War II.

1955–1956
- Montgomery, Alabama, bus boycott by African Americans focuses national attention on civil rights.

1956
- Interstate Highway and Defense System Act provides federal funds for road-building activities previously done by state and local governments.
- Eisenhower reelected by landslide to second term.
- Allen Ginsberg publishes poem *Howl*, expressing rebelliousness of Beat generation.

1957
- Martin Luther King Jr. and others found Southern Christian Leadership Conference (SCLC) to organize protests against segregation.
- Soviets launch *Sputnik*, first satellite to orbit Earth.
- Labor union membership peaks at 27.1 percent of labor force.
- Jack Kerouac publishes *On the Road*, best-selling novel of the Beat generation.

1958
- Eisenhower establishes the National Aeronautics and Space Administration (NASA).

1959
- American National Exhibition in Moscow is scene of "kitchen debate" between Nixon and Khrushchev.

1960
- Soviets shoot down U.S. U-2 spy plane, causing rift in U.S.-Soviet relations.
- Women represent one-third of labor force; 35 percent of women work outside the home.
- One-quarter of Americans live in suburbs.

BIBLIOGRAPHY

General Works

William Chafe, *The Unfinished Journey: America since World War II* (1986).

John Patrick Diggins, *The Proud Decades: America in War and Peace, 1941–1960* (1988).

Alan Ehrenhalt, *The Lost City: Discovering the Forgotten Virtues of Community in the Chicago of the 1950s* (1995).

David Halberstam, *The Fifties* (1993).

Douglas T. Miller and Marion Nowak, *The Fifties: The Way We Really Were* (1977).

J. Ronald Oakley, *God's Country: America in the Fifties* (1986).

William L. O'Neill, *American High: The Years of Confidence, 1945–1960* (1986).

James T. Patterson, *Grand Expectations: The United States, 1945–1974* (1996).

Michael S. Sherry, *In the Shadow of War: The United States since the 1930s* (1995).

Domestic Politics and Policies

Charles C. Alexander, *Holding the Line: The Eisenhower Era, 1952–1961* (1975).

Craig Allen, *Eisenhower and the Mass Media: Peace, Prosperity, and Prime-Time TV* (1993).

Stephen E. Ambrose, *Eisenhower*, vol. 2, *The President* (1984).

Jeff Broadwater, *Eisenhower and the Anti-Communist Crusade* (1992).

Robert F. Burk, *Dwight D. Eisenhower: Hero and Politician* (1986).

Fred I. Greenstein, *The Hidden-Hand Presidency: Eisenhower as Leader* (1982).

Chester J. Pach Jr. and Elmo Richardson, *The Presidency of Dwight D. Eisenhower* (rev. ed., 1991).

Geoffrey Perret, *Eisenhower* (1999).

Gary W. Reichard, *The Reaffirmation of Republicanism* (1975).

Foreign Policy

Stephen E. Ambrose, *Ike's Spies: Eisenhower and the Espionage Establishment* (1981).

Michael R. Beschloss, *Mayday: Eisenhower, Khrushchev, and the U-2 Affair* (1986).

Gunter Bischof and Saki Dockrill, eds., *Cold War Respite: The Geneva Summit of 1955* (2000).

Blanche Wiesen Cook, *The Declassified Eisenhower: A Divided Legacy of Peace and Political Warfare* (1981).

Robert A. Divine, *The Sputnik Challenge* (1993).

Michael S. Foley, *American Orientalism: The United States and the Middle East since 1945* (2002).

Steven Z. Freiberger, *Dawn over Suez: The Rise of American Power in the Middle East, 1953–1957* (1992).

George C. Herring, *America's Longest War: The United States and Vietnam, 1950–1975* (2nd rev. ed., 1986).

Richard H. Immerman, *The CIA in Guatemala* (1982).

Richard H. Immerman, *John Foster Dulles and the Diplomacy of the Cold War* (1990).

Stanley Karnow, *Vietnam: A History* (rev. ed., 1991).

Stephen Kinzer, *All the Shah's Men: An American Coup and the Roots of Middle East Terror* (2003).

Walter LaFeber, *Inevitable Revolutions: The United States in Central America* (1983).

Donald Neff, *Warriors at Suez: Eisenhower Takes America into the Middle East* (1981).

Stephen G. Rabe, *Eisenhower and Latin America: The Foreign Policy of Anticommunism* (1988).

Andrew J. Rotter, *The Path to Vietnam: Origins of the American Commitment to Southeast Asia* (1987).

David L. Snead, *The Gaither Committee, Eisenhower, and the Cold War* (1999).

Philip Taubman, *Secret Empire: Eisenhower, the C.I.A., and the Hidden Story of America's Space Espionage* (2003).

Lawrence S. Wittner, *The Struggle against the Bomb*, 2 vols. (1993, 1997).

Women, Gender Roles, and the Family

Wini Breines, *Young, White, and Miserable: Growing Up Female in the Fifties* (1992).

Stephanie Coontz, *The Way We Never Were: American Families and the Nostalgia Trip* (1992).

Barbara Ehrenreich, *The Hearts of Men: American Dreams and the Flight from Commitment* (1983).

Betty Friedan, *The Feminine Mystique* (1963).

James Howard Jones, *Alfred C. Kinsey: A Public/Private Life* (1998).

Elaine Tyler May, *Homeward Bound: American Families in the Cold War Era* (1988).

Joanne Meyerowitz, ed., *Not June Cleaver: Women and Gender in Postwar America, 1945–1960* (1994).

Steven Mintz and Susan Kellogg, *Domestic Revolutions: A Social History of American Family Life* (1988).

Arlene Skolnick, *Embattled Paradise: The American Family in an Age of Uncertainty* (1991).

Rickie Solinger, *Wake Up Little Susie: Single Pregnancy and Race before Roe v. Wade* (1992).

Economic and Social Developments

Rosalyn Baxandall and Elizabeth Ewen, *Picture Windows: How the Suburbs Happened* (2000).

Lizabeth Cohen, *A Consumers' Republic: The Politics of Mass Consumption in Postwar America* (2003).

Gail Cooper, *Air-Conditioning America: Engineers and the Controlled Environment, 1900–1960* (1998).

Ruth Schwartz Cowan, *A Social History of American Technology* (1997).

Richard O. Davies, *The Age of Asphalt: The Automobile, the Freeway, and the Condition of Metropolitan America* (1975).

Herbert Gans, *The Levittowners: Ways of Life and Politics in a New Suburban Community* (2nd ed., 1982).

Kenneth T. Jackson, *Crabgrass Frontier: The Suburbanization of the United States* (1985).

Barbara Kelly, *Expanding the American Dream: Building and Rebuilding Levittown* (1993).

Tom Lewis, *Divided Highways: Building the Interstate Highways, Transforming American Life* (1999).

Michael P. Malone and Richard W. Etulain, *The American West: A Twentieth-Century History* (1989).

Raymond A. Mohl, *Searching for the Sunbelt: Historical Perspectives on a Region* (1993).

Gerald D. Nash, *The American West in the Twentieth Century* (1973).

Adam Rome, *The Bulldozer in the Countryside: Suburban Sprawl and the Rise of American Environmentalism* (2001).

Mark H. Rose, *Interstate: Express Highway Politics, 1941–1956* (1979).

Bruce J. Schulman, *From Cotton Belt to Sunbelt: Federal Policy, Economic Development, and the Transformation of the South, 1938–1980* (1994).

Jon C. Teaford, *The Twentieth-Century American City* (1993).

Religion and Culture

Erik Barnouw, *Tube of Plenty: The Evolution of American Television* (rev. ed., 1982).

James L. Baughman, *The Republic of Mass Culture: Journalism, Film-making, and Broadcasting in America since 1941* (1997).

William Boddy, *Fifties Television: The Industry and Its Critics* (1994).

Paul Boyer, *By the Dawn's Early Light: American Thought and Culture at the Dawn of the Atomic Age* (1985).

James Campbell, *This Is the Beat Generation: New York–San Francisco–Paris* (2001).

Robert Ellwood, *The Fifties Spiritual Marketplace: American Religion in a Decade of Conflict* (1997).

Simon Frith, *Sound Effects: Youth, Leisure, and the Politics of Rock and Roll* (1981).

Serge Guilbaut, *How New York Stole the Idea of Modern Art: Abstract Expressionism, Freedom, and the Cold War* (1983).

Peter Guralnick, *Last Train to Memphis: The Rise of Elvis Presley* (1994).

Peter Guralnick, *Careless Love: The Unmaking of Elvis Presley* (1999).

James Hudnut-Beumler, *Looking for God in the Suburbs: The Religion of the American Dream and Its Critics, 1945–1965* (1994).

David Mark, *Democratic Vistas: Television in American Culture* (1984).

Karal Ann Marling, *As Seen on TV: The Visual Culture of Everyday Life in the 1950s* (1994).

Lary May, ed., *Recasting America: Culture and Politics in the Age of the Cold War* (1989).

James Miller, *Flowers in the Dustbin: The Rise of Rock and Roll, 1947–1977* (1999).

Lynn Spigel, *Make Room for TV: Television and the Family Ideal in Postwar America* (1992).

Cecelia Tichi, *Electronic Hearth: Creating an American Television Culture* (1991).

Steven Watson, *The Birth of the Beat Generation: Visionaries, Rebels, and Hipsters, 1944–1960* (1995).

Stephen J. Whitfield, *The Culture of the Cold War* (1991).

Robert Wuthnow, *The Restructuring of American Religion: Society and Faith since World War II* (1988).

Minorities and Civil Rights

Melba Patillo Beals, *Warriors Don't Cry: A Searing Memoir of the Battle to Integrate Little Rock's Central High* (1994).

Thomas Borstelmann, *The Cold War and the Color Line: American Race Relations in the Global Arena* (2001).

Taylor Branch, *Parting the Waters: America in the King Years, 1954–1963* (1988).

Robert Fredrick Burk, *The Eisenhower Administration and Black Civil Rights* (1984).

Mary L. Dudziak, *Cold War Civil Rights: Race and the Image of American Democracy* (2000).

John Egerton, *Speak Now against the Day: The Generation before the Civil Rights Movement in the South* (1994).

Adam Fairclough, *To Redeem the Soul of America: The Southern Christian Leadership Conference and Martin Luther King Jr.* (1987).

Donald L. Fixico, *Termination and Relocation: Federal Indian Policy, 1945–1960* (1986).

David J. Garrow, *Bearing the Cross: Martin Luther King Jr. and the Southern Christian Leadership Conference* (1986).

David J. Garrow, ed., *The Montgomery Boycott and the Women Who Started It: The Memoir of Jo Ann Gibson Robinson* (1987).

Arnold R. Hirsch, *Making the Second Ghetto: Race and Housing in Chicago, 1940–1960* (1998).

Richard Kluger, *Simple Justice: The History of* Brown v. Board of Education *and Black America's Struggle for Equality* (1976).

Doug McAdam, *Political Process and the Development of Black Insurgency, 1930–1970* (1982).

R. Warren Metcalf, *Termination's Legacy: The Discarded Indians of Utah* (2002).

Aldon D. Morris, *The Origins of the Civil Rights Movement: Black Communities Organizing for Change* (1984).

E. Frederick Morrow, *Black Man in the White House* (1963).

James T. Patterson, Brown v. Board of Education: *A Civil Rights Milestone and Its Troubled Legacy* (2001).

Barbara Ransby, *Ella Baker and the Black Freedom Movement* (2003).

Thomas J. Sugrue, *The Origins of the Urban Crisis: Race and Inequality in Postwar Detroit* (1996).

Mark V. Tushnet, *Making Civil Rights Law: Thurgood Marshall and the Supreme Court, 1936–1961* (1995).

Juan Williams, *Thurgood Marshall: American Revolutionary* (1998).

"COUNTRY JOE" McDONALD'S GUITAR

Music was an omnipresent element of protest movements in the 1960s. Civil rights demonstrators sang "We Shall Overcome," antiwar rallies featured folk singers, and hippies turned on to acid rock. The guitar was the central musical instrument for each kind of music: traditional African American, folk, and rock. This wooden acoustic guitar, adorned with a peace symbol, belonged to "Country Joe" McDonald, who started his band, Country Joe and the Fish, at a draft protest in Oakland, California, in 1965. The band was one of many that originated in the San Francisco Bay area, but its popularity soon spread across the country.

The Oakland Museum of California.

Reform, Rebellion, and Reaction

1960–1974

O N AUGUST 31, 1962, Fannie Lou Hamer boarded a bus carrying eighteen African Americans from Ruleville, Mississippi, to the county seat in Indianola, where they intended to register to vote. Blacks made up more than 60 percent of Sunflower County's population but only 1.2 percent of registered voters. Before young civil rights activists arrived in Ruleville to start a voter registration drive, Hamer recalled, "I didn't know that a Negro could register and vote." Her forty-five years of poverty, exploitation, and political disfranchisement typified the lives of most blacks in the rural South. The daughter of sharecroppers, Hamer began work in the cotton fields at age six, attending school in a one-room shack from December to March and only until she was twelve. In her late twenties, she married Perry Hamer and moved onto the plantation where he sharecropped. She worked in the fields, did domestic work for the plantation owner, and recorded the cotton share-croppers brought in to be weighed.

At Indianola, Hamer and her companions defied a hostile, white, gun-carrying crowd to enter the county courthouse. Using a common practice to keep blacks from the voting booth, the registrar tested Hamer on an obscure section of the state constitution. Since her schooling had not included Mississippi's constitution, she, predictably, failed the test but resolved to try again. When she arrived home, her plantation-owner boss ordered her to withdraw her registration application or get off his land. Refusing to back down, Hamer left the plantation. Ten days later, sixteen bullets flew into the home of friends who had taken her in. Refusing to be intimidated, she tried again to register (and succeeded on the third attempt), attended a civil rights leadership training conference, and began to mobilize others to vote. In 1963, she and other activists were arrested in Winona, Mississippi, and beaten so brutally that Hamer went from the jail to the hospital, refusing to see her family, except for one sister, who could not recognize her battered face.

Fannie Lou Hamer's courage and determination made her a prominent figure in a movement that shook the nation's conscience, raised hopes for change, provided a model of protest for other groups, and transformed national policy. Although the federal government often tried to curb civil rights activists, the two Democratic presidents of the 1960s favored a **progressive** government and—helped by a prosperous economy—put solving social and economic problems high on the national agenda. After John F. Kennedy was assassinated in November 1963, Lyndon B. Johnson launched the **Great Society**—a multitude of efforts to promote racial justice, education, medical

Mississippi Freedom Democratic Party Rally
Fannie Lou Hamer (left foreground) and other activists sing at a rally outside the Democratic National Convention hall in 1964, supporting the Mississippi Freedom Democratic Party (MFDP) in its challenge to the all-white delegation sent by the regular Mississippi Democratic Party. Next to Hamer is Eleanor Holmes Norton, a civil rights lawyer, and Ella Baker (far right), who helped organize the Southern Christian Leadership Conference and later managed MFDP headquarters in Washington, D.C.
Matt Herron/Take Stock.

care, urban development, and environmental and economic health. Those who struggled for racial justice lost property, personal safety, and sometimes their lives, but by the end of the decade, law had caught up with the American ideal of equality.

Yet legal change did not go far enough. Strong civil rights legislation and pathbreaking Supreme Court decisions affected little the deplorable economic conditions of African Americans, on which Hamer and others increasingly focused after 1965. Nor was the political establishment a consistently reliable ally, as Hamer found out in 1964 when President Johnson and his allies rebuffed black Mississippi Democrats' efforts to be represented at the Democratic National Convention. "We followed all the laws that the white people themselves made," she said, only to find that "the white man is not going to give up his power to us. . . . We have to take for ourselves." By 1966, a minority

of African American activists were demanding black power; the movement soon splintered, and white support sharply declined. A growing number of **conservatives** protested that the Great Society went too far and condemned the challenge to American values and institutions mounted by blacks, students, and others.

Although disillusioned and often frustrated, Fannie Lou Hamer remained an activist until her death in 1977, mingling with new social movements stimulated by the black freedom struggle. In 1969, she supported Mississippi Valley State College students' demands for black studies courses and a greater voice in campus decisions. In 1972, she attended the founding conference of the National Women's Political Caucus, established to achieve greater representation for women in government. The caucus was part of a much broader feminist movement emerging during the period, one that promoted a revolution in women's legal status as well as important changes in the everyday relationships between women and men.

Feminists and other groups, including ethnic minorities, environmentalists, and gays and lesbians, benefited and borrowed from the ideas, tactics, and policy precedents of the civil rights movement. These movements helped to carry the tide of reform into the 1970s and to push the Republican administration of Richard M. Nixon to sustain the **liberalism** of the 1960s with its emphasis on a strong government role in regulating the economy and guaranteeing the welfare and rights of all individuals. Despite its conservative rhetoric designed to ride a backlash against increasing the authority of government to solve social problems, the Nixon administration would implement school desegregation and **affirmative action** and adopt pathbreaking measures in such areas as environmental regulation, equality for women, and justice for Native Americans. The years between 1960 and 1974 contained the greatest efforts to reconcile America's promise with reality since the New Deal.

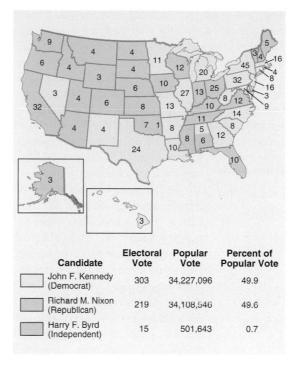

Candidate	Electoral Vote	Popular Vote	Percent of Popular Vote
John F. Kennedy (Democrat)	303	34,227,096	49.9
Richard M. Nixon (Republican)	219	34,108,546	49.6
Harry F. Byrd (Independent)	15	501,643	0.7

MAP 28.1 The Election of 1960

Liberalism at High Tide

At the Democratic National Convention in 1960, John F. Kennedy announced that the United States faced "a New Frontier . . . of unfulfilled hopes and threats," and he promised to confront "unsolved problems of peace and war, unconquered pockets of ignorance and prejudice, unanswered questions of poverty and surplus." Four years later, Lyndon B. Johnson invoked the ideal of a "Great Society, [which] rests on abundance and liberty for all [and] demands an end to poverty and racial injustice." Acting under the liberal faith that government could and should use its power to solve social and economic problems, end injustice, and promote the welfare of all citizens, the Democratic administrations of the 1960s won legislation on civil rights, poverty, education, medical care, housing, consumer protection, and environmental protection.

The Promise and Substance of Kennedy's New Frontier

John F. Kennedy grew up in privilege, the child of an Irish Catholic businessman who served in Franklin D. Roosevelt's administration and nourished political ambitions for his sons. Helped by a distinguished World War II navy record, Kennedy won election to the House of Representatives in 1946 and the Senate in 1952. His record in Congress was unremarkable, but with a powerful political machine, his family's fortunes, and a handsome and dynamic appearance, Kennedy won the Democratic presidential nomination in 1960. He stunned many Democrats by choosing as his running mate Lyndon B. Johnson of Texas, who had bid for the presidency himself and was detested by liberals who viewed him as a typical southern conservative.

Kennedy defeated his Republican opponent, Vice President Richard M. Nixon, in an excruciatingly close election (Map 28.1). African American voters contributed to his victory, helping to offset the 52 percent of the white vote cast for Nixon and contributing to his 120,000-vote margin overall and to close victories in such key states as Illinois and Michigan. Lyndon Johnson helped the ticket carry most of the South, and a rise in unemployment in 1960 also favored the Democrats. Finally, Kennedy benefited from the nation's first televised presidential debates, appearing cool, confident, and in command of the issues, beside a nervous, sweaty, and pale Nixon.

The Kennedy administration projected energy, idealism, and glamour, though in fact Kennedy was a cautious, pragmatic politician.

The first president to hold live televised press conferences, Kennedy charmed the press corps and the people with his grace, vigor, and self-mocking wit. He kept hidden from the public serious health problems as well as affairs with several women, recklessly making himself vulnerable to blackmail and risking the dignity of his office. Journalists turned a blind eye, instead projecting warm images of an energetic, youthful president with his chic and cultured wife, Jacqueline.

At his inauguration, the forty-three-year-old Kennedy declared that a "new generation" was assuming leadership and called on Americans to cast off complacency and self-indulgence and serve the common good. "Ask not what your country can do for you," he implored, "ask what you can do for your country." Though Kennedy's idealism inspired many, especially the young, to replace self-interest with service to a larger cause, he failed to redeem campaign promises to expand the **welfare state**. Nor did he assume leadership on behalf of racial justice until late in his term, when civil rights activists gave him no choice. Referring to a book by Kennedy, *Profiles in Courage* (1956), liberals jokingly disparaged his leadership by suggesting that he show "less profile and more courage."

Kennedy did win support for a $2 billion slum clearance and urban renewal program; for the Area Redevelopment Act of 1961, offering incentives to businesses to locate in depressed areas; and for the Manpower Development and Training Act of 1962, which provided training for the unemployed. But two important items on the Democratic agenda since the Truman administration, federal aid to education and health care for the elderly, got nowhere.

Kennedy had promised to "get this country moving again," making economic growth a key objective. "A rising tide lifts all boats" expressed Kennedy's belief that economic growth could eradicate poverty and solve most social problems. He also focused on growth to make the nation more competitive with the Soviet Union. Economic advisers argued that infusing money into the economy by reducing taxes would increase demand, boost production, and decrease unemployment. To that end, Kennedy asked Congress to pass an enormous tax cut in 1963. This use of fiscal policy to stimulate the economy even when there was no recession gained the name "the new economics."

> Though Kennedy's idealism inspired many to replace self-interest with service to a larger cause, he failed to redeem campaign promises to expand the welfare state. Nor did he assume leadership on behalf of racial justice until late in his term.

The Kennedy Appeal
The youth and glamour of the Kennedy administration are apparent in this photo of the president and his wife attired for his inauguration gala. The gown that Jacqueline Kennedy had designed by Oleg Cassini for the occasion bore a cockade at the waist, indicating her French ancestry and keen interest in history and culture, which were reflected in White House social events that elevated Washington's cultural scene by featuring artists, writers, scholars, and musicians throughout the Kennedy presidency. The president was well aware of his wife's appeal to the public, asking the driver of their limousine to "turn on the lights so they can see Jackie."
© Bettmann/Corbis.

John F. Kennedy's Funeral
For a few days following November 22, 1963, normal life stopped in the United States. Schools and businesses were closed, and tens of thousands of Americans traveled to Washington, D.C., to file past Kennedy's coffin in the rotunda of the Capitol. The relatively new medium of television unified the nation, as it allowed millions of viewers to experience every moment of that long, terrible weekend, culminating in the funeral procession, shown here. The president's widow, Jacqueline Kennedy, is escorted in the procession by the president's brothers Robert (left) and Edward (right).
© Henri Dauman, 1963, NYC.

Kennedy did not live to see approval of his bill. Passed in February 1964, the law contributed to the greatest economic boom since World War II. Unemployment dropped to 4.1 percent, and the gross national product shot up by 7 to 9 percent annually between 1964 and 1966. Some liberal critics of the tax cut, however, maintained that economic growth alone would not eliminate poverty, arguing instead for increased spending on social programs.

Poverty had gained Kennedy's attention in 1960, when he campaigned in Appalachia for the votes of the rural poor. In 1962, he read *The Other America*, in which the political activist Michael Harrington described the poverty of more than one in every five Americans "maimed in body and spirit, existing at levels beneath those necessary for human decency." During the summer of 1963, Kennedy asked aides to plan an attack on poverty, and he also issued a dramatic call for a comprehensive civil rights bill, marking a turning point in his attitude toward domestic problems. Whether he could have achieved these breakthroughs was left unanswered by his assassination on November 22, 1963.

Assassination of a President

The murder of the president touched Americans as had no other event since the end of World War II. Within minutes of the shooting—which occurred as the Kennedy motorcade passed through Dallas, Texas, on November 22, 1963— radio and television broadcast the unfolding horror to the nation. Millions watched the return of *Air Force One* to Washington bearing the president's coffin, his widow in her bloodstained suit, and the new president, Lyndon Baines Johnson.

Stunned Americans struggled with what had happened and why. Soon after the assassination, police arrested Lee Harvey Oswald and concluded that he had fired the shots from a nearby building. Two days later, as a television audience watched Oswald being transferred from one jail to another, a local nightclub operator, Jack Ruby, killed him. Suspicions arose that Ruby murdered Oswald to cover up a conspiracy by ultraconservative Texans who hated Kennedy, or by Communists who supported Castro's Cuba. To get at the truth, President

Johnson appointed a commission headed by Chief Justice Earl Warren, which concluded in September 1964 that both Oswald and Ruby had acted alone. Although several experts pointed to errors and omissions in the report, and some contested the lone-killer explanation, most scholars agreed that no conspiracy had existed.

Debate continued over how to assess Kennedy's domestic record. It had been unremarkable in his first two years, but his initiatives on taxes, civil rights, and poverty in 1963 suggested an important shift. Whether Kennedy could have persuaded Congress to enact his proposals cannot be known. In the words of journalist James Reston, "What was killed was not only the president but the promise. . . . He never reached his meridian: We saw him only as a rising sun."

Johnson Fulfills the Kennedy Promise

Lyndon Johnson assumed the presidency with a wealth of political experience. A self-made man from the Texas hill country, he had won election to the House of Representatives in 1937 and to the Senate in 1948. By 1955, he had secured the top post of Senate majority leader, which he used brilliantly to forge a Democratic consensus on the Civil Rights Acts of 1957 and 1960 and other programs.

Johnson's coarse wit, extreme vanity, and Texas accent repulsed those who preferred the sophisticated Kennedy style. Lacking his predecessor's eloquence, Johnson excelled behind the scenes, where he could entice or threaten legislators into support of his objectives. The famous "Johnson treatment" became legendary (see photograph to the right). In his ability to

The "Johnson Treatment"
Abe Fortas, a distinguished lawyer who had argued a major criminal rights case, *Gideon v. Wainwright* (1963), before the Supreme Court, was a close friend and adviser to President Lyndon Johnson. This photograph of the president and Fortas taken in July 1965 illustrates how Johnson used his body as well as his voice to bend people to his will.
Yoichi R. Okamoto/LBJ Library Collection.

achieve consensus around his goals—and in the means to which he was willing to resort—he had few peers in American history.

"I had to take the dead man's program and turn it into a martyr's cause," Johnson declared, entreating Congress to act so that "John Fitzgerald Kennedy did not live or die in vain." By trimming the federal budget and promising government frugality, he won over fiscal conservatives and signed Kennedy's tax cut bill in February 1964. Still more revolutionary was the Civil Rights Act of July 1964, the strongest such measure since Reconstruction, and one requiring every ounce of Johnson's political skills to pry sufficient votes from Republicans to balance the "nays" of southern Democrats.

Fast on the heels of the Civil Rights Act came a response to Johnson's call for "an unconditional war on poverty." The Economic Opportunity Act of 1964 authorized ten programs under a newly created Office of Economic Opportunity, allocating $800 million for the first year (about 1 percent of the federal budget). Many provisions targeted impoverished youth—from Head Start, a preschool program, to work-study grants for college students and a Job Corps providing job training. There were also loans to businesses willing to hire the long-term unemployed; aid to small farmers; and the Volunteers in Service to America (VISTA) program, which paid modest wages to volunteers working with the disadvantaged. A legal services program provided lawyers for the poor, leading to lawsuits that enforced their rights to welfare programs.

The most novel and controversial part of the law, the Community Action Program (CAP), required "maximum feasible participation" of the poor themselves in antipoverty programs, thus challenging the system itself. Poor people began to organize community action programs to take control of their neighborhoods and to make welfare agencies, school boards, police departments, and housing authorities more accountable to the people they served. When mayors complained that activists were challenging local governments and "fostering class struggle," Johnson backed off from pushing genuine representation for the poor. Nonetheless, CAP gave people usually excluded from government an opportunity to act on their own behalf and to develop leadership skills. To a Mississippi sharecropper who left school to work before he learned to read and write, a local CAP literacy program provided basic skills and self-respect. It "has meant more to me than I can express," he said. "I can now write my name and I will be able to help my younger children when they start school."

Completing the Great Society Agenda

Having steered the nation through the assassination trauma and established his capacity for national leadership, Johnson projected stability and security in the midst of a booming economy. Few voters wanted to risk the dramatic change promised by his Republican opponent in the 1964 election, Arizona senator Barry M. Goldwater, who attacked the welfare state and suggested using nuclear weapons if necessary to crush **communism** in Vietnam. Although Goldwater captured five southern states, Johnson achieved a record-breaking landslide of 61 percent of the popular vote, and Democrats won resounding majorities in the House (295–140) and Senate (68–32). Yet, as we shall see in chapter 30, Goldwater's campaign aroused considerable grassroots support, contributing to the growth and ultimate ascendancy of conservatism in national politics.

"I want to see a whole bunch of coonskins on the wall," Johnson told his aides, using a hunting analogy to stress his ambitious legislative goals that would usher in what he called the "Great Society." In the sheer amount and breadth of new laws, Johnson succeeded mightily, persuading Congress to act on discrimination, poverty, education, medical care, housing, consumer and environmental protections, and more. Public opinion polls gave unusually high marks to both the president and Congress. Reporters called the legislation of the Eighty-ninth Congress (1965–1966) "a political miracle."

The Economic Opportunity Act of 1964 was the opening shot in the war on poverty. Congress doubled the program's funding in 1965 and passed two new initiatives—the Appalachian Regional Development Act and the Public Works and Economic Development Act. Targeting depressed regions that the general economic boom had bypassed, these measures—like the tax cut of 1964—sought to help the poor indirectly by stimulating economic growth and providing jobs through road building and other public works projects.

A second approach endeavored to equip the poor with the skills necessary to find jobs. The largest assault on poverty through education was the Elementary and Secondary Education Act of 1965, which for the first time authorized federal funds to aid school districts. The law allocated dollars based on the number of poor children whom districts educated, and it provided equipment and supplies to private and parochial schools to be used for poor children. That same year, Congress passed the Higher Education Act, vastly expanding federal assistance to colleges and universities for buildings, programs, scholarships, and low-interest student loans.

Other antipoverty efforts provided direct aid, like a new food stamp program that largely replaced surplus food distribution, giving poor people greater choice in obtaining food. Rent supplements also allowed some poor families more options, enabling them to avoid public housing projects. In addition, with the Model Cities Act, Congress authorized more than $1 billion to improve conditions in the nation's slums.

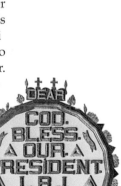

The federal government's responsibility for health care grew even more. Trimming Truman's proposed plan for government-sponsored universal care, Johnson focused on the elderly, who constituted a large portion of the nation's poor. Congress responded with the Medicare program, providing the elderly with universal compulsory medical insurance financed largely through Social Security taxes. A separate program, Medicaid, authorized federal grants to supplement state-paid medical care for poor people under sixty-five.

A Tribute to Johnson for Medicare
George Niedermeyer, who lived in Hollywood, Florida, and received a Social Security pension, painted wood pieces and glued them together to create this thank-you to President Johnson for establishing Medicare. He entrusted his congressional representative, Claude Pepper, known for his support for the interests of the elderly, to deliver the four-foot tall tribute to Johnson in 1967.
LBJ Library, photo by Henry Groskinsky.

The assumption of national responsibility for social justice also underlay key civil rights legislation. Pressured by the black freedom struggle, Johnson got Congress to pass the Voting Rights Act of 1965, which banned literacy tests like the one that stymied Fannie Lou Hamer, and authorized federal intervention to ensure access to the voting booth. Another form of discrimination fell with the Immigration and Nationality Act of 1965, which abolished fifty-year-old quotas based on national origins that were biased against immigrants from areas outside northern and western Europe. It maintained caps on the number of immigrants and for the first time limited those from the Western Hemisphere; yet the law made possible a tremendous—and unanticipated—surge of immigration near the end of the century (see chapter 31).

> Measured by statistics, the reduction in poverty in the 1960s was considerable.

Great Society benefits reached well beyond the poverty-stricken and victims of discrimination. Medicare covered the elderly, regardless of income. In 1965, liberal activist and future Green Party presidential candidate Ralph Nader published *Unsafe at Any Speed*, an exposé and indictment of the automobile industry; he and others led a growing consumer movement that won legislation to make automobiles safer and to raise standards for the food, drug, and cosmetics industries. In 1965, Johnson became the first president to send Congress a special message on the environment, obtaining measures to control water and air pollution and to preserve the natural beauty of the American landscape. The National Arts and Humanities Act of 1965 funded artists, musicians, writers, and scholars and brought their work to public audiences.

The flood of reform legislation dwindled to a trickle after 1966, when midterm elections trimmed the Democrats' majorities in Congress and a backlash against government programs arose. Even though most poor people were white, whites tended to associate antipoverty programs with African Americans and expressed their opposition with buttons reading "I fight poverty—I work." The Vietnam War dealt the largest blow to Johnson's ambitions, diverting his attention from domestic affairs, spawning an antiwar movement that crippled his leadership, devouring tax dollars, increasing the **federal deficit**, and fueling inflation.

Against these odds, in 1968 Johnson pried out of Congress one more civil rights law, which banned discrimination in housing and jury service. He also signed the National Housing Act of 1968, which authorized an enormous increase in construction of low-income housing—1.7 million units over three years—and by leaving construction and ownership in private hands, a new way of providing it. Government-guaranteed low-interest loans spurred developers to build housing for the needy and enabled poor people to purchase those houses.

Assessing the War on Poverty

Measured by statistics, the reduction in poverty in the 1960s was considerable. The number of impoverished Americans fell from forty million in 1959 to twenty-five million in 1968, from over 20 percent of the population to around 13 percent (Figure 28.1). Especially through the community action programs, those whom Johnson had said "lived on the outskirts of hope" gained more control of their circumstances and a sense of their right to a fairer share of America's bounty. One observer remarked on a new "mood of applicants in welfare waiting rooms. . . . They were no longer as humble, as self-effacing, as pleading." Rosemary Bray described another new attitude, writing about her family that "five people on welfare for eighteen years had become five working, taxpaying adults" by 1980. Attributing that achievement to a number of factors, including her mother's sheer will and ability to stretch a handful of coins into an adequate meal, she concluded, "What fueled our dreams and fired our belief that our lives could change for the better was the promise of the civil rights movement and the war on poverty."

Certain groups fared much better than others, however. Large numbers of the aged and members of male-headed families rose out of poverty, while the plight of female-headed families actually worsened. Although African American family income grew from 54 percent of white family income to 61 percent, whites escaped poverty at a faster rate than blacks, who constituted one-third of the poor population in the 1970s. Moreover, as Johnson had intended, no significant redistribution of income resulted, despite large increases in subsidies for food stamps, housing, medical care, and the **New Deal** program Aid to Families with Dependent Children (AFDC). The poorest 20 percent of the population received 5.1 percent of total national income in 1964 and 5.4 percent in 1974.

Conservatives charged that Great Society programs discouraged initiative by giving the poor "handouts." George Gilder, for example, insisted, "The only dependable route from poverty is always work, family, and faith." Critics on the left claimed that the emphasis on training and education placed the responsibility for poverty on the poor themselves rather than on an economic system that could not provide enough adequately paying jobs. Most training programs prepared graduates for low-level jobs and could not guarantee employment. Surveys in 1966 and 1967, for example, found 28 percent of Job Corps graduates unemployed six months after finishing their training.

Who reaped the greatest benefits from Great Society programs? Most of the funds for economically depressed areas built highways and thus helped the construction industry. Real estate developers, investors, and moderate-income families benefited most from the National Housing Act of 1968. As commercial development and high-income housing often displaced the poor in slum clearance programs, blacks called urban renewal "Negro removal." Physicians' fees and hospital costs soared after enactment of Medicare and Medicaid.

Some critics argued that ending poverty required a redistribution of income—raising taxes and using those funds to create jobs, overhaul social welfare systems, and rebuild slums. Great Society programs did invest more heavily in the public sector, but Johnson's antipoverty efforts relied on economic growth rather than new taxes on the rich or middle class to increase revenues. Determined to avoid conflict, Johnson would not take from the advantaged to provide for the poor. Economic prosperity allowed spending for the poor to rise and significantly improved the lives of millions, but that spending never approached the amounts necessary to claim victory in the War on Poverty. Johnson himself conceded as much, but he insisted, "no one would ever again be able to ignore the poverty in our midst."

The Judicial Revolution

A key element of liberalism's ascendency during the Kennedy and Johnson years emerged in the

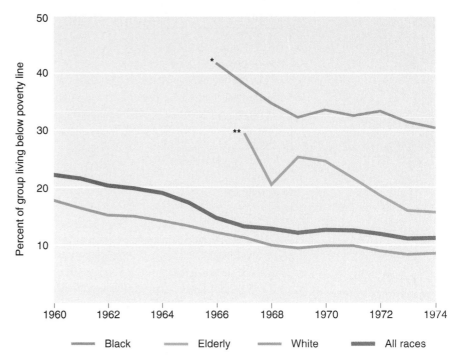

*Statistics on blacks for years 1960–1965 not available.
**Statistics on the elderly for years 1960–1966 not available.

FIGURE 28.1 Poverty in the United States, 1960–1974
The short-term effects of economic growth and the Great Society's attack on poverty are seen here. Which groups experienced the sharpest decline in poverty, and what might account for the differences?

Supreme Court under Chief Justice Earl Warren, who presided from 1953 to 1969. Expanding the Constitution's promise of equality and individual rights, the Court's decisions supported an activist government to prevent injustice and discrimination and provided new protections to disadvantaged groups and accused criminals. Following the path-breaking *Brown* school desegregation decision of 1954 (see chapter 27), the Court ruled against all-white public facilities and struck down educational plans devised by southern states to avoid integration. The Court also upheld the rights of freedom of assembly and speech, thereby enabling the black freedom struggle to continue sit-ins, mass marches, and other tactics critical to its success.

Chief Justice Warren considered *Baker v. Carr* (1963) his most important decision. The case grew out of a complaint that Tennessee electoral districts were so inequitably drawn that sparsely

> The Court's decisions supported an activist government to prevent injustice and discrimination and provided new protections to disadvantaged groups and accused criminals.

Reforms of the Great Society, 1964–1968

1964

Twenty-fourth Amendment	Abolishes poll tax as prerequisite for voting.
Tax Reduction Act	Provides $10 billion in tax cuts over 1964–1965.
Civil Rights Act	Bans discrimination in public accommodations, public education, and employment and extends protections to Indians on reservations.
Economic Opportunity Act	Creates programs for the disadvantaged, including Head Start, VISTA, Job Corps, and CAP.
Wilderness Preservation Act	Sets aside 9.1 million acres of national forest for protection.

1965

Elementary and Secondary Education Act	Provides $1.3 billion in aid to elementary and secondary schools.
Medical Care Act	Provides health insurance (Medicare) for all citizens age 65 and over. Extends federal health benefits to welfare recipients (Medicaid).
Voting Rights Act	Bans literacy tests and other voting tests and authorizes the federal government to act directly to enable African Americans to register and vote.
Executive Order 11246	Bans discrimination on the basis of race, religion, and national origin by employers awarded government contracts and requires them to "take affirmative action to ensure equal opportunity."
Department of Housing and Urban Development (HUD)	New government department created to provide programs to address housing and community issues.
National Arts and Humanities Act	Creates National Endowment for the Humanities (NEH) and National Endowment for the Arts (NEA) to support the work of artists, musicians, writers, and scholars.
Water Quality Act	Requires states to set and enforce water quality standards.
Immigration and Nationality Act	Abolishes fifty-year-old quotas based on national origins, increasing the number of non-Western and southern and eastern European immigrants.
Air Quality Act	Imposes air pollution standards for motor vehicles.
Higher Education Act	Expands federal assistance to colleges and universities.

1966

National Traffic and Motor Vehicle Safety Act	Establishes federal safety standards.
Highway Safety Act	Requires federally approved safety programs at the state level.
Department of Transportation	New government department created to administer transportation programs and policies.
Model Cities Act	Authorizes more than $1 billion to ameliorate nation's slums.

1967

Executive Order 11375	Extends earlier executive order banning discrimination and requiring affirmative action by federal contractors to cover women.

1968

Civil Rights Act of 1968	Bans discrimination in housing and in jury service.
National Housing Act	Subsidizes the private construction of 1.7 million units of low-income housing.

populated rural districts had far more representatives than densely populated urban areas. Using the Fourteenth Amendment guarantee of "equal protection of the laws," the Court in *Baker* and companion cases established the principle of "one person, one vote" both for state legislatures and for the House of Representatives. President Kennedy publicly endorsed the decision, claiming that "the right to have each vote count equally is basic to the successful operation of a democracy." Most states were required to redraw electoral districts, helping to make state legislatures more responsive to metropolitan interests.

The egalitarian thrust of the Warren Court also touched the criminal justice system as it overturned a series of convictions on the grounds that the accused had been deprived of "life, liberty, or property, without due process of law," a denial of their Fourteenth Amendment rights. Furthermore, the Court decided that states as well as the federal government were subject to the Bill of Rights, with rulings that transformed law enforcement practices and the treatment of individuals accused of crime. In *Gideon v. Wainwright* (1963) (see appendix, page A-43), the Court ruled that when accused criminals could not afford to hire lawyers, states must provide them without charge. In *Escobedo v. Illinois* (1964), the justices extended the right to counsel to the period when suspects are being questioned by police officers. Two years later, in *Miranda v. Arizona* (see appendix, page A-43), the Court ruled that officers must inform suspects of their rights upon arrest; and it overturned convictions based on evidence obtained by unlawful arrest, by electronic surveillance, or without a search warrant.

As Supreme Court decisions overturned judicial precedents and often moved ahead of public opinion, critics accused the justices of obstructing law enforcement and letting criminals go free. Sam Yorty, the mayor of Los Angeles, for example, equated *Miranda* with "handcuffing the police." Liberals, however, argued that these rulings promoted equal treatment in the criminal justice system: The wealthy always had access to legal counsel, and practiced criminals were well aware of their right to remain silent. The beneficiaries of the decisions were the poor and the ignorant, as well as the general population, whose right to privacy was strengthened by the Court's stricter guidelines for admissible evidence.

The Warren Court also fortified protections for people suspected of being Communists or subversives, setting limits, for example, on government officials who investigated and prosecuted them. Like the criminal justice cases, these rulings guaranteed the rights of people on the margins of American society and aroused opposition.

The Court's decisions on prayer and Bible reading in public schools provoked even greater outrage. In *Abington School District v. Schempp* (1963), it overturned a Pennsylvania law requiring Bible reading and prayer in the schools as a violation of the First Amendment principle of separation of church and state. The evangelist Billy Graham charged that the Court was "taking God and moral teaching from the schools." Later decisions ruled out official prayer in public schools even if students were not required to participate. Even though these decisions left students free to pray on their own, an infuriated Alabama legislator cried, "They put Negroes in the schools and now they've driven God out." The Court's supporters, however, declared that the religion cases protected the rights of non-Christians and atheists.

Two or three justices who believed that the Court was overstepping its authority often issued sharp dissents. Outside the Court, opponents worked to pass laws or constitutional amendments that would upset despised decisions, and billboards demanded, "Impeach Earl Warren." Nonetheless, the Court's major decisions withstood Warren's retirement in 1969 and the test of time.

The Second Reconstruction

Before the Great Society reforms of the mid-1960s—and, in fact, contributing to them—African Americans had already mobilized a movement that struck down legal separation and discrimination in the South. While the first Reconstruction in the aftermath of the Civil War reflected the power of northern Republicans, the second Reconstruction depended heavily on the courage and determination of black people themselves. In the words of Sheyann Webb, one of thousands of marchers in the 1965 Selma, Alabama, campaign for voting rights, "We were just people, ordinary people, and we did it."

The early black freedom struggle, focused on legal rights in the South, won widespread acceptance. But when African Americans began to attack racial injustice in the rest of the country as well as the deplorable economic conditions that equal rights left untouched, a strong backlash developed as the movement itself lost cohesion.

The Flowering of the Black Freedom Struggle

The Montgomery bus boycott of 1955–1956 gave racial issues national visibility, produced a leader in Martin Luther King Jr., and demonstrated the effectiveness of mass organization. In the 1960s, protest expanded dramatically, mobilizing blacks into direct and personal confrontation with the people and institutions that segregated and discriminated against them: lunch counters, department stores, public parks and libraries, buses and depots, voting registrars, and police forces.

Massive direct action began in February 1960, when four African American students at North Carolina A&T College in Greensboro requested service at the whites-only Woolworth's lunch counter. Within days, hundreds of young people joined their demonstration, and others launched sit-ins in thirty-one cities in eight southern states. In April, Ella Baker, executive secretary of the Southern Christian Leadership Conference (SCLC), called activists together from campuses across the South. Choosing independence from the older civil rights organizations, they founded the Student Nonviolent Coordinating Committee (SNCC, pronounced "snick"), creating a decentralized, nonhierarchical structure that encouraged leadership and decision making at the grassroots level.

Lunch Counter Sit-in
John Salter Jr., a professor at Tougaloo College, and students Joan Trumpauer and Anne Moody take part in a 1963 sit-in at the Woolworth's lunch counter in Jackson, Mississippi. Shortly before this photograph was taken, whites had thrown two students to the floor, and police had arrested one student. Salter was spattered with mustard and ketchup. Moody would publish a popular book in 1968 about her experiences in the black freedom struggle, *Coming of Age in Mississippi*.
State Historical Society of Wisconsin.

FOR MORE HELP ANALYZING THIS IMAGE, see the visual activity for this chapter in the Online Study Guide at bedfordstmartins.com/roark.

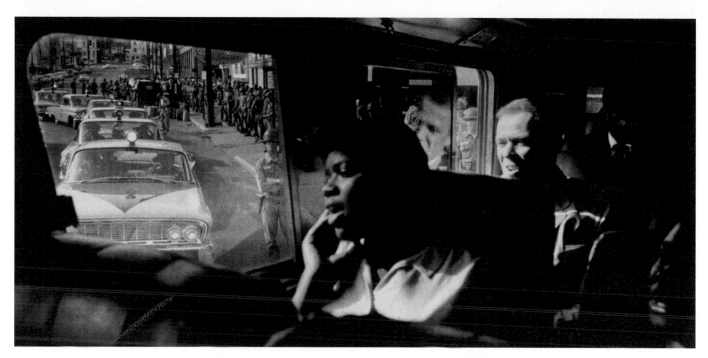

Freedom Riders

In 1961, black and white activists embarked on Freedom Rides into the South in an effort to implement the Supreme Court decision that declared segregation in interstate travel unconstitutional. When angry whites in Alabama attacked them with clubs, iron bars, and smoke bombs, the Kennedy administration sent agents to investigate and pressed state officials to protect the riders, while at the same time urging activists to stop the rides for a while. In this photo, the Freedom Riders sing while Alabama state police and national guardsmen escort their bus. Protection was sporadic, however. After a bus carrying SNCC activists arrived in Montgomery, the escort disappeared, and a white mob set upon the riders. The riders persisted, nonetheless. Several hundred reached Jackson, Mississippi, where they were arrested; 300 served time in Mississippi jails.

Bruce Davidson/Magnum Photos, Inc.

SNCC initially embraced civil disobedience and the nonviolence principles of Martin Luther King Jr. Students would directly confront their oppressors and stand up for their rights, but they would not respond if attacked. At SNCC's founding conference, James Lawson explained how that strategy could change the hearts of racists: "We affirm . . . nonviolence as a foundation of our purpose, the presupposition of our faith, and the manner of our action." With its appeal to human conscience, "nonviolence nurtures the atmosphere in which reconciliation and justice become actual possibilities."

The activists' optimism and commitment to nonviolence soon underwent severe testing. Although some cities quietly met student demands, more typically the students encountered violence. Hostile whites poured food over demonstrators, burned them with cigarettes, called them "niggers," and pelted them with rocks. Local police went after protesters with dogs, clubs, fire hoses, and tear gas; they arrested more than 3,600 civil rights demonstrators in the year following the Greensboro sit-in.

In May 1961, the Congress of Racial Equality (CORE) organized Freedom Rides to integrate interstate transportation in the South. Six whites and seven blacks boarded two buses in Washington, D.C., bound for New Orleans. When they got to Alabama, white hoodlums bombed a bus and beat the riders with baseball bats. After a huge mob attacked the activists in Montgomery, Attorney General Robert Kennedy dispatched federal marshals to restore order. But when the buses reached Jackson, Mississippi, the Freedom Riders

Civil Rights Freedom Rides, May 1961

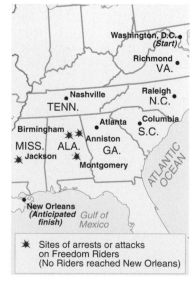

were promptly arrested, and several hundred spent part of the summer in Mississippi jails.

Encouraged by Kennedy administration officials who viewed voter registration as less controversial than civil disobedience (and more likely to benefit the Democratic Party), SNCC and other groups began a Voter Education Project in the summer of 1961. Seeking to register black voters in the Deep South, they too met violence. Whites bombed black churches, threw tenant farmers out of their homes, and beat and jailed activists like Fannie Lou Hamer. In June 1963, a white man gunned down Mississippi NAACP leader Medgar Evers in front of his house in Jackson; the murderer eluded conviction until the 1990s.

Television revealed to the world the brutality of southern resistance to racial equality in April 1963, when Martin Luther King Jr. launched a campaign in Birmingham, Alabama, to integrate public facilities and open jobs to African Americans. The city's police chief, Eugene "Bull" Connor, responded with police dogs, electric cattle prods, and high-pressure hoses. Hundreds of demonstrators, including children, went to jail, and firebombs exploded at King's motel and his brother's house. Four months later, a bomb killed four black girls attending Sunday school in Birmingham.

The largest demonstration drew 250,000 blacks and whites to the nation's capital in August 1963, where King put his indelible stamp on the day. Speaking from the Lincoln Memorial and invoking the Bible, Negro spirituals, and the nation's patriotic anthems, King drew on all the passion and skills that made him the greatest orator of his day. "I have a dream," he repeated again and again, that "the sons of former slaves and the sons of former slave owners will be

> The largest civil rights demonstration drew 250,000 blacks and whites to the nation's capital in August 1963, where King put his indelible stamp on the day.

The March on Washington

More than a quarter of a million Americans, including 50,000 whites, gathered on the Mall in the nation's capital on August 28, 1963, to pressure the government to support African Americans' civil rights. Here, Martin Luther King Jr. is about to mesmerize the crowd with his "I have a dream" speech. Afterward, Malcom X said to march organizer Bayard Rustin, "You know this dream of King's is going to be a nightmare before it's over."

Francis Miller/TimePix/Getty.

The Selma March for Voting Rights
In 1963, the Student Nonviolent Coordinating Committee (SNCC) began a campaign for voting rights in Selma, Alabama, where white officials had registered only 335 of the 15,000 African Americans of voting age. As often happened, after younger activists had gotten things started, Martin Luther King Jr. came to Selma in January 1965. He planned a fifty-four-mile march from Selma to Montgomery, the state capital, to insist that blacks be registered, but, warned of a serious threat on his life, he did not lead the march. In this photo, young African Americans carrying the flag march with nuns, priests, and other supporters. During the march, Juanita Williams wore out her shoes (shown here), which are now displayed at the National Museum of History in Washington, D.C. What do you think motivated the marchers to carry the American flag?
Steve Shapiro/TimePix/Getty; Smithsonian Institution, Washington, D.C.

able to sit down together at the table of brotherhood." With the crowd roaring in support, he imagined the day "when all of God's children . . . will be able to join hands and sing . . . 'Free at last, free at last; thank God Almighty, we are free at last.'"

Yet the euphoria of the March on Washington quickly faded as activists returned to continued violence in the South. In 1964, the Mississippi Freedom Summer Project mobilized more than a thousand northern black and white college students to conduct a voter education registration drive. Resistance was fierce. By the end of the summer, only twelve hundred new voters had been allowed to register; whites had killed several activists, beaten eighty, arrested more than a thousand, and burned thirty-five black churches. Less apparent resistance came from the federal government itself, as the FBI spied on King and other leaders and expanded its activities to "expose, disrupt, misdirect, discredit, or otherwise neutralize" black protest.

Still the movement persisted. In March 1965, Alabama troopers used such fierce force to turn back a fifty-four-mile march from Selma to the state capitol in Montgomery that the incident earned the name "Bloody Sunday." After several days, President Johnson called up the Alabama National Guard to protect the marchers. Before the Selma campaign was over, whites had killed three demonstrators. Battered and hospitalized on Bloody Sunday, John Lewis, chairman of SNCC (and later a congressman), managed to make the final march to the capitol, which he counted as one of the most meaningful events in his life: "In October of that year the Voting Rights bill was passed and we all felt we'd had a part in it."

The Response in Washington

Civil rights leaders would have to wear sneakers, Lyndon Johnson said, if they were going to keep up with him. But both Kennedy and

Johnson acted more in response to the black freedom struggle than on their own initiative, moving only when events gave them little choice. Kennedy sent federal marshals to Montgomery to protect the Freedom Riders, dispatched troops to enable air force veteran James H. Meredith to enroll in the all-white University of Mississippi in 1962, and called up the Alabama National Guard during the Birmingham demonstrations in May 1963. But, well aware of the political costs of deploying federal force, he told activists pleading for more federal protection that law enforcement was a local matter.

In June 1963, Kennedy finally made good on his promise to seek strong antidiscrimination legislation. Pointing to the injustice suffered by blacks, Kennedy asked white Americans, "Who among us would then be content with the counsels of patience and delay?" Johnson took up Kennedy's commitment with passion, assisted by a number of factors. Scenes of violence against peaceful demonstrators appalled many television viewers across the nation. The resulting public support, the "Johnson treatment," and the president's ability to turn the measure into a memorial to the martyred Kennedy all produced the most important civil rights law since Reconstruction.

> Public support, the "Johnson treatment," and the president's ability to turn the measure into a memorial to the martyred Kennedy all produced the most important civil rights law since Reconstruction.

The Civil Rights Act of 1964 guaranteed access for all Americans to public accommodations, public education, employment, and voting, thus sounding the death knell for the South's system of segregation and discrimination. The law also extended constitutional protections to Indians on reservations. Title VII of the measure, banning discrimination in employment, not only attacked racial inequality outside the South but also outlawed job discrimination against women. Introduced by a conservative southerner in hopes of defeating the entire bill, the sex provision was pushed by a small group of women's rights advocates. Because Title VII applied not just to wages but to every aspect of employment, including hiring and promotion, it represented a giant step toward equal employment opportunity for white women as well as racial minorities.

Responding to black voter registration drives in the South, Johnson soon demanded a law that would remove "every remaining obstacle to the right and the opportunity to vote." In August 1965, he signed the Voting Rights Act, which empowered the federal government to intervene directly to enable African Americans to register and vote. A major transformation began in southern politics. (See Map 28.2 and "Historical Question," page 1038.)

Two more measures completed Johnson's civil rights record. The Civil Rights Act of 1968 banned racial discrimination in housing and jury selection and authorized federal intervention when states failed to protect civil rights workers from violence. In addition, Johnson used his presidential authority in September 1965 to issue Executive Order 11246, banning discrimination by employers holding government contracts (affecting about one-third of the labor force) and also obligating them to take affirmative action to ensure equal opportunity. Extended to cover women in 1967, the controversial affirmative action program was called "reverse discrimination" by many people who incorrectly thought that affirmative action required rigid quotas and hiring unqualified candidates. In fact, it required employers to counter the effects of centuries of oppression by acting forcefully to align their labor force with the available pool of qualified candidates. Most large businesses came to see affirmative action as a good employment practice.

Black Nationalism

By 1966, civil rights activism had undergone dramatic changes. Black protest extended from the South to the entire nation, demanded not just legal equality but also economic justice, and no longer held nonviolence as its basic principle. None of these developments was entirely new. For example, some African Americans had armed themselves in self-defense since Reconstruction, and even in the 1950s and early 1960s many activists doubted that demonstrators' passive suffering in the face of violence would change the hearts of racists. Still, the black freedom struggle began to show a different face, one more threatening to the white majority.

In part the new emphases resulted from earlier successes, as legal oppression receded only to reveal other injustices more subtle but no less pervasive. Integration and legal equality did little to improve the material conditions of blacks; and black rage at oppressive conditions erupted in waves of urban riots from 1964 to 1968. The Watts district of Los Angeles in August 1965, Newark and Detroit in July 1967, and the nation's capital in April 1968 saw the most destruction, but

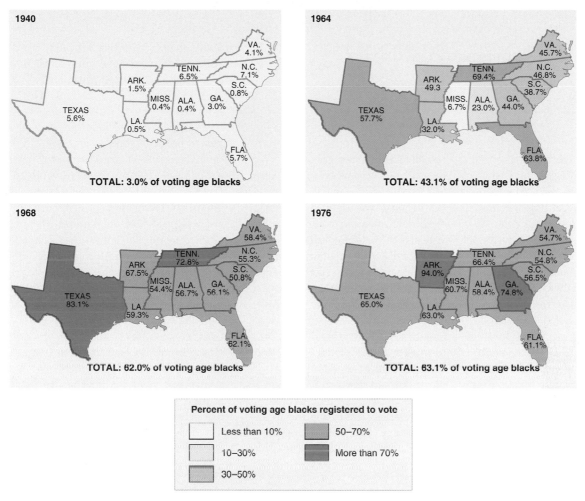

1940

VA. 4.1%
TENN. 6.5%
N.C. 7.1%
ARK. 1.5%
S.C. 0.8%
MISS. 0.4%
ALA. 0.4%
GA. 3.0%
TEXAS 5.6%
LA. 0.5%
FLA. 5.7%

TOTAL: 3.0% of voting age blacks

1964

VA. 45.7%
TENN. 69.4%
N.C. 46.8%
ARK. 49.3
S.C. 38.7%
MISS. 6.7%
ALA. 23.0%
GA. 44.0%
TEXAS 57.7%
LA. 32.0%
FLA. 63.8%

TOTAL: 43.1% of voting age blacks

1968

VA. 58.4%
TENN. 72.8%
N.C. 55.3%
ARK 67.5%
S.C. 50.8%
MISS. 54.4%
ALA. 56.7%
GA. 56.1%
TEXAS 83.1%
LA. 59.3%
FLA. 62.1%

TOTAL: 62.0% of voting age blacks

1976

VA. 54.7%
TENN. 66.4%
N.C. 54.8%
ARK. 94.0%
S.C. 56.5%
MISS. 60.7%
ALA. 58.4%
GA. 74.8%
TEXAS 65.0%
LA. 63.0%
FLA. 61.1%

TOTAL: 63.1% of voting age blacks

Percent of voting age blacks registered to vote

☐ Less than 10%   ▨ 50–70%
☐ 10–30%   ▨ More than 70%
▨ 30–50%

MAP 28.2   The Rise of the African American Vote, 1940–1976
Voting rates of southern blacks increased gradually in the 1940s and 1950s but shot up dramatically in the deep South after the Voting Rights Act of 1965 provided for federal agents to enforce African Americans' right to vote.

READING THE MAP: When did the biggest change in African American voter registration occur in the South? Which states had the highest and which had the lowest voter registration rates in 1968?
CONNECTIONS: What role did African American voters play in the 1960 election? What were the targets of three major voting drives in the 1960s?

FOR MORE HELP ANALYZING THIS MAP, see the map activity for this chapter in the Online Study Guide at bedfordstmartins.com/roark.

violence visited hundreds of cities, usually after an incident between white police and local blacks. Rioting in Detroit brought 43 deaths (30 at the hands of law enforcement personnel and most of them black), 7,000 arrests, 1,300 destroyed buildings, and 2,700 looted shops. "Our nation is moving toward two societies, one black, one white—separate and unequal," warned the Kerner Commission, appointed by Johnson to investigate the turmoil, but little was done about the basic conditions from which riots sprang.

In the North, a powerful new challenge to the ethos of nonviolence arose. Malcolm Little grew up in poverty and went to prison at the age of twenty-one for attempted burglary. There he educated himself, joined the Nation of Islam, whose adherents called themselves Black Muslims, and changed his name to Malcolm X, to symbolize the African identity stripped from his ancestors. Released from jail in 1952, he went to work for the Nation of Islam, which drew on the long tradition of **black nationalism** and its emphasis on racial

What Difference Did Black Voting Rights Make?

Born to poor black sharecroppers in the Mississippi Delta, Unita Blackwell hearkened in church one Sunday in 1964 when a SNCC worker talked about voter registration. The very next day she went to the courthouse where, as had happened to Fannie Lou Hamer and hundreds of other African Americans, officials refused her application. Undeterred, she succeeded on the third try, threw herself into activism as a SNCC organizer, and saw her share of jail cells. In fact, she and her husband planned their protest activities so that only one would risk arrest and the other would remain free to care for their child. A founder of the Mississippi Freedom Democratic Party, established to challenge the all-white state organization, Blackwell saw the challenge fall to compromise at the 1964 Democratic National Convention. But four years later, she participated in the national convention with Mississippi's reconfigured biracial delegation. Subsequently, she served as vice chair of the state Democratic Party and on the Democratic National Committee. When her small town of Mayersville incorporated in 1976, Blackwell won election as its first mayor and the first black female mayor in Mississippi.

Blackwell's career is but one measure of the transformations generated by African Americans' struggle for the most basic right of citizenship. Their determination to register to vote and the resulting resistance and violence of southern whites created a crisis that the federal government could not ignore. Its response—the Voting Rights Act of 1965 and subsequent extensions—suspended the literacy tests that had been used to disqualify blacks but not whites, and it brought electoral operations in most southern states under federal supervision. The law required the Justice Department to approve in advance any changes in state procedures that might disadvantage black voters, and it empowered the attorney general to send federal agents to observe registration and election processes and even to register voters in areas of continued white resistance.

"Legislation is not self-implementing," warned NAACP leader Roy Wilkins. "There is work to be done." As was the case with its passage, implementation of the Voting Rights Act depended on the efforts of African Americans themselves. More than two hundred voter registration drives between 1966 and 1968 paid off in dramatic increases in the numbers of blacks registered. Throughout the South, the proportion of African Americans on voter rolls jumped from 43 percent in 1964 to 62 percent in 1968. In Mississippi, the total leaped from just 6.7 percent in 1964 to 68 percent in 1968. African Americans also gained political offices in unprecedented numbers. Fewer than two dozen blacks held elective office in the South in 1964. In 1970, they claimed almost 500 elected government posts, and two years later the number reached nearly 1,200. Just seven years after whites bludgeoned civil rights activists during the Selma voting drive, black candidates won half of the ten seats on Selma's city council. With the victories of Barbara Jordan from Houston, Texas, and Andrew Young from Atlanta, Georgia, in 1972, the former Confederacy sent its first African Americans to the House of Representatives since the late nineteenth century.

Black electoral success was not limited to the South. Across the nation, African Americans held 1,500 elected positions in 1970, and by 1990 that number exceeded 7,000. The greatest progress came at the local level. The number of black city council members vaulted from 552 in 1970 to nearly 3,000 in 1989, and the number of black mayors grew sixfold, to more than 300, in the 1990s. The total of black representatives in Congress inched up from 10 in 1970 to 25 in 1990 and to 37 in the 1996 elections. Electoral success translated into tangible benefits. When black officials took office, their constituents saw improvements in public facilities,

pride, black autonomy and enterprise, and separation from the dominant white culture and institutions. Malcolm X attracted a large following, especially in urban ghettos, calling for black pride and autonomy, separation from the "corrupt [white] society," and self-defense against white violence. In 1964, he left the Nation, began to cultivate a wider constituency, and expressed an openness to working with whites. At a Harlem rally in February 1965, three Black Muslims shot and killed him.

The ideas espoused by Malcolm X resonated with younger activists. At a June 1966 rally in Greenwood, Mississippi, SNCC chairman Stokely police protection, roads, trash collection, and other basic services. Referring to Unita Blackwell's accomplishments as mayor, a Mayersville resident noted, "She brought in the water tower. Mostly it was pumps then. . . . Sewage, too. There wasn't nothing but those little old outdoor houses." Another constituent pointed to "old folks' houses. And paved streets. I grew up here when they wasn't paved." Black local officials also awarded more government jobs to African Americans and contracts to minority businesses. Elected mayor of Atlanta in 1973, Maynard Jackson appointed a black police chief and increased blacks' share of city jobs from 42 to 51 percent.

Most black officials had far less power than Jackson, but even when they were outnumbered by whites, they could at least introduce issues of concern to blacks that whites had ignored, and they gained access to information about behind-the-scenes government. An African American serving on a city council in Florida pointed out that "no matter what happened, [my white colleagues] knew I was listening to everything that went on." Activist Fannie Lou Hamer noted the psychological benefits of electoral progress. When blacks had no political voice, she recalled, "some white

Registering to Vote
Two civil rights volunteers during the 1964 Mississippi Freedom Summer campaign help a couple fill out voter registration forms. The form included a question asking the applicant to interpret a portion of the state's constitution, one of the ways white officials kept African Americans from voting in southern states before passage of the Voting Rights Act in 1965.
Charles Moore/Black Star/Stockphoto.com.

folks would drive past your house in a pickup truck with guns hanging up on the back and give you hate stares. . . . Those same people now call me Mrs. Hamer."

Yet increased political power did not guarantee African

Americans economic equality or even material security. Their minority status in the population and their residential dispersion, combined with many whites' disinclination to vote for blacks, meant that even by 1990 African Americans occupied fewer than 2 percent of all elected positions in the nation. As African Americans looked to increase their political force and shape policy to meet their needs, they sought to revive grassroots activism and form coalitions with other racial and ethnic groups. In addition, they considered a number of electoral strategies to solidify black and minority strength in a majoritarian system: reducing the number of at-large elections, which dilute minorities' power, and increasing the number of single-member district systems; monitoring electoral redistricting to ensure as many black-majority districts as possible; and supporting proportionate or cumulative voting.

Despite the limited reach of black enfranchisement, most experts nonetheless view the voting rights revolution as the most successful of all civil rights initiatives. As Unita Blackwell put it, "We didn't have nothing, and we changed the whole world with nothing. We changed a whole outlook."

Carmichael gave those principles a new name when he shouted, "We want black power." "Black power" quickly became the rallying cry in SNCC and CORE, and the black power movement riveted national attention in the late 1960s. A young autoworker in Detroit enthused, "I dig what Stokely Carmichael said . . . whites appear to be friendly by passing a few laws, but my basic situation gets worse and worse."

Carmichael called integration "a subterfuge for the maintenance of white supremacy" and rejected assimilation because it implied the superiority of white institutions and values. African Americans were encouraged to develop independent businesses, control their own schools and communities, and form all-black political organizations. The phrase "Black is beautiful" emphasized pride in African American culture and connections to blacks around the world. Referring to revolutionary movements in Africa and elsewhere, Carmichael declared, "We see that our freedom, our liberation, depends on these people and vice versa, their liberation depends on us, so we must wage the same struggle."

According to black power advocates, nonviolence brought only more beatings and killings. Malcolm X had once said, "If someone puts a hand on you, send him to the cemetery." Carmichael agreed: "Black people should and must fight back." After police killed an unarmed black teenager in San Francisco in 1966, Huey Newton and Bobby Seale organized the Black Panther Party for Self-Defense in 1966 and armed its members for self-defense against police brutality. The press paid an inordinate amount of attention to black radicals, and the black power movement encountered a severe white backlash. Although the urban riots of the mid-1960s erupted spontaneously, triggered by specific incidents usually involving abusive treatment of blacks by police, horrified whites blamed the riots on black power militants. By 1966, a full 85 percent of the white population thought that African Americans were pressing for too much too quickly, up from 34 percent two years earlier. A woman from Orange County, California, asserted her belief that "integration depends considerably on the Negro himself. If he will straighten up and live right he'll naturally be accepted." White autoworkers in St. Louis displayed anxiety about African American competition for their jobs when they set up a can of shoe polish by a sign stating, "Paint your face black and you can get anything."

Malcolm X in Egypt
Malcolm X stands in front of the pyramids in Egypt during a trip to Africa and the Middle East in 1964. Partly as a result of meeting Muslims of all colors as well as whites who were committed to ending racism, he no longer equated whites with the devil. "The white man is not inherently evil," he concluded, "but America's racist society influences him to act evilly."
John Launois/Black Star/Stockphoto.com.

Afro Rake
In a movement that paralleled the white counterculture in the 1960s and 1970s, young African Americans began to reject middle-class blacks' tendency to fashion their appearance after that of whites. They adopted African styles of dress and let their hair grow into a natural Afro style. In her poem "Homage to My Hair," Lucille Clifton celebrated the expression of authentic black identity: "when I feel her jump up and dance i hear the music! my God i'm talking about my nappy hair!" African Americans used combs like this Afro rake or pik, which makes further political statements with its clenched fist and peace symbol.
Salamandu, courtesy National Afro-American Museum and Cultural Center; Courtesy Antonio's Manufacturing Inc., Cresson, PA.

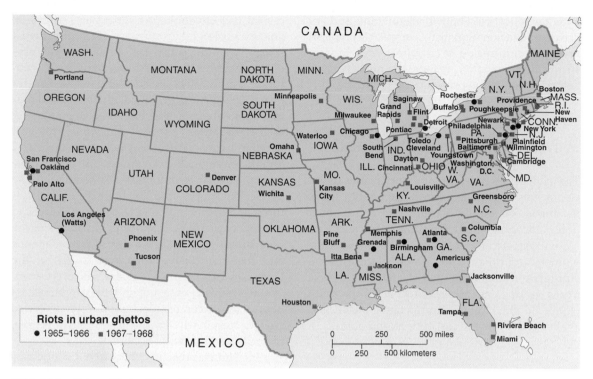

MAP 28.3   Urban Riots, 1965–1968
As black residents of the Watts district of Los Angeles watched a white police officer strike a twenty-one-year-old African American, whom he had just pulled over for driving drunk, one of the onlookers shouted, "We've got no rights at all—it's just like Selma." The altercation escalated into a full-scale five-day riot, during which young blacks set fires, looted, and attacked police and firefighters. When thousands of national guardsmen and police finally quelled the riot, 34 people were dead, 900 blacks had been injured and 4,000 arrested, hundreds of families had lost their homes, and scores of businesses had been wiped out. Although usually not on so large a scale, similar violence erupted in dozens of cities across the nation during the next three summers, as this map indicates. The urban violence provoked an intense backlash among whites against black aspirations, yet rioting and looting seemed to many young blacks the only means available to protest the poverty, lack of opportunity, and official insensitivity that they experienced daily in the ghettos. As one government worker commented when parts of Washington, D.C., went up in flames after Martin Luther King's death in 1968, "The black people in this city were really happy for three days. They have been kicked so long, and this is the one high spot in their life."

READING THE MAP: In what regions and cities of the United States were the 1960s riots concentrated? What years saw the greatest unrest?

CONNECTIONS: What were some of the causes of racial unrest in America's cities during this period? Whom did whites generally hold responsible for the riots and why?

FOR MORE HELP ANALYZING THIS IMAGE, see the map activity for this chapter in the Online Study Guide at bedfordstmartins.com/roark.

Martin Luther King Jr. agreed with black power advocates on the need for "a radical reconstruction of society." He himself expanded the scope of the struggle, mounting in 1965 a drive for better jobs, schools, and housing in Chicago and planning a Poor People's March to Washington in 1968 to seek greater antipoverty efforts. Yet he clung to nonviolence and integration as the means to this end. In 1968, the thirty-nine-year-old leader went to Memphis to support striking municipal garbage workers. There, on April 4, King was shot and killed by an escaped white convict.

Although they made the headlines, black power organizations failed to capture the massive support that African Americans gave King and other earlier leaders. Black militants were harassed by the FBI and jailed; some encounters with law officers left both black militants and police dead. Black nationalism's emphasis on racial pride and culture and its critique of American institutions, however, resonated broadly and helped to shape the protest of other groups.

A Multitude of Movements

The civil rights movement's undeniable moral claims helped to make protest respectable, while its impact on public opinion and government policy encouraged other groups with grievances. Native Americans, Latinos, college students, women, and others drew on the black freedom struggle for inspiration and models of activism. These groups engaged in direct-action protests, expressed their own cultural nationalism, and challenged dominant institutions and values.

Native American Protest

Protest was not new to the group of Americans with the oldest grievances, but Native American activism took on fresh militancy and goals in the 1960s. Contrary to the intention of Indian policy established in the 1940s and 1950s to assimilate Native Americans, the termination policy stirred Indian resistance, and the relocation programs stimulated a sense of Indian identity across tribal lines and a desire to preserve traditional culture among those who moved to cities. In 1961, a new, more militant generation of Native Americans expressed growing discontent with the government and with the older Indian leadership by forming the National Indian Youth Council (NIYC). Johnson's War on Poverty encouraged Native Americans to expect funds for and control over projects to ameliorate desperate living conditions in the cities and on reservations. The cry "red power" reflected the influence of black radicalism on Native Americans who rejected the goal of assimilation and sought the freedom to control their own circumstances. As NIYC founding member Clyde Warrior put it, "For the sake of the spiritual and material well-being of our total community, we must be able to demonstrate competence to ourselves. . . . We must make decisions about our own destinies."

Native Americans demonstrated and occupied land and public buildings, claiming rights to natural resources and territory that they had owned collectively before European settlement. For example, beginning in 1963 Northwest Indians mounted "fish-ins" to enforce century-old treaty rights. Native American militancy captured world attention in 1969, when several dozen seized Alcatraz Island, an abandoned federal penitentiary in San Francisco Bay, claiming their right to this "surplus" land under the Fort Laramie Treaty of 1868. They held on to the island for nineteen months, using the occupation to publicize the injustices Indians had suffered, promote pan-Indian cooperation, celebrate traditional cultures, and inspire other activists. (See "American Places," page 1043.) One of the organizers of the occupation, Dr. LaNada Boyer, a Shosone-Bannock and the first Native American to attend the University of California, Berkeley, said of Alcatraz, "We were able to raise, not only the consciousness of other American people, but our own people as well, to reestablish our identity as Indian people, as a culture, as political entities."

In Minneapolis in 1968, two Chippewas, Dennis Banks and George Mitchell, founded the American Indian Movement (AIM) to attack problems in cities, where about 300,000 Indians lived. AIM sought to protect Indians from police harassment, secure antipoverty funds, and establish "survival schools" to teach Indian history and values. The new movement's appeal quickly spread beyond urban areas and seized many Indians, especially young people, with a sense of purpose. AIM members did not have "that hangdog reservation look I was used to," Lakota activist and author Mary Crow Dog wrote, and their visit to her South Dakota reservation "loosened a sort of earthquake inside me." Recalling that her early life had been "just one endless vicious cycle of drinking and fighting, drinking and fighting," Crow Dog was able to break out of that cycle with her commitment to AIM.

AIM leaders helped organize the "Trail of Broken Treaties" caravan to the nation's capitol in 1972, when some of the activists took over the Bureau of Indian Affairs. The occupiers expressed their outrage at the bureau's paternalism, policies, and bureaucratic interference in Indians' lives by destroying the offices when the government announced its intention to remove the protesters. A much longer siege occurred on the Lakota Sioux reservation in South Dakota, where conflicts between AIM militants and older

AMERICAN PLACES

Alcatraz Island, San Francisco, California

Alcatraz Island and San Francisco Bay
© Gerald French/Corbis.

In 1854, the U.S. army installed the first fortifications on the seventeen-acre Alcatraz Island in San Francisco Bay, and within a few years it also began to house military prisoners there. From time to time, other groups were incarcerated there, including Southern loyalists during the Civil War, conscientious objectors during World War I, and Native Americans. In 1895, seventeen Hopis were imprisoned when they refused government efforts to turn them into farmers (traditionally the work of Hopi women) and resisted the educating of Indian children in government boarding schools. After 1907, Alcatraz was used exclusively as a military prison. Recognizing how the turbulent waters surrounding the island made it nearly escape-proof, in 1934 the government converted it into a maximum security prison to house what it considered the most hard-

ened criminals, including the Chicago gangster Al Capone.

After the government closed the prison in 1963, local Indian activists began to view the island as surplus federal property and subject to treaties promising such land to Native Americans. On November 20, 1969, seventy-eight Indians, mostly college students, braved harsh winds and waves in several boats to make a successful landing on the island. John Trudell, a Sioux, expressed the excitement of the occupiers: "When I got . . . on that island, here's all these Native people. I didn't know any of them, but yet I did. It was like going home." The group was led by Richard Oakes, a Mohawk and former ironworker, now a student at San Francisco State College in its brand-new Native American studies program. Members of many tribes, the occupiers called themselves "Indians of All Tribes" and issued a proclamation declaring that "we

reclaim the land . . . in the name of all American Indians by right of discovery." Referring mockingly to the Dutch colonists who had paid Indians for Manhattan Island in 1626, the proclamation declared, "We will purchase said Alcatraz Island for twenty-four dollars in glass beads and red cloth."

Although severely challenged by internal dissension and the difficulty of obtaining supplies, protesters managed to hold the island for nineteen months, gaining enormous publicity for their cause. For a time the Nixon administration took a hands-off approach, hoping that the occupiers would give up their demands for title to the island and creation of a university and cultural center. Eventually the government removed a barge that had supplied fresh water to the island and shut down electric power. On June 10, 1971, government agents landed on Alcatraz and removed the fifteen Native Americans who were left. While the occupiers failed in their ultimate goals, they energized Native American protest. "Alcatraz encouraged young people to become themselves, as opposed to hiding their Indianness," said Blackfoot longshoreman Joseph Myers. Even a government memo acknowledged that Alcatraz was a "symbol of the lack of attention to [their] unmet needs."

Today visitors can experience the history of Alcatraz Island as military fort, penitentiary, and site of the Indian occupation in person or on the Web. Both sites are operated by the National Park Service. A stroll or scroll through provides a detailed history of the occupation, natural features of the island, dramatic photographs, and passionate expressions of the people who defied the government to reclaim their heritage and rights as American citizens.

For Web links related to this site and other American Places, see "PlaceLinks" at bedfordstmartins.com/roark.

Occupation of the Bureau of Indian Affairs
Native American activists despised the Bureau of Indian Affairs (BIA), an agency of the Department of the Interior that supervised and provided services to recognized tribes. The bureau was a symbol of all the injustices they endured. Although President Nixon nearly tripled the BIA's budget, his administration spent little on off-reservation Indians. Representing these urban Indians, the American Indian Movement organized the "Trail of Broken Treaties" caravan to Washington, D.C., and on November 2, hundreds of Indians occupied the BIA. Pressured by the Nixon administration and fearful that riot police would attack them, the occupiers agreed to leave after six days, with promises that the government would create a task force to study their grievances, that it would not prosecute them, and that it would finance their travels home. Like the much longer seizure of Alcatraz (see "American Places," page 1043), the demonstrators failed to win their demands but gained attention for their cause. What is the significance of the flag in this photo?
© Bettmann/Corbis.

tribal leaders led AIM to take over—for seventy-two days—the village of Wounded Knee, where U.S. troops had massacred more than 100 Sioux in 1890.

Although these dramatic occupations failed to achieve their specific goals, the wave of Indian protest produced the end of relocation and termination policies; greater tribal sovereignty and control over community services; enhanced health, education, and other services; and protection of Indian religious practices. A number of laws and court decisions restored rights to ancestral lands or compensated Indian tribes for land seized in violation of treaties. Native Americans recovered a measure of identity and pride, greater respect for and protection of their culture, and, in the words of President Johnson's special message on the "Forgotten American" in 1968, recognition of "the right of the First Americans to remain Indians while exercising their rights as Americans."

Latino Struggles for Justice

The fastest-growing minority group in the 1960s was Latinos, or Hispanic Americans, an extraordinarily varied population encompassing people of Mexican, Puerto Rican, Caribbean, and other Latin American origins. (The term *Latino* stresses their common bonds as a minority group in the United States; the less political term *Hispanic* also includes those with origins in Spain.) People of Puerto Rican and Caribbean descent tended to live in East Coast cities, but more than half of the

Latino population of the United States—some six million Mexican Americans—lived in California, Texas, Arizona, New Mexico, and Colorado. In addition, thousands illegally crossed the two-thousand-mile border between Mexico and the United States in search of economic opportunity.

Mexican Americans had always organized to push for political power and economic rights. As we saw in chapter 26, middle-class Mexican Americans had formed the League of United Latin-American Citizens (LULAC) in 1929, which provided aid to newer immigrants and, like the NAACP, fought segregation and discrimination through litigation. In the 1960s, however, young Mexican Americans, like African Americans and Native Americans, increasingly rejected traditional politics in favor of direct action. One symbol of this generational challenge was young activists' adoption of the term *Chicano* (from *mejicano*, the Spanish word for "Mexican").

Chicano protest drew national attention to California, where Cesar Chavez and Dolores Huerta organized a movement to improve the wretched conditions of migrant agricultural workers. As a child moving from farm to farm with his family, often crowded into soggy tents or tarpaper cabins, exploited by labor contractors, Chavez had to change schools frequently and stopped after the eighth grade. He encountered indifference and discrimination in the educational system, where speaking Spanish was forbidden. One teacher, he recalled, "hung a sign on me that said, 'I am a clown, I speak Spanish.'" After serving in the navy during World War II and starting a family, Chavez began to organize voter registration drives among Mexican Americans and to study labor history and the ideas of Catholic reformers and Mahatma Gandhi.

In contrast to Chavez, Dolores Huerta grew up in an integrated urban neighborhood and avoided the farmworkers' grinding poverty and exploitation, but she witnessed subtle forms of discrimination. Once, for example, a high school teacher challenged her authorship of an essay because it was so well written. After completing community college and starting a family, at the age of twenty-five she met Chavez; determined that a union was the key to improving the lives of farmworkers, they founded the United Farm Workers (UFW) in 1962. Although Chavez headed the union until his death in 1993, Huerta was indispensable to its vitality. According to Luis Valdez, who headed the Farm Workers Theater, "Dolores was a thirty-five-year-old firebrand in 1965, and she was commanding crusty

Cesar Chavez in the Vineyards
Cesar Chavez, whose grandfather had migrated to the United States in the nineteenth century, experienced the plight of farmworkers when his family lost its business and farm in Arizona during the depression. Here he meets with grape pickers in California during the national grape boycott of 1965. The boycott's proclamation listed these aims: "just wages, humane working conditions, protection from the misuse of pesticides, and the fundamental right of collective bargaining."
Arthur Schatz/TimePix/Getty.

macho *campesinos* twenty years her senior." UFW marches and strikes gained widespread support, and a national boycott of California grapes helped the union win a wage increase for the workers in 1970. Although the UFW struggled and lost membership, it helped politicize Mexican Americans and improved the lives of thousands of farmworkers. In 1999, California made Chavez's birthday a state holiday.

Chicanos mobilized elsewhere to end discrimination in employment and education, gain political power, and combat police brutality. In southwestern cities in 1968, high school students launched a wave of strikes, called "Blow Outs," to protest racism in the public schools. "Teachers, Sí, Bigots, No!" their signs declared. In Denver, Colorado, Rodolfo "Corky"

> Chicanos mobilized to end discrimination in employment and education, gain political power, and combat police brutality.

Gonzales set up "freedom schools," where Chicano children studied Spanish and Mexican American history and chanted, "Chicano power." The nationalist strains of Chicano protest were evident in La Raza Unida (the United Race), a political party founded by José Angel Gutierrez in Texas and based on cultural pride and brotherhood. With blacks and Native Americans, Chicanos continued to be overrepresented among the poor but gradually won more political offices, more effective enforcement of antidiscrimination legislation, and greater respect for their culture.

Student Rebellion, the New Left, and the Counterculture

Although materially and legally more secure than their African American, Indian, and Latino counterparts, white youth joined them in expressing dissent, supporting the black freedom struggle, and launching student protests, the antiwar movement, and the new **feminist** movement. Challenging establishment institutions and traditional values, these movements, along with those of racial and ethnic minorities, formed part of a reinvigorated political left and helped change higher education, the family, the national government, and other key institutions.

> Although materially and legally more secure than their African American, Indian, and Latino counterparts, white youth joined them in expressing dissent, supporting the black freedom struggle, and launching student protests, the antiwar movement, and the new feminist movement.

The central organization of white student protest was Students for a Democratic Society (SDS), formed in 1960 by a remnant of an older **socialist**-oriented student organization. In 1962, some sixty members met in Port Huron, Michigan, to draft a statement of purpose. "We are people of this generation, bred in at least modest comfort, housed now in universities, looking uncomfortably at the world we inherit," the statement began. The idealistic students criticized the complacency of their elders, the remoteness of decision makers from the people, and the powerlessness and alienation generated in a society run by impersonal bureaucratic institutions. SDS aimed to mobilize a "New Left," around the goals of civil rights, peace, and universal economic security. It remained small until 1965, but other forms of student activism soon followed.

A free speech movement, the first large-scale white student protest, arose at the University of California, Berkeley, in 1964, when university officials banned student organizations from setting up tables to recruit support for various causes. Led by whites back from civil rights work in the South, the students claimed the right to freedom of expression and political action. Jack Weinberg, one of the leaders, recalled the students' reaction to the university ban: "They may prohibit it, but we're not going to stop doing it." They occupied the administration building, and more than seven hundred were arrested before the California Board of Regents overturned the new restrictions.

Hundreds of student rebellions followed on campuses across the country. Opposition to the Vietnam War activated the largest number of students, who held rallies and took over buildings to protest universities' links to the war. But they also demanded curricular reforms, more financial aid for minority and poor students, independence from paternalistic rules, and a larger voice in campus decision making. (See "Documenting the American Promise," page 1048.) Protesting a variety of restrictions on student behavior, radicals at the University of Florida equated their campus to a ghetto. "Like all ghettos, it has its managers (the administration), its Uncle Toms (the intimidated, status-berserk faculty), its raw natural resources processed for outside exploitation and consumptions (the students)," their underground paper declared.

Growing up alongside and often overlapping the New Left and student movements was the counterculture, a rebellion that drew on the ideas of the Beats of the 1950s. Cultural radicals, or "hippies," as they were called, rejected many mainstream values, such as the work ethic, materialism, rationality, order, and sexual control. Seeking personal rather than political change, they advocated "Do your own thing" and drew attention with their long hair and wildly colorful clothing. The Haight-Ashbury district of San Francisco harbored the most famous hippie community, but thousands of radicals established communes in cities or on farms, where they renounced private property and shared everything, often including sex partners. They sought to discard inhibitions and elevate their senses with illegal drugs such as marijuana and LSD. As counterculture guru Timothy Leary advised, "Turn on, tune in, drop out."

Rock and folk music defined both the counterculture and the political left. English groups

Woodstock
The Woodstock Music Festival, held on a farm near Bethel, New York, in August 1969, featured the greatest rock and folk musicians of the era and epitomized the values and hopes of the counterculture. Despite terrible conditions created by bad weather and the failure of festival organizers to plan for so many people, the youthful crowd of 400,000 created a loving, peaceful community for three days filled with music, sex, and drugs. What symbols of the counterculture can you pick out in this photo?
John Dominis / Image Works.

such as the Beatles and the Rolling Stones and homegrown products such as Bob Dylan, Janis Joplin, the Jefferson Airplane, and Jerry Garcia's Grateful Dead took American youth by storm. Music during the 1960s often carried insurgent political and social messages. Despairing of the violence around the world and the threat of nuclear annihilation, "Eve of Destruction," a top hit of 1965, reminded young men, "You're old enough to kill but not for votin'." Other popular songs derided authority, touted drug use and sexual freedom, and called for peace, love, and revolution.

The hippies faded away in the 1970s, but many elements of the counterculture—from rock music to jeans and long hair—filtered into the mainstream. Sex outside marriage and tolerant attitudes about sexual morality spawned what came to be called a "sexual revolution," with help from the birth-control pill newly available in the 1960s. Self-fulfillment became a dominant concern of many Americans, and questioning of authority became much more widespread.

A New Movement to Save the Environment

Although it differed from the identity-based politics of racial, ethnic, and youth-oriented groups, environmentalism likewise contributed to a redefinition of liberalism in the 1960s and beyond. One aspect of the new environmental movement resembled the conservation movement born in the Progressive era and championed by Theodore Roosevelt to preserve portions of the natural world for recreational and aesthetic purposes (see chapter 21). Such efforts seemed all the more necessary with the post–World War II explosion

Student Protest

The waves of student protest that rolled across college campuses in the 1960s were all the more surprising because observers had found the "silent generation" of the 1950s so complacent and conformist. Although the majority of college students did not participate in the rebellions, a sizable number at all kinds of colleges and universities challenged traditional authorities, criticized established institutions, and demanded a voice for themselves in the decisions that affected their lives.

DOCUMENT 1
Edward Schwartz on Student Power, October 1967

This statement was written by student activist Edward Schwartz to represent the views of the National Student Association, the largest college-student organization in the 1960s. It was ironic that this association, which contributed to the student upheaval in the 1960s, had been founded a decade earlier, with secret funding from the CIA, as a liberal group to counter communism.

The educational premise behind demands for student power reflects the notion that people learn through living, through the process of integrating their thoughts with their actions, through testing their values against those of a community, through a capacity to act. College presidents who invoke legal authority to prove educational theory assume that growth is the ability to accept what the past has created. Student power is a medium through which people integrate their own experience with a slice of the past which seems appropriate, with their efforts to intensify the relationships between the community within the university.

Let this principle apply—he who must obey the rule should make it.

Students should make the rules governing dormitory hours, boy-girl visitation, student unions, student fees, clubs, newspapers, and the like. Faculty and administrators should advise—attempt to persuade, even. Yet the student should bear the burden of choice.

Students and faculty should co-decide curricular policy.

Students, faculty, and administration should co-decide admissions policy, overall college policy affecting the community, even areas like university investment. . . . Student power should not be argued on legal grounds. It is not a legal principle. It is an educational principle.

Student power is threatening to those who wield power now, but this is understandable. A student should threaten his administrators outside of class, just as bright students threaten professors inside of class. Student power ultimately challenges everyone in the university—the students who must decide; the faculty and administrators who must rethink their own view of community relations in order to persuade.

People who say that student power means anarchy imply really that students are rabble who have no ability to form community and to adhere to decisions made by community. Student power is not the negation of rules—it is the creation of a new process for the enactment of rules. Student power is not the elimination of authority, it is the development of a democratic standard of authority.

SOURCE: Edward Schwartz, "He Who Must Obey the Rule Should Make It," in Immanuel Wallerstein and Paul Starr, eds., *The University Crisis Reader*, vol. 1, *The Liberal University under Attack* (New York: Random House, 1971), 482–84. Copyright © 1971 by Random House, Inc. Reprinted with permission.

DOCUMENT 2
Demands of Howard University Students, February 1968

African American students launched campus protests even at universities where most faculty and administrators were black, like Howard University in Washington, D.C. Following are demands of black students at Howard, printed in the campus newspaper, The Spear and Shield.

1. We demand the immediate resignation of the following Howard administrators on the grounds of their incompetence and obvious unwillingness to work toward a black Howard University. [There followed names of the president, vice president, and liberal arts dean.]
2. We demand the institution of the following curriculum changes by next semester:

   a. We demand that Howard should be the center of Afro-American thought. We demand that the economics, government, literature, and social science departments begin to place more emphasis on how these disciplines may be used to effect the liberation of black people in this country.
   b. We demand the institution of non-prerequisite courses in Negro History.
   c. We demand the immediate abolishment of Freshman Assembly. Black students are not culturally deprived.

3. We demand the immediate reinstatement of all Howard instructors who have been unjustifiably dismissed for their political activism.
4. We demand a Black Awareness Research Institute at Howard University.
5. Students are trained to be leaders only by learning to accept responsibility. We demand therefore . . . student control in matters that concern only students.

   a. The student judiciary and codification of rules presently submitted to the Faculty Senate Steering Committee should be immediately instituted.
   b. That students must be authorized to control the budgeting and expenditure of the student activity fee.

6. Howard must be made relevant to the black community. The University campus must be made more available to all black people and programs must be instituted to aid the black community in the struggle against oppression.
7. We demand that Howard personnel begin to treat students like black people should treat black people, with respect and courtesy.

SOURCE: Howard University: February 1968, "The Spear and Shield," in Immanuel Wallerstein and Paul Starr, eds., *The University Crisis Reader,* vol. 2, *Confrontation and Counterattack* (New York: Random House, 1971), 485–86. Copyright © 1971 by Random House, Inc. Reprinted with permission.

DOCUMENT 3
SDS Explanation of the Columbia Strike, September 1968

One of the longest and most violent student protests occurred in New York City at Columbia University in April and May 1968, when white and black students occupied five buildings for a week; a subsequent student strike closed the university for the rest of the academic year. One of the key issues arose from the university's practice of expanding by buying up land in neighboring Harlem and evicting black tenants. The members of the Columbia SDS chapter, one of various factions among the protesters, rationalized their actions in the following statement.

When we seized five buildings at Columbia University, we engaged the force of wealth, privilege, property—and the force of state violence that always accompanies them—with little more than our own ideals, our fears, and a vague sense of outrage at the injustices of our society. Martin Luther King had just been shot, his name demeaned by Columbia officials who refused to grant a decent wage to Puerto Rican workers, and who had recently grabbed part of Harlem for a student gym. . . .

For years Columbia Trustees had evicted tenants from their homes, taken land through city deals, and fired workers for trying to form a union. For years they had trained officers for Vietnam who, as ROTC literature indicates, killed Vietnamese peasants in their own country. In secret work for the IDA [Institute for Defense Analysis] and the CIA, in chemical-biological war research for the Department of War, the Trustees implicated their own University in genocide. They had consistently . . . lied to their own constituents and published CIA books under the guise of independent scholarship. . . . We lived in an institution that channeled us, marked us, ranked us, failed us, used us, and treated masses of humanity with class contempt. . . .

The collegiate wing of privilege could not shield us from the decay and violence in our society. The University was not, as we first believed, a sanctuary from the world; it was, in fact, a proponent of the most violent system the centuries have created—the system of capital. . . .

Columbia, standing at the top of a hill, looked down on Harlem. . . . People who survived in Harlem had been evicted by the Trustees from Morningside or still paid rent to Columbia. . . . We walked to our classrooms across land that had been privatized; we studied in buildings that had once been homes in a city that is underhoused; and we listened to the apologies for Cold War and capital in our classes.

Columbia professors often claim that the University is a neutral institution. . . . Many professors pursue all sides of a question as an end in itself. They find a certain refuge in the difficulty of defining good and evil. The result is a clogging of their moral sense, their capacity for collective justice. . . . What liberals call neutrality is really one of the ways by which the faculty protects its special status in society.

A University could not, even if it wanted, choose to be really value-free. It can choose good values; it can choose bad values; or it can remain ignorant of the values on which it acts. . . . A social institution should at least articulate its own perspective, so that its own values may be consciously applied or modified. It is a typical fallacy of American teaching, that to remain silent on crucial issues is to be objective with your own constituents. Actually a "neutral" institution is far more manipulative than a University committed to avowed goals and tasks.

(continued)

DOCUMENT 4
Chicago Women's Liberation on Sexism in Higher Education, February 1969

In January 1969, the University of Chicago refused to reappoint Dr. Marlene Dixon, an assistant professor of sociology who had incorporated the study of women into her teaching. While officials insisted that Dixon did not meet the university's academic standards, her supporters believed that she was fired for her radical beliefs and because she was female. SDS and other factions of radical students protested for two weeks but failed to save Dixon's job. Chicago Women's Liberation, one of the radical groups that grew out of women's activism in the New Left, issued this statement addressing broader issues.

What does women's freedom mean? . . . It means the freedom to be one's own person in an integrated life of work, love, play, motherhood: the freedoms, rights and privileges of first class citizenship, of equality in relationships of love and work: the right to choose to make decisions or not to: the right to full self-realization and to full participation in the life of the world. . . . To achieve these rights we must struggle as all other oppressed groups must struggle: one only has the rights one fights for. . . .

At the U of C we see the first large action, the first important struggle of women's liberation. This university—all universities—discriminate against women, impede their full intellectual development, deny them places on the faculty, exploit talented women and mistreat women students.

DOCUMENT 5
Counterthrust on Student Power, Spring 1967

While the majority of students simply avoided involvement in campus rebellions, some students actively criticized the protesters. The largest conservative student organization was Young Americans for Freedom, which more than doubled in size during the 1960s. The following selection, from a leaflet entitled "Student Power Is a Farce," reflected the views of Counterthrust, a conservative group at Wayne State University in Michigan.

Our University is being treated to the insanity of Left-Wing students demanding the run of the University. . . . Wayne students are told by the Left that "student power" merely means more democracy on campus. This is an outright lie! Student power is a Left-Wing catchword symbolizing campus militancy and radicalism. In actuality, the Left-Wing, spearheaded by the SDS [Students for a Democratic Society] want to radically alter the university community. . . .

The Leftists charge a sinister plot by private enterprise to train students for jobs at taxpayers' expense. Evidently it never occurred to the SDS that private enterprise is also the biggest single taxpayer for schools. But, of course, that would require a little thought on the part of the SDS which they have already demonstrated they are incapable of. . . .

The byword of student power-union advocates is Radicalism. . . . Fraternities and student Governments will have no place in student power-unions since both are considered allies of the status quo and thus useless. . . . As responsible Wayne students, we cannot allow our University to be used by Leftists for their narrow purposes. We were invited to this campus by the Michigan Taxpayer to receive an education. Let us honor that invitation.

of economic growth. In the West especially, the expanding economy and mushrooming population necessitated greater supplies of water and power, and environmental groups mobilized to stop construction of dams that would disrupt national parks and wilderness areas.

The new environmentalists, however, dramatically broadened the agenda of the conservationists; now the focus turned to the ravaging effects of industrial development on human life and health. The polluted air and water and spread of deadly chemicals attending economic growth threatened wildlife, plants, and the delicate ecological balance that sustained human life. To the leaders of a new organization, Friends of the Earth, unlimited economic growth was "no longer healthy, but a

DOCUMENT 6
George F. Kennan's Speech on Student Protest, December 1967

*George F. Kennan, the foreign policy expert who had articulated the **containment** policy in 1947, reflected the views of many critics of student protest when he gave this speech at Swarthmore College in Pennsylvania.*

There is an ideal that has long been basic to the learning process, one that stands at the very center of our modern institutions of higher education. It is the ideal of the association of the process of learning with a certain remoteness from the contemporary scene—a certain detachment and seclusion, a certain voluntary withdrawal and renunciation of participation in contemporary life in the interests of the achievement of a better perspective on that life when the period of withdrawal is over. It is an ideal that does not predicate any total conflict between thought and action, but recognizes that there is a time for each. . . .

What strikes one first about the angry militancy [among current students] is the extraordinary degree of certainty by which it is inspired: certainty of one's own rectitude, certainty of the correctness of one's own answers, certainty of the accuracy and profundity of one's own analysis of the problems of contemporary society, certainty as to the iniquity of those who disagree. . . . One is struck to see such massive certainties already present in the minds of people who not only have not studied very much but presumably are not studying a great deal, because it is hard to imagine that the activities to which this aroused portion of our student population gives itself are ones readily compatible with quiet and successful study. . . .

I am not saying that students should not be concerned, should not have views, should not question what goes on in the field of national policy. . . . Some of us, who are older, share many of their misgivings, many of their impulses. . . .

I have seen more harm done in this world by those who tried to storm the bastions of society in the name of utopian beliefs, who were determined to achieve the elimination of all evil . . . than by all the humble efforts of those who have tried to create a little order and civility and affection within their own intimate entourage, even at the cost of tolerating a great deal of evil in the public domain. Behind this modesty, after all, there has been the recognition of a vitally important truth—a truth that the Marxists, among others, have never brought themselves to recognize; namely that the decisive seat of evil in this world is not in social and political institutions, and not even, as a rule, in the ill will or iniquities of statesmen, but simply in the weakness and imperfection of the human soul itself.

SOURCE: George F. Kennan, "Rebels without a Program," *The University Crisis Reader*, vol. 1, *The Liberal University under Attack* (New York: Random House, 1971), 12–23. Copyright © 1971 by Random House, Inc. Reprinted with permission.

QUESTIONS FOR ANALYSIS AND DEBATE

1. What different ideas about the nature and purposes of the university do these writers present? How do they differ in their view of students' capabilities and rights?

2. Do you agree or disagree with George Kennan's insistence that universities should maintain "a certain remoteness from the contemporary scene" in order to achieve "a better perspective" on current issues? Why or why not?

3. Consider the different backgrounds and circumstances of the authors of these writings. Are factors such as age, race, gender, and economic class important to the viewpoints expressed? Why or why not?

4. To what extent do your own campus policies and practices suggest that student protest made a difference? What changes that the protesters demanded do not appear at your college? Should they?

---

cancer." An oil spill from a drilling operation off the coast of Santa Barbara, California, blackened hundreds of square miles of ocean and thirty miles of beaches in January 1969 and provided a dramatic image of pollution. President Nixon's adviser on the environment considered it "comparable to tossing a match into a gasoline tank: it exploded into the environmental revolution."

Biologist Rachel Carson had already drawn national attention to environmental concerns in 1962 with her best seller *Silent Spring*, which described the harmful effects of toxic chemicals, particularly dioxin and the pesticide DDT. Older conservation organizations such as the Sierra Club and the Wilderness Society expanded their agendas, and a host of new organizations arose.

Millions of Americans expressed environmental concerns on the first observation of Earth Day in April 1970. In Wisconsin, students distributed fliers encouraging recycling, and a group of Detroit women picketed a steel plant that polluted a river with industrial waste. Girl Scouts cleaned garbage from the Potomac River, African Americans in St. Louis dramatized the effects of poisons in lead paint, students in Michigan smashed a Ford to protest auto emissions, and people all over the country planted trees. Harvard law student Denis Hayes, who organized a teach-in on Earth Day, reported that environmentalists were prepared to do "whatever it takes. This may be our last chance."

Responding to these concerns, the federal government staked out a broad role in environmental regulation in the 1960s and 1970s. Lyndon Johnson became the first president to send Congress a special message on the environment, obtaining measures to control air and water pollution and to preserve the American landscape. In 1970, President Richard Nixon's

State of the Union message called "clean air, clean water, open spaces . . . the birthright of every American," and he created the Environmental Protection Agency (EPA) to enforce clean air and water policies and regulate pesticides. That same year, Congress passed the Occupational Safety and Health Act (OSHA), protecting workers against workplace accidents and disease. The Clean Air Act of 1970 set national standards for air quality and restricted factory and automobile emissions of carbon dioxide and other pollutants. Despite challenges from industry and lenient enforcement, and even in the face of population and economic growth, by 1990 air pollutants had decreased by one-third in major cities.

Environmentalism challenged the dominant values of consumption and growth that characterized the post–World War II era. But, especially by the late 1970s, when antigovernment sentiment rose and the economy slumped, it was not unusual for the imperative of economic growth to trump environmental concerns. Corporations seeking to expand, apply new technologies, or exploit natural resources resisted restrictions. "If you're hungry and out of work, eat an environmentalist," read a union bumper sticker reflecting fears that regulations threatened jobs. Many Americans who expressed support for protecting the environment at the same time valued economic expansion, personal acquisition, and convenience. Yet, despite these struggles and contradictions, the environmental movement achieved cleaner air and water, a reduction in toxic wastes, and some preservation of endangered species and wilderness. And Americans now recognized that human ingenuity had developed the power to destroy life on earth.

The New Wave of Feminism

On August 26, 1970, fifty years after women won the right to vote, tens of thousands of women across the country took to the streets. Participants included radical women in jeans and conservatively dressed suburbanites, peace activists and politicians, and a sprinkling of women of color. They carried signs reading "Sisterhood Is Powerful" and "Don't Cook Dinner—Starve a Rat Today." Some of the banners opposed the war in Vietnam, and others demanded racial justice, but women's own liberation stood at the forefront.

Beginning in the 1960s, the women's movement reached high tide in the 1970s and persisted in various forms into the twenty-first century. By that time women had experienced tremendous transformations in their legal status, public opportunities, and personal and sexual relationships; and popular expectations about appropriate gender roles had shifted dramatically.

A Movement Emerges

After women won the right to vote in 1920, feminism receded from national attention, but small groups of women continued to work for women's rights and opportunities in such areas as employment, jury service, and electoral politics. Beginning in the 1940s, large demographic changes laid the preconditions for a resurgence of feminism. Women did not abandon the workplace after World War II, as more and more women, especially wives and mothers, took jobs. Consequently, the importance of their paid work to the economy and to their families belied the idea of women as dependent, domestic beings and awakened their recognition of the inferior conditions of their employment. Moreover, the democratization of higher education brought more and more women to college campuses,

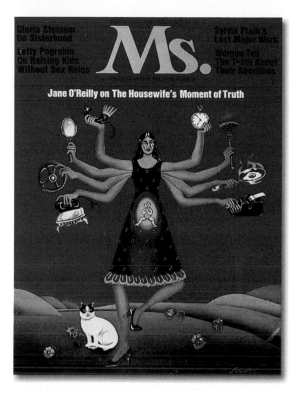

First Issue of _Ms._ Magazine

In 1972, Gloria Steinem and other journalists and writers published the premier issue of the first mass-circulation magazine for and controlled by women. _Ms.: The New Magazine for Women_ ignored the recipes and fashion tips of typical women's magazines. It featured literature by women writers and articles on a broad range of feminist issues. A scholar later wrote that it was "mind-blowing. Here was, written down, what [women] had not yet admitted they felt, had always feared to say out loud, and could not believe was now before their eyes, in public, for all to read."

What concerns are suggested by this cover of the first issue? What is the significance of the woman's multiple arms?

Courtesy, Lang Communications.

where their aspirations expanded beyond the confines of domesticity and of routine, subordinate work.

Policy initiatives in the early 1960s reflected both these larger transformations and the specific efforts of small bands of women's rights activists in the 1940s and 1950s, and sparked new activism. In 1961, Assistant Secretary of Labor Esther Peterson persuaded Kennedy to strengthen his support among women by appointing a President's Commission on the Status of Women (PCSW). Chaired by Eleanor Roosevelt, the commission reported its findings in October 1963, eight months after Betty Friedan

attacked sex discrimination in _The Feminine Mystique_ (see chapter 27). Although not challenging women's traditional roles, the commission reported widespread discrimination against women and recommended remedies. Spawning counterparts in all the states, the PCSW created networks of motivated women eager for action who would launch a grassroots women's movement a few years later.

The PCSW highlighted a practice that women's organizations and labor unions had sought to eliminate for two decades: the age-old custom of paying women less than men for the same work. They achieved that goal when Kennedy signed the Equal Pay Act in June 1963, making wage disparities based solely on gender illegal. Within a few years, women began to win pay increases and back pay worth millions of dollars, although forty years later, women still had not closed the income gap.

Just as it inspired other protests, the black freedom struggle also gave an immense boost to the rise of a new women's movement, by creating a moral climate sensitive to injustice and providing precedents and strategies that feminists followed. For example, by piggybacking onto civil rights measures, feminists gained the ban against sex discrimination in Title VII of the Civil Rights Act of 1964 and the extension of affirmative action to women. Their expectations raised by these new policies, feminists grew impatient when the government failed to take them seriously and moved slowly to enforce them. The head of the Equal Employment Opportunity Commission (EEOC), enforcement agency for Title VII, called the provision "a fluke . . . conceived out of wedlock" and told reporters that men were entitled to have female secretaries. Outraged by such attitudes and deciding that they needed a "civil rights organization for women," in 1966 Betty Friedan and others founded the National Organization for Women (NOW) "to bring women into full participation in the mainstream of American society now, exercising all the privileges and responsibilities thereof in truly equal partnership with men."

Simultaneously, a more radical feminism grew among women in the black freedom struggle and the New Left. In 1964, two white women in SNCC, Mary King and Casey Hayden, recognized the contradiction between the ideal of equality and women's actual status in the movement, and in 1965 they began circulating their ideas to other New Left women. King and Hayden argued that, like blacks, women were subject to a "caste system . . . forcing them to work around or outside hierarchical structures of power which may exclude them" and were also subordinated in personal relations. When most male radicals reacted with indifference or ridicule to such ideas, women began to walk out of male-dominated political meetings, and by 1967 they had created an independent women's liberation movement composed of small groups across the nation.

Women's liberation demonstrations began to gain public attention, especially when dozens of women picketed the Miss America beauty pageant in 1968, protesting against being forced "to compete for male approval [and] enslaved by ludicrous 'beauty' standards." They crowned a sheep Miss America and set up a "freedom trash can," inviting women to throw away their "bras, girdles, curlers, false eyelashes, wigs, and *Cosmopolitan*," which they called "objects of female torture." The range of feminist activism ran the gamut from lobbying Congress and state legislatures to direct action. Women began to speak publicly about personal experiences that had always been shrouded in secrecy, such as rape and abortion. They marched by the tens of thousands for a variety of causes, and a handful of women illegally occupied state capital buildings and went on hunger strikes. Throughout the country, women joined consciousness-raising groups where they discovered that what they had considered "personal" problems reflected an entrenched system of discrimination against and devaluation of women.

The Many Facets and Achievements of Feminism

Radical feminists, who called their movement "women's liberation," differed from feminists in NOW and other more mainstream groups in several ways, particularly in the early years of feminism's resurgence. NOW focused on achieving equal treatment for women in the public sphere, while women's liberation emphasized women's subordination in the family and other personal relationships. Groups like NOW wanted to integrate women into existing institutions, while radical groups, ranging from New York City's Radical Feminists to Dayton, Ohio's Women's Liberation, insisted that women would never achieve justice until economic, political, and social institutions were totally transformed. On the national level, NOW existed as a typical hierar-

chical organization, while radical women met throughout the country in small groups where decision by consensus prevailed. Differences between these two strands of feminism blurred in the 1970s, as NOW and other mainstream groups embraced many of the issues raised by radicals.

A protest that occurred simultaneously with the Miss America contest, the NAACP-sponsored Miss Black America contest, indicated the complicated relationships between black women and feminism that arose from their interlocking racial and gender identities. On the one hand, by opposing the exclusion of African Americans from the mainstream contest, the Miss Black America contest seemed to support conventional gender norms that valued women in terms of their appearance. Yet the alternative pageant also expressed racial pride, as Saundra Williams, the winner, wore her hair in a natural Afro style, performed an African dance, and discussed her participation in civil rights demonstrations. Because the gender of black women was shaped by race, and because some African American men saw feminism as "an attempt by the power structure to divide black men and women," black women could not easily identify with feminist aims that were defined by white women.

Although NOW elected a black president, Aileen Hernandez, in 1970, white middle-class women predominated in the new feminism's national leadership and much of its constituency. Women of color criticized white women's organizations for their frequent indifference to the concerns of women unlike themselves, such as the disproportionate poverty experienced by minority women, their greater risk of being sterilized without their consent, and their vulnerability to additional layers of discrimination based on race or ethnicity. Cellestine Ware, an African American writer and a founder of New York Radical Feminists, insisted that black and white women could work together "only if the movement changes its priorities to work on issues that affect the lives of minority group women."

Yet support for feminism was exceedingly multifaceted. Most African American women worked through their own groups such as the older National Council of Negro Women and the National Black Feminist Organization, founded in 1973. Similarly, in the early 1970s American Indian women and Mexican American women founded national organizations, and Asian American women formed their own local movements. Blue-collar women organized the National

Coalition of Labor Union Women in 1974. Lesbians established collectives throughout the country as well as their own caucuses in organizations such as NOW. Women founded a host of other groups that focused on single issues such as health, abortion rights, education, and violence against women. Finally, U.S. feminists interacted with and learned from their sisters abroad, joining a movement that crossed national borders. (See "Beyond America's Borders," page 1056.)

Common threads underlay the great diversity of organizations, issues, and activities. Above all, feminism represented the belief that women were barred from, unequally treated in, or poorly served by the male-dominated public arena, encompassing politics, medicine, law, education, and religion. Feminists also sought equality in the private sphere, challenging traditional norms that identified women primarily as wives and mothers or sex objects, subservient to men.

Although more an effect than a cause of women's rising employment, feminism lifted female aspirations and helped lower barriers to jobs and offices monopolized by men. Women made some inroads into skilled crafts and management positions. Between 1970 and 2000, their share of law degrees shot up from 5 percent to nearly 50 percent, and their proportion of medical degrees from less than 10 percent to more than 35 percent. Women gained political offices very slowly; yet by 2000, they constituted more than 10 percent of Congress and more than 20 percent of all state executives and legislators.

Feminist activism produced the most sweeping changes in laws and policies concerning women since they had won the right to vote in 1920. In 1972, Congress passed an Equal Rights Amendment to the Constitution (ERA) that would outlaw differential treatment of men and women under all state and federal laws. Title IX of the Education Amendments Act of 1972 banned sex discrimination in all aspects of education, such as admissions, athletics, and faculty hiring. Congress also outlawed sex discrimination in the granting of loans in 1974, opened U.S. military academies to women in 1976, and prohibited discrimination against pregnant workers in 1978. Moreover, the Supreme Court struck down laws that treated men and women differently in Social Security, welfare and military benefits, and workers' compensation.

At the state and local levels, radical feminists won laws forcing police departments and the legal system to treat rape victims more justly and humanely. Activists set up shelters for battered women and their children, and they won state laws ensuring greater protection for victims of domestic violence and more effective prosecution of offenders. Feminists pressured state legislatures to end restrictions on abortion, and many testified publicly about their own illegal abortions. "Without the full capacity to limit her own reproduction," abortion rights activist Lucinda Cisler insisted, "a woman's other 'freedoms' are tantalizing mockeries that cannot be exercised." In 1973, the Supreme Court issued the landmark *Roe v. Wade* (see appendix, page A-44) decision, ruling that the Constitution protects the right to abortion, which states cannot prohibit in the early stages of pregnancy. However, later decisions allowed state governments to impose restrictions on that right, such as denying coverage under Medicaid and other government-financed health programs, thereby making it harder for poor women to obtain abortions.

A Counter Movement Arises

Public opinion polls registered majority support for most feminist goals, yet by the mid-1970s feminism faced a strong counter movement focused on preventing ratification of the ERA. Most states rushed to ratify the amendment, yet by 1973 a powerful opposition developed, led by Phyllis Schlafly, a conservative activist in the Republican Party and a Goldwater supporter in 1964. Schlafly mobilized a highly effective host of women at the grassroots level who believed that traditional gender roles were God-given and feared that feminism would devalue their own roles as wives and mothers. These women, marching on state capitols, persuaded some male legislators to block ratification. When the time limit ran out in 1982, only thirty-five states had ratified the amendment, three short of the necessary three-fourths majority. (See "Historical Question" in chapter 30, page 1118, and Map 30.3.)

Opposition to the right to abortion was even more intense. Many Americans believed that human life begins with conception, equating abortion with murder. The Catholic Church and other

> Feminist activism produced the most sweeping changes in laws and policies concerning women since they had won the right to vote in 1920.

Transnational Feminisms

When large numbers of American women began to protest sex discrimination in the 1960s, most were unaware that they belonged to a movement stretching more than one hundred years back in history and across oceans. In 1850, Ernestine Rose, who had been born in Poland and lived in Berlin, Paris, and London, told a women's rights convention in Massachusetts, "We are not contending here for the rights of the women of New England, or of old England, but of the world." Her statement affirmed the connections among women from France, Germany, England, Hungary, Finland, Belgium, and the United States, who wrote and visited each other and exchanged ideas and inspiration in the first international women's movement.

By the early twentieth century, women had formalized such connections. For example, the International Alliance of Women, founded in 1904 initially to promote global woman **suffrage**, expanded its agenda to include equal pay and employment, prostitution, peace, married women's citizenship, and more. By 1929, the Alliance claimed national organizations in fifty-one countries, including the United States and most of Europe, China, Egypt, India, Japan, Palestine, and several Latin American nations.

The search for a "universal sisterhood" revealed deep cleavages among the women who represented the nations of the Alliance. At its 1935 conference in Istanbul, Shareefeh Hamid Ali, representing India, warned that "any arrogant assumption of superiority or of patronage on the part of Europe or America . . . will alienate . . . the womanhood of Asia and Africa." White, Christian women from the United States and Europe dominated the organization and all too readily assumed that they could speak for all women. But oppression and discrimination looked quite different to women in other parts of the world. For example, in **colonized** countries such as India and Egypt, feminism arose alongside movements for independence from the very **imperial** nations that were home to most Alliance leaders. Egyptian feminist and nationalist Huda Sha'arawi was the only Muslim among the international leadership. She worked closely with the Alliance on many issues, but she realized the need to address the particular interests of Arab women overlooked or opposed by Euro-American feminists, and she established an Arab Feminist Union in 1945.

Temporarily disrupted by World War II, global connections among women increased dramatically with the creation of the United Nations. In a pathbreaking move, nations signing the UN Charter in 1945 affirmed "the equal rights of men and women" and "fundamental freedoms for all without distinction as to race, sex, language, or religion." Two years later, the UN established a Commission on the Status of Women, creating a forum for women from around the globe to meet and be heard; and in 1948 it adopted a Universal Declaration of Human Rights, which enumerated an extensive set of rights and explicitly rejected sex discrimination. Women pressed hard for such guarantees—including Eleanor Roosevelt, U.S. delegate to the UN who chaired the commission that drafted the declaration; Hansa Mehta, legislator and women's rights advocate from India; and Minerva Bernardino of the Dominican Republic.

These and other international commitments to justice for women went far beyond any rights guaranteed to women by the American legal system or those of most other nations, thereby setting standards and raising expectations. The UN, for example, asserted women's right to equal pay in 1951, twelve years before the U.S. Congress passed the Equal Pay Act of 1963, and the international body attacked discrimination in education a decade before Congress passed Title IX. While the dominant nations in the UN concentrated on security concerns, not women's issues, women around the world used these bold UN commitments to equality to advocate for rights in their own countries.

The UN helped launch a global feminist movement of unparalleled size and diversity when it declared 1975 International Women's Year and sponsored a conference in Mexico City. The unprecedented decision reflected a number of factors: growing concern about a rapidly increasing world population; rising interest in women's roles in economic development; the surge of feminism in member nations; and pressures from delegates to the UN's Commission on the Status of Women. Six thousand women came to Mexico City on their own, while official delegates from 125 nations approved a World Plan of Action for Women and prompted the UN to declare the UN Decade for Women (1976–1985).

International Women's Year Tribune

A majority of delegates at the UN International Women's Year Conference in Mexico City in July 1975 were women, but men provided the leadership and most of the speeches, and delegates frequently took positions mandated by their government but not necessarily representing the interests of women. In contrast, nongovernmental organizations associated with the UN sponsored a Tribune on the other side of the city, where 6,000 women, most of whom came to the conference on their own, attended workshops that they or their organizations designed. The Tribune was chaotic and confrontational, reflecting differences between Western women promoting equal rights and women from developing countries demading attention to poverty, and disagreements over whether such issues as apartheid in South Africa or the lack of self-government for Palestinians were women's issues. Yet most women were enlightened and energized by the gathering. A woman from Nigeria emphasized the "sharing and participation. You have pain for so many years, and now I know that women all over the world have this same pain. If this is all I get out of the Tribune, then that's enough."

© Bettye Lane.

In response to the Mexico City meeting's call for action in individual countries, the U.S. government sponsored a National Women's Conference in Houston, Texas, in 1977. More than 2,000 state delegates, representing a cross section of American womanhood, attended. They adopted a National Plan of Action, not only supporting such typical feminist goals as ratification of the ERA and reproductive freedom, but also addressing the needs of specific groups of women, including the elderly, lesbians, racial minorities, rural women, and homemakers. For the first time, the U.S. women's movement had a comprehensive national agenda setting goals for decades to come.

The three themes established for the UN Decade for Women—equality, development, peace—reflected an effort to address the enormously diverse needs of women throughout the world. Feminists from the United States and Europe who focused on equal rights met criticism from women representing impoverished **third world** countries—home to two-thirds of the world's women—who often took the position that "to talk feminism to a woman who has no water, no food, and no home is to talk nonsense." Ever larger UN-sponsored meetings followed Mexico City—Copenhagen in 1980, Nairobi in 1985, and Beijing in 1995, where 20,000 convened in an unofficial forum. From these global exchanges American feminists learned that they would have to revise their Western-centered perspective on women's needs if they hoped to participate in a truly international movement.

The UN Convention on the Elimination of All Forms of Discrimination against Women

(continued)

(continued)

(CEDAW), passed by the General Assembly in 1979, reflected the broadening definition of feminism and a new understanding of what constituted "women's issues." The most sweeping declaration of women's rights by any official body, CEDAW proclaimed not only women's right to work, education, and political participation, but also the obligation to safeguard women's interests in economic development programs and to eliminate all forms of colonialism. By 2002, more than 165 nations had ratified the treaty. Among the major nations, the only country not to approve was the United States, where conservatives charged that it would promote abortion and weaken the family.

American feminists also learned that the United States was not always the most advanced nation when it came to women's welfare and status.

For example, employed women in most other industrialized countries were entitled to paid maternity leave, and their children had access to public child care. By 2000, women had headed governments in more than 30 other countries, including Indira Gandhi in India, Golda Meir in Israel, and Margaret Thatcher in England. Many other nations, such as Argentina, Egypt, France, India, and the European Union, had some form of affirmative action to increase the numbers of women in government. And while American women held 13.8 percent of the seats in the House of Representatives, women constituted 20 percent of the lower house in South Korea, 25 percent in Mozambique, 30 percent in Germany, and more than 35 percent in Norway, Denmark, and Sweden. Yet, despite enormous differences among women around the world, internationally minded feminists were determined

to find common ground. For, as Gertrude Mongella, secretary general of the Beijing conference, insisted in 1995, "A revolution has begun and there is no going back. . . . This revolution is too just, too important, and too long overdue."

BIBLIOGRAPHY

Bonnie Anderson, *"Joyous Greetings": The First International Women's Movement, 1830–1860* (2000).

Arvonne S. Fraser, *The U.N. Decade for Women* (1987).

Estelle B. Freedman, *No Turning Back: The History of Feminism and the Future of Women* (2002).

Angela Miles, *Integrative Feminisms: Building Global Visions, 1960s–1990s* (1996).

Hilkka Pietilä and Jeanne Vickers, *Making Women Matter: The Role of the United Nations* (1994).

Leila J. Rupp, *Worlds of Women: The Making of an International Women's Movement* (1997).

Deborah Stienstra, *Women's Movements and International Organizations* (1994).

religious organizations provided institutional support for their protest; conservative politicians and their supporters constituted another segment of the right-to-life movement. Like ERA opponents with whom they often overlapped, the right-to-life movement mobilized thousands of women who believed that abortion disparaged motherhood and who saw feminism as a threat to their traditional roles.

Feminists faced a host of other challenges. Despite some inroads into male-dominated occupations, most women still worked in low-paying, traditionally female jobs. Employed women continued to bear primary responsibility for their homes and families, thereby working a "double day." Congress's effort to ease this burden with a comprehensive child care bill fell to President Nixon's veto in 1971. As the number of female-headed families doubled from 10 percent to 20 percent of all American families by the end of the century, the situation of working mothers became even more critical.

The Persistence of Liberal Reform in the Nixon Administration

Feminism was not the only movement to arouse strong antagonism. Opposition to civil rights measures, Great Society reforms, protest groups, and changing gender roles and sexual mores—along with frustrations surrounding the war in Vietnam (see chapter 29)—spawned a third-party challenge in 1968 and delivered the White House to Republican Richard M. Nixon. As presidential candidate, Nixon attacked the Great Society for "pouring billions of dollars into programs that have failed," and he promised to represent the "forgotten Americans, the non-shouters, the non-demonstrators."

Yet, despite Nixon's desire to attract southern whites and other Democrats disaffected by Johnson's reforms and by Democrat support for

Nixon's 1968 Campaign

Seeking the presidency in the turbulent year of protests, riots, and assassinations, Richard Nixon tried to appeal to a broad constituency of voters, reflected in this campaign poster. Prominent Republicans of all stripes appear, including the liberal Nelson Rockefeller and conservative Barry Goldwater. While the sign "Champion of Forgotten America" spoke to white Americans alienated by the Great Society's programs for minorities and the poor, the appearance of the black Republican senator Edward Brooke and Wilt Chamberlain of the Los Angeles Lakers nodded to African Americans. Nixon also appealed to youth by supporting the vote for eighteen-year-olds and promising to end the draft.

Collection of Janice L. and David J. Frent.

minority group causes, liberal policies persisted during his tenure as president. The Nixon administration either promoted or at least accepted substantially greater federal assistance to the poor, new protections for African Americans, Native Americans, women, and other groups, major environmental regulations, and financial policies deviating sharply from traditional Republican economics. As we shall see in chapter 30, Nixon's rhetoric and some of his policies played to a growing conservatism in American politics; yet the liberalism of the 1960s persisted into the early 1970s.

Extending the Welfare State and Regulating the Economy

The liberal policies of the Nixon administration reflected a number of forces. Not only did the Democrats retain control of Congress, but Nixon wanted to preserve support from moderates in his party and achieve Republican ascendancy by attracting some traditional Democrats. He could not entirely ignore grassroots movements, and his body of advisers included several who were sympathetic to environmentalism, Indian rights, and other reforms. Serious economic problems also compelled new approaches, and although Nixon's real passion lay in foreign rather than domestic policy, he knew that history's approving gaze would depend in part on how he handled problems at home.

Under Nixon, government assistance programs actually grew. Congress resisted many of his attacks on antipoverty programs, refusing, for example, to eliminate the Office of Economic Opportunity. Key programs such as Medicare and Medicaid, Head Start, Legal Services, and job training remained intact. Indeed, the federal budget for social services exceeded defense spending for the first time since World War II. Social Security benefits—now required to rise with the cost of living—increased; subsidies for low income housing tripled; and a new billion-dollar program provided Pell grants (named for the bill's sponsor) for low-income students to attend college. In response to growing public concern about undernourishment, Nixon supported a huge expansion of the food stamp program, which benefited 12.5 million recipients. Noting the disparity between Nixon's political speeches designed to gain votes and his actual practice as president, his disgruntled speechwriter, the archconservative Pat Buchanan, grumbled, "Vigorously did we inveigh against the Great Society, enthusiastically did we fund it."

Nixon also acted contrary to his rhetoric against a growing federal bureaucracy by expanding controls over the economy when economic crises and energy shortages induced him to increase the federal government's power in the marketplace. Throughout the post–World War II economic boom, the nation's abundant oil deposits and access to cheap Middle Eastern oil had encouraged the building of large cars and glass-enclosed skyscrapers with no concern for fuel efficiency. The traditional American assumption that energy resources were boundless and the resulting wasteful practices meant that by the 1970s the United States, with just 6 percent of the world's population, consumed one-third of its fuel resources.

In the fall of 1973, the United States faced its first energy crisis when Arab nations, furious at the nation's support of Israel during the Yom Kippur War (see chapter 29), cut off oil shipments to the United States. As oil supplies fell in the winter of 1973–74, long lines formed at gas stations, where prices had nearly doubled, many homes were cold, and some schools closed. In response, Nixon authorized temporary emergency measures allocating petroleum and establishing a national 55-mile-per-hour speed limit to save gasoline. By the spring of 1974, the crisis had eased, but the United States had yet to come to grips with its seemingly unquenchable demand for fuel and dependence on foreign oil.

> Nixon expanded the government's regulatory role with a host of environmental protection measures.

Soaring energy prices contributed to severe economic problems. Fueled by the Vietnam War, by 1969 inflation had risen to 7 percent, an enormous increase for Americans used to rates of about 2 percent. In 1970, unemployment hit the economy hard. This unprecedented combination of a stagnant economy and inflation was dubbed "stagflation." Domestic troubles were compounded by the decline of American dominance in the international economy. Having fully recovered from World War II, the economies of Japan and Western Europe grew faster than that of the United States in the 1970s. Foreign cars, electronic equipment, and other products competed favorably with American goods throughout the world. In 1971, for the first time in decades, the United States imported more than it exported. Because the amount of dollars in foreign hands exceeded U.S. gold reserves, the nation could no longer back up its currency with gold.

The president's response to these economic problems diverged from conventional Republican doctrine. With an eye to the 1972 election, Nixon announced a "New Economic Policy" in August 1971. He abandoned the convertibility of dollars into gold, devalued the dollar to make American goods cheaper in foreign markets and thus increase exports, and imposed a 10 percent surcharge on most imports. Nixon also froze wages and prices, thus enabling the government to stimulate the economy without fueling more inflation. In the short run, these policies worked. Exports surged ahead of imports, inflation subsided, unemployment fell below 5 percent, and Nixon was resoundingly reelected in 1972. Yet the New Economic Policy treated the economy only superficially. The lifting of price and wage controls in 1973, the Arab oil embargo, and rising food prices sent the consumer price index soaring by 11 percent by 1974. Unemployment also crept back up, and Nixon's successor inherited the most severe economic crisis since the depression of the 1930s.

More successfully, Nixon expanded the government's regulatory role with a host of environmental protection measures. Influenced especially by his domestic policy chief, John Ehrlichman, Nixon responded to growing public concern for the environment, proclaiming in 1970 that the nation must make "reparations for the damage we have done to our air, to our land and to our water." In addition to establishing the Environmental Protection Agency, Nixon signed strong clean-air legislation and measures to regulate noise pollution, oil spill cleanup, and the dumping of pesticides into the oceans. Although environmentalists claimed that Nixon failed to do enough, pointing particularly to his veto—for budgetary reasons—of the Clean Water Act of 1972, which Congress overrode, no previous administration had matched the initiatives undertaken under Nixon.

Responding to Demands for Social Justice

Nixon's 1968 campaign had exploited antipathy to black protest and new civil rights policies in order to woo white southerners and northern workers away from the Democratic Party, yet his administration had to answer to the courts and Congress. In 1968, fourteen years after the *Brown* decision, school desegregation had barely touched the South: Two-thirds of African American children did not have a single white schoolmate. Like Eisenhower, Nixon was reluctant to use federal power to compel integration, but the Supreme Court overruled efforts by the Justice Department to delay court-ordered desegregation and compelled the administration to enforce the law. By the time Nixon left office, fewer than one in ten southern black children attended totally segregated schools.

The Nixon administration also began to implement affirmative action, requiring contractors and unions to employ more minority workers on federally funded construction projects and awarding more government contracts and loans to minority businesses. Congress took the initiative in other areas. In 1970, it extended the Voting Rights Act of 1965 by five years; and in 1972, Congress strengthened the Civil Rights Act of 1964 by enlarging the enforcement powers of the EEOC and authorizing it to initiate lawsuits against employers suspected of discrimination.

While women as well as minority groups benefited from the implementation of affirmative action and the strengthened EEOC, several measures of the Nixon administration specifically attacked sex discrimination. The president had quite conventional—and patronizing—attitudes about women's capabilities and appropriate roles, responding to criticism that he had not appointed many women to federal jobs as "Much ado about *nothing!*" Yet again he confronted a growing popular movement and listened to more open-minded advisers and Republican feminists. Nixon vetoed a child care bill and publicly opposed abortion, but he signed the pathbreaking Title IX, banning sex discrimination in education, and a measure providing women equal access to credit.

President Nixon gave more public support for justice to Native Americans than to any other protest group. While not giving in to radical demands, the administration dealt cautiously with extreme protests, such as the occupations of Alcatraz Island, the Bureau of Indian Affairs, and Wounded Knee. Nixon denounced termination and forced assimilation, calling for "self-determination among the Indian people." He signed measures recognizing claims of Alaskan and New Mexican Indians and restoring tribal status to the Menominee, whose status had been terminated in 1961, and he set in motion legislation restoring additional tribal lands and granting Indians more control over their schools and other service institutions.

Conclusion: Achievements and Limitations of Liberalism

Senate majority leader Mike Mansfield was not alone in concluding that Lyndon Johnson "has done more than FDR ever did, or ever thought of doing." Yet opposition to his leadership grew so strong by 1968 that Johnson abandoned hopes for reelection. As his liberal vision lay in ruins,

he asked, "How was it possible that all these people could be so ungrateful to me after I have given them so much?"

Fannie Lou Hamer could have provided a number of reasons. Support from the federal government was minimal when local officials arrested and beat her and others who were organizing Mississippi blacks to obtain their rights. "We learned the hard way that even though we had all the law and all the righteousness on our side—that white man is not going to give up his power to us," Hamer concluded. Moreover, her efforts to use Johnson's antipoverty programs to help poor blacks in Mississippi eventually ended in failure. Internal problems hampered her projects, but they also reflected some of the more general shortcomings of the War on Poverty. Inadequately planned and funded, many antipoverty programs ended up benefiting industry and the nonpoor as much as or more than the impoverished. Because Johnson refused to ask for sacrifices from prosperous Americans, the Great Society never approached the redistribution of wealth and resources that would have been necessary for the elimination of poverty.

Black aspirations exceeded white Americans' commitment to genuine equality. It was easy for northerners to be sympathetic when the civil rights movement focused on crude and blatant forms of racism in the South. But when it attacked the subtler racism that existed throughout the nation and sought equality in fact as well as in rights, the black freedom struggle confronted a powerful backlash. By the end of the 1960s, the revolution in the legal status of African Americans was complete, but the black freedom struggle had lost much of its momentum, and African Americans remained, with Native Americans and Chicanos, at the bottom of the economic ladder.

Critics of Johnson's Great Society on the left as well as on the expanding right overlooked its more successful and lasting elements. Medicare and Medicaid provided access to health care for the elderly and the poor and contributed to a sharp decline in poverty among aged Americans. Programs of federal aid for education and housing became permanent elements of national policy. Moreover, even though swept into the White House on a backlash against the liberalism of the 1960s, Richard Nixon's administration implemented school desegregation in the South and affirmative action, expanded government assistance to the disadvantaged, initiated substantial environmental regulations, and secured new rights for Native Americans and women. Although the material status of minorities remained below that of white Americans, new policies provided greater opportunities for those able to take advantage of them. Women especially benefited from the decline of discrimination, and significant numbers of African Americans and other minority groups began to enter the middle class.

Yet the perceived shortcomings of government programs contributed to social turmoil and fueled the resurgence of conservative politics. Young radicals launched direct confrontations with the government and universities that, together with racial conflict, escalated into political discord and social disorder not seen since the union wars of the 1930s. The war in Vietnam polarized American society as much as did racial issues or the behavior of young people, and Johnson's and Nixon's conduct of the war undermined faith in presidential leadership. The war starved the Great Society, devouring revenues that might have been used for social reform and eclipsing the substantial progress that had actually been achieved.

For additional firsthand accounts of this period, see Chapter 28 in Michael Johnson, ed., *Reading the American Past*, Third Edition.

To assess your mastery of the material in this chapter, see the Online Study Guide at bedfordstmartins.com/ roark.

For Web links related to the topics in this chapter, see "HistoryLinks," "DocLinks," and "PlaceLinks" at bedfordstmartins.com/roark.

CHRONOLOGY

1960
- African American college students in Greensboro, North Carolina, stage sit-in at whites-only lunch counter.
- Democrat John F. Kennedy elected president.
- Student Nonviolent Coordinating Committee (SNCC) established to mobilize young people for direct action for civil rights.
- Students for a Democratic Society (SDS) founded to promote participatory democracy, economic justice, and peace.

1961
- Congress of Racial Equality (CORE) sponsors Freedom Rides to desegregate interstate transportation in South.

1962
- Michael Harrington's *The Other America* published, exposing widespread poverty in the United States.
- Cesar Chavez and Dolores Huerta found United Farm Workers (UFW) to better conditions for Chicano migrant laborers.
- Rachel Carson's *Silent Spring* published, exposing the dangers of dioxin, DDT, and other poisons to the environment.

1963
- Betty Friedan's best-selling book *The Feminine Mystique* published.

- President's Commission on the Status of Women issues report documenting widespread sex discrimination.
- Equal Pay Act makes wage disparities based solely on gender illegal.
- *Baker v. Carr* mandates electoral redistricting to enforce "one person, one vote" principle.
- *Abington School District v. Schempp* outlaws prayer in public schools.
- Mississippi NAACP leader Medgar Evers assassinated in Jackson.
- March on Washington becomes largest civil rights demonstration in U.S. history.
- President Kennedy assassinated in Dallas, Texas; Vice President Lyndon B. Johnson becomes president.

1964
- Congress enacts Civil Rights Act, the strongest such measure since Reconstruction.
- Economic Opportunity Act launches Lyndon Johnson's War on Poverty.
- Free speech movement, first large-scale white student protest of 1960s, organized at University of California, Berkeley.
- Malcolm X breaks from Nation of Islam and attracts wide following.

- President Johnson elected to full term in landslide over Republican senator Barry Goldwater.
- Tax cut bill proposed by Kennedy administration passes.

1965
- Malcolm X assassinated in New York City.
- Selma-to-Montgomery march for voting rights; Johnson orders federal protection for marchers after they are attacked.
- Congress passes Voting Rights Act, establishing protections for minorities' access to the ballot.
- **August**. The Watts district of Los Angeles erupts in riots protesting police brutality.

1965–1966

- 89th Congress passes most of Johnson's Great Society domestic programs, including antipoverty measures, public works acts, aid to education, and Medicare/Medicaid.

1966
- Black Panther Party founded, advocating African American economic and political autonomy.
- In *Miranda v. Arizona*, Supreme Court requires police to inform suspects of their rights.
- National Organization for Women (NOW) founded.

1967
- **July**. Riots break out in Detroit.

1968
- Martin Luther King Jr. assassinated in Memphis, Tennessee; riots erupt in Washington, D.C., and elsewhere.
- American Indian Movement (AIM) founded.
- Republican Richard M. Nixon elected president.

1969
- Native Americans occupy Alcatraz Island.

1970
- Earth Day demonstrations held to support environmental goals.
- Congress passes Occupational Safety and Health Act to improve workplace conditions.
- Environmental Protection Agency established by Nixon.
- Clean Air Act sets standards, imposes restrictions on emissions of pollutants.
- Native American Women's Association founded.
- Women Strike for Peace and Equality demonstrations take place nationwide.

1971
- First national Mexican American women's conference held.
- Nixon's New Economic Policy abandons gold standard, imposes price and wage controls.

1972
- Title IX of Education Amendments bans sex discrimination in education.
- Congress passes Equal Rights Amendment, sends it to states for ratification.
- American Indians' "Trail of Broken Treaties" caravan to Washington, D.C., and seizure of the Bureau of Indian Affairs.

1973
- AIM members occupy Wounded Knee to press Indian claims against the U.S. government.
- National Black Feminist Organization founded.
- In *Roe v. Wade*, Supreme Court rules that abortion is constitutionally protected.

BIBLIOGRAPHY

General Works

John Morton Blum, *Years of Discord: American Politics and Society, 1961–1974* (1991).

David Burner, *Making Peace with the 60s* (1996).

David Farber, *The Age of Great Dreams: America in the 1960s* (1994).

Hugh Davis Graham, *The Civil Rights Era: Origins and Development of National Policy, 1960–1972* (1990).

Maurice Isserman and Michael Kazin, *America Divided: The Civil War of the 1960s* (2000).

Allen J. Matusow, *The Unraveling of America: A History of Liberalism in the 1960s* (1984).

Douglas T. Miller, *On Our Own: Americans in the Sixties* (1996).

Edward P. Morgan, *The Sixties Experience: Hard Lessons about Modern America* (1991).

William L. O'Neill, *Coming Apart: An Informal History of America in the 1960s* (1971).

Barbara L. Tischler, ed., *Sights on the Sixties* (1992).

The Black Freedom Struggle

Peter J. Albert and Ronald Hoffman, eds., *We Shall Overcome: Martin Luther King Jr. and the Black Freedom Struggle* (1990).

Jervis Anderson, *Bayard Rustin: Troubles I've Seen* (1997).

Taylor Branch, *Parting the Waters: America in the King Years, 1954–63* (1988).

Taylor Branch, *Pillar of Fire: America in the King Years, 1963–65* (1998).

James W. Button, *Black Violence: Political Impact of the 1960s Riots* (1978).

Clayborne Carson, *In Struggle: SNCC and the Black Awakening of the 1960s* (1981).

David L. Chappell, *Inside Agitators: White Southerners in the Civil Rights Movement* (1994).

John Dittmer, *Local People: The Struggle for Civil Rights in Mississippi* (1994).

Michael Eric Dyson, *Making Malcolm: The Myth and Meaning of Malcolm X* (1995).

David J. Garrow, *Protest at Selma: Martin Luther King Jr. and the Voting Rights Act of 1965* (1978).

David J. Garrow, *Bearing the Cross: Martin Luther King Jr. and the Southern Christian Leadership Conference* (1986).

Peter L. Goldman, *The Death and Life of Malcolm X* (1979).

Ralph G. Gomes and Linda Faye Williams, eds., *From Exclusion to Inclusion: The Long Struggle for African American Political Power* (1992).

Steven F. Lawson, *Running for Freedom: Civil Rights and Black Politics in America since 1941* (1991).

Chana Kai Lee, *For Freedom's Sake: The Life of Fannie Lou Hamer* (1999).

John Lewis with Michael D'Orso, *Walking with the Wind: A Memoir of the Movement* (1998).

Doug McAdam, *Freedom Summer* (1989).

August Meier and Elliott M. Rudwick, *CORE: A Study in the Civil Rights Movement, 1942–1968* (1973).

Stephen B. Oates, *Let the Trumpet Sound: The Life of Martin Luther King Jr.* (1982).

Kenneth O'Reilly, *"Racial Matters": The FBI's Secret File on Black America, 1960–1972* (1989).

Frank R. Parker, *Black Votes Count: Political Empowerment in Mississippi after 1965* (1990).

Charles Payne, *I've Got the Light of Freedom: The Organizing Tradition and the Mississippi Freedom Struggle* (1995).

Bruce Perry, *Malcolm: The Life of a Man Who Changed Black America* (1991).

James R. Ralph Jr., *Northern Protest: Martin Luther King Jr., Chicago, and the Civil Rights Movement* (1993).

Barbara Ransby, *Ella Baker and the Black Freedom Movement: A Radical Democratic Vision* (2003).

Belinda Robnett, *How Long? How Long? African-American Women in the Struggle for Civil Rights* (1997).

Timothy Tyson, *Radio Free Dixie: Robert F. Williams and the Roots of Black Power* (1999).

Frederick M. Wirt, *"We Ain't What We Was": Civil Rights in the New South* (1997).

Politics and Policies

David Burner, *John F. Kennedy and a New Generation* (1988).

Robert Caro, *The Years of Lyndon Johnson*, vols. 1, 2, and 3 (1982, 1990, and 2002).

Paul K. Conkin, *Big Daddy from the Pedernales: Lyndon Baines Johnson* (1986).

Robert Dallek, *Flawed Giant: Lyndon B. Johnson, 1960–1973* (1998).

Robert Dallek, *An Unfinished Life: John F. Kennedy, 1917–1963* (2003).

James N. Giglio, *The Presidency of John F. Kennedy* (1992).

Robert Alan Goldberg, *Barry Goldwater* (1995).

Joan Hoff, *Nixon Reconsidered* (1994).

Michael B. Katz, *The Undeserving Poor: From the War on Poverty to the War on Welfare* (1989).

Doris Kearns, *Lyndon Johnson and the American Dream* (1976).

Robert Mann, *The Walls of Jericho: Lyndon Johnson, Hubert Humphrey, Richard Russell, and the Struggle for Civil Rights* (1996).

Rick Perlstein, *Before the Storm: Barry Goldwater and the Unmaking of the American Consensus* (2001).

Gerald Posner, *Case Closed: Lee Harvey Oswald and the Assassination of JFK* (1993).

Jill Quadagno, *The Color of Welfare: How Racism Undermined the War on Poverty* (1994).

Richard Reeves, *President Kennedy: Profile of Power* (1993).

Mark Stern, *Calculating Visions: Kennedy, Johnson, and Civil Rights* (1992).

Irwin Unger, *The Best of Intentions: The Triumph and Failure of the Great Society* (1996).

Tom Wicker, *One of Us: Richard Nixon and the American Dream* (1991).

Protest Movements

Terry H. Anderson, *The Movement and the Sixties* (1995).

Stewart Burns, *Social Movements of the 1960s: Searching for Democracy* (1990).

David Chalmers, *And the Crooked Places Made Straight: The Struggle for Social Change in the 1960s* (1991).

Martha F. Davis, *Brutal Need: Lawyers and the Welfare Rights Movement, 1960–1973* (1993).

Vine Deloria Jr., *Behind the Trail of Broken Treaties* (1974).

Ignacio M. Garcia, *United We Win: The Rise and Fall of La Raza Unida Party* (1989).

Todd Gitlin, *The Sixties: Years of Hope, Days of Rage* (1987).

Juan Gómez-Quiñones, *Chicano Politics: Reality and Promise, 1940–1990* (1990).

Manuel G. Gonzales, *Mexicanos: A History of Mexicans in the United States* (1999).

Richard Griswold del Castillo and Richard A. Garcia, *Cesar Chavez: A Triumph of Spirit* (1995).

Laurence M. Hauptman, *The Iroquois Struggle for Survival: World War II to Red Power* (1986).

Maurice Isserman, *If I Had a Hammer . . . : The Death of the Old Left and the Birth of the New Left* (1987).

George Katsiaficas, *The Imagination of the New Left: A Global Analysis of 1968* (1987).

Cyril Levitt, *Children of Privilege: Student Revolt in the Sixties* (1984).

Peter B. Levy, *The New Left and Labor in the 1960s* (1994).

Peter Matthiessen, *In the Spirit of Crazy Horse* (1983).

James Miller, *"Democracy Is in the Streets": From Port Huron to the Siege of Chicago* (1987).

Joan Moore and Harry Pachon, *Hispanics in the United States* (1985).

Donald L. Parman, *Indians and the American West in the Twentieth Century* (1994).

Doug Rossinow, *The Politics of Authenticity: Liberalism, Christianity, and the New Left in America* (1998).

John D. Skrentny, *The Minority Rights Revolution* (2002).

William Wei, *The Asian American Movement* (1993).

Cultural Change, Sexual Revolution, and Feminism

David Allyn, *Make Love, Not War: The Sexual Revolution, an Unfettered History* (2000).

Beth Bailey, *Sex in the Heartland* (1999).

Maxine Leeds Craig, *Ain't I a Beauty Queen? Black Women, Beauty, and the Politics of Race* (2002).

Flora Davis, *Moving the Mountain: The Women's Movement since 1960* (1991).

Alice Echols, *Daring to Be Bad: Radical Feminism in America, 1967–1975* (1989).

Sara Evans, *Personal Liberation: The Roots of Women's Liberation in the Civil Rights Movement and the New Left* (1978).

Sara Evans, *Tidal Wave: How Women Changed America at Century's End* (2003).

Judith Ezekiel, *Feminism in the Heartland* (2002).

Jo Freeman, *The Politics of Liberation* (1975).

David Garrow, *Liberty and Sexuality: The Right to Privacy and the Making of* Roe v. Wade (1994).

Cynthia Harrison, *On Account of Sex: The Politics of Women's Issues, 1945–1968* (1988).

Susan M. Hartmann, *The Other Feminists: Activists in the Liberal Establishment* (1998).

Daniel Horowitz, *Betty Friedan and the Making of* The Feminine Mystique (1998).

James Miller, *Flowers in the Dustbin: The Rise of Rock and Roll, 1947–1977* (1999).

Ruth Rosen, *The World Split Open: How the Modern Women's Movement Changed America* (2000).

William L. Van Deburg, *New Days in Babylon: The Black Power Movement and American Culture, 1965–1975* (1993).

The Supreme Court

Archibald Cox, *The Warren Court: Constitutional Decision as an Instrument of Reform* (1968).

Richard Y. Funston, *Constitutional Counterrevolution? The Warren Court and the Burger Court: Judicial Policy Making in Modern America* (1977).

Philip B. Kurland, *Politics and the Warren Court* (1970).

Paul L. Murphy, *The Constitution in Crisis Times, 1918–1969* (1972).

Lucas A. Powe Jr., *The Warren Court and American Politics* (2000).

Bernard Schwartz, *Super Chief: Earl Warren and His Supreme Court, a Judicial Biography* (1983).

Bernard Schwartz, ed., *The Warren Court: A Retrospective* (1996).

Melvin I. Urofsky, *The Continuity of Change: The Supreme Court and Individual Liberties, 1953–1986* (1991).

FATIGUE HAT WITH BUTTONS
The button on this fatigue hat belonging
to a veteran who served two tours of duty
demonstrates veterans' response to the many Americans who just wanted to forget the war that the United States
failed to win. Because their war was so different from other American wars, Viet-
nam veterans often returned home to hostility or indifference. The POW-MIA pin refers to prisoners of war and those
missing in action. This man was unusual in serving two tours of duty in Vietnam; most soldiers served only one year.
Why might he have gone back for a second tour? How might his experiences have differed in the two periods separated by five years?

Nancy Gewitz / Antique Textile Resource / Picture Research Consultants & Archives.

Vietnam and the Limits of Power

1961–1975

AS CHARLES ANDERSON'S PLANE prepared to land, the pilot announced, "Gentlemen, we'll be touching down in Da Nang, Vietnam, in about ten minutes. . . . Fasten your seat belts, please. On behalf of the entire crew and staff, I'd like to say we've enjoyed having you with us . . . and we hope to see all of you again next year on your way home. Goodbye and good luck." Like most soldiers after 1966, Charles Anderson went to war on a commercial jetliner, complete with stewardesses (as they were called then) in miniskirts.

Military personnel traveling to battle like business executives or tourists only hints at how different the Vietnam War was from America's previous wars. Marine infantry officer Philip Caputo landed at Da Nang in March 1965 confident that the enemy "would be quickly beaten and that we were doing something altogether noble and good." But in just a few months, "what had begun as an adventurous expedition had turned into an exhausting, indecisive war of attrition in which we fought for no other cause than our own survival."

Another soldier discovered even more quickly that "something was wrong." Wondering why the bus taking him from the air base to the compound had wire mesh over the windows, he was told, "The gooks will throw grenades through the windows." Soldiers in Vietnam initially used the racist word *gook* to refer to the enemy—the North Vietnamese or their supporters in the south—but it quickly became a term used for any Vietnamese. "From one day to the next, you could see for yourself changes coming over guys on our side—decent fellows, who wouldn't dream of calling an Oriental a 'gook' back home," reported one American. The problem was that "they couldn't tell who was their friend and who wasn't. Day after day, out on patrol we'd come to . . . a shabby village, and the elders would welcome us and the children come running with smiles on their faces, waiting for the candy we'd give them. But . . . just as we were leaving the village behind, the enemy would open up on us, and there was bitterness among us that the villagers hadn't given us warning."

Americans' horrifying and bewildering experiences in Vietnam grew out of **cold war** commitments made in the 1940s and 1950s by Presidents Harry S. Truman and Dwight D. Eisenhower. John F. Kennedy wholeheartedly took on those commitments, promising more flexible and vigorous efforts to thwart **communism**. In the most memorable words of his 1961 inauguration, he declared, "Let every nation know, whether it wishes us well or ill, that we shall pay any price, bear any burden, meet any hardship, support any friend, oppose any foe to assure the survival and the success of liberty."

Fighting the Climate and Geography
Steamy tropical conditions and inhospitable terrain were among the nonhuman enemies U.S. troops faced in Vietnam. Soldiers like this one making his way under fire through a rice paddy in 1966 were soaked for weeks on end. Veteran Philip Caputo wrote about "being pounded numb by ceaseless rain" during the monsoon; "at night we squatted in muddy holes, picked off the leeches that sucked on our veins."

Henri Gilles Huet/World Wide Photos, Inc.

Vietnam became the foremost test of Kennedy's pledge. He sent increasing amounts of American arms and personnel to sustain the South Vietnamese government, and Lyndon B. Johnson dramatically escalated that commitment. By 1965, the civil war in Vietnam had become America's war, with 543,000 military personnel serving there at peak strength in 1968 and more than 3 million total throughout the war's duration. Yet this massive intervention not only failed to defeat North Vietnam but also added a new burden to the costs of fighting the cold war—intense discord at home. The Vietnam War cost President Johnson another term in office and contributed to the political demise of his Republican successor, Richard M. Nixon. Some Americans lauded the U.S. goal in Vietnam and decried only the nation's unwillingness to pursue it effectively. Others believed that preserving a non-Communist South Vietnam was neither in the best interests of the United States nor within its capacity or moral right to achieve.

But none could deny the war's enormous costs. "The promises of the Great Society have been shot down on the battlefield of Vietnam," said Martin Luther King Jr. In addition to derailing domestic reform, the war exacted a heavy toll in American lives and dollars, kindled internal conflict, and led to the violation of the rights of antiwar protesters. Like the African American freedom struggle, Vietnam had a deep and lasting effect on the nation.

Even as the United States incurred tremendous costs in fighting communism in Vietnam (and intervened on a much smaller scale in other **third world** countries), its leaders moved to ease cold war tensions with the major Communist powers—the Soviet Union and China. The United States and Russia cooperated during the 1960s to limit nuclear testing and the spread of nuclear weapons; in 1972, they agreed to the first restrictions on the development of new weapons since the beginning of the nuclear age. In addition, Nixon's historic visit to China in 1972 marked abandonment of the policy of isolating China and paved the way for normal diplomatic relations by the end of the 1970s.

New Frontiers in Foreign Policy

John F. Kennedy moved quickly to fulfill his promise to pursue **containment** with a more aggressive yet more flexible foreign policy, expanding the nation's ability to wage nuclear, conventional, or **guerrilla warfare**. His secretary of defense, Robert S. McNamara, and several other advisers shared the president's youth, Ivy League education, and competitiveness. Exuding confidence and eager to apply technology to problem solving, they welcomed danger and risk—characteristics that sometimes contributed to foreign policy crises under both Kennedy and Johnson.

In order to ensure U.S. superiority over the Soviet Union in every domain, Kennedy accelerated the nation's space exploration program and increased attention to the third world. In his unflinching determination to halt communism, Kennedy took the United States to the brink of nuclear war during the 1962 Cuban missile crisis. Less dramatically but no less tenaciously, Kennedy stepped up American arms and personnel to save the government of South Vietnam from Communist insurgents.

Meeting the "Hour of Maximum Danger"

Kennedy and other Democrats criticized the Eisenhower administration for relying too heavily on nuclear weapons. They wanted to build up conventional ground forces as well, to provide the nation a **flexible response** to Communist expansion. They also charged that limits on defense spending had allowed the United States to fall behind even in nuclear capability. In January 1961, Kennedy warned that the nation faced a grave peril: "Each day the crises multiply. . . . Each day we draw nearer the hour of maximum danger."

Although the president exaggerated the actual threat to national security, several developments in 1961 heightened the sense of crisis and provided rationalization for a military buildup. In a speech made shortly before Kennedy's inauguration, Soviet premier Nikita Khrushchev had encouraged "wars of national liberation," thereby aligning the Soviet Union with independence movements (usually anti-Western) in the third world. Khrushchev wanted to bolster Soviet leadership of the Communist world against challenges by the People's Republic of China, and to shore up his political position at home by projecting forcefulness abroad. U.S. officials, however, saw in his words a threat to the status quo of containment.

Nowhere was the perceived threat closer to home than in Cuba, just ninety miles from the United States. Fidel Castro's revolution had already moved Cuba into the Soviet orbit; and under Eisenhower, the CIA had been planning an invasion by anti-Castro exiles. Kennedy ordered the invasion to proceed even though his military advisers gave it only a fair chance of success. To do otherwise, the president believed, would create an appearance of weakness.

MAP 29.1 U.S. Involvement in Latin America and the Caribbean, 1954–1994
During the cold war, the United States frequently intervened in Central American and Caribbean countries to suppress Communist or leftist movements.

READING THE MAP: How many and which Latin American countries did the United States directly invade? What was the extent of U.S. indirect involvement in other upheavals in the region?
CONNECTIONS: What role did geographic proximity play in U.S. policy toward the region? What was the significance of the Cuban missile crisis for U.S. foreign policy? Did the political party of the intervening administration make a difference? Why or why not?

FOR MORE HELP ANALYZING THIS MAP, see the map activity for this chapter in the Online Study Guide at bedfordstmartins.com/roark.

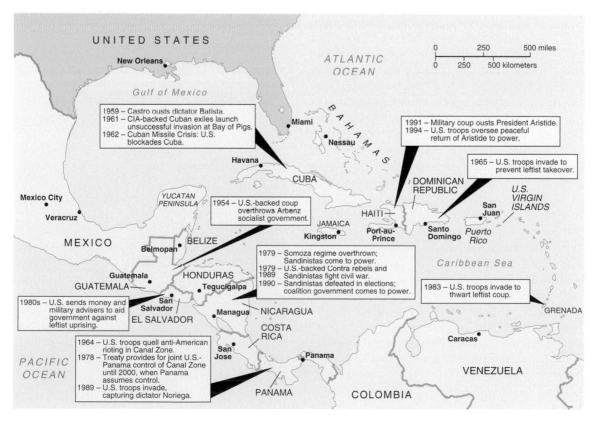

On April 17, 1961, about 1,300 anti-Castro exiles who had been trained and armed by the CIA landed at the Bay of Pigs on the south shore of Cuba (Map 29.1). Contrary to expectations, no popular uprising materialized to support the anti-Castro brigade. Kennedy refused to supply direct military support, and the invaders quickly fell to Castro's forces, who through intelligence leaks knew about the invasion and were prepared. The disaster was humiliating for Kennedy and the United States, posing a stark contrast to Kennedy's inaugural promise of a new, more effective foreign policy. The attempted armed interference in another nation compromised the moral authority of the United States, evoked memories of **Yankee imperialism** among Latin American countries, aligned Cuba even more closely with the Soviet Union, and helped Castro consolidate his power.

> The attempted armed interference in another nation compromised the moral authority of the United States, evoked memories of Yankee imperialism, aligned Cuba even more closely with the Soviet Union, and helped Castro consolidate his power.

Shortly before the Bay of Pigs invasion, the United States had suffered a psychological blow when a Soviet astronaut became the first human to orbit the earth. In May 1961, Kennedy called for a huge new commitment to the space race. "If we are to win the battle that is now going on around the world between freedom and tyranny," the United States must "take a clearly leading role in space achievement." His goal: an American on the moon within six to eight years. Congress authorized the Apollo program and boosted appropriations for space exploration. In 1962, John H. Glenn orbited the earth. Then in 1969, the United States surpassed the Soviet Union when Neil A. Armstrong and Edwin E. "Buzz" Aldrin Jr. became the first humans to set foot on the moon.

Early in his presidency, Kennedy sought a meeting with Khrushchev "to show him that we can be as tough as he is." The two met in June 1961, in Vienna, Austria, but contrary to Kennedy's expectations, Khrushchev was belligerent and threatening and shook the president's confidence. The stunned president reported to a journalist, "He just beat [the] hell out of me. . . . If he thinks I'm inexperienced and have no guts . . . we won't get anywhere with him." Khrushchev demanded an agreement recognizing the existence of two Germanys; otherwise, he warned, the Soviets would sign a separate treaty with East Germany, a move that would threaten America's occupation rights in West Berlin and its access to the city, which lay some one hundred miles within East Germany. Kennedy responded by substantially increasing U.S. military forces in Europe.

The massive exodus of East Germans into West Berlin, which had begun shortly after Berlin was partitioned following World War II, caused the Communists major embarrassment. To stop this flow of escapees from behind the **iron curtain**, on August 13, 1961, East Germany erected a wall between East and West Berlin, shocking the world. With the Berlin Wall stemming the tide of migration, Khrushchev backed off from his threats. But not until 1972 did the superpowers recognize East and West Germany as separate nations and guarantee Western access to West Berlin.

Humans Reach the Moon
In July 1969, less than a decade after President John F. Kennedy announced the goal of "landing a man on the moon and returning him safely to earth," the space capsule *Apollo 11* carried astronauts Edwin E. ("Buzz") Aldrin Jr. and Neil A. Armstrong to the moon. As millions of people watched on television, Armstrong became the first human to step on the moon's surface, saying, "That's one small step for a man, one giant leap for mankind." Armstrong and Aldrin collected rock samples and conducted scientific experiments. In this photo, Aldrin appears with a flag that had to be stretched on supports because the moon is windless.
NASA/Johnson Space Center.

Kennedy used the Berlin crisis to add $3.2 billion to the defense budget and to expand the military by 300,000 troops. This buildup of conventional forces met Kennedy's demand for "a wider choice than humiliation or all-out nuclear action" by providing a "flexible reponse" strategy. When the Soviet Union terminated its three-year moratorium on nuclear testing, the United States followed suit and vigorously developed new weapons and delivery systems.

New Approaches to the Third World

The Kennedy administration sought to complement its hard-line policy toward the Soviet Union with fresh approaches to the independence movements that had convulsed the world since the end of World War II. In 1960 alone, seventeen African nations gained their independence. Much more than his predecessors, the president publicly supported third world **democratic** and **nationalist** aspirations, believing that the United States could win over developing nations by helping to fulfill hopes for independence and democracy. To that end, Kennedy created the Alliance for Progress, promising $20 billion in aid for Latin America over the next decade. Like the Marshall Plan, the Alliance for Progress was designed to thwart communism and hold nations within the American sphere by fostering economic development. Likewise, the new Agency for International Development (AID) emphasized economic aid over military aid in foreign assistance programs.

In 1961, Kennedy launched his most dramatic third world initiative: the Peace Corps. Exemplifying the personal sacrifice summoned by Kennedy in his inaugural address, the program attracted idealistic volunteers, such as one who expressed his discomfort at having been "born between clean sheets when others were issued into the dust with a birthright of hunger." After studying a country's language and culture, Peace Corps volunteers went to work directly with its people, opening schools, providing basic health care, and assisting with agriculture, nutrition, and small economic enterprises. By the mid-1970s, more than 60,000 volunteers had fanned out around the globe, serving two-year stints in Latin America, Africa, and Asia.

Nevertheless, Kennedy's foreign aid initiatives fell far short of their objectives. Though generally welcomed, Peace Corps projects numbered too few to make a dent in the poverty and suffering in third world countries. By 1969, the

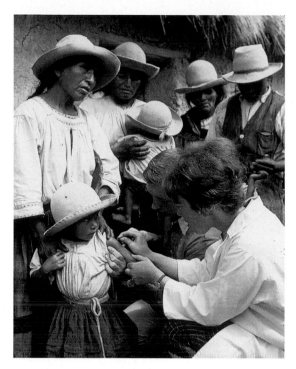

Peace Corps Volunteers in Bolivia
The majority of Peace Corps volunteers worked on educational projects in developing countries. Others helped increase food production, build public works, and curb diseases, as did these volunteers, Rita Helmkamp and Ed Dennison, vaccinating a young Bolivian girl. President John F. Kennedy saw the Peace Corps volunteers, with their dedication to freedom, "overcoming the efforts of Mr. Khrushchev's missionaries who are dedicated to undermining that freedom." In the course of their missions, however, some volunteers came to question the single-minded focus of U.S. policy on anticommunism.
David S. Boyer © National Geographic Society.

United States had provided only half of the $20 billion promised to the Alliance for Progress, and much of that funded military projects or was skimmed off by corrupt ruling elites. In addition, a soaring birthrate in Latin America counteracted economic gains, and these nations increasingly bore heavy foreign debt.

Kennedy also reverted to direct military means to bring political stability to the third world. Although he supported popular movements' efforts to gain independence and better living conditions, he drew the line at uprisings that appeared to have Communist connections or goals. Even though a growing split between the Soviet Union and Communist China suggested otherwise, Kennedy clung to the basic cold war tenet: Communism was a monolithic force and had to be contained, no matter what form it took.

To that end, he promoted counterinsurgency forces to put down insurrections that smacked of communism. The showcase of the administration's counterinsurgency strategy was an elite military corps trained to wage guerrilla warfare. Called "special forces," the corps had been established under Eisenhower to aid groups sympathetic to the United States and opposed to Communist-leaning national liberation movements. Kennedy rapidly expanded the special forces, called them the Green Berets (after their official headgear), and equipped them with the latest technology.

The Arms Race and the Nuclear Brink

The final piece of Kennedy's defense strategy was to strengthen American nuclear superiority over the Soviet Union. This drive for nuclear dominance increased the number of U.S. nuclear weapons based in Europe from 2,500 to 7,200 and multiplied fivefold the supply of intercontinental ballistic missiles (ICBMs). Concerned that this buildup would enable the United States to launch a first strike and wipe out Soviet missile sites before the Soviets could respond, the Kremlin stepped up its own ICBM program. Thus began the most intense arms race in history.

The superpowers came perilously close to using their weapons of terror in 1962, when Khrushchev decided to install nuclear missiles in Cuba, probably intending to get the United States to withdraw from Berlin in exchange for the Soviets withdrawing the missiles from Cuba. On October 16, the CIA showed Kennedy aerial photographs of launching sites under construction in Cuba for missiles with ranges of 1,000 and 2,200 miles. Considering this an intolerable threat to the United States, the president met daily in secret with a small group of advisers to manage the ensuing thirteen-day Cuban missile crisis. On October 22, he told a television audience that he had placed the military on full alert and was imposing a "strict quarantine on all offensive military equipment" headed from the Soviet Union to Cuba. The U.S. navy would turn back any Soviet vessel suspected of carrying offensive missiles to Cuba. (Only later did the United States find out that offensive missiles were already there.) Kennedy warned Khrushchev that any attack launched from Cuba would trigger a full nuclear assault against the Soviet Union. The number of bomb shelters Americans built leaped during those tense days.

Projecting the appearance of toughness was paramount to Kennedy, who called the missiles an "unjustified change in the status quo which cannot be accepted . . . if our courage and our commitments are ever to be trusted again by either friend or foe." According to his speechwriter, Theodore Sorensen, although the missiles did not "alter the strategic balance in fact . . . that balance would have been substantially altered in appearance; and in matters of national will and world leadership such appearances contribute to reality." But if Kennedy was willing to risk nuclear war for appearances, he also exercised caution. He refused advice from the military to bomb the missile sites and instead ordered the quarantine to allow time for negotiations. On October 24, some of the Russian ships carrying nuclear warheads toward Cuba suddenly turned back. Kennedy matched Khrushchev's restraint. When one ship crossed the blockade line, he ordered the navy to follow it rather than attempt to stop it. "We don't want to push him [Khrushchev] to a precipitous action," he said.

While Americans experienced the cold war's most fearful days, Kennedy and Khrushchev exchanged offers and counteroffers. Finally, the Soviets removed the missiles and pledged not to

Cuban Missile Crisis, 1962

U.S. blockade zone

— Range of Soviet missiles

⚓ Soviet missile and jet bomber bases

Preparing for the Worst during the Cuban Missile Crisis

Waiting out the tense days after President Kennedy issued the ultimatum to the Soviet Union to halt shipments of missile materials to Cuba, many Americans tried to prepare for the worst possible outcome. Owners of Chalet Suzanne, a hotel in Lake Wales, Florida, canned several thousand cases of well water, labeled NASK for Nuclear Attack Survival Kit. Courtesy Chalet Suzanne Foods, Inc., Lake Wales, Florida. Photo by David Woods.

introduce new offensive weapons into Cuba. The United States promised not to invade the island. Secretly, Kennedy also agreed to remove U.S. missiles based in Turkey and aimed at the Soviet Union.

In miscalculating Kennedy's resolution, the Soviets lost ground in their contest with China for the allegiance of third world countries, and the missile crisis contributed to Khrushchev's fall from power two years later. Kennedy emerged triumphant. The image of an inexperienced president fumbling the Bay of Pigs invasion and being bullied by Khrushchev in Vienna gave way to that of a brilliant leader combining firmness with restraint, bearing the United States through its "hour of maximum danger."

Having proved his toughness, Kennedy could afford to be conciliatory. After the Cuban missile crisis, Kennedy acted to prevent future confrontations. He and Khrushchev installed a special telephone "hot line" to speed top-level communication at critical moments. In a major speech at American University in June 1963, Kennedy called for a reexamination of cold war assumptions, asking Americans "not to see conflict as inevitable." Acknowledging the superpowers' immense differences, Kennedy stressed what they had in common: "We all inhabit this small planet. We all breathe the same air. We all cherish our children's future and we are all mortal."

Responding to pressures from scientists and other Americans alarmed by the dangers of nuclear weapons, Kennedy also called for an end to "a vicious cycle" in which "new weapons beget counterweapons." In August 1963, the United States, the Soviet Union, and Great Britain signed a limited test ban treaty. Because France and China refused to sign, the agreement failed to stop the proliferation of nuclear weapons. Nonetheless, it reduced the threat of radioactive fallout from nuclear testing and raised hopes for superpower accord on other issues.

Venturing into a Quagmire in Vietnam

The new approach that Kennedy outlined at American University did not mean abandoning South Vietnam to communism. He had criticized the idea of "a Pax Americana enforced on the world by American weapons of war," but he increased the flow of those weapons into South Vietnam. His early foreign policy setbacks suggested the need to make a strong stand somewhere, and he also remembered the political

blows to the Democratic Party when China was "lost" in 1949.

Kennedy's strong anticommunism, his interpretation of the lessons of history, and his commitment to an activist foreign policy prepared him to take a stand in Vietnam. The new counterinsurgency program provided the means. Kennedy's key military adviser, General Maxwell

U.S. Involvement in Vietnam

1954 **May** French colonial presence ends with Vietnamese victory at Dien Bien Phu.

July Geneva accords establish temporary division of North and South Vietnam at the seventeenth parallel and provide for free elections.

September United States joins with European, East Asian, and other nations to form the Southeast Asia Treaty Organization (SEATO).

Eisenhower administration begins to send weapons and military advisers to South Vietnam to bolster Diem government.

1955–1961 United States sends $8 million in aid to South Vietnamese army (ARVN) to support its struggle with North Vietnamese government.

1961–1963 Under Kennedy administration, military aid to South Vietnam doubles, and number of military advisers reaches 9,000.

1963 South Vietnamese military overthrows Diem's government.

1964 President Johnson uses Gulf of Tonkin incident to escalate the war.

1965 Johnson administration initiates Operation Rolling Thunder, intensifies bombing of North Vietnam.

1965–1967 Number of U.S. troops in Vietnam increases, reaching 543,000 in 1968, but U.S. and ARVN forces make only limited progress against the guerrilla forces, resulting in a stalemate.

1968 **January 30** Tet Offensive causes widespread destruction and heavy casualties.

March 31 Johnson announces reduction in bombing of North Vietnam, plans for peace talks, and his decision not to run for another presidential term.

1969 Nixon administration initiates secret bombing of Cambodia, increases bombing of the North while reducing U.S. troops in the South, and pursues peace talks.

1970 Nixon orders joint U.S.-ARVN invasion of Cambodia.

1970–1971 U.S. troops in Vietnam decrease from 334,600 to 140,000.

1972 With peace talks stalled in December, Nixon administration orders the most devastating bombing of North Vietnam that would occur throughout the conflict.

1973 On January 27, the United States, North Vietnam, and South Vietnam sign formal accord in Paris marking end of U.S. involvement.

1975 North Vietnam launches a new offensive in South Vietnam, defeating ARVN. Vietcong troops occupy Saigon and rename it Ho Chi Minh City.

Taylor, thought that Vietnam would be a good testing ground for the Green Berets. Holding firm in Vietnam would show the Soviets that sponsoring wars of national liberation would be "costly, dangerous, and doomed to failure."

Two major problems, however, undercut Taylor's analysis. First, the South Vietnamese insurgents—called Vietcong, short for *Vietnam Cong-san* ("Vietnamese Communists"), by the Americans—were an indigenous force whose initiative came from within, not from the Soviet Union or China. Even Ho Chi Minh's Communist government in North Vietnam did not supply weapons or soldiers to the rebels in the south until 1959, after those rebels had initiated guerrilla activities against the South Vietnamese government on their own. Because the Saigon government refused to hold the elections promised in the Geneva accords and was determined to exterminate its opponents, the rebels saw no choice but to take up arms.

The second problem lay in the South Vietnamese government and army (the Army of the Republic of Vietnam, or ARVN), which proved to be ineffective at containing communism. Ngo Dinh Diem, South Vietnamese premier from 1954 to 1963, chose self-serving military leaders merely for their personal loyalty. The government's corruption and repression of opponents alienated many South Vietnamese, not just the Communists.

Intervention by North Vietnam made matters worse. In 1960, the Hanoi government established the National Liberation Front (NLF), composed of South Vietnamese rebels but directed by the northern army. In addition, Hanoi constructed a network of infiltration routes (called the "Ho Chi Minh Trail") in neighboring Laos and Cambodia, through which it sent people and supplies to help liberate the south (Map 29.2). Violence escalated between 1960 and 1963, bringing the Saigon government close to collapse.

When Kennedy took office, more than $1 billion of aid and seven hundred U.S. military advisers had failed to stabilize South Vietnam. He resisted pressure from some advisers for an all-out effort, but he began to escalate the American

MAP 29.2 The Vietnam War, 1964–1975
The United States sent more than two million soldiers to Vietnam and spent more than $150 billion on the longest war in American history, but it was unable to prevent the unification of Vietnam under a Communist government.

READING THE MAP: What accord divided Vietnam into two nations? When was it signed, and where was the line of division drawn? Through what countries did the Ho Chi Minh Trail go?

CONNECTIONS: What was the Gulf of Tonkin incident, and how did the United States respond? What was the Tet Offensive, and how did it affect the war?

FOR MORE HELP ANALYZING THIS MAP, see the map activity for this chapter in the Online Study Guide at bedfordstmartins.com/roark.

commitment. At the same time he worried that each step was "like taking a drink. . . . The effect wears off, and you have to take another." By spring 1963, military aid doubled, and the nine thousand Americans who were serving in Vietnam as military advisers occasionally participated in actual combat. Although the United States extracted new promises of reform from Diem, the South Vietnamese government never made good on them.

American officials assumed that the military's superior technology and sheer power could stem the Communist tide in South Vietnam. Yet advanced weapons were ill suited to the guerrilla warfare practiced by the enemy, who launched on U.S. and ARVN forces sporadic surprise attacks that were designed to weaken support for the South Vietnamese government rather than to gain territory. In addition, U.S. weapons and strategy harmed the very people they were intended to save. Thousands of peasants were uprooted and resettled in "strategic hamlets" supposedly secure from the Communists. Those left in the countryside fell victim to bombs—containing the highly flammable substance napalm—dropped by the U.S.-backed ARVN in an effort to quell the Vietcong. In January 1962, U.S. planes began to spray herbicides to destroy the Vietcong's jungle hideouts and food supply.

South Vietnamese military leaders effected a coup on November 2, 1963, brutally executing Premier Diem and his brother who headed the secret police. Although shocked by the killings, Kennedy indicated no change in policy. In a speech to be given on the day he was assassinated, Kennedy called Americans to their responsibilities as "the watchmen on the walls of world freedom." Referring specifically to Southeast Asia, his undelivered speech warned, "We dare not weary of the task." At his death, 16,000 Americans had served in Vietnam and 100 had died there.

Lyndon Johnson's War against Communism

The cold war assumptions that shaped Kennedy's foreign policy underlay the new president's approach to Southeast Asia and Latin America as well. Retaining Kennedy's key advisers, Lyndon Johnson continued his massive buildup of nuclear weapons and conventional and counter-

insurgency forces. In 1965, when the South Vietnamese government approached collapse, Johnson made the fateful decisions to order U.S. troops into combat and initiate sustained bombing of the north. That same year, Johnson sent U.S. marines to the Dominican Republic to crush a leftist rebellion.

Toward an All-Out Commitment in Vietnam

Having sent more military advisers, weapons, and economic aid to South Vietnam during his first year as president, in August 1964 Lyndon Johnson seized an opportunity to increase the pressure on North Vietnam. American ships routinely engaged in espionage in the Gulf of Tonkin off the coast of North Vietnam, and two U.S. destroyers reported that North Vietnamese gunboats had fired on them on August 2 and 4 (see Map 29.2). Johnson quickly ordered air strikes on North Vietnamese torpedo bases and oil storage facilities, and he sought authority from Congress to take "all necessary measures to repel any armed attacks against the forces of the United States and to prevent further aggression." His portrayal of the situation was at best misleading, revealing neither the uncertainty about whether the second attack had even occurred nor the provocative U.S. actions (staging covert raids and operating close to the North Vietnamese coast). Congress supported Johnson's plan by passing the Gulf of Tonkin Resolution on August 7, 1964, with just two senators voting no.

> In 1965, when the South Vietnamese government approached collapse, Johnson made the fateful decisions to order U.S. troops into combat and initiate sustained bombing of the north.

Johnson's tough stance only two months before the 1964 elections helped counter the charges made by his opponent, Arizona's Senator Barry Goldwater, that he was "soft on communism." Yet the president also presented himself as the peace candidate. When Goldwater proposed massive bombing of North Vietnam, Johnson assured Americans that "we are not going to send American boys nine or ten thousand miles away from home to do what Asian boys ought to be doing for themselves."

Soon after winning reelection, however, Johnson did widen the war. He rejected peace overtures from North Vietnam, which insisted on American withdrawal and a coalition government in South Vietnam as steps toward ultimate

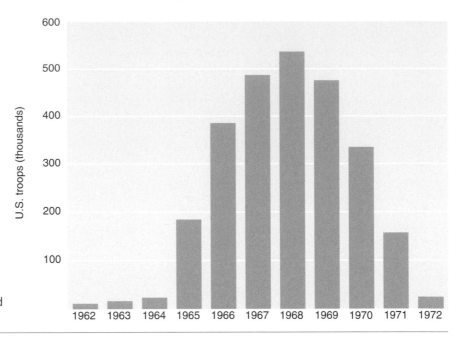

FIGURE 29.1   U.S. Troops in Vietnam, 1962–1972
The steepest increases in the American military presence in Vietnam came in 1965 and 1966. Although troop levels declined in 1971 and 1972, the United States continued massive bombing attacks.

unification of the country. Instead he accepted the advice of Secretary of Defense Robert S. McNamara and other officials to begin a bombing campaign against the North. Operation Rolling Thunder, a strategy of gradually intensified bombing of North Vietnam, began in February 1965. Less than a month later, the first U.S. combat troops landed near Da Nang, South Vietnam. In July, Johnson shifted U.S. troops from defensive to offensive operations and authorized the dispatch of 50,000 more soldiers (Figure 29.1). Those decisions, whose import was downplayed for Congress and the public, marked a critical turning point. Now it was genuinely America's war.

Preventing Another Castro in Latin America

Closer to home, Johnson faced perpetual problems in Latin America despite the efforts of the Alliance for Progress. Thirteen times during the 1960s, military coups toppled Latin American governments, and local insurgencies grew apace. The administration's response to such turmoil varied from case to case but centered on the determination to prevent any more Castro-type revolutions.

In 1964, riots erupted in the Panama Canal Zone, which the United States had seized and made a U.S. territory early in the century.

> Johnson's Latin American policy generated new cries of "Yankee imperialism."

Instigated by Panamanian nationalists who viewed the United States as a colonial power, the riots left four U.S. soldiers and more than twenty Panamanians dead. Johnson sent troops to quell the disturbance, but he also initiated negotiations that eventually led to Panamanian authority over the canal in 2000.

Meanwhile, Johnson's Latin American policy generated new cries of "Yankee imperialism," an ongoing complaint about U.S. interference in the region. In 1961, voters in the Dominican Republic ousted a longstanding dictator and elected a constitutional government headed by Juan Bosch, who was overthrown by a military coup two years later. In 1965, when Bosch supporters rallied in an uprising against the military government, Johnson sent more than 20,000 soldiers to take control of the island. After a truce was arranged, Dominicans voted in a constitutional government under a moderate rightist in 1966.

This first outright show of Yankee force in Latin America in forty years damaged the administration at home and abroad. Although the administration had justified intervention on the grounds that Communists were among the rebels, it quickly became clear that they had played no significant role, and U.S. intervention kept the reform-oriented Boschists from returning to power. Moreover, the president had not consulted the Dominicans or the Organization of American States (OAS), to which the United States had pledged to respect national sovereignty in Latin America. Once the troops had landed in the Dominican Republic, Johnson asked for approval from the OAS, but Mexico, Chile, Venezuela, and other nations refused to grant it.

The Americanized War

The apparent success in the Dominican Republic no doubt encouraged the president to press on in Vietnam. From Operation Rolling Thunder in 1965 to early 1968, the United States gradually escalated attacks against the North Vietnamese and their Vietcong allies, endeavoring to break their will while avoiding provoking intervention by the Chinese, as they had done in Korea. Johnson himself scrutinized military plans, boasting, "They can't even bomb an outhouse without my approval."

Over the course of the war, U.S. pilots dropped 3.2 million tons of explosives, more than the United States had launched in all of World War II. Claiming monthly death tolls of more than 2,000 North Vietnamese, the intensive bombing nonetheless failed to dampen the Hanoi government's commitment. (See "Historical Question," page 1078.) In the South, the United States rained down more than twice the tonnage of bombs dropped on North Vietnam.

Because there was no battlefront as in previous wars, General William Westmoreland's strategy of attrition was designed to search out and kill the Vietcong and North Vietnamese regular army. The military used helicopters extensively to conduct offensives all over South Vietnam. (See "The Promise of Technology," page 1082.) Officials calculated progress not in territory seized but in "body counts" and "kill ratios"— the number of enemies killed relative to the cost in American and ARVN lives. According to U.S. army officer Colin Powell, who served in Vietnam in 1962 and again in 1968–69, "The Army desperately needed something to measure. What military objectives could we claim in this week's report? A hill? A valley? A hamlet? Rarely. Consequently, bodies became the measure." In this situation, American soldiers did not always distinguish between military combatants and civilians; according to Lieutenant Philip Caputo, the operating rule was "if it's dead and Vietnamese, it's VC [Vietcong]." A helicopter pilot summed up the attrition strategy when, after a brutal battle, his comrade asked, "What did we win? We don't have any more real estate, no new villages are under American control, and

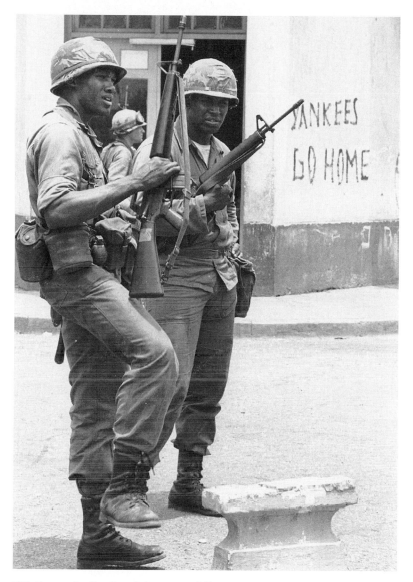

U.S. Troops in the Dominican Republic
These U.S. paratroopers were among the 20,000 troops sent to the Dominican Republic in April and May 1965. The American invasion helped restore peace but kept the popularly elected government of Juan Bosch from regaining office. Dominicans expressed their outrage in anti-American slogans that greeted troops throughout the capital, Santo Domingo. Bosch himself said, "This was a democratic revolution smashed by the leading democracy in the world."
© Bettmann/Corbis.

it took everything we had to stop them." The pilot responded, "More of them got killed than us. It's that simple."

In contrast to World War II, when the average soldier was twenty-six years old, teenagers fought the Vietnam War. Until the Twenty-sixth Amendment reduced the voting age from twenty-one to eighteen in 1971, most soldiers, whose average age was nineteen, could not even

Why Couldn't the United States Bomb Its Way to Victory in Vietnam?

World War II demonstrated the critical importance of airpower in modern war. According to the official U.S. study of strategic bombing during World War II, "No nation can long survive the free exploitation of air weapons over its homeland." In the Vietnam War, U.S. planes delivered even more explosives than they had in World War II. Why, then, did strategic bombing not bring victory in Vietnam?

"Our airpower did not fail us; it was the decision makers," asserted Admiral U. S. Grant Sharp, World War II veteran and commander in chief of the Pacific Command during the Vietnam War. Military officials welcomed President Johnson's order to begin bombing North Vietnam in February 1965 as a means to destroy the North's capacity and will to support the Communist insurgents in South Vietnam. But they chafed at Johnson's strategy of gradual escalation and the restrictions he imposed on Operation Rolling Thunder, the three-and-a-half-year bombing campaign. Military officials believed that the United States should have begun Operation Rolling Thunder with all-out massive bombing and continued until the devastation brought North Vietnam to its knees. Instead, they charged, civilian decision makers compelled the military to fight with one hand tied behind its back. Their arguments echoed General Douglas MacArthur's criticism of Truman's policy during the Korean War—though these officials did not repeat MacArthur's insubordination.

Unlike military officials, who could single-mindedly focus on defeating the enemy, the president needed to balance military objectives against political considerations and found compelling reasons to limit the application of airpower. Recalling the Korean War, Johnson noted that "China is there on the [North Vietnamese] border with 700 million men," and he studiously avoided action that might provoke intervention by the Chinese, who now possessed nuclear weapons. Johnson's strategy also aimed to keep the Soviet Union out of the war, to avoid inflaming antiwar sentiment at home, and to avert international criticism of the United States.

Consequently, the president would not permit bombing of areas where high civilian casualties might result and areas near the Chinese border. He banned strikes on airfields and missile sites that were under construction and thus likely to contain Chinese or Soviet advisers, and he refused to mine North Vietnam's harbors, through which Soviet ships imported goods to North Vietnam. But Johnson did escalate the pressure, increasing the intensity of the bombing fourfold by 1968. In all, Operation Rolling Thunder rained 643,000 tons of bombs on North Vietnam between 1965 and 1968.

Military leaders agreed with Johnson's desire to spare civilians. The Joint Chiefs of Staff never proposed, for example, strikes against a system of dikes and dams that could have disrupted food production and flooded Hanoi under twenty feet of water. Rather, they focused on destroying North Vietnam's industry and transportation system. Noncombatant casualties in North Vietnam contrasted sharply with those in World War II, when Anglo-American bombing of Dresden, Germany, alone took more than 35,000 civilian lives and the firebombing of Japan caused 330,000 civilian deaths. In three and a half years, Operation Rolling Thunder's bombing claimed an estimated 52,000 civilian lives.

The relatively low level of economic development in North Vietnam and the North Vietnamese government's ability to mobilize its citizens counteracted the military superiority of the United States. Sheer man-, woman-, and child-power compensated for the demolition of transportation sources, industry sites, and electric power plants. When bombs struck a rail line, civilians rushed with bicycles to unload a train's cargo, carry it beyond the break, and load it onto a second train. Three hundred thousand full-time workers and 200,000 farmers labored in their spare time to keep the Ho Chi Minh Trail usable in spite of heavy bombing. When bridges were destroyed, the North Vietnamese resorted to ferries and pontoons made from bamboo, and they rebuilt bridges slightly

The B-52 Bomber

After 1965, B-52 bombers constantly filled the skies over Vietnam, and at times over Laos and Cambodia. Designed originally to deliver nuclear bombs, a single B-52 carried thirty tons of explosives. A mission of six planes could destroy an area one-half mile wide by three miles long. The B-52 flew too high to be heard on the ground, but its bombs hit with such force that they could kill people in underground shelters.

Co Rentmeester, *Life* magazine/TimePix/Getty.

underwater to make them harder to detect from the air. They dispersed oil storage facilities and production centers throughout the countryside, and when bombs knocked out electric power plants, the Vietnamese turned to more than two thousand portable generators and used oil lamps and candles in their homes.

North Vietnam's military needs were relatively small, and officials found ample means to meet them. In 1967, North Vietnam had only about 55,000 soldiers in South Vietnam, and because they waged a guerrilla war with only sporadic fighting, the insurgents in the South did not require huge amounts of supplies.

Even after Communist forces in the South increased, the total nonfood needs of these soldiers were estimated at just one-fifth of what a single U.S. division required. What U.S. bombs destroyed, the North Vietnamese replaced with Chinese and Soviet imports. China provided 600,000 tons of rice in 1967 alone, and it supplied small arms and ammunition, vehicles, and other goods throughout the war. Competing with China for influence in North Vietnam and favor in the third world, the Soviets contributed tanks, fighter planes, surface-to-air missiles, and other sophisticated weapons. An estimated $2 billion of foreign aid

substantially curtailed the effect of Operation Rolling Thunder, and the Soviet-installed modern defense systems made the bombing more difficult and dangerous for U.S. pilots.

In July 1969, Seventh Air Force commander General William W. Momyer commented on Operation Rolling Thunder to the retiring air force chief of staff: "We had the force, skill, and intelligence, but our civilian betters wouldn't turn us loose." Johnson refused to turn the military loose because in addition to the goal he shared with the military—breaking Hanoi's ability to support insurgency in the South—he also wanted to keep China and the Soviet Union (and nuclear weapons) out of the war and to contain domestic and international criticism of U.S. policy. Whether a more devastating air war would have provoked Chinese or Soviet intervention can never be known.

Nor can we know whether all-out bombing of the North could have guaranteed an independent non-Communist government in the South. We do know that Johnson's military advisers imposed their own restraints, never recommending the wholesale attacks on civilians that took place in World War II. Short of decimating the civilian population, it is questionable whether more intense bombing could have completely halted North Vietnamese support for the Vietcong, given the nature of the North Vietnamese economy, the determination and ingenuity of its people, and the plentiful assistance from China and the Soviet Union. Whether the strategic bombing that worked so well in a world war against major industrial powers could be effective in a third world guerrilla war remained in doubt after the Vietnam War.

vote for the officials who sent them to war. Men of all classes had fought World War II, but Vietnam was the war of the poor and working class, who constituted about 80 percent of the troops. More privileged youth found ways to avoid the **draft**, usually through college deferments or by using family connections to get into the National Guard. Sent from Plainville, Kansas, to Vietnam in 1965, Mike Clodfelter could not recall "a single middle-class son of the town's businessmen, lawyers, doctors, or ranchers from my high school graduating class who experienced the Armageddon of our generation."

> Men of all classes had fought World War II, but Vietnam was the war of the poor and working class, who constituted about 80 percent of the troops.

Much more than World War II, the Vietnam War was a men's war; women's share of all military personnel during the Vietnam era was just half what it was during World War II. The United States did not undergo full mobilization for the war in Vietnam; consequently, officials did not seek women's sacrifices for the war effort. In response to a journalist who said that some military women were distressed because they had not been called to serve in Vietnam, President Johnson joked, "Well there is always a chance of anything taking place when our women are sufficiently distressed," and the reporters guffawed. Still, estimates of 7,500 to 10,000 women served in Vietnam, the vast majority of them nurses. Although women were not allowed to carry weapons, they did come under enemy fire, and eight lost their lives. Most difficult for most of the women was their helplessness in the face of the dead and maimed bodies they tended. "When you finally saved a life," said Peggy DuVall, "you wondered what kind of life you had saved."

Early in the war, African Americans constituted 31 percent of combat troops, often choosing the military over the meager opportunities in the civilian economy. Special forces ranger Arthur E. Woodley Jr. believed, "I was just what my country needed. A black patriot. . . . The only way I could possibly make it out of the ghetto was to be the best soldier I possibly could." Death rates among black soldiers were disproportionately high until 1966, when the military adjusted personnel assignments to produce a more racially balanced distribution of sacrifice.

The young American troops faced extremely difficult conditions. Soldiers fought in thick jungles and swamps filled with leeches, in oppressive heat, rain, and humidity. Lieutenant Caputo remembered "weeks of expectant waiting and, at random intervals, conducting vicious manhunts through jungles and swamps where snipers harassed us constantly and booby traps cut us down one by one." Soldiers in previous wars had served "for the duration," but Vietnam warriors had one-year tours of duty; a commander called it "the worst personnel policy in history," because men had less incentive

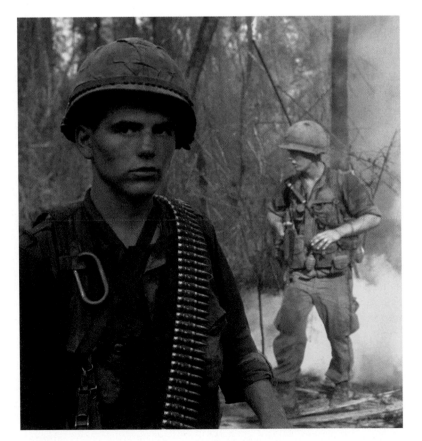

Vietnam: The War of the Young
The faces of these soldiers in the jungle near Hue in 1968 reflect the youth of the soldiers who fought the Vietnam War, in which the average age was nineteen. When one young marine received his supplies, he wondered "What did I need with shaving equipment? I was only seventeen. I didn't have hair under my *arms*, let alone my face." The youth of the soldiers intensified the emotional trauma felt by the military nurses who cared for them. One nurse remembered a dying soldier "in so much pain and so scared, asking for his mom." Another sobbed over a snapshot that fell out of a dying soldier's pocket: "It is a picture of the soldier and his girl—dressed for a prom." Kyoichi Savada/Corbis.

to fight near the end of their tour, wanting merely to stay alive and whole. The U.S. military inflicted great losses on the enemy, estimated at more than 200,000 by the end of 1967. Yet it could claim no more than a stalemate. In the words of infantryman Tim O'Brien, who later became an award-winning author, "We slay one of them, hit a mine, kill another, hit another mine. . . . And each piece of ground left behind is his [the enemy's] from the moment we are gone on our next hunt."

The South Vietnamese government itself was an obstacle to victory. After a series of coups and short-lived regimes, in 1965 the government settled into a period of stability led by Air Marshal Nguyen Cao Ky and General Nguyen Van Thieu. But graft and corruption continued to flourish, and Ky and Thieu failed to rally popular support. In the intensified fighting and inability to distinguish friend from foe, thousands of South Vietnamese civilians were killed and wounded, their farms and villages bombed and burned. By 1968, five million people, nearly 30 percent of the population, had become refugees. Huge infusions of American dollars and goods produced rampant inflation, hurt local industries, and increased dependence on foreign aid.

Johnson's decisions that Americanized the war flowed logically from the commitments of three presidents before him. All the same, 1965 marked a critical turning point: The rationale for involvement in the war shifted from the need to contain communism in Southeast Asia to the need to prove to the world the ability of the United States to make good on its commitments.

A Nation Polarized

Soon President Johnson was fighting a war on two fronts. Domestic opposition to the war grew significantly after 1965, and the United States experienced internal conflict unparalleled since the Civil War. Television brought the carnage of Vietnam into American homes day after day, making it the first "living-room war." Torn between his domestic critics and the military's clamor for more troops, in March 1968 Johnson announced restrictions on the bombing, a new

effort at negotiations, and his decision not to pursue reelection. Throughout 1968, demonstrations, violence, and assassinations convulsed the nation. Vietnam took center stage in the election, and voters narrowly favored the Republican candidate, former vice president Richard Nixon, who promised to "bring Americans together again" and to achieve "peace with honor."

The Widening War at Home

Before 1965, American actions in Vietnam evoked little domestic criticism. But Johnson's authorization of Operation Rolling Thunder sparked a mass movement against the war. In April 1965, Students for a Democratic Society (SDS) recruited 20,000 people for the first major protest, a rally in Washington, D.C., and SDS chapters sprang up on more than 300 college campuses across the country. Thousands of young people joined campus protests against Reserve Officers Training Corps (ROTC) programs, CIA recruiters, manufacturers of war materials, and university departments that conducted research for the Department of Defense. In 1967, Martin Luther King Jr. rebuked his government as "the greatest purveyor of violence in the world today," calling opposition to the war "the privilege and burden of all of us who deem ourselves bound by allegiances and loyalties which are broader and deeper than nationalism." Environmentalists attacked the use of chemical weapons, such as the deadly dioxin-product Agent Orange that the military was raining on Vietnam to destroy foliage where the enemy might hide. A new draft policy in 1967 ended deferments for postgraduate education and upped male students' stake in ending the war. In the spring of 1968, as many as one million college and high school students participated in a nationwide strike.

Antiwar sentiment also entered society's mainstream. The *New York Times* began questioning administration policy in 1965, and by 1968 media critics included the *Wall Street Journal, Life* magazine, and popular TV journalist Walter Cronkite. Clergy, businesspeople, scientists, and physicians formed their own groups to pressure Johnson to stop the bombing and start negotiations. Though most of organized labor supported the president, some union members joined the peace movement.

> Domestic opposition to the war grew significantly after 1965, and the United States experienced internal conflict unparalleled since the Civil War.

The Military Helicopter

Reflecting on how the Vietnam War would have been fought without helicopters, General William C. Westmoreland concluded, "We would have been fighting a different war, for a smaller area, at a greater cost, with less effectiveness." Waging war in Vietnam without helicopters, he maintained, would have been like fighting Hitler's army in Europe without tanks.

It took more than three decades after the first successful airplane flight for engineers to develop an aircraft that could take off and land vertically, move in any direction, and remain stationary in the air. The man frequently identified as the inventor of the helicopter in the United States, Russian engineer Igor Sikorsky, developed two helicopters in 1909 and 1910, but neither succeeded. After the Russian Revolution of 1917, Sikorsky emigrated to the United States and organized a company that produced airplanes while he continued to work on the helicopter. German engineers produced the first practical helicopter in 1936, but the United States was not far behind.

As was true of much new technology in the twentieth century, federal dollars supported research and development. In 1938, Congress first appropriated funds to develop the helicopter, and Sikorsky and his associates produced the first helicopter for the Army Air Corps in 1942. During World War II, the United States used helicopters for some rescue operations in the Pacific theater, and Germany used them for artillery spotting and reconnaissance. The American military employed helicopters for medical evacuations in Korea, but not until manufacturers replaced piston engines with smaller, lighter gas-turbine engines did helicopters play a central role in military operations.

Although the army developed its plans for the use of helicopters in the 1950s within the context of nuclear warfare, once the United States began to assist with military operations of the South Vietnamese, the helicopter became a central feature of the war. The particular nature of the conflict in Vietnam—the guerrilla tactics of the enemy, the conduct of fighting all over South Vietnam rather than across a fixed battlefront, and the mountains and dense jungles, with limited landing areas—put a premium on the helicopter's mobility and maneuverability. Already in December 1961, long before U.S. troops actually saw combat in Vietnam, the army employed thirty-two of its helicopters to transfer some one thousand South Vietnamese paratroopers for an attack on suspected Vietcong headquarters. To U.S. army captain Colin Powell serving as an adviser to a South Vietnamese army battalion in a remote spot near the Laotian border in 1962, the helicopter "became my closest link to the world I had left." One piloted by a U.S. marine came every two weeks, and at those times, Powell remembered, "my anticipation was almost sexual. This flier brought my latest batch of paperbacks, my carton of Salems, and my mail."

The UH-1 Iroquois (known as "Huey") was the most widely used helicopter; thousands of them carried infantry units all over South Vietnam. One marine commented that "we commuted to and from the war," though it was hardly an ordinary commute when helicopters had to land in the midst of enemy fire. Choppers also transported artillery and ammunition, performed reconnaissance, picked up downed pilots, and evacuated the dead and wounded. Mounted with machine guns and grenade launchers, helicopters served as attack vehicles. The largest, the CH-47 ("Chinook"), could carry thirty-three soldiers or considerable amounts of cargo and even rescue smaller downed aircraft. Chinooks also dropped two and a

---

Increasing numbers of prominent Democratic senators, including J. William Fulbright, George McGovern, and majority leader Mike Mansfield, urged Johnson to substitute negotiation for force. Fulbright's book, *The Arrogance of Power*, warned against "the tendency of great nations to equate power with virtue" and urged American leaders not to think of the country as "God's chosen saviour of mankind."

Opposition to the war took diverse forms: letter-writing campaigns to officials, teach-ins on college campuses, mass marches, student strikes, withholding of federal taxes, draft card burnings, civil disobedience against military centers and producers of war materials, and attempts to stop trains carrying troops. Although the peace movement never claimed a majority of the population, it focused media attention on the war

Helicopters in Vietnam

This helicopter brings ammunition in 1968 to U.S. soldiers in Khe Sanh, in the far northwest region of South Vietnam. Before and during the Tet Offensive, thousands of North Vietnamese forces surrounded and shelled the garrison of six thousand marines, making the ability to supply Khe Sanh from helicopters essential. This photo was taken by Larry Burrows, who died three years later during the invasion of Laos. The helicopter in which he and three other well-known combat photographers were traveling exploded after being hit by a North Vietnamese antiaircraft gun.

Photograph by Larry Burrows, LIFE © Timo, Inc., 1968.

half tons of napalm on the enemy in just one delivery.

Helicopters enabled military personnel to receive unprecedented support. In Vietnam it was not unusual for American soldiers in the field to be provided with hot meals rather than cold C rations. More important was the medical evacuation helicopter, called the "Dust-off," which could hoist to safety injured soldiers without touching land. Most of those wounded in Vietnam were promptly evacuated to hospitals, and those with grave injuries were sped to base facilities in the Pacific region or the United States. The improvements in medical evacuation, combined with advances in medicine, helped to raise the ratio of surviving wounded to dead to 6:1, in contrast to a World War II ratio of 2.6:1. So central were helicopters to a soldier's experience that, one man noted, "When the helicopters flew off, a feeling of abandonment came over us."

Journalists hitched rides on helicopters "like taxis" to see the war firsthand. Michael Herr, who wrote for *Esquire* and other magazines, flew on hundreds of them, remembering "choppers rising straight out of small cleared jungle spaces, wobbling down onto city rooftops, cartons of rations and ammunition thrown off, dead and wounded loaded on. Sometimes they were so plentiful and loose that you could touch down at five or six places a day."

The massive use of helicopters, of course, failed to defeat the enemy in Vietnam. Although air mobility played a key role in the successes that the United States and South Vietnamese armies did achieve, it could not win the war alone. In the words of one military adviser, "After all, when you come to think of it, the use of helicopters is a tacit admission that we don't control the ground. And in the long run, it's control of the ground that wins or loses the war." Helicopters remained important to the very end of the U.S. presence in Vietnam. As Saigon fell to the Communists in 1975, choppers carried the last Americans out of danger.

and severely limited the administration's options. The twenty-year-old consensus about cold war foreign policy had broken down.

Many would not fight in the war. The World Boxing Association stripped Muhammad Ali of his world heavyweight title when he refused to serve in what he called a "white man's war." More than 170,000 men who opposed the war on moral or religious grounds gained conscientious objector status and performed nonmilitary duties at home or in Vietnam. About 60,000 fled the country to escape the draft, and more than 200,000 were accused of failing to register or committing other draft offenses.

When he got his induction notice in 1968, Tim O'Brien agonized over what to do. He opposed the war, yet to avoid the draft would bring criticism and embarrassment to his family in his

Chemical Weapons

The U.S. military began to employ the tear gas CS (o-chlorobenzylidenemalononitrile) in grenades in Vietnam in 1964 and was discharging more than two million pounds of CS a year by 1969. It was used in operations such as the one shown here. The marine has just thrown a CS gas grenade into a tunnel to flush out the enemy and make the tunnel unusable for several months. Military planes also dropped or sprayed CS from the air to rid large areas of land of enemy forces. CS is usually not lethal but has incapacitating effects. Nonetheless, its use evoked criticism at home and from abroad. The *New York Times* noted that "no other country has employed such a weapon in recent warfare." The Political Committee of the UN General Assembly maintained that generally recognized rules of warfare prohibited the use of any chemical agents.

James H. Pickerell/Stock Connection; Ordinance Museum/Aberdeen Proving Grounds.

small-town Minnesota community, whose leaders expected young men to serve their country. In addition, he said, "I owed the prairie something. For twenty-one years I'd lived under its laws, accepted its education . . . wallowed in its luxuries, played on its Little League teams." In the end, he could not bring himself to desert the country that he had never before thought of leaving. Though he held to his belief that "the war was wrong," O'Brien served in the army.

Opponents of the war held far from unanimous views. Some condemned the war on moral grounds, insisting that their country had no right to interfere in another country and stressing the suffering of the Vietnamese people. Their goal was total withdrawal. As American intervention esca- lated with no tangible results, a larger segment of antiwar sentiment reflected practical considerations—that the war could not be won or that the cost would be too great to bear. Not demanding withdrawal, those activists wanted Johnson to stop bombing North Vietnam and seek negotiations.

The antiwar movement outraged millions of Americans who supported the war. Some members of the generation who had fought against Hitler could not understand younger men's refusal to support the government. Working-class people were no more pro-war than other groups, but they were especially conscious of the class dimensions of the war and the public opposition to it. A firefighter whose son had died in Vietnam said bitterly, "It's people like us who give up our sons for the country. The businesspeople, they run the country and make money from it. The college types . . . go to Washington and tell the government what to do. . . . But their sons don't end up in the swamps over there, in Vietnam."

President Johnson tried a number of means to silence critics. To avoid focusing attention on the war's burdens, he eschewed price and wage controls, imposed in other wars to control inflation, and delayed asking for a tax increase to pay for the war. Congress passed a 10 percent surcharge on federal income taxes in June 1968, after Johnson promised to cut domestic spending. The Great Society programs suffered, but the surcharge failed to reverse the inflationary surge.

The president agonized over casualty reports and felt personally wounded when protesters chanted outside the White House, "Hey, hey, LBJ, how many kids have you killed today?" Reacting harshly to antiwar sentiment, he misled the public about the war's progress, tried to discredit opponents by labeling them "nervous Nellies" or Communists, and ordered the CIA to spy on peace advocates. Without the president's specific authorization, the FBI infiltrated the peace movement, disrupted its work, and spread false information about activists. However, even the resort to illegal measures failed to subdue the opposition.

1968: Year of Upheaval

By late 1967—two years after the Americanization of the war—public impatience and frustration had intensified. On one side were the so-called **hawks**, who charged that the United States was fighting with one hand tied behind its

Pro-War Demonstrators

Advocates as well as opponents of the war in Vietnam took to the streets, as these New Yorkers did in support of the U.S. invasion of Cambodia in May 1970. Construction workers—called "hard hats"—and other union members marched with American flags and posters championing President Nixon's policies and blasting New York Mayor John Lindsay for his antiwar position. Following the demonstration, sympathetic union leaders presented Nixon with an honorary hard hat. Paul Fusco/Magnum Photos, Inc.

FOR MORE HELP ANALYZING THIS IMAGE, see the visual activity for this chapter in the Online Study Guide at bedfordstmartins.com/roark.

Mothers against the War

Women played an active role in the opposition to the Vietnam War—and not just college students or radicals. In 1961, years before Vietnam became an issue, Women Strike for Peace (WSP) was founded to work for nuclear disarmament. Identifying themselves as "concerned housewives" and mothers, an estimated 50,000 women throughout the country staged a one-day protest, calling on President Kennedy to "End the Arms Race—Not the Human Race." As early as 1963, WSP began to "alert the public to the dangers and horrors of the war in Vietnam," and throughout the war it played a vigorous role in the antiwar movement, mobilizing around the slogan "Not Our Sons, Not Your Sons, Not Their Sons." In February 1967, WSP became the first group to take the antiwar protest to the Pentagon. The women in this photograph were among more than 2,000 women who gathered at the Pentagon, using their shoes to bang against the doors that were locked as they approached. Newspaper readers in the United States and around the world saw dramatic images of these women outraged at the refusal of officials to meet with them. © Bettmann/Corbis.

back and called for the government to apply more power against North Vietnam. The **doves** wanted de-escalation or withdrawal. Most people were torn between weariness with the war and worry about abandoning the American commitment. As one woman said to a pollster, "I want to get out but I don't want to give up."

Grave doubts about the war penetrated the administration itself in 1967. Secretary of Defense Robert McNamara, a principal architect of U.S. involvement, now believed that the North Vietnamese "won't quit no matter how much bombing we do." And he feared for the image of the United States, "the world's greatest superpower killing or seriously injuring 1,000 noncombatants a week, while trying to pound a tiny, backward nation into submission on an issue whose merits are hotly disputed." McNamara kept those views to himself until thirty years later, but in early 1968 he left the administration.

The critical turning point came with the Tet Offensive, which began on January 30, 1968. Just a few weeks after General Westmoreland had reported that "the enemy has been driven away from the population centers [and] has been compelled to disperse," the North Vietnamese and Vietcong attacked key cities and every major American base in South Vietnam. This was the biggest surprise of the war, and not simply because both sides had customarily observed a truce during the Vietnamese New Year holiday

> The Tet Offensive underscored the credibility gap between official statements and the war's actual progress.

(called Tet). The offensive displayed the Communists' vitality and refusal to be intimidated by the presence of half a million American soldiers. Militarily, the enemy suffered a defeat, losing more than 30,000 men, ten times as many as ARVN and U.S. forces. Psychologically, however, Tet was devastating to the United States.

The Tet Offensive underscored the credibility gap between official statements and the war's actual progress. TV anchorman Walter Cronkite wondered, "What the hell is going on? I thought we were winning the war." The attacks created a million more South Vietnamese refugees as well as widespread destruction, especially in the ancient city of Hue, whose **archaeological** treasures were reduced to rubble. Explaining how he had defended a village, a U.S. army official said, "We had to destroy the town to save it." The statement epitomized for more and more Americans the brutality and senselessness of the war.

In the aftermath of Tet, Johnson considered a request from Westmoreland for 200,000 more troops. He conferred with advisers in the Defense Department and an unofficial group of foreign policy experts, dubbed the "Wise Men," who had been key architects of cold war policies since World War II. Dean Acheson, secretary of state under Truman, summarized their conclusion: "We can no longer do the job we set out to do in the time we have left and we must begin to take steps to disengage."

On March 31, 1968, Lyndon Johnson announced in a televised speech that the United States would reduce its bombing of North Vietnam and that he was prepared to begin peace talks with its leaders. Then he stunned his audience by declaring that he would not run for reelection. The announcement marked the end of the gradual escalation that had begun in 1965. What followed was a shift from "Americanization" to "Vietnamization" of the war, but it was a shift in strategy, not in policy. The United States maintained its goal of a non-Communist South Vietnam; it simply aimed to reach that goal by relying more heavily on the South Vietnamese.

Negotiations began in Paris in May 1968. But the United States would not agree to recognition of the Hanoi government's National Liberation Front, to a coalition government, or to American withdrawal. The North Vietnamese would agree to nothing less. Although the talks continued, so did the fighting.

Meanwhile, violence escalated at home. In June, two months after the murder of Martin Luther King Jr. and the ensuing riots, another assassination shook the nation. Running for the Democratic presidential nomination, Senator Robert F. Kennedy, the late president's brother, had just celebrated his triumph in the California primary when he was shot by a Palestinian Arab refugee, Sirhan B. Sirhan, who was outraged by Kennedy's support for Israel.

Spring 1968 also saw campus demonstrations intensify around the world as well as in the United States, where some two hundred protests occurred before summer. In the bloodiest action, students took over buildings at Columbia University in New York City, demanding that the university stop uprooting African Americans

The Tet Offensive

Launched by the North Vietnamese in January 1968, the Tet Offensive took the war to major cities for the first time. NLF troops quickly occupied Hue, the ancient imperial city, and held it for nearly a month. Supported by aerial bombing, U.S. marines finally took back the city, street by street. A journalist who had also covered the Korean War reported, "Nothing I saw . . . has been as terrible, in terms of destruction and despair, as what I saw in Hue." More than half of its 17,000 houses were leveled. Here, marines fight from rubble that was once part of the Citadel of Hue.

John Olson, U.S. Army/National Archives.

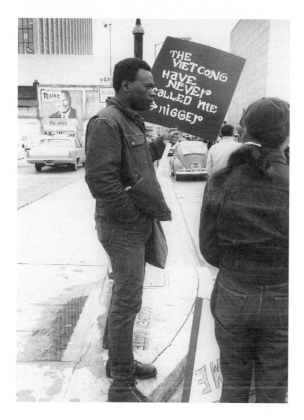

African American Antiwar Protest

The first expression of African American opposition to the war in Vietnam occurred in Mississippi in July 1965 when a group of civil rights workers called for draft resistance. Blacks should not fight for freedom in Vietnam "until all the Negro People are free in Mississippi," and they should not "risk our lives and kill other Colored People in Santo Domingo and Viet Nam." This protester on the West Coast in April 1967 expresses similar sentiments.

Joe Flowers/Black Star/Stockphoto.com.

International Party (Yippies), a splinter group of SDS. Its leaders, Abbie Hoffman and Jerry Rubin, urged students to demonstrate their hatred of the establishment by provoking the police to violence and creating chaos in the backyard of the Democratic convention. The Yippies brought a live pig to Chicago as their candidate. "Our concept of revolution," Hoffman declared, "is that it's fun."

Chicago's leading Democrat, Mayor Richard J. Daley, issued a ban on rallies and marches, ordered a curfew, and mobilized thousands of police. On August 25, demonstrators responded to police orders to disperse with insults and jeers, whereupon police attacked protesters with tear gas and clubs. Street battles continued for three days, culminating in what an official commission later termed a "police riot" on the night of August 28. Taunted by the crowd, the police

Protest in Chicago

The worst violence surrounding the 1968 Democratic National Convention in Chicago came on August 28 when protesters decided to assemble in Grant Park and march to the convention site. Mayor Daley refused them a parade permit and dispatched the police and the Illinois National Guard to the park to keep them from marching. As protesters listened to speeches in the park, a group of young men tore down the American flag and replaced it with a red T-shirt, prompting the police to go after the demonstrators with their clubs. Later that night when activists tried to march to the convention, the police struck out widely and wildly, bloodying and teargassing many people who were not connected to the radicals.

Jeffrey Blankfort/Jeroboam.

in the neighboring community, do more to meet black students' needs, stop research for the Department of Defense, and grant amnesty to student demonstrators. When negotiations failed, university officials called in the city police, who cleared the buildings, injuring more than one hundred demonstrators and arresting more than seven hundred others. An ensuing student strike prematurely ended the academic year. (See "Documenting the American Promise," chapter 28, page 1048.)

In August, protesters battled the police in Chicago, where the Democratic Party had convened to nominate its presidential ticket. Several thousand demonstrators came to the city, some to support the peace candidate Senator Eugene McCarthy, others to act more aggressively. Many of the latter had been mobilized by the Youth

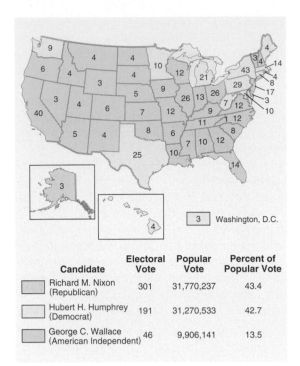

Candidate	Electoral Vote	Popular Vote	Percent of Popular Vote
Richard M. Nixon (Republican)	301	31,770,237	43.4
Hubert H. Humphrey (Democrat)	191	31,270,533	42.7
George C. Wallace (American Independent)	46	9,906,141	13.5

MAP 29.3   The Election of 1968

used mace and nightsticks, clubbing not only those who had come to provoke violence but also reporters, peaceful demonstrators, and convention delegates.

The bloodshed in Chicago and upheaval across the country had little effect on the outcome of either major party's convention. Peace Democrats lost the presidential nomination, as Vice President Hubert H. Humphrey trounced Eugene McCarthy by nearly three to one. McCarthy's refusal to share the podium with Humphrey as the convention ended underscored the bitter split within the party. In contrast, the Republican convention peacefully nominated former vice president Richard Nixon on the first ballot. For his running mate, Nixon chose Maryland governor Spiro T. Agnew, hoping to gather southern support while not alienating northern and western voters.

For the first time in nearly fifty years, a strong third party entered the electoral scene. Staunch segregationist former Alabama governor George C. Wallace ran on the ticket of the American Independent Party. Wallace appealed to Americans nationwide who believed that civil rights and antipoverty programs benefited the

> The 1968 elections revealed deep cracks in the coalition that had, except during the Eisenhower years, kept the Democrats in power for thirty years.

undeserving at their expense and who were outraged by assaults on traditional values by students and others. Nixon guardedly played on resentments that fueled the Wallace campaign, appealing to "the forgotten Americans, the non-shouters, the non-demonstrators."

Few differences separated the two major-party candidates on the central issue of Vietnam. Nixon promised to "bring an honorable end" to the war but did not indicate how he would do it. Humphrey had strong reservations about U.S. policy in Vietnam, yet as vice president he wanted to avoid a break with Johnson. Finally Johnson boosted Humphrey's campaign when he announced a halt to the bombing of North Vietnam. By election eve, Nixon and Humphrey were neck-and-neck.

With nearly ten million votes (13 percent of the total), the American Independent Party produced the strongest third-party finish since 1924. Nixon edged out Humphrey by just half a million popular votes, prevailing more strongly in the electoral college, with 301 votes to Humphrey's 191 and Wallace's 46. The Democrats lost a few seats in Congress but kept control of both the House and the Senate (Map 29.3).

The 1968 elections revealed deep cracks in the coalition that had, except during the Eisenhower years, kept the Democrats in power for thirty years. The Democrats' policies on race moved most of the former "solid South" behind Nixon or Wallace, shattering a century of Democratic Party dominance in that region. Large numbers of blue-collar workers broke union ranks to vote for Wallace or Nixon, along with other groups associating the Democrats with racial turmoil, inflation, antiwar protesters, changing sexual mores, urban riots, and America's impotence in Vietnam. These resentments continued to simmer, soon to be mobilized into a resurging right in American politics (see chapter 30).

New Opportunities and Dangers in a Multipolar World

Vietnam may have dominated the 1968 election campaigns, but Richard Nixon's ambitious foreign policy goals extended far beyond ending that war. The challenges of foreign policy captured Nixon's greatest enthusiasm, and he hoped to make his mark on history by applying his broad understanding of international relations to a changing world. Nixon believed that the "rigid and bipolar world of the 1940s and 1950s" was giving way to "the fluidity of a new era of multi-lateral diplomacy." Diverging from Republican orthodoxy, his dramatic overtures to the Soviet Union and China reduced decades-old hostilities.

Yet, as reflected in Nixon's aggressive pursuit of the war in Vietnam, anticommunism remained central to American policy. In Latin America, Africa, and the Middle East, the administration threw its support behind repressive regimes when the alternative appeared too close to communism.

Moving toward Détente with the Soviet Union and China

Even while fighting against communism in Vietnam, the United States reached some accord with the major Communist nations. In 1968, building on negotiations that began under Eisenhower and included Kennedy's 1963 nuclear test ban treaty, the United States, the Soviet Union, and sixty other nations agreed to a Nuclear Non-Proliferation Treaty. American ratification of the treaty was delayed when the Soviets invaded Czechoslovakia in 1968 to put down an opposition movement; but in 1969, Nixon asked the Senate for approval, and the treaty became effective in 1970. Designed to prevent the spread of nuclear weapons, the treaty lacked adherence from such key nations as China, France (both of whom eventually signed), India, Israel, and Pakistan. The nuclear superpowers, on the one hand, gave up little by agreeing not to help other nations acquire nuclear bombs; non-nuclear signatories, on the other hand, committed themselves to retaining that status.

While the nonproliferation treaty was largely the work of his predecessors, Nixon took the initiative in a dramatic move toward China. The president's most important adviser was national security assistant Henry A. Kissinger, a German-born refugee from Hitler's Holocaust and a Harvard professor of international relations. Both men saw opportunity in the growing Soviet-Chinese discord. If these two nations checked each other's power, their threat to the United States would lessen; thus, according to Nixon, Soviet-Chinese hostility "served our purpose best if we maintained closer relations with

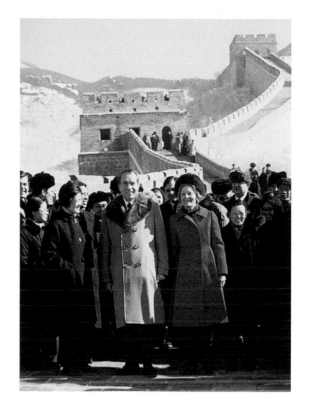

Nixon in China

"This was the week that changed the world," proclaimed President Richard M. Nixon in February 1972, emphasizing the stunning turnaround in relations with America's former enemy, the People's Republic of China. Nixon's trip was meticulously planned to dramatize the event on television and, aside from criticism from some conservatives, won overwhelming support from Americans. The Great Wall of China forms the setting for this photograph of Nixon and his wife Pat.

Nixon Presidential Materials Project, National Archives and Record Administration.

each side than they did with each other." Working with Kissinger and often in secret, Nixon exploited the deterioration in Soviet-Chinese relations that had begun in the early 1960s.

Following two years of secret negotiations, in February 1972, Nixon became the nation's first president to set foot on Chinese soil—an astonishing act by a man who had climbed the political ladder as a fervent anti-Communist. Recognizing that his anti-Communist credentials were what enabled him to conduct this shift in U.S.-Chinese relations with no significant objections at home, Nixon remarked to Chinese leader Mao Zedong, "Those on the right can do what those on the left only talk about." Although the act was largely symbolic, cultural and scientific exchanges followed, and American manufacturers began to find markets in China—small steps in the process of **globalization** that would take giant strides in the 1990s (see chapter 31).

As Nixon and Kissinger hoped, the warming of U.S.-Chinese relations increased Soviet responsiveness to their strategy of **détente**, their term for easing conflict with the Soviet Union. Détente did not mean abandoning containment but instead focusing on issues of common concern, such as arms control and trade. Containment would be achieved not only by military threat but also by ensuring that Russian and Chinese stakes in a stable international order would restrain Russia and China from precipitating crises. Nixon's goal was "a stronger healthy United States, Europe, Soviet Union, China, Japan, each balancing the other."

> Even while applying practical politics rather than ideology to U.S. relations with China and the Soviet Union, in Vietnam and elsewhere Nixon and Kissinger actively resisted social revolutions that might lead to communism.

In May 1972, three months after his trip to China, Nixon visited Moscow, signing several agreements on trade and cooperation in science and space. Most significantly, Soviet and U.S. leaders concluded arms limitation treaties that had grown out of the Strategic Arms Limitation Talks (SALT) begun in 1969. Both sides agreed to limit antiballistic missile systems (ABMs) to two each. Giving up pursuit of a defense against nuclear weapons was a move of crucial importance, because it prevented either nation from building so secure an ABM defense against a nuclear attack that it would risk a first strike.

Gerald Ford, who became president when Nixon resigned in 1974 (see chapter 30), failed to sustain widespread support of détente. The secrecy of the Nixon-Kissinger initiatives had alienated legislators, and some Democrats charged that détente ignored Soviet violations of human rights. Members of both parties worried that Soviet strength was overtaking that of the United States. In response,

Congress derailed trade agreements with the Soviet Union, refusing economic favors unless the Soviets stopped their harsh treatment of internal dissidents and Jews.

Further negotiations on limiting strategic arms went nowhere, but U.S., Soviet, and European leaders signed a historic agreement in 1975 in Helsinki, Finland, formally recognizing the existing post–World War II boundaries in Europe and also committing the signers to respect the human rights of their citizens. The agreement outraged **conservatives** at home because it meant U.S. acceptance of the Soviets' domination over their satellite countries in Eastern Europe—a condition to which American leaders had objected so bitterly thirty years earlier as the cold war began.

Shoring Up Anticommunism in the Third World

Nixon promised in 1973, "The time has passed when America will make every other nation's conflict our own . . . or presume to tell the people of other nations how to manage their own affairs." Yet even while applying practical politics rather than ideology to U.S. relations with China and the Soviet Union, in Vietnam and elsewhere Nixon and Kissinger continued to equate Marxism with a threat to U.S. interests and actively resisted social revolutions that might lead to communism.

The Nixon administration found such a threat in Salvador Allende, a self-proclaimed Marxist who was elected president of Chile in 1970. Since 1964, the Central Intelligence Agency (CIA) and U.S. corporations concerned about nationalization of their Chilean properties had assisted Allende's opponents. When Allende won the election, Nixon ordered the CIA director to make the Chilean economy "scream" and thus destabilize his government. In 1973, with the help of the CIA, the Chilean military engineered a coup, killed Allende, and established a brutal dictatorship under General Augusto Pinochet, who twenty-five years later was

Chile

found guilty of torture, murder, and terrorism by an international court.

In other parts of the world, too, the Nixon administration stood by repressive governments. It eased pressures on white minority governments that tyrannized blacks in southern Africa, believing that, as a National Security Council (NSC) memorandum put it, the "whites are here to stay. . . . There is no hope for the blacks to gain the political rights they seek through violence, which will lead only to chaos and increased opportunities for Communists." In the Middle East, the United States supported the harsh regime of the shah of Iran—whom the CIA had helped regain power in 1953—because it considered Iran a stable anti-Communist ally with enormous petroleum reserves. Nixon secretly began massive arms shipments to the shah in 1972, cementing a relationship that would ignite a new crisis when the shah was overthrown in 1979 (see chapter 30).

Like his predecessors, Nixon pursued a delicate balance between defending Israel's security and seeking the goodwill of Arab nations strategically and economically important to the United States. Conflict between Israel and the Arab nations had escalated into the all-out Six-Day War in 1967, when Egypt massed troops on Israel's border and Israel launched a preemptive strike. Although Syria and Jordan joined the war on Egypt's side, Israel won a stunning victory, seizing territory that amounted to twice its original size. Israeli forces took control of the Sinai Peninsula and Gaza Strip from Egypt, the Golan Heights from Syria, and the West Bank from Jordan, which included the Arab sector of Jerusalem, a city sacred to Jews, Christians, and Muslims alike.

That decisive victory did not quell Middle Eastern turmoil. In October 1973, on the Jewish holiday Yom Kippur, Egypt and Syria surprised Israel with a full-scale attack. When the Nixon administration sided with Israel, the Arab nations retaliated with an oil embargo that created severe shortages in the United States and height-

Israeli Territorial Gains in the Six-Day War, 1967

ened environmentalists' concerns about the nation's wasteful use of energy. After Israel repulsed the attack, Kissinger attempted to mediate between Israel and Arab nations, efforts that continued for the next three decades with only limited success. The Arab countries refused to recognize Israel's right to exist; Israel would not withdraw from the territories occupied during the Six-Day War and began to settle Israelis there; and no solution could be found for the Palestinian refugees who had been displaced by the creation of Israel in the late 1940s. The simmering conflict contributed to anti-American sentiment among Arabs who viewed the United States as Israel's supporter.

Nixon's Search for Peace with Honor in Vietnam

"I'm not going to end up like LBJ, holed up in the White House afraid to show my face on the street," the new president asserted. "I'm going to stop that war. Fast." Although he began a gradual withdrawal of U.S. ground troops, Nixon was no more willing than Johnson to allow South Vietnam to fall to the Communists. Neither was he more able to prevent it, despite expanding military operations into Cambodia and Laos and sporadically but ferociously bombing North Vietnam. In January 1973, the administration concluded a truce that ended the direct involvement of the United States and led to total victory for the North Vietnamese in April 1975.

Vietnamization and Negotiations

Nixon and Kissinger embraced the overriding goal of the three preceding administrations: a non-Communist South Vietnam. By 1969, however, that goal had become almost incidental to the larger objective of maintaining American credibility. Regardless of the wisdom of the initial intervention, Kissinger asserted, "the commitment of 500,000 Americans has settled the importance of Vietnam. For what is involved now is confidence in American promises."

From 1969 to 1972, Nixon and Kissinger pursued a four-pronged approach. First, they tried to strengthen the South Vietnamese military and government. Second, to disarm the antiwar movement at home, Nixon gradually replaced U.S. forces with South Vietnamese soldiers and American technology and bombs. Third, Nixon and Kissinger negotiated with both North Vietnam and the Soviet Union. Fourth, the military applied enormous firepower to persuade Hanoi to accept American terms at the bargaining table.

As part of the Vietnamization of the war, ARVN forces grew to over one million, supported with the latest American equipment and training. The South Vietnamese air force became the fourth largest in the world. U.S. advisers and funds also promoted land reform, village elections, and the building of schools, hospitals, and transportation facilities.

The other side of Vietnamization was the withdrawal of U.S. forces. The number of GIs decreased from 543,000 in 1968 to 140,000 by the end of 1971. Tim O'Brien boarded the plane back home in March 1971 wondering, "What kind of war is it that begins and ends this way, with a pretty girl [the stewardess], cushioned seats, and magazines." Despite reduced draft calls and casualties (from nearly 800 deaths a month in 1969 to 352 in 1970), more than 20,000 Americans perished in Vietnam during the last four years of the war. Having been exposed to the antiwar movement at home, many of the remaining soldiers had less faith in the war than their predecessors had. In addition to mounting racial tensions among soldiers, hundreds of incidents of "fragging" (attacks on officers by enlisted men) occurred, more than in any previous wars, and many soldiers sought escape in illegal drugs. In a 1971 report, "The Collapse of the Armed Forces," a retired Marine Corps colonel described the lack of discipline: "Our army that now remains in Vietnam [is] near mutinous."

Nixon and Kissinger also endeavored to link Soviet interest in expanded trade and arms reductions with U.S. goals in Vietnam. However, their breakthroughs in summit diplomacy with the Soviet Union and China failed to change the course of the war. Nor did intensification of bombing achieve its objective. Echoing Johnson, Kissinger believed that a "fourth-rate power like North Vietnam" had to have a "breaking point," but the hundreds of thousands of tons of bombs delivered by U.S. pilots failed to find it. Fierce application of American power bought time, but little else. (See "Historical Question," page 1078.)

Nixon's War

In the spring of 1969, Nixon began a ferocious air war in Cambodia, carefully hiding it from Congress and the public for more than a year. Seeking to knock out North Vietnamese sanctuaries in Cambodia, the campaign dropped more than 100,000 tons of bombs but succeeded only in sending the North Vietnamese to other hiding places. To support a new, pro-Western Cambodian government installed through a military coup in 1970 and "to show the enemy that we were still serious about our commitment in Vietnam," in April 1970 Nixon ordered a joint U.S.-ARVN invasion of Cambodia.

That order made Vietnam "Nixon's war" and provoked outrage at home. Nixon made a belligerent speech defending his move and emphasizing the importance of U.S. credibility: "If when the chips are down, the world's most powerful nation acts like a pitiful helpless giant, the forces of totalitarianism and anarchy will threaten free nations" everywhere. Upon reading Nixon's speech, a cabinet member predicted, "This will make the students puke." They did more. More than 100,000 people protested in Washington, and students demonstrated and boycotted classes on hundreds of campuses. At Kent State University in Ohio, National Guard troops were dispatched after protesting students burned an old ROTC building. Then, at a peaceful rally on May 4, 1970, nervous troops being pelted by rocks fired at students, killing four and wound-

U.S. Invasion of Cambodia, 1970

THAILAND

LAOS

CAMBODIA

Phnom Penh

SOUTH VIETNAM

Saigon

→ U.S. invasion of Cambodia

ing ten others. "They're starting to treat their own children like they treat us," commented a black woman in Harlem. In a confrontation at Jackson State College in Mississippi on May 14, police shot into a dormitory, killing two black students. In August, police used tear gas and clubs against protesters at a Chicano antiwar rally in Los Angeles.

Upon learning of the bombing and invasion of Cambodia, furious legislators attempted to curb the president. The Senate voted to terminate the Gulf of Tonkin Resolution, which had given the president virtually a blank check in Vietnam, and to cut off funds for the Cambodian operation. The House of Representatives refused to go along, but Congress was clearly becoming an obstacle to the Nixon administration's plans. By the end of June, Nixon pulled out all U.S. soldiers from Cambodia.

The invasion of Cambodia failed to break the will of the North Vietnamese, but it set in motion a terrible tragedy for the Cambodian people. The North Vietnamese moved further into Cambodia and increased their support of the Khmer Rouge, an organization of Communist insurgents attempting to overthrow the U.S.-supported government of Lon Nol. A brutal civil war raged until 1975, when the Khmer Rouge triumphed and imposed a savage rule, slaughtering millions of Cambodians and giving the name "killing fields" to the land of this historically peaceful people.

In 1971, Vietnam veterans themselves became a visible part of the peace movement, the first men in U.S. history to organize against a war in which they had fought. Veterans held a public investigation of "war crimes" in Vietnam, rallied in front of the Capitol, and cast away their war medals. In May 1971, veterans numbered among the 40,000 protesters who engaged in civil disobedience in an effort to shut down Washington. Officials made more than 12,000 arrests, which courts later ruled violations of protesters' rights.

My Lai Massacre
When U.S. forces attacked My Lai in March 1968, they believed that the village was a Vietcong stronghold and expected a fierce fight. Even though they encountered no enemy forces, the men of Charlie Company systematically killed every inhabitant, nearly all of whom were old men, women, and children. Estimates put the death toll at more than 400 villagers. Twelve officers and enlisted men were charged with murder or assault to commit murder, but only one, First Lieutenant William Calley, was convicted. Though convicted of premeditated murder, Calley was paroled after serving less than four years in prison. This photograph of murdered villagers was taken by an army photographer.
Ron Haeberle/TimePix/Getty.

After the spring of 1971, there were fewer massive antiwar demonstrations, but protest continued. Public attention focused on the court-martial of Lieutenant William Calley, which began in November 1970 and resulted in his conviction. During the trial, Americans learned that Calley's company had massacred more than 400 civilians in the hamlet of My Lai in March 1968. Among those murdered were children and women, an atrocity that the military had covered up for more than a year.

Administration policy suffered another blow in June 1971 with publication of the *Pentagon Papers*, a secret government study critical of U.S. policy in Vietnam. Daniel Ellsberg, once a civilian adviser in Vietnam and an aide to Henry Kissinger, had worked on the study. Frustrated in his attempts to persuade officials of the war's futility, Ellsberg copied the papers and gave them to the *New York Times*. Administration efforts to prevent their publication were defeated

> In 1971, Vietnam veterans themselves became a visible part of the peace movement, the first men in U.S. history to organize against a war in which they had fought.

by the Supreme Court as a violation of freedom of the press. The *Pentagon Papers* heightened disillusionment with the war by casting doubts on the government's credibility. More than 60 percent of respondents to a public opinion poll in 1971 considered it a mistake to have sent American troops to Vietnam; 58 percent believed the war to be immoral (Figure 29.2).

The Peace Accords and the Fall of Saigon

Nixon and Kissinger continued to combine military force and negotiation. In March 1972, responding to a strong North Vietnamese offensive, the United States resumed sustained bombing of the North, mined Haiphong and other harbors for the first time, and announced a naval blockade. With peace talks stalled, in December Nixon ordered the most devastating bombing of North Vietnam yet: In twelve days, U.S. planes dropped more bombs than they had in all of 1969–1971.

The ferocious bombing, called "jugular diplomacy" by Kissinger, was costly to both sides, and resumed talks brought agreement.

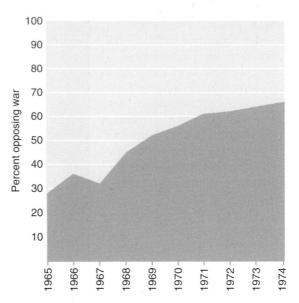

FIGURE 29.2 Public Opinion about the Vietnam War, 1965–1974
This chart reflects the percentage of people answering "yes" to a Gallup poll question: "In view of the developments since we entered the fighting in Vietnam, do you think the United States made a mistake in sending troops to fight in Vietnam?"

Evacuating South Vietnam

As Communist troops rolled south toward Saigon in the spring of 1975, desperate South Vietnamese attempted to flee along with the departing Americans. Here a CIA employee helps Vietnamese board a helicopter from the top of a building a half mile from the U.S. embassy. Thousands of Vietnamese who wanted to be evacuated were left behind. But even though space for evacuees was desperately limited, South Vietnamese president Nguyen Van Thieu fled with fifteen tons of baggage on a U.S. plane to Taiwan.

© Bettmann/Corbis.

On January 27, 1973, representatives of the United States, North Vietnam, the South Vietnamese government, and the Vietcong (now called the People's Revolutionary Government) signed a formal accord in Paris. The agreement required removal of all U.S. troops and military advisers but allowed North Vietnamese forces to remain. Both sides agreed to return prisoners of war. Nixon announced that the agreement brought "peace with honor," but it actually

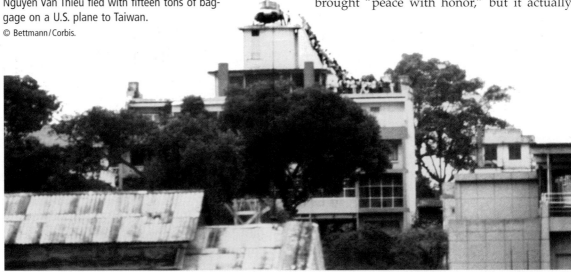

allowed only a face-saving withdrawal for the United States. The South Vietnamese government remained in power for just a little more than two years.

Fighting resumed immediately among the Vietnamese. Nixon's efforts to support the South Vietnamese government, and indeed his ability to govern at all, were increasingly eroded by what came to be known as the Watergate scandals (discussed in chapter 30). In 1975, North Vietnam launched a new offensive in South Vietnam and on May 1 occupied Saigon and renamed it Ho Chi Minh City to honor the Communist leader.

Confusion, humiliation, and tragedy marked the hasty evacuation of Americans and their South Vietnamese allies. The United States got its own citizens out, along with 150,000 South Vietnamese, but it lacked sufficient transport and time to evacuate all those who wanted to leave. U.S. marines beat back desperate Vietnamese trying to escape through the U.S. Embassy. Some South Vietnamese troops, frightened and angry at being left behind, fired on departing Americans.

The Legacy of Defeat

It took Nixon four years to end the war. During that time, the conflict expanded into Cambodia and Laos, Southeast Asia endured massive bombing campaigns, and with a Republican president now conducting it, the Vietnam War became genuinely bipartisan. Although increasing numbers of legislators criticized the war, Congress never denied the funds to fight it.

Only after the peace accords did the legislative branch stiffen its constitutional authority over the making of war. In November 1973, Congress passed the War Powers Act requiring the president to report to Congress within forty-eight hours of deploying military forces abroad. If Congress failed to endorse the president's action within sixty days, the troops would have to be withdrawn.

The dire predictions of three presidents that a Communist victory in South Vietnam would set the dominoes cascading did not materialize. Although Vietnam, Laos, and Cambodia all fell within the Communist camp in the spring of 1975, Thailand, Burma, Malaysia, and the rest of Southeast Asia did not. When China and Vietnam reverted to their historically hostile relationship, the myth of a monolithic Communist power overrunning Asia evaporated.

TABLE 29.1	VIETNAM WAR CASUALTIES
United States	
Killed in action	47,382
Wounded	153,303
Died, noncombat	1,811
Missing, captured	10,753
South Vietnam	
Killed in action	110,357
Military wounded	499,026
Civilians killed	415,000
Civilians wounded	913,000
Communist Regulars and Guerrillas	
Killed in action	666,000

Source: U.S. Department of Defense.

While most Americans wanted simply to forget defeat in Vietnam, veterans and those who lost loved ones could not so easily put the war behind them. The nation had always honored its soldiers' sacrifices, but three unique elements of the Vietnam War denied veterans the traditional homecoming: its lack of strong support at home, its character as a guerrilla war, and its ultimate failure. As one veteran remarked, "The left hated us for killing, and the right hated us for not killing enough."

Because the Vietnam War was in large part a civil, guerrilla war, combat was especially brutal (Table 29.1). The terrors of conventional warfare were multiplied, and so were the opportunities and motivations to commit atrocities. The massacre at My Lai was only the most publicized war crime. To demonstrate the immorality of the war, peace advocates stressed the atrocities, contributing to an image of the Vietnam War veteran as dehumanized and violent and thus deserving of public hostility or indifference.

> Three unique elements of the Vietnam War denied veterans the traditional homecoming: its lack of strong support at home, its character as a guerrilla war, and its ultimate failure.

Veterans largely expressed two kinds of reactions to the defeat. Many regarded the commitment as an honorable one and felt betrayed by the government for not letting them and their now-dead comrades win the war. Others blamed the government for sacrificing the nation's youth in an immoral or useless war. These soldiers best expressed their sense of the war's futility in

AMERICAN PLACES

The Vietnam Veterans Memorial, Washington, D.C.

Deciding how to memorialize the men and women who served in Vietnam was nearly as controversial as the war itself. In 1979, a group of Vietnam veterans, led by Jan C. Scruggs, who had been wounded and decorated as an infantry corporal, formed the Vietnam Veterans Memorial Fund (VVMF). The Memorial Fund received authorization from Congress in 1980 to raise money to erect a memorial on national park land in commemoration of the men and women who served with the U.S. Armed Forces during the Vietnam War. Well aware that "so many veterans met with ridicule and contempt upon returning home," VVWF intended the memorial to "be a place where that injustice could at long last be rectified."

The Memorial Fund conducted a national competition for design of the monument. Eight experts judged nearly fifteen hundred designs, unanimously selecting the one by Maya Ying Lin of Athens, Ohio, whose parents had fled China in 1948. The twenty-one-year-old architecture major at Yale University imagined a 500-foot sloping, V-shaped wall of polished black granite, ten feet high at the vertex and inscribed with the names of every serviceman and servicewoman who perished in Vietnam, in the order of their deaths. The chronological order gives each one a place in history; and, as Lin explained in her design entry, "these names, seemingly infinite in number, convey the sense of overwhelming numbers, while unifying these individuals into a whole."

The VVMF had wanted to separate "the issue of the service of the individual men and women from the issue of U.S. policy in Vietnam [and thus] to begin a process of national reconciliation." But there were immediate objections to Lin's design. Marine lieutenant James Webb, who was wounded three times and had won many decorations, hated the design; he found it negative, unpatriotic, symbolic of failure, a "black ditch," "a black gash of shame." To appease critics who wanted a more positive, heroic, lifelike monument, a traditional sculpture of three servicemen was added to the site. In 1993, the memorial received another statue, this one showing three uniformed women tending a fallen soldier, to honor all of the women who served.

A number of Web sites allow visitors to get a close view of the wall and a feel for the emotions that continue to surround the memorial and the war. There is a "virtual wall" site, where you can focus in on particular sections to read the names etched into the granite. Other sites feature pictures, recollections, poems, and a message board where veterans and their families and friends write in to locate com-

the slang term they used for a comrade's death: He was "wasted." Often identifying with the Vietnamese more than with their white comrades, veterans belonging to minority groups had more reason to doubt the nobility of their purpose. A Native American soldier assigned to resettle Vietnamese civilians found it to be "just like when they moved us to the rez [reservation]. We shouldn't have done that."

"We would not return to cheering crowds, parades, and the pealing of great cathedral bells," wrote Philip Caputo. Most veterans came home to public neglect, while some faced harassment from antiwar activists who did not distinguish the war from the warriors. A veteran remembered the "feelings of rejection and scorn that a bunch of depressed and confused young men experienced when they returned home from doing what their country told them to do." Government benefits were less generous to Vietnam War veterans than they had been to World War II and Korean War soldiers. The women who had served felt even more isolated and ignored by the government, the public, and veterans' groups. Yet two-thirds of Vietnam veterans said that they would serve again, and most veterans readjusted well to civilian life under difficult circumstances.

Nonetheless, the Veterans Administration (VA) estimated that nearly one-sixth of the three million veterans suffered from post-traumatic stress disorder, with its symptoms of fear, recurring nightmares, feelings of guilt and shame, violence, drug and alcohol abuse, and suicidal tendencies. Thirty years after doing army intelligence work in Saigon, Doris Allen "still hit the

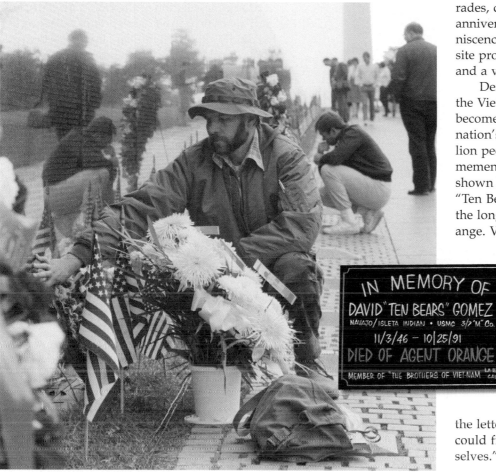

rades, commemorate birthdays or anniversaries, and exchange reminiscences. The memorial's official site provides a history of its creation and a visitor's guide.

Despite the initial controversy, the Vietnam Veterans Memorial has become the most popular site in the nation's capital, visited by 4.4 million people each year. Many leave mementos, such as the small plaque shown here memorializing David "Ten Bears" Gomez, who died from the long-term effects of Agent Orange. Veterans especially appreciate the opportunity to connect in a tangible way with their lost comrades and to heal themselves. As one explained at the memorial's dedication in 1982, they came "to find the names of those we lost in the war, as if by tracing the letters cut into the granite we could find what was left of ourselves."

The Vietnam Veterans Memorial
© Bettmann/Corbis; National Archives.

FOR WEB LINKS RELATED TO THIS SITE AND OTHER AMERICAN PLACES, see "PlaceLinks" at bedfordstmartins.com/roark.

floor sometimes when I hear loud bangs." In the late 1970s, many of those who had served in Vietnam began to display a different set of symptoms: They produced deformed children and fell ill themselves with cancer, severe skin disorders, and other ailments. Veterans claimed a link between these illnesses and Agent Orange, an herbicide that contained the deadly poison dioxin, which the military had sprayed by the millions of gallons over Vietnam. Scientists disagreed about the chemical's effects, and not until 1991 did Congress provide assistance to veterans with diseases linked to the poison.

The government's new position on Agent Orange coincided with a shift in the climate surrounding Vietnam War veterans. "It wasn't until the early 1980s," one veteran observed, "that it became 'all right' to be a combat veteran." The Vietnam War began to enter the realm of popular culture with novels, TV shows, and hit movies depicting a broad range of military experience—from soldiers reduced to brutality to men and women serving with courage and integrity.

The incorporation of the Vietnam War into the collective experience was symbolized most dramatically in the Vietnam Veterans Memorial unveiled in Washington, D.C., in November 1982. Designed by Yale architect student Maya Lin, the black, V-shaped wall inscribed with the names of 58,000 men and women lost to the war became the second most visited site in the capital. In an article describing the memorial's dedication, a Vietnam combat veteran spoke to and for his former comrades: "Welcome home. The war is over." (See "American Places," above.)

Conclusion: An Unwinnable War

Vietnam was America's longest war. The United States spent $150 billion and sent 2.6 million of its young men and women to Vietnam. Of those, 58,000 never returned, and 150,000 suffered serious injury. The war shattered consensus at home and contributed to the most severe internal disorder in a century. It increased presidential power at the expense of congressional authority and public accountability and led to the downfall of two presidents.

The Vietnam War was a logical extension of the nation's post–World War II commitment to containment everywhere on the planet. Yet even as Nixon and Kissinger took steps to ease cold war tensions with the major Communist powers, the Soviet Union and China (who were also the main suppliers of the North Vietnamese), they relentlessly pursued a war to keep South Vietnam from falling to communism. To do otherwise, they believed, would threaten the credibility of American policy and make the United States appear weak. Defeat in Vietnam did not make the United States the "pitiful helpless giant" predicted by Nixon, but it did suggest the relative decline of U.S. power and the impossibility of containment on a global scale.

One of the constraints on U.S. power was the tenacity of revolutionary movements that were determined to achieve national independence. Marine lieutenant Philip Caputo recalled the surprise at discovering "that the men we had scorned as peasant guerrillas were, in fact, a lethal, determined enemy." U.S. officials badly underestimated the sacrifices that the enemy was willing to make to achieve national liberation. Policymakers overestimated the effectiveness of American technological superiority, and they failed to realize how easily the United States could be perceived as a colonial intruder, no more welcome than the French had been.

A second constraint on Eisenhower, Kennedy, Johnson, and Nixon was their resolve to avoid a major confrontation with the Soviet Union or China. For Johnson, who conducted the largest escalation of the war, caution was especially critical so as not to provoke direct intervention by the Communist superpowers. After China exploded its first atomic bomb in 1964, the potential heightened for the Vietnam conflict to escalate into worldwide disaster.

Third, in Vietnam the United States faced the problem of containment by means of an extremely weak ally. The South Vietnamese government never won the support of its people, and the intense devastation and suffering the war brought to civilians only made things worse. Short of taking over the South Vietnamese government and military, the United States could do little to strengthen South Vietnam's ability to resist communism.

Finally, domestic opposition to the war constrained the options of Johnson and Nixon. From its origin in 1965, the antiwar movement grew to include significant portions of mainstream America by 1968. As the war dragged on, with increasing American casualties and growing evidence of the damage being inflicted on innocent Vietnamese, more and more civilians wearied of the conflict. Even some who had fought the war joined the movement, including Philip Caputo, who sent his campaign ribbons and a bitter letter of protest to the White House. By 1968, distinguished experts who had fashioned and implemented the containment policy recognized that erosion of support for the war made its continuation untenable. Five years later, Nixon and Kissinger bowed to the resolution of the enemy and the limitations of U.S. power. As the war wound down, passions surrounding it contributed to a rising conservative movement that would substantially alter the post–World War II political order.

For additional firsthand accounts of this period, see Chapter 29 in Michael Johnson, ed., *Reading the American Past,* Third Edition.

To assess your mastery of the material in this chapter, see the Online Study Guide at bedfordstmartins.com/roark.

For Web links related to the topics in this chapter, see "HistoryLinks," "DocLinks," and "PlaceLinks" at bedfordstmartins.com/roark.

CHRONOLOGY

1961
- CIA-backed Cuban exiles launch unsuccessful invasion of Cuba at Bay of Pigs.
- Berlin Wall erected, dividing East and West Berlin.
- Kennedy administration increases military aid and military advisers in South Vietnam.

- Kennedy administration creates Alliance for Progress and Peace Corps.

1962
- Cuban missile crisis results in Soviet removal of missiles in Cuba.

1963
- Limited nuclear test ban treaty signed by United States and Soviet Union.
- South Vietnamese military overthrows President Ngo Dinh Diem.

1964
- U.S. troops quell anti-American rioting in Panama Canal Zone.
- President Johnson uses Gulf of Tonkin incident to get congressional resolution of support for escalating the war in Vietnam.

1965
- First major protest demonstration in Washington, D.C., against Vietnam War attracts 20,000 people.
- Johnson administration initiates Operation Rolling Thunder, intensifies bombing of North Vietnam.
- Johnson orders increase in number of U.S. troops in Vietnam; peak is 543,000 in 1968.
- U.S. troops invade Dominican Republic to prevent leftist government from taking power.

1968
- Hundreds of thousands of Americans demonstrate against Vietnam War.

- Vietnamese Communists' Tet Offensive leads Johnson administration to reverse its policy in Vietnam and seek negotiated settlement.
- In wake of Tet Offensive, Johnson decides not to seek second term.
- Republican Richard Nixon elected president.

1969
- Neil Armstrong and "Buzz" Aldrin become first humans to land on the moon.

- Nixon orders secret bombing of Cambodia to eliminate enemy sanctuaries and supply lines.

1970
- Nixon orders joint U.S.–South Vietnamese invasion of Cambodia.
- Students killed by national guardsmen and police during campus protests at Kent State and Jackson State.
- Nuclear Non-Proliferation Treaty signed by United States, Soviet Union, and 60 other nations goes into effect.

1971
- *New York Times* publishes *Pentagon Papers*, a secret government study critical of U.S. policy in Vietnam.

1972
- Nixon becomes first U.S. president to visit China.

- Nixon visits Moscow to sign arms limitation treaties with Soviets.

1973
- Paris accords between the United States, North and South Vietnam, and Vietcong bring formal end to U.S. role in Vietnam.
- Congress enacts War Powers Act, limiting president's ability to send Americans to war without congressional consent.
- CIA-backed military coup in Chile topples leftist president Salvador Allende, bringing military dictatorship of Augusto Pinochet to power.
- Arab oil embargo in retaliation for U.S. support of Israel in the Yom Kippur War.

1975
- North Vietnam launches final offensive and takes over all of South Vietnam, ending war in Vietnam.
- Helsinki accords signed by United States, Soviet Union, and European nations recognize post–World War II boundaries of Europe and promise human rights to their citizens.

BIBLIOGRAPHY

General Works

David Halberstam, *The Best and the Brightest* (1972).

George C. Herring, *America's Longest War: The United States and Vietnam, 1950–1975* (1986).

Walter A. McDougall, *The Heavens and the Earth: A Political History of the Space Age* (1985).

Kim McQuaid, *The Anxious Years: America in the Vietnam and Watergate Era* (1989).

Charles Murray and Catherine Bly Cox, *Apollo: The Race to the Moon* (1989).

James S. Olson and Randy Roberts, *Where the Domino Fell: America and Vietnam, 1945–1990* (1996).

Irwin Unger and Debi Unger, *Turning Point: 1968* (1988).

Marilyn B. Young, *The Vietnam Wars, 1945–1990* (1991).

Foreign Policy in the 1960s

Warren Bass, *Support Any Friend: Kennedy's Middle East and the Making of the U.S.-Israel Alliance* (2003).

William Bundy, *A Tangled Web: The Making of Foreign Policy in the Nixon Presidency* (1998).

Elizabeth Cobbs Hoffman, *All You Need Is Love: The Peace Corps and the Spirit of the 1960s* (1998).

Walter Isaacson, *Kissinger: A Biography* (1992).

Keith L. Nelson, *The Making of Détente: Soviet-American Relations in the Shadow of Vietnam* (1995).

Thomas G. Paterson, ed., *Kennedy's Quest for Victory: American Foreign Policy, 1962–1963* (1989).

Gerald T. Rice, *The Bold Experiment: JFK's Peace Corps* (1986).

Robert D. Schulzinger, *Henry Kissinger: Doctor of Diplomacy* (1989).

Thomas Alan Schwartz, *Lyndon Johnson and Europe: In the Shadow of Vietnam* (2003).

D. Michael Shafe, *Deadly Paradigms: The Failure of the U.S. Counterinsurgency Policy* (1988).

Deborah Shapley, *Promise and Power: The Life and Times of Robert McNamara* (1993).

The United States and Latin America

Graham T. Allison and Philip Zelikow, *Essence of Decision: Explaining the Cuban Crisis* (2nd ed., 1999).

James G. Blight and Philip Brenner, *Sad and Luminous Days: Cuba's Struggle with the Superpowers after the Missile Crisis* (2002).

Aleksandr Fursenko and Timothy J. Naftali, *One Hell of a Gamble: The Secret History of the Cuban Missile Crisis* (1998).

Trumball Higgins, *The Perfect Failure: Kennedy, Eisenhower, and the CIA at the Bay of Pigs* (1987).

Lester D. Langley, *America and the Americans: The United States in the Western Hemisphere* (1989).

Jerome Levinson and Juan de Onis, *The Alliance That Lost Its Way* (1970).

Abraham Lowenthal, *The Dominican Intervention* (1972).

James A. Nathan, ed., *The Cuban Missile Crisis Revisited* (1992).

Thomas G. Paterson, *Contesting Castro: The United States and the Triumph of the Cuban Revolution* (1994).

Stephen G. Rabe, *The Most Dangerous Area in the World: John F. Kennedy Confronts Communist Revolution in Latin America* (1999).

Robert Smith Thompson, *The Missiles of October: The Declassified Story of John F. Kennedy and the Cuban Missile Crisis* (1992).

Robert Weisbrot, *Maximum Danger: Kennedy, the Missiles, and the Crisis of American Confidence* (2001).

Mark J. White, *Missiles in Cuba: Kennedy, Khrushchev, Castro, and the 1962 Crisis* (1997).

The War in Vietnam

David L. Anderson, *Shadow on the White House: Presidents and the Vietnam War* (1993).

Loren Baritz, *Backfire: A History of How American Culture Led Us into Vietnam and Made Us Fight the Way We Did* (1985).

Larry Berman, *Lyndon Johnson's War: The Road to Stalemate in Vietnam* (1989).

Robert Buzzanco, *Masters of War: Military Dissent and Politics in the Vietnam Era* (1996).

Mark Clodfelter, *The Limits of Air Power: The American Bombing of North Vietnam* (1989).

Bernard Fall, *The Two Vietnams: A Political and Military Analysis* (1967).

Frances FitzGerald, *Fire in the Lake: The Vietnamese and the Americans in Vietnam* (1972).

Lloyd C. Gardner, *Pay Any Price: Lyndon Johnson and the Wars for Vietnam* (1995).

James William Gibson, *The Perfect War: Technowar in Vietnam* (1986).

Allan E. Goodman, *The Lost Peace: America's Search for a Negotiated Settlement of the Vietnam War* (1978).

Ellen J. Hammer, *A Death in November: America in Vietnam, 1973* (1987).

Michael H. Hunt, *Lyndon Johnson's War: America's Cold War Crusade in Vietnam* (1996).

Arnold R. Isaacs, *Without Honor: Defeat in Vietnam and Cambodia* (1983).

Arnold R. Isaacs, *Vietnam Shadows: The War, Its Ghosts, and Its Legacy* (1997).

David Kaiser, *American Tragedy: Kennedy, Johnson, and the Origins of the Vietnam War* (2000).

Stanley Karnow, *Vietnam: A History* (rev. ed., 1991).

Jeffrey P. Kimball, *Nixon's Vietnam War* (1998).

Gabriel Kolko, *Anatomy of a War: Vietnam, the United States, and the Modern Historical Experience* (1985).

A. J. Langguth, *Our Vietnam/Nuoc Viet Ta: A History of the War, 1954–1975* (2000).

Michael Lind, *Vietnam, the Necessary War: A Reinterpretation of America's Most Disastrous Military Conflict* (1999).

Fredrik Logevall, *Choosing War: The Lost Chance for Peace and the Escalation of the War in Vietnam* (1999).

Robert S. McNamara, *In Retrospect: The Tragedy and Lessons of Vietnam* (1995).

Robert S. McNamara, et al., *Argument without End: In Search of Answers to the Vietnam Tragedy* (1999).

Edwin E. Moïse, *Tonkin Gulf and the Escalation of the Vietnam War* (1996).

John M. Newman, *JFK and Vietnam: Deception, Intrigue, and the Struggle for Power* (1992).

John Prados, *The Hidden History of the Vietnam War* (1995).

Jeffrey Record, *The Wrong Way: Why We Lost in Vietnam* (1998).

Ronald H. Spector, *After Tet: The Bloodiest Year in Vietnam* (1993).

Roger Warner, *Shooting at the Moon: The Story of America's Clandestine War in Laos* (1997).

Those Who Served

Christian G. Appy, *Working-Class War: American Combat Soldiers in Vietnam* (1993).

Lawrence M. Baskir and William A. Strauss, *Chance and Circumstance: The Draft, the War, and the Vietnam Generation* (1978).

Alfred S. Bradford, *Some Even Volunteered: The First Wolfhounds Pacify Vietnam* (1994).

Philip Caputo, *A Rumor of War* (1977).

David Donovan, *Once a Warrior King: Memories of an Officer in Vietnam* (1985).

Bernard Edelman, ed., *Dear America: Letters Home from Vietnam* (1985).

Peter Goldman, *Charlie Company: What Vietnam Did to Us* (1983).

Bob Greene, *Homecoming: When the Soldiers Returned from Vietnam* (1989).

Ron Kovic, *Born on the Fourth of July* (1976).

Myra MacPherson, *Long Time Passing: Vietnam and the Haunted Generation* (1984).

Kathryn Marshall, *In the Combat Zone: Vivid Personal Recollections of the Vietnam War from the Women Who Served There* (1987).

Harry Maurer, *Strange Ground: Americans in Vietnam, 1945–1975, an Oral History* (1998).

Harold G. Moore, *We Were Soldiers Once—and Young: Ia Drang, the Battle That Changed the War in Vietnam* (1992).

Stewart O'Nan, ed., *The Vietnam Reader* (1998).

Al Santoli, *Everything We Had: An Oral History of the Vietnam War* (1981).

Neil Sheehan, *A Bright Shining Lie: John Paul Vann and America in Vietnam* (1988).

James E. Westheider, *Fighting on Two Fronts: African Americans and the Vietnam War* (1997).

John Wheeler, *Touched with Fire: The Future of the Vietnam Generation* (1984).

The Antiwar Movement

Charles DeBenedetti, with Charles Chatfield, *An American Ordeal: The Antiwar Movement in the Vietnam Era* (1990).

Michael S. Foley, *Confronting the War Machine: Draft Resistance during the Vietnam War* (2003).

Adam Garfinkle, *Telltale Hearts: The Origins and Impact of the Vietnam Antiwar Movement* (1995).

Todd Gitlin, *The Whole World Is Watching* (1980).

Andrew E. Hunt, *The Turning: A History of Vietnam Veterans against the War* (1999).

Rhodri Jeffreys-Jones, *Peace Now! American Society and the Ending of the Vietnam War* (1999).

Thomas Powers, *Vietnam: The War at Home* (1973).

Melvin Small, *Johnson, Nixon, and the Doves* (1988).

Melvin Small and William D. Hoover, eds., *Give Peace a Chance: Exploring the Vietnam Antiwar Movement* (1992).

Amy Swerdlow, *Women Strike for Peace: Traditional Motherhood and Radical Politics in the 1960s* (1993).

Michael Useem, *Conscription, Protest, and Social Conflict: The Life and Death of a Draft Resistance Movement* (1983).

Nancy Zaroulis and Gerald Sullivan, *Who Spoke Up? American Protests against the War in Vietnam* (1984).

Domestic Politics

Dan T. Carter, *The Politics of Race: George Wallace, the Origins of the New Conservatism, and the Transformation of American Politics* (1995).

Stephan Lesher, *George Wallace: American Populist* (1994).

David Rudenstine, *The Day the Presses Stopped: A History of the Pentagon Papers Case* (1996).

Jonathan Schell, *The Time of Illusion* (1976).

Theodore H. White, *The Making of the President, 1968* (1970).

Jules Witcover, *Eighty-Five Days: The Last Campaign of Robert Kennedy* (1969).

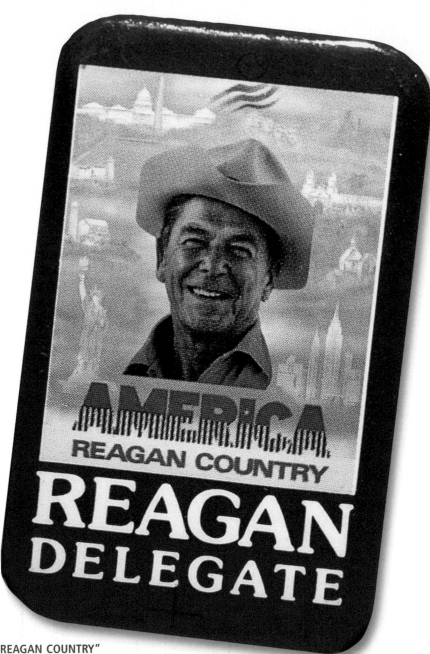

MAKING AMERICA "REAGAN COUNTRY"

This delegate badge from the 1980 Republican National Convention
played on themes that would characterize Ronald Reagan's presidential campaigns and the
politics and policies of the 1980s. Just as the badge appealed to patriotic sentiments with the flag, the
Statue of Liberty, and the space program, Reagan encouraged Americans to take pride in their nation and
celebrate its achievements rather than to focus on its shortcomings. His image as a cowboy brought to
mind some of the movies he had acted in and his favorite recreation—working on the ranch he owned in
California—as well as the independence and rugged individualism in the West, where he had made his
home since the 1940s. The West produced a key element in the surge of conservatism that ensured Reagan's victory in 1980, shaped his administration's antigovernment, anti-Communist agenda, and reversed
the liberal direction that national politics had taken in the 1960s.

National Museum of American History, Smithsonian Institution, Behring Center.

CHAPTER 30

America Moves to the Right

1969–1989

W HEN CONSERVATIVE REPUBLICAN BARRY GOLDWATER spoke to the National Federation of Republican Women in 1963, Phyllis Schlafly, who had invited him, experienced "one of the most exciting days of my life." Like Goldwater, she opposed the moderate Republicanism that had guided the Eisenhower administration and still captured the party leadership. Both Schlafly and Goldwater called for the United States to go beyond simply containing **communism** and to eliminate that evil threat entirely. And both wanted to cut back the government in Washington, especially its role in providing social welfare and enforcing civil rights. Disappointed by Goldwater's loss to Lyndon Johnson in the presidential race of 1964, Schlafly nevertheless took heart in the ability of the **conservatives** to engineer his nomination and continued her efforts to move the Republican Party to the right. Capitalizing on opposition to the policy innovations and turmoil of the 1960s, she added new issues to the conservative agenda and helped to build a grassroots movement on the right that would redefine not only the Republican Party, but American politics and policy into the twenty-first century.

Phyllis Stewart was born in St. Louis in 1924, attended Catholic schools and Washington University, and earned an M.A. in government from Radcliffe College in 1945. Four years later she married Fred Schlafly, an Alton, Illinois, attorney whose anticommunism and antigovernment passions equaled hers. The mother of six children, Schlafly claimed, "I don't think there's anything as much fun as taking care of a baby," and she asserted, "I'd rather scrub bathroom floors than write the newsletter." Yet while she insisted that caring for home and family was women's most important career, Schlafly spent much of her time in politics—writing, speaking, testifying before legislative committees, and losing two bids for Congress in her heavily Democratic district, in 1952, when she was already a mother, and in 1970. Her book, *A Choice Not an Echo*, which she self-published in 1964, excoriated the control of the Republican Party by a **liberal** elite eastern establishment, pushed Barry Goldwater as "the obvious choice" for president, and sold over a million copies. Beginning in 1967, she also published *The Phyllis Schlafly Report*, a monthly newsletter dealing with current political issues. Throughout the 1950s and 1960s, Schlafly focused on the need for stronger efforts against communism at home and abroad, a more powerful military, and a less active government in domestic affairs—all traditional conservative goals.

In the 1970s, however, Schlafly began to pay attention to a host of new issues, including **feminism** and the Equal Rights Amendment, abortion, gay

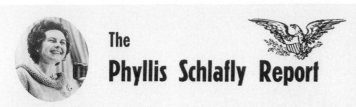

The Phyllis Schlafly Report

Phyllis Schlafly's monthly newsletter to members of her conservative Eagle Forum began in 1967 with articles attacking federal social programs and calling for stronger measures and weapons to fight the cold war against communism. When Congress passed the Equal Rights Amendment in 1972, the *Report* began to add antifeminism and other concerns of the New Right to its agenda, including opposition to abortion rights, sex education in the schools, and protections for gays and lesbians. Schlafly's attacks on feminism appealed to many people; subscribers to her newsletter numbered more than 35,000 in the mid-1970s. The feminist leader Betty Friedan told Schlafly, "I consider you a traitor to your sex. I consider you an Aunt Tom." Courtesy of Phyllis Schlafly.

rights, busing for racial integration, and religion in the schools. Her positions resonated with many Americans who were fed up with the protest movements, the expansion of government, and the challenges to authority and tradition that seemed to define the 1960s. Moreover, the votes of those Americans began to reshape American politics—in Richard Nixon's victories in the presidential elections of 1968 and 1972; in the presidency of Jimmy Carter, whose policies stood substantially to the right of the Democratic administrations of the 1960s; and in conservative Ronald Reagan's capture of the Republican Party, the presidency, and the political agenda in 1980.

Although Richard Nixon did not embrace the entire conservative agenda, he sought to make the Republicans the dominant party by appealing to disaffected blue-collar and southern white Democrats. Nixon resigned the presidency in disgrace in 1974, and his Republican successor, Gerald Ford, occupied the Oval Office for little more than two years; but the shift of the political spectrum to the right continued even when the Democrats captured the White House in 1976. Antigovernment sentiment grew out of the deceptions of the Johnson administration, Nixon's abuse of presidential powers, and the inability of Presidents Ford and Carter to resolve domestic and foreign crises. As Americans saw their incomes decline because of surging unemployment and inflation, many lost confidence in government and became convinced that their taxes were too high.

In 1980, Phyllis Schlafly saw her call for "a choice, not an echo" realized when Ronald Reagan won the presidency. Cutting taxes and government regulations, attacking social programs, expanding the nation's military capacity, and putting pressure on the Soviet Union and communism in the **third world**, Reagan addressed the hopes of traditional conservatives. Like Schlafly, he also championed the concerns of the **New Right**, opposing abortion and sexual permissiveness and supporting a larger role for religion in public life. Reagan's goals encountered resistance from feminists, civil rights groups, environmentalists, and others who fought to keep what they had won in the 1960s. Although his administration failed to enact the entire conservative agenda, left the government with an enormous national debt, and engaged in illegal activities to thwart communism in Latin America, Reagan's popularity helped send another Republican, his vice president, George H. Bush, to the White House at the end of his second term. And Reagan's determined optimism and spirited leadership contributed to a revival in national pride and confidence.

Nixon and the Rise of Postwar Conservatism

Although, as we have seen in chapter 28, Nixon acquiesced in the continuation of most **Great Society** programs and even approved pathbreaking new measures in such areas as the environment, Native American rights, and women's rights, his public rhetoric and certain of his actions as president signified the country's rightward move in both politics and sentiment. During Nixon's years in office, a new strand of conservatism began to join the older movement that focused on anticommunism, a strong national defense, and a limited role for the federal government in domestic affairs. The new conservatism, which Phyllis Schlafly helped promote, condemned much of the Great Society and other developments of the 1960s, including antiwar protests, civil rights demonstrations, liberal Supreme Court decisions, the sexual revolution, and feminism.

The Emergence of a Grassroots Conservative Movement

Although Lyndon Johnson's landslide victory over Barry Goldwater in 1964 appeared to signify liberalism triumphant, those election results actually concealed a rising conservative movement. Defining his purpose as "enlarging freedom at home and safeguarding it from the forces of tyranny abroad," Goldwater echoed the ideas of conservative intellectuals who argued that government intrusion into economic life hindered prosperity, stifled personal responsibility, and interfered with individuals' rights to determine their own values. While they assailed big government in domestic affairs, they demanded a strong military to eradicate "Godless communism."

A growing grassroots movement, vigorous especially in the South and West and including middle-class suburban women and men, members of the rabidly anti-Communist John Birch Society, and college students in the new Young Americans for Freedom had enabled Goldwater, an Arizona senator, to win the nomination. They did not give up when he lost the election. Margaret Minek, who had organized for Goldwater in her community, insisted, "We have a . . . flame . . . burning and the energy it gives off needs to be utilized." Newly energized conservatives like Minek in California contributed to Ronald

Reagan's defeat of the incumbent liberal governor, Edmund Brown, in 1966, another sign of the rising strength of the right. Linking his opponent with the student disruptions at the University of California at Berkeley (Reagan called them "the filthy speech movement") and the Watts riot, Reagan capitalized on popular fears about rising taxes, student challenges to authority, and black demands for justice. He claimed in one campaign speech that "if an individual wants to discriminate against Negroes or others in selling or renting his house he has a right to do so."

Although the rise of grassroots conservatism was not limited to the West and South, a number of elements in the **Sun Belt** were conducive to its growth in areas such as Orange County, California; Dallas, Texas; Scottsdale, Arizona; and Jefferson Parish, Louisiana. Areas that hosted strong conservative movements contained relatively homogeneous, skilled, and affluent populations, and their economies depended heavily on military bases and defense production. The West harbored a long-standing tradition of **Protestant** morality, individualism, and opposition to interference by a remote federal government. That tradition continued with the emergence of the New Right, even though it was hardly consistent with the western states' economic dependence on military and defense spending.

> Although the rise of grassroots conservatism was not limited to the West and South, a number of elements in the Sun Belt were conducive to its growth there.

The South shared the West's antipathy to the federal government, but there hostility to racial change was much more central to the new conservatism. After signing the Civil Rights Act of 1964, President Lyndon Johnson remarked to a friend, "I think we just delivered the South to the Republican Party." Indeed, Barry Goldwater won a majority in five southern states in 1964.

Grassroots movements emerged around a number of issues that conservatives believed marked the "moral decline" of their nation. For example, in 1968, Eleanor Howe mobilized her community to eliminate sex education from the schools in Anaheim, California, when she examined the curriculum and found that "nothing depicted my values. . . . It wasn't so much the information. It was the shift in values." In 1970, Alice Moore launched a campaign in Charleston, West Virginia, against a sex education curriculum that she found anti-American and anti-Christian and based on an "atheistic and relativistic view of morality." Decisions by the Warren Court on such issues as school prayer, obscenity, and birth control also galvanized conservatives to restore "traditional values" to the nation.

Nixon Courts the Right

In the 1968 campaign, Nixon's "southern strategy" had exploited antipathy to black protest and new civil rights policies, wooing white southerners away from the Democratic Party as well as considerable numbers of northern voters. Republicans hoped to use the "southern strategy" to make further inroads into traditional Democratic strongholds in the 1972 election.

> School segregation was widespread in northern and western cities, where residential patterns left half of all African American children attending virtually all-black schools.

The Nixon administration reluctantly enforced court orders to achieve high degrees of integration in southern schools, but it stymied efforts to deal with segregation outside the South. School segregation was widespread in northern and western cities, where residential patterns left half of all African American children attending virtually all-black schools. After courts began to order the transfer of students between schools in white and black neighborhoods to achieve desegregation, and the Supreme Court assented in *Swann v. Charlotte-Mecklenburg Board of Education* in 1971, busing became "political dynamite," according to a Gallup poll. Phyllis Schlafly spoke for many busing opponents when she wrote in 1972, "We've had all we can take of judicial interference with local schools."

Although children had been riding buses to school for decades, especially in rural areas, busing for racial integration provoked outrage. Such fury erupted in Boston in 1974 when black students began to attend the formerly all-white South Boston High School. Nearly all the white students boycotted classes, and angry white crowds threw rocks at black students disembarking from buses. The whites most affected came from working-class families, who remained in cities abandoned by the more affluent and whose children were usually the ones riding buses to predominantly black schools where overcrowding and deficient facilities often meant inferior education. Clarence McDonough fingered the liberal officials who bused his "kid half way around Boston so that a bunch of politicians can end up their careers with a clear conscience." Phyllis Schlafly echoed the sentiment, pointing out, "None of the justices who ordered busing ever sent their children to inner-city schools or allowed them to be the victims of forced busing." African Americans themselves were conflicted about the benefits of sending their children on long rides to schools where teachers might not welcome or respect them. Nixon failed to persuade Congress to end court-ordered busing, but after he had appointed four new justices, the Supreme Court moved in the president's direction in 1974. In a five-to-four decision concerning the Detroit public schools (*Milliken v. Bradley*), the Court imposed strict limits on the use of busing to achieve racial balance.

Nixon also sought to implement the southern strategy and ride the backlash against liberalism through his judicial appointments. He believed that the Supreme Court under Chief Justice Earl Warren had been "unprecedentedly politically active . . . too often using their interpretation of the law to remake American society according to their own social, political, and ideological precepts." Appealing to Americans outraged by the Warren Court's liberal decisions, Nixon planned to reverse the Court's direction. When Warren resigned in June 1969, Nixon replaced him with Warren E. Burger, a federal appeals court judge who was seen as a **strict constructionist**—someone inclined to interpret the Constitution narrowly and to limit government intervention to protect individual rights.

Unions and civil rights groups, however, mounted strong campaigns against Nixon's next two nominees, conservative southern judges, and the Senate forced him to settle on more moderate candidates. The Burger Court proved more sympathetic than the Warren Court to the president's agenda, restricting somewhat the protections of individual rights established by the previous Court. For example, the Court limited the range of **affirmative action** in *Regents of the University of California v. Bakke* (1978) (see "Significant Supreme Court Cases," page A-44). Yet that decision did allow affirmative action programs to attack the results of past discrimination as long as strict quotas or racial classifications were not involved. (The Court reaffirmed this position in 2003.) In *Bakke* and other cases,

Integration of Public Schools, 1968

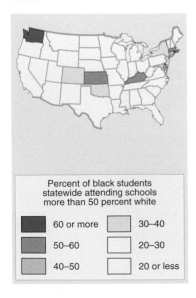

Percent of black students statewide attending schools more than 50 percent white

- 60 or more
- 50–60
- 40–50
- 30–40
- 20–30
- 20 or less

School Busing

Controversy over busing as a means to integrate public schools erupted in Boston when the school year started in autumn 1974. Opposition was especially high in white ethnic neighborhoods like South Boston. Residents there resented liberal judges from the suburbs assigning them the burden of integration. Clashes between blacks and whites in South Boston, such as this one in February 1975 outside Boston's Hyde Park High School, prompted authorities to dispatch police to protect black students.

AP / Wide World.

the Burger Court continued to uphold liberal programs of the 1960s.

Nixon's southern strategy and the backlash against the civil rights revolution of the 1960s ended the Democratic hold on the "solid South." In 1964, Senator Strom Thurmond of South Carolina, who had headed the Dixiecrat challenge to Truman in 1948, changed his party affiliation to Republican. North Carolina senator Jesse Helms followed suit in 1971, and aspirants for office throughout the South began to realize that Democratic candidates had a dim future in that region. Although Republicans never realized the dominance held by the Democrats in 1950, when only two southern Republican representatives sat in Congress, by 2002 Republicans held the majority of southern seats in the House and Senate and four of the seven governorships in the South.

In addition to courting the votes of Americans uncomfortable with the pace of racial change, Nixon aligned himself with those fearful about women's changing roles and new demands. In 1971, he vetoed a bill providing federal funds for day care centers with a message that combined the old and new conservatism. Parents should purchase child care services "in the private, open market," he insisted, not through a fiscally irresponsible program requiring "a new army of bureaucrats." At the same time, he played to concerns of social conservatives by warning about the "family-weakening

implications" of the measure that would replace "the family-centered approach [with] communal approaches to child rearing." And, in response to the movement to liberalize abortion laws, Nixon took the side of the "defenders of the right to life of the unborn." He did not comment publicly on *Roe v. Wade* (1973), but his earlier stance against abortion anticipated the Republican Party's eventual embrace of an issue that Phyllis Schlafly and others would use to mobilize forces on the right.

Constitutional Crisis and Restoration

Nixon's ability to attract Democrats resulted in a resounding landslide victory in the 1972 election. Two years later, however, the so-called Watergate scandals caused him to abandon his office. Nixon's abuse of power and efforts to cover up crimes committed by subordinates betrayed the public trust and forced the first presidential resignation in history. His handpicked successor, Gerald Ford, helped to restore confidence in the presidency, but the aftermath of Watergate and severe economic

Nixon's abuse of power and efforts to cover up crimes committed by subordinates betrayed the public trust and forced the first presidential resignation in history.

problems returned the White House to the Democrats in 1976. Nonetheless, so robust was the conservative tide that it not only survived the temporary setback when Nixon resigned the presidency, it quickly challenged the Democratic administration that followed.

The Election of 1972

Nixon's most spectacular foreign policy initiatives, **détente** with the Soviet Union and the opening of relations with China (see chapter 29), heightened his prospects for reelection in 1972. Although the war in Vietnam continued, antiwar protests diminished with the decrease in American ground forces and casualties. Nixon's New Economic Policy had temporarily checked inflation and unemployment, and his attacks on busing and antiwar protesters had appealed to the right, positioning him favorably for the 1972 election.

A large field of contenders vied for the Democratic nomination, including New York representative Shirley Chisholm, the first African American politician to make a serious bid for the presidency, who won 151 delegate votes. On the right, Governor George Wallace of Alabama captured a series of southern primaries as well as those in Michigan and Maryland, but his campaign was cut short when a deranged man shot him, leaving Wallace paralyzed below the waist. Democratic senator George S. McGovern of South Dakota, who had defeated a large field of contenders, came to the Democratic convention as the clear leader, and the composition of the convention delegates made his position even stronger.

After the bitter 1968 convention, the Democrats had initiated key reforms, requiring delegations to represent the relative proportions of minorities, women, and youth in their states. These newcomers displaced many regular Democrats—officeholders, labor leaders, and representatives of traditional ethnic groups. One party regular thought that "the Democratic Party was taken over by the kooks," and another, referring to the considerable numbers of young people and women, remarked that there was "too much hair, and not enough cigars at this convention." Though easily nominated, McGovern struggled against Nixon from the outset. Republicans portrayed him as a left extremist; and his support for busing, his call for immediate withdrawal from Vietnam, and his pledge to cut $30 billion from the Pentagon's budget alienated conservative Democrats.

Nixon gained 60.7 percent of the popular vote, carrying every state except Massachusetts in a landslide victory second only to Johnson's in 1964. Although the Democrats maintained control of Congress, Nixon won a majority of votes among southerners, Catholics, urbanites, and blue-collar workers, all traditionally strong supporters of the Democratic Party. The president had little time to savor his triumph, however, as revelations began to emerge about crimes and misdemeanors that had been committed to ensure the victory.

Watergate

During the early morning hours of June 17, 1972, five men working for Nixon's reelection campaign crept into Democratic Party headquarters in the Watergate complex in Washington. Intending to repair a bugging device installed in an earlier break-in, they were discovered and arrested on the scene. In trying to

Shirley Chisholm Runs for President

From an active political career in the Democratic Party, grassroots community groups, the League of Women Voters, and the New York State Assembly, Shirley Chisholm became the first African American woman elected to the House of Representatives in 1968. She won that election against James Farmer, a founder of CORE, whose campaign stressed the need for "a strong male image" and a "man's voice in Washington." Chisholm entered the race for the Democratic presidential nomination in 1972 knowing that her chances were slim but asserting that minority women were "used to taking up seemingly impossible challenges . . . and in the process increas[ing] the chance that success would come, someday." Here she announces her candidacy at the Concord Baptist Church in Brooklyn in January 1972.

Dan Hogan Charles/New York Times/Getty Images.

The Gap in the Watergate Tapes

Franklin Roosevelt installed the first recording apparatus in the White House under his desk in 1940, but neither he, Truman, nor Eisenhower recorded conversations extensively. John F. Kennedy was the first president to put in a complete taping network; and Richard Nixon was the first to use a voice-activated system, which taped about 2,800 hours of conversations in which most participants did not know they were being recorded. When Nixon was compelled to turn over the tapes during the Watergate investigation, an 18½-minute gap was discovered in a conversation between Nixon and his chief of staff, H. R. Haldeman, just three days after the Watergate break-in. Nixon's secretary Rose Mary Woods said that her foot must have slipped while she was transcribing the tape, using the transcription machine pictured above; but others, noting that the 18 minutes contained several separate erasings, suggested that the clumsiness of the deed linked it to Nixon.

Nixon Presidential Materials Project, National Archives and Records Administration.

cover up the connection between those arrested and administration officials, Nixon and his aides set in motion the most serious constitutional crisis since the Civil War. Reporters dubbed it "Watergate."

Over the next two years, Americans learned that Nixon and his associates had engaged in other abuses, such as accepting illegal campaign contributions, using so-called dirty tricks to sabotage Democratic candidates, and unlawfully attempting to silence critics of the Vietnam War. Nixon was not the first president to lie to the public or to misuse power. Every president since Franklin D. Roosevelt had enlarged the powers of the presidency, justifying his actions as necessary to protect national security. This expansion of executive powers, often called the "imperial presidency," weakened some of the traditional **checks and balances** on the executive branch and opened the door to abuses.

Watergate began when White House adviser Charles Colson established a secret unit nicknamed the "plumbers" to stop the kinds of "leaks" that had led to publication of the *Pentagon Papers* in 1971. These men soon turned to projects to disrupt the Democratic presidential nomination process and discredit potential candidates, and in 1972 they staged the Watergate break-in to bug the Democratic Party's phones. After the arrest of the Watergate burglars, Nixon secretly plotted to conceal links between the burglars and the White House, while publicly denying any connection to the break-in. When investigations by a grand jury and the Senate suggested that White House aides had been involved, Nixon decided that it was time to act.

In April 1973, the president accepted official responsibility for Watergate but denied any personal knowledge of the break-in or of a cover-up. He also announced the resignations of three White House aides and Attorney General Richard Kleindienst. In May, he authorized the appointment of an independent special prosecutor, Archibald Cox, to conduct an investigation. Meanwhile, sensational revelations exploded in the Senate investigating committee, headed by Democrat Samuel J. Ervin of North Carolina. Counsel to the President John Dean described projects to harass "enemies" through tax audits and other illegal means and asserted that the president had long known of efforts to cover up the Watergate burglary. The most damaging blow struck when a White House aide disclosed that all conversations in the Oval Office were taped. Both Cox and the Ervin committee immediately asked for tapes related to Watergate. When Nixon refused, citing executive privilege and separation of powers, Cox and Ervin took their case to federal district court.

At the same time, more disclosures revealed Nixon's misuse of federal funds and tax evasion. In August 1973, Vice President Spiro Agnew was compelled to resign after an investigation revealed that he had taken bribes while governor of Maryland. Although Nixon's choice of House minority leader Gerald Ford of Michigan to succeed Agnew won widespread approval, the vice president's resignation further tarnished the administration.

On October 19, 1973, Nixon ordered special prosecutor Cox to cease his efforts to obtain the Oval Office tapes. When Cox refused, Nixon ordered Attorney General Elliot Richardson to fire Cox. Richardson instead resigned, as did the next man in line at the Justice Department. Finally, the solicitor general, Robert Bork, agreed to carry out the president's order. The press called the series of dismissals and resignations the "Saturday night massacre," 250,000 telegrams

Nixon's Farewell
The first president in Amercian history to resign the presidency, Nixon did not admit guilt, even though tapes of his conversations indicated that he had obstructed justice, abused his power, and lied. In the decades after his resignation, he gradually rehabilitated his reputation and became an elder statesman and foreign-policy adviser. All the living presidents attended his funeral in 1994. In this photo, he and his family say goodbye to his successor, Gerald Ford, and Betty Ford, and prepare to board the helicopter that would take them away from the White House for the last time.
Nixon Presidential Materials Project, National Archives and Records Administration (E3398-09).

condemning Nixon's action flooded the White House, and his popular support plummeted to 27 percent.

In February 1974, the House of Representatives voted to begin an **impeachment** investigation. In April, Nixon began to release edited transcripts of the tapes. As the public read passages sprinkled with "expletive deleted," the House Republican leader Hugh Scott of Penn-

sylvania abandoned his support of the president, calling the transcripts a "deplorable, shabby, disgusting, and immoral performance by all." The transcripts included Nixon's orders to John Mitchell, his former attorney general and head of his reelection committee, and Dean in March 1973: "I don't give a shit what happens. I want you all to stonewall it, let them plead the Fifth Amendment, cover up or anything else, if it'll save it—save the plan."

In July 1974, the House Judiciary Committee began debate over specific charges for impeachment: (1) obstruction of justice, (2) abuse of power, (3) contempt of Congress, (4) unconstitutional waging of war by the secret bombing of Cambodia, and (5) tax evasion and the selling of political favors. While the last two counts failed to get a majority, the committee voted to take the first three charges to the House, where a vote of impeachment seemed certain. On July 24, a unanimous Supreme Court ordered the president to hand over the remaining tapes. Transcripts of tapes released August 5 revealed that just six days after the break-in, Nixon and aides had discussed manipulating the CIA to hinder the FBI's investigation of the burglary. This was sufficient evidence to seal his fate.

Nixon announced his resignation to a national television audience on August 8, 1974. Acknowledging some incorrect judgments, he insisted that he had always tried to do what was best for the nation. The next morning, Nixon ended a rambling, emotional farewell to his staff with some advice: "Always give your best, never get discouraged, never get petty; always remember, others may hate you, but those who hate you don't win unless you hate them, and then you destroy yourself." Had he practiced that advice, he might have saved his presidency.

The Ford Presidency and the Election of 1976

Gerald R. Ford, who had represented Michigan in the House of Representatives since 1948, had built a reputation as a conservative party loyalist who treated opponents with respect. Not a brilliant thinker, Ford was known for his integrity, humility, and dedication to public office. "I'm a Ford, not a Lincoln," he acknowledged. Most of official Washington and the American public looked favorably on his succession as president.

Upon taking office, Ford announced, "Our long nightmare is over," but he shocked many Americans when he ended the particular nightmare of the former president. On September 8, 1974, Ford granted Nixon a pardon "for all offenses against the United States which he . . . has committed or may have committed or taken part in" during his presidency. It was the most generous presidential pardon ever issued, saving Nixon from nearly certain indictment and trial. Thirty of his associates ultimately were convicted or pleaded guilty. The pardon provoked a tremendous outcry from Congress and the public. Capitalizing on revulsion over Watergate and the pardon, Democrats made impressive gains in the November congressional elections.

With the Democrats in control, Congress sought to guard against the types of abuses revealed in the Watergate investigations. The Federal Election Campaign Act of 1974, for example, established public financing of presidential campaigns, though it failed to stop the ever-larger campaign donations that candidates found ways to solicit from interest groups, corporations, labor unions, and wealthy individuals. In 1978, Congress passed an independent counsel law establishing a nonpartisan procedure for the appointment of special prosecutors who could not be fired. The law was used to investigate possibly criminal actions by Presidents Reagan and Clinton (see chapter 31) as well as more than a dozen lesser officials before it expired in 1998.

Special investigating committees in Congress discovered a host of illegal FBI and CIA activities stretching back to the 1950s. Both agencies had harassed political dissenters, and the CIA had made plans to assassinate Fidel Castro and other foreign leaders. In response to these revelations, President Ford established new controls on covert operations, and Congress created permanent committees to oversee the intelligence agencies. Yet these measures did little to diminish the public cynicism and lack of trust in government that had been developing since the Johnson years.

Ford carried a number of burdens into the 1976 presidential race. Underlying weaknesses in the U.S. economy remained: a low growth rate, high unemployment, a foreign trade deficit, and high energy prices tied to dependence on oil from abroad. Ford also faced a major challenge from the Republican right, as California governor Ronald Reagan came close to capturing the nomination.

The Democrats nominated James Earl "Jimmy" Carter Jr., former state senator and governor of Georgia. A graduate of the U.S. Naval Academy, Carter spent seven years in the navy before his father's death called him back to Plains, Georgia, to run the family peanut farming business. Highly intelligent and well prepared on the issues, the soft-spoken Carter stressed his small-town roots, deep religious commitment, and distance from the suspect national government. Although Carter selected liberal senator Walter F. Mondale of Minnesota as his running mate and accepted a platform compatible with traditional Democratic principles, his nomination nonetheless represented a decided rightward turn in the party.

After the revelations of corruption in the Nixon administration, the candidate who carried his own bags, lived modestly, and went home from the campaign trail almost every week to teach a Bible class at his Baptist church had considerable appeal. Carter also benefited from the country's economic problems and from his ability to attract votes from the traditional Democratic coalition of blacks, southerners, organized labor, and ethnic groups. Yet, although Democrats retained substantial margins in Congress, Carter received just 49.9 percent of the popular vote to Ford's 47.9 percent (Map 30.1).

MAP 30.1 The Election of 1976

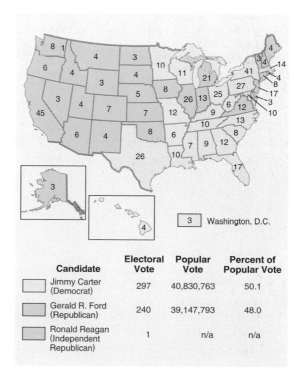

Candidate	Electoral Vote	Popular Vote	Percent of Popular Vote
Jimmy Carter (Democrat)	297	40,830,763	50.1
Gerald R. Ford (Republican)	240	39,147,793	48.0
Ronald Reagan (Independent Republican)	1	n/a	n/a

The "Outsider" Presidency of Jimmy Carter

Carter promised that he would lead a government that was "competent," as well as "honest, decent, open, fair, and compassionate." He also warned Americans that "we can neither answer all questions nor solve all problems." His personal honesty and decency helped to revive trust in the presidency but did not inspire confidence in his own ability to lead the nation through domestic and foreign crises. He faced at more intense levels the energy shortages and stagflation (see chapter 28) that had confounded his predecessors, and he presided over deteriorating Soviet-American relations and renewed instability in the Middle East.

> Carter faced at more intense levels the energy shortages and stagflation that had confounded his predecessors, and he presided over deteriorating Soviet-American relations and renewed instability in the Middle East.

Retreat from Liberalism

Jimmy Carter vowed "to help the poor and aged, to improve education, and to provide jobs" but at the same time "not to waste money." He wanted a government that would help those in need, but one that also was efficient and prudent in its spending. When these aims conflicted, especially when inflation threatened economic stability, Carter's commitment to reform took second place. Americans seeing their material status eroded by stagflation became less willing to see their tax dollars used to benefit the disadvantaged, though their opposition to government programs did not extend to those such as Social Security and Medicare that helped the middle class. As Carter leaned in the direction of fiscal stringency, liberal Democrats accused him of deserting the Democratic reform tradition that stretched back to Franklin D. Roosevelt.

Although Carter's outsider status helped him win the presidency, it left him without strong ties to party insiders or prominent legislators.

Jimmy Carter's Inauguration
After his inauguration in January 1977, Jimmy Carter eschewed the customary presidential limousine and instead walked with his wife, daughter, and two sons and their wives down Pennsylvania Avenue from the Capitol to the White House. He wanted to emphasize his opposition to some of the trappings of office that separated government from the people. Ordering cabinet heads to drive their own cars, he said, "Government officials can't be sensitive to your problems if we are living like royalty here."
Jimmy Carter Presidential Library.

Moreover, his comprehensive proposals went against the congressional tendency to tackle problems with a piecemeal, incremental approach. Legislators complained of inadequate consultation and Carter's tendency to flood them with a mass of unprioritized proposals.

Even a president without those liabilities might not have done much better than Carter, as Congress itself diminished the ability of party leaders to deliver a united front. While it flexed its muscles in response to Watergate and abuses of presidential power, Congress reduced the power of committee chairs, weakened party control over legislators, and decentralized the decision-making process. In addition, because primary elections rather than party conventions now controlled the nominating process, candidates depended less on party support and more on campaign funds from interest groups, which they used to appeal directly to voters through television.

The Carter administration did little better with the formidable problems that had plagued the Nixon and Ford administrations—unemployment, inflation, and slow economic growth. With new tax cuts and increased federal spending on public works and public service jobs programs, unemployment receded for a time. But in 1978, rising inflation impelled Carter to curtail federal spending and the Federal Reserve Board to increase interest rates and tighten the money supply. These policies not only failed to halt inflation, which surpassed 13 percent in 1980, but also contributed to rising unemployment, reversing gains made in Carter's first two years.

Nor did Carter achieve much progress on traditional Democratic issues. His commitment to holding down the federal budget frustrated Democrats pushing for comprehensive welfare reform and a national health insurance program. To ensure solvency in Social Security, Carter and Congress agreed to raise employer and employee contributions, but this also increased the tax burden of lower- and middle-income Americans.

In contrast, corporations and wealthy individuals gained from new legislation. A sharp cut in the capital gains tax benefited high-income individuals. When the Chrysler Corporation approached bankruptcy in 1979, Congress provided $1.5 billion worth of loan guarantees to ensure the survival of the tenth largest corporation in the country. Pleasing to conservatives were Carter's proposals to give greater rein to free enterprise. Congress complied, deregulating airlines in 1978 and the banking, trucking, and railroad industries in 1980.

"We are struggling with a profound transition from a time of abundance to a time of growing scarcity in energy," Carter insisted in 1979, pointing to the nation's enormous consumption of energy and its dependence on oil from the unstable Middle East. The president fought for a comprehensive program and gave that issue cabinet status by creating a Department of Energy. Although the United States was even more dependent on foreign oil than it had been during the energy crisis linked to the Yom Kippur War of 1973, Carter's efforts fell victim to his poor relationship with Congress and to competing demands among energy producers and consumers. Congress did pass legislation to penalize gas-guzzling automobiles and provide other incentives to conserve energy. And in 1979, when another Middle Eastern crisis created the most severe energy shortage yet, Congress authorized more measures to limit consumption and decrease the need for foreign oil. Still, they fell short of Carter's comprehensive proposal, and American industry and individuals continued to devour energy. At the end of the century, the United States, with only about 6 percent of the world's population, consumed more than 25 percent of global oil production.

Carter Promotes Human Rights

Campaigning for president in 1976, Jimmy Carter charged his predecessors' foreign policy with violating the nation's principles of freedom and human dignity. "We've seen a loss of morality . . . and we're ashamed of what our government is as we deal with other nations around the world," he said. The cynical support of dictators, the secret diplomacy, the interference in the internal affairs of other countries, and the excessive reliance on military solutions— Carter promised to reverse them all.

Human rights formed the cornerstone of his approach. Administration officials chastised governments that denied their citizens basic political and civil rights. They also applied economic pressure, denying aid or trading privileges to such nations as Argentina, Chile, and El Salvador, and to the white minority governments of Rhodesia and South Africa, which blatantly violated the rights of their black majorities. Yet glaring inconsistencies appeared in the human rights policy. Concluding the process that Nixon and Kissinger had begun, Carter established formal

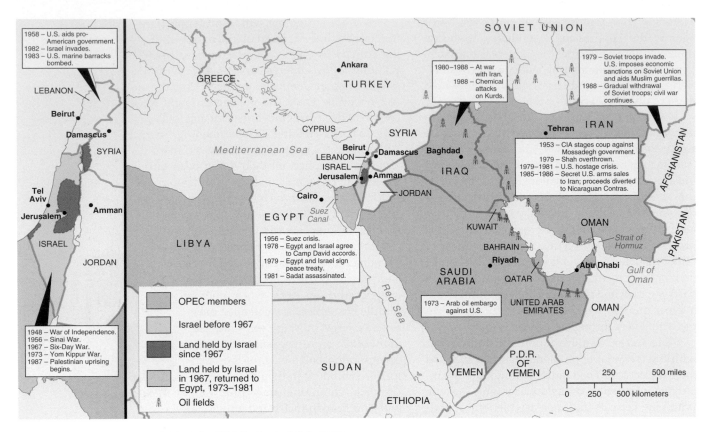

1958 – U.S. aids pro-
American government.
1982 – Israel invades.
1983 – U.S. marine barracks
bombed.

1980–1988 – At war
with Iran.
1988 – Chemical
attacks
on Kurds.

1979 – Soviet troops invade.
U.S. imposes economic
sanctions on Soviet Union
and aids Muslim guerrillas.
1988 – Gradual withdrawal
of Soviet troops; civil war
continues.

1953 – CIA stages coup against
Mossadegh government.
1979 – Shah overthrown.
1979–1981 – U.S. hostage crisis.
1985–1986 – Secret U.S. arms sales
to Iran; proceeds diverted
to Nicaraguan Contras.

1956 – Suez crisis.
1978 – Egypt and Israel agree
to Camp David accords.
1979 – Egypt and Israel sign
peace treaty.
1981 – Sadat assassinated.

1973 – Arab oil embargo
against U.S.

1948 – War of Independence.
1956 – Sinai War.
1967 – Six-Day War.
1973 – Yom Kippur War.
1987 – Palestinian uprising
begins.

OPEC members

Israel before 1967

Land held by Israel
since 1967

Land held by Israel
in 1967, returned to
Egypt, 1973–1981

Oil fields

MAP 30.2   The Middle East, 1948–1989

Determination to preserve access to the rich oil reserves of the Middle East and commitment to the security of Israel were the fundamental—and often conflicting—principles of U.S. foreign policy in that region.

READING THE MAP: Where did the United States become involved diplomatically or militarily in the Middle East between 1948 and 1989? Which countries are members of OPEC?

CONNECTIONS: What role did U.S. foreign policy regarding the Middle East and events in Israel play in provoking the 1973 Arab oil embargo against the United States? What precipitated the taking of U.S. hostages in Iran in 1979? Was U.S. intervention in the country a factor? If so, why?

FOR MORE HELP ANALYZING THIS MAP, see the map activity for this chapter in the Online Study Guide at bedfordstmartins.com/roark.

diplomatic relations with the People's Republic of China in 1979, even though the Chinese government blatantly refused to grant **democratic** rights to its people. Moreover, the administration invoked no sanctions against repressive governments in Iran, South Korea, and the Philippines, thus sacrificing human rights ideals to strategic and security considerations.

Cold war considerations vied with human rights concerns in Carter's approach to Nicaragua, which had been ruled since 1936 by the corrupt and viciously oppressive Somoza regime. U.S. officials complained about the dictatorship's excesses and invoked some economic sanctions, but when a rebellion erupted, their greatest concern was to contain Communist influence in the anti-Somoza movement. Officials were particularly uneasy about the Sandinistas, a leading element in the opposition with ties to Cuba. Nonetheless, when the Somoza regime fell in 1979 and Sandinista leader Daniel Ortega assumed power, Carter extended recognition and economic aid to the new government. Critics attacked Carter for pressuring the Somoza regime on human rights and recognizing the Ortega government, demanding instead the more typical test for U.S. support during the cold war years—whether a country was anti-Communist and friendly to American interests, not how it treated its citizens.

Applying moral principles to relations with Panama, Carter sped up negotiations over control of the Panama Canal—the most conspicuous symbol of **Yankee imperialism**. In 1977, the United States and Panama signed treaties providing for joint control of the canal until 2000, when Panama would take over. Treaty supporters viewed the agreement as recompense for the blatant use of U.S. power to obtain the canal in 1903. Angry opponents insisted on retaining the vital waterway. "We bought it, we paid for it, it's ours," claimed Ronald Reagan during the presidential primaries of 1976. Only after the Carter administration undertook a massive campaign to rally support did the Senate ratify the treaties by the narrowest margins.

Seeking to apply his moral authority toward peace in the Middle East, Carter seized on the courage of Egyptian president Anwar Sadat, the first Arab leader to risk his political career by talking directly with Israeli officials. When initial discussions between Sadat and Israeli prime minister Menachem Begin faltered, Carter invited them to the presidential retreat at Camp David, Maryland, and spent thirteen days there mediating between the two. The Camp David accords led to an agreement that Begin and Sadat signed at the White House in March 1979: Egypt became the first Arab state to recognize Israel, and Israel agreed to gradual withdrawal from the Sinai Peninsula, territory that it had seized in the 1967 war (Map 30.2). Although the issues of Palestinian self-determination in other Israeli-occupied territories—the West Bank and Gaza—and the plight of Palestinian refugees remained unresolved, the first meaningful steps toward peace in the Middle East had been taken.

The Cold War Intensifies

Elsewhere, Carter was unable to duplicate his success with the Panama treaties and the Egypt-Israel accord. Preferring to pursue national security through nonmilitary means, Carter initially sought accommodation with the Soviet Union. But in 1979, he abandoned efforts to obtain Senate ratification of a new strategic arms limitation treaty and began development of intermediate-range missiles to be deployed in Western Europe and an enormous new missile system for the United States.

Carter's decision for the military buildup, which conservatives like Phyllis Schlafly had been pushing for years, came in 1979 when the Soviet Union invaded its neighbor Afghanistan, whose recently installed Communist government was threatened by Muslim opposition (see Map 30.2). Insisting that the Soviet aggression "could pose the greatest threat to peace since the Second World War," Carter also imposed economic sanctions on the Soviet Union, barred U.S. participation in the 1980 Olympic Games in Moscow, and obtained legislation requiring all nineteen-year-old men to register for the **draft**.

The president claimed that Soviet actions jeopardized oil supplies from the Middle East and announced his own "Carter Doctrine," threatening the use of any means necessary to prevent an outside force from gaining control of the Persian Gulf. His human rights policy fell by the wayside as the United States stepped up aid to Afghanistan's neighbor, Pakistan, then under a military dictatorship. Finally, Carter called for hefty increases in defense spending over the next five years.

Events in Iran encouraged this reversion to a hard-line, militaristic approach. All the U.S. arms and aid had not enabled the shah to quash Iranian dissidents who still resented the CIA's role in the overthrow of the Mossadegh government in 1953 (see chapter 27), condemned the shah's savage attempts to silence opposition, and detested his adoption of Western culture and values. In 1979, a revolution forced the shah out of Iran and gave Ayatollah Ruholla Khomeini and other Shiite Islamic **fundamentalists** control of the government. These forces were intensely hostile to the United States, which they blamed for supporting the shah's brutalities and undermining the religious foundations of their country.

When Carter permitted the shah to enter the United States for medical treatment, anti-American demonstrations escalated in Teheran. On November 4, 1979, a crowd broke into the U.S. Embassy and seized more than 60 Americans, demanding that the shah be returned for trial. When Khomeini supported the captors, Carter froze Iranian assets in U.S. banks and placed an embargo on Iranian oil. He sent a small military operation into Iran in April 1980, but the rescue mission failed and the hostages remained prisoners until January 1981.

The aborted mission fed Americans' feelings of impotence, simmering since the nation's defeat in Vietnam. Those frustrations in turn produced support for a more militaristic foreign policy. Opposition to Soviet-American détente, combined with the Soviet invasion of

American Hostages in Iran
Iranian militants display one of the hostages they took when they occupied the U.S. Embassy in Teheran on November 4, 1979. Until the hostages were released in January 1981, Americans regularly watched TV images of the captives being paraded before angry Iranian crowds. Many Americans tied yellow ribbons around trees and car antennas or wore them to demonstrate their concern for the hostages and hopes for their safe return. Because the hostages served as humiliating symbols of the limitations of American power, a surge of celebration accompanied their release. "I am overjoyed. I feel proud again," said a New Hampshire police officer.
Ph. Ledru/Sygma; Collection of Janice L. and David J. Frent.

Afghanistan, nullified the thaw in relations that Nixon and Kissinger had begun. The American hostages in Iran filled the news during the 1980 presidential campaign and contributed to Carter's defeat. Iran released the hostages on the day he left office, but relations with the United States remained tense.

Ronald Reagan and the Conservative Ascendancy

Ronald Reagan's victory in 1980 marked the most important turning point in politics since Franklin D. Roosevelt won the presidency in 1932. Eisenhower and Nixon had campaigned as middle-of-the-road Republicans, but Reagan's success established conservatism's dominance in the Republican Party. Since the 1930s, the Democratic Party had defined the major issues; in the 1980s, the Republicans assumed that ini-

tiative, while the Democrats moved toward the right in their search for voter support. On the domestic front, the Reagan administration left its most important mark on the economy: victory over inflation, deregulation of industry, a moratorium on social spending, enormous tax cuts, and a staggering budget deficit. Economic expansion brought great wealth to some, but the percentage of Americans in poverty increased, and income distribution became more unequal.

Appealing to the New Right and Beyond

The oldest candidate ever nominated for the presidency, Ronald Reagan was born in Tampico, Illinois, in 1911. After attending Eureka, a small religious college, he worked as a sportscaster before becoming a movie actor and, later, president of the Screen Actors Guild. He initially shared the politics of his staunchly Democratic father but moved to the right in the 1940s and

1950s and campaigned for Goldwater in 1964. Reagan's political career took off when he was elected governor of California in 1966. Although he ran as a conservative, in office he displayed considerable flexibility, approving a major tax increase, a strong water pollution bill, and a liberal abortion law. Displaying similar agility in his 1980 presidential campaign, he softened earlier attacks on issues such as Social Security and chose the moderate Republican George H. Bush as his running mate.

Despite this move to the center, some Republicans balked at his nomination and at the party platform, which reflected the domination of the party's right wing. For example, Phyllis Schlafly persuaded the party to reverse its forty-year support for the Equal Rights Amendment, sparking moderate and liberal Republican women to march in protest outside the convention hall. (See "Historical Question," page 1118). Some of them, along with other anti-Reagan Republicans, found a more acceptable candidate in John B. Anderson, congressman from Illinois, who deserted his party to run as an independent.

The economic recession and the country's declining international stature—symbolized by the dozens of Americans held hostage in Iran—provided ample weapons for Reagan's campaign. Repeatedly Reagan reminded voters of the "misery index"—the combined rates of unemployment and inflation—asking, "Are you better off now than you were four years ago?" He promised to "take government off the backs of the people" and to restore Americans' morale and other nations' respect. A narrow majority of voters, 51 percent, responded to Reagan's upbeat message. Carter won 41 percent of the vote, and 7 percent went to Anderson. The Republicans picked up thirty-three new seats in the House and won control of the Senate for the first time since the 1950s.

While the economy and Iran sealed Reagan's victory, he also benefited from the burgeoning grassroots conservatism. An extraordinarily adept politician, Reagan appealed to a wide spectrum of groups and sentiments: free-market advocates, militant anti-Communists, fundamentalist Christians, southerners, and white working-class Democrats disenchanted with the Great Society and suffering from the high inflation and unemployment rates of the last years of the Carter administration.

A critical portion of Reagan's support came from religious conservatives, who constituted a relatively new phenomenon in politics, known

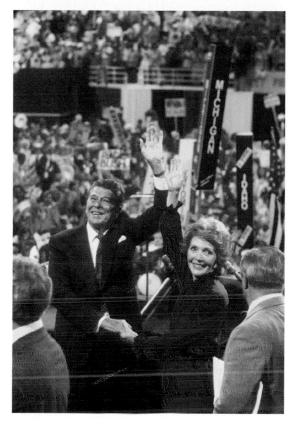

Ronald Reagan Nominated for President
Nancy and Ronald Reagan respond to cheers at the Republican National Convention where he was nominated for president in the summer of 1980. Reagan became one of the most popular presidents of the twentieth century, though his wife did not always share his high ratings from the American people.
Lester Sloan / Woodfin Camp & Associates.

as the New Right or New Christian Right. During the 1970s, **evangelical** and fundamentalist Christianity claimed thousands of new adherents and made adept use of sophisticated mass-mailing techniques and the "electronic ministry." Evangelical ministers such as Jim Bakker and Pat Robertson preached to huge television audiences, attacking feminism, abortion, homosexuality, and pornography and calling for restoration of old-fashioned "family values." They wanted prayer back in, and sex education out of, the schools. Robertson, for example, believed that "non-Christian people and atheistic people" were using the Constitution "to destroy the very

> Reagan reminded voters of the "misery index"—the combined rates of unemployment and inflation—asking, "Are you better off now than you were four years ago?"

Why Did the ERA Fail?

The proposed Equal Rights Amendment to the U.S. Constitution guaranteed briefly and simply that women and men would be treated equally under the law: "Equality of rights under the law shall not be denied or abridged by the United States or by any State on account of sex." Two more short sections provided that Congress would have enforcement powers and that the ERA would take effect two years after ratification. By the 1970s it had become the symbol of the late-twentieth-century women's movement.

Members of a small militant feminist organization, the National Woman's Party, first proposed an equal rights amendment to the Constitution in 1923, but it won little support either in Congress or among the public before the resurgence of feminism in the mid-1960s. In 1968, the National Organization for Women made it a key objective and, armed with support from traditional women's organizations and liberal groups, began to pressure Congress. The pressure took many forms, including civil disobedience. In early 1970, for example, NOW members disrupted a Senate subcommittee hearing on extending the vote to eighteen-year-olds, demanding that the Senate schedule hearings on the ERA. Initially fearing arrest, according to Wilma Scott Heide, who would become NOW president in 1971, the women soon learned that "we could do almost anything and get away with it . . . they didn't want to make martyrs out of us." Feminists and their allies lobbied Congress, and women in both political parties mobilized a letter-writing campaign, flooding some congressional offices with 1,500 letters a month.

Despite opposition in committee hearings, both houses of Congress passed the amendment by overwhelming margins, 354 to 23 in the House and 84 to 8 in the Senate. Within three hours of Senate passage in March 1972, Hawaii rushed to become the first state to ratify. By the end of 1972, 23 states had done so. Public opinion heavily favored ratification, peaking at 74 percent in favor in 1974 and never falling below 52 percent, while the opposition never surpassed 31 percent. Yet even after Congress extended the time period for ratification until 1982, the ERA failed. The Constitution requires approval of amendments by three-fourths of the states, and only 35 states ratified, three short of the minimum needed (see Map 30.3). Why did a measure with so much congressional and popular support fail?

The ERA encountered well-organized and passionate opposition linked to the growing conservative forces in the 1970s. Opponents ranged from religious organizations, such as the National Council of Catholic Women, to local groups such as HOTDOGS (Humanitarians Opposed to the Degradation of Our Girls), sponsored by the John Birch Society in Utah. Leading the resistance was Phyllis Schlafly.

Conservatives' opposition to the ERA reflected in part their traditional distaste for big government and their demand for a strong defense system to counter communism. Schlafly predicted that the amendment would transfer power from state legislatures and even from families to the federal government. Putting women in foxholes alongside men, she warned, would surely result from ratification of the ERA and that in turn would weaken the military and make the United States more vulnerable to communism. To a large extent, it was this linking of antifeminist goals with issues of long-standing concern to conservatives that made the New Right "new" as it developed a "pro-family" focus in the late 1970s.

The strategy of ERA opponents was to raise fears about the effects of the amendment. They could make extravagant arguments because its brevity and simplicity precluded anyone from saying with absolute certainty how courts would interpret it. Senator Samuel J. Ervin Jr., nationally known and highly respected for his chairing of the Watergate hearings, claimed that the ERA would eliminate laws against rape, require male and female prisoners to be housed together, and deprive women of alimony and child support. Others claimed that it would legalize homosexual marriage. Overall, the anti-ERA forces emphasized sex differences. By destroying the distinct sex roles on which the family was based, Erwin claimed, ERA would destroy the family and produce "increased rates of alcoholism, suicide, and possible sexual deviation."

Anti-ERA leaders were adept at framing arguments that spoke to many women's religious beliefs and their definitions of their own self-interest. In contrast to feminists who viewed traditional sex roles as constructed by society, anti-ERA men and women believed that they were God given. Evangelical minister and politician Jerry Falwell declared the ERA "a definite violation of holy Scripture [and its] mandate that 'the

Marching for Ratification of the ERA
About three thousand marchers parade down Pennsylvania Avenue in Washington, D.C., on August 26, 1977. On the fifty-seventh anniversary of ratification of the Nineteenth Amendment, which extended the right to vote to women, these advocates expressed their demand for ratification of the Equal Rights Amendment, carrying its words on their banner.
© Bettye Lane © Photo Researchers.

Phyllis Schlafly
The most prominent antifeminist, Phyllis Schlafly, is shown in her home in Alton, Illinois, in 1987. Despite time-consuming and energetic political activities that involved traveling and speaking all over the country, she insisted on calling herself a housewife. She poses with a pillow that signals her domesticity and political aim.
© Bettmann/Corbis.

husband is the head of the wife.'" Many ERA opponents were full-time housewives who had no stake in equal treatment in the marketplace and who feared that the amendment would eliminate the duty of men to support their families. They had entered traditional marriages where, in exchange for raising children and caring for home and husbands, they expected economic support. Schlafly stressed the unfairness of changing the rules in the middle of the game, noting that "ERA does not even include a 'grandmother' clause." Women in both camps recognized the precariousness of economic security; but while feminists wanted to render women self-sustaining, antifeminists wanted men to bear responsibility for their support.

Phyllis Schlafly and other conservative leaders skillfully mobilized women who saw their traditional roles threatened. In October 1972, she established a national movement, STOP (Stop Taking Our Privileges) ERA, so carefully organized that it could respond immediately when action was necessary. Thus when a state legislature began to consider ratification, STOP ERA women deluged legislators with letters and lobbied them personally in state capitals. In Illinois, for example, they gave lawmakers apple pies with notes attached that read: "My heart and my hand went into this dough / For the sake of the family please vote 'no.'" Opponents also brought baby girls to the legislature wearing signs that pleaded, "Please don't draft me." Another opposition group, Happiness of Womanhood (HOW), presented California legislators with mice bearing the message, "Do you want to be a man or a mouse?" And housewives in North Carolina took home-baked bread to members of the state legislature with notes reading, "To the breadwinners from the breadbakers."

ERA opponents had an easier task than supporters, for all they had to do was to convince a minority of legislators in a minority of states to preserve the status quo. The framers of the Constitution had stacked the odds against revision. Supporters, by contrast, had to persuade a majority of lawmakers in three-quarters of the states that the need to guarantee

(continued)

1119

women equal rights was urgent and that it could not be accomplished without a constitutional amendment. In addition, in contrast to the suffrage movement, which for decades gradually built up support through local and state campaigns, the ERA forces concentrated on winning Congress and did so in less than ten years. Amendment supporters were not prepared for the state campaigns, and the intensity of the opposition took them by surprise. By the time ERA proponents got organized on the state level, the momentum for ratification had already stalled.

Feminists still had to overcome the tendency of men to trivialize women's issues or to take them less seriously than other concerns. For example, when the House initially passed the ERA in 1970, the *New York Times* printed an editorial criticizing it under the title "The Henpecked House." The conservative syndicated columnist James J. Kilpatrick said that the ERA was "the contrivance of a gang of professional harpies" and that congressmen had voted for it simply to "get these furies off their backs." The very gains feminists made in the 1960s and 1970s also worked against approval of the ERA. Congress had already banned sex discrimination in employment, education, credit, and other areas; and the Supreme Court used the equal protection clause of the Fourteenth Amendment to strike down several state and federal laws that treated men and women differently. Even though the Court did not ban all distinctions based on sex, its decisions made it harder for ERA advocates to demonstrate the urgency of constitutional revision.

So why did the ERA fail? It failed because a handful of men in a handful of state legislatures voted against it. The shift of only a few votes in states such as Illinois and North Carolina would have meant ratification. Phyllis Schlafly's forces played a key role in the defeat, because men could vote "no" and take cover behind the many women who opposed it. And those women proved willing to commit time, energy, and money to block ratification because conservative leaders convinced them that the ERA threatened their very way of life.

Feminists did not leave the ERA battle empty-handed, however. The National Organization for Women grew enormously during the struggle for ratification. Thousands of women were mobilized across the political spectrum and participated in the political arena for the first time. Fourteen states passed their own equal rights amendments after 1970. And feminists continued to struggle in the legislative and judicial arenas for the expansion of women's rights, struggles that continue to bear fruit in the twenty-first century.

foundation of our society." Although the Christian Right was predominately Protestant, some Catholics, like Phyllis Schlafly, shared the fundamentalists' goal of a return to their version of "Christian values."

Conservatives created a raft of political organizations, such as the Moral Majority, founded by minister Jerry Falwell in 1979 with the goals of fighting "left-wing, social-welfare bills . . . pornography, homosexuality, the advocacy of immorality in school textbooks," and pushing for a "Family Protection Agency." The Christian Coalition, which Pat Robertson formed in 1989, claimed 1.6 million members and control of the Republican Party in more than a dozen states within a few years. The instruments of more traditional conservatives— those who advocated limited government at home and militant anticommunism abroad— likewise flourished. These included publications such as the *National Review*, edited by William F. Buckley Jr., and think tanks such as the

American Enterprise Institute and the Heritage Foundation, which supported experts who developed new policy approaches. The monthly *Phyllis Schlafly Report* (see photo on page 1104) continued to merge the sentiments of the old and new right, which were also manifest in its publisher's organization, Eagle Forum.

Reagan embraced the full spectrum of conservatism, ignoring certain inconsistencies. For example, the New Right's demand for the government to intervene in private matters by outlawing abortion and homosexuality conflicted with the traditional conservative attachment to **laissez-faire**. Reagan avowed agreement on abortion, school prayer, and other New Right issues, yet he was careful not to alienate the more traditional conservatives by pushing hard on so-called moral or social issues. Rather, his major achievements lay in areas most important to the older right—strengthening the nation's anti-Communist posture and reducing taxes and government restraints on free enterprise. "In the present crisis," Reagan argued, "government is not the solution to our problem, government is the problem."

Reagan's admirers, however, stretched far beyond conservatives. The extraordinarily popular president was liked even by Americans who opposed his policies and even when he made glaring mistakes. At one meeting, he failed to recognize his own secretary of housing and urban development, calling him "Mr. Mayor." On another occasion, he proclaimed that vegetation caused 90 percent of all air pollution. He made so many misstatements that aides tried to keep him away from reporters, and they carefully scripted the former actor's public appearances.

Democratic representative Patricia Schroeder tagged Reagan the "Teflon President" because none of his administration's mistakes, even his own errors and falsehoods, seemed to stick to him. His confidence and easygoing humor were a large part of his appeal. Ignoring darker aspects of the nation's past, he presented a version of history that Americans could feel good about. Listeners understood Reagan's declaration that it was "morning in America" as a promise that the best was yet to come for the nation. He also gained public sympathy after being shot by a would-be assassin in March 1981. Just before surgery for removal of the bullet, Reagan joked to physicians, "I hope you're Republicans." So great was Reagan's appeal that his popularity withstood serious charges of executive branch misconduct in foreign policy in his second term.

Unleashing Free Enterprise

Reagan's first domestic objective was a massive tax cut. Although tax reduction, especially in the face of a large budget deficit, contradicted traditional Republican economic doctrine, Reagan relied on a new theory called **supply-side economics**, which held that cutting taxes would actually increase revenue. Supply-siders insisted that lower taxes would enable businesses to expand, that individuals would work harder because they could keep more of their earnings, and that tax reduction would increase the production of goods and services—the supply—which in turn would boost demand. To allay worries about the budget deficit, Reagan promised to cut federal expenditures, a position fully compatible with his antigovernment views.

In the summer of 1981, Congress passed the Economic Recovery Tax Act, resulting in the largest tax reduction in U.S. history. The legislation cut the tax rate of individuals with the low-est incomes from 14 to 11 percent and lowered the rate of individuals with the highest incomes from 70 to 50 percent. Corporations also received tax breaks, and taxes on capital gains, gifts, and inheritances fell. A second measure, the Tax Reform Act of 1986, reduced tax rates even more, lowering the maximum rate on individual income to 28 percent and on business income to 35 percent. The entire tax structure became more regressive—that is, affluent Americans saved far more on their tax bills than did average taxpayers, and the distribution of wealth was further skewed in favor of the rich.

"Hack, chop, crunch!" were *Time* magazine's words for the administration's efforts to free private enterprise from government restraints. Carter had confined deregulation to particular industries, such as air transportation and banking, while increasing regulation in health, safety, and environmental protection. The Reagan administration, by contrast, pursued across-the-board deregulation. It declined to enforce the Sherman Antitrust Act—the 1890 law designed to reduce **monopoly** and promote competition (see chapter 17)—against an unprecedented number of business mergers and takeovers. Reagan also loosened restraints on business imposed by employee health and safety measures, and he weakened organized labor. When thirteen thousand members of the Professional Air Traffic Controllers Organization (PATCO) struck in 1981, Reagan fired them, destroying their union. Blaming environmental laws for the nation's sluggish economic growth, Reagan targeted them too for deregulation, but popular support for environmental protection blocked the complete realization of Reagan's goals.

Deregulation of the banking industry, begun under Carter and supported by Democrats and Republicans alike, created a crisis in the savings and loan industry. Some of the newly deregulated savings and loan institutions (S&Ls) extended enormous loans to real estate developers and invested in other high-yield but risky ventures. S&L owners reaped lavish profits, and their depositors enjoyed high interest rates. But then real estate values began to plunge, and hundreds of S&Ls went bankrupt. After Congress voted to bail out the S&L industry in 1989, the burden of the largest financial scandal in U.S. history fell on American taxpayers.

> Deregulation of the banking industry, begun under Carter and supported by Democrats and Republicans alike, created a crisis in the savings and loan industry.

The S&L crisis deepened the **federal deficit**, which soared during the 1980s despite Reagan's pledge to pare federal spending. When the administration cut funds for food stamps, job training, aid to low-income students, health services, and other welfare programs, hundreds of thousands of people lost benefits, and those with incomes just around the poverty line were hardest hit. Increases in defense spending, however, far exceeded the budget cuts, and the deficit continued to climb: from $74 billion when Carter left office in 1981 to a high of $220 billion in 1986. Under Reagan, the nation's debt grew from $834 billion to $2.3 trillion, and interest on the debt consumed one-seventh of all federal expenditures.

It took the severest recession since the 1930s to squeeze inflation out of the U.S. economy. Beginning in 1981, unemployment rose sharply, approaching 11 percent late in 1982. Record numbers of banks and businesses closed, and 12 million workers could not find jobs. The threat of unemployment further undermined organized labor, forcing unions to make concessions that management insisted were necessary for industry's survival. The economy recovered in 1983 and entered an unprecedented period of growth, yet unemployment never fell below 5 percent during the decade.

The economic upswing and Reagan's own popularity posed a formidable challenge for the Democrats in the 1984 election. Walter F. Mondale, vice president under Carter, won the Democratic nomination. Although he electrified the Democratic National Convention by choosing as his running mate New York representative Geraldine A. Ferraro, the first woman on a major party ticket, it failed to save the Democrats from a humiliating defeat. Reagan charged his opponents with concentrating on America's failures, while he emphasized success and possibility. Democrats, he claimed, "see an America where every day is April 15th [the due date for income tax returns] . . . we see an America where every day is the Fourth of July."

Voters responded to the president's sunny vision and to the economic comeback, giving him a landslide 59 percent of the vote. Winning only the state of Minnesota, the Democrats pondered how to stem the exodus of longtime loyalists—particularly southern white males—to the Republican Party. Stung by Republican charges that the Democratic Party was captive to "special interests" such as labor, women, and minorities, some Democratic leaders urged that the party shift more toward the right.

Winners and Losers in a Flourishing Economy

After the recession of 1981–82, the economy took off, bringing great fortunes to some as popular culture celebrated making money and displaying wealth. Books by business wizards topped bestseller lists, the press described lavish parties costing millions of dollars, and popular magazines featured articles such as "They're like Us, except They're Rich." College students told poll takers that their primary ambition was to make money.

Participating conspicuously in the affluence of the 1980s were members of the baby boom generation known popularly as "yuppies," short for "young urban professionals." These mostly white, well-educated young men and women tended to live in urban condominiums and to pursue fast-track careers; in their leisure time, they consumed lavishly—fancy cars, gourmet food, expensive vacations, and electronic gadgets. Though definitely a minority, they established consumption standards that many tried to emulate.

Many of the newly wealthy achieved success from moving assets around rather than from producing goods. Notable exceptions included Steven Jobs, who invented the Apple computer in his garage, and Liz Claiborne, who in thirteen years turned a $250,000 investment into a billion-dollar fashion enterprise. But many others got rich—or richer—by manipulating debt and restructuring corporations through mergers and takeovers. "To say these guys are entrepreneurs is like saying Jesse James was an entrepreneur," opined Texas businessman Ross Perot, who defined entrepreneurship as making things, not money. Most financial wizards operated within the law, but occasionally greed led to criminal convictions. Michael Milken pioneered in issuing junk bonds, so called because they offered high risk and high yield. He took home well over $50 million a year, but he and others landed in jail for using insider information to maximize their financial manipulations.

Other problems remained, even in an abundant economy. The steel, automobile, and electronics industries were surpassed by those of Germany and Japan; Americans bought more Volkswagens and Hondas and fewer Fords and

Chevrolets. With Americans purchasing more foreign-made goods than domestic producers were able to sell abroad, the nation's trade deficit (the difference between imports and exports) soared to $126 billion by 1988.

International competition forced the collapse of some older companies, while others moved factories and jobs abroad to be closer to foreign markets or to benefit from the low wage standards of such countries as Mexico and Korea. Service industries expanded during this process of **de-industrialization** and created new jobs at home, but former blue-collar workers forced to take those jobs found their wages substantially lower. When David Ramos was laid off in 1982 from his $12.75-an-hour job in a steel plant, his wages fell to $5 an hour as a security guard, forcing his family to rely on food stamps. Overall, the number of full-time workers earning wages below the poverty level ($12,195 for a family of four in 1990) rose sharply from 12 to 18 percent of all workers in the 1980s.

The weakening of organized labor combined with the decline in manufacturing to erode the position of blue-collar workers like David Ramos and Chicago steelworker Ike Mazo. "They're telling you you're not a good citizen if you're not willing to accept less," Mazo fumed, contemplating the $6-an-hour jobs available to him. "It's an attack on the living standards of workers." Increasingly, a second income was needed to stave off economic decline. By 1990, nearly 60 percent of married women with young children worked outside the home. Yet even with two incomes, fewer young families could purchase their first home or provide a good life for their children. "I worry about their future every day," Mazo's wife confessed. "Will we be able to put them through college? . . . Will they be out in the workforce working for four dollars an hour?" The average $10,000 disparity between male and female annual earnings made things even harder for the nearly 20 percent of female-headed families. One mother of two, divorced from an abusive husband, supplemented her paycheck by selling her blood and accepting help from her church. Mark Burke, who had worked at a rubber plant in Barberton, Ohio, lost his job in 1980 when the plant closed. Among the 80 percent of workers displaced from the rubber industry and unable to find jobs that paid as well, he lamented, "There's a big difference between what I could be and what I am."

In keeping with conservative philosophy, Reagan avoided substantial government efforts

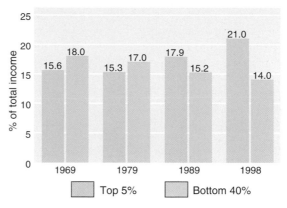

FIGURE 30.1 The Growth of Inequality: Changes in Family Income, 1969–1998
For three decades after World War II, income increased for all groups on the economic ladder. After 1979, the income of the poorest families declined, while the income of the richest 20 percent of the population grew substantially.

to reverse this growing income inequality (which his tax policies encouraged), insisting that a booming economy would benefit everyone. Average personal income did rise during his tenure, but the trend toward greater economic inequality that had begun in the 1970s intensified in the 1980s, in part because of the new tax policies. The rich got richer, a portion of the middle class did well, and the poor got poorer. Personal income shot up sharply for the wealthiest 20 percent of Americans while it fell for the poorest by 9.8 percent between 1979 and 1987. No longer could all Americans expect, as they had in the two decades following World War II, that their children would do better than they had done (Figure 30.1).

Poverty statistics, too, revealed a reversal of the trend toward greater equality. Between 1980 and 1988, poor people increased from 11.7 to 13.5 percent of total U.S. population—the highest poverty rate in the industrialized world. A relatively low poverty rate among the elderly testified to the lasting success of Social Security and Medicare. Less fortunate were large segments of other groups that the economic boom had bypassed: racial minorities, female-headed families, and children. One child in every five lived in poverty.

Even before the 1990 recession, affluent urbanites walked past numerous men and women sleeping in subway stations, on grates over steam vents, and on park benches. Experts debated the total number of homeless Americans—

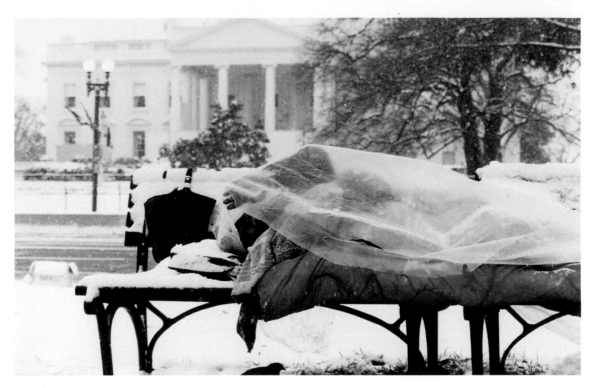

Homelessness

The increased presence of homeless people in cities across the nation challenged the view of the 1980s as a decade of prosperity. Hundreds of homeless people could be found on the sidewalks of the nation's capital every night. In November 1987, during the first snowfall of the season, a homeless man sleeps in Lafayette Square across from the White House. What might the location of this homeless man suggest to viewers of the photograph?

© Bettmann / Corbis.

estimates ranged from 350,000 upward—but no one doubted that homelessness had increased. Women and children constituted the fastest-growing population without shelter. Those without homes included the victims of long-term unemployment, erosion of welfare benefits, and slum clearance as well as individuals suffering from mental illness, drug abuse, and alcoholism.

Continuing Struggles over Rights and the Environment

The dominance of conservatism and the laissez-faire inclination of the Reagan administration threw social movements on the defensive. As the Reagan administration, often supported by the increasingly conservative federal courts, moved away from the national commitment to equal opportunity undertaken in the 1960s, feminists and minority groups fought to defend protections they had won in the 1960s and 1970s. They

achieved some limited gains. A newer movement advocating rights for gay men and lesbians gained visibility and helped to edge attitudes toward greater tolerance for homosexuality. Environmentalists, too, clashed with the Reagan administration, as they sought to maintain regulations enacted in the 1970s and as the world faced new threats to human life and health.

The Conservative Shift in the Federal Courts

Since the 1950s, liberals had grown accustomed to counting on the federal judiciary as a powerful ally in their struggles for civil rights and social justice. But in the 1980s, they saw their allies slipping away as more and more conservative justices populated the Supreme Court and lower federal courts. Given the opportunity to appoint half of the 761 federal court judges and three new Supreme Court justices, President Reagan carefully selected candidates who had strongly conservative views. With these appointments, the tide began to turn in favor of strict construction—the literal application of the original aims of the Constitution's authors that limits judicial power to protect individual rights.

The Supreme Court did not execute an abrupt about-face: It upheld important affirmative action and antidiscrimination policies and ruled that sexual harassment in the workplace constituted sex discrimination. And, in one key case, Congress stepped in to defend antidiscrimination policy. In 1984, the Justice Department persuaded the Supreme Court to severely weaken Title IX of the Education Amendments Act of 1972, a crucial law promoting equal opportunity in education. *Grove City v. Bell* (1984) allowed the Justice Department to abandon dozens of civil rights cases against schools and colleges, but it also galvanized a coalition of civil rights organizations and groups representing women, the aged and disabled, and their allies. In 1988, Congress passed the Civil Rights Restoration Act, which reversed the administration's victory in *Grove City* and—going further—banned any organization that practiced discrimination on the basis of race, color, national origin, sex, disability, or age from receiving government funds.

Nonetheless, Reagan's Supreme Court appointees tipped the balance to the right. Sandra Day O'Connor was a moderate conservative, but the appointments of Antonin Scalia and Anthony M. Kennedy gave strict constructionists a slim majority. The full impact of these appointments continued after Reagan left office. The Court allowed states to impose restrictions that limited access to abortion for poor and uneducated women and those living in rural areas. Other rulings weakened protections against employment discrimination and whittled away at legal safeguards against the death penalty.

Feminism on the Defensive

One of the signal achievements of the New Right was capturing the Republican Party's position on women's rights. For the first time in its history, the Republican Party took an explicitly antifeminist tone, opposing both the Equal Rights Amendment and a woman's right to abortion, key goals of women's rights activists. When the time limit for ratification of the ERA ran out in 1982 (Map 30.3), Phyllis Schlafly could claim victory on the issue that first galvanized her antifeminist campaign. (See chapter 28 and "Historical Question," page 1118.)

Cast on the defensive, feminists began to focus more on women's economic and family problems; and they found some common ground with the Reagan administration in two measures that addressed women's economic distress. The Child Support Enforcement Amendments Act helped single and divorced mothers to collect court-ordered child support payments from absent parents. The Retirement Equity Act of 1984 benefited divorced and older women by strengthening their claims to their husbands' pensions and enabling women to qualify more easily for private retirement pensions.

The Reagan administration had its own concerns about women, specifically about the **gender gap**—women's tendency to vote for liberal and Democratic candidates in larger numbers

> With Reagan's judicial appointees, the tide began to turn in favor of strict construction—the literal application of the original aims of the Constitution's authors that limits judicial power to protect individual rights.

Confrontations over Abortion
Failing to win a constitutional amendment banning abortion, in the late 1970s and 1980s some groups in the right-to-life movement adopted more militant tactics, picketing abortion clinics, yelling at patients and employees, and trying to block entrance into clinics. The pro-choice activists shown here defend clinic access and the right to abortion.
Paul S. Howell / Gamma Liaison.

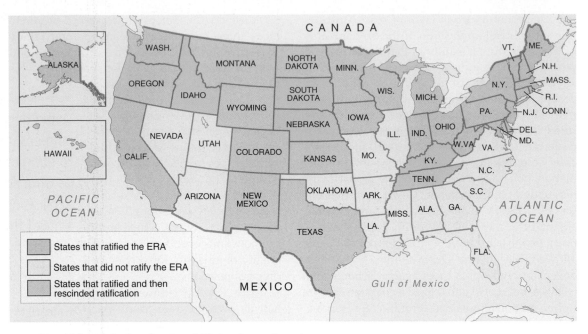

MAP 30.3   The Fight for the Equal Rights Amendment

Many states that failed to ratify the Equal Rights Amendment had previously refused to ratify the woman suffrage amendment (or ratified it decades later, as did North Carolina in 1971).

READING THE MAP: How many states ratified the amendment, and how many did not? Did any regions overwhelmingly support or oppose the ERA?

CONNECTIONS: What was the goal of the ERA? Who were its opponents, and what were their main points of opposition?

FOR MORE HELP ANALYZING THIS MAP, see the map activity for this chapter in the Online Study Guide at bedfordstmartins.com/roark.

than men did. (Party leaders welcomed the opposite element of that trend: white men's movement into Republican ranks.) Reagan appointed three women to cabinet posts and, in 1981, selected the first woman, Sandra Day O'Connor, for the Supreme Court. But these actions accompanied a general decline in the number of women and minorities in high-level positions. And with higher poverty rates than men, women suffered most from Reagan's budget cuts in social programs.

Although court decisions placed restrictions on women's ability to obtain abortions, feminists successfully fought to retain the basic principles of *Roe v. Wade*. The women's movement, however, hit a stone wall in efforts to improve day care services and promote pay equity—equal pay for traditionally female jobs that were comparable in worth to jobs performed primarily by men. Like other pressure groups, the women's movement pursued locally what it failed to achieve at the federal level. The pay equity movement took hold in several states, and many states strengthened their laws against rape.

States also increased funding for domestic violence programs and stepped up efforts to protect victims and prosecute abusers.

The Gay and Lesbian Rights Movement

Influenced by minority struggles, the New Left, the counterculture, and feminism, gay men and lesbians began to claim equal rights and to express pride in their sexual identities. Although an organization for homosexual rights had existed as early as 1924, and small groups like the Mattachine Society and the Daughters of Bilitis mobilized in the 1950s, not until the 1980s did a national mass movement emerge. It grew out of the social upheaval of the 1960s and was sparked by the Stonewall riot of 1969, when gay men and lesbians fought back against a police raid on the Stonewall Inn, a gay bar in New York City's Greenwich Village. Linking their cause with that of other minorities, they asserted, "A common struggle will bring common triumph."

Lesbians and gay men began to organize across the nation in the 1970s, demonstrating and lobbying for an end to discrimination and affirmation of their own decisions about whom to love. One result of their efforts came in 1973 when the American Psychiatric Association ended its categorization of homosexuality as a mental disease. Although the Supreme Court upheld the right of states to enforce laws against sodomy until 2003, most states had taken such laws off the books by the 1980s.

The acquired immune deficiency syndrome (AIDS) epidemic, which researchers identified in 1981, further mobilized the gay and lesbian rights movement in the 1980s, because initially male homosexuals were disproportionately afflicted. As the disease swept through communities of gay men in New York, San Francisco, and elsewhere, gay men and lesbians organized to promote public funding for AIDS education, prevention, and treatment.

The gay and lesbian rights movement helped thousands of closeted homosexuals experience the relief of "coming out." Their visibility helped to increase awareness (if not always acceptance) of homosexuality among the larger population. Activists organized gay rights and gay pride marches throughout the country and began to win local victories, gaining some protections against discrimination. (See "Documenting the American Promise," page 1128.) Beginning with the election of Elaine Noble to the Massachusetts legislature in 1974, several openly gay politicians won offices from mayor to member of Congress; and the Democrats began to include gay rights in their party platforms.

Popular attitudes about homosexuality moved toward greater tolerance but remained complex. For example, by the end of the century 84 percent of respondents to public opinion polls supported equal job opportunities for gays and lesbians, but 59 percent thought homosexuality was morally wrong. These diverse attitudes were reflected in uneven changes in policies. In some states and cities, lesbians and gay men won protections that were enjoyed by heterosexual citizens. Dozens of cities banned job discrimination against homosexuals, and beginning with Wisconsin in 1982, eleven states made sexual orientation a protected category under civil rights laws. Nearly one hundred cities and many large corporations began to offer health insurance and other benefits to domestic partners. After the Vermont Supreme Court ruled that gay couples were unconstitutionally discriminated against in 1999, the Vermont legislature created for same-sex couples a category called "civil unions," which entitled them to rights available to married couples in areas such as inheritance, taxes, and medical decisions.

Even as popular TV shows and movies increasingly featured gay men and lesbians, most

> Influenced by minority struggles, the New Left, the counterculture, and feminism, gay men and lesbians began to claim equal rights and to express pride in their sexual identities.

Gay Pride Parades

In June 1970, gays and lesbians marched in New York City to commemorate the first anniversary of the Stonewall riot. Since then, gay pride parades have taken place throughout the United States and in other countries every year in June. A history professor, Robert Dawidoff, pointed out that the parades were not about "flaunting private things in public," as some people charged, but a way for gay men and lesbians to express "pride in our history . . . in having survived the thousand petty harassments and reminders of a special status we neither seek nor merit." Increasingly, friends, supporters, and families of homosexuals participate in the parades, as these family members do in a Los Angeles parade.
© Bettmann / Corbis.

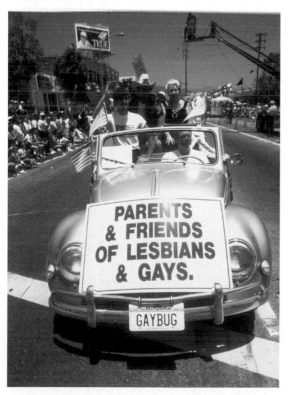

PARENTS & FRIENDS OF LESBIANS & GAYS.

GAYBUG

Antidiscrimination Laws for Gays and Lesbians, 2000

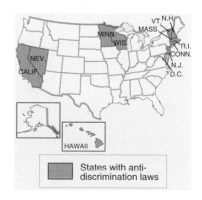

States with anti-discrimination laws

Protecting Gay and Lesbian Rights

Since the 1970s, the gay and lesbian rights movement has worked for passage of laws and ordinances to protect homosexuals from discrimination. In 1982, Wisconsin became the first state to ban discrimination on the basis of sexual orientation, following the lead of several cities throughout the United States that passed gay rights ordinances in the 1970s. By the mid-1990s, nine states and more than eighty cities had such legislation on the books. These measures ignited controversy that surrounded the issue into the twenty-first century.

eral welfare; such discriminatory practices threaten the rights, privileges, and opportunities of all inhabitants of the city and such rights, privileges, and opportunities are hereby to be declared civil rights, and the adoption of this Chapter is deemed to be an exercise of the policy power of the City to protect such rights.

SOURCE: Norman Dorsen and Aryeh Neier, eds., *The Rights of Gay People: The Basic ACLU Guide to a Gay Person's Rights* (New York: Dutton, 1992), 251.

justice and love, which is the message of the word of God.

As a New Yorker I find it incredible that this great city, populated by more gay persons than any other city in the world, still denies them basic human rights. They make an enormous contribution to the commercial, artistic, and religious life of our city.

SOURCE: Paul Moore, letter to the editor, *New York Times*, December 8, 1981.

DOCUMENT 1
Ordinance of the City of Minneapolis, 1974

In 1974, the city council of Minneapolis amended its civil rights ordinance to cover discrimination based on sexual preference. The law provided a rationale for banning discrimination and, unlike some laws focusing exclusively on employment, encompassed a broad range of activities.

It is determined that discriminatory practices based on race, color, creed, religion, national origin, sex, or affectional or sexual preference, with respect to employment, labor union membership, housing accommodations, property rights, education, public accommodations, and public services, or any of them, tend to create and intensify conditions of poverty, ill health, unrest, civil disobedience, lawlessness, and vice and adversely affect the public health, safety, order, convenience, and gen-

DOCUMENT 2
Letter to the Editor of the *New York Times* from Paul Moore, November 23, 1981

Paul Moore, Episcopal bishop of New York, made a religious argument for gay rights in his letter to the editor of the New York Times.

I quote our diocesan resolution: "Whereas this Convention, without making any judgment on the morality of homosexuality, agrees that homosexuals are entitled to full civil rights. Now therefore be it resolved this Convention supports laws guaranteeing homosexuals all civil rights guaranteed to other citizens."

The Bible stands for justice and compassion for all of God's children. To deny civil rights to anyone for something he or she cannot help is against the clear commandment of

DOCUMENT 3
Vatican Congregation for the Doctrine of the Faith, August 6, 1992

The following statement from the Roman Catholic Church reflects the views of many religious groups that take positions against gay rights.

"Sexual orientation" does not constitute a quality comparable to race, ethnic background, etc., in respect to nondiscrimination. Unlike these, homosexual orientation is an objective disorder and evokes moral concern.

There are areas in which it is not unjust discrimination to take sexual orientation into account, for example, in the placement of children for adoption or foster care, in employment of teachers or athletic coaches, and in military recruitment.

SOURCE: Vatican Congregation for the Doctrine of the Faith, *Origins*, August 6, 1992.

DOCUMENT 4
Testimony of Charles Cochrane Jr. before the House Subcommittee on Employment Opportunities of the Committee on Education and Labor, January 27, 1982

Although the U.S. Congress has never enacted legislation banning discrimination on the basis of sexual orientation, it has considered a number of bills for that purpose. Charles Cochrane Jr., an army veteran and police sergeant, testified on behalf of such a bill in 1982.

I am very proud of being a New York City policeman. And I am equally proud of being gay. I have always been gay.

I have been out of the closet for 4 years. November 6 was my anniversary. It took me 34 years to muster enough courage to declare myself openly.

We gays are loathed by some, pitied by others, and misunderstood by most. We are not cruel, wicked, cursed, sick, or possessed by demons. We are artists, business people, police officers, and clergymen. We are scientists, truck drivers, politicians; we work in every field. We are loving human beings who are in some ways different. . . .

During the early years of my association with the New York City Police Department a great deal of energy did go into guarding and concealing my innermost feelings. I believed that I would be subjected to ridicule and harassment were my colleagues to learn of my sexual orientation. Happily, when I actually began to integrate the various aspects of my total self, those who knew me did not reject me.

Then what need is there for such legislation as H.R. 1454? The crying need of others, still trapped in their closets, who must be protected, who must be reassured that honesty about themselves and their lives will not cost them their homes or their jobs. . . .

The bill before you will not act as a proselytizing agent in matters of sexual orientation or preference. It will not include affirmative action provisions. Passage of this bill will protect the inherent human rights of all people of the United States, while in no way diminishing the rights of those who do not see the need for such legislation. Finally, it will signify, quite clearly, recognition and compassion for a group which is often maligned without justification.

SOURCE: U.S. House Subcommittee on Employment Opportunities of the Committee on Education and Labor, *Hearing on H.R. 1454*, 97th Cong., 2nd sess., 1982, 54–56.

DOCUMENT 5
Carl F. Horowitz, "Homosexuality's Legal Revolution," May 1991

Carl Horowitz, a policy analyst at a conservative think tank, the Heritage Foundation, expresses arguments of those opposed to government protection of homosexual rights.

Homosexual activists have all but completed their campaign to persuade the nation's educational establishment that homosexuality is normal "alternative" behavior, and thus any adverse reaction to it is akin to a phobia, such as fear of heights, or an ethnic prejudice, such as anti-Semitism.

The movement now stands on the verge of fully realizing its use of law to . . . intimidate heterosexuals uncomfortable about coming into contact with it. . . .

The movement seeks to win sinecures through the state, and over any objections by "homophobic" opposition. With a cloud of a heavy fine or even a jail sentence hanging over a mortgage lender, a rental agent, or a job interviewer who might be discomforted by them, homosexuals under these laws can win employment, credit, housing, and other economic entitlements. Heterosexuals would have no right to discriminate against homosexuals, but apparently, not vice versa. . . .

These laws will create market bottlenecks. Heterosexuals and even "closeted" homosexuals will be at a competitive disadvantage for jobs and housing. . . .

The new legalism will increase heterosexual anger—and even violence—toward homosexuals.

SOURCE: Carl F. Horowitz, "Homosexuality's Legal Revolution," *Freeman*, May 1991.

QUESTIONS FOR ANALYSIS AND DEBATE

1. According to these documents, how would heterosexuals be affected by laws protecting gay and lesbian rights?

2. Which of these documents suggest that the civil rights movement influenced the authors' views on homosexual rights?

3. What do you think is the strongest argument for government protection of homosexual rights? What do you think is the strongest argument against government protection?

remained vulnerable to intolerance and some-times violence. The Christian Right targeted gays and lesbians as symbols of national im-morality and succeeded in overturning some ho-mosexual rights measures, which in any case lagged far behind the civil rights guarantees that racial minorities and women had achieved.

Conflicts over Environmental Protections

While feminists and the gay and lesbian rights movement battled the "family values" wing of conservatism, environmentalists struggled against conservatives hostile to federal regulations on free enterprise. In the late 1970s, environmen-talists won new protections, aided by crises and disasters that brought national attention to the costs of unregulated economic develop-ment. Residents at Love Canal in Niagara Falls, New York, for exam-ple, discovered that their houses and school sat atop highly toxic waste products from a nearby chemical company and fought to get officials to recognize the dan-ger. The state finally agreed to help the families relocate in 1978. Lois Gibbs, a Love Canal resident who eventually headed a national move-ment against toxic wastes, ex-plained how she and many other women became environmentalists: "I never thought of myself as an activist or an organizer. I was a housewife, a mother, but all of a sudden it was my family, my children, and my neighbors."

Warning of radiation leakage, potential acci-dents, and the hazards of nuclear wastes, envi-ronmentalists also targeted nuclear power plants, which by 1977 produced about 11 percent of the country's electricity. French and German citizens demonstrated against nuclear plants in 1971, and Americans followed suit. In 1976, hun-dreds of members of the Clamshell Alliance went to jail for attempting to block construction of a nuclear plant in Seabrook, New Hampshire. Groups such as Abalone Alliance in California, Citizen Alert in Nevada, and SHAD (Sound and Hudson Against Atomic Development) on Long Island, New York, sprung up across the United States to demand an environment safe from nu-clear radiation and waste.

The perils of nuclear energy came into dra-matic focus in March 1979, when an accident occurred at the Three Mile Island nuclear facility near Harrisburg, Pennsylvania, and technicians worked for days to prevent a meltdown of the reactor core. Popular opposition and the great expense of building nuclear power plants stalled further development of the industry; but antinu-clear activism endured as part of the environ-mental movement, especially after the explosion of a nuclear reactor and the spread of deadly ra-diation in Chernobyl, Ukraine, in 1986.

The Carter administration responded to the Love Canal disaster by sponsoring legislation in 1980 to create the so-called Superfund, $1.6 bil-lion for cleanup of hazardous wastes left by the

> While feminists and the gay and lesbian rights movement battled the "family values" wing of conservatism, environmen-talists struggled against conservatives hostile to federal regulations on free enterprise.

Controversy over the Environment

Secretary of the Interior James Watt joined the Reagan cabinet committed to dismantling much of the environ-mental regulation of the previous two decades. His efforts drew considerable opposition, and he failed to turn back the clock substantially. In 1983, President Reagan ap-pointed a more moderate replacement. What exactly does this *Newsweek* cover suggest that Watt wants to do to the environment?

FOR MORE HELP ANALYZING THIS IMAGE, see the visual activity for this chapter in the Online Study Guide at bedfordstmartins.com/roark.

Illustration by Wilson McLean. Reprinted with permission of the artist and *Newsweek* magazine.

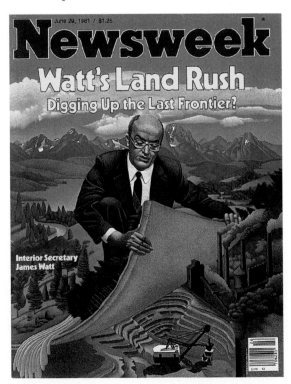

chemical industry. Carter also signed laws to improve clean air and water programs; to preserve vast areas of Alaska from commercial exploitation; and to control strip mining, which left ugly scars on the land. During the gasoline shortage brought on by the Iranian revolution in 1979, Carter attempted to balance the development of domestic fuel sources with environmental concerns; acknowledging that "some of the new technologies we will need to develop pose environmental risks," he angered some in the environmental movement. But he also won legislation to conserve energy and to provide incentives for the development of environmentally friendly alternative fuels, such as solar energy. (See "The Promise of Technology," page 1132.)

Although Ronald Reagan loved the outdoors and relished his retreats to his isolated ranch in the mountains of southern California during his presidency, in contrast to Carter he blamed environmental laws for the nation's sluggish economic growth and targeted them for deregulation. His first secretary of the interior, James Watt, declared, "We will mine more, drill more, cut more timber," and released federal lands to private exploitation, while the head of the Environmental Protection Agency eased enforcement of air and water pollution measures. The popular outcry that resulted led to the resignation of several environmental officials and the failure of other deregulatory goals, and it indicated that the concerns and values of the environmental movement had to some extent become part of the public consciousness.

Ronald Reagan Confronts an "Evil Empire"

Running for president in 1980, Ronald Reagan had capitalized on the Soviet invasion of Afghanistan and the Iranian hostage crisis, accusing Carter of weakening the military and losing the confidence of the nation's allies and its enemies' respect. As president, he accelerated the arms buildup begun by Carter and harshly censured the Soviet Union, calling it "an evil empire." Yet despite the new aggressiveness—or, as some argued, because of it—Reagan presided over the most impressive thaw in superpower conflict since the shattering of the World War II alliance. On the periphery of the cold war, however, Reagan practiced militant anticommunism, authorizing aid to antileftist movements in Asia,

Africa, and Central America and dispatching troops to both the Middle East and the Caribbean. When Congress blocked Reagan's efforts to assist opponents of the leftist Sandinista government in Nicaragua, administration officials resorted to secret and illegal means to effect their agenda.

Militarization and Interventions Abroad

Reagan sought to expand the military with new bombers and missiles, an enhanced nuclear force in Europe, a larger navy, and a rapid-deployment force. Despite the growing budget deficit, Congress approved most of these programs, and military expenditures shot up by one-third in the first half of the 1980s. Throughout Reagan's presidency, defense spending averaged $216 billion a year, up from $158 billion in the Carter years and higher even than in the Vietnam era.

Justifying the military buildup as a means to negotiate with the Soviets from a position of strength, Reagan provoked an outburst of pleas to halt the arms race. A rally demanding a freeze on additional nuclear weapons drew 700,000 people in New York City in 1982.

> On the periphery of the cold war, Reagan practiced militant anticommunism, authorizing aid to antileftist movements in Asia, Africa, and Central America and dispatching troops to both the Middle East and the Caribbean.

Hundreds of thousands demonstrated across Europe, stimulated by fears of new U.S. missiles scheduled for deployment in **North Atlantic Treaty Organization (NATO)** countries in 1983.

Reagan startled many of his own advisers in March 1983 by announcing plans for research on the Strategic Defense Initiative (SDI). Immediately dubbed "Star Wars" by critics who doubted its feasibility, the project would deploy lasers in space to destroy enemy missiles before they could reach their targets. Reagan conceded that SDI could appear as "an aggressive policy" allowing the United States to strike first and not fear retaliation. The Soviets reacted angrily because SDI development violated the 1972 ABM treaty and would require the Soviets to invest huge sums in their own Star Wars technology. SDI research continued under future administrations, but with no workable results despite more than $60 billion in funding.

The U.S. military buildup placed the Soviets on the defensive but did not guarantee American

Solar Energy

"We want to inherit a clean earth," read a child's appeal to a conference on energy and the environment in Norway in 1990. "Why shouldn't we be allowed to live as you did when you were little? Play in fresh forests, fish in any water, drink clean water from the river. . . . We must find energy that does not pollute." The oil crises of the 1970s and growing concerns about the environmental effects of energy generated by coal, oil, and nuclear reactions had already sparked American interest in renewable energy, especially solar energy, an endless and environmentally clean source of fuel for homes and businesses.

Solar rays can be used directly for heating and lighting buildings by means of solar-thermal technologies, which concentrate the sun's rays to heat a liquid. That fluid is then used to warm buildings or create steam to turn a generator and create electricity. A Swiss scientist built the world's first solar collector in 1767, and in 1891 the Baltimore inventor Clarence Kemp patented the first commercial solar water heater. By the end of the twentieth century, more than 1.2 million buildings in the United States had solar water heating systems, and more than 250,000 swimming pools were warmed by the sun's rays. President Jimmy Carter put solar water heating panels on the White House to symbolize the importance of energy in his domestic program.

The other most common way to transfer sunlight into power is through photovoltaic systems (PVs), a process observed by a French physicist in 1839. Bell Telephone Laboratories developed a silicon PV cell in 1954; and in 1958, the American space program began to pioneer in the development of PVs when it used solar energy to power the *Vanguard* space satellite's radio. When sunlight hits the panels that make up photovoltaic systems, a chemical reaction occurs, releasing electricity. During the energy crises of the 1970s, the Federal Photovoltaic Utilization Program tested more than 3,000 PV systems.

Environmental advocates predicted that the sun could provide nearly one-fifth of the country's electricity by 2000; and the price of individual solar cells fell rapidly. Yet solar power has not reached its fullest potential. As the energy crises of the 1970s passed, opposition to government spending for research and subsidies increased, especially from corporations producing energy from fossil fuels. President Bill Clinton initiated a program in 1997 aimed at adding one million residential solar power systems by 2010, but the program was dependent on state subsidies, and the responses of most states were lukewarm. California was an exception. A program called PV Pioneers in Sacramento, for example, recruited a waiting list of more than 700 volunteers who agreed to pay a small surcharge on their electric bill to install solar panels on their roofs.

The greatest use of solar energy occurred in private homes. Although

---

security. Although Iran released the American hostages, terrorism continued to threaten the United States. In October 1983, an Islamic extremist drove a bomb-filled truck into a U.S. marine barracks in Lebanon, killing 241 Americans (see Map 30.2). The attack caused Reagan to pull out U.S. troops sent to Lebanon as part of a peacekeeping mission to monitor the withdrawal of Israeli and Palestinian Liberation Organization forces. Faced with other incidents of murder, kidnapping, and hijacking by various Middle Eastern extremist groups, Reagan refused to negotiate, insisting that to bargain with terrorists would only encourage more assaults.

The Reagan administration sought to contain leftist movements close to home and across the globe. In October 1983, U.S. troops invaded Grenada, a small island nation in the Caribbean that had succumbed to a left-wing, Marxist coup. In Asia, the United States moved more quietly, aiding the Afghan rebels' war against Afghanistan's Soviet-backed government. In the African nation of Angola, the United States armed rebel forces against the Soviet- and Cuban-backed government. Reagan also sided with the South African government that was brutally suppressing black protest against apartheid. In 1985, Congress had to override Reagan's veto such housing cost more to build and construction was not compatible with mass-production methods used in many housing developments, demand for "green" houses grew gradually. A retired couple in Maine, Debbi and Bill Lord, paid about 15 percent more to build their house with solar panels and other energy-smart features. Their designer Steven Strong had gone into the solar energy business after working as a consultant on the Alaska pipeline, which prompted him to shift his career to finding better ways than "going to the ends of the Earth to extract the last drop of fossil fuel." Although the Lords paid only $7.55 a month to the electric company, they didn't expect to make up for the extra cost of their house. Still, Bill Lord favored solar power because it was "practical," and "I like the idea of minimally impacting the environment." His wife agreed: "I think you walk softly on the Earth when you do this."

As Americans turned slowly to solar energy, by 2003 Japan had replaced the United States as the leading producer of solar panels. Having almost no domestic sources of fuel and depending on imported and expensive energy, Japan generated half of the world's solar power; the government subsidized about one-third of the cost of the solar panels. By the twenty-first century, the United States was drawing about 11 percent of its electricity from renewable sources such as solar power, but its future depended on the reliability and cost of more traditional forms of energy and on Americans' willingness to trade off short-term costs for energy independence and a healthier and cleaner environment.

Solar Home
The house of Bill and Debbi Lord in Kennebunkport, Maine, employs both of solar energy's key technologies. On one side of the south-facing roof shown here, photovoltaic panels collect the sun's rays, which are converted to electricity for the house. On the other side of the roof are solar thermal collector panels, which heat water for direct use and for warming the house through radiant tubing in the floors. The Lords also practice "green" transportation. Instead of using gasoline or petrodiesel, their Volkswagen runs on biodiesel, a soybean product.
Maine Solar House/www.solarhouse.com.

in order to impose economic sanctions against South Africa.

Administration officials were most fearful of left-wing movements in Central America that, according to Reagan, threatened to "destabilize the entire region from the Panama Canal to Mexico." When a leftist uprising occurred in 1981 in El Salvador, the United States sent money and military advisers to prop up the government even though it had committed murderous human rights violations and opposed social reform.

In neighboring Nicaragua, where Reagan aimed to unseat the left-wing Sandinistas, the administration aided the Contras (literally, "opposers"), a coalition of armed opposition to the Sandinistas that included many individuals from the ousted Somoza regime. Fearing another Vietnam, many Americans opposed aligning the United States with reactionary forces not supported by the majority of Nicaraguans; and Congress repeatedly instructed the president to stop aid to the Contras or limit it to nonmilitary purposes.

Deliberately violating congressional will, the administration secretly provided weapons and training to the Contras. The CIA directed assaults on economic targets and helped to mine Nicaraguan harbors in 1984. Through legal and

Terrorist Bombing of Marines in Beirut

In 1982, President Reagan sent U.S. troops to join a multinational force to quell fighting between Israelis and Palestinians in Lebanon. On October 23, 1983, members of Islamic Jihad, a group of anti-American fanatics sponsored by Iran, demonstrated their hostility to an American presence in the Middle East by exploding a car bomb outside the U.S. marine compound near the Beirut airport and killing 241 Americans. Secretary of Defense Caspar Weinberger then moved to withdraw the marines, supported by his assistant, army colonel Colin Powell, who believed that "America [was] sticking its hand into a thousand-year-old hornet's nest" in the Middle East. The question of whether and when to risk American lives abroad for peacekeeping or humanitarian purposes would be one of the most difficult problems facing policymakers in the ensuing decades.

Bill Pierce © Bettmann/Corbis/Sygma.

El Salvador and Nicaragua

NSC aide marine lieutenant colonel Oliver North, and CIA director William Casey arranged to sell arms to Iran, then at war with neighboring Iraq. In exchange, Iranians were to pressure Muslim terrorists to release seven American hostages being held in Lebanon (see Map 30.1). Funds from the arms sales were then channeled through Swiss bank accounts to aid the Nicaraguan Contras. Over the objections of Secretary of State George Shultz and Defense Secretary Caspar Weinberger, Reagan approved the arms sales, but the three subsequently denied knowing that the proceeds were diverted to the Contras.

When news of the affair surfaced in November 1986, the Reagan administration faced serious charges. The president who had pledged never to bargain with terrorists had allowed his aides to do so, violating U.S. neutrality in the Iran-Iraq War. Even worse, the administration had defied Congress's express ban on military aid for the Contras. Although North and others destroyed incriminating documents, enough remained to demonstrate the culpability of seven individuals. Brought to trial by an independent prosecutor appointed by Reagan, all pleaded guilty or were convicted of lying to Congress and destroying evidence. North's felony conviction was later overturned on a technicality, and President George H. Bush pardoned the other six officials in December 1992. The independent prosecutor's final report, issued in 1994, found no evidence that Reagan had broken the law; but it concluded that both Reagan and Vice President Bush had known about the diversion of funds to the Contras and that Reagan had "knowingly participated or at least acquiesced" in covering up the scandal— the most serious case of executive branch misconduct since Watergate.

A Thaw in Soviet-American Relations

Reagan weathered Iran-Contra in part because Americans applauded a momentous thaw in the cold war. The new Soviet-American accord depended on Reagan's flexibility and an innovative Soviet head of state who recognized that his country's domestic problems demanded a relaxation of cold war antagonism. Mikhail Gorbachev assumed power in 1985 determined to revitalize an inefficient Soviet economy incapable of delivering basic consumer goods. Hoping to stimulate production and streamline distribution, Gorbachev

illegal means, the Reagan administration sustained the Contras and helped wreck the Nicaraguan economy, thereby undermining support for the Sandinista government. After nine years of civil war, Nicaragua's president, Daniel Ortega, agreed to a political settlement, and when he was defeated by a coalition of all the opposition groups, he stepped aside.

The Iran-Contra Scandal

Secret aid to the Contras was part of a larger project that came to be known as the Iran-Contra scandal. It began in 1985, when heads of the National Security Council, introduced some elements of free enterprise and proclaimed a new era of *glasnost* (greater freedom of expression), eventually allowing new political parties, contested elections, and challenges to Communist rule.

Concerns about immense defense budgets moved both Reagan and Gorbachev to the negotiating table. Enormous military expenditures stood between the Soviet premier and his goal of economic revival. With Congress increasingly criticizing the arms race and growing popular support for arms reductions, Reagan made disarmament a major goal in his last years in office and readily responded when Gorbachev took the initiative.

A positive personal chemistry developed between Reagan and Gorbachev, who met four times between 1985 and 1988. By December 1987, the superpowers had completed an intermediate-range nuclear forces (INF) agreement, eliminating all short- and medium-range missiles from Europe and providing for on-site inspection for the first time. George H. Bush, Reagan's successor, achieved another breakthrough in June 1990, with a strategic arms reduction treaty (START) that cut about 30 percent of each superpower's nuclear arsenal.

In 1988, Gorbachev further reduced tensions by announcing a gradual withdrawal from Afghanistan, which had become the Soviet equivalent of America's Vietnam. In Africa, the Soviet Union, the United States, and Cuba agreed on a political settlement for the civil war in Angola. And in the Middle East, both superpowers supported a cease-fire and peace talks in the eight-year war between Iran and Iraq.

> The new Soviet-American accord depended on Reagan's flexibility and an innovative Soviet head of state who recognized that his country's domestic problems demanded a relaxation of cold war antagonism.

Nuclear Freeze Campaign
Sixteen-year-old Justin Martino made this mask to wear in a march on the Pentagon in 1985 supporting disarmament and world peace. Martino wanted to symbolize his belief that "the arms race has no end except the end of life," and he later contributed the mask to the Smithsonian Museum of American History. The worldwide demonstrations for nuclear disarmament achieved limited success when the United States and Soviet Union signed arms limitation agreements in 1987.
Smithsonian Institution, Washington, D.C.

Conclusion: Reversing the Course of Government

"Ours was the first revolution in the history of mankind that truly reversed the course of government," boasted Ronald Reagan in his farewell address in 1989. The word *revolution* exaggerated the change, but his administration did mark the slowdown or reversal of expanding federal budgets, programs, and regulations that had taken off in the 1930s. Although he did not deliver on the social or moral issues dear to the heart of the New Right, to Phyllis Schlafly, Reagan represented the "choice not an echo" that she had called for in 1964, as he used his skills as "the Great Communicator" to cultivate antigovernment sentiment and undo the liberal assumptions of the **New Deal**.

Hostility toward and distrust of the federal government grew along with the backlash against the reforms of the 1960s and the conduct of the Vietnam War. Watergate and other misdeeds of the Nixon administration further disillusioned Americans. Presidents Ford and Carter restored morality to the White House, but neither could solve the gravest economic problems since the Great Depression—a low rate of economic growth, stagflation, and an increasing trade deficit. Even the Democrat Carter gave higher priority to fiscal austerity than to social reform, and he began the government's retreat from regulation of key industries.

The Cold War Thaws
U.S. president Ronald Reagan and Soviet premier Mikhail Gorbachev shake hands as they meet at a
five-day summit in June 1988 for a round of Strategic Arms Reduction Talks (START). Moving beyond
the Strategic Arms Limitation Talks (SALT) agreements of the 1970s, these negotiations aimed to reduce
rather than limit nuclear warheads and the bombers that carried them. The talks culminated with a
comprehensive treaty signed by Reagan's successor George H. Bush and Gorbachev in July 1991.
David Burnett / Contact Press Images.

During the Reagan years, as a new conservative movement flourished, the United States turned explicitly away from the assumptions that had shaped domestic policy since the New Deal. Republican presidents Eisenhower and Nixon had attempted to curb the role of the federal government, but no president before Ronald Reagan had so castigated its activities. His tax cuts, combined with hefty increases in defense spending, created a federal deficit crisis that justified cuts in social welfare spending and made new federal initiatives unthinkable. Many Americans continued to approve of specific federal programs at the end of the Reagan years, but public sentiment about the government in general had undergone a U-turn from the Roosevelt era. Instead of seeing the government as a helpful and problem-solving institution, they believed it was not only ineffective at solving national problems but often made things worse. As Reagan appointed new Supreme Court justices, that body also retreated from its earlier liberalism, in which it had upheld the government's authority to protect individual rights and regulate the economy.

With his optimistic rhetoric, Ronald Reagan also lifted the confidence of Americans about their nation and its promise, confidence that had eroded with the economic and foreign-policy blows of the 1970s. Beginning his presidency with harsh rhetoric against the Soviet Union and a huge military buildup, Reagan left office having helped move the two superpowers to the highest level of cooperation since the cold war began. Although that accord was not welcome to strong anti-Communist conservatives like Phyllis Schlafly, it signaled developments that would transform American-Soviet relations—and the world—in the next decade.

For additional firsthand accounts of this period, see Chapter 30 in Michael Johnson, ed., *Reading the American Past*, Third Edition.

To assess your mastery of the material in this chapter, see the Online Study Guide at bedfordstmartins.com/roark.

For Web links related to topics in this chapter, see "HistoryLinks," "DocLinks," and "PlaceLinks" at bedfordstmartins.com/roark.

CHRONOLOGY

1964
- Conservatives capture Republican presidential nomination for Barry Goldwater.

1966
- Ronald Reagan wins election to California governorship as a conservative.

1968
- Richard Nixon elected president.

1969
- Nixon appoints Warren E. Burger chief justice of U.S. Supreme Court.
- Stonewall riot in New York City helps spark gay and lesbian rights movement.

1971
- Nixon vetoes comprehensive child care bill.
- In *Swann v. Charlotte-Mecklenburg Board of Education*, U.S. Supreme Court affirms transfer of students between schools in white and black neighborhoods to achieve desegregation.

1972
- Nixon campaign aides apprehended breaking into Democratic Party headquarters in Watergate complex.
- Nixon reelected by landslide to a second term.

1974
- Nixon resigns as president in face of certain impeachment by House of Representatives over his role in Watergate affair; Gerald Ford becomes president.
- Ford pardons Nixon of any crimes he may have committed while president.
- In *Milliken v. Bradley*, U.S. Supreme Court imposes some limitations on use of busing to achieve racial integration in schools.

1976
- Jimmy Carter elected president.

1977
- United States signs treaties providing for return of Panama Canal to Panama in 2000.

1978
- Carter helps negotiate peace agreement between Egypt and Israel (Camp David accords).
- In *Bakke case*, U.S. Supreme Court rules against racial quotas but upholds use of affirmative action to remedy effects of past discrimination.
- Discovery of toxic wastes in the Love Canal neighborhood of Niagara Falls, New York, brings national attention to environmental effects of industrial dumping.

1978–1980
- Congress passes bills deregulating airlines, banking, trucking, and railroad industries.

1979
- Carter establishes formal diplomatic relations with the People's Republic of China.

- Soviet Union invades Afghanistan; United States imposes economic sanctions.
- Hostage crisis in Iran begins.
- Rev. Jerry Falwell founds Moral Majority to involve evangelical Christians in politics.

1979–1980
- Congress enacts measures to conserve energy and increase its production.

1980
- Congress passes Superfund legislation to clean up toxic wastes.
- Ronald Reagan elected president, defeating incumbent Jimmy Carter.

1981
- Researchers identify a virus as the cause of AIDS epidemic.
- Congress passes Economic Recovery Tax Act, resulting in the largest tax cut in U.S. history.
- Reagan appoints first female justice to U.S. Supreme Court: Sandra Day O'Connor.

1981–1982
- Economic recession pushes unemployment rate above 10 percent.

1982
- Large peace marches held in the United States and Europe to limit nuclear weapons.

1983
- United States invades Grenada and topples its Marxist government.
- United States terminates peacekeeping mission in Lebanon after a terrorist bombs U.S. marine barracks and kills 241 Americans.
- Reagan announces plans for Strategic Defense Initiative ("Star Wars"), a space-based missile defense system.

1984
- Reagan reelected to a second term.

1986
- Iran-Contra scandal shakes Reagan administration.
- Federal budget deficit reaches all-time high of $220 billion.

1987
- Soviet premier Mikhail Gorbachev and President Reagan sign INF agreement, eliminating all short- and medium-range missiles from Europe.

1988
- Congress passes Civil Rights Restoration Act, strengthening safeguards against discrimination on the basis of race, color, national origin, sex, disability, or age.

BIBLIOGRAPHY

Foreign Policy

Zbigniew Brzezinski, *Power and Principle: Memoirs of the National Security Adviser, 1977–1981* (1983).

Beth A. Fischer, *The Reagan Reversal: Foreign Policy and the End of the Cold War* (1997).

Frances FitzGerald, *Way Out There in the Blue: Reagan, Star Wars, and the End of the Cold War* (2000).

Raymond I. Garthoff, *Détente and Confrontation: American-Soviet Relations from Nixon to Reagan* (rev. ed., 1994).

David Kyvig, ed., *Reagan and the World* (1990).

Sanford Lakoff and Herbert F. York, *A Shield in Space?* (1989).

Peter Schweizer, *Victory: The Reagan Administration's Secret Strategy That Hastened the Collapse of the Soviet Union* (1995).

George P. Shultz, *Turmoil and Triumph: My Years as Secretary of State* (1993).

Gaddis Smith, *Morality, Reason, and Power: American Diplomacy in the Carter Years* (1986).

Strobe Talbott, *The Master of the Game: Paul Nitze and the Nuclear Peace* (1988).

Cyrus Vance, *Hard Choices: Critical Years in America's Foreign Policy* (1983).

Daniel Wirls, *Buildup: The Politics of Defense in the Reagan Era* (1992).

The United States and the Middle East

James A. Bill, *The Eagle and the Lion: The Tragedy of American-Iranian Relations* (1988).

Theodore Draper, *A Very Thin Line: The Iran-Contra Affair* (1991).

Mark J. Gasiorowski, *U.S. Foreign Policy and the Shah: Building a Client State in Iran* (1991).

Douglas Little, *American Orientalism: The United States and the Middle East since 1945* (2002).

Benny Morris, *Righteous Victims: A History of the Zionist-Arab Conflict, 1881–1999* (1999).

The United States and Latin America

Cynthia J. Arnson, *Crossroads: Congress, the Reagan Administration, and Central America* (1989).

Thomas Carothers, *In the Name of Democracy: U.S. Policy toward Latin America in the Reagan Years* (1991).

J. Michael Hogan, *The Panama Canal in American Politics* (1986).

Robert Kagan, *A Twilight Struggle: American Power and Nicaragua, 1977–1990* (1996).

William M. LeoGrande, *Our Own Backyard: The United States in Central America, 1977–1992* (1998).

Energy and the Environment

Thomas R. Dunlap, *DDT: Scientists, Citizens, and Public Policy* (1981).

J. Brooks Flippen, *Nixon and the Environment* (2000).

Samuel P. Hays, *A History of Environmental Politics since 1945* (2000).

Martin V. Melosi, *Coping with Abundance: Energy and Environment in Industrial America* (1985).

Roderick Frazier Nash, *American Environmentalism: Readings in Conservation History* (1990).

Hal K. Rothman, *The Greening of a Nation? Environmentalism in the United States since 1945* (1998).

Philip Shabecoff, *A Fierce Green Fire: The American Environmental Movement* (1993).

Daniel Yergin, *The Prize: The Epic Quest for Oil, Money, and Power* (1990).

Conservatism and Right-Wing Movements

John A. Andrew, *The Other Side of the Sixties: Young Americans for Freedom and the Rise of Conservative Politics* (1997).

William C. Berman, *America's Right Turn: From Nixon to Clinton* (1998).

Earl Black and Merle Black, *The Rise of Southern Republicans* (2002).

Matthew Dallek, *The Right Moment: Ronald Reagan's First Victory and the Decisive Turning Point in American Politics* (2000).

Thomas Byrd Edsall with Mary D. Edsall, *Chain Reaction: The Impact of Race, Rights, and Taxes on American Politics* (1992).

Lee Edwards, *The Conservative Revolution: The Movement That Remade America* (1999).

Carol Felsenthal, *Sweetheart of the Silent Majority* (1981).

Thomas Ferguson and Joel Rogers, *Right Turn: The Decline of the Democrats and the Future of American Politics* (1986).

Godfrey Hodgson, *The World Turned Right Side Up: A History of the Conservative Ascendancy in America* (1996).

William Martin, *With God on Our Side: The Rise of the Religious Right in America* (1996).

Lisa McGirr, *Suburban Warriors: The Origins of the New American Right* (2001).

Jonathan M. Schoenwald, *A Time for Choosing: The Rise of Modern Conservatism* (2001).

Social Movements, Rights, and the Supreme Court

Barry D. Adam, *The Rise of a Gay and Lesbian Movement* (rev. ed., 1995).

Norman C. Amaker, *Civil Rights and the Reagan Administration* (1988).

John D'Emilio, Urvashi Vaid, and William B. Turner, *Creating Change: Sexuality, Public Policy, and Civil Rights* (2000).

Susan M. Hartmann, *The Other Feminists: Activists in the Liberal Establishment* (1998).

Lisa Keen and Suzanne B. Goldberg, *Strangers to the Law: Gay People on Trial* (1998).

Dean J. Kotlowski, *Nixon's Civil Rights: Politics, Principle, and Policy* (2001).

Jane J. Mansbridge, *Why We Lost the ERA* (1986).

Donald G. Mathews and Jane Sherron De Hart, *Sex, Gender, and the Politics of the ERA* (1990).

Herman Schwartz, *Packing the Courts: The Conservative Campaign to Rewrite the Constitution* (1988).

Randy Shilts, *And the Band Played On: Politics, People, and the AIDS Epidemic* (1987).

James F. Simon, *The Center Holds: The Power Struggle inside the Rehnquist Court* (1995).

Melvin Urofsky, *A Conflict of Rights: The Supreme Court and Affirmative Action* (1991).

The Economy and Its Casualties

Michael Bernstein, David E. Adler, and Robert Heilbroner, *Understanding American Economic Decline* (1994).

W. Carl Biven, *Jimmy Carter's Economy: Policy in an Age of Limits* (2003).

Jefferson Cowie, *Capital Moves: RCAs Seventy-year Quest for Cheap Labor* (1999).

Kathleen Day, *S&L Hell: The People and the Politics behind the $1 Trillion Savings and Loan Scandal* (1993).

Kathryn Marie Dudley, *The End of the Line: Lost Jobs, New Lives in Postindustrial America* (1994).

Bennett Harrison and Barry Bluestone, *The Great U-Turn: Corporate Restructuring and the Polarizing of America* (1988).

Jennifer L. Hochschild, *Facing Up to the American Dream: Race, Class, and the Soul of the Nation* (1995).

Christopher Jencks, *The Homeless* (1994).

Kevin Phillips, *The Politics of Rich and Poor: Wealth and the American Electorate in the Reagan Aftermath* (1990).

Robert J. Samuelson, *The American Dream in the Age of Entitlement, 1945–1995* (1996).

John E. Schwartz and Thomas J. Volgy, *The Forgotten Americans* (1993).

John W. Sloan, *The Reagan Effect: Economics and Presidential Leadership* (1999).

Adam Smith, *The Roaring '80s* (1988).

Watergate

Carl Bernstein and Bob Woodward, *All the President's Men* (1974).

Stanley I. Kutler, *The Wars of Watergate: The Last Crisis of Richard Nixon* (1990).

Stanley I. Kutler, ed., *Abuse of Power: The New Nixon Tapes* (1997).

Kathryn S. Olmstead, *Challenging the Secret Government: The Post-Watergate Investigations of the CIA and FBI* (1996).

Keith W. Olson, *Watergate: The Presidential Scandal That Shook America* (2003).

Presidents and Politics

Lou Cannon, *President Reagan: The Role of a Lifetime* (1991).

Gary M. Fink and Hugh Davis Graham, eds., *The Carter Presidency: Policy Choices in the Post–New Deal Era* (1998).

Haynes Johnson, *Sleepwalking through History: America in the Reagan Years* (1992).

Burton I. Kaufmann, *The Presidency of James Earl Carter* (1993).

Michael Schaller, *Reckoning with Reagan: America and Its President of the 1980s* (1992).

Melvin Small, *The Presidency of Richard Nixon* (1999).

Tom Wicker, *One of Us: Richard Nixon and the American Dream* (1991).

A SHRINKING WORLD

The cellular telephone is one of the new technologies contributing to the process of globalization that intensified with the end of the cold war in 1990. Connecting users to conventional telephone networks through microwave radio frequencies, wireless phones began to be used in Tokyo in 1979, and the first American system began in 1983. By the end of the century, hundreds of millions of people used cell phones around the world, not only to call friends and business associates but also to connect to the Internet and send and receive e-mail. Cellular systems have improved communication for people in countries that lack a good wire-based telephone system, facilitating commerce as well as connecting far-flung family members and other individuals. By 2003, cell phones comprised 43 percent of all phones in the United States; in European and other countries, cell phones outnumbered traditional phones. Terrorists who struck the World Trade Center towers and the Pentagon on September 11, 2001, used mobile devices to coordinate the attacks, and many victims of the terror spoke their last words to loved ones over cell phones. Wireless phones decorated with the American flag became popular expressions of patriotism in the aftermath of the attacks.

Kit Hinricks/Pentagon Design.

The End of the Cold War and the Challenges of Globalization

Since 1989

O N APRIL 22, 1988, Ronald Reagan's national security adviser, army general Colin L. Powell, returned to his Moscow hotel from the Kremlin, where he had heard Premier Mikhail Gorbachev announce plans that would dramatically alter the government and economy of the Soviet Union. "Lying there in bed," Powell recalled, "I realized that one phase of my life had ended, and another was about to begin. Up until now, as a soldier, my mission had been to confront, contain, and if necessary, combat communism. Now I had to think about a world without a Cold War." For the next sixteen years, Powell would be a key figure helping to define his country's new role in a world transformed.

Colin Powell was born in New York City's Harlem in 1937 and grew up in the Bronx, the son of parents who had immigrated from Jamaica in 1920. His father had begun as a gardener and ultimately became head of the shipping department of a garment manufacturer, where his mother worked as a seamstress. Powell attended public schools and then City College of New York, where he joined the army's Reserve Officers Training Corps program (ROTC), which became the center of his collegiate experience. "The discipline, the structure, the camaraderie, the sense of belonging," he said, "were what I craved." Commissioned as a lieutenant when he graduated in 1958, Powell began a lifelong career in military and public service, rising to the highest rank of four-star general. He chose to stay in the army after fulfilling his ROTC obligation primarily because "I loved what I was doing." But he also recognized that "for a black, no other avenue in American society offered so much opportunity."

The two tours of duty that he served in Vietnam were defining experiences for Powell, just as the war was for many Americans. Powell learned from Vietnam that "you do not squander courage and lives without clear purpose, without the country's backing, and without full commitment." In his subsequent capacities as national security adviser to Ronald Reagan, as chairman of the Joint Chiefs of Staff in the George H. W. Bush and William Jefferson Clinton administrations, and as secretary of state under George W. Bush, Powell endeavored to ensure that his country did not engage in "half-hearted warfare for half-baked reasons that the American people could not understand or support."

Secretary of State Colin Powell

Among the many characteristics that helped Colin Powell rise through the ranks of the army and serve in four presidential administrations were his loyalty and discretion. The decision by George W. Bush to invade Iraq in March 2003 ran counter to his secretary of state's commitment to acting through the international community and sacrificing American lives only when a vital interest was at stake and a plan for ending the intervention had been established. Although Powell's position lost out to the more hawkish Vice President Dick Cheney and Secretary of Defense Donald Rumsfeld, Powell stayed in his job and defended administration policy. In this photo taken in the White House in February 2003, he listens to Rumsfeld; National Security Adviser Condoleezza Rice stands behind them. Charles Ommanney/Contact Press Images for Newsweek.

Powell's sense that Gorbachev's reforms would bring about the end of the **cold war** became reality more quickly than anyone anticipated. Eastern Europe broke free from **Communist** control in 1989, and the Soviet Union disintegrated in 1991. As the lone superpower, throughout the 1990s the United States deployed both military and diplomatic power during episodes of instability in Latin America, the Middle East, Eastern Europe, and Asia, almost always in concert with the major nations of Europe and Asia. In 1991, in its first full-fledged war since Vietnam, it led a United Nations–authorized force of twenty-eight nations to repel Iraq's invasion of Kuwait.

In the mid-1990s during a temporary retirement from public service, Powell remarked that "neither of the two major parties fits me comfortably." Many Americans seemed to agree: They turned Republican George H. W. Bush out of office in 1992 but elected Republican Congresses during Democrat Bill Clinton's administration; when Republican George W. Bush entered the White House in 2001, he faced a nearly evenly divided Congress. Between 1989 and 2000, domestic policies reflected a slight retreat from the **conservatism** of the Reagan years: The Bush administration saw tighter environmental protections and new rights for people with disabilities, and Clinton signed measures strengthening gun control and aiding low wage earners. But the pendulum swung back in the early years of the second Bush presidency.

All three presidents shared a commitment to economic growth and to hastening the globalizing processes that were linking nations together in an increasingly connected economy. As capital, products, and people crossed national boundaries at greater speed, the United States itself became more diverse with a surge of immigration rivaling that of a century earlier, which had brought Powell's parents to the United States. Powell cheered **globalization**, predicting in the 1990s that the world would become "defined by trade relations, by the flow of information, capital, technology, and goods, rather than by armies glaring at each other across borders."

Powell was not so naive as to anticipate a world "without war or conflict," and he pointed to challenges such as nuclear proliferation, **nationalist** passions in areas of former Soviet dominance, civil wars in Africa, and Islamic **fundamentalism.** But he was as shocked as other Americans when in September 2001 deadly terrorist attacks on New York City, the nation's economic center, and Washington, D.C., its political and military core, exposed American vulnerability to new and horrifying international threats. The administration's response to terrorism overwhelmed Secretary of State Powell's commitments to internationalism, multilateralism, and military restraint, as George W. Bush began a second war against Iraq, implementing a radical shift in U.S. foreign policy based on preemptive attacks against presumed threats and going it alone if necessary.

Domestic Stalemate and Global Upheaval: The Presidency of George H. W. Bush

When Vice President George H. W. Bush announced his candidacy for the presidency in 1987, he declared, "We don't need radical new directions." Generally satisfied with the agenda set by Ronald Reagan and facing a Democratic-controlled Congress, Bush proposed few domestic initiatives. His dispatch of troops to oust the corrupt dictator of Panama represented a much longer continuity, following a century of American intervention in Latin America. Yet, as the most dramatic changes since the 1940s swept through the world, his government confronted situations that did not fit the simpler free-world versus communism framework that had guided foreign policy since World War II. Most Americans approved of Bush's handling of two challenges to American foreign policy and military capacity: disintegration of the Soviet Union and its hold over Eastern Europe and Iraq's invasion of neighboring Kuwait. But voters' concern over a sluggish economy and other domestic problems limited Bush to one term in the White House.

Gridlock in Government

The son of a wealthy New England senator, George Herbert Walker Bush grew up in a privileged milieu that put a premium on public service. He fought in World War II, earned a Yale degree, and then settled in Texas to make his own way in the oil industry and politics. He served in Congress during the 1960s and headed the CIA during the Nixon-Ford years. When Ronald Reagan achieved a commanding lead in the 1980 primaries, Bush put his own presidential ambitions on hold, adjusted his more moderate policy positions to fit Reagan's conservative agenda, and accepted second place on the Republican ticket.

Michael Dukakis, governor of Massachusetts, won the Democratic Party nomination, defeating several candidates. An important contender was the Reverend Jesse Jackson, who had fought civil rights battles with Martin Luther King Jr, and whose Rainbow Coalition campaign centered on the needs of minorities, women, working-class families, and the poor. He won several primaries, gathering 7 million votes, but his race, lack of government experience, and position on the left of the party proved to be insuperable obstacles. On election day, half the eligible voters stayed home, indicating the electorate's general disgust with the negative campaigning or their satisfaction with the Republican record on peace and prosperity. Divided government would remain, however: 54 percent of the voters chose Bush, but the Democrats gained seats in the House and Senate.

Although President Bush saw himself primarily as guardian and beneficiary of the Reagan legacy, he promised "a kinder, gentler nation" and was more inclined than Reagan to approve government activity in the private sphere. For example, he signed the Clean Air Act of 1990, the strongest, most comprehensive environmental law in history; it required power plants to cut sulfur dioxide emissions by more than half by the year 2000 and oil companies to develop cleaner-burning gasoline. Some 40 million Americans reaped the benefits of another regulatory measure, the 1991 Americans with Disabilities Act, which banned job discrimination against the disabled and required that private businesses, public accommodations, and transportation be made handicapped-accessible. Cynthia Jones, publisher of *Mainstream Magazine*, which reported on disability politics, attended the bill's signing on the White House lawn. When a breeze stirred the crowd, she remembered with jubilation, "It was kind of like a new breath of air was sweeping across America. . . . People knew they had rights. That was wonderful."

Yet Bush needed to satisfy party conservatives. His most famous campaign pledge was "Read my lips: No new taxes," and he opposed most proposals requiring additional federal funds. "If you're looking for George Bush's domestic program, and many people are, this is

> Most Americans approved of George H. W. Bush's handling of two challenges to American foreign policy and military capacity. But voters' concern over a sluggish economy and other domestic problems limited Bush to one term.

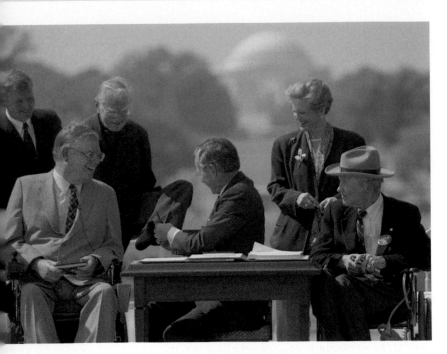

President George H. W. Bush Signs the Americans with Disabilities Act
After signing the landmark measure guaranteeing civil rights for people with disabilities on July 26, 1990, President Bush presented a pen to the Reverend Dr. Harold Wilke. A minister, professor, and disability rights leader, Wilke accepted the pen with his foot because he was born without arms. On the left, Vice President Daniel Quayle watches.

© Bettmann/Corbis.

it: the veto pen," charged Democratic House majority leader Richard Gephardt in 1991. Bush blocked Congress thirty-six times, vetoing bills that would have lifted abortion restrictions, extended unemployment benefits, raised taxes, mandated family and medical leave for workers, and reformed campaign financing. By the end of his term, press reports were filled with the words *stalemate, gridlock,* and *divided government.*

Continuing a trend begun during the Reagan administration, states tried to compensate for this paralysis, becoming more innovative than Washington. "Our federal politics are gridlocked, and governors have become the ones who have to have the courage to put their necks out," said a spokesperson for governors. States passed bills to block corporate takeovers, establish parental leave policies, require equal pay for jobs of equal worth, improve food labeling, and protect the environment. Beginning in the 1980s, a few states began to pass measures guaranteeing gay and lesbian rights. (See "Documenting the American Promise," page 1128.) In the 1990s, dozens of cities passed ordinances requiring businesses with tax abatements or other benefits

from cities to pay wages well above the federal minimum wage. And in 1999, California passed a gun control bill with much tougher restrictions on assault weapons than reformers had been able to get through Congress.

A huge **federal budget deficit** inherited from the Reagan administration impelled the president and Congress to break their deadlock. In 1990, Bush reluctantly abandoned his "no new taxes" pledge and agreed to modest tax increases for high-income Americans and higher levies on gasoline, cigarettes, alcohol, and luxury items. Although the budget agreement brought in new revenues and Congress limited spending, three years later the deficit soared even higher, boosted by rising costs in entitlement programs such as Social Security and Medicare-Medicaid as well as by spending on unforeseen emergencies of war and natural disasters. The new taxes affected only slightly the massive tax reductions of the early 1980s, leaving intact a key element of Reagan's legacy.

Bush also continued Reagan's efforts to create a more conservative Supreme Court. His first nominee, federal appeals judge David Souter, won easy confirmation by the Senate. But in 1991, when the only African American on the Court, Justice Thurgood Marshall, retired, Bush set off a national controversy by nominating Clarence Thomas, a conservative black appeals judge, who had opposed **affirmative action** as head of the Equal Employment Opportunity Commission (EEOC) under Reagan. Charging that Thomas would not protect minority rights, the National Association for the Advancement of Colored People (NAACP) and other **liberal** organizations fought the nomination. Then Anita Hill, a law professor and former EEOC employee, stunned the nation by accusing Thomas of sexual harassment.

The Senate Judiciary Committee investigated the charges during three days of nationally televised hearings. Thomas angrily denied the alleged incidents, and Hill's testimony failed to sway the Senate, which voted narrowly to confirm him. The hearings did sensitize the public to sexual harassment, and they angered many women, including a dozen House members, who expressed outrage at the shabby treatment that Hill received from senators seeking to discredit her. **Feminists** complained that men "still don't get it" and redoubled their efforts to get more women into office. But Thomas's confirmation solidified the Supreme Court's shift to the right.

The End of the Cold War

The forces of change that Gorbachev had encouraged in the Communist world (see chapter 30) swept through Eastern Europe in 1989, where popular uprisings demanded an end to state repression, official corruption, and economic bureaucracies unable to deliver an acceptable standard of living. Communist governments toppled like dominoes (Map 31.1). East Germany opened its border with West Germany, and in November 1989, ecstatic Germans danced on the Berlin Wall, which had separated East and West since 1961, using whatever was at hand to demolish that dominant symbol of the cold war. An amazed East Berliner crossed over the line exclaiming, "They just let us go. I can't believe it."

Unification of East and West Germany into one nation sped to completion in 1990. The Warsaw Pact dissolved, and by 2000 three former **iron curtain** countries—the Czech Republic, Hungary, and Poland—had joined **NATO**, and more were in line to become members. Although U.S. military forces remained in Europe as part of NATO, the commanding role of the United States had been eclipsed. The same was true of its economic clout: Western Europe, including unified Germany, formed a common economic market in 1992. The destiny of Europe, to which the United States and the Soviet Union had held the key for forty-five years, now lay in European hands.

By the end of 1991, Gorbachev's initiatives had brought his own downfall. Inspired by the liberation of Eastern Europe, republics within the Soviet Union sought their own independence, while Moscow's efforts at economic change brought widespread destitution. According to one Muscovite, "Gorbachev knew how to bring us freedom but he did not know how to make sausage." In December, Boris Yeltsin, president

> On November 12, 1989, ecstatic Germans danced on the Berlin Wall, using whatever was at hand to demolish that dominant symbol of the cold war.

Fall of the Berlin Wall
After 1961, the Berlin Wall stood as the prime symbol of the cold war and the iron grip of communism over Eastern Europe and the Soviet Union. More than four hundred easterners were killed trying to flee. After Communist authorities opened the wall on November 9, 1989, permitting free travel between East and West Germany, Berliners from both sides gathered at the wall to celebrate.
Eric Bouvet/Gamma Press Images.

For more help analyzing this image, see the visual activity for this chapter in the Online Study Guide at bedfordstmartins.com/roark.

MAP 31.1   Events in Eastern Europe, 1989–2002
The overthrow of Communist governments throughout eastern and central Europe and the splintering of the Soviet Union into more than a dozen separate nations were the most momentous changes in world history since World War II.

READING THE MAP: Which country was the first to overthrow its Communist government? Which was the last? In which nations did elections usher in change in government?
CONNECTIONS: What problems did Mikhail Gorbachev try to solve, and how did he try to solve them? What policy launched by Ronald Reagan contributed to Soviet dilemmas? Did it create any problems in the United States?

FOR MORE HELP ANALYZING THIS MAP, see the map activity for this chapter in the Online Study Guide at bedfordstmartins.com/roark.

of the Russian Republic, announced that Russia and eleven other republics had formed a new entity, the Commonwealth of Independent States (CIS), and other former Soviet states declared independence. With nothing left to govern, Gorbachev resigned.

China and North Korea resisted the liberalizing tides sweeping the world. In 1989, the Chinese military killed hundreds of pro-democracy demonstrators in Tiananmen Square in Beijing, and the Communist government arrested some 10,000 citizens as it cracked down on advocates of reform. North Korea remained under a Communist dictatorship that threatened

to develop nuclear weapons and to deliver materials that could help other nations achieve a nuclear capacity.

"The post–cold war world is decidedly not postnuclear," declared one U.S. official. In 1996, the world took a small step back from the nuclear brink when the UN General Assembly overwhelmingly approved a total nuclear test ban treaty. Yet India and Pakistan, hostile neighbors, refused to sign and both exploded atomic devices in 1998, increasing the nuclear risk in South Asia. Moreover, in a highly partisan vote, the Republican-controlled Senate defeated U.S. ratification of the treaty in October 1999, halting a decade of progress on nuclear weapons control.

Going to War in Central America and the Persian Gulf

Despite the diminishing threat of the Soviet Union during his four years in office, President Bush twice sent U.S. soldiers into battle. Nearly every cold war president before him had dispatched aid or troops to Central America and the Caribbean in the name of suppressing communism; but Bush intervened in Panama in 1989 for different reasons. The United States had tolerated the repressive regime of Panamanian dictator Manuel Noriega when he served as a CIA informer about Communist activities in the 1980s. But in 1989, after Noriega was indicted for drug trafficking by a grand jury in Miami, Florida, and after his troops killed an American marine, President Bush ordered 25,000 military personnel into Panama to capture the dictator. In an invasion labeled "Operation Just Cause," U.S. forces quickly overcame Noriega's troops, at the cost of 23 Americans and hundreds of Panamanians, many of them civilians. Chairman of the Joint Chiefs of Staff Colin Powell noted that "our euphoria over our victory in Just Cause was not universal": Both the United Nations and the Organization of American States censured the unilateral action by the United States.

If the resort to military intervention in Panama fit within the century-old tradition of **Yankee imperialism**, Bush's second military engagement represented a decided break with the past, demonstrating how much the cold war's end had changed the world. Former cold war enemies worked together when, in August 1990, Iraq occupied the small, oil-rich country of Kuwait to its south (Map 31.2). Struggling with an enormous debt from ten years of war against Iran, Iraqi dictator Saddam Hussein desperately needed revenues and sought control of Kuwait. Within days of invading Kuwait, Iraqi troops moved toward the Saudi Arabian border, threatening the world's largest oil reserves.

President Bush reacted quickly. He invoked principles of national self-determination and international law, but the need to maintain access to oil drove the U.S. response. As the largest importer of oil, the United States consumed one-fourth of the world supply. With the consent of Saudi Arabia, Bush ordered a massive mobilization of land, air, and naval forces and assembled more than thirty nations in an international coalition to stand up to Iraq. "The community of nations has resolutely gathered to condemn and repel lawless aggression," Bush announced. "With few exceptions, the world now stands as one."

Reflecting the end of superpower conflict in the Middle East, the Soviet Union joined the United States in condemning Hussein and cut off arms shipments to Iraq. The UN declared an embargo on Iraqi oil and authorized the use of force if Iraq did not withdraw from Kuwait by January 15, 1991. By early January, the United States had deployed 400,000 soldiers to Saudi Arabia, joined by 265,000 troops from some two dozen nations, including Egypt, Syria, and several other Arab states.

When Bush asked Congress to approve war in January 1991, considerable public and legislative

> By early January 1991, the United States had deployed 400,000 soldiers to Saudi Arabia, joined by 265,000 troops from some two dozen nations, including Egypt, Syria, and several other Arab states.

The Gulf War

These soldiers from the Twenty-fourth Infantry arrived in Saudi Arabia in August 1990 as part of the U.S.-led effort to drive Iraq out of Kuwait. For the first time, women served in combat-support positions: More than 33,000 were stationed throughout the Gulf; 11 died, and 2 were held as prisoners of war. Among their duties were piloting planes and helicopters, directing artillery, and fighting fires. Reuters Newmedia/Corbis.

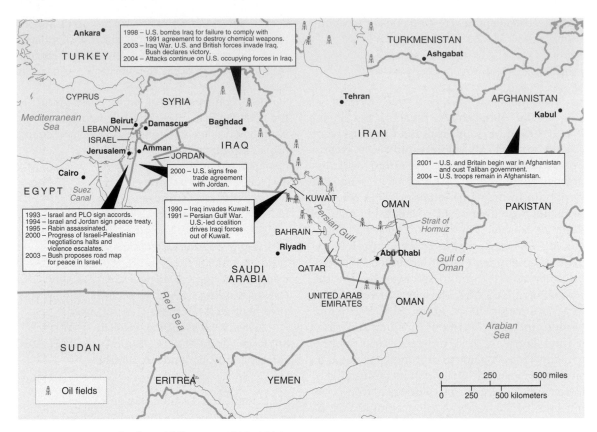

1998 – U.S. bombs Iraq for failure to comply with 1991 agreement to destroy chemical weapons.
2003 – Iraq War. U.S. and British forces invade Iraq. Bush declares victory.
2004 – Attacks continue on U.S. occupying forces in Iraq.

2001 – U.S. and Britain begin war in Afghanistan and oust Taliban government.
2004 – U.S. troops remain in Afghanistan.

2000 – U.S. signs free trade agreement with Jordan.

1993 – Israel and PLO sign accords.
1994 – Israel and Jordan sign peace treaty.
1995 – Rabin assassinated.
2000 – Progress of Israeli-Palestinian negotiations halts and violence escalates.
2003 – Bush proposes road map for peace in Israel.

1990 – Iraq invades Kuwait.
1991 – Persian Gulf War. U.S.-led coalition drives Iraqi forces out of Kuwait.

⚒ Oil fields

MAP 31.2 Events in the Middle East, 1989–2004

During the Persian Gulf War of 1991, Egypt, Syria, and other Middle Eastern nations joined the coalition against Iraq, and the 22-member Arab League supported the war as a means to liberate Kuwait. After September 11, 2001, the Arab League approved of U.S. military operations in Afghanistan because the attacks "were an attack on the common values of the world, not just on the United States." Yet, except for the countries where the United States had military bases—Bahrain, Kuwait, Qatar, and Saudi Arabia—no Arab country supported the American invasion and occupation of Iraq in 2003. Arab hostility to the United States also reflected the deterioration of Israeli-Palestinian relations from 2000 to 2004, as Arabs charged that the United States allowed Israel to deny Palestinians land and liberty.

sentiment favored waiting to see whether the embargo would force Hussein to back down. Within the administration, Colin Powell quietly urged such restraint. In Congress, Democratic senator George J. Mitchell agreed on the need to free Kuwait but asked, "Should we start with war, before other means have been fully exhausted?" Linking the crisis to the failure of U.S. energy conservation, Democratic senator Edward M. Kennedy insisted, "Not a single American life should be sacrificed in a war for the price of oil." Congress debated for three days and then authorized war by margins of five votes in the Senate and sixty-seven in the House. On January 17, 1991, the U.S.-led coalition launched Operation Desert Storm, a forty-day air war against Iraq, bombing military targets, power plants, oil refineries, and transportation networks. Having severely crippled Iraq, the coalition stormed into Kuwait with massive ground forces on February 23, and within one hundred hours Hussein announced that he would withdraw from Kuwait (see Map 31.2).

"By God, we've kicked the Vietnam syndrome once and for all," President Bush exulted on March 1. Most Americans found no moral ambiguity in the Persian Gulf War and took pride in the display of military competence. In contrast to the loss of 50,000 American lives in Vietnam, 270 U.S. servicemen and women perished in Desert Storm. The United States stood at the apex of global leadership, steering a coalition in which Arab nations fought beside their former colonial rulers.

Yet victory did not bring stability to the Middle East. Israel, which had endured Iraqi missile attacks, was more secure, but the Israeli-Palestinian conflict remained intractable. Despite military losses, Saddam Hussein remained in power and turned his war machine on Iraqi Kurds and Shiite Muslims whom the United States had encouraged to rebel. Hussein continued to develop chemical, biological, and nuclear weapons, while Iraqi citizens suffered malnutrition, disease, and death caused by the continuing embargo and the destruction of the nation's fuel, communications, and transportation systems.

The 1992 Election

Despite ongoing instability in the Middle East, in March 1991 Bush's chances for reelection in 1992 looked golden. The Gulf War victory catapulted his approval rating to 88 percent, causing the most prominent Democrats to opt out of the presidential race. But that did not deter William Jefferson "Bill" Clinton, who at age forty-five had served as governor of Arkansas for twelve years. Like Jimmy Carter in 1976 and Michael Dukakis in 1988, Clinton and his running mate, Tennessee senator Albert Gore Jr., presented themselves as "New Democrats." Both belonged to the Democratic Leadership Council, which Clinton had helped found in 1985 to rid the party of its liberal image.

In an approach reminiscent of Richard Nixon's appeal to the "silent majority" in 1968, Clinton promised to work for the "forgotten middle class," who "do the work, pay the taxes, raise the kids, and play by the rules." Clinton deliberately distanced himself from Jesse Jackson and his Rainbow Coalition and appealed to voters who believed that some Americans were getting a free ride at their expense. "We're going to put an end to welfare as we know it," Clinton claimed. Disavowing the "tax and spend" label that Republicans pinned on his party, he promised a tax cut for the middle class and pledged to reinvigorate government and the economy.

With no new crises to display his talents in foreign policy, Bush was vulnerable to voters' concerns about the economy. As foreign competition drove businesses to trim budgets, victims of corporate downsizing worried about finding new jobs while other workers worried about keeping theirs. Unemployment edged over 7 percent in 1992. A sign at Clinton headquarters

insisting "It's the economy, stupid" reflected the campaign's focus on bread-and-butter issues.

The popularity of a third candidate revealed Americans' frustrations with government and the major parties. In announcing his candidacy on the popular TV talk show *Larry King Live*, self-made Texas billionaire H. Ross Perot set the tone of his unconventional campaign. Although he gave no press conferences, he had plenty of money, used television extensively, and attracted a sizable grassroots movement with his down-to-earth personality and appeals to voters' disgust with Washington. Perot's candidacy hurt the president more than it hurt Clinton, and it established the federal budget deficit as a key campaign issue.

Fifty-five percent of those eligible showed up at the polls, just barely reversing the thirty-year decline in voter turnout. Americans gave Clinton 43 percent of their votes, Bush 38 percent, and Perot 19 percent—the strongest third-party finish since Theodore Roosevelt's Progressive Party candidacy in 1912. Although casting two-thirds of their votes against Bush

Clinton and Gore on Tour

The gregarious Bill Clinton excelled at political campaigning, and the youth of the first baby-boomer candidates appealed to many. During the 1992 presidential election campaign, Clinton and his wife, Hillary—accompanied by running mate Al Gore and his wife, Tipper—went out on several bus tours as a way of demonstrating the Democrats' connection to ordinary people. Not far from this campaign stop in Sylvester, Georgia, the bus caravan passed by a handmade sign that read "Bubbas for Clinton/Gore."

© Ira Wyman/Sygma/Corbis.

demonstrated a mandate for change, voters formed no majority around a particular direction that change should take.

The Clinton Administration's Search for the Middle Ground

The president who asserted "The era of big government is over" was not Ronald Reagan but Bill Clinton, reflecting the Democratic Party's move to the right that had begun with Jimmy Carter in the 1970s. Clinton did not completely abandon the principles that had guided the party in the 1960s. He signed important measures benefiting the working poor, delivered incremental reforms to feminists, environmentalists, and other groups, and spoke out in favor of affirmative action and gay rights. Yet his administration attended more to the concerns of middle-class Americans than to the needs of the poor and restrained federal programs and appropriations for the disadvantaged.

> The Clinton administration attended more to the concerns of middle-class Americans than to the needs of the poor and restrained federal programs and appropriations for the disadvantaged.

The Clinton administration ended its eight years with a surplus in the federal budget and the longest economic boom in history. Although various factors generated the prosperity, many Americans identified Clinton with the buoyant economy, returned him to office for a second term, and continued to support him even when his reckless sexual behavior resulted in **impeachment**. Although the Senate did not find sufficient cause to remove him from office, the scandal crippled Clinton's leadership in his last years in office.

Clinton's Promise of Change

Clinton wanted to restore confidence in government as a force for good but avoid alienating antigovernment voters by proposing new large federal programs, and in any case, the budget deficit—$4.4 trillion in 1993—precluded such spending. Just as Clinton was short on cash for using government in positive ways, he also lacked political capital, for the Republicans controlled Congress for all but his first two years in office. Moreover, the end of the cold war de-prived the president of a national agenda around which to unite Americans and eliminated the rationale that domestic reform was necessary to combat communism abroad.

The popular mandate for change, nonetheless, allowed the New Democrat president to exert some federal authority to solve national problems. Using his executive powers to reverse Reagan and Bush policies, Clinton eased restrictions on abortion and signed several bills that Republicans had previously blocked. In 1993, Congress enacted gun control legislation; a $30 billion anticrime program; and the Family and Medical Leave Act, which enabled workers in larger companies to take time off for childbirth, adoption, and family medical emergencies. The Violence against Women Act of 1994 authorized $1.6 billion and new remedies for combating sexual assault and domestic violence. Clinton vetoed measures that would have weakened environmental standards, and he achieved stricter air pollution controls and protection for wilderness areas, national forests, and national parks. Other liberal measures of the Clinton administration included an increase of the minimum wage, expansion of aid to low- and moderate-income college students, and creation of AmeriCorps, a program enabling students to pay for their education with community service. "I know that I have made a difference in my community and the individuals that live in it," Maria Moore reported proudly after working on a neighborhood development project in Mesa, Arizona. Others helped to meet needs in education, housing, health, and the environment; and when fires raged through southern California in October 2003, dozens of AmeriCorps members helped feed firefighters and set up shelters for people driven from their homes.

Most significantly, to fulfill his campaign promise that no full-time worker should live in poverty, Clinton pushed through a substantial increase in the Earned Income Tax Credit (EITC) for low wage earners, a program begun in 1975. EITC gave tax reductions to people who worked full-time at meager wages or, if they paid no taxes, a government subsidy to lift their family income above the poverty line. By 2000, 15 million low-income families were benefiting from EITC, almost one-half of them minorities. One expert called it "the largest antipoverty program since the Great Society."

Even before Clinton took office, the economy had begun to rebound, and the boom that followed helped boost his popularity through the 1990s. Economic expansion, along with budget cuts, tax increases, and declining unemployment, reduced the federal budget deficit by about half between 1992 and 1996 and in 1998 produced the first surplus since 1969. Despite the biggest tax cut since 1981—a 1997 law reducing levies on estates and capital gains and providing tax credits for families with children and for higher education—the surplus grew. The seemingly inexorable growth of government debt had turned around.

Clinton stumbled badly, however, over an ambitious health care reform plan to provide universal coverage that would have included the 39 million Americans without health insurance and to curb steeply rising medical costs. Under the direction of First Lady Hillary Rodham Clinton, the administration presented a complex bill that much of the health care industry charged would mean higher taxes and government interference in health care decisions. Although the bill failed, Congress did enact piecemeal reform by enabling workers who changed jobs to retain health insurance and by passing a new health care program for 5 million uninsured children. Yet the number of uninsured Americans surpassed 40 million, about 15 percent of the population, in 2004; and health care became an even more critical issue in the twenty-first century.

Changing the Face of Government

Along with promoting a more active federal government, Clinton wanted to choose his appointments to create a government that "looked like America." In so doing, he built on the gradual progress made by women and minorities during the previous decades. By 1990, more than 7,000 African Americans held public office, an increase of nearly 50 percent from 1980. Cities registered the most impressive gains. Black mayors presided over Atlanta, Chicago, Los Angeles, Philadelphia, and other large cities. David Dinkins's election as mayor of New York City in 1989 epitomized the rise of black leaders even among predominantly white electorates. The presidential campaigns of Jesse Jackson in 1984 and 1988 inspired African Americans and demonstrated white willingness to support a minority candidate. In 1989, Democrat L. Douglas Wilder of Virginia became the first black governor since Reconstruction, joining the only Hispanic governor, Republican Bob Martinez of Florida. Women similarly had been edging slowly into the corridors of political power. By the end of the 1980s, they had made their marks as governors of Kentucky, Vermont, and Nebraska; and several large cities boasted women mayors, including Jane Byrne of Chicago and Dianne Feinstein of San Francisco, who later became one of California's two female senators.

In the executive branch, Clinton appointed the most diverse group of department heads ever assembled. Of twenty-three key appointments, six were women, three African American, and two Latino; as Secretary of Commerce he chose the first Asian American to serve in the cabinet, Norman Y. Mineta, who had spent part of his childhood in a Japanese American internment camp. Janet Reno became the first female attorney general, and Madeleine K. Albright the first female secretary of state. Clinton's judicial appointments had a similar cast. Of his first 129 appointments to federal courts, nearly one-third were women, 31 were black, and 11 were Hispanic. In June 1993, he appointed the second woman to the Supreme Court, Ruth Bader Ginsburg, a self-identified feminist who had planned legal strategy and won key women's rights rulings from the Supreme Court before she became an appeals court judge in 1980.

The appointments of Clinton's successor, George W. Bush, would continue to reflect diversity in the highest levels of the executive branch. He chose Colin Powell for secretary of state and appointed African American Condoleezza Rice as his national security adviser. Five of his top-level appointees were women, including Secretary of Labor Elaine L. Chao, the first Asian American woman to serve in the cabinet; and Housing and Urban Development secretary Mel Martinez was a Latino. Gains for women and minorities came more slowly in Congress. When the 107th Congress convened in January 2001, two Asian Americans and one American Indian were the only ethnic minorities in the Senate. Thirty-six African Americans served in the 435-member House of Representatives, along with nineteen Hispanics and four Asian Americans. Women held seventy-two seats in Congress, 13.5 percent of the total, and less than in nearly every European assembly. One of these was Hillary Rodham Clinton, the new senator from New York and the first First Lady to run for political office.

> The number of uninsured Americans surpassed 40 million, about 15 percent of the population, in 2000; and health care became an even more critical issue in the twenty-first century.

The Clinton Administration Moves Right

While parts of Clinton's agenda sustained the traditional Democratic turn to government to help the disadvantaged, his presidency in general moved the party to the right. The 1994 elections swept away the Democratic majorities in both houses of Congress and contributed to Clinton's embrace of Republican issues such as reforming welfare and downsizing government. Led by Representative Newt Gingrich of Georgia, Republicans considered the 1994 elections a mandate for their "contract with America," a conservative platform that included drastic contraction of the federal government, deep tax cuts, and a constitutional amendment to ban abortions. Opposition from Democrats and more moderate Republicans stymied most of the contract pledges, but Gingrich succeeded in moving the debate to the right.

Far from Washington, a more extreme antigovernment movement emerged in the form of grassroots armed militias claiming the need to defend themselves from government tyranny. Anticipating government repression, they stockpiled, according to one militia leader, "the four Bs: Bibles, bullets, beans, and bandages," and they embraced a variety of sentiments including opposition to taxes, to gun control, and to the United Nations, and a defense of white Christian supremacy. Their ranks grew with passage of gun control legislation and after government agents stormed the headquarters of an armed religious cult in Waco, Texas, in April 1993, resulting in more than 80 deaths. On the second anniversary of that event, in the worst terrorist attack in the nation's history up to then, a bomb leveled a federal building in Oklahoma City, taking 169 lives. Authorities quickly arrested two militia members, who were tried and convicted in 1997.

Clinton bowed to conservative views on issues relating to homosexual rights. In 1993, opposition from military leaders, including his chairman of the Joint Chiefs of Staff, Colin Powell, enlisted men, and key legislators, caused him to back away from a campaign promise to lift the ban on homosexuals in the military. Instead, he announced the "don't ask, don't tell" policy, forbidding officials from asking military personnel about their sexuality but allowing dismissal of men and women who admitted they were gay or engaged in homosexual behavior. According to Cathleen Glover, who was discharged for being a lesbian, "The military preaches integrity, integrity, integrity but asks you to lie to everyone around you." What began as an effort to promote tolerance ended in a 67 percent jump in discharges of gay men and lesbians. In 1996, Clinton also signed the Defense of Marriage Act, prohibiting the federal government from recognizing state-licensed marriages between same-sex couples.

Clinton's determination to cast himself as a centrist was nowhere more apparent than in his handling of welfare reform. Since Lyndon Johnson's War on Poverty in the 1960s (see chapter 28), public sentiment had shifted. Instead of blaming poverty on a shortage of adequate jobs, poor education, and other external circumstances, more people were inclined to place responsibility on the poor themselves and on government welfare programs, which they charged kept people in cycles of dependency. Nearly everyone considered work better than welfare but disagreed about whether the economy could provide sufficient jobs at decent wages and how much government assistance poor people needed in the transition from welfare to work. Most estimates showed that it cost less to support a family on welfare than to provide job training, child care, and other supports necessary for that transition.

Clinton vetoed two measures on welfare reform, thereby forcing a less punitive bill, which he signed as the 1996 election approached. The Personal Responsibility and Work Opportunity Reconciliation Act abolished Aid to Families with Dependent Children (AFDC) and with it the nation's pledge to provide a minimum level of subsistence for all its children. In place of AFDC, the law authorized grants to the states along with two-year limits on welfare payments whether or not the recipient could find a job. The law set a lifetime limit of aid at five years, barred legal immigrants who had not become citizens from obtaining food stamps and other benefits, and allowed states to stop Medicaid to legal immigrants.

A "moment of shame," cried Marian Wright Edelman, president of the Children's Defense Fund, when Clinton signed the bill. State and local officials across the country scrambled to understand the law and how to implement it. "We certainly endorse the overall direction toward work," a Minnesota official said, while ex-

> Clinton's determination to cast himself as a centrist was nowhere more apparent than in his handling of welfare reform.

pressing grave concern about how the law would operate. "A child could very well have to go to foster care," predicted a Louisiana social worker. Critics proved wrong in their most severe predictions. By 2000, welfare rolls had been cut nearly in half, and because of the strong economy the poverty rate fell to 11.4 percent, its lowest in more than two decades. That did not mean, however, that all former welfare recipients were now self-supporting. Forty percent of former welfare mothers were not working regularly after being cut from the rolls, and those with jobs earned on average only about $12,000 a year.

Clinton's signature on the new law denied the Republicans a partisan issue. In the 1996 election campaign, the president ran as a moderate who would save the country from extremist Republicans. In fact, the Republican Party also moved to the center, passing over a field of conservatives to nominate Kansan Robert Dole, a World War II hero and former Senate majority leader who had served in Washington for more than two decades.

Whether out of satisfaction with a favorable economy or boredom with the candidates, about half of the electorate stayed home. Fifty percent of voters chose Clinton, while 41 percent favored Dole, and 9 percent Perot, who ran again as a third-party candidate. The largest **gender gap** to date appeared in the election: Women gave 54 percent of their votes to Clinton and 38 percent to Dole, while men split their votes nearly evenly. Although Clinton won reelection with room to spare, voters sent a Republican majority back to Congress.

Impeaching the President

Clinton's ability to capture the middle ground of the electorate, along with the nation's economic resurgence, enabled the self-proclaimed "comeback kid" to survive scandals and an impeachment trial in 1998. Early in the first Clinton administration, charges of illegalities related to firings of White House staff, political use of FBI records, and the Clintons' involvement in a real estate deal in Arkansas nicknamed "Whitewater" led to an official investigation by an independent prosecutor. Clinton also faced a sexual harassment lawsuit filed in 1994 by a state employee, who asserted that in 1991 the Arkansas governor had made unwanted sexual advances. A federal court threw out her suit in April 1998, but Clinton's sexual recklessness continued to threaten his presidency.

Clinton's Impeachment

This cartoon expresses the consternation of Republicans when President Clinton's approval ratings remained high despite the revelation of his affair with Monica Lewinsky and his subsequent impeachment. Many Americans, though not condoning the president's behavior, separated what they considered his private actions from his public duties and criticized prosecutor Kenneth Starr and the Republicans for not doing the same.

In January 1998, independent prosecutor Kenneth Starr, who had taken over the Whitewater probe in 1994, began to investigate the most inflammatory charge—that Clinton had had sexual relations with a twenty-one-year-old White House intern, Monica Lewinsky, and then lied about it to a federal grand jury. Clinton first vehemently denied the charge but subsequently bowed to the mounting evidence against him. Starr took his case for impeachment to the House of Representatives, which in December 1998 voted, mostly along party lines, to impeach the president on two counts: perjury and obstruction of justice. Clinton became the second president—after Andrew Johnson, in 1868—to be impeached by the House and tried by the Senate.

Most Americans believed that the president had acted inappropriately with Lewinsky, yet they continued to approve his presidency and to oppose impeachment. Some saw Starr as a fanatic invading individuals' privacy; most people separated what they considered the president's private actions from his public duties. One man said, "Let him get a divorce from his wife. Don't take him out of office and disrupt the country." Those favoring impeachment insisted that the president was not above the law, that he must set a high moral standard for the nation, and that lying to a grand jury, even over a private matter, was a serious offense.

The Senate conducted the impeachment trial with much less partisanship than that displayed in the House. A number of senators believed that Clinton had committed perjury and obstruction of justice but did not find those actions to constitute the high crimes and misdemeanors required by the Constitution for his removal. With a two-thirds majority needed for that result, the Senate voted 45 to 55 on the perjury count and 50 to 50 on the obstruction of justice count. A majority of senators, including some Republicans, seemed to agree with a Clinton advocate that the president's behavior, while "indefensible, outrageous, unforgivable, shameless," was insufficient to warrant his removal from office.

The investigation that triggered events leading up to impeachment culminated in 2000 with the independent counsel's finding of insufficient evidence that the Clintons disobeyed the law in the Whitewater land deals. The investigation had lasted six years and cost almost $60 million of federal funds. In the face of widespread dissatisfaction with Whitewater and other investigations by special prosecutors, Congress let the independent counsel act expire in 1998.

The Booming Economy of the 1990s

Clinton's ability to weather the impeachment crisis drew incalculable help from the prosperous economy, which took off in 1991 and began the longest period of economic growth in U.S. history. During the 1990s, the gross domestic product grew by more than one-third, thirteen million new jobs were created, unemployment reached its lowest point in twenty-five years, inflation remained in check, and the stock market soared.

Clinton eagerly took credit for the thriving economy, and his policies did contribute to the boom. He made deficit reduction a priority, and in exchange the Federal Reserve Board and bond market traders lowered interest rates, which in turn encouraged economic expansion by making money easier to borrow. Businesses also prospered because they had squeezed down their costs through restructuring

> Clinton's ability to weather the impeachment crisis drew incalculable help from the prosperous economy, which took off in 1991 and began the longest period of economic growth in U.S. history.

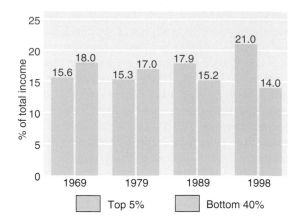

FIGURE 31.1   The Growth of Inequality: Changes in Family Income, 1969–1998
For most of the post–World War II period, income increased for all groups on the economic ladder. But after 1979, the income of the poorest families actually declined, while the income of the richest 20 percent of the population grew substantially.

and laying off workers. Economic problems in Europe and Asia helped American firms become more competitive in the international market. Above all, the computer revolution and the application of information technology to the production and distribution of goods and services tremendously boosted productivity. By the end of the century, half the workforce used computers on the job.

People at all income levels benefited from the economic boom, but it had uneven effects. In contrast to the economic expansion of the 1950s and 1960s, gaps between rich and poor and between the rich and the middle class that had been growing since the 1970s failed to narrow (Figure 31.1). This persistence of inequality in a rising economy was linked in part to what fueled the boom—the growing use of information technology, which increased demand for highly skilled workers while the movement of manufacturing jobs abroad lessened opportunities and wages for those not trained in the requisite skills. In addition, deregulation, globalization, and the continuing decline of unions hurt lower-skilled workers, and the national minimum wage failed to keep up with inflation.

Although more minorities than ever attained middle-class status, in general people of color remained lowest on the economic ladder. Reflecting Colin Powell's observation that "race still casts a shadow over our society," when the median income for white families surpassed

$44,000 in 2001, it stood at just $29,500 and $33,565 for African American and Hispanic American households, respectively. Overall, median family income for Asian Americans surpassed that of whites, but only because Asian families had more wage earners. In 2001, poverty afflicted about 23 percent of blacks and Latinos and 25 percent of American Indians, more than double the white rate of 10 percent.

The United States in a Globalizing World

America's economic success in the 1990s was linked to its dominance in the world economy. From that position, President Clinton tried to shape the tremendous economic transformations occurring in a process that came to be called globalization, the growing integration and interdependence of national citizens and economies. His administration lowered a number of barriers that impeded trade across national borders, but it also faced stiff opposition from those who pointed out the economic deprivation and environmental devastation that often resulted from the liberalization of international trade.

In contrast to his clear vision about the U.S. role in the global economy, Clinton and his advisers seemed less certain about the use of military and diplomatic power. Clinton took military action in Somalia, Haiti, the Middle East, and eastern Europe, and he pushed hard to ease the conflict between Israel and the Palestinians. Yet no new global strategy emerged to replace **containment** of communism as the decisive factor in the exercise of American power abroad.

Defining America's Place in a New World Order

In 1991, President George H. W. Bush had declared a "new world order" emerging from the ashes of the cold war. As the sole superpower, the United States was determined to lead the nations of the world and serve as its model of freedom and **democracy**. Without the overarching goal of containing communism, however, policymakers struggled to define a guiding principle that would determine where and how the nation would use its military and diplomatic power in a post–cold war world of some 190 nations. Acting in the face of Saddam Hussein's naked aggres-

sion and threat to vital oil reserves seemed the obvious course to Bush and his advisers in 1991. Determining the appropriate action in other areas of instability, however, proved much more difficult, and the United States under both Bush and Clinton applied its force inconsistently throughout the 1990s.

Africa was a case in point, where civil wars, famine, and extreme human suffering rarely evoked a strong American response. Bush had ended economic sanctions against South Africa in 1991, as it began to recognize the rights of its black majority. In 1994, that nation elected its first black president, Nelson Mandela, who had spent twenty-seven years in prison for fighting apartheid. Guided largely by humanitarian concern, in 1992 President Bush had attached U.S. forces to a U.N. operation in the small northern African country of Somalia, where famine and civil war raged. In 1993, when President Clinton allowed the humanitarian mission to turn into "nation building"—an effort to establish a stable government— eighteen U.S. soldiers were killed. The outcry at home suggested that most Americans were unwilling to sacrifice lives when no vital economic or political interest seemed threatened. Indeed, both the United States and the United Nations stood by in 1994 when more than a half million people were massacred in a brutal civil war in the central African nation of Rwanda.

> Without the overarching goal of containing communism, policymakers struggled to define a guiding principle that would determine where and how the nation would use its military and diplomatic power in a post–cold war world of some 190 nations.

As always, the United States was more inclined to use force nearer its borders, but it did so in the case of Haiti as part of an international effort. When a military coup overthrew their democratically elected president, Jean-Bertrand Aristide, thousands of Haitians tried to escape political violence and poverty, many on flimsy boats heading for Florida. With anti-immigrant sentiment already high in the nation, President Clinton was pressed hard to stop the refugee flow. (See "Historical Question," page 1156.) He got the United Nations to impose economic sanctions on Haiti, and when that failed, Clinton threatened the military regime with a UN-authorized intervention of U.S. troops. In September 1994, hours before 20,000 troops were to invade Haiti, the military leaders promised to step down. U.S. forces peacefully landed and began disarming Haitian troops, and Aristide was

Still a Promised Land?

"The United States is our land. . . . We intend to maintain it so. The day of unalloyed welcome to all peoples, the day of indiscriminate acceptance of all races, has definitely ended." So spoke Washington senator Albert Johnson in 1924, just after Congress severely limited immigration with passage of the National Origins Act, which Johnson had sponsored. Thereafter, immigration, which had forcefully shaped American society since its beginning, ebbed for several decades as the restrictive law combined with the Great Depression and World War II to discourage potential newcomers. In fact, during the worst years of the depression, more people abandoned the United States than chose to migrate there. Yet the immigration question had not been finally settled. By the 1980s, large numbers of immigrants once more were entering the United States, reigniting old debates about whether Americans should share their promise of political freedom and economic opportunity with people from other lands.

What reopened the door to immigration after World War II? Economic considerations always loomed large in prompting migration to the United States and in determining how welcome immigrants would be: The twenty-five-year economic boom that followed World War II exerted a positive force on both ends. In fact, until 1964 the U.S. government actively encouraged the temporary migration of Mexicans by continuing the so-called *bracero program* begun during World War II to fill a shortage of agricultural workers. Hundreds of thousands of

Mexicans established social networks in the United States and grew accustomed to crossing the border for jobs, even when the jobs were backbreaking and low paying by U.S. standards. When the *bracero* program ended, many Mexicans continued to come north for work, with or without legal authorization.

In addition to a prosperous economy, a growing tolerance toward people of different races and ethnic groups in the decades following World War II contributed to the increase in immigration. Like the key civil rights laws passed around the same time, the Immigration Act of 1965 reflected a belief that people should be treated as individuals rather than as members of a particular group. The new immigration law ended the national quotas that were so insulting to non–Western European groups, although it for the first time placed limits on newcomers from the Western Hemisphere. It made possible a tremendous rise in the volume of immigration and facilitated a huge increase in migrants from Asia and Latin America, a result that the law's sponsors did not anticipate.

The 1965 law set an annual ceiling of 270,000, but the actual volume was much higher. Besides those who came illegally, hundreds of thousands fell into special categories that gained them legal admission above and beyond the limit. In 1986, for example, the United States admitted 335,000 immigrants over the ceiling; about two-thirds of these were children, spouses, or parents of U.S. citizens, and the rest were political refugees and asylum seekers. Migration chains were thus estab-

lished by which, once newcomers became citizens, their sisters, brothers, and adult children received special preference, while even closer relatives gained entry without regard to the limit.

The new waves of immigration also grew directly from foreign policy after World War II. The cold war spread U.S. military and other personnel throughout the world, enabling foreigners to learn about the United States and make personal contacts with Americans. Once the cold war identified communism as an unmitigated evil, the United States could hardly refuse asylum to its enemy's victims. In the twenty-five years following Fidel Castro's revolution in 1959, for example, more than 800,000 Cubans fled to the United States. The Vietnam War and its aftermath brought more than 600,000 Vietnamese, Laotians, and Cambodians in the decade following 1974.

Not all refugees entered the United States so easily, for refugee policy bore a distinct anti-Communist bias. Haitians, Salvadorans, and others fleeing right-wing dictatorships were frequently turned back or, having reached the United States, were denied asylum and deported. "Why let Poles stay but not Salvadorans?" demanded one advocate for these refugees, pointing out the more favorable treatment given to immigrants from Communist countries.

Even though U.S. policy failed to accommodate all who wanted to immigrate, by the 1980s immigration was once more a major force in American society. During that decade, the 6 million legal and estimated 2 million undocumented immigrants accounted for more than one-third of total population growth. Seventy-five percent of the immigrants settled in just seven states,

Cuban Refugees
These Cubans are being towed by the U.S. Coast Guard into port at Miami, Florida. Their desire for the expected economic opportunity and political freedom of the United States is evinced in their willingness to flee Cuba on a crowded, makeshift vessel. Some "boat people" drowned in these risky ventures.
Jon Kral/Miami Herald.

with California, New York, Texas, and Florida receiving the most. After the 1990 census, California won five additional seats in the House of Representatives solely on the basis of immigrant additions to the population. A 1983 *Time* magazine article called Los Angeles "the new Ellis Island" because of its large Asian and Hispanic populations.

The higher volume of immigration, its **third world** sources, and the economy's recession combined to reactivate nativist sentiment in the 1980s. Increasingly, Americans saw immigrants as taking jobs from the native-born and acting as a drain on schools, health care, police, and other services; and Congress sought to reduce illegal immigration with the Immigration Reform and Control Act of 1986. In the 1990s, anti-immigrant sentiment grew especially strong in California, then reeling from an economic slump owing to the downsiz-

ing of defense production. That state took in more than one-third of the nation's immigrants in the 1980s and an estimated one-half of the undocumented ones. Congress reflected national anti-immigrant feelings by restricting health care, food stamps, and other benefits to immigrants in the welfare reform legislation of 1996.

Greatest hostility focused on people who entered without legal documentation, a phenomenon that the 1986 law penalizing employers of such people had not significantly curtailed. Some states, including California, Florida, and New Jersey, filed lawsuits charging the federal government with failure to stop the flow of illegal immigration and suing for the costs it added to state budgets. In 1994, California voters passed a referendum that barred the children of illegal immigrants from attending public schools, although the courts later ruled it unconstitutional.

Economic and political crises elsewhere and the continuing appeal of the United States meant that high levels of immigration—legal and illegal—persisted into the twenty-first century. Anti-immigrant sentiment diminished somewhat as jobs became plentiful during the spectacular economic boom at the end of the twentieth century. The chief executive of a semiconductor firm who filled more than one-third of his administrative and engineering positions with immigrants, lashed out at restrictionist legislators: "They want to send back the first-round draft choices of the intellectual world so that they can compete against us in their homelands."

The terrorist attacks in 2001, by contrast, made things more difficult for immigrants, especially Muslims or those who looked as though they might be Muslims. Seeking to deter terrorists, the Immigration and Naturalization Service increased border surveillance and required documentation that complicated the application process for visas, for example, increasing the obstacles to foreign students who wanted to attend American colleges. Moreover, the pendulum of anti-immigrant sentiment swung back again with the recession that began in 2001 and saw the loss of 2.6 million jobs. Still, there seemed no end to the desires of people around the world to enjoy the economic opportunity and freedoms of the United States. America entered the twenty-first century as it had the twentieth, with a rapidly diversifying society, continuing to make itself, as sociologist Nathan Glazer put it, a "permanently unfinished country."

restored to power. Initially a huge success, U.S. policy would continue to be tested as Haiti faced grave economic and political challenges and a new rebellion in 2004.

In eastern Europe, the collapse of communism ignited the most severe crisis on the continent since the 1940s. During the cold war, the Communist government of Yugoslavia, a federation of six republics, had held ethnic tensions in check, and many Muslims, Croats, and Serbs had grown accustomed to living and working together. After the Communists were swept out in 1989, Yugoslavia splintered into separate states and fell into civil war as ruthless leaders exploited ethnic differences to bolster their power. The Serbs' aggression against the Bosnian Muslims in particular horrified much of the world.

As reports of terror, rape, and torture in Bosnia increased, American leaders worried about the image of the world's strongest nation unwilling to use its power to stop the violence. In November 1995, the United States brought the leaders of Serbia, Croatia, and Bosnia to Dayton, Ohio, where they hammered out a peace treaty. President Clinton then agreed to send 20,000 American troops to Bosnia as part of a NATO peacekeeping mission.

In 1998, new fighting broke out in the southern Serbian province of Kosovo, where ethnic Albanians, who constituted 90 percent of the population, were making a bid for independence. The Serbian army brutally retaliated, driving out one-third of Kosovo's 1.8 million Albanian Muslims. When Serbian president Slobodan Milosevic refused to agree to a peace settlement in 1999, NATO launched a U.S.-led bombing attack on Serbian military and government targets. Three months of bombing forced Serbia to agree to a settlement. Serbians voted Milosevic out of office in October 2000, and he was brought before an international tribunal in 2002 for genocide.

Breakup of Yugoslavia

President Clinton was less hesitant to deploy American power when he could send missiles rather than men and women, and he also proved willing to act without international support or UN sanction. In August 1998, bombs exploded in U.S. embassies in Kenya and Tanzania, killing 12 Americans and more than 250 Africans. In response, Clinton ordered missile attacks on terrorist training camps in Afghanistan and facilities in Sudan controlled by Osama bin Laden, a Saudi-born millionaire who financed an Islamic-extremist terrorist network and had directed the embassy bombings.

A few months later, in December 1998, Clinton launched air strikes against Iraqi military installations. At the end of the Gulf War in 1991, Saddam Hussein had agreed to eliminate Iraq's chemical, germ, and nuclear weapons and to allow UN inspections. But he resisted full compliance with the agreement and tried to block inspection officials, prompting the U.S. attacks. Whereas Bush had acted in the Gulf War with the support of an international force that included Arab states, Clinton acted unilaterally and in the face of Arab opposition.

Elsewhere in the Middle East, Clinton used diplomatic rather than military power, continuing the decades-long efforts to ameliorate the Israeli-Palestinian conflict. In 1993, Yasir Arafat, head of the Palestine Liberation Organization (PLO), and Yitzhak Rabin, Israeli prime minister, for the first time recognized the existence of the other's state and agreed to Israeli withdrawal from and Palestinian self-government in the Gaza Strip and Jericho. Less than a year later, in July 1994, Clinton presided over another turning point as Rabin and King Hussein of Jordan signed a declaration of peace. Yet obdurate issues remained to be settled: control of Jerusalem, with sites sacred to Christians, Jews, and Muslims alike; the fate of Palestinian refugees; and the more than 200,000 Israeli settlers living in the West

Events in Israel since 1989

1993 – Israel and PLO sign accords.
1994 – Israel and Jordan sign peace treaty.
1995 – Rabin assassinated.
2000 – Progress of Israeli-Palestinian negotiations halts and violence escalates.
2003 – Bush proposes road map for peace in Israel.

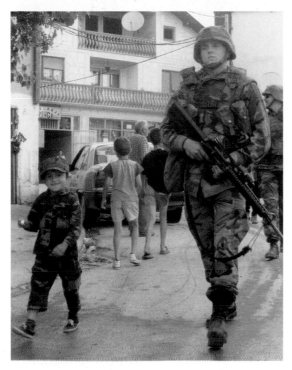

U.S. Troops in Kosovo

In 1999, American troops joined a NATO peacekeeping unit in the former Yugoslav province of Kosovo after a U.S.-led NATO bombing campaign forced the Serbian army to withdraw. The NATO soldiers were dispatched to monitor the departure of Serbian troops, assist the return of ethnic Albanians who had fled the Serb army, and reestablish civil governments. Here, an ethnic Albanian boy walks beside Specialist Brent Baldwin from Jonesville, Michigan, as he patrols the town of Gnjilane in southeast Kosovo in May 2000.

Wide World Photos, Inc.

Bank, the land seized by Israel in 1967, where 3 million Palestinians were determined to establish their own state. Negotiations between the two parties broke down in 2000, and violence between Israelis and Palestinians consumed the area. A year after the George W. Bush administration proposed a "roadmap" to peace in April 2003, casualties continued to mount on both sides.

Debates over Globalization

Although the Clinton administration sometimes seemed uncertain about the use of military force, it moved energetically on the economic side to speed up the growth of a "global marketplace." The process of globalization had begun in the fifteenth century, when Europeans began to trade with and populate other parts of the world.

Between the U.S. Civil War and World War I, the flow of products, capital, and labor crossed national boundaries in ever larger numbers. In that era, globalization was based on **imperialism**, as Western nations took direct control of foreign territories, extracted their natural resources, and restricted manufacturing.

In contrast, late-twentieth-century globalization advanced among sovereign nations and involved the industrialization of less developed areas, such as Korea and China. Other distinguishing marks of the more recent globalization were its scope and intensity: The Internet, cell phones, and other new communications technology connected nations, corporations, and individuals—nearly the entire planet—at much greater speed and much less cost than at any previous time (see "The Promise of Technology," page 1160).

As Clinton worked to diminish impediments to the free flow of products and capital across national borders, debates over globalization in the United States and elsewhere raged over which trade barriers to eliminate and under what conditions. In a world economy characterized by **laissez-faire** capitalism, who would protect workers' health and security, human rights, and the environment?

Tens of thousands of activists dramatized the debate when they assembled in Seattle, Washington, in November 1999 to protest at a meeting of the World Trade Organization (WTO), an international economic body established in 1994 to liberalize trading policies and practices and mediate economic disputes between some 135 member nations. Most of the demonstrators marched peacefully, but police used tear gas and arrested hundreds who practiced civil disobedience and blocked traffic. Activists charged the WTO with promoting a global economy that undercut standards and wages for workers, destroyed the environment, and devastated poorer, developing nations. These protesters reflected new alliances: Referring to some environmentalists dressed as sea turtles, an endangered species, one sign read, "Teamsters and Turtles—Together at Last." Gauging the profound impact of the demonstrations, California state senator Tom Hayden, the former student radical from the 1960s, proclaimed, "These protests have made WTO a household word."

Tico Almeida, a new college graduate, was thrilled in Seattle to hear "workers and unions from rich and poor countries alike stand together

The Internet

The network that links millions of computers throughout the world began to alter the lives of millions of Americans in the 1990s. Just 313,000 computers were linked to the Internet in 1990; six years later, 10 million were connected. By the year 2000, a majority of Americans logged on to the Internet at home or at work to e-mail coworkers, friends, and relatives, shop, chat with strangers around the world, listen to music, play games, buy and sell stocks, do homework assignments, and more.

Like many technological innovations of the post–World War II era, the Internet was a product of government funding inspired by the cold war. Shortly after the Soviets launched *Sputnik*, in 1958 President Eisenhower created the Advanced Research Projects Agency (ARPA) to push research on technology. In 1969, the U.S. Department of Defense established ARPANET, which developed a system called packet switching, a technology first invented by MIT graduate student Leonard Kleinrock to route digitized messages between computers. Not only would such a system be able to handle vast amounts of information—allowing many users to share computers and communications lines—but it would provide security for military secrets and enable communication to continue even if some computers were damaged by an enemy attack. By 1971, ARPANET linked twenty-three computers, most of them at research universities.

Universities and research centers rushed to join ARPANET, but some were turned down because the military restricted access for security reasons. New networks soon developed, and the military created its own separate network in 1982. Meanwhile, the National Science Foundation (NSF) took over much of the technology and sponsored development of a civilian "backbone network" called NSFNET. With technology developed under ARPA, disparate networks could now connect with one another through Transmission Control Protocol/Internet Protocol (TCP/IP), or sets of instructions that translated each network's system for other networks' systems. In 1980, fewer than 200 networks were connected, but by 1988 what had come to be called the Internet connected more than 50,000 host computers.

Electronic mail had not been on the minds of defense officials when they developed packet switching, but it quickly surpassed all other forms of traffic on ARPANET. It was much faster than "snail mail," the scornful term computer users applied to mail sent via the postal service, and it was much cheaper than long-distance telephone conversations. Moreover, two people could communicate on the same day without having to be at their phones at the same time, and they could do so easily across different time zones.

As ownership of personal computers spread, people not only exchanged e-mail but also began to put entire documents on the Net. Two key inventions helped users to find and retrieve such material. In 1991, researchers at the University of Minnesota launched a retrieval system called "gopher," a slang term for one who fetches things and also the university's mascot. Then came the World Wide Web, first proposed in 1989 by researchers at a physics institute in Geneva, Switzerland. Through the Web, users gained access to billions of documents connected to each other by hyperlinks, which take the user from one text to another.

The Internet and Web were central to what journalist Thomas Friedman calls "the democratization of information." Dictatorships could no longer keep their subjects ignorant of what was going on in the rest of the world or restrain dissidents from communicating with one another. As President Bill Clinton asserted in 1998, "In this global information age, when economic success is built on ideas, personal freedom is essential to the greatness of any modern nation." The Internet carried the potential to empower people even in democratic nations: Organizers of the protests against globalization carried out much of their mobilization via the Internet, and the high speed and low cost of communication enabled international movements to organize around other issues much more easily than ever before. In the United States, "distance learning" via the Internet began to breach geographical and financial barriers to formal education, and the Internet became a popular recruitment and campaigning tool during the 2004 presidential race.

By offering nearly instant, cheap communication around the globe, the Internet tremendously facilitated the growth of a global economy. It quickly spread capital around the world, made it easier for companies to manage operations abroad, and even enabled employees to work together while thousands of miles separated them. In 1997, for example, computer programmers in Beijing developing a project for IBM sent their work at the end of the day via the Internet to IBM workers in Seattle, who built on it and then passed it on to programmers in Belarus and Latvia, who did the same and relayed it on to counterparts in India, who passed it on to the Beijing group, who started the process all over again until the project was finished. According to IBM executive John Patrick, "It's like we've created a forty-eight-hour day through the Internet."

Although the Internet has enabled people to exchange news, knowledge, photographs, music, and money rapidly, it is not without critics. Some observers worry that the Internet is taking the place of human relationships. A 2000 survey found that 20 percent of the people who went online five or more hours a week spent less time with family and friends or at social events than they had spent before gaining access to the Net. Respondents had even more sharply reduced their time devoted to reading the newspaper or watching television. The availability of pornography on the Web and the exposure of users' personal and financial information are also concerns,

The Internet Links the World
By the end of the twentieth century, even the poorest countries had some access to the Internet, the network that links millions of computers throughout the world. President Bill Clinton displayed his fervent faith in the promise of technology to encourage democracy, claiming that "when over 100 million people in China can get on the Net, it will be impossible to maintain a closed political and economic society." In Iran, where the theocratic government tightly restricted women, young girls turned to the Internet for discussions about sex and marriage. As a seventeen-year-old declared, "What else can we do when we cannot have a normal social life?" These Buddhist monks stand outside an Internet café in the Cambodian capital of Phnom Penh in December 2000.
© Bettmann/Corbis.

along with the daily irritation of an electronic mailbox filled with spam, or junk e-mail.

Other critics have pointed to the disparate access to information technology, a "digital divide" across class and racial lines. As costs of hardware and software plummeted during the 1990s, computers and access to the Internet grew dramatically but unevenly. By 2000, more than 50 percent of all U.S. households had computers, and 41 per-

cent could log on to the Internet, in contrast to fewer than 25 percent of African American and Latino households. Even so, the Internet is well on its way to becoming as ubiquitous as television but with a much greater and varied impact. A computer software engineer who helped develop the Internet remarked, "It has already changed everything we do and changed it for good."

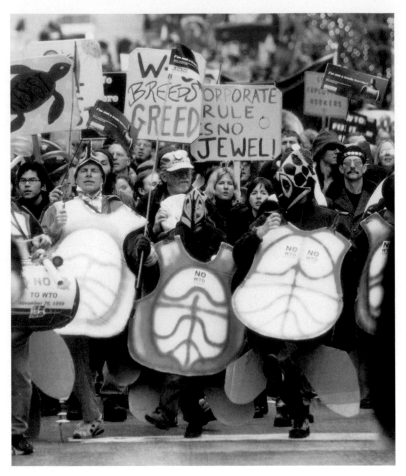

Protests against the WTO

Environmentalists and animal protection advocates were among the varied groups demonstrating against the World Trade Organization when it attempted to meet in Seattle, Washington, in November 1999. These activists dressed as sea turtles to protest WTO agreements permitting economic actions that they believed threatened the survival of the animals.

Wide World Photos, Inc.

wanted trade treaties requiring other countries to enforce decent wage and labor standards. Environmentalists similarly wanted countries seeking increased commerce with the United States to adopt measures that would eliminate or reduce pollution and prevent the destruction of endangered species.

Globalization controversies often centered on relationships between the United States, which dominated the world's industrial core, and the developing nations on the periphery, whose cheap labor and lax environmental standards attracted investment. United Students Against Sweatshops, for example, attacked the international conglomerate Nike, which paid Chinese workers $1.50 per pair to produce shoes that sold for more than $100 in the United States. Yet many leaders of developing nations actively sought foreign investment and manufacturing jobs for their workers, insisting that wages deemed pitiful by American standards offered people in poor nations a much better living than they could otherwise obtain. At the same time developing countries often pointed to the hypocrisy of the United States in advocating free trade in industry while heavily subsidizing its own agricultural sector. "We are kept out of the world market," complained John Nagenda, a farmer in Uganda. "When countries like America, Britain and France subsidize their farmers, we get hurt."

The demonstrations in Seattle, and the protests that followed in Washington, D.C., Prague (capital of the Czech Republic), Genoa, Italy, and Mexico City, targeted international financial institutions such as the WTO and the International Monetary Fund (IMF). Protesters charged that the WTO and IMF forced devastating regulations on developing nations, which had little voice in trade policy decisions. For example, the IMF often required poor nations to privatize state industries, deregulate their economies, and cut government spending for social welfare in order to obtain loans. While globalization's cheerleaders argued that in the long run everyone would benefit, critics focused on the short-term victims and destruction of traditional cultures that accompanied economic modernization. "International trade and global financial markets are very good at generating wealth," conceded American businessman George Soros, "but they cannot take care of other social needs, such as the preservation of peace, alleviation of poverty, protection of the environment, labor conditions, or human rights."

and say, 'We want rules for workers' rights to be integrated into the global economy.'" At the WTO demonstrations and elsewhere, U.S. labor unions emphasized the flight of factory jobs to developing nations as corporate executives sought cheaper labor to lower production costs. (See "Beyond America's Borders," page 1164.) For example, General Motors, one of the nation's largest manufacturers, produced its Pontiac Le Mans in South Korea, with parts manufactured in Japan, Germany, Taiwan, Singapore, Britain, Ireland, and Barbados. Critics linked globalization to the weakening of unions, the erosion of the safety net provided for workers since the 1930s, and the growing gap between rich and poor in the United States. Demanding "fair trade" rather than simply free trade, they

Liberalizing Foreign Trade

Building on steps taken by Presidents Reagan and Bush, Bill Clinton sought new measures to ease restrictions on international commerce. In November 1993, Congress approved the North American Free Trade Agreement (NAFTA), which eliminated all tariffs and trade barriers among the United States, Canada, and Mexico. Organized labor and other groups, fearing loss of jobs and industries to Mexico, lobbied vigorously against NAFTA. But proponents argued that all three trading partners would benefit from greater export opportunities, more jobs in the long run, and global clout. With 360 million people and a $6 billion economy, the NAFTA trio constituted the largest trading bloc in the world. A year later, the Senate ratified the General Agreement on Tariffs and Trade (GATT), establishing the WTO to enforce substantial tariff reductions, elimination of import quotas, and other provisions of the treaty.

The China trade bill of 2000, which added China to the vast majority of countries that enjoyed normal trade relations with the United States, aroused another controversy over free trade. Conservatives attacked the deal with Communist China as "selling out the very moral and spiritual principles that made America great," while liberals expressed concerns about Chinese labor standards and human rights violations. In contrast, supporters of the bill argued that increased trade would promote human rights and humane working conditions. Clinton himself advocated trade not just for its economic benefits but as a means of promoting international peace and security. Opening China to outside competition, he asserted, would "speed the information revolution there . . . speed the demise of China's huge state industries . . . spur the enterprise of private-sector involvement . . . and diminish the role of government in people's daily lives."

Although advocates of globalization prevailed on NAFTA, GATT, and the China bill, in 2000 opponents won an executive order from President Clinton requiring an environmental impact review before the signing of any trade agreement. And globalization's critics had an impact beyond the United States. In September 2000, officials from the World Bank and IMF along with representatives from wealthy nations promised to provide poor nations more debt relief and a greater voice in decisions about loans and grants. According to World Bank president James D. Wolfensohn, "Our challenge is to make globalization an instrument of opportunity and inclusion—not fear."

The Internationalization of the United States

Globalization was typically associated with the expansion of American enterprise and culture to—or its imposition on—other countries, yet the United States itself experienced the dynamic forces creating a global economy. Already in the 1980s, Japanese, European, and Middle Eastern investors had purchased American stocks and bonds, real estate, and corporations, such as Firestone, Brooks Brothers, and 20th Century Fox. By the twenty-first century, the Royal Bank of Scotland owned more than fifteen U.S. banks, and the German media giant Bertelsmann had acquired the publisher Random House. Local communities welcomed foreign capital, and several states outdid themselves in recruiting foreign automakers to establish plants within their boundaries. American non-union workers began to produce Hondas in Marysville, Ohio, and BMWs in Spartanburg, South Carolina. By 2002, the paychecks of nearly 4 million American workers came from European-owned companies.

> Although the Clinton administration sometimes seemed uncertain about the use of military force, it moved energetically on the economic side to speed up the growth of a "global marketplace."

Globalization was transforming not just the economy but American society as well, as the United States experienced a tremendous surge of immigration in the late twentieth century. (See "Historical Question," page 1156, and appendix, page A-51.) By 2002, one out of every ten Americans was an immigrant. Sixteen million foreign-born arrived between 1980 and 2000, surpassing immigration during the first two decades in the twentieth century, when Colin Powell's parents had come to America, and exhibiting a striking difference in country of origin. Eighty-five percent of the previous immigrants had come from Europe; by the 1980s, almost half of the new arrivals were Asians and nearly 40 percent came from Latin America and the Caribbean. Consequently, immigration changed the racial and ethnic composition of the nation. By 2002, the Asian and Pacific Islander population had grown to 13 million, and the number of Latinos increased to nearly 39 million. At 13 percent of the popula-

Jobs in a Globalizing Era

In November 2001, Paul Sufronko, a supervisor at Rocky Shoes and Boots in the small town of Nelsonville, Ohio, handed out final paychecks to the company's last sixty-seven employees in the United States, ending a process of outsourcing jobs that had begun in the 1980s. His own job was not quite over. Before receiving his last check, he traveled to Rocky plants in Puerto Rico and the Dominican Republic to complete the transfer of production and to train a local worker to do his job. Asked about his job loss, the thirty-six-year-old said, "I had other plans. Things just didn't work out."

Many Americans did not take the loss of their jobs to foreign workers so philosophically. One, a son of Mexican American sharecroppers, who had been laid off when Chrysler shut down its Jeep production in Kenosha, Wisconsin, in 1988, saw his fifteen years on the assembly line as "a habit that's your life" and mourned the loss of "pride in being an autoworker." One of his coworkers believed that "greed" drove the shutdown, pointing out that Chrysler had "plants down in Mexico" where workers were "making $1.25 a day." Another assembler agreed that "corporations are looking for a disposable workforce. . . . No commitment to community; no commitment to country."

In 1960, American workers made 96 percent of shoes bought in the United States; by 2000, as the number of American workers in the industry plummeted from hundreds of thousands to fewer than 25,000, nearly all shoes came from abroad.

The globalizing process was not a new experience for Julio Lopez, a temporary beneficiary of Rocky's transfer of labor abroad. Born in Puerto Rico, he went to New York as a young man to work in a toy factory, until it moved its operations overseas. Returning to Puerto Rico, he spent twenty-three years making shoes and boots for another company but lost his job when it sought cheaper labor elsewhere. In 2001, he found work at Rocky's Puerto Rico plant at the minimum wage of $5.15 an hour, less than half of what the company had paid Nelsonville workers. Lopez hoped that the factory would stay there for eight more years. "Then I will be 62, and I can retire." His hopes were not unusual, and his concerns were not unfounded. Lillian Chaparro, the plant manager, spoke about the perpetual motion of jobs: "It's like a chain, you know? The jobs leave the U.S. They come here. Then they go to the Dominican, to China. That's why I push people—we have to be able to compete."

Construction of a single pair of Rocky hiking boots in 2001 illustrates the web of connections that define the global economy. Leather produced in Australia was shipped to the Dominican Republic, where the uppers were cut and sewed and then sent to Puerto Rico. Puerto Rican workers like Julio Lopez assembled those materials along with outsoles that had been purchased in China and Gore-Tex waterproofing material made in the United States. Finally, the finished boots were transported to Rocky's warehouse near Nelsonville, Ohio.

The athletic shoe manufacturer Nike was one of the first companies to exploit the advantages of production abroad. Nike first turned to Japan, in the 1960s, but when labor costs there began to rise, it began to sign contracts with South Korean businessmen, who by the 1990s were turning out 4 million pairs of shoes. When South Korean workers began to demand higher wages and better working conditions, Nike moved production to China, Indonesia, and Thailand. Nike did not employ foreign workers directly but contracted their labor through local entrepreneurs, who in Indonesia, for example, paid workers as little as fifteen cents an hour as they churned out 70 million pairs of shoes in 1996.

Charles Seitz, who lost his job at Eastman Kodak in Rochester, New York, when the company moved some operations to China and Mexico, was not entirely wrong when he said, "There's nothing made here anymore." In the 1950s, one-third of all American workers were employed in manufacturing; by the twenty-first century just 10 percent produced goods. Of course, not all the job losses resulted from the transfer of work overseas. At Kodak, for example, a machine took the place of fourteen workers who previously had mixed film-making ingredients. In the 1980s and 1990s, American corporations devoted intense energy to increasing production so that they could downsize their workforces, in addition to looking abroad as a way of cutting labor costs. Moreover, some companies decided to build plants abroad in order to be close to burgeoning markets there, as foreign automakers had done when they began operations in the United States. Because so many companies, like Nike, contracted out production to foreign companies

U.S. Products Made Abroad

This woman, who is working on a mechanical part at a *maquiladora* (assembly plant) in Tijuana, Mexico, is part of one process by which manufacturing jobs left the United States. The Mexican government allowed foreign-owned companies to establish operations in Mexico, where they could take advantage of low labor costs, lax environmental protection measures, and close proximity to U.S. consumers. Beginning in the 1960s, but especially in the 1980s and 1990s, home appliance, electronics, automobile, and other U.S. manufacturers took advantage of these conditions to locate assembly plants in Mexico near the U.S. border. In 2002, more than 3,500 plants employed nearly one million workers. For Mexico, the program proved an important source of employment, but it also contributed to environmental degradation by enormously increasing population in the borderland area and encouraging the dumping of hazardous wastes. The manufacturing labels illustrate the global dispersal of garment manufacturing as the number of apparel jobs in the United States was cut in half between 1994 and 2003.

Worker: © Annie Griffiths Belt/Corbis; labels: Picture Research Consultants & Archives.

rather than employing foreign workers directly, statistics on the number of U.S. jobs lost through outsourcing do not exist.

The outsourcing of work for U.S. companies did not end with manufacturing jobs. By 2003, many corporations were relying on workers abroad, and especially in India, for a wide range of service and professional work. For example, 1,700 engineers and scientists conducted research for General Electric in Bangalore, India, which became the South Asian equivalent of California's Silicon Valley. Avis employed East Indians to manage its online car rentals; technology experts in Bangalore provided telephone help for customers flummoxed by their Dell computers; and the business consulting firm Accenture employed more than 4,000 workers in India, China, Russia, and the Philippines.

An executive in a research firm outlined the rationale: "You can get crackerjack Java programmers in India right out of college for $5,000 a year versus $60,000." Pointing to the power of technology to overcome distance, she asked, "Why be in New York City when you can be 9,000 miles away with far less expense?" An executive of IBM, which employed hundreds of researchers and developers in Haifa, Israel, agreed, adding, "Our competitors are doing it and we have to do it." Others worried about not just the immediate loss of jobs at home but also the long-term consequences for the American economy. "If we continue losing these jobs," argued the head of a computer software company, "our schools will stop producing the computer engineers and programmers we need for the future."

The flight of jobs has not been entirely one-way. Seeking to move production closer to its market, in 1982 Honda became the first Japanese company to manufacture cars in the United States, hiring more

(continued)

1165

(continued)

than 150,000 American workers by 2003. Other automakers followed—South Carolinians began making BMWs, and Toyota opened a plant in Kentucky. Pointing to a factory in Lafayette, Indiana, college professor John Larson remarked that "in the 1950s, it was America that was doing all the outreaching. We did all the globalizing. But when the Japanese car people were looking for a site for the Subaru factory, they came in here the way Americans go into India." In all, about 5 percent of all American workers in 2003 received their paychecks from foreign companies operating in the United States.

Nonetheless, the vast majority of jobs moved in the opposite direction. In 2003, one of the most distinctive American products rolled off a U.S. production line for the last time. The blue jeans company founded in 1853 by Levi Strauss, a Bavarian immigrant, closed its last plants in the United States, contracting out its work to suppliers in fifty other countries from Latin America to Asia. The company's president refused to see any significance in the move. "Consumers are used to buying products from all over the world," he said. "The issue is not where they're made." But Clara Flores, who had sewn hems for twenty-four years and headed her union local in San Antonio, Texas, wondered, "Where are we ever going to find something like this?" Marivel Gutierez, a side-seam operator, acknowledged that workers in Mexico and elsewhere would benefit, suggesting the globalization of the American dream. "But, what happens to our American dream?" Workers like these stood as stark reminders that as the benefits of the free flow of economic enterprise across national borders reached many, globalization left multitudes of victims in its wake.

BIBLIOGRAPHY

Jefferson Cowie, *Capital Moves: RCA's Seventy-Year Quest for Cheap Labor* (1999).

Jefferson Cowie and Joseph Heathcott, eds., *Beyond the Ruins: The Meanings of Deindustrialization* (2003).

Kathryn Marie Dudley, *The End of the Line: Lost Jobs, New Lives in Postindustrial America* (1994).

Bennett Harrison and Barry Bluestone, *The Great U-Turn: Corporate Restructuring and the Polarizing of America* (1988).

Walter LaFeber, *Michael Jordan and the New Global Capitalism* (1999).

Theodore H. Moran, *Beyond Sweatshops: Foreign Direct Investment and Globalization in Developing Countries* (2002).

Ellen Israel Rosen, *Making Sweatshops: The Globalization of the U.S. Apparel Industry* (2002).

tion, Latinos outnumbered African Americans for the first time.

The racial composition of the new immigration revived the century-old wariness of the native-born toward recent arrivals. Pressure for more restrictive policies stemmed from beliefs (generally unfounded) that immigrants took jobs from the native-born and fears that immigrants would erode the dominant culture and language. Americans expressed particular hostility to immigrants who entered the country illegally, even though the economy depended on their cheap labor. Estimated to number as many as 6 million by 2001, undocumented immigrants were primarily Latin Americans fleeing civil war and economic deprivation. The Immigration Reform and Control Act of 1986, which penalized employers who hired undocumented aliens but also granted amnesty to some two million illegal immigrants who had been in the country before 1982, did little to stem the tide. In California, with the largest numbers of illegal immigrants, voters passed an initiative denying public schooling to their children. Nor were legal immigrants immune from **nativist** policy. In 1996, Congress denied food stamps, Medicaid, and other benefits to those who had not become citizens.

The new immigration was again making America an international, interracial society, and not just along the coasts. American culture reflected growing diversity: Tortillas rivaled white bread in total sales, sushi bars and Thai food restaurants appeared in midwestern cities, cable TV companies added Spanish-language stations, Latinos became the largest minority in major league baseball, and a truly international sport, soccer, soared in popularity. Mixed marriages displayed a growing fusion of cultures, recognized by the Census Bureau in 2000 when it let Americans check more than one racial category on their forms. Demographers predicted that by 2050 the American population would be just over 50 percent white, 16 percent black, 24 percent Hispanic, and 9 percent Asian.

Like their predecessors a hundred years earlier, the majority of post-1965 immigrants were unskilled and poor. They took the lowest-paying jobs, providing farm labor, yard work, child and elder care, and cleaning services. Yet a significant number were highly skilled workers, sought after by burgeoning high-tech industries. For example, in 1999 about one-third of the scientists and engineers who worked in California's Silicon Valley had been born abroad. One small 31-person biotech company seeking cures for prostate diseases employed two Vietnamese, two Canadians, one Pole, two Lebanese, three Chinese, one Korean, one Indian, one Israeli, one Scot, one English, and two Latinos. Emphasizing American society's unique multiculturalism at the turn of the twenty-first century, the company's owner boasted, "I cannot think of another country in the world where you could so easily put such a team together."

President George W. Bush: Conservatism at Home and Radical Initiatives Abroad

The second son of a former president to gain that office himself, George W. Bush pushed an agenda that in many respects resembled Ronald Reagan's more than it did his father's, George H. W. Bush. The second Bush got Congress to pass tax cuts that helped send the federal budget into a huge deficit, and he reduced environmental protections. As Islamist terrorism replaced communism as the primary threat to U.S. security, the Bush administration launched a war in Afghanistan in 2001 and expanded government's powers to monitor, investigate, arrest, and detain individuals. In distinct contrast to his father's multilateral and cautious approach in

The New Immigration

These employees at UroGenesys, Inc., in Santa Monica, California, provide one example of America's increasingly diverse workforce at the start of the twenty-first century, the result of the highest immigration rates in a hundred years and of the economy's increasing need for a technologically skilled workforce. This biotechnology company conducts research aimed at discovering and developing therapeutic and diagnostic products for urological cancers, especially prostate cancer.

Courtesy UroGenesys. Photo by Deidre Davidson.

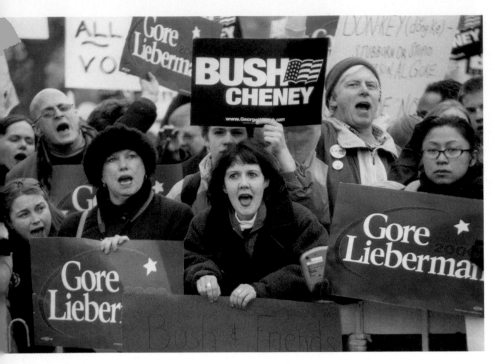

The Disputed Election

While attorneys representing presidential candidates George W. Bush and Al Gore pursued lawsuits over the counting of ballots that would determine who won Florida's 25 electoral college votes, partisan supporters took to the streets. Here backers of both sides rally outside the Supreme Court in Washington, D.C., on Monday, December 11, 2000, a day before the Court issued its five-to-four ruling that ended the hand recounts of ballots and consequently secured the presidency for Bush. Critics charging that the five justices who voted to stop the recounts had applied partisanship rather than objectivity to the case pointed out that the decision went against those justices' custom of preferring state over federal authority.

Wide World Photos, Inc.

foreign and military policy, George W. Bush adopted a policy of unilateralism and preemption by going to war against Iraq in 2003.

The Disputed Election of 2000

Even though the Clinton administration ended with a flourishing economy, Democratic candidate Vice President Albert Gore failed to retain the White House for his party in the election of 2000. His choice of running mate, Connecticut senator Joseph Lieberman, the first Jew to run on a major party ticket, was popular, and polls indicated that a majority of Americans agreed with the Democratic nominees on most issues. Yet Gore's personal style appeared stiff to many voters, and he seemed too willing to change his positions to gain political advantage. The Clinton administration scandals also burdened Gore's election campaign.

Texas governor George W. Bush emerged as the Republican nominee from a series of hard-

fought primaries financed with the most money ever raised in a presidential campaign. The oldest son of former president George H. W. Bush had attended Yale and Harvard and then worked in the oil industry in Texas and as managing partner of the Texas Rangers baseball team. In 1994, Texans elected him governor. Criticized for his lack of Washington and international experience and his unfamiliarity with certain policy issues, Bush chose for his running mate a seasoned official, Richard B. Cheney, who had served in the Nixon, Ford, and first Bush administrations.

Both candidates ran cautious campaigns, accommodating their positions to what polls indicated voters wanted. Bush's strategy mirrored Clinton's in 1992. Calling himself a "compassionate conservative," he separated himself from the extreme right wing of his party and tried to co-opt Democratic issues such as education. Like Republicans before him, he promised a substantial cut in taxes and federal spending.

Many observers predicted that the amazingly strong economy would give Gore the edge in the close race, and he did surpass Bush by more than a half million votes. Once the polls closed, however, it became clear that whoever won Florida's 25 electoral college votes would capture the election. Bush's margin was so tiny in that state, where his brother served as governor, that it prompted an automatic recount of the votes, which eventually gave Bush an edge of 537 votes.

Meanwhile, the Democrats asked for hand-counting of Florida ballots in several heavily Democratic counties where machine errors may have left hundreds of votes unrecorded. The Republicans, in turn, went to court to try to stop the hand-counts. As the dispute unfolded, Americans discovered that some counties used voting systems that were especially prone to error. Punch-card ballots were most unreliable, and they were used more in counties with large numbers of minority and poor voters.

The outcome of the 2000 election hung in the balance for more than a month as court cases went all the way up to the Supreme Court. Finally, a bitterly divided Supreme Court ruled

The Stability of American Constitutionalism
A week after the Supreme Court stopped the recount of votes in Florida and Gore conceded the presidency to Bush, the two met in Washington, D.C., at the vice president's residence. Their public handshake in the snow symbolized Americans' willingness to abide by the rules governing their political institutions even when the electoral process was flawed and bitterly contested.
Wide World Photos, Inc.

Although Bush had campaigned as a "compassionate conservative," his policies were more conservative than compassionate, at least in terms of who benefited. He claimed that the tax cuts would promote economic growth and jolt the economy out of a recession that had begun in 2001 and had sent the unemployment rate above 6 percent in 2003. But opponents stressed that the tax cuts favored the rich and pointed to a mushrooming federal deficit that reached some $500 billion in 2004, the highest in U.S. history. According to Senator Joseph Lieberman, Bush's tax cuts were "giving the most to those who need it least, piling more debt on the backs of our children and robbing Social Security and Medicare to pay for it." Republicans had traditionally railed against budget deficits, but some now saw them as a way to limit the size of the federal government. Representative Sue Myrick from North Carolina, for example, came to Congress in 1996 as a vigorous critic of deficits; six years later she said, "Anything that will help us stop spending money, I'm in favor of. And if there's a deficit, that may help us."

> Gore conceded the presidency to Bush on December 13, 2000. For the first time since 1888, a president who failed to win the popular vote took office.

five to four against further recounts of the Florida vote, and Gore conceded the presidency to Bush on December 13, 2000. For the first time since 1888, a president who failed to win the popular vote took office (Map 31.3). Despite the lack of a popular mandate, the Bush administration set out to make dramatic policy changes.

The Domestic Policies of a "Compassionate Conservative"

Bush moved quickly to implement his domestic agenda. He signed two tax-cut measures, one in 2001 reducing taxes over the following ten years by $1.35 trillion, followed by a 2003 bill slashing another $320 billion. The laws reduced income taxes, phased out estate taxes, cut rates on capital gains and dividends, provided benefits for married couples and families with children, provided deductions for college expenses, and gave immediate relief to all taxpayers through rebates of up to $300 each. House Majority Leader Dick Armey of Texas crowed over the bill: "The party is over. . . . We're no longer going to get stoned on other people's money."

MAP 31.3 The Election of 2000

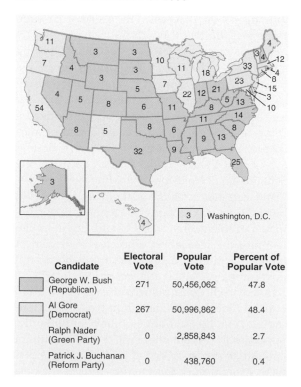

Candidate	Electoral Vote	Popular Vote	Percent of Popular Vote
George W. Bush (Republican)	271	50,456,062	47.8
Al Gore (Democrat)	267	50,996,862	48.4
Ralph Nader (Green Party)	0	2,858,843	2.7
Patrick J. Buchanan (Reform Party)	0	438,760	0.4

As Clinton had done, Bush altered environmental policy by issuing regulations that did not require congressional approval. But whereas Clinton had moved in the direction of greater controls, Bush subordinated environmental protection to larger goals of reducing government regulation, promoting economic growth, and increasing energy production. The Senate blocked Bush's efforts to allow drilling for oil in the Arctic National Wildlife Refuge, but elsewhere the administration withdrew 200 million acres of public land from consideration for wilderness protection, opening the way to mining, oil, and timber industries. Bush relaxed requirements of the Clean Air Act and issued new rules under the Clean Water Act that allowed coal companies to dump waste into rivers and streams. He imposed new restrictions on diesel pollutants but rejected higher standards for carbon dioxide emissions and, to worldwide dismay, withdrew from the Kyoto Protocol on global warming, signed in 1997 by 178 nations to reduce greenhouse gas emissions. While environmentalists pushed for measures to limit American energy consumption, the administration called for more rapid development of energy resources.

In contrast to the partisan conflict that attended tax and environmental policy, Bush mobilized bipartisan support behind his education initiative, the "No Child Left Behind" law of 2002, which marked the greatest change in federal education policy since the 1960s. Promising to end, in Bush's words, "the story of children being just shuffled through the system," the law required every school to meet annual testing standards and publish the results, provided penalties for—including the eventual closing of—failing schools and allowed parents to transfer their children out of them, and authorized a 20 percent increase in federal aid aimed primarily at the poorest districts.

One of the few critics of the education bill, Senator Paul Wellstone of Minnesota, asked, "How can you reach the goal of leaving no child behind on a tin cup budget?", a query that anticipated problems that states would face in implementing the legislation, since just 7 percent of their education budgets came from the federal government. Democratic senator Edward M. Kennedy, who had helped pass the law, complained that the administration was underfunding it: The Bush budget "may provide the resources to test our children," he said, "but not enough to teach them." By 2004, most states were straining to meet the demands of the new education standards as they struggled with severe budget crises brought on in part by the recession.

The Bush administration's second major domestic effort to co-opt Democratic Party issues constituted what the president hailed as "the greatest advance in health care coverage for America's seniors" since Medicare was established in 1965. In December 2003, he signed a bill that for the first time would provide prescription drug benefits to the elderly and at the same time expanded the role of private insurers in the Medicare system. Most Democrats opposed the bill, warning that it left big gaps in coverage, subsidized private insurers with federal funds to compete with Medicare, banned imports of cheaper drugs from abroad, and prohibited the government from negotiating with drug companies to reduce prices. Legislators of both parties worried about the cost of the new drug benefit, estimated to surpass $500 billion after it took effect in 2006. Fiscal concerns mounted as the federal budget deficit mushroomed, the result of Bush's huge tax cuts, the recession, two wars, and an urgent new need to protect domestic security.

The Globalization of Terrorism

Immigrants and citizens from sixty nations shared the fate of more than 2,000 Americans killed on the morning of September 11, 2001, when U.S. civilian airplanes crashed into the twin towers of the World Trade Center in lower Manhattan and the Pentagon in Washington, D.C. In the most deadly and shocking attack ever launched on American soil, nineteen members of Osama bin Laden's Al Qaeda international terrorist organization had hijacked four planes and flown three of them into the buildings, the fourth crashing in a field in Pennsylvania. The nation, indeed the world, was stunned. As one commentator observed in the days immediately following the events, "It took hours to comprehend their magnitude; it is taking days for the defensive numbness they induced to wear off; it will take months—or years—to measure their impact and meaning."

The attacks, organized from Osama bin Laden's sanctuaries in Afghanistan, where the radical Muslim Taliban government had taken control after the Soviet departure (see chapter 30), related to globalization in several ways. The spread of Western goods, culture, and values into the Muslim world, along with the 1991 Gulf

War against Iraq and the stationing of American troops in Saudi Arabia, bin Laden's homeland, enraged Islamic extremists. Acting on a distorted interpretation of one of the world's great religions, bin Laden sought to rid the Middle East of Western influence and install puritanical Muslim control. High levels of poverty ignored by undemocratic and corrupt governments provided bin Laden a pool of disaffected young Muslims who saw the United States as the evil source of their misery and the supporter of Israel's oppression of Palestinian Muslims. The technological advances accompanying globalization and people's increased mobility facilitated bin Laden's worldwide coordination of his Al Qaeda network and eased the hijackers' entrance into and activities in the United States.

In the wake of the September 11 attack, President George W. Bush sought a global alliance against terrorism and won at least verbal support from most governments. On October 11, the United States and Britain began bombing Afghanistan, and American special forces aided the Northern Alliance, the Taliban government's main opposition. By December the Taliban were routed, but bin Laden had not been captured and numerous Al Qaeda forces had escaped or remained in hiding throughout the world. Although 12,000 U.S. troops were still stationed in Afghanistan three years later, economic stability and physical security for its people remained out of reach.

Afghanistan

At home, the balance between **liberty** and security tilted as authorities arrested more than 1,000 Arabs and Muslims, holding more than 300 on immigration violations for months even though they had not been charged with any crimes related to the attacks. As one security official stated, "It doesn't mean we're going to profile Arabs, but we are going to look at people who come from a certain culture with a certain background." An internal study by the Justice Department later reported that many people with no connections to terrorism spent months in jail denied their rights. "I think America overreacted . . . by singling out Arab-named men like myself," said Shanaz Mohammed, who was jailed for eight months for an immigration violation. Throughout the country, anti-immigrant

sentiment revived, and anyone appearing to be Middle Eastern or practicing Islam was likely to arouse suspicion.

"The smoke was still coming out of the rubble in New York City when we passed the law," said Republican representative from Idaho C. L. Otter, referring to the USA Patriot Act, which Congress approved by huge margins in October 2001. The law gave the government new powers to monitor suspected terrorists and their associates, including the ability to pry personal information about suspected individuals from libraries, universities, businesses, and the like, while allowing more exchange of information between criminal investigators and those investigating foreign threats. It soon provoked calls for revision from both conservatives and liberals. One hundred fifty cities and three states passed resolutions objecting to the Patriot Act. Ann Arbor councilwoman Kathleen MacKenzie explained that "as awful as we feel about September 11 and as concerned as we were about national safety, we felt that giving up [rights] was too high a price to pay." But a security official countered, "If you don't violate someone's human rights some of the time, you probably aren't doing your job."

The government also sought to protect Americans from future terrorist attacks by a major reorganization of the executive branch, the biggest since 1948. In November 2002, Congress authorized a new Department of Homeland Security combining 170,000 federal employees from 22 agencies through which responsibilities for different aspects of domestic security had been dispersed. Chief among the duties of the new department were intelligence analysis; overseeing immigration and border security; chemical, biological, and nuclear countermeasures; and emergency preparedness and response.

> On many international issues, the Bush administration adopted a go-it-alone approach, shattering a fifty-year-old tradition of multilateralism.

Unilateralism, Preemption, and the Iraq War

In contrast to the administration's search for a collective action against the Taliban, on many other international issues the Bush administrathe space-based missile-defense system—SDI—first proposed by Ronald Reagan. Bush also withdrew the United States from the UN's International Criminal Court, arguing that it would make U.S. citizens vulnerable to politically motivated prosecution. And the United States rejected an agreement to enforce bans on development and possession of biological weapons that was signed by all its European allies.

Nowhere was the new policy of unilateralism more striking than in a new war against Iraq, a war pushed by Vice President Dick Cheney and Secretary of Defense Donald H. Rumsfeld but not Secretary of State Colin Powell. In his State of the Union message in January 2002, Bush identified Iraq, Iran, and North Korea as constituting an "axis of evil," alarming leaders of European and Asian nations alike, who insisted that these three nations posed entirely different challenges. Bush's opponents in Europe and Asia preferred to emphasize diplomacy rather than confrontation, and they objected to America's unilateral decisions about what countries constituted the greatest threats to world order. Nonetheless, addressing West Point graduates in June, President Bush proclaimed a new policy for American security that scuttled a defense strategy based on containment for one based on preemption.

According to the president, "Traditional concepts of deterrence will not work against a terrorist enemy whose avowed tactics are wanton destruction and the targeting of innocents; whose so-called soldiers seek martyrdom in death and whose most potent protection is statelessness." Because nuclear, chemical, and biological weapons enabled "even weak states and small groups [to] attain a catastrophic power to strike great nations," it was necessary for the United States to "be ready for preemptive action." Even though the United States had intervened militarily and unilaterally in the affairs of small nations for a century, it had not gone to war except to repel aggression against itself or its allies. Claiming the right of the United States to start a war defied many Americans' understanding of their nation's ideals and distressed most of its great-power allies.

Nonetheless, the Bush administration moved deliberately to apply the doctrine of preemption to Iraq, whose dictator Saddam Hussein had violated UN resolutions from the 1991 Gulf War requiring Iraq to destroy and stop further development of nuclear, chemical, and biological

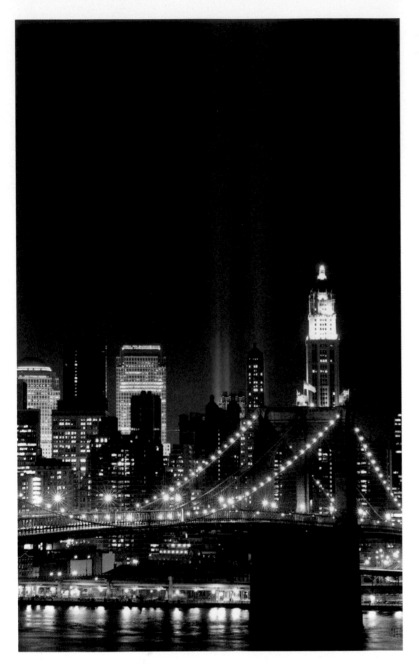

The "Tribute in Light"
Twin pillars of light, projected by 88 searchlights in the place where the World Trade Center twin towers had stood, soared as a monument to the victims of the terrorist attacks of September 11, 2001. Sharon Weicman, who worked as a volunteer for a month on the site of the destruction, was drawn by the illumination, remarking, "The closer I got, the more at peace I felt." Turned on at the six-month anniversary of the attack, the "Tribute in Light" was dimmed one month later.
Daniel Derella/AP/Wide World Photos, Inc.

tion adopted a go-it-alone approach, shattering a fifty-year-old tradition of multilateralism. In addition to withdrawing from the Kyoto Protocol on global warming, it scrapped the 1972 Antiballistic Missile Treaty in order to develop weapons. In November 2002, the United States got the UN Security Council to pass a resolution requiring Iraq to disarm or face "serious consequences." When Iraq failed to comply fully with new UN inspections, the administration decided on war. Claiming that Hussein had links to Al Qaeda and harbored terrorists and that Iraq possessed weapons of mass destruction, Bush insisted that the threat was immediate and great enough to justify preemptive action. Despite opposition from the Arab world and most major nations—including France, Germany, China, and Russia—which preferred to give inspections more time, the United States and Britain invaded Iraq on March 19, 2003, supported by what the administration called the "coalition of the willing" (see Map 31.2). That coalition represented some thirty nations, including Australia, Italy, Japan, and Spain, but few major powers or traditional allies. Although Saddam Hussein remained at large until December 2003, the coalition forces won an easy and decisive victory, and Bush declared the end of the war on May 1.

The Bush administration believed that destroying the regime of Saddam Hussein would create a model for democracy and freedom throughout the Middle East, but while Arabs were glad to see the end of Hussein, many did not welcome American troops. As the publisher of a Lebanese newspaper put it, "They [Iraqis] have to choose between the night of tyranny and the night of humiliation stemming from foreign occupation." Moreover, the damage from U.S. bombing and the massive looting resulting from the inability of U.S. and British forces to secure order and provide basic necessities once the regime had fallen left Iraqis wondering how much they had gained. "With Saddam there was tyranny, but at least you had a salary to put food on your family's table," said a young father from Hussein's hometown of Tikrit. Tha'ar Abdul Qader, who worked at a children's hospital in Baghdad, complained, "They can take our oil, but at least they should let us have electricity and water."

By September 2003, three months after Bush had declared the war over, the United States had 150,000 troops in Iraq and was spending $3.9 billion a month. Iraqis still lacked basic necessities such as water and electricity; oil production, on which the administration had counted to help pay for the occupation, remained at a near standstill; and the dearth of security forces subjected Iraqis to crime and violence. "Yes, of course we are free," conceded Hisham Abbas, an unemployed laborer, but "what good is freedom if we do not feel safe?" One defense official commented on the increasing Iraqi resentment of the U.S. occupation: "To a lot of Iraqis, we're no longer the guys who threw out Saddam, but the ones who are busting down doors and barging in on their wives and daughters."

American forces came under attack almost daily from remnants of the Hussein regime, religious extremists, and foreign terrorists now entering the chaotic country. As the American death toll surpassed 900 in July 2004, six times as many soldiers had been killed during the occupation as during the war. Terrorists launched deadly assaults on other targets, such as the UN mission in Baghdad, Red Cross headquarters, and a major Shiite mosque in Najaf, seeking to divide Iraqis and undermine the occupation. Some observers spoke of **guerrilla warfare** and "quagmire," evoking comparisons with the U.S. experience in Vietnam. By September 2003, the enormity of the task of reconstructing Iraq was apparent. "There is suddenly a new appreciation

The Iraq War

"The Americans did a great thing when they got rid of that tyrant," rejoiced Hassan Naji, a Shiite Muslim who worked at a hospital in southern Iraq. While he acknowledged that the occupation's inability to provide steady electricity increased the infant death rate at his hospital, he still insisted, "Things could even get worse here and I would still feel that way." Most Iraqis shared that initial jubilation, but the disorder and bloodshed that followed the defeat of Saddam Hussein's government threatened the Bush administration's plans to bring democracy and stability to the Middle East. In the first days of the American invasion, many Iraqis joined U.S. soldiers in removing Hussein's omnipresent image throughout the country. "We wanted to send a message that Saddam is done," reported U.S. marine major David Gurfein as he tore down a poster in the southern town of Safwan. Chris Hondras/Getty Images.

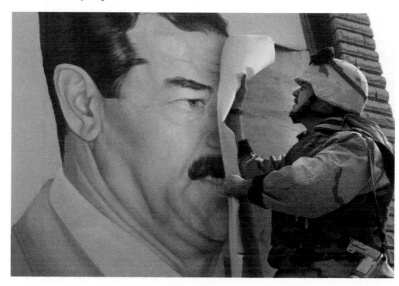

for alliances around here," said one foreign policy official as the Bush administration turned away from unilateralism and began to seek help from the very nations that had opposed the invasion.

The president's father, George H. W. Bush, had refused to invade Iraq at the end of the 1991 Gulf War. He, Colin Powell, and other advisers had believed that "unilaterally exceeding the United Nations' mandate would have destroyed the precedent of international response to aggression that we hoped to establish." The first Bush administration resisted making the nation "an occupying power in a bitterly hostile land," refusing to incur the "incalculable human and political costs" that such an invasion would produce.

Whether his son's decisions in the second Iraq war would serve American interests remained in question. To be sure, the U.S. military had felled a brutal dictator supported by few anywhere in the world. Yet coalition forces did not find the weapons of mass destruction that administration officials had insisted made the war necessary. The administration failed to prove its case that Iraq was linked to the terrorism of Osama bin Laden. In the war-induced chaos, more than a thousand terrorists entered Iraq—the place, according to one expert, "for fundamentalists to go . . . to stick it to the West." Although the war and occupation took relatively few American lives, they bore a steep price, not in dollars alone but also in U.S. relations with the other great powers and the nation's credibility and image in the world, especially among Arab nations. The war and occupation not only swelled the budget deficit but also diverted energies from the stabilization of Afghanistan and elimination of bin Laden and Al Qaeda and from dealing with the threat posed by North Korea's development of nuclear weapons. How quickly and how effectively Iraq became the model of democracy and freedom that President Bush had promised would determine whether the cost was worth it.

Conclusion: Defining the Government's Role at Home and Abroad

On March 21, 2003, some 225 years after the birth of the United States, Colin Powell referred to the unfinished nature of the American promise when he declared that the question of America's role in the world "isn't answered yet." In fact,

the end of the cold war, the rise of international terrorism, and the George W. Bush administration's radically new doctrines of preemption and unilateralism sparked new debates over the long-standing question of how the United States should act beyond its borders.

Nor had Americans set to rest questions about the role of government at home. In a population so greatly derived from people fleeing oppressive governments, Americans had debated for more than two centuries what responsibilities the government could or should shoulder, and what was best left to private enterprise, families, churches, and other voluntary institutions. Far more than other democracies, the United States had taken the path of private rather than public obligation, individual rather than collective solutions. In the twentieth century, Americans had significantly enlarged the federal government's powers and responsibilities, but the last three decades of the twentieth century had seen a decline of trust in government's ability to improve people's lives, even as a poverty rate of 20 percent among children and a growing gap between rich and poor survived the economic boom of the 1990s.

The shifting of control of the government back and forth between Republicans and Democrats from 1989 to 2004 revealed a dynamic contestation over the role of the government in domestic affairs. The protections enacted for people with disabilities during the first Bush administration and Bill Clinton's incremental reforms built on a deep-rooted reform tradition that sought to realize the American promise of justice and human well-being. Those who demonstrated at Seattle and elsewhere against the ravages of globalization worked internationally for what the **populists** and **progressives**, the **New Deal** reformers, and many activists of the 1960s had sought for the domestic population—protection of individual rights, curbs on laissez-faire capitalism, assistance for victims of rapid economic change, and fiscal policies that placed greater responsibility on those best able to pay for the collective good. The second Bush administration, however—with a few exceptions such as the Patriot Act—pushed the pendulum back to a more limited role for the federal government.

As it entered the twenty-first century, the United States became ever more deeply embedded in the global economy as products, information, and people crossed borders with amazing speed and frequency. While the end of the cold war brought about unanticipated cooperation between the United States and its former enemies, globalization also contributed to international instability and the threat of deadly terrorism to a nation unaccustomed to foreign attacks within its own borders. In response to those dangers, the second Bush administration began to chart a departure from the multilateral approach to foreign policy that had been built up by Republican and Democratic administrations alike since World War II. Yet as the United States became mired in reconstruction efforts in Iraq, Americans continued to debate how the nation could best maintain domestic security while still exercising its economic and military power on a rapidly changing planet.

FOR ADDITIONAL FIRSTHAND ACCOUNTS OF THIS PERIOD, see Chapter 31 in Michael Johnson, ed., *Reading the American Past,* Third Edition.

TO ASSESS YOUR MASTERY OF THE MATERIAL IN THIS CHAPTER, see the Online Study Guide at bedfordstmartins.com/roark.

FOR WEB LINKS RELATED TO TOPICS IN THIS CHAPTER, see "HistoryLinks," "DocLinks," and "PlaceLinks" at bedfordstmartins.com/roark.

CHRONOLOGY

1988 • Republican Vice President George H. W. Bush elected president.

1989 • Communism collapses in eastern Europe; Berlin Wall falls.
• United States invades Panama and arrests dictator Manuel Noriega.

1990 • Bush and Congress agree to tax increase because of mounting federal deficit.

1991 • United States commits more than 400,000 troops to oust Iraqi army from Kuwait in Persian Gulf War.
• Clarence Thomas becomes second African American to sit on U.S. Supreme Court.
• Congress passes Americans with Disabilities Act, protecting people with disabilities from discrimination.

1992 • Democrat William Jefferson (Bill) Clinton elected president.

1993 • Israeli prime minister Yitzhak Rabin and PLO leader Yasir Arafat sign peace accords.
• Eighteen U.S. soldiers killed in UN peacekeeping operation in Somalia.
• Congress approves North American Free Trade Agreement (NAFTA).
• Clinton announces "don't ask, don't tell" policy for gays in military.
• Congress passes gun control and anticrime bills.
• Clinton signs Family and Medical Leave Act.

1994 • U.S. troops oversee peaceful return of Haitian president Jean-Bertrand Aristide to power.
• Senate ratifies General Agreement on Tariffs and Trade (GATT).
• Republicans recapture House and Senate in congressional elections.

1995 • Domestic terrorists bomb federal building in Oklahoma City.
• U.S. leaders broker peace accords, temporarily ending civil war in former Yugoslavia.

1996 • Clinton signs Personal Responsibility and Work Opportunity Reconciliation Act, replacing the Aid to Families with Dependent Children (AFDC) federal welfare program with state grants and two year limits on payments.
• Clinton elected to a second term.

1997 • Clinton signs largest tax cut since 1981.

1998 • United States bombs terrorist sites in Afghanistan and Sudan in retaliation for embassy bombings.
• United States bombs Iraq for failure to comply with 1991 agreement to destroy chemical, germ, and nuclear weapons.
• Federal budget shows surplus for first time since 1969.
• President Clinton impeached for perjury and obstruction of justice in the Monica Lewinsky case.

1999 • Senate trial fails to approve articles of impeachment.
• United States, with NATO, bombs Serbia for more than two months to force an end to Serbian atrocities against ethnic Albanians in Kosovo.
• U.S. Senate defeats ratification of UN comprehensive nuclear test ban treaty.
• Protesters disrupt meeting of the World Trade Organization in Seattle.

2000 • Congress approves China trade bill, normalizing trade relations.
• Republican George W. Bush becomes president in disputed election.

2001
- **September 11.** Terrorists fly airplanes into World Trade Center buildings in New York City and the Pentagon in Washington, D.C., killing nearly 3,000 people.

- United States attacks Afghanistan, driving out its Taliban government, which had harbored terrorists involved in the September 11 attacks.
- USA Patriot Act gives government new powers to investigate suspected terrorists and their associates.
- Congress passes $1.3 trillion tax cut.

2002
- "No Child Left Behind" Act requires all public schools receiving federal funding to meet achievement standards.
- Newly created Department of Homeland Security effects comprehensive reorganization of federal government's units dealing with domestic security.

2003
- United States attacks Iraq, driving out the regime of Saddam Hussein.
- Congress enacts major revision of Medicare.

BIBLIOGRAPHY

Domestic Politics and Policies

Sidney Blumenthal, *The Clinton Wars* (2003).

Frank Bruni, *Ambling into History: The Unlikely Odyssey of George W. Bush* (2002).

James MacGregor Burns and Georgia Sorenson, *Dead Center: The Clinton-Gore Leadership and the Perils of Moderation* (1999).

Alan M. Dershowitz, *Supreme Injustice: How the Supreme Court Hijacked the Election of 2000* (2001).

Greg J. Duncan et al., eds., *For Better and for Worse: Welfare Reform and the Well-Being of Children and Families* (2002).

David Frum, *The Right Man: An Inside Account of the Bush White House* (2003).

Colin Gordon, *Dead on Arrival: The Politics of Health Care in Twentieth-Century America* (2003).

John Robert Greene, *The Presidency of George Bush* (2000).

Haynes Johnson, *The Best of Times: America in the Clinton Years* (2001).

Joe Klein, *The Natural: The Misunderstood Presidency of Bill Clinton* (2002).

Bruce D. Meyer and Douglas Holtz-Eakin, *Making Work Pay: The Earned Income Tax Credit and Its Impact on America's Families* (2002).

Herbert S. Parmet, *George Bush: The Life of a Lone Star Yankee* (1997).

Gerald Posner, *Citizen Perot: His Life and Times* (1996).

Richard A. Posner, *An Affair of State: The Investigation, Impeachment, and Trial of President Clinton* (1999).

Richard A. Posner, *Breaking the Deadlock: The 2000 Election, the Constitution, and the Courts* (2001).

Richard K. Scotch, *From Good Will to Civil Rights: Transforming Federal Disability Policy* (rev. ed., 2001).

Jeffrey Toobin, *A Vast Conspiracy: The Real Story of the Sex Scandal That Nearly Brought Down a President* (2001).

Jeffrey Toobin, *Too Close to Call: The Thirty-Six-Day Battle to Decide the 2000 Election* (2001).

The Domestic Economy

Martin Campbell-Kelly and William Aspray, *Computer: A History of the Information Machine* (1996).

John Cassidy, *Dot.con: How America Lost Its Mind and Money in the Internet Era* (2003).

Alfred D. Chandler Jr., *Inventing the Electronic Century: The Epic Story of the Consumer Electronics and Computer Science Industries* (2001).

Roger Lowenstein, *Origins of the Crash: The Great Bubble and Its Undoing* (2004).

Maggie Mahar, *Bull!: A History of the Boom, 1982–1999* (2003).

David K. Shipler, *The Working Poor: Invisible in America* (2004).

Beth Shulman, *The Betrayal of Work: How Low-Wage Jobs Fail Thirty Million Americans and Their Families* (2003).

Joseph E. Stiglitz, *The Roaring Nineties: A New History of the World's Most Prosperous Decade* (2003).

A Multicultural Society

Frank D. Bean and Gillian Stevens, *America's Newcomers and the Dynamics of Diversity* (2003).

George J. Borjas, *Heaven's Door: Immigration Policy and the American Economy* (1999).

Juan Gonzalez, *Harvest of Empire: A History of Latinos in America* (2001).

Andrew Hacker, *Two Nations: Black and White, Separate, Hostile, Unequal* (1992).

S. Mitra Kalita, *Suburban Sahibs: Three Immigrant Families and Their Passage from India to America* (2003).

Sarah J. Mahler, *American Dreaming: Immigrant Life on the Margins* (1995).

David M. Reimers, *Still the Golden Door: The Third World Comes to America* (rev. ed., 1992).

David M. Reimers, *Unwelcome Strangers: American Identity and the Turn against Immigration* (1998).

Al Santoli, *New Americans: An Oral History* (1988).

Peter Skerry, *Mexican Americans: The Ambivalent Minority* (1993).

Roberto Suro, *Strangers among Us: Latinos' Lives in a Changing America* (1999).

Ronald Takaki, *Strangers from a Different Shore: A History of Asian Americans* (1989).

Sanford J. Ungar, *Fresh Blood: The New American Immigrants* (1995).

William Wei, *The Asian American Movement* (1993).

Helen Zia, *Asian American Dreams: The Emergence of an American People* (2001).

Foreign Policy after the Cold War

Michael R. Beschloss and Strobe Talbott, *At the Highest Levels: The Inside Story of the End of the Cold War* (1993).

Ivo H. Daalder and James M. Lindsay, *America Unbound: The Bush Revolution in Foreign Policy* (2003).

Raymond I. Garthogg, *The Great Transition: America-Soviet Relations and the End of the Cold War* (1994).

David Halberstam, *War in a Time of Peace: Bush, Clinton, and the Generals* (2001).

Michael Hirsh, *At War with Ourselves: Why America Is Squandering Its Chance to Build a Better World* (2003).

Stanley Hoffmann, *World Disorders: Troubled Peace in the Post–Cold War Era* (1998).

Michael J. Hogan, ed., *The End of the Cold War: Its Meaning and Implications* (1992).

Robert L. Hutchings, *American Diplomacy and the End of the Cold War: An Insider's Account of U.S. Policy in Europe, 1989–1992* (1997).

William Hyland, *Clinton's World* (1999).

Robert Kagan, *Of Paradise and Power: America and Europe in the New World Order* (2003).

Richard Ned Lebow and Janice Gross Stein, *We All Lost the Cold War* (1994).

James Mann, *Rise of the Vulcans: The History of Bush's War Cabinet* (2004).

Joseph S. Nye Jr., *The Paradox of American Power: Why the World's Only Superpower Can't Go It Alone* (2002).

Clyde Prestowitz, *Rogue Nation: American Unilateralism and the Failure of Good Intentions* (2003).

James M. Scott, ed., *After the End: Making U.S. Foreign Policy in the Post–Cold War World* (1998).

The United States and Latin America

John Dinges, *Our Man in Panama: How General Noriega Used the United States and Made Millions in Drugs and Arms* (1990).

Frederick Kempe, *Divorcing the Dictator: America's Bungled Affair with Noriega* (1990).

W. Dirk Raat, *Mexico and the United States: Ambivalent Vistas* (1997).

Peter H. Smith, *Talons of the Eagle: Dynamics of U.S.–Latin American Relations* (2nd ed., 1999).

The United States and the Middle East

Rick Atkinson, *Crusade: The Untold Story of the Persian Gulf War* (1994).

Rick Atkinson, *In the Company of Soldiers: A Chronicle of Combat* (2004).

Richard Butler, *The Greatest Threat: Iraq, Weapons of Mass Destruction, and the Crisis of Global Security* (2000).

Lawrence Freedman and Efraim Karsh, *The Gulf Conflict, 1990–1991: Diplomacy and War in the New World Order* (1993).

Lawrence F. Kaplan and William Kristol, *The War over Iraq: Saddam's Tyranny and America's Mission* (2003).

Douglas Little, *American Orientalism: The United States and the Middle East since 1945* (2002).

Benny Morris, *Righteous Victims: A History of the Zionist-Arab Conflict, 1881–1999* (1999).

Williamson Murray and Robert H. Scales Jr., *The Iraq War: A Military History* (2003).

Donald Neff, *Fallen Pillars: U.S. Policy towards Palestine and Israel since 1945* (1995).

Todd S. Purdum, *A Time of Our Choosing: America's War in Iraq* (2003).

Elaine Sciolino, *The Outlaw State: Saddam Hussein's Quest for Power and the Gulf Crisis* (1991).

Milton Viorst, *In the Shadow of the Prophet: The Struggle for the Soul of Islam* (2001).

Globalization

Richard J. Barnet and John Cavanagh, *Global Dreams: Imperial Corporations and the New World Order* (1994).

Jeremy Brecher, Tim Costello, and Brendan Smith, *Globalization from Below* (2000).

Stephen Castles, ed., *Citizenship and Migration: Globalization and the Politics of Belonging* (2000).

Thomas L. Friedman, *The Lexus and the Olive Tree: Understanding Globalization* (1999).

Robert Gilpin and Jean M. Gilpin, *The Challenge of Global Capitalism* (2000).

John Gray, *The Delusions of Global Capitalism* (1999).

Evelyn Hu-Dehart, ed., *Across the Pacific: Asian Americans and Globalization* (1999).

Philippe Legrain, *Open World: The Truth about Globalization* (2004).

John R. MacArthur, *The Selling of "Free Trade": NAFTA, Washington, and the Subversion of American Democracy* (2000).

Douglas S. Massey, *Worlds in Motion: Understanding International Migration at Century's End* (1998).

Joseph E. Stiglitz, *Globalization and Its Discontents* (2002).

Terrorism

Peter L. Bergen, *Holy War, Inc.: Inside the Secret World of Osama bin Laden* (2001).

Yossef Bodansky, *Bin Laden: The Man Who Declared War on America* (1999).

Philip B. Heymann, *Terrorism, Freedom, and Security: Winning without War* (2003).

Bruce Hoffman, *Inside Terrorism* (1998).

James F. Hoge Jr. and Gideon Rose, *How Did This Happen? Terrorism and the New War* (2001).

Gilles Kepel, *Jihad: The Trail of Political Islam* (2002).

Walter Laqueur, *The New Terrorism: Fanaticism and the Arms of Mass Destruction* (2000).

Daniel Levitas, *The Terrorist Next Door: The Militia Movement and the Radical Right* (2002).

Paul R. Pillar, *Terrorism and U.S. Foreign Policy* (2001).

Gerald Posner, *Why America Slept: The Failure to Prevent 9/11* (2003).

Ahmed Rashid, *Taliban: Militant Islam, Oil, and Fundamentalism in Central Asia* (2000).

Simon Reeve, *The New Jackals: Ramzi Yousef, Osama bin Laden and the Future of Terrorism* (1999).

Richard A. Serrano, *One of Ours: Timothy McVeigh and the Oklahoma City Bombing* (1998).

Documents

For additional documents see the DocLinks feature at bedfordstmartins.com/roark.

THE DECLARATION OF INDEPENDENCE

In Congress, July 4, 1776,

THE UNANIMOUS DECLARATION OF THE THIRTEEN UNITED STATES OF AMERICA

When in the course of human events, it becomes necessary for one people to dissolve the political bands which have connected them with another, and to assume, among the powers of the earth, the separate and equal station to which the laws of nature and of nature's God entitle them, a decent respect to the opinions of mankind requires that they should declare the causes which impel them to the separation.

We hold these truths to be self-evident, that all men are created equal; that they are endowed by their Creator with certain unalienable rights; that among these, are life, liberty, and the pursuit of happiness. That, to secure these rights, governments are instituted among men, deriving their just powers from the consent of the governed; that, whenever any form of government becomes destructive of these ends, it is the right of the people to alter or to abolish it, and to institute a new government, laying its foundation on such principles, and organizing its powers in such form, as to them shall seem most likely to effect their safety and happiness. Prudence, indeed, will dictate that governments long established, should not be changed for light and transient causes; and, accordingly, all experience hath shown, that mankind are more disposed to suffer, while evils are sufferable, than to right themselves by abolishing the forms to which they are accustomed. But, when a long train of abuses and usurpations, pursuing invariably the same object, evinces a design to reduce them under absolute despotism, it is their right, it is their duty, to throw off such government and to provide new guards for their future security. Such has been the patient sufferance of these colonies, and such is now the necessity which constrains them to alter their former systems of government. The history of the present King of Great Britain is a history of repeated injuries and usurpations, all having, in direct object, the establishment of an absolute tyranny over these States. To prove this, let facts be submitted to a candid world:

He has refused his assent to laws the most wholesome and necessary for the public good.

He has forbidden his governors to pass laws of immediate and pressing importance, unless suspended in their operation till his assent should be obtained; and, when so suspended, he has utterly neglected to attend to them.

He has refused to pass other laws for the accommodation of large districts of people, unless those people would relinquish the right of representation in the legislature; a right inestimable to them, and formidable to tyrants only.

He has called together legislative bodies at places unusual, uncomfortable, and distant from the depository of their public records, for the sole purpose of fatiguing them into compliance with his measures.

He has dissolved representative houses repeatedly for opposing, with manly firmness, his invasions on the rights of the people.

He has refused, for a long time after such dissolutions, to cause others to be elected; whereby the legislative powers, incapable of annihilation, have returned to the people at large for their exercise; the state remaining in the mean-time exposed to all the danger of invasion from without, and convulsions within.

He has endeavoured to prevent the population of these States; for that purpose, obstructing the laws for naturalization of foreigners, refusing to pass others to encourage their migration hither, and raising the conditions of new appropriations of lands.

He has obstructed the administration of justice, by refusing his assent to laws for establishing judiciary powers.

He has made judges dependent on his will alone, for the tenure of their offices, and the amount and payment of their salaries.

He has erected a multitude of new offices, and sent hither swarms of officers to harass our people, and eat out their substance.

He has kept among us, in times of peace, standing armies, without the consent of our legislature.

He has affected to render the military independent of, and superior to, the civil power.

He has combined, with others, to subject us to a jurisdiction foreign to our Constitution, and unacknowledged by our laws; giving his assent to their acts of pretended legislation:

For quartering large bodies of armed troops among us:

For protecting them by a mock trial, from punishment, for any murders which they should commit on the inhabitants of these States:

For cutting off our trade with all parts of the world:

For imposing taxes on us without our consent:

For depriving us, in many cases, of the benefit of trial by jury:

For transporting us beyond seas to be tried for pretended offences:

For abolishing the free system of English laws in a neighboring province, establishing therein an arbitrary government, and enlarging its boundaries, so as to render it at once an example and fit instrument for introducing the same absolute rule into these colonies:

For taking away our charters, abolishing our most valuable laws, and altering, fundamentally, the powers of our governments:

For suspending our own legislatures, and declaring themselves invested with power to legislate for us in all cases whatsoever.

He has abdicated government here, by declaring us out of his protection, and waging war against us.

He has plundered our seas, ravaged our coasts, burnt our towns, and destroyed the lives of our people.

He is, at this time, transporting large armies of foreign mercenaries to complete the works of death, desolation, and tyranny, already begun, with circumstances of cruelty and perfidy scarcely paralleled in the most barbarous ages, and totally unworthy the head of a civilized nation.

He has constrained our fellow citizens, taken captive on the high seas, to bear arms against their country, to become the executioners of their friends, and brethren, or to fall themselves by their hands.

He has excited domestic insurrections amongst us, and has endeavored to bring on the inhabitants of our frontiers, the merciless Indian savages, whose known rule of warfare is an undistinguished destruction of all ages, sexes, and conditions.

In every stage of these oppressions, we have petitioned for redress; in the most humble terms; our repeated petitions have been answered only by repeated injury. A prince, whose character is thus marked by every act which may define a tyrant, is unfit to be the ruler of a free people.

Nor have we been wanting in attention to our British brethren. We have warned them, from time to time, of attempts made by their legislature to extend an unwarrantable jurisdiction over us. We have reminded them of the circumstances of our emigration and settlement here. We have appealed to their native justice and magnanimity, and we have conjured them, by the ties of our common kindred, to disavow these usurpations, which would inevitably interrupt our connections and correspondence. They, too, have been deaf to the voice of justice and consanguinity. We must, therefore, acquiesce in the necessity which denounces our separation, and hold them as we hold the rest of mankind, enemies in war, in peace, friends.

We, therefore, the representatives of the United States of America, in general Congress assembled, appealing to the Supreme Judge of the world for the rectitude of our intentions, do, in the name, and by authority of the good people of these colonies, solemnly publish and declare, that these united colonies are, and of right ought to be, free and independent states: that they are absolved from all allegiance to the British Crown, and that all political connection between them and the state of Great Britain is, and ought to be, totally dissolved; and that, as free and independent states, they have full power to levy war, conclude peace, contract alliances, establish commerce, and to do all other acts and things which independent states may of right do. And, for the support of this declaration, with a firm reliance on the protection of Divine Providence, we mutually pledge to each other our lives, our fortunes, and our sacred honor.

The foregoing Declaration was, by order of Congress, engrossed, and signed by the following members:

JOHN HANCOCK

New Hampshire
Josiah Bartlett
William Whipple
Matthew Thornton

Massachusetts Bay
Samuel Adams
John Adams
Robert Treat Paine
Elbridge Gerry

Rhode Island
Stephen Hopkins
William Ellery

Connecticut
Roger Sherman
Samuel Huntington
William Williams
Oliver Wolcott

New York
William Floyd
Phillip Livingston
Francis Lewis
Lewis Morris

New Jersey
Richard Stockton
John Witherspoon
Francis Hopkinson
John Hart
Abraham Clark

Pennsylvania
Robert Morris
Benjamin Rush
Benjamin Franklin
John Morton
George Clymer
James Smith
George Taylor
James Wilson
George Ross

Delaware	North Carolina	Virginia	Georgia
Caesar Rodney	William Hooper	George Wythe	Button Gwinnett
George Read	Joseph Hewes	Richard Henry Lee	Lyman Hall
Thomas M'Kean	John Penn	Thomas Jefferson	George Walton
		Benjamin Harrison	
Maryland	**South Carolina**	Thomas Nelson, Jr.	
Samuel Chase	Edward Rutledge	Francis Lightfoot Lee	
William Paca	Thomas Heyward, Jr.	Carter Braxton	
Thomas Stone	Thomas Lynch, Jr.		
Charles Carroll,	Arthur Middleton		
of Carrollton			

Resolved, That copies of the Declaration be sent to the several assemblies, conventions, and committees, or councils of safety, and to the several commanding officers of the continental troops; that it be proclaimed in each of the United States, at the head of the army.

THE ARTICLES OF CONFEDERATION AND PERPETUAL UNION

Agreed to in Congress, November 15, 1777.
Ratified March 1781.

BETWEEN THE STATES OF NEW HAMPSHIRE, MASSACHU-SETTS BAY, RHODE ISLAND AND PROVIDENCE PLANTA-TIONS, CONNECTICUT, NEW YORK, NEW JERSEY, PENN-SYLVANIA, DELAWARE, MARYLAND, VIRGINIA, NORTH CAROLINA, SOUTH CAROLINA, GEORGIA.*

Article 1

The stile of this confederacy shall be "The United States of America."

Article 2

Each State retains its sovereignty, freedom and independence, and every power, jurisdiction, and right, which is not by this confederation expressly delegated to the United States, in Congress assembled.

Article 3

The said states hereby severally enter into a firm league of friendship with each other for their common defence, the security of their liberties and their mutual and general welfare; binding themselves to assist each other against all force offered to, or attacks made upon them, or any of them, on account of religion, sovereignty, trade, or any other pretence whatever.

---

* This copy of the final draft of the Articles of Confederation is taken from the *Journals,* 9:907–925, November 15, 1777.

Article 4

The better to secure and perpetuate mutual friendship and intercourse among the people of the different states in this union, the free inhabitants of each of these states, paupers, vagabonds, and fugitives from justice excepted, shall be entitled to all privileges and immunities of free citizens in the several states; and the people of each State shall have free ingress and regress to and from any other State, and shall enjoy therein all the privileges of trade and commerce, subject to the same duties, impositions, and restrictions, as the inhabitants thereof respectively; provided, that such restrictions shall not extend so far as to prevent the removal of property, imported into any State, to any other State of which the owner is an inhabitant; provided also, that no imposition, duties, or restriction, shall be laid by any State on the property of the United States, or either of them.

If any person guilty of, or charged with treason, felony, or other high misdemeanor in any State, shall flee from justice and be found in any of the United States, he shall, upon demand of the governor or executive power of the State from which he fled, be delivered up and removed to the State having jurisdiction of his offence.

Full faith and credit shall be given in each of these states to the records, acts, and judicial proceedings of the courts and magistrates of every other State.

Article 5

For the more convenient management of the general interests of the United States, delegates shall be annually appointed, in such manner as the legislature of each State shall direct, to meet in Congress, on the 1st Monday in November in every year, with a power reserved to each State to recall its delegates, or any of them, at any time within the year, and to send others in their stead for the remainder of the year.

No State shall be represented in Congress by less than two, nor by more than seven members; and no person shall be capable of being a delegate for more than three years in any term of six years; nor shall any person, being a delegate, be capable of holding any office under the United States, for which he, or any other for his benefit, receives any salary, fees, or emolument of any kind.

Each State shall maintain its own delegates in a meeting of the states, and while they act as members of the committee of the states.

In determining questions in the United States, in Congress assembled, each State shall have one vote.

Freedom of speech and debate in Congress shall not be impeached or questioned in any court or place out of Congress: and the members of Congress shall be protected in their persons from arrests and imprisonments, during the time of their going to and from, and attendance on Congress, except for treason, felony, or breach of the peace.

Article 6

No State, without the consent of the United States, in Congress assembled, shall send any embassy to, or receive any embassy from, or enter into any conference, agreement, alliance, or treaty with any king, prince, or state; nor shall any person, holding any office of profit or trust under the United States, or any of them, accept of any present, emolument, office or title, of any kind whatever, from any king, prince, or foreign state; nor shall the United States, in Congress assembled, or any of them, grant any title of nobility.

No two or more states shall enter into any treaty, confederation, or alliance, whatever, between them, without the consent of the United States, in Congress assembled, specifying accurately the purposes for which the same is to be entered into, and how long it shall continue.

No state shall lay any imposts or duties which may interfere with any stipulations in treaties entered into by the United States, in Congress assembled, with any king, prince, or state, in pursuance of any treaties already proposed by Congress to the courts of France and Spain.

No vessels of war shall be kept up in time of peace by any State, except such number only as shall be deemed necessary by the United States, in Congress assembled, for the defence of such State or its trade; nor shall any body of forces be kept up by any State, in time of peace, except such number

only as, in the judgment of the United States, in Congress assembled, shall be deemed requisite to garrison the forts necessary for the defence of such State; but every State shall always keep up a well regulated and disciplined militia, sufficiently armed and accoutred, and shall provide, and constantly have ready for use, in public stores, a due number of field pieces and tents, and a proper quantity of arms, ammunition and camp equipage.

No State shall engage in any war without the consent of the United States, in Congress assembled, unless such State be actually invaded by enemies, or shall have received certain advice of a resolution being formed by some nation of Indians to invade such State, and the danger is so imminent as not to admit of a delay till the United States, in Congress assembled, can be consulted; nor shall any State grant commissions to any ships or vessels of war, nor letters of marque or reprisal, except it be after a declaration of war by the United States, in Congress assembled, and then only against the kingdom or state, and the subjects thereof, against which war has been so declared, and under such regulations as shall be established by the United States, in Congress assembled, unless such State be infested by pirates, in which case vessels of war may be fitted out for that occasion, and kept so long as the danger shall continue, or until the United States, in Congress assembled, shall determine otherwise.

Article 7

When land forces are raised by any State for the common defence, all officers of or under the rank of colonel, shall be appointed by the legislature of each State respectively, by whom such forces shall be raised, or in such manner as such State shall direct; and all vacancies shall be filled up by the State which first made the appointment.

Article 8

All charges of war and all other expences, that shall be incurred for the common defence or general welfare, and allowed by the United States, in Congress assembled, shall be defrayed out of a common treasury, which shall be supplied by the several states, in proportion to the value of all land within each State, granted to or surveyed for any person, as such land and the buildings and improvements thereon shall be estimated according to such mode as the United States, in Congress assembled, shall, from time to time, direct and appoint.

The taxes for paying that proportion shall be laid and levied by the authority and direction of the legislatures of the several states, within the time agreed upon by the United States, in Congress assembled.

Article 9

The United States, in Congress assembled, shall have the sole and exclusive right and power of determining on peace and war, except in the cases mentioned in the 6th article; of sending and receiving ambassadors; entering into treaties and alliances, provided that no treaty of commerce shall be made, whereby the legislative power of the respective states shall be restrained from imposing such imposts and duties on foreigners as their own people are subjected to, or from prohibiting the exportation or importation of any species of goods or commodities whatsoever; of establishing rules for deciding, in all cases, what captures on land or water shall be legal, and in what manner prizes, taken by land or naval forces in the service of the United States, shall be divided or appropriated; of granting letters of marque and reprisal in times of peace; appointing courts for the trial of piracies and felonies committed on the high seas, and establishing courts for receiving and determining, finally, appeals in all cases of captures; provided, that no member of Congress shall be appointed a judge of any of the said courts.

The United States, in Congress assembled, shall also be the last resort on appeal in all disputes and differences now subsisting, or that hereafter may arise between two or more states concerning boundary, jurisdiction or any other cause whatever; which authority shall always be exercised in the manner following: whenever the legislative or executive authority, or lawful agent of any State, in controversy with another, shall present a petition to Congress, stating the matter in question, and praying for a hearing, notice thereof shall be given, by order of Congress, to the legislative or executive authority of the other State in controversy, and a day assigned for the appearance of the parties by their lawful agents, who shall then be directed to appoint, by joint consent, commissioners or judges to constitute a court for hearing and determining the matter in question; but, if they cannot agree, Congress shall name three persons out of each of the United States, and from the list of such persons each party shall alternately strike out one, the petitioners beginning, until the number shall be reduced to thirteen; and from that number not less than seven, nor more than nine names, as Congress shall direct, shall, in the presence of Congress, be drawn out by lot; and the persons whose names shall be so drawn, or any five of them, shall be commissioners or judges to hear and finally determine the controversy, so always as a major part of the judges who shall hear the cause shall agree in the determination; and if either party shall neglect to attend at the day appointed, without shewing reasons which Congress shall judge sufficient, or, being present, shall refuse to strike, the Congress shall proceed to nominate three persons out of each State, and the secretary of Congress shall strike in behalf of such party absent or refusing; and the judgment and sentence of the court to be appointed, in the manner before prescribed, shall be final and conclusive; and if any of the parties shall refuse to submit to the authority of such court, or to appear or defend their claim or cause, the court shall nevertheless proceed to pronounce sentence or judgment, which shall, in like manner, be final and decisive, the judgment or sentence and other proceedings begin, in either case, transmitted to Congress, and lodged among the acts of Congress for the security of the parties concerned: provided, that every commissioner, before he sits in judgment, shall take an oath, to be administered by one of the judges of the supreme or superior court of the State where the cause shall be tried, "well and truly to hear and determine the matter in question, according to the best of his judgment, without favour, affection, or hope of reward:" provided, also, that no State shall be deprived of territory for the benefit of the United States.

All controversies concerning the private right of soil, claimed under different grants of two or more states, whose jurisdictions, as they may respect such lands and the states which passed such grants, are adjusted, the said grants, or either of them, being at the same time claimed to have originated antecedent to such settlement of jurisdiction, shall, on the petition of either party to the Congress of the United States, be finally determined, as near as may be, in the same manner as is before prescribed for deciding disputes respecting territorial jurisdiction between different states.

The United States, in Congress assembled, shall also have the sole and exclusive right and power of regulating the alloy and value of coin struck by their own authority, or by that of the respective states; fixing the standard of weights and measures throughout the United States; regulating the trade and managing all affairs with the Indians not members of any of the states; provided that the legislative right of any State within its own limits be not infringed or violated; establishing and regulating post offices from one State to another throughout all the United States, and exacting such postage on the papers passing through the same as may be requisite to defray the expences of the said office; appointing all officers of the land forces in the service of the United States, excepting regimental officers; appointing all the officers of the naval forces, and commissioning all officers whatever in the service of the United States; making rules for the government and regulation of the said land and naval forces, and directing their operations.

The United States, in Congress assembled, shall have authority to appoint a committee to sit in the recess of Congress, to be denominated "a Committee of the States," and to consist of one delegate from each State, and to appoint such other committees and civil officers as may be necessary for managing the general affairs of the United States, under their direction; to appoint one of their number to preside; provided that no person be allowed to serve in the office of president more than one year in any term of three years; to ascertain the necessary sums of money to be raised for the service of the United States, and to appropriate and apply the same for defraying the public expences; to borrow money or emit bills on the credit of the United States, transmitting, every half year, to the respective states, an account of the sums of money so borrowed or emitted; to build and equip a navy; to agree upon the number of land forces, and to make requisitions from each State for its quota, in proportion to the number of white inhabitants in such State; which requisitions shall be binding; and thereupon, the legislature of each State shall appoint the regimental officers, raise the men, and cloathe, arm, and equip them in a soldier-like manner, at the expence of the United States; and the officers and men so cloathed, armed, and equipped, shall march to the place appointed and within the time agreed on by the United States, in Congress assembled; but if the United States, in Congress assembled, shall, on consideration of circumstances, judge proper that any State should not raise men, or should raise a smaller number than its quota, and that any other State should raise a greater number of men than the quota thereof, such extra number shall be raised, officered, cloathed, armed, and equipped in the same manner as the quota of such State, unless the legislature of such State shall judge that such extra number cannot be safely spared out of the same, in which case they shall raise, officer, cloathe, arm, and equip as many of such extra number as they judge can be safely spared. And the officers and men so cloathed, armed, and equipped, shall march to the place appointed and within the time agreed on by the United States, in Congress assembled.

The United States, in Congress assembled, shall never engage in a war, nor grant letters of marque and reprisal in time of peace, nor enter into any treaties or alliances, nor coin money, nor regulate the value thereof, nor ascertain the sums and expences necessary for the defence and welfare of the United States, or any of them: nor emit bills, nor borrow money on the credit of the United States, nor appropriate money, nor agree upon the number of vessels of war to be built or purchased, or the number of land or sea forces to be raised, nor appoint a commander in chief of the army or navy, unless nine states assent to the same; nor shall a question on any other point, except for adjourning from day to day, be determined, unless by the votes of a majority of the United States, in Congress assembled.

The Congress of the United States shall have power to adjourn to any time within the year, and to any place within the United States, so that no period of adjournment be for a longer duration than the space of six months, and shall publish the journal of their proceedings monthly, except such parts thereof, relating to treaties, alliances or military operations, as, in their judgment, require secrecy; and the yeas and nays of the delegates of each State on any question shall be entered on the journal, when it is desired by any delegate; and the delegates of a State, or any of them, at his, or their request, shall be furnished with a transcript of the said journal, except such parts as are above excepted, to lay before the legislatures of the several states.

Article 10

The committee of the states, or any nine of them, shall be authorized to execute, in the recess of Congress, such of the powers of Congress as the United States, in Congress assembled, by the consent of nine states, shall, from time to time, think expedient to vest them with; provided, that no power be delegated to the said committee, for the exercise of which, by the articles of confederation, the voice of nine states, in the Congress of the United States assembled, is requisite.

Article 11

Canada acceding to this confederation, and joining in the measures of the United States, shall be admitted into and entitled to all the advantages of this union; but no other colony shall be admitted into the same, unless such admission be agreed to by nine states.

Article 12

All bills of credit emitted, monies borrowed and debts contracted by, or under the authority of Congress before the assembling of the United States, in pursuance of the present confederation, shall be deemed and considered as a charge against the United States, for payment and satisfaction whereof the said United States and the public faith are hereby solemnly pledged.

Article 13

Every State shall abide by the determinations of the United States, in Congress assembled, on all questions which, by this confederation, are submitted to them. And the articles of this confederation shall be inviolably observed by every State, and the union shall be perpetual; nor shall any alteration at any time hereafter be made in any of them, unless such alteration be agreed to in a Congress of the United States, and be afterwards confirmed by the legislatures of every State.

These articles shall be proposed to the legislatures of all the United States, to be considered, and if approved of by them, they are advised to authorize their delegates to ratify the same in the Congress of the United States; which being done, the same shall become conclusive.

THE CONSTITUTION OF THE UNITED STATES*

Agreed to by Philadelphia Convention, September 17, 1787. Implemented March 4, 1789.

Preamble

We the people of the United States, in order to form a more perfect union, establish justice, insure domestic tranquility, provide for the common defense, promote the general welfare, and secure the blessings of liberty to ourselves and our posterity, do ordain and establish this Constitution for the United States of America.

Article I

Section 1 All legislative powers herein granted shall be vested in a Congress of the United States, which shall consist of a Senate and a House of Representatives.

Section 2 The House of Representatives shall be composed of members chosen every second year by the people of the several States, and the electors in each State shall have the qualifications requisite for electors of the most numerous branch of the State Legislature.

No person shall be a Representative who shall not have attained to the age of twenty-five years, and been seven years a citizen of the United States, and who shall not, when elected, be an inhabitant of that State in which he shall be chosen.

Representatives and direct taxes shall be apportioned among the several States which may be included within this Union, according to their respective numbers, *which shall be determined by adding to the whole number of free persons, including those bound to service for a term of years and excluding Indians not taxed, three-fifths of all other persons.* The actual enumeration shall be made within three years after the first meeting of the Congress of the United States, and within every subsequent term of ten years, in such manner as they shall by law direct. The number of Representatives shall not exceed one for every thirty thousand, but each State shall have at least one Representative; *and until such enumeration shall be made, the State of New Hampshire shall be entitled to choose three, Massachusetts eight, Rhode Island and Providence Plantations one, Connecticut five, New York six, New Jersey four, Pennsylvania eight, Delaware one, Maryland six, Virginia ten, North Carolina five, South Carolina five, and Georgia three.*

When vacancies happen in the representation from any State, the Executive authority thereof shall issue writs of election to fill such vacancies.

The House of Representatives shall choose their Speaker and other officers; and shall have the sole power of impeachment.

Section 3 The Senate of the United States shall be composed of two Senators from each State, *chosen by the legislature thereof,* for six years; and each Senator shall have one vote.

Immediately after they shall be assembled in consequence of the first election, they shall be divided as equally as may be into three classes. The seats of the Senators of the first class shall be vacated at the expiration of the second year, of the second class at the expiration of the fourth year, and of the third class at the expiration of the sixth year, so that one-third may be chosen every second year; *and if vacancies happen by resignation or otherwise, during the recess of the legislature of any State, the Executive thereof may make temporary appointments until the next meeting of the legislature, which shall then fill such vacancies.*

No person shall be a Senator who shall not have attained to the age of thirty years, and been nine years a citizen of the United States, and who shall not, when elected, be an inhabitant of that State for which he shall be chosen.

The Vice-President of the United States shall be President of the Senate, but shall have no vote, unless they be equally divided.

The Senate shall choose their other officers, and also a President *pro tempore,* in the absence of the Vice-President, or when he shall exercise the office of President of the United States.

The Senate shall have the sole power to try all impeachments. When sitting for that purpose, they shall be on oath or affirmation. When the President of the United States is tried, the Chief Justice shall preside: and no person shall be convicted without the concurrence of two-thirds of the members present.

Judgment in cases of impeachment shall not extend further than to removal from the office, and disqualification to hold and enjoy any office of honor, trust or profit under the United States: but the party convicted shall nevertheless be liable and subject to indictment, trial, judgment and punishment, according to law.

Section 4 The times, places and manner of holding elections for Senators and Representatives shall be prescribed in each State by the legislature thereof; but the Congress may at any time by law make or alter such regulations, except as to the places of choosing Senators.

The Congress shall assemble at least once in every year, and such meeting *shall be on the first*

---

*Passages no longer in effect are in italic type.

Monday in December, unless they shall by law appoint a different day.

Section 5   Each house shall be the judge of the elections, returns and qualifications of its own members, and a majority of each shall constitute a quorum to do business; but a smaller number may adjourn from day to day, and may be authorized to compel the attendance of absent members, in such manner, and under such penalties, as each house may provide.

Each house may determine the rules of its proceedings, punish its members for disorderly behavior, and with the concurrence of two-thirds, expel a member.

Each house shall keep a journal of its proceedings, and from time to time publish the same, excepting such parts as may in their judgment require secrecy; and the yeas and nays of the members of either house on any question shall, at the desire of one-fifth of those present, be entered on the journal.

Neither house, during the session of Congress, shall, without the consent of the other, adjourn for more than three days, nor to any other place than that in which the two houses shall be sitting.

Section 6   The Senators and Representatives shall receive a compensation for their services, to be ascertained by law and paid out of the treasury of the United States. They shall in all cases except treason, felony and breach of the peace, be privileged from arrest during their attendance at the session of their respective houses, and in going to and returning from the same; and for any speech or debate in either house, they shall not be questioned in any other place.

No Senator or Representative shall, during the time for which he was elected, be appointed to any civil office under the authority of the United States, which shall have been created, or the emoluments whereof shall have been increased, during such time; and no person holding any office under the United States shall be a member of either house during his continuance in office.

Section 7   All bills for raising revenue shall originate in the House of Representatives; but the Senate may propose or concur with amendments as on other bills.

Every bill which shall have passed the House of Representatives and the Senate, shall, before it become a law, be presented to the President of the United States; if he approve he shall sign it, but if not he shall return it with objections to that house in which it shall have originated, who shall enter the objections at large on their journal, and proceed to reconsider it. If after such reconsideration two-thirds of that house shall agree to pass the bill, it shall be sent, together with the objections, to the other house, by which it shall likewise be reconsidered, and, if approved by two-thirds of that house,

it shall become a law. But in all such cases the votes of both houses shall be determined by yeas and nays, and the names of the persons voting for and against the bill shall be entered on the journal of each house respectively. If any bill shall not be returned by the President within ten days (Sundays excepted) after it shall have been presented to him, the same shall be a law, in like manner as if he had signed it, unless the Congress by their adjournment prevent its return, in which case it shall not be a law.

Every order, resolution, or vote to which the concurrence of the Senate and House of Representatives may be necessary (except on a question of adjournment) shall be presented to the President of the United States; and before the same shall take effect, shall be approved by him, or being disapproved by him, shall be repassed by two-thirds of the Senate and House of Representatives, according to the rules and limitations prescribed in the case of a bill.

Section 8   The Congress shall have power

To lay and collect taxes, duties, imposts, and excises, to pay the debts and provide for the common defense and general welfare of the United States; but all duties, imposts and excises shall be uniform throughout the United States;

To borrow money on the credit of the United States;

To regulate commerce with foreign nations, and among the several States, and with the Indian tribes;

To establish an uniform rule of naturalization, and uniform laws on the subject of bankruptcies throughout the United States;

To coin money, regulate the value thereof, and of foreign coin, and fix the standard of weights and measures;

To provide for the punishment of counterfeiting the securities and current coin of the United States;

To establish post offices and post roads;

To promote the progress of science and useful arts by securing for limited times to authors and inventors the exclusive right to their respective writings and discoveries;

To constitute tribunals inferior to the Supreme Court;

To define and punish piracies and felonies committed on the high seas and offences against the law of nations;

To declare war, grant letters of marque and reprisal, and make rules concerning captures on land and water;

To raise and support armies, but no appropriation of money to that use shall be for a longer term than two years;

To provide and maintain a navy;

To make rules for the government and regulation of the land and naval forces;

THE CONSTITUTION OF THE UNITED STATES

To provide for calling forth the militia to execute the laws of the Union, suppress insurrections and repel invasions;

To provide for organizing, arming, and disciplining the militia, and for governing such part of them as may be employed in the service of the United States, reserving to the States respectively the appointment of the officers, and the authority of training the militia according to the discipline prescribed by Congress;

To exercise exclusive legislation in all cases whatsoever, over such district (not exceeding ten miles square) as may, by cession of particular States, and the acceptance of Congress, become the seat of the government of the United States, and to exercise like authority over all places purchased by the consent of the legislature of the State, in which the same shall be, for erection of forts, magazines, arsenals, dock-yards, and other needful buildings;—and

To make all laws which shall be necessary and proper for carrying into execution the foregoing powers, and all other powers vested by this Constitution in the government of the United States, or in any department or officer thereof.

Section 9 *The migration or importation of such persons as any of the States now existing shall think proper to admit shall not be prohibited by the Congress prior to the year one thousand eight hundred and eight; but a tax or duty may be imposed on such importation, not exceeding ten dollars for each person.*

The privilege of the writ of habeas corpus shall not be suspended, unless when in cases of rebellion or invasion the public safety may require it.

No bill of attainder or ex post facto law shall be passed.

No capitation, or other direct, tax shall be laid, unless in proportion to the census or enumeration herein before directed to be taken.

No tax or duty shall be laid on articles exported from any State.

No preference shall be given by any regulation of commerce or revenue to the ports of one State over those of another; nor shall vessels bound to, or from, one State be obliged to enter, clear, or pay duties in another.

No money shall be drawn from the treasury, but in consequence of appropriations made by law; and a regular statement and account of the receipts and expenditures of all public money shall be published from time to time.

No title of nobility shall be granted by the United States: and no person holding any office of profit or trust under them, shall, without the consent of the Congress, accept of any present, emolument, office, or title, of any kind whatever, from any king, prince, or foreign state.

Section 10 No State shall enter into any treaty, alliance, or confederation; grant letters of marque and reprisal; coin money; emit bills of credit; make anything but gold and silver coin a tender in payment of debts; pass any bill of attainder, ex post facto law, or law impairing the obligation of contracts, or grant any title of nobility.

No State shall, without the consent of Congress, lay any imposts or duties on imports or exports, except what may be absolutely necessary for executing its inspection laws: and the net produce of all duties and imposts, laid by any State on imports or exports, shall be for the use of the treasury of the United States; and all such laws shall be subject to the revision and control of the Congress.

No State shall, without the consent of Congress, lay any duty of tonnage, keep troops, or ships of war in time of peace, enter into any agreement or compact with another State, or with a foreign power, or engage in war, unless actually invaded, or in such imminent danger as will not admit of delay.

Article II

Section 1 The executive power shall be vested in a President of the United States of America. He shall hold his office during the term of four years, and, together with the Vice-President, chosen for the same term, be elected as follows:

Each State shall appoint, in such manner as the legislature thereof may direct, a number of electors, equal to the whole number of Senators and Representatives to which the State may be entitled in the Congress; but no Senator or Representative, or person holding an office of trust or profit under the United States, shall be appointed an elector.

The electors shall meet in their respective States, and vote by ballot for two persons, of whom one at least shall not be an inhabitant of the same State with themselves. And they shall make a list of all the persons voted for, and of the number of votes for each; which list they shall sign and certify, and transmit sealed to the seat of government of the United States, directed to the President of the Senate. The President of the Senate shall, in the presence of the Senate and House of Representatives, open all the certificates, and the votes shall then be counted. The person having the greatest number of votes shall be the President, if such number be a majority of the whole number of electors appointed; and if there be more than one who have such majority, and have an equal number of votes, then the House of Representatives shall immediately choose by ballot one of them for President; and if no person have a majority, then from the five highest on the list said house shall in like manner choose the President. But in choosing the President the votes shall be taken by States, the representation from each State having one vote; a quorum for this purpose shall consist of a member or members from two-thirds of the States, and a majority of all the States shall be necessary to a choice. In every case, after the choice of the President, the person having the greatest number of votes of the electors shall be the Vice-President. But if there should remain two or more who have equal votes, the Senate shall choose from them by ballot the Vice-President.

The Congress may determine the time of choosing the electors, and the day on which they shall give their votes; which day shall be the same throughout the United States.

No person except a natural-born citizen, *or a citizen of the United States at the time of the adoption of this Constitution*, shall be eligible to the office of President; neither shall any person be eligible to that office who shall not have attained to the age of thirty-five years, and been fourteen years a resident within the United States.

In cases of the removal of the President from office or of his death, resignation, or inability to discharge the powers and duties of the said office, the same shall devolve on the Vice-President, and the Congress may by law provide for the case of removal, death, resignation, or inability, both of the President and Vice-President, declaring what officer shall then act as President, and such officer shall act accordingly, until the disability be removed, or a President shall be elected.

The President shall, at stated times, receive for his services a compensation, which shall neither be increased nor diminished during the period for which he shall have been elected, and he shall not receive within that period any other emolument from the United States, or any of them.

Before he enter on the execution of his office, he shall take the following oath or affirmation:—"I do solemnly swear (or affirm) that I will faithfully execute the office of the President of the United States, and will to the best of my ability preserve, protect and defend the Constitution of the United States."

Section 2 The President shall be commander in chief of the army and navy of the United States, and of the militia of the several States, when called into the actual service of the United States; he may require the opinion, in writing, of the principal officer in each of the executive departments, upon any subject relating to the duties of their respective offices, and he shall have power to grant reprieves and pardons for offenses against the United States, except in cases of impeachment.

He shall have power, by and with the advice and consent of the Senate, to make treaties, provided two-thirds of the Senators present concur; and he shall nominate, and by and with the advice and consent of the Senate, shall appoint ambassadors, other public ministers and consuls, judges of the Supreme Court, and all other officers of the United States, whose appointments are not herein otherwise provided for, and which shall be established by law: but Congress may by law vest the appointment of such inferior officers, as they think proper, in the

President alone, in the courts of law, or in the heads of departments.

The President shall have power to fill up all vacancies that may happen during the recess of the Senate, by granting commissions which shall expire at the end of their next session.

Section 3 He shall from time to time give to the Congress information of the state of the Union, and recommend to their consideration such measures as he shall judge necessary and expedient; he may, on extraordinary occasions, convene both houses, or either of them, and in case of disagreement between them, with respect to the time of adjournment, he may adjourn them to such time as he shall think proper; he shall receive ambassadors and other public ministers; he shall take care that the laws be faithfully executed, and shall commission all the officers of the United States.

Section 4 The President, Vice-President and all civil officers of the United States shall be removed from office on impeachment for, and on conviction of, treason, bribery, or other high crimes and misdemeanors.

Article III

Section 1 The judicial power of the United States shall be vested in one Supreme Court, and in such inferior courts as the Congress may from time to time ordain and establish. The judges, both of the Supreme and inferior courts, shall hold their offices during good behavior, and shall, at stated times, receive for their services a compensation which shall not be diminished during their continuance in office.

Section 2 The judicial power shall extend to all cases, in law and equity, arising under this Constitution, the laws of the United States, and treaties made, or which shall be made, under their authority;—to all cases affecting ambassadors, other public ministers and consuls;—to all cases of admiralty and maritime jurisdiction;—to controversies to which the United States shall be a party;—to controversies between two or more States;—*between a State and citizens of another State;*—between citizens of different States;—between citizens of the same State claiming lands under grants of different States, and between a State, or the citizens thereof, and foreign states, citizens or subjects.

In all cases affecting ambassadors, other public ministers and consuls, and those in which a State shall be party, the Supreme Court shall have original jurisdiction. In all the other cases before mentioned, the Supreme Court shall have appellate jurisdiction, both as to law and fact, with such exceptions, and under such regulations, as the Congress shall make.

The trial of all crimes, except in cases of impeachment, shall be by jury; and such trial shall be held in the State where said crimes shall have been committed; but when not committed within any State, the trial shall be at such place or places as the Congress may by Law have directed.

Section 3 Treason against the United States shall consist only in levying war against them, or in adhering to their enemies, giving them aid and comfort. No person shall be convicted of treason unless on the testimony of two witnesses to the same overt act, or on confession in open court.

The Congress shall have power to declare the punishment of treason, but no attainder of treason shall work corruption of blood, or forfeiture except during the life of the person attainted.

Article IV

Section 1 Full faith and credit shall be given in each State to the public acts, records, and judicial proceedings of every other State. And the Congress may by general laws prescribe the manner in which such acts, records, and proceedings shall be proved, and the effect thereof.

Section 2 The citizens of each State shall be entitled to all privileges and immunities of citizens in the several States.

A person charged in any State with treason, felony, or other crime, who shall flee from justice, and be found in another State, shall on demand of the executive authority of the State from which he fled, be delivered up, to be removed to the State having jurisdiction of the crime.

No Person held to service or labor in one State, under the laws thereof, escaping into another, shall, in consequence of any law or regulation therein, be discharged from such service or labor, but shall be delivered up on claim of the party to whom such service or labor may be due.

Section 3 New States may be admitted by the Congress into this Union; but no new State shall be formed or erected within the jurisdiction of any other State; nor any State be formed by the junction of two or more States, or parts of States, without the consent of the legislatures of the States concerned as well as of the Congress.

The Congress shall have power to dispose of and make all needful rules and regulations respecting the territory or other property belonging to the United States; and nothing in this Constitution shall be so construed as to prejudice any claims of the United States, or of any particular State.

Section 4 The United States shall guarantee to every State in this Union a republican form of government, and shall protect each of them against invasion; and on application of the legislature, or of the executive (when the legislature cannot be convened), against domestic violence.

Article V

The Congress, whenever two-thirds of both houses shall deem it necessary, shall propose amendments to this Constitution, or, on the application of the legislatures of two-thirds of the several States, shall call a convention for proposing amendments, which, in either case, shall be valid to all intents and purposes, as part of this Constitution, when ratified by the legislatures of three-fourths of the several States, or by conventions in three-fourths thereof, as the one or the other mode of ratification may be proposed by the Congress; provided *that no amendments which may be made prior to the year one thousand eight hundred and eight shall in any manner affect the first and fourth clauses in the ninth section of the first article*; and that no State, without its consent, shall be deprived of its equal suffrage in the Senate.

Article VI

All debts contracted and engagements entered into, before the adoption of this Constitution, shall be as valid against the United States under this Constitution, as under the Confederation.

This Constitution, and the laws of the United States which shall be made in pursuance thereof; and all treaties made, or which shall be made, under the authority of the United States, shall be the supreme law of the land; and the judges in every State shall be bound thereby, anything in the Constitution or laws of any State to the contrary notwithstanding.

The Senators and Representatives before mentioned, and the members of the several State legislatures, and all executive and judicial officers, both of the United States and of the several States, shall be bound by oath or affirmation to support this Constitution; but no religious test shall ever be required as a qualification to any office or public trust under the United States.

Article VII

The ratification of the conventions of nine States shall be sufficient for the establishment of this Constitution between the States so ratifying the same.

Done in convention by the unanimous consent of the States present, the seventeenth day of September in the year of our Lord one thousand seven hundred and eighty-seven and of the Independence of the United States of America the twelfth. In witness whereof we have hereunto subscribed our names.

GEORGE WASHINGTON

PRESIDENT AND DEPUTY FROM VIRGINIA

New Hampshire
John Langdon
Nicholas Gilman

Massachusetts
Nathaniel Gorham
Rufus King

Connecticut
William Samuel
   Johnson
Roger Sherman

New York
Alexander Hamilton

New Jersey
William Livingston
David Brearley
William Paterson
Jonathan Dayton

Pennsylvania
Benjamin Franklin
Thomas Mifflin
Robert Morris
George Clymer
Thomas FitzSimons
Jared Ingersoll
James Wilson
Gouverneur Morris

Delaware
George Read
Gunning Bedford, Jr.
John Dickinson
Richard Bassett
Jacob Broom

Maryland
James McHenry
Daniel of St. Thomas
   Jenifer
Daniel Carroll

Virginia
John Blair
James Madison, Jr.

North Carolina
William Blount
Richard Dobbs Spaight
Hugh Williamson

South Carolina
John Rutledge
Charles Cotesworth
   Pinckney
Charles Pinckney
Pierce Butler

Georgia
William Few
Abraham Baldwin

AMENDMENTS TO THE CONSTITUTION WITH ANNOTATIONS
(including the six unratified amendments)

IN THEIR EFFORT TO GAIN Antifederalists' support for the Constitution, Federalists frequently pointed to the inclusion of Article 5, which provides an orderly method of amending the Constitution. In contrast, the Articles of Confederation, which were universally recognized as seriously flawed, offered no means of amendment. For their part, Antifederalists argued that the amendment process was so "intricate" that one might as easily roll "sixes an hundred times in succession" as change the Constitution.

The system for amendment laid out in the Constitution requires that two-thirds of both houses of Congress agree to a proposed amendment, which must then be ratified by three-quarters of the legislatures of the states. Alternatively, an amendment may be proposed by a convention called by the legislatures of two-thirds of the states. Since 1789, members of Congress have proposed thousands of amendments. Besides the seventeen amendments added since 1789, only the six "unratified" ones included here were approved by two-thirds of both houses and sent to the states for ratification.

Among the many amendments that never made it out of Congress have been proposals to declare dueling, divorce, and interracial marriage unconstitutional as well as proposals to establish a national university, to acknowledge the sovereignty of Jesus Christ, and to prohibit any person from possessing wealth in excess of $10 million.*

Among the issues facing Americans today that might lead to constitutional amendment are efforts to balance the federal budget, to limit the number of terms elected officials may serve, to limit access to or prohibit abortion, to establish English as the official language of the United States, and to prohibit flag burning. None of these proposed amendments has yet garnered enough support in Congress to be sent to the states for ratification.

Although the first ten amendments to the Constitution are commonly known as the Bill of Rights, only Amendments 1–8 actually provide guarantees of individual rights. Amendments 9 and 10 deal with the structure of power within the constitutional system. The Bill of Rights was promised to appease Antifederalists who refused to ratify the Constitution without guarantees of individual liberties and limitations to federal power. After studying more than two hundred amendments recommended by the ratifying conventions of the states, Federalist James Madison presented a list of seventeen to Congress, which used Madison's list as the foundation for the twelve amendments that were sent to the states for ratification. Ten of the twelve were adopted in 1791. The first on the list of twelve,

---

*Richard B. Bernstein, *Amending America* (New York: Times Books, 1993), 177–81.

known as the Reapportionment Amendment, was never adopted (see page A-15). The second proposed amendment was adopted in 1992 as Amendment 27 (see page A-24).

Amendment I

Congress shall make no law respecting an establishment of religion, or prohibiting the free exercise thereof; or abridging the freedom of speech, or of the press; or the right of the people peaceably to assemble, and to petition the government for a redress of grievances.

♦♦♦

The First Amendment is a potent symbol for many Americans. Most are well aware of their rights to free speech, freedom of the press, and freedom of religion and their rights to assemble and to petition, even if they cannot cite the exact words of this amendment.

The First Amendment guarantee of freedom of religion has two clauses: the "free exercise clause," which allows individuals to practice or not practice any religion, and the "establishment clause," which prevents the federal government from discriminating against or favoring any particular religion. This clause was designed to create what Thomas Jefferson referred to as "a wall of separation between church and state." In the 1960s, the Supreme Court ruled that the First Amendment prohibits prayer (see Engel v. Vitale, *online) and Bible reading in public schools.*

Although the rights to free speech and freedom of the press are established in the First Amendment, it was not until the twentieth century that the Supreme Court began to explore the full meaning of these guarantees. In 1919, the Court ruled in Schenck v. United States *(online) that the government could suppress free expression only where it could cite a "clear and present danger." In a decision that continues to raise controversies, the Court ruled in 1990, in* Texas v. Johnson, *that flag burning is a form of symbolic speech protected by the First Amendment.*

Amendment II

A well-regulated militia being necessary to the security of a free State, the right of the people to keep and bear arms shall not be infringed.

♦♦♦

Fear of a standing army under the control of a hostile government made the Second Amendment an important part of the Bill of Rights. Advocates of gun ownership claim that the amendment prevents the government from regulating firearms. Proponents of gun control argue that the amendment is designed only to protect the right of the states to maintain militia units.

In 1939, the Supreme Court ruled in United States v. Miller *that the Second Amendment did not protect the right of an individual to own a sawed-off shotgun, which*

it argued was not ordinary militia equipment. Since then, the Supreme Court has refused to hear Second Amendment cases, while lower courts have upheld firearms regulations. Several justices currently on the bench seem to favor a narrow interpretation of the Second Amendment, which would allow gun control legislation. The controversy over the impact of the Second Amendment on gun owners and gun control legislation will certainly continue.

Amendment III

No soldier shall, in time of peace, be quartered in any house without the consent of the owner, nor in time of war, but in a manner to be prescribed by law.

♦♦♦

The Third Amendment was extremely important to the framers of the Constitution, but today it is nearly forgotten. American colonists were especially outraged that they were forced to quarter British troops in the years before and during the American Revolution. The philosophy of the Third Amendment has been viewed by some justices and scholars as the foundation of the modern constitutional right to privacy. One example of this can be found in Justice William O. Douglas's opinion in Griswold v. Connecticut *(online).*

Amendment IV

The right of the people to be secure in their persons, houses, papers, and effects, against unreasonable searches and seizures, shall not be violated, and no warrants shall issue but upon probable cause, supported by oath or affirmation, and particularly describing the place to be searched, and the persons or things to be seized.

♦♦♦

In the years before the Revolution, the houses, barns, stores, and warehouses of American colonists were ransacked by British authorities under "writs of assistance" or general warrants. The British, thus empowered, searched for seditious material or smuggled goods that could then be used as evidence against colonists who were charged with a crime only after the items were found.

The first part of the Fourth Amendment protects citizens from "unreasonable" searches and seizures. The Supreme Court has interpreted this protection as well as the words search *and* seizure *in different ways at different times. At one time, the Court did not recognize electronic eavesdropping as a form of search and seizure, though it does today. At times, an "unreasonable" search has been almost any search carried out without a warrant, but in the two decades before 1969, the Court sometimes sanctioned warrantless searches that it considered reasonable based on "the total atmosphere of the case."*

The second part of the Fourth Amendment defines the procedure for issuing a search warrant and states the requirement of "probable cause," which is generally viewed as evidence indicating that a suspect has committed an offense.

The Fourth Amendment has been controversial because the Court has sometimes excluded evidence that has been seized in violation of constitutional standards. The justification is that excluding such evidence deters violations of the amendment, but doing so may allow a guilty person to escape punishment.

Amendment V

No person shall be held to answer for a capital, or otherwise infamous crime, unless on a presentment or indictment of a grand jury, except in cases arising in the land or naval forces, or in the militia, when in actual service in time of war or public danger; nor shall any person be subject for the same offence to be twice put in jeopardy of life or limb; nor shall be compelled in any criminal case to be a witness against himself, nor be deprived of life, liberty, or property, without due process of law; nor shall private property be taken for public use without just compensation.

♦ ♦ ♦

The Fifth Amendment protects people against government authority in the prosecution of criminal offenses. It prohibits the state, first, from charging a person with a serious crime without a grand jury hearing to decide whether there is sufficient evidence to support the charge and, second, from charging a person with the same crime twice. The best-known aspect of the Fifth Amendment is that it prevents a person from being "compelled . . . to be a witness against himself." The last clause, the "takings clause," limits the power of the government to seize property.

Although invoking the Fifth Amendment is popularly viewed as a confession of guilt, a person may be innocent yet still fear prosecution. For example, during the Red-baiting era of the late 1940s and 1950s, many people who had participated in legal activities that were associated with the Communist Party claimed the Fifth Amendment privilege rather than testify before the House Un-American Activities Committee because the mood of the times cast those activities in a negative light. Since "taking the Fifth" was viewed as an admission of guilt, those people often lost their jobs or became unemployable. (See chapter 26.) Nonetheless, the right to protect oneself against self-incrimination plays an important role in guarding against the collective power of the state.

Amendment VI

In all criminal prosecutions, the accused shall enjoy the right to a speedy and public trial, by an impartial jury of the State and district wherein the crime shall have been committed, which district shall have been previously ascertained by law, and to be informed of the nature and cause of the accusation; to be confronted with the witnesses against him; to have compulsory process for obtaining witnesses in his favor, and to have the assistance of counsel for his defence.

♦ ♦ ♦

The original Constitution put few limits on the government's power to investigate, prosecute, and punish crime. This process was of great concern to the early Americans, however, and of the twenty-eight rights specified in the first eight amendments, fifteen have to do with it. Seven rights are specified in the Sixth Amendment. These include the right to a speedy trial, a public trial, a jury trial, a notice of accusation, confrontation by opposing witnesses, testimony by favorable witnesses, and the assistance of counsel.

Although this amendment originally guaranteed these rights only in cases involving the federal government, the adoption of the Fourteenth Amendment began a process of applying the protections of the Bill of Rights to the states through court cases such as Gideon v. Wainwright *(online).*

Amendment VII

In suits at common law, where the value in controversy shall exceed twenty dollars, the right of trial by jury shall be preserved, and no fact tried by a jury shall be otherwise reexamined in any court of the United States, than according to the rules of the common law.

♦ ♦ ♦

This amendment guarantees people the same right to a trial by jury as was guaranteed by English common law in 1791. Under common law, in civil trials (those involving money damages) the role of the judge was to settle questions of law and that of the jury was to settle questions of fact. The amendment does not specify the size of the jury or its role in a trial, however. The Supreme Court has generally held that those issues be determined by English common law of 1791, which stated that a jury consists of twelve people, that a trial must be conducted before a judge who instructs the jury on the law and advises it on facts, and that a verdict must be unanimous.

Amendment VIII

Excessive bail shall not be required, nor excessive fines imposed, nor cruel and unusual punishments inflicted.

♦ ♦ ♦

The language used to guarantee the three rights in this amendment was inspired by the English Bill of Rights of

AMENDMENTS TO THE CONSTITUTION WITH ANNOTATIONS

1689. *The Supreme Court has not had a lot to say about "excessive fines." In recent years it has agreed that despite the provision against "excessive bail," persons who are believed to be dangerous to others can be held without bail even before they have been convicted.*

Although opponents of the death penalty have not succeeded in using the Eighth Amendment to achieve the end of capital punishment, the clause regarding "cruel and unusual punishments" has been used to prohibit capital punishment in certain cases (see Furman v. Georgia, *online) and to require improved conditions in prisons.*

Amendment IX

The enumeration in the Constitution, of certain rights, shall not be construed to deny or disparage others retained by the people.

♦ ♦ ♦

Some Federalists feared that inclusion of the Bill of Rights in the Constitution would allow later generations of interpreters to claim that the people had surrendered any rights not specifically enumerated there. To guard against this, Madison added language that became the Ninth Amendment. Interest in this heretofore largely ignored amendment revived in 1965 when it was used in a concurring opinion in Griswold v. Connecticut *(online). While Justice William O. Douglas called on the Third Amendment to support the right to privacy in deciding that case, Justice Arthur Goldberg, in the concurring opinion, argued that the right to privacy regarding contraception was an unenumerated right that was protected by the Ninth Amendment.*

In 1980, the Court ruled that the right of the press to attend a public trial was protected by the Ninth Amendment. While some scholars argue that modern judges cannot identify the unenumerated rights that the framers were trying to protect, others argue that the Ninth Amendment should be read as providing a constitutional "presumption of liberty" that allows people to act in any way that does not violate the rights of others.

Amendment X

The powers not delegated to the United States by the Constitution, nor prohibited by it to the States, are reserved to the States respectively, or to the people.

♦ ♦ ♦

The Antifederalists were especially eager to see a "reserved powers clause" explicitly guaranteeing the states control over their internal affairs. Not surprisingly, the Tenth Amendment has been a frequent battleground in the struggle over states' rights and federal supremacy. Prior to the Civil War, the Democratic Republican Party and Jacksonian Democrats invoked the Tenth Amendment to prohibit the federal government from making decisions about whether people in individual states could own slaves. The Tenth Amendment was virtually suspended during Reconstruction following the Civil War. In 1883, however, the Supreme Court declared the Civil Rights Act of 1875 unconstitutional on the grounds that it violated the Tenth Amendment. Business interests also called on the amendment to block efforts at federal regulation.

The Court was inconsistent over the next several decades as it attempted to resolve the tension between the restrictions of the Tenth Amendment and the powers the Constitution granted to Congress to regulate interstate commerce and levy taxes. The Court upheld the Pure Food and Drug Act (1906), the Meat Inspection Acts (1906 and 1907), and the White Slave Traffic Act (1910), all of which affected the states, but struck down an act prohibiting interstate shipment of goods produced through child labor. Between 1934 and 1935, a number of New Deal programs created by Franklin D. Roosevelt were declared unconstitutional on the grounds that they violated the Tenth Amendment. (See chapter 24.) As Roosevelt appointees changed the composition of the Court, the Tenth Amendment was declared to have no substantive meaning. Generally, the amendment is held to protect the rights of states to regulate internal matters such as local government, education, commerce, labor, and business, as well as matters involving families such as marriage, divorce, and inheritance within the state.

Unratified Amendment

Reapportionment Amendment (proposed by Congress September 25, 1789, along with the Bill of Rights)

After the first enumeration required by the first article of the Constitution, there shall be one Representative for every thirty thousand, until the number shall amount to one hundred, after which the proportion shall be so regulated by Congress, that there shall be not less than one hundred Representatives, nor less than one Representative for every forty thousand persons, until the number of Representatives shall amount to two hundred; after which the proportion shall be so regulated by Congress, that there shall not be less than two hundred Representatives, nor more than one Representative for every fifty thousand persons.

♦ ♦ ♦

If the Reapportionment Amendment had passed and remained in effect, the House of Representatives today would have more than 5,000 members rather than 435.

Amendment XI
[Adopted 1798]

The judicial power of the United States shall not be construed to extend to any suit in law or equity, commenced or prosecuted against one of the United States by citizens of another State, or by citizens or subjects of any foreign state.

◆ ◆ ◆

In 1793, the Supreme Court ruled in favor of Alexander Chisholm, executor of the estate of a deceased South Carolina merchant. Chisholm was suing the state of Georgia because the merchant had never been paid for provisions he had supplied during the Revolution. Many regarded this Court decision as an error that violated the intent of the Constitution.

Antifederalists had long feared a federal court system with the power to overrule a state court. When the Constitution was being drafted, Federalists had assured worried Antifederalists that section 2 of Article 3, which allows federal courts to hear cases "between a State and citizens of another State," did not mean that the federal courts were authorized to hear suits against a state by citizens of another state or a foreign country. Antifederalists and many other Americans feared a powerful federal court system because they worried that it would become like the British courts of this period, which were accountable only to the monarch. Furthermore, Chisholm v. Georgia *prompted a series of suits against state governments by creditors and suppliers who had made loans during the war.*

In addition, state legislators and Congress feared that the shaky economies of the new states, as well as the country as a whole, would be destroyed, especially if loyalists who had fled to other countries sought reimbursement for land and property that had been seized. The day after the Supreme Court announced its decision, a resolution proposing the Eleventh Amendment, which overturned the decision in Chisholm v. Georgia, *was introduced in the U.S. Senate.*

Amendment XII

[Adopted 1804]

The electors shall meet in their respective States, and vote by ballot for President and Vice-President, one of whom, at least, shall not be an inhabitant of the same State with themselves; they shall name in their ballots the person voted for as President, and in distinct ballots the person voted for as Vice-President, and they shall make distinct lists of all persons voted for as President, and of all persons voted for as Vice-President, and of the number of votes for each, which lists they shall sign and certify, and transmit sealed to the seat of government of the United States, directed to the President of the Senate;—the President of the Senate shall, in the presence of the Senate and House of Representatives, open all the certificates and the votes shall then be counted;—the person having the greatest number of votes for President

shall be the President, if such number be a majority of the whole number of electors appointed; and if no person have such majority, then from the persons having the highest numbers not exceeding three on the list of those voted for as President, the House of Representatives shall choose immediately, by ballot, the President. But in choosing the President, the votes shall be taken by States, the representation from each State having one vote; a quorum for this purpose shall consist of a member or members from two-thirds of the States, and a majority of all the States shall be necessary to a choice. And if the House of Representatives shall not choose a President whenever the right of choice shall devolve upon them, before *the fourth day of March* next following, then the Vice-President shall act as President, as in the case of the death or other constitutional disability of the President.

The person having the greatest number of votes as Vice-President shall be the Vice-President, if such number be a majority of the whole number of electors appointed; and if no person have a majority, then from the two highest numbers on the list the Senate shall choose the Vice-President; a quorum for the purpose shall consist of two-thirds of the whole number of Senators, and a majority of the whole number shall be necessary to a choice. But no person constitutionally ineligible to the office of President shall be eligible to that of Vice-President of the United States.

◆ ◆ ◆

The framers of the Constitution disliked political parties and assumed that none would ever form. Under the original system, electors chosen by the states would each vote for two candidates. The candidate who won the most votes would become president, while the person who won the second-highest number of votes would become vice president. Rivalries between Federalists and Antifederalists led to the formation of political parties, however, even before George Washington had left office. Though Washington was elected unanimously in 1789 and 1792, the elections of 1796 and 1800 were procedural disasters because of party maneuvering (see chapters 9 and 10). In 1796, Federalist John Adams was chosen as president, and his great rival, the Antifederalist Thomas Jefferson (whose party was called the Republican Party), became his vice president. In 1800, all the electors cast their two votes as one of two party blocs. Jefferson and his fellow Republican nominee, Aaron Burr, were tied with 73 votes each. The contest went to the House of Representatives, which finally elected Jefferson after 36 ballots. The Twelfth Amendment prevents these problems by requiring electors to vote separately for the president and vice president.

Unratified Amendment

Titles of Nobility Amendment (proposed by Congress May 1, 1810)

If any citizen of the United States shall accept, claim, receive or retain any title of nobility or honor or shall, without the consent of Congress, accept and retain any present, pension, office or emolument of any kind whatever, from any emperor, king, prince or foreign power, such person shall cease to be a citizen of the United States, and shall be incapable of holding any office of trust or profit under them or either of them.

♦ ♦ ♦

This amendment would have extended Article 1, section 9, clause 8 of the Constitution, which prevents the awarding of titles by the United States and the acceptance of such awards from foreign powers without congressional consent. Historians speculate that general nervousness about the power of the emperor Napoleon, who was at that time extending France's empire throughout Europe, may have prompted the proposal. Though it fell one vote short of ratification, Congress and the American people thought the proposal had been ratified and it was included in many nineteenth-century editions of the Constitution.

The Civil War and Reconstruction Amendments (Thirteenth, Fourteenth, and Fifteenth Amendments)

In the four months between the election of Abraham Lincoln and his inauguration, more than 200 proposed constitutional amendments were presented to Congress as part of a desperate attempt to hold the rapidly dissolving Union together. Most of these were efforts to appease the southern states by protecting the right to own slaves or by disfranchising African Americans through constitutional amendment. None were able to win the votes required from Congress to send them to the states. The relatively innocuous Corwin Amendment seemed to be the only hope for preserving the Union by amending the Constitution.

The northern victors in the Civil War tried to restructure the Constitution just as the war had restructured the nation. Yet they were often divided in their goals. Some wanted to end slavery; others hoped for social and economic equality regardless of race; others hoped that extending the power of the ballot box to former slaves would help create a new political order. The debates over the Thirteenth, Fourteenth, and Fifteenth Amendments were bitter. Few of those who fought for these changes were satisfied with the amendments themselves; fewer still were satisfied with their interpretation. Although the amendments put an end to the legal status of slavery, it took nearly a hundred years after the amendments' passage before most of the descendants of former slaves could begin to experience the economic, social, and political equality the amendments had been intended to provide.

Unratified Amendment

Corwin Amendment (proposed by Congress March 2, 1861)

No amendment shall be made to the Constitution which will authorize or give to Congress the power to abolish or interfere, within any State, with the domestic institutions thereof, including that of persons held to labor or service by the laws of said State.

♦ ♦ ♦

Following the election of Abraham Lincoln, Congress scrambled to try to prevent the secession of the slaveholding states. House member Thomas Corwin of Ohio proposed the "unamendable" amendment in the hope that by protecting slavery where it existed, Congress would keep the southern states in the Union. Lincoln indicated his support for the proposed amendment in his first inaugural address. Only Ohio and Maryland ratified the Corwin Amendment before it was forgotten.

Amendment XIII

[Adopted 1865]

Section 1   Neither slavery nor involuntary servitude, except as a punishment for crime whereof the party shall have been duly convicted, shall exist within the United States, or any place subject to their jurisdiction.

Section 2   Congress shall have power to enforce this article by appropriate legislation.

♦ ♦ ♦

Although President Lincoln had abolished slavery in the Confederacy with the Emancipation Proclamation of 1863, abolitionists wanted to rid the entire country of slavery. The Thirteenth Amendment did this in a clear and straightforward manner. In February 1865, when the proposal was approved by the House, the gallery of the House was newly opened to black Americans who had a chance at last to see their government at work. Passage of the proposal was greeted by wild cheers from the gallery as well as tears on the House floor, where congressional representatives openly embraced one another.

The problem of ratification remained, however. The Union position was that the Confederate states were part of the country of thirty-six states. Therefore, twenty-seven states were needed to ratify the amendment. When Kentucky and Delaware rejected it, backers realized that without approval from at least four former Confederate states, the amendment would fail. Lincoln's successor, President Andrew Johnson, made ratification of the Thirteenth Amendment a condition for southern states to rejoin the Union. Under those terms, all the former Confederate states except Mississippi accepted the Thirteenth Amendment, and by the end of 1865 the amendment had become part of the Constitution and slavery had been prohibited in the United States.

Amendment XIV

[Adopted 1868]

Section 1 All persons born or naturalized in the United States, and subject to the jurisdiction thereof, are citizens of the United States and of the State wherein they reside. No State shall make or enforce any law which shall abridge the privileges or immunities of citizens of the United States; nor shall any State deprive any person of life, liberty, or property, without due process of law; nor deny to any person within its jurisdiction the equal protection of the laws.

Section 2 Representatives shall be appointed among the several States according to their respective numbers, counting the whole number of persons in each State, excluding Indians not taxed. But when the right to vote at any election for the choice of Electors for President and Vice-President of the United States, Representatives in Congress, the executive and judicial officers of a State, or the members of the legislature thereof, is denied to any of the male inhabitants of such State, being twenty-one years of age and citizens of the United States, or in any way abridged, except for participation in rebellion, or other crime, the basis of representation therein shall be reduced in the proportion which the number of such male citizens shall bear to the whole number of male citizens twenty-one years of age in such State.

Section 3 No person shall be a Senator or Representative in Congress, or Elector of President and Vice-President, or hold any office, civil or military, under the United States, or under any State, who, having previously taken an oath, as a member of Congress, or as an officer of the United States, or as a member of any State legislature, or as an executive or judicial officer of any State, to support the Constitution of the United States, shall have engaged in insurrection or rebellion against the same, or given aid or comfort to the enemies thereof. Congress may, by a vote of two-thirds of each house, remove such disability.

Section 4 The validity of the public debt of the United States, authorized by law, including debts incurred for payment of pensions and bounties for services in suppressing insurrection or rebellion, shall not be questioned. But neither the United States nor any State shall assume or pay any debt or obligation incurred in aid of insurrection or rebellion against the United States, or any claim for the loss or emancipation of any slave; but all such debts, obligations, and claims shall be held illegal and void.

Section 5 The Congress shall have power to enforce, by appropriate legislation, the provisions of this article.

◆ ◆ ◆

Without Lincoln's leadership in the reconstruction of the nation following the Civil War, it soon became clear that the Thirteenth Amendment needed additional constitutional support. Less than a year after Lincoln's assassination, Andrew Johnson was ready to bring the former Confederate states back into the Union with few changes in their governments or politics. Anxious Republicans drafted the Fourteenth Amendment to prevent that from happening. The most important provisions of this complex amendment made all native-born or naturalized persons American citizens and prohibited states from abridging the "privileges or immunities" of citizens; depriving them of "life, liberty, or property, without due process of law"; and denying them "equal protection of the laws." In essence, it made all ex-slaves citizens and protected the rights of all citizens against violation by their own state governments.

As occurred in the case of the Thirteenth Amendment, former Confederate states were forced to ratify the amendment as a condition of representation in the House and the Senate. The intentions of the Fourteenth Amendment, and how those intentions should be enforced, have been the most debated point of constitutional history. The terms due process *and* equal protection *have been especially troublesome. Was the amendment designed to outlaw racial segregation? Or was the goal simply to prevent the leaders of the rebellious South from gaining political power?*

The framers of the Fourteenth Amendment hoped Article 2 would produce black voters who would increase the power of the Republican Party. The federal government, however, never used its power to punish states for denying blacks their right to vote. Although the Fourteenth Amendment had an immediate impact in giving black Americans citizenship, it did nothing to protect blacks from the vengeance of whites once Reconstruction ended. In the late nineteenth and early twentieth centuries, section 1 of the Fourteenth Amendment was often used to protect business interests and strike down laws protecting workers on the grounds that the rights of "persons," that is, corporations, were protected by "due process." More recently, the Fourteenth Amendment has been used to justify school desegregation and affirmative action programs, as well as to dismantle such programs.

Amendment XV

[Adopted 1870]

Section 1   The right of citizens of the United States to vote shall not be denied or abridged by the United States or by any State on account of race, color, or previous condition of servitude.

Section 2   The Congress shall have power to enforce this article by appropriate legislation.

♦ ♦ ♦

The Fifteenth Amendment was the last major piece of Reconstruction legislation. While earlier Reconstruction acts had already required black suffrage in the South, the Fifteenth Amendment extended black voting rights to the entire nation. Some Republicans felt morally obligated to do away with the double standard between North and South since many northern states had stubbornly refused to enfranchise blacks. Others believed that the freedman's ballot required the extra protection of a constitutional amendment to shield it from white counterattack. But partisan advantage also played an important role in the amendment's passage, since Republicans hoped that by giving the ballot to northern blacks, they could lessen their political vulnerability.

Many women's rights advocates had fought for the amendment. They had felt betrayed by the inclusion of the word male *in section 2 of the Fourteenth Amendment and were further angered when the proposed Fifteenth Amendment failed to prohibit denial of the right to vote on the grounds of sex as well as "race, color, or previous condition of servitude." In this amendment, for the first time, the federal government claimed the power to regulate the franchise, or vote. It was also the first time the Constitution placed limits on the power of the states to regulate access to the franchise. Although ratified in 1870, the amendment was not enforced until the twentieth century.*

The Progressive Amendments (Sixteenth–Nineteenth Amendments)

No amendments were added to the Constitution between the Civil War and the Progressive Era. America was changing, however, in fundamental ways. The rapid industrialization of the United States after the Civil War led to many social and economic problems. Hundreds of amendments were proposed, but none received enough support in Congress to be sent to the states. Some scholars believe that regional differences and rivalries were so strong during this period that it was almost impossible to gain a consensus on a constitutional amendment. During the Progressive Era, however, the Constitution was amended four times in seven years.

Amendment XVI

[Adopted 1913]

The Congress shall have power to lay and collect taxes on incomes, from whatever source derived, without apportionment among the several States, and without regard to any census or enumeration.

♦ ♦ ♦

Until passage of the Sixteenth Amendment, most of the money used to run the federal government came from customs duties and taxes on specific items, such as liquor. During the Civil War, the federal government taxed incomes as an emergency measure. Pressure to enact an income tax came from those who were concerned about the growing gap between rich and poor in the United States. The Populist Party began campaigning for a graduated income tax in 1892, and support continued to grow. By 1909, thirty-three proposed income tax amendments had been presented in Congress, but lobbying by corporate and other special interests had defeated them all. In June 1909, the growing pressure for an income tax, which had been endorsed by Presidents Roosevelt and Taft, finally pushed an amendment through the Senate. The required thirty-six states had ratified the amendment by February 1913.

Amendment XVII

[Adopted 1913]

Section 1   The Senate of the United States shall be composed of two Senators from each State, elected by the people thereof, for six years; and each Senator shall have one vote. The electors in each State shall have the qualifications requisite for electors of [voters for] the most numerous branch of the State legislatures.

Section 2   When vacancies happen in the representation of any State in the Senate, the executive authority of such State shall issue writs of election to fill such vacancies: Provided, that the Legislature of any State may empower the executive thereof to make temporary appointments until the people fill the vacancies by election as the Legislature may direct.

Section 3   This amendment shall not be so construed as to affect the election or term of any Senator chosen before it becomes valid as part of the Constitution.

♦ ♦ ♦

The framers of the Constitution saw the members of the House as the representatives of the people and the members of the Senate as the representatives of the states. Originally senators were to be chosen by the state legislators. According to reform advocates, however, the growth of private industry and transportation conglomerates during the Gilded Age had created a network of corruption in which wealth and power were exchanged for influence and votes in the Senate. Senator Nelson Aldrich, who represented Rhode Island in the late nineteenth and early twentieth centuries, for example, was known as "the senator from Standard Oil" because of his open support of special business interests.

Efforts to amend the Constitution to allow direct election of senators had begun in 1826, but since any proposal had to be approved by the Senate, reform seemed impossible. Progressives tried to gain influence in the Senate by instituting party caucuses and primary elections, which gave citizens the chance to express their choice of a senator who could then be officially elected by the state legislature. By 1910, fourteen of the country's thirty senators received popular votes through a state primary before the state legislature made its selection. Despairing of getting a proposal through the Senate, supporters of a direct-election amendment had begun in 1893 to seek a convention of representatives from two-thirds of the states to propose an amendment that could then be ratified. By 1905, thirty-one of forty-five states had endorsed such an amendment. Finally, in 1911, despite extraordinary opposition, a proposed amendment passed the Senate; by 1913, it had been ratified.

Amendment XVIII

[Adopted 1919; repealed 1933
by Amendment XXI]

Section 1   After one year from the ratification of this article the manufacture, sale, or transportation of intoxicating liquors within, the importation thereof into, or the exportation thereof from the United States and all territory subject to the jurisdiction thereof, for beverage purposes, is hereby prohibited.

Section 2   The Congress and the several States shall have concurrent power to enforce this article by appropriate legislation.

Section 3   This article shall be inoperative unless it shall have been ratified as an amendment to the Constitution by the legislatures of the several States, as provided by the Constitution, within seven years from the date of the submission thereof to the States by the Congress.

♦♦♦

The Prohibition Party, formed in 1869, began calling for a constitutional amendment to outlaw alcoholic beverages in 1872. A prohibition amendment was first proposed in the Senate in 1876 and was revived eighteen times before 1913. Between 1913 and 1919, another thirty-nine attempts were made to prohibit liquor in the United States through a constitutional amendment. Prohibition became a key element of the progressive agenda as reformers linked alcohol and

drunkenness to numerous social problems, including the corruption of immigrant voters. While opponents of such an amendment argued that it was undemocratic, supporters claimed that their efforts had widespread public support. The admission of twelve "dry" western states to the Union in the early twentieth century and the spirit of sacrifice during World War I laid the groundwork for passage and ratification of the Eighteenth Amendment in 1919. Opponents added a time limit to the amendment in the hope that they could thus block ratification, but this effort failed. (See also Amendment XXI.)

Amendment XIX

[Adopted 1920]

Section 1   The right of citizens of the United States to vote shall not be denied or abridged by the United States or by any State on account of sex.

Section 2   Congress shall have the power to enforce this article by appropriate legislation.

♦♦♦

Advocates of women's rights tried and failed to link woman suffrage to the Fourteenth and Fifteenth Amendments. Nonetheless, the effort for woman suffrage continued. Between 1878 and 1912, at least one and sometimes as many as four proposed amendments were introduced in Congress each year to grant women the right to vote. While over time women won very limited voting rights in some states, at both the state and federal levels opposition to an amendment for woman suffrage remained very strong. President Woodrow Wilson and other officials felt that the federal government should not interfere with the power of the states in this matter. Others worried that granting suffrage to women would encourage ethnic minorities to exercise their own right to vote. And many were concerned that giving women the vote would result in their abandoning traditional gender roles. In 1919, following a protracted and often bitter campaign of protest in which women went on hunger strikes and chained themselves to fences, an amendment was introduced with the backing of President Wilson. It narrowly passed the Senate (after efforts to limit the suffrage to white women failed) and was adopted in 1920 after Tennessee became the thirty-sixth state to ratify it.

Unratified Amendment

Child Labor Amendment (proposed by Congress June 2, 1924)

Section 1   The Congress shall have power to limit, regulate, and prohibit the labor of persons under eighteen years of age.

Section 2   The power of the several States is unimpaired by this article except that the operation of

State laws shall be suspended to the extent necessary to give effect to legislation enacted by Congress.

♦ ♦ ♦

Throughout the late nineteenth and early twentieth centuries, alarm over the condition of child workers grew. Opponents of child labor argued that children worked in dangerous and unhealthy conditions, that they took jobs from adult workers, that they depressed wages in certain industries, and that states that allowed child labor had an economic advantage over those that did not. Defenders of child labor claimed that children provided needed income in many families, that working at a young age developed character, and that the effort to prohibit the practice constituted an invasion of family privacy.

In 1916, Congress passed a law that made it illegal to sell goods made by children through interstate commerce. The Supreme Court, however, ruled that the law violated the limits on the power of Congress to regulate interstate commerce. Congress then tried to penalize industries that used child labor by taxing such goods. This measure was also thrown out by the courts. In response, reformers set out to amend the Constitution. The proposed amendment was ratified by twenty-eight states, but by 1925, thirteen states had rejected it. Passage of the Fair Labor Standards Act in 1938, which was upheld by the Supreme Court in 1941, made the amendment irrelevant.

Amendment XX

[Adopted 1933]

Section 1   The terms of the President and Vice-President shall end at noon on the 20th day of January, and the terms of Senators and Representatives at noon on the 3rd day of January, of the years in which such terms would have ended if this article had not been ratified; and the terms of their successors shall then begin.

Section 2   The Congress shall assemble at least once in every year, and such meeting shall begin at noon on the 3rd day of January, unless they shall by law appoint a different day.

Section 3   If, at the time fixed for the beginning of the term of the President, the President-elect shall have died, the Vice-President-elect shall become President. If a President shall not have been chosen before the time fixed for the beginning of his term, or if the President-elect shall have failed to qualify, then the Vice-President-elect shall act as President until a President shall have qualified; and the Congress may by law provide for the case wherein neither a President-elect nor a Vice-President-elect shall have qualified, declaring who shall then act as President, or the manner in which one who is to act shall be selected, and such person shall act accordingly until a President or Vice-President shall have qualified.

Section 4   The Congress may by law provide for the case of the death of any of the persons from whom the House of Representatives may choose a President whenever the right of choice shall have devolved upon them, and for the case of the death of any of the persons from whom the Senate may choose a Vice-President whenever the right of choice shall have devolved upon them.

Section 5   Sections 1 and 2 shall take effect on the 15th day of October following the ratification of this article.

Section 6   This article shall be inoperative unless it shall have been ratified as an amendment to the Constitution by the Legislatures of three-fourths of the several States within seven years from the date of its submission.

♦ ♦ ♦

Until 1933, presidents took office on March 4. Since elections are held in early November and electoral votes are counted in mid-December, this meant that more than three months passed between the time a new president was elected and when he took office. Moving the inauguration to January shortened the transition period and allowed Congress to begin its term closer to the time of the president's inauguration. Although this seems like a minor change, an amendment was required because the Constitution specifies terms of office. This amendment also deals with questions of succession in the event that a president- or vice president-elect dies before assuming office. Section 3 also clarifies a method for resolving a deadlock in the electoral college.

Amendment XXI

[Adopted 1933]

Section 1   The eighteenth article of amendment to the Constitution of the United States is hereby repealed.

Section 2   The transportation or importation into any State, Territory, or Possession of the United States for delivery or use therein of intoxicating liquors, in violation of the laws thereof, is hereby prohibited.

Section 3   This article shall be inoperative unless it shall have been ratified as an amendment to the Constitution by conventions in the several States, as provided in the Constitution, within seven years from the date of the submission thereof to the States by the Congress.

♦ ♦ ♦

Widespread violation of the Volstead Act, the law enacted to enforce prohibition, made the United States a nation of lawbreakers. Prohibition caused more problems than it solved by encouraging crime, bribery, and corruption. Further, a coalition of liquor and beer manufacturers, personal liberty advocates, and constitutional scholars joined forces to challenge the amendment. By 1929, thirty proposed repeal amendments had been introduced in Congress, and the Democratic Party made repeal part of its platform in the 1932 presidential campaign. The Twenty-first Amendment was proposed in February 1933 and ratified less than a year later. The failure of the effort to enforce prohibition through a constitutional amendment has often been cited by opponents to subsequent efforts to shape public virtue and private morality.

Amendment XXII

[Adopted 1951]

Section 1   No person shall be elected to the office of the President more than twice, and no person who has held the office of President, or acted as President, for more than two years of a term to which some other person was elected President shall be elected to the office of President more than once. But this article shall not apply to any person holding the office of President when this Article was proposed by the Congress, and shall not prevent any person who may be holding the office of President, or acting as President, during the term within which this Article becomes operative from holding the office of President or acting as President during the remainder of such term.

Section 2   This article shall be inoperative unless it shall have been ratified as an amendment to the Constitution by the legislatures of three-fourths of the several States within seven years from the date of its submission to the States by the Congress.

◆ ◆ ◆

George Washington's refusal to seek a third term of office set a precedent that stood until 1912, when former President Theodore Roosevelt sought, without success, another term as an independent candidate. Democrat Franklin Roosevelt was the only president to seek and win a fourth term, though he did so amid great controversy. Roosevelt died in April 1945, a few months after the beginning of his fourth term. In 1946, Republicans won control of the House and the Senate, and early in 1947 a proposal for an amendment to limit future presidents to two four-year terms was offered to the states for ratification. Democratic critics of the Twenty-second Amendment charged that it was a partisan posthumous jab at Roosevelt.

Since the Twenty-second Amendment was adopted, however, the only presidents who might have been able to seek a third term, had it not existed, were Republicans Dwight Eisenhower and Ronald Reagan, and Democrat Bill Clinton. Since 1826, Congress has entertained 160 proposed amendments to limit the

president to one six-year term. Such amendments have been backed by fifteen presidents, including Gerald Ford and Jimmy Carter.

Amendment XXIII

[Adopted 1961]

Section 1   The District constituting the seat of Government of the United States shall appoint in such manner as the Congress may direct: A number of electors of President and Vice-President equal to the whole number of Senators and Representatives in Congress to which the District would be entitled if it were a State, but in no event more than the least populous State; they shall be in addition to those appointed by the States, but they shall be considered for the purposes of the election of President and Vice-President, to be electors appointed by a State; and they shall meet in the District and perform such duties as provided by the twelfth article of amendment.

Section 2   The Congress shall have the power to enforce this article by appropriate legislation.

◆ ◆ ◆

When Washington, D.C., was established as a federal district, no one expected that a significant number of people would make it their permanent and primary residence. A proposal to allow citizens of the district to vote in presidential elections was approved by Congress in June 1960 and was ratified on March 29, 1961.

Amendment XXIV

[Adopted 1964]

Section 1   The right of citizens of the United States to vote in any primary or other election for President or Vice-President, for electors for President or Vice-President, or for Senator or Representative in Congress, shall not be denied or abridged by the United States or any State by reason of failure to pay any poll tax or other tax.

Section 2   The Congress shall have the power to enforce this article by appropriate legislation.

◆ ◆ ◆

In the colonial and Revolutionary eras, financial independence was seen as necessary to political independence, and the poll tax was used as a requirement for voting. By the twentieth century, however, the poll tax was used mostly to bar poor people, especially southern blacks, from voting. While conservatives complained that the amendment interfered with states' rights, liberals thought that the amendment did not go far enough because it barred the poll tax only in national elections and not in state or local elections. The amendment was ratified in 1964, however, and two years later, the Supreme Court ruled that poll taxes in state and local elections also violated the equal protection clause of the Fourteenth Amendment.

Amendment XXV

[Adopted 1967]

Section 1   In case of the removal of the President from office or of his death or resignation, the Vice-President shall become President.

Section 2   Whenever there is a vacancy in the office of the Vice-President, the President shall nominate a Vice-President who shall take office upon confirmation by a majority vote of both Houses of Congress.

Section 3   Whenever the President transmits to the President pro tempore of the Senate and the Speaker of the House of Representatives his written declaration that he is unable to discharge the powers and duties of his office, and until he transmits to them a written declaration to the contrary, such powers and duties shall be discharged by the Vice-President as Acting President.

Section 4   Whenever the Vice-President and a majority of either the principal officers of the executive departments or of such other body as Congress may by law provide, transmit to the President pro tempore of the Senate and the Speaker of the House of Representatives their written declaration that the President is unable to discharge the powers and duties of his office, the Vice-President shall immediately assume the powers and duties of the office as Acting President.

Thereafter, when the President transmits to the President pro tempore of the Senate and the Speaker of the House of Representatives his written declaration that no inability exists, he shall resume the powers and duties of his office unless the Vice-President and a majority of either the principal officers of the executive department[s] or of such other body as Congress may by law provide, transmit within four days to the President pro tempore of the Senate and the Speaker of the House of Representatives their written declaration that the President is unable to discharge the powers and duties of his office. Thereupon Congress shall decide the issue, assembling within forty-eight hours for that purpose if not in session. If the Congress, within twenty-one days after receipt of the latter written declaration, or, if Congress is not in session, within twenty-one days after Congress is required to assemble, determines by two-thirds vote of both Houses that the President is unable to discharge the powers and duties of his office, the Vice-President shall continue to discharge the same as Acting President; otherwise, the President shall resume the powers and duties of his office.

♦ ♦ ♦

The framers of the Constitution established the office of vice president because someone was needed to preside over the Senate. The first president to die in office was William Henry Harrison, in 1841. Vice President John Tyler had himself sworn in as president, setting a precedent that was followed when seven later presidents died in office. The assassination of President James A. Garfield in 1881 posed a new problem, however. After he was shot, the president was incapacitated for two months before he died; he was unable to lead the country, while his vice president, Chester A. Arthur, was unable to assume leadership. Efforts to resolve questions of succession in the event of a presidential disability thus began with the death of Garfield.

In 1963, the assassination of President John F. Kennedy galvanized Congress to action. Vice President Lyndon Johnson was a chain smoker with a history of heart trouble. According to the 1947 Presidential Succession Act, the two men who stood in line to succeed him were the seventy-two-year-old Speaker of the House and the eighty-six-year-old president of the Senate. There were serious concerns that any of these men might become incapacitated while serving as chief executive. The first time the Twenty-fifth Amendment was used, however, was not in the case of presidential death or illness, but during the Watergate crisis. When Vice President Spiro T. Agnew was forced to resign following allegations of bribery and tax violations, President Richard M. Nixon appointed House Minority Leader Gerald R. Ford vice president. Ford became president following Nixon's resignation eight months later and named Nelson A. Rockefeller as his vice president. Thus, for more than two years, the two highest offices in the country were held by people who had not been elected to them.

Amendment XXVI

[Adopted 1971]

Section 1   The right of citizens of the United States, who are eighteen years of age or older, to vote shall not be denied or abridged by the United States or by any State on account of age.

Section 2   The Congress shall have power to enforce this article by appropriate legislation.

♦ ♦ ♦

Efforts to lower the voting age from twenty-one to eighteen began during World War II. Recognizing that those who were old enough to fight a war should have some say in the government policies that involved them in the war, Presidents Eisenhower, Johnson, and Nixon endorsed the idea. In 1970, the combined pressure of the antiwar movement and the demographic pressure of the baby boom generation led to a Voting Rights Act lowering the voting age in federal, state, and local elections.

In Oregon v. Mitchell (1970), the state of Oregon challenged the right of Congress to determine the age at which people could vote in state or local elections. The Supreme Court agreed with Oregon. Since the Voting Rights Act was ruled unconstitutional, the Constitution had to be amended to allow passage of a law that would lower the voting age. The amendment was ratified in a little more than three months, making it the most rapidly ratified amendment in U.S. history.

Unratified Amendment

Equal Rights Amendment (proposed by Congress March 22, 1972; seven-year deadline for ratification extended June 30, 1982)

Section 1   Equality of rights under the law shall not be denied or abridged by the United States or by any State on account of sex.

Section 2   The Congress shall have the power to enforce, by appropriate legislation, the provisions of this article.

Section 3   This amendment shall take effect two years after the date of ratification.

♦♦♦

In 1923, soon after women had won the right to vote, Alice Paul, a leading activist in the woman suffrage movement, proposed an amendment requiring equal treatment of men and women. Opponents of the proposal argued that such an amendment would invalidate laws that protected women and would make women subject to the military draft. After the 1964 Civil Rights Act was adopted, protective workplace legislation was removed anyway.

The renewal of the women's movement, as a by-product of the civil rights and antiwar movements, led to a revival of the Equal Rights Amendment (ERA) in Congress. Disagreements over language held up congressional passage of the proposed amendment, but on March 22, 1972, the Senate approved the ERA by a vote of 84 to 8, and it was sent to the states. Six states ratified the amendment within two days, and by the middle of 1973 the amendment seemed well on its way to adoption, with thirty of the needed thirty-eight states having ratified it. In the mid-1970s, however, a powerful "Stop ERA" campaign developed. The campaign portrayed the ERA as a threat to "family values" and traditional relationships between men and women. Although thirty-five states ultimately ratified the ERA, five of those state legislatures voted to rescind ratification, and the amendment was never adopted.

Unratified Amendment

D.C. Statehood Amendment (proposed by Congress August 22, 1978)

Section 1   For purposes of representation in the Congress, election of the President and Vice-President, and article V of this Constitution, the District constituting the seat of government of the United States shall be treated as though it were a State.

Section 2   The exercise of the rights and powers conferred under this article shall be by the people of the District constituting the seat of government, and as shall be provided by Congress.

Section 3   The twenty-third article of amendment to the Constitution of the United States is hereby repealed.

Section 4   This article shall be inoperative, unless it shall have been ratified as an amendment to the Constitution by the legislatures of three-fourths of the several states within seven years from the date of its submission.

♦♦♦

The 1961 ratification of the Twenty-third Amendment, giving residents of the District of Columbia the right to vote for a president and vice president, inspired an effort to give residents of the district full voting rights. In 1966, President Lyndon Johnson appointed a mayor and city council; in 1971, D.C. residents were allowed to name a nonvoting delegate to the House; and in 1981, residents were allowed to elect the mayor and city council. Congress retained the right to overrule laws that might affect commuters, the height of federal buildings, and selection of judges and prosecutors. The district's nonvoting delegate to Congress, Walter Fauntroy, lobbied fiercely for a congressional amendment granting statehood to the district. In 1978, a proposed amendment was approved and sent to the states. A number of states quickly ratified the amendment, but, like the ERA, the D.C. Statehood Amendment ran into trouble. Opponents argued that section 2 created a separate category of "nominal" statehood. They argued that the federal district should be eliminated and that the territory should be reabsorbed into the state of Maryland. Although these theoretical arguments were strong, some scholars believe that racist attitudes toward the predominantly black population of the city was also a factor leading to the defeat of the amendment.

Amendment XXVII
[Adopted 1992]

No law, varying the compensation for the services of the Senators and Representatives, shall take effect, until an election of Representatives shall have intervened.

♦ ♦ ♦

While the Twenty-sixth Amendment was the most rapidly ratified amendment in U.S. history, the Twenty-seventh Amendment had the longest journey to ratification. First proposed by James Madison in 1789 as part of the package that included the Bill of Rights, this amendment had been ratified by only six states by 1791. In 1873, however, it was ratified by Ohio to protest a massive retroactive salary increase by the federal government. Unlike later proposed amend-ments, this one came with no time limit on ratification. In the early 1980s, Gregory D. Watson, a University of Texas economics major, discovered the "lost" amend-ment and began a single-handed campaign to get state legislators to introduce it for ratification. In 1983, it was accepted by Maine. In 1984, it passed the Colorado legislature. Ratifications trickled in slowly until May 1992, when Michigan and New Jersey became the thirty-eighth and thirty-ninth states, respectively, to ratify. This amendment prevents members of Congress from raising their own salaries without giving voters a chance to vote them out of office before they can benefit from the raises.

THE CONSTITUTION OF THE CONFEDERATE STATES OF AMERICA

In framing the Constitution of the Confederate States, the authors adopted, with numerous small but signifi-cant changes and additions, the language of the Con-stitution of the United States, and followed the same order of arrangement of articles and sections. The revi-sions that they made to the original Constitution are shown here. The parts stricken out are enclosed in brack-ets, and the new matter added in framing the Confed-erate Constitution is printed in italics.

Adopted March 11, 1861

WE, the People of the [United States] *Confederated States, each State acting in its sovereign and independent character,* in order to form a [more perfect Union] *permanent Federal government,* establish Justice, in-sure domestic Tranquillity [provide for the common defense, promote the general Welfare], and secure the Blessings of Liberty to ourselves and our Posterity, *invoking the favor and guidance of Almighty God,* do ordain and establish this Constitution for the [United] *Confederate* States of America.

Article I

Section I All legislative Powers herein [granted] *delegated,* shall be vested in a Congress of the [United] *Confederate* States, which shall consist of a Senate and House of Representatives.

Section II The House of Representatives shall be composed of Members chosen every second Year by the People of the several States, and the Electors in each State shall *be citizens of the Confederate States, and* have the Qualifications requisite for Electors of the most numerous Branch of the State Legislature; *but no person of foreign birth, and not a citizen of the Confederate States, shall be allowed to vote for any offi-cer, civil or political, State or federal.*

No Person shall be a Representative who shall not have attained to the Age of twenty-five Years, and [been seven Years a Citizen of the United] *be a citizen of the Confederate* States, and who shall not, when elected, be an Inhabitant of that State in which he shall be chosen.

Representatives and direct Taxes shall be ap-portioned among the several States which may be included within this [Union] *Confederacy,* according to their respective Numbers, which shall be deter-mined by adding to the whole Number of free Persons, including those bound to Service for a Term of Years, and excluding Indians not taxed, three-fifths of all [other Persons] *slaves.* The actual Enumeration shall be made within three Years after the first Meeting of the Congress of the [United] *Confederate* States, and within every subsequent Term of ten Years, in such Manner as they shall by Law direct. The Number of Representatives shall not exceed one for every [thirty] *fifty* Thousand, but each State shall have at Least one Representative; and until such enumeration shall be made, the State of [New Hampshire shall be entitled to choose three, Massachusetts eight, Rhode Island and Providence Plantations one, Connecticut five, New York six, New Jersey four, Pennsylvania eight, Delaware one, Maryland six, Virginia ten, North Carolina five, South Carolina five, and Georgia three] *South Carolina shall be entitled to choose six, the State of Georgia ten, the State of Alabama nine, the State of Florida two, the State of Mississippi seven, the State of Louisiana six, and the State of Texas six.*

When vacancies happen in the Representation from any State, the Executive Authority thereof shall issue Writs of Election to fill such Vacancies.

The House of Representatives shall choose their Speaker and other Officers; and shall have the sole Power of Impeachment; *except that any judicial or other federal officer resident and acting solely within the limits of any State, may be impeached by a vote of two-thirds of both branches of the Legislature thereof.*

Section III   The Senate of the [United] *Confederate* States shall be composed of two Senators from each State, chosen by the Legislature thereof, for six Years, *at the regular session next immediately preceding the commencement of the term of service;* and each Senator shall have one Vote.

Immediately after they shall be assembled in Consequence of the first Election, they shall be divided as equally as may be into three Classes. The Seats of the Senators of the first Class shall be vacated at the Expiration of the second Year, of the second Class at the Expiration of the fourth Year, and of the third Class at the Expiration of the sixth Year, so that one-third may be chosen every second Year; and if Vacancies happen by Resignation, or otherwise, during the Recess of the Legislature of any State, the Executive thereof may make temporary Appointments until the next Meeting of the Legislature, which shall then fill such Vacancies.

No Person shall be a Senator who shall not have attained to the Age of thirty Years, and [been nine Years a Citizen of the United] *be a citizen of the Confederate* States, and who shall not, when elected, be an Inhabitant of that State for which he shall be chosen.

The Vice President of the [United] *Confederate* States shall be President of the Senate, but shall have no Vote, unless they be equally divided.

The Senate shall choose their other Officers, and also a President *pro tempore,* in the Absence of the Vice President, or when he shall exercise the Office of President of the United States.

The Senate shall have the sole Power to try all Impeachments. When sitting for that Purpose, they shall be on Oath or Affirmation. When the President of the [United] *Confederate* States is tried, the Chief Justice shall preside: And no Person shall be convicted without the Concurrence of two-thirds of the Members present.

Judgment in Cases of Impeachment shall not extend further than to removal from Office, and Disqualification to hold and enjoy any Office of honour, Trust or Profit under the [United] *Confederate* States; but the Party convicted shall nevertheless be liable and subject to Indictment, Trial, Judgment and Punishment, according to Law.

Section IV   The Times, Places and Manner of holding Elections for Senators and Representatives, shall be prescribed in each State by the Legislature thereof, *subject to the provisions of this Constitution;* but the Congress may at any time by Law make or alter such Regulations, except as to the *times and* places of choosing Senators.

The Congress shall assemble at least once in every Year, and such Meeting shall be on the first Monday in December, unless they shall by Law appoint a different Day.

Section V   Each House shall be the Judge of the Elections, Returns and Qualifications of its own Members, and a Majority of each shall constitute a Quorum to do Business; but a smaller Number may adjourn from day to day, and may be authorized to compel the Attendance of absent Members, in such Manner, and under such Penalties as each House may provide.

Each House may determine the Rules of its Proceedings, punish its Members for disorderly Behaviour, and, with the Concurrence of two-thirds *of the whole number* expel a Member.

Each House shall keep a Journal of its Proceedings, and from time to time publish the same, excepting such Parts as may in their Judgment require Secrecy; and the Yeas and Nays of the Members of either House on any question shall, at the Desire of one-fifth of those Present, be entered on the Journal.

Neither House, during the Session of Congress, shall, without the Consent of the other, adjourn for more than three days, nor to any other Place than that in which the two Houses shall be sitting.

Section VI   The Senators and Representatives shall receive a Compensation for their Services, to be ascertained by Law, and paid out of the Treasury of the [United] *Confederate* States. They shall in all Cases, except Treason [Felony] and Breach of the Peace, be privileged from Arrest during their Attendance at the Session of their respective Houses, and in going to and returning from the same; and for any Speech or Debate in either House, they shall not be questioned in any other Place.

No Senator or Representative shall, during the Time for which he was elected, be appointed to any civil Office under the Authority of the [United] *Confederate* States, which shall have been created, or the Emoluments whereof shall have been increased during such time; and no Person holding any Office under the [United] *Confederate* States, shall be a Member of either House during his Continuance in Office. *But Congress may, by law, grant to the principal officers in each of the executive departments a seat upon the floor of either House, with the privilege of discussing any measures appertaining to his department.*

Section VII   All Bills for raising Revenue shall originate in the House of Representatives; but the Senate may propose or concur with Amendments as on other Bills.

Every Bill which shall have passed [the House of Representatives and the Senate] *both Houses,* shall, before it become a Law, be presented to the President of the [United] *Confederate* States; If he approve he shall sign it, but if not he shall return it, with his Objections to that House in which it shall have originated, who shall enter the Objections at

THE CONSTITUTION OF THE CONFEDERATE STATES OF AMERICA

large on their Journal, and proceed to reconsider it. If after such Reconsideration two-thirds of that House shall agree to pass the Bill, it shall be sent, together with the Objections, to the other House, by which it shall likewise be reconsidered, and if approved by two-thirds of that House, it shall become a Law. But in all *such* Cases the Votes of both Houses shall be determined by Yeas and Nays, and the Names of the Persons voting for and against the Bill shall be entered on the Journal of each House respectively. If any Bill shall not be returned by the President within ten Days (Sundays excepted) after it shall have been presented to him, the Same shall be a law, in like Manner as if he had signed it, unless the Congress by their Adjournment prevent its return, in which Case it shall not be a Law. *The President may approve any appropriation and disapprove any other appropriation in the same bill. In such case he shall, in signing the bill, designate the appropriation disapproved, and shall return a copy of such appropriation, with his objections, to the House in which the bill shall have originated; and the same proceedings shall then be had as in case of other bills disapproved by the President.*

Every Order, Resolution, or Vote to which the Concurrence of [the Senate and House of Representatives] *both Houses* may be necessary (except on a question of Adjournment), shall be presented to the President of the [United] *Confederate* States; and before the Same shall take Effect, shall be approved by him, or being disapproved by him, [shall] *may* be repassed by two-thirds of [the Senate and House of Representatives] *both Houses*, according to the Rules and Limitations prescribed in the Case of a Bill.

Section VIII   The Congress shall have Power

To lay and collect Taxes, Duties, Imposts and *Excises, for revenue necessary* to pay the Debts [and], provide for the common Defense [and general Welfare of the United States; but], *and carry on the government of the Confederate States; but no bounties shall be granted from the treasury, nor shall any duties, or taxes, or importation from foreign nations be laid to promote or foster any branch of industry; and* all Duties, Imposts and Excises shall be uniform throughout the [United] *Confederate* States;

To borrow Money on the credit of the [United] *Confederate* States;

To regulate Commerce with foreign Nations, and among the several States, and with the Indian Tribes; *but neither this, nor any other clause contained in this Constitution, shall ever be construed to delegate the power to Congress to appropriate money for any internal improvement intended to facilitate commerce; except for the purpose of furnishing lights, beacons, and buoys, and other aids to navigation upon the coasts, and the improvement of harbors, and the removing of obstructions in river navigation; in all such cases such duties shall be laid on the navigation facilitated thereby, as may be necessary to pay the costs and expenses thereof;*

To establish an uniform Rule of Naturalization, and uniform Laws on the subject of Bankruptcies throughout the [United] *Confederate* States; *but no law of Congress shall discharge any debt contracted before the passage of the same;*

To coin Money, regulate the Value thereof, and of foreign Coin, and fix the Standard of Weights and Measures;

To provide for the Punishment of counterfeiting the Securities and current Coin of the [United] *Confederate* States;

To establish Post Offices and post [Roads] *routes; but the expenses of the Postoffice Department, after the first day of March, in the year of our Lord eighteen hundred and sixty-three, shall be paid out of its own revenues;*

To promote the progress of Science and useful Arts, by securing for limited Times to Authors and Inventors the exclusive Right to their respective Writings and Discoveries;

To constitute Tribunals inferior to the supreme Court;

To define and punish Piracies and Felonies committed on the high Seas, and Offences against the Law of Nations;

To declare War, grant Letters of Marque and Reprisal, and make Rules concerning Captures on Land and Water;

To raise and support Armies, but no Appropriation of Money to that Use shall be for a longer Term than two Years;

To provide and maintain a Navy;

To make Rules for the Government and Regulation of the land and naval Forces;

To provide for calling forth the Militia to execute the Laws of the [Union] *Confederate States,* suppress Insurrections and repel Invasions;

To provide for organizing, arming, and disciplining the Militia and for governing such Part of them as may be employed in the Service of the [United] *Confederate* States, reserving to the States respectively, the Appointment of the Officers, and the Authority of training the Militia according to the Discipline prescribed by Congress;

To exercise exclusive Legislation in all Cases whatsoever, over such District (not exceeding ten Miles square) as may, by Cession of particular States, and the Acceptance of Congress, become the Seat of the Government of the [United] *Confederate* States, and to exercise like Authority over all Places purchased by the Consent of the Legislature of the State in which the Same shall be, for the Erection of Forts, Magazines, Arsenals, Dock Yards, and other needful Buildings;—And

To make all Laws which shall be necessary and proper for carrying into Execution the foregoing Powers, and all other Powers vested by this Constitution in the Government of the [United] *Confederate* States or in any Department or Officer thereof.

Section IX [The Migration or Importation of such Persons as any of the States now existing shall think proper to admit, shall not be prohibited by the Congress prior to the Year one thousand eight hundred and eight, but a Tax or Duty may be imposed on such Importation, not exceeding ten dollars for each Person.] *The importation of negroes of the African race from any foreign country other than the slaveholding States or territories of the United States of America, is hereby forbidden; and Congress is required to pass such laws as shall effectually prevent the same. Congress shall also have power to prohibit the introduction of slaves from any State not a member of, or territory not belonging to, this Confederacy.*

The Privilege of the Writ of Habeas Corpus shall not be suspended, unless when in Cases of Rebellion or Invasion the public Safety may require it. No Bill of Attainder or ex post facto Law, *or law denying or impairing the right of property in negro slaves,* shall be passed.

No Capitation, or other direct, Tax shall be laid, unless in Proportion to the Census or Enumeration herein before directed to be taken.

No Tax or Duty shall be laid on Articles exported from any State, *except by a vote of two-thirds of both Houses.*

No Preference shall be given by any Regulation of Commerce or Revenue to the Ports of one State over those of another; nor shall Vessels bound to, or from, one State, be obliged to enter, clear, or pay Duties in another.

No Money shall be drawn from the Treasury, but in Consequence of Appropriations made by Law; and a regular Statement and Account of the Receipts and Expenditures of all public Money shall be published from time to time.

Congress shall appropriate no money from the Treasury except by a vote of two-thirds of both Houses, taken by yeas and nays, unless it be asked and estimated for by some one of the heads of departments and submitted to Congress by the President; or for the purpose of paying its own expenses and contingencies; or for the payment of claims against the Confederate States, the justice of which shall have been officially declared by a tribunal for the investigation of claims against the Government, which it is hereby made the duty of Congress to establish.

All bills appropriating money shall specify in Federal currency the exact amount of each appropriation and the purposes for which it is made; and Congress shall grant no extra compensation to any public contractor, officer, agent or servant, after such contract shall have been made or such service rendered.

No Title of Nobility shall be granted by the [United] *Confederate* States; and no Person holding any Office of Profit or Trust under them, shall, without the Consent of the Congress, accept of any present, Emolument, Office, or Title, of any kind whatever, from any King, Prince or foreign State.

[Here the framers of the Confederate Constitution insert the U.S. Bill of Rights.]

Congress shall make no law respecting an establishment of religion, or prohibiting the free exercise thereof; or abridging the freedom of speech, or of the press; or the right of the people peaceably to assemble, and to petition the Government for a redress of grievances.

A well-regulated Militia, being necessary to the security of a free State, the right of the people to keep and bear Arms shall not be infringed.

No Soldier shall, in time of peace, be quartered in any house, without the consent of the Owner, nor in time of war, but in a manner to be prescribed by law.

The right of the people to be secure in their persons, houses, papers, and effects, against unreasonable searches and seizures, shall not be violated, and no Warrants shall issue, but upon probable cause, supported by Oath or affirmation, and particularly describing the place to be searched, and the persons or things to be seized.

No person shall be held to answer for a capital, or otherwise infamous crime, unless on a presentment or indictment of a Grand Jury, except in cases arising in the land or naval forces, or in the Militia, when in actual service in time of War or public danger; nor shall any person be subject for the same offence to be twice put in jeopardy of life or limb; nor shall be compelled in any Criminal Case to be a witness against himself, nor be deprived of life, liberty or property without due process of law; nor shall private property be taken for public use, without just compensation.

In all criminal prosecutions, the accused shall enjoy the right to a speedy and public trial, by an impartial jury of the State and district wherein the crime shall have been committed, which district shall have been previously ascertained by law, and to be informed of the nature and cause of the accusation; to be confronted with the witnesses against him; to have Compulsory process for obtaining Witnesses in his favour, and to have the Assistance of Counsel for his defence.

In Suits at common law, where the value in controversy shall exceed twenty dollars, the right of trial by jury shall be preserved, and no fact tried by a jury shall be otherwise reexamined in any Court of the [United] *Confederate* States, than according to the rules of the common law.

Excessive bail shall not be required, nor excessive fines imposed, nor cruel and unusual punishments inflicted.

Every law or resolution having the force of law, shall relate to but one subject, and that shall be expressed in the title.

Section X No State shall enter into any Treaty, Alliance, or Confederation; grant Letters of Marque and Reprisal; coin Money; [emit Bills of Credit;] make any Thing but gold and silver Coin a Tender in Payment of Debts; pass any Bill of Attainder, *or*

THE CONSTITUTION OF THE CONFEDERATE STATES OF AMERICA

ex post facto Law, or Law impairing the Obligation of Contracts, or grant any Title of Nobility.

No State shall, without the consent of the Congress, lay any Imposts or Duties on Imports or Exports, except what may be absolutely necessary for executing its inspection Laws: and the net Produce of all Duties and Imposts, laid by any State on Imports or Exports, shall be for the Use of the Treasury of the [United] *Confederate* States; and all such Laws shall be subject to the Revision and Control of the Congress.

No State shall, without the Consent of Congress, lay any Duty of Tonnage, *except on sea-going vessels, for the improvement of its rivers and harbors navigated by the said vessels; but such duties shall not conflict with any treaties of the Confederate States with foreign nations; and any surplus of revenue thus derived shall, after making such improvement, be paid into the common treasury; nor shall any State* keep Troops, or Ships of War in time of Peace, enter into any Agreement or Compact with another State, or with a foreign Power, or engage in War, unless actually invaded, or in such imminent Danger as will not admit of Delay. *But when any river divides or flows through two or more States, they may enter into compacts with each other to improve the navigation thereof.*

Article II

Section I   [The executive Power shall be vested in a President of the United States of America. He shall hold his Office during the Term of four Years, and, together with the Vice President, chosen for the same Term, be elected, as follows:] *The executive power shall be vested in a President of the Confederate States of America. He and the Vice President shall hold their offices for the term of six years; but the President shall not be re-eligible. The President and Vice President shall be elected as follows:*

Each State shall appoint in such Manner as the Legislature thereof may direct, a Number of Electors, equal to the whole Number of Senators and Representatives to which the State may be entitled in the Congress; but no Senator or Representative, or Person holding an Office of Trust or Profit under the [United] *Confederate* States, shall be appointed an Elector.

The Electors shall meet in their respective States, and vote by ballot for President and Vice President, one of whom, at least, shall not be an inhabitant of the same State with themselves; they shall name in their ballots the person voted for as President, and in distinct ballots the person voted for as Vice President, and they shall make distinct lists of all persons voted for as President, and of all persons voted for as Vice President, and of the number of votes for each, which lists they shall sign and certify, and transmit sealed to the seat of the government of the [United] *Confederate* States, directed to the President of the Senate;—The President of the Senate shall, in the presence of the Senate and House of Representatives, open all the certificates and the votes shall then be counted;—The person having the greatest number of votes for President shall be the President, if such number be a majority of the whole number of Electors appointed; and if no person have such majority, then from the persons having the highest numbers not exceeding three on the list of those voted for as President, the House of Representatives shall choose immediately, by ballot, the President. But in choosing the President, the votes shall be taken by States, the representation from each State having one vote; a quorum for this purpose shall consist of a member or members from two-thirds of the States, and a majority of all the States shall be necessary to a choice. And if the House of Representatives shall not choose a President whenever the right of choice shall devolve upon them, before the fourth day of March next following, then the Vice President shall act as President, as in the case of the death or other constitutional disability of the President. The person having the greatest number of votes as Vice President shall be the Vice President, if such number be a majority of the whole number of Electors appointed, and if no person have a majority, then from the two highest numbers on the list the Senate shall choose the Vice President; a quorum for the purpose shall consist of two-thirds of the whole number of Senators, and a majority of the whole number shall be necessary to a choice. But no person constitutionally ineligible to the office of President shall be eligible to that of Vice President of the [United] *Confederate* States.

The Congress may determine the Time of choosing the Electors, and the Day on which they shall give their Votes; which Day shall be the same throughout the [United] *Confederate* States.

No Person except a natural-born Citizen [or a Citizen of the United States] *of the Confederate States, or a citizen thereof,* at the time of the Adoption of this Constitution, *or a citizen thereof born in the United States prior to the 20th of December, 1860,* shall be eligible to the Office of President; neither shall any Person be eligible to that Office who shall not have attained to the Age of thirty-five Years, and been fourteen Years a Resident within the [United States] *limits of the Confederate States, as they may exist at the time of his election.*

In Cases of the Removal of the President from Office, or of his Death, Resignation, or Inability to discharge the Powers and Duties of the said Office, the same shall devolve on the Vice President, and the Congress may by Law provide for the Case of Removal, Death, Resignation, or Inability, both of the President and Vice President, declaring what Officer shall then act as President, and such Officer shall act accordingly, until the Disability be removed, or a President shall be elected.

The President shall, at stated Times, receive for his Services, a Compensation, which shall neither be increased nor diminished during the Period for which he shall have been elected, and he shall not receive within that Period any other Emolument from the [United] *Confederate* States or any of them.

Before he enters on the Execution of his Office, he shall take the following Oath or Affirmation—"I do solemnly swear (or affirm) that I will faithfully execute the Office of President of the [United] *Confederate* States, and will to the best of my Ability, preserve, protect and defend the Constitution [of the United States] *thereof."*

Section II   The President shall be Commander in Chief of the Army and Navy of the [United] *Confederate* States, and of the Militia of the several States, when called into the actual Service of the [United] *Confederate* States; he may require the Opinion, in writing, of the principal Officer in each of the executive Departments, upon any Subject relating to the Duties of their respective Offices, and he shall have Power to grant Reprieves and Pardons for Offenses against the [United] *Confederate* States, except in Cases of Impeachment.

He shall have Power, by and with the Advice and Consent of the Senate, to make Treaties, provided two-thirds of the Senators present concur; and he shall nominate, and by and with the Advice and Consent of the Senate, shall appoint Ambassadors, other public Ministers and Consuls, Judges of the supreme Court, and all other Officers of the [United] *Confederate* States, whose Appointments are not herein otherwise provided for, and which shall be established by Law: but the Congress may by Law vest the Appointment of such inferior Officers, as they think proper, in the President alone, in the Courts of Law, or in the Heads of Departments. *The principal officer in each of the executive departments, and all persons connected with the diplomatic service, may be removed from office at the pleasure of the President. All other civil officers of the executive department may be removed at any time by the President, or other appointing power, when their services are unnecessary, or for dishonesty, incapacity, inefficiency, misconduct, or neglect of duty; and when so removed, the removal shall be reported to the Senate, together with the reasons therefor.*

The President shall have Power to fill [up] all Vacancies that may happen during the Recess of the Senate, by granting Commissions which shall expire at the End of their next Session.

Section III   [He] *The President* shall from time to time give to the Congress Information of the State of the [Union] *Confederacy,* and recommend to their Consideration such Measures as he shall judge necessary and expedient; he may, on extraordinary Occasions, convene both Houses, or either of them, and in Case of Disagreement between them, with Respect to the Time of Adjournment, he may adjourn them to such Time as he shall think proper;

he shall receive Ambassadors and other public Ministers; he shall take Care that the Laws be faithfully executed, and shall Commission all the officers of the [United] *Confederate* States.

Section IV   The President, Vice President and all civil Officers of the [United] *Confederate* States, shall be removed from Office or Impeachment for, and Conviction of, Treason, Bribery, or other high Crimes and Misdemeanors.

Article III

Section I   The judicial Power of the [United] *Confederate* States shall be vested in one [supreme] *Superior* Court, and in such inferior Courts as the Congress may from time to time ordain and establish. The Judges, both of the supreme and inferior Courts, shall hold their Offices during good Behavior, and shall, at stated Times, receive for their Services a Compensation, which shall not be diminished during their Continuance in Office.

Section II   The judicial Power shall extend to all cases [in Law and Equity, arising under this Constitution], *arising under this Constitution, in law and equity,* the Laws of the [United] *Confederate* States, and Treaties made, or which shall be made, under their Authority;—to all Cases affecting Ambassadors, other public Ministers, and Consuls;—to all Cases of admiralty and maritime Jurisdiction;—to Controversies to which the [United] *Confederate* States shall be a Party;—to Controversies between two or more States;—between a State and Citizens of another State *where the State is plaintiff;*—*between* Citizens *claiming lands under grants* of different States,—[between Citizens of the same State claiming Lands under Grants of different States,] and between a State, or the Citizens thereof, and foreign States, Citizens or Subjects; *but no State shall be sued by a citizen or subject of any foreign State.*

In all Cases affecting Ambassadors, other public Ministers and Consuls, and those in which a State shall be Party, the supreme Court shall have original Jurisdiction. In all the other Cases before mentioned, the supreme Court shall have appellate Jurisdiction, both as to Law and Fact, with such Exceptions, and under such Regulations as the Congress shall make.

The Trial of all Crimes, except in Cases of Impeachment, shall be by Jury; and such Trial shall be held in the State where the said Crime[s] shall have been committed; but when not committed within any State, the Trial shall be at such Place or Places as the Congress may by Law have directed.

Section III   Treason against the [United] *Confederate* States shall consist only in levying War against them, or in adhering to their Enemies, giving them Aid and Comfort. No Person shall be convicted of Treason unless on the Testimony of two Witnesses to the same overt Act, or on Confession in open Court.

The Congress shall have Power to declare the Punishment of Treason, but no Attainder of Treason shall work Corruption of Blood, or Forfeiture except during the Life of the Person attainted.

Article IV

Section I   Full Faith and Credit shall be given in each State to the public Acts, Records, and judicial Proceedings of every other State. And the Congress may by general Laws prescribe the Manner in which such Acts, Records and Proceedings shall be proved, and the Effect thereof.

Section II   The Citizens of each State shall be entitled to all Privileges and Immunities of Citizens in the several States, *and shall have the right of transit and sojourn in any State of this Confederacy, with their slaves and other property; and the right of property in such slaves shall not be impaired.*

A Person charged in any State with Treason, Felony, or other Crime, who shall flee from Justice, and be found in another State, shall on Demand of the executive Authority of the State from which he fled, be delivered up, to be removed to the State having Jurisdiction of the Crime.

No *slave or* Person held to Service or Labor in [one State] *any State or Territory of the Confederate States* under the Laws thereof, *escaping or unlawfully carried* into another, shall, in Consequence of any Law or Regulation therein, be discharged from such Service or Labor, but shall be delivered up on Claim of the Party to whom such *slave belongs, or to whom such* Service or Labor may be due.

Section III   [New States may be admitted by the Congress into this Union;] *Other States may be admitted into this Confederacy by a vote of two-thirds of the whole House of Representatives and two-thirds of the Senate, the Senate voting by States;* but no new State shall be formed or erected within the Jurisdiction of any other State; nor any State be formed by the Junction of two or more States, or Parts of States, without the Consent of the Legislatures of the States concerned as well as of the Congress.

The Congress shall have Power to dispose of and make all needful Rules and Regulations [respecting the Territory or other Property belonging to the United States; and nothing in this Constitution shall be so construed as to Prejudice any Claims of the United States, or of any particular State] *concerning the property of the Confederate States, including the lands thereof.*

The Confederate States may acquire new territory, and Congress shall have power to legislate and provide governments for the inhabitants of all territory belonging to the Confederate States lying without the limits of the several States, and may permit them, at such times and in such manner as it may by law provide, to form States to be admitted into the Confederacy. In all such territory the institution of negro slavery as it now exists in the Confederate States shall be recognized and protected by Congress and by the territorial government, and the inhabitants of the several Confederate States and territories shall have the right to take to such territory any slaves lawfully held by them in any of the States or Territories of the Confederate States.

[Section IV]   The [United] *Confederate* States shall guarantee to every State [in this Union] *that now is, or hereafter may become, a member of this Confederacy,* a Republican Form of Government, and shall protect each of them against Invasion; and on Application of the Legislature, or of the Executive (when the Legislature [cannot be convened] *is not in session*) against domestic Violence.

Article V

[The Congress, whenever two-thirds of both Houses shall deem it necessary, shall propose Amendments to this Constitution, or on the Application of the Legislatures of two-thirds of the several States, shall call a Convention for proposing Amendments, which, in either Case, shall be valid to all Intents and Purposes, as Part of this Constitution, when ratified by the Legislatures of three-fourths of the several States, or by Conventions in three-fourths thereof, as the one or the other Mode of Ratification may be proposed by the Congress: Provided that no Amendment which may be made prior to the Year one thousand eight hundred and eight shall in any Manner affect the first and fourth Clauses in the Ninth Section of the first Article; and that no State, without its Consent, shall be deprived of its equal Suffrage in the Senate.]

Upon the demand of any three States, legally assembled in their several Conventions, the Congress shall summon a Convention of all the States, to take into consideration such amendments to the Constitution as the said States shall concur in suggesting at the time when the said demand is made; and should any of the proposed amendments to the Constitution be agreed on by the said Convention—voting by States—and the same be ratified by the Legislatures of two-thirds of the several States, or by Conventions in two-thirds thereof—as the one or the other mode of ratification may be proposed by the general Convention—they shall henceforward form a part of this Constitution. But no State shall, without its consent, be deprived of its equal representation in the Senate.

Article VI

The Government established by this Constitution is the successor of the Provisional Government of the

Confederate States of America, and all laws passed by the latter shall continue in force until the same shall be repealed or modified; and all the officers appointed by the same shall remain in office until their successors are appointed and qualified or the offices abolished.

All Debts contracted and Engagements entered into, before the Adoption of this Constitution, shall be as valid against the [United] *Confederate* States under this Constitution, as under the [Confederation] *Provisional Government.*

This Constitution and the Laws of the [United] *Confederate* States [which shall be] made in Pursuance thereof; and all Treaties made, or which shall be made, under the authority of the [United] *Confederate* States, shall be the supreme Law of the Land; and the Judges in every State shall be bound thereby, any Thing in the Constitution or Laws of any State to the Contrary notwithstanding.

The Senators and Representatives before mentioned, and the Members of the several State Legislatures, and all executive and judicial Officers, both of the [United] *Confederate* States and of the several States, shall be bound by Oath or Affirmation, to support this Constitution; but no religious Test shall ever be required as a Qualification to any Office or public Trust under the [United] *Confederate* States.

The enumeration in the Constitution, of certain rights, shall not be construed to deny or disparage others retained by the people *of the several States.*

The powers not delegated to the [United] *Confederate* States by the Constitution, nor prohibited by it to the States, are reserved to the States respectively, or to the people.

Article VII

The Ratification of the Conventions of [nine] *five* States shall be sufficient for the Establishment of this Constitution between the States so ratifying the same.

When five States shall have ratified this Constitution, in the manner before specified, the Congress under the Provisional Constitution shall prescribe the time for holding the election of President and Vice President; and for the meeting of the electoral college; and for counting the votes and inaugurating the President. They shall also prescribe the time for holding the first election of members of Congress under this Constitution, and the time for assembling the same. Until the assembling of such Congress, the Congress under the Provisional Constitution shall continue to exercise the legislative powers granted them, not extending beyond the time limited by the Constitution of the Provisional Government.

[Done in Convention by the Unanimous Consent of the States present, the Seventeenth Day of September in the Year of our Lord one thousand seven hundred and eighty-seven and of the Independence of the United States of America the Twelfth.] *Adopted unanimously March 11, 1861.*

Facts and Figures: Government, Economy, and Demographics

U.S. Politics and Government

PRESIDENTIAL ELECTIONS

Year	Candidates	Parties	Popular Vote	Percentage of Popular Vote	Electoral Vote	Percentage of Voter Participation
1789	**GEORGE WASHINGTON (Va.)***				69	
	John Adams				34	
	Others				35	
1792	**GEORGE WASHINGTON (Va.)**				132	
	John Adams				77	
	George Clinton				50	
	Others				5	
1796	**JOHN ADAMS (Mass.)**	Federalist			71	
	Thomas Jefferson	Democratic-Republican			68	
	Thomas Pinckney	Federalist			59	
	Aaron Burr	Dem.-Rep.			30	
	Others				48	
1800	**THOMAS JEFFERSON (Va.)**	Dem. Rep.			73	
	Aaron Burr	Dem.-Rep.			73	
	John Adams	Federalist			65	
	C. C. Pinckney	Federalist			64	
	John Jay	Federalist			1	
1804	**THOMAS JEFFERSON (Va.)**	Dem.-Rep.			162	
	C. C. Pinckney	Federalist			14	
1808	**JAMES MADISON (Va.)**	Dem.-Rep.			122	
	C. C. Pinckney	Federalist			47	
	George Clinton	Dem.-Rep.			6	
1812	**JAMES MADISON (Va.)**	Dem.-Rep.			128	
	De Witt Clinton	Federalist			89	
1816	**JAMES MONROE (Va.)**	Dem.-Rep.			183	
	Rufus King	Federalist			34	
1820	**JAMES MONROE (Va.)**	Dem.-Rep.			231	
	John Quincy Adams	Dem.-Rep.			1	
1824	**JOHN Q. ADAMS (Mass.)**	Dem.-Rep.	108,740	30.5	84	26.9
	Andrew Jackson	Dem.-Rep.	153,544	43.1	99	
	William H. Crawford	Dem.-Rep.	46,618	13.1	41	
	Henry Clay	Dem.-Rep.	47,136	13.2	37	
1828	**ANDREW JACKSON (Tenn.)**	Democratic	647,286	56.0	178	57.6
	John Quincy Adams	National Republican	508,064	44.0	83	

*State of residence when elected president.

Year	Candidates	Parties	Popular Vote	Percentage of Popular Vote	Electoral Vote	Percentage of Voter Participation
1832	**ANDREW JACKSON (Tenn.)**	Democratic	687,502	55.0	219	55.4
	Henry Clay	National Republican	530,189	42.4	49	
	John Floyd	Independent			11	
	William Wirt	Anti-Mason	33,108	2.6	7	
1836	**MARTIN VAN BUREN (N.Y.)**	Democratic	765,483	50.9	170	57.8
	W. H. Harrison	Whig			73	
	Hugh L. White	Whig	739,795	49.1	26	
	Daniel Webster	Whig			14	
	W. P. Mangum	Independent			11	
1840	**WILLIAM H. HARRISON (Ohio)**	Whig	1,274,624	53.1	234	80.2
	Martin Van Buren	Democratic	1,127,781	46.9	60	
	J. G. Birney	Liberty	7,069		—	
1844	**JAMES K. POLK (Tenn.)**	Democratic	1,338,464	49.6	170	78.9
	Henry Clay	Whig	1,300,097	48.1	105	
	J. G. Birney	Liberty	62,300	2.3	—	
1848	**ZACHARY TAYLOR (La.)**	Whig	1,360,967	47.4	163	72.7
	Lewis Cass	Democratic	1,222,342	42.5	127	
	Martin Van Buren	Free-Soil	291,263	10.1	—	
1852	**FRANKLIN PIERCE (N.H.)**	Democratic	1,601,117	50.9	254	69.6
	Winfield Scott	Whig	1,385,453	44.1	42	
	John P. Hale	Free-Soil	155,825	5.0	—	
1856	**JAMES BUCHANAN (Pa.)**	Democratic	1,832,995	45.3	174	78.9
	John C. Frémont	Republican	1,339,932	33.1	114	
	Millard Fillmore	American	871,731	21.6	8	
1860	**ABRAHAM LINCOLN (Ill.)**	Republican	1,865,593	39.8	180	81.2
	Stephen A. Douglas	Democratic	1,382,713	29.5	12	
	John C. Breckinridge	Democratic	848,356	18.1	72	
	John Bell	Union	592,906	12.6	39	
1864	**ABRAHAM LINCOLN (Ill.)**	Republican	2,206,938	55.0	212	73.8
	George B. McClellan	Democratic	1,803,787	45.0	21	
1868	**ULYSSES S. GRANT (Ill.)**	Republican	3,012,833	52.7	214	78.1
	Horatio Seymour	Democratic	2,703,249	47.3	80	
1872	**ULYSSES S. GRANT (Ill.)**	Republican	3,597,132	55.6	286	71.3
	Horace Greeley	Democratic; Liberal Republican	2,834,125	43.9	66	
1876	**RUTHERFORD B. HAYES (Ohio)**	Republican	4,036,572	48.0	185	81.8
	Samuel J. Tilden	Democratic	4,284,020	51.0	184	
1880	**JAMES A. GARFIELD (Ohio)**	Republican	4,454,416	48.5	214	79.4
	Winfield S. Hancock	Democratic	4,444,952	48.1	155	
1884	**GROVER CLEVELAND (N.Y.)**	Democratic	4,879,507	48.5	219	77.5
	James G. Blaine	Republican	4,850,293	48.2	182	
1888	**BENJAMIN HARRISON (Ind.)**	Republican	5,439,853	47.9	233	79.3
	Grover Cleveland	Democratic	5,540,309	48.6	168	
1892	**GROVER CLEVELAND (N.Y.)**	Democratic	5,555,426	46.1	277	74.7
	Benjamin Harrison	Republican	5,182,690	43.0	145	
	James B. Weaver	People's	1,029,846	8.5	22	
1896	**WILLIAM McKINLEY (Ohio)**	Republican	7,104,779	51.1	271	79.3
	William J. Bryan	Democratic-People's	6,502,925	47.7	176	
1900	**WILLIAM McKINLEY (Ohio)**	Republican	7,207,923	51.7	292	73.2
	William J. Bryan	Dem.-Populist	6,358,133	45.5	155	

U.S. POLITICS AND GOVERNMENT

Year	Candidates	Parties	Popular Vote	Percentage of Popular Vote	Electoral Vote	Percentage of Voter Participation
1904	**THEODORE ROOSEVELT (N.Y.)**	Republican	7,623,486	57.9	336	65.2
	Alton B. Parker	Democratic	5,077,911	37.6	140	
	Eugene V. Debs	Socialist	402,283	3.0	—	
1908	**WILLIAM H. TAFT (Ohio)**	Republican	7,678,908	51.6	321	65.4
	William J. Bryan	Democratic	6,409,104	43.1	162	
	Eugene V. Debs	Socialist	420,793	2.8	—	
1912	**WOODROW WILSON (N.J.)**	Democratic	6,293,454	41.9	435	58.8
	Theodore Roosevelt	Progressive	4,119,538	27.4	88	
	William H. Taft	Republican	3,484,980	23.2	8	
	Eugene V. Debs	Socialist	900,672	6.1	—	
1916	**WOODROW WILSON (N.J.)**	Democratic	9,129,606	49.4	277	61.6
	Charles E. Hughes	Republican	8,538,221	46.2	254	
	A. L. Benson	Socialist	585,113	3.2	—	
1920	**WARREN G. HARDING (Ohio)**	Republican	16,143,407	60.5	404	49.2
	James M. Cox	Democratic	9,130,328	34.2	127	
	Eugene V. Debs	Socialist	919,799	3.4	—	
1924	**CALVIN COOLIDGE (Mass.)**	Republican	15,725,016	54.0	382	48.9
	John W. Davis	Democratic	8,386,503	28.8	136	
	Robert M. La Follette	Progressive	4,822,856	16.6	13	
1928	**HERBERT HOOVER (Calif.)**	Republican	21,391,381	58.2	444	56.9
	Alfred E. Smith	Democratic	15,016,443	40.9	87	
	Norman Thomas	Socialist	267,835	0.7	—	
1932	**FRANKLIN D. ROOSEVELT (N.Y.)**	Democratic	22,809,638	57.4	472	56.9
	Herbert Hoover	Republican	15,758,901	39.7	59	
	Norman Thomas	Socialist	881,951	2.2	—	
1936	**FRANKLIN D. ROOSEVELT (N.Y.)**	Democratic	27,751,597	60.8	523	61.0
	Alfred M. Landon	Republican	16,679,583	36.5	8	
	William Lemke	Union	882,479	1.9	—	
1940	**FRANKLIN D. ROOSEVELT (N.Y.)**	Democratic	27,244,160	54.8	449	62.5
	Wendell Willkie	Republican	22,305,198	44.8	82	
1944	**FRANKLIN D. ROOSEVELT (N.Y.)**	Democratic	25,602,504	53.5	432	55.9
	Thomas E. Dewey	Republican	22,006,285	46.0	99	
1948	**HARRY S. TRUMAN (Mo.)**	Democratic	24,105,695	49.5	303	53.0
	Thomas E. Dewey	Republican	21,969,170	45.1	189	
	J. Strom Thurmond	States'-Rights Democratic	1,169,021	2.4	38	
	Henry A. Wallace	Progressive	1,156,103	2.4	—	
1952	**DWIGHT D. EISENHOWER (N.Y.)**	Republican	33,936,252	55.1	442	63.3
	Adlai Stevenson	Democratic	27,314,992	44.4	89	
1956	**DWIGHT D. EISENHOWER (N.Y.)**	Republican	35,575,420	57.6	457	60.6
	Adlai Stevenson	Democratic	26,033,066	42.1	73	
	Other	—	—		1	
1960	**JOHN F. KENNEDY (Mass.)**	Democratic	34,227,096	49.9	303	62.8
	Richard M. Nixon	Republican	34,108,546	49.6	219	
	Other	—	—		15	
1964	**LYNDON B. JOHNSON (Texas)**	Democratic	43,126,506	61.1	486	61.7
	Barry M. Goldwater	Republican	27,176,799	38.5	52	
1968	**RICHARD M. NIXON (N.Y.)**	Republican	31,770,237	43.4	301	60.9
	Hubert H. Humphrey	Democratic	31,270,533	42.7	191	
	George Wallace	American Indep.	9,906,141	13.5	46	
1972	**RICHARD M. NIXON (N.Y.)**	Republican	47,169,911	60.7	520	55.2
	George S. McGovern	Democratic	29,170,383	37.5	17	
	Other	—	—		1	

Year	Candidates	Parties	Popular Vote	Percentage of Popular Vote	Electoral Vote	Percentage of Voter Participation
1976	**JIMMY CARTER (Ga.)**	Democratic	40,828,587	50.0	297	53.5
	Gerald R. Ford	Republican	39,147,613	47.9	241	
	Other	—	1,575,459	2.1	—	
1980	**RONALD REAGAN (Calif.)**	Republican	43,901,812	50.7	489	54.0
	Jimmy Carter	Democratic	35,483,820	41.0	49	
	John B. Anderson	Independent	5,719,722	6.6	—	
	Ed Clark	Libertarian	921,188	1.1	—	
1984	**RONALD REAGAN (Calif.)**	Republican	54,455,075	59.0	525	53.1
	Walter Mondale	Democratic	37,577,185	41.0	13	
1988	**GEORGE H. W. BUSH (Texas)**	Republican	47,946,422	54.0	426	50.2
	Michael S. Dukakis	Democratic	41,016,429	46.0	112	
1992	**WILLIAM J. CLINTON (Ark.)**	Democratic	44,908,254	42.3	370	55.9
	George H. W. Bush	Republican	39,102,282	37.4	168	
	H. Ross Perot	Independent	19,721,433	18.9	—	
1996	**WILLIAM J. CLINTON (Ark.)**	Democratic	47,401,185	49.2	379	49.0
	Robert Dole	Republican	39,197,469	40.7	159	
	H. Ross Perot	Independent	8,085,294	8.4	—	
2000	**GEORGE W. BUSH (Texas)**	Republican	50,456,062	47.8	271	51.2
	Al Gore	Democratic	50,996,862	48.4	267	
	Ralph Nader	Green Party	2,858,843	2.7	—	
	Patrick J. Buchanan	—	438,760	.4	—	

PRESIDENTS, VICE PRESIDENTS, AND SECRETARIES OF STATE

The Washington Administration (1789–1797)

Vice President	John Adams	1789–1797
Secretary of State	Thomas Jefferson	1789–1793
	Edmund Randolph	1794–1795
	Timothy Pickering	1795–1797

The John Adams Administration (1797–1801)

Vice President	Thomas Jefferson	1797–1801
Secretary of State	Timothy Pickering	1797–1800
	John Marshall	1800–1801

The Jefferson Administration (1801–1809)

Vice President	Aaron Burr	1801–1805
	George Clinton	1805–1809
Secretary of State	James Madison	1801–1809

The Madison Administration (1809–1817)

Vice President	George Clinton	1809–1813
	Elbridge Gerry	1813–1817
Secretary of State	Robert Smith	1809–1811
	James Monroe	1811–1817

The Monroe Administration (1817–1825)

Vice President	Daniel Tompkins	1817–1825
Secretary of State	John Quincy Adams	1817–1825

The John Quincy Adams Administration (1825–1829)

Vice President	John C. Calhoun	1825–1829
Secretary of State	Henry Clay	1825–1829

The Jackson Administration (1829–1837)

Vice President	John C. Calhoun	1829–1833
	Martin Van Buren	1833–1837
Secretary of State	Martin Van Buren	1829–1831
	Edward Livingston	1831–1833
	Louis McLane	1833–1834
	John Forsyth	1834–1837

The Van Buren Administration (1837–1841)

Vice President	Richard M. Johnson	1837–1841
Secretary of State	John Forsyth	1837–1841

The William Harrison Administration (1841)

Vice President	John Tyler	1841
Secretary of State	Daniel Webster	1841

The Tyler Administration (1841–1845)

Vice President	None	
Secretary of State	Daniel Webster	1841–1843
	Hugh S. Legaré	1843
	Abel P. Upshur	1843–1844
	John C. Calhoun	1844–1845

U.S. POLITICS AND GOVERNMENT

The Polk Administration (1845–1849)

Vice President	George M. Dallas	1845–1849
Secretary of State	James Buchanan	1845–1849

The Taylor Administration (1849–1850)

Vice President	Millard Fillmore	1849–1850
Secretary of State	John M. Clayton	1849–1850

The Fillmore Administration (1850–1853)

Vice President	None	
Secretary of State	Daniel Webster	1850–1852
	Edward Everett	1852–1853

The Pierce Administration (1853–1857)

Vice President	William R. King	1853–1857
Secretary of State	William L. Marcy	1853–1857

The Buchanan Administration (1857–1861)

Vice President	John C. Breckinridge	1857–1861
Secretary of State	Lewis Cass	1857–1860
	Jeremiah S. Black	1860–1861

The Lincoln Administration (1861–1865)

Vice President	Hannibal Hamlin	1861–1865
	Andrew Johnson	1865
Secretary of State	William H. Seward	1861–1865

The Andrew Johnson Administration (1865–1869)

Vice President	None	
Secretary of State	William H. Seward	1865–1869

The Grant Administration (1869–1877)

Vice President	Schuyler Colfax	1869–1873
	Henry Wilson	1873–1877
Secretary of State	Elihu B. Washburne	1869
	Hamilton Fish	1869–1877

The Hayes Administration (1877–1881)

Vice President	William A. Wheeler	1877–1881
Secretary of State	William M. Evarts	1877–1881

The Garfield Administration (1881)

Vice President	Chester A. Arthur	1881
Secretary of State	James G. Blaine	1881

The Arthur Administration (1881–1885)

Vice President	None	
Secretary of State	F. T. Frelinghuysen	1881–1885

The Cleveland Administration (1885–1889)

Vice President	Thomas A. Hendricks	1885–1889
Secretary of State	Thomas F. Bayard	1885–1889

The Benjamin Harrison Administration (1889–1893)

Vice President	Levi P. Morton	1889–1893
Secretary of State	James G. Blaine	1889–1892
	John W. Foster	1892–1893

The Cleveland Administration (1893–1897)

Vice President	Adlai E. Stevenson	1893–1897
Secretary of State	Walter Q. Gresham	1893–1895
	Richard Olney	1895–1897

The McKinley Administration (1897–1901)

Vice President	Garret A. Hobart	1897–1901
	Theodore Roosevelt	1901
Secretary of State	John Sherman	1897–1898
	William R. Day	1898
	John Hay	1898–1901

The Theodore Roosevelt Administration (1901–1909)

Vice President	Charles Fairbanks	1905–1909
Secretary of State	John Hay	1901–1905
	Elihu Root	1905–1909
	Robert Bacon	1909

The Taft Administration (1909–1913)

Vice President	James S. Sherman	1909–1913
Secretary of State	Philander C. Knox	1909–1913

The Wilson Administration (1913–1921)

Vice President	Thomas R. Marshall	1913–1921
Secretary of State	William J. Bryan	1913–1915
	Robert Lansing	1915–1920
	Bainbridge Colby	1920–1921

The Harding Administration (1921–1923)

Vice President	Calvin Coolidge	1921–1923
Secretary of State	Charles E. Hughes	1921–1923

The Coolidge Administration (1923–1929)

Vice President	Charles G. Dawes	1925–1929
Secretary of State	Charles E. Hughes	1923–1925
	Frank B. Kellogg	1925–1929

The Hoover Administration (1929–1933)

Vice President	Charles Curtis	1929–1933
Secretary of State	Henry L. Stimson	1929–1933

The Franklin D. Roosevelt Administration (1933–1945)

Vice President	John Nance Garner	1933–1941
	Henry A. Wallace	1941–1945
	Harry S. Truman	1945
Secretary of State	Cordell Hull	1933–1944
	Edward R. Stettinius Jr.	1944–1945

The Truman Administration (1945–1953)

Vice President	Alben W. Barkley	1949–1953
Secretary of State	Edward R. Stettinius Jr.	1945
	James F. Byrnes	1945–1947
	George C. Marshall	1947–1949
	Dean G. Acheson	1949–1953

The Eisenhower Administration (1953–1961)

Vice President	Richard M. Nixon	1953–1961
Secretary of State	John Foster Dulles	1953–1959
	Christian A. Herter	1959–1961

The Kennedy Administration (1961–1963)

Vice President	Lyndon B. Johnson	1961–1963
Secretary of State	Dean Rusk	1961–1963

The Lyndon Johnson Administration (1963–1969)

Vice President	Hubert H. Humphrey	1965–1969
Secretary of State	Dean Rusk	1963–1969

The Nixon Administration (1969–1974)

Vice President	Spiro T. Agnew	1969–1973
	Gerald R. Ford	1973–1974
Secretary of State	William P. Rogers	1969–1973
	Henry A. Kissinger	1973–1974

The Ford Administration (1974–1977)

Vice President	Nelson A. Rockefeller	1974–1977
Secretary of State	Henry A. Kissinger	1974–1977

The Carter Administration (1977–1981)

Vice President	Walter F. Mondale	1977–1981
Secretary of State	Cyrus R. Vance	1977–1980
	Edmund Muskie	1980–1981

The Reagan Administration (1981–1989)

Vice President	George H. W. Bush	1981–1989
Secretary of State	Alexander M. Haig	1981–1982
	George P. Shultz	1982–1989

The George H. W. Bush Administration (1989–1993)

Vice President	J. Danforth Quayle	1989–1993
Secretary of State	James A. Baker III	1989–1992
	Lawrence S. Eagleburger	1992–1993

The Clinton Administration (1993–2001)

Vice President	Albert Gore	1993–2001
Secretary of State	Warren M. Christopher	1993–1997
	Madeleine K. Albright	1997–2001

The George W. Bush Administration (2001–)

Vice President	Richard Cheney	2001–
Secretary of State	Colin Powell	2001–

ADMISSION OF STATES TO THE UNION

State	Date of Admission	State	Date of Admission
Delaware	December 7, 1787	Rhode Island	May 29, 1790
Pennsylvania	December 12, 1787	Vermont	March 4, 1791
New Jersey	December 18, 1787	Kentucky	June 1, 1792
Georgia	January 2, 1788	Tennessee	June 1, 1796
Connecticut	January 9, 1788	Ohio	March 1, 1803
Massachusetts	February 6, 1788	Louisiana	April 30, 1812
Maryland	April 28, 1788	Indiana	December 11, 1816
South Carolina	May 23, 1788	Mississippi	December 10, 1817
New Hampshire	June 21, 1788	Illinois	December 3, 1818
Virginia	June 25, 1788	Alabama	December 14, 1819
New York	July 26, 1788	Maine	March 15, 1820
North Carolina	November 21, 1789	Missouri	August 10, 1821

ADMISSION OF STATES TO THE UNION

State	Date of Admission	State	Date of Admission
Arkansas	June 15, 1836	Colorado	August 1, 1876
Michigan	January 16, 1837	North Dakota	November 2, 1889
Florida	March 3, 1845	South Dakota	November 2, 1889
Texas	December 29, 1845	Montana	November 8, 1889
Iowa	December 28, 1846	Washington	November 11, 1889
Wisconsin	May 29, 1848	Idaho	July 3, 1890
California	September 9, 1850	Wyoming	July 10, 1890
Minnesota	May 11, 1858	Utah	January 4, 1896
Oregon	February 14, 1859	Oklahoma	November 16, 1907
Kansas	January 29, 1861	New Mexico	January 6, 1912
West Virginia	June 19, 1863	Arizona	February 14, 1912
Nevada	October 31, 1864	Alaska	January 3, 1959
Nebraska	March 1, 1867	Hawaii	August 21, 1959

SUPREME COURT JUSTICES

Name	Service	Appointed by	Name	Service	Appointed by
John Jay*	1789–1795	Washington	Philip P. Barbour	1836–1841	Jackson
James Wilson	1789–1798	Washington	John Catron	1837–1865	Van Buren
John Blair	1789–1796	Washington	John McKinley	1837–1852	Van Buren
John Rutledge	1790–1791	Washington	Peter V. Daniel	1841–1860	Van Buren
William Cushing	1790–1810	Washington	Samuel Nelson	1845–1872	Tyler
James Iredell	1790–1799	Washington	Levi Woodbury	1845–1851	Polk
Thomas Johnson	1791–1793	Washington	Robert C. Grier	1846–1870	Polk
William Paterson	1793–1806	Washington	Benjamin R. Curtis	1851–1857	Fillmore
John Rutledge†	1795	Washington	John A. Campbell	1853–1861	Pierce
Samuel Chase	1796–1811	Washington	Nathan Clifford	1858–1881	Buchanan
Oliver Ellsworth	1796–1799	Washington	Noah H. Swayne	1862–1881	Lincoln
Bushrod Washington	1798–1829	J. Adams	Samuel F. Miller	1862–1890	Lincoln
			David Davis	1862–1877	Lincoln
Alfred Moore	1799–1804	J. Adams	Stephen J. Field	1863–1897	Lincoln
John Marshall	1801–1835	J. Adams	**Salmon P. Chase**	1864–1873	Lincoln
William Johnson	1804–1834	Jefferson	William Strong	1870–1880	Grant
Henry B. Livingston	1806–1823	Jefferson	Joseph P. Bradley	1870–1892	Grant
Thomas Todd	1807–1826	Jefferson	Ward Hunt	1873–1882	Grant
Gabriel Duval	1811–1836	Madison	**Morrison R. Waite**	1874–1888	Grant
Joseph Story	1811–1845	Madison	John M. Harlan	1877–1911	Hayes
Smith Thompson	1823–1843	Monroe	William B. Woods	1880–1887	Hayes
Robert Trimble	1826–1828	J. Q. Adams	Stanley Matthews	1881–1889	Garfield
John McLean	1829–1861	Jackson	Horace Gray	1882–1902	Arthur
Henry Baldwin	1830–1844	Jackson	Samuel Blatchford	1882–1893	Arthur
James M. Wayne	1835–1867	Jackson	Lucius Q. C. Lamar	1888–1893	Cleveland
Roger B. Taney	1836–1864	Jackson	**Melville W. Fuller**	1888–1910	Cleveland
			David J. Brewer	1889–1910	B. Harrison
			Henry B. Brown	1890–1906	B. Harrison
			George Shiras	1892–1903	B. Harrison
			Howell E. Jackson	1893–1895	B. Harrison

*Chief Justices appear in bold type.
†Acting Chief Justice; Senate refused to confirm appointment.

Name	Service	Appointed by	Name	Service	Appointed by
Edward D. White	1894–1910	Cleveland	Harold H. Burton	1945–1958	Truman
Rufus W. Peckham	1896–1909	Cleveland	**Frederick M. Vinson**	1946–1953	Truman
Joseph McKenna	1898–1925	McKinley			
Oliver W. Holmes	1902–1932	T. Roosevelt	Tom C. Clark	1949–1967	Truman
William R. Day	1903–1922	T. Roosevelt	Sherman Minton	1949–1956	Truman
William H. Moody	1906–1910	T. Roosevelt	**Earl Warren**	1953–1969	Eisenhower
Horace H. Lurton	1910–1914	Taft	John Marshall Harlan	1955–1971	Eisenhower
Charles E. Hughes	1910–1916	Taft	William J. Brennan Jr.	1956–1990	Eisenhower
Willis Van Devanter	1910–1937	Taft	Charles E. Whittaker	1957–1962	Eisenhower
Edward D. White	1910–1921	Taft	Potter Stewart	1958–1981	Eisenhower
Joseph R. Lamar	1911–1916	Taft	Byron R. White	1962–1993	Kennedy
Mahlon Pitney	1912–1922	Taft	Arthur J. Goldberg	1962–1965	Kennedy
James C. McReynolds	1914–1941	Wilson	Abe Fortas	1965–1969	L. Johnson
			Thurgood Marshall	1967–1991	L. Johnson
Louis D. Brandeis	1916–1939	Wilson	**Warren E. Burger**	1969–1986	Nixon
John H. Clarke	1916–1922	Wilson	Harry A. Blackmun	1970–1994	Nixon
William H. Taft	1921–1930	Harding	Lewis F. Powell Jr.	1972–1988	Nixon
George Sutherland	1922–1938	Harding	William H. Rehnquist	1972–1986	Nixon
Pierce Butler	1923–1939	Harding	John Paul Stevens	1975–	Ford
Edward T. Sanford	1923–1930	Harding	Sandra Day O'Connor	1981–	Reagan
Harlan F. Stone	1925–1941	Coolidge			
Charles E. Hughes	1930–1941	Hoover	**William H. Rehnquist**	1986–	Reagan
Owen J. Roberts	1930–1945	Hoover			
Benjamin N. Cardozo	1932–1938	Hoover	Antonin Scalia	1986–	Reagan
Hugo L. Black	1937–1971	F. Roosevelt	Anthony M. Kennedy	1988–	Reagan
Stanley F. Reed	1938–1957	F. Roosevelt			
Felix Frankfurter	1939–1962	F. Roosevelt	David H. Souter	1990–	G. H. W. Bush
William O. Douglas	1939–1975	F. Roosevelt			
Frank Murphy	1940–1949	F. Roosevelt	Clarence Thomas	1991–	G. H. W. Bush
Harlan F. Stone	1941–1946	F. Roosevelt			
James F. Byrnes	1941–1942	F. Roosevelt	Ruth Bader Ginsburg	1993–	Clinton
Robert H. Jackson	1941–1954	F. Roosevelt			
Wiley B. Rutledge	1943–1949	F. Roosevelt	Stephen Breyer	1994–	Clinton

SIGNIFICANT SUPREME COURT CASES

Marbury v. Madison (1803)

This case established the right of the Supreme Court to review the constitutionality of laws. The decision involved judicial appointments made during the last hours of the administration of President John Adams. Some commissions, including that of William Marbury, had not yet been delivered when President Thomas Jefferson took office. Infuriated by the last-minute nature of Adams's Federalist appointments, Jefferson refused to send the undelivered commissions out, and Marbury decided to sue. The Supreme Court, presided over by John Marshall, a Federalist who had assisted Adams in the judicial appointments, ruled that although

Marbury's commission was valid and the new president should have delivered it, the Court could not compel him to do so. The Court based its reasoning on a finding that the grounds of Marbury's suit, resting in the Judiciary Act of 1789, were in conflict with the Constitution.

For the first time, the Court had overturned a national law on the grounds that it was unconstitutional. John Marshall had quietly established the concept of judicial review: The Supreme Court had given itself the authority to nullify acts of the other branches of the federal government. Although the Constitution provides for judicial review, the Court had not exercised this power before and did not use it again until 1857. It seems likely that if the Court had waited until 1857 to use this power, it would have been difficult to establish.

McCulloch v. Maryland (1819)

In 1816, Congress authorized the creation of a national bank. To protect its own banks from competition with a branch of the national bank in Baltimore, the state legislature of Maryland placed a tax of 2 percent on all notes issued by any bank operating in Maryland that was not chartered by the state. McCulloch, cashier of the Baltimore branch of the Bank of the United States, was convicted for refusing to pay the tax. Under the leadership of Chief Justice John Marshall, the Court ruled that the federal government had the power to establish a bank, even though that specific authority was not mentioned in the Constitution.

Marshall maintained that the authority could be reasonably implied from Article 1, section 8, which gives Congress the power to make all laws that are necessary and proper to execute the enumerated powers. Marshall also held that Maryland could not tax the national bank because in a conflict between federal and state laws, the federal law must take precedence. Thus he established the principles of implied powers and federal supremacy, both of which set a precedent for subsequent expansion of federal power at the expense of the states.

Scott v. Sandford (1857)

Dred Scott was a slave who sued for his own and his family's freedom on the grounds that, with his master, he had traveled to and lived in free territory that did not allow slavery. When his case reached the Supreme Court, the justices saw an opportunity to settle once and for all the vexing question of slavery in the territories. The Court's decision in this case proved that it enjoyed no special immunity from the sectional and partisan passions of the time. Five of the nine justices were from the South and seven were Democrats.

Chief Justice Roger B. Taney hated Republicans and detested racial equality; his decision reflects those prejudices. He wrote an opinion not only declaring that Scott was still a slave but also claiming that the Constitution denied citizenship or rights to blacks, that Congress had no right to exclude slavery from the territories, and that the Missouri Compromise was unconstitutional. While southern Democrats gloated over this seven-to-two decision, sectional tensions were further inflamed and the young Republican Party's claim that a hostile "slave power" was conspiring to destroy northern liberties was given further credence. The decision brought the nation closer to civil war and is generally regarded as the worst decision ever rendered by the Supreme Court.

Butchers' Benevolent Association of New Orleans v. Crescent City Livestock Landing and Slaughterhouse Co. (1873)

The *Slaughterhouse* cases, as the cases docketed under the *Butchers'* title were known, were the first legal test of the Fourteenth Amendment. To cut down on cases of cholera believed to be caused by contaminated water, the state of Louisiana prohibited the slaughter of livestock in New Orleans except in one slaughterhouse, effectively giving that slaughterhouse a monopoly. Other New Orleans butchers claimed that the state had deprived them of their occupation without due process of law, thus violating the Fourteenth Amendment.

In a five-to-four decision, the Court upheld the Louisiana law, declaring that the Fourteenth Amendment protected only the rights of federal citizenship, like voting in federal elections and interstate travel. The federal government thus was not obliged to protect basic civil rights from violation by state governments. This decision would have significant implications for African Americans and their struggle for civil rights in the twentieth century.

United States v. E. C. Knight Co. (1895)

Also known as the *Sugar Trust* case, this was among the first cases to reveal the weakness of the Sherman Antitrust Act in the hands of a pro-business Supreme Court. In 1895, American Sugar Refining Company purchased four other sugar producers, including the E. C. Knight Company, and thus took control of more than 98 percent of the sugar refining in the United States. In an effort to limit monopoly, the government brought suit against all five of the companies for violating the Sherman Antitrust Act, which outlawed trusts and other business combinations in restraint of trade. The Court dismissed the suit, however, arguing that the law applied only to commerce and not to manufacturing, defining the latter as a local concern and not part of the interstate commerce that the government could regulate.

Plessy v. Ferguson (1896)

African American Homer Plessy challenged a Louisiana law that required segregation on trains passing through the state. After ensuring that the railroad and the conductor knew that he was of mixed race (Plessy appeared to be white but under the racial code of Louisiana was classified as "colored" because he was one-eighth black), he refused to move to the "colored only" section of the coach. The Court ruled against Plessy by a vote of seven to one, declaring that "separate but equal" facilities were permissible according to section 1 of the Fourteenth Amendment, which calls upon the states to provide "equal protection of the laws" to anyone within their jurisdiction. Although the case was viewed as relatively insignificant at the time, it cast a long shadow over several decades.

Initially, the decision was viewed as a victory for segregationists, but in the 1930s and 1940s civil rights advocates referred to the doctrine of "separate but equal" in their efforts to end segregation. They argued that segregated institutions and accommodations were often *not* equal to those available to whites, and finally succeeded in overturning *Plessy* in *Brown v. Board of Education* in 1954 (see below).

Lochner v. New York (1905)

In this case, the Court ruled against a New York state law that prohibited employees from working in bakeries more than ten hours a day or sixty hours a week. The purpose of the law was to protect the health of workers, but the Court ruled that it was unconstitutional because it violated "freedom of contract" implicitly protected by the due process clause of the Fourteenth Amendment. Most of the justices believed strongly in a laissez-faire economic system that favored survival of the fittest. They felt that government protection of workers interfered with this system. In a dissenting opinion, Justice Oliver Wendell Holmes accused the majority of distorting the Constitution and of deciding the case on "an economic theory which a large part of the country does not entertain."

Muller v. Oregon (1908)

In 1905, Curt Muller, owner of a Portland, Oregon, laundry, demanded that one of his employees, Mrs. Elmer Gotcher, work more than the ten hours allowed as a maximum workday for women under Oregon law. Muller argued that the law violated his "freedom of contract" as established in prior Supreme Court decisions.

Progressive lawyer Louis D. Brandeis defended the Oregon law by arguing that a state could be justified in abridging freedom of contract when the health, safety, and welfare of workers was at issue. His innovative strategy drew on ninety-five pages of excerpts from factory and medical reports to substantiate his argument that there was a direct connection between long hours and the health of women and thus the health of the nation. In a unanimous decision, the Court upheld the Oregon law, but later generations of women fighting for equality would question the strategy of arguing that women's reproductive role entitled them to special treatment.

Schenck v. United States (1919)

During World War I, Charles Schenck and other members of the Socialist Party printed and mailed out flyers urging young men who were subject to the draft to oppose the war in Europe. In upholding the conviction of Schenck for publishing a pamphlet urging draft resistance, Justice Oliver Wendell Holmes established the "clear and present danger" test for freedom of speech. Such utterances as Schenck's during a time of national peril, Holmes wrote, could be considered the equivalent of shouting "Fire!" in a crowded theater. Congress had the right to protect the public against such an incitement to panic, the Court ruled in a unanimous decision. But the analogy was a false one. Schenck's pamphlet had little power to provoke a public firmly opposed to its message. Although Holmes later modified his position to state that the danger must relate to an immediate evil and a specific action, the "clear and present danger" test laid the groundwork for those who later sought to limit First Amendment freedoms.

Schechter Poultry Corp. v. United States (1935)

During the Great Depression, the National Industrial Recovery Act (NIRA), which was passed under President Franklin D. Roosevelt, established fair competition codes that were designed to help businesses. The Schechter brothers of New York City, who sold chickens, were convicted of violating the codes. The Supreme Court ruled that the NIRA unconstitutionally conferred legislative power on an administrative agency and overstepped the limits of federal power to regulate interstate commerce. The decision was a significant blow to the New Deal recovery program, demonstrating both historic American resistance to economic planning and the refusal of the business community to yield its autonomy unless it was forced to do so.

Brown v. Board of Education (1954)

In 1950, the families of eight Topeka, Kansas, children sued the Topeka Board of Education. The children were blacks who lived within walking distance of a whites-only school. The segregated school system required them to take a time-consuming, inconvenient, and dangerous route to get to a black school, and their parents argued that there was no reason their children should not be allowed to attend the nearest school. By the time the case reached the Supreme Court, it had been joined with similar cases regarding segregated schools in other states and the District of Columbia. A team of lawyers from the National Association for the Advancement of Colored People (NAACP), led by Thurgood Marshall (who would later be appointed to the Supreme Court), urged the Court to overturn the fifty-eight-year-old precedent established in *Plessy v. Ferguson*, which had enshrined "separate but equal" as the law of the land. A unanimous Court, led by Chief Justice Earl Warren, declared that "separate educational facilities are inherently unequal" and thus violate the Fourteenth Amendment. In 1955, the Court called for desegregation "with all deliberate speed" but established no deadline.

Roth v. United States (1957)

In 1957, New Yorker Samuel Roth was convicted of sending obscene materials through the mail in a case that ultimately reached the Supreme Court. With a six-to-three vote, the Court reaffirmed the historical view that obscenity is not protected by the First Amendment. Yet it broke new ground by declaring that a work could be judged obscene only if, "taken as a whole," it appealed to the "prurient interest" of "the average person."

Prior to this case, work could be judged obscene if portions were thought able to "deprave and corrupt" the most susceptible part of an audience (such as children). Thus, serious works of literature such as Theodore Dreiser's *An American Tragedy*, which was banned in Boston when first published, had received no protection. Although this decision continued to pose problems of definition, it did help to protect most works that attempt to convey ideas, even if those ideas have to do with sex, from the threat of obscenity laws.

Engel v. Vitale (1962)

In 1959, five parents with ten children in the New Hyde Park, New York, school system sued the school board. The parents argued that the so-called Regents' Prayer that public school students in New York recited at the start of every school day violated the doctrine of separation of church and state outlined in the First Amendment. In 1962, the Supreme Court voted six to one in favor of banning the Regents' Prayer.

The decision threw the religious community into an uproar. Many religious leaders expressed dismay and even shock; others welcomed the decision. Several efforts to introduce an amendment allowing school prayer have failed. Subsequent Supreme Court decisions have banned reading of the Bible in public schools. The Court has also declared mandatory flag saluting to be an infringement of religious and personal freedoms.

Gideon v. Wainwright (1963)

When Clarence Earl Gideon was tried for breaking into a poolroom, the state of Florida rejected his demand for a court-appointed lawyer as guaranteed by the Sixth Amendment. In 1963, the Court upheld his demand in a unanimous decision that established the obligation of states to provide attorneys for indigent defendants in felony cases. Prior to this decision, the right to an attorney had applied only to federal cases, not state cases. In its ruling in *Gideon v. Wainwright*, the Supreme Court applied the Sixth through the Fourteenth Amendments to the states. In 1972, the Supreme Court extended the right to legal representation to all cases, not just felony cases, in its decision in *Argersinger v. Hamlin*.

Griswold v. Connecticut (1965)

With a vote of seven to two, the Supreme Court reversed an "uncommonly silly law" (in the words of Justice Potter Stewart) that made it a crime for anyone in the state of Connecticut to use any drug, article, or instrument to prevent conception. *Griswold* became a landmark case because here, for the first time, the Court explicitly invested with full constitutional status "fundamental personal rights," such as the right to privacy, that were not expressly enumerated in the Bill of Rights. The majority opinion in the case held that the law infringed on the constitutionally protected right to privacy of married persons.

Although the Court had previously recognized fundamental rights not expressly enumerated in the Bill of Rights (such as the right to procreate in *Skinner v. Oklahoma* in 1942), *Griswold* was the first time the Court had justified, at length, the practice of investing such unenumerated rights with full constitutional status. Writing for the majority, Justice William O. Douglas explained that the First, Third, Fourth, Fifth, and Ninth Amendments imply "zones of privacy" that are the foundation for the general right to privacy affirmed in this case.

Miranda v. Arizona (1966)

In 1966, the Supreme Court, by a vote of five to four, upheld the case of Ernesto Miranda, who appealed a murder conviction on the grounds that police had gotten him to confess without giving him access to an attorney. The *Miranda* case was the culmination of the Court's efforts to find a meaningful way of determining whether police had used due process in extracting confessions from people accused of crimes. The *Miranda* decision upholds the Fifth Amendment protection against self-incrimination outside the courtroom and requires that suspects be given what came to be known as the "Miranda warning," which advises them of their right to remain silent and warns them that anything they say might be used against them in a court of law. Suspects must also be told that they have a right to counsel.

New York Times Co. v. United States (1971)

With a six-to-three vote, the Court upheld the right of the *New York Times* and the *Washington Post* to print materials from the so-called *Pentagon Papers*, a secret government study of U.S. policy in Vietnam, leaked by dissident Pentagon official Daniel Ellsberg. Since the papers revealed deception and secrecy in the conduct of the Vietnam War, the Nixon administration had quickly obtained a court injunction against their further publication, claiming that suppression was in the interests of national security. The Supreme Court's decision overturning the injunction strengthened the First Amendment protection of freedom of the press.

Furman v. Georgia (1972)

In this case, the Supreme Court ruled five to four that the death penalty for murder or rape violated the cruel and unusual punishment clause of the Eighth Amendment because the manner in which the death penalty was meted out was irregular, "arbitrary," and "cruel." In response, most states enacted new statutes that allow the death penalty to be imposed only after a postconviction hearing at which evidence must be presented to show that "aggravating" or "mitigating" circumstances were factors in the crime. If the postconviction hearing hands down a death sentence, the case is automatically reviewed by an appellate court.

In 1976, the Court ruled in *Gregg v. Georgia* that these statutes were not unconstitutional. In 1977, the Court ruled in *Coker v. Georgia* that the death penalty for rape was "disproportionate and excessive," thus allowing the death penalty only in murder cases. Between 1977 and 1991, some 150 people were executed in the United States. Public opinion polls indicate that about 70 percent of Americans favor the death penalty for murder. Capital punishment continues to generate controversy, however, as opponents argue that there is no evidence that the death penalty deters crime and that its use reflects racial and economic bias.

Roe v. Wade (1973)

In 1973, the Court found, by a vote of seven to two, that state laws restricting access to abortion violated a woman's right to privacy guaranteed by the due process clause of the Fourteenth Amendment. The decision was based on the cases of two women living in Texas and Georgia, both states with stringent antiabortion laws. Upholding the individual rights of both women and physicians, the Court ruled that the Constitution protects the right to abortion and that states cannot prohibit abortions in the early stages of pregnancy.

The decision stimulated great debate among legal scholars as well as the public. Critics argued that since abortion was never addressed in the Constitution, the Court could not claim that legislation violated fundamental values of the Constitution. They also argued that since abortion was a medical procedure with an acknowledged impact on a fetus, it was inappropriate to invoke the kind of "privacy" argument that was used in *Griswold v. Connecticut* (see page A-43), which was about contraception. Defenders suggested that the case should be argued as a case of gender discrimination, which did violate the equal protection clause of the Fourteenth Amendment. Others said that the right to privacy in sexual matters was indeed a fundamental right.

Regents of the University of California v. Bakke (1978)

When Allan Bakke, a white man, was not accepted by the University of California Medical School at Davis, he filed a lawsuit alleging that the admissions program, which set up different standards for test scores and grades for members of certain minority groups, violated the Civil Rights Act of 1964, which outlawed racial or ethnic preferences in programs supported by federal funds. Bakke further argued that the university's practice of setting aside spaces for minority applicants denied him equal protection as guaranteed by the Fourteenth Amendment. In a five-to-four decision, the Court ordered that Bakke be admitted to the medical school, yet it sanctioned affirmative action programs to attack the results of past discrimination as long as strict quotas or racial classifications were not involved.

Webster v. Reproductive Health Services (1989)

By a vote of five to four, the Court upheld several restrictions on the availability of abortions as imposed by Missouri state law. It upheld restrictions on the use of state property, including public hospitals, for abortions. It also upheld a provision requiring physicians to perform tests to determine the viability of a fetus that a doctor judged to be twenty weeks of age or older. Although the justices did not go so far as to overturn the decision in *Roe v. Wade* (see at left), the ruling galvanized interest groups on both sides of the abortion issue. Opponents of abortion pressured state legislatures to place greater restrictions on abortions; those who favored availability of abortion tried to mobilize public action by presenting the decision as a major threat to the right to choose abortion.

SIGNIFICANT SUPREME COURT CASES

Cipollone v. Liggett (1992)

In a seven-to-two decision, the Court ruled in favor of the family of Rose Cipollone, a woman who died of lung cancer after smoking for forty-two years. The Court rejected arguments that health warnings on cigarette packages protected tobacco manufacturers from personal injury suits filed by smokers who contract cancer and other serious illnesses.

Miller v. Johnson (1995)

In a five-to-four decision, the Supreme Court ruled that voting districts created to increase the voting power of racial minorities were unconstitutional. The decision threatens dozens of congressional, state, and local voting districts that were drawn to give minorities more representation as had been required by the Justice Department under the Voting Rights Act. If states are required to redraw voting districts, the number of black members of Congress could be sharply reduced.

Romer v. Evans (1996)

In a six-to-three decision, the Court struck down a Colorado amendment that forbade local governments from banning discrimination against homosexuals.

Writing for the majority, Justice Anthony Kennedy said that forbidding communities from taking action to protect the rights of homosexuals and not of other groups unlawfully deprived gays and lesbians of opportunities that were available to others. Kennedy based the decision on the guarantee of equal protection under the law as provided by the Fourteenth Amendment.

Bush v. Palm Beach County Canvassing Board (2000)

In a bitterly argued five-to-four decision, the Court reversed the Florida Supreme Court's previous order for a hand recount of contested presidential election ballots in several counties of that battleground state, effectively securing the presidency for Texas Republican governor George W. Bush. The ruling ended a protracted legal dispute between presidential candidates Bush and Vice President Al Gore while inflaming public opinion: For the first time since 1888, a president who failed to win the popular vote took office. Critics charged that the Supreme Court had applied partisanship rather than objectivity to the case, pointing out that the decision went against this Court's customary interpretation of the Constitution to favor state over federal authority.

The American Economy

THESE FIVE "SNAPSHOTS" of the U.S. economy show significant changes over the past century and a half. In 1849, the agricultural sector was by far the largest contributor to the economy. By the turn of the century, with advances in technology and an abundance of cheap labor and raw materials, the country had experienced remarkable industrial expansion and the manufacturing industries dominated. By 1950, the service sector had increased significantly, fueled by the consumerism of the 1920s and the post–World War II years, and the economy was becoming more diversified. Note that by 1990, the government's share in the economy had grown to more than 10 percent and activity in both the trade and manufacturing sectors had declined, partly as a result of competition from Western Europe and Asia. Manufacturing continued to decline, and by 2001 the service and finance, real estate, and insurance sectors had all grown steadily to eclipse it.

Main Sectors of the U.S. Economy: 1849, 1899, 1950, 1990, 2001

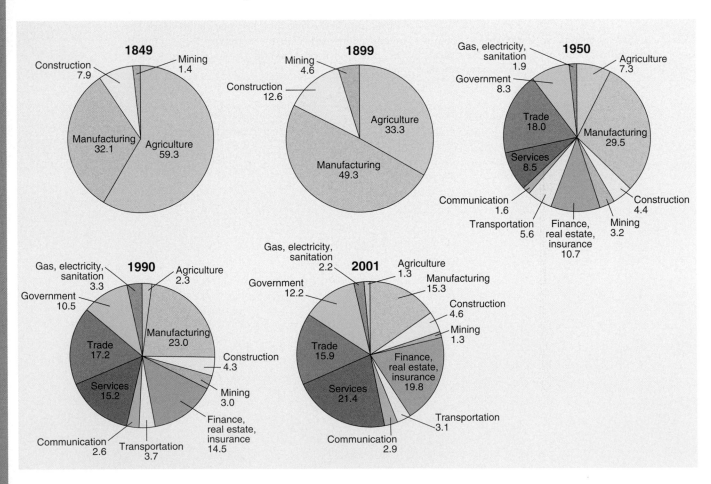

SOURCE: Data from *Historical Statistics of the United States, Colonial Times to 1970* (1975); *Statistical Abstract of the United States, 1998;* U.S. Bureau of Economic Analysis, *Industry Accounts Data, 2001.*

FEDERAL SPENDING AND THE ECONOMY, 1790–2002

Year	Gross National Product (in billions)	Foreign Trade (in millions) Exports	Imports	Federal Budget (in billions)	Federal Surplus/Deficit (in billions)	Federal Debt (in billions)
1790	NA	20	23	0.004	0.00015	0.076
1800	NA	71	91	0.011	0.0006	0.083
1810	NA	67	85	0.008	0.0012	0.053
1820	NA	70	74	0.018	−0.0004	0.091
1830	NA	74	71	0.015	0.100	0.049
1840	NA	132	107	0.024	−0.005	0.004
1850	NA	152	178	0.040	0.004	0.064
1860	NA	400	362	0.063	−0.01	0.065
1870	7.4	451	462	0.310	0.10	2.4
1880	11.2	853	761	0.268	0.07	2.1
1890	13.1	910	823	0.318	0.09	1.2
1900	18.7	1,499	930	0.521	0.05	1.2
1910	35.3	1,919	1,646	0.694	−0.02	1.1
1920	91.5	8,664	5,784	6.357	0.3	24.3
1930	90.4	4,013	3,500	3.320	0.7	16.3
1940	99.7	4,030	7,433	9.6	−2.7	43.0
1950	284.8	10,816	9,125	43.1	−2.2	257.4
1960	503.7	19,600	15,046	92.2	0.3	286.3
1970	977.1	42,700	40,189	195.6	−2.8	371.0
1980	2,631.7	220,600	244,871	590.9	−73.8	907.7
1990	5,832.2	393,600	495,300	1,253.2	−221.2	3,266.1
2000	9,848.0	1,070,054	1,445,438	1,788.8	236.4	5,701.9
2002	10,436.7	974,107	1,392,145	2,011.0	−157.8	6,255.4

SOURCE: *Historical Statistics of the U.S., Colonial Times to 1970* (1975), *Statistical Abstract of the U.S., 1996* (1996), *Statistical Abstract of the U.S., 1999* (1999), and *Statistical Abstract of the U.S., 2003* (2003).

A Demographic Profile of the United States and Its People

Population

FROM AN ESTIMATED 4,600 white inhabitants in 1630, the country's population grew to a total of just under 250 million in 1990. It is important to note that the U.S. census, first conducted in 1790 and the source of these figures, counted blacks, both free and slave, but did not include American Indians until 1860. The years 1790 to 1900 saw the most rapid population growth, with an average increase of 25 to 35 percent per decade. In addition to "natural" growth—birthrate exceeding death rate—immigration was also a factor in that rise, especially between 1840 and 1860, 1880 and 1890, and 1900 and 1910 (see table on page A-51). The twentieth century witnessed slower growth, partly a result of 1920s immigration restrictions and a decline in the birthrate, especially during the depression era and the 1960s and 1970s. The U.S. population is expected to reach almost 300 million by the year 2010.

POPULATION GROWTH, 1630–2000

Year	Population	Percent Increase	Year	Population	Percent Increase
1630	4,600	—	1820	9,638,453	33.1
1640	26,600	473.3	1830	12,866,020	33.5
1650	50,400	89.1	1840	17,069,453	32.7
1660	75,100	49.0	1850	23,191,876	35.9
1670	111,900	49.1	1860	31,443,321	35.6
1680	151,500	35.4	1870	39,818,449	26.6
1690	210,400	38.9	1880	50,155,783	26.0
1700	250,900	19.3	1890	62,947,714	25.5
1710	331,700	32.2	1900	75,994,575	20.7
1720	466,200	40.5	1910	91,972,266	21.0
1730	629,400	35.0	1920	105,710,620	14.9
1740	905,600	43.9	1930	122,775,046	16.1
1750	1,170,800	30.0	1940	131,669,275	7.2
1760	1,593,600	36.1	1950	150,697,361	14.5
1770	2,148,100	34.8	1960	179,323,175	19.0
1780	2,780,400	29.4	1970	203,302,031	13.4
1790	3,929,214	41.3	1980	226,542,199	11.4
1800	5,308,483	35.1	1990	248,718,302	9.8
1810	7,239,881	36.4	2000	281,422,509	13.1

Source: Historical Statistics of the U.S. (1960), Historical Statistics of the U.S., Colonial Times to 1970 (1975), Statistical Abstract of the U.S., 1996 (1996), and Statistical Abstract of the U.S., 2003 (2003).

A DEMOGRAPHIC PROFILE OF THE UNITED STATES AND ITS PEOPLE

Birthrate, 1820–2000

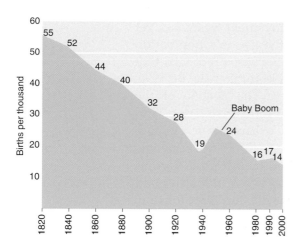

SOURCE: Data from *Historical Statistics of the U.S., Colonial Times to 1970* (1975) and *Statistical Abstract of the U.S., 2003* (2003).

Death Rate, 1900–2000

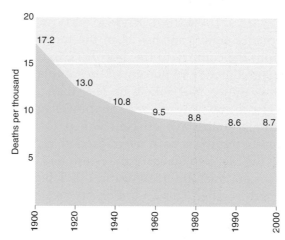

SOURCE: Data from *Historical Statistics of the U.S., Colonial Times to 1970* (1975) and *Statistical Abstract of the U.S., 2003* (2003).

Life Expectancy, 1900–2000

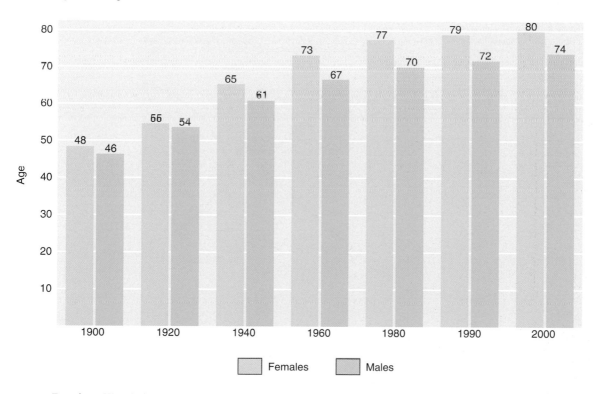

SOURCE: Data from *Historical Statistics of the U.S., Colonial Times to 1970* (1975) and *Statistical Abstract of the U.S., 2003* (2003).

MIGRATION AND IMMIGRATION

WE TEND TO ASSOCIATE INTERNAL MIGRATION with movement westward, yet equally significant has been the movement of the nation's population from the country to the city. In 1790, the first U.S. census recorded that approximately 95 percent of the population lived in rural areas. By 1990, that figure had fallen to less than 25 percent. The decline of the agricultural way of life, late-nineteenth-century industrialization, and immigration have all contributed to increased urbanization. A more recent trend has been the migration, especially since the 1970s, of people to the Sun Belt states of the South and West, lured by factors as various as economic opportunities in the defense and high-tech industries and good weather. This migration has swelled the size of cities like Houston, Dallas, Tucson, Phoenix, and San Diego, all of which in recent years ranked among the top ten most populous U.S. cities.

Rural and Urban Population, 1750–2000

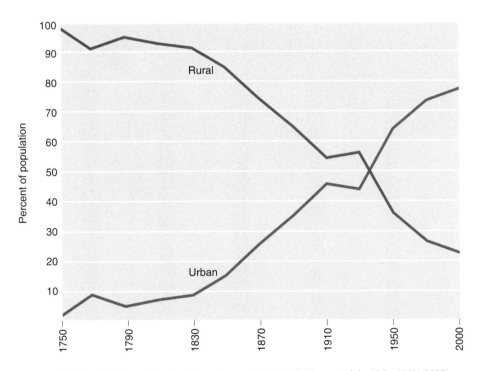

SOURCE: *Statistical Abstract of the U.S., 1991* (1991), *Statistical Abstract of the U.S., 2002* (2002).

MIGRATION AND IMMIGRATION

THE QUANTITY AND CHARACTER OF IMMIGRATION to the United States has varied greatly over time. During the first major influx, between 1840 and 1860, newcomers hailed primarily from northern and western Europe. From 1880 to 1915, when rates soared even more dramatically, the profile changed, with 80 percent of the "new immigration" coming from central, eastern, and southern Europe. Following World War I, strict quotas reduced the flow considerably. Note also the significant falloff during the years of the Great Depression and World War II. The sources of immigration during the last half century have changed significantly, with the majority of people coming from Latin America, the Caribbean, and Asia. The latest surge during the 1980s and 1990s brought more immigrants to the United States than in any decade except 1901–1910.

RATES OF IMMIGRATION, 1821–2002

Year	Number	Rate per Thousand of Total Resident Population
1821–1830	151,824	1.6
1831–1840	599,125	4.6
1841–1850	1,713,521	10.0
1851–1860	2,598,214	11.2
1861–1870	2,314,824	7.4
1871–1880	2,812,191	7.1
1881–1890	5,246,613	10.5
1891–1900	3,687,546	5.8
1901–1910	8,795,386	11.6
1911–1920	5,735,811	6.2
1921–1930	4,107,209	3.9
1931–1940	528,431	0.4
1941–1950	1,035,039	0.7
1951–1960	2,515,479	1.6
1961–1970	3,321,677	1.8
1971–1980	4,493,300	2.2
1981–1990	7,338,100	3.0
1991	1,827,167	7.2
1992	973,977	3.8
1993	904,292	3.5
1994	804,416	3.1
1995	720,461	2.7
1996	915,900	3.4
1997	798,378	2.9
1998	654,451	2.4
1999	646,568	2.3
2000	849,807	3.0
2001	1,064,318	3.7
2002	1,063,732	3.7

Source: Historical Statistics of the U.S., Colonial Times to 1970 (1975), Statistical Abstract of the U.S., 1996 (1996), Statistical Abstract of the U.S., 1999 (1999), 2002 Yearbook of Immigration Statistics (2002), and Statistical Abstract of the U.S., 2003. (2003).

Major Trends in Immigration, 1820–2000

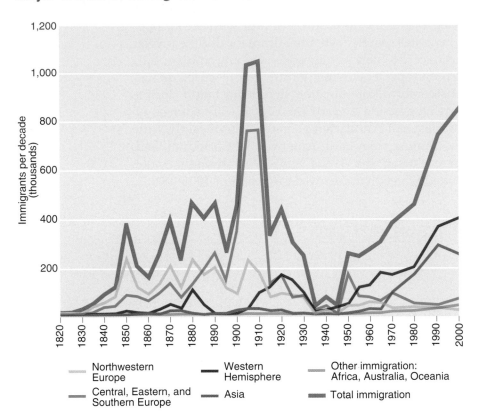

SOURCE: Data from *Historical Statistics of the U.S., Colonial Times to 1970* (1975), *Statistical Abstract of the U.S., 1999* (1999), and *Statistical Abstract of the U.S., 2003* (2003).

Research Resources in U.S. History

For help refining your research skills, finding what you need on the Web, and using it effectively, see "Other Resources at Bedford/St. Martin's" at bedfordstmartins.com/roark.

WHILE DOING RESEARCH IN HISTORY, you will use the library to track down primary and secondary sources and to answer questions that arise as you learn more about your topic. This appendix suggests helpful indexes, references, periodicals, and sources of primary documents. It also offers an overview of electronic resources available through the Internet. The materials listed here are not carried at all libraries, but they will give you an idea of the range of sources available. Remember, too, that librarians are an extremely helpful resource. They can direct you to useful materials throughout your research process.

Bibliographies and Indexes

American Historical Association Guide to Historical Literature. 3rd ed. New York: Oxford University Press, 1995. Offers 27,000 citations to important historical literature, arranged in forty-eight sections covering theory, international history, and regional history. An indispensable guide recently updated to include current trends in historical research.

American History and Life. Santa Barbara: ABC-Clio, 1964–. Covers publications of all sorts on U.S. and Canadian history and culture in a chronological/regional format, with abstracts and alphabetical indexes. Available in computerized format. The most complete ongoing bibliography for American history.

Freidel, Frank Burt. *Harvard Guide to American History.* Cambridge: Harvard University Press, Belknap Press, 1974. Provides citations to books and articles on American history published before 1970. The first volume is arranged topically, the second chronologically. Though it does not cover current scholarship, it is a classic and remains useful for tracing older publications.

Prucha, Francis Paul. *Handbook for Research in American History: A Guide to Bibliographies and Other Reference Works.* 2nd rev. ed. Lincoln: University of Nebraska Press, 1994. Introduces a variety of research tools, including electronic ones. A good source to consult when planning an in-depth research project.

General Overviews

Dictionary of American Biography. New York: Scribner's, 1928–1937, with supplements. Gives substantial biographies of prominent Americans in history.

Dictionary of American History. New York: Scribner's, 1976. An encyclopedia of terms, places, and concepts in U.S. history; other more specialized sets include the *Encyclopedia of North American Colonies* and the *Encyclopedia of the Confederacy.*

Dictionary of Concepts in History. New York: Greenwood, 1986. Contains essays defining concepts in historiography and describing how the concepts were formed; excellent bibliographies.

Encyclopedia of American Social History. New York: Scribner's, 1993. Surveys topics such as religion, class, gender, race, popular culture, regionalism, and everyday life from pre-Columbian to modern times.

Encyclopedia of the United States in the Twentieth Century. New York: Scribner's, 1996. An ambitious overview of American cultural, social, and intellectual history in broad articles arranged topically. Each article is followed by a thorough and very useful bibliography for further research.

Specialized Information

Black Women in America: An Historical Encyclopedia. Brooklyn: Carlson, 1993. A scholarly compilation of biographical and topical articles that constitute a definitive history of African American women.

Carruth, Gordon. *The Encyclopedia of American Facts and Dates.* 10th ed. New York: HarperCollins, 1997. Covers American history chronologically from 1986 to the present, offering information on treaties, battles, explorations, popular culture, philosophy, literature, and so on, mixing significant events with telling trivia. Tables allow for reviewing a year from a variety of angles. A thorough index helps pinpoint specific facts in time.

Cook, Chris. *Dictionary of Historical Terms*. 2nd ed. New York: Peter Bendrick, 1990. Covers a wide variety of terms—events, places, institutions, and topics—in history for all periods and places in a remarkably small package. A good place for quick identification of terms in the field.

Dictionary of Afro-American Slavery. New York: Greenwood, 1985. Surveys important people, events, and topics, with useful bibliographies; similar works include *Dictionary of the Vietnam War*, *Historical Dictionary of the New Deal*, and *Historical Dictionary of the Progressive Era*.

Knappman-Frost, Elizabeth. *The ABC-Clio Companion to Women's Progress in America*. Santa Barbara: ABC-Clio, 1994. Covers American women who were notable for their time as well as topics and organizations that have been significant in women's quest for equality. Each article is brief; there are a chronology and a bibliography at the back of the book.

United States Bureau of the Census. *Historical Statistics of the United States, Colonial Times to 1970*. Washington, D.C.: Government Printing Office, 1975. Offers vital statistics, economic figures, and social data for the United States. An index at the back helps locate tables by subject. For statistics since 1970, consult the annual *Statistical Abstract of the United States*.

Primary Resources

There are many routes to finding contemporary material for historical research. You may search your library catalog using the name of a prominent historical figure as an author; you may also find anthologies covering particular themes or periods in history. Consider also the following special materials for your research.

THE PRESS

American Periodical Series, 1741–1900. Ann Arbor: University Microfilms, 1946–1979. Microfilm collection of periodicals from the colonial period to 1900. An index identifies periodicals that focused on particular topics.

Herstory Microfilm Collection. Berkeley: Women's History Research Center, 1973. A microfilm collection of alternative feminist periodicals published between 1960 and 1980. Offers an interesting documentary history of the women's movement.

New York Times. New York: New York Times, 1851–. Many libraries have this newspaper on microfilm going back to its beginning in 1851. An index is available to locate specific dates and pages of news stories; it also provides detailed chronologies of events as they were reported in the news.

Readers' Guide to Periodical Literature. New York: Wilson, 1900–. This index to popular magazines started in 1900; an earlier index, *Poole's Index to Periodical Literature*, covers 1802–1906, though it does not provide such thorough indexing.

DIARIES, PAMPHLETS, BOOKS

The American Culture Series. Ann Arbor: University Microfilms, 1941–1974. A microfilm set, with a useful index, featuring books and pamphlets published between 1493 and 1875.

American Women's Diaries. New Canaan: Readex, 1984–. A collection of reproductions of women's diaries. There are different series for different regions of the country.

The March of America Facsimile Series. Ann Arbor: University Microfilms, 1966. A collection of more than ninety facsimiles of travel accounts to the New World published in English or English translation from the fifteenth through the nineteenth century.

Women in America from Colonial Times to the Twentieth Century. New York: Arno, 1974. A collection of reprints of dozens of books written by women describing women's lives and experiences in their own words.

GOVERNMENT DOCUMENTS

Congressional Record. Washington, D.C.: Government Printing Office, 1874–. Covers daily debates and proceedings of Congress. Earlier series were called *Debates and Proceedings in the Congress of the United States* and *The Congressional Globe*.

Foreign Relations of the United States. Washington, D.C.: Department of State, 1861–. A collection of documents from 1861, including diplomatic papers, correspondence, and memoranda, that provides a documentary record of U.S. foreign policy.

Public Papers of the Presidents. Washington, D.C.: Office of the Federal Register, 1957–. Includes major documents issued by the executive branch from the Hoover administration to the present.

Serial Set. Washington, D.C.: Government Printing Office, 1789–1969. A huge collection of congressional documents, available in many libraries on microfiche, with a useful index.

LOCAL HISTORY COLLECTIONS

State and county historical societies often house a wealth of historical documents; consider their resources when planning your research—you may find yourself working with material that no one else has analyzed before.

Internet Resources

The Internet has been a useful place for scholars to communicate and publish information in recent years. Electronic discussion lists, electronic journals,

INTERNET RESOURCES

and primary texts are among the resources available to historians. The following sources are good places to find historical information. You can also search the World Wide Web using any of a number of search engines. However, bear in mind that there is no board of editors screening Internet sites for accuracy or usefulness, and the search engines generally rely on free-text searches rather than subject headings. Be critical of all of your sources, particularly those found on the Internet. Note that when this book went to press, the sites listed below were active and maintained.

American Memory: Historical Collections for the National Digital Library Program. <http://rs6.loc.gov/amhome.html> An Internet site that features digitized primary source materials from the Library of Congress, among them African American pamphlets, Civil War photographs, documents from the Continental Congress and the Constitutional Convention of 1774–1790, materials on woman suffrage, and oral histories.

Douglass Archives of American Public Address. <http://douglassarchives.org> An electronic archive of American speeches and documents by a variety of people from Jane Addams to Jonathan Edwards to Theodore Roosevelt.

Historical Text Archive. <http://historicaltextarchive.com/> A Web interface for the oldest and largest Internet site for historical documents. Includes sections on Native American, African American, and U.S. history, in which can be found texts of the Declaration of Independence, the U.S. Constitution, the Constitution of Iroquois Nations, World War II surrender documents, photograph collections, and a great deal more. These can be used online or saved as files.

History Links from Yahoo! <http://dir.yahoo.com/arts/humanities/history/> A categorically arranged and frequently updated site list for all types of history. Some of the sources are more useful than others, but this can be a helpful gateway to some good information.

Index of Civil War Information on the Internet. <http://www.cwc.lsu.edu/cwc/civlink.htm> Compiled by the United States Civil War Center, this index lists everything from diaries to historic battlefields to reenactments.

Index of Native American Resources on the Internet. <http://www.hanksville.org/NAresources> A vast index of Native American resources organized by category. Within the history category, links are organized under subcategories: oral history, written history, geographical areas, timelines, and photographs and photographic archives. A central place to come in the search for information on Native American history.

Internet Resources for Students of Afro-American History and Culture. <http://www.libraries.rutgers.edu/rul/rr_gateway/research_guides/history/afrores.shtml> A good place to begin research on topics in African American history. The site is indexed and linked to a wide variety of sources, including primary documents, text collections, and archival sources on African American history. Individual documents such as slave narratives and petitions, the Fugitive Slave Acts, and speeches by W. E. B. Du Bois, Booker T. Washington, and Martin Luther King Jr. are categorized by century.

The Martin Luther King Jr. Papers Project. <http://www.stanford.edu/group/King> Organized by Stanford University, this site gives information about Martin Luther King Jr. and offers some of his writings.

NativeWeb. <http://www.nativeweb.org> One of the best organized and most accessible sites available on Native American issues, *NativeWeb* combines an events calendar and message board with history, statistics, a list of news sources, archives, new and updated related sites each week, and documents. The text is indexed and can be searched by subject, nation, and geographic region.

Perry-Castañeda Library Map Collection. <http://www.lib.utexas.edu/maps/index.html> The University of Texas at Austin library has put over seven hundred United States maps on the Web for viewing by students and professors alike.

Smithsonian Institution. <http://www.si.edu> Organized by subject, such as military history or Hispanic/Latino American resources, this site offers selected links to sites hosted by Smithsonian Institution museums and organizations. Content includes graphics of museum pieces and relevant textual information, book suggestions, maps, and links.

Supreme Court Collection. <http://supct.law.cornell.edu/supct/> This database can be used to search for information on various Supreme Court cases. Although the site primarily covers cases that occurred after 1990, there is information on some earlier historic cases. The justices' opinions, as originally written, are also included.

United States History Index. <http://www.ukans.edu/history/VL/USA> Maintained by a history professor and arranged by subject, such as women's history, labor history, and agricultural history, this index provides links to a variety of other sites. Although the list is extensive, it does not include a synopsis of each site, which makes finding specific information a time-consuming process.

United States Holocaust Memorial Museum. <http://www.ushmm.org> This site contains information about the Holocaust Museum in Washington, D.C., in particular and the Holocaust in general, and it lists links to related sites.

Women's History Resources. <http://www.mcps.k12 .md.us/curriculum/socialstd/Women_Bookmarks .html> An extensive listing of women's history sources available on the Internet. The site indexes resources on subjects as diverse as woman suffrage, women in the workplace, and celebrated women writers. Some of the links are to equally vast indexes, providing an overwhelming wealth of information.

WWW-VL History Index. <http://www.ukans.edu/ history/VL> A vast list of more than 1,700 links to sites of interest to historians, arranged alphabetically by general topic. Some links are to sources for general reference information, but most are on historical topics. A good place to start an exploration of Internet resources.

GLOSSARY OF HISTORICAL VOCABULARY

A Note to Students: This list of terms is provided to help you with historical and economic vocabulary. Many of these terms refer to broad, enduring concepts that you may encounter not only in further studies of history but also when following current events. The terms appear in bold at their first use in each chapter. In the glossary, the page numbers of those chapter-by-chapter appearances are provided so you can look up the terms' uses in various periods and contexts. For definitions and discussions of words not included here, consult a dictionary and the book's index, which will point you to topics covered at greater length in the book.

affirmative action   Policies established in the 1960s and 1970s by governments, businesses, universities, and other institutions to overcome the effects of past discrimination against specific groups such as racial and ethnic minorities and women. Measures to ensure equal opportunity include setting goals for admission, hiring, and promotion, considering minority status when allocating resources, and actively encouraging victims of past discrimination to apply for jobs and other resources. (pp. 1023, 1106, 1144)

agribusiness   Farming on a large scale, using the production, processing, and distribution methods of modern business. Farming became a big business, not just a way to feed a family and make a living, in the late nineteenth century as farms got larger and more mechanized. In the 1940s and 1950s, specialized commercial farms replaced many family-run operations and grew to an enormous scale. (pp. 652, 996)

alliance system   The military and diplomatic system formulated in an effort to create a balance of power in pre–World War I Europe. Nations were bound together by rigid and comprehensive treaties that promised mutual aid in the case of attack by specific nations. The system swung into action after the Austrian archduke Francis Ferdinand was assassinated in Sarajevo on June 28, 1914, dragging most of Europe into war. (p. 793)

anarchist   A person who rebels against established order and authority. An anarchist is someone who believes that government of any kind is unnecessary and undesirable and should be replaced with voluntary cooperation and free association. Anarchists became increasingly visible in the United States in the late nineteenth and early twentieth centuries. They advocated revolution and grew in numbers through appeals to discontented laborers. Anarchists frequently employed violence in an attempt to achieve their goals. In 1901, anarchist Leon Czolgosz assassinated President William McKinley. (pp. 687, 718, 759, 851)

antebellum   A term that means "before a war" and commonly refers to the period prior to the Civil War. (pp. 402, 438, 541, 573)

antinomian   A person who does not obey societal or religious law. In colonial Massachusetts, Puritan authorities accused Anne Hutchinson of antinomianism because she believed that Christians could achieve salvation by faith alone; they further asserted, incorrectly, that Hutchinson also held the belief that it was not necessary to follow God's laws as set forth in the Bible. (p. 118)

archaeology   A social science devoted to learning about people who lived in the past through the study of physical artifacts created by humans. Most but not all archaeological study focuses on the history of people who lived before the use of the written word. (pp. 3, 79, 271, 533, 1086)

Archaic America   Various hunting and gathering cultures that descended from Paleo-Indians. The term also refers to the period of time when these cultures dominated ancient America, roughly from 8000 BC to between 2000 and 1000 BC. (p. 11)

artifacts   Material remains studied and used by archaeologists and historians to support their interpretations of human history. Examples of artifacts include bones, pots, baskets, jewelry, furniture, tools, clothing, and buildings. (pp. 3, 73, 271)

artisan   A term commonly used prior to 1900 to describe a skilled craftsman, such as a cabinetmaker. (pp. 57, 126, 139, 218, 270, 413, 447, 682)

Bill of Rights   The commonly used term for the first ten amendments to the U.S. Constitution. The Bill of Rights (the last of which was ratified in 1791) guarantees individual liberties and defines limitations to federal power. Many states made the promise of the prompt addition of a bill of rights a precondition for their ratification of the Constitution. (pp. 279, 287)

black nationalism   A term linked to several African American movements emphasizing racial pride, separation from whites and white institutions, and black autonomy. Black nationalism gained in popularity with the rise of Marcus Garvey and the Universal Negro Improvement Association (1917–1927) and later with the Black Panther Party, Malcolm X, and other participants of the black power movements of the 1960s. (pp. 845, 1037)

bloody shirt   A refrain used by Republicans in the late nineteenth century to remind the voting public that the Democratic Party, dominated by the South, was largely responsible for the Civil War and that the Republican

Party had led the victory to preserve the Union. Republicans urged their constituents to "Vote the way you shot." (pp. 585, 616)

bracero program   A policy begun during World War II to help with wartime agriculture in which Mexican laborers (*braceros*) were permitted to enter the United States and work for a limited period of time but not to gain citizenship or permanent residence. The program officially ended in 1964. (pp. 1001, 1156)

brinksmanship   A cold war practice of appearing willing and able to resort to nuclear war in order to make an enemy back down. Secretary of State John Foster Dulles was the foremost proponent of this policy. (p. 991)

Calvinism   The religious doctrine of which the primary tenet is that salvation is predestined by God. Founded by John Calvin of Geneva during the Protestant Reformation, Calvinism required its adherents to live according to a strict religious and moral code. The Puritans who settled in colonial New England were devout Calvinists. (p. 112) *See also* predestination.

checks and balances   A system in which the executive, legislative, and judicial branches of the government curb each other's power. Checks and balances were written into the U.S. Constitution during the Constitutional Convention of 1787. (pp. 280, 1109)

civil service   The administrative service of a government. This term often applies to reforms following passage of the Pendleton Act in 1883, which set qualifications for U.S. government jobs and sought to remove such jobs from political influence. (pp. 585, 623) *See also* spoils system.

closed shop   An establishment in which every employee is required to join a union. (p. 832)

cold war   The hostile and tense relationship that existed between the Soviet Union on the one hand and the United States and other Western nations on the other from 1947 to 1989. This war was said to be "cold" because the hostility stopped short of armed (hot) conflict, which was warded off by the strategy of nuclear deterrence. (pp. 952, 985, 1067, 1114, 1142) *See also* deterrence.

collective bargaining   Negotiation by a group of workers (usually through a union) and their employer concerning rates of pay and working conditions. (pp. 801, 883, 971, 997)

collective security   An association of independent nations that agree to accept and implement decisions made by the group, including going to war in defense of one or more members. The United States resolutely avoided such alliances until after World War II, when it created the North Atlantic Treaty Organization (NATO) in response to the threat posed by the Soviet Union. (pp. 811, 833, 961) *See also* North Atlantic Treaty Organization.

colonization   The process by which a country or society gains control over another, primarily through settlement. (pp. 39, 69, 107, 376, 533, 731, 791, 1056)

Columbian exchange   The transatlantic exchange of goods, peoples, and ideas that began when Columbus arrived in the Caribbean, ending the age-old separation of the hemispheres. (p. 44)

communism (Communist Party)   A system of government and political organization, based on Marxist-Leninist ideals, in which a single authoritarian party controls the economy through state ownership of production, as a means toward reaching the final stage of Marxist theory in which the state dissolves and economic goods are distributed evenly for the common good. Communists around the globe encouraged the spread of communism in other nations in hopes of fomenting worldwide revolution. At its peak in the 1930s, the Communist Party of the United States worked closely with labor unions and insisted that only the overthrow of the capitalist system by its workers could save the victims of the Great Depression. After World War II, the Communist power and aspirations of the Soviet Union were held to be a direct threat to American democracy, prompting the cold war. (pp. 814, 861, 868, 913, 951, 985, 1027, 1067, 1103, 1142) *See also* cold war.

conscription   Compulsory military service. Americans were first subject to conscription during the Civil War. The Draft Act of 1940 marked the first peacetime use of conscription. (pp. 536, 673, 798) *See also* draft.

conservatism   A political and moral outlook dating back to Alexander Hamilton's belief in a strong central government resting on a solid banking foundation. Currently associated with the Republican Party, conservatism today places a high premium on military preparedness, free-market economics, low taxes, and strong sexual morality. (pp. 478, 534, 568, 610, 713, 762, 831, 870, 932, 978, 986, 1022, 1090, 1103, 1142)

consumer culture (consumerism)   A society that places high value on and devotes substantial resources to the purchase and display of material goods. Elements of American consumerism were evident in the nineteenth century but really took hold in the twentieth century with installment buying and advertising in the 1920s and again with the postwar prosperity of the 1950s. (pp. 701, 844, 986)

containment   The U.S. foreign policy developed after World War II to hold in check the power and influence of the Soviet Union and other groups or nations espousing communism. The strategy was first fully articulated by diplomat George F. Kennan in 1946–1947. (pp. 952, 985, 1051, 1068, 1155)

covenant   An agreement or pact; in American history, this refers to a religious agreement. The Pilgrims used this term in the Mayflower Compact to refer to the agreement among themselves to establish a law-abiding community in which all members would work together for the common good. Later, New England Puritans used this term to refer to the agreement they made with God and each other to live according to God's will as revealed through Scripture. (pp. 104, 139) *See also* Halfway Covenant.

cult of domesticity The nineteenth-century belief that women's place was in the home, where they should create a haven for harried men of the household working in the outside world. This ideal was made possible by the separation of the workplace and the home and was used to sentimentalize the home and women's role in it. (pp. 692, 724) *See also* separate spheres.

de-industrialization A long period of decline in the industrial sector. This term often refers specifically to the decline of manufacturing and the growth of the service sector of the economy in post–World War II America. This shift and the loss of manufacturing resulting from it were caused by more efficient and automated production techniques at home, increased competition from foreign-made goods, and the use of cheap labor abroad by U.S. manufacturers. (p. 1123)

democracy A system of government in which the people have the power to rule, either directly or indirectly through their elected representatives. Believing that direct democracy was dangerous, the framers of the Constitution created a government that gave direct voice to the people only in the House of Representatives and that placed a check on that voice in the Senate by offering unlimited six-year terms to senators, elected by the state legislatures to protect them from the whims of democratic majorities. The framers further curbed the perceived dangers of democracy by giving each of the three branches of government (legislative, executive, and judicial) the ability to check the power of the other two. (pp. 219, 254, 287, 340, 366, 468, 478, 519, 578, 608, 654, 709, 758, 791, 871, 912, 953, 1071, 1114, 1155) *See also* checks and balances.

détente French for "loosening." The term refers to the easing of tensions between the United States and the Soviet Union during the Nixon administration. (pp. 1090, 1108)

deterrence The linchpin of U.S. military strategy during the cold war. The strategy of deterrence dictated that the United States would maintain a nuclear arsenal so substantial that the Soviet Union would refrain from attacking the United States and its allies out of fear that the United States would retaliate in devastating proportions. The Soviets pursued a similar strategy. (pp. 961, 1016)

domino theory The assumption underlying U.S. foreign policy from the early cold war until the end of the Vietnam conflict that if one country fell to communism, neighboring countries would also fall under Communist control. (pp. 959, 991)

doves Peace advocates, particularly during the Vietnam War. (p. 1085)

draft (draftee) A system for selecting individuals for compulsory military service. A draftee is an individual selected through this process. (pp. 221, 535, 798, 920, 961, 1080, 1115) *See also* conscription.

emancipation The act of freeing from slavery or bondage. The emancipation of American slaves, a goal shared by slaves and abolitionists alike, occurred with the passage of the Thirteenth Amendment in 1865. (pp. 261, 344, 376, 462, 515, 559, 818)

English Reformation *See* Reformation.

Enlightenment An eighteenth-century philosophical movement that emphasized the use of reason to reevaluate previously accepted doctrines and traditions. (p. 159)

evangelicalism The trend in Protestant Christianity stressing salvation through conversion, repentance of sin, adherence to Scripture, and the importance of preaching over ritual. During the Second Great Awakening, in the 1830s, evangelicals worshipped at camp meetings and religious revivals led by exuberant preachers. (pp. 342, 356, 426, 459, 622, 1117) *See also* Second Great Awakening.

fascism An authoritarian system of government characterized by dictatorial rule, disdain for international stability, and a conviction that warfare is the only means by which a nation can attain greatness. Nazi Germany and Mussolini's Italy are the prime examples of fascism. (pp. 871, 908)

federal budget deficit The situation resulting when the government spends more money than it takes in. (pp. 1028, 1122, 1144)

feminism The belief that men and women have the inherent right to equal social, political, and economic opportunities. The suffrage movement and second-wave feminism of the 1960s and 1970s were the most visible and successful manifestations of feminism, but feminist ideas were expressed in a variety of statements and movements as early as the late eighteenth century and continue to be expressed in the twenty-first. (pp. 292, 576, 779, 841, 1004, 1046, 1103, 1144)

flexible response Military strategy employed by the Kennedy and Johnson administrations designed to match a wide range of military threats by complementing nuclear weapons with the buildup of conventional and special forces and employing them all in a gradual and calibrated way as needed. Flexible response was a departure from the strategy of massive retaliation used by the Eisenhower administration. (p. 1069)

franchise The right to vote. The franchise was gradually widened in the United States to include groups such as women and African Americans, who had no vote when the Constitution was ratified. (pp. 429, 577, 723) *See also* suffrage.

free labor Work conducted free from constraint and in accordance with the laborer's personal inclinations and will. Prior to the Civil War, free labor became an ideal championed by Republicans (who were primarily Northerners) to articulate individuals' right to work how and where they wished, and to accumulate property in their own name. The ideal of free labor lay at the heart of the North's argument that slavery should not be extended into the western territories. (pp. 377, 421, 443, 493, 541, 562)

free silver The late-nineteenth-century call by silver barons and poor American farmers for the widespread coinage of silver and for silver to be used as a base upon which to expand the paper money supply. The coinage of silver created a more inflationary monetary system that benefited debtors. (pp. 627, 713) *See also* gold standard.

free soil The idea advanced in the 1840s that Congress should prohibit slavery within western territories. "Free soil, free speech, free labor, and free men" became the rallying cry of the short-lived Free-Soil Party. (pp. 477, 531)

frontier A borderland area. In U.S. history this refers to the borderland between the areas primarily inhabited by Europeans or their descendants and the areas solely inhabited by Native Americans. (pp. 40, 85, 119, 137, 174, 220, 302, 334, 355, 396, 476, 663, 711)

fundamentalism Strict adherence to core, often religious beliefs. The term has varying meanings for different religious groups. Protestant fundamentalists adhere to a literal interpretation of the Bible and thus deny the possibility of evolution. Muslim fundamentalists believe that traditional Islamic law should govern nations and that Western influences should be banned. (pp. 852, 1115, 1142)

gender gap An electoral phenomenon that became apparent in the 1980s when men and women began to display different preferences in voting. Women tended to favor liberal candidates, and men tended to support conservatives. The key voter groups contributing to the gender gap were single women and women who worked outside the home. (pp. 1125, 1153)

globalization The spread of political, cultural, and economic influences and connections among countries, businesses, and individuals around the world through trade, immigration, communication, and other means. In the late twentieth century, globalization was intensified by new communications technology that connected individuals, corporations, and nations with greater speed at low prices. This led to an increase in political and economic interdependence and mutual influence among nations. (pp. 1090, 1142)

gold standard A monetary system in which any circulating currency was exchangeable for a specific amount of gold. Advocates for the gold standard believed that gold alone should be used for coinage and that the total value of paper banknotes should never exceed the government's supply of gold. The triumph of gold standard supporter William McKinley in the 1896 presidential election was a big victory for supporters of this policy. (pp. 629, 710) *See also* free silver.

gospel of wealth The idea that wealth garnered from earthly success should be used for good works. Andrew Carnegie promoted this view in an 1889 essay in which he maintained that the wealthy should serve as stewards and act in the best interests of society as a whole. (pp. 615, 750)

government bonds Promissory notes issued by a government in order to borrow money from members of the public. Such bonds are redeemable at a set future date. Bondholders earn interest on their investment. (p. 229)

Great Awakening The widespread movement of religious revitalization in the 1730s and 1740s that emphasized vital religious faith and personal choice. It was characterized by large, open-air meetings at which emotional sermons were given by itinerant preachers. (pp. 159, 342)

Great Society President Lyndon Johnson's domestic program, which included civil rights legislation, antipoverty programs, government subsidy of medical care, federal aid to education, consumer protection, and aid to the arts and humanities. (pp. 1021, 1104)

guerrilla warfare Fighting carried out by an irregular military force usually organized into small, highly mobile groups. Guerrilla combat was common in the Vietnam War and during the American Revolution. Guerrilla warfare is often effective against opponents who have greater material resources. (pp. 212, 496, 518, 580, 661, 734, 992, 1068, 1173)

Halfway Covenant A Puritan compromise that allowed the unconverted children of the "visible saints" to become "halfway" members of the church and to baptize their own children even though they were not full members of the church themselves because they had not experienced full conversion. Massachusetts ministers accepted this compromise in 1662, though the compromise remained controversial throughout the seventeenth century. (p. 120)

hard currency (hard money) Money coined directly from, or backed in full by, precious metals (particularly gold). (pp. 229, 262, 294, 364)

hawks Advocates of aggressive military action or all-out war, particularly during the Vietnam War. (p. 1084) *See also* War Hawks.

holding company A system of business organization whereby competing companies are combined under one central administration in order to curb competition and ensure profit. Pioneered in the late 1880s by John D. Rockefeller, holding companies, such as Standard Oil, exercised monopoly control even as the government threatened to outlaw trusts as a violation of free trade. (p. 605) *See also* monopoly; trust.

impeachment The process by which formal charges of wrongdoing are brought against a president, a governor, or a federal judge. (pp. 575, 888, 1110, 1150)

imperialism The system by which great powers gain control of overseas territories. The United States became an imperialist power by gaining control of Puerto Rico, Guam, the Philippines, and Cuba as a result of the Spanish-American War. (pp. 491, 586, 710, 792, 962, 1056, 1159)

indentured servitude A system that committed poor immigrants to four to seven years of labor in exchange for passage to the colonies and food and shelter after they arrived. An indenture is a type of contract. (pp. 71, 138)

iron curtain A metaphor coined by Winston Churchill during his commencement address at Westminster College in Fulton, Missouri, in 1946, to refer to the political, ideological, and military barriers that separated Soviet-controlled Eastern Europe from the rest of Europe and the West following World War II. (pp. 954, 991, 1070, 1145)

isolationism A foreign policy perspective characterized by a desire to have the United States withdraw from the conflicts of the world and enjoy the protection of two vast oceans. (pp. 731, 812, 833, 909, 951)

Jim Crow The system of racial segregation that developed in the post–Civil War South and extended well into the twentieth century; it replaced slavery as the chief instrument of white supremacy. Jim Crow laws segregated African Americans in public facilities such as trains and streetcars and denied them basic civil rights, including the right to vote. It was also at this time that the doctrine of "separate but equal" became institutionalized. (pp. 582, 677, 783, 931)

jingoism (jingoes) Extreme nationalism marked by belligerent foreign policy, an attitude held by many late-nineteenth-century Americans. Jingoism was epitomized by Theodore Roosevelt, who believed that nations and individuals needed warfare to maintain their virility. (p. 737)

Keynesian economics A theory, developed by economist John Maynard Keynes, that guided U.S. economic policy from the New Deal to the 1970s. According to Keynesians, the federal government has a duty to stimulate and manage the economy by spending money on public works projects and by making general tax cuts in order to put more money into the hands of ordinary people, thus creating demand. (p. 900)

laissez-faire The doctrine, based on economic theory, that government should not interfere in business or the economy. Laissez-faire ideas guided American government policy in the late nineteenth century and conservative politics in the twentieth. Business interests that supported laissez-faire in the late nineteenth century accepted government interference when it took the form of tariffs or subsidies that worked to their benefit. Broader uses of the term refer to the simple philosophy of abstaining from interference. (pp. 615, 710, 748, 870, 1120, 1159)

land grant A gift of land from a government, usually intended to encourage settlement or development. The British government issued several land grants to encourage development in the American colonies. In the mid-nineteenth century the U.S. government issued land grants to encourage railroad development and through passage of the Land-Grant College Act (also known as the Morrill Act) in 1863 set aside public lands to support universities. (pp. 72, 121, 175, 220, 421, 491, 600, 648)

liberalism The political doctrine that government rests on the consent of the governed and is duty-bound to protect the freedom and property of the individual. In the

twentieth century, liberalism became associated with the idea that the government should regulate the economy and ensure the material well-being and individual rights of all people. (pp. 714, 748, 824, 871, 932, 969, 987, 1023, 1103, 1144)

liberty The condition of being free or enjoying freedom from control. This term also refers to the possession of certain social, political, or economic rights such as the right to own and control property. Eighteenth-century American colonists evoked the principle to argue for strict limitations on government's ability to tax its subjects. (pp. 104, 174, 211, 254, 290, 322, 356, 430, 443, 493, 520, 566, 794, 1171)

manifest destiny A term coined by journalist John O'Sullivan in 1845 to express the popular nineteenth-century belief that the United States was destined to expand westward to the Pacific Ocean and had an irrefutable right and God-given responsibility to do so. This idea provided an ideological shield for westward expansion and masked the economic and political motivations of many of those who championed it. (pp. 397, 486, 731)

McCarthyism The practice of searching out suspected Communists and others outside mainstream American society, discrediting them, and hounding them from government and other employment. The term derives from Senator Joseph McCarthy, who gained notoriety for leading such repressive activities from 1950 to 1954. (p. 973)

mercantilism A set of policies that regulated colonial commerce and manufacturing for the enrichment of the mother country. Mercantilist policies ensured that the American colonies in the mid-seventeenth century produced agricultural goods and raw materials to be shipped to Britain, where they would increase wealth in the mother country through reexportation or manufacture into finished goods that would then be sold to the colonies and elsewhere. (p. 89)

Middle Passage The crossing of the Atlantic (as a slave destined for auction) in the hold of a slave ship in the eighteenth and nineteenth centuries. Conditions were unimaginably bad, and many slaves died during these voyages. (pp. 97, 149)

military-industrial complex A term first used by President Dwight D. Eisenhower to refer to the aggregate power and influence of the armed forces in conjunction with the aerospace, munitions, and other industries that produced supplies for the military in the post–World War II era. (p. 995)

miscegenation The sexual mixing of races. In slave states, despite social stigma and legal restrictions on interracial sex, masters' almost unlimited power over their female slaves meant that liaisons inevitably occurred. Many states maintained laws against miscegenation into the 1950s. (pp. 450, 620, 845)

monopoly Exclusive control and domination by a single business entity over an entire industry through ownership, command of supply, or other means. Gilded

Age businesses monopolized their industries quite profitably, often organizing holding companies and trusts to do so. (pp. 37, 357, 592, 605, 651, 709, 759, 884, 945, 1121) *See also* holding company; trust.

Monroe Doctrine   President James Monroe's 1823 declaration that the Western Hemisphere was closed to any further colonization or interference by European powers. In exchange, Monroe pledged that the United States would not become involved in European struggles. Although Monroe could not back his policy with action, it was an important formulation of national goals. (pp. 347, 731, 767, 791)

nationalism   A strong feeling of devotion and loyalty toward one nation over others. Nationalism encourages the promotion of the nation's common culture, language, and customs. (pp. 340, 407, 540, 790, 993, 1071, 1142)

nativism   Bias against immigrants and in favor of native-born inhabitants. American nativists especially favor persons who come from white, Anglo-Saxon, Protestant lines over those from other racial, ethnic, and religious heritages. Nativists may include former immigrants who view new immigrants as incapable of assimilation. Many nativists, such as members of the Know-Nothing Party in the nineteenth century and the Ku Klux Klan through the contemporary period, voice anti-immigrant, anti-Catholic, and anti-Semitic sentiments. (pp. 492, 657, 752, 821, 850, 1166)

New Deal   The group of social and economic programs that President Franklin Roosevelt developed to provide relief for the needy, speed economic recovery, and reform economic and governmental institutions. The New Deal was a massive effort to bring the United States out of the Great Depression and ensure its future prosperity. (pp. 713, 869, 909, 951, 985, 1028, 1135, 1174)

New Right   Politically active religious conservatives who became particularly vocal in the 1980s. The New Right criticized feminism, opposed abortion and homosexuality, and promoted "family values" and military preparedness. (p. 1104)

New South   A vision of the South, promoted after the Civil War by Henry Grady, editor of the *Atlanta Constitution,* that urged the South to abandon its dependence on agriculture and use its cheap labor and natural resources to compete with northern industry. Many Southerners migrated from farms to cities in the late nineteenth century, and northerners and foreigners invested a significant amount of capital in railroads, cotton and textiles, mining, lumber, iron, steel, and tobacco in the region. (pp. 560, 617)

North Atlantic Treaty Organization (NATO)   A post–World War II alliance that joined the United States, Canada, and Western European nations into a military coalition designed to counter efforts to expand by the Soviet Union. Each NATO member pledged to go to war if any member was attacked. Since the end of the cold war, NATO has been expanding to include the formerly Communist countries of Eastern Europe. (pp. 952, 1131, 1145)

nullification   The idea that states can disregard federal laws when those laws represent an overstepping of congressional powers. The controversial idea was first proposed by opponents of the Alien and Sedition Acts of 1798 and later by South Carolina politicians in 1828 as a response to the Tariff of Abominations. (pp. 311, 325, 386, 480)

oligopoly   A competitive system in which several large corporations dominate an industry by dividing the market so each business has a share of it. More prevalent than outright monopolies during the late 1800s, the oligopolies of the Gilded Age successfully muted competition and benefited the corporations that participated in this type of arrangement. (pp. 612, 640)

paternalism   The idea that slavery was a set of reciprocal obligations between masters and slaves, with slaves providing labor and obedience and masters providing basic care and direction. The concept of paternalism denied that the slave system was brutal and exploitative. While paternalism did provide some protection against the worst brutality, it did not guarantee decent living conditions, reasonable work, or freedom from physical punishment. (pp. 448, 540)

planters   Owners of large farms (or more specifically plantations) that were worked by twenty or more slaves. By 1860, planters had accrued a great deal of local, statewide, and national political power in the South despite the fact that they represented a minority of the white electorate in those states. Planters' dominance of southern politics demonstrated both the power of tradition and stability among southern voters and the planters' success at convincing white voters that the slave system benefited all whites, even those without slaves. (pp. 80, 128, 149, 183, 213, 305, 335, 376, 443, 477, 520, 562, 617)

popular sovereignty   The idea that government is subject to the will of the people; before the Civil War, this was the idea that the residents of a territory should determine, through their legislatures, whether to allow slavery. (p. 478)

Populism   A political movement that led to the creation of the People's Party, primarily comprising southern and western farmers who railed against big business and advocated business and economic reforms, including government ownership of the railroads. The movement peaked in the late nineteenth century. The Populist ticket won more than one million votes in the presidential election of 1892 and 1.5 million in the congressional elections of 1894. The term *populism* has come to mean any political movement that advocates on behalf of the common person, particularly for government intervention against big business. (pp. 630, 710, 755, 1174)

predestination   The idea that individual salvation or damnation is determined by God at, or just prior to, a person's birth. The concept of predestination invalidated the idea that salvation could be obtained through either faith or good works. (p. 112) *See also* Calvinism.

progressivism (progressive movement)   A wide-ranging twentieth-century reform movement that advocated government activism to mitigate the problems created by urban industrialism. Progressivism reached its peak in 1912 with the creation of the Progressive Party, which ran Theodore Roosevelt for president. The term *progressivism* has come to mean any general effort advocating for social welfare programs. (pp. 682, 713, 748, 790, 829, 872, 932, 1021, 1174)

Protestant Reformation   *See* Reformation.

Protestantism   A powerful Christian reform movement that began in the sixteenth century with Martin Luther's critiques of the Roman Catholic Church. Over the centuries, Protestantism has taken many different forms, branching into numerous denominations with differing systems of worship. (pp. 62, 87, 106, 138, 199, 276, 342, 373, 425, 438, 492, 616, 752, 850, 871, 1105)

Puritanism   The ideas and religious principles held by dissenters from the Church of England, including the belief that the church needed to be purified by eliminating the elements of Catholicism from its practices. (pp. 87, 104, 138)

reform Darwinism   A social theory, based on Charles Darwin's theory of evolution, that emphasized activism, arguing that humans could speed up evolution by altering the environment. A challenge to social Darwinism, reform Darwinism condemned laissez-faire and demanded that the government take a more active approach to solving social problems. It became the ideological basis for progressive reform in the late nineteenth and early twentieth centuries. (p. 755) *See also* laissez-faire; social Darwinism.

Reformation   The reform movement that began in 1517 with Martin Luther's critiques of the Roman Catholic Church, which led to the formation of Protestant Christian groups. The English Reformation began with Henry VIII's break with the Roman Catholic Church, which established the Protestant Church of England. Henry VIII's decision was politically motivated; he had no particular quarrel with Catholic theology and remained an orthodox Catholic in most matters of religious practice. (pp. 60, 105)

republicanism   The belief that the unworkable model of European-style monarchy should be replaced with a form of government in which supreme power resides in the hands of citizens with the right to vote and is exercised by a representative government answerable to this electorate. In Revolutionary-era America, republicanism became a social philosophy that embodied a sense of community and called individuals to act for the public good. (pp. 219, 250, 287, 321, 469, 510)

scientific management   A system of organizing work, developed by Frederick Winslow Taylor in the late nineteenth century, to increase efficiency and productivity by breaking tasks into their component parts and training workers to perform specific parts. Labor resisted this effort because it deskilled workers and led to the speedup of production lines. Taylor's ideas were most popular at the height of the Progressive Era. (pp. 755, 834)

Second Great Awakening   A popular religious revival that preached that salvation was available to anybody who chose to take it. The revival peaked in the 1830s, and its focus on social perfection inspired many of the reform movements of the Jacksonian era. (p. 373) *See also* evangelicalism.

separate spheres   A concept of gender relations that developed in the Jacksonian era and continued well into the twentieth century, holding that women's proper place was in the private world of hearth and home (the private sphere) and men's was in the public world of commerce and politics (the public sphere). The doctrine of separate spheres eroded slowly over the nineteenth and twentieth centuries as women became more and more involved in public activities. (pp. 369, 620, 692, 844) *See also* cult of domesticity.

social Darwinism   A social theory, based on Charles Darwin's theory of evolution, that argued that all progress in human society came as the result of competition and natural selection. Gilded Age proponents such as William Graham Sumner and Herbert Spencer claimed that reform was useless because the rich and poor were precisely where nature intended them to be and intervention would retard the progress of humanity. (pp. 612, 676, 726, 755) *See also* reform Darwinism.

social gospel movement   A religious movement in the late nineteenth and early twentieth centuries founded on the idea that Christians have a responsibility to reform society as well as individuals. Social gospel adherents encouraged people to put Christ's teachings to work in their daily lives by actively promoting social justice. (pp. 749, 873)

social purity movement   A movement to end prostitution and eradicate venereal disease, often accompanied by censorship of materials deemed "obscene." (p. 749)

socialism   A governing system in which the state owns and operates the largest and most important parts of the economy. (pp. 690, 713, 753, 805, 861, 873, 932, 960, 1046)

spoils system   An arrangement in which party leaders reward party loyalists with government jobs. This slang term for *patronage* comes from the phrase "To the victor go the spoils." Widespread government corruption during the Gilded Age spurred reformers to curb the spoils system through the passage of the Pendleton Act in 1883, which created the Civil Service Commission to award government jobs on the basis of merit. (pp. 369, 585, 615, 643) *See also* civil service.

state sovereignty   A state's autonomy or freedom from external control. The federal system adopted at the Constitutional Convention in 1787 struck a balance between state sovereignty and national control by creating a strong central government while leaving the states intact as political entities. The states remained in possession of many important powers on which the federal government cannot intrude. (p. 522)

states' rights A strict interpretation of the Constitution that holds that federal power over states is limited and states hold ultimate sovereignty. First expressed in 1798 through the passage of the Virginia and Kentucky Resolutions, which were based on the assumption that states have the right to judge the constitutionality of federal laws, the states' rights philosophy became a cornerstone of the South's resistance to federal control of slavery. (pp. 272, 347, 385, 537, 566, 773, 842)

strict constructionism An approach to constitutional law that attempts to adhere to the original intent of the writers of the Constitution. Strict construction often produces Supreme Court decisions that defer to the legislative branch and to the states and restrict the power of the federal government. Opponents of strict construction argue that the Constitution is an organic document that must be interpreted to meet conditions unimagined when it was written. (p. 1106)

suffrage The right to vote. The term *suffrage* is most often associated with the efforts of American women to secure voting rights. (pp. 256, 366, 428, 468, 561, 620, 709, 748, 790, 1056) *See also* franchise.

Sun Belt The southern and southwestern regions of the United States, which grew tremendously in industry, population, and influence after World War II. (pp. 999, 1105)

supply-side economics An economic theory based on the premise that tax cuts for the wealthy and for corporations encourage investment and production (supply), which in turn stimulate consumption. Embraced by the Reagan administration and other conservative Republicans, this theory reversed Keynesian economic policy, which assumes that the way to stimulate the economy is to create demand through federal spending on public works and general tax cuts that put more money into the hands of ordinary people. (p. 1121) *See* Keynesian economics.

temperance movement The reform movement to end drunkenness by urging people to abstain from the consumption of alcohol. Begun in the 1820s, this movement achieved its greatest political victory with the passage of a constitutional amendment in 1919 that prohibited the manufacture, sale, and transportation of alcohol. That amendment was repealed in 1933. (pp. 375, 426, 621, 723, 751)

third world Originally a cold war term linked to decolonization, "third world" was first used in the late 1950s to describe newly independent countries in Africa and Asia that were not aligned with either Communist nations (the second world) or non-Communist nations (the first world). Later, the term was applied to all poor, nonindustrialized countries, in Latin America as well as in Africa and Asia. Many international experts see "third world" as a problematic category when applied to such a large and disparate group of nations, and they criticize the discriminatory hierarchy suggested by the term. (pp. 962, 1057, 1068, 1104, 1157)

trickle-down economics The theory that financial benefits and incentives given to big businesses in the top tier of the economy will flow down to smaller businesses and individuals and thus benefit the entire nation. President Herbert Hoover unsuccessfully used the trickle-down strategy in his attempt to pull the nation out of the Great Depression, stimulating the economy through government investment in large economic enterprises and public works such as construction of the Boulder (Hoover) Dam. In the late twentieth century, conservatives used this economic theory to justify large tax cuts and other financial benefits for corporations and the wealthy. (p. 857)

Truman Doctrine President Harry S. Truman's assertion that American security depended on stopping any Communist government from taking over any non-Communist government—even nondemocratic and repressive dictatorships—anywhere in the world. Beginning in 1947 with American aid to help Greece and Turkey stave off Communist pressures, this approach became a cornerstone of American foreign policy during the cold war. (p. 952)

trust A corporate system in which corporations give shares of their stock to trustees who coordinate the industry to ensure profits to the participating corporations and curb competition. Pioneered by Standard Oil Company, such business practices were deemed unfair, were moderated by the Sherman Antitrust Act (1890), and were finally abolished by the combined efforts of Presidents Theodore Roosevelt and William Howard Taft and the sponsors of the 1914 Clayton Antitrust Act. The term *trust* is also loosely applied to all large business combinations. (pp. 604, 749, 891) *See also* holding company.

vertical integration A system in which a single person or corporation controls all processes of an industry from start to finished product. Andrew Carnegie first used vertical integration in the 1870s, controlling every aspect of steel production from the mining of iron ore to the manufacturing of the final product, thereby maximizing profits by eliminating the use of outside suppliers or services. (pp. 604, 654)

virtual representation The notion, propounded by British Parliament in the eighteenth century, that the House of Commons represented all British subjects—wherever they lived and regardless of whether they had directly voted for their representatives. Prime Minister George Grenville used this idea to argue that the Stamp Act and other parliamentary taxes on colonists did not constitute taxation without representation. American colonists rejected this argument, insisting that political representatives derived authority only from explicit citizens' consent indicated by elections, and that members of a distant government body were incapable of adequately representing their interests. (p. 187)

War Hawks Young Republicans elected to the U.S. Congress in the fall of 1810 who were eager for war with England in order to legitimize attacks on Indians, end impressment, and avenge foreign insults. (p. 336) *See also* hawks.

welfare capitalism The idea that a capitalistic, industrial society can operate benevolently to improve the lives of workers. The notion of welfare capitalism became popular in the 1920s as industries extended the benefits of scientific management to improve safety and sanitation in the workplace as well as institute paid vacations and pension plans. (p. 835) *See also* scientific management.

welfare state A nation or state in which the government assumes responsibility for some or all of the individual and social welfare of its citizens. Welfare states commonly provide education, health care, food programs for the poor, unemployment compensation, and other social benefits. The United States dramatically expanded its role as a welfare state with the provisions of the New Deal in the 1930s. (pp. 890, 987, 1024)

Yankee imperialism A cry raised in Latin American countries against the United States when it intervened militarily in the region without invitation or consent from those countries. (pp. 1070, 1115, 1147)

yeoman A farmer who owned a small plot of land sufficient to support a family and tilled by family members and perhaps a few servants. (pp. 88, 153, 388, 464, 477, 536, 578, 654)

Spot Artifact Credits

p. 18 (mica hand) Ohio Historical Society; p. 23 (dolls) Photo courtesy of the Oakland Museum, California; p. 39 (caravel) National Maritime Museum, London; p. 55 (crucifix) Courtesy of the Historical Archaeology Collections of the Florida Museum of Natural History; p. 75 (pot) Valentine Museum, Cook Collection; p. 88 (pipe) Niemeyer Nederlands Tabacologisch Museum; p. 94 (stirrup) © George H. H. Huey; p. 113 (die) Courtesy of Association for the Preservation of Virginia Antiquities; p. 120 (cradle) Wadsworth Atheneum, Hartford, Wallace Nutting Collection, Gift of J. Pierpont Morgan; p. 128 (scales) Concord Musuem; p. 139 (pitcher) Pocumtuck Valley Memorial Association, Memorial Hall Museum, Deerfield, MA; p. 147 (*Poor Richard's Almanack*) Courtesy, American Antiquarian Society; p. 152 (slave's doll) The Stagville Center, Division of Archives and History, North Carolina Department of Cultural Resources; p. 155 (mirror) Concord Museum; p. 186 (stamps) Courtesy of the Trustees of the British Library; p. 190 (teapot) Peabody Essex Museum, Salem, MA; p. 203 (pistol) Concord Museum; p. 203 (musket) Concord Museum; p. 205 (Wheatley title page) Library of Congress; p. 216 (drum) Massachusetts Historical Society; p. 226 (broadside) Courtesy, American Antiquarian Society; p. 229 (currency) Smithsonian Institution, Washington, D.C., photo by Douglas Mudd; p. 233 (Howitzer) West Point Museum, United States Military Academy, West Point, N.Y.; p. 262 (penny note) Library of Congress; p. 274 (inkwell) Independence National Historic Park; p. 290 (ballot box) Independence National Historic Park; p. 291 (barrel) Peabody Essex Museum, Salem, MA; p. 305 (kettle) Ohio Historical Society; p. 326 (compass) Smithsonian Institution, Washington, D.C.; p. 349 (telescope) Thomas Jefferson Memorial Foundation, Inc.; p. 368 (spittoon) Courtesy, The Henry Francis du Pont Winterthur Museum; p. 388 (bank note) Miriam and Ira D. Wallach Division of Art, Prints and Photographs, The New York Public Library, Astor, Lenox and Tilden Foundations; p. 389 (miniature log cabin) National Museum of American History, Smithsonian Institution, Behring Center; p. 405 (flag) Texas Memorial Museum; p. 417 (plow) Smithsonian Institution, Washington, D.C.; p. 418 (watch) Smithsonian Institution, Washington, D.C.; p. 426 (sheet music) Special Collections, Milton S. Eisenhower Library, The Johns Hopkins University; p. 449 (shoe) Valentine Museum, Cook Collection; p. 467 (fiddle) National Museum of American History, Smithsonian Institution, Washington, D.C.; p. 479 (poster) Courtesy, American Antiquarian Society; p. 496 (cane) Collection of McKissick Museum, University of South Carolina; p. 502 (shackles) Private Collection; p. 506 (revolver) Ohio Historical Society; p. 523 (jacket) Smithsonian Institution, Washington, D.C.; p. 543 (potholder) Chicago Historical Society; p. 563 (Bible) Anacostia Museum, Smithsonian Institution, Washington, D.C.; p. 575 (ticket) Collection of Janice L. and David J. Frent; p. 584 (plow) Courtesy Deere & Company; p. 599 (watch) Union Pacific Museum Collection; p. 606 (*McClure's*) Special Collections, The Ida Tarbell Collection, Pelletier Library, Allegheny; p. 607 (telephone) Smithsonian Institution, Washington, D.C.; p. 618 (tobacco) Duke Homestead; p. 638 (silver bar) The Oakland Museum; p. 648 (bucket) Kansas State Historical Society; p. 662 (moccasins) Photo Addison Doty, Santa Fe, NM; p. 683 (sewing machine) National Museum of American History, Smithsonian Institution, Washington, D.C.; p. 686 (typewriter) National Museum of American History, Smithsonian Institution, Washington, D.C.; p. 694 (baseball, card, and glove) Smithsonian Institution, Washington, D.C.; p. 697 (faucet) Picture Research Consultants & Archives; p. 718 (dagger) Library & Archives Division, Historical Society of Western Pennsylvania; p. 720 (paycheck) Chicago Historical Society, Archives and Manuscript Department; p. 729 (button) Collection of Janice L. and David J. Frent; p. 729 (hat) National Museum of American History, Smithsonian Institution, Washington, D.C.; p. 752 (postcard) Chicago Historical Society; p. 779 (IWW poster) Library of Congress; p. 795 (recruiting poster) Library of Congress; p. 798 (machine gun) National Museum of American History, Smithsonian Institution, Behring Center; p. 801 ("Save Wheat" poster) Herbert Hoover Presidential Library; p. 837 (refrigerator) From the Collection of The Henry Ford; p. 845 (Hughes book) Picture Research Consultants & Archives; p. 848 (button) Private Collection; p. 849 (*This Side of Paradise*) Matthew J. & Arlyn Bruccoli Collection of F. Scott Fitzgerald, University of South Carolina; p. 860 (movie poster) Collection of Hershenson-Allen Archives; p. 870 (wheelchair) FDR Library/photo by Hudson Valley Photo Studio; p. 871 (1932 buttons) Collection of Janice L. and David J. Frent; p. 916 (Good Neighbor button) Collection of Colonel Stuart S. Corning, Jr./Picture Research Consultants, Inc.; p. 930 (Double V button) Private Collection; p. 945 (atomic bomb) National Archives; p. 954 (Truman and Churchill button) Collection of Janice L. and David J. Frent; p. 969 (NAACP button) Collection of Janice L. and David J. Frent; p. 969 (banner) Dr. Hector P. Garcia Papers, Special Collections & Archives, Texas A & M University, Corpus Christi, Bell Library; p. 975 (helmet) West Point Museum, United States Military Academy, West Point, N.Y.; p. 987 (sign) NEW Traffic Safety; p. 1005 (*The Feminine Mystique*) W. W. Norton & Company, Inc. N.Y.C. © 1963; p. 1008 (album cover) Private Collection; p. 1010 (NAACP button) Collection of Janice L. and David J. Frent; p. 1027 (food stamps) Getty Images; p. 1034 (pennant) Private Collection; p. 1042 (Indian resistance button) Collection of Janice L. and David J. Frent; p. 1052 (flag) Smithsonian Institution, Washington, D.C.; p. 1072 (beret) West Point Museum, United States Military Academy, West Point, N.Y.; p. 1081 (Vietnam button) Picture Research Consultants & Archives; p. 1084 (antiwar button) Collection of Janice L. and David J. Frent; p. 1105 (magazine) Young Americans for Freedom; p. 1113 (VW with sign) © Dennis Brack; p. 1120 (bumper sticker) Courtesy, Christian Coalition; p. 1122 (Yuppie handbook) Book cover from *The Yuppies Handbook: The State-of-the-Art Manual for Young Urban Professionals* by Marissa Piesman and Marilee Hartley. Copyright © 1984 Marissa Piesman and Marilee Hartley; p. 1145 (piece of Berlin Wall) Patton Museum of Cavalry & Armor; p. 1163 (Green Card document) Nolo; p. 1168 (ballots) © Reuters NewMedia Inc./Corbis.

A note about the index:

Names of individuals appear in boldface; biographical dates are included for major historical figures.

Letters in parentheses following pages refer to:
(i) illustrations, including photographs and artifacts, as well as information in picture captions
(f) figures, including charts and graphs
(m) maps
(b) boxed features (such as "Historical Question")
(t) tables

St. Augustine (Florida), 60, 61
St. Clair, Arthur, 302, 303
Saint Domingue, 306
Sainthood, Puritan concept of, 112, 120
St. Lawrence River, 63
St. Louis, 346(i)
Saipan, 943(i)
Salado culture, ritual figure, 27(i)
Salem (Massachusetts), 104
    witch trials in, 121, 122–123(b), 123(i)
Saleswomen, 687
Saloons, 375
SALT (Strategic Arms Limitation Talks),
    1090
Saltcellar, ivory, 38(i)
Salter, John, Jr., 1032(i)
Salt Lake City (Utah), 656
    U.S. invasion of (1857), 403
Salvation, Puritan view of, 108, 112,
    117, 118
Samoan Islands, 734, 734(m)
Samoset, 107
Samuel, Rebecca, 276
Samuelson, Robert, 1004
San Carlos Reservation (Arizona
    Territory), 661
Sand Creek (Colorado), massacre at
    (1864), 529, 658
San Diego (California), mission, 164,
    165(i), 166(b)
Sandinistas, 1114
Sandoz, Jules, 663
San Francisco, 697
    Chinatown, 677
    Chinese immigrants, 677
    Chinese immigrants in, 413(b), 414(b)
    gold rush (1849–1852) and, 412–413
Sanger, Margaret (1879–1966), 780–781,
    780(i), 844
San Juan Hill, Battle of (1898), 737(i)
San Miguel de Gualdape, 49
San Salvador, 35
Santa Anna, Antonio López de
    (1794–1876), 404, 409–411
Santa Fe (New Mexico), 60, 403, 409
Santa Fe Trail, 399(m), 403
Santamaria, Juan, 491
Santa Fe (New Mexico), Confederate
    capture of (1862), 528
Santo Domingo, Grant's proposed
    annexation of, 586
Saratoga, Battle of (1777), 222(m),
    234, 234(m)
Satan, Puritans' view of, 115, 121–123(b),
    123(i)
Saturday Evening Post, The, 805, 841
Saudi Arabia, 1147
Savages, use of the term, 90
Savage's Station, Battle of (Seven Days
    Battle; 1862), 525(i), 526, 549(i)
Savannah (Georgia), 238, 545(t), 550
Savings and loan institutions (S&Ls),
    1121–1122
Scalia, Antonin, 1125
Schenck, Charles, 818
Schenck v. United States, 818

Schlafly, Phyllis, 1055, 1103, 1104,
    1104(i), 1105–1107, 1117–1119,
    1119(i), 1120, 1125
Schneiderman, Rose, 753
Schools, 698
    desegregation (integration) of
        1950s–1960s, 1010, 1011(i),
        1012–1013(b)
    in 1970s, 1060
    busing for, 1106, 1107(i)
    Nixon administration, 1106
    Indian boarding, 635–636
    segregation in, 969–970, 969(i), 1106
Schreiber, Marie, 964–965
Schroeder, Patricia, 1121
Schurz, Carl, 559–560, 624
Schuyler, Philip, 295–296
Schuylkill (Pennsylvania), 360
Schwachheim, Carl, 3
Schwartz, Edward, 1048(b)
Science. *See* Technology
Scientific management, 755, 834–835
SCLC (Southern Christian Leadership
    Conference), 1016
Scopes trial (1925), 852–853
Scots-Irish immigrants, 137, 141, 142, 147
Scott, Dred, 496, 497(i), 498–500
Scott, Hugh D., 975–976, 1110
Scott, Tom, 602
Scott, Winfield (1786–1866), 408(i), 411, 486
Scottsboro Boys, 861(i), 862
Scriven, Abream, 459
SDI (Strategic Defense Initiative;
    "Star Wars"), 1131, 1172
SDS (Students for a Democratic Society),
    1046, 1049–1050(b)
Seale, Bobby, 1040
Seal of Andrew Oliver, 189(i)
SEATO (Southeast Asia Treaty
    Organization), 992, 1073(t)
Seattle, 1919 strike, 813
Seattle (Washington), 1999 anti-
    globalization protests, 1159,
    1162, 1162(i)
Secession from the Union, 340, 480, 504,
    507–509, 508(m), 519(m)
    Johnson's program of reconciliation
        and, 567
    Lincoln on, 509
    nullification doctrine in 1830s and, 386
Second Bank of the United States, 364,
    365, 387
Second Continental Congress
    (1775–1781), 222, 224, 274. *See also*
        Confederation government;
        Constitutional Convention
    "A Declaration on the Causes and
        Necessity of Taking Up Arms," 213
    Articles of Confederation, 248(i), 250–253
    assumption of political and military
        authority by, 213, 216
    currency (paper money) and, 213, 229
    economic policies of, 229, 232
    reconciliation with England, 216
Second Great Awakening, 373–375
Secotan, 71(i)

Secretaries, 686–687
Sectionalism (sectional conflict), 476, 481
    undoing of sectional balance, 482–488
Sectionalism, New South and, 617–619
Securities and Exchange Commission
    (SEC), 876
Sedition Act (1798), 311, 312–313(b)
Sedition Act (1918), 805
Segregation, 432, 784
    Jim Crow laws, 582, 677
    New Deal and, 901
    in Progressive era, 783
    residential, 680
    in schools, 969–970, 969(i), 1106
    "separate but equal" doctrine, 783, 895,
        1010, 1012
Selective Service Act (1917), 798
Selective Service Act (1940), 920
Self-determination, principle of
    Franklin D. Roosevelt and, 910, 916, 940
    Truman and, 962
    Wilson and, 809, 810
Self-discipline (self-control), 426
Selma (Alabama), march for voting rights
    (1963), 1035, 1035(i)
Seminole Indians, 261, 528(i)
Seminole War (1836–1837), 384
Senate, Constitutional Convention and
    (1787), 272, 273
Senators, election of, 623, 771
Seneca Falls Declaration of Sentiments
    (1848), 428–429
Seneca Falls (New York) national women's
    rights convention (1848), 428
Seneca Indians, 23, 182, 227, 233, 234
"Separate but equal" doctrine, 783, 895,
    1010, 1012
Separate spheres, doctrine of, 369–370,
    620, 692, 844
Separatism, 107
September 11, 2001, terrorist attacks, 1170
Sequoyah, 384(i)
Serra, Junípero (1713–1784), 164, 165,
    167(b)
Servants (servant labor system), 84–87
    domestic, 370
        1870s–1890s, 693
    in plantations, 457, 457(i)
    indentured, seventeenth century, 81,
        84–88, 85(i), 93, 97, 98
    women, in Chesapeake colonies, 85, 86
Service industries, 997–998, 1123
Servicemen's Readjustment Act (GI Bill;
    1944), 965, 968, 1003
Settlement house movement, 748, 749,
    749(i), 750–751(b). *See also* Hull
    House
Settlements (settlers). *See also* Colonies;
    Westward expansion; Westward
    migration; *and specific settlements*
    agricultural (before 1492), 16–19, 23
    Archaic, 11, 13–16
    patterns of, seventeenth century, 87(m)
    Spanish, 44, 49, 57, 60, 61
    trans-Mississippi West, 644
        areas settled before 1862, 648(m)

ATLAS OF THE TERRITORIAL GROWTH OF THE UNITED STATES

Lake Superior

Lake Michigan

Lake Huron

Lake Ontario

Lake Erie

St. Lawrence R.

N.H.

MASS.

NEW YORK

RHODE ISLAND

CONNECTICUT

Connecticut R.

Hudson R.

PENN.

Delaware R.

NEW JERSEY

Susquehanna R.

DELAWARE

MARYLAND

THE ORIGINAL THIRTEEN COLONIES

Proclamation Line of 1763

Potomac R.

Chesapeake Bay

James R.

VIRGINIA

Missouri R.

Ohio R.

NORTH CAROLINA

Cape Fear R.

Cumberland R.

Tennessee R.

ATLANTIC OCEAN

SOUTH CAROLINA

Arkansas R.

Mississippi R.

Savannah R.

GEORGIA

Gulf of Mexico

THE ORIGINAL
THIRTEEN COLONIES
IN 1776

| 0 | 150 | 300 miles |
| 0 | 150 | 300 kilometers |

M-2

Lake Superior

Lake Huron

Lake Michigan

Lake Ontario

Lake Erie

St. Lawrence R.

Connecticut R.

N.H.

MASS.

NEW YORK

Hudson R.

RHODE
ISLAND

CONNECTICUT

PENN.

Delaware R.

Susquehanna R.

NEW JERSEY

DELAWARE

MARYLAND

Potomac R.

THE ORIGINAL THIRTEEN COLONIES

Chesapeake
Bay

Missouri R.

Ohio R.

James R.

**Gained by treaty
with Britain, 1783**

VIRGINIA

Proclamation Line of 1763

NORTH
CAROLINA

Cumberland R.

Tennessee R.

Cape Fear R.

Arkansas R.

Mississippi R.

ATLANTIC
OCEAN

SOUTH
CAROLINA

Savannah R.

GEORGIA

**THE UNITED STATES
IN 1783**

0   150   300 miles

0   150   300 kilometers

Gulf of Mexico

M-3

Area ceded by Great Britain, 1818

Area ceded by the United States to Great Britain, 1818

Columbia R.

Missouri R.

LOUISIANA PURCHASE from France, 1803

Snake R.

N. Platte R.

Platte R.

S. Platte R.

Sacramento R.

San Joaquin R.

Colorado R.

Red R.

PACIFIC OCEAN

Rio Grande

Lake Superior

Lake Michigan

Lake Huron

Lake Ontario

Lake Erie

(MICHIGAN TERRITORY)

St. Lawrence R.

Maine
(part of Mass.)

VERMONT
(1791)

NEW YORK
(1788)

N.H.
(1788)

MASS.
(1788)

Connecticut R.

Hudson R.

RHODE
ISLAND
(1790)

CONNECTICUT
(1788)

PENN.
(1787)

Susquehanna R.

Delaware R.

NEW JERSEY
(1787)

DELAWARE
(1787)

MARYLAND
(1788)

Chesapeake
Bay

OHIO
(1803)

INDIANA
(1816)

ILLINOIS
(1818)

Missouri R.

Potomac R.

James R.

VIRGINIA
(1788)

Ohio R.

KENTUCKY
(1792)

**Gained by treaty
with Britain, 1783**

Proclamation Line of 1763

THE ORIGINAL THIRTEEN COLONIES

NORTH
CAROLINA
(1789)

Cape Fear R.

Cumberland R.

Tennessee R.

TENNESSEE
(1796)

SOUTH
CAROLINA
(1788)

Savannah R.

*ATLANTIC
OCEAN*

Mississippi R.

MISSISSIPPI
(1817)

ALABAMA
(1819)

GEORGIA
(1788)

LOUISIANA
(1812)

THE UNITED STATES
IN 1819

0 — 150 — 300 miles

0 — 150 — 300 kilometers

**Areas taken from Spain
in 1810, 1813**

**FLORIDA
Treaty with Spain,
1819**

Gulf of Mexico

(1789) Date of statehood

Area ceded by
Great Britain,
1818

Area ceded by
the United States
to Great Britain,
1818

Missouri R.

Columbia R.

OREGON COUNTRY
Agreement with Britain,
1846

(OREGON TERRITORY)

Snake R.

LOUISIANA
PURCHASE
from France, 1803

N. Platte R.

Platte R.

S. Platte R.

Sacramento R.

(UTAH TERRITORY)

MEXICAN CESSION,
1848

San Joaquin R.

CALIFORNIA
(1850)

Colorado R.

(NEW MEXICO TERRITORY)

(Claim waived by
Texas, 1850)

Red R.

TEXAS
Annexed, 1845

PACIFIC
OCEAN

TEXAS
(1845)

GADSDEN PURCHASE
from Mexico, 1853

Rio Grande

Areas ceded by Britain, 1842 (Webster-Ashburton Treaty)

Lake Superior

(MINNESOTA TERRITORY)

WISCONSIN (1848)

Lake Huron

Lake Michigan

MICHIGAN (1837)

MAINE (1820)

VERMONT (1791)

St. Lawrence R.

Connecticut R.

N.H. (1788)

MASS. (1788)

Lake Ontario

NEW YORK (1788)

Hudson R.

RHODE ISLAND (1790)

CONNECTICUT (1788)

IOWA (1846)

Missouri R.

ILLINOIS (1818)

INDIANA (1816)

OHIO (1803)

Lake Erie

PENN. (1787)

THE ORIGINAL THIRTEEN COLONIES

Susquehanna R.

Delaware R.

NEW JERSEY (1787)

DELAWARE (1787)

MARYLAND (1788)

Proclamation Line of 1763

Potomac R.

Chesapeake Bay

MISSOURI (1821)

Ohio R.

KENTUCKY (1792)

Gained by treaty with Britain, 1783

James R.

VIRGINIA (1788)

Cumberland R.

Tennessee R.

NORTH CAROLINA (1789)

Cape Fear R.

ATLANTIC OCEAN

ARKANSAS (1836)

Mississippi R.

TENNESSEE (1796)

SOUTH CAROLINA (1788)

(INDIAN TERRITORY)

Savannah R.

MISSISSIPPI (1817)

ALABAMA (1819)

GEORGIA (1788)

THE UNITED STATES IN 1853

LOUISIANA (1812)

0   150   300 miles

0   150   300 kilometers

FLORIDA (1845)

FLORIDA Treaty with Spain, 1819

Areas taken from Spain in 1810, 1813

Gulf of Mexico

(1789)   Date of statehood

M-7

Area ceded by
the United States
to Great Britain,
1818

Area ceded by
Great Britain,
1818

WASHINGTON
(1889)
★ Olympia

Missouri R.

Helena ★

NORTH DAKOTA
(1889)

Bismarck ★

MONTANA
(1889)

Columbia R.

★ Salem

OREGON COUNTRY
Agreement with Britain,
1846

IDAHO
(1890)

OREGON
(1859)

★ Boise

Snake R.

SOUTH DAKOTA
(1889)

Pierre ★

L O U I S I A N A
P U R C H A S E

WYOMING
(1890)

from France, 1803

NEBRASKA
(1867)

N. Platte R.

Platte R.

Sacramento R.

★ Salt Lake
City

Cheyenne ★

Carson City ★

S. Platte R.

★ Sacramento

NEVADA
(1864)

UTAH
(1896)

Denver ★

COLORADO
(1876)

KANSAS
(1861)

San Joaquin R.

MEXICAN CESSION
1848

Colorado R.

CALIFORNIA
(1850)

PACIFIC
OCEAN

ARIZONA
(1912)

Santa Fe ★

NEW
MEXICO
(1912)

TEXAS
Annexed, 1845

Red R.

★ Phoenix

GADSDEN PURCHASE
from Mexico, 1853

TEXAS
(1845)

Rio Grande

ARCTIC OCEAN

RUSSIA

ALASKA
(1959)
Purchased from
Russia, 1867

CANADA

Yukon R.

Bering
Sea

Gulf of
Alaska

★ Juneau

HAWAII
(1959)
Annexed,
1898

★ Honolulu

PACIFIC
OCEAN

MEXICO

0   250   500 miles

0   250   500 kilometers

0   50   100 miles

0   50   100 kilometers

M-8

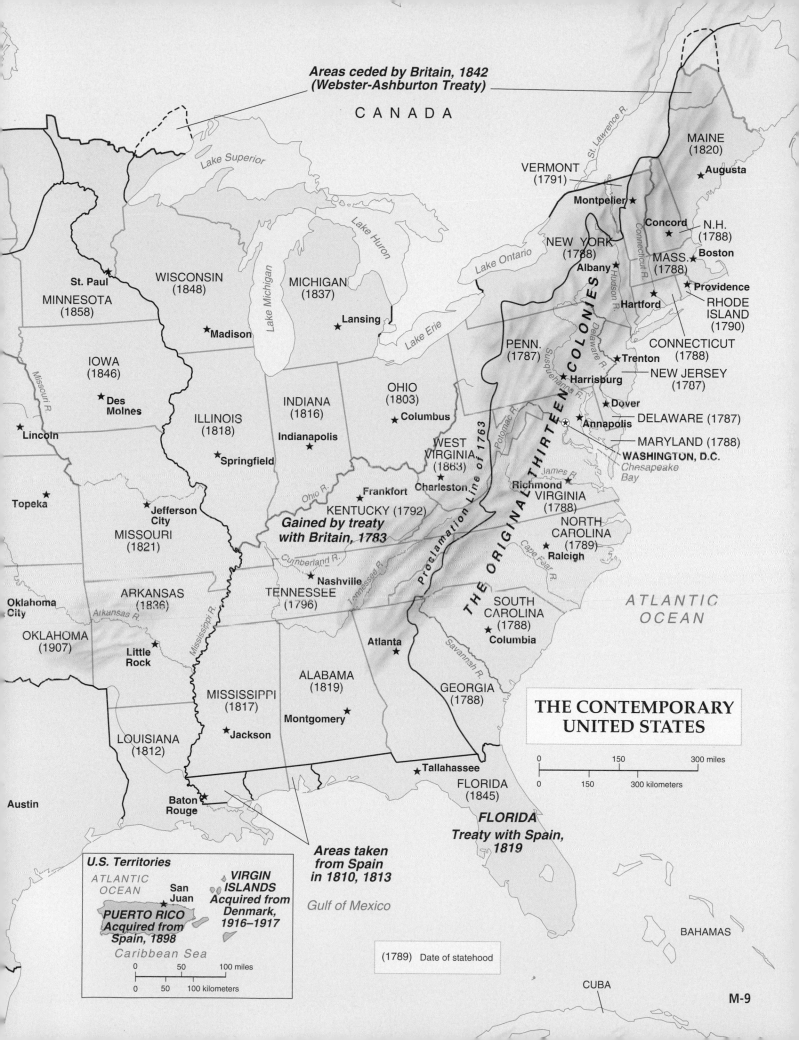

Areas ceded by Britain, 1842
(Webster-Ashburton Treaty)

CANADA

St. Lawrence R.

Lake Superior

MAINE
(1820)

★ Augusta

VERMONT
(1791)

Montpelier ★

Lake Huron

Lake Michigan

WISCONSIN
(1848)

MICHIGAN
(1837)

St. Paul ★

MINNESOTA
(1858)

NEW YORK
(1788)

Albany ★

Concord
★

N.H.
(1788)

★ Boston

MASS.
(1788)

Connecticut R.

Hartford ★

★ Providence

RHODE
ISLAND
(1790)

Lake Ontario

Hudson R.

★ Lansing

Lake Erie

PENN.
(1787)

Susquehanna R.

Delaware R.

CONNECTICUT
(1788)

IOWA
(1846)

Madison ★

★ Trenton

NEW JERSEY
(1787)

OHIO
(1803)

INDIANA
(1816)

Harrisburg ★

Dover ★

★ Des Moines

Missouri R.

★ Columbus

Lincoln ★

ILLINOIS
(1818)

Indianapolis ★

Springfield ★

WEST
VIRGINIA
(1863)

Annapolis ★

DELAWARE (1787)

MARYLAND (1788)

WASHINGTON, D.C.

Potomac R.

Chesapeake Bay

Topeka ★

Jefferson
City ★

MISSOURI
(1821)

Ohio R.

Frankfort ★

KENTUCKY (1792)

Charleston ★

Richmond ★

James R.

VIRGINIA
(1788)

THE ORIGINAL THIRTEEN COLONIES

Proclamation Line of 1763

**Gained by treaty
with Britain, 1783**

Cumberland R.

Nashville ★

NORTH
CAROLINA
(1789)

Cape Fear R.

Raleigh ★

ATLANTIC
OCEAN

ARKANSAS
(1836)

TENNESSEE
(1796)

Tennessee R.

Oklahoma
City

Arkansas R.

OKLAHOMA
(1907)

Little
Rock ★

SOUTH
CAROLINA
(1788)

Columbia ★

Atlanta ★

Mississippi R.

Savannah R.

THE CONTEMPORARY
UNITED STATES

0   150   300 miles

0   150   300 kilometers

ALABAMA
(1819)

MISSISSIPPI
(1817)

Jackson ★

Montgomery ★

GEORGIA
(1788)

LOUISIANA
(1812)

★ Tallahassee

FLORIDA
(1845)

Austin

Baton
Rouge ★

**Areas taken
from Spain
in 1810, 1813**

FLORIDA
**Treaty with Spain,
1819**

U.S. Territories

*ATLANTIC
OCEAN*

San
Juan
★

*VIRGIN
ISLANDS*
**Acquired from
Denmark,
1916–1917**

PUERTO RICO
**Acquired from
Spain, 1898**

Caribbean Sea

0   50   100 miles

0   50   100 kilometers

Gulf of Mexico

(1789)   Date of statehood

BAHAMAS

CUBA

M-9

THE CONTEMPORARY WORLD